Hoover's Handbook of

Private Companies 2004

HOOVER'S
BUSINESS PRESS

Austin, Texas

Hoover's Handbook of Private Companies 2004 is intended to provide readers with accurate and authoritative information about the enterprises covered in it. Hoover's asked all companies and organizations profiled to provide information. Many did so; a number did not. The information contained herein is as accurate as we could reasonably make it. In many cases we have relied on third-party material that we believe to be trustworthy, but were unable to independently verify. We do not warrant that the book is absolutely accurate or without error. Readers should not rely on any information contained herein in instances where such reliance might cause loss or damage. The publisher, the editors, and their data suppliers specifically disclaim all warranties, including the implied warranties of merchantability and fitness for a specific purpose. This book is sold with the understanding that neither the publisher, the editors, nor any content contributors are engaged in providing investment, financial, accounting, legal, or other professional advice.

The financial data (Historical Financials sections) in this book are from the companies profiled or from trade sources deemed to be reliable. Hoover's, Inc., is solely responsible for the presentation of all data.

Many of the names of products and services mentioned in this book are the trademarks or service marks of the companies manufacturing or selling them and are subject to protection under US law. Space has not permitted us to indicate which names are subject to such protection, and readers are advised to consult with the owners of such marks regarding their use. Hoover's is a trademark of Hoover's, Inc.

HOOVER'S
BUSINESS PRESS

10 9 8 7 6 5 4 3 2 1

Publishers Cataloging-in-Publication Data

Hoover's Handbook of Private Companies 2004

Includes indexes.

ISBN 1-57311-090-6

ISSN 1073-6433

1. Business enterprises — Directories. 2. Corporations — Directories.

HF3010 338.7

Hoover's Company Information is also available on the Internet at Hoover's Online (www.hoovers.com). A catalog of Hoover's products is available on the Internet at www.hooversbooks.com.

The Hoover's Handbook series is edited by George Sutton and is produced for Hoover's Business Press by:

Sycamore Productions, Inc.
5808 Balcones Drive, Suite 205
Austin, Texas 78731
info@sycamoreproductions.com

Cover design is by John Baker. Electronic prepress and printing are by Sheridan Books, Inc., Ann Arbor, Michigan.

U.S. AND WORLD BOOK SALES

Hoover's, Inc.
5800 Airport Blvd.
Austin, TX 78752
Phone: 512-374-4500
Fax: 512-374-4538
e-mail: orders@hoovers.com
Web: www.hooversbooks.com

EUROPEAN BOOK SALES

William Snyder Publishing Associates
5 Five Mile Drive
Oxford OX2 8HT
England
Phone & fax: +44-186-551-3186
e-mail: snyderpub@aol.com

Hoover's, Inc.

EDITORIAL

HOOVER'S BUSINESS PRESS

ABOUT HOOVER'S, INC. — THE BUSINESS INFORMATION AUTHORITY™

Hoover's, Inc., a subsidiary of D&B (NYSE: DNB), is a leading provider of business information. Hoover's provides authoritative, updated information for sales, marketing, business development, and other professionals who need intelligence on U.S. and global companies, industries, and the people who shape them. This information, along with powerful tools to search, sort, download, and integrate the content, is available through Hoover's Online (www.hoovers.com), the company's premier online service. Hoover's business information is also available through corporate intranets and distribution agreements with licensees, as well as via print from Hoover's Business Press. Hoover's is headquartered in Austin, Texas.

Abbreviations

AFL-CIO – American Federation of Labor and Congress of Industrial Organizations
AMA – American Medical Association
AMEX – American Stock Exchange
ARM – adjustable-rate mortgage
ASP – application services provider
ATM – asynchronous transfer mode
ATM – automated teller machine
CAD/CAM – computer-aided design/ computer-aided manufacturing
CD-ROM – compact disc – read-only memory
CD-R – CD-recordable
CEO – chief executive officer
CFO – chief financial officer
CMOS – complimentary metal oxide silicon
COO – chief operating officer
DAT – digital audiotape
DOD – Department of Defense
DOE – Department of Energy
DOS – disk operating system
DOT – Department of Transportation
DRAM – dynamic random-access memory
DSL – digital subscriber line
DVD – digital versatile disc/digital video disc
DVD-R – DVD-recordable
EPA – Environmental Protection Agency
EPROM – erasable programmable read-only memory
EPS – earnings per share
ESOP – employee stock ownership plan
EU – European Union
EVP – executive vice president
FCC – Federal Communications Commission
FDA – Food and Drug Administration
FDIC – Federal Deposit Insurance Corporation
FTC – Federal Trade Commission
FTP – file transfer protocol
GATT – General Agreement on Tariffs and Trade
GDP – gross domestic product
HMO – health maintenance organization
HR – human resources
HTML – hypertext markup language
ICC – Interstate Commerce Commission
IPO – initial public offering
IRS – Internal Revenue Service
ISP – Internet service provider
kWh – kilowatt-hour
LAN – local-area network
LBO – leveraged buyout
LCD – liquid crystal display
LNG – liquefied natural gas
LP – limited partnership
Ltd. – limited
mips – millions of instructions per second
MW – megawatt
NAFTA – North American Free Trade Agreement
NASA – National Aeronautics and Space Administration
NASDAQ – National Association of Securities Dealers Automated Quotations
NATO – North Atlantic Treaty Organization
NYSE – New York Stock Exchange
OCR – optical character recognition
OECD – Organization for Economic Cooperation and Development
OEM – original equipment manufacturer
OPEC – Organization of Petroleum Exporting Countries
OS – operating system
OSHA – Occupational Safety and Health Administration
OTC – over-the-counter
PBX – private branch exchange
PCMCIA – Personal Computer Memory Card International Association
P/E – price to earnings ratio
RAID – redundant array of independent disks
RAM – random-access memory
R&D – research and development
RBOC – regional Bell operating company
RISC – reduced instruction set computer
REIT – real estate investment trust
ROA – return on assets
ROE – return on equity
ROI – return on investment
ROM – read-only memory
S&L – savings and loan
SCSI – Small Computer System Interface
SEC – Securities and Exchange Commission
SEVP – senior executive vice president
SIC – Standard Industrial Classification
SOC – system on a chip
SVP – senior vice president
USB – universal serial bus
VAR – value-added reseller
VAT – value-added tax
VC – venture capitalist
VoIP – Voice over Internet Protocol
VP – vice president
WAN – wide-area network
WWW – World Wide Web

Contents

Companies Profiled

Companies Profiled (continued)

Companies Profiled (continued)

Companies Profiled (continued)

About Hoover's Handbook of Private Companies 2004

Hoover's Handbook of Private Companies 2004 continues this year in its long tradition as one of America's premier sources of business information on privately held enterprises, with two major changes: It has a new look, and we have greatly expanded the information found inside.

We have redesigned the cover and the inside pages and moved to a larger format so that we can pack even more information into the book. This has allowed us to drop the past distinction between companies with in-depth profiles and those with shorter, capsule profiles. Some larger and more visible companies will continue to have an additional History section, but now all companies will have up to 10 years of financial information, product information where available, and a longer list of company executives.

By doing this, we have achieved our goal of adding even more value to this already valuable resource.

Publishing current, relevant information about nonpublic companies can be a challenge, as many of them see secrecy as a competitive strategy, but in this ninth edition of *Hoover's Handbook of Private Companies*, we have compiled the hard-to-find facts on 900 of the largest and most influential enterprises in the US.

HOOVER'S ONLINE FOR BUSINESS NEEDS

In addition to the 2,550 companies featured in our handbooks, coverage of some 35,000 business enterprises is available in electronic format on our Web site, Hoover's Online (www.hoovers.com). Our goal is to provide one site that offers authoritative, updated intelligence on US and global companies, industries, and the people who shape them. Hoover's has partnered with other prestigious business information and service providers to bring you all the right business information, services, and links in one place. We welcome the recognition we have received as the premier provider of high-quality company information — online, electronically, and in print — and continue to look for ways to make our products more available and more useful to you.

Hoover's Handbook of Private Companies is one of our four-title series of handbooks that covers, literally, the world of business. The series is available as an indexed set, and also includes *Hoover's Handbook of American Business* (in two volumes), *Hoover's Handbook of World Business*, and *Hoover's Handbook of Emerging Companies*. This series brings you information on the biggest, fastest-growing, and most influential enterprises in the world.

We believe that anyone who buys from, sells to, invests in, lends to, competes with, interviews with, or works for a company should know all there is to know about that enterprise. Taken together, this book and the other Hoover's products and resources represent the most complete source of basic corporate information readily available to the general public.

HOW TO USE THIS BOOK

This book has four sections:

1. "Using Hoover's Handbooks" describes the contents of our profiles and explains the ways in which we gather and compile our data.
2. "A List-Lover's Compendium" contains lists of the largest and fastest-growing private companies. The lists are based on the information in our profiles, or compiled from well-known sources.
3. The company profiles section makes up the largest and most important part of the book — 900 profiles of major private enterprises, arranged alphabetically.
4. Three indexes complete the book. The first sorts companies by industry groups, the second by headquarters location. The third index is a list of all the executives found in the Executives section of each company profile.

As always, we hope you find our books useful. We invite your comments via phone (512-374-4500), fax (512-374-4538), mail (5800 Airport Boulevard, Austin, Texas 78752), or e-mail (custsupport@hoovers.com).

The Editors,
Austin, Texas,
December 2003

Using Hoover's Handbooks

SELECTION OF THE COMPANIES PROFILED

The 900 enterprises profiled in this book include the largest and most influential private enterprises in America. Among them are:

- private companies, from the giants (Cargill and Koch) to the colorful and prominent (King Ranch and L.L. Bean)
- mutuals and cooperative organizations owned by their customers (State Farm Insurance, Ace Hardware, Ocean Spray Cranberries)
- not-for-profits (American Red Cross, Kaiser Foundation Health Plan, Smithsonian Institution)
- joint ventures (Motiva Enterprises, Dow Corning)
- partnerships (Baker & McKenzie, Kohlberg Kravis Roberts & Co.)
- universities (Columbia, Harvard, University of California)
- government-owned corporations (US Postal Service and New York City's Metropolitan Transportation Authority)
- and a selection of other enterprises (National Basketball Association, AFL-CIO, Texas Lottery Commission).

ORGANIZATION

The profiles are presented in alphabetical order. We have shown the full legal name of the enterprise at the top of the profile, unless it is too long, in which case you will find it above the address in the Where section of the profile. If a company name is also a person's name, such as Edward J. DeBartolo or Mary Kay, it will be alphabetized under the first name; if the company name starts with initials, for example, L.L. Bean or S.C. Johnson, look for it under the combined initials (in the above examples, LL and SC, respectively).

Basic financial data are listed under the heading Historical Financials. The annual financial information contained in the profiles is current through fiscal year-ends occurring as late as October 2003. We have included certain nonfinancial developments, such as officer changes, through November 2003.

OVERVIEW

In the first section of the profile, we have tried to give a thumbnail description of the company and what it does. The description will usually include information on the company's strategy, reputation, and ownership. We recommend that you read this section first.

HISTORY

This extended section, which is available for some of the larger and more well known companies, reflects our belief that every enterprise is the sum of its history and that you have to know where you came from in order to know where you are going. While some companies have limited historical awareness and were unable to help us much and other companies are just plain boring, we think the vast majority of the enterprises in this book have colorful backgrounds. We have tried to focus on the people who made the enterprises what they are today. We have found these histories to be full of twists and ironies; they make fascinating reading.

EXECUTIVES

Here we list the names of the people who run the company, insofar as space allows. In the few cases where available, we have shown the ages and pay of key officers. In some instances the published data is for the previous year although the company has announced promotions or retirements since year-end. The pay represents cash compensation, including bonuses, but excludes stock option programs.

Although companies are free to structure their management titles any way they please, most modern corporations follow standard practices. The ultimate power in any corporation lies with the shareholders, who elect a board of directors, usually including officers or "insiders" as well as individuals from outside the company. The chief officer, the person on whose desk the buck stops, is usually called the chief executive officer (CEO). Often, he or she is also the chairman of the board.

As corporate management has become more complex, it is common for the CEO to have a "right-hand person" who oversees the day-to-day operations of the company, allowing the CEO plenty of time to focus on strategy and long-term issues. This right-hand person is usually designated the chief operating officer (COO) and is often the president of the company. In other cases one person is both chairman and president.

A multitude of other titles exists, including chief

financial officer (CFO), chief administrative officer, and vice chairman. We have always tried to include the CFO, the chief legal officer, and the chief human resources or personnel officer.

The people named in the Executives section are indexed at the back of the book.

The Executives section also includes the name of the company's auditing (accounting) firm, where available.

LOCATIONS

Here we include the company's headquarters, street address, telephone and fax numbers, and Web site, as available. The back of the book includes an index of companies by headquarters locations.

In some cases we have also included information on the geographic distribution of the company's business, including sales and profit data. Note that these profit numbers, like those in the Products/Operations section below, are usually operating or pretax profits rather than net profits. Operating profits are generally those before financing costs (interest income and payments) and before taxes, which are considered costs attributable to the whole company rather than to one division or part of the world. For this reason the net income figures (in the Historical Financials section) are usually much lower, since they are after interest and taxes. Pretax profits are after interest but before taxes.

Headquarters for companies which are incorporated in Bermuda, but whose operational headquarters are in the US, are listed under their US address. The same applies for companies with joint US and non-US headquarters (such as KPMG International).

PRODUCTS/OPERATIONS

This section lists as many of the company's products, services, brand names, divisions, subsidiaries, and joint ventures as we could fit. We have tried to include all its major lines and all familiar brand names.

The nature of this section varies by company and the amount of information available. If the company publishes sales and profit information by type of business, we have included it.

COMPETITORS

In this section we have listed companies that compete with the profiled company. This feature is included as a quick way to locate similar companies and compare them. The universe of competitors includes all public companies and all private companies with sales in excess of $500 million. In a few instances we have identified smaller private companies as key competitors.

HISTORICAL FINANCIALS

Here we have tried to present as much data about each enterprise's financial performance as we could compile in the allocated space. The information varies somewhat from industry to industry and is less complete in the case of private companies that do not release data (although we have always tried to provide annual sales and employment). There are a few industries, venture capital and investment banking, for example, for which revenue numbers are not reported as a rule. In the case of private companies that do not publicly disclose financial information, we have gathered estimates of sales and other statistics from numerous sources.

The following information is generally present.

A 10-year table, with relevant annualized compound growth rates, covers:

- Sales — fiscal year sales (year-end assets for most financial companies)
- Net income — fiscal year net income (before accounting changes)
- Income as a percent of sales — fiscal year net income as a percent of sales (as a percent of assets for most financial firms)
- Employees — fiscal year-end or average number of employees

The information on the number of employees is intended to aid the reader interested in knowing whether a company has a long-term trend of increasing or decreasing employment. As far as we know, we are the only company that publishes this information in print format.

The numbers on the left in each row of the Historical Financials section give the month and the year in which the company's fiscal year actually ends. Thus, a company with a February 28, 2003, year-end is shown as 2/03. The last item in the Financials section is a graph, which for private companies, shows net income, or, if that is unavailable, sales.

Key year-end statistics are included in this section for insurance companies and companies required to file reports with the SEC. They generally show the financial strength of the enterprise, including:

- Debt ratio (long-term debt as a percent of shareholders' equity)
- Return on equity (net income divided by the average of beginning and ending common shareholders' equity)
- Cash and cash equivalents
- Current ratio (ratio of current assets to current liabilities)
- Total long-term debt (including capital lease obligations)
- Fiscal year sales for financial institutions.

Hoover's Handbook of

Private Companies

A List-Lover's Compendium

The 300 Largest Companies by Sales in *Hoover's Handbook of Private Companies 2004*

Rank	Company	Sales ($ mil.)
1	Blue Cross and Blue Shield	162,800
2	United States Postal Service	66,463
3	Cargill, Incorporated	59,894
4	State Farm Insurance	49,700
5	Koch Industries, Inc.	40,000
6	Nationwide	29,421
7	New York Life Insurance	25,678
8	Kaiser Foundation Health Plan	22,500
9	IGA, INC.	21,000
10	TIAA-CREF	19,791
11	Motiva Enterprises LLC	19,446
12	Cellco Partnership	19,260
13	Massachusetts Mutual Life	16,253
14	Publix Super Markets, Inc.	16,027
15	Northwestern Mutual	16,024
16	University of California	15,980
17	Deloitte Touche Tohmatsu	15,100
18	Mars, Incorporated	15,000
19	Cingular Wireless LLC	14,727
20	Liberty Mutual Insurance	14,544
21	PricewaterhouseCoopers	13,800
22	Ernst & Young International	13,136
23	Penske Corporation	12,000
24	Blue Cross Blue Shield of Michigan	11,883
25	Bechtel Group, Inc.	11,600
26	The ASCII Group, Inc.	11,000
27	Meijer, Inc.	10,900
28	KPMG International	10,720
29	Carlson Wagonlit Travel, Inc.	10,700
30	Cox Enterprises, Inc.	9,900
31	H. E. Butt Grocery Company	9,900
32	C&S Wholesale Grocers, Inc.	9,700
33	USAA	9,222
34	FMR Corp.	8,900
35	The Trump Organization	8,500
36	Swift & Company	8,432
37	Ascension Health	7,666
38	JM Family Enterprises, Inc.	7,600
39	Highmark Inc.	7,400
40	Guardian Life Insurance	7,192
41	Army and Air Force Exchange	7,133
42	Tennessee Valley Authority	6,835
43	Carlson Companies, Inc.	6,700
44	Farmland Industries, Inc.	6,574
45	Enterprise Rent-A-Car Company	6,500
46	Dairy Farmers of America, Inc.	6,448
47	Wakefern Food Corporation	6,200
48	Health Care Service Corporation	6,198
49	Rosenbluth International	6,000
50	Science Applications International Corporation	5,903
51	Catholic Health Initiatives	5,900
52	Land O'Lakes, Inc.	5,847
53	The Marmon Group, Inc.	5,756
54	MacAndrews & Forbes	5,700
55	Equistar Chemicals, LP	5,537
56	Duke Energy Field Services, LLC	5,492
57	Chevron Phillips	5,473
58	American Family Insurance Group	5,307
59	Menard, Inc.	5,300
60	VT Inc.	5,299
61	United Way of America	5,000
62	CCA Global Partners	5,000
63	S.C. Johnson & Son, Inc.	5,000
64	MidAmerican Energy Holdings	4,968
65	The University of Texas System	4,806
66	Trinity Health	4,800
67	Visa International	4,800
68	Flying J Inc.	4,600
69	Huntsman International LLC	4,518
70	Catholic Healthcare West	4,500
71	Alticor Inc.	4,500
72	Giant Eagle, Inc.	4,415
73	Dole Food Company, Inc.	4,392
74	Catholic Health East	4,300
75	New York City Health and Hospitals Corporation	4,300
76	MBM Corporation	4,236
77	Sutter Health	4,216
78	National Football League Inc.	4,200
79	Advance Publications, Inc.	4,200
80	Hallmark Cards, Inc.	4,200
81	New York State Lottery	4,185
82	Levi Strauss & Co.	4,137
83	Mayo Foundation	4,135
84	The American Red Cross	4,117
85	Hy-Vee, Inc.	4,100
86	Horizon Blue Cross Blue Shield	4,098
87	MTA	4,052
88	California State University	4,050
89	Blue Cross and Blue Shield of Massachusetts, Inc.	4,043
90	NRT Incorporated	4,039
91	TAP Pharmaceutical Products Inc.	4,037
92	Partners HealthCare System, Inc.	4,002
93	Guardian Industries Corp.	4,000
94	YMCA of the USA	4,000
95	Delta Dental Plan of California	4,000
96	Graybar Electric Company, Inc.	3,975
97	Hyatt Corporation	3,950
98	Reyes Holdings LLC	3,900
99	Thrivent Financial for Lutherans	3,871
100	Pacific Mutual Holding Company	3,816
101	Gulf States Toyota, Inc.	3,800
102	The Lefrak Organization	3,800
103	WorldTravel BTI	3,800
104	Southern Wine & Spirits	3,750
105	Peter Kiewit Sons', Inc.	3,699
106	Milliken & Company Inc.	3,600
107	Eby-Brown Company	3,600
108	Auto-Owners Insurance Group	3,514
109	Major League Baseball	3,500
110	State University of New York	3,476
111	Roundy's, Inc.	3,450
112	The Hearst Corporation	3,300
113	ContiGroup Companies, Inc.	3,300
114	Topco Associates LLC	3,300
115	McKinsey & Company	3,300
116	North Shore-Long Island Jewish Health System	3,200
117	Raley's Inc.	3,200
118	Associated Wholesale Grocers	3,097
119	University of Wisconsin System	3,059
120	QuikTrip Corporation	3,050
121	Ace Hardware Corporation	3,029
122	RaceTrac Petroleum, Inc.	3,000
123	Wegmans Food Markets, Inc.	3,000
124	NASCAR	3,000
125	Chemoil Corporation	3,000
126	The Martin-Brower Company	3,000
127	J.R. Simplot Company	3,000
128	Kohler Co.	3,000
129	George E. Warren Corporation	3,000
130	Allegis Group, Inc.	3,000
131	Bloomberg L.P.	3,000
132	The University of Michigan	2,944
133	Stanford University	2,940
134	Kemper Insurance Companies	2,848
135	Texas Lottery Commission	2,826
136	Harbour Group Industries, Inc.	2,800
137	Unified Western Grocers, Inc.	2,793
138	Gilbane, Inc.	2,771
139	Brown Automotive Group Ltd.	2,750
140	Gordon Food Service	2,750
141	Alliance Capital Management L.P.	2,742
142	Perdue Farms Incorporated	2,700
143	Keystone Foods LLC	2,700
144	The Port Authority of New York and New Jersey	2,671
145	Stater Bros. Holdings Inc.	2,666
146	Tenaska, Inc.	2,665
147	Intermountain Health Care, Inc.	2,652
148	Hendrick Automotive Group	2,639
149	Schneider National, Inc.	2,627
150	Dow Corning Corporation	2,610

SOURCE: HOOVER'S, INC., DATABASE, OCTOBER 2003

The 300 Largest Companies by Sales in *Hoover's Handbook of Private Companies 2004* (continued)

Rank	Company	Sales ($ mil.)
151	Catholic Healthcare Partners	2,602
152	Bill Heard Enterprises	2,600
153	Clark Retail Group, Inc.	2,600
154	International Data Group	2,580
155	The Connell Company	2,525
156	St. Joseph Health System	2,514
157	CARQUEST Corporation	2,500
158	NextiraOne, LLC	2,500
159	Kinray Inc.	2,500
160	H.T. Hackney Co.	2,500
161	Clark Enterprises, Inc.	2,500
162	Quality King Distributors Inc.	2,450
163	Transammonia, Inc.	2,434
164	Whiting-Turner	2,400
165	Consolidated Electrical Distributors	2,400
166	Parsons Corporation	2,400
167	Harvard University	2,357
168	Do it Best Corp.	2,308
169	A-Mark Financial Corporation	2,300
170	Sinclair Oil Corporation	2,300
171	Bon Secours Health System, Inc.	2,300
172	The Jones Financial Companies	2,270
173	The Texas A&M University System	2,254
174	Belk, Inc.	2,242
175	Lumbermens Merchandising	2,200
176	BJC HealthCare	2,200
177	Booz Allen Hamilton Inc.	2,200
178	JohnsonDiversey, Inc.	2,196
179	SIRVA, Inc.	2,186
180	84 Lumber Company	2,177
181	TruServ Corporation	2,176
182	Renco Group, Inc.	2,175
183	National Basketball Association	2,164
184	ESPN, Inc.	2,120
185	MedStar Health	2,110
186	Schnuck Markets, Inc.	2,107
187	Holman Enterprises	2,105
188	Springs Industries, Inc.	2,100
189	Red Apple Group, Inc.	2,100
190	Amtrak	2,100
191	Kinko's, Inc.	2,100
192	The Structure Tone Organization	2,100
193	The Golub Corporation	2,100
194	Banner Health	2,100
195	Power Authority of the State of New York	2,060
196	Goodwill Industries International	2,055
197	The Mutual of Omaha Companies	2,053
198	Bill & Melinda Gates Foundation	2,048
199	CalPERS	2,023
200	Wawa, Inc.	2,010
201	Columbia University	2,009
202	Gores Technology Group	2,000
203	H Group Holding Inc.	2,000
204	Quexco Incorporated	2,000
205	Grant Thornton International	2,000
206	Black & Veatch	2,000
207	Henry Ford Health System	2,000
208	Micro Warehouse, Inc.	2,000
209	KB Toys	2,000
210	Fry's Electronics, Inc.	2,000
211	JELD-WEN, inc.	2,000
212	Tufts Associated Health Plans	2,000
213	CH2M HILL Companies, Ltd.	1,999
214	Westcon Group, Inc.	1,993
215	Quintiles Transnational Corp.	1,992
216	Alex Lee, Inc.	1,980
217	J.F. Shea Co., Inc.	1,968
218	Zachry Construction Corporation	1,940
219	TravelCenters of America, Inc.	1,935
220	Ingram Industries Inc.	1,929
221	Sheetz, Inc.	1,920
222	The Scoular Company	1,900
223	Demoulas Super Markets Inc.	1,900
224	UniGroup, Inc.	1,896
225	MasterCard Incorporated	1,892
226	Sentry Insurance	1,880
227	Gold Kist Inc.	1,864
228	Emory University	1,860
229	Dr Pepper/Seven Up Bottling Group, Inc.	1,820
230	University of Washington	1,814
231	Aera Energy LLC	1,807
232	Ag Processing Inc	1,802
233	Minnesota Mutual Companies	1,801
234	Allina Hospitals and Clinics	1,800
235	Quad/Graphics, Inc.	1,800
236	Golden State Foods	1,800
237	Software House International, Inc.	1,797
238	Metaldyne Corporation	1,793
239	EPIX Holdings Corporation	1,782
240	Forever Living Products	1,773
241	Hensel Phelps Construction Co.	1,771
242	Lincoln Property Company	1,766
243	Leprino Foods Company	1,750
244	Follett Corporation	1,733
245	Houchens Industries Inc.	1,727
246	The University of Iowa	1,721
247	Haworth, Inc.	1,710
248	Discovery Communications, Inc.	1,710
249	SSM Health Care System Inc.	1,705
250	Rich Products Corporation	1,702
251	Crown Central Petroleum	1,700
252	AECOM Technology Corporation	1,700
253	Pilot Corporation	1,700
254	Cumberland Farms, Inc.	1,700
255	E. & J. Gallo Winery	1,700
256	National Distributing Company	1,700
257	Brookshire Grocery Company	1,700
258	Southwire Company	1,700
259	Central National-Gottesman Inc.	1,700
260	National Hockey League	1,697
261	Gulf Oil Limited Partnership	1,680
262	Vertis Inc.	1,675
263	Cornell University	1,666
264	Massachusetts Institute of Technology	1,665
265	The Ohio State University	1,661
266	Services Group of America	1,650
267	General Parts, Inc.	1,650
268	The University of Chicago	1,617
269	Save Mart Supermarkets	1,600
270	Bashas' Inc.	1,600
271	Sentara Healthcare	1,600
272	Purity Wholesale Grocers, Inc.	1,600
273	Burger King Corporation	1,600
274	Glazer's Wholesale Drug	1,600
275	Bose Corporation	1,600
276	Vanderbilt University	1,590
277	The Vanguard Group	1,568
278	Mary Kay Inc.	1,560
279	Di Giorgio Corporation	1,560
280	Larry H. Miller Group	1,550
281	Swinerton Incorporated	1,549
282	Dresser, Inc.	1,546
283	WinCo Foods, Inc.	1,540
284	ACT Manufacturing, Inc.	1,536
285	Dunn Industries, Inc.	1,533
286	Sammons Enterprises, Inc.	1,510
287	Frank Consolidated Enterprises	1,500
288	Purdue Pharma L.P.	1,500
289	The Irvine Company Inc.	1,500
290	Retail Brand Alliance, Inc.	1,500
291	Builders FirstSource	1,500
292	Hunt Consolidated Inc.	1,500
293	Maritz Inc.	1,500
294	Mashantucket Pequot Gaming	1,500
295	Lucasfilm Ltd.	1,500
296	Nikken Global Inc.	1,500
297	The Grocers Supply Co., Inc.	1,500
298	Young's Market Company, LLC	1,490
299	University of Southern California	1,480
300	BE&K Inc.	1,478

The 300 Largest Employers in *Hoover's Handbook of Private Companies 2004*

Rank	Company	Employees
1	United States Postal Service	854,376
2	Express Personnel Services	224,000
3	Carlson Companies, Inc.	180,000
4	Blue Cross and Blue Shield	150,000
5	Goodwill Industries	140,023
6	Kaiser Foundation Health Plan	125,000
7	PricewaterhouseCoopers	124,563
8	Publix Super Markets, Inc.	123,000
9	Deloitte Touche Tohmatsu	119,237
10	University of California	114,282
11	Ernst & Young International	103,000
12	KPMG International	98,000
13	Cargill, Incorporated	98,000
14	IGA, INC.	92,000
15	Ascension Health	83,412
16	Meijer, Inc.	83,402
17	Hyatt Corporation	80,000
18	State Farm Insurance	79,400
19	Cox Enterprises, Inc.	77,000
20	Catholic Health Initiatives	67,000
21	The University of Texas System	65,689
22	MTA	64,169
23	H. E. Butt Grocery Company	60,000
24	Dole Food Company, Inc.	57,000
25	NRT Incorporated	52,801
26	Army and Air Force Exchange	52,400
27	Enterprise Rent-A-Car Company	50,000
28	Wakefern Food Corporation	50,000
29	Bechtel Group, Inc.	47,000
30	Hy-Vee, Inc.	46,000
31	Mayo Foundation	45,536
32	Chick-fil-A Inc.	45,000
33	Trinity Health	44,500
34	Catholic Health East	43,000
35	H Group Holding Inc.	41,000
36	California State University	40,000
37	The American Red Cross	40,000
38	The Salvation Army	40,000
39	Cellco Partnership	39,300
40	Science Applications International Corporation	38,700
41	Penske Corporation	36,000
42	Catholic Healthcare West	36,000
43	Sutter Health	36,000
44	Liberty Mutual Insurance	35,000
45	Cingular Wireless LLC	33,800
46	Providence Health System	33,000
47	The Ohio State University	32,000
48	New York City Health and Hospitals Corporation	31,544
49	Burger King Corporation	31,000
50	Centerplate	30,200
51	Nationwide	30,000
52	Wegmans Food Markets, Inc.	30,000
53	North Shore-Long Island Jewish Health System	30,000
54	Catholic Healthcare Partners	30,000
55	The City University of New York	30,000
56	Mars, Incorporated	30,000
57	Metromedia Company	29,500
58	FMR Corp.	29,000
59	The Jones Financial Companies	28,469
60	Bon Secours Health System, Inc.	27,000
61	24 Hour Fitness Worldwide Inc.	27,000
62	University of Missouri System	26,316
63	Giant Eagle, Inc.	26,000
64	BJC HealthCare	25,801
65	Delaware North Companies, Inc.	25,000
66	Texas A&M University System	25,000
67	Kohler Co.	25,000
68	University of Wisconsin System	25,000
69	KB Toys	25,000
70	YMCA of the USA	25,000
71	Inter-Con Security Systems, Inc.	25,000
72	KinderCare Learning Centers, Inc.	25,000
73	RTM Restaurant Group	25,000
74	Amtrak	24,600
75	The Schwan Food Company	24,000
76	Asplundh Tree Expert Co.	24,000
77	University of Washington	23,680
78	Buffets, Inc.	23,000
79	Intermountain Health Care, Inc.	23,000
80	Advance Publications, Inc.	22,785
81	Allina Hospitals and Clinics	22,347
82	MedStar Health	22,000
83	SSM Health Care System Inc.	22,000
84	USAA	22,000
85	The Trump Organization	22,000
86	Federal Prison Industries, Inc.	21,778
87	Grant Thornton International	21,500
88	Banner Health	21,500
89	Swift & Company	21,300
90	Schneider National, Inc.	20,756
91	The Day & Zimmermann Group	20,000
92	Perdue Farms Incorporated	20,000
93	Kinko's, Inc.	20,000
94	American Golf Corporation	20,000
95	ClubCorp, Inc.	20,000
96	JELD-WEN, inc.	20,000
97	Hallmark Cards, Inc.	20,000
98	MacAndrews & Forbes Holdings	19,800
99	The Golub Corporation	19,700
100	Emory University	19,288
101	Guardian Industries Corp.	19,000
102	St. Joseph Health System	18,930
103	Schnuck Markets, Inc.	18,000
104	Gold Kist Inc.	18,000
105	Viasystems Group, Inc.	18,000
106	Belk, Inc.	17,800
107	Guardsmark, Inc.	17,369
108	Adventist Health	17,200
109	The Hearst Corporation	17,170
110	NPC International, Inc.	17,000
111	Raley's Inc.	17,000
112	University of Southern California	17,000
113	Vanderbilt University	16,679
114	Indiana University	16,500
115	Loews Cineplex Entertainment	16,500
116	The Lefrak Organization	16,200
117	Carrols Corporation	16,100
118	BREED Technologies, Inc.	16,000
119	Quintiles Transnational Corp.	15,548
120	AECOM Technology Corporation	15,500
121	Sentara Healthcare	15,200
122	United Way of America	15,166
123	Harvard University	15,000
124	Hobby Lobby Stores, Inc.	15,000
125	Peter Kiewit Sons', Inc.	15,000
126	Henry Ford Health System	15,000
127	ContiGroup Companies, Inc.	14,500
128	Zachry Construction Corporation	14,000
129	Milliken & Company Inc.	14,000
130	Taylor Corporation	14,000
131	General Parts, Inc.	14,000
132	Farmland Industries, Inc.	13,800
133	Domino's, Inc.	13,800
134	JohnsonDiversey, Inc.	13,530
135	Renco Group, Inc.	13,500
136	Roundy's, Inc.	13,451
137	Stater Bros. Holdings Inc.	13,400
138	Cornell University	13,319
139	International Data Group	13,050
140	Inova Health System	13,000
141	NextiraOne, LLC	13,000
142	Wawa, Inc.	13,000
143	J.R. Simplot Company	13,000
144	Tennessee Valley Authority	13,000
145	White Castle System, Inc.	12,900
146	Booz Allen Hamilton Inc.	12,600
147	Cinemark, Inc.	12,500
148	Levi Strauss & Co.	12,400
149	Princeton University	12,238
150	The University of Iowa	12,000

SOURCE: HOOVER'S, INC., DATABASE, OCTOBER 2003

The 300 Largest Employers in *Hoover's Handbook of Private Companies 2004* (continued)

Rank	Company	Employees
151	New York Life Insurance	12,000
152	The University of Chicago	12,000
153	Whataburger, Inc.	12,000
154	Boscov's Department Store	12,000
155	McKinsey & Company	12,000
156	Turner Industries, Ltd.	12,000
157	Ritz Camera Centers, Inc.	12,000
158	The University of Nebraska	11,530
159	Flying J Inc.	11,500
160	Brookshire Grocery Company	11,500
161	University of Rochester	11,200
162	MediaNews Group, Inc.	11,200
163	Foster Poultry Farms	11,000
164	Cushman & Wakefield, Inc.	11,000
165	Quad/Graphics, Inc.	11,000
166	Highmark Inc.	11,000
167	Koch Industries, Inc.	11,000
168	MidAmerican Energy Holdings	10,985
169	CH2M HILL Companies, Ltd.	10,600
170	Group Health Cooperative of Puget Sound	10,500
171	Alticor Inc.	10,500
172	TravelCenters of America, Inc.	10,255
173	Concentra Inc.	10,254
174	Mohegan Tribal Gaming	10,203
175	MSX International, Inc.	10,142
176	Retail Brand Alliance, Inc.	10,036
177	Gores Technology Group	10,000
178	University of Pittsburgh	10,000
179	Haworth, Inc.	10,000
180	The Vanguard Group	10,000
181	Stevedoring Services of America	10,000
182	Allegis Group, Inc.	10,000
183	Follett Corporation	10,000
184	United Space Alliance	10,000
185	Barnes & Noble College Bookstores, Inc.	9,500
186	NESCO, Inc.	9,500
187	S.C. Johnson & Son, Inc.	9,500
188	CBRE Holding, Inc.	9,500
189	Massachusetts Institute of Technology	9,400
190	Parsons Brinckerhoff Inc.	9,294
191	Menard, Inc.	9,200
192	Estes Express Lines	9,160
193	HBE Corporation	9,100
194	Parsons Corporation	9,100
195	SAS Institute Inc.	9,023
196	Alex Lee, Inc.	9,000
197	Nypro Inc.	9,000
198	AMSTED Industries Incorporated	9,000
199	Massachusetts Mutual Life Insurance Company	9,000
200	Kemper Insurance Companies	9,000
201	BE&K Inc.	8,822
202	Bass Pro Shops, Inc.	8,800
203	Dr Pepper/Seven Up Bottling Group, Inc.	8,800
204	UIS, Inc.	8,800
205	Vertis Inc.	8,700
206	Battelle Memorial Institute	8,700
207	R. B. Pamplin Corp.	8,500
208	Atlantic Express Transportation	8,500
209	Sheetz, Inc.	8,500
210	Dresser, Inc.	8,500
211	Andersen Corporation	8,500
212	Discount Tire Co.	8,415
213	Graybar Electric Company, Inc.	8,300
214	Variety Wholesalers, Inc.	8,300
215	J. Crew Group, Inc.	8,200
216	Dow Corning Corporation	8,200
217	Automobile Club of Southern California	8,000
218	IASIS Healthcare Corporation	8,000
219	Motiva Enterprises LLC	8,000
220	Washington University in St. Louis	8,000
221	Huntsman International LLC	8,000
222	Duchossois Industries, Inc.	8,000
223	Towers Perrin	8,000
224	Mark IV Industries, Inc.	8,000
225	NCH Corporation	8,000
226	Baker & McKenzie	8,000
227	Land O'Lakes, Inc.	8,000
228	Bose Corporation	8,000
229	Bloomberg L.P.	8,000
230	Memorial Sloan-Kettering Cancer Center	7,953
231	Big Y Foods, Inc.	7,850
232	Horseshoe Gaming Holding Corp.	7,780
233	Yale University	7,577
234	Colliers International Property Consultants Inc.	7,572
235	Carlson Wagonlit Travel, Inc.	7,504
236	Red Apple Group, Inc.	7,500
237	Ilitch Holdings, Inc.	7,500
238	American Family Insurance Group	7,500
239	The Holmes Group, Inc.	7,500
240	C&S Wholesale Grocers, Inc.	7,500
241	SIRVA, Inc.	7,500
242	Clark Retail Group, Inc.	7,400
243	The Longaberger Company	7,300
244	Save Mart Supermarkets	7,300
245	Colson & Colson Construction	7,300
246	Contran Corporation	7,300
247	Coast Casinos, Inc.	7,259
248	Presbyterian Healthcare Services	7,253
249	Pilot Corporation	7,200
250	Outsourcing Solutions Inc.	7,200
251	Jordan Industries, Inc.	7,200
252	Metaldyne Corporation	7,100
253	National Service Industries, Inc.	7,100
254	Columbia University	7,100
255	Cabela's Inc.	7,041
256	United Supermarkets, Ltd.	7,000
257	Lanoga Corporation	7,000
258	Crown Equipment Corporation	7,000
259	Quexco Incorporated	7,000
260	VT Inc.	7,000
261	Oxford Automotive, Inc.	7,000
262	Black & Veatch Holding Company	7,000
263	Beaulieu of America, LLC	7,000
264	EnerSys Inc.	7,000
265	Cumberland Farms, Inc.	6,976
266	Pella Corporation	6,945
267	Klaussner Furniture Industries	6,900
268	Sinclair Oil Corporation	6,900
269	Team Health, Inc.	6,800
270	Northwestern University	6,800
271	Jostens, Inc.	6,700
272	Keystone Foods LLC	6,700
273	QuikTrip Corporation	6,575
274	TIAA-CREF	6,500
275	WinCo Foods, Inc.	6,500
276	American Cancer Society, Inc.	6,500
277	McKee Foods Corporation	6,500
278	Rich Products Corporation	6,500
279	Genmar Holdings, Inc.	6,500
280	Greenville Hospital System	6,500
281	Sealy Corporation	6,480
282	Arctic Slope Regional	6,413
283	The SF Holdings Group, Inc.	6,370
284	Lane Industries, Inc.	6,350
285	Delco Remy International, Inc.	6,338
286	Williamson-Dickie Manufacturing	6,300
287	PeaceHealth	6,230
288	Carpenter Co.	6,200
289	Ingram Industries Inc.	6,148
290	Builders FirstSource	6,100
291	Marc Glassman Inc.	6,100
292	Carter Holdings, Inc.	6,083
293	Ashley Furniture Industries, Inc.	6,000
294	Averitt Express, Inc.	6,000
295	Safelite Group, Inc.	6,000
296	Visa International	6,000
297	GeoLogistics Corporation	6,000
298	Les Schwab Tire Centers	6,000
299	Underwriters Laboratories Inc.	6,000
300	Russell Stover Candies Inc.	6,000

The *Inc.* 500 Fastest-Growing Private Companies in America

Rank	Company	Headquarters	1998-2002 Sales Growth Increase (%)
1	American Biophysics	East Greenwich, RI	25,615
2	Under Armour Performance Apparel	Baltimore, MD	12,753
3	Áegis Assisted Living	Redmond, WA	12,449
4	Rent Rite	Boca Raton, FL	12,359
5	Cross Match Technologies	Palm Beach Gardens, FL	11,517
6	Blackboard	Washington, DC	11,047
7	Proflowers	San Diego, CA	10,783
8	Technology and Management Associates	Galloway, NJ	9,508
9	180s	Baltimore, MD	9,249
10	The Access Group	Atlanta, GA	9,058
11	Floorgraphics	Princeton, NJ	7,480
12	Coventry First	Fort Washington, PA	7,112
13	edocs	Natick, MA	7,082
14	Vesta	Portland, OR	6,330
15	4life Research	Sandy, UT	6,108
16	Network Telephone	Pensacola, FL	6,093
17	Tastefully Simple	Alexandria, MN	5,710
18	United Underwriters Insurance	Provo, UT	5,657
19	SupplyCore	Rockford, IL	5,612
20	TPi Billing Solutions	Tulsa, OK	5,197
21	AnswerNet Network	Princeton, NJ	4,954
22	Epsilon Systems Solutions	San Diego, CA	4,921
23	Advanced Business Fulfillment	Earth City, MO	4,895
24	Tesoro	Virginia Beach, VA	4,705
25	Atlantic Credit & Finance	Roanoke, VA	4,386
26	Sterling Financial Group	Boca Raton, FL	4,370
27	Magnet Communications	Atlanta, GA	4,291
28	Y2 Marketing	DeSoto, TX	4,009
29	ForeRunner	Lakewood, CO	3,974
30	Preferred Systems Solutions	Fairfax, VA	3,961
31	Motive Communications	Austin, TX	3,748
32	Pangea	Chesterfield, MO	3,683
33	TruStar Solutions	Fishers, IN	3,379
34	Clover Technologies Group	Ottawa, IL	3,320
35	Outsource Group, The	Walnut Creek, CA	3,303
36	Mythic Entertainment	Fairfax, VA	3,198
37	CCBN	Boston, MA	3,171
38	Orange Glo International	Greenwood Village, CO	3,156
39	World Development	Palm Desert, CA	3,139
40	Ikano Communications	Salt Lake City, UT	3,120
41	Speakeasy	Seattle, WA	3,041
42	Synhrgy HR Technologies	Houston, TX	2,978
43	Starmark International	Fort Lauderdale, FL	2,929
44	Conquest	Annapolis Junction, MD	2,898
45	Ace Mortgage Funding	Indianapolis, IN	2,801
46	Mercury Online Solutions	Brainbridge Island, WA	2,789
47	iProspect	Arlington, MA	2,758
48	CaseStack	Los Angeles, CA	2,721
49	Auction Systems Auctioneers & Appraisers	Phoenix, AZ	2,516
50	Prometheus Laboratories	San Diego, CA	2,499
51	Cooktek	Chicago, IL	2,496
52	Argon Engineering Associates	Fairfax, VA	2,465
53	Ed Necco & Associates	South Point, OH	2,446
54	CRAssociates	Newington, VA	2,442
55	Electronic Cash Systems	Rancho Santa Margarita, CA	2,412
56	bigdough.com	Bethesda, MD	2,374
57	Portage Environmental	Espanola, NM	2,207
58	Kortec	Beverly, MA	2,178
59	Carteret Mortgage	Centreville, VA	2,169
60	Chadco Enterprises	Sarasota, FL	2,160
61	The Scooter Store	New Braunfels, TX	2,147
62	Vision Systems Group	Somerset, NJ	2,043
63	BankServ	San Francisco, CA	2,026
64	Noodles & Co.	Boulder, CO	2,011
65	Wireless Retail	Scottsdale, AZ	2,003
66	Newtel Holdings	Minneapolis, MN	1,979
67	Cultural Experiences Abroad	Tempe, AZ	1,921
68	The Diamond Group	Dallas, TX	1,911
69	Denali Ventures	Cheyenne, WY	1,896
70	IntraLinks	New York, NY	1,895
71	Color Kinetics	Boston, MA	1,885
72	Research Pharmaceutical Services	Plymouth Meeting, PA	1,882
73	Sierra Design Group	Reno, NV	1,881
74	3t Systems	Denver, CO	1,867
75	Marlin Leasing	Mount Laurel, NJ	1,846
76	Diversitech	Cincinatti, OH	1,844
77	Automated License Systems	Nashville, TN	1,816
78	Oakleaf Waste Management	East Hartford, CT	1,796
79	eCopy	Nashua, NH	1,776
80	Columbia Data Products	Altamonte Springs, FL	1,756
81	iDirect Technologies	Reston, VA	1,755
82	Cardtronics	Houston, TX	1,742
83	ISite Design	Portland, OR	1,729
84	Global Brand Marketing	Santa Barbara, CA	1,708
85	Proven Direct	Menomonee Falls, WI	1,683
86	Noble Fiber Technologies	Clarks Summit, PA	1,658
87	SecureInfo	San Antonio, TX	1,628
88	Performance Software	Phoenix, AZ	1,625
89	Massini Group	Hillsboro, OR	1,609
90	Red Peacock International	Glendale, CA	1,582
91	MasiMax Resources	Rockville, MD	1,568
92	Shred First	Spartanburg, SC	1,551
93	Restaurant Partners	Orlando, FL	1,550
94	Casabyte	Renton, WA	1,545
95	C&A Industries	Omaha, NE	1,538
96	Refinery	Huntingdon Valley, PA	1,527
97	Aelita Software	Dublin, OH	1,520
98	HSU Development	Rockville, MD	1,511
99	Freedom Medical	Exton, PA	1,510
100	Legal Network	Pittsburgh, PA	1,496

SOURCE: *INC.*; OCTOBER 15, 2003

The *Inc.* 500 Fastest-Growing Private Companies in America (continued)

Rank	Company	Headquarters	1998-2002 Sales Growth Increase (%)
101	LTM	Havelock, NC	1,491
102	The Artery Group	Bethesda, MD	1,473
103	PowerLight	Berkeley, CA	1,469
104	PlayNetwork	Redmond, WA	1,466
105	AmeriPay Payroll	Elk Grove Village, IL	1,466
106	Liberty Tax Service	Virginia Beach, VA	1,462
107	No Brainer Enterprises	Houston, TX	1,452
108	American Ironhorse Motorcycle	Fort Worth, TX	1,445
109	httprint	San Francisco, CA	1,434
110	Spotfire	Somerville, MA	1,400
111	Catapult Technology	Bethesda, MD	1,389
112	Electronic Consulting Services	Reston, VA	1,381
113	Integrated DisAbility Resources	Bloomfield, CT	1,372
114	DrinkWorks!	Newport Beach, CA	1,360
115	RetroBox	Columbus, OH	1,358
116	Professional Placement Resources	Jacksonville Beach, FL	1,350
117	Honest Tea	Bethesda, MD	1,333
118	Hat World	Indianapolis, IN	1,312
119	CSI Network Services	Broadview Heights, OH	1,306
120	Milestone Group	Arlington, VA	1,297
121	Family First Mortgage	Palm Coast, FL	1,292
122	Rochester MicroSystems	Rochester, NY	1,276
123	Open Systems of Cleveland	Cleveland, OH	1,271
124	The Myers Group	Snellville, GA	1,266
125	Blue Pumpkin	Sunnyvale, CA	1,266
126	Paradigm Solutions	Rockville, MD	1,247
127	Quality Assured Services	Orlando, FL	1,246
128	Landmark Protection	San Jose, CA	1,246
129	AES Consulting	San Francisco, CA	1,244
130	Keurig	Wakefield, MA	1,242
131	Trios Associates	Lanham, MD	1,232
132	International Software Systems	Greenbelt, MD	1,201
133	Defender Security	Indianapolis, IN	1,194
134	Meridian Knowledge Solutions	Chantilly, VA	1,191
135	Gameplan Financial Marketing	Woodstock, GA	1,183
136	Wood Flooring International	Delran, NJ	1,167
137	PharmaFab	Grand Prairie, TX	1,145
138	Laboratory Management Systems	New Castle, DE	1,137
139	Capitol	Sacramento, CA	1,135
140	ProClarity	Boise, ID	1,126
141	Stake Center Locating	Salt Lake City, UT	1,126
142	Eze Castle Software	Boston, MA	1,123
143	Support Services of America	Norwalk, CA	1,117
144	Extra Mile Transportation	Buffalo, NY	1,114
145	National Bankcard Systems	Austin, TX	1,110
146	Advanced Data Services	Mt. Pleasant, SC	1,106
147	Commercial Energy of Montana	Cut Bank, MT	1,105
148	Quorum Business Solutions	Dallas, TX	1,101
149	C3i	New York, NY	1,100
150	Milestone Construction Services	Sterling, VA	1,096
151	Human Capital	Southfield, MI	1,082
152	Bridgeway Capital Management	Houston, TX	1,079
153	The ASI Show	Trevose, PA	1,071
154	Brightstar	Miami, FL	1,064
155	Zoup! Fresh Soup	Ferndale, MI	1,055
156	Logistics Management Services	Eagan, MN	1,055
157	Card USA	Hollywood, FL	1,052
158	MRE Consulting	Houston, TX	1,051
159	ActiveLight	Poulsbo, WA	1,046
160	CourtSmart Digital Systems	N. Chelmsford, MA	1,045
161	Powercom Electrical Services	Bronx, NY	1,039
162	SafeHome Security	Provo, UT	1,032
163	MyFamily.com	Provo, UT	1,026
164	Wolf Electronix	Orem, UT	1,009
165	Trasys	Cincinnati, OH	1,004
166	FurnitureFind	Buchanan, MI	1,003
167	ITS Corporation	Oxnard, CA	998
168	New York Staffing Services	New York, NY	997
169	Plexus Com/Group	Baltimore, MD	980
170	ScriptSave	Tuscon, AZ	968
171	Campbell Alliance	Raleigh, NC	962
172	Cafe Rio	Orem, UT	961
173	Beacon Technologies	Nashville, TN	960
174	car.com	Troy, MI	943
175	Business Plus	Hampton, VA	938
176	Court Reporter's Clearinghouse	Houston, TX	937
177	Fetch Logistics	Amherst, NY	937
178	SubZero Constructors	Lake Forest, CA	935
179	Capella Education Company	Minneapolis, MN	922
180	Co-Advantage Resources	Orlando, FL	914
181	Tommy Bahama Footwear	Phoenix, AZ	912
182	Envision Telephony	Seattle, WA	911
183	IMS Engineers	Jackson, MS	908
184	Earth Sun Moon Trading Company	Grove City, PA	895
185	Omniture	Orem, UT	892
186	Comfort Research	Grand Rapids, MI	890
187	Enterprise Computing Solutions	Mission Viejo, CA	887
188	Managed Care Network	Niagara Falls, NY	880
189	Complex Litigation Integrators	Tinton Falls, NJ	870
190	Adea Solutions	Dallas, TX	863
191	Gray Hawk Systems	Alexandria, VA	862
192	Health Dialog Services	Boston , MA	860
193	Unica	Waltham, MA	857
194	GHR Systems	Wayne, PA	848
195	Innovative Lighting	Roland, IA	842
196	Intrasphere Technologies	New York, NY	840
197	Click Wine Group	Seattle, WA	840
198	Joseph Sheairs Associates	Shamong, NJ	834
199	Schoollink	Fayetteville, NC	831
200	Lenco Marine	Stuart, FL	830

The *Inc.* 500 Fastest-Growing Private Companies in America (continued)

Rank	Company	Headquarters	1998-2002 Sales Growth Increase (%)
201	Trinity Springs	Ketchum, ID	826
202	Belzon	Huntsville, AL	820
203	Quotable Cards	New York, NY	819
204	American Pie	Syosset, NY	815
205	IVCi	Hauppauge, NY	813
206	Questar Capital	Ann Arbor, MI	808
207	American Megacom	Livonia, MI	808
208	Softscape	Wayland, MA	807
209	Timber Blind and Shutter	McKinney, TX	806
210	StoneTech Professional	Walnut Creek, CA	804
211	Superchips	Longwood, FL	801
212	Afterburner, Inc.	Atlanta, GA	801
213	For Any Occasion	Tampa, FL	800
214	Partners of Progress	Bloomfield Hills, MI	799
215	Arrow Financial Services	Niles, IL	797
216	Windmill International	Nashua, NH	793
217	QSS Group	Lanham, MD	788
218	Royal Mortgage	Princeton, NJ	786
219	Maui Wowi	Littleton, CO	779
220	Fionda	Santa Barbara, CA	777
221	Resort Golf Group	Scottsdale, AZ	776
222	Potbelly Sandwich Works	Chicago, IL	770
223	Spectrum Communications Cabling Services	Corona, CA	761
224	Navarro Research & Engineering	Oak Ridge, TN	759
225	Simply Certificates	Guilderland, NY	758
226	Republic State Mortgage	Houston, TX	754
227	E. A. Technologies	Hauppauge, NY	753
228	Texas Residential Mortgage/Bankers Alliance	Dallas, TX	750
229	Pepperweed Consulting	Pittsburgh, PA	749
230	Links Medical Products	Irvine, CA	740
231	Valley Oak Systems	Alamo, CA	738
232	Back to Basics Products	Bluffdale, UT	738
233	American Services Technology	Cocoa, FL	736
234	StreetGlow	Wayne, NJ	733
235	SoftArtisans	Brookline, MA	733
236	Ho-Chunk	Winnebago, NE	731
237	Integra Telecom	Beaverton, OR	728
238	Flake-Wilkerson Market Insights	Little Rock, AR	727
239	AdminSolutions	Charlotte, NC	725
240	ProtoTest	Englewood, CO	724
241	Airborne 1	Los Angeles, CA	723
242	Recovered Capital	Fort Walton Beach, FL	717
243	Micro Solutions Enterprises	Chatsworth, CA	717
244	The Good Home Co.	New York, NY	712
245	Contract Recruiting	Palos Verdes Estates, CA	708
246	Access Communications	Summit, NJ	707
247	AutoComm	Appleton, WI	702
248	TeleChem International	Sunnyvale, CA	697
249	BCC	Glen Burnie, MD	693
250	BCS Industries	Memphis, TN	692

Rank	Company	Headquarters	1998-2002 Sales Growth Increase (%)
251	Network Management Resources	Severna Park, MD	691
252	Royal Buying Group	Hindsdale, IL	691
253	ComFrame Software	Birmingham, AL	691
254	Blue Star Food Products	Miami, FL	689
255	Omega Insurance Services	St. Petersburg, FL	689
256	Soneticom	West Melbourne, FL	688
257	Project Assistants	Wilmington, DE	687
258	Marlabs	Edison, NJ	684
259	V2	Blue Bell, PA	682
260	Unicru	Beaverton, OR	682
261	W. Ray Wallace & Associates	Alpharetta, GA	680
262	Asset Acceptance	Warren, MI	677
263	National Heritage Acadamies	Grand Rapids, MI	673
264	Digital Visual Display Technologies	Atlanta, GA	671
265	Strategic Data Systems	San Diego, CA	670
266	Connected Corporation	Framingham, MA	665
267	Redbarn Pet Products	Long Beach, CA	664
268	ReyHan PGF	Eagan, MN	659
269	Scott Pipitone Design	Pittsburgh, PA	656
270	AccuForce Staffing Services	Kingsport, TN	653
271	Thinknicity	San Francisco, CA	653
272	Melton Franchise Systems	Carpinteria, CA	647
273	Spenser Communications	Irwindale, CA	647
274	USA Funding	Brookfield, WI	644
275	Conquest Systems	Washington, DC	642
276	MindWorks	Santa Clara, CA	641
277	Entology	Bedminster, NJ	641
278	MicroTek	Oakbrook Terrace, IL	636
279	Comm-Works	Plymouth, MN	634
280	Avino Construction	E. Northport, NY	631
281	Burgess Construction Consultants	Richardson, TX	629
282	Obsidian Software	Austin, TX	628
283	Creditors Interchange	Buffalo, NY	625
284	AmeriQuest Transportation and Logistics Resources	Cherry Hill, NJ	624
285	Kaizen Direct	Rochester, NY	624
286	CareerStaff	Irvine, CA	623
287	Gold Crest Distributing	Mexico, MO	620
288	Sigma Analytics and Consulting	Atlanta, GA	620
289	L.E.M. Products	Harrison, OH	615
290	Employees Only	Troy, MI	613
291	Church Hill Classics	Danbury, CT	612
292	Custom Shop Clothiers, The	Sylvania, OH	611
293	Techni-Glass	Surgoinsville, TN	606
294	FlavorX	Bethesda, MD	605
295	Angie's List	Indianapolis, IN	605
296	Tourico Holiday Flights	Altamonte Springs, FL	604
297	Foremark	Dallas, TX	598
298	Capstone	Dallas, TX	596
299	Global Science and Technology	Greenbelt, MD	590
300	HealthScribe	Sterling, VA	589

The *Inc.* 500 Fastest-Growing Private Companies in America (continued)

Rank	Company	Headquarters	1998-2002 Sales Growth Increase (%)
301	Alexander Global Promotions	Bellevue, WA	588
302	VoiceLog	Gaithersburg, MD	587
303	Vitacost.com	Boynton Beach, FL	586
304	ZonePerfect Nutrition	Beverly, MA	584
305	Palm Beach Tan	Carrollton, TX	581
306	D&D Consulting	Albany, NY	581
307	Resulté Universal	Dallas, TX	580
308	Money Clip Magazine	Virginia Beach, VA	578
309	MapFrame	Dallas, TX	572
310	Gulf Coast Laundry Services	Gulfport, MS	571
311	Alogent	Alpharetta, GA	570
312	Open Software Solutions	Greensboro, NC	567
313	K & Company	Parkville, MO	563
314	Palladian Partners	Silver Spring, MD	562
315	Career Step	Springville, UT	562
316	DJM Sales & Marketing	Boise, ID	561
317	Staff Tech	Roseville, CA	559
318	Perseus Development Corporation	Braintree, MA	559
319	ABCO Maintenance	Staten Island, NY	558
320	Caliber Collision Centers	Irvine, CA	557
321	Trek Equipment	Sausalito, CA	557
322	CapTech Ventures	Richmond, VA	557
323	Insyght Interactive	Beverly Hills, CA	557
324	REI Systems	Annandale, VA	556
325	RTI Insurance Services of Florida	Fort Myers Beach, FL	556
326	Thinsolutions	Cleveland, OH	555
327	Decisionmark	Cedar Rapids, IA	555
328	Execuscribe	Rochester, NY	553
329	CNSI	Rockville, MD	553
330	LocalNet	Williamsville, NY	551
331	ScripNet	Las Vegas, NV	551
332	HomeRoute	Howell, MI	549
333	Advanced Technologies Group	West Des Moines, IA	549
334	Petron Pacific	Manassas, VA	548
335	Fiberlink Communications	Blue Bell, PA	545
336	Educational Directories Unlimited	Chester, PA	541
337	Stone Brewing	San Marcos, CA	540
338	WCI	Seattle, WA	540
339	Cardinal Cartridge	Elmhurst, IL	540
340	The Mosaic Co.	Renton, WA	538
341	Parksite	Batavia, IL	535
342	Network Outsource	New Hyde Park, NY	533
343	Atlantic Bay Mortgage Group	Virginia Beach, VA	532
344	Smartsoft International	Norcross, GA	530
345	Horizon Datacom Solutions	Columbus, OH	527
346	Mindbridge Software	Norristown, PA	523
347	Gryphon Technologies	Riverdale, MD	516
348	Spindustry Systems	Des Moines, IA	514
349	MicroPact Engineering	Herndon, VA	512
350	SmartOffice Services	Millersville, MD	512
351	Swiss Watch International	Hollywood, FL	510
352	AnviCom	Vienna, VA	509
353	Noble Logos	Cicero, IN	509
354	Ultimus	Cary, NC	506
355	Contract Counsel	Madison Heights, MI	504
356	Summit Products	Parker, CO	503
357	Calamos Investments	Naperville, IL	500
358	Randall Mortgage Services	Dublin, OH	500
359	Schaller Anderson	Phoenix, AZ	496
360	Luminex Software	Riverside, CA	496
361	ath Power Consulting	Andover, MA	494
362	Z Corp.	Burlington, MA	493
363	Cherokee Information Services	Arlington, VA	492
364	Bolt Staffing Service	Vallejo, CA	490
365	Tilson HR	Greenwood, IN	484
366	Heartland Payment Systems	Princeton, NJ	483
367	Authoria	Waltham, MA	482
368	DrinkMore Water	Gaithersburg, MD	481
369	HKS Medical Information Systems	Omaha, NE	481
370	Smartronix	California, MD	477
371	Network Presence	Los Angeles, CA	475
372	Quantum Logistics	Denver, CO	475
373	Maverick Technologies	Columbia, IL	474
374	Global Data Systems	Lafayette, LA	474
375	Strategic Management Initiatives	Gaithersburg, MD	473
376	Timberlane Woodcrafters	North Wales, PA	472
377	Heartland Dental Care	Effingham, IL	472
378	GRT	Stamford, CT	470
379	Integrity Staffing Solutions	Newark, DE	470
380	VIPdesk	Alexandria, VA	468
381	All Copy Products	Denver, CO	467
382	Franklin American Mortgage	Franklin, TN	465
383	Cambridge Home Health Care	Akron, OH	465
384	C&B Services	Port Neches, TX	465
385	Schultz Engineering Services	Poplar Bluff, MO	463
386	Franklin Financial Group	Southfield, MI	463
387	Socket Internet	Columbia, MO	462
388	McKeough Land Company	Grand Haven, MI	461
389	ProfitLine	San Diego, CA	461
390	Governor's Distributors	Miami, FL	460
391	Round Table Group	Chicago, IL	457
392	ArchivesOne	Waterbury, CT	454
393	Morgan Research	Huntsville, AL	454
394	USAData	New York, NY	453
395	Advanced Facilities Services	Cheektowaga, NY	453
396	TSE Sports & Entertainment	New York, NY	452
397	The Benecon Group	Leola, PA	452
398	Linksys	Irvine, CA	451
399	Momentum Marketing Services	Alexandria, VA	450
400	ReNew Life Formulas	Clearwater, FL	448

The *Inc.* 500 Fastest-Growing Private Companies in America (continued)

Rank	Company	Headquarters	1998-2002 Sales Growth Increase (%)
401	Cleaner Image Maintenance	Clackamas, OR	448
402	Future Computer Technologies	Sparks, NV	448
403	Pro2Serve	Oak Ridge, TN	442
404	Mathis, Earnest & Vandeventer	Cedar Falls, IA	439
405	Maverick Construction	Boston, MA	438
406	ATA Services	Salt Lake City, UT	438
407	Network Hardware Resale	Santa Barbara, CA	438
408	Jelec USA	Lafayette, LA	436
409	Just Marketing	Indianapolis, IN	436
410	Interactive Solutions	Memphis, TN	435
411	WRG Services	Willoughby, OH	435
412	NetAppl	San Ramon, CA	435
413	V-Span	King of Prussia, PA	430
414	InTouch	Vadnais Heights, MN	430
415	Diamond Drugs	Indiana, PA	429
416	Dancor	Columbus, OH	427
417	Blue Angel Technologies	Valley Forge, PA	424
418	Norstar Office Products	Commerce, CA	420
419	Blue Ridge Numerics	Charlottesville, VA	420
420	Radiant Research	Kirkland, WA	419
421	Shelko Consulting	Ridgewood, NJ	418
422	Advanced Vision Research	Woburn, MA	414
423	Bowman Consulting Group	Chantilly, VA	413
424	In Zone	Austell, GA	409
425	The Service Source	Adrian, MI	407
426	Savela & Associates	Birmingham, AL	405
427	Advanced Health Education Center	Houston, TX	405
428	Tropical Oasis	McKinney, TX	404
429	Great Lakes Media Technology	Mequon, WI	402
430	Mortgage Sources	Overland Park, KS	401
431	Beyond Now Technologies	Overland Park, KS	397
432	Great Works Internet	Biddeford, ME	396
433	ASG	Naples, FL	394
434	Engineering Solid Solutions	Southfield, MI	393
435	Juxtamark	Louisville, CO	393
436	Extreme Pizza	San Francisco, CA	388
437	Long Wave	Oklahoma City, OK	387
438	Lane Marketing Communications	Portland, OR	386
439	Staff One	Woodridge, IL	386
440	Coastal Capital Markets	Wilmington, NC	384
441	The Lloyd Group	New York, NY	383
442	Pride Products Distributors	Springfield, NJ	383
443	Advantage Credit International	Pensacola, FL	380
444	Software Professionals	Irving, TX	380
445	Network Express	Largo, FL	380
446	Amerisource Funding	Houston, TX	376
447	Paisley Consulting	Cokato, MN	376
448	A.M.E.'s Uniforms	Fort Lauderdale, FL	373
449	Mid-Atlantic Car Wash Technology	Charlottesville, VA	373
450	Pacific Data Designs	San Francisco, CA	372
451	Topics Entertainment	Renton, WA	371
452	Thunder Creek	Baltimore, MD	370
453	Heartlab	Westerly, RI	367
454	Dankoff Solar Products	Santa Fe, NM	366
455	Service Link	Aliquippa, PA	361
456	Adonix	Reston, VA	360
457	Mister Sparky	Marietta, GA	359
458	Advanced Vending Systems	Ringgold, GA	359
459	Interface Software	Oak Brook, IL	357
460	Grant Harrison Advertising	Houston, TX	357
461	Beador Construction	Newport Beach, CA	355
462	Direct Data	Horsham, PA	354
463	Chocoholics Divine Desserts	Stockton, CA	354
464	Virtium Technology	Irvine, CA	354
465	Print-Tech	Madison, WI	352
466	Elite Exteriors	Sandy, UT	351
467	J. C. Malone Associates	Louisville, KY	348
468	Southern Homes of the Upstate	Central, SC	348
469	Kraft Construction	Naples, FL	344
470	Berbee Information Networks	Madison, WI	343
471	Patterson Ventilation	Blythewood, SC	343
472	Marketing Resources	Chicago, IL	342
473	Maxons Restorations	New York, NY	342
474	NetTV	San Rafael, CA	341
475	Door to Door Storage	Kent, WA	339
476	Associated Business Systems	Portland, OR	338
477	Quantum Loyalty Systems	Incline Village, NV	336
478	GTS Refreshment Services	Kingsport, TN	336
479	Four Hands	Austin, TX	335
480	Randy's Ring & Pinion	Everett, WA	335
481	Monitronics International	Dallas, TX	334
482	PPM Consulting	West Monroe, LA	334
483	Isa Consulting	Blue Bell, PA	334
484	Campaigners	Redondo Beach, CA	331
485	Career Control Group	Dallas, TX	329
486	Home Instead Senior Care	Omaha, NE	328
487	Recom Group, The	San Dimas, CA	328
488	Fisher Mortgage	Vernon Hills, IL	328
489	Banfe	Barrington, NJ	327
490	Impulse Communications	Fountain Valley, CA	324
491	Stinger Industries	Murfreesboro, TN	326
492	Progressive Medical	Westerville, OH	326
493	Baci Fresh	Pompano Beach, FL	324
494	ConferenceCall.com	Carrollton, TX	324
495	S2Tech	Chesterfield, MO	323
496	Prosys Information Systems	Norcross, GA	321
497	SPL Integrated Solutions	Columbia, MD	319
498	DB Professionals	Portland, OR	319
499	Advertising Ventures	Providence, RI	319
500	Berks and Beyond Employment Services	West Reading, PA	312

The *Forbes* Largest Private Companies in the US

Rank	Company	Sales ($ mil.)
1	Cargill	59,894
2	Koch Industries	40,000
3	Mars	16,800
4	Publix Super Markets	16,027
5	PricewaterhouseCoopers	15,900
6	Ernst & Young	13,100
7	Bechtel	11,600
8	C&S Wholesale Grocers	11,300
9	Meijer	10,900
10	H.E. Butt Grocery	10,700
11	TRW Automotive	10,630
12	Huntsman	9,000
13	Fidelity Investments	8,937
14	Swift & Co.	8,380
15	JM Family Enterprises	7,600
16	Enterprise Rent-A-Car	6,900
17	Science Applications Intl.	5,902
18	Unisource	5,900
19	Marmon Group	5,756
20	Advance Publications	5,565
21	Menard	5,500
22	S.C. Johnson & Son	5,372
23	MDFC Holding	5,105
24	International Steel Group	5,000
25	Alticor	4,900
26	Giant Eagle	4,739
27	Cox Enterprises	4,444
28	Southern Wine & Spirits	4,400
29	MBM	4,236
30	Hy-Vee	4,230
31	Reyes Holdings	4,180
32	Levi Strauss & Co.	4,137
33	Hallmark Cards	4,039
34	Platinum Equity	4,000
35	Graybar Electric	3,975
36	Guardian Industries	3,940
37	Gulf States Toyota	3,750
38	InterTech Group	3,700
39	Peter Kiewit Sons'	3,699
40	Eby-Brown	3,670
41	Roundy's	3,638
42	Hearst	3,565
43	The Schwan Food Co.	3,500
44	Milliken & Co.	3,419
45	Flying J	3,417
46	Raley's	3,200
47	J.R. Simplot	3,100
48	Wegmans Food Markets	3,020
49	Bloomberg	3,000
50	Gordon Food Service	3,000

Rank	Company	Sales ($ mil.)
51	McKinsey & Co.	3,000
52	Kohler	2,940
53	QuikTrip	2,815
54	Apex Oil	2,800
55	Clark Enterprises	2,800
56	Gilbane	2,771
57	Quality King Distributors	2,700
58	Stater Bros. Markets	2,700
59	Capital Group of Cos.	2,665
60	JohnsonDiversey	2,659
61	HT Hackney	2,650
62	Keystone Foods	2,600
63	Schneider National	2,600
64	Kinray	2,500
65	Perdue Farms	2,500
66	International Data Group	2,410
67	Transammonia	2,309
68	Consolidated Elec. Distributors	2,300
69	OSI Group	2,300
70	Springs Industries	2,300
71	Sinclair Oil	2,290
72	Wawa	2,272
73	Edward Jones	2,270
74	Ingram Industries	2,250
75	RaceTrac Petroleum	2,250
76	Belk	2,242
77	Tenaska Energy	2,231
78	A-Mark Financial	2,200
79	Booz Allen Hamilton	2,200
80	Schnuck Markets	2,200
81	Services Group of America	2,200
82	84 Lumber	2,177
83	Sirva	2,177
84	Alex Lee	2,170
85	Golub	2,100
86	Gulf Oil	2,100
87	Renco Group	2,100
88	H Group Holding	2,047
89	Allegis Group	2,035
90	Grant Thornton International	2,010
91	Andersen	2,000
92	Black & Veatch	2,000
93	ContiGroup Cos.	2,000
94	Cumberland Farms	2,000
95	Fry's Electronics	2,000
96	Jeld-Wen Holding	2,000
97	KB Toys	2,000
98	Kinko's	2,000
99	Schreiber Foods	2,000
100	CH2M Hill Companies	1,999

Rank	Company	Sales ($ mil.)
101	JF Shea	1,994
102	Quintiles Transnational	1,992
103	Tishman Realty & Construction	1,980
104	Sammons Enterprises	1,950
105	Hunt Consolidated/Hunt Oil	1,930
106	Houchens Industries	1,913
107	DeMoulas Super Markets	1,900
108	Leprino Foods	1,900
109	Sheetz	1,900
110	Nortek Holdings	1,888
111	Brookshire Grocery	1,884
112	Software House Intl.	1,875
113	Whiting-Turner Contracting	1,874
114	Hensel Phelps Construction	1,872
115	TravelCenters of America	1,870
116	Follett	1,851
117	Aecom Technology	1,850
118	Dr Pepper/7 Up Bottling Group	1,820
119	Hunt Construction Group	1,820
120	DreamWorks SKG	1,813
121	Quad/Graphics	1,800
122	Scoular	1,800
123	Rich Products	1,784
124	E&J Gallo Winery	1,760
125	Walsh Group	1,754
126	Purity Wholesale Grocers	1,750
127	Carlson Cos.	1,745
128	Crown Central Petroleum	1,737
129	DeBruce Grain	1,729
130	Musicland Group	1,727
131	UniGroup	1,708
132	Golden State Foods	1,700
133	AG Spanos Cos.	1,700
134	Structure Tone	1,700
135	WinCo Foods	1,700
136	Zachry Construction	1,700
137	Asplundh Tree Expert	1,678
138	Venture Industries	1,676
139	Vertis	1,675
140	Dunn Industries	1,655
141	Save Mart Supermarkets	1,655
142	General Parts	1,651
143	Glazer's Wholesale Drug	1,615
144	Bashas'	1,600
145	Bose	1,600
146	Central National-Gottesman	1,600
147	Delaware North Cos.	1,600
148	Mary Kay	1,600
149	National Distributing	1,600
150	Dresser	1,595

SOURCE: *FORBES*; NOVEMBER 6, 2003

The *Forbes* Largest Private Companies in the US (continued)

Rank	Company	Sales ($ mil.)
151	DiGiorgio	1,560
152	Swinerton	1,560
153	Purdue Pharma	1,551
154	Parsons	1,534
155	Builders FirstSource	1,533
156	Frank Consolidated Enterprises	1,500
157	Grocers Supply	1,500
158	McWane	1,500
159	Metaldyne	1,500
160	Colonial Group	1,480
161	Life Care Centers of America	1,460
162	Medline Industries	1,454
163	Lanoga	1,453
164	Flint Ink	1,450
165	Towers Perrin	1,441
166	Maritz	1,440
167	Metromedia	1,435
168	Foster Farms	1,434
169	National Gypsum	1,430
170	ABC Supply	1,425
171	Discount Tire	1,417
172	Amsted Industries	1,415
173	Reinhart Foodservice	1,411
174	Dot Foods	1,410
175	Ashley Furniture Industries	1,400
176	Ebsco Industries	1,400
177	Heico Cos.	1,400
178	Kingston Technology	1,400
179	Southwire	1,400
180	Ergon	1,380
181	Bass Pro	1,370
182	Parsons Brinckerhoff	1,370
183	The F. Dohmen Co.	1,368
184	G-I Holdings	1,361
185	Day & Zimmermann	1,351
186	Barton Malow	1,350
187	Battelle Memorial Institute	1,350
188	Love's Travel Stops	1,350
189	Vanguard Health Systems	1,341
190	Ben E. Keith	1,335
191	W.L. Gore & Associates	1,330
192	Sierra Pacific Industries	1,330
193	Haworth	1,320
194	Skadden, Arps	1,310
195	Ardent Healthcare Services	1,305
196	Rooms to Go	1,300
197	VarTec Telecom	1,300
198	Sweetheart Holdings	1,286
199	Domino's Pizza	1,275
200	Taylor	1,269
201	Barnes & Noble College Bookstores	1,264
202	Rooney Brothers	1,262
203	Cabela's	1,250
204	Holiday Cos.	1,250
205	Borden Chemical	1,248
206	Sunbelt Beverage	1,240
207	JM Huber	1,231
208	Wilbur-Ellis	1,223
209	TIC Holdings	1,221
210	Ritz Camera Centers	1,219
211	Houghton Mifflin	1,211
212	Baker & Taylor	1,203
213	Columbia House	1,200
214	Esselte	1,200
215	Lucasfilm	1,200
216	Rosen's Diversified	1,200
217	Truman Arnold Cos.	1,200
218	Vought Aircraft Industries	1,200
219	Big Y Foods	1,190
220	Sealy	1,189
221	FHC Health Systems	1,188
222	Shamrock Foods	1,186
223	SAS Institute	1,180
224	Conair	1,176
225	Michael Foods	1,168
226	U.S. Oil	1,166
227	Hobby Lobby Stores	1,164
228	National Waterworks	1,162
229	Horizon Natural Resources	1,155
230	Young's Market	1,155
231	Red Apple Group	1,150
232	Baker & McKenzie	1,134
233	North Pacific Group	1,132
234	SSA Marine	1,131
235	Goodman Manufacturing	1,130
236	Anderson News	1,128
237	Dart Container	1,127
238	Gould Paper	1,125
239	Burger King	1,120
240	Carpenter	1,114
241	Golden Rule Financial	1,109
242	Boar's Head Provisions	1,100
243	Dick Corp.	1,100
244	Key Safety Systems	1,100
245	Maines Paper & Foodservice	1,100
246	New Balance Athletic Shoe	1,100
247	Primus	1,100
248	Dunavant Enterprises	1,099
249	BE&K	1,098
250	Modern Continental Cos.	1,098
251	Herbalife International	1,094
252	Iasis Healthcare	1,073
253	L.L. Bean	1,070
254	Genmar Holdings	1,070
255	Ingram Entertainment Hldgs.	1,070
256	Delco Remy International	1,069
257	Noveon	1,069
258	K-VA-T Food Stores	1,063
259	American Tire Distributors	1,060
260	Austin Industries	1,056
261	Printpack	1,053
262	Bellco Health	1,050
263	Boscov's	1,050
264	Fiesta Mart	1,050
265	Meridian Automotive Systems	1,050
266	DPR Construction	1,049
267	Watkins Associated Industries	1,038
268	Menasha	1,025
269	Pella	1,025
270	McCarthy Building Cos.	1,024
271	M. A. Mortenson	1,024
272	Yates Cos.	1,022
273	Boston Consulting Group	1,020
274	Klein Wholesale Distributors	1,015
275	Icon Health & Fitness	1,012
276	Brasfield & Gorrie	1,011
277	Connell Limited Partnership	1,000
278	HP Hood	1,000
279	Levitz Home Furnishings	1,000
280	Oxford Automotive	1,000
281	Swagelok	1,000

Top 20 Universities

Rank	School
1	Harvard University
1	Princeton University
3	Yale University
4	Massachusetts Institute of Technology
5	California Institute of Technology
5	Duke University
5	Stanford University
5	University of Pennsylvania
9	Dartmouth College
9	Washington University in St. Louis
11	Columbia University
11	Northwestern University
13	University of Chicago
14	Cornell University
14	Johns Hopkins University
16	Rice University
17	Brown University
18	Emory University
19	University of Notre Dame
19	Vanderbilt University

*Ranked by composite score, including such factors as graduation and retention rates, faculty resources, and student-to-faculty ratio.

SOURCE: *U.S. NEWS AND WORLD REPORT*, SEPTEMBER 1, 2003

Top 20 US Foundations

Rank	Name	State	Assets ($ mil.)
1	Bill & Melinda Gates Foundation	WA	24,082.1
2	Lilly Endowment Inc.	IN	10,054.0
3	The Ford Foundation	NY	9,300.1
4	J. Paul Getty Trust	CA	8,623.8
5	The Robert Wood Johnson Foundation	NJ	8,012.4
6	The David and Lucile Packard Foundation	CA	6,196.5
7	The William and Flora Hewlett Foundation	CA	6,080.7
8	W. K. Kellogg Foundation	MI	5,530.5
9	The Starr Foundation	NY	4,781.1
10	John D. and Catherine T. MacArthur Foundation	IL	4,215.9
11	The Pew Charitable Trusts	PA	3,753.6
12	The Andrew W. Mellon Foundation	NY	3,600.6
13	The California Endowment	CA	3,366.3
14	The Annie E. Casey Foundation	MD	2,709.4
15	The Rockefeller Foundation	NY	2,679.1
16	The Annenberg Foundation	PA	2,354.8
17	Casey Family Programs	WA	2,349.8
18	Robert W. Woodruff Foundation, Inc.	GA	2,210.2
19	The Kresge Foundation	MI	2,164.5
20	The Duke Endowment	NC	2,084.8

SOURCE: THE FOUNDATION CENTER (WWW.FDNCENTER.ORG), OCTOBER 27, 2003

Top 20 US Law Firms

Rank	Law Firm	Gross Revenue ($ mil.)	Number of Lawyers
1	Skadden, Arps, Slate, Meagher & Flom	1,310.0	1,632
2	Baker & McKenzie	1,060.0	3,156
3	Jones Day	908.0	1,698
4	Latham & Watkins	906.0	1,393
5	Sidley Austin Brown & Wood	831.0	1,377
6	Mayer, Brown, Rowe & Maw	705.0	1,181
7	Shearman & Sterling	700.0	969
8	Weil, Gotshal & Manges	688.0	925
9	White & Case	675.0	1,463
10	McDermott, Will & Emery	628.0	897
11	Sullivan & Cromwell	624.0	643
12	Kirkland & Ellis	611.0	765
13	Akin Gump Strauss Hauer & Feld	575.0	864
14	Davis Polk & Wardwell	570.0	595
15	Gibson, Dunn & Crutcher	569.0	721
16	O'Melveny & Myers	565.0	792
17	Morgan, Lewis & Bockius	557.5	1,055
18	Simpson Thacher & Bartlett	543.5	626
19	Cleary, Gottlieb Steen & Hamilton	531.0	695
20	Holland & Knight	514.5	1,162

SOURCE: *AMERICAN LAWYER*, JULY 2003

Top 20 Tax & Accounting Firms by US Revenue

Rank	Firm	Headquarters	2002 US Revenue ($ mil.)
1	Deloitte & Touche	New York	5,933.0
2	PricewaterhouseCoopers	New York	5,174.0
3	Ernst & Young	New York	4,515.0
4	KPMG	New York	3,400.0
5	H&R Block Inc.	Kansas City, MO	3,317.7
6	RSM McGladrey /McGladrey & Pullen	Bloomington, MN	584.6
7	Grant Thornton	Chicago	400.7
8	American Express Tax & Business Services	New York	367.5
9	Century Business Services	Cleveland	360.0
10	BDO Seidman	Chicago	353.0
11	Jackson Hewitt Inc.	Parsippany, NJ	330.2
12	BKD	Springfield, MO	210.9
13	Crowe, Chizek and Co.	Indianapolis	204.6
14	Moss Adams	Seattle	174.5
15	Centerprise Advisors Inc.	Chicago	168.0
16	Plante & Moran	Southfield, MI	161.4
17	Clifton Gunderson	Peoria, IL	136.7
18	Fiducial Inc.	New York	101.1
19	Virchow, Krause & Co.	Madison, WI	96.4
20	Gilman + Clocia Inc.	Poughkeepsie, NY	91.7

SOURCE: *ACCOUNTING TODAY*, MARCH 17-APRIL 6, 2003

Hoover's Handbook of

Private Companies

The Companies

24 Hour Fitness Worldwide Inc.

If you're holding too much weight, 24 Hour Fitness Worldwide has the solution. It owns and operates more than 300 fitness centers that offer aerobic, cardiovascular, and weight lifting activities. Some facilities also feature squash, racquetball, and basketball courts; swimming pools; steam and sauna rooms; tanning rooms; and whirlpools. The centers are located in 16 states in the US, as well as in Europe and Asia. Investment partnership McCown De Leeuw & Co. is the leading investor in the firm, which was founded in 1983 by CEO Mark Mastrov. The company has bought the Q Clubs and Hart's Athletic Clubs chains, which it converted to 24 Hour Fitness locations.

EXECUTIVES

Chairman and CEO: Mark S. Mastrov
EVP and CFO: Colin Heggie
EVP Sales and Marketing: Craig Pepin-Donat
VP Health Services and Corporate Accounts: Kevin Steele
VP Human Resources: John Putereaugh
VP and Assistant General Counsel: Joseph Freschi
President, 24 Hour Fitness USA: Brian Bouma
CIO: Lee Kennedy
Corporate Director, Group Exercise: Donna Meyer
Director of Corporate Group Sales, Midwest Division: Stefani Hoery
Director of Corporate Group Sales, Northern California: Ben Midgley
Director of Corporate Group Sales, Pacific Northwest Division: Michelle Briede
Director of Corporate Group Sales, Southern California: Daryl Hawkins
Director of Corporate Group Sales, Texas: Eric Frazier
Director of Team Sports Marketing: Chris Feder
Corporate Account Director, Central California Division: Jad Hassan
Public Relations Manager: Shannon May
Auditors: Deloitte & Touche

LOCATIONS

HQ: 12647 Alcosta Blvd., 5th Fl., San Ramon, CA 94583
Phone: 925-543-3100 **Fax:** 925-543-3229
Web: www.24hourfitness.com

24 Hour Fitness Worldwide operates clubs in China, Denmark, Germany, South Korea, Norway, Singapore, Spain, Sweden, Taiwan, Thailand, and the US.

COMPETITORS

Bally Total Fitness
Curves International
Gold's Gym
Jazzercise
Lift Club
Physical Spa & Fitness
The Sports Club
World Gym
YMCA
YWCA

HISTORICAL FINANCIALS

Company Type: Private

Income Statement FYE December 31

	REVENUE ($ mil.)	NET INCOME ($ mil.)	NET PROFIT MARGIN	EMPLOYEES
12/01	1,029	—	—	27,000
12/00	911	—	—	26,794
12/99	736	—	—	19,500
12/98	330	—	—	15,000
12/97	262	—	—	11,500
12/96	180	—	—	—
12/95	98	—	—	—
12/94	41	—	—	—
12/93	33	—	—	—
Annual Growth	53.7%	—	—	23.8%

Revenue History

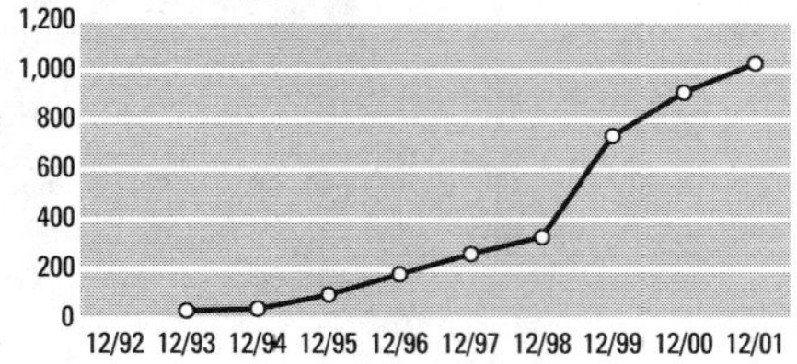

84 Lumber Company

With its no-frills stores (most don't have air conditioning or heating), 84 Lumber has built itself to be a low-cost provider of lumber and building materials. Through more than 430 stores, the company, which is the nation's largest privately held building-materials supplier, sells lumber, siding, drywalls, windows, and other supplies, as well as kits to make barns, playsets, decks, and even homes. Its stores are in about 35 states, mainly in the East, Southeast, and Midwest; 84 Lumber also sells products internationally. CEO Joseph Hardy Sr. founded 84 Lumber in 1956; his daughter, president Maggie Hardy Magerko, owns about 80% of the firm.

Founded to serve professionals, 84 Lumber expanded its product offering to attract more DIY consumers. It has since re-shifted its focus to professional builders and remodelers, who account for about 80% of sales. A sister company, 84 Components, operates 10 truss and wall-panel plants in eight states with plans to build another 10. While the professional market is less profitable and more cyclic than the DIY segment, it has the advantage of being less crowded with heavy competitors such as The Home Depot and Lowe's.

84 Lumber is also reconfiguring stores for individual markets; this includes adding more lumber inventory and specialty services, as well as expanding its 84-Plus store format (lumberyard *plus* hardware store).

HISTORY

In 1956 Joseph Hardy Sr. opened the first 84 Lumber store in Eighty Four, Pennsylvania, a town near Pittsburgh. Hardy epitomized the bare-bones approach, keeping a tight rein on his company and paying cash for new building sites.

The strategy was successful, and for the next two decades 84 Lumber prospered, growing steadily to more than 350 stores in the early 1980s. But the 1980s brought trouble, not only for 84 Lumber but also within the Hardy family. Paul Hardy, the second-eldest son, left the company after continued sparring with Hardy Sr. Another son, Joe Hardy Jr., seemed to be his father's handpicked successor: He had worked for 84 Lumber since 1967, rising to the level of COO. However, Joe Jr. and Joe Sr. clashed and under pressure from his father, Joe Jr. resigned in 1988.

Joe Sr. also underwent a transformation during this time, opening his once-tight purse strings to buy himself an honorary English title — lord of the manor of Henley-in-Arden — for about $170,000. In 1987 he paid $3.1 million to purchase a retreat in southwestern Pennsylvania, the Nemacolin Woodlands. He placed the renovation of the resort (at the cost of some $100 million) in the hands of his daughter Maggie, who was in her early twenties at the time.

While Hardy was transforming, so was 84 Lumber. The company started moving away from its traditional approach in an attempt to gain a piece of the budding yuppie market. This approach, along with an ill-timed expansion, led to a loss of customers and falling profits. Earnings fell from $52 million in 1987 to $22 million in 1989.

84 Lumber started to right itself in 1991. Hardy transferred stock to Maggie, his heir apparent. While running luxury resort Nemacolin Woodlands, Maggie strove to emulate her father's business style, including obscenity-laced staff meetings. 84 Lumber shut stores and returned to its basic operating scheme as a low-cost provider of lumber in small towns. The company also added do-it-yourself (DIY) building kits for kitchens and baths that year, and it expanded that DIY concept a year later in 1992, with home building kits.

Under new president Maggie, 84 Lumber's sales topped the $1 billion mark in 1993 and the company refocused on its professional contractor customers. The company first shipped its building materials internationally in 1996 (to New Zealand) and added customers in China, Korea, Switzerland, and Australia in the late 1990s.

In 1997 84 Lumber opened Maggie's Building Solutions Showroom, a 7,500-sq.-ft. remodeling center featuring upscale home products. By 1997 84 Lumber was the US's largest dealer of building supplies to professional contractors.

In a further effort to attract contractors' business, 84 Lumber introduced a builder financing program in 1999 and began converting some of its stores to an 84-Plus store format, in which its traditional lumberyard setup is matched with a 10,000-sq.-ft. hardware store.

In an effort to reach more professionals, the company increased outside sales staff by 25% in 2000.

The next year the company bought 15 stores from Payless Cashways, which went out of business, a move that extended 84 Lumber's operations to Oklahoma, Nevada, and Nebraska.

The company added two red-letter dates to its company history in 2002. On April 3 of that year, 84 Lumber opened 20 new stores throughout the US, increasing its store count by 5%. Thanks in part to added revenue from those stores, on December 7, 2002, company cash registers went past the $2 billion mark in sales for the year.

EXECUTIVES

CEO: Joseph A. Hardy Sr., age 80
President: Maggie Hardy Magerko
COO: Bill Myrick
CFO: Dan Wallach
VP Human Resources: Steve Cherry
VP Marketing and Advertising: Terry Carter

LOCATIONS

HQ: 1019 Route 519, Eighty Four, PA 15330
Phone: 724-228-8820 **Fax:** 724-228-8058
Web: www.84lumber.com

84 Lumber operates stores in about 35 states and sells its products in Australia, China, South Korea, and Switzerland.

PRODUCTS/OPERATIONS

Selected Products

Doors
Drywall
Flooring
Insulation
Lumber
Plywood
Project kits
Barns (pole and storage)
Decks
Garages
Houses
Kitchens
Playsets
Roofing
Room additions
Siding
Skylights
Trim
Trusses
Ventilation
Windows

COMPETITORS

Ace Hardware
Builder Marts
Builders FirstSource
Building Materials Holding
Carter Lumber
Contractors' Warehouse
Do it Best
Foxworth-Galbraith Lumber
Futter Lumber
Grossman's
Home Depot
Lanoga
Lowe's
McCoy
Menard
Stock Building Supply
Sutherland Lumber
TruServ
Wickes
Wolohan Lumber

HISTORICAL FINANCIALS

Company Type: Private

Income Statement

FYE: December 31

	REVENUE ($ mil.)	NET INCOME ($ mil.)	NET PROFIT MARGIN	EMPLOYEES
12/02	2,177	—	—	5,800
12/01	1,904	—	—	5,400
12/00	1,850	—	—	5,000
12/99	1,800	—	—	4,500
12/98	1,625	—	—	4,400
12/97	1,600	—	—	4,815
12/96	1,590	—	—	4,500
12/95	1,275	—	—	3,500
12/94	1,275	—	—	3,500
12/93	1,060	—	—	3,500
Annual Growth	8.3%	—	—	5.8%

Revenue History

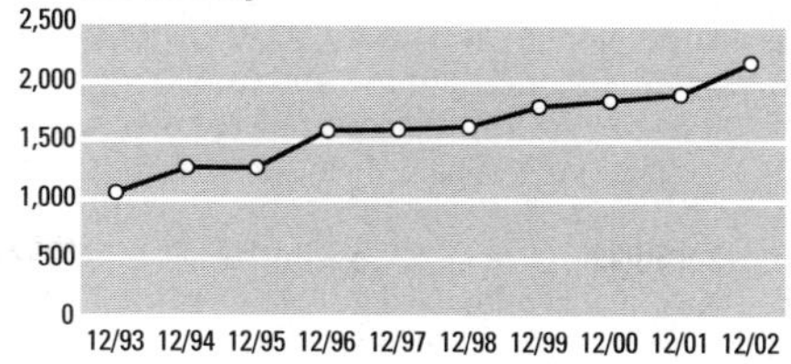

A&E Television Networks

A&E Television Networks is defying the notion that TV rots the brain. It offers a smorgasbord of programming in history, the arts, current events, and nature through its two main cable networks: A&E (more than 84 million subscribers) and The History Channel (more than 85 million subscribers). The company's flagship program is A&E's *Biography.* A&E Television also operates two digital cable channels (Biography Channel, History Channel International) and a handful of Web sites. A&E is a joint venture of media giants Hearst (37.5%), Walt Disney's ABC Cable (37.5%), and General Electric's NBC (25%).

A&E has turned its *Biography* into a media juggernaut, expanding into videos, books, and magazines. In addition, the company plans to expand its Internet-related activities, which include a handful of Web sites (biography.com, mysteries.com, historytravel.com); it acquired Genealogy.com in 2001.

In spite of its success with *Biography,* A&E's flagship cable channel has suffered from lagging ratings. It lost its stable *Law and Order* syndicated program to competitor TNT and replaced it with rescue drama *Third Watch,* which has attracted less-than-stellar ratings. The company has also been unsuccessful with its original programming (*Nero Wolf, 100 Centre Street),* which won critical acclaim but few viewers.

EXECUTIVES

President and CEO: Nickolas Davatzes
EVP Sales and Marketing: Whitney Goit II
EVP Finance and CFO: Gerard Gruosso
EVP and General Manager, History Channel: Daniel E. Davids
EVP and General Manager, A&E Network: Abbe Raven
EVP Enterprises: Jim Greiner
SVP and General Manager, Biography Channel: Thomas Heymann
SVP and General Manager, International: Maria Komodikis
SVP Human Resources: Rosalind Clay Carter
SVP Marketing: Artie Scheff
SVP Programming, A&E Network: Robert DiBitetto, age 46
VP and General Counsel: Anne Atkinson
VP Documentary Development, A&E Network: Nancy Dubuc
VP, Interactive Production: Will Corbin
VP Internet Sales: William Jennings
VP Legal and Business Affairs: Stephen Stander
VP, Programming & Production, International: Michael Katz
Director, Network Operations and Traffic Services: Paul Damp
Director of Public Affairs and Communication: Michael Feeney

LOCATIONS

HQ: 235 E. 45th St., New York, NY 10017
Phone: 212-210-1400 **Fax:** 212-850-9370
Web: www.aande.com

PRODUCTS/OPERATIONS

Media Products

Audio books
CD-ROMs
Compact discs
DVDs
Home video
Magazines
TV programming
Web sites

Operating Units

A&E Network
AETN Enterprises (home videos, magazines, CDs)
AETN Interactive (e-commerce & Web site operation)
AETN International
The Biography Channel
The History Channel
History Channel International

COMPETITORS

ABC
Advance Publications
CBS
CPB
Crown Media
Discovery Communications
Fox Entertainment
HBO
Lifetime
NBC
National Geographic
PBS
Rainbow Media
Turner Broadcasting
Viacom

HISTORICAL FINANCIALS

Company Type: Joint venture

Income Statement

FYE: December 31

	REVENUE ($ mil.)	NET INCOME ($ mil.)	NET PROFIT MARGIN	EMPLOYEES
12/02	550	—	—	500
12/01	804	—	—	600
12/00	770	—	—	600
12/99	499	—	—	570
12/98	394	—	—	450
12/97	349	—	—	425
12/96	304	—	—	400
12/95	284	—	—	315
12/94	214	—	—	260
12/93	174	—	—	215
Annual Growth	13.6%	—	—	9.8%

Revenue History

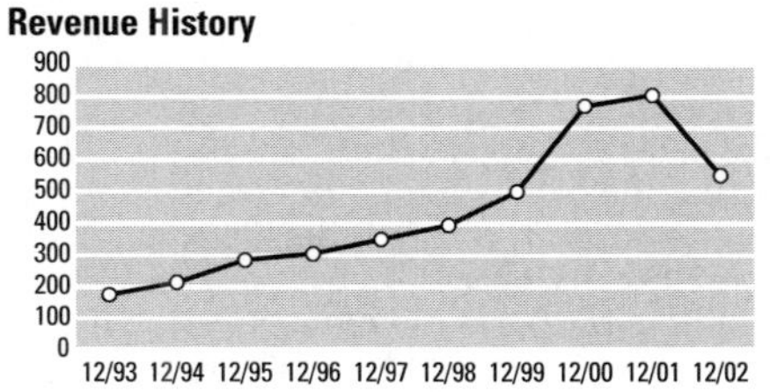

AARP

AARP is gearing up for the geezer boom. Open to anyone age 50 or older (dues are $12.50 per year), the not-for-profit organization is the largest organization of older adults in the US with more than 35 million members and is also the largest lobbyist for the elderly (it spends about $57 million on lobbying and related activities). On a mission to enhance the quality of life for older Americans, AARP is active in four areas: information and education, community service, advocacy, and member services. It also publishes the monthly *AARP Bulletin* and has combined its bimonthly *Modern Maturity* and *My Generation* magazines into a single publication, *AARP The Magazine*.

AARP disseminates information in a variety of formats (a Web site, public policy agendas, and radio and TV spots) and pursues educational and research efforts through the AARP Andrus Foundation, the Research Information Center, and the Public Policy Institute.

AARP may not be the most exclusive club around, but it is one of the most powerful. AARP is attempting to transform itself by adapting to its changing demographics. The organization has initiated a $100 million, five-year marketing plan to attract aging baby boomers who are becoming eligible for membership.

AARP members are eligible for services, including savings on prescription drugs, travel, investment opportunities, and health, life, and auto insurance. Retired educators who join the National Retired Teachers Association (a division of AARP) can receive both AARP services and other benefits designed specifically for them.

HISTORY

Ethel Andrus, a retired Los Angeles high school principal who founded the National Retired Teachers Association (NRTA) in 1947, founded the American Association of Retired Persons (AARP) in 1958 with the help of Leonard Davis, a New York insurance salesman who had helped her find an underwriter for the NRTA. The new organization's goal: to "enhance the quality of life" for older Americans and "improve the image of aging."

Andrus offered members the same low rates for health and accident insurance provided to NRTA members. She also started publishing AARP's bimonthly magazine, *Modern Maturity,* in 1958. The organization's first local chapter opened in Youngstown, Arizona, in 1960. Still an insurance man, Davis formed Colonial Penn Insurance in 1963 to take over the AARP account. Andrus led the AARP and its increasingly powerful lobby for the elderly until her death in 1967.

With criticism of Colonial Penn mounting in the 1970s (critics charged the organization was little more than a front for the insurance company), Prudential won AARP's insurance business in 1979. The NRTA merged with AARP in 1982, and the following year it lowered the membership eligibility age from 55 to 50. The organization continued to expand its offerings, adding an auto club and financial products such as mutual funds and expanded insurance policies. The organization also started a federal credit union for members in 1988, but despite rosy projections, it ceased operations two years later.

AARP forked over $135 million to the IRS in 1993 as part of a settlement regarding the tax status of profits from some of its activities, but the dispute remained unresolved. AARP switched insurance providers again in 1996 (New York Life) and started offering discounted legal services. Also that year, AARP said it would let HMOs offer managed-care services to members. The plan drew objections over its potential violation of Medicare anti-kickback laws, and AARP developed a revised payment plan in 1997.

AARP's image was bruised in 1998 when Dale Van Atta wrote a scathing account of the organization, *Trust Betrayed: Inside the AARP.* The book accused the organization of operating out of lavish accommodations, acting as a shill for businesses to hawk their wares, and concealing a drop in membership. Also in 1998, recognizing that nearly a third of its members were working, the organization dropped the American Association of Retired Persons moniker and began to refer to itself by the AARP abbreviation.

To end the long-running dispute with the IRS, AARP reached a settlement over its alleged profit-making enterprises by creating a new taxable subsidiary called AARP Services in 1999. The following year AARP initiated a five-year plan to attract aging baby boomers. AARP launched its new *My Generation* magazine 2001. In 2003 the organization combined *My Generation* with its *Modern Maturity* magazine to form a single publication: *AARP The Magazine*.

EXECUTIVES

Executive Director and CEO: William D. (Bill) Novelli
President: James G. Parkel
COO: Thomas C. Nelson
CFO: Robert Hagans Jr.
VP, Secretary, and Treasurer: Charles Leven
VP Membership and Member Services: Charles J. Mendoza
President, AARP Services: Dawn Sweeney
Associate Executive Director, Operations: Richard Henry
Associate Executive Director, State and National Initiatives: Chris Hansen
Director Human Resources: Russ Consaul
Director Policy and Strategy: John Rother
General Counsel: Joan Wise

LOCATIONS

HQ: 601 E St. NW, Washington, DC 20049
Phone: 202-434-2277 **Fax:** 202-434-6548
Web: www.aarp.org

AARP has offices in all 50 states, the District of Columbia, Puerto Rico, and the Virgin Islands.

PRODUCTS/OPERATIONS

Selected Operations and Programs

55 ALIVE/Mature Driving
AARP Andrus Foundation (gerontology research)
AARP Bulletin (monthly news update)
AARP Legal Services Network
AARP Services (taxable product management, marketing, and e-commerce subsidiary)
AARP The Magazine (bimonthly magazine)
Financial Planning
Mature Focus Radio (daily news program)
National Retired Teachers Association
Public Policy Institute
Research Information Center
Senior Community Service Employment Program
Tax-Aide

HISTORICAL FINANCIALS

Company Type: Association

Income Statement FYE: December 31

	REVENUE ($ mil.)	NET INCOME ($ mil.)	NET PROFIT MARGIN	EMPLOYEES
12/02	636	—	—	1,800
12/01	595	—	—	1,800
12/00	580	—	—	2,000
12/99	486	—	—	2,000
12/98	541	—	—	2,000
12/97	529	—	—	1,900
12/96	475	—	—	1,850
12/95	506	—	—	1,800
12/94	469	—	—	1,752
12/93	369	—	—	1,793
Annual Growth	6.2%	—	—	0.0%

Revenue History

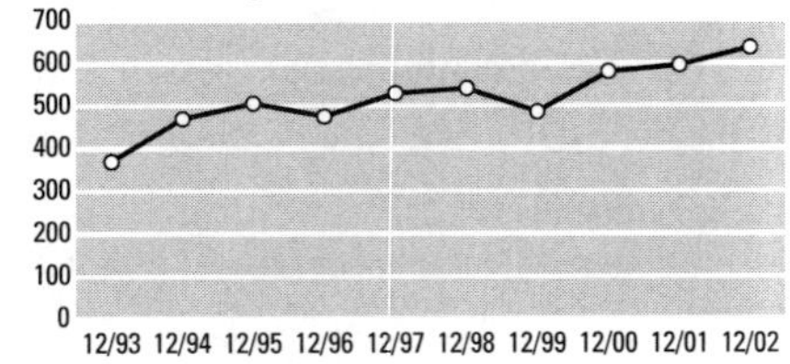

Academy Sports & Outdoors, Ltd.

Academy Sports & Outdoors is near the head of the class among sporting goods retailers. The company is the third-largest full-line sporting goods chain in the US (behind The Sports Authority and Gart Sports) with over 60 stores located throughout the South and Southwest. Academy's low-frills stores carry clothing, shoes, and equipment for almost any sport and outdoor activity, including camping, hunting, fishing, and boating. The company dates back to a San Antonio tire shop opened by Max Gochman in 1938. The business moved into military surplus items and during the 1980s began focusing on sports and outdoor merchandise. The Gochman family still owns Academy.

EXECUTIVES

Chairman, President, and CEO: David Gochman
EVP and COO: James Pierce
EVP, Apparel: Robert Frennea
EVP, Footwear: Beth Menuet
EVP, Hardgoods: A. J. Blanchard
VP and CFO: Michael Ondruch
VP and General Counsel: Elise Neal
VP, Human Resources: Sylvia Barrera
VP, Information Technology: Mike Marrie
VP, Logistics and Distribution: Kal Patel
VP, Marketing: Casey Ramm
VP, Store Operations: Allen McConnell
Senior Controller: Gary Winkler

LOCATIONS

HQ: 1800 N. Mason Rd., Katy, TX 77449
Phone: 281-646-5200 **Fax:** 281-646-5204
Web: www.academy.com

Academy Sports & Outdoors operates stores in Alabama, Florida, Louisiana, Mississippi, Oklahoma, Tennessee, and Texas.

COMPETITORS

Athlete's Foot
Bass Pro Shops
Finish Line
Foot Locker
Footstar
Hibbett Sporting Goods
Kmart
Sports Authority
Target
Wal-Mart

HISTORICAL FINANCIALS

Company Type: Private

Income Statement FYE: January 31

	REVENUE ($ mil.)	NET INCOME ($ mil.)	NET PROFIT MARGIN	EMPLOYEES
1/02	775	—	—	5,000
1/01	720	—	—	4,748
1/00	612	—	—	4,745
1/99	499	—	—	4,500
1/98	435	—	—	3,200
1/97	367	—	—	2,800
1/96	315	—	—	2,500
1/95	268	—	—	1,700
1/94	210	—	—	1,700
1/93	154	—	—	—
Annual Growth	19.7%	—	—	14.4%

Revenue History

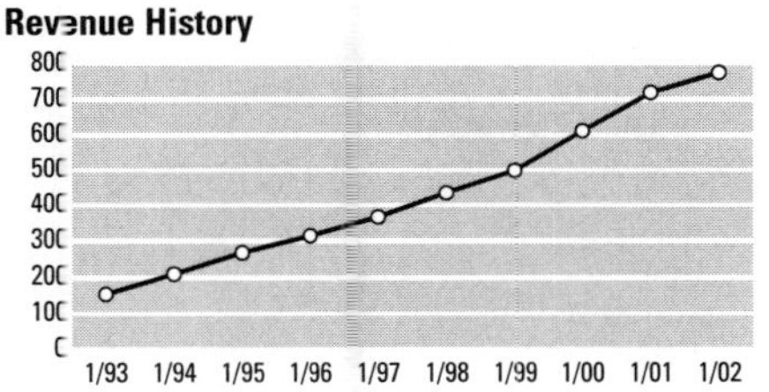

Ace Hardware Corporation

Luckily, Ace has John Madden up its sleeve. Despite the growth of warehouse-style competitors, Ace Hardware has remained a household name, thanks to ads featuring Madden, a former Oakland Raiders football coach and TV commentator. The company is the #1 hardware cooperative in the US, ahead of Do It Best, which operates about 4,400 member-owned stores in the US and more than 40 other countries. Ace dealer-owners operate more than 5,100 Ace Hardware stores throughout the US and in about 70 other countries. The co-op distributes to its retailers from more than 20 wholesale warehouses.

Ace distributes products such as electrical and plumbing supplies, garden equipment, hand tools, housewares, and power tools. It also makes its own brand of paint and offers thousands of other Ace-brand products. Subsidiary Ace Insurance Agency offers dealers insurance for their stores and employees. Ace also provides training programs and advertising campaigns.

Challenged by big-box chains such as The Home Depot and Lowe's, Ace has unveiled its Next Generation store concept, which calls for signage with detailed product descriptions and different flooring to set off departments, among other features. Ace dealers own the company and receive dividends from Ace's profits.

HISTORY

A group of Chicago-area hardware dealers — William Stauber, Richard Hesse, Gern Lindquist, and Oscar Fisher — decided in 1924 to pool their hardware buying and promotional costs. In 1928 the group incorporated as Ace Stores, named in honor of the superior WWI fliers dubbed aces. Hesse became president the following year, retaining that position for the next 44 years. The company also opened its first warehouse in 1929, and by 1933 it had 38 dealers.

The organization had 133 dealers in seven states by 1949. In 1953 Ace began to allow dealers to buy stock in the company through the Ace Perpetuation Plan. During the 1960s Ace expanded into the South and West, and by 1969 it had opened distribution centers in Georgia and California — its first such facilities outside Chicago. In 1968 it opened its first international store in Guam.

By the early 1970s the do-it-yourself market began to surge as inflation pushed up plumber and electrician fees. As the market grew, large home center chains gobbled up market share from independent dealers such as those franchised through Ace. In response, Ace and its dealers became a part of a growing trend in the hardware industry — cooperatives.

Hesse sold the company to its dealers in 1973 for $6 million (less than half its book value), and the following year Ace began operating as a cooperative. Hesse stepped down in 1973. In 1976 the dealers took full control when the company's first Board of Dealer-Directors was elected.

After signing up a number of dealers in the eastern US, Ace had dealers in all 50 states by 1979. The co-op opened a plant to make paint in Matteson, Illinois, in 1984. By 1985 Ace had reached $1 billion in sales and had initiated its Store of the Future Program, allowing dealers to borrow up to $200,000 to upgrade their stores and conduct market analyses. Former head coach John Madden of the National Football League's Oakland Raiders signed on as Ace's mouthpiece in 1988.

A year later the co-op began to test ACENET, a computer network that allowed Ace dealers to check inventory, send and receive e-mail, make special purchase requests, and keep up with prices on commodity items such as lumber. In 1990 Ace established an International Division to handle its overseas stores. (It had been exporting products since 1975.) EVP and COO David Hodnik became president in 1995. That year the co-op added a net of 67 stores, including a three-store chain in Russia. Expanding further internationally, Ace signed a five-year joint-supply agreement in 1996 with Canadian lumber and hardware retailer Beaver Lumber. Hodnik added CEO to his title in 1996.

Ace fell further behind its old rival, True Value, in 1997 when ServiStar Coast to Coast and True Value merged to form TruServ, a hardware giant that operated more than 10,000 outlets at the completion of the merger.

Late in 1997 Ace launched an expansion program in Canada. (The co-op already operated distribution centers in Ontario and Calgary.) In 1999 Ace merged its lumber and building materials division with Builder Marts of America to form a dealer-owned buying group to supply about 2,700 retailers. In 2000, Ace gained 208 member outlet stores, but saw 279 member outlets terminated. The next year it gained 220, but lost 255.

Sodisco-Howden bought all the shares of Ace Hardware Canada in February 2003.

EXECUTIVES

President and CEO: David F. Hodnik, age 55, $744,800 pay
EVP, Strategic Planning: Rita D. Kahle, age 46, $492,080 pay
EVP, Retail: Ray A. Griffith, age 49, $438,100 pay
SVP, International and Technology: Paul M. Ingevaldson, age 57, $433,100 pay
SVP, Retail Support and Logistics: David F. Myer, age 57, $420,500 pay
VP and Controller: Ronald J. (Ron) Knutson, age 39
VP, Human Resources: Jimmy Alexander, age 45
VP, Information Technology: Michael J. Altendorf, age 45
VP, Marketing, Advertising, Retail Development, and Company Stores: Michael C. Bodzewski, age 53
VP, Merchandising: Lori L. Bossmann, age 42
VP, Retail Operations: Kenneth L. (Ken) Nichols, age 54
VP, Retail Support — East: Daniel C. Prochaska, age 45
VP, Retail Support — West: William J. Bauman, age 54
Treasurer: Sandy Brandt
Director, Application Development: Jay Heubner
Director, International Licensees: Maurice Ademe
Director, People Development and Learning Systems: Ron Wagner
Director, Retail Operations for the Midwest Division: Bob Guido
General Counsel: Donna Flenard
Customer Service: Tim Schubert
Auditors: KPMG LLP

LOCATIONS

HQ: 2200 Kensington Ct., Oak Brook, IL 60523
Phone: 630-990-6600 **Fax:** 630-990-6838
Web: www.acehardware.com

Ace Hardware wholesales products to dealers with retail operations in the US and about 70 other countries.

PRODUCTS/OPERATIONS

Subsidiaries

Ace Corporate Stores, Inc. (operation of company-owned stores)
Ace Hardware de México, S.A. de C.V. (hardware wholesaler)
Ace Insurance Agency, Inc. (dealer insurance program)
A.H.C. Store Development Corp. (operation of company-owned stores)
Loss Prevention Services, Inc. (security training and loss prevention services for dealers)
National Hardlines Supply, Inc. (sells to retailers outside the Ace dealer network)

COMPETITORS

84 Lumber
Akzo Nobel
Benjamin Moore
Building Materials Holding
Costco Wholesale
Do it Best
Fastenal
Grossman's
Handy Hardware Wholesale
Home Depot
ICI American
Kmart
Lanoga
Lowe's
McCoy
Menard
Northern Tool
Réno-Dépôt
Sears
Sherwin-Williams
Stock Building Supply
Sutherland Lumber
TruServ
United Hardware Distributing
Wal-Mart
Wickes
Wolohan Lumber

HISTORICAL FINANCIALS

Company Type: Cooperative

Income Statement FYE: Saturday nearest December 31

	REVENUE ($ mil.)	NET INCOME ($ mil.)	NET PROFIT MARGIN	EMPLOYEES
12/02	3,029	82	2.7%	5,268
12/01	2,894	73	2.5%	5,229
12/00	2,945	80	2.7%	5,513
12/99	3,182	93	2.9%	5,180
12/98	3,120	88	2.8%	4,672
12/97	2,907	76	2.6%	4,685
12/96	2,743	72	2.6%	4,352
12/95	2,436	64	2.6%	3,917
12/94	2,326	65	2.8%	3,664
12/93	2,018	57	2.8%	3,405
Annual Growth	4.6%	4.1%	—	5.0%

2002 Year-End Financials

Debt ratio: 58.2%
Return on equity: 29.3%
Cash ($ mil.): 42
Current ratio: 1.39
Long-term debt ($ mil.): 163

Net Income History

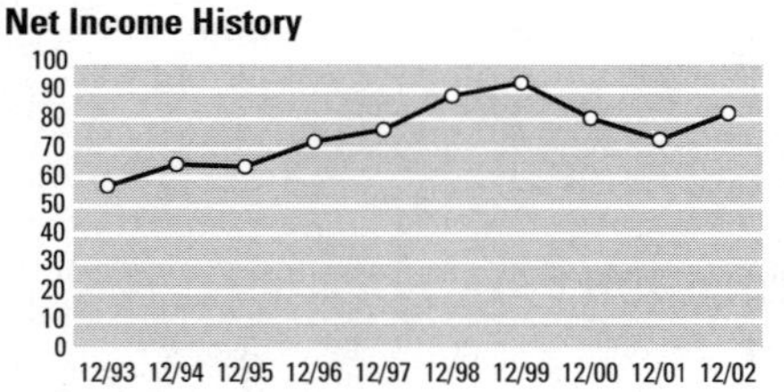

ACF Industries

ACF Industries (ACF) has been around for more than a century, but it is still on track. The company makes railroad tank and covered hopper cars (a category that it revolutionized with its Center Flow design). Through ACF Acceptance, the company also provides financing for its customers. ACF Industries has manufacturing operations in Pennsylvania and West Virginia. Formed in 1899 and originally known as American Car & Foundry, ACF is the oldest builder of railcars in the US and is owned by billionaire financier Carl Icahn, who also is ACF's chairman.

EXECUTIVES

Chairman: Carl C. Icahn, age 67
President: Roger Wynkoop
VP and Controller: Harry McKinstry
VP, Finance: Laura Parli
VP, Manufacturing: Larry Stewart
VP, Marketing: Brian Evdoe
Senior Director of Human Resources: Gary Rager

LOCATIONS

HQ: ACF Industries, Inc.
620 N. 2nd St., St. Charles, MO 63301
Phone: 636-940-5000 **Fax:** 636-940-5020
Web: www.acfindustries.com

ACF Industries has manufacturing plants in Milton, Pennsylvania and Huntington, West Virginia.

COMPETITORS

Duchossois Industries
GATX
Greenbrier
Johnstown America
L. B. Foster
Marmon Group
Meridian Rail
Miner Enterprises
Pioneer Railcorp
Siemens Transportation Systems
Trinity Industries

HISTORICAL FINANCIALS

Company Type: Private

Income Statement FYE: December 31

	REVENUE ($ mil.)	NET INCOME ($ mil.)	NET PROFIT MARGIN	EMPLOYEES
12/02	600	—	—	2,800
12/01	620	—	—	3,000
12/00	623	—	—	2,900
12/99	604	—	—	2,700
12/98	638	—	—	2,700
12/97	891	—	—	2,600
12/96	720	—	—	2,200
12/95	550	—	—	2,400
12/94	430	—	—	2,200
Annual Growth	4.3%	—	—	3.1%

Revenue History

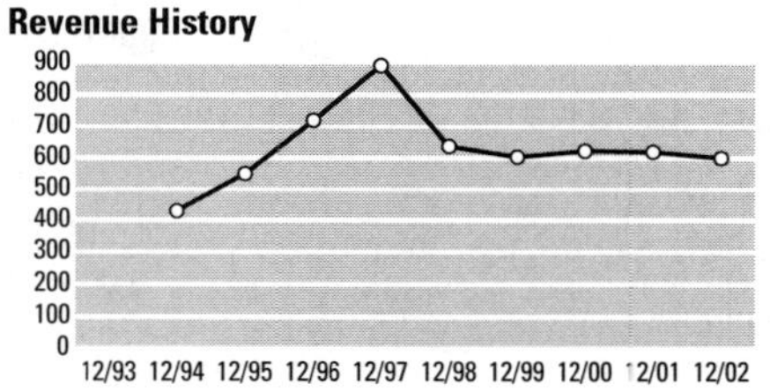

ACG Holdings

Paperboys and papergirls everywhere can thank ACG Holdings for giving them a workout. The company's American Color Graphics makes your newspaper pudgy by printing advertising inserts for about 270 retailers and Sunday comics for more than 200 newspapers. American Color Graphics also prints comic books for Marvel Publishing comic books, local newspapers, and other publications. Through its American Color division, the company provides digital imaging and pre-press services. Morgan Stanley Leveraged Equity Fund owns about 60% of the company. The company was founded in 1926.

EXECUTIVES

Chairman, President, and CEO: Stephen M. Dyott, age 50, $1,275,000 pay
President, Graphics: Malcolm J. Anderson, age 63, $675,000 pay
President, American Color: Kathleen A. DeKam, age 41
EVP Purchasing of Graphics: Larry R. Williams, age 61, $525,000 pay
EVP, Operations of Graphics: Stuart R. Reeve, age 38, $500,000 pay
SVP and CFO: Patrick W. Kellick, age 44
SVP Administration, Secretary, and General Counsel: Timothy M. Davis, age 47, $500,000 pay
VP Human Resources: Lance Ikard
Auditors: Ernst & Young LLP

LOCATIONS

HQ: ACG Holdings, Inc.
100 Winners Circle, Brentwood, TN 37027
Phone: 615-377-0377 **Fax:** 615-377-0370
Web: www.amcg.com

ACG Holdings has operations in the US and Canada.

PRODUCTS/OPERATIONS

Selected Services

Creative services
Digital photography
Facilities and asset management
Packaging pre-press services
Plate making
Pre-press services
Printing
Comic books
Large format publications
Newspaper comics
Retail advertising inserts
Telecommunications services

COMPETITORS

Banta
Berlin Industries
Black Dot Group
Cadmus Communications
Quad/Graphics
Quebecor
R. R. Donnelley
Segerdahl
Seven Worldwide
Solar Communications
Transcontinental
Valassis
Vertis

HISTORICAL FINANCIALS

Company Type: Private

Income Statement FYE: March 31

	REVENUE ($ mil.)	NET INCOME ($ mil.)	NET PROFIT MARGIN	EMPLOYEES
3/03	520	(0)	—	2,465
3/02	542	1	0.1%	2,430
3/01	587	24	4.2%	2,810
3/00	547	10	1.7%	2,835
3/99	520	(13)	—	2,760
3/98	533	(30)	—	2,800
3/97	525	(29)	—	2,880
3/96	530	(26)	—	2,893
3/95	433	(4)	—	2,020
3/94	415	(23)	—	2,300
Annual Growth	2.6%	—	—	0.8%

2003 Year-End Financials

Debt ratio: —
Return on equity: —
Cash ($ mil.): 0
Current ratio: 0.71
Long-term debt ($ mil.): 200

Net Income History

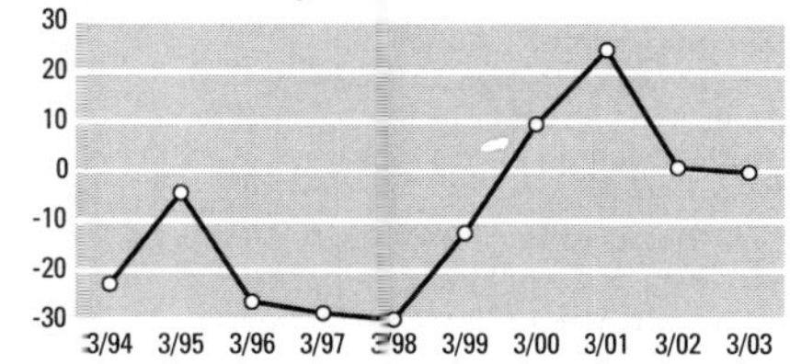

ACT Manufacturing

ACT Manufacturing is trying to keep its PCB act together long enough to sell it. Most of ACT's business comes from printed circuit board, or PCB, assemblies, though it also makes cable and harness assemblies and electromechanical subassemblies. It also offers advanced manufacturing, product testing, and order fulfillment services. Top customers include Efficient Networks, EMC, and Nortel Networks. In the face of brutal market conditions and a steep decline in its business, ACT has filed for Chapter 11 bankruptcy protection and announced plans to sell the company. Chairman John Pino and his family own 28% of ACT.

Most of the company's sales come from manufacturers in the networking and telecommunications markets; ACT also serves computer, industrial, and medical instrumentation customers.

EXECUTIVES

Chairman: John A. Pino
Acting President and CEO: John Young
Acting Treasurer: Pauline E. Taylor
Auditors: Deloitte & Touche LLP

LOCATIONS

HQ: ACT Manufacturing, Inc.
2 Cabot Rd., Hudson, MA 01749
Phone: 978-567-4000 **Fax:** 978-562-8395
Web: www.actmfg.com

ACT Manufacturing has operations in France, Ireland, Mexico, Singapore, Taiwan, Thailand, the UK, and the US.

PRODUCTS/OPERATIONS

Services

Manufacturing
- Cable and harness assemblies (including ribbon, multiconductor, coaxial, and fiber-optic cable assemblies, and discrete wire harness assemblies)
- Electromechanical subassemblies (combining circuit boards, cable and harness assemblies, and other components)
- Printed circuit board assemblies (custom manufacturing and in-circuit testing using surface-mount technology)
- Total system assemblies and integration

Value-Added
- Advanced manufacturing and test engineering
- Materials management
- New product introductions
- Order fulfillment and distribution
- Packaging
- Product configuration
- Product diagnostics and repair
- Test services

COMPETITORS

Benchmark Electronics
Celestica
Flextronics
IEC Electronics
Jabil
Manufacturers' Services
Merix
PEMSTAR
Photocircuits
Plexus
Sanmina-SCI
Solectron
SYNNEX
Viasystems
Volex

HISTORICAL FINANCIALS

Company Type: Private

Income Statement FYE: December 31

	REVENUE ($ mil.)	NET INCOME ($ mil.)	NET PROFIT MARGIN	EMPLOYEES
12/01	1,536	—	—	—
12/00	1,371	29	2.1%	8,800
12/99	696	6	0.9%	2,816
12/98	291	1	0.4%	1,042
12/97	265	(4)	—	985
12/96	226	10	4.5%	799
12/95	116	6	5.0%	655
12/94	86	7	8.2%	510
12/93	45	2	4.9%	417
12/92	27	1	3.7%	331
Annual Growth	56.5%	52.3%	—	50.7%

Revenue History

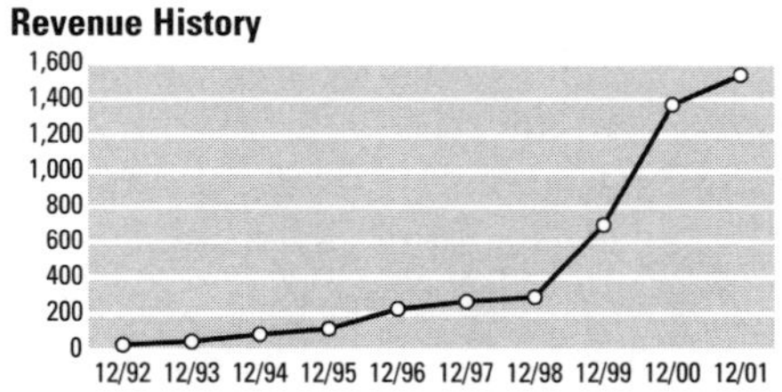

Advance Publications

Advance Publications gets its marching orders from the printed page. One of the top US newspaper publishers, Advance owns some 25 daily newspapers around the country, including *The Star-Ledger* (New Jersey), *The Cleveland Plain Dealer,* and its namesake *Staten Island Advance.* It also owns American City Business Journals (41 weekly papers) and Parade Publications (*Parade Magazine* Sunday insert). Advance is the #2 magazine publisher in the US (behind Time, Inc.) through units Condé Nast Publications, with its popular titles such as *Allure, Glamour,* and *Vanity Fair,* and trade journal publisher Fairchild Publications (*Women's Wear Daily*). Samuel "Si" Newhouse Jr. and his brother Donald own the company.

Aside from print publishing, Advance is a major online publisher with 10 regional news Web sites. Its CondéNet unit runs Web versions of Condé Nast's magazines and other Internet properties, including Epicurious (food and dining) and Concierge (travel). The company also has stakes in cable TV systems (33%, with Time Warner), broadband ISP Road Runner (9%), and cable broadcaster Discovery Communications (about 25%).

Advance has boosted its magazine portfolio, acquiring The New York Times Company's Golf Properties unit (*Golf Digest*), Miami-based Ideas Publishing Group (Spanish language versions of US magazines), and PRIMEDIA's *Modern Bride.*

HISTORY

Solomon Neuhaus (later Samuel I. Newhouse) got started in the newspaper business after dropping out of school at age 13. He went to work at the *Bayonne Times* in New Jersey and was put in charge of the failing newspaper in 1911; he managed to turn the paper around within a year. In 1922 he bought the *Staten Island Advance* and formed the Staten Island Advance Company in 1924. After buying up more papers, he changed the name of the company to Advance Publications in 1949. By the 1950s the company had local papers in New York, New Jersey, and Alabama.

In 1959 Newhouse bought magazine publisher Condé Nast as an anniversary gift for his wife. (He joked that she had asked for a fashion magazine, so he bought her *Vogue.*) His publishing empire continued to grow with the addition of the *Times-Picayune* (New Orleans) in 1962 and *The Cleveland Plain Dealer* in 1967. In 1976 the company paid more than $300 million for Booth Newspapers, publisher of eight Michigan papers and *Parade Magazine.*

Newhouse died in 1979, leaving his sons Si and Donald to run the company, which encompassed more than 30 newspapers, a half-dozen magazines, and 15 cable systems. The next year Advance bought book publishing giant Random House from RCA. Si resurrected the Roaring Twenties standard *Vanity Fair* in 1983 and added *The New Yorker* under the Condé Nast banner in 1985. The Newhouses scored a victory over the IRS in 1990 after a long-running court battle involving inheritance taxes. Condé Nast bought Knapp Publications (*Architectural Digest*) in 1993 and Advance later acquired American City Business Journals in 1995.

In 1998 the company sold the increasingly unprofitable Random House to Bertelsmann for about $1.2 billion. It later bought hallmark Internet magazine *Wired* (though it passed on Wired Ventures' Internet operations). That year revered *New Yorker* editor Tina Brown, credited with jazzing up the publication's content and increasing its circulation, left the magazine; staff writer and Pulitzer Prize winner David Remnick was named as Brown's replacement.

In 1999 Advance joined Donrey Media Group (now called Stephens Media Group), E.W. Scripps, Hearst Corporation, and MediaNews Group to purchase the online classified advertising network AdOne (later named PowerOne Media). It also bought Walt Disney's trade publishing unit, Fairchild Publications, for $650 million. In 2000 the company shifted *Details* from Condé Nast to Fairchild and relaunched the magazine as a fashion publication. Later that year the company announced it would begin creating Web versions of its popular magazine titles.

In 2001 Condé Nast bought a majority stake in Miami-based Ideas Publishing Group (Spanish language versions of US magazines). Also that year Advance bought four golf magazines, including *Golf Digest,* from the New York Times Company for $430 million. Condé Nast picked up *Modern Bride* magazine from PRIMEDIA in 2002 for $52 million.

EXECUTIVES

Chairman and CEO; Chairman, Condé Nast Publications: Samuel I. (Si) Newhouse Jr., age 74
President: Donald E. Newhouse, age 72
COO, Advance Magazine Publishers; EVP and COO, Condé Nast: Charles H. (Chuck) Townsend
VP Finance and Human Resources; Comptroller, Staten Island Advance: Arthur Silverstein
Chairman and Editorial Director, Golf Digest Companies: Jerry Tarde
Chairman and CEO, American City Business Journals: Ray Shaw
Chairman, CEO, and Publisher, Parade Publications: Walter Anderson
President and CEO, Condé Nast Publications: Steven T. Florio
President and CEO, Golf Digest Companies: Mitchell Fox
President and CEO, Fairchild Publications: Mary G. Berner
President and Creative Director, Advance.net: Jeff Jarvis
President, Advance Internet: Peter Weinberger
President, CondéNet: Sarah Chubb
Publisher, *Staten Island Advance*: Richard E. Diamond
Director of Retail, Classified, and National Sales, *Staten Island Advance*: Gary Cognetta
VP Marketing, *Staten Island Advance*: Jack Furnari
Human Resources: Pammy Brooks

LOCATIONS

HQ: Advance Publications, Inc.
950 Fingerboard Rd., Staten Island, NY 10305
Phone: 212-286-2860 **Fax:** 718-981-1456
Web: www.advance.net

Advance Publications publishes 41 business weeklies in 22 states.

PRODUCTS/OPERATIONS

Selected Operations

Broadcasting and Communications
Cartoonbank.com (database of cartoons from Discovery Communications; 25%, cable TV channel)
Newhouse Broadcasting (33%, cable TV joint venture with Time Warner)
Newhouse News Service
Religion News Service
Road Runner (9%, broadband Internet service)

Magazine Publishing
Condé Nast Publications
Allure
Architectural Digest
Bon Appetit
Bride's
Condé Nast Traveler
Glamour
Gourmet
GQ
House & Garden
Modern Bride
The New Yorker
Self
Vanity Fair
Vogue
Wired
Fairchild Publications
Details
Jane
Supermarket News
W
Women's Wear Daily
The Golf Digest Companies
Golf Digest
Golf for Women
Golf World
Golf World Business

Newspaper Publishing
American City Business Journals (41 weekly titles in 22 states)
Street & Smith's Sports Business Group
Newhouse Newspapers (25 papers across the US)
Parade Publications

Online Publishing
Advance Internet
CondéNet

Selected Newspapers
The Birmingham News (Alabama)
The Oregonian (Portland)
The Plain Dealer (Cleveland)
The Star-Ledger (Newark, NJ)
Staten Island Advance (New York)
The Times-Picayune (New Orleans)

COMPETITORS

American Express
Crain Communications
Dow Jones
E. W. Scripps
Freedom Communications
Gannett
Gruner + Jahr
Hachette Filipacchi Médias
Hearst
Knight-Ridder
MSO
McClatchy Company
Meredith
New York Times
Newsweek
North Jersey Media
PRIMEDIA
Reader's Digest
Reed Elsevier Group
Time
Tribune
Washington Post

HISTORICAL FINANCIALS

Company Type: Private

Income Statement FYE: December 31

	REVENUE ($ mil.)	NET INCOME ($ mil.)	NET PROFIT MARGIN	EMPLOYEES
12/01	4,200	—	—	22,785
12/00	4,542	—	—	23,000
12/99	4,228	—	—	26,300
12/98	3,859	—	—	24,000
12/97	3,669	—	—	24,000
12/96	4,250	—	—	24,000
12/95	5,349	—	—	24,000
12/94	4,855	—	—	19,000
12/93	4,690	—	—	19,000
12/92	4,416	—	—	19,000
Annual Growth	(0.6%)	—	—	2.0%

Revenue History

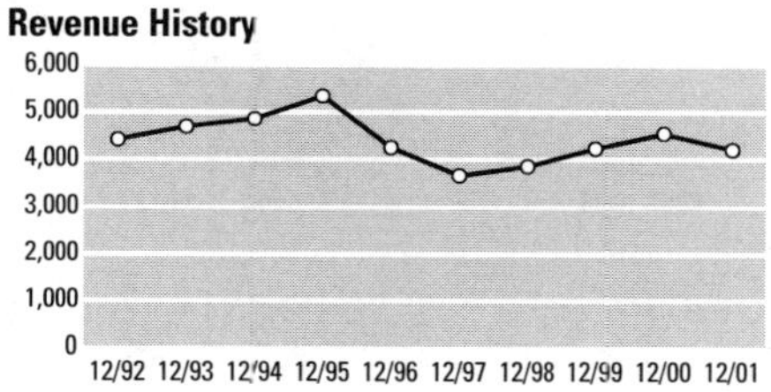

Adventist Health

Adventist Health is a not-for-profit health care system with strong ties to the Seventh-Day Adventist Church.

The West Coast wing of an international organization operating more than 160 Adventist health care operations, Adventist Health runs about 20 hospitals (with some 3,200 beds), almost 20 home health services agencies, and various other outpatient facilities and hospices in California, Hawaii, Oregon, and Washington.

The organization also works with its own churches and those of other denominations to offer such preventative health services as medical screenings, immunizations, and health education.

EXECUTIVES

Chairman: Thomas J. Mostert Jr.
President and CEO: Donald R. Ammon
EVP: Robert G. Carmen
SVP, Finance: Douglas E. Rebok
SVP: Alan Rice
VP and Treasurer: Rodney Wehtje
VP, Delivery of Care: Wynelle J. Huff
COO, Central Valley General Hospital: Roger Rieger
VP: Everett Gooch
Director, Human Resources: Roger Ashley
Director, Corporate Communication: Rita Waterman
CIO, Southern California Facilities: Mark D. Amey
President and CEO, South Coast Medical Center: Gary G. Irish
Auditors: Ernst & Young LLP

LOCATIONS

HQ: 2100 Douglas Blvd., Roseville, CA 95661
Phone: 916-781-2000 **Fax:** 916-783-9909
Web: www.adventisthealth.org

PRODUCTS/OPERATIONS

Selected Operations

Clinics and outpatient facilities
Home health agencies
Home medical equipment agencies
Hospices
Hospitals
Infusion/pharmacy services
Physician medical foundations and groups
Private-duty agencies

COMPETITORS

Catholic Healthcare West
HCA
Kaiser Foundation
Legacy Health System
LifePoint
Los Angeles County Health Department
Memorial Health Services
PacifiCare
Providence Health
Province Healthcare
Sisters of Charity of Leavenworth
Sutter Health
Tenet Healthcare
Triad Hospitals
Trinity Health
Vitas Healthcare

HISTORICAL FINANCIALS

Company Type: Not-for-profit

Income Statement FYE: December 31

	REVENUE ($ mil.)	NET INCOME ($ mil.)	NET PROFIT MARGIN	EMPLOYEES
12/02	3,822	—	—	17,200
12/01	2,869	—	—	16,500
12/00	2,510	—	—	16,500
12/99	2,045	—	—	16,477
12/98	1,740	—	—	17,129
12/97	1,090	—	—	16,567
12/96	980	—	—	15,351
12/95	981	—	—	14,610
12/94	952	—	—	13,799
12/93	1,350	—	—	13,000
Annual Growth	12.3%	—	—	3.2%

Revenue History

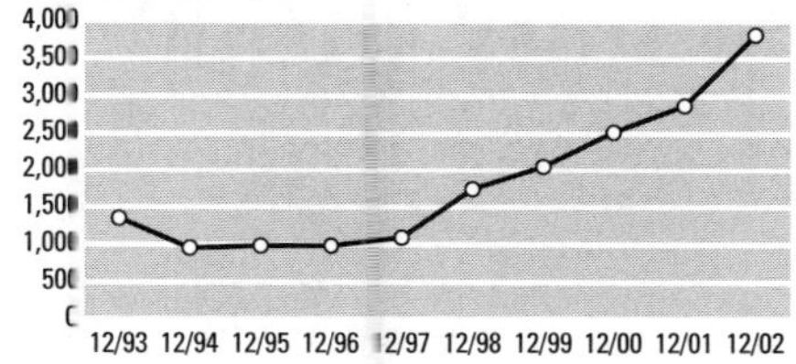

AECOM Technology

AECOM Technology means never having to say Architecture, Engineering, Consulting, Operations, and Maintenance. One of the world's leading engineering and design groups, the company offers a range of professional technical services mostly to government agencies and large corporations. AECOM is a top design firm in Asia and the Middle East and a global leader in the water, transportation, and wastewater sectors. It has expanded in Europe by acquiring UK-based companies such as transportation infrastructure groups Maunsell and Oscar Faber and water and wastewater construction group Metcalf & Eddy UK. AECOM employees control the company with a 44% stake.

EXECUTIVES

Chairman and CEO: Richard G. Newman, age 68, $1,182,000 pay
Vice Chairman: Joseph A. Incaudo, age 61, $516,250 pay (prior to promotion)
President; CEO, Americas Group: Raymond W. Holdsworth, age 58, $535,000 pay
CFO: Glenn Robson
EVP Corporate Operations, Corporate Development, and Strategic Planning: Grant G. McCullagh, age 50, $508,720 pay
SVP Strategic Planning and Operations: Beverly L. Thelander, age 46
VP Controller/Treasurer: Dennis W. Tons
Director; Chairman of Australia and Asia: Francis S. Y. Bong, age 59, $594,950 pay
President, DMJM DESIGN: Ray Landy
CEO, Global Group: David N. Odgers, age 59, $482,075 pay
Director of Corporate Communications: Jill Groswirth
Auditors: Ernst & Young LLP

LOCATIONS

HQ: AECOM Technology Corporation
555 S. Flower St., Ste. 3700, Los Angeles, CA 90071
Phone: 213-593-8000 **Fax:** 213-593-8729
Web: www.aecom.com

AECOM Technology has 25 major operating offices worldwide.

PRODUCTS/OPERATIONS

Selected Operations

Consoer Townsend Envirodyne (CTE, transportation and environmental engineering)
DMJM Aviation (consulting and engineering for aviation industry)
Daniel, Mann, Johnson, Mendenhall, Holmes & Narver (architecture, engineering, construction services)
DMJM + Harris (construction and engineering)
Maunsell Ltd. (transportation infrastructure, water and wastewater facilities, engineering, UK)
McClier Corporation (architectural engineering, construction, and consulting)
Metcalf & Eddy Ltd. (wastewater engineering and environmental consulting, UK)
Turner Collie & Braden Inc. (engineering and project management)

COMPETITORS

ABB
AMEC
Bechtel
Black & Veatch
Earth Tech
Fluor
Foster Wheeler
Henkels & McCoy
HLM Design
Jacobs Engineering
Lockwood Greene
Louis Berger
MWH Global
Parsons Brinckerhoff
Parsons
Perini
Skidmore Owings
STV
URS

HISTORICAL FINANCIALS

Company Type: Private

Income Statement FYE: September 30

	REVENUE ($ mil.)	NET INCOME ($ mil.)	NET PROFIT MARGIN	EMPLOYEES
9/02	1,700	—	—	15,500
9/01	904	—	—	12,700
9/00	691	—	—	12,100
Annual Growth	56.8%	—	—	13.2%

Revenue History

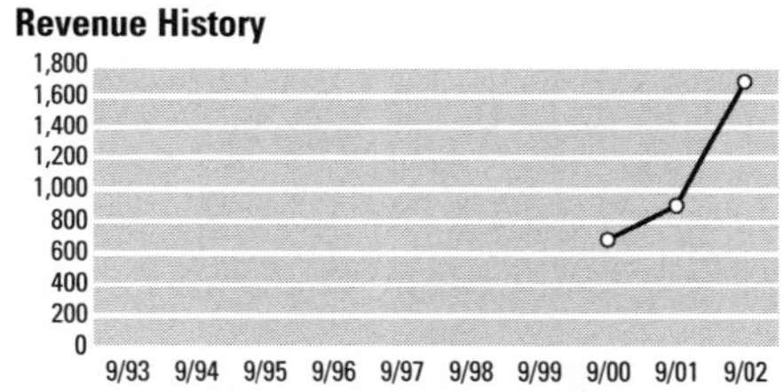

Aera Energy

Aera Energy covers a large area, California. The state's leading oil and gas producer, Aera Energy's properties extend from the Los Angeles Basin in the south to Coalinga in the north. It has daily production of 250,000 barrels of oil and 90 million cubic feet of natural gas equivalent and boasts proved onshore and offshore reserves of about 1 billion barrels of oil equivalent. The company is a joint venture of Exxon Mobil and Shell.

EXECUTIVES

President and CEO: Eugene J. (Gene) Voiland
CFO: Len Fox
CIO: David Walker
Manager Operations: Frank Dominguez
Auditors: PricewaterhouseCoopers LLP

LOCATIONS

HQ: Aera Energy LLC
10000 Ming Ave., Bakersfield, CA 93311
Phone: 661-665-5000 **Fax:** 661-665-5042
Web: www.aeraenergy.com

COMPETITORS

BP
ChevronTexaco
Greka Energy
PYR

HISTORICAL FINANCIALS

Company Type: Joint venture

Income Statement FYE: December 31

	REVENUE ($ mil.)	NET INCOME ($ mil.)	NET PROFIT MARGIN	EMPLOYEES
12/02	1,807	—	—	1,100

The Aerospace Corporation

The Aerospace Corporation definitely knows its space from its aero. Established in 1960, the not-for-profit organization provides research, development, and advisory services to space-related programs of the US government, international organizations, and commercial businesses. Its primary customers are the US Air Force's Space and Missile Systems Center and the National Reconnaissance Office, but it also works with NASA and other international space organizations, and runs a federally funded research and development center for the Department of Defense. Among the corporation's areas of expertise are launch certification, systems engineering, process implementation, and satellite control systems.

EXECUTIVES

President and CEO: Wiliam F. Ballhaus Jr.
EVP: Joe M. Straus
SVP, Engineering and Technology Group: Wanda M. Austin
SVP, General Counsel, and Secretary: Gordon J. Louttit
SVP, National Systems Group: Jon H. Bryson
SVP, Space Systems Group: John R. Parsons
SVP, Systems Planning and Engineering: Rodney C. Gibson
VP, CFO, and Treasurer: Dale E. Wallis
VP, Human Resources and Administration: Marlene M. Dennis
VP, Laboratory Operations: Lawrence T. Greenberg
VP, National Space Systems Engineering: Donald R. Walker
VP, Space Launch Operations: Ray F. Johnson
VP, Space Program Operations: Stephen E. Burrin

LOCATIONS

HQ: 2350 E. El Segundo Blvd., El Segundo, CA 90245
Phone: 310-336-5000 **Fax:** 310-336-7055
Web: www.aero.org

The Aerospace Corporation has offices in California, Colorado, the District of Columbia, Florida, Maryland, Nebraska, New Mexico, Pennsylvania, Texas, and Virginia.

PRODUCTS/OPERATIONS

Selected Areas of Expertise

Environmental applications
Launch certification
Launch vehicles and support
Materials, component design, and analysis
Process implementation
Satellite and launch control systems
Signal collection and processing
Software assessment
Space debris
Space environment
System architecture, engineering, and design
Task integration
Technology development

COMPETITORS

Alliant Techsystems
Battelle Memorial
Boeing
Charles Stark Draper Laboratory
Computer Sciences
Lockheed Martin
MITRE
Northrop Grumman
Orbital Sciences
Raytheon
Research Triangle Institute
SAIC
Southwest Research Institute
SRI International

HISTORICAL FINANCIALS

Company Type: Not-for-profit

Income Statement FYE: September 30

	REVENUE ($ mil.)	NET INCOME ($ mil.)	NET PROFIT MARGIN	EMPLOYEES
9/02	506	—	—	3,000
9/01	476	—	—	3,000
9/00	434	—	—	3,000
9/99	350	—	—	3,000
9/98	339	—	—	3,000
9/97	346	—	—	3,000
9/96	327	—	—	—
Annual Growth	7.5%	—	—	0.0%

Revenue History

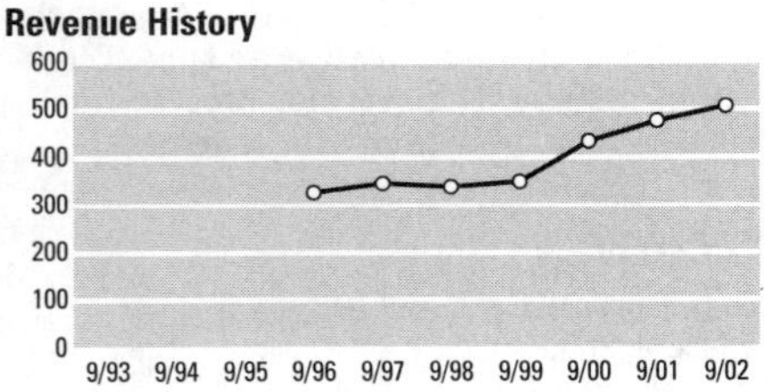

Affiliated Foods Incorporated

Actually, it's the stores — 700 of them — that are affiliated with grocery distributor Affiliated Foods. The cooperative distributes food and non-food items to its member-owners' stores in Arizona, Colorado, Kansas, New Mexico, Oklahoma, Texas, and Wyoming. Founded in 1946 as Panhandle Associated Grocers, Affiliated Foods also helps retailers implement computer systems and software. In addition, the co-op operates Tri-State Baking (TenderCrust and Always Fresh brands) and owns the Plains Dairy, which produces 60,000 gallons of milk a day and bottles water, juice, tea, and fruit drinks. It also owns a stake in private-label products supplier Western Family Foods (Western Family and Shurfine brands).

EXECUTIVES

President and COO: George Lankford
CFO: Wayne Smith
EVP: Mark Griffin
President, Plains Dairy Products: Dub Garlington
President, Tri State Baking Company: Jim Ravenscraft
General Manager Southwest: Randy Arceneaux
Day Director Warehouse Operations: Paul Siebenthal
Evening Director Warehouse Operations: Joe Moore
Director of Human Resources: Gene Blackburn
Auditors: Johnson Moore & Associates, PC

LOCATIONS

HQ: 1401 Farmers Ave., Amarillo, TX 79118
Phone: 806-372-3851 **Fax:** 806-372-3647
Web: www.afiama.com

COMPETITORS

AWG
Fleming Companies
GSC Enterprises
IGA
Nash Finch
SUPERVALU

HISTORICAL FINANCIALS

Company Type: Cooperative

Income Statement FYE: September 30

	REVENUE ($ mil.)	NET INCOME ($ mil.)	NET PROFIT MARGIN	EMPLOYEES
9/02	854	—	—	1,000
9/01	700	—	—	962
9/00	697	—	—	1,100
9/99	671	—	—	1,100
9/98	655	—	—	1,000
9/97	640	—	—	920
9/96	608	—	—	875
9/95	570	—	—	840
9/94	530	—	—	850
9/93	500	—	—	900
Annual Growth	6.1%	—	—	1.2%

Revenue History

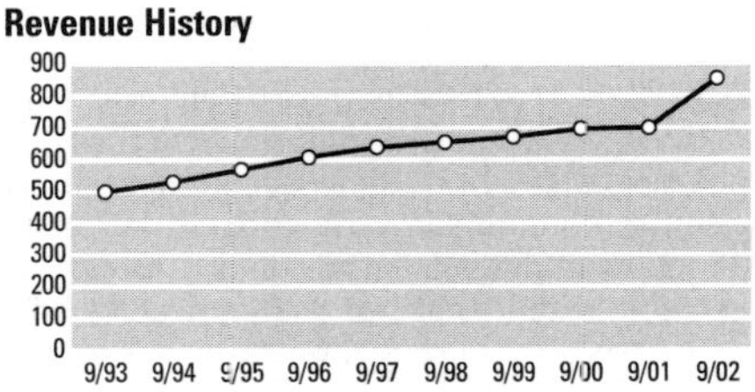

Affinity Group Holding, Inc.

Recreation is serious business for Affinity Group Holding, Inc. (AGHI). The direct marketing company sells goods and services through four clubs: Good Sam, Coast to Coast, and President's (which provide discounts for the RV crowd), and Golf Card (discounts for green fees). Nearly 2 million people pay membership fees ranging from $12 to $90 to join the clubs. AGHI also runs Camping World, a 30-store chain in some 18 states, which sells RV products (refrigerators, sanitation products) not usually found in general merchandise stores. In addition, AGHI publishes about 30 magazines and travel guides, from which it derives subscription fees and ad sales revenue. Chairman Stephen Adams owns about 95% of the company.

EXECUTIVES

Chairman; Chairman of Affinity Group, Inc.: Stephen Adams, age 65, $2,425,022 pay
President, CEO and Director; President and CEO of Affinity Group, Inc.: Joe McAdams, age 59, $675,010 pay
COO of Affinity Group, Inc.: Michael Schneider, age 48, $497,505 pay
VP and CFO; SVP and CFO of Affinity Group, Inc.: Mark J. Boggess, age 47
SVP of Affinity Group, Inc.: Michael Blumer, age 57
SVP, Marketing of Affinity Group, Inc.: Murray S. Coker, age 62, $385,753 pay
President and CEO, Camping World, and Director: Mark T. Gilman, age 38, $377,650 pay
Human Resources Manager: Mavis Rieck
Auditors: Ernst & Young LLP

LOCATIONS

HQ: 64 Inverness Dr. East, Englewood, CO 80112
Phone: 303-792-7284 **Fax:** 303-728-7322

PRODUCTS/OPERATIONS

2002 Sales

	$ mil.	% of total
Retail	239.9	56
Membership services	124.5	29
Publications	66.7	15
Total	**431.1**	**100**

COMPETITORS

Cendant
International Leisure
KOA
REI
Thousand Trails

HISTORICAL FINANCIALS

Company Type: Private

Income Statement FYE: December 31

	REVENUE ($ mil.)	NET INCOME ($ mil.)	NET PROFIT MARGIN	EMPLOYEES
12/02	431	12	2.8%	1,627
12/01	405	1	0.1%	1,514
12/00	405	3	0.8%	1,608
12/99	382	7	1.7%	1,565
12/98	359	(5)	—	1,471
12/97	301	4	1.2%	—
12/96	139	(2)	—	—
Annual Growth	20.8%	—	—	2.6%

2002 Year-End Financials

Debt ratio: —
Return on equity: —
Cash ($ mil.): 2
Current ratio: 0.65
Long-term debt ($ mil.): 215

Net Income History

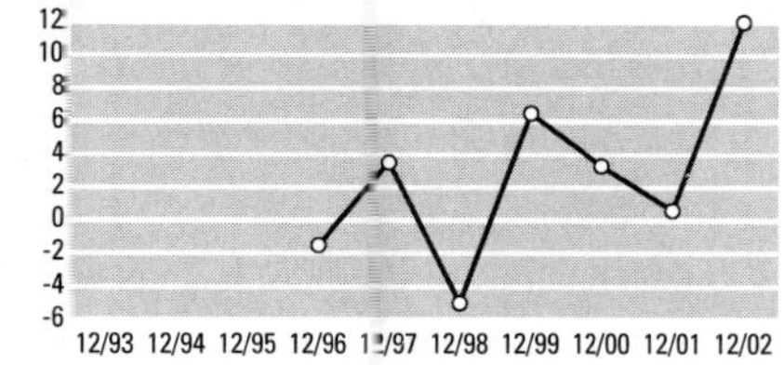

AFL-CIO

Talk about spending a long time in labor: The AFL-CIO (American Federation of Labor and Congress of Industrial Organizations) has been at it for more than a century. The AFL-CIO is an umbrella organization for 65 autonomous national and international unions representing more than 13 million workers — ranging from actors and airline pilots to teachers and Teamsters — and works to improve wages and working conditions. The organization charters 51 state federations and nearly 580 central labor councils. Union members generally receive about 33% higher pay and more benefits than nonmembers.

The organization's membership has been decreasing because of the decline in manufacturing jobs and the increased use of temporary workers and automation. However, the AFL-CIO is reviving under the leadership of John Sweeney, primarily because of his aggressive emphasis on recruiting.

HISTORY

The American Federation of Labor (AFL) was formed in 1886 in Columbus, Ohio, by the merger of six craft unions and a renegade craft section of the Marxist-oriented Knights of Labor. Samuel Gompers, a New York cigar factory worker who headed the AFL until his death in 1924, initiated the AFL's pragmatic focus: to work within the economic system to increase wages, improve working conditions, and abolish child labor.

Gompers' successes incensed employers, whose arsenal, supported by the US courts and public opinion, included injunctions, government-backed police forces to crush strikes, and the Sherman Anti-Trust Act (used to assail union monopoly powers).

WWI's production needs boosted AFL membership to 4 million by 1919. Labor clashes with management were widespread in the 1920s amid the fear of Bolsheviks. As part of open-shop drives, employers replaced strikers with southern African-Americans and Mexican workers.

The Great Depression brought more supportive public and pro-labor laws, including the National Industrial Recovery Act (NIRA, 1933), which allowed union organizing and collective bargaining. After NIRA was declared unconstitutional, the Wagner Act (1936) restated many of NIRA's provisions and established the legal basis for unions.

Union power split in 1935 when AFL coal miner John L. Lewis began organizing unskilled workers. Lewis and his allies, expelled from the AFL, formed the Congress of Industrial Organizations (CIO, 1938) and enjoyed success in unionizing the auto, steel, textile, and other industries. By 1946 the AFL and CIO had 9 million and 5 million members, respectively.

Amid postwar concern over rising prices, communist infiltration, and union corruption, Congress passed the Taft-Hartley Act in 1947 (which outlawed closed shops). The new climate of hostility led the AFL (headed by plumber George Meany) and the CIO (headed by autoworker Walter Reuther) to merge in 1955. The AFL-CIO soon expelled the Teamsters and other unions on charges of corruption. (The Teamsters reaffiliated in 1987.)

AFL-CIO membership jumped after President Kennedy gave federal employees the right to unionize (1962); state, county, and municipal workers soon followed.

Union membership, which peaked in the mid-1940s with more than a third of the US labor force, was particularly hurt by a jump in imported goods in the 1970s and automation's triumph over manual labor in the 1980s. Legislation supported by the AFL-CIO included a law requiring 60 days' notice for plant closings (1988) and the Family Leave Act (1993). But labor lost its battle against NAFTA (North American Free Trade Agreement), which it feared would export jobs to Mexico.

In 1995 John Sweeney, former head of the Service Employees International Union, became president of the AFL-CIO in its first contested election. Under Sweeney the union spent $35 million in advertising in 1996 to draw attention to issues. After years with little focus on organizing, in 1997 the AFL-CIO launched a massive campaign to organize construction, hospital, and hotel workers in Las Vegas, and committed a third of its budget to recruiting and reorganizing. It supported the Teamsters' successful strike against UPS in 1997 and in 1998 threw its weight behind the Air Line Pilots Association's walkout on Northwest Airlines. It approved a restructuring plan in 1999 and the next year spent significant time and money rallying members all across the US in support of losing presidential candidate Al Gore. In 2002 AFL-CIO announced its pledge of $750 million to create affordable housing in New York City.

EXECUTIVES

President: John J. Sweeney, age 69
EVP: Linda Chavez-Thompson, age 59
Secretary and Treasurer: Richard L. Trumka, age 54
VP; President, American Federation of State, County, and Municipal Employees: Gerald W. McEntee
VP; President, American Federation of Teachers: Sandra Feldman
VP; President, International Association of Machinists and Aerospace Workers: R. Thomas Buffenbarger
VP; President, International Brotherhood of Teamsters: James P. Hoffa
VP; President, International Brotherhood of Electrical Workers: Edwin D. Hill
VP; President Sheet Metal Wokers Union: Mike Sullivan
VP; President, U.A.W.: Stephen P. Yokich
Director Corporate Affairs: Ron Blackwell
Director International Affairs: Barbara Shailor
Director Human Resources: Karla Garland
Director Legislative: Peggy Taylor
Director Office of Investment: Bill Patterson
General Counsel: Jonathan Hiatt

LOCATIONS

HQ: 815 16th St. NW, Washington, DC 20006
Phone: 202-637-5000 **Fax:** 202-637-5058
Web: www.aflcio.org

The AFL-CIO encompasses 65 national and international unions.

PRODUCTS/OPERATIONS

Selected Trades and Workers Represented

Acting
Airline pilots
Broadcasting
Building trades
Education
Electrical trades
Engineering
Farmworkers
Firefighters
Flight attendants
Food trades
Government workers
Hotel employees
Industrial trades
Maritime trades
Metal trades
Mining
Music
Office employees
Police
Postal employees
Restaurant employees
Teachers
Transportation trades
Utility workers
Writers

Ag Processing

Soy far, soy good for Ag Processing (AGP), one of the largest soybean processors in the US. AGP's chief soybean products include vegetable oil and commercial animal feeds. It also provides grain marketing and transportation services. The co-operative is promoting its corn-based ethanol and soybean oil-based bio-fuels, fuel additives, and solvents. AGP processes some 15,000 acres of soybeans a day from its members' farms. The co-op's owners include 250,000 members from 16 states and Canada. The members, mostly in the Midwest, are represented through 243 local co-ops and eight regional co-ops.

AGP also turns its products into food ingredients, such as lecithin and meat extenders for ground beef.

To capitalize on new EPA emission limits and mandates, the co-op is lobbying to increase retail demand for ethanol. Additionally, AGP is promoting methyl ester, a by-product of soy oil refining, for use as a clean fuel and fuel additive, agricultural spray, and non-toxic solvent to replace petroleum-based products.

Fire shut down the co-op's soybean crusher in Mason City, Iowa, in February 2001. Customers were routed to crushing facilities in Eagle Grove and Emmetsburg, Iowa, while repairs were made. As of the end of 2002, the soybean crusher was still undergoing repair and upgrading.

HISTORY

Seeking strength in numbers, Ag Processing (AGP) was formed in 1983 when agricultural cooperatives Land O' Lakes and Farmland Industries merged their money-losing soybean operations into similarly struggling Boone Valley Cooperative.

Separately, AGP's six soybean mills had been unable to compete successfully against each other and larger corporations. The entire industry had been hampered by the Soviet grain embargoes imposed by the US in 1973 and 1979, and US government policies had contributed to increased competition from heavily subsidized soy producers in Argentina and Brazil. Soy exports from the US had fallen dramatically, leading to a production capacity surplus.

Collectively, AGP was able to attract a stronger management staff than its predecessors had; it hired 21-year Archer Daniels Midland (ADM) veteran James Lindsay as CEO and general manager. With operations scattered over four states, AGP placed its headquarters in Omaha, Nebraska — chosen for its central location and close proximity to the co-op's main bank.

In its first two years, AGP cut employee rolls by 20% and scaled back production, thus trimming costs and squeezing higher prices for finished products. A turnaround came quickly, and in 1985 members received a dividend from the co-op's $8 million pretax profit. That year AGP purchased two Iowa plants from AGRI Industries.

AGP dismantled two plants in 1987. By the next year the co-op witnessed an increase in domestic demand and had resumed selling to the Soviet Union. It generated additional sales by further processing soybean oil into food-grade products like hydrogenated oil and lecithin.

With an eye on diversification and value-added products, by 1991 AGP had expanded to eight soybean plants and two vegetable oil refineries; it also acquired the feed and grain business of International Multifoods that year through an 80%-owned joint venture with ADM. The acquisition included 29 feed plants in the US and Canada, 26 retail centers, 18 grain elevators, and the brands Supersweet and Masterfeeds. In 1994 AGP formed feed manufacturer Consolidated Nutrition, a 50-50 joint-venture with ADM.

Consolidated Nutrition introduced a Swine Operations program in 1996. The program quickly grew through the development of PORK PACT, a partnership to serve pork producers. (The co-op has since exited the swine business.) The next year AGP's grain division sold nine grain elevators in Ohio and Indiana to Cargill. That year the co-op gained control of Venezuelan feed manufacturer Proagro.

By 1998 passage of the Freedom to Farm Act and growing demand had spurred soybean planting. The co-op in 1998 opened an additional processing plant in Emmetsburg, Iowa, followed by another in Eagle Grove, Iowa. AGP sold off its pet food operations in 1998 to Windy Hill, which was later acquired by Doane Pet Care Enterprises. Also that year Consolidated Nutrition combined its Master Mix and Supersweet feed brands into the Consolidated Nutrition label.

In 1999 the company added the Garner-Klemme-Meservey cooperative to its grain operations. It opened a new plant late that year in St. Joseph, Missouri, to make value-added products such as hardfat (used in emulsifiers).

In June 2001 AGP sold its 50% share of Consolidated Nutrition to ADM. In 2002 the co-op's Masterfeeds business acquired four feed mills and a merchandising operation from Saskatchewan Wheat Pool.

EXECUTIVES

Chairman: Bradley T. Davis
Vice Chairman: Lowell D. Wilson
CEO and General Manager: Martin P. Reagan
CFO: J. Keith Spackler
SVP and Corporate Controller: Tim E. Witty
SVP, Corporate & Member Relations: Mike Maranell
SVP, Human Resources: Judy Ford
SVP, Transportation: Terry J. Voss
Group VP, Animal Nutrition: Robert J. Flack
Group VP, Food and Industrial: George L. Hoover
Group VP, Grain: Michael J. Knobbe
VP and Corporate General Counsel: Larry Steier
VP, Government Relations and Industrial Products: John B. Campbell
VP, Hedging: Daryl D. Dahl
VP, Information Systems: Michael Reed
VP, Nutrition & Technical Service: Wayne L. Stockland
VP, Soybean/Corn Operations: Gary L. Olsen
VP, Research, Process Development and Technical Operations, Food & Industrial: Richard P. Copeland
VP, Technology Marketing and Applications: Blake Hendrix
Treasurer, Secretary, and Director: Ronald R. Ross
Director International: Glen Heitritter
Manager Communications: Ed Woll
Manager Purchasing: Gary Chestnut

LOCATIONS

HQ: Ag Processing Inc.
12700 W. Dodge Rd., Omaha, NE 68154
Phone: 402-496-7809 **Fax:** 402-498-2215
Web: www.agp.com

Ag Processing has operations in 16 states in the US and Canada.

PRODUCTS/OPERATIONS

Selected Operations

Commercial feeds
Food (lecithin, soybean oil, vegetable oil)
Grain
Industrial products (ethanol, methyl ester)
Soybean processing
Transportation (barge, rail, truck)

Selected Brands

Masterfeeds (feeds, Canada)
SOYGOLD (bio-diesel, solvents, fuel additives)

Selected Subsidiaries

Ag Environmental Products (soybean methyl ester products)
AGP Grain Cooperative
AGP Grain, Ltd.
Intellectual Property Holdings LLC

COMPETITORS

Abengoa Bioenergy
Agway
Andersons
ADM
Bunge Limited
Cargill
CHS
ConAgra
Corn Products International
DeBruce Grain
Farmland Industries
Griffin Industries
MFA
Riceland Foods
Southern States
Stake Technology

HISTORICAL FINANCIALS

Company Type: Cooperative

Income Statement FYE: August 31

	REVENUE ($ mil.)	NET INCOME ($ mil.)	NET PROFIT MARGIN	EMPLOYEES
8/02	1,802	32	1.8%	2,500
8/01	1,789	27	1.5%	2,500
8/00	1,962	—	—	2,500
8/99	2,095	—	—	2,500
8/98	2,615	—	—	2,550
8/97	2,948	—	—	3,000
8/96	2,765	—	—	3,050
8/95	2,132	—	—	—
8/94	1,377	—	—	—
8/93	1,219	—	—	—
Annual Growth	4.4%	20.4%	—	(3.3%)

2002 Year-End Financials

Debt ratio: 21.6%
Return on equity: 8.2%
Cash ($ mil.): 9
Current ratio: 1.76
Long-term debt ($ mil.): 87

Net Income History

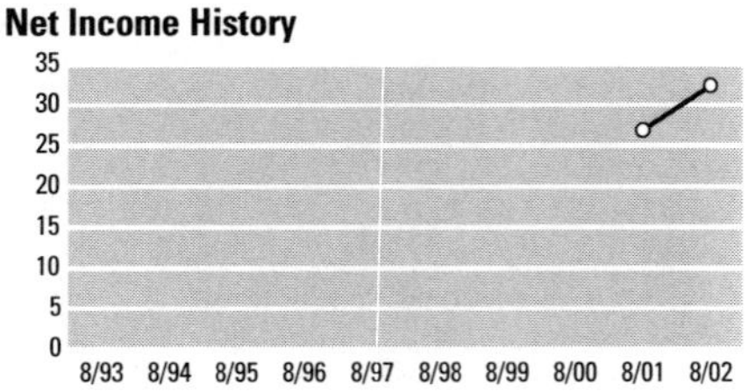

A. G. Spanos Companies

Spanning the land from California to Florida, A.G. Spanos Companies bridges many operations: building, managing, and selling multi-family housing units to constructing master-planned communities, to developing land. The firm has built more than 80,000 apartments in 18 states since its founding in 1960. Major projects include Spanos Park, a $1 billion master-planned community on 3,000 acres in founder and chairman Alex Spanos' hometown of Stockton, California, as well as the construction of luxury apartments across the nation. Alex Spanos, owner of the NFL's San Diego Chargers, stills owns the firm, which is operated by sons Dean (president and CEO) and Michael Spanos (EVP).

EXECUTIVES

Chairman: Alexander G. (Alex) Spanos, age 80
President and CEO: Dean A. Spanos, age 53
EVP: Michael A. Spanos, age 43
CFO: Jeremiah T. Murphy
Financial Officer and CTO: Steven L. Cohen
Director, Public Relations: Natalia Orfanos
Manager, Florida and Texas Division: Charlie Raffo
Manager, Georgia Division: Jim Kourafas
Manager, Human Resources: Charlene Flynn
Manager, Land Development Division: Jim Panagopoulos
Manager, Nevada Division: George Filios
Manager, Property Management Division: Jean Lobsinger
Manager, Property Management Division: Michael Meath
Manager, Southern California, Arizona, and New Mexico Division: Ray Hanes

LOCATIONS

HQ: 1341 W. Robinhood Dr., Ste. A-1,
Stockton, CA 95207
Phone: 209-478-7954 **Fax:** 209-473-3703
Web: www.agspanos.com

The A.G. Spanos Companies has offices in Arizona (Phoenix/Tempe), California (Sacramento and Stockton), Florida (Tampa), Georgia (Atlanta/Marietta), Indiana (Carmel), Kansas (Overland), Nevada (Las Vegas), North Carolina (Charlotte), and Texas (Austin, Dallas/Irving).

PRODUCTS/OPERATIONS

Selected Subsidiaries

A. G. Spanos Construction
A. G. Spanos Development, Inc.
A. G. Spanos Enterprises, Inc.
A. G. Spanos Management, Inc.
A. G. Spanos Realty, Inc.
A. G. Spanos Securities
AGS Financial Corporation
The Spanos Corporation

Other Ownership Interests

A. G. Spanos Jet Center (Stockton, California)
San Diego Chargers National Football League Team

COMPETITORS

Barratt Developments
Calprop
Centex
Del Webb
Edward Rose
Irvine Company
Lennar
Morrison Homes
Perini
Pinnacle West
Pulte Homes
Schuler Homes
William Lyon Homes

HISTORICAL FINANCIALS

Company Type: Private

Income Statement FYE: September 30

	ESTIMATED REVENUE ($ mil.)	NET INCOME ($ mil.)	NET PROFIT MARGIN	EMPLOYEES
9/02	1,400	—	—	600
9/01	1,560	—	—	600
9/00	1,590	—	—	600
9/99	1,440	—	—	600
9/98	1,175	—	—	600
9/97	964	—	—	600
9/96	950	—	—	600
9/95	947	—	—	—
Annual Growth	5.8%	—	—	0.0%

Revenue History

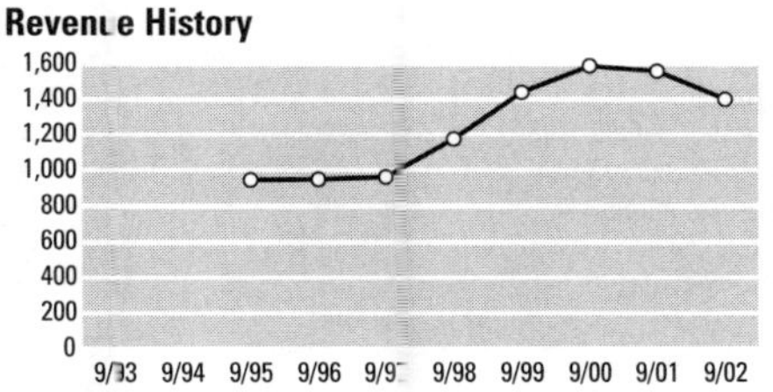

AgAmerica, FCB

AgAmerica aggrandizes farm credit in the western US. The cooperative recently merged with AgriBank, making the new entity one of the largest of five regional banks in the federal Farm Credit System, which provides loans and banking services to local Farm Credit offices. AgAmerica offers operating and land loans, rural home mortgages, crop insurance, and financial services including record-keeping and financial planning to such borrowers as aquatic producers, farmers, ranchers, rural homeowners, timber harvesters, and rural utility providers. The bank raises its funds through the sale of securities.

EXECUTIVES

Chairman: Alan Dillman
Vice Chairman: Robert E. Epler
President and CEO: William J. Collins
VP and CFO: Diane M. Cole
VP, Secretary, and General Counsel: William J. Thone
VP, Credit: Ross B. Anderson
VP, Information and Business Services: Rodney A. Nelsestuen
VP, Government Affairs: John J. O'Day
VP, Audit and Review: Donald W. Theuninck
VP, Human Resources and Administrative Services: John E. Lovstad
Auditors: PricewaterhouseCoopers LLP

LOCATIONS

HQ: 375 Jackson St., St. Paul, MN 55101
Phone: 651-282-8800 **Fax:** 651-282-8666
Web: www.agamericafcb.com

COMPETITORS

Acceptance Insurance
Ag Services
AgFirst
Farmland Mutual Insurance Company
National Rural Utilities Cooperative Finance

HISTORICAL FINANCIALS

Company Type: Cooperative

Income Statement FYE: December 31

	ASSETS ($ mil.)	NET INCOME ($ mil.)	INCOME AS % OF ASSETS	EMPLOYEES
12/01	11,568	186	1.6%	—
12/00	10,689	197	1.8%	—
12/99	9,792	138	1.4%	—
12/98	9,105	124	1.4%	—
12/97	7,986	140	1.8%	—
12/96	7,764	127	1.6%	—
12/95	7,462	147	2.0%	—
Annual Growth	7.6%	4.0%	—	—

2001 Year-End Financials

Equity as % of assets: —
Return on assets: 1.7%
Return on equity: —
Long-term debt ($ mil.): —
Sales ($ mil.): 822

Net Income History

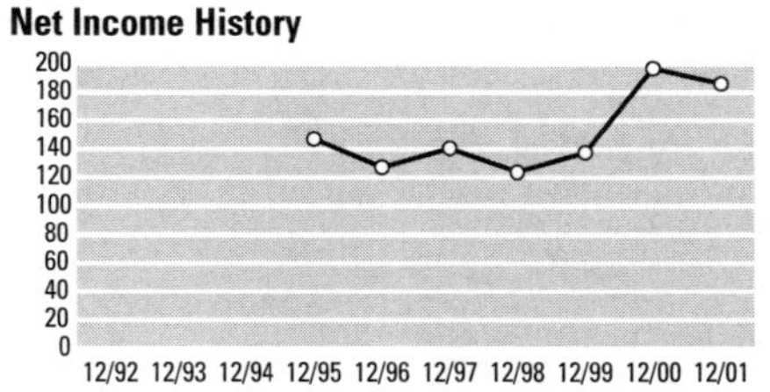

AgFirst Farm Credit Bank

AgFirst puts farmers first. A large and growing agricultural lender, AgFirst Farm Credit Bank operates in 15 eastern states and Puerto Rico, offering more than $10 billion in loans to some 80,000 farmers, ranchers, rural homeowners, and agribusiness owners. AgFirst originates real estate, operating, and rural home mortgage loans. Additionally, it offers crop, life, and timber insurance; equipment leasing; tax services; record keeping; and other products and services designed to meet customers' business and personal needs. The bank does not accept deposits; it raises money by selling bonds and notes on the capital markets.

AgFirst is a member of the largest agricultural lending organization in the U.S., Farm Credit System (FCS), with assets eclipsing $100 billion. The bank finances farmers, agribusinesses, and rural homeowners through affiliated retail lenders. Through its Capital Markets unit, it arranges and participates in loans for agribusinesses. Its Secondary Mortgage Market unit buys, sells, and services agricultural and rural home loans.

EXECUTIVES

Chairman: F. Merrel Lust
Vice Chairman: Richard Kriebel
President and CEO: F. A. (Andy) Lowrey, $390,810 pay
EVP and CFO: Larry R. Doyle
EVP: Thomas S. Welsh
VP, Capital Markets: Felicia Morant
VP, Marketing: Joy M. Upchurch
Director of Advertising and Communications: Donna J. Camacho
Senior Human Resources Specialist: Pat N. Roche
Auditors: PricewaterhouseCoopers LLP

LOCATIONS

HQ: 1401 Hampton St., Columbia, SC 29202
Phone: 803-799-5000 **Fax:** 803-254-1776
Web: www.agfirst.com

AgFirst Farm Credit Bank operates in Alabama, Delaware, Florida, Georgia, Kentucky, Louisiana, Maryland, Mississippi, Ohio, North Carolina, Pennsylvania, Puerto Rico, South Carolina, Tennessee, Virginia, and West Virginia.

PRODUCTS/OPERATIONS

2001 Sales

	$ mil.	% of total
Loan interest	636.1	84
Securities interest	104.5	14
Other	13.5	2
Total	**754.1**	**100**

COMPETITORS

Acceptance Insurance
Ag Services
AgAmerica
AgriBank
Alabama Farmers Cooperatives
National Rural Utilities Cooperative Finance

HISTORICAL FINANCIALS

Company Type: Cooperative

Income Statement FYE: December 31

	ASSETS ($ mil.)	NET INCOME ($ mil.)	INCOME AS % OF ASSETS	EMPLOYEES
12/01	13,233	131	1.0%	—
12/00	13,522	235	1.7%	—
12/99	12,726	218	1.7%	—
12/98	11,987	218	1.8%	—
12/97	11,053	209	1.9%	—
12/96	10,544	201	1.9%	—
12/95	10,355	172	1.7%	—
Annual Growth	4.2%	(4.5%)	—	—

2001 Year-End Financials

Equity as % of assets: —
Return on assets: 1.0%
Return on equity: —
Long-term debt ($ mil.): —
Sales ($ mil.): 754

Net Income History

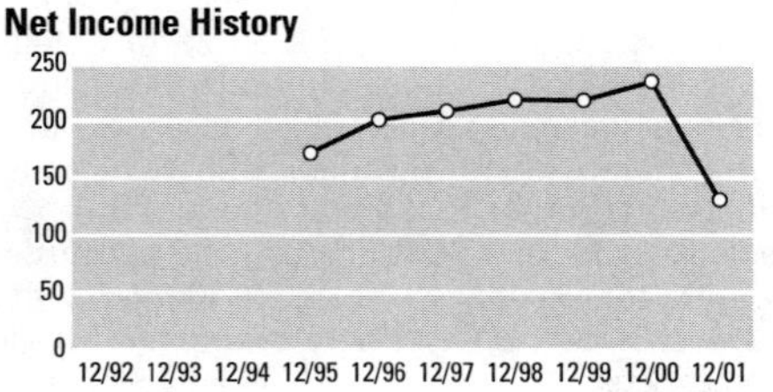

AgriBank, FCB

AgriBank puts the "green" in green acres. A financial intermediary, AgriBank provides wholesale lending and business services to Farm Credit System (FCS) associations in America's heartland. Established by Congress, the FCS is a nationwide network of cooperatives that provides loans and financial services for some 200,000 farmers, ranchers, agribusiness owners, timber producers, and rural homeowners. Farm Credit Service's co-ops write loans for land, equipment, and other farm operating costs; they in turn own AgriBank. AgriBank also provides credit to rural electric, water, and telephone systems. The company merged with AgAmerica in 2003.

Located in St Paul, Minnesota, AgriBank serves the Seventh Farm Credit District, which operates in primarily mid-western states. It is organized along three lines of business: wholesale, business services, and retail. Providing district associations with wholesale products and services is its primary focus; however, it also offers a wide range of business services including information technology, portfolio risk management, retail product and processing support, and human resources.

EXECUTIVES

Chairman: Douglas Felton, $25,475 pay
CEO: William J. Collins, $501,000 pay
VP and CFO: Diane M. Cole
VP, Audit and Review: Donald W. Theuninck
VP, Credit: Ross B. Anderson
VP, Government Affairs: John J. O'Day
VP, Human Resources and Administrative Services: John E. Lovstad
VP, Information and Business Services: Rodney A. Nelsestuen
VP, Secretary, and General Counsel: William J. Thone
Auditors: PricewaterhouseCoopers LLP

LOCATIONS

HQ: 375 Jackson St., St. Paul, MN 55164
Phone: 651-282-8800 **Fax:** 651-282-8666
Web: www.agribank.com

AgriBank operates in Arkansas, Illinois, Indiana, Iowa, Kentucky, Michigan, Minnesota, Missouri, Nebraska, North Dakota, Ohio, South Dakota, Tennessee, Wisconsin, and Wyoming.

PRODUCTS/OPERATIONS

2002 Sales

	$ mil.	% of total
Loan interest	752.2	85
Securities interest	95.4	11
Business services	25.1	3
Loan prepayment fees & other	9.4	1
Total	**882.1**	**100**

COMPETITORS

Acceptance Insurance
Ag Services
AgFirst
Alabama Farmers Cooperatives
CHS
Farmland Mutual Insurance Company
National Rural Utilities Cooperative Finance

HISTORICAL FINANCIALS

Company Type: Cooperative

Income Statement FYE: December 31

	ASSETS ($ mil.)	NET INCOME ($ mil.)	INCOME AS % OF ASSETS	EMPLOYEES
12/02	24,074	180	0.7%	3,300
12/01	21,465	146	0.7%	3,300
12/00	22,767	316	1.4%	3,200
12/99	21,343	218	1.0%	3,200
12/98	21,246	266	1.2%	3,200
12/97	19,416	265	1.4%	3,160
12/96	18,649	256	1.4%	—
12/95	16,253	251	1.5%	—
12/94	15,646	222	1.4%	—
12/93	14,905	268	1.8%	—
Annual Growth	5.5%	(4.3%)	—	0.9%

2002 Year-End Financials

Equity as % of assets: 6.6%
Return on assets: 0.8%
Return on equity: 11.5%
Long-term debt ($ mil.): 22,214
Sales ($ mil.): 882

Net Income History

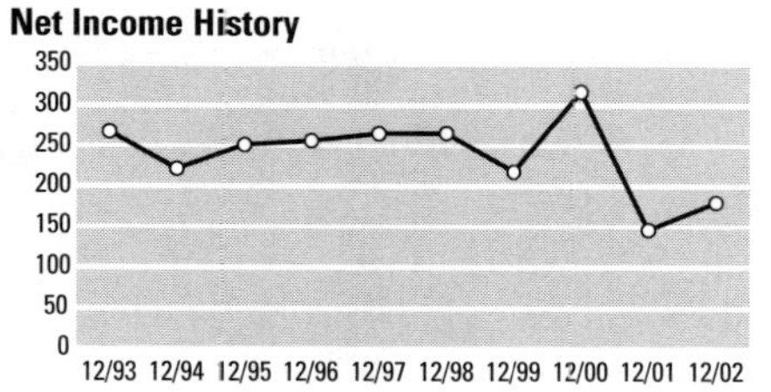

Agri-Mark, Inc.

Cheese lovers who make a habit of Cabot ought to know Agri-Mark, the northeastern dairy cooperative that makes Cabot-brand cheese, butter, and cultured dairy products, and McCadam-brand cheese. Formed in 1980, Agri-Mark has more than 1,450 member-owners who operate farms throughout New England and New York, producing 2.7 billion pounds of milk a year. The company merged with Cabot Creamery in 1992 and purchased the McCadam Cheese business in 2003. Agri-Mark also sells milk to bottlers and manufacturers in the eastern US. It owns four processing plants: two in Vermont and one each in Massachusetts and New York.

EXECUTIVES

Chairman: Carl Peterson
President and General Manager: Paul P. Johnston
EVP and COO; CEO, Cabot Creamery: Richard W. Stammer
SVP Finance and Administration: Margaret H. Bertolino
SVP Economics, Communications, and Legislative Affairs: Robert D. Wellington
SVP Sales, Cabot Creamery: Charlie Green
VP Human Resources: Robert Porter
VP Information Services: Ralph Viscomi
Director of Communications: Douglas DiMento

LOCATIONS

HQ: 100 Milk St., Methuen, MA 01844
Phone: 978-689-4442 **Fax:** 978-794-8304
Web: www.agrimark.net

PRODUCTS/OPERATIONS

Selected Products

Bovine lactoferrin (nutritional whey protein found in cow's milk)
Butter
Cheese
Condensed skim milk
Condensed whey
Cottage cheese
Cream
Milk powder
Skim milk
Sour cream and dips
Sweet cream
Yogurt

COMPETITORS

Dairy Farmers of America
Dairylea
Dean Foods
Great Lakes Cheese
Keller's
Kraft Foods
Land O'Lakes
Lucille Farms

HISTORICAL FINANCIALS

Company Type: Cooperative

Income Statement FYE: November 30

	REVENUE ($ mil.)	NET INCOME ($ mil.)	NET PROFIT MARGIN	EMPLOYEES
11/02	550	7	1.2%	700
11/01	570	6	1.0%	600
11/00	520	2	0.4%	600
11/99	556	—	—	500
11/98	575	—	—	500
11/97	462	—	—	—
11/96	479	—	—	—
11/95	396	—	—	—
Annual Growth	4.8%	89.2%	—	8.8%

Net Income History

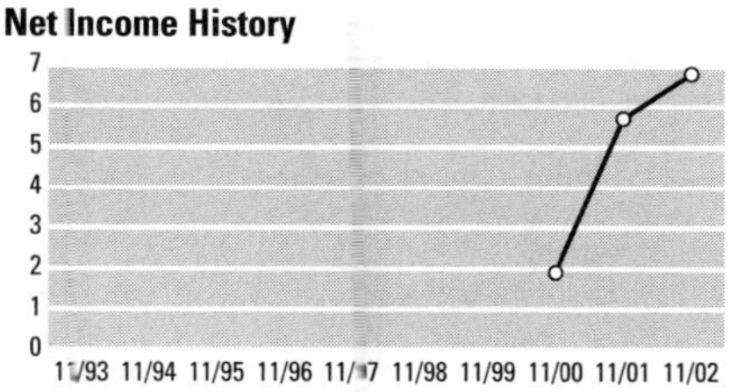

Agway Inc.

It's either Agway or the highway for many farmers. The agricultural co-op has 69,000 members, primarily in the Northeast. The co-op's Agricultural Group sells feeds, seeds, fertilizers, and other farm supplies to members and other growers. Agway's largest revenue producer is its Agway Energy Products unit, which sells fuel and HVAC systems and markets electricity and gas in deregulated states. Agway's Country Products Group processes and markets fresh produce (mostly under the Country Best label). It also invests in new agricultural technology. The co-op also offers leasing services. In 2002 Agway filed for bankruptcy.

Serving more than 500,000 customers, Agway Energy Products sells natural gas, electricity, heating oil, propane, and diesel fuel to farms, homes, and small businesses; it also sells and services heating and air-conditioning equipment and provides consulting and financing services.

The Agway Agricultural Group offers feed for livestock and poultry and seed, fertilizers, herbicides, and soil preparation products for crops. It primarily sells directly to farmers through its own sales force.

The co-op's Country Products Group processes, packages, and markets fresh produce, birdfood, and edible beans. That group also makes bags and oversees the co-op's investments in a pet food manufacturer (ProPet) and companies that develop agricultural technology. Agway also finances buildings, equipment, and vehicles for its rural customers.

In 2002, the company announced it was concentrating on three business segments: agriculture, energy, and its Country Products Group. The company then sold its insurance business, its sunflower seed and edible products business, and its Agronomy and Seedway units.

The company is exploring its options for restructuring, including the possibility of liquidating its remaining operations.

EXECUTIVES

Chairman: Gary K. Van Slyke, age 59, $60,000 pay
Vice Chairman: Andrew J. Gilbert, age 43, $46,000 pay
President and CEO; President, Agway Energy Products: Michael R. Hopsicker, age 37 $746,618 pay (prior to promotion)
SVP and Chief Administrative Officer; Chairman and President, Agway Insurance Group: Gerald R. (Jerry) Seeber, age 55, $402,620 pay
SVP, Finance and Control: Peter J. O'Neill, age 55
SVP, General Counsel, and Secretary: Christopher W. Fox, age 54
SVP, Public Affairs: Stephen H. Hoefer, age 47
VP and CIO: William L. Parker, age 55
VP and Chief Investment Officer: G. Leslie Smith, age 59
President, Country Products Group: Roy S. Lubetkin, age 45, $787,579 pay
President, Telmark: Daniel J. Edinger, age 51, $528,022 pay
Treasurer: Karen J. Ohliger, age 40
Corporate Controller: John F. Feeney, age 41
Director, Human Resources: Richard Opdyke
Auditors: PricewaterhouseCoopers LLP

LOCATIONS

HQ: 333 Butternut Dr., DeWitt, NY 13214
Phone: 315-449-7061 **Fax:** 315-449-6008
Web: www.agway.com

PRODUCTS/OPERATIONS

Major Operating Units

Agriculture
Agway Agricultural Group (animal feeds, crop seeds, fertilizers, crop protectants, and farm supplies)

Country Products Group
The Produce Group (packaging and marketing of fresh produce)
The Business Group (commodity processing and distribution, bag manufacturing, investment in pet food)
The Investment Group (CPG Nutrients; LifeRights Foods LLC; Planet Polymer Technologies Inc.)

Energy
Agway Energy Products LLC (fuel oil, kerosene, propane, and motor vehicle fuel; heating and air-conditioning equipment; gas and electricity in certain markets)

Leasing
Telmark Inc. (lease financing for buildings, equipment, and vehicles)

COMPETITORS

Able Energy
Ag Processing
Ag Services
AmeriGas Partners
ADM
Cargill
CH Energy
CHS
ConAgra
DeBruce Grain
Energy East
Farmland Industries
GROWMARK
Rochester Gas and Electric
Saskatchewan Wheat Pool
Southern States
Star Gas Partners
Wilbur-Ellis

HISTORICAL FINANCIALS

Company Type: Cooperative

Income Statement

FYE: Last Saturday in June

	REVENUE ($ mil.)	NET INCOME ($ mil.)	NET PROFIT MARGIN	EMPLOYEES
6/02	900	(98)	—	4,200
6/01	1,548	9	0.6%	4,700
6/00	1,427	(9)	—	5,600
6/99	1,484	2	0.1%	7,200
6/98	1,563	13	0.8%	7,000
6/97	1,671	11	0.6%	7,100
6/96	1,663	13	0.8%	7,500
6/95	1,592	(16)	—	9,000
6/94	1,695	(3)	—	7,900
6/93	1,720	20	1.2%	6,600
Annual Growth	(6.9%)	—	—	(4.9%)

2002 Year-End Financials

Debt ratio: 1,265.7%
Return on equity: —
Cash ($ mil.): 0
Current ratio: 0.68
Long-term debt ($ mil.): 406

Net Income History

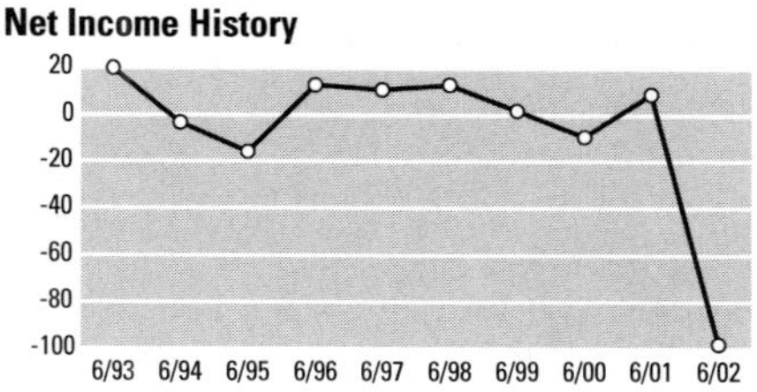

Akin, Gump, Strauss, Hauer & Feld, L.L.P.

Lobbying is as lobbying does. Akin, Gump, Strauss, Hauer & Feld is known for its work inside Washington's Beltway and has a staff peppered with political insiders such as Robert Strauss (co-founder and former chairman of the Democratic National Committee) and Vernon Jordan (friend and adviser to former President Clinton). The firm has about 1,000 attorneys in ten US offices as well as four international locations. Although known for its prominent lobbying contingent, Akin Gump's expertise ranges from corporate law to white-collar criminal defense.

Over the last few years, the firm has enhanced its intellectual property and technology practices and other standard practice areas. It moved into entertainment law with a 2000 acquisition of Troop Steuber Pasich Reddick & Tobey. The firm recently expanded its litigation practice by adding attorneys from the Austin office of Brobeck, Phleger & Harrison LLP.

EXECUTIVES

Chairman: R. Bruce McLean
CFO: Janet Campion
Senior Executive Partner: Robert S. Strauss
Senior Executive Partner: Alan D. Feld, age 66
CIO: Bradley Christmas
Chief Human Resources Officer: Julie Dressing
Chief Marketing Officer: Wendy Loder
Controller: David Staub
Communications Manager: Kristin M. White
Investor Relations: Ronald Adee

LOCATIONS

HQ: Robert S. Strauss Building, 1333 New Hampshire Ave. NW, Washington, DC 20036
Phone: 202-887-4000 **Fax:** 202-887-4288
Web: www.akingump.com

Akin, Gump, Strauss, Hauer & Feld has offices in Austin, Dallas, Houston, and San Antonio, Texas; Denver; Los Angeles; McLean, Virginia; New York City; Philadelphia; and Washington, DC; as well as in Brussels, London, and Moscow. It also has an affiliate office in Riyadh, Saudi Arabia.

PRODUCTS/OPERATIONS

Selected Practice Areas

Antitrust
Corporate and securities
Energy
Entertainment
Environmental
Government contracts
Health care
Insurance
Intellectual property
International
Investment management
Labor and employment
Litigation
Mergers and acquisitions
Public law and policy
Real estate
Tax
Technology (Akin Gump Technology Ventures)
White-collar criminal defense

COMPETITORS

Arnold & Porter
Covington & Burling
Hogan & Hartson
Howrey Simon Arnold & White
Kaye Scholer
O'Melveny & Myers
Williams & Connolly
Wilson Sonsini

HISTORICAL FINANCIALS

Company Type: Partnership

Income Statement FYE: December 31

	REVENUE ($ mil.)	NET INCOME ($ mil.)	NET PROFIT MARGIN	EMPLOYEES
12/01	553	—	—	1,000
12/00	430	—	—	1,000
12/99	360	—	—	2,000
12/98	301	—	—	1,800
12/97	246	—	—	1,700
12/96	218	—	—	1,550
12/95	190	—	—	1,400
12/94	163	—	—	1,235
12/93	137	—	—	1,000
12/92	132	—	—	—
Annual Growth	17.3%	—	—	0.0%

Revenue History

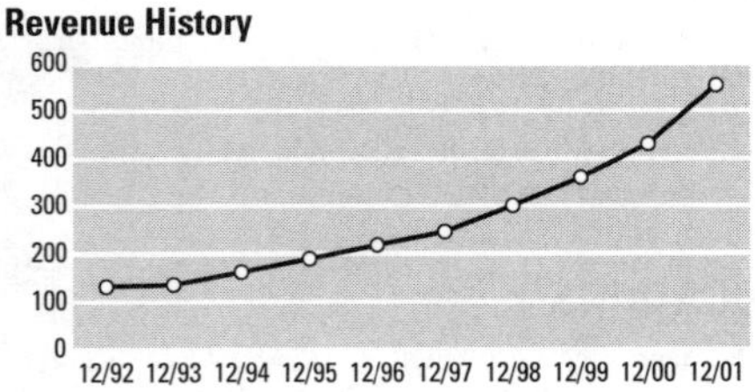

Alberici Corporation

Alberici helped shape the St. Louis skyline; it now sets its sights — its construction sites — on the world. Alberici Corp., parent company of Alberici Constructors (formerly J.S. Alberici Construction Co.), encompasses a group of enterprises with a presence in Brazil, Canada, Germany, Mexico, and the US. Operations include construction services, construction equipment, building materials, and steel fabrication units. The group also has a travel division. Alberici offers general contracting, construction management, design/build, and heavy demolition and other specialty contracting services. The Alberici family still holds the largest share of the employee-owned firm, founded in 1918 by John S. Alberici.

EXECUTIVES

President; President and CEO, Alberici Constructors, Inc.; President, Alberici Group: Robert F. (Bob) McCoole
Secretary-Treasurer; SVP Alberici Group: John S. Alberici
SVP Business Acquisition and Estimating, Alberici Group: Steven E. (Steve) Olson
SVP Contract Risk Management, Alberici Group: James E. (Jim) Frey
VP Corporate Finance and Controller, Alberici Group: Gregory T. (Greg) Hesser
VP Quality Management, Alberici Group: Ronald T. Rogge
VP Information Technology, Alberici Group: Frank C. Kropiunik
Director Employment Resources, Alberici Group: Denay Davis
Creative Director, Alberici Group: Scott A. Tripp
COO, Alberici Constructors, Inc.: Leroy J. Stromberg
VP Labor Relations, Alberici Constructors, Inc.: Robert C. Fritz
SVP and General Manager, Great Lakes Region, Alberici Constructors, Inc.: Paul H. Lemley
VP and General Manager, Southeast Region, Alberici Constructors, Inc.: Kenneth W. Robuck
VP Special Projects, Alberici Constructors, Inc.: Thomas A. Taylor
Warehouse and Equipment Manager, Alberici Constructors, Inc.: Steven W. Bodine
Leader, Alberici Healthcare: Donald E. Wojtkowski
VP, Hillsdale Fabricators: Shawn Pitt
Manager, Alberici Travel: Deborah A. Weber
President, Alberici Constructors, Ltd. (Canada): Gregory J. Kozciz

LOCATIONS

HQ: 2150 Kienlen Ave., St. Louis, MO 63121
Phone: 314-261-2611 **Fax:** 314-261-4225
Web: www.alberici.com

PRODUCTS/OPERATIONS

Selected Affiliated Companies

Alberici Construcciones, S.A. de C.V. (construction services, Mexico)
Alberici Constructors, Inc. (construction services)
Alberici Constructors, Ltd. (construction services, Canada)
Alberici do Brasil Ltda. (construction services, Brazil)
Alberici Healthcare (construction services for the health care market)
Alberici Projektmanagement GmbH (construction services, Germany)
Alberici Travel (full-service travel agency)
Gabriel Equipment (construction equipment leasing)
Gunther-Nash, Inc. (shaft, slope, and tunnel construction for mining industry)
Hillsdale Building Materials (raw materials and steel supplier)
Hillsdale Fabricators (steel fabrication)
Marhnos-Alberici Construcciones S.A. de C.V. (joint venture, Mexico)
North/South Constructors (joint venture)

COMPETITORS

ABB
Bechtel
Black & Veatch
DPR Construction
Duke/Fluor Daniel
Fluor
Hensel Phelps Construction
Hoffman Corporation
Hyundai Engineering and Construction
Jacobs Engineering
Parsons
Peter Kiewit Sons'
Raytheon
TIC Holdings
Walbridge Aldinger
Washington Group
Zachry

HISTORICAL FINANCIALS

Company Type: Private

Income Statement FYE: December 31

	REVENUE ($ mil.)	NET INCOME ($ mil.)	NET PROFIT MARGIN	EMPLOYEES
12/01	837	—	—	480
12/00	837	—	—	430
12/99	866	—	—	1,500
12/98	531	—	—	1,500
12/97	645	—	—	1,500
12/96	563	—	—	1,500
12/95	451	—	—	1,200
12/94	659	—	—	1,500
Annual Growth	3.5%	—	—	(15.0%)

Revenue History

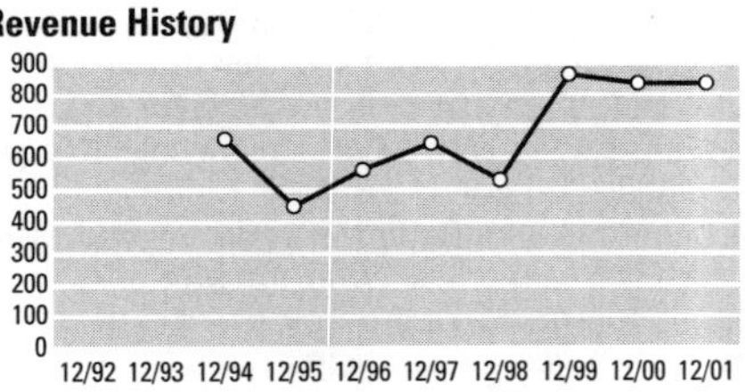

Albert Trostel & Sons Co.

A luxury car needs a luxurious leather interior, and automakers turn to Albert Trostel & Sons for leather seats and interior fixtures. The company's main subsidiary, Eagle Ottawa Leather (founded in 1865), provides leather products for more than 90 car and truck models. Eagle Ottawa's customers include GM, Ford, DaimlerChrysler, and Toyota. Albert Trostel & Sons' other subsidiaries include Trostel, Ltd., which produces custom seals, custom rubber compounds, and precision-molded rubber components for the automotive, appliance, and agricultural markets, and Trostel SEG, which makes polyurethane wheels and thermoplastics. Holding company Everett Smith Group owns Albert Trostel & Sons.

EXECUTIVES

Chairman and CEO: Anders Segerdahl
President: Randall Perry
VP and CFO: Bruce Betters
Director, Human Resources: Mike Toye

LOCATIONS

HQ: 330 E. Kilbourn Ave., Ste. 750,
Milwaukee, WI 53202
Phone: 414-223-1560 **Fax:** 414-225-0025

Through Eagle Ottawa Leather and its other subsidiaries, Albert Trostel & Sons has operations in Michigan and Wisconsin.

PRODUCTS/OPERATIONS

Selected Subsidiaries and Products

Eagle Ottawa Leather Co.
- Automobile upholstery

Trostel, Ltd.
- Cartridge seals
- Custom shapes
- Dynamic seals
- Face seals (appliances)
- General industrial products
- Grease seals
- Integral seal assemblies
- Impellers
- Oil seals
- Pressure seals
- Radial lip seals
- Reciprocating seals
- Rotary seals
- Shaft seals
- Unitized seals
- Vacuum seals
- Valve seals

Trostel Specialty Elastomers Group, Inc.
- Cast polyurethanes
- Thermoplastics

COMPETITORS

3M
Collins & Aikman
Federal-Mogul
Gates Rubber
Crespi
Harbour Group
Johnson Controls
Kaydon
Lear
Magna International
Manuli Rubber
Sumitomo Rubber

HISTORICAL FINANCIALS

Company Type: Private

Income Statement FYE: November 30*

	REVENUE ($ mil.)	NET INCOME ($ mil.)	NET PROFIT MARGIN	EMPLOYEES
12/02	623	—	—	4,750
12/01	560	—	—	4,606
12/00	490	—	—	4,500
12/99	500	—	—	3,500
12/98	500	—	—	3,500
Annual Growth	5.7%	—	—	7.9%

*Fiscal year change

Revenue History

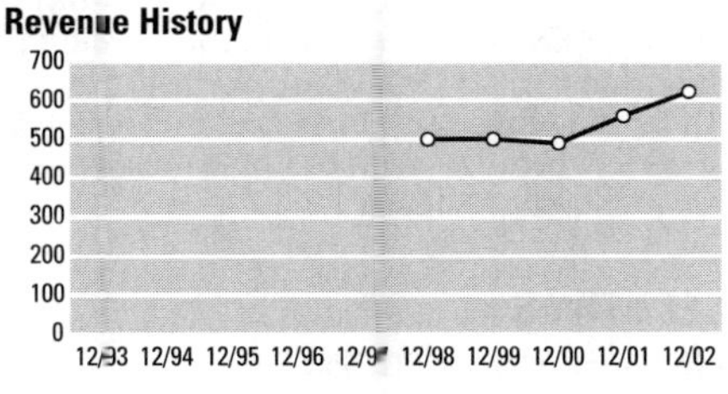

Alex Lee, Inc.

The George family mixed food wholesaling and retail well before it became a trend among consolidators. Founded by Alex and Lee George, Alex Lee has been distributing food to retailers through Merchants Distributors, Inc. (MDI) since 1931. MDI serves more than 600 retailers in the Mid-Atlantic and Southeast, including IGA stores and Galaxy Food Centers. The company became a food service supplier in the 1960s through Institution Food House, and in 1984 it bought the Lowes Foods chain, which has more than 100 stores in North Carolina and Virginia. In 1998 Alex Lee started Consolidation Services to provide logistic services to vendors, distributors, and manufacturers. The George family controls Alex Lee.

EXECUTIVES

Chairman and CEO: Boyd L. George, age 61
President: Dennis Hatchell
EVP and CFO: Ronald W. Knedlik
President, Lowes Foods: Curtis Oldenkamp
VP, Human Resources: Glenn DeBiasi

LOCATIONS

HQ: 120 4th St. SW, Hickory, NC 28602
Phone: 828-323-4424 **Fax:** 828-323-4435
Web: www.alexlee.com

COMPETITORS

Ahold USA
ARAMARK
Fleming Companies
Ingles Markets
Kroger
K-VA-T Food Stores
McLane Foodservice
Nash Finch
Ruddick
SUPERVALU
SYSCO
U.S. Foodservice
Winn-Dixie

HISTORICAL FINANCIALS

Company Type: Private

Income Statement FYE: September 30

	REVENUE ($ mil.)	NET INCOME ($ mil.)	NET PROFIT MARGIN	EMPLOYEES
9/02	1,980	—	—	9,000
9/01	1,890	—	—	8,500
9/00	1,690	—	—	8,500
9/99	1,588	—	—	7,154
9/98	1,516	—	—	7,482
9/97	1,315	—	—	6,143
9/96	1,300	—	—	5,400
9/95	1,270	—	—	5,400
9/94	1,159	—	—	3,000
9/93	1,073	—	—	—
Annual Growth	7.0%	—	—	14.7%

Revenue History

Allegis Group

Clients in need of highly skilled technical and other personnel might want to take the pledge of Allegis. Allegis Group is one of the world's largest staffing and recruitment firms, with more than 300 offices in North America and Europe. Its operating companies include Aerotek (engineering, automotive, and scientific professionals for short- and long-term assignments), Mentor 4 (recruitment for accounting, human resources, and customer support positions), and TEKsystems (IT staffing and consulting). In 1983 Steve Bisciotti and Jim Davis established Aerotek to provide contract engineering personnel to two clients in the aerospace industry; Bisciotti and Davis still control Allegis.

EXECUTIVES

CEO: Steve Bisciotti
CFO: Dave Seandeven
EVP Human Resources: Neil Mann
CEO, Mentor 4: Mike McSally
CEO, TEKsystems: Mike Salandra
President, Onsite Companies: Tom Thornton
CIO: Kevin Apperson
General Counsel: Randy Sones

LOCATIONS

HQ: Allegis Group, Inc.
7301 Parkway Dr., Hanover, MD 21076
Phone: 410-579-4800 **Fax:** —
Web: www.allegisgroup.com

PRODUCTS/OPERATIONS

Operating Companies

Aerotek (engineering, automotive, and scientific personnel for short- and long-term assignments)
Mentor 4
- Contacteam (call center personnel)
- M4 Accounting Support
- Mentor 4 Accounting and Financial Search
- Option One (management level and non-technical personnel)

Onsite Companies (technical and specialty personnel for the aviation, construction, and manufacturing industries, among others)
TEKsystems (IT staffing and consulting)

COMPETITORS

Adecco
CDI
Kelly Services
Manpower
MPS
Randstad
Robert Half
Snelling and Snelling
Spherion
Vedior
Volt Information

HISTORICAL FINANCIALS

Company Type: Private

Income Statement FYE: December 31

	ESTIMATED REVENUE ($ mil.)	NET INCOME ($ mil.)	NET PROFIT MARGIN	EMPLOYEES
12/02	3,000	—	—	10,000
12/01	2,700	—	—	8,000
12/00	3,700	—	—	8,800
Annual Growth	(10.0%)	—	—	6.6%

Revenue History

Alliance Capital Management

Alliance Capital Management has tons of funds. As one of the world's largest investment managers, Alliance Capital Management primarily serves such institutional investors as pension funds, foundations, endowments, government entities, and insurance companies. Alliance offers more than 300 domestic and international mutual funds. It also offers individuals managed accounts, retirement plans, and college savings plans. Alliance owns money manager and research firm Sanford C. Bernstein. French insurer AXA holds nearly 55% of Alliance Capital Management; publicly traded Alliance Capital Management Holding owns about 30%.

Institutional customers — which include public retirement funds in more than 40 states and nearly half of the *FORTUNE* 100 companies — account for about 55% of Alliance's more than $430 billion in assets under management.

Alliance Capital and Sanford C. Bernstein utilize in-house research staffs to cover international and domestic stocks and bonds for their own funds and for institutional investors.

Long known as a growth investor, Alliance Capital is trying to cast itself in a more conservative light. But the company has taken a hit from troubled telecommunications concern WorldCom, in which it holds a 10% stake. It was also one of the largest shareholders of collapsed energy firm Enron.

EXECUTIVES

Chairman: Bruce W. Calvert, age 56, $6,275,002 pay
Vice Chairman: Alfred Harrison, age 65
Vice Chairman: Roger Hertog, age 61, $1,500,002 pay
Vice Chairman and CEO: Lewis A. (Lew) Sanders, age 56, $2,500,002 pay
President and COO: John D. Carifa, age 58, $6,275,002 pay
EVP and Chief Investment Officer, International Value Equities: Andrew S. Adelson, age 47
EVP and Co-Head, Growth Equities: John L. Blundin, age 62
EVP; CEO, Alliance Fixed Income Investors: Kathleen A. Corbet, age 43, $2,785,000 pay
EVP and Chief Investment Officer, US Value Equities: Marilyn G. Fedak, age 56
EVP; President, Bernstein Investment Research and Management: Thomas S. Hexner, age 46
EVP; Chairman, Alliance Fund Distributors: Michael J. Laughlin, age 56
EVP, Finance and Operations: Gerald M. Liebermann, age 56
EVP; Senior Managing Director, AllianceBernstein Institutional Investment Management: Marc O. Mayer, age 45
EVP and Large Cap Growth Portfolio Manager: James G. Reilly, age 42
EVP, Director of Global Growth Equity Research, and Portfolio Manager: Paul C. Rissman, age 46
EVP; Chairman and CEO, Sanford C. Bernstein & Co.: Lisa A. Shalett, age 39
EVP and Co-Head of Growth Equities: Christopher M. Toub, age 43
SVP and General Counsel: David R. Brewer Jr., age 57
SVP and CFO: Robert H. Joseph Jr., age 55
VP and Director, Investor Relations: Valerie Haertel
Auditors: KPMG LLP

LOCATIONS

HQ: Alliance Capital Management L.P.
1345 Avenue of the Americas, New York, NY 10105
Phone: 212-969-1000 **Fax:** 212-969-2229
Web: www.alliancecapital.com

Alliance Capital Management has offices in Australia, Austria, Bahrain, Brazil, Canada, France, Germany, Hong Kong, India, Japan, Luxembourg, New Zealand, Singapore, South Africa, South Korea, Spain, Taiwan, the UK, and the US.

2002 Sales

	$ mil.	% of total
US	2,339	85
International	403	15
Total	**2,742**	**100**

PRODUCTS/OPERATIONS

Selected Mutual Fund Families

AllianceBernstein Value Funds
Asset Allocation Funds
Cash Management Funds
Global & International Stock Funds
Money Market Funds
Select Investor Series
Taxable Bond Funds
Tax-Exempt Bond Funds
US Stock Funds

Selected Subsidiaries

ACM Investments Limited (UK)
Alliance Capital Asset Management (India) Private Ltd. (75%)
Alliance Capital Australia Limited
Alliance Capital Management Australia Limited (50%)
Alliance Capital Management New Zealand Limited (50%)
Alliance Capital Management (Asia) Ltd.
Alliance Capital Management Canada, Inc.
AllianceBernstein Investment Research and Management, Inc. (formerly Alliance Fund Distributors, Inc.)
Alliance Capital Management (Singapore) Ltd.
Alliance Capital Management (Proprietary) Limited (South Africa; 80%)
Alliance Capital Management Corporation of Delaware
Alliance Capital Management LLC
  Sanford C. Bernstein & Co., LLC
  Sanford C. Bernstein Limited (UK)
Alliance Capital Services Limited (UK)
Alliance Capital Whittingdale Limited (UK)
Alliance SBS-AGRO Capital Management Company (Russia; 49%)
Alliance-Odyssey Capital Management (Namibia)(Proprietary) Limited
Alliance-MBCA Capital (Private) Limited (Zimbabwe; 50%)
Cursitor Alliance LLC
Meiji-Alliance Capital Corporation (50%)
New-Alliance Asset Management (Asia) Limited (Hong Kong; 50%)

COMPETITORS

Affiliated Managers Group
AIG SunAmerica
American Century
AIG
AMVESCAP
BlackRock
Eaton Vance
Federated Investors
FMR
Franklin Resources
Gabelli Asset Management
ING
Janus Capital
Legg Mason
MFS
Merrill Lynch
Neuberger Berman
Nuveen
Principal Financial
Raymond James Financial
T. Rowe Price
UBS Financial Services
Vanguard Group
Waddell & Reed Financial

HISTORICAL FINANCIALS

Company Type: Private

Income Statement FYE: December 31

	ASSETS ($ mil.)	NET INCOME ($ mil.)	INCOME AS % OF ASSETS	EMPLOYEES
12/02	7,218	611	8.5%	4,172
12/01	8,175	615	7.5%	4,542
12/00	8,271	669	8.1%	4,438
12/99	1,661	462	27.8%	2,396
Annual Growth	63.2%	9.8%	—	20.3%

2002 Year-End Financials

Equity as % of assets: 54.9%
Return on assets: 7.9%
Return on equity: 15.4%
Long-term debt ($ mil.): 427
Sales ($ mil.): 2,742

Net Income History

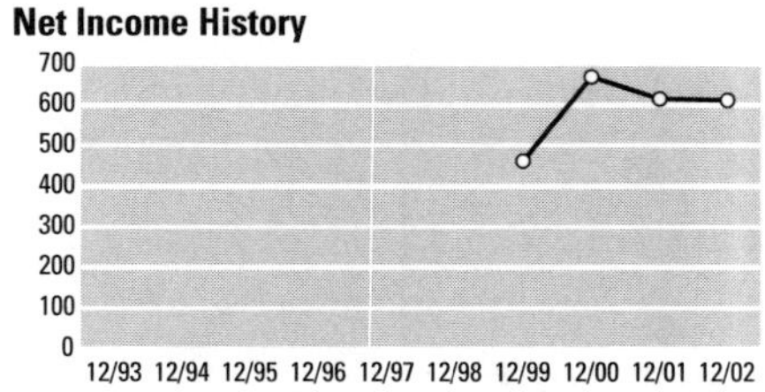

Alliance Entertainment

Alliance Entertainment rolls out the rock 'n' roll. The company distributes more than 300,000 music and video items — CDs, videos, DVDs, games, and related products — to home entertainment retailers (both online retailers and brick-and-mortar stores). Alliance also provides support services (including e-commerce software) and operates the All-Media Guide, an online database of entertainment information with three consumer guides: All-Movie Guide, All-Music Guide, and All-Game Guide. Alliance owns Digital On-Demand, a distributor of digital music, movies, and games. A planned merger with Liquid Audio was abandoned in late 2002. Investment firm The Yucaipa Companies owns a majority stake in Alliance.

EXECUTIVES

Chairman and Interim CEO: Tony Schnug
President and COO: Alan Tuchman
EVP and CFO: Darren Karst
EVP Corporate Development and Strategic Planning: Lonnie Chenkin

SVP and General Counsel: Isabel Barney
SVP Sales: Mike Donohue
VP Marketing: Beth Stefani
VP Public Relations: Sue D'Agostino
President, All Media Guide: Vladmir Bogdanov
President, Digital On-Demand/RedDotNet: Tim Sexton
President, Innovative Distribution Network: Todd Van Gorp
President, One Way Records: David Schlang
COO, Distribution and Fulfillment Services Group: Peter Blei
HR Director: Maureen Linehan

LOCATIONS

HQ: Alliance Entertainment Corp.
4250 Coral Ridge Dr., Coral Springs, FL 33065
Phone: 954-255-4000 **Fax:** 954-255-4078
Web: www.aent.com

COMPETITORS

Baker & Taylor	Ingram Entertainment
Diamond Entertainment	KOCH Entertainment
Handleman	Navarre
Image Entertainment	Rentrak

HISTORICAL FINANCIALS

Company Type: Private

Income Statement FYE: December 31

	REVENUE ($ mil.)	NET INCOME ($ mil.)	NET PROFIT MARGIN	EMPLOYEES
12/02	600	—	—	1,250
12/01	589	—	—	1,200
12/00	466	—	—	1,000
12/99	450	—	—	900
12/98	400	—	—	800
12/97	391	—	—	700
12/96	691	—	—	1,850
12/95	720	—	—	—
12/94	535	—	—	—
12/93	201	—	—	—
Annual Growth	13.0%	—	—	(6.3%)

Revenue History

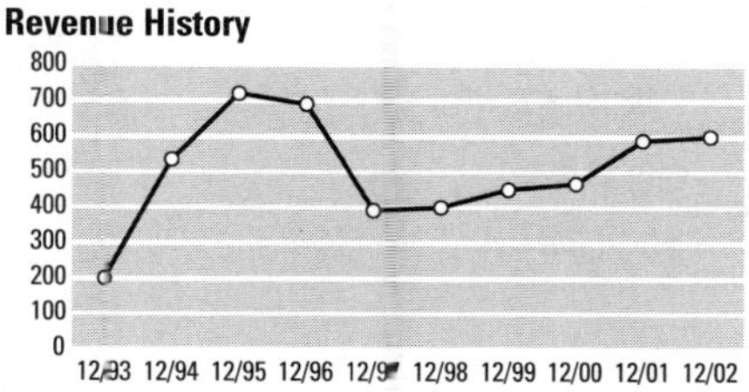

Allina Hospitals and Clinics

Allina Hospitals and Clinics is a not-for-profit health care system that focuses on protecting people's number one asset — "Their Good Health." Allina Hospitals and Clinics owns and operates 11 hospitals, and more than 40 clinics offering inpatient and ambulatory care. Its doctors and hospitals serve Minnesota and western Wisconsin. Allina Hospitals and Clinics also provides disease prevention, hospice, medical equipment, medical transportation, and pharmacy services.

EXECUTIVES

Chairman: Michael E. Dougherty, age 62
Vice Chairman: James Campbell
Vice Chairman: John M. Morrison
President and CEO: Richard Pettingill
EVP, Compliance and Public Policy, and Chief Compliance Officer: David B. Orbuch
EVP Finance: Larry Kryzaniak
EVP, Hospital & Specialty Operations: Rickie Ressler
EVP, Human Resources and Chief Talent Officer: Michael W. Howe
EVP, Safety and Quality Systems: Barbara Balik
CFO: Mark Harrison
Chief Medical Officer: Brian Anderson
Chief Information Officer: Bruce Smith
Corporate VP, Communications/PR/Marketing: Kendra Calhoun
President, Abbott Northwestern Hospital: Denny DeNarvaez
President, Allina Medical Clinic: Thomas D. Holets
President, Mercy & Unity Hospitals: Venetia Kudrle
President, Phillips Eye Institute: Shari Levy
President, United Hospital: Mark Mishek
VP Care Improvement, Mercy & Unity Hospitals: Charles O. Gensmer
VP, Medical Affairs, Abbott Northwestern Hospital: Richard R. Sturgeon
VP Medical Affairs, United Hospital: Dan Foley
District Medical Director, Allina Medical Clinic: Dennis C. O'Hare
Chief Medical Officer, Allina Medical Clinic: Bruce McCarthy
Auditors: Deloitte & Touche LLP

LOCATIONS

HQ: 710 East 24th St., Minneapolis, MN 55404
Phone: 612-775-5000 **Fax:** 612-863-5667
Web: www.allina.com

PRODUCTS/OPERATIONS

Selected Hospitals

Abbott Northwestern Hospital (Minneapolis, MN)
Buffalo Hospital (Buffalo, MN)
Cambridge Medical Center (Cambridge, MN)
Mercy Hospital (Coon Rapids, MN)
New Ulm Medical Center (New Ulm, MN)
Owatonna Hospital (Owatonna, MN)
Phillips Eye Institute (Minneapolis, MN)
River Falls Area Hospital (River Falls, WI)
St. Francis Regional Medical Center (Shakopee, MN)
United Hospital (St. Paul, MN)
Unity Hospital (Fridley, MN)

COMPETITORS

Alexian Brothers Health System	HCA
Catholic Health Initiatives	Mayo Foundation
	SSM Health Care

HISTORICAL FINANCIALS

Company Type: Not-for-profit

Income Statement FYE: December 31

	REVENUE ($ mil.)	NET INCOME ($ mil.)	NET PROFIT MARGIN	EMPLOYEES
12/02	1,800	—	—	22,347
12/01	1,700	—	—	22,102
12/00	2,600	—	—	21,500
12/99	2,600	—	—	22,546
12/98	2,550	—	—	22,000
12/97	2,500	—	—	21,200
12/96	2,400	—	—	20,800
12/95	2,100	—	—	20,000
Annual Growth	(2.2%)	—	—	1.6%

Revenue History

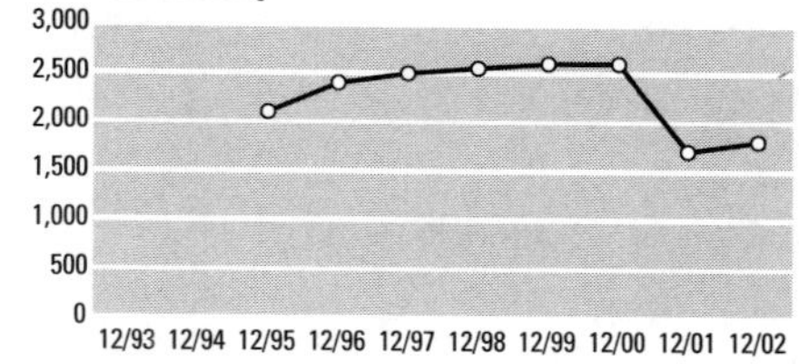

Alticor Inc.

At the core of Alticor, there is Amway. Alticor was formed in 2000 as a holding company for four businesses: direct-selling giant Amway, Web-based sales firm Quixtar, Pyxis Innovations (corporate development for Alticor and affiliates), and Access Business Network (manufacturing, logistics services). Access Business' biggest customers are Amway and Quixtar, but Access also serves outsiders. Amway, which accounts for the bulk of Alticor's revenues, sells more than 450 different products through 3 million independent distributors. Quixtar sells Amway and other products online. Alticor is owned by Amway founders, the DeVos and Van Andel families.

EXECUTIVES

Chairman: Steve Van Andel
President and Director; President, Amway; and President, Quixtar: Doug DeVos, age 37
VP and CFO: Lynn Lyall
Chief of Staff: William R. Payne
COO, Access Business Group: Al Koop
Director of Human Resources: Robin Horder-Koop

LOCATIONS

HQ: 7575 Fulton St. East, Ada, MI 49355
Phone: 616-787-1000 **Fax:** 616-682-4000
Web: www.alticor.com

Alticor operates in more than 80 countries worldwide. It has manufacturing facilities in the US, China, and South Korea and farming operations in the US, Mexico, and Brazil.

PRODUCTS/OPERATIONS

Selected Amway Products

Catalog Products
Appliances
Electronics
Fashions
Home furnishings
Office supplies
Toys

Home Care Products
Dishwashing liquid
Laundry detergent
Multi-purpose cleaner

Home Living/Home Tech Products
Cookware
Water-treatment systems

Nutrition and Wellness Products
Beverages
Dietary supplements
Meals
Snacks
Weight-control products

Personal Care Products
Body washes
Deodorants
Hair care products
Lotions
Toothpaste

Skin Care and Cosmetics Products
Cleansers
Color cosmetics
Moisturizers
Toners

Subsidiaries

Access Business Group (manufacturing, distribution, and outsourcing)
Amway (direct sales)
Pyxis (corporate development)
Quixtar (online product sales)

COMPETITORS

Avon
Bath & Body Works
Brown-Forman
CCL Industries
Clorox
Colgate-Palmolive
Daiei
Dial
Estée Lauder
Fingerhut
Forever Living
GNC
Gillette
Henkel
Herbalife
Johnson & Johnson
Kao
L'Oréal
MacAndrews & Forbes
Mary Kay
Newell Rubbermaid
Nikken
Nu Skin
PFSweb
Procter & Gamble
S.C. Johnson
Shaklee
Tom's of Maine
Tupperware
Unilever

HISTORICAL FINANCIALS

Company Type: Private

Income Statement FYE: August 31

	REVENUE ($ mil.)	NET INCOME ($ mil.)	NET PROFIT MARGIN	EMPLOYEES
8/02	4,500	—	—	10,500
8/01	3,500	—	—	10,500
8/00	3,500	—	—	10,000
8/99	3,000	—	—	10,000
8/98	2,900	—	—	14,000
8/97	5,780	—	—	13,000
8/96	5,352	—	—	13,000
8/95	4,958	—	—	13,000
8/94	4,309	—	—	12,500
8/93	3,465	—	—	11,000
Annual Growth	2.9%	—	—	(0.5%)

Revenue History

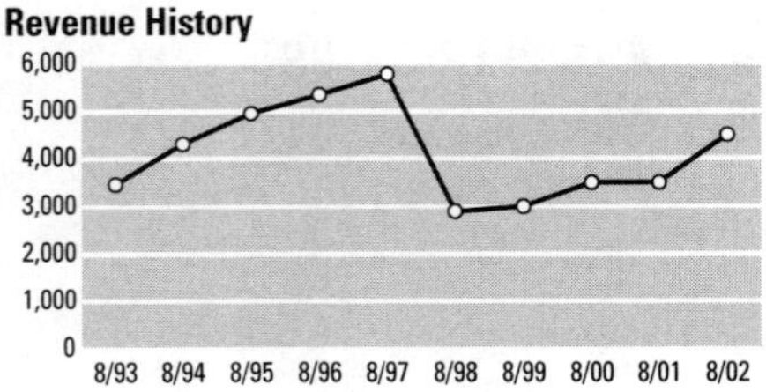

A-Mark Financial

Calling all gold bugs: A-Mark Financial trades, markets, and finances rare coins, precious metals, and collectibles. A-Mark Precious Metals trades in gold, silver, platinum, and palladium coins, bars, ingots, and medallions for central banks, corporations, and individuals around the world. A-Mark Financial distributes coins for government mints, including those of Australia, Canada, South Africa, and the US. Subsidiary A-M Handling provides melting and assay services. Chairman, president, and owner Steven Markoff founded A-Mark Financial in 1965.

EXECUTIVES

President and CEO: Steven C. Markoff
Controller, Treasurer, and Secretary: Joseph Ozaki
Auditors: Deloitte & Touche LLP

LOCATIONS

HQ: A-Mark Financial Corporation
100 Wilshire Blvd., 3rd Fl., Santa Monica, CA 90401
Phone: 310-319-0200 **Fax:** 310-319-0346
Web: www.amark.com

PRODUCTS/OPERATIONS

Selected Services

Deferred pricing transactions
Inventory financing
Leasing and consignment
Market making
Marketing support
New product announcements
Order execution
Platinum market updates
Refining
Storage

COMPETITORS

Anglo American
Degussa
DGSE Companies
Tumba Bruk

HISTORICAL FINANCIALS

Company Type: Private

Income Statement FYE: July 31

	ESTIMATED REVENUE ($ mil.)	NET INCOME ($ mil.)	NET PROFIT MARGIN	EMPLOYEES
7/02	2,300	—	—	104
7/01	2,600	—	—	102
7/00	1,812	—	—	106
7/99	2,446	—	—	120
7/98	1,000	—	—	100
7/97	1,000	—	—	120
7/96	1,000	—	—	110
7/95	1,000	—	—	121
7/94	1,000	—	—	104
7/93	1,000	—	—	—
Annual Growth	9.7%	—	—	0.0%

Revenue History

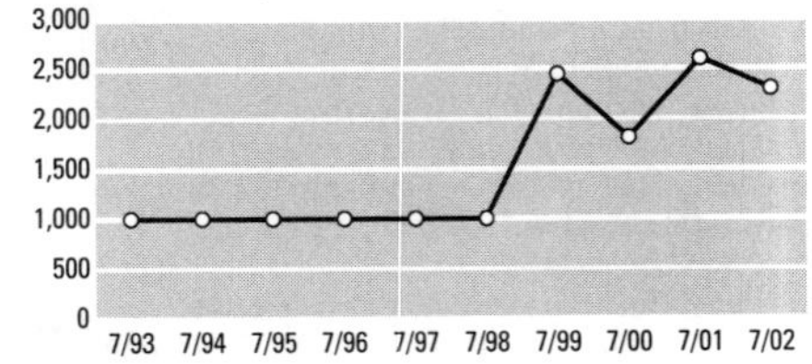

ABC Supply

American Builders & Contractors Supply Co. (which operates as ABC Supply) has put roofs over millions of heads. A leading supplier of roofing, siding, windows, and related builder's supplies, ABC Supply has more than 250 outlets in more than 44 states. It carries its own brand of products (Amcraft, Mule-Hide), and it offers doors, windows, tools and such from vendors. In 2002 the company purchased about 30 distribution centers, primarily in the Western US, from Wm. Cameron & Co. ABC Supply, which markets its products mostly to small- and medium-sized professional contractors, was founded in 1982 by CEO Kenneth Hendricks. Hendricks and his wife, EVP Diane, own the company.

EXECUTIVES

Chairman and CEO: Kenneth A. (Ken) Hendricks, age 62, $1,592,308 pay
President, COO, and Director: David A. Luck, age 53, $1,143,406 pay
CFO, Treasurer, and Director: Kendra A. Story, age 43, $509,208 pay
EVP, Secretary, and Director: Diane M. Hendricks, age 55, $275,002 pay
SVP Manufacturing Operations: Robert Bartels, age 54, $504,593 pay
VP Branch Operations: Kevin Hendricks, age 38
VP Strategic Marketing and Planning: Keith Rozolis, age 43
CIO: Kathy Murray
Director Human Resources: Lisa Indgjer, age 40
Development Supervisor: John Homer
Auditors: Ernst & Young LLP

LOCATIONS

HQ: American Builders & Contractors Supply Co., Inc.
1 ABC Pkwy., Beloit, WI 53511
Phone: 608-362-7777 **Fax:** 608-362-2717
Web: www.abc-supply.com

PRODUCTS/OPERATIONS

2002 Sales

	$ mil.	% of total
Steep slope roofing	817	57
Low slope roofing	275	19
Siding	218	15
Windows	67	5
Other	48	4
Total	**1,425**	**100**

COMPETITORS

Bracco Supply
Eagle Supply Group
Emco Limited
Georgia-Pacific Corporation
Guardian Building Products
Huttig Building Products
North Pacific Group
Pacific Coast Building Products
PrimeSource Building

HISTORICAL FINANCIALS

Company Type: Private

Income Statement FYE: December 31

	REVENUE ($ mil.)	NET INCOME ($ mil.)	NET PROFIT MARGIN	EMPLOYEES
12/02	1,425	41	2.9%	3,711
12/01	1,382	42	3.1%	3,188
12/00	1,239	14	1.1%	3,121
12/99	1,198	7	0.6%	3,239
12/98	1,162	(3)	—	3,100
Annual Growth	5.2%	—	—	4.6%

2002 Year-End Financials

Debt ratio: 292.0%
Return on equity: 46.5%
Cash ($ mil.): 7
Current ratio: 2.50
Long-term debt ($ mil.): 297

Net Income History

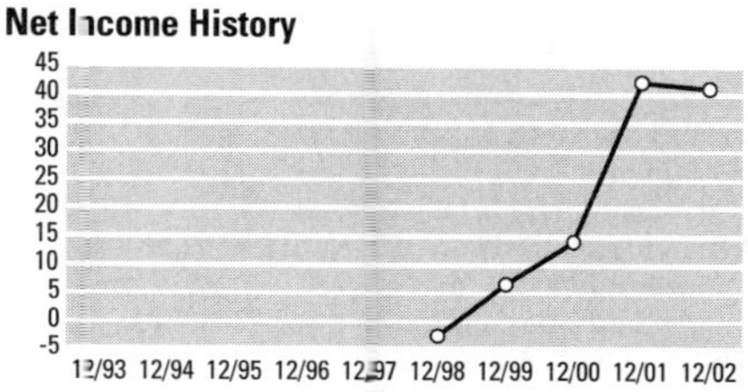

American Cancer Society

The American Cancer Society (ACS) works as a firefighter for your lungs. Dedicated to the elimination of cancer, the not-for-profit organization is staffed by professionals and more than 2 million volunteers at some 3,400 local units across the country. ACS is the largest source of private cancer research funds in the US. Recipients of the society's funding include 32 Nobel Prize laureates. In addition to research, the ACS supports detection, treatment, and education programs. The organization encourages prevention efforts with programs such as the Great American Smokeout. Patient services include moral support, transportation to and from treatment, and camps for children who have cancer.

The ACS has generated considerable income by marketing its name for antismoking nicotine patches and orange juice, and is contemplating even more lucrative deals. Programs account for 73% of expenses; 27% goes to administration and fund raising.

HISTORY

Concerned over the lack of progress in detecting and treating cancer, a group of 10 physicians and five laymen met in New York City in 1913 to form the American Society for the Control of Cancer (ASCC). Because public discussion of cancer was taboo, the group struggled with how to educate people without raising unnecessary fears. Some physicians even preferred keeping knowledge of the disease from the public. In the 1920s the ASCC began sponsoring cancer clinics and collecting statistics on the disease. By 1923 some states reported improvements in early diagnosis and treatment. In 1937 the ASCC started its first nationwide public education program, with the help of volunteers known as the Women's Field Army. President Franklin Roosevelt named April National Cancer Control Month, a practice since followed by every president.

By 1944 some cancer rates were rising but the word "cancer" still couldn't be mentioned on radio. Mary Lasker, wife of prominent ad executive Albert Lasker, was instrumental in getting information about cancer broadcast. At her insistence, in 1945 the newly renamed American Cancer Society began donating at least 25% of its budget to research. The society raised $4 million in its first major national fund-raising campaign.

The link between smoking and lung cancer became known after a study in the early 1950s by ACS medical director Charles Cameron. That information became part of the Surgeon General's Report of 1964. In 1973 an ACS branch in Minnesota held the first Great American Smokeout to encourage people to quit smoking.

The ACS backed the 1971 congressional bill that inaugurated the War on Cancer. The society was attacked in the 1970s for emphasizing cures rather than prevention because, critics claimed, research would reveal environmental causes from industrial products made by companies with connections to ACS directors. In the 1970s and 1980s, the ACS backed tougher restrictions on tobacco and, in response to earlier criticism, directed research toward prevention as well as treatment. The society played a major role in the 1989 airline smoking ban.

John Seffrin, a former Indiana University professor, was named CEO of ACS in 1992. The first of several genetic breakthroughs came in the 1990s when ACS grantees isolated genes believed to be responsible for triggering various types of cancer. In 1995 the ACS accused the tobacco industry of infiltrating its offices in the 1970s and using its papers to aid in the early marketing of low-tar cigarettes.

In 1996 the ACS announced that new data showed a drop in the US cancer death rate for the first time ever. The ACS entered agreements with SmithKline Beecham (NicoDerm antismoking patches) and the Florida Department of Citrus in 1996 to allow the use of the American Cancer Society name in marketing.

The proposed $369 billion settlement between the attorneys general of 40 states and the tobacco industry was big news in 1997. The ACS had wanted more concessions, such as a $2-per-pack tax increase, more power for industry regulation by the FDA, and underage use rate-reduction targets for smokeless tobacco products as stringent as those for cigarettes.

In 1998 the ACS launched a $5 million national advertising campaign to combat what it sees as "misleading" information spread by the tobacco industry. It argued in Supreme Court in 1999 to help the FDA gain control over cigarette production and distribution. In 2000 ACS restructured its $50-million-a-year research program to increase the size of individual grants; it also awarded its largest-ever award, $1.7 million, to study the side effects of cancer treatment. In 2001 ACS filed petitions to the FDA urging them to regulate new tobacco products marketed as being safer than traditional cigarettes. In 2002 ACS and The Robert Wood Johnson Foundation launched the Center for Tobacco Cessation to help people quit smoking. In 2003 ACS published strategic guides to help countries in early stages of tobacco control.

EXECUTIVES

Chairman: David M. Zacks
Chairman-Elect: Gary J. Streit
Vice Chairman: Thomas G. Burish
CEO: John R. Seffrin
President: Mary Simmonds
President-Elect: Ralph B. Vance
CFO: Peter Tartikoff
First VP: Mark Clanton
Second VP: Stephen F. Sener
National VP Corporate Communications: A. Gregory Donaldson
National VP Federal and State Governmental Affairs: Daniel E. Smith
National VP Human Resources: Aurelia C. Stanley
National VP Strategic Marketing Alliances: Cynthia Currence
CIO: Vic Ayers
Chief Counsel: William Dalton
Secretary: Anna Johnson-Winegar
Treasurer: Jean B. McGill

LOCATIONS

HQ: American Cancer Society, Inc.
1599 Clifton Rd. NE, Atlanta, GA 30345
Phone: 404-320-3333 **Fax:** 404-982-3677
Web: www.cancer.org

PRODUCTS/OPERATIONS

Selected Patient Services Programs

Children's Camps (for children and teens with cancer; some for siblings)
Hope Lodge (housing assistance)
I Can Cope (education and support classes on living with cancer)
Look Good . . . Feel Better (cosmetics and beauty techniques for women experiencing side effects of cancer treatment)
Man To Man Prostate Cancer Support
Pamphlets and brochures for cancer patients and their families
Reach to Recovery (support for women with breast cancer and their families)
Road to Recovery (transportation services)

Selected Public Education Programs and Publications

Great American Smokeout (national stop-smoking-for-a-day event)
Making Strides Against Breast Cancer (fund-raiser)
Relay for Life (fund-raiser)

Selected Research Grants and Awards

Clinical Research Professorships
Clinical Research Training Grants
Institutional research grants
Postdoctoral fellowships
Research Opportunity Grants
Research Professorships

HISTORICAL FINANCIALS

Company Type: Not-for-profit

Income Statement FYE: August 31

	REVENUE ($ mil.)	NET INCOME ($ mil.)	NET PROFIT MARGIN	EMPLOYEES
8/01	822	—	—	6,500
8/00	812	—	—	6,000
8/99	672	—	—	4,500
8/98	677	—	—	4,500
8/97	602	—	—	4,418
8/96	458	—	—	4,500
8/95	420	—	—	4,656
8/94	392	—	—	4,100
8/93	388	—	—	4,200
8/92	358	—	—	4,650
Annual Growth	9.7%	—	—	3.8%

Revenue History

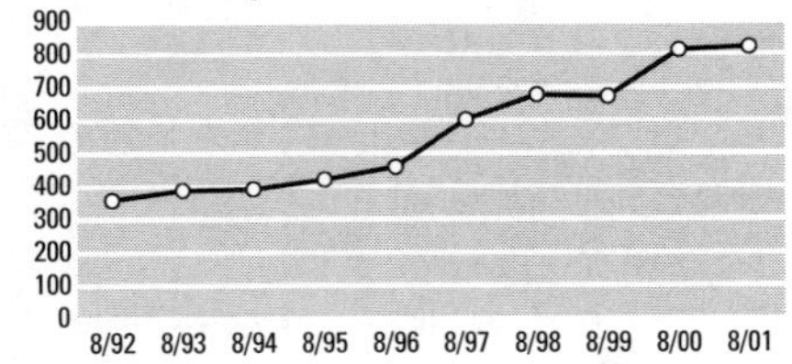

American Cast Iron Pipe

American Cast Iron Pipe Co. (ACIPCO) has one of the largest individual ductile iron pipe casting plants in the world. Its divisions — American Centrifugal, American Ductile Iron Pipe, American Flow Control, and American Steel Pipe — make ductile iron pipe and fittings, cast steel tubes, electric resistance welded steel pipes, fire hydrants and fire truck pumps, and valves for water treatment and energy production. ACIPCO's newest subsidiary, American SpiralWeld Pipe, produces spiral-welded steel pipe. John Joseph Eagan founded ACIPCO in 1905, and in 1922 placed all of the company's stock into a beneficial trust for ACIPCO employees. Employees also receive generous quarterly bonuses.

EXECUTIVES

President and CEO: Van L. Richey, age 53
CFO and Treasurer: J. M. Cook
VP, Corporate Communications: Cynthia Lovoy
VP, Human Resources: LeAnn Barr
VP, Sales and Secretary: J. Michael O'Brien
Sales Manager, American Ductile Iron Pipe: Jerry N. Burns
Sales Manager, American Flow Control: Walter L. Cooper
Manager Marketing Services, American Ductile Iron Pipe: Philip A. Selig
Assistant Sales Manager, American Ductile Iron Pipe: W.D. (Skip) Benton
Plant Manager: H. Arthur Edge
Purchasing Agent: B. W. Erwin
Auditors: KPMG LLP

LOCATIONS

HQ: American Cast Iron Pipe Company
1501 N. 31st Ave. North, PO Box 2727,
Birmingham, AL 35202
Phone: 205-325-7701 **Fax:** 205-325-1942
Web: www.acipco.com

American Cast Iron Pipe has operations in Alabama, Minnesota, South Carolina, and Texas.

PRODUCTS/OPERATIONS

Selected Divisions and Products

ACIPCO International
Coatings and primers
Ductile iron pipe
Flanged pipe and fittings
Joints
Linings
Restrained pipe and fittings

American Centrifugal
Casting
Fabrication
Machining

American Ductile Iron Pipe
Coatings and linings
Ductile iron pipe and fittings
Special pipe and fittings

American Flow Control
Check valves
Fire hydrants
Gate valves
Tapping sleeves and saddles
Trench adapters

American Steel Pipe
Electric-resistance weld line pipe

COMPETITORS

AK Steel Holding Corporation
Ameron
CIRCOR International
Dalmine
Kubota
Lone Star Technologies
Maverick Tube
McWane
Northwest Pipe
Oregon Steel Mills
Siderca
Valve Research & Manufacturing
Walter Industries
Webco
Wilson Industries
Darley & Co.

HISTORICAL FINANCIALS

Company Type: Private

Income Statement FYE: December 31

	REVENUE ($ mil.)	NET INCOME ($ mil.)	NET PROFIT MARGIN	EMPLOYEES
12/02	650	—	—	3,000
12/01	600	—	—	2,313
12/00	600	—	—	2,800
12/99	550	—	—	2,800
12/98	500	—	—	2,800
12/97	405	—	—	3,000
12/96	402	—	—	2,366
Annual Growth	8.3%	—	—	4.0%

Revenue History

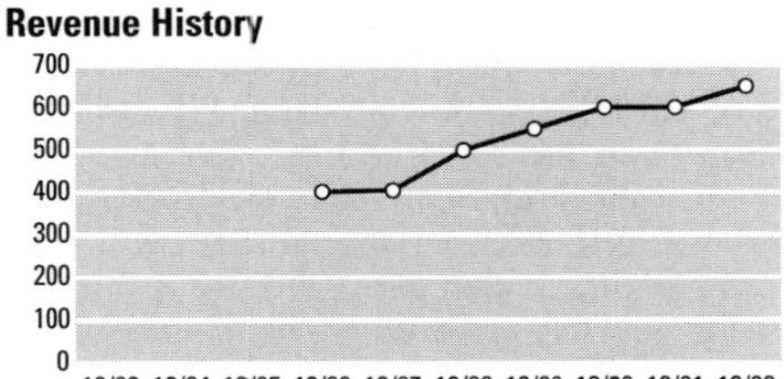

American Crystal Sugar Company

Call it saccharine, but for American Crystal Sugar, business is all about sharing. The sugar beet cooperative is owned by more than 3,000 growers in the Red River Valley of North Dakota and Minnesota. American Crystal, formed in 1899 and converted into a co-op in 1973, divides the 35-mile-wide valley into five districts, each served by a processing plant. During an annual eight-month "campaign," the plants operate continuously, producing sugar, molasses, and beet pulp. Its products (under the Crystal name, the licensed Pillsbury brand, and private labels) are sold through marketing co-ops United Sugars and Midwest Agri-Commodities. American Crystal also owns 46% of corn sweeteners joint venture ProGold.

EXECUTIVES

Chairman: Robert Vivatson, age 52
President and CEO: James J. Horvath, age 57, $776,015 pay
VP, Administration: Tom Astrup, age 33, $234,162 pay
VP, Agriculture: David A. Berg, age 48, $309,413 pay
VP, Finance: Joseph J. Talley, age 42, $329,257 pay
VP, Operations: David A. Walden, age 49, $301,464 pay
Secretary: Dan Mott, age 43
Treasurer and Assistant Secretary: Samuel S. M. Wai, age 48
Corporate Controller, Assistant Secretary, and Assistant Treasurer: Brian Ingulsrud, age 39
Director, Business Development: David L. Malmskog, age 45
Director, Human Resources: Randy Johnson
Manager, Accounting & Systems: Ronald K. Peterson, age 47
Auditors: Eide Bailly LLP

LOCATIONS

HQ: 101 N. Third St., Moorhead, MN 56560
Phone: 218-236-4400 **Fax:** 218-236-4422
Web: www.crystalsugar.com

COMPETITORS

Alberto-Culver
Alexander & Baldwin
Amalgamated Sugar
Cargill
Cumberland Packing
Florida Crystals
Imperial Sugar
Sterling Sugars
Sugar Foods
U.S. Sugar

HISTORICAL FINANCIALS

Company Type: Cooperative

Income Statement FYE: August 31

	REVENUE ($ mil.)	NET INCOME ($ mil.)	NET PROFIT MARGIN	EMPLOYEES
8/02	775	399	51.4%	1,243
8/01	866	389	44.9%	1,250
8/00	731	358	49.0%	1,294
8/99	844	370	43.8%	1,292
8/98	677	306	45.2%	1,263
8/97	677	367	54.2%	1,202
8/96	688	310	45.1%	2,437
8/95	606	321	52.9%	2,000
8/94	563	274	48.6%	—
8/93	543	304	56.0%	—
Annual Growth	4.0%	3.1%	—	(6.6%)

2002 Year-End Financials

Debt ratio: 79.2%
Return on equity: 178.0%
Cash ($ mil.): 0
Current ratio: 1.41
Long-term debt ($ mil.): 182

Net Income History

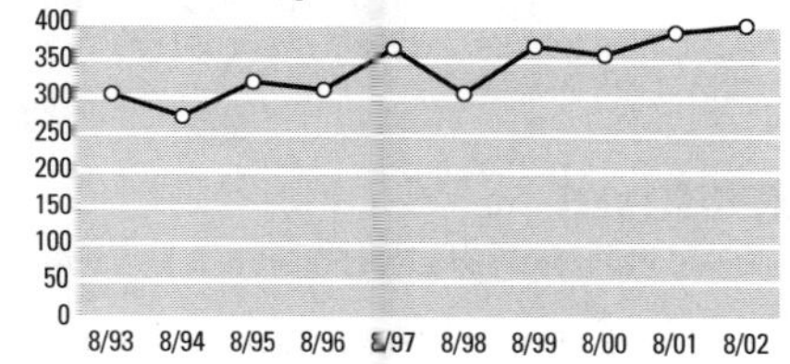

American Family Insurance Group

Even singles can get insured through American Family Insurance Group. The company specializes in property & casualty insurance, but also offers life, health, and homeowners coverage, as well as investment and retirement-planning products. It is among the largest US mutual companies that concentrates on auto insurance (State Farm is the biggest). American Family also provides coverage for apartment owners, restaurants, contractors, and other businesses. Through the company's consumer finance division, agents can also offer their customers home equity and personal lines of credit.

The company has around 4,000 agents operating primarily in the Midwest. Unlike many of its competitors, American Family has said it has no plans to demutualize.

American Family grew its policy count by almost 10% in 2002 but the volatile stock market hurt the company's net result.

HISTORY

In 1927 Herman Wittwer founded Farmers Mutual Automobile Insurance to sell coverage to Wisconsin farmers. As farms became mechanized in the 1920s, the insurance market grew. Low-density rural traffic reduced the potential for accidents, a fact that attracted Wittwer and others, such as State Farm (founded in 1922) to serve the similar markets. Wittwer also noted that rural Wisconsin's severe winters made cars unusable for a good part of the year, further reducing risk.

Farmers Mutual grew despite the Depression and WWII, spreading to Minnesota (1933); Missouri (1939); Nebraska and the Dakotas (1940); and Indiana, Iowa, and Kansas (1943). The war years were generous to insurers: Rising incomes allowed people to insure their cars, but rationing programs limited use of the cars. The postwar suburban boom — when cars became a necessity rather than a luxury — also helped auto insurers.

Growing prosperity for single-earner households in the 1950s helped boost the demand for life insurance. In 1958 Farmers Mutual formed American Family Life Insurance. The company wrote $1.6 million in insurance on its first day in the life insurance business. During that decade, Farmers Mutual moved into Illinois.

The 1960s brought growth and change. To capture more auto business, it founded American Standard Insurance to write nonstandard auto insurance. The firm also launched consumer finance operations for insurance customers and noncustomers alike, departing from standard industry practice by selling through agents rather than offices. In 1963, in recognition of its growing diversification, Farmers Mutual changed its name to American Family Mutual Insurance.

During the 1970s and 1980s, the firm strengthened its infrastructure and added regional offices. It moved into Arizona and later formed American Family Brokerage to fill in gaps in its own coverage by obtaining insurance for clients through other insurers.

During this period American Family suffered cultural pains. It moved beyond its traditional rural clientele and into the urban unknown as it sought to increase its market share. In 1981 community groups questioned whether the company was adequately serving racially mixed neighborhoods. In 1988 the US Justice Department began investigating allegations that the firm engaged in redlining (offering inferior or no service for minority neighborhoods); a class-action suit based on similar claims was filed in 1990. The suit went all the way to the Supreme Court, which ruled that insurance sales must comply with the Fair Housing Act.

The company had begun rectifying its practices before the case was decided. Nevertheless, when American Family settled the case in 1995, it agreed to pay a $14.5 million settlement plus about $2 million in court costs. Part of the settlement was to compensate people who had suffered from the company's discrimination. But most of the money went to fund community programs begun in 1996 to promote home ownership among minorities. In 1997 trouble came from within and without: One lawsuit claimed the company falsely promised to shrink premiums as policies earned dividends, and two dissident agents filed a civil complaint for wrongful termination (the latter case was settled the next year).

The company's profits tumbled in 1998 due to severe storms in Minnesota and Wisconsin. The next year American Family expanded its operations in Colorado and moved into Cleveland.

In 2000 Wisconsin was again pounded by hail, high winds, and floods. American Family Insurance announced $100 million in expected losses from the event. Streamlining claims processing, the company closed nine of its offices in 2001.

EXECUTIVES

Chairman and CEO: Harvey R. Pierce
President, COO, and Director: David R. Anderson
EVP, Secretary, and Corporate Legal: James F. Eldridge
EVP, Finance and Treasurer: J. Brent Johnson
EVP, Administration: Darnell Moore
EVP, Sales: Daniel R. DeSalvo
VP and Controller: Daniel R. Schultz
VP, Actuarial: Bradley J. Gleason
VP, American Family Financial Services: R.D. Boschulte
VP, American Family Life Insurance: Jack C. Salzwedel
VP, Claims: Terese A. Taarud
VP, Commercial, Farm/Ranch: Jerry G. Rekowski
VP, Education: Nancy M. Johnson
VP, Government Affairs and Compliance: Mark V. Afable
VP, Human Resources: Vicki L. Chvala
VP, Information Services: Byrne W. Chapman
VP, Investments: Thomas S. King
VP, Legal: Christopher S. Spencer
VP, Marketing: Alan E. Meyer
VP, Office Administration: Richard J. Haas
VP, Personal Lines: Joseph J. Zwettler
VP, Public Relations: Richard A. Fetherston
VP, Sales, Great Lakes Region: David N. Krueger
VP, Sales, Midland Region: Michael G. Duran
VP, Sales, Mountain Region: Donald D. Alfermann
VP, Sales, Northwest Region: Jeffrey E. Burke
VP, Sales, Valley Region: M. Jeffrey Bosco
VP, Variable Products: Joseph W. Tisserand
Auditors: PricewaterhouseCoopers LLP

LOCATIONS

HQ: 6000 American Pkwy., Madison, WI 53783
Phone: 608-249-2111 **Fax:** 608-243-4921
Web: www.amfam.com

American Family Insurance Group operates in Arizona, California, Colorado, Illinois, Indiana, Iowa, Kansas, Minnesota, Missouri, Nebraska, Nevada, North Dakota, Ohio, Oregon, South Dakota, Washington, and Wisconsin.

PRODUCTS/OPERATIONS

Selected Subsidiaries

American Family Mutual Insurance Co.
American Family Financial Services, Inc.
American Family Insurance Co.
American Family Life Insurance Co.
American Standard Insurance Company of Ohio
American Standard Insurance Company of Wisconsin

COMPETITORS

21st Century
AIG American General
Allstate
American Financial
AIG
Berkshire Hathaway
Chubb
CIGNA
Cincinnati Financial
Citigroup
CNA Financial
GeneralCologne Re
The Hartford
Kemper Insurance
Liberty Mutual
Lincoln National
Loews
Mutual of Omaha
Nationwide
Ohio Casualty
Old Republic
Progressive Corporation
Prudential
SAFECO
St. Paul Companies
State Farm
USAA

HISTORICAL FINANCIALS

Company Type: Mutual company

Income Statement FYE: December 31

	ASSETS ($ mil.)	NET INCOME ($ mil.)	INCOME AS % OF ASSETS	EMPLOYEES
12/02	10,840	58	0.5%	7,500
12/01	10,275	100	1.0%	7,431
12/00	9,970	237	2.4%	7,300
12/99	9,569	282	2.9%	7,247
12/98	8,949	40	0.4%	6,940
12/97	8,348	252	3.0%	6,800
12/96	6,836	55	0.8%	6,506
12/95	6,256	219	3.5%	6,411
12/94	5,706	163	2.9%	6,365
12/93	5,228	159	3.0%	6,373
Annual Growth	8.4%	(10.6%)	—	1.8%

2002 Year-End Financials

Equity as % of assets: 29.0%
Return on assets: 0.6%
Return on equity: 1.8%
Long-term debt ($ mil.): 1,732
Sales ($ mil.): 5,307

Net Income History

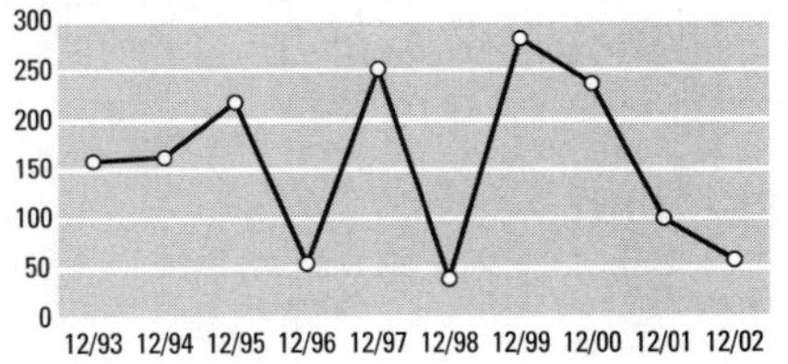

American Golf Corporation

American Golf Corporation (AGC) is in the rough. The company — one of the largest golf course management firms in the world with more than 250 public, private, and resort courses in the US, Australia, Japan, and the UK — is struggling with the weak US economy and increased competition. The firm has fallen behind in rental payments to sister firm National Golf Properties, from which it leases half its properties. National Golf had agreed to acquire AGC, although some National Golf shareholders challenged the deal on claims that the primary beneficiary would be David Price (chairman of both AGC and National Golf). Instead, an investor group led by Goldman Sachs purchased both National Golf and ACG in 2003.

EXECUTIVES

Chairman Emeritus: David G. Price, age 68
CEO: Roland C. Smith, age 48
CFO: Edward R. Sause
VP Human Resources: Tom Norton
VP Sales: Jim Allison
Regional Director of Sales, Dallas: J.C. Hernandez
Regional Director of Sales, Midwest, Northeast, and Atlantic: Mary Grover
National Accounts Manager: David Sandlin
Auditors: PricewaterhouseCoopers LLP

LOCATIONS

HQ: 2951 28th St., Santa Monica, CA 90405
Phone: 310-664-4000 **Fax:** 310-664-6160
Web: www.americangolf.com

PRODUCTS/OPERATIONS

Selected Properties

Addington Court Golf Course (Surrey, UK)
Arrowhead Country Club (Glendale, AZ)
Bobby Jones Golf Course (Atlanta)
The Classics Country Club (Naples, FL)
Cotgrave Place Golf & Country Club (Nottingham, UK)
The Foothills Golf Club (Phoenix)
Highland Park Country Club (Illinois)
Ivy Hills Country Club (Cincinnati)
Las Vegas Golf Club
Mission Trails Golf Course (San Diego)
Oyster Reef Golf Club (Hilton Head, SC)
Paradise Springs (Queensland, Australia)
Park Hill Golf Club (Denver)
Plantation Country Club (Boise, ID)
Reynolds Park Golf Course (Winston-Salem, NC)
Riverside Golf Course (Austin, TX)
Silver Lake Golf Course (Staten Island, NY)
Skylinks Municipal Golf Course (Long Beach, CA)
Tilden Park Golf Course (Berkeley, CA)
Woodlake Country Club (San Antonio)
World Houston Golf Course

COMPETITORS

ClubCorp
Golf Trust of America

HISTORICAL FINANCIALS

Company Type: Private

Income Statement FYE: December 31

	REVENUE ($ mil.)	NET INCOME ($ mil.)	NET PROFIT MARGIN	EMPLOYEES
12/01	731	(60)	—	20,000
12/00	746	2	0.3%	22,000
12/99	698	9	1.2%	20,000
12/98	576	5	0.8%	20,000
12/97	525	19	3.7%	15,000
12/96	440	14	3.3%	13,000
12/95	359	10	2.7%	10,344
12/94	307	10	3.4%	10,000
Annual Growth	13.2%	—	—	10.4%

2001 Year-End Financials

Debt ratio: —
Return on equity: —
Cash ($ mil.): 12
Current ratio: 0.35
Long-term debt ($ mil.): 1

Net Income History

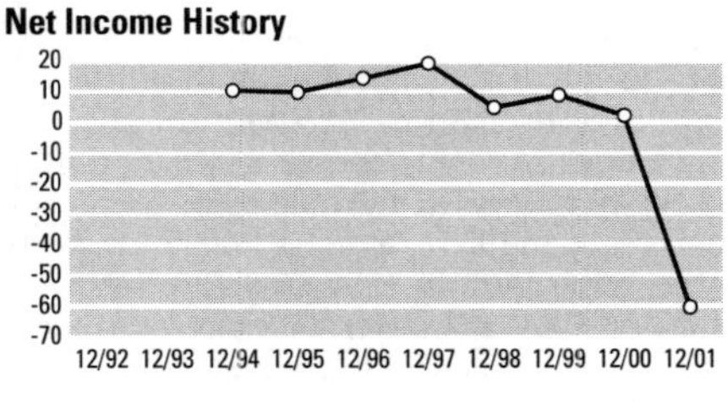

American Plumbing and Mechanical, Inc.

To avoid pulling the plug on its operations, American Plumbing and Mechanical (AMPAM) has filed for bankruptcy protection. AMPAM provides contract plumbing services, as well as HVAC and mechanical services, in more than a dozen states. It provides services for single-family and multifamily residential structures, as well as for commercial and institutional projects. Founded in 1998 to acquire 10 regional contracting companies, AMPAM began operations in 1999 and continued to acquire or create similar companies in new service areas. The firm's subsidiaries operate as separate entities, with AMPAM providing financial and accounting support. Officers and directors control more than 80% of AMPAM.

EXECUTIVES

Chairman, President, and CEO: Robert A. Christianson, age 58, $331,369 pay
Vice Chairman; CEO, AMPAM J.A. Croson: James A. (Jim) Croson, age 71
President and COO, Multifamily Operations; CEO, AMPAM LDI Mechanical: Lloyd C. Smith, age 59, $336,570 pay
President, Single-Family Plumbing Operations, California, Nevada, and Arizona: Robert C. (Bob) Richey
President, AMPAM Parks: Charles E. (Buddy) Parks III, age 44
CEO, AMPAM Atlas Plumbing: Stephen F. (Steve) Turner, age 46
VP, General Counsel, and Corporate Secretary: Carl Wimberley
VP Human Resources: Phil Thompson
Auditors: Deloitte & Touche

LOCATIONS

HQ: 1950 Louis Henna Blvd., Round Rock, TX 78664
Phone: 512-246-5260 **Fax:** 512-246-5290
Web: www.ampam.com

American Plumbing and Mechanical has operations in Arizona, California, Colorado, Florida, Georgia, Indiana, Maryland, Nevada, New Jersey, North Carolina, Ohio, Texas, and Virginia.

PRODUCTS/OPERATIONS

Selected AMPAM Companies

AMPAM Atlas Plumbing, LLC
AMPAM Christianson, LP
AMPAM Colorado, Inc.
AMPAM Commercial Midwest, LLP
AMPAM Commercial Sherwood Mechanical, Inc.
AMPAM Commercial Southeast, Inc.
AMPAM Dallas, LP
AMPAM J.A. Croson Company
AMPAM LDI Mechanical, Inc.
AMPAM Management Company, Inc.
AMPAM Miller Mechanical, Inc.
AMPAM Parks Mechanical, Inc.
AMPAM Partners, LLC
AMPAM Power Plumbing, LP
AMPAM RCR Companies
AMPAM Riggs Plumbing, Inc.
AMPAM Services, Inc.
Franklin Fire Sprinkler Company
J.A. Croson Company
Teepe's River City Mechanical, Inc.

COMPETITORS

ACCO
American Residential Services
APi Group
EMCOR
Integrated Electrical Services
NorthWestern
Roto-Rooter
Scott Co.
Southland Industries
TDIndustries

HISTORICAL FINANCIALS

Company Type: Private

Income Statement FYE: December 31

	REVENUE ($ mil.)	NET INCOME ($ mil.)	NET PROFIT MARGIN	EMPLOYEES
12/02	575	(55)	—	5,500
12/01	606	8	1.3%	5,600
12/00	558	15	2.6%	5,200
12/99	334	3	0.9%	4,000
12/98	322	9	2.8%	2,700
Annual Growth	15.6%	—	—	19.5%

2002 Year-End Financials

Debt ratio: 870.2%
Return on equity: —
Cash ($ mil.): 3
Current ratio: 1.60
Long-term debt ($ mil.): 155

Net Income History

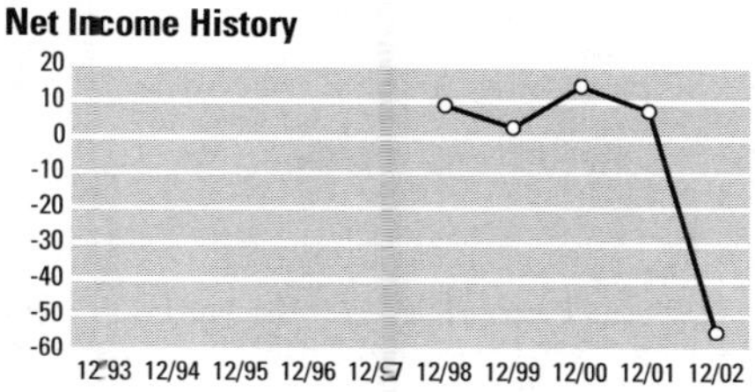

The American Red Cross

When it comes to disaster, the Red Cross is the master. The American Red Cross is a member of the International Red Cross and Red Crescent Movement, a not-for-profit organization that helps victims, especially after disasters. Chartered by Congress in 1905, the American Red Cross isn't a government agency. Its staff is largely volunteer — more than 1 million strong. Aside from helping victims of more than 67,000 disasters each year, the Red Cross teaches CPR, first aid, and AIDS awareness courses; provides counseling for US military personnel; and maintains some of the nation's largest blood, plasma, and tissue banks.

The mission of the American Red Cross was highlighted after the 2001 terrorist attacks on New York City and Washington, DC, gaining praise for its quick response immediately afterwards. Soon after, however, it drew fire from critics about the handling of donations given for attack victims and their families.

HISTORY

The Red Cross traces its start to a trip made in 1859 by Jean-Henri Dunant, a Swiss businessman. Dunant was traveling in northern Italy when he saw the aftermath of the Battle of Solferino — 40,000 dead or wounded troops, left without help. He published a pamphlet three years later calling for the formation of international volunteer societies to aid wounded soldiers.

In 1863 a five-member committee (including Dunant) formed the International Committee of the Red Cross in Geneva. Delegates of 16 countries attended the first conference, which resulted in the formation of national Red Cross societies across Europe. A red cross on a white background (the reverse of the Swiss flag) was chosen as the organization's symbol; the Red Crescent symbol was added in 1876 by Muslim relief workers during the Russo-Turkish War. In 1864 the group's principles were codified into international law — initially signed by 12 nations — through the Geneva Convention.

Clara Barton, famous for her aid to soldiers during the US Civil War, learned about the Red Cross when she assisted with relief efforts during the Franco-Prussian War (1870-71). After the war, Barton returned home and persuaded Congress to support the Geneva Convention. In 1881 she and some friends founded the American Association of the Red Cross, with the first chapter in Dansville, New York. The US signed the Geneva Convention in 1882.

Barton soon expanded the Red Cross' mission to include aiding victims of natural disasters. The group received a congressional charter in 1905, making it responsible for providing assistance to the US military and disaster relief in the US and overseas.

Membership soared during WWI as the number of chapters jumped from 107 to 3,864, and volunteers from the US and other nations served with the armed forces in Europe. After the war, the American Red Cross helped refugees in Europe, recruited thousands of nurses to improve the health and hygiene of rural Americans, and provided food and shelter to millions during the Depression.

The Red Cross established its first blood center, in New York's Presbyterian Hospital, in 1941. During WWII the American Red Cross again mobilized massive relief efforts. At home, volunteers taught nutrition courses, served in hospitals, and collected blood.

In 1956 the Red Cross began research to increase the safety of its blood supply. It also continued to provide assistance during natural disasters, as well as during the Korean and Vietnam Wars and other US military conflicts.

During the 1980s the Red Cross was criticized for moving too slowly to improve testing of its blood supply for the HIV virus. Elizabeth Dole, named the organization's president in 1991, reorganized the blood collection program. (Dole took a leave of absence in 1996 to help her husband, Bob Dole, in his unsuccessful bid for the US presidency.)

In 1996 *Money* magazine reported that the Red Cross spent more than 91 cents of every dollar on programs, the best ratio of any major charity. The next year HemaCare settled a blood-product-pricing lawsuit against the Red Cross without disclosing terms, and Ellis & Associates challenged the organization's hold on lifeguard training (certifying about 32,000 guards versus 185,000 for the Red Cross).

In 1998 the organization ran up against its costliest year ever, spending more than $162 million to fight some 240 disasters across the US. The next year Dole resigned from the Red Cross and followed in her husband's footsteps by making her own bid for the US presidency in 2000 (she later dropped out of the race). Dole was succeeded by Dr. Bernadine Healy, a former dean of the Ohio State University College of Medicine and the first physician to head the association.

Healy was given her walking papers less than two months after the September 11 attacks amid disagreements with the Red Cross board and ire from critics over a proposal to use some donations for a blood bank reserve instead of it all going to families of those killed and injured in the attacks.

General Counsel Harold Decker was tapped to replace Healy at the end of 2001. That same year the FDA announced that the Red Cross had failed to be in compliance with safety laws in its blood collection program, despite being under a consent decree since 1993. The American Red Cross appointed Marsha Johnson Evans as president and CEO in 2002. In 2003 the organization provided humanitarian aid to military personnel and their families during and after the war in Iraq.

EXECUTIVES

Chairman: David T. McLaughlin
President and CEO: Marsha Johnson Evans
COO: Alan McCurry
EVP and CEO, Biomedical Services: Ramesh Thadani
EVP Chapter Services: James Krueger
EVP Disaster Services: Terry Sicilia
Acting EVP Human Resources: Carol Miller
SVP and CFO: John D. Campbell
National Chair of Volunteers: Mary H. DeKuyper
CIO: Tom Schwaninger
Chief Diversity Officer: Anthony J. Polk
General Counsel: Larry Moore
Auditors: KPMG LLP

LOCATIONS

HQ: 430 17th St. NW, Washington, DC 20006
Phone: 202-737-8300 **Fax:** 202-942-2024
Web: www.redcross.org

The American Red Cross has more than 1,100 chapters worldwide.

PRODUCTS/OPERATIONS

Selected Activities

Armed Forces Emergency Services
Counseling
Emergency assistance
Veterans assistance

Biomedical Services
Blood
Dental programs
Plasma operations
Research and development
Stem cell
Tissue

Disaster Services
Disaster mitigation
Emergency assistance
Long-term assistance
Mass care

Health and Safety Education
Babysitting courses
CPR courses
First-aid courses
HIV/AIDS education
Nurse assistant training

COMPETITORS

America's Blood Centers
Daxor
HemaCare
Tissue Banks

HISTORICAL FINANCIALS

Company Type: Not-for-profit

Income Statement FYE: June 30

	REVENUE ($ mil.)	NET INCOME ($ mil.)	NET PROFIT MARGIN	EMPLOYEES
6/02	4,117	—	—	40,000
6/01	2,743	—	—	35,000
6/00	2,529	—	—	35,000
6/99	2,422	—	—	35,000
6/98	2,080	—	—	30,000
6/97	1,940	—	—	29,850
6/96	1,814	—	—	30,021
6/95	1,724	—	—	31,000
6/94	1,740	—	—	32,169
6/93	1,796	—	—	25,000
Annual Growth	9.7%	—	—	5.4%

Revenue History

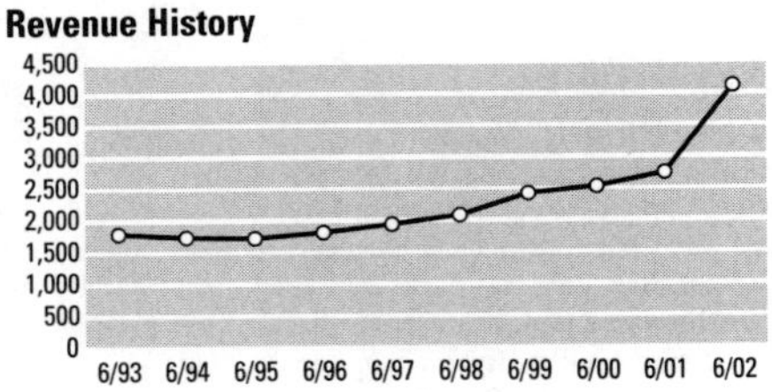

American Society of Composers

While Frank Sinatra got the glory, Johnny Mercer got some of the money, and his estate still does, thanks to the American Society of Composers, Authors and Publishers (ASCAP). ASCAP is the #1 performance rights organization in the world. The group protects the rights of composers, songwriters, lyricists, and music publishers by licensing and distributing royalties for the public performances of their copyrighted works. Be they played in a stadium, on the radio or Internet, on an airplane, or in a bar, songs of more than 150,000 members are covered.

ASCAP no longer charges annual membership dues. Founded in 1914, the not-for-profit organization is run entirely by members who serve on the board of directors.

EXECUTIVES

Chairman and President: Marilyn Bergman
Vice Chairman: Cy Coleman
Vice Chairman: Jay Morgenstern
CEO: John LoFrumento
VP and CFO: Bob Candela
EVP Membership Group, Los Angeles: Todd Brabec
EVP Performing Rights Group: Al Wallace
SVP Licensing, Performing Rights Group: Vincent Candilora
SVP and Chief Economist, Performing Rights Group: Peter Boyle
SVP International, Headquarters Group: Roger Greenaway
SVP Marketing, Headquarters Group: Philip Crosland
VP Human Resources, Headquarters Group: Diane Pfadenhauer

LOCATIONS

HQ: American Society of Composers, Authors and Publishers
1 Lincoln Plaza, New York, NY 10023
Phone: 212-621-6000 **Fax:** 212-724-9064
Web: www.ascap.com

PRODUCTS/OPERATIONS

Selected Past and Present Members

Beck
Leonard Bernstein
Garth Brooks
Duke Ellington
George Gershwin
James Horner
Lyle Lovett
Madonna
Henry Mancini
Tito Puente
Stevie Wonder

COMPETITORS

BMI
SESAC

HISTORICAL FINANCIALS

Company Type: Not-for-profit

Income Statement FYE: December 31

	REVENUE ($ mil.)	NET INCOME ($ mil.)	NET PROFIT MARGIN	EMPLOYEES
12/01	600	—	—	600
12/00	500	—	—	500
12/99	500	—	—	500
12/98	500	—	—	600
12/97	500	—	—	583
12/96	483	—	—	588
12/95	437	—	—	566
12/94	423	—	—	688
12/93	386	—	—	814
12/92	380	—	—	907
Annual Growth	5.2%	—	—	(4.5%)

Revenue History

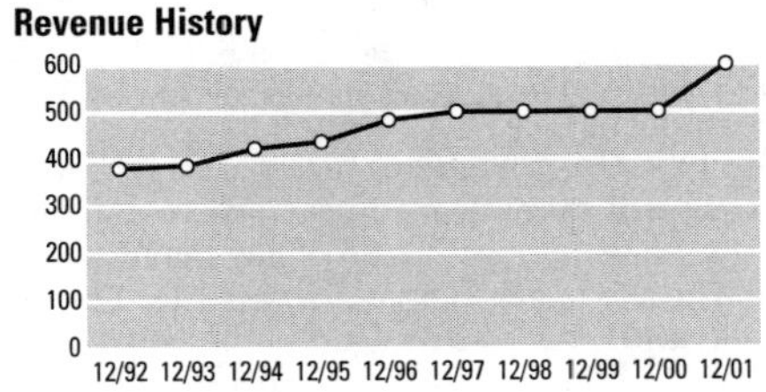

American Tire Distributors, Inc.

American Tire Distributors' business starts where the rubber meets the road. The company, formerly Heafner Tire, is the largest independent distributor of tires and related products in the US. Tire brands include industry leaders Michelin and Bridgestone/Firestone as well as Goodyear, which also makes American Tire's Monarch house brand through its Kelly-Springfield subsidiary. American Tire's distribution business is split into four divisions, which operate 62 distribution centers that serve 35 states. To focus on national distribution, American Tire has sold 130 Winston Tire Centers on the West Coast and about 30 T.O. Haas Tire outlets. Charlesbank Equity Fund IV owns more than 97% of the company.

EXECUTIVES

Chairman and CEO: Richard P. (Dick) Johnson, age 55, $541,730 pay
President and COO: William E. Berry, age 48, $271,291 pay
EVP, General Counsel, Treasurer, and Secretary: J. Michael Gaither, age 50, $317,291 pay
SVP, Procurement: Daniel K. Brown, age 49, $308,767 pay
SVP, Sales and Marketing: Phillip E. Marrett, age 52, $246,291 pay
VP, Credit and Financial Services: Jack Phillips
VP, Equipment and Supply: Gary Reed
VP, Heafner Worldwide: Lee Fishkin
Auditors: PricewaterhouseCoopers LLP

LOCATIONS

HQ: 12200 Herbert Wayne Ct., Ste. 150, Huntersville, NC 28070
Phone: 704-992-2000 **Fax:** 704-992-1384
Web: www.americantiredistributors.com

PRODUCTS/OPERATIONS

Selected Products and Brands

Equipment
- Ammco
- Hunter
- Lincoln
- Magnum

Supplies

Tires
- BF Goodrich
- Bridgestone
- Carlisle
- Dunlop
- DynaTrac
- Firestone
- Gillette
- Goodyear
- Kumho
- Lee
- Michelin
- Modi
- Monach
- Nitto
- Pirelli
- Powermark
- Regul
- SteelMark
- Titan
- UniRoyal
- Winston
- Wynstar
- Yokohama

Wheels

COMPETITORS

Cooper Tire & Rubber
Discount Tire
Sears
TBC

HISTORICAL FINANCIALS

Company Type: Private

Income Statement FYE: December 31

	REVENUE ($ mil.)	NET INCOME ($ mil.)	NET PROFIT MARGIN	EMPLOYEES
12/02	1,060	37	3.5%	1,915
12/01	1,108	(31)	—	2,025
12/00	1,087	(43)	—	2,600
12/99	908	(7)	—	—
Annual Growth	5.3%	—	—	(14.2%)

2002 Year-End Financials

Debt ratio: —
Return on equity: —
Cash ($ mil.): 3
Current ratio: 1.44
Long-term debt ($ mil.): 193

Net Income History

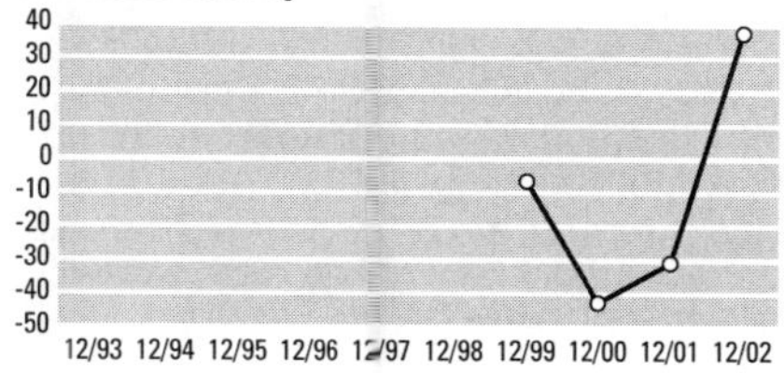

American United Mutual Insurance

American United Mutual Insurance Holding Company specializes in pensions and annuities, and also offers individual and group life insurance and disability coverage. The company touts its reinsurance unit (which dates from 1904) as the oldest in the US. American United was formed from the 1936 merger of United Mutual Life Insurance and American Central Life Insurance. Licensed in 49 states and the District of Columbia, it also does business in Latin America. The company has restructured into a mutual holding company, which gives it a more favorable tax status as well as allowing it to form publicly traded subsidiaries.

EXECUTIVES

Chairman and CEO: Jerry D. Semler
President: R. Stephen Radcliffe
SVP, Corporate Finance: Constance E. Lund
SVP, Group Division; President, CNL Financial Corporation: John R. Barton
SVP, Individual Operations: Dayton H. Molendorp
SVP, Investments: G. David Sapp
SVP, Retirement Services: William L. Tindall
SVP, Reinsurance Division; President and CEO, AUL Reinsurance Management Services: Charles D. Lineback
SVP and General Manager, AUL International: Michael D. Ogdon
VP, Human Resources and Corporate Support: Mark Roller
General Counsel and Secretary: William R. Brown, age 51
Auditors: PricewaterhouseCoopers LLP

LOCATIONS

HQ: American United Mutual Insurance Holding Company, 1 American Sq., Indianapolis, IN 46206
Phone: 317-285-1877 **Fax:** —
Web: www.aul.com

PRODUCTS/OPERATIONS

2002 Sales

	$ mil.	% of total
Premiums	608	51
Investment income	467	39
Policy & contract charges	106	9
Other	13	1
Realized investment losses	(11)	—
Total	**1,183**	**100**

Selected Subsidiaries

American United Life Insurance Company
AUL Reinsurance Management Services, LLC
CNL Financial Corporation
OneAmerica Financial Partners, Inc.
OneAmerica Securities, Inc.
The State Life Insurance Company

COMPETITORS

Aetna
AXA Financial
Citigroup
CNA Financial
GeneralCologne Re
John Hancock Financial Services
Lincoln National
MassMutual
MetLife
Minnesota Mutual
New York Life
Northwestern Mutual
Principal Financial
Prudential

HISTORICAL FINANCIALS

Company Type: Mutual company

Income Statement FYE: December 31

	ASSETS ($ mil.)	NET INCOME ($ mil.)	INCOME AS % OF ASSETS	EMPLOYEES
12/02	12,208	9	0.1%	1,700
12/01	12,092	53	0.4%	1,700
12/00	10,933	80	0.7%	1,634
12/99	10,578	68	0.6%	1,400
12/98	9,336	67	0.7%	1,500
12/97	8,598	74	0.9%	1,475
12/96	7,852	52	0.7%	1,300
12/95	7,328	46	0.6%	1,152
Annual Growth	7.6%	(20.6%)	—	5.7%

2002 Year-End Financials

Equity as % of assets: 9.0%
Return on assets: 0.1%
Return on equity: 0.9%
Long-term debt ($ mil.): 75
Sales ($ mil.): 1,183

Net Income History

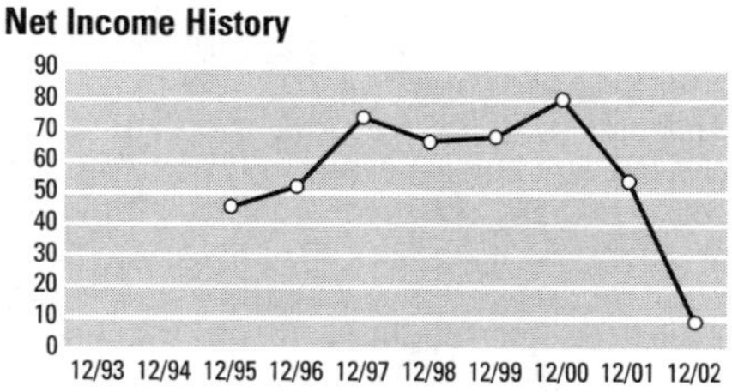

America's Second Harvest

For those not fortunate enough to reap the first harvest, there's America's Second Harvest, the largest US hunger-relief charity. The not-for-profit organization collects nearly 2 billion pounds of surplus food (donated by food growers, distributors, manufacturers, and retailers) and distributes it to more than 50,000 charities through a network of more than 200 food banks in the US and Puerto Rico. The food and groceries help some 23 million recipients every year. Second Harvest is stepping up its online relief efforts, promoting several hunger relief Web sites and charity campaigns. It also has boosted its reach through a merger with fellow charity Foodchain.

EXECUTIVES

Chair: William A. Rudnick
President and CEO: Robert H. Forney, age 61
CFO and Treasurer: Roberta Lane
SVP Affiliate Services: Al Brislain
VP Affiliate Services: Chris Rebstock
VP Business Development and Logistics: Mike Halligan
VP Public Policy and Research: Doug O'Brien
VP Technology: David Preudergast
Secretary: Sandra L. Hensley
Director Communications: Carol Gifford
Director Human Relations: Daphne E. Powell
Auditors: KPMG LLP

LOCATIONS

HQ: 35 E. Wacker Dr., Ste. 2000, Chicago, IL 60601
Phone: 312-263-2303 **Fax:** 312-263-5626
Web: www.secondharvest.org

America's Second Harvest has food banks in all 50 US states and Puerto Rico.

PRODUCTS/OPERATIONS

Selected Agencies Served

Food banks and pantries
Soup kitchens
Women's shelters

HISTORICAL FINANCIALS

Company Type: Not-for-profit

Income Statement FYE: June 30

	REVENUE ($ mil.)	NET INCOME ($ mil.)	NET PROFIT MARGIN	EMPLOYEES
6/02	488	—	—	80
6/01	422	—	—	80
6/00	668	—	—	70
6/99	392	—	—	69
6/98	395	—	—	54
6/97	403	—	—	41
6/96	354	—	—	40
6/95	371	—	—	38
6/94	427	—	—	42
6/93	439	—	—	—
Annual Growth	1.2%	—	—	8.4%

Revenue History

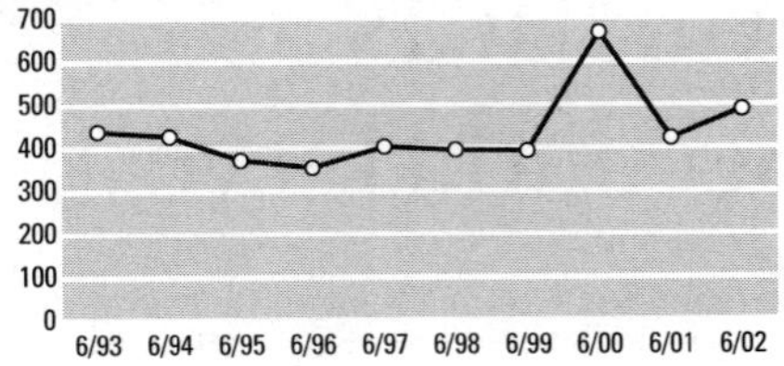

Amica Mutual Insurance Company

Amica is an amicable source for your insurance needs. Amica Mutual Insurance Company provides a variety of personal insurance products, including auto, home, marine, personal liability, and life policies. Amica sells its policies directly to customers through about 60 offices throughout the US. Its roots as an auto insurer go back to 1907 (when fire coverage was a car owner's most important need, due to exploding gas tanks). Amica was formed in 1973 through the consolidation of Automobile Mutual Insurance Company of America and Factory Mutual Liability Insurance Company of America.

EXECUTIVES

President and CEO: Thomas A. Taylor
SEVP: Andrew M. Erickson, age 61
SVP; General Manager, Amica Life: James E. McDermott Jr.
SVP, CFO, and Treasurer: Robert A. DiMuccio
SVP and Chief Investment Officer: Robert K. Benson
SVP Human Resources: Patricia A. Talin
SVP Production Division: Ronley Bates
VP Accounting: Maribeth Williamson
Senior Assistant VP, Claims Division: Peter Reid
Auditors: KPMG LLP

LOCATIONS

HQ: 100 Amica Way, Lincoln, RI 02865
Phone: 800-242-6422 **Fax:** 401-333-4610
Web: www.amica.com

PRODUCTS/OPERATIONS

Selected Subsidiaries

Amica Life Insurance Company
Amica Lloyds of Texas

COMPETITORS

ACE Limited
Allstate
AIG
Chubb
CNA Financial
GEICO
The Hartford
Liberty Mutual
Progressive Corporation
Prudential
State Farm
Travelers
USAA

HISTORICAL FINANCIALS

Company Type: Mutual company

Income Statement FYE: December 31

	ASSETS ($ mil.)	NET INCOME ($ mil.)	INCOME AS % OF ASSETS	EMPLOYEES
12/02	2,826	16	0.6%	3,700
12/01	2,909	40	1.4%	3,600
12/00	3,007	78	2.6%	3,300
12/99	2,953	58	2.0%	3,000
12/98	2,787	73	2.6%	3,000
12/97	2,531	82	3.3%	3,000
12/96	2,249	41	1.8%	3,300
12/95	2,093	81	3.9%	—
Annual Growth	4.4%	(20.7%)	—	1.9%

2002 Year-End Financials

Equity as % of assets: 44.8%
Return on assets: 0.6%
Return on equity: 1.2%
Long-term debt ($ mil.): —
Sales ($ mil.): 1,060

Net Income History

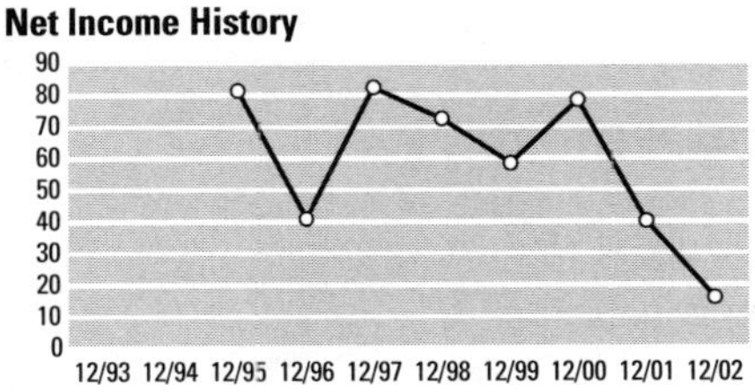

Ampacet Corporation

Ampacet helps manufacturers of plastic products show their true hues with its custom color and additive concentrates. Using polyethylene, polypropylene, polystyrene, polyamide, and polyester resins, Ampacet makes compounds and concentrates that enable plastics manufacturers to produce consistent colors and chemical characteristics for their extruded and molded products. The company's additives are used in food and industrial packaging, pipe and conduit, wire and cable, and other plastic products. Founded in 1937, Ampacet is one of the largest color compound and concentrate makers in North America. Norman Alexander, chairman and CEO of Sequa Corporation, owns the firm.

Alexander bought Ampacet, then known as American Molding Powder Co., in 1954. (Ampacet is actually short for American Molding Powder acetate.)

The company has cut costs by seeking cheaper foreign suppliers. It also has added more capacity by opening plants in Italy and Ohio and is seeking small acquisitions in specialized concentrates.

Ampacet has about 17% of the North American market for color concentrates. Globally, the company is #2 behind Ciba Specialty Chemicals. About 60% of Apacet's sales come from the US, 25% come from Europe, and the rest are from Asia and South America.

EXECUTIVES

Chairman: David S. Weil
President and CEO: Robert A. DeFalco
SVP and General Manager, North America: Robert Fielding
SVP, Finance: Joel Slutsky
SVP, Technical: Victor J. Mimeault
VP, Human Resources: Bob Oakes
VP, Sales, North America and Export: Robert J. Lammie
VP, Strategic Accounts, North America: James L. Brockwell
General Manager, Ampacet Asia: Christian Carnevali
General Manager, Ampacet Canada: Mike Firek
General Manager, Ampacet Europe: Daniel Peruzzo
General Manager, Ampacet South America: Yves Carette
Manager, Safety and Environmental: Denise R. Holl
National Sales Manager, Ampacet Australia Pty. Ltd.: Michael Kiely
Latin American Sales Manager: Guillermo Quijano

LOCATIONS

HQ: 660 White Plains Rd., Tarrytown, NY 10591
Phone: 914-631-6600 **Fax:** 914-631-7197
Web: www.ampacet.com

Ampacet has manufacturing plants in Georgia, Indiana, Louisiana, Ohio, and Texas in the US, and in Argentina, Belgium, Canada, Chile, Italy, and Thailand.

PRODUCTS/OPERATIONS

Selected Applications

Agricultural films
Coated boxboard, paper, and foil
Extrusion lamination
Fibers (for upholstery, carpets, rugs, and draperies)
Food packaging
Industrial packaging
Injection molded articles
Paper-like products
Photographic paper coatings
Pipe and conduit
Wire and cable

COMPETITORS

A. Schulman
Ciba Specialty Chemicals
Clariant International
DuPont
Ferro
PolyOne
Spartech

HISTORICAL FINANCIALS

Company Type: Private

Income Statement FYE: December 31

	REVENUE ($ mil.)	NET INCOME ($ mil.)	NET PROFIT MARGIN	EMPLOYEES
12/01	503	—	—	1,250
12/00	450	—	—	850
12/99	450	—	—	850
12/98	415	—	—	830
12/97	350	—	—	750
12/96	335	—	—	700
12/95	306	—	—	700
12/94	335	—	—	665
12/93	315	—	—	610
12/92	300	—	—	—
Annual Growth	5.9%	—	—	9.4%

Revenue History

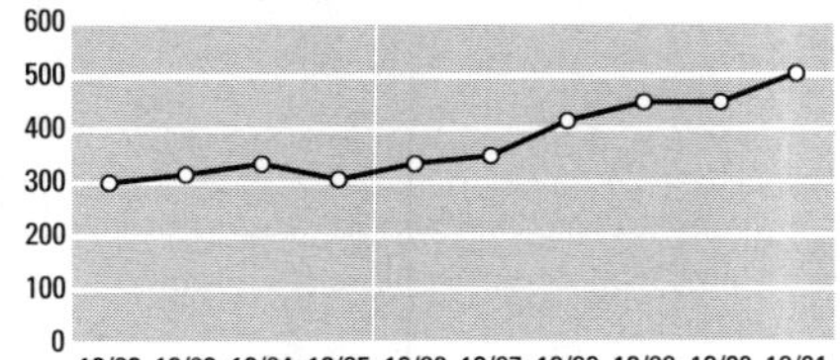

AMSTED Industries Incorporated

Wilbur and Orville Wright's first flight might never have succeeded without an assist from Amsted's Diamond Chain subsidiary. A maker of roller chains for a variety of equipment and machinery, Diamond Chain also produced the propeller chain for the Wright brothers' aircraft. AMSTED's other subsidiaries include ASF-Keystone (side frames, bolsters, and cast steel freight car components), Griffin Pipe Products (ductile iron pressure and sewer pipe), and Means Industries (automotive steering and transmission components). Customers include industrial distributors, locomotive and railcar manufacturers, and automotive OEMs. Employee-owned, AMSTED has roughly 50 plants worldwide.

EXECUTIVES

Chairman Emeritus: Gordon R. Lohman, age 68
Chairman, President, and CEO: W. Robert Reum, age 60
VP and CFO: Stephen Gregory
VP, General Counsel, and Secretary: Thomas G. Berg
President ASF-Keystone, North America: John Wories Jr.
President, Baltimore Aircoil: Steven S. Duerwachter
President, Burgess-Norton Mfg. Co.: John F. Carroll
President, Brenco Incorporated: J. Craig Rice
President, Consolidated Metco: Ed Oeltjen
President, Diamond Chain Company: James E. Humphrey
President, Griffin Pipe Products: Paul T. Ciolino
President, Griffin Wheel Company: William J. Demmert
President, Means Industries, Inc.: D. W. (Bill) Shaw
Director, Human Resources: Shirley Whitesell
Auditors: PricewaterhouseCoopers

LOCATIONS

HQ: 205 N. Michigan Ave., 44th Fl., Chicago, IL 60601
Phone: 312-645-1700 **Fax:** 312-819-8494
Web: www.amsted.com

AMSTED has manufacturing plants in Alabama, Arkansas, Delaware, Illinois, Indiana, Iowa, Kansas, Kentucky, Maryland, Michigan, Nevada, New Jersey, North Carolina, Ohio, Oklahoma, Oregon, Virginia, and Wisconsin. The company also has factories in Australia, Belgium, Canada, the Czech Republic, France, Germany, Italy, Mexico, South Africa, and the UK.

PRODUCTS/OPERATIONS

Selected Divisions

ASF-Keystone (cast steel freight car components, hot coiled steel springs and buffers, discharge gates, draft and draw gears, dynamic brake components, valves)
Baltimore Aircoil Company (cooling towers, evaporative condensers, heat exchangers, ice thermal storage systems, industrial fluid coolers)
Brenco, Incorporated (railroad track anchoring systems, tapered roller bearings)
Burgess-Norton Mfg. Co. (gray and ductile iron castings, piston pins, powder metal parts, rocker arms and assemblies)
Consolidated Metco, Inc. (aluminum permanent mold and die castings, axle hubs, door sill assemblies, fifth wheels and assemblies, instrument panels, sleeper cab accessories, spring brake flanges and pistons, structural molded plastic products, suspension components, transmission housings)
Diamond Chain Company (roller chain)
Griffin Pipe Products Co. (ductile iron pressure pipe and fittings, ductile iron sewer pipe)
Griffin Wheel Co. (cast steel railroad wheels)
Means Industries, Inc. (automatic transmission reaction plates, one-way clutches, stamped metal components, steering column components, transmission components)

COMPETITORS

ALSTOM
American Standard
Japan Steel Works
Meridian Rail
Newcor
Trinity Industries

HISTORICAL FINANCIALS

Company Type: Private

Income Statement FYE: September 30

	REVENUE ($ mil.)	NET INCOME ($ mil.)	NET PROFIT MARGIN	EMPLOYEES
9/02	1,360	—	—	9,000
9/01	1,650	—	—	10,300
9/00	1,774	—	—	11,200
9/99	1,370	—	—	12,600
9/98	1,252	—	—	9,100
9/97	1,105	—	—	8,500
9/96	1,140	—	—	8,700
9/95	1,165	—	—	9,300
9/94	1,030	—	—	9,000
9/93	868	—	—	7,900
Annual Growth	5.1%	—	—	1.5%

Revenue History

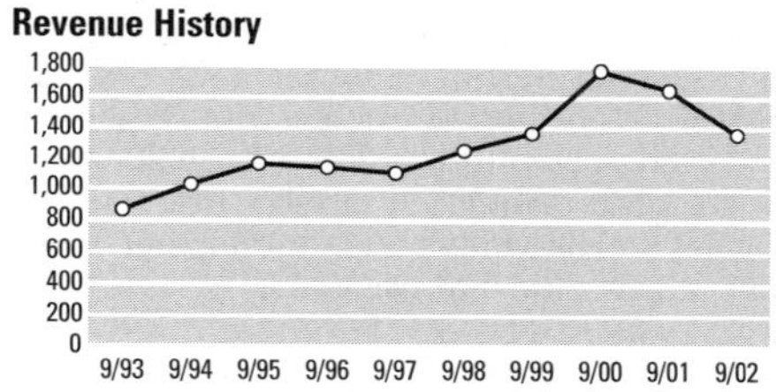

Ancira Enterprises

Ancira Enterprises wants to help Texans hit the road: It sells cars, trucks, and recreational vehicles exclusively in the Lone Star State. The company's dealerships feature new vehicles under the Buick, Chevrolet, Chrysler, Ford, Jeep, Kia, Nissan, Pontiac, and Volkswagen brands, as well as used cars and trucks. Ancira Enterprises also sells new and used campers, motor homes, and recreational vehicles under the Fleetwood, American Dream, and Winnebago names, among others. The company is one of the nation's top fleet dealers and operates on-site parts and service departments. Ancira Enterprises, which was founded in 1984, is owned by president Ernesto Ancira Jr.

EXECUTIVES

President and CEO: Ernesto Ancira Jr.
CFO: Betty Ferguson
Director of Human Resources: Valerie Tackett

LOCATIONS

HQ: 6111 Bandera Rd., San Antonio, TX 78238
Phone: 210-681-4900 **Fax:** 210-681-9413
Web: www.ancira.com

COMPETITORS

Allen Samuels Enterprises
AutoNation
Coast Distribution
Cruise America
Curtis Gunn
Don Davis Auto Group
DriveTime
Gillman
Group 1 Automotive
Gunn Automotive
McCombs Automotive
McCombs Enterprises
McDavid Auto Group

HISTORICAL FINANCIALS

Company Type: Private

Income Statement FYE: December 31

	REVENUE ($ mil.)	NET INCOME ($ mil.)	NET PROFIT MARGIN	EMPLOYEES
12/02	556	—	—	675
12/01	648	—	—	675
12/00	589	—	—	625
12/99	525	—	—	600
12/98	450	—	—	550
12/97	412	—	—	520
12/96	358	—	—	483
12/95	300	—	—	450
12/94	261	—	—	434
12/93	181	—	—	325
Annual Growth	13.3%	—	—	8.5%

Revenue History

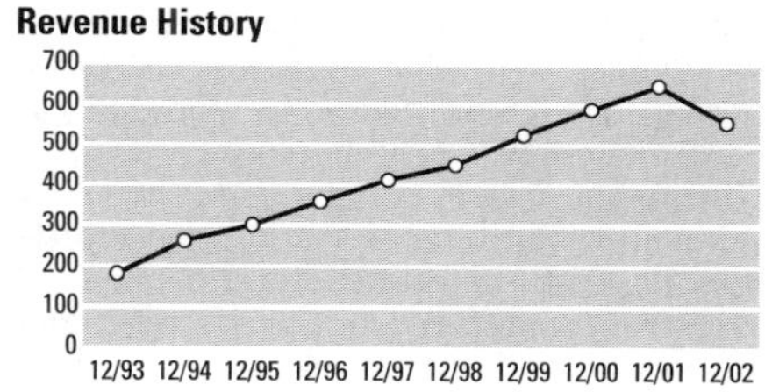

Andersen Corporation

Windows of opportunity open and shut daily for Andersen, a leading and well-known maker of wood-clad windows and patio doors in the US. Andersen offers window designs from hinged, bay, and double-hung to skylight, gliding, and picture windows. It operates 50 Renewal by Andersen window replacement stores in more than 20 states. Andersen's EMCO subsidiary makes storm and screen doors. Through independent and company-owned distributorships, the company sells to architects, general contractors, and building owners throughout the Americas, Europe, Asia, and the Middle East. Andersen Logistics operates in 16 states. The company is owned equally by the Andersen family, company employees, and the Andersen Foundation.

Andersen competes in the marketplace by building strong brand recognition for its products. Acquisitions play an important role in the company's growth strategy, and Andersen has been buying many of the independent distributorships that carry its products, including Morgan Products, the largest US distributor of its products.

The company celebrates its 100th year in 2003. It is publishing a book on its history and initiating a community project to build 100 Habitat for Humanity homes over a five-year period, along with special events and exhibits during the year.

HISTORY

Danish immigrant Hans Andersen and his two sons, Fred and Herbert, founded Andersen in 1903. Andersen's first words in English, "All together, boys," became the company motto. Andersen arrived in Portland, Maine, in 1870 and worked as a lumber dealer and manufacturer. In the 1880s he bought a sawmill in St. Cloud, Minnesota, and later managed one in Hudson, Wisconsin. When the Hudson mill owners asked him to let workers go during the off season, Andersen refused and then resigned. He subsequently launched his own lumber business — Andersen Lumber Company — in 1903 and hired some of the men who had been laid off. He opened a second lumberyard, in Afton, Minnesota, in 1904. Andersen and his sons revolutionized the window industry in the early 1900s by introducing a standardized window frame with interchangeable parts. Buoyed by success, the Andersens sold their lumberyards in 1908 to focus on the window-frame business. (Andersen purchased lumberyards again in 1916 before exiting the lumberyard business for good in the 1930s.) Around 1913 the company moved from Hudson to South Stillwater (now Bayport), Minnesota.

Thrifty Hans launched the company's first (and the US's third) profit-sharing plan shortly before his death in 1914. Herbert became VP, secretary, treasurer, and factory manager, and Fred became president. Herbert died in 1921 (at age 36), but Fred proved to be a versatile and capable successor. Among his accomplishments, Fred came up with the tag line "Only the rich can afford poor windows."

In 1929 the company changed its name to Andersen Frame Corporation. In the following decade Andersen introduced a number of innovations, including Master Frame (a frame with a locked sill joint, 1930); a casement window, the industry's first complete factory-made window unit (1932); and a basement window (1934). The company adopted its current name in 1937.

Andersen introduced the gliding window concept in the early 1940s. It also launched the Home Planners Scrap Book consumer ad campaign in 1943. During the 1950s Andersen's new products included the Flexivent awning window, which featured welded insulating glass that served as an alternative to traditional storm windows. In the 1960s the company produced a gliding door and introduced the Perma-Shield system. The system featured easy-to-maintain vinyl cladding to protect wood frames from weathering. By 1978 Perma-Shield products accounted for three-quarters of sales. Fred, who had run the company as president until 1960 and had subsequently held the positions of chairman and chairman emeritus, died in 1979 at age 92.

Between 1984 and 1994 the company increased its sales threefold by introducing additional customized and state-of-the-art products, including patio doors. In 1995 it launched Renewal by Andersen, a retail window-replacement business that has expanded to about 40 US locations.

Andersen acquired former long-term strategic partner Aspen Research (materials testing, research, and product development) in 1997. Among its jointly developed products is Fibrex, a composite material used in replacement windows. Also in 1997 the company moved its international division office from Bayport, Minnesota, to the Minnesota World Trade Center in St. Paul to help boost its export drive.

In 1998 company veteran Donald Garofalo succeeded Andersen's president and CEO Jerold Wulf, who retired after 39 years with the company. Andersen reinforced its company-owned distributorships in 1999 when it bought millwork distributors Morgan Products and Independent Millwork.

Expanding its product offerings, Andersen purchased privately held EMCO Enterprises (storm doors and accessories, Iowa) in 2001. Other acquisitions from about 1993 to 2003 have included Dashwood Industries (windows, skylights, roof windows, doors; Canada), Aspen Research (product development), and KML Windows (architectural windows and doors, Canada). The company also opened a new production facility in Menomonie, Wisconsin.

At the close of 2002, Andersen's COO James Humphrey was promoted to president, becoming the company's ninth president. Garofalo retained the position of vice chair of the board. Andersen celebrated its 100th year in 2003 and kicked off a community project to build 100 Habitat for Humanity homes throughout North America over the next five years.

EXECUTIVES

Chairwoman: Sarah J. Andersen
Vice Chairman: Donald L. Garofalo
President and CEO: James E. (Jim) Humphrey, age 57
EVP and CFO: Michael O. (Mike) Johnson
SVP and CFO: Phil Donaldson
SVP Operations: Pat Riley
SVP Human Resources and Communications: Mary D. Carter
SVP Advanced Technology: Kurt Heikkila
SVP Research, Engineering, and Quality and Advanced Technology: Mary J. Schumacher, age 46
SVP Sales and Marketing: Jay Lund
VP and General Counsel: Alan Bernick
VP Engineering and Quality: James (Jim) Brett
VP Marketing; President, EMCO Enterprises: J. Glasnapp
VP Sales: Steve Mog
President, Renewal by Andersen: Craig Evanich
Director of Corporate Communications: Maureen McDonough
Technology and Business Development Project Manager: Jay Libby

LOCATIONS

HQ: 100 4th Ave. North, Bayport, MN 55003
Phone: 651-264-5150 **Fax:** 651-264-5107
Web: www.andersencorp.com

Andersen markets its products throughout the Americas, Asia, Europe, and the Middle East.

PRODUCTS/OPERATIONS

Selected Products and Brands

Doors
- Patio doors
  - Art glass (Frank Lloyd Wright designs)
  - Frenchwood Collection (gliding, hinged, and outswing)
  - Narroline gliding patio doors
  - Perma-Shield gliding patio doors
- Screen doors
- Storm doors

Windows
- Art glass
- Awning
- Basement
- Bay and bow
- Casement
- Double-hung
- Fixed
- Gliding
- Horizontal sliding
- Picture
- Skylights and roof windows
- Transom
- Utility

COMPETITORS

Bocenor
JELD-WEN
Marshfield DoorSystems
Overhead Door
Pella
Royal Group Technologies
Sierra Pacific Industries
Simonton Windows
Thermal Industries
Weru

HISTORICAL FINANCIALS

Company Type: Private

Income Statement

FYE: December 31

	ESTIMATED REVENUE ($ mil.)	NET INCOME ($ mil.)	NET PROFIT MARGIN	EMPLOYEES
12/02	2,000	—	—	8,000
12/01	1,800	—	—	7,000
12/00	1,700	—	—	6,000
12/99	1,500	—	—	6,000
12/98	1,400	—	—	3,700
12/97	1,300	—	—	3,700
12/96	1,250	—	—	3,700
12/95	1,200	—	—	3,700
12/94	1,100	—	—	3,700
12/93	1,000	—	—	—
Annual Growth	8.0%	—	—	10.1%

Revenue History

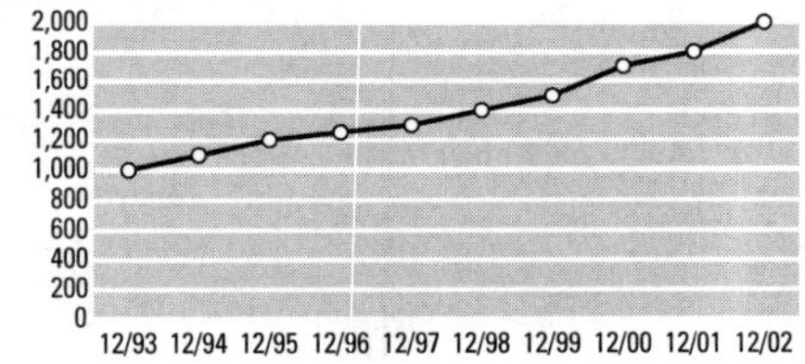

The Angelo Iafrate Companies

Included among the largest US private firms, The Angelo Iafrate Companies also ranks among the nation's top environmental construction firms. The group's subsidiaries are engaged in surface paving and heavy civil and highway construction projects, turnkey industrial contracting, underground utility infrastructure installation, site preparation and excavation, and environmental construction and remediation. The company also has a materials division that processes and sells crushed concrete, sand and gravel, limestone, and asphalt. Founded in 1960, the company is owned by the Iafrate family, who developed a state-of-the-art process to crush and recycle concrete.

EXECUTIVES

Vice Chairman: Angelo E. Iafrate Sr.
Vice Chairman: Dominic Iafrate
President: Angelo E. Iafrate Jr.
CFO and Treasurer: George Ihm
SVP: Duane Laurila
VP Engineering/Estimating: Don Statler
VP Legal Affairs/General Counsel: Christopher O. Corden
VP Operations: Dave Michael
Director Human Resources: Eugene Polk

LOCATIONS

HQ: 26400 Sherwood, Warren, MI 48091
Phone: 586-756-1070 **Fax:** 586-756-0467
Web: www.iafrate.com

COMPETITORS

Bechtel
Earth Tech
Jacobs Engineering
Lane Construction
MWH Global
Shaw Group
Washington Group

HISTORICAL FINANCIALS

Company Type: Private

Income Statement FYE: December 31

	REVENUE ($ mil.)	NET INCOME ($ mil.)	NET PROFIT MARGIN	EMPLOYEES
12/01	688	—	—	4,410
12/00	675	—	—	2,000
Annual Growth	1.9%	—	—	120.5%

Revenue History

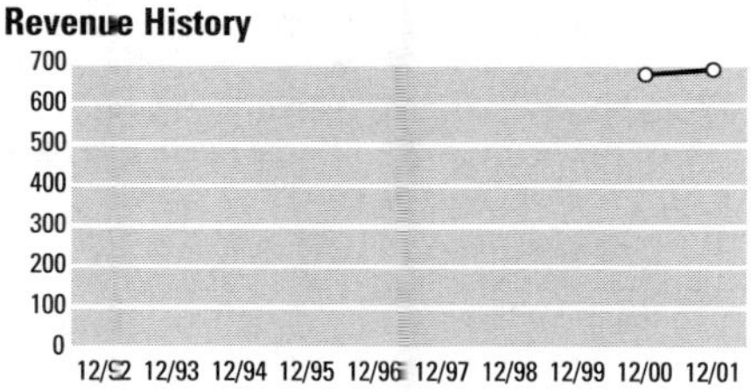

Apex Oil Company, Inc.

At the top of its game, Apex Oil is engaged in the wholesale sales, storage, and distribution of petroleum products. Its range of refined products includes asphalt, kerosene, fuel oil, diesel fuel, heavy oil, gasoline, and bunker fuels. The company's terminals are located on the East Coast and Gulf Coast, in California, and in the Midwest. Internationally, Apex Oil has a terminal in Caracas, Venezuela, and has additional activities in Bermuda, Monaco, and the Netherlands. The company is also engaged in a tug boat and barge business and has a storage and truck rack operation. Founded in 1932 by Samuel Goldstein, Apex Oil is controlled by CEO Tony Novelly.

EXECUTIVES

CEO: P. Anthony (Tony) Novelly
President: Ed Wahl
CFO: John L. Hank Jr.
VP and Terminal Manager: Tom Depke
CIO: John Diderrich
General Counsel: Neil Miller
Credit: Laura Seymour
Human Resources and Benefits: Julie Cook

LOCATIONS

HQ: 8235 Forsyth Blvd., Ste. 400, Clayton, MO 63105
Phone: 314-889-9600 **Fax:** 314-854-8539
Web: www.apexoil.com

Apex Oil operates terminals in Arkansas, California, Florida, Illinois, Louisiana, Maryland, Missouri, New York, North Carolina, Tennessee, Texas, Virginia, and West Virginia. It also has operations in Bermuda, Monaco, the Netherlands, and Venezuela.

PRODUCTS/OPERATIONS

Major Products

Asphalt
Bunker fuels
Diesel fuel
Fuel oil
Gasoline
Heavy oil
Kerosene

Subsidiaries and Affiliates

Apex Towing Co. (tug boats and barges)
Clark Oil Trading Co. (wholesale oil trading)
Edgington Oil Co. (asphalt and fuel refinery)
Enjet Incorporated (fuel oil marketing and refinery)
Petroleum Fuel and Terminal Co. (storage and truck racks)

COMPETITORS

Chemoil
Crown Central Petroleum
Getty Petroleum Marketing
Global Companies
Koch
Marathon Oil
Premcor
Tauber Oil
U.S. Oil

HISTORICAL FINANCIALS

Company Type: Private

Income Statement FYE: September 30

	REVENUE ($ mil.)	NET INCOME ($ mil.)	NET PROFIT MARGIN	EMPLOYEES
9/02	1,400	—	—	175
9/01	2,000	—	—	175
9/00	1,700	—	—	—
Annual Growth	(9.3%)	—	—	0.0%

Revenue History

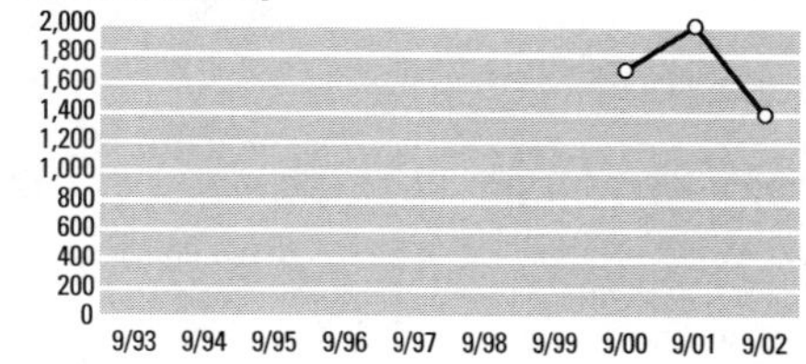

APi Group, Inc.

Holding company APi Group has a piece of the action in five business sectors: construction services, fire protection, systems, manufacturing, and materials distribution. APi has more than 25 subsidiaries, which operate as independent companies. Services provided by the company's construction subsidiaries include energy conservation; electrical, industrial, and mechanical contracting; industrial insulation; and overhead door installation. Other units install fire protection systems, fabricate structural steel, and distribute building materials. The family-owned company was founded in 1926 by Reuben Anderson, father of CEO Lee Anderson.

EXECUTIVES

Chairman and CEO: Lee R. Anderson Sr., age 62
President: Russell Becker
EVP, CFO, and Treasurer: Loren Rachey
CTO: Brad Bechel
Secretary: William M. Beadie
Marketing: Kathy Anderson

LOCATIONS

HQ: 2366 Rose Place, St. Paul, MN 55113
Phone: 651-636-4320 **Fax:** 651-636-0312
Web: www.apigroupinc.com

APi Group has US offices primarily in midwestern and western states; through its Vipond Fire Protection subsidiary, APi Group also operates in Canada, Ireland, and the UK.

PRODUCTS/OPERATIONS

Selected Subsidiaries

Construction Services
APi Construction Co. (industrial insulation)
APi Supply, Inc. (rental, sales, service of aerial work platforms)
Doody Mechanical, Inc. (mechanical contracting, including heating, ventilation, and air-conditioning)
The Jamar Co. (mechanical and specialty contracting)
Thompson Electric (electrical contracting)

Fire Protection
Northern Fire & Communications, Inc.
Security Fire Protection Co., Inc.
Viking Automatic Sprinkler Co.

Manufacturing
Anco Products, Inc. (flexible air ducts)
LeJeune Steel Co. (structural steel)

Materials Distribution
ASDCO (wholesale distributor of construction materials)
APi Distribution (insulation products)

Systems
API Systems Group (fire and gas detection and security systems provider)
Communications Systems, Inc. (security systems integration)
Halon Banking Systems

COMPETITORS

AMPAM
Comfort Systems USA
CPT Holdings
EMCOR
Integrated Electrical Services
Irex
John E Green Company
Scott Co.
TDIndustries
Team, Inc.
Turner Industries
Tyco Fire and Security Services

HISTORICAL FINANCIALS

Company Type: Private

Income Statement FYE: December 31

	REVENUE ($ mil.)	NET INCOME ($ mil.)	NET PROFIT MARGIN	EMPLOYEES
12/02	675	—	—	5,000
12/01	750	—	—	5,000
12/00	726	—	—	5,000
12/99	535	—	—	4,000
12/98	537	—	—	3,500
12/97	540	—	—	3,000
12/96	530	—	—	3,000
Annual Growth	4.1%	—	—	8.9%

Revenue History

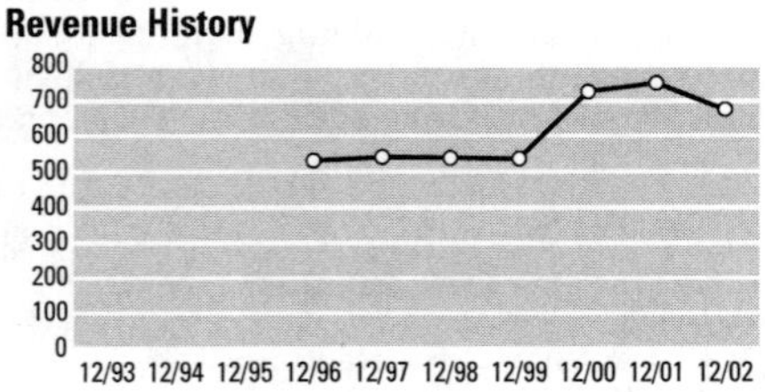

Arctic Slope Regional Corporation

The Inupiat people have survived the Arctic for centuries, and now they're surviving in the business world. The Inupiat-owned Arctic Slope Regional Corporation (ASRC) was set up to manage 5 million acres on Alaska's North Slope after the Alaska Native Claims Settlement Act in 1971 cleared the way for oil development in the area.

ASRC gets about two-thirds of sales from its energy services subsidiaries (ASRC Energy Services) and its petroleum refining and marketing units (Petro Star).

Other operations include construction, engineering, and governmental services.

EXECUTIVES

Chairman and VP Government Affairs: Oliver Leavitt
President and CEO: Jacob Adams
COO: Conrad Bagne
VP and CFO: Frank Zirnkilton
VP and General Counsel: Alma McClellan Upicksoun
VP Administration and Shareholder Relations: Flossie Chrestman
VP Barrow Operations: Forrest (Deano) Olemaun
VP Human Resources: Karen Burnell
VP Lands: Richard Glenn
Corporate Secretary: Mary Ellen Ahmaogak
Corporate Treasurer: Patsy Aamodt
Auditors: Deloitte & Touche LLP

LOCATIONS

HQ: 3900 C St., Ste. 801, Anchorage, AK 99503
Phone: 907-339-6000 **Fax:** 907-339-6028
Web: www.asrc.com

Arctic Slope Regional Corporation has US offices in Alaska, Arizona, California, Maryland, New Mexico, and Oregon. It also has operations in Mexico and Venezuela.

PRODUCTS/OPERATIONS

Selected Operations
Engineering and Construction
Manufacturing
Petroleum Refining and Marketing
Technical Services

COMPETITORS

Alaska Communications Systems
Baker Hughes
Halliburton
Nabors Industries
Noble
Schlumberger
Smith International
Tesoro Petroleum
T-Mobile USA

HISTORICAL FINANCIALS

Company Type: Private

Income Statement FYE: December 31

	REVENUE ($ mil.)	NET INCOME ($ mil.)	NET PROFIT MARGIN	EMPLOYEES
12/01	1,062	—	—	6,413
12/00	1,038	—	—	5,973
12/99	888	—	—	3,000
12/98	888	—	—	3,000
Annual Growth	6.1%	—	—	28.8%

Revenue History

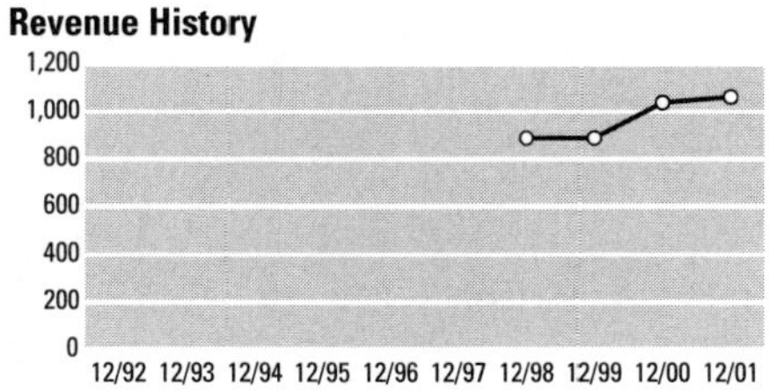

Army and Air Force Exchange

Be all that you can be and buy all that you can buy at the PX (Post Exchange). The Army and Air Force Exchange Service (AAFES) runs thousands of facilities — including PXs and BXs (Base Exchanges) — at US Army and Air Force bases worldwide. Its outlets range from tents to shopping centers that have retail stores, fast-food outlets (including 180-plus Burger King restaurants worldwide), movie theaters, beauty shops, and gas stations. AAFES serves active-duty military personnel, reservists, retirees, and their family members. A government agency under the Department of Defense (DoD), it receives no funding from the DoD.

While the AAFES receives no federal money, it pays neither taxes nor rent to occupy US government property. More than 70% of AAFES's profits go into Morale, Welfare, and Recreation Programs for amenities such as libraries and youth centers. Other profits are used to renovate or build stores. Active military personnel head AAFES, but its staff consists mostly of military family members and other civilians.

HISTORY

During the American Revolution, peddlers known as sutlers followed the Army, selling items such as soap, razors, and tobacco. The practice lasted until after the Civil War, when post traders replaced sutlers. This system was replaced in 1889 when the War Department authorized canteens at military bases.

The first US military exchanges were established in 1895, creating a system to supply military personnel with personal items on US Army bases around the world. The exchanges were run independently, with each division creating a Post Exchange (PX) to serve its unit. The post commander would assign an officer to run the PX (usually along with other duties) and would decide how profits were spent.

In 1941 the Army Exchange Service was created, and the system was reorganized. A five-member advisory committee made up of civilian merchandisers was created to provide recommendations for the reorganization. The restructuring made the system more like a chain store business. The independent PXs were bought by the War Department from the individual military organizations that ran them. Civilian personnel were brought in to staff the PXs, and a brigadier general was named to head an executive staff made up of Army officers and civilians that provided centralized control of the system. The Army also created a special school to train officers to run the PXs.

Sales at the PXs skyrocketed during WWII; a catalog business was added so soldiers could order gifts to send home to their families. The Department of the Air Force was established in 1947, and the exchange system organization was renamed the Army and Air Force Exchange Service (AAFES) the next year.

In 1960 the government allowed the overseas exchanges to provide more luxury items in an effort to keep soldiers from buying foreign-made goods. By the time the military had been cranked up again for the Vietnam War, big-ticket items such as TVs, cameras, and tape recorders were among the exchanges' best-sellers. In 1967 AAFES moved its headquarters from New York City to Dallas.

By 1991 the exchanges were open to the National Guard and the Reserve; AAFES's customer base had grown to 14 million. When the military began downsizing during the 1990s following the end of the Cold War, AAFES's customer base shrank by 35%.

AAFES stores sold more than $12 million of pornographic materials in 1995. The following year the House of Representatives passed the Military Honor and Decency Act prohibiting the sale of pornography on US military property, including AAFES stores; this ban was struck down as unconstitutional in 1997. That year AAFES was approved as a provider of medical equipment covered by federal CHAMPUS/TRICARE insurance. It also created a Web site to offer online shopping in 1997.

The Supreme Court upheld the 1996 porn ban in 1998; the Pentagon banned the sale of more than 150 sexually explicit magazines (such as *Penthouse*), while a military board permitted the continued sale of certain publications (including *Playboy*). Maj. Gen. Barry Bates took over as AAFES's Commander and CEO in 1998. To better battle other retailers, that year AAFES announced its stores would offer best-price guarantees, matching prices of local stores and refunding price differences if customers found lower prices within 30 days of buying products.

In 1999 AAFES expanded to Macedonia and Kosovo, providing its services to military personnel in Operation Joint Guardian. In 2000 Bates was replaced as AAFES commander and CEO by Maj. Gen. Charles J. Wax.

Wax stepped down as commander and CEO in August 2002 and was replaced by Maj. Gen. Katherine Frost of the US Army.

EXECUTIVES

Chairman: Lt. Gen. Charles S. Mahan Jr.
Commander: Maj. Gen. Katherine Frost, USA
Vice Commander and Director, Equal Opportunity: Brig. Gen. Toreraser A. Steele, USAF
COO: Marilyn Iverson
CFO: Jerry Justus
SVP, Management Information Systems: Terry B. Corley
SVP, Human Resources: Ronnie Compton
SVP, Sales: Mary Ellen Gillespie
VP, Food and Theater Division: Richard Sheff
Director, Food Programs: Butch Freed
General Counsel: Col. Athena Jones, USAF
Purchasing Manager, Restaurant Operations: Beverly Hopp
AAFES Burger King Restaurant Program Manager: Lee Wiederkeht
Senior Buyer: Ken Warden
Auditors: Ernst & Young LLP

LOCATIONS

HQ: Army and Air Force Exchange Service
3911 S. Walton Walker Blvd., Dallas, TX 75236
Phone: 214-312-2011 **Fax:** 214-312-3000
Web: www.aafes.com

The Army and Air Force Exchange Service has operations in all 50 states and in 25 countries and overseas areas.

PRODUCTS/OPERATIONS

Selected Merchandise and Services

Barber and beauty shops
Books, newspapers, and magazines
Catalog services
Class Six stores
Concessions
Food facilities (mobile units, snack bars, name-brand fast-food franchises, and concession operations)
Gas stations and auto repair
Military clothing stores
Movie theaters
Retail stores
Vending centers

COMPETITORS

7-Eleven
Best Buy
Costco Wholesale
J. C. Penney
Kmart
Kroger
METRO AG
Sears
Target
Wal-Mart

HISTORICAL FINANCIALS

Company Type: Government agency

Income Statement FYE: January 31

	REVENUE ($ mil.)	NET INCOME ($ mil.)	NET PROFIT MARGIN	EMPLOYEES
1/02	7,133	373	5.2%	52,400
1/01	7,369	381	5.2%	52,400
1/00	6,992	362	5.2%	54,000
1/99	6,783	343	5.1%	54,000
1/98	6,620	337	5.1%	53,946
1/97	6,874	348	5.1%	57,583
1/96	6,710	228	3.4%	56,495
1/95	6,746	269	4.0%	58,556
1/94	7,276	315	4.3%	60,000
1/93	6,763	301	4.5%	72,562
Annual Growth	0.6%	2.4%	—	(3.6%)

2002 Year-End Financials

Debt ratio: —
Return on equity: 12.3%
Cash ($ mil.): 147
Current ratio: 2.27
Long-term debt ($ mil.): 0

Net Income History

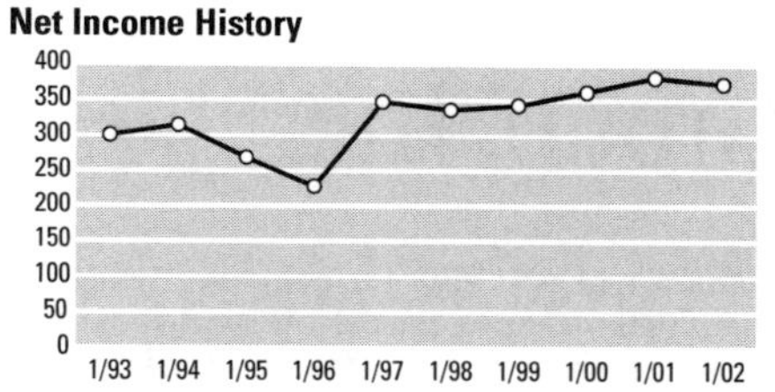

Ascension Health

Things are looking up for Ascension Health. Formed in the 1999 merger of the Daughters of Charity National Health System and the Sisters of St. Joseph Health System, Ascension Health's network consists of nearly 70 Roman Catholic hospitals, as well as nursing homes, psychiatric wards, long-term care centers, and other health care facilities in about 20 states and the District of Columbia. Ascension Health is the largest Catholic hospital system the United States. Ascension Health is also the largest not-for-profit health care provider in the United States.

Ascension's facilities are primarily located in the southern, midwestern, and northeastern areas of the US.

The system takes to heart the words of St. Vincent de Paul, co-founder of the Daughters of Charity, who advised the order to serve "the poor sick bodily, ministering to them in all their needs, and spiritually also so that they will live and die well."

As such, Nuns from Ascension's sponsoring religious orders sit on its governing board, which is led by non-clergy CEO Douglas French.

In this age of high-cost health care, Ascension realizes the need for fiscal health. In addition to selling money-losing hospitals, Ascension has reorganized its facilities by geographic regions, with each region headed by a VP who controls costs and speeds decision making.

In response to rising health care costs, Ascension merged with national Catholic health care provider Carondelet Health System in 2003.

HISTORY

The Daughters of Charity order was formed in France in 1633 when St. Vincent de Paul recruited a rich widow (St. Louise de Marillac) to care for the sick on battlefields and in their homes.

Elizabeth Ann Seton, America's first saint (canonized 1974), brought the order to the US. In 1809 Seton earned the title of Mother and started the Sisters of Charity. The Sisters adopted the vows of the Daughters of Charity, adding "service" to them in 1812.

The Sisters officially became part of the Daughters of Charity in 1850. The Daughters cared for soldiers during the Civil War and were responsible for training Florence Nightingale. In the late 1800s the Daughters pioneered exclusive provider arrangements (similar to today's managed care contracts) with railroads, lumber camps, and the like. During the next 100 years, the order furthered its mission of caring for the sick and the poor. To support their efforts, the nuns founded hospitals (44 by 1911), schools, and other charity centers.

In 1969 the charity association formed a health care services cooperative, which became the Daughters of Charity National Health System (DCNHS).

DCNHS operated as two regional institutions (one based in Maryland, the other in Missouri) until 1986, when the systems merged. The first task was to balance their holy mission with the need to make money. With competition from managed care companies increasing, DCNHS responded by cutting staff and diversifying into nursing homes and retirement centers.

The Daughters of Charity's western unit combined its six hospitals in California with Mullikin Centers (a physician-owned medical group) in 1993 to form one of the largest health care associations in the state.

DCNHS expanded its network in 1995 by merging its hospitals with and becoming a co-sponsor of San Francisco-based Catholic Healthcare West. That year it joined with Catholic Relief Services to operate a hospital in war-torn Angola.

In 1996 DCNHS dropped a proposed merger of its struggling 221-bed Carney Hospital in Boston with Quincy Hospital because the municipally owned Quincy facility was required by law to provide abortions. Instead, DCNHS sold Carney Hospital to Caritas Christi Health Care System (owned by the Boston Roman Catholic archdiocese), one of about a dozen hospital sales by DCNHS in the mid-1990s.

DCNHS reorganized its leadership in 1997, creating SVP positions for system direction and policy and for program development to strengthen and update its programs. In 1998 Sister Irene Kraus, who had founded DCNHS and led it through its expansion, died.

In 1999 DCNHS merged with fellow Catholic caregiver Sisters of St. Joseph Health System, then Michigan's largest health care system.

In 2000 Ascension saw the collapse of a five-hospital merger in Florida between subsidiary St. Vincent's Health System and Baptist Health System. The organization also launched the Voice for the Voiceless initiative, which combines private monies and federal grants to fund programs for the uninsured in Detroit, New Orleans, and Austin, Texas.

EXECUTIVES

Chairperson: Sister Joyce DeShano
President and CEO: Douglas D. French, age 49
COO and Strategy Leader for Well-Run Organization: Anthony R. Tersigni
SVP and CFO: Anthony Speranzo
SVP Strategic Business Development and Innovation; President, Ascension Health Ventures: John D. Doyle
SVP Great Lakes and Mid-Atlantic States Operating Group: Robert J. Henkel
SVP Legal Services and General Counsel: Rex P. Killian
SVP, Advocacy and External Relations, and Strategy Leader for Voice for the Voiceless: Susan Nestor Levy
SVP; Acting CEO, Catholic Health Partners: Matthias D. Maguire
SVP Clinical Excellence: David Pryor
SVP Leadership Development: Tom Thibault
SVP, Mission Integration: Sister Maureen McGuire
VP and CIO: Sherry L. Browne
VP Risk Management: Steve Gillen
VP and Associate General Counsel: Steven H. Pratt
VP, Communications: Elaine Moore
President, Seton Healthcare Network: Charles J. Barnett, age 56
CEO Supply Chain Initiative: Arnie Kimmel
Executive Director Shared Services/Operations Support and Corporate Responsibility Officer: John Nusbaum
Senior Executive Advisor to the President: Sister Bernice Coreil
Chief Administrative Officer, Organizational Effectiveness and Strategy Leader for Work Life Community: Deborah A. Proctor
Human Resources Manager: Kate Brandt
Auditors: Ernst & Young LLP

LOCATIONS

HQ: 4600 Edmundson Rd., St. Louis, MO 63134
Phone: 314-733-8000 **Fax:** 314-733-8013
Web: www.ascensionhealth.org

PRODUCTS/OPERATIONS

2003 Facilities

	No.
Acute care hospitals	67
Long-term care facilities	37
Community health centers	14
Adult residential facilities	13
Psychiatric hospitals	4
Rehabilitation facilities	4
Long-term acute care hospitals	2
Total	**141**

COMPETITORS

Beverly Enterprises
Catholic Health East
Catholic Health Initiatives
Catholic Healthcare Partners
HCA
Health Management Associates
HEALTHSOUTH
Kindred
Life Care Centers
Tenet Healthcare
Triad Hospitals
Trinity Health
Universal Health Services

HISTORICAL FINANCIALS

Company Type: Not-for-profit

Income Statement FYE: June 30

	REVENUE ($ mil.)	NET INCOME ($ mil.)	NET PROFIT MARGIN	EMPLOYEES
6/02	7,666	111	1.4%	83,412
6/01	6,853	—	—	83,412
6/00	6,400	—	—	67,000
6/99	6,400	—	—	67,000
6/98	6,170	—	—	65,000
6/97	5,700	—	—	60,000
6/96	5,700	—	—	61,100
6/95	6,200	—	—	62,300
6/94	7,000	—	—	67,400
6/93	6,500	—	—	—
Annual Growth	1.9%	—	—	2.7%

2002 Year-End Financials

Debt ratio: 49.7%
Return on equity: —
Cash ($ mil.): 505
Current ratio: 1.18
Long-term debt ($ mil.): 2,382

Revenue History

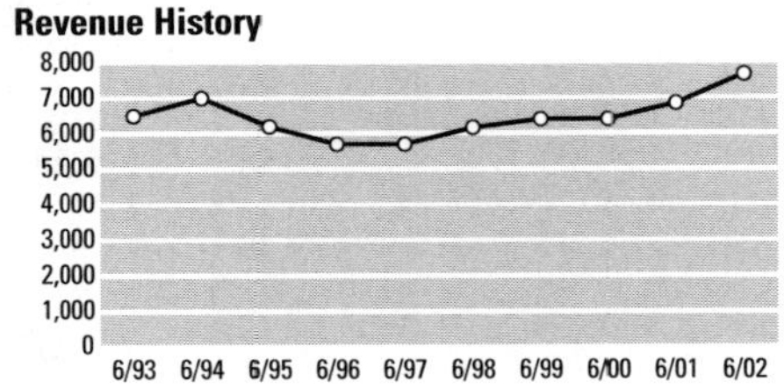

The ASCII Group, Inc.

ASCII makes it easy for computer resellers. The ASCII Group is one of the world's largest buying consortiums for independent, full-service computer resellers, representing more than 2,000 US and Canadian members. Paying a monthly fee entitles members to buy volume products and negotiate better deals with hardware and software distributors, such as D&H Distributing and Ingram Micro, and from vendors, including Iomega and Seagate Technology. ASCII also offers discounts on credit card processing and leasing rates, online pricing, financing, health and business insurance, training, and other business service program offerings. Chairman and CEO Alan Weinberger founded the group in 1984.

ASCII members range from local mom-and-pop computer stores to $100 million enterprises. Altogether, they buy nearly $1 billion worth of products from preferred distributors each year. ASCII has invested in an e-commerce processing facility so its members can sell their products online without the heavy costs of setting up their own Internet sites.

EXECUTIVES

Chairman and CEO: Alan D. Weinberger
CFO: Steve Reynolds
Director, Business Development: Jerry Koutavas
Director, E-Commerce Services: Doug Young
Marketing Programs Manager: Suzanne Elbaum
National Account Manager: Christina Ottey
National Sales Manager: Trevor L. Estelle
Office Administrator: Margaret Burris
Office Coordinator: Naomi Coleman

LOCATIONS

HQ: 7101 Wisconsin Ave., Ste. 1000, Bethesda, MD 20814
Phone: 301-718-2600 **Fax:** 301-718-0435
Web: www.ascii.com

The ASCII Group has operations in Canada and the US.

PRODUCTS/OPERATIONS

Selected Distributors

D&H Distributing
Ingram Micro
SYNNEX Information Technologies

Selected Member Services

Credit card processing
Financing
Insurance (business and health)
Online pricing
Payroll services
Product leasing
Training

COMPETITORS

Agilysys
Arrow Electronics
ASI Corp.
Avnet
Future Electronics
Optical Laser
Software Spectrum

HISTORICAL FINANCIALS

Company Type: Consortium

Income Statement FYE: December 31

	ESTIMATED REVENUE ($ mil.)	NET INCOME ($ mil.)	NET PROFIT MARGIN	EMPLOYEES
12/02	11,000	—	—	30
12/01	10,600	—	—	25
12/00	10,300	—	—	—
12/99	9,900	—	—	—
12/98	9,600	—	—	—
12/97	9,200	—	—	22
12/96	6,500	—	—	18
12/95	5,100	—	—	—
12/94	4,650	—	—	—
12/93	3,875	—	—	—
Annual Growth	12.3%	—	—	8.9%

Revenue History

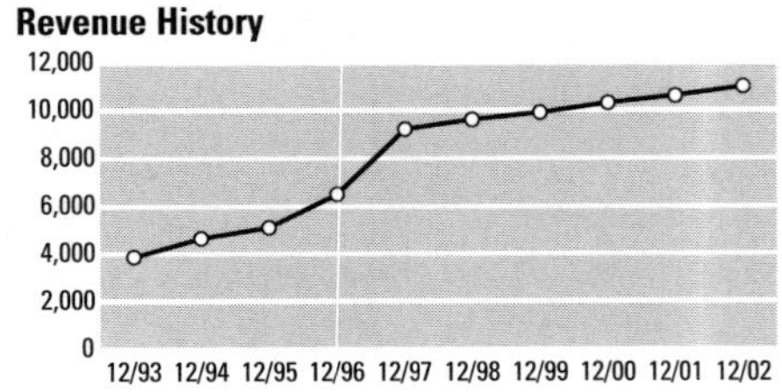

Ashley Furniture Industries, Inc.

Furniture buyers took a shine to Ashley Furniture Industries when it added a tough, high-gloss polyester finish to its furniture in 1986. The company is one of the nation's largest furniture manufacturers. Ashley Furniture makes and imports upholstered, leather, and hardwood furniture, as well as bedding. It has manufacturing plants and distribution centers spread throughout the country and overseas. It runs more than 90 Ashley Furniture HomeStores — independently owned shops that sell only Ashley Furniture products. The firm was founded by Carlyle Weinberger in 1945. Father-and-son duos Ron and Todd Wanek and Chuck and Ben Vogel own Ashley Furniture.

In 2002 the Vogels (who own 25% of Ashley Furniture) filed a lawsuit against the Waneks (who own 75%), alleging that the Waneks were trying to squeeze the Vogel father and son out of the business.

EXECUTIVES

Chairman: Ronald (Ron) Wanek
CEO: Todd Wanek
CFO: Richard Barclay
EVP and Chief International Operations Officer: Ben Vogel
EVP: Charles (Chuck) Vogel
Human Resources Manager: Jim Dotta

LOCATIONS

HQ: 1 Ashley Way, Arcadia, WI 54612
Phone: 608-323-3377 **Fax:** 608-323-6008
Web: www.ashleyfurniture.com

COMPETITORS

Bassett Furniture
Bombay Company
Brown Jordan International
Ethan Allen
Euromarket Designs
Furniture Brands International
Hooker Furniture
IKEA
Kimball International
Klaussner Furniture
La-Z-Boy
Natuzzi
Pulaski Furniture
Rowe Companies
Williams-Sonoma

HISTORICAL FINANCIALS

Company Type: Private

Income Statement FYE: December 31

	REVENUE ($ mil.)	NET INCOME ($ mil.)	NET PROFIT MARGIN	EMPLOYEES
12/01	1,090	—	—	6,000
12/00	952	—	—	5,000
12/99	816	—	—	5,691
12/98	650	—	—	4,567
12/97	540	—	—	2,100
12/96	450	—	—	—
Annual Growth	19.4%	—	—	30.0%

Revenue History

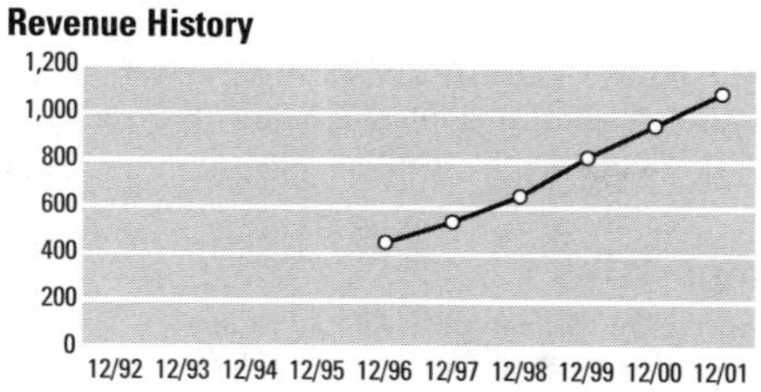

ASI Corp.

ASI has a whole lotta sales going on. The company, a wholesale distributor of computer software, hardware, and accessories, sells more than 3,000 products, including CD-ROM drives, modems, monitors, PCs, networking equipment, and storage devices.

ASI also boasts a dedicated motherboard catalog site, motherboardmaster.com, and offers standard and custom configurations. The company sells to systems integrators and resellers throughout North America. Vendor partners include 3Com, Microsoft, Samsung, and Toshiba. President Christine Liang, who founded ASI in 1987, owns 51% of the company.

EXECUTIVES

Chairman and CEO: Marcel Liang
President: Christine Liang
Administrator, Human Resources: Crystal Yuan

LOCATIONS

HQ: 48289 Fremont Blvd., Fremont, CA 94538
Phone: 510-226-8000 **Fax:** 510-226-8858
Web: www.asipartner.com

ASI has sales offices and warehouses in California, Colorado, Florida, Georgia, Illinois, Kansas, New Jersey, Oregon, and Texas, as well as in Canada.

PRODUCTS/OPERATIONS

Selected Products

Cameras
CD-ROM drives
Hard drives
Keyboards
Memory
Mice
Modems
Monitors
Motherboards
MP3 players
Notebooks
Optical drives
PCs
Printers
Projectors
Scanners
Software
Speakers
Storage devices
Video cards
Zip drives

COMPETITORS

Arrow Electronics
ASCII Group
Avnet
Comark
CompuCom
D&H Distributing
Dell
En Pointe
Gateway
Hewlett-Packard
Ingram Micro
IBM
Merisel
Micro Warehouse
Software House
Supercom
Tech Data

HISTORICAL FINANCIALS

Company Type: Private

Income Statement FYE: December 31

	REVENUE ($ mil.)	NET INCOME ($ mil.)	NET PROFIT MARGIN	EMPLOYEES
12/02	866	—	—	530
12/01	1,000	—	—	500
12/00	818	—	—	500
12/99	730	—	—	610
12/98	730	—	—	560
12/97	540	—	—	400
12/96	426	—	—	350
12/95	326	—	—	300
12/94	300	—	—	250
12/93	185	—	—	200
Annual Growth	18.7%	—	—	11.4%

Revenue History

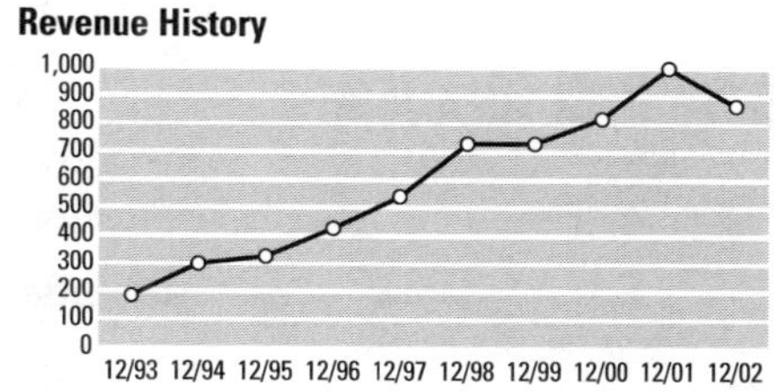

Asplundh Tree Expert Co.

How much wood would a woodchuck chuck, if a woodchuck could chuck wood? A lot, if the woodchuck were named Asplundh. The company is the world's largest tree-trimming business, clearing tree limbs from power lines for utilities and municipalities in Australia, Canada, New Zealand, and the US. The company also offers utility-related services such as meter reading, pipeline maintenance, storm emergency services, street light maintenance and construction, underground pipeline location, and utility pole maintenance. The Asplundh family owns and manages the company, which was founded in 1928.

EXECUTIVES

Chairman and CEO: Christopher B. Asplundh
President: Scott Asplundh
EVP: George Graham
Treasurer and Secretary: Joseph P. Dwyer
Director of Human Resources: Jean Nichols

LOCATIONS

HQ: 708 Blair Mill Rd., Willow Grove, PA 19090
Phone: 215-784-4200 **Fax:** 215-784-4493
Web: www.asplundh.com

Asplundh has operations in Australia, Canada, New Zealand, and the US.

PRODUCTS/OPERATIONS

Selected Subsidiaries

American Lighting & Signalization (traffic signal services)
Asplundh Construction (utility and heavy construction)
Blume Tree Services (line clearance and vegetation management)
Central Locating Service (locating underground utility pipes and lines)
Compass Equipment Leasing (utility equipment rentals)
Utility Meter Services (meter reading and installation)
Utility Pole Technologies (pole inspection and restoration)

COMPETITORS

Davey Tree
Monroe and Lewis Tree Service
Wright Tree Service

HISTORICAL FINANCIALS

Company Type: Private

Income Statement FYE: December 31

	REVENUE ($ mil.)	NET INCOME ($ mil.)	NET PROFIT MARGIN	EMPLOYEES
12/01	1,400	—	—	24,000
12/00	1,473	—	—	25,500
12/99	1,251	—	—	24,000
12/98	1,026	—	—	25,000
12/97	1,000	—	—	22,000
12/96	936	—	—	18,000
12/95	868	—	—	18,500
12/94	856	—	—	19,200
12/93	560	—	—	14,500
12/92	560	—	—	14,500
Annual Growth	10.7%	—	—	5.8%

Revenue History

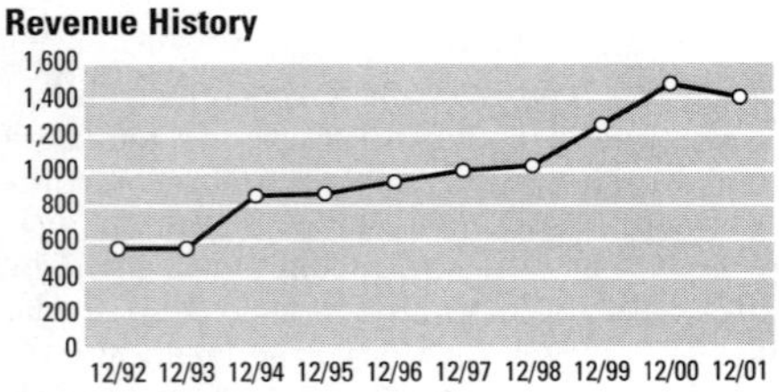

Associated Electric Cooperative Inc.

Associated Electric Cooperative is an association of associated power cooperatives. The utility provides transmission and generation services to its six member-owner companies, which in turn provide power supply services to 51 distribution cooperatives in three Midwest states. (The distribution cooperatives have a combined customer count of nearly 800,000.) Associated Electric operates some 9,000 miles of power transmission lines and has 5,000 MW of generating capacity from interests in coal- and gas-fired power plants; it also engages in wholesale energy transactions with other regional utilities.

EXECUTIVES

General Manager and CEO: James J. Jura
Director Accounting and Finance and CFO: Michael M. (Mike) Miller
Director Business and Technical Services: Patrick L. Mills
Director Engineering and Operations: Gary L. Fulks
Director Human Resources: David P. Stump
Director Member Services and Corporate Communications: Keith E. Hartner
Auditors: PricewaterhouseCoopers LLP

LOCATIONS

HQ: 2814 S. Golden, Springfield, MO 65801
Phone: 417-881-1204 **Fax:** 417-885-9252
Web: www.aeci.org

HISTORICAL FINANCIALS

Company Type: Cooperative

Income Statement FYE: December 31

	REVENUE ($ mil.)	NET INCOME ($ mil.)	NET PROFIT MARGIN	EMPLOYEES
12/02	661	16	2.5%	583
12/01	693	7	1.1%	572
12/00	669	—	—	563
12/99	624	—	—	572
12/98	590	—	—	585
12/97	541	—	—	640
12/96	557	—	—	—
12/95	464	—	—	—
12/94	484	—	—	—
12/93	431	—	—	—
Annual Growth	4.9%	123.3%	—	(1.8%)

Net Income History

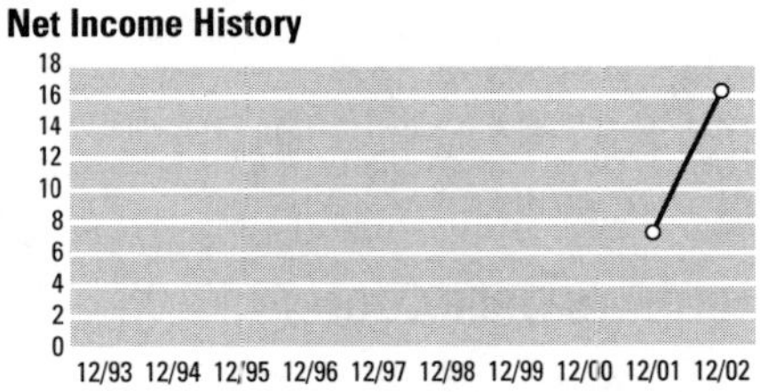

Associated Food Stores, Inc.

Associated Food Stores, a regional cooperative wholesale distributor, goes to extremes — mountain cold and desert heat — in supplying more than 500 independent supermarkets.

Member stores (and the cooperative's owners) are located in eight western states. Associated owns about 20% of Western Family Foods, a grocery wholesalers' partnership that produces Western Family private-label goods. It acquired three of its four largest customers (Dan's, Lin's, and Macey's) in 1999 to avoid losing them to acquisition-hungry supermarket chains. Associated owns and operates about 20 retail stores.

The co-op was formed in 1940 by Donald Lloyd, president of the Utah Retail Grocers Association, and 34 other retailers.

EXECUTIVES

Chairman: Jack Shaum
President and CEO: Richard A. (Rich) Parkinson
SVP and CFO: S. Neal Berube
SVP Merchandising: Richard Hardy
VP and Manager, Helena Division: Kelly Atkins
VP Marketing and Communication: Steve Reich
VP Operations: Dave Jonckowski
VP, Procurement: Brian Duff
VP Store Development: Steve Miner
Director Human Resources: Fred Ferguson
Head of Corporate Stores: Richard (Dick) King
Auditors: Deloitte & Touche LLP

LOCATIONS

HQ: 1850 W. 2100 South, Salt Lake City, UT 84119
Phone: 801-973-4400 **Fax:** 801-978-8551
Web: www.afstores.com

Associated Food Stores has operations in Idaho, Montana, and Utah.

PRODUCTS/OPERATIONS

Wholly Owned Subsidiaries

AFS Insurance Services, Inc.
Associated Pharmacies, Inc.
Dan's Supermarkets, Inc
Lin's Supermarkets, Inc.
Macey's, Inc.
Market Development, Inc.

COMPETITORS

Albertson's
AMCON Distributing
AWG
Costco Wholesale
Fleming Companies
IGA
Kroger
Shurfine International
Smith's Food & Drug
SUPERVALU
Topco Associates
Unified Western Grocers
Wal-Mart

HISTORICAL FINANCIALS

Company Type: Cooperative

Income Statement FYE: Saturday nearest March 31

	ESTIMATED REVENUE ($ mil.)	NET INCOME ($ mil.)	NET PROFIT MARGIN	EMPLOYEES
3/02	1,184	1	0.1%	1,400
3/01	1,190	6	0.5%	1,400
3/00	1,085	2	0.2%	1,400
3/99	925	—	—	1,500
3/98	1,000	—	—	1,500
3/97	925	—	—	1,500
3/96	850	—	—	—
Annual Growth	5.7%	(26.4%)	—	(1.4%)

Net Income History

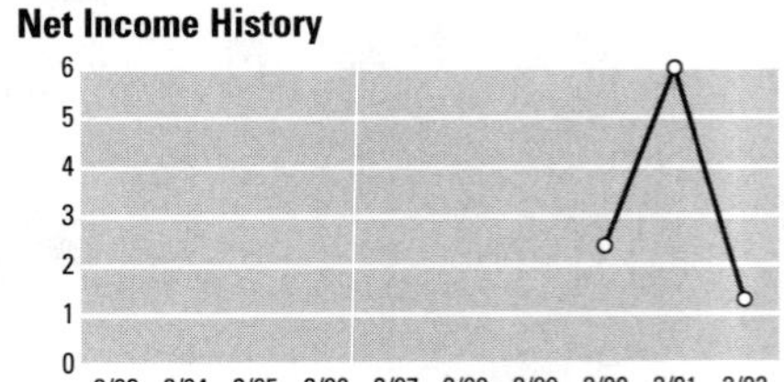

Associated Grocers, Inc.

Associated Grocers (AG) feeds the ability of its member/owners to remain competitive. The co-operative distributes food and nonfood goods and provides support services to more than 300 independent grocery retailers in the Northwest, Hawaii, Alaska, Guam, and the Pacific Rim. It distributes more than 12,000 items, including products under the Western Family, Ovenworks, and Javaworks names. AG (not to be confused with Associated Grocers in other regions) was formed in 1934 to support 11 Seattle-based neighborhood grocers. Financial trouble led to a 15-month-long restructuring effort that resulted in asset sales and a new management team led by CEO Robert Hermanns, formerly the COO of Weis Markets.

EXECUTIVES

President and CEO: Robert P. Hermanns
Chief Financial Officer: John L. Carrosino
VP, Human Resources: Dick Harding
VP, Nonperishables: Craig E. Calton
VP, Perishables: Paul Kennedy
CIO: Gene Puhrmann
General Counsel: Craig Palm
Director of Business Development, Oregon and Alaska: John Santos

LOCATIONS

HQ: 3301 S. Norfolk, Seattle, WA 98118
Phone: 206-762-2100 **Fax:** 206-764-7731
Web: agsea.com

PRODUCTS/OPERATIONS

Selected Members
Admiral Thriftway
Alaska Commercial Company
Larry's Markets
Market Place
Proctor Thriftway
Queen Anne Thriftway
Ralph's Bayview Thriftway
Red Apple Markets
Roth's
Thriftway
Zupan's Markets

Private-Label Brands
Javaworks
Ovenworks
Western Family

COMPETITORS

Albertson's
Fleming Companies
Kroger
Nash Finch
Safeway
SUPERVALU
Topco Associates
Unified Western Grocers
Wal-Mart

HISTORICAL FINANCIALS

Company Type: Private

Income Statement FYE: Friday nearest September 30

	REVENUE ($ mil.)	NET INCOME ($ mil.)	NET PROFIT MARGIN	EMPLOYEES
9/02	900	—	—	1,100
9/01	1,000	—	—	1,100
9/00	1,100	—	—	1,500
9/99	1,100	—	—	1,400
9/98	1,090	—	—	1,300
9/97	1,092	—	—	1,360
9/96	1,090	—	—	1,350
9/95	1,055	—	—	1,340
9/94	1,107	—	—	1,340
9/93	1,073	—	—	1,381
Annual Growth	(1.9%)	—	—	(2.5%)

Revenue History

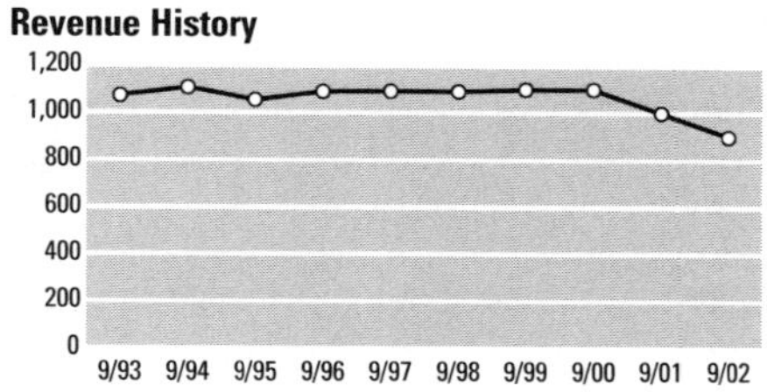

Associated Materials Incorporated

Associated Materials Incorporated (AMI) is quick to side with its customers. Through its Alside division (more than 95% of sales), the company makes vinyl siding and vinyl windows for the new construction and home remodeling markets. Other Alside products include vinyl fencing, decking, railing, and garage doors. Alside operates 90 company-owned supply centers and distributes metal siding and other building products made by other OEMs. AMI sold its AmerCable division (jacketed electrical cable) to AmerCable Incorporated and members of AmerCable's management in 2002. Investment firm Harvest Partners controls AMI through Associated Materials Holdings.

In 2003 Associated Materials acquired Gentek Holdings, Inc. (vinyl, aluminum, and steel siding and vinyl windows), including its Gentek Building Products, Inc., and Gentek Building Products Limited subsidiaries, for about $118 million.

EXECUTIVES

President, CEO, and Director; President and CEO, Alside: Michael J. (Mike) Caporale Jr., age 50, $766,913 pay (prior to promotion)
VP, CFO, Secretary, and Treasurer: D. Keith LaVanway, age 37
VP Human Resources: John Haumesser
Group VP, Window Products, Alside: Wayne D. Fredrick, age 55
President, Alside Window Co.: Kenneth L. Bloom, age 38
Auditors: Ernst & Young LLP

LOCATIONS

HQ: 3773 State Rd., Cuyahoga Falls, OH 44223
Phone: 330-929-1811 **Fax:** 330-922-2354
Web: www.associatedmaterials.com

Associated Materials has plants in Arkansas, Iowa, North Carolina, Ohio, Texas, and Washington.

PRODUCTS/OPERATIONS

Selected Alside Products
Vinyl fencing, decking, and railing
Vinyl garage doors
Vinyl siding
Vinyl windows

COMPETITORS

Andersen Corporation
CertainTeed
General Cable
JELD-WEN
Louisiana-Pacific
MMI Products
Nortek
Owens Corning
Royal Group Technologies
Superior TeleCom
ThermoView Industries

HISTORICAL FINANCIALS

Company Type: Private

Income Statement FYE: December 31

	REVENUE ($ mil.)	NET INCOME ($ mil.)	NET PROFIT MARGIN	EMPLOYEES
12/02	630	6	1.0%	2,550
12/01	596	25	4.3%	2,140
12/00	499	24	4.7%	2,000
12/99	453	21	4.5%	1,800
12/98	408	9	2.2%	2,440
12/97	398	13	3.3%	1,500
12/96	357	9	2.5%	2,215
12/95	350	1	0.4%	2,310
12/94	353	8	2.2%	2,400
12/93	313	6	1.9%	—
Annual Growth	8.1%	1.1%	—	0.8%

2002 Year-End Financials

Debt ratio: 136.4%
Return on equity: 4.6%
Cash ($ mil.): 13
Current ratio: 2.35
Long-term debt ($ mil.): 242

Net Income History

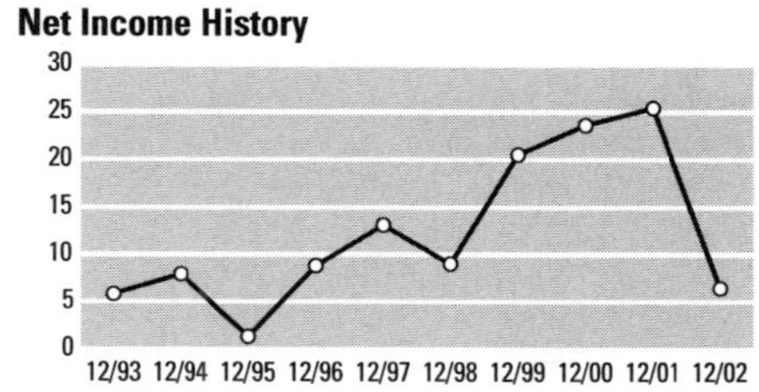

Associated Milk Producers Inc.

Associated Milk Producers Incorporated might wear a cheesy grin, but it churns up solid sales. Shying away from the liquid stuff, it transforms more than 5 billion pounds of milk into butter, cheese, and other solid milk products each year. A regional cooperative of 4,600 dairy farms from Iowa, Minnesota, Missouri, Nebraska, North and South Dakota, and Wisconsin, AMPI operates 14 manufacturing plants. The co-op produces 60% of all the instant milk sold in the US and is a major cheddar producer. Aside from its own State brand of cheese and butter, AMPI primarily makes private-label products for retailers and food service customers.

AMPI has upgraded its 14 plants to produce additional value-added dairy products such as shredded cheese, aseptic-packaged cheese sauces (in coated cardboard containers for stable shelf life), and individually wrapped butter pats. Only one plant produces fluid milk. In addition, AMPI's 93,000-sq.-ft. plant in New Ulm, Minnesota, is the biggest butter barn in the US, whipping up nearly 20,000 pounds of butter per hour.

EXECUTIVES

President of the Board: Paul Toft
General Manager: Mark Furth
CFO: Steve Sorenson
Director of Information Technology: Chip Collum
Director of Marketing: Jim Walsh
Human Resources Manager: Leigh Heilman

LOCATIONS

HQ: 315 N. Broadway, New Ulm, MN 56073
Phone: 507-354-8295 **Fax:** 507-359-8651
Web: www.ampi.com

Associated Milk Producers Incorporated has 14 milk processing plants in Iowa, Minnesota, Missouri, Nebraska, North Dakota, South Dakota, and Wisconsin.

PRODUCTS/OPERATIONS

Selected Products

Butter
Cheese
Cheese Sauce
Dry milk
Fluid milk
Pudding

COMPETITORS

California Dairies Inc.
Dairy Farmers of America
Dairylea
Dean Foods
Foremost Farms
Great Lakes Cheese
Land O'Lakes
Leprino Foods
Marathon Cheese
MMPA
Prairie Farms Dairy
Saputo
Schreiber Foods

HISTORICAL FINANCIALS

Company Type: Cooperative

Income Statement FYE: December 31

	REVENUE ($ mil.)	NET INCOME ($ mil.)	NET PROFIT MARGIN	EMPLOYEES
12/02	1,000	—	—	1,700
12/01	1,200	—	—	1,600
12/00	1,000	—	—	1,600
12/99	1,100	—	—	1,600
12/98	1,100	—	—	1,600
12/97	928	—	—	1,600
12/96	2,189	—	—	4,500
12/95	2,555	—	—	4,500
12/94	2,629	—	—	4,500
12/93	2,692	—	—	4,199
Annual Growth	(10.4%)	—	—	(9.6%)

Revenue History

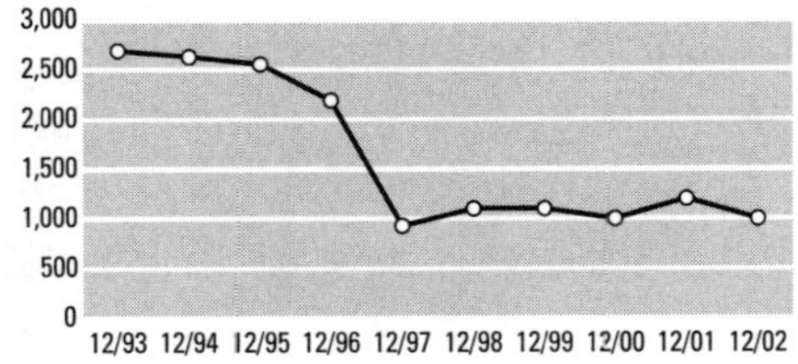

The Associated Press

This just in: The Associated Press (AP) is reporting tonight and every night wherever news is breaking. AP is the world's largest newsgathering organization, with about 240 news bureaus serving more than 120 countries. It provides news, photos, graphics, and audiovisual services that reach people daily through print, radio, television, and the Web. In addition to its traditional news services, the not-for-profit cooperative, which is owned by its 1,550 member newspapers, runs several other operations including an international television division (APTN), a digital ad delivery service (AP AdSEND), an ad processing and billing service, photo archives, and a continuous online news service (The WIRE).

AP's news reports are translated into five languages (Dutch, English, French, German, and Spanish) and reach more than 1 billion people daily. Its AP Digital division sells news to the Internet and wireless markets. The cooperative has been in operation for more than 150 years.

In 2003 previous president and publisher of *USA TODAY* and Gannett SVP Tom Curley replaced the retiring Louis Boccardi as president and CEO of AP, becoming the 12th person to lead the news organization since its founding in 1848. Curley's older brother John is AP's vice chairman. AP is also moving its headquarters from Manhattan's Rockefeller Plaza (its home for the last 65 years) to 450 W. 33rd St.

HISTORY

The Associated Press was formed in 1848 when six New York City newspapers joined to share news that arrived by telegraph wire. Two years later AP began selling wire reports to other papers and before long started creating regional associations. Adapting to changing technologies and public interests, AP began covering sports, financial, and public interest stories in the 1920s and was selling news reports to radio stations in the 1940s. Advancements during WWII included using transatlantic cable and radio-teletype circuits to deliver news and photos.

In the late 1960s AP and Dow Jones introduced services to improve business and financial reporting. AP improved photo delivery, reception, and storage in the 1970s with the advent of Laserphoto and the Electronic Darkroom. It began transmitting news by satellite and offering color photographs to newspapers in the 1980s. In 1985 Louis Boccardi took over the job as president and CEO of AP.

AP adjusted to the media-heavy culture of the 1990s by launching the APTV international news video service and the All News Radio network in 1994. It then moved onto the Internet with The WIRE in 1996 and began offering online access to its Photo Archive in 1997. It bought Worldwide Television News in 1998, combining it with APTV to form APTN (Associated Press Television News). The following year it purchased the radio news contracts of UPI after the rival organization announced it was getting out of broadcast news.

In 2000 AP created an Internet division, AP Digital, to focus on marketing news to online providers. The cooperative continued its Internet focus the following year, launching AP Online en Español (news for Spanish-language Web sites) and AP Entertainment Online (multimedia entertainment news for Web sites). Also that year AP bought the Newspaper Industry Communication Center from the Newspaper Association of America.

In 2002 the company launched an expanded editorial partnership with Dow Jones Newswires, increasing the amount of financial news distributed on AP wires. Later that year it acquired Capitolwire, a provider of state government news.

EXECUTIVES

Chairman: Robert Osborne
Vice Chairman: John J. Curley
President and CEO: Tom Curley, age 54
SVP and CFO: Patrick T. O'Brien
SVP: Jonathan P. Wolman
VP and Director, AP Broadcast: James R. William, III
VP and Director, AP Digital: Thomas E. Slaughter
VP and Director, Business Development: Tom Brettingen
VP and Director, Corporate Communications: Kelly Smith Tunney
VP, Communication and Technology: John Reid
VP, Human Resources and Secretary: James M. Donna
Assistant Secretary and Director, Corporate Events: Lilo Jedelhauser
Treasurer: Daniel M. Boruch
Director, Media Relations: Jack Stokes
Executive Editor: Kathleen Carroll, age 46
Managing Editor: Mike Silverman
Chief Executive, AP Television News: Ian Ritchie
Director, Administration, AP Broadcast: Greg Groce
Deputy Director of Broadcast Division and Director of Broadcast Technology: Lee Perryman
Deputy Director and Managing Editor, AP Broadcast: Brad Kalbfeld
General Manager, AP Radio: Thomas P. Callahan
Auditors: Ernst & Young

LOCATIONS

HQ: 50 Rockefeller Plaza, New York, NY 10020
Phone: 212-621-1500 **Fax:** 212-621-5447
Web: www.ap.org

The Associated Press has about 240 news bureaus serving 121 countries.

PRODUCTS/OPERATIONS

Selected Products and Services

AP AdSEND (digital transmission of advertisements)
AP Digital (news for Internet and wireless markets)
AP Information Services (news products for corporations, government, and online distributors)
AP Photo Archive (more than 750,000 online photos)
AP Telecommunications (land-based and satellite information networks)
AP Wide World Photos (20th-century historical photos for professional photographers)
APTN (Associated Press Television Network, international television news service)
ENPS (electronic news production system)
NICC (Newpaper Industry Communication Center; ad placement, billing and tear sheet processing)
The WIRE (24-hour news service for the Internet)

COMPETITORS

Agence France-Presse
Bloomberg
Business Wire
COMTEX
Corbis
Dow Jones
Gannett
Getty Images
Knight-Ridder
New York Times
PR Newswire
Reuters
Tribune
UPI

HISTORICAL FINANCIALS

Company Type: Cooperative

Income Statement FYE: December 31

	REVENUE ($ mil.)	NET INCOME ($ mil.)	NET PROFIT MARGIN	EMPLOYEES
12/02	554	—	—	3,500
12/01	575	—	—	3,500
12/00	574	—	—	3,700
12/99	572	—	—	3,500
12/98	495	—	—	3,500
12/97	441	—	—	3,500
12/96	418	—	—	3,000
12/95	390	—	—	3,150
12/94	406	—	—	3,150
12/93	382	—	—	3,150
Annual Growth	4.2%	—	—	1.2%

Revenue History

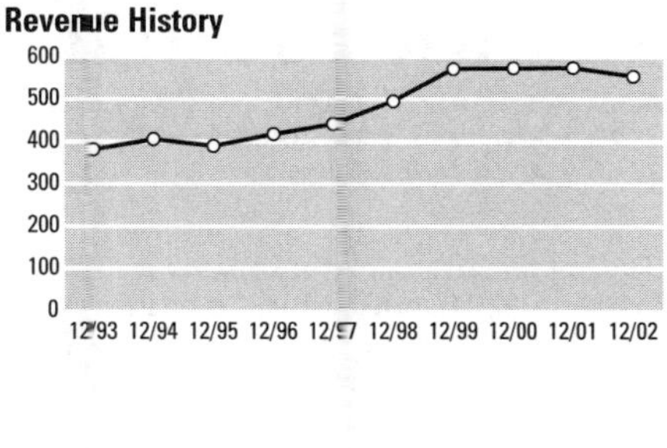

Associated Wholesale Grocers, Inc.

Associated Wholesale Grocers (AWG) knows its customers can't live by bread and milk alone. The AWG cooperative supplies more than 850 member-stores with wholesale grocery sales, advertising and market support, store decorating and design, and selecting appropriate technology. The co-op's territory covers primarily Arkansas, Kansas, Missouri, and Oklahoma, but also six other midwestern and southern states. The co-op offers its members the use of such banners as Country Mart, Thriftway, Price Chopper, and Sun Fresh. AWG also operates more than 30 of its own Falley's and Food 4 Less stores in Kansas and Missouri, as well as 43 Homeland stores throughout Oklahoma.

AWG acquired Homeland Stores in September 2002 and formed a new subsidiary, Associated Retail Grocers, to oversee Homeland and its Falley's chain. (Wholesaler AWG moved into food retailing in 1998 with its acquisition of Falley's.)

AWG supplies members with brand-name and private-label food (Always Save and Best Choice) and nonfood items; other services the co-op provides include property and casualty insurance, employee benefits packages, loan programs, and real estate lease assistance. It also helps its members appeal to Hispanic customers with its "Authentic Hispanic" product line of more than 300 items.

Other AWG banners include Apple Market, Cash Saver, and Price Mart (a food warehouse format).

HISTORY

About 20 Kansas City, Kansas-area grocers met in a local grocery in 1924 and organized the Associated Grocers Company to get better deals on purchases and advertising. They elected J. C. Harline president, and each chipped in a few hundred dollars to make their first purchases. It took a while to find a manufacturer who would sell directly to them; a local soap maker was finally convinced, and others gradually followed.

In 1926 the group was incorporated as Associated Wholesale Grocers (AWG). It outgrew two warehouses in four years, finally moving to a 16,000-sq.-ft. facility big enough to add new lines and more products. Membership doubled between 1930 and 1932 as grocers moved from ordering products a year ahead to the new wholesale concept, and members took seriously the slogan: "Buy, Sell, Buy Some More." They met every week to plan how to sell their products, and buyer and advertising manager Harry Small gave sales presentations and advertising ideas (his trade-in plan for old brooms sold more than two train-carloads of brooms in two weeks). Heavy newspaper advertising also paid off; AWG topped $1 million in sales in 1933.

The cooperative made its first acquisition in 1936, buying Progressive Grocers, a warehouse in Joplin, Missouri; a second warehouse named Associated Grocers was acquired the next year in Springfield, Missouri. AWG continued building and expanding warehouses, and annual sales were at $11 million by 1951.

Louis Fox became CEO in 1956. Fox maximized year-end rebates for members, led several acquisitions, and formed a new subsidiary for financing stores and small shopping centers where AWG members had a presence (Supermarket Developers). Sales increased nearly fifteenfold to over $200 million in his first 15 years.

James Basha, who succeeded Fox when he retired in 1984, saw sales reach $2.4 billion by his own retirement in 1992. Basha was followed by former COO Mike DeFabis, once a deputy mayor of Indianapolis. DeFabis orchestrated several acquisitions, including 41 Kansas City-area stores — most of which were quickly bought by members — from bankrupt Food Barn Stores in 1994 and 29 Oklahoma stores and a warehouse from Safeway spinoff Homeland Stores in 1995 (members bought all the stores).

AWG's nonfood subsidiary, Valu Merchandisers Co., was established in 1995; its new Kansas warehouse began shipping health and beauty aids and housewares the following year to help members battle big discounters. Members narrowly defeated a proposal in late 1996 to convert the cooperative into a public company. Proponents promptly petitioned for a second vote, which was defeated early the next year.

AWG veteran Doug Carolan succeeded DeFabis in 1998, becoming only the fifth CEO in the co-operative's history. The company bought five Falley's and 33 Food 4 Less stores in Kansas and Missouri from Fred Meyer in 1998 for $300 million. In a break with tradition, AWG is operating the stores rather than selling them to members.

In 2000, after a months-long labor dispute with the Teamsters was resolved, Carolan left AWG. The company's CFO, Gary Phillips, was named president and CEO later that year. In 2001 the company debuted a new format, ALPS (Always Low Price Stores) — small stores that carry a limited selection of grocery top-sellers. Also that year AWG's Kansas City division began distributing to more than 10 new stores that had formerly been served by Fleming, the #1 US wholesale food distributor.

In 2002 supermarket operator Homeland Stores, which operates 43 stores throughout Oklahoma, emerged from bankruptcy as a fully owned subsidiary of AWG.

From the August 2003 sale of Fleming Companies' wholesale distribution business, AWG picked up food distribution centers in Nebraska (two), Oklahoma (one), and Tennessee (two) and general merchandise distribution centers in Tennessee and Kansas.

EXECUTIVES

Chairman: J. Fred Ball
President and CEO: Gary Phillips
EVP and CFO: Robert C. Walker
EVP, Marketing: Jerry Garland
SVP and General Manager, KC Division: Mike Rand
SVP, Real Estate: Scott Wilmoski
VP and General Counsel: Chi Chi Puhl
VP, Corporate Sales: Bill Lancaster
VP, Human Resources: Frank Tricamo
VP, Procurement: Dennis Kinser
VP, Secretary, and Treasurer: Joe Campbell
President and CEO, Benchmark Insurance Companies: William R. Morrison
President and CEO, Homeland Stores: Larry Willis
President, Valu Merchandisers: Ken Nemeth
Executive Director, AWG Brands: Scott Richey

LOCATIONS

HQ: 5000 Kansas Ave., Kansas City, KS 66106
Phone: 913-288-1000 **Fax:** 913-288-1508
Web: www.awginc.com

Associated Wholesale Grocers serves grocers in Arkansas, Illinois, Iowa, Kansas, Kentucky, Missouri, Nebraska, Oklahoma, Tennessee, and Texas. The cooperative has four distribution centers in Kansas, Missouri, and Oklahoma.

PRODUCTS/OPERATIONS

Selected Private-Label Brands

Always Save
Best Choice

Selected Services

Advertising
Category management
Employee training
Financial planning
In-store marketing
Insurance
Market research and analysis
Merchandising advice
Private-label products
Product positioning
Real estate lease assistance
Reclamation
Site acquisition
Store engineering and construction
Store financing
Store franchise formats
Store remodeling

Selected Store Formats

Apple Market (15,000-25,000-sq.-ft. grocery stores designed for neighborhood locations in both rural and metropolitan areas)
Cash Saver (designed with fewer perishables to serve rural areas)
Country Mart (25,000-45,000-sq.-ft. value-priced stores designed for county-seat and medium-sized towns)
Falley's (conventional supermarkets)
Food 4 Less (warehouse stores)
Price Chopper and Price Mart (50,000-92,000-sq.-ft. value-priced warehouse stores designed for high-volume areas)
Sun Fresh (40,000-63,000-sq.-ft. stores designed to serve medium-to-upper-income customers)
Thriftway (neighborhood locations)

COMPETITORS

Affiliated Foods
Albertson's
Delhaize America
Fleming Companies
GSC Enterprises
H.T. Hackney
Hy-Vee
IGA
Kroger
Nash Finch
Roundy's
S. Abraham & Sons
Schnuck Markets
Shurfine International
Spartan Stores
SUPERVALU
Topco Associates
Wal-Mart

HISTORICAL FINANCIALS

Company Type: Cooperative

Income Statement FYE: Last Saturday in December

	REVENUE ($ mil.)	NET INCOME ($ mil.)	NET PROFIT MARGIN	EMPLOYEES
12/01	3,097	53	1.7%	3,300
12/00	3,267	46	1.4%	3,300
12/99	3,370	65	1.9%	3,300
12/98	3,180	66	2.1%	3,100
12/97	3,129	64	2.0%	3,000
12/96	3,096	—	—	2,797
12/95	2,970	—	—	—
12/94	2,600	—	—	—
12/93	2,540	—	—	—
12/92	2,404	—	—	—
Annual Growth	2.9%	(4.5%)	—	3.4%

2001 Year-End Financials

Debt ratio: 34.1%
Return on equity: 32.4%
Cash ($ mil.): 12
Current ratio: 1.05
Long-term debt ($ mil.): 55

Net Income History

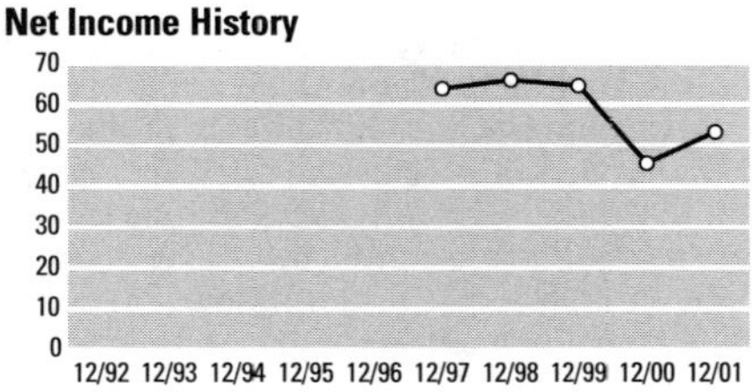

Atlantic Express Transportation

Driving with thousands of schoolchildren doesn't intimidate Atlantic Express Transportation — but insurance costs are another matter. The school bus operator has a fleet of about 7,000 buses that serve 150 school districts in the US; it also sells school buses. The company cited increases in its insurance and pension obligations when it filed for bankruptcy protection in 2002. Besides its school bus operations, Atlantic Express runs an express bus line between New York City and Atlantic City and provides paratransit services in New York City, New Jersey, and Phoenix. President and CEO Domenic Gatto founded Atlantic Express in 1964. An affiliate of Greenwich Street Capital Partners owns 90% of the company.

EXECUTIVES

Chairman: Sanjay Patel, age 42
President and CEO: Domenic Gatto
EVP, CFO, Secretary, and Treasurer: Nathan Schlenker
COO: Jerome (Jerry) Dente
EVP: Noel Cabrera
Controller: Richard Dineburg
CIO: Ken Rosiello
Human Resources Manager: Diane Turcotte

LOCATIONS

HQ: Atlantic Express Transportation Corp.
7 North St., Staten Island, NY 10302
Phone: 718-442-7000 **Fax:** 718-442-7672
Web: www.atlanticexpress.com

PRODUCTS/OPERATIONS

Selected Services

Bus sales
Charter and tour bus operations
Express commuter transit
Paratransit services
Pre-kindergarten transportation
School bus transportation

COMPETITORS

Coach USA
FirstGroup
Laidlaw International
National Express Corp.

HISTORICAL FINANCIALS

Company Type: Private

Income Statement FYE: June 30

	REVENUE ($ mil.)	NET INCOME ($ mil.)	NET PROFIT MARGIN	EMPLOYEES
6/02	427	—	—	8,500
6/01	442	—	—	8,500
6/00	402	—	—	7,200
6/99	322	—	—	6,850
6/98	262	—	—	5,800
6/97	166	—	—	5,600
6/96	143	—	—	—
6/95	114	—	—	—
Annual Growth	20.8%	—	—	8.7%

Revenue History

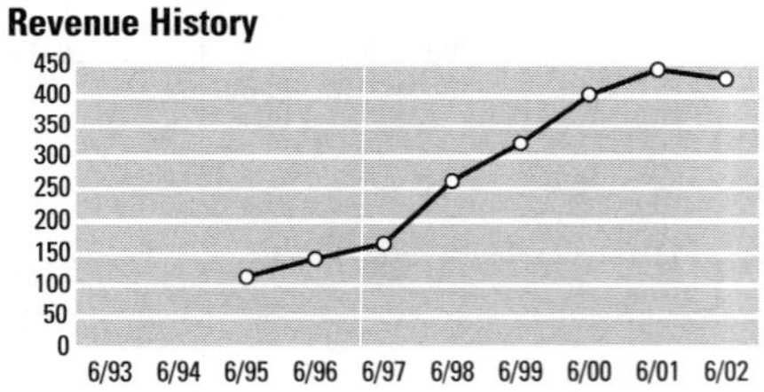

Atlantic Mutual Companies

Having set sail as a marine insurer more than 150 years ago, Atlantic Mutual Companies today provides commercial, personal, and marine property/casualty insurance to individuals and businesses. Through its subsidiaries (including Atlantic Mutual Insurance, Centennial Insurance, and Atlantic Specialty Insurance), the company offers insurance programs and loss control for large firms and specialty coverage for small to mid-sized companies such as financial institutions, retailers, and wholesalers. Atlantic Mutual also provides auto and homeowners coverage for individuals. Independent agents and brokers sell the company's products throughout the US.

Atlantic Mutual has expanded into Europe with the formation of Atlantic Mutual International; the subsidiary will primarily serve US businesses in the European Union.

EXECUTIVES

Chairman and CEO: Klaus G. Dorfi
President and COO: Kermit C. Smith
SVP and CFO: Cornelius E. (Neal) Golding
SVP, Claims Services Division and Corporate Counsel: Theodore R. Henke
SVP, Commercial Insurance Division: Robert G. Himmer
SVP, Customer Service Division: John G. Heitz
SVP, Information Systems Division: David P. Mitchell Jr.
SVP, Marine and Surety Division: Thomas P. Gorke
SVP, Personal Insurance Division: Daniel H. Olmsted
Human Resources Manager: Lisa Reciniti

LOCATIONS

HQ: 140 Broadway, New York, NY 10005
Phone: 212-943-1800 **Fax:** 212-428-6566
Web: www.atlanticmutual.com

PRODUCTS/OPERATIONS

Group Companies
Atlantic Companies Holding Corp.
Atlantic Mutual Insurance Company
Atlantic Mutual International Limited (UK)
Atlantic Mutual of Bermuda Limited
Atlantic Risk Services, Inc.
Atlantic Specialty Insurance Company
Centennial Insurance Company

COMPETITORS

ACE Limited
AIG
Capitol Transamerica
Chubb
Kemper Insurance
Royal & SunAlliance USA
St. Paul Companies
Travelers Bond
W. R. Berkley

HISTORICAL FINANCIALS

Company Type: Mutual company

Income Statement FYE: December 31

	ASSETS ($ mil.)	NET INCOME ($ mil.)	INCOME AS % OF ASSETS	EMPLOYEES
12/02	1,845	18	1.0%	1,800
12/01	1,764	(14)	—	1,800
12/00	1,785	11	0.6%	1,800
12/99	1,753	2	0.1%	—
Annual Growth	1.7%	127.7%	—	0.0%

2002 Year-End Financials

Equity as % of assets: 24.7%
Return on assets: 1.0%
Return on equity: 4.0%
Long-term debt ($ mil.): —
Sales ($ mil.): 1,078

Net Income History

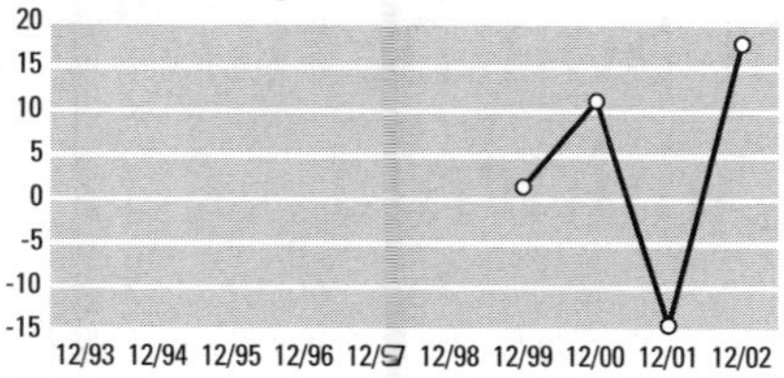

Atlas World Group, Inc.

Willing to carry the weight of the world, Atlas World Group is the holding company for one of the largest moving companies in the US, Atlas Van Lines.

Atlas Van Lines operates through its Relocation Services Group, which moves household goods, and its Specialized Transportation Group, which moves items such as trade show exhibits, fine art, and electronics, as well as general commodities. Atlas World Group also provides international freight forwarding services and operates Atlas Canada, a major household and corporate moving business in that country.

Atlas Van Lines was formed in 1948 by a group of 33 local movers; Atlas World Group was formed in 1994. The company is owned by its agents.

EXECUTIVES

Chairman and CEO: Michael L. Shaffer
CFO, Atlas World Group and Atlas Van Lines: Richard J. (Rick) Olson
VP, General Counsel, and Corporate Secretary; Atlas World Group and Atlas Van Lines: Marian Weilert Sauvey
President and COO, Atlas Van Lines: James A. Stamm
President and COO, Atlas Van Lines (Canada): Doug Auld
SVP Operations, Specialized Transportation Group, Atlas Van Lines: Glen Dunkerson
SVP Sales, Relocation Services Group, Atlas Van Lines: Michael N. Scavuzzo
SVP Sales Development, Relocation Services Group, Atlas Van Lines: Greg L. Hoover
SVP Transportation, Relocation Services Group, Atlas Van Lines: Dennie D. Lynn
Corporate Counsel: Todd Suter
Auditors: Ernst & Young

LOCATIONS

HQ: 1212 St. George Rd., Evansville, IN 47711
Phone: 812-424-2222 **Fax:** 812-421-7125
Web: www.atlasworldgroup.com

PRODUCTS/OPERATIONS

Selected Subsidiaries

Atlas Terminal Company, Inc. (sells, finances, and repairs transportation equipment)
Atlas Van Lines (Canada) Ltd.
Atlas Van Lines International Corp.

COMPETITORS

AMERCO
Bekins
Graebel
Penske Truck Leasing
SIRVA
UniGroup

HISTORICAL FINANCIALS

Company Type: Private

Income Statement FYE: December 31

	REVENUE ($ mil.)	NET INCOME ($ mil.)	NET PROFIT MARGIN	EMPLOYEES
12/01	586	—	—	800
12/00	607	—	—	804
12/99	522	—	—	750
12/98	512	—	—	750
12/97	490	—	—	731
12/96	485	—	—	730
Annual Growth	3.9%	—	—	1.8%

Revenue History

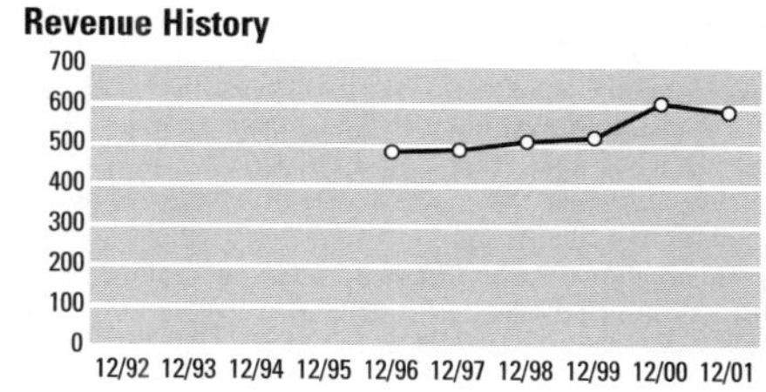

Atrium Companies, Inc.

Atrium Companies produces aluminum and vinyl windows (more than 75% of sales) and patio doors, and "woodn't" have it any other way. After selling its wood window and door business, Atrium now makes vinyl and aluminum products. Customers include retail centers, lumberyards, builders, and wholesalers for both new construction and remodeling markets. Atrium also offers installation and repair services. Since its founding in 1948, Atrium has grown to include window and door making facilities and distribution centers in the US and Mexico, vinyl and aluminum extrusion operations in the US, and joint ventures in North Carolina and China. GE Investment Private Placement Partners II owns about 73% of Atrium.

Major customers for Atrium's products include retail centers (Home Depot and Lowe's) and national homebuilders (Pulte Homes, D.R. Horton, and Centex). The company's joint ventures include vinyl compounding operations in North Carolina and a vinyl extrusion operation in China.

As part of its plan to vertically integrate its operations, in 2003 Atrium acquired Texas-based zinc die-casting supplier Miniature Die Casting of Texas, LP for $3.25 million; it operates the company as MD Casting, Inc., a stand-alone operating unit that sells metal hardware to Atrium and to third parties. Atrium also agreed to acquire Texas-based aluminum and vinyl window and door maker Danvid Window Company, a subsidiary of American Architectural Products Corporation, for $5.8 million. Also in 2003 Atrium formed subsidiary Aluminum Screen Manufacturers, Inc., and purchased Aluminum Screen Manufacturing, Ltd., L.L.P.; Aluminum Screen Products, Inc.; and Aztex Screen Products, L.L.C.

Atrium's plan for growth includes maintaining and developing its markets in the US, cross-selling its vinyl products in traditional aluminum markets and vice-versa, leveraging the Atrium brand name across its product lines, increasing operational efficiencies, refining its product offerings, and acquiring complementary businesses.

EXECUTIVES

Chairman: Daniel T. Morley, age 50
President, CEO, and Director: Jeff L. Hull, age 37, $655,000 pay
EVP and CFO: Eric W. Long, age 34, $273,000 pay
EVP and Co-COO: Robert E. Burns, age 37, $340,625 pay
EVP and Co-COO: C. Douglas Cross, age 47, $278,750 pay
SVP, General Counsel, and Secretary: Philip J. (Phil) Ragona, age 41
SVP, Human Resources: D. D. (Gus) Agostinelli, age 57
VP, Information Systems: Michael Lynch
Treasurer and Asst. Secretary: Patrick Coffee
President, Atrium Door and Window Company of the Rockies: Donald Sloane
President, R. G. Darby Company, Inc., and Total Trim, Inc.: Cliff Darby, age 38, $300,000 pay
Auditors: PricewaterhouseCoopers LLP

LOCATIONS

HQ: 1341 W. Mockingbird Ln., Ste. 1200W, Dallas, TX 75247
Phone: 214-630-5757 **Fax:** 214-630-5001
Web: www.atriumcompanies.com

Atrium Companies has 45 manufacturing facilities and distribution centers in 22 states; it also operates a distribution center in Mexico City, Mexico.

PRODUCTS/OPERATIONS

Selected Divisions and Subsidiaries and Affiliates

Atrium Aluminum Products Division
Atrium Door and Window of Arizona & Nevada
Atrium Door and Window of New England
Atrium Door and Window of the Northeast
Atrium Door and Window of the Rockies
Atrium Door and Window of the West Coast
Atrium Patio Doors (a division of Woodgrain Millwork)
Atrium Vinyl Products Division
Best Built Window, Inc.
Dow Tech Plastics Division
Extruders Division
H-R Windows Division
Kel-Star Building Products Division
MD Casting, Inc.
North Texas Die & Tool Co.
R. G. Darby Division (aluminum products)
Thermal Industries, Inc.

COMPETITORS

Andersen Corporation
Bocenor
Drew Industries
International Aluminum
JELD-WEN
Masco
Masonite International
MI Home Products
MW Manufacturers
Nortek
Novar
Pella
Sierra Pacific Industries
Silver Line Building Products
Therma-Tru

HISTORICAL FINANCIALS

Company Type: Private

Income Statement FYE: December 31

	REVENUE ($ mil.)	NET INCOME ($ mil.)	NET PROFIT MARGIN	EMPLOYEES
12/01	525	(5)	—	4,350
12/00	496	(74)	—	4,100
12/99	499	2	0.4%	4,200
12/98	211	(3)	—	3,200
12/97	187	6	3.3%	1,885
12/96	156	4	2.7%	1,675
12/95	136	2	1.3%	—
12/94	124	9	7.4%	—
12/93	99	10	10.2%	—
Annual Growth	23.2%	—	—	21.0%

2001 Year-End Financials

Debt ratio: 261.3%
Return on equity: —
Cash ($ mil.): 1
Current ratio: 1.15
Long-term debt ($ mil.): 304

Net Income History

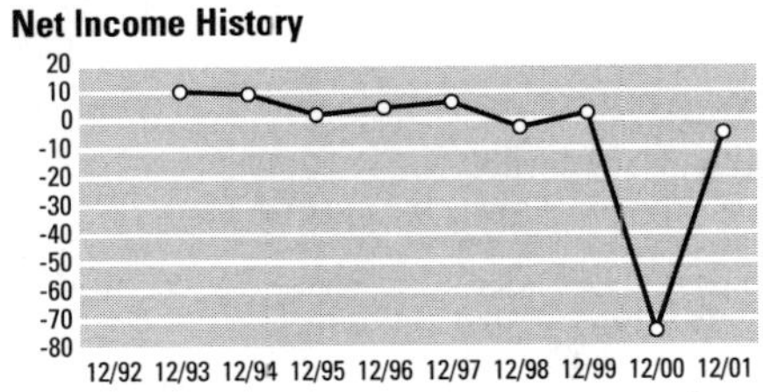

Austin Industries, Inc.

Paving the way for progress, Austin Industries provides civil, commercial, and industrial construction services. Its oldest subsidiary, Austin Bridge & Road, provides road, bridge, and parking lot construction across Texas. Subsidiary Austin Commercial, known for its high-rises, builds corporate headquarters, technology sites, and hospitals in the central and southwestern US. Austin Commercial tackled its first major sports arena project with American Airlines Center in Dallas. The group's Austin Industrial provides construction, maintenance, and electrical services for the chemical, refining, power, and manufacturing industries, mostly in the US South and Southeast. The employee-owned firm was founded in 1918.

EXECUTIVES

Chairman: William T. (Bill) Solomon, age 60
Vice Chairman: Charles M. Solomon
President and CEO: Ronald J. (Ron) Gafford, age 53
VP Finance and CFO: Paul W. Hill
President, Austin Bridge & Road: James R. (Jim) Andoga
President, Austin Commercial: David B. Walls, age 40
President, Austin Industrial: Henry G. Kelly
Director of Human Resources: Brad Brown
Director Corporate Communications: Lori Elise
Auditors: Ernst & Young LLP

LOCATIONS

HQ: 3535 Travis St., Ste. 300, Dallas, TX 75204
Phone: 214-443-5500 **Fax:** 214-443-5581
Web: www.austin-ind.com

Austin Industries and its operating companies have offices in Albuquerque, New Mexico; Augusta, Georgia; Austin, Beaumont, Dallas, Fort Worth, Houston, and San Antonio, Texas; Miami; Phoenix; Richmond, Virginia; and Sulphur, Louisiana.

COMPETITORS

Balfour Beatty
Bechtel
Beck Group
Brasfield & Gorrie
Choate Construction
Flint Industries
Fluor
Granite Construction
Halliburton
Hardin Construction
Hensel Phelps Construction
Hunt Construction
J.F. Shea
JGC
MYR Group
Peter Kiewit Sons'
Rooney Brothers
Shaw Group
Skanska
Sundt
Swinerton
Turner Corporation
Turner Industries
Zachry

HISTORICAL FINANCIALS

Company Type: Private

Income Statement FYE: December 31

	REVENUE ($ mil.)	NET INCOME ($ mil.)	NET PROFIT MARGIN	EMPLOYEES
12/02	1,056	—	—	6,000
12/01	1,257	—	—	6,000
12/00	1,217	—	—	6,000
12/99	836	—	—	6,000
12/98	808	—	—	6,300
12/97	619	—	—	6,000
12/96	741	—	—	5,400
12/95	608	—	—	5,100
12/94	613	—	—	5,000
12/93	509	—	—	5,500
Annual Growth	8.4%	—	—	1.0%

Revenue History

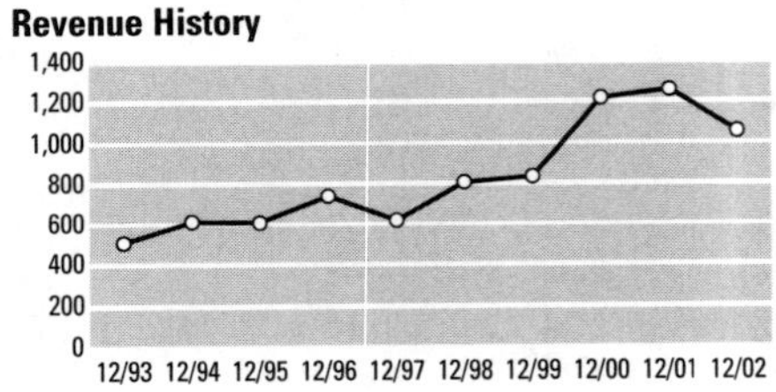

Automobile Club of Southern California

Ready to ride to the rescue for cars that have gone south in the Southland is the Automobile Club of Southern California. The largest US affiliate of the American Automobile Association (AAA), the Auto Club of Southern California has more than 70 district offices in 13 counties and boasts about 5 million members. It provides 24-

hour roadside assistance, travel planning, auto pricing, buying, and maintenance services, as well as a host of insurance plans. In addition, members can renew vehicle registrations, plates, and stickers at club offices. The club also publishes *Westways* magazine, which offers travel tips and discounts. Ten auto enthusiasts founded the club in 1900.

EXECUTIVES

President and CEO: Thomas V. McKernan Jr.
CFO: John F. Boyle
VP, Human Resources: James Philipp

LOCATIONS

HQ: 2601 S. Figueroa St., Los Angeles, CA 90007
Phone: 213-741-3686 **Fax:** 213-741-4890
Web: www.aaa-calif.com

Automobile Club of Southern California has offices in 13 counties: Imperial, Inyo, Kern, Los Angeles, Mono, Orange, Riverside, San Bernardino, San Diego, San Luis Obispo, Santa Barbara, Tulare, and Ventura.

COMPETITORS

21st Century
Allstate
APCC
Mercury General
Miller Industries
State Farm

HISTORICAL FINANCIALS

Company Type: Not-for-profit

Income Statement FYE: December 31

	ESTIMATED REVENUE ($ mil.)	NET INCOME ($ mil.)	NET PROFIT MARGIN	EMPLOYEES
12/01	750	—	—	8,000
12/00	500	—	—	5,700
12/99	550	—	—	5,700
12/98	500	—	—	5,700
Annual Growth	14.5%	—	—	12.0%

Revenue History

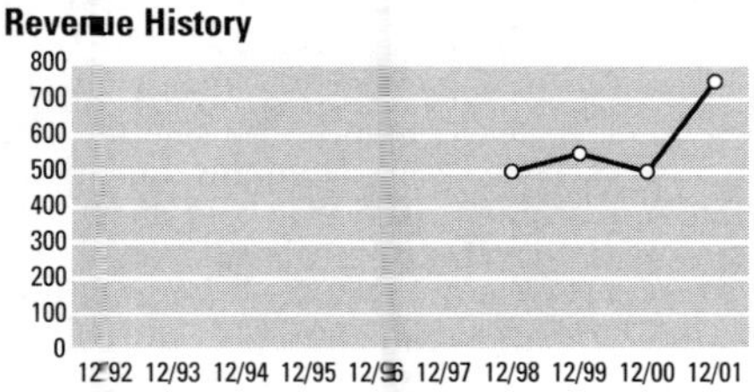

Auto-Owners Insurance Group

There's more to Auto-Owners Insurance Group than the name implies. In addition to auto coverage, the company provides personal products such as universal and whole life, homeowners, and long-term care insurance through its predictably named subsidiaries (including Home-Owners Insurance Company and Property-Owners Insurance Company). Auto-Owners Insurance Group also sells commercial auto, liability, and workers' compensation policies. With almost 30,000 independent agents in 5,000 different locations, the company operates in some 25 states nationwide.

EXECUTIVES

Chairman and CEO: Herman J. Arends
President: John W. Fisher
EVP: Roger L. Looyenga
SVP and Treasurer: Greg L. Cornell
SVP, Personnel: Doug Marsh

LOCATIONS

HQ: 6101 Anacapri Blvd., Lansing, MI 48917
Phone: 517-323-1200 **Fax:** 517-323-8796
Web: www.auto-owners.com

Auto-Owners has full-service offices in Lansing, MI; Traverse City, MI; White Bear Lake, MN; Peoria, IL; Montgomery, AL; Marion, IN; Lima, OH; Lakeland, FL; Brentwood, TN; West Des Moines, IA; Charlotte, NC; Mesa, AZ; Appleton, WI; Duluth, GA; and Columbia, SC. It has claim offices in 59 cities.

PRODUCTS/OPERATIONS

Selected Subsidiaries

Auto-Owners Insurance Company
Auto-Owners Life Insurance Company
Home-Owners Insurance Company
Owners Insurance Company
Property-Owners Insurance Company
Southern-Owners Insurance Company

COMPETITORS

ACE Limited
Allstate
AIG
Farmers Group
GEICO
MetLife
Progressive Corporation
Prudential
SAFECO
St. Paul Companies
State Farm
Travelers

HISTORICAL FINANCIALS

Company Type: Private

Income Statement FYE: December 31

	REVENUE ($ mil.)	NET INCOME ($ mil.)	NET PROFIT MARGIN	EMPLOYEES
12/02	3,514	—	—	3,000
12/01	3,016	—	—	3,000
Annual Growth	16.5%	—	—	0.0%

Revenue History

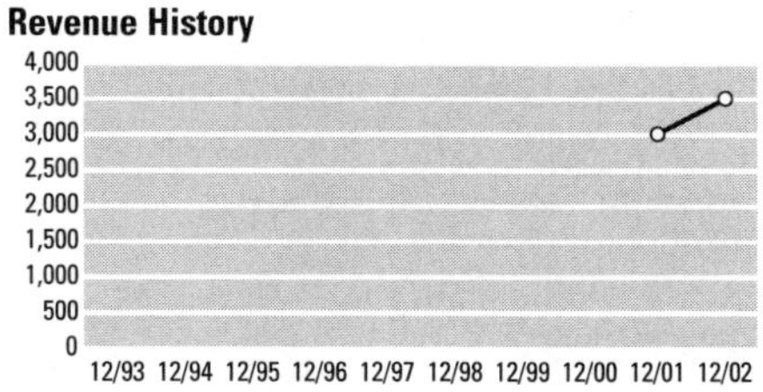

Averitt Express

Averitt Express provides less-than-truckload (LTL), truckload, and expedited freight transportation service, primarily in the southern US. The company operates a fleet of about 3,000 tractors and 9,000 trailers. CEO Gary Sasser owns Averitt Express.

EXECUTIVES

President and CEO: Gary D. Sasser
EVP and COO: Wayne Spain
EVP and CFO: George Johnson
EVP Sales and Marketing: Phil Pierce

LOCATIONS

HQ: Averitt Express, Inc.
1415 Neal St., Cookeville, TN 38501
Phone: 931-526-3306 **Fax:** 931-520-5603
Web: www.averittexpress.com

COMPETITORS

Arkansas Best
Con-Way
Estes Express
FedEx Freight
Old Dominion Freight
Overnite Transportation
Roadway
USF
Watkins Associated Industries
Yellow

HISTORICAL FINANCIALS

Company Type: Private

Income Statement FYE: December 31

	REVENUE ($ mil.)	NET INCOME ($ mil.)	NET PROFIT MARGIN	EMPLOYEES
12/02	582	18	3.2%	6,485
12/01	553	16	2.9%	6,000
Annual Growth	5.3%	14.3%	—	8.1%

Net Income History

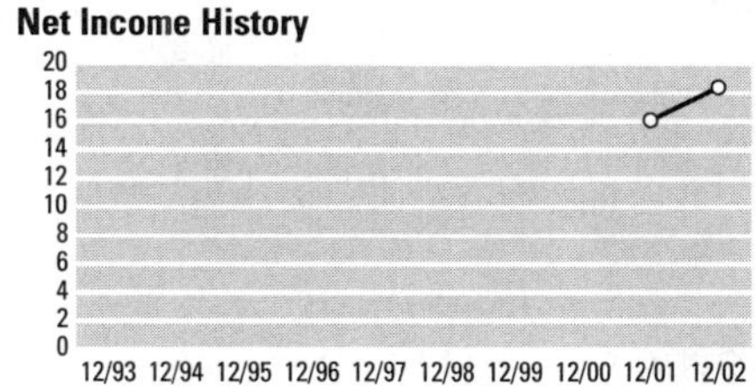

Avondale Incorporated

Family-owned Avondale has fabric in its genes . . . er, jeans. The vertically integrated company makes apparel fabrics (cotton and cotton-blend piece-dyed fabrics, indigo-dyed denim), greige fabrics (undyed, unfinished cotton and cotton blends), specialty fabrics (such as coated materials for awnings, boat covers, and tents), and yarns. Leading apparel makers such as VF Corporation (maker of Lee and Wrangler jeans, among others) buy from Avondale. The company operates about 20 manufacturing facilities in Alabama, Georgia, and North and South Carolina. Avondale was founded in Georgia in 1895 and is headed by G. Stephen Felker, great-grandson of the founder.

VF accounts for about 20% of sales. Due to its unprofitable yarn operations, Avondale was forced to close two open-end yarn manufacturing plants in North Carolina in 2002.

EXECUTIVES

Chairman, President, and CEO, Avondale and Avondale Mills: G. Stephen Felker, age 50, $1,200,016 pay
Vice Chairman and CFO, Avondale and Avondale Mills: Jack R. Altherr Jr., age 53, $455,008 pay
VP, Avondale Mills; President, Manufacturing Operations: T. Wayne Spraggins, age 65, $371,016 pay
VP, Avondale Mills; President, Marketing and Sales: Keith M. Hull, age 50, $373,032 pay
VP, Planning and Development, Avondale Mills: Craig S. Crockard, age 60, $159,520 pay
VP, Secretary, and Controller, Avondale Mills and Avondale: M. Delen Boyd, age 46
VP, Human Resources, Avondale Mills: Sharon L. Rodgers, age 46
Auditors: Crisp Hughes Evans LLP

LOCATIONS

HQ: 506 S. Broad St., Monroe, GA 30655
Phone: 770-267-2226 **Fax:** 770-267-5196

Avondale operates about 20 manufacturing facilities in Alabama, Georgia, North Carolina, and South Carolina.

PRODUCTS/OPERATIONS

2003 Sales

	$ mil.	% of total
Apparel fabric	502.9	68
Yarns	167.6	23
Other fabric	66.1	9
Adjustments	(145.7)	—
Total	**590.9**	**100**

COMPETITORS

Burlington Industries
Concord Fabrics
Cone Mills
Galey & Lord
Greenwood Mills
Guilford Mills
Johnston Industries
Milliken
Parkdale Mills
R. B. Pamplin
Springs Industries

HISTORICAL FINANCIALS

Income Statement FYE: Last Friday in August

	REVENUE ($ mil.)	NET INCOME ($ mil.)	NET PROFIT MARGIN	EMPLOYEES
8/03	591	(8)	—	5,000
8/02	660	(0)	—	5,700
8/01	773	1	0.2%	5,800
8/00	837	33	3.9%	—
8/99	881	10	1.1%	6,800
8/98	1,056	34	3.2%	7,000
8/97	1,050	23	2.2%	7,500
8/96	706	14	1.9%	—
8/95	539	21	3.9%	—
8/94	482	14	2.9%	—
Annual Growth	2.3%	—	—	(6.5%)

Net Income History

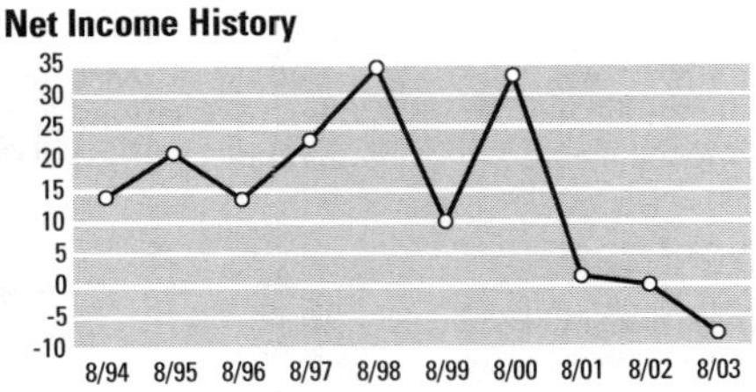

2003 Year-End Financials

Debt ratio: 144.0%
Return on equity: —
Cash ($ mil.): 14
Current ratio: 2.91
Long-term debt ($ mil.): 164

Bad Boy Entertainment

This empire is run by a bad boy with more names than Prince. Sean Combs (also known as Puff Daddy, Puffy, and P. Diddy) wears many hats as the entrepreneur behind the multiple business lines of Bad Boy Entertainment. Bad Boy Records has produced artists such as Faith Evans, Puff Daddy, and the late Notorious B.I.G. The company expanded with interests in apparel (Sean John), restaurants (Justin's in New York and Atlanta), and music publishing (a co-publishing agreement with EMI). Subsidiary Janice Combs Management manages music producers. Sean Combs owns Bad Boy Entertainment.

Bad Boy Entertainment began in 1994 as a record label joint venture between Combs and Arista Records. Arista dropped Bad Boy Records in 2002 due to lagging sales. Combs had considered selling the label, but instead inked a three-year distribution deal with Universal in 2003. Music, however, is no longer Bad Boy's bread and butter as sales of the Sean John clothing line have skyrocketed, now comprising more than half of the company's estimated revenues. Sean John has become one of the top-selling men's clothing lines in the US, and Combs' high-profile fashion shows have elevated him to the ranks of the fashion elite.

EXECUTIVES

Chairman and CEO: Sean (P. Diddy) Combs, age 32
CFO: Derek Ferguson
VP A&R: Harve Pierre
VP Marketing: Tracey Waples
VP Promotions: Mel Smith
President, Blue Flame Marketing and Advertising: Jameel Spencer, age 34
General Manager: Tucker Lewis
Associate VP Marketing: Allison Peters
Publicity: Donna Torrence

LOCATIONS

HQ: Bad Boy Entertainment, Inc.
1540 Broadway, 30th Fl., New York, NY 10036
Phone: 212-381-1540 **Fax:** 212-381-1599
Web: www.badboyonline.com

COMPETITORS

Atlantic
Capitol Records
Columbia Records
Elektra
Epic Records
Interscope
Island Def Jam
TVT Records
Tha Row
Tommy Boy Music
Zomba Records

HISTORICAL FINANCIALS

Company Type: Private

Income Statement FYE: December 31

	ESTIMATED REVENUE ($ mil.)	NET INCOME ($ mil.)	NET PROFIT MARGIN	EMPLOYEES
12/02	500	—	—	600
12/01	300	—	—	600
12/00	300	—	—	—
12/99	200	—	—	—
12/98	150	—	—	—
12/97	122	—	—	—
Annual Growth	32.6%	—	—	0.0%

Revenue History

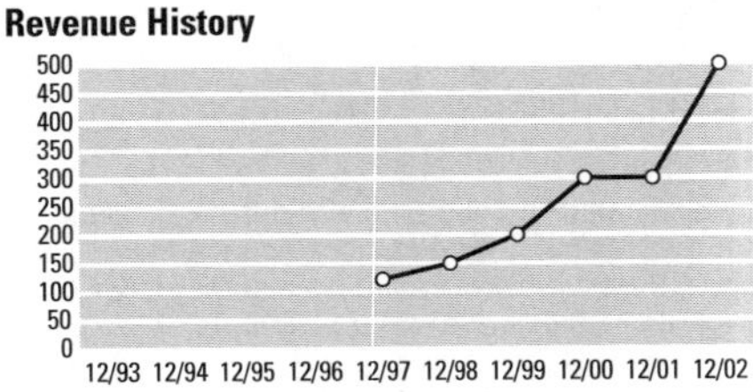

Bain & Company

"Bainies" are always ready when corporate titans need a little direction. One of the world leaders in strategic consulting, Bain & Company (whose consultants are called Bainies) offers services such as business unit, organizational, and corporate strategy; distribution and logistics advice; mergers, acquisitions, and divestiture consulting; and sales and marketing strategy. It works for clients in a variety of industries, including consumer products, financial services, technology, media and communications, and telecommunications. The firm also offers services for startups through its bainlab unit.

Bain was one of the many consulting firms riding high on the wave of Internet mania, helping both startups and offline companies develop business strategies for the New Economy. While the post dot-com boom world might not be as exciting, a softening economy has created an increased demand for efficiency and cost analysis services. Its bainlab incubator unit has also shifted its focus to performing due diligence for other VCs. Bain is also facing increased competition from consulting units spawned by the Big 5 accounting firms. But, Bain & Company judges its success in terms of its clients' financial results and is not shy in noting that its clients have outperformed the stock market by a factor of three.

The firm has 26 offices in nearly 20 countries. Although founded by the same individuals, Bain & Company and investment firm Bain Capital are separate entities.

EXECUTIVES

Chairman: Orit Gadiesh, age 50
Worldwide Managing Director: John Donahoe
CFO: Len Banos
Director and Head of Worldwide Health Care Practice: Michael Steiner, age 47

Head of Worldwide Information Technology Practice: David Shpilberg, age 51
Director of Human Resources: Elizabeth Corcoran
Worldwide Public Relations Director: Cheryl Krauss
Public Relations: Lori Shaley

LOCATIONS

HQ: 2 Copley Place, Boston, MA 02116
Phone: 617-572-2000 **Fax:** 617-572-2427
Web: www.bain.com

Bain & Company has operations in Australia, Belgium, Brazil, Canada, China, France, Germany, Italy, Japan, Mexico, the Netherlands, Singapore, South Africa, South Korea, Spain, Sweden, Switzerland, the UK, and the US.

PRODUCTS/OPERATIONS

Selected Consulting Services

Business unit strategy
Corporate strategy
Distribution and logistics
Organizational strategy
Post-merger integration
Marketing strategy

Selected Industries Served

Aerospace and defense
Business services
Consumer products
Financial services
Government agencies
Healthcare and medical services
Media and entertainment
Natural resources
Non-profits
Retail
Technology
Telecommunications
Utilities

COMPETITORS

Accenture
A.T. Kearney
BearingPoint
Booz Allen
Boston Consulting
Cap Gemini
Deloitte Consulting
McKinsey & Company
Mercer

HISTORICAL FINANCIALS

Company Type: Partnership

Income Statement

FYE: December 31

	REVENUE ($ mil.)	NET INCOME ($ mil.)	NET PROFIT MARGIN	EMPLOYEES
12/01	825	—	—	2,800
12/00	810	—	—	2,700
12/99	700	—	—	2,400
12/98	499	—	—	2,100
12/97	480	—	—	1,700
12/96	450	—	—	1,500
12/95	375	—	—	1,200
12/94	300	—	—	1,000
12/93	213	—	—	900
Annual Growth	18.4%	—	—	15.2%

Revenue History

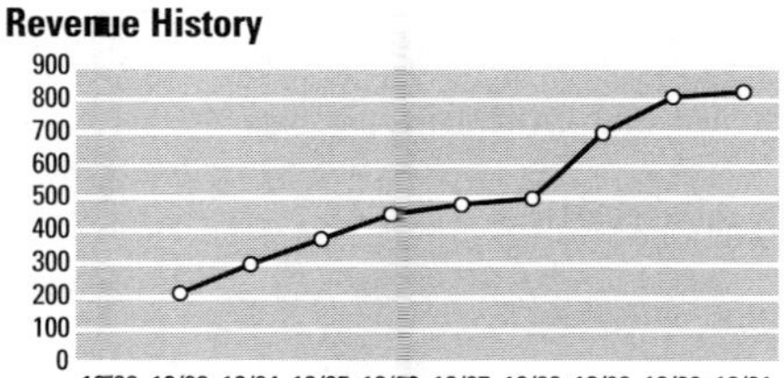

Baker & McKenzie

Baker & McKenzie knows that size has its advantages (and disadvantages). Baker is one of the world's largest law firms with more than 3,000 lawyers serving in more than 60 offices across some 35 countries. It offers expertise in such areas as international trade and tax. Although Baker's size helps attract attorneys as well as clients, the firm also has had to fight the image that it is focused more on franchising than quality legal work. Russell Baker and John McKenzie founded the firm in 1949 with a focus on building an international practice; Baker has become one of the first major practices to appoint a woman as its top partner.

Christine Lagarde was chosen in 1999 to replace outgoing chairman John Klotsche. In addition to closing the gender gap, Lagarde is also one of the youngest partners, age 43 when she was elected, to lead the firm.

Baker is a full-service firm offering legal advice in areas such as banking, securities, labor, international trade, and tax. The half-century-old firm has handled the legal affairs of such heavy-duty clients as Chase Manhattan (now J.P. Morgan Chase), Honeywell, and Ingersoll-Rand.

The firm is known for the global scale of its practice, with some 80% of Baker attorneys practicing outside the US. However, it is beginning to face new competition on the global scene from firms such as Clifford Chance (which merged with two other practices in 2000 to create a network larger than Baker's).

HISTORY

Russell Baker traveled from his native New Mexico to Chicago on a railroad freight car to attend law school. Upon graduation in 1925 he started practicing law with his classmate Dana Simpson under the name Simpson & Baker. Inspired by Chicago's role as a manufacturing and agricultural center for the world and influenced by the international focus of his alma mater, the University of Chicago, Baker dreamed of creating an international law practice. He began developing an expertise in international law, and in 1934 Abbott Laboratories retained him to handle its worldwide legal affairs. Baker was on his way to fulfilling his dream.

Baker joined forces with Chicago litigator John McKenzie in 1949, forming Baker & McKenzie. In 1955 the firm opened its first foreign office in Caracas, Venezuela, to meet the needs of its expanding US client base. Over the next 10 years it branched out into Asia, Australia, and Europe, with offices in London, Manila, Paris, and Tokyo. Baker's death in 1979 neither slowed the firm's growth nor changed its international character. The next year it expanded into the Middle East and opened its 30th office in 1982 (Melbourne). To manage the sprawling law firm, Baker & McKenzie created the position of chairman of the executive committee in 1984.

In late 1991 the firm dropped the Church of Scientology as a client, losing an estimated $2 million in business. It was speculated that pressure from client Eli Lilly (maker of the drug Prozac, which Scientologists actively oppose) influenced the decision. In 1992 Baker & McKenzie was ordered to pay $1 million for wrongfully firing an employee who later died of AIDS. (The case became the basis for the 1993 film *Philadelphia.*) The firm fought the verdict but eventually settled for an undisclosed amount in 1995.

In 1994 Baker & McKenzie closed its Los Angeles office (the former MacDonald, Halsted & Laybourne; acquired 1988) amid considerable rancor. Also that year a former secretary at the firm received a $7.1 million judgment for sexual harassment by a partner. (A San Francisco Superior Court judge later reduced the award to $3.5 million.)

John Klotsche, a senior partner from the firm's Palo Alto, California, office was appointed chairman in 1995. The following year the firm began a major expansion into California's Silicon Valley as part of an initiative to serve technology companies around the world. It also expanded its Warsaw, Poland, office through a merger with the Warsaw office of Dickinson, Wright, Moon, Van Dusen & Freman.

In 1998 Baker & McKenzie formed a special unit in Singapore to deal with business generated by the financial troubles in Asia. The opening of offices in Taiwan and Azerbaijan in 1998 brought the firm's total number of offices to 59. Klotsche stepped down in 1999 as the firm celebrated its 50th anniversary; Christine Lagarde replaced him. In early 2001 Baker & McKenzie created a joint venture practice with Singapore-based associate firm Wong & Leow. Also that year it merged with Madrid-based Briones Alonso y Martin to create the largest independent law firm in Spain.

EXECUTIVES

Chairman Executive Committee: Christine Lagarde, age 46
COO: Peter Smith
CFO: Robert S. Spencer
CTO: Craig Courter
General Counsel: Edward J. Zulkey
Director, Professional Development: Anne Waldron
Global Director Marketing: Roberta Montafia

LOCATIONS

HQ: 1 Prudential Plaza, 130 E. Randolph Dr., Ste. 2500, Chicago, IL 60601
Phone: 312-861-8800 **Fax:** 312-861-8823
Web: www.bakernet.com

Baker & McKenzie has more than 60 offices throughout Asia, Australia, Europe, Latin America, the Middle East, and North America.

PRODUCTS/OPERATIONS

Selected Practice Areas

Banking and finance
Corporate and securities
E-commerce
International commercial arbitration
International trade
IP, IT, and Communications
Labor and employment
Tax
US Litigation

COMPETITORS

Clifford Chance
Deloitte Touche Tohmatsu
Ernst & Young
Jones Day
Kirkland & Ellis
KPMG
Mayer, Brown, Rowe & Maw
McDermott, Will
PricewaterhouseCoopers
Sidley Austin Brown & Wood
Skadden, Arps

HISTORICAL FINANCIALS

Company Type: Partnership

Income Statement FYE: June 30

	REVENUE ($ mil.)	NET INCOME ($ mil.)	NET PROFIT MARGIN	EMPLOYEES
6/02	1,000	—	—	8,000
6/01	1,000	—	—	8,000
6/00	940	—	—	8,000
6/99	818	—	—	6,900
6/98	785	—	—	6,700
6/97	697	—	—	6,100
6/96	646	—	—	5,680
6/95	594	—	—	5,248
6/94	546	—	—	5,114
6/93	512	—	—	5,054
Annual Growth	7.7%	—	—	5.2%

Revenue History

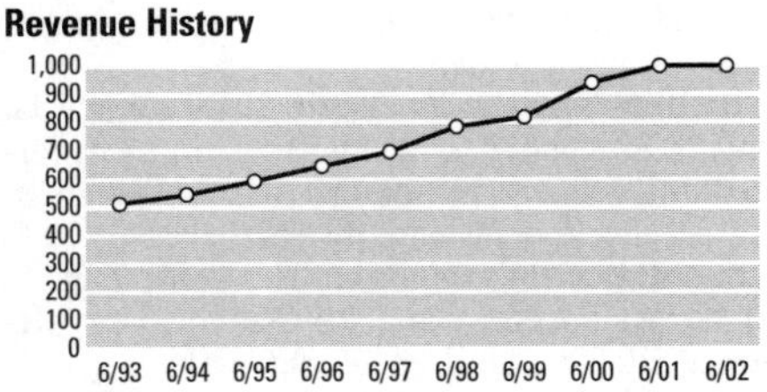

Baker & Taylor Corporation

If you've strolled through a library recently, you likely saw a lot of Baker & Taylor (B&T) without knowing it. The #1 book supplier to libraries, B&T maintains three operating units. Its institutional segment distributes books, calendars, music, and DVDs to about 8,000 school, public, and specialty libraries around the world. Its retail unit supplies storefront and Internet retailers, as well as independent booksellers, with nearly 4 million book titles and more than 135,000 video, DVD, and CD titles. Its Informata.com unit is B&T's business-to-business e-commerce arm. The Carlyle Group (who owned about 85% of B&T) sold the company to Chicago-based investment firm Willis Stein & Partners in July 2003.

B&T's institutional unit also offers acquisition and collection management support services to libraries through its YBP Library Services subsidiary. In addition, B&T Retail provides fulfillment for companies such as Amazon.com and barnesandnoble.com, as well as handling the company's international operations. Its Informata.com unit distributes electronic content and licenses database services and applications.

B&T also offers automatic shipping of books and books-on-tape by popular authors (mailed as soon as they are published), and its Replica Books publishes out-of-print and paperback titles on demand.

EXECUTIVES

President and CEO: Richard Willis
EVP, Distribution: Marshall A. (Arnie) Wight
SVP and CIO: Matt Carroll
SVP and Chief Marketing Officer, Informata: Pamela Smith
SVP and General Counsel: Bradley D. Murchison
SVP, A/V Library Services: William Hartman
SVP, Customized Library Services: Livia Bitner
SVP, Finance and Corporate VP: David Finlon
SVP, Human Resources: Claudette Hampton
SVP, Merchandising: Jean Srnecz
SVP, Operations: James Benjamin
SVP, Retail Sales and Marketing: William Preston

LOCATIONS

HQ: 2709 Water Ridge Pkwy., Charlotte, NC 28217
Phone: 704-357-3500 **Fax:** 704-329-8989
Web: www.btol.com

Baker & Taylor has operations in Colorado, Georgia, Illinois, Nevada, New Hampshire, New Jersey, and North Carolina, and sales offices in Australia and Japan, although it supplies books and services to libraries and retailers worldwide.

PRODUCTS/OPERATIONS

Selected Products and Services

Accessories
Audiocassettes
Calendars
Cataloging database (B&T MARC)
CD-ROM and Internet database and ordering software (Title Source II)
CDs
DVDs
Hardcover and paperback books
Library automation system (Libris 2020)
On-demand printing (Replica Books)
Online prepublication information (B&T Express Wired)
Spoken-word audiocassettes
Standing-order service (Compass)
Videos

Operating Units and Subsidiaries

Baker & Taylor Institutional
Professional Media Services Corp.
YBP Library Services
Baker & Taylor Retail
Informata.com

COMPETITORS

Advanced Marketing
Alliance Entertainment
BH Blackwell Ltd.
Book Wholesalers
Brodart
Chas. Levy
Dawson Holdings
East Texas Distributing
Educational Development
Follett
Handleman
Ingram Entertainment
Ingram Industries
LDI
Ludington News
Major Video Concepts
Midwest Library Service
Navarre
Rentrak

HISTORICAL FINANCIALS

Company Type: Private

Income Statement FYE: Last Friday in June

	REVENUE ($ mil.)	NET INCOME ($ mil.)	NET PROFIT MARGIN	EMPLOYEES
6/02	1,122	—	—	2,750
6/01	1,000	—	—	2,500
6/00	1,130	—	—	2,700
6/99	1,021	—	—	2,500
6/98	883	—	—	—
6/97	829	—	—	—
6/96	751	—	—	—
6/95	784	—	—	—
Annual Growth	5.3%	—	—	3.2%

Revenue History

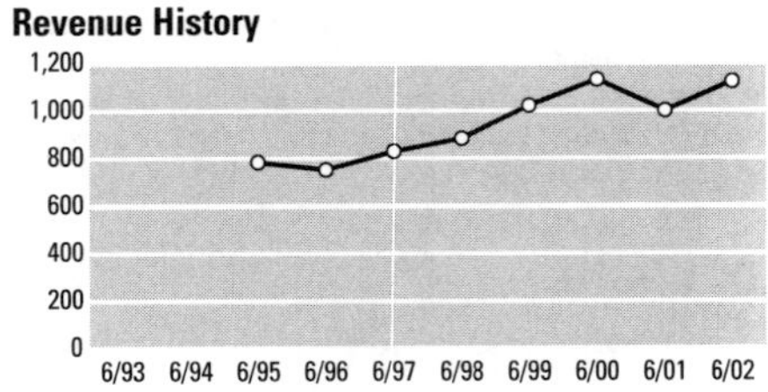

Banner Health

Formed from the merger of Lutheran Health Systems and Samaritan Health System, Banner Health is one of the largest non-church-affiliated, not-for-profit health systems in the country. The organization operates about 20 hospitals, six long-term care centers, and family clinics in seven states. Banner Health provides a wide variety of services that consist of home care, heart care, cancer care, organ transplants, and women's health, along with behavioral health and rehabilitation services. Banner Health also participates in medical research in areas such as Alzheimer's and spinal cord injuries.

EXECUTIVES

Chairman: Wilford A. Cardon
President and CEO: Peter S. Fine
SVP and CFO: Ron Bunnell
SVP, People Resources: Gerri Twomey
SVP, Quality and Care Management: John Hensing
SVP Strategy: Susan Doria
President, Banner Health Arizona Region: Susan Edwards
President, Banner Health Colorado Region: Scott Bosch
Senior Network Analyst: Phil Bosen

LOCATIONS

HQ: 1441 N. 12th St., Phoenix, AZ 85006
Phone: 602-495-4000 **Fax:** 602-495-4559
Web: www.bannerhealth.com

Banner Health has operations in Alaska, Arizona, California, Colorado, Nebraska, Nevada, and Wyoming.

PRODUCTS/OPERATIONS

Selected Facilities

Banner Desert Medical Center (Mesa, AZ)
Banner Baywood Medical Center (Mesa, AZ)
Banner Baywood Heart Hospital (Mesa, AZ)
Banner Churchill Community Hospital (Fallon, NV)
Banner Good Samaritan Medical Center (Phoenix, AZ)
Banner Lassen Community Hospital (Susanville, CA)
Banner Mesa Medical Center (Mesa, AZ)
Banner Thunderbird Medical Center (Glendale, AZ)
East Morgan County Hospital (Brush, CO)
McKee Medical Center (Loveland, CO)
North Colorado Medical Center (Greeley, CO)
Page (Arizona) Hospital
Sterling (Colorado) Regional MedCenter

COMPETITORS

Catholic Healthcare West
HCA
Iasis Healthcare
Presbyterian Healthcare Services
Province Healthcare
Tenet Healthcare
Triad Hospitals
Vanguard Health Systems

HISTORICAL FINANCIALS

Company Type: Not-for-profit

Income Statement FYE: December 31

	REVENUE ($ mil.)	NET INCOME ($ mil.)	NET PROFIT MARGIN	EMPLOYEES
12/02	2,100	—	—	22,000
12/01	1,900	—	—	23,000
12/00	1,735	—	—	24,500
12/99	1,561	—	—	22,500
12/98	1,476	—	—	—
Annual Growth	9.2%	—	—	(0.7%)

Revenue History

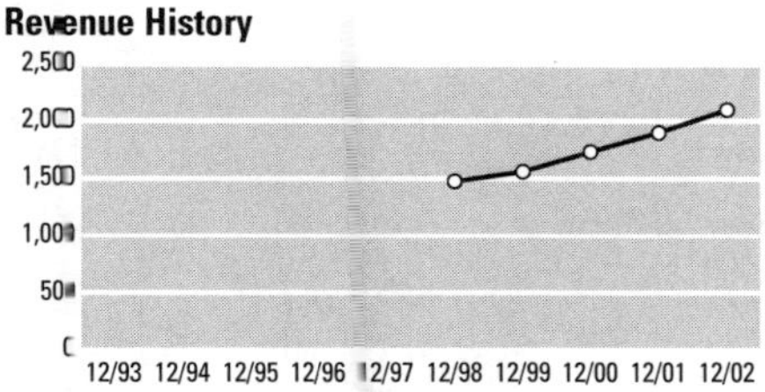

Barnes & Noble College Bookstores, Inc.

Barnes & Noble College Bookstores is the scholastic sister company of Barnes & Noble (B&N), the US's largest bookseller. Started in 1873, the company operates more than 500 campus bookstores nationwide, selling textbooks, trade books, school supplies, collegiate clothing, and emblematic merchandise. Universities, medical and law schools, and community colleges hire Barnes & Noble College Bookstores to replace traditional campus cooperatives. (The schools get a cut of the sales.) Its College Marketing Network division offers on-campus marketing opportunities to businesses. The company also runs online retailer textbooks.com. B&N's chairman, Leonard Riggio, owns a controlling interest in the company.

EXECUTIVES

Chairman; Chairman, Barnes & Noble, Inc.: Leonard S. Riggio, age 62
President and CEO: Max J. Roberts
CFO: Barry Brover
SVP Marketing: Bill Maloney
VP and General Merchandise Manager: Jade Roth
VP, General Merchandise and Stores: Joel Friedman
VP, Human Resources: Gail Gittleson
VP, Marketing: Janine von Juergensonn
Auditors: BDO Seidman, LLP

LOCATIONS

HQ: 33 E. 17th St., New York, NY 10003
Phone: 212-539-2000 **Fax:** 212-780-1866
Web: www.bkstore.com

COMPETITORS

Amazon.com
Borders
Ecampus.com
Follett
Nebraska Book
Varsity Group
Wallace's Bookstores
Wal-Mart

HISTORICAL FINANCIALS

Company Type: Private

Income Statement FYE: April 30

	ESTIMATED REVENUE ($ mil.)	NET INCOME ($ mil.)	NET PROFIT MARGIN	EMPLOYEES
4/02	1,250	—	—	9,500
4/01	1,200	—	—	9,000
4/00	920	—	—	6,500
4/99	830	—	—	6,000
4/98	800	—	—	5,500
4/97	725	—	—	5,000
4/96	700	—	—	4,000
4/95	700	—	—	—
Annual Growth	8.6%	—	—	15.5%

Revenue History

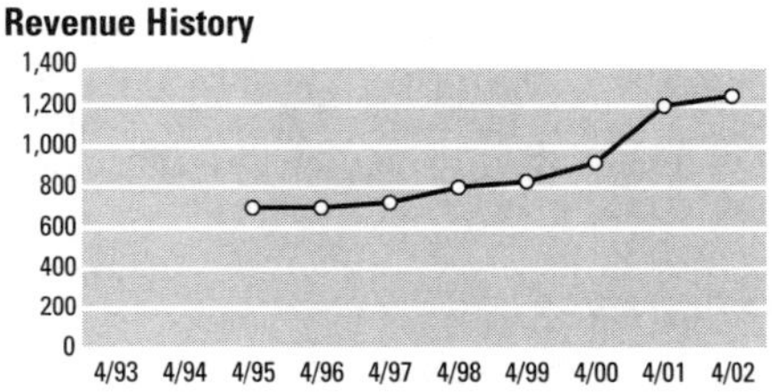

Bartlett and Company

When the cows come home, Bartlett and Company will be ready. The company's primary business is grain merchandising, but it also runs cattle feedlots and mills flour. Bartlett operates grain storage facilities in Kansas City, Kansas; St. Joseph and Waverly, Missouri; and Nebraska City, Nebraska. It has terminal elevators in Iowa, Kansas, and Missouri, as well as more than 10 country elevators. Bartlett's cattle operations are based in Texas; its flour mills are in Kansas, North Carolina, and South Carolina. The Bartlett and Company Grain Charitable Foundation makes financial gifts to local causes. Founded in 1907 as Bartlett Agri Enterprises, the company is still owned by the founding Bartlett family.

EXECUTIVES

Chairman: Paul D. Bartlett Jr., age 83
President and CEO: James B. Heberstreit
VP and CFO: Arnie Wheeler
VP, Personnel: Bill Webster

LOCATIONS

HQ: 4800 Main St., Ste. 600, Kansas City, MO 64112
Phone: 816-753-6300 **Fax:** 816-753-0062
Web: www.bartlettandco.com

COMPETITORS

Ag Processing
ADM
AzTx Cattle
Cactus Feeders
Cargill
CHS
ContiGroup
DeBruce Grain
Friona Industries
GROWMARK
King Ranch
Scoular

HISTORICAL FINANCIALS

Company Type: Private

Income Statement FYE: December 31

	ESTIMATED REVENUE ($ mil.)	NET INCOME ($ mil.)	NET PROFIT MARGIN	EMPLOYEES
12/01	800	—	—	600
12/00	810	—	—	575
12/99	705	—	—	600
12/98	720	—	—	575
12/97	750	—	—	575
12/96	866	—	—	560
12/95	825	—	—	525
12/94	700	—	—	525
12/93	708	—	—	525
12/92	758	—	—	—
Annual Growth	0.6%	—	—	1.7%

Revenue History

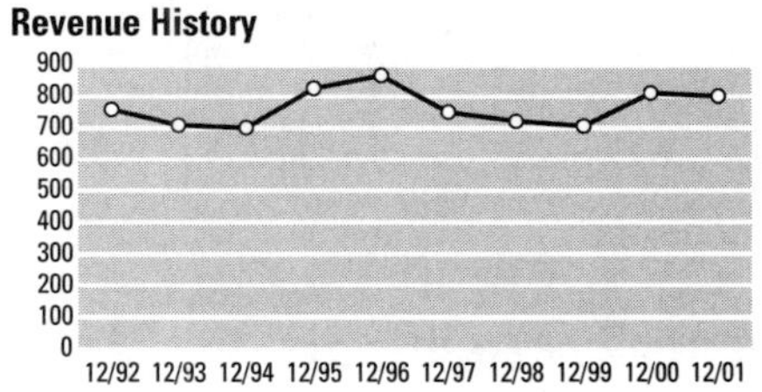

Barton Malow Company

Barton Malow scores by building end zones and home plates. The construction management and general contracting firm also makes points for its schools, hospitals, offices, and plants. Barton Malow's services range from planning to completion on projects located in 37 states and the District of Columbia, including Atlanta's Phillips Arena, Boston's Shriners Hospital, and General Motors' Truck Product Center.

Barton Malow Design provides architecture and engineering services, and the company's Barton Malow Rigging unit installs process equipment and machinery. Chairman Ben Maibach Jr. and his family own a majority stake in the firm, which was founded in 1924 by C. O. Barton.

EXECUTIVES

Chairman: Ben C. Maibach Jr.
President: Ben C. Maibach III
EVP and Secretary: Mark A. Bahr
SVP and General Counsel: Thomas (Tom) Porter
VP and Treasurer: Edward R. (Ed) Jarchow
VP Marketing: Sheryl B. Maibach
VP Human Resources: Judith Willard
Auditors: Grant Thornton LLP

LOCATIONS

HQ: 26500 American Dr., Southfield, MI 48034
Phone: 248-436-4500 **Fax:** 248-436-5001
Web: www.bmco.com

Barton Malow has offices in Atlanta; Baltimore; Charlottesville, Virginia; Detroit and Southfield, Michigan; and Phoenix.

PRODUCTS/OPERATIONS

Primary Services

Architecture/planning
Construction management
Design/build
Facility audits
Facility services
General contracting
Interior design
Program management
Rigging/millwright
Technology consulting

COMPETITORS

Alberici
BE&K
Brasfield & Gorrie
Clark Enterprises
Dunn Industries
Flint Industries
Fluor
Gilbane
Hardin Construction
Hensel Phelps Construction
H.J. Russell
Hoffman Corporation
Hunt Construction
M. A. Mortenson
McCarthy Building
Rooney Brothers
Walbridge Aldinger
Walsh Group
Whiting-Turner
Zachry

HISTORICAL FINANCIALS

Company Type: Private

Income Statement FYE: March 31

	REVENUE ($ mil.)	NET INCOME ($ mil.)	NET PROFIT MARGIN	EMPLOYEES
3/03	1,000	—	—	1,550
3/02	1,251	—	—	1,264
3/01	1,160	—	—	1,640
3/00	1,026	—	—	1,500
3/99	821	—	—	1,350
3/98	727	—	—	1,300
3/97	565	—	—	896
3/96	669	—	—	754
3/95	634	—	—	762
3/94	466	—	—	759
Annual Growth	8.9%	—	—	8.3%

Revenue History

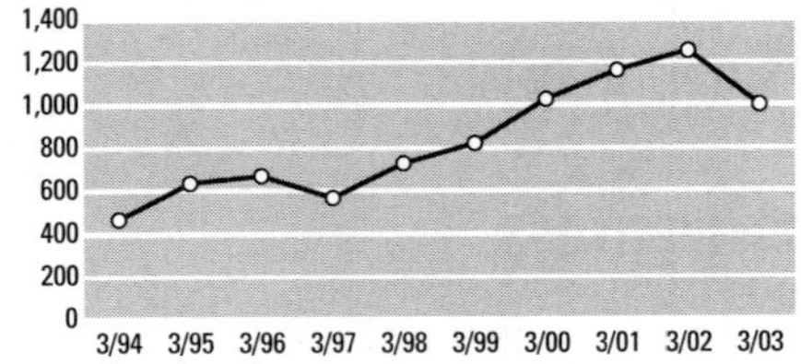

Bashas' Inc.

Bashas' has blossomed in the Arizona desert. Founded in 1932 and owned by the Basha family, the food retailer has grown to about 135 stores. These are located primarily throughout Arizona, but with one store each in California and New Mexico. Its holdings include Bashas' traditional supermarkets, AJ's Fine Foods (gourmet-style supermarkets), Bashas' Dine Markets, and Food City supermarkets, which cater to Hispanics in southern Arizona. Bashas' has opened 32 Natural Choice in-store departments that feature natural and organic items. It also operates a handful of supermarkets (including its New Mexico store) in the Navajo Nation. The company offers online grocery shopping through its Groceries On The Go service.

EXECUTIVES

Chairman and CEO: Edward N. (Eddie) Basha Jr., age 65
President: Wayne C. Manning
EVP and COO: Mike Proulx
SVP, Administration, Finance, and CFO: Darl J. Andersen
SVP, Human Resources: Michael Gantt
VP, Food Service: Jay Volk
VP, General Merchandise: George Fiscus
VP, Retail Operations, Northern Arizona Division: Ralph Woodward
VP, Sales Promotion and Customer Loyalty: Christie Coleman

LOCATIONS

HQ: 22402 S. Basha Rd., Chandler, AZ 85248
Phone: 480-895-9350 **Fax:** 480-895-5394
Web: www.bashas.com

COMPETITORS

Albertson's
Fleming Companies
Kroger
Safeway
Smart & Final
SUPERVALU
Trader Joe's Co
Wal-Mart
Whole Foods
Wild Oats Markets

HISTORICAL FINANCIALS

Company Type: Private

Income Statement FYE: December 31

	ESTIMATED REVENUE ($ mil.)	NET INCOME ($ mil.)	NET PROFIT MARGIN	EMPLOYEES
12/02	1,600	—	—	12,500
12/01	1,359	—	—	10,500
12/00	1,200	—	—	8,800
12/99	1,210	—	—	8,000
12/98	1,000	—	—	7,600
12/97	870	—	—	7,600
12/96	800	—	—	6,600
12/95	675	—	—	5,600
12/94	650	—	—	5,000
12/93	580	—	—	5,000
Annual Growth	11.9%	—	—	10.7%

Revenue History

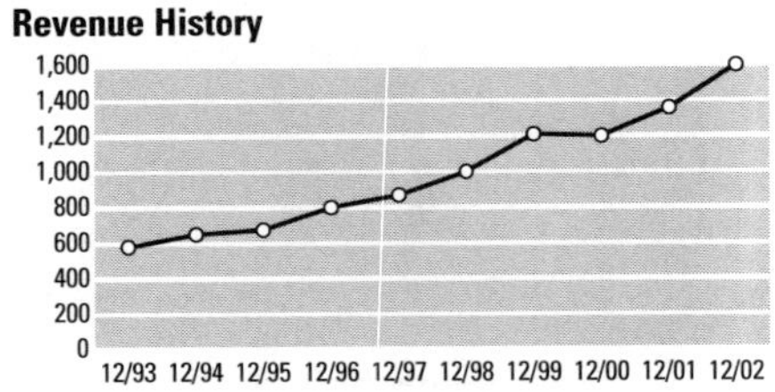

Basin Electric Power Cooperative

Ranges at home on the range depend on Basin Electric Power Cooperative, as do other electric-powered items in nine states from Montana to Iowa to New Mexico. The regional, consumer-owned power generation and transmission co-op generates about 2,400 MW of capacity (mostly coal-fired) for 124 rural electric member systems, which serve 1.7 million people. It generates an additional 1,000 MW for participants in the Missouri Basin Power Project. Basin Electric's subsidiaries include Dakota Gasification (produces natural gas from coal), Dakota Coal (markets lignite and limestone), Basin Telecommunications (Internet access), Basin Cooperative Services (property management), and Granite Peak Energy (power marketing).

EXECUTIVES

CEO and General Manager, Basin Electric and Basin Cooperative Services; President and CEO, Dakota Coal, Dakota Gasification, and Basin Telecommunications: Ronald R. (Ron) Harper, age 53
President and Director; Chairman, Basin Telecommunications: Wayne L. Child
SVP and Deputy General Manager: Paul Sukut, age 47
SVP and CFO: Clifton T. Hudgins, age 56
SVP Administration: Tom Fischer, age 48
SVP External Relations and Communications: Alan Edwards, age 52

SVP Generation: Wayne Backman, age 50
SVP Transmission: Ted Humann, age 58
Secretary, Treasurer, and Director: Kermit Pearson
Manager Human Resources: Sharon Klein
Auditors: Deloitte & Touche LLP

LOCATIONS

HQ: 1717 E. Interstate Ave., Bismarck, ND 58503
Phone: 701-223-0441 **Fax:** 701-224-5336
Web: www.basinelectric.com

Basin Electric Power Cooperative provides electricity in Colorado, Iowa, Minnesota, Montana, Nebraska, New Mexico, North Dakota, South Dakota, and Wyoming.

PRODUCTS/OPERATIONS

2002 Sales

	% of total
Utility	59
Synthetic gas	18
Lignite coal	10
Byproducts & other	13
Total	**100**

Regional Member Cooperatives

Central Montana Electric Power Cooperative
Central Power Electric Cooperative
Corn Belt Power Cooperative (Humboldt, IA)
East River Electric Power Cooperative
Flathead Electric Cooperative (Kalispell, MT)
L & O Power Cooperative
Northwest Iowa Power Cooperative (NIPCO)
Powder River Energy Corp. (Sundance, WY)
Rushmore Electric Power Cooperative
Tri-State Generation and Transmission Association
Upper Missouri Generation and Transmission Electric Cooperative

COMPETITORS

Alliant Energy
Aquila
Black Hills
MDU Resources
MidAmerican Energy
Nebraska Public Power
NorthWestern
Omaha Public Power
Otter Tail
Xcel Energy

HISTORICAL FINANCIALS

Company Type: Cooperative

Income Statement FYE: December 31

	REVENUE ($ mil.)	NET INCOME ($ mil.)	NET PROFIT MARGIN	EMPLOYEES
12/02	830	37	4.4%	1,768
12/01	863	27	3.1%	1,775
12/00	512	43	8.3%	1,750
12/99	757	4	0.5%	1,661
12/98	763	(5)	—	1,684
12/97	784	(3)	—	1,790
12/96	774	(3)	—	1,735
12/95	733	—	—	1,761
12/94	783	—	—	—
12/93	764	—	—	—
Annual Growth	0.9%	—	—	0.1%

2002 Year-End Financials

Debt ratio: 175.6%
Return on equity: 5.9%
Cash ($ mil.): 65
Current ratio: 1.16
Long-term debt ($ mil.): 1,058

Net Income History

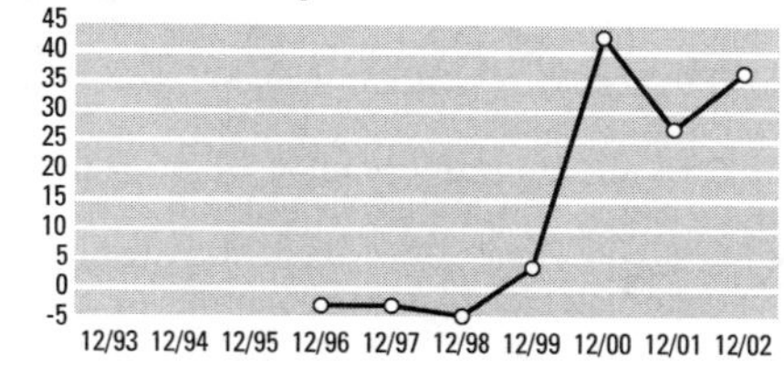

Bass Pro Shops

Bass Pro Shops (BPS) knows how to reel in the shoppers. Each of its 15 Outdoor World stores (in 10 states) covers about 280,000 sq. ft. The cavernous outlets sell boats, campers, equipment, and apparel for most outdoor activities and offer features such as archery ranges, fish tanks, snack bars, and video arcades. The first Outdoor World store, in Missouri, has been one of the state's biggest tourist attractions since it opened in 1981. BPS catches shoppers at home with its seasonal and specialty catalogs and through its TV and radio programs. It owns Tracker Marine (boat manufacturing) and American Rod & Gun (sporting goods wholesale) and runs a resort in the Ozark Mountains. Founder John Morris owns BPS.

EXECUTIVES

Founder: John L. Morris
President and COO: James Hagale
CFO: Toni Miller
VP of Human Resources: Mike Roland
Director of Corporate Public Relations: Martin Mac Donald
Corporate Public Relations: Larry Whitely

LOCATIONS

HQ: Bass Pro Shops, Inc.
2500 E. Kearney, Springfield, MO 65898
Phone: 417-873-5000 **Fax:** 417-873-4672
Web: www.basspro.com

Bass Pro Shops has stores in Florida, Georgia, Illinois, Maryland, Michigan, Missouri, North Carolina, Ohio, Tennessee, and Texas.

PRODUCTS/OPERATIONS

Selected Merchandise Categories

Apparel
Camping and auto
Fishing
Fly fishing
Footwear
Gifts and home decor
Hunting
Marine and electronics
Saltwater fishing

Other Operations

American Rod & Gun (sporting goods wholesale)
Bass Pro Shops (sporting goods catalog)
Bass Pro Shops Outdoor World (magazine and radio and TV programs)
Big Creek Lodge (resort)
Outdoor World (retail stores)
Tracker Marine (sport boat manufacturing)

COMPETITORS

Academy
Athlete's Foot
Cabela's
Camping World
Cruise America
Dick's Sporting Goods
Finish Line
Foot Locker
Footstar
Galyans Trading
Hibbett Sporting Goods
Holiday RV Superstores
Kmart
MarineMax
REI
Sears
Sports Authority
Sportsman's Guide
Target
Travis Boats & Motors
Wal-Mart
West Marine
Winmark

HISTORICAL FINANCIALS

Company Type: Private

Income Statement FYE: December 31

	ESTIMATED REVENUE ($ mil.)	NET INCOME ($ mil.)	NET PROFIT MARGIN	EMPLOYEES
12/01	1,100	—	—	8,800
12/00	990	—	—	8,200
12/99	950	—	—	7,900
12/98	311	—	—	—
12/97	270	—	—	—
Annual Growth	42.1%	—	—	5.5%

Revenue History

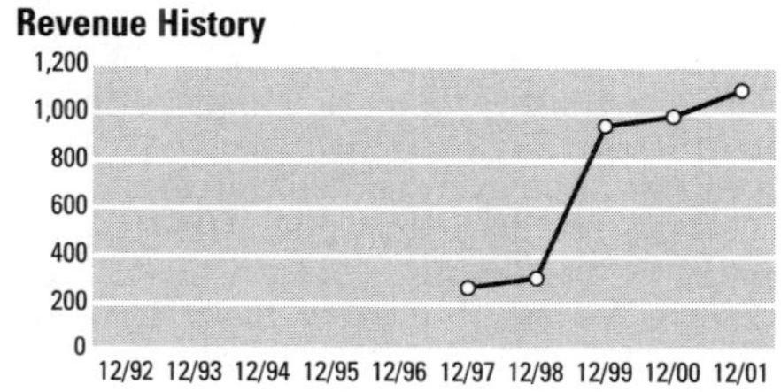

Battelle Memorial Institute

When you use a copier, hit a golf ball, or listen to a CD, you're using technologies developed by Battelle Memorial Institute. The nonprofit trust operates one of the world's largest research enterprises. Originally formed to promote metallurgy and related industries, the institute has diversified into research and development for agriculture, automobiles, chemicals, energy, software, and medicine. Battelle is also a major source of research and development expertise for the US government. It serves the departments of Energy, Defense, and Health and Human Services; the Environmental Protection Agency; and nearly 800 other government organizations.

The institute, which works with corporations and governments in nearly 30 countries, was instrumental in developing the photocopy machine, optical digital recording (used with compact discs), and bar codes. Primarily a contract research provider, the institute continues to explore next-generation technologies including advanced medical products, alternative fuels, and recycling processes.

Battelle is spinning off for-profit companies to benefit its nonprofit cause; it has shed its medical, flat-panel display, and software units as subsidiaries. Current development projects include cancer prevention, crude oil extraction, and paper mill waste recycling.

HISTORY

Battelle Memorial Institute was founded with a $1.5 million trust willed by Gordon Battelle, who died in 1923. Battelle was a champion of research for the advancement of humankind, and before taking his father's place as president of several Ohio steel mills, he had funded a former university professor's successful work to extract useful chemicals from mine waste. Battelle's mother, upon her death in 1925, left the institute an additional $2.1 million. The institute opened in 1929.

The institute took on perhaps the most important project in its history in 1944 when it helped an electronics company's patent lawyer, Chester Carlson, find practical uses for his invention, called xerography. Eventually Battelle developed the first photocopy machine, and in 1955 it sold the patent rights for the machine to Haloid (now Xerox) in exchange for royalties.

During WWII Battelle worked on uranium refining for the Manhattan Project, and in the early 1950s it established the world's first private nuclear research facility. The company also set up operations in Germany and Switzerland.

The tax man came knocking in 1961, questioning the tax-free status of some of Battelle's activities. The organization eventually had to pay $47 million. In 1965 Battelle developed a coin with a copper core and a copper-and-nickel-alloy cladding for the US Treasury.

As the result of a ruling that reinterpreted a clause in Gordon Battelle's will, in 1975 the institute gave $80 million to philanthropic enterprises. This ruling, coupled with the taxes that the organization was still unaccustomed to paying, forced Battelle to reexamine its strategy.

Battelle co-developed the Universal Product Code (the bar code symbol found today on nearly all consumer goods packaging) in the 1970s. The institute also landed a lucrative contract from the US Department of Energy (DOE) to manage its commercial nuclear waste isolation program.

In 1987 Battelle chose Douglas Olesen — a 20-year veteran of the institute — to replace retiring CEO Ronald Paul. The company signed an extension with the DOE in 1992 to run its Pacific Northwest Laboratory (which it has operated since 1965).

An Ohio court in 1997 approved a seven-page agreement with the institute outlining the key principles that must be followed according to Gordon Battelle's will. This agreement replaced the 1975 decree and ended more than 20 years of scrutiny by the state Attorney General's Office.

In 1998 the DOE contracted Brookhaven Science Associates — a partnership between the State University of New York and Battelle — to operate Brookhaven National Laboratory. That year a Battelle contract to dispose of Vietnam War-era napalm drew national attention when subcontractor Pollution Control Industries backed out of the project, citing safety concerns. Under Battelle's direction, Houston-based GNI Group took the 3.4 million gallons of napalm off the US Navy's hands.

Battelle and the University of Tennessee in 1999 won a five-year contract to operate the US government's Oak Ridge National Laboratory. That year the institute made several breakthroughs in cancer research, including FDA approval to test an inhalation delivery system for treating lung cancer.

In 2000 the company spun off OmniViz (data mining software) and Battelle Pulmonary Therapeutics (pulmonary and drug delivery technology) as wholly owned subsidiaries. In 2001 Battelle chose former Kodak EVP and chief technology officer Carl Kohrt to replace Olesen.

EXECUTIVES

Chairman: John B. McCoy Jr.
First Vice Chairman: John J. Hopfield
Second Vice Chairman: W. George Meredith
President and CEO: Carl F. Kohrt, age 59
EVP, Laboratory Operations Market Sector; Director, Oak Ridge National Laboratory: William J. Madia
SVP and CTO, Core Technology Development: Richard C. Adams
SVP and COO, Laboratory Operations Market Sector: Donald P. McConnell
SVP, CFO, and Treasurer: Mark W. Kontos
SVP; General Manager, Army/Marines/Office of Secretary of Defense Market Sector: Stephen E. Kelly
SVP; General Manager, Chemical Products Market Sector: Benjamin G. Maiden
SVP; General Manager, Energy Products Market Sector: Henry J. Cialone
SVP; General Manager, Pharmaceutical and Medical Products Market Sector: Richard D. Rosen
SVP, Administration, General Counsel, and Secretary: Jerome R. Bahlmann
SVP, Department of Energy Science Programs: Jeffrey Wadsworth
SVP, Organizational Development: Robert W. Smith Jr.

LOCATIONS

HQ: 505 King Ave., Columbus, OH 43201
Phone: 614-424-6424 **Fax:** 614-424-5263
Web: www.battelle.org

Battelle Memorial Institute manages programs in nearly 30 countries.

PRODUCTS/OPERATIONS

Selected Inventions

Automobile cruise control (1960s)
Exploded-tip paintbrush (nylon brush for Wooster Brush Co., 1950)
Golf ball coatings (1965)
Heat Seat (microwaveable heated stadium cushion, 1990s)
Holograms (work began in the 1970s)
Insulin injection pen (for Eli Lilly, 1990s)
Oil spill outline monitor (1992)
PCB-cleaning chemical process (1992)
Photocopy machine (with Haloid, 1940s)
Plastic breakdown process (1990s)
"Sandwich" coins (copper/copper and nickel alloy cladding design for US Treasury, 1965)
SenSonic toothbrush (with Teledyne/WaterPik, 1990s)
Smart cards (cards embedded with tiny computer chips that store information, 1980s)
SnoPake (correction fluid, 1955)
Universal Product Code (co-creator; bar code, 1970s)

Subsidiaries

Battelle Pulmonary Therapeutics, Inc.
Geosafe Corporation
Global Transaction Company, Inc.
OmniViz, Inc.
Research Insurance Company Ltd.
Scientific Advances, Inc.
State Science and Technology Institute
Vitex Systems, Inc.

COMPETITORS

Altran Technologies
Charles Stark Draper Laboratory
Kendle
MIT
MITRE
PAREXEL
Quintiles Transnational
Research Triangle Institute
SAIC
Southwest Research Institute
SRI International
University of California

HISTORICAL FINANCIALS

Company Type: Not-for-profit

Income Statement FYE: September 30

	REVENUE ($ mil.)	NET INCOME ($ mil.)	NET PROFIT MARGIN	EMPLOYEES
9/02	1,176	—	—	8,700
9/01	1,029	—	—	7,607
9/00	950	—	—	7,100
9/99	901	—	—	7,060
9/98	710	—	—	7,250
9/97	946	—	—	7,060
9/96	945	—	—	7,163
9/95	974	—	—	7,500
9/94	958	—	—	8,583
9/93	869	—	—	8,400
Annual Growth	3.4%	—	—	0.4%

Revenue History

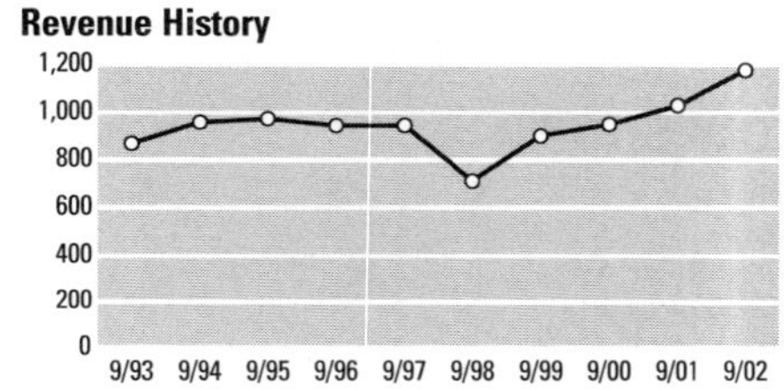

BE&K Inc.

Like a busy bee building hives for the queen, BE&K keeps up its reputation as a top US engineering and construction contractor. Through a network of subsidiaries, BE&K provides engineering, procurement, and construction and maintenance services worldwide for industrial process facilities, including the cement, chemical, petrochemical, pharmaceutical, and pulp and paper industries. It also serves the telecommunications, manufacturing, environmental, energy, and commercial sectors. The company was founded in 1972 by partners Peter Bolvig, William Edmonds, and Chairman Ted Kennedy (who retain ownership). Overseas operations began in Poland in 1984 through a strategic relationship with International Paper.

EXECUTIVES

Chairman: Theodore C. (Ted) Kennedy
President and CEO: T. Michael (Mike) Goodrich, age 57
EVP and COO; President, BE&K Construction: John W. Redmon
EVP and CFO: Clyde M. Smith

SVP Human Resources: Kimberly S. Patterson
VP Sales and Marketing: Tom Freeland
Controller: W. H. Rubar
Director Corporate Communications: Robin Paulding
General Counsel: Ed Cassady
Auditors: Ernst & Young LLP

LOCATIONS

HQ: 2000 International Park Dr., Birmingham, AL 35243
Phone: 205-972-6000 **Fax:** 205-972-6651
Web: www.bek.com

BE&K has offices in Alabama, Delaware, Georgia, New York North Carolina, Oregon, Pennsylvania, and Texas.

PRODUCTS/OPERATIONS

Selected Services

Bio-pharmaceutical facility design and construction
Boiler and auxiliary equipment installation, repair, and replacement
Computer-aided design (CAD) engineering
Construction design, engineering, and building
Environmental consulting and engineering
Industrial contract maintenance and plant support
International industrial design, engineering, and construction
Process industries design, construction, and maintenance

COMPETITORS

AMEC
ARCADIS
Bechtel
Black & Veatch
CH2M HILL
Day & Zimmermann
Dick Corporation
Eichleay Corporation
EMC Engineers
Fluor
Foster Wheeler
Gilbane
Halliburton
HOCHTIEF
Jacobs Engineering
McClier
Parsons Brinckerhoff
Parsons
Perini
Peter Kiewit Sons'
Philipp Holzmann
Skanska
Tetra Tech
URS
Washington Group

HISTORICAL FINANCIALS

Company Type: Private

Income Statement FYE: March 31

	REVENUE ($ mil.)	NET INCOME ($ mil.)	NET PROFIT MARGIN	EMPLOYEES
3/02	1,478	—	—	8,822
3/01	1,776	—	—	10,799
3/00	1,370	—	—	10,525
3/99	960	—	—	8,617
3/98	1,061	—	—	8,159
3/97	960	—	—	7,872
3/96	807	—	—	7,600
3/95	828	—	—	7,303
3/94	580	—	—	6,917
3/93	491	—	—	3,300
Annual Growth	13.0%	—	—	11.5%

Revenue History

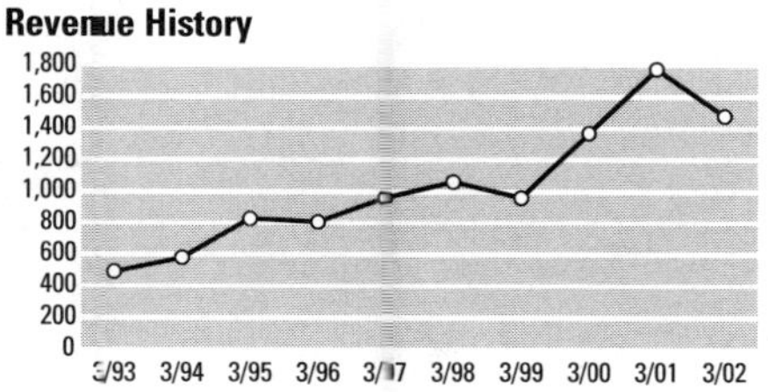

Beaulieu of America, LLC

Beaulieu of America (BOA) is rolling into a room near you with products that primarily include berber, commercial, and indoor/outdoor (nonwoven, turf) carpet. Chances are you may have had BOA underfoot at some point; the company is the third-largest carpet manufacturer. Major customers for its carpets include home improvement chains The Home Depot and Lowe's Companies. BOA sold its area rug division to Springs Industries and is currently closing and consolidating other operations. Chairman and CEO Carl Bouckaert and his wife, Mieke, whose family made carpets in Europe, founded Beaulieu in 1978; the Bouckaerts control BOA.

EXECUTIVES

Chairman and CEO: Carl M. Bouckaert
President and COO: Ralph Boe
CFO: Tim Devries
Chief Administrative Officer: Clint Hubbard

LOCATIONS

HQ: 1502 Coronet Dr., Dalton, GA 30720
Phone: 706-695-4624 **Fax:** 706-695-6237
Web: www.beaulieu-usa.com

Beaulieu Of America operates facilities in Canada, Mexico, and the US.

PRODUCTS/OPERATIONS

Selected Products

Berber carpet
Cut loops
Cut piles
Indoor/outdoor carpet
Natural nylon BCF nylon fibers
Needle-punched carpet
Nylon intermediates
Outdoor artificial grass
Polypropylene BCF fibers
Polypropylene resin
Polypropylene staple fiber
Solution-dyed nylon BCF fibers

COMPETITORS

Armstrong World Industries
Burlington Industries
Dakotah, Incorporated
Interface
Milliken
Mohawk Industries
Shaw Industries

HISTORICAL FINANCIALS

Company Type: Private

Income Statement FYE: December 31

	REVENUE ($ mil.)	NET INCOME ($ mil.)	NET PROFIT MARGIN	EMPLOYEES
12/02	1,100	—	—	7,000
12/01	1,400	—	—	10,000
12/00	1,800	—	—	11,000
12/99	1,700	—	—	10,000
12/98	1,130	—	—	9,347
12/97	961	—	—	6,413
12/96	863	—	—	6,617
12/95	868	—	—	6,500
12/94	833	—	—	6,500
12/93	744	—	—	5,900
Annual Growth	4.4%	—	—	1.9%

Revenue History

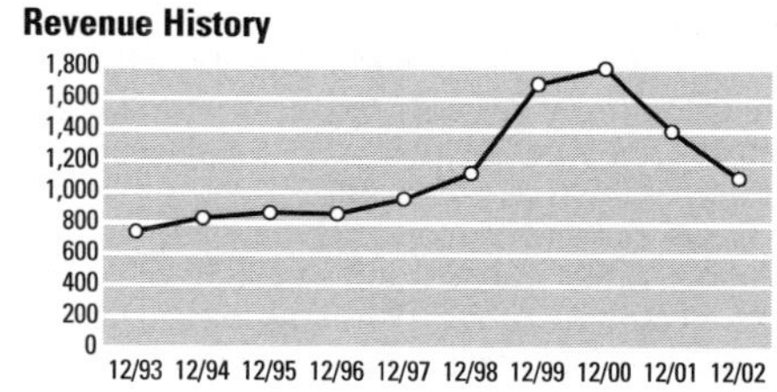

Bechtel Group

Whether it's raising an entire city or razing a nuclear power plant, you can bet the Bechtel Group will be there to bid on the business. The firm is the US's #1 contractor (ahead of Fluor). The engineering, construction, and project management firm operates worldwide, participating in such notable projects as the construction of Hoover Dam and the cleanup of the Chernobyl nuclear plant. Subsidiary Bechtel Enterprises invests in infrastructure projects and arranges financing for its clients. The group is in its fourth generation of leadership by the Bechtel family, with chairman and CEO Riley Bechtel at the helm. The billionaire Bechtel family owns a controlling stake in the firm.

Bechtel has made a name for itself by participating in mega-projects. It completes more than 1,000 projects a year. The services Bechtel offers are as broad as the industries it serves. Besides project management and design, it offers such services as environmental restoration and remediation, telecommunications infrastructure (installing cable-optic networks and constructing data centers), and e-business infrastructure (including design, systems integration, and commissioning).

Among Bechtel's more traditional infrastructure projects has been its involvement in the Big Dig, Boston's Central Artery/Tunnel project. Bechtel, in a joint venture with Parsons Brinckerhoff, has served as lead contractor on the $14.6 billion project, which has been the subject of much dispute over cost overruns.

Another major project of the group is its expansion of AT&T Wireless Services' US network. With a downturn in the telecommunications industry, however, Bechtel has looked to other areas of infrastructure. In Europe it is expanding its rail business by participating in the construction of the Channel Tunnel Rail Link, the UK's first major new railroad project in a century.

Bechtel National has also won a US Army contract to destroy mustard agent weapons stored in a Pueblo, Colorado, chemical depot, and the group beat out Fluor and other rivals to win a contract worth up to $680 million from the U.S. Agency for International Development to repair Iraq's war-damaged infrastructure.

HISTORY

In 1898 25-year-old Warren Bechtel left his Kansas farm to grade railroads in the Oklahoma Indian territories, then followed the rails west. Settling in Oakland, California, he founded his own contracting firm. Foreseeing the importance of roads, oil, and power, he won big projects such as the Northern California Highway and the Bowman Dam. By 1925, when he incorporated his company as W.A. Bechtel & Co., it ranked as the West's largest construction company. In 1931 Bechtel helped found the consortium that built Hoover Dam.

Under the leadership of Steve Bechtel (president after his father's death in 1933), the company obtained contracts for large infrastructure projects such as the San Francisco-Oakland Bay Bridge. Noted for his friendships with influential people, including Dwight Eisenhower, Adlai Stevenson, and Saudi Arabia's King Faisal, Steve developed projects that spanned nations and industries, such as pipelines in Saudi Arabia and numerous power projects. By 1960, when Steve Bechtel Jr. took over, the company was operating on six continents.

In the next two decades, Bechtel worked on transportation projects — such as San Francisco's Bay Area Rapid Transit (BART) system and the Washington, DC, subway system — and power projects, including nuclear plants. After the 1979 Three Mile Island accident, Bechtel tried its hand at nuclear cleanup. With nuclear power no longer in vogue, it focused on other markets, such as mining in New Guinea (gold and copper, 1981-84) and China (coal, 1984). Bechtel's Jubail project in Saudi Arabia, begun in 1976, raised an entire industrial port city on the Persian Gulf.

The US recession and rising developing-world debt of the early 1980s sent Bechtel reeling. It cut its workforce by 22,000 and stemmed losses by piling up small projects.

Riley Bechtel, great-grandson of Warren, became CEO in 1990. After the 1991 Gulf War, Bechtel extinguished Kuwait's flaming oil wells and worked on the oil-spill cleanup. During the decade it also worked on such projects as the Channel tunnel (Chunnel) between England and France, the new airport in Hong Kong, and pipelines in the former Soviet Union.

Bechtel was part of the consortium contracted in 1996 to build a high-speed passenger rail line between London and the Chunnel. International Generating (InterGen), Bechtel's joint venture with Pacific Gas and Electric (PG&E), was chosen to help build Mexico's first private power plant. In 1996 Bechtel bought PG&E's share of InterGen, then sold a 50% stake in InterGen to a unit of Royal Dutch/Shell in early 1997.

That year Bechtel began a venture, Netcon (Thailand), with Lucent to build telecom systems abroad. Bechtel also joined with other companies to buy interests in energy projects in developing regions. In 1998 it won a major contract to construct a gas production plant with Technip in Abu Dhabi. That year it joined Battelle and Electricité de France in project management of a long-term plan to stabilize the damaged reactor of the Chernobyl nuclear plant in Ukraine.

In 1999 Bechtel was hired to decommission the Connecticut Yankee nuclear plant. It also won contracts with Internet companies, including failed online grocer Webvan, to build a series of 26 automated grocery warehouses in the US in a deal worth nearly $1 billion. However, only four were completed before Webvan fizzled in mid-2001. The next year Bechtel teamed up with Shell Oil to build a $400 million power plant in Baja California to meet the high demands of the US-Mexico border region. It also formed Nexant, an energy consulting service for the oil and gas industry and utilities.

Bechtel expanded its telecommunications operations in 2001 to provide turnkey network implementation services in Europe, the Middle East, and Asia. In 2002 Bechtel was once again called on to work on the UK's rail system, taking over management of the upgrade of the West Coast main line from financially troubled Railtrack. As part of a consortium with UK facilities management giants Jarvis and Amey, Bechtel began work that year on a 30-year project to modernize part of London's aging subway system.

EXECUTIVES

Chairman Emeritus: Steve Bechtel Jr., age 78
Chairman and CEO: Riley P. Bechtel, age 51
President and COO: Adrian Zaccaria
EVP and Deputy COO: Jude Laspa
EVP; President, Bechtel Enterprises: Tim Statton
EVP; President, Civil Global Business Unit: Lee McIntire
EVP: Mike Thiele
SVP and CFO: Peter Dawson
SVP and General Counsel: Rick Burt
SVP; President, Bechtel National; President, Bechtel Systems and Infrastructure: Thomas F. (Tom) Hash
SVP; President, Bechtel Infrastructure: John McDonald
SVP; President, Mining and Metals Global Business Unit: Andy Greig
SVP; President, Petroleum and Chemical Global Business Unit; President, Pipeline Global Business Unit: Bill Dudley
SVP; President, Power Global Business Unit: Scott Ogilvie
SVP; President, Telecommunications and Industrial Global Business Unit: George Conniff
SVP; President, Europe, Africa, Middle East, and Southwest Asia Regions: Chuck Redman
SVP; Manager Construction: Cliff Mumm
SVP; Manager Corporate and External Affairs: Jock Covey
SVP; Manager Engineering: Ed Richardson
SVP; Manager EPC Functions: Carl Rau
SVP; Manager Procurement: Jack Futcher
President, Latin America Region: José Ivo
President and General Manager, Bechtel SAIC: John T. Mitchell
CIO: Geir Ramleth
Manager Human Resources: Jim Illich
Public Communications Manager: Jeff H. Berger
Auditors: PricewaterhouseCoopers LLP

LOCATIONS

HQ: Bechtel Group, Inc.
50 Beale St., San Francisco, CA 94105
Phone: 415-768-1234 **Fax:** 415-768-9038
Web: www.bechtel.com

Bechtel Group operates worldwide from offices in 11 states in the US, along with international offices in Argentina, Australia, Brazil, Canada, Chile, China, Egypt, France, India, Indonesia, Japan, Korea, Malaysia, Mexico, Oman, Peru, the Philippines, Russia, Saudi Arabia, Singapore, Spain, Taiwan, Thailand, Turkey, United Arab Emirates, the UK, and Venezuela.

PRODUCTS/OPERATIONS

Selected Services

Automation technology
Community relations
Environmental health and safety
Equipment operations
International consulting
Labor relations
Project management, engineering, and financing
Worldwide procurement

Selected Industries Served

Civil infrastructure
Defense and space
e-Business
Environmental
Government services
Hazardous waste cleanup
Hotels, resorts, and theme parks
Manufacturing
Mining and metals
Petroleum and chemicals
Pipelines
Ports and harbors
Power (fossil and nuclear)
Surface transportation
Telecommunications
Water and wastewater treatment

COMPETITORS

ABB Lummus Global
aker Kvaerner
AMEC
Black & Veatch
Bouygues
Centerline Piping
CH2M HILL
Chiyoda Corp.
Eiffage
Fluor
Foster Wheeler
Halliburton
HOCHTIEF
Hyundai Engineering and Construction
ITOCHU
Jacobs Engineering
Kajima
Parsons
Perini
Peter Kiewit Sons'
RWE
Schneider
Shaw Group
Siemens
Skanska
Technip
URS
VINCI
Washington Group
Weston

HISTORICAL FINANCIALS

Company Type: Private

Income Statement FYE: December 31

	REVENUE ($ mil.)	NET INCOME ($ mil.)	NET PROFIT MARGIN	EMPLOYEES
12/02	11,600	—	—	47,000
12/01	13,400	—	—	50,000
12/00	15,108	—	—	40,000
12/99	12,600	—	—	40,000
12/98	12,645	—	—	30,000
12/97	11,329	—	—	30,000
12/96	8,157	—	—	30,000
12/95	8,504	—	—	29,400
12/94	7,885	—	—	29,200
12/93	7,337	—	—	29,400
Annual Growth	5.2%	—	—	5.4%

Revenue History

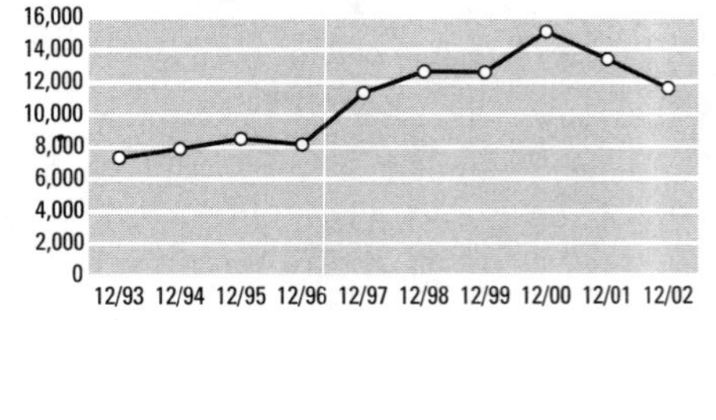

Belk, Inc.

Belk has shed a lot of bulk. Now a relatively svelte 210-plus-store retailer operating in 13 states, the chain was a confederation of 112 separate companies, formed over the past century, before its 1998 reorganization. Belk stores, located in the Southeast and Mid-Atlantic (primarily in the Carolinas and Georgia), offer mid-priced brand-name and private-label apparel, shoes, cosmetics, gifts, and home furnishings. Its stores usually anchor malls or shopping centers in small to medium-sized markets. The Belk family runs the show and owns most of the company, which is the largest privately owned department store chain in the US.

Larger Belk stores may also have hair salons, restaurants, and optical centers.

While some might say a public offering is the logical next step, chairman and octogenarian John Belk has vowed that will not happen while he is alive. The Belk brood has not always brimmed with brotherly love, but there is no need to call in Richard Dawson to settle the Belk family feud.

The company plans to open eight new stores this year (focusing on medium-size markets) and remodel four others.

HISTORY

William Henry Belk didn't mind being known as a cheapskate. At 26 he opened his first store, New York Racket, in 1888 in Monroe, North Carolina. He nicknamed the tiny shop "The Cheapest Store on Earth" and created the slogan "Cheap Goods Sell Themselves." In 1891 Belk convinced his brother John to give up a career as a doctor and join him in the retail business.

The new company, Belk Brothers, opened stores in North and South Carolina, often with partners who were family members or former employees, resulting in many two-family store names such as Belk-Harry and Hudson-Belk.

The Belks formed a partnership with the Leggett family (John's in-laws) in 1920. But feuding between the two families led to a split in 1927. The Leggetts agreed that the Belk family could keep a 20% share of the Leggett stores. John died the next year.

A strict no-credit policy worked in William's favor during the Depression, when he was able to buy out his more lenient competitors for rock-bottom prices. The shrewd businessman grew the chain from 29 stores in 1929 to about 220 stores by 1945, employing concepts such as a no-haggling policy and easy returns. William died in 1952.

That year one of his six children, William Henry Jr., opened a Belk-Lindsey store in Florida using a new format that featured, among other things, an Oriental design. Most of his siblings balked at the store's new look, but William Jr. opened another store in 1953 following the same format.

Two years later four of William Jr.'s siblings — John, Irwin, Tom, and Sarah — cut ties with the Florida stores and formed Belk Stores Services to organize their other stores. Angry at the rebuke, William Jr. and another brother, Henderson, sued the rest of the family, but they later dropped the lawsuit. In 1956 Belk Stores, with John at the helm, bought out 50-store rival chain Effird.

John had political ambitions and was elected mayor of Charlotte, North Carolina, in 1969, despite attempts by his brother William Jr. to foil the campaign. He remained mayor until 1977. Tom became the company's president in 1980.

Belk Stores continued to hold its own in the 1980s against larger department store chains on the prowl for acquisitions, but the company was stung by family discord and a loose ownership structure. Some relatives sold Belk stores to competitors such as Proffitt's (now Saks Inc.) and Dillard's. Irwin and his family, discouraged about the company's direction, sold their stock to John. In 1996 the Leggetts came back into the fold when Belk Stores bought out their 30-store chain.

Tom died in 1997 after complications from gall bladder surgery. His three sons, Tim, Johnny, and McKay, stepped up as co-presidents but continued to answer to their uncle John, the CEO. Also in 1997 Belk Stores closed its struggling 13 Tags off-price outlets.

A year later the firm reorganized and brought all 112 separate corporations under one company, streamlining the company's accounting (previously it had to fill out tax forms for all 112 businesses) and other operations. Soon after, Belk consolidated its 13 divisional offices into four regional units. Also in 1998 it traded several store locations with Dillard's.

In 1999 Belk formed Belk National Bank in Georgia to manage its credit card operations. In 2001 the company closed four of its distribution centers, consolidating their operations into its new Blythewood, South Carolina center.

The company opened nine new department stores in 2002 and shut down two others.

EXECUTIVES

Chairman and CEO: John M. Belk, age 83, $1,134,667 pay
Vice Chairman: B. Frank Matthews II, age 75
President, Finance Systems and Operations, and Director: John R. (Johnny) Belk, age 44, $778,391 pay
President, Merchandising and Marketing: Mary R. Delk, age 53
President, Merchandising, Marketing, and Merchandise Planning, and Director: H. W. McKay Belk, age 46, $778,391 pay
President, Store Divisions and Real Estate, and Director: Thomas M. (Tim) Belk Jr., age 48, $778,391 pay
EVP, Finance: Brian T. Marley, age 46
EVP, General Counsel and Secretary: Ralph A. Pitts, age 49, $579,782 pay
EVP, Human Resources: Stephen J. Pernotto
EVP, Systems: Robert K. (Roddy) Kerr Jr., age 53
SVP and Controller: Edward J. Record, age 35
Auditors: KPMG LLP

LOCATIONS

HQ: 2801 W. Tyvola Rd., Charlotte, NC 28217
Phone: 704-357-1000 **Fax:** 704-357-1876
Web: www.belk.com

2003 Stores

	No.
North Carolina	75
Georgia	41
South Carolina	37
Florida	19
Virginia	19
Alabama	4
Kentucky	4
Tennessee	4
Arkansas	3
Texas	3
Maryland	2
West Virginia	2
Mississippi	1
Total	**214**

PRODUCTS/OPERATIONS

Private Labels

Home Accents
J.Khaki
Kim Rogers
Madison Studio
Meeting Street
Saddlebred

COMPETITORS

Dillard's
Elder-Beerman Stores
Federated
J. C. Penney
Kohl's
May
Saks Inc.
Sears
Stein Mart
Target
TJX
Wal-Mart

HISTORICAL FINANCIALS

Company Type: Private

Income Statement FYE: Saturday closest to January 31

	REVENUE ($ mil.)	NET INCOME ($ mil.)	NET PROFIT MARGIN	EMPLOYEES
1/03	2,242	84	3.7%	17,800
1/02	2,243	63	2.8%	18,500
1/01	2,270	57	2.5%	21,000
1/00	2,145	71	3.3%	21,000
1/99	2,091	57	2.7%	22,000
1/98	1,974	54	2.8%	29,000
1/97	1,773	101	5.7%	25,000
1/96	1,686	44	2.6%	—
1/95	1,694	49	2.9%	—
1/94	1,674	54	3.2%	—
Annual Growth	3.3%	5.1%	—	(5.5%)

2003 Year-End Financials

Debt ratio: 37.3%
Return on equity: 9.1%
Cash ($ mil.): 91
Current ratio: 3.58
Long-term debt ($ mil.): 356

Net Income History

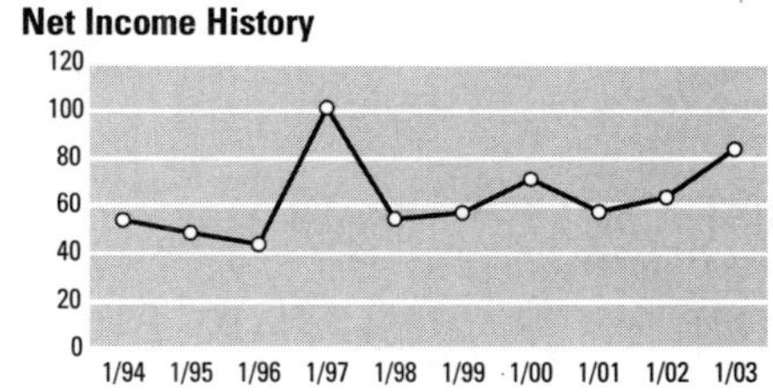

Belkin Corporation

Where do all of those multiplying wires under your feet come from? Belkin could be the source. The company makes a variety of connectivity and power products. A leading manufacturer of universal serial bus (USB) devices, Belkin also provides surge protectors, uninterruptible power supplies (UPS), and computer cables. Other products include FireWire digital video editing and connectivity products, LAN cabling and networking hardware, and accessories for cell phones and personal digital assistants. The company, which was founded in 1983, sells its products worldwide, primarily through resellers and distributors.

EXECUTIVES

President: Chet Pipkin
VP, Marketing and Sales: Steve Bellow
Director, Marketing and Product Development: Eric Tong
Senior Business Unit Manager: Megan Daley
Manager, Public Relations: James Little

LOCATIONS

HQ: 501 W. Walnut St., Compton, CA 90220
Phone: 310-898-1100 **Fax:** 310-898-1111
Web: www.belkin.com

Belkin has offices in Australia, the Netherlands, the UK, and the US. It sells its products worldwide.

PRODUCTS/OPERATIONS

Selected Products

Cables (audio, digital video interface, modem, monitor, networking, printer)
Computer accessories (laptop cases, keyboards, mice, mouse pads)
Gaming accessories (gamepads, mice)
KVN (keyboard, video, mouse) switches
Networking components (interface cards, racks, routers, switches)
Personal digital assistant accessories (cases, chargers, power cords)
Power and surge protectors
Telephone accessories (cords, couplers, jacks, splitters, stands)
Wireless telephone accessories (batteries, cases, chargers, faceplates, power cords)

COMPETITORS

2Wire
3Com
Adaptec
American Power Conversion
Avocent
Belden
Cisco Systems
D-Link
Katy Industries
NETGEAR
Powerware
Rose Electronics
SIIG
Xircom

HISTORICAL FINANCIALS

Company Type: Private

Income Statement FYE: December 31

	REVENUE ($ mil.)	NET INCOME ($ mil.)	NET PROFIT MARGIN	EMPLOYEES
12/02	460	—	—	1,000
12/01	450	—	—	1,000
12/00	400	—	—	1,000
Annual Growth	7.2%	—	—	0.0%

Revenue History

Bellco Health

Bellco Health is no baby. The company operates through three divisions. Its Bellco Drug division is an independent drug distributor selling primarily to pharmacies and retailers on Long Island and in New York City. The company distributes various name-brand and generic pharmaceutical products, as well as over-the-counter drugs and sundries. Its American Medical Distributors division sells professional products to specialty clinics and physicians. The company's third division, Dialysis Purchasing Alliance, is a group purchasing organization focusing on dialysis equipment and supplies. The Schuss family, which founded Bellco in 1955, owns the company.

EXECUTIVES

Chairman: Eric Schuss
CEO: Neal Goldstein
President and CFO: Vincent Russo

LOCATIONS

HQ: Bellco Health Corp.
5500 New Horizons Blvd.,
North Amityville, NY 11701
Phone: 631-789-6300 **Fax:** 631-841-6185
Web: www.bellcohealth.com

COMPETITORS

Allou
AmerisourceBergen
Cardinal Health
Caremark
McKesson
Quality King

HISTORICAL FINANCIALS

Company Type: Private

Income Statement FYE: June 30

	REVENUE ($ mil.)	NET INCOME ($ mil.)	NET PROFIT MARGIN	EMPLOYEES
6/02	877	—	—	165
6/01	775	—	—	156
6/00	659	—	—	215
6/99	560	—	—	145
6/98	462	—	—	145
6/97	345	—	—	100
6/96	210	—	—	—
Annual Growth	26.9%	—	—	10.5%

Revenue History

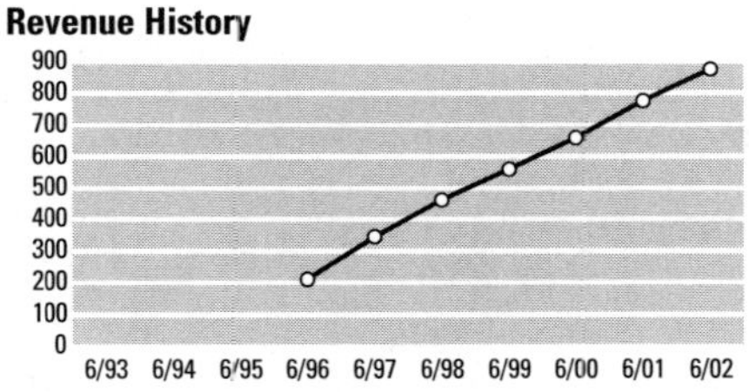

Ben E. Keith Company

Ben E. Keith is your bud if you like eating out and drinking Bud. The company delivers a full line of foods (produce, dry groceries, frozen food, meat), paper goods, equipment, and supplies to more than 12,000 customers in Arkansas, Kansas, Louisiana, New Mexico, Oklahoma, and Texas. It is one of the world's largest Anheuser-Busch distributors, delivering beer in 54 Texas counties. Ben E. Keith's customers include restaurants, hospitals, schools, and other institutional businesses. Founded in 1906 as Harkrider-Morrison, the company assumed its current name in 1931 in honor of Ben E. Keith, who served as the company's president until 1959. Its owners include Robert and Howard Hallam.

EXECUTIVES

Chairman and CEO: Robert Hallam
President and COO: Howard Hallam
CFO: Mel Cockrell
President, Ben E. Keith Beers: Kevin Bartholomew
President, Ben E. Keith Foods: Mike Roach
Corporate Secretary and General Counsel: David Greenlee
Director of Human Resources: Sam Reeves

LOCATIONS

HQ: 601 E. 7th St., Fort Worth, TX 76102
Phone: 817-877-5700 **Fax:** 817-338-1701
Web: www.benekeith.com/main.html

COMPETITORS

Gambrinus
MBM
McLane Foodservice
Morrison Management Specialists
Southern Wine & Spirits
SYSCO
U.S. Foodservice

HISTORICAL FINANCIALS

Company Type: Private

Income Statement FYE: June 30

	REVENUE ($ mil.)	NET INCOME ($ mil.)	NET PROFIT MARGIN	EMPLOYEES
6/02	1,185	—	—	2,526
6/01	1,068	—	—	2,347
6/00	959	—	—	2,160
6/99	787	—	—	2,000
6/98	682	—	—	1,800
6/97	630	—	—	1,626
6/96	580	—	—	1,600
6/95	542	—	—	1,513
6/94	513	—	—	1,446
6/93	508	—	—	1,382
Annual Growth	9.9%	—	—	6.9%

Revenue History

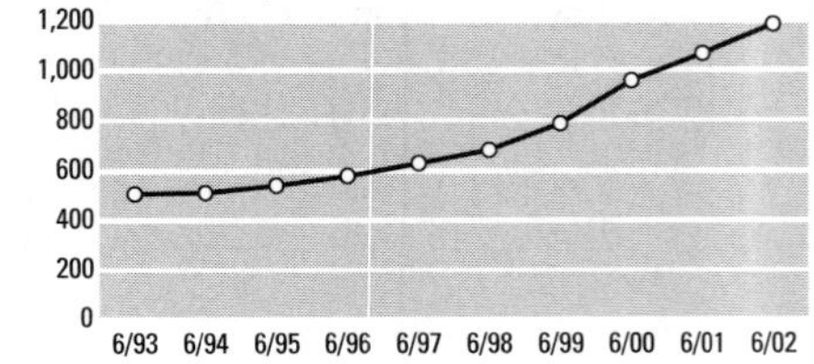

Berry Plastics Corporation

Berry Plastics is a leading maker of injection-molded plastic products. It has three business segments: containers (about half of sales), closures, and consumer products such as plastic drink cups and housewares. Berry's containers package items such as dairy products and pool chemicals. Its closures unit makes overcaps for aerosol cans and caps for mouthwash and detergents. Fast-food restaurants, convenience stores, and stadiums use its plastic drink cups. Berry also makes plastic housewares like plates, bowls, pitchers, and flowerpots. Berry has about 12,000 customers, including major retail, beverage, and fast-food companies. First Atlantic Capital sold Berry Plastics to a unit of The Goldman Sachs Group in 2002.

Berry Plastics has grown primarily through acquisitions. Internationally, the company operates facilities in the UK, Italy, and Mexico.

EXECUTIVES

Chairman: Joseph H. Gleberman, age 45
President, CEO, and Director: Ira G. Boots, age 49
EVP, CFO, Secretary, and Treasurer: James M. Kratochvil, age 45
EVP and General Manager, Closures: William J. Herdrich, age 52
EVP and General Manager, Consumer Products: Bruce J. Sims, age 52, $307,055 pay
EVP and General Manager, Containers: R. Brent Beeler, age 48
VP, Global Purchasing: Scott Farmer
VP, Human Resources: Martha Jochem
VP, Resin Purchasing: John Rathbun
VP and Plant Manager, Evansville: Fred Heseman
Auditors: Ernst & Young LLP

LOCATIONS

HQ: 101 Oakley St., Evansville, IN 47710
Phone: 812-424-2904 **Fax:** 812-424-0128
Web: www.berryplastics.com

COMPETITORS

Berlin Packaging
Dart Container
Huhtamäki
Kerr Group
Letica
Owens-Illinois
Polytainers
SF Holdings

HISTORICAL FINANCIALS

Company Type: Private

Income Statement FYE: Last Saturday in December

	REVENUE ($ mil.)	NET INCOME ($ mil.)	NET PROFIT MARGIN	EMPLOYEES
12/02	494	(33)	—	3,250
12/01	462	(2)	—	3,100
12/00	409	(23)	—	3,100
12/99	329	(9)	—	2,800
12/98	272	(8)	—	2,300
12/97	227	(14)	—	2,100
12/96	151	(3)	—	1,040
12/95	141	6	4.5%	1,100
12/94	106	2	2.1%	930
12/93	88	(2)	—	—
Annual Growth	21.2%	—	—	16.9%

2002 Year-End Financials

Debt ratio: 800.0%
Return on equity: —
Cash ($ mil.): 16
Current ratio: 1.80
Long-term debt ($ mil.): 601

Net Income History

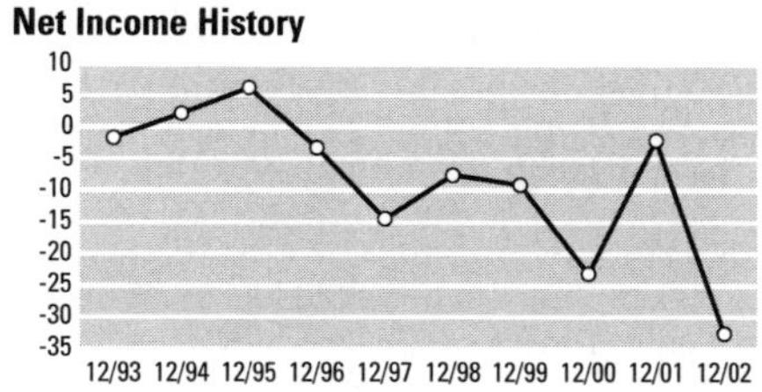

Berwind Group

Berwind Group isn't workin' in a coal mine anymore. Founded in 1874 to mine Appalachian coal, the firm began leasing its mining operations in 1962 to fund investments in new ventures. Berwind's Interlogix subsidiary makes items such as intrusion and fire detection sensors, facility integration control systems, and surveillance equipment. Berwind Property Group owns commercial, retail, and residential real estate nationwide, and Berwind Financial Group provides investment banking services. Berwind Natural Resources and Berwind Pharmaceutical Services round out the group's operations. The Berwind family owns the company.

EXECUTIVES

President and CEO: James L. Hamling
Chief Financial Officer: Van Billet
Director, Human Resources: Catherine Warrin

LOCATIONS

HQ: 3000 Centre Square West, 1500 Market St., Philadelphia, PA 19102
Phone: 215-563-2800 **Fax:** 215-563-8347
Web: www.berwind.com

PRODUCTS/OPERATIONS

Selected Operations

Berwind Pharmaceutical Services, Inc. (pharmaceutical and biotechnology products and services)
- CRC Industries, Inc. (specialty chemical products)
- Perfect Equipment Company, LLC (wheel-balancing weights)
- Synventive Molding Solutions, Inc. (manufacturer of hot runner injection molding systems)
- Venture Measurement Company, LLC (instrumentation products)
- Zymark Corp. (laboratory automation and robotic solutions)

Berwind Property Group, Inc. (real estate investment management)
Berwind Natural Resources Corp. (land and resource management)
Eureka Growth Capital (a Berwind sponsored, non-control investment fund)
Hunt Corporation (manufacturer and marketer of office supplies and art and framing products)

COMPETITORS

Aventis
Bosch
Dover
Dow Chemical
DuPont
FMC
Illinois Tool Works
Ingersoll-Rand
W.W. Grainger

HISTORICAL FINANCIALS

Company Type: Private

Income Statement FYE: December 31

	ESTIMATED REVENUE ($ mil.)	NET INCOME ($ mil.)	NET PROFIT MARGIN	EMPLOYEES
12/02	1,000	—	—	3,500
12/01	1,000	—	—	7,500
12/00	850	—	—	4,150
12/99	1,000	—	—	7,500
12/98	1,300	—	—	4,800
12/97	1,156	—	—	4,500
12/96	850	—	—	5,000
12/95	725	—	—	5,000
12/94	654	—	—	4,000
12/93	515	—	—	4,000
Annual Growth	7.7%	—	—	(1.5%)

Revenue History

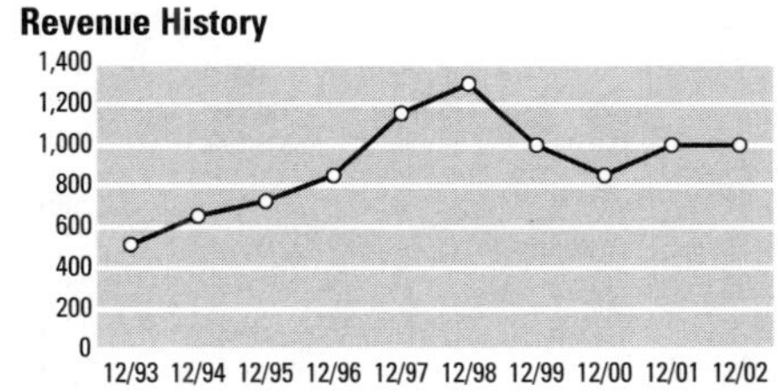

Big Y Foods, Inc.

Why call it Big Y? Big Y Foods began as a 900-sq.-ft. grocery at a Y intersection in Chicopee, Massachusetts. It now operates about 50 supermarkets in Massachusetts and Connecticut. More than half of its stores are Big Y World Class Markets, offering specialty areas such as bakeries and floral shops, as well as banking. The rest consist of Big Y Supermarkets and one Table & Wine store, which sells gourmet food, wine, and liquor. Some Big Y stores provide child care, dry cleaning, photo processing, and even propane sales, and their delis and Food Courts offer to-go foods. Big Y is owned and run by the D'Amour family; Paul D'Amour bought the original store in 1936 and was quickly joined by teenage brother Gerald.

EXECUTIVES

Chairman and CEO: Donald H. D'Amour
EVP and COO: Charles L. D'Amour
SVP, CFO: Herbert T. (Herb) Dotterer
SVP, Merchandising: Daniel (Dan) Lescoe
VP, Center Store: Phill Schneider
VP, Corporate Communications: Claire H. D'Amour-Daley
VP, Employee Services: Jack Henry
VP, Information Systems: John N. Sarno
VP, Operations: David Brunelle
Auditors: Deloitte & Touche LLP

LOCATIONS

HQ: 2145 Roosevelt Ave., Springfield, MA 01102
Phone: 413-784-0600 **Fax:** 413-732-7350
Web: www.bigy.com

PRODUCTS/OPERATIONS

Selected Products And Services

Babysitting
Bakery
Banking
Deli
Dry cleaning
Florist
Gourmet food
Liquor
Lottery tickets
Meat
Photo processing
Produce
Propane
Seafood
Wine

COMPETITORS

Cumberland Farms
DeMoulas Super Markets
Golub
Hannaford Bros.
Shaw's
Stop & Shop
SUPERVALU
Wal-Mart

HISTORICAL FINANCIALS

Company Type: Private

Income Statement FYE: June 30

	REVENUE ($ mil.)	NET INCOME ($ mil.)	NET PROFIT MARGIN	EMPLOYEES
6/02	1,200	—	—	7,850
6/01	1,200	—	—	7,800
6/00	1,083	—	—	7,600
6/99	1,010	—	—	7,000
6/98	1,009	—	—	7,200
6/97	914	—	—	7,173
6/96	789	—	—	6,253
6/95	735	—	—	3,940
6/94	630	—	—	3,305
6/93	550	—	—	4,500
Annual Growth	9.1%	—	—	6.4%

Revenue History

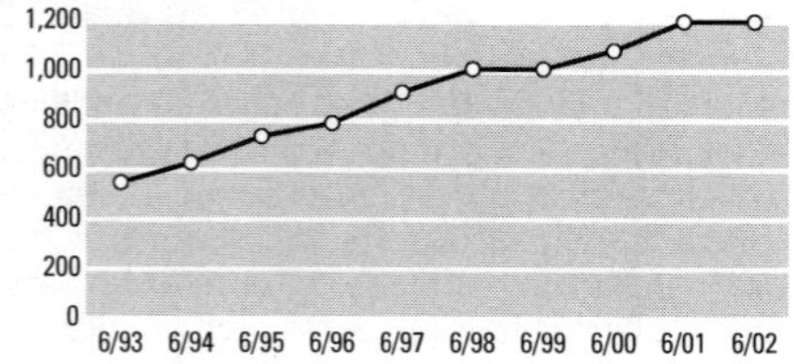

Bill & Melinda Gates Foundation

You don't have to be one of the richest men in the world to attract attention to your charitable foundation, but it doesn't hurt. Established in 1994, The William H. Gates Foundation was thrust into the spotlight in 1999 after receiving more than $2 billion from Microsoft chairman and foundation namesake Bill Gates. Later that year it combined with affiliate Gates Learning Foundation to form the Bill & Melinda Gates Foundation. Its contributions fund work in the areas of world health (vaccine research) and education; it also supports community service initiatives in the Pacific Northwest. William Gates Sr. runs the foundation, which is the largest in the US, with an endowment of about $24 billion.

The foundation also has the Gates Millennium Scholars Program, which plans to provide scholarships to minority students over the next 20 years. Gates has said he would like to give away most of his fortune while he is still living.

HISTORY

Bill Gates created the William H. Gates Foundation in 1994 with $106 million. During the next four years, he added about $2 billion to the charity. He appointed his father the head of the foundation, and the foundation at first was housed in Bill Gates Sr.'s basement. In 1997 Gates established the Gates Learning Foundation (originally called the Gates Library Foundation), a philanthropic effort to improve library systems. It was Gates' goal to improve technology and Internet access at libraries, which some critics saw as a way for him to plant Microsoft software at libraries nationwide. Patty Stonesifer, a former executive at Microsoft, ran the organization from an office above a pizza parlor.

Bill and his wife Melinda contributed some $16 billion to the foundation in 1999. That year Gates decided to merge his two charity programs into one entity: the Bill & Melinda Gates Foundation, to be run by the elder Gates and Stonesifer.

In early 2000 Gates made another $5 billion gift of stock to the foundation. That year a federal judge ordered that Microsoft be split up — the effect, if any, on the foundation is unclear. (Most of its donations come in the form of stock that is then converted to cash.) In 2000 the foundation pledged $10 million toward construction of an underground visitors center at Capitol Hill in Washington, DC. The Bill & Melinda Gates Foundation donated another $10 million in 2001 to be awarded over three years to the Hope for African Children Initiative, which will help African children affected by AIDS. In 2002 the Bill & Melinda Gates Foundation pledged more than $100 million over 10 years to reduce the spread of AIDS in India. The foundation awarded a $70 million grant to the departments of genome sciences and bioengineering at the University of Washington in 2003.

EXECUTIVES

Co-Chair: William H. (Bill) Gates III, age 47
Co-Chair and President: Patricia Q. (Patty) Stonesifer, age 46
COO and Executive Director, Libraries, Pacific Northwest and Special Projects: Sylvia Mathews
Executive Director, Education: Tom Vander Ark
Executive Director, Global Health: Richard D. Klausner
Executive Director, International Library Initiatives: Richard Akeroyd
Director, Human Resources: Julie Olson
Director, Public Affairs: Joe Cerrell
CFO and Administrative Officer: Allan C. Golston
Senior Program Officer, Pacific Northwest Giving: Jaime García Rioseco

LOCATIONS

HQ: 1551 Eastlake Ave. East, Seattle, WA 98102
Phone: 206-709-3100 **Fax:** 206-709-3180
Web: www.gatesfoundation.org

PRODUCTS/OPERATIONS

Selected Beneficiaries

Alliance for Cervical Cancer Prevention ($3.9 million over two years)
Gay City Health Project ($30,000 over three years)
Global Health Council ($4.8 million over three years)
Helen Keller International ($5 million over five years)
International Planned Parenthood Federation ($8.8 million over five years)
International Tuberculosis Foundation ($1.9 million over five years)
International Vaccine Institute ($40 million over five years)
Library and Information Commission ($4.2 million over one year)
National Institute of Child Health and Human Development ($15 million over five years)
Oxfam ($2.9 million over four years)
Pacific Institute for Women's Health ($1 million over three years)
Population Council ($4 million over two years)
Portland Children's Museum ($600,000 over three years)
United Negro College Fund ($1 billion over 20 years)
US Fund for UNICEF ($15 million over five years)

HISTORICAL FINANCIALS

Company Type: Foundation

Income Statement FYE: December 31

	REVENUE ($ mil.)	NET INCOME ($ mil.)	NET PROFIT MARGIN	EMPLOYEES
12/02	2,048	—	—	—
12/01	1,182	—	—	—
12/00	304	—	—	6
12/99*	276	—	—	4
3/98	128	—	—	2
Annual Growth	100.2%	—	—	73.2%

*Fiscal year change

Revenue History

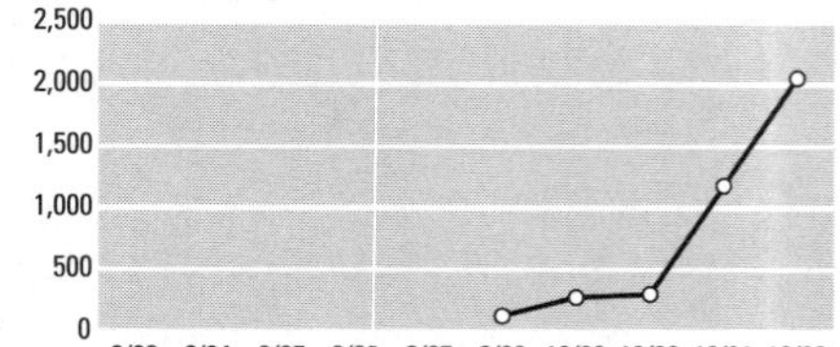

Bill Heard Enterprises

The Southern hills (and Western deserts) are alive with the sound of Chevys — music to the ears of Bill Heard Enterprises. The nation's leading chain of Chevrolet franchises, Bill Heard has more than 15 dealerships in Alabama, Arizona, Florida, Georgia, Nevada, Tennessee, and Texas. The dealer sells both new and used vehicles and auto supplies and offers repair services; it also owns Oldsmobile and Cadillac franchises in Georgia and sells Hyundais at its Memphis location. William Heard Sr. opened his first dealership in 1919. He switched to selling Chevrolets exclusively in 1932, and his son and grandsons, who now run the family-owned business, continue to focus on Chevy sales.

EXECUTIVES

CEO: William T. Heard
CFO: Ronald A. (Ron) Feldner
Corporate Services Administrator: Jim Matthews

LOCATIONS

HQ: 200 Brookstone Center Pkwy., Ste. 205, Columbus, GA 31904
Phone: 706-323-1111 **Fax:** 706-321-9488
Web: www.billheard.com

COMPETITORS

AutoNation
CarMax
Charlie Thomas Dealer Group
Gulf States Toyota
Hendrick Automotive
JM Family Enterprises
McCombs Enterprises
Morse Operations
United Auto Group

HISTORICAL FINANCIALS

Company Type: Private

Income Statement FYE: December 31

	ESTIMATED REVENUE ($ mil.)	NET INCOME ($ mil.)	NET PROFIT MARGIN	EMPLOYEES
12/01	2,600	—	—	4,000
12/00	1,796	—	—	3,100
12/99	1,433	—	—	3,100
12/98	1,200	—	—	2,000
12/97	1,100	—	—	2,000
12/96	950	—	—	1,800
12/95	875	—	—	1,600
12/94	800	—	—	1,600
12/93	613	—	—	1,300
12/92	432	—	—	—
Annual Growth	22.1%	—	—	15.1%

Revenue History

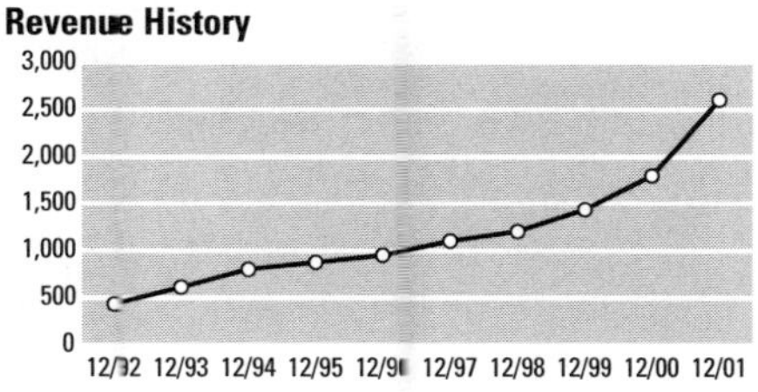

Bingham McCutchen LLP

Ambitious law firm Bingham McCutchen (formerly Bingham Dana) has its eye on expansion. Bingham McCutchen successfully courted Hartford's Hebb & Gitlin in 1999, a firm that had declined merger invitations from other firms, and added New York City firm Richards & O'Neil in 2001. In May 2002, the firm agreed to merge with McCutchen, Doyle, Brown & Enersen. Bingham McCutchen also lured former New Hampshire governor Stephen Merrill to its practice from a competing firm. Founded in 1891, the firm has more than 800 attorneys serving regional, national, and international clients. Areas of expertise include banking and finance, corporate and securities law, real estate, tax, and mergers and acquisitions.

EXECUTIVES

Chairman: Jay Zimmerman
Vice Chairman: Donn Pickett
Executive Director: William A. Bachman
CIO: David L. Furey
Director of Finance: Joseph J. Hinderhofer
Director Human Resources: Lesley A. Ficarri
Business Development: Margaret H. Child
Information Technology: C. Janice Ferguson
Public/Media Relations: Hank Shafran
Operations: Toni S. Belding

LOCATIONS

HQ: 150 Federal St., Boston, MA 02110
Phone: 617-951-8000 **Fax:** 617-951-8736
Web: www.bingham.com

The firm has offices in Boston; Hartford, Connecticut; London; Los Angeles, San Francisco, Silicon Valley, and Walnut Creek, California; New York City; Singapore; and Washington, DC.

PRODUCTS/OPERATIONS

Selected Areas of Practice

Antitrust/franchise
Banking and finance
Commercial technology
Employee benefits
Entrepreneurial services
Environmental
Estate planning
Intellectual property
Internal investigations
International trade
Investment management
Japanese practice
Latin American practice
Mergers and acquisitions
Project finance
Real estate
Securities litigation
Sports, entertainment, and media
Tax
White-collar defense

COMPETITORS

Baker & McKenzie
Clifford Chance
Debevoise & Plimpton
Gibson, Dunn & Crutcher
Goodwin Procter
Hale and Dorr
Jones Day
Kirkland & Ellis
Latham & Watkins
Mintz, Levin
O'Melveny & Myers
Orrick, Herrington
Ropes & Gray
Skadden, Arps
Wilson Sonsini

HISTORICAL FINANCIALS

Company Type: Partnership

Income Statement FYE: December 31

	REVENUE ($ mil.)	NET INCOME ($ mil.)	NET PROFIT MARGIN	EMPLOYEES
12/02	434	—	—	1,870
12/01	252	—	—	1,000
12/00	209	—	—	500
12/99	162	—	—	400
12/98	133	—	—	400
12/97	106	—	—	350
Annual Growth	32.5%	—	—	39.8%

Revenue History

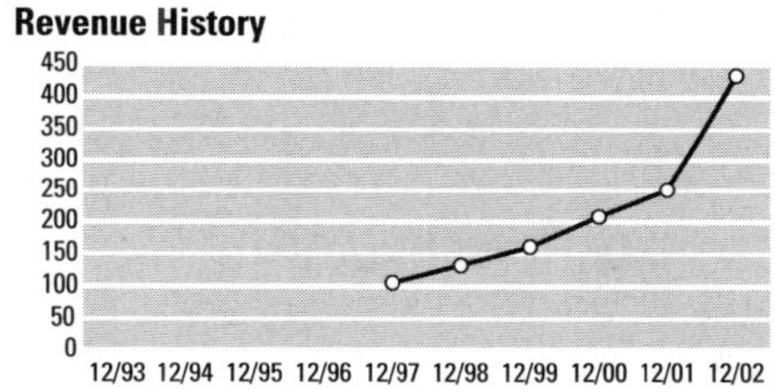

Birds Eye Foods

Whether from a bird's eye or with eyes on the bottom line, the view is excellent at Birds Eye Foods. As the #1 US maker of frozen vegetables, company brands include its flagship brand Birds Eye, as well as Freshlike and McKenzie's. The company also makes branded canned vegetables, pie fillings, chili and chili ingredients, salad dressings, and snacks. In addition, it offers private-label, food service, and industrial market foods. In 2002 Vestar Holdings acquired control of Birds Eye from Pro-Fac Cooperative. Vestar and Pro-Fac hold approximately 56% and 41% of Birds Eye, respectively. In 2002 the company changed its name from Agrilink Foods to Birds Eye Foods.

The company has 30 production facilities across the US. Its more than 40 brands include Comstock and Wilderness canned pie fillings; Brooks and Nalley chili and chili ingredients; Bernstein's salad dressings; and Husman's, Tim's, and Snyder of Berlin snacks. Its Birds Eye brands include Birds Eye Voila!, Birds Eye Simply Grillin', and Birds Eye Hearty Spoonfuls. The Birds Eye brands were named after company founder Clarence Birdseye. The company's name change reflected the company's high visibility of and continued success with the Birdseye brands.

Birds Eye's private label and industrial products include canned and frozen vegetables, salad dressings, salsa, fruit fillings and toppings, and frozen vegetable specialty products.

EXECUTIVES

Chairman, President, and CEO: Dennis M. Mullen, $600,000 pay
EVP, Finance, CFO, and Treasurer: Earl L. Powers, $305,250 pay
EVP, Member/Investor Relations: Stephen R. Wright, $225,000 pay
EVP, Operations: Carl W. Caughran, $240,000 pay
EVP, Sales: Bernhard H. (Ben) Frega
EVP, Sales, Marketing, and Business Development: David (Dave) Hogbert
VP, Corporate Communications: Bea Slizewski
VP, Human Resources: Lois Warlick-Jarvie
VP, Marketing: Randy Zeno
Auditors: PricewaterhouseCoopers LLP

LOCATIONS

HQ: Birds Eye Foods, Inc.
90 Linden Oaks, Rochester, NY 14602
Phone: 585-383-1850 **Fax:** 585-383-9153
Web: www.birdseyefoods.com

COMPETITORS

Chiquita Brands	General Mills
ConAgra	Hanover Foods
Del Monte Foods	Kraft Foods
Dole	Nestlé
Fyffes	Unilever

HISTORICAL FINANCIALS

Company Type: Private

Income Statement FYE: Last Saturday in June

	REVENUE ($ mil.)	NET INCOME ($ mil.)	NET PROFIT MARGIN	EMPLOYEES
6/03	878	21	2.4%	3,200
6/02	1,011	(131)	—	4,000
6/01	1,303	0	0.0%	4,685
6/00	1,183	6	0.5%	5,289
6/99	1,239	17	1.4%	—
6/98	720	17	2.4%	—
Annual Growth	4.1%	4.0%	—	(15.4%)

Net Income History

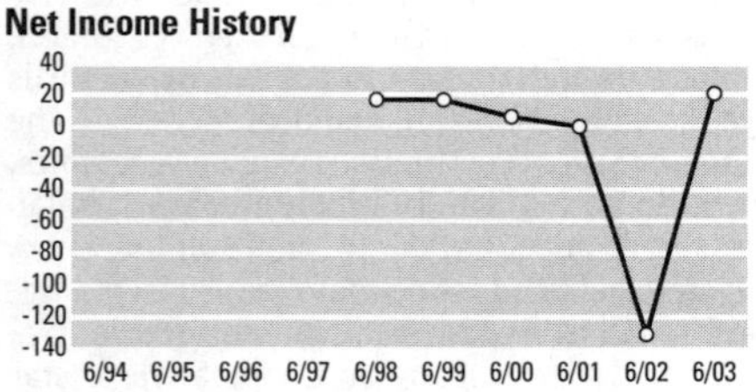

BISSELL Inc.

A pioneer in the carpet-cleaning industry, BISSELL produces a full line of vacuum cleaners, floor sweepers, steam cleaners, and cleaning chemicals for the home. Its models include the PowerSteamer, Little Green, and Spot Lifter machines. The company sells its products worldwide under the BISSELL brand name, mostly to mass merchandisers including Best Buy, Sears, Target, and Wal-Mart. Founded in 1876 by Melville and Anna Bissell, it is still owned and operated by the Bissell family. BISSELL also makes state, world, and specialty flags and related hardware through Bissell Outdoor Products.

The company has shed its health care unit (rehabilitation and patient-assistance products), as well as its graphics businesses (imaging, check-reading).

EXECUTIVES

Chairman: John M. Bissell, age 72
President and CEO: Mark J. Bissell
EVP Product Development, Sales and Marketing: James A. (Jim) Krzeminski
SVP Administration and CFO: Daniel T. Caldon
SVP Operations: Lawrence W. McDonough
VP and Corporate Controller: Timothy E. Bosscher
VP and General Counsel: William J. Brennan
Director Human Resources: Thomas P. McInerney

LOCATIONS

HQ: 2345 Walker St. NW, Grand Rapids, MI 49544
Phone: 616-453-4451 **Fax:** 616-453-1383
Web: www.bissell.com

PRODUCTS/OPERATIONS

Selected Products

Accessories and replacement parts (bags, belts, filters)
Cleaning formulas
Deep cleaners (uprights, canisters, portables)
Sweepers
Vacuums (uprights, canisters, car vacs, stick vacs, hand vacs)

COMPETITORS

Aerus	Matsushita Electric Corporation of America
Black & Decker	Maytag
Candy	Royal Appliance
Electrolux AB	
Kirby Company	

HISTORICAL FINANCIALS

Company Type: Private

Income Statement FYE: December 31

	ESTIMATED REVENUE ($ mil.)	NET INCOME ($ mil.)	NET PROFIT MARGIN	EMPLOYEES
12/01	500	—	—	1,700
12/00	500	—	—	1,700
12/99	500	—	—	2,500
12/98	450	—	—	2,250
12/97	450	—	—	2,250
12/96	443	—	—	2,250
12/95	425	—	—	2,450
12/94	400	—	—	2,600
Annual Growth	3.2%	—	—	(5.9%)

Revenue History

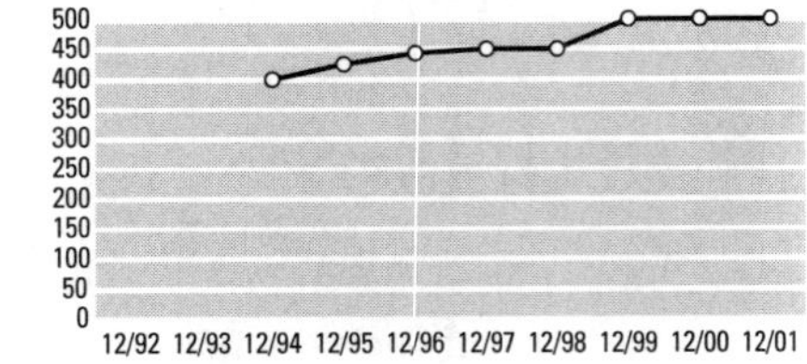

BJC HealthCare

BJC brings Jews and Christians together for the good of its patients. BJC HealthCare is the product of the 1993 merger of Barnes-Jewish, Inc., and Christian Health System. The system operates 12 hospitals and about 100 primary care and home health facilities in and around St. Louis — both in Missouri and Illinois. Specialized services include hospice care, rehabilitation services, and occupational health and workers' compensation. BJC also offers a dental plan with HMO, PPO, and fee-for-service options through Delta Dental Plan of Missouri, which acquired BJC's dental plan in 2003. BJC Health System is affiliated with Washington University Medical Center.

EXECUTIVES

Chairman: John Dubinsky
President and CEO: Steven H. Lipstein
Senior Executive Officer: Mark A. Eustis
Senior Executive Officer; President, Barnes-Jewish Hospital: Ronald G. Evens
Senior Executive Officer; President, Boone Hospital Center: Michael B. Shirk
Senior Executive Officer; President, St. Louis Children's Hospital: Lee Fetter
SVP and General Counsel: Michael A. DeHaven
VP and CFO: Edward Stiften
VP Human Resources: JoAnn Shaw

LOCATIONS

HQ: 4444 Forest Park Ave., St. Louis, MO 63108
Phone: 314-286-2000 **Fax:** 314-286-2060
Web: www.bjc.org

BJC HealthCare operates five nursing homes, 12 hospitals, and about 100 ambulatory care centers in Illinois and Missouri.

PRODUCTS/OPERATIONS

Hospitals

Alton Memorial Hospital (Alton, IL)
Barnes-Jewish Hospital (St. Louis, MO)
Barnes-Jewish St. Peters Hospital (St. Peters, MO)
Barnes-Jewish West County Hospital (St. Louis, MO)
Boone Hospital Center (Columbia, MO)
Christian Hospital (St. Louis, MO)
Clay County Hospital (Flora, IL)
Fayette County Hospital (Vandalia, IL)
Missouri Baptist Medical Center (St. Louis, MO)
Missouri Baptist Hospital-Sullivan (Sullivan, MO)
Parkland Health Center (Farmington, MO)
St. Louis Children's Hospital (St. Louis, MO)

COMPETITORS

Alexian Brothers Health System
Ascension
Catholic Health Initiatives
HCA
Sisters of Mercy
SSM Health Care
Tenet Healthcare
Universal Health Services

HISTORICAL FINANCIALS

Company Type: Not-for-profit

Income Statement FYE: December 31

	REVENUE ($ mil.)	NET INCOME ($ mil.)	NET PROFIT MARGIN	EMPLOYEES
12/01	2,200	—	—	25,801
12/00	2,100	—	—	26,038
12/99	1,608	—	—	27,071
12/98	1,561	—	—	25,853
12/97	1,587	—	—	25,500
12/96	1,553	—	—	23,696
12/95	1,530	—	—	24,975
12/94	1,413	—	—	—
12/93	1,340	—	—	—
Annual Growth	6.4%	—	—	0.5%

Revenue History

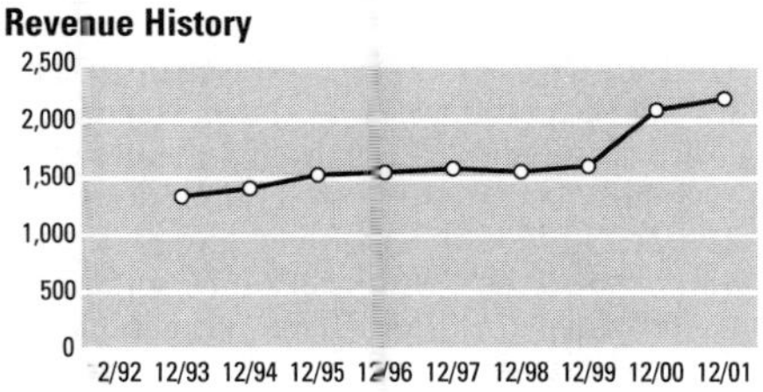

Black & Veatch

From Argentina to Zimbabwe, Black & Veatch provides the ABCs of construction, engineering, and consulting. Although a global firm, it is one of the largest private companies in the US, where it receives 78% of its revenues. Targeting infrastructure development for the energy, water, and information markets, the group engages in all phases of building projects, including design and engineering, financing and procurement, and construction. Among its services are environmental consulting, operations and maintenance, security design and consulting, and management consulting. Founded in 1915 in Kansas City by engineers E. B. Black and Tom Veatch, the firm is now employee-owned and has more than 90 offices worldwide.

EXECUTIVES

Chairman, President, and CEO: Leonard C. (Len) Rodman
Vice Chairman: Wayne F. Hall
CFO: Karen L. Daniel
EVP, General Counsel, and Secretary: G. Christian (Chris) Hedemann
Chief Human Resources Officer: Shirley Gaufin
President, Energy Engineering & Construction: Ronald R. Wood
President, Energy Services: Kim I. Mastalio
President, Power Delivery: Dean H. Oskvig
President, Process: Dwane R. Stone
President, Telecommunications: Howard G. Withey
Chief Administration Officer and President, Federal Services Division: David F. Guyot
CTO: John Voeller
Media Relations Manager: Neal Thurman

LOCATIONS

HQ: Black & Veatch Holding Company
8400 Ward Pkwy., Kansas City, MO 64114
Phone: 913-458-2000 **Fax:** 913-458-2934
Web: www.bv.com

Black & Veatch has offices in the following countries: Argentina, Australia, Botswana, Brazil, China, the Czech Republic, Egypt, Germany, Hong Kong, India, Indonesia, Kuwait, Malaysia, Mexico, the Philippines, Poland, Saudi Arabia, Singapore, South Africa, South Korea, Swaziland, Taiwan, Thailand, Turkey, the United Arab Emirates, the UK, the US, Vietnam, Zambia, and Zimbabwe.

PRODUCTS/OPERATIONS

Major Divisions

Energy Sector
Energy Engineering & Construction
Energy Services
Power Delivery
Process

Information Sector
BV Solutions Group
Enterprise Consulting
Federal Services
Telecommunications

Water Sector
Americas Division
Asia Pacific Division
Europe Division

COMPETITORS

ABB
ALSTOM
AMEC
Bechtel
CH2M HILL
Duke/Fluor Daniel
EA Engineering
Fluor
Foster Wheeler
Halliburton
HNTB
Louis Berger
Malcolm Pirnie
McDermott
Michael Baker
MWH Global
Parsons Brinckerhoff
Parsons
Shaw Group
TIC Holdings
Washington Group
Zachry

HISTORICAL FINANCIALS

Company Type: Private

Income Statement FYE: December 31

	REVENUE ($ mil.)	NET INCOME ($ mil.)	NET PROFIT MARGIN	EMPLOYEES
12/02	2,000	—	—	7,000
12/01	2,224	—	—	8,500
12/00	2,358	—	—	8,500
12/99	2,375	—	—	9,000
12/98	2,100	—	—	9,000
12/97	1,860	—	—	8,000
12/96	1,400	—	—	6,500
12/95	1,102	—	—	4,400
12/94	985	—	—	4,900
12/93	693	—	—	4,900
Annual Growth	12.5%	—	—	4.0%

Revenue History

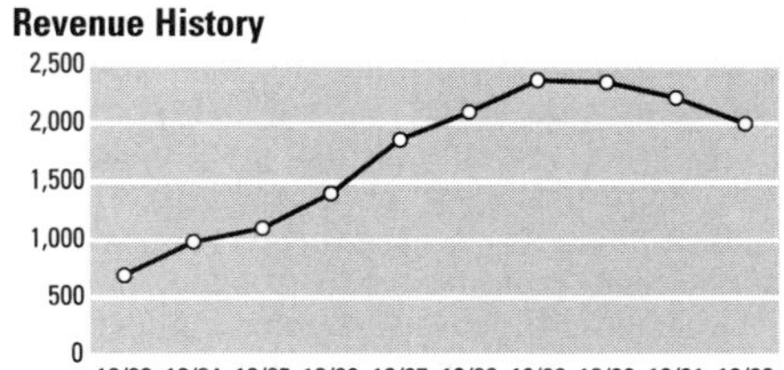

Bloomberg L.P.

What do you do when you've conquered Wall Street? You become mayor of the city the famous financial district calls home. After leading his financial news and information company to success, founder Michael Bloomberg left Bloomberg to lead the Big Apple. The Bloomberg Professional service's terminals provide real-time, around-the-clock financial news, market data, and analysis. With some 170,000 terminals installed, Bloomberg is among the world's largest providers of such devices. The company also has a syndicated news service; publishes books and magazines; and disseminates business information via TV, radio, and the Web. Michael Bloomberg, inaugurated mayor in 2002, still owns 72% of the company.

Bloomberg serves more than 200,000 customers in some 100 countries. Although terminals generate most of the company's sales (Bloomberg charges a monthly fee of $1,285 per terminal), the company distributes financial news and information through many other media channels in an effort to build its brand and keep up with the intense competition. In addition to the company's media products, Bloomberg also offers an order-matching system, the Bloomberg Tradebook. The company's Bloomberg Index License creates and licenses indices to fund managers, stock exchanges, and other clients.

Merrill Lynch also has an ownership stake in the company.

HISTORY

By the mid-1970s Michael Bloomberg had worked his way up to head of equity trading and sales at New York investment powerhouse Salomon Brothers. He left Salomon in 1981, just after the firm went private, cashing out with $10 million for his partnership interest.

Bloomberg founded Innovative Marketing Systems and spent the next year developing the Bloomberg terminal, which allowed users to manipulate bond data. In 1982 he pitched it to Merrill Lynch, which bought 20 machines. Regular production of the terminals began in 1984, and in 1985, Merrill Lynch invested $39 million in the company to gain a 30% stake. The company prospered during the 1980s boom, and over time the data, not the machines, became the heart of the business, which was renamed Bloomberg L.P. in 1986.

The company weathered the stock market crash of 1987, opening offices in London and Tokyo. Bloomberg made its entry into newsgathering and delivery in 1990 when Bloomberg News began broadcasting on its terminals. The company built its news organization from scratch, hiring away reporters from such publications as *The Wall Street Journal* and *Forbes*. Bloomberg bought a New York radio station in 1992 and converted it to an all-news format. The next year it built an in-house TV studio and created a business news show for PBS. A satellite TV station followed in 1994, along with the *Bloomberg Personal Finance* magazine.

In 1995 Bloomberg began offering business information via its Web site. The company also introduced the Bloomberg Tradebook, an electronic securities-trading venue designed to compete with Reuters' Instinet. (In 1997 Tradebook was approved by the SEC for use in connection with some Nasdaq-listed stocks.) Bloomberg also started offering its services to subscribers in a PC-compatible format and selling its data to other news purveyors, such as LexisNexis (an online information service).

In 1996 the company went further into financial publishing, issuing *Swap Literacy: A Comprehensive Guide* and *A Common Sense Guide to Mutual Funds.* That year Michael Bloomberg bought back 10% of the company from Merrill Lynch for $200 million, giving Bloomberg L.P. an estimated market value of $2 billion. The company agreed in 1997 to supply the daytime programming for Paxson Communications' New York TV station WPXN.

When Bridge Information Systems bought Dow Jones Markets from Dow Jones in 1998, Bridge surpassed Bloomberg in number of financial information terminals installed, bumping Bloomberg from the #2 spot into third place. But Bloomberg continued expanding its offerings through strategic agreements with Internet companies such as America Online and CNET Networks, and through the introduction of new magazines such as *Bloomberg Money* in 1998 as well as *On Investing* and *Bloomberg Wealth Manager* in 1999.

Also in 1999 Bloomberg secured a deal with the Australian stock exchange that would allow its terminals to facilitate international order routing into the Australian market. The company also expanded its presence in the Spanish-language market through its agreement with CBS Telenoticias to produce a TV news program (*Noticiero Financiero*). In 2000 Bloomberg joined with Merrill Lynch to make Merrill Lynch's institutional e-commerce portal available to Bloomberg customers. The company shuttered its *Bloomberg Personal Finance* magazine in early 2003.

EXECUTIVES

Founder: Michael R. Bloomberg, age 61
Chairman: Peter T. Grauer, age 57
CEO: Lex Fenwick
Director of Public Relations: Chris Taylor
Head of Ad Sales: Michael Rosen
Head of Affiliate Relations & Marketing: David Wachtel
Human Resources: Linda Norris

LOCATIONS

HQ: 499 Park Ave., New York, NY 10022
Phone: 212-318-2000 **Fax:** 212-369-5000
Web: www.bloomberg.com

Bloomberg has offices in New York City; Princeton, New Jersey; and San Francisco; as well as Frankfurt; Hong Kong; London; Sao Paulo; Singapore; Sydney; and Tokyo.

PRODUCTS/OPERATIONS

Selected Products and Services

Bloomberg Data License (financial database service)
Bloomberg Energy (Web site focusing on energy)
Bloomberg Index License (indices creation and licensing)
Bloomberg Investimenti (financial publication focusing on Italian finance)
Bloomberg Magazine (financial magazine)
Bloomberg Money (financial magazine for European investors)
Bloomberg News (syndicated news service)
Bloomberg Portfolio Trading System (asset management tool)
Bloomberg Press (book publishing)
Bloomberg Pro (wireless access to news and information)
Bloomberg Professional (24-hour, real-time financial information system)
Bloomberg Radio (syndicated radio news service)
Bloomberg Television (24-hour news channel and syndicated reports)
Bloomberg Tradebook (equities trading technology)
Bloomberg Trading System (Bloomberg information combined with trading technology)
Bloomberg Wealth Manager (magazine for financial planners and investment advisers)
Bloomberg.com (Web site)
On Investing (financial magazine, custom published for Charles Schwab's wealthiest clients)

COMPETITORS

Agence France-Presse
Associated Press
Dow Jones
FactSet
Forbes
Interactive Data
Intuit
MarketWatch.com
Media General
Reuters
TheStreet.com
Thomson Corporation

HISTORICAL FINANCIALS

Company Type: Private

Income Statement FYE: December 31

	ESTIMATED REVENUE ($ mil.)	NET INCOME ($ mil.)	NET PROFIT MARGIN	EMPLOYEES
12/02	3,000	—	—	8,000
12/01	2,600	—	—	7,200
12/00	2,800	—	—	7,200
12/99	2,300	—	—	5,150
12/98	1,500	—	—	4,900
12/97	1,300	—	—	4,000
12/96	760	—	—	3,000
12/95	650	—	—	2,500
12/94	550	—	—	2,000
12/93	370	—	—	1,800
Annual Growth	26.2%	—	—	18.0%

Revenue History

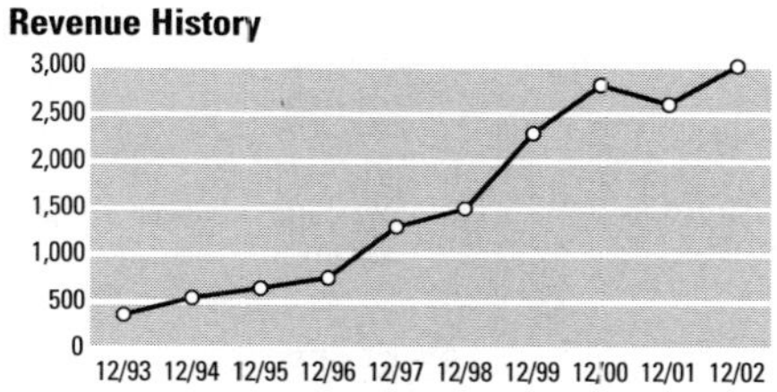

Blue Cross and Blue Shield

The rise of managed health care has had some of its members singing the blues, but the Blue Cross and Blue Shield Association still has major market power. The Blue Cross and Blue Shield Association coordinates about 45 chapters that provide health care coverage to more than 80 million Americans through indemnity insurance, Health Maintenance Organizations (HMOs), preferred provider organizations (PPOs), point-of-service (POS) plans, and fee-for-service plans. Blue Cross and Blue Shield Association chapters also administer Medicare plans for the federal government.

While some Blues always faced competition head-on, most received tax benefits for taking all comers. But as lower-cost plans attracted the hale and hearty, the Blues' customers became older, sicker, and more expensive. With their quasi-charitable status and outdated rate structures, many Blues lost market share.

They have fought back by merging among themselves, creating for-profit subsidiaries, forming alliances with for-profit enterprises, or dropping their not-for-profit status and going public — while still using the Blue Cross Blue Shield name. A history of tax breaks complicates these efforts and usually requires the creation of charitable foundations. As a result, the umbrella association is becoming a licensing and brand-marketing entity. The conversion of the Blues to for-profit status is sparking a backlash by consumer organizations.

HISTORY

Blue Cross was born in 1929, when Baylor University official Justin Kimball offered schoolteachers 21 days of hospital care for $6 a year. A major plan feature was a community rating system that based premiums on the community claims experience rather than members' conditions.

The Blue Cross symbol was devised in 1933 by Minnesota plan executive E. A. van Steenwyck. By 1935 many of the 15 plans in 11 states used the symbol. Many states gave the plans nonprofit status, and in 1936 the American Hospital Association formed the Committee on Hospital Service (renamed the Blue Cross Association in 1948) to coordinate them.

As Blue Cross grew, state medical societies sponsored prepaid plans to cover doctors' fees. In 1946 they united under the aegis of the American Medical Association (AMA) as the Associated Medical Care Plans (later the Association of Blue Shield Plans).

In 1948 the AMA thwarted a Blue Cross attempt to merge with Blue Shield. But the Blues increasingly cooperated on public policy matters while competing for members, and each Blue formed a not-for-profit corporation to coordinate its plan's activities.

By 1960 Blue Cross insured about a third of the US. Over the next decade the Blues started administering Medicare and other government health plans, and by 1970 half of Blue Cross' premiums came from government entities.

In the 1970s the Blues adopted such cost-control measures as review of hospital admissions; many plans even abandoned the community rating system. Most began emphasizing preventive care in HMOs or PPOs. The two Blues finally merged in 1982, but this had little effect on the associations' bottom lines as losses grew.

By the 1990s the Blues were big business. Some of the state associations offered officers high salaries and perks but still insisted on special regulatory treatment.

Blue Cross of California became the first chapter to give up its tax-free status when it was bought by WellPoint Health Networks, a managed care subsidiary it had founded in 1992. In a 1996 deal, WellPoint became the chapter's parent and converted it to for-profit status, assigning all of the stock to a public charitable foundation which received the proceeds of its subsequent IPO. WellPoint also bought the group life and health division of Massachusetts Mutual Life Insurance.

The for-profit switches picked up in 1997. Blue Cross of Connecticut merged with insurance provider Anthem, and other mergers followed. Half the nation's Blues formed an alliance called BluesCONNECT, competing with national health plans by offering employers one nationwide benefits organization. The association also pursued overseas licensing agreements in Europe, South America, and Asia, assembling a network of Blue Cross-friendly caregivers aiming for worldwide coverage.

In 1998 Blues in more than 35 states sued the nation's big cigarette companies to recoup the costs of treating smoking-related illnesses. In a separate lawsuit, Blue Cross and Blue Shield of Minnesota received nearly $300 million from the tobacco industry. In 1999, Anthem moved to acquire or affiliate with Blues in Colorado, Maine, and New Hampshire.

In 2000, after years of discussions, the New York Attorney General permitted Empire Blue Cross and Blue Shield to convert to for-profit status.

EXECUTIVES

Chairman: Robert L. Shoptaw, age 55
President and CEO: Scott P. Serota
SVP, Corporate Secretary, and General Counsel: Roger G. Wilson
SVP, Strategic Services: Maureen Sullivan
SVP and Chief Medical Officer: Allan M. Korn
VP, Finance and Administration: Ralph Rambach
VP, Human Resources: Bill Colbourne
VP, Deputy General Counsel, and Assistant Corporate Secretary: Paul F. Brown
National Antifraud Director: Byron Hollis
Auditors: PricewaterhouseCoopers LLP

LOCATIONS

HQ: Blue Cross and Blue Shield Association
225 N. Michigan Ave., Chicago, IL 60601
Phone: 312-297-6000 **Fax:** 312-297-6609
Web: www.bcbs.com

The Blue Cross and Blue Shield Association has offices in Chicago and Washington, DC, with licensees operating throughout the US as well as in Africa, Australia, Asia, Canada, Latin America, the Middle East, and western Europe.

PRODUCTS/OPERATIONS

Selected Operations

BlueCard Worldwide (care of US members in foreign countries)
BluesCONNECT (nationwide alliance)
Federal Employee Health Benefits Program (federal employees and retirees)
Health maintenance organizations
Medicare management
Point-of-service programs
Preferred provider organizations

COMPETITORS

Aetna
CIGNA
Health Net
Humana
Kaiser Foundation
Oxford Health Plans
PacifiCare
Prudential
UniHealth
UnitedHealth Group

HISTORICAL FINANCIALS

Company Type: Association

Income Statement FYE: December 31

	REVENUE ($ mil.)	NET INCOME ($ mil.)	NET PROFIT MARGIN	EMPLOYEES
12/02	162,800	—	—	150,000
12/01	143,200	—	—	150,000
12/00	126,000	—	—	150,000
12/99	93,700	—	—	150,000
12/98	94,700	—	—	150,000
12/97	76,500	—	—	150,000
12/96	75,200	—	—	150,000
12/95	74,400	—	—	146,000
12/94	71,414	—	—	146,352
12/93	71,161	—	—	135,883
Annual Growth	9.6%	—	—	1.1%

Revenue History

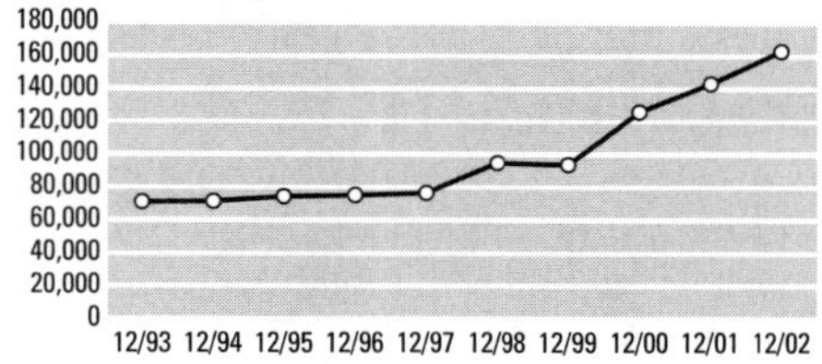

Blue Cross and Blue Shield of Massachusetts

Hobbled by its past, Blue Cross and Blue Shield of Massachusetts has worked its way back into the race. Serving more than 2.4 million members, it offers indemnity insurance, HMOs, preferred provider organizations, and Medicare extension programs. The not-for-profit organization runs HMO Blue, HMO Blue New England, and Blue Choice New England, as well as Medex, a Medicare supplemental plan. Blue Cross and Blue Shield of Massachusetts also teams up with other regional Blues to offer plans HMO Blue New England and Blue Choice New England, which feature discounts at some health clubs.

Blue Cross and Blue Shield of Massachusetts has battled its way back to financial health by selling noncore businesses and reducing staff after spending recent years in the red.

Like Blues nationwide, it has been hit hard by competition. The company is now refocusing on its core business (health insurance) through divestitures and new products. Blue Cross and Blue Shield of Massachusetts also entered the risky business of reinsurance.

HISTORY

The predecessor of the Blue Cross Association was founded in Dallas in 1929 to allow teachers to prepay for hospitalization. The idea spread quickly during the Depression. By 1937, when its 26th affiliate was founded in Massachusetts, the organization had become associated with the Blue Cross logo. Fairly priced by Depression standards, Blue Cross pegged its premiums to care costs in each region rather than underwriting each policyholder or group individually.

Seeing the success of Blue Cross, doctors joined up to offer similar prepayment plans known together as the Blue Shield Association. Doctor participation in Massachusetts was so widespread that members had a nearly unlimited choice of physicians.

Blue Cross and Blue Shield worked almost as one unit in Massachusetts but remained legally separate. At first they limited memberships to groups, but during the 1940s they began accepting individuals. In the 1960s the groups became co-administrators of the state's Medicare program. The Medex program was started in 1966 to supplement Medicare, but later evolved to encompass a state-mandated program for the medically indigent elderly. During the 1970s the companies began creating HMOs, but mostly for rural areas.

The groups continued to dominate Massachusetts health care in the 1980s. By the decade's end, however, the Massachusetts Blues had hit hard times, suffering lost market share, bloated management, and antiquated systems. As Blues in other states merged, competitors repeatedly blocked efforts to join the two Massachusetts organizations. Both Blues lost money from 1986 to 1988.

Efforts to help the situation only made matters worse (a failed upgrade of Blue Cross' information systems was abandoned in 1992 after six years and $100 million). The groups' efforts to drive harder bargains with hospitals led to cries that the plans were trying to force rejected hospitals out of business.

In 1988 the organizations were at last allowed to merge. William Van Faasen became CEO in 1990, charged with reengineering BCBSMA. For five years his efforts seemed to work. But the Medex segment was an earnings vacuum, and the new management drew criticism for hefty pay raises.

Blaming Medex, BCBSMA lost $90 million in 1996, which led the state insurance commissioner to step in and oversee its operations.

To make money like a regular health care company, BCBSMA started acting like a regular health care company — it slashed 16% of its workforce, enforced 10% pay cuts for those executives who survived a year-long purge, sold 10 clinics (to what is now Caremark Rx), and attempted to cancel 7,000 policies.

In 1998 BCBSMA agreed to pay $9.5 million to settle lawsuits that it overcharged Massachusetts subscribers for medical care. It also agreed in 1999 to pay $4.75 million to reimburse the US government for claims paid on people who were actually covered by BCBSMA. In the meantime, it created a new health insurance plan, Access Blue (launched in 2000), that lets patients see specialists without referrals. The plan has met resistance from hospitals and doctors, who consider its premiums too low to be financially viable.

BCBSMA filed to divide its operations into three companies, a move shot down by state legislators in 1998. Meanwhile, for-profit Blues licensees like Anthem continue to buy Blues (including those in Connecticut and New Hampshire). BCBSMA is pursuing affiliation with other not-for-profit regional Blues, although its attempt to do so in Rhode Island was rejected by the state's attorney general. In 2000, BCBSMA got state permission to enter the reinsurance business.

EXECUTIVES

Chairman Emeritus: Milton L. Glass
Chairman, President and CEO: William C. Van Faasen, age 54
Vice Chairman: Robert J. Haynes
COO: Arthur E. Banks
CFO: Allen P. Maltz
EVP and Chief Legal Officer: Sandra L. Jesse
EVP, Healthcare Services: Sharon L. Smith
EVP, Sales, Marketing, and Services: Stephen R. Booma
EVP, Corporate Affairs: Peter G. Meade
SVP, Corporate Relations: Fredi Shonkoff
SVP, Corporate Planning and Development: Phyllis L. Baron
SVP, Human Resources: Joseph Patrnchak
SVP and Chief Information Officer: Carl J. Ascenzo
Chief Actuary: Bruce W. Butler
Chief Medical Officer: James Fanale
Auditors: Ernst & Young LLP

LOCATIONS

HQ: Blue Cross and Blue Shield of Massachusetts
LandMark Center, 401 Park Dr., Boston, MA 02215
Phone: 617-246-5000 **Fax:** 617-246-4832
Web: www.bcbsma.com

PRODUCTS/OPERATIONS

Selected Services

Blue Care Elect Preferred (managed care plan)
Blue Choice (managed care plan)
Blue Choice New England (regional managed care)
Comprehensive Major Medical (traditional plan)
Dental Blue
Dental Blue PPO
Direct Blue (nongroup plans)
HMO Blue (statewide managed care)
HMO Blue New England (regional managed care)
Medex (Medicare supplement)

COMPETITORS

Aetna
Anthem
CIGNA
Harvard Pilgrim
Prudential
Tufts Health Plan

HISTORICAL FINANCIALS

Company Type: Not-for-profit

Income Statement FYE: December 31

	REVENUE ($ mil.)	NET INCOME ($ mil.)	NET PROFIT MARGIN	EMPLOYEES
12/02	4,043	104	2.6%	3,424
12/01	3,725	132	3.5%	3,396
12/00	2,883	110	3.8%	3,045
12/99	2,120	61	2.9%	2,601
12/98	2,041	64	3.1%	2,579
12/97	2,123	13	0.6%	2,756
12/96	3,504	(90)	—	5,500
12/95	3,575	11	0.3%	5,630
12/94	3,595	43	1.2%	5,865
12/93	3,792	54	1.4%	6,171
Annual Growth	0.7%	7.6%	—	(6.3%)

2002 Year-End Financials

Debt ratio: —
Return on equity: 15.4%
Cash ($ mil.): 1,626
Current ratio: —
Long-term debt ($ mil.): —

Net Income History

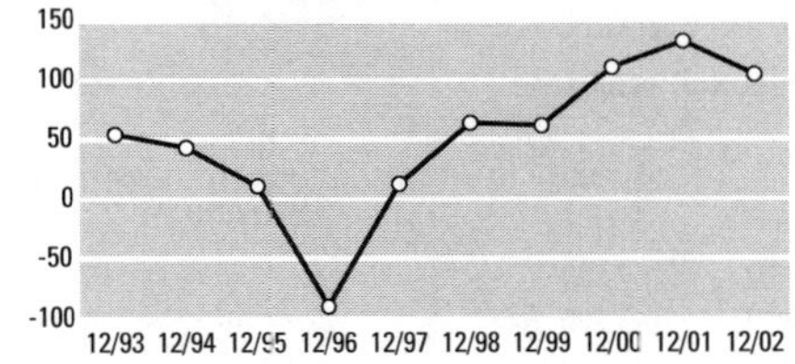

Blue Cross Blue Shield of Michigan

Blue Cross Blue Shield of Michigan is one of the nation's top Blue Cross Blue Shield health insurance associations, serving more than 4.8 million members, including autoworkers for GM and Ford. The company's insurance plans include traditional indemnity, Blue Preferred (PPO), and Blue Care Network (HMO). Blue Cross Blue Shield of Michigan also offers dental, vision, and Medicare supplement coverage, as well as workers' compensation insurance, health assessment, and health care management services. For-profit subsidiary Preferred Provider Organization of Michigan offers private health care management services.

For Blue Cross Blue Shield of Michigan, operating a "profitable" not-for-profit is a constant struggle.

While other Blues have converted to for-profit status or have teamed up with for-profit companies to become more competitive, BCBSM is committed to remaining not-for-profit. Rate hikes have helped get the company's insurance operations back into the black, and it plans to continue raising rates to keep up with the skyrocketing costs of health care.

HISTORY

The history of prepaid medical care began in 1929, when Baylor University Hospital administrator Justin Kimball developed a plan to offer schoolteachers 21 days of hospital care for $6 a year. Fundamental to the plan was a community rating system, which based premiums on the community's claims experience rather than subscribers' conditions.

A similar program was started in Michigan in 1938 when a group of hospitals formed the Michigan Society for Group Hospitalization, which became the Michigan Hospital Service and later became a chapter of the national Blue Cross association. The health care plan was funded by local hospitals and private grants. (A group of private donors, including Oldsmobile automotive founder Ransom Olds, loaned the group $5,000.)

The state insurance commission approved tax-exempt status for the Michigan Blue Cross in 1939. Nine days after opening a three-person office in Detroit, Blue Cross landed its first customer, insurance company John Hancock Mutual Life. John Hancock's Detroit branch manager became the first subscriber, paying $1.90 per month for 21 days of hospitalization coverage for his family of eight.

Due in part to the addition of Chrysler, Ford, and General Motors to its health plans, Blue Cross grew from less than 1 million members in the 1940s to more than 3 million in the 1950s. In 1945 it began to offer coverage for individuals; 14 years later the association started to offer policies to seniors who were ineligible for group coverage. Blue Cross took over operation of Michigan's Medicare program in 1966.

Michigan's Blue Cross merged with longtime partner Blue Shield in 1975 to create Blue Cross Blue Shield of Michigan, with a total of 5 million subscribers. Blue Shield, a prepayment plan that covered doctors' services, had been started in 1939 by the Michigan State Medical Society (a group of Michigan physicians).

As overseas competition forced automakers to cut their employment rolls, Blue Cross Blue Shield of Michigan's membership contracted. BCBSM chairman John McCabe, realizing the need to generate additional revenue, pushed for an end to the company's not-for-profit status in the 1980s but was rejected by the Michigan legislature. This failure was at least partially behind McCabe's resignation in 1987.

The struggling Michigan Blues moved toward profitability in 1994 when the state legislature specially authorized its $291 million purchase of the for-profit State Accident Fund, the state's workers' compensation program. It also lost its large but hard-to-manage state Medicare contract to Blue Cross Blue Shield of Illinois (now Health Care Service Corporation). In 1996 the company reorganized, with a division for Michigan residents and one for nationwide accounts. In 1997 BCBSM continued its efforts to increase revenue by acquiring private health management company Preferred Provider Organization of Michigan, which operates in Michigan and nearby states. BCBSM president and CEO Richard Whitmer announced that he was willing to compete with other Blues in bordering states.

In 1998 Blue Cross Blue Shield of Michigan consolidated four regional HMOs into a single statewide HMO, the Blue Care Network. Costs of the merger and growing losses in drug coverage constrained earnings, but were counterweighted by returns on assets invested in the stock market. In 1999 and 2000 the company rankled Detroit's small business owners with double-digit premium hikes.

EXECUTIVES

Chairman: Greg Sudderth
Vice Chairman: John MacKeigan
President and CEO: Richard E. Whitmer
SVP and CFO: Mark R. Bartlett
SVP and CIO: Raymond R. Khan
SVP, General Counsel, and Secretary: Steven C. Hess
SVP, Auto/National Business Unit: Leslie A. Viegas
SVP, Health Care Products and Provider Services: Marianne Udow
SVP, Human Resources, and Chief Administration Officer: George F. Francis III
SVP, Michigan Sales and Services: J. Paul Austin
SVP, Corporate Communications: Richard T. Cole
Auditors: Deloitte & Touche LLP

LOCATIONS

HQ: 600 E. Lafayette Blvd., Detroit, MI 48226
Phone: 313-225-9000 **Fax:** 313-225-5629
Web: www.bcbsm.com

PRODUCTS/OPERATIONS

Selected Health Care Plans

Blue Care Network (health maintenance)
Blue Choice (point of service)
Blue MedSave (prescription plan)
Blue Preferred PPO (preferred provider for auto industry workers)
Blue Traditional (prepayment)
Blue Vision PPO
Community Blue PPO
Community Dental
Medicare Blue HMO
Personal Plus HMO
Preferred Rx (prescription plan)
Traditional Dental
Traditional Rx (prescription plan)
Traditional Vision Coverage

COMPETITORS

Aetna
Anthem
CIGNA
Henry Ford Health System
Humana
United American Healthcare
UnitedHealth Group

HISTORICAL FINANCIALS

Company Type: Not-for-profit

Income Statement FYE: December 31

	REVENUE ($ mil.)	NET INCOME ($ mil.)	NET PROFIT MARGIN	EMPLOYEES
12/02	12,511	161	1.3%	8,500
12/01	11,883	56	0.5%	8,500
12/00	10,507	65	0.6%	8,500
12/99	9,487	89	0.9%	8,500
12/98	8,432	83	1.0%	8,500
12/97	7,731	43	0.6%	8,827
12/96	7,001	101	1.4%	7,980
12/95	6,926	154	2.2%	6,500
12/94	6,411	71	1.1%	8,415
12/93	6,193	120	1.9%	8,417
Annual Growth	8.1%	3.3%	—	0.1%

2002 Year-End Financials

Debt ratio: —
Return on equity: 11.4%
Cash ($ mil.): 492
Current ratio: —
Long-term debt ($ mil.): —

Net Income History

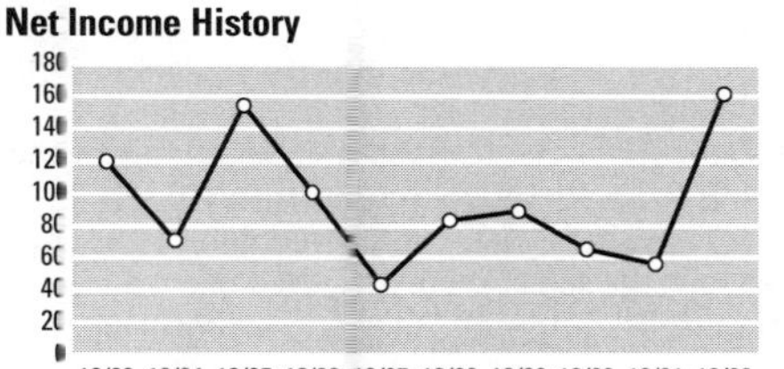

Bob Rohrman Auto Group

With about 35 dealerships in Indiana and around Chicago, Bob Rohrman Auto Group is after the lion's share of area car sales. The company sells more than 36,000 new and used vehicles annually from its dealerships in Chicago and in Indianapolis, Fort Wayne, and Lafayette, Indiana. Bob Rohrman offers new vehicles from most major auto manufacturers, including DaimlerChrysler, Ford, Honda, Hyundai, Isuzu, Kia, Mitsubishi, Nissan, and Toyota. It also sells auto parts and offers financing services. Its Web site features an inventory search for new and used cars. President and namesake Bob Rohrman owns the company, which he founded in 1963.

EXECUTIVES

President and CEO: Bob Rohrman
Comptroller and CFO: Tom Hanlan
Director of Fixed Operations: Ryan Turner
Director of Human Resources: Kim Sharp
Director of Operations: Craig Gipson

LOCATIONS

HQ: 701 Sagamore Pkwy. South, Lafayette, IN 47905
Phone: 765-448-1000 **Fax:** 765-449-2266
Web: www.rohrman.com

COMPETITORS

AutoNation
Continental Motors
Frank Consolidated Enterprises
Jeff Wyler Automotive
Jordan Automotive
Kelley Automotive
Loeber Motors
Motor Werks of Barrington
Patrick Dealer
Rizza Automotive Group
Steve Foley
Wolfe Automotive Group

HISTORICAL FINANCIALS

Company Type: Private

Income Statement FYE: December 31

	REVENUE ($ mil.)	NET INCOME ($ mil.)	NET PROFIT MARGIN	EMPLOYEES
12/02	633	—	—	1,000
12/01	694	—	—	1,000
12/00	649	—	—	1,000
12/99	639	—	—	1,000
12/98	509	—	—	900
12/97	494	—	—	1,000
12/96	450	—	—	900
Annual Growth	5.9%	—	—	1.8%

Revenue History

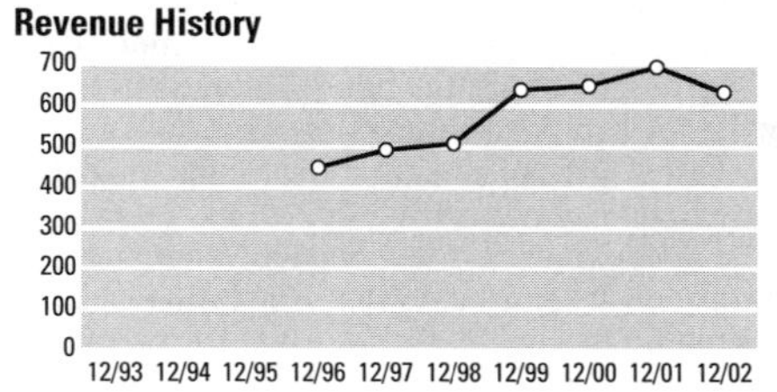

Boler Co.

Smooth is how Boler wants truck drivers to describe their ride. The holding company, which operates as Hendrickson International, makes truck and trailer suspension systems and auxiliary axle systems for the commercial heavy-duty vehicle market. The Hendrickson stamping division makes truck bumpers and stamped components. Hendrickson's spring division manufactures steel flat-leaf and parabolic taper-leaf springs. The company sells to OEMs in Europe and Latin America, as well as Australia, Japan, and the US. Chairman, president, and founder John Boler bought Hendrickson International in 1977 and continues to own the company.

EXECUTIVES

Chairman and President: John M. Boler
CFO: John Gaynor
VP, Sales: Keith Stevenson
Director, Human Resources: Peter Quagliana

LOCATIONS

HQ: 500 Park Blvd., Ste.1010, Itasca, IL 60143
Phone: 630-773-9111 **Fax:** 630-773-9121

Boler Co. has 14 manufacturing facilities and two product development centers in Asia, Europe, North America, and South America.

PRODUCTS/OPERATIONS

Selected Products

Bumpers
Lift axles
Springs
Tractor suspension systems
Trailer suspension systems
Truck suspension systems
Vehicle controls

COMPETITORS

ArvinMeritor, Inc.
Tower Automotive
Transportation Components
Transportation Technologies
Wozniak Industries

HISTORICAL FINANCIALS

Company Type: Private

Income Statement FYE: December 31

	ESTIMATED REVENUE ($ mil.)	NET INCOME ($ mil.)	NET PROFIT MARGIN	EMPLOYEES
12/01	600	—	—	500
12/00	675	—	—	3,600
12/99	675	—	—	3,500
12/98	550	—	—	3,000
12/97	450	—	—	2,500
12/96	500	—	—	3,000
12/95	625	—	—	3,000
12/94	600	—	—	3,000
Annual Growth	0.0%	—	—	(22.6%)

Revenue History

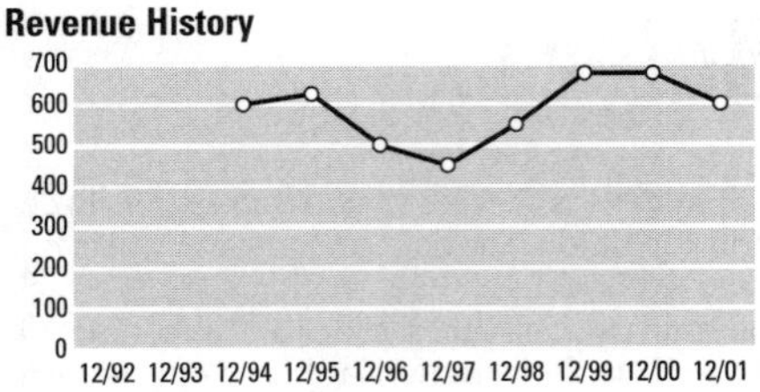

Bon Secours Health System

Bon Secours Health System succors the poor and sick. A not-for-profit organization dedicated to providing health care services to all, Bon Secours Health System was created in 1983 by the Sisters of Bon Secours, an international Roman Catholic order established in 1824 in Paris. Bon Secours Health System is composed of 24 acute-care hospitals, nine long-term-care facilities, and a psychiatric hospital. Bon Secours Health System also operates ambulatory sites, nursing care centers, assisted-living facilities, hospices, and home health care services.

Acquisitive Bon Secours has operations in nine states, primarily on the East Coast.

EXECUTIVES

Chairperson: Sister Patricia A. Eck
President and CEO: Christopher M. Carney
COO: Stephanie S. McCutcheon
SVP Finance and CFO: Michael W. Cottrell
SVP Business Development: John T. Shea
SVP Fund Development: Henry DeVries Jr.
SVP Corporate Services: Edward Boyer
SVP Operations, Northeast Division: Donald E. Strange
VP Human Resources: David D. Jones
VP Non Acute Services: Mary Anne Wilson
CEO, Bon Secours St. Francis Health System, Greenville, SC: Vanita Rutledge

LOCATIONS

HQ: Bon Secours Health System, Inc.
1505 Marriottsville Rd., Marriottsville, MD 21104
Phone: 410-442-5511 **Fax:** 410-442-1082
Web: www.bshsi.com

Selected Locations

Bon Secours & Canterbury Partnership for Care (NJ)
Bon Secours Baltimore Health System (MD)
Bon Secours Charity Health System (NY)
Bon Secours Charity Health System (PA)
Bon Secours Cottage Health Services (MI)
Bon Secours Hampton Roads Health System (VA)
Bon Secours Holy Family Regional Health System (PA)
Bon Secours Kentucky Health System (KY)
Bon Secours New York Health System (NY)
Bon Secours Richmond Health System (VA)
Bon Secours St. Francis Health System (SC)
Bon Secours St. Petersburg Health System (FL)
Bon Secours St. Joseph Healthcare Group (FL)
Bon Secours Venice Health Care Corporation (FL)
CareAlliance Health System (SC)

COMPETITORS

Carilion Health System
Catholic Health East
Inova
Johns Hopkins Medicine
MedStar
North Broward Hospital District
Novant Health
Sentara Healthcare
Trinity Health

HISTORICAL FINANCIALS

Company Type: Not-for-profit

Income Statement FYE: August 31

	REVENUE ($ mil.)	NET INCOME ($ mil.)	NET PROFIT MARGIN	EMPLOYEES
8/02	2,305	—	—	27,000
8/01	1,998	—	—	20,000
8/00	1,654	—	—	27,000
8/99	1,100	—	—	20,000
8/98	1,190	—	—	20,000
8/97	1,098	—	—	19,000
8/96	761	—	—	19,000
8/95	634	—	—	14,100
8/94	562	—	—	—
8/93	541	—	—	—
Annual Growth	17.5%	—	—	9.7%

Revenue History

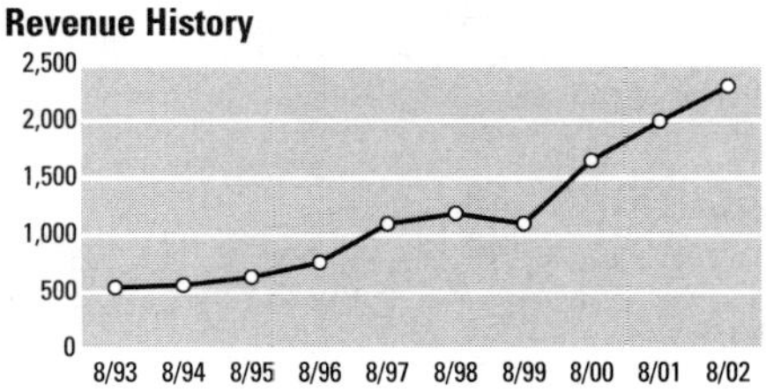

Booz Allen Hamilton Inc.

Booz Allen Hamilton has been on a big consulting bender for more than 80 years. Founded in 1914, the consultancy provides government agencies and *FORTUNE* 500 companies with international management and technology expertise. The firm operates in two segments: worldwide technology business and worldwide commercial business. Its technology business unit covers such areas as defense and national security, the environment, transportation, and space. The commercial unit includes consumer and engineered products; communications, media, and technology; energy; and financial services.

Booz Allen's staff of more than 12,000 covers the US and 30 other countries through more than 100 offices. The rising tide of privatization in many foreign governments has provided an increasing source of consulting work for the company, and Booz has plenty of experience working with governments: the US government is the company's largest customer. Booz Allen is also leveraging its government work in the commercial sector, specifically in such areas as strategic and information security as well as its experience in transportation and food and drug safety.

Despite the scaled back demand for consulting services that the company has faced in 2001 and 2002, Booz Allen Hamilton has continued to invest in growth opportunities such as its 2003 purchase of Gemini Consulting Japan.

HISTORY

Edwin Booz graduated from Northwestern University in 1914 with degrees in economics and psychology and started a statistical analysis firm in Chicago. After serving in the army during WWI, he returned to his firm, renamed Edwin Booz Surveys. In 1925 Booz hired his first full-time assistant, George Fry, and in 1929 he hired a second, James Allen. By then the company had a long list of clients, including U.S. Gypsum, the *Chicago Tribune,* and Montgomery Ward, which was losing a retail battle with Sears, Roebuck and Co.

In 1935 Carl Hamilton joined the partnership, and a year later it was renamed Booz, Fry, Allen & Hamilton. The firm prospered well into the next decade by providing advice based on "independence that enables us to say plainly from the outside what cannot always be said safely from within," according to a company brochure.

During WWII the firm worked increasingly on government and military contracts. Fry opposed the pursuit of such work for consultants and left in 1942. The firm was renamed Booz, Allen & Hamilton. Hamilton died in 1946, and the following year Booz retired (he died in 1951), leaving Allen as chairman. He successfully steered the firm into lucrative postwar work for clients such as Johnson Wax, RCA, and the US Air Force.

A separate company, Booz, Allen Applied Research, Inc. (BAARINC), was formed in 1955 for technical and government consulting, including missile and weaponry work, as well as consulting with NASA. By the end of the decade, *Time* had dubbed Booz Allen "the world's largest, most prestigious management consultant firm." The partnership was incorporated as a private company in 1962, and in 1967 commissioner Pete Rozelle requested its services for the merger of the National Football League and American Football League.

When Allen retired in 1970, Charlie Bowen became the new chairman, and the company went public. However, as the economy stalled during the energy crisis, spending for consultants plunged. Jim Farley replaced Bowen in 1975, and the company was taken private again in 1976. A turnaround was engineered, and the firm was soon helping Chrysler through its historic bailout and developing strategies for the breakup of AT&T.

Booz Allen again experienced troubles in the 1980s as Farley set up a competition to select his successor. In 1984 Michael McCullough was chosen, but the selection process had taken a toll on morale. McCullough began restructuring the firm along industry lines, creating a department store of services in an industry characterized by boutique houses. The turmoil was too much, and by 1988 nearly a third of the partners had quit.

William Stasior became chairman in 1991 and reorganized Booz Allen yet again, splitting it down public and private sector lines. James Allen died in 1992, the same year the firm moved to McLean, Virginia. The company began privatization work in the former Soviet Union and in Eastern Europe in 1992 and continued to emphasize government business, including contracts with the IRS (1995) for technology modernization and with the General Services Administration (1996) to provide technical and management support for all federal telecommunications users.

In 1998 the company won a 10-year, $200 million contract with the US Defense Department to establish a scientific and technical data warehouse. Ralph Shrader was appointed CEO in early 1999; Stasior retired as chairman later that year. Booz Allen acquired Scandinavian consulting firm Carta in 1999 and formed a venture capital firm for startups with Lehman Brothers in 2000. The company announced in late 2000 that it would spin off Aestix, its e-commerce business, but reconsidered amid a general economic slowdown and hostile IPO market.

EXECUTIVES

Chairman and CEO: Ralph W. Shrader
CFO: Doug Swenson
SVP: Keith Oliver
VP and Co-Leader, Global Security Practice: Mark Gerencser
VP and Director Infrastructure Assurance Center: Mike McConnell
President, Worldwide Commercial Business: Daniel C. Lewis
President, Worldwide Technology Business: Dennis Doughty
Chief Personnel Officer: DeAnne Aguirre
Senior Director Marketing and Communications: Marie Lerch

LOCATIONS

HQ: 8283 Greensboro Dr. McLean, VA 22102
Phone: 703-902-5000 **Fax:** 703-902-3333
Web: www.boozallen.com

Booz Allen Hamilton has more than 100 offices in the US and more than 30 other countries.

PRODUCTS/OPERATIONS

Selected Consulting Services

Commercial services
Corporate strategy
E-business strategy
Innovation
Knowledge management
Productivity improvement
Strategic security

Technology Business Services

Engineering
Information technology
Management consulting (systems development/systems integration)

COMPETITORS

Accenture
AMS
A.T. Kearney
Bain & Company
BearingPoint
Boston Consulting
Cap Gemini
Computer Sciences
Day & Zimmermann
Deloitte Consulting
IBM
Management Network Group
MAXIMUS
McKinsey & Company
PA Consulting
SRI International
Towers Perrin

HISTORICAL FINANCIALS

Company Type: Private

Income Statement

FYE: March 31

	REVENUE ($ mil.)	NET INCOME ($ mil.)	NET PROFIT MARGIN	EMPLOYEES
3/03	2,200	—	—	12,600
3/02	2,100	—	—	11,510
3/01	2,100	—	—	11,045
3/00	1,800	—	—	9,800
3/99	1,600	—	—	9,000
3/98	1,400	—	—	8,000
3/97	1,300	—	—	7,500
3/96	1,100	—	—	6,700
3/95	989	—	—	6,000
3/94	804	—	—	5,481
Annual Growth	11.8%	—	—	9.7%

Revenue History

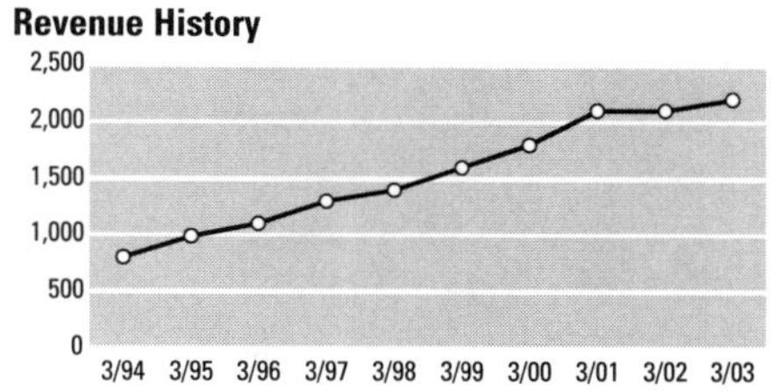

Borden Chemical, Inc.

A restructured (and renamed) Borden Chemical, Inc., has moved on from Cracker Jacks and dairy products and turned to the hard stuff: industrial chemicals. Since being bought by Kohlberg Kravis Roberts & Co. (KKR), the company (formerly Borden) has changed its focus. Borden Chemical's operations now consist of the production of formaldehyde, forest product resins, industrial resins, UV coatings, and oilfield products (proppants). Customers include businesses in the forest products, foundry, automotive, construction, composites, electronics, and oilfield industries.

Borden Chemical finally gave the last of its edibles the heave-ho late in 2001 when it jettisoned the remainder of its food interests (it had maintained management of certain operations even after their sale) and changed its name to Borden Chemical, Inc. It then got out of the consumer products business by selling the remainder of its Elmer's Products (consumer adhesives) division — one of the largest producers of household and school glues (Elmer's and Krazy Glue) in the US — in 2002.

In April 2003 Borden sold its Melamine Chemicals unit to Mississippi Chemical.

EXECUTIVES

Chairman: C. Robert Kidder, age 58, $1,736,280 pay (prior to title change)
President, CEO, and Director: Craig O. Morrison, age 47
EVP, CFO, Treasurer, and Director: William H. (Bill) Carter, age 49, $702,140 pay
EVP, Global Resins: John M. Kaestle, age 47
EVP, Performance Resins: Joseph P. (Jody) Bevilaqua, age 47
EVP, General Counsel, and Director: William F. (Bill) Stoll Jr., age 54, $589,068 pay
VP, Finance: George F. Knight
VP, Human Resources: Judy A. Sonnett, age 46
Auditors: Deloitte & Touche LLP

LOCATIONS

HQ: 180 E. Broad St., Columbus, OH 43215
Phone: 614-225-4000 **Fax:** —
Web: www.bordenchem.com

Borden has 21 production and manufacturing facilities in Australia, Canada, Europe, Malaysia, and South America and nearly 30 in the US.

2002 Sales

	$ mil.	% of total
US	813	65
Canada	171	14
Other countries	264	21
Total	**1,248**	**100**

PRODUCTS/OPERATIONS

Selected Operations

North American Forest Products:
Forest product resins
Formaldehyde

North American Performance Resins:
Foundry resins
Industrial resins
Laminate resins
Nonwoven resins
Oilfield resins
Specialty resins
UV coatings

International:
Forest product resins
Formaldehyde
Performance resins

COMPETITORS

Akzo Nobel
Ashland
BASF AG
Celanese
Dow Chemical
Dynea
DuPont
Georgia Gulf
Georgia-Pacific Corporation
Huntsman International
ICI
Lancaster Colony
Rohm and Haas
TOTAL
Valspar

HISTORICAL FINANCIALS

Company Type: Private

Income Statement

FYE: December 31

	REVENUE ($ mil.)	NET INCOME ($ mil.)	NET PROFIT MARGIN	EMPLOYEES
12/02	1,248	(37)	—	2,600
12/01	1,372	(125)	—	2,800
12/00	1,524	34	2.2%	4,000
12/99	1,360	53	3.9%	4,000
12/98	1,400	63	4.5%	4,200
12/97	3,482	278	8.0%	15,000
12/96	5,765	82	1.4%	20,000
12/95	5,944	(366)	—	27,500
12/94	5,626	(598)	—	32,300
12/93	5,506	(631)	—	41,900
Annual Growth	(15.2%)	—	—	(26.6%)

2002 Year-End Financials

Debt ratio: —
Return on equity: —
Cash ($ mil.): 15
Current ratio: 0.04
Long-term debt ($ mil.): 523

Net Income History

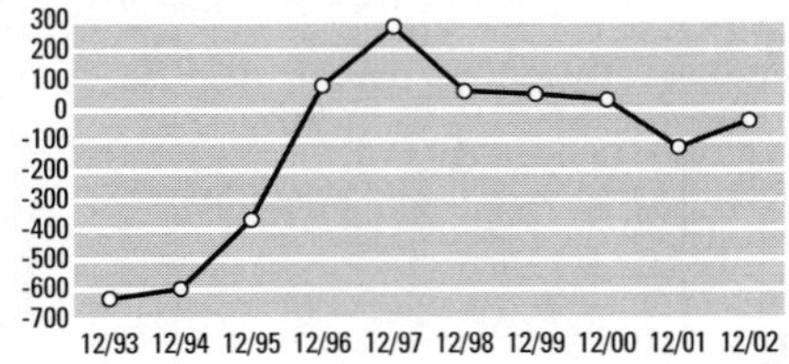

Boscov's Department Store

Outlet mall capital Reading, Pennsylvania, has conceived more than bargain shopping. It's given us Boscov's Department Store, which operates more than 35 department stores that anchor malls mainly in Pennsylvania, but also in Delaware, Maryland, New Jersey, and New York. The stores sell men's, women's, and children's apparel, shoes, and accessories; also jewelry, cosmetics, housewares, appliances, toys, and sporting goods. Some stores also feature travel agencies, vision centers, hair salons, and restaurants. The firm's charge card services are handled by its Boscov's Receivable Finance subsidiary. Boscov's was founded by Solomon Boscov in 1911 and is owned by the families of Albert Boscov and Edwin Lakin.

EXECUTIVES

Chairman, Boscov's, Inc.: Albert R. (Al) Boscov
President, Boscov's, Inc.: Edwin A. Lakin
Chairman and CEO, Boscov's Department Store, LLC: Kenneth S. Lakin
President and Chief Merchandising Officer, Boscov's Department Store, LLC: Burton C. Krieger
SVP and General Merchandise Manager: William H. Gallagher
SVP and General Merchandise Manager: Robert Oppenheimer
SVP, Operations: Larry Bergman
SVP, Human Resources: Ed Elko
SVP, Finance and Administration: Peter Lakin
Auditors: PricewaterhouseCoopers LLP

LOCATIONS

HQ: 4500 Perkiomen Ave., Reading, PA 19606
Phone: 610-779-2000 **Fax:** 610-370-3495
Web: www.boscovs.com

COMPETITORS

Bon-Ton Stores	Kohl's	Toys "R" Us
Federated	May	Wal-Mart
J. C. Penney	Sears	
Kmart	Target	

HISTORICAL FINANCIALS

Company Type: Private

Income Statement FYE: January 31

	REVENUE ($ mil.)	NET INCOME ($ mil.)	NET PROFIT MARGIN	EMPLOYEES
1/03	1,050	—	—	10,500
1/02	1,000	—	—	12,000
1/01	1,000	—	—	10,000
1/00	958	—	—	10,000
1/99	1,000	—	—	10,000
1/98	846	—	—	9,000
1/97	811	—	—	8,500
1/96	783	—	—	8,500
1/95	750	—	—	6,500
1/94	720	—	—	5,500
Annual Growth	4.3%	—	—	7.4%

Revenue History

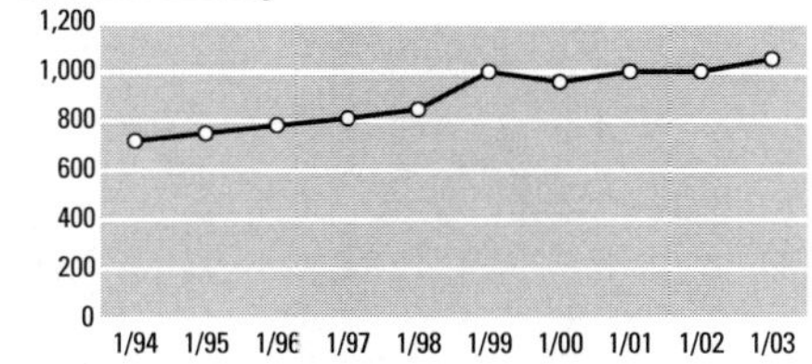

Bose Corporation

Bose doesn't subscribe to the theory that bigger is better. One of the world's leading speaker makers, the company has been concentrating on making its speakers smaller to better blend into home and office decors. Bose makes a variety of audio products, including auto sound systems and speakers, home stereo speakers, music systems, PC sound systems, aviation headsets, and professional loudspeakers. Its critically acclaimed Wave radio (compact in size but not in sound) has been a success despite its $350 price tag. Bose makes its goods in North America and Ireland and sells them through retailers and about 100 of its own stores worldwide. Founder Amar Bose, an MIT professor, is the company's largest shareholder.

Bose keeps his company sharp with unconventional products and methods. The firm stands out by offering tiny, yet technologically advanced, products such as palm-sized cube speakers and compact radios with rich sound. To stay on the cutting edge, Bose invests much of its profits in research and development. The company has operations in Australia, Canada, Europe, Japan, and the US and is entering markets in Russia, China, and India.

HISTORY

Music and electronics struck a chord in Amar Bose, the son of an Indian emigrant from Calcutta. As a youngster he studied violin and liked fixing electronic gadgets. A teenaged Bose started a radio repair shop in his basement during WWII that turned out to be the family's main source of income when his father's import business faltered during the war. Bose's interest in electronics led him to college at MIT in 1947.

His quest to develop a better sound system began nearly a decade later when the hi-fi stereo he bought as a reward for doing well in his graduate studies made his violin record sound shrill. MIT allowed Bose to research the topic while he taught there. He formed his namesake company in 1964 and hired as its first employee Sherwin Greenblatt, a former student who later became company president.

Bose discovered that most speaker systems funneled sound directly at the listener, while live concerts sent sound directly and indirectly by bouncing it off walls, floors, and ceilings. He designed a system in which only some speakers are aimed at the listener while others reflect the sounds around the room. Calling the concept "reflected sound," Bose began selling his 901 stereo speakers in 1968.

A feud with *Consumer Reports* showed the arrogant side of the self-made entrepreneur. After the magazine concluded in a 1970 review that Bose speakers created a sound that tended to "wander around the room," Bose sued, claiming product disparagement. (The lawsuit was settled 13 years later when the Supreme Court ruled in favor of *Consumer Reports*.) Bose began making professional loudspeakers in 1972.

After trying and failing to gain market share in Japan throughout the 1970s, in 1978 Bose hired sales executive Sumi Sakura, who convinced 400 Japanese dealers to find space in their jam-packed stores for Bose products. Sales jumped within months. Bose also turned his attention to car stereos in the 1970s. After promising talks with General Motors in 1979, he risked $13 million and four years developing a stereo that could be custom-designed for cars. The first one was offered in 1983 in a Cadillac Seville. Contracts with other major carmakers followed, usually for their top-of-the-line models.

In the 1980s the company took its technology to TV sets. With an agreeable guinea pig in Zenith, Bose developed a speaker tube that could coil inside the set without adding much bulk. The set was a hit, even with a price tag of more than $1,400 (in 1987). The firm's speakers were also used in several space shuttle flights, beginning in 1992 with *Endeavour*.

The critically acclaimed Wave radio was introduced in 1993 and has been a huge success, even though it is primarily offered through direct mail. A year later Bose acquired professional loudspeaker maker US Sound from Carver. In 1996 it teamed up with satellite TV firm PRIMESTAR to offer the home theater Companion systems. (The systems were discontinued in 1999, dissolving the partnership.) The next year Bose and IBM paired up to upgrade the quality of PC sound systems.

Bose upped the ante on its retail operations in 1997 when it began opening more upscale showcase stores where audiophiles can test sound systems at in-store music theaters. The company began making its sound systems for more mainstream cars, such as the Chevrolet Blazer, the following year. In 1999 Bose began selling its products online and introduced a new version of its popular Wave radio (with a CD player). In 2001 Bose introduced the Bose Wave/PC interactive system that provides one-touch access to Internet radio, digital audio files, AM/FM radio, and CDs through a personal computer.

EXECUTIVES

Chairman and CEO: Amar G. Bose, age 73
President: John Coleman
VP, Engineering: Joseph Veranth
VP, Europe: Nic A. Merks
VP, Finance and CFO: Daniel A. Grady, age 67
VP, Human Resources: John Ferrie
VP, Manufacturing: Thomas Beeson
VP, Research: Thomas Froeschle
VP, Sales: David Wood
VP: Sumiyoshi Sakura
Secretary: Alexander Bernhard
Assistant Secretary: Mark E. Sullivan
Treasurer: William R. Swanson
Director of Public Relations: Carolyn Cinotti
Director of Retail Development: Linda Pilla
Auditors: PricewaterhouseCoopers LLP

LOCATIONS

HQ: The Mountain, Framingham, MA 01701
Phone: 508-879-7330 **Fax:** 508-766-7543
Web: www.bose.com

Bose has plants in Canada, Ireland, Mexico, and the US.

PRODUCTS/OPERATIONS

Selected Products

Aircraft entertainment systems
Auto sound systems and speakers
Aviation headsets
Custom home audio systems
Home stereo speakers
Marine speakers
Multimedia speakers
Music systems
Outdoor audio systems
PC sound systems
Professional loudspeakers
Radios
Speaker accessories

COMPETITORS

Aiwa
Allen Organ Company
Bang & Olufsen
Boston Acoustics
Cambridge SoundWorks
Creative Technology
Emerson Radio
Harman International
Jamo
Kenwood
Koss
Matsushita
Mitek Corp.
Paradigm Electronics
Philips Electronics
Phoenix Gold
Pioneer
Polk Audio
QSC
Rockford
Ruark Acoustics
Sharp
Snell Acoustics
Sony
Stanton Group
Telex Communications
Victor Company of Japan
Yamaha

HISTORICAL FINANCIALS

Company Type: Private

Income Statement FYE: March 31

	REVENUE ($ mil.)	NET INCOME ($ mil.)	NET PROFIT MARGIN	EMPLOYEES
3/03	1,600	—	—	8,000
3/02	1,300	—	—	7,000
3/01	1,250	—	—	7,000
3/00	1,100	—	—	6,000
3/99	950	—	—	4,000
3/98	850	—	—	4,000
3/97	750	—	—	4,000
3/96	700	—	—	3,500
3/95	600	—	—	3,100
3/94	500	—	—	3,100
Annual Growth	13.8%	—	—	11.1%

Revenue History

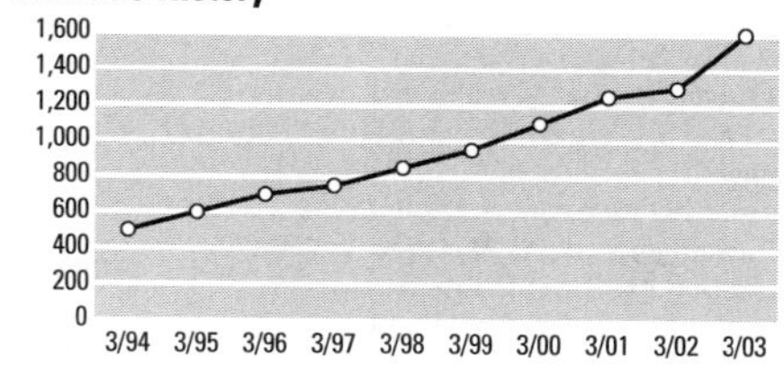

The Boston Consulting Group

Global corporations are willing to give much more than a penny for the thoughts of management consulting firm Boston Consulting Group (BCG). Founded in 1963 by consulting pioneer Bruce Henderson, BCG is one of the top ranked consulting practices in the world, serving leading firms in such industries as consumer goods, financial services, and telecommunications. Its nearly 3,000 consultants assist clients in developing and implementing corporate strategies, improving efficiencies, and integrating new technologies. The firm is noted for developing and applying its own original consulting concepts, such as "time-based competition" (rapid response to change) and "deconstruction" (an end to vertical integration).

Although the employee-owned firm is nearly 40 years old, BCG remains on the cutting edge of the technology-fueled economy and is regarded as one of the premier e-commerce consultancies. BCG has established several "Web labs" to create e-commerce sites and other online products for its clients. The next great frontier for the group is China, where the firm is growing its business. It has announced plans to expand its staff there within three years.

However, like most firms, BCG has felt the strain of the weakening economy and strategy consultants have taken an even bigger hit as companies cut consulting from their budgets. As a result BCG has laid off 12% of its staff.

EXECUTIVES

Chairman: John S. Clarkeson, age 60
President and CEO: Carl Stern, age 57
CFO: Hugh Simons
Media Relations: Erol (K.C.) Munuz

LOCATIONS

HQ: Exchange Place, 31st Fl., Boston, MA 02109
Phone: 617-973-1200 **Fax:** 617-973-1399
Web: www.bcg.com

Boston Consulting Group has 55 offices in more than 30 countries.

PRODUCTS/OPERATIONS

Selected Practice Areas

Branding
Corporate development
E-commerce
Energy
Financial services
Globalization
Health care
Industrial goods
Information technology
Operational effectiveness
Organization
Pricing
Technology communications
Travel and tourism

COMPETITORS

Accenture
A.T. Kearney
Bain & Company
BearingPoint
Booz Allen
Deloitte Consulting
Marsh & McLennan
McKinsey & Company
PricewaterhouseCoopers
Towers Perrin

HISTORICAL FINANCIALS

Company Type: Private

Income Statement FYE: December 31

	REVENUE ($ mil.)	NET INCOME ($ mil.)	NET PROFIT MARGIN	EMPLOYEES
12/02	1,020	—	—	4,000
12/01	1,050	—	—	4,450
12/00	1,100	—	—	4,300
12/99	948	—	—	4,334
12/98	730	—	—	3,000
12/97	655	—	—	2,000
12/96	600	—	—	1,550
12/95	550	—	—	1,320
12/94	430	—	—	1,246
12/93	340	—	—	—
Annual Growth	13.0%	—	—	15.7%

Revenue History

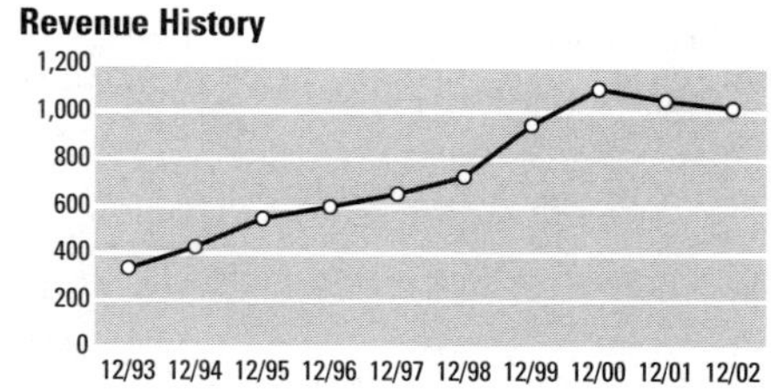

Bozzuto's Inc.

If you shop at an IGA supermarket within 250 miles of Cheshire, Connecticut, then Bozzuto's will keep you grinning. The company distributes food and other items to independent supermarkets belonging to the IGA network. The wholesaler supplies more than 100 stores with food, tobacco products, and household items under national brands as well as the IGA and Bestway labels. It also provides store design, administrative, marketing, and inventory management services. Bozzuto's owns Adams Super Food Stores, a Cheshire-based supermarket chain. Founded in

1945 as John Bozzuto & Sons, Bozzuto's serves stores in New England, New York, New Jersey, and Pennsylvania. Founder Adam Bozzuto passed away in mid-2002.

EXECUTIVES

Chairman, President, and CEO: Michael A. Bozzuto
EVP, Finance and CFO: Mark G. Kindig
EVP, Retail Development: George Motel
VP and General Counsel: Kevin Daly
VP, Finance: Robert H. Wood
VP, Sales: Dan Brock
Corporate Secretary and Assistant Treasurer: Patricia S. Houle
Director, Human Resources: Doug Vaughn

LOCATIONS

HQ: 275 School House Rd., Cheshire, CT 06410
Phone: 203-272-3511 **Fax:** 203-250-2953
Web: www.bozzutos.com

COMPETITORS

C&S Wholesale
Di Giorgio
Fleming Companies
Krasdale Foods
Nash Finch
Shaw's
Stop & Shop
SUPERVALU
Wakefern Food

HISTORICAL FINANCIALS

Company Type: Private

Income Statement FYE: September 30

	REVENUE ($ mil.)	NET INCOME ($ mil.)	NET PROFIT MARGIN	EMPLOYEES
9/02	900	—	—	1,050
9/01	850	—	—	1,025
9/00	777	—	—	1,000
9/99	685	—	—	900
9/98	650	—	—	800
Annual Growth	8.5%	—	—	7.0%

Revenue History

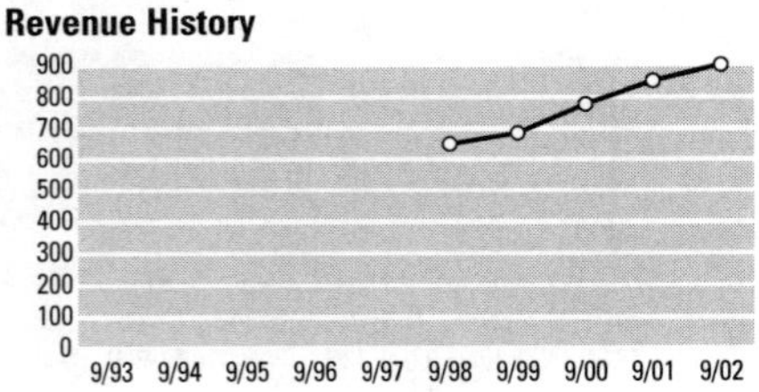

Bradco Supply

Bradco Supply offers construction contractors everything they need to put a roof over their clients' heads. The company distributes roofing, siding, windows, and other building materials through more than 100 locations in 25 states. Founded in 1966, Bradco Supply is one of the nation's largest distributors of roofing materials for commercial use. It also exports its construction materials to Africa, the Caribbean, Europe, Latin America, and the Middle East. The company has been acquiring smaller roofing material businesses. CEO Barry Segal owns Bradco Supply.

EXECUTIVES

CEO: Barry Segal
President: Bradley (Brad) Segal
CFO and Treasurer: Steven (Steve) Feinberg
Controller: Joe Stacy
Accounting Manager: Susan Biunno
Information Systems Manager: Joe Hradil
Marketing Manager: Elaine Ferrie
Marketing Manager: Fran Frank
General Counsel: Michael L. Weinberger

LOCATIONS

HQ: Bradco Supply Corp.
13 Production Way, Avenel, NJ 07001
Phone: 732-382-3400 **Fax:** 732-382-6577
Web: www.bradcosupply.com

COMPETITORS

ABC Supply
Builder Marts
CRH
Georgia-Pacific Corporation
Guardian Building Products
Huttig Building Products
North Pacific Group
PrimeSource Building

HISTORICAL FINANCIALS

Company Type: Private

Income Statement FYE: December 31

	REVENUE ($ mil.)	NET INCOME ($ mil.)	NET PROFIT MARGIN	EMPLOYEES
12/02	850	—	—	1,770
12/01	800	—	—	1,450
12/00	700	—	—	1,425
12/99	600	—	—	1,300
12/98	523	—	—	1,200
12/97	475	—	—	1,100
Annual Growth	12.3%	—	—	10.0%

Revenue History

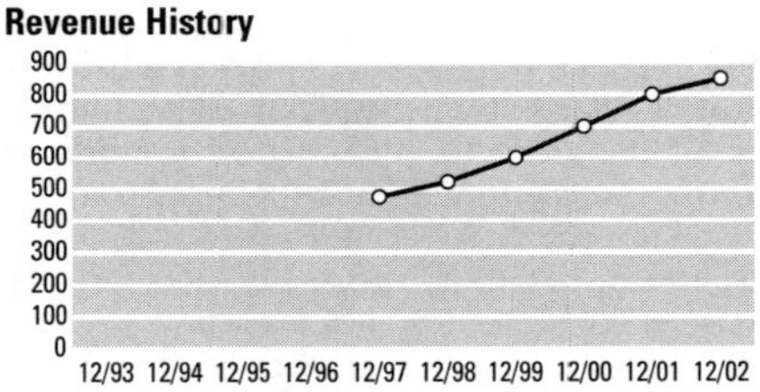

Braman Management Association

It's no bull to say that Braman Management sells cars fit for Brahmans. Braman Management operates four dealerships in Florida and three in Colorado. The company's dealerships, most of which operate under the Braman name, sell upscale makes such as Acura, Audi, Bentley, BMW, Cadillac, Mercedes, Porsche, and Rolls-Royce; it also sells new Hondas, MINIs, and Mitsubishis and a variety of used cars. Each Braman location offers parts and service departments. Owner and CEO Norman Braman, who once owned the Philadelphia Eagles, formed Braman Management in 1972.

EXECUTIVES

President and CEO: Norman Braman
CFO: Robert E. Bernstein
Director of Human Resources: Linda Brickman

LOCATIONS

HQ: 2060 Biscayne Blvd., 2nd Fl., Miami, FL 33137
Phone: 305-576-1889 **Fax:** 305-576-9898
Web: www.braman.com

COMPETITORS

AutoNation
Buchanan Automotive
Ferman Automotive
Germain Motor
Group 1 Automotive
JM Family Enterprises
Kuni Automotive
March/Hodge
Morse Operations
Phil Long Dealerships
Scott-McRae Group

HISTORICAL FINANCIALS

Company Type: Private

Income Statement FYE: December 31

	REVENUE ($ mil.)	NET INCOME ($ mil.)	NET PROFIT MARGIN	EMPLOYEES
12/01	500	—	—	1,100
12/00	500	—	—	950
12/99	500	—	—	900
12/98	500	—	—	850
12/97	536	—	—	806
12/96	480	—	—	800
12/95	423	—	—	750
12/94	392	—	—	750
12/93	600	—	—	830
12/92	600	—	—	850
Annual Growth	(2.0%)	—	—	2.9%

Revenue History

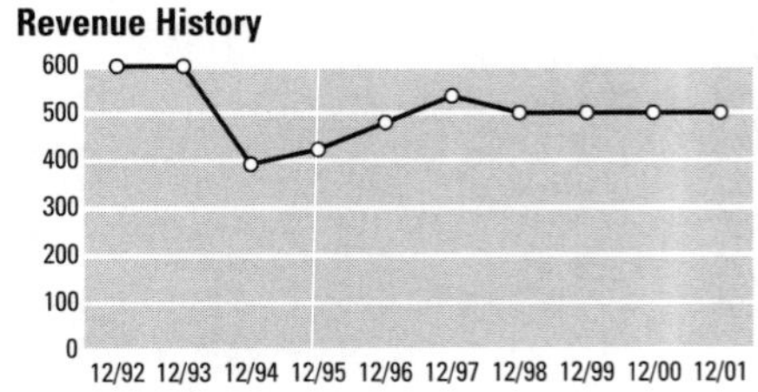

Brasfield & Gorrie, LLC

Brasfield & Gorrie makes a big splash in the southeastern US. Among the construction company's projects are the Georgia Aquarium and the VisionLand amusement and water park in Alabama. Other projects include health care facilities, hotels, industrial plants, multistory offices, retail complexes, schools, and water-treatment plants. Commercial and industrial construction together account for most of its revenues. It provides general contracting, design/build, and construction management services through 12 operating divisions and offices in Alabama, Florida, Georgia, North Carolina, and Tennessee. Founded in 1922 by Thomas C. Brasfield, the company was sold to owner Miller Gorrie (chairman and CEO) in 1964.

EXECUTIVES

Chairman and CEO: M. Miller Gorrie, age 67
President: Jim Gorrie
VP and COO: Jeff Stone
CFO: Randall J. Freeman
CIO: Tom Garrett
Controller: Earl Whatley
Director Marketing: Missy Mauk
Director Human Resources: Kelly Crane
Corporate Accounting: Gail Black
Auditors: PricewaterhouseCoopers

LOCATIONS

HQ: 729 S. 30th St., Birmingham, AL 35233
Phone: 205-328-4000 **Fax:** 205-251-1304
Web: www.brasfieldgorrie.com

Brasfield & Gorrie has offices in Atlanta; Birmingham, Alabama; Nashville; Orlando; and Raleigh, North Carolina.

PRODUCTS/OPERATIONS

Major Sectors

Auto and industrial
Commercial
Health care
Institutional
Retail
Treatment plants

COMPETITORS

Alberici
BE&K
Bechtel
Beck Group
Bovis Lend Lease
Choate Construction
Hardin Construction
H.J. Russell
McCarthy Building
Peter Kiewit Sons'
Skanska USA Building
Turner Corporation
Whiting-Turner

HISTORICAL FINANCIALS

Company Type: Private

Income Statement FYE: December 31

	REVENUE ($ mil.)	NET INCOME ($ mil.)	NET PROFIT MARGIN	EMPLOYEES
12/01	943	—	—	2,000
12/00	849	—	—	2,000
12/99	646	—	—	1,765
12/98	566	—	—	1,375
12/97	477	—	—	1,539
Annual Growth	18.6%	—	—	6.8%

Revenue History

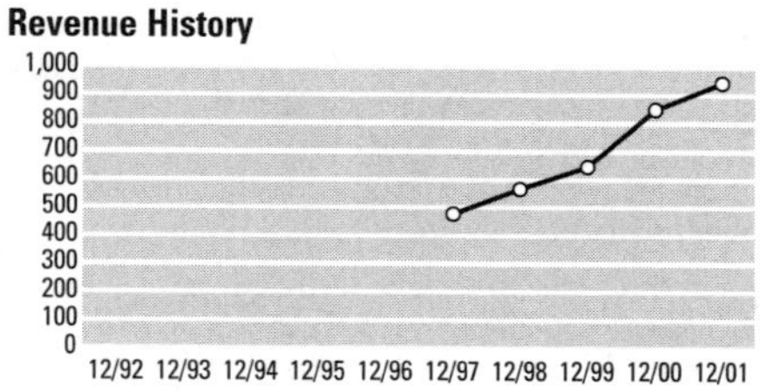

Brazos Electric Power

Brazos means "arms" in Spanish, and the generation and transmission arms of Brazos Electric Power Cooperative reach across 66 Texas counties. Founded in 1941, the utility was the state's first electricity generation and transmission cooperative. It serves 17 member/owner distribution cooperatives, three municipalities, and one university in northern and Central Texas. Brazos Electric Power has 700 MW of fossil-fueled generating capacity; it also purchases about 1,300 MW from other utilities and marketers. Pipeline subsidiary Brazos Fuel purchases and distributes the cooperative's natural gas supply.

EXECUTIVES

President, Board of Directors: John Hartgraves
VP, Board of Directors: Ronnie Robinson
EVP and General Manager: Clifton B. Karnei
VP Accounting Services: Khaki Bordovsky
VP Generation: David Murphy
VP Power Supply and Marketing: Hugh F. Lewox
VP Transmission: Johnny A. York
Secretary, Treasurer, and Director: Loyd Jackson
Director Human Resources: J. Thomas (Tom) Yows Jr.
Auditors: PricewaterhouseCoopers LLP

LOCATIONS

HQ: Brazos Electric Power Cooperative, Inc.
2404 La Salle Ave., Waco, TX 76706
Phone: 254-750-6500 **Fax:** 254-750-6292
Web: www.brazoselectric.com

Brazos Electric Power Cooperative has operations in 66 counties in northern and Central Texas.

PRODUCTS/OPERATIONS

Member/Owners

Barlett Electric Cooperative
Belfalls Electric Cooperative
Comanche Electric Cooperative
Cooke County Electric Cooperative
CoServ Electric
Fort Belknap Electric Cooperative
Hamilton County Electric Cooperative
HILCO Electric Cooperative
J-A-C Electric Cooperative
McLennan County Electric Cooperative
Mid-South Electric Cooperative
Navarro County Electric Cooperative
Navasota Valley Electric Cooperative
South Plains Electric Cooperative
Tri-County Electric Cooperative
United Cooperative Services
Wise Electric Cooperative

COMPETITORS

AEP
Cap Rock Energy
CenterPoint Energy
El Paso Electric
Entergy
LCRA
TNP Enterprises
TXU

HISTORICAL FINANCIALS

Company Type: Cooperative

Income Statement FYE: December 31

	REVENUE ($ mil.)	NET INCOME ($ mil.)	NET PROFIT MARGIN	EMPLOYEES
12/02	433	—	—	315
12/01	456	—	—	309
12/00	290	—	—	295
12/99	300	—	—	275
12/98	287	—	—	300
12/97	278	—	—	300
12/96	260	—	—	—
12/95	235	—	—	—
12/94	217	—	—	300
12/93	220	—	—	290
Annual Growth	7.8%	—	—	0.9%

Revenue History

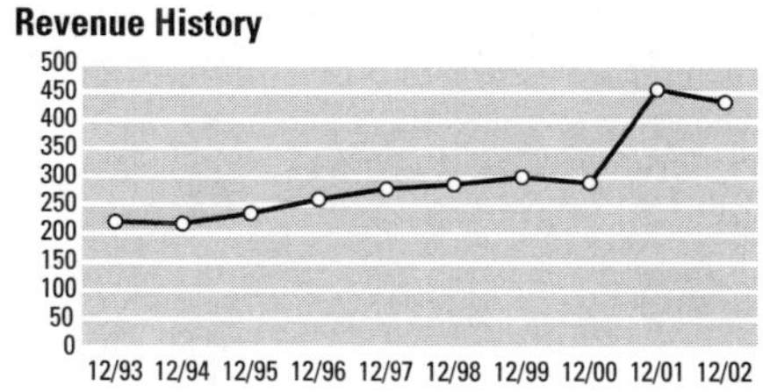

BREED Technologies

BREED Technologies is a leading manufacturer of air bags and air bag components. The company also makes steering wheels and seat belts. BREED's line of air bag products includes sensors, inflators, driver-side and steering-wheel air bag combinations, and side-impact air bag systems. The company supplies air bag systems to most of the world's carmakers. BREED also makes a line of interior trim products including automatic and manual shift knobs, park brake handles, shift and brake boots, armrest covers, pull handles, and other assorted trim components. The Carlyle Group's Key Automotive Group controls the company.

After a mid-1990s buying spree left BREED awash in debt, the company found itself under bankruptcy protection. The company emerged from Chapter 11 in late 2000 and has been taken private. Carlyle principal B. Edward Ewing became CEO of BREED in early 2003 and soon announced plans to achieve $200 million in cost savings for fiscal 2003. To this end the company has plans to lay off 3,500 people across the company's global operations by the end of 2004 (27% of the workforce), and is seeking price breaks from its suppliers.

The company also has plans to lose the BREED name. The company will be folded into the operations of Key Automotive Group and do business as Key Safety Systems.

EXECUTIVES

Chairman and CEO: B. Edward Ewing
SVP and CFO: Larry Schwentor
SVP, Engineering and CTO: Craig W. White
SVP, Human Resources: Rick Blough
SVP, Legal: Stuart D. Boyd
President and COO, Asia: Jason Luo
President and COO, Europe: Giulio Zambeletti
President and COO, North America: Douglas Nyhoff

LOCATIONS

HQ: BREED Technologies, Inc.
5300 Allen K. Breed Hwy., Lakeland, FL 33811
Phone: 863-668-6000 **Fax:** 863-668-6007
Web: www.breedtech.com

BREED Technologies operates facilities in Alabama, California, Tennessee, Texas, and Wisconsin; as well as in China, France, Germany, Italy, Japan, Korea, Mexico, Thailand, and the UK.

PRODUCTS/OPERATIONS

Selected Products

Airbag systems, inflators, and modules
Armrest covers
Electronics (crash sensors)
Park brake handles
Seat-belt systems
Shift and brake boots
Shift knobs
Steering wheels

COMPETITORS

Analog Devices
Autoliv
Denso
Fondmetal
Honeywell International
Motorola
Oki Electric
OZ Italy Wheel
PerkinElmer
Robert Bosch
SensoNor
Siemens
Temic
Texas Instruments
Tokai Rika

HISTORICAL FINANCIALS

Company Type: Private

Income Statement FYE: June 30

	REVENUE ($ mil.)	NET INCOME ($ mil.)	NET PROFIT MARGIN	EMPLOYEES
6/02	1,100	—	—	16,000
6/01	1,422	—	—	16,000
6/00	1,400	—	—	16,100
6/99	1,400	—	—	16,200
6/98	1,385	—	—	16,300
6/97	795	—	—	11,100
6/96	432	—	—	7,000
6/95	401	—	—	4,800
6/94	278	—	—	3,200
6/93	154	—	—	1,804
Annual Growth	24.5%	—	—	27.4%

Revenue History

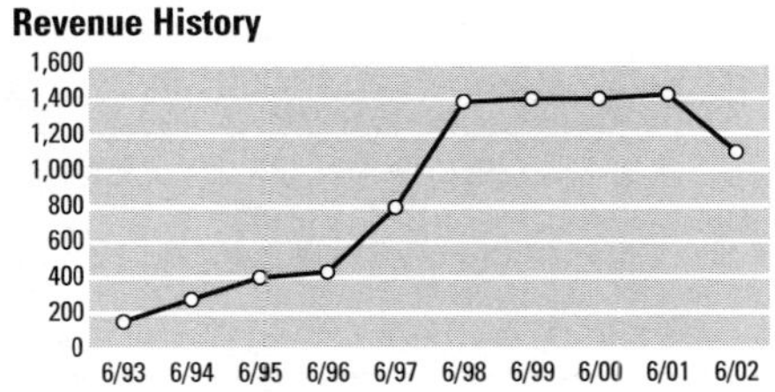

Broder Bros. Co.

Selling clothes is in the genes of sportswear distributor Broder Bros. Co. Begun as a haberdashery in 1919, the company evolved from hats and gloves to distributing imprintable sportswear such as golf shirts, T-shirts, sweatshirts, and jerseys. Broder Bros. also offers its private-label Luna Pier outerwear. Customers, mostly small retailers in the US, can view and order merchandise through seasonal catalogs or online. Broder Bros. bought rival Full Line Distributors in August 2001, and it agreed in September 2003 to acquire Philadelphia-based Alpha Shirt. Private investment firm Bain Capital acquired a majority interest of the company in May 2000.

EXECUTIVES

President: Vincent Tyra
CFO: Howard Morof
VP, Controller: Diane Miller
VP, Finance: David Hollister
VP, IT: Daniel (Dan) Abell
VP, Operations: Norman Hollinger
Director, Purchasing: Kurt Schloss
Director, Human Resources: Linda MacEllven

LOCATIONS

HQ: 45555 Port St., Plymouth, MI 48170
Phone: 734-454-4800 **Fax:** 800-521-1251
Web: www.broderbros.com

Broder Bros. Co. has distribution centers in Albany, New York; Atlanta, Georgia; Charlotte, North Carolina; Cleveland; Dallas; Detroit; Fresno, California; Fullerton, California; Houston; Louisville, Kentucky; Miami; Orlando, Florida; St. Louis, Missouri; Wadesboro, North Carolina; and Plymouth, Michigan.

COMPETITORS

Delta Apparel
Dickie Walker Marine
Drew Pearson Marketing
Gildan Activewear
PremiumWear
Russell Corporation

HISTORICAL FINANCIALS

Company Type: Private

Income Statement FYE: December 31

	REVENUE ($ mil.)	NET INCOME ($ mil.)	NET PROFIT MARGIN	EMPLOYEES
12/01	486	—	—	815
12/00	439	—	—	797
12/99	344	—	—	675
12/98	328	—	—	552
12/97	270	—	—	500
Annual Growth	15.8%	—	—	13.0%

Revenue History

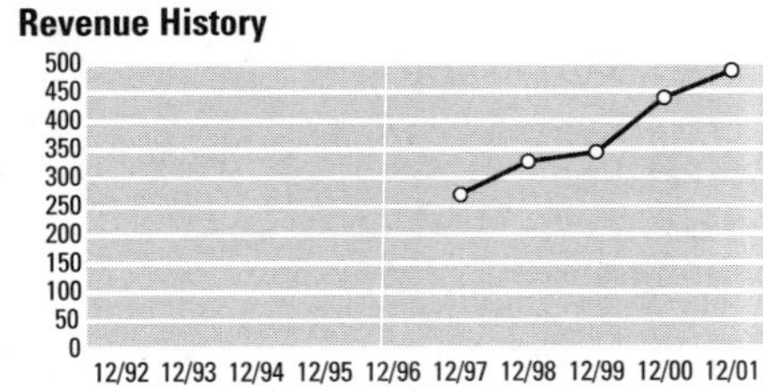

Brookshire Brothers, Ltd.

From its roots in East Texas the Brookshire Brothers supermarket chain now has 70-plus locations stretching from Louisiana to Central Texas. The company primarily operates under the Brookshire Brothers banner, although a few fly the B&B Foods, Budget Chopper, and Celebration Foods flags. Nearly all of the stores feature outlets selling Conoco gasoline (the company is one of Conoco's largest distributors). Brookshire Brothers is not affiliated with Brookshire Grocery of Tyler, Texas. The companies share a common ancestry dating back to 1921, but a split between the founding brothers in the late 1930s resulted in separate grocery chains. Formerly family-owned, Brookshire Brothers is now 67%-owned by employees.

EXECUTIVES

EVP and CFO: Donny Johnson
EVP and Chief Administrative Officer: Jerry Johnson
EVP, Retail Operations: Jack Gabriel
VP, Human Resource and Risk Management: Robert Gilmer

LOCATIONS

HQ: 1201 Ellen Trout Dr., Lufkin, TX 75902
Phone: 936-634-8155 **Fax:** 936-633-4611
Web: www.brookshirebrothers.com

2003 Stores

	No.
Texas	67
Louisiana	5
Total	**72**

PRODUCTS/OPERATIONS

2003 Stores

	No.
Brookshire Brothers	60
B&B	9
Budget Chopper	1
Celebration Foods	1
Petro Barn	1
Total	**72**

COMPETITORS

Albertson's
Fiesta Mart
Gerland's Food Fair
H-E-B
Kroger
Randall's
Wal-Mart

HISTORICAL FINANCIALS

Company Type: Private

Income Statement FYE: April 30

	ESTIMATED REVENUE ($ mil.)	NET INCOME ($ mil.)	NET PROFIT MARGIN	EMPLOYEES
4/02	700	—	—	6,000
4/01	750	—	—	6,000
4/00	700	—	—	5,500
4/99	675	—	—	5,500
4/98	700	—	—	5,500
4/97	725	—	—	5,563
4/96	690	—	—	5,300
4/95	675	—	—	5,200
4/94	650	—	—	5,000
4/93	600	—	—	5,000
Annual Growth	1.7%	—	—	2.0%

Revenue History

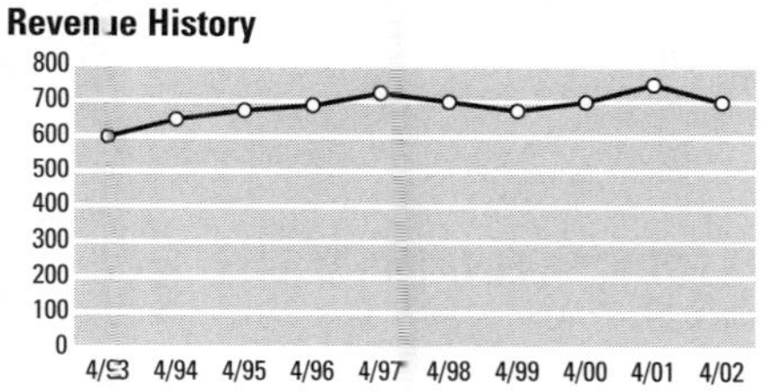

Brookshire Grocery

By selling staples, specialties, and Southern hospitality, Brookshire Grocery Company has grown into a chain of about 135 Brookshire's and Super 1 Food supermarkets in Texas, Arkansas, Louisiana, and Mississippi. The company also owns two distribution centers, a dairy, a fleet of nearly 350 trucks, and bakery, ice cream, drink, and ice manufacturing facilities. Brookshire's stores average about 40,000 sq. ft., while its warehouse-style Super 1 Foods stores average 60,000 sq. ft. More than 40 of Brookshire Grocery's stores sell gasoline. Originally part of the Brookshire Brothers grocery chain (dating back to 1921), the company split from it in 1939. The Brookshire family is still among the company's owners.

EXECUTIVES

Chairman: Bruce G. Brookshire
President Corporate Development Group: Brad Brookshire
President Human Resources and Finance Group: Tim Brookshire
President Marketing Group: Mark Brookshire
President Retail Operations Group: Britt Brookshire
EVP and CFO: Marvin Massey
EVP: Ronnie Horton
VP, Information Technology: Gary Butler

LOCATIONS

HQ: Brookshire Grocery Company
1600 W. South West Loop 323, Tyler, TX 75701
Phone: 903-534-3000 **Fax:** 903-534-2206
Web: www.brookshires.com

COMPETITORS

Albertson's
E-Z Mart Stores
Fleming Companies
H-E-B
Kmart
Kroger
Minyard Food Stores
Randall's
SUPERVALU
Target
Wal-Mart
Winn-Dixie

HISTORICAL FINANCIALS

Company Type: Private

Income Statement FYE: September 30

	ESTIMATED REVENUE ($ mil.)	NET INCOME ($ mil.)	NET PROFIT MARGIN	EMPLOYEES
9/02	1,700	—	—	11,500
9/01	1,700	—	—	10,750
9/00	1,600	—	—	10,500
9/99	1,650	—	—	10,700
9/98	1,550	—	—	10,700
9/97	1,500	—	—	10,500
9/96	1,300	—	—	9,500
9/95	1,200	—	—	8,500
9/94	800	—	—	8,000
9/93	700	—	—	7,500
Annual Growth	10.4%	—	—	4.9%

Revenue History

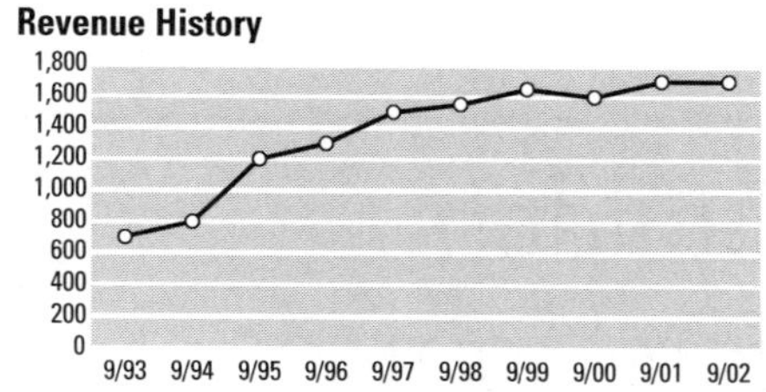

Brown Automotive

Color them diverse. Brown Automotive Group, a leading auto dealer in the mid-Atlantic region, sells about fifteen makes of automobiles from more than 20 dealerships in the Washington, DC, and Baltimore areas, as well as in Charlottesville and Richmond, Virginia. The company's new-car makes include DaimlerChrysler, General Motors, Honda, Jaguar, Mazda, Mercedes-Benz, Nissan, Saab, Subaru, Toyota, and Volkswagen. It also sells used cars and provides collision-repair services. Although the company was formed by William Schuiling in 1983, it traces its origins to Schuiling's purchase of one of Brown Automotive's Pontiac dealerships in Arlington, Virginia, in the early 1970s.

EXECUTIVES

CEO: Charles S. Stringfellow Jr.
President: Daniel Legge
VP, Accounting: Larry Palsha
VP, Sales: Jeffrey Best
Corporate Secretary: Lee Nicholaus
IT Manager: Chris Faber

LOCATIONS

HQ: Brown Automotive Group Ltd.
10287 Lee Hwy., Fairfax, VA 22030
Phone: 703-352-5555 **Fax:** 703-352-5591
Web: www.brownscar.com

COMPETITORS

AutoNation
CarMax
Darcars
Jim Koons Automotive
Ourisman Automotive
Planet Automotive Group
Rosenthal Automotive
Sheehy Auto

HISTORICAL FINANCIALS

Company Type: Private

Income Statement FYE: December 31

	ESTIMATED REVENUE ($ mil.)	NET INCOME ($ mil.)	NET PROFIT MARGIN	EMPLOYEES
12/01	2,750	—	—	3,100
12/00	2,500	—	—	3,000
12/99	2,400	—	—	3,200
12/98	2,300	—	—	3,400
12/97	2,200	—	—	3,700
12/96	2,000	—	—	3,600
12/95	2,000	—	—	3,600
12/94	1,750	—	—	—
Annual Growth	6.7%	—	—	(2.5%)

Revenue History

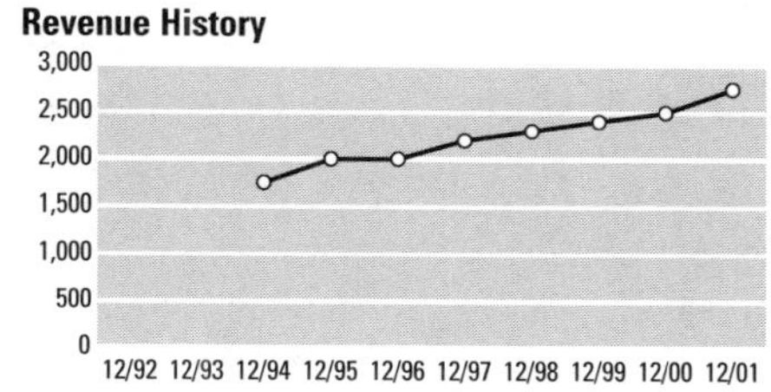

Buffets, Inc.

You don't have to worry about getting seconds at Buffets. The company operates one of the country's largest portfolios of buffet restaurants, with about 370 locations in 35 states. Operating mostly under the Old Country Buffet and HomeTown Buffet brands, the company's locations are self-service buffets featuring entrees, sides, and desserts for an all-inclusive price. Its other brands include Granny's Buffet, Country Roadhouse Buffet & Grill, and Tahoe Joe's Famous Steakhouse. In addition to its company-owned restaurant operations, Buffets franchises about 20 locations. Private equity firm Caxton-Iseman Capital owns 77% of the company.

Once a public company, Buffets was taken private in 2000 by a management group led by CEO Kerry Kramp and backed by Caxton-Iseman. Since the $643 million buyout, the company has reorganized its operations, closing or selling several underperforming locations, and has paid down a substantial part of its debt. It is also revamping and updating many of its existing restaurants. As the company starts to see signs of success and a return of profits, it is gearing up to begin expanding once again.

Sentinel Capital owns an additional 7% of Buffets, while vice chairman and co-founder Roe Hatlen has a 5% stake.

EXECUTIVES

Chairman: Frederick J. (Fred) Iseman, age 51
Vice Chairman: Roe H. Hatlen, age 59
President and CEO: Kerry A. Kramp, age 48, $522,500 pay
EVP and CFO: R. Michael Andrews Jr., age 39, $291,000 pay
EVP, General Counsel, and Secretary: H. Thomas Mitchell, age 46, $242,400 pay
EVP Human Resources: K. Michael Shrader, age 60
EVP Marketing: Glenn D. Drasher, age 52, $222,560 pay
EVP Purchasing: Jean C. Rostollan, $192,400 pay
VP Development: Janet Astor
VP Workforce Excellence: Nancy Rich
COO, Tahoe Joe's Famous Steakhouse: Loret Carbone
Senior Director of Field Training: Linda Allison
Human Resources, Tahoe Joe's Famous Steakhouse: Lorie Ruth
Public Relations: Chris Fodor
Auditors: Deloitte & Touche

LOCATIONS

HQ: 1460 Buffet Way, Eagan, MN 55121
Phone: 651-994-8608 **Fax:** 651-365-2356
Web: www.buffet.com

Buffets, Inc., operates and franchises about 400 restaurants in nearly 40 states. It also has a cabinet shop in Marshfield, Wisconsin.

2003 Locations

	No.
California	95
Illinois	33
Michigan	22
Pennsylvania	22
Ohio	21
New York	16
Washington	16
Minnesota	15
Colorado	14
Indiana	13
Arizona	12
Missouri	12
Wisconsin	12
Virginia	11
Massachusetts	10
Other states	71
Total	**395**

PRODUCTS/OPERATIONS

2003 Locations

	No.
Company-owned	372
Franchised	23
Total	**395**

COMPETITORS

Applebee's
Bob Evans
Boston Market
Buffet Partners
Carlson Restaurants
CBRL Group
Denny's
Garden Fresh Restaurants
Golden Corral
Luby's
Metromedia Restaurant Group
Piccadilly Cafeterias
Ryan's
Shoney's
VICORP Restaurants
Worldwide Restaurant Concepts

HISTORICAL FINANCIALS

Company Type: Private

Income Statement FYE: Wednesday nearest June 30

	REVENUE ($ mil.)	NET INCOME ($ mil.)	NET PROFIT MARGIN	EMPLOYEES
6/03	985	13	1.3%	23,000
6/02*	527	(7)	—	24,000
12/01	1,045	13	1.2%	25,000
12/00	1,021	32	3.1%	25,200
12/99	937	42	4.5%	25,000
12/98	869	39	4.5%	24,350
12/97	809	29	3.5%	24,830
12/96	751	(7)	—	24,100
12/95	510	27	5.3%	15,540
12/94	410	23	5.5%	15,915
Annual Growth	10.2%	(5.9%)	—	4.2%

*Fiscal year change

2003 Year-End Financials

Debt ratio: 6,932.3%
Return on equity: —
Cash ($ mil.): 16
Current ratio: 0.51
Long-term debt ($ mil.): 392

Net Income History

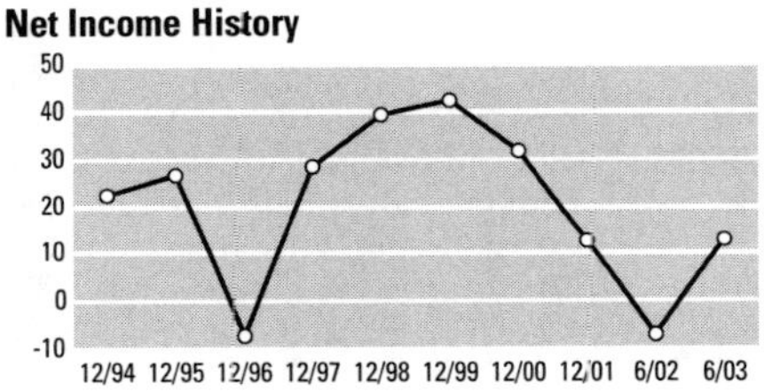

Builders FirstSource

Builders FirstSource, like an ambitious weight lifter, is bulking up an already well-built form. It aims to be a leading supplier to professional builders — it sells doors, hardware, windows, lumber, and other building products. Since its founding in 1997 as Stonegate Resources, the company has grown, primarily through acquisitions, to include more than 80 distribution centers and more than 85 manufacturing plants in 12 states. The company is focusing more on value-added products, such as wall panels, trusses, and specialty millwork. Builders FirstSource was founded by a management team headed by former CEO John Roach and private investment firm JLL Partners (formerly Joseph, Littlejohn & Levy).

EXECUTIVES

Chairman and CEO: Floyd F. Sherman
COO: Kevin P. O'Meara
SVP and CFO: Charles L. Horn
SVP and General Counsel: Donald F. McAleenan
VP, National Sales and Marketing: Richard J. Chapman
VP, Process Improvement: Rich TerHaar
VP, Purchasing: Dan Carver
VP, Sales and Business Development, Central Group: Brian Reed
Director, Human Resources: Bobby Quinten
Director, Information Technology: John Hogg
Auditors: PricewaterhouseCoopers LLP

LOCATIONS

HQ: 2001 Bryan St., Ste. 1600, Dallas, TX 75201
Phone: 214-880-3500 **Fax:** 214-880-3599
Web: www.buildersfirstsource.com

Builders FirstSource has plants and distribution facilities in Colorado, Florida, Georgia, Kentucky, Maryland, New Jersey, North Carolina, Ohio, Tennessee, Texas, South Carolina, and Virginia.

PRODUCTS/OPERATIONS

Selected Products

Building Materials
Interior Items
Lumber and Related Products
Manufactured Components
Millwork
Tools

COMPETITORS

84 Lumber
Ace Hardware
Building Materials Holding
Carter Lumber
CertainTeed
Home Depot
Lanoga
Lowe's
McCoy
Menard
TruServ
Wickes
Wolohan Lumber

HISTORICAL FINANCIALS

Company Type: Private

Income Statement FYE: December 31

	REVENUE ($ mil.)	NET INCOME ($ mil.)	NET PROFIT MARGIN	EMPLOYEES
12/02	1,500	—	—	6,100
12/01	1,561	—	—	6,800
12/00	1,710	—	—	6,800
12/99	1,900	—	—	5,160
12/98	1,220	—	—	5,200
Annual Growth	5.3%	—	—	4.1%

Revenue History

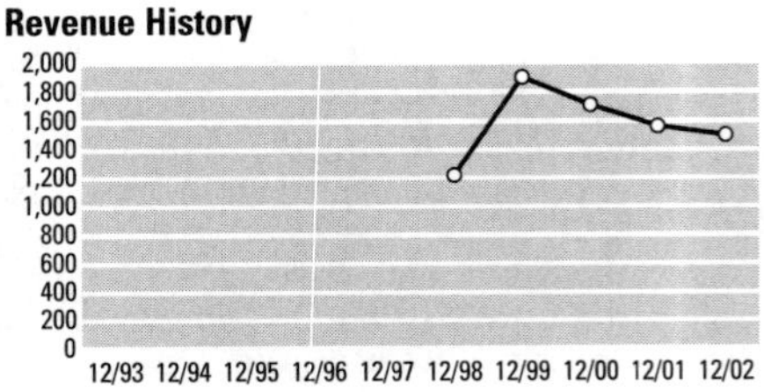

Burger King Corporation

This king commands a whopper of a fast food empire. Burger King operates the #2 hamburger chain (behind McDonald's) with more than 11,300 restaurants across the US and in more than 55 other countries. In addition to its popular Whopper sandwich, the chain offers a variety of burgers, chicken sandwiches, salads, and breakfast items. Most of Burger King's freestanding units offer drive-through service as well as dine-in seating; about 90% of its restaurants are operated by franchisees. Founded by James McLamore and David Edgerton in 1954, Burger King was owned by UK-based Diageo until 2002 when an investment group led by Texas Pacific Group bought the company and took it private.

The fast food giants have been embroiled in a down-and-dirty price war trying to steal market share while consumers have started to abandon greasy menus in search of healthier alternatives. And while all the big chains have experienced declining same-store sales, Burger King has also suffered from a revolving door in the board room (it has welcomed eight CEOs since 1989) and several failed attempts to redesign its brand. Now free from its UK parent, Burger King's latest management team (led by former Darden Restaurants vice chairman Brad Blum) is banking that better food quality, rather than lower prices, will help it turn the corner.

Switching its $350 million advertising business from Deutsch to Young & Rubicam in 2003, the company has started to emphasize its open-flame grilling process by replacing its age-old "flame broiled" tag with "fire grilled." It also brought in 7-Eleven's chief marketer Russ Klein to help with its brand repositioning. Meanwhile, the company is shedding some items from its crowded menu offerings in an effort to simplify restaurant operations for its franchisees.

Texas Pacific Group and its partners acquired Burger King for about $1.5 billion.

HISTORY

In 1954 restaurant veterans James McLamore and David Edgerton opened the first Burger King in Miami. Three years later the company added the Whopper sandwich, which then sold for 37 cents, to its menu of hamburgers, shakes, and sodas. Burger King used television to help advertise the Whopper (its first TV commercial appeared in 1958). During its infancy Burger King was the first chain to offer dining rooms.

Looking to expand nationwide, Burger King turned to franchising in 1959. McLamore and Edgerton took a hands-off approach, allowing franchises to buy large territories and operate with autonomy. Although their technique spurred growth, it also created large service inconsistencies among Burger Kings across the US; this bugaboo would haunt the company for years. Having grown to 274 stores in the US and abroad, Burger King was sold to Pillsbury in 1967.

During the early 1970s Burger King continued to add locations. The company did well during this time, launching its successful "Have It Your Way" campaign in 1974 and introducing drive-through service a year later. Yet parent Pillsbury had to fight to rein in large franchisees who argued they could run their Burger Kings better than a packaged-goods company. In 1977 Pillsbury handed control of Burger King to Donald Smith, a McDonald's veteran, who soon silenced the insurrection. Smith tightened franchising regulations, created 10 regional management offices, and instituted annual visits.

Smith left for Pizza Hut in 1980, and by 1982 Burger King had reached the #2 fast-food plateau, trailing only McDonald's. The company struggled through the rest of the 1980s, though, hurt by high management turnover and a string of unsuccessful ad campaigns. (Remember "Herb the Nerd"?) Pillsbury became the target of a hostile takeover by UK-based Grand Metropolitan, and in 1988 Grand Met acquired Pillsbury along with its 5,500 Burger King restaurants.

Grand Met bolstered Burger King's foreign operations in 1990 by converting about 200 recently acquired UK-based Wimpey hamburger stores into Burger Kings. International expansion increased, with new restaurants in Mexico (1991), Saudi Arabia (1993), and Paraguay (1995).

In 1997 Grand Met and Guinness combined their operations to form Diageo, making Burger King a subsidiary. That year Dennis Malamatinas left GrandMet's Asian beverage division to become Burger King's CEO. In 1999 the company joined rival TRICON (now YUM! Brands) in shucking out $150 million to help food distributor AmeriServe stay afloat following AmeriServe's filing for bankruptcy.

Late in 2000 Diageo announced plans to spin off Burger King, but the burger chain's slow sales delayed action. Malamatinas resigned as CEO and was replaced in 2001 by John Dasburg, former CEO of Northwest Airlines. Late that year Burger King took its cue from McDonald's popular New Tastes Menu and introduced 14 new items to its menu, including a vegetarian burger.

An investment group led by Texas Pacific Group acquired Burger King for $1.5 billion in 2002. Earlier that year the group had agreed to pay $2.26 billion but renegotiated amid falling sales and a downturn in the burger market. Shortly after the purchase, Dasburg was ousted and Brad Blum, vice chairman of Darden Restaurants, was named as his replacement.

EXECUTIVES

CEO: Bradley D. (Brad) Blum, age 48
President: Robert T. (Bob) Nilsen, age 43
EVP and CFO: Bennett L. Nussbaum
EVP and Chief Development Officer: Michael (Mike) Ellis, age 40
EVP Franchise Operations and Chief Development Officer for North America: Paul Novak, age 57
EVP and General Counsel: Richard B. (Ben) Hirst, age 56
EVP Strategic Projects and Capital Management: Adam Gray
Chief Marketing Officer: Russ Klein, age 45
SVP Consumer Insights and Strategic Branding: Glad Markunas
SVP Diversity: Clyde Rucker
SVP Franchise Operations, Eastern Division: Enrique (Rick) Silva
SVP Franchise Operations, Western Division: Joe Soraci
SVP Marketing Programs and Sales: Rick N. Brown
SVP Operations Excellence Programs and Services: Jim Hyatt
SVP Restaurant Operations, US: Dave Gagnon
VP and Corporate Counsel: Elsie Romero
VP Corporate Communications: Rob Doughty
VP Global Advertising and Promotions: Craig Braasch
President, Burger King International: Nish Kankiwala, age 45
President, Latin America: Julio Ramirez

LOCATIONS

HQ: 5505 Blue Lagoon Dr., Miami, FL 33126
Phone: 305-378-3000 **Fax:** 305-378-7262
Web: www.burgerking.com

Burger King operates and franchises more than 11,300 restaurants in about 60 countries.

2003 Locations

	No.
US	7,978
International	3,389
Total	**11,367**

PRODUCTS/OPERATIONS

2003 Locations

	No.
Franchised	10,309
Company-owned	1,058
Total	**11,367**

COMPETITORS

AFC Enterprises
Chick-fil-A
CKE Restaurants
Subway
Domino's
Dairy Queen
Jack in the Box
Little Caesar's
McDonald's
Papa John's
Triarc
Wendy's
YUM!

HISTORICAL FINANCIALS

Company Type: Private

Income Statement FYE: June 30

	REVENUE ($ mil.)	NET INCOME ($ mil.)	NET PROFIT MARGIN	EMPLOYEES
6/03	1,600	—	—	31,000
6/02	1,721	—	—	31,000
6/01	1,474	—	—	30,166
6/00	1,427	—	—	28,432
6/99	1,379	—	—	26,000
6/98	1,449	—	—	27,149
6/97	1,396	—	—	29,590
6/96	1,342	—	—	—
Annual Growth	2.5%	—	—	0.8%

Revenue History

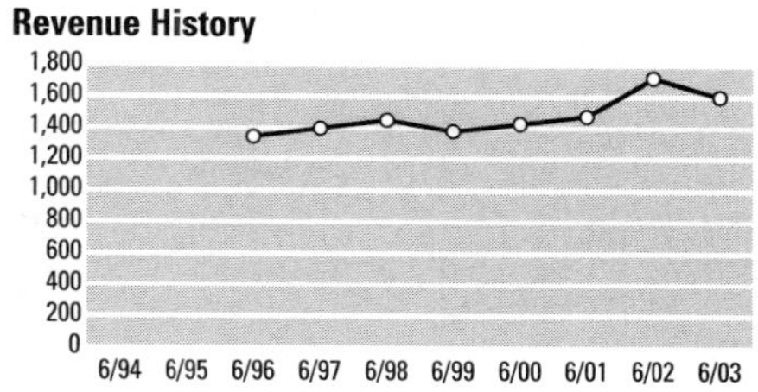

Burt Automotive Network

John Elway may have retired, but Burt Automotive Network is still trying to sack him. In Denver Burt goes head-to-head with the John Elway AutoNation dealerships once owned (and still named for) the former Broncos star. Burt operates nine dealerships in Colorado that sell new cars from Ford, GM, Toyota, and Subaru. It also sells commercial trucks and used cars, and offers parts and repair services. With Kuni Group, Burt operates Burt Kuni Honda Oldsmobile in Denver. Burt, owned by CEO Lloyd G. Chavez, is one of the largest Hispanic-owned businesses in the US. A salesman with Burt since 1950, Chavez became the majority owner in 1982 and bought the rest of the company in 1987.

EXECUTIVES

Chairman: Lloyd G. Chavez Sr.
President and CEO: Lloyd G. Chavez Jr., age 53
CFO: Robin Helms
SVP, General Manager, and Corporate Legal Counsel: John Held
Corporate Development Director: Deborah Brown Garrity
Marketing Director: Jennifer Brown
Human Resources Manager: Todd van Maldeghem
Executive Administrative Assistant: Patty Hara

LOCATIONS

HQ: 10301 E. Arapahoe Rd., Centennial, CO 80112
Phone: 303-789-6700 **Fax:** 303-789-6706
Web: www.burt.com

COMPETITORS

AutoNation
Larry H. Miller Group
MNL, Inc.
Phil Long Dealerships

HISTORICAL FINANCIALS

Company Type: Private

Income Statement FYE: December 31

	REVENUE ($ mil.)	NET INCOME ($ mil.)	NET PROFIT MARGIN	EMPLOYEES
12/02	1,478	—	—	1,032
12/01	1,317	—	—	1,350
12/00	1,130	—	—	1,200
12/99	1,004	—	—	1,184
12/98	838	—	—	1,019
12/97	867	—	—	875
12/96	813	—	—	849
12/95	576	—	—	790
12/94	423	—	—	719
12/93	529	—	—	600
Annual Growth	12.1%	—	—	6.2%

Revenue History

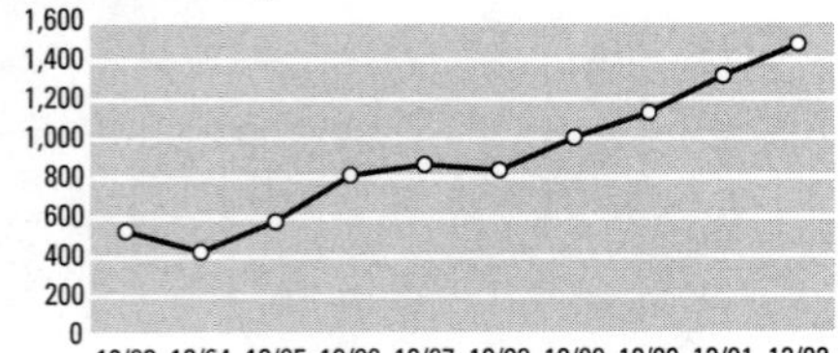

BWAY Corporation

BWAY helps keep coffee fresh and ammo dry. The company manufactures steel containers such as aerosol cans, pails, specialty cans, oblong cans, and ammunition boxes. Its products package items from paints, lubricants, and roof and driveway sealants to food, coffee, vegetable oil, and aerosol products. The company also provides material center services such as coating, lithography, and metal shearing. BWAY Manufacturing is the company's main subsidiary. Private investment firm Kelso & Co. has acquired the company for about $330 million in cash and debt in partnership with Jean-Pierre Ergas, BWAY's chairman and CEO, vice chairman Warren Hayford, and other members of management.

The US accounts for more than 95% of sales. The company has shut down some facilities in Ohio and Illinois. It is concentrating on reducing its debt and revitalizing its material center operations (coating and lithography services).

EXECUTIVES

Chairman and CEO: Jean-Pierre M. Ergas, age 63, $1,218,750 pay
Vice Chairman: Warren J. Hayford, age 73
COO: Kenneth Roessler, age 39, $252,500 pay
EVP, Manufacturing and Engineering: Thomas Eagleson, age 61, $589,229 pay
VP, Administration and CFO: Kevin C. Kern, age 42, $362,141 pay
VP, Marketing and National Accounts: Robert C. Coleman
VP, Human Resources: Joe Frabotta
VP, Information Technology Services: Patrick F. Hodges
VP and Treasurer: Jeffrey M. O'Connell, age 49
Auditors: Deloitte & Touche LLP

LOCATIONS

HQ: 8607 Roberts Dr., Ste. 250, Atlanta, GA 30350
Phone: 770-645-4800 **Fax:** 770-645-4810
Web: www.bwaycorp.com

BWAY has manufacturing facilities in California, Georgia, Illinois, Mississippi, New Jersey, Ohio, Pennsylvania, Tennessee, and Texas.

PRODUCTS/OPERATIONS

Selected Products and Services

Aerosol cans
Ammunition boxes
Coffee cans
Material centers (cut, coil, coat, and lithograph sheets of steel)
Oblong cans
Pails
Paint cans
Specialty cans (utility cans with screw-cap tops and applicator brushes; cone top cans)

Principal Subsidiary

BWAY Manufacturing, Inc.

COMPETITORS

Amcor
Ball Corporation
CLARCOR
Consolidated Container
Crown
Jarden
Silgan
U.S. Can

HISTORICAL FINANCIALS

Company Type: Private

Income Statement FYE: Sunday nearest September 30

	REVENUE ($ mil.)	NET INCOME ($ mil.)	NET PROFIT MARGIN	EMPLOYEES
9/02	528	12	2.3%	1,868
9/01	475	(17)	—	1,726
9/00	461	(3)	—	1,954
9/99	467	6	1.2%	2,176
9/98	401	2	0.4%	1,898
9/97	402	13	3.3%	2,097
9/96	283	1	0.4%	1,695
9/95	248	9	3.6%	1,155
9/94	225	5	2.3%	1,145
9/93	181	5	2.9%	—
Annual Growth	12.6%	10.0%	—	6.3%

2002 Year-End Financials

Debt ratio: 137.7%
Return on equity: 18.5%
Cash ($ mil.): 20
Current ratio: 1.20
Long-term debt ($ mil.): 100

Net Income History

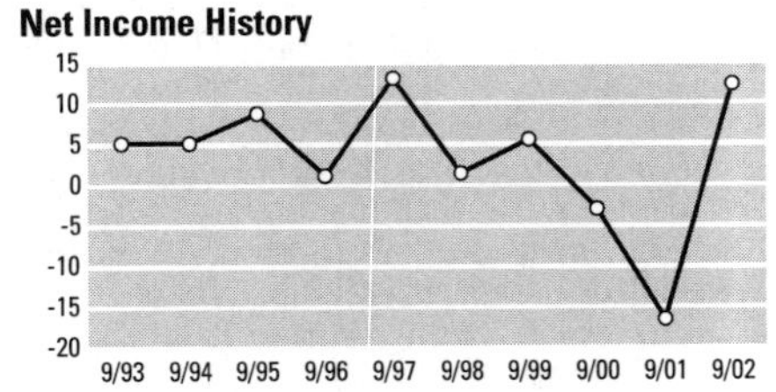

Cabela's Inc.

Cabela's is a hunter's and fisherman's Disneyland. The seller of outdoor sporting goods operates mainly through the 60 million-plus catalogs it mails each year, but its eight stores are big attractions, too. Located in Kansas, Michigan, Minnesota, Nebraska, South Dakota, and Wisconsin, the stores are as big as 150,000 sq. ft. and include such features as waterfalls, mountain replicas, and exotic game trophies. Founded in 1961 by Dick Cabela, he and his younger brother James own 80% of the company (J.P. Morgan Partners owns close to 20%) which sells footwear, clothing, and gear for fishing, hunting, camping, and other outdoor activities. Cabela's also sells merchandise online and has an outdoors show on ESPN2.

EXECUTIVES

Chairman: Dick Cabela
President: James Cabela
VP Customer Service: Ron Spath
VP Finance: Dave Roehr
Director of Human Resources: Larry Hiers
Manager of eCommerce: Tom Rosdail

LOCATIONS

HQ: One Cabela Dr., Sidney, NE 69160
Phone: 308-254-5505 **Fax:** 308-254-4800
Web: www.cabelas.com

PRODUCTS/OPERATIONS

Selected Products

Archery equipment
Automotive and ATV accessories
Camping gear
Clothing
Fishing and marine equipment
Footwear
Gifts and furnishings
Hunting equipment
Optical items
Snowmobile accessories

COMPETITORS

Academy
Bass Pro Shops
L.L. Bean
North Face
Orvis Company
REI
Sportsman's Guide
Wal-Mart

HISTORICAL FINANCIALS

Company Type: Private

Income Statement FYE: December 31

	REVENUE ($ mil.)	NET INCOME ($ mil.)	NET PROFIT MARGIN	EMPLOYEES
12/01	875	—	—	7,041
12/00	775	—	—	5,000
12/99	666	—	—	3,265
12/98	288	—	—	3,265
12/97	275	—	—	—
Annual Growth	33.6%	—	—	29.2%

Revenue History

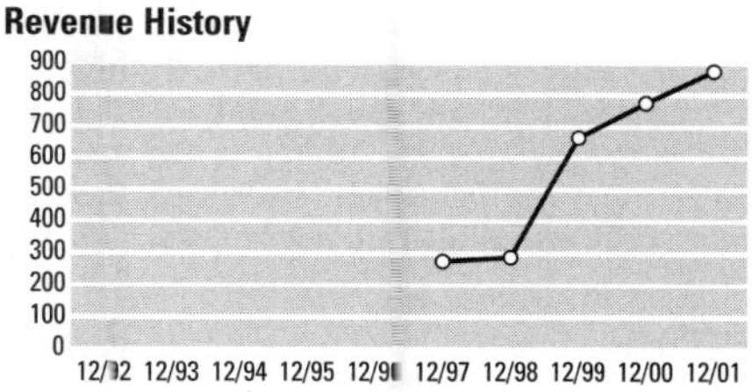

Calcot, Ltd.

With a crop of 1,639 members in California and Arizona, Calcot is one of the top cotton-marketing cooperatives in the US. Members of the co-op, which started in 1927, grow premium-grade Far Western cottons, including California/Arizona, California Upland, Pima, Sacramento Valley, and San Joaquin Acala varieties. Member-owned Calcot also markets raw almonds. More than 85% of Calcot's annual crops are exported to textile mills worldwide, mostly to Pacific Rim countries. Calcot and three other major US co-ops together comprise Amcot, a worldwide cotton marketer.

EXECUTIVES

President: David D. Farley, age 45
SVP Finance and Administration: Robert Norris
VP Arizona and Southern California Operations: Lon Emerson
VP Grower Relations: Gene Lundquist
Assistant VP Call Pool Operations and Economics: Jarral Neeper
Assistand VP Export Sales: John Burch
Assistant VP Futures: Cindy Walters
Assistant VP Administrative Services and Human Resources: Mary Joe Pasek
Treasurer and General Accountant: Larry Nichols
Director Communications: Mark Bagby
Director Sales Administration: Ron Nickell
Auditors: Eadie & Payne LLP

LOCATIONS

HQ: 1900 E. Brundage Ln., Bakersfield, CA 93307
Phone: 661-327-5961 **Fax:** 661-861-9870
Web: www.calcot.com

COMPETITORS

Cargill
Dunavant Enterprises
King Ranch
Plains Cotton
Staplcotn

HISTORICAL FINANCIALS

Company Type: Cooperative

Income Statement FYE: July 31

	REVENUE ($ mil.)	NET INCOME ($ mil.)	NET PROFIT MARGIN	EMPLOYEES
7/02	535	—	—	100
7/01	455	—	—	99
7/00	567	—	—	100
7/99*	435	—	—	100
8/98	652	—	—	155
8/97	685	—	—	185
8/96	642	—	—	115
8/95	739	—	—	115
8/94	800	—	—	110
8/93	600	—	—	—
Annual Growth	(1.3%)	—	—	(1.2%)

*Fiscal year change

Revenue History

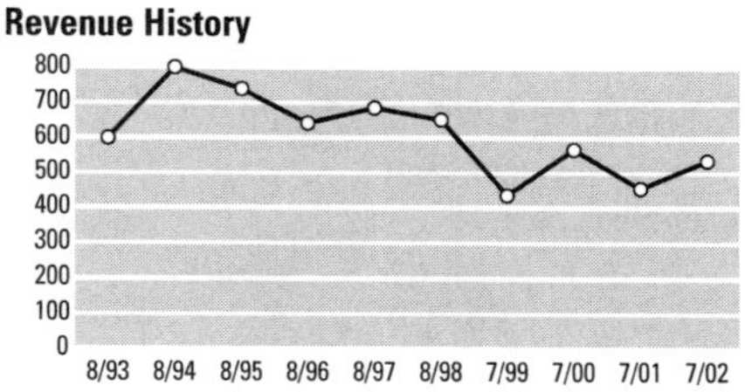

CalPERS

California's public-sector retirees already have a place in the sun; CalPERS gives them the money to enjoy it. CalPERS is the California Public Employees' Retirement System, one of the largest public pension systems in the US. It manages retirement and health plans for approximately 1.4 million beneficiaries (employees, retirees, and their dependents) from nearly 2,500 government agencies and school districts. Even though all of the system's beneficiaries are from the Golden State, CalPERS brings its influence to bear in all 50 states and beyond.

With nearly $145 billion in assets, CalPERS uses its clout to sway such corporate governance issues as company performance, executive compensation, and even social policy. In the absence of a strong federal effort to purge corporations of corruption, CalPERS often acts as a force for reform; urging companies to remove conflicts of interest and make themselves more accountable to shareholders, employees, and the public. CalPERS is also a powerful negotiator for such services as insurance; rates established by the system serve as benchmarks for employers throughout the nation.

Most of CalPERS' revenue comes from its enormous investment program: It has interests in US and foreign securities, real estate development and investment, and even hedge funds and venture capital activities. CalPERS has steadily increased its investments in private equity, looking to take ownership stakes in more firms. (It already owns 10% of investment bank Thomas Weisel.)

Over the next few years CalPERS may be forced to sell assets, as it is expected to be hit with a wave of early retirements by middle-aged workers. In the meantime it is eyeing more short-term investments with higher returns.

CalPERS' board consists of six elected, three appointed, and four designated members (the director of the state's Department of Personnel Administration, the state controller, the state treasurer, and a member of the State Personnel Board). An abysmal performance in 2001 (the fund's worst in nearly two decades) and several public and sometimes nasty donnybrooks have led to the exodus of several key personnel, including former CEO James Burton and former chief investment officer Daniel Szente.

HISTORY

The state of California founded CalPERS in 1931 to administer a pension fund for state employees. By the 1940s the system was serving other public agencies and educational institutions on a contract basis.

When the Public Employees' Medical and Hospital Care Act was passed in 1962, CalPERS added health coverage. The fund was conservatively managed in-house, with little exposure to stocks. Despite slow growth, the state used the system's funds to meet its own cash shortfalls.

CalPERS became involved in corporate governance issues in the mid-1980s, when California treasurer Jesse Unruh became outraged by corporate greenmail schemes. In 1987 he hired as CEO Wisconsin pension board veteran Dale Hanson, who led the movement for corporate accountability to institutional investors.

In the late 1980s CalPERS moved into real estate and Japanese stocks. When both crashed around 1990, Hanson came under pressure. CalPERS was twice forced to take major write-downs for its real estate holdings and turned to expensive outside fund managers, but its investment performance deteriorated and member services suffered.

Legislation in 1990 enabled CalPERS to offer long-term health insurance. Governor Pete Wilson's 1991 attempt to use $1.6 billion from CalPERS to help meet a state budget shortfall resulted in legislation banning future raids. CalPERS made its first direct investment in 1993, an energy-related infrastructure partnership with Enron.

CalPERS suffered in the 1994 bond crash. That year Hanson resigned amid criticism that his focus on corporate governance had depressed fund performance. The system moved to an indexing strategy.

CalPERS eased its corporate relations stance, creating a separate office to handle investor issues and launching an International Corporate Governance Program. However, the next year CalPERS was uninvited from a KKR investment pool because of criticism of its fund management and fee structure.

In 1996 the system teamed with the Asian Development Bank to invest in the Asia/Pacific region; it took a major hit in the Asian financial crisis the next year, but used the downturn as an opportunity to expand its position there in undervalued stocks. In 1998 CalPERS pressured foreign firms to adopt more transparent financial reporting methods.

In 2000 the system raised health care premiums almost 10% to keep up with rising care costs. It widened the scope of its direct investments with stakes in investment bank Thomas Weisel Partners (10%) and asset manager Arrowstreet Capital (15%); it also moved into real estate development, buying Genstar Land Co. with Newland Communities, and announcing plans to invest in high-tech firms focused on B2B online real estate services. CalPERS said that year it would sell off more than $500 million in tobacco holdings; it then invested the same amount in five biotech funds (including one from what is now GlaxoSmithKline), its first foray into the sector.

In 2001 California state controller and CalPERS board member Kathleen Connell successfully sued the system for not following state-sanctioned rules regarding pay increases. CalPERS was forced to cut salaries for investment managers, a move that prompted chief investment officer Daniel Szente to resign.

In 2003 CalPERS agreed to a record $250 million settlement relating to an age-discrimination suit brought by the Equal Employment Opportunity Commission. Also in 2003, CalPERS clamored for (and got) the resignation of New York Stock Exchange Chairman Richard Grasso. CalPERS and others claimed Grasso's pay of about $140 million a year made it impossible for him to effectively monitor the exchange's member companies for corruption.

EXECUTIVES

CEO: Fred R. Buenrostro Jr., age 51
President, Board of Administration; Director: Sean Harrigan
VP, Board of Administration; Director: Rob Feckner
Deputy Executive Officer: Loren Suter
Assistant Executive Officer, Financial and Administration Services: Vincent P. Brown
Assistant Executive Officer, Member and Benefit Services: Barbara D. Hegdal
Assistant Executive Officer, Governmental Affairs, Planning, and Research: Robert D. Walton
Chief Investment Officer: Mark J.P. Anson
Chief, Fiscal Services Division: Holly Fong
Chief, Change Management Office: Allen Goldstein
Chief, Office of Public Affairs: Patricia K. Macht
Chief, Office of Governmental Affairs: Karen Neuwald
Chief, Human Resources: Tom Pettey
Chief Actuary: Ronald L. Seeling
General Counsel: Peter H. Mixon
Deputy General Counsel: Carol McConnell
Auditors: PricewaterhouseCoopers LLP

LOCATIONS

HQ: California Public Employees' Retirement System
Lincoln Plaza, 400 P St., Sacramento, CA 95814
Phone: 916-326-3000 **Fax:** 916-558-4001
Web: www.calpers.ca.gov

PRODUCTS/OPERATIONS

2002 Assets

	% of total
Stocks	60
Bonds	27
Real estate	8
Private equity	5
Total	**100**

Selected Retirement Plans

Defined Benefit Plans
Judges' Retirement Fund
Judges' Retirement Fund II
Legislators' Retirement System
Public Employees' Retirement Fund
Volunteer Firefighters' Length of Service Award System

Defined Contribution Plans
State Peace Officers' and Firefighters' Defined Contribution Plan Fund

Health Care Plans
Public Employees' Health Care Fund
Public Employees' Contingency Reserve Fund

Others
Replacement Benefit Fund
Public Employees Long-Term Care Fund
Public Employees' Deferred Compensation Fund
Old Age & Survivors' Insurance Revolving Fund

COMPETITORS

A.G. Edwards
AIG SunAmerica
Alliance Capital Management
AXA Financial
Charles Schwab
Citigroup Global Markets
FMR
Franklin Resources
Janus Capital
Legg Mason
MFS
Mellon Financial
Merrill Lynch
Morgan Stanley
Nationwide Financial
Principal Financial
Putnam
Raymond James Financial
State Street
T. Rowe Price
TIAA-CREF
UBS Financial Services
USAA
Vanguard Group

HISTORICAL FINANCIALS

Company Type: Government-owned

Income Statement FYE: June 30

	ASSETS ($ mil.)	NET INCOME ($ mil.)	INCOME AS % OF ASSETS	EMPLOYEES
6/02	162,167	—	—	1,614
6/01	173,717	—	—	1,614
6/00	191,157	—	—	1,594
6/99	172,446	—	—	1,500
6/98	156,643	—	—	1,247
6/97	128,880	—	—	1,089
6/96	102,797	—	—	1,037
6/95	90,417	—	—	1,000
6/94	76,935	—	—	900
6/93	69,484	—	—	—
Annual Growth	9.3%	—	—	7.6%

Asset History

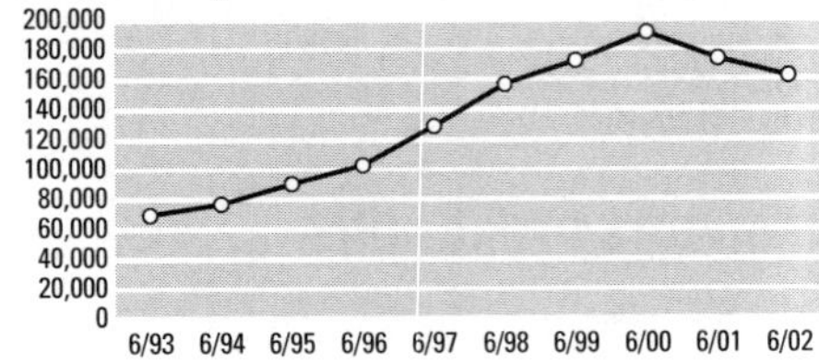

California State University

California State University (CSU) turns students into teachers. The university traces its roots to the state's teaching colleges and trains some 60% of California's teachers. CSU is also neck and neck with the State University of New York (SUNY) as the nation's largest university system. With some baby boomers' children reaching college age and college participation increasing among adults, CSU's student body has grown to around 400,000. The system has campuses in 23 cities, including Bakersfield, Los Angeles, San Francisco, and San Jose. The university primarily awards bachelor's and master's degrees in about 240 subject areas, leaving higher levels of study to the University of California (UC) system.

CSU is developing strategies to cope with an expected enrollment increase of about 40% through 2010 — what it calls Tidal Wave II. The first waves are starting already, with more than 20,000 additional students flooding the system in the fall of 2001. To battle the crippling influx of new students, CSU has begun offering distance-education programs in which students are taught via teleconferencing and the Internet. Other strategies involve adding a summer semester to create year-long schooling, and expanding the use of off-campus centers.

HISTORY

In 1862 San Francisco's Normal School, a training center for elementary teachers, became California's first state-founded school for higher education. Six students attended its first classes, but there were 384 by 1866. It later moved to San Jose to escape the bustle of San Francisco.

In the late 1880s State Normal Schools opened in Chico, San Diego, and San Francisco, followed in 1901 by California State Polytechnic Institute, which offered studies in agriculture, business, and engineering. Other new colleges included Fresno State (1911) and Humboldt State (1913). Most of the schools offered four-year programs and admitted any student with eight years of grammar school education.

The Normal Schools were renamed Teachers Colleges in 1921 to reflect their role in teacher education. Two years later the colleges began awarding bachelor of arts degrees in education.

In 1935 the schools were renamed State Colleges and expanded into liberal arts. In 1947 they were authorized to confer master's degrees in education.

After WWII, students on the GI Bill helped increase enrollment, and campuses opened in Los Angeles, Sacramento, and Long Beach. The prospect of the first baby boomers reaching college age prompted the founding of more campuses in the late 1950s. Russia's 1957 launch of Sputnik spurred additional focus on science and math at all education levels. The next year the colleges began awarding master's degrees in subjects unrelated to teacher education.

During the Red Scare, the system's first chancellor, Buell Gallagher, was accused by the press of being soft on communism. Other faculty were subpoenaed to appear before the House Committee on Un-American Activities.

In 1961 the system became the California State Colleges (CSC) and the board of trustees was created, giving the schools more independence from state government. In 1969 student and faculty groups seeking ethnic studies departments went on strike in San Francisco; the unrest closed the campus.

In 1972 CSC became known as the California State University and Colleges. Ten years later it adopted the name California State University.

Barry Munitz became chancellor in 1991, taking over a system that had become oppressive due to a heavy-handed administration. Munitz, who came from corporate America, brought his business sense to the university and increased private fund raising, among other activities. He used words like "consumer" and "product" to describe his job. Munitz also increased tuition, which caused enrollments to drop from 1991-1995.

CSU added two new campuses in 1995, including CSU Monterey Bay, the first military base to be converted into a university since the end of the Cold War.

In 1997 Charles Reed was named to replace Munitz as chancellor, effective the following year. That year CSU proposed the California Educational Technology Initiative (CETI), a plan to build high-speed computer and telephone networks linking its campuses. CETI failed in 1998 after Microsoft and other investors pulled out. In 1999, after lengthy contract negotiations between Reed and faculty members failed to produce accord over teacher salaries and employment conditions, Reed imposed his own merit-based plan. The faculty responded with official rebukes and a vote of no confidence in Reed. The two sides eventually settled on a new three-year contract with provisions that salary and benefits may be negotiated annually.

The rancor over pay continued in 2000 when the California Faculty Association issued a report claiming women were discriminated against and the merit system was inherently unfair. CSU issued its own report denying the charges. In 2001 Reed, stirring up more controversy, began a new quest that would allow CSU to offer doctorate degrees. The move is bitterly opposed by the competing University of California system.

EXECUTIVES

Chair: Debra Farar
Chancellor: Charles B. Reed, age 62
Executive Vice Chancellor and Chief Academic Officer: David S. Spence
Executive Vice Chancellor and CFO: Richard P. West
Vice Chancellor Human Resources: Jackie McClain
Vice Chancellor University Advancement; President, CSU Foundation: Louis E. Caldera, age 46
General Counsel: Christine Helwick, age 56
President, California Maritime Academy: William B. Eisenhardt
President, California State Polytechnic University, Pomona: Bob Suzuki, age 67
President, California Polytechnic State University, San Luis Obispo: Warren J. Baker, age 65
President, CSU, Bakersfield: Tomas A. Arciniega, age 66
President, CSU, Channel Islands: Richard Rush
President, CSU, Chico: Manuel A. Esteban, age 63
President, CSU, Dominguez Hills: James E. Lyons Sr.
President, CSU, Fresno: John D. Welty, age 59
President, CSU, Fullerton: Milton A. Gordon, age 68
President, CSU, Haywood: Norma S. Rees
President, CSU, Long Beach: Robert C. Maxson
President, CSU, Los Angeles: James M. Rosser, age 64
President, CSU, Monterey Bay: Peter P. Smith, age 57
President, CSU, Northridge: Jolene Koester
President, CSU, Sacramento: Donald R. Gerth, age 74
President, CSU, San Bernardino: Albert K. Karnig
President, CSU, San Marcos: Alexander Gonzalez
President, CSU, Stanislaus: Marvalene Hughes
President, San Diego State University: Stephen L. (Steve) Weber, age 60
President, San Francisco State University: Robert A. (Bob) Corrigan, age 68
President, San Jose State University: Robert L. Caret
President, Sonoma State University: Ruben Arminana, age 56
President, Humboldt State University: Rollin C. Richmond
Auditors: KPMG LLP

LOCATIONS

HQ: Trustees of the California State University
401 Golden Shore, Long Beach, CA 90802
Phone: 562-951-4000 **Fax:** 562-951-4949
Web: www.calstate.edu

California State University has campuses in 23 cities.

California State University Campuses

California Maritime Academy
California Polytechnic State University, San Luis Obispo
California State Polytechnic University, Pomona
California State University
Bakersfield
Channel Islands
Chico
Dominguez Hills
Fresno
Fullerton
Hayward
Long Beach
Los Angeles
Monterey Bay
Northridge
Sacramento
San Bernardino
San Marcos
Stanislaus
Humboldt State University
San Diego State University
San Francisco State University
San Jose State University
Sonoma State University

HISTORICAL FINANCIALS

Company Type: School

Income Statement FYE: June 30

	REVENUE ($ mil.)	NET INCOME ($ mil.)	NET PROFIT MARGIN	EMPLOYEES
6/01	4,050	—	—	40,000
6/00	3,804	—	—	40,000
6/99	3,272	—	—	40,323
6/98	2,612	—	—	39,000
6/97	2,522	—	—	38,512
6/96	3,889	—	—	37,360
6/95	3,121	—	—	33,000
6/94	2,121	—	—	34,779
6/93	2,085	—	—	33,859
6/92	2,131	—	—	—
Annual Growth	7.4%	—	—	2.1%

Revenue History

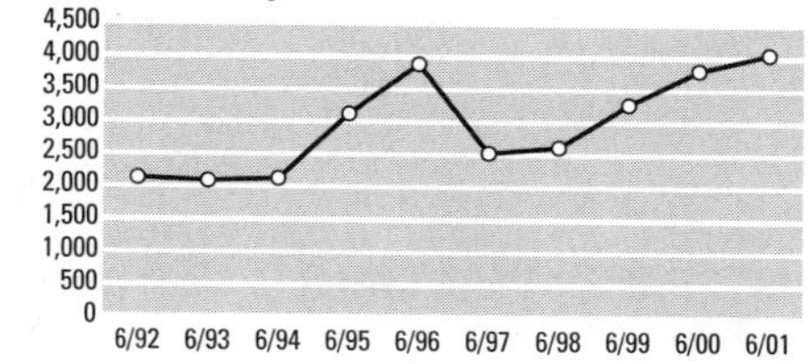

California Steel Industries, Inc.

California Steel Industries (CSI) is into slab and steel slab. The company uses steel slab produced by third parties to manufacture steel products such as hot-rolled and cold-rolled steel, galvanized coils and sheets, and electric resistance weld (ERW) pipe. Its customers include construction and building suppliers, oil and gas producers, wheel and rim manufacturers, and packaging and container companies. CSI serves the western region of the US; about half of its flat-rolled steel is consumed by customers in Las Vegas, Phoenix, and Southern California. Japan's JFE Holdings and Brazilian iron ore miner Companhia Vale do Rio Doce (CVRD) each own 50% of CSI.

The majority of sales come from within the US; CSI does sell to foreign customers, primarily in Canada and Mexico (about 1% of sales).

CSI also offers additional services like engineering and metallurgical advice. The company operates slitting, shearing, coating, and single-billing services for third parties.

EXECUTIVES

Chairman: Tatsuhiko Hamamoto, age 62
President and CEO: Vicente Wright, $262,370 pay (prior to promotion)
EVP, Operations: Tashiyuki (Ted) Tamai, age 52, $282,149 pay
VP, Administration and Corporate Secretary: Brett Guge, age 48, $260,050 pay
VP, Sales: James Wilson, age 52, $223,650 pay
Controller and Treasurer: Robert McPherson
Communications Manager: Kyle Schulty
Auditors: KPMG LLP

LOCATIONS

HQ: 14000 San Bernardino Ave., Fontana, CA 92335
Phone: 909-350-6200 **Fax:** 909-350-6223
Web: www.californiasteel.com

California Steel Industries sells steel products in 11 US states located west of the Rocky Mountains.

PRODUCTS/OPERATIONS

2002 Sales

	% of total
Hot-rolled steel	47
Galvanized steel	36
Cold-rolled steel	11
Electric resistance weld pipe	6
Total	**100**

COMPETITORS

AK Steel Holding Corporation
Geneva Steel
Imsa
Nucor
Slater Steel
Steel Dynamics

HISTORICAL FINANCIALS

Company Type: Joint venture

Income Statement FYE: December 31

	REVENUE ($ mil.)	NET INCOME ($ mil.)	NET PROFIT MARGIN	EMPLOYEES
12/02	754	35	4.6%	929
12/01	640	(4)	—	952
12/00	721	35	4.8%	973
12/99	687	47	6.8%	952
12/98	673	20	2.9%	—
12/97	723	29	4.0%	—
Annual Growth	0.9%	4.0%	—	(0.8%)

2002 Year-End Financials

Debt ratio: 66.0%
Return on equity: 14.7%
Cash ($ mil.): 3
Current ratio: 2.92
Long-term debt ($ mil.): 163

Net Income History

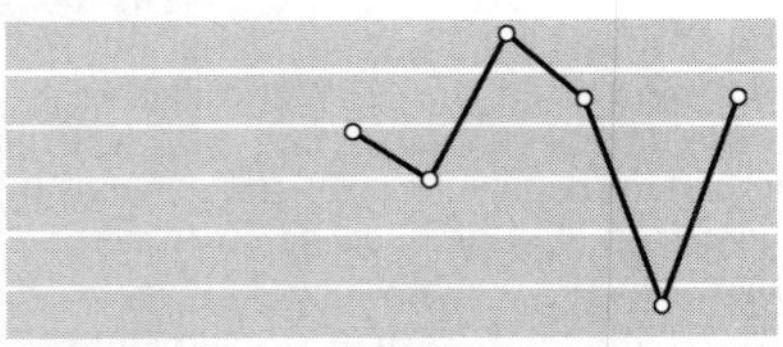

C&S Wholesale Grocers, Inc.

C&S Wholesale Grocers is at the bottom of the food chain — and likes it that way. The company is New England's largest food wholesaler and second in the US (behind SUPERVALU), delivering groceries to some 4,000 independent supermarkets, major supermarket chains (including Safeway), mass marketers, and wholesale clubs from Maine to Maryland. The company distributes more than 53,000 items, including groceries, produce, and nonfood items. It runs facilities in Connecticut, Maryland, Massachusetts, New Jersey, New York, Ohio, Pennsylvania, and Vermont. C&S also sells groceries through Grand Union supermarkets. Chairman and CEO Richard Cohen owns the company, which his grandfather started in 1918.

Under pressure from the rapid growth of self-distributing grocery chains (most notably Wal-Mart Supercenters), C&S Wholesale has grown its business by providing outsourced distribution and logistics services to its retailer customers through its logistics service provider ES3. The wholesaler has taken over the facilities and runs distribution and logistics for customers including the Stop & Shop, Pathmark, Safeway's Eastern Division, and the Tops Markets supermarket chains. The 2002 acquisition of Tops' distribution operations, with facilities in Buffalo, NY and the Cleveland area, opens up new markets for C&S Wholesale.

To avoid losing one of its top customers, the company, through affiliate GU Markets, bought bankrupt supermarket chain The Grand Union Company's assets in March 2001, expanding C&S Wholesale into retailing. However, C&S Wholesale has since closed or sold off most of Grand Union's 170 stores.

C&S is moving its headquarters and 400 jobs from Brattleboro to Keene, New Hampshire. The wholesaler will build new offices in Keene, and keep its warehouse operations and about 800 workers in Brattleboro.

In keeping with its buying surge, C&S in 2003 purchased parts of the wholesale grocery division of Fleming Companies.

HISTORY

Israel Cohen and Abraham Siegel began C&S Wholesale Grocers in 1918 in Worcester, Massachusetts. Cohen ran the company for more than 50 years after buying out Siegel in 1921. It became a family concern in 1972 when Cohen turned the company over to his son Lester, who soon brought in his sons, Jim and Rick.

C&S Wholesale expanded over the years, growing along with its customers. It had $98 million in sales in 1981, the year its skyrocketing growth began. Also in 1981 Rick, now the company's chairman, president, and CEO, engineered a move to Brattleboro, in southern Vermont, where it had better access to interstate highways and a larger workforce.

After attending a seminar hosted by management whiz Tom Peters, in 1987 Cohen set up self-managed teams of three to eight employees who would act as small business units responsible for a customer's order from the time it was received to when it was delivered. Team members were paid for the amount of time they worked and were given bonuses for error-free operations and penalties for errors or damaged goods. His plan saw an immediate response in terms of increased sales, and by 1992 C&S Wholesale had more than $1 billion in sales. Rick bought out his father in 1989 and the next year became the company's single shareholder when he bought out his brother.

C&S Wholesale started its produce business in 1990 (by 1994 it was the major purchaser of locally grown fruits and vegetables) and began making plans to build an 800,000-sq.-ft. refrigerated warehouse near a scenic highway in Brattleboro. However, it ran up against environmentalists and Vermont's Act 250 environmental impact law, and eventually dropped its original plan, opting instead to expand at its headquarters.

In 1992 the wholesaler offered plans for a smaller, revised warehouse, but again met opposition. After a two-year battle, C&S Wholesale gave up and said it would build elsewhere. (Most of its employees and warehouses are now in Massachusetts and New Jersey.)

The following year C&S Wholesale welcomed 127 Grand Union stores and several East Coast Wal-Mart stores as customers. The next year the company picked up another 103 Grand Union stores; Grand Union said it was closing two distribution centers and shifting distribution to C&S Wholesale in a deal worth $500 million a year. A $650 million-per-year contract with Edwards stores was inked in 1996, the year C&S Wholesale's sales topped $3 billion.

The company acquired ice-cream distributor New England Frozen Foods in 1997. Continuing its move toward the Mid-Atlantic, C&S Wholesale took over the distribution and supply operations of New Jersey-based grocery chain Pathmark Stores in 1998 for $60 million. In 1999 C&S Wholesale purchased Shaw's Supermarkets' Star Markets' wholesale division and moved into Pennsylvania with a facility in York.

In 2001 the company, through affiliate GU Markets, bought most of the assets of one of its biggest customers, bankrupt The Grand Union Company. C&S acquired about 170 of Grand Union's 197 stores in the purchase. It transferred most of the stores to third-party purchasers, but will continue operating about 20 of them.

In June 2002 C&S Wholesale formed a new holding company, called C&S Holdings, and reorganized its management to better oversee its various businesses. Also that summer the company acquired the grocery distribution operations of Tops Markets, a division of Dutch supermarket giant Royal Ahold.

EXECUTIVES

Chairman and CEO: Richard B. (Rick) Cohen
Vice Chairman: Reuben T. Harris
President: Edward Albertian
EVP and CFO, General Counsel: Mark Gross
SVP, Deputy General Counsel: Carl G. Wistreich
SVP, Finance: James Weidenheimer
SVP, Human Resources: Charlotte Edwards
SVP, Procurement: Bob Palmer
SVP, Retail Services: Ken Ferrera
SVP, Strategic Planning: William Hamlin
VP, Marketing and Merchandising: Russell Zwanka
President, C&S Holdings; Acting President, ES3: Ronald (Ron) Wright
Director of Corporate Giving: Gina Goff
Director of Special Projects: Perry Cohen

LOCATIONS

HQ: 47 Old Ferry Rd., Brattleboro, VT 05302
Phone: 802-257-4371 **Fax:** 802-257-6810
Web: www.cswg.com

C&S Wholesale Grocers services more than 4,000 stores from Maine to Maryland. It has warehouses and distribution facilities in Aberdeen and Collingwood, Maryland; Brattleboro, Vermont; Hatfield and Westfield, Massachusetts; Chester, Montgomery, and Newburgh, New York; Windsor Locks, Connecticut; Woodbridge, New Brunswick, North Brunswick, and Dayton, New Jersey; Cleveland, Ohio; and Harrisburg, Pennsylvania.

PRODUCTS/OPERATIONS

Selected Customers

A&P
Big Y Foods
BJ's Wholesale Club
Foodtown
Giant-Carlisle (owned by Royal Ahold)
Giant-Landover (owned by Royal Ahold)
Pathmark
Safeway
Shaw's
Stop and Shop
Tops Markets

COMPETITORS

Associated Wholesalers
Bozzuto's
Di Giorgio
Fleming Companies
IGA
Krasdale Foods
McLane
Nash Finch
Richfood
SUPERVALU
Wakefern Food

HISTORICAL FINANCIALS

Company Type: Private

Income Statement FYE: September 30

	REVENUE ($ mil.)	NET INCOME ($ mil.)	NET PROFIT MARGIN	EMPLOYEES
9/02	9,700	—	—	7,500
9/01	8,500	—	—	7,000
9/00	7,000	—	—	5,000
9/99	6,050	—	—	4,000
9/98	5,120	—	—	3,800
9/97	3,665	—	—	3,000
9/96	3,348	—	—	2,850
9/95	2,650	—	—	2,000
9/94	1,837	—	—	1,500
9/93	1,867	—	—	1,300
Annual Growth	20.1%	—	—	21.5%

Revenue History

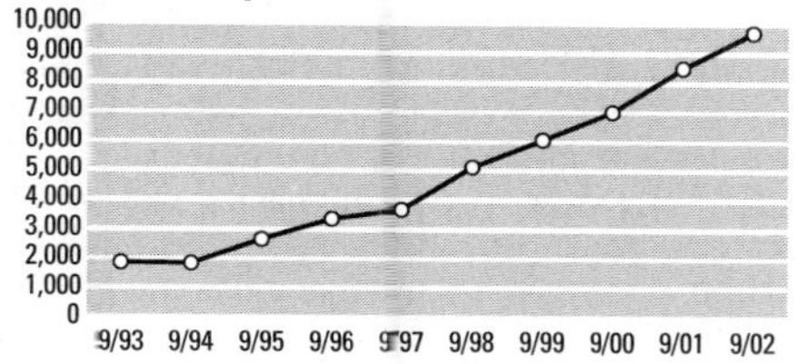

Cargill, Incorporated

Cargill may be private but all of its parts are highly visible. The US's largest private corporation, Cargill's diversified operations include grain, cotton, sugar, and petroleum trading; financial trading; food processing; futures brokering; feed and fertilizer production; and steelmaking. The company is the leading grain producer in the US, and its Excel unit is one of the top US meatpackers. Cargill's brands include Diamond Crystal (salt), Gerkens (cocoa), Honeysuckle White (poultry), and Sterling Silver (fresh meats). Descendants of the founding Cargill and MacMillan families own about 85% of Cargill.

Being private doesn't mean Cargill is cut off from the world. The agribusiness giant has operations in 67 countries throughout the world. Along with its grain and meatpacking businesses, Cargill is a commodity trader and a producer of animal feed and crop fertilizers. It is also a global supplier of oils, syrups, flour, and other products used in food processing.

Cargill also is involved in petroleum trading, financial trading, futures brokering, and shipping. Its North Star subsidiary is a major minimill steelmaker in the US. To focus on processing, Cargill sold its seed operations and coffee trading business and is selling part of its steel business. It is forming a joint venture with Hormel Foods to market fresh beef, along with pork, under the brand name Always Tender.

In order to expand its sweetener segment, in 2002 Cargill announced a marketing alliance with Southern Minnesota Beet Sugar Cooperative and in 2003 it announced another such agreement with Wyoming Sugar. Later in 2003 the company announced a joint venture with Hain Celestial to develop healthy functional foods and beverages using Cargill's isoflavones, inulin, and chondroitin products. That year it also announced it was acquiring The Duckworth Group, a UK Flavor company with facilities in Africa, China, India, and the UK.

HISTORY

William W. Cargill founded Cargill in 1865 when he bought his first grain elevator in Conover, Iowa. He and his brother Sam bought grain elevators all along the Southern Minnesota Railroad in 1870, just as Minnesota was becoming an important shipping route. Sam and a third brother, James, expanded the elevator operations while William worked with the railroads to monopolize transport of grain to markets and coal to farmers.

Around the turn of the century, William's son William S. invested in a number of ill-fated projects. William W. found that his name had been used to finance the projects; shortly afterward, he died of pneumonia. Cargill's creditors pressed for repayment, which threatened to bankrupt the company. John MacMillan, William W.'s son-in-law, took control and rebuilt Cargill. It had recovered by 1916 but lost its holdings in Mexico and Canada. MacMillan opened offices in New York (1922) and Argentina (1929), expanding grain trading and transport operations.

In 1945 Cargill bought Nutrena Mills (animal feed) and entered soybean processing; corn processing began soon after and grew with the demand for corn sweeteners. In 1954 Cargill benefited when the US began making loans to help developing countries buy American grain. Subsidiary Tradax, established in 1955, became one of the largest grain traders in Europe. A decade later Cargill began trading sugar by purchasing sugar and molasses in the Philippines and selling them abroad.

Cargill made its finances public in 1973 (as a requirement for its unsuccessful takeover bid of Missouri Portland Cement), revealing it to be one of the US's largest companies, with $5.2 billion in sales. In the 1970s it expanded into coal, steel, and waste disposal and became a major force in metals processing, beef, and salt production.

In the early 1990s Cargill began selling branded meats and packaged foods directly to supermarkets. To placate family heirs who wanted to take Cargill public, CEO Whitney MacMillan, grandson of John, created an employee stock plan in 1991 that allowed shareholders to cash in their shares. He also boosted dividends and reorganized the board, reducing the family's control. MacMillan retired in 1995 and non-family member Ernest Micek became CEO and chairman.

The firm bought Akzo Nobel's North American salt operations in 1997, becoming the #2 US salt company. Cargill bulked up its grain trading business by acquiring the grain export operations of Continental Grain in 1999. Micek resigned as CEO that year and was replaced by Warren Staley. Also in 1999 Cargill fessed up to misappropriating some genetic seed material from rival Pioneer Hi-Bred, killing the $650 million sale of its North American seed assets to Germany's AgrEvo.

Cargill sold its coffee trading unit in 2000 and sought buyers for its rubber business. Also, Cargill sold its North American hybrid seed business to Dow Chemical (Cargill had sold its foreign seed operations to Monsanto in 1998) and bought Agribrands International (Purina and Checkerboard animal feeds sold outside the US).

In 2001 the company bought family-held turkey and chicken processor Rocco Enterprises. That year the North Star Steel subsidiary agreed to sell off its tubing business and laid off employees in other divisions, citing high energy costs and lower demands for steel.

In 2002 Cargill Health & Food Technologies introduced trehalose, a naturally occurring type of sugar made from cornstarch. Trehalose has a blunted insulin response relative to other sugars and helps preserve food flavor, color, and texture. Cargill also launched Oliggo-Fiber, a line of natural soluble fiber ingredients that increases calcium absorption as well as the number of beneficial bacteria in the body. Both are marketed to the food industry for use in nutrition bars, sports drinks, bakery products, ice cream, and confections. That same year Cargill purchased a 56% stake in Cerestar (starches, syrups, feeds) from Montedison SpA, the Italian agriculture and energy conglomerate. It subsequently purchased the bulk of the company's publicly held stock, increasing its ownership of Cerestar to approximately 97%.

While its Wilbur Chocolate subsidiary is generally quiet, Cargill plumped it up by acquiring Peter's Chocolate from Nestlé USA in late 2002.

EXECUTIVES

Chairman and CEO: Warren R. Staley, age 60
Vice Chairman and CFO: Robert L. Lumpkins, age 59
Vice Chairman: F. Guillaume (Bassy) Bastiaens
Vice Chairman: David W. Raisbeck, age 55
President and COO: Gregory R. Page
EVP: Fredric W. Corrigan
EVP: David M. Larson
SVP: David W. Rogers
SVP, Director of Corporate Affairs: Robbin S. Johnson
Corporate VP: William A. (Bill) Buckner
Corporate VP: John E. Geisler
Corporate VP: James N. Haymaker
Corporate VP: John D. March
Corporate VP: K. Scott Portnoy
Corporate VP and Controller: Galen G. Johnson
Corporate VP and CTO: Ronald L. Christenson
Corporate VP and Treasurer: William W. Veazey
Corporate VP, General Counsel and Corporate Secretary: Steven C. Euller
Corporate VP, Human Resources: Nancy P. Siska
Corporate VP, Information Technology: Rita J. Heise
Corporate VP, Procurement: James T. Prokopanko
Corporate VP, Public Affairs: Bonnie E. Raquet
Corporate VP, Transportation & Product Assurance: Frank L. Sims
Director, Stakeholder and Investor Relations: Lisa Clemens
Auditors: KPMG LLP

LOCATIONS

HQ: 15407 McGinty Rd. West, Wayzata, MN 55391
Phone: 952-742-7575 **Fax:** 952-742-7393
Web: www.cargill.com

PRODUCTS/OPERATIONS

Selected Divisions and Products

Agriculture
Animal feed
Aquaculture feed
Biosciences
Caprock Industries (cattle feedlots)
Cargill AgHorizons
Cargill Animal Nutrition
Champions Choice (agricultural salt products)
Feed phosphates
Fertilizer
Pet food

Financial Markets
Financial Markets Group (financial instrument trading, money markets, value investing and trade, and structured finance)
Cargill Technical Services (agricultural consultancy, management, natural resource management, rural development, and technical assistance)

Food Processing
Apples
Bulk and packaged oils (baking, frying, margarine, and salad dressing)
Cargill Cacau (cocoa and cocoa products)
Cargill Foods
Cargill Malts
Cargill Salt
Citric acid
Copra (dried coconut meat)
Corn (including dextrose and starch production)
Corn- and wheat- wet milling (produce corn syrups, glucose, and dry sweeteners)
Cottonseed
Diamond Crystal (salt products)
Dry Corn Ingredients
Emmpak Foods (meat packing)
Erythritol
Ethanol
Excel Corporation (beef and pork processing and sales)
Gerkens (cocoa and cocoa products)
Hazelnuts
High fructose corn syrups
Honeysuckle White (turkey)
Lactic acid polymers
Masa flour (tortillas, tortilla chips, and taco shells)
Nutraceuticals
Oliggo-Fiber (soluble fiber food ingredient)
Oranges
Palm oil
Peanuts
Poultry (production, processing, marketing)
Progressive Baker
Protein products (flavored soy protein, soy flour, and textured vegetable protein)
Rapeseed
Riverside (turkey)
Sodium citrate
Soybeans
Sun Valley Foods (chicken and turkey)
Sunflower seeds
Sunny Fresh (processed egg products)
Trehalose (cornstarch sugar)
Wilbur Chocolate Company

Industrial
Cargill Corn Milling (industrial-grade starches)
Cargill Industrial Oils & Lubricants
Cargill Steel and Wire (chain link fencing, concrete reinforcing wire, flat-rolled steel, industrial wire, and wire mesh)
North Star Recycling (supplies metal to parent North Star Steel's minimills)
North Star Steel (steel minimills)
Phosphate mining and fertilizer manufacturing
Salt (process evaporated, rock, and solar)

Trading
Cargill Investor Services (CIS, futures/futures options broker and risk management consultant)
Cargill Marine and Terminal
Cargo Carriers (operates jumbo dry and liquid cargo barges)
G&M Stevedoring
Greenwich Marine (ocean shipping)
Hohenberg Bros (cotton trading)
Rogers Terminal & Shipping (stevedoring services)

COMPETITORS

Ag Processing
ADM
BASF AG
Bunge Limited
Cereol
COFCO
CHS
ConAgra
ContiGroup
Corn Products International
Dow Chemical
DuPont
Farmland Industries
General Mills
Hormel
King Arthur Flour
Koch
Land O'Lakes Farmland Feed
Morton Salt
Nippon Steel
Nucor
Perdue
Rohm and Haas
Saskatchewan Wheat Pool
Smithfield Foods
Tate & Lyle
Tyson Foods
Tyson Fresh Meats
United States Steel

HISTORICAL FINANCIALS

Company Type: Private

Income Statement FYE: May 31

	REVENUE ($ mil.)	NET INCOME ($ mil.)	NET PROFIT MARGIN	EMPLOYEES
5/03	59,894	1,290	2.2%	98,000
5/02	50,826	827	1.6%	97,000
5/01	49,204	358	0.7%	90,000
5/00	47,602	480	1.0%	84,000
5/99	45,697	597	1.3%	84,000
5/98	51,418	468	0.9%	80,600
5/97	56,000	814	1.5%	79,000
5/96	56,000	902	1.6%	76,000
5/95	51,000	671	1.3%	73,300
5/94	47,135	571	1.2%	70,700
Annual Growth	2.7%	9.5%	—	3.7%

Net Income History

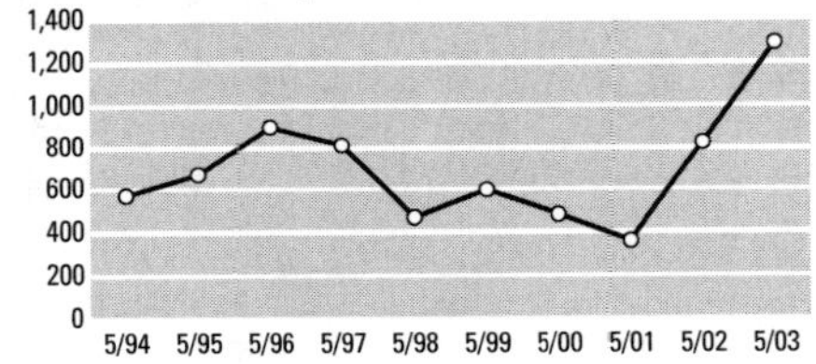

Carlson Companies, Inc.

Carlson Companies began in 1938 as the Gold Bond Stamp Company but has evolved into a leisure services juggernaut. The company owns 50% of travel giant Carlson Wagonlit (French hotelier Accor owns the rest). It also owns more than 800 hotels under brands such as Radisson, Country Inns & Suites By Carlson, Park Inn, and Park Plaza. Carlson's restaurant empire includes the 700-unit T.G.I. Friday's chain. A specialist in relationship marketing, Carlson Marketing Group offers services such as sales promotion and customer loyalty programs. CEO Marilyn Carlson Nelson and director Barbara Carlson Gage, the daughters of late founder Curtis Carlson, each own half of the company.

Carlson Companies' travel operations include Carlson Wagonlit Travel, its 50/50 joint venture with Accor. One of the largest business travel firms in the world, Carlson Wagonlit has more than 3,000 locations worldwide and counts AT&T, General Electric, and IBM among its clients.

Carlson's lodging empire includes the 430-unit Radisson chain, as well as the Country Inns & Suites By Carlson (300 hotels), Park Inn and Park Plaza Hotels (100), and Regent International (about a dozen). In 2002 the company announced it was building about 20 new hotels, largely Radisson and Country Inns & Suites, in India. Carlson also is active in cruise operations through its Radisson Seven Seas Cruises, which offers one all-suite and five deluxe ships sailing to about 485 destinations.

In 2002 Marilyn Carlson Nelson was appointed by President Bush to chair the National Women's Business Council.

HISTORY

Curtis Carlson, the son of Swedish immigrants, graduated from the University of Minnesota in 1937 and went to work selling soap for Procter & Gamble in the Minneapolis area. In 1938 he borrowed $55 and formed Gold Bond Stamp Company to sell trading stamps. His wife, Arleen, dressed as a drum majorette and twirled a baton to promote the concept. By 1941 the company had 200 accounts. Business was slowed by WWII but took off in the 1950s. During the 1960s the company began diversifying into other enterprises such as travel, marketing, hotels, and real estate.

In 1962 Gold Bond Stamp bought the Radisson Hotel in Minneapolis and began expanding the chain. The company adopted the Carlson Companies name in 1973. Carlson Companies continued expanding its holdings during the 1970s, buying the 11-unit T.G.I. Friday's chain, as well as Country Kitchen International, a string of family restaurants.

In 1979 Carlson bought First Travel Corp., which owned travel agency Ask Mr. Foster and Colony Hotels. Carlson Companies slowed the pace of its acquisitions in the 1980s. Hired in 1984, Juergen Bartels changed the hospitality division's strategy from building and owning hotels to franchising and managing them. This enabled Carlson to weather the crash that followed the 1980s hotel building boom.

The company took T.G.I. Friday's public to fund expansion in 1983, but it reacquired all outstanding shares in 1989. Carlson launched its cruise ship business in 1992, when the luxury liner SSC *Radisson Diamond* set sail.

The company made a major international advance in 1994 when it formed joint venture Carlson Wagonlit Travel, with France's Accor. In 1997 Carlson expanded into the luxury hotel business when it bought Regent International from Four Seasons. In a nod to its roots, the company also unveiled the Gold Points Reward guest loyalty system to reward customers who frequent its hotels and restaurants.

In 1998 Curtis Carlson appointed his daughter, Marilyn Carlson Nelson, as the company's chief executive (he remained chairman). The following year Carlson Companies merged its UK leisure travel business with UK-based travel and financial services firm Thomas Cook. Founder Curtis Carlson died that year and Nelson added chairman to her title. The company later filed to spin off its T.G.I. Friday's unit as Carlson Restaurants Worldwide, but decided to put that offering on hold until market conditions improved.

In 2001 Carlson Companies sold its 22% stake in Thomas Cook Holdings to German tour company C&N (which then changed its name to Thomas Cook AG). In mid-2001 the company bought 52-unit Asian restaurant chain Pick up Stix. That year it also added a sixth ship to its cruise line.

EXECUTIVES

Chairman and CEO: Marilyn Carlson Nelson, age 63
President and COO; Chairman and CEO, Carlson Restaurants Worldwide; President and CEO, Carlson Hospitality Worldwide; COO, Carlson Consumer Group: Curtis C. Nelson
EVP and CFO: Martyn R. Redgrave, age 50
SVP and CIO: Stephen S. Brown
SVP and General Counsel: William A. Van Brunt
SVP Human Resources: Rosalyn (Roz) Mallet
VP and Treasurer: John M. Diracles Jr.
VP Corporate Audit and Consulting: Vicki Rasmusen
VP Corporate Financial Services and Business Risk Management: Anita Phillips
VP Corporate Human Resources: Charles Montreuil
VP Corporate Public Relations and Communications: Douglas R. Cody
VP Legal and Corporate Secretary: Ralph Beha
VP Tax: Darrel M. Hamann
Director of Public Relations: Sam Macalus
President and CEO, Carlson Leisure Group: Michael Batt
President and CEO, Carlson Marketing Group: James J. (Jim) Ryan
President, Carlson Restaurants Worldwide: Richard T. Snead
President and CEO, Carlson Wagonlit Travel: Hervé Gourio
President and CEO, Radisson Seven Seas Cruises: Mark S. Conroy
President and Managing Director of Carlson Hotels Worldwide Asia-Pacific: Paul S. Kirwin
President, Carlson Family Foundation: Barbara Carlson Gage
President, Carlson Hotels Worldwide; President, Carlson Hotels — The Americas; President and COO, Radisson Hotels and Resorts: Jay Witzel
President, Carlson Real Estate Company: Matt Van Slooten

LOCATIONS

HQ: 1405 Xenium Ln. North, Plymouth, MN 55441
Phone: 763-212-1000 **Fax:** 763-212-2219
Web: www.carlson.com

Carlson Companies has operations in more than 140 countries.

PRODUCTS/OPERATIONS

Selected Operations

Cruises
Radisson Seven Seas Cruises

Hotels
Country Inns & Suites By Carlson
Park Inn and Park Plaza hotels
Radisson Hotels & Resorts
Regent International Hotels

Marketing
Carlson Marketing Group
Gold Points Rewards

Restaurants
Pick up Stix
T.G.I. Friday's

Travel
Carlson Destination Marketing Services
Carlson Leisure Fulfillment Services
Carlson Wagonlit Travel (50%)
CarlsonTravel.com
Neiman Marcus Travel Services
Travel Agents International

Other
Carlson Leasing Group (equipment lease financing)
Carlson Vacation Ownership (vacation ownership properties)
Provisions (food and beverage distribution)

COMPETITORS

American Express
Applebee's
Brinker
Carnival
Darden
Denny's
Fairmont Hotels
Four Seasons Hotels
Gage Marketing
Hilton
Hyatt
Interpublic Group
Maritz
Marriott International
Metromedia
Mitchells & Butlers
O'Charley's
Omnicom
Outback Steakhouse
Ritz-Carlton
Rosenbluth International
Royal Caribbean Cruises
Starwood Hotels & Resorts
Sunterra
TRT Holdings
WorldTravel
WPP Group
Wyndham

HISTORICAL FINANCIALS

Company Type: Private

Income Statement FYE: December 31

	ESTIMATED REVENUE ($ mil.)	NET INCOME ($ mil.)	NET PROFIT MARGIN	EMPLOYEES
12/02	6,700	—	—	180,000
12/01	6,800	—	—	188,000
12/00	9,800	—	—	192,000
12/99	9,800	—	—	188,000
12/98	7,800	—	—	147,000
12/97	6,600	—	—	68,530
12/96	4,900	—	—	65,462
12/95	4,500	—	—	69,000
12/94	3,900	—	—	65,000
12/93	3,500	—	—	41,000
Annual Growth	7.5%	—	—	17.9%

Revenue History

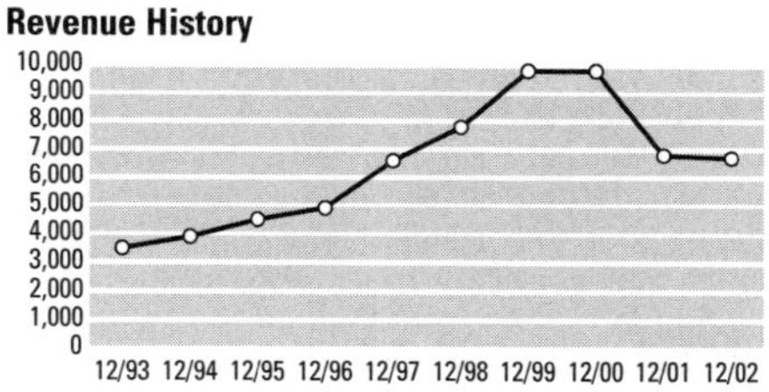

Carlson Wagonlit Travel

No, Carlson Wagonlit Travel did not get its middle name from Indians trying to explain to pioneers that their covered wagons were on fire. The company is descended from both the creator of the Orient Express (Wagons-Lits) and the oldest US travel agency chain (Ask Mr. Foster). It manages business travel from more than 3,000 travel offices in more than 140 countries. The company is the #2 travel firm in the world behind American Express. It is co-owned by the US firm Carlson Companies (whose US leisure and franchise operations also fall under the Carlson Wagonlit brand) and France's Accor.

Carlson Companies is a service conglomerate with nonbusiness travel operations such as hospitality (it franchises Radisson Hotels, T.G.I. Friday's and Italianni's restaurants, and luxury cruise lines) and marketing services (motivational and incentive programs for businesses). The company's two parents have invested $100 million to get Carlson Wagonlit (pronounced Vah-gon-LEE) online with business-to-consumer and business-to-business sites. Accor also is reaping the benefits of training the company's travel agents in booking Accor hotel rooms.

At the beginning of 2003, the company was granted permission by China to form a joint venture project with China Air Service for a corporate travel management company.

HISTORY

Belgian inventor Georges Nagelmackers' first enterprise was adding sleeping compartments to European trains in 1872. Nagelmackers later created the Orient Express. Over the years his Wagons-Lits company expanded its mission to become Wagonlit Travel.

While Nagelmackers was establishing his business in Europe, Ward G. Foster was giving out steamship and train schedules from his gift shop facing the stately Ponce de Leon Hotel in St. Augustine, Florida. As legend has it, hotel patrons with travel questions were directed to Foster's shop with: "Ask Mr. Foster. He'll know." In 1888 he founded Ask Mr. Foster Travel (it became the oldest travel agency in the US). By 1913 the company had offices located in pricey department stores and in the lobbies of upscale hotels and resorts throughout the country. After 50 years at the helm, Foster sold his business in 1937, three years before his death.

After suffering hard times during WWII and into the 1950s, the company changed hands again in 1957 when Donald Fisher and Thomas Orr, two Ask Mr. Foster shareholders, bought controlling interests for $157,000. In 1972 Peter Ueberroth (future Major League Baseball commissioner and Los Angeles Olympic Organizing Committee president) bought the company, then sold it in 1979 to Carlson Companies, Inc. In 1990 Ask Mr. Foster became Carlson Travel Network. Also that year Carlson Companies acquired the UK's A.T. Mays, the Travel Agents — a leading UK seller of vacation and tour packages. By 1992 Carlson Companies, besides adding a travel agency a day to the 2,000-plus it already owned, was adding a new hotel every 10 days.

Europe's Wagonlit Travel and the US's Carlson Travel Network joined forces in 1994 to pursue expansion efforts. Under a dual-president ownership, the parent companies owned operations in specific world regions. The two companies began developing new business technology and expanded into new global business markets. In 1994 the venture acquired Germany's Brune Reiseburo travel agency and opened a branch office in Moscow. Through 1995 and 1996 acquisitions targeted the Asia/Pacific region, including Hong Kong's and Japan's Dodwell Travel and the corporate travel business of Singapore's Jetset Travel. It also formed a partnership with Traveland, an Australian travel agency.

In 1997 Wagonlit Travel and Carlson Travel Network finalized the merger of their business activities operations, renamed Carlson Wagonlit Travel. The following year the new company acquired Florida's Travel Agents International, with more than 300 franchised operations and $600 million in annual sales. In 1999 three travel agencies in eastern Canada consolidated under the Carlson Wagonlit Travel brand, creating the largest travel network in that region. Also, Carlson Companies founder and Carlson Wagonlit Travel chairman Curtis Carlson died. In 2000 the company agreed to form a Japan-based joint venture with Japan Travel Bureau (now JTB Corp.). The arrangement will increase Carlson Wagonlit's presence in Asia while increasing the number of JTB locations in North America.

In 2001 Carlson Wagonlit cut jobs because of a slowdown in business travel.

EXECUTIVES

President and CEO; President, Europe, Middle East, and Africa: Hervé Gourio
CFO: Tim Hennessy
EVP Business Travel: Dan Miles
EVP Global Sales and Account Management: Liliana Frigerio
EVP Supplier Relations: Robert (Rob) Deliberto
CIO: Loren Brown
President, Asia Pacific: Geoffrey Marshall
President, North America: Robin Schleien
EVP, France: Georges Sampeur
EVP Business Development and Marketing, North America: Robert (Bob) Briggs
EVP Europe, Middle East, and Africa: Richard Lovell
EVP Human Resources, Europe, Middle East, and Africa: Philippe Vinay
EVP Information Technology, Europe, Middle East, and Africa: Len Blackwood
CFO, Europe, Middle East, and Africa: Nicholas Francou
VP Finance, Americas: Nick Bluhm
VP Human Resources, North America: David Moran
Public Relations Specialist: Laurie Alexander

LOCATIONS

HQ: Carlson Wagonlit Travel, Inc.
1405 Xenium Ln. North, Plymouth, MN 55441
Phone: 763-212-4000 **Fax:** 763-212-2219
Web: www.carlsonwagonlit.com

COMPETITORS

American Express
JTB
Kuoni Travel
Maritz
Rosenbluth International
Thomas Cook AG
TUI
World Travel Specialists
WorldTravel

HISTORICAL FINANCIALS

Company Type: Joint venture

Income Statement FYE: December 31

	REVENUE ($ mil.)	NET INCOME ($ mil.)	NET PROFIT MARGIN	EMPLOYEES
12/02	10,700	—	—	7,504
12/01	11,000	—	—	8,083
12/00	12,000	—	—	7,702
12/99	11,000	—	—	7,015
12/98	11,000	—	—	20,100
12/97	10,600	—	—	20,000
12/96	9,500	—	—	20,000
Annual Growth	2.0%	—	—	(15.1%)

Revenue History

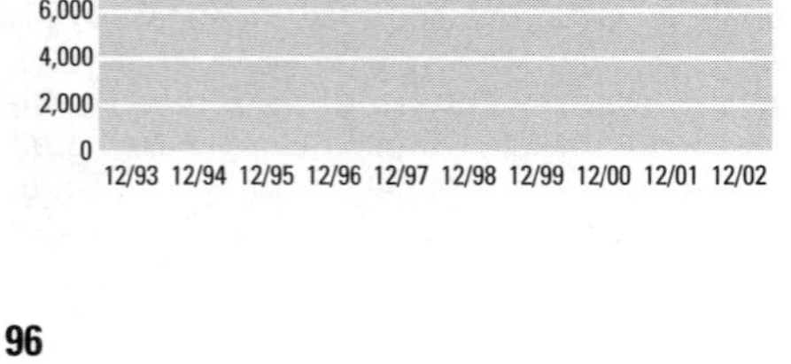

The Carlyle Group

Can you say military-industrial complex? The Carlyle Group takes part in management-led buyouts (MBOs), acquires minority stakes, and provides other investment capital for companies. It is particularly hawkish on the aerospace and defense industries, putting to good use the experience of its chairman emeritus Frank Carlucci, a former Secretary of Defense. Firms in this arena make up a significant share of the portfolio at Carlyle, one of the world's largest private equity firms. The company has also engineered MBOs and other capital deals for firms in such industries as consumer products, energy, health care, information technology, real estate, beverages, and telecommunications.

Carlyle's directorship reads like George W. Bush's inaugural ball invite list. Reagan Secretary of the Treasury James Baker serves as a senior counselor, and Richard Darman, former director of the Office of Management and Budget under George Bush (the elder), is a managing director. Former President George Bush has served with Carlyle and Colin Powell, before becoming Secretary of State, made an appearance on behalf of the firm.

The company has more than $13 billion in assets under management and has invested in such names as United Defense Industries of Crusader artillery fame, Dr Pepper/Seven Up Bottling Group, and MedPointe.

Although the majority of the firm's money is in North America, it is also pushing more intensely overseas, launching funds aimed at Asia, Europe, Latin America, and Russia. The firm (along with Apax Partners and UK-based cinven) bought a 28% share of France-based health care and business publisher Vivendi Universal Publishing. One of the company's larger moves overseas is the purchase of the transportation business of The Daiei, Japan's #2 retailer in which the company has a 90% stake, worth $28 million.

Its moves overseas haven't all been as easy as picking up the phone or as lucrative, however. Carlyle, along with investment firm Welsh, Carson, Anderson & Stowe, are planning to buy the yellow pages business of the financially strapped Qwest Communications while navigating the lawsuit filed by Milberg Weiss Bershad Hynes & Lerach LLP. The firm also returned portions of its European venture capital group funds to investors after the values of its investments lessened and the availability of target acquisitions decreased.

Carlyle is keeping an eye on the transportation and health care industries as possible candidates for deal making, but the maturing buy-out market creates fewer prize deals and more competitors.

California Public Employees' Retirement System, or CalPERS, owns more than 5% of Carlyle.

HISTORY

In 1987 T. Rowe Price director Edward Mathias brought together David Rubenstein, a former President Carter aide; Stephen Norris and Daniel D'Aniello, both executives with Marriott Corp.; William Conway Jr., the CFO of MCI; and Greg Rosenbaum, a VP with a New York investment firm. They pooled their experience along with a load of money from T. Rowe Price Associates, Alex. Brown & Sons (now Deutsche Banc Alex. Brown), First Interstate (now part of Wells Fargo), and Pittsburgh's Mellon family to form a buyout firm.

Named after the Carlyle Hotel in New York, the firm opted to make Washington, DC, its headquarters so it wouldn't get lost in the crowd of New York investment firms. The company spent its first years investing in a mish-mash of companies, using Norris' and D'Aniello's Marriott experience to focus primarily on restaurant and food service companies (including Mexican restaurant chain Chi-Chi's).

In 1989 it wooed the well-connected Frank Carlucci, who had served as President Reagan's secretary of defense, to join the group. Soon thereafter, Carlyle began making more high-profile deals. That year it acquired Coldwell Banker's commercial real estate operations (sold 1996) and Caterair International, Marriott's airline food services (sold 1995).

Carlucci helped redirect the firm's focus to the downsizing defense industry. Among its targets were Harsco Corp. (1990), BDM International (1991), and LTV Corp.'s missile and aircraft units (1992). Carlyle helped overhaul their operations and make them attractive (for the right price) to the industry's elite, including Boeing and Lockheed Martin.

As the company's reputation grew, so did its cast of players. Among its new backers were James Baker and Richard Darman (both Reagan and Bush administration alums), and investor George Soros, who chipped in some $100 million into the Carlyle Partners L.P. buyout fund. With the help of its "access capitalists" such as Baker and Saudi Prince al-Waleed bin Talal (whom the firm helped add to his fortune in a 1991 Citicorp stock transaction), Carlyle made deals in the Middle East and Western Europe (including a bailout of Euro Disney) in the mid-1990s.

While the firm continued to be a side in the iron triangle, acquiring such defense companies as aircraft castings maker Howmet in 1995, it picked up a grab bag of holdings, such as natural food grocer Fresh Fields Markets (1994; sold in 1996); the quick turnaround helped build Carlyle's war chest. The firm also began investing in industrial-cleanup companies, seeing increased government spending as a major opportunity for profit.

As Carlyle's esteem rose, so did the number of its investors. In the late 1990s the firm launched buyout funds targeting Asia (closed 1999), Europe (closed 1998), Russia, and Latin America. At home, it faced a dwindling number of opportunities as the long-running bull market drove up prices and more investors chased fewer deals. Among those was its partnership with Cadbury Schweppes to buy the Dr Pepper Bottling Co. of Texas and merge it with its own American Bottling Co.

Carlyle began the new century by launching Carlyle Asset Management Group, selling its stake in Le Figaro to Socpresse, acquiring Rexnord and a majority stake in CSX Lines. Extending its reach, the company partnered with GMT Communications Partners and acquired Casema in 2003. The firm went on to buy automotive parts manufacturer United Components from UIS, Inc., in the same year.

EXECUTIVES

Chairman Emeritus: Frank C. Carlucci, age 73
Chairman: Louis V. Gerstner Jr., age 61
Chairman, Carlyle Europe: Rt. Hon. John Major
Senior Counselor: James A. (Jim) Baker III, age 72
Managing Director and CEO, Carlyle Management Group: B. Edward Ewing
Founder and Managing Director: William E. Conway Jr., age 53
Founder and Managing Director: Daniel A. D'Aniello
Founder and Managing Director: David M. Rubenstein
Senior Advisor: Arthur Levitt Jr., age 71
Managing Director and CFO: John F. Harris
Manager, Human Resources: Lori Sabet
Principal, Carlyle Asset Management Group: David Kupperman
Carlyle Asset Management Group: Eric Edell
Principal: Ted Hobart
Director of External Communications, Europe: Daniela Zuin
Director, Carlyle Asia Venture Partners: Kandasamy Chandrasekar
Director, Carlyle Asia Venture Partners: Sean He
Director, European Real Estate: Marc Demumieux
Director, Carlyle Japan Partners: Shigeru Fukunaga
Principal, Carlyle Partners: Steve Owens
Director, Carlyle Carlyle: Dennis Schulze
VP Corporate Communications: Chris Ullman

LOCATIONS

HQ: 1001 Pennsylvania Ave. NW, Ste. 220 South, Washington, DC 20004
Phone: 202-347-2626 **Fax:** 202-347-1818
Web: www.thecarlylegroup.com

US Offices

Bellevue, WA	Newport Beach, CA
Charlotte, North Carolina	San Francisco
Dallas	Tysons Corner, VA
Greenwich, CT	Washington, DC
New York	

International Offices

Bangalore, India	Munich
Barcelona, Spain	Paris
Frankfurt	Riyadh, Saudi Arabia
Hong Kong	Seoul
London	Singapore
Milan	Tokyo
Moscow	

COMPETITORS

Bain Capital	Investcorp
Blackstone Group	J.P. Morgan Partners
Credit Suisse First Boston (USA), Inc.	KKR
Forstmann Little	Lehman Brothers
Goldman Sachs	Texas Pacific Group
Hicks, Muse	Thomas Lee

Carpenter Co.

It's a cushy job for Carpenter Co., making polyurethane foam and chemicals and polyester fiber used as cushioning by the automotive, bedding, floor covering, and furniture industries, among others. The company started out making foam rubber; it now manufactures air filter media, expanded polystyrene building materials, and a tire fill product as a replacement for air in off-road construction vehicles. Carpenter has facilities throughout the US, as well as in Canada, Denmark, France, Germany, Spain, Sweden, and the UK. The company also sells consumer products — which include craft fiber products, mattress pads, and pillows — through retailers. Carpenter is owned by chairman and CEO Stanley Pauley.

EXECUTIVES

Chairman and CEO: Stanley F. Pauley
CFO: Dave Moorman
VP, Sales and Marketing, Consumer Division: Dan Schecter
Director, MIS: Tim Lester
Personnel Recruiter: Tom Newport

LOCATIONS

HQ: 5016 Monument Ave., Richmond, VA 23220
Phone: 804-359-0800 **Fax:** 804-353-0694
Web: www.carpenter.com

Carpenter has manufacturing facilities throughout the US, as well as in Canada, Denmark, France, Germany, Spain, Sweden, and the UK.

PRODUCTS/OPERATIONS

Selected Products

Air filter media	Consumer products
Automotive	Polystyrene
Bedding	Flexible foam packaging
Carpet cushion	Furniture
Chemicals	Polyester fiber
Chemical systems	Tire products

COMPETITORS

Acordis	PMC Global
Advanced Materials Group	RBX
British Vita	Reliance Industries
Foamex	Sealed Air
Owens Corning	Wellman

HISTORICAL FINANCIALS

Company Type: Private

Income Statement FYE: December 31

	REVENUE ($ mil.)	NET INCOME ($ mil.)	NET PROFIT MARGIN	EMPLOYEES
12/02	1,000	—	—	6,200
12/01	1,035	—	—	6,200
12/00	1,075	—	—	6,200
12/99	977	—	—	5,500
12/98	950	—	—	6,500
12/97	879	—	—	6,325
12/96	800	—	—	6,500
12/95	745	—	—	6,900
12/94	691	—	—	6,901
12/93	619	—	—	6,905
Annual Growth	5.5%	—	—	(1.2%)

Revenue History

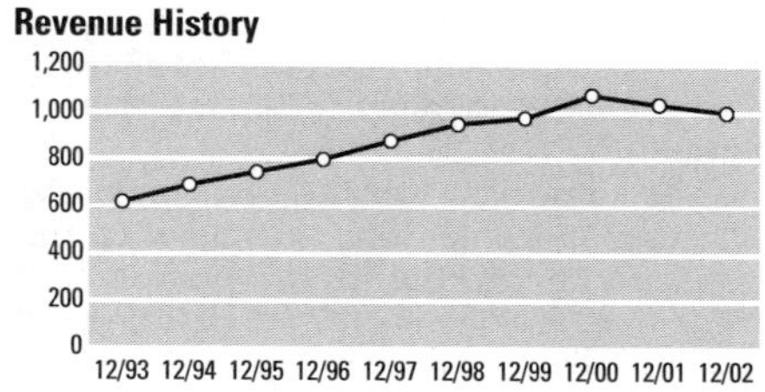

CARQUEST Corporation

Searching for a sensor, solenoid, or switches? CARQUEST can steer you in the right direction. The replacement auto parts distribution group is owned by its seven member warehouse distributors (the largest is North Carolina-based General Parts). The CARQUEST group includes a network of about 60 distribution centers serving about 4,000 distributor-owned and independent jobbers in the US and Canada. The company sells its own line of auto parts (made by Moog Automotive, Dana, Gabriel, and others) to the jobbers, as well as wholesalers, for eventual resale to professional repair centers, service stations, dealerships, and, to a lesser degree, do-it-yourself (DIY) customers.

General Parts owns more than 1,200 stores across the US and Canada. The average CARQUEST store carries about 18,000 parts, while a distribution center carries some 150,000 items.

To strengthen ties with service shops, CARQUEST offers the Tech-Net Professional Auto Service program. The program provides a national computer base of more than 600,000 repair records as well as a full guarantee on parts; signage and other marketing tools are also included.

Consolidation in the aftermarket industry has blurred the lines of distribution between wholesalers and retailers, causing all segments of the industry to scramble for ways to gain or maintain market share. CARQUEST focuses on professional mechanics, but it is being squeezed as retailers such as AutoZone look beyond their regular DIY customers for a piece of the commercial pie. At the same time, chains such as The Pep Boys — Manny, Moe & Jack are chipping away at service stations' business by offering parts and service.

HISTORY

Even though he didn't know the auto parts business, Temple Sloan recognized America's infatuation with the automobile and started distributor General Parts in 1961 at age 21. By 1972 he had acquired enough warehouse space to supply the entire state of North Carolina. Determined to get bigger faster, Sloan studied auto parts kingpin Genuine Parts, digging through its annual reports and uncovering tricks of the trade, while working on a few of his own. To compete in what was then a fast-growing industry, Genuine Parts had created a marketing alliance, NAPA, that used mass buying power to garner better pricing and service from manufacturers that often wouldn't recognize individual companies.

Sloan recruited friends and fellow distributors Dan Bock, president of Bobro Products, and Joe Hughes, president of Indiana Parts Warehouse, and together they formed CARQUEST in 1974. The company was designed to help jobbers (middlemen between distributors and mechanics) being threatened by retailers attempting to get a piece of the commercial business market traditionally served by jobbers. CARQUEST began recruiting other distributors and achieved first-year sales of $29 million. In the first five years, almost 1,500 jobbers committed to CARQUEST. Leadership rotated among distributor members until Bock became president in 1984.

As CARQUEST grew, the need for a unifying private-label line became apparent. In the 1970s it developed the Proven Value line of do-it-yourself-oriented products such as oils and filters. The establishment of the CARQUEST brand in the mid-1980s gave the company complete control over quality, coverage, price, and promotions, giving CARQUEST jobbers an advantage in the marketplace. Private-label sales grew from 20%-25% of business to 70% by 1996.

That year CARQUEST relocated its national headquarters from Tarrytown, New York, to Lakewood, Colorado, and Peter Kornafel became president and CEO, replacing Bock. Kornafel had been president of Hatch Grinding, a Denver distributor that merged with General Parts in 1996. The next year the firm moved into Canada, as General Parts bought half of the McKerlie-Millen subsidiary of Acklands (more than 400 parts stores). In 1998 CARQUEST launched its Tech-Net Professional Service program.

Also in 1998 CARQUEST added about 150 new stores to its network when General Parts bought bankrupt APS Holding; it also added 75 stores and eight DCs from Republic Auto. In 1999 General Parts bought The Parts Source, which included 41 Ace Auto Parts stores in Florida.

In January 2000 General Parts bought Acktion Corp's 50% interest in CARQUEST Canada, giving them complete ownership. Later in the year, General Parts also bought St. Louis-based distributor; A.E. Lottes Co. In 2001 the company moved its headquarters to Raleigh, North Carolina, and Art Lottes III succeeded Kornafel as president.

EXECUTIVES

Chairman: Neil Stockel
Vice Chairman, Secretary, and Treasurer: Pete Kornafel
President: A.E. Lottes III
EVP: Todd Hack
CFO, CARQUEST and General Parts: John Gardner
Director of Human Resources, CARQUEST and General Parts: Ted Pattison

LOCATIONS

HQ: 2635 E. Millbrook Rd., Raleigh, NC 27604
Phone: 919-573-3000 **Fax:** 919-573-2501
Web: www.carquest.com

CARQUEST operates some 60 warehouse distribution centers serving about 4,000 stores in the US and Canada.

PRODUCTS/OPERATIONS

Member Warehouse Distributors

Auto Parts Wholesale
Automotive Warehouse, Inc.
BWP Distributors, Inc.
CAP Warehouse
CARQUEST Canada, Ltd. (owned by General Parts)
General Parts, Inc.
Muffler Warehouse
Straus-Frank Co.

Selected Manufacturers of CARQUEST Products

Airtex
American Driveline
Cardone Industries
Dana
Federal
Federal Mogul Corporation
Gates
Maremont/Gabriel
Melling
Moog Automotive
NEAPCO
Standard Motor Products
Wells Manufacturing Corp.
WIX

COMPETITORS

Advance Auto Parts
AutoZone
CSK Auto
Genuine Parts
Hahn Automotive
Pep Boys
Sears
Target
Wal-Mart

HISTORICAL FINANCIALS

Company Type: Private

Income Statement FYE: December 31

	ESTIMATED REVENUE ($ mil.)	NET INCOME ($ mil.)	NET PROFIT MARGIN	EMPLOYEES
12/02	2,500	—	—	36,500
12/01	2,200	—	—	36,000
12/00	2,000	—	—	36,000
12/99	2,000	—	—	36,000
12/98	1,400	—	—	35,000
12/97	1,300	—	—	35,000
12/96	1,200	—	—	26,000
12/95	940	—	—	26,000
12/94	860	—	—	—
12/93	860	—	—	—
Annual Growth	12.6%	—	—	5.0%

Revenue History

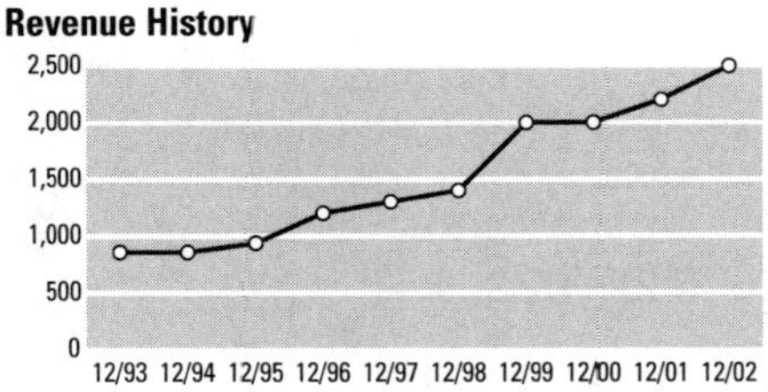

Carrols Corporation

You might say Carrols has some quick-service royalty in its blood. The company is the #1 Burger King franchisee in the US, with more than 350 units in about a dozen states. The company also owns and franchises its own quick-service chains, Taco Cabana and Pollo Tropical. Its 126 Taco Cabana units (10 are franchised) offer Tex-Mex and traditional Mexican dishes, such as tacos, fajitas, and quesadillas. The 82-unit Pollo Tropical chain (24 are franchised) serves fresh grilled chicken and Caribbean side dishes, such as fried yucca and black beans and rice. The company, started in 1968 by Herbert Slotnick, is controlled by investment firms BIB Holdings (42%) and Madison Dearborn Partners (21%).

While more than half the company's sales come from its Burger King operations, Carrols is focused on growing its two quick-service chains. In 2002 it brought in John Haywood, formerly with Jerrico (which once owned the Long John Silver's chain), to lead the development of the two concepts. Carrols acquired Pollo Tropical for $95 million in 1998 and bought Taco Cabana for $155 million in 2000.

The company had formerly operated the Carrols fast-food chain, acquired by Slotnick in 1968. He combined it with his movie theater chain to form Carrols Development Corporation, which went public the next year. Beginning in 1976, however, the company began converting its Carrols locations into Burger King restaurants. Within two years the Carrols chain had disappeared, but the company retained the name. Carrols was forced by anti-trust regulators to shed the theaters in 1981. Chairman Alan Vituli, who has a 9% stake in Carrols, led an $88 million buyout to take the company private in 1986.

EXECUTIVES

Chairman and CEO: Alan Vituli, age 61, $1,076,250 pay
President and COO; President, Taco Cabana: Daniel T. Accordino, age 52, $760,015 pay
VP and CFO: Paul R. Flanders, age 46, $380,008 pay
VP, General Counsel, and Secretary: Joseph A. Zirkman, age 42, $380,008 pay
VP and Controller: Timothy J. LaLonde, age 46
VP Human Resources: Jerry Digenova, age 45
VP Information Services: John Lukas, age 41
President and COO, Pollo Tropical: Nicholas A. Castaldo, age 51, $347,288 pay
EVP, Taco Cabana: Michael A. Biviano, age 45
Chief Concept Officer, Hispanic Brands: John W. Haywood
Auditors: PricewaterhouseCoopers LLP

LOCATIONS

HQ: 968 James St., Syracuse, NY 13203
Phone: 315-424-0513 **Fax:** 315-425-8874
Web: www.carrols.com

2002 Burger King Locations

	No.
New York	147
Ohio	82
North Carolina	40
Michigan	27
South Carolina	21
Pennsylvania	12
Kentucky	10
Indiana	5
Maine	5
Massachusetts	2
New Jersey	2
Connecticut	1
Vermont	1
Total	**355**

PRODUCTS/OPERATIONS

2002 Sales

	$ mil.	% of total
Burger King	380.1	58
Taco Cabana	175.4	27
Pollo Tropical	101.5	15
Total	**657.0**	**100**

COMPETITORS

AFC Enterprises
California Pizza Kitchen
Checkers Drive-In
Chick-fil-A
CKE Restaurants
Consolidated Restaurant Operations
Subway
Dairy Queen
Jack in the Box
La-Van Hawkins Food
McDonald's
Pancho's Mexican Buffet
Triarc
Wendy's
YUM!

HISTORICAL FINANCIALS

Company Type: Private

Income Statement FYE: Sunday nearest December 31

	REVENUE ($ mil.)	NET INCOME ($ mil.)	NET PROFIT MARGIN	EMPLOYEES
12/02	657	12	1.8%	16,100
12/01	656	(4)	—	16,100
12/00	467	4	0.9%	17,200
12/99	457	1	0.2%	13,200
12/98	417	0	0.1%	12,725
12/97	295	2	0.7%	11,700
12/96	241	3	1.3%	8,400
12/95	226	15	6.6%	7,500
12/94	204	(2)	—	7,800
12/93	171	(9)	—	7,200
Annual Growth	16.1%	—	—	9.4%

2002 Year-End Financials

Debt ratio: 1,307.7%
Return on equity: 55.6%
Cash ($ mil.): 3
Current ratio: 0.44
Long-term debt ($ mil.): 349

Net Income History

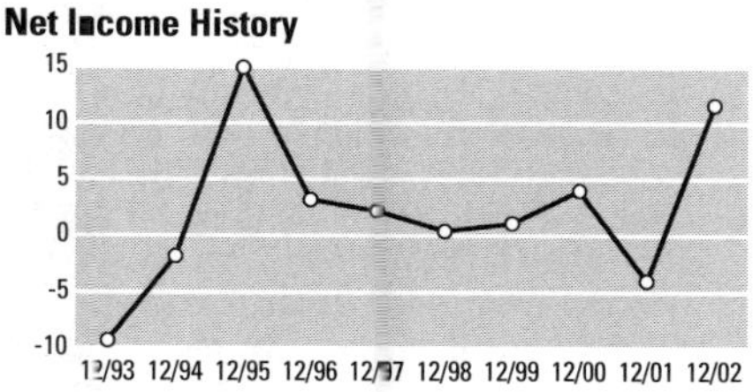

Carter Lumber

Who says you can't teach an old log new tricks? Founded in 1932 by Warren Carter, Carter Lumber owns about 250 lumber and home-improvement stores in Ohio and eight other states from Michigan to South Carolina. The company caters to both contractors and do-it-yourselfers, supplying them with lumber, plywood, roofing, kitchen and bath products, windows, doors, plumbing and electrical products, heating equipment, tools, siding, and other products. The home-improvement retailer also operates two building supply centers and 72,000 acres of timberland in Arkansas. Warren Carter died in 2000, at the age of 101, but Carter Lumber continues to be a family-owned business.

EXECUTIVES

CEO: Bryan Carter
President: Neil C. Sackett
SVP and CFO: Jeff Donley
VP, Marketing and Director, Human Resources: David McCafferty
VP, Technology: Jeff Seder

LOCATIONS

HQ: Carter Lumber Company
601 Tallmadge Rd., Kent, OH 44240
Phone: 330-673-6100 **Fax:** 330-678-6134
Web: www.carterlumber.com

Carter Lumber operates stores in Illinois, Indiana, Kentucky, Michigan, North Carolina, Ohio, Pennsylvania, South Carolina, and Virginia.

COMPETITORS

84 Lumber
Home Depot
Lowe's
Menard
Stock Building Supply
Weekes Forest Products
Wickes
Wolohan Lumber

HISTORICAL FINANCIALS

Company Type: Private

Income Statement FYE: December 31

	ESTIMATED REVENUE ($ mil.)	NET INCOME ($ mil.)	NET PROFIT MARGIN	EMPLOYEES
12/01	590	—	—	4,400
12/00	570	—	—	4,300
12/99	560	—	—	4,100
12/98	550	—	—	4,000
12/97	450	—	—	—
Annual Growth	7.0%	—	—	3.2%

Revenue History

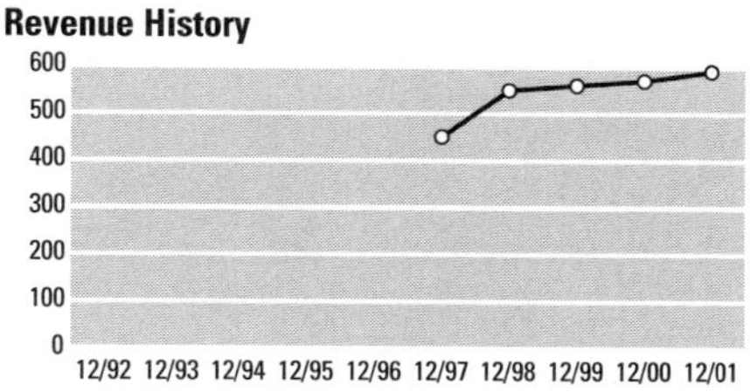

Catholic Health East

Catholic Health East doesn't believe prayers to St. Jude are necessary to continue providing health care to any person in need. Catholic Health East is one of the top religious health systems in the US. The company carries out its mission of serving the poor and the old by offering health care through more than 30 hospitals, about 40 nursing homes, and some 20 independent- and assisted-living facilities, primarily on the East Coast. The network also operates behavioral health facilities and offers adult day care, home health services, and hospice care.

Catholic Health East is governed by a board composed of 10 sisters, eight secular health care professionals, and one reverend.

Like many religious health care systems, Catholic Health East continues to struggle with the problem of keeping both the faith and the bottom line intact. Providing indigent care is becoming increasingly difficult thanks to the ever-rising costs of health care coupled with cuts in reimbursements that have hurt not only the system's hospital services but its nursing home and outpatient services as well.

HISTORY

It was three easy pieces that made up Catholic Health East in 1997. Allegany Health System, Eastern Mercy Health System, and Sisters of Providence Health System operated almost entirely in separate, but adjacent, geographic areas on the East Coast, overlapping only in Florida.

Catholic Health East's history goes as far back as 1831, when the Sisters of Mercy was founded in Dublin, Ireland, by Catherine McAuley, who established a poorhouse using her inheritance. Some of the sisters hopped the Pond in 1843, establishing the first Catholic hospital in the US, the Mercy Hospital of Pittsburgh, four years later. Over the years the Sisters of Mercy expanded throughout the US. By 1991 there were 25 Sisters of Mercy congregations; they united that year under the newly formed Institute of the Sisters of Mercy of the Americas.

The Sisters of Providence came from Kingston, Ontario, to found the first hospital in Holyoke, Massachusetts. Having established their own ministry, the sisters in Holyoke became a separate congregation in 1892. The congregation expanded slowly, moving into North Carolina in 1956, eventually forming the Sisters of Providence Health System.

A Polish nun, Mother Colette Hilbert, formed a new congregation in Pittsburgh in 1897 after the other members of her former parish were recalled to Poland. The new congregation entered health care in 1926, establishing a home for the elderly in New York. In honor of Hilbert's favorite saint, the order became the Franciscan Sisters of St. Joseph in 1934.

The Franciscan Sisters of St. Joseph and the Sisters of Mercy united to form the ministry that became Pittsburgh Mercy Health System in 1983. In 1986 the congregations formed Eastern Mercy Health System as a holding company for the health concern. The consolidation served to cut costs, as well as to preserve the organization's religious mission.

The Franciscan Sisters of Allegany congregation got its start in 1859 teaching children in Buffalo, New York. In 1883 the order took over St. Elizabeth Hospital in Boston, expanding its health care services ministry throughout New York, New Jersey, and Florida by the 1930s. In 1986 the sisters organized the operations as Allegany Health System.

In the early 1990s Catholic health care systems underwent a round of consolidation. Allegany Health Systems and Eastern Mercy Health Systems combined services, aiming to lower costs through economies of scale.

The mid-1990s also brought consolidation, but this time operational costs weren't the major problem; Catholic health systems across the nation were facing a shortage of sisters. To have a sufficient number of sisters to keep the "Catholic" in Catholic health care, the three health systems merged in 1997, becoming Catholic Health East.

After the merger, the company continued to build its network through acquisitions, including Mercy Health in Miami (1998) and a suffering, secular Cooper Health System in Camden, New Jersey (1999). In 2000 it gained control of two troubled hospitals in Palm Beach, Florida, only to sell them the following year. Catholic Health East remains focused on reducing costs as it expands.

EXECUTIVES

President and CEO: Daniel F. Russell
EVP and COO: Robert V. Stanek
EVP and CFO: C. Kent Russell
EVP, Continuing Care: Robert H. Morrow
EVP, Mission Integration: Sister Juliana Casey
EVP and Chief Administration Officer: Stanley T. Urban
EVP and Chief Medical Officer: Richard F. Afable
EVP, Mid-Atlantic Division: Mark O'Neil
EVP, Northeast Division: Sister Kathleen Popko

EVP, Southeast Division: Howard Watts
VP, Advocacy and Government Relations: Kenneth A. Becker
VP, Communications: Salvatore C. Foti
VP, Corporate Compliance and Legal Services: Michael C. Hemsley
VP, Financial Services: Patricia Gathers
VP, Financial Services: Randal Schultz
VP, Information Technology and CIO: Jack Hueter
VP, Leadership Formation and Human Resources: George F. Longshore
VP, Mission Services: Mary Ann Carter
VP, Quality and Patient Safety: Diane S. Denny
VP, Risk Management Services and Chief Risk Officer: Theodore Schlert
VP, Strategy Development: Elaine Bauer
VP, Materiels Management: Thomas Gruber
VP, Treasury Services: Paul Klinck
VP, Claims Services: Kathleen Murphy
VP Information Technology and Chief Information Officer, Mid Atlantic Region: William Nicholas
VP, Clinical Improvement: Ellen Reap
VP, Information Technology, Southeast Region: Doris Crain
Manager, Information Technology: Steven Basile
President and CEO, Global Health: Sister Elizabeth Scanlon

LOCATIONS

HQ: 14 Campus Blvd., Ste. 300,
Newtown Square, PA 19073
Phone: 610-355-2000 **Fax:** 610-355-2050
Web: www.che.org

PRODUCTS/OPERATIONS

Divisions

Northeast
Catholic Health System (Buffalo, NY)
Mercy Health System of Maine (Portland)
Mercycare Corporation (Albany, NY)
Sisters of Providence Health System (Springfield, MA)
St. James Mercy Health System (Hornell, NY)

Mid-Atlantic
Lourdes Health System (Camden, NJ)
Mercy Health System (Conshohocken, PA)
Pittsburgh Mercy Health System

Southeast
BayCare Health Systems (Clearwater, FL)
Holy Cross Health Ministries (Fort Lauderdale, FL)
Intracoastal Health System (West Palm Beach, FL)
Mercy Hospital (Miami)
Saint Joseph's Health System (Atlanta)
St. Mary's Health Care System, Inc. (Athens, GA)

Long-Term Care
Mercy Community Health (West Hartford, CT)
Mercy Medical (Daphne, AL)
Mercy Uihlein Health Corporation (Lake Placid, NY)
St. Joseph of the Pines (Pinehurst, NC)

Other
Franciscan Health Foundation (Tampa, FL)
Catholic Managed Care Consortium (St. Louis)
Catholic Health Association (St. Louis)
Children's Health Matters (Alexandria, VA)
Mercy Resource Management, Inc. (Naperville, IL)
NewCap Insurance Company, Limited (Cayman Islands)
Premier (California, Illinois, and North Carolina)

Supporting Congregations

Franciscan Sisters of Allegany (St. Bonaventure, NY)
Franciscan Sisters of St. Joseph (Hamburg, NY)
Hope Ministries (Newtown Square, PA)
Sisters of Mercy (Albany, NY)
Sisters of Mercy (Baltimore)
Sisters of Mercy (Buffalo, NY)
Sisters of Mercy (Hartsdale, NY)
Sisters of Mercy (Merion, PA)
Sisters of Mercy (Pittsburgh)
Sisters of Mercy (Portland, ME)
Sisters of Mercy (Rochester, NY)
Sisters of Mercy (West Hartford, CT)
Sisters of Providence (Holyoke, MA)
Sisters of St. Joseph (St. Augustine, FL)

COMPETITORS

Ascension
Bon Secours Health
Catholic Health Initiatives
HCA
Triad Hospitals

HISTORICAL FINANCIALS

Company Type: Not-for-profit

Income Statement FYE: December 31

	REVENUE ($ mil.)	NET INCOME ($ mil.)	NET PROFIT MARGIN	EMPLOYEES
12/01	4,300	—	—	43,000
12/00	4,300	—	—	44,000
12/99	4,300	—	—	45,000
12/98	3,800	—	—	45,000
12/97	3,000	—	—	31,838
12/96	2,700	—	—	—
Annual Growth	9.8%	—	—	7.8%

Revenue History

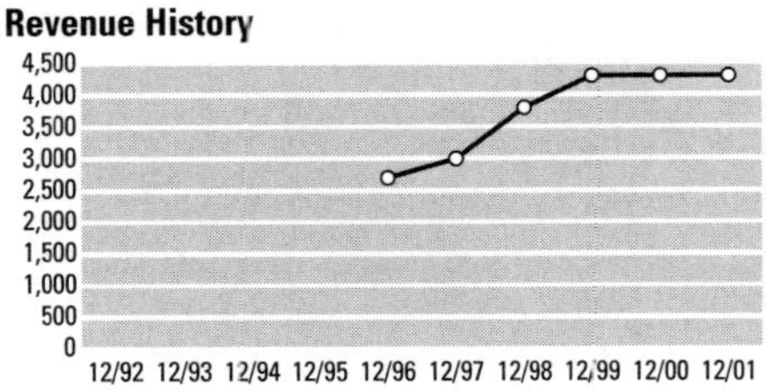

Catholic Health Initiatives

Giant not-for-profit Catholic Health Initiatives is an amalgamation of four Roman Catholic health care systems (Catholic Health Corporation of Omaha, Nebraska; Franciscan Health System of Aston, Pennsylvania; Sisters of Charity Health Care Systems of Cincinnati; and Sisters of Charity of Nazareth Health Care System of Bardstown, Kentucky). A leading Roman Catholic health system, Catholic Health Initiatives operates nearly 70 hospitals and more than 40 long-term care, assisted-living, and residential facilities. The organization is sponsored by 12 different congregations and serves communities in some 20 states.

"And he sent them out to preach the Kingdom of God and to heal the sick" (Luke 9:2). Catholic Health Initiatives hopes to make those words the driving force behind its initiative.

As a reflection of its divine purpose in a mundane health care market, the company's governing board is made up of both religious and lay officers.

Catholic Health Initiatives has to deal with the conundrum facing many Catholic health systems: Their religious mission — to care for the "unserved and underserved" (and underinsured) members of its communities — is financially uncompetitive. CHI offsets the expense of its mission by also providing health care to the general public and by making business decisions more often associated with secular business (cutting staff, centralizing functions, and joining with other Catholic health care institutions to drive harder bargains with medical suppliers).

HISTORY

In 1860 the Sisters of St. Francis established a hospital in Philadelphia, laying the foundation for a larger health care organization. In 1981 Franciscan Health System was formally established to be a national holding company for Catholic hospitals and related organizations. By the mid-1990s the system consisted of 12 member and two affiliate hospitals and 11 long-term-care facilities located in the mid-Atlantic states and the Pacific Northwest.

Sisters of Charity of Cincinnati and the Sisters of St. Francis Perpetual Adoration of Colorado Springs co-sponsored The Sisters of Charity Health Care Systems, incorporated in 1979 as a multi-institutional health care network. By the mid-1990s the system included 20 hospitals in Colorado, Kentucky, Nebraska, New Mexico, and Ohio.

Three congregations collaborated to form Catholic Health Corporation in 1980, one of the first such health care partnerships between religious communities within the Roman Catholic Church in the US. By 1996 this coalition operated 100 health care facilities in 12 states.

The development of modern managed care health care systems put pressure on the smaller Catholic hospital operations, so the three systems established Catholic Health Initiatives (CHI) in 1996 as a national entity serving five geographic regions. Patricia Cahill, a lay health care veteran who previously served the Archdiocese of New York, was appointed president and CEO of CHI. The following year CHI absorbed the 10-hospital Sisters of Charity of Nazareth Health Care System, based in Bardstown, Kentucky (founded in a log cabin in 1812).

That year CHI continued to seek new partnerships to improve efficiency. With Alegent Health it formed provider network Midwest Select with nearly 200 hospitals, marketing discounted rates to businesses. CHI allied with the Daughters of Charity to form for-profit joint venture Catholic Healthcare Audit Network to provide operational, financial, compliance, and information systems audits, as well as due diligence reviews. CHI also joined insurance joint venture NewCap Insurance with the Daughters of Charity and Catholic Health East; the firm allowed CHI to operate independently of commercial insurers.

CHI made a secular tie-in with the University of Pennsylvania Health System in 1998, whereby the university's system would offer care through five Catholic hospitals (CHI made plans to transfer these hospitals to Catholic Health East in 2001). The next year CHI announced its first loss, due to lackluster performance in the Midwest. During 2000 the company responded by streamlining operations and changing management, resulting in a positive bottom line. In 2001 it sold three hospitals in Pennsylvania, one in Delaware, and one in New Jersey.

EXECUTIVES

Chairman: Maryanna Coyle
President and CEO: Kevin Lofton
SVP, Finance and Treasury: Sister Geraldine Hoyler

SVP and Chief Medical Officer: Harold E. Ray
SVP, Human Resources, and Chief Administrative Officer: Michael Fordyce
Auditors: Ernst & Young LLP

LOCATIONS

HQ: 1999 Broadway, Ste. 2605, Denver, CO 80202
Phone: 303-298-9100 **Fax:** 303-298-9690
Web www.catholichealthinit.org

PRODUCTS/OPERATIONS

Sponsoring Congregations

Benedictine Sisters of Mother of God Monastery (Watertown, SD)
Congregation of the Dominican Sisters of St. Catherine of Siena (Kenosha, WI)
Franciscan Sisters of Little Falls (Little Falls, MN)
Nuns of the Third Order of St. Dominic (Great Bend, KS)
Sisters of Charity of Cincinnati
Sisters of Charity of Nazareth (Bardstown, KY)
Sisters of the Holy Family of Nazareth (Philadelphia, PA)
Sisters of Mercy of the Americas, Regional Community of Omaha (Omaha, NE)
Sisters of the Presentation of the Blessed Virgin Mary (Fargo, ND)
Sisters of St. Francis of Colorado Springs
Sisters of St. Francis of the Immaculate Heart of Mary (Hankinson, ND)
Sisters of St. Francis of Philadelphia

COMPETITORS

Allina Hospitals
Ascension
Beverly Enterprises
BJC HealthCare
Catholic Healthcare Partners
HCA
Health Management Associates
Health Midwest
Life Care Centers
Mayo Foundation
OhioHealth
Presbyterian Healthcare Services
Tenet Healthcare

HISTORICAL FINANCIALS

Company Type: Not-for-profit

Income Statement FYE: June 30

	REVENUE ($ mil.)	NET INCOME ($ mil.)	NET PROFIT MARGIN	EMPLOYEES
6/03	6,072	203	3.3%	67,000
6/02	5,900	117	2.0%	67,000
6/01	5,742	167	2.9%	66,000
6/00	5,551	97	1.7%	56,100
6/99	5,000	—	—	50,000
6/98	4,500	—	—	44,000
6/97	4,002	—	—	—
6/96	3,755	—	—	—
6/95	3,800	—	—	—
6/94	1,116	—	—	—
Annual Growth	20.7%	28.1%	—	8.8%

2003 Year-End Financials

Debt ratio: 55.0%
Return on equity: 5.5%
Cash ($ mil.): 298
Current ratio: 1.56
Long-term debt ($ mil.): 2,070

Net Income History

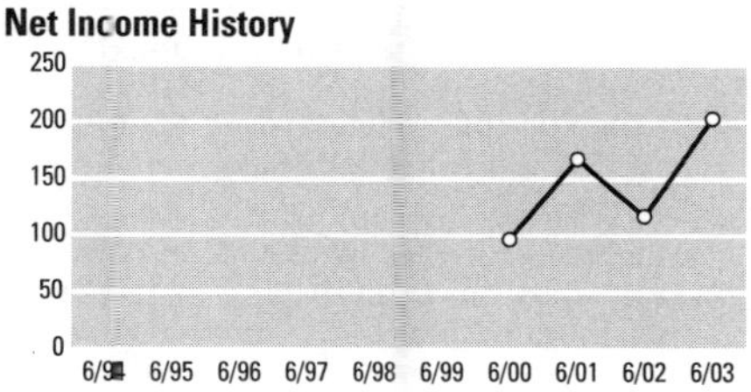

Catholic Healthcare Partners

Catholic Healthcare Partners offers health care services, primarily in Ohio but also in Indiana, Kentucky, Pennsylvania, and Tennessee through the more than 100 corporations that make up its system. Facilities include about 30 hospitals, some 30 long-term-care facilities, housing sites for the elderly, and wellness centers. The system also offers physician practices, hospice and home healthcare, and outreach services. Catholic Healthcare Partners is co-sponsored by the Sisters of Mercy in Cincinnati and in Dallas, Pennsylvania; The Sisters of the Humility of Mary in Villa Maria, Pennsylvania; The Franciscan Sisters of the Poor; and Covenant Health Systems.

EXECUTIVES

Chairman: Raymond R. Clark
Vice Chairman: Sister Mildred Ely
President, CEO, and Board Member: Michael D. Connelly
EVP: Jane Durney Crowley
EVP: Susan Smith Makos
EVP: A. David Jimenez
SVP and CFO: William Shuttleworth
SVP and Chief Medical Officer: Donald E. Casey Jr.
SVP and CIO: Rebecca Sykes
SVP and General Counsel: Michael A. Bezney
SVP, Human Resources and Organizational Learning: Jon C. Abeles
SVP, Mission and Values Integration: Sister Doris Gottemoeller
Auditors: Ernst & Young LLP

LOCATIONS

HQ: 615 Elsinore Place, Cincinnati, OH 45202
Phone: 513-639-2800 **Fax:** 513-639-2700
Web: www.health-partners.org

COMPETITORS

Ascension
Catholic Health Initiatives
Genesis Health Ventures
HCA
Kindred
OhioHealth
Tenet Healthcare
Universal Health Services

HISTORICAL FINANCIALS

Company Type: Not-for-profit

Income Statement FYE: December 31

	REVENUE ($ mil.)	NET INCOME ($ mil.)	NET PROFIT MARGIN	EMPLOYEES
12/01	2,602	—	—	30,000
12/00	2,373	—	—	27,941
12/99	1,984	—	—	30,800
12/98	1,821	—	—	29,000
12/97	1,778	—	—	23,920
12/96	1,909	—	—	24,000
12/95	2,246	—	—	18,100
12/94	1,045	—	—	15,739
12/93	1,076	—	—	—
12/92	1,025	—	—	—
Annual Growth	10.9%	—	—	9.7%

Revenue History

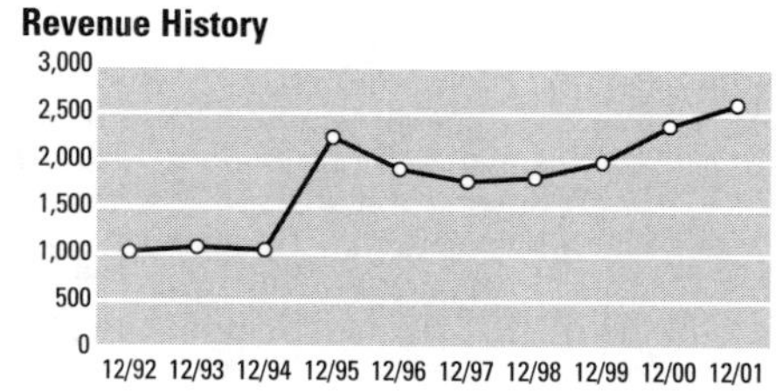

Catholic Healthcare West

Catholic Healthcare West (CHW) has found it takes a lot of nunsense to become one of the largest private, not-for-profit health care providers in the state of California. CHW has a network of more than 40 facilities in California, Arizona, and Nevada. CHW's health care system consists of acute care hospitals, skilled nursing facilities, and medical centers. CHW also has an alliance with Scripps, a major San Diego-based health care provider. The organization was formed when the hospital operations of several Roman Catholic women's religious orders consolidated, along with some non-Catholic community hospitals.

With both clergy and laity on its governing board, CHW has grown by consolidating hospitals owned by Roman Catholic women's religious orders. Additional affiliations with non-Catholic institutions have raised some hackles because Catholic doctrine opposes abortion, most forms of birth control, and in vitro fertilization.

The rapid expansion that made CHW a name in the California health care industry also left it bloated. Rising health care costs and trouble with its physician management groups cut deeply into earnings. Management casualties occurred as CHW reorganized.

HISTORY

Catholic Healthcare West traces its roots to 1857, when the Sisters of Mercy founded St. Mary's Hospital in San Francisco. The order expanded in that area, and in 1986 two different communities of the Sisters of Mercy merged their hospitals into an organization with one retirement home and 10 hospitals from the Bay Area to San Diego. Declining membership in Roman Catholic religious orders, combined with consolidation in the field, led the orders to see merger as their only route to survival.

Rising medical costs, slow payers, and merger expenses dropped the organization's combined net income to $20 million in 1988 (from nearly $58 million in 1986). One of the hardest-hit CHW affiliates was Mercy Healthcare Sacramento, which lost $4.2 million between 1986 and 1987. In 1988 Mercy Healthcare restructured along regional lines.

The next year the Sisters of St. Dominic brought two hospitals into the alliance. CHW launched the Community Economic Assistance program, which provided $220,000 in grants to 16 human service and health care agencies in its first year.

CHW continued to add facilities, including

AMI Community Hospital in Santa Cruz, California, in 1990. Since CHW already owned the area's only other acute care hospital, Dominican Santa Cruz Hospital, CHW in 1993 was ordered not to acquire any more acute care hospitals in Santa Cruz County without FTC approval.

As the trend to managed care became a stampede in the 1990s, CHW moved more into preventive care and began reining in costs through productivity improvement plans. It continued to add hospitals, including tax-supported institutions trying to compete with national for-profit systems.

The network increased its medical clout in 1994 by allying with San Diego-based ScrippsHealth, one of the state's largest HMO systems. In 1995 the Daughters of Charity Province of the West realigned its six-hospital operation with CHW. The next year the Dominican Sisters (California), the Dominican Sisters of St. Catherine of Siena (Wisconsin), and the Sisters of Charity of the Incarnate Word allied their California hospitals with CHW. New community hospitals included Bakersfield Memorial, Sierra Nevada Memorial (Grass Valley), Sequoia Hospital (Redwood City), and Woodland Healthcare.

Charity and cost-consciousness clashed in 1996 when union members staged a walkout to protest nonunion outsourcing of vocational nursing, housekeeping, and kitchen jobs. This dispute was settled, but CHW continued to be a target for union organizers, with a bitter battle against the Service Employees International Union (SEIU) starting in 1998.

CHW agreed in 1996 to merge with Samaritan Health Systems (now Banner Health System) in a move that would have made CHW one of the US's top five providers, but the deal fell apart in 1997. In 1998 CHW merged with UniHealth, a group with eight facilities in Los Angeles and Orange counties. Mounting costs forced CHW to post a loss, and in 1999 it cut some managerial positions and reorganized to recover.

The year 2000 brought CHW more problems with labor relations: SEIU argued that the organization was resistant to unionization. Continued losses led the organization to implement major restructuring the following year, as its 10 regional divisions were consolidated into four.

In 2001, CHW stepped up donations, grants, and other sponsorship efforts designed to benefit areas served by its hospitals and clinics.

EXECUTIVES

Chairperson: Diane Grassilli
President and CEO: Lloyd H. Dean
COO: Michael Erne
EVP and CFO: Michael Blaszyk
SVP Legal Services and General Counsel: Derrick Covert
SVP and Chief Medical Officer: George Bo-Linn
SVP Mission Services: Bernita McTernan
VP Finance: Mary Connick
VP Human Resources: Ernie Urquhart
Chief Information Officer: Gayle Simpkin
Chief Administrative Officer: Elizabeth Shih
Division President, Northern California Region: Edward G. Schroeder

LOCATIONS

HQ: 185 Berry St., Ste. 300, San Francisco, CA 94107
Phone: 415-438-5500 **Fax:** 415-438-5724
Web: www.chw.edu

Catholic Healthcare West operates hospitals in Arizona, California, and Nevada.

PRODUCTS/OPERATIONS

CHW Network

Arizona
Barrow Neurological Institute, Phoenix
Chandler Regional Hospital, Phoenix
Chandler Regional Medical Center, Phoenix
CHW Business Services Center, Phoenix
St. Joseph's Hospital and Medical Center, Phoenix

California
Bakersfield Memorial Hospital, Bakersfield
California Hospital Medical Center, Los Angeles
Community Hospital of San Bernardino, San Bernardino
Dominican Hospital, Santa Cruz
Glendale Memorial Hospital & Health Center, Glendale
Marian Medical Center, Santa Maria
Mark Twain St. Joseph's Hospital, San Andreas
Mercy General Hospital, Sacramento
Mercy Hospital of Folsom, Folsom
Mercy Hospital, Bakersfield
Mercy Medical Center Merced, Merced
Mercy Medical Center Mt. Shasta, Mt. Shasta
Mercy Medical Center Redding, Redding
Mercy San Juan Medical Center, Carmichael
Mercy Southwest Hospital, Bakersfield
Mercy Westside Hospital, Taft
Methodist Hospital of Sacramento, Sacramento
Northridge Hospital — Sherman Way Campus, Van Nuys
Northridge Hospital Medical Center, Northridge
Oak Valley Hospital District, Oakdale
Roscoe Boulevard Campus, Northridge
Saint Francis Memorial Hospital, San Francisco
San GabrielValley Medical Center, San Gabriel
Sequoia Hospital, Redwood City
Sierra Nevada Memorial Hospital, Grass Valley
St. Bernardine Medical Center, San Bernardino
St. Dominic's Hospital, Manteca
St. Elizabeth Community Hospital, Red Bluff
St. Francis Medical Center, Santa Barbara
St. John's Pleasant Valley Hospital, Camarillo
St. John's Regional Medical Center, Oxnard
St. Joseph's Behavioral Health Center, Stockton
St. Joseph's Medical Center, Stockton
St. Mary Medical Center, Long Beach
St. Mary's Medical Center, San Francisco
Woodland Healthcare, Woodland

Nevada
St. Rose Dominican Hospital, Henderson

Sponsoring Organizations

Daughters of Charity, Province of the West
Dominican Sisters of San Rafael
Franciscan Sisters of the Sacred Heart of Frankfort, Illinois
Sisters of Charity of the Incarnate Word of Houston, Texas
Sisters of Mercy, Auburn and Burlingame Regional Communities
Sisters of St. Catherine of Siena of Kenosha, Wisconsin
Sisters of St. Dominic of Adrian, Michigan
Sisters of St. Francis of Penance and Christian Charity of Redwood City

COMPETITORS

Adventist Health
Catholic Health Initiatives
HCA
Los Angeles County Health Department
Memorial Health Services
Sutter Health
Tenet Healthcare
Triad Hospitals

HISTORICAL FINANCIALS

Company Type: Not-for-profit

Income Statement

FYE: June 30

	REVENUE ($ mil.)	NET INCOME ($ mil.)	NET PROFIT MARGIN	EMPLOYEES
6/02	4,500	(54)	—	36,000
6/01	4,807	(87)	—	36,000
6/00	4,513	(47)	—	40,000
6/99	4,200	82	2.0%	38,000
6/98	3,301	73	2.2%	20,000
6/97	2,749	36	1.3%	17,451
6/96	2,688	161	6.0%	21,495
6/95	2,674	99	3.7%	20,000
6/94	2,584	91	3.5%	17,618
6/93	1,633	45	2.8%	17,451
Annual Growth	11.9%	—	—	8.4%

Net Income History

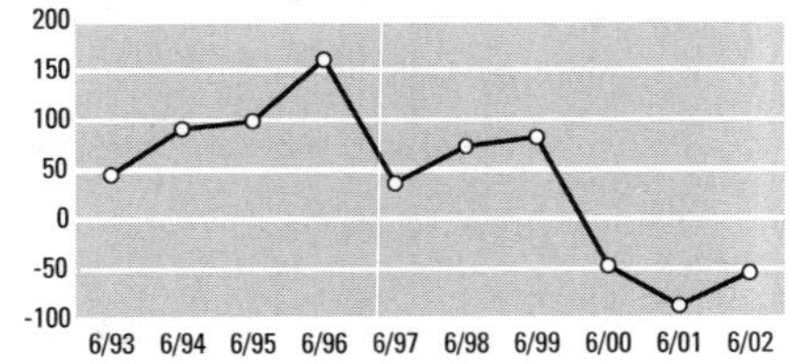

CBRE Holding

CBRE Holding is all about location, location, location — not to mention *ubicacion, l'emplacement, posizione,* and *Standort.* Better known by the name of its primary operating subsidiary CB Richard Ellis, it is the largest commercial real estate services company in the US and a powerhouse throughout the world, with operations in 48 countries. Its recent acquisition of fellow real estate giant Insignia Financial has made CBRE the largest commercial property manager in the world, overseeing a whopping 850 million sq. ft. The firm's other offerings include real estate brokerage, market research, mortgage banking (L. J. Melody), and asset management and advisory services for private pension funds and large investors.

CBRE has expanded to about 250 offices, about half of which are outside the US in nearly 50 countries in Africa, Asia, Europe, and South America. The company has moved strongly into construction in Japan, where it hopes land values have hit rock bottom. However, the vast majority of sales still come from the US, where the company is streamlining its operations and investing in Internet real estate services.

Originally a product of the merger of the commercial portion of Coldwell Banker and the non-UK based operations of Richard Ellis, the company has been taken private by a group of investors led by chairman Richard Blum's BLUM Capital Partners and CEO Ray Wirta. They bought the 60% of publicly traded CB Richard Ellis that they did not already own, and took the company private.

The company's merger with a pared-down Insignia Financial (terms of the deal dictated that firms' residential brokerage and investment properties be dumped before consummation of the merger) has put CBRE at the top of the heap in the real estate services sector.

EXECUTIVES

Chairman: Richard C. Blum
CEO: Raymond E. Wirta, age 57
President, CB Richard Ellis: W. Brett White, age 41
CFO: Kenneth J. Kay
President, EMEA (Europe, Middle East, Africa): Vaughn Thomas
Chairman and CEO, Asia Pacific: Robert Blain
President, Brokerage Western Division: William Chillingworth
President, Brokerage Eastern Division: James A. Reid
President, CBRE Investors: Robert Zerbst
COO, Americas: Calvin Frese
Chairman, Global Brokerage: Stephen B. Siegel, age 58
SVP Human Resources: Pam Perry
General Counsel: Ellis Reiter
Auditors: Deloitte & Touche LLP

LOCATIONS

HQ: CBRE Holding, Inc.
355 S. Grand Ave., Ste. 3100, Los Angeles, CA 90071
Phone: 213-613-3333 **Fax:** 213-613-3100
Web: www.cbre.com

PRODUCTS/OPERATIONS

Selected Subsidiaries

CB Richard Ellis Services, Inc.
CB Commercial Ltd. (United Kingdom)
CB Richard Ellis Investors KK (Japan)
CB Richard Ellis Investors, L.L.C.
CB Richard Ellis, Inc.
CBRE Stewardship (United Kingdom)
L.J. Melody & Company

COMPETITORS

CarrAmerica
Cendant
Colliers International
Cushman & Wakefield
DTZ
FirstService
Forest City Enterprises
Grubb & Ellis
Hines Interests
Inland Group
JMB Realty
Jones Lang LaSalle
Studley
Lend Lease
Lincoln Property
Mitsui Fudosan
Shorenstein
Staubach
Tishman Realty
Trammell Crow

HISTORICAL FINANCIALS

Company Type: Private

Income Statement

FYE: December 31

	REVENUE ($ mil.)	NET INCOME ($ mil.)	NET PROFIT MARGIN	EMPLOYEES
12/02	1,170	19	1.6%	9,500
12/01	1,171	(17)	—	9,700
12/00	1,324	33	2.5%	9,600
12/99	1,213	23	1.9%	9,853
12/98	1,035	25	2.4%	9,400
12/97	730	26	3.6%	6,700
12/96	583	71	12.1%	4,100
12/95	469	7	1.6%	4,000
12/94	429	7	1.7%	3,899
12/93	392	9	2.3%	—
Annual Growth	12.9%	8.2%	—	11.8%

2002 Year-End Financials

Debt ratio: 203.4%
Return on equity: 7.4%
Cash ($ mil.): 80
Current ratio: 0.85
Long-term debt ($ mil.): 511

Net Income History

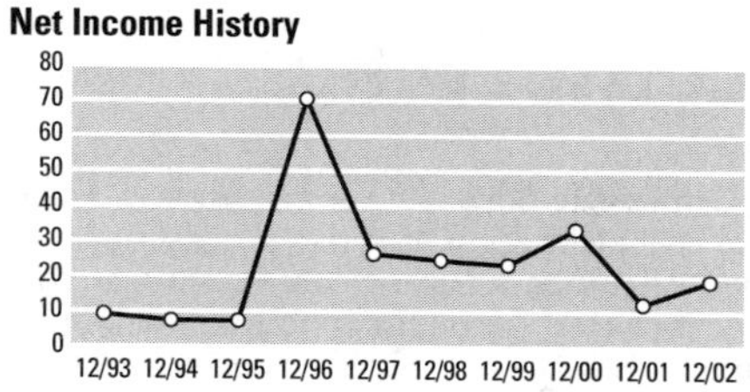

CCA Global Partners

Business is "floor"ishing at CCA Global Partners. Formerly Carpet Co-op, the firm has about 2,400 locations selling name-brand carpets and floor coverings such as ceramic tile, laminates, and hardwoods. While most stores operate under the Carpet One name, other names include Stone Mountain Carpet Mill Outlets, ProSource, and International Design Guild (high-end showrooms). Carpet One is the world's largest floor covering retailer, with stores in the US, Canada, Australia, and New Zealand. It's the exclusive US marketer of Bigelow and Lees carpet brands. Executives Howard Brodsky and Alan Greenberg founded the co-op in 1984.

CCA Global's Lighting One division (lamps, ceiling fans, accessories) has about 80 locations. The flooring group is also looking to increase its market share in the hard window treatment business. In 2003 CCA Global expanded into formalwear with Tuxedo America, a cooperative of more than 300 independently owned retailers of men's formalwear.

EXECUTIVES

Co-Chairman and Co-CEO: Howard Brodsky
Co-Chairman and Co-CEO: Alan Greenberg
President: Sandy Mishkin
Co-COO and President, Carpet One Canada: Charlie Dilks
Co-COO and SVP Marketing: Dean Marcarelli
CFO: Ed Muchnick
VP and CTO: Alan Tortorella
VP Hard Surfaces: Sandy Bone
President, Tuxedo America: Christopher Ramey
Director Human Resources: Lisa Miles

LOCATIONS

HQ: 4301 Earth City Expwy., Earth City, MO 63045
Phone: 314-506-0000 **Fax:** 314-291-6674
Web: www.carpetone.com

COMPETITORS

Abbey Carpet
After Hours
Federated
Formal Specialist
Gingiss
Home Depot
L.D. Brinkman
Lowe's
May
Menard

HISTORICAL FINANCIALS

Company Type: Cooperative

Income Statement

FYE: September 30

	ESTIMATED REVENUE ($ mil.)	NET INCOME ($ mil.)	NET PROFIT MARGIN	EMPLOYEES
9/02	5,000	—	—	550
9/01	4,000	—	—	450
9/00	3,140	—	—	350
9/99	2,800	—	—	300
9/98	2,450	—	—	265
9/97	2,000	—	—	150
Annual Growth	20.1%	—	—	29.7%

Revenue History

Cellco Partnership

Cellco Partnership, which does business as Verizon Wireless, is the #1 US mobile phone operator serving 32.5 million customers nationwide. Verizon Wireless began operations in 2000 when Bell Atlantic and Vodafone combined their US wireless assets, including their PrimeCo partnership. Verizon Wireless gained GTE's US wireless operations when Bell Atlantic bought GTE to form Verizon Communications, which owns 55% of the company; Vodafone owns 45%. Plans for an IPO, postponed in 2001, were revived but finally withdrawn in 2003 citing lack of funding needs.

The company is developing third-generation wireless services based on CDMA (code division multiple access) technology. It also has teamed up with Microsoft to develop and market wireless data services.

In late 2002 Verizon Wireless reached an agreement with Northcoast Communications, a unit of Cablevision Systems, to acquire 50 radio wave spectrum licenses in a cash deal valued at about $750 million. The licenses cover several lucrative markets including Boston and New York City. Following the deal's completion in 2003 Verizon Wireless announced plans to introduce a national service in direct competition with rival Nextel's "push to talk" feature.

EXECUTIVES

Chairman: Ivan G. Seidenberg, age 56
President, CEO, and Director; EVP, Verizon Communications: Dennis F. (Denny) Strigl, age 57, $2,000,000 pay
EVP, COO, and Director: Lowell C. McAdam, age 48, $1,124,100 pay
EVP and CTO: Richard J. (Dick) Lynch, age 54, $725,525 pay
VP and CFO: Andrew Halford, age 44, $687,835 pay
VP and CIO: Roger Gurnani, age 42
VP Human Resources: Marc C. Reed, age 44
VP Legal and External Affairs, General Counsel, and Secretary: S. Mark Tuller, age 54, $661,050 pay
VP Corporate Communications: James J. (Jim) Gerace, age 39
VP and Chief Marketing Officer: John G. Stratton, age 42
Auditors: Deloitte & Touche LLP

LOCATIONS

HQ: 180 Washington Valley Rd., Bedminster, NJ 07921
Phone: 908-306-7000 **Fax:** 908-306-6927
Web: www.verizonwireless.com

PRODUCTS/OPERATIONS

Selected Services

Cellular
Equipment sales
Paging
PCS (personal communications services)
Wireless data and Internet

COMPETITORS

ALLTEL
Arch Wireless
AT&T Wireless
Cingular Wireless
Metrocall
Nextel
SkyTel Communications
Sprint PCS
T-Mobile USA
U.S. Cellular
Western Wireless

HISTORICAL FINANCIALS

Company Type: Joint venture

Income Statement FYE: December 31

	REVENUE ($ mil.)	NET INCOME ($ mil.)	NET PROFIT MARGIN	EMPLOYEES
12/02	19,260	2,584	13.4%	39,300
12/01	17,393	1,300	7.5%	40,000
12/00	14,222	1,528	10.7%	38,000
12/99	7,659	932	12.2%	32,500
12/98	6,641	906	13.6%	—
12/97	6,196	737	11.9%	—
Annual Growth	25.5%	28.5%	—	6.5%

2002 Year-End Financials

Debt ratio: 26.4%
Return on equity: 13.3%
Cash ($ mil.): 124
Current ratio: 0.28
Long-term debt ($ mil.): 5,350

Net Income History

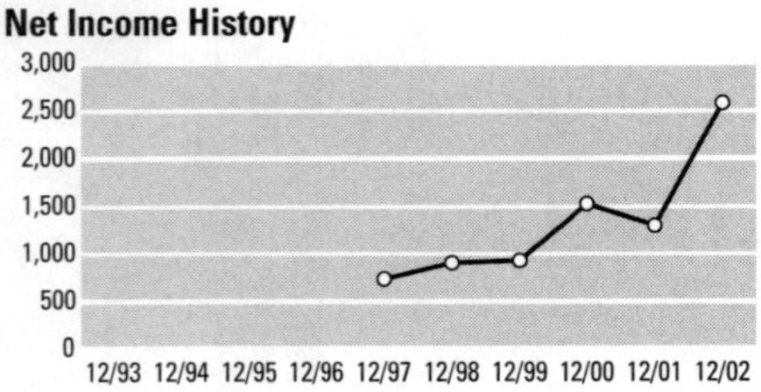

Centerplate

Centerplate (formerly Volume Services America) isn't picky about placement; it just hopes its food will make an appearance somewhere on consumers' plates. The service contractor is one of the largest providers of food, merchandise, and facility management at sports, convention, and entertainment venues in the US. Centerplate provides food services, specialized catering, and facility design and management. It has about 130 clients, including more than 20 professional football, baseball, and basketball teams. Among its 30 convention and civic center clients are the San Diego Convention Center and the Jacob K. Javits Center. Centerplate was formed through the 1998 merger of Volume Services and Service America.

In 2000 Centerplate lost out to ARAMARK in a battle for the food services business of Ogden, now known as Covanta Energy.

EXECUTIVES

CEO and Director: Lawrence E. Honig, age 54
EVP and CFO: Kenneth R. Frick, age 46, $303,596 pay
EVP, Secretary, and General Counsel: Janet Steinmayer, age 46, $341,713 pay
VP Purchasing: Paul F. Daly
VP Sales: Andy Gustafson
VP Sales/Marketing, Convention Centers: Pia Brown
VP Sales/Marketing, Sport and Entertainment: Wayne Tolleson
Auditor: Bob Pacletti
Manager, Human Resources: Jeff Witt
Public Relations: Elaine Gosnell
Auditors: Deloitte & Touche LLP

LOCATIONS

HQ: 201 E. Broad St., Spartanburg, SC 29306
Phone: 864-598-8600 **Fax:** 864-598-8695
Web: www.centerplate.com

COMPETITORS

ARAMARK
Covanta
Delaware North
HMSHost
Levy Restaurants
Sodexho

HISTORICAL FINANCIALS

Company Type: Private

Income Statement FYE: December 31

	REVENUE ($ mil.)	NET INCOME ($ mil.)	NET PROFIT MARGIN	EMPLOYEES
12/02	577	5	0.8%	28,600
12/01	543	(4)	—	30,200
12/00	523	(4)	—	33,200
12/99	283	(5)	—	26,000
12/98	196	—	—	10,800
12/97	190	—	—	10,000
Annual Growth	24.8%	—	—	23.4%

2002 Year-End Financials

Debt ratio: —
Return on equity: —
Cash ($ mil.): 10
Current ratio: 0.81
Long-term debt ($ mil.): 224

Net Income History

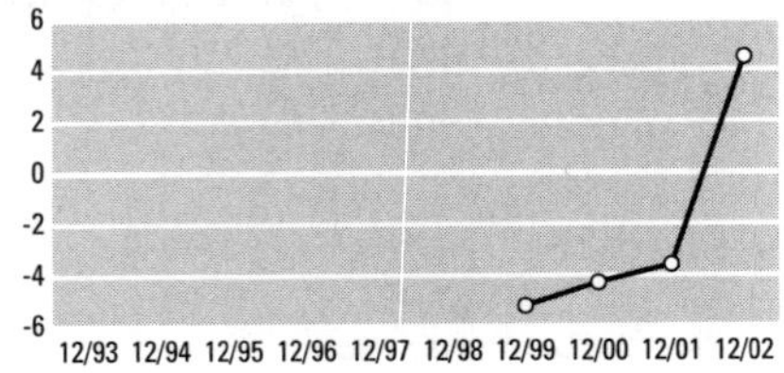

Central National-Gottesman Inc.

Got pulp? Central National-Gottesman does. Founded in 1886, the family-owned company distributes pulp, paper, paperboard, and newsprint in about 75 countries worldwide. In addition to its North American operations, the company operates about 25 overseas offices in 22 countries located in Asia, Europe, and Latin America. The Central National-Gottesman network includes the Lindenmeyr family of companies, which specialize in the distribution of fine paper as well as papers for books and magazines. The company's extensive list of suppliers includes paper industry leaders International Paper (#1) and Weyerhaeuser.

EXECUTIVES

President and CEO: Kenneth L. Wallach
Treasurer: Joshua J. (Josh) Eisenstein
VP, Human Resources: Louise Caputo
Marketing Manager: Jay Norris

LOCATIONS

HQ: 3 Manhattanville Rd., Purchase, NY 10577
Phone: 914-696-9000 **Fax:** 914-696-1066

Central National-Gottesman has operations in the Americas, Asia, Australia, and Europe including 24 overseas sales offices.

COMPETITORS

Clifford Paper
International Paper
Midland Paper
Pope & Talbot
Ris Paper
Smurfit-Stone Container
Unisource

HISTORICAL FINANCIALS

Company Type: Private

Income Statement FYE: December 31

	ESTIMATED REVENUE ($ mil.)	NET INCOME ($ mil.)	NET PROFIT MARGIN	EMPLOYEES
12/01	1,700	—	—	900
12/00	1,825	—	—	900
12/99	1,660	—	—	900
12/98	1,600	—	—	900
12/97	2,000	—	—	900
12/96	2,000	—	—	900
12/95	2,000	—	—	900
12/94	2,000	—	—	900
12/93	1,500	—	—	700
Annual Growth	1.6%	—	—	3.2%

Revenue History

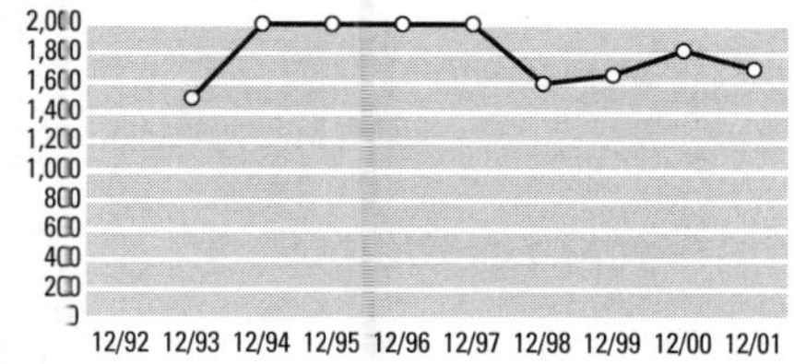

CF Industries

The grass is always greener at CF Industries. Organized in 1946 as Central Farmers Fertilizer Company, CF Industries is an interregional agricultural cooperative that manufactures and markets fertilizers, including nitrogen products (ammonia, granular urea, and UAN solutions), phosphates, and potash (potassium) products to its members in 48 states and two Canadian provinces. The co-op is owned by nine regional agricultural co-ops, including GROWMARK, Land O'Lakes, and CENEX Harvest States Cooperative. CF Industries operates nitrogen and phosphate plants, a phosphate mine, and a network of distribution terminals and storage facilities by which it offers products worldwide.

EXECUTIVES

Interim President and CEO; SVP and CFO: Stephen R. Wilson
SVP, Marketing and Sales: John H. Sultenfuss
VP and Controller: Robert D. Webb
VP and General Counsel: Paul R. Obert
VP, Planning and Business Development: Stephen Chase
VP, Public Affairs: Rosemary O'Brien
Treasurer: Dennis Baker
Recruiting Advisor: Francie Lucente

LOCATIONS

HQ: CF Industries, Inc.
1 Salem Lake Dr., Long Grove, IL 60047
Phone: 847-438-9500 **Fax:** 847-438-0211
Web: www.cfindustries.com

CF Industries has facilities in Florida, Illinois, Indiana, Iowa, Louisiana, Minnesota, Missouri, Nebraska, North Dakota, Ohio, and Washington, and in Alberta, Canada.

PRODUCTS/OPERATIONS

Selected Members

Agway, Inc.
CENEX Harvest States Cooperative
Cooperative federee de Quebec
GROWMARK, Inc.
Intermountain Farmers Association
Land O'Lakes, Inc.
MFA Incorporated
Southern States Cooperative, Inc.
Tennessee Farmers Cooperative

Selected Products

Anhydrous ammonia
Diammonium phosphate
Granular triple super phosphate
Granular urea
Monoammonium phosphate
Urea ammonium nitrate

COMPETITORS

Agrium
Farmland Industries
IMC Global
Koch
Mississippi Chemical
PCS
Terra Industries

HISTORICAL FINANCIALS

Company Type: Cooperative

Income Statement FYE: December 31

	REVENUE ($ mil.)	NET INCOME ($ mil.)	NET PROFIT MARGIN	EMPLOYEES
12/01	1,087	(67)	—	1,700
12/00	1,101	—	—	1,474
12/99	1,095	—	—	1,519
12/98	1,200	—	—	1,600
12/97	1,432	—	—	1,652
12/96	1,468	—	—	1,609
12/95	1,383	—	—	1,548
12/94	1,183	—	—	1,471
12/93	906	—	—	1,478
12/92	898	—	—	—
Annual Growth	2.1%	—	—	1.8%

Revenue History

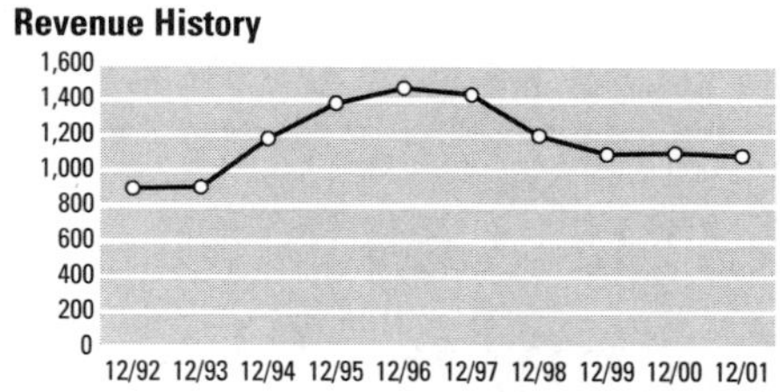

CH2M HILL Companies, Ltd.

CH2M's name is a company (not a chemical) compound derived from the initials of its founders — Cornell, Howland, Hayes, and Merryfield — plus HILL, from its first merger. The group offers engineering consulting related to industrial facility design, transportation, water treatment, and environmental remediation. Specialties include sewer and waste-treatment design, hazardous-waste cleanup, and transportation projects such as highways and bridges. CH2M HILL is also involved in federal nuclear waste cleanup projects, facilities operations and management, and security and emergency management services. Founded in 1946 in Corvallis, Oregon, the firm is employee-owned and operates from about 200 offices worldwide.

EXECUTIVES

Chairman, President, and CEO: Ralph R. Peterson, age 58, $1,127,862 pay
Vice Chairman and SVP: Joseph A. (Bud) Ahearn, age 66
EVP, CFO, and Secretary: Samuel H. Iapalucci, age 49, $627,066 pay
SVP and Director; President, CH2M HILL Water Business Group and Operations and Maintenance Business Group: Donald S. Evans, age 52, $628,954 pay
SVP and Director; President, Energy, Environment, and Systems Business Group and CH2M HILL Constructors, Inc.: James J. (Jim) Ferris, age 59, $654,646 pay
VP and Controller: Vern L. Nelson
VP and Treasurer: Stanley W. (Stan) Vinson
VP Human Resources: Robert C. (Bob) Allen
Director Marketing Communications: Cary Baird
Media Relations Manager: Karen Steeper
Public Relations Team Manager: Patty Keck
Auditors: KPMG

LOCATIONS

HQ: 9191 S. Jamaica St., Englewood, CO 80112
Phone: 303-771-0900 **Fax:** 720-286-9250
Web: www.ch2m.com

CH2M HILL Companies operates from 136 offices in the US and 60 offices abroad.

PRODUCTS/OPERATIONS

Selected Subsidiaries

CH2M HILL Capital Services, Inc. (CAPCO, infrastructure financing)
CH2M HILL Canada Limited (Canadian division; energy, environment and systems, water, and transportation services)
CH2M HILL Hanford Group, Inc. (prime contractor for US Department of Energy; treating waste at underground tanks at Hanford site in Washington State)
CH2M HILL Inc. (engineering, program management, and construction services)
CH2M HILL International, Ltd. (construction project management outside the US)
Industrial Design and Construction (IDC, high-technology facilities design)
Kaiser-Hill Company, LLC (50%, joint venture with Kaiser Group International for closure of Rocky Flats nuclear weapons production site)
Operations Management International, Inc. (OMI, utilities support services and maintenance)

COMPETITORS

AECOM
Bechtel
Black & Veatch
Earth Tech
ERM
Fluor
Foster Wheeler
Jacobs Engineering
MWH Global
Parsons Brinckerhoff
Parsons
Shaw Group
Tetra Tech
URS

HISTORICAL FINANCIALS

Company Type: Private

Income Statement FYE: December 31

	REVENUE ($ mil.)	NET INCOME ($ mil.)	NET PROFIT MARGIN	EMPLOYEES
12/02	1,999	30	1.5%	10,600
12/01	1,941	28	1.4%	10,500
12/00	1,707	25	1.4%	10,600
12/99	1,185	14	1.1%	9,200
12/98	932	6	0.6%	7,000
12/97	918	5	0.5%	7,200
12/96	937	5	0.5%	7,026
12/95	805	5	0.7%	6,876
12/94	676	3	0.5%	6,559
Annual Growth	14.5%	31.6%	—	6.2%

2002 Year-End Financials

Debt ratio: 5.1%
Return on equity: 17.1%
Cash ($ mil.): 106
Current ratio: 1.26
Long-term debt ($ mil.): 9

Net Income History

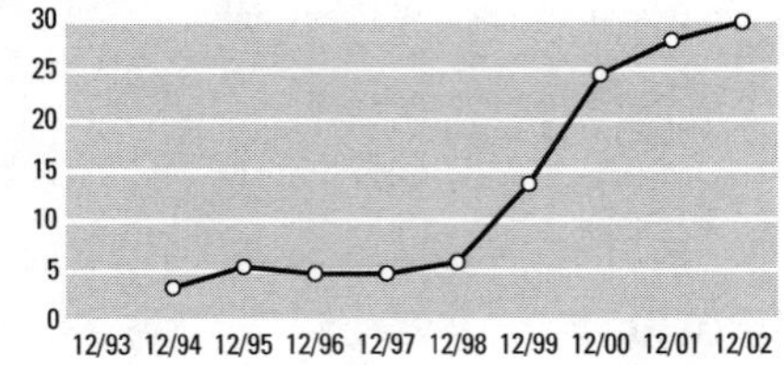

Chapman Automotive Group, LLC

Spend a few hours with a dealer in Vegas and you might lose your shirt — or end up with a new car. Chapman Automotive Group sells about 18,000 new and used automobiles from about 10 dealerships in Nevada and Arizona. The group sells General Motors, DaimlerChrysler, BMW, Isuzu, Lincoln, Mercury, and Volkswagen automobiles. The company's dealerships also offer parts and service departments. In addition to selling to individual consumers, Chapman Automotive also supplies cars, trucks, and parts to government and corporate fleet buyers. CEO Jerry Chapman founded the group in 1978.

EXECUTIVES

CEO: Jerry B. Chapman
COO: Edward (Eddie) Davault
Controller: Allen Elggren
Internet Manager, Chapman Auto Center: Bill Mansoor
Internet Fleet Manager, Chapman BMW, Chapman Dodge, and Chapman Volkswagen: David Robinson
Internet Fleet Manager, Chapman BMW on Camelback: Matt Bertone
Internet Fleet Manager, Chapman BMW on Camelback: Jose Martinez
Internet Fleet Manager, Chapman Chevrolet Chandler: Christine Lambert
Internet Fleet Manager, Chapman Chevrolet Isuzu: Nick Bruce
Internet Fleet Manager, Chapman Lincoln Mercury: Patrick Heigl

LOCATIONS

HQ: PO Box 11550, Scottsdale, AZ 85271
Phone: 480-970-0740 **Fax:** 480-994-4096
Web: www.chapmanchoice.com

COMPETITORS

AutoNation
Findlay Automotive
Fletcher Jones
Lithia Motors
Tuttle-Click
VT

HISTORICAL FINANCIALS

Company Type: Private

Income Statement FYE: December 31

	ESTIMATED REVENUE ($ mil.)	NET INCOME ($ mil.)	NET PROFIT MARGIN	EMPLOYEES
12/01	612	—	—	—
12/00	522	—	—	—
12/99	500	—	—	—
12/98	450	—	—	—
12/97	440	—	—	—
12/96	450	—	—	—
Annual Growth	6.4%	—	—	—

Revenue History

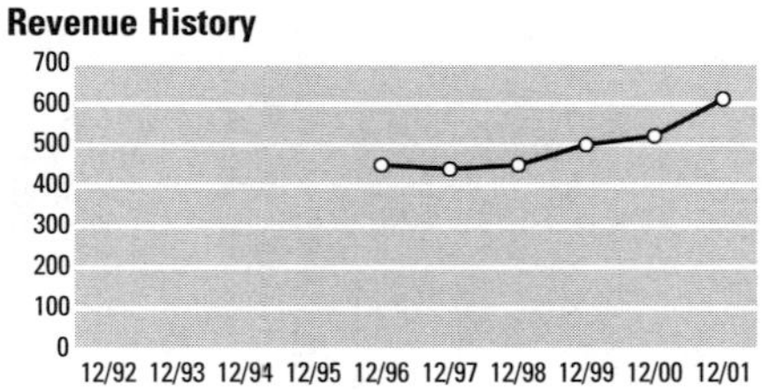

Chas. Levy Company LLC

Chas. Levy keeps racking up sales. The wholesaler distributes magazines and books throughout the US, primarily in several midwestern states. It is one of four companies that control nearly 90% of single-copy sales at US magazine racks. Having grown through acquisitions of other distributors, Chas. Levy distributes books through its Levy Home Entertainment subsidiary to retail chains including Best Buy, Kmart, Meijer, ShopKo, Stop & Shop, Target, and Wal-Mart. The company has shut down its newspaper distribution operation. Chair Barbara Levy Kipper owns the company her grandfather founded in 1893.

EXECUTIVES

Chairman: Barbara Levy Kipper
Vice Chairman: James (Jim) Levy
President and CEO: Carol G. Kloster
President and COO, Levy Home Entertainment: Howard F. Reese
EVP and COO, Chas. Levy Circulating Company: George Lampros
VP and CFO: William Nelson
VP and General Counsel: Beth Corvino
Acting Director, HR: John Zilm
Auditors: Deloitte & Touche

LOCATIONS

HQ: 1200 N. North Branch St., Chicago, IL 60622
Phone: 312-440-4400 **Fax:** 312-440-7414
Web: www.chaslevy.com

PRODUCTS/OPERATIONS

Subsidiaries

Chas. Levy Circulating Co. (magazine distribution)
Levy Home Entertainment (book distribution)

COMPETITORS

Advanced Marketing
Anderson News
Baker & Taylor
Hudson News
Ingram Industries
Jim Pattison Group

HISTORICAL FINANCIALS

Company Type: Private

Income Statement FYE: September 30

	REVENUE ($ mil.)	NET INCOME ($ mil.)	NET PROFIT MARGIN	EMPLOYEES
9/02*	750	—	—	6,500
3/01	715	—	—	6,000
3/00	615	—	—	5,000
3/99	381	—	—	4,500
3/98	362	—	—	4,240
3/97	310	—	—	3,168
3/96	284	—	—	2,234
3/95	320	—	—	2,000
3/94	280	—	—	1,885
3/93	265	—	—	1,800
Annual Growth	12.3%	—	—	15.3%

*Fiscal year change

Revenue History

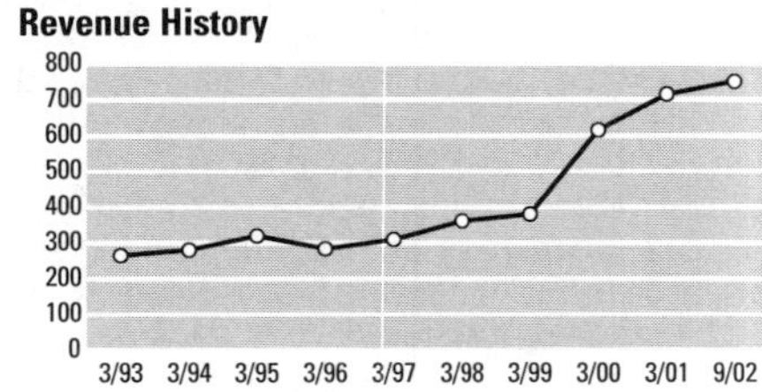

Charles Pankow Builders, Ltd.

Charles Pankow Builders has some concrete ideas on how to construct high-rises. The design/build general contractor specializes in quake-resistant concrete frames, putting up department stores, hotels, condominiums, medical facilities, and office buildings, primarily in California and Hawaii. Pankow's new framing system, developed with researchers at the University of Washington and the National Institute of Standards and Technology, has been used for San Francisco's tallest precast concrete building. Affiliate Pankow Special Projects focuses on small-scale projects such as renovations and seismic upgrades. The company, founded by chairman Charles Pankow in 1963, helped pioneer the design/build delivery system.

EXECUTIVES

Chairman: Charles J. Pankow Jr.
President and CEO: Rik Kunnath
SVP: Thomas (Tom) Verti
President, Pankow Special Projects: Richard G. (Dick) Walterhouse
CFO: Kim Petersen
Area Manager, Honolulu: Kirk Clagstone
Area Manager, Los Angeles: Chris Turner
Area Manager, Oakland: Kim Lum
Project Development, Los Angeles: Chip McCorkle
Product Development, Oakland: Andy Robertson
Director Human Resources: Patty Bevans

LOCATIONS

HQ: 2476 N. Lake Ave., Altadena, CA 91001
Phone: 626-791-1125 **Fax:** 626-794-1539
Web: www.pankow.com

Charles Pankow Builders operates from offices in California (Altadena and Oakland) and Hawaii (Honolulu). Pankow Special Projects maintains offices in Honolulu and in Newport Beach, Oakland, Pasadena, and San Francisco, California.

PRODUCTS/OPERATIONS

Selected Construction Markets

Hospitality
Medical/technology
Office
Parking
Residential
Retail/entertainment

Selected Renovation and Seismic Upgrade Markets

Commercial
Hospitality
Medical
Office
Retail

COMPETITORS

Beck Group
Hathaway Dinwiddie Construction
Hensel Phelps Construction
M. A. Mortenson
McCarthy Building
Pepper Construction
Rudolph & Sletten
S. J. Amoroso Construction
Sundt
Swinerton
Turner Corporation
Webcor Builders

HISTORICAL FINANCIALS

Company Type: Private

Income Statement FYE: December 31

	ESTIMATED REVENUE ($ mil.)	NET INCOME ($ mil.)	NET PROFIT MARGIN	EMPLOYEES
12/01	600	—	—	220
12/00	1,000	—	—	135
Annual Growth	(40.0%)	—	—	63.0%

Revenue History

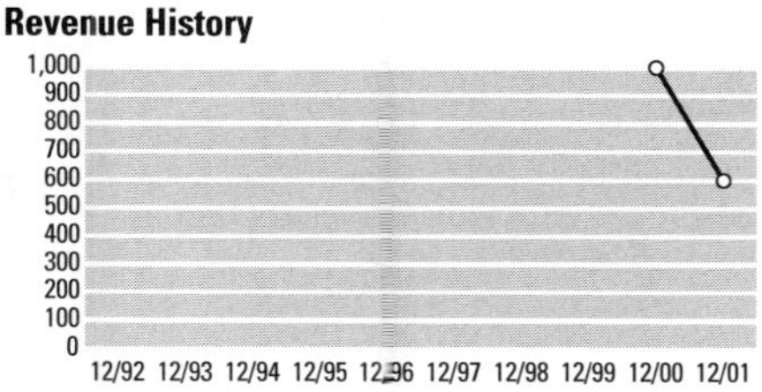

Charmer Industries, Inc.

Not easily shaken by competition, Charmer Industries has not stirred from its top spot as New York State's #1 wine and liquor wholesaler. It is the state's exclusive distributor for Schieffelin & Sommerset (a joint venture between Diageo's United Distillers & Vintners and Moët-Hennessy), and Brown-Forman (maker of Jack Daniel's and Southern Comfort). Charmer Industries also owns Connecticut Distributors and Washington (DC) Wholesale Liquor. The company is owned by the Merinoff family and run by CEO Herman Merinoff. Charmer Industries is part of the Maryland-based Charmer-Sunbelt Group, the second-largest wine and spirits wholesaler in the US.

EXECUTIVES

Chairman: Charles Merinoff
CEO: Herman I. Merinoff
CFO: Steve Meresmen
Director Human Resources: Annette Perry
Manager, Greater Metropolitan Area: John Paladino

LOCATIONS

HQ: 19-50 48th St., Astoria, NY 11105
Phone: 718-726-2500 **Fax:** 718-726-4428
Web: www.charmer.com

COMPETITORS

Allied Domecq
Gallo
Johnson Brothers
National Distributing
Peerless Importers
Southern Wine & Spirits

HISTORICAL FINANCIALS

Company Type: Private

Income Statement FYE: December 31

	ESTIMATED REVENUE ($ mil.)	NET INCOME ($ mil.)	NET PROFIT MARGIN	EMPLOYEES
12/01	790	—	—	1,500
12/00	790	—	—	1,500
12/99	725	—	—	1,300
12/98	670	—	—	1,300
12/97	675	—	—	1,300
12/96	650	—	—	1,300
12/95	650	—	—	1,000
12/94	605	—	—	1,230
12/93	580	—	—	1,230
Annual Growth	3.9%	—	—	2.5%

Revenue History

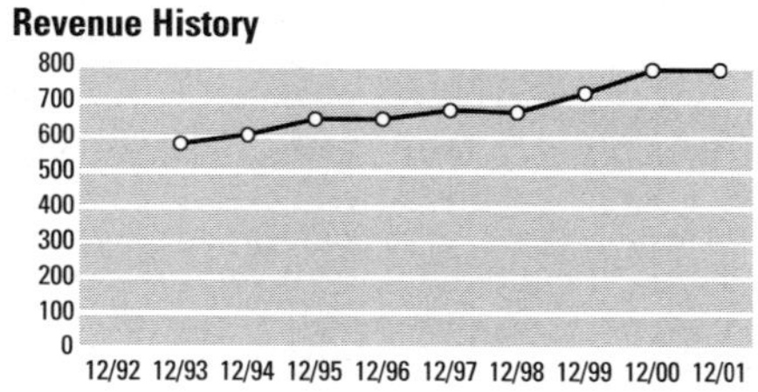

CHEM-CENTRAL Corporation

CHEMCENTRAL is in the center of a chemically dependent world. The company is one of the top chemical distributors in North America. It carries products made by BASF, Dow Chemical, DuPont, and others. Key customers for CHEMCENTRAL's more than 8,000 chemical products include companies that manufacture adhesives, caulks, and sealants; cleaning agents; cosmetics and personal care products; inks and paint coatings; and plastic and rubber compounds. Established in 1926 as the William J Hough Company of Chicago, CHEMCENTRAL now has more than 100 warehouse, distribution, and sales units worldwide.

EXECUTIVES

President and COO: John R. Yanney
VP and CFO: John G. LaBahn
VP, Finance and Treasurer: Lloyd Tarrh
VP, Marketing: William R. Hough
VP, Personnel: Ken Krausz

LOCATIONS

HQ: 7050 W. 71st St., Bedford Park, IL 60499
Phone: 708-594-7000 **Fax:** 708-594-6382
Web: www.chemcentral.com

CHEMCENTRAL operates distribution facilities in the US, Canada, and Mexico. The company has joint ventures in Asia.

PRODUCTS/OPERATIONS

Selected Products

Adhesives
Amines
Caulks
Glycerin
Glycols
Paint coatings
Personal care product additives
Polymers
Printing ink products
Rubber and plastic compounds
Sealants
Silicones
Solvents
Surfactants

COMPETITORS

Aceto
Air Products
Arrow-Magnolia
Ashland
Cytec
Dow Chemical
DuPont
HELM U.S.
Hercules
K.A. Steel Chemicals
Ondeo Nalco
Royal Vopak
Seegott
Stinnes
Univar
Yule Catto

HISTORICAL FINANCIALS

Company Type: Private

Income Statement FYE: December 31

	REVENUE ($ mil.)	NET INCOME ($ mil.)	NET PROFIT MARGIN	EMPLOYEES
12/02	885	—	—	1,000
12/01	860	—	—	982
12/00	917	—	—	1,050
12/99	881	—	—	1,000
12/98	880	—	—	918
12/97	875	—	—	870
12/96	825	—	—	865
12/95	850	—	—	897
12/94	745	—	—	834
12/93	675	—	—	810
Annual Growth	3.0%	—	—	2.4%

Revenue History

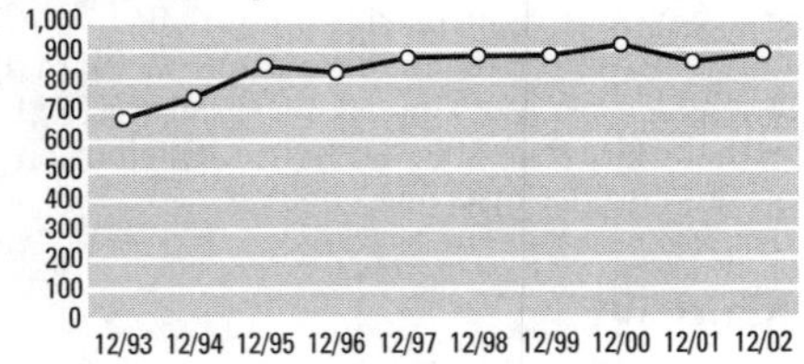

Chemoil Corporation

Chemoil is hunkered down in the bunker fuel distribution business. Founded in 1981, the company supplies marine bunker fuels to shipping companies worldwide. Chemoil operates refineries and terminals and distributes fuel from five US ports (including New York and Los Angeles), the Netherlands, Singapore, and Turkey. The company supplies more than 4,000 vessels a year. Fuel is delivered mostly by tankers, barges, and tugboats owned and operated by Chemoil or its affiliates, which include AFT-Chemoil (Rotterdam) and Chemoil-ITC (Singapore). Chemoil is 50%-owned by Japanese trading company ITOCHU, which is helping to fund its expansion to new ports. The remaining 50% is owned by president and CEO Robert Chandran.

EXECUTIVES

President and CEO: Robert V. Chandran
VP Administration and Secretary: Lucius C. Conrad
VP Global Marketing: Adrian H. Tolson
Treasurer: Manolete Gonzalez
General Counsel: Helen Surh
Auditors: PricewaterhouseCoopers LLP

LOCATIONS

HQ: 4 Embarcadero Center, Ste. 1100,
San Francisco, CA 94111
Phone: 415-268-2700 **Fax:** 415-268-2701
Web: www.chemoil.com

Chemoil operates from five US ports (Houston, Los Angeles, New Orleans, New York, and San Francisco), and in the Netherlands, Singapore, and Turkey.

COMPETITORS

Apex Oil
BP
Exxon Mobil
Hunting
Motiva Enterprises
Royal Dutch/Shell Group
Tesoro Petroleum
Transammonia
World Fuel Services

HISTORICAL FINANCIALS

Company Type: Private

Income Statement FYE: December 31

	REVENUE ($ mil.)	NET INCOME ($ mil.)	NET PROFIT MARGIN	EMPLOYEES
12/01	3,000	—	—	100
12/00	1,100	—	—	70
12/99	500	—	—	65
12/98	350	—	—	100
12/97	400	—	—	100
12/96	390	—	—	100
12/95	297	—	—	90
12/94	276	—	—	—
12/93	386	—	—	—
Annual Growth	29.2%	—	—	1.8%

Revenue History

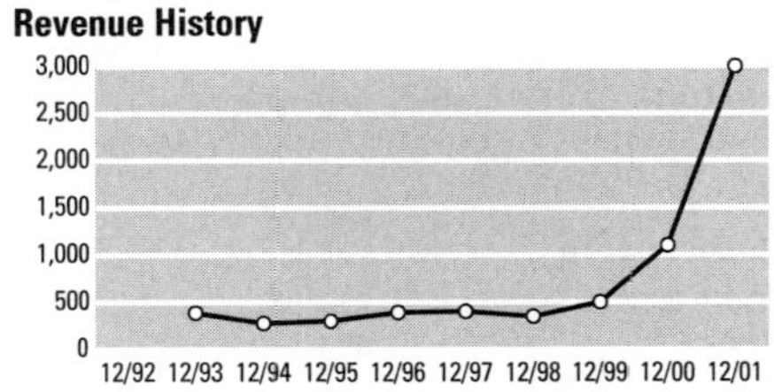

Chevron Phillips Chemical

A coin toss determined which name would go first when Chevron (now ChevronTexaco) and Phillips Petroleum (now ConocoPhillips) formed a new 50-50 joint venture, Chevron Phillips Chemical Company (CPChem). A major US petrochemical firm, CPChem produces ethylene, propylene, polyethylene, and polypropylene — sometimes used as building blocks for the company's other products such as pipe. CPChem also produces aromatics such as benzene and styrene, as well as specialty chemicals such as acetylene black and chemicals used in drilling and mining. The company has formed several petrochemicals joint ventures in the Middle East. Most of CPChem's operations are located in the US.

The company is North America's largest producer of high-density polyethylene (HDPE) — used in blow/injection molding, plastic bags and pipes, and films. CPChem is also near the top in styrene, ethylene, and aromatics production.

Chevron Phillips Chemical Company LP is the US operating subsidiary of CPChem, which also includes foreign ventures, mainly those in Asia and the Middle East. Chevron Phillips Chemical Company LP accounts for about 85% of its parent's revenues.

EXECUTIVES

President and CEO: James L. (Jim) Gallogly, age 51, $794,348 pay
SVP and CFO: C. K. (Kent) Potter, age 56, $412,091 pay
SVP, Aromatics and Styrenics: J. M. (Mike) Parker, age 56
SVP, Manufacturing: R. L. (Rick) Roberts, age 48
SVP, Olefins and Polyolefins: Timothy G. (Tim) Taylor, age 49, $397,549 pay
SVP, Planning and Specialty Projects: Greg C. Garland, age 45, $376,240 pay
VP and Controller: Greg G. Maxwell, age 46
VP, General Counsel, and Secretary: Craig B. Glidden, age 44, $446,825 pay
VP and Treasurer: Joseph M. (Joe) McKee, age 52
VP, Environment, Health, and Safety: A. S. (Scott) Meyer
VP, Human Resources: C. D. (Sherry) Richard
VP, Technology: Mary Jane Hagenson
Auditors: Ernst & Young LLP

LOCATIONS

HQ: Chevron Phillips Chemical Company LLC
10001 Six Pines Dr., The Woodlands, TX 77380
Phone: 832-813-4100 **Fax:** 800-231-3890
Web: www.cpchem.com

Chevron Phillips Chemical Company LLC operates 35 manufacturing facilities and five research and technical centers, including facilities in Belgium, China, Mexico, Qatar, Saudi Arabia, Singapore, South Korea, and the US.

2002 Sales

	$ mil.	% of total
US	4,678	85
Other countries	711	13
Adjustments	84	2
Total	**5,473**	**100**

PRODUCTS/OPERATIONS

Selected Products

Olefins and Polyolefins
Ethylene
Polyethylene
Polyethylene pipe
Polypropylene
Propylene

Aromatics
Benzene
Cumene
Cyclohexane
Paraxylene
Styrene

Specialty Chemicals and Plastics
Acetylene black
Alpha olefins
Dimethyl sulfide
Drilling specialty chemicals
High-purity hydrocarbons and solvents
Mining chemicals
Neohexene
Performance and reference fuels
Polyalpha olefins
Polystyrene

COMPETITORS

BASF AG
BP Chemicals
BP
Dow Chemical
DuPont
Equistar Chemicals
ExxonMobil Chemical
KRATON
NOVA Chemicals
Shell
Sterling Chemicals

HISTORICAL FINANCIALS

Company Type: Joint venture

Income Statement FYE: December 31

	REVENUE ($ mil.)	NET INCOME ($ mil.)	NET PROFIT MARGIN	EMPLOYEES
12/02	5,473	(30)	—	5,517
12/01	6,010	(480)	—	6,056
Annual Growth	(8.9%)	—	—	(8.9%)

2002 Year-End Financials

Debt ratio: 31.7%
Return on equity: —
Cash ($ mil.): 39
Current ratio: 1.49
Long-term debt ($ mil.): 1,190

Net Income History

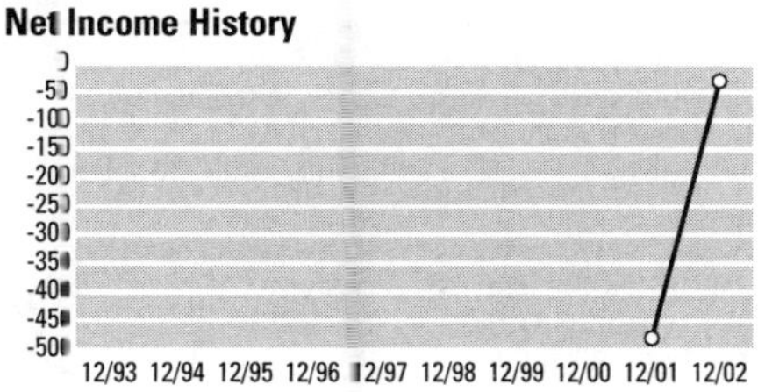

Chick-fil-A Inc.

Beloved by bovines, Chick-fil-A is the nation's #3 fast-food chicken restaurant company (behind YUM! Brands' KFC and the dual-brand AFC Enterprises). It serves chicken entrees, sandwiches, and salads (as well as its famous waffle fries and fresh-squeezed lemonade) at almost 1,100 stores in more than 30 US states. Although nearly 40% of its restaurants are located in shopping malls, the company is focusing most of its expansion efforts on freestanding outlets. Chick-fil-A also licenses units inside hospitals, schools, airports, and other nontraditional locations.

Truett Cathy, the company's founder and owner, is a devout Baptist and requires all stores to close on Sundays. Cathy also emphasizes employee care; the company claims a relatively low management-turnover rate for its industry.

Chick-fil-A also operates one 1950s retro Truett's Grille in Morrow, Georgia.

EXECUTIVES

Chairman, CEO, and Founder: S. Truett Cathy
President and COO: Dan T. Cathy
SVP; President, Dwarf House: Donald M. (Bubba) Cathy
SVP Design and Construction: Perry A. Ragsdale
SVP Finance and CFO: James B. (Buck) McCabe
SVP Marketing: Steve A. Robinson
SVP Operations: Timothy P. Tassopoulos
SVP Public Relations: Don Perry
SVP Real Estate and General Counsel: Bureon E. Ledbetter Jr.
Human Resources Administrator: Renea Boozer

LOCATIONS

HQ: 5200 Buffington Rd., Atlanta, GA 30349
Phone: 404-765-8000 **Fax:** 404-765-8971
Web: www.chick-fil-a.com

COMPETITORS

AFC Enterprises
Burger King
CKE Restaurants
Subway
Dairy Queen
Jack in the Box
KFC
Krystal
McDonald's
Quizno's
Triarc
Wendy's
YUM!

HISTORICAL FINANCIALS

Company Type: Private

Income Statement FYE: December 31

	REVENUE ($ mil.)	NET INCOME ($ mil.)	NET PROFIT MARGIN	EMPLOYEES
12/02	1,373	—	—	45,000
12/01	1,242	—	—	43,000
12/00	1,082	—	—	40,000
12/99	750	—	—	35,000
12/98	650	—	—	35,000
12/97	672	—	—	28,500
12/96	570	—	—	25,000
12/95	502	—	—	—
12/94	451	—	—	—
Annual Growth	14.9%	—	—	10.3%

Revenue History

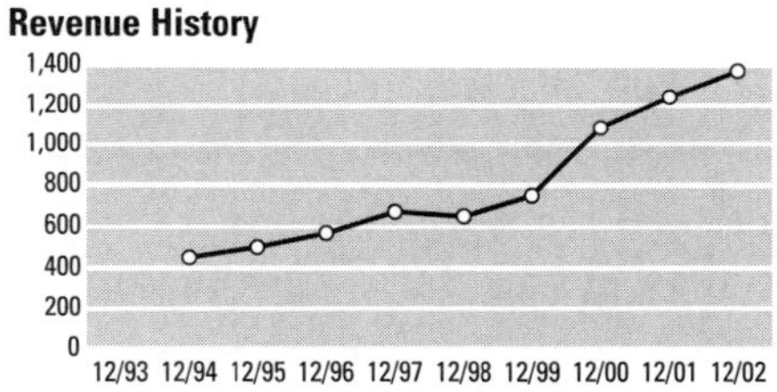

CIC International

Like a veteran goalie, CIC International holds its own on defense. The company makes military equipment and systems for governments and defense industries worldwide. It makes military products for land, sea, and air. The company's main products include night vision and optical devices, munitions, helicopters, and avionics components (jet engines, fuel systems, headup displays). CIC also upgrades tanks and armored personnel carriers. Its naval services include upgrading weapon systems and providing engineering for surface warfare problems. The defense contractor began in 1930 as a silk and fur trader. Company executives and employees control CIC.

EXECUTIVES

Chairman and CEO: Satiris G. Fassoulis
CFO: Robert C. Perry
VP, CIO/CTO: James Chladek
VP, Human Resources; Customer Service: Robert Volvo
President, Columbia Technology: Joseph Ceva
International Operations: Dino Seferian
Legal: Richard Zaroff
Purchasing: Robert Thompson
Secretary; Business Development: Larry Thompson
Treasurer: Marie Couvaras

LOCATIONS

HQ: CIC International Ltd.
5 Marine View Plaza, Hoboken, NJ 07030
Phone: 201-792-1800 **Fax:** 201-792-5755
Web: www.cic-international.com

CIC International has plants in Honolulu and Philadelphia.

COMPETITORS

Alliant Techsystems
Allied Defense Group
Alvis
Anteon
Elbit Systems
General Dynamics
Lockheed Martin
Lockheed Martin Missiles
Northrop Grumman
United Defense Industries
Venturian

HISTORICAL FINANCIALS

Company Type: Private

Income Statement FYE: August 31

	REVENUE ($ mil.)	NET INCOME ($ mil.)	NET PROFIT MARGIN	EMPLOYEES
8/02	773	6	0.8%	735
8/01	709	—	—	624
8/00	563	—	—	514
8/99	505	—	—	502
8/98	438	—	—	252
8/97	426	—	—	—
Annual Growth	12.7%	—	—	30.7%

Revenue History

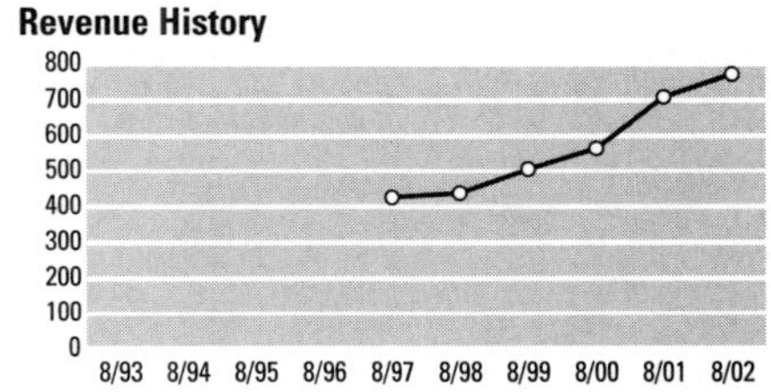

Cinemark, Inc.

Cinemark has left its mark on the cinema landscape. The third-largest movie exhibitor in the US (following Regal Entertainment and AMC) has more than 3,000 screens in 280 theaters in the US and several other countries, mostly in Latin America. Cinemark operates multiplex theaters (the ratio of screens to theaters is about 11 to 1) in smaller cities and in suburban areas of major metropolitan markets. Some larger theaters operate under the Tinseltown name; other Cinemark theaters are "discount" theaters, as opposed to the houses which exhibit first-run movies. Chairman and CEO Lee

Roy Mitchell owns about 92% of the company's voting stock.

All of Cinemark's theaters are multiplexes, many of which sport neon color schemes not found in nature. About 15% of its theaters are "discount" cinemas. The company prefers to build new theaters in midsized markets or in suburbs of major cities where the Cinemark theater is the only game in town. Cinemark's theaters can be found in 33 US states and 14 other countries.

The company spent the late nineties upgrading into one of the most modern and technologically advanced movie chains. (About two-thirds of the current screens have been built since 1996; about 65% of its North American first run screens and 75% of its international screens feature stadium seating — a trend that began in the 1990s.) Cinemark, along with the rest of the movie theater industry, struggled through the late 1990s as numerous bankruptcies abounded thanks to overbuilding. Things seemed to be on the upswing in early 2002, and Cinemark responded by filing to go public. However, the overall decline of the stock market forced the firm to postpone its offering later that year.

EXECUTIVES

Chairman and CEO: Lee Roy Mitchell, age 66, $1,547,870 pay
Vice Chairman, EVP, and Secretary: Tandy Mitchell, age 52
President, COO, and Director: Alan W. Stock, age 42, $615,453 pay
SVP Operations: Robert F. Carmony, age 45, $433,240 pay
SVP, Treasurer, CFO, Assistant Secretary, and Director: Robert D. Copple, age 44, $449,400 pay
SVP; President, Cinemark International: Tim Warner, age 58, $499,086 pay
VP, General Counsel, and Assistant Secretary: Michael Cavalier, age 36
VP Marketing and Communications: Terrell Falk, age 52
Director Human Resources: Brad Smith
Auditors: Deloitte & Touche LLP

LOCATIONS

HQ: 3900 Dallas Pkwy., Ste. 500, Plano, TX 75093
Phone: 972-665-1000 **Fax:** 972-665-1004
Web: www.cinemark.com

Cinemark has theaters in Argentina, Brazil, Canada, Chile, Colombia, Costa Rica, Ecuador, El Salvador, Honduras, Nicaragua, Mexico, Panama, Peru, the UK, and 33 states in the US.

2002 Sales

	$ mil.	% of total
US and Canada	727.9	77
Mexico	84.4	9
Brazil	65.2	7
Other countries	62.7	7
Adjustments	(0.9)	—
Total	**939.3**	**100**

PRODUCTS/OPERATIONS

2002 Sales

	$ mil.	% of total
Admissions	597.4	64
Concessions	292.8	31
Other	49.1	5
Total	**939.3**	**100**

COMPETITORS

AMC Entertainment
Carmike Cinemas
CCG Holdings
Famous Players
Hoyts Cinemas
Loews Cineplex
National Amusements
Pacific Theatres
Regal Entertainment

HISTORICAL FINANCIALS

Company Type: Private

Income Statement FYE: December 31

	REVENUE ($ mil.)	NET INCOME ($ mil.)	NET PROFIT MARGIN	EMPLOYEES
12/02	939	39	4.2%	12,500
12/01	854	(4)	—	8,000
12/00	786	(10)	—	8,000
12/99	713	1	0.1%	8,000
12/98	571	11	1.9%	8,000
12/97	435	15	3.5%	7,000
12/96	342	15	4.3%	6,500
12/95	299	13	4.4%	7,000
12/94	283	7	2.5%	5,500
12/93	240	10	4.0%	5,100
Annual Growth	16.4%	16.7%	—	10.5%

2002 Year-End Financials

Debt ratio: 2,385.7%
Return on equity: 146.6%
Cash ($ mil.): 64
Current ratio: 0.55
Long-term debt ($ mil.): 662

Net Income History

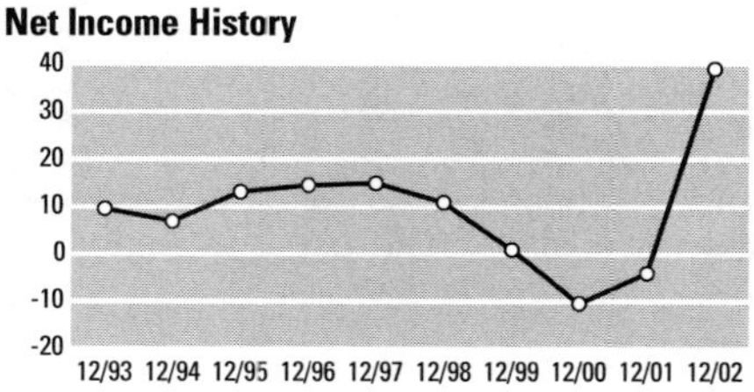

Cingular Wireless LLC

BellSouth *plus* SBC *times* wireless assets *equals* Cingular Wireless. With a name chosen to emphasize unity and the individual customer, the two regional Bell companies have combined assets to create the #2 wireless carrier in the US, behind Verizon Wireless. With about 22 million customers, the joint venture is 60%-owned by SBC and 40% by BellSouth, according to the contributions made by the two companies, which share control. Eleven brand names used by the SBC and BellSouth wireless units have been replaced by the Cingular Wireless brand. The company, which has held talks to merge with VoiceStream Wireless, now T-Mobile USA, has announced cuts in 7% of its workforce, or more than 2,500 jobs.

Competition aside, Cingular Wireless has formed a joint venture with rival AT&T Wireless to work jointly on the development of advanced networks. The two wireless carriers use the same network technology.

Cingular Wireless also has agreed to buy some additional licenses from bankrupt NextWave Telecom. The deal, valued at $1.4 billion, would send licenses for 34 markets to Cingular mostly providing additional spectrum in areas where it already operates. The agreement is subject to bankruptcy court approval. In another deal, Cingular has agreed to swap some cellular properties in northwest Michigan to Dobson Communications in exchange for properties along the eastern Maryland shore.

EXECUTIVES

Chairman: Randall L. Stephenson, age 42
President and CEO: Stanley T. (Stan) Sigman, age 55, $1,821,000 pay
COO: Mark L. Feidler, age 46, $1,608,192 pay
CFO: Richard G. (Rick) Lindner, age 48, $522,827 pay
President, Cingular Interactive: Charles Nelson
President, Network Operations: Edgar L. (Ed) Reynolds, age 54
President, Wireless Operations: Robert W. Shaner, age 54, $444,000 pay
President, Wireless Operations East: Steve Sitton
Regional President, West: LeAnn Priebe
EVP and General Counsel, Legal and Regulatory: Joaquin R. Carbonell III, age 50
EVP Human Resources: Rickford D. (Rick) Bradley, age 51
VP, Assistant General Counsel, Corporate Secretary, and Chief Compliance Officer: Carol L. Tacker, age 54
Chief Marketing Officer: Marc Lefar
CTO: W.E. (Bill) Clift
Auditors: Ernst & Young LLP

LOCATIONS

HQ: Glenridge Highlands Two, 5565 Glenridge Connector, Atlanta, GA 30342
Phone: 404-236-6000 **Fax:** 404-236-6005
Web: www.cingular.com

Cingular Wireless has operations in 38 states, the District of Columbia, and two US territories.

PRODUCTS/OPERATIONS

Selected Services

Analog wireless access
Digital wireless access
Interactive messaging
Short text messaging
Wireless data
Wireless Internet access

COMPETITORS

ALLTEL
Arch Wireless
AT&T Wireless
Cellco Partnership
Centennial Communications
CenturyTel
Nextel
Sprint PCS
Telephone & Data Systems
T-Mobile USA
U.S. Cellular
Western Wireless

HISTORICAL FINANCIALS

Company Type: Joint venture

Income Statement FYE: December 31

	REVENUE ($ mil.)	NET INCOME ($ mil.)	NET PROFIT MARGIN	EMPLOYEES
12/02	14,727	1,207	8.2%	33,800
12/01	14,108	1,692	12.0%	—
12/00	3,055	127	4.2%	—
12/99	9,042	—	—	—
12/98	7,988	—	—	—
12/97	7,433	—	—	—
Annual Growth	14.7%	208.3%	—	—

2002 Year-End Financials

Debt ratio: 166.4%
Return on equity: 18.0%
Cash ($ mil.): 908
Current ratio: 0.98
Long-term debt ($ mil.): 12,546

Net Income History

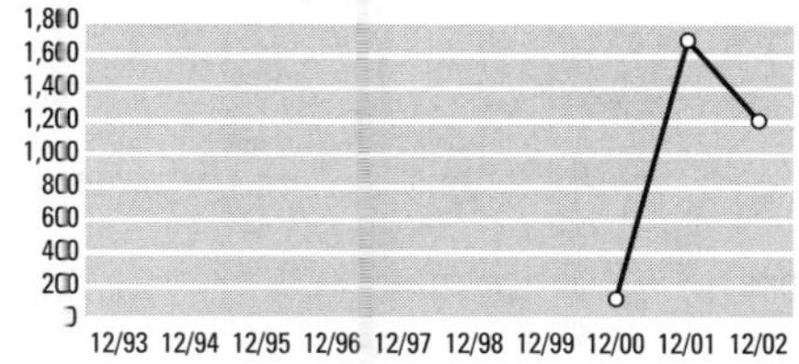

The City University of New York

The City University of New York (CUNY) is the big "U" in the Big Apple. The college has 20 campuses in the five boroughs of New York City and is the US's largest urban university system. About 200,000 undergraduate and graduate students are enrolled at CUNY. The university also teaches some 204,000 students in adult and continuing education programs. CUNY has 10 senior colleges, six community colleges, a doctoral-granting graduate school, a four-year technical school, and medical and law schools. Its 1,230 programs range from specialized, career-oriented courses to traditional liberal arts curricula. CUNY's 12,000-person faculty is split almost evenly between full- and part-time members and its student body includes students from 145 countries.

CUNY has made some big changes, including tougher admission standards that critics feared would hurt the university's ethnic diversity, a hallmark of the school (enrollment numbers have proven otherwise). Notable CUNY alumni include novelist Oscar Hijuelos, General Colin Powell, comedian Jerry Seinfeld, and 11 Nobel laureates.

As with many public universities throughout the US, CUNY is enduring tough times economically. In order to free up the money to hire more full-time professors, the university has had to end a 10-year tradition: not charging four-year students for the last semester of their senior year. Tuition and fees account for about 36% of funds for the university.

HISTORY

The New York State Legislature first created a municipal college system in New York City in 1926, when it formed the New York City Board of Higher Education to manage the operations of the City College of New York and Hunter College. City College's roots were established in 1847 when New York passed a referendum creating the Free Academy, a tuition-free school. Hunter College was founded in 1870 as a women's college, and it was the first free teacher's college in the US.

The Board of Higher Education authorized City College to create the Brooklyn Collegiate Center (a two-year men's college) in 1926; Hunter established a similar two-year women's branch in Brooklyn. Four years later the schools merged to create the Brooklyn College of the City of New York, the city's first public, coed liberal arts college. Other schools added to the municipal system included Queens College (1937), New York City Community College (1947), Staten Island Community College (1955), Bronx Community College (1957), and Queensborough Community College (1958).

The state legislature renamed New York City's municipal college system The City University of New York (CUNY) in 1961 and ordered its board of trustees to expand the system's facilities and scope. One of the first actions was to create a graduate school. CUNY chartered a number of new schools during the 1960s, including Richmond College (1965), York College (1966), Medgar Evers College (1968), and several community colleges. CUNY took over management of the New York State Institute of Applied Arts and Sciences (renamed New York City Technical College) in 1964 and established the John Jay College of Criminal Justice. CUNY became affiliated with Mount Sinai School of Medicine in 1967.

Despite its expansion, the university system had difficulty keeping up with demand, particularly after 1970, when it established an open admissions policy for all New York City high school graduates. Richmond College and Staten Island Community College became the College of Staten Island in 1976. Both CUNY and the City of New York ran into serious financial problems in the mid-1970s, spelling the end of CUNY's tradition of free undergrad tuition for New York City residents. To increase state financial support for CUNY, the legislature signed the City University Governance and Financing Act in 1979.

The City University School of Law held its first classes in 1983. The following year the state board of regents authorized CUNY to offer a doctor of medicine degree. CUNY's law school received accreditation from the American Bar Association in 1992. Since abandoning the free enrollment policy in the 1970s, the university's tuition continued to increase. In 1992, after presenting a nearly $600 increase in tuition, CUNY initiated its "last semester free" program, whereby four-year students did not have to pay tuition for the last semester of their senior year.

After several years of budget cuts and steadily increasing enrollment, CUNY declared a state of financial emergency in 1995. The following year New York's Governor George Pataki proposed new budget cuts, and in 1997 he called for tuition hikes. CUNY's board of trustees introduced a resolution calling for the elimination of remedial education programs at the senior college level in 1998. The state Board of Regents approved the plan in 1999 (most remedial classes were phased out by 2001). Matthew Goldstein was appointed chancellor in 1999 and has worked to increase CUNY's budget to hire more full-time faculty.

Belt-tightening continued in 2002. The university was forced to begin charging four-year students for the last semester of their senior year in order to earn more money.

EXECUTIVES

Chancellor: Matthew Goldstein
Executive Vice Chancellor for Academic Affairs: Louise Mirrer
Vice Chancellor for Facilities Planning, Construction, and Management: Emma Espino Macari
Vice Chancellor for Faculty and Staff Relations: Brenda Richardson Malone
Vice Chancellor for University Relations: Jay Hershenson
Interim Vice Chancellor for Budget and Finance: Ernesto Malave
General Counsel and Vice Chancellor for Legal Affairs: Frederick P. Schaffer
University Dean for Student Services and Enrollment Management: Otis Hill
University Dean for Instructional Technology and Information Services: Michael Ribaudo
University Dean for The-Executive Office: Robert Ptachik
University Dean for Research: Spiro D. Alexandratos
University Dean for Academic Affairs and Deputy to the Executive Vice Chancellor: John Mogulescu
Special Counsel to the Chancellor: Dave Fields
Auditors: KPMG LLP

LOCATIONS

HQ: 535 E. 80th St., New York, NY 10021
Phone: 212-794-5555 **Fax:** 212-209-5600
Web: www.cuny.edu

The City University of New York has schools serving the Bronx, Brooklyn, Manhattan, Queens, and Staten Island boroughs of New York City.

PRODUCTS/OPERATIONS

Senior Colleges

Bernard M. Baruch College
Brooklyn College
City College
City University School of Law at Queens College
The College of Staten Island
The Graduate School and University Center
Herbert H. Lehman College
Hunter College
John Jay College of Criminal Justice
Medgar Evers College
New York City College of Technology
Queens College
York College

Community Colleges

Borough of Manhattan Community College
Bronx Community College
Hostos Community College
Kingsborough Community College
LaGuardia Community College
Queensborough Community College

HISTORICAL FINANCIALS

Company Type: School

Income Statement FYE: June 30

	REVENUE ($ mil.)	NET INCOME ($ mil.)	NET PROFIT MARGIN	EMPLOYEES
6/02	1,041	—	—	30,000
6/01	1,927	—	—	30,000
6/00	1,900	—	—	30,000
6/99	1,873	—	—	28,000
6/98	1,784	—	—	28,000
6/97	1,729	—	—	27,900
6/96	1,756	—	—	25,800
6/95	1,722	—	—	25,800
6/94	1,655	—	—	—
Annual Growth	(5.6%)	—	—	2.2%

Revenue History

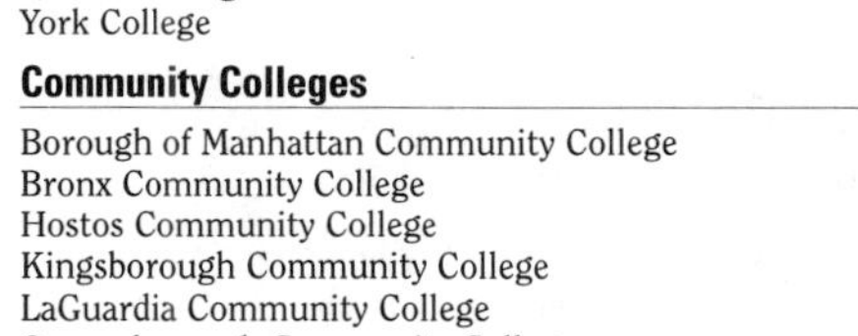

Clark Enterprises, Inc.

Convention does not bind Clark Enterprises. The Clark Construction Group, Clark Enterprises' main subsidiary, is known for constructing convention centers, but it also builds hotels, office buildings, prisons, stadiums, and transportation facilities. Projects include Chicago's McCormick Place, the Los Angeles Convention Center, and a new ballpark for the San Diego Padres. Services include general contracting, construction management, materials procurement, and project development. Through other units Clark Enterprises also provides heavy construction, multifamily residential construction, road building, and real estate development and management. Chairman and CEO James Clark owns Clark Enterprises.

EXECUTIVES

Chairman and CEO: A. James Clark
President and COO: Lawrence C. Nussdorf, age 56
EVP: Robert J. (Bob) Flanagan, age 47
VP and Treasurer: Sandy R. Garchik
VP: Terri D. Klatzkin
VP and General Counsel: Rebecca L. Owen
Chairman, Clark Construction Group: Peter C. Forster
President, Clark Construction Group: Dan T. Montgomery
CFO, Clark Construction Group: Dale Rosenthal
CIO, Clark Construction Group: David (Dave) Golden

LOCATIONS

HQ: 7500 Old Georgetown Rd., 15th Fl., Bethesda, MD 20814
Phone: 301-657-7100 **Fax:** 301-657-7263
Web: www.clarkenterprisesinc.com

COMPETITORS

Barton Malow
Bechtel
Bovis Lend Lease
Centex
Fluor
Gilbane
Hensel Phelps Construction
Hunt Construction
Perini
Peter Kiewit Sons'
Skanska
Turner Corporation
Tutor-Saliba
Webcor Builders
Whiting-Turner

HISTORICAL FINANCIALS

Company Type: Private

Income Statement FYE: December 31

	ESTIMATED REVENUE ($ mil.)	NET INCOME ($ mil.)	NET PROFIT MARGIN	EMPLOYEES
12/01	2,500	—	—	4,000
12/00	2,400	—	—	4,500
12/99	1,800	—	—	5,000
12/98	1,500	—	—	5,000
12/97	1,330	—	—	3,500
12/96	1,400	—	—	4,500
12/95	1,500	—	—	5,000
12/94	1,500	—	—	5,000
12/93	1,600	—	—	5,000
12/92	1,009	—	—	5,000
Annual Growth	10.6%	—	—	(2.4%)

Revenue History

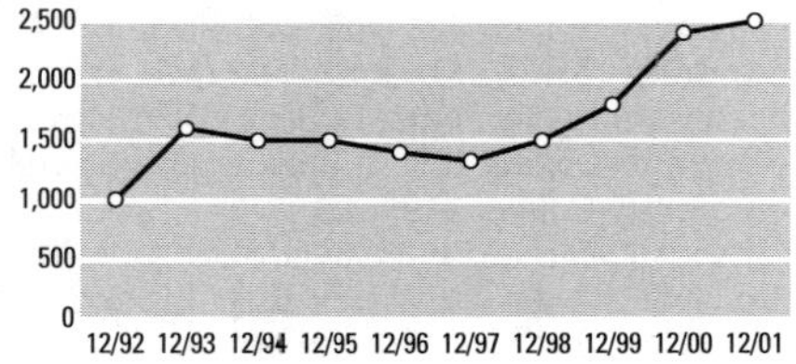

Clark Retail Group, Inc.

Clark Retail Group's hopes to reach out to those on the go are all but gone. Through its struggling subsidiary, Clark Retail Enterprises, the company has sold off some 585 Clark gas stations to more than 200 separate buyers since filing for reorganization under Chapter 11 bankruptcy protection in October 2002. Clark Retail is also negotiating the sale of its 250-store White Hen Pantry Chicago-area convenience store chain, which was excluded from Clark's bankruptcy filing, to raise cash. Clark Retail Enterprises was formed when an affiliate of investment firm Apollo Management bought the retail assets of oil refiner Clark USA in 1999.

EXECUTIVES

President and CEO: Brandon K. Barnholt
EVP and CFO: Jeffrey W. Jones
EVP and COO: John I. Hanner
VP and Controller: Paula A. Kuykendall
VP, Franchise Operations: Douglas J. Fritsch
VP, Petroleum and Business Development: Karl E. Goodhouse
VP, Retail Operations: Richard A. Nelsen
Director of Corporate Accounting and Reporting: Timothy Hughes
Director of Corporate Human Resources: Lou Kartsimas
Director, Legal: Joe Sullivan

LOCATIONS

HQ: 3003 Butterfield Rd., Ste. 300, Oak Brook, IL 60523
Phone: 630-366-3000 **Fax:** 630-366-3465
Web: www.clarkretail.com

COMPETITORS

7-Eleven
BP
Casey's General Stores
ChevronTexaco
CITGO
Exxon Mobil
Flying J
Holiday Companies
Pilot
Royal Dutch/Shell Group
TravelCenters of America

HISTORICAL FINANCIALS

Company Type: Private

Income Statement FYE: December 31

	REVENUE ($ mil.)	NET INCOME ($ mil.)	NET PROFIT MARGIN	EMPLOYEES
12/01	2,600	—	—	7,400
12/00	2,600	—	—	6,000
12/99	1,450	—	—	6,000
12/98	1,400	—	—	6,000
Annual Growth	22.9%	—	—	7.2%

Revenue History

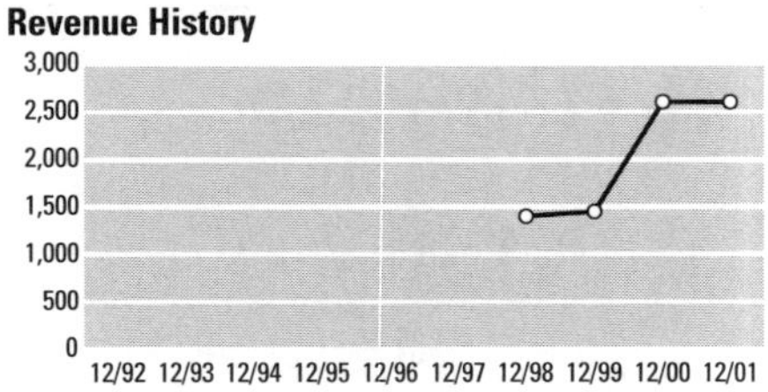

Cleary, Gottlieb, Steen & Hamilton

Cleary, Gottlieb, Steen & Hamilton may be a big cheese in the Big Apple, but the law firm also has made a name for itself in the international arena. Cleary, Gottlieb's attorneys work from 11 offices scattered across the globe and are known for specializing in practice areas such as corporate finance, mergers and acquisitions, litigation, and intellectual property. The firm has more than 700 attorneys, with a third of those outside the US. It has represented British Airways and Deutsche Telekom. It was founded in 1946 by former Root Clark Buckner partners George Cleary, Leo Gottlieb, Fowler Hamilton, and Mel Steen.

EXECUTIVES

Managing Partner: Peter Karasz
Administrative Director: John H. Slattery
Director of Finance: Adrienne E. Boan
Director of Administrative Personnel: Nancy J. Roberts
Manager Media Relations: Nidhi Agrawal

LOCATIONS

HQ: 1 Liberty Plaza, New York, NY 10006
Phone: 212-225-2000 **Fax:** 212-225-3999
Web: www.cgsh.com

Cleary, Gottlieb, Steen & Hamilton has offices in Belgium, France, Germany, Hong Kong, Italy, Japan, the UK, and the US.

PRODUCTS/OPERATIONS

Selected Practice Areas

Corporate
Employee benefits
Energy
Environmental law
Individual clients and charitable organizations
Intellectual property
International trade
Litigation
Tax
US antitrust and European competition

COMPETITORS

Baker & McKenzie
Clifford Chance
Cravath, Swaine
Davis Polk
Debevoise & Plimpton
Dewey Ballantine
Fried, Frank, Harris
Jones Day
LeBoeuf, Lamb
Morgan, Lewis
Shearman & Sterling
Simpson Thacher
Skadden, Arps
Weil, Gotshal

HISTORICAL FINANCIALS

Company Type: Partnership

Income Statement FYE: December 31

	REVENUE ($ mil.)	NET INCOME ($ mil.)	NET PROFIT MARGIN	EMPLOYEES
12/02	531	—	—	—
12/01	492	—	—	—
12/00	460	—	—	—
12/99	412	—	—	1,300
12/98	366	—	—	1,400
12/97	341	—	—	1,430
12/96	310	—	—	—
12/95	286	—	—	—
12/94	265	—	—	—
12/93	263	—	—	—
Annual Growth	8.1%	—	—	(4.7%)

Revenue History

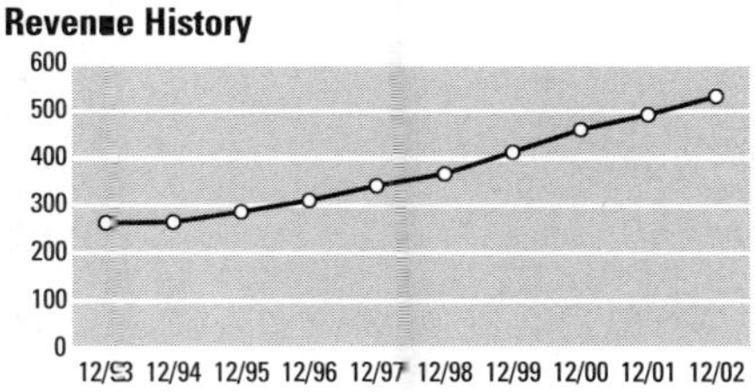

ClubCorp, Inc.

ClubCorp makes its green from the green — the golf green, that is. The world's largest operator of golf courses, country clubs, private business clubs, and resorts, the company owns and operates almost 200 properties in the US and four other countries. Its holdings include Mission Hills Country Club near Palm Springs, California, and North Carolina's Pinehurst Resort and Country Club (site of the 1999 US Open). The company has sold its interests in ClubLink, a leading Canadian developer and operator of golf courses, and PGA European Tour Courses, an operator of tournament golf courses across Europe. The family of late founder Robert Dedman owns 47% of ClubCorp.

Striving to stay on top of the game, the company has been acquiring new properties and is building new ones through Bear's Best, a joint venture with golf legend Jack Nicklaus. Robert Dedman, who was named by *Forbes* magazine as one of the 400 wealthiest Americans, died in 2002. His son, Robert Jr., took over as CEO. ClubCorp's other shareholders include The Cypress Group, which owns about 16%.

HISTORY

Though his childhood in Depression-era Arkansas was dominated by intense poverty, ClubCorp founder Robert Dedman knew how to dream big. At a young age he vowed to become "very, very rich," and the scrappy Dedman embarked on achieving that goal by earning a college scholarship, obtaining a law degree, and eventually launching a flourishing Dallas law practice.

Dedman's law firm was successful, but he realized that it wouldn't bring him the $50 million he wanted to earn by age 50. In 1957 he formed Country Clubs, Inc., to venture into the country club business. At that time, doctors and lawyers working on a volunteer basis were managing most clubs, and Dedman believed his new company could bring professional management expertise to these facilities. The company opened its first country club, Dallas' Brookhaven Country Club, in 1957. Through the subsequent purchase of 20 more clubs, Country Clubs refined its management style, implementing unique practices such as reducing playing time on the golf course and developing specialized training for club staff.

In 1965 the company expanded into city and athletic clubs and assumed the Club Corporation of America name. The expansion drive that followed fueled a 30% growth rate that the company maintained from the 1960s through the 1980s. In 1985 the company was restructured and divided into a handful of separate companies owned by the newly formed Club Corporation International holding company.

In 1988 the company bought an 80% interest in Franklin Federal Bancorp. The bank's club properties had initially caught his eye, but Dedman also believed that the 400,000 members of his clubs might prove fertile ground for the marketing of financial services. In 1996, however, Club Corporation International sold the financial institution to Norwest. Although Franklin Federal was turning a profit, losses from investment in derivatives, coupled with the bank's inability to compete with larger competitors, prompted the company to sell the bank and refocus on its core club and resort business.

In 1996 Japanese cookie-maker Tohato sued the company, claiming that it intentionally mismanaged the Pinewild Country Club. Pinewild was owned by Tohato, managed by Club Corporation International, and located next door to Club Corporation International's Pinehurst Resort and Country Club. Tohato alleged that the company's mismanagement was part of a scheme to eventually buy Pinewild at a reduced price. The case was eventually settled, but the nasty legal wrangling that ensued cast a pall over the impending 1999 US Open at Pinehurst.

In 1998 the company was reincorporated as ClubCorp International, Inc. It expanded its international base that year by purchasing nearly 30% of PGA European Tour Courses. The company also entered into a joint venture with Jack Nicklaus to develop three dozen new golf courses.

The company shortened its moniker to ClubCorp in 1999. Among the additions ClubCorp made to its holdings that year were 22 properties acquired from The Meditrust Companies. The company also increased its ownership of Canadian club developer ClubLink to 25%. An influx of funds for further expansion came in 1999 after investment firm The Cypress Group took a stake. In 2001 the company sold its interests in ClubLink and PGA European Tour Courses.

Robert Dedman passed away in 2002. His son, Robert Dedman Jr., took over as CEO.

EXECUTIVES

Chairman and CEO: Robert H. Dedman Jr., age 45, $779,092 pay
President and COO: John A. Beckert, age 49
CFO: Jeffrey P. Mayer, age 46, $434,200 pay
EVP Growth and Development: Douglas T. Howe, age 45
EVP Sales: Frank C. Gore, age 53, $341,817 pay
EVP Strategic Operations: Murray S. Siegel, age 56
EVP, Secretary and General Counsel: Terry A. Taylor, age 47
EVP: Mark W. Dietz, age 48
EVP: James E. Maser, age 64
SVP Food and Beverage: John Hornsby
SVP Marketing: Lisa H. Kislak
SVP and Chief Accounting Officer: John D. Bailey, age 44
President, The Pinehurst Company: Patrick A. (Pat) Corso, age 52, $365,940 pay
CIO: Colby H. Springer, age 54
Director, Human Resources: Lori Park
Managing Director, Asia/Pacific: David McMann
Auditors: KPMG LLP

LOCATIONS

HQ: 3030 LBJ Fwy., Ste. 700, Dallas, TX 75234
Phone: 972-243-6191 **Fax:** 972-888-7700
Web: www.clubcorp.com

ClubCorp has operations in Australia, China, Mexico, Switzerland, and the US.

PRODUCTS/OPERATIONS

Selected Clubs

Aspen Glen Country Club (Colorado)
The Athletic and Swim Club at Equitable Center (New York)
Columbia Tower Club (Washington)
Golden Bear Golf Club (South Carolina)
The Hills Country Club (Texas)
Mission Hills Country Club (California)
Pinehurst Resort and Country Club (North Carolina)
Tampa Palms Golf and Country Club (Florida)
Teal Bend Golf Club (California)

COMPETITORS

American Golf
Club Med
Four Seasons Hotels
Golf Trust of America
Hillman
Hilton
Hyatt
Marriott International
National Golf Properties
ResortQuest International
Sandals Resorts
Silverleaf Resorts
Starwood Hotels & Resorts

HISTORICAL FINANCIALS

Company Type: Private

Income Statement FYE: Last Wednesday in December

	REVENUE ($ mil.)	NET INCOME ($ mil.)	NET PROFIT MARGIN	EMPLOYEES
12/02	947	(62)	—	20,000
12/01	1,015	(106)	—	23,000
12/00	1,069	(17)	—	24,000
12/99	1,028	12	1.1%	23,000
12/98	851	38	4.5%	21,000
12/97	840	122	14.5%	20,000
12/96	784	29	3.7%	19,000
12/95	761	(11)	—	19,800
12/94	773	15	1.9%	19,200
12/93	1,200	41	3.4%	13,000
Annual Growth	(2.6%)	—	—	4.9%

2002 Year-End Financials

Debt ratio: 137.9%
Return on equity: —
Cash ($ mil.): 2
Current ratio: 0.68
Long-term debt ($ mil.): 597

Net Income History

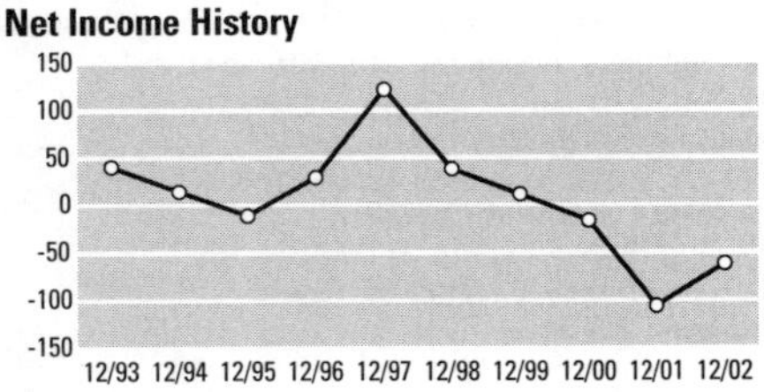

Coast Casinos

Placing its bets off the beaten path, Coast Casinos (formerly Coast Resorts) is now gliding toward the jackpot. With three of its four hotel-casinos located off the Las Vegas strip, the company primarily attracts local gamblers who seek a more casual alternative to the bustle of the strip. In addition to gaming tables, slot machines, and video poker, the hotel-casinos offer amenities such as live music, movie theaters, bowling alleys, and restaurants. The company is forging ahead, making $275 million worth of improvements to its existing properties and announcing plans to begin construction on a new hotel-casino. Chairman and CEO Michael J. Gaughan owns 31% of the company.

EXECUTIVES

Chairman and CEO: Michael J. Gaughan, age 59, $300,000 pay
President, COO, and Director: Harlan Braaten, age 51, $487,500 pay
VP, CFO, Assistant Secretary, and Director: Gage Parrish, age 48, $275,000 pay
VP Casino Operations and Director: Franklin Toti, age 63
VP Slot Operations: Marcus Suann
Secretary and Director: J. Tito Tiberti, age 57
Treasurer and Director: Jerry Herbst, age 64
Auditors: PricewaterhouseCoopers LLP

LOCATIONS

HQ: Coast Casinos, Inc.
4500 W. Tropicana Ave., Las Vegas, NV 89103
Phone: 702-365-7000 **Fax:** 702-365-7566
Web: www.coastcasinos.com

PRODUCTS/OPERATIONS

Properties

The Barbary Coast Hotel and Casino (197 rooms, 609 machines, 36 tables)
The Gold Coast Hotel and Casino (712 rooms, 2,203 machines, 52 tables)
The Orleans Hotel and Casino (840 rooms, 2,893 machines, 64 tables)
The Suncoast Hotel and Casino (419 rooms, 2,271 machines, 58 tables)

COMPETITORS

Aztar
Boyd Gaming
Harrah's Entertainment
Las Vegas Sands
Mandalay Resort Group
MGM Mirage
Park Place Entertainment
Riviera Holdings
Station Casinos

HISTORICAL FINANCIALS

Company Type: Private

Income Statement FYE: December 31

	REVENUE ($ mil.)	NET INCOME ($ mil.)	NET PROFIT MARGIN	EMPLOYEES
12/02	545	32	5.8%	7,286
12/01	518	36	7.0%	7,259
12/00	409	27	6.6%	—
12/99	358	(6)	—	—
Annual Growth	15.0%	—	—	0.4%

2002 Year-End Financials

Debt ratio: 238.3%
Return on equity: 18.5%
Cash ($ mil.): 38
Current ratio: 0.71
Long-term debt ($ mil.): 449

Net Income History

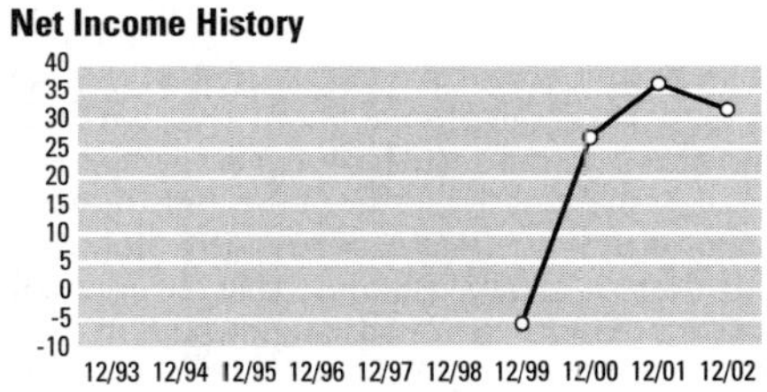

Coca-Cola Bottling Co. United, Inc.

Coca-Cola Bottling Co. United brings icy-cold Cokes to the sunny South. Founded in 1902, it is the third-largest Coca-Cola bottler (the world's #1 soft drink) in the US. The company serves franchises in Alabama, Georgia, Louisiana, Mississippi, South Carolina, and Tennessee, rolling out Coca-Cola's bottled water, iced teas, fruit drinks, and sports drinks, as well as soft drinks. Brands include Coca-Cola Classic, Diet Coke, Fresca, Sprite, and the new Vanilla Coke. Its 101-year-old subsidiary, Chattanooga Coca-Cola Bottling Co., is the world's oldest Coca-Cola bottler. The bottler was the subject of a 1987 book, *Coca-Cola Bottling Company United, Inc.: A Pause to Reflect*.

EXECUTIVES

Chairman: Crawford T. Johnson III
President and CEO: Claude B. Nielsen, age 53
VP and CFO: Hafiz Chandinwala
VP, Marketing: Robert B. (Bob) Lovell
VP, Human Resources: Debbie Myles
President, United Packers, Inc.: Edward (Ed) Mizell
President, Eastern Region: John Sherman
President, Gulf Region: Gary Sligar
Corporate Secretary: Dixie A. Bauder
Director, Engineering and Operations: Dick Morrette

LOCATIONS

HQ: 4600 E. Lake Blvd., Birmingham, AL 35217
Phone: 205-841-2653 **Fax:** 205-841-9168

COMPETITORS

Buffalo Rock
Coca-Cola Bottling Consolidated
Coca-Cola Enterprises
Cott
Dr Pepper/Seven Up Bottling
National Beverage
Nestlé
Pepsi Bottling
PepsiAmericas
PepsiCo
Snapple
Suntory

HISTORICAL FINANCIALS

Company Type: Private

Income Statement FYE: December 31

	ESTIMATED REVENUE ($ mil.)	NET INCOME ($ mil.)	NET PROFIT MARGIN	EMPLOYEES
12/02	500	—	—	2,900
12/01	500	—	—	2,900
12/00	495	—	—	3,000
12/99	501	—	—	3,000
12/98	450	—	—	3,000
12/97	449	—	—	3,300
12/96	425	—	—	2,600
12/95	425	—	—	2,500
Annual Growth	2.3%	—	—	2.1%

Revenue History

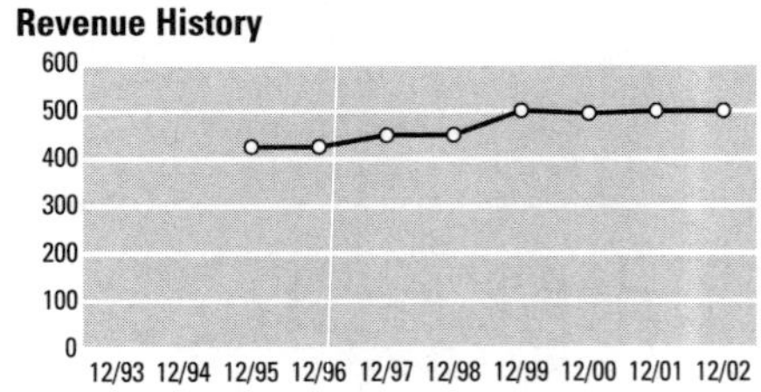

Coinmach Corporation

You won't find much dirty laundry at Coinmach. The leading US supplier of coin- and card-operated laundry equipment and related services has helped customers do millions of loads of laundry. Leasing laundry rooms in apartments and dormitories, Coinmach owns and operates some 855,000 washing machines and dryers at about 80,000 locations nationwide. The company also owns Appliance Warehouse, which rents machines to apartment residents and management companies, and more than 160 Kwik Wash laundromats in Texas and Arizona. Subsidiary Super Laundry designs and builds or retrofits retail laundromats and distributes laundry equipment. GTCR Golder Rauner owns about two-thirds of Coinmach Corporation.

Coinmach's LaundriMate service notifies apartment and dormitory residents when machines are available and when their laundry is finished.

Coinmach has been rapidly increasing its machine count, which stood at about 55,000 in 1995. Operating in a largely fragmented industry, Coinmach folds newly purchased operations into its national organization to achieve economies of scale. The company maintains more than 60 regional offices in about 20 states.

EXECUTIVES

Chairman and CEO: Stephen R. Kerrigan
President, COO, and Director: Mitchell Blatt
SVP, CFO, Treasurer, Secretary, and Director: Robert M. (Bob) Doyle, age 46
SVP, Corporate Development: John E. Denson, age 65
SVP: Stephen P. Close
SVP: Michael E. Stanky, age 51
VP: James P. McDonnell
VP: R. Daniel Osborne
VP: Charles Prato
VP: Harold Sazzmann
VP: David A. Siegel
Human Resources Manager: Cathy Chambers
Assistant to the President: Carol Ann Siebuhr
Auditors: Ernst & Young LLP

LOCATIONS

HQ: 303 Sunnyside Blvd., Ste. 70, Plainview, NY 11803
Phone: 516-349-8555 **Fax:** 516-349-9125
Web: www.coinmach.com

COMPETITORS

Alliance Laundry Systems
Clean Rite Centers
Dryclean USA
Mac-Gray
SpinCycle
Web Service Company

HISTORICAL FINANCIALS

Company Type: Private

Income Statement FYE: March 31

	REVENUE ($ mil.)	NET INCOME ($ mil.)	NET PROFIT MARGIN	EMPLOYEES
3/03	535	(2)	—	2,015
3/02	539	(41)	—	2,049
3/01	528	(30)	—	2,119
3/00	527	(17)	—	2,226
3/99	505	(12)	—	2,045
3/98	325	(15)	—	1,850
3/97	207	(11)	—	1,180
3/96	89	(3)	—	689
3/95	90	(6)	—	—
3/94	74	(5)	—	—
Annual Growth	24.6%	—	—	16.6%

2003 Year-End Financials

Debt ratio: 1,441.9%
Return on equity: —
Cash ($ mil.): 27
Current ratio: 1.68
Long-term debt ($ mil.): 718

Net Income History

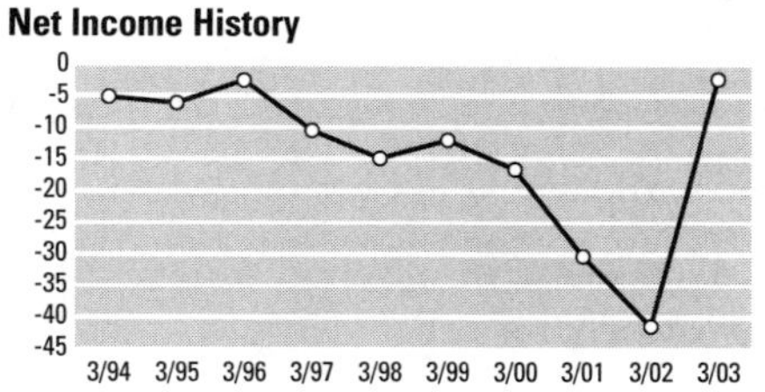

Colfax Corporation

Colfax Corporation is primed to stay pumped. The company has two operating segments: a power transmission group (Warner Electric, Boston Gear, Ameridrives), and a pump group (Allweiler, Imo Pump). Warner Electric makes industrial clutches and brakes for applications ranging from lawn tractors to tractor-trailer rigs. Boston Gear manufactures motion control products and components, while Ameridrives produces power transmission products such as gear couplings and universal joints. Its Germany-based subsidiary, Allweiler, offers an array of industrial pumps designed to move everything from soft drinks to sewage. Imo Pumps makes pumps used in chemical processing, marine, and power generation machinery.

The company typically looks to acquire companies with brand name recognition and an established place in the market. Colfax acts as the parent company, which allows its business units to act independently and market their products more effectively. The company has developed Colfax Business System, a customer-driven management system that utilizes aspects of six sigma for product development and delivery. The company has filed a petition with the SEC to withdraw its 1998 IPO registration.

EXECUTIVES

President, CEO, and Director: John Young
VP and CFO: Doug Barnett
VP and Comptroller: Scott Faison
VP, General Counsel, and Secretary: Thomas M. O'Brien
VP, Colfax Business System and Global Sourcing: Michael K. Dwyer
VP, Human Resources: Steve Weidenmueller
President, Colfax Power Transmission Group: Charles W. Nims
President, Colfax Pump Group: T. Campbell Walton

LOCATIONS

HQ: 8730 Stony Point Parkway, Ste. 150, Richmond, VA 23235
Phone: 804-560-4070 **Fax:** 804-560-4076
Web: www.colfaxcorp.com

Colfax Corporation has manufacturing facilities in Asia, Europe, and North America.

PRODUCTS/OPERATIONS

Selected Divisions and Products

Power Transmission Group
Ameridrives Couplings (gear couplings, mill spindles, and universal joints)
Bay City Forge (carbon and alloy steel open die forgings)
Boston Gear (enclosed gear drives, open gearing, motors, overhead release clutches, and power transmission components)
Delroyd Worm Gear (parallel shaft and in-line helical speed reducers)
Fincor Electronics (AC and DC motor controls, motors, and accessories)
Formsprag Clutch (overrunning clutches and holdbacks)
Industrial Clutch (dry and oil immersed clutches and brakes, hydraulic and pneumatic controls)
Marland Clutch (roller ramp and sprag type overrunning clutches and backstops)
Nuttall Gear (worm and worm gear sets)
Stieber Clutch (overrunning clutches)
Warner Electric (clutches, brakes, clutch/brake controls, and accessories)
Wichita Clutch (pneumatic clutches and brakes)

Pump Group
Allweiler (centrifugal pumps, two-screw pumps, three-screw pumps, progressing cavity pumps, propeller pumps, macerators, castings, and pump skids)
Houttuin (low pressure two-screw pumps)
Imo Pump (two-screw pumps, three-screw pumps, gear pumps, and pump skids)
Warren Pumps (engineered two-screw pumps)

COMPETITORS

Ampco-Pittsburgh
Control Chief Holdings
Crane
Emerson Electric
Flowserve
Gorman-Rupp
Graco
IDEX
Ingersoll-Rand
ITT Industries
Lord Corporation
Parker Hannifin
Regal-Beloit
Robbins & Myers
Roper Industries
Sauer
SpiraxSarco
TB Wood's
Weir Group

HISTORICAL FINANCIALS

Company Type: Private

Income Statement FYE: December 31

	ESTIMATED REVENUE ($ mil.)	NET INCOME ($ mil.)	NET PROFIT MARGIN	EMPLOYEES
12/02	500	—	—	3,500
12/01	525	—	—	3,500
12/00	900	—	—	3,500
12/99	1,000	—	—	3,500
12/98	500	—	—	3,500
12/97	107	—	—	3,800
Annual Growth	36.2%	—	—	(1.6%)

Revenue History

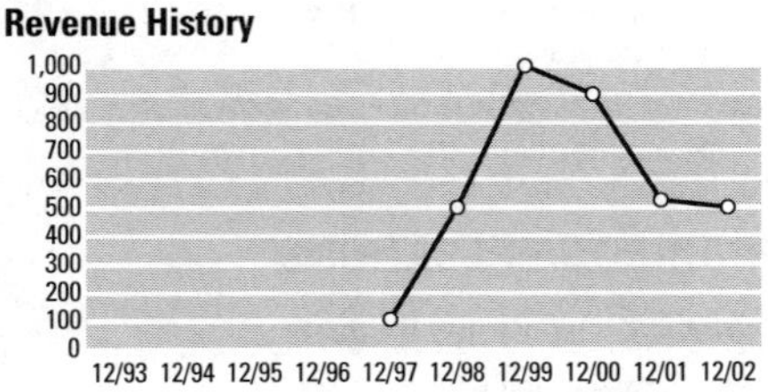

Colliers International

Colliers International Property Consultants is one of the largest commercial real estate dealers in the world. With more than 230 offices in about 50 countries, the company is a partnership of more than 40 independently owned firms. Colliers International agencies provide brokerage, construction consulting, investment sales, and property development and management services to tenants, owners, and investors. Colliers Macauley Nicolls (dba Colliers International) is the group's largest member, with offices in nearly 90 cities worldwide. Originally founded in 1832, Colliers Jardine represents the Asia/Pacific region. Colliers International firms manage about 450 million sq. ft. of property on six continents.

EXECUTIVES

President: Margaret Wigglesworth
SVP Operations: Margaret Carlson
SVP and Director, Corporate Services Group: Richard B. Kimball
Chief Technology Officer: Joshua Fost
Manager, Accounting: Connie Prestera
Manager, Internet and Intranet Services: Dustin Turner
Manager, Specialty Groups and Projects: Laura Cuddihy
Office Administrator: Amanda Mayo
Systems Administrator: Jennifer McCarron

LOCATIONS

HQ: Colliers International Property Consultants Inc.
84 State St., 3rd Fl., Boston, MA 02019
Phone: 617-722-0221 **Fax:** 617-722-0224
Web: www.colliers.com

COMPETITORS

CB Richard Ellis
Cushman & Wakefield
DTZ
Gale Company
Grubb & Ellis
JMB Realty
Jones Lang LaSalle
NRT Inc.
Trammell Crow

HISTORICAL FINANCIALS

Company Type: Private

Income Statement FYE: December 31

	REVENUE ($ mil.)	NET INCOME ($ mil.)	NET PROFIT MARGIN	EMPLOYEES
12/02	880	—	—	7,572
12/01	800	—	—	6,600
12/00	1,000	—	—	9,000
12/99	900	—	—	8,000
Annual Growth	(0.7%)	—	—	(1.8%)

Revenue History

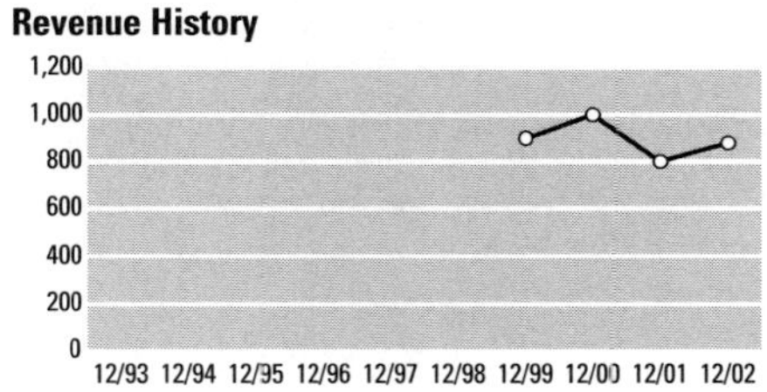

Colson & Colson Construction

Colson & Colson Construction builds retirement communities for senior citizens worldwide. The company primarily develops affordable retirement properties nationwide for Holiday Retirement Corp. (HRC), the #1 owner and manager of retirement homes in the US and Canada; it also operates in France and the UK. Colson & Colson has interests in some 20,000 HRC units. Generally located in a midsized town, the typical property is a traditional retirement facility of about 115 units. The company uses a prefabrication process to speed construction and keep costs down. William Colson is head of both Colson & Colson and HRC. The Colson family owns the majority of Colson & Colson and also holds a significant stake in HRC.

EXECUTIVES

President and Managing General Partner: William E. (Bill) Colson, age 61
SVP: Norman Brendan
Treasurer: Gregory Tibbot
Secretary: Bruce Thorn
Human Resources: Linda Livermore

LOCATIONS

HQ: Colson & Colson Construction Company
2250 McGilchrist SE, Ste. 200, Salem, OR 97302
Phone: 503-370-7070 **Fax:** 503-364-5716

Colson & Colson Construction develops property for Holiday Retirement Corp.'s operations in 39 states in the US, six provinces in Canada, and in France and the UK.

COMPETITORS

Centex
Del Webb
Embree Construction
John Wieland Homes
KB Home
Lennar
Marriott International
Morrison Homes
Pulte Homes

HISTORICAL FINANCIALS

Company Type: Private

Income Statement FYE: December 31

	REVENUE ($ mil.)	NET INCOME ($ mil.)	NET PROFIT MARGIN	EMPLOYEES
12/02	900	—	—	7,300
12/01	888	—	—	7,100
12/00	690	—	—	6,800
12/99	707	—	—	6,800
12/98	675	—	—	6,500
12/97	600	—	—	6,000
12/96	500	—	—	—
Annual Growth	10.3%	—	—	4.0%

Revenue History

Colt's Manufacturing Company, Inc.

The Colt .45 may have won the West, but it took a New York investment firm to save Colt's Manufacturing from a post-Cold War decline in weapons sales and tough foreign competition. Through its subsidiaries, Colt's Manufacturing makes handguns (Cowboy, Defender) and semi-automatic rifles for civilian use and military weapons (M-16, M-4 Carbine) for the US and other governments. Colt's also licenses its name to a variety of other companies, such as Encore Software (for Encore's Wild West Shootout game). Founded in 1836 by Samuel Colt, the company is about 83%-owned by investment firm Zilkha & Co.

With the firearms industry taking cover from safety and health care expense-related lawsuits filed by cities and counties across the US, Colt's is discontinuing a number of handguns it makes for the consumer market. The company spun off its "smart gun" division as iColt but the division soon closed. Colt's sold its military weapons manufacturer Saco Defense to General Dynamics in mid 2000.

Zilkha & Co. has been working to revive the company since 1994 when it bought the firm out of bankruptcy.

HISTORY

After waiting four years for a patent, Samuel Colt started the Patent Arms Manufacturing Company in 1836 to make his revolutionary handgun, a revolver. The newfangled gun was slow to catch on (the company went bankrupt in 1842), but it gained fame after being adopted by the Texas Rangers. The US Army delegated Capt. Samuel Walker to work with Colt to improve the design, and sales of the resulting "Walker Colt" enabled Colt to set up a factory in Hartford, Connecticut.

In 1851 Patent Arms became the first American manufacturer to open a plant in England. The company was renamed Colt's Patent Fire Arms Manufacturing Co. four years later. Colt was a millionaire when he died in 1862 at age 47.

Colt's introduced the six-shot Colt .45 Army Model, "the gun that won the West," in 1873. More products followed, including machine guns and automatic pistols designed by inventor John Browning. Colt's widow sold the firm to an investor group in 1901.

Business boomed during both world wars, but by the 1940s labor strife and outmoded equipment began to take a toll, and Colt's lost money during the last years of WWII. In 1955 the struggling firm was acquired by conglomerate Penn-Texas. In 1959 Colt's patented the M-16 rifle; in 10 years it sold a million units to the US military.

During the Vietnam War the company flourished, but the 1980s brought low-end competition and shrinking defense orders. Colt's sales were hurt when the US government replaced the Colt .45 as the standard-issue sidearm for the armed forces. A three-year strike prompted the Army to shift its M-16 contract to Belgium's FN Herstal in 1988.

Two years later Colt's was acquired by private investors and a Connecticut state pension fund and was renamed Colt's Manufacturing. Sales remained flat, however, forcing the company to seek bankruptcy protection in 1992. There Colt's remained until New York investment firm Zilkha & Co. bailed it out in 1994, reorganizing the company. The new management made an offer for rival FN Herstal in 1997, but the deal was blocked by the Belgian government and fell through. Late that year the company won a contract to supply M-4 rifles to the Army.

Colt's bought military weapons specialist Saco Defense, maker of MK 19 and Striker grenade launchers, in 1998. Also that year Steven Sliwa succeeded retiring CEO Ronald Stewart.

As US cities began suing Colt's and other makers of firearms in attempts to recover safety and health expenses attributed to gun violence, the company stepped up lobbying in 1999 and said it would increase gun safety efforts, including development of its "smart gun" technology.

A restructuring in 1999 ended most of Colt's consumer handgun business. It also spun off its smart gun technology as a separate company, iColt. Sliwa left to head iColt, and retired US Marine Lieutenant General William Keys was named president and CEO of Colt's. Also in 1999 Colt's bought Ultra-Light Arms, a maker of upscale hunting rifles, and said it would buy Heckler & Koch, a small arms manufacturer based in Germany. By 2000 the company had withdrawn iColt (investors didn't seem interested in a lawsuit laden industry) and stepped away from the Heckler & Koch deal. The company continues to focus on weapons for the military and police, but in 2001 it lost out to CAPCO Inc. in a bid for a contract to upgrade M16 rifles used by the Air Force.

EXECUTIVES

Chairman: Donald Zilkha
President and CEO: William M. (Bill) Keys
CFO: Tom Moore
Director, Human Resources: Mike Magouirk
Director, Marketing: Mike Reissig

LOCATIONS

HQ: 545 New Park Ave., West Hartford, CT 06110
Phone: 860-236-6311 **Fax:** 860-244-1442
Web: www.colt.com

PRODUCTS/OPERATIONS

Selected Products and Brands

Classics
Anaconda
Python

Commercial rifles
Colt accurized rifles
Match target rifles

Law enforcement
AR15
Carbine
Colt accurized rifles
Commando
M-16A2
M203 Grenade Launchers
M-4 Carbine
Match target rifles
Submachine guns

Performance products
Colt Gunsite Pistol
Colt XSE Series
Gold Cup Trophy
Special Combat Government Competition

Personal protection
Colt Defender
M1991A1

Western
Colt Cowboy
Model Ps

COMPETITORS

Action Arms
BAE SYSTEMS
Browning
Crosman
Beretta
FN Manufacturing
Glock
Mauser-Werke
Navegar
Remington Arms
Saf T Lok
SIG
Smith & Wesson Holding
Springfield Inc.
Ruger
U.S. Repeating Arms

HISTORICAL FINANCIALS

Company Type: Private

Income Statement

FYE: December 31

	ESTIMATED REVENUE ($ mil.)	NET INCOME ($ mil.)	NET PROFIT MARGIN	EMPLOYEES
12/00	100	—	—	700
12/99	100	—	—	700
12/98	96	—	—	700
12/97	92	—	—	700
Annual Growth	2.8%	—	—	0.0%

Revenue History

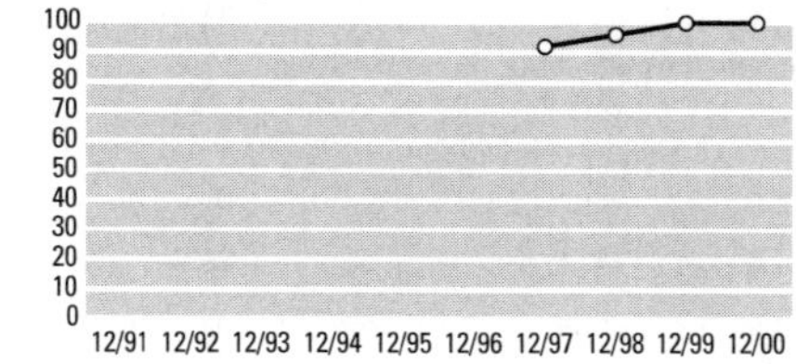

Columbia Forest Products Inc.

Columbia Forest Products is a clear-cut leader as North America's largest manufacturer of hardwood plywood, veneer, and laminated products. The employee-owned company makes products used in flooring, cabinets, architectural millwork, and commercial fixtures. Columbia Forest Products specializes in Northern Appalachian hardwoods. Its rotary veneer is used by the cabinetry, door, furniture, and decorative plywood industries. The company sells its products to OEMs, wholesale distributors, and mass merchandisers. Columbia Forest Products began in 1957 with a plywood plant in Oregon and has grown to operate 20 plants throughout the US and Canada.

Columbia Forest Products purchased Weyerhaeuser's Nipigon Multiply hardwood plywood underlayment operation (Ontario, Canada) in 2002, and enlists Weyerhaeuser Building Materials as a sales and distribution agent to its customers in North America. The company also has an exclusive agreement with Halex Corporation to head up sales of the Multiply flooring underlayment to wholesale flooring distributors in North America. (Multiply is three-ply aspen, one-fourth inch plywood for use under vinyl, ceramic and laminate flooring.)

EXECUTIVES

Chairman: Arnold Curtis
President and CEO: Harry L. Demorest, age 61
CFO: Cliff Barry
CTO: Frank Leipzig
EVP Sales and Marketing: Ed Woods
Director of Organizational Development and Human Resources: Rick Howell

LOCATIONS

HQ: 222 SW Columbia, Ste. 1575, Portland, OR 97201
Phone: 503-224-5300 **Fax:** 503-224-5294
Web: www.columbiaforestproducts.com

Columbia Forest Products operates manufacturing plants in Arkansas, Georgia, Kentucky, Maine, North Carolina, Oregon, Texas, Vermont, Virginia, West Virginia, and Wisconsin in the US, as well as plants in Ontario and Quebec, Canada.

PRODUCTS/OPERATIONS

Selected Products

Flooring
Hardwood plywood
Hardwood plywood flooring underlayment
Hardwood veneers
Veneer raised panels and door inserts

COMPETITORS

Armstrong Holdings
Boise Cascade
Dal-Tile
Georgia-Pacific Corporation
Louisiana-Pacific
Mohawk Industries
Nexfor
Plum Creek Timber
Potlatch
Roseburg Forest Products
Shaw Industries
Sierra Pacific Industries
Temple-Inland
West Fraser Timber
Weyerhaeuser

HISTORICAL FINANCIALS

Company Type: Private

Income Statement FYE: December 31

	ESTIMATED REVENUE ($ mil.)	NET INCOME ($ mil.)	NET PROFIT MARGIN	EMPLOYEES
12/02	700	—	—	3,000
12/01	750	—	—	3,300
12/00	800	—	—	3,500
12/99	725	—	—	3,300
12/98	650	—	—	3,214
12/97	600	—	—	3,042
Annual Growth	3.1%	—	—	(0.3%)

Revenue History

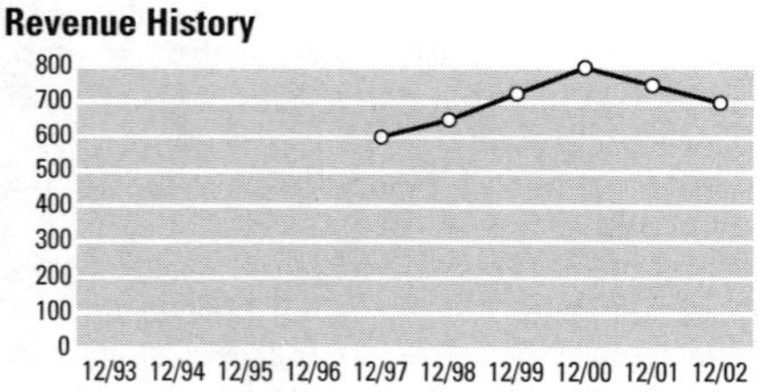

Columbia House

If the house is a-rockin', it's probably Columbia House. Initially a fifty-fifty joint venture between entertainment giants Sony and Time Warner, Columbia House is the top club-based direct marketer (with some 14 million members in the US, Canada, and Mexico) of music, videos, DVDs, and video games in North America. The company sells more than 12,000 music selections and 7,000 video titles via mail order and online. The company agreed to merge with online music retailer CDnow in 1999, but the deal was called off in 2000. Merger talks with rental giant Blockbuster are currently underway. Investment firm Blackstone Group bought 85% of Columbia House in June 2002 (Sony and Time Warner retain a 15% stake).

EXECUTIVES

Chairman and CEO: Scott Flanders, age 45
President: Brian S. Wood
COO: Terry Dwyer
SVP and CFO: Frank Mergenthaler
SVP and General Manager: Neil Pennington
SVP, Human Resources: Michael E. Pilnick
SVP, Music Club: Jim Litwak
SVP, Video Clubs: Michelle Jehle
VP, Marketing: Ann Marie Resnick
Chief Administrative Officer and General Counsel: Andrea Hirsch
Chief Marketing Officer: Bill Ostroff

LOCATIONS

HQ: Columbia House Company
1221 Avenue of the Americas, New York, NY 10020
Phone: 212-596-2000 **Fax:** 212-596-2213
Web: www.columbiahouse.com

COMPETITORS

Amazon.com
barnesandnoble.com
Bertelsmann
Best Buy
Borders
CDnow
EMusic.com
Hastings Entertainment
Image Entertainment
MP3.com
MTS
Musicland
Netflix
Trans World Entertainment
Wal-Mart

HISTORICAL FINANCIALS

Company Type: Private

Income Statement FYE: December 31

	REVENUE ($ mil.)	NET INCOME ($ mil.)	NET PROFIT MARGIN	EMPLOYEES
12/02	1,200	—	—	4,000
12/01	1,100	—	—	4,000
12/00	1,200	—	—	4,000
12/99*	1,000	—	—	3,000
3/98	1,400	—	—	3,000
Annual Growth	(3.8%)	—	—	7.5%

*Fiscal year change

Revenue History

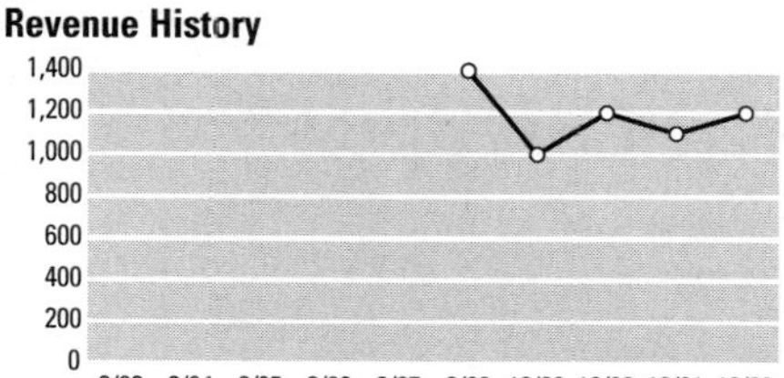

Columbia University

Predating the American Revolution, Columbia University (founded as King's College in 1754) is the fifth-oldest institution of higher learning in the US. With almost 23,000 students and a campus spread across 36 acres in Manhattan, Columbia's 16 schools and colleges grant undergraduate and graduate degrees in about 100 disciplines, including its well-known programs in journalism, law, and medicine. The Ivy League university's 7,700-member faculty has included 64 Nobel laureates and former Vice President Al Gore. Columbia also has a strong reputation for research and ranks #1 among universities earning funds through patents and royalties.

Columbia has forged affiliations with nearby institutions such as Barnard College, Teachers College, and Union Theological Seminary. Columbia-Presbyterian Medical Center, the result of more than 70 years of partnership between Columbia and The Presbyterian Hospital, helped pioneer the concept of academic medical centers.

Columbia's list of alumni includes such luminaries as Yankee great Lou Gehrig, Supreme Court Justice Ruth Bader Ginsberg, and President Franklin Roosevelt. Columbia has gone to the alumni well (and others sources) often over the past 10 years, collecting a record $4.3 billion in fund-raising. In 2003 the university announced plans to close its unprofitable Fathom e-Learning unit.

HISTORY

Created by royal charter of King George II of England, the university was founded in 1754 as King's College. Its first class of eight students met in a schoolhouse adjacent to Trinity Church (in what is now Manhattan). Some of the university's earliest students included Alexander Hamilton and John Jay. King's College was renamed Columbia College in 1784, a name that symbolized the patriotic mind-set of the age.

The college moved to 49th Street and Madison Avenue in 1849. The School of Law was founded in 1858, followed by the predecessor to the School of Engineering and Applied Science in 1864. The Graduate School of Arts and Sciences was established in 1880, and Columbia became affiliated with Barnard College in 1889.

Columbia College became Columbia University in 1896, and the following year it moved to its present location, the former site of the Bloomingdale Insane Asylum. (Columbia retained its original site, on which Rockefeller Center was built, until selling it in 1985.) Columbia continued to expand during the early 20th century. It added the School of Journalism in 1912 with funding from publishing magnate Joseph Pulitzer. Other additions included the School of Business (1916), the School of Public Health (1921), and the School of International and Public Affairs (1946).

Dwight Eisenhower became president of Columbia in 1948, retaining the position until becoming President of the United States in 1953. During the late 1960s Columbia gained a reputation for student political action, and in 1968 students closed down the university for several days in protest of the Vietnam War.

Facing financial woes, an escalating New York

City crime rate, and contention among its faculty, Columbia struggled to maintain its reputation during the 1970s and 1980s. With this challenge as a backdrop, the university continued to evolve, welcoming its first coed freshman class in 1983.

Still facing economic pressures and reductions in government research spending, Columbia was forced to cut costs, eliminating its linguistics and geography departments in 1991. George Rupp became Columbia's president in 1993. Columbia took over operation of the controversial Biosphere 2 laboratory in Arizona in 1996 (the university had been associated with the lab since 1994, when it formed a consortium with other universities to overhaul the ailing science experiment).

By the late 1990s Columbia had begun to recover from its financial and academic decline. Under the leadership of president Rupp, the university improved its fund-raising efforts and became more selective in student admissions. Microsoft founder Bill Gates donated $150 million to Columbia's School of Public Health in 1999 for research into the prevention of death and disability from childbirth in developing countries. That year Columbia created Morningside Ventures, a for-profit company focused on producing educational materials.

The university partnered in 2000 with the British Library, Cambridge University Press, the London School of Economics, the New York Public Library, and the Smithsonian to form another for-profit venture, Fathom.com, a site offering online access to various scholarly resources from each institution. The next year, the National Science Foundation awarded Columbia a $90,000 grant to gather personal accounts and create an oral history piece on the World Trade Center attacks of September 11. In 2002 Columbia University received a pledge of $8 million from Bernard Spitzer for stem cell research to develop new treatments for Parkinson's disease and other neurological disorders. Also that year Lee Bollinger replaced Rupp as president.

EXECUTIVES

Chairman: David J. Stern, age 61
President: Lee C. Bollinger
Provost and Dean of Faculties: Jonathan R. Cole
EVP Administration: Emily Lloyd
EVP Finance: John Masten
VP and Dean Arts and Sciences: David Cohen
VP Human Resources: Colleen M. Crooker
Secretary: R. Keith Walton
Treasurer and Controller: Patricia L. Francy, age 57
Vice Provost for Academic Administration: Stephen Rittenberg
Auditors: Deloitte & Touche LLP

LOCATIONS

HQ: 2960 Broadway, New York, NY 10027
Phone: 212-854-1754 **Fax:** 212-749-0397
Web: www.columbia.edu

Columbia University in the City of New York is located in the Morningside Heights section of Manhattan.

PRODUCTS/OPERATIONS

Selected Schools, Colleges, and Programs

Continuing Education

Graduate and Professional Schools
College of Physicians and Surgeons
  Human Nutrition
  Occupational Therapy
  Physical Therapy
The Fu Foundation School of Engineering & Applied Science
Mailman School of Public Health
School of Architecture, Planning & Preservation
School of the Arts
School of Arts and Sciences
School of Business
  Executive Education Program
  Executive MBA Program
School of Dental & Oral Surgery
School of International and Public Affairs
School of Journalism
School of Law
School of Nursing
School of Social Work

Undergraduate Schools
Columbia College
The Fu Foundation School of Engineering and Applied Science
School of General Studies

HISTORICAL FINANCIALS

Company Type: School

Income Statement FYE: June 30

	REVENUE ($ mil.)	NET INCOME ($ mil.)	NET PROFIT MARGIN	EMPLOYEES
6/02	2,009	—	—	15,300
6/01	1,934	—	—	7,072
6/00	1,790	—	—	15,000
6/99	1,574	—	—	15,000
6/98	1,448	—	—	15,300
6/97	1,339	—	—	17,930
6/96	1,234	—	—	16,300
6/95	1,160	—	—	16,565
6/94	1,103	—	—	14,639
6/93	1,032	—	—	—
Annual Growth	7.7%	—	—	0.6%

Revenue History

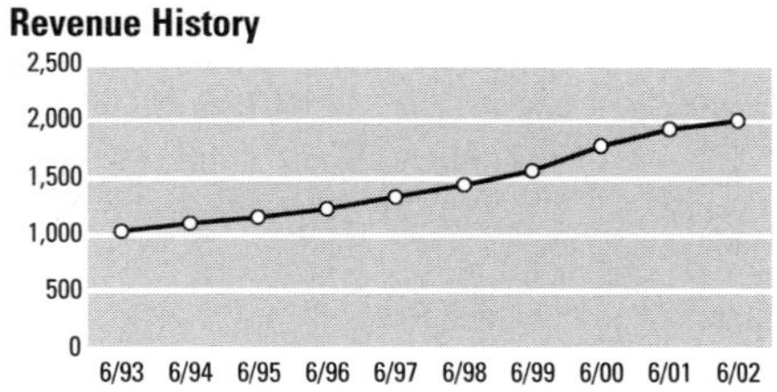

Community Newspaper Holdings, Inc.

Community Newspaper Holdings, Inc. (CNHI) might be holding your community's newspaper. Founded in 1997 to acquire community papers, the company owns more than 200 daily and weekly publications in 22 states with a combined circulation of more than 1 million. Nearly 30% of CNHI's publications are in Oklahoma and Texas. Most of the company's papers fall in the 13,000-25,000 circulation range. CNHI, which is backed by Retirement Systems of Alabama, focuses on cutting costs by building newspaper clusters.

EXECUTIVES

President, CEO, and CFO: Michael E. Reed
VP and COO: Kevin Kampman
VP and Publisher, *The Weatherford Democrat*: Jim Wilson
VP, Plains Newspaper Division: David Gentry
CTO: Brenda Cole
Publisher, Indiana division: Michael C. Casuscelli
Head of Human Resources: Yvette Northcutt

LOCATIONS

HQ: 3500 Colonnade Pkwy., Ste. 600, Birmingham, AL 35243
Phone: 205-298-7100 **Fax:** 205-298-7101
Web: www.cnhi.com

Community Newspaper Holdings has newspaper operations in 22 US states, with the largest concentration of papers in Oklahoma and Texas.

PRODUCTS/OPERATIONS

Selected Newspapers
The Apex Herald (North Carolina)
Big Spring Herald (Texas)
Clinton Herald (Iowa)
The Cullman Times (Alabama)
The Daily Independent (Ashland, KY)
Enid News and Eagle (Oklahoma)
The Free Press (Mankato, MN)
The Herald (Sharon, PA)
Jackson Progress-Argus (Georgia)
The Joplin Globe (Missouri)
Kane Republican (Pennsylvania)
Macon County Times (Lafayette, TN)
The Norman Transcript (Oklahoma)
The Orange Leader (Texas)
Penny Saver Times (South Bend, IN)
Picayune Item (Mississippi)
The Richmond Register (Kentucky)
The Robesonian (Lumberton, NC)
Union-Sun & Journal (Lockport, NY)

COMPETITORS

E. W. Scripps
Gannett
Knight-Ridder
Landmark Communications
Lee Enterprises
Liberty Group Publishing
Media General
Morris Communications
Tribune

HISTORICAL FINANCIALS

Company Type: Private

Income Statement FYE: December 31

	REVENUE ($ mil.)	NET INCOME ($ mil.)	NET PROFIT MARGIN	EMPLOYEES
12/01	454	—	—	—
12/00	470	—	—	—
12/99	350	—	—	—
12/98	200	—	—	—
12/97	120	—	—	—
Annual Growth	39.5%	—	—	—

Revenue History

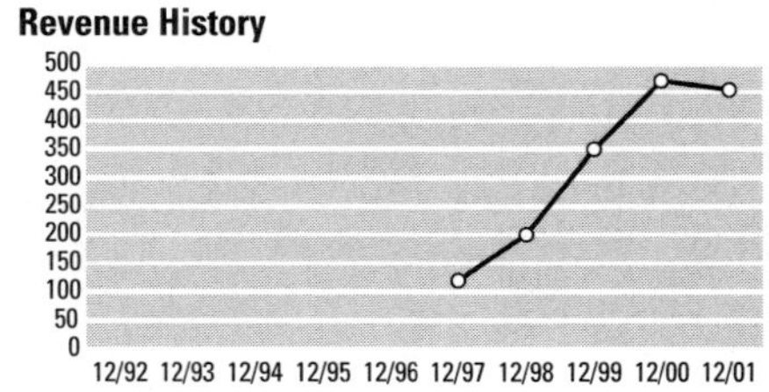

Computer Sales International

Founded in 1972, Computer Sales International (CSI) provides computer leasing for customers in Brazil, Canada, Costa Rica, Germany, Mexico, the UK, and the US. Charlesbank Capital Partners of Boston invested about $30 million in the company in 2002, taking a minority equity position.

EXECUTIVES

Chairman and CEO: Kenneth B. (Ken) Steinback, age 60
Vice Chairman: Albert (Al) Smith, age 60
President and COO: E. William (Bill) Gillula, age 57
EVP and Co-CFO: J. Philip (Phil) Cagney, age 47
EVP and Co-CFO: Frederick (Fred) O'Neal, age 46
EVP and Director of Acquisitions and International Operations: Steve G. Hamilton, age 47
EVP, Marketing: Lawrence (Larry) Schinsky
SVP, General Counsel, and Secretary: Lorraine Cherrick
Auditors: Ernst & Young LLP

LOCATIONS

HQ: Computer Sales International, Inc.
9990 Old Olive Street Rd., Ste. 101,
St. Louis, MO 63141
Phone: 314-997-7010 **Fax:** 314-997-7844
Web: www.csileasing.com

HISTORICAL FINANCIALS

Company Type: Private

Income Statement FYE: June 30

	REVENUE ($ mil.)	NET INCOME ($ mil.)	NET PROFIT MARGIN	EMPLOYEES
6/02	502	14	2.7%	400
6/01	577	11	1.9%	—
6/00	521	—	—	—
6/99	464	—	—	—
6/98	309	—	—	—
Annual Growth	12.9%	24.5%	—	—

Net Income History

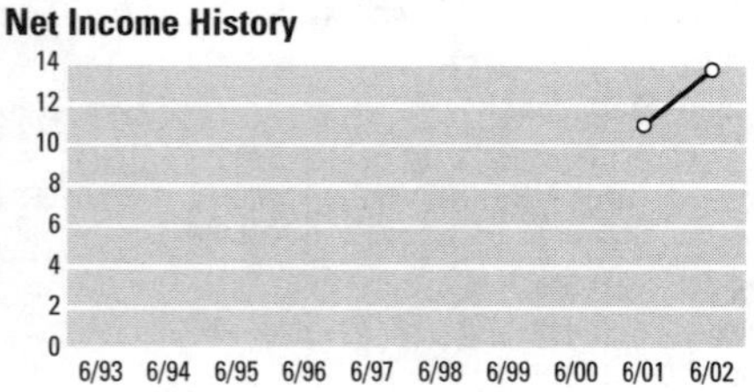

Conair Corporation

Counterintelligence has shown that Conair has a place in many bathrooms and kitchens. Personal products by Conair include curling irons, hair dryers, mirrors, shavers, and salon products (Jheri Redding, Rusk) designed for both home and professional salon use. Its small appliances include food blenders, food processors, and other kitchen appliances produced by its Cuisinart unit. Conair also sells answering machines, the Interplak electric toothbrush, and telephones. Products are sold at discount chains, department stores, and mass merchants (Bed Bath & Beyond, Target, Wal-Mart) throughout the US. Lee Rizzuto, who founded Conair in 1959 with his parents, pleaded guilty to tax evasion in 2002.

EXECUTIVES

Co-President: Ronald T. Diamond
Co-President: Barry Haber
CFO: Pat Yannotta
SVP Administration: John Mayorek
VP Marketing: Frank Lindsey

LOCATIONS

HQ: 1 Cummings Point Rd., Stamford, CT 06902
Phone: 203-351-9000 **Fax:** 203-351-9180
Web: www.conair.com

PRODUCTS/OPERATIONS

Selected Brands

BaByliss
Conair
Cuisinart
Forfex
Grand Finale
Interplak
Jheri Redding
Pollenex
Raje
Rusk
Waring

Selected Divisions and Products

Conair Packaging (health and beauty aid products)
Consumer Electronics (telephones)
Consumer Toiletries (hair and skin care)
Cuisinart (kitchen appliances)
Interplak (electric toothbrushes)
Personal Care (hair dryers, curling irons, health and fitness appliances)
Professional Products (toiletries and appliances)

COMPETITORS

Alberto-Culver
American Household
Applica
Gillette
Helen of Troy
Holmes Group
John Paul Mitchell
L'Oréal
National Presto Industries
Newell Rubbermaid
Philips Electronics
Philips Oral
Procter & Gamble
Professional Dental Technologies
Remington Products
Revlon
Salton
SEB
Shiseido

HISTORICAL FINANCIALS

Company Type: Private

Income Statement FYE: December 31

	REVENUE ($ mil.)	NET INCOME ($ mil.)	NET PROFIT MARGIN	EMPLOYEES
12/01	1,151	—	—	4,592
12/00	1,082	—	—	4,461
12/99	928	—	—	3,676
12/98	787	—	—	3,898
12/97	716	—	—	3,652
12/96	655	—	—	3,175
12/95	614	—	—	3,431
Annual Growth	11.0%	—	—	5.0%

Revenue History

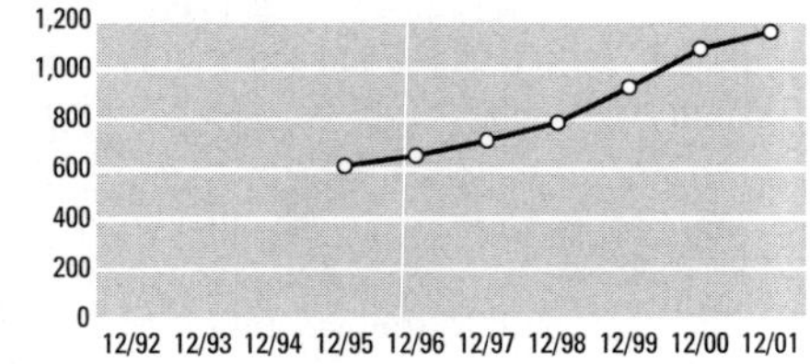

Concentra Inc.

Concentra (formerly CONCENTRA Managed Care) concentrates on getting people back to work cheaper. It is the holding company for Concentra Operating Corporation, which provides cost containment and case management services to employers and to occupational, auto, and group health payors throughout the US. Concentra offers specialized cost-containment services for occupational and auto injury cases, preferred provider network management, telephone case management, and medical bill review. The company also operates more than 200 medical centers in about 30 states, providing occupational health care including pre-employment screening, injury care, and loss prevention.

EXECUTIVES

Chairman: Paul B. Queally II, age 39
CEO and Director: Daniel J. Thomas
President and COO: Fredrick C. Dunlap
EVP, CFO, and Treasurer: Thomas E. Kiraly
EVP, Secretary, and General Counsel: Richard A. Parr II
EVP, Corporate Development: James M. Greenwood
SVP and Chief Medical Officer: W. Tom Fogarty
SVP and Chief Marketing Officer: Andrew R. Daniels, age 46
SVP and CIO: Laura Ciavola
SVP, National Sales: Ken Loffredo
Medical Examinations: David Moules
Human Resources: Tammy Jackson
Auditors: PricewaterhouseCoopers

LOCATIONS

HQ: 5080 Spectrum Dr., Ste. 400W, Addison, TX 75001
Phone: 972-364-8000 **Fax:** 972-387-1938
Web: www.concentra.com

PRODUCTS/OPERATIONS

Divisions

Concentra Case Management Services
Concentra Health Services
Concentra Medical Examinations
Concentra Preferred Systems
First Notice Systems
FOCUS HealthCare Management

COMPETITORS

COPE
CorVel
Crawford & Company
First Health Group
NDCHealth
Per-Se Technologies
RTW

HISTORICAL FINANCIALS

Company Type: Private

Income Statement FYE: December 31

	REVENUE ($ mil.)	NET INCOME ($ mil.)	NET PROFIT MARGIN	EMPLOYEES
12/02	999	(4)	—	10,254
12/01	843	(23)	—	10,276
12/00	752	(7)	—	8,800
12/99	681	(27)	—	8,800
12/98	617	23	3.6%	7,800
12/97	459	3	0.6%	7,270
12/96	170	11	6.5%	2,725
12/95	109	6	5.6%	2,125
12/94	60	2	3.7%	1,900
12/93	101	4	4.2%	—
Annual Growth	29.1%	—	—	23.5%

Net Income History

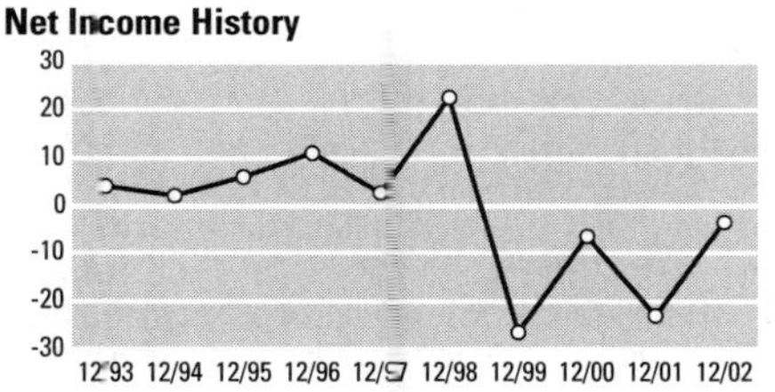

ConnectiCare

To profit or not to profit? That is no longer a question for ConnectiCare. The company, one of the largest HMOs in Connecticut, has converted to for-profit status in order to raise capital. In 1979 a group of doctors at Hartford Hospital planted the seeds for what would become ConnectiCare; today, the company's nearly 280,000 members in Connecticut and western Massachusetts choose from HMO or point-of-service options. The company has a network of more than 30 hospitals and about 9,000 care providers. ConnectiCare established a charitable foundation as part of its reorganization to for-profit status.

Conservative investment firm The Carlyle Group partnered with private equity firm Liberty Partners to buy ConnectiCare.

EXECUTIVES

Chair: Eileen S. Kraus
President and CEO: Marcel L. (Gus) Gamache
SVP, CFO and Treasurer: Thomas L. Tran
SVP and Chief Medical Officer: Paul A. Bluestein
VP and Medical Director: Ronald Blumenfeld
VP, Network Operations: William F. Carroll
VP, Human Resources: Dick Rogers
VP, Operations: Ida M. Schnipper
Chief Marketing Officer: Paul Philpott, age 53
VP and General Counsel: Gail Bogossian
Chief Information Officer: Mark Dixon

LOCATIONS

HQ: ConnectiCare, Inc.
30 Batterson Park Rd., Farmington, CT 06032
Phone: 860-674-5700 **Fax:** 860-674-2030
Web: www.connecticare.com

ConnectiCare operates in Connecticut, and in the Massachusetts counties of Hampden, Hampshire, and Franklin.

PRODUCTS/OPERATIONS

Subsidiaries

ConnectiCare Insurance Company
ConnectiCare of Massachusetts, Inc.

COMPETITORS

Aetna
Anthem
Blue Cross
CIGNA
Harvard Pilgrim
Health Net
Oxford Health Plans
Tufts Health Plan
UnitedHealth Group

HISTORICAL FINANCIALS

Company Type: Private

Income Statement FYE: December 31

	REVENUE ($ mil.)	NET INCOME ($ mil.)	NET PROFIT MARGIN	EMPLOYEES
12/01	654	21	3.2%	540
12/00	541	—	—	530
12/99	440	—	—	450
12/98	354	—	—	450
12/97	291	—	—	400
12/96	264	—	—	—
Annual Growth	19.9%	—	—	7.8%

Revenue History

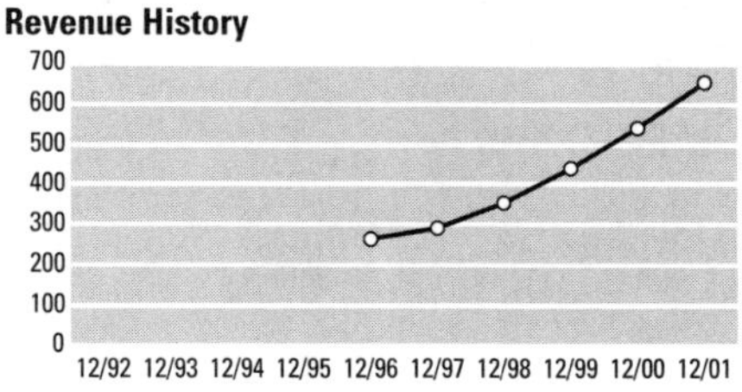

The Connell Company

The Connell Company can sell you a boatload of rice or lend you money for that power plant you've been meaning to install. Connell's core business is rice distribution, conducted through subsidiary Connell Rice & Sugar. The company's support operations have grown into full subsidiaries including brokerage of flour and sweeteners, export sales of food manufacturing equipment, commercial real estate development, heavy equipment leasing, exporting, and financial services (such as underwriting airlines' purchases of aircraft). The company has offices in Taiwan, Thailand, and the US. Connell has remained a family-owned business since it was founded in 1926.

EXECUTIVES

President: Grover Connell
CFO: Terry Connell
VP, Human Resources: Maureen Waldron

LOCATIONS

HQ: 1 Connell Dr., Berkeley Heights, NJ 07922
Phone: 908-673-3700 **Fax:** 908-673-3800
Web: www.connellco.com

PRODUCTS/OPERATIONS

Selected Divisions and Subsidiaries

Connell & Co. (flour, sugar brokerage services)
Connell Finance Company, Inc. (financial advisory services)
  Connell Equipment Leasing Company
  Connell Technologies Company (asset management services)
Connell GATCO Company (heavy equipment distribution)
Connell International Co. (exporting)
Connell Realty & Development Co. (commercial and corporate buildings)
Connell Rice & Sugar Co.

COMPETITORS

American Rice
Atlas Copco
Cargill
Deere
Man Group
Merrill Lynch
Riceland Foods
Riviana Foods

HISTORICAL FINANCIALS

Company Type: Private

Income Statement FYE: December 31

	ESTIMATED REVENUE ($ mil.)	NET INCOME ($ mil.)	NET PROFIT MARGIN	EMPLOYEES
12/01	2,525	—	—	245
12/00	2,425	—	—	240
12/99	2,300	—	—	220
12/98	2,100	—	—	225
12/97	1,275	—	—	225
12/96	1,300	—	—	220
12/95	1,200	—	—	200
12/94	1,100	—	—	200
12/93	1,050	—	—	200
12/92	1,050	—	—	200
Annual Growth	10.2%	—	—	2.3%

Revenue History

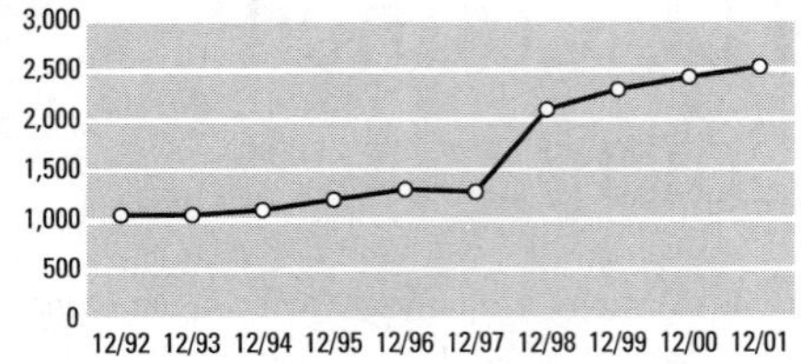

Connell Limited Partnership

The die was cast in 1987 when several subsidiaries organized to create Connell Limited Partnership, a maker of aluminum alloy and industrial equipment. Connell's wholly owned businesses, Wabash Alloys, Danly IEM, and Yuba Heat Transfer, serve customers in the automotive, appliance, aerospace, electronics, and power and process industries. The company also makes die sets and supplies for die makers. The company operates some 30 facilities in the US, Mexico, and Canada, and has grown through acquisitions. Connell sold its Mayville Metal products to APW Limited for about $225 million in 2001.

EXECUTIVES

President and CEO: Francis A. Doyle, age 55
VP and CFO: Kurt J. Keady
Director, Taxes: Catherine Gallagher

LOCATIONS

HQ: 1 International Place, Boston, MA 02110
Phone: 617-737-2700 **Fax:** 617-737-1617
Web: www.connell-lp.com

Connell Limited Partnership has manufacturing plants and other facilities in Canada, Mexico, and the US.

COMPETITORS

Anchor Lamina
Bethlehem Corporation
Commercial Metals
Envirosource
Harsco
IMCO Recycling
Metallurg
Productivity Technologies
Tang Industries
United States Steel

HISTORICAL FINANCIALS

Company Type: Private

Income Statement FYE: December 31

	REVENUE ($ mil.)	NET INCOME ($ mil.)	NET PROFIT MARGIN	EMPLOYEES
12/02	1,100	—	—	1,700
12/01	1,000	—	—	1,700
12/00	1,185	—	—	2,000
12/99	1,160	—	—	3,114
12/98	1,110	—	—	2,836
12/97	1,190	—	—	2,620
12/96	1,238	—	—	3,123
12/95	1,257	—	—	3,000
12/94	1,163	—	—	2,923
12/93	913	—	—	3,100
Annual Growth	2.1%	—	—	(6.5%)

Revenue History

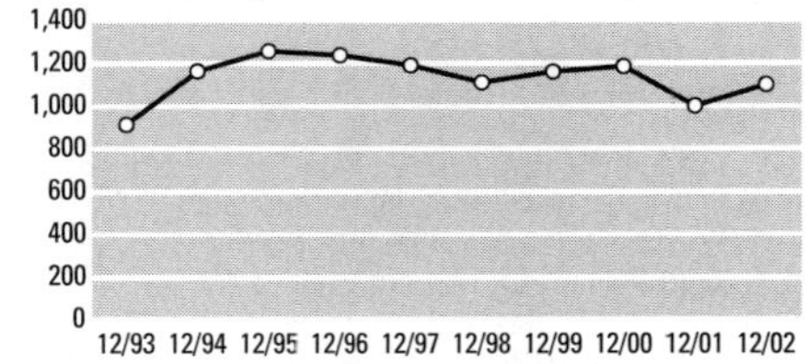

Conn's, Inc.

Conn's has managed to outlive human life expectancy. With more than 100 years under its belt, the retailer sells appliances (refrigerators, freezers, washers, dryers) and electronics (VCRs, DVD players, camcorders, computers, LCD and plasma-screen TVs) through about 40 stores in Texas and Louisiana, and via its Web site. Conn's also offers home office equipment, lawn and garden products, and other home products such as bedding. The retailer began as a small plumbing and heating business in 1890. Conn's filed to go public in September 2003. A trust established by Stephens Group will control most of the company's voting power after its IPO.

EXECUTIVES

Chairman of the Board: Thomas J. Frank Sr., age 63, $1,302,750 pay
President and COO: William C. Nylin Jr., age 60, $516,000 pay
SVP Advertising: Robert B. Lee Jr., age 55
SVP Merchandising: David W. Trahan, age 42, $348,500 pay
SVP Store Operations: Walter M. Broussard, age 43, $297,000 pay
SVP and Secretary/Treasurer: David R. Atnip, age 56
EVP and CFO: C. William (Bill) Frank, age 56, $480,000 pay
Auditors: Ernst & Young LLP

LOCATIONS

HQ: 3295 College St., Beaumont, TX 77701
Phone: 409-832-1696 **Fax:** 409-832-4344
Web: www.conns.com

COMPETITORS

Ace Hardware
Bed Bath & Beyond
Best Buy
Circuit City Stores
CompUSA
Costco Wholesale
Home Depot
J. C. Penney
Kmart
Linens 'n Things
Lowe's
Office Depot
OfficeMax
RadioShack
SAM'S CLUB
Sears
Staples
Target
TruServ
Ultimate Electronics
Wal-Mart

HISTORICAL FINANCIALS

Company Type: Private

Income Statement FYE: January 31

	REVENUE ($ mil.)	NET INCOME ($ mil.)	NET PROFIT MARGIN	EMPLOYEES
1/03	450	21	4.6%	1,890
1/02*	209	11	5.1%	—
7/01	330	17	5.2%	—
7/00	280	15	5.2%	—
Annual Growth	17.2%	12.2%	—	—

*Fiscal year change

2003 Year-End Financials

Debt ratio: 54.2%
Return on equity: 35.8%
Cash ($ mil.): 2
Current ratio: 2.29
Long-term debt ($ mil.): 37

Net Income History

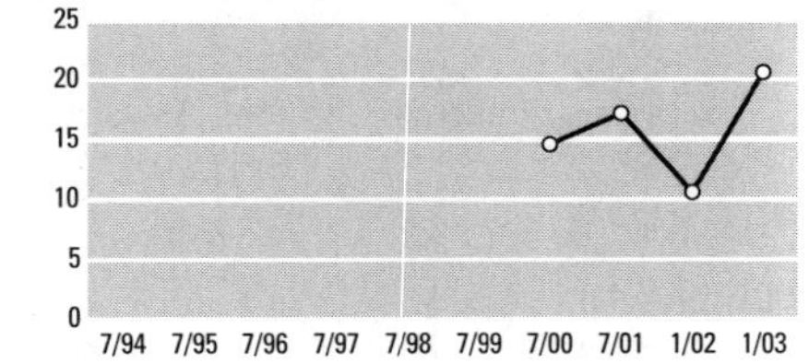

Conrail Inc.

Conrail is the holding company for Consolidated Rail, a freight railroad in the heavily industrialized Northeast. Most of its former lines and facilities have been divided between its joint owners, rail operators CSX (42%) and Norfolk Southern (58%), following an agreement that took effect in 1999. Conrail, however, continues to manage and operate some lines and facilities in the Philadelphia and Detroit metropolitan areas and in much of New Jersey. To serve customers along those lines, both CSX and Norfolk Southern pay a fee to Conrail for line access; Conrail acts as the local switching and terminal management agent.

EXECUTIVES

President and CEO: Gregory R. Weber
SVP Operations: Ronald L. Batory
VP Corporate Affairs and Corporate Secretary: James McGeehan
VP Finance: Joseph Rogers
VP Human Resources: Anthony Carlini
VP Law and General Counsel: Jonathan Broder
Auditors: Ernst & Young LLP; KPMG LLP

LOCATIONS

HQ: 2001 Market St., 16th Fl., Philadelphia, PA 19103
Phone: 215-209-2000 **Fax:** 215-209-4819
Web: www.conrail.com

Conrail operates rail facilities in Detroit, Philadelphia, and much of New Jersey.

COMPETITORS

Burlington Northern Santa Fe
Canadian National Railway
Canadian Pacific Railway
Genesee & Wyoming
Guilford Transportation
Heartland Express
Landstar System
Old Dominion Freight
Schneider National
Transtar
Union Pacific
USF
Werner Enterprises
Yellow

HISTORICAL FINANCIALS

Company Type: Private

Income Statement FYE: December 31

	REVENUE ($ mil.)	NET INCOME ($ mil.)	NET PROFIT MARGIN	EMPLOYEES
12/02	893	80	20.2%	—
12/01	903	74	19.3%	—
12/00	985	70	17.3%	—
12/99	2,200	26	1.2%	—
12/98	3,863	267	6.9%	—
12/97	3,765	7	0.2%	—
12/96	3,714	342	9.2%	—
12/95	3,686	264	7.2%	—
12/94	3,733	324	8.7%	—
12/93	3,438	234	6.8%	—
Annual Growth	(13.9%)	(2.9%)	—	—

2002 Year-End Financials

Debt ratio: 26.6%
Return on equity: 4.3%
Cash ($ mil.): 23
Current ratio: 0.91
Long-term debt ($ mil.): 1,123

Net Income History

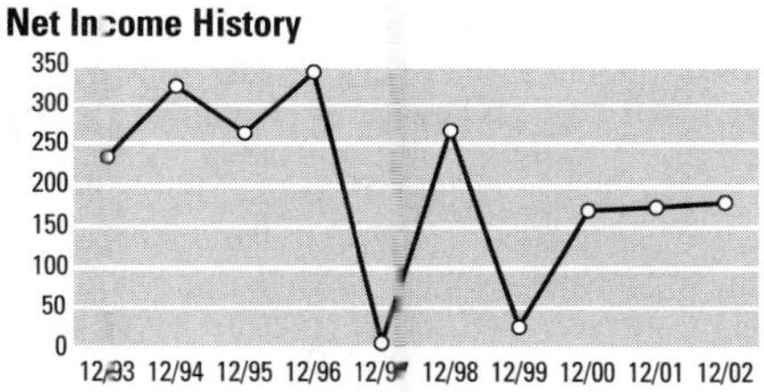

Consolidated Electrical Distributors Inc.

Electrical equipment wholesaler Consolidated Electrical Distributors (CED) has US distribution wired. With more than 500 locations nationwide, the family-owned business is one of the largest distributors of electrical products in the country. CED supplies load centers, panelboards, transformers, switches, motor controls, drives, and similar products to residential and commercial contractors and industrial customers. Founded in 1957 as The Electric Corporation of San Francisco, the company has grown by acquiring electrical distributors; since it usually keeps the acquired firm's name and management team, CED now does business under about 80 names. The Colburn family owns CED.

EXECUTIVES

Chairman and CEO: Keith W. Colburn
President: H. Dean Bursch
CFO: Thomas A. Lullo
Human Resources: Marie Lipp

LOCATIONS

HQ: 31356 Via Colinas, Ste. 107, Westlake Village, CA 91362
Phone: 818-991-9000 **Fax:** 818-991-6842
Web: www.cedcareers.com

Consolidated Electrical Distributors has more than 500 US locations in 44 states.

PRODUCTS/OPERATIONS

Selected Products

Adjustable frequency drives
Busway
Circuit breakers
Control transformers
Load centers
Metering equipment
Motor control centers
Open starters/contractors
Panelboards
Power logic
Power outlet panels
Pushbuttons
Relays
Safety switches
Starters
Switchboards
Switchgear
Timers
Transformers

COMPETITORS

Anixter International
Cameron & Barkley
Electrocomponents
General Cable
Graybar Electric
Hubbell
Hughes Supply
McJunkin
McNaughton-McKay
Rexel Canada
Rexel, Inc.
Sonepar USA
Stuart C. Irby
SUMMIT Electric Supply
Thomas & Betts
WESCO International
W.W. Grainger

HISTORICAL FINANCIALS

Company Type: Private

Income Statement FYE: December 31

	ESTIMATED REVENUE ($ mil.)	NET INCOME ($ mil.)	NET PROFIT MARGIN	EMPLOYEES
12/02	2,400	—	—	5,350
12/01	2,400	—	—	5,350
12/00	2,500	—	—	5,500
12/99	2,700	—	—	5,000
12/98	2,600	—	—	4,500
12/97	1,925	—	—	4,500
12/96	1,900	—	—	4,000
12/95	1,600	—	—	4,000
12/94	1,600	—	—	3,700
12/93	1,500	—	—	2,800
Annual Growth	5.4%	—	—	7.5%

Revenue History

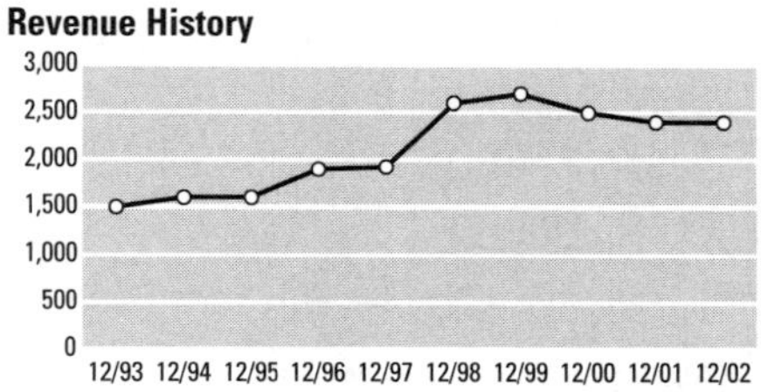

Consumers Union

Consumers Union of United States (CU) inspires both trust and fear. Best known for publishing *Consumer Reports* magazine (4 million subscribers), the not-for-profit organization also serves as a consumer watchdog through newsletters, books, TV and radio programming, and the *Consumer Reports for Kids Online* site. Its subscriber Web site (1 million paid subscribers) rates products ranging from candy bars to cars. The company tests and rates thousands of products annually. Its Consumer Policy Institute conducts research and education projects on issues such as air pollution, biotechnology, food safety, and right-to-know laws.

It maintains 50 laboratories within its National Testing and Research Center in Yonkers, New York. In addition to conducting its own product testing, CU gathers product information by surveying the readers of its publications.

CU derives revenue from sales of its publications, from car and insurance pricing services, and from contributions, grants, and fees.

The company has revamped its *Consumer Reports* publication with additional content and a new look aimed at improving the magazine's layout and organization.

The organization testifies before legislative and regulatory entities and files lawsuits on behalf of consumers. CU is governed by an 18-member board. To preserve its independence, CU accepts no advertising and does not permit its ratings or comments to be used commercially.

HISTORY

In 1926 engineer Frederick Schlink organized a "consumer club" (in White Plains, New York), which distributed lists of recommended and non-recommended products. The lists led to the founding of Consumers' Research and a magazine devoted to testing products.

Schlink moved the group to Washington, New Jersey, in 1933. In 1935 three employees formed a union. Schlink fired them. Faced with another strike that year, Schlink accused the strikers of being "Red" and responded with strikebreakers and armed detectives. The next year the strikers set up their own organization, the Consumers Union of United States (CU).

CU's first magazine, *Consumers Union Reports*, came out three months later and rated products that the fledgling organization could afford to test, such as soap and breakfast cereals. Subsequent issues focused on food and drug regulation and working conditions for women in textile mills.

The organization drew the wrath of both *Reader's Digest* and *Good Housekeeping* (which accused it in 1939 of prolonging the Depression). The next year the House Un-American Activities Committee put CU on its list of suspect organizations. CU cut staff and dropped "Union" from its magazine title, but circulation remained low until after WWII.

By 1950, however, Americans began consuming again, helping to boost circulation to almost 400,000. During the 1950s CU published a series of reports on the health hazards of smoking.

In 1960 CU helped found the International Organization of Consumers Unions (now Consumers International) to foster the consumer movement worldwide. Rhoda Karpatkin was hired as publisher in 1974. During the 1970s CU established consumer advocacy offices in California, Texas, and Washington, DC.

Recession and an increase in not-for-profit mailing rates caused the organization to lose money in the early 1980s. CU looked to its readers, who donated more than $3 million. The organization was hit by a 13-week strike in 1984 by union members calling for more say in management.

In 1996 CU slapped "not acceptable" ratings on the Isuzu Trooper and the Acura SLX. The next year the National Highway Traffic Safety Administration declared that CU's testing procedure of the Trooper was flawed, but CU stood by its tests of the vehicle.

CU hit another bump in 1998 when it was compelled to retract a story on the nutritional value of Iams and Eukanuba pet food. Admitting its test results were incorrect, CU's retraction of the story was something of a rarity — its last retraction had occurred almost 20 years earlier when the organization retracted a story on condoms.

In 1999 the company defended itself in court against allegations by Isuzu and Suzuki that their companies were defamed through negative reviews by Consumer Reports. The following year a jury found CU guilty of falsely reporting on the Isuzu but declined to impose fines on the publisher. Also in 2000 a district court upheld the dismissal of Suzuki's suit against CU (based on CU's 1988 rating of the Suzuki Samurai as "not acceptable" due to rollover risks); Suzuki is appealing. Karpatkin announced she would step down as president in 2001. Later that year CU agreed to license its content to Internet portal Yahoo! James Guest, CU's chairman since 1980, took over as president in 2001.

EXECUTIVES

Chairman and President: James Guest
CFO: Richard Gannon
SVP, Technical Policy: R. David Pittle
Director, Consumer Policy Institute: Jean Halloran
Director, Washington, DC Office: Gene Kimmelman
Director, Southwest Regional Office: Reggie James
Project Director, Eco-labeling Project: Urvashi Rangan
Research Associate, Consumer Policy Institute: Michael K. Hansen
Senior Scientist: Edward (Ned) Groth
Health Policy Editor, *Consumer Reports*: Trudy Lieberman
Project Leader, Consumers Union Technical Division, Public Service Projects: Deborah Wallace
Auditors: KPMG LLP

LOCATIONS

HQ: Consumers Union of United States, Inc.
101 Truman Ave., Yonkers, NY 10703
Phone: 914-378-2000 **Fax:** 914-378-2900
Web: www.consumersunion.org

Consumers Union of United States performs most product tests at a renovated warehouse in Yonkers, New York. It tests cars and trucks in East Haddam, Connecticut, and has consumer advocacy offices in Austin, Texas; San Francisco; and Washington, DC.

PRODUCTS/OPERATIONS

Selected Products and Services

Auto Services
CR New Car Price Service
CR Used Car Price Service

Books and Buying Guides
Auto Books
New Car Buying Guide
New Car Preview
Used Car Buying Guide
Used Car Yearbook
House and Home
Best Buys for Your Home 2003
Buying Guide 2003
Home Computer Buying Guide 2003
Money
Consumer Reports Money Book
How to Plan for a Secure Retirement
Personal and Leisure
Consumer Drug Reference 2003
Guide to Baby Products
Guide to Health Care for Seniors
Home Computer Buying Guide 2003
Travel Well for Less 2003

Magazines and Newsletters
Consumer Reports Magazine
Consumer Reports on Health
Consumer Reports Travel Letter

TV and Radio
Consumer Reports on TV (video segments)
CR Radio (daily radio feature)

Web Sites
ConsumerReports.org
Consumer Reports for Kids Online (zillions.org)

COMPETITORS

Consumers' Research
Epinions
Hearst
International Data Group
J.D. Power
National Technical Systems
PRIMEDIA
Reader's Digest
Reed Elsevier Group
Underwriters Labs

HISTORICAL FINANCIALS

Company Type: Not-for-profit

Income Statement FYE: May 31

	REVENUE ($ mil.)	NET INCOME ($ mil.)	NET PROFIT MARGIN	EMPLOYEES
5/00	140	—	—	450
5/99	140	—	—	482
5/98	140	—	—	475
5/97	135	—	—	461
5/96	136	—	—	451
5/95	129	—	—	453
5/94	124	—	—	451
Annual Growth	2.1%	—	—	(0.0%)

Revenue History

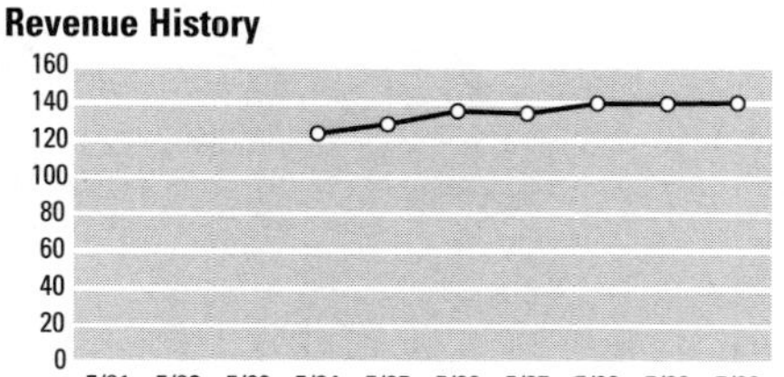

ContiGroup Companies, Inc.

It's farther up the food chain now, but ContiGroup Companies (CGC, formerly Continental Grain) is still a big name in agribusiness. CGC has exited the grain export business and now operates through ContiBeef (the #2 cattle feedlot operator, behind Cactus Feeders), PSF Group Holdings (the #2 US fresh pork producer, after Smithfield Foods), and Wayne Farms, a major poultry processor. Overseas the company has interests in feed milling, aquaculture, shipping, and energy trading. CGC's investment arm, ContiInvestments, manages diverse holdings. Chairman Paul Fribourg (the founder's great-great-great-grandson) and his family own CGC.

In China, the Caribbean, and Latin America, CGC has interests in flour milling, animal feed, poultry processing, and aquaculture. In the Far East, ContiChem-LPG handles about 12% of the world's trade in liquid petroleum gas (LPG) and charters shipping.

Despite its size and scope, the company remains genteelly private about its business.

HISTORY

Simon Fribourg founded a commodity trading business in Belgium in 1813. It operated domestically until 1848, when a drought in Belgium caused it to buy large stocks in Russian wheat.

As the Industrial Revolution swept across Europe and populations shifted to cities, people consumed more traded grain. In the midst of such rapid changes, the company prospered. After WWI, Russia, which had been Europe's primary grain supplier, ceased to be a major player in the trading game, and Western countries picked up the slack. Sensing the shift, Jules and Rene Fribourg reorganized the business as Continental Grain and opened its first US office in Chicago in 1921.

Throughout the Depression the company bought US grain elevators, often at low prices. Through its purchases, Continental Grain built a North American grain network that included major locations like Kansas City, Missouri; Nashville, Tennessee; and Toledo, Ohio.

In Europe, meanwhile, the Fribourgs were forced to endure constant political and economic upheaval, often profiting from it (they supplied food to Republican forces during the Spanish Civil War). When Nazis invaded Belgium in 1940, the Fribourgs were forced to flee, but they reorganized the business in New York City after the war.

Following the war, Continental Grain pioneered US grain trade with the Soviets. The company went on a buying spree in the 1960s and 1970s, acquiring Allied Mills (feed milling, 1965) and absorbing many agricultural and transport businesses, including Texas feedlots, a bakery, and the Quaker Oats agricultural products unit.

During the 1980s Continental Grain sold its baking units (Oroweat and Arnold) and its commodities brokerage house. Amid an agricultural bust, it formed ContiFinancial and other financial units.

Michel Fribourg stepped down as CEO in 1988 and was succeeded by Donald Staheli, the first outside CEO. The company entered a grain-handling and selling joint venture with Scoular in 1991. Three years later Staheli added the title of chairman, and Michel's son Paul became president. Continental Grain sold a stake in ContiFinancial (home equity loans and investment banking) to the public in 1996. Also in 1996 the firm formed ContiInvestments, an investment arm geared toward the parent company's areas of expertise.

That year Continental Grain and an overseas affiliate (Arab Finagrain) agreed to pay the US government $35 million, which included a $10 million fine against Arab Finagrain, to settle a fraud case involving commodity sales to Iraq.

Paul succeeded Staheli as CEO in 1997. The company bought Campbell Soup's poultry processing units that year, and in 1998 it bought a 51% stake in pork producer/processor Premium Standard Farms. Meanwhile, ContiFinancial diversified into retail home mortgage and home equity lending.

Continental Grain sold its commodities marketing business in July 1999 to #1 grain exporter Cargill. With its grain operations gone, in 1999 the company renamed itself ContiGroup Companies.

During 2000 ContiFinancial declared bankruptcy, and ContiGroup sold its Animal Nutrition Division (Wayne Foods) to feed manufacturer Ridley Inc for $37 million. In mid-2000, Premium Standard Farms doubled its processing capacity with the purchase of Lundy Packing Company. Chairman emeritus Michel Fribourg, the founder's great-great-grandson, died in 2001. That same year ContiSea, the salmon and seafood processing joint venture between ContiGroup and Seaboard, was sold to Norway's Fjord Seafood, giving ContiGroup a significant share of Fjord.

EXECUTIVES

Chairman, President, and CEO: Paul J. Fribourg, age 49
EVP and COO: Vart K. Adjemian, age 59
EVP, Investments and Strategy and CFO; President, ContiInvestments: Michael J. Zimmerman, age 52
EVP, Human Resources and Information Systems: Teresa E. McCaslin
CEO, ContiBeef: John Rakestraw
CEO, Premium Standard Farms: John M. Meyer, age 40
CEO, Wayne Farms: Elton Maddox
SVP and Managing Director, Asian Industries Division: Michael A. Hoer
VP and General Manager, ContiLatin: Brian Anderson

LOCATIONS

HQ: 277 Park Ave., New York, NY 10172
Phone: 212-207-5100 **Fax:** 212-207-2910
Web: www.contigroup.com

ContiGroup Companies operates in the Caribbean, China, Latin America, and the US.

PRODUCTS/OPERATIONS

Major Business Units

Asian Industries
Feed milling (China)
Pork production (China)
Poultry production (China)

ContiBeef, LLC
Cattle feedlots

ContiInvestments, LLC
Investment management

ContiLatin
Feed and flour milling
Poultry operations
Salmon farming
Seafood processing
Shrimp farming

PSF Group Holdings, Inc.
Premium Standard Farms (hog and pork production)

Wayne Farms, LLC
Poultry production

COMPETITORS

Cactus Feeders
Cargill
CHS
ConAgra
Farmland Industries
Seaboard
Smithfield Foods
Tyson Foods

HISTORICAL FINANCIALS

Company Type: Private

Income Statement FYE: March 31

	ESTIMATED REVENUE ($ mil.)	NET INCOME ($ mil.)	NET PROFIT MARGIN	EMPLOYEES
3/03	2,000	—	—	13,500
3/02	3,300	—	—	14,500
3/01	4,000	—	—	14,500
3/00	10,000	—	—	13,500
3/99	10,500	—	—	14,000
3/98	15,000	—	—	17,500
3/97	16,000	—	—	16,800
3/96	15,000	—	—	16,000
3/95	14,000	—	—	16,000
3/94	15,000	—	—	15,500
Annual Growth	(20.1%)	—	—	(1.5%)

Revenue History

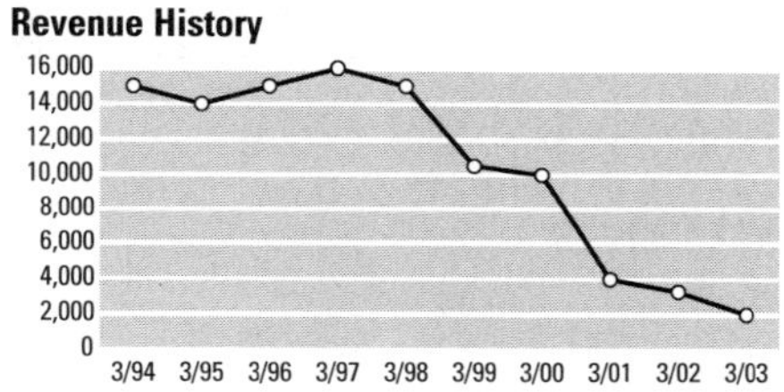

Contran Corporation

Give Texas billionaire Harold Simmons a 10-yard penalty, because the company he founded, Contran, is a holding company. Through subsidiaries and affiliations, Valhi, Inc. (a publicly traded company controlled by Contran) conducts diversified operations in chemicals (NL Industries), metals (Titanium Metals Corporation), waste management (Waste Control Specialties), computer support systems, and precision ball bearing slides and locking systems (CompX International). Contran also has a controlling interest in Keystone Consolidated Industries, a maker of fencing and wire products. Trusts benefiting Simmons' family (with Simmons as the sole trustee) own pretty much all of Contran.

EXECUTIVES

Chairman, President, and CEO: Harold C. Simmons, age 72
VP and Treasurer: Bob D. O'Brien
VP: Robert D. Graham
Employee Benefits Manager: Keith A. Johnson
Secretary: Andrew Louis

LOCATIONS

HQ: Three Lincoln Centre, 5430 LBJ Fwy., Ste. 1700, Dallas, TX 75240
Phone: 972-233-1700 **Fax:** 972-448-1444

COMPETITORS

DuPont
Huntsman International
ICI
Kerr-McGee
Millennium Chemicals
Minebea
Nachi-Fujikoshi
RTI International Metals
Timken
Waste Management

HISTORICAL FINANCIALS

Company Type: Private

Income Statement FYE: December 31

	REVENUE ($ mil.)	NET INCOME ($ mil.)	NET PROFIT MARGIN	EMPLOYEES
12/02	1,100	—	—	7,300
12/01	1,100	—	—	7,300
12/00	1,200	—	—	9,000
12/99	1,160	—	—	9,000
12/98	1,077	—	—	8,500
12/97	1,112	—	—	3,800
12/96	1,094	—	—	4,100
12/95	1,125	—	—	4,100
12/94	1,213	—	—	4,000
12/93	1,148	—	—	—
Annual Growth	(0.5%)	—	—	7.8%

Revenue History

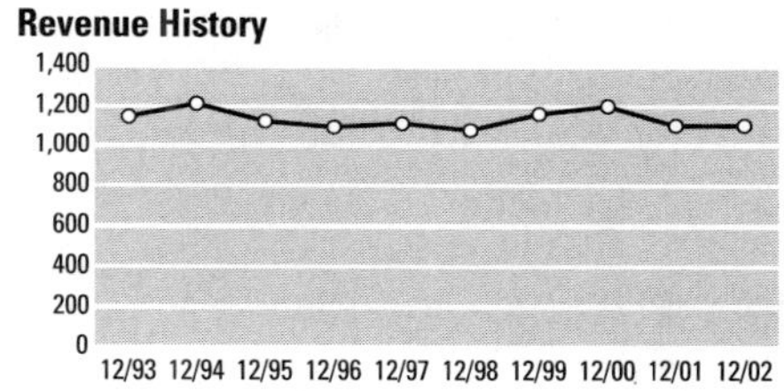

The Copley Press, Inc.

There's no business like the news business for The Copley Press. The newspaper publisher has holdings that include *The San Diego Union-Tribune, The Daily Breeze* (Torrance, California), and about 20 other newspapers — mostly in Illinois (the *Journal Star*), Ohio (*The Independent*), and Southern California (the *Borrego Sun*). Its Copley News Service operates six news bureaus in the US and Mexico. In addition, Copley owns the La Casa del Zorro Desert Resort in Borrego Springs, California, and has a stake in a newsprint mill.

The company is owned and operated by descendants of James Copley, adopted son of founder Colonel Ira Copley. In 2001 Helen Copley turned over the day-to-day operations of the company and her title of chairman to her son David.

EXECUTIVES

Chairman Emeritus: Helen K. Copley
Chairman, President, CEO, and Publisher *San Diego Union-Tribune*: David C. Copley
EVP and COO: Charles F. Patrick
VP Finance, CFO, and Treasurer: Dean P. Dwyer
VP and Chief Legal Officer: Harold W. Fuson Jr.
VP and CIO: Milton J. Goldwasser Jr.
VP and Chief Human Resources Officer: James F. Vargas
Controller: Jessica W. Walker
Manager of Sales and Marketing, Copley News Service: Timothy Cien

LOCATIONS

HQ: 7776 Ivanhoe Ave., La Jolla, CA 92037
Phone: 858-454-0411 **Fax:** 858-729-7689

The Copley Press has newspapers in California, Illinois, and Ohio, as well as news bureaus in California, Illinois, Mexico, and Washington, DC.

PRODUCTS/OPERATIONS

Selected Newspapers

Borrego Sun (Borrego Springs, CA)
The Courier (Lincoln, IL)
The Daily Breeze (Torrance, CA)
The Independent (Massillon, OH)
Journal Star (Peoria, IL)
The Register-Mail (Galesburg, IL)
The Repository (Canton, OH)
The San Diego Union-Tribune
The State Journal-Register (Springfield, IL)
The Times-Reporter (New Philadelphia, OH)

Selected Other Operations

Copley News Service (news distribution service)
La Casa del Zorro (resort; Borrego Springs, CA)
Newsprint manufacturing

COMPETITORS

Advance Publications
Associated Press
Cox Enterprises
Dow Jones
E. W. Scripps
Freedom Communications
Gannett
Hearst
Hollinger
Hollinger International
Knight-Ridder
Liberty Group Publishing
Media General
MediaNews
New York Times
Paddock Publications
Pulitzer
Tribune

HISTORICAL FINANCIALS

Company Type: Private

Income Statement FYE: December 31

	REVENUE ($ mil.)	NET INCOME ($ mil.)	NET PROFIT MARGIN	EMPLOYEES
12/01	534	—	—	4,500
12/00	565	—	—	4,654
12/99	550	—	—	4,700
12/98	500	—	—	4,654
12/97	477	—	—	4,200
12/96	423	—	—	3,800
12/95	398	—	—	3,232
12/94	384	—	—	3,800
12/93	365	—	—	3,500
12/92	363	—	—	3,500
Annual Growth	4.4%	—	—	2.8%

Revenue History

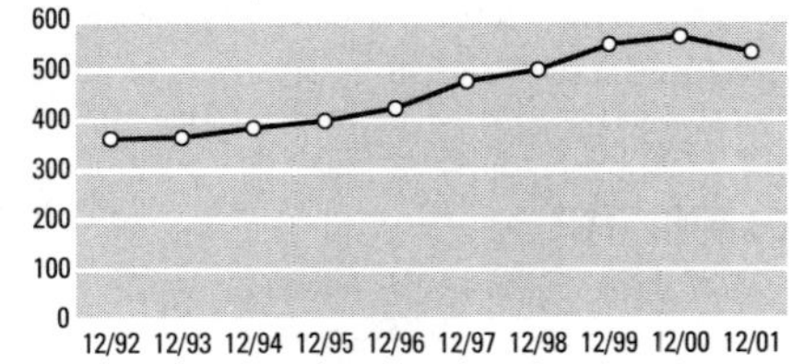

Corky McMillin

The Corky McMillin Companies, formerly McMillin Companies, develops and sells properties in California's San Diego and Riverside counties (near Los Angeles). McMillin Land Development and McMillin Commercial focus on master-planned communities and commercial development, respectively, while McMillin Homes builds single-family homes, primarily in McMillin communities. The company also offers real estate and relocation services (McMillin Realty) and mortgage financing (McMillin Mortgage) and manages residential, commercial, and industrial properties. Founded in 1960 by Corky McMillin as a custom home-building company, the company is owned and run by the McMillin family.

EXECUTIVES

CEO: Macey L. (Corky) McMillin
Vice Chairman; President, McMillin Homes: Mark McMillin
Vice Chairman; President, McMillin Realty and Mortgage: Scott McMillin
CFO: Gary Beason
Staffing Specialist: Cassie Harding

LOCATIONS

HQ: The Corky McMillin Companies
2727 Hoover Ave., National City, CA 91950
Phone: 619-447-4117 **Fax:** 619-336-3119
Web: www.mcmillin.com

COMPETITORS

Brookfield Homes
CB Richard Ellis
Cendant
Centex
Colliers International
D.R. Horton
Fieldstone Communities
Greystone Homes
Grubb & Ellis
Hovnanian Enterprises
Irvine Company
J.F. Shea
KB Home
Majestic Realty
Marcus & Millichap
Staubach
William Lyon Homes

HISTORICAL FINANCIALS

Company Type: Private

Income Statement FYE: December 31

	REVENUE ($ mil.)	NET INCOME ($ mil.)	NET PROFIT MARGIN	EMPLOYEES
12/02	445	—	—	—
12/01	464	—	—	—
12/00	445	—	—	—
12/99	507	—	—	—
12/98	445	—	—	—
12/97	190	—	—	—
12/96	180	—	—	—
12/95	132	—	—	—
12/94	129	—	—	—
12/93	110	—	—	—
Annual Growth	16.8%	—	—	—

Revenue History

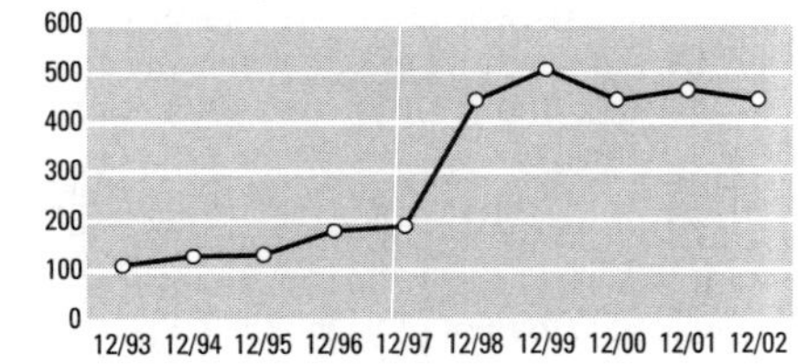

Cornell University

To excel at Cornell University, you'll need every one of your brain cells. The Ivy League university has been educating young minds since its founding in 1865. Its more than 20,000 students can select from seven undergraduate and four graduate and professional colleges and schools. In addition to its Ithaca, New York, campus, the university also offers two medical graduate and professional colleges and schools in New York City and has set up education-outreach centers in every county and borough of New York. Cornell's faculty includes a handful of Nobel laureates, and the university has a robust research component studying everything from animal health to space to waste management.

EXECUTIVES

President: Hunter R. Rawlings III, age 58
Provost: C. Biddy Martin
Provost Medical Affairs: Antonio M. Gotto Jr., age 67
Vice Provost Life Sciences: Kraig K. Adler
Vice Provost Research: Robert C. Richardson
Vice Provost: Walter I. Cohen
VP Alumni Affairs and Development: Inge T. Reichenbach
VP Budget and Planning: Carolyn N. Ainslie
CFO and VP Administration: Harold D. Craft Jr.
VP Information Technologies: Polley Ann McClure
VP Human Resources: Mary G. Opperman
VP Student and Academic Services: Susan H. Murphy, age 51
VP University Relations: Henrik N. Dullea
University Counsel and Secretary: James J. Mingle
Auditors: KPMG LLP

LOCATIONS

HQ: Cornell University Campus, 305 Day Hall, Ithaca, NY 14853
Phone: 607-255-2000 **Fax:** 607-255-5396
Web: www.cornell.edu

Cornell University has operations across the state of New York.

PRODUCTS/OPERATIONS

Selected Undergraduate Colleges and Schools

College of Agriculture and Life Sciences
College of Architecture, Art, and Planning
College of Arts and Sciences
College of Engineering
College of Human Ecology
School of Hotel Administration
School of Industrial and Labor Relations

Selected Graduate and Professional Colleges and Schools

College of Veterinary Medicine
Graduate School
Johnson Graduate School of Management
Law School
Weill Graduate School of Medical Sciences (New York City)
Weill Medical College (New York City)

HISTORICAL FINANCIALS

Company Type: School

Income Statement FYE: June 30

	REVENUE ($ mil.)	NET INCOME ($ mil.)	NET PROFIT MARGIN	EMPLOYEES
6/02	1,666	—	—	13,319
6/01	1,459	—	—	12,866
6/00	2,352	—	—	12,468
6/99	1,856	—	—	12,207
6/98	1,899	—	—	11,873
6/97	1,709	—	—	11,757
6/96	1,747	—	—	11,481
6/95	1,378	—	—	9,600
6/94	1,315	—	—	9,500
Annual Growth	3.0%	—	—	4.3%

Revenue History

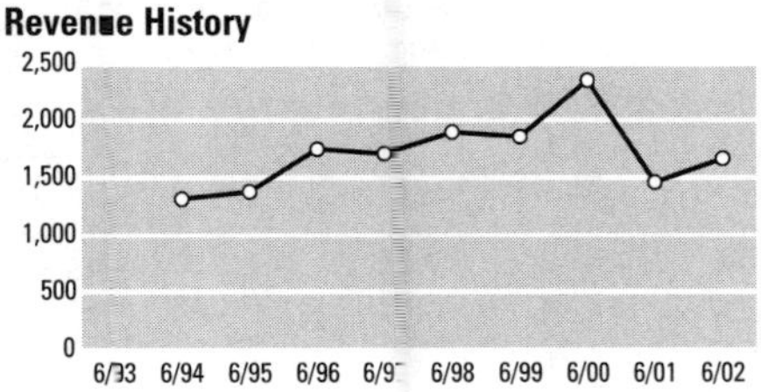

Corporation for Public Broadcasting

This organization is made possible by a grant from the federal government and by support from viewers like you. The Corporation for Public Broadcasting (CPB) is an independent, not-for-profit government organization (not a government agency) that receives appropriations from Congress to help fund programming for more than 1,000 member-owned stations of the Public Broadcasting Service, National Public Radio, Public Radio International, and other organizations. The organization's funding is often a political hot potato (frequently a target of Republicans who are opposed to government funding of educational, informational, and cultural programming).

Funding has been approved through 2003, despite a 1999 investigation that revealed some PBS stations had given their mailing lists to the Democratic party for fundraising purposes. CPB's funding was approved at $350 million for 2002 and $365 million for 2003.

HISTORY

As commercial radio began to fill the radio dial, the FCC in 1945 reserved 20 channels from 88 FM to 92 FM for noncommercial, educational broadcasts. The first public television station started broadcasting in 1953, and by 1965 there were 124 public TV stations across the country. To help allocate government funds to these public TV and radio stations, Congress created the Corporation for Public Broadcasting (CPB) in 1967.

CPB has always been politically controversial; critics have often charged it with elitism, cultural bias, and liberalism. When Republicans gained control of Congress in 1994, their laundry list of grievances included government cultural spending. They were foiled in their effort to eliminate funding for CPB, however, in part because of public support for public television. Congress still cut funding by $100 million, forcing CPB to reduce its staff by almost 25% and introduce performance criteria for stations seeking grant money, including listenership and community financial support minimums.

Robert Coonrod was promoted to CEO in 1997. The following year Congress approved additional funding to help public television's transition from analog to digital broadcasting. Frank Cruz was appointed chairman of CPB in 1999. At about the same time, increased funding for 2003 (funding is approved two years in advance) was threatened when it was discovered that some PBS stations were giving their mailing lists to the Democratic party for fundraising purposes. Nevertheless, funding for CPB was increased in the 2001 budget. In late 2001 businesswoman Katherine Milner Anderson was voted in as chairman, taking over for Cruz. (Cruz remained on the board.) After serving two consecutive terms as chairman, Anderson was replaced by veteran journalist Kenneth Y. Tomlinson in 2003.

EXECUTIVES

Chairman: Katherine Milner Anderson
Vice Chairman: Ritajean Hartung Butterworth
President and CEO: Robert T. Coonrod, $159,212 pay
EVP and Senior Adviser to the President: Frederick L. DeMarco
EVP and COO: Kathleen Cox
SVP Media: Andrew Russell
SVP Radio: Vincent Curren
VP, General Counsel, and Corporate Secretary: Donna Coleman Gregg
VP Business Affairs: Steven Altman
VP Communications: Carole Florman
VP Education: Cheryl Scott Williams
VP Finance and Administration, Treasurer: Elizabeth A. Griffith
VP Government Relations: Deborah Kilmer
VP Program Operations: Yoko Arthur
VP Strategic Development: Douglas A. Weiss
VP Television and Digital Media: Terry Bryant
Inspector General: Ken Konz
Director Human Resources and Assistant to the President for EEO: Alicia Schoshinski
Director, Information Technology: David Creekmore
Director, Budget: Luis Guardia
Controller: Aiman Sadeq
Auditors: Deloitte & Touche LLP

LOCATIONS

HQ: 401 9th St., NW, Washington, DC 20004
Phone: 202-879-9600 **Fax:** 202-879-9700
Web: www.cpb.org

PRODUCTS/OPERATIONS

Selected Affiliations

American Public Television (programs for public television)
The Annenberg/CPB Projects (telecourses and education programs)
Association of America's Public Television Stations (organization of public TV stations)
Independent Television Service (independent creative programming for public TV)
National Public Radio (radio programming distribution)
Public Broadcasting Service (TV distribution)
Public Radio International (international radio distribution)

COMPETITORS

A&E Networks
BBC
Discovery Communications
Ford Foundation
Fox Entertainment
NBC
National Geographic
NPR
Viacom
Walt Disney
Westwood One

HISTORICAL FINANCIALS

Company Type: Not-for-profit

Income Statement FYE: September 30

	REVENUE ($ mil.)	NET INCOME ($ mil.)	NET PROFIT MARGIN	EMPLOYEES
9/01	398	—	—	110
9/00	384	—	—	100
9/99	283	—	—	90
9/98	285	—	—	90
9/97	282	—	—	90
9/96	296	—	—	85
9/95	286	—	—	95
9/94	275	—	—	100
9/93	339	—	—	900
9/92	341	—	—	101
Annual Growth	1.7%	—	—	1.0%

Revenue History

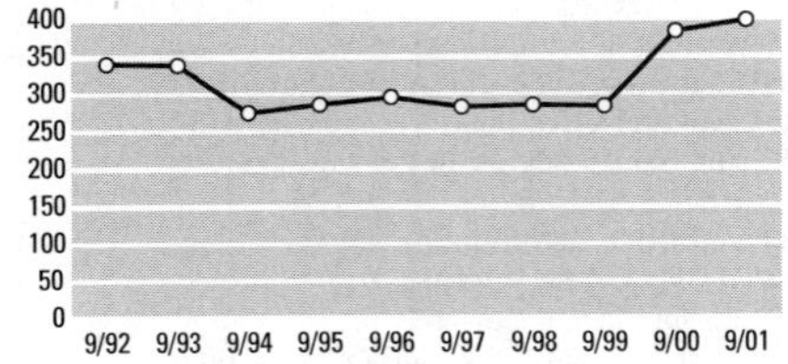

Cox Enterprises

The Cox family has been working at this enterprise for more than 100 years. One of the largest media conglomerates in the US, family-owned Cox Enterprises publishes 17 daily newspapers (including *The Atlanta Journal-Constitution*) and about 25 weeklies and shoppers and owns 15 TV stations through Cox Television. It also owns about 62% of Cox Radio (more than 80 radio stations) and controls 63% of Cox Communications, one of the US's largest cable systems, with more than 6.5 million subscribers in about 20 states. Cox's Manheim Auctions runs 115 automobile auctions worldwide and owns a majority-stake in AutoTrader.com, and Cox Interactive Media operates about 20 city-specific Web sites.

While Cox Communications is the company's biggest revenue generator, Cox Enterprises has been spending a lot of money and time, like many other media conglomerates, on the Internet. AutoTrader.com, which the company operates in conjunction with Manheim, is one of the few profitable Internet companies. Manheim is the world's largest used-car auctioneer and the combination of the businesses has proved lucrative for Cox.

However, Cox has also learned the hard lesson that other media companies have been taught as they try to be successful on the Internet. Cox scrapped a plan for an AutoTrader.com IPO in 2000 when the market soured. And in 2002 the company cut about 75 jobs from its Cox Interactive unit and dropped a plan to develop a nationwide network of local city Web sites.

Barbara Cox Anthony (mother of chairman and CEO James Kennedy) and Anne Cox Chambers, daughters of founder James Cox, control 98% of the company. The sisters were recently ranked high on *Forbes'* list of the richest Americans.

HISTORY

James Middleton Cox, who dropped out of school in 1886 at 16, had worked as a teacher, reporter, and congressional secretary before buying the *Dayton Daily News* in 1898. After acquiring the nearby *Springfield Press-Republican* in 1905, he took up politics, serving two terms in the US Congress (1909-1913) and three terms as Ohio governor (1913-1915; 1917-1921). He even ran for president in 1920 (his running mate was future President Franklin Roosevelt) but lost to rival Ohio publisher Warren G. Harding.

Once out of politics, Cox began building his media empire. He bought the *Miami Daily News* in 1923 and founded WHIO (Dayton, Ohio's first radio station). He bought Atlanta's WSB ("Welcome South, Brother"), the South's first radio station, in 1939 and added WSB-FM and WSB-TV, the South's first FM and TV stations, in 1948. Cox founded Dayton's first FM and TV stations (WHIO-FM and WHIO-TV) the next year, and *The Atlanta Constitution* joined his collection in 1950. Cox died in 1957.

The company continued to expand its broadcasting interests in the late 1950s and early 1960s. It was one of the first major broadcasting companies to expand into cable TV when it purchased a system in Lewistown, Pennsylvania, in 1962. The Cox family's broadcast properties were placed in publicly held Cox Broadcasting in 1964. Two years later its newspapers were placed into privately held Cox Enterprises, and the cable holdings became publicly held Cox Cable Communications. The broadcasting arm diversified, buying Manheim Services (auto auctions, 1968), Kansas City Automobile Auction (1969), and TeleRep (TV ad sales, 1972).

Cox Cable had 500,000 subscribers in nine states when it rejoined Cox Broadcasting in 1977. Cox Broadcasting was renamed Cox Communications in 1982, and the Cox family took the company private again in 1985, combining it with Cox Enterprises. James Kennedy, grandson of founder James Cox, became chairman and CEO in 1987.

Expansion became the keyword for Cox in the 1990s. The company merged its Manheim unit with the auto auction business of Ford Motor Credit and GE Capital in 1991. It also formed Sprint Spectrum in 1994, a partnership with Sprint, TCI (now part of AT&T), and Comcast to bundle telephone, cable TV, and other communications services (Sprint bought out Cox in 1999). Then, in one of its biggest transactions, Cox bought Times Mirror's cable TV operations for $2.3 billion in 1995 and combined them with its own cable system into a new, publicly traded company called Cox Communications. The following year it spun off its radio holdings into a public company called Cox Radio.

To expand its online presence, the company formed Cox Interactive Media in 1996, establishing a series of city Web sites and making a host of investments in various Internet companies, including CareerPath, ExciteHome, iVillage, MP3.com, and Tickets.com. Cox also applied the online strategy to its automobile auction businesses, establishing AutoTrader.com in 1998 and placing the Internet operations of Manheim Auctions into a new company, Manheim Interactive, in 2000.

In 2002 the company dropped plans to expand its local Internet city guide business nationwide.

EXECUTIVES

Chairman and CEO: James Cox Kennedy, age 56
President and COO: G. Dennis Berry, age 59
EVP and CFO: Robert C. O'Leary, age 64
SVP Administration: Timothy W. Hughes
SVP Public Policy: Alexander V. Netchvolodoff
VP and CIO: Gregory B. Morrison, age 43
VP and General Tax Counsel: Preston B. Barnett
VP and Treasurer, Cox Enterprises and Cox Radio: Richard J. Jacobson, age 45
VP Direct Marketing and Database Management: Tom Whitfield
VP Human Resources: Marybeth H. Leamer, age 45
VP Legal Affairs and Secretary: Andrew A. Merdek
VP Marketing and Communications: John C. Williams
VP Materials Management: Michael J. Mannheimer, age 54
VP Public Policy: Alexandra M. Wilson
President and CEO, AutoTrader.com: Victor A. (Chip) Perry III
President and CEO, Cox Communications, Inc.: James O. (Jim) Robbins, age 60
President and CEO, Cox Radio: Robert F. Neil, age 44
President and CEO, Manheim Auctions: Dean H. Eisner, age 44
President, Cox Newspapers Inc.: Jay R. Smith, age 52
President, Cox Television: Andrew S. Fisher, age 54

LOCATIONS

HQ: Cox Enterprises, Inc.
6205 Peachtree Dunwoody Rd., Atlanta, GA 30328
Phone: 678-645-0000 **Fax:** 678-645-1079
Web: www.coxenterprises.com

PRODUCTS/OPERATIONS

2002 Sales

	$ mil.	% of total
Cable TV	5,040	51
Auctions	2,405	24
Newspapers	1,350	14
TV stations	684	7
Radio stations	421	4
Total	**9,900**	**100**

COMPETITORS

Advance Publications
Austin Chronicle
Belo
Clear Channel
Columbus Fair Auto Auction
Comcast
Dow Jones
E. W. Scripps
Gannett
Hearst
Knight-Ridder
Media General
Morris Communications
New York Times
News Corp.
Ticketmaster
Time Warner Cable
Tribune
Viacom
Walt Disney
Washington Post

HISTORICAL FINANCIALS

Company Type: Private

Income Statement FYE: December 31

	REVENUE ($ mil.)	NET INCOME ($ mil.)	NET PROFIT MARGIN	EMPLOYEES
12/02	9,900	—	—	77,000
12/01	8,693	—	—	76,000
12/00	7,824	—	—	74,000
12/99	6,097	—	—	61,000
12/98	5,355	—	—	55,500
12/97	4,936	—	—	50,000
12/96	4,591	—	—	43,000
12/95	3,806	—	—	38,000
12/94	2,939	—	—	37,000
12/93	2,675	—	—	31,000
Annual Growth	15.7%	—	—	10.6%

Revenue History

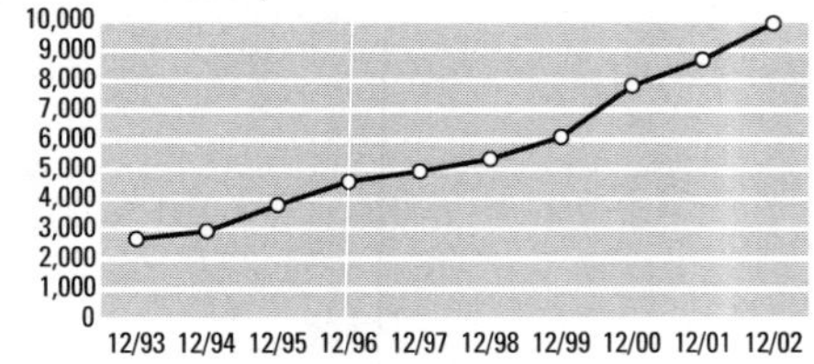

CP Kelco ApS

CP Kelco makes money with consistency: The company makes additives used to give food, industrial, personal care, and pharmaceutical products texture and stability. Formed in 2000 by the combination of Hercules' Copenhagen Pectin/Food Gums Division and the Kelco Biopolymers unit of Monsanto/Pharmacia, CP Kelco's products include carrageenan, pectin, gellan gum, xanthan gum, and microparticulated whey protein. These additives give everything from jam and ketchup to paint and cosmetics their desired texture and viscosity characteristics. Lehman Brothers and Hercules Incorporated own 71% and 29% of CP Kelco, respectively.

EXECUTIVES

President and CEO: Robert B. Toth
SVP, CFO, and Information Technology (Interim): Andrew Hines
SVP and Corporate Secretary: Charles A. Oswald
SVP, Business Management: Jack H. Koberstine
SVP, Global Operations and Technology: Jurgen G. Dominik
SVP, Human Resources: John Falcetta
SVP, Sales: George W. Littlecott

LOCATIONS

HQ: 1313 N. Market Street, Wilmington, DE 19894
Phone: 866-821-1325 **Fax:** 302-594-6260
Web: www.cpkelco.com

CP Kelco has manufacturing facilities in Brazil, Denmark, Germany, the Philippines, the UK, and the US (Danville, Pennsylvania; Okmulgee, Oklahoma; and San Diego).

PRODUCTS/OPERATIONS

Selected Products

Carrageenan (thickening agent with food applications)
Gellan gum (gelling agent with food, personal care, pharmaceutical, and industrial applications)
Pectin (gelling agent used in products such as jams and jellies)
Welan gum (used in cement and gypsum-based products)
Whey protein concentrate (dairy product with food applications)
Xanthan gum (thickening agent used in syrups and powdered juice drinks)

COMPETITORS

ADM
Degussa
Donlar
Dow Chemical
FMC
Leprino Foods
MGP Ingredients
Rohm and Haas
Saputo

HISTORICAL FINANCIALS

Company Type: Private

Income Statement FYE: December 31

	REVENUE ($ mil.)	NET INCOME ($ mil.)	NET PROFIT MARGIN	EMPLOYEES
12/02	450	—	—	1,850
12/01	450	—	—	1,850
12/00	450	—	—	1,850
12/99	450	—	—	1,850
Annual Growth	0.0%	—	—	0.0%

Revenue History

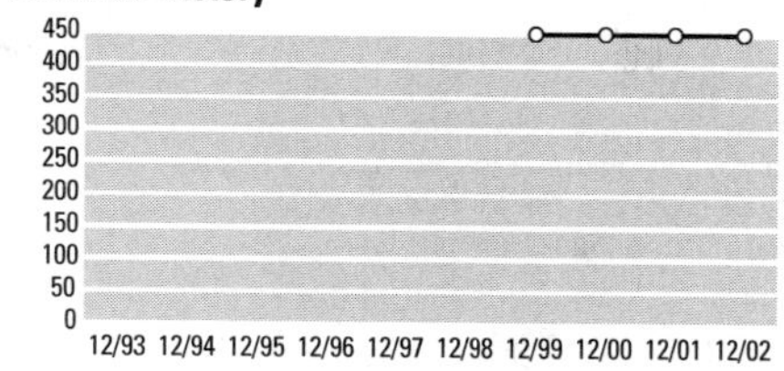

Crescent Electric Supply Company

Crescent Electric Supply Company always plays it straight with its customers. The company was founded in 1919 by Titus Schmid as a lamp agent for General Electric. Today Crescent Electric distributes electrical supplies from leading manufacturers such as GE Lighting, Hubbell, Siemens, and Thomas & Betts. The company also offers bin management and other inventory services. Orders can be placed through Crescent Electric's online order system at any hour of the day. Customers include John Deere, Caterpillar, Mitsubishi, and various government agencies. Members of the Schmid family continue to own Crescent Electric.

EXECUTIVES

President: James R. (Jim) Etheredge
VP and General Manager: Martin S. (Marty) Burbridge
VP, Sales: Carl A. Otterness
VP, Operations and Quality: Ronald D. (Ron) Schlader
VP, Marketing and Strategic Development: Richard T. (Dick) Schmid
VP, Finance: Alice R. Vontalge
Secretary and Treasurer: Carol M. Hoffman
Director, Human Resources: Dan Philippi
Manager, Information Services and Technologies: Ken Snodgrass

LOCATIONS

HQ: 7750 Dunleith Dr., East Dubuque, IL 61025
Phone: 815-747-3145 **Fax:** 815-747-7720
Web: www.cesco.com

Crescent Electric Supply has more than 100 stocking facilities in 24 states across the US.

PRODUCTS/OPERATIONS

Selected Products

Ballasts
Builders' products
Conduit
Connecting materials
Electric heaters
Factory automation systems
Lamps
Lighting
Line construction material
Motor controls
Tools
Voice, data, and video equipment
Wire, cords, and cables
Wiring devices

COMPETITORS

Anixter International
Border States
C&H Distributors
Communications Supply
Graybar Electric
Hughes Supply
Kirby Risk
Mayer Electric
McNaughton-McKay
Sammons Enterprises
SUMMIT Electric Supply
WESCO International
W.W. Grainger

HISTORICAL FINANCIALS

Company Type: Private

Income Statement FYE: December 31

	REVENUE ($ mil.)	NET INCOME ($ mil.)	NET PROFIT MARGIN	EMPLOYEES
12/01	609	—	—	—
12/00	632	—	—	—
Annual Growth	(3.6%)	—	—	—

Revenue History

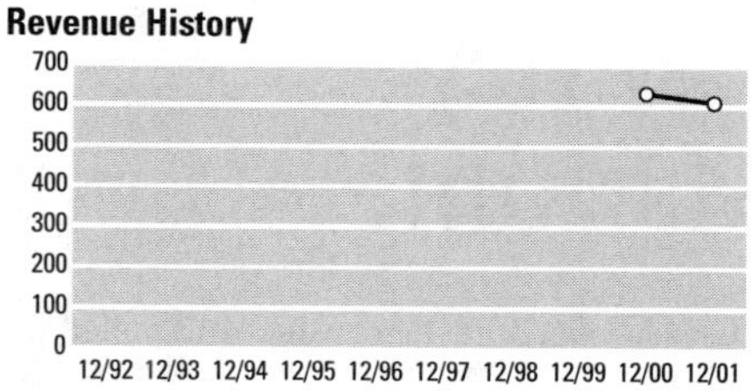

Crete Carrier Corporation

Crete Carrier keeps customers' goods moving. The flagship of a group of truckload carriers controlled by chairman Duane Acklie, Crete Carrier provides dry van freight transportation services in the 48 contiguous states. It operates from more than 15 terminals, mainly in the eastern half of the US. The company's Shaffer Trucking unit transports temperature-controlled cargo, and Hunt Transportation (no relation to J.B. Hunt Transport Services) hauls heavy equipment and other cargo on flatbed trailers. Collectively, the companies operate about 5,400 tractors and more than 13,000 trailers. Other Crete affiliates provide insurance, real estate development, and warehousing services.

EXECUTIVES

Chairman: Duane W. Acklie, age 71
President and CEO: Tonn M. Ostergard
VP Operations: Lee Hoffman
President and CEO, Shaffer Trucking: Matt Stoll

LOCATIONS

HQ: 400 NW 56th St., Lincoln, NE 68501
Phone: 402-475-9521 **Fax:** 402-479-2075
Web: www.cretecarrier.com

COMPETITORS

Celadon
CFI
Covenant Transport
Heartland Express
J. B. Hunt
Landstar System
Schneider National
Swift Transportation
U.S. Xpress
Werner Enterprises

HISTORICAL FINANCIALS

Company Type: Private

Income Statement FYE: September 30

	REVENUE ($ mil.)	NET INCOME ($ mil.)	NET PROFIT MARGIN	EMPLOYEES
9/02	725	—	—	5,000

Crowley Maritime

Crowley Maritime has pushed and pulled its way into prominence as one of the largest tug and barge operators in the world. The company transports containers, trailers, petroleum products, and breakbulk (structures that cannot be broken down) by ship. It provides ship assists, towing, logistics, and marine salvage. The company's fleet of more than 300 vessels includes tugboats, tankers, barges, and specialized cargo carriers. Crowley Maritime has about 100 offices worldwide. CEO Thomas Crowley (grandson of the founder), his family, and employees own about 85% of the company, which was founded in 1892.

EXECUTIVES

Chairman, President, and CEO: Thomas B. (Tom) Crowley Jr., age 36, $1,424,505 pay
Vice Chairman and EVP: William A. Pennella, age 58, $569,110 pay
SVP and General Counsel: William P. Verdon, $357,655 pay
SVP and General Manager, Logistics: John Hourihan
SVP and General Manager, Marine Transport: Rockwell (Rocky) Smith
SVP and General Manager, Puerto Rico and Caribbean Services: John Douglass
SVP and General Manager, Latin America Services: Rinus Schepen
VP Human Resources: Susan Rodgers
Corporate Secretary: Bruce Love
Auditors: Deloitte & Touche LLP

LOCATIONS

HQ: Crowley Maritime Corporation
155 Grand Ave., Oakland, CA 94612
Phone: 510-251-7500 **Fax:** 510-251-7788
Web: www.crowley.com

PRODUCTS/OPERATIONS

2002 Sales

	$ mil.	% of total
Liner	535.4	55
Oil & chemical distribution & transportation	283.4	29
Energy & marine	88.6	9
Ship assist & escort	70.5	7
Total	**977.9**	**100**

Major Subsidiaries

Crowley Liner Services, Inc.
Crowley Logistics Inc.
Crowley Marine Services, Inc.
Crowley Petroleum Transport, Inc.
Marine Transport Corporation
Vessel Management Services, Inc.

COMPETITORS

Alexander & Baldwin
A.P. Møller — Maersk
APL
Evergreen Marine
Hamburg Süd
Hanjin Shipping
International Shipholding
Kirby
Maritrans
Overseas Shipholding Group
P&O
Compañía Sud Americana de Vapores

HISTORICAL FINANCIALS

Company Type: Private

Income Statement FYE: December 31

	ESTIMATED REVENUE ($ mil.)	NET INCOME ($ mil.)	NET PROFIT MARGIN	EMPLOYEES
12/02	978	17	1.8%	3,913
12/01	1,001	20	2.0%	3,800
12/00	799	20	2.5%	5,000
12/99	775	—	—	3,300
12/98	1,100	—	—	5,000
12/97	1,100	—	—	5,000
12/96	1,100	—	—	5,000
12/95	1,100	—	—	5,000
12/94	1,100	—	—	5,000
12/93	1,100	—	—	5,000
Annual Growth	(1.3%)	(7.7%)	—	(2.7%)

2002 Year-End Financials

Debt ratio: 102.8%
Return on equity: 6.1%
Cash ($ mil.): 44
Current ratio: 1.21
Long-term debt ($ mil.): 296

Net Income History

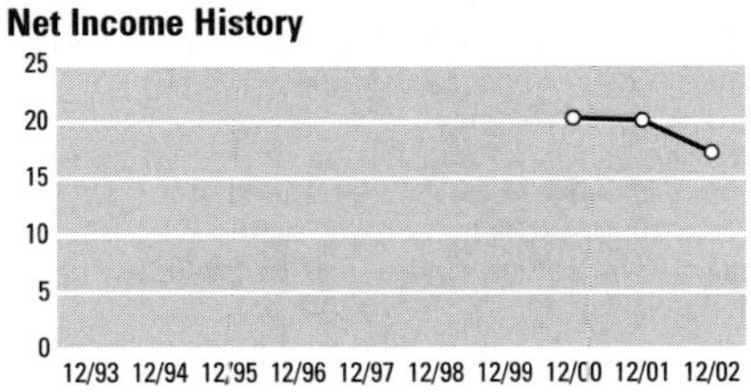

Crown Central Petroleum

Independent oil refiner and marketer Crown Central Petroleum's family jewels include two refineries in Texas with a total capacity of 152,000 barrels per day, 314 retail service stations in the mid-Atlantic and southeastern US, and 10 product terminals. Crown Central also offers fleet fueling services. The company has come under attack for a four-year labor lockout at its Houston-area refinery, civil rights violations, and excessive toxic releases. It is considering selling its refineries and its terminals. Rosemore, the holding company of Henry Rosenberg and his family, took full ownership of Crown Central in 2001 after beating out a competing bid for control from rival Apex Oil.

EXECUTIVES

President: Thomas L. Owsley
EVP and CFO: John E. Wheeler Jr.
SVP Human Resources: J. Michael Mims
VP Retail Marketing; President, CrownCen Marketing: James R. Evans
General Counsel and Corporate Secretary: Andrew Lapayowker
Auditors: Ernst & Young LLP

LOCATIONS

HQ: Crown Central Petroleum Corporation
1 North Charles St., Baltimore, MD 21201
Phone: 410-539-7400 **Fax:** 410-659-4747
Web: www.crowncentral.com

Crown Central Petroleum owns two refineries in Texas, as well as 346 service stations in Alabama, Georgia, Maryland, North Carolina, Pennsylvania, South Carolina, and Virginia.

PRODUCTS/OPERATIONS

Products

Diesel fuel
Fleet fueling services
Fuel oil
Gasoline
Heating oil
Jet fuel
Kerosene
Telephone calling cards

COMPETITORS

Apex Oil
BP
ConocoPhillips
Exxon Mobil
George Warren
Giant Industries
Marathon Ashland Petroleum
Motiva Enterprises
Premcor
Sunoco
Valero Energy
Williams Companies

HISTORICAL FINANCIALS

Company Type: Private

Income Statement FYE: December 31

	REVENUE ($ mil.)	NET INCOME ($ mil.)	NET PROFIT MARGIN	EMPLOYEES
12/01	1,700	—	—	2,600
12/00	1,961	—	—	2,636
12/99	1,270	—	—	2,695
12/98	1,264	—	—	3,028
12/97	1,603	—	—	2,819
12/96	1,635	—	—	2,900
12/95	1,451	—	—	3,009
12/94	1,319	—	—	2,971
12/93	1,451	—	—	3,344
12/92	1,576	—	—	3,894
Annual Growth	0.8%	—	—	(4.4%)

Revenue History

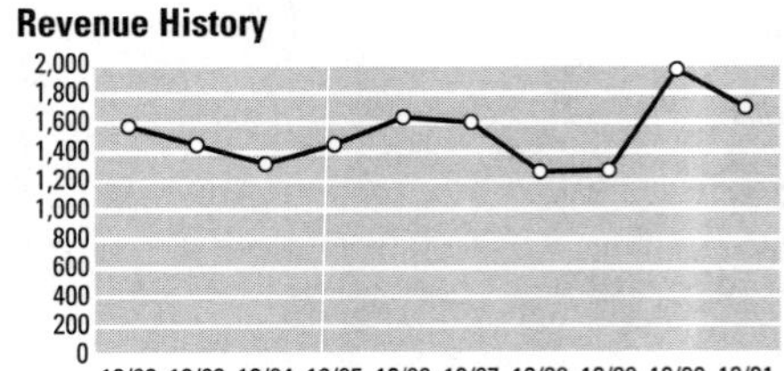

Crown Equipment

Crown Equipment Corporation is a leading maker of electric heavy-duty lift trucks for maneuvering goods in warehouses and distribution centers. The company's products include narrow-aisle stacking equipment, powered pallet trucks, order-picking equipment, and forklift trucks. Its equipment can move four-ton loads and stack pallets nearly 45 feet high. Crown Equipment sells its products globally through retailers. The company, founded in 1945 by brothers Carl and Allen Dicke, originally made temperature controls for coal furnaces. It began making material-handling equipment in the 1950s. The Dicke family still controls Crown Equipment.

EXECUTIVES

Chairman: James F. Dicke
President and CEO: James F. Dicke II, age 57
EVP: James F. Dicke III
SVP: Donald E. Luebrecht
SVP: James D. Moran
VP and General Counsel: John G. Maxa
VP, Branch Operations: James B. Ellis
VP, Design Center: Michael P. Gallagher
VP, Engineering: Timothy S. Quellhorst
VP, Europe Operations: John Tate
VP, Finance: Kent Spille
VP, Human Resources: Randy Niekamp

LOCATIONS

HQ: Crown Equipment Corporation
44 S. Washington St., New Bremen, OH 45869
Phone: 419-629-2311 **Fax:** 419-629-2900
Web: www.crownlift.com

Crown Equipment has 26 factory-owned sales and service facilities and about 150 independent dealers across North America. It also maintains a worldwide retail network.

PRODUCTS/OPERATIONS

Selected Products

Counterbalanced trucks
Order pickers
Reach trucks
Rider pallet trucks
Tow tractors
Walkie pallet trucks
Walkie stackers

COMPETITORS

Caterpillar
Hyundai Heavy Industries
Ingersoll-Rand Infrastructure
Komatsu
Mack Trucks
Mitsubishi Heavy Industries
NACCO Industries
Sammons Enterprises

HISTORICAL FINANCIALS

Company Type: Private

Income Statement FYE: March 31

	REVENUE ($ mil.)	NET INCOME ($ mil.)	NET PROFIT MARGIN	EMPLOYEES
3/02	966	—	—	7,000
3/01	1,127	—	—	7,290
3/00	1,010	—	—	6,510
3/99	968	—	—	6,440
3/98	855	—	—	6,050
3/97	781	—	—	5,975
3/96	707	—	—	5,800
3/95	607	—	—	5,000
3/94	486	—	—	4,200
Annual Growth	9.0%	—	—	6.6%

Revenue History

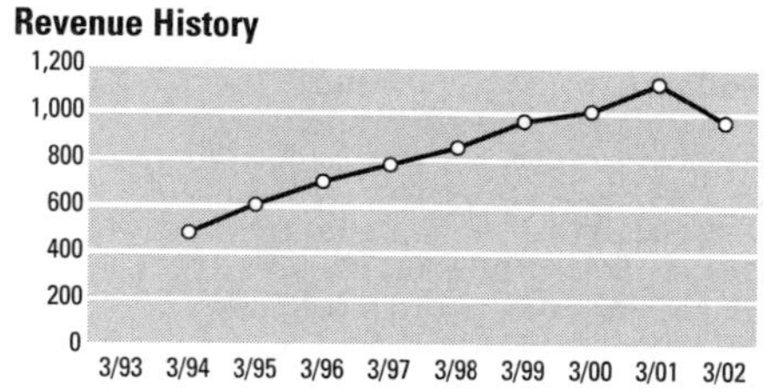

Cumberland Farms, Inc.

Beginning as a one-cow dairy, Cumberland Farms now owns and operates more than 1,000 convenience stores (three-fourths of which sell gasoline) in 11 eastern seaboard states from Maine to Florida. The company has its own grocery distribution and bakery operations to supply its stores. Cumberland Farms owns a two-thirds limited partnership in petroleum wholesaler Gulf Oil, giving it the right to use and license Gulf trademarks in Delaware, New Jersey, New York, most of Ohio, Pennsylvania, and the New England states. The company, the first convenience-store operator in New England, was founded in 1938 by Vasilios and Aphrodite Haseotes. The Haseotes' children, including CEO Lily Haseotes Bentas, own the company.

EXECUTIVES

Chairman, President, and CEO: Lily Haseotes Bentas
EVP and COO: Harry J. Brenner
SVP, Retail Operations: Daniel D. Phaneuf
VP, Human Resources: Foster G. Macrides
VP, Marketing: Alvin McKay
VP, Wholesale Petroleum: George P. Haseotes
Controller: Kevin Johnson
General Counsel: Michael A. Kelly

LOCATIONS

HQ: 777 Dedham St., Canton, MA 02021
Phone: 781-828-4900 **Fax:** 781-828-9624
Web: www.cumberlandfarms.com

Cumberland Farms operates about 1,000 convenience stores in Connecticut, Delaware, Florida, Maine, Massachusetts, New Hampshire, New Jersey, New York, Pennsylvania, Rhode Island, and Vermont.

COMPETITORS

7-Eleven
BP
ChevronTexaco
DeMoulas Super Markets
Exxon Mobil
Gate Petroleum
Getty Realty
Golub
Motiva Enterprises
Racetrac Petroleum
Sheetz
Stewart's Shops
Wawa

HISTORICAL FINANCIALS

Company Type: Private

Income Statement FYE: September 30

	REVENUE ($ mil.)	NET INCOME ($ mil.)	NET PROFIT MARGIN	EMPLOYEES
9/02	1,700	—	—	6,976
9/01	1,500	—	—	6,545
9/00	950	—	—	6,200
9/99	1,140	—	—	6,900
9/98	1,387	—	—	6,800
9/97	1,469	—	—	7,100
9/96	1,396	—	—	7,100
9/95	1,321	—	—	7,200
9/94	1,188	—	—	7,500
9/93	1,100	—	—	—
Annual Growth	5.0%	—	—	(0.9%)

Revenue History

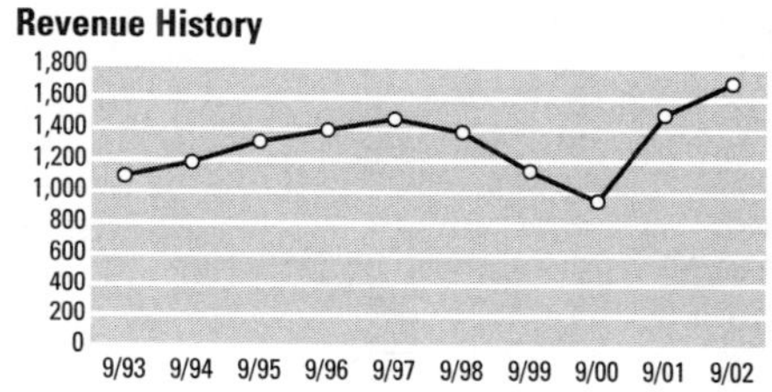

Cupertino Electric, Inc.

Old Economy meets New in Cupertino Electric. The electrical contractor builds and maintains electrical power and data infrastructure systems for commercial, industrial, and institutional facilities, including semiconductor plants, biotech installations, data centers, network systems, and schools. It provides generation facilities for companies that are not on a grid or need additional power. The company operates under three divisions: Cascade Controls, Frank Electric, and Ceitronics. Cupertino Electric, whose clients include Intel, Microsoft, and Oracle, withdrew its IPO in 2001 because of an unfavorable market. Cupertino is 33%-owned by the family of chairman Eugene Ravizza, who founded the company in 1954.

EXECUTIVES

Chairman: Eugene A. Ravizza
President and CEO: James S. (Jim) Ryley
COO: Walter E. (Gene) Ryley
SVP and CFO: Earl C. Charles
SVP Engineering: Rudy G. Bergthold
SVP Production: Bruce Baxter
SVP Purchasing: Darrell Bender
SVP Energy Solutions: James (Jim) Medefesser

VP, General Counsel, and Secretary: Jan Kang
Director Human Resources: Rose Baldwin
Auditors: Deloitte & Touche LLP

LOCATIONS

HQ: 1132 N. 7th St., San Jose, CA 95112
Phone: 408-808-8000 **Fax:** 408-275-8575
Web: www.cei.com

Cupertino Electric has locations in Milpitas, Sacramento, San Francisco, and San Jose, California; it also operates in Mesa, Arizona.

COMPETITORS

Bechtel
Dycom
EMCOR
Fluor
Integrated Electrical Services
MasTec
Quanta Services
Rosendin Electric
SASCO

HISTORICAL FINANCIALS

Company Type: Private

Income Statement FYE: December 31

	REVENUE ($ mil.)	NET INCOME ($ mil.)	NET PROFIT MARGIN	EMPLOYEES
12/01	509	—	—	1,201
12/00	746	—	—	3,075
12/99	325	—	—	2,726
12/98	235	—	—	—
12/97	153	—	—	—
12/96	123	—	—	—
12/95	116	—	—	—
Annual Growth	28.0%	—	—	(33.6%)

Revenue History

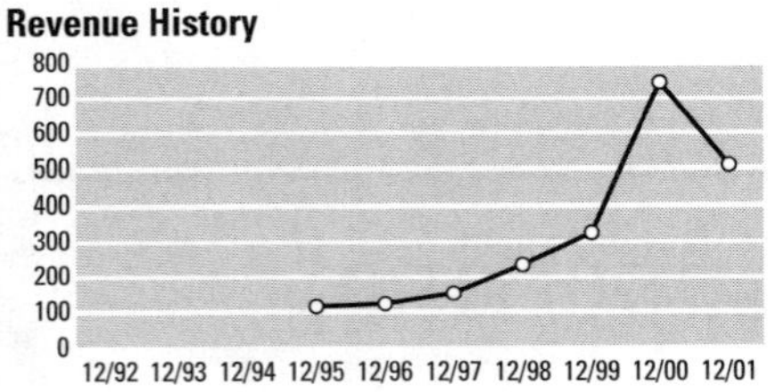

Cushman & Wakefield, Inc.

Cushman & Wakefield serves the real estate needs of corporations and financial institutions around the globe. The commercial real estate brokerage and services company, founded in 1917 by J. Clydesdale Cushman and Bernard Wakefield, has some 160 offices in about 50 countries. In addition to property management (for about 5,500 properties totaling nearly 350 million sq. ft.) and brokerage services, Cushman & Wakefield also provides research and analysis on 85 major markets worldwide. It has partnered with Business Integration Group and Yardi Systems to develop Web-based real estate management services software. The Rockefeller Group, a Mitsubishi Estate subsidiary, owns about 80% of Cushman & Wakefield.

The firm's Asian operations have expanded to include property management and leasing in China via a joint venture with PREMAS International, a Singapore-based firm.

Mindful of tenants' security concerns after the terrorist attacks of September 11, 2001, Cushman & Wakefield has also partnered with Kroll to provide security consulting services.

Cushman & Wakefield has focused its global efforts on European (where it operates as Cushman & Wakefield Healey & Baker) and Asian markets. Domestically, growth plans entail the retail brokerage and multifamily investment businesses.

EXECUTIVES

Chairman: John C. Cushman III, age 62
Vice Chairman: Louis B. Cushman
Vice Chairman: Charles R. Borrok
Vice Chairman: John Cefaly
Vice Chairman: August A. DiRenzo
Vice Chairman: Timothy D. Relyea
Vice Chairman: Donald A. DiRenzo Sr.
Vice Chairman: Edward J. Weiss
President and CEO: Arthur J. Mirante II
EVP and CFO: Thomas P. Dowd
EVP Advisory Group: Christopher J. Lowery
EVP Asset Services: John C. Santora
EVP Brokerage: Mitchell L. Konsker
Executive Managing Director, Human Resources: Carolyn F. Sessa
Executive Managing Director and General Counsel: Kenneth P. Singleton
Senior Managing Director, Corporate Communications: Celine T. Clarke

LOCATIONS

HQ: 51 W. 52nd St., New York, NY 10019
Phone: 212-841-7500 **Fax:** 212-841-7767
Web: www.cushwake.com

PRODUCTS/OPERATIONS

Selected Projects

American Express Tower, New York (managing agent)
Bank of America, San Francisco (project consultant)
Centro Insurgentes, Mexico City (leasing agent)
Chrysler Building, New York (project management)
Citicorp Center, San Francisco (leasing and managing agent)
Georgia-Pacific, Atlanta (development consultant and later leasing and managing agent)
McGraw Hill, Ryder Court, London (lease negotiation)
Pan Am Building, New York (project management)
Sears Tower, Chicago (project consultant and leasing and managing agent)
World Bank, Washington, DC (strategic planning and advisory services)

Selected Services

Acquisition
Administration
Agency leasing
Analysis
Appraisal
Consulting
Corporate advisory
Demographic studies
Disposition
Due diligence
Facilities management
Finance
Investment
Investment research
Landlord representation
Location and incentives
Market analysis
Portfolio strategy
Project management
Property management
Repositioning consulting
Strategic occupancy
Strategic programming
Tenant representation
Transaction management
Underwriting
Valuation consulting

COMPETITORS

CB Richard Ellis
Colliers International
Grubb & Ellis
Jones Lang LaSalle
Lend Lease
Trammell Crow

HISTORICAL FINANCIALS

Company Type: Private

Income Statement FYE: December 31

	REVENUE ($ mil.)	NET INCOME ($ mil.)	NET PROFIT MARGIN	EMPLOYEES
12/01	870	—	—	11,000
12/00	820	—	—	11,500
12/99	700	—	—	9,500
12/98	700	—	—	7,700
12/97	400	—	—	5,500
Annual Growth	21.4%	—	—	18.9%

Revenue History

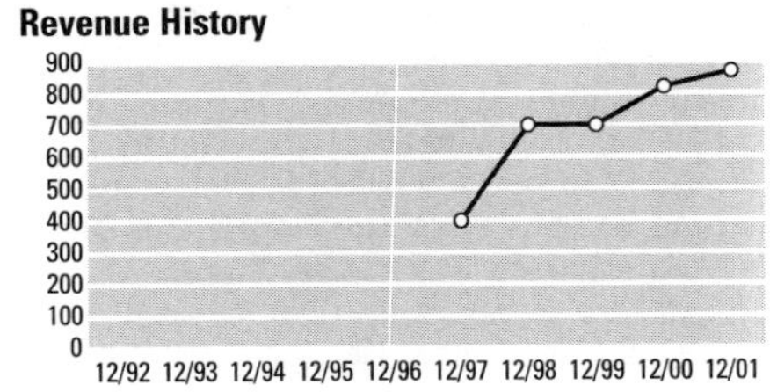

Dairy Farmers of America, Inc.

Dairy Farmers of America (DFA) are partners in cream. DFA is now the world's largest dairy cooperative, with more than 24,000 members in 48 states. The co-op produces nearly 30% of the US milk supply with an annual pool of more than 47 billion pounds of milk. Along with fresh and shelf-stable fluid milk, the co-op also produces cheese, butter, and other products for industrial, wholesale, and retail customers worldwide. DFA is seeking strength in value-added products and joint ventures to distribute its milk and milk-based food ingredients to wider regions.

While DFA is a major supplier to the #1 US milk processor, Dean Foods, it also owns half of what will likely become the #2 US milk processor, National Dairy Holdings. DFA's American Dairy Brands makes and markets Borden cheeses, and its Formulated Dairy Food Products group bottles up Starbucks' Frappuccino coffee drink. In addition, the co-op provides marketing, research and development, and legislative lobbying on behalf of its members.

American dairy farmers have had to come to terms with consolidation in the retail industry, dissolving government milk price supports, and increased foreign competition. To better compete with other dairy processors and soften the swings of the commodity markets, DFA has invested heavily in facilities and joint ventures to process its fluid milk into value-added products and high-end dairy-based ingredients.

HISTORY

Mid-America Dairymen (Mid-Am), the largest of the cooperatives that merged to form Dairy Farmers of America (DFA), was born in 1968. At that time, several midwestern dairy co-ops banded together to attack common economic problems, such as reduced government subsidies, price drops resulting from a rising milk surplus, dealer consolidation, and improvements in production, processing, and packaging. The merging organizations — representing 15,000 dairy farmers — were Producers Creamery Company (Springfield, Missouri), Sanitary Milk Producers (St. Louis), Square Deal Milk Producers (Highland, Illinois), Mid-Am (Kansas City, Missouri), and Producers Creamery Company of Chillicothe (north central Missouri).

During the early 1970s Mid-Am struggled with internal restructuring. Most dairy farmers and co-ops were hit hard by the energy crisis and the government's decision to allow increased dairy imports in 1973, the same year the US Justice Department filed an antitrust suit against Mid-Am. (A judge cleared the co-op 12 years later.)

In 1974 Mid-Am lost almost $8 million on revenues of $625 million, chalked up to record-high feed prices, a weakened economy, a milk surplus, and a massive inventory loss. Co-op veteran Gary Hanman was named CEO that year. Over the next two years, Mid-Am cut costs, sold corporate frills, downsized management, and began marketing more of its own products under the Mid-America Farms label, thus reducing dependency on commodity sales.

Mid-Am expanded its research and development efforts throughout the 1980s. The co-op opened its services to farmers in California and New Mexico in 1993, and a series of mergers in 1994 and 1995 nearly doubled its size. In 1997 it purchased some of Borden's dairy operations, including rights to the valuable Elsie the Cow and Borden's trademarks.

Wary of falling milk prices, Mid-Am merged with Western Dairymen Cooperative, Milk Marketing, and the Southern Region of Associated Milk Producers at the end of 1997 to form DFA. Hanman moved into the seat of CEO at the new co-op. DFA began a series of joint ventures with the #1 US dairy processor, Suiza Foods.

DFA added California Gold (more than 330 farmers, 1998) and Independent Cooperative Milk Producers Association (730 dairy farmer members in Michigan and parts of Ohio and Indiana, 1999). In another joint venture with Suiza in early 2000 DFA sold its 50% stake in the US's #3 fluid milk processor, Southern Foods, in exchange for 34% of a new company named Suiza Dairy Group.

After mollifying the government's antitrust fears, DFA acquired the butter operations of Sodial North America in mid-2000. It then molded all its butter businesses into a new entity, Keller's Creamery, LLC.

During 2001 the cooperative went in with Land O'Lakes 50/50 to purchase a cheese plant from Kraft. Later in the year as Suiza Foods acquired Dean Foods (and took on its name), DFA sold back its stake in Suiza Dairy Group to the new Dean Foods. DFA then teamed up with a group of dairy investors to form a new 50/50 joint venture, National Dairy Holdings, which received 11 processing plants from Dean Foods as part of the exchange for Suiza Dairy.

Weak milk prices and a drop in demand during 2002 caused DFA's revenues to slide. DFA has typically grown by inviting smaller dairy co-ops to merge with it, including the Black Hills Milk Producers Cooperative in 2002. However, to better secure milk sources for its customers in the northeastern US, that same year DFA welcomed two regional co-ops, Dairylea and St. Albans, to join as members. The two co-ops remain as separate but affiliated organizations.

EXECUTIVES

Chairman: Tom Camerlo
President and CEO: Gary E. Hanman
EVP: Don H. Schriver
CFO: Gerald (Jerry) Bos
Corporate VP, Human Resources & Administration: Harold Papen
Corporate VP, Legal Counsel: David A. Geisler
Corporate VP, Marketing and Economic Analysis: John J. Wilson
SVP; COO, Southwest Area, Mountain Area: David C. Jones
SVP Southeast Area, Mideast Area, and Central Area; COO, Southeast Area: John I. Collins
VP, Accounting & Information Systems: Joel Clark
VP; COO, Mideast Area: James F. (Jim) Carroll
VP; COO, Western Area: David L. Parrish
VP; COO, Central Area: Randall S. (Randy) McGinnis
VP, Communications and Public Relations: Agnes Schafer
President, Dairy Food Products: Sam E. McCroskey
President, American Dairy Brands; VP, DFA Dairy Food Products Group: Mark Korsmeyer
COO, Northeast Area; CEO, Dairylea: Richard P. (Rick) Smith
Auditors: Deloitte & Touche LLP

LOCATIONS

HQ: 10220 N. Ambassador Dr., Kansas City, MO 64153
Phone: 816-801-6455 **Fax:** 816-801-6456
Web: www.dfamilk.com

Dairy Farmers of America includes more than 24,000 members from 48 states.

PRODUCTS/OPERATIONS

Selected Products

Butter (Breakstone's, Hotel Bar, Keller's, Plugra)
Cheese dips
Cheeses (Borden)
Coffee creamer
Condensed milk
Cream
Dehydrated dairy products
Infant formula
Nonfat dry milk powder
Shelf-stable nutritional beverages (Sport Shake)
Whey products

COMPETITORS

Arla
AMPI
California Dairies Inc.
Dean Foods
Fonterra
Foremost Farms
Glanbia
Kraft Foods North America
Lactalis
Land O'Lakes
Northwest Dairy
Parmalat
Prairie Farms Dairy
Quality Chekd
Saputo
Schreiber Foods
Unilever
WestFarm Foods

HISTORICAL FINANCIALS

Company Type: Cooperative

Income Statement FYE: December 31

	REVENUE ($ mil.)	NET INCOME ($ mil.)	NET PROFIT MARGIN	EMPLOYEES
12/02	6,448	50	0.8%	4,000
12/01	7,902	62	0.8%	4,000
12/00	6,586	39	0.6%	4,000
12/99	7,483	43	0.6%	5,000
12/98	7,284	70	1.0%	5,300
12/97	3,818	26	0.7%	5,300
12/96	4,085	17	0.4%	3,200
12/95	3,681	14	0.4%	3,100
12/94	2,491	12	0.5%	3,000
12/93	1,826	1	0.1%	3,500
Annual Growth	15.0%	54.5%	—	1.5%

Net Income History

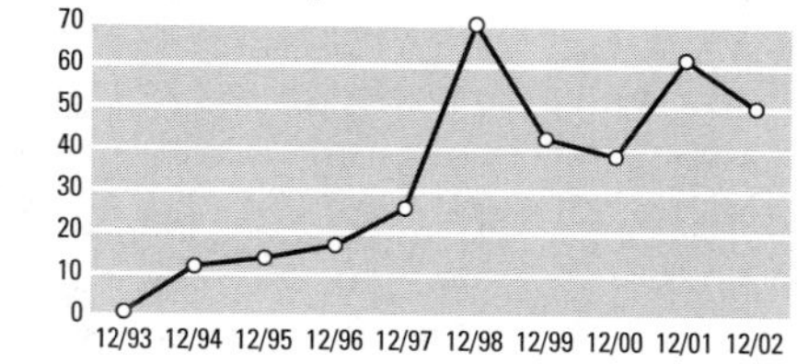

Dairylea Cooperative Inc.

Yes, the farmer takes a wife, then hi-ho, the derry-o, the farmer takes membership in milk marketing organizations such as Dairylea Cooperative. Owned by more than 2,500 dairy farmers in the northeastern US, Dairylea markets 5.2 billion pounds of milk for its farmers annually to customers such as Kraft Foods, Dean Foods, and Leprino Foods. The cooperative invests in dairy companies and provides members with financial and farm management services, as well as insurance. Its Empire Livestock subsidiary operates a livestock auction market. Dairylea, the largest milk marketer in the Northeast, has a joint marketing venture with Dairy Farmers of America.

EXECUTIVES

Chairman and President: Clyde E. Rutherford
CEO: Richard P. (Rick) Smith
COO: Greg Wickham
CFO and Director of Human Resources: Edward Bangel
VP of Finance: Ellen Gall
Secretary: William Beeman
Treasurer: David M. Chamberlain
Director of Communications: Monica Coleman

LOCATIONS

HQ: 5001 Brittonfield Pkwy., East Syracuse, NY 13057
Phone: 315-433-0100 **Fax:** 315-433-2345
Web: www.dairylea.com

COMPETITORS

Agri-Mark
AMPI
eMerge Interactive
Foremost Farms
Horizon Organic
Land O'Lakes
Quality Chekd

HISTORICAL FINANCIALS

Company Type: Cooperative

Income Statement FYE: March 31

	REVENUE ($ mil.)	NET INCOME ($ mil.)	NET PROFIT MARGIN	EMPLOYEES
3/03	852	1	0.1%	115
3/02	941	1	0.1%	115
3/01	803	1	0.1%	107
3/00	812	—	—	205
3/99	881	—	—	250
3/98	750	—	—	200
3/97	699	—	—	150
3/96	594	—	—	80
Annual Growth	5.3%	5.4%	—	5.3%

Net Income History

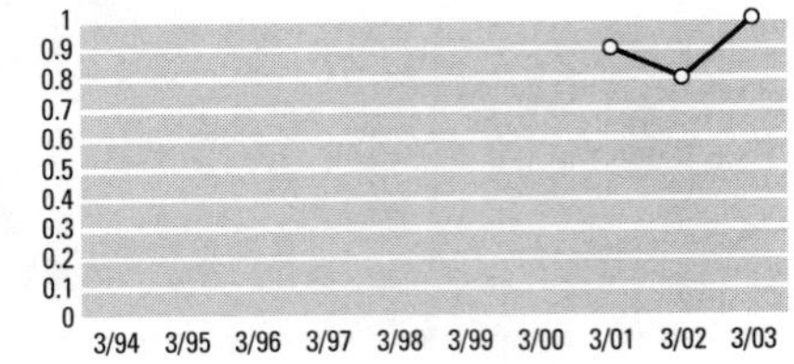

Darby Group Companies, Inc.

The Darby Group can help you take care of your canines or your canine teeth. The group's Darby-Spencer-Mead Dental Supply uses more than 200 phone operators to take orders and distribute some 40,000 products in stock for dentists. Its Burns Veterinary Supply unit provides veterinary supplies and services through about 150 field and phone sales representatives. Darby Drug provides health care professionals with pharmaceuticals and disposable supplies. Other companies within the Darby Group include Bedford Chiropractic Supply, which distributes chiropractic equipment, nutritional supplements, and other items.

EXECUTIVES

Chairman: Michael Ashkin
CEO: Carl Ashkin
CFO: Justina Sorraci
Director, Human Resources: Susan Scanlon

LOCATIONS

HQ: 865 Merrick Ave., Westbury, NY 11590
Phone: 516-683-1800 **Fax:** 516-832-7101
Web: www.darbygroup.com

Darby Group Companies has offices in Colorado, Florida, Georgia, Maryland, Michigan, Minnesota, Missouri, Nevada, New York, Texas, and Washington.

PRODUCTS/OPERATIONS

Selected Subsidiaries

Dental Division
Darby Dental Laboratory Supply Co., Inc.
Darby-Spencer-Mead Dental Supply Company
OIS

Medical Division
Bedford Chiropractic Supply
Darby Drug Co., Inc.

Veterinary Division
Burns Veterinary Supply, Inc.

COMPETITORS

Allegiance
Caremark
Henry Schein
McKesson
Owens & Minor
Patterson Dental
PETsMART
PSS World Medical
Suzuken

HISTORICAL FINANCIALS

Company Type: Private

Income Statement FYE: December 31

	ESTIMATED REVENUE ($ mil.)	NET INCOME ($ mil.)	NET PROFIT MARGIN	EMPLOYEES
12/01	625	—	—	1,500
12/00	675	—	—	1,400
12/99	675	—	—	2,100
12/98	625	—	—	2,100
12/97	565	—	—	2,000
12/96	500	—	—	2,000
12/95	450	—	—	2,000
12/94	430	—	—	2,000
Annual Growth	5.5%	—	—	(4.0%)

Revenue History

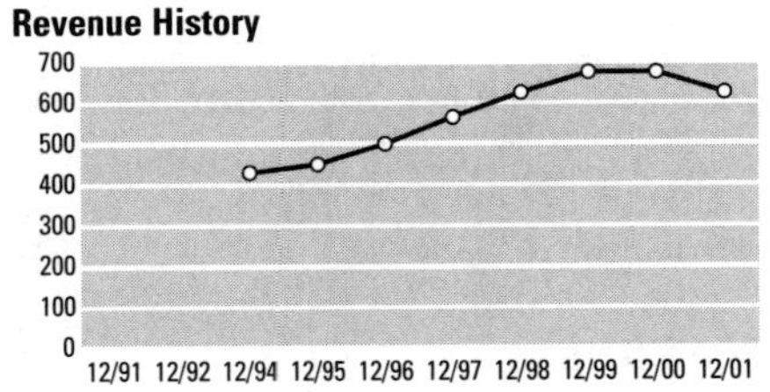

Darcars Automotive

Buying a new vehicle in the Washington, DC, area can expose you to the Darcars side of human nature. Darcars Automotive Group, an automobile dealership holding company, has about 30 automobile dealerships in Maryland and Virginia. Its dealerships sell a variety of new and used automobiles, including cars made by DaimlerChrysler, Ford Motor, General Motors, Kia Motors, Mitsubishi, Toyota, Volkswagen, and Volvo. Darcars offers a full range of automotive services, including parts and service departments and car body repair. Darcars Automotive Group was founded in 1977 by John Darvish, whose family still owns and runs the company.

EXECUTIVES

Chairman: John R. Darvish, age 63
CFO: Michael Hancheruk
VP; General Manager, Darcars Toyota: Tammy Darvish, age 38
Finance Director: Mike Quinn
Personnel Director: Sam Bruner

LOCATIONS

HQ: Darcars Automotive Group
12210 Cherry Hill Rd., Silver Spring, MD 20904
Phone: 301-622-0300 **Fax:** 301-622-4915
Web: www.darcars.com

COMPETITORS

Atlantic Automotive
AutoNation
Brown Automotive
CarMax
Jim Koons Automotive
Ourisman Automotive
pohanka automotive
Rosenthal Automotive
Sheehy Auto
Sonic Automotive

HISTORICAL FINANCIALS

Company Type: Private

Income Statement FYE: December 31

	REVENUE ($ mil.)	NET INCOME ($ mil.)	NET PROFIT MARGIN	EMPLOYEES
12/02	813	—	—	1,800
12/01	845	—	—	1,800
12/00	783	—	—	1,700
12/99	732	—	—	1,600
12/98	592	—	—	1,500
12/97	546	—	—	1,521
12/96	521	—	—	1,612
12/95	491	—	—	1,245
12/94	446	—	—	1,000
12/93	320	—	—	950
Annual Growth	10.9%	—	—	7.4%

Revenue History

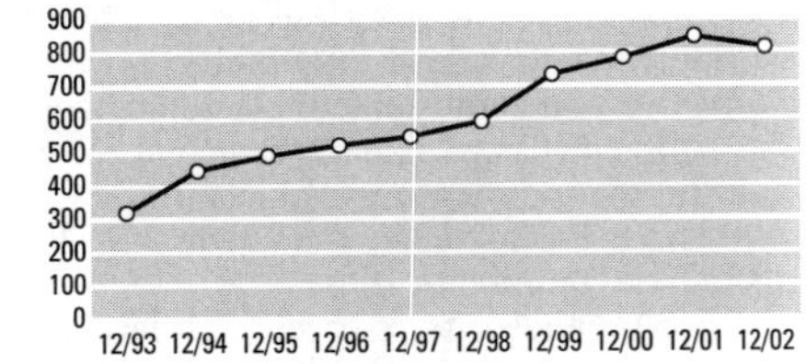

Dart Container Corporation

Dart Container is a world cup winner — maybe not in soccer, but it is the world's top maker of foam cups and containers, with about half of the global market in cups. The company uses a secret method of molding expandable polystyrene to make its products, which include cups, lids, dinnerware, and cutlery for customers such as hospitals, schools, and restaurants. To cut costs, Dart Container builds its own molding machinery and operates its own distribution trucks. The firm sells its recycled polystyrene to companies that make such items as insulation material and egg cartons. Although often embroiled in litigation, the Dart family continues to own the company.

The king of cups has a simple strategy — secrecy. The cup-making machine developed by the Darts was never patented to avoid revealing how it works. Most of its factory workers have never seen the machines, and the firm's salespeople are not allowed inside the plants. After years of legal battles, the Darts have reached an agreement regarding alleged discrepancies in the family inheritance. The terms of the settlement are, naturally, secret.

In terms of Dart's products, the company is moving into foam lid and plastic containers for industrial or retail use.

The company runs four polystyrene-recycling plants and operates in the US and through subsidiaries in Argentina, Australia, Canada, Mexico, and the UK.

HISTORY

William F. Dart founded a Michigan firm to make steel tape measures in 1937. Dart's son William A. started experimenting with plastics in 1953, and in the late 1950s the two devised a cheap way to mold expandable polystyrene and built a cup-making machine. Dart Container was incorporated in Mason, Michigan, in 1960 and shipped its first cups that year. By the late 1960s the rising demand for plastic-foam products sparked an increase in R&D. In 1970 the company built a plant in Corona, California.

It was a family feud in the making in 1974, as William F. divided the business among his grandsons — Tom, Ken, and Robert — in separate trusts that named William A. trustee for all. Tom branched out in 1975 and founded oil and gas company Dart Energy, which was later absorbed into Dart Container. William F. died the next year. Following the oil market crash of the early 1980s, Tom went through a sticky divorce and admitted to cocaine abuse. His father temporarily removed him as head of Dart Energy in 1982, and the next year the entire family underwent group psychiatric counseling.

The family reorganized its assets in 1986, giving Ken and Robert the cup business and Tom the energy business plus $58 million in cash. In 1987 Ken began to swell the family fortune with a series of successful investments. Better tax rates motivated Dart family members to move to Sarasota, Florida, in 1989. They set up shop in an unmarked building behind a sporting-goods store. By the late 1980s Dart Container commanded more than 50% of the worldwide market for foam cups.

In 1990 the company paid $250,000 to settle a factory worker's minority discrimination lawsuit. The next year Ken bought 11% of the Federal Home Loan Mortgage Corp. (Freddie Mac), as well as portions of Salomon and Brazil's foreign debt. According to Tom, that year Ken also financed brain research in hopes of finding a way to keep his brain alive after the death of his body in an attempt to avoid future estate taxes.

Tom sued his brothers and father in 1992 for allegedly cheating him out of millions in trust money in the 1986 reorganization. Ken turned a $300 million investment into $1 billion by selling the Freddie Mac shares. The next year he and Robert renounced their US citizenship to avoid paying taxes. Ken also made a failed attempt to block the restructuring of Brazil's debt (of which Dart owned 4%). That year Ken's new $1 million Sarasota home was firebombed (the case remains unsolved), and Robert moved to Britain, where he soon filed for divorce.

Ken began hiring bodyguards, and he moved his family to the Cayman Islands in 1994. Dart then shelled out $230,000 to settle yet another discrimination case. In 1995 Tom was fired from Dart Energy, and Ken tried — and failed — to return to the US as a diplomat of Belize. In 1996 Tom accused Judge Donald Owens of being biased in favor of William A. The judge succumbed to the pressure in 1997 and removed himself from the proceedings, only to be ordered back on the case by Michigan's Court of Appeals. The lawsuit was settled in 1998 before going to trial, but the terms were kept secret. The following year saw yet another series of lawsuits for the container company. In 1999 Dart Container filed an appeal to an IRS demand to pay $31 million in back taxes from 1994 and late penalties. The legal wrangling continued through 2001, but in 2002 the company agreed to pay $26 million to settle the issue. Meanwhile, the company has expanded their foam lid and container products for wholesale industrial or retail use.

EXECUTIVES

President: Kenneth B. Dart
CFO and Treasurer: William Myer
VP: Robert C. Dart
VP, Administration and General Counsel: Jim Lammers
Director, Human Resources: Mark Franks

LOCATIONS

HQ: 500 Hogsback Rd., Mason, MI 48854
Phone: 517-676-3800 **Fax:** 517-676-3883
Web: www.dartcontainer.com

Dart Container has four recycling centers in Canada and the US, and manufacturing operations in Argentina, Australia, Canada, Mexico, the UK, and the US.

PRODUCTS/OPERATIONS

Selected Products

Clear containers
Container lids
Deli containers and lids
Dinnerware
Foam cups
Hinged containers
Paper cups and lids
Plastic cups and lids
Plastic cutlery

Selected Services

CARE (Cups Are REcyclable) Program (provides densifier to larger customers to compact their polystyrene, which Dart then picks up)
Foam-Recycling (four plants in Canada, Florida, Michigan, and Pennsylvania and a drop-off site in Georgia)
Recycla-Pak (provides small-volume businesses with cup-shipping containers that double as recycling bins)

COMPETITORS

Berry Plastics
Huhtamäki
NOVA Chemicals
Radnor Holdings
SF Holdings
Smurfit-Stone Container
Sonoco Products
Sweetheart
Temple-Inland

HISTORICAL FINANCIALS

Company Type: Private

Income Statement FYE: December 31

	ESTIMATED REVENUE ($ mil.)	NET INCOME ($ mil.)	NET PROFIT MARGIN	EMPLOYEES
12/02	1,100	—	—	4,950
12/01	1,170	—	—	5,000
12/00	1,200	—	—	5,000
12/99	1,100	—	—	5,000
12/98	1,150	—	—	5,000
12/97	1,000	—	—	5,000
12/96	1,000	—	—	4,300
12/95	1,000	—	—	4,300
12/94	800	—	—	3,600
12/93	600	—	—	3,750
Annual Growth	7.0%	—	—	3.1%

Revenue History

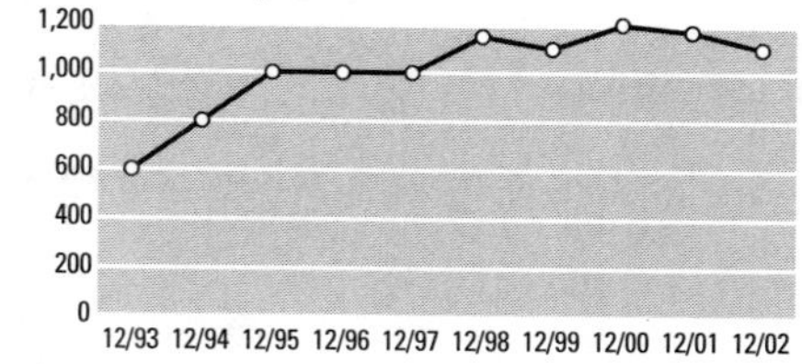

David Weekley Homes

A development home developed to *your* taste? David Weekley Homes will do it. Founded in 1976, it is the second-largest privately owned homebuilder in the US, annually building more than 3,400 single-family detached homes that range in size from about 1,500 sq. ft. to more than 4,000 sq. ft. Weekley builds homes from hundreds of floor plans and offers custom upgrades. Prices range from $120,000 to about $650,000. The company builds in its own planned communities in Texas, Colorado, and in the Southeast, as well as on buyers' lots. For the past three years, it has been listed among the "Top 100 Companies to Work for in America" in *FORTUNE* magazine. Founder and chairman David Weekley owns the firm.

EXECUTIVES

Chairman and CEO: David M. Weekley
President: John Johnson
VP and CFO: Jim Alexander
VP Design: Bob Rhode
VP Human Resources: Mike Gentry
VP Information Technology: Heather Humphrey
VP Operations: Mike Humphrey
VP Sales and Marketing: Gian Hasbrook
Marketing Director: Natalie Harris
Auditors: Ernst & Young LLP

LOCATIONS

HQ: 1111 N. Post Oak Rd., Houston, TX 77055
Phone: 713-963-0500 **Fax:** 713-963-0322
Web: www.davidweekleyhomes.com

Markets Served

Atlanta
Austin, TX
Charleston, SC
Charlotte, NC
Dallas/Fort Worth
Denver
Fort Myers, FL
Houston
Jacksonville
Nashville, TN
Orlando, FL
Raleigh, NC
San Antonio
Tampa

COMPETITORS

Centex
D.R. Horton
Engle Homes
KB Home
Lennar
M/I Schottenstein Homes
NVR
Pulte Homes
Rottlund
Ryland
Standard Pacific
Toll Brothers
Town and Country Homes

HISTORICAL FINANCIALS

Company Type: Private

Income Statement FYE: December 31

	REVENUE ($ mil.)	NET INCOME ($ mil.)	NET PROFIT MARGIN	EMPLOYEES
12/02	855	—	—	1,037
12/01	937	—	—	1,037
12/00	828	—	—	1,010
12/99	711	—	—	900
12/98	608	—	—	820
12/97	503	—	—	790
12/96	474	—	—	638
12/95	427	—	—	600
12/94	428	—	—	600
Annual Growth	9.0%	—	—	7.1%

Revenue History

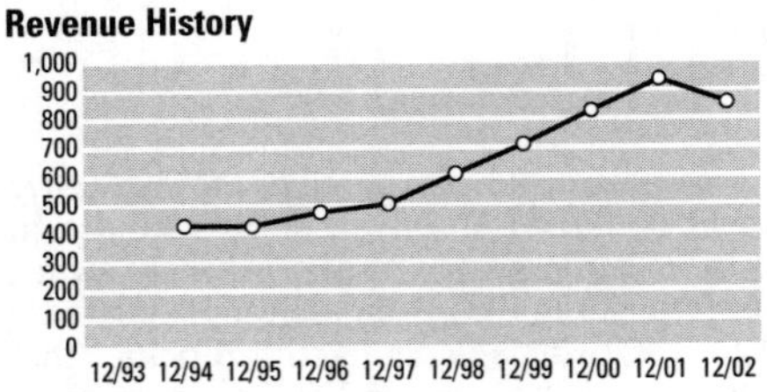

David Wilson's Automotive Group

First Orange County, then the world — or at least Arizona. David Wilson's Automotive Group has its roots in Orange County, California. In 1985 owner David Wilson bought Toyota of Orange, the first of his 12 dealerships, which are all located in California and Arizona and sell Acura, Ford, and Honda cars as well as Toyotas. David Wilson's Automotive Group didn't expand eastward until 1998 when it opened a Honda dealership in Scottsdale, Arizona. The company then added a Toyota location in Arizona in 1999. The dealerships run by David Wilson's Automotive Group, which together sell more than 42,000 new and used cars annually, also offer parts and service departments; some offer fleet services.

EXECUTIVES

Chairman and CEO: David Wilson
President: Randy Rooney
CFO: Ted Tomasek
EVP: Craig Whetter
VP Human Resources: Vicki Murphy

LOCATIONS

HQ: 1400 N. Tustin, Orange, CA 92867
Phone: 714-639-6750 **Fax:** 714-771-0363

COMPETITORS

AutoNation
Holman Enterprises
Marty Franich
Penske Automotive
Prospect Motors
Tuttle-Click

HISTORICAL FINANCIALS

Company Type: Private

Income Statement FYE: December 31

	REVENUE ($ mil.)	NET INCOME ($ mil.)	NET PROFIT MARGIN	EMPLOYEES
12/01	1,073	—	—	450
12/00	1,033	—	—	450
12/99	395	—	—	420
12/98	391	—	—	413
12/97	409	—	—	500
12/96	388	—	—	472
12/95	296	—	—	393
12/94	262	—	—	—
Annual Growth	22.3%	—	—	2.3%

Revenue History

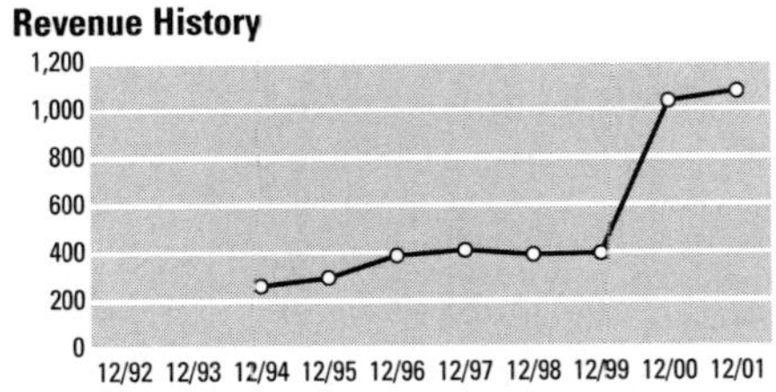

Davis Polk & Wardwell

Founded in 1849, Davis Polk & Wardwell is one of the oldest law firms in the US. Having built a notable corporate practice early on, it helped J. P. Morgan (now J.P. Morgan Chase) form General Electric. With some 660 lawyers, the firm is known for its skill in litigation, securities, and mergers and acquisitions; other practice areas include real estate, tax, and technology. Davis Polk serves such high-profile clients as AT&T (it was involved in the record-breaking stock offering of AT&T's wireless unit in 2000), Comcast, EMI Group, RJR Nabisco, and Philip Morris. In addition, more than one-third of the firm's clients are non-US companies or governments. Davis Polk has nine offices in seven countries.

EXECUTIVES

Managing Partner: John R. Ettinger
Director Recruiting: Bonnie Hurry
Business Development Administrator: Kevin Cavanaugh

LOCATIONS

HQ: 450 Lexington Ave., New York, NY 10017
Phone: 212-450-4000 **Fax:** 212-450-4800
Web: www.dpw.com

Davis Polk & Wardwell has US offices in Menlo Park, California; New York City; and Washington, DC. It has international offices in Frankfurt, Hong Kong, London, Madrid, Paris, and Tokyo.

PRODUCTS/OPERATIONS

Selected Practice Areas

Antitrust
Corporate
Employment
Estate planning
Mergers and acquisitions
Real estate
Securities
Tax
Technology
White-collar crime

COMPETITORS

Baker & McKenzie
Cleary, Gottlieb
Coudert Brothers
Cravath, Swaine
Debevoise & Plimpton
Dewey Ballantine
Hughes Hubbard
Kelley Drye
Proskauer Rose
Simpson Thacher
Skadden, Arps
Sullivan & Cromwell
Wachtell, Lipton

HISTORICAL FINANCIALS

Company Type: Partnership

Income Statement FYE: December 31

	REVENUE ($ mil.)	NET INCOME ($ mil.)	NET PROFIT MARGIN	EMPLOYEES
12/01	570	—	—	—
12/00	525	—	—	—
12/99	460	—	—	—
12/98	435	—	—	—
12/97	390	—	—	—
12/96	346	—	—	—
12/95	282	—	—	—
12/94	254	—	—	—
12/93	270	—	—	—
12/92	267	—	—	—
Annual Growth	8.8%	—	—	—

Revenue History

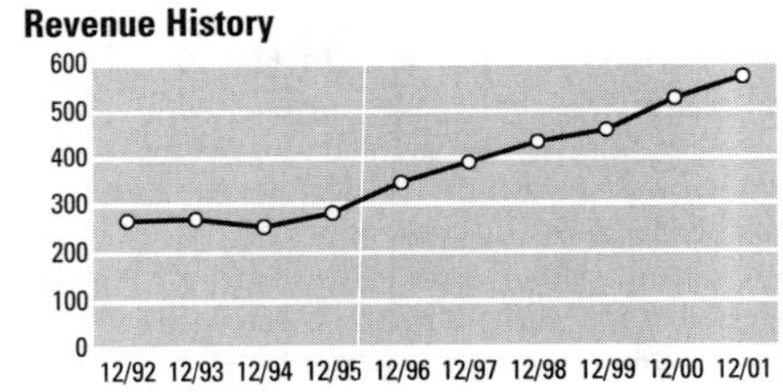

Dawn Food Products, Inc.

A muffin at Starbucks, a cookie from Mrs. Fields, or a doughnut from Krispy Kreme — all just another day in the kitchen for Dawn Food Products. The company provides pre-baked and fully baked products — as well as bases, equipment, fillings, frozen dough, icings, ingredients, and mixes — to the food industry. Its customers include food service companies, institutional bakeries, restaurants, retail outlets, and supermarkets. Dawn Food Products also offers support services such as merchandising and marketing. Owned by the Jones family, Dawn Food Products was founded in 1920 in Jackson, Michigan, and operates throughout the US and in 13 other countries.

EXECUTIVES

Chairman, President and CEO: Ronald L. (Ron) Jones
CFO, Treasurer, and Director: Peter J. (Pete) Staelens
EVP; Director of Research and Development and Director: Miles E. Jones
VP, Operations: Rick Dahlin
President, Dawn Foods North America and Director: John C. Nally
President, Dawn International and Director: Carrie L. Barber
Director of UK Operations: Dave Kowal
HR Manager: William (Bill) Lambkin

LOCATIONS

HQ: 2021 Micor Dr., Jackson, MI 49203
Phone: 517-789-4400 **Fax:** 517-789-4465
Web: www.dawnfoods.com

COMPETITORS

Bridgford Foods
Flowers Foods
General Mills
George Weston
Gonnella Baking
International Multifoods
Interstate Bakeries
Maple Leaf Foods
Otis Spunkmeyer
Rich Products
Sara Lee Bakery Group

HISTORICAL FINANCIALS

Company Type: Private

Income Statement FYE: December 31

	REVENUE ($ mil.)	NET INCOME ($ mil.)	NET PROFIT MARGIN	EMPLOYEES
12/02	750	—	—	2,800
12/01	655	—	—	2,100
12/00	650	—	—	2,100
12/99	649	—	—	2,101
12/98	603	—	—	2,150
Annual Growth	5.6%	—	—	6.8%

Revenue History

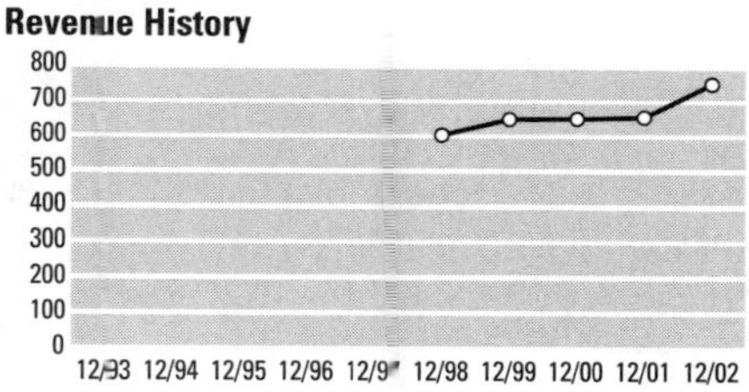

Day & Zimmermann

The Day & Zimmermann Group offers services as distinct as day and night. The company provides engineering and construction, security, munitions products and services, and technical and administrative staffing services worldwide. Day & Zimmermann provides government operations and maintenance services to US and foreign governments and commercial customers. The group has sold three divisions (transportation construction, infrastructure, and public buildings) to integrate its operations and focus on its strategic businesses, particularly technical staffing unit H. L. Yoh Company (Yoh Co.). Founded in 1901, Day & Zimmermann is owned and managed by the Yoh family, which has headed the firm for three generations.

EXECUTIVES

Chairman and CEO: Harold L. (Hal) Yoh III, age 42
VP Finance and CFO: Joseph W. (Joe) Ritzel
SVP Administration: William R. (Bill) Hamm
VP and CIO: Anthony J. Bosco Jr.
VP and Group Controller: Joseph E. McKinney
VP Corporate Marketing and Communications: Sharon Gosdeck
VP Human Resources: Belen J. Acosta
Auditors: Deloitte & Touche

LOCATIONS

HQ: The Day & Zimmermann Group, Inc.
1818 Market St., Fl. 22, Philadelphia, PA 19103
Phone: 215-299-8000 **Fax:** 215-299-8030
Web: www.dayzim.com

The Day & Zimmermann Group operates from more than 150 locations worldwide.

COMPETITORS

Adecco
Alliant Techsystems
AMEC
Bechtel
CDI
Fluor
Foster Wheeler
Halliburton
Jacobs Engineering
Johnson Controls
Louis Berger
Manpower
McCarthy Building
McDermott
Parsons
Peter Kiewit Sons'
URS
Washington Group
WS Atkins

HISTORICAL FINANCIALS

Company Type: Private

Income Statement FYE: December 31

	REVENUE ($ mil.)	NET INCOME ($ mil.)	NET PROFIT MARGIN	EMPLOYEES
12/01	1,300	—	—	20,000
12/00	1,554	—	—	26,000
12/99	1,650	—	—	24,000
12/98	1,080	—	—	16,500
12/97	995	—	—	15,000
12/96	812	—	—	14,000
12/95	766	—	—	13,800
12/94	706	—	—	12,000
12/93	726	—	—	11,600
12/92	650	—	—	—
Annual Growth	8.0%	—	—	7.0%

Revenue History

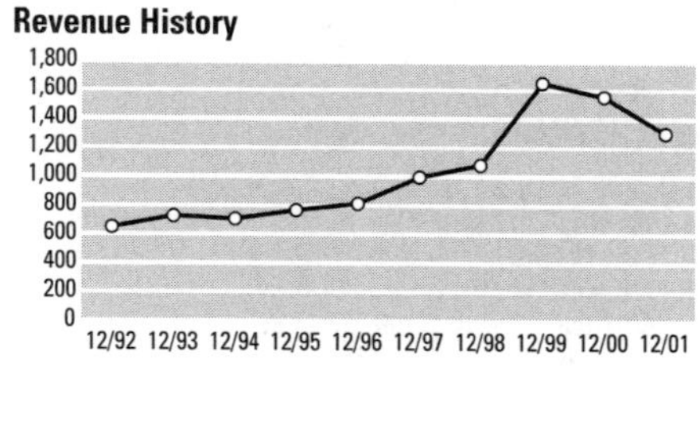

The DeBartolo Corporation

Real estate holdings, gambling, horse racing, a felony conviction, and warring siblings surrounded by a storied NFL franchise — sounds like an old episode of *Dallas*. But the story of The DeBartolo Corporation takes place in Youngstown, Ohio (where the company is based), via San Francisco (where the company owns the 49ers football team). The company also provides management services to the Louisiana Downs racetrack in Bossier City. The firm's other interests include a software firm in Tennessee and a few health care companies in Oklahoma and Pennsylvania. DeBartolo Corp. is also trying to bring an Arena Football League team to San Francisco.

The saga of the DeBartolo family concerns chairman and CEO Denise DeBartolo York and her brother, former CEO Eddie DeBartolo Jr., children of the company's founder. Eddie's guilty plea to charges of failing to report a felony led to his ouster and a lawsuit from his sister to recover a $94 million debt he owed the company. Eddie countersued, and after much wrangling, the siblings reached an agreement whereby Denise took the company name, the 49ers, and the racetrack (which it later sold but still operates), and Eddie received real estate and the firm's minority stake in Simon Property Group, one of North America's largest public real estate companies.

HISTORY

Edward J. DeBartolo left his stepfather's paving business in 1944 and established the eponymous Edward J. DeBartolo Corporation. DeBartolo's foresight about the growth of the suburbs led him to build one of the first strip-style malls outside California, the Belmont Plaza, near Youngstown, Ohio, in 1949. Over the next 15 years, the company built 45 more strip centers throughout the US. In the 1960s DeBartolo became one of the first to develop large, covered regional malls in many parts of the nation. DeBartolo opened the Louisiana Downs racetrack in 1974 and moved the company into the sports business in 1977 when he helped his son, Edward Jr. (Eddie), buy the San Francisco 49ers.

When the management of Allied Stores asked DeBartolo to help fend off a bid by real estate developer Robert Campeau, DeBartolo thought that control of Allied's department store chains would provide anchor stores for his mall developments and loaned Campeau $150 million for the takeover instead. Two years later DeBartolo borrowed $480 million and lent it to Campeau for his acquisition of Federated Department Stores.

The company reached its zenith in the late 1980s (opening the Rivercenter in San Antonio and Lakeland Square in Florida), but Campeau was in trouble — the highly leveraged Allied and Federated went bankrupt and threatened to take DeBartolo with them. As part of the bankruptcy settlement, DeBartolo took a 60% interest in California-based Ralphs supermarket (since sold) and started selling off assets in 1991 to cover the loan he made to Campeau and the company's own $4 billion debt. The fire sale included his private jet, three malls, two office buildings, a 50% stake in Higbee's department stores, and the Rivercenter.

Edward died in 1994. His daughter, Denise

DeBartolo York, became chairman, and his son, Eddie (who was also chairman and CEO of the 49ers) became president and CEO. Eddie reshuffled the company's assets with most of its real estate holdings turned into DeBartolo Realty, a real estate investment trust that went public that year, raising $575 million. Mounting tensions between the siblings intensified in 1995 when Eddie formed DeBartolo Entertainment, his own separate company in the gaming business (Denise tried to distance the family business from Eddie's new company in a press release). DeBartolo Realty merged with Simon Property Group the following year.

Eddie ran into trouble in 1997 when an investigation revealed that he had paid former Louisiana governor Edwin Edwards $400,000 in an effort to obtain a riverboat gambling license for DeBartolo Entertainment. (Before the gambling fraud probe became public, San Francisco voters approved a $100 million bond issue to help finance a $525 million stadium/shopping mall for the 49ers. Those plans were put on ice.) Eddie pleaded guilty to felony charges of concealing wrongdoing the next year, was fined $2 million, and stepped down from DeBartolo Corp. (His later testimony against Gov. Edwards helped lead to the government official's conviction on extortion charges.) The NFL then fined Eddie another $1 million and banned him from the 49ers in 1999. Later that year Denise sued Eddie for debt owed to the company and he countersued. DeBartolo Corp. also sold two of its racetracks (Thistledown and Remington Park).

In 2001 the DeBartolos completed the division of the company's assets between them. DeBartolo York also shortened the company's name to The DeBartolo Corporation.

EXECUTIVES

Chairman and CEO: Marie Denise DeBartolo York, age 52
President; Director and Owner's Representative, San Francisco 49ers: John C. York II
CFO: Tim Ciple
VP: Anthony Nasrallah
President and CEO, 49ers: Peter Harris
General Manager, 49ers: Terry Donahue, age 59
Head Coach, 49ers: Dennis Erickson

LOCATIONS

HQ: 7620 Market St., Youngstown, OH 44512
Phone: 330-965-2000 **Fax:** 330-965-2077
Web: http://www.49ers.com/team/OfficeBio.asp-?FrontOfficeID=82

The DeBartolo Corporation has operations in California, Louisiana, Ohio, Oklahoma, Pennsylvania, and Tennessee.

COMPETITORS

Fair Grounds
Golden State Warriors
Harrah's Entertainment
Oakland Raiders
San Jose Sharks

HISTORICAL FINANCIALS

Company Type: Private

Income Statement FYE: June 30

	ESTIMATED REVENUE ($ mil.)	NET INCOME ($ mil.)	NET PROFIT MARGIN	EMPLOYEES
6/01	250	—	—	4,000
6/00	250	—	—	4,000
6/99	254	—	—	4,000
6/98	250	—	—	4,000
6/97	250	—	—	3,000
6/96	220	—	—	3,000
6/95	230	—	—	3,000
6/94	550	—	—	3,800
6/93	525	—	—	—
6/92	500	—	—	—
Annual Growth	(7.4%)	—	—	0.7%

Revenue History

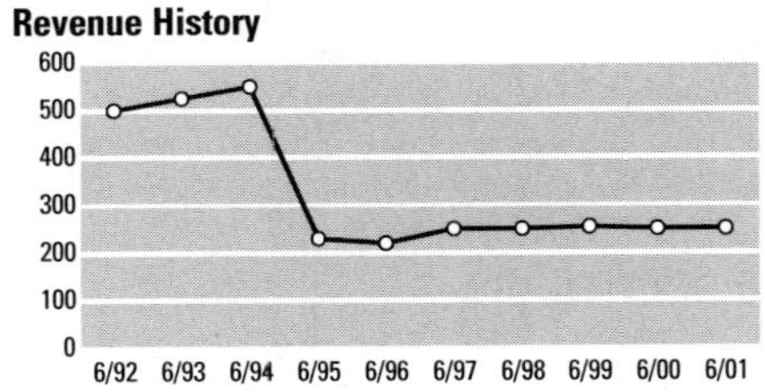

DeBruce Grain, Inc.

Got a few tons of wheat and no place to keep it? DeBruce Grain stores, handles, and sells grain and fertilizer for the agribusiness industry. The company runs 13 grain elevators in Iowa, Kansas, Nebraska, and Texas with a combined capacity of 60 million bushels of grain. DeBruce Grain's office in Mexico merchandises grain grown in both countries. The company also markets fertilizer (by the bag, truck, or barge-load), and it brokers truck freight through subsidiary DeBruce Transportation. DeBruce paid a $685,000 fine in relation to the 1998 explosion, which killed seven workers, of its Haysville, Kansas, facility — the largest grain elevator in the world. Owner and CEO Paul DeBruce founded the company in 1978.

EXECUTIVES

CEO: Paul DeBruce
President: Larry Kittoe
CFO: Curt Heinz
VP, DeBruce Fertilizer: Denny Gibeson
VP, DeBruce Transportation: Dale Feitz
Executive Secretary: Patty Piburn
Corporate Controller: Roger Lawrence
Director, Operations: Dick Wilbur
Director, Transportation: Jeff Hicks
Manager, Ag Service: Terry Meyers
Manager, Feed Ingredients: Robert Clair
Manager, MIS: Ron Lentz
Benefits Coordinator: Joni Hawn

LOCATIONS

HQ: 4100 N. Mulberry Dr., Kansas City, MO 64116
Phone: 816-421-8182 **Fax:** 816-584-2350
Web: www.debruce.com

DeBruce Grain operates 13 grain elevators in Iowa, Kansas, Nebraska, and Texas with a combined capacity of 60 million bushels of grain.

Grain Elevators

Iowa
Percival

Kansas
Abilene
Clay Center
Wichita

Nebraska
Clarks
Fremont
Lexington
Nebraska City
Thumel

Texas
Amarillo
Dimmitt
Etter

COMPETITORS

Ag Processing
Agway
ADM
Bartlett and Company
Bunge Limited
Cargill
CHS
ConAgra
Farmland Industries
Scoular

HISTORICAL FINANCIALS

Company Type: Private

Income Statement FYE: March 31

	REVENUE ($ mil.)	NET INCOME ($ mil.)	NET PROFIT MARGIN	EMPLOYEES
3/02	1,378	—	—	400
3/01	1,201	—	—	330
3/00	879	—	—	300
3/99	772	—	—	250
3/98	723	—	—	200
3/97	865	—	—	200
3/96	688	—	—	150
3/95	507	—	—	130
3/94	472	—	—	130
Annual Growth	14.3%	—	—	15.1%

Revenue History

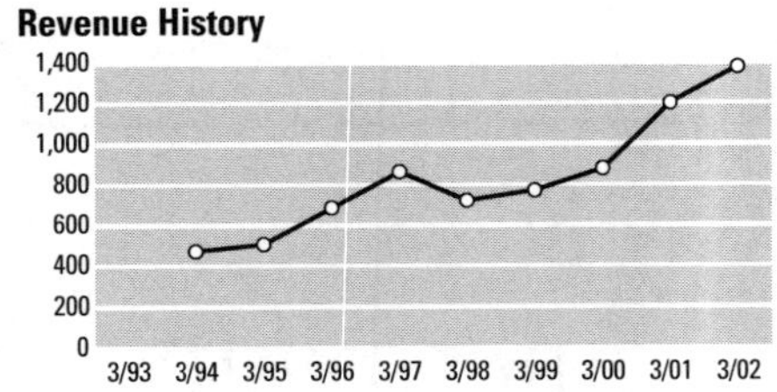

DecisionOne Corporation

Haven't decided which computer technology support services to use? Try DecisionOne. With some 4,000 technicians working out of more than 150 North American offices, DecisionOne offers computer maintenance and technology support services for large businesses, manufacturers, Internet service providers, and software developers. DecisionOne's services include planning and consulting, call center support, deployment, network support, and logistics. The company was founded in 1969 as Decision Data, a provider of keypunch machines. In 2000 a group of investors, including Bear Stearns and Goldman Sachs, took DecisionOne private as it emerged from Chapter 11 bankruptcy.

EXECUTIVES

Chairman and CEO: George W. de Sola
EVP and CFO: Paul H. Snyder, age 55
EVP, Operations: Robert Schultz
SVP and CIO: Gilbert (Gil) Piddington
SVP, Corporate Resources: Dwight T. Wilson
SVP, Field Operations: Gregory G. Martin
VP, Marketing: Frank Tait
Auditors: Deloitte & Touche LLP

LOCATIONS

HQ: 50 E. Swedesford Rd., Frazer, PA 19355
Phone: 610-296-6000 **Fax:** 610-296-2910
Web: www.decisionone.com

DecisionOne has offices in Canada and the US.

PRODUCTS/OPERATIONS

Services

Call center support
Deployment
Logistics
Network support
Planning and consulting
Technical support

COMPETITORS

Affiliated Computer Services
Aquent
CIBER
CHC
Computer Sciences
CTG
Data Systems & Software
EDS
Getronics
IBM
Perot Systems
Sapient
u1.net
Unisys

HISTORICAL FINANCIALS

Company Type: Private

Income Statement FYE: June 30

	REVENUE ($ mil.)	NET INCOME ($ mil.)	NET PROFIT MARGIN	EMPLOYEES
6/02	450	—	—	4,000
6/01	490	—	—	4,000
6/00	528	—	—	4,000
6/99	726	—	—	5,110
6/98	806	—	—	6,500
6/97	786	—	—	6,560
6/96	540	—	—	5,600
6/95	163	—	—	5,900
6/94	108	—	—	—
6/93	114	—	—	—
Annual Growth	16.5%	—	—	(5.4%)

Revenue History

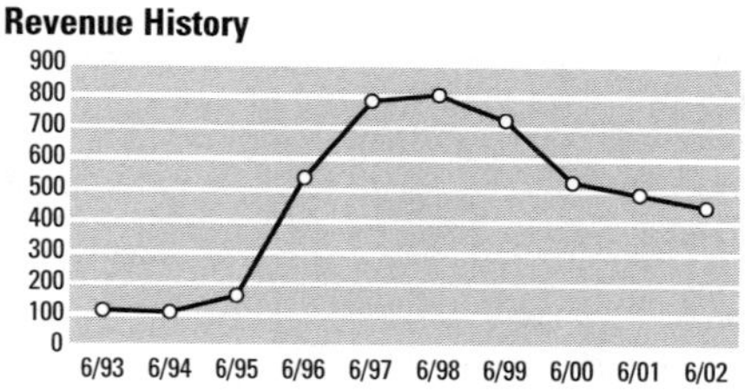

Delaware North Companies, Inc.

When it comes to corn dogs and nachos, Delaware North makes a lot of concessions. A giant in the food concession industry, the company has a string of subsidiaries ready to make hungry folks happy. Among the company's holdings are Sportservice (food service at sports stadiums), CA One Services (airport food service), and Delaware North Parks Services (visitor services for national parks and tourist attractions). It also operates Boston's FleetCenter and owns a handful of pari-mutuel racetracks across the US. Delaware North was founded in 1915 by brothers Charles, Louis, and Marvin Jacobs. The Jacobs family (including CEO Jeremy Jacobs, owner of the NHL's Boston Bruins) still controls the company.

EXECUTIVES

Chairman and CEO: Jeremy M. Jacobs
President and COO: Richard T. Stephens, age 60
EVP: Jeremy Jacobs Jr.
EVP: Louis M. (Lou) Jacobs
VP and CFO: Charles E. (Chuck) Moran Jr.
VP and Controller: Bruce W. Carlson
VP Corporate Communications and Public Relations: Wendy Watkins
VP Finance and Treasurer: Ellen Ott
VP, General Counsel, and Secretary: Bryan J. Keller
VP Human Resources: Eileen Morgan

LOCATIONS

HQ: 40 Fountain Plaza, Buffalo, NY 14202
Phone: 716-858-5000 **Fax:** 716-858-5479
Web: www.delawarenorth.com

Delaware North has operations in Canada, Europe, the Pacific Rim, and the US.

PRODUCTS/OPERATIONS

Selected Operations

American Park 'n Swap (open air markets)
Boston Bruins (pro hockey team)
CA One Services (airport food service operator)
Delaware North Parks Services (visitor services for national parks, state parks, and tourist attractions)
FleetCenter (venue operation)
Sportservice (sports stadium food service)
Sportsystems (pari-mutuel facility operator)
The Delta Queen Steamboat Company (paddlewheel boat trips)

Selected Customers

Austin-Bergstrom International Airport
Boston Celtics
Chicago White Sox
Colonial Stadium (Melbourne)
Grand Canyon
John F. Kennedy International Airport
Kennedy Space Center
Melbourne Zoo
St. Louis Cardinals
Sydney Entertainment Center
Texas Rangers
Yosemite National Park

COMPETITORS

ARAMARK
Centerplate
Compass Group
Creative Host Services
HMSHost
Levy Restaurants
Sodexho Alliance
Sodexho

HISTORICAL FINANCIALS

Company Type: Private

Income Statement FYE: December 31

	REVENUE ($ mil.)	NET INCOME ($ mil.)	NET PROFIT MARGIN	EMPLOYEES
12/02	1,300	—	—	25,000
12/01	1,600	—	—	25,000
12/00	1,500	—	—	25,000
12/99	1,400	—	—	25,000
12/98	1,224	—	—	25,000
12/97	1,200	—	—	25,000
12/96	1,214	—	—	25,000
12/95	1,200	—	—	20,000
12/94	1,165	—	—	20,000
12/93	1,300	—	—	20,000
Annual Growth	0.0%	—	—	2.5%

Revenue History

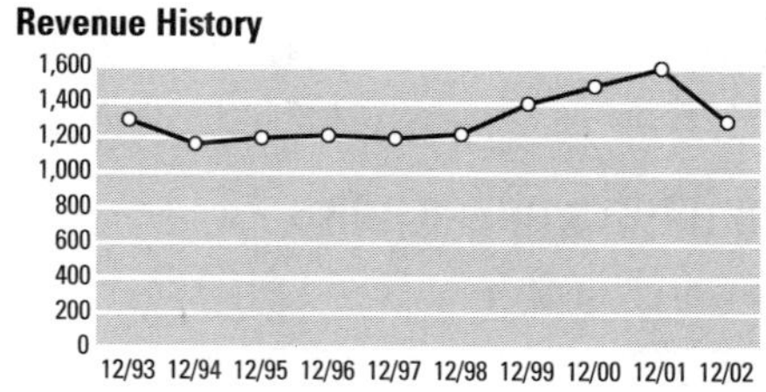

Delco Remy International

Carmakers get cranked up with the help of Delco Remy International, which manufactures and distributes starters and alternators for carmakers and light- and heavy-duty truck makers. The company, which is owned by Citicorp Venture Capital, also remanufactures engines, fuel systems, starters, transmissions, alternators, and torque converters for the automotive aftermarket. Delco's OEM customers include companies such as General Motors, Delphi, Navistar, and Caterpillar; aftermarket customers include O'Reilly, AutoZone, and other automotive parts chains.

Acquisitions boosted Delco Remy's sales, but they failed to do much for the company's stock price, which consistently traded below its IPO price. The company was finally acquired by Citicorp Venture Capital in 2001. Berkshire Hathaway holds about a 20% stake.

EXECUTIVES

Chairman: Harold K. Sperlich, age 73
Vice Chairman: Erwin H. (Bill) Billig, age 76
President, CEO, and Director: Thomas J. Snyder, age 58, $579,100 pay
EVP and CFO: Raj Shah, age 51, $567,700 pay
SVP, Human Resources and Communications: Roderick English, age 51, $302,500 pay
VP and Operations Controller: Allen R. Wilkie, age 52
VP; Managing Director, Europe: Patrick C. Mobouck, age 48
VP, Secretary, and Treasurer: David E. Stoll, age 60
President, Delco Remy America: Richard L. Stanley, age 46, $340,400 pay
President, Aftermarket: Richard L. Keister, age 57, $325,700 pay
SVP Global Operations, Delco Remy America: Matt Mullarkey
SVP Sales and Marketing, Aftermarket Group: Joe Tori
Auditors: Ernst & Young LLP

LOCATIONS

HQ: Delco Remy International, Inc.
2902 Enterprise Dr., Anderson, IN 46013
Phone: 765-778-6499 **Fax:** 765-778-6404
Web: www.delcoremy.com

Delco Remy International has manufacturing facilities in Belgium, Brazil, Canada, Hungary, Mexico, Poland, South Korea, Tunisia, the UK, and the US.

2002 Sales

	$ mil.	% of total
US	915	86
Europe	95	9
Latin America	33	3
Asia Pacific	22	2
Canada	4	—
Total	**1,069**	**100**

PRODUCTS/OPERATIONS

Selected Products

Alternators
Engines
Fuel systems
Starter motors
Torque converters
Traction control systems
Transmissions

COMPETITORS

Champion Parts
Dana
Federal-Mogul
General Parts
Genuine Parts
Hahn Automotive
Mitsubishi Motors
Motorcar Parts
Prestolite Electric
Robert Bosch
Valeo

HISTORICAL FINANCIALS

Company Type: Private

Income Statement FYE: December 31

	REVENUE ($ mil.)	NET INCOME ($ mil.)	NET PROFIT MARGIN	EMPLOYEES
12/02	1,069	(133)	—	6,338
12/01	1,054	(73)	—	7,422
12/00*	443	10	—	7,424
7/00	1,091	12	—	7,707
7/99	954	28	—	6,845
7/98	815	(4)	—	4,833
7/97	690	(14)	—	4,949
7/96	637	(5)	—	3,000
7/95	573	7	—	3,000
7/94	—	—	—	2,800
Annual Growth	8.1%	—	—	9.5%

*Fiscal year change

2002 Year-End Financials

Debt ratio: —
Return on equity: —
Cash ($ mil.): 13
Current ratio: 1.86
Long-term debt ($ mil.): 596

Net Income History

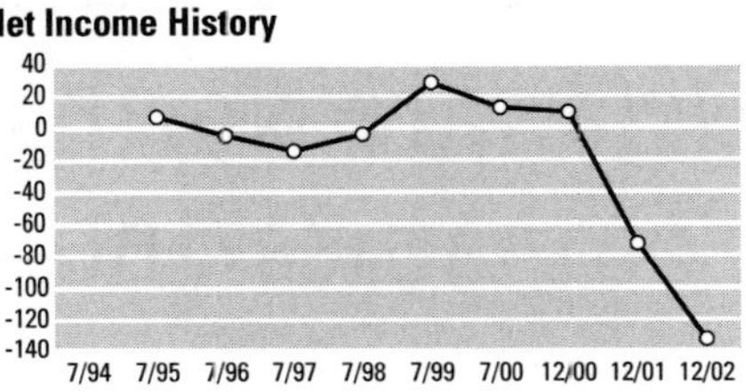

Deloitte Touche Tohmatsu

This company is "deloitted" to make your acquaintance, particularly if you're a big business in need of accounting services. Deloitte Touche Tohmatsu (which now does business simply as Deloitte) is one of accounting's Big Four, along with Ernst & Young, KPMG, and PricewaterhouseCoopers. Deloitte offers traditional audit and fiscal-oversight services to a multinational clientele. It also provides human resources and tax consulting services, as well as services to governments and international lending agencies working in emerging markets. Units include Deloitte & Touche (the US accounting arm) and Deloitte Consulting.

Deloitte spent the 1980s and 1990s pursuing a strategy of using accountants and consultants in concert to provide seamless service in auditing, accounting, strategic planning, information technology, financial management, and productivity. Deloitte Consulting became Deloitte's fastest-growing line, offering strategic and management consulting, in addition to information technology and human resources consulting services.

Increasingly, though, Deloitte and its peers were coming under fire for their combined accounting/consulting operations; regulators and observers wondered whether accountants could maintain objectivity when they were auditing clients for whom they also provided consulting services. Criticism mounted after Enron's collapse capsized Arthur Andersen and put the entire accounting industry under scrutiny. (Deloitte picked up new business and members in Andersen's wake.)

Deloitte in 2002 announced it would spin off its consulting business, becoming the last of the big accountants to do so; a year later it called off the split, citing a weakened market for consulting, among other woes.

HISTORY

In 1845 William Deloitte opened an accounting office in London, at first soliciting business from bankrupts. The growth of joint stock companies and the development of stock markets in the mid-19th century created a need for standardized financial reporting and fueled the rise of auditing, and Deloitte moved into the new field. The Great Western Railway appointed him as its independent auditor (the first anywhere) in 1849.

In 1890 John Griffiths, who had become a partner in 1869, opened the company's first US office in New York City. Four decades later branches had opened throughout the US. In 1952 the firm partnered with Haskins & Sells, which operated 34 US offices.

Deloitte aimed to be "the Cadillac, not the Ford" of accounting. The firm, which became Deloitte Haskins & Sells in 1978, began shedding its conservatism as competition heated up; it was the first of the major accountancy firms to use aggressive ads.

In 1984 Deloitte Haskins & Sells tried to merge with Price Waterhouse, but the agreement fell through after Price Waterhouse's partners in the UK objected.

In 1989 Deloitte Haskins & Sells joined the flamboyant Touche Ross (founded 1899) to become Deloitte & Touche. Touche Ross's Japanese affiliate, Ross Tohmatsu (founded 1968) rounded out the current name. The merger was engineered by Deloitte's Michael Cook and Touche's Edward Kangas, in part to unite the former firm's US and European strengths with the latter's Asian presence. Cook continued to oversee US operations, with Kangas presiding over international operations. Many affiliates, particularly in the UK, rejected the merger and defected to competing firms.

As auditors were increasingly held accountable for the financial results of their clients, legal action soared. In the 1990s Deloitte was sued because of its actions relating to Drexel Burnham Lambert junk bond king Michael Milken, the failure of several savings and loans, and clients' bankruptcies.

Nevertheless, in 1995 the SEC chose Michael Sutton, the firm's national director of auditing and accounting practice, as its chief accountant. That year Deloitte formed Deloitte & Touche Consulting to consolidate its US and UK consulting operations; its Asian consulting operations were later added to facilitate regional expansion.

In 1996 the firm formed a corporate fraud unit (with special emphasis on the Internet) and bought PHH Fantus, the leading corporate relocation consulting company. The next year Deloitte and Thurston Group (a Chicago-based merchant bank) teamed up to form NetDox, a system for delivering legal, financial, and insurance documents via the Internet. In 1997, amid a new round of industry mergers, rumors swirled that a Deloitte and Ernst & Young union had been scrapped because the firms could not agree on ownership issues. Deloitte disavowed plans to merge and launched an ad campaign directly targeted against its rivals.

The Asian economic crisis hurt overseas expansion in 1998, but provided a boost in restructuring consulting. In 1999 the firm sold its accounting staffing service unit (Resources Connection) to its managers and Evercore Partners, citing possible conflicts of interest with its core audit business. Also that year Kangas (now chairman emeritus) stepped down as CEO to be succeeded by James Copeland, and Deloitte Consulting decided to sell its computer programming subsidiary to CGI Group.

In 2001 the SEC forced Deloitte & Touche to restate the financial results of Pre-Paid Legal Services. In an unusual move, Deloitte & Touche publicly disagreed with the SEC's findings.

The accountancy put some old trouble to bed in 2003 when it agreed to pay $23 million to settle claims it had been negligent in its auditing of failed Kentucky Life Insurance, a client in the 1980s. Later that year the UK's High Court found Deloitte negligent in audits related to the failed Barings Bank; however, the ruling was considered something of a victory for the accountancy because it essentially cleared Deloitte of the majority of charges against it and effectively limited its financial liability in the matter. Copeland retired from the global CEO's office that year and handed the reins over to Bill Parrett, who had formerly served as managing director for the US and the Americas.

EXECUTIVES

Chairman: Piet Hoogendoorn
CEO; Senior Partner, US: William G. (Bill) Parrett, age 57
CFO and Managing Partner, Global Office: William A. Fowler
CIO: Wolfgang Richter
Global Managing Partner, Reputation, Excellence, and Practice Protection; Managing Partner, Netherlands: Willy A. Biewinga
Global Managing Partner, Innovation and Investment; Managing Partner, Germany and Regional Managing Partner, Europe/Middle East/Africa: Wolfgang Grewe
Global Managing Partner, Client Service Excellence; Tohmatsu Representative to DTT, and Regional Managing Partner, Japan: Shuichiro Sekine
Global Managing Partner, Brand and Eminence; Chief Executive and Managing Managing Partner, Canada and Regional Managing Partner, North America: Colin Taylor
Global Managing Partner, Intellectual Capital, Inclusion, and Development; Chief Executive, France: Philippe Vassor
Global Managing Partner, Financial Advisory Services: Ralph G. Adams
Global Managing Partner, Audit: Stephen Almond
Global Managing Partner, Regulation and Risk: Jeffrey K. (Jeff) Willemain
CEO, Deloitte Consulting: Paul Robinson, age 50
Chairman, Deloitte & Touche LLP: Sharon L. Allen, age 51
CEO, Deloitte & Touche LLP: James H. (Jim) Quigley, age 50
Global Managing Partner, Clients & Markets: Jerry Leamon
Global Managing Partner, Tax & Legal Services: Alan Schneier
Global Managing Partner, Human Resources: Conrad Venter
General Counsel: Joseph J. Lambert

LOCATIONS

HQ: 1633 Broadway, New York, NY 10019
Phone: 212-489-1600 **Fax:** 212-492-4154
Web: www.deloitte.com

Deloitte Touche Tohmatsu operates through about 700 offices in nearly 150 countries.

PRODUCTS/OPERATIONS

Selected Services

Accounting and auditing
Corporate finance
Emerging markets consulting
Forensic services
Human resources, actuarial, insurance, and managed care consulting
Legal services
Management consulting
Outsourcing
Reorganization services
Risk management
Tax advice and planning
Transaction services

Selected Industry Specializations

Aviation and transport services
Banking and securities
Consumer products
Consumer services
Gas and oil
Insurance
Investment management
Manufacturing
Mining
Retail/wholesale and distribution
Technology, media, and telecommunications
Utilities

COMPETITORS

Accenture
BDO International
Booz Allen
Boston Consulting
Cap Gemini
EDS
Ernst & Young
Grant Thornton International
H&R Block
KPMG
Marsh & McLennan
McKinsey & Company
PricewaterhouseCoopers
Towers Perrin
Watson Wyatt

HISTORICAL FINANCIALS

Company Type: Partnership

Income Statement FYE: May 31

	REVENUE ($ mil.)	NET INCOME ($ mil.)	NET PROFIT MARGIN	EMPLOYEES
5/03	15,100	—	—	119,237
5/02	12,500	—	—	98,000
5/01	12,400	—	—	95,000
5/00*	11,200	—	—	90,000
8/99	10,600	—	—	90,000
8/98	9,000	—	—	82,000
8/97	7,400	—	—	65,000
8/96	6,500	—	—	63,440
8/95	5,950	—	—	59,000
8/94	5,200	—	—	56,600
Annual Growth	12.6%	—	—	8.6%

*Fiscal year change

Revenue History

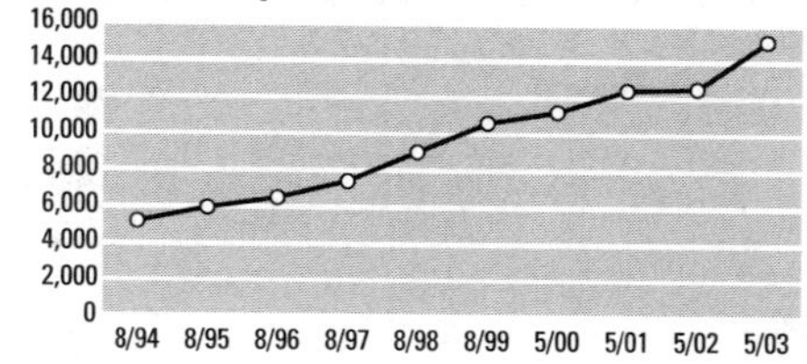

Delta Dental

Delta Dental Plan of California doesn't just help keep the mouths of movie stars clean. A not-for-profit organization, the company is a member of the Delta Dental Plans Association and has affiliates nationwide. Delta Dental provides dental coverage through HMOs, preferred provider plans (PPOs), and such government programs as California's Denti-Cal. The company serves some 17 million enrollees in California; its programs cover more than one-third of California residents. Together with Delta Dental of Pennsylvania, Delta Dental of California formed Dentegra Group, a holding company that serves nearly 20 million members throughout the US.

EXECUTIVES

President and CEO: Gary D. Radine, age 54
CFO: Elizabeth Russell
SVP and Chief Administrative Officer: Jerry Holcombe
SVP and General Manager, California Commercial Business Unit: Anthony S. Barth, age 40
SVP and CIO: Martin Whelan
SVP, Government Programs: Michael Kaufmann
SVP, Professional Services: Marilyn Belek
SVP, Health Care Affiliates: Robert B. Elliot
Director, Human Resources: Teri Forestieri
COO, Delta Dental of Pennsylvania: Thomas Toons, age 40
COO, Delta Dental Insurance; SVP and COO, PMI Dental Health Plan: Belinda Martinez, age 38

LOCATIONS

HQ: Delta Dental Plan of California
100 1st St., San Francisco, CA 94105
Phone: 415-972-8300 **Fax:** 415-972-8466
Web: www.deltadentalca.org

PRODUCTS/OPERATIONS

Selected Products

DeltaCare (dental plans for groups in more than one state)
DeltaCare USA (group and individual dental HMOs)
DeltaVision (group vision HMO)

COMPETITORS

Aetna
CIGNA
Health Net
MetLife
PacifiCare
SafeGuard Health Enterprises
WellPoint Health Networks

HISTORICAL FINANCIALS

Company Type: Not-for-profit

Income Statement FYE: December 31

	REVENUE ($ mil.)	NET INCOME ($ mil.)	NET PROFIT MARGIN	EMPLOYEES
12/02	4,000	—	—	2,500
12/01	3,300	—	—	2,400
12/00	2,800	—	—	2,400
12/99	2,700	—	—	2,400
12/98	2,440	—	—	2,400
12/97	2,315	—	—	2,115
12/96	2,114	—	—	1,960
12/95	2,145	—	—	1,800
12/94	2,025	—	—	1,649
12/93	1,792	—	—	—
Annual Growth	9.3%	—	—	5.3%

Revenue History

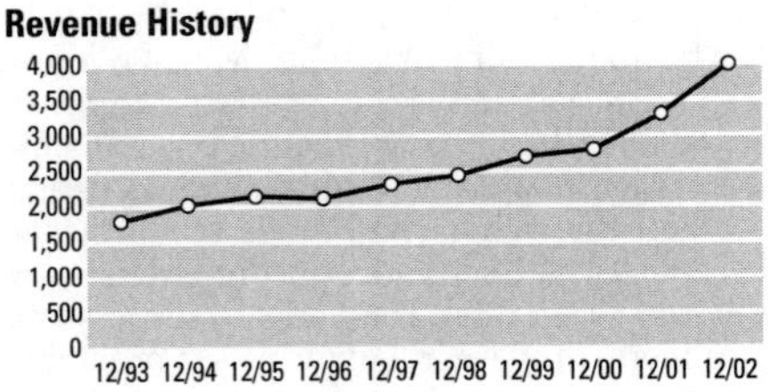

Demoulas Super Markets Inc.

Supermarket or soap opera? Demoulas Super Markets runs nearly 60 grocery stores under the Market Basket and Demoulas Super Market names in Massachusetts and New Hampshire. The firm also has real estate interests. The company was founded in 1954 when brothers George and Mike Demoulas bought their parents' mom-and-pop grocery. The men agreed that, upon one brother's death, the other would care for the deceased's family and maintain the firm's 50-50 ownership. In 1990 George's family alleged that Mike had defrauded them of all but 8% of the company's stock; the 10-year court battle was decided in favor of George's family, giving it 51% of the company. By then Mike had resigned as CEO; the post remains vacant.

EXECUTIVES

EVP: Julien Lacourse
EVP: James Miamis
VP of Finance, Treasurer: Donald Mulligan
VP, Grocery Sales and Merchandising: Joseph Rockwell
VP, Real Estate: Michael Kettenbach
Corporate Counsel: Sumner Darman
Payroll Administrator: Lucille Lopez

LOCATIONS

HQ: 875 East St., Tewksbury, MA 01876
Phone: 978-851-8000 **Fax:** 978-640-8390

COMPETITORS

Big Y Foods
BJs Wholesale Club
Costco Wholesale
Cumberland Farms
Golub
Hannaford Bros.
IGA
Shaw's
Stop & Shop
SUPERVALU
Wal-Mart

HISTORICAL FINANCIALS

Company Type: Private

Income Statement FYE: December 31

	ESTIMATED REVENUE ($ mil.)	NET INCOME ($ mil.)	NET PROFIT MARGIN	EMPLOYEES
12/02	1,900	—	—	12,700
12/01	2,000	—	—	12,700
12/00	1,800	—	—	12,500
12/99	1,800	—	—	12,500
12/98	1,700	—	—	12,350
12/97	1,850	—	—	12,300
12/96	1,760	—	—	11,900
12/95	1,650	—	—	11,700
12/94	1,338	—	—	10,000
12/93	1,200	—	—	—
Annual Growth	5.2%	—	—	3.0%

Revenue History

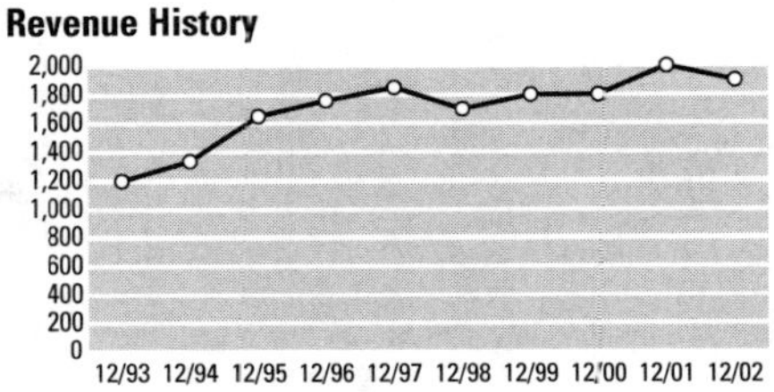

Deseret Management Corporation

While the Church of Jesus Christ of Latter-day Saints handles the spiritual, Deseret Management takes care of the worldly. The holding company oversees a portfolio of for-profit ventures for the Mormon Church, including about 20 radio stations, several TV stations, and Salt Lake City's *Deseret News* newspaper. Its Deseret Book Company publishes primarily inspirational books under four imprints and operates a chain of more than 30 book stores in about a dozen states. Deseret also houses life insurance, hotel and restaurant management, and property management services. Founded in 1932, Deseret Management does not accept advertising for alcohol or other goods objectionable to the church.

EXECUTIVES

President and CEO: Rodney H. Brady, age 69
VP and Controller: Dale G. Bailey
VP Administration: Roland A. Radack
VP Tax and Treasurer: Scott C. Florence
CIO: Stephen J. Tolman
Director of Audit: Ivan R. Briggs
General Counsel and Secretary: Robert W. Edwards

LOCATIONS

HQ: 60 E. South Temple, Ste. 575, Salt Lake City, UT 84111
Phone: 801-538-0651 **Fax:** 801-538-0655
Web: www.deseretmanagement.com

Selected Broadcasting Markets

Chicago
Salt Lake City
San Francisco
St. Louis, MO
Washington, DC

PRODUCTS/OPERATIONS

Selected Operations

Broadcasting
Bonneville Communications (media services for not-for-profit organizations)
Bonneville International Corp.
Bonneville International Radio Network
Bonneville Satellite
Video West Productions

Financial Services
Beneficial Life Insurance, Inc.
Zion Securities Corp.

Publishing
Deseret Book Company
Deseret News *(Salt Lake City)*

Real Estate
Hawaii Reserves
Hotel Temple Square

COMPETITORS

Amazon.com
Barnes & Noble
Borders
Christian Science Publishing
Clear Channel
Cox Enterprises
Family Christian Stores
Gospel Communications International
Infinity Broadcasting
Integrity Media
Nightingale-Conant
R. B. Pamplin
Reader's Digest
Salem Communications
Standex
Thomas Nelson

HISTORICAL FINANCIALS

Company Type: Private

Income Statement FYE: December 31

	ESTIMATED REVENUE ($ mil.)	NET INCOME ($ mil.)	NET PROFIT MARGIN	EMPLOYEES
12/01	800	—	—	3,200
12/00	780	—	—	3,100
12/99	665	—	—	3,000
12/98	715	—	—	3,000
12/97	725	—	—	3,000
12/96	600	—	—	3,000
12/95	700	—	—	3,000
12/94	630	—	—	3,000
12/93	615	—	—	3,000
Annual Growth	3.3%	—	—	0.8%

Revenue History

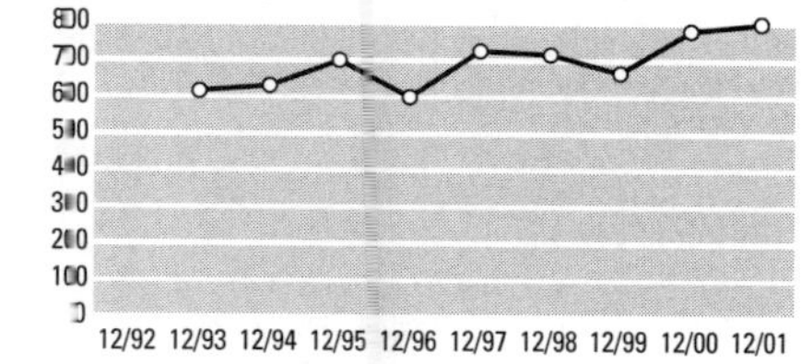

Devcon Construction

The dot-com deathwatch hasn't stopped Devcon Construction — it's still riding the coattails of Silicon Valley's business boom. One of the area's top general building contractors, Devcon has constructed more than 35 million sq. ft. of office, industrial, and commercial space in Northern California. Founded in 1976, Devcon specializes in high-tech projects, including industrial research and development facilities for clients such as Cisco Systems and Silicon Graphics. Devcon also provides engineering, design/build, and interior design services. In addition to building company facilities and offices, Devcon works on projects such as hotels, restaurants retail stores, and schools.

EXECUTIVES

President: Gary Filizetti
VP Architecture and Secretary: Barry L. Ludwig
Controller: Bret Sisney
CIO: Jeremy Holland
Safety Officer: Ken Sullivan
Human Resources/Payroll Accountant: Jennifer Cooke

LOCATIONS

HQ: Devcon Construction Incorporated
690 Gibraltar Dr., Milpitas, CA 95035
Phone: 408-942-8200 **Fax:** 408-262-2342
Web: www.devcon-const.com

Devcon Construction has offices in Milpitas and Santa Cruz, California, and operates primarily in the San Francisco Bay Area and Silicon Valley.

COMPETITORS

Charles Pankow Builders
DPR Construction
Hathaway Dinwiddie Construction
Hensel Phelps Construction
Obayashi
Rudolph & Sletten
Swinerton
Turner Corporation
Webcor Builders

HISTORICAL FINANCIALS

Company Type: Private

Income Statement FYE: March 31

	REVENUE ($ mil.)	NET INCOME ($ mil.)	NET PROFIT MARGIN	EMPLOYEES
3/02	520	—	—	600
3/01	1,351	—	—	550
3/00	1,300	—	—	600
3/99	780	—	—	600
3/98	560	—	—	500
3/97	443	—	—	400
Annual Growth	3.3%	—	—	8.4%

Revenue History

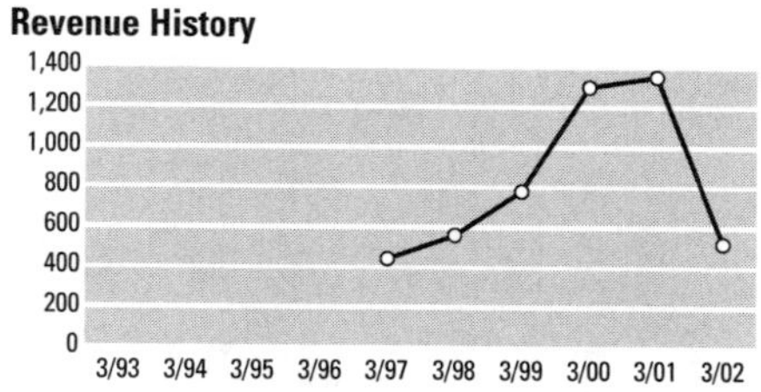

Di Giorgio Corporation

Di Giorgio delivers little apples (and other foods) to the Big Apple. Founded in 1920, the firm is a food wholesaler and distributor primarily in New York City, Long Island, New Jersey, and the greater Philadelphia area. It offers more than 18,000 products to food retailers ranging from independents and members of co-ops to regional chains. (A&P accounts for 25% of sales.) Although Di Giorgio distributes national brands, it also supplies frozen and refrigerated products under its White Rose brand, a name known in New York for well over a century. Di Giorgio co-chairman and CEO Richard Neff owns approximately 99% of the company, primarily through his sole general partnership in Rose Partners.

EXECUTIVES

Co-Chairman and CEO: Richard B. Neff, age 54, $950,000 pay
Co-Chairman, President, and COO: Stephen R. Bokser, age 60, $950,000 pay
SVP and CFO: Lawrence S. (Larry) Grossman, $292,000 pay
EVP, Finance and Treasurer: Robert A. Zorn, age 48, $330,600 pay
SVP, Distribution: Joseph R. DeSimone, age 63
SVP and General Manager, White Rose Dairy Division: Joseph Fantozzi, age 41, $298,000 pay
SVP and General Manager, White Rose Frozen: John Annetta, age 51
SVP: John J. Zumba, age 65
VP, General Counsel, and Secretary: Harlan Levine, age 41
Assistant VP, Human Resources: Jackie Simmons
Auditors: Deloitte & Touche LLP

LOCATIONS

HQ: 380 Middlesex Ave., Carteret, NJ 07008
Phone: 732-541-5555 **Fax:** 732-541-3590
Web: www.whiterose.com

PRODUCTS/OPERATIONS

Selected Customers

A&P
Associated Foods Stores
Bravo
C-Town
Food Basics
Food Emporium
Foodtown
Grande (Puerto Rico)
Gristede's Foods
King Kullen
Kings Super Markets
Met
Pioneer
Quick Chek
Scaturros
Sloans Supermarkets
Super Food
Superfresh
Waldbaums
Western Beef

COMPETITORS

Associated Wholesalers
Bozzuto's
C&S Wholesale
Fleming Companies
General Trading
Key Food
Krasdale Foods
Richfood
SGA Sales & Mktg
SUPERVALU
Topco Associates
Wakefern Food

HISTORICAL FINANCIALS

Company Type: Private

Income Statement FYE: Saturday nearest December 31

	REVENUE ($ mil.)	NET INCOME ($ mil.)	NET PROFIT MARGIN	EMPLOYEES
12/02	1,560	13	0.8%	1,288
12/01	1,539	12	0.8%	1,353
12/00	1,488	11	0.7%	1,373
12/99	1,414	10	0.7%	1,275
12/98	1,197	4	0.4%	1,229
12/97	1,072	(3)	—	1,156
12/96	1,050	5	0.5%	1,123
12/95	1,020	0	—	1,135
12/94	934	(1)	—	1,305
12/93	772	4	0.5%	600
Annual Growth	8.1%	14.8%	—	8.9%

2002 Year-End Financials

Debt ratio: 533.3%
Return on equity: 53.7%
Cash ($ mil.): 1
Current ratio: 1.67
Long-term debt ($ mil.): 150

Net Income History

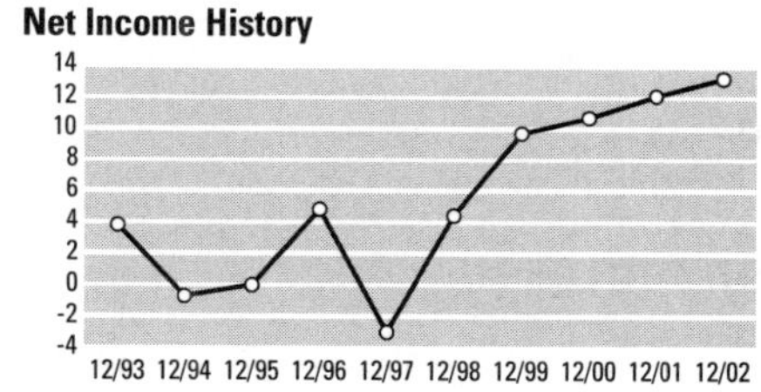

Dick Corporation

Without any help from Tom or Harry, Dick Corp., a general contracting, construction, and construction management firm, builds commercial, institutional, power, industrial, bridge, and highway structures. Some of its landmark projects include PNC Park, home of the Pittsburgh Pirates, and the preservation of Fallingwater, a home designed by Frank Lloyd Wright. Current projects include contracts to help construct a military complex at the Navy base at Guantanamo Bay. The firm founded by Noble Dick in 1922 is still owned by his descendants, including co-chairmen Douglas and David Dick.

EXECUTIVES

Co-Chairman: Douglas E. Dick
Co-Chairman: David E. Dick
President: Stephen (Steve) D'Angelo
CFO: John G. Borman
SVP, Corporate Counsel, and Secretary: Roger J. Peters
SVP; President, National Building Operations: Don F. Cooper
SVP; President, Construction Management Operations: Frank J. Cservak
SVP; President, Bridge and Highway Operations: John J. Stanich
SVP Strategic Planning: Ellsworth F. Vines
SVP Human Resources: Janet A. Love
Corporate Communications: David Rearick
Auditors: Deloitte & Touche LLP

LOCATIONS

HQ: 1900 State Rt. 51, Large, PA 15236
Phone: 412-384-1000 **Fax:** 412-384-1150
Web: www.dickcorp.com

Dick Corporation has offices in the metro areas of Chicago; Fairbanks, Alaska; Honolulu; Las Vegas; Pittsburgh (Large, Pennsylvania); and Washington, DC. It also has offices in Barrigada, Guam, and San Juan, Puerto Rico.

PRODUCTS/OPERATIONS

Divisions

Building
Construction management
Dick Carribbean
Dick Pacific
Heavy/industrial

COMPETITORS

BE&K
Bechtel
Beck Group
Black & Veatch
Brown and Caldwell
CH2M HILL
Choate Construction
Devcon International
Duke/Fluor Daniel
Dyckerhoff & Widmann
Embree Construction
Fluor
Foster Wheeler
Gilbane
Granite Construction
Graycor
Hardin Construction
Hensel Phelps Construction
HBG
Impregilo
Jacobs Engineering
Louis Berger
Malcolm Pirnie
Michael Baker
MWH Global
Parsons
Peter Kiewit Sons'
Philipp Holzmann
Raytheon
TIC Holdings
Turner Corporation
Tutor-Saliba
URS
Washington Group
Zachry

HISTORICAL FINANCIALS

Company Type: Private

Income Statement FYE: December 31

	ESTIMATED REVENUE ($ mil.)	NET INCOME ($ mil.)	NET PROFIT MARGIN	EMPLOYEES
12/02	1,100	—	—	3,500
12/01	1,100	—	—	3,500
12/00	1,050	—	—	3,000
12/99	689	—	—	5,000
12/98	550	—	—	5,000
12/97	540	—	—	5,000
12/96	550	—	—	5,000
12/95	450	—	—	5,000
12/94	500	—	—	3,000
12/93	450	—	—	3,000
Annual Growth	10.4%	—	—	1.7%

Revenue History

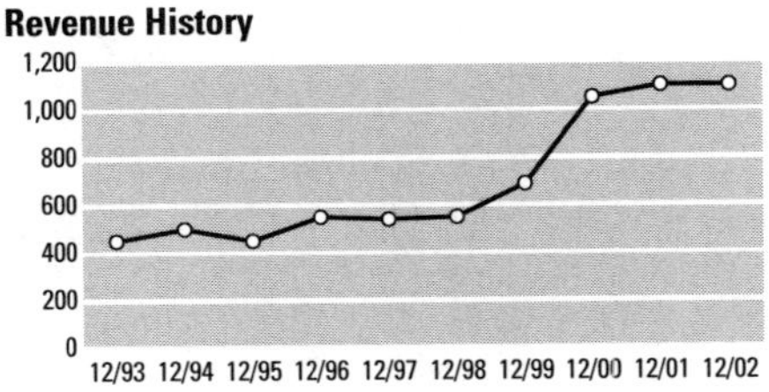

Dierbergs Markets Inc.

Dierbergs Markets has a taste of what folks in St. Louis like to eat. Dierbergs operates nearly 20 upscale supermarkets in the St. Louis area, where rival Schnuck Markets is the market leader. Dierbergs' stores offer food, drugs, photo processing, video centers, as well as cooking schools, banks, self-service checkout, Krispy Kreme donuts, and made-to-order Chinese food at some locations. Dierbergs Florist and Gifts, affiliated with FTD, offers gift baskets and floral services at its stores and over the Internet for local and international delivery. Founded as a trading outpost in 1854, the Dierberg family has owned and operated Dierbergs since 1914.

EXECUTIVES

Chairman, President and CEO: Robert J. (Bob) Dierberg
Vice Chairman: Roger Dierberg
EVP: Greg Dierberg
VP, CFO: Connie Holley
VP, Human Resources: Linda Ryan
Controller: Laura Schneider
Director, Information Technology: Robert Sanabria

LOCATIONS

HQ: 16690 Swingley Ridge Rd., Chesterfield, MO 63017
Phone: 636-532-8884 **Fax:** 636-532-8759
Web: www.dierbergs.com

COMPETITORS

7-Eleven
ALDI
AWG
IGA
Kmart
Kroger
Schnuck Markets
SUPERVALU
Walgreen
Wal-Mart

HISTORICAL FINANCIALS

Company Type: Private

Income Statement FYE: December 31

	ESTIMATED REVENUE ($ mil.)	NET INCOME ($ mil.)	NET PROFIT MARGIN	EMPLOYEES
12/01	550	—	—	4,300
12/00	525	—	—	4,300
12/99	500	—	—	4,230
12/98	450	—	—	4,200
12/97	475	—	—	4,134
12/96	446	—	—	4,300
Annual Growth	4.3%	—	—	0.0%

Revenue History

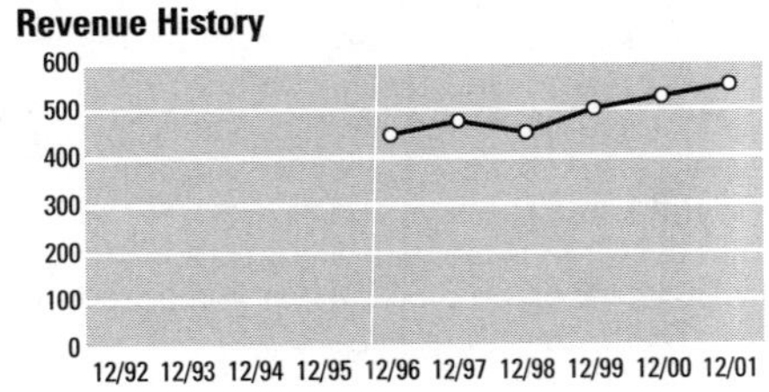

Discount Drug Mart Inc.

Drugs are just part of the story at Discount Drug Mart. One of the largest drugstore chains in northeastern Ohio, primarily in the Cleveland area, the company offers pharmacy services, nonprescription medications, and medical supplies, as well as food, housewares, beauty products, video rentals, photo developing, stamps, pet supplies, hardware, and more. Its 60 stores offer, on average, 25,000 sq. ft. of selling space, about twice the size of rival drugstores. Discount Drug also runs mail-order and online prescription services through subsidiary Immediate Pharmaceutical Services. The company is expanding into central Ohio. Chairman and CEO Parviz Boodjeh owns Discount Drug, which was founded in 1970.

EXECUTIVES

Chairman and CEO: Parviz Boodjeh
Co-COO: Donald Boodjeh
Co-COO: John Wright
SVP and CFO: Thomas McConnell
SVP Marketing: David Baytosh
VP Human Resources: Michael Eby
VP Pharmacy: Pete Ratcyz

President, Retail Division: John Gans
Treasurer, Chief Administrative Officer: Douglas Boodjeh
Auditors: Grant Thornton

LOCATIONS

HQ: 211 Commerce Dr., Medina, OH 44256
Phone: 330-725-2340 **Fax:** 330-722-2990
Web: www.discount-drugmart.com

COMPETITORS

Ahold USA
Costco Wholesale
CVS
Giant Eagle
Kmart
Marc Glassman
Rite Aid
Snyder's Drug Stores
Target
Walgreen
Wal-Mart

HISTORICAL FINANCIALS

Company Type: Private

Income Statement FYE: March 31

	REVENUE ($ mil.)	NET INCOME ($ mil.)	NET PROFIT MARGIN	EMPLOYEES
3/03	525	—	—	2,450
3/02	480	—	—	2,300
3/01	442	—	—	2,100
3/00	400	—	—	2,100
3/99	400	—	—	2,100
3/98	327	—	—	1,250
Annual Growth	9.9%	—	—	14.4%

Revenue History

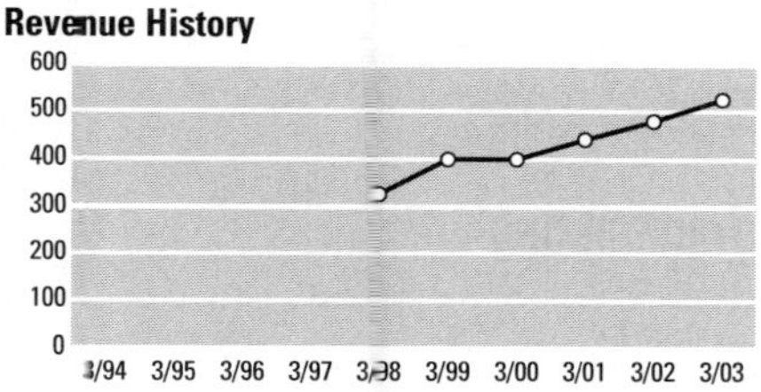

Discount Tire Co.

Concerned about that upcoming "re-tirement"? Discount Tire Co., one of the largest independent tire dealers in the US, can provide several options. With more than 500 stores in some 20 states, the company sells leading brands (Michelin, Goodyear, Uniroyal) and private-label tires, as well as wheels and suspension products. Discount Tire operates mostly in the Midwest and Southwest and fixes flat tires for free, regardless of where they were bought. Some of the company's West Coast stores operate as America's Tire Co. because of a name conflict. Discount Tire also sells tires online through Discount Tire Direct. Owner Bruce Halle founded the company in 1960 with six tires — four of them recaps.

EXECUTIVES

CEO: Gary T. Van Brunt
CFO: Christian Roe
EVP of Finance and Administration: Bob Holman
Director of Human Resources: Staci Adams

LOCATIONS

HQ: 20225 N. Scottsdale Rd., Scottsdale, AZ 85255
Phone: 480-606-6000 **Fax:** 480-606-4401
Web: www.discounttire.com

Discount Tire Co. and America's Tire Co. have stores in Arizona, California, Colorado, Florida, Georgia, Illinois, Indiana, Michigan, Minnesota, Nevada, New Mexico, North Carolina, Ohio, Oregon, South Carolina, Texas, Utah, Virginia, and Washington.

COMPETITORS

Les Schwab Tire Centers
Penske
Pep Boys
Sears
TBC
Tire Centers
Wal-Mart

HISTORICAL FINANCIALS

Company Type: Private

Income Statement FYE: December 31

	REVENUE ($ mil.)	NET INCOME ($ mil.)	NET PROFIT MARGIN	EMPLOYEES
12/01	1,320	—	—	8,415
12/00	1,192	—	—	8,987
12/99	1,031	—	—	8,100
12/98	900	—	—	6,500
12/97	864	—	—	6,200
12/96	739	—	—	5,154
12/95	658	—	—	4,714
12/94	590	—	—	4,200
Annual Growth	12.2%	—	—	10.4%

Revenue History

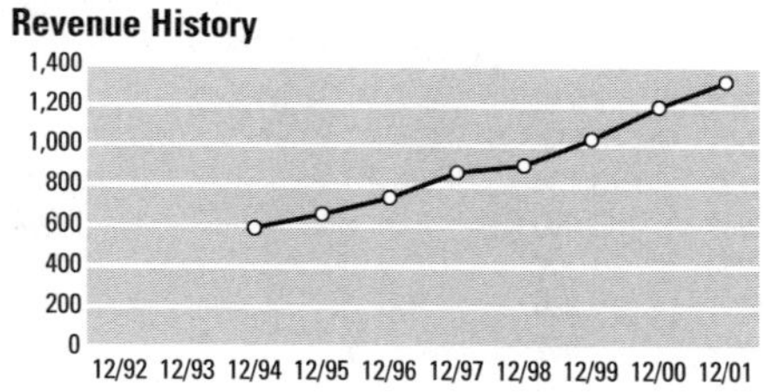

Discovery Communications

Discover science and nature in the comfort of your living room with Discovery Communications (DCI). Reaching more than 85 million households, its Discovery Channel is one of the top-rated cable networks in the US. DCI owns other cable networks as well, including The Learning Channel (with its popular *Trading Spaces* program), Travel Channel, and Animal Planet. DCI also operates Discovery Channel retail stores, and its Internet unit, Discovery.com, houses various nature and science Web sites. Liberty Media Corp. (49%), Cox Communications (25%), and Advance/Newhouse Communications (25%) own DCI.

The company also operates five digital Discovery cable channels focused on specific topics such as science and home and health. In a joint venture, Discovery and The New York Times Company have launched the news-oriented Discovery Times Channel, which will take the place of the Discovery Civilization Channel. The company also launched a new digital cable network called Discovery HD Theater, which features high-definition quality television.

Building on its name brand, DCI creates original programming, games, and activities for a series of science and nature Web sites under the Discovery.com name and publishes videos, books, and CD-ROMs. It also operates about 170 Discovery Channel retail stores.

Speculation about whether DCI would be acquired has made headlines in recent times, but CEO and founder John Hendricks has denied all reports of a sale.

HISTORY

John Hendricks, a history graduate who wanted to expand the presence of educational programming on TV, founded Cable Educational Network in 1982. Three years later he introduced the Discovery Channel. Devoted entirely to documentaries and nature shows, the channel premiered in 156,000 US homes. After dodging bankruptcy (it had $5,000 cash and $1 million in debt to the BBC), within a year the Discovery Channel had 7 million subscribers and a host of new investors, including Cox Cable Communications and TCI (now AT&T Broadband). It expanded its programming from 12 hours to 18 hours a day in 1987.

Discovery continued to attract subscribers, reaching more than 32 million by 1988. The next year it launched Discovery Channel Europe to more than 200,000 homes in the UK and Scandinavia. The company began selling home videos in 1990 and entered the Israeli market. The following year Discovery Communications, Inc. (DCI) was formed to house the company's operations, and it bought The Learning Channel (TLC, founded in 1980). The company revamped TLC's programming, and in 1992 introduced a daily, six-hour, commercial-free block of children's programs. The next year it introduced its first CD-ROM title, *In the Company of Whales,* based on the Discovery Channel documentary.

DCI increased its focus on international expansion in 1994, moving into Asia, Latin America, the Middle East, North Africa, Portugal, and Spain. The next year the company introduced its Web site and began selling company merchandise such as CD-ROMs and videos. DCI solidified its move into the retail sector in 1996 with the acquisition of The Nature Company and Scientific Revolution chains (renamed Discovery Channel Store). Also that year it launched its third major cable channel, Animal Planet.

The company continued expanding internationally throughout the mid-1990s, establishing operations in Australia, Canada, India, New Zealand, and South Korea (1995); Africa, Brazil, Germany, and Italy (1996); and Japan and Turkey (1997). DCI also added to its stable of cable channels with the purchase of 70% of Paxson Communications' Travel Channel in 1997 (it acquired the rest in 1999). The company's 1997 original production "Titanic: Anatomy of a Disaster" attracted 3.2 million US households, setting a network ratings record.

The following year DCI and the British Broadcasting Corporation launched Animal Planet in Asia through a joint venture and agreed to market and distribute new cable channel BBC America. It also bought CBS's Eye on People, renaming the channel Discovery People (DCI shut the channel down in 2000). DCI spent $330 million launching its new health and fitness channel, Discovery Health, in 1999 and formed partnerships with high-speed online service Road Runner (to provide interactive information and services to Road Runner customers) and Rosenbluth Travel (to provide vacation packages based on DCI programming).

DCI reorganized its Internet activities into one unit called Discovery.com in 2000 with plans to eventually take it public. Later that year the Discovery Channel set back-to-back records with the two highest-rated documentaries ever on cable, "Raising the Mammoth" (10.1 million people) and "Walking With Dinosaurs" (10.7 million people). In 2001 the company cut about 50 jobs as part of a restructuring. Later that year Discovery Communications struck a three-year deal to lease time from NBC on Saturday mornings (paying $6 million per season) to show its Discovery Kids programs.

In 2002 the company launched a 24-hour high-definition television network called Discovery HD Theater.

EXECUTIVES

Chairman and CEO, Discovery Communications and Discovery.com: John S. Hendricks, age 50
President and COO: Judith A. McHale, age 56
CFO: Barbara (Barb) Bennett
EVP Advertising Sales: Scott McGraw
EVP Corporate Operations and General Counsel: Mark Hollinger
EVP Human Resources and Administration: Pandit Wright
EVP Research and Planning: Daniel Fischer
EVP Strategy & Development: Donald A. Baer
EVP and General Manager, Travel Channel: Rick Rodriguez
President, Discovery Networks, US: William M. (Billy) Campbell III
President, Discovery Consumer Products: Michela A. English, age 52
President, Ad Sales: Joe Abruzzese
President, Discovery Networks International: Dawn L. McCall
SVP and Chief Information Officer, Technology: Diane Duggan
SVP and General Manager, Discovery Digital Networks: David Karp
SVP and General Manager, Discovery HD Theater: Clint Stinchcomb
SVP and General Manager, Discovery Times Channel: Vivian Schiller
SVP; Division CFO, Discovery Networks International: Nathan Fong
SVP Marketing Resources, New York: Beth Rockwood
SVP National Advertising Sales: Ben Price
SVP National Advertiser Sales: Evan Sternschein
SVP Production, Operations & Engineering, Discovery Channel: Jay Schneider

LOCATIONS

HQ: Discovery Communications, Inc.
1 Discovery Place, Silver Spring, MD 20910
Phone: 240-662-0000 **Fax:** 301-771-4064
Web: www.discovery.com

PRODUCTS/OPERATIONS

Selected Operations

Discovery Consumer Products
- Discovery Channel Catalog (product catalog)
- Discovery Channel School (educational programs)
- Discovery Channel Stores (approximately 170 Discovery Channel retail outlets)
- Disovery.com (online store)

Discovery HD Theater (digital channel featuring high-definition TV programming)
Discovery Networks International (32 languages, 154 countries)
Discovery Networks US
- Animal Planet (78 million households)
- BBC America (27 million households, markets and distributes for the BBC)
- Discovery Channel (85 million)
- Discovery en Español (digital)
- Discovery Health Channel (40 million)
- Discovery Home & Leisure Channel (digital, joint venture with The New York Times Company)
- Discovery Times Channel (digital)
- Discovery Wings Channel (digital)
- The Learning Channel (83 million)
- The Science Channel (digital)
- Travel Channel (64 million)

COMPETITORS

A&E Networks
CPB
Crown Media
E. W. Scripps
F.A.O.
Lifetime
NBC
National Geographic
News Corp.
Oxygen Media
PBS
Space Holdings
Time Warner
Univision
Viacom
Walt Disney

HISTORICAL FINANCIALS

Company Type: Joint venture

Income Statement FYE: December 31

	REVENUE ($ mil.)	NET INCOME ($ mil.)	NET PROFIT MARGIN	EMPLOYEES
12/02	1,710	—	—	5,000
12/01	1,800	—	—	4,000
12/00	1,730	—	—	4,000
12/99	1,400	—	—	3,500
12/98	1,100	—	—	3,000
12/97	860	—	—	3,000
12/96	662	—	—	1,900
12/95	452	—	—	500
12/94	200	—	—	400
12/93	52	—	—	—
Annual Growth	47.4%	—	—	37.1%

Revenue History

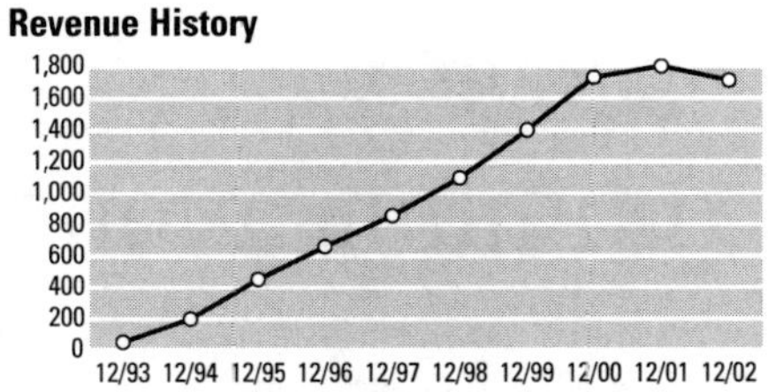

Do it Best Corp.

If you're building a house or fixing one up, you might as well Do it Best — at least, that's the hope of the hardware industry's second-largest cooperative after Ace Hardware. Do it Best has about 4,400 member-owned stores in the US and more than 40 other countries. The stores stock some 70,000 hardware and building products, which are also sold online. (Its Web site offers advice for do-it-yourselfers.) The co-op, whose buying power enables members to get retail products at competitive prices, also offers unifying branding programs using the Do it Best and Do it center names. Do it Best (formerly Hardware Wholesalers) began in 1945; it bought the Our Own Hardware co-op in 1998.

EXECUTIVES

Chairman: Steve Hawkinson
Vice Chairman: Bruce Ellis
President and CEO: Bob Taylor
EVP and COO: David (Dave) Haist
VP of Finance: Dave Dietz
VP of Marketing and International Development: William Zielke
Secretary and Director: Brenda Ward
Treasurer and Director: Myron Andersen
Manager of Communications: Heather Martin
Manager of Human Resources: Nancy Harris
Auditors: Crowe, Chizek and Company LLP

LOCATIONS

HQ: 6502 Nelson Rd., Fort Wayne, IN 46801
Phone: 260-748-5300 **Fax:** 260-748-5620
Web: www.doitbest.com

COMPETITORS

84 Lumber
Ace Hardware
Home Depot
Lowe's
Menard
Northern Tool
Sears
Sutherland Lumber
TruServ
Wal-Mart
Wickes

HISTORICAL FINANCIALS

Company Type: Cooperative

Income Statement FYE: June 30

	REVENUE ($ mil.)	NET INCOME ($ mil.)	NET PROFIT MARGIN	EMPLOYEES
6/02	2,308	—	—	1,625
6/01	2,191	—	—	1,350
6/00	2,445	—	—	1,307
6/99	2,215	—	—	1,300
6/98	1,900	—	—	1,250
6/97	1,830	—	—	1,100
6/96	1,620	—	—	1,100
6/95	1,705	—	—	1,100
6/94	1,628	—	—	—
6/93	1,400	—	—	—
Annual Growth	5.7%	—	—	5.7%

Revenue History

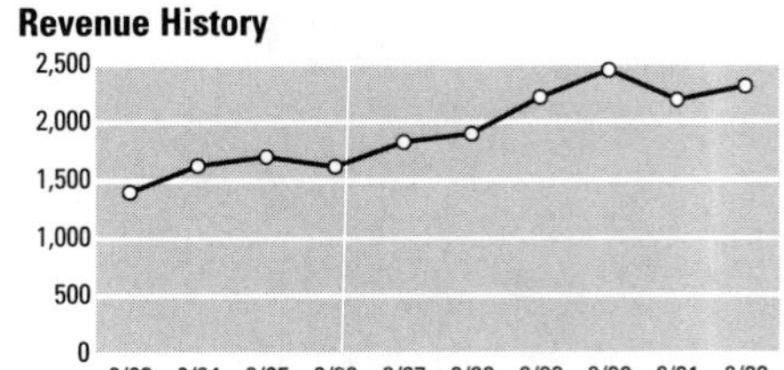

Doane Pet Care Company

Doane Pet Care has no quibble with kibble. The largest maker of private-label dog and cat food in Europe and North America, the company makes dry (nearly 75% of sales) and semi-moist foods, soft treats, and dog biscuits. Doane also makes products for other pet food companies. Its customers include Wal-Mart (more than 40% of sales), mass merchandisers, grocery and pet store chains, and farm and feed stores. The company has expanded into Asia, Europe, and Latin America through acquisitions. Doane is owned by a group of private equity investors, as well as investment companies, including J.P. Morgan Partners, and buyout firm Bruckmann, Rosser, Sherrill.

EXECUTIVES

Chairman: George B. Kelly, age 53
President, CEO, and Director: Douglas J. (Doug) Cahill, age 43, $400,000 pay
VP and Managing Director, European Operations: Tonny F. Carstensen, age 47
VP and General Manager, North American Operations: David L. Horton, age 42, $225,000 pay
VP, Co-Manufacturing and Specialty: Richard A. Hannasch, age 49
VP, Finance and CFO: Philip K. Woodlief, age 49, $225 000 pay
VP, People: Debra J. Shecterle, age 50
VP, Supply Chain, Quality and CIO: Joseph J. Meyers, age 41, $200,000 pay
Controller and Principal Accounting Officer: Stephen P. Havala
Auditors: KPMG LLP

LOCATIONS

HQ: 210 Westwood Place South, Ste. 400, Brentwood, TN 37027
Phone: 615-373-7774 **Fax:** 615-309-1187
Web: www.doanepetcare.com

Doane Pet Care has about 25 manufacturing and distribution facilities in Alabama, California, Colorado, Georgia, Indiana, Iowa, Minnesota, New York, Ohio, Oklahoma, Pennsylvania, South Carolina, Tennessee, Texas, Virginia, and Wisconsin. It also has facilities in Austria, Denmark, Spain, and the UK.

2002 Sales

	% of total
Domestic	78
International	
Denmark	17
Spain	4
UK	1
Total	**100**

PRODUCTS/OPERATIONS

Brand Names

Bonkers	Ol' Roy
Canine Club	Pathmark
Dura Lite	Pet Club
Exceed	Pet Lovers
Hy Vee	PMI-Nutrition
Kozy Kitten	Retriever
Maxximum Nutrition	Special Kitty
NutraCare	TrailBlazer

COMPETITORS

Colgate-Palmolive	Mars
Del Monte Foods	Nestlé Purina PetCare
Hartz Mountain	Royal Canin
Iams	

HISTORICAL FINANCIALS

Company Type: Private

Income Statement FYE: December 31

	REVENUE ($ mil.)	NET INCOME ($ mil.)	NET PROFIT MARGIN	EMPLOYEES
12/02	887	15	1.7%	2,707
12/01	896	(22)	—	2,730
12/00	892	(5)	—	3,585
12/99	771	21	2.8%	2,286
12/98	687	(22)	—	2,453
12/97	565	6	1.1%	2,330
12/96	513	(2)	—	—
Annual Growth	9.6%	—	—	3.0%

2002 Year-End Financials

Debt ratio: 937.2%
Return on equity: 31.7%
Cash ($ mil.): 8
Current ratio: 1.38
Long-term debt ($ mil.): 548

Net Income History

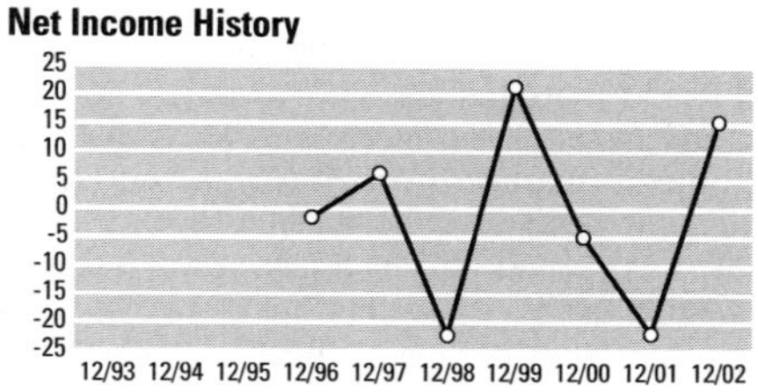

Doctor's Associates Inc.

You don't have to go underground to catch this subway. The #3 fast-food company by sales (behind McDonald's and YUM! Brands), Doctor's Associates owns and franchises the Subway sandwich shop chain. It boasts more than 18,000 locations in 70 countries, with more US locations than the Golden Arches. Virtually all Subway restaurants are franchised and offer such fare as hot and cold sandwiches, turkey wraps, and salads. Subways are located in freestanding buildings, as well as in airports, convenience stores, sports facilities, and other locations. The company is owned by co-founders Fred DeLuca and Peter Buck, who opened the first Subway in 1965.

With a low initial franchise cost and simple operations (minimum space requirements and little on-premises cooking), Subway has been one of the fastest-growing franchises in the world. Doctor's Associates sold some 4,500 franchises in 2002. Its popularity as a healthy alternative to burgers and fries has also increased with the help of an advertising campaign featuring Jared Fogle, a customer who claims to have lost 245 pounds on a diet of Subway sandwiches. Subway now controls about a third of the sandwich market.

The company is focused on increasing its international presence, having opened more than 100 locations in the UK and 400 in Australia. It is also seeking to outpace its competition in key US markets, including deli-rich New York City.

HISTORY

In 1965 17-year-old Fred DeLuca dreamed of becoming a doctor and worked as a stockboy in a Bridgeport, Connecticut, hardware store to earn college tuition. It wasn't enough, so he cornered family friend Peter Buck at a backyard barbecue and asked for advice. Buck, a nuclear physicist, suggested DeLuca open a submarine sandwich shop and put up $1,000 to get him started.

As the summer of 1965 was coming to an end, DeLuca rented a small location in a remote area of Bridgeport, opened Pete's Super Submarines, and began selling foot-long sandwiches. On the first day the sandwiches were so popular that DeLuca hired customers to work behind the counter; by the end of the day, he had sold out of all his supplies. The sandwiches continued to be popular for a while, but within a few months the shop started losing money, and DeLuca and Buck found that selling submarine sandwiches was a seasonal business. They decided they could create an illusion of success by opening a second location and then a third. The third store was finally successful, partly because of its more visible location and increased marketing and partly because of a new name — Subway.

DeLuca and Buck had set a goal of 32 shops opened by 1975, but they had only 16 by 1974. They realized that the only way they could reach their goal in one year was to license the Subway name. The first franchise opened that year, in Wallingford, Connecticut, and there were 32 by the end of 1975. The partners hit 100 by 1978 and 200 by 1983, and DeLuca set a new goal: 5,000 Subway shops by 1994. The first international Subway opened in Bahrain in 1984, and DeLuca hit his goal of 5,000 shops by 1990.

During the 1990s, DeLuca experimented with several other franchise concepts, including We Care Hair (budget styling salons), Cajun Joe's (spicy fried chicken), and Q Burgers. But none of these ventures fared as well as his sandwich empire. As Subway grew, however, controversy surrounding its treatment of franchisees began to surface. A Federal Trade Commission investigation of the company was dropped in 1993, but Subway continued to battle franchisees complaining about broken contracts, market over-saturation (and, therefore, too much competition), and what the franchisees viewed as unreasonably high royalty fees.

In spite of its franchising troubles, Subway kept growing. It expanded into Russia and China in the mid-1990s, and opened its 11,000th restaurant in 1995. In 1997 Subway inked deals with the Army, Navy, and Air Force exchange services to bring Subway units to military bases. Two years later the company opened its 14,000th restaurant in Mount Gambier, Australia, an event that coincided with Subway's renewed push to expand internationally.

The company got some unexpected publicity in 1999 when 22-year-old Jared Fogle claimed that he dropped 245 pounds from his 425-pound frame by subsisting on a diet of Subway turkey sandwiches. Subway helped Fogle extend his 15 minutes of fame by featuring him and his oversized pants in a TV commercial. (The company has since built an entire campaign around Fogle which features other weight watchers attributing their success to Jared and Subway.) Subway introduced its largest menu initiative ever in 2000 when it unveiled its Subway Selects Gourmet Sandwiches, adding 13 items to the menu. In April of 2001 the company opened its 15,000th store.

Also that year, Buck retired as chairman, but stayed on as a member of the board of directors. In March 2002 Subway opened its 16,000th location; it passed 17,000 in October of that year.

EXECUTIVES

President: Frederick A. (Fred) DeLuca
Chief Marketing Officer: Bill Schettini
Controller: David Worroll
Director of Corporate Communications: Michele Klotzer
Director of Development and Franchise Sales: Don Fertman
Director of International Development: Patricia Demarais
Director of Research and Development: Suzanne Greco
Director of Creative Services: Ruth Woyciesjes
Senior National Accounts Manager: Janet Bencivenga
Public Relations Coordinator: Les Winograd

LOCATIONS

HQ: 325 Bic Dr., Milford, CT 06460
Phone: 203-877-4281 **Fax:** 203-876-6695
Web: www.subway.com

2002 Locations

	No.
US	14,976
Canada	1,729
Australia	455
Puerto Rico	148
UK	134
Japan	99
Other countries	650
Total	**18,191**

COMPETITORS

Blimpie
Burger King
Chick-fil-A
CKE Restaurants
Dairy Queen
Jack in the Box
McDonald's
Papa John's
Quizno's
Schlotzsky's
Triarc
Wendy's
YUM!

HISTORICAL FINANCIALS

Company Type: Private

Income Statement FYE: December 31

	ESTIMATED REVENUE ($ mil.)	NET INCOME ($ mil.)	NET PROFIT MARGIN	EMPLOYEES
12/02	500	—	—	730
12/01	400	—	—	730
12/00	350	—	—	730
12/99	300	—	—	—
12/98	300	—	—	—
12/97	300	—	—	—
12/96	250	—	—	—
12/95	250	—	—	—
12/94	200	—	—	—
12/93	200	—	—	—
Annual Growth	10.7%	—	—	0.0%

Revenue History

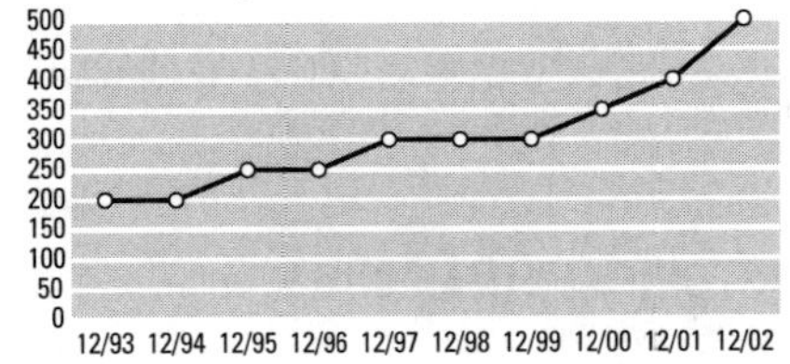

Dole Food Company, Inc.

Bananas might be Dole Food's favorite fruit because they have "a-peel," but as the world's largest producer of fresh fruits and vegetables, it grows and markets much more. The company is one of the world's leading producers of bananas and pineapples, and also markets citrus, table grapes, dried fruits, and nuts. Dole has added value-added products (packaged salads, novelty canned pineapple shapes) to insulate itself from commodity markets. Cost-cutting measures, including job cuts, have helped boost Dole's earnings. CEO David Murdock took the company private in 2003.

Dole is the #1 banana brand in North America and Japan with approximately 33% and 28%, respectively, of the market share. The company is the #2 world producer of fresh pineapples (behind Fresh Del Monte Produce). It has begun introducing convenience-oriented products such as bagged vegetables and individual fruit servings packaged in plastic cups, as well as niche products such as organic bananas.

Dole is adding to its distribution channels, with a signficant share of its products now available in drug and convenience stores, club stores, and mass merchandisers.

HISTORY

James Dole embarked on an unlikely career in a faraway land when he graduated from Harvard College in 1899 and sailed to Hawaii. He bought 61 acres of farmland for $4,000 in 1900 and the next year organized the Hawaiian Pineapple Company, announcing that the island's pineapples would eventually be in every US grocery store.

Others had tried and failed to sell fresh fruit to the mainland. Dole decided he would succeed by canning pineapples. He built his first cannery in 1903 and introduced a national magazine advertising campaign in 1908 designed to make consumers associate Hawaii with pineapples (then considered exotic fruits).

In 1922 Dole expanded his production by buying the island of Lanai, where he set up a pineapple plantation. He financed the purchase by selling a third interest in Hawaiian Pineapple to Waialua Agricultural Company, which was part of Castle & Cooke (C&C). Samuel Castle and Amos Cooke, missionaries to Hawaii, formed C&C in 1851 to manage their church's failing depository, which supplied outlying mission posts with staple goods. In 1858 they entered the sugar business and within 10 years served as agents for several Hawaiian sugar plantations and the ships that carried their cargoes.

C&C gained control of Hawaiian Pineapple in 1932 when it acquired an additional 21% interest in the business. The company began using the Dole name on packaging the next year. Dole became chairman of the board of the reorganized company in 1935 but pursued other business interests until he retired in 1948.

Hawaiian Pineapple was run separately until C&C bought the remainder in 1961. The company started pineapple and banana farms in the Philippines in 1963 to supply markets in East Asia. C&C began importing bananas when it purchased 55% of Standard Fruit of New Orleans in 1964. (It purchased the remainder four years later.)

Heavily in debt and limping from two hostile takeover attempts, C&C agreed in 1985 to merge with Flexi-Van, a container leasing company. The merger brought with it needed capital, Flexi-Van owner David Murdock (who became C&C's CEO), and a fleet of ships to transport produce. Murdock began trimming back, leaving C&C with its fruit and real estate operations. He then decided to end all pineapple operations on Lanai to concentrate on tourist properties. (The company took a $168 million writeoff on them in 1995, when it spun off its real estate and resort operations as Castle & Cooke.)

C&C became Dole Food in 1991. The company expanded at home and internationally, adding SAMICA (dried fruits and nuts, Europe, 1992), Dromedary (dates, US, 1994), Chiquita's New Zealand produce operations (1995), and SABA Trading (60%, produce importing and distribution, Sweden, 1998).

In 1995 Dole sold its juice business to Seagram's Tropicana Products division, keeping its pineapple juices and licensing the Dole name to Seagram (PepsiCo bought Tropicana in 1998.) Dole entered the fresh-flower trade in 1998 by acquiring four major growers and marketers and has become the world's largest producer of freshly cut flowers.

A worldwide banana glut, Hurricane Mitch, and severe freezes in California hit the company hard in late 1998. The next year Dole launched cost-cutting measures, which by early 2000 had ripened into better earnings. Nonetheless, cutbacks and disposals continued throughout 2001.

In 2002 Murdock made a cash and debt takeover bid for the company worth about $2.5 billion. However, at least one minority shareholder was dissatisfied with the offer and filed a proposal calling for Murdock's resignation. The company rejected Murdock's $29.50 per share offer and negotiated with him regarding a larger price-per-share offer. In December Dole and Murdock finally signed a merger agreement. The deal, which gave stockholders $33.50 per share in cash, was approved by company stockholders in March 2003 and left Murdock in sole control of the company.

EXECUTIVES

Chairman and CEO: David H. Murdock, age 79, $2,124,423 pay
President and COO: Lawrence A. Kern, age 55, $1,513,846 pay
VP and CFO: Richard J. Dahl, age 51, $654,482 pay
VP, Administration and Support Operations: George R. Horne, age 66
VP, General Counsel, and Corporate Secretary: C. Michael Carter, age 59, $778,077 pay
VP: Roberta Wieman, age 58
President, Dole Fresh Flowers: John T. Schouten
President, Dole North America Tropical Fresh Fruit: Michael J. Cavallero, age 56

President, Dole Worldwide Packaged Foods: Peter M. Nolan, age 60
President, Dole Worldwide Vegetables: Eric M. Schwartz, age 4[illegible]
Treasurer: Beth Potillo, age 43
Corporate Controller and Chief Accounting Officer: Yoon J. Hugh, age 32
Director, Consumer Services: Donna Skidmore
Corporate Communications: Freya Maneki
Auditors: Deloitte & Touche LLP

LOCATIONS

HQ: 1 Dole Dr., Westlake Village, CA 91362
Phone: 818-879-6600 **Fax:** 818-879-6615
Web: www.dole.com

Dole Food distributes its more than 200 products in more than 90 countries worldwide.

2002 Sales

	$ mil.	% of total
US	2,118	48
Japan	559	13
Sweden	366	8
Germany	311	7
France	134	4
Italy	101	2
Other countries	803	18
Total	**4,392**	**100**

PRODUCTS/OPERATIONS

Divisions and Selected Products

Dried Fruit and Nuts
Almonds
Dates
Pistachios
Prunes
Raisins
Raspberries
Strawberries
Tangelos

Fresh Flowers
Carnations
Chrysanthemums
Roses

Fresh Fruit
Apples
Bananas
Cherries
Cranberries
Grapefruit
Grapes
Kiwi
Lemons
Mangoes
Melons
Oranges
Papayas
Pears
Pineapples

Fresh Vegetables
Artichokes
Asparagus
Broccoli
Carrots
Celery
Lettuce
Onions
Snow peas
Spinach

Freshly Cut Vegetables
Coleslaw
Peeled mini-carrots
Salad mixes
Shredded lettuce

Packaged Foods
Canned mandarin-orange segments
Canned mixed fruits
Canned pineapple
Pineapple juice

COMPETITORS

Blue Diamond Growers
Chiquita Brands
Cirio
Del Monte Foods
Earthbound Farm
Fresh Del Monte Produce
Fyffes
Geest
Global Berry Farms
John Sanfilippo & Son
Maui Land & Pineapple
Ocean Spray
Seneca Foods
Sun Growers
Sunkist
UniMark Group
United Foods

HISTORICAL FINANCIALS

Company Type: Private

Income Statement FYE: Saturday closest to December 31

	REVENUE ($ mil.)	NET INCOME ($ mil.)	NET PROFIT MARGIN	EMPLOYEES
12/02	4,392	36	0.8%	57,000
12/01	4,449	150	3.4%	59,000
12/00	4,763	68	1.4%	61,000
12/99	5,061	49	1.0%	59,500
12/98	4,424	12	0.3%	53,500
12/97	4,336	160	3.7%	44,000
12/96	3,840	89	2.3%	46,000
12/95	3,804	23	0.6%	43,000
12/94	3,842	68	1.8%	46,000
12/93	3,431	78	2.3%	45,300
Annual Growth	2.8%	(8.1%)	—	2.6%

2002 Year-End Financials

Debt ratio: 118.4%
Return on equity: 4.9%
Cash ($ mil.): 647
Current ratio: 1.72
Long-term debt ($ mil.): 883

Net Income History

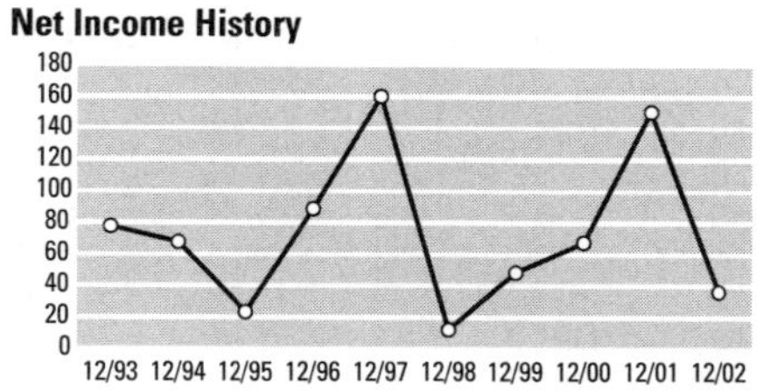

Domino's, Inc.

Domino's knows the rules of the pizza delivery game. The company is the world's #2 pizza chain (behind YUM! Brands' Pizza Hut division) with more than 7,200 locations in 50 countries. It features several different styles of pizza with a wide array of topping options, as well as additional items such as bread sticks, cheese bread, and chicken wings. Domino's stores are principally delivery locations and generally do not have any dine-in seating. More than 90% of its locations are franchised. Bain Capital controls 49% of the company; Thomas Monaghan, who founded Domino's with his brother James in 1960, has 25% voting control.

Domino's trails Pizza Hut in the quick-service pizza segment with almost 12% of the overall market compared to its rival's 20% market share, but the company is #1 in the pizza delivery business, controlling about 20% of that market. Its stores deliver about 400 million pizzas each year. Domino's gets more than half of its revenue from sales of food and other supplies to its franchisees. Its company-owned stores account for a third of its business.

Since its stores have no need for seating, they tend to be smaller with less start-up and maintenance costs than other types of restaurants, making them especially attractive to potential franchisees. Domino's has focused on expanding its international operations in recent years while holding the number of its domestic locations fairly even.

As with any of the large fast-food chains, Domino's spends a hefty amount on advertising to maintain and increase its market share. The company's franchisees each contribute a percentage of their sales to fund both national marketing efforts and local advertising. Domino's also places a lot of emphasis on new-product development to steal customers away from other pizzerias. It launched Domino's Dots, balls of pizza dough covered with cinnamon and vanilla icing, in 2003.

HISTORY

Thomas Monaghan's early life was one of hardship. After growing up in an orphanage and numerous foster homes, Monaghan spent his young-adult life experimenting, trying everything from a Catholic seminary to a stint in the Marine Corps.

In 1960 Monaghan borrowed $500 and bought DomiNick's, a failed pizza parlor in Ypsilanti, Michigan, which he operated with the help of his brother James. In 1961 James traded his share in the restaurant to his brother for a Volkswagen Beetle, but Thomas pressed on, learning the pizza business largely by trial and error. After a brief partnership with an experienced restaurateur with whom he later had a falling out, Monaghan developed a strategy to sell only pizza and to locate stores near colleges and military bases. In 1965 the company changed its name to Domino's.

In the 1960s and 1970s, Monaghan endured setbacks that brought the company to the brink of bankruptcy. Among these were a 1968 fire that destroyed the Domino's headquarters and a 1975 lawsuit from Domino Sugar maker Amstar (now Tate & Lyle) for trademark infringement. But the company won the ensuing legal battles, and by 1978 it was operating 200 stores.

In the 1980s Domino's grew phenomenally. Between 1981 and 1983 the company doubled its number of US stores to 1,000; it went international in 1983, opening a store in Canada. The company's growth brought Monaghan a personal fortune. In 1983 he bought the Detroit Tigers baseball team and amassed one of the world's largest collections of Frank Lloyd Wright objects.

Domino's expansion continued in the mid-1980s with the help of a national advertising campaign featuring the red-suited Noid, an animated character meant to represent customers' concerns about pizza delivery ("Avoid the Noid"). With sales figures mounting, the company introduced pan pizza (its first new product) in 1989. That year Monaghan put Domino's up for sale, but his practice of linking his personal and professional finances had gotten both the founder and company into such dire fiscal straits that no one wanted to buy the chain. Monaghan installed a new management group and removed himself from day-to-day involvement.

Monaghan returned to the business in 1991 when its performance began to slide. Having experienced a religious rebirth, he sold off many of his private holdings (including his resort island and his baseball team, which went to cross-town pizza rival Michael Ilitch of Little Caesar). Monaghan also moved to reorganize management and reinvigorate the company. The next year Domino's introduced its first non-pizza menu item, bread sticks.

In 1993 a $79 million judgment was levied against the company resulting from a 1989 case in which a Domino's driver, trying to fulfill the company's 30-minute delivery guarantee, ran a red light and collided with another car. The incident prompted Domino's to drop its 30-

minute delivery pledge and replace it with a satisfaction guarantee.

The company revamped its logo and updated its stores in 1997. The following year it introduced a patented delivery bag designed to keep pies hot and crispy. Also in 1998, prompted by his decision to devote more time to religious pursuits, Monaghan announced he would retire from the business he had guided for nearly 40 years. He sold 93% of his stake in the company to investment firm Bain Capital for $1 billion. (The deal left Monaghan sizable voting control in the firm, however.) David Brandon, former CEO of sales promotion company Valassis Communications, replaced Monaghan as chairman and CEO.

In 1999 the company restructured its operations once again, eliminating 100 managers and closing or selling to franchisees 142 stores. It also introduced the first in its line of Italian Originals — specialty pizzas featuring Italian spices — and began selling pizza online through a number of franchisees.

In 2001 Domino's bought a majority stake in Dutch Pizza Beheer B.V., an operator of 52 Domino's restaurants in the Netherlands. The acquisition gave the company a base to manage future expansion in Europe.

EXECUTIVES

Chairman and CEO: David A. Brandon, age 50, $1,800,000 pay
EVP, General Counsel, and Secretary: Elisa D. Garcia, age 45
EVP Build the Brand: Ken C. Calwell
EVP Communications and Investor Relations: Lynn M. Liddle
EVP Finance and CFO: Harry J. Silverman, age 44, $820,000 pay
EVP Flawless Execution – Domestic Stores: Patrick W. Knotts, age 48, $750,000 pay
EVP Franchise Relations: James G. Stansik, age 47
EVP International: J. Patrick Doyle, age 39, $675,000 pay
EVP Maintain High Standards – Distribution: Michael D. Soignet, age 43, $755,000 pay
EVP People First: Patricia A. Wilmot, age 53
VP and Associate General Counsel: Edwina W. Divins
VP and Corporate Controller: Jeffrey D. Lawrence, age 28
VP and Treasurer: Joseph Donovan
VP Brand Growth: Terri Snyder
VP Corporate Communications: Tim McIntyre
VP Purchasing: Jim Caldwell
CIO: Timothy J. Monteith, age 60
National Marketing Director, Domino's Pizza of Canada: Glenn Quast
Public Relations Manager: Holly Ryan
Auditors: PricewaterhouseCoopers LLP

LOCATIONS

HQ: 30 Frank Lloyd Wright Dr., Ann Arbor, MI 48106
Phone: 734-930-3030 **Fax:** 734-747-6210
Web: www.dominos.com

2002 Locations

	No.
US	
Franchises	4,271
Company-owned	577
International	2,382
Total	**7,230**

PRODUCTS/OPERATIONS

2002 Sales

	$ mil.	% of total
Domestic distribution	676	53
Store operations		
Company-owned	376	30
Domestic franchises	141	11
International	82	6
Total	**1,275**	**100**

COMPETITORS

Bertucci's
Burger King
Subway
Godfather's Pizza
Jack in the Box
Little Caesar's
McDonald's
Papa John's
Papa Murphy's
Pizza Hut
Round Table Pizza
Wendy's

HISTORICAL FINANCIALS

Company Type: Private

Income Statement FYE: Sunday nearest December 31

	REVENUE ($ mil.)	NET INCOME ($ mil.)	NET PROFIT MARGIN	EMPLOYEES
12/02	1,275	36	2.8%	13,800
12/01	1,258	37	2.9%	12,600
12/00	1,166	25	2.2%	14,600
12/99	1,157	2	0.2%	14,400
12/98	1,177	77	6.5%	14,200
12/97	1,045	61	5.8%	—
12/96	970	20	2.0%	—
12/95	905	25	2.8%	—
12/94	875	0	0.0%	—
Annual Growth	4.8%	108.6%	—	(0.7%)

2002 Year-End Financials

Debt ratio: —
Return on equity: —
Cash ($ mil.): 22
Current ratio: 0.92
Long-term debt ($ mil.): 599

Net Income History

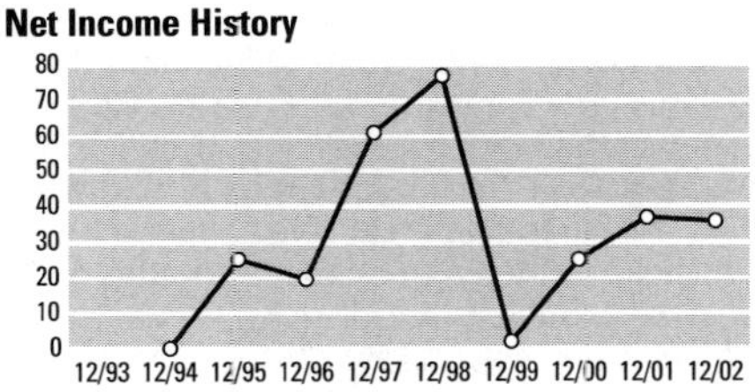

Dow Corning Corporation

Cosmetic surgery has caused major health problems at Dow Corning. A 50-50 joint venture of chemical titan Dow Chemical and glass giant Corning, Dow Corning is operating under bankruptcy protection as a result of thousands of claims by women alleging the company's silicone-gel breast implants harmed them. Dow Corning produces about 7,000 silicone-based products such as adhesives, insulating materials, and lubricants for aerospace, automotive, and electrical uses. Because silicone does not conduct electricity, it is also used in its hard polycrystalline form (silicon) as the material on which semiconductors are built. With manufacturing plants worldwide, the company sells about 55% of its products outside the US.

Having filed for bankruptcy protection in 1995, Dow Corning appeared close to a settlement that would help it emerge from bankruptcy protection in 1998. The settlement would provide $3.2 billion for breast implant claims over a 16-year period. A bankruptcy court approved the deal in 1999 (paving the road for the company's exit from bankruptcy), but the deal fell through when the judge ruled that women who did not agree to the settlement could still sue Dow Corning's corporate parents. Dow Corning and about 94% of the women who have sued it appealed the judge's ruling. Another court since has recommended releasing Dow Chemical and Corning from liability.

Corning, Inc., has been suffering from weak sales in telecommunications markets, and Dow Corning's expected exit from bankruptcy in 2003 could help Corning back to profitability.

HISTORY

Dow Corning was founded in 1943 as a joint venture between Dow Chemical and Corning Glass Works. Corning, founded by Amory Houghton in 1875, provided Thomas Edison with glass for the first lightbulbs. It developed Pyrex heat-resistant glass in 1915.

Corning made its first silicone resin samples in 1938. It teamed with a group of Dow Chemical scientists who were also working on silicone products in 1940. Dow Chemical president Willard Dow and Corning Glass Works president Glen Cole shook hands on the idea of a joint venture in 1942, and 10 months later Dow Corning was formed. Its first product, the engine grease DOW CORNING 4, enabled B-17s to fly at 35,000 feet (a major contribution to the Allied war effort). In 1945 DOW CORNING 35 (an emulsifier used in tire molds) and Pan Glaze (which made baking pans stick-proof and easier to clean) were instant successes on the home front.

Dow Corning expanded rapidly in international markets and in 1960 set up Dow Corning International to handle sales and technical service in markets outside North America. By 1969 the company had operations worldwide.

Dow Corning's first breast implants went on the market in 1964. Since then Dow Corning and other silicone makers have sold silicone breast implants to more than a million women in the US. In the early 1980s breast-implant recipients began suing Dow Corning and other implant makers, claiming that the silicone gel in the implants leaked and caused health problems. Dow Corning, the leading implant maker, defended the devices as safe. Dow Corning stopped making implants in 1992, after the Food and Drug Administration called for a moratorium on silicone-gel implants.

In 1993 Baxter International, Bristol-Myers Squibb, and Dow Corning offered $4.2 billion to settle thousands of claims. The corporation declared bankruptcy in 1995 to buy time for financial reorganization. A federal judge stripped Dow Chemical of its protection from direct liability, and the company was later ordered to pay a Nevada couple $4.1 million in damages (other jurisdictions did not follow suit). Dow Corning sold its Polytrap polymer technology to Advanced Polymer, maker of polymer-based pharmaceutical delivery systems, in 1996. The following year the company sold Bisco Products, its silicone-foam business, to Rogers Corporation for $12 million.

Dow Corning's $3.7 billion bankruptcy reorganization plan, offered in 1997, allowed for $2.4 billion to be set aside to settle most implant lawsuits against the corporation. However, a federal bankruptcy judge found legal flaws in the proposal and refused to allow claimants to vote on it. In 1998 Dow Corning upped the ante to $4.4 billion — $3 billion to the silicone claimants and the rest to creditors.

Both sides later agreed to a $3.2 billion compensation package, and in 1999 the plan received approval from a bankruptcy judge and creditors. However, the settlement stalled when the judge ruled that women who disagreed with the settlement could sue Dow Corporation and Corning (Dow Corning is appealing). Despite its court battles, in 2000 the company acquired the 51% of Universal Silicones & Lubricants (high-tech lubricants and silicone sealants) it did not own and renamed the company Dow Corning India.

EXECUTIVES

Chairman and CEO: Gary E. Anderson
President and COO: Stephanie A. Burns
CFO: Joseph Donald (Don) Sheets
SVP; President, Americas; and General Manager, Specialty Chemicals Industry Business: Jere D. Marciniak
VP and Chief Human Resources Officer: Derek A. O'Malley-Keyes
VP and Executive Director, Supply Chains: Alex Royez
VP, Communications and Chief Communications Officer: Barbara S. Carmichael
VP, General Counsel, and Secretary: Sue K. McDonnell
VP; General Manager, Construction Industry and Core Products Business Unit: Chris J. Bowyer
VP; General Manager, Life Sciences Industry and Life Sciences Product Business IBU: Endvar Rossi
VP; General Manager, New Ventures Business Unit: Jean-Marc Gilson
VP; General Manager, Service Enterprise Unit: Allan C. (Harry) Ludgate
VP, Geographic Development; President, Asia; and Chairman, Dow Corning Toray Silicones: Bruno Sulmon
VP; President, Dow Corning China; and General Manager, Electronics Industry and Advanced Materials: Ian Thackwray
CIO and Executive Director, Information Technology/Knowledge Management: Abbe Mulders
Executive Director, Marketing and Sales: Scott Fuson
Auditors: PricewaterhouseCoopers LLP

LOCATIONS

HQ: 2200 W. Salzburg Rd., Midland, MI 48686
Phone: 989-496-4000 **Fax:** 989-496-4393
Web: www.dowcorning.com

Dow Corning has about 22 manufacturing sites worldwide. Its principal manufacturing facilities in the US are located in Kentucky and Michigan. Its principal non-US manufacturing facilities are located in Belgium, Germany, Japan, and the UK.

2002 Sales

	$ mil.	% of total
US	1,069	41
Japan	318	12
Germany	136	5
South Korea	131	5
UK	119	5
Other countries	837	32
Total	**2,610**	**100**

PRODUCTS/OPERATIONS

Selected Products and Applications

Aerospace
Adhesives
Encapsulants
Exotic composite materials
Greases
High-purity fluids
Protective coatings
Sealants

Automotive
Body components
Brake systems
Chassis
Electrical components
Electronic components
Engine/drivetrain
Exterior lighting
Fuel systems

Chemical and Material Manufacturing
Agrochemicals
Auto appearance chemicals
Industrial release agents
Materials treatment
Oil and gas
Process aid antifoams
Pulp manufacturing

Cleaning Products
Hand cleaners
Janitorial floor waxes
Laundry detergents

Coatings and Plastics
Caulks
Coatings
Sealants

Electrical/Electronics
Adhesives and sealants
Conformal coatings
Dielectric gels
High-voltage insulators
Hyperpure polycrystalline silicon
Interlayer dielectric and passivation materials
Liquid transformer fluid
Silicone encapsulants
Silicone grease for insulators
Silicone RTV coating for insulators
Silicone rubber insulators
Thermally conductive adhesives

Food and Beverage
Defoamers
Packaging

Health Care
Hydrocephalus shunts
Pacemaker leads
Tubing for dialysis

Paper Manufacturing & Finishing
Release coatings for label-backing paper, pressure-sensitive adhesives, and paper coatings

Personal Care
Materials for deodorants, cosmetics, and lotions

Plastics

Textiles
Waterproofing agents

COMPETITORS

3M
BASF AG
Bostik Findley
Crompton
Cytec
Degussa
Dynea
Eastman Chemical
Goldschmidt
H.B. Fuller
ICI
National Starch and Chemical
Shin-Etsu Chemical
Wacker
Witco Corporation

HISTORICAL FINANCIALS

Company Type: Joint venture

Income Statement FYE: December 31

	REVENUE ($ mil.)	NET INCOME ($ mil.)	NET PROFIT MARGIN	EMPLOYEES
12/02	2,610	59	2.2%	8,200
12/01	2,438	(23)	—	7,500
12/00	2,751	105	3.8%	9,000
12/99	2,603	110	4.2%	9,000
12/98	2,568	207	8.0%	9,000
12/97	2,644	238	9.0%	9,100
12/96	2,532	222	8.8%	8,900
12/95	2,493	(31)	—	8,500
12/94	2,205	(7)	—	8,300
12/93	2,044	(287)	—	8,000
Annual Growth	2.8%	—	—	0.3%

2002 Year-End Financials

Debt ratio: 10.1%
Return on equity: 11.5%
Cash ($ mil.): 1,117
Current ratio: 1.85
Long-term debt ($ mil.): 55

Net Income History

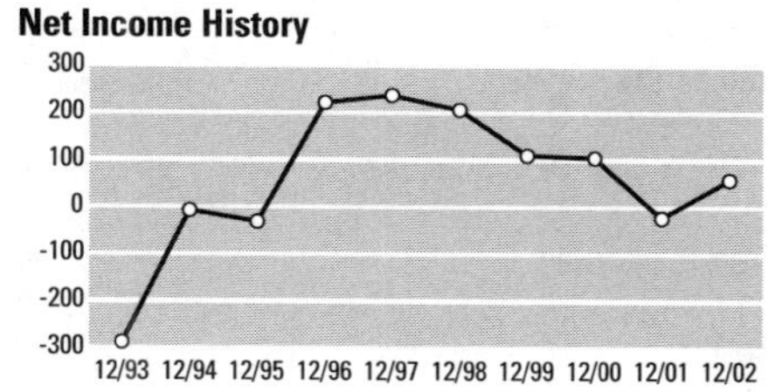

DPR Construction

From bio labs to wafer fabs, the projects of DPR Construction reflect the diversity of its commercial building. The general contractor/construction manager, one of the largest in the US, focuses on projects for the biotechnology, pharmaceutical, health care, education, and semiconductor markets. DPR also specializes in corporate office and entertainment projects (such as theme parks and studios) and warehouses and distribution centers. Clients include Apple Computer, Banner Health, Pixar Animation, and PricewaterhouseCoopers. President Doug Woods, CEO Peter Nosler, and secretary/treasurer Ron Davidowski (the D, P, and R) founded the company in 1990. The employee-owned group has 15 offices across the US.

EXECUTIVES

CEO: Peter Nosler
President: Doug Woods
CFO: Sandra Waechter
Secretary and Treasurer: Ron Davidowski
EVP: Jim Dolen
EVP: Eric Lamb
EVP: Peter Salvati
Marketing and Corporate Communications: Yumi Sera
Human Resources: Jorinne Liberatore

LOCATIONS

HQ: DPR Construction, Inc.
1450 Veterans Blvd., Redwood City, CA 94063
Phone: 650-474-1450 **Fax:** 650-474-1451
Web: www.dprinc.com

DPR Construction has offices in Atlanta; Austin, Texas; Denver; Fairfax and Richmond, Virginia; Newport Beach, Pleasanton, Redwood City, Sacramento, San Diego, San Francisco, and San Jose, California; Phoenix; Portland, Oregon; and Seattle.

COMPETITORS

Alberici
Austin Industries
Beck Group
Devcon Construction
Fluor
Hathaway Dinwiddie Construction
Hensel Phelps Construction
Hoffman Corporation
Jacobs Engineering
Rudolph & Sletten
Skanska USA Building
Swinerton
Turner Corporation
Webcor Builders
Whiting-Turner
WorkPlaceUSA

HISTORICAL FINANCIALS

Company Type: Private

Income Statement FYE: December 31

	REVENUE ($ mil.)	NET INCOME ($ mil.)	NET PROFIT MARGIN	EMPLOYEES
12/02	1,100	—	—	2,100
12/01	1,800	—	—	3,100
12/00	1,958	—	—	3,100
12/99	1,200	—	—	2,000
12/98	1,300	—	—	2,500
12/97	890	—	—	1,200
12/96	620	—	—	1,149
12/95	257	—	—	656
12/94	175	—	—	350
12/93	100	—	—	110
Annual Growth	30.5%	—	—	38.8%

Revenue History

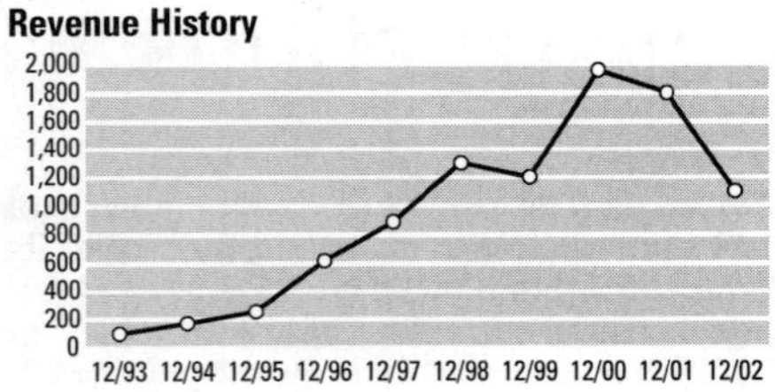

Dr Pepper/Seven Up Bottling Group, Inc.

Dr Pepper/Seven Up Bottling Group (DPSUBG) rings up sweet results for Cadbury Schweppes, the world's #3 soft-drink firm. It is a leading bottler of soft drinks in the US, distributing in 21 states. Besides the Dr Pepper and 7 UP brands (owned by Cadbury Schweppes), it also bottles the lesser-known Big Red and Crush brands. DPSUBG was formed in 1999 when Dr Pepper Bottling Company of Texas and American Bottling merged. Cadbury Schweppes and The Carlyle Group own 40% and 53% of the company, respectively. CEO Jim Turner, who owns 5%, joined Dr Pepper Bottling Company of Texas in 1982 and built it by acquiring franchises. The company continues to grow by acquiring other bottlers.

EXECUTIVES

President and CEO: Jim L. Turner, age 57
CFO: Holly Lowvorn
EVP, Administration: Tom Taszarek
VP, Human Resources: Kellie Defratus
VP, Information Systems: Jerry Mecca
VP, Sales and Marketing: Guy Mueller

LOCATIONS

HQ: 5950 Sherry Ln., Ste. 500, Dallas, TX 75225
Phone: 214-530-5000 **Fax:** 214-530-5036

COMPETITORS

Buffalo Rock
Coca-Cola Bottling Consolidated
Coca-Cola United
Coca-Cola
Coca-Cola Enterprises
Cott
National Beverage
Pepsi Bottling
Pepsi Bottling Ventures
PepsiAmericas
PepsiCo
Philadelphia Coca-Cola

HISTORICAL FINANCIALS

Company Type: Private

Income Statement FYE: December 31

	REVENUE ($ mil.)	NET INCOME ($ mil.)	NET PROFIT MARGIN	EMPLOYEES
12/01	1,820	—	—	8,800
12/00	1,900	—	—	8,000
12/99	1,900	—	—	3,000
12/98	878	—	—	2,700
12/97	709	—	—	2,500
12/96	523	—	—	1,567
12/95	496	—	—	1,535
12/94	532	—	—	1,400
12/93	475	—	—	1,320
Annual Growth	18.3%	—	—	26.8%

Revenue History

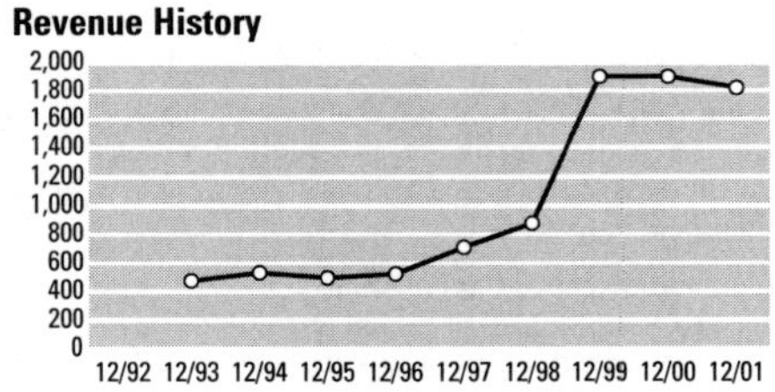

DreamWorks SKG

DreamWorks SKG has moguls times three. Created in 1994 by Steven Spielberg (famed film director/producer), Jeffrey Katzenberg (former Disney film executive and animation guru), and David Geffen (recording industry maven), DreamWorks has established itself in the entertainment industry after a rocky start. The company produces films (*Catch Me if You Can*), TV shows (*Boomtown* and *Oliver Beene*), and music, including the soundtracks to DreamWorks films and record deals with artists such as Toby Keith. DreamWorks pulled out of the GameWorks video arcade business it started with SEGA and Universal Pictures. The three founders collectively own 66% of DreamWorks; Microsoft co-founder Paul Allen owns about 26%.

The division of labor is spread out among DreamWorks founders. Spielberg oversees the live-action movie unit, which includes films such as *Minority Report*, *Old School*, and *Road to Perdition*. Former Disney head of production Katzenberg leads the animation division, responsible for such hits as *Chicken Run* and *Shrek* (one of 2001's highest grossing films) and misses (2003's failed *Sinbad: Legend of the Seven Seas*). Geffen runs DreamWorks Records, producing the soundtracks to all DreamWorks films and albums for popular artists.

The company's progress has been marked by a few obstacles: its television division has produced only one notable hit (*Spin City*, whose six-year series-run ended in 2002); its first animated feature (*Prince of Egypt*) and early live-action films (*Amistad, Almost Famous*) flopped at the box office; and DreamWorks scuttled plans for a Web entertainment division. In addition, the company's bid to build a new film studio in LA failed. (DreamWorks has offices at Universal Pictures, where Spielberg's Amblin Pictures production studio operates.) In contrast to its major studio rivals Paramount and Universal that produce about 2 dozen films annually, the smaller DreamWorks makes eight to ten films a year.

DreamWorks has cut about 150 jobs, and in 2002 the company received a cash infusion through refinancing from J.P. Morgan Chase and FleetBoston Financial Corp, which it is using to expand its animation facilities as well as its live-action film production. Its TV division has signed a development pact with NBC.

HISTORY

Before pooling their collective talents in 1994, Steven Spielberg, Jeffrey Katzenberg, and David Geffen had each established an impressive track record. Spielberg had spawned such blockbusters as *Jaws, The Indiana Jones Trilogy*, and *Jurassic Park*. Katzenberg had guided Walt Disney's return to animation (*The Lion King, Aladdin*) before a falling out with Disney CEO Michael Eisner. Music guru Geffen had helped make superstars of the Eagles and Nirvana.

A high-tech who's who embraced the SKG dream. Microsoft invested around $30 million to develop video games, while Microsoft co-founder Paul Allen shelled out nearly $500 million for a stake in the new company. Soon DreamWorks had arranged a $100 million programming deal with ABC, a 10-year HBO licensing agreement worth an estimated $1 billion, and co-founded a $50 million animation studio with Silicon Graphics. DreamWorks then announced plans in 1995 to build the first new studio since the 1930s, just outside of Los Angeles in Playa Vista.

DreamWorks produced a string of TV flops before finding success with the Michael J. Fox comedy *Spin City* in 1996. Later that year the company released the first record under its new label, a dud from pop star George Michael, and it announced its partnership with SEGA and MCA (now Universal Studios) to develop SEGA GameWorks (video arcade super-centers featuring SEGA titles and games designed by Spielberg). The company finally released its first three movies in 1997 (*The Peacemaker, Amistad,* and *Mouse Hunt*) to mixed critical reviews and mediocre box office performance. Combined with DreamWorks' less-than-stellar offerings in TV and music, buzz circulated that the meeting of the minds at DreamWorks wasn't all it was cracked up to be.

But DreamWorks started showing signs of life in 1998 with the comet disaster film *Deep Impact* and Spielberg's Oscar-winning *Saving Private Ryan,* the highest grossing film of the year. It also introduced its first animated films that year, which included the successful *Antz*. DreamWorks finished the year with the highest average gross per film of all the major studios.

After facing a multitude of environmental protests, cost overruns, and construction delays, DreamWorks scrapped its Playa Vista studio plans in 1999. Around the same time, Katzenberg settled his high-profile lawsuit against Disney over a bonus owed him when he resigned. Later that year DreamWorks joined with Imagine Entertainment and Paul Allen's Vulcan Ventures to create POP.com, a Web site offering digital short films and streaming video features. It also announced a five-picture deal with Academy Award-winning animation firm Aardman Animations, with which it co-produced *Chicken Run* (released in 2000).

DreamWorks and Microsoft sold DreamWorks Interactive, their video game joint venture, to Electronic Arts in 2000. Later that year *American Beauty* took home the Oscar for Best Picture of 1999, and the studio continued its successful box-office run with three films that grossed more than $100 million (*Gladiator,* which scored the studio its second Best Picture Oscar, *Chicken Run,* and *What Lies Beneath*). After Allen failed to merge the struggling, unlaunched POP.com with iFilm.com (in which he is also a major investor), DreamWorks and Imagine shut down the netcaster.

The studio scored an early summer hit in 2001 with *Shrek,* which became one of that year's highest grossing films with more than $265 million at the box office. *A Beautiful Mind,* its co-production with Universal Pictures won one of the company's films yet another Best Picture Oscar. Also that year the company exited the GameWorks venture when the arcades failed to catch on quickly. In 2002 another round of financing injected DreamWorks with a cash infusion that the company is using to increase its live-action film production and expand its animation production facilities.

EXECUTIVES

Principal: David Geffen, age 60
Principal: Jeffrey Katzenberg, age 52
Principal: Steven Spielberg, age 56
Head of Consumer Products: Brad Globe
Head of DreamWorks Records: Mo Ostin
Head of DreamWorks Records: Michael Ostin
Head of DreamWorks Records: Lenny Waronker
Head of DreamWorks Television: Justin Falvey
Head of DreamWorks Television: Darryl Frank
Head of Feature Animation: Ann Daly
Head of Marketing and Public Relations: Terry Press
Head of Motion Picture Division: Laurie MacDonald
Head of Motion Picture Division: Walter Parkes, age 52
Head of PDI/DreamWorks: Patti Burke
Head of Production: Michael De Luca, age 37
Head of Technology: Andy Hendrickson
Head of Theatrical Distribution: Jim Tharp
Head of Worldwide Pay Television: Hal Richardson
Finance Executive: Tony Hull

LOCATIONS

HQ: 1000 Flower St., Glendale, CA 91201
Phone: 818-733-7000 **Fax:** 818-695-7574
Web: www.dreamworks.com

DreamWorks SKG has offices in Glendale, Los Angeles, and Universal City, California.

PRODUCTS/OPERATIONS

Selected Films, Recording Artists, and Television Shows

DreamWorks Pictures
A Beautiful Mind (2001, co-produced with Universal Studios)
Almost Famous (2000)
American Beauty (1999)
Amistad (1997)
Antz (1998)
Catch Me if You Can (2002)
Chicken Run (2000, co-produced with Aardman Animation)
Deep Impact (1998, co-produced with Paramount Pictures)
Galaxy Quest (1999)
Gladiator (2000, co-produced with Universal Studios)
The Legend of Bagger Vance (2000)
Minority Report (2002)
Mouse Hunt (1997)
Old School (2003)
The Peacemaker (1997)
The Prince of Egypt (1998)
The Ring (2002)
Road to Perdition (2002)
Road Trip (2000)
Saving Private Ryan (1998, co-produced with Paramount Pictures)
Shrek (2001)
Sinbad: Legend of the Seven Seas (2003)
Small Time Crooks (2000)
What Lies Beneath (2000, co-produced with 20th Century Fox)

DreamWorks Records
Buckcherry
Eels
Nelly Furtado
Toby Keith
Len
Papa Roach
Chris Rock
Elliott Smith
Rufus Wainwright

DreamWorks Television
Boomtown (2002-2003)
Freaks and Geeks (1999-2000)
The Job (2001)
Oliver Beene (2003)
Spin City (1996-2002)
Undeclared (2001)

COMPETITORS

Alliance Atlantis Communications
Artisan Entertainment
Carsey-Werner-Mandabach
Fox Entertainment
Lions Gate Entertainment
Lucasfilm
MGM
Miramax
Paramount Pictures
Pixar
Sony Pictures Entertainment
VUE
Warner Bros.

HISTORICAL FINANCIALS

Company Type: Private

Income Statement FYE: December 31

	REVENUE ($ mil.)	NET INCOME ($ mil.)	NET PROFIT MARGIN	EMPLOYEES
12/02	1,813	—	—	1,600
12/01	2,219	—	—	1,500
12/00	1,873	—	—	1,500
12/99	1,242	—	—	1,500
12/98	1,000	—	—	1,600
Annual Growth	16.0%	—	—	0.0%

Revenue History

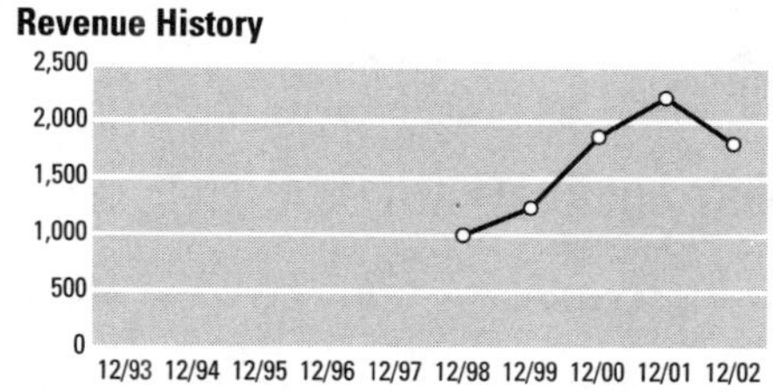

The Drees Co.

A family-operated enterprise since its founding by Theodore Drees in 1928, The Drees Co. builds more than 2,700 homes annually. Customers may choose from more than 100 floor plans for homes that range in price from about $95,000 to $500,000. Drees is a leading homebuilder in Cincinnati. It also builds condominiums, apartments, and commercial buildings through its nine divisions. The company is expanding through acquisitions such as the additions of the homebuilding assets of Zaring National in Cincinnati (Zaring Premier Homes), Indianapolis, and Nashville, and Ausherman Homes in the Washington, DC, area. Drees offers financing through its First Equity Mortgage subsidiary.

EXECUTIVES

Chairman: Ralph Drees
President and CEO: David Drees
EVP and CFO: Mark Williams
SVP Marketing: Jack Miller
VP Human Resources: Effie McKeehan
Director, IS: Mike Rulli
Director Marketing: Barbara Drees
Secretary and Treasurer: Lawrence G. Herbst

LOCATIONS

HQ: 211 Grandview Dr., Ste. 300, Fort Mitchell, KY 41017
Phone: 859-578-4200 **Fax:** 859-341-5854
Web: www.dreeshomes.com

The Drees Co. has operations in Indianapolis, Indiana; northern Kentucky; Maryland; Raleigh, North Carolina; Cincinnati, Cleveland and Dayton, Ohio; Nashville, Tennessee; Austin and Dallas/Fort Worth, Texas; Virginia; and Washington DC.

Division Office Locations

Austin Division — Austin, Texas
Cincinnati Division — Ft. Mitchell, Kentucky
Cleveland — North Canton, Ohio
Dallas Division — Irving, Texas
Dayton Division — Centerville, Ohio
Indianapolis Division — Indianapolis, Indiana
Nashville Division — Brentwood, Tennessee
Raleigh Division — Raleigh, North Carolina
Washington DC Division — Alexandria, Virginia

COMPETITORS

Centex
D.R. Horton
Engle Homes
Fischer Homes
KB Home
Lennar
M/I Schottenstein Homes
Pulte Homes
Ryland

HISTORICAL FINANCIALS

Company Type: Private

Income Statement FYE: March 31

	REVENUE ($ mil.)	NET INCOME ($ mil.)	NET PROFIT MARGIN	EMPLOYEES
3/03	822	80	9.7%	1,232
3/02	848	66	7.8%	1,100
3/01	527	—	—	850
3/00	515	—	—	—
3/99	366	—	—	700
3/98	343	—	—	685
3/97	301	—	—	675
3/96	253	—	—	675
3/95	236	—	—	625
Annual Growth	16.9%	21.6%	—	8.9%

Net Income History

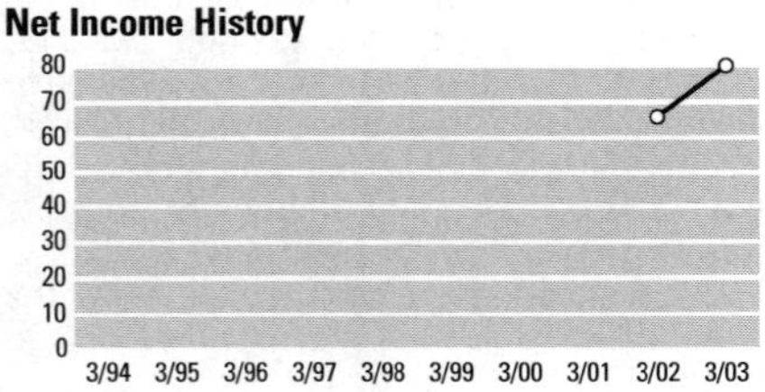

Dresser, Inc.

All dressed up and no place to flow? Not Dresser. The company, formerly Dresser Industries (and once a part of Halliburton), makes flow control products, measurement systems, and power systems. In addition to diagnostic equipment, injection pumps, and valves, Dresser's flow control segment now oversees the products once manufactured by the company's measurement systems division (gas pumps and outdoor payment systems, pressure and temperature gauges, natural gas meters, and regulators). Dresser's power systems include natural gas-powered engines, rotary blowers, and vacuum pumps bearing the Waukesha and ROOTS brands. DEG Acquisitions, a US-based investment firm, owns more than 90% of Dresser.

EXECUTIVES

Chairman: William E. Macaulay, age 57
CEO and Director: Patrick M. Murray, age 60
President and Director: Steven G. Lamb
EVP and CFO: James A. Nattier, age 42
SVP, Corporate Development: J. Scott Matthews
VP; President, Waukesha Engine: William E. O'Connor, age 55
VP; President, Dresser Wayne: John P. Ryan, age 49
VP, General Counsel, and Secretary: Frank P. Pittman, age 55
VP, Finance and Chief Accounting Officer: Dale B. Mikus, age 37
VP, Human Resources: James F. Riegler, age 52
Treasurer: Richard T. Kernan, age 54
Director, Corporate Communications: Stewart P. Yee
Auditors: PricewaterhouseCoopers

LOCATIONS

HQ: 15455 Dallas Pkwy., Ste. 1100, Addison, TX 75001
Phone: 972-361-9800 **Fax:** 972-361-9929
Web: www.dresser.com

Dresser has manufacturing facilities around the globe.

COMPETITORS

Caterpillar
Cooper Cameron
Danaher
Datamarine
Dover
Emerson Electric
Flowserve
IDEX
ITT Industries
Pentair
Rotork
SPX
Tokheim
Tyco International

HISTORICAL FINANCIALS

Company Type: Private

Income Statement FYE: December 31

	REVENUE ($ mil.)	NET INCOME ($ mil.)	NET PROFIT MARGIN	EMPLOYEES
12/02	1,595	—	—	7,500
12/01	1,546	—	—	8,500
Annual Growth	3.2%	—	—	(11.8%)

Revenue History

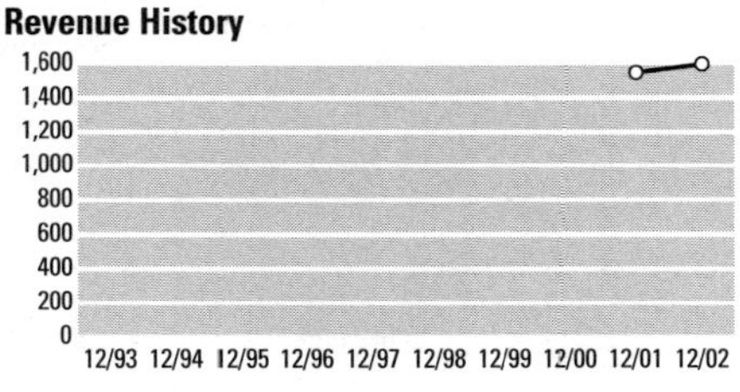

DriveTime Automotive

In this story the ugly duckling changes into DriveTime. DriveTime Automotive, formerly known as Ugly Duckling, is a leading used-car dealership chain, primarily targeting low-income customers and those with credit problems. To cater to these subprime customers, the company is a "buy here-pay here" dealer, meaning it finances and services car loans rather than using outside lenders (interest rates range from 20% to 30%). DriveTime operates about 80 dealerships in metropolitan areas in eight states, selling more than 3,500 cars a month. The cars undergo a 52-point inspection and are run through AutoCheck, an auto history database. The company was taken private by a group led by chairman Ernest Garcia.

EXECUTIVES

Chairman: Ernest C. Garcia II, age 44
President and CEO: Gregory B. Sullivan, age 43, $266,275 pay
VP and CFO: Mark G. Sauder, age 41
VP, Secretary, and General Counsel: Jon D. Ehlinger, age 44, $160,000 pay
VP and Treasurer: C. Robert Fulton, age 36, $150,000 pay
Director, Human Resources: Brandie Anslow
Auditors: KPMG LLP

LOCATIONS

HQ: DriveTime Automotive Group, Inc.
4020 E. Indian School Rd., Phoenix, AZ 85018
Phone: 602-852-6600 **Fax:** 602-852-6686
Web: www.drivetime.com

2001 Dealerships by Market

	No.
Los Angeles	13
Atlanta	9
Dallas	9
San Antonio	9
Tampa	9
Orlando	7
Phoenix	7
Richmond	5
Albuquerque	3
Tucson	3
Las Vegas	2
Total	**76**

COMPETITORS

America's Car-Mart
AutoNation
CarMax
Driver's Mart Worldwide
Gillman
Gunn Automotive
Hall Auto World
McCombs Automotive
Sonic Automotive
VT

HISTORICAL FINANCIALS

Company Type: Private

Income Statement FYE: December 31

	REVENUE ($ mil.)	NET INCOME ($ mil.)	NET PROFIT MARGIN	EMPLOYEES
12/01	434	(10)	—	2,300
12/00	483	9	1.9%	2,600
12/99	390	9	2.4%	2,700
12/98	288	(6)	—	2,500
12/97	124	9	7.6%	2,300
12/96	54	6	11.0%	652
12/95	56	(4)	—	425
12/94	34	(2)	—	—
12/93	17	1	4.2%	—
Annual Growth	50.5%	—	—	32.5%

2001 Year-End Financials

Debt ratio: 316.9%
Return on equity: —
Cash ($ mil.): 9
Current ratio: 13.98
Long-term debt ($ mil.): 461

Net Income History

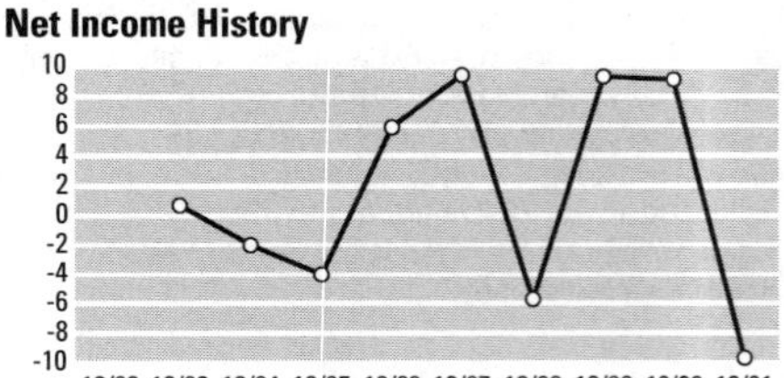

Drummond Company, Inc.

Drummond Company is building its business from the ground down. The company's Shoal Creek coal mine in Alabama is one of the US's largest underground mines. Shoal Creek produces more than 4 million tons of coal annually, most of which it sells to electric utility Alabama Power. Drummond also operates a surface coal mine in Colombia. Its ABC Coke unit has an annual capacity of some 750,000 tons. In addition, the company develops housing communities and office parks in Alabama, California, and Florida. Heman Drummond began his namesake company in 1935 on land homesteaded by his mother; eventually his five sons entered the business. The Drummond family still owns and manages the company.

EXECUTIVES

Chairman and CEO: Garry N. Drummond, age 64
Vice Chairman: E. A. (Larry) Drummond
SEVP, External Affairs and Treasurer: Walter F. Johnsey
SVP and CFO: Jack Stillwell
VP, Human Resources: Andy Slentz
President, ABC Coke Division: John M. Pearson
President, Drummond Coal Sales, Inc.: George E. Wilbanks
President, Drummond, Ltd.: Agusto Jimenez
President, Mining Division: Mike Zervos

LOCATIONS

HQ: 530 Beacon Pkwy. W., Ste. 900, Birmingham, AL 35209
Phone: 205-945-6500 **Fax:** 205-945-6251
Web: www.drummondco.com

Drummond Company has mining operations in the US (in Alabama) and in Colombia, and a coke facility in Alabama. The company is also involved in real estate projects in Alabama, California, and Florida.

PRODUCTS/OPERATIONS

Selected Operations

ABC Coke (coke plant; Jefferson County, Alabama)
La Loma Mine (coal, Colombia)
Liberty Park (real estate development; Birmingham, Alabama)
Oakbridge (real estate development; Lakeland, Florida)
Rancho La Quinta (real estate development; La Quinta, California)
Shoal Creek Mine (coal; Jefferson County, Alabama)

Selected Subsidiaries and Affiliates

Drummond Coal Sales, Inc. (Japan, the UK, and the US)
Drummond Ltd. (Colombia)
Perry Supply, Inc. (mining and foundry supply business)

COMPETITORS

Alliance Resource Partners
Arch Coal
Black Hills
CONSOL Energy
Grupo México
Horizon Natural Resources
Level 3 Communications
Massey Energy
NACCO Industries
Oxbow
Peabody Energy
Penn Virginia
Sherritt International
Walter Industries
Westmoreland Coal

HISTORICAL FINANCIALS

Company Type: Private

Income Statement FYE: December 31

	REVENUE ($ mil.)	NET INCOME ($ mil.)	NET PROFIT MARGIN	EMPLOYEES
12/02	600	—	—	2,500
12/01	600	—	—	2,500
12/00	615	—	—	2,800
12/99	720	—	—	3,300
12/98	734	—	—	2,900
12/97	746	—	—	2,850
12/96	750	—	—	2,800
12/95	725	—	—	3,350
12/94	687	—	—	2,800
12/93	730	—	—	2,800
Annual Growth	(2.2%)	—	—	(1.3%)

Revenue History

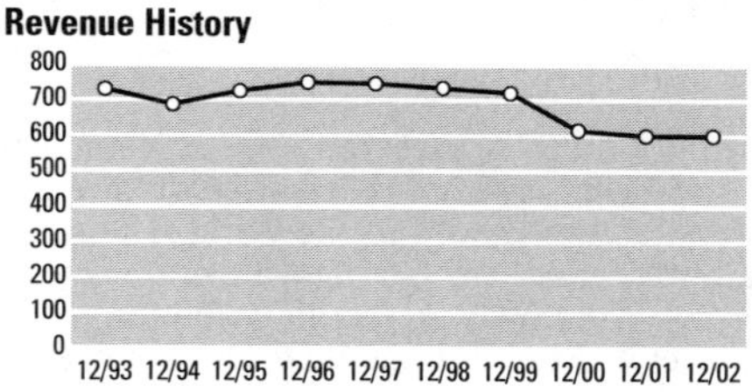

Duchossois Industries, Inc.

Business is no longer a horse race for holding company Duchossois Industries. The former owner of Chicago's Arlington International Racecourse, Duchossois Industries (pronounced Deshy-swa) sold its interests in the track to Churchill Downs. The Chamberlain Group, a Duchossois subsidiary, is the world's largest maker of residential and commercial door openers, and it is a leading maker of access control products. Duchossois also has interests in the consumer products, transportation, defense, and entertainment industries. Duchossois sold its railroad car unit (Thrall) to Trinity Industries in 2001. Chairman Richard Duchossois and his family own the company; he also holds a 24% stake in Churchill Downs.

EXECUTIVES

Chairman: Richard L. Duchossois, age 80
President and CEO: Craig J. Duchossois, age 58
CFO: Robert L. Fealy, age 50
VP Data Processing: David Gillhouse
VP Taxes: Mary Wong, age 47
CEO, The Chamberlain Group, Inc.: J. David Rolls
Hiring Manager: Melanie Ditore
Assistant General Counsel: David L. Filkin

LOCATIONS

HQ: 845 N. Larch Ave., Elmhurst, IL 60126
Phone: 630-279-3600 **Fax:** 630-530-6091

PRODUCTS/OPERATIONS

Selected Subsidiaries

Automatic Gate Supply
The Chamberlain Group, Inc.
M & S Systems, Inc.
Sentex Systems

COMPETITORS

General American Door
GE
Griffon
Microchip Technology
Nortek
Overhead Door
Stanley Works

HISTORICAL FINANCIALS

Company Type: Private

Income Statement FYE: December 31

	ESTIMATED REVENUE ($ mil.)	NET INCOME ($ mil.)	NET PROFIT MARGIN	EMPLOYEES
12/02	1,000	—	—	8,000
12/01	1,105	—	—	6,500
12/00	1,200	—	—	7,000
12/99	1,500	—	—	8,000
12/98	1,250	—	—	8,000
12/97	1,250	—	—	7,000
12/96	1,260	—	—	8,000
12/95	1,070	—	—	8,000
12/94	1,000	—	—	8,000
12/93	1,000	—	—	8,000
Annual Growth	0.0%	—	—	0.0%

Revenue History

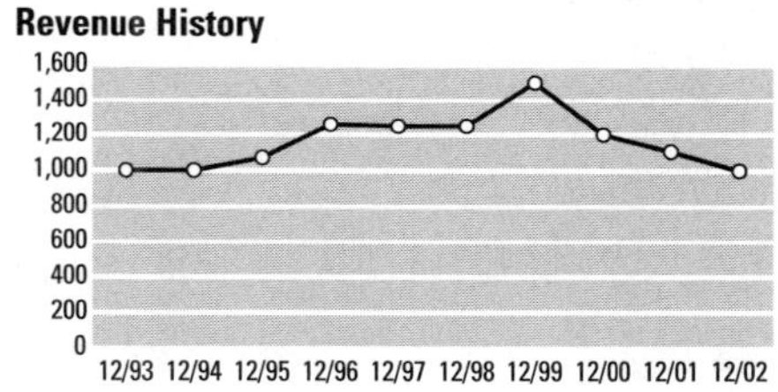

Duke Energy Field Services

Duke Energy Field Services (DEFS) is a midstream maven. Formed when Duke Energy and Phillips Petroleum (later ConocoPhillips) combined their gas gathering, processing, and marketing operations, the company is one of the largest midstream natural gas operators in the US, with 60,000 miles of gathering pipeline and 71 processing plants. DEFS also owns several NGL processing facilities and is the US's #1 NGL producer, at 392,000 barrels per day. The firm sells about 40% of its NGL production to ConocoPhillips under a long-term contract. Duke Energy owns about 70% of DEFS; ConocoPhillips owns 30%. DEFS is the general partner of TEPPCO Partners, L.P., which owns a network of refined products and crude oil pipelines.

EXECUTIVES

Chairman, President, and CEO: Jim W. Mogg, age 54, $490,072 pay
EVP: William W. Slaughter, age 55, $339,128 pay
EVP Marketing and Corporate Development: Mark A. Borer, age 48, $329,146 pay
EVP Gathering and Processing: Michael J. Bradley, age 48, $329,116 pay
SVP Northern Division: Robert F. Martinovich, age 48, $304,687 pay
VP and CFO: Rose M. Robeson, age 42
VP, General Counsel, and Secretary: Brent L. Backes, age 43
Human Resources: David Goode
Investor Relations: Tom Long
Auditors: Deloitte & Touche LLP

LOCATIONS

HQ: Duke Energy Field Services, LLC
370 17th St., Ste. 900, Denver, CO 80202
Phone: 303-595-3331 **Fax:** 303-595-0480
Web: www.defieldservices.com

Duke Energy Field Services operates in Colorado, Kansas, New Mexico, Texas, and Wyoming and in northwestern Alberta, Canada. It also operates along the US Gulf Coast and in the Gulf of Mexico.

PRODUCTS/OPERATIONS

2002 Sales

	$ mil.	% of total
Natural gas	5,187	95
Transportation, storage & processing	291	5
Other	14	—
Total	**5,492**	**100**

COMPETITORS

ChevronTexaco
Dynegy
El Paso
Enterprise Products
Kerr-McGee
Kinder Morgan Energy Partners
Koch
Nuevo Energy
Plains All American Pipeline
Western Gas
Williams Companies

HISTORICAL FINANCIALS

Company Type: Joint venture

Income Statement FYE: December 31

	REVENUE ($ mil.)	NET INCOME ($ mil.)	NET PROFIT MARGIN	EMPLOYEES
12/02	5,492	(47)	—	3,800
12/01	9,598	364	3.8%	3,600
12/00	9,093	680	7.5%	3,400
12/99	3,458	43	1.3%	2,700
12/98	1,584	2	0.1%	—
12/97	1,802	51	2.8%	—
Annual Growth	25.0%	—	—	12.1%

2002 Year-End Financials

Debt ratio: 92.0%
Return on equity: —
Cash ($ mil.): 7
Current ratio: 0.79
Long-term debt ($ mil.): 2,256

Net Income History

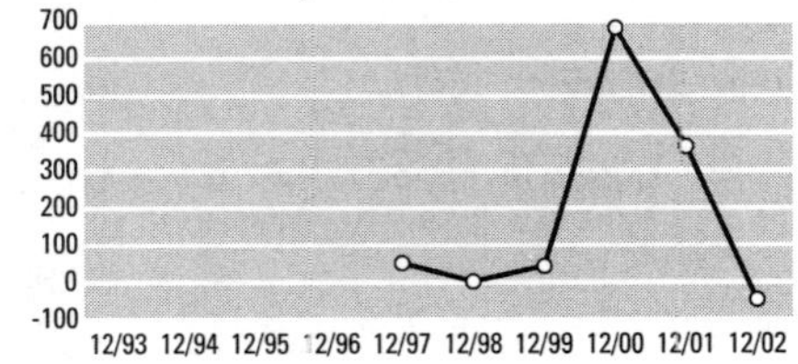

Revenue History

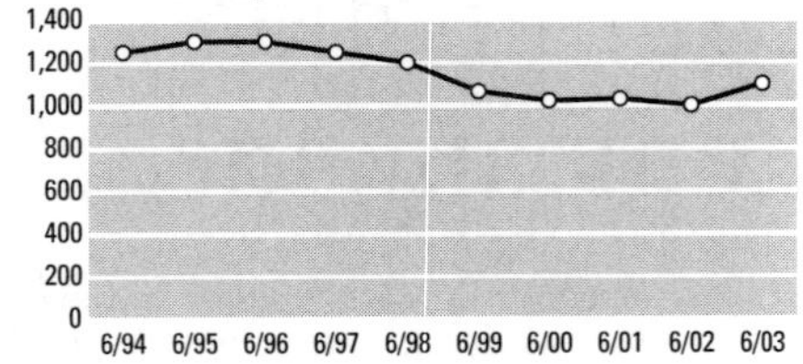

Dunavant Enterprises, Inc.

King Cotton is alive and well in Memphis. Homegrown Dunavant Enterprises is one of the largest cotton traders in the world. The company was founded in 1960 by William Dunavant, his son Billy (who is allergic to cotton), and Samuel T. Reeves. (The elder Dunavant died shortly after the founding, and Reeves left in 1995 to form Pinnacle Trading.) The company, which grew by selling aggressively to China and the Soviet Union, maintains offices in Asia, Australia, Europe, Mexico, South America, the former Soviet Union, and the southern US. The company's other business interests include cotton ginning, trucking, and warehousing. Dunavant Enterprises is owned by the Dunavant family and company employees.

EXECUTIVES

Chairman and CEO: William B. (Billy) Dunavant Jr.
President, Dunavant of California: Roger Glaspey
Manager, Human Resources: Mike Andereck

LOCATIONS

HQ: 3797 New Getwell Rd., Memphis, TN 38118
Phone: 901-369-1500 **Fax:** 901-369-1608
Web: www.dunavant.com

COMPETITORS

Calcot
Cargill
Cotton Inc.
King Ranch
Plains Cotton
Southwestern Irrigated Cotton
Staplcotn
Weil Brothers Cotton

HISTORICAL FINANCIALS

Company Type: Private

Income Statement FYE: June 30

	ESTIMATED REVENUE ($ mil.)	NET INCOME ($ mil.)	NET PROFIT MARGIN	EMPLOYEES
6/03	1,099	—	—	2,000
6/02	1,000	—	—	2,000
6/01	1,030	—	—	2,400
6/00	1,022	—	—	950
6/99	1,065	—	—	700
6/98	1,200	—	—	700
6/97	1,250	—	—	950
6/96	1,300	—	—	920
6/95	1,300	—	—	—
6/94	1,250	—	—	—
Annual Growth	(1.4%)	—	—	11.7%

Dunn Industries, Inc.

Although its beginnings date back to 1924, this company is far from done. Dunn Industries, owned by descendants of founder John E. Dunn, holds construction companies, including flagship J.E. Dunn Construction and Witcher Construction and R.J. Griffin Construction. The group builds institutional, commercial, and industrial structures; it also provides construction and program management and design/build services. J.E. Dunn Construction, which ranks among the top 10 US general builders, was one of the first contractors to offer the construction management delivery method. Projects include Sprint's world headquarters near Kansas City, one of the Midwest's largest construction projects.

EXECUTIVES

Chairman Emeritus: William H. Dunn Sr.
Chairman: Steve Dunn
Vice Chairman: Robert A. Long
President and CEO: Terrence P. Dunn
SVP and CFO, J.E. Dunn Construction: Gordon Lansford
SVP Corporate Development: Charles J. (Chuck) Cianciaruso
VP Human Resources: Rick Beyer
VP Information Services: Kent Immenschuh
VP Marketing: John Brake
Secretary: Barbara Hachey
Financial Analyst and Auditor: John Conley

LOCATIONS

HQ: 929 Holmes, Kansas City, MO 64106
Phone: 816-474-8600 **Fax:** 816-391-2510
Web: www.jedunn.com

COMPETITORS

Alberici
Bovis Lend Lease
Clark Enterprises
Hensel Phelps Construction
Rudolph & Sletten
Skanska USA Building
Turner Corporation
Washington Group

HISTORICAL FINANCIALS

Company Type: Private

Income Statement FYE: December 31

	REVENUE ($ mil.)	NET INCOME ($ mil.)	NET PROFIT MARGIN	EMPLOYEES
12/01	1,533	—	—	3,000
12/00	1,311	—	—	3,000
12/99	1,063	—	—	2,000
12/98	871	—	—	2,000
12/97	386	—	—	2,000
12/96	632	—	—	1,700
Annual Growth	19.4%	—	—	12.0%

Revenue History

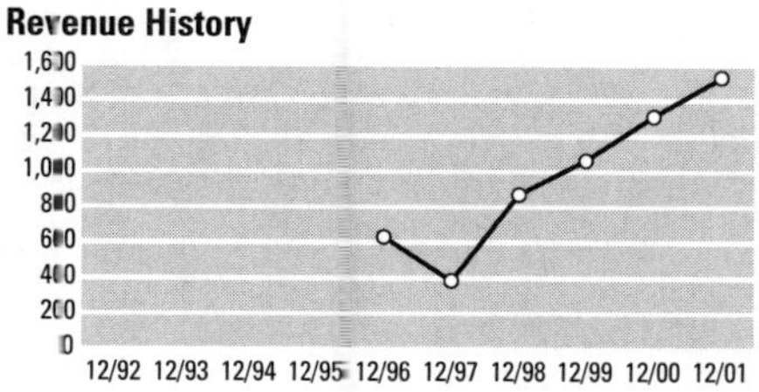

Eagle-Picher Industries, Inc.

From batteries to boron, Eagle-Picher Industries (EPI) provides products for the automotive, aerospace, telecommunications, pharmaceutical, and food and beverage industries. EPI's automotive group leads in sales with products that include precision-machined components, rubber-coated parts, and fluid systems. The company's technologies segment makes batteries for satellites, launch vehicles, and missiles, as well as boron for nuclear applications. Eagle-Picher has sold its machinery segment that made elevating wheel tractor scrapers (exclusively for Caterpillar). Its filtration and minerals segment produces diatomaceous earth and perlite filter aids. Dutch investment firm Granaria Holdings owns EPI.

EXECUTIVES

Chairman: Joel P. Wyler, age 52
President and CEO: John H. Weber, age 47, $225,000 pay
SVP and CFO: Thomas R. Pilholski
SVP, Human Resources: Jeffrey D. Sisson, age 45
VP and Controller: John F. Sullivan, age 59
VP, Director of Taxes: David N. Evans, $215,000 pay
VP, General Counsel, and Secretary: David G. Krall, age 39, $336,666 pay
Treasurer: Tom B. Scherpenberg, $165,000 pay
Auditors: Deloitte & Touche LLP

LOCATIONS

HQ: 11201 N. Tatum Blvd., Ste. 110, Phoenix, AZ 85028
Phone: 602-923-7200 **Fax:** 602-923-7951
Web: www.epcorp.com

Eagle-Picher Industries has facilities primarily in the US. Other operations are located in Canada, Germany, Mexico, and the UK.

PRODUCTS/OPERATIONS

Selected Divisions and Products

Automotive
Hillsdale Division (components for engine, transmission, and driveline applications)
Wolverine Division (sealing solutions for engines, transmissions, and compressors)

Technologies
Batteries for satellites, launch vehicles, and missiles
Boron
Germanium

Minerals
Diatomaceous earth
Functional filters
Industrial absorbants
Perlite filter aids
Soil amendments and conditioners

COMPETITORS

Alleghany Corporation
Exide
Federal-Mogul
JCI
Linamar
Newcor
Powerware
Precision Castparts

HISTORICAL FINANCIALS

Company Type: Private

Income Statement FYE: November 30

	REVENUE ($ mil.)	NET INCOME ($ mil.)	NET PROFIT MARGIN	EMPLOYEES
11/02	697	(37)	—	3,800
11/01	693	(54)	—	4,100
11/00	838	(6)	—	5,400
11/99	913	(18)	—	6,925
11/98	826	—	—	6,600
11/97	906	—	—	6,700
11/96	891	—	—	7,700
11/95	849	—	—	—
11/94	757	—	—	—
11/93	662	—	—	—
Annual Growth	0.6%	—	—	(11.1%)

2002 Year-End Financials

Debt ratio: —
Return on equity: —
Cash ($ mil.): 32
Current ratio: 1.01
Long-term debt ($ mil.): 355

Net Income History

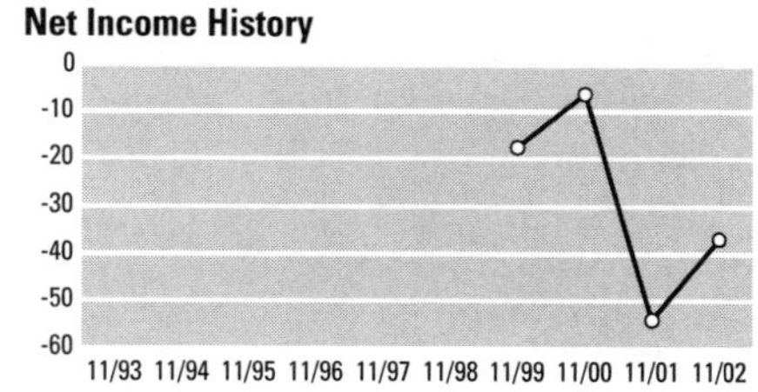

E. & J. Gallo Winery

Let them drink wine! E. & J. Gallo Winery brings merlot to the masses. The world's largest wine maker produces about 30% of the wine sold in the US, thanks in part to its inexpensive jug and box brands Carlo Rossi and Peter Vella. It also makes the fortified Thunderbird brand. The vintner cultivates more than 3,000 acres in the Napa and Sonoma valleys in California. Gallo also makes its own labels and bottles and is the leading US wine exporter. It also produces premium wines, imports and sells Italian wine Ecco Domani, and is a leading brandy producer. The Gallo family owns the vintner.

Gallo sells nearly 35 brands over a wide price range, from alcohol-added wines and wine coolers to upscale varietals that fetch more than $50 a bottle. Gallo once only sold wine in the low-to-moderate price range, but has successfully expanded into premium wines such as Turning Leaf and Gossamer Bay, which don't have the Gallo name on the label. The vintner's strong affiliation with Wal-Mart has boosted wine sales in new Wal-Mart markets such as Germany and the UK.

Gallo also buys grapes from other Sonoma County growers. Its 2002 purchase of fellow Sonoma County vintner Louis M. Martini Winery marks the first time Gallo has bought another winery; it usually buys land and labels. Gallo plans to allow Martini, also family owned, to continue as an autonomous operation. Since the purchase, Gallo has invested about $1 million in capital improvements at the winery and reportedly plans to ramp up production in 2004 of cabernet under the Martini label.

HISTORY

Giuseppe Gallo, the father of Ernest and Julio Gallo, was born in 1882 in the wine country of northwest Italy. Around 1900 he and his brother, Michelo (they called themselves Joe and Mike), traveled to America seeking their fame and fortune in the San Francisco area. Both brothers became wealthy by growing grapes and anticipating the growth of the market during Prohibition. (Home winemaking was legal and popular.)

Giuseppe's eldest sons, Ernest and Julio, worked with their father from the beginning. Their relationship was strained, and the father was reluctant to help his sons, particularly Ernest, in business. However, the mysterious murder-suicide that ended the lives of Giuseppe and his wife in 1933 eliminated that problem: The sons inherited the business their father had been unwilling to share.

From then on Ernest ran the business end, assembling a large distribution network and building a national brand, while Julio made the wine and Joe Jr., the third, much younger, brother, worked for them. In the early 1940s Gallo opened bottling plants in Los Angeles and New Orleans, using screw-cap bottles, which then seemed more hygienic and modern than corks. Gallo lagged during WWII, when alcohol was diverted for the military. Under Julio's supervision, it upgraded its planting stock and refined its technology.

In an attempt to capitalize on the sweet wines popular in the 1950s, Gallo introduced Thunderbird, a fortified wine (its alcohol content boosted to 20%), in 1957. In the 1960s Gallo spurred its growth by advertising heavily and keeping prices low. It introduced Hearty Burgundy, a jug wine, in 1964, along with Ripple. Gallo introduced the carbonated, fruit-flavored Boone's Farm Apple Wine in 1969, creating an interest in "pop" wines that lasted for a few years.

The company introduced its first varietal wines in 1974. In the 1970s Gallo field workers switched unions, from the United Farm Workers to the Teamsters. Repercussions included protests and boycotts, but sales were largely unaffected. From 1976 to 1982 Gallo operated under an FTC order limiting its control over wholesalers. The order was lifted after the industry's competitive balance changed.

Through the 1970s and 1980s, Gallo expanded its production of varietals; in 1988 it began adding vintage dates to the wines' labels. But it also kept a hand in the lower levels of the market, introducing Bartles & Jaymes wine coolers.

Gallo began a legal battle in 1986 with Joe, who had been eased out of the business, over the use of the Gallo name. In 1992 Joe lost the use of his name for commercial purposes. Julio died the next year when his Jeep overturned on a family ranch.

In 1996 rival Kendall-Jackson sued Gallo for trademark infringement over Gallo's new wine brand, Turning Leaf, claiming Gallo copied its Vintner's Reserve bottle and label. A jury ruled in Gallo's favor in 1997; a federal appeals court supported that decision in 1998.

In May 2000 Gallo announced plans to promote wine-cooler market leader Bartles & Jaymes with a new advertising campaign, although the category continues to wane.

In 2001 Gallo's research team patented a number of diagnostic tools that can be licensed to winemakers around the world; one tool, for example, can spot an infected vine in a matter of hours, rather than years.

In 2002 Gallo bought the Louis M. Martini Winery in Napa Valley, furthering its expansion into the premium wine business. It also bought the brand name and stocks of San Jose-based wine producer Mirassou Vineyards, one of the oldest wineries in California.

EXECUTIVES

Chairman: Ernest Gallo
Co-President: James E. Coleman
Co-President: Joseph E. Gallo
Co-President: Robert J. Gallo
EVP and General Counsel: Jack B. Owens
EVP, Marketing: Albion Fenderson
CFO: Tony Youga
VP, Human Resources: Mike Chase
VP, Information Systems: Kent Kushar
VP, Media: Sue McClelland
VP, National Sales: Gary Ippolito

LOCATIONS

HQ: 600 Yosemite Blvd., Modesto, CA 95354
Phone: 209-341-3111 **Fax:** 209-341-3569
Web: www.gallo.com

E. & J. Gallo Winery has four wineries in the California counties of Fresno, Livingston, Modesto, and Sonoma, and vineyards throughout the region. Its wine is sold throughout the US and in more than 85 countries.

PRODUCTS/OPERATIONS

Selected Products and Labels

Bargain generic and varietals (Carlo Rossi, Livingston Cellars, Peter Vella, Twin Valley, Wild Vines)
Brandy (E & J, E&J Cask & Cream, E&J VSOP)
Flagship (Gallo of Sonoma — County, Estate, and Single Vineyard series)
Fortified and jug (Night Train, Ripple, Thunderbird)
Hospitality industry (Burlwood, Copperidge by E&J Gallo, Liberty Creek, William Wycliff Vineyards)
Imported varietals (Bella Sera, Ecco Domani, McWilliams Hanwood Estate)
Mid-priced varietals (Redwood Creek, Turning Leaf)
Sparkling (André, Ballatore, Indigo Hills, Tott's)
Premium (Anapamu, Frei Brothers Reserve, Indigo Hills, Marcelina, Rancho Zabaco, Turning Leaf Coastal Reserve)

COMPETITORS

Allied Domecq
Asahi Breweries
Bacardi
Bacardi USA
Beringer Blass
Brown-Forman
Chalone Wine
Constellation Brands
Diageo
Foster's
Heaven Hill Distilleries
GIV
Jim Beam Brands
Kendall-Jackson
Kirin
LVMH
Pernod Ricard
Ravenswood Winery
R.H. Phillips
Robert Mondavi
Sebastiani Vineyards
Taittinger
Terlato Wine
Trinchero Family Estates
UST
Concha y Toro
Vincor
Wine Group

HISTORICAL FINANCIALS

Company Type: Private

Income Statement FYE: December 31

	ESTIMATED REVENUE ($ mil.)	NET INCOME ($ mil.)	NET PROFIT MARGIN	EMPLOYEES
12/01	1,700	—	—	3,500
12/00	1,610	—	—	3,600
12/99	1,520	—	—	5,250
12/98	1,500	—	—	5,000
12/97	1,300	—	—	5,000
12/96	1,200	—	—	5,000
12/95	1,100	—	—	4,000
12/94	980	—	—	4,000
12/93	1,100	—	—	4,000
12/92	1,000	—	—	3,000
Annual Growth	6.1%	—	—	1.7%

Revenue History

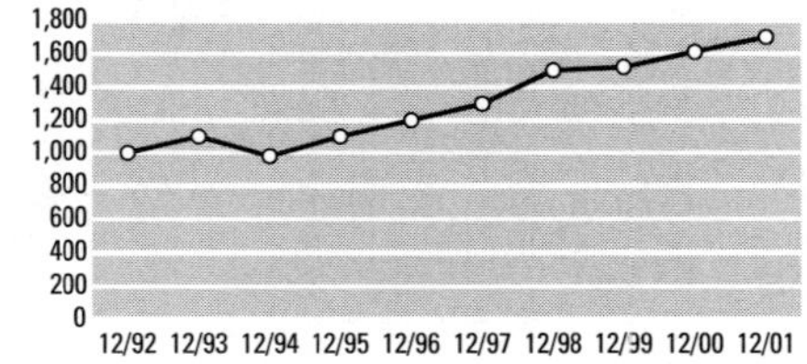

Earle M. Jorgensen

Earle M. Jorgensen Company (EMJ) is one of the US's largest independent steel distributors. The company sells tubing, pipes, and bar, as well as structural, plate, and sheet metal products. EMJ makes its products from carbon steel, alloy steel, stainless steel, and aluminum. It markets to the automotive, agriculture, chemical, medical, oil, defense, food, petrochemical, and machinery-manufacturing industries. The company operates a cutting center, a tube-honing facility, and 35 service centers throughout North America. Employees own about 25% of EMJ; investment firm Kelso & Company owns most of the rest.

EXECUTIVES

Chairman: David M. Roderick, age 79
President, CEO, COO, and Director: Maurice S. Nelson Jr., age 65, $930,150 pay
EVP: R. Neil McCaffery, age 53, $350,568 pay
VP, CFO, and Secretary: William S. Johnson, age 44
VP, Chicago Region: Kenneth L. Henry, age 56, $371,603 pay
VP, Eastern Region: James D. Hoffman, age 44, $352,105 pay
VP, Merchandising: Frank D. Travetto, age 50, $387,174 pay
Director, Human Resources: Inger Dickinson
Auditors: Ernst & Young LLP

LOCATIONS

HQ: Earle M. Jorgensen Company
3050 E. Birch St., Brea, CA 92821
Phone: 714-579-8823 **Fax:** 714-577-3784
Web: www.emjmetals.com

Earle M. Jorgensen Company operates facilities in Canada and the US.

PRODUCTS/OPERATIONS

2002 Sales

	% of total
Bars	
Carbon & alloy	37
Stainless	11
Aluminum	8
Tubing	
Carbon & alloy	25
Stainless	3
Aluminum	3
Plate	
Carbon & alloy	4
Aluminum	2
Stainless	1
Other	6
Total	**100**

COMPETITORS

AK Steel Holding Corporation
Alcoa
Chaparral Steel
Dalmine
Gerdau AmeriSteel
Japan Steel Works
Lone Star Technologies
LTV
MAXXAM
Metals USA
Nippon Steel
O'Neal Steel
Reliance Steel
Rouge Industries
Russel Metals
Ryerson Tull
Siderca
Superior Group
TXI
Ulbrich Stainless Steels
United States Steel

HISTORICAL FINANCIALS

Company Type: Private

Income Statement FYE: March 31

	REVENUE ($ mil.)	NET INCOME ($ mil.)	NET PROFIT MARGIN	EMPLOYEES
3/03	920	2	0.3%	1,674
3/02	895	5	0.6%	1,725
3/01	1,060	18	1.7%	2,010
3/00	938	24	2.6%	1,920
3/99	916	25	2.7%	1,900
3/98	1,050	16	1.5%	2,200
3/97	1,024	(27)	—	2,300
3/96	1,026	(29)	—	2,600
3/95	1,023	20	1.9%	2,800
3/94	843	(4)	—	2,561
Annual Growth	1.0%	—	—	(4.6%)

2003 Year-End Financials

Debt ratio: —
Return on equity: —
Cash ($ mil.): 20
Current ratio: 1.80
Long-term debt ($ mil.): 328

Net Income History

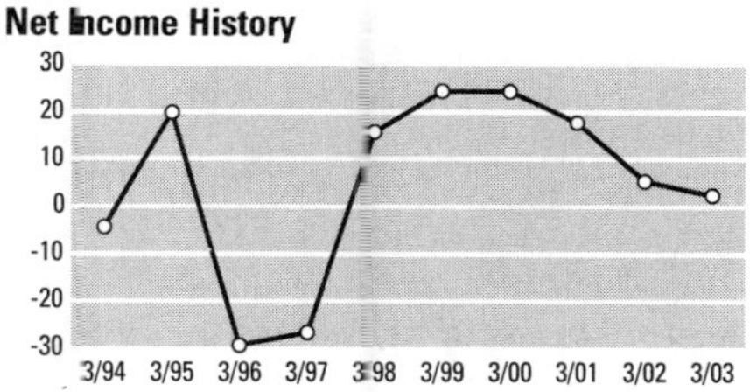

Earnhardt's Auto Centers

Milking the Southwest for all it's worth, Earnhardt's Auto Centers (and its bull-riding founder) sell more than 25,000 new and used vehicles each year. The company's nine auto dealerships in Arizona feature Chrysler, Dodge, Ford, Honda, Hyundai, Jeep, Kia, Mazda, Suzuki, and Volkswagen autos. The outlets also operate parts and service departments and offer financing. The company also sells new and used RVs. Earnhardt's Web site allows customers to "build" their next car online: Shoppers can select from a complete list of options before submitting it electronically. Established in 1951 by Tex Earnhardt, the company is family-owned and -operated.

EXECUTIVES

Chairman: Hal J. (Tex) Earnhardt Jr.
President: Hal J. Earnhardt III
CFO: Bobbyn McDowell
Secretary and Treasurer: Jim B. Earnhardt
Director of Human Resources: Sue Camrud
Director of Special Finance: Kevin Murphy

LOCATIONS

HQ: 1301 N. Arizona Ave., Gilbert, AZ 85233
Phone: 480-926-4000 **Fax:** 480-632-7712
Web: www.earnhardt.com

Earnhardt's Auto Centers has dealerships in Apache Junction, Chandler, Gilbert, Glendale, Mesa, and Tempe, Arizona.

COMPETITORS

Autobytel
AutoNation
AutoTrader
carOrder.com
CarsDirect.com
Chapman Automotive
David Wilson's
Larry H. Miller Group
StoneAge.com
Tuttle-Click
United Auto Group
VT

HISTORICAL FINANCIALS

Company Type: Private

Income Statement FYE: December 31

	ESTIMATED REVENUE ($ mil.)	NET INCOME ($ mil.)	NET PROFIT MARGIN	EMPLOYEES
12/01	685	—	—	2,000
12/00	680	—	—	1,500
12/99	800	—	—	1,500
12/98	800	—	—	1,500
12/97	650	—	—	1,400
12/96	560	—	—	1,112
12/95	475	—	—	—
12/94	400	—	—	—
Annual Growth	8.0%	—	—	12.5%

Revenue History

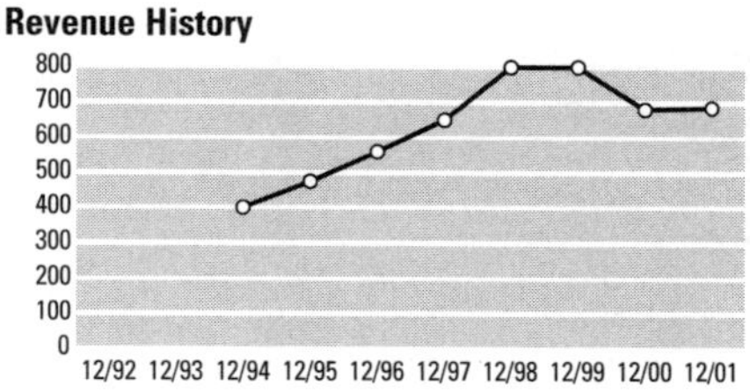

EBSCO Industries Inc.

Few portfolios are more diverse than that of EBSCO Industries (short for Elton B. Stephens Company). Among the conglomerate's information services, manufacturing, and sales subsidiaries are magazine subscription and fulfillment firms, a fishing lure manufacturer, a rifle manufacturer, a specialty office and computer furniture retailer, and a real estate company. Its main businesses revolve around the publishing industry: EBSCO operates a subscription management agency and is one of the largest publishers of information online and on CD-ROM. The family of founder Elton B. Stephens Sr. owns the company.

EBSCO provides bulk subscription services for print and electronic journals, technical reports, books, and other publications to schools, libraries, and professional offices. It offers sales, promotion, telemarketing, and fulfillment services to publishers, and it owns commercial printers and supplies bindery and packaging products.

Among EBSCO's eclectic subsidiaries are promotional products manufacturers Four Seasons and Vitronic; PRADCO, which makes fishing tackle; Valley Joist, which produces steel construction materials; Vulcan Industries, which makes point-of-purchase displays; Knight & Hale, which makes hunting accessories; specialty furniture makers H. Wilson and Luxor; and real estate unit EBSCO Development.

In 2003 EBSCO acquired the European operations of RoweCom, a company that provided libraries with an online service giving subscribers access to more than 240,000 periodicals.

EXECUTIVES

Chairman Emeritus: Elton B. Stephens
Chairman, President, and CEO: James T. Stephens
VP and CFO: Richard L. Bozzelli
VP and Chief Accounting Officer: Carol Matthews Johnson
VP; General Manager, Information Systems and Services: John R. Fitts
VP Corporate Communications: Joe K. Weed
VP HR: John Thompson

LOCATIONS

HQ: 5724 Hwy. 280 East, Birmingham, AL 35242
Phone: 205-991-6600 **Fax:** 205-995-1636
Web: www.ebscoind.com

PRODUCTS/OPERATIONS

Selected Operations

Information Services
EBSCO Information Services (reference databases, online journals, and subscription services)
EBSCO Publishing (database publishing and information retrieval services)
EBSCO Subscription Services (subscription services for libraries and institutions)

Manufacturing
EBSCO Media (commercial printer)
Four Seasons (promotional products)
H. Wilson Co. (audiovisual and computer products and furniture)
Luxor (specialty furniture for offices, schools, libraries, and health care facilities)
PRADCO Outdoor Brands (fishing lures, fishing line, and related products)
Valley Joist (steel joists, girders, and metal decks for the construction industry)
Vitronic (promotional products)
Wayne Industries (point-of-purchase advertising and signs)

Sales
EBSCO Development Co. (real estate development)
EBSCO Magazine Express (direct-marketing subscription agency)
EBSCO Realty (real estate broker)
EBSCO TeleServices (telemarketing services)
Military Service Company (producer and manufacturers' representative serving military base exchanges)
Publisher Promotion and Fulfillment (promotion and fulfillment services)
S.S. Nesbitt & Co. (insurance)
Vulcan Service (magazine subscription sales)

COMPETITORS

ACI Telecentrics
AMREP
APAC Customer Services
Black Dot Group
Bowne
Brunswick
Dai Nippon Printing
divine
General Binding
HA-LO Industries
Johnson Outdoors
McGraw-Hill
Moore Corporation
Quebecor
Reed Elsevier Group
Roanoke Electric Steel
R. R. Donnelley
Scholastic
Simon Worldwide
SITEL
TeleSpectrum
Thomson Corporation

HISTORICAL FINANCIALS

Company Type: Private

Income Statement FYE: June 30

	ESTIMATED REVENUE ($ mil.)	NET INCOME ($ mil.)	NET PROFIT MARGIN	EMPLOYEES
6/02	1,400	—	—	5,000
6/01	1,375	—	—	4,500
6/00	1,375	—	—	4,200
6/99	1,210	—	—	4,200
6/98	1,000	—	—	4,000
6/97	1,000	—	—	4,000
6/96	900	—	—	4,000
Annual Growth	7.6%	—	—	3.8%

Revenue History

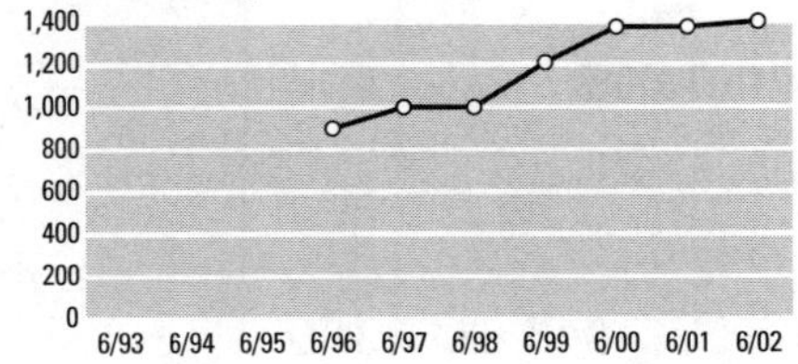

Eby-Brown Company

Eby-Brown makes its money on vices such as munchies and nicotine. The company is a leading convenience-store supplier of more than 11,000 name-brand products, including tobacco, candy, snacks, health and beauty aids, and general merchandise. The company's eight distribution centers serve 28 midwestern and southeastern states and more than 25,000 stores, including the Speedway and SuperAmerica chains owned by Marathon Ashland Petroleum. Eby-Brown also has a marketing division that offers its customers advertising and promotion services. The century-old company is family owned and run. Co-CEOs Tom and Dick Wake succeeded their father, chairman William Wake Jr., in 1983.

EXECUTIVES

Chairman: William S. (Bill) Wake Jr.
Co-President and Co-CEO: Richard (Dick) Wake
Co-President and Co-CEO: Thomas G. (Tom) Wake
CFO: Mark Smetana
EVP Sales: Al Palma
VP Advertising and Sales Promotions: Ralph Kallmann
VP, Business Development: Ron Coppel
VP, Merchandising: Jode Bunce
VP, Merchandising: Curt O'Rourke
VP, Merchandising: John Scardina
VP Merchandising: Mike Wierzbicki
Director of Human Resources: Rick Thorgesen

LOCATIONS

HQ: 280 W. Shuman Blvd., Ste. 280, Naperville, IL 60566
Phone: 630-778-2800 **Fax:** 630-778-2830
Web: www.eby-brown.com

COMPETITORS

AMCON Distributing
C.D. Hartnett
Fleming Companies
GSC Enterprises
H.T. Hackney
McLane
Nash Finch
Purity Wholesale Grocers
S. Abraham & Sons
Spartan Stores

HISTORICAL FINANCIALS

Company Type: Private

Income Statement FYE: September 30

	REVENUE ($ mil.)	NET INCOME ($ mil.)	NET PROFIT MARGIN	EMPLOYEES
9/02*	3,600	—	—	2,100
12/01	3,670	—	—	2,100
12/00	3,400	—	—	2,011
12/99	2,773	—	—	2,011
12/98	1,700	—	—	1,550
12/97	1,650	—	—	1,450
12/96	1,670	—	—	1,395
12/95	1,550	—	—	1,411
12/94	1,450	—	—	1,327
12/93	1,040	—	—	1,300
Annual Growth	14.8%	—	—	5.5%

*Fiscal year change

Revenue History

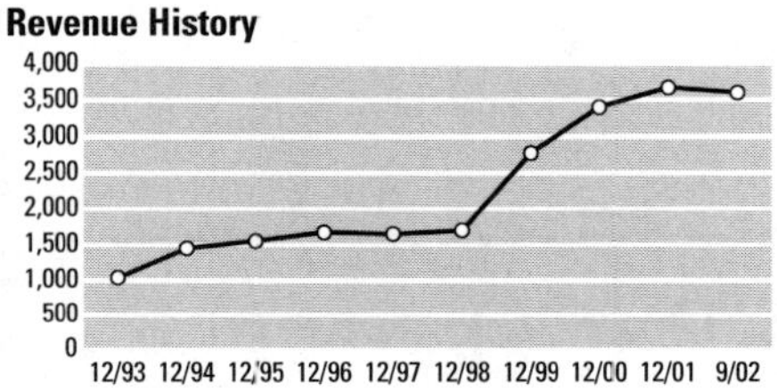

Educational Testing Service

Educational Testing Service (ETS) produces as many sweaty palms as the words, "We're from the IRS." The creator of the Scholastic Assessment Test (SAT) administers more than 12 million achievement, occupational, and admissions tests a year. Founded in 1947, the not-for-profit group is one of the nation's largest testing organizations. The ETS Research division conducts research projects focusing on education. For-profit subsidiary The Chauncey Group International designs, develops, and administers occupational certification and professional assessment tests. ETS closed about 84 of its testing centers outside the US.

EXECUTIVES

President and CEO: Kurt M. Landgraf, age 56
CFO: Frank R. Gatti
SVP and General Counsel: Stanford H. von Mayrhauser
SVP and General Manager, Elementary and Secondary Education: John H. Oswald
SVP Research and Development: Drew Gitomer
SVP School and College Services: Paul A. Ramsey
VP Communications and Public Affairs: Leslie C. Francis
VP Human Resources: Yvette Donado
Chief Information and Strategy Officer: Arthur C. Chisholm

LOCATIONS

HQ: Rosedale Road, Princeton, NJ 08541
Phone: 609-921-9000 **Fax:** 609-734-5410
Web: www.ets.org

Educational Testing Service administers tests in about 200 countries and has operations in California, Florida, New Jersey, and Washington, DC, as well as Puerto Rico. Subsidiary The Chauncey Group International operates in Canada, Europe, and the US.

PRODUCTS/OPERATIONS

Selected ETS Testing Programs

Advanced Placement Test (AP)
College-Level Examination Program (CLEP)
Graduate Management Admission Test (GMAT)
Graduate Record Examinations (GRE)
The Praxis Series: Professional Assessments for Beginning Teachers
Preliminary SAT/National Merit Scholarship Qualifying Test (PSAT/NMSQT)
Scholastic Assessment Test Program (SAT)
Test of English as a Foreign Language (TOEFL)

Selected Chauncey Group Products and Services

Basic and advanced skills assessment
Candidate screening
Certification examinations
Computer-based testing
Diagnostic assessment
English language examination
Internet testing
Job analysis
Paper and pencil testing
Program audits
Recertification assessment
Training needs analysis
Test development

COMPETITORS

ACT
Harcourt Education
Houghton Mifflin
Kaplan
McGraw-Hill
NCS Pearson
Princeton Review
Touchstone Applied Science

HISTORICAL FINANCIALS

Company Type: Not-for-profit

Income Statement FYE: June 30

	REVENUE ($ mil.)	NET INCOME ($ mil.)	NET PROFIT MARGIN	EMPLOYEES
6/03	600	—	—	2,500
6/02	700	—	—	2,500
6/01	600	—	—	2,500
6/00	500	—	—	2,500
6/99	494	—	—	2,100
6/98	496	—	—	2,300
6/97	432	—	—	2,300
6/96	411	—	—	2,300
6/95	386	—	—	2,300
Annual Growth	5.7%	—	—	1.0%

Revenue History

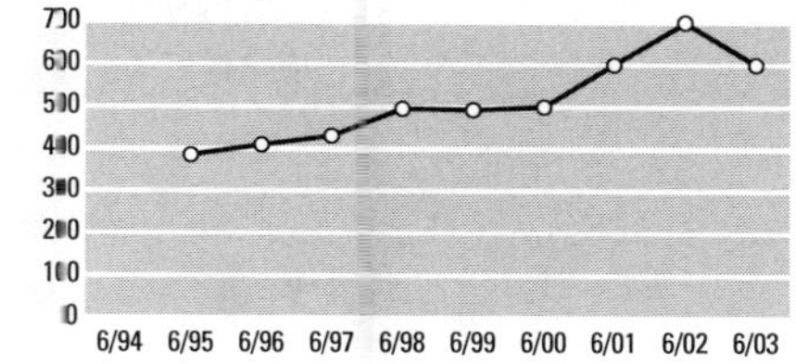

Elder Automotive

Being respectful to Elders is job one at the Elder Ford dealership and other lots in the Elder Automotive Group. It owns a leading Jaguar dealership in North America, Jaguar of Troy (Michigan), as well as Elder Ford, Aston Martin of Troy, and Saab of Troy; and in Tampa, Flordia, Aston Martin of Tampa and Jaguar of Tampa. The company sells new and used cars and offers repairs and maintenance through its parts and service departments. Elder Automotive Group was founded in 1967 by the Elder family; Irma Elder, owner and CEO, took over after her husband's death in 1983.

EXECUTIVES

CEO: Irma Elder
President: Tony Elder
Controller: Sandy Foster

LOCATIONS

HQ: Elder Automotive Group
777 John R. Rd., Troy, MI 48083
Phone: 248-585-4000 **Fax:** 248-583-0815
Web: www.elderautomotivegroup.com

COMPETITORS

AutoNation
March/Hodge
Meade Group
Mel Farr Automotive
Serra Automotive

HISTORICAL FINANCIALS

Company Type: Private

Income Statement FYE: December 31

	REVENUE ($ mil.)	NET INCOME ($ mil.)	NET PROFIT MARGIN	EMPLOYEES
12/01	539	—	—	111
12/00	484	—	—	280
12/99	486	—	—	250
12/98	437	—	—	213
12/97	381	—	—	229
Annual Growth	9.0%	—	—	(16.6%)

Revenue History

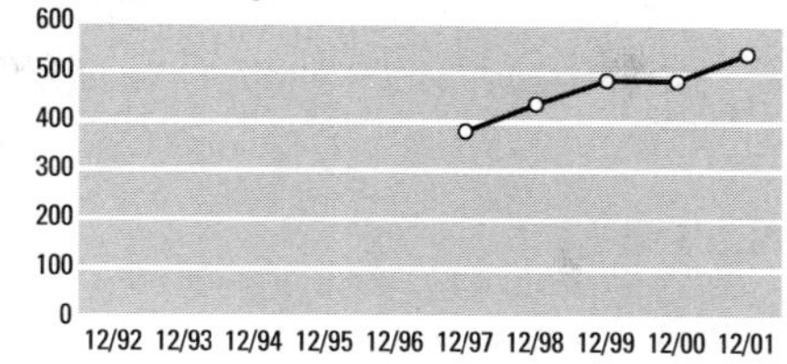

Elkay Manufacturing

Elkay Manufacturing doesn't make everything, but they do make the kitchen sink — along with cabinets, drinking fountains, faucets, water coolers, and water filtration products. The Katz family founded Elkay in the early 1920s to make sinks for butlers' pantries and sculleries. Elkay now sells residential and commercial stainless steel sinks under such names as Celebrity, Lustertone, and Gourmet. The company also offers kitchen accessories (colanders, cutting boards, soap dispensers). Elkay's cabinetmaking holdings include Yorktowne Cabinets, Medallion Cabinetry, and MasterCraft Cabinets. Elkay is the parent company of E.B. Tecnica Mexicana and Elkay Canada. Chairman Ronald Katz owns Elkay Manufacturing.

EXECUTIVES

Chairman and CEO: Ronald C. (Ron) Katz
President and COO: John P. Edl
EVP Marketing and Sales: John Heilstedt
VP and CFO: Timothy J. Bondy
VP Sales: William (Bill) Blaine
VP Human Resources: Walter E. Reilly
Division President: James (Jim) Scott
Division VP, Operations: Cary B. Wood
Division Director, Quality: Jeff Sharp

LOCATIONS

HQ: Elkay Manufacturing Company
2222 Camden Ct., Oak Brook, IL 60523
Phone: 630-574-8484 **Fax:** 630-574-5012
Web: www.elkay.com

Elkay Manufacturing has facilities in Europe, North America, and the Pacific Rim region.

PRODUCTS/OPERATIONS

Selected Products

Drinking fountains
Faucets
Kitchen cabinets
Residential and commercial sinks
Sink accessories (including colanders, cutting boards, drain trays, soap dispensers)
Sink tops, countertops, and drainboards
Water coolers
Water filters

Selected Subsidiaries

E.B. Tecnica Mexicana
Elkay Canada
MasterCraft Cabinets, Inc.
Medallion Cabinetry, Inc.
Yorktowne Cabinets

COMPETITORS

American Standard
American Woodmark
AquaCell
Armstrong World Industries
Black & Decker
Jacuzzi Brands
Kohler
MAAX
Masco
MasterBrand Cabinets
Moen
Novar

HISTORICAL FINANCIALS

Company Type: Private

Income Statement FYE: December 31

	REVENUE ($ mil.)	NET INCOME ($ mil.)	NET PROFIT MARGIN	EMPLOYEES
12/02	560	—	—	3,700
12/01	527	—	—	3,700
12/00	515	—	—	3,800
12/99	470	—	—	3,650
12/98	422	—	—	3,300
12/97	370	—	—	2,950
12/96	320	—	—	2,634
12/95	273	—	—	2,260
12/94	264	—	—	2,375
12/93	197	—	—	—
Annual Growth	12.3%	—	—	5.7%

Revenue History

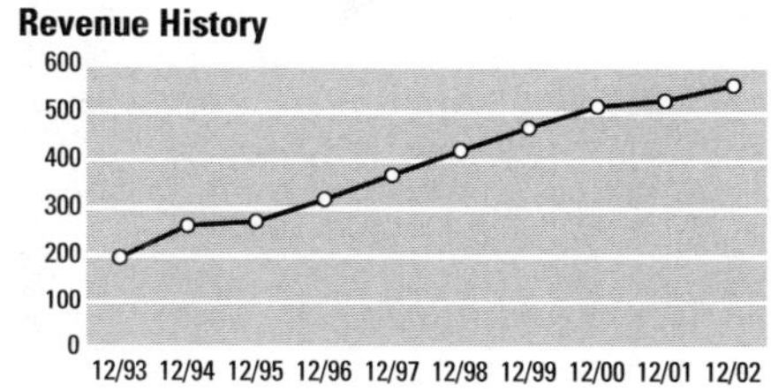

eMachines, Inc.

They're not cheap — they're *inexpensive*. eMachines' bargain PCs are designed for word processing, e-mail, and Web surfing. It sells its products through distributors and retailers such as Best Buy, Circuit City, and Office Depot. The company also sells products directly. eMachines saw early success as a pioneer seller of cut-rate PCs bundled with Internet service contracts, but it has struggled against larger PC makers with competitively priced products. Founded in 1998 by former CEO Steven Dukker, eMachines was acquired by director Lap Shun (John) Hui through a holding company and taken private in 2001.

Bargain-priced PCs allowed the company to become a top seller of computers through US retailers in its first year of business, but razor-thin margins and a quick competitive response to the low-end deals caused eMachines' sales and stock to plummet. Its efforts to restructure — including job cuts, a management overhaul, and the streamlining of its product line — failed to keep it from being delisted, but the company has found new life as a private entity. With a revamped line of low-cost PCs and an increased focus on customer service, eMachines has managed to hold on to a significant slice of the retail PC market.

EXECUTIVES

President and CEO: Wayne R. Inouye
SVP and COO: Adam Andersen
SVP, Customer Care: Mike Zimmerman
SVP, Global Product Marketing and Channel Development: Bob Davidson

LOCATIONS

HQ: 14350 Myford Rd., Ste. 100, Irvine, CA 92606
Phone: 714-481-2828 **Fax:** 714-505-5049
Web: www.emachines.com

PRODUCTS/OPERATIONS

Products

Desktop PCs
Monitors

COMPETITORS

Acer
Apple Computer
Dell
Fujitsu
Gateway
Hewlett-Packard
IBM
MPC Computers
NEC
Sony
Toshiba

HISTORICAL FINANCIALS

Company Type: Private

Income Statement FYE: December 31

	REVENUE ($ mil.)	NET INCOME ($ mil.)	NET PROFIT MARGIN	EMPLOYEES
12/02	700	—	—	150
12/01	540	—	—	150
12/00	684	—	—	134
12/99	814	—	—	61
12/98	58	—	—	49
Annual Growth	86.1%	—	—	32.3%

Revenue History

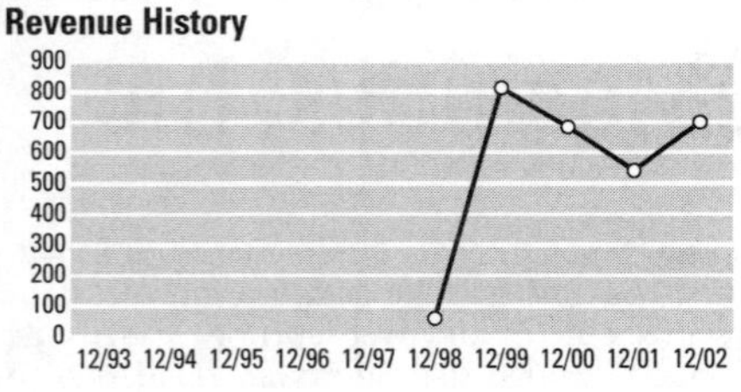

Emory University

"Have a Coke and a smile" means a little more to Emory University than it does to the rest of the world. The school, which boasts more than 11,400 students and 2,500 faculty members, was transformed from Emory College to Emory University in 1915 by a $1 million donation from Coca-Cola Company owner Asa Candler. Today, about 40% of Emory's endowment consists of Coca-Cola stock. The university offers undergraduate, graduate, and professional degrees in a wide range of fields, including medicine, theology, law, nursing, and business. Founded in 1836, the private university also maintains several research centers and operates a joint venture with HCA to offer managed health care.

EXECUTIVES

President Emeritus: Sanford S. Atwood
President Emeritus: James T. Laney
President: William M. Chace
Provost and EVP Academic Affairs: Howard Hunter
EVP Finance and Business and COO: John L. Temple
EVP Health Affairs and Director, Robert W. Woodruff Health Sciences Center: Michael M. E. Johns, age 61
SVP and General Counsel: Kent Alexander
SVP Institutional Advancement: William H. Fox
SVP for Campus Life: John Ford
Interim Dean Emory College: Robert A. Paul
VP Finance and Treasurer: Frank H. Huff
VP Human Resources: Alice R. Miller
VP and Secretary of the University: Gary S. Hauk

LOCATIONS

HQ: 1380 S. Oxford Rd. SE, Atlanta, GA 30322
Phone: 404-727-6123 **Fax:** 404-727-0646
Web: www.emory.edu

Emory University has campuses in Atlanta and Oxford, Georgia.

PRODUCTS/OPERATIONS

Selected Schools and Colleges

Candler School of Theology
Emory College
Goizueta Business School
Graduate School of Arts and Sciences
Law School
Nell Hodgson Woodruff School of Nursing
Oxford College
Rollins School of Public Health
School of Medicine

Selected Research Centers

The Carter Center
Center for Ethics
Center for the Study of Health, Culture, and Society
Cherry L. Emerson Center for Scientific Computation
Institute of African Studies
The Lewis H. Beck Center for Electronic Collections
ScienceNet
Winship Cancer Institute
Yerkes Regional Primate Center

HISTORICAL FINANCIALS

Company Type: School

Income Statement FYE: August 31

	REVENUE ($ mil.)	NET INCOME ($ mil.)	NET PROFIT MARGIN	EMPLOYEES
8/02	1,860	—	—	19,288
8/01	1,800	—	—	19,000
8/00	1,759	—	—	17,382
8/99	1,627	—	—	16,000
8/98	1,739	—	—	15,491
8/97	1,408	—	—	15,481
8/96	1,200	—	—	14,000
8/95	1,110	—	—	16,000
8/94	988	—	—	15,000
8/93	862	—	—	—
Annual Growth	8.9%	—	—	3.2%

Revenue History

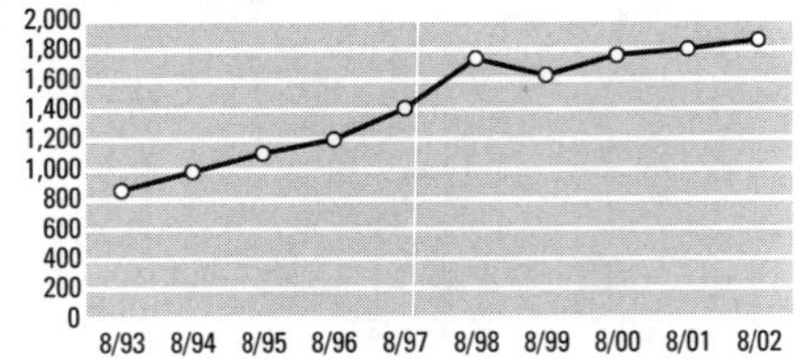

Empire Beef Company, Inc.

Protein has given Empire Beef its bulk. The wholesale meat and food service distributor ships more than six million pounds of meat each week. Purchased from major packers such Hormel and Perdue Farms, Empire Beef distributes beef, lamb, pork, poultry, seafood, and veal. The firm also makes portion-controlled marinated and flavor-enhanced fresh and frozen meat products for food service and retail sale. Empire Beef serves customers east of the Mississippi, primarily in the Northeast, with its fleet of multi-temperature trucks. Harry Levine started the firm as a small slaughtering plant in 1937; slaughter operations later stopped. The Levine family (Harry's grandson Steve is CEO) owns Empire Beef.

EXECUTIVES

CEO: Steve H. Levine
Controller: Michael Quinn
General Manager: Christopher Carretta
Manager, HR: Marybeth Serone
Manager, IT: Jason Torchia

LOCATIONS

HQ: 171 Weidner Rd., Rochester, NY 14624
Phone: 585-235-7350 **Fax:** 585-235-1776
Web: www.empirebeef.com

COMPETITORS

GFI America
Performance Food
Sherwood Food
Stock Yards Packing
SYSCO
U.S. Foodservice

HISTORICAL FINANCIALS

Company Type: Private

Income Statement FYE: December 31

	REVENUE ($ mil.)	NET INCOME ($ mil.)	NET PROFIT MARGIN	EMPLOYEES
12/01	703	—	—	200
12/00	682	—	—	230
12/99	701	—	—	215
12/98	600	—	—	220
12/97	548	—	—	240
12/96	522	—	—	170
Annual Growth	6.1%	—	—	3.3%

Revenue History

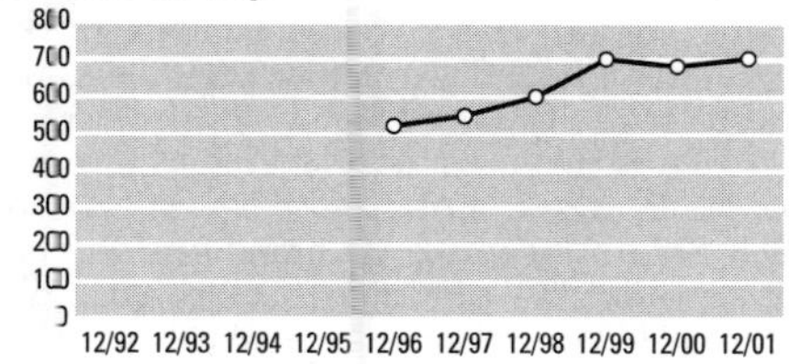

Encyclopaedia Britannica, Inc.

Encyclopaedia Britannica thinks it knows everything, and it probably does. The company publishes reference works including its flagship 32-volume *Encyclopaedia Britannica* (first published in 1768), *The Annals of America,* and *Great Books of the Western World.* It also publishes a variety of dictionaries (*Merriam Webster's Collegiate Dictionary, Merriam Webster's Biographical Dictionary*) through its Merriam-Webster subsidiary. Most of the company's products are available online, as well as on CD-ROM and DVD. Swiss financier Jacob Safra (a nephew of the late banking king Edmond Safra) owns the company.

Its Britannica.com Web site offers access for a fee to its entire collection of encyclopedia articles, an editorially reviewed Web site directory and third-party content from *The New York Times* and other providers. Britannica's site also features an online store where users can buy its print and interactive products.

After initially being late to the CD-ROM and dot-com party, Encyclopaedia Britannica decided to commit to Britannica.com, a sister firm devoted to electronic content which was to be spun off in an IPO. But the idea turned out to be disastrous (in part because of bad publicity over traffic jams at the site and a downturn in online advertising), and the company has since focused back on its core business with a renewed interest in print products under new CEO Ilan Yeshua. The company is considering selling its Merriam-Webster subsidiary to raise capital.

HISTORY

Engraver Andrew Bell and printer and bookseller Colin Macfarquhar created the first edition of the *Encyclopaedia Britannica* in Scotland, releasing the three-volume set in weekly installments between 1768 and 1771. Benjamin Franklin and John Locke were among early contributors. The second edition, completed in 1784 expanded to 10 volumes; the fourth (1809) contained 20. The ninth edition (1889) captured the scientific spirit of the age with articles by Thomas Henry Huxley and James Clerk Maxwell.

American businessmen Horace Hooper and Walter Jackson purchased the *Encyclopaedia* in 1901 and established the Encyclopaedia Britannica Company in the US. It published the first *Britannica Book of the Year* in 1913. Sears chairman Julius Rosenwald bought the company in 1920 and tried to market *Britannica* through Sears' retail operations as well as with door-to-door sales. William Benton (of Benton & Bowles Advertising) bought the business from Sears in 1941 and built a nationwide sales force with a hard-sell reputation. Britannica released its first foreign-language encyclopedia, *Enciclopedia Barsa,* in 1957 and acquired dictionary publisher G. & C. Merriam in 1964.

When Benton died in 1974, he bequeathed the operation to the non-profit William Benton Foundation, the sole beneficiary of which was the University of Chicago. Britannica later bought out rival Compton's Encyclopedia in the mid-1970s. The 1989 CD-ROM release of *Compton's MultiMedia Encyclopedia* was a first for the industry, but Britannica sold Compton's NewMedia division to Chicago's Tribune Company in 1993 just before the CD-ROM market exploded. The company also promised not to release a competing multimedia version of Encyclopaedia Britannica for two years. Not realizing that the electronic revolution was upon them and reluctant to change its established and profitable door-to-door sales techniques, the conservative company fell behind challengers who offered CD-ROMs including Microsoft and its *Funk & Wagnalls* product (later relaunched as *Encarta*).

Jacob Safra, a *Britannica* lover since childhood, led a group that paid $135 million for the struggling company in 1996. With book sales dwindling and heavy competition, Britannica cut its prices and ceased its door-to-door marketing that year. It agreed to sell both its CD-ROM and print encyclopedias in retail stores in 1997, and lured publisher Paul Hoffman away from Walt Disney's successful *Discover* magazine. Britannica Internet Guide (BIG), a free Internet search engine, launched that year. Britannica added guest columns and other features to BIG in 1998 and renamed it eBlast (it changed the site's name again to Britannica the following year).

Encyclopaedia Britannica Holdings (Safra's umbrella firm for the publisher) launched a sister firm, Britannica.com, in 1999 to oversee the company's electronic and Internet products and services. CEO Don Yannias resigned his post with the print company and took the reins of the new digital firm, allowing Hoffman to take over as the publisher's president. Britannica.com struggled with the rest of the Internet industry in 2000, laying off almost 25% of its staff.

In 2001 Yannias left the company entirely and was replaced by Ilan Yeshua, an executive from an Israeli educational technology firm. Later that year, the company integrated Britannica.com back into the encyclopedia unit of Encyclopaedia Britannica, a move that involved severely downsizing the Web staff.

EXECUTIVES

Chairman: Jacob E. Safra
CEO: Ilan Yeshua
SVP Sales and Marketing: Patti Ginnis
EVP, Secretary, and General Counsel: William J. Bowe
SVP and Editor: Dale Hoiberg
VP Operations and Finance: Richard Anderson
CTO: Dave Becker
President and Publisher, Merriam-Webster: John Morse
Corporate Communications: Tom Panelas
Auditors: PricewaterhouseCoopers

LOCATIONS

HQ: 310 S. Michigan Ave., Chicago, IL 60604
Phone: 312-347-7000 **Fax:** 312-347-7399
Web: corporate.britannica.com

Encyclopaedia Britannica makes its headquarters in Chicago and maintains offices in London; New Delhi; Paris; Seoul; Sydney; Taipei; Taiwan; and Tokyo.

PRODUCTS/OPERATIONS

Selected Products

Dictionaries
Merriam Webster's Biographical Dictionary
Merriam Webster's Collegiate Dictionary
Merriam Webster's Collegiate Thesaurus
Merriam Webster's Dictionary of Law

Encyclopedias
Britannica First Edition Replica Set
Encyclopaedia Britannica
The Encyclopedia of Popular Music

Other Reference Works
The Annals of America
Gray's Anatomy
Great Books of the Western World

COMPETITORS

Berkshire Hathaway
Dow Jones
Franklin Electronic Publishers
Harcourt Education
LexisNexis
McGraw-Hill
Microsoft
National Geographic
Pearson
Random House
Scholastic Library Publishing
Thomson Corporation
Time
Vivendi Universal Publishing

HISTORICAL FINANCIALS

Company Type: Private

Income Statement FYE: December 31

	REVENUE ($ mil.)	NET INCOME ($ mil.)	NET PROFIT MARGIN	EMPLOYEES
12/01	225	—	—	260
12/00	275	—	—	300
12/99*	279	—	—	350
9/98	300	—	—	400
9/97	325	—	—	400
9/96	375	—	—	700
9/95	400	—	—	800
9/94	453	—	—	900
9/93	540	—	—	1,000
9/92	586	—	—	1,100
Annual Growth	(10.1%)	—	—	(14.8%)

*Fiscal year change

Revenue History

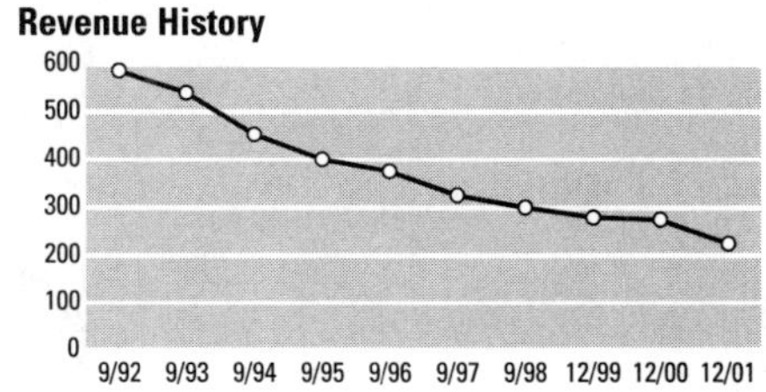

EnerSys Inc.

EnerSys' battery operations are charging off in different directions. The company, formerly Yuasa Inc., makes stationary industrial batteries that provide uninterruptible power and backup power for electronic systems and motive power batteries for big equipment such as forklifts. Other products include battery chargers and accessories. Its Hawker subsidiary makes batteries with industrial and military applications. Company management and Morgan Stanley acquired

Yuasa's Motive Power and Stationary Power operations in 2000 and renamed the company EnerSys. EnerSys has also acquired Invensys' Energy Storage products group.

EXECUTIVES

Chairman, President, and CEO: John D. Craig
CFO and EVP, Finance: Michael T. Philion
EVP, North America Reserve Power and Worldwide Marketing: Charles K. (Charlie) McManus
EVP, North America Motive Power: John A. Shea
EVP, Administration: Richard W. (Dick) Zuidema
VP, Procurement and Operations Planning: Larry B. Axt
VP, Strategic Planning and Asia: Cheryl A. Duiguid
VP, Engineering and Technology, Americas and Asia: Steven J. Weik
President, Asian Operations: Jean-Luc Dubrulle
President, European Operations: Ray Kubis
Director, Human Resources: Ted Fries

LOCATIONS

HQ: 2366 Bernville Rd., Reading, PA 19605
Phone: 610-208-1991 **Fax:** 610-372-8628
Web: www.enersysinc.com

EnerSys has manufacturing operations in Argentina, Brazil, Canada, Mexico, and the US.

PRODUCTS/OPERATIONS

Selected Products and Brands

Diesel engine starting batteries (LMUD-500, UB-510)
Flooded batteries (General, Heritage)
Lift truck batteries (Exide, Hup)
Rail signal batteries (EMF-R)
Sealed gel maintenance-free batteries (Renegade, Smarthog)
Valve-regulated lead-acid batteries (Independence)
Wet-cell batteries (Loadhog, Superhog, Workhog)

COMPETITORS

C&D Technologies
Delphi
Duracell
Exide
General Motors
Johnson Controls
Key Components
Matsushita
Rayovac
Schumacher

HISTORICAL FINANCIALS

Company Type: Private

Income Statement

FYE: March 31

	REVENUE ($ mil.)	NET INCOME ($ mil.)	NET PROFIT MARGIN	EMPLOYEES
3/02	900	—	—	7,000
3/01	400	—	—	2,500
3/00	427	—	—	3,000
3/99	425	—	—	2,750
3/98	396	—	—	2,707
3/97	358	—	—	2,712
3/96	358	—	—	—
3/95	329	—	—	—
3/94	296	—	—	—
3/93	281	—	—	—
Annual Growth	13.8%	—	—	20.9%

Revenue History

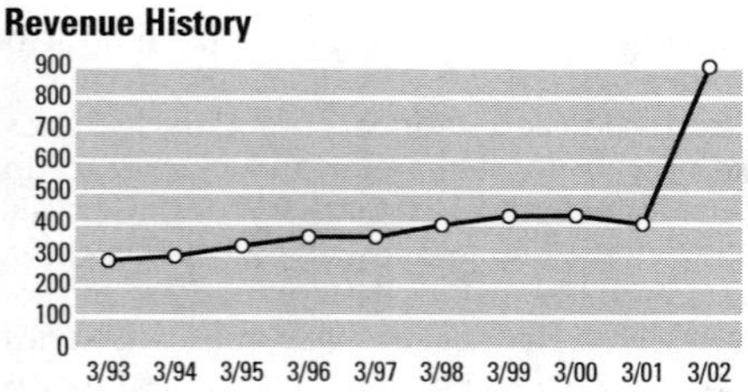

Enterprise Rent-A-Car Company

This Enterprise is boldly going where it has not gone before — the airport. The company, which offers to ferry customers to the rental office, says it is the largest car rental firm in the US. With more than 530,000 cars in its fleet, Enterprise operates in the US, Canada, Germany, Ireland, and the UK. The company targets customers whose own cars are in the shop or who need a rental for short trips; it also has begun serving the airport market. Controlled by founder Jack Taylor and his family, Enterprise has spun off its non-automotive operations (balloons, footwear, a golf course, hotel amenities, and prison supplies) as Centric Group.

Enterprise also leases vehicles and manages fleets for other companies (Enterprise Fleet Services), and when it's ready to refresh its fleet, Enterprise sells its cars (Enterprise Car Sales) through a nationwide program. Potential customers can shop by make and model through the Enterprise Web site.

The company recently published a report saying business travelers are increasingly choosing to drive rather than fly when it comes to regional trips. These "short-haul" trips are defined as 300 miles or less.

Founder Taylor's son Andrew is Enterprise's chairman and CEO.

HISTORY

In 1957 Jack Taylor, the sales manager for a Cadillac dealership in St. Louis, hit on the idea that leasing cars might be an easier way to make money than selling them. Taylor's idea sounded good to his boss, Arthur Lindburg, who agreed to set Taylor up in the leasing business. In return for a 50% pay cut, Taylor received 25% of the new enterprise, called Executive Leasing, which began in the walled-off body shop of a car dealership.

In the early 1960s Taylor started renting cars for short periods as well as leasing them. When his leasing agents expressed annoyance with the rental operation, Taylor turned that business over to Don Holtzman. Holtzman realized that his 17-car rental operation was too little to take on industry giants like Hertz and Avis; instead, he concentrated on the "home city" or replacement market. He offered competitive rates to insurance adjusters who needed to find cars for policyholders whose cars were damaged or stolen. Propelled by court decisions that required casualty companies to pay for loss of transportation, Taylor expanded from his St. Louis base in 1969 with a branch office in Atlanta. Since another car leasing outfit in Georgia was already named Executive, Taylor changed the name of his company to Enterprise Rent-A-Car.

The company expanded into Florida and Texas in the early 1970s, targeting garages and body shops that performed repairs for insured drivers. Oil price shocks of that period compelled Taylor to diversify his operations. In 1974 Enterprise acquired Keefe Coffee and Supply, a supplier of coffee, packaged foods, and beverages to prison commissaries. To service *FORTUNE* 1000 companies wanting to lease or buy more than 50 vehicles, the company started Enterprise Fleet Services in 1976.

Enterprise acquired Courtesy Products (coffee and tea for hotel guests) in 1980, and the following year sales reached the $100 million mark. It acquired ELCO Chevrolet in 1986, the same year it formed Crawford Supply (hygiene products for prisons). Taylor bought out the Lindburg family's interest in Enterprise the next year. In 1989 Enterprise raised its brand recognition with a national TV campaign that focused on an older and higher-income audience by showing its commercials exclusively on CBS. Also in the late 1980s, the company began targeting "discretionary rentals" to families with visiting relatives or with children home for the holidays.

Taylor's son, Andrew, became CEO of Enterprise in 1991, and sales topped $1 billion for the first time. By 1994 sales had passed $2 billion, and the company had expanded into Canada and the UK. By 1996 Enterprise had a fleet of more than 300,000 vehicles. That year it opened several locations in the UK. In 1997 the company opened locations in Ireland, Munich, Scotland, and Wales.

In 1998 Enterprise battled other rental firms over use of the advertising tagline, "We'll pick you up," which it had trademarked. Rent-A-Wreck lost a court case over the matter; Hertz settled with Enterprise over use of the phrase.

In 1999 the company more than doubled the number of its airport locations in an attempt to woo occasional travelers (rather than hard-core corporate fliers). That year the Taylor family split off their non-automotive operations (including companies involved in prison supplies, hotel amenities, a golf course, mylar balloons, and athletic shoes) as Centric Group.

In 2001 the company's COO, Donald Ross, became the first non-Taylor to be promoted to president after Jack Taylor was named chairman emeritus and Andrew gave up the president title to assume the company's chairmanship while remaining as CEO.

EXECUTIVES

Chairman and CEO: Andrew C. (Andy) Taylor, age 56
President and COO: Donald L. Ross
CFO and SVP: William W. (Bill) Snyder
EVP, North American Operations: Pamela M. (Pam) Nicholson
SVP and CIO: Craig Kennedy
SVP, Corporate Strategy: M.W. (Sandy) Rogers
SVP, Fleet Services: Steven E. Bloom
SVP, Human Resources: Edward (Ed) Adams
VP, ELCO Chevrolet: Mark S. Hadfield
VP, International Operations: Mike Robertson
VP, Marketing Communications: Steve Smith
VP, New Business Development: Kurt Kohler
VP, Remarketing: Greg Dart
VP, Rental: Jim Runnels
Assistant VP, Corporate Communications: Christy Conrad
Manager, Public Relations: Lee Broughton
Auditors: Ernst & Young LLP

LOCATIONS

HQ: 600 Corporate Park Dr., St. Louis, MO 63105
Phone: 314-512-5000 **Fax:** 314-512-4706
Web: www.enterprise.com

Enterprise Rent-A-Car has more than 5,000 offices in the US, Canada, Germany, Ireland, and the UK.

PRODUCTS/OPERATIONS

Operations

ELCO Chevrolet Inc. (car dealership, St. Louis)
Enterprise Car Sales (used car sales)
Enterprise Fleet Services (vehicle leasing)
Enterprise Rent-A-Car

COMPETITORS

Airways Transportation Group
Alamo
AMERCO
AutoNation
Budget
Cendant
Dollar Thrifty Automotive
Hertz
Penske
Rent-A-Wreck
Ryder
Sixt

HISTORICAL FINANCIALS

Company Type: Private

Income Statement FYE: July 31

	REVENUE ($ mil.)	NET INCOME ($ mil.)	NET PROFIT MARGIN	EMPLOYEES
7/02	6,500	—	—	50,000
7/01	6,300	—	—	50,000
7/00	5,600	—	—	45,000
7/99	4,730	—	—	40,000
7/98	4,180	—	—	37,000
7/97	3,680	—	—	35,182
7/96	3,127	—	—	28,806
7/95	2,464	—	—	21,703
7/94	2,108	—	—	18,500
7/93	1,659	—	—	14,000
Annual Growth	16.4%	—	—	15.2%

Revenue History

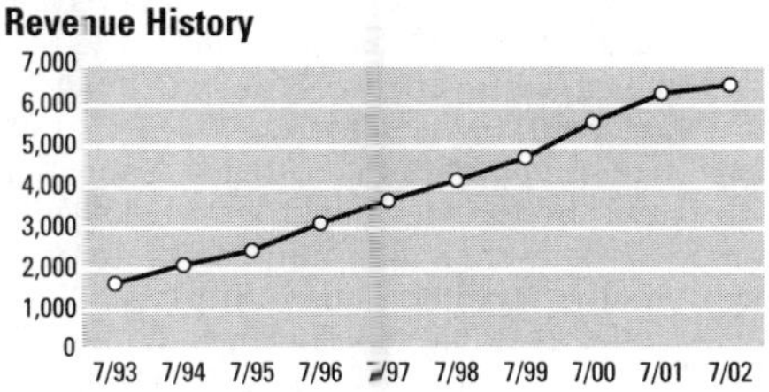

Environmental Systems Research Institute, Inc.

Environmental Systems Research Institute (ESRI) maps out a successful mix of geography and software. The company is a leading developer of geographic information systems (GIS) software used to create and label digital maps, publish maps on the Internet, and build related databases. Founded in 1969 with $1,100 by consultants Jack (president) and Laura Dangermond, ESRI has customers in fields such as government, forestry, oil and gas, and transportation. Its products and services have been used by the state of Wyoming to plan highway and bridge programs, by the Australian government to build an interactive environmental resources Web site, and to track the spread of fire ants in Texas. The Dangermonds own ESRI.

In early 2003, ESRI acquired ALIDA, a French cartography software company that marketed the DataDraw product. ALIDA was founded in 1996 as Hémisphères by Thierry Kressmann and Marc-Olivier Briat, who combined their expertise in desktop publishing, database management systems, and geographic information systems (GIS). The company was renamed ALIDA in 2002.

EXECUTIVES

President: Jack Dangermond
CFO: Tom Pickett
Director, Marketing: Linda Hecht
Director, Products, Solutions, and International: David Maguire
Director, Software Products: Clint Brown
Defense Market Manager: David Swann
Human Resources Manager: Cathy Mueller
Manager, Marketing Communications: Karen Hurlbut

LOCATIONS

HQ: 380 New York St., Redlands, CA 92373
Phone: 909-793-2853 **Fax:** 909-307-3025
Web: www.esri.com

Environmental Systems Research Institute has offices throughout the US and distributors in more than 75 countries.

PRODUCTS/OPERATIONS

Selected Software

AM/FM utilities (ArcFM)
Business geographic information systems (ArcView Business Analyst, Atlas GIS)
Cartography (Maplex, Military Overlay Editor, MOLE, PLTS)
Developer tools (MapObjects, MapObjects LT, NetEngine)
Field geographic information systems (ArcPad)
Geographic information systems tools (ArcCAD, Data Automation Kit, PC/ARC/INFO)
Internet mapping (ArcIMS)
Routing and logistics software (ArcLogistics Route)

Selected Services

Consulting and database design
Database automation and conversion
Data publishing
Product implementation
Programming

COMPETITORS

Analytical Surveys
Autodesk
Auto-trol
DeLorme
Intergraph
Landmark Graphics
MapInfo
NavTech
ObjectFX
PlanGraphics

HISTORICAL FINANCIALS

Company Type: Private

Income Statement FYE: December 31

	REVENUE ($ mil.)	NET INCOME ($ mil.)	NET PROFIT MARGIN	EMPLOYEES
12/02	469	—	—	2,600
12/01	427	—	—	2,500
12/00	370	—	—	2,500
12/99	341	—	—	2,530
12/98	278	—	—	1,375
12/97	259	—	—	1,300
12/96	224	—	—	2,000
12/95	174	—	—	2,000
12/94	132	—	—	760
12/93	109	—	—	630
Annual Growth	17.6%	—	—	17.1%

Revenue History

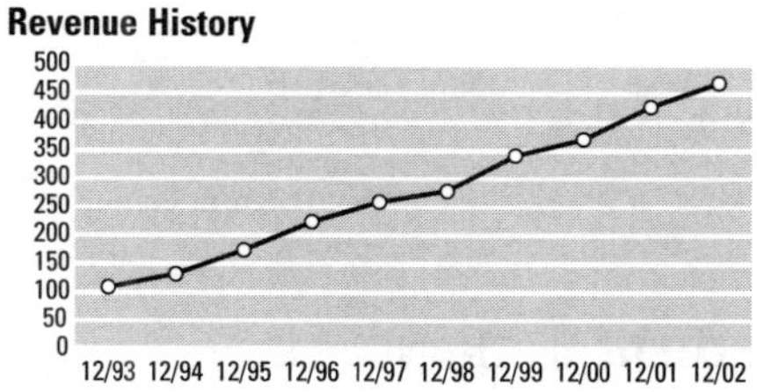

EPIX Holdings Corporation

When it comes to epic human resources concerns, more and more employers are using EPIX solutions. EPIX Holdings (formerly Payroll Transfers) is one of the nation's leading professional employer organizations, providing human resources management for its clients' permanent full-time workers. The company's services include insurance, tax administration, employee benefits programs, regulatory compliance, and payroll processing. The company provides administrative services for more than 50,000 employees from some 3,500 small and midsized businesses throughout the US. EPIX, which was founded in 1989, is backed by Texas financier Robert Bass' Keystone group, among other investment firms.

EXECUTIVES

Chairman: Thomas C. Wajnert, age 59
President and CEO: Thomas S. Taylor, age 44
CFO: James O'Deobinak, age 42
EVP and General Counsel: Peter Deutsch, age 39
VP Human Resources: Karen Droz, age 39
VP Quality and Assurance: Alexandra Lange, age 38
VP Renewal and Pricing: Jeff Hecht, age 39
VP Sales and Marketing: John Gibson, age 36
VP Sales Operations: Judy Levine, age 33
VP Strategy and Treasury: Edwin Shepherdson, age 41
CIO: Larry Witt, age 39
Director Corporate Communications and Public Relations: Janet Gillis, age 46

LOCATIONS

HQ: 3710 Corporex Park Dr., Tampa, FL 33619
Phone: 813-664-0404 **Fax:** 813-621-6816
Web: www.epixweb.com

EPIX Holdings has main offices in Tampa, Florida, and Woodbridge, New Jersey, and about 10 sales offices across the US.

PRODUCTS/OPERATIONS

Selected Services

401(k) and pensions
Employee benefits
Human resources
Lifestyle benefits
Payroll administration
Risk management

COMPETITORS

Administaff
ADP TotalSource
ADP
Exult
Gevity HR
Paychex
TEAM America
TeamStaff
United Benefit Consulting

HISTORICAL FINANCIALS

Company Type: Private

Income Statement FYE: December 31

	REVENUE ($ mil.)	NET INCOME ($ mil.)	NET PROFIT MARGIN	EMPLOYEES
12/02	1,782	—	—	300
12/01	1,842	—	—	400
12/00	1,300	—	—	450
12/99	1,000	—	—	380
12/98	734	—	—	325
12/97	392	—	—	—
12/96	350	—	—	—
12/95	300	—	—	—
12/94	229	—	—	—
12/93	175	—	—	—
Annual Growth	29.4%	—	—	(2.0%)

Revenue History

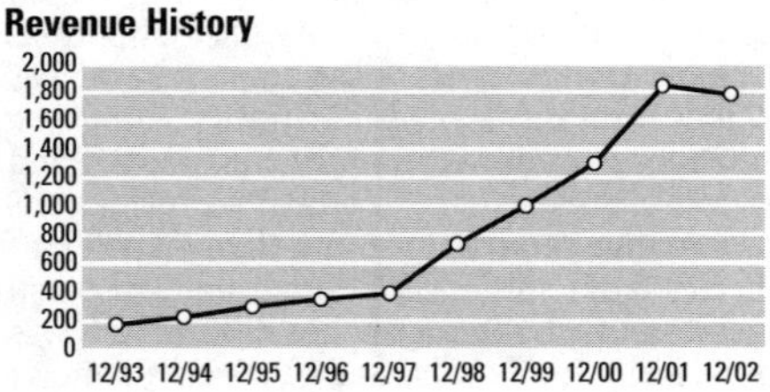

Equistar Chemicals, LP

Petrochemicals are used to make polymers, and Equistar Chemical — a partnership of Lyondell Chemical (which owns 70.5%) and Millennium Chemicals (29.5%) — makes a lot of both. Equistar's largest business segment, petrochemicals, makes olefins (ethylene, propylene, and butadiene), oxygenated products (ethylene oxide, ethylene glycol), and aromatics (benzene and toluene). Equistar's polymers segment makes polyolefins (polyethylenes, polypropylene) and performance polymers. Polyethylene is used in plastic bags and bottles; polypropylene is used in plastic caps, rigid packaging, automotive components, and carpet. Lyondell recently acquired Occidental's 30% stake in the company.

EXECUTIVES

Co-Chairman, President, and CEO: Dan F. Smith, age 56
Co-Chairman: William M. (Bill) Landuyt, age 47
EVP and COO: Morris Gelb, age 56
SVP, Chemicals and Polymers: Edward J. Dineen, age 48
SVP, Fuels and Raw Materials: W. Norman Phillips Jr., age 48, $392,226 pay
VP and Controller: Charles L. Hall
VP, Human Resources: John A. Hollinshead
VP, Research and Development: J. Rick Fontenot, $366,775 pay
VP, Polymers Sales: Vaughn Deasy
Manager, Corporate Communications: Anne Knisely
Manager, Marketing Communications: Kelly McCarthy
Manager, Public Affairs: David Harpole
Auditors: PricewaterhouseCoopers LLP

LOCATIONS

HQ: 1221 McKinney St., Ste. 700, Houston, TX 77010
Phone: 713-652-7200 **Fax:** 713-652-4151
Web: www.equistarchem.com

Equistar Chemicals operates 16 major plants in Illinois, Iowa, Louisiana, New Jersey, Ohio, and Texas.

PRODUCTS/OPERATIONS

Selected Products

Petrochemicals
Aromatics
Olefins
Oxygenated products
Specialty products
Polymers

COMPETITORS

A. Schulman
AEP Industries
BP Chemicals
BP
CPChem
Dow Chemical
ExxonMobil Chemical
Formosa Plastics USA
Huntsman International
PMC Global
PolyOne
PVC Container
Royal Dutch/Shell Group
W. R. Grace

HISTORICAL FINANCIALS

Company Type: Partnership

Income Statement FYE: December 31

	REVENUE ($ mil.)	NET INCOME ($ mil.)	NET PROFIT MARGIN	EMPLOYEES
12/02	5,537	(1,299)	—	3,400
12/01	5,909	(283)	—	3,400
12/00	7,495	153	2.0%	3,700
12/99	5,436	32	0.6%	4,500
12/98	4,363	143	3.3%	5,000
12/97	365	7	1.9%	4,000
Annual Growth	72.3%	—	—	(3.2%)

2002 Year-End Financials

Debt ratio: 114.3%
Return on equity: —
Cash ($ mil.): 27
Current ratio: 1.58
Long-term debt ($ mil.): 2,196

Net Income History

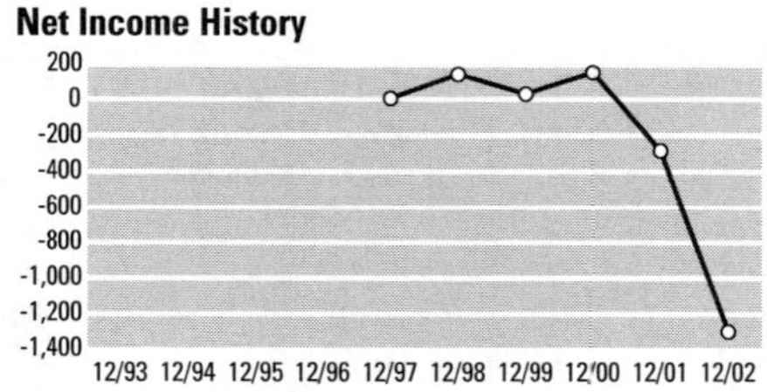

Equity Group Investments

Equity Group Investments is the apex of financier Sam Zell's pyramid of business holdings. The Chicago-based private investment group controls a multi-billion-dollar mix of businesses, including real estate investment trusts (REITs), restaurants, and cruise ships. Zell's REIT portfolio makes him the US's largest owner of property leased by manufactured homeowners (Manufactured Home Communities), office buildings (Equity Office Properties Trust), and apartments (Equity Residential Properties Trust). Sam Zell has a controlling interest in Equity Group Investments.

Equity Office Properties is one of the largest landlords in San Francisco and Seattle. Zell has made his niche — and a lot of money — by purchasing distressed properties and turning them into profitable investments (for which he earned the nickname "Grave Dancer").

Equity Group Investments has rescued many companies floundering in bankruptcy and often buys during downturns. Many acquisitions are made through the Zell/Chilmark Fund. Zell's Equity Residential Properties continues to build its portfolio through acquisitions.

Zell has made forays into other investments with mixed success. He bought into sugar mills in Mexico that were nationalized by the government. Another holding, American Classic Voyages, suffered a combo of misfortune with the soft Hawaiian cruise industry on one side and the aftermath of September 11 on travel on the other. It has filed for Chapter 11 reorganization. As bargains dry up in the US, Zell is rediscovering a junk-bond investing strategy.

HISTORY

Sam Zell's first business endeavor was photographing his eighth-grade prom. In 1953 he graduated to reselling 50-cent *Playboy* magazines to schoolmates at a 200% markup.

While at the University of Michigan in the 1960s, Zell teamed with fraternity brother Robert Lurie to manage off-campus student housing. In graduate school, they invested in residential properties and formed Equity Financial and Management Co. after graduation. Their collection of distressed properties grew in the 1970s as Zell made the deals and Lurie made them work. Zell's hands-off management style had its drawbacks, however: In 1976 Zell and three others (including his brother-in-law) were indicted on federal tax-related charges after selling a Reno, Nevada, hotel and apartment complex. The charges were later dropped against Zell and another defendant (only the brother-in-law was convicted).

In the 1980s tax-law changes led the team to begin buying troubled companies. They started in 1983 with Great American Management and Investment, a foundering real estate manager they turned into an investment vehicle. Other targets included Itel (1984, now Anixter International) and oil and gas company Nucorp (1988, now part of insurer CNA Surety). The true attraction in many of these acquisitions, however, lay in tax-loss carryforwards that could be applied against future earnings.

Lurie died in 1990, after which Zell began to

consolidate his power and ease out old friends. (Lurie's estate still owns shares of many Zell enterprises.) That year Zell and David Schulte formed the Zell/Chilmark Fund, which soon owned or controlled such companies as Schwinn (sold 1997), Sealy (sold 1997), and Revco (sold 1997). Among the fund's failures was West Coast retailer Broadway Stores, which Zell bought out of bankruptcy in 1992; when California's slumping economy prevented a rapid turnaround, Zell sold it (once again near bankruptcy) in 1995.

Starting in 1987, Zell formed four real estate funds with Merrill Lynch; six years later, both Equity Residential Properties Trust and Manufactured Home Communities went public. As REITs became popular with investors, more trusts began vying for distressed assets — Zell's traditional lifeblood. In 1997 Zell melded four of his commercial real estate funds into another REIT, Equity Office Properties Trust, and took it public.

In 1998, as investors and financiers looked for fresh opportunities, Zell launched Equity International Properties, a fund targeting acquisitions in Latin America and elsewhere. That year a civil racketeering suit brought against Zell by former executive Richard Perlman shed light on "handshake" loans to top executives and other informal business deals. In 1999 Zell sold Jacor Communications to radio industry consolidator Clear Channel Communications. Equity Group Investments remains diversified, however: That year Equity Office Properties teamed with venture capital firm Kleiner Perkins Caufield & Byers to form Broadband Office to offer Internet and phone services to Zell's tenants and those of other property owners.

Equity Office Properties Trust continued its buying into the 21st century, claiming New York-based Cornerstone Properties (2000) and California's Spieker Properties (2001).

EXECUTIVES

Chairman: Samuel (Sam) Zell, age 61
Co-Chairman: Sheli Z. Rosenberg, age 61
President: Donald J. Liebentritt, age 51

LOCATIONS

HQ: Equity Group Investments, L.L.C.
2 N. Riverside Plaza, Ste. 600, Chicago, IL 60606
Phone: 312-454-1800 **Fax:** 312-454-0610

PRODUCTS/OPERATIONS

Selected Affiliates

American Classic Voyages Co. (36%, cruises)
Angelo & Maxie's, Inc. (38%, restaurants)
Anixter International, Inc. (14%, communications network equipment)
Capital Trust, Inc. (commercial real estate finance)
Davel Communications, Inc. (14%, pay-telephone operator)
Equity International Properties (overseas buyout fund)
Equity Office Properties Trust (4%, office property REIT)
Equity Residential Properties Trust (3%, apartments REIT)
Manufactured Home Communities, Inc. (15%, mobile home communities REIT)
Transmedia Network (40%, consumer savings programs)
Zell/Chilmark Fund L.P. (investment vulture fund)

COMPETITORS

Apollo Advisors
Blackstone Group
Carlyle Group
Clayton, Dubilier
Goldman Sachs
JMB Realty
KKR
Thomas Lee
Trump

Ergon, Inc.

When it comes to work, Ergon (named after the Greek word for work) has it covered. The diversified company operates in seven major business segments: asphalt and emulsions; information technology; oil and gas; real estate; refining; specialty petroleum products; and transportation and terminaling. In addition to providing a range of petroleum products and services, the company manufactures and markets computer technology services and sells road maintenance systems, including emulsions and special coatings. Ergon also provides truck, rail, and marine transport services and sells residential and commercial real estate properties.

EXECUTIVES

President: Leslie Lampton Sr.
VP Data Processing: Ron Washington
VP Finance, Treasurer, and Secretary: Kathy Stone
VP Human Resources: Lance Maserov
VP Sales: Leslie Lampton III

LOCATIONS

HQ: 2829 Lakeland Dr., Ste. 2000, Jackson, MS 39232
Phone: 601-933-3000 **Fax:** 601-933-3350
Web: www.ergon.com

PRODUCTS/OPERATIONS

Major Operations

Asphalt and Emulsions
Crafco, Inc.
DRM Systems
Ertech Technical Coating Products
PASS System

Information Technology
Diversified Technology, Inc.

Oil and Gas
Lampton-Love, Inc.

Real Estate
Ergon Properties

Refining
Ergon Refining

Specialty Petroleum Products
Petroleum Specialties Marketing

Transportation and Terminaling
Ergon Rail
Ergon Terminals
Ergon Trucking, Inc.
Magnolia Marine Transport Company

COMPETITORS

AmeriGas Partners
Ferrellgas Partners
Kirby
Koch
Marathon Oil

HISTORICAL FINANCIALS

Company Type: Private

Income Statement FYE: December 31

	ESTIMATED REVENUE ($ mil.)	NET INCOME ($ mil.)	NET PROFIT MARGIN	EMPLOYEES
12/01	1,460	—	—	2,000
12/00	1,900	—	—	2,000
12/99	1,400	—	—	2,000
Annual Growth	2.1%	—	—	0.0%

Revenue History

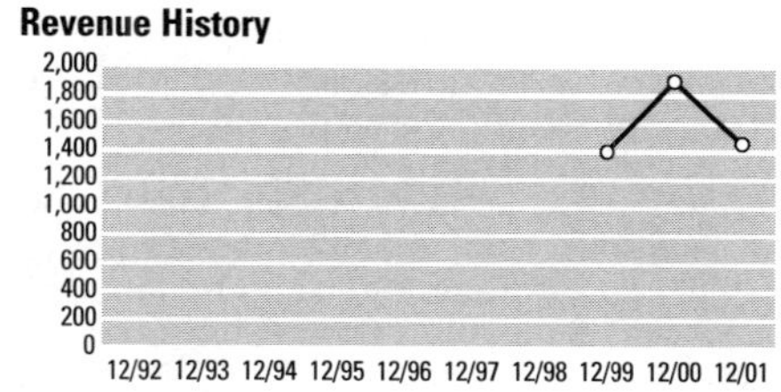

Ernst & Young International

Accounting may actually be the *second*-oldest profession, and Ernst & Young is one of the oldest practitioners. Ernst & Young is also one of the world's largest accounting firms, offering auditing and accounting services around the globe. The firm also provides legal services and services relating to emerging growth companies, human resources issues, and corporate transactions (mergers and acquisitions, IPOs, and the like). Ernst & Young has one of the world's largest tax practices, serving multinational clients that have to comply with multiple local tax laws.

After spending decades building them, the big accountancies have all moved toward shedding their consultancies, because of internal and regulatory pressures, as well as the perceived conflict of interest in providing auditing and consulting services to the same clients. Ernst & Young was the first to split off its consultancy, selling it in 2000 to what is now Cap Gemini Ernst & Young.

Ernst & Young, which gained an impressive amount of weight in former rival Andersen's diaspora, has also boosted its legal services, assembling some 2,000 lawyers in dozens of countries.

Ernst & Young has faced Andersen-style trouble of its own. Federal regulators in 2002 sued the firm for its alleged role in the failure of Superior Bank FSB, and threatened civil charges for purported fraud relating to Cendant. In the UK, insurer Equitable Life in 2003 sued the accountancy for professional negligence related to work performed when Ernst & Young was its auditor. More problems followed with clients Healthsouth and America Online.

Rick Bobrow retired as the firm's global CEO after a year on the job, presumably because of the airing of previously unpublicized Ernst & Young financial information during Bobrow's divorce proceedings.

HISTORY

In 1494 Luca Pacioli's *Summa di Arithmetica* became the first published text on double-entry bookkeeping, but it was almost 400 years before accounting became a profession.

In 1849 Frederick Whinney joined the UK firm of Harding & Pullein. His ledgers were so clear that he was advised to take up accounting, which was a growth field as stock companies proliferated. Whinney became a name partner in 1859 and his sons followed him into the business. The firm became Whinney, Smith & Whinney (WS&W) in 1894. After WWII, WS&W formed an alliance with Ernst & Ernst (founded in Cleveland in 1903 by brothers Alwin and Theodore Ernst), with each firm operating on the other's behalf across the Atlantic.

Whinney merged with Brown, Fleming & Murray in 1965 to become Whinney Murray. In 1979 Whinney Murray, Turquands Barton Mayhew (also a UK firm), and Ernst & Ernst merged to form Ernst & Whinney.

But Ernst & Whinney wasn't done merging. Ten years later, when it was the fourth-largest accounting firm, it merged with #5 Arthur Young, which had been founded by Scotsman Arthur Young in 1895 in Kansas City. Long known as "old reliable," Arthur Young fell on hard times in the 1980s because its audit relationships with failed S&Ls led to expensive litigation (settled in 1992 for $400 million).

Thus the new firm of Ernst & Young faced a rocky start. In 1990 it fended off rumors of collapse. The next year it slashed payroll, even thinning its partner roster. Exhausted by the S&L wars, in 1994 the firm replaced its pugnacious general counsel, Carl Riggio, with the more cost-conscious Kathryn Oberly.

In the mid-1990s Ernst & Young concentrated on consulting, particularly in software applications, and grew through acquisitions. In 1996 the firm bought Houston-based Wright Killen & Co., a petroleum and petrochemicals consulting firm, to form Ernst & Young Wright Killen. It also entered new alliances that year, including ones with Washington-based ISD/Shaw, which provided banking industry consulting, and India's Tata Consulting.

In 1997 Ernst & Young was sued for a record $4 billion for its alleged failure to effectively handle the 1993 restructuring of the defunct Merry-Go-Round Enterprises retail chain (it settled for $185 million in 1999.) On the heels of a merger deal between Coopers & Lybrand and Price Waterhouse, Ernst & Young agreed in 1997 to merge with KPMG International. But Ernst & Young called off the negotiations in 1998, citing the uncertain regulatory process they faced.

In 1999 the firm reached a settlement in lawsuits regarding accounting errors at Informix and Cendant and sold its UK and Southern African trust and fiduciary businesses to Royal Bank of Canada (now RBC Financial Group).

In 2000 Ernst & Young became the first of the (then) Big Five firms to sell its consultancy, dealing it to France's Cap Gemini Group for about $11 billion. The following year the UK accountancy watchdog group announced it would investigate Ernst & Young for its handling of the accounts of UK-based The Equitable Life Assurance Society. The insurer was forced to close to new business in 2000 because of massive financial difficulties.

E&Y made headlines and gave competitors plenty to talk about in 2002 when financial records that had been closely held were made public during a divorce case involving executive Rick Bobrow (who in 2003 abruptly retired as global CEO after just a year on the job). The firm in 2002 also formed an alliance with former New York City mayor Rudy Giuliani to help launch a business consultancy and an investment firm bearing the Giuliani name.

EXECUTIVES

Global Chairman and CEO; Chairman for the Americas: James S. (Jim) Turley
CFO and Global Managing Partner – Finance and Infrastrucure: Norbert R. Becker
COO: Paul J. Ostling
Global Managing Partner – Quality & Risk Management: Michael N.M. Boyd
Global Managing Partner – Markets: Mike Cullen
Global Managing Partner – People: Timothy T. (Tim) Griffy
Global Managing Partner – Practice Integration: Jean-Charles Raufast
Deputy Global Managing Partner – Infrastructure; VC of Knowledge & Technology, Ernst & Young LLP: John G. Peetz Jr.
Global Director – Business Risk Services: Thomas Bussa
Vice Chairman – Strategy: Beth A. Brooke
Vice Chairman – Assurance and Advisory Business Services: James A. Hassett
Vice Chairman – Global Financial Services: Robert W. Stein
Vice Chairman – Tax: Karl Johansson
Vice Chairman – Technology, Communications and Entertainment: Stephen E. Almassy
Vice Chairman – Law: Patrick Bignon
Vice Chairman – Emerging Growth Markets Accounts: Roger F. Dunbar
Vice Chairman – Sales: Patrick J.P. Flochel
Vice Chairman – Corporate Finance: Francis Small
Director, Entrepreneur of the Year Program: Nancy Clark

LOCATIONS

HQ: 5 Times Square, New York, NY 10036
Phone: 212-773-3000 **Fax:** 212-773-6350
Web: www.eyi.com

Ernst & Young International has approximately 670 offices in more than 140 countries.

PRODUCTS/OPERATIONS

2003 Sales

	$ mil.	% of total
Assurance & advisory business services	7,736	59
Tax & law services	4,165	32
Transaction advisory services	960	7
Other	275	2
Total	**13,136**	**100**

Industry Specializations

Chemicals
Communications
Construction
Energy
Entertainment
Financial services
Health sciences
Hospitality
Industrial products
Real estate
Retail and consumer products
Technology
Utilities

Selected Services

Assurance and Advisory
- Actuarial services
- Audits
- Accounting advisory
- Business risk services
- Internal audit
- Real estate advisory services
- Technology and security risk services
- Transaction support services

Emerging Growth Companies
- Corporate finance services
- IPO services
- Mergers and acquisitions advisory
- Operational consulting
- Strategic advisory

Human Capital
- Compensation and benefits consulting
- Cost optimization and risk management
- Transaction support services

Law
- Corporate and M&A
- Employment
- Finance
- Information technology services
- Intellectual property
- International trade and anti-trust
- Litigation and arbitration
- Real estate

Tax
- Customs and international trade
- Electronic VAT assurance
- International tax
- Partial exemption evaluation process
- Tax outsourcing

Transactions
- Capital management
- Due diligence and transaction support
- Financial and business modeling
- M&A advisory
- Post-deal advisory
- Strategic finance
- Valuation

COMPETITORS

AMS
Bain & Company
BDO International
Deloitte Touche Tohmatsu
Grant Thornton International
IBM
KPMG
PricewaterhouseCoopers

HISTORICAL FINANCIALS

Company Type: Partnership

Income Statement

FYE: June 30

	REVENUE ($ mil.)	NET INCOME ($ mil.)	NET PROFIT MARGIN	EMPLOYEES
6/03	13,136	—	—	103,000
6/02	10,124	—	—	87,206
6/01	9,900	—	—	82,000
6/00*	9,500	—	—	88,625
9/99	12,500	—	—	97,800
9/98	10,900	—	—	85,000
9/97	9,100	—	—	79,750
9/96	7,800	—	—	72,000
9/95	6,867	—	—	68,452
9/94	6,020	—	—	61,287
Annual Growth	9.1%	—	—	5.9%

*Fiscal year change

Revenue History

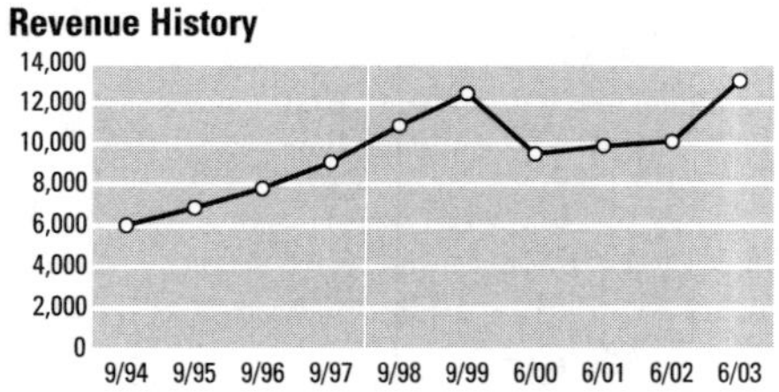

ESPN, Inc.

ESPN is a superstar of the sports broadcasting world. The company is the leading cable sports broadcaster with seven domestic networks — including its flagship ESPN, ESPN2 (sporting events and news), ESPN Classic (historical sports footage), ESPN HD, and ESPNEWS (24-hour news and information) — that reach more than 87 million US homes. It also reaches another 119 million homes worldwide with its ESPN International unit. In addition, ESPN creates content for TV and radio and operates one of the most popular sports sites on the Internet. ESPN also has lent its name to a magazine and a chain of eight sports-themed restaurants. ESPN is 80% owned by Walt Disney (through ABC Cable); Hearst has a 20% stake.

After buying domestic rights from the National Basketball Association in 2002, ESPN became the first network ever to have contracts with and televise all four professional sports leagues — baseball, football, basketball, and hockey. The company launched a high definition service, called ESPN HD, in spring 2003. In addition to its heavily watched sports wrap-up shows, the company has tried its hand at original programming including movies *Season on the Brink* and *The Junction Boys*.

For those curious about the roots of the company's name: the network's original name was the Entertainment and Sports Programming Network when it was formed in 1979. The network adopted the new name — ESPN, Inc. — in 1985.

EXECUTIVES

President; President, ABC Sports: George W. Bodenheimer
EVP and CFO: Christine Driessen, age 46
EVP Affiliate Sales and Marketing: Sean H. R. Bratches
EVP Event Marketing and National Sales: David Rotem
EVP Programming and Production: Mark Shapiro
EVP espn.com and *ESPN The Magazine*: John Skipper
SVP and Editor-In-Chief, *ESPN The Magazine*: John Papanek
SVP and Executive Editor, ESPN Inc. and ESPN Internet Group: John Walsh
SVP and General Manager, ESPN Enterprises: Rick Alessandri
SVP Advertising, Marketing, and Promotion: Lee Ann Daly
SVP, Consumer Communications: Chris LaPlaca
SVP Information Services: Tony Tamburo
SVP Programming and Production: Mark Quenzel

LOCATIONS

HQ: 935 Middle St., Bristol, CT 06010
Phone: 860-766-2000 **Fax:** 860-766-2213
Web: espn.go.com

ESPN has offices in Bristol, Connecticut, as well as New York City.

PRODUCTS/OPERATIONS

Selected TV Operations
ESPN (sporting events and news channel)
ESPN Classic (archival sports footage channel)
ESPN Classic Sport (70%, European network)
ESPN Extra (pay-per-view events)
ESPN Original Programming (original content for cable channels)
ESPN2 (sporting events and news channel)
ESPNEWS (24-hour sports news channel)

Web Operations
espn.go.com (sports information site)

Other Operations
B.A.S.S. (bass fishing organization)
ESPN The Magazine (magazine)
ESPN Zone (sports-themed restaurants)
SportsTicker (provider of sports news and scores)

COMPETITORS

CBS
Comcast Spectacor
Fox Entertainment
Fox Sports
NBC
SportsLine.com
Turner Broadcasting
Yahoo!

HISTORICAL FINANCIALS

Company Type: Joint venture

Income Statement FYE: September 30

	REVENUE ($ mil.)	NET INCOME ($ mil.)	NET PROFIT MARGIN	EMPLOYEES
9/02	2,120	—	—	—
9/01	2,500	—	—	—
9/00	2,600	—	—	2,500
Annual Growth	(9.7%)	—	—	—

Revenue History

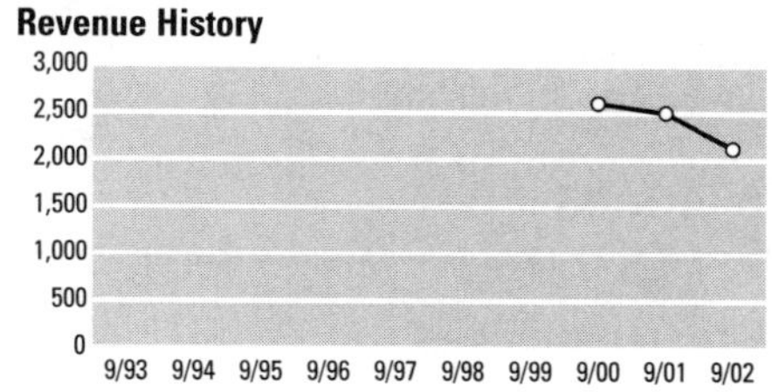

Estes Express Lines

Estes Express Lines is a multiregional less-than-truckload (LTL) freight hauler. (LTL carriers consolidate freight from multiple shippers into a single trailer.) The company operates a fleet of about 3,800 tractors and 11,800 trailers from a network of more than 100 terminals, mainly in the eastern half of the US. It provides services to the rest of the US and Canada through its partners in the ExpressLINK regional LTL alliance: G.I. Trucking, Lakeville Motor Express, and TST Overland Express. Estes Express also offers warehousing, domestic airfreight forwarding, and truck and trailer leasing. Founded by W. W. Estes in 1931, the company is owned and operated by the Estes family.

EXECUTIVES

Chairman: Robey W. Estes Sr.
President: Robey W. (Rob) Estes Jr., age 51
EVP: William T. (Billy) Hupp
VP; General Manager, Southwest Division: John D. Rogers
VP Corporate Communications: Trish Garland
VP Human Resources: Thomas Donahue
VP Operations: John T. (Junior) Johnson
VP Sales: Chuck Parker
Corporate Secretary: Stephen E. Hupp
Treasurer and CFO: Gary D. Okes
Information Services: Hugh Camden
Auditors: Joyner, Kirkham, Keel & Robertson, P. C.

LOCATIONS

HQ: 3901 W. Broad St., Richmond, VA 23230
Phone: 804-353-1900 **Fax:** 804-358-5900
Web: www.estes-express.com

COMPETITORS

Arkansas Best
J. B. Hunt
Old Dominion Freight
Overnite Transportation
Roadway
Schneider National
SCS Transportation
USF
Watkins Associated Industries
Yellow

HISTORICAL FINANCIALS

Company Type: Private

Income Statement FYE: December 31

	REVENUE ($ mil.)	NET INCOME ($ mil.)	NET PROFIT MARGIN	EMPLOYEES
12/02	800	—	—	9,160
12/01	695	—	—	8,531
12/00	691	—	—	8,000
12/99	603	—	—	7,800
12/98	519	—	—	7,000
Annual Growth	11.4%	—	—	7.0%

Revenue History

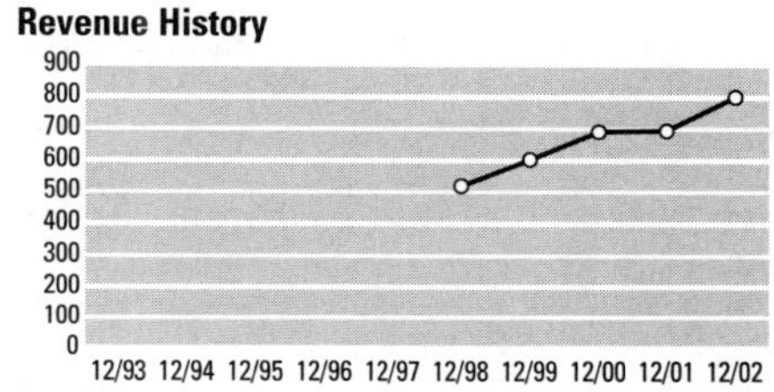

Everett Smith Group, Ltd.

From skins to steel, Everett Smith Group has you covered. The investment firm owns Albert Trostel & Sons, the parent of Eagle Ottawa Leather, which makes upholstery leather for major carmakers. Albert Trostel & Sons also is parent of Trostel, Ltd., a manufacturer of rubber molded seals for the appliance and automotive industries, and Trostel SEG, which makes thermoplastic products for the automotive and hand tool industries. Other Everett Smith investments include OEM Worldwide, which manufactures electronic assemblies for medical and industrial applications, and Maysteel, which makes power distribution equipment and enclosures for the utility industry. Descendants of Everett G. Smith control the firm.

EXECUTIVES

Chairman and CEO: Anders Segerdahl
Vice Chairman: Thomas Hauske Jr.
VP and CFO: James Orth
VP and General Counsel: Steven Hartung
VP: Randall Perry

LOCATIONS

HQ: 800 N. Marshall St., Milwaukee, WI 53202
Phone: 414-273-3421 **Fax:** —
Web: www.esmithgroup.com

Everett Smith Group has operations in Argentina, Hungary, Ireland, Mexico, South Africa, the UK, and the US.

PRODUCTS/OPERATIONS

Selected Operations

Albert Trostel & Sons Co.
Maysteel Corp.
Eagle Ottawa Leather Company
OEM Worldwide
Trostel, Ltd.
Trostel SEG

COMPETITORS

Federal-Mogul
Giddings & Lewis
Kawasho
ROHN Industries
Tandy Brands

HISTORICAL FINANCIALS

Company Type: Private

Income Statement FYE: November 30*

	REVENUE ($ mil.)	NET INCOME ($ mil.)	NET PROFIT MARGIN	EMPLOYEES
12/02	730	—	—	5,900
12/01	685	—	—	5,300
12/00	677	—	—	5,300
12/99	635	—	—	6,000
12/98	700	—	—	6,000
Annual Growth	1.1%	—	—	(0.4%)

*Fiscal year change

Revenue History

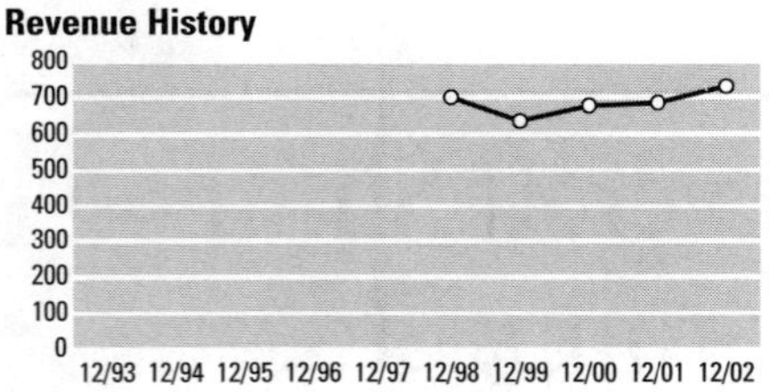

Express Personnel Services

When you need a worker fast, Express Personnel Services delivers. The professional staffing company provides work for some 225,000 employees from more than 400 offices in the US, Canada, and South Africa. In addition to temporary staffing, it provides professional placement and contract staffing through Express Professional Staffing and offers workplace services (consulting, training, development) through Express Business Solutions. The company is owned by founder and CEO Robert Funk, who also owns the Oklahoma City Blazers hockey team and Express Ranches, one of the nation's largest cattle breeders.

EXECUTIVES

Chairman and CEO: Robert A. Funk
Vice Chairman: William H. Stoller
EVP and CFO: Thomas N. Richards
EVP Sales: Bob Fellinger
SVP Franchising: Tom Gunderson
VP and Controller: Sharon Patric
VP Administration and Personnel: Carol Lane
VP Human Resources: Larry Ferree
VP Marketing and Communications: Linda C. Haneborg

LOCATIONS

HQ: 8516 Northwest Expwy., Oklahoma City, OK 73162
Phone: 405-840-5000 **Fax:** 405-717-5669
Web: www.expresspersonnel.com

PRODUCTS/OPERATIONS

Selected Staffing Fields

Express Personnel
Accounting
General labor
Industrial
Legal
Medical
Office and clerical
Sales and marketing
Technical

Express Professional
Accounting and financial
Engineering and manufacturing
Health care
Human resources
Information technology
Sales and marketing
Technical

COMPETITORS

Adecco
Administaff
ADP TotalSource
Barrett Business Services
Butler International
EPIX
Gevity HR
Kelly Services
Manpower
MPS
Randstad
Robert Half
Spherion
Uniforce Staffing
Volt Information

HISTORICAL FINANCIALS

Company Type: Private

Income Statement FYE: December 31

	REVENUE ($ mil.)	NET INCOME ($ mil.)	NET PROFIT MARGIN	EMPLOYEES
12/01	781	—	—	224,000
12/00	916	—	—	262,000
Annual Growth	(14.7%)	—	—	(14.5%)

Revenue History

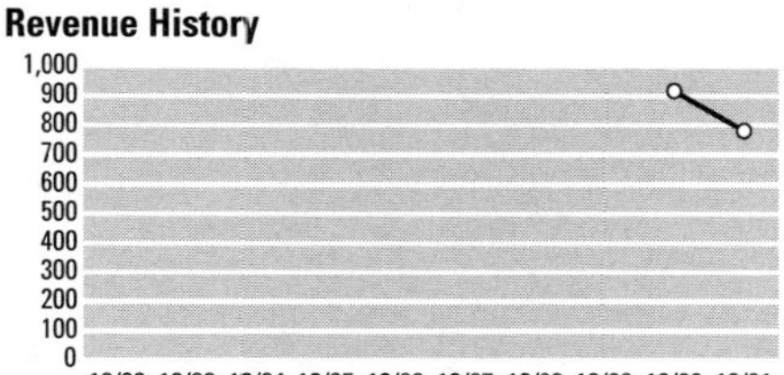

F. Dohmen Co.

The F. Dohmen Co. helps pharmacists with just about everything except interpreting handwriting. The company is one of the largest private pharmaceutical wholesalers in the US. Its Dohmen Medical division distributes brand name and generic products, including medical and surgical supplies. F. Dohmen also makes pharmaceutical management systems that perform an array of services, including prescription processing, physician and insurer information management, and chronic disease management. The company's additional services include advertising assistance; it sells National Brand Equivalent products that permit pharmacies to use their own store labels. German immigrant Frederick Dohmen founded the firm in 1858.

EXECUTIVES

President and CEO: John Dohmen
CFO: Tracy Pearson
EVP, Human Resources: Robert Dohmen
VP, Marketing and Sales: Doug Rewerts

LOCATIONS

HQ: The F. Dohmen Co.
W194 N11381 McCormick Dr.,
Germantown, WI 53022
Phone: 262-255-0022 **Fax:** 262-255-0041
Web: www.dohmen.com

PRODUCTS/OPERATIONS

Selected Company Divisions
DDN Pharmaceutical Logistics (pharmaceutical distribution)
Dohmen Distribution Partners, LLC (pharmacy management services)
jASCorp (pharmaceutical management systems)
RESTAT (prescription benefits management)

Selected Products
DotConnect (central prescription editing, messaging, and data analysis system)
Encounter Pro (disease management system)
Encounter Rx (prescription processing system)
Enhance Pro (pharmacy counseling system)
HealthCare America Ad Program (advertising assistance)
HealthCare America private labels (National Brand Equivalent products)
Impact (insurer/physician/patient information management system)
Infonet EC (electronic ordering system)
P3 Performance Plan (program that assists pharmacists with marketing and provides product information)

COMPETITORS

AmerisourceBergen
Cardinal Health
D & K Healthcare Resources
Kinray
McKesson
Owens & Minor
QK Healthcare

HISTORICAL FINANCIALS

Company Type: Private

Income Statement FYE: April 30

	REVENUE ($ mil.)	NET INCOME ($ mil.)	NET PROFIT MARGIN	EMPLOYEES
4/02	838	—	—	450
4/01	748	—	—	450
4/00	655	—	—	480
4/99	524	—	—	430
Annual Growth	16.9%	—	—	1.5%

Revenue History

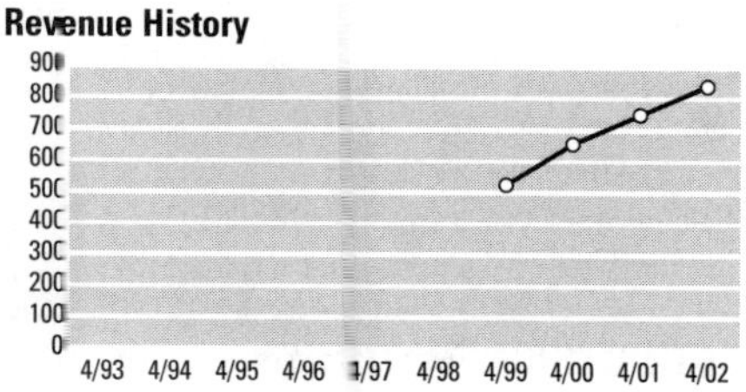

COMPETITORS

American Homestar
Cavalier Homes
Cavco
Champion Enterprises
Clayton Homes
Coachmen
Fleetwood Enterprises
Horton Industries
Liberty Homes
Monaco Coach
National RV
Oakwood Homes
Palm Harbor
Patriot Homes
Skyline
Southern Energy Homes
Thor Industries
Winnebago

HISTORICAL FINANCIALS

Company Type: Private

Income Statement FYE: December 31

	ESTIMATED REVENUE ($ mil.)	NET INCOME ($ mil.)	NET PROFIT MARGIN	EMPLOYEES
12/02	500	—	—	900

Fairmont Homes, Inc.

Fairmont Homes really knows how to put the mobile in mobile homes, since it makes recreational vehicles as well as manufactured housing. Brothers Jim and John Shea acquired Fairmont Homes in 1971. Fairmont manufactures both single- and multi-section homes with up to 2,340 sq. ft. from floor plans that feature two to five bedrooms. Jim bought his brother's share of the company in 1975 and founded subsidiary Gulf Stream Coach, a builder of RVs, in 1983. Gulf Stream offers big slide-out rooms as standard features in its smaller, economically priced vehicles, as well as in its luxury motorhomes. Fairmont's suppliers include General Electric (appliances), Georgia-Pacific (plywood), and Owens Corning (insulation).

EXECUTIVES

CEO: James Foster Shea
CFO: Carlos Macau
Director, Human Resources: Rick Jones
President, Gulf Stream Motorized Division: Brian Shea
VP Sales and Marketing, Gulf Stream Motorized Division: Claude Donati

LOCATIONS

HQ: 502 S. Oakland Ave., Nappanee, IN 46550
Phone: 574-773-7941 **Fax:** 574-773-2185
Web: www.fairmonthomes.com

PRODUCTS/OPERATIONS

Selected Brand Names

Manufactured Housing
Celebrity series
Fairpoint
Foxwood series
Friendship Cape Cod series
Happy House series
Triumph series
Windsor series

Gulf Stream Motorhomes, Trailers, Towables, and Fifth Wheels
Atrium (motorhome)
B Touring Cruiser (motorhome)
Conquest (trailer and fifth wheel)
Friendship (motorhome)
Independence (motorhome)
Innsbruck (trailer and fifth wheel)
Mako (fifth wheel)
Scenic Cruiser (motorhome)
Sea Hawk (trailer)
Tour Master (motorhome)

Farmland Industries, Inc.

Farmland Industries helps its members farm land industriously. Farmland was the #1 farmer-owned agricultural cooperative in North America for years. It filed for bankruptcy in 2002, after having lost $90 million in 2001, and began selling off segments. Before its financial woes, Farmland had been a major US beef packer and pork producer. It still is a competitor in international agribusiness, exporting products (mainly grain) worldwide. Farmland Industries is owned by about 1,700 local co-ops that are made up of about 600,000 farmers in Canada, Mexico, and the US. The co-op still provides its member-farmers with feed, fertilizer, and pesticides; it also processes, stores, and markets their crops and livestock.

After declaring bankruptcy Farmland sought court approval to pay approximately $8 million to 96 employees so that they would stay with the company through its reorganization. In order to raise funds to pay its creditors, Farmland in 2003 sold its nitrogen fertilizer business to Koch Nitrogen.

In August 2003 Farmland announced it was selling its remaining assets including its Midwestern grain elevators and its interests in the joint ventures it has with Agriliance, Land O'Lakes Feed, and SF Phosphates.

EXECUTIVES

Chairman: Harry Fehrenbacher, age 54
Vice Chairman and VP: Jody Bezner, age 61
President and CEO: Robert B. (Bob) Terry, age 46, $311,026 pay
EVP and CFO: Steve Rhodes, age 48
EVP; President, Crop Production: Stanley A. Riemann, age 51, $295,000 pay
EVP; President, Refrigerated Foods: William G. Fielding, age 55, $350,000 pay
VP and Treasurer: J. Randall Vance, age 41
VP, Administration: Tim R. Daugherty, age 49, $235,728 pay
VP, General Counsel, and Secretary: Robert W. Schuller
VP, Human Resources: Holly D. McCoy
Auditors: KPMG LLP

LOCATIONS

HQ: 12200 N. Ambassador Dr., Kansas City, MO 64163
Phone: 816-713-7000 **Fax:** 816-713-6323
Web: www.farmland.com

More than 600,000 farmers and their cooperatives, located in the US, Canada, and Mexico, form Farmland Industries, which conducts business worldwide.

PRODUCTS/OPERATIONS

Selected Subsidiaries and Joint Ventures

Agriliance, LLC (with Land O'Lakes and Cenex Harvest States to supply fertilizer, pesticides, herbicides, and seed to farmers)
Farmland MissChem Limited (anhydrous ammonia manufacturing)
Land O'Lakes Farmland Feed
SF Phosphates, Limited Liability Company (fertilizer manufacturing)
Southern Farm Fish Processors
WILFARM, LLC (with Wilbur-Ellis Co.; pesticides)

Selected Consumer Product Brands

Carando (bread, specialty meats)
Cider House (bacon)
Farmland (processed pork products)
OhSe (hot dogs, sandwich meats, and bacon)
Roegelein (processed pork products)

COMPETITORS

Ag Processing
Agway
American Foods
ADM
Cargill
CF Industries
CHS
ConAgra
ContiGroup
DeBruce Grain
Exxon Mobil
Gold Kist
GROWMARK
Hormel
IMC Global
JR Simplot
Rose Packing
Rosen's Diversified
Royal Dutch/Shell Group
Scoular
Seaboard
Smithfield Foods
Southern States
Transammonia
Tyson Foods
Tyson Fresh Meats

HISTORICAL FINANCIALS

Company Type: Cooperative

Income Statement FYE: August 31

	REVENUE ($ mil.)	NET INCOME ($ mil.)	NET PROFIT MARGIN	EMPLOYEES
8/02	6,574	(347)	—	13,800
8/01	11,763	(90)	—	14,500
8/00	12,239	(29)	—	15,000
8/99	10,709	14	0.1%	17,700
8/98	8,775	59	0.7%	16,100
8/97	9,148	135	1.5%	14,600
8/96	9,789	126	1.3%	14,700
8/95	7,257	163	2.2%	12,700
8/94	6,678	74	1.1%	12,000
8/93	4,723	(30)	—	8,155
Annual Growth	3.7%	—	—	6.0%

2002 Year-End Financials

Debt ratio: 42.5%
Return on equity: —
Cash ($ mil.): 0
Current ratio: 1.40
Long-term debt ($ mil.): 140

Net Income History

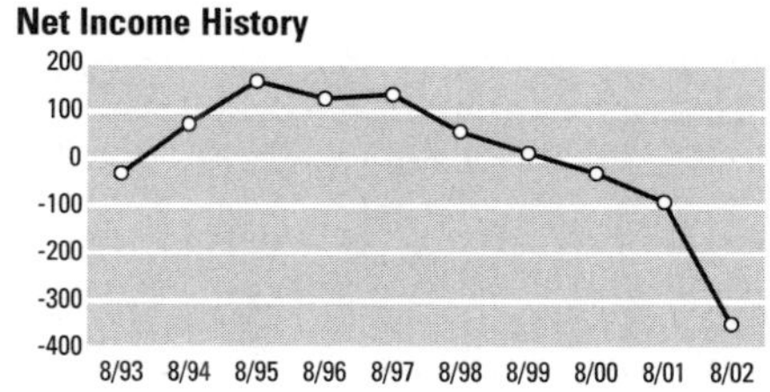

The Faulkner Organization

The sound and the fury of Buicks moving off the lot is coming from The Faulkner Organization, one of the Delaware Valley's largest-volume automotive dealers. The company operates more than 20 automobile dealerships in Pennsylvania. Its domestic car franchises include Pontiac, Buick, GMC, Cadillac, Ford, Chevrolet, Mercury, and Saturn; its import franchises sell Toyotas, Hondas, Mitsubishis, and Mazdas. In addition to new and used cars, the company sells auto parts and offers automotive repairs and car financing. Founded in 1932 by Henry Faulkner, the company is still owned and operated by the Faulkner family.

EXECUTIVES

President and CEO: Hank Faulkner
COO: Bob Lewis
CFO and Director of Human Resources: Bill Sebald
Director of Fixed Operations: Walt Huber

LOCATIONS

HQ: 4437 Street Rd., Trevose, PA 19053
Phone: 215-364-3980 **Fax:** 215-364-0706
Web: www.tobesure.com

COMPETITORS

Asbury Automotive
AutoNation
Brown Automotive
Budget
CarMax
Darcars
Holman Enterprises
Jim Koons Automotive
Ourisman Automotive
Pacifico
Planet Automotive Group
Rosenthal Automotive
Sonic Automotive

HISTORICAL FINANCIALS

Company Type: Private

Income Statement FYE: December 31

	REVENUE ($ mil.)	NET INCOME ($ mil.)	NET PROFIT MARGIN	EMPLOYEES
12/01	818	—	—	1,100
12/00	821	—	—	1,100
12/99	806	—	—	1,100
12/98	735	—	—	1,100
12/97	711	—	—	1,000
12/96	630	—	—	1,200
12/95	625	—	—	1,200
12/94	550	—	—	1,100
12/93	400	—	—	1,288
Annual Growth	9.4%	—	—	(2.0%)

Revenue History

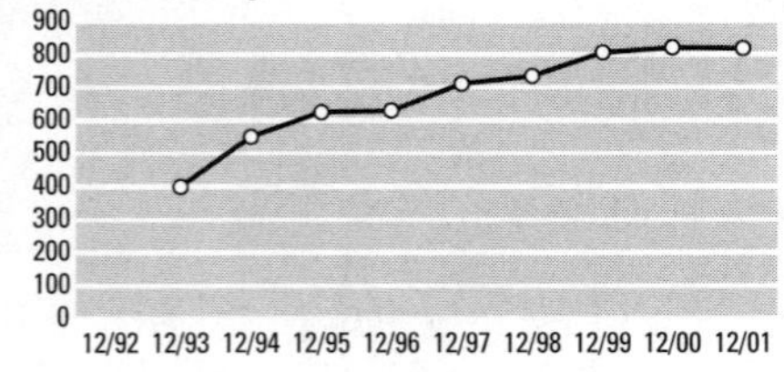

Federal Prison Industries, Inc.

Some businesses benefit from captive audiences; this company benefits from captive employees. Federal Prison Industries (FPI), better known by its trade name UNICOR, uses prisoners to make products and provide services, mainly for the US government. More than 21,000 inmates (about 18% of the total federal inmate population) are employed in over 100 FPI factories. UNICOR, which is part of the Justice Department's Bureau of Prisons, manufactures such products as office furniture, work clothing, beds and linens, electronics equipment, and eyewear. It also offers such services as data entry, bulk mailing, laundry services, printing, recycling, and refurbishing vehicle components.

Federal law mandates that government buyers consider UNICOR products first; the company is allowed to sell services (but not products) to the private sector. FPI already produces most of the products the federal government buys, and it is benefitting from a growing prison population. The company is also tapping into the commercial market by offering services. Self-supporting, UNICOR is overseen by a governing board that is appointed by the US president.

HISTORY

FPI was established by President Franklin Roosevelt in 1934 to teach job skills at men's and women's federal prisons. During WWII, 95% of FPI's output was dedicated to the war effort — the company's products included parachutes and munitions. In the late 1950s and early 1960s, FPI built or renovated structures at 18 of the 31 federal prisons. In 1974 it established regional sales offices, and in 1977 it took the name UNICOR.

Although self-supporting, UNICOR remained necessarily inefficient because of its goal to put as many inmates as possible to work. However, as the prison population increased, the company underwent rapid expansion and added skilled services in the 1980s.

UNICOR put its product catalog online in 1996. The next year the Senate authorized a study of ways to make UNICOR more competitive, after private businesses had complained that the booming prison population, low wages (23 cents to $1.15 per hour), and government preferential treatment gave UNICOR an unfair advantage. Legislation to force FPI to bid against the private sector for government contracts was brought before Congress in 1999; at the same time, a bill was introduced to allow the company to offer its products to the private sector. Meanwhile, FPI began selling services such as data entry to private-sector customers.

In 2003 Dell Computer dropped UNICOR as the vendor for its computer recycling program.

EXECUTIVES

Director, Federal Bureau of Prisons: Kathleen M. Hawk-Sawyer
COO: Steve Schwalb
Controller: Bruce Long
Assistant Director (Human Resources): Keith Hall
Ombudsman: Jan Hynson
Auditors: PricewaterhouseCoopers LLP

LOCATIONS

HQ: 320 1st St. NW, Washington, DC 20534
Phone: 202-305-3500 **Fax:** 202-305-7340
Web: www.unicor.gov

Federal Prison Industries operates 111 factories at 71 prisons in the US.

PRODUCTS/OPERATIONS

Selected Products

Office furniture
Casegoods and training table products
Filing and storage products
Office furniture and accessories
Office system products
Packaged office solutions
Seating products

Clothing & textiles
Apparel
Embroidery and screenprinting on textiles
Draperies and curtains
Mattresses, bedding, linens, and towels

Electronics
Electrical cables (both braided and cord assemblies)
Electrical components and connectors
Lighting systems
Wire harness assemblies and circuit boards

Fleet management
Fleet management customized services
New vehicle retrofit services
Rebuild and refurbish vehicle components

Industrial products
Custom fabricated industrial products, lockers, and storage cabinets
Dorm and quarters furnishings and packaged room solutions
Industrial racking catwalks, mezzanines, and shelving
Optical eyewear (safety and prescription)
Replacement filters
Security fencing

Graphics
Custom engraving and printing on awards, promotional gifts, and license plates
Interior and exterior architectural, safety, and recreational signs
Printing and creative design services
Remanufacturing of toner cartridges

Services
Assembly and packing services
Call center and order fulfillment services
Distribution and mailing services
Document conversion
Laundry services
Recycling activities
Recycling of electronic components
Reuse and recovery of usable components for resale

COMPETITORS

Anderson Hickey
Avnet
CPAC
Deere
Federal Signal
Global Furniture
Haworth
Herman Miller
HighPoint Furniture
HON INDUSTRIES
Kimball International
Matthews International
Mine Safety Appliances
Molex
Steelcase
Tyco International
WestPoint Stevens

HISTORICAL FINANCIALS

Company Type: Government agency

Income Statement FYE: September 30

	REVENUE ($ mil.)	NET INCOME ($ mil.)	NET PROFIT MARGIN	EMPLOYEES
9/02	679	9	1.3%	21,778
9/01	584	5	0.8%	22,560
9/00	546	(12)	—	21,688
9/99	566	17	2.9%	20,966
9/98	534	(2)	—	21,800
9/97	513	3	0.6%	18,414
9/96	496	12	2.4%	17,379
9/95	459	—	—	16,780
9/94	395	—	—	16,200
Annual Growth	7.0%	(4.5%)	—	3.8%

2002 Year-End Financials

Debt ratio: 6.9%
Return on equity: 3.2%
Cash ($ mil.): 108
Current ratio: 2.21
Long-term debt ($ mil.): 20

Net Income History

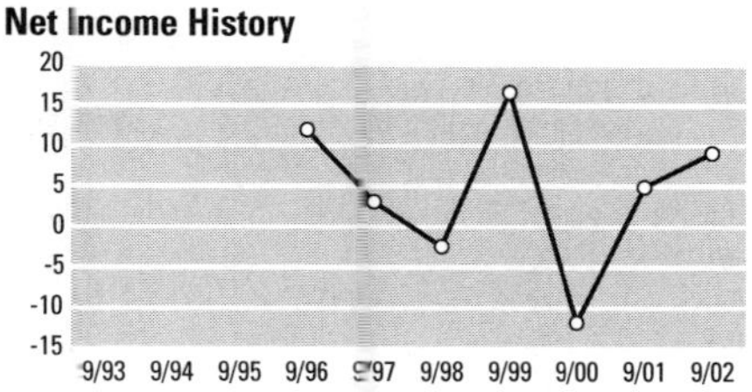

Feld Entertainment

A lot of clowning around has helped Feld Entertainment become one of the largest live entertainment producers in the world. The company entertains some 10 million people each year through its centerpiece, Ringling Bros. and Barnum & Bailey Circus, which visits about 90 locations. In addition, Feld also produces several touring ice shows, including Disney On Ice shows such as *Beauty and the Beast* and *Toy Story,* and it owns the Siegfried & Roy show at The Mirage in Las Vegas (the show's future is uncertain after Roy Horn was mauled by a tiger in 2003). Chairman and CEO Kenneth Feld, whose father, Irvin, began managing the circus in 1956, owns the company and personally oversees most of its productions. He also produces Broadway plays.

Feld has engaged in some high-profile battles lately with animal rights activists. In 2001 a district court judge dismissed a complaint filed against the company by several animal activist groups, who claimed that Feld Entertainment didn't comply with federal regulations regarding the care of Asian elephants. The lawsuit was reinstated in early 2003 due to a procedural technicality.

HISTORY

When five-year-old Irvin Feld found a $1 bill in 1923, he told his mother, "I'm going to buy a circus." He started by working the sideshows of traveling circuses before settling in Washington, DC, in 1940. Feld, who was white, opened the Super Cut-Rate Drugstore in a black section of the segregated city with the backing of the NAACP. In 1944 he opened the Super Music City record store and started his own record company, Super Disc. Feld and his brother Israel also began promoting outdoor concerts. When rock and roll became popular in the 1950s, Feld promoted Chubby Checker and Fats Domino, among others.

Feld came a step closer to his dream in 1956 when he began managing the Ringling Bros. and Barnum & Bailey Circus for majority owner John Ringling North. North's circus traced its roots back to 1871 and P. T. Barnum's Grand Traveling Museum, Menagerie, Caravan, and Circus. Barnum's circus merged with James Bailey's circus in 1881, creating Barnum & Bailey. In 1907 Bailey's widow sold Barnum & Bailey to North's uncles, the Ringling brothers, who had started their circus in 1884.

Among Feld's suggestions to North was moving the circus into air-conditioned arenas, saving $50,000 a week because 1,800 roustabouts were no longer needed to set up tents. Feld continued to promote music acts, but he suffered a serious blow in 1959 when three of his stars — Buddy Holly, Ritchie Valens, and J. P. Richardson (the Big Bopper) — died in a plane crash.

Feld's dream of owning a circus finally was realized in 1967 when he and investors paid $8 million for Ringling Brothers. He fired most of the circus' performers and opened a Clown College to train new ones. Feld bought a German circus the following year to obtain animal trainer Gunther Gebel-Williams (who then spent spent the next 30 years with Ringling Brothers). Feld split Ringling into two units in 1969, so he could book it in two parts of the country at the same time and double his profits. Feld took the company public that year.

Feld and the other stockholders sold the circus to Mattel in 1971 for $47 million in stock; Feld stayed on as manager and held on to the lucrative concession business, Sells-Floto. He persuaded Mattel to buy the Ice Follies, Holiday on Ice, and the Siegfried & Roy magic show in 1979. Mattel sold the circus back to Feld in 1982 for $22.5 million, along with the ice shows and the magic show. Feld died two years later, and his son Kenneth became head of the company. A chip off the old block, Kenneth fired almost all the circus performers when he took over.

In an attempt to leverage the Barnum & Bailey brand, the company opened four retail store locations in 1990, but the venture failed and the stores were closed two years later. A constant target of animal rights activists, Feld began backing conservation efforts on behalf of the endangered Asian elephant and established the Center for Elephant Conservation in Florida in 1995. The next year the company changed its name to Feld Entertainment.

Under increasing pressure as the company's creative guru and managerial boss, Feld hired Turner Home Entertainment executive Stuart Snyder as president and COO in 1997, so he could focus on the creative side of the business. That focus produced Barnum's Kaleidoscape in 1999, an upscale version of the original circus, featuring specialty acts, gourmet food, plush seats, and audience interaction. Plus, for the first time since 1956, a Feld circus was performed under a tent. (The company later shut down the tour of the Kaleidoscape, but claims it will return.) Snyder resigned later that year.

In an effort to inject new life into the 130-year-old Ringling Bros. and Barnum & Bailey Circus, Feld Entertainment launched two new marketing campaigns (one aimed at adults, the other aimed at children) in 2001.

Feld Entertainment's popular Siegfried & Roy show suffered a potential permanent setback in 2003 when Roy Horn was mauled by a white tiger during a performance. He is expected to recover, but there has been no word on whether the show will continue.

EXECUTIVES

Chairman and CEO: Kenneth Feld, age 54
CFO: Mike Ruch
SVP Field Marketing and Sales, North America: Jeff Meyer
SVP Marketing: Julie Robertson
VP Creative Development: Jerry Bilik
VP International Sales and Business Development: Robert McHugh
Director of Human Resources: Kirk McCoy
Director of Corporate Communications: Catherine Ort-Mabry
Executive Director of Animal Stewardship, Ringling Bros. and Barnum & Bailey: John Kirtland
Public Relations, Siegfried & Roy: Frank H. Lieberman

LOCATIONS

HQ: Feld Entertainment, Inc.
8607 Westwood Center Dr., Vienna, VA 22182
Phone: 703-448-4000 **Fax:** 703-448-4100
Web: www.feldentertainment.com

Feld Entertainment produces shows in 45 countries on six continents.

COMPETITORS

Cirque du Soleil
Clear Channel Entertainment
Harlem Globetrotters
HIT Entertainment
Corporación Interamericana de Entretenimiento
On Stage Entertainment
Renaissance Entertainment
Six Flags
TBA
Tom Collins

HISTORICAL FINANCIALS

Company Type: Private

Income Statement FYE: January 31

	ESTIMATED REVENUE ($ mil.)	NET INCOME ($ mil.)	NET PROFIT MARGIN	EMPLOYEES
1/01	776	—	—	2,500
1/00	675	—	—	2,500
1/99	645	—	—	2,500
1/98	630	—	—	2,500
1/97	550	—	—	2,500
1/96	625	—	—	2,500
1/95	600	—	—	2,500
1/94	570	—	—	2,500
1/93	500	—	—	2,500
Annual Growth	5.6%	—	—	0.0%

Revenue History

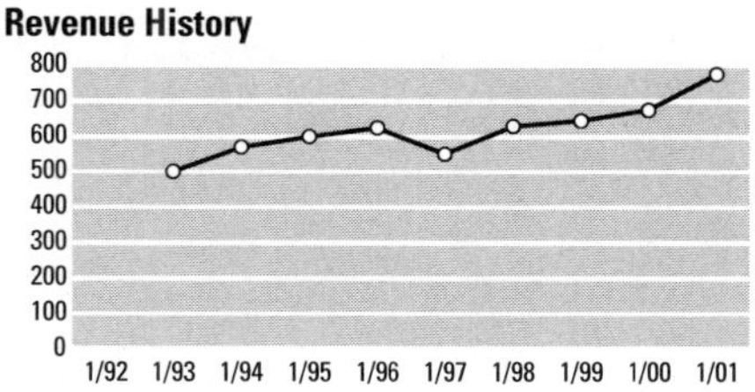

Fellowes, Inc.

Fellowes, Inc. (formerly Fellowes Manufacturing Company) produces office products that can organize or obliterate. A leading maker of paper shredders (Powershred, Shredmate), it also makes office storage boxes, computer accessories (such as ergonomic wrist rests and glare filters), and office desk accessories. The company has moved further into the digital age with new offerings such as notebook security locks and PDA accessories. Fellowes' products are sold through office products stores and mass merchandisers in more than 100 countries. Still owned and run by the Fellowes family, the company was started in 1917 when Harry Fellowes paid $50 for Bankers Box, a maker of storage boxes for bank records.

EXECUTIVES

CEO: James (Jim) Fellowes
COO; President, Fellowes Europe: Peter Fellowes
CFO: Joseph T. (Joe) Koch
VP and General Manager: Jim Lewis
VP and General Manager: Mark Naidoff
VP and General Manager: John Smith
VP, Human Resources: Lyn Bulman
President, Fellowes North America: Bob Compagno
Director of Corporate Marketing Communications: Maureen Moore
Manager of Corporate Marketing: Julie Garrard

LOCATIONS

HQ: 1789 Norwood Ave., Itasca, IL 60143
Phone: 630-893-1600 **Fax:** 630-893-1648
Web: www.fellowes.com

Fellowes has operations in Africa, Asia, Australia, the Benelux countries, Canada, France, Germany, Italy, Japan, Latin America, the Middle East, Poland, the UK, and the US.

PRODUCTS/OPERATIONS

Selected Products

Backrests
Cables
CD storage and wallets
Cellular accessories
Cleaning supplies
Copyholders
Document binding equipment and supplies
Drawer files
Dust covers
Footrests
Glare filters
Headsets
Keyboards and keyboard managers
Labeling equipment and supplies
Laminating machines and supplies
Laptop cases
Media storage (CDs, DVDs, cassettes, videos)
Mice and mouse pads
Monitor and CPU accessories
PDA accessories
Printer stands
Shredders and accessories
Storage boxes
Surge protectors
Tool kits
Wrist rests

COMPETITORS

ACCO
Avery Dennison
CompX International
Cummins-American
Escalade
Esselte
Fortune Brands
General Binding
Iron Mountain
Knape & Vogt
Lane Industries
Newell Rubbermaid
Optical Coating Lab
Relax the Back
Smead
TAB Products
Targus

HISTORICAL FINANCIALS

Company Type: Private

Income Statement FYE: March 31

	REVENUE ($ mil.)	NET INCOME ($ mil.)	NET PROFIT MARGIN	EMPLOYEES
3/02	700	—	—	1,750
3/01	650	—	—	1,800
3/00	607	—	—	1,800
3/99	523	—	—	1,773
3/98	500	—	—	1,450
3/97	358	—	—	1,474
3/96	310	—	—	1,461
3/95	220	—	—	1,258
3/94	191	—	—	—
Annual Growth	17.7%	—	—	4.8%

Revenue History

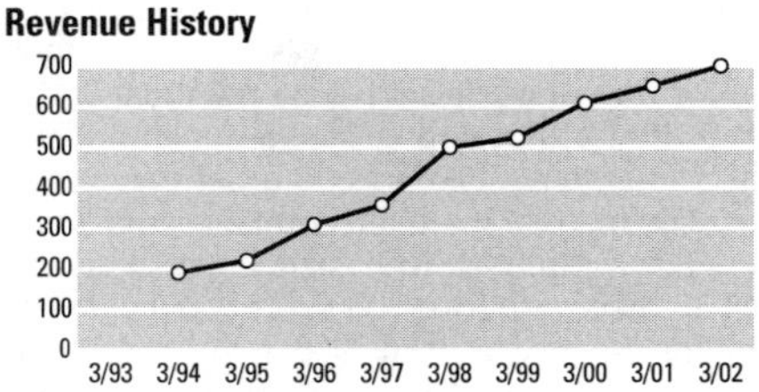

Ferolie Group

A food broker serving the entire US, the Ferolie Group broke into the business on the East Coast in 1948. The company provides sales and marketing services for packaged food and packaged goods companies. Through exclusive area and regional contracts, the group arranges distribution to warehouse stores, drugstores, supermarkets, and mass merchandisers. Some of Ferolie's biggest clients are Gillette's Duracell, Georgia-Pacific's Fort James, Kraft Foods, Unilever's Lipton, and McCormick & Company. The company is affiliated with Advantage Sales & Marketing, a partnership of food brokerages operating across the US. Founded by A. Joseph Ferolie, the company remains family-owned.

EXECUTIVES

Chairman and CEO: Lawrence J. Ferolie Sr.
COO: Paul Nadel
CIO: James (Jim) Ferolie
EVP, Business Teams and SVP, Grocery: Anthony (Tony) Ferolie
EVP, Customer Teams and VP, Frozen Foods: Frank Tomanelli
VP, Corporate Development: Tony Scuderi
VP, Finance: Catherine (Cathy) Ross
VP, Human Resources: Julie Shasteen
VP, Sales: Robert (Bob) Martin
Director, Marketing: Steven Nadel
General Counsel: Daryl Fox

LOCATIONS

HQ: 2 Van Riper Rd., Montvale, NJ 07645
Phone: 201-307-9100 **Fax:** 201-782-0878
Web: www.feroliegroup.com

COMPETITORS

Affiliated Foods
Atlantic Mktg
C&S Wholesale
Carrefour
CROSSMARK
Di Giorgio
Fleming Companies
Nash Finch
Richfood
Royal Ahold
Wal-Mart

HISTORICAL FINANCIALS

Company Type: Private

Income Statement FYE: December 31

	ESTIMATED REVENUE ($ mil.)	NET INCOME ($ mil.)	NET PROFIT MARGIN	EMPLOYEES
12/02	2,200	—	—	850
12/01	1,200	—	—	615
12/00	1,100	—	—	615
12/99	1,100	—	—	615
12/98	970	—	—	615
12/97	800	—	—	610
12/96	750	—	—	—
Annual Growth	19.6%	—	—	6.9%

Revenue History

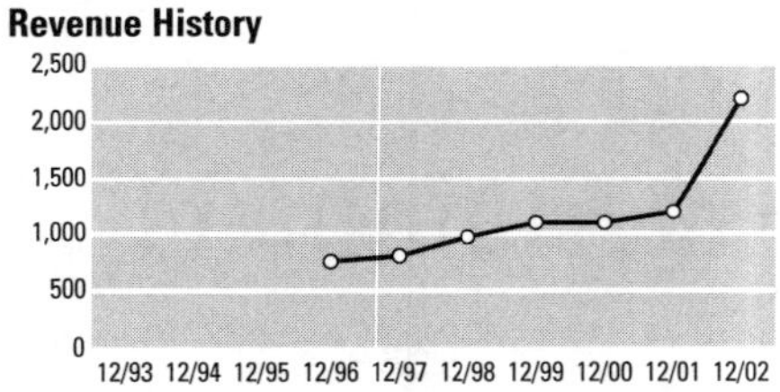

FFP Marketing Company, Inc.

FFP Marketing Company is a roadside respite, operating about 425 convenience stores (under the names Kwik Pantry, Nu-Way, Economy Drive-Ins, and Taylor Food Mart), self-service gas outlets, and truck stops (Drivers Travelmarts). The company's outlets are located primarily in Texas, but also in 10 other central, southern, and southwestern states. FFP Marketing also sells fuel wholesale, provides fuel-management systems, and owns a money-order business that operates through its outlets. The company is selling about 160 of its convenience stores and gas stations in secondary markets. CEO John Harvison and his family own 41% of FFP Marketing; they also own FFP Partners. The company went private in late 2002.

EXECUTIVES

Chairman and CEO: John H. Harvison, age 68, $135,000 pay
President, COO, and Director: Robert J. Byrnes, age 61, $135,000 pay
VP, Finance, General Counsel, Secretary, Treasurer, and CFO: Craig T. Scott, $150,000 pay
VP, Fuel Supply and Distribution, and Director: J. D. St. Clair, age 67
VP, Retail Operations, and Director: Michael Triantafellou, age 48, $115,000 pay
Payroll Supervisor: Linda Bickerstaff
Auditors: Grant Thornton LLP

LOCATIONS

HQ: 2801 Glenda Ave., Fort Worth, TX 76117
Phone: 817-838-4700 **Fax:** 817-838-4799
Web: www.ffpmarketing.com

COMPETITORS

7-Eleven
Ace Cash Express
Allsup's
Casey's General Stores
ChevronTexaco
Exxon Mobil
E-Z Mart Stores
Flying J
Hale-Halsell
Kroger
Petro Stopping Centers
Pilot
TravelCenters of America

HISTORICAL FINANCIALS

Company Type: Private

Income Statement FYE: Sunday nearest December 31

	REVENUE ($ mil.)	NET INCOME ($ mil.)	NET PROFIT MARGIN	EMPLOYEES
12/01	622	(5)	—	1,693
12/00	688	1	0.1%	1,622
12/99	504	(1)	—	1,865
12/98	416	(1)	—	1,839
12/97	379	0	0.0%	1,688
12/96	390	(0)	—	1,138
12/95	370	4	1.1%	—
12/94	356	4	1.0%	—
12/93	327	1	0.2%	—
12/92	279	1	0.2%	—
Annual Growth	9.3%	—	—	8.3%

2001 Year-End Financials

Debt ratio: 213.7%
Return on equity: —
Cash ($ mil.): 8
Current ratio: 1.01
Long-term debt ($ mil.): 31

Net Income History

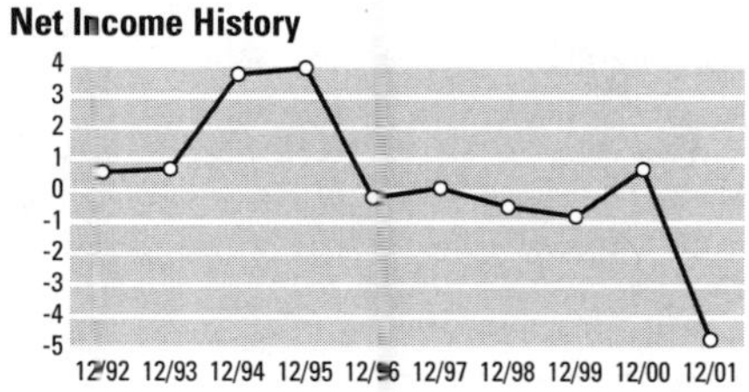

Field Container Company, L.P.

Field Container Company is always ready for a boxing match. The company manufactures and prints folding cartons, gift boxes, retail packaging, and gift wrap. It is a major supplier to the food concession (popcorn, ice cream) and deli markets. Field Container's paperboard mills recycle more than 180,000 tons of light-core paperboard annually into products such as toilet paper tubes. The company's Handschy Industries subsidiary develops environmentally friendly inks and paper coatings. Field Container's products are made at nine carton plants, two paperboard mills, an ink factory, and a gift wrap plant, primarily in the midwestern US. CEO Larry Field runs the family-owned company, which was established in 1942.

EXECUTIVES

Chairman: Eli Field
CEO: Larry Field
President and COO: Michael Nussbaum
CFO: Craig LaPlante
VP, Human Resources: Tony Grassi

LOCATIONS

HQ: 1500 Nicholas Blvd., Elk Grove Village, IL 60007
Phone: 847-437-1700 **Fax:** 847-956-9250
Web: www.fieldcontainer.com

Field Container has plants in Alabama, Illinois, Indiana, Michigan, and Ohio.

PRODUCTS/OPERATIONS

Selected Subsidiaries and Divisions

Gift Box Division (gift boxes for retail outlets)
Handschy Industries (development of ink and coating technologies)
J.G. Clark Division (folding cartons, carryout cartons, popcorn boxes, and retail packaging)
LaPorte Division (web offset printing)
Michigan Paperboard Division (recycled clay-coated newsboard)
Pekin Paperboard Co., LP (recycled paperboard)
Southfield Division (in-line flexographic printing)
St. Clair Packwell (gift wrapping and packaging)
Westfield Division (fulfillment of short-run carton and specialty printing orders)

COMPETITORS

Boise Cascade
Caraustar
International Paper
Jefferson Smurfit
MOD-PAC
Potlatch
Sonoco Products
Stora Enso North America
Temple-Inland
Weyerhaeuser

HISTORICAL FINANCIALS

Company Type: Private

Income Statement FYE: April 30

	REVENUE ($ mil.)	NET INCOME ($ mil.)	NET PROFIT MARGIN	EMPLOYEES
4/02	500	—	—	2,100
4/01	500	—	—	2,100
4/00	500	—	—	2,100
4/99	480	—	—	2,100
4/98	485	—	—	2,100
4/97	475	—	—	2,200
4/96	472	—	—	2,125
4/95	450	—	—	2,400
4/94	425	—	—	2,232
4/93	405	—	—	—
Annual Growth	2.4%	—	—	(0.8%)

Revenue History

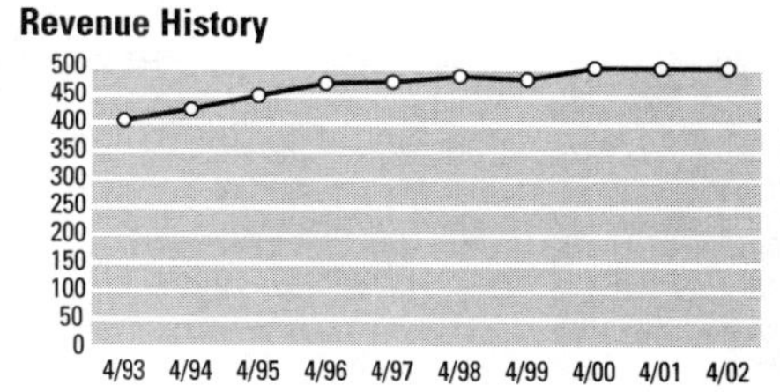

Findlay Industries, Inc.

Findlay Industries doesn't need a room to show off its interior designs. The automotive interiors supplier makes door and sidewall trim panels (quarter-trim panels), seat back and trunk covers, headliners, and sleeper cabs. It makes these components for customers including General Motors, Ford, BMW, Toyota, and other car and heavy truck makers around the world. Findlay Industries' brands include the ProBond family of molded headliner material. The company has 24 manufacturing facilities in Europe and North America. The company, founded by Philip D. Gardner in 1959, is controlled by Gardner and former president Philip J. Gardner.

EXECUTIVES

CEO: Thomas Zigler
CFO: Raymond Lowry
Human Resources: Geneva Frennell
Marketing Manager: Tom Leffler

LOCATIONS

HQ: 4000 Fostoria Rd., Findlay, OH 45840
Phone: 419-422-1302 **Fax:** 419-427-3390
Web: www.findlayindustries.com

Findlay Industries has 24 manufacturing facilities in seven countries throughout North America and Europe.

PRODUCTS/OPERATIONS

Selected Products, Services, and Systems

Aftermarket
Assembly, sequencing, and logistics
Door panel systems
Overhead systems
Rear compartment systems
Seat systems

COMPETITORS

Delphi
Delta USA
Dura Automotive
Faurecia
Honeywell International
Intier
Johnson Controls
Lear
Magna International
Siemens

HISTORICAL FINANCIALS

Company Type: Private

Income Statement

FYE: April 30

	ESTIMATED REVENUE ($ mil.)	NET INCOME ($ mil.)	NET PROFIT MARGIN	EMPLOYEES
4/02	800	—	—	3,500
4/01	776	—	—	3,400
4/00	845	—	—	5,400
4/99	525	—	—	3,300
Annual Growth	15.1%	—	—	2.0%

Revenue History

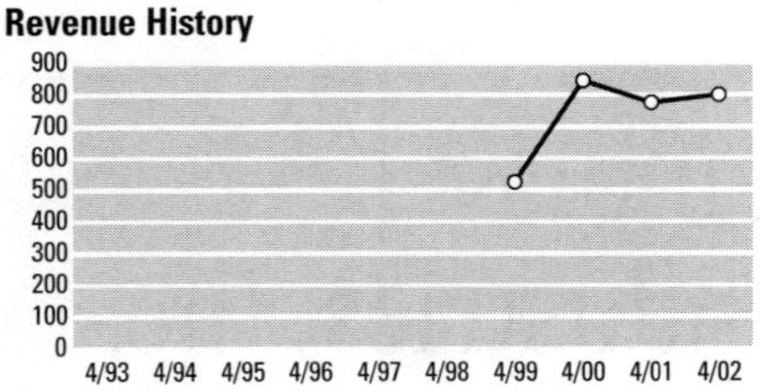

First Banks, Inc.

First Banks is the holding company for Union Financial Group, which owns First Bank and equipment leasing outfit First Capital Group. First Bank has more than 90 locations in Illinois and Missouri, while First Capital operates a single office in Albuquerque, New Mexico. First Banks also owns First Banks America, the parent of First Bank & Trust, which has about 50 branches in California and Texas. To complement its core business and real estate lending operations, First Banks is also engaged in securities brokerage, insurance brokerage, and institutional asset management. First Banks is owned by chairman and CEO James Dierberg and his family, including son Michael, who is a director of the company.

Commercial, financial, and agricultural loans account for almost a third of First Banks' loan book, as do commercial mortgages. Its portfolio is rounded out by residential mortgages and construction loans, as well as a relatively small amount of consumer loans.

EXECUTIVES

Chairman and CEO: James F. Dierberg, age 65, $685,000 pay
President, COO, CFO, Secretary, and Director: Allen H. Blake, age 59, $401,700 pay
SEVP, Chief Credit Officer, and Director: Donald W. Williams, age 55, $345,000 pay
EVP and CIO: Michael F. Hickey, age 44
EVP, First Banks and First Banks America; Chairman, President, and CEO, First Bank & Trust: Terrance M. McCarthy, age 47, $258,000 pay
EVP, Banking Support: Michael F. McWhortor, age 50
EVP, Mortgage Banking; Chairman, President, and CEO, First Banc Mortgage; EVP, First Bank: Mark T. Turkcan, age 46, $200,000 pay
Retail Marketing Officer: Ellen D. Schepman, age 27
Auditors: KPMG LLP

LOCATIONS

HQ: 135 N. Meramec Ave., Clayton, MO 63105
Phone: 314-854-4600 **Fax:** 314-592-6840
Web: www.firstbanks.com

PRODUCTS/OPERATIONS

Selected Subsidiaries and Affiliates

First Banc Insurors Agency (insurance brokerage)
First Banks America, Inc.
  The San Francisco Company
First Brokerage America L.L.C.
Union Financial Group, Ltd.
  First Bank
  First Capital Group, Inc. (equipment leasing)

COMPETITORS

Bank of America
Cass Information Systems
Commerce Bancshares
Marshall & Ilsley
Pulaski Financial
UMB Financial
Union Planters
U.S. Bancorp

HISTORICAL FINANCIALS

Company Type: Private

Income Statement

FYE: December 31

	ASSETS ($ mil.)	NET INCOME ($ mil.)	INCOME AS % OF ASSETS	EMPLOYEES
12/01	6,779	65	1.0%	2,350
12/00	5,877	56	1.0%	1,985
12/99	4,868	44	0.9%	1,670
12/98	4,555	34	0.7%	1,739
Annual Growth	14.2%	24.4%	—	10.6%

2001 Year-End Financials

Equity as % of assets: 6.6%
Return on assets: 1.0%
Return on equity: 16.1%
Long-term debt ($ mil.): 28
Sales ($ mil.): 543

Net Income History

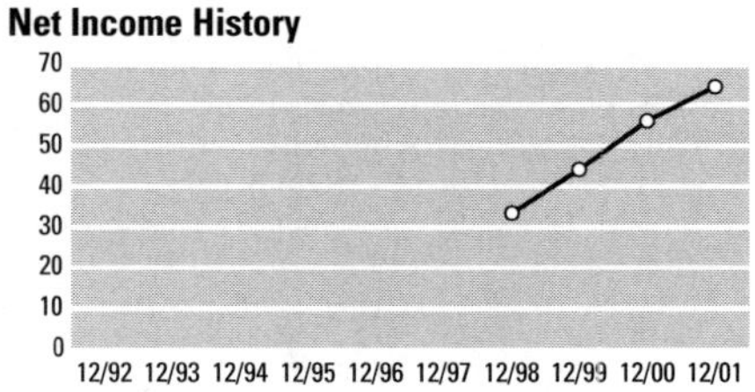

Flint Ink Corporation

The world's #2 ink maker (behind Sun Chemical), Flint Ink produces inks and coatings for a variety of applications, including packaging, publication, commercial uses, and digital printing. It operates six divisions: North America, Latin America, Asia/Pacific, Flint-Schmidt (which serves Europe), Digital (inkjet inks), and CDR Pigments and Dispersions (colorants used in ink and for other uses). The company's products include sheetfed and web offset, gravure, ultraviolet and electronic beam (UV/EB) curable, and digital inks. The Flint family owns the company and Howard Flint II represents the third generation of the family to head the firm.

Flint Ink has plants throughout the Americas, Australasia, and Europe. The company's primary customers include printing facilities that produce magazines, newspapers, catalogs, and packaging materials. Flint Ink also makes specialty inks (for example, for printing lottery tickets) and environment-friendly vegetable oil-based inks.

Although the world's #1 privately held maker of inks, Flint Ink has drawn a bull's-eye on becoming the #1 ink maker, regardless of ownership. The company has been growing through acquisitions, joint ventures, and partnerships. Flint Ink acquired one of Europe's largest ink makers, German-based Gebr. Schmidt GmbH, in 2002.

H. Howard Flint founded Flint Ink in 1920.

EXECUTIVES

Chairman and CEO: H. Howard Flint II
President and COO: Leonard D. (Dave) Frescoln
EVP: David B. Flint
SVP, Finance and CFO: Michael J. Gannon
SVP, Research and New Product Development: Joseph W Raksis
VP and General Manager, Digital Division: Kenneth Stack
VP and General Manager, North American Publication and Commercial Ink Divisions: Susan Kuchta
VP, Human Resources: Glenn T. Autry
VP, Research & Development: Graham Battersby
Director, Corporate Communications: Rita Conrad

LOCATIONS

HQ: 4600 Arrowhead Dr., Ann Arbor, MI 48105
Phone: 734-622-6000 **Fax:** 734-622-6131
Web: www.flintink.com

Flint Ink has operations in the Americas, Australasia, and Europe.

PRODUCTS/OPERATIONS

Selected Products and Brands

Commercial inks
Flexo/Gravure packaging inks
Flexographic news inks
High-performance inks and coatings
Inkjet inks
Offset news inks
Packaging inks
Publication gravure inks
Sheetfed inks
UV/EB curable inks
Web offset heatset inks

COMPETITORS

Akzo Nobel
BASF AG
Dainippon Ink
Eastman Resins
Field Container

HISTORICAL FINANCIALS

Company Type: Private

Income Statement FYE: December 31

	REVENUE ($ mil.)	NET INCOME ($ mil.)	NET PROFIT MARGIN	EMPLOYEES
12/01	1,400	—	—	4,000
12/00	1,080	—	—	3,700
12/99	1,200	—	—	3,500
12/98	1,216	—	—	3,500
12/97	924	—	—	3,500
12/96	836	—	—	2,730
12/95	875	—	—	2,700
12/94	634	—	—	2,613
12/93	546	—	—	2,585
12/92	515	—	—	—
Annual Growth	11.8%	—	—	5.6%

Revenue History

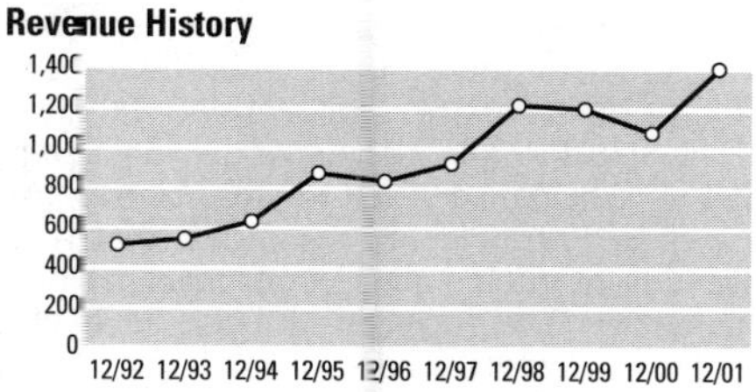

Florida's Natural Growers

Florida's Natural Growers (formerly Citrus World) is known for squeezing out profits. It is the third largest citrus juice seller (behind Tropicana and Minute Maid), producing more than 20 million boxes of oranges from 60,000 acres of citrus groves. The cooperative produces frozen concentrated and not-from-concentrate juices (orange, apple, grapefruit, lemonade, and fruit blends) under the Florida's Natural, Grower's Pride, Donald Duck, Bluebird, Adams, and Texsun brand names. The company was founded in 1933 by a group of citrus growers in order to process grapefruit.

The co-op's products are sold to the food service (about 30% of sales), retail, and vending industries, and it exports to more than 40 countries (including Japan and some in Europe).

EXECUTIVES

CEO: Stephen Caruso
CFO: W. J. Hendry
VP Sales and Marketing: Walt Lincer
Director of Human Resources: Susan Langley

LOCATIONS

HQ: 650 Hwy. 27, Lake Wales, FL 33853
Phone: 863-676-1411 **Fax:** 863-676-5744
Web: floridanatural.com

COMPETITORS

Chiquita Brands
Coca-Cola North America
Gatorade/Tropicana
Horizon Organic
Smucker
Louis Dreyfus Citrus
Naked Juice
National Grape Cooperative
Northland Cranberries
Ocean Spray
Odwalla
Procter & Gamble
Sunkist
Tree Top
Vitality Beverages

HISTORICAL FINANCIALS

Company Type: Cooperative

Income Statement FYE: August 31

	REVENUE ($ mil.)	NET INCOME ($ mil.)	NET PROFIT MARGIN	EMPLOYEES
8/02	600	—	—	1,000
8/01	620	—	—	—
8/00	605	—	—	—
8/99	550	—	—	—
8/98	469	—	—	—
Annual Growth	6.4%	—	—	—

Revenue History

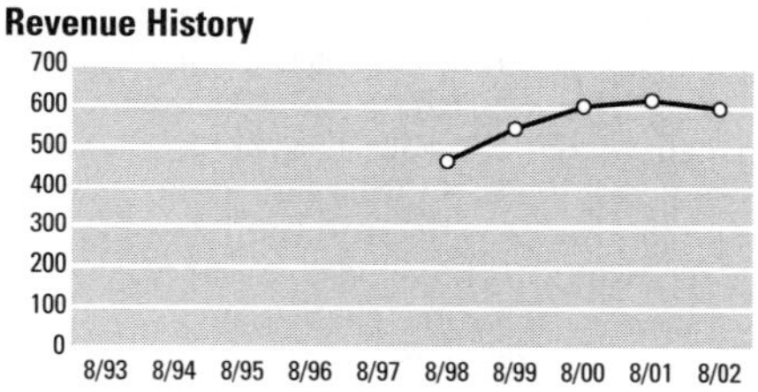

Flying J Inc.

Flying J puts out a welcome mat for truckers in North America. From its beginnings in 1968 with four locations, the company is now the #1 distributor of diesel fuel and a leading truck-stop operator in the US — with more than 160 amenity-loaded Flying J Travel Plazas in 41 states and Canada. Flying J and its subsidiaries go beyond the usual truck-stop fare (food, fuel, showers) by offering extra services, including advertising, banking, bulk-fuel programs, fuel cost analysis, insurance, and truck fleet sales. The company also owns oil and gas reserves and a 25,000-barrel-a-day refinery. Founder and Chairman Jay Call died in a plane crash in March 2003. Flying J plans to add about 30 new locations by 2004.

EXECUTIVES

President and CEO: J. Phillip Adams
CFO and Treasurer: Paul F. Brown
SVP, Legal and Secretary: Barre G. Burgon
VP, Financial and Communications Services: J. J. Singh
VP, Fuel Marketing: Richard Peterson
VP, Operations: James (Jim) Baker
VP, Real Estate: Ronald R. Parker
CIO: Bron McCall
Controller: Scott Clayson
Director, Personnel: Jerry Beckman

LOCATIONS

HQ: 1104 Country Hills Dr., Ogden, UT 84403
Phone: 801-624-1000 **Fax:** 801-624-1587
Web: www.flyingj.com

Flying J has truck stops in the US and Canada, an oil refinery in Utah, and oil and gas reserves in Montana, North Dakota, Utah, and Wyoming.

PRODUCTS/OPERATIONS

Selected Products and Services

Advertising services
ATMs
Banking
Bulk-fuel programs
Calling cards
Credit cards
Fleet financing
Food
Freight matching
Fuel
Insurance
Laundry facilities
Load and equipment postings
Lube centers
Motels
Restaurants
Showers
Truck washes

COMPETITORS

Exxon Mobil
FFP Marketing
Inland Resources
Love's Country Stores
Marathon Oil
Petro Stopping Centers
Pilot
Rip Griffin Truck Service Center
Stuckey's
TravelCenters of America

HISTORICAL FINANCIALS

Company Type: Private

Income Statement FYE: January 31

	REVENUE ($ mil.)	NET INCOME ($ mil.)	NET PROFIT MARGIN	EMPLOYEES
1/03	4,600	—	—	11,500
1/02	3,150	—	—	11,500
1/01	4,349	—	—	11,000
1/00	2,953	—	—	10,000
1/99	2,344	—	—	9,000
1/98	1,600	—	—	8,000
1/97	1,558	—	—	8,000
1/96	1,282	—	—	7,600
1/95	1,031	—	—	6,952
1/94	895	—	—	5,831
Annual Growth	19.9%	—	—	7.8%

Revenue History

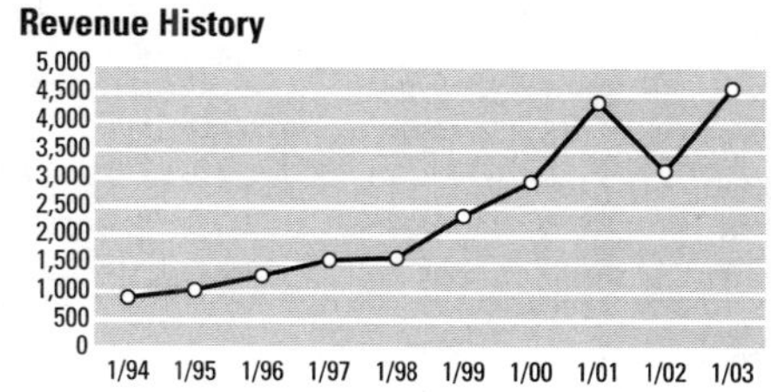

FM Global

If you're looking to protect your corporation, turn your insurance dial to FM Global. The insurer provides commercial and industrial property insurance and a variety of risk management services, ranging from all-risk programs to specialized products for ocean cargo and machinery equipment. FM Global operates through such subsidiaries as Factory Mutual Insurance, Mutual Boiler Re, Affiliated FM Insurance, and Bermuda-based New Providence Mutual (which offers alternative risk financing for hard-to-find coverage). In addition to the US, the company has offices in Australia, Asia, Canada, Europe, and South America.

EXECUTIVES

Chairman and CEO: Shivan S. Subramaniam
EVP, Staff Operations and Planning: Ruud H. Bosman
EVP and Manager, North American Operations: Brian J. Hurley
SVP, Finance and CFO: Jeffrey A. Burchill
SVP, Investments: Norman D. Baker Jr.
SVP, Commercial Lines: Carol G. Barton
SVP, Underwriting: Robert Bean
SVP, Marketing: Roland Bonitati
SVP, Research and Approvals: Thomas Lawson
SVP, Law and Governmental Affairs: John J. Pomeroy
SVP, Human Resources: Enzo Rebula
SVP, Information Services: William J. Stella
Auditors: Ernst & Young LLP

LOCATIONS

HQ: 1301 Atwood Ave., Johnston, RI 02919
Phone: 401-275-3000 **Fax:** 401-275-3029
Web: www.fmglobal.com

PRODUCTS/OPERATIONS

Selected Subsidiaries

Affiliated FM Insurance
FM Global Research
FM Insurance Company, Limited
Mutual Boiler Re
New Providence Mutual
TSB Loss Control Consultants, Inc.

COMPETITORS

ACE Limited
Allianz
AIG
CNA Financial
GE Global Insurance Holding
Gerling
Royal & SunAlliance USA
St. Paul Companies
Travelers

HISTORICAL FINANCIALS

Company Type: Mutual company

Income Statement FYE: December 31

	ASSETS ($ mil.)	NET INCOME ($ mil.)	INCOME AS % OF ASSETS	EMPLOYEES
12/02	7,189	244	3.4%	4,400
12/01	6,516	(132)	—	4,000
12/00	5,673	345	6.1%	—
Annual Growth	12.6%	(15.9%)	—	10.0%

2002 Year-End Financials

Equity as % of assets: 28.9%
Return on assets: 3.6%
Return on equity: 12.0%
Long-term debt ($ mil.): 125
Sales ($ mil.): 2,016

Net Income History

FMR Corp.

FMR Corp. is *semper fidelis* (ever faithful) to its core business. The financial services conglomerate, better known as Fidelity Investments, is the world's #1 mutual fund company. Serving some 18 million individual and institutional clients, Fidelity manages nearly 340 funds and has approximately $775 billion of assets under management. Among its notable offerings is the Magellan Fund, which was for many years the US's largest. The founding Johnson family controls most of FMR; Abigail Johnson, CEO Ned's daughter and heir apparent, is the largest single shareholder with about 25%.

Fidelity's nonfund offerings include life insurance, trust services, securities clearing, retirement services, and a leading online discount brokerage. It is one of the largest administrators of 401(k) plans, and the firm continues to grow this segment, which includes other services related to benefits outsourcing.

FMR has major holdings in telecommunications (COLT Telecom Group) and transportation (BostonCoach). Like many institutional investors, Fidelity uses its clout to sway the boards of companies in which it has significant holdings.

HISTORY

Boston money management firm Anderson & Cromwell formed Fidelity Fund in 1930. Edward Johnson became president of the fund in 1943, when it had $3 million invested in Treasury bills. Johnson diversified into stocks, and by 1945 the fund had grown to $10 million. In 1946 he established Fidelity Management and Research to act as its investment adviser.

In the early 1950s Johnson hired Gerry Tsai, a young immigrant from Shanghai, to analyze stocks. He put Tsai in charge of Fidelity Capital Fund in 1957. Tsai's brash, go-go investment strategy in such speculative stocks as Xerox and Polaroid paid off; by the time he left to form his own fund in 1965, he was managing more than $1 billion.

The Magellan Fund started in 1962. The company entered the corporate pension plans market (FMR Investment Management) in 1964, and retirement plans for self-employed individuals (Fidelity Keogh Plan) in 1967. It began serving investors outside the US (Fidelity International) in 1968.

Holding company FMR was formed in 1972, and that year Johnson gave control of Fidelity to his son Ned, who vertically integrated FMR by selling directly to customers rather than through brokers. The next year he formed Fidelity Daily Income Trust, the first money market fund to offer check writing.

Peter Lynch was hired as manager of the Magellan Fund in 1977. During his 13-year tenure, Magellan grew from $20 million to $12 billion in assets and outperformed all other mutual funds. Fidelity started Fidelity Brokerage Services in 1978, becoming the first mutual fund company to offer discount brokerage.

In 1980 the company launched a nationwide branch network and in 1986 entered the credit card business. The Wall Street crash of 1987 forced its Magellan Fund to liquidate almost $1 billion in stock in a single day. That year FMR moved into insurance by offering variable life, single premium, and deferred annuity policies. In 1989 the company introduced the low-expense Spartan Fund, targeted toward large, less-active investors.

Magellan's performance faded in the early 1990s, dropping from #1 performer to #3. Most of Fidelity's best performers were from its 36 select funds, which focus on narrow industry segments. FMR founded London-based COLT Telecom in 1993. In 1994 Ned Johnson gave his daughter and heir apparent, Abigail, a 25% stake in FMR.

Jeffrey Vinik resigned as manager of Magellan in 1996, one of more than a dozen fund managers to leave the firm that year and the next. Robert Stansky took the helm of the $56 billion fund, which FMR decided to close to new investors in 1997. Fidelity had a first that year when it went with an outside fund manager, hiring Bankers Trust (now part of Deutsche Bank) to manage its index funds.

FMR did some housecleaning in the late 1990s. It sold its Wentworth art galleries (1997) and *Worth* magazine (1998). Despite continued management turnover, it entered Japan and expanded its presence in Canada.

In 1999 the firm formed a joint venture with Charles Schwab; Donaldson, Lufkin & Jenrette, known now as Credit Suisse First Boston (USA); and Spear, Leeds & Kellogg to form electronic communications network REDIBook ECN (now part of Archipelago) to trade Nasdaq stocks online. That year Fidelity teamed with Internet portal Lycos (now part of Terra Lycos) to develop its online brokerage.

FMR opened savings and loan Fidelity Personal Trust Co. in 2000. That year the Magellan Fund for a time lost its longtime title as the US's largest mutual fund to the Vanguard Index 500 Fund. In 2001 the company teamed up with Frank Russell to offer a new fund for wealthy clients.

EXECUTIVES

Chairman and CEO: Edward C. (Ned) Johnson III, age 71
Vice Chairman and COO: Robert L. (Bob) Reynolds
Director; President, Fidelity Management and Research: Abigail P. (Abby) Johnson, age 41
Chief Administrative Officer and Director: Stephen P. Jonas
EVP and CFO: Laura B. Cronin
Vice Chairman, Fidelity Management & Research: Peter S. Lynch
Managing Partner, Fidelity Ventures: Robert C. Ketterson
Managing Director, Pembroke Real Estate: Peter E. Madsen
Managing Director, Fidelity Leveraged Acquisitions Group: William P. (Bill) Wall
EVP, Fidelity Institutional Retirement Services: William Carey
EVP, Defined Benefits Practice, Fidelity Management & Research: Brian A. Cooke
EVP, Corporate Affairs: Thomas E. Eidson
EVP, HR/Payroll Practice, Fidelity Management & Research: Teresa A. Hassara

EVP, Fidelity Institutional Retirement Services: David L. Liebrock
EVP, Human Resources: Guy L. Patton
EVP, Risk Oversight: Kenneth A. Rathgeber
EVP, Health and Welfare Practice, Fidelity Management & Research: Surinder Singh
EVP, Public Policy and Regional Affairs: David C. Weinstein
SVP, Fidelity Management & Research: Philip L. Bullen
SVP and General Counsel: Lena G. Goldberg
SVP, Fidelity Management & Research: Bart A. Grenier
Auditors: PricewaterhouseCoopers LLP

LOCATIONS

HQ: 82 Devonshire St., Boston, MA 02109
Phone: 617-563-7000 **Fax:** 617-476-6150
Web: www.fidelity.com

FMR has offices in about 70 US cities, as well as in Australia, Bermuda, Canada, France, Germany, Hong Kong, India, Japan, Luxembourg, the Netherlands, Spain, Sweden, Switzerland, Taiwan, and the UK.

PRODUCTS/OPERATIONS

Selected Subsidiaries

Fidelity Capital
Fidelity Financial Intermediary Services
 Fidelity Investments Canada Limited
 Fidelity Investments Institutional Services Company, Inc.
Fidelity International Limited (Bermuda)
Fidelity Investments Institutional Retirement Group
 Fidelity Benefits Center
 Fidelity Group Pensions International
 Fidelity Institutional Retirement Services Company
 Fidelity Investments Public Sector Services Company
 Fidelity Investments Tax-Exempt Services Company
 Fidelity Management Trust Company
Fidelity Investments Life Insurance Company
Fidelity Personal Investments and Brokerage Group
 Fidelity Brokerage Technology Group
 Fidelity Capital Markets
 Fidelity Investment Advisor Group
 National Financial Correspondent Services
Fidelity Technology & Processing Group
Strategic Advisers, Inc.

COMPETITORS

Alliance Capital
American Century
Ameritrade
AXA Financial
Barclays
Charles Schwab
Citigroup
Dow Jones
E*TRADE Financial
Goldman Sachs
John Hancock Financial Services
Lehman Brothers
Marsh & McLennan
MassMutual
Merrill Lynch
MetLife
Morgan Stanley
Northwestern Mutual
Prudential
Putnam
Quick & Reilly
Raymond James Financial
T. Rowe Price
TD Waterhouse
TIAA-CREF
UBS Financial Services
Vanguard Group

HISTORICAL FINANCIALS

Company Type: Private

Income Statement FYE: December 31

	REVENUE ($ mil.)	NET INCOME ($ mil.)	NET PROFIT MARGIN	EMPLOYEES
12/02	8,900	808	9.1%	29,000
12/01	9,800	1,320	13.5%	31,033
12/00	11,096	2,170	19.6%	33,186
12/99	8,845	1,008	11.4%	30,000
12/98	6,776	446	6.6%	28,000
12/97	5,878	536	9.1%	25,000
12/96	5,080	423	8.3%	23,300
12/95	4,277	431	10.1%	18,000
12/94	3,530	315	8.9%	14,600
12/93	2,570	225	8.8%	12,900
Annual Growth	14.8%	15.3%	—	9.4%

Net Income History

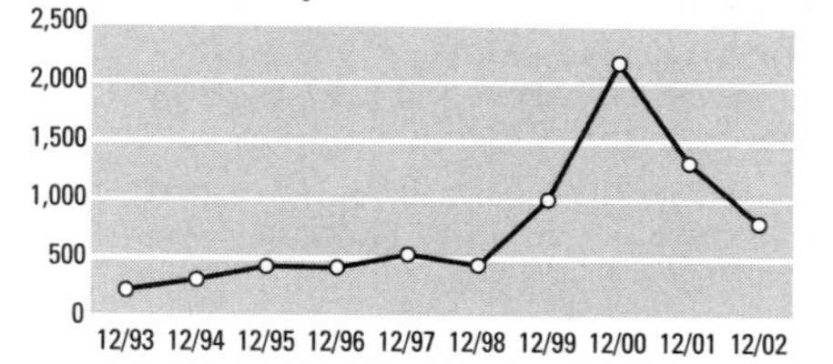

Foley & Lardner

Though most famous for its cheese, Wisconsin has another thing going for it: lawyers. Foley & Lardner, the largest and oldest law firm in Wisconsin, has nearly 1,000 lawyers and has expanded far beyond its Milwaukee base with offices in 15 other US cities (including five in Florida and four in California). In addition, Foley & Lardner is affiliated with an office in Brussels and another in Japan. The firm, founded in 1842, has one of the nation's leading health law practices and is focusing on strengthening its intellectual property practice; other areas of expertise include business law, litigation, regulatory issues, and tax planning.

EXECUTIVES

Chairman and CEO: Ralf R. Böer
Managing Partner: Stanley S. Jaspan
CFO: Tom L. Budde
CIO: Douglas D. Caddell
Executive Director and COO: Darrell R. Ohlhauser
National Director Human Resources: Marilyn L. Lagerman
National Director Marketing: Kyle Heath
Director Legal Recruitment and Professional Development: Patti Dixon

LOCATIONS

HQ: 777 E. Wisconsin Ave., Milwaukee, WI 53202
Phone: 414-271-2400 **Fax:** 414-297-4900
Web: www.foleylardner.com

PRODUCTS/OPERATIONS

Selected Practice Areas

Antitrust
Environmental
Estates and trusts
Family law
Financial institutions
Health law payments
Intellectual property
Managed care
Mergers and acquisitions
Public affairs
Public hospitals
Real estate
Tax
Trademark and copyright

COMPETITORS

Baker & McKenzie
Jones Day
Shearman & Sterling
Skadden, Arps

HISTORICAL FINANCIALS

Company Type: Partnership

Income Statement FYE: January 31

	REVENUE ($ mil.)	NET INCOME ($ mil.)	NET PROFIT MARGIN	EMPLOYEES
1/03	490	—	—	—
1/02	453	—	—	—
1/01	363	—	—	—
1/00	313	—	—	1,900
1/99	277	—	—	1,800
1/98	234	—	—	1,700
1/97	204	—	—	—
1/96	162	—	—	—
1/95	145	—	—	—
1/94	143	—	—	—
Annual Growth	14.7%	—	—	5.7%

Revenue History

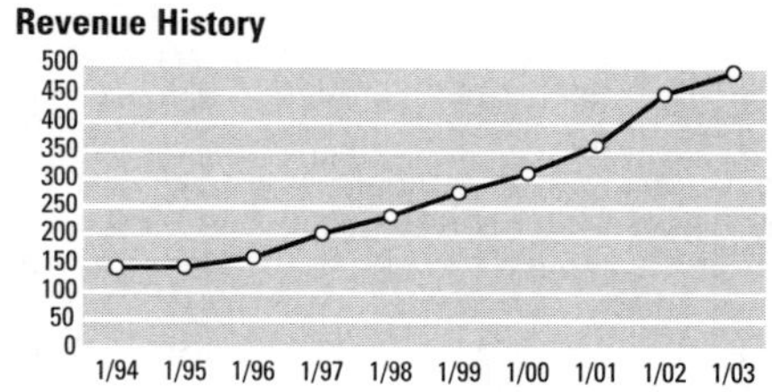

Follett Corporation

Not all kids like to read, but (fortunately for Follett) by the time they reach college, they don't have a choice. Follett is the #1 operator of US college bookstores and has about 600 campus bookstores throughout the US and Canada. The company's business groups, which operate in about 60 countries, also provide books and audiovisual materials to grade school and public libraries, library automation and management software, textbook reconditioning, and other services. Its efollett.com Web site sells new and used college textbooks (its database has about 16 million titles). The Follett family has owned and managed the company for four generations.

In addition to books, campus stores sell items such as clothing, school supplies, and software. The company has capitalized on the growing trend of universities farming out operations to independent operators.

HISTORY

Follett began in 1873 as a small bookstore opened by the Rev. Charles Barnes in his Wheaton, Illinois, home. By 1893 a recession had rocked the business, and Barnes sought investment from his wife's family, for which he gave up controlling interest. Sales topped $237,000 in 1899.

Initially hired by Barnes in 1901 to help move the store to a new location in Chicago, 18-year-old C. W. Follett stayed on as both salesman and stock clerk. Barnes retired the following year and left the business to his son William and his father-in-law, John Wilcox, who was a major shareholder. In 1917 C. W. bought into the company when William moved to New York (he started what became one of Follett's biggest competitors, Barnes & Noble), and he renamed it J. W. Wilcox & Follett Company. Wilcox died in 1923, and C. W. bought the Wilcox family shares and shortened the name to Wilcox & Follett.

C. W.'s sons were brought into the business, and each was instrumental in shaping the company's future. Garth created Follett Library Resources, a wholesale service for libraries. Dwight started the elementary textbook publishing division. But Robert would have the most influence: He began wholesaling college textbooks, which led to the establishment of Follett College Stores and Follett Campus Resources.

Wilcox & Follett expanded throughout the Depression. During WWII it began publishing kids' books, which were in demand because of a metal toy shortage. C. W. died in 1952 and Dwight took over. Five years later the firm organized into divisions; Follett was created as the parent company. During the 1960s Follett developed the first multiracial textbook series. Dwight built the company to $50 million in annual sales by 1977, when he retired. His son Robert succeeded him and led Follett through tremendous growth in the 1980s.

In 1983 the company sold its publishing division to Esquire Education Group; using funds from this sale, it began acquiring college bookstore chains such as Campus Services. In 1989 Follett developed Tom-Tracks, a computerized textbook system for college bookstores. A year later the company acquired Brennan College Service, adding 57 stores to its chain. Robert's son-in-law Richard Traut, named chairman in 1994, was the first person without the Follett name to hold that position. By 1994 Tom-Tracks had been installed in over 500 bookstores across the country. Also in 1994 Follett introduced Sneak Preview Plus, a CD-ROM product designed to enhance the acquisition process in libraries.

The company acquired used-textbook reseller Western Textbook Exchange (1996), juvenile-book distributor Book Wholesalers (1997), and coursepack printer CAPCO (1998). In early 1998 Follett reorganized its corporate structure by market segments, establishing three divisions: the Elementary/High School Group, the Higher Education Group, and Library Group. Also in 1998 the Follett Campus Resources unit agreed to pay the University of Tennessee $380,000 after the school discovered that the firm had been underpaying students in a book-buyback program for several years. Adding to its bevy of campus bookstores, it signed a contract that year to build a $5 million bookstore at the University of Texas at Arlington.

Also in 1998 CFO Kenneth Hull replaced Richard Litzsinger as CEO. Follett launched efollett.com in early 1999 to sell college textbooks online. That year CEO Kenneth Hull became chairman upon Richard Traut's departure. In November 2000 Christopher Traut became CEO; Hull remained chairman.

In April 2001 Hull retired, and Mark Litzsinger succeeded him as chairman.

EXECUTIVES

Chairman: R. Mark Litzsinger
President and CEO: Christopher Traut
EVP Finance and CFO: Kathryn A. Stanton
EVP Human Resources: Richard Ellspermann
SVP: Gary Shapiro
President and CEO, Follett School and Library Group: Ross Follett
EVP, Follett School and Library Group: Chuck Follett
EVP Marketing, Follett Higher Education Group: Scott Deaton

LOCATIONS

HQ: 2233 West St., River Grove, IL 60171
Phone: 708-583-2000 **Fax:** 708-452-9347
Web: www.follett.com

Follett has operations in more than 60 countries, including more than 110,000 schools in the US and Canada.

PRODUCTS/OPERATIONS

Company Divisions

Elementary/High School Group
Follett Educational Services (K-12 textbook and workbooks)
Follett Software Company (library automation)
Library Systems & Services (library management)

Higher Education Group

Library Group
Book Wholesalers, Inc. (public libraries)
Follett Audiovisual Resources (comprehensive audiovisual products and services, academic and public libraries)
Follett Library Resources (school libraries)

COMPETITORS

Baker & Taylor
Barnes & Noble College Bookstores
Barnes & Noble
barnesandnoble.com
Borders
D&H Distributing
Ecampus.com
Educational Development
Indigo Books & Music
Ingram Industries
Kinko's
Nebraska Book
Varsity Group
Wallace's Bookstores
Wal-Mart

HISTORICAL FINANCIALS

Company Type: Private

Income Statement FYE: March 31

	REVENUE ($ mil.)	NET INCOME ($ mil.)	NET PROFIT MARGIN	EMPLOYEES
3/02	1,733	—	—	10,000
3/01	1,554	—	—	8,000
3/00	1,401	—	—	8,000
3/99	1,200	—	—	8,000
3/98	1,073	—	—	7,500
3/97	916	—	—	8,000
3/96	811	—	—	7,500
3/95	713	—	—	7,200
3/94	646	—	—	6,800
3/93	612	—	—	6,500
Annual Growth	12.3%	—	—	4.9%

Revenue History

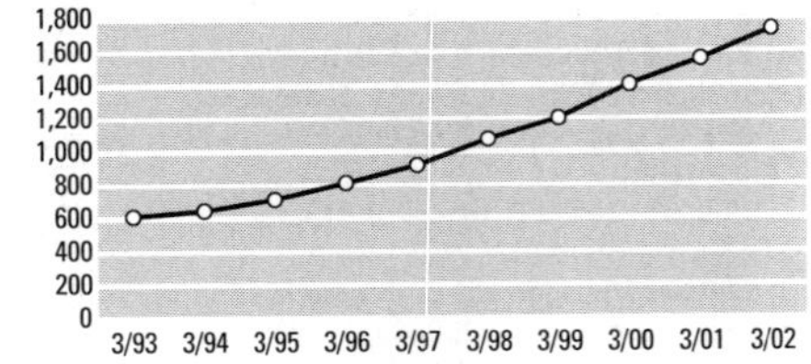

The Ford Foundation

As one of the US's largest philanthropic organizations with a more than $9 billion diversified investment portfolio, The Ford Foundation can afford to be generous. The not-for-profit foundation offers grants to individuals and institutions in the US and abroad that meet its stated goals of strengthening democratic values, reducing poverty and injustice, promoting international cooperation, and advancing human achievement. The Ford Foundation's charitable giving covers a wide spectrum, from A (Association for Asian Studies) to Z (Zanzibar International Film Festival).

The Ford Foundation gives to a variety of causes in one of three areas: Asset Building and Community Development (designed to help expand opportunities for the poor and reduce hardship); Peace and Social Justice (promotes peace and the rule of law, human rights, and freedom); and Education, Media, Arts, and Culture (aimed at strengthening education and the arts and at building identity and community). Following the September 11 terrorist attacks in 2001, The Ford Foundation joined other philanthropic organizations in providing disaster relief.

The foundation is governed by an international board of trustees and no longer has stock in Ford Motor Company or ties to the Ford family. Funds are derived from a diversified investment portfolio that includes publicly traded equity and fixed-income securities.

HISTORY

Henry Ford and his son Edsel gave $25,000 to establish The Ford Foundation in Michigan in 1936, followed the next year by 250,000 shares of nonvoting stock in the Ford Motor Company. The foundation's activities were limited mainly to Michigan until the deaths of Edsel (1943) and Henry (1947) made the foundation the owner of 90% of the automaker's nonvoting stock (catapulting the endowment to $474 million, the US's largest).

In 1951, under a new mandate and president (Paul Hoffman, former head of the Marshall Plan), Ford made broad commitments to the promotion of world peace, the strengthening of democracy, and the improvement of education. Early education program grants overseen by University of Chicago chancellor Robert Maynard Hutchins ($100 million between 1951 and 1953) helped establish major international programs (e.g., Harvard's Center for International Legal Studies) and the National Merit Scholarships.

Under McCarthy-era criticism for its experimental education grants, the foundation in 1956 granted $550 million (after selling 22% of its Ford shares) to noncontroversial recipients such as liberal arts colleges and not-for-profit hospitals. The organization's money set up the Radio and Television Workshop (1951); public TV support became a foundation trademark.

International work, begun in Asia and the Middle East (1950) and extended to Africa (1958) and Latin America (1959), focused on education and rural development. The foundation also supported the Population Council and research in high-yield agriculture with The Rockefeller Foundation.

In the early 1960s Ford targeted innovative approaches to employment and race relations. McGeorge Bundy (former national security adviser to President John F. Kennedy), named president of the foundation in 1966, increased the activist trend with grants for direct voter registration; the NAACP; public-interest law centers serving consumer, environmental, and minority causes; and housing for the poor.

The early 1970s saw support for black colleges and scholarships, child care, and job training for women, but by 1974 inflation, weak stock prices, and overspending had eroded assets. Programs were cut, but continued support for social justice issues led Henry Ford II to quit the board in 1976.

Under lawyer Franklin Thomas (named president in 1979), Ford established the nation's largest community development support organization, Local Initiatives Support. Thomas, the first African-American to lead the foundation, was a catalyst in a series of meetings between white and black South Africans in the mid-1980s.

Thomas stepped down in 1996, and new president Susan Berresford, formerly EVP, consolidated the foundation's grant programs into three areas: Asset Building and Community Development; Peace and Social Justice; and Education, Media, Arts, and Culture. In the late 1990s Ford was surpassed by various other foundations and had to relinquish its 30-year title as the biggest charitable organization in the US.

In 2000 the foundation announced its largest grant ever, the 10-year, $330 million International Fellowship Program to support graduate students studying in 20 countries. The Ford Foundation provided aid to people affected by the September 11 attacks in 2001, committing grants of $10 million in New York City and more than $1 million in Washington, DC.

EXECUTIVES

Chairman: Paul A. Allaire, age 64
President: Susan V. Berresford
EVP, Secretary, and General Counsel: Barron M. Tenny
SVP: Barry D. Gaberman
VP and Chief Investment Officer: Linda B. Strumpf
VP Asset Building and Community Development: Melvin L. Oliver
VP Communications: Alexander Wilde
VP Education, Media, Arts, and Culture: Alison R. Bernstein
VP Peace and Social Justice: Bradford K. Smith
Controller, Treasurer, and Director Financial Services: Nicholas M. Gabriel
Senior Director Office Management Services: Natalia Kanem
Director Community and Resource Development: Cynthia Duncan
Director Economic Development: Frank F. DeGiovanni
Director Education, Knowledge, and Religion: Janice Petrovich
Director Governance and Civil Society: Michael A. Edwards
Director Human Development and Reproductive Health: Virginia Davis Floyd
Director Human Resources: Bruce D. Stuckey
Director Human Rights and International Cooperation: Alan Jenkins
Assistant Secretary and Associate General Counsel: Nancy P. Feller
Auditors: PricewaterhouseCoopers LLP

LOCATIONS

HQ: 320 E. 43rd St., New York, NY 10017
Phone: 212-573-5000 **Fax:** 212-351-3677
Web: www.fordfound.org

The Ford Foundation has representatives in New York City, as well as Beijing; Cairo; Hanoi, Vietnam; Jakarta, Indonesia; Johannesburg; Lagos, Nigeria; Manila, Philippines; Mexico City; Moscow; Nairobi, Kenya; New Delhi; Rio de Janeiro; and Santiago, Chile.

PRODUCTS/OPERATIONS

Program Area Grants

Asset Building and Community Development
- Community and Resource Development
- Economic Development
- Human Development and Reproductive Health

Education, Media, Arts, and Culture
- Education, Knowledge, and Religion
- Media, Arts, and Culture

Peace and Social Justice
- Governance and Civil Society
- Human Rights and International Cooperation

HISTORICAL FINANCIALS

Company Type: Foundation

Income Statement FYE: September 30

	REVENUE ($ mil.)	NET INCOME ($ mil.)	NET PROFIT MARGIN	EMPLOYEES
9/02	289	—	—	400
9/01	992	—	—	500
9/00	2,432	—	—	600
9/99	1,785	—	—	576
9/98	1,087	—	—	580
9/97	1,005	—	—	574
9/96	899	—	—	570
9/95	586	—	—	587
9/94	489	—	—	597
9/93	797	—	—	590
Annual Growth	(10.7%)	—	—	(4.2%)

Revenue History

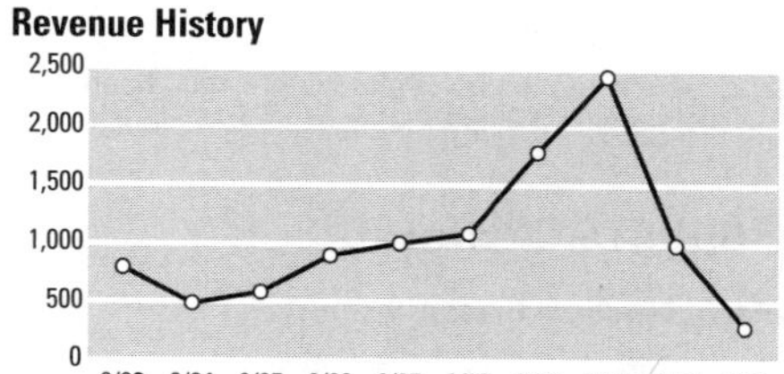

Ford of Santa Monica, Inc.

You can get a new car from Ford of Santa Monica if the other Santa doesn't bring one. Ford of Santa Monica is one of the top-selling Ford dealers in the US, selling about 24,000 vehicles a year. The dealership sells new Ford cars and trucks, with most of its business from fleet sales (mass quantities to corporate customers). Ford of Santa Monica also operates a parts and service department and a body shop. Established in 1948, Ford of Santa Monica offers a customer satisfaction program that includes surveys, follow-up phone calls, and keep-in-touch letters. L. Wayne Harding owns the company.

EXECUTIVES

President: Ronald Davis
Secretary-Treasurer: Dean Chow
Director Human Resources: Ricky Berardy

LOCATIONS

HQ: 1230 Santa Monica Blvd., Santa Monica, CA 90404
Phone: 310-451-1588 **Fax:** 310-394-8115

COMPETITORS

AutoNation
David Wilson's
Galpin Motors
Sonic Automotive
Tuttle-Click

HISTORICAL FINANCIALS

Company Type: Private

Income Statement FYE: December 31

	REVENUE ($ mil.)	NET INCOME ($ mil.)	NET PROFIT MARGIN	EMPLOYEES
12/01	800	—	—	100
12/00	800	—	—	100
12/99	750	—	—	100
12/98	582	—	—	100
12/97	510	—	—	100
12/96	550	—	—	100
12/95	572	—	—	100
12/94	442	—	—	96
12/93	489	—	—	100
12/92	778	—	—	110
Annual Growth	0.3%	—	—	(1.1%)

Revenue History

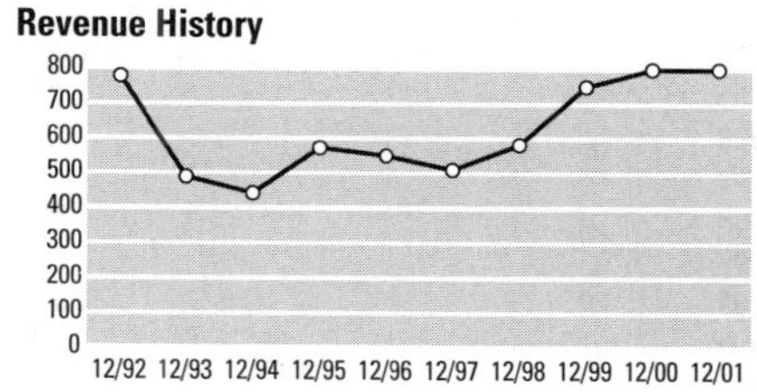

Foremost Farms

No jokes about "herd mentality," please. Foremost Farms USA — owned by about 4,300 dairy farmers in seven midwestern states, mainly Wisconsin — is a major dairy cooperative in the US.

From 24 plants the cooperative churns more than 5 billion pounds of milk into solid and fluid dairy products for industrial, retail, and food service customers.

Foremost's retail brands include Golden Guernsey Dairy and Morning Glory Dairy; it also produces private label products for retailers.

To reduce dependence on commodity products, the co-op is developing new products (flavored milk drinks, pharmaceutical-grade lactose), and has expanded its mozzarella capacity to meet consumer demand.

EXECUTIVES

Chairman: Edward Brooks
President: Dave Fuhrmann
VP, Finance: Duaine Kamenick
VP, Fluid Milk, Employee and Member Services: Jim Kasten
VP, Cheese Division: Doug Wilke
VP, Fluid Products Division: Joseph Weis
VP, Ingredient Division: Jim Geyer
VP, Planning and Marketing Analyst: Curtis Kurth
Director of Communications: Joan Behr
Auditors: PricewaterhouseCoopers LLP

LOCATIONS

HQ: Foremost Farms USA, Cooperative
E10889A Penny Lane, Baraboo, WI 53913
Phone: 608-355-8700 **Fax:** 608-355-8699
Web: www.foremostfarms.com

Foremost Farms serves farmers in Illinois, Indiana, Iowa, Michigan, Minnesota, Ohio, and Wisconsin.

COMPETITORS

Alto Dairy
AMPI
Century Foods
Dairy Farmers of America
Dairylea
Dean Foods
Horizon Organic
Land O'Lakes
Leprino Foods
MMPA
National Dairy Holdings
Prairie Farms Dairy
Quality Chekd
Saputo
Schreiber Foods

HISTORICAL FINANCIALS

Company Type: Cooperative

Income Statement FYE: December 31

	REVENUE ($ mil.)	NET INCOME ($ mil.)	NET PROFIT MARGIN	EMPLOYEES
12/02	1,167	2	0.2%	1,766
12/01	1,332	10	0.8%	1,705
12/00	1,093	10	0.9%	1,646
12/99	1,302	19	1.5%	1,716
12/98	1,376	27	2.0%	1,800
12/97	1,193	5	0.4%	1,750
12/96	1,357	17	1.2%	2,000
12/95	822	13	1.5%	2,000
12/94	548	—	—	1,000
12/93	536	—	—	946
Annual Growth	9.0%	(22.1%)	—	7.2%

2002 Year-End Financials

Debt ratio: 47.4%
Return on equity: 1.3%
Cash ($ mil.): 0
Current ratio: 1.36
Long-term debt ($ mil.): 75

Net Income History

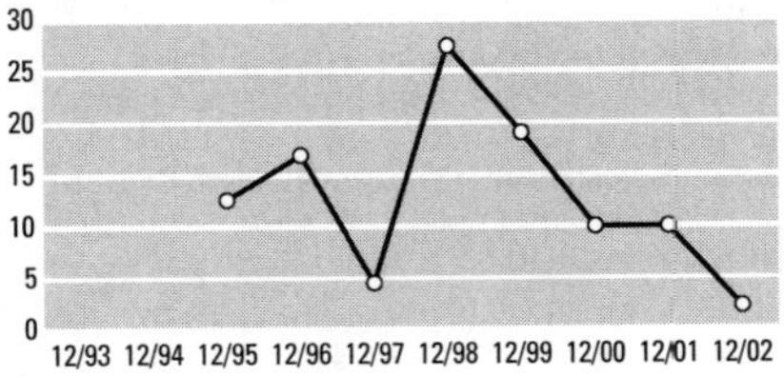

Forever Living Products

Forever Living Products International might not lead you to immortality, but its aloe vera-based health care products are intended to improve your well-being. The firm sells aloe vera drinks, as well as aloe vera-based aromatherapy products, cosmetics, dietary and nutritional supplements, lotion, soap, and tooth gel products. Owner Rex Maughan also owns aloe vera plantations in the Dominican Republic, Mexico, and Texas; Aloe Vera of America, a processing plant; and Forever Resorts' US resorts and marinas, including Dallas-area South Fork Ranch (of *Dallas* TV show fame). Forever Living Products sells its goods through a global network of independent distributors.

EXECUTIVES

Chairman, President, and CEO: Rex Maughan
CFO and Controller: David Hall
VP, Human Resources: Glen B. Banks

LOCATIONS

HQ: Forever Living Products International, Inc.
7501 E. McCormick Pkwy., Ste. 135S,
Scottsdale, AZ 85258
Phone: 480-998-8888 **Fax:** 480-998-8887
Web: www.foreverliving.com

Forever Living Products has distributors throughout the US and on all five continents. Subsidiary Forever Resorts has more than twenty locations (lodges and marinas) in Alaska, Arizona, California, Colorado, Georgia, Kentucky, Missouri, Nevada, Texas, Washington, and Wyoming.

PRODUCTS/OPERATIONS

Selected Product Categories

Aloe vera drinks
Bee products
Cosmetics
Nutrition
Skin care
Weight loss

COMPETITORS

Advanced Nutraceuticals
Alticor
Avon
Body Shop
Burt's Bees
GNC
Herbalife
Mannatech
Nature's Sunshine
NBTY
Nu Skin
Shaklee
Sunrider
Weider Nutrition International
Whole Foods
Wild Oats Markets

HISTORICAL FINANCIALS

Company Type: Private

Income Statement FYE: December 31

	REVENUE ($ mil.)	NET INCOME ($ mil.)	NET PROFIT MARGIN	EMPLOYEES
12/02	1,773	—	—	4,000
12/01	1,489	—	—	2,000
12/00	1,200	—	—	1,901
12/99	1,100	—	—	932
12/98	1,000	—	—	1,700
12/97	950	—	—	1,200
12/96	900	—	—	1,360
12/95	800	—	—	750
12/94	750	—	—	—
12/93	700	—	—	—
Annual Growth	10.9%	—	—	27.0%

Revenue History

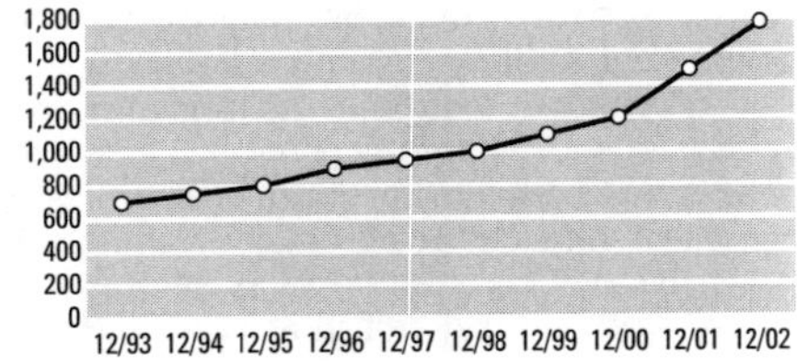

Forsythe Technology, Inc.

Forsythe Technology believes it has the foresight to provide businesses with the right computer equipment and network technology. Its Forsythe Solutions Group helps companies select, install, and manage computer systems and software, and its Forsythe McArthur subsidiary leases computer equipment. Forsythe Technology also owns a stake in management service provider SevenSpace. The company offers an Information Technology Risk Management Practice, helping clients plan for disaster recovery. In 2003 Forsythe launched a new venture, Forsythe Biotechnology, to provide equipment financing for biotech firms. CEO Richard Forsythe holds a majority interest in the employee-owned company, which he founded in 1971.

Forsythe was started with $200 and a telephone on a dining room table. The company now works with vendors such as Cisco Systems, Hewlett-Packard, and Sun Microsystems, and it serves more than 3,000 clients from offices throughout the US. Customers include D&B (formerly Dun & Bradstreet), Deere, McDonald's, and Walt Disney.

EXECUTIVES

Chairman and President; Chairman and CEO, Forsythe McArthur; Chairman, Forsythe Solutions: Richard A. (Rick) Forsythe
SVP; President and CEO, Forsythe Solutions Group: Eva T. Losacco
SVP, Finance and Administration; President, Forsythe McArthur Associates: Albert L. (Al) Weiss
SVP, Sales: John Carcone
SVP, Sales: Robert D. (Bob) Dvorak

VP and Chief Accounting Officer: Thomas R. Ehmann
VP and CIO: Mitchell G. (Mitch) Germaine
VP, General Counsel, and Secretary: R. Thomas (Tom) Hoffman
VP, Human Resources: Julie A. Fusco
VP, Marketing: Sally K. Buchanan
Treasurer: Raymond L. Ellingsen
Director, Corporate Communications: Stacy R. Reineking
Auditors: KPMG LLP

LOCATIONS

HQ: 7500 Frontage Rd., Skokie, IL 60077
Phone: 847-675-8000 **Fax:** 847-763-7557
Web: www.forsythetech.com

Forsythe Technology has 25 offices in 25 states in the US.

PRODUCTS/OPERATIONS

Services

Forsythe Solutions
Back-up and recovery
Database and application development
Internet application integration
Network design and security
Software and systems benchmarking
Storage systems integration
Systems analysis and management
Systems consolidation
Training

Forsythe McArthur
Computer equipment leasing

COMPETITORS

Affiliated Computer Services
AMS
ATEL
Black Box
Comdisco
Computer Sciences
Dell
Electro Rent
EDS
ePlus
FAEF
GATX
GCI Systems
HP Services
IBM Global Services
ICON Holdings
Keane
Meridian Group
ORIX
Perot Systems
Sayers Group
Unisys

HISTORICAL FINANCIALS

Company Type: Private

Income Statement

FYE: December 31

	REVENUE ($ mil.)	NET INCOME ($ mil.)	NET PROFIT MARGIN	EMPLOYEES
12/02	569	20	3.5%	535
12/01	691	34	5.0%	521
12/00	631	24	3.8%	562
12/99	536	25	4.6%	393
12/98	448	22	4.9%	363
12/97	280	14	5.1%	302
12/96	189	12	6.3%	230
12/95	151	8	5.0%	150
12/94	160	8	4.7%	141
12/93	158	—	—	148
Annual Growth	15.3%	13.0%	—	15.3%

Net Income History

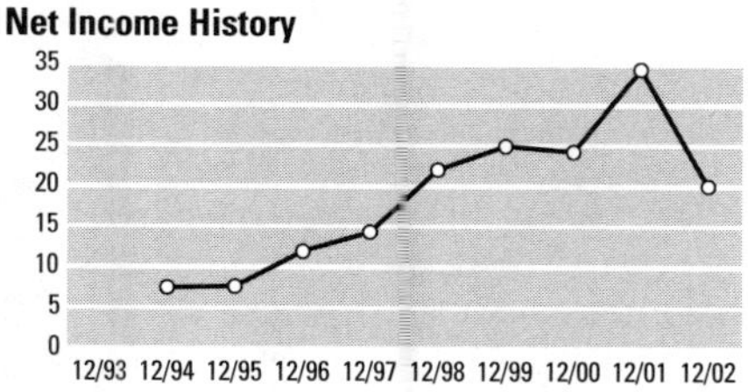

Fortunoff

Fortunoff wants to bedeck your body, as well as your home. Two related firms owned by members of the Fortunoff family make up the company. Fortunoff Fine Jewelry & Silverware, founded in 1922, sells fine and antique jewelry, silver, and watches, plus housewares and cookware products. M. Fortunoff of Westbury sells home furnishings, furniture, domestics, small appliances, gifts, luggage, and tabletop accessories. Fortunoff also operates a Baby Fortunoff shop and offers seasonal retail outlets — outdoor furniture in the summer and trim-a-tree shops at Christmas. The two Fortunoff companies (with nine stores in New York and New Jersey) share some retail spaces and operate some stand-alone stores.

EXECUTIVES

CIO, Fortunoff Fine Jewelry & Silverware, Inc.: David Fortunoff
President and CEO, Fortunoff Fine Jewelry & Silverware, Inc.: Helene Fortunoff
EVP and Human Resources Director, Fortunoff Fine Jewelry & Silverware, Inc.: Louis Fortunoff
EVP, Jewelry Merchandising, Fortunoff Fine Jewelry & Silverware, Inc.: Esther Fortunoff
EVP, Jewelry Merchandising, Fortunoff Fine Jewelry & Silverware, Inc.: Ruth Fortunoff
VP and Treasurer, M. Fortunoff of Westbury Corp.: Elliot Mayrock
VP, M. Fortunoff of Westbury Corp.: Isidore Mayrock
VP and Secretary, M. Fortunoff of Westbury Corp.: Rachel Mayrock Sands
CFO, Fortunoff Fine Jewelry & Silverware, Inc. and M. Fortunoff of Westbury Corp.: Leonard Tabs

LOCATIONS

HQ: 70 Charles Lindbergh Blvd., Uniondale, NY 11553
Phone: 516-832-9000 **Fax:** 516-237-1703
Web: www.fortunoff.com

2003 Stores

	No.
New York	6
New Jersey	3
Total	**9**

PRODUCTS/OPERATIONS

Store Names

Baby Fortunoff
Backyard Store
Fortunoff
Fortunoff Clearance Center
M. Fortunoff of Westbury
Watch Store

COMPETITORS

Ashford.com
Barneys
Bed Bath & Beyond
Blue Nile
Bulgari
Burlington Coat Factory
Crescent Jewelers
Federated
Helzberg Diamonds
Linens 'n Things
May
Neiman Marcus
Pier 1 Imports
Saks Fifth Avenue
Signet
Stein Mart
Tiffany
Toys "R" Us
Ultra Stores
Whitehall Jewellers
Williams-Sonoma
Zale

HISTORICAL FINANCIALS

Company Type: Private

Income Statement

FYE: January 31

	ESTIMATED REVENUE ($ mil.)	NET INCOME ($ mil.)	NET PROFIT MARGIN	EMPLOYEES
1/02	425	—	—	2,500
1/01*	411	—	—	2,500
7/00	400	—	—	3,500
7/99	400	—	—	2,500
7/98	390	—	—	2,500
7/97	375	—	—	2,500
7/96	365	—	—	2,500
7/95	360	—	—	2,500
7/94	350	—	—	2,500
Annual Growth	2.5%	—	—	0.0%

*Fiscal year change

Revenue History

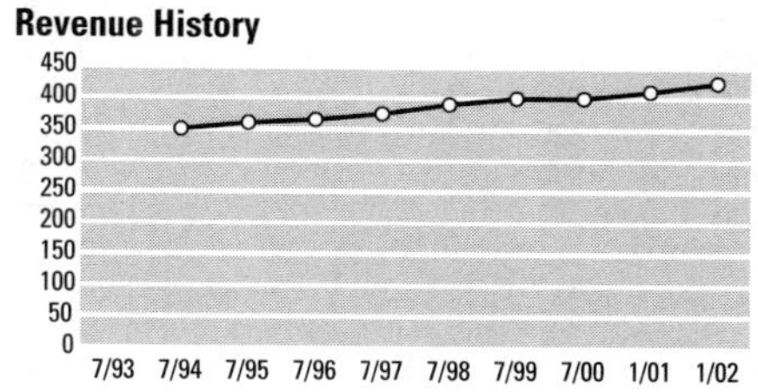

Foster Poultry Farms

As the West Coast's top poultry company, Foster Poultry Farms has a secure place in the pecking order. The company's vertically integrated operations see chickens and turkeys from the incubator to grocers' meat cases (under the Foster Farms brand). In addition to hatching, raising, slaughtering, and processing chickens and turkeys for the grocery and food service industries, the company grinds its own feeds. Already #1 in its home state, Foster Poultry Farms bought the chicken operations of local rival Zacky Farms, making it even larger. Max and Verda Foster founded the company in 1939; it is still owned by the Foster family, which also operates sister company Foster Dairy Farms.

EXECUTIVES

CEO: Paul Carter
President: Don Jackson
CFO: Larry Keillor
VP Human Resources: Tim Walsh
VP Sales: Bob Kellert
VP Marketing: David Schanzer
Auditors: Deloitte & Touche LLP

LOCATIONS

HQ: 1000 Davis St., Livingston, CA 95334
Phone: 209-394-7901 **Fax:** 209-394-6342
Web: www.fosterfarms.com

Foster Poultry Farms has operations in Alabama, California, Oregon, and Washington.

COMPETITORS

Cagle's
ConAgra
Gold Kist
Hormel
Murphy-Brown
Pilgrim's Pride
Randall Foods
Tyson Foods
Zacky Farms

HISTORICAL FINANCIALS

Company Type: Private

Income Statement FYE: December 31

	REVENUE ($ mil.)	NET INCOME ($ mil.)	NET PROFIT MARGIN	EMPLOYEES
12/02	1,400	—	—	11,000
12/01	1,269	—	—	11,000
12/00	1,127	—	—	9,500
12/99	1,100	—	—	7,500
12/98	990	—	—	7,000
12/97	1,000	—	—	7,200
12/96	925	—	—	6,800
12/95	825	—	—	6,700
12/94	800	—	—	6,600
12/93	580	—	—	6,200
Annual Growth	10.3%	—	—	6.6%

Revenue History

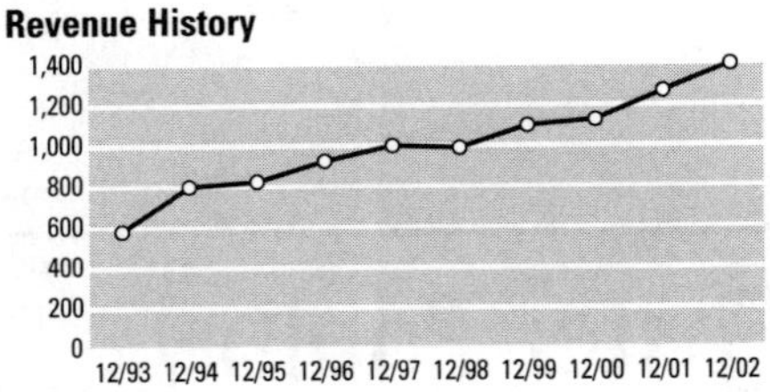

Foxworth-Galbraith Lumber

It might be a mouthful to say, but Foxworth-Galbraith Lumber Company sells more than a handful of building materials to customers in the Southwest. Through more than 70 locations in Arizona, Colorado, New Mexico, and Texas, it sells hardware, lumber, paint, plumbing equipment, and tools. Foxworth-Galbraith's main customers are residential and commercial builders; other clients include do-it-yourselfers, retailers, specialty contractors, and federal and state agencies. The company acquired Brookhart's Building Centers in Colorado in 1999. Foxworth-Galbraith is still owned and operated by the families of W. L. Foxworth and H. W. Galbraith, who founded the company in Dalhart, Texas, in 1901.

EXECUTIVES

Chairman and CEO: Walter L. Foxworth
President and COO: Jimmy Galbraith III
EVP and CFO: Jack Foxworth
EVP: Grant P. Foxworth
EVP and Internet Director: Ted Galbraith
VP and Director of Human Resources: R. Lynn Guillory
Human Resources Recruiter: Eileen Nichols

LOCATIONS

HQ: Foxworth-Galbraith Lumber Company, 17111 Waterview Pkwy., Dallas, TX 75252
Phone: 972-437-6100 **Fax:** 972-454-4251
Web: www.foxgal.com

PRODUCTS/OPERATIONS

Selected Product Categories

Building materials
Cabinets
Electrical
Hardware
Lawn & garden
Lumber
Paint
Plumbing
Tools

COMPETITORS

84 Lumber
A.C. Houston Lumber
Ace Hardware
Building Materials Holding
Do it Best
Home Depot
Lowe's
McCoy
Sears
Sherwin-Williams
Stock Building Supply
Sutherland Lumber
TruServ

HISTORICAL FINANCIALS

Company Type: Private

Income Statement FYE: December 31

	REVENUE ($ mil.)	NET INCOME ($ mil.)	NET PROFIT MARGIN	EMPLOYEES
12/02	515	—	—	2,250
12/01	500	—	—	2,500
12/00	540	—	—	2,500
12/99	450	—	—	2,300
12/98	375	—	—	1,550
12/97	350	—	—	1,471
12/96	340	—	—	1,522
12/95	339	—	—	1,479
12/94	350	—	—	1,800
12/93	250	—	—	1,100
Annual Growth	8.4%	—	—	8.3%

Revenue History

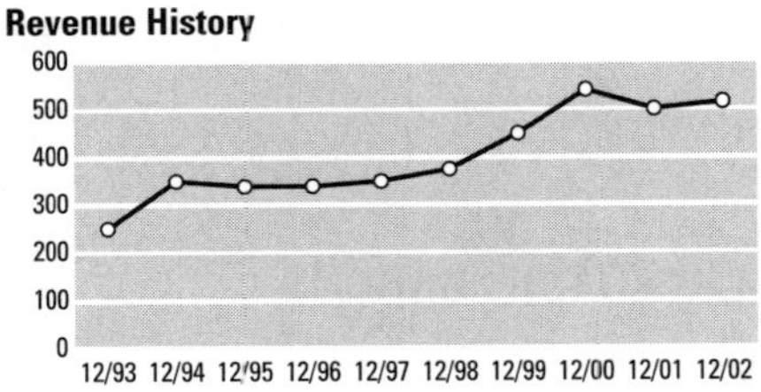

Frank Consolidated Enterprises

Frank Consolidated Enterprises has an old lease on life. Its Wheels subsidiary, which claims to have pioneered the auto leasing concept, provides administrative, management, and financing services to help corporations manage their vehicle fleets. The company manages more than 240,000 vehicles. It operates in the US as Wheels and in other countries through Interleasing, an alliance of international fleet management and leasing companies. Wheels was founded in 1939 by Zollie Frank. Frank's family still owns the parent company; his widow serves as its chair and son Jim is its president and CEO.

EXECUTIVES

Chairman: Elaine S. Frank
President and CEO; President and CEO, Wheels: James S. (Jim) Frank, age 60
EVP and COO, Wheels: Ford Pearson
SVP, Finance and Operations and CFO, Wheels: Mary Ann O'Dwyer
SVP, Sales and Marketing, Wheels; General Manager, Four Wheels: Scott Pattullo
VP, Human Resources, Wheels: Joan Richards
VP, MAP Operations and Wheels Maintenance Assistance Program, Wheels: John Frank
VP, Sales, Wheels: Michael Christian
VP, International Sales, Wheels: Peter Egan
Manager, Wheels Maintenance Assistance Program: Bob Clark

LOCATIONS

HQ: 666 Garland Place, Des Plaines, IL 60016
Phone: 847-699-7000 **Fax:** 847-699-6494
Web: www.wheels.com

COMPETITORS

Accessity Corp.
Continental Motors
Donlen
Emkay
Enterprise Rent-A-Car
Ford
General Motors
Holman Enterprises
Jordan Automotive
Patrick Dealer
PHH Arval
Sixt

HISTORICAL FINANCIALS

Company Type: Private

Income Statement FYE: August 31

	REVENUE ($ mil.)	NET INCOME ($ mil.)	NET PROFIT MARGIN	EMPLOYEES
8/03	1,500	—	—	550
8/02	1,575	—	—	550
8/01	1,500	—	—	600
8/00	1,431	—	—	591
8/99	1,364	—	—	562
8/98	1,181	—	—	574
8/97	1,025	—	—	600
8/96	1,200	—	—	675
8/95	1,165	—	—	675
8/94	1,045	—	—	700
Annual Growth	4.1%	—	—	(2.6%)

Revenue History

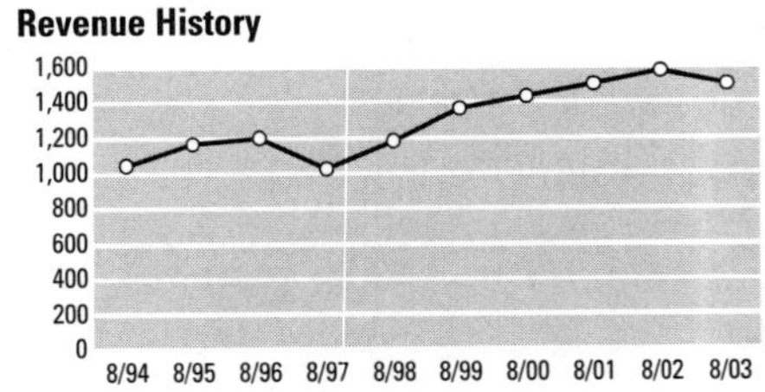

Freedom Communications

Southern California is the real cradle of Freedom. Media conglomerate Freedom Communications owns more than two dozen daily newspapers, including *The Gazette* in Colorado Springs, Colorado, and the company's flagship, California's *Orange County Register,* with a circulation of about 320,000. In addition, the company owns 37 weekly papers and eight television stations. Freedom Communications also operates a number of Web sites, which range from online versions of its printed properties to regional information guides.

The family of founder R. C. Hoiles has had some clashes over the company's future. Tim Hoiles, grandson of the company's founder, threatened to sue his relatives if he was not able to cash out his 8.6% share in the company. The company explored selling all or part of the business to raise the monies necessary to buy out certain family shareholders, and big newspaper companies were salivating over the prospect. In the end, Freedom Communications approved a recapitalization plan in 2003 that will allow the company to remain in family hands, while allowing relatives who want to sell their shares to do so.

EXECUTIVES

Chairman: R. D. Threshie
President and CEO: Alan J. Bell
SVP and CFO: David Kuykendall
President, Freedom Broadcasting: Doreen Wade
President, Freedom Community Newspapers: Jonathan Segal
President, Freedom Metro Newspapers: N. Christian Anderson III
VP Human Resources and Organizational Development: Marcy Bruskin
VP and CFO of Shared Services: Jeff Whitton
VP and CIO: Mike Brown
VP and Controller: Nancy Trillo

LOCATIONS

HQ: Freedom Communications, Inc.
17666 Fitch Ave., Irvine, CA 92614
Phone: 949-253-2300 **Fax:** 949-474-7675
Web: www.freedom.com

PRODUCTS/OPERATIONS

Selected Newspapers

Brownsville Herald (Texas)
Clovis News Journal (New Mexico)
The Daily News (Jacksonville, NC)
The Gaston Gazette (Gastonia, NC)
The Gazette (Colorado Springs, CO)
The Lima News (Ohio)
The Monitor (McAllen, TX)
The News Herald (Panama City, FL)
Odessa American (Texas)
The Orange County Register (Santa Ana, CA)
The Tribune (Seymour, IN)
Valley Morning Star (Harlingen, TX)

Television Stations

KFDM-TV (Beaumont, TX)
KTVL-TV (Medford, OR)
WLAJ-TV (Lansing, MI)
WLNE-TV (Providence, RI)
WPEC-TV (West Palm Beach, FL)
WRGB-TV (Albany, NY)
WTVC-TV (Chattanooga, TN)
WWMT-TV (Grand Rapids, MI

COMPETITORS

Advance Publications
Belo
Copley Press
Cox Enterprises
Daily Journal
E. W. Scripps
Gannett
Hearst
Journal Communications
Media General
MediaNews
Meredith
New York Times
Stephens Media Group
Tribune
Young Broadcasting

HISTORICAL FINANCIALS

Company Type: Private

Income Statement FYE: December 31

	ESTIMATED REVENUE ($ mil.)	NET INCOME ($ mil.)	NET PROFIT MARGIN	EMPLOYEES
12/01	760	—	—	8,000
12/00	850	—	—	8,000
12/99	750	—	—	8,100
12/98	673	—	—	7,000
12/97	645	—	—	7,200
12/96	605	—	—	6,900
12/95	525	—	—	5,500
12/94	501	—	—	6,800
12/93	479	—	—	6,800
12/92	477	—	—	5,500
Annual Growth	5.3%	—	—	4.3%

Revenue History

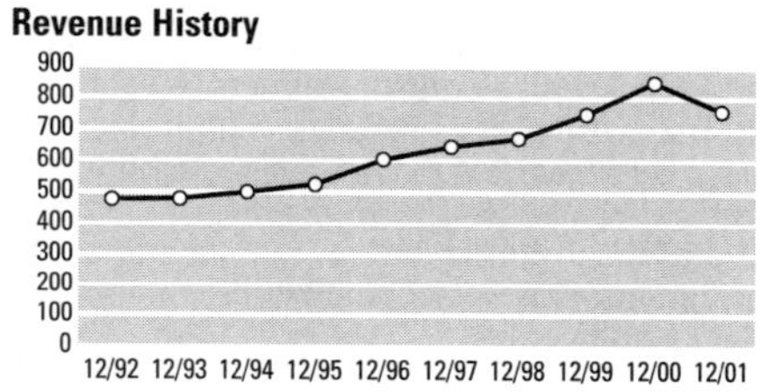

Fry's Electronics, Inc.

Service may be heavy-handed, but where else can you buy appliances, build a computer, grab some Ho-Ho's or Maalox, and find the latest *Playboy* or *Byte*? The 22-store Fry's Electronics chain offers all that plus low prices, extensive inventory (including Crock-Pots, vacuums, stereos, TVs, and computer software and hardware), and whimsically themed displays (such as Wild West motifs). The technogeek's superstore — whose notoriously bad service is chronicled on unaffiliated Web pages — began in 1985 as the brainchild of CEO John Fry (with brothers Randy and Dave) and EVP Kathryn Kolder. The Fry brothers, who got their start at Fry's Food Stores, still own the company.

Its mammoth stores, some swallowing almost 200,000 sq. ft., cater to the intensely technical shopper. Fry's outlets (a regular stop on bus tours) stock more than 50,000 low-priced electronic items and are known for their decor and displays. Each follows a theme, from *Alice in Wonderland* to a UFO crash site. The geek-gaws range from silicon chips to potato chips, from *Byte* to *Playboy,* and high-speed PCs (plus software and peripherals) to No-Doz (and other over-the-counter drugs).

But Fry's unfriendly reputation has left it a target of gripe-filled Web sites. Employees are searched at the end of each day as an antitheft measure (a concern that also keeps Fry's products stacked on the sales floor due to the elimination of stock rooms). Customers hoping to return items must abide by a process known internally as the "double H," for hoops and hurdles. One manager of an anti-Fry's Web site has likened the experience to a bizarre game of S&M.

Fry's also owns tech products e-tailer Cyberian Outpost. CEO John Fry, a mathematician who collects the writings of Nobel Prize winners for fun, is known for hiring computer-illiterate sales clerks for a pittance.

HISTORY

The Fry brothers — David, John, and Randy — wear genes stitched of retailing. Their father, Charles, started Fry's Food Stores supermarket chain in the 1950s in South Bay, California. The 40-store chain was sold for $14 million in 1972 before Charles' progeny heard the retail calling.

Charles gave each of his sons $1 million from the sale of the supermarkets. His oldest, John, who had gained technical expertise while running the supermarket's computer system, convinced his siblings of the viability of a hard-core computer retail store. The brothers pooled their funds and in 1985 started the first in Sunnyvale, California, along with Kathryn Kolder (now EVP). They added a store in Fremont in 1988; the Palo Alto store was completed two years later.

John mixed his supermarket sales experience with a sharp marketing acumen, selling prime shelf space at smart prices to suppliers. He stocked the stores with everything for a computer user's survival and slashed prices. The first Los Angeles-area store opened in 1992; a second one opened the following year.

Hiring an ex-Lucasfilm designer, John spent $1 million on each location, decorating stores like medieval castles, Mayan temples, Wild West saloons, and other individual fantasy themes.

In 1994 the Los Angeles computer retail market began to see increased competition from nationwide discount computer superstores. The next year Fry's responded by opening a new store in Woodland Hills with an *Alice in Wonderland* motif. It was the first Southern California Fry's Electronics store to offer appliances and an expanded music department.

The chain continued to gain notoriety for the contempt it seemed to show its customers. Local Better Business Bureaus started ranking Fry's "unsatisfactory" because the stores would not respond to complaints. Visitors were usually met by security guards, scores of hidden surveillance cameras, and employees who were promised bonuses for talking customers out of cash returns.

Still the company thrived, turning over its inventories twice as fast as competitors. One customer who sued Fry's for injuries allegedly received at the hands of store security guards went back for deals soon thereafter. Fry's went on an expansion frenzy in 1996, opening new California stores in Burbank, San Jose, and Anaheim. Moving beyond its Pacific roots, the company in 1997 spent $118 million to buy six of Tandy's failed Incredible Universe retail mega-outlets in Arizona, Oregon, and Texas. The company also won a legal battle with Frenchy Frys, a Seattle vending machine maker, for the right to own and use the frys.com URL. The company in 1998 continued to restructure its new stores into Fry's outlets.

Fry's opened a new store (complete with gushing oil derricks) in Houston in 2001. That year Fry's pulled out of a deal it had made to acquire all of the assets of technology products marketer Egghead.com and bought competitor Cyberian Outpost instead. In January 2003 Fry's set up shop in Las Vegas; the entrance features a two-story neon slot machine.

EXECUTIVES

CEO: John Fry
President: William R. (Randy) Fry
CFO and CIO: David (Dave) Fry
EVP Business Development: Kathryn Kolder
VP Merchandising and Advertising: Ohmar Siddiqui
Director of Human Resources: Karen Schultz

LOCATIONS

HQ: 600 E. Brokaw Rd., San Jose, CA 95112
Phone: 408-487-4500 **Fax:** 408-487-4700
Web: www.frys.com

Fry's Electronics has stores in Arizona, California, Nevada, Oregon, and Texas.

PRODUCTS/OPERATIONS

Selected Computer Products

Computer chips
Motherboards
PCs
Peripherals
Software

Other Products

Audio CDs
Beer
Coffeemakers
Digital mixers
Fax machines
Magazines
Over-the-counter medicines
Potato chips
Razors
Soda
Stereos
Telephones
Telescopes
Televisions
Video systems

COMPETITORS

Best Buy
Beyond
BUY.COM
CDW
Circuit City Stores
CompUSA
Cyberian Outpost
Dell
Gateway
Good Guys
Insight Enterprises
Micro Electronics
Micro Warehouse
Office Depot
PC Connection
PC Mall
RadioShack
Staples
Systemax
Zones

HISTORICAL FINANCIALS

Company Type: Private

Income Statement FYE: December 31

	ESTIMATED REVENUE ($ mil.)	NET INCOME ($ mil.)	NET PROFIT MARGIN	EMPLOYEES
12/02	2,000	—	—	5,650
12/01	1,900	—	—	4,900
12/00	1,500	—	—	4,450
12/99	1,420	—	—	4,100
12/98	1,250	—	—	4,000
12/97	950	—	—	4,000
12/96	535	—	—	2,000
12/95	414	—	—	1,500
12/94	327	—	—	1,500
12/93	250	—	—	1,300
Annual Growth	26.0%	—	—	17.7%

Revenue History

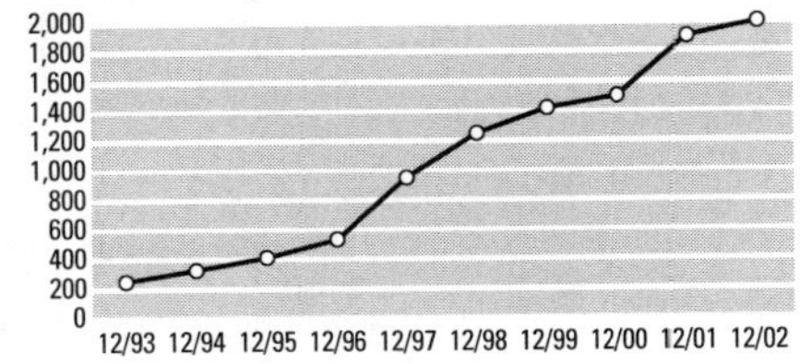

Galpin Motors, Inc.

Galpin Motors will do just about anything to get you to buy a car, even jolt you with joe at the full-service Starbucks shops attached to its dealerships. Claiming to have sold the first Saturn, it also sells Aston Martin, Ford, Jaguar, Lincoln, Mazda, Mercury, Th!nk, and Volvo models, as well as used cars, from four dealerships and a Web site. It also rents and customizes — or "Galpinizes" — vehicles, such as the Tailgate Party Truck with a built-in stainless steel barbecue and refrigerated beer kegs. Galpin Motors' dealerships have featured a King Tut exhibit and a miniature circus. The company also donated $1 million to Mother Teresa. Founded in 1946, Galpin Motors is owned and run by the Boeckmann family.

President Bert Boeckmann is a member of the Los Angeles Police Department's governing Police Commission.

EXECUTIVES

President: Herbert F. (Bert) Boeckmann II
CFO: Phil Marshall
VP: Beau Boeckmann
VP: Brad Boeckmann
VP: Karl Boeckmann
Director Human Resources: Joyce McNeely
Director, Information Technology: Lynn Shurley

LOCATIONS

HQ: 15505 Roscoe Blvd., North Hills, CA 91343
Phone: 818-787-3800 **Fax:** 818-778-2210
Web: www.gogalpin.com

COMPETITORS

AutoNation
Conant Auto Retail
David Wilson's
Fletcher Jones
Ford of Santa Monica
Penske Automotive
Tuttle-Click

HISTORICAL FINANCIALS

Company Type: Private

Income Statement FYE: December 31

	REVENUE ($ mil.)	NET INCOME ($ mil.)	NET PROFIT MARGIN	EMPLOYEES
12/01	666	—	—	750
12/00	655	—	—	750
12/99	616	—	—	741
12/98	550	—	—	715
12/97	533	—	—	682
12/96	502	—	—	675
12/95	434	—	—	620
12/94	394	—	—	595
12/93	308	—	—	—
Annual Growth	10.1%	—	—	3.4%

Revenue History

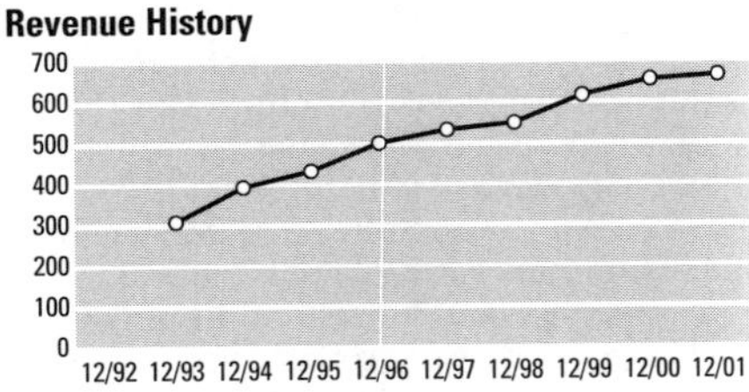

The Gambrinus Company

Named after a medieval Belgian duke credited with inventing the toast as a social custom, The Gambrinus Company brews, imports, and distributes beer. Among the brews it distributes are Corona Extra (the #1 imported beer in the US; Heineken is #2), Modelo Especial, Negra-Modelo, Pacifico, and Moosehead Beer. Imports pour in from Mexico and Canada and are sold primarily in the eastern US, Texas, Bermuda, and the Caribbean. Gambrinus also owns the Spoetzl Brewery (Shiner Bock, the #1 selling bock in the US) of Shiner, Texas; Oregon's oldest microbrewery, BridgePort Brewing Company; and Pete's Brewing Company (Pete's Wicked Ale). Owner Carlos Alvarez founded Gambrinus in 1986 and serves as its president and CEO.

EXECUTIVES

President and CEO; President and CEO, Pete's Brewing: Carlos Alvarez, age 52
CFO; CFO, Pete's Brewing: James Bolz
Director of Brewery Operations: Jaime Jurado
Director of Marketing: Ron Christesson
Director of National Sales: Don Lake
Manager of Human Resources; Manager of Human Resources, Pete's Brewing: Brad Kohanke

LOCATIONS

HQ: 14800 San Pedro Ave., San Antonio, TX 78232
Phone: 210-490-9128 **Fax:** 210-490-9984
Web: www.gambrinusco.com

The Gambrinus Company distributes Grupo Modelo beers (Corona, Modelo, and Pacifico) in Bermuda, the Caribbean, Texas, 24 eastern states, and Washington, DC. It exclusively distributes Canada's Moosehead Beer across the US. The company's Pete's Brewing Company markets its specialty beers in 49 states; Washington, DC; and the UK; and its Spoetzl Brewery products are sold in 23 states across the southern US.

PRODUCTS/OPERATIONS

Selected Distributed Brands

Grupo Modelo
Corona Extra
Corona Light
Modelo Especial
Negra-Modelo
Pacifico

Moosehead Breweries
Moosehead Beer

Selected Brewers and Brands

BridgePort Brewing Company
BridgePort Amber
BridgePort IPA (India Pale Ale)
BridgePort Old Knucklehead

Pete's Brewing Company
Pete's Oktoberfest
Pete's Signature Pilsner
Pete's Summer Brew
Pete's Wicked Ale

Spoetzl Brewery
Shiner Blonde
Shiner Bock
Shiner Winter Ale

COMPETITORS

Adolph Coors
Anchor Brewing
Anheuser-Busch
Asahi Breweries
Boston Beer
Carlsberg
Diageo
Foster's
Heineken
Interbrew
Kirin
Miller Brewing
Molson
Pyramid Breweries
Redhook Ale
Grolsch
Sapporo
Scottish & Newcastle

HISTORICAL FINANCIALS

Company Type: Private

Income Statement FYE: December 31

	ESTIMATED REVENUE ($ mil.)	NET INCOME ($ mil.)	NET PROFIT MARGIN	EMPLOYEES
12/01	500	—	—	300
12/00	425	—	—	300
12/99	425	—	—	300
12/98	400	—	—	300
12/97	350	—	—	147
12/96	250	—	—	95
12/95	125	—	—	—
12/94	75	—	—	—
Annual Growth	31.1%	—	—	25.9%

Revenue History

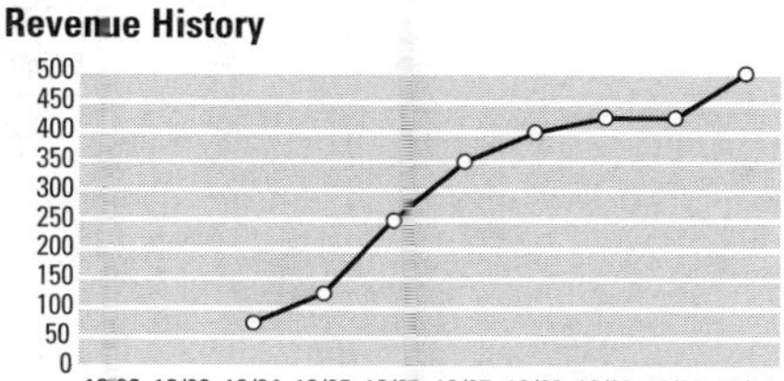

General Parts, Inc.

Feel free to salute General Parts, distributor of replacement automotive parts, supplies, and tools for every make and model of foreign and domestic car, truck, bus, and farm or industrial vehicle. The largest member of the CARQUEST network, employee-owned General Parts, with more than 1,200 company-owned stores, distributes its products to about 4,000 CARQUEST and other auto parts stores across North America through 35 distribution centers. The company, which has been growing through acquisitions, sells its parts to do-it-yourself mechanics, professional installers, body shops, farmers, and fleet owners (commercial customers account for about 85% of sales). The company owns CARQUEST Canada.

EXECUTIVES

Chairman and CEO: O. Temple Sloan Jr., age 64
Vice Chairman: Joe Owen
President: O. Temple Sloan III
CFO: John Gardner
VP of Administration and Accounting: Bill Kuykendall
President, Stores Group: Wayne Lavrack
Director of Personnel: Ed Wharty

LOCATIONS

HQ: 2635 Millbrook Rd., Raleigh, NC 27604
Phone: 919-573-3000 **Fax:** 919-573-3553

COMPETITORS

Advance Auto Parts
AutoZone
CSK Auto
Genuine Parts
Hahn Automotive
Pep Boys
TBC

HISTORICAL FINANCIALS

Company Type: Private

Income Statement FYE: December 31

	REVENUE ($ mil.)	NET INCOME ($ mil.)	NET PROFIT MARGIN	EMPLOYEES
12/02	1,650	—	—	14,000
12/01	1,562	—	—	13,000
12/00	1,459	—	—	12,000
12/99	1,462	—	—	12,700
12/98	1,248	—	—	10,150
12/97	1,060	—	—	6,700
12/96	818	—	—	6,700
12/95	680	—	—	4,700
12/94	612	—	—	4,670
12/93	500	—	—	3,750
Annual Growth	14.2%	—	—	15.8%

Revenue History

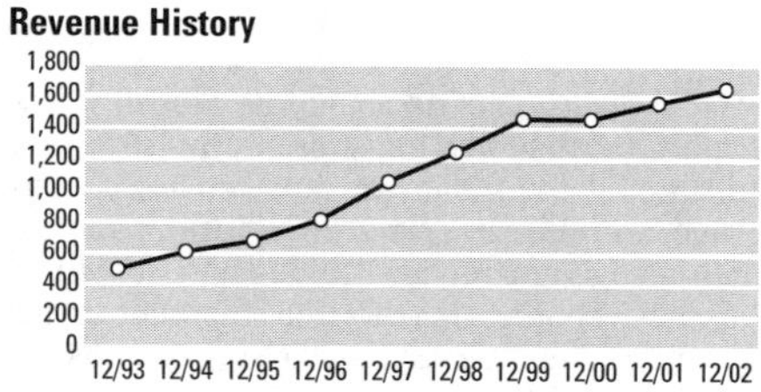

Genlyte Thomas Group LLC

At the marriage of The Genlyte Group and Thomas Industries, which formed Genlyte Thomas Group, they must have played "You Light Up My Life." The joint venture — of which Genlyte owns 68%, Thomas 32% — plays a leading role in the North American lighting market. Genlyte Thomas' lighting fixtures and controls are used both indoors and outdoors, for decoration, landscaping, and tracking. Brand names include Bronzelite, Capri, Lightolier, and ZED. The company markets to distributors, who resell the products for use in the construction and remodeling of residential, commercial, and industrial facilities. Genlyte Thomas' flagship Lightolier division is teaming up with Steelcase to develop workplace lighting.

Genlyte Thomas will continue to diversify its lighting interests. Recent acquisitions include the manufacturing and sales divisions of entertainment lighting specialist Vari-Lite Inc. from the US-based VLPS Lighting Services International (formerly Vari-Lite International). The company's Lightolier division is developing new safety lighting products that feature nickel metal hydride batteries for use in the event of power failures. Genlyte Thomas' Canada-based division, Canlyte, has introduced Symmetry Thermoplastic LED Exit emergency signage products.

EXECUTIVES

Chairman, President, and CEO: Larry K. Powers, age 60, $200,000 pay
CFO: William G. (Bill) Ferko, age 48
President, Lightolier Division: Zia Eftekhar, age 57, $200,000 pay
Director, Human Resources: Manny Cadima
VP, Sales, Central and East Region, Canlyte Division: Pierre Vincent
VP, Sales, Central and West Region, Canlyte Division: Terry Madden
CIO: Rick Blanchard
Auditors: Ernst & Young LLP

LOCATIONS

HQ: 10350 Ormsby Park Place, Ste. 601, Louisville, KY 40223
Phone: 502-420-9500 **Fax:** 502-420-9540
Web: www.genlytethomas.com

Genlyte Thomas Group operates facilities in Canada, Mexico, and the US.

2002 Sales

	$ mil.	% of total
US	814.2	84
Other countries	156.1	16
Total	**970.3**	**100**

PRODUCTS/OPERATIONS

Selected Brands

Bronzelite
Canlyte
Capri
Day-Brite
Emco
Gardco
Hadco
Ledalite
Lightolier
Lite-Energy
Lumec
Matrix
mcPhilben
Stonco
Translite
Thomas Lighting
ZED

COMPETITORS

Catalina Lighting
Cooper Industries
Dann Dee
GE
Hubbell
Jacuzzi Brands
Juno Lighting
Leviton
LSI Industries
Luminex Lighting
Philips Electronics
Sonepar USA
VLPS
WKI Holding

HISTORICAL FINANCIALS

Company Type: Joint venture

Income Statement FYE: December 31

	REVENUE ($ mil.)	NET INCOME ($ mil.)	NET PROFIT MARGIN	EMPLOYEES
12/02	970	41	4.2%	5,076
12/01	985	85	8.6%	5,314
12/00	1,008	36	3.6%	3,317
12/99	978	79	8.1%	1,060
12/98	624	27	4.2%	—
Annual Growth	11.7%	11.6%	—	68.6%

2002 Year-End Financials

Debt ratio: 11.2%
Return on equity: 12.1%
Cash ($ mil.): 112
Current ratio: 2.58
Long-term debt ($ mil.): 33

Net Income History

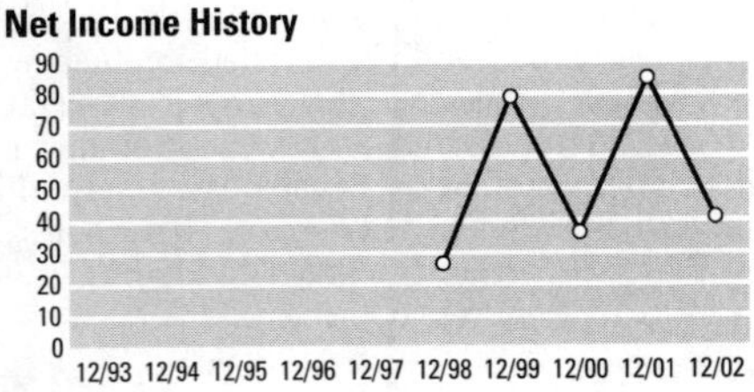

Genmar Holdings, Inc.

Genmar Holdings trolls for sales by cruising the pleasure boat market with a line of luxury yachts, recreational powerboats, and fishing boats. The company builds more than 400 different boat models ranging in size from 60-foot yachts (servants not included) to fishing skiffs. Its brands include Glastron, Ranger, and Wellcraft. Genmar markets its boats through about 1,800 independent dealers in the US and 30 other countries. The company — which is a combination of 16 different boat manufacturers acquired over 25 years — is controlled by chairman Irwin Jacobs (investor and former corporate raider). In 2001, through JTC Acquisitions, Genmar acquired bankrupt Outboard Marine's US boating and trailer assets.

EXECUTIVES

Chairman: Irwin L. Jacobs
President and CEO: Grant E. Oppegaard
EVP and CFO: Roger R. Cloutier II
EVP, Operations: David Vigdal
SVP and Controller: Mark W. Peters
SVP, Marketing: George E. Sullivan
SVP, Operations: Marcia M. Kull

LOCATIONS

HQ: 80 S. 8th St., Minneapolis, MN 55402
Phone: 612-339-7600 **Fax:** 612-337-1930
Web: www.genmar.com

Genmar Holdings has manufacturing facilities in Arkansas, Florida, Kansas, Minnesota, North Carolina, Wisconsin, and Canada.

PRODUCTS/OPERATIONS

Selected Brands

Aquasport
Carver
Champion
Crestliner
Four Winns
Genmar by Zodiac
Glastron
Hydra Sports
Larson
Lowe
Lund
Ranger
Seaswirl
Stratos
Triumph
Trojan
Wellcraft

COMPETITORS

Bénéteau
Brunswick
Cigarette Racing Team
Fountain Powerboat
Yamaha Motor

HISTORICAL FINANCIALS

Company Type: Private

Income Statement FYE: June 30

	REVENUE ($ mil.)	NET INCOME ($ mil.)	NET PROFIT MARGIN	EMPLOYEES
6/02	1,200	—	—	6,500
6/01	990	—	—	7,000
6/00	858	—	—	6,500
6/99	705	—	—	4,600
6/98	586	—	—	4,700
6/97	261	—	—	4,700
6/96	618	—	—	4,900
6/95	549	—	—	5,200
6/94	499	—	—	5,100
6/93	409	—	—	—
Annual Growth	12.7%	—	—	3.1%

Revenue History

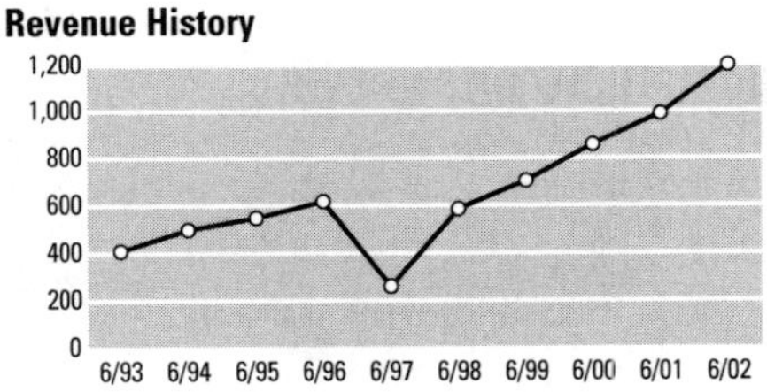

GeoLogistics Corporation

GeoLogistics gets goods going, globally. The company's integrated logistics offerings include multimodal freight forwarding, customs brokerage, warehousing and distribution, supply chain management, and trade-show logistics. GeoLogistics provides real-time shipment tracking through its Internet-based GeoVista logistics software system. The company has operations in 140 countries. To focus on core logistics operations, GeoLogistics has sold its moving van unit, The Bekins Company. Investment firms Questor Management, William E. Simon & Sons, and Oaktree Capital Management control GeoLogistics, which was founded in 1996.

EXECUTIVES

President and CEO: William J. (Bill) Flynn
EVP Finance: Steve Davison
SVP and Chief Logistics Officer: Scott T. Brinks
SVP Marketing: Christopher Logan
VP Finance: Michael Bible
VP and General Counsel: Ronald (Ron) Jackson
Regional CEO, GeoLogistics Asia/Pacific: Wolfgang Hollermann
Regional CEO, Europe, Middle East, and Africa: Karl Nutzinger
Regional Director, Eastern Europe: Rainer Haverkamp
CEO, GeoLogistics SpA: Domenico Tafuro
CEO, Benelux: Thomas Egbers
CEO, Indonesia: Jeremy Foxon
President, Matrix International Logistics: Abe Ranish
CIO: Joseph R. (Joe) Szmadzinski
Director, Human Resources, GeoLogistics Americas: Bob Westman
Auditors: Ernst & Young LLP

LOCATIONS

HQ: 1251 E. Dyer Rd., Ste. 200, Santa Ana, CA 92705
Phone: 714-513-3000 **Fax:** 714-513-3120
Web: www.geo-logistics.com

PRODUCTS/OPERATIONS

Selected Services

Air and ocean freight forwarding
Customs brokerage
Distribution and warehousing
Inventory management
Packaging, transportation, unpacking
Packing and crating
Real-time shipment tracking
Trade show and exhibition services

COMPETITORS

APL
APL Logistics
BAX Global
C.H. Robinson Worldwide
CNF
EGL
Exel
Expeditors
Panalpina
Stinnes

HISTORICAL FINANCIALS

Company Type: Private

Income Statement FYE: December 31

	REVENUE ($ mil.)	NET INCOME ($ mil.)	NET PROFIT MARGIN	EMPLOYEES
12/02	1,200	—	—	6,000
12/01	1,000	—	—	6,000
12/00	1,500	—	—	6,000
12/99	1,558	—	—	6,200
12/98	1,600	—	—	6,300
12/97	1,525	—	—	6,000
12/96	1,639	—	—	6,352
Annual Growth	(5.1%)	—	—	(0.9%)

Revenue History

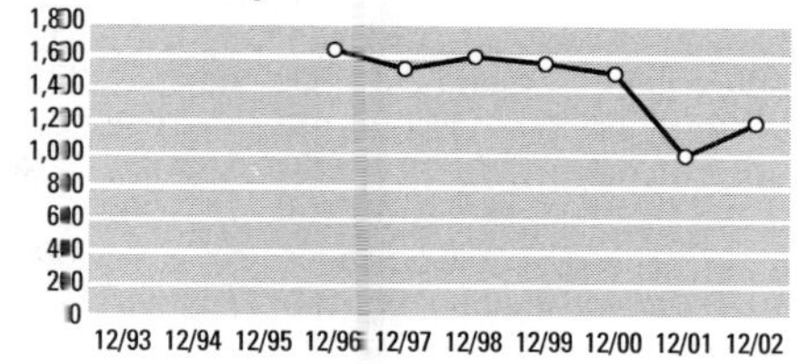

George E. Warren Corporation

By barge, by pipeline, by tank truck, by George, George E. Warren is a major private wholesale distributor of petroleum in the eastern US. Founded in Boston by George E. Warren in 1907 as a coal and oil distributor, it moved to Florida in the early 1990s. The company distributes product mostly by barge and pipeline, though it uses some tank trucks as well. Warren has distribution facilities in the southeastern and southwestern US. It distributes products including ethylene and heating oil to various industries. President and CEO Thomas Corr owns the company.

EXECUTIVES

President and CEO: Thomas L. Corr
CFO and Controller: Michael E. George
Director Human Resources: Martin Paris

LOCATIONS

HQ: 605 17th St., Vero Beach, FL 32960
Phone: 772-778-7100 **Fax:** 772-778-7171
Web: www.gewarren.com

COMPETITORS

ConocoPhillips
Crown Central Petroleum
Entergy
Exxon Mobil
Koch
Lyondell Chemical
Martin Resource Management
Penn Octane
Sun Coast Resources
Valley National Gases
Western Gas
Williams Companies

HISTORICAL FINANCIALS

Company Type: Private

Income Statement FYE: December 31

	REVENUE ($ mil.)	NET INCOME ($ mil.)	NET PROFIT MARGIN	EMPLOYEES
12/02	3,000	—	—	25
12/01	3,200	—	—	25
12/00	2,000	—	—	25
12/99	1,281	—	—	25
12/98	1,406	—	—	25
12/97	2,602	—	—	24
12/96	2,313	—	—	23
Annual Growth	4.4%	—	—	1.4%

Revenue History

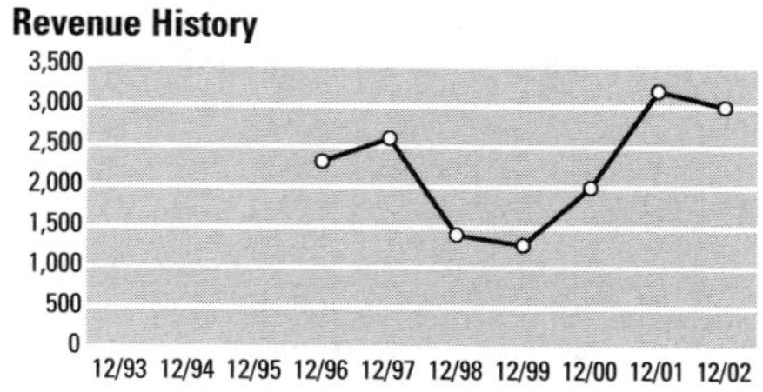

Georgia Crown Distributing

Aptly named Fate D. Leebern may have died for Georgia Crown Distributing, a beverage bottler and distributor. He founded Georgia Crown as Columbus Wine Company Distributor in 1938, the same year Georgia prohibition was repealed. After the first rail shipment of legal liquor was received, someone — reportedly the Dixie Mafia — murdered Leebern. Today the family-owned company distributes beer, wine, liquor, bottled water, juices, and soft drinks to Georgia, Alabama, and Tennessee. The bottler also distributes its brand of bottled water, Melwood Springs. CEO Donald Leebern Jr. is the grandson of the company's founder. The Leebern family owns the business.

Georgia Crown is moving its headquarters northeast from Columbus, Georgia, to a $12 million facility in Henry County.

EXECUTIVES

Chairman and CEO: Donald M. Leebern Jr., age 63
President: Donald M. Leebern III
CFO: Orlene Bovaird
VP Human Resources: Mary Beth Gibbon

LOCATIONS

HQ: Georgia Crown Distributing Company
7 Crown Cir., Columbus, GA 31907
Phone: 706-568-4580 **Fax:** 706-561-1647
Web: www.georgiacrown.com

Georgia Crown Distributing Company has facilities throughout Georgia in Albany, Atlanta, Augusta, and Savannah as well as operations in Alabama and Tennessee.

COMPETITORS

Buffalo Rock
Coca-Cola Bottling Consolidated
Coca-Cola Enterprises
Constellation Brands
Gambrinus
Johnson Brothers
Molson
National Beverage
National Distributing
Nestlé
Pernod Ricard
Rémy Cointreau
Southern Wine & Spirits
Sunbelt Beverage
Suntory

HISTORICAL FINANCIALS

Company Type: Private

Income Statement FYE: July 31

	REVENUE ($ mil.)	NET INCOME ($ mil.)	NET PROFIT MARGIN	EMPLOYEES
12/02*	730	—	—	1,600
7/01	730	—	—	1,665
7/00	710	—	—	1,600
7/99	700	—	—	1,600
7/98	675	—	—	1,600
7/97	670	—	—	1,600
7/96	656	—	—	1,600
7/95	648	—	—	1,600
7/94	645	—	—	1,600
7/93	—	—	—	1,700
Annual Growth	1.6%	—	—	(0.7%)

*Fiscal year change (since changed back to July)

Revenue History

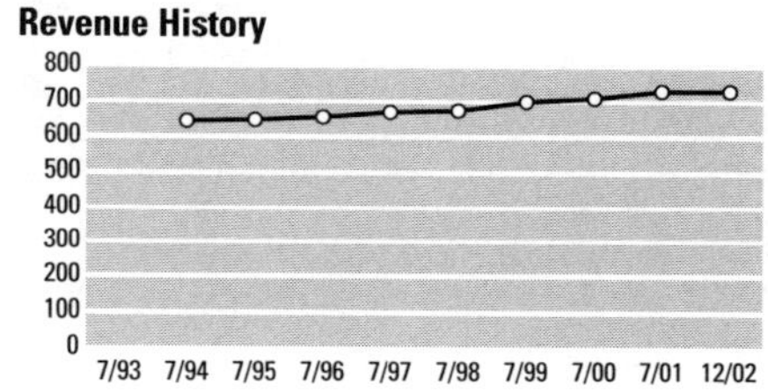

G-I Holdings

G-I Holdings (formerly GAF Corporation) works to keep a roof over your head. It is one of the US's oldest sources for commercial and residential roofing materials, with more than 25 plants. Subsidiary Building Materials Corporation of America makes flashing, vents, and complete roofing systems. Other products include residential shingles (Timberline and Sovereign brands) and GAF CompositeRoof for commercial asphalt roofing. Customers include contractors, distributors, and retail outlets such as The Home Depot. G-I Holdings has filed for bankruptcy protection due to asbestos liability claims. Chairman Samuel Heyman owns 99% of the company and all of affiliate International Specialty Products Inc.

EXECUTIVES

Chairman: Samuel J. Heyman, age 64
President, CEO, General Counsel, and Secretary: Richard A. Weinberg, age 43
SVP, CFO, and Treasurer: Susan B. Yoss, age 44
VP Human Resources: Gary Schneid

LOCATIONS

HQ: G-I Holdings, Inc.
1361 Alps Rd., Wayne, NJ 07470
Phone: 973-628-3000 **Fax:** 973-628-3326

G-I Holdings operates 26 plants throughout the US.

PRODUCTS/OPERATIONS

Selected Residential Products

Laminated shingles (Timberline)
Roofing systems (Weather Stopper)
Specialty shingles (Slateline)
Strip shingles (Sovereign)

COMPETITORS

Bridgestone
Carlisle Companies
ElkCorp
Formica
Johns Manville
NCI Building Systems
Owens Corning

HISTORICAL FINANCIALS

Company Type: Private

Income Statement FYE: December 31

	REVENUE ($ mil.)	NET INCOME ($ mil.)	NET PROFIT MARGIN	EMPLOYEES
12/02	1,300	—	—	3,400
12/01	1,293	—	—	3,400
12/00	1,200	—	—	3,500
12/99	1,140	—	—	3,500
12/98	1,088	—	—	3,300
12/97	945	—	—	3,000
12/96	1,568	—	—	5,209
12/95	1,339	—	—	5,400
12/94	1,156	—	—	4,500
12/93	1,069	—	—	4,350
Annual Growth	2.2%	—	—	(2.7%)

Revenue History

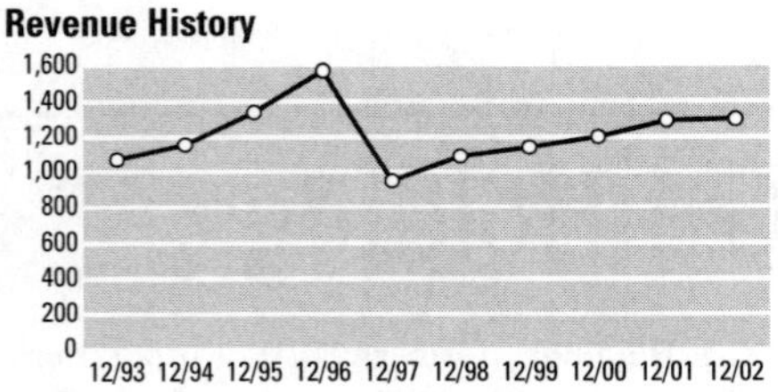

Giant Eagle, Inc.

With its talons firmly wrapped around western Pennsylvania, Giant Eagle is eyeing new territory. The grocery chain is the #1 food retailer in Pittsburgh, and it has about 130 corporate and 83 franchised supermarkets (about 60,000 sq. ft. in size) throughout Maryland, western Pennsylvania, Ohio, and north central West Virginia. In addition to food, many Giant Eagle stores feature video rental, banking, photo processing, and ready-to-eat meals. Giant Eagle is also a wholesaler to the licensed stores and sells groceries to other retail chains. Chairman and CEO David Shapira is the grandson of one of the five men who founded the company in 1931. The founders' families own Giant Eagle.

As with other birds of the retailing feather, Giant Eagle's supermarkets carry private-label brands (Eagle Valley and Giant Eagle) and nonfood items; many have pharmacies.

Giant Eagle became the #1 food seller in eastern Ohio through a 1997 acquisition, and the supermarket chain has expanded to Cleveland, Toledo, and Columbus. The company's goal is to grow Giant Eagle food and drug sales through a combination of acquisitions and organic growth to $9 billion by 2007. To that end, in 2002 Giant Eagle launched a successful bid for the remaining assets of bankrupt discount durgstore chain Phar-Mor.

The company is launching a new convenience store chain called GetGo from Giant Eagle. Of the initial 30 GetGo stores, some are located next to Giant Eagle supermarkets, while others are larger (4,500 sq. ft.) stand-alone structures. Both formats feature fresh foods and sell gas.

HISTORY

When Joe Porter, Ben Chait, and Joe Goldstein sold their chain of 125 Eagle grocery stores in Pittsburgh to Kroger in 1928, the agreement stated that the men would have to leave the grocery business for three years. In retrospect, Kroger should have made the term last for the length of their lives, because in 1931 the three men joined the owners of OK Grocery — Hyman Moravitz and Morris Weizenbaum — and launched a new chain of grocery stores called Giant Eagle. Eventually, the chain would knock Kroger out of the Pittsburgh market.

Although slowed by the Great Depression, the chain expanded, fighting such large rivals as Acme, A&P, and Kroger for Pittsburgh's food shoppers. The stores were mom-and-pop operations with over-the-counter service until they began converting to self-service during the 1940s. Store sizes expanded to nearly 15,000 sq. ft. in the 1950s. During that time Giant Eagle, with about 30 stores, launched Blue Stamps in answer to Green Stamps and other loyalty programs.

It phased out trading stamps in the 1960s in lieu of everyday low prices. To accommodate its growth, in 1968 Giant Eagle acquired a warehouse in Lawrenceville, Pennsylvania, that more than doubled its storage area. Also that year the firm opened its first 20,000-sq.-ft. Giant Eagle store.

During the inflationary 1970s Giant Eagle introduced generic items and began offering the Food Club line, a private-label brand, in conjunction with wholesaler Topco. It continued its expansion, and by 1979 it had become Pittsburgh's #1 supermarket chain, as chains such as Kroger, Acme, and A&P were leaving the city. In 1981 Giant Eagle, with 52 stores, acquired Tamarkin, a wholesale and retail chain in Youngstown, Ohio, part-owned by the Monus family. The purchase moved it into the franchise business, and later that year the first independent Giant Eagle store opened in Monaca (outside Pittsburgh).

The Tamarkin purchase brought together Mickey Monus and Giant Eagle CEO David Shapira, grandson of founder Goldstein. In 1982 they created Phar-Mor, a deep-discount drugstore chain (Wal-Mart's Sam Walton once said it was the only competitor he truly feared). From a single store in Niles, Ohio, Phar-Mor grew rapidly to 310 outlets in 32 states in the early 1990s.

Phar-Mor president Monus helped found the World Basketball League (WBL) in 1987 and became the owner of three teams. In 1992 an auditor discovered two unexplainable Phar-Mor checks to the WBL totaling about $100,000. Investigators soon uncovered three years of overstated inventories and a false set of books; Shapira (who was also CEO of Phar-Mor), Giant Eagle owners (which held a 50% stake in Phar-Mor until 1992), and other investors had been duped of more than $1 billion. Shapira fired Monus and his cronies on July 31, 1992. The next day the WBL folded; about two weeks after that Phar-Mor filed for Chapter 11 bankruptcy. A mistrial in 1994 couldn't save Monus from prison; he was reindicted in 1995 and sentenced to 20 years (later reduced to 12).

Giant Eagle made its largest acquisition in 1997, paying $403 million for Riser Foods, a wholesaler (American Seaway Foods) with 35 company-owned stores under the Rini-Rego Stop-n-Shop banner. The stores were converted to the Giant Eagle banner in 1998 (another 18 independent Stop-n-Shop stores were also converted).

In 2000 Giant Eagle opened several stores in Columbus, Ohio. The grocer moved into Maryland in 2001 when it acquired six Country Market stores in Maryland and Pennsylvania. Also in 2001, the grocer founded ECHO Real Estate Services Co. to develop retail, housing, and golf course projects.

In 2002 Giant Eagle was among the winning bidders for the remaining assets of bankrupt Phar-Mor, acquiring leases to 10 Phar-Mor stores and the inventory and prescription lists for 27 stores.

The retailer scrapped its plan to sell its transportation business and signed a new five-year contract with its union delivery drivers in September 2003.

EXECUTIVES

Chairman and CEO: David S. (Dave) Shapira, age 61
Vice Chairman: Anthony C. Rego
President and COO: Raymond Burgo
EVP, Business Systems: Jack Flanagan
SVP and CFO: Mark Minnaugh
SVP, Distribution: Larry Baldauf
SVP, Information Services: Russ Ross
SVP, Marketing: Laura Karet
SVP, Meat and Seafood: Ed Steinmetz
VP, Advertising and Corporate Brand Marketing: Kevin Srigley
VP, Logistics: Bill Parry
VP, Personnel: Raymond A. Huber
VP, Pharmacy: Randy Heiser
Director, Communications: Rob Borella
Director, Floral and Greeting Cards: Tina Flowers
Director, Iggle Entertainment and Video: Chuck Porter
Director, Knowledge Strategies: Robert (Bob) Guy
Director, Prepared Foods: Lou Coppola

LOCATIONS

HQ: 101 Kappa Dr., Pittsburgh, PA 15238
Phone: 412-963-6200 **Fax:** 412-968-1617
Web: www.gianteagle.com

2003 Stores

	No.
Ohio	
Cleveland	46
Youngstown	29
Akron/Canton	26
Columbus	5
Toledo	2
Pennsylvania	
Pittsburgh	71
Johnstown	11
Erie	9
Lake	5
West Virginia	6
Maryland	4
Total	**214**

PRODUCTS/OPERATIONS

Private Labels

Eagle Valley
Giant Eagle

Selected Services

Bakery	Greeting cards
Banking services	Pharmacy
Childcare	Photo developing
Deli department	Ready-to-eat meals
Dry cleaning	Ticketmaster outlet
Fresh seafood	Video rental

COMPETITORS

Ahold USA	Kroger
Giant Food	SUPERVALU
A&P	Wal-Mart
Heinen's	Wegmans
IGA	Weis Markets

HISTORICAL FINANCIALS

Company Type: Private

Income Statement

FYE: June 30

	ESTIMATED REVENUE ($ mil.)	NET INCOME ($ mil.)	NET PROFIT MARGIN	EMPLOYEES
6/02	4,415	—	—	26,000
6/01	4,435	—	—	25,600
6/00	4,221	—	—	25,600
6/99	4,360	—	—	25,600
6/98	4,050	—	—	25,000
6/97	3,800	—	—	19,200
6/96	2,200	—	—	12,000
6/95	2,100	—	—	7,200
6/94	2,000	—	—	7,200
6/93	2,000	—	—	11,800
Annual Growth	9.2%	—	—	9.2%

Revenue History

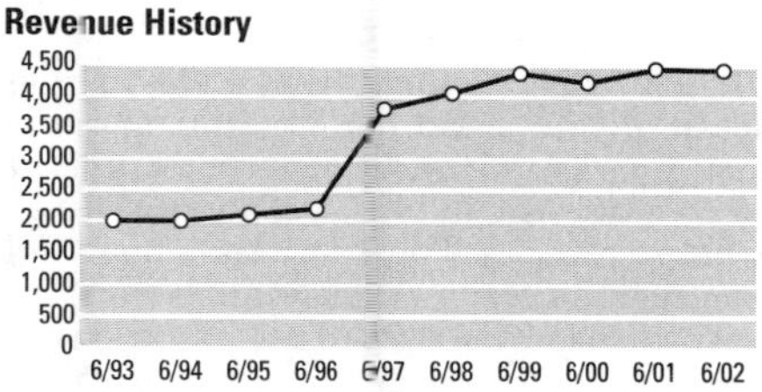

Gilbane, Inc.

Family-owned Gilbane has been the bane of its rivals for four generations. Subsidiary Gilbane Building provides construction management, contracting, and design and build services to construct office buildings, manufacturing plants, schools, prisons, and more for the firm's governmental, commercial, and industrial clients. Landmark projects include work on the National Air and Space Museum, Lake Placid's 1980 Winter Olympics facilities, and the new WWII memorial in Washington, DC. Another subsidiary, Gilbane Properties, develops and finances public and private projects and acts as a property manager. Chairman and CEO Paul Choquette is a descendant of William and Thomas Gilbane, who founded the firm in 1873.

EXECUTIVES

Chairman and CEO, Gilbane and Gilbane Building Company: Paul J. Choquette Jr., age 64
SVP and CFO: Ken Alderman
SVP Advanced Technologies Sector: J. Philip Southerland Jr.
SVP Sales and Marketing: Alfred K. Potter
VP and CIO: Keith Authelet
VP Human Resources: Dan M. Kelly
President and CEO, Gilbane Properties: Robert V. Gilbane
President and COO, Gilbane Building Company: Thomas F. Gilbane Jr.
EVP, Gilbane Building Company: William J. Gilbane Jr.
Director Corporate Communications: Wesley C. Cotter
Director Marketing: Geff Bottomley

LOCATIONS

HQ: 7 Jackson Walkway, Providence, RI 02903
Phone: 401-456-5800 **Fax:** 401-456-5936
Web: www.gilbaneinc.com

PRODUCTS/OPERATIONS

Selected Markets

Aviation	Infrastructure
Corporate	Library
Criminal justice	Life sciences
Education	Public assembly
Government	Waste and wastewater
Health care	

Subsidiaries

Gilbane Building Company
Gilbane Properties, Inc.

COMPETITORS

BE&K	McCarthy Building
Bechtel	Parsons
Black & Veatch	Perini
Bovis Lend Lease	Skanska
Clark Enterprises	Structure Tone
Fluor	Swinerton
Hunt Construction	Turner Corporation
Jacobs Engineering	Whiting-Turner
M. A. Mortenson	York Hunter

HISTORICAL FINANCIALS

Company Type: Private

Income Statement

FYE: December 31

	REVENUE ($ mil.)	NET INCOME ($ mil.)	NET PROFIT MARGIN	EMPLOYEES
12/02	2,771	—	—	1,700
12/01	2,658	—	—	1,700
12/00	2,388	—	—	1,510
12/99	2,179	—	—	900
12/98	2,200	—	—	1,200
12/97	1,923	—	—	1,148
12/96	1,848	—	—	993
12/95	1,371	—	—	1,000
12/94	1,249	—	—	958
12/93	936	—	—	843
Annual Growth	12.8%	—	—	8.1%

Revenue History

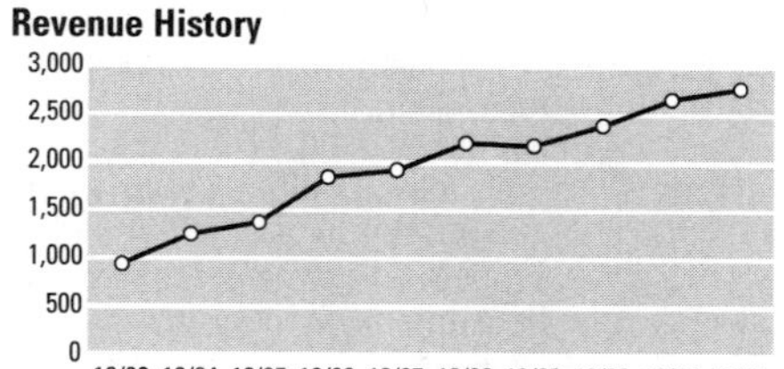

Gilster-Mary Lee Corporation

Breakfast is the most important meal of the day, especially at Gilster-Mary Lee. One of the largest private-label cereal manufacturers in the US (along with Ralcorp Holdings), Gilster-Mary Lee makes nearly 500 private-label products including cereal, cake, cocoa, dinner, and drink mixes; pasta; and popcorn. The company's customers include major US grocery chains and food wholesalers. The firm also offers products under its own Hospitality brand. The Gilster family founded the company as a flour mill in 1895 and began making cake mixes in the 1950s. Gilster-Mary Lee is led by president and CEO Donald Welge and his brother, CFO Michael Welge; the two are great-nephews of the company's founders.

EXECUTIVES

President and CEO: Donald Welge, age 67
CFO: Michael Welge, age 62
SVP, Sales and Marketing: Sheldon Geitelman
Director, Human Resources: Robert Welge

LOCATIONS

HQ: 1037 State St., Chester, IL 62233
Phone: 618-826-2361 **Fax:** 618-826-2973
Web: www.gilstermarylee.com

COMPETITORS

American Italian Pasta
Aurora Foods
Barilla
Borden Chemical
ConAgra
General Mills
Hershey
Kellogg
Kraft Foods
Malt-O-Meal
New World Pasta
Ralcorp

HISTORICAL FINANCIALS

Company Type: Private

Income Statement

FYE: December 31

	REVENUE ($ mil.)	NET INCOME ($ mil.)	NET PROFIT MARGIN	EMPLOYEES
12/01	615	—	—	4,000
12/00	585	—	—	3,800
12/99	500	—	—	3,600
12/98	483	—	—	3,500
Annual Growth	8.4%	—	—	4.6%

Revenue History

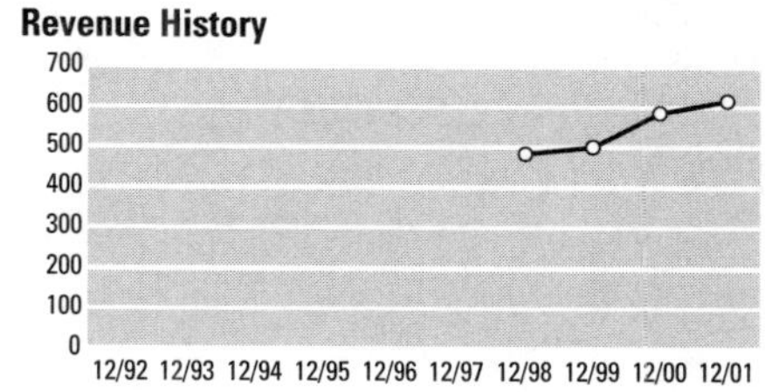

Glazer's Wholesale Drug Company, Inc.

Glazer's Wholesale Drug, named during Prohibition when only drugstores and drug wholesalers could deal in liquor, is a wholesale distributor of alcoholic beverages. It is the largest distributor of malts, spirits, and wines in Texas and one of the largest US wine and spirits distributors. It also operates in Arizona (Alliance Beverage), Arkansas, Indiana (Olinger Distributing), Iowa, Kansas, Louisiana, Missouri, and Ohio. The company distributes Robert Mondavi wines, Brown-Forman and Bacardi spirits, and Diageo products, among others. Glazer's has been acquiring wholesalers and distributors in the Midwest, including Mid-Continent Distributor (Missouri). CEO Bennett Glazer and family own Glazer's.

In 2003 Glazer's bought a 50% stake in Union Beverage Co. (a subsidiary of National Wine & Spirits Inc.) to move distribution into Illinois. In June 2003 the company became the sole provider of Diageo brands in Dallas and Houston as part of Diageo's consolidation of its Texas distributors.

EXECUTIVES

Chairman and CEO: Bennett Glazer
President: Jerry Cargill
VP and CFO: Cary Rossel
EVP and COO: Barkley J. Stuart
EVP and Secretary: Mike Glazer
VP, Operations: Jack Westenborg
VP, Sales and Marketing: Don Pratt
VP, Business Development: Mike Maxwell
VP and CIO: Mike Adams
VP, Business and Marketing: George Trilikis
Director of Corporate Account Sales: Jim Grace
Director of Domaines and Estates: James Gunter
Director of Training: Bill Saul
Director of Chain Account Sales: Mike Williams
Director of Human Resources: Rusty Harmount

LOCATIONS

HQ: 14860 Landmark Blvd., Dallas, TX 75254
Phone: 972-702-0900 **Fax:** 972-702-8508
Web: www.glazers.com

COMPETITORS

Ben E. Keith
Block Distributing
Constellation Brands
Gallo
Gambrinus
Johnson Brothers
National Distributing
National Wine & Spirits
Rémy Cointreau
Southern Wine & Spirits
Tarrant Distributors
Wirtz

HISTORICAL FINANCIALS

Company Type: Private

Income Statement FYE: December 31

	REVENUE ($ mil.)	NET INCOME ($ mil.)	NET PROFIT MARGIN	EMPLOYEES
12/01	1,600	—	—	3,600
12/00	1,480	—	—	3,200
12/99	1,110	—	—	2,700
12/98	855	—	—	2,700
12/97	758	—	—	2,500
12/96	670	—	—	1,850
12/95	590	—	—	1,100
12/94	520	—	—	1,000
12/93	470	—	—	1,000
12/92	385	—	—	1,050
Annual Growth	17.1%	—	—	14.7%

Revenue History

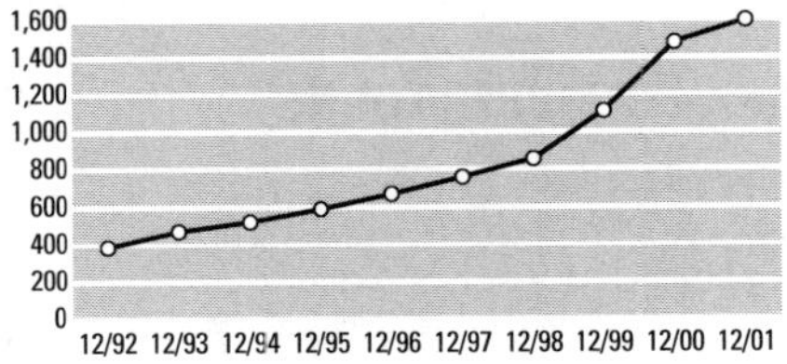

Gold Kist Inc.

At Gold Kist, the chickens don't even get to see the road, much less cross it. An agricultural cooperative of 2,500 farmers (mainly in the South), Gold Kist is a major processor and plucker in the US poultry industry. It markets whole and cut-up chickens, chicken parts, and other processed products under brands such as Gold Kist Farms and Young 'n Tender to grocery chains, the food service and institutional food industries, and export markets. It also markets hogs, provides financing for farmers, and builds and installs industrial wastewater treatment systems.

The company divides its operations geographically into cooperative broiler divisions, each with its own chicken flocks, hatcheries, feed mill, and processing plant.

Gold Kist has seen an increase in demand owing to concerns about mad cow disease and to a weakened economy that favors chicken over its more expensive rival, beef. However, the Russian embargo on US chicken challenged the company on two counts. First it meant losses of export sales to that country, and secondly it meant an oversupply of chicken parts in domestic markets that drove overall prices down.

HISTORY

Georgia native David Brooks, a University of Georgia agronomy professor from the age of 19, left teaching to form Georgia Cooperative Cotton Producers Association in 1933. A Depression-era creation, Brooks saw the Carrollton, Georgia, cotton marketing cooperative as a way to improve the economic well-being of its members through collective price bargaining and the elimination of middlemen. By the end of its first year, Georgia Cotton Producers had grown from 13 members to about 7,000. The co-op expanded into neighboring states during the 1930s and dropped "Georgia" from its name.

The cooperative diversified in the 1940s and 1950s. During WWII the enterprise made ammunition at its fertilizer plants. Cotton Producers moved into pecan and peanut production in 1950s under the Gold Kist label. It also established itself as a major exporter of agricultural products, setting up sales offices in Europe in the late 1940s and Asia and the Middle East in the 1950s. The Gold Kist moniker was slowly adopted as the co-op's name over the next 20 years. When Brooks stepped down from full-time leadership in 1968, Gold Kist was the South's largest farm cooperative.

In the late 1970s the energy crisis, bad harvests, and other factors led to a decline in cooperatives, including Gold Kist, which posted a loss in 1980. The co-op founded Golden Poultry in 1982 to run the Georgia-based broiler complex acquired earlier that year by Agri International, another of its subsidiaries. In 1986 Gold Kist spun off 27% of Golden Poultry, the first farmer-owned cooperative to make such a move. North Carolina-based Carolina Golden Products (a poultry processor partnership between Gold Kist and Golden Poultry) was merged into the company that year.

Gold Kist combined its peanut operations with Archer Daniels Midland's in 1987, forming Golden Peanut Company. Alimenta Processing, the Georgia-based unit of a Swiss firm, became part of Golden Peanut two years later.

The co-op opened its Russellville, Alabama, facility in 1990, increasing its processed-chicken production capacity by half and entering the fast-food market. The co-op moved into pork and pet food processing and catfish farming. Gold Kist merged its pecan operations into Young Pecan Company in 1992. It also beefed up exports (from about $46 million in 1990 to more than $70 million in 1995).

In 1997 Gold Kist bought back the stake in Golden Poultry it did not own. Although low poultry prices and troubled foreign markets hit the company hard in 1998, it continued its plan to focus on food, selling its wholesale and retail farm supply assets — including 100 stores, as well as grain buying stations and cotton gins — to the Southern States agricultural cooperative. After reporting a $26 million loss in sales, Gold Kist announced cost-cutting measures in 2000 that included cutbacks in production and a salary freeze.

In 2001 the company recalled more than 420,000 pounds of chicken that may have been contaminated with an insecticide, but it did make a profit that year of more than $33 million, thanks in part to more export sales as a result of concerns about mad cow disease. Also that year the company divested its 25% stake in Golden Peanut Company and discontinued its aquaculture operations.

During 2002 Golden Kist continued to exit non-core businesses by ending its relationship with a pecan processor.

EXECUTIVES

Chairman: Douglas A. Reeves Sr., age 62
President and CEO: John Bekkers, age 58, $522,115 pay
CFO and Treasurer: Stephen O. West, age 57, $207,211 pay
SVP Planning and Administration: Michael A. Stimpert, age 58, $284,000 pay
VP, General Counsel, and Secretary: J. David Dyson, age 56
VP, Human Resources: Harry T. McDonald, age 58

VP, Information Services: Sandra W. Kearney, age 44
VP, Marketing and Sales: Jerry L. Stewart, age 62, $240,769 pay
VP, Operations: Donald W. Mabe, age 49, $210,769 pay
VP, Purchasing: Marshall Smitherman, age 61
VP, Science and Technology: Allen C. Merritt, age 57
Controller: W. F. Pohl Jr., age 53
Sales Manager, National Accounts: Kevin Ledford
Auditors: KPMG LLP

LOCATIONS

HQ: 244 Perimeter Center Pkwy. NE, Atlanta, GA 30346
Phone: 770-393-5000 **Fax:** 770-393-5262
Web: goldkist.com

Gold Kist has operations in Alabama, Florida, Georgia, North Carolina, and South Carolina.

PRODUCTS/OPERATIONS

Selected Brands

Big Value
Early Bird
Gold Kist Farms
Medallion
Young 'n Tender

COMPETITORS

Alabama Farmers Cooperatives
Cagle's
ConAgra Poultry
Perdue
Pilgrim's Pride
Sanderson Farms
Townsends
Tyson Foods
Wayne Farms LLC

HISTORICAL FINANCIALS

Company Type: Cooperative

Income Statement

FYE: Sunday nearest June 30

	REVENUE ($ mil.)	NET INCOME ($ mil.)	NET PROFIT MARGIN	EMPLOYEES
6/02	1,864	34	1.8%	18,000
6/01	1,811	33	1.8%	18,000
6/00	1,707	(26)	—	18,000
6/99	1,766	61	3.5%	17,500
6/98	1,651	(103)	—	18,000
6/97	2,289	12	0.5%	17,500
6/96	1,956	37	1.9%	16,500
6/95	1,689	12	0.7%	15,700
6/94	1,561	34	2.2%	14,000
6/93	1,401	27	1.9%	14,000
Annual Growth	3.2%	2.5%	—	2.8%

2002 Year-End Financials

Debt ratio: 88.5%
Return on equity: 12.3%
Cash ($ mil.): 9
Current ratio: 1.84
Long-term debt ($ mil.): 251

Net Income History

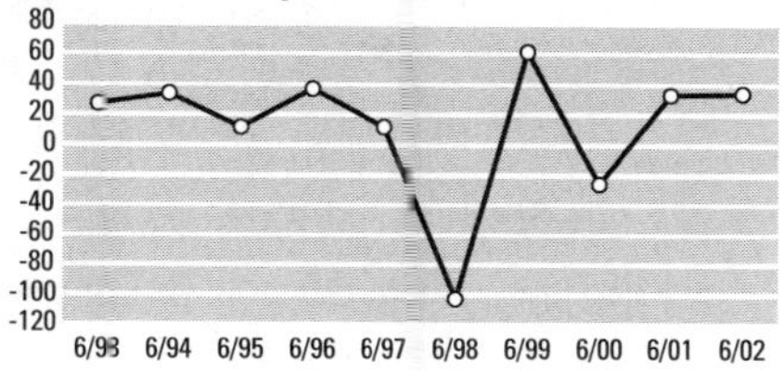

Golden Rule Insurance

Follow the golden rule and you will find insurance. Golden Rule Insurance provides health insurance, life insurance, and annuities. Other products include Asset-Care (a long-term care insurance policy that combines life insurance and asset management), ValuTerm (term life insurance), and WealthBuilder (fixed-rate annuities). Golden Rule Insurance operates across the US except in New York. Throughout the 1980s and 90s the company was accused of hardball tactics aimed at denying policyholder claims and denying sick and therefore high-risk customers.

The company focuses on group and individual health plans, which include employer-sponsored health plans and medical savings account plans.

EXECUTIVES

CEO: John Whelan
CFO: Patrick F. Carr
VP: Lee Tooman
Chief Investment Officer: Steven Pollack
President, Financial Services Division: Richard L. Merrill
Director of Human Resources: Rick Lane

LOCATIONS

HQ: Golden Rule Insurance Company
712 11th St., Lawrenceville, IL 62439
Phone: 618-943-8000 **Fax:** 618-943-8031
Web: www.goldenrule.com

COMPETITORS

Aetna
Fortis Health
UnitedHealth Group
WellPoint Health Networks

HISTORICAL FINANCIALS

Company Type: Private

Income Statement

FYE: December 31

	REVENUE ($ mil.)	NET INCOME ($ mil.)	NET PROFIT MARGIN	EMPLOYEES
12/02	893	—	—	650
12/01	829	—	—	700
12/00	829	—	—	1,084
12/99	729	—	—	1,000
12/98	742	—	—	1,500
Annual Growth	4.7%	—	—	(18.9%)

Revenue History

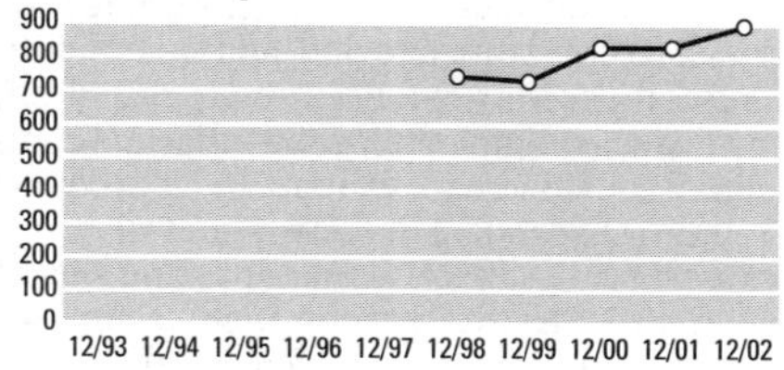

Golden State Foods

Did somebody say McDonald's? Food processor and distributor Golden State Foods is listening. The company is the fast-food giant's largest full-line supplier, providing its restaurants with more than 130 products. These include beef patties, the Big Mac sauce (which it helped formulate), buns, ketchup, mayonnaise, and salad dressing. Golden State Foods has 11 distribution centers in the US and overseas (Australia, Egypt, and Mexico) and operates two food processing plants in the US. The company was founded in 1947 by the late William Moore. Investment firm Yucaipa owns a majority of Golden State, while CEO Mark Wetterau's family-owned management company Wetterau Associates owns most of the rest.

Yucaipa and Wetterau Associates bought Golden State in 1998 from its management, which kept a small stake in the company.

Golden State Foods supplies more than 2,900 McDonald's restaurants throughout the US and worldwide. McDonald's and its suppliers have established a symbiotic relationship. Golden State Foods adheres to McDonald's standards and gears its operations toward furthering the restaurant chain's interests. The company serves McDonald's without the benefit of a long-term, written contract, but McDonald's is known for its loyalty to its suppliers.

EXECUTIVES

Chairman and CEO: Mark S. Wetterau
SEVP, Liquid Products Group: Frank Listi
EVP and CFO: Mike Waitukaitis
VP, Accounting and Information Services: Richard D. Moretti
VP, Human Resources: Steve Becker
VP, International: Phillip Crane
VP, Legal Affairs, General Counsel and Assistant Secretary: Michael J. Hoppe Jr.
President, Distribution: Robert (Bob) Jorge
President, Meat Group: David H. Gilbert
Assistant VP, Technical Services: T. Webber Neal
Director of Development: John Walter
West Coast Director, Liquid Products: Kevin Deary
West Coast Director, Meat Operations: Lenny Goler

LOCATIONS

HQ: 18301 Von Karman Ave., Ste. 1100, Irvine, CA 92612
Phone: 949-252-2000 **Fax:** 949-252-2080
Web: www.goldenstatefoods.com

Golden State Foods has distribution and processing facilities in Arizona, California, Georgia, Hawaii, New York, North Carolina, Oregon, South Carolina, Virginia, and Washington as well as Australia, Egypt, and Mexico.

PRODUCTS/OPERATIONS

Selected Products

Beef patties
Buns
Ketchup
Jelly
Lettuce
Mayonnaise
Onions
Salad dressing
Sundae toppings

COMPETITORS

JR Simplot
Keystone Foods
Martin-Brower
MBM
McLane Foodservice
Reyes Holdings
Services Group
Shamrock Foods
SYSCO
U.S. Foodservice

HISTORICAL FINANCIALS

Company Type: Private

Income Statement FYE: December 31

	ESTIMATED REVENUE ($ mil.)	NET INCOME ($ mil.)	NET PROFIT MARGIN	EMPLOYEES
12/01	1,800	—	—	2,000
12/00	1,764	—	—	2,000
12/99	1,750	—	—	2,000
12/98	1,600	—	—	1,800
12/97	1,500	—	—	2,000
12/96	1,450	—	—	2,000
12/95	1,340	—	—	1,700
12/94	1,260	—	—	1,700
12/93	1,160	—	—	1,700
12/92	1,032	—	—	1,700
Annual Growth	6.4%	—	—	1.8%

Revenue History

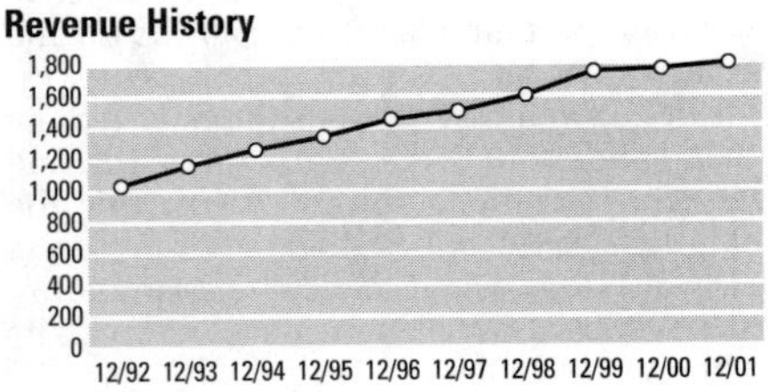

The Golub Corporation

Supermarket operator The Golub Corporation offers tasty come-ons such as table-ready meals, gift certificates, automatic discount cards, and a hotline where cooks answer food-related queries. Golub operates 100-plus Price Chopper supermarkets in Connecticut, Massachusetts, New Hampshire, upstate New York, northeastern Pennsylvania, and Vermont. It also runs Mini Chopper service stations and convenience stores. Golub has discontinued its HouseCalls home delivery service. Brothers Bill and Ben Golub founded the company in 1932. The Golub family owns 45% of the firm and has turned down offers to sell it. Employees own the other 55% of Golub.

EXECUTIVES

Chairman: Lewis Golub
President and CEO, Director: Neil M. Golub
CFO: John Endres
EVP and COO: Lawrence Zettle
EVP, Secretary and General Counsel: William Kenneally
SVP, Information Systems and CIO, Price Chopper: Tom Nowak
SVP, Sales and Merchandising: Tom Robbins
VP and Treasurer, Price Chopper: Jennifer Kenneally
VP, Human Resources: Margaret Davenport
Corporate Controller: Carol L. Cillis
Manager, Public Relations and Consumer Services: Mona Golub
Auditors: PricewaterhouseCoopers LLP

LOCATIONS

HQ: 501 Duanesburg Rd., Schenectady, NY 12306
Phone: 518-355-5000 **Fax:** 518-379-3597
Web: www.pricechopper.com

COMPETITORS

7-Eleven
Ahold USA
Big Y Foods
Cumberland Farms
DeMoulas Super Markets
A&P
Hannaford Bros.
Penn Traffic
Shaw's
Wal-Mart
Wegmans

HISTORICAL FINANCIALS

Company Type: Private

Income Statement FYE: April 30

	ESTIMATED REVENUE ($ mil.)	NET INCOME ($ mil.)	NET PROFIT MARGIN	EMPLOYEES
4/02	2,100	—	—	19,700
4/01	2,000	—	—	19,500
4/00	1,800	—	—	18,500
4/99	1,710	—	—	18,000
4/98	1,610	—	—	18,000
4/97	1,600	—	—	17,500
4/96	1,375	—	—	15,500
4/95	1,200	—	—	9,000
4/94	1,140	—	—	8,000
4/93	1,120	—	—	7,855
Annual Growth	7.2%	—	—	10.8%

Revenue History

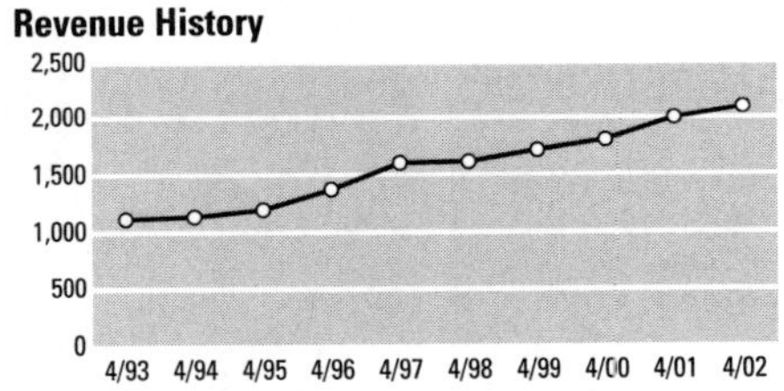

Goodman Manufacturing

Goodman knows how to cool off a hot situation. Goodman Manufacturing Company, through its Amana Heating and Air Conditioning, Goodman Manufacturing, and Quietflex divisions, makes air-conditioning, ventilation, and heating equipment for residential and commercial use. Goodman, which sells its products through independent installers and distributors worldwide, is among the top US makers of air conditioners. Its brands include Amana, Caloric, Goodman, GmC, Modern Maid, and Janitrol. The company sold its Amana Appliance division (washers, dryers, microwaves, and refrigerators) to Maytag. Goodman is owned by the family of Harold Goodman, who founded the company in 1977.

EXECUTIVES

Chairman: John B. Goodman
President and CEO: Charles A. Carroll
CFO: Larry Blackburn
EVP Human Resources: Donald R. King

LOCATIONS

HQ: Goodman Manufacturing Company, L.P.
2550 N. Loop West, Ste. 400, Houston, TX 77092
Phone: 713-861-2500 **Fax:** 713-861-2176
Web: www.goodmanmfg.com

Goodman Manufacturing Company has factories in Houston, Texas, and Dayton, Tennessee.

PRODUCTS/OPERATIONS

Selected Products

Air handlers
Cooling split systems
Ductless split systems
Evaporator coils
Gas furnaces
Heat pump split systems
Multi-family and apartment systems
Package heating/cooling systems
Room air conditioners

COMPETITORS

AAON
American Standard
Carrier
Continental Materials
Electrolux AB
Fedders
GE Consumer Products
Lennox
Maytag
Nortek
Paloma Industries
Samsung Electronics
Whirlpool
York International

HISTORICAL FINANCIALS

Company Type: Private

Income Statement FYE: December 31

	ESTIMATED REVENUE ($ mil.)	NET INCOME ($ mil.)	NET PROFIT MARGIN	EMPLOYEES
12/01	1,150	—	—	3,750
12/00	1,100	—	—	3,750
12/99	2,160	—	—	7,500
12/98	2,055	—	—	7,500
12/97	1,900	—	—	7,500
12/96	1,850	—	—	7,200
12/95	500	—	—	1,700
12/94	450	—	—	1,700
12/93	400	—	—	1,500
Annual Growth	14.1%	—	—	12.1%

Revenue History

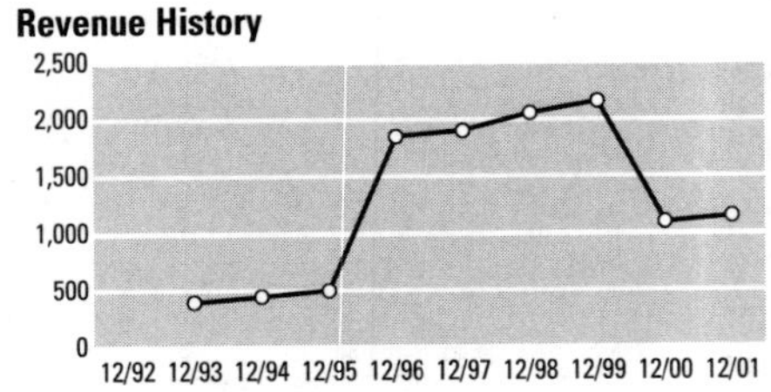

GT Brands

GT Brands (formerly GoodTimes Entertainment) hopes you find its celebrity-endorsed products Dy-No-Mite! The company sells videos and DVDs in niches such as animated features (*Rudolph the Red-Nosed Reindeer*), Christian entertainment (*Charlton Heston Presents The Bible*), and fitness instruction (Richard Simmons). GTE, which also has licensing and merchandising operations, distributes its products through retail outlets as well as TV (infomercials, home shopping channels), telemarketing, catalogs, direct mail, and the Web. The company was founded in 1984. Private investment firm Quadrangle Capital Partners (who counts InterActiveCorp CEO Barry Diller among its investors) purchased the company in 2003.

EXECUTIVES

CEO: Andrew Greenberg
COO: Gerard Love
CFO: Jonathan Boon
SVP, Legal and Business Affairs: Karen Charal Gross
VP, Licensing and Consumer Products: Pamela Ferris
President, GT Direct: Lynn Hamlin
President, Retail and Entertainment: William (Bill) Sondheim
Director, International: Myriam Diaz
Manager, Customer Services: Virginia Arias

LOCATIONS

HQ: 16 E. 40th St., New York, NY 10016
Phone: 212-951-3000 **Fax:** 212-951-9319
Web: www.goodtimes.com

PRODUCTS/OPERATIONS

Selected Brands

Beatrix Potter's Peter Rabbit and Friends, The Wind in the Willows, Berenstein Bears, Heroes and Legends of the Bible, Jekyll & Hyde, and Smokey Joe's Café
Cableflex
Charlton Heston's Bible Series
Cindy Crawford's exercise products
Debbie Allen's COPA hair care products
Joan Rivers' beauty, fashion, and decorative products
Leslie Sansone's fitness products
Richard Simmons' weight loss products
Rudolph the Red Nosed Reindeer
The Turbo Cooker

COMPETITORS

Aloette
CINAR
Cybex International
DIC Entertainment
Fitness Quest
GenesisIntermedia
Guthy-Renker
HIT Entertainment
Hydron
ICON Health
Jim Henson Co.
Ronco
Saban
Sesame Workshop
Thane International

HISTORICAL FINANCIALS

Company Type: Private

Income Statement FYE: December 31

	ESTIMATED REVENUE ($ mil.)	NET INCOME ($ mil.)	NET PROFIT MARGIN	EMPLOYEES
12/01	760	—	—	800
12/00	475	—	—	500
12/99	475	—	—	500
12/98	475	—	—	500
12/97	475	—	—	600
12/96	475	—	—	600
12/95	500	—	—	600
Annual Growth	7.2%	—	—	4.9%

Revenue History

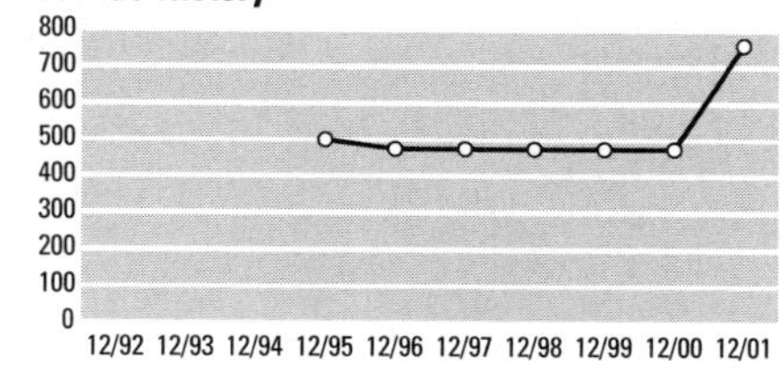

Goodwill Industries

Founded to give those in need "a hand up, not a handout," Goodwill Industries International supports the operations of about 210 independent Goodwill chapters worldwide. Though known mainly for its some 1,900 thrift stores, Goodwill focuses on providing rehabilitation, training, placement, and employment services for those with disabilities and other barriers to employment. Goodwill is one of the world's largest providers of such services, as well as one of the world's largest employers of the disabled. Funding comes primarily from the retail stores, contract services provided to local employers, and grants. Nearly 86% of revenues go to job training and rehabilitation programs.

EXECUTIVES

President and CEO: George W. Kessinger
VP Administration: Ginette Colot
VP Membership and Enterprise Development: James Van Erden
Comptroller: Peter Gibson
Director, Contracts and Industrial Services: Ellen Brown
Director, Goodwill Global, Inc.: Howard Wallack
Director, Media Relations: Christine Bragale
Director, Retail and Donated Goods: Renee Weippert
HR Developer: Alison Jenkens
Auditors: Deloitte & Touche

LOCATIONS

HQ: Goodwill Industries International, Inc.
9200 Rockville Pike, Bethesda, MD 20814
Phone: 301-530-6500 **Fax:** 301-530-1516
Web: www.goodwill.org

Goodwill Industries International has about 210 member organizations throughout the US, Canada, and 22 other countries.

HISTORICAL FINANCIALS

Company Type: Not-for-profit

Income Statement FYE: December 31

	REVENUE ($ mil.)	NET INCOME ($ mil.)	NET PROFIT MARGIN	EMPLOYEES
12/02	2,055	—	—	140,023
12/01	1,940	—	—	61,766
12/00	1,850	—	—	77,895
12/99	1,650	—	—	60,000
12/98	1,507	—	—	60,000
12/97	1,361	—	—	60,000
12/96	1,200	—	—	60,679
12/95	1,038	—	—	64,403
Annual Growth	10.3%	—	—	11.7%

Revenue History

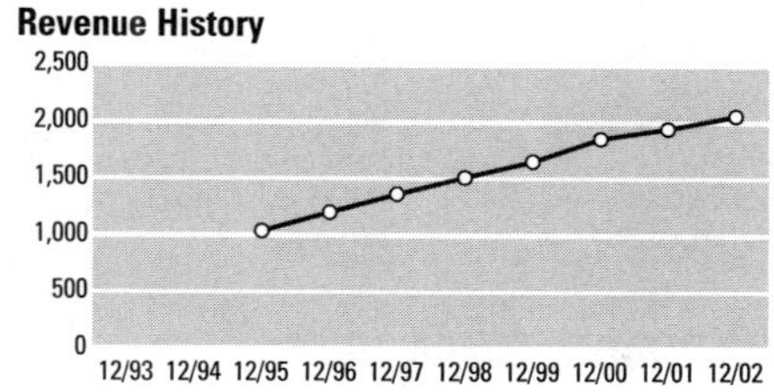

Gordon Food Service

Gordon Food Service (GFS) caters to the tastes of Midwesterners and Canadians. A food distributor serving schools, restaurants, and other institutions, GFS boasts more than 12,000 products ranging from fresh produce to sanitation systems. The company also makes its own foods under names such as Triumph Packaging and Ready, Set, Serve, and it sells food in bulk through some 85 GFS Marketplace stores in four states. GFS acquired in 2002 the Pacific Division of SERCA Foodservice from Sobeys and renamed it Neptune Food Service. The late Isaac VanWestenbrugge (great-grandfather of CEO Dan Gordon) founded the company as a butter and egg distributor in 1897. GFS is still owned and run by the Gordon family.

EXECUTIVES

President and CEO: Dan Gordon
COO: Steve Plakmeyer
CFO: Steve Whitteberry
Secretary and Treasurer: John Gordon Jr.
Operations Manager: Jim Gordon
Director, Human Resources: David Vickery

LOCATIONS

HQ: 333 50th St. SW, Grand Rapids, MI 49501
Phone: 616-530-7000 **Fax:** 616-261-7600
Web: www.gfs.com

Gordon Food Service has operations in Michigan and Ohio and distributes food across the midwestern US and in Canada (Ontario and Quebec). GFS Marketplace stores are located in Illinois, Indiana, Michigan, and Ohio.

PRODUCTS/OPERATIONS

Selected Products

Beverage systems
Dairy
Disposables
Fresh produce
Frozen foods
Groceries
Meats
Poultry
Sanitation systems
Seafood
Tabletop and supplies

Selected Brand Names

GFS
Primo Gusto Italian Specialities
Ready, Set, Serve
Signature Coffee
Triumph Packaging

COMPETITORS

Clark Products
ConAgra
Costco Wholesale
MBM
McLane Foodservice
Performance Food
Services Group
Sherwood Food
Sobeys
SYSCO
U.S. Foodservice
Wal-Mart

HISTORICAL FINANCIALS

Company Type: Private

Income Statement FYE: October 31

	REVENUE ($ mil.)	NET INCOME ($ mil.)	NET PROFIT MARGIN	EMPLOYEES
10/02	2,750	—	—	5,000
10/01	2,600	—	—	5,000
10/00	2,150	—	—	4,400
10/99	2,000	—	—	3,600
10/98	1,700	—	—	3,400
10/97	1,600	—	—	3,300
10/96	1,400	—	—	3,000
10/95	1,250	—	—	2,450
10/94	1,115	—	—	2,300
10/93	910	—	—	2,300
Annual Growth	13.1%	—	—	9.0%

Revenue History

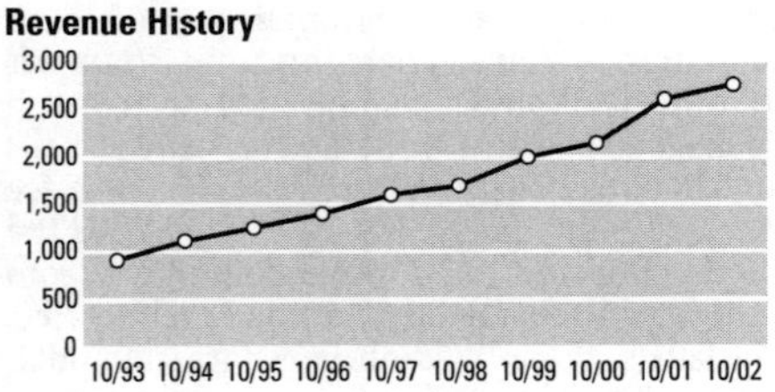

Gores Technology

In the gory aftermath of the Tech Wreck, Gores Technology Group can probably find a bargain. The company buys and manages software, hardware, technology services, and telecommunications concerns. Targets typically have revenues between $10 million and $1 billion and are often spinoffs of noncore operations from Global 2000 companies. Gores Technology usually takes full ownership. Since its founding by chairman Alec Gores in 1992, it has bought some 35 companies around the world. These include the personal computer operations of Micron Electronics (now Interland) and software maker The Learning Company, which subsequently sold its education business to Ireland's Riverdeep software firm.

EXECUTIVES

Chairman: Alec Gores, age 50
President: Vance Diggins
CFO: Cathy Scanlon
EVP and General Counsel: Eric Hattler
Director of Business Development: Dan Gray
Director of Human Resources: Liz Davis
President and CEO, Adventa Control Technologies: Dan M. Schell
President and CEO, Riverdeep: Barry O'Callaghan
President and CEO, MicronPC: Michael S. Adkins
President and CEO, Revere: Steve Pak
CEO, SSA Global Technologies: Michael Greenough
CEO, VeriFone: Douglas G. (Doug) Bergeron

LOCATIONS

HQ: Gores Technology Group
10877 Wilshire Blvd., Ste. 1805,
Los Angeles, CA 90024
Phone: 310-209-3010 **Fax:** 310-209-3310
Web: www.gores.com

Gores Technology Group has operations in Asia, Europe, South America, and the US.

PRODUCTS/OPERATIONS

Selected Investments

Adventa Control Technologies, Inc.
Aonix
Artemis
Connection Machines Services
Encore Real Time Computing, Inc.
Farallon
Information Dimensions
MicronPC, LLC
Quortech Solutions, Inc.
Revere, Inc.
Software Productivity Research, Inc.
The Learning Company
VeriFone, Inc.
Vicorp

COMPETITORS

Bain Capital
Carlyle Group
Clayton, Dubilier
Forstmann Little
Hicks, Muse
KKR
Platinum Equity

HISTORICAL FINANCIALS

Company Type: Private

Income Statement FYE: December 31

	REVENUE ($ mil.)	NET INCOME ($ mil.)	NET PROFIT MARGIN	EMPLOYEES
12/01	2,000	—	—	10,000
12/00	1,200	—	—	3,000
12/99	800	—	—	1,200
12/98	300	—	—	900
12/97	200	—	—	850
12/96	150	—	—	700
Annual Growth	67.9%	—	—	70.2%

Revenue History

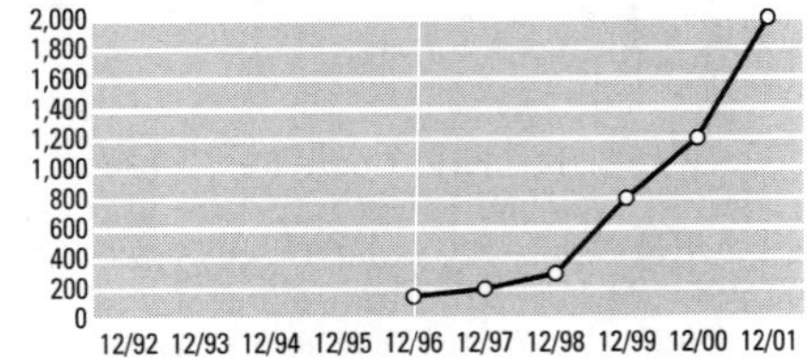

Goss International

Goss International always has some pressing news. The company operates through its Goss Graphic Systems subsidiary, making web-offset printing presses for newspapers and commercial printers, as well as advertising insert presses. Goss offers its presses, related parts, and services (sensitive to publishing schedules) through sales offices and plants in North America, Europe, and Asia. The company serves newspaper publishers in more than 120 countries. Customers have included *The Asahi Shimbun* (Japan), *The People's Daily* (China), and *The Financial Times* (UK). Goss has emerged from Chapter 11 bankruptcy, and investment firm Stonington Partners controls 91% of the company.

The company is one of three companies still manufacturing web-presses in the US.

EXECUTIVES

CEO: Bob Brown
EVP and CFO: Joseph P. Gaynor III
SVP, Global Sales: Dick Schultz
SVP, Americas Parts and Service and Aftermarket Sales: Tom Hojnicki
Recruiting, Human Resources: Angela Lewis
Director, Aftermarket Sales and Product Development: Michael Ide
General Sales Manager, UK and Eire: Ian McLeod
Regional Sales Manager, Northeast Region, The Americas: Bruce Barna
Director of Training and Technical Publications: Peter Farmer

LOCATIONS

HQ: Goss International Corporation
3 Territorial Court, Bolingbrook, IL 60440
Phone: 630-755-9300 **Fax:** 630-755-9301
Web: www.gossgraphic.com

Goss International has US manufacturing operations in Cedar Rapids, Iowa, and international operations in China, France, Germany, Japan, and the UK.

PRODUCTS/OPERATIONS

Selected Products

Advertising-insert presses (C700, Magnum)
Aftermarket parts
Commercial presses (G18, G25, M16)
Large newspaper presses (Colorliner, Newsliner)
Small newspaper presses (Community, Universal)

COMPETITORS

Baldwin Technology
Enovation Graphics Systems
Heidelberg
Indigo N.V.
Koenig & Bauer
MAN
Mitsubishi Heavy Industries
Pamarco Technologies

HISTORICAL FINANCIALS

Company Type: Private

Income Statement FYE: December 31

	REVENUE ($ mil.)	NET INCOME ($ mil.)	NET PROFIT MARGIN	EMPLOYEES
12/01	650	—	—	2,700
12/00	623	—	—	2,689
12/99*	608	—	—	2,845
9/98	764	—	—	3,313
9/97	633	—	—	2,386
9/96	698	—	—	2,300
9/95	709	—	—	2,800
9/94	648	—	—	—
9/93	627	—	—	—
9/92	688	—	—	—
Annual Growth	(0.6%)	—	—	(0.6%)

*Fiscal year change

Revenue History

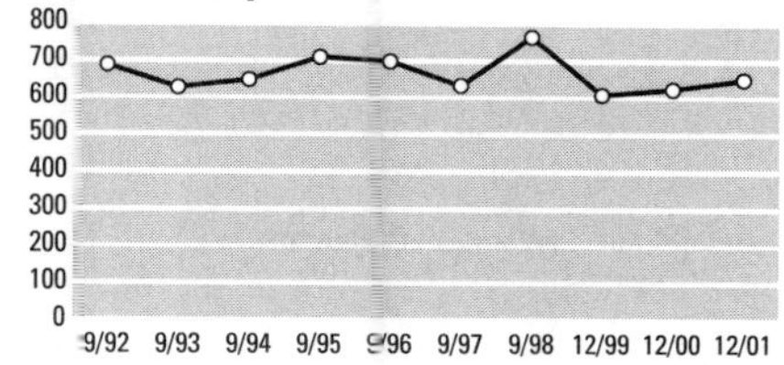

Gould Paper Corporation

Paper is as good as gold for Gould Paper, one of the largest privately owned distributors of printing and fine papers in the US. The company distributes and sells paper for multiple markets including fine papers, commercial printing, lithography, newsprint, direct mail, catalogs, envelopes, and specialty papers. The Gould North America division oversees business within the US and Canada, while Gould National produces paper rolls (wholesale) Its International Packaging Group makes specialty packaging (paperboard, plastics). Harry Gould Sr. (father of chairman, president, CEO, and company owner Harry Gould Jr.) formed the company in 1924. Gould Paper has expanded over the years by acquiring other paper companies.

EXECUTIVES

Chairman, President, and CEO: Harry E. Gould Jr.
EVP and CFO: Carl Matthews
VP and CIO: Robert Bunsick
VP, Secretary & Treasurer: Pat Mullen
President, Gould National Division: Robert Anderson
President, Gould International Packaging Group: John Curtin
President, Gould Business Products Division: Michael Negri
Chairman, Gould North America: Thomas Ryan
President, Gould North America Division: Robert Kralik
President, Gould Communications & Business Products Division: Robert Simone
President, Gould Distribution: Robert Weil

LOCATIONS

HQ: 11 Madison Ave., New York, NY 10010
Phone: 212-301-0000 **Fax:** 212-481-0067
Web: www.gouldpaper.com

Gould Paper has divisions and locations in California, Florida, Illinois, Massachusetts, Maryland, New Jersey, and New York.

COMPETITORS

Bradner Central
Clifford Paper
Crane & Co.
International Paper
Midland Paper
National Envelope
Ris Paper

HISTORICAL FINANCIALS

Company Type: Private

Income Statement FYE: December 31

	REVENUE ($ mil.)	NET INCOME ($ mil.)	NET PROFIT MARGIN	EMPLOYEES
12/02	1,100	—	—	485
12/01	820	—	—	455
12/00	810	—	—	455
12/99	805	—	—	450
12/98	855	—	—	450
12/97	740	—	—	525
12/96	700	—	—	525
12/95	790	—	—	450
12/94	830	—	—	425
12/93	510	—	—	375
Annual Growth	8.9%	—	—	2.9%

Revenue History

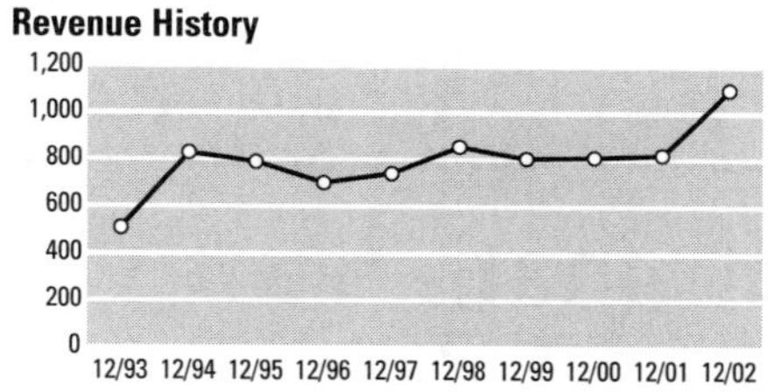

Goya Foods, Inc.

Called frijoles or hibicuelas, beans are beans, and Goya's got 'em. Goya Foods produces about 1,000 Hispanic and Caribbean grocery items, including canned and dried beans, canned meats, olives, rice, seasonings, plantain and yuca chips, and frozen entrees. It sells more than 20 rice products and 30 types of beans and peas. Brands include Goya and Canilla. It also sells beverages such as tropical fruit nectars and juices, tropical sodas, and coffee. Goya is owned by one of the richest Hispanic *familias* in the US, the Unanues, who founded the company in 1936.

Goya has historically served the Hispanic communities in the Northeast and Florida with mostly Cuban, Dominican, and Puerto Rican customers. The company now has products geared toward the tastes of Hispanics in California and the Southwest with roots in Mexico and Central and South America. A growing taste for ethnic foods across the US has fueled Goya's growth beyond its Hispanic roots. In addition, its "all-in-one-aisle" product placement in food stores has proven very successful.

Yet it faces competition from food giants such as Kraft Foods, which have lines of Hispanic specialty products. It's also challenged by food manufacturers from Mexico who are turning north to tap the pocketbooks of US consumers.

Goya is one of the largest Hispanic-owned companies in the US.

HISTORY

Immigrants from Spain by way of Puerto Rico, husband and wife Prudencio Unanue and Carolina Casal founded Unanue & Sons in New York City in 1936. The couple imported sardines, olives, and olive oil from Spain, but when the Spanish Civil War (1936-1939) interrupted supply lines, they began importing from Morocco.

In 1949 the company established a cannery in Puerto Rico; the Puerto Rican imports were distributed to local immigrants from the West Indies. Each of the couple's four sons eventually joined the family business, and in 1958 the firm relocated to Brooklyn. The company took its current name, Goya Foods, in 1962 when the family bought the Goya name — originally a brand of sardines — for $1.

The oldest Unanue son, CEO Charles, was fired from Goya in 1969 — and subsequently cut out of Prudencio's will — when he spoke out about an alleged tax evasion scheme. (Legal wrangling between Charles and the rest of the family continued into the late 1990s.) Goya moved to its present New Jersey headquarters in 1974.

Another son, Anthony, died in 1976, as did Prudencio. That year Joseph, another sibling, was named president and CEO. Along with his brother Francisco (Frank), president of Goya Foods de Puerto Rico, he began a cautious expansion campaign by adding traditional products to the company's existing line of Latin Caribbean and Spanish favorites.

Buoyed by the growing popularity of Mexican food, in 1982 Goya began distributing its products in Texas, targeting the region's sizable Mexican and Central American population. At first, the move proved a disaster. Goya's products were not suited to the Mexican palate, which generally preferred spicier food. Likewise, a similar strategy to capture a portion of Florida's huge Cuban market share initially met with only moderate success, but Goya persevered, eventually turning the tables in its favor.

During the 1980s the company also attempted to woo the non-Hispanic market. While Goya's cream of coconut — a key ingredient in piña coladas — found a broader market, its ad campaign featuring obscure actress Zohra Lampert did little to attract a large following of non-Hispanic customers.

Success in that market came in the 1990s. America's interest in the reportedly healthier "Mediterranean diet" boosted sales of Goya's extra-virgin olive oil. Recommendations for low-fat, high-fiber diets prompted the company's launch of the "For Better Meals, Turn to Goya" advertising campaign — its first in English — in 1992.

Three years later the company released a line of juice-based beverages. In 1996 Goya sponsored an exhibition of the works of the Spanish master Goya at the New York Metropolitan Museum of Art. Continuing its efforts to reach out to non-

Hispanics and English-dominant Hispanics, in 1997 the company began including both English and Spanish on the front of its packaging.

To lure more snackers, the next year Goya added yuca (a.k.a. cassava) chips to its line. In 1999 Goya began packaging its frozen entrees in microwaveable trays. In 2001 it bought a new factory in Spain.

In 2002 Goya added 12 flavors (including guava, mandarin orange, and tamarind) to its line of Refresco Goya Fruit Sodas, thus joining the beverage industry trend toward offering more diverse flavors.

Francisco Unanue died in late 2002.

EXECUTIVES

President and CEO: Joseph A. Unanue
EVP and COO: Andrew Unanue
VP, Computer Information Services: David Kinkela
VP, Purchasing: Joseph Perez
VP, Sales & Marketing: Conrad O. Colon
Controller: Tony Diaz
Director, Finance: Miguel Lugo
Director, Human Resources: Johana Soco
Director, Marketing: Esperanza Carrion
Director, Public Relations: Rafael Toro
Director, Sales: Richard Gonzales
General Counsel: Carlos Ortiz
Deputy Counsel: Ira Matestsky
Corporate Secretary: Maribel Alvarez
Assistant, Public Relations: Evanessa Mangual
General Manager, California: Francisco Ahummada
General Manager, West Coast Operations: Francisco Javier Ahumada
Manager, Secaucus plant: Benjamin Spinnickie

LOCATIONS

HQ: 100 Seaview Dr., Secaucus, NJ 07096
Phone: 201-348-4900 **Fax:** 201-348-6609
Web: www.goya.com

Goya Foods has 13 facilities located in the Caribbean, Europe, and the US.

PRODUCTS/OPERATIONS

Selected Products

Beverages
Café Goya
Coconut Water
Malta (malt beverage)
Nectars and juices (apple, apricot, banana, guanabana, guava, mango, passion fruit, papaya, peach, pear, pear/passion, pineapple, pineapple/guava, pineapple/passion, strawberry, strawberry/banana, tamarind, tropical fruit punch)
Tropical sodas (apple, coconut, cola champagne, fruit punch, ginger beer, grape, guaraná, guava, lemon lime, mandarin orange, pineapple, strawberry, tamarind)

Foods and Other Products
Beans (black-eyed peas, chick peas, lentils, refried)
Bouillon
Cooking sauces
Cooking wine
Cornmeal
Devotional candles
Flour
Frozen foods
Marinades
Meat (chorizo, corned beef, potted, vienna sausage)
Olive oil
Olives
Pasta
Plantain chips
Rice
Seafood
Seasonings
Spices
Yuca chips

COMPETITORS

American Rice	Kraft Foods
Authentic Specialty Foods	McCormick
Bimbo	Nestlé
Chiquita Brands	Pinnacle Foods Corporation
ConAgra	Pro-Fac
Del Monte Foods	Riceland Foods
Dole	Riviana Foods
Frito-Lay	Seneca Foods
Herdez	Unilever
Hormel	

HISTORICAL FINANCIALS

Company Type: Private

Income Statement FYE: May 31

	REVENUE ($ mil.)	NET INCOME ($ mil.)	NET PROFIT MARGIN	EMPLOYEES
5/02	750	—	—	2,500
5/01	715	—	—	2,500
5/00	695	—	—	2,500
5/99	653	—	—	2,200
5/98	620	—	—	3,000
5/97	600	—	—	3,000
5/96	560	—	—	2,200
5/95	528	—	—	2,000
5/94	480	—	—	2,000
5/93	453	—	—	1,800
Annual Growth	5.8%	—	—	3.7%

Revenue History

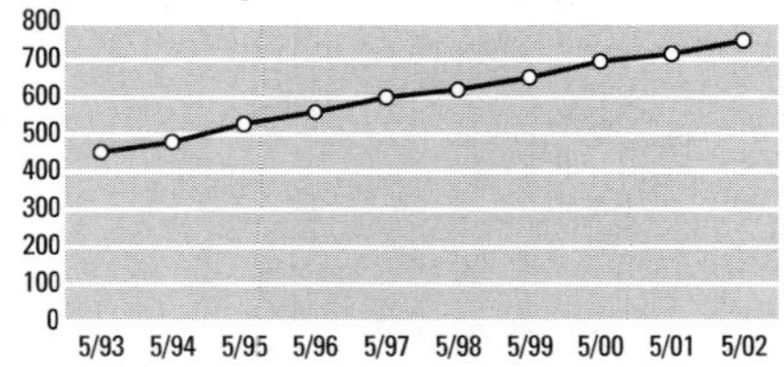

Graham Packaging

Grocery stockers and mechanics handle Graham Packaging's products every day. The company makes blow-molded plastic containers for food and beverages, household and personal care products, and automotive lubricants. Customers such as Hershey Foods, Procter & Gamble, and Pennzoil-Quaker State use the containers for juices, sauces, teas, fabric and dish detergents, and motor oil. One-third of Graham Packaging's manufacturing plants are located on the grounds of its customers' production facilities. The company, which is controlled by Blackstone Group, has postponed its IPO until market conditions improve.

North America accounts for about 80% of sales.

EXECUTIVES

Chairman and CEO: Philip R. Yates, age 55, $1,252,397 pay
President and COO: Roger M. Prevot, age 44, $813,220 pay
CFO: John E. Hamilton, age 44, $508,181 pay
SVP and General Manager, North America Automotive and South America: G. Robinson Beeson, age 55, $500,474 pay
SVP and General Manager, Household and Personal Care: Scott G. Booth, age 45, $478,492 pay
SVP and General Manager, Europe and North America Food and Beverage Polyolefins: Ashok Sudan, age 49, $412,022 pay
SVP, Global People Resources: George Lane
SVP and General Manager, North America Food and Beverage PET: John A. Buttermore, age 56, $417,565 pay
Auditors: Deloitte & Touche LLP

LOCATIONS

HQ: Graham Packaging Company, Inc.
2401 Pleasant Valley Rd., York, PA 17402
Phone: 717-849-8500 **Fax:** 717-848-4836
Web: www.grahampackaging.com

Graham Packaging Holdings Company has 55 plants in Europe, Latin America, and North America.

PRODUCTS/OPERATIONS

Selected Products

Food and Beverage Containers
Frozen juices
Jellies and jams
Non-carbonated juice drinks
Pasta sauce and other sauces
Soups
Teas
Toppings
Yogurt and nutritional drinks

Household and Personal Care Containers
Body wash
Dish care
Hair care
Hard surface cleaners
Liquid automatic dishwashing detergents
Liquid fabric care

Automotive Lubricant Containers
Antifreeze
Motor oils

COMPETITORS

Amcor
Ball Corporation
Chesapeake Corporation
Consolidated Container
Constar International
Owens-Illinois
Pechiney
Plastipak Holdings, Inc.
RPC Group
Silgan

HISTORICAL FINANCIALS

Company Type: Private

Income Statement FYE: December 31

	REVENUE ($ mil.)	NET INCOME ($ mil.)	NET PROFIT MARGIN	EMPLOYEES
12/02	907	8	0.8%	3,900
12/01	923	(44)	—	4,100
12/00	825	(46)	—	4,000
12/99	716	1	0.2%	4,000
12/98	588	(28)	—	—
12/97	522	11	2.0%	—
12/96	460	21	4.6%	—
12/95	467	19	4.0%	—
Annual Growth	9.9%	(12.2%)	—	(0.8%)

2002 Year-End Financials

Debt ratio: —
Return on equity: —
Cash ($ mil.): 7
Current ratio: 1.05
Long-term debt ($ mil.): 1,063

Net Income History

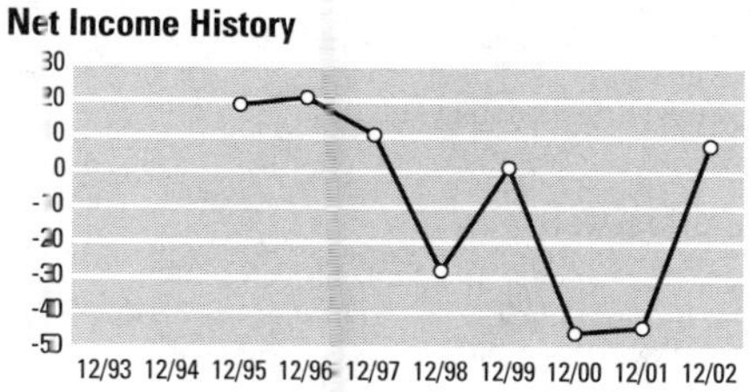

Grant Thornton International

Grant Thornton International is a kid brother to the Big Four. The umbrella organization of accounting and management consulting firms operates from more than 580 offices around the world, making it one of the top second-tier companies that trail around behind the biggest of the big guys (Deloitte Touche Tohmatsu, Ernst & Young International, KPMG International, and PricewaterhouseCoopers). Grant Thornton International's member firms elect representatives to an international policy board that runs the day-to-day operations of the accounting company.

Industry consolidation prompted Grant Thornton International and other second-tier firms to enter such niche areas as information technology and corporate finance. And while the Big Four focus on large corporations, Grant Thornton locks in on owner-managed companies, helping them with accounting, audit, and tax issues, as well as growth strategies. It is facing new competitors for its target market; such firms as H&R Block and American Express have been adding accounting, tax planning, and consulting services.

With the lowering of trade barriers in Latin America and Europe, Grant Thornton has been focusing on developing business in emerging markets. Member firms have been working to increase cross-border cooperation by pooling resources and cutting costs. The organization also helped pick up the pieces as Andersen crumbled, acquiring clients, offices, and clients from the felled giant.

HISTORY

Cameron, Missouri accountant Alexander Grant founded Alexander Grant & Co. in 1924 with William O'Brien. They built their firm in Chicago and concentrated on providing services to midwestern clients.

In the 1950s and 1960s, the firm began expanding both domestically and internationally. Alexander Grant & Co. continued to focus on manufacturing and distribution companies.

In 1973 O'Brien died. In 1979 the company began publishing its well-known (and sometimes controversial) index of state business climates. An attempt to merge with fellow second-tier accounting firm Laventhol & Horwath failed that year. The next year Grant Thornton International was formed when Alexander Grant & Co. and its British affiliate, Thornton Baker, combined their offices around the world to form a network. The UK and US branches, however, kept their respective names.

The 1980s brought turmoil and change for the firm. Financial scandals led investors and the government to hold accounting firms liable for their audits. Along with the (then) Big Six, Alexander Grant & Co. was hit with several lawsuits alleging fraud and cover-ups. One case marred the firm's squeaky-clean image and caused dozens of clients to jump ship: Just days after Alexander Grant issued it a clean audit, a Florida trading firm was shut down by the SEC. Jilted investors sued to reclaim lost money; Alexander Grant settled for $160 million. Chairman Herbert Dooskin and other leaders also left the company; although they denied it was because of the scandal, their departures left Alexander Grant rudderless during a critical time.

Meanwhile, the company merged with Fox & Co. to create the US's #9 accounting firm. With scandal-scared partners leaving (and taking clients), Fox looked to the merger to shore up its reputation. But Alexander Grant's auditing troubles led some Fox partners and clients to flee from the merged company.

After the fallout from the lawsuits and the merger, the company began rebuilding, taking on new clients, reclaiming lost ones, and refocusing on midsized companies. In 1986 both Alexander Grant & Co. and Thornton Baker took the Grant Thornton name.

The early 1990s recession reduced accounting revenues but increased demand for management consulting. As political and economic barriers fell during the decade, Grant Thornton International grew. The firm entered emerging markets in Africa, Asia, Europe, and Latin America. In 1998 the Big Six became the Big Five; Grant Thornton added refugee firms and partners to its global network. In 1999 the firm's US branch entertained merger offers from H&R Block and PricewaterhouseCoopers, but instead announced plans to reposition itself as a corporate services firm to better compete.

In 2000 the company pulled out of its advisory position to companies involved in controversial diamond mining in war-torn portions of Africa. It also agreed to merge its UK operations with those of HLB Kidsons; the merged firm retained the Grant Thornton name.

The following year, after disagreements about strategy, US CEO Dom Esposito resigned. UK partner David McDonnell was named the global CEO. In 2002, Grant Thornton grew by picking up pieces of Andersen that fell away as a result of the Enron scandal. Anderson's fall also winnowed out Grant Thornton's competitors (at least in the numeric sense), as the Big Five became the Big Four.

EXECUTIVES

Chairman: Leonard Brehm
Global CEO: David C. McDonnell
Divisional Director, Asia Pacific: Gabriel Azedo
Divisional Director, Europe, Middle East and Africa: Clive Bennett
Divisional Director, The Americas: Shelley Stein
Worldwide Director, Audit and Quality Control: Barry Barber
Worldwide Director, Client Services: Soren Carlsson
International Director, Marketing Communication: Sue Palmer
Treasurer and Director of Administration: Louis A. Fanchi
Director of Administration: Ricky Lawrence
Director of Human Resources, Grant Thornton LLP: Jill Osborn

LOCATIONS

HQ: 1 Prudential Plaza, Ste. 800, 130 E. Randolph Dr., Chicago, IL 60601
Phone: 312-856-0001 **Fax:** 312-616-7142
Web: www.gti.org

Grant Thornton International has offices in 110 countries worldwide.

PRODUCTS/OPERATIONS

Selected Services

Assurance
Corporate finance
Corporate recovery and business reorganization
International tax
PRIMA (people and relationship issues in management)

COMPETITORS

American Express Tax and Business Services
Baker Tilly International
BDO International
Deloitte Touche Tohmatsu
Ernst & Young
H&R Block
KPMG
McGladrey & Pullen
McKinsey & Company
Moores Rowland
PricewaterhouseCoopers
RSM McGladrey, Inc.

HISTORICAL FINANCIALS

Company Type: Not-for-profit

Income Statement FYE: July 31

	REVENUE ($ mil.)	NET INCOME ($ mil.)	NET PROFIT MARGIN	EMPLOYEES
7/03	2,000	—	—	21,500
7/02	1,840	—	—	21,500
7/01	1,700	—	—	21,879
7/00	1,690	—	—	20,300
7/99	1,800	—	—	20,000
7/98	1,600	—	—	20,160
7/97	1,405	—	—	18,562
7/96	1,285	—	—	18,300
Annual Growth	6.5%	—	—	2.3%

Revenue History

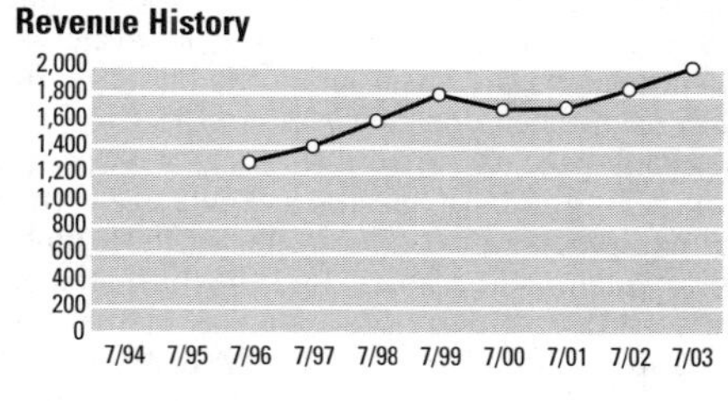

Graybar Electric Company, Inc.

Keeping you connected is no problem for Graybar Electric, one of the largest distributors of electrical products in the US. Purchasing from thousands of manufacturers, the employee-owned company distributes nearly 1 million electrical and communications components, including wire, cable, and lighting products. Its customers include electrical contractors, industrial plants, power utilities, and telecommunications providers. Subsidiary Graybar Financial Services offers equipment leasing and financing alternatives as well as complete project funding.

The construction industry has been the company's traditional market, but changes in telecommunications have prompted it to solidify relationships with major vendors such as GE, Lucent, and Thomas & Betts.

Graybar has reorganized its sales force, setting up districts throughout the US. To help bring supply, distribution, and inventory costs down, the company uses electronic data interchange and supplier-assisted inventory management, and urges its suppliers to have bar codes on all products. Graybar Electric has grown by targeting both national and international accounts.

HISTORY

After serving as a telegrapher during the Civil War, Enos Barton borrowed $400 from his widowed mother in 1869 and started an electrical equipment shop in Cleveland with George Shawk. Later that year Elisha Gray, a professor of physics at Oberlin College who had several inventions (including a printing telegraph) to his credit, bought Shawk's interest in the shop, and the firm moved to Chicago, where a third partner joined.

The company incorporated as the Western Electric Manufacturing Co. in 1872, with two-thirds of the company's stock held by two Western Union executives. As the telegraph industry took off, the enterprise grew rapidly, providing equipment to towns and railroads in the western US.

Gray and his company missed receiving credit for inventing the telephone in 1875 when Gray's patent application for a "harmonic telegraph" reached the US Patent Office a few hours after Bell's application for his telephone. However, the telephone and the invention of the lightbulb in 1879 opened new doors for Western Electric. The company began to grow into a major corporation, selling and distributing a variety of electrical equipment, including batteries, telegraph keys, and fire-alarm boxes. By 1900 the firm was the world's #1 maker of telephone equipment.

Western Electric formed a new distribution business in 1926, Graybar Electric Co. (from "Gray" and "Barton"), the world's largest electrical supply merchandiser. In 1929 employees bought the company from Western Electric for $3 million in cash and $6 million in preferred stock. During the 1930s it marketed a line of appliances and sewing machines under the Graybar name.

In 1941 the company bought the outstanding shares of stock from Western Electric for $1 million. Graybar Electric was a vital link between manufacturers and US defense needs during WWII. Its men and equipment wired the Panama Canal with telephone cable; it also helped the US military during the Korean conflict and the Vietnam War.

By 1980 Graybar Electric had reached nearly $1.5 billion in sales. Business was hurt when construction slowed in the late 1980s and the early 1990s, and the company reorganized in 1991, closing regional offices and cutting jobs. Rebounding in 1992 as the US economy improved, Graybar acquired New Jersey-based Square Electric Co.

The company acquired a minority interest in R.E.D. Electronics, a Canadian data communications and computer networking company, and realigned its operations into two business segments: electrical products and communications and data products in 1994.

In 1995 Graybar Electric formed the Solutions Providers Alliance with wholesale distributors Kaman Industrial Technologies, VWR Scientific Products, and Vallen Corporation. The national and international network provides products and services to the companies' maintenance, repair, and operations customers. In 1996 AT&T's Global Procurement Group named the company as one of only three suppliers for its electrical products. The next year Graybar Electric upped its stake in one of its Canadian operations, Harris & Roome Supply Limited.

Graybar Electric in 1998 opened a subsidiary in Chile and formed a joint venture, Graybar Financial Services, with Newcourt Financial (formerly AT&T Capital). The next year Graybar Electric bought the Connecticut-based electrical wholesaler Frank A. Blesso, Inc., and it expanded its distribution partnership with wire and cable manufacturer, Belden Electronics, in 2000.

In 2001 Graybar opened a new distribution location in northeastern Pennsylvania. The following year Graybar increased its presence in the telecommunication industry when it inked a deal to distribute products made by Copper Mountain Networks, a US-based broadband solutions manufacturer.

EXECUTIVES

President, CEO, and Chairman: Robert A. Reynolds, age 54, $518,976 pay
SVP, CFO, and Director: Juanita H. Hinshaw, age 58, $294,607 pay
SVP, Operations, and Director: Lawrence R. (Larry) Giglio
SVP, Business Management and Director: Charles R. Udell, age 58, $260,043 pay
SVP, Sales and Marketing and Director: Dennis E. DeSousa, $258,478 pay
Group VP, Atlanta, Tampa, and Southeastern Comm/Data Districts, and Director: Richard D. Offenbacher, age 52
Group VP, California Electrical, and California Comm/Data Districts, and Director: Gary D. Hodges
Group VP, Minneapolis, Cincinnati, Chicago, and North Central Comm/Data Districts, and Director: Richard A. Cole
Group VP (New York, Boston, and Northeastern Comm/Data Districts): Donald M. Block
Group VP, Seattle, Phoenix, Western Comm/Data, and Aurora Districts, and Director: Kenneth B. Sparks, age 57
Group VP, Pittsburgh, Richmond, and Mid-Atlantic Comm/Data Districts, and Director: Thomas S. Gurganous
Group VP, SPN District: John C. Mansfield
Group VP., St. Louis, Dallas, and Houston Districts and Director: John C. Loff
VP, Human Resources and Director: Jack F. Van Pelt, age 64, $255,965 pay
VP, Secretary, General Counsel, and Director: Thomas F. Dowd
Auditors: Ernst & Young LLP

LOCATIONS

HQ: 34 N. Meramec Ave., St. Louis, MO 63105
Phone: 314-573-9200 **Fax:** 314-512-9453
Web: www.graybar.com

Graybar Electric Company has offices and distribution facilities in Canada, Mexico, Puerto Rico, Singapore, and the US.

PRODUCTS/OPERATIONS

Selected Products and Services

Ballasts
Batteries
Cable
Conduit
Connectors
Emergency lighting
Enclosures
Fiber optic cable
Fittings
Fluorescent lighting
Fuses
Hand tools
Hangers/fasteners
Heating and ventilating
Industrial fans
Lighting
Lubricants
Paints
Patch cords
Smoke detectors
Testing and measuring instruments
Timers
Transfer switches
Transformers
Utility products
Wire

COMPETITORS

Agilysys
Anixter International
Arrow Electronics
Avnet
Communications Supply
Consolidated Electrical
Cooper Industries
Eaton
Emerson Electric
GE
Hagemeyer
Matsushita
Molex
Premier Farnell
Rexel, Inc.
Siemens
Sonepar
Sonepar USA
SPX
SUMMIT Electric Supply
Tech Data
Tyco International
WESCO International
W.W. Grainger

HISTORICAL FINANCIALS

Company Type: Private

Income Statement

FYE: December 31

	REVENUE ($ mil.)	NET INCOME ($ mil.)	NET PROFIT MARGIN	EMPLOYEES
12/02	3,975	11	0.3%	8,300
12/01	4,815	32	0.7%	9,800
12/00	5,214	66	1.3%	10,500
12/99	4,300	65	1.5%	8,900
12/98	3,744	60	1.6%	7,900
12/97	3,338	53	1.6%	7,200
12/96	2,991	45	1.5%	6,600
12/95	2,765	37	1.3%	6,200
12/94	2,356	19	0.8%	5,500
12/93	2,033	15	0.7%	5,100
Annual Growth	7.7%	(2.8%)	—	5.6%

2002 Year-End Financials

Debt ratio: 68.8%
Return on equity: 2.9%
Cash ($ mil.): 21
Current ratio: 1.73
Long-term debt ($ mil.): 267

Net Income History

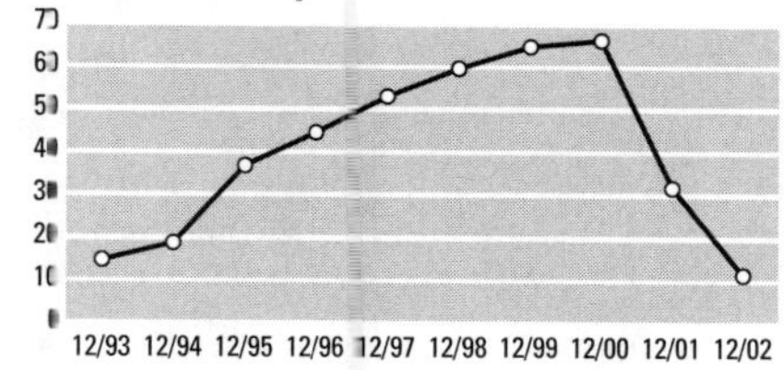

Great Dane Limited Partnership

Great Dane is really going places — the company is one of the largest manufacturers of truck trailers in North America. Great Dane makes refrigerated (reefer) and freight vans and platform trailers. The company has nine manufacturing plants in the US and sales, parts, and service centers across the US, Canada, Mexico, and South America. It also sells used trailers. Great Dane is a unit of Chicago-based investment group CC Industries, which is controlled by the Henry Crown family. The company started in 1900 as a maker of steel products and switched to trailer making in 1931.

EXECUTIVES

President: C. F. (Kit) Hammond III
COO; President, Pines Trailer Division: Phillip Pines
SVP, Finance, CFO, and Secretary: Tom Horan
SVP, Manufacturing: Mike Thomas
SVP, Sales and Marketing: H. T. (Skip) Skipper
VP, Human Resources: Thor Egede-Nissen

LOCATIONS

HQ: 602 E. Lathrop Ave., Savannah, GA 31402
Phone: 912-644-2100 **Fax:** 912-644-2166
Web: www.greatdanetrailers.com

Great Dane has nine manufacturing plants in the US.

PRODUCTS/OPERATIONS

Selected Products

Freight Vans
Aluminum
Customized
Stainless steel

Platform Trailers
All steel
Drop deck
Extendable platform
Steel/aluminum combo

Reefers
Classic aluminum
Stainless steel
SuperSeal
Thermacube

COMPETITORS

Carlisle Companies
Featherlite
Lufkin Industries
RailAmerica
Supreme Industries
Trailmobile
Utility Trailer
Wabash National

HISTORICAL FINANCIALS

Company Type: Private

Income Statement FYE: December 31

	ESTIMATED REVENUE ($ mil.)	NET INCOME ($ mil.)	NET PROFIT MARGIN	EMPLOYEES
12/02	1,000	—	—	4,000
12/01	1,000	—	—	3,400
12/00	1,310	—	—	5,000
12/99	1,400	—	—	4,000
12/98	1,000	—	—	4,700
12/97	1,000	—	—	4,715
Annual Growth	0.0%	—	—	(3.2%)

Revenue History

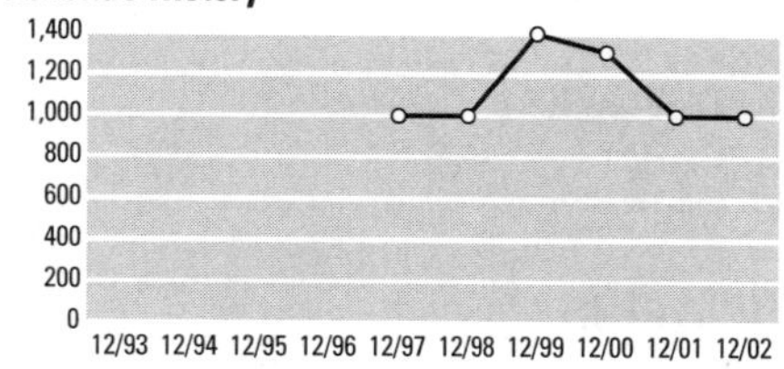

Great Lakes Cheese

Great Lakes Cheese Company understands the power of provolone and the charm of cheddar. The firm manufactures and distributes natural and processed cheeses, including cheddar, Swiss, mozzarella, and provolone. The company packages shredded, chunk, and sliced cheese under retailers' private labels. Additionally it imports cheeses, and produces cheese for deli, bulk, and food service sale. The firm has six plants in New York, Ohio, Utah, and Wisconsin. It sells directly to consumers through a store in its New York plant and its website. Hans Epprecht, a Swiss immigrant, founded the company in 1958 as a bulk-cheese distributor in Cleveland. Chairman Epprecht and Great Lakes Cheese employees own the company.

EXECUTIVES

Chairman: Hans Epprecht
President and CEO: Gary Vanic
CFO: Russell (Russ) Mullins
VP, Sales: Bill Andrews
Director of Information Services: Ron Barlow
Manager, Personnel: Beth Wendell

LOCATIONS

HQ: Great Lakes Cheese Company, Inc.
17825 Great Lakes Pkwy., Hiram, OH 44234
Phone: 440-834-2500 **Fax:** 440-834-1002
Web: www.greatlakescheese.com

COMPETITORS

Agri-Mark
AMPI
ConAgra
Dairy Farmers of America
Kraft Foods
Land O'Lakes
Leprino Foods
Lucille Farms
Marathon Cheese
Saputo
Schreiber Foods

HISTORICAL FINANCIALS

Company Type: Private

Income Statement FYE: December 31

	REVENUE ($ mil.)	NET INCOME ($ mil.)	NET PROFIT MARGIN	EMPLOYEES
12/01	800	—	—	1,200
12/00	717	—	—	1,200
12/99	770	—	—	1,200
12/98	700	—	—	1,000
12/97	625	—	—	950
12/96	612	—	—	900
12/95	473	—	—	830
12/94	414	—	—	659
12/93	361	—	—	—
Annual Growth	10.4%	—	—	8.9%

Revenue History

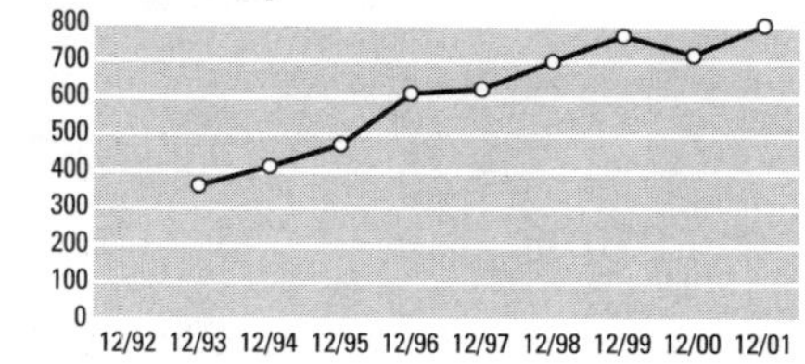

Grede Foundries, Inc.

Many industries would be lost without Grede Foundries. The company produces gray iron, ductile iron, and steel castings for use in farm and construction equipment, motor vehicles, and a host of other products. Grede's cast products include axles, brackets, crankshafts, hydraulic end caps, and sprockets. The company also offers services such as design assistance, painting, machining, and subassembly. William Grede founded the company as Liberty Foundry in 1920. The business is still owned by Grede's descendants, including chairman Burleigh Jacobs.

Grede manufactures castings for the construction machinery, farm machinery and equipment, and the automotive industries. The company also makes additional products such as compressor parts, exhaust manifolds, transmission rings, and wheel cylinders.

Grede operates 11 foundries in the US and one in the UK. In a partnership with Grupo Proeza (an industrial and technology service provider), the company is constructing a ductile iron foundry near Monterrey, Mexico, which will produce about 80,000 tons of castings for customers in the automotive, agricultural, and construction industries.

EXECUTIVES

Chairman: Burleigh E. Jacobs
President and CEO: Bruce E. Jacobs, age 55
EVP and COO: Peter E. Sohlden
VP and CFO: Kristen Z. Reilly
VP, Engineering Services: Dale A. Weeldreyer
VP, Human Resources: W. Stewart Davis
VP, Sales and Marketing: Dennis R. Lauber
Sales Administrator: Barbara Taczala

LOCATIONS

HQ: 9898 W. Bluemound Rd., Milwaukee, WI 53226
Phone: 414-257-3600 **Fax:** 414-256-9399
Web: www.grede.com

Grede Foundries has facilities in the US (Indiana, Kansas, Kentucky, Michigan, Minnesota, Oklahoma, South Carolina, and Wisconsin), as well as the UK.

PRODUCTS/OPERATIONS

Selected Cast Products

Axles
Bearing caps
Brackets
Brake parts (drums)
Calipers
Cases/carriers/housings
Compressor parts
Crankshafts
Disc and antiskid systems
Exhaust manifolds
Frame segments
Gear blanks
Hubs
Hydraulic end caps
Spool valves
Sprockets
Transmission rings
Turbos
Water pumps
Wheel cylinders

COMPETITORS

Atchison Casting
Chief Industries
Citation
INTERMET
Jernberg Industries
Lufkin Industries
Margate Industries
Metalcraft
ThyssenKrupp Budd
Transportation Technologies
United Defense Steel Products

HISTORICAL FINANCIALS

Company Type: Private

Income Statement FYE: December 31

	REVENUE ($ mil.)	NET INCOME ($ mil.)	NET PROFIT MARGIN	EMPLOYEES
12/02	539	—	—	4,200
12/01	591	—	—	4,500
12/00	633	—	—	5,000
12/99	601	—	—	5,000
12/98	633	—	—	6,000
12/97	525	—	—	5,000
12/96	486	—	—	4,400
12/95	461	—	—	—
12/94	395	—	—	—
Annual Growth	4.0%	—	—	(0.8%)

Revenue History

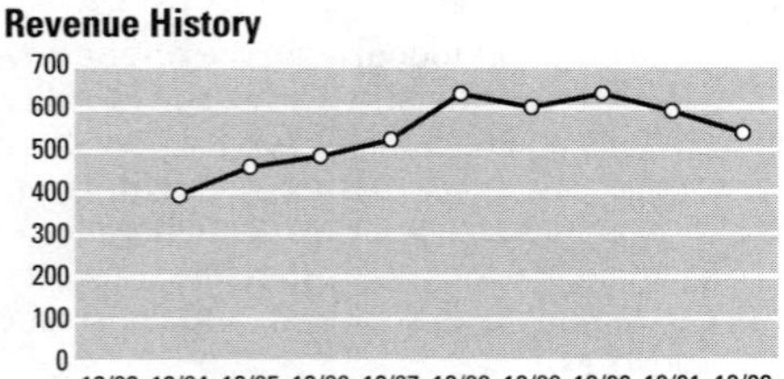

Green Bay Packaging Inc.

Green Bay Packaging is always packed and ready to go. The company is an integrated and diversified paperboard packaging manufacturer. In addition to corrugated containers, the company makes pressure-sensitive label stock, folding cartons, linerboard, and lumber products. Its Fiber Resources division in Arkansas manages more than 210,000 acres of company-owned forests and, through contractors, produces lumber, woodchips, recycled paper, and wood fuel. Green Bay Packaging also offers fiber procurement, wastepaper brokerage, and paper-slitting services. Founded by corrugated paper pioneer George Kress in 1933, the company operates about 30 divisions in 14 states. The Kress family controls Green Bay Packaging.

EXECUTIVES

President: William F. Kress
CFO and Treasurer: Joseph Baemmert

LOCATIONS

HQ: 1700 N. Webster Ct., Green Bay, WI 54307
Phone: 920-433-5111 **Fax:** 920-433-5337
Web: www.gbp.com

Green Bay Packaging operates about 30 divisions in 14 states.

PRODUCTS/OPERATIONS

Selected Products and Services

Corrugated containers
Fiber procurement
Folding cartons
Linerboard
Lumber
Paper slitting
Wastepaper brokerage and procurement

COMPETITORS

Boise Cascade
Caraustar
Chesapeake Corporation
Rock-Tenn
Shorewood Packaging
Smurfit-Stone Container
Temple-Inland

HISTORICAL FINANCIALS

Company Type: Private

Income Statement FYE: December 31

	REVENUE ($ mil.)	NET INCOME ($ mil.)	NET PROFIT MARGIN	EMPLOYEES
12/02	800	—	—	2,750
12/01	800	—	—	2,800
12/00	826	—	—	3,025
12/99	738	—	—	3,000
12/98	650	—	—	2,700
12/97	500	—	—	2,700
12/96	650	—	—	2,600
12/95	650	—	—	2,560
12/94	533	—	—	2,557
Annual Growth	5.2%	—	—	0.9%

Revenue History

The Green Bay Packers, Inc.

On the frozen tundra of Lambeau Field, the legendary Green Bay Packers battle for pride in the National Football League. The team, founded in 1919 by Earl "Curly" Lambeau, has been home to such football icons as Bart Starr, Ray Nitschke, and legendary coach Vince Lombardi. The Packers boast a record 12 championship titles, including three Super Bowl victories. The team is also the NFL's only community-owned franchise, being a not-for-profit corporation with about 110,000 shareholders. The shares do not increase in value nor pay dividends, and can only be sold back to the team. No individual is allowed to own more than 200,000 shares.

After a couple of poor seasons, both athletically and financially, the Packers organization has high hopes for the future. Green Bay voters approved public financing for a $295 million renovation of historic Lambeau Field (which the city owns) in 2000. The completed project added 10,000 seats to the stadium, as well as additional luxury seats. The team's waiting list for season tickets boasts more than 56,000 names.

HISTORY

In 1919 Earl "Curly" Lambeau helped organize a professional football team in Green Bay, Wisconsin, with the help of George Calhoun, the sports editor of the *Green Bay Press-Gazette.* At 20 years old, Lambeau was elected team captain and convinced the Indian Packing Company to back the team, giving the squad its original name, the Indians. The local paper, however, nicknamed the team the Packers and the name stuck. Playing on an open field at Hagemeister Park, the team collected fees by passing the hat among the fans. In 1921 the team was admitted into the American Professional Football Association (later called the National Football League), which had been organized the year before.

The Packers went bankrupt after a poor showing its first season in the league, and Lambeau and Calhoun bought the team for $250. With debts continuing to mount, *Press-Gazette* general manager Andrew Turnbull helped reorganize the team as the not-for-profit Green Bay Football Corporation and sold stock at $5 a share. Despite winning three straight championships from 1929-31, the team again teetered on the brink of bankruptcy, forcing another stock sale in 1935. With fortunes on and off the field dwindling, Lambeau retired in 1950. A third stock sale was called for that year, raising $118,000. City Stadium (renamed Lambeau Field in 1965) was opened in 1957. In 1959 the team hired New York Giants assistant Vince Lombardi as head coach.

Under Lombardi, the Packers dominated football in the 1960s, winning five NFL titles. With players such as Bart Starr and Ray Nitschke, the team defeated the Kansas City Chiefs in the first Super Bowl after the 1966 season. Lombardi resigned after winning Super Bowl II (he passed away in 1970), and the team again fell into mediocrity. Former MVP Starr was called upon to coach in 1974 but couldn't turn the tide before he was released in 1983.

Bob Harlan, who had joined the Packers as assistant general manager in 1971, became president and CEO in 1989. He hired Ron Wolf as general manager in 1991, who in turn hired Mike Holmgren as head coach early the next year. With a roster including Brett Favre, Reggie White, and Robert Brooks, the Packers posted six straight playoff appearances and won its third Super Bowl in 1997. A fourth stock sale (preceded by a 1,000:1 stock split) netted the team more than $24 million.

After Holmgren resigned in 1999 (he left to coach the Seattle Seahawks), former Philadelphia Eagles coach Ray Rhodes tried to lead the team but lasted only one dismal season. In 2000 Mike Sherman, a former Holmgren assistant, was named the team's 13th head coach. Prompted by falling revenue, the team announced plans to renovate Lambeau Field, and voters in Brown County later approved a sales tax increase to help finance the $295 million project. (The project was completed in 2003.) The next year Wolf retired and coach Sherman was tapped as general manager. The team also signed quarterback Favre to a 10-year, $100 million contract extension.

EXECUTIVES

President and CEO: Robert E. Harlan, age 67
EVP and COO: John M. Jones, age 51
EVP, General Manager, and Head Coach: Michael F. (Mike) Sherman, age 48
VP Football Operations: Mark Hatley, age 54
VP Player Finance and General Counsel: Andrew Brandt, age 43
Executive Director of Public Relations: Lee Remmel, age 79
Corporate Counsel: Jason Wied
Corporate Sales Executive: Jason Hartlund
Secretary: Peter M. Platten III, age 63
Treasurer: John R. Underwood
Director of Accounting: Duke Copp
Director of Administrative Affairs: Mark Schiefelbein
Director of College Scouting: John Dorsey, age 43
Director of Corporate Security: Jerry Parins
Director of Corporate Sponsorships: Craig Benzel
Director of Information Technology: Wayne Wichlacz
Director of Facility Operations: Ted Eisenreich
Director of Finance: Vicki Vannieuwenhoven
Director of Player Development: Edgar Bennett, age 34
Director of Premium Guest Services: Jennifer Ark
Director of Pro Personnel: Reggie McKenzie, age 40
Director of Public Relations: Jeff Blumb
Director of Research and Development: Mike Eayrs, age 52
Director of Special Events: Lee Geurts-Bengtson
Director of Ticket Operations: Mark Wagner
Assistant Director of Public Relations and Travel Coordinator: Aaron Popkey
Assistant to the General Manager and Director of Football Administration: Bruce Warwick, age 36
Manager of Community Relations: Cathy Dworak
Marketing Entertainment Coordinator: Kandi Goltz
Marketing and Corporate Sales Coordinator: Shea Greil
Auditors: Wipfli Ullrich Bertelson LLP

LOCATIONS

HQ: 1265 Lombardi Ave., Green Bay, WI 54304
Phone: 920-496-5700 **Fax:** 920-496-5712
Web: www.packers.com

The Green Bay Packers play at Lambeau Field in Green Bay, Wisconsin. The team holds its training camp at St. Norbert College in De Pere, Wisconsin.

PRODUCTS/OPERATIONS

Championship Titles

Super Bowl I (1967)
Super Bowl II (1968)
Super Bowl XXXI (1997)
NFC Championships (1996-97)
NFC Central Division (1972, 1995-97)
NFC North Division (2002)
NFL Championships (1929-31, 1936, 1939, 1944, 1961-62, 1965)
NFL Western Conference (1936, 1938-39, 1944, 1960-62, 1965-67)

COMPETITORS

Chicago Bears
Detroit Lions
Minnesota Vikings

HISTORICAL FINANCIALS

Company Type: Not-for-profit

Income Statement FYE: March 31

	REVENUE ($ mil.)	NET INCOME ($ mil.)	NET PROFIT MARGIN	EMPLOYEES
3/03	153	19	12.3%	150
3/02	132	7	5.3%	150
3/01	124	9	7.0%	140
3/00	109	3	2.5%	95
3/99	103	7	6.3%	95
3/98	82	6	7.7%	92
3/97	75	—	—	90
3/96	70	—	—	82
3/95	62	—	—	80
3/94	66	—	—	74
Annual Growth	9.9%	24.4%	—	8.2%

Net Income History

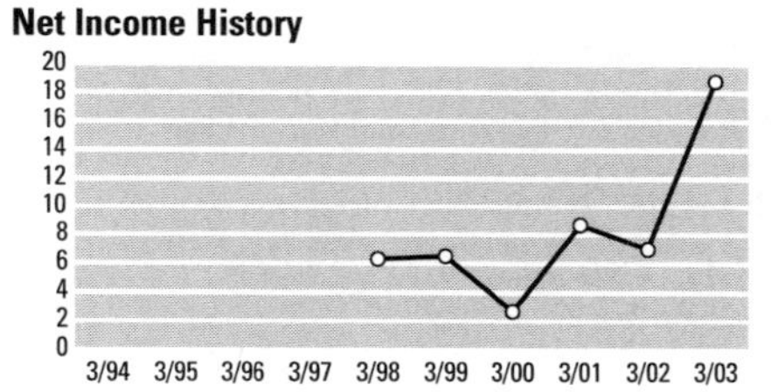

Greenville Hospital System

Greenville Hospital System is a not-for-profit community hospital system serving South Carolina's "Golden Strip" (the I-85 corridor connecting Charlotte, North Carolina, and Atlanta). Founded in 1912 as a community hospital, the system today includes four acute-care hospitals (about 900 beds), as well as a children's hospital, a cancer center, and a nursing home. Greenville Hospital System offers a full range of services, including a primary-care physician network, a health plan, and outpatient care. The company, which also operates a charitable foundation, has teaching affiliations with two medical schools and a research affiliation with Clemson University.

EXECUTIVES

President: Frank D. Pinckney
Executive Director Financial Services and Treasurer: Susan Bichel
CIO: Doran Dunaway
VP Human Resources: Douglas Dorman
Auditors: Ernst & Young LLP

LOCATIONS

HQ: 701 Grove Rd., Greenville, SC 29605
Phone: 864-455-7000 **Fax:** 864-455-6218
Web: www.ghs.org

Greenville Hospital System operates in South Carolina.

PRODUCTS/OPERATIONS

Selected Operations

Allen Bennett Hospital (Greer, acute care)
Greenville Memorial Hospital (acute care)
Hillcrest Hospital (Simpsonville, acute care)
Marshall I. Pickens Hospital (Greenville, psychiatric care)
North Greenville Hospital (Travelers Rest, acute care)
Roger C. Peace Rehabilitation Hospital (Greenville, rehab)
Roger Huntington Nursing Center (Greer, assisted living)

COMPETITORS

Bon Secours Health
Health Management Associates
Novant Health

HISTORICAL FINANCIALS

Company Type: Not-for-profit

Income Statement FYE: September 30

	REVENUE ($ mil.)	NET INCOME ($ mil.)	NET PROFIT MARGIN	EMPLOYEES
9/02	710	33	4.7%	6,500
9/01	691	34	4.9%	6,500
9/00	592	35	5.9%	6,200
9/99	541	10	1.8%	6,000
9/98	494	—	—	5,700
9/97	453	—	—	5,500
9/96	430	—	—	5,500
9/95	399	—	—	5,000
9/94	373	—	—	5,000
9/93	347	—	—	5,000
Annual Growth	8.3%	50.6%	—	3.0%

2002 Year-End Financials

Debt ratio: 104.6%
Return on equity: 11.5%
Cash ($ mil.): 65
Current ratio: 1.65
Long-term debt ($ mil.): 320

Net Income History

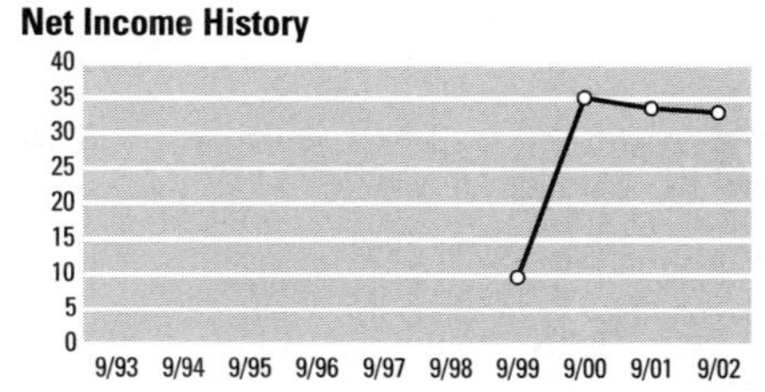

The Grocers Supply Co., Inc.

Need crackers in Caracas or vanilla in Manila? Grocers Supply Co. distributes groceries near and far. The company (not to be confused with fellow Texas distributor GSC Enterprises) distributes food, health and beauty items, household products, and school and office supplies to more than 1,200 convenience stores, 650 supermarkets, and 200 schools within a 350-mile radius of Houston. Its Grocers Supply International (GSI) division ships supplies to oil company operations, other commercial customers, and US embassies around the world. GSI boasts that it will buy anything to ship anywhere for anyone, including macaroons in Rangoon, or even oleo in Tokyo. Grocers Supply is owned by the Levit family.

In August 2003 Grocers Supply Co. acquired the Garland, Texas, division of Fleming Companies when Fleming sold its wholesale distribution business.

EXECUTIVES

CEO: Milton Levit
President: Max Levit
SVP, Financial Services: Jim Nelson
SVP, Sales: Dave Hoffman
VP, Accounting: Michael Castleberry
VP, Buying: Tom Becker
VP, Human Resources: Terry Collins
VP, Management Information Systems: David Bash
VP, Sales: Jim Davenport
Secretary: Tracy Levit-Larner
Controller: Bill Stewart
Auditors: PricewaterhouseCoopers

LOCATIONS

HQ: 3131 E. Holcombe Blvd., Houston, TX 77021
Phone: 713-747-5000 **Fax:** 713-746-5611
Web: www.grocerssupply.com

COMPETITORS

Affiliated Foods
Brenham Wholesale
C.D. Hartnett
Fleming Companies
GSC Enterprises
Hale-Halsell
McLane
Nash Finch
SUPERVALU
Topco Associates

HISTORICAL FINANCIALS

Company Type: Private

Income Statement FYE: December 31

	REVENUE ($ mil.)	NET INCOME ($ mil.)	NET PROFIT MARGIN	EMPLOYEES
12/02	1,500	—	—	2,538
12/01*	1,500	—	—	2,400
5/00	1,400	—	—	2,000
5/99	1,400	—	—	1,800
5/98	1,400	—	—	1,938
5/97	1,300	—	—	1,200
5/96	1,200	—	—	1,200
5/95	1,500	—	—	1,200
5/94	1,450	—	—	1,200
5/93	1,400	—	—	1,275
Annual Growth	0.8%	—	—	7.9%

*Fiscal year change

Revenue History

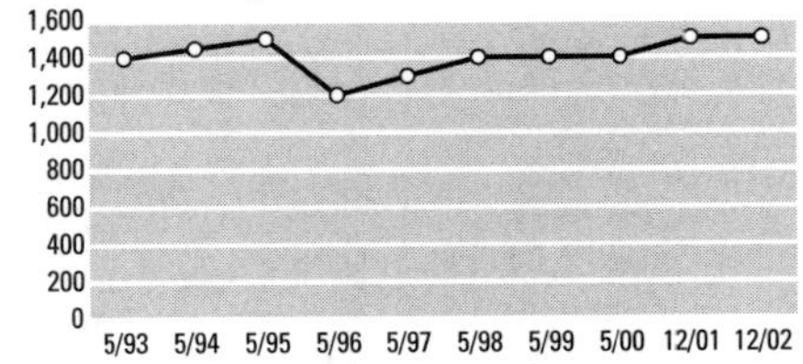

Group Health Cooperative of Puget Sound

Group Health Cooperative of Puget Sound is a not-for-profit managed health care group serving counties in Washington and northern Idaho. Members may participate in HMO, PPO, or point-of-service health plans. The co-op is governed by an 11-person board elected by the organization's members. Specialized services include mental health and substance abuse treatment, hospice services, and HIV/AIDS case management. Group Health Cooperative of Puget Sound has an alliance with Virginia Mason Medical Center (to share medical centers and hospitals), as well as with Kaiser Permanente, one of the nation's largest nonprofit health care systems. The organization is owned by its nearly 600,000 members.

EXECUTIVES

Chairman: Grant Hendrickson
Vice Chairman: Ruth Ballweg
President and CEO: Cheryl M. Scott
EVP and CFO: Jim Truess
EVP and COO: Scott Armstrong
EVP and Chief Marketing Officer; President and CEO, Group Health Options: Maureen McLaughlin
EVP, Group Practice Division: Peter G. Adler
VP and General Counsel: Rick Woods
VP and Chief Information Officer: Janice Newell
VP Public Affairs and Governance: Pam MacEwan
VP, Human Resources: Brenda Tolbert
Auditors: Deloitte & Touche

LOCATIONS

HQ: 521 Wall St., Seattle, WA 98121
Phone: 206-448-5600 **Fax:** 206-448-4010
Web: www.ghc.org

PRODUCTS/OPERATIONS

Selected Services

The Adolescent Center
The Care Center at Kelsey Creek (long-term care)
Center for Attention Deficit Disorders
Consulting Nurse Service
Group Health Credit Union
Group Health Fitness Network
The Group Health Resource Line
The Hear Centers
Language translators
Nutrition Clinics
See Centers/Contact Lens Clinics
Speech, Language and Learning Centers
Take Care stores (wellness products)
Weight Management Programs

COMPETITORS

Aetna
CIGNA
PacifiCare
UnitedHealth Group

HISTORICAL FINANCIALS

Company Type: Not-for-profit

Income Statement FYE: December 31

	REVENUE ($ mil.)	NET INCOME ($ mil.)	NET PROFIT MARGIN	EMPLOYEES
12/01	1,436	21	1.5%	10,500
12/00	1,400	—	—	9,873
12/99	1,400	—	—	9,746
12/98	1,323	—	—	9,602
12/97	1,016	—	—	8,300
12/96	927	—	—	7,179
12/95	1,039	—	—	7,100
12/94	1,013	—	—	7,100
12/93	934	—	—	7,100
12/92	854	—	—	—
Annual Growth	5.9%	—	—	5.0%

Revenue History

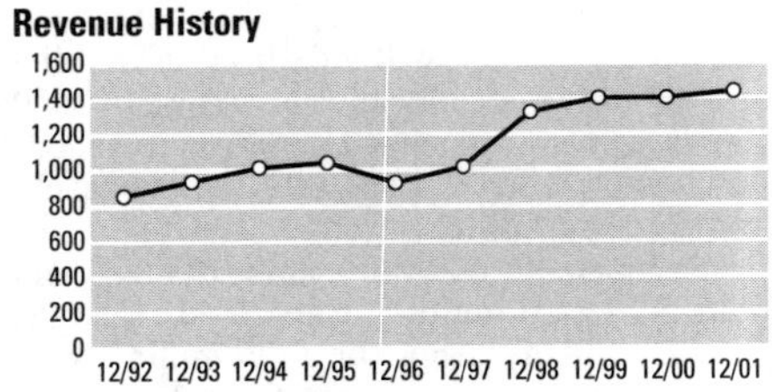

GROWMARK

Retail farm-supply and grain-marketing cooperative GROWMARK can mark its growth by the grain. Through its member-owner co-ops — about 100 in retail and 250-plus in grain marketing — GROWMARK serves farmers in the midwestern US and Ontario, Canada. Operating under the Fast Stop name, the co-op runs fuel stations and convenience stores. Its FS- and NK-brand grains include alfalfa, corn, wheat, and soybeans. GROWMARK also offers fertilizer, seeds, and buildings such as grain bins. GROWMARK partners with Archer Daniels Midland, fertilizer maker and distributor CF Industries, and pet food producer PRO-PET, and it has an energy alliance with Countrymark Cooperative and Land O'Lakes.

EXECUTIVES

CEO: Bill Davisson
VP, Corporate Marketing and Operations: Steve Barwick
VP, Energy Marketing and Operations: Sid Messamore
VP, Finance: Jeff Solberg
VP, Grain Marketing: Davis Anderson
VP, Member Services: Dennis Farmer
VP, Strategic Planning and Corporate Services: Vern McGinnis
VP and General Counsel: Steve Carr
Corporate Employment Specialist: Wes Ehler
Auditors: Ernst & Young LLP

LOCATIONS

HQ: GROWMARK, Inc.
1701 Towanda Ave., Bloomington, IL 61701
Phone: 309-557-6000 **Fax:** 309-829-8532
Web: www.growmark.com

GROWMARK has member cooperatives in Illinois, Iowa, and Wisconsin, and in Ontario, Canada.

COMPETITORS

Ag Processing
Agway
ADM
Cargill
CHS
ConAgra
Farmland Industries
Southern States
Terra Nitrogen

HISTORICAL FINANCIALS

Company Type: Cooperative

Income Statement FYE: August 31

	REVENUE ($ mil.)	NET INCOME ($ mil.)	NET PROFIT MARGIN	EMPLOYEES
8/03	1,679	19	1.1%	626
8/02	1,242	18	1.4%	697
8/01	1,461	18	1.3%	745
8/00	1,392	(0)	—	1,000
8/99	1,156	(10)	—	—
8/98	1,300	37	2.8%	966
8/97	1,570	53	3.4%	875
8/96	1,350	—	—	845
8/95	1,100	—	—	900
8/94	950	—	—	—
Annual Growth	6.5%	(15.5%)	—	(4.4%)

2003 Year-End Financials

Debt ratio: 24.9%
Return on equity: 6.1%
Cash ($ mil.): 7
Current ratio: 1.13
Long-term debt ($ mil.): 81

Net Income History

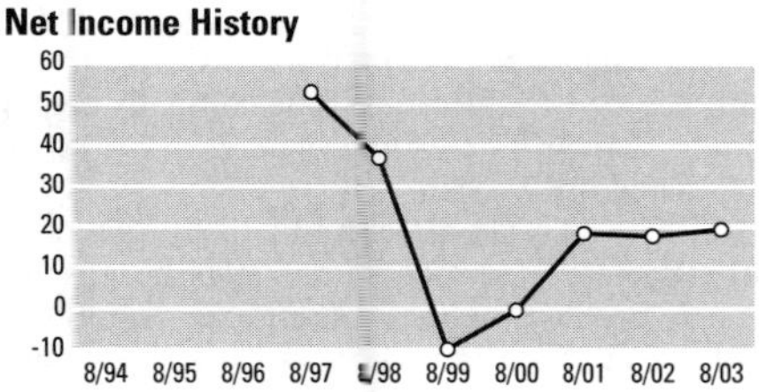

GSC Enterprises

GSC Enterprises brings the groceries to the grocery store. The wholesale distributor (whose name stands for "Grocery Supply Company," not to be confused with Grocers Supply Co.) supplies independently owned convenience stores, grocers, discounters, and other retailers and wholesalers. It serves some 15,000 stores in about 15 states in the Southwest, Southeast, and Midwest. GSC stocks and distributes tobacco, candy, grocery items, prepared foods (Chicago Style Pizza, Chester Fried Chicken, Deli-Fast Foods), and other items. The firm also owns Fidelity Express, which sells money orders in stores. GSC is owned by the McKenzie family, descendants of two of the men who founded it in 1947.

EXECUTIVES

Chairman and CEO: Michael K. (Mickey) McKenzie
President and COO: Larry D. Kerns
VP, Finance and CFO: Kerry Law
VP, Information Technology: Jerry Donaho
VP, Distribution: Michael J. Bain
VP, Marketing and Trade Relations: Steve Shing
VP, Risk Management and Employee Services: Janet Price
VP, Sales: Monty Covington
Secretary: Melissa Bernard
Director, Human Resources: Theresa Patterson

LOCATIONS

HQ: GSC Enterprises, Inc.
130 Hillcrest Dr., Sulphur Springs, TX 75482
Phone: 903-885-0829 **Fax:** 903-885-6928
Web: www.grocerysupply.com

COMPETITORS

Affiliated Foods
AWG
Brenham Wholesale
C.D. Hartnett
Eby-Brown
First Data
Fleming Companies
Grocers Supply
H.T. Hackney
McLane
MoneyGram
Nash Finch
Spartan Stores
SUPERVALU

HISTORICAL FINANCIALS

Company Type: Private

Income Statement FYE: Saturday nearest December 31

	REVENUE ($ mil.)	NET INCOME ($ mil.)	NET PROFIT MARGIN	EMPLOYEES
12/01	1,100	—	—	1,100
12/00	1,082	—	—	1,100
12/99	1,111	—	—	2,000
12/98	1,050	—	—	1,550
12/97	1,082	—	—	1,650
12/96	1,225	—	—	1,840
12/95	1,066	—	—	1,939
12/94	789	—	—	1,600
12/93	757	—	—	1,400
12/92	703	—	—	—
Annual Growth	5.1%	—	—	(3.0%)

Revenue History

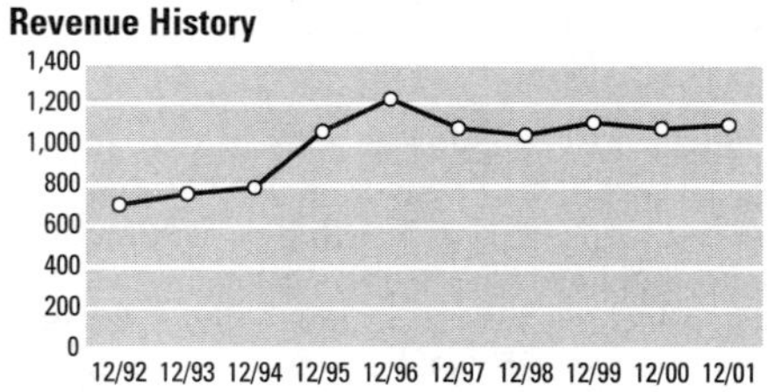

Guardian Industries Corp.

Giving its customers a break would never occur to Guardian Industries, one of the world's largest glassmakers. With facilities on five continents, Guardian primarily produces float glass and fabricated glass products for the automobile and construction markets. It also makes architectural glass, fiberglass, and automotive trim parts. Through its Guardian Building Products Group, the company operates Guardian Fiberglass, Builder Marts of America (which is 20% owned by Ace Hardware), and Cameron Ashley Building Products. President and CEO William Davidson took Guardian Industries public in 1968 and bought it back for himself in 1985. Davidson is also the managing partner of the Detroit Pistons NBA team.

Guardian has been expanding primarily through international acquisitions and by increasing its already significant position in the building materials business. In 2002 the company announced plans to build new float glass plants in Brazil and the UK.

HISTORY

Guardian Glass began as a small maker of car windshields in Detroit in 1932 during the Great Depression. The company spent the 1930s and 1940s building its business to gain a foothold in glassmaking, historically one of the world's most monopolized industries. In 1949 PPG Industries and Libbey-Owens-Ford (now owned by the UK's Pilkington) agreed to stop their alleged monopolistic activity. William Davidson took over Guardian Glass from his uncle in 1957. As president, he tried to boost the enterprise's standing in the windshield niche, but PPG and Libbey-Owens-Ford refused to sell him raw glass. That year Guardian Glass filed for bankruptcy to reorganize.

The company emerged from bankruptcy in 1960 (the same year Pilkington developed the float process for glassmaking), and in 1965 it was hit with its first patent-infringement lawsuit. Three years later the company went public, changed its name to Guardian Industries, and was refused a license to use Pilkington's float technology. Guardian began an aggressive acquisition strategy in 1969, and in 1970 it hired Ford's top glass man (who knew the float process) and proceeded to build its first float-glass plant in Michigan. PPG sued Guardian in 1972. Davidson bought the Detroit Pistons in 1974. He applied a do-or-die style that might best be illustrated by the 1979 firing of Piston's coach Dick Vitale, who claims Davidson axed him on his own front doorstep while a curbside limo waited with the motor running.

In 1980 Guardian started making fiberglass and began hiring former workers from insulation maker Manville to duplicate that company's patented technology for fiberglass insulation. Manville successfully sued Guardian in 1981. Guardian opened a Luxembourg plant that year. Pilkington sued Guardian in 1983, but the case was settled out of court three years later. Davidson took Guardian private in 1985, and in 1988 he bought an Indiana auto trim plant. He also built The Palace of Auburn Hills sports arena in 1988.

The 1990s brought more international expansion for Guardian, with plants added in India, Spain, and Venezuela. It also set up a distribution center in Japan, a country known for its tight control of the glass industry. In 1992 Guardian bought OIS Optical Imaging Systems, a maker of computer display screens. Guardian moved its headquarters to Auburn Hills, Michigan, in 1995. Its 1996 purchase of Automotive Moulding boosted its position in the auto plastics and trim market. In 1997 some 30 class-action lawsuits that alleged price-fixing were filed against the top five US glassmakers, including Guardian. The US Justice Department began investigating the matter.

Guardian booted its OIS Optical Imaging Systems unit in 1998, citing ongoing losses. That year the company's fiberglass subsidiary bought 50% of building materials buying group Builder Marts of America, giving Guardian a foothold in the markets for lumber and roofing products. Also in 1998 Davidson made a failed attempt to buy the Tampa Bay Lightning hockey team.

In 1999 Guardian bought Siam Guardian Glass Ltd. from Siam Cement Plc, the company's partner in Thailand. The next year Guardian acquired Cameron Ashley Building Products, a distributor with more than 160 branches in the US and Canada. Cameron Ashley distributes pool and patio enclosures, roofing, siding, insulation, industrial metals, and millwork materials to independent building materials dealers, builders, large contractors, and mass retailers.

EXECUTIVES

President and CEO: William M. Davidson
EVP: Ralph J. Gerson, age 47
President and CEO, Automotive Products Group: D. James Davis
President, Building Products Group: Duane H. Faulkner
President, Glass Group: Russell J. Ebeid
Director of Communications: Gayle A. Joseph

LOCATIONS

HQ: 2300 Harmon Rd., Auburn Hills, MI 48326
Phone: 248-340-1800 **Fax:** 248-340-9988
Web: www.guardian.com

Guardian Industries operates worldwide manufacturing and distribution facilities.

PRODUCTS/OPERATIONS

Selected Products and Services

Architectural Glass
Custom fabrication
Float glass
Insulating glass
Laminated glass
Mirrors
Patterned glass
Reflective coated glass
Tempered glass

Automotive Systems
Bodyside (mud flaps, wheel covers)
Front and rear end (grilles, rub strips)
Side window (door-frame moldings)
Windshield (window-surround moldings)

Cameron Ashley
Aluminum screen doors
Carports
Ceiling tile
Door frames
Doors
Fiberglass insulation
Formica
Metal roofing
Patio covers
Plywood
Rebar
Sheetrock
Storm doors
Windows

Guardian Fiberglass
Fiberglass insulation

Retail Auto Glass
Auto glass
Auto glass repair and replacement
Insurance claim processing

COMPETITORS

Apogee Enterprises
Asahi Glass
Corning
CRH
Donnelly
Johns Manville
Nippon Sheet Glass
Owens Corning
Pilkington
PPG
Safelite Group
Saint-Gobain
Vitro

HISTORICAL FINANCIALS

Company Type: Private

Income Statement FYE: December 31

	ESTIMATED REVENUE ($ mil.)	NET INCOME ($ mil.)	NET PROFIT MARGIN	EMPLOYEES
12/01	4,000	—	—	19,000
12/00	4,000	—	—	20,000
12/99	3,650	—	—	15,000
12/98	2,200	—	—	15,000
12/97	2,000	—	—	14,000
12/96	1,900	—	—	13,000
12/95	1,700	—	—	12,000
12/94	1,500	—	—	10,000
12/93	1,200	—	—	9,000
12/92	1,200	—	—	10,000
Annual Growth	14.3%	—	—	7.4%

Revenue History

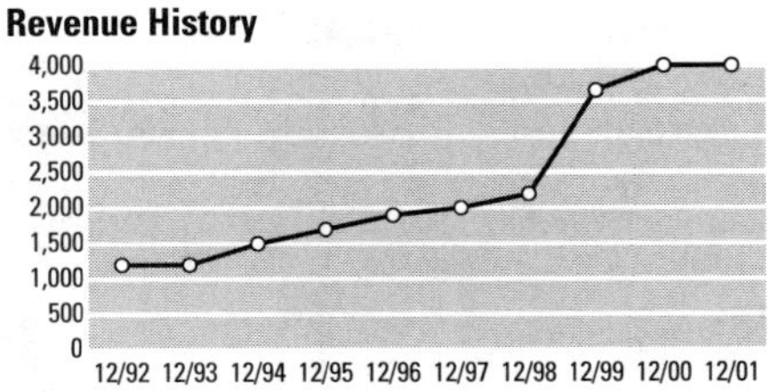

Guardian Life Insurance

When your guardian angel fails you, there's Guardian Life Insurance Company of America. The mutual company, boasting nearly 3 million policy-holding owners, offers life insurance, disability income insurance, and — more recently — retirement programs. Guardian Life Insurance Company of America's employee health indemnity plans provide HMO, PPO, and dental and vision plans, as well as disability plans. In the retirement area, Guardian has long offered the Park Avenue group of mutual funds and annuity products, managed by its Guardian Investor Services.

To meet competition in the quickly deregulating financial services area, the company is building its wealth management capabilities to target baby boomers getting ready for retirement. It created broker-dealer Park Avenue Securities and launched Guardian Trust Company to offer trust and investment management services.

As part of these initiatives, Guardian has been on the move to improve customer service and to raise its profile through national advertising. It has also continued acquiring complementary insurers including the acquisition of disability insurance (one of the company's designated growth areas) specialist Berkshire Life Insurance.

Guardian's life insurance and annuity products had a strong year in 2002 but like so many of its peers, losses on investments dragged its net results down in the red. Due to the poorly performing stock market, the company has stopped selling new group pension products.

HISTORY

Hugo Wesendonck came to the US from Germany in 1850 to escape a death sentence for his part in an abortive 1848 revolution. After working in the silk business in Philadelphia, he moved to New York, which was home to more ethnic Germans than any city save Berlin and Vienna.

In 1860 Wesendonck and other expatriates formed an insurance company to serve the German-American community. Germania Life Insurance was chartered as a stock mutual, which paid dividends to shareholders and policy owners. Wesendonck was its first president.

The Civil War blocked the company's growth in the South, but it expanded in the rest of the US and by 1867 even operated in South America.

After the Civil War, many insurers foundered from high costs. Wesendonck battled this by implementing strict cost controls and limiting commissions, allowing the company to continue issuing dividends and rebates on its policyholders' premiums.

In the 1870s Germania opened offices in Europe, and for the next few decades much of the company's growth was there. By 1910, 46% of sales originated in Europe. The company's target clientele in the US decreased between the 1890s and WWI as German immigration slowed, and its market share dropped from ninth in 1880 to 21st in 1910.

During WWI the company lost contact with its German business. Prodded by anti-German sentiment in the US, the company changed its name to The Guardian Life Insurance Company of America in 1917. After WWI the company began winding down its German business (a process that lasted until 1952).

In 1924 Guardian began mutualizing but could not complete the process until 1944 because of probate problems with a shareholder's estate.

After WWII, Guardian offered noncancelable medical insurance (1955) and group insurance (1957). The company formed Guardian Investor Services in 1969 to offer mutual funds; two years later it established Guardian Insurance & Annuity to sell variable contracts. In 1989 it organized Guardian Asset Management to handle pension funds.

In 1993, as indemnity health costs rose, the company moved into managed care via its membership in Private Health Care Systems, a consortium of commercial insurance carriers offering managed health care products and services. This allowed Guardian to offer HMO and PPO products.

Guardian entered a joint marketing agreement in 1995 with HMO Physicians Health Services, which contracts with physicians and hospitals in the New York tri-state area. In 1996 the company acquired Managed Dental Care of California and an interest in Physicians Health Services.

Facing deregulation and consolidation in the financial services area, as well as the demutualization of some of its largest competitors, Guardian in the late 1990s decided to add depth to its employee benefits lines and breadth to its wealth management lines.

In 1999 Guardian formed its broker-dealer subsidiary and received a thrift license to facilitate creation of a trust business. Acquisitions included

Innovative Underwriters Services, Fiduciary Insurance Co. of America, and managed dental care companies First Commonwealth and First Choice Dental Network. In 2001 the company moved to boost its disability business with the purchase of Berkshire Life Insurance.

EXECUTIVES

President, CEO, and Director: Dennis J. Manning
EVP and CFO: Robert E. Broatch, age 49
EVP and Chief Investment Officer: Thomas G. Sorell
EVP and Chief Actuary: Armand M. dePalo
EVP and CIO: Dennis S. Callahan
EVP, Equity Products: Bruce C. Long
EVP, Risk Management Products: Gary B. Lenderink
EVP and Director: Edward K. Kane
SVP and Corporate Secretary: Joseph A. Caruso
SVP, Corporate Marketing: Nancy E. Rogers
SVP, Group Insurance: Richard A. White
SVP, Human Resources: Douglas C. Kramer
SVP, Individual Markets: Anthony T. Mazzei Sr.
VP and General Counsel: John Peluso
VP, Group Pensions: Dennis P. Mosticchio
VP, Reinsurance: Jeremy Starr
Auditors: PricewaterhouseCoopers LLP

LOCATIONS

HQ: The Guardian Life Insurance Company of America
7 Hanover Sq., New York, NY 10004
Phone: 212-598-8000 **Fax:** 212-919-2170
Web: www.glic.com

Guardian Life Insurance Company of America has operations in all 50 states, the District of Columbia, and Puerto Rico.

PRODUCTS/OPERATIONS

Selected Services

Employee benefits
Group pensions and 401(k) products
Individual life and disability income insurance
Investment products (stocks, bonds, mutual funds, and variable annuities & life insurance)

Selected Subsidiaries

Berkshire Life Insurance Company of America
First Commonwealth, Inc.
Guardian Baillie Gifford, Ltd. (Scotland)
The Guardian Insurance & Annuity Company, Inc.
Guardian Investor Services LLC
Guardian Trust Company, FSB
Innovative Underwriters, Inc.
Managed Dental Care of California
Managed DentalGuard of Texas
Park Avenue Life Insurance Company
Park Avenue Securities LLC

COMPETITORS

Aetna
AIG American General
Allstate
Anthem
AXA Financial
Charles Schwab
CIGNA
Citigroup
CNA Financial
FMR
GeneralCologne Re
The Hartford
John Hancock Financial Services
Liberty Mutual
MassMutual
Merrill Lynch
MetLife
New York Life
Northwestern Mutual
Oxford Health Plans
Pacific Mutual
Principal Financial
Prudential
UBS Financial Services
UnitedHealth Group
USAA
WellPoint Health Networks

HISTORICAL FINANCIALS

Company Type: Mutual company

Income Statement FYE: December 31

	ASSETS ($ mil.)	NET INCOME ($ mil.)	INCOME AS % OF ASSETS	EMPLOYEES
12/02	34,074	(283)	—	5,500
12/01	34,333	170	0.5%	6,000
12/00	32,359	563	1.7%	6,000
12/99	31,696	325	1.0%	5,465
12/98	25,854	160	0.6%	—
12/97	22,089	299	1.4%	4,800
12/96	18,196	173	1.0%	5,155
12/95	15,811	125	0.8%	5,322
12/94	13,567	144	1.1%	7,602
12/93	12,336	249	2.0%	7,126
Annual Growth	12.0%	—	—	(2.8%)

2002 Year-End Financials

Equity as % of assets: 16.7%
Return on assets: —
Return on equity: —
Long-term debt ($ mil.): 18,223
Sales ($ mil.): 7,192

Net Income History

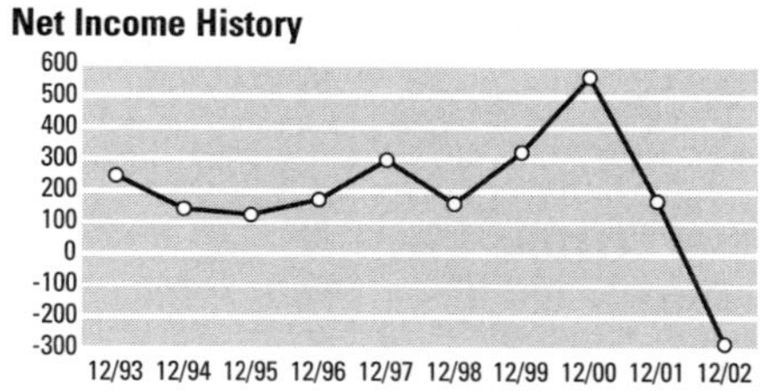

Guardsmark

When FBI agents leave Quantico, they go to Guardsmark. The world's largest employer of former FBI agents is also one of the largest security firms in the US. Guardsmark operates in some 400 cities in North America, where it provides security services to the financial, utility, transportation, and health care industries. The company offers security guards, private investigation, and drug testing services. It consults with architects and builders to design security programs. Guardsmark also conducts background checks (employment, education, and criminal history) and provides outsourcing services (Peoplemark). Chairman and president Ira Lipman owns the company, which he founded in 1963.

EXECUTIVES

Chairman, President, and CEO: Ira A. Lipman
Vice Chairman: Weldon L. Kennedy
Vice Chairman: Jeffrey B. Westcott
SVP, CFO, and Treasurer: Jerome C. Jacques
SVP External Government Affairs: Howard B. Spector
SVP Security Division Sales: John F. Clark
SVP: Jeffrey D. Landreth
SVP: Gustave K. Lipman
SVP: Don K. Pettus
VP and CIO: Edward S. Rothman
Auditors: PricewaterhouseCoopers LLP

LOCATIONS

HQ: Guardsmark, Inc.
10 Rockefeller Plaza, New York, NY 10020
Phone: 212-765-8226 **Fax:** 212-603-3854
Web: www.guardsmark.com

COMPETITORS

Allied Security
ADP Screening and Selection Services
Barton Protective Services
ChoicePoint
Command Security
Employee Information Services
Kroll
Kroll Laboratory Specialists
LabOne
PharmChem
TransNational Security
Wackenhut

HISTORICAL FINANCIALS

Company Type: Private

Income Statement FYE: June 30

	REVENUE ($ mil.)	NET INCOME ($ mil.)	NET PROFIT MARGIN	EMPLOYEES
6/02	454	—	—	17,369
6/01	400	—	—	17,000
6/00	342	—	—	15,500
6/99	300	—	—	14,000
6/98	279	—	—	13,000
Annual Growth	12.9%	—	—	7.5%

Revenue History

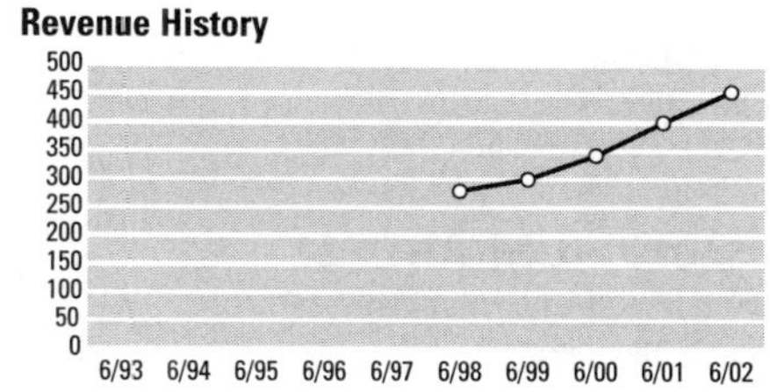

Guide Corporation

This Guide shows motorists the way through the dark. Guide makes auto and truck exterior lighting systems: headlamps, turn signals, tail lamps, and license plate lamps. The company took its name from Guide Motor Lamp Manufacturing, which developed the first electric headlamp before it was acquired by GM in 1928. Guide's ownership became a corporate "hot potato" after GM sold the company to investment firm Palladium Equity Partners in 1998. Despite a $50 million infusion of cash, a restructuring plan, and the installation of fresh management, Guide remained in the red. In 2001 Guide was acquired by turnaround specialist B.N. Bahadur's Vehicle Lighting, Inc.

EXECUTIVES

President and CEO: Dennis E. Hiller
EVP and CFO: Fran Corby
EVP, Engineering and Development: Jeff Mickel
EVP, Quality and Human Resources: Steve Murray
EVP, Sales and Marketing: Dan Dobbins
EVP, Worldwide Operations: Keith Merrill
VP and CIO: Jim Johnson
VP, Industrial Relations: Bob Stearns
VP, Salaried Personnel and Employee Benefits: Carlton Montague
COO, North American Operations: Robert Anders
Director, Materials Management: Chuck Wittum

LOCATIONS

HQ: 600 Corporation Dr., Pendleton, IN 46064
Phone: 765-221-7000 **Fax:** 765-221-7904
Web: www.guidecorp.com

Guide Corporation has manufacturing operations in Indiana, Louisiana, and Mexico, as well as joint venture operations in India, South Korea, and Poland.

PRODUCTS/OPERATIONS

Selected Products

Cornering lamps
Fog lamps
Halogen infrared lamps
Head lights
High-intensity discharge headlamps
High-mounted third brake lights
LED lamps
License plate lamps
Neon lighting
Reflex panels
Tail lamps
Turn signal lamps

COMPETITORS

Catalina Lighting
Federal-Mogul
Philips Electronics
Robert Bosch
UIS
Visteon

HISTORICAL FINANCIALS

Company Type: Private

Income Statement FYE: December 31

	REVENUE ($ mil.)	NET INCOME ($ mil.)	NET PROFIT MARGIN	EMPLOYEES
12/02	450	—	—	3,500
12/01	401	—	—	3,000
12/00	597	—	—	3,200
12/99	600	—	—	3,100
12/98	665	—	—	4,000
Annual Growth	(9.3%)	—	—	(3.3%)

Revenue History

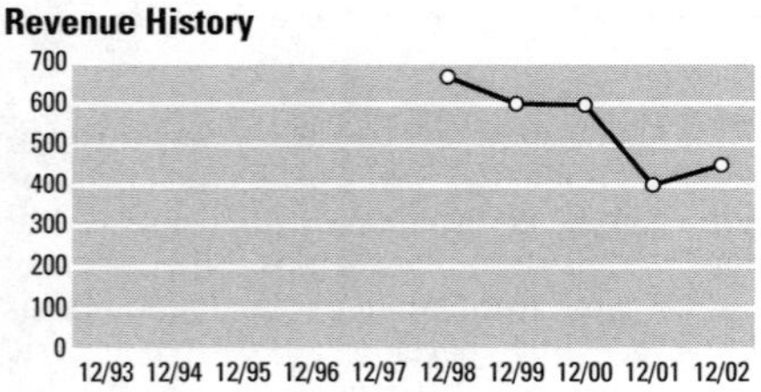

Gulf Oil Limited Partnership

Gulf Oil bridges the gap between petroleum producers and retail sales outlets. The petroleum wholesaler distributes gasoline and diesel fuel to 1,800 Gulf-branded stations in 11 northeastern states. Gulf Oil, which owns and operates 12 storage terminals, also distributes motor oils, lubricants, and heating oil to commercial, industrial, and utility customers. The company has alliances with terminal operators in areas in the Northeast where it does not have a proprietary terminal. Noteworthy for providing the world's first drive-in service station, Gulf Oil was established in 1901 with an oil strike in Spindletop, Texas. The oil company restructured into seven operating companies in the 1970s.

EXECUTIVES

CEO: John Kaneb
President: Gary Kaneb
Controller: Alice Kuhne
Director Human Resources: Karen Channel

LOCATIONS

HQ: 90 Everett Ave., Chelsea, MA 02150
Phone: 617-889-9000 **Fax:** 617-884-0637
Web: www.gulfoil.com

Gulf Oil operates in northeastern US states.

PRODUCTS/OPERATIONS

Selected Products

Antifreeze
Gasoline
Grease
Heating oil
Kerosene
Synthetic lubricants
Transmission fluid
Zinc-free oils

COMPETITORS

Amerada Hess
BP
CITGO
Exxon Mobil
Getty Petroleum Marketing
Global Companies
Motiva Enterprises
Premcor
Sunoco

HISTORICAL FINANCIALS

Company Type: Partnership

Income Statement FYE: September 30

	ESTIMATED REVENUE ($ mil.)	NET INCOME ($ mil.)	NET PROFIT MARGIN	EMPLOYEES
9/02	1,680	—	—	150
9/01	1,970	—	—	200
9/00	1,800	—	—	185
9/99	1,808	—	—	185
9/98	1,800	—	—	185
9/97	2,300	—	—	200
9/96	1,900	—	—	200
9/95	2,000	—	—	200
9/94	1,800	—	—	200
9/93	1,650	—	—	150
Annual Growth	0.2%	—	—	0.0%

Revenue History

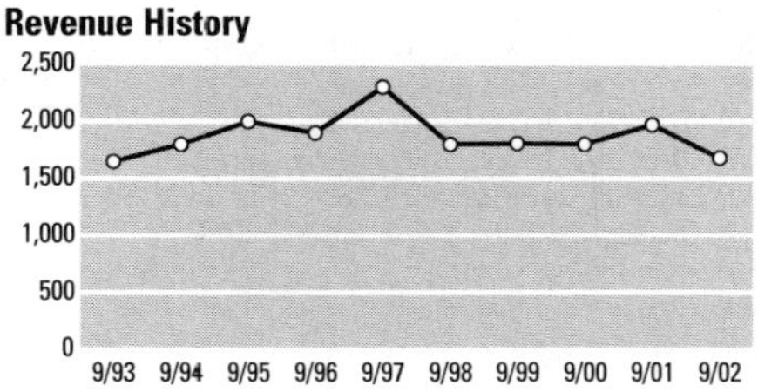

Gulf States Toyota, Inc.

Even good ol' boys buy foreign cars from Gulf States Toyota. One of only two US Toyota distributors not owned by Toyota Motor Sales (the other is JM Family Enterprises' Southeast Toyota Distributors), the company distributes Toyota and Lexus cars, trucks, and sport utility vehicles in Arkansas, Louisiana, Mississippi, Oklahoma, and Texas. Founded in 1969 by Thomas Friedkin and still owned by The Friedkin Companies, Gulf States distributes new Toyotas, parts, and accessories to around 140 dealers in its region. Gulf States Toyota has acquired Metrix Holdings in New York.

EXECUTIVES

President and General Manager: Toby Hynes
CFO: Frank Gruen
Director of Administration: David Copeland
VP of Human Resources: Dominic Gallo

LOCATIONS

HQ: 7701 Wilshire Place Dr., Houston, TX 77040
Phone: 713-580-3300 **Fax:** 713-580-3332

COMPETITORS

BMW
DaimlerChrysler
Ford
General Motors
Honda
JM Family Enterprises
Kia Motors
Mazda
McDavid Auto Group
Nissan North America
Volkswagen
Volvo

HISTORICAL FINANCIALS

Company Type: Private

Income Statement FYE: December 31

	ESTIMATED REVENUE ($ mil.)	NET INCOME ($ mil.)	NET PROFIT MARGIN	EMPLOYEES
12/01	3,800	—	—	3,000
12/00	3,250	—	—	1,650
12/99	3,158	—	—	1,600
12/98	2,500	—	—	1,600
12/97	2,300	—	—	1,600
12/96	1,700	—	—	1,500
12/95	1,600	—	—	1,500
12/94	1,800	—	—	1,500
12/93	1,534	—	—	1,500
12/92	1,190	—	—	—
Annual Growth	13.8%	—	—	9.1%

Revenue History

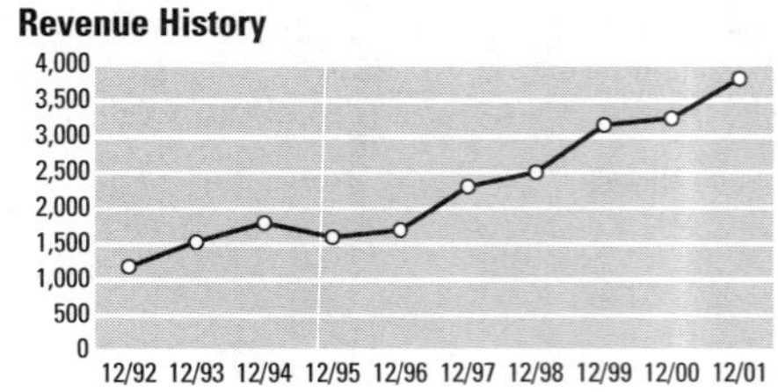

Guthy-Renker

What do Kathie Lee Gifford, Cindy Crawford, Victoria Principal, and Tony Robbins have in common? Each has starred in an infomercial produced by Guthy-Renker, one of the largest infomercial producers in the US. The firm's pitchpeople hawk a variety of goods and services, including skin care products and cosmetics (the company's primary category), fitness equipment, and motivational tapes. In addition, Guthy-Renker sells *The Dean Martin Celebrity Roasts*. The company also pursues marketing opportunities through direct mail, retail, and telemarketing. Guthy-Renker was founded in 1988 by Bill Guthy and Greg Renker, after being spun off from Guthy's Cassette Productions Unlimited (CPU).

EXECUTIVES

Co-CEO: William Guthy
Co-CEO: Greg Renker
EVP, CFO, and COO: Kevin Knee
EVP Business Development: Ben Van De Bunt

LOCATIONS

HQ: Guthy-Renker Corp.
41-550 Eclectic St., Ste. 200, Palm Desert, CA 92260
Phone: 760-773-9022 **Fax:** 760-836-1013
Web: www.guthy-renker.com

PRODUCTS/OPERATIONS

Selected Infomercials

Meaningful Beauty skin care (hosted by Cindy Crawford)
Natural Advantage skin care (hosted by Kathie Lee Gifford)
Personal Power motivational tapes (hosted by Anthony Robbins)
Principal Secret skin care (hosted by Victoria Principal)
Pro-Activ Solutions skin care (hosted by Vanessa Williams and Judith Light)
Sellecca Solution skin care (hosted by Connie Sellecca)
Victoria Jackson Cosmetics
Youthful Essence skin care (hosted by Susan Lucci)

COMPETITORS

Aloette
GenesisIntermedia
GT Brands
Hydron
IAC
QVC
Ronco
Thane International
ValueVision Media

HISTORICAL FINANCIALS

Company Type: Private

Income Statement FYE: December 31

	REVENUE ($ mil.)	NET INCOME ($ mil.)	NET PROFIT MARGIN	EMPLOYEES
12/01	700	—	—	175
12/00	500	—	—	—
12/99	350	—	—	200
12/98	350	—	—	200
12/97	350	—	—	190
12/96	300	—	—	126
12/95	270	—	—	67
12/94	125	—	—	63
Annual Growth	27.9%	—	—	15.7%

Revenue History

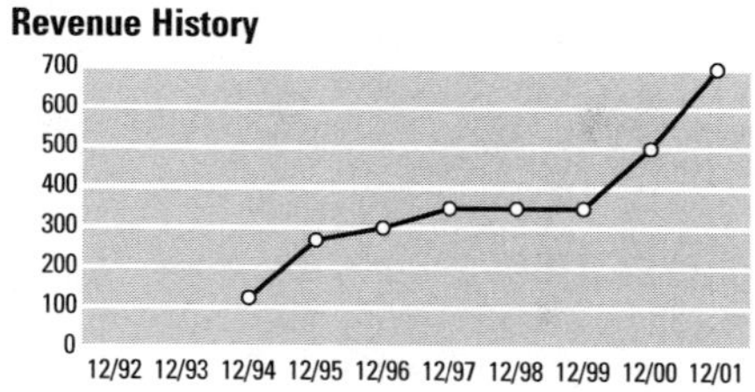

H Group Holding Inc.

Owned and operated by the Pritzkers, Chicago's financial super-family, H Group Holding is the holding company for Hyatt Hotels, Conwood tobacco company, and Classic Residence senior communities. Since the death of Jay Pritzker in 1999, family squabbles over their vast $15 billion fortune have led to talks of breaking up the empire and taking Hyatt public. The Pritzker portfolio also includes the Marmon Group (including credit check subsidiary Trans Union), Pritzker Realty, and a 25% stake in the Royal Caribbean cruise ship line. The family is active in philanthropic circles through the Pritzker Foundation.

H Group Holding sold its stake in joint venture (with Israel Aircraft Industries) Galaxy Aerospace to General Dynamics in 2001.

EXECUTIVES

CEO: Thomas J. Pritzker, age 52
CFO: Frank Borg

LOCATIONS

HQ: 200 W. Madison St., 39th Fl., Chicago, IL 60606
Phone: 312-750-1234 **Fax:** 312-750-8550

COMPETITORS

Cendant
Four Seasons Hotels
GE
Hilton
Host Marriott
ITT Industries
Marriott International
Starwood Hotels & Resorts
Swisher International
UST
Wyndham

HISTORICAL FINANCIALS

Company Type: Private

Income Statement FYE: December 31

	REVENUE ($ mil.)	NET INCOME ($ mil.)	NET PROFIT MARGIN	EMPLOYEES
12/01	2,000	—	—	41,000
12/00	2,300	—	—	70,000
12/99	2,200	—	—	70,000
12/98	2,000	—	—	70,000
12/97	1,378	—	—	43,000
12/96	869	—	—	—
Annual Growth	18.1%	—	—	(1.2%)

Revenue History

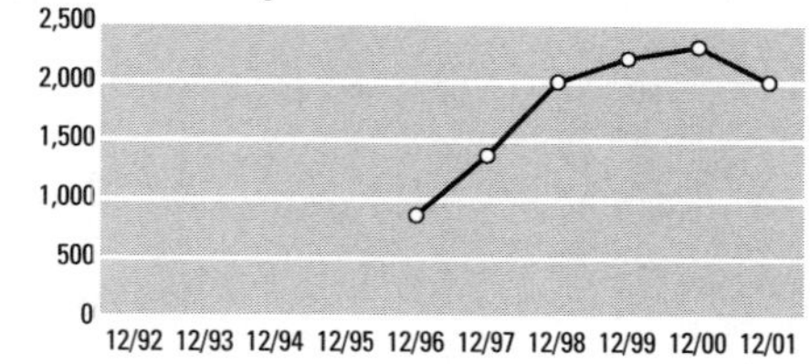

Haggen, Inc.

Haggen showers shoppers in the Pacific Northwest with salmon, coffee, and other essentials. The area's largest independent grocer, Haggen operates nearly 30 combination supermarket/drugstores in Washington and Oregon. Most upscale Haggen Food & Pharmacy stores feature specialty departments, while the TOP Food & Drug outlets emphasize savings; however, both may offer such amenities as Starbucks Coffee shops, Blockbuster Video outlets, or child-care centers. To keep up with the Joneses of supermarket fame and fortune, Haggen partnered with ShopEaze.com (an e-commerce service provider), which failed, leaving Haggen without an online store. Brothers and co-chairmen Don and Rick Haggen own the chain.

EXECUTIVES

Co-Chairman: Donald E. Haggen
Co-Chairman: Richard R. Haggen, age 57
President and CEO: Dale C. Henley
SVP, Information Technology and Corporate Services: Fred Byrum
SVP, Sales and Merchandising: Dave Norton
VP, Administration: Jeff Wood
VP, Finance: Tom Kenney
VP, Marketing: Scott Smith
Controller: Gary Hall
Director, Human Resources: Janel Ernster

LOCATIONS

HQ: 2211 Rimland Dr., Bellingham, WA 98226
Phone: 360-733-8720 **Fax:** 360-650-8235
Web: www.haggen.com

Haggen operates Haggen Food & Pharmacy stores in Washington and Oregon and TOP Food & Drug stores in Washington.

PRODUCTS/OPERATIONS

Selected Departments and Services

Bakery
Banking
Blockbuster Video
Cash machines
Dry cleaning
Full-service floral department
Garden supplies
In-store home economist
Just for Kids child-care center
Library book drop off
Market Street Café
Parcel pickup
Pharmacy
Seafood
Starbucks Coffee shop
Sushi

COMPETITORS

Albertson's
Brown & Cole Stores
Costco Wholesale
Fred Meyer Stores
Quality Food
Safeway
Trader Joe's Co
Wal-Mart
WinCo Foods

HISTORICAL FINANCIALS

Company Type: Private

Income Statement FYE: December 31

	REVENUE ($ mil.)	NET INCOME ($ mil.)	NET PROFIT MARGIN	EMPLOYEES
12/02	760	—	—	4,100
12/01	700	—	—	4,000
12/00	666	—	—	4,000
12/99	579	—	—	3,500
12/98	521	—	—	3,200
12/97	450	—	—	2,850
12/96	436	—	—	3,000
12/95	420	—	—	2,600
12/94	400	—	—	2,400
Annual Growth	8.4%	—	—	6.9%

Revenue History

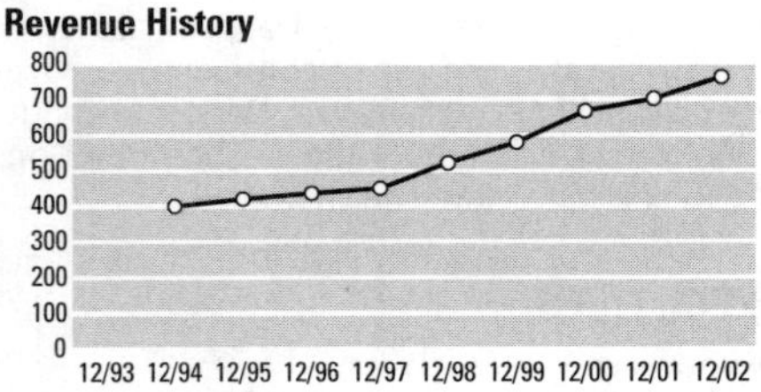

Hale-Halsell Co.

Hale-Halsell Co. doesn't make cattle drives, but the food retailer and wholesaler does round up and move out grocery goods throughout Arkansas, Kansas, Missouri, Oklahoma, and Texas. On the retail side, the company operates some 120 Git-N-Go convenience stores and about 10 Super H Foods supermarkets, primarily in small Oklahoma towns. Hale-Halsell also runs a restaurant supply business. Tom Hale and Hugh Halsell started the company in 1901 to supply settlers in the newly opened Native American lands in Oklahoma. Hale-Halsell is majority-owned by Hale's descendant, Elmer Hale Jr.

EXECUTIVES

Chairman and CEO: Robert D. Hawk
President and COO: James O. Lewis
VP, Operations: Jim Scivally
Secretary and Treasurer: Michael Owens
Director of Personnel: Ron Stacey

LOCATIONS

HQ: 9111 E. Pine St., Tulsa, OK 74115
Phone: 918-835-4484 **Fax:** 918-641-5471
Web: www.hale-halsell.com

COMPETITORS

7-Eleven
Affiliated Foods
Albertson's
AWG
ChevronTexaco
Exxon Mobil
E-Z Mart Stores
Fleming Companies
Grocers Supply
GSC Enterprises
Homeland Stores
IGA
Kroger
Nash Finch
QuikTrip
SUPERVALU
Wal-Mart

HISTORICAL FINANCIALS

Company Type: Private

Income Statement FYE: December 31

	REVENUE ($ mil.)	NET INCOME ($ mil.)	NET PROFIT MARGIN	EMPLOYEES
12/01	950	—	—	4,500
12/00	859	—	—	4,531
12/99	837	—	—	4,683
12/98	815	—	—	4,674
12/97	731	—	—	4,660
12/96	756	—	—	5,129
12/95	715	—	—	5,300
12/94	697	—	—	5,281
12/93	403	—	—	5,320
12/92	380	—	—	4,079
Annual Growth	10.7%	—	—	1.1%

Revenue History

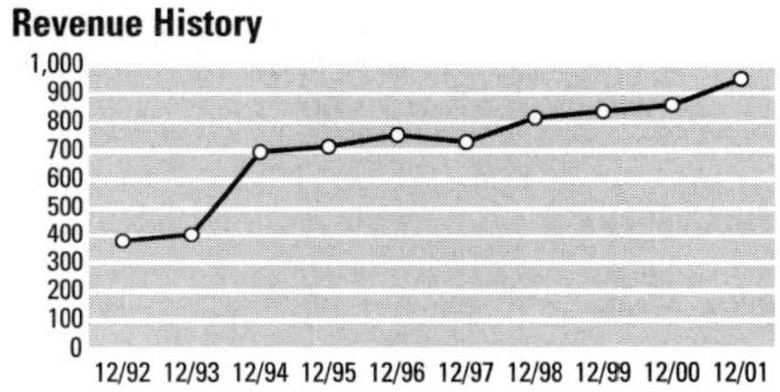

Hallmark Cards, Inc.

As the #1 producer of warm fuzzies, Hallmark Cards is the Goliath of greeting cards. The company's cards are sold under brand names such as Hallmark, Shoebox, and Ambassador and can be found in more than 42,000 US retail stores (about 4,300 of these stores bear the Hallmark Gold Crown name; the majority of these stores are franchised). Hallmark also owns Binney & Smith (maker of Crayola brand crayons) and portrait studio chain The Picture People. It offers electronic greeting cards and flowers through its Web site, Hallmark.com, and produces television movies through Hallmark Entertainment and its majority-owned Crown Media unit. Members of the founding Hall family own two-thirds of Hallmark.

Not resting on well-engraved laurels, Hallmark has announced its intention to triple its revenue by 2010. While it plans to continue expanding its greeting card empire, the company is also intent on stretching its reach in markets such as personal development and family entertainment. Hallmark is bringing a literary slant to its products with a new line of cards and products developed by Pulitzer Prize nominee and poet Maya Angelou.

HISTORY

Eighteen-year-old Joyce Hall started selling picture postcards from two shoe boxes in his room at the Kansas City, Missouri, YMCA in 1910. His brother Rollie joined him the next year, and the two added greeting cards to their line in 1912. The brothers opened Hall Brothers, a store that sold postcards, gifts, books, and stationery, but it was destroyed in a 1915 fire. The Halls got a loan, bought an engraving company, and produced their first original cards in time for Christmas.

In 1921 a third brother, William, joined the firm, which started stamping the backs of its cards with the phrase "A Hallmark Card." By 1922 Hall Brothers had salespeople in all 48 states. The firm began selling internationally in 1931.

Hall Brothers patented the "Eye-Vision" display case for greeting cards in 1936 and sold it to retailers across the country. The company aired its first radio ad in 1938. The next year it introduced a friendship card, displaying a cart filled with purple pansies. The card became the company's best-seller. During WWII Joyce Hall persuaded the government not to curtail paper supplies, arguing that his greeting cards were essential to the nation's morale.

The company opened its first retail store in 1950. The following year marked the first production of *Hallmark Hall of Fame,* TV's longest-running dramatic series and winner of more Emmy awards than any other program. Hall Brothers changed its name to Hallmark Cards in 1954 and introduced its Ambassador line of cards five years later.

Hallmark introduced paper party products and started putting *Peanuts* characters on cards in 1960. Donald Hall, Joyce Hall's son, was appointed CEO in 1966. Two years later Hallmark opened Crown Center, which surrounded company headquarters in Kansas City. Disaster struck in 1981 when two walkways collapsed at Crown Center's Hyatt Regency hotel, killing 114 and injuring 225.

Joyce Hall died in 1982, and Donald Hall became both chairman and CEO. Hallmark acquired Crayola Crayon maker Binney & Smith in 1984. It introduced Shoebox Greetings, a line of nontraditional cards, in 1986. Irvine Hockaday replaced Donald Hall as CEO the same year (Hall continued as chairman).

The company joined with Information Storage Devices in 1993 to market recordable greeting cards. It unveiled its Web site, Hallmark.com, in 1996 and began offering electronic greeting cards. Hallmark's 1998 acquisition of UK-based Creative Publications boosted the company into the top spot in the British greeting card market. The following year the company acquired portrait studio chain The Picture People and Christian greeting card maker DaySpring Cards. Hallmark also introduced Warm Wishes, a line of 99-cent cards, and unveiled the Hallmark Home Collection, a line of home furnishings.

The company began testing overnight flower delivery in the US just in time for Valentine's Day 2000. Hallmark Entertainment subsidiary

Crown Media went public in that same year. Hockaday retired as president and CEO at the end of 2001; vice chairman Donald Hall Jr. took the additional title of CEO in early 2002.

EXECUTIVES

Chairman: Donald J. Hall
Vice Chairman, President, and CEO: Donald J. (Don) Hall Jr., age 47
EVP and CFO: Robert J. Druten, age 56
EVP, General Counsel, and Secretary: Judith C. Whittaker, age 64
EVP Worldwide Marketing and Brand Strategy: Chris R. Moseley, age 52
SVP Corporate Strategy: Anil Jagtiani
SVP Creative Product Development: Paul Barker
SVP Human Resources: David E. Hall, age 40
SVP Marketing: James Welch
SVP Public Affairs and Communication: Steve Doyal
SVP Sales: Steve Paoletti
VP Operations: Wayne Herran
VP Trade Development: Vince G. Burke
Director of Employee Benefits: Tresia Franklin
Director of Marketing: Jen Weiss
Director of Performance Management and Rewards: Jeff Blair
President and CEO, Binney & Smith: Mark Schwab
President and CEO, Crown Media: David J. Evans
President, Hallmark Entertainment; Chairman, Crown Media and Hallmark Entertainment Investments: Robert A. Halmi Jr., age 46
President, Hallmark North America: Donald H. Fletcher
President, Hallmark Loyalty Marketing: Scott Robinette

LOCATIONS

HQ: 2501 McGee St., Kansas City, MO 64108
Phone: 816-274-5111 **Fax:** 816-274-5061
Web: www.hallmark.com

Hallmark Cards has operations in Australia, Belgium, Canada, Denmark, Japan, Mexico, the Netherlands, New Zealand, Puerto Rico, Spain, the UK, and the US.

PRODUCTS/OPERATIONS

Selected Product Lines

Ambassador (greeting cards)
Fresh Ink (greeting cards)
Life Mosaic (cards and gifts by poet Maya Angelou)
Hallmark.com (electronic greeting cards, gifts, flowers)
Hallmark Flowers (flower delivery)
Keepsake (holiday ornaments and other collectibles)
Mahogany (products celebrating African-American heritage)
Maxine (greeting cards)
Nature's Sketchbook (gifts)
Shoebox (greeting cards)
Sinceramente (Spanish-language greeting cards)
Tree of Life (products celebrating Jewish heritage)

Selected Subsidiaries

Binney & Smith (Crayola brand crayons and markers)
Crown Center Redevelopment (retail complex)
DaySpring Cards (Christian greeting cards)
Gift Certificate Center (business and consumer certificates)
Hallmark Entertainment (television, movies, and home video production)
Crown Media Holdings (67%, pay television channels)
Halls Merchandising (department store)
Image Arts (discount greeting card distribution)
InterArt (specialized cards)
Irresistible Ink (handwriting and marketing service)
Litho-Krome (lithography)
The Picture People (portrait studio chain)
William Arthur (invitations, stationery)

COMPETITORS

1-800-FLOWERS.COM
American Greetings
Amscan
Andrews McMeel Universal
Blyth
CPI Corp.
CSS Industries
Dixon Ticonderoga
Enesco Group
Faber-Castell
Lifetouch
Olan Mills
Party City
PCA International
SPS Studios
Syratech
Thomas Nelson
Time Warner
Viacom
Walt Disney

HISTORICAL FINANCIALS

Company Type: Private

Income Statement FYE: December 31

	REVENUE ($ mil.)	NET INCOME ($ mil.)	NET PROFIT MARGIN	EMPLOYEES
12/02	4,200	—	—	20,000
12/01	4,000	—	—	20,000
12/00	4,200	—	—	24,500
12/99	4,200	—	—	21,000
12/98	3,900	—	—	20,945
12/97	3,700	—	—	12,554
12/96	3,600	—	—	12,600
12/95	3,400	—	—	12,100
12/94	3,800	—	—	12,800
12/93	3,400	—	—	12,600
Annual Growth	2.4%	—	—	5.3%

Revenue History

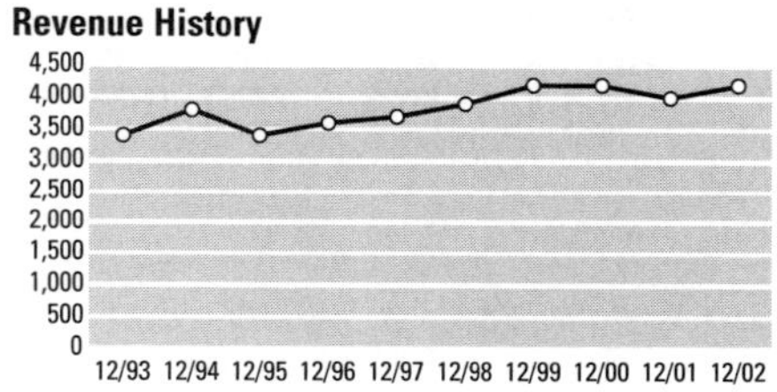

Hampton Affiliates

As a vertically integrated lumber company, Hampton Affiliates knows trees from the seedling to the stud. One of Oregon's top timber firms, Hampton produces about 900 million board feet of lumber annually. The company has more than 180,000 acres of timberland and owns tree farms and mills in Oregon and Washington. Through its Hampton Distribution Companies division, it distributes doors, windows, and other building materials; its Lane Stanton Vance division produces lumber from imported and domestic hardwood. Hampton has added stud lumber and distribution operations to supply home-building centers. L. M. "Bud" Hampton founded the company in 1942, and the Hampton family still owns it.

Hampton Affiliates has grown primarily by adding timberland and increasing its manufacturing capacity and distribution operations. Its plan for future growth includes expanding its resource base, adding manufacturing plants, and investing in new technologies and equipment upgrades. The company also plans to diversify into new market segments and opportunities throughout the Pacific Rim region.

During 2002 the company acquired Darrington Lumber Mills and completed a timberland exchange of 92,000 acres.

EXECUTIVES

President and CEO: Ronald C. (Ron) Parker
EVP and CFO: Steven J. Zika
CTO: Andy McNiece
VP Manufacturing: Bob Schutte
General Sales Manager: Carter Stinton
Treasurer and Controller: Robert Bluhm
President, HLS: Mike Phillips

LOCATIONS

HQ: 9600 SW Barnes Rd., Ste. 200, Portland, OR 97225
Phone: 503-297-7691 **Fax:** 503-203-6607
Web: www.hamptonlumber.com

Hampton Affiliates owns sawmills in Oregon and Washington, and distribution facilities in California.

PRODUCTS/OPERATIONS

Selected Products

Clear and industrial lumber
Dimensional lumber
Domestic and imported hardwood lumber
Engineered wood
Panel products
Residential doors
Siding and trim
Stud lumber
Timbers
Wood windows

COMPETITORS

Boise Cascade
Crown Pacific Partners
Doman Industries
Georgia-Pacific Corporation
International Paper
Louisiana-Pacific
Roseburg Forest Products
Sierra Pacific Industries
Simpson Investment
TreeSource
West Fraser Timber
Weyerhaeuser

HISTORICAL FINANCIALS

Company Type: Private

Income Statement FYE: January 31

	REVENUE ($ mil.)	NET INCOME ($ mil.)	NET PROFIT MARGIN	EMPLOYEES
1/02	700	—	—	1,300
1/01	721	—	—	1,300
1/00	715	—	—	1,100
1/99	525	—	—	900
1/98	500	—	—	800
1/97	—	—	—	900
1/96	—	—	—	850
Annual Growth	8.8%	—	—	7.3%

Revenue History

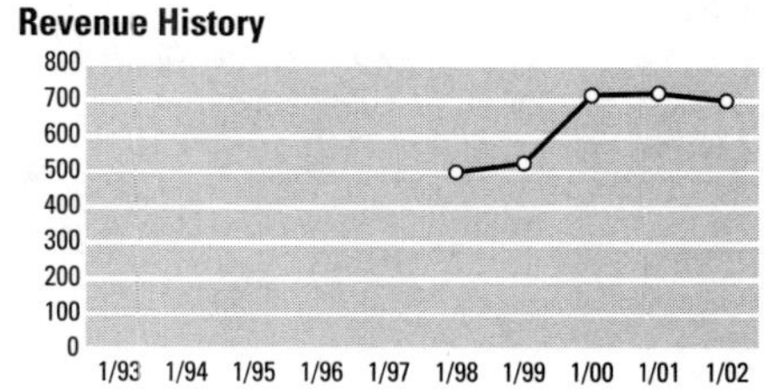

Harbour Group Industries, Inc.

Troubled manufacturers can seek refuge with Harbour Group Industries, a conglomerate that acquires and consolidates manufacturing companies in fragmented industries. Harbour's current portfolio includes companies in about 30 different industries, including auto accessories, chimney and fireplace products, industrial cleaning, paint sundries, plastics-processing equipment, heat exchangers, and textile machinery. Since its founding in 1976, Harbour Group has acquired about 130 companies; most have been combined with similar acquisitions.

Experts in the acquisition game, the folks at Harbour Group look for companies in mature but fragmented industries, which they build and fortify by continually re-investing in them and combining them with newly acquired complementary companies. In this way Harbour Group creates clusters of companies within a given industry to create operational efficiencies. When the company enters a new business segment, the first acquisition is known as the "platform" company, and from there the buy-and-build strategy begins anew. Harbour Group takes a long-term approach with its acquisitions, retaining existing management and assisting them with operational needs and investments.

In 2002 Harbour Group bought Merit Industries, the largest developer and manufacturer of touch-screen entertainment systems in North America and the worldwide leader in countertop video game systems (card games, trivia, and the like) seen in bars and restaurants. Merit is the platform company of the newly created Entertainment Products Group. Auto Meter Industries, another 2002 purchase, is the platform company for Harbour Group's new Performance Products Group. Auto Meter makes gauges, tachometers, and similar products for professional auto racing industry as well as your everyday hot rodders.

Other company segments include industrial springs, specialty distribution, and building products. Chairman and CEO Sam Fox controls the company.

EXECUTIVES

Chairman and CEO: Sam Fox, age 73
President and COO: Jeff Fox
SVP and CFO: William (Bill) Willhite
VP and Treasurer: Mike Santoni
Corporate Communications: Mark Leeker
Corporate Communications: Ashley Shih
Office Administrator: Harriet Lovins

LOCATIONS

HQ: 7701 Forsyth Blvd., Ste. 600, St. Louis, MO 63105
Phone: 314-727-5550 **Fax:** 314-727-9912
Web: www.harbourgroup.com

PRODUCTS/OPERATIONS

Selected Divisions

Automotive Accessories
Building Products Group
Chimney and Fireplace Products
Entertaiment Products Group
Heat Exchangers
Industrial Cleaning
Industrial Springs
Paint Sundries
Performance Products Group
Plastics-Processing Equipment
Specialty Distribution Group
Textile machinery

COMPETITORS

Albert Trostel & Sons
AptarGroup
Baxter
Federal Signal
Flow
Giddings & Lewis
Haskel
Ingersoll-Rand Industrial Solutions
Kennametal
Milacron
Rieter Holding
Swagelok
United States Surgical

HISTORICAL FINANCIALS

Company Type: Private

Income Statement FYE: December 31

	ESTIMATED REVENUE ($ mil.)	NET INCOME ($ mil.)	NET PROFIT MARGIN	EMPLOYEES
12/02	2,800	—	—	—
12/01	2,800	—	—	—
Annual Growth	0.0%	—	—	—

Revenue History

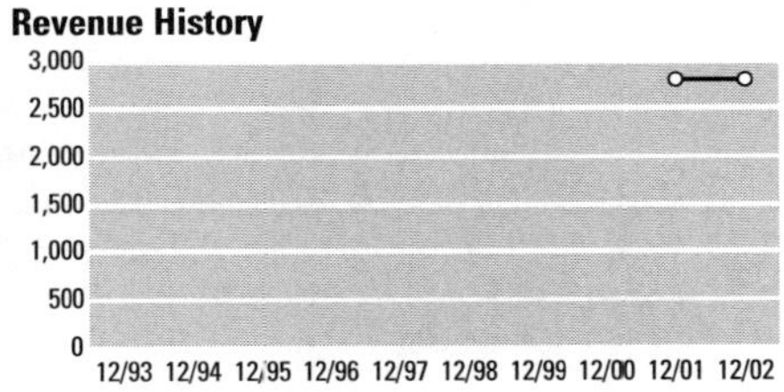

Hardin Construction

Working hard has worked out for Hardin Construction Company, which is in the top tier of US private general contractors. Hardin's services include general and interior construction, as well as construction management and renovation. Most of the company's sales are for new commercial buildings, including malls, office complexes, multifamily residences, and hotels. The firm also constructs institutional buildings such as education, government, and public assembly facilities. Founded in 1946 by Ira Hardin, the family-owned business was acquired by employees in 1993. Majority shareholders are chairman and CEO Earl Shell, EVP and CFO Brantley Barrow, and group presidents William Pinto and Robert Smith.

EXECUTIVES

Chairman and CEO: Earl L. Shell Jr.
Group President: Robert D. Smith
Group President: William A. (Bill) Pinto
EVP and CFO: M. Brantley Barrow
Director Corporate Communications: JoAnn Weinberg
VP Human Resources: Lisa Fanto

LOCATIONS

HQ: Hardin Construction Company, LLC
1380 W. Paces Ferry Rd., NW, Atlanta, GA 30327
Phone: 404-264-0404 **Fax:** 404-264-3514
Web: www.hardinconstruction.com

Hardin Construction Company has offices in Atlanta and in Jacksonville, Orlando, and Tampa, Florida; it serves clients throughout the US, as well as in the Caribbean.

PRODUCTS/OPERATIONS

Selected Clients

Ben Carter Properties
Capital One Financial Corporation
Carter & Associates
Citicorp North America, Inc.
City of North Charleston, South Carolina
Georgia World Congress Center Authority
Hilton Hotels Corporation
Hyatt Development Corporation
IBM Corporation
Marriott International, Inc.
Maryland Stadium Authority
Nordstrom, Inc.
Orange County, Florida
Pennsylvania Convention Center Authority
Sears, Roebuck and Co.

COMPETITORS

Abrams Industries
Alberici
Austin Industries
Barton Malow
Beck Group
Bovis Lend Lease
Brasfield & Gorrie
Choate Construction
Clark Enterprises
Dick Corporation
Fisher Development
Gilbane
H.J. Russell
Hunt Construction
Perini
Skanska
Structure Tone
Turner Corporation
Walsh Group
Whiting-Turner

HISTORICAL FINANCIALS

Company Type: Private

Income Statement FYE: December 31

	REVENUE ($ mil.)	NET INCOME ($ mil.)	NET PROFIT MARGIN	EMPLOYEES
12/02	545	—	—	433
12/01*	641	—	—	433
6/01	559	—	—	600
6/00	500	—	—	700
6/99	531	—	—	700
Annual Growth	0.7%	—	—	(11.3%)

*Fiscal year change

Revenue History

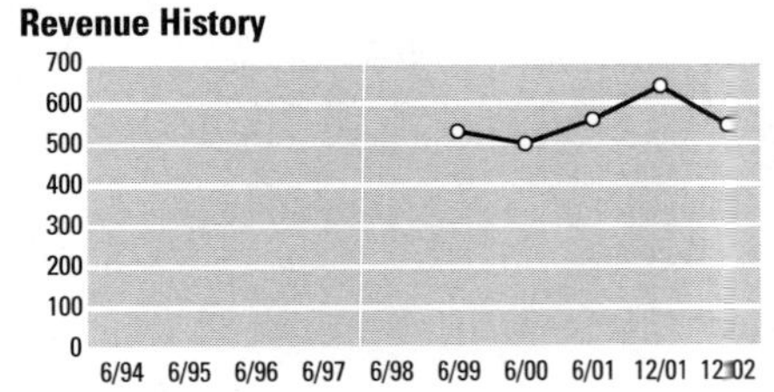

Harold Levinson Associates

Harold Levinson Associates (HLA) can soothe your nicotine fit with a fat cigar, satisfy your sweet tooth, and even help you make a long-distance phone call. HLA distributes more than 17,000 products, including its own proprietary coffee (Island Coffee), candy, cigarettes, phone cards and prepaid wireless coupons, snacks, and tobacco, to more than 20,000 convenience stores in Connecticut, Massachusetts, New Jersey, New York, and Rhode Island. With a fleet of more than 100 trucks, HLA distributes from centers in Farmingdale and Albany, New York, and Naugatuck, Connecticut. Boasting one of the largest walk-in humidors in North America, HLA also ships high-grade cigars to all 50 states. HLA was founded in 1975.

EXECUTIVES

CEO: Edward (Ed) Berro
CFO: Andrew P. DeFrancesco
VP, Sales: Marty Glick
Director, Purchasing: Ira Mark
Human Resource Manager: Mirella Barrasso

LOCATIONS

HQ: 21 Banfi Plaza, Farmingdale, NY 11735
Phone: 631-962-2400 **Fax:** 631-962-9000
Web: www.hladistributors.com

PRODUCTS/OPERATIONS

Selected Product Categories

Automotive
Candy
Cigarettes
Foodservice programs
Groceries
Phone cards
Prepaid wireless coupons
Snacks
Tobacco & accessories

COMPETITORS

800-JR Cigar
Davidoff International
Havana Group
Holt's Cigar
Synergy Brands

HISTORICAL FINANCIALS

Company Type: Private

Income Statement FYE: December 31

	REVENUE ($ mil.)	NET INCOME ($ mil.)	NET PROFIT MARGIN	EMPLOYEES
12/01	1,000	—	—	350
12/00	730	—	—	300
12/99	640	—	—	300
12/98	526	—	—	260
12/97	434	—	—	160
Annual Growth	23.2%	—	—	21.6%

Revenue History

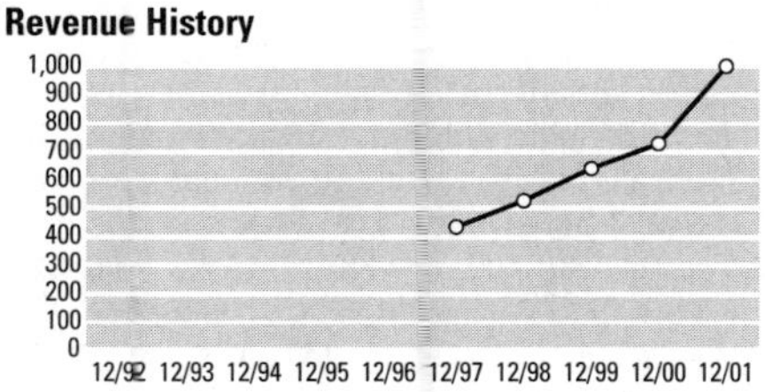

Harpo, Inc.

Everyone knows Oprah Winfrey is an exceptional businesswoman; there's no need to Harpo on it. Unrelated to the silent Marx brother, Harpo controls the entertainment interests of talk show host/actress/producer extraordinaire Oprah Winfrey. *The Oprah Winfrey Show* is the highest-rated TV talk show in history, seen in almost every US market and in 105 countries. Winfrey's show has ranked number one among all talk shows for the past 17 seasons (it is currently in its 17th season). Harpo also produces feature films (*Beloved,* which also starred Winfrey) and made-for-TV movies (*Oprah Winfrey Presents: Tuesdays with Morrie*) and publishes *O, The Oprah Magazine* with Hearst at a circulation of about 2.5 million.

Winfrey is worth about $1 billion according to *Forbes* magazine's list of billionaires. (She is the first black woman to join the ranks.) Her innovative ideas (such as Oprah's Book Club, which sent many previously little known titles to the top of bestseller lists) have earned *The Oprah Winfrey Show* more than 30 Emmys. Each week her show has some 21 million viewers in the US, about three-fourths of whom are women. The talk show icon had previously announced that her show would end in 2006, the 20th anniversary of the program; however, she has since signed a new contract to keep it on the air into 2008. Winfrey founded Harpo (Oprah spelled backwards) in 1986.

Winfrey also owns about 8% of women's cable company Oxygen Media. The Oxygen network airs her *Oprah After the Show* program, where viewers can see the candid conversations Oprah has with her studio audience.

HISTORY

Oprah Winfrey began her broadcasting career in 1973 at age 19 as a news anchor at Nashville's WTVF-TV. She became an evening news co-anchor in Baltimore in 1976, where she was recruited to co-host WJZ-TV's local talk show *People Are Talking.* She moved to Chicago in the early 1980s to host ABC affiliate WLS-TV's *AM Chicago,* which quickly became the city's top morning talk show. It was renamed *The Oprah Winfrey Show* in 1985.

Winfrey's performance in Steven Spielberg's *The Color Purple* in 1985 (her first ever acting role) won her an Oscar nomination and boosted her ratings when *The Oprah Winfrey Show* debuted nationally in 138 cities the following year thanks to a syndication deal with King World Productions secured by her agent (later Harpo's president and COO) Jeffrey Jacobs. Harpo was founded that year.

Winfrey obtained full ownership of her program in 1988. Two years later Harpo Films was created, and Winfrey bought a Chicago studio to produce *Oprah,* becoming only the third woman to own her own production studio (Mary Pickford and Lucille Ball were the others). She introduced the popular Oprah's Book Club in 1996. Also that year Texas cattlemen filed a lawsuit claiming she had caused a drop in beef future prices after a show on the UK outbreak of mad cow disease (Winfrey didn't emphasize that the disease had not appeared in the US). But jurors ruled in her favor in early 1998. Winfrey also renewed her contract that year until the 2001-2002 TV season.

In 1998, Winfrey agreed to produce original programming for Oxygen, a new cable network for women, in exchange for an equity stake. CBS bought King World in 1999, and the deal gave King World stockholder Winfrey a $100 million stake in CBS (which is now a stake in Viacom following its buy of CBS). The following year Winfrey launched with Hearst her own magazine (*O, The Oprah Magazine*) that focuses on relationships, health, and fashion.

In 2002 the talk show diva decided that Oprah's Book Club would be an occasional, instead of a regular, segment on her TV program (much to the dismay of many book publishers). In addition, a spinoff talk show hosted by Dr. Phil McGraw (a regular on the Oprah show) premiered that year. In 2003 Winfrey announced that she was reviving her book club (with an emphasis on classic literature rather than books authored by contemporary writers). She also signed a contract to keep her TV program on the air into 2008.

EXECUTIVES

Chairman: Oprah Winfrey, age 49
CFO: Doug Pattison
President, Harpo Productions: Tim Bennett
President, Harpo Films: Kate Forte
Director of Media and Corporate Relations: Lisa Halliday
Director of Human Resources: Bernice Smith

LOCATIONS

HQ: 110 N. Carpenter St., Chicago, IL 60607
Phone: 312-633-1000 **Fax:** 312-633-1976
Web: www.oprah.com

PRODUCTS/OPERATIONS

Selected Operations

Harpo Entertainment Group
Harpo Films
- *Beloved* (1998)
- *Oprah Winfrey Presents: Before Women Had Wings* (1997)
- *Oprah Winfrey Presents: The Wedding* (1998)
- *Overexposed* (1992)
- *There Are No Children Here* (1993)

Harpo Productions
- *Oprah Winfrey Presents: Amy & Isabelle* (2001)
- *Oprah Winfrey Presents: David and Lisa* (1998)
- *Oprah Winfrey Presents: Tuesdays with Morrie* (1999)
- *The Oprah Winfrey Show*
- *The Women of Brewster Place* (1989)

Harpo Video

COMPETITORS

Hallmark
iVillage
Lifetime
MSO
News Corp.
Rainbow Media
Sony Pictures Entertainment
Time Warner
Universal Television
Viacom

HISTORICAL FINANCIALS

Company Type: Private

Income Statement FYE: December 31

	REVENUE ($ mil.)	NET INCOME ($ mil.)	NET PROFIT MARGIN	EMPLOYEES
12/02	225	—	—	240
12/01	200	—	—	221
12/00	180	—	—	200
12/99	170	—	—	200
12/98	162	—	—	190
12/97	150	—	—	175
12/96	140	—	—	176
12/95	130	—	—	166
12/94	120	—	—	141
12/93	110	—	—	135
Annual Growth	8.3%	—	—	6.6%

Revenue History

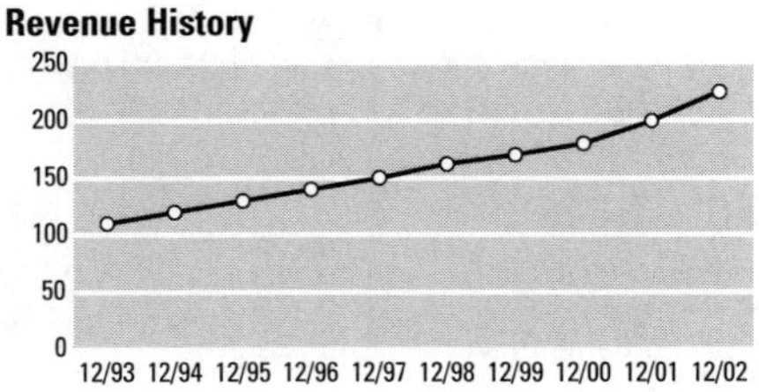

Hartz Mountain Corporation

Hartz Mountain has something for pets of all sizes. The company markets about 1,500 pet care products including nutritional products for small pets, birds, and fish; over-the-counter animal health products (including flea and tick treatments); and toys and accessories for dogs, cats, and birds. Hartz Mountain is buying the Alley Cat and Meow Mix brands from Nestlé Purina PetCare. Max Stern founded the company in 1926 after emigrating from Germany. The Stern family operated the company for more than 75 years under the Hartz Group umbrella along with the family's real estate operations. An investment group, including members of Hartz management, bought the Hartz Mountain pet products business in 2000.

EXECUTIVES

President and CEO: Robert Devine
CFO: Chris Bridgnell
Staffing Specialist: Kelly Shevlin

LOCATIONS

HQ: The Hartz Mountain Corporation
400 Plaza Dr., Secaucus, NJ 07094
Phone: 201-271-4800 **Fax:** 201-271-0164
Web: www.hartz.com

PRODUCTS/OPERATIONS

Selected Pet Products

Aquarium kits
Aquarium pumps, filters, and accessories
Birds
Bird accessories
Bird food and treats
Cat flea and tick products
Cat health and beauty care products
Cat toys
Cat treats
Dog and cat collars and leads
Dog flea and tick products
Dog health and beauty care products
Dog toys
Dog treats
Feeding dishes
Fish
Fish food
Pond products
Reptiles
Reptile accessories
Reptile food
Small-animal food and treats
Small-animal health and beauty care
Small-animal kits
Small-animal litter and accessories

COMPETITORS

Central Garden & Pet
Doane Pet Care Company
Iams
Mars
Nestlé Purina PetCare

HISTORICAL FINANCIALS

Company Type: Private

Income Statement FYE: December 31

	ESTIMATED REVENUE ($ mil.)	NET INCOME ($ mil.)	NET PROFIT MARGIN	EMPLOYEES
12/01	1,100	—	—	2,200
12/00	975	—	—	2,100
12/99	300	—	—	2,400
Annual Growth	91.5%	—	—	(4.3%)

Revenue History

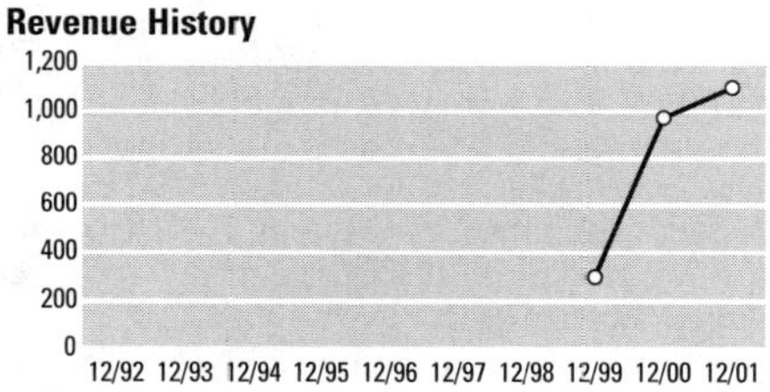

Harvard University

Many parents dream of sending their children to Harvard; some even dream of being able to afford it at more than $27,400 a year (undergrad). The oldest institution of higher learning in the US, Harvard is home to Harvard College (undergraduate studies) and 10 graduate schools (John F. Kennedy School of Government, the Harvard Business School, Harvard Law School, Harvard Medical School). The Radcliffe Institute for Advanced Study at Harvard was created when Radcliffe College and Harvard University merged in 1999. Harvard has more than 19,500 students, nearly two-thirds of whom are enrolled in graduate programs. At more than $18 billion, Harvard's endowment is the largest of any US university (Yale ranks #2).

It's usually a toss-up whether Harvard or one of its Ivy League rivals Princeton or Yale will rank at the top of the list of America's premiere schools or programs, but the university's reputation for academic excellence is well-founded. More than 30 Harvard faculty members have won Nobel Prizes over the years. Additionally, among Harvard's alumni are six US presidents — John Adams, John Quincy Adams, Rutherford B. Hayes, John F. Kennedy, Franklin Delano Roosevelt, and Theodore Roosevelt.

HISTORY

In 1636 the General Court of Massachusetts appropriated 400 pounds sterling for the establishment of a college. The first building was completed at Cambridge in 1639 and was named for John Harvard, who had willed his collection of about 400 books and half of his land to the school. The first freshman class had four students.

During its first 150 years, Harvard adhered to the education standards of European schools, with emphasis on classical literature and languages, philosophy, and mathematics. It established its first professorship in 1721 (the Hollis Divinity Professorship) and soon after added professorships in mathematics and natural philosophy. In 1783 the school appointed its first professor of medicine.

Harvard updated its curriculum in the early 1800s, after professor Edward Everett returned from studying abroad with reports of the modern teaching methods in Germany. The university established the Divinity School in 1816, the Law School in 1817, and two schools of science in the 1840s.

In 1869 president Charles Eliot began engineering the development of graduate programs in arts and sciences, engineering, and architecture. He raised standards at the medical and law schools and laid the groundwork for the Graduate School of Business Administration and the School of Public Health. Radcliffe College was founded as "Harvard Annex" in 1879, 15 years after a group of women had begun studying privately with Harvard professors in rented rooms.

Harvard's enrollment, faculty, and endowment grew tremendously throughout the 20th century. The Graduate School of Education opened in 1920, and the first undergraduate residential house opened in 1930. In the 1930s and 1940s, the school established a scholarship program and a general education curriculum for undergraduates. During WWII Harvard and Radcliffe undergraduates began attending the same classes.

A quota limiting the number of female students was abolished in 1975, and in 1979 Harvard introduced a new core curriculum. Princeton-educated Neil Rudenstine became president in 1991 and vowed to cut costs and to seek additional funding so that no one would be denied a Harvard education for financial reasons.

Harvard made dubious headlines during its 1994-95 academic year, enduring a bank robbery in Harvard Square, three student suicides, and one murder-suicide. The following year Harvard paid a fine of $775,000 after the US Attorney's Office claimed the school's pharmacy had not properly controlled drugs, including antidepressants and codeine cough syrup. The fine was the largest ever paid in the US under the Controlled Substance Act.

In 1998 Harvard's endowment fund acquired insurance services firm White River in one of the largest direct investments ever made by a not-for-profit institution. Also that year the school altered some of its graduation processes and introduced stress-reducing programs in the wake of another student suicide.

In 1999 Radcliffe College merged with Harvard and the Radcliffe Institute for Advanced Study at Harvard was established. In 2000 president Neil Rudenstine announced he would step down in June 2001. Former Treasury Secretary Lawrence Summers replaced him.

EXECUTIVES

President: Lawrence H. Summers, age 47
Provost: Steven E. Hyman
VP Administration: Sally H. Zeckhauser
VP Alumni Affairs and Development: Thomas M. Reardon, age 54
VP Government, Community, and Public Affairs: Alan Stone
VP and General Counsel: Anne Taylor
Treasurer: D. Ronald Daniel
Auditors: PricewaterhouseCoopers LLP

LOCATIONS

HQ: Massachusetts Hall, Cambridge, MA 02138
Phone: 617-495-1000 **Fax:** 617-495-0754
Web: www.harvard.edu

PRODUCTS/OPERATIONS

Selected Programs and Schools

Undergraduate
Harvard College

Graduate
Graduate School of Arts and Sciences
Graduate School of Design
Graduate School of Education
Harvard Business School
Harvard Divinity School
Harvard Law School
Harvard Medical School
Harvard School of Public Health
John F. Kennedy School of Government
School of Dental Medicine

HISTORICAL FINANCIALS

Company Type: School

Income Statement FYE: June 30

	REVENUE ($ mil.)	NET INCOME ($ mil.)	NET PROFIT MARGIN	EMPLOYEES
6/02	2,357	—	—	15,000
6/01	2,228	—	—	15,000
6/00	2,023	—	—	11,360
6/99	1,788	—	—	10,500
6/98	1,679	—	—	9,701
6/97	1,565	—	—	12,782
6/96	1,519	—	—	12,150
6/95	1,467	—	—	11,100
6/94	1,377	—	—	11,000
6/93	1,306	—	—	11,000
Annual Growth	6.8%	—	—	3.5%

Revenue History

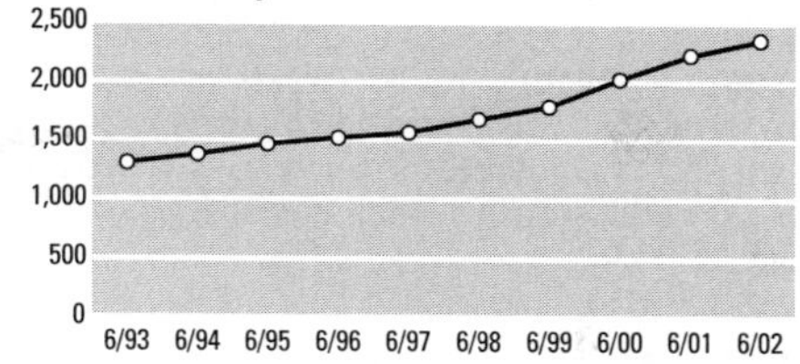

The Haskell Company

Design-build services lie at the heart of Haskell. The company ranks among the US's top design-build firms, which oversee not only the architectural and engineering design but also the construction of a project. Haskell also offers construction management, facility management, interior design, and real estate services. Projects include industrial, commercial, and institutional facilities and range from a Krispy Kreme Doughnuts factory to a federal medium-security prison. Chairman Preston Haskell founded the employee-owned firm in 1965 and also led the establishment of the Design-Build Institute of America in 1993.

EXECUTIVES

Chairman: Preston H. Haskell
President and CEO: Steven T. (Steve) Halverson
EVP and COO: John R. Cobb
EVP and CFO; President and CEO, Haskell Enterprise Group: Edward W. (Ted) Mullinix
SVP and Chief Architect: David L. (Dave) Engdahl
President, Civil Group: John H. Patton
President, Industrial Group: Gregory (Greg) Ferrell
President, Institutional/Commercial Group: James A. (Jim) Gray
EVP and COO, Haskell Management Services: William L. (Bill) Mason
VP, Human Resources: John B. (Jack) Morgan
Auditors: KPMG

LOCATIONS

HQ: 111 Riverside Ave., Jacksonville, FL 32202
Phone: 904-791-4500 **Fax:** 904-791-4699
Web: www.thehaskellco.com

Haskell has offices in the US in California, Florida, North Carolina, and Texas and operates in North America, Latin America, and the Caribbean region.

PRODUCTS/OPERATIONS

Industry Divisions

Aviation
Criminal Justice
Distribution
Diversified
Education
Food & Beverage
General Commercial
Healthcare
Latin America
Manufacturing & Technology
Senior Living
Site
Transportation
Water & Wastewater

COMPETITORS

BE&K
Hensel Phelps Construction
Kimley-Horn and Associates
Parsons
Peter Kiewit Sons'
Skanska USA Building
Turner Corporation
Washington Group

HISTORICAL FINANCIALS

Company Type: Private

Income Statement FYE: December 31

	REVENUE ($ mil.)	NET INCOME ($ mil.)	NET PROFIT MARGIN	EMPLOYEES
12/02	651	—	—	1,325
12/01	700	—	—	1,300
Annual Growth	(7.0%)	—	—	1.9%

Revenue History

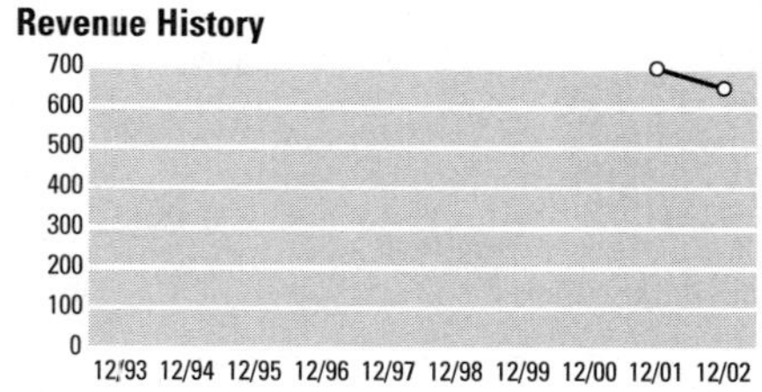

Haworth, Inc.

Designers at Haworth sit at their cubicles and think about . . . more cubicles. The company is one of the top office furniture manufacturers in the US (behind #1 Steelcase and neck and neck with HON INDUSTRIES). Haworth offers a full range of furniture known for its innovative design, including partitions, desks, chairs, tables, and storage products. Brands include Berlin, if, PLACES, and X99. Dilbert and other long-suffering office drones have Haworth to thank for inventing the pre-wired partitions that make today's cubicled workplace possible.

Haworth is owned by the family of Gerrard Haworth, who founded the company in 1948. The company sells its products in more than 120 countries worldwide through some 800 dealers.

Haworth, known as an aggressive competitor, has been expanding its presence in Europe, mostly through acquisitions. Operations include Germany's Roeder, Spain's Kemen, and Canada's SMED International and Groupe Lacasse.

Though the company has a reputation for being efficient, the soft market for furniture has hit Haworth as hard as its competitors and it has had to lay off some employees.

EXECUTIVES

Chairman: Richard G. Haworth
President and CEO: Robert Krasa
VP, Asia/Pacific: Frank Rexach
VP, European Operations: Gerhard Rolf
VP, Finance and CFO: Calvin W. Kreuze
VP, Global Information Systems: Michael Moon
VP, Global Manufacturing; President, SMED International: Craig Speck
VP, Global Sales: Al Lanning
VP, Human Resources: Nancy Teutsch
CEO, SMED International: Mogens F. Smed

LOCATIONS

HQ: 1 Haworth Center, Holland, MI 49423
Phone: 616-393-3000 **Fax:** 616-393-1570
Web: www.haworth.com

Haworth operates in more than 120 countries throughout Asia, the Caribbean, Europe, the Middle East, and North, Central, and South America.

PRODUCTS/OPERATIONS

Products

Desks and casegoods	Systems
Files and storage	Tables
Seating	Work tools

COMPETITORS

Boise Office Solutions	Knoll
Bush Industries	Neutral Posture
Facom	O'Sullivan Industries
Falcon Products	Sauder Woodworking
Herman Miller	Shelby Williams
HON INDUSTRIES	Steelcase
Jami	Teknion
KI	Vitra
Kimball International	

HISTORICAL FINANCIALS

Company Type: Private

Income Statement FYE: December 31

	REVENUE ($ mil.)	NET INCOME ($ mil.)	NET PROFIT MARGIN	EMPLOYEES
12/01	1,710	—	—	10,000
12/00	2,065	—	—	14,500
12/99	1,580	—	—	10,000
12/98	1,540	—	—	10,000
12/97	1,510	—	—	10,000
12/96	1,370	—	—	9,000
12/95	1,150	—	—	8,900
12/94	1,005	—	—	7,400
12/93	848	—	—	7,000
12/92	650	—	—	6,000
Annual Growth	11.3%	—	—	5.8%

Revenue History

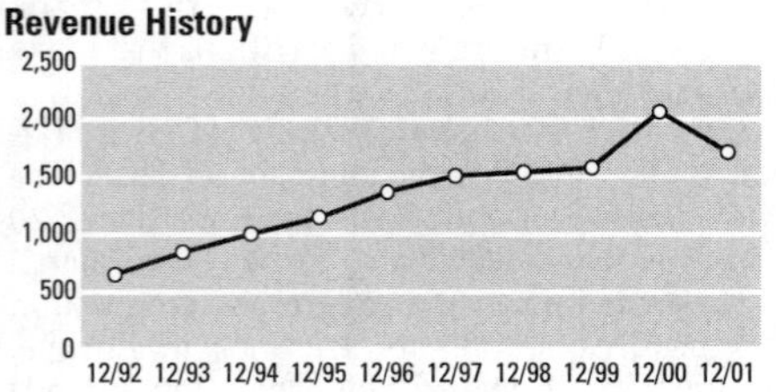

HBE Corporation

HBE derives a healthy business out of designing and building health care facilities. The firm provides planning, architectural, engineering, management, interior design, and construction services throughout the US. Hospital Building & Equipment is the group's chief operating division. HBE also designs and builds financial institutions and hotels and is engaged in the hospitality industry through its operation and ownership of Adam's Mark Hotels & Resorts properties. HBE is owned by chairman, president, and CEO Fred Kummer, who founded the design/build firm as a small construction company in 1960.

EXECUTIVES

Chairman, President, and CEO: Fred S. Kummer
EVP and COO: Fred S. Kummer III
EVP and CFO: Gene Kemp
VP Hospital Marketing: Dennis Oerly
VP Purchasing: Howard Ackerman
Director Personnel: Jim O'Daniel

LOCATIONS

HQ: 11330 Olive Street Rd., St. Louis, MO 63141
Phone: 314-567-9000 **Fax:** 314-567-0602
Web: www.hbecorp.com

COMPETITORS

Bovis Lend Lease	Marriott International
Centex	Pepper Construction
DPR Construction	Skanska USA Building
Gilbane	Starwood Hotels & Resorts
Hyatt	Turner Corporation
M. A. Mortenson	Walsh Group

HISTORICAL FINANCIALS

Company Type: Private

Income Statement FYE: December 31

	REVENUE ($ mil.)	NET INCOME ($ mil.)	NET PROFIT MARGIN	EMPLOYEES
12/02	625	—	—	9,100
12/01	614	—	—	9,100
12/00	658	—	—	11,000
12/99	650	—	—	10,000
12/98	658	—	—	7,000
12/97	575	—	—	7,000
Annual Growth	1.7%	—	—	5.4%

Revenue History

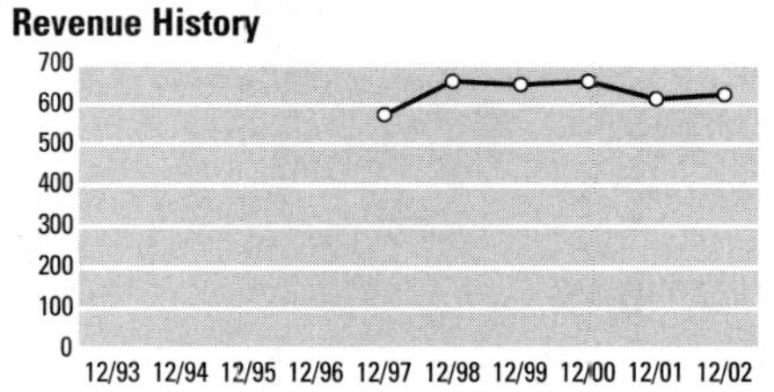

HDR, Inc.

One night under a big Montana sky, a cowboy named Henning H. Henningson must have thought, "I could have been an engineer." As quick as he could say "git along, little dogie," Henningson scurried back home to Iowa to get an engineering degree. HDR has grown from the civil engineering firm he started in 1917 for municipal plants in the rural Midwest to become a leading architecture and engineering consulting firm with experience worldwide. Engineers Charles Durham and Willard Richardson provided the "R" and the "D" to add to the "H" for Henningson in the firm's name. The employee-owned group offers design/build services and works on projects such as bridges, hospitals, and water and wastewater-treatment plants.

EXECUTIVES

Chairman, President, and CEO: Richard R. Bell
Vice Chairman and EVP Corporate Development: James H. Suttle
President, HDR Architecture: Robert Cavigli
President, HDR Engineering: George A. Little
CFO: Terry Cox
SVP and Director Human Resources: Roger L. Parkins
VP Marketing Services (Architecture): Pamm Killeen
VP Marketing Services (Engineering): Nancy Gruwell
Treasurer: Wendy Lacey
Secretary and General Counsel: Louis Pachman
National Director, Dams and Hydraulic Structures: Peter J. Hradilek
National Director, Environmental and Resource Management: Elwin Larson
Auditors: Deloitte & Touche LLP

LOCATIONS

HQ: 8404 Indian Hills Dr., Omaha, NE 68114
Phone: 402-399-1000 **Fax:** 402-399-1238
Web: www.hdrinc.com

HDR has more than 70 offices worldwide.

PRODUCTS/OPERATIONS

Major Service Areas

Consulting	Justice
Design/build	Planning
Environmental and resource	Program management
Management	Science and technology
Federal	Security and technology
Health care	Sustainable design
International	Transportation
	Water

COMPETITORS

AECOM	Leo A. Daly
Black & Veatch	Malcolm Pirnie
Brown and Caldwell	Michael Baker
CH2M HILL	MWH Global
Earth Tech	STV
HBE Corporation	Tetra Tech
Jacobs Engineering	URS
Kimley-Horn and Associates	Washington Group

HISTORICAL FINANCIALS

Company Type: Private

Income Statement FYE: December 31

	REVENUE ($ mil.)	NET INCOME ($ mil.)	NET PROFIT MARGIN	EMPLOYEES
12/02	470	—	—	3,167
12/01	438	—	—	3,030
Annual Growth	7.4%	—	—	4.5%

Revenue History

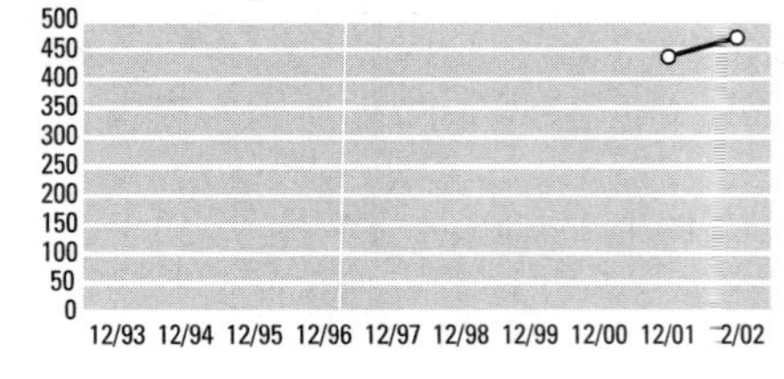

H. E. Butt Grocery

The Muzak bounces between Tejano and country, and the warm tortillas and ribs are big sellers at H. E. Butt Grocery (H-E-B). Texas' largest private company and the #1 food retailer in South and Central Texas, H-E-B owns more than 300 supermarkets, including a growing number of large (70,000 sq. ft.) gourmet Central Market stores in major metropolitan areas and more than 80 smaller (24,000-30,000 sq. ft.) Pantry Foods stores, often in more rural areas. H-E-B also has one store in Louisiana and about 20 upscale and discount stores in Mexico. H-E-B processes some of its own meat, dairy products, bread, and tortillas. The company is owned by the Butt family, which founded H-E-B in Kerrville, Texas, in 1905.

To cement its #1 spot in Central Texas and fend off Wal-Mart, which is expanding in the region, H-E-B recently lowered prices on some 12,000 items in the Austin market. H-E-B is also acquiring nine stores in Texas from rival Albertson's.

The Texas grocery chain plans to invest $150 million in the Houston market in 2003 to add 11 large combination food and drug stores, while closing some of its smaller Pantry supermarkets in the area. The company aims to become a major player in and around Houston, where Kroger is #1. To gain an edge on its competition, H-E-B plans to incorporate aspects of its upscale Central Market format, including cafes, into the new Houston stores.

H-E-B is familiar with the tastes of Latinos as about half of its market is Hispanic. South of the border H-E-B has moved into Monterrey's more affluent neighborhoods, with stores operating under the H-E-B banner and the Economax name (a discount supermarket format). The company plans to have about 40 stores in Mexico by 2004.

More than 40% of the H-E-B stores have gasoline outlets, and most have pharmacies. The retailer recently opened its first Payless Express shoe department in a Laredo store, and has plans to open more.

HISTORY

Charles C. Butt and his wife, Florence, moved to Kerrville, in the Texas Hill Country, in 1905, hoping the climate would help Charles' tuberculosis. Since Charles was unable to work, Florence began peddling groceries door-to-door for A&P. Later that year she opened a grocery store, C. C. Butt Grocery. However, Florence, a dyed-in-the-wool Baptist, refused to carry such articles of vice as tobacco. The family lived over the store, and all three of the Butt children worked there. The youngest son, Howard, began working in the business full-time in his teens and took over the business after WWI.

By adopting modern marketing methods such as price tagging (and deciding to sell tobacco), the Butts earned enough to begin expanding. In 1927 Howard opened a second store in Del Rio in West Texas, and over the next few years he opened other stores in the Rio Grande Valley. The company gained patron loyalty by making minimal markups on staples. It moved from Kerrville to Harlingen, Texas, in 1928 (it moved to Corpus Christi, Texas, in 1940 and to San Antonio in 1985).

The company began manufacturing foods in the 1930s, and it invested in farms and orchards. In 1935 Howard (who had adopted the middle name Edward) rechristened the chain the H. E. Butt Grocery Company (H-E-B). He put his three children to work for the company, grooming son Charles for the top spot after Howard Jr. took over the H. E. Butt Foundation from his mother.

While other chains updated their stores during the 1960s, H-E-B plodded. Howard Sr. resigned in 1971 and Charles took over, bringing in fresh management. But this was not enough. Studies showed that the reasons for its lagging market share were its refusal to stock alcohol and its policy of Sunday closing; it abandoned these policies in 1976. It also drastically undercut competitors, driving many independents out of business. Winning the price wars, H-E-B emerged the dominant player in its major markets.

H-E-B's first superstore, a 56,000-sq.-ft. facility offering general merchandise, photofinishing, and a pharmacy, opened in Austin, Texas, in 1979, and it concentrated on building more superstores over the next decade. It also installed in-store video rentals and added 35 freestanding Video Central locations (sold to Hollywood Entertainment in 1993).

In 1988 H-E-B launched its H-E-B Pantry division, which remodeled and built smaller supermarkets, mostly in rural Texas towns. Three years later it launched another format, the 93,000-sq.-ft. H-E-B Marketplace in San Antonio, which included restaurants. It also opened the upscale Central Market in Austin with extensive cheese, produce, and wine departments in 1994 (it later opened similar stores in San Antonio and Houston).

Chairman and CEO Charles retired as president in 1996, and James Clingman became the first non-family member to assume the office. That year H-E-B opened its first non-Texas store, in Lake Charles, Louisiana. In 1997 it opened its first Mexican store in an affluent area of Monterrey, followed the next year by a discount supermarket there under the Economax banner. In 1999 the company said it would expand further in Mexico with six to eight new stores per year (it opened seven in 2001). Also in 2001 H-E-B opened its first store — a Central Market — in the Dallas/Ft. Worth area.

In mid-2002 H-E-B opened a new Central Market in Dallas, its seventh Central Market in Texas and the company's 300th store. The company also acquired five San Antonio stores from Albertson's and reopened them as H-E-B stores in August and September.

EXECUTIVES

Chairman and CEO: Charles C. Butt
COO: Robert D. (Bob) Loeffler, age 52
Chief Administration Officer and CFO: Jack C. Brouillard
SVP, Fresh Merchandising, Procurement and Product Development: Steve Harper
SVP, General Manager, South Texas: Jeff Thomas
SVP, Human Resources: Todd Piland
SVP, Information Solutions and Chief Information Officer: Don Beaver
VP, E-Commerce: Alan Markert
VP, General Manager of Store Operations: Paul Madura
VP, Operations, Central Market, and Dallas-Fort Worth Region: Stephen Butt
VP, Procurement/Merchandising, Central Market: John Campbell
VP, Public Affairs and Diversity: Winell Herron
VP, Quality Control: Bill Fry
VP, Selling and Customer Service: Jaren Shaw
President, H-E-B Houston and Central Market Stores: Scott McClelland
Director, Employee Benefits: Kathy Durbin
Director, Foodservice Marketing: Ed Howie
Director, Produce Procurement: Hugh Topper
Director, Public Affairs: Greg Flores
Manager, Promotions: Jodi Brasiola
Manager, Quality Assurance: Richard Parker

LOCATIONS

HQ: H. E. Butt Grocery Company
646 S. Main Ave., San Antonio, TX 78204
Phone: 210-938-8000 **Fax:** 210-938-8169
Web: www.heb.com

H. E. Butt Grocery Company operates grocery stores and gas stations throughout Texas and in Louisiana and Mexico. The company also operates bakeries; a photo processing lab; and meat, milk, and ice cream plants.

2002 Stores

	No.
US	
Central Texas	63
San Antonio and West Texas	58
Houston Metro	55
Border	42
Gulf Coast	29
Houston Rural East	24
Houston Rural West	23
Mexico	17
Total	**311**

PRODUCTS/OPERATIONS

Private Labels

H-E-B Own Brand
Hill Country Fare

Store Formats

Central Market (about 70,000 sq. ft., upscale supermarkets with expanded organic and gourmet foods; located in major metropolitan markets)
Economax (discount supermarkets, Mexico)
Gas 'N Go (gas stations)
H-E-B (large supermarkets)
H-E-B Marketplace (large supermarkets with specialty departments)
H-E-B Pantry (24,000-30,000 sq. ft., no-frills supermarkets with basic groceries; often located in rural or suburban areas)

COMPETITORS

7-Eleven
Albertson's
Brookshire Brothers
Chedraui
Comerci
Grupo Corvi
Costco Wholesale
Eckerd
Fiesta Mart
Gerland's Food Fair
Gigante
IGA
Kmart
Kroger
Minyard Food Stores
Randall's
Rice Food Markets
Soriana
Walgreen
Wal-Mart de México
Wal-Mart
Whole Foods
Winn-Dixie

HISTORICAL FINANCIALS

Company Type: Private

Income Statement FYE: October 31

	REVENUE ($ mil.)	NET INCOME ($ mil.)	NET PROFIT MARGIN	EMPLOYEES
10/02	9,900	—	—	60,000
10/01	8,965	—	—	60,000
10/00	8,200	—	—	50,000
10/99	7,500	—	—	45,000
10/98	7,000	—	—	45,000
10/97	6,500	—	—	45,000
10/96	5,800	—	—	42,000
10/95	5,137	—	—	25,000
10/94	4,844	—	—	25,000
10/93	4,500	—	—	19,772
Annual Growth	9.2%	—	—	13.1%

Revenue History

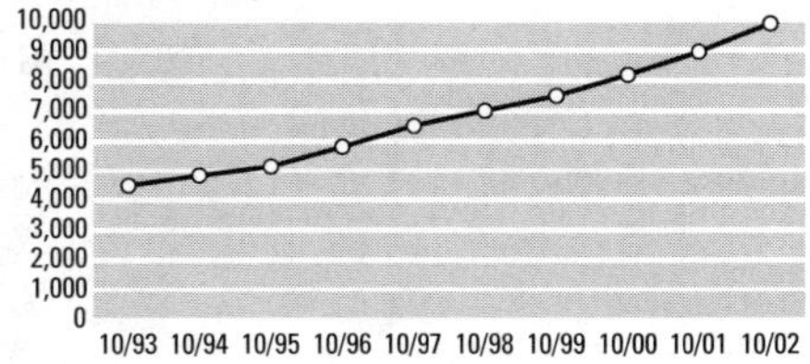

Health Care Service

Health Care Service Corporation (HCSC) has the Blues. HCSC is made up of Blue Cross Blue Shield of Illinois (that state's oldest and largest health insurer), Blue Cross and Blue Shield of Texas, and Blue Cross and Blue Shield of New Mexico. A licensee of the Blue Cross and Blue Shield Association, the mutual company provides a range of group and individual insurance and medical plans to some 8 million members, including indemnity insurance and managed care programs. HCSC also offers prescription drug plans, Medicare supplement insurance, dental and vision coverage, life and disability insurance, workers' compensation, retirement services, and medical financial services through subsidiaries.

HCSC also covers federal employees in its three states through the Federal Employee Program, a contract with the US government.

To better compete in the health care industry and to benefit from economies of scale, HCSC had planned an alliance with The Regence Group, which owns the Blues of Idaho, Utah, Oregon, and Washington, to serve some 10 million members and be the largest not-for-profit health insurance organization in the US. However, the two organizations changed their minds and instead teamed to cooperate on initiatives aimed at reducing administrative expenses.

HISTORY

The seeds of the Blue Cross organization were sown in 1929, when an official at Baylor University Hospital in Dallas began offering schoolteachers 21 days of hospital care for $6 a year. Fundamental to its coverage was a community rating system, which based premiums on the community's claims experience rather than subscribers' conditions.

In 1935 Elgin Watch Co. owner Taylor Strawn, Charles Schweppe, and other Chicago civic leaders pooled resources to form Hospital Services Corporation to provide the same type of coverage. (The firm adopted the Blue Cross symbol in 1939.) Employees of the Rand McNally cartography company were the first to be covered by the plan.

Soon, four similar plans were launched in other Illinois towns. Between 1947 and 1952, Hospital Services Corp. and these other four joined forces, offering coverage nearly statewide.

Meanwhile, Blue Shield physician's fee plans in several cities were incorporated as Illinois Medical Service. Hospital Services Corp. and Illinois Medical Service operated independently but shared office space and personnel.

A 1975 change in state legislation let the entities merge to become Health Care Service Corp. (HCSC), which offered both Blue Cross and Blue Shield coverage. Following the merger, the company's board of directors (which had been primarily composed of care providers) became dominated by consumers, which helped HCSC become more responsive to its members.

For the next six years, the state denied HCSC any rate increases, leaving it with a frighteningly low $12 million in reserves in 1982.

HCSC achieved statewide market presence in 1982 when it merged with Illinois' last independent Blue Cross plan, Rockford Blue Cross. In 1986, as managed care swept through the health care industry, only 14% of HCSC's members were enrolled in managed care plans. HCSC created its Managed Care Network Preferred point-of-service plan in 1991; the idea caught on with both employers and individuals and enrollment skyrocketed. By 1994 more than two-thirds of the firm's subscribers participated in some sort of managed care plan. That year it picked up Medicare payment processing for the state of Michigan.

In 1995 HCSC and Blue Cross and Blue Shield of Texas (BCBST) formed an affiliation they hoped would culminate in a merger giving the combined company $6 billion in sales and reserves of more than $1 billion. Texas consumer groups objected to the merger, claiming that Texas residents own BCBST and that Texans should be compensated for the transfer of ownership — especially since BCBST had received state tax breaks for decades in exchange for accepting all applicants. (A Texas judge ruled in favor of the merger in 1998.)

Citing high risks and low margins, HCSC in 1997 dropped its Medicare payment processing contract, which it had held for some 30 years. The next year HCSC agreed to pay $144 million after it pleaded guilty to covering up its poor performance in processing Medicare claims.

In 1999 HCSC agreed to buy Aetna's NylCare of Texas, giving it large, profitable HMOs in Houston and Dallas (completed in 2000). The next year it bested Anthem and Wellmark in wooing the troubled Blue Cross Blue Shield of New Mexico (completed in 2001).

EXECUTIVES

Chairman: Milton Carroll, age 52
President and CEO: Raymond F. McCaskey
SVP, Finance and CFO: Sherman M. Wolff
SVP, Information Technology and Subscriber Services: Joanne M. Rounds
SVP and Chief Information Officer: Patrick E. Moroney, age 48
President of Blue Cross and Blue Shield of Illinois: Gail Boudreaux, age 42
President, Blue Cross and Blue Shield of New Mexico: Liz Watrin
President, Blue Cross and Blue Shield of Texas: Patricia A. Hemingway Hall, age 50
Corporate VP, Marketing and Commercial Accounts, Blue Cross Blue Shield of Illinois: Paula Steiner
VP, Health Care Division, Blue Cross and Blue Shield of New Mexico: Thomas A. (Tom) MacLean
Director, Human Resources: Robert Ernst
Auditors: Ernst & Young LLP

LOCATIONS

HQ: Health Care Service Corporation
300 E. Randolph, Chicago, IL 60601
Phone: 312-653-6000 **Fax:** 312-819-1220
Web: www.bcbsil.com

PRODUCTS/OPERATIONS

Selected Subsidiaries

Group Medical and Surgical Service
Preferred Financial Group
Colorado Bankers Life Insurance Company
Fort Dearborn Life Insurance Co.
Medical Life Insurance Company
Rio Grande HMO, Inc.
Texas Gulf Coast HMO, Inc.
Texas Health Plan, Inc.
West Texas Health Plans, L.C.

COMPETITORS

Aetna
AFLAC
Anthem
CIGNA
Guardian Life
Humana
Kaiser Foundation
Mutual of Omaha
New York Life
Prudential
UnitedHealth Group

HISTORICAL FINANCIALS

Company Type: Mutual company

Income Statement FYE: December 31

	REVENUE ($ mil.)	NET INCOME ($ mil.)	NET PROFIT MARGIN	EMPLOYEES
12/02	7,312	246	3.4%	—
12/01	6,198	387	6.2%	—
12/00	10,430	174	1.7%	—
12/99	8,980	111	1.2%	—
12/98	7,819	50	0.6%	—
12/97	5,107	71	1.4%	[illegible],700
12/96	4,478	89	2.0%	[illegible],650
12/95	4,201	139	3.3%	[illegible],600
12/94	3,930	166	4.2%	—
12/93	3,441	98	2.8%	—
Annual Growth	8.7%	10.8%	—	0.9%

2002 Year-End Financials

Debt ratio: 27.4%
Return on equity: 18.6%
Cash ($ mil.): 541
Current ratio: —
Long-term debt ($ mil.): [illegible]00

Net Income History

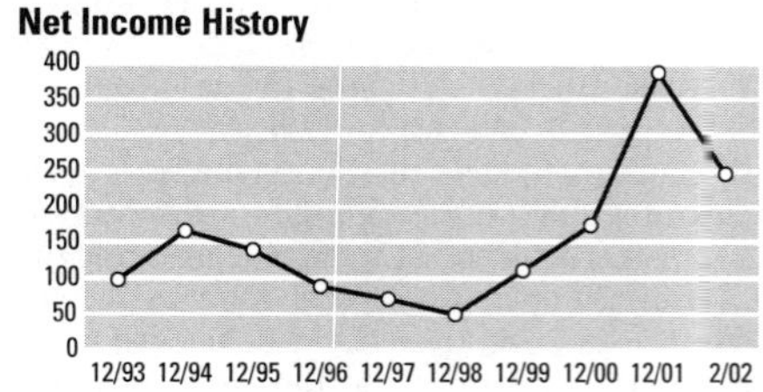

The Hearst Corporation

Like legendary founder William Randolph Hearst's castle, The Hearst Corporation is sprawling. The company owns 12 daily newspapers (including the *San Francisco Chronicle* and the *Houston Chronicle*) and 14 weekly newspapers, 17 US consumer magazines (such as *Cosmopolitan* and *Esquire*), TV and radio stations (through 40%-owned Hearst Argyle Television), and a cartoon and features service (King Features). Hearst is also active in cable networks through stakes in A&E, Lifetime, and ESPN; and online services through its 30% stake in iVillage, the Web network aimed at women. The company is owned by the Hearst family, but managed by a board of trustees.

Hearst sold the *San Francisco Examiner* to the Fang family to satisfy antitrust regulators in conjunction with its 2000 purchase of the larger *San Francisco Chronicle*. Although it no longer owns Hearst Castle (deeded to the State of California in 1951), the company has extensive real estate holdings.

Using the selling power of its popular *Cosmopolitan* magazine, the company has capitalized with a TV channel in Spain and Portugal based on the magazine. The company is adding another one in Latin America and is considering a US launch. Hearst also turned a TV channel into a magazine; the company launched *Lifetime* magazine in 2003 in a joint venture with women's cable channel Lifetime. Hearst hopes the move takes some of the sting out of its high-profile failure of *Talk* magazine, a joint venture with movie studio Miramax. Led by Tina Brown, the famous former editor of *The New Yorker*, the magazine only lasted two years before the partners shut it down, citing the downturn in the economy and poor circulation.

Hearst further expanded its potent stable of magazines in 2003 by purchasing *Seventeen* magazine from PRIMEDIA. In addition to the magazine, the deal (valued at $182 million) includes the purchase of *Teen* magazine, seventeen.com and teenmag.com, and school marketing business Cover Concepts.

Upon his death, William Randolph Hearst left 99% of the company's common stock to two charitable trusts controlled by a 13-member board that includes five family and eight non-family members. The will includes a clause that allows the trustees to disinherit any heir who contests the will.

HISTORY

William Randolph Hearst, son of a California mining magnate, started as a reporter — having been expelled from Harvard in 1884 for playing jokes on professors. In 1887 he became editor of the *San Francisco Examiner*, which his father had obtained as payment for a gambling debt. In 1895 he bought the *New York Morning Journal* and competed against Joseph Pulitzer's *New York World*. The "yellow journalism" resulting from that rivalry characterized American-style reporting at the turn of the century.

Hearst branched into magazines (1903), film (1913), and radio (1928). Also during this time it created the Hearst International News Service (it was sold to E.W. Scripps' United Press in 1958 to form United Press International). By 1935 Hearst was at its peak, with newspapers in 19 cities, the largest syndicate (King Features), international news and photo services, 13 magazines, eight radio stations, and two motion picture companies. Two years later Hearst relinquished control of the company to avoid bankruptcy, selling movie companies, radio stations, magazines, and, later, most of his San Simeon estate. (Hearst's rise and fall inspired the 1941 film *Citizen Kane*.)

In 1948 Hearst became the owner of one of the US's first TV stations, WBAL-TV in Baltimore. When Hearst died in 1951, company veteran Richard Berlin became CEO. Berlin sold off failing newspapers, moved into television, and acquired more magazines.

Frank Bennack, CEO since 1979, expanded the company, acquiring newspapers, publishing firms (notably William Morrow, 1981), TV stations, magazines (*Redbook*, 1982; *Esquire*, 1986), and 20% of cable sports network ESPN (1991). Hearst branched into video via a joint venture with Capital Cities/ABC (1981) and helped launch the Lifetime and Arts & Entertainment cable channels (1984).

In 1991 Hearst launched a New England news network with Continental Cablevision. The following year it brought on board former Federal Communications Commission chairman Alfred Sikes, who quickly moved the company onto the Internet. In 1996 Randolph A. Hearst passed the title of chairman to nephew George Hearst (the last surviving son of the founder, Randolph died in 2000). Broadcaster Argyle Television merged with Hearst's TV holdings in 1997 to form publicly traded Hearst-Argyle Television.

In 1999 Hearst combined its HomeArts Web site with Women.com to create one of the largest online networks for women. It also joined with Walt Disney's Miramax Films to publish entertainment magazine *Talk* (shut down in 2001) and Oprah Winfrey's Harpo Entertainment to publish *O, The Oprah Magazine* (launched in 2000). In 1999 the company sold its book publishing operations to News Corp.'s HarperCollins unit. It also agreed to buy the *San Francisco Chronicle* from rival Chronicle Publishing. That deal was called into question over concerns that the *San Francisco Examiner* would not survive and the city would be left with one major paper. To resolve the issue, the next year Hearst sold the *Examiner* to ExIn (a group of investors affiliated with the Ted Fang family and other owners of the *San Francisco Independent*). Also in 2000 Hearst bought the UK magazines of Gruner + Jahr, the newspaper and magazine unit of German media juggernaut Bertelsmann.

The following year Hearst gained a 30% stake in iVillage following that company's purchase of rival Women.com Networks. In mid-2002 Victor Ganzi took over as CEO and president following Bennack's retirement from those positions. Hearst expanded further into entertaining the younger generation with the purchase of *Seventeen* magazine from PRIMEDIA.

EXECUTIVES

Chairman: George R. Hearst Jr., age 75
Vice Chairman: Frank A. Bennack Jr., age 70
President and CEO; Chairman, Hearst-Argyle Television: Victor F. Ganzi, age 56
EVP, Hearst Newspapers: Steven R. Swartz
SVP and CFO: Ronald J. Doerfler
SVP; President, Hearst Newspapers: George B. Irish
SVP; Group Head, Hearst Entertainment and Syndication: Raymond E. Joslin
VP and General Counsel: Eve Burton
VP; President and CEO, Hearst Magazines International; EVP, Hearst Magazines: George Green
VP; VP and Deputy Group Head, Hearst Entertainment and Syndication; President, Hearst Entertainment: Bruce Paisner
President and CEO, Hearst-Argyle Television: David J. Barrett, age 54
President, Hearst Business Media: Richard P. Malloch
President, Hearst Interactive Media: Kenneth A. Bronfin, age 46
President, Hearst Magazines: Cathleen P. Black, age 58
VP and General Manager, Hearst Interactive Sudios: Jay Bobowicz
VP, Hearst Interactive Media: Michael Dunn, age 44

LOCATIONS

HQ: 959 8th Ave., New York, NY 10019
Phone: 212-649-2000 **Fax:** 212-765-3528
Web: www.hearstcorp.com

Hearst newspapers are located throughout the US. Hearst Magazines are distributed in more than 110 countries.

PRODUCTS/OPERATIONS

Selected Operations

Broadcasting
Hearst-Argyle Television (40%)

Business Publications
Black Book
Diversion
Electronic Products
First DataBank
Motor Magazine

Entertainment and Syndication
A&E Television Networks (37.5%, with ABC & NBC)
The History Channel
Cosmopolitan Television Iberia (Spain & Portugal)
ESPN (20%)
King Features Syndicate
Lifetime Entertainment Services (50%, with ABC)
Locomotion (with Cisneros Group; all animation TV)
New England Cable News (with Comcast)
Tevecap (10%, pay-TV; Brazil)

Interactive Media
Circles (invested in online loyalty solutions company)
drugstore.com (invested in online pharmacy site)
Hire.com (invested in career job site)
iVillage (30%, Internet site geared toward women)

Magazines
Best (UK magazine)
Company (UK magazine)
CosmoGIRL!
Cosmopolitan
Country Living
Esquire
Good Housekeeping
Harper's Bazaar
House Beautiful
Lifetime (50%)
Marie Claire (with Marie Claire Album)
O, The Oprah Magazine (with Harpo)
Popular Mechanics
Prima (UK magazine)
Redbook
Seventeen
She (UK magazine)
SmartMoney (with Dow Jones)
Teen
Town & Country
Veranda
Your Home (UK magazine)
Zest (UK magazine)

Major Newspapers
Albany Times Union (New York)
Houston Chronicle
Huron Daily Tribune (Michigan)
Laredo Morning Times (Texas)
Midland Daily News (Michigan)
San Antonio Express-News
San Francisco Chronicle
Seattle Post-Intelligencer

Real Estate
Hearst Realties
San Francisco Realties
Sunical Land & Livestock Division

Other Operations
Cover Concepts (in-school marketing)

COMPETITORS

Advance Publications
Andrews McMeel Universal
Belo
Bertelsmann
Bloomberg
Cox Enterprises
Dennis Publishing
Emap
E. W. Scripps
Freedom Communications
Gannett
Hachette Filipacchi Médias
IPC Media
Knight-Ridder
Liberty Media
McGraw-Hill
MediaNews
Meredith
New York Times
News Corp.
PRIMEDIA
Reader's Digest
Reed Elsevier Group
Rodale
Seattle Times
Time Warner
Tribune
Viacom
Walt Disney
Washington Post

HISTORICAL FINANCIALS

Company Type: Private

Income Statement FYE: December 31

	REVENUE ($ mil.)	NET INCOME ($ mil.)	NET PROFIT MARGIN	EMPLOYEES
12/01	3,300	—	—	17,170
12/00	3,400	—	—	18,300
12/99	2,740	—	—	14,000
12/98	2,200	—	—	13,555
12/97	2,833	—	—	15,000
12/96	2,568	—	—	14,000
12/95	2,513	—	—	14,000
12/94	2,299	—	—	14,000
12/93	2,174	—	—	13,500
12/92	1,973	—	—	13,000
Annual Growth	5.9%	—	—	3.1%

Revenue History

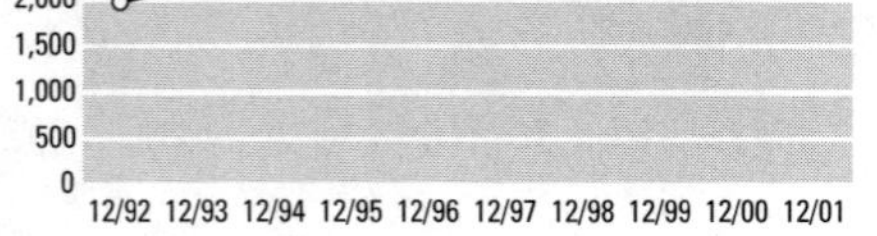

Helmsley Enterprises, Inc.

What word rhyming with "itch" describes Leona Helmsley? Rich! Helmsley Enterprises is the repository of the real estate empire amassed by the late Harry Helmsley over a period of 50 years. Helmsley's widow and heir, Leona, has interests in such high-profile properties as the Helmsley Park Lane, the Helmsley Windsor, and the Carlton House. Other holdings include apartment buildings and millions of square feet of primarily New York real estate, not to mention a lease held on the Empire State Building (which is owned by Donald Trump and others) until 2075.

The portfolio was valued at $5 billion before Leona Helmsley began to sell properties from it after her husband's death in 1997; the company still controls real estate valued at about half that amount.

Helmsley has ended a relatively quiet half-decade of staying out of the limelight. After quietly selling off a number of properties, many at a premium in New York's stratospheric real estate market, the "Queen of Mean" is grabbing headlines again: She appears to be winning a public fight with Donald Trump over the terms of the Empire State Building lease, but she's lost a lawsuit involving the alleged mistreatment of gay hotel employees (a judge reduced the jury-rewarded damages from $11.1 million to a mere $554,000), and is now being sued by former Helmsley Enterprises COO Patrick Ward, for allegedly firing him when he wouldn't become romantically involved with her.

Leona's holdings may be eroding even further; the Helmsley Middletowne is up for sale, Helmsley hotels no longer hold coveted slots on the *Zagat Survey of Top U.S. Hotels*, and occupancy levels are below those of Manhattan's new trendy boutique hotels.

At its apex, Helmsley's real estate empire included interests in more than 25 million sq. ft. of office space, more than 20,000 apartments, some 7,500 hotel rooms, 50 retail projects, warehouse space, land, garages, restaurants, and real estate companies. To keep the money in the family, the properties were managed by Helmsley-Spear (then 99%-owned by Helmsley, sold in 1997) and Helmsley-Noyes.

Helmsley has sold more than $2 billion worth of property since her husband's death.

HISTORY

In 1925 Harry Helmsley began his career as a Manhattan rent collector; the work, then done in person, taught him to evaluate buildings and acquainted him with their owners. During the Depression, Helmsley obtained property at bargain prices. He paid $1,000 down for a building with a $100,000 mortgage and later quipped that he did so to provide a job for his father, whom he hired as superintendent. In 1946 he sold the building for $165,000.

In the late 1940s Helmsley teamed up with lawyer Lawrence Wien. Helmsley located properties; Wien financed them through a device of his own invention, the loan syndicate. Prominent properties Helmsley bought into in the 1950s included the Flatiron (1951), Berkeley (1953), and Equitable (1957) buildings. He moved into management in 1955 with the purchase of Leon Spear's property management firm. In 1961 Helmsley bought the Empire State Building for $65 million and sold it to Prudential for $29 million with a 114-year leaseback (which expires in 2075); a public offering for the newly created Empire State Building Co. made up the balance.

In the mid-1960s Helmsley moved into property development, erecting office buildings and shopping centers. He bought the 30-building Furman and Wolfson trust, borrowing $78 million of the $165 million price on the strength of his reputation — the largest signature loan ever.

In 1969 Spear introduced Helmsley to Leona Roberts, a real estate broker who had sold Spear an apartment. Helmsley hired Leona and promoted her to SVP at his Brown, Harris, Stevens real estate brokerage. He divorced his wife and married Leona in 1971. In 1974 he leased an historic building and delegated the renovation to Leona (who built the company's hotel business). The Helmsley Palace opened in 1980 (now the New York Palace, sold 1993).

As Harry's health began to fail in the 1980s, Leona gained control of the empire. Maintenance deteriorated, bookkeeping went lax, and the couple's lavish spending became notorious. In 1988 they were charged with tax evasion. Harry was ruled incompetent to stand trial, but in 1989 Leona was convicted, fined $7.1 million, and sentenced to jail. She spent 21 months incarcerated, the last part of it in a halfway house.

After her 1994 release, Leona was banned from management of the hotels by laws forbidding felon involvement in businesses that serve liquor. She became more involved in the management of Harry's interests and began reshuffling assets, moving management contracts from Helmsley-Spear to Helmsley-Noyes, and selling buildings.

A 1995 suit brought by Harry's partners in Helmsley-Spear accused Leona of looting the company by depriving it of management contracts and loading it with debt to render worthless their right to buy the company under a 1970 option agreement.

In 1997 Harry died, and Leona announced she would sell the 125-property Helmsley portfolio. Wien's son-in-law Peter Malkin, partner in 13 top-notch Manhattan buildings, contested the control granted to her by Harry's will. They resolved their differences late that year. Leona also settled her differences with the Helmsley-Spear partners in 1997, agreeing to sell them the firm for less than $1 million.

Leona sold her favorite, the Helmsley Building on 230 Park Place, in 1998 to the Bass family on condition the building retain the name. That year, partly to avoid estate taxes, she formed the Harry and Leona Helmsley Foundation, a charity to which she contributed more than $30 million in 1999.

Leona moved closer to a deal in 2000 to buy back the Empire State Building from current owner Donald Trump and partners. The following year Malkin moved to challenge her, forming a plan to buy the skyscraper himself; Leona vowed to block his proposal.

EXECUTIVES

Chairman and CEO: Leona Helmsley, age 82
CFO: Abe Wolf
VP and General Counsel: Harold Meriam
Human Resources Director: Yogesh Mathur
Auditors: Eisner & Lubin LLP

LOCATIONS

HQ: 230 Park Ave., New York, NY 10169
Phone: 212-679-3600 **Fax:** 212-953-2810

Helmsley Enterprises operates primarily in New York City.

PRODUCTS/OPERATIONS

Selected Owned and/or Managed Properties

Empire State Building (office building, New York City)
Helmsley Carlton House (hotel, New York City)
Helmsley Middletowne (hotel, New York City)
Helmsley Park Lane (hotel, New York City)
Helmsley Sandcastle (hotel, Sarasota, Florida)
Helmsley Windsor (hotel, New York City)
Lincoln Building (office building, New York City)
New York Helmsley (hotel, New York City)

COMPETITORS

Accor
Four Seasons Hotels
Hyatt
JMB Realty
Lefrak Organization
Lincoln Property
Macklowe Properties
Marriott International
Ritz-Carlton
Shorenstein
SL Green Realty
Tishman Realty
Trammell Crow
Trizec Properties
Trump
Vornado Realty Trust

HISTORICAL FINANCIALS

Company Type: Private

Income Statement FYE: December 31

	ESTIMATED REVENUE ($ mil.)	NET INCOME ($ mil.)	NET PROFIT MARGIN	EMPLOYEES
12/01	1,000	—	—	3,000
12/00	1,000	—	—	3,000
12/99	1,000	—	—	3,000
12/98	1,000	—	—	7,800
12/97	1,000	—	—	7,800
12/96	1,900	—	—	13,000
12/95	1,770	—	—	13,000
12/94	1,700	—	—	13,000
12/93	1,200	—	—	13,000
12/92	1,200	—	—	13,000
Annual Growth	(2.0%)	—	—	(15.0%)

Revenue History

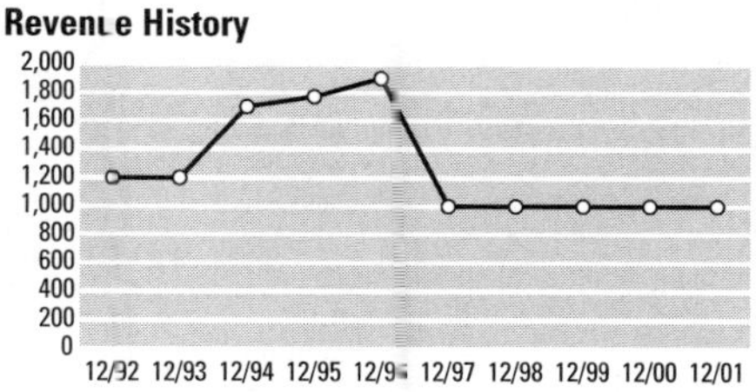

Hendrick Automotive

For megadealer Hendrick Automotive Group, variety is the spice of life. The company sells new and used cars and light trucks from more than 20 automakers, including General Motors, Honda, and Porsche. Hendrick has a network of about 70 dealerships in nine states ranging from the Carolinas to California. The company also offers financing, as well as automobile parts, accessories, service, and body repair. Founder Rick Hendrick pleaded guilty in 1997 to mail fraud relating to alleged bribes of American Honda executives; he was later pardoned by President Bill Clinton. Hendrick owns the company, which began in 1976 as a single dealership in Bennettsville, South Carolina.

EXECUTIVES

CEO: Jim C. Perkins
EVP and CFO: James F. Huzl
VP of Accounting, Audits, and Taxes: Veronica Zayatz
Director of Human Resources: Tim Taylor

LOCATIONS

HQ: Hendrick Automotive Group
6000 Monroe Rd., Charlotte, NC 28212
Phone: 704-568-5550 **Fax:** 704-566-3295
Web: www.hendrickauto.com

Hendrick Automotive Group operates in California, Georgia, Kansas, Missouri, North Carolina, South Carolina, Tennessee, Texas, and Virginia.

COMPETITORS

Asbury Automotive
AutoNation
Bill Heard
CarMax
Holman Enterprises
Morse Operations
Penske
Serra Automotive
Sonic Automotive
United Auto Group
VT

HISTORICAL FINANCIALS

Company Type: Private

Income Statement FYE: December 31

	REVENUE ($ mil.)	NET INCOME ($ mil.)	NET PROFIT MARGIN	EMPLOYEES
12/01	2,639	—	—	4,700
12/00	2,483	—	—	4,500
12/99	2,522	—	—	4,500
12/98	2,434	—	—	4,300
12/97	2,455	—	—	4,500
12/96	2,250	—	—	4,500
12/95	2,315	—	—	4,500
12/94	1,800	—	—	4,500
12/93	1,690	—	—	4,500
12/92	1,500	—	—	3,500
Annual Growth	6.5%	—	—	3.3%

Revenue History

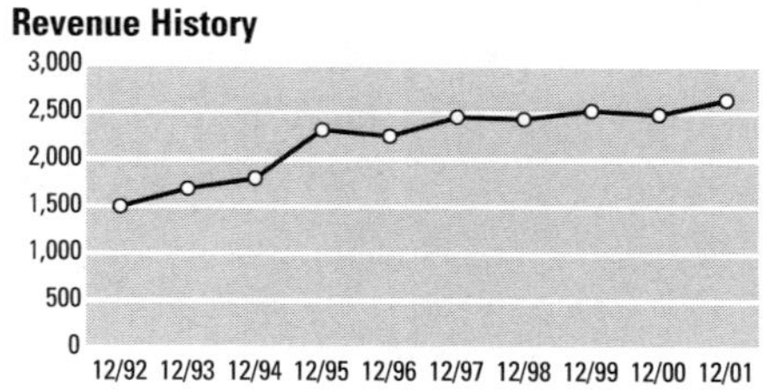

Henkels & McCoy, Inc.

When utilities, communications companies, or governments need the real McCoy to install or repair their transmission networks, they can call on Henkels & McCoy. The specialty contractor provides engineering, construction, and network development services. About 75% of its employees are engaged in communications operations, providing design, installation, and maintenance services worldwide. The company installs aerial and underground electrical distribution systems, fiber-optic networks on electric transmission towers or along railroad rights-of-way, and gas transmission lines. John Henkels Jr. founded the company in 1923 as a tree-trimming and landscaping firm. Employees and the Henkels family own the company.

EXECUTIVES

Chairman: Paul M. Henkels
Vice Chairman and Co-CEO: Kenneth L. Rose
President and Co-CEO: T. Roderick (Rod) Henkels
EVP and COO: Jonathon C. Schoff
VP and CFO: Robert Delark
Regional VP: James M. (Jim) Dillahunty
Regional VP: Denis J. Palermo
VP, General Counsel, and Secretary:
Christine A. Crawford
Treasurer: Robert M. Severi
Director Human Resources: Vincent Benedict
Manager Marketing Communications: Paul DeMara
Auditors: Ernst & Young

LOCATIONS

HQ: 985 Jolly Rd., Blue Bell, PA 19422
Phone: 215-283-7600 **Fax:** 215-283-7659
Web: www.henkelsandmccoy.com

Henkels & McCoy has 80 offices in Arizona, California, Colorado, Hawaii, Illinois, Indiana, Georgia, Massachusetts, Michigan, North Carolina, New Jersey, New York, Oklahoma, Ohio, Oregon, Pennsylvania, Texas, Virginia, and Washington.

PRODUCTS/OPERATIONS

Selected Services

Communications
Customized networks
Labor management
Material logistics

Electric Transmission
Aerial distribution
Extra high voltage (EHV)
Storm restoration
Substations
Switching stations
Underground distribution

Engineering
Design
Planning
Project management
Staffing

Gas Transmission
Engineering
Maintenance
Pipeline installation
Service line installation

General Construction
Demolition
Electrical systems
Engineering
Foundations
HVAC systems
Mechanical systems
Steel erection

Training
Broadband systems installation
Computer assembly
LAN installation

COMPETITORS

AMEC
Dycom
EMC Engineers
EMCOR
Goldfield
Integrated Electrical Services
MasTec
MDU Resources
MYR Group
Quanta Services
RailWorks
Rosendin Electric
Willbros

HISTORICAL FINANCIALS

Company Type: Private

Income Statement FYE: September 30

	REVENUE ($ mil.)	NET INCOME ($ mil.)	NET PROFIT MARGIN	EMPLOYEES
9/02	604	—	—	5,000
9/01	675	—	—	5,000
9/00	748	—	—	5,647
9/99	570	—	—	5,200
9/98	500	—	—	4,800
9/97	425	—	—	4,500
9/96	380	—	—	4,400
9/95	375	—	—	4,150
Annual Growth	7.0%	—	—	2.7%

Revenue History

Henry Ford Health System

In 1915 automaker Henry Ford founded the hospital that would be the starting point for southeastern Michigan's not-for-profit Henry Ford Health System, a hospital network that is also involved in medical research and education. The system includes six hospitals with about 2,000 beds, more than 30 other health care facilities, and over 2,000 physicians representing a wide range of specialties. The system's Health Alliance Plan provides managed care and health insurance to some 540,000 members. The Henry Ford Health Sciences Center Research Institute, the Josephine Ford Cancer Center, and other research centers and affiliated hospitals are also part of the health care system.

EXECUTIVES

President and CEO, Henry Ford Health System and Henry Ford Hospital: Nancy M. Schlichting, age 48
EVP and Chief Medical Officer; CEO, Henry Ford Medical Group: Mark A. Kelly
SVP Strategic Planning and Development: Vinod K. Sahney
CFO: James M. Connelly
Corporate VP, Human Resources: Robert Rieny
Chief Information Officer: Arthur Gross
System Treasurer: David Mazurkiewicz
Chair, Ophthalmology (Henry Ford Eye Care Services): Paul A. Edwards

LOCATIONS

HQ: 1 Ford Place, Detroit, MI 48202
Phone: 313-876-8700 **Fax:** 313-876-9243
Web: www.henryfordhealth.org

PRODUCTS/OPERATIONS

Selected Facilities
Bi-County Hospital (osteopathic hospital)
Cottage Hospital
Henry Ford Hospital
Henry Ford Wyandotte Hospital
Kingswood Hospital (mental health care)
Riverside Osteopathic Hospital

COMPETITORS

Ascension
Blue Cross (MI)
Detroit Medical Center
Trinity Health
William Beaumont Hospital

HISTORICAL FINANCIALS

Company Type: Not-for-profit

Income Statement FYE: December 31

	ESTIMATED REVENUE ($ mil.)	NET INCOME ($ mil.)	NET PROFIT MARGIN	EMPLOYEES
12/01	2,000	—	—	15,000
12/00	1,900	—	—	16,000
12/99	1,229	—	—	16,000
12/98	1,303	—	—	17,000
12/97	2,200	—	—	17,000
12/96	1,980	—	—	17,000
12/95	1,750	—	—	17,000
12/94	1,525	—	—	15,000
12/93	1,417	—	—	12,898
12/92	1,255	—	—	12,703
Annual Growth	5.2%	—	—	1.9%

Revenue History

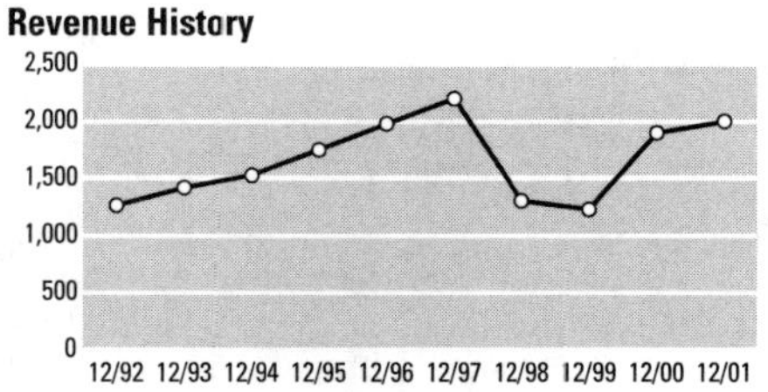

Henry Modell & Company, Inc.

Modell's colors change from city to city. Henry Modell & Company sells sporting goods, apparel (including local team apparel), and brand-name athletic footwear at more than 90 Modell's Sporting Goods stores in the Northeast. Founded in 1889 by Morris Modell (who first sold menswear from a Lower East Side pushcart in New York City), the chain is the oldest family-owned and -operated sports retailer in the country; it is in its fourth generation of Modell management. Best known for offering branded products at reasonable prices, Modell has stores in malls, regional shopping centers, and busy urban areas.

EXECUTIVES

Chairman: William Modell
CEO: Mitchell B. Modell
President and COO: Robert Stevenish
CFO: Lawrence E. (Larry) Long
VP, Information Technology: Hans Kantor
Director, Human Resources: Phyllis Siegel
Director, Real Estate and General Counsel: Douglas Epstein

LOCATIONS

HQ: 498 7th Ave., 20th Fl., New York, NY 10018
Phone: 212-822-1000 **Fax:** 212-822-1025
Web: www.modells.com

Modell's has locations in Delaware, Maryland, New Jersey, New York, Pennsylvania, Virginia, and Washington, DC.

PRODUCTS/OPERATIONS

Selected Products
Apparel
Baseball
Basketball
Camping/hiking
Cycling
Electronics/optics
Fan shop-pro/college
Field hockey
Fishing
Fitness
Football
Footwear
Golf
Ice/roller hockey
In-line/roller skating
Lacrosse
Outdoor recreation
Paintball
Racquetball/squash
Roller hockey
Rugby
Running
Scooters
Skateboarding
Snow sports
Soccer
Softball
Squash
Tennis
Treadmills
Volleyball
Winter recreation
Wrestling
Yoga

COMPETITORS

Dick's Sporting Goods
Foot Locker
Hat World
Wal-Mart

HISTORICAL FINANCIALS

Company Type: Private

Income Statement FYE: January 31

	ESTIMATED REVENUE ($ mil.)	NET INCOME ($ mil.)	NET PROFIT MARGIN	EMPLOYEES
1/03	500	—	—	3,500
1/02	465	—	—	3,500
1/01	436	—	—	3,500
1/00	370	—	—	3,200
1/99	370	—	—	3,200
1/98	340	—	—	3,000
1/97	320	—	—	3,000
1/96	229	—	—	3,000
1/95	238	—	—	2,300
1/94	200	—	—	1,800
Annual Growth	10.7%	—	—	7.7%

Revenue History

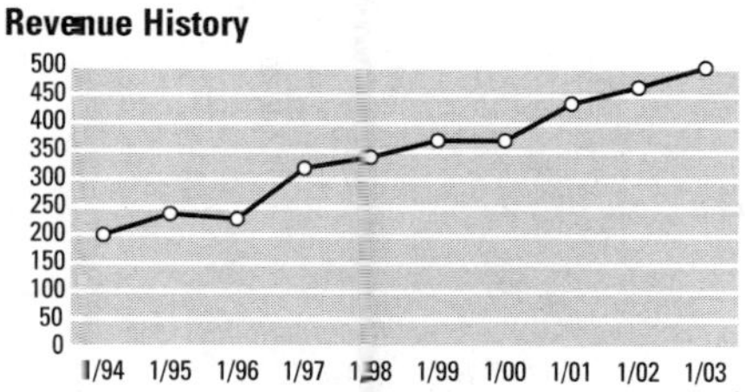

Hensel Phelps Construction Co.

Hensel Phelps Construction builds it all, from the courthouse to the Big House. Launched as a homebuilding firm by Hensel Phelps in 1937, the employee-owned general contractor now focuses on institutional and commercial projects: prisons, airport facilities, hotels, government and corporate complexes, convention centers, sport arenas, and department stores. It also works on mass transportation, educational, residential, and health care projects. Hensel Phelps offers design/build and construction management services. Recent projects include the Hyatt Denver Convention Center Hotel and the new headquarters for Whole Foods Market in Austin, Texas.

EXECUTIVES

President and CEO: Jerry L. Morgensen
EVP and Manager, Eastern Division and Mid-Atlantic District: Robert E. Daniels
EVP and Manager, Western Division; President, Phelps Program Management: Robert J. (Bob) Pesavento
VP Finance and CFO: Stephen J. (Steve) Carrico
VP and General Counsel: Eric L. Wilson
VP, Mid Atlantic District: Scott V. Conrad
VP, Northern California District: Jon W. Ball
VP Plains District; EVP, Phelps Program Management (PPM): Ronald G. (Ron) Norby
VP, South Central District: Mark Baugh
VP, Southeast District: Jeffrey (Jeff) Wenaas
VP, Southern California District: Wayne S. Lindholm
VP, Southwest District: Edwin L. Calhoun
Auditors: KPMG LLP

LOCATIONS

HQ: 420 6th Ave., Greeley, CO 80632
Phone: 970-352-6565 **Fax:** 970-352-9311
Web: www.henselphelps.com

Hensel Phelps Construction has offices in Arkansas, California, Colorado, Florida, Texas, and Virginia.

PRODUCTS/OPERATIONS

Selected Services

Building operation
Commissioning
Estimating
Feasibility studies
Financing
Land acquisition
Leasing
Moving services
Scheduling
Subcontractor management
Warranty programs
Zoning and code compliance

Selected Projects

Capital Square Office Tower (Sacramento)
Colorado Convention Center Expansion and Renovation Project (Denver)
Denver Center of the Performing Arts
Excelsior Hotel & Convention Center (Little Rock, AR)
J.D. Edwards Corporate Headquarters (Denver)
Neiman Marcus (Palo Alto, CA)
Paseo Nuevo Shopping Center (Santa Barbara, CA)
Pentagon Renovation Wedges 2-5 (Arlington, VA)
Riverport Casino Center (Maryland Heights, MO)
Sahara Hotel and Casino (Las Vegas)
San Antonio International Airport
Sea World New Friends Stadium (San Antonio)
University of Texas at Dallas School of Management
New Midfield Concourse, Washington Dulles Airport
Youth Services Center (Washington, DC)

COMPETITORS

Clark Enterprises
Dick Corporation
Hunt Construction
M. A. Mortenson
McCarthy Building
PCL
Perini
Rooney Brothers
Skanska USA Building
Turner Corporation
Walbridge Aldinger
Walsh Group
Whiting-Turner

HISTORICAL FINANCIALS

Company Type: Private

Income Statement FYE: May 31

	REVENUE ($ mil.)	NET INCOME ($ mil.)	NET PROFIT MARGIN	EMPLOYEES
5/03	1,872	—	—	2,500
5/02	1,771	—	—	2,200
5/01	1,368	—	—	2,200
5/00	1,357	—	—	2,200
5/99	1,165	—	—	2,151
5/98	934	—	—	1,926
5/97	876	—	—	1,535
5/96	726	—	—	1,540
5/95	734	—	—	1,400
5/94	692	—	—	1,650
Annual Growth	11.7%	—	—	4.7%

Revenue History

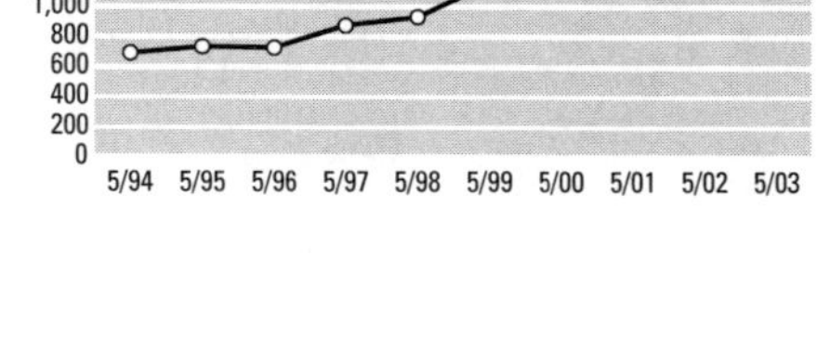

Herb Chambers Companies

Step into the chambers of Herb Chambers Companies and you'll find a wide range of cars. The company runs more than 20 dealerships in New England that sell just about everything from pricey new cars from BMW, Cadillac, Lexus, Mercedes-Benz, and Porsche to more affordable offerings from Honda, Hyundai, Kia, Mazda, Saturn, and Toyota; dealerships also offer used cars. All of its cars are available online. Herb Chambers also offers parts and service and runs three body shops. Owner and CEO Herb Chambers started his automotive empire with a Cadillac/Oldsmobile dealership in New London, Connecticut, in 1985.

EXECUTIVES

President and CEO: Herbert G. (Herb) Chambers, age 61
CFO: Bruce Spatz

LOCATIONS

HQ: The Herb Chambers Companies
259 McGrath Hwy., Somerville, MA 02145
Phone: 617-666-8333 **Fax:** 617-666-8448
Web: www.chamberscars.com

COMPETITORS

AutoNation
Group 1 Automotive
March/Hodge
Planet Automotive Group
United Auto Group

HISTORICAL FINANCIALS

Company Type: Private

Income Statement FYE: December 31

	REVENUE ($ mil.)	NET INCOME ($ mil.)	NET PROFIT MARGIN	EMPLOYEES
12/01	987	—	—	1,000
12/00	974	—	—	1,000
12/99	801	—	—	1,000
12/98	674	—	—	1,000
12/97	607	—	—	822
12/96	562	—	—	798
12/95	461	—	—	703
Annual Growth	13.5%	—	—	6.0%

Revenue History

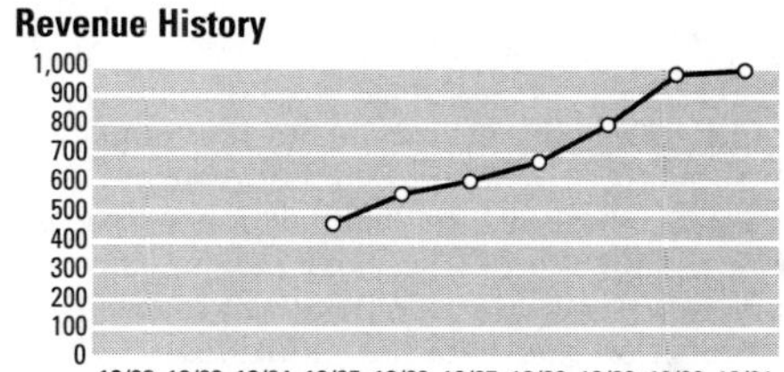

Herbalife International

Rooted in the medicinal value provided by Mother Nature, Herbalife International sells more than 160 products containing herbal and other natural ingredients. Products include weight-control mixes and tablets, nutritional supplements specifically designed for men and women, food, shampoos, lotions, sunscreens, and body oils. The multi-level marketer sells its products through a network of independent distributors in more than 50 countries; salespeople earn money from their own efforts, as well as from the sales of those whom they have recruited into the organization.

Distributors in emerging markets in Africa, Asia, and Eastern Europe have been attracted to Herbalife by the low startup costs. After buying promotional materials (average cost: $60), distributors buy products from Herbalife at a discount of up to 50% and resell them at retail prices. Nearly two-thirds of the company's gross sales are made outside the US.

The company's sales were hit hard by the economic crises in Asia and Russia, two key sales areas. Herbalife's continued struggle with slumping sales and industrywide questions of product efficacy were exacerbated by challenges brought on by the unexpected death of then-chairman and CEO Mark Hughes. The company, hoping to turn the tables on its troubles, was acquired by a group of venture capital firms including Whitney & Co. and Golden Gate Capital.

HISTORY

Mark Hughes' mother's death from an overdose of prescription diet pills was the catalyst for Herbalife. Hughes, a high-school dropout, founded the company with diet supplement maker Richard Marconi in 1980. Herbalife went public in 1986 after rapid growth, but it got into trouble for some of its product claims. Following federal and state investigations and US Senate hearings, Herbalife paid a hefty fine and removed some of its products from the market. Hughes was able to resurrect the firm by taking it overseas. Sales also got a boost from the success of the Thermojetics weight-control systems.

In 1995 Herbalife introduced a line of herbal and botanical skin care products (Dermajetics). In 1997 insider selling of stock prompted a major slide in the price of Herbalife shares. Earnings tanked in 1998 when economic crises hit such big revenue contributors as Russia and Asia.

In 1999 Hughes planned to buy the company's outstanding shares and take the company private; investors sued. In 2000 he dropped the attempt. That year 44-year-old Hughes died in what was ruled an accidental death caused by a combination of alcohol and antidepressant medication. Hughes' longtime associate and former Herbalife COO Christopher Pair moved into the positions of president and CEO. He stepped down a year later after the company's board criticized his management.

Later that year, the Mark Hughes Family Trust turned down a $173 million bid for control of the company from Internet retailer Rbid.com. A group of investment firms bought the company in 2002 and Hughes' hopes to take the company private came to fruition without him.

EXECUTIVES

Chairman: Peter M. Castleman, age 47
Co-President: Carol Hannah, age 54, $1,544,500 pay (prior to promotion)
Co-President: Brian L. Kane, age 57, $1,492,000 pay (prior to promotion)
SVP, Finance and Treasury: William D. Lowe
Auditors: Deloitte & Touche LLP

LOCATIONS

HQ: Herbalife International, Inc.
1800 Century Park East, Los Angeles, CA 90067
Phone: 310-410-9600 **Fax:** 310-216-5169
Web: www.herbalife.com

Herbalife International sells its products in nearly 50 countries worldwide.

2001 Sales

	% of total
Asia/Pacific Rim	35
Americas	37
Europe	28
Total	**100**

PRODUCTS/OPERATIONS

Selected Products

Nutritional Supplements
Aminogen
A.M. Replenishing
Cell-U-Loss
Dinomins
DinoShakes
Echinacea Plus
Extreme C
Florafiber
Herbal Calmative
Herbal-Aloe
Herbalifeline
Kindermins
Male Factor 1000
Male Performance Complex
P.M. Cleansing
RoseOx
Schizandra Plus
Sleep Now
Tang Kuei Plus
Thermo-bond
Ultimate Prostate Formula
Woman's Choice
Women's Advantage
Xtra-Cal

Personal Care
Colour cosmetics
Dermajetics
AromaVie
Good Hair Day
Nature's Mirror
Parfums Vitessences
Skin Survival Kit

Weight Management
Formula 1 Protein Mix
Thermojetics
Thermojetics Gold Herbal Supplement Tablets
Thermojetics Herbal Concentrate
Thermojetics High-Protein, Low-Carb Program

COMPETITORS

Alticor
GNC
Jenny Craig
Mannatech
Nature's Sunshine
NBTY
Nu Skin
Reliv'
Rexall Sundown
Shaklee
Slim-Fast
Sunrider
Vitamin Shoppe Industries
Weider Nutrition International
Whole Living
Wyeth

HISTORICAL FINANCIALS

Company Type: Private

Income Statement

FYE: December 31

	REVENUE ($ mil.)	NET INCOME ($ mil.)	NET PROFIT MARGIN	EMPLOYEES
12/01	1,020	43	4.2%	2,445
12/00	944	37	3.9%	2,391
12/99	956	57	6.0%	2,170
12/98	867	49	5.6%	1,742
12/97	783	55	7.0%	1,459
12/96	632	45	7.1%	1,180
12/95	489	20	4.0%	1,060
12/94	467	46	9.9%	862
12/93	365	41	11.3%	638
12/92	214	20	9.4%	464
Annual Growth	18.9%	8.7%	—	20.3%

2001 Year-End Financials

Debt ratio: 0.5%
Return on equity: 17.6%
Cash ($ mil.): 179
Current ratio: 2.08
Long-term debt ($ mil.): 1

Net Income History

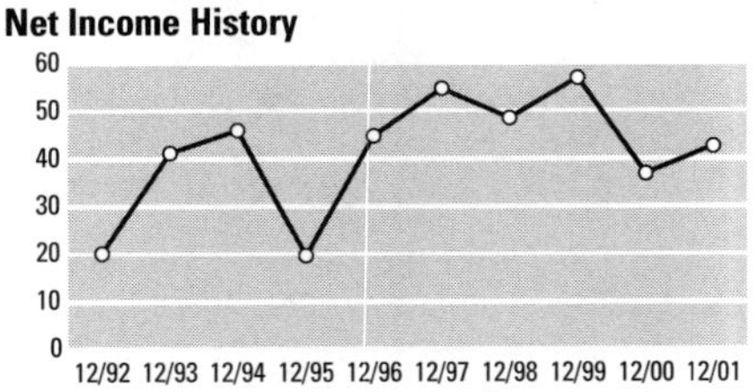

Hicks, Muse, Tate & Furst

These Texas Hicks know an investment pool ain't no cement pond and like to buy, buy & buy. (They sell sometimes, too.) Hicks, Muse, Tate & Furst creates investment pools in the form of limited partnerships. Investors are mostly pension funds but also include financial institutions and wealthy private investors. The leveraged buyout firm assembles limited partnership investment pools, targets underperforming companies in specific niches, builds them up, and uses them to form a nucleus for other investments. Hicks, Muse also has holdings in manufacturing and real estate.

As its target industries consolidated — making US acquisitions scarce — Hicks, Muse increasingly turned to foreign markets. The firm (which sold its AMFM to Clear Channel Communications to create the US's largest radio, television, and outdoor advertising group) began exporting its media mogul strategy through investments in Europe and Latin America. Hicks, Muse, along with US-based Liberty Media International, owns Cablevision SA, Argentina's largest cable operator. Hicks, Muse's late 1990s hopes for a tidy profit on the more than $1 billion it invested in the South American nation turned into a 2002 headache as that country wades through an economic depression.

At home, Hicks, Muse has suffered losses in telecommunications and has considered closing funds before they reach their original target amounts. It abandoned plans to buy out manufacturing firm Johns Manville with Bear Stearns when its stock took a dive. Hicks, Muse also closed down offices in Argentina and New York.

The company turned its strategy to focus more on due diligence in efforts to emerge from the off-message period of the late 1990s. Hicks, Muse, along with Colorado-based Booth Creek Management, bought a 54% share of ConAgra's meatpacking operations as a part of its "back to basics" approach to reaffirm their three money making areas: media, branded food, and basic component manufacturing. Hicks, Muse also owns the North American assets of bankrupt Vlasic Foods International Inc., including Vlasic pickles, Open Pit barbecue sauces, and Swanson Frozen Food.

HISTORY

The son of a Texas radio station owner, Thomas Hicks became interested in leveraged buyouts as a member of First National Bank's venture capital group. Hicks and Robert Haas formed Hicks & Haas in 1984 the next year that firm bought Hicks Communications, a radio outfit run by Hicks' brother Steven. (This would be the first of many media companies bought or created by the buyout firm, often with Steven Hicks' involvement.)

Hicks & Haas' biggest coup was its mid-1980s buy of several soft drink makers, including Dr Pepper and Seven-Up. The firm took Dr Pepper/Seven-Up public just 18 months after merging the two companies. In all, Hicks & Haas turned $88 million of investor funding into $1.3 billion. The pair split up in 1989; Hicks wanted to raise a large pool to invest, but Haas preferred to work deal by deal.

Hicks raised $250 million in 1989 and teamed with former Prudential Securities banker John Muse. Early investments included Life Partners Group (life insurance, 1990; sold 1996). In 1991 Morgan Stanley's Charles Tate and First Boston's Jack Furst became partners.

As part of its buy-and-build strategy, Hicks, Muse bought DuPont's connector systems unit in 1993, renamed it Berg Electronics, added six more companies to it, and doubled its earnings before selling it in 1998. Not every move was a star in the Hicks, Muse crown. Less-than-successful purchases included bankrupt brewer G. Heileman, bought in 1994 and sold two years later for an almost $100 million loss.

The buyout firm's Chancellor Media radio company went public in 1996. That year Hicks, Muse gained entry into Latin America with its purchases of cash-starved Mexican companies, including Seguros Commercial America, one of the country's largest insurers. That year also brought International Home Foods (Jiffy Pop, Chef Boyardee) into the Hicks, Muse fold.

In 1997 Chancellor and Evergreen Media merged to form Chancellor Media (renamed AMFM in 1999). The next year Hicks, Muse continued buying US and Latin American media companies, as well as a few oddities (a UK software maker, a Danish seed company, and US direct-seller Home Interiors & Gifts). Hicks, Muse and Kohlberg Kravis Roberts merged their cinema operations to form the US's largest theater chain. The company that year also moved into the depressed energy field (Triton Energy) and formed a $1.5 billion European fund.

Buys in 1999 included UK food group Hillsdown Holdings, one-third of Mexican flour maker Grupo Minsa, and just in time for millennial celebrations) popular champagne brands Mumm and Perrier-Jouët (it quadrupled its investment when it sold the champagne houses in late 2000). Lured by low stock prices on real estate investment trusts (REITs), the company agreed to buy Walden (formerly Walden Residential Properties) that year.

Hicks, Muse, along with UK-based Apax Partners, bought British Telecommunication's yellow pages firm Yell for roughly $3.5 billion, making it the largest non-corporate LBO in European history. Yell bought US directories publisher McLeodUSA Publishing for about $600 million. Hicks, Muse then smelled a good deal and bought Nestle's Ambient Food Business in 2002.

EXECUTIVES

Chairman and CEO: Thomas O. Hicks, age 57
President: John R. Muse, age 52
Chief Operating Officer: Jack D. Furst, age 43
CFO: Darron Ash
Partner: Dan H. Blanks
Partner: John P. Civantos
Partner: Joe Colonnetta
Partner: Lyndon Lea
Partner: Eric C. Neuman, age 56
Partner: Stephan Lobmeyer
Partner: Philippe von Stauffenberg
Principal: Marcos Clutterbuck
Principal: Robert Darwent
Principal: Edward Herring
Principal: Eric Lindberg
Principal: Andrew Rosen
Principal: Luca Velussi

LOCATIONS

HQ: Hicks, Muse, Tate & Furst Incorporated
200 Crescent Ct., Ste. 1600, Dallas, TX 75201
Phone: 214-740-7300 **Fax:** 214-720-7888

Hicks, Muse, Tate & Furst has offices in Dallas and London.

PRODUCTS/OPERATIONS

Selected Holdings

Ambient Food Business (food business)
CCI/Triad Systems Corp. (computer systems)
CEI Citicorp Holding (40%, telecommunications and publishing)
Glass Group (automotive information services software)
Grupo Minsa, S.A. de C.V. (32%, corn flour producer, Mexico)
Grupo MVS SA (23%, pay-TV provider and radio station owner, Mexico)
Grupo Vidrio Formas (69%, glass container supplier, Mexico)
Hedstrom Corp. (playground equipment)
Hillsdown Holdings PLC (food production, office furniture)
Home Interiors & Gifts, Inc. (80%, direct-selling of decorative accessories and gift items)
Ibero-American Media Partners (50%, Latin American media buyout fund)
International Outdoor Advertising (97%; billboards in Argentina, Chile, and Uruguay)
International Wire Holdings Corp. (60%; wire, wire harnesses, and cable)
LIN Holdings (69%, television stations)
Metrocall Inc. (paging systems)
Olympus Real Estate Corp. (real estate equity and mortgage investments)
OmniAmerica Wireless LP (45%, broadcast towers)
Pan-American Sports Network (80%, regional cable sports network)
RCN Corp. (fiber-optic telecommunications networks)
Rhythms NetConnections (8%, high-speed Internet access)
Sunrise Television Corp. (87%, small-market television stations)
Traffic (49%, broadcasting, Brazil)
United Biscuits (Holdings) plc (87%, with Finalrealm; food products; UK)
Viasystems Group (printed circuit boards)
Yell (directories)
Walden (REIT)

COMPETITORS

Bain Capital
Berkshire Hathaway
Boston Ventures
Clayton, Dubilier
CVC Capital Partners
Equity Group Investments
Haas Wheat
Heico
Investcorp
Jordan Company
KKR
Leonard Green
Maseca
Texas Pacific Group
Thomas Lee
Vestar Capital Partners
Vsm Investors
Vulcan Northwest
Wingate Partners

Highmark Inc.

Highmark is walking the tightrope between high-minded and high income. Highmark provides health-related coverage to some 23 million customers, primarily in Pennsylvania. Highmark offers medical, dental, vision, life, casualty, and other health insurance, as well as such community service programs as the Western Pennsylvania Caring Foundation, which offers free health care coverage to children whose parents earn too much to qualify for public aid but too little to afford private programs. Highmark also processes Medicare claims (Veritus Medicare and HGSAdministrators Medicare Services) and offers administrative and information services (Alliance Ventures).

Highmark continues to operate in western Pennsylvania under the Highmark Blue Cross Blue Shield name and as Pennsylvania Blue Shield statewide. National subsidiaries include United Concordia Companies (dental coverage) and Highmark Life and Casualty Group (disability and life insurance).

HISTORY

Highmark was created from the merger of Blue Cross of Western Pennsylvania (founded in 1937) and Pennsylvania Blue Shield, created in 1964 when the Medical Service Association of Pennsylvania (MSAP) adopted the Blue Shield name.

The Pennsylvania Medical Society, in conjunction with the state of Pennsylvania, had formed MSAP to provide medical insurance to the poor and indigent. MSAP borrowed $25,000 from the Pennsylvania Medical Society to help set up its operations, and Chauncey Palmer (who had originally proposed the organization) was named president. Individuals paid 35 cents per month, and families paid $1.75 each month to join MSAP, which initially covered mainly obstetrical and surgical procedures.

In 1945 Arthur Daugherty replaced Palmer as president (he served until his death in 1968) and helped MSAP recruit major new accounts, including the United Mine Workers and the Congress of Industrial Organizations. MSAP in 1946 became a chapter of the national Blue Shield association, which was started that year by the medical societies of several states to provide prepaid health insurance plans.

In 1951 MSAP signed up the 150,000 employees of United States Steel, bringing its total enrollment to more than 1.6 million. Growth did not lead to prosperity, though, as the organization had trouble keeping up with payments to its doctors. This shortfall in funds led MSAP to raise its premiums in 1961, at which point the state reminded the association of its social mission and suggested it concentrate on controlling costs instead of raising rates.

MSAP changed its name to Pennsylvania Blue Shield in 1964. Two years later the association began managing the state's Medicare plan and started the 65-Special plan to supplement Medicare coverage. In the 1970s Pennsylvania Blue Shield again could not keep up with the cost of paying its doctors, which led to more rate increases and closer scrutiny of its expenses. Competition increased in the 1980s as HMOs cropped up around the state. Pennsylvania Blue Shield fought back by creating its own HMO plans — some of which it owned jointly with Blue Cross of Western Pennsylvania — in the 1980s.

After years of slowly collecting noninsurance businesses, Blue Cross of Western Pennsylvania changed its name to Veritus in 1991 to reflect the growing importance of its for-profit operations.

In 1996 Pennsylvania Blue Shield overcame physicians' protests and state regulators' concerns to merge with Veritus. The company adopted the name Highmark to represent its standards for high quality; it took a loss as it failed to meet cost-cutting goals and suffered early-retirement costs related to the merger consolidation. To gain support for the merger, Highmark sold for-profit subsidiary Keystone Health Plan East to Independence Blue Cross in 1997.

In 1999 Highmark teamed with Mountain State Blue Cross Blue Shield to become West Virginia's primary licensee. Rate hikes and investment returns helped propel the company into the black as the decade closed.

In 2001 Highmark announced that it had uncovered almost $5 million in health care insurance fraud against the company over the course of the previous year.

EXECUTIVES

Chairman: John N. Shaffer
Vice Chairman: John A. Carpenter
President, CEO, and Director: Kenneth R. Melani, age 48
Group EVP, Health Insurance Operations: James Klingensmith
EVP, Government Business and Corporate Affairs: George F. Grode
SVP, CFO, and Treasurer: Robert C. Gray
SVP, Corporate Secretary, and General Counsel: Gary R. Truitt
SVP and General Auditor: Elizabeth A. Farbacher
SVP, Human Resources and Administrative Services: S. Tyrone Alexander
Assistant Secretary: Carrie J. Pecht
Assistant Treasurer: Joseph F. Reichard
Corporate Compliance Officer: George A. Welsh
Auditors: PricewaterhouseCoopers LLP

LOCATIONS

HQ: Fifth Avenue Place, 120 5th Ave., Pittsburgh, PA 15222
Phone: 412-544-7000 **Fax:** 412-544-8368
Web: www.highmark.com

PRODUCTS/OPERATIONS

Selected Health Plans and Divisions

Alliances Ventures
Clarity Vision
Davis Vision
HealthGuard (managed care organization)
HGSAdministrators
Highmark Life & Casualty Group
Insurer Physician Services Organization
Keystone Health Plan Central (HMO; central Pennsylvania)
Keystone Health Plan West (HMO; western Pennsylvania)
United Concordia (dental)
Veritus Medicare Services

COMPETITORS

Aetna
CIGNA
Coventry Health Care
Guardian Life
Humana
New York Life
Prudential
UnitedHealth Group
U.S. Healthcare, Inc.

HISTORICAL FINANCIALS

Company Type: Not-for-profit

Income Statement FYE: December 31

	REVENUE ($ mil.)	NET INCOME ($ mil.)	NET PROFIT MARGIN	EMPLOYEES
12/02	7,400	(83)	—	11,000
12/01	6,799	132	1.9%	11,000
12/00	9,000	242	2.7%	11,000
12/99	8,190	69	0.8%	11,000
12/98	7,544	62	0.8%	12,000
12/97	7,405	101	1.4%	12,000
12/96	6,619	(50)	—	10,500
12/95	3,367	43	1.3%	8,000
12/94	3,221	128	4.0%	7,200
12/93	3,113	132	4.2%	—
Annual Growth	10.1%	—	—	5.4%

Net Income History

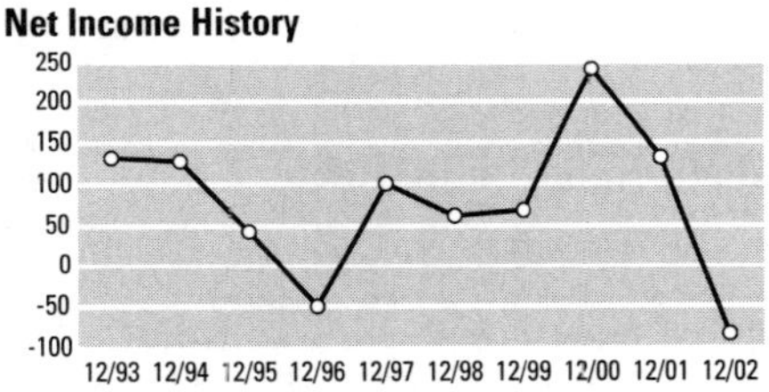

Hines Interests L.P.

Hines Interests has been involved in many developments, but none of them include ketchup. Founded by Gerald Hines in 1957, the company is a private commercial real estate development company. Hines handles most aspects of real estate development, including site selection, rezoning, design, construction management, and financing. Its 700 property investment portfolio includes corporate headquarters, industrial facilities, and master-planned residential communities. Hines also manages almost 80 million sq. ft. of real estate in the US and 11 other countries. Management services include public relations, tenant relations, and vendor contract-negotiation services. Hines Interests is controlled by the Hines family.

EXECUTIVES

Chairman and CEO: Gerald D. Hines
President: Jeffery C. Hines
CFO: C. Hastings (Hasty) Johnson
SVP and Chief Administration Officer: David LeVrier
EVP, Capital Markets: Charles M. Baughn
SVP Corporate Finance: Kay P. Forbes
EVP Conceptual Construction: John A. Harris
VP Human Resources: Stephanie Fore
VP Corporate Communication: George C. Lancaster
VP and CTO: Gerhard Karba

LOCATIONS

HQ: Williams Tower, 2800 Post Oak Blvd., Houston, TX 77056
Phone: 713-621-8000 **Fax:** 713-966-2053
Web: www.hines.com

Hines Interests has offices California, Colorado, Georgia, Illinois, New York, and Texas; and in Argentina, Brazil, China, France, Germany, Italy, Mexico, Poland, Russia, Spain, and the UK.

PRODUCTS/OPERATIONS

Selected Services

Acquisition and Disposition Services
Asset Management Services
Development Services
Marketing and Leasing Services

COMPETITORS

CarrAmerica
CB Richard Ellis
Equity Office Properties Trust
Grubb & Ellis
Jones Lang LaSalle
Lincoln Property
Mack-Cali
Opus
Staubach
Trammell Crow

HISTORICAL FINANCIALS

Company Type: Private

Income Statement FYE: December 31

	ESTIMATED REVENUE ($ mil.)	NET INCOME ($ mil.)	NET PROFIT MARGIN	EMPLOYEES
12/02	750	—	—	2,800
12/01	750	—	—	2,800
12/00	750	—	—	2,800
12/99	750	—	—	2,800
12/98	750	—	—	2,800
12/97	700	—	—	2,700
12/96	650	—	—	2,500
12/95	600	—	—	2,500
12/94	600	—	—	1,300
12/93	—	—	—	1,100
Annual Growth	2.8%	—	—	10.9%

Revenue History

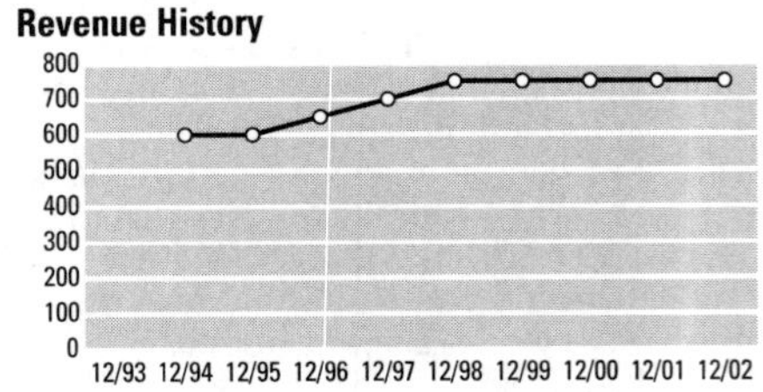

Hitchcock Automotive Resources

It's no mystery: Hitchcock Automotive Resources owns five automotive dealerships and Puente Hills Body Shop, all located in central California. A multiple-brand car dealer, the company sells new cars made by BMW, Ford, Mazda, Toyota, Volkswagen; more than 14,100 were sold in 2002. All dealerships offer parts and service departments. Frederick "Fritz" Hitchcock opened his first car dealership in 1971, and in 1980 he founded Hitchcock Automotive Resources to oversee his growing dealership network. Hitchcock, who is also the company's chairman and CEO, owns the business.

EXECUTIVES

Chairman and CEO: Frederick E. (Fritz) Hitchcock Jr.
CFO: Barry Wasserman
SVP Human Resources: David K. Hall
SVP Information Systems: Rich Morris
VP: Howard Hakes
General Sales Manager: Sam Miranda

LOCATIONS

HQ: 17340 E. Gale Ave., City of Industry, CA 91748
Phone: 626-839-8401 **Fax:** 626-965-4983
Web: www.phford.com

COMPETITORS

AutoNation
David Wilson's
Galpin Motors
Kuni Automotive
Marty Franich
Prospect Motors
Tuttle-Click
Vista

HISTORICAL FINANCIALS

Company Type: Private

Income Statement FYE: December 31

	REVENUE ($ mil.)	NET INCOME ($ mil.)	NET PROFIT MARGIN	EMPLOYEES
12/01	503	—	—	575
12/00	499	—	—	575
12/99	429	—	—	550
12/98	470	—	—	550
12/97	400	—	—	550
12/96	358	—	—	550
12/95	478	—	—	550
12/94	450	—	—	500
Annual Growth	1.6%	—	—	2.0%

Revenue History

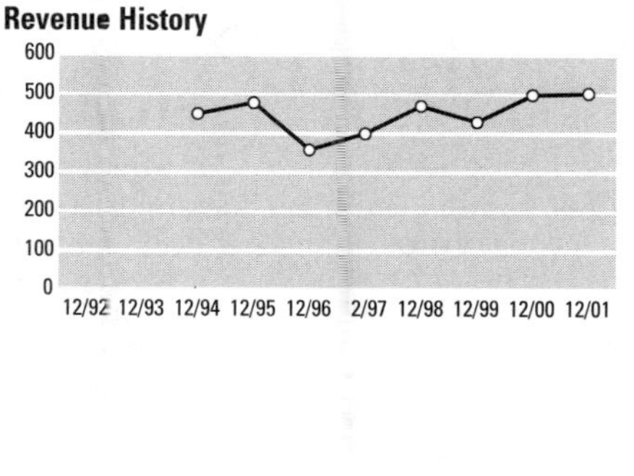

HNTB Ltd.

HNTB leads the pack of "pure designers" — engineering or architectural firms that derive most of their revenues from architecture, engineering, or environmental design operations. From 60 locations across the US, HNTB provides civil and environmental engineering services and urban design and planning for industry and government agencies worldwide. A transportation specialist, HNTB has worked on most of the highways and transit systems in the US. The company is also known for its airport projects and its sports arena and stadium designs (Coors Field and Invesco Field at Mile High are among its projects). Employee-owned HNTB (which once stood for Howard Needles Tammen & Berendoff) traces its roots to 1914.

EXECUTIVES

Chairman: Harvey K. Hammond Jr.
CEO, HNTB Companies: Paul A. Yarossi
Director Corporate Development: Edward (Ed) McSpedon
COO: W. Scott Butzen
CFO: Terry M. Campbell
Corporate Risk Officer: Robert L. (Bob) Fogle
CIO: Daniel S. Wolgemuth
President, HNTB Corporation: Kenneth R. Graham
Director Client Development and Chief Sales Officer, HNTB Corp.: James P. Anglin
Director, Corporate Planning and Communication: Gary F. Link

LOCATIONS

HQ: 715 Kirk Dr., Kansas City, MO 64105
Phone: 816-472-1201 **Fax:** 816-472-4060
Web: www.hntb.com

COMPETITORS

AECOM
Black & Veatch
Duke Energy
Earth Tech
Ellerbe Beckett
HOK
Jacobs Engineering
Kimley-Horn and Associates
Louis Berger
Gensler
Parsons Brinckerhoff
URS

HISTORICAL FINANCIALS

Company Type: Private

Income Statement FYE: December 31

	ESTIMATED REVENUE ($ mil.)	NET INCOME ($ mil.)	NET PROFIT MARGIN	EMPLOYEES
12/01	541	—	—	700
12/00	461	—	—	2,800
Annual Growth	17.3%	—	—	(75.0%)

Revenue History

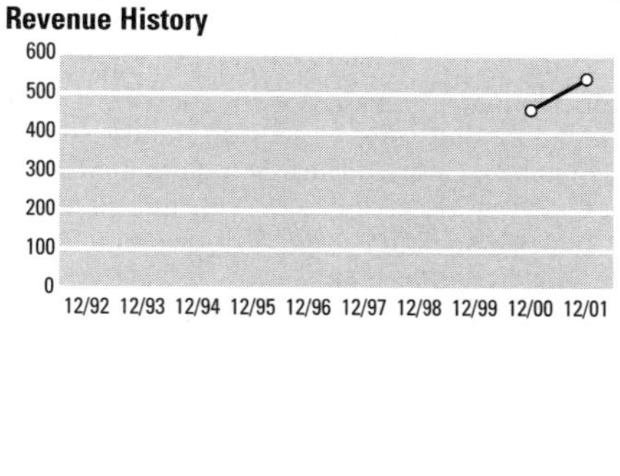

Hobby Lobby Stores, Inc.

If something wicker this way comes, Hobby Lobby Stores may be the source. The company runs nearly 300 stores in 26 southern and midwestern states, selling arts and craft supplies, baskets, candles, frames, home decorating accessories, and silk flowers. The #3 craft retailer (after Michaels Stores and Jo-Ann Stores), Hobby Lobby prefers to set up shop in second-generation retail sites (such as vacated supermarkets and Wal-Marts). Sister companies supply Hobby Lobby with merchandise, which is distributed through a center in Oklahoma City. CEO David Green, who owns the company with his wife, Barbara, founded the company in 1972 and operates it according to biblical principles, including closing stores on Sunday.

EXECUTIVES

President and CEO: David Green
CFO: John Cargill
EVP: Steve Green
SVP Operations: Ken Haywood
VP Advertising: Bill Hane
VP Construction: Steve Seay
VP Legal: Peter Dobelbower
VP and Director of Real Estate: Bill Darrow
Director of Recruiting: Bill Owens

LOCATIONS

HQ: 7707 SW 44th St., Oklahoma City, OK 73179
Phone: 405-745-1100 **Fax:** 405-745-1636
Web: www.hobbylobby.com

Hobby Lobby Stores has stores in Alabama, Arkansas, Colorado, Florida, Georgia, Illinois, Indiana, Iowa, Kansas, Kentucky, Louisiana, Michigan, Minnesota, Mississippi, Missouri, Nebraska, New Mexico, North Carolina, Ohio, Oklahoma, South Carolina, South Dakota, Tennessee, Texas, Wisconsin, and Wyoming.

PRODUCTS/OPERATIONS

Selected Products

Arts and crafts supplies
Baskets
Candles
Cards
Furniture
Home accent pieces
Jewelry-making supplies
Memory books
Model kits
Needlework
Party supplies
Picture frames and framing
Rubber stamping supplies
Seasonal items
Sewing materials (fabric, patterns, notions)
Silk flowers
Wearable art

COMPETITORS

A.C. Moore
Family Christian Stores
Frank's Nursery & Crafts
Garden Ridge
Hancock Fabrics
HobbyTown USA
Home Interiors & Gifts
Jo-Ann Stores
Kirkland's
Longaberger
Michaels Stores
Old Time Pottery
Rag Shops
Wal-Mart

HISTORICAL FINANCIALS

Company Type: Private

Income Statement FYE: December 31

	REVENUE ($ mil.)	NET INCOME ($ mil.)	NET PROFIT MARGIN	EMPLOYEES
12/01	1,015	—	—	15,000
12/00	905	—	—	13,500
12/99	798	—	—	12,000
12/98	664	—	—	11,000
12/97	590	—	—	7,500
12/96	540	—	—	7,500
Annual Growth	13.5%	—	—	14.9%

Revenue History

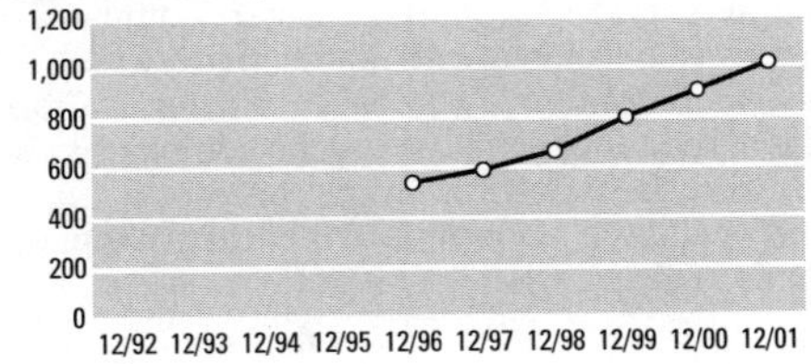

Hoffman Corporation

Hoffman cherishes a challenge — such as building the nation's deepest subway station in Portland, Oregon, or the snakelike, metal-clad Experience Music Project in Seattle. The general contractor and construction manager's main subsidiary, Hoffman Construction, builds civic, commercial, and industrial facilities, primarily in the western US. It is a leading builder of semiconductor facilities and serves such sectors as education, health care, sports, transportation, and government. The group also provides plumbing and HVAC (heating, ventilation, and air-conditioning) installation, electrical wiring, surveying, and concrete contracting services. Employees own the company, which was founded in 1922.

EXECUTIVES

Co-Chairman: Eric Hoffman
Co-Chairman: Cecil W. Drinkward
President and CEO: Wayne A. Drinkward
CFO: Scott Fredricks
VP Marketing: Barton Eberwein
Purchasing Manager: Jon Grasle
IT Manager: Anne Belle
HR: Sheri Sundstrom

LOCATIONS

HQ: 805 SW Broadway, Ste. 2100, Portland, OR 97205
Phone: 503-221-8811 **Fax:** 503-221-8934
Web: www.hoffmancorp.com

Hoffman has offices in Portland, Oregon, and Seattle, Washington.

PRODUCTS/OPERATIONS

Selected Markets

Advanced technology
Athletic
Corrections
Cultural/museums
Destination/hotel
Education
Government
Health care
Industrial
Office
Parking facilities
Renovation
Residential
Transportation

COMPETITORS

Alberici
Bechtel
Black & Veatch
Bovis Lend Lease
DPR Construction
Fluor
Gilbane
Hensel Phelps Construction
McCarthy Building
Peter Kiewit Sons'
Skanska
Structure Tone
Swinerton
Turner Corporation
Washington Group
Webcor Builders
Whiting-Turner

HISTORICAL FINANCIALS

Company Type: Private

Income Statement FYE: December 31

	REVENUE ($ mil.)	NET INCOME ($ mil.)	NET PROFIT MARGIN	EMPLOYEES
12/01	1,165	—	—	1,200
12/00	954	—	—	1,460
12/99	400	—	—	500
12/98	527	—	—	466
12/97	1,175	—	—	154
12/96	990	—	—	850
Annual Growth	3.3%	—	—	7.1%

Revenue History

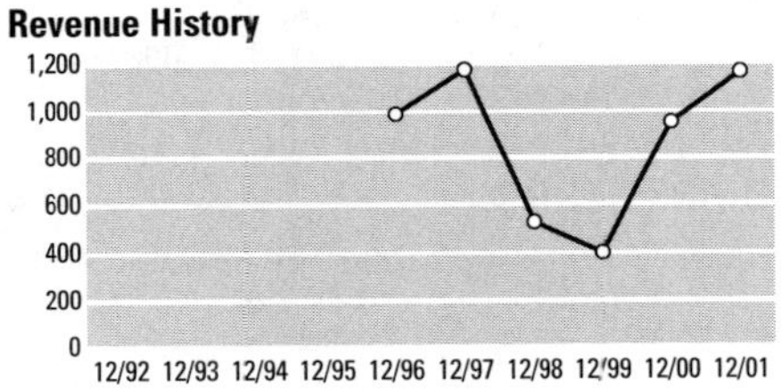

Holiday Companies

Wholesaling has taken a vacation at Holiday Companies. It sold its Fairway Foods distributions business to Fleming Companies in 2000 and now owns convenience stores and sporting good stores in the upper Midwest and Northwest. Holiday Companies owns more than 250 Holiday Stationstores in 11 states and also has 37 franchised stores. These sell gas supplied by the company's Erickson Petroleum subsidiary as well as Blue Planet gasoline, low-sulfur fuel available in Minnesota. Holiday Companies also owns about 55 Gander Mountain sporting goods stores. The company was founded in 1928 as a general store in a small Wisconsin town by two Erickson brothers, whose descendants still own and operate the company.

EXECUTIVES

CEO: Ronald A. (Ron) Erickson, age 66
VP, Human Resources: Bob Nye
VP, Holiday Stationstores: George Townsend
VP, Petroleum Supply and Distribution, Holiday Stationstores: Dick Mills
CEO, Gander Mountain: Mark R. Baker
CFO, Gander Mountain: Dennis Lindahl
COO, Gander Mountain: Al Dittrich
EVP, Gander Mountain: Gary Hauger
Regional VP and District Manager, Iowa and Minnesota: Andy Carlin

LOCATIONS

HQ: 4567 American Blvd. West, Bloomington, MN 55437
Phone: 952-830-8700 **Fax:** 952-830-8864
Web: holidaystationstores.com

COMPETITORS

7-Eleven
Bass Pro Shops
Cabela's
Casey's General Stores
Clark Retail
Exxon Mobil
Kroger
Marathon Ashland Petroleum
QuikTrip
Sports Authority

HISTORICAL FINANCIALS

Company Type: Private

Income Statement FYE: December 31

	ESTIMATED REVENUE ($ mil.)	NET INCOME ($ mil.)	NET PROFIT MARGIN	EMPLOYEES
12/02	1,250	—	—	6,000
12/01	1,300	—	—	5,500
12/00	1,200	—	—	5,500
12/99	1,100	—	—	5,500
12/98	1,700	—	—	6,000
12/97	1,100	—	—	5,000
12/96	1,000	—	—	5,000
12/95	1,250	—	—	5,100
12/94	1,600	—	—	5,000
12/93	1,000	—	—	5,000
Annual Growth	2.5%	—	—	2.0%

Revenue History

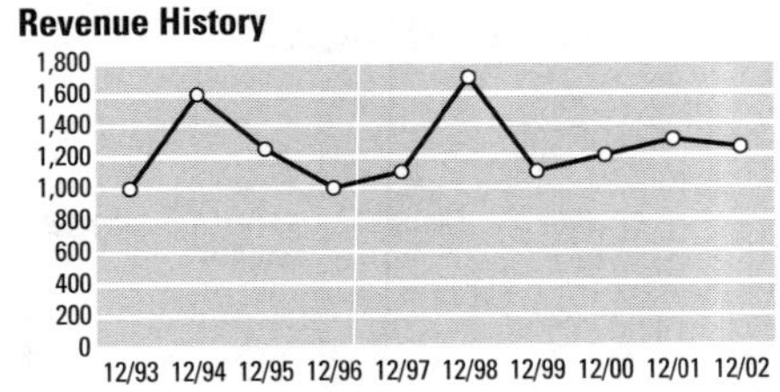

Holland & Knight LLP

Your legal knight in shining armor is just around the corner. Holland & Knight is one of the largest law firms in the US, operating in more than 100 practice areas of law organized into four major departments (business law; litigation; public law; and real estate, environmental and land use). Holland & Knight was founded in the 1880s and has more than 20 offices in nine US states, with five international offices. The firm has been growing through acquisitions, adding Levine & Associates, a leading firm in Native American affairs; the Los Angeles and Tokyo offices of Whitman Breed Abbott & Morgan; and Gilbert, Segall & Young to its stable of more than 1,200 lawyers.

The firm combined with Chicago-based firm McBride Baker & Coles in August 2002.

EXECUTIVES

Chairman: Martha W. Barnett
Managing Partner: Howell W. Melton Jr.
Executive Director: Herb Albritton
CFO: Carl Culler
CIO: Ralph Barber
Director Human Resources: Andrew Petterson
Director Marketing: Martha (Marty) Duvall
Public Relations Manager: Karen Schoening

LOCATIONS

HQ: 195 Broadway, 24th Fl., New York, NY 10007
Phone: 212-513-3200 **Fax:** 212-385-9010
Web: www.hklaw.com

Holland & Knight has US offices in California, Florida, Georgia, Illinois, Maryland, Massachusetts, New York, Rhode Island, Virginia, and Washington, DC. The firm has international offices in Brazil, Finland, Mexico, and Japan.

PRODUCTS/OPERATIONS

Selected Practice Groups

Business law
Litigation
Public law
Real estate, environmental, and land use

Selected Practice Areas

Agriculture
Appropriations
Bankruptcy
Class action
Communications
Criminal defense
Education
Energy
Estates and trusts
Health care
Native American affairs
Marital and family law
Maritime and shipping
Product liability
REITs
Telecommunications
Trusts and estates
White-collar crime

COMPETITORS

Baker & Hostetler
Baker & McKenzie
Greenberg Traurig
Jones Day
Proskauer Rose
Schulte Roth & Zabel
Skadden, Arps
White & Case

HISTORICAL FINANCIALS

Company Type: Partnership

Income Statement FYE: December 31

	REVENUE ($ mil.)	NET INCOME ($ mil.)	NET PROFIT MARGIN	EMPLOYEES
12/02	515	—	—	2,800
12/01	466	—	—	2,722
12/00	364	—	—	—
12/99	298	—	—	2,600
12/98	228	—	—	—
12/97	169	—	—	—
12/96	138	—	—	—
12/95	115	—	—	—
12/94	99	—	—	—
12/93	77	—	—	—
Annual Growth	23.5%	—	—	2.5%

Revenue History

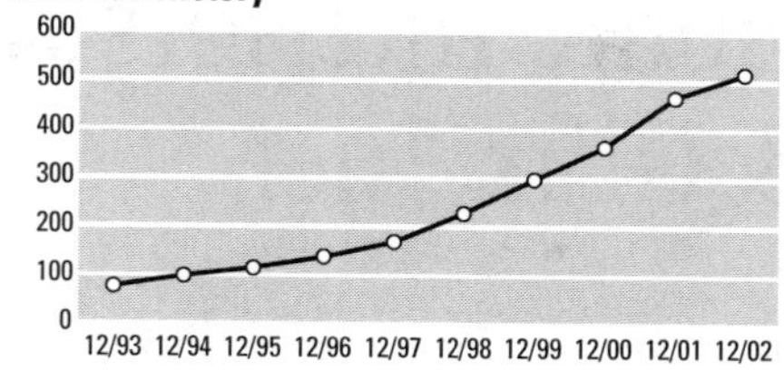

Holman Enterprises

Holman sells a whole lot of cars. Family-owned Holman Enterprises owns more than 20 car and truck dealerships in southern New Jersey and southern Florida. Founded in 1924, Holman sells BMW, Ford, Infiniti, Jaguar, Lincoln, Mercury, Rolls-Royce, and Saturn cars, as well as Ford, Kenworth, and Sterling trucks. The company also offers collision repair services. Holman's RMP engine and parts distributor sells small parts and engines authorized by Ford. Its Automotive Resources International unit, one of the largest independently owned vehicle fleet leasing management groups in the world, also operates a truck parts and accessories company.

EXECUTIVES

Chairman and CEO: Joseph S. Holman
President: Mindy Holman
VP: Bill Cariss
VP Finance: Robert Campbell
Manager Human Resources: Paul Toepel

LOCATIONS

HQ: 7411 Maple Ave., Pennsauken, NJ 08109
Phone: 856-663-5200 **Fax:** 856-665-3444
Web: www.holmanauto.com

COMPETITORS

AMERCO
AutoNation
CarMax
Cendant
Enterprise Rent-A-Car
Frank Consolidated Enterprises
Hendrick Automotive
JM Family Enterprises
Morse Operations
Penske
Planet Automotive Group
Ryder
Sansone Auto Network
Toresco Enterprises
United Auto Group

HISTORICAL FINANCIALS

Company Type: Private

Income Statement FYE: December 31

	REVENUE ($ mil.)	NET INCOME ($ mil.)	NET PROFIT MARGIN	EMPLOYEES
12/01	2,105	—	—	2,600
12/00	2,200	—	—	2,800
12/99	2,146	—	—	2,718
12/98	1,870	—	—	2,700
12/97	1,870	—	—	2,800
12/96	1,800	—	—	2,700
12/95	1,600	—	—	2,500
12/94	1,350	—	—	2,870
12/93	1,073	—	—	2,370
12/92	1,028	—	—	2,300
Annual Growth	8.3%	—	—	1.4%

Revenue History

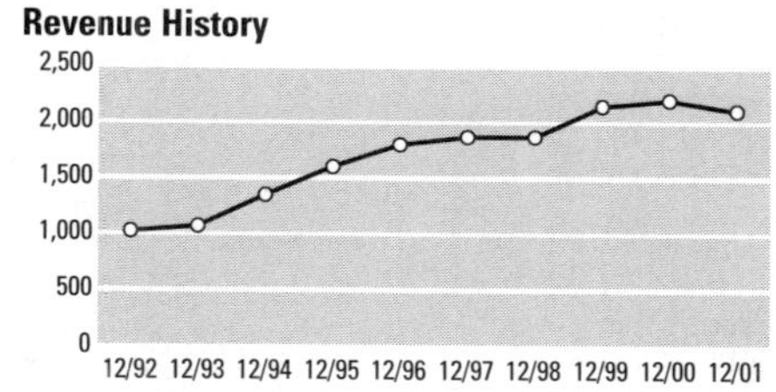

The Holmes Group, Inc.

The Holmes Group makes what it takes to condition the air, open canned goods, and slow-cook meals. The company (formerly Holmes Products) makes Bionaire, Family Care, Holmes, and other brands of air purifiers, fans, filters, heaters, and humidifiers. Holmes also distributes decorative lighting products. Its Rival kitchen appliances division offers can openers, Crock-Pots, toasters, and more. Holmes has shut down all US manufacturing operations and is utilizing its alliances in the Far East. Goods are sold in Asia, Europe, North America, and South America. Wal-Mart, Kmart, and Target ring up nearly half of Holmes' sales. Investment firm Berkshire Partners owns about 75% of the firm.

Founder and chairman Jerry Kahn owns more than 10% of Holmes.

EXECUTIVES

Chairman: Jordan A. (Jerry) Kahn, age 60, $616,430 pay
President, CEO, and Director: Peter J. Martin, age 46, $267,300 pay
EVP, Sales and Marketing and Director: Gregory F. White, age 38, $388,977 pay
SVP and CFO: John M. Kelliher, age 50
SVP, Human Resources and Organizational Performance: Louis F. Cimini, age 47
Managing Director, Far East Operations and Director: Woon Fai (Tommy) Liu, age 49, $319,800 pay
Auditors: PricewaterhouseCoopers LLP

LOCATIONS

HQ: 1 Holmes Way, Milford, MA 01757
Phone: 508-634-8050 **Fax:** 508-634-1211
Web: www.theholmesgroup.com

PRODUCTS/OPERATIONS

Selected Products

Air purifiers
Air filters
Can openers
Crock-Pots
Deep fryers
Electric knives
Electric skillets and griddles
Fans
Fondue pots
Grinders
Hand makers
Heaters
Humidifiers
Ice cream makers
Lighting products
Popcorn makers
Slow cookers
Toasters
Vaporizers

COMPETITORS

American Household
Applica
Catalina Lighting
Conair
Craftmade
Electrolux AB
Fedders
HMI Industries
Honeywell International
Juno Lighting
Kaz
Masco
NACCO Industries
National Presto Industries
Philips
Salton
SEB
Toastmaster Inc.
Water Pik Technologies
Whirlpool

HISTORICAL FINANCIALS

Company Type: Private

Income Statement FYE: December 31

	REVENUE ($ mil.)	NET INCOME ($ mil.)	NET PROFIT MARGIN	EMPLOYEES
12/02	609	(58)	—	7,300
12/01	628	(16)	—	7,500
12/00	513	(32)	—	7,500
12/99	507	2	0.4%	7,500
12/98	215	9	4.2%	4,300
12/97	192	4	2.0%	4,150
12/96	194	6	3.2%	—
12/95	178	3	1.8%	—
Annual Growth	19.2%	—	—	12.0%

2002 Year-End Financials

Debt ratio: —
Return on equity: —
Cash ($ mil.): 8
Current ratio: 2.20
Long-term debt ($ mil.): 266

Net Income History

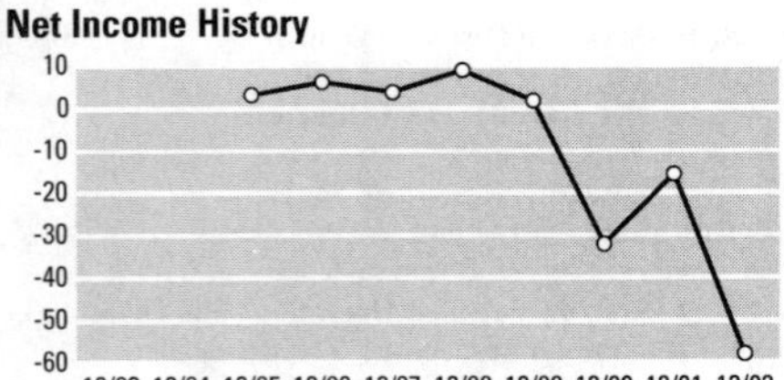

Home Interiors & Gifts, Inc.

Home Interiors & Gifts is knocking. The company makes decorating accessories, which are sold by more than 70,000 representatives through home parties in the US, Canada, and Mexico. Its product lines include artificial flowers, candles, framed artwork, lighting sconces, mirrors, plaques, and shelves. The firm buys virtually all of its products from subsidiaries such as Dallas Woodcraft Company and Laredo Candle Company. Mary Crowley, sister-in-law of makeup maven Mary Kay Ash, founded Home Interiors in 1957. Executives led by Joey Carter (Crowley's grandson) and buyout firm Hicks, Muse, Tate & Furst recapitalized Home Interiors & Gifts in 1998. Hicks, Muse, which owns about 75%, is seeking buyers for the firm.

EXECUTIVES

Chairman and CEO: Donald J. (Joey) Carter Jr., age 42, $1,693,750 pay
Vice Chairman: Christina L. (Christi) Carter Urschel, age 39
President and COO: Michael D. (Mike) Lohner, age 40, $1,631,168 pay
SVP Finance and CFO: Kenneth J. (Ken) Cichocki, age 49, $379,138 pay
SVP International: Eugenia B. (Jeannie) Price, age 37, $269,090 pay
SVP Sales: Nora I. Serrano, age 37, $341,064 pay
VP IT: Alan Boyer
Associate VP Human Resources: Pat Sinclair
Auditors: PricewaterhouseCoopers LLP

LOCATIONS

HQ: 1649 Frankford Rd. West, Carrollton, TX 75007
Phone: 972-695-1000 **Fax:** 972-695-1112
Web: www.homeinteriors.com

PRODUCTS/OPERATIONS

Selected Products

Artificial floral displays
Candle holders
Candles
Figurines
Framed artwork and mirrors
Planters
Plaques
Sconces
Wall shelves

COMPETITORS

Alticor
Avon
Blyth
Garden Ridge
Hanover Direct
Hobby Lobby
Lancaster Colony
Lillian Vernon
Mary Kay
Michaels Stores
Pier 1 Imports
Pinnacle
Wal-Mart
Wicks'N'Sticks
Yankee Candle

HISTORICAL FINANCIALS

Company Type: Private

Income Statement FYE: December 31

	REVENUE ($ mil.)	NET INCOME ($ mil.)	NET PROFIT MARGIN	EMPLOYEES
12/02	575	36	6.2%	2,400
12/01	462	4	0.8%	1,300
12/00	460	10	2.1%	1,200
12/99	503	52	10.3%	1,400
12/98	490	48	9.9%	1,400
12/97	469	62	13.3%	—
12/96	434	54	12.5%	—
12/95	483	50	10.2%	—
12/94	515	71	13.7%	—
Annual Growth	1.4%	(8.2%)	—	14.4%

2002 Year-End Financials

Debt ratio: —
Return on equity: —
Cash ($ mil.): 64
Current ratio: 1.29
Long-term debt ($ mil.): 323

Net Income History

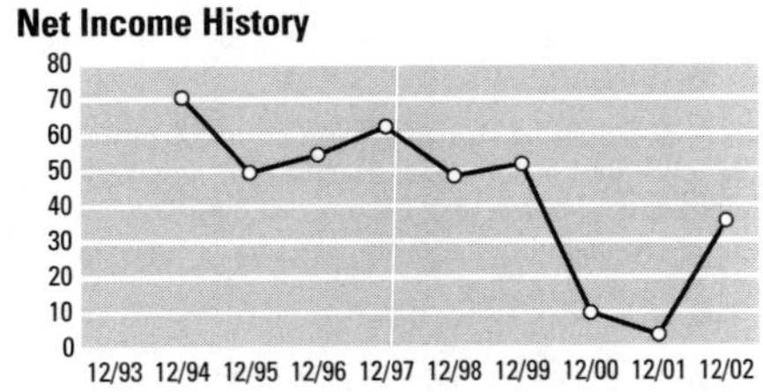

Honickman Affiliates

Honickman Affiliates doesn't mind bottling its creative juices. The firm is one of the nation's largest private bottlers — bottling and distributing soft drinks primarily in Maryland, New Jersey, New York, Ohio, and Virginia through more than 10 plants. A major bottler of Pepsi-Cola and Cadbury Schweppes brands including 7 UP, it also sells Canada Dry, Mott's, Snapple, and South Beach Beverage Company's SoBe beverages. It distributes Coors beers in New York and brews up private-label soft drinks. Chairman and owner Harold Honickman started the company in 1957 when his father-in-law built a bottling plant for him.

EXECUTIVES

Chairman: Harold Honickman
CEO: Jeffrey Honickman
CFO: Walt Wilkinson
President of Pepsi-Cola and Canada Dry: Robert Brockway
Director of Human Resources: June Raufer
Data Processing: Gwen Dolceamore

LOCATIONS

HQ: 8275 Rte. 130, Pennsauken, NJ 08110
Phone: 856-665-6200 **Fax:** 856-661-4684

COMPETITORS

Coca-Cola Bottling Consolidated
Coca-Cola Enterprises
Cott
National Beverage
Nestlé
Odwalla
Philadelphia Coca-Cola
Snapple
Suntory

HISTORICAL FINANCIALS

Company Type: Private

Income Statement

FYE: December 31

	ESTIMATED REVENUE ($ mil.)	NET INCOME ($ mil.)	NET PROFIT MARGIN	EMPLOYEES
12/01	1,100	—	—	5,000
12/00	980	—	—	5,000
12/99	1,000	—	—	5,200
12/98	1,005	—	—	5,200
12/97	1,000	—	—	5,200
12/96	1,000	—	—	5,200
12/95	975	—	—	—
12/94	912	—	—	—
Annual Growth	2.7%	—	—	(0.8%)

Revenue History

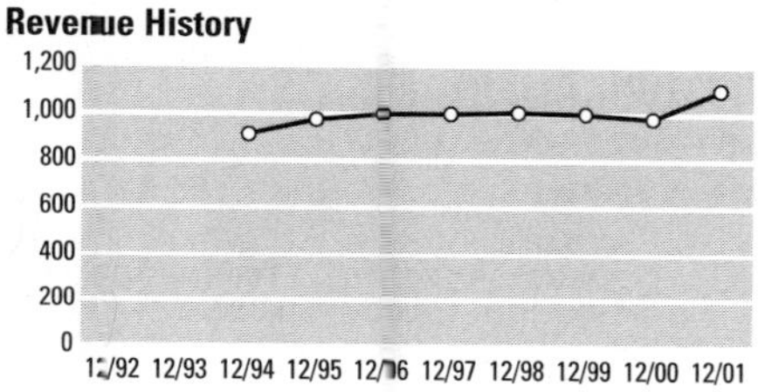

Horizon Blue Cross Blue Shield

Horizon Blue Cross Blue Shield of New Jersey is New Jersey's top not-for-profit health insurance provider, serving nearly 3 million members. The company's insurance plans include traditional indemnity, Horizon HMO, Horizon PPO, and Horizon Direct Access (Open Access). Horizon Blue Cross Blue Shield of New Jersey also offers dental, Medicare, and behavioral health coverage, as well as workers' compensation insurance. The company's Horizon Healthcare Insurance Agency subsidiary provides life, long-term disability, and long-term care coverage. The company's Horizon/Mercy subsidiary participates in the state of New Jersey's Medicaid program.

EXECUTIVES

President and CEO: William J. Marino, age 59
SVP of Administration, CFO and Treasurer: Robert J. Pures
SVP of Information Systems and CIO: Charles C. Emery Jr.
VP Corporate Marketing and Corporate Communications: Lawrence B. Altman
VP, Human Resources: Carole Czar Soldo
Auditors: PricewaterhouseCoopers LLP

LOCATIONS

HQ: Horizon Blue Cross Blue Shield of New Jersey
3 Penn Plaza East, Newark, NJ 07101
Phone: 973-466-4000 **Fax:** 973-466-4317
Web: www.horizon-bcbsnj.com

Horizon Blue Cross Blue Shield of New Jersey's operations area includes the state of New Jersey and ten counties in lower New York state.

PRODUCTS/OPERATIONS

2002 Sales

	$ mil.	% of total
Premiums	3,814	94
Administrative service fees	225	6
Other	59	—
Total	**4,098**	**100**

Subsidiaries

Horizon Casualty Services (workers' comp and TPA services)
Horizon Healthcare (managed care plans and services)
Horizon/Mercy (Medicaid HMO)
Horizon Healthcare Dental (managed dental care plans and services)
Horizon Healthcare Insurance Agency (Life, LTD, and LTC)

COMPETITORS

Aetna
CIGNA
UnitedHealth Group

HISTORICAL FINANCIALS

Company Type: Not-for-profit

Income Statement

FYE: December 31

	REVENUE ($ mil.)	NET INCOME ($ mil.)	NET PROFIT MARGIN	EMPLOYEES
12/02	4,098	114	2.8%	4,600
12/01	3,534	106	3.0%	—
12/00	3,079	117	3.8%	—
Annual Growth	15.4%	(1.4%)	—	—

2002 Year-End Financials

Debt ratio: —
Return on equity: 17.3%
Cash ($ mil.): 269
Current ratio: 0.76
Long-term debt ($ mil.): —

Net Income History

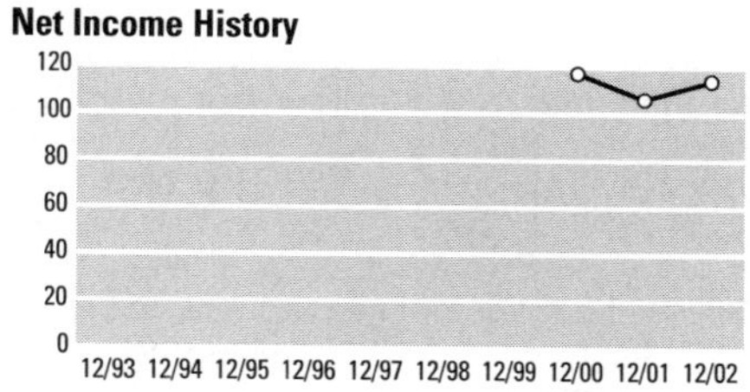

Horizon Natural Resources

Horizon Natural Resources (formerly AEI Resources) is one of the US's largest producers of steam (bituminous) coal. The company operates mines in five states. It sells mainly to electric utilities in the eastern US. Horizon's Mining Technologies subsidiary makes Addcar-brand highwall mining equipment, while its Mining Machinery subsidiary provides trucking services, major equipment rebuilds, and mining equipment. Horizon's ties to the founding Addington family were severed as part of a reorganization that bought the company out of bankruptcy in 2002; however, later that year it again filed to reorganize under Chapter 11. Horizon's heavy debt was caused in part by numerous acquisitions during the late 1990s.

EXECUTIVES

Chairman: John J. Delucca, age 59
Acting CEO and Director: Scott M. Tepper, age 41
Acting CFO: Steven Cohn, age 48
EVP, Human Resources and Administration: Lance G. Sogan, age 55
SVP, Sales and Marketing: Marc R. Merritt, age 49
VP and Treasurer: Paul H. Buckholz, age 54
VP and Controller: Richard A. Boone, age 48
General Counsel: Daniel L. Stickler, age 56

LOCATIONS

HQ: Horizon Natural Resources Company
2000 Ashland Dr., Ashland, KY 41101
Phone: 606-920-7400 **Fax:** 606-920-7720
Web: www.horizonnr.com

Horizon Natural Resources mines and markets steam coal from mines in Colorado, Indiana, Illinois, Kentucky, and West Virginia. It also owns subsidiaries that produce mining machinery and offer related services in Kentucky.

PRODUCTS/OPERATIONS

Selected Operations

Mining Machinery (trucking services, equipment and component rebuilding services, equipment rental)
Mining Technologies, Inc. (ADDCAR Highwall Mining System)
Zeigler Coal Holding Company (underground and surface coal mining)

COMPETITORS

Arch Coal
CONSOL Energy
Drummond
Ingersoll-Rand
Joy Global
Massey Energy
Peabody Energy
RAG
Westmoreland Coal

HISTORICAL FINANCIALS

Company Type: Private

Income Statement FYE: December 31

	REVENUE ($ mil.)	NET INCOME ($ mil.)	NET PROFIT MARGIN	EMPLOYEES
12/02	1,200	—	—	3,500
12/01	1,413	—	—	4,000
12/00	1,500	—	—	4,000
12/99	1,331	—	—	4,000
12/98	733	—	—	4,081
12/97	175	—	—	—
12/96	123	—	—	—
Annual Growth	46.1%	—	—	(3.8%)

Revenue History

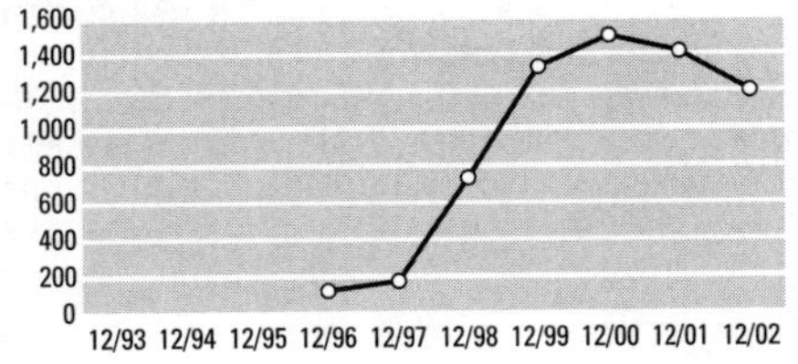

Horseshoe Gaming Holding

Bring your lucky charms to casinos owned by Horseshoe Gaming Holding Corp. The company owns a Horseshoe Casino and Hotel in Bossier City, Louisiana, as well as one in Tunica, Mississippi. In 2001 Horseshoe Gaming sold its Empress Casino riverboat and hotel in Joliet, Illinois, but it retains an Empress location in Hammond, Indiana. Illinois officials denied the company a license to operate the Empress riverboat in Joliet, alleging that owner and CEO Jack Binion failed to comply with state regulations after buying the casino. The company appealed the decision, but later struck a deal that forced it to sell the location to Argosy Gaming. Horseshoe has agreed to be acquired by Harrah's for $1.45 billion.

EXECUTIVES

Chairman, CEO, and Secretary: Jack B. Binion, age 65, $1,000,000 pay
Vice Chairperson: Peri N. Howard, age 41
President and COO: Robert Wagner, age 54, $750,000 pay
SVP, CFO, and Treasurer: Kirk C. Saylor, age 45, $405,000 pay
SVP Government Affairs: Floyd B. Hannon, age 60, $401,300 pay
SVP Human Resources: David S. Carroll, age 47
SVP and CIO: Jon C. Wolfe, age 34
SVP and General Counsel: Dominic F. Polizzotto, age 36, $461,200 pay

LOCATIONS

HQ: Horseshoe Gaming Holding Corp.
18454 S. West Creek Dr., Tinley Park, IL 60477
Phone: 708-429-8300 **Fax:** 708-429-8315
Web: www.horseshoegaming.com

2002 Sales

	$ mil.	% of total
Hammond	309.1	38
Bossier City	255.7	32
Tunica	247.7	30
Total	**812.6**	**100**

COMPETITORS

Casino Magic
Harrah's Entertainment
Isle of Capri Casinos
Lakes Entertainment
Mandalay Resort Group
Park Place Entertainment
Pinnacle Entertainment

HISTORICAL FINANCIALS

Company Type: Private

Income Statement FYE: December 31

	REVENUE ($ mil.)	NET INCOME ($ mil.)	NET PROFIT MARGIN	EMPLOYEES
12/02	813	60	7.4%	7,780
12/01	933	232	24.9%	7,843
12/00	1,013	61	6.0%	9,699
12/99	526	32	6.2%	8,920
12/98	461	25	5.4%	—
12/97	335	27	8.2%	—
Annual Growth	19.4%	17.0%	—	(4.5%)

2002 Year-End Financials

Debt ratio: 242.6%
Return on equity: 27.1%
Cash ($ mil.): 102
Current ratio: 1.18
Long-term debt ($ mil.): 557

Net Income History

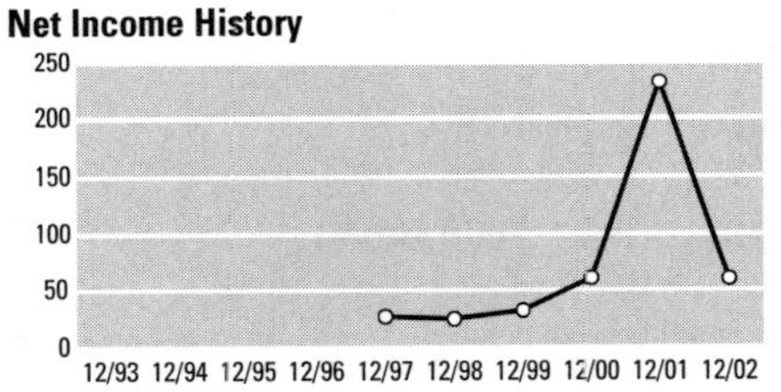

Houchens Industries Inc.

Houchens Industries operates stores for shoppers more interested in supper than super. Eschewing the industry trend toward massive superstores, the company's 31 Houchens Markets in Kentucky average less than 20,000 sq. ft. Its nearly 200 Save-A-Lot stores (licensed from SUPERVALU) offer limited selections and cover 15,000 sq. ft. or less. Houchens has stores in 13 states from eastern Texas to New York. The company also owns more than 40 Jr. Foods convenience stores and 23 Tobacco Shoppe discount cigarette outlets, mostly in Kentucky and Tennessee. It bought cigarette maker Commonwealth Brands in 2001. Founded as BG Wholesale in 1918 by Ervin Houchens, the company is entirely owned by its employees.

EXECUTIVES

President and CEO: Jim Gipson
CFO: Mark Iverson
Director of Advertising: Venus Popplewell
Director of Benefits: Sharon Grooms

LOCATIONS

HQ: 900 Church St., Bowling Green, KY 42101
Phone: 270-843-3252 **Fax:** 270-781-6377

Houchens Industries has stores in Alabama, Georgia, Illinois, Indiana, Kentucky, New York, North Carolina, Ohio, South Carolina, Tennessee, Texas, Virginia, and West Virginia.

COMPETITORS

7-Eleven
Alliance Tobacco
Cigarettes Cheaper
Cumberland Farms
Delhaize America
Fleming Companies
Kroger
K-VA-T Food Stores
Meijer
Sheetz
Smokin Joes
Vector
Wal-Mart
Weis Markets
Winn-Dixie

HISTORICAL FINANCIALS

Company Type: Private

Income Statement FYE: September 30

	ESTIMATED REVENUE ($ mil.)	NET INCOME ($ mil.)	NET PROFIT MARGIN	EMPLOYEES
9/02	1,727	—	—	5,850
9/01	820	—	—	5,200
9/00	735	—	—	4,800
9/99	585	—	—	4,200
9/98	515	—	—	3,860
9/97	450	—	—	3,600
9/96	400	—	—	3,100
Annual Growth	27.6%	—	—	11.2%

Revenue History

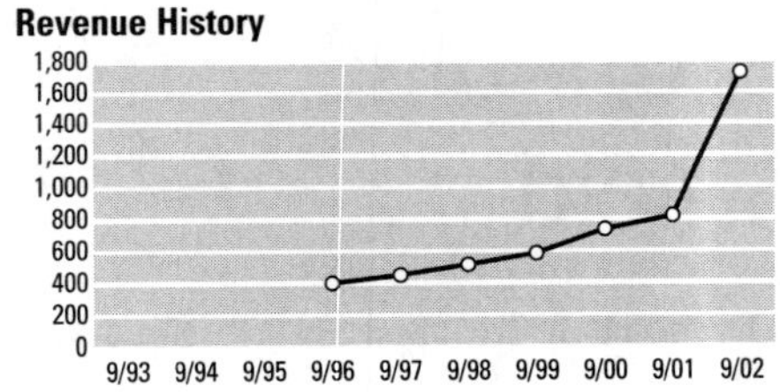

Houghton Mifflin

Alice Cooper's 1972 album *School's Out* probably doesn't get much play around the offices of Houghton Mifflin. A top publisher of textbooks for the K-12 and college markets, the company also offers fiction and nonfiction books for adults and children and reference works such as the *American Heritage Dictionary.* Major divisions include

McDougal Littell (secondary school textbooks), Riverside Publishing (educational testing), and Great Source Education Group (supplemental school materials for grades K-12). It also operates a digital publishing business. Vivendi Universal Publishing, the publishing arm of French media giant Vivendi Universal, sold Houghton to several investment firms in 2002.

The company's trade fiction and nonfiction lines, although small, still produce the occasional best seller (such as 2001's *Fast Food Nation* by Eric Schlosser).

Houghton Mifflin is working on building up the company's college, trade and reference, and workplace assessments units. The publisher currently relies heavily on its K-12 publishing business, which makes up 65% of sales.

After 150 years in business as an independent company, the company has had several changes of ownership in recent years. Houghton Mifflin was acquired by French media giant Vivendi Universal in 2001 for $2.2 billion (which included the assumption of $500 million in debt). Houghton Mifflin was placed under Vivendi Universal's publishing unit, which in 2002 decided to sell off most of its assets as part of Vivendi Universal's $9.8 billion sale of assets. Two investment firms (Thomas H. Lee and Bain Capital) bought Houghton Mifflin. Vivendi Universal Publishing sold off its non-US-based publishing assets to an investment bank firm, which then sold the assets to Lagardère.

EXECUTIVES

CEO: Anthony (Tony) Lucki
EVP and COO: Sylvia Metayer
EVP, College Division: June Smith, age 57
EVP, School Division: George A. Logue, age 50
SVP Administration: Gary L. Smith, age 56
SVP, President, The Riverside Publishing Company: John E. Laramy, age 56, $390,750 pay
SVP Trade and Reference: Theresa Kelly
VP, Executive Managing Editor, Adult Trade: Becky Saikia-Wilson
VP Corporate Development and Technology Initiatives: Iwan Streichenberger
Auditors: Ernst & Young LLP

LOCATIONS

HQ: Houghton Mifflin Company
222 Berkeley St., Boston, MA 02116
Phone: 617-351-5000 **Fax:** 617-351-1105
Web: www.hmco.com

PRODUCTS/OPERATIONS

Selected Operations

Calabash (professional development resources)
Classwell (online pre K-12 educational resources)
College Division
Great Source Education Group (supplemental education materials)
McDougal Littell (secondary textbooks)
Promissor (test administration technology and services)
The Riverside Publishing Company (testing materials)
School Division
Trade and Reference Division

COMPETITORS

Educational Testing Service
Everyday Learning
Goodheart-Willcox
Harcourt Education
HarperCollins
John Wiley
McGraw-Hill
Pearson
Random House
Scholastic
Scholastic Library Publishing
Time Warner Book Group
Touchstone Applied Science
Verlagsgruppe Georg von Holtzbrinck
W.W. Norton

HISTORICAL FINANCIALS

Company Type: Private

Income Statement

FYE: December 31

	REVENUE ($ mil.)	NET INCOME ($ mil.)	NET PROFIT MARGIN	EMPLOYEES
12/02	1,000	—	—	4,400
12/01	1,000	—	—	4,000
12/00	1,028	—	—	3,500
12/99	920	—	—	3,300
12/98	862	—	—	2,830
12/97	797	—	—	2,550
12/96	718	—	—	2,420
12/95	529	—	—	2,350
12/94	483	—	—	2,023
12/93	463	—	—	1,920
Annual Growth	8.9%	—	—	9.7%

Revenue History

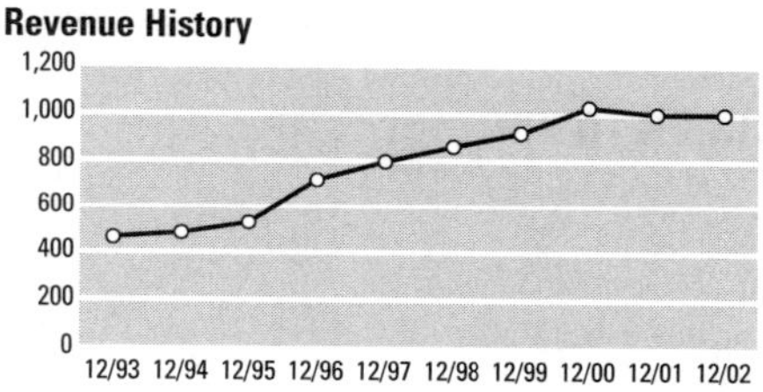

HP Hood Inc.

HP Hood is busily trying to cream its competition — with ice cream, sour cream, and whipping cream. The company, one of New England's leading dairies, also produces milk, cottage cheese, and juices. Besides its own brands, HP Hood makes private-label, licensed, and franchise products. It specializes in extended-shelf-life products, which are distributed nationally under licensing agreements. Founded in 1846 by Harvey P. Hood as a one-man milk delivery service, the company still offers home delivery. The family of CEO John Kaneb owns the company. HP Hood has announced that it intends to acquire a minority portion of the much larger National Dairy Holdings and share leadership.

EXECUTIVES

Chairman, President, and CEO: John A. Kaneb
CFO: Gary R. Kaneb
SVP, Sales: James F. Walsh
VP, Human Resources: Bruce W. Bacon
VP, Licensed Marketing: Kevin Donavan
VP, Operations Services: Francis V. Torgerson
General Counsel: Paul F. Beatty

LOCATIONS

HQ: 90 Everett Ave., Chelsea, MA 02150
Phone: 617-887-3000 **Fax:** 617-887-8484
Web: www.hphood.com

HP Hood has plants in Connecticut, Maine, Massachusetts, New York, Vermont, and Virginia.

PRODUCTS/OPERATIONS

Selected Brands

Booth Brothers
Hood
Lactaid

COMPETITORS

Organic Valley
Dean Foods
Dreyer's
National Dairy Holdings
Parmalat North America
Stew Leonard's
Stonyfield Farm
Unilever

HISTORICAL FINANCIALS

Company Type: Private

Income Statement

FYE: December 31

	REVENUE ($ mil.)	NET INCOME ($ mil.)	NET PROFIT MARGIN	EMPLOYEES
12/01	800	—	—	1,600
12/00	700	—	—	1,439
12/99	600	—	—	1,450
12/98	500	—	—	1,300
12/97	500	—	—	1,200
Annual Growth	12.5%	—	—	7.5%

Revenue History

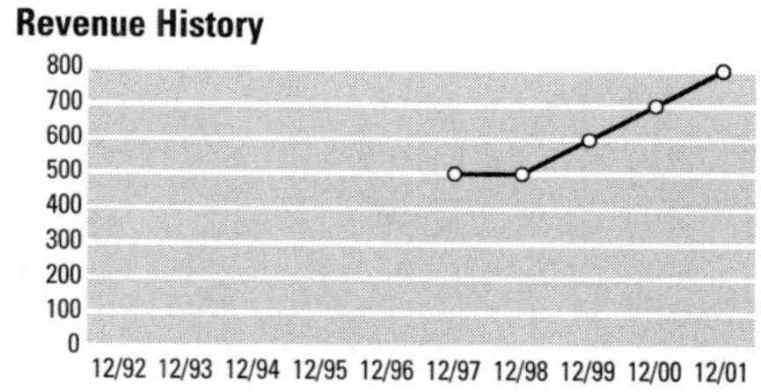

H.T. Hackney Co.

The H.T. Hackney Company began delivering goods to small grocers by horse and buggy in 1891; it now supplies more than 20,000 independent grocers and convenience stores in about 20 states east of the Mississippi. H.T. Hackney distributes more than 30,000 items, including frozen food, tobacco products, health and beauty items, and deli products. In addition it owns Tennessee-based Natural Springs Water Group and has furniture-making operations (Volunteer Fabricators). Looking to expand its convenience store business, in 2000 the company acquired six gas stations from Aztex Enterprises and two supply centers from Spartan Stores in 2003. Chairman and CEO Bill Sansom owns H.T. Hackney.

EXECUTIVES

Chairman and CEO: William B. (Bill) Sansom, age 61
VP Finance: Mike Morton

LOCATIONS

HQ: 502 S. Gay St., Knoxville, TN 37902
Phone: 865-546-1291 **Fax:** 865-546-1501
Web: www.hthackney.com

COMPETITORS

Alex Lee
AWG
Eby-Brown
Fleming Companies
GSC Enterprises
McLane
Nash Finch
S. Abraham & Sons
Spartan Stores
SUPERVALU

HISTORICAL FINANCIALS

Company Type: Private

Income Statement FYE: December 31

	REVENUE ($ mil.)	NET INCOME ($ mil.)	NET PROFIT MARGIN	EMPLOYEES
12/01	2,500	—	—	3,100
12/00	2,300	—	—	3,100
12/99	2,000	—	—	3,000
12/98	1,818	—	—	2,900
12/97	1,623	—	—	2,643
12/96	1,800	—	—	1,900
Annual Growth	6.8%	—	—	10.3%

Revenue History

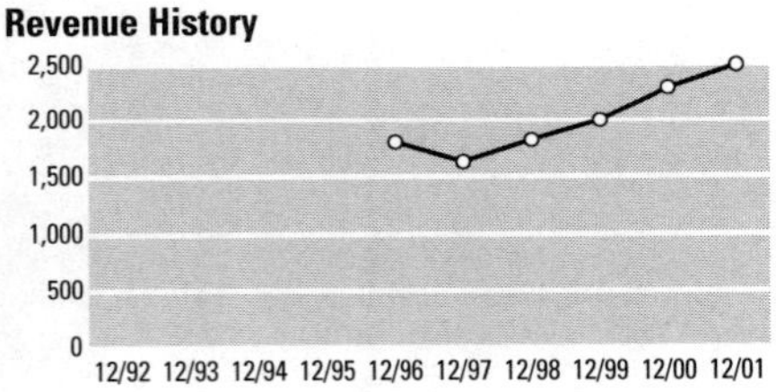

Hubbard Broadcasting

This Hubbard's cupboard is full of broadcasting treats. Hubbard Broadcasting owns eight TV stations and three radio stations, mainly in Minnesota and New York. Hubbard Broadcasting also owns TV production company Diamond P Sports. Since selling its 51% stake in United States Satellite Broadcasting to Hughes Electronics (DIRECTV) in 1999 for $1.25 billion, Hubbard has launched several satellite and cable channels of its own, like the All News Channel and Moviewatch. Hubbard sold its Conus Communications (video archive service) unit to a group of former employees. Late founder Stanley E. Hubbard began his broadcasting empire when he launched a Minneapolis radio station in 1923. Hubbard's family owns the company.

EXECUTIVES

Chairman, President, and CEO: Stanley S. Hubbard
VP; Chairman and CEO, Hubbard Media Group: Stanley E. Hubbard II
President, Television: Robert W. Hubbard
President, Radio: Virginia Hubbard (Ginny) Morris
CFO: Ronald Lindwall
CTO: Bill Langley
Director of Sales: Trey Fabacher
Director Human Resources: Suzanne Cook

LOCATIONS

HQ: Hubbard Broadcasting Inc.
3415 University Ave., St. Paul, MN 55114
Phone: 651-646-5555 **Fax:** 651-642-4172

PRODUCTS/OPERATIONS

Selected Operations

Diamond P Sports (TV production)
Radio stations
- KSTP-AM (Minneapolis-St. Paul, MN)
- KSTP-FM (Minneapolis-St. Paul, MN)
- WIXK-FM (New Richmond, WI)

TV stations
- KAAL-TV (Rochester/Austin, MN)
- KDIO-TV (Duluth, MN)
- KOB-TV (Albuquerque, NM)
- KSAX-TV (Minnesota)
- KSTP-TV (Minneapolis-St. Paul, MN)
- WDIO-TV (Duluth, MN)
- WHEC-TV (Rochester, NY)
- WNYT-TV (Albany, Schenectady, and Troy, New York)

COMPETITORS

ACME Communications
Clear Channel
CNN
Gannett
Granite Broadcasting
Hearst-Argyle Television
Infinity Broadcasting
LIN TV
Sinclair Broadcast Group
Young Broadcasting

HISTORICAL FINANCIALS

Company Type: Private

Income Statement FYE: December 31

	ESTIMATED REVENUE ($ mil.)	NET INCOME ($ mil.)	NET PROFIT MARGIN	EMPLOYEES
12/01	600	—	—	1,344
12/00	600	—	—	1,450
12/99	600	—	—	1,450
12/98	600	—	—	1,450
Annual Growth	0.0%	—	—	(2.5%)

Revenue History

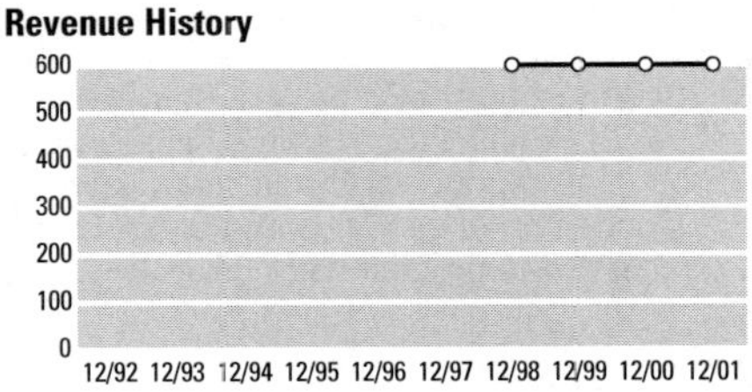

Hudson News Company

As a large distributor and retailer of magazines and books in the New York area, Hudson News has been keeping people up-to-date on current events for years. The company distributes *Talk*, *Business Week*, and other publications. Its retail business, Hudson Group, operates about 250 newsstands, cafes, and specialty shops, in airports and other transportation terminals across the US. Hudson News sold its Metropolitan News and holdings in the Newark Newsdealer Supply Company to The New York Times Company in 1992. Formerly Hudson County News, the firm was renamed in 1997. The company is purchasing UK magazine and book retailer WH Smith's US airport retailing business. Hudson News is owned by chairman Robert Cohen.

EXECUTIVES

Chairman: Robert B. Cohen
President and CEO: James Cohen
CFO: Catherine Oberg
EVP, Hudson Group: Joseph DiDomizio
SVP, Book Corner: Michael Joachim
SVP, Merchandising, Hudson Group: Lisa Strollo-Caruna
SVP, Operations, Hudson Group: Brian Quinn
SVP, Operations, Hudson Group: Roger Fordyce
SVP, Sales and Marketing, Hudson Group: Hope Remoundos
Director, Human Resources: Cynthia Simmons

LOCATIONS

HQ: 1305 Paterson Plank Rd., North Bergen, NJ 07047
Phone: 201-867-3600 **Fax:** 201-867-0067
Web: www.hudsongroupusa.com

PRODUCTS/OPERATIONS

Selected Retail Operations

Book Corner
Discover Stores
Euro Cafe
Hudson News

COMPETITORS

AMREP
Anderson News
Baker & Taylor
Barnes & Noble
Borders
Chas. Levy
Ingram Industries
Jim Pattison Group

HISTORICAL FINANCIALS

Company Type: Private

Income Statement FYE: December 31

	ESTIMATED REVENUE ($ mil.)	NET INCOME ($ mil.)	NET PROFIT MARGIN	EMPLOYEES
12/01	600	—	—	2,225
12/00	598	—	—	2,225
12/99	586	—	—	2,200
12/98	508	—	—	2,200
12/97	430	—	—	1,800
12/96	420	—	—	1,800
12/95	350	—	—	—
12/94	360	—	—	—
12/93	352	—	—	—
12/92	310	—	—	—
Annual Growth	7.6%	—	—	4.3%

Revenue History

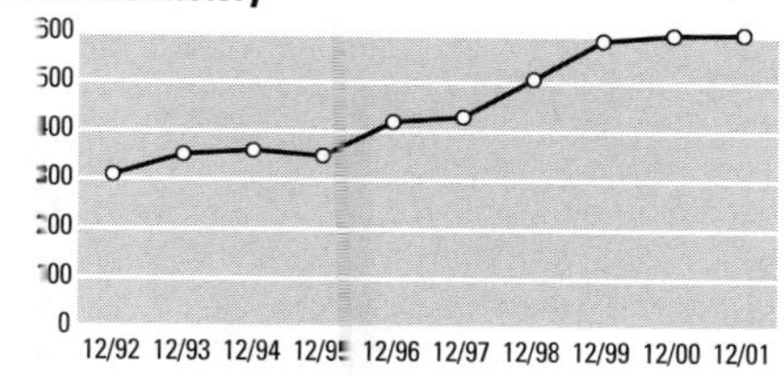

Hunt Consolidated

Hunt Consolidated is a holding company for the oil and real estate businesses of Ray Hunt, son of legendary Texas wildcatter and company founder H.L. Hunt. Founded in 1934 (reportedly with H.L.'s poker winnings), Hunt Oil is an oil and gas production and exploration company with primary interests in North and South America. Hoping to repeat huge discoveries in Yemen, Hunt is exploring in Canada, Ghana, Madagascar, and Oman. It has also teamed up with Repsol YPF and SK Corporation on an exploration project in Peru, and has expanded its Canadian operations through the acquisition of Chieftain International. Hunt Realty handles commercial and residential real estate development and investment management activities.

EXECUTIVES

Chairman and CEO: Ray L. Hunt, age 59
SVP and CFO: Donald (Don) Robillard
VP Human Resources: Laura S. Weaver

LOCATIONS

HQ: Hunt Consolidated Inc.,
Fountain Place, 1445 Ross at Field, Ste. 1400,
Dallas, TX 75202
Phone: 214-978-8000 **Fax:** 214-978-8888

PRODUCTS/OPERATIONS

Selected Subsidiaries

Hunt Oil Company (integrated oil company)
Hunt Oil Company of Canada
Hunt Power Corporation (utility projects and services)
Hunt Private Equities Group
Hunt Realty Corporation (acquires real estate and manages investments)
Hunt Refining Co. Inc.
Hunt Ventures, L.P. (diversified investments)
Yemen Hunt Oil Co.

COMPETITORS

Anadarko Petroleum
BP
Exxon Mobil
Houston Exploration
Kerr-McGee
Lincoln Property
Murphy Oil
Nexen
Royal Dutch/Shell Group
TOTAL

HISTORICAL FINANCIALS

Company Type: Private

Income Statement FYE: December 31

	REVENUE ($ mil.)	NET INCOME ($ mil.)	NET PROFIT MARGIN	EMPLOYEES
12/01	1,500	—	—	2,600
12/00	2,000	—	—	2,500
12/99	1,200	—	—	2,600
12/98	700	—	—	2,600
12/97	1,000	—	—	2,600
12/96	1,000	—	—	2,600
12/95	1,000	—	—	2,600
12/94	1,000	—	—	2,600
12/93	1,000	—	—	2,600
12/92	720	—	—	—
Annual Growth	8.5%	—	—	0.0%

Revenue History

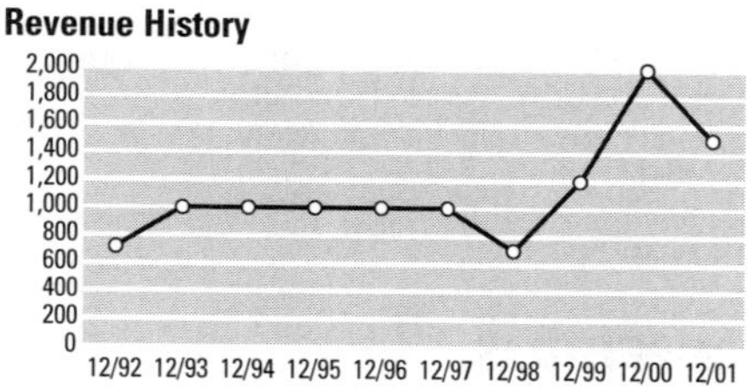

Huntsman International

Huntsman International has gathered together enough business to become the world's largest privately held chemical company. Huntsman is a major producer of basic chemicals and petrochemicals like ethylene and propylene. The company also produces surfactants (used in cleaning and personal care products) and specialty chemicals such as polyurethanes, propylene oxides, and propylene glycol. Huntsman is the largest maker of titanium dioxide, the world's most commonly used white pigment, with about 15% of the world market. Having completed its takeover of a portion of Imperial Chemical Industries (ICI), Huntsman has crawled out of its massive debt and the Huntsman family again controls 100% of the company.

In June 2002 Huntsman restructured its debt through Credit Suisse First Boston's Global Opportunities Partners (now MatlinPatterson Global Opportunity Partners) by creating a holding company that owns Huntsman International and Huntsman Polymers. MatlinPatterson owns 49.9% equity of the newly created HMP Equity Holdings. The Huntsman family owns the rest and continues to run the company.

Also in 2002 Huntsman International restructured its business segments. The new categories are: polyurethanes (polyurethanes and PO), base chemicals (olefins and aromatics), pigments (titanium dioxide), and performance products (surfactants, ethyleneamines, and other performance chemicals). The most significant change was the split of the former specialty chemicals segment into two: polyurethanes and performance products. The former tioxide segment was renamed pigments, and the former petrochemicals segment was renamed base chemicals.

In May 2003 Huntsman completed its purchase of four of ICI's chemical groups by buying the British chemical giant's 30% stake in Huntsman International for about $400 million in senior discount notes. That was the deal (along with the buyout of the remaining 9% of Huntsman International from JP Morgan Partners and MidOcean Capital Investors) that again gave the Huntsman family 100% control of all Huntsman companies.

Founder and chairman Jon Huntsman, a cancer survivor, has directed hundreds of millions of dollars of company profits and his own money to educational and charitable causes and medical research. He donated $100 million to fund the Huntsman Cancer Institute at the University of Utah and has pledged an additional $125 to fund research.

HISTORY

First exposed to the use of plastics in the manufacture of egg cartons, Jon Huntsman spent three frustrating years at Dow Chemical. Then he and his brother Blaine raised $300,000 and received a $1 million loan from Hambrecht & Quist to found Huntsman Container in 1970. When chemical supplies began to run short, Huntsman sold the company to Keyes Fiber in 1976.

After six years, half of which had been spent doing missionary work for the Mormon Church, Huntsman took over polystyrene operations and set his sights on an underused Shell plant in Ohio. With oil and gas titan Atlantic Richfield's backing, Huntsman convinced Shell and a bank to lend him the balance of the purchase price and formed Huntsman Chemical in 1982.

With the acquisition of Hoechst Celanese's polystyrene business in 1986, Huntsman became the #1 producer of styrene in the US. In 1987 Huntsman sold 40% of Huntsman Chemical for $52 million and then acquired a New Jersey polypropylene plant from Shell. Huntsman reentered the packaging business in 1989 by acquiring Keyes, the European firm that had once been a part of Huntsman Container.

In 1991 hamburger dynasty McDonald's succumbed to environmentalist pressure and ceased to use the Huntsman-developed polystyrene clamshell containers; as a result, Huntsman lost about 10% of its business. The company acquired packaging assets from Goodyear Tire & Rubber in 1992 and named the new subsidiary Huntsman Packaging. The next year Huntsman bought 50% of Chemplex Australia Limited from Consolidated Press Holdings (controlled by Australian tycoon Kerry Packer).

Huntsman and Packer joined forces again in 1994 to buy most of Texaco's unprofitable petrochemical operations (renamed Huntsman Corporation) for $1 billion, which doubled Huntsman's size and added 24 plants in 12 countries. Also that year Huntsman bought Eastman Chemical's worldwide polypropylene business. The next year it formed a joint venture with Texaco to operate Texaco's worldwide lubricant-additives line, and Huntsman reacquired the 17% stake held by Great Lakes Chemical, which had been the only stock in the company held by outsiders at that time.

In 1996 Huntsman placed all of his businesses under a single entity, the Huntsman Corporation. The company bought the last of Texaco's chemicals operations in 1997, moving Huntsman into the propylene oxide market. Huntsman also bought packaging maker Rexene that year.

Huntsman sold its polystyrene and styrene monomer businesses in the US and Europe to NOVA Chemicals in 1998; it retained its expandable polystyrene unit when federal regulators objected to its sale. In 1999 the company doubled its size with the purchase of Imperial Chemical Industries' polyurethane, aromatics, titanium dioxide, petrochemical, and olefins businesses. (Huntsman established Huntsman International, a joint venture with ICI in which Huntsman owns a 70% stake, to manage these assets. Huntsman later agreed to buy ICI's 30% stake; the transaction was completed in 2003.)

In 2000 Huntsman sold Huntsman Packaging to J. P. Morgan Partners in a deal worth $1 billion. Also, Jon Huntsman stepped down as CEO (but remained as chairman). He was succeeded by his son, Peter Huntsman. Late in the year Huntsman acquired Rohm and Haas' thermoplastic polyurethane (TPU) business for about $120 million.

Hamstrung by about $2 billion in debt, higher raw material costs, and a depressed chemicals market, Huntsman stopped paying interest on debt and sought a financial restructuring. Credit Suisse First Boston's Global Opportunities Partners held much of Huntsman's debt but swapped its bonds for a 49.9% equity in a holding company that owns the Huntsman companies.

EXECUTIVES

Chairman: Jon M. Huntsman Sr., age 65
President, CEO, and Director: Peter R. Huntsman, age 40, $947,000 pay
EVP and COO: Donald J. Stanutz, age 51
EVP and CFO: J. Kimo Esplin, age 40, $398,659 pay
EVP, General Counsel, and Secretary: Samuel D. Scruggs, age 43
SVP, Environmental, Health, and Safety: Michael J. Kern, age 53
SVP, Base Chemical: Thomas J. Keenan, age 49
SVP, Global Public Affairs: Don H. Olsen, age 56
VP: Karen H. Huntsman, age 64
VP, Corporate Development: John R. Heskett, age 34
VP, Finance: L. Russell Healy, age 47
VP, Marketing: Monte G. Edlund, age 46
VP and Treasurer: Sean Douglas, age 38
VP and Controller: Richard H. Johnigan Jr., age 56
President, Performance Products: Tony Hankins
President, Pigments: Douglas A.L. (Doug) Coombs, age 62, $1,366,155 pay
President, Polyurethanes: Patrick W. Thomas, $936,680 pay
SVP, Pigments: Rob Louw
SVP, Sales and Marketing, Pigments: Wayne Barnacal
SVP, Base Chemicals Manufacturing: Kevin J. Ninow, $314,213 pay
SVP, Purchasing: Brian V. Ridd, age 45
VP and Deputy General Counsel: James R. Moore, age 58
VP, European Base Chemicals Sales: James H. Huntsman, age 32
VP, Purchasing: David S. Parkin, age 30
VP, Surface Sciences: Curtis C. Dowd, age 43
VP, Tax: Kevin Hardman, age 39

LOCATIONS

HQ: Huntsman International LLC
500 Huntsman Way, Salt Lake City, UT 84108
Phone: 801-584-5700 **Fax:** 801-584-5781
Web: www.huntsman.com

Huntsman International has manufacturing facilities located in Africa, Asia, Europe, and North America, and its products are sold throughout the world.

2002 Sales

	$ mil.	% of total
US	1,742	31
UK	1,538	27
Netherlands	895	16
Other	1,458	26
Adjustments & eliminations	(1,115)	—
Total	**4,518**	**100**

PRODUCTS/OPERATIONS

Business Segments

Polyurethanes (polyurethanes and propylene oxide)
Base Chemicals (olefins and aromatics)
Pigments (titanium dioxide)
Performance Products (surfactants and other performance chemicals)

Selected Joint Ventures

CONDEA-Huntsman GmbH & Co. KG (automobile parts, boat hulls, and marble bath fixtures; Germany)
Huntsman Chemical Company Australia Limited (joint venture with Consolidated Press Holdings)
Polystyrene Australia (joint venture with Dow Chemical (Australia) Ltd.)
Rubicon, Inc. (manufacturing joint venture with Crompton Corp.)

COMPETITORS

Akzo Nobel
ATOFINA
ATOFINA Chemicals
BASF AG
Bayer AG
BP Chemicals
BP
ChevronTexaco
Clariant International
Cognis
Degussa
Dow Chemical
Eastman Chemical
DuPont
Enichem Augusta
Exxon Mobil
FPC
Hercules
Houghton Chemical
ICI
Kerr-McGee
Lyondell Chemical
Millennium Chemicals
NL Industries
OxyChem
Occidental Petroleum
Owens Corning
PPG
Rohm and Haas
Sasol
Shell Chemicals
Sinopec Shanghai Petrochemical
Teknor Apex

HISTORICAL FINANCIALS

Company Type: Private

Income Statement FYE: December 31

	REVENUE ($ mil.)	NET INCOME ($ mil.)	NET PROFIT MARGIN	EMPLOYEES
12/02	4,518	20	0.4%	8,000
12/01	4,575	(61)	—	8,050
12/00	4,448	151	3.4%	6,600
12/99	4,500	—	—	7,500
12/98	4,600	—	—	8,500
12/97	4,750	—	—	9,550
12/96	4,500	—	—	8,000
12/95	4,300	—	—	8,000
12/94	3,400	—	—	8,100
12/93	1,850	—	—	5,000
Annual Growth	10.4%	(63.5%)	—	5.4%

2002 Year-End Financials

Debt ratio: 256.3%
Return on equity: 2.0%
Cash ($ mil.): 75
Current ratio: 1.35
Long-term debt ($ mil.): 2,730

Net Income History

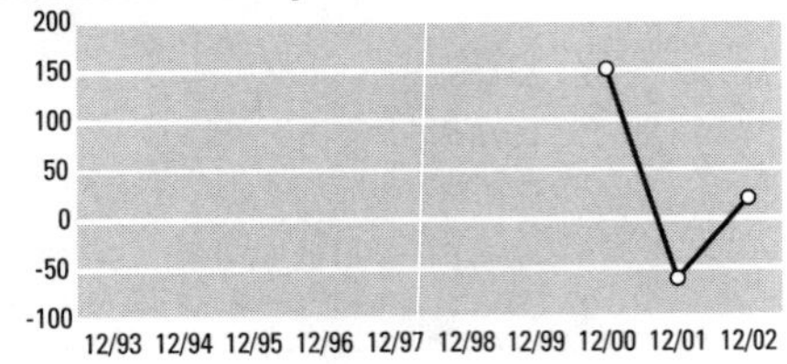

Hyatt Corporation

Hyatt is at your service. One of the nation's largest hotel operators, the company has more than 120 full-service luxury hotels and resorts in North America and the Caribbean (Hyatt International, its overseas branch, operates some 80 hotels and resorts in 39 countries outside its domestic and Caribbean properties). Many of Hyatt's hotels and resorts feature professionally designed golf courses and supervised activities for children (Camp Hyatt). The company also operates casinos and luxury retirement communities (Classic Residence by Hyatt). Led by chairman and CEO Thomas Pritzker, the company is owned by the Pritzker family, one of the wealthiest in the US.

Hyatt caters to business travelers, conventiongoers, and upscale vacationers. The company offers specially designed Business Plan rooms with fax machines and 24-hour access to copiers, printers, and other business necessities. Camp Hyatt targets family travelers with educational games, activities, and programs for children. The company, through Hyatt International, is doing much of its growing outside the US. It has some 15 hotels under construction in places such as China, India, Poland, Thailand, and the United Arab Emirates.

The Pritzker family has been a roller coaster of unhappiness based on family differences over the last few years. As part of a financial settlement within the family, there are plans to liquidate holdings and possibly even take the company public over the next ten years.

HISTORY

Nicholas Pritzker left Kiev for Chicago in 1881, where his family's ascent to the ranks of America's wealthiest families began. His son A. N. left the family law practice in the 1930s and began investing in a variety of businesses. He turned a 1942 investment (Cory Corporation) worth $25,000 into $23 million by 1967. A. N.'s son Jay followed in his father's wheeling-and-dealing footsteps. In 1953, with the help of his father's banking connections, Jay purchased Colson Company and recruited his brother Bob, an industrial engineer, to restructure a company that made tricycles and US Navy rockets. By 1990 Jay and Bob had added 60 industrial companies, with annual sales exceeding $3 billion, to the entity they called the Marmon Group.

The family's connection to Hyatt hotels was established in 1957 when Jay Pritzker bought a hotel called Hyatt House, located near the Los

Angeles airport, from Hyatt von Dehn. Jay added five locations by 1961 and hired his gregarious youngest brother, Donald, to manage the hotel company. Hyatt went public in 1967, but the move that opened new vistas for the hotel chain was the purchase that year of an 800-room hotel in Atlanta that both Hilton and Marriott had turned down. John Portman's design, incorporating a 21-story atrium, a large fountain, and a revolving rooftop restaurant, became a Hyatt trademark.

The Pritzkers formed Hyatt International in 1969 to operate hotels overseas, and the company grew rapidly in the US and abroad during the 1970s. Donald Pritzker died in 1972, and Jay assumed control of Hyatt. The family decided to take the company private in 1979. Much of Hyatt's growth in the 1970s came from contracts to manage, under the Hyatt banner, hotels built by other investors. When Hyatt's cut on those contracts shrank in the 1980s, the company launched its own hotel and resort developments under Nick Pritzker, a cousin to Jay and Bob. In 1988, with US and Japanese partners, it built the Hyatt Regency Waikoloa on Hawaii's Big Island for $360 million — a record at the time for a hotel.

The Pritzkers took a side-venture into air travel in 1983 when they bought bedraggled Braniff Airlines through Hyatt subsidiaries as it emerged from bankruptcy. After a failed 1987 attempt to merge the airline with PanAm, the Pritzkers sold Braniff in 1988.

Hyatt opened Classic Residence by Hyatt, a group of upscale retirement communities, in 1989. The company joined Circus Circus (now Mandalay Resort Group) in 1994 to launch the Grand Victoria, the nation's largest cruising gaming vessel, at Elgin Illinois. The next year, as part of a new strategy to manage both freestanding golf courses and those near Hyatt hotels, the company opened its first freestanding course: an 18-hole par 71 championship course in Aruba.

President Thomas Pritzker, Jay's son, took over as chairman and CEO of Hyatt following his father's death in early 1999. In 2000 Hyatt announced plans to join rival Marriott International in launching an independent company to provide an online procurement network to serve the hospitality industry. The following year the company announced plans to build a 47-story skyscraper in downtown Chicago. Construction for the new building, named the Hyatt Center, began at the end of 2002.

EXECUTIVES

Chairman and CEO; Chairman, Hyatt International Corporation: Thomas J. Pritzker, age 52
Vice Chairman; Chairman and President, Hyatt Development Corporation; President, Hyatt Equities: Nicholas J. (Nick) Pritzker
President: Douglas G. Geoga, age 47
Chairman, Classic Residence by Hyatt: Penny S. Pritzker, age 43
President, Classic Residence by Hyatt: Randal J. Richardson
President, Hyatt International Corporation: Bernd Chorengel
President, Hyatt Hotels Corporation: Edward W. Rabin
SVP, Human Resources, Hyatt Hotels Corporation: Linda Olson
SVP Marketing, Hyatt Hotels Corporation: Thomas F. O'Toole, age 44
SVP Operations, Hyatt Hotels Corporation: Chuck Floyd
VP Finance: Kirk A. Rose
Divisional VP (Southern), Hyatt Hotels Corporation: Tim Lindgren
Divisional VP (Resorts), Hyatt Hotels Corporation: Victor Lopez, age 52
Divisional VP (Western), Hyatt Hotels Corporation: John Orr
Divisional VP (Central), Hyatt Hotels Corporation: Steve Sokal

LOCATIONS

HQ: 200 W. Madison St., Chicago, IL 60606
Phone: 312-750-1234 **Fax:** 312-750-8550
Web: www.hyatt.com

Hyatt Corporation and Hyatt International, a separate entity also controlled by the Pritzker family, own and operate hotels in Argentina, Australia, Azerbaijan, Canada, Chile, China, Egypt, France, Germany, Greece, Guatemala, Hungary, India, Indonesia, Israel, Japan, Jordan, Kazakhstan, Kyrgyzstan, Malaysia, Mexico, Micronesia, Morocco, Nepal, New Zealand, Oman, the Philippines, Puerto Rico, Saudi Arabia, Serbia and Montenegro, Singapore, South Africa, South Korea, Spain, Taiwan, Thailand, Turkey, the UK, the United Arab Emirates, the US, and the West Indies.

PRODUCTS/OPERATIONS

Selected Operations

Camp Hyatt (activities for children)
Classic Residence by Hyatt (upscale retirement communities)
Hyatt Hotels and Resorts
Regency Casinos

COMPETITORS

Accor
Cendant
Four Seasons Hotels
Helmsley
Hilton
Host Marriott
InterContinental Hotels
Marriott International
Ritz-Carlton
Sandals Resorts
Starwood Hotels & Resorts
Trump

HISTORICAL FINANCIALS

Company Type: Private

Income Statement FYE: January 31

	ESTIMATED REVENUE ($ mil.)	NET INCOME ($ mil.)	NET PROFIT MARGIN	EMPLOYEES
1/00	3,950	—	—	80,000
1/99	3,400	—	—	80,000
1/98	3,000	—	—	80,000
1/97	2,900	—	—	80,000
1/96	2,500	—	—	65,000
1/95	1,240	—	—	54,000
1/94	950	—	—	47,000
1/93	1,460	—	—	52,275
1/92	1,350	—	—	51,275
1/91	2,915	—	—	49,820
Annual Growth	3.4%	—	—	5.4%

Revenue History

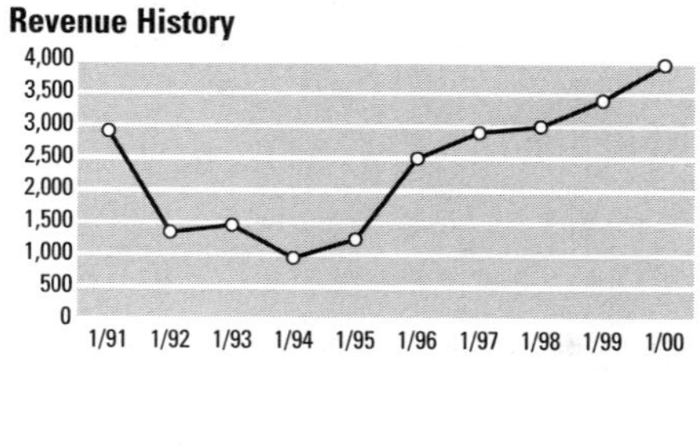

Hy-Vee, Inc.

Give Hy-Vee a high five for being one of the largest privately owned US supermarket chains, despite serving some modestly sized midwestern towns. The company runs more than 200 Hy-Vee supermarkets in Illinois, Iowa, Kansas, Minnesota, Missouri, Nebraska, and South Dakota. About half of its supermarkets are in Iowa, as are most of its 25-plus Drug Town drugstores. It distributes products to its stores through several subsidiaries, including Lomar Distributing (specialty foods), Perishable Distributors of Iowa (fresh foods), and Florist Distributing (flowers). Charles Hyde and David Vredenburg founded the employee-owned firm in 1930. The company's moniker is a combination of the founders' names.

EXECUTIVES

Chairman, CEO, and COO: Ronald D. (Ron) Pearson
President and Chief Administrative Officer: Ric Jurgens
EVP: Charlie Bell
EVP: Ray Stewart
EVP: Ken Waller
SVP, CFO, and Treasurer: John Briggs
VP, General Merchandise: Jon Wendel
VP, Human Resources: Jane Knaack-Esbeck
VP, Purchasing and Marketing: Ron Taylor

LOCATIONS

HQ: 5820 Westown Pkwy., West Des Moines, IA 50266
Phone: 515-267-2800 **Fax:** 515-267-2817
Web: www.hy-vee.com

PRODUCTS/OPERATIONS

Selected Subsidiaries

D & D Foods, Inc.
Florist Distributing, Inc.
Hy-Vee Weitz Construction, L.C.
Lomar Distributing
Meyocks & Priebe Advertising, Inc.
Midwest Heritage Bank, FSB
Perishable Distributors of Iowa, Ltd.

COMPETITORS

Albertson's
AWG
Casey's General Stores
CVS
Eagle Food
Fareway Stores
Fleming Companies
Kmart
Kroger
Nash Finch
Rite Aid
Roundy's
SUPERVALU
Target
Walgreen
Wal-Mart

HISTORICAL FINANCIALS

Company Type: Private

Income Statement FYE: September 30

	ESTIMATED REVENUE ($ mil.)	NET INCOME ($ mil.)	NET PROFIT MARGIN	EMPLOYEES
9/02	4,100	—	—	46,000
9/01	3,900	—	—	46,000
9/00	3,600	—	—	44,000
9/99	3,500	—	—	42,900
9/98	3,200	—	—	41,200
9/97	2,900	—	—	38,400
9/96	2,800	—	—	36,000
9/95	2,700	—	—	30,000
9/94	2,480	—	—	30,000
9/93	2,500	—	—	30,000
Annual Growth	5.7%	—	—	4.9%

Revenue History

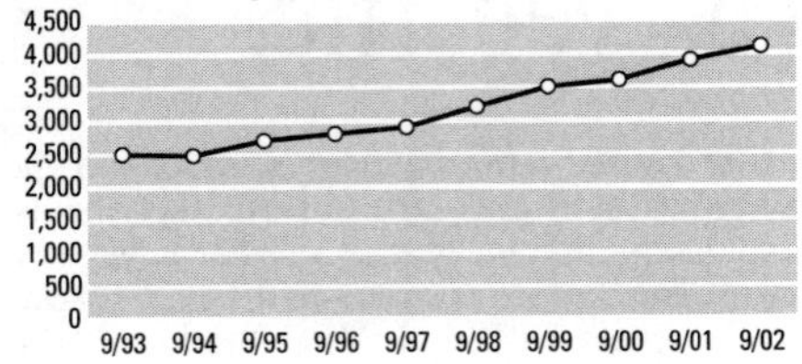

IASIS Healthcare Corporation

If you're sick in the suburbs, IASIS Healthcare provides a medical oasis. Formed largely from castoffs of hospital operators Tenet Healthcare and Paracelsus Healthcare (now Clarent Hospital Corporation) and a series of management buyouts in 1999, the company owns and operates 14 hospitals in Arizona, Florida, Texas, and Utah. IASIS also operates four outpatient surgical centers, and Health Choice, a Medicaid-managed health plan that serves nearly 60,000 individuals in Arizona. Private equity firm Joseph Littlejohn & Levy owns more than 85% of the company.

IASIS focuses on building networks of midsized hospitals in growing urban and suburban regions.

EXECUTIVES

Chairman, President, and CEO: David R. White, age 55, $521,733 pay
COO: Sandra K. McRee, age 46
CFO: W. Carl Whitmer, age 38, $220,887 pay (prior to promotion)
Secretary and General Counsel: Frank A. Coyle, age 38
Chief Nursing Officer; Division President and COO, Arizona: Dolores Horvath
President, Utah Market: David L. Jones
Division President, Florida and Texas: Phillip J. Mazzuca, age 43, $206,637 pay
Director of Human Resources: Russ Follis
Auditors: Ernst & Young LLP

LOCATIONS

HQ: 113 Seaboard Ln., Ste. A200, Franklin, TN 37067
Phone: 615-844-2747 **Fax:** 615-846-3006
Web: www.iasishealthcare.com

Facilities

Hospitals
- Mesa General Hospital Medical Center (Mesa, AZ)
- St. Luke's Medical Center (Phoenix, AZ)
- St. Luke's Behavioral Health Center (Phoenix, AZ)
- Tempe St. Luke's Hospital (Tempe, AZ)
- Memorial Hospital of Tampa (Tampa, FL)
- Palms of Pasadena Hospital (St. Petersburg, FL)
- Town & Country Hospital (Tampa, FL)
- Mid-Jefferson Hospital (Nederland, TX)
- Odessa Regional Hospital (Odessa, TX)
- Park Place Medical Center (Port Arthur, TX)
- Southwest General Hospital (San Antonio, TX)
- Davis Hospital and Medical Center (Layton, UT)
- Jordan Valley Hospital (West Jordan, UT)
- Pioneer Valley Hospital (West Valley City, UT)
- Salt Lake Regional Medical Center (Salt Lake City, UT)

Surgery Centers
- Arizona Diagnostic and Surgery Center (Mesa, AZ)
- Biltmore Surgery Center (Phoenix, AZ)
- Care Center (Phoenix, AZ)
- Metro Surgery Center (Mesa, AZ)

COMPETITORS

Ascension
Banner Health
Catholic Health East
Catholic Healthcare West
CHRISTUS Health
Community Health Systems
HCA
Intermountain Health Care
Mayo Foundation
Tenet Healthcare
Triad Hospitals

HISTORICAL FINANCIALS

Company Type: Private

Income Statement FYE: September 30

	REVENUE ($ mil.)	NET INCOME ($ mil.)	NET PROFIT MARGIN	EMPLOYEES
9/02	950	(11)	—	8,000
9/01	890	—	—	8,100
9/00	815	—	—	8,100
9/99*	137	—	—	—
12/98	178	—	—	—
Annual Growth	51.9%	—	—	(0.6%)

*Fiscal year change

Revenue History

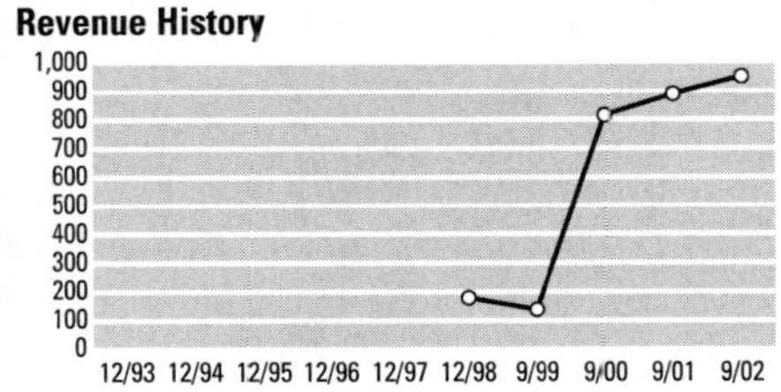

ICC Industries

ICC Industries keeps pharmaceutical companies supplied with the raw materials used in manufacturing drugs. An international maker and marketer of chemicals, plastics, and pharmaceutical products, ICC also trades and distributes nutritional supplements and food ingredients. Its main subsidiary, ICC Chemical Corporation, maintains trading and marketing offices in Asia, Europe, South America, and the US. ICC Industries also owns a majority of Pharmaceutical Formulations, a manufacturer and distributor of generic over-the-counter drugs. The Farber family, including chairman John Farber, owns ICC.

EXECUTIVES

Chairman: John J. Farber
President: John Oram
VP and Treasurer: Susan Abinder
VP and General Counsel: Paul Falick
VP, Human Resources: Sandra Farber
VP, Taxation: Gerald Unger
President and CEO, ICC Chemical: William Brunger
Manager, Information Services: Dan Burghardt

LOCATIONS

HQ: ICC Industries Inc.
460 Park Ave., New York, NY 10022
Phone: 212-521-1700 **Fax:** 212-521-1970
Web: www.iccchem.com

ICC Industries has offices in Asia, Europe, and North and South America.

PRODUCTS/OPERATIONS

Selected Subsidiaries and Operations

ICC Chemical Corporation
- Chemicals (chemical distribution and trading)
- Pharmaceuticals (raw materials for pharmaceuticals)
- Plastics (distribution and trading)

Prior Energy Corporation (natural gas marketing and distribution)

COMPETITORS

Brenntag
FPC
HELM U.S.
IFF
IVAX
Lyondell Chemical
Nagase & Co.
Novartis
Roche
Synthetech

HISTORICAL FINANCIALS

Company Type: Private

Income Statement FYE: December 31

	REVENUE ($ mil.)	NET INCOME ($ mil.)	NET PROFIT MARGIN	EMPLOYEES
12/01	1,249	—	—	2,300
12/00	1,300	—	—	1,900
12/99	1,200	—	—	3,000
12/98	1,000	—	—	3,000
12/97	1,030	—	—	2,729
12/96	955	—	—	2,550
12/95	1,062	—	—	2,500
12/94	1,050	—	—	2,466
12/93	887	—	—	2,343
12/92	616	—	—	2,058
Annual Growth	8.2%	—	—	1.2%

Revenue History

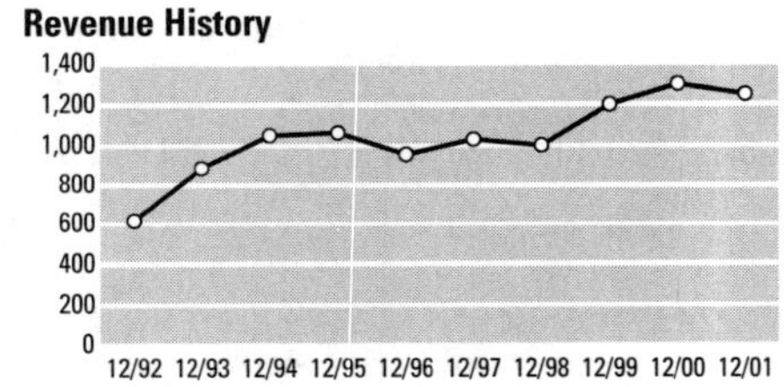

ICON Health & Fitness, Inc.

ICON Health & Fitness has brawn as the leading US maker of home fitness equipment. Its products include treadmills, elliptical trainers, and weight benches. Brands include Weider, HealthRider, IMAGE, NordicTrack, ProForm, JumpKing, Weslo, and the licensed Reebok name. ICON also offers fitness accessories, spas, and commercial fitness gear. It makes most of its products in Utah and sells them through retailers, infomercials, the Web, and its catalog, Workout Warehouse. Sears has an exclusive license to sell NordicTrack-brand apparel. Bain Capital, Credit Suisse, and founders Scott Watterson and Gary Stevenson collectively own more than 90% of ICON. The company plans to license its brands to other manufacturers.

EXECUTIVES

Chairman and CEO: Scott R. Watterson
President and COO: Gary E. Stevenson
VP, CFO, and Treasurer: S. Fred Beck
VP, Marketing and Research and Development: David J. Watterson, $209,459 pay
Secretary and General Counsel: Brad H. Bearnson
Director, Human Resources: Doug Younker
Director, Information Technology: Richard Crosbie
Director, Marketing: Colleen Logan
Corporate Communications: Jay Wright
Auditors: PricewaterhouseCoopers LLP

LOCATIONS

HQ: 1500 S. 1000 West, Logan, UT 84321
Phone: 435-750-5000 **Fax:** 435-750-3917
Web: www.iconfitness.com

ICON has facilities in Canada, China, Europe, and the United States.

COMPETITORS

Amer Group
Bell Sports
Brunswick
Cybex International
Escalade
Fitness Quest
Keys Fitness
Life Fitness
The Nautilus Group
Soloflex

HISTORICAL FINANCIALS

Company Type: Private

Income Statement FYE: May 31

	REVENUE ($ mil.)	NET INCOME ($ mil.)	NET PROFIT MARGIN	EMPLOYEES
5/02	896	—	—	5,000
5/01	850	—	—	5,000
5/00	733	—	—	3,952
5/99	710	—	—	4,328
5/98	749	—	—	4,200
5/97	836	—	—	5,400
5/96	748	—	—	4,300
5/95	531	—	—	3,437
5/94	403	—	—	—
5/93	315	—	—	—
Annual Growth	12.3%	—	—	5.5%

Revenue History

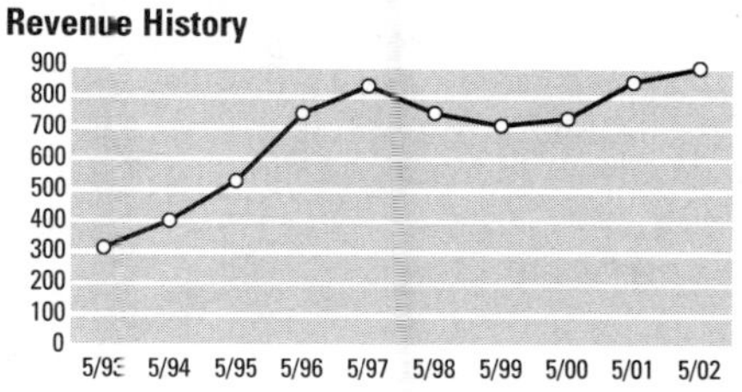

IGA, INC.

IGA grocers are independent, but not that independent. The world's largest voluntary supermarket network, IGA has more than 4,000 stores, including members in nearly all 50 states and more than 40 other countries. Collectively, its members are among North America's leaders in terms of supermarket sales. IGA (for either International or Independent Grocers Alliance, the company says) is owned by 36 worldwide distribution companies, including Fleming Companies and SUPERVALU. Members can sell IGA Brand private-label products (2,300 items) and take advantage of joint operations and services such as advertising and volume buying. Some stores in the alliance, which primarily caters to smaller towns, also sell gas.

The first US grocer in China and Singapore, IGA has moved into Europe with its operations in Poland and Spain. Its international operations account for more than 60% of its total sales. IGA realigned its corporate structure in 2001, setting up IGA North America, IGA Southern Hemisphere/Europe/Caribbean, and IGA Asia, each with its own president.

HISTORY

IGA was founded in Chicago in 1926 by a group led by accountant Frank Grimes. During the 1920s chains began to dominate the grocery store industry. Grimes, an accountant for many grocery wholesalers, saw an opportunity to develop a network of independent grocers that could compete with the burgeoning chains. Grimes and five associates — Gene Flack, Louis Groebe, W. K. Hunter, H. V. Swenson, and William Thompson — created IGA.

Their idea was to "level the playing field" for independent grocers and chain stores by taking advantage of volume buying and mass marketing. IGA originally acted as a purchasing agent for its wholesalers but eventually passed that duty to the wholesalers. The group's first members were Poughkeepsie, New York-based grocery distributor W. T. Reynolds Company and the 69 grocery stores it serviced.

IGA focused on adding distributors and retailers, and it soon added wholesaler Fleming-Wilson (now Fleming Companies) and Winston & Newell (now SUPERVALU). In 1930 it hired Babe Ruth as a spokesman; other celebrity endorsers during the period included Jackie Cooper, Jack Dempsey, and Popeye. IGA also sponsored a radio program called the IGA Home Town Hour.

In 1945 the company introduced the Foodliner format, a design for stores larger than 4,000 sq. ft. The next year IGA introduced the 30-foot-by-100-foot Precision Store — designed so customers had to pass all the other merchandise in the store to get to the dairy and bread sections.

Grimes retired as president in 1951. He was succeeded by his son, Don, who continued to expand the company. Don was succeeded in 1968 by Richard Jones, head of IGA member J. M. Jones Co.

Thomas Haggai was named chairman of the company in 1976. A Baptist minister, radio commentator, and former CIA employee, Haggai had come to the attention of Grimes in 1960 when he praised Christian Scientists in one of his radio broadcasts. Grimes, a Christian Scientist, asked Haggai to speak at an IGA convention and eventually asked him to join the IGA board. Haggai, who became CEO in 1986, tightened the restrictions for IGA members, weeding out many of the smaller, low-volume mom-and-pop stores making up much of the group's network.

Haggai also began a push for international expansion. In 1988 the organization signed a deal with Japanese food company C. Itoh (now ITOCHU) to open a distribution outlet in Tokyo.

The 1990s saw expansion into Australia, Papua New Guinea, the Caribbean, China, Singapore, South Africa, and Brazil. IGA also expanded outside the continental US when it entered Hawaii. In 1993 IGA began an international television advertising campaign, a first for the supermarket industry. The next year the company launched its first line of private-label products for an ethnic food market, introducing several Mexican food products. In 1998 the group developed a new format for its stores that included on-site gas pumps.

SUPERVALU signed 54 independent grocery stores (primarily in Mississippi and Arkansas and Trinidad in the Caribbean) to the IGA banner in August 1999.

With more than 60% of sales coming from international operations, IGA realigned its corporate structure in 2001, setting up three new business units, each with its own president: IGA North America, IGA Asia, and IGA Southern Hemisphere/Europe/Caribbean.

EXECUTIVES

Chairman and CEO: Thomas S. Haggai
EVP and Chief Growth Officer: William (Bill) Benzing
President, IGA Institute and Director, IGA International: Paulo Goelzer
CFO: Robert (Bob) Grottke
VP, Administration, Events and Communications: Barbara G. Wiest
VP, Information Technology: Nick Liakopulos
VP, Red Oval Family Relations: Thomas (Tom) Zatina
Controller: John Collins
Director, Human Resources: Pat Smiftana
Director, Packaging: Tim Considine
Director, Midwest Region: Bill Overman
Director, North Central Area: Ricky St. John
Director, South Central Area: George Beaver
Director, Southeast Area: Doug Blanton
Marketing Events Coordinator: Zorona Chapman
IGA Australia, Brand Manager: Neil Vincett

LOCATIONS

HQ: 8725 W. Higgins Rd., Chicago, IL 60631
Phone: 773-693-4520 **Fax:** 773-693-4532
Web: www.igainc.com

IGA has operations in 48 states and more than 40 countries, including Anguilla, Antigua, Barbuda, Aruba, Australia, Barbados, Botswana, Brazil, Cambodia, Canada, Cayman Islands, China, the Czech Republic, Dominica, the Dominican Republic, Grenada, Indonesia, Jamaica, Japan, Kenya, Lesotho, Malawi, Malaysia, Mauritius, Mozambique, Namibia, Papua New Guinea, Philippines, Poland, St. Kitts, Singapore, South Africa, South Korea, Spain, Swaziland, Thailand, Trinidad and Tobago, the Turks and Caicos, Vietnam, Zambia, and Zimbabwe, and is served by 37 independent distribution companies.

PRODUCTS/OPERATIONS

Distributors/Owners

Bozzuto's Inc.
C.I. Foods Systems Co., Ltd. (Japan)
The Copps Corporation
Davids Limited (Australia)
Fleming Companies, Inc.
Foodland Associated Limited (Australia)
Great North Foods
IGA Brasil (includes 16 individual companies)
Ira Higdon Grocery Company
Laurel Grocery Company
Martahari Putra Prima Tbk (Indonesia)
McLane Polska (Poland)
Merchants Distributors, Inc.
Metro Cash & Carry (Africa)
Nash Finch Company
NTUC Fairprice (Singapore)
Pearl River Distribution Ltd. (China)
SUPERVALU INC.
Tasmania Independent Wholesalers (Australia)
Tripifoods, Inc.
Villa Market JP Co., Ltd. (Thailand)
W. Lee Flowers & Co., Inc.
WALTERMART SUPERMARKETS (Philippines)

Affiliates

H.Y. Louie (fraternal relationship, Canada)
Sobey's (fraternal relationship, Canada)

Selected Joint Operations and Services

Advertising
Community service programs
Equipment purchase
IGA Brand (private-label products)
IGA Grocergram (in-house magazine)
Internet services
Marketing
Merchandising
Red Oval Family (manufacturer/IGA collaboration on sales, marketing, and other activities)
Volume buying

COMPETITORS

Albertson's
AWG
BJs Wholesale Club
C&S Wholesale
Carrefour
Casino Guichard
Coles Myer
Daiei
Dairy Farm International
Delhaize
George Weston
A&P
Hannaford Bros.
H-E-B
Ito-Yokado
Kroger
Meijer
Metro Cash and Carry
Penn Traffic
Publix
Roundy's
Royal Ahold
Safeway
Spartan Stores
Topco Associates
Wakefern Food
Wal-Mart
Winn-Dixie

HISTORICAL FINANCIALS

Company Type: Holding company

Income Statement FYE: December 31

	ESTIMATED REVENUE ($ mil.)	NET INCOME ($ mil.)	NET PROFIT MARGIN	EMPLOYEES
12/01	21,000	—	—	92,000
12/00	21,000	—	—	92,000
12/99	19,000	—	—	92,000
12/98	18,000	—	—	92,000
12/97	18,000	—	—	135,000
12/96	16,800	—	—	128,000
12/95	17,100	—	—	130,000
12/94	17,000	—	—	—
12/93	16,500	—	—	—
12/92	15,900	—	—	—
Annual Growth	3.1%	—	—	(5.6%)

Revenue History

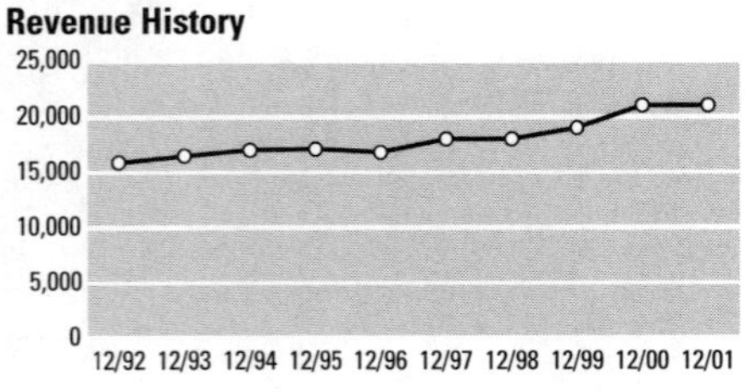

Ilitch Holdings

How do you get to the Big Leagues? Pizza. Ilitch Holdings was formed by Mike and Marian Ilitch in 1999 to bring their numerous businesses under a single umbrella. Among the holding company's subsidiaries are Little Caesar Enterprises (the pizza chain the Ilitches launched with a single restaurant in 1959), the NHL's Detroit Red Wings, and Major League Baseball's Detroit Tigers. Other operations include Olympia Entertainment (management and concessions at Comerica Park, Joe Louis Arena, and Cobo Arena), the Second City — Detroit (comedy theatre, with its Hockeytown Cafe), and Olympia Development (real estate). The Ilitch portfolio also includes Detroit's historic Fox Theatre building, which houses the firm's offices.

EXECUTIVES

Chairman: Michael Ilitch
Vice Chairman: Marian Ilitch
Co-President: Christopher Ilitch
Co-President; Vice Chairwoman, Little Caesar Enterprises; and President, Olympia Development: Denise Ilitch, age 47
VP Finance and Administration: Scott Fisher
VP Tax Affairs: John Kotlar
CIO: Todd Seroka
Controller: Tonya Cousino
General Counsel: Jay Bielfield
Internal Audit: Charlie Christ
Director of Community Affairs and Public Relations: Alexander Sebastian
Director of Risk Management: C. Michael Healy

LOCATIONS

HQ: Ilitch Holdings, Inc., 2211 Woodward Ave., Detroit, MI 48201
Phone: 313-983-6600 **Fax:** 313-983-6094
Web: www.ilitchholdings.com

PRODUCTS/OPERATIONS

Selected Operations

Blue Line Distributing (food service distribution and restaurant equipment and supplies)
Detroit Red Wings (professional hockey team)
Detroit Tigers (professional baseball team)
Fox Theatre (theater and office building)
Little Caesar Pizza Enterprises (pizza chain)
Little Caesars Pizza Kit (school fund-raising program)
Olympia Development (Detroit business development)
Olympia Entertainment (arena management and concessions firm)
The Second City — Detroit (comedy club)
Hockeytown Cafe
Uptown Entertainment (film theaters)

COMPETITORS

Chicago Blackhawks
Chicago White Sox
Cleveland Indians
Domino's
Kansas City Royals
Minnesota Twins
Nashville Predators
Papa John's
Pizza Hut
St. Louis Blues

HISTORICAL FINANCIALS

Company Type: Holding company

Income Statement FYE: December 31

	REVENUE ($ mil.)	NET INCOME ($ mil.)	NET PROFIT MARGIN	EMPLOYEES
12/02	800	—	—	7,500
12/01	800	—	—	7,500
12/00	777	—	—	7,500
12/99	800	—	—	7,700
12/98	800	—	—	8,000
Annual Growth	0.0%	—	—	(1.6%)

Revenue History

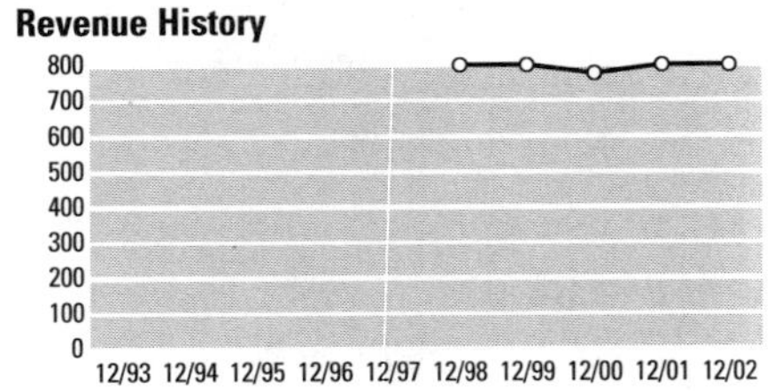

Indiana University

Indiana University has been educating residents of the Hoosier State since its founding in 1820. With a total student population of almost 99,000, the university has eight campuses including flagship institution IU-Bloomington and seven commuter campuses in Fort Wayne, Gary, Indianapolis, Kokomo, New Albany, Richmond, and South Bend. IU-Bloomington offers students more than 100 undergraduate majors. Its graduate schools offer advanced degrees in a variety of areas ranging from business to music to law. IU-Bloomington also is home to a string of centers and institutes including the Advanced Research & Technology Institute and the Center for International Business Education and Research.

EXECUTIVES

President: Adam W. Herbert Jr.
VP and Chief Administrative Officer: J. Terry Clapacs
VP and CFO: Judith G. Palmer
VP Research and Dean Graduate School: George E. Walker
VP Academic Affairs and Chancellor IU Bloomington: Sharon Brehm
VP Information Technology and CIO: Michael A. McRobbie
VP Public Affairs and Government Relations: William B. Stephan
VP Student Development and Diversity: Charlie Nelms
Associate VP Human Resources: Daniel Rives
Treasurer: Steven A. Miller
Auditors: Indiana State Board of Accounts

LOCATIONS

HQ: 107 S. Indiana Ave., Bloomington, IN 47405
Phone: 812-855-4848 **Fax:** 812-855-7002
Web: www.indiana.edu

Indiana University has campuses in Bloomington, Fort Wayne, Gary, Indianapolis, Kokomo, New Albany, Richmond, and South Bend, Indiana.

PRODUCTS/OPERATIONS

Selected Colleges and Schools

College of Arts and Sciences
Honors College
Graduate School
School of Business
School of Continuing Studies
School of Education
School of Fine Arts
School of Informatics
School of Journalism
School of Library and Information Science
School of Medicine
School of Music
School of Nursing
School of Optometry
School of Public and Environmental Affairs
School of Social Work

HISTORICAL FINANCIALS

Company Type: School

Income Statement FYE: June 30

	REVENUE ($ mil.)	NET INCOME ($ mil.)	NET PROFIT MARGIN	EMPLOYEES
6/02	1,261	—	—	16,500
6/01	1,783	—	—	16,070
6/00	1,658	—	—	16,000
6/99	1,541	—	—	15,000
6/98	1,470	—	—	14,458
6/97	1,379	—	—	15,000
6/96	1,280	—	—	17,000
6/95	1,216	—	—	17,000
6/94	1,173	—	—	16,875
6/93	1,118	—	—	—
Annual Growth	1.3%	—	—	(0.3%)

Revenue History

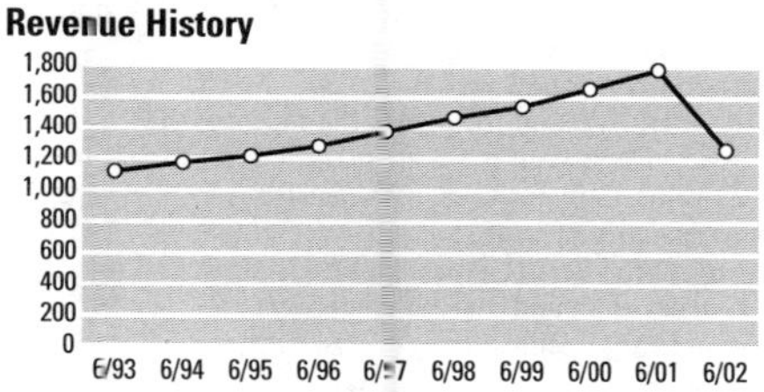

Inductotherm Industries, Inc.

The heat is on at Inductotherm Industries, the parent of an international group of more than 50 engineering and technology companies that produce a variety of products primarily for the metals industry. Inductotherm is a leading maker of induction-heating equipment, with more than 10,000 units installed worldwide. Group companies produce welding equipment, electrical components, electronics, engineered products, metal components, and plastic products. Services range from metals fabrication to silkscreen printing. Chairman and majority owner Hank Rowan (namesake of New Jersey's Rowan University) and his late wife Betty financed the company's startup in 1953 from the sale of their home.

EXECUTIVES

Chairman and President: Henry M. (Hank) Rowan, age 78
President and CEO, Induction and Technology Companies: John H. Mortimer
VP, Finance: Frank D. Manley
VP, Corporate Advertising: Virginia R. Smith
Group VP, Diversified Products and Corporate Development and Treasurer: Manning J. Smith III
Group VP, Electronic Products: Joseph T. Sroka
Group VP, Heating: Byron L. Taylor
General Counsel and Secretary: L. A. Krupnick
Personnel Director: David L. Braddock
Auditors: KPMG LLP

LOCATIONS

HQ: 10 Indel Ave., Rancocas, NJ 08073
Phone: 609-267-9000 **Fax:** 609-267-5705
Web: www.inductothermindustries.com

Inductotherm Industries operates manufacturing plants in Australia, Belgium, Brazil, France, Germany, India, Japan, Mexico, South Korea, Taiwan, Turkey, the UK, and the US.

PRODUCTS/OPERATIONS

Selected Products

Electrical component systems
Electronics
Engineered products
Heating equipment
Melting equipment
Metal products and components
Plastics
Specialized printing equipment
Welding equipment

COMPETITORS

Astronics
Commercial Metals
Dover
Elgin National Industries
Emerson Electric
Herr-Voss
Illinois Tool Works
Ingersoll-Rand
Invensys
Lincoln Electric
Milacron
Morton Industrial Group
Park-Ohio Holdings
SPX
Tang Industries
Thermadyne Holdings
Watsco

HISTORICAL FINANCIALS

Company Type: Private

Income Statement FYE: April 30

	REVENUE ($ mil.)	NET INCOME ($ mil.)	NET PROFIT MARGIN	EMPLOYEES
4/02	700	—	—	5,000
4/01	735	—	—	5,048
4/00	750	—	—	5,142
4/99	800	—	—	5,320
4/98	808	—	—	5,334
4/97	779	—	—	5,288
4/96	674	—	—	4,974
4/95	638	—	—	4,823
4/94	552	—	—	4,384
4/93	482	—	—	4,163
Annual Growth	4.2%	—	—	2.1%

Revenue History

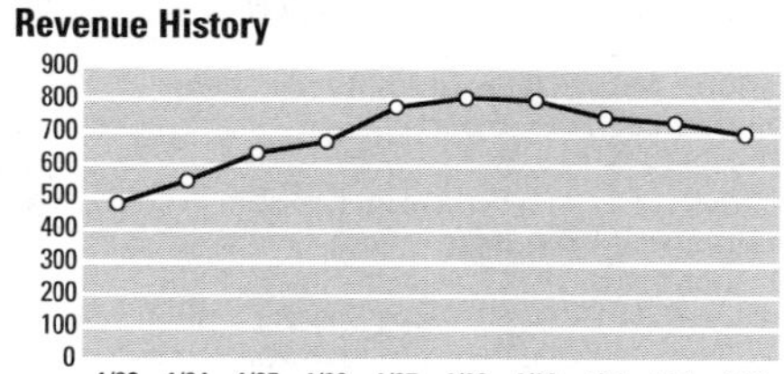

Ingram Entertainment

Companies selling books and CDs might get the star treatment, but Ingram Entertainment Holdings doesn't mind a supporting role. Ingram is the #1 independent video, DVD, and computer game distributor in the US. It also distributes software, audio books, electronics, and used videos and games. From 22 US locations, Ingram serves more than 10,000 video stores, mass retailers, e-tailers, drugstores, and supermarkets (including Blockbuster, Tower Records, and Circuit City). Ingram offers direct-to-consumer fulfillment services for e-commerce sites and has a majority stake in ad agency Frank, Best & Ingram. Chairman David Ingram owns 95% of Ingram Entertainment, which was spun off from family-owned Ingram Industries in 1997.

EXECUTIVES

Chairman and President: David B. Ingram, age 40
EVP and CFO: William D. (Donnie) Daniel
EVP, Purchasing and Operations: Robert W. (Bob) Webb
SVP, Finance and Treasurer: Jeffrey D. (Jeff) Skinner
SVP, Interactive Media: Bob Geistman
SVP, Sales and Marketing: John Reding
VP and CIO: Mark D. Ramer
VP, Human Resources: Andy Grossberg
VP, Sales: Bill Bryant
Auditors: PricewaterhouseCoopers

LOCATIONS

HQ: Ingram Entertainment Holdings Inc.
2 Ingram Blvd., La Vergne, TN 37089
Phone: 615-287-4000 **Fax:** 615-287-4982
Web: www.ingramentertainment.com

COMPETITORS

Alliance Entertainment
Baker & Taylor
East Texas Distributing
Handleman
Image Entertainment
KOCH Entertainment
Navarre
Rentrak

HISTORICAL FINANCIALS

Company Type: Private

Income Statement FYE: December 31

	REVENUE ($ mil.)	NET INCOME ($ mil.)	NET PROFIT MARGIN	EMPLOYEES
12/01	871	—	—	928
12/00	1,057	—	—	1,200
12/99	1,155	—	—	1,083
12/98	1,048	—	—	1,030
12/97	914	—	—	1,033
12/96	904	—	—	1,039
12/95	856	—	—	—
12/94	804	—	—	—
12/93	829	—	—	—
12/92	687	—	—	—
Annual Growth	2.7%	—	—	(2.2%)

Revenue History

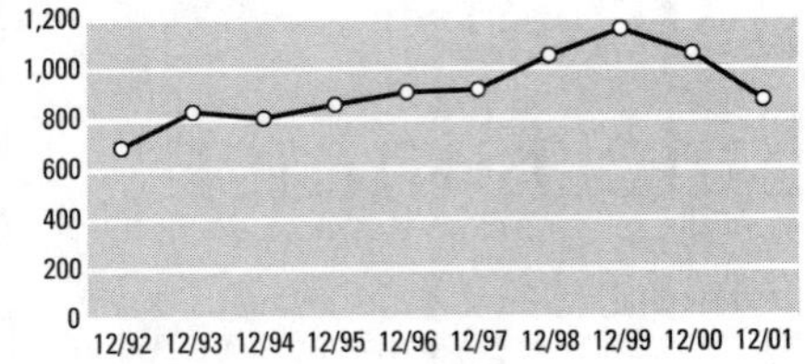

Ingram Industries Inc.

Ingram Industries is heavy into books, boats, and bad drivers. Ingram Book Group is one of the largest wholesale book distributors in the US; it ships more than 175 million books and audiotapes annually, serving some 32,000 retail outlets and 13,000 publishers. Ingram Marine Group operates Ingram Materials and ships grain, ore, and other products through about 4,100 barges. Ingram Insurance Group covers high-risk drivers in seven states through Permanent General Insurance. The Ingram family, led by chairman Martha Ingram (one of America's wealthiest active businesswomen), owns and runs Ingram Industries and controls about 75% of the voting shares of Ingram Micro (a top computer products wholesaler).

Ingram Book Group (operating out of four fulfillment centers) is also a leading distributor to libraries, and the entire book division accounts for over half of Ingram Industries' total sales. Its Lightning Source subsidiary is a leader in print on demand services with over 250,000 titles (including e-books) and a printing count of 12,000 titles a day.

Ingram Industries spun off its largest segment, Ingram Micro, in 1996. Ingram Entertainment (the US's top distributor of videotapes) was spun off the following year and is now owned by Martha's son, David.

HISTORY

Orrin Ingram and two partners founded the Dole, Ingram & Kennedy sawmill in 1857 in Eau Claire, Wisconsin, on the Chippewa River, about 50 miles upstream from the Mississippi River. By the 1870s the company, renamed Ingram & Kennedy, was selling lumber as far downstream as Hannibal, Missouri.

Ingram's success was noticed by Frederick Weyerhaeuser, a German immigrant in Rock Island, Illinois, who, like Ingram, had worked in a sawmill before buying one of his own. In 1881 Ingram and Weyerhaeuser negotiated the formation of Chippewa Logging (35%-owned by up-river partners, 65% by down-river interests), which controlled the white pine harvest of the Chippewa Valley. In 1900 Ingram paid $216,000 for 2,160 shares in the newly formed Weyerhaeuser Timber Company. Ingram let his sons and grandsons handle the investment and formed O.H. Ingram Co. to manage the family's interests. He died in 1918.

In 1946 Ingram's descendants founded Ingram Barge, which hauled crude oil to the company's refinery near St. Louis. After buying and then selling other holdings, in 1962 the family formed Ingram Corp., consisting solely of Ingram Barge. Brothers Bronson and Fritz Ingram (the great-grandsons of Orrin) bought the company from their father, Hank, before he died in 1963, and in 1964 they bought half of Tennessee Book, a textbook distributing company founded in 1935. In 1970 they formed Ingram Book Group to sell trade books to bookstores and libraries.

Ingram Barge won a $48 million Chicago sludge-hauling contract in 1971, but later the company was accused of bribing city politicians with $1.2 million in order to land the contract. The brothers stood trial in 1977 for authorizing the bribes; Bronson was acquitted, but the court convicted Fritz on 29 counts. Before Fritz entered prison (he served 16 months of a four-year sentence), he and his brother split their company. Fritz took the energy operations and went bust in the 1980s. Bronson took the barge and book businesses and formed Ingram Industries.

The new company formed computer products distributor Ingram Computer in 1982 and between 1985 and 1989 bought all the stock of Micro D, a computer wholesaler. Ingram Computer and Micro D merged to form Ingram Micro. In 1992 it acquired Commtron, the world's #1 wholesaler of prerecorded videocassettes, and merged it into Ingram Entertainment.

When Bronson died in mid-1995, his wife Martha (the PR director) became chairman and began a restructuring. Ingram Industries closed its non-bookstore rack distributor (Ingram Merchandising) in 1995 and sold its oil-and-gas machinery subsidiary (Cactus Co.) in 1996. It spun off Ingram Micro in 1996, followed in 1997 by Ingram Entertainment. Ingram Industries purchased Christian books distributor Spring Arbor that year and also introduced an on-demand book publishing service (Lightning Print).

The company in late 1998 agreed to sell its book group to Barnes & Noble for $600 million, but FTC pressure killed the deal in mid-1999. With customers and competitors increasing distribution capacity in the western US, a resulting drop in business led Ingram Industries to cut more than 100 jobs at an Oregon warehouse in 1999.

In early 2000 Ingram renamed Lightning Print as Lightning Source. Also that year Ingram announced plans to distribute products other than books for e-tailers (starting with gifts). In March 2001 Ingram took over the specialty-book distribution for Borders.

In July 2002 Ingram completed its acquisition of Midland Enterprises LLC, a leading US inland marine transportation company that includes The Ohio River Company LLC and Orgulf Transport LLC. In an effort to streamline its distribution network, in mid-2002 Ingram Book Group consolidated its eight distribution centers into four super centers, including a new facility in Pennsylvania.

EXECUTIVES

Chairman: Martha Ingram
Vice Chairman; Chairman, Ingram Book Group: John R. Ingram, age 41
President and CEO; Chairman, Ingram Barge Company: Orrin H. Ingram II
EVP and CFO: Mary K. Cavarra
Chairman and CEO, Permanent General: Steven Mason
President and CEO, Ingram Book Group: Michael Lovett
President and CEO, Lightning Source: J. Kirby Best
President and COO, Permanent General: Randy Parker
President, Ingram International: Peter Clifton
President, Spring Arbor Distributors: Julie Burns
Managing Director, Lightning Source UK: Malcolm Allen
Chief Commercial Officer, Ingram Book Group: Jim Chandler
EVP, Ingram Library Services: Larry C. Price
VP, Human Resources: Dennis Delaney
VP, Product Database Development, Ingram Library Services: Wendell Lotz
VP, Sales and Marketing, Ingram Library Services: Shannon H. McGuire
VP, Technical Services, Ingram Library Services: Rebecca James
Merchandising Director, Ingram Book Group: George Tattersfield

LOCATIONS

HQ: 1 Belle Meade Place, 4400 Harding Rd., Nashville, TN 37205
Phone: 615-298-8200 **Fax:** 615-298-8242

PRODUCTS/OPERATIONS

Selected Operations

Ingram Book Group
Ingram Book Company (wholesaler of trade books and audiobooks)
Ingram Customer Systems (computerized systems and services)
Ingram International (international distribution of books and audiobooks)
Ingram Library Services (distributes books, audiobooks, and videos to libraries)
Ingram Periodicals (direct distributor of specialty magazines)
Ingram Publisher Relations (publishing services for publishers)
Lightning Source (on-demand printing and electronic publishing)
Specialty Retail (book distributor to nontraditional book market)
Spring Arbor Distributors (product and services for Christian retailers)
Ingram Insurance Group
Permanent General Insurance Co. (automobile insurance in California, Florida, Georgia, Ohio, South Carolina, Tennessee, and Wisconsin)
Ingram Marine Group
Custom Fuel Services (provides midstream fueling services to inland marine operations)
Ingram Barge (ships grain, ore, and other products)
Ingram Materials Co. (produces construction materials such as sand and gravel)

COMPETITORS

Advanced Marketing
Allstate
American Commercial Lines
American Financial
Baker & Taylor
Chas. Levy
Follett
Hudson News
Kirby
Media Source
Progressive Corporation
SAFECO
State Farm
TECO Energy
Thomas Nelson
Times Publishing

HISTORICAL FINANCIALS

Company Type: Private

Income Statement FYE: December 31

	REVENUE ($ mil.)	NET INCOME ($ mil.)	NET PROFIT MARGIN	EMPLOYEES
12/01	1,929	—	—	6,148
12/00	2,075	—	—	6,494
12/99	2,135	—	—	6,080
12/98	2,000	—	—	6,500
12/97	1,796	—	—	6,362
12/96	1,463	—	—	5,300
12/95	11,000	—	—	13,000
12/94	8,010	—	—	10,000
12/93	6,163	—	—	9,658
12/92	4,657	—	—	8,407
Annual Growth	(9.3%)	—	—	(3.4%)

Revenue History

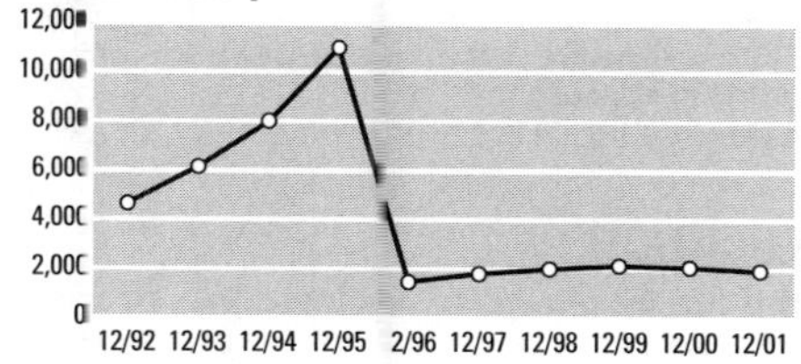

Inova Health System

Inova keeps NoVa healthy. Founded in 1956 as a country hospital in Fairfax, Virginia, Inova Health System is a not-for-profit health care provider, offering acute care, long-term care, home health care, mental health, and satellite emergency care services in the northern Virginia suburbs of Washington, DC. Inova's network consists of five hospitals (including a children's hospital) with about 1,400 beds, as well as assisted living centers for seniors and several family practice locations. Through the Inova Health System Foundation, the company coordinates philanthropy programs for the community.

EXECUTIVES

President and CEO: Knox Singleton
COO and EVP Hospital Operations: Jolene Tornabeni
SVP Financial Affairs: Richard Magenheimer
SVP Legal Affairs: James Hughes
SVP Human Resources: Ellen Menard

LOCATIONS

HQ: 2990 Telestar Ct., Falls Church, VA 22042
Phone: 703-289-2000 **Fax:** 703-205-2161
Web: www.inova.org

PRODUCTS/OPERATIONS

Selected Facilities

Inova Alexandria Hospital (Alexandria, VA)
Inova Fair Oaks Hospital (Fairfax, VA)
Inova Fairfax Hospital (Falls Church, VA)
Inova Fairfax Hospital for Children (Fairfax, VA)
Inova Mount Vernon Hospital (Alexandria, VA)

COMPETITORS

Bon Secours Health
Carilion Health System
HCA
Integrated Health Services
Johns Hopkins Medicine
Manor Care, Inc.
MedStar

HISTORICAL FINANCIALS

Company Type: Not-for-profit

Income Statement FYE: December 31

	REVENUE ($ mil.)	NET INCOME ($ mil.)	NET PROFIT MARGIN	EMPLOYEES
12/02	1,280	—	—	13,000
12/01	1,150	—	—	13,000
12/00	1,009	—	—	13,000
12/99	963	—	—	13,000
12/98	908	—	—	13,000
12/97	900	—	—	13,000
12/96	700	—	—	9,500
12/95	644	—	—	9,500
Annual Growth	10.3%	—	—	4.6%

Revenue History

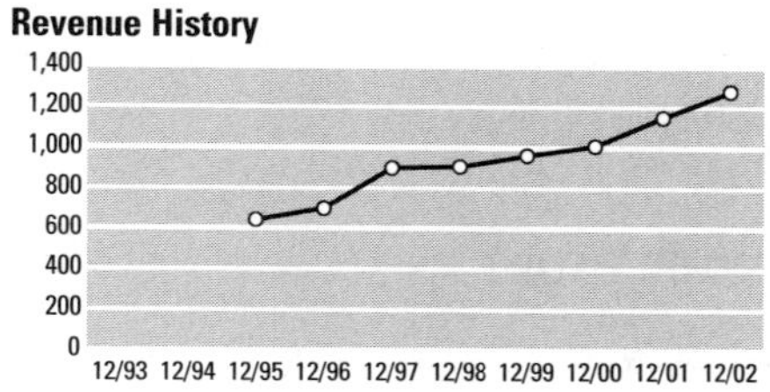

Inserra Supermarkets

The Big Apple need never be short of apples (or oranges, for that matter), thanks to Inserra Supermarkets. Inserra owns and operates more than 20 ShopRite supermarkets and superstores in northern New Jersey and southeastern New York State (most are in Westchester and Rockland counties). Inserra's superstores feature bagel bakeries, cafes, and pharmacies. The company also offers banking services in selected stores through agreements with Poughkeepsie Savings Bank, Statewide Savings Bank, and others. Owned by the Inserra family, the retailer is one of 40-plus members that make up cooperative Wakefern Food, the owner of the ShopRite name.

EXECUTIVES

Chairman and CEO: Lawrence R. Inserra
President: Lawrence R. Inserra Jr.
CFO: Theresa Inserra
VP; Director of Operations: Steve Chalas
Director of Human Resources: Marie Larson

LOCATIONS

HQ: Inserra Supermarkets, Inc.
20 Ridge Rd., Mahwah, NJ 07430
Phone: 201-529-5900 **Fax:** 201-529-1189

COMPETITORS

D'Agostino Supermarkets
A&P
Gristede's Foods
Hannaford Bros.
Key Food
King Kullen Grocery
Kings Super Markets
Man-dell Food Stores
Pathmark
Royal Ahold
Trader Joe's Co
Western Beef

HISTORICAL FINANCIALS

Company Type: Private

Income Statement FYE: December 31

	REVENUE ($ mil.)	NET INCOME ($ mil.)	NET PROFIT MARGIN	EMPLOYEES
12/02	900	—	—	3,900
12/01	800	—	—	3,900
12/00	834	—	—	3,900
12/99	785	—	—	3,500
12/98	750	—	—	4,000
12/97	530	—	—	2,300
12/96	500	—	—	2,300
12/95	500	—	—	2,300
12/94	500	—	—	2,300
12/93	456	—	—	2,100
Annual Growth	7.8%	—	—	7.1%

Revenue History

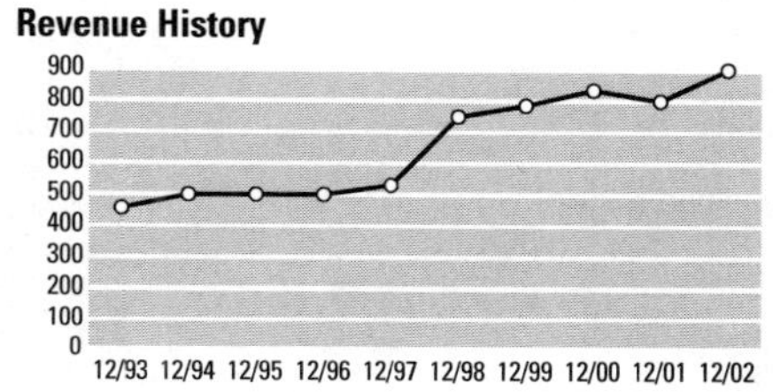

Insurance Services Office

Insurance Services Office (ISO) is a leading provider of statistical, actuarial, and underwriting information for the property/casualty insurance and risk management industries. The company gathers premium, claim, and loss data that it files with state regulators; the data is used to evaluate the price of insurance in each state. ISO's other services include developing standardized policy language, formulating rating and underwriting rules, and conducting site surveys of individual properties, and fraud identification. ISO has replaced state, regional, and national bureaus for property/casualty lines of business. Insurance companies own some 85% of ISO; employees control the rest.

EXECUTIVES

Chairman, President, and CEO: Frank J. Coyne
EVP and CFO: Kenneth G. Geraghty, age 51
SVP and Secretary: James D. Langell
SVP, Insurance Services: Kevin B. Thompson
Public Relations Officer: Christopher Guidette
Manager, Media Relations: Dave Dasgupta
Auditors: Deloitte & Touche LLP

LOCATIONS

HQ: Insurance Services Office, Inc.
Newport World Business Center, 545 Washington Blvd., Jersey City, NJ 07310
Phone: 201-469-2000 **Fax:** 201-748-1670
Web: www.iso.com

Insurance Services Office has operations in Israel, the UK, and the US.

COMPETITORS

ChoicePoint
Computer Sciences
Crawford & Company
Fair Isaac
INSpire Insurance Solutions
NCCI Holdings

HISTORICAL FINANCIALS

Company Type: Private

Income Statement FYE: December 31

	REVENUE ($ mil.)	NET INCOME ($ mil.)	NET PROFIT MARGIN	EMPLOYEES
12/02	425	—	—	2,400
12/01	400	—	—	2,400
12/00	400	—	—	2,200
12/99	350	—	—	2,050
12/98	307	—	—	2,223
12/97	270	—	—	2,102
Annual Growth	9.5%	—	—	2.7%

Revenue History

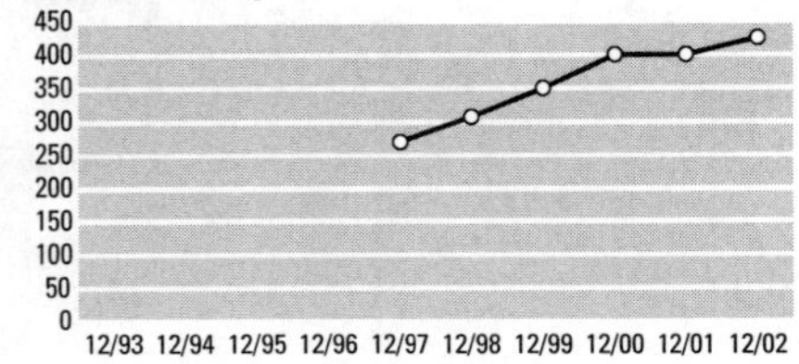

Integris Metals

Metals are an integral part of Integris Metals. The company, a joint venture between Alcoa and BHP Billiton, provides processing services that include cut-to-length leveling, precision blanking, heat treating, polishing, and slitting. Integris Metals sells aluminum, stainless steel, alloy steel, brass and copper, carbon steel, and building products to more than 35,000 customers in the transportation, building and construction, machinery and equipment, and general manufacturing markets. Its products include copper roofing and the AlumaKlad and ColorKlad lines of prepainted architectural metals.

EXECUTIVES

President and CEO: Harrison P. (Harry) Jones
COO: Michael H. Goldberg
CFO: Everett P. Chesley
VP, Information Systems: David Cagle
VP, Human Resources: John Smith

LOCATIONS

HQ: Integris Metals, Inc.
455 85th Ave. NW, Minneapolis, MN 55433
Phone: 763-717-9000 **Fax:** 763-717-7168
Web: www.integrismetals.com

Integris Metals has more than 60 facilities in Canada and the US.

PRODUCTS/OPERATIONS

Selected Products and Processes

Commercial Products
Alloy steel
Aluminum
Brass and copper
Carbon steel
Nickel alloys
Stainless steel

Building Products
Prepainted architectural metals (AlumaKlad, ColorKlad, and MEGAKlad)
Roofing copper

Processes
Cut-to-length leveling
Flame cutting
Heat treating
Polishing
Precision blanking
Sawing
Slitting
Traverse winding
Trepanning

COMPETITORS

Metals USA
Reliance Steel
Ryerson Tull

HISTORICAL FINANCIALS

Company Type: Joint venture

Income Statement FYE: June 30

	REVENUE ($ mil.)	NET INCOME ($ mil.)	NET PROFIT MARGIN	EMPLOYEES
6/03	1,341	—	—	2,385
6/02	2,000	—	—	3,000
Annual Growth	(33.0%)	—	—	(20.5%)

Revenue History

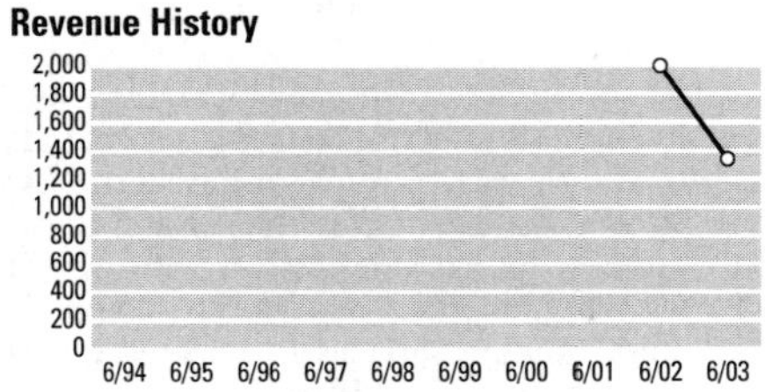

Intelsat, Ltd.

Intelsat's geostationary satellites enjoy a bird's-eye view of earth. The former International Telecommunications Satellite Organization, set up by governments around the world in 1964, reorganized in 2001 as a private company and has plans to conduct a US public offering by the end of 2003. Intelsat is owned by the telecom companies that are its major customers, accounting for more than 75% of sales. The Intelsat system provides Internet, broadcast, telephony, and corporate network services worldwide. The company is upgrading its satellite fleet, which it plans to expand to 24 by 2003, and it is developing a terrestrial infrastructure to complement its "birds." Lockheed Martin owns a 24% stake in Intelsat.

EXECUTIVES

Chairman: John Sponyoe, age 64
CEO: Conny L. Kullman, age 52
EVP and CFO: Joseph (Joe) Corbett
President and COO, Intelsat Global Service: Ramu Potarazu, age 41
President, Intelsat Global Service Corporation: Kevin Mulloy, age 44
President, Intelsat Data, Carrier & Internet (DC&I) Business Unit: John Stanton
SVP and Chief Administration Officer, Intelsat Global Service: Tony Trujillo
SVP and General Counsel, Intelsat Global Service: David B. Meltzer, age 43
Auditors: KPMG LLP

LOCATIONS

HQ: 3400 International Dr. NW, Washington, DC 20008
Phone: 202-944-7877 **Fax:** 202-944-7661
Web: www.intelsat.com

Intelsat has offices in Australia, Brazil, France, Germany, Hong Kong, India, Norway, Singapore, South Africa, the UK, and the US.

2002 Sales

	% of total
Europe	29
North America & Caribbean	24
Asia Pacific	17
Latin America	13
Sub-Saharan Africa	11
Middle East & North Africa	6
Total	**100**

PRODUCTS/OPERATIONS

2002 Sales

	% of total
Customer Segment	
Carriers	37
Corporate Network	30
Broadcast	17
Internet	15
Other	1
Total	**100**

COMPETITORS

APT Satellite
Eutelsat
FLAG Telecom
Global Crossing
Globalstar
Hughes Electronics
Inmarsat
Level 3 Communications
Loral Space
Mobile Communications
ICO
Pasifik Satelit
SES GLOBAL
Tyco Telecommunications
WorldCom

HISTORICAL FINANCIALS

Company Type: Private

Income Statement FYE: December 31

	REVENUE ($ mil.)	NET INCOME ($ mil.)	NET PROFIT MARGIN	EMPLOYEES
12/02	992	274	27.6%	905
12/01	1,084	499	46.0%	875
12/00	1,097	505	46.0%	792
12/99	977	356	36.5%	750
12/98	1,020	547	53.6%	700
12/97	962	367	38.2%	650
12/96	911	341	37.5%	650
12/95	805	299	37.1%	—
12/94	706	281	39.8%	—
12/93	658	309	47.0%	—
Annual Growth	4.7%	(1.3%)	—	5.7%

2002 Year-End Financials

Debt ratio: 58.5%
Return on equity: 13.2%
Cash ($ mil.): 9
Current ratio: 0.89
Long-term debt ($ mil.): 1,258

Net Income History

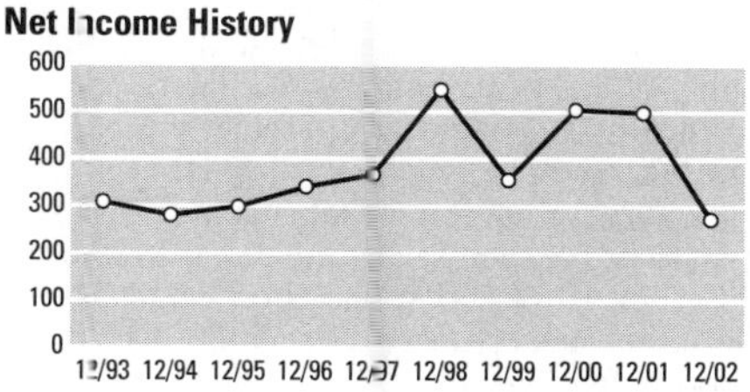

Interactive Brokers Group

Interactive Brokers Group serves investors wanting to interact with world markets. The company (formerly The Timber Hill Group) executes more than 200,000 trades daily in stocks, options, futures, and foreign exchange. Customers may trade on more than 40 different markets in 16 countries. Interactive Brokers caters to individual and institutional investors who execute their trades via the Internet or with the company's IB Trader Workstation software. The firm's affiliate, Timber Hill LLC, acts as a market maker. Interactive Brokers, the Bourse de Montréal, and the Boston Stock Exchange have formed a partnership to launch the Boston Options Exchange (BOX). The company is owned by chairman Thomas Peterffy.

EXECUTIVES

Chairman: Thomas Peterffy
CFO: Paul Brody
CTO: Thomas Frank
VP, Business Development and Marketing: Steve Sanders
Director of Media Relations: Carla Cavaletti
Human Resources Manager: Tammy Silby
Auditors: Deloitte & Touche LLP

LOCATIONS

HQ: Interactive Brokers Group LLC
1 Pickwick Plaza, Greenwich, CT 06830
Phone: 203-618-5700 **Fax:** 203-618-5770
Web: www.interactivebrokers.com

In addition to its Greenwich, Connecticut, headquarters, Interactive Brokers Group LLC operates through offices in Chicago, Hong Kong, London, Montreal, Sydney, and Zug, Switzerland.

COMPETITORS

Charles Schwab
CIBC World Markets
Citigroup Global Markets
Goldman Sachs
ICAP
Instinet
Jefferies Group
Knight Trading
Lehman Brothers
Man Group
Merrill Lynch
Morgan Stanley
Scottrade
UBS Financial Services
William Blair

HISTORICAL FINANCIALS

Company Type: Private

Income Statement FYE: December 31

	REVENUE ($ mil.)	NET INCOME ($ mil.)	NET PROFIT MARGIN	EMPLOYEES
12/02	643	—	—	419
12/01	746	—	—	479
12/00	707	—	—	400
Annual Growth	(4.6%)	—	—	2.3%

Revenue History

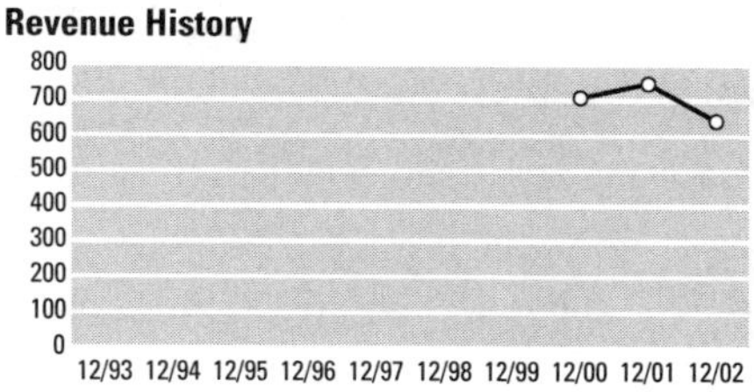

Inter-Con Security Systems

There is no conning Inter-Con Security Systems. The company, one of the largest private security consulting firms in the US, provides custom designed security programs for commercial, governmental, and industrial clients in 25 countries on four continents. Its services include security consulting, protection, investigations, and training. It also provides security guard and patrol services. Inter-Con's clients have included NASA, The Academy Awards, and the US government. The company, founded in 1973, is owned by CEO Rick Hernandez and the Hernandez family.

EXECUTIVES

Chairman, President, and CEO: Enrique (Rick) Hernandez Jr., age 47
VP Administration: Neil Martau
Client Services Director: Edward Ternan
General Manager: Jim Clark

LOCATIONS

HQ: Inter-Con Security Systems, Inc.
210 S. De Lacey Ave., Pasadena, CA 91105
Phone: 626-535-2200 **Fax:** 626-685-9111
Web: www.icsecurity.com

Inter-Con provides security services to customers in 25 countries on four continents.

COMPETITORS

Gavin de Becker
Guardsmark
Kroll
Securicor
Securitas Security Services USA
TransNational Security
Vance International

HISTORICAL FINANCIALS

Company Type: Private

Income Statement FYE: December 31

	REVENUE ($ mil.)	NET INCOME ($ mil.)	NET PROFIT MARGIN	EMPLOYEES
12/02	1,000	—	—	25,000

Interline Brands, Inc.

When something breaks, bursts, or drips, you can call Interline Brands (formerly Wilmar Industries), a national distributor of repair and maintenance products. The firm sells more than 30,000 plumbing, hardware, electrical, janitorial, and related products under private labels (including Wilmar, Sexauer, Barnett). The company more than doubled its size in October 2000 with its purchase of plumbing supplier Barnett (Premier, ProPlus, Barnett, Rx, U.S. Lock, and Legend brands). Interline Brands runs some 60 distribution centers. Interline Brands is primarily owned by General Motors Pension Fund, JPMorgan Partners, Parthenon Capital, Sterling Investment Partners, and management.

EXECUTIVES

President and CEO: Michael J. Grebe
EVP and CFO: William E. Sanford
SVP and Chief Merchandising Officer: William R. Pray, age 52
VP, Customer Service and Special Projects: Tony Faralli
VP, Field Sales: Fred Bravo
VP, Finance and Treasurer: Thomas J. Tossavainen
VP, Human Resources: Annette A. Ricciuti
VP, Marketing: Pamela L. Maxwell
VP, Operations: Jim Spahn
CIO: Hugh Bryan
Controller: Dave Serrano
Auditors: Deloitte & Touche

LOCATIONS

HQ: 801 W. Bay St., Jacksonville, FL 32204
Phone: 904-421-1400 **Fax:** 904-358-2486
Web: www.interlinebrands.com

COMPETITORS

Hughes Supply	Waxman
Noland	Wolseley
Turtle & Hughes	W.W. Grainger

HISTORICAL FINANCIALS

Company Type: Private

Income Statement FYE: Friday before December 31

	REVENUE ($ mil.)	NET INCOME ($ mil.)	NET PROFIT MARGIN	EMPLOYEES
12/02	638	—	—	2,200
12/01	609	—	—	2,200
12/00	597	—	—	2,200
12/99	226	—	—	1,338
12/98	193	—	—	903
12/97	151	—	—	764
12/96	101	—	—	606
12/95	61	—	—	361
12/94	48	—	—	327
Annual Growth	38.3%	—	—	26.9%

Revenue History

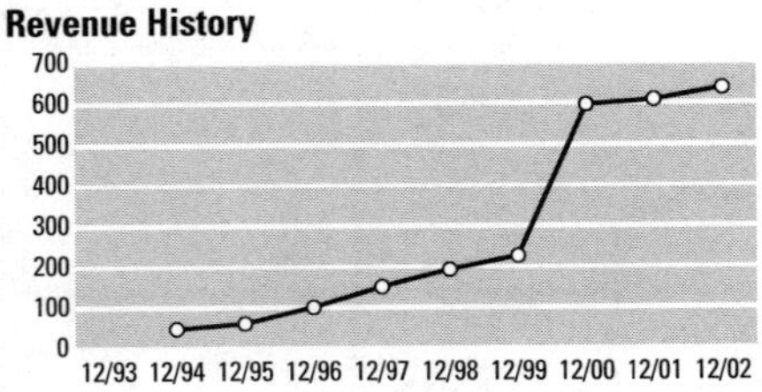

Intermountain Health Care, Inc.

Intermountain Health Care (IHC) is a not-for-profit health care organization operating more than 20 hospitals, 16 home health care agencies, an air ambulance service, and some 75 physician and urgent care clinics in Utah and Idaho. IHC has affiliations with more than 2,000 physicians, including about 400 in its IHC Physician Group. IHC Health Plans offers health insurance programs to large and small employers. The company was formed in 1975 when the Church of Jesus Christ of Latter Day Saints (the Mormons) decided to donate 15 of its hospitals to the communities they served.

EXECUTIVES

Chairman: Richard J. Galbraith
President and CEO: William H. Nelson
CFO: Everett Goodwin
Director, Human Resources: Phyllis A. Domm, age 56

LOCATIONS

HQ: 36 S. State St., Salt Lake City, UT 84111
Phone: 801-442-2000 **Fax:** 801-442-3327
Web: www.ihc.com

PRODUCTS/OPERATIONS

Hospitals

Alta View Hospital (Utah)
American Fork Hospital (Utah)
Bear River Valley Hospital (Utah)
Cassia Regional Medical Center (Idaho)
Cottonwood Hospital (Utah)
Delta Community Medical Center (Utah)
Dixie Regional Medical Center (Utah)
Fillmore Community Medical Center (Utah)
Garfield Memorial Hospital and Clinics (Utah)
Heber Valley Medical Center (Utah)
LDS Hospital (Utah)
Logan Regional Hospital (Utah)
McKay-Dee Hospital Center (Utah)
Orem Community Hospital (Utah)
The Orthopedic Specialty Hospital (Utah)
Pocatello Regional Medical Center (Idaho)
Primary Children's Medical Center (Utah)
Sanpete Valley Hospital (Utah)
Sevier Valley Hospital (Utah)
Utah Valley Regional Medical Center (Utah)
Valley View Medical Center (Utah)

COMPETITORS

Aetna
Blue Cross
CHRISTUS Health
HCA
Iasis Healthcare
LifePoint
Sierra Health
Trinity Health
UnitedHealth Group

HISTORICAL FINANCIALS

Company Type: Not-for-profit

Income Statement FYE: December 31

	REVENUE ($ mil.)	NET INCOME ($ mil.)	NET PROFIT MARGIN	EMPLOYEES
12/01	2,652	—	—	23,000
12/00	2,552	—	—	23,000
12/99	2,390	—	—	23,000
12/98	2,156	—	—	23,000
12/97	2,009	—	—	22,000
12/96	1,758	—	—	20,000
12/95	1,589	—	—	20,000
12/94	1,380	—	—	19,000
12/93	1,318	—	—	18,000
Annual Growth	9.1%	—	—	3.1%

Revenue History

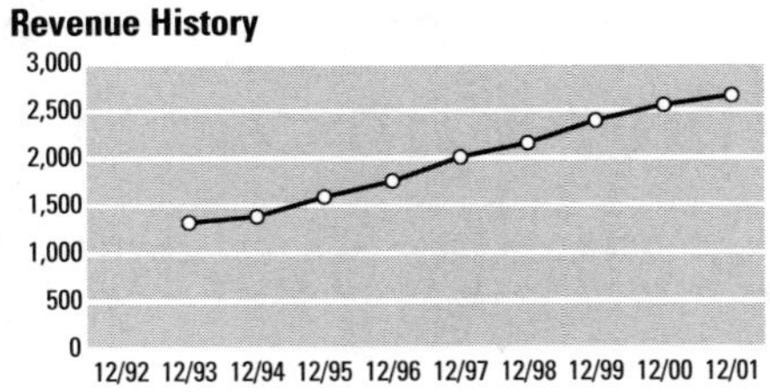

International Brotherhood of Teamsters

The International Brotherhood of Teamsters is the largest and arguably most (in)famous labor union in the US. With about 1.4 million members, the Teamsters represents 16 trade groups, including truckers, UPS workers, warehouse employees, cab drivers, airline workers, construction crews, and other workers. The union negotiates with employers for contracts that guarantee members fair wages and raises, health coverage, job security, paid time off, promotions, and other benefits. The Teamsters union has about 570 local chapters in the US and Canada.

Elected in 1998, Teamsters chief James P. Hoffa (son of assumed-dead union leader Jimmy Hoffa) is working to shed the union's notorious image and has proposed ethics policies aimed at rooting out internal corruption and ties to organized crime. Hoffa wants the Teamsters to police themselves and put an end to the close governmental supervision under which the union has operated since 1988. He also is working to re-establish the union as a power in national politics, lobbying against plans to allow trucks from Mexico to traverse US highways.

HISTORY

Two rival team-driver unions, the Drivers International Union and the Teamsters National Union, merged to form the International Brotherhood of Teamsters in 1903. Led by Cornelius Shea, the Teamsters established headquarters in Indianapolis. Daniel Tobin (president for 45 years, starting in 1907) demanded that union locals obtain executive approval before striking. Membership expanded from the team-driver base, prompting the union to add Chauffeurs, Stablemen, and Helpers to its name (1909).

Following the first transcontinental delivery by motor truck (1912), the Teamster deliverymen traded their horses for trucks. The union then recruited food processing, brewery, and farm workers, among others, to augment Teamster effectiveness during strikes. It joined the American Federation of Labor in 1920.

Until the Depression the Teamsters was still a small union of predominantly urban deliverymen. Then Farrell Dobbs, a Trotskyite Teamster from Minneapolis, organized the famous Minneapolis strikes in 1934 to protest local management's refusal to allow the workers to unionize. Workers clashed with police and National Guard units for 11 days before management acceded to the workers' demands. The strikes demonstrated the potential strength of unions, and Teamsters membership swelled. Although union power ebbed during WWII, the union continued to grow. It moved its headquarters to Washington, DC, in 1953.

The AFL-CIO expelled the Teamsters in 1957 when Teamster ties to the mob became public during a US Senate investigation. New Teamsters boss Jimmy Hoffa eluded indictment and took advantage of America's growing dependence on trucking to negotiate the powerful National Master Freight Agreement (1964). Hoffa also organized industrial workers. He used a union pension fund to make mob-connected loans and was later convicted of jury tampering and sent to prison. In 1975, four years after his release, Hoffa vanished without a trace and is believed to have been the victim of a Mafia hit.

The Teamsters rejoined the AFL-CIO in 1987 and the following year settled a racketeering lawsuit filed by the US Justice Department by allowing government appointees to discipline corrupt union leaders, help run the union, and oversee its elections. The election of self-styled reformer Ronald Carey in 1991 (he received 49% of the vote) seemed to portend real changes for the union; each of his six predecessors had been accused of or imprisoned for criminal activities. However, membership dropped by 40,000 in both 1991 and 1992.

Carey won re-election as union president in 1996 over rival, and son of former boss Jimmy Hoffa, James P. Hoffa (whom Carey accused of having ties to organized crime). A 15-day strike by the Teamsters' UPS employees in 1997 led to the delivery company's agreement to combine part-time jobs into 10,000 new full-time positions. That year Carey's re-election was overturned amid a campaign finance investigation that netted guilty pleas from three Carey associates, and the Teamsters leader was disqualified from running for re-election in 1998. Carey was officially expelled from the Teamsters by the federal government, and Hoffa won the 1998 election over Tom Leedham (who was backed by the union's reform wing).

Promising to fight corruption, Hoffa hired former federal prosecutor Edwin Stier and several former FBI agents to help him operate Project RISE (respect, integrity, strength, and ethics), a new in-house anti-corruption program. In 2002 the union began lobbying against plans to allow Mexican trucking companies to transport goods across the US.

EXECUTIVES

General President: James P. Hoffa, age 62
General Secretary-Treasurer: C. Thomas (Tom) Keegel
VP At-Large: Randy Cammack
VP At-Large: Fred Gegare
VP At-Large: Carl E. Haynes
VP At-Large: Thomas R. O'Donnell
VP At-Large: Ralph J. Taurone
VP, Canada; President, Teamsters Canada: Robert Bouvier
VP, Canada: Joseph McLean
VP, Canada: Garnet Zimmerman
VP, Central Region: Patrick Flynn
VP, Central Region: Walter Lytle
VP, Central Region: Dotty W. Malinsky
VP, Central Region: Lester A. Singer
VP, Central Region: Philip E. Young
VP, Eastern Region: Jack Cipriani
VP, Eastern Region: John Murphy
VP, Eastern Region: Dan De Santi
VP, Eastern Region: Richard Volpe
VP, Southern Region: Tyson Johnson
VP, Southern Region: Ken Wood
VP, Western Region: Al Hobart
VP, Western Region: Chuck Mack
VP, Western Region: Jim Santangelo
Director of Human Resources Department: Lynda Sist

LOCATIONS

HQ: 25 Louisiana Ave. NW, Washington, DC 20001
Phone: 202-624-6800 **Fax:** 202-624-6918
Web: www.teamster.org

2002 Membership

	% of total
United States	
Central	32
East	28
West	26
South	7
Canada	7
Total	**100**

PRODUCTS/OPERATIONS

Trade Divisions

Airline
Bakery and Laundry
Brewery and Soft Drink
Building Material and Construction
Carhaul
Dairy
Freight
Industrial Trades
Motion Picture and Theatrical Trade
Newspaper, Magazine, and Electronic Media
Parcel and Small Package
Port
Public Services
Tankhaul
Trade Show and Convention Centers
Warehouse

HISTORICAL FINANCIALS

Company Type: Labor union

Income Statement

FYE: December 31

	REVENUE ($ mil.)	NET INCOME ($ mil.)	NET PROFIT MARGIN	EMPLOYEES
12/97	89	—	—	—
12/96	90	—	—	—
12/95	90	—	—	—
12/94	82	—	—	—
12/93	74	—	—	—
12/92	78	—	—	—
12/91	83	—	—	—
Annual Growth	1.2%	—	—	—

Revenue History

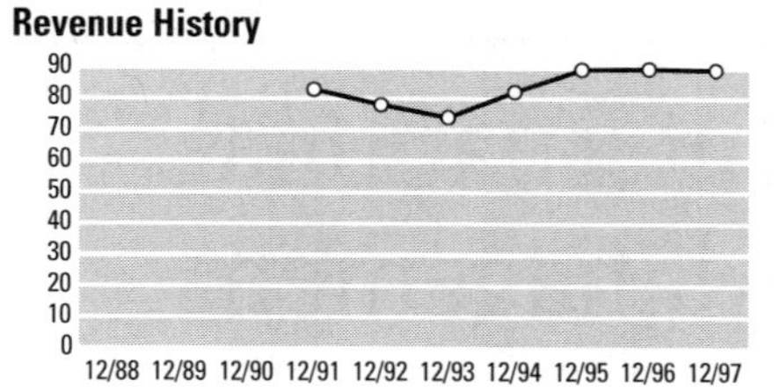

International Data Group

International Data Group (IDG) is a publishing giant with digital appeal. The world's top technology publisher, IDG produces some 300 magazines and newspapers in 85 countries, including *PC World* and *CIO*. In addition to publishing, IDG provides technology market research through its IDC unit and produces a number of industry events. In 2001 the firm sold its 75% stake in Hungry Minds (formerly IDG Books Worldwide), the oracle for the tech-unsavvy with its *For Dummies* series of books. Chairman Patrick McGovern, who founded IDG in 1964, holds a majority stake in the company; an employee stock plan owns the rest.

While a downturn in the economy hurt publishers in 2000 and 2001, IDG weathered the storm in part by concentrating on growing its market research and event marketing businesses. The company's IDC unit has hundreds of analysts in 43 countries, and its industry events include Macworld Expo and the BioITWorld Conference & Expo. It also offers career services through JobUniverse.com and ITcareers.com and operates 330 Web sites featuring technology content. IDG has acquired some assets of *Industry Standard* publisher Standard Media (subscriber lists, trademarks, newsletters) following that company's bankruptcy liquidation.

HISTORY

Patrick McGovern began his career in publishing as a paperboy for the *Philadelphia Bulletin*. As a teenager in the 1950s, McGovern was inspired by Edmund Berkeley's book *Giant Brains; or Machines That Think*. He later built a computer and won a scholarship to MIT. There he edited the first computer magazine, *Computers and Automation*. McGovern started market research firm International Data Corporation in 1964 after interviewing the president of computer pioneer UNIVAC. Three years later he launched *Computerworld*, and within a few weeks the eight-page tabloid had 20,000 subscribers. Combined under the name International Data Group, McGovern's company reached $1 million in sales by 1968.

Taking the "International" in its name to heart, IDG began publishing in Japan in 1971 and expanded to Germany in 1975. Following the collapse of communism, the company had 10 publications in Russia and Eastern Europe by 1990. That year two teenage hackers broke into the company's voice mail system and erased orders from customers and messages from writers. The prank cost IDG about $2.4 million. Also in 1990, IDG launched IDG Books Worldwide (renamed Hungry Minds in 2000), which hit it big the next year with *DOS for Dummies*.

With the technology boom of the 1990s, competition in tech publishing heated up. By 1993 several of IDG's magazines, including *InfoWorld*, *Macworld*, and *PC World*, began losing ad pages to rivals Ziff-Davis and CMP Media. To help stem advertiser attrition, IDG started an incentive program tied to its new online service. In 1995 IDG bought a stake in software companies Architect Software (now ExciteHome) and Netscape (now owned by America Online) as part of its move toward Internet-based services.

In 1996 IDG launched *Netscape World: The Web,* a magazine covering the Internet, and introduced more than 30 industry newsletters delivered by e-mail. The company also bought *PC Advisor,* the UK's fastest-growing computer magazine. IDG kicked off its online ad placement service, Global Web Ad Network, in 1997. That year IDG merged *Macworld* with rival Ziff-Davis' *MacUser* in a joint venture called Mac Publishing.

In 1998 IDG pledged $1 billion in venture capital for high-tech startups in China. It also introduced new publications in China, including a Chinese edition of *Cosmopolitan* (with Hearst Magazines) and *China Computer Reseller World.* Later that year the company launched *The Industry Standard* and spun off 25% of IDG Books to the public.

In 1999 it sold a 20% stake in Industry Standard Communications (renamed Standard Media International) to private investors and began laying plans for a possible spinoff in 2000. However, a weakening economy and slowing ad sales in 2000 quieted those plans.

The next year both Standard Media and Hungry Minds announced staff cuts and restructuring. IDG eventually sold its majority interest in Hungry Minds to John Wiley & Sons for about $90 million. Standard Media filed for bankruptcy and liquidated its assets, some of which were bought by IDG. The company also purchased Ziff Davis' 50% stake in their joint venture Mac Publishing. In 2002 IDG CEO Kelly Conlin left the business and was replaced by company executive Pat Kenealy.

EXECUTIVES

Chairman: Patrick J. McGovern
CEO: Pat Kenealy
CFO: Ted Bloom
VP Finance: Jim Ghirardi
VP Human Resources: Karen Budreau
President and CEO, Bio-IT World Inc.: Morris R. Levitt
President, CXO Media: Walter Manninen
President and CEO, IDG World Expo: Charlie Greco, age 50
VP New Business Development and Operations: Colin Crawford
VP Sales, Marketing and Product Development, IDG World Expo: Rob Scheschareg
VP Software Partnering and Alliances Research: Steve McHale
Public Relations: Sarah Hansen
Auditors: Deloitte & Touche LLP

LOCATIONS

HQ: 1 Exeter Plaza, 15th Fl., Boston, MA 02116
Phone: 617-534-1200 **Fax:** 650-524-5730
Web: www.idg.com

International Data Group publishes more than 300 magazines and newspapers in 85 countries.

PRODUCTS/OPERATIONS

Selected Operations

IDC (market research)
IDG Events & Conferences
IDG Publications (periodical publishing)
IDG Recruitment Solutions (employment services)
IDG.net (online publications hub)

Selected Events

BioITWorld Conference & Expo
ComNet
LinuxWorld Conference & Expo
Macworld Expo

Selected Periodicals

CIO
Computerworld
Games
InfoWorld
Macworld
Network World
PC World
Publish

COMPETITORS

CNET Networks
Forrester Research
Freeman Companies
Future Network
Gartner
Jupitermedia
McGraw-Hill
MediaLive International
Microsoft
Pearson
Penton Media
Reed Elsevier Group
SYS-CON Media
United Business Media
Vivendi Universal Publishing
VNU
Ziff Davis Media

HISTORICAL FINANCIALS

Company Type: Private

Income Statement FYE: September 30

	REVENUE ($ mil.)	NET INCOME ($ mil.)	NET PROFIT MARGIN	EMPLOYEES
9/02	2,580	—	—	13,050
9/01	3,010	—	—	13,200
9/00	3,100	—	—	13,400
9/99	2,560	—	—	12,000
9/98	2,050	—	—	11,500
9/97	1,876	—	—	9,500
9/96	1,700	—	—	8,500
9/95	1,400	—	—	8,200
9/94	1,100	—	—	7,200
9/93	880	—	—	5,000
Annual Growth	12.7%	—	—	11.2%

Revenue History

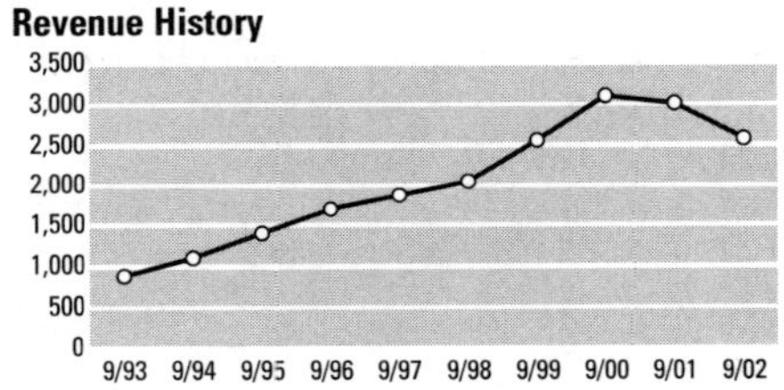

International Management Group

Show me the money! Founded by the late pioneer of sports marketing Mark McCormack, International Management Group (IMG) is the world's largest sports talent and marketing agency. The firm's list of clients includes the hippest athletes of the day, including Venus and Serena Williams, Tiger Woods, and Wayne Gretzky. In addition to representing sports idols, IMG also counts artists (Placido Domingo), models (Tyra Banks), and broadcasters (Bob Costas) among its clients. Its Trans World International division produces more than 4,000 hours of sports TV programming each year. In addition, IMG represents corporate clients (Cisco Systems), acts as a literary agent, and is active in real estate and golf course design.

IMG is credited with having invented the field of sports management. While representing VIP clients may be how IMG gained its fame, the company is involved in several other aspects of sports promotion as well. It gives many of its clients venues in which to compete by promoting sporting events, and when athletes need training, they can take advantage of IMG's various sports academies.

The company is active in financial consulting through a joint venture with Merrill Lynch (McCormack Advisors International). IMG continues to expand internationally, organizing sporting events such as basketball, baseball, golf, and rugby across Asia, Australia, and Europe.

After having been in a coma for several months following a heart attack, the 72-year-old McCormack passed away in 2003.

HISTORY

When former amateur golfer Mark McCormack went to Yale Law School in the 1950s, he didn't desert golf entirely. In his free time he set up paid exhibitions for pro golfers he knew from his days on the links, and in 1960 one of these players, Arnold Palmer, asked McCormack to manage his finances so he could concentrate on his game. McCormack went above and beyond the call of duty, signing Palmer to endorsement deals and licensing his name and image. In two years Palmer's annual income skyrocketed from $60,000 to more than $500,000 — a fiscal triumph that would be the bedrock of IMG's business. Throughout the early and mid-1960s, IMG signed up more big-name golfers, as well as stars from other sports such as Jackie Stewart (car racing) and Jean-Claude Killy (skiing).

The addition of foreign stars such as Stewart (Scotland), Killy (France), and Gary Player (South Africa) allowed IMG access to global markets. In the late 1960s as television began to bring sports and its stars into living rooms around the world, IMG used its clients to promote products and services internationally. In 1967 McCormack created a new division of IMG — a TV production company that filmed and distributed sporting events called Trans World International (TWI). The next year IMG signed a contract with Wimbledon's organizers to coordinate video and television licensing.

IMG's entrepreneurial spirit came to the forefront with a vengeance in the 1980s. In addition to managing athletes, sporting events, and sponsors, the company began to skip the middleman and create the sports event itself. IMG debuted the Skins Game in 1983, a golf invitational featuring four of the sport's top athletes playing for high stakes. IMG also created Saturday afternoon sports staples such as *The Battle of the Network Stars,* shows that featured sports or TV stars competing in a series of events such as the tug-o-war and obstacle courses.

By the 1990s McCormack had situated IMG to take advantage of almost every aspect of televised sports events: Typically, an IMG event involved working with the athletes, the sponsor or sponsors, the event itself, and the television distribution rights. The company continued to expand its clientele beyond sports, adding names such as musician Placido Domingo. By 1997 IMG also counted the Rock and Roll Hall of Fame, the Americas Cup, and the Mayo Clinic as clients.

IMG teamed up with Chase Capital Partners (now J.P. Morgan Partners) in 1998 to form

IMG/Chase Sports Capital, a private equity fund expected to raise some $200 million to invest in the sports industry. The next year IMG demonstrated a well-honed knack for capitalizing on its clients' appeal by staging a televised golf match between clients Tiger Woods and David Duval, and again in 2000 between Woods and Sergio Garcia. Also that year IMG tried to create a new cable network between TWI and the New York Yankees, but the New York Supreme Court blocked the deal, saying it violated the Yankees' current deal with MSG Network. In 2001 the Yankees broke ties with MSG, paying them $30 million, to do its own network. McCormack died in 2003.

EXECUTIVES

President and COO of IMG International: Alastair Johnston
President and COO of IMG North and South America: Robert D. Kain
President, IMG Academies: Nick Bollettieri
SVP, Golf; President Basketball: Mark Steinberg, age 35
SVP, Golf Course Design: Mike Rielly
SVP and Managing Director, IMG Artists: Ed Landau
SVP and Associate Director, IMG Artists: Elizabeth Sobol
SVP and Director, Vocal Division, IMG Artists: Alex C. Treuhaft
SVP, Business Development, IMG West Coast: Sam Peck
VP and Director, Dance Division, IMG Artists: Nancy Gabriel
VP and Director, Attractions, IMG Artists: Mark S. Maluso
VP, National Sales Group, IMG West Coast: Jim McIver
VP, Los Angeles Sales, IMG West Coast: Gus Sampras
VP, San Francisco Sales, IMG West Coast: Paul Siri
VP, San Francisco Sales, IMG West Coast: Steve Tseng
VP, Western Region Events IMG West Coast: Peter Tatum
VP, X Sports, IMG West Coast: James Leitz
VP, Consulting, TWI: Nathan Kerry
Director, Business Development and Sponsorship Sales, IMG West Coast: David Potovsky
Director, Regional Sales and Marketing, IMG West Coast: Nancy Young

LOCATIONS

HQ: 1360 E. 9th St., Ste. 100, Cleveland, OH 44114
Phone: 216-522-1200 **Fax:** 216-522-1145
Web: www.imgworld.com

IMG has 85 offices in 33 countries.

PRODUCTS/OPERATIONS

Selected Clients

All England Lawn Tennis & Croquet Club (Wimbledon)
Tyra Banks
Jose Carreras
Cisco Systems
Bob Costas
Placido Domingo
David Duval
Sergio Garcia
Wayne Gretzky
Stephen Hawking
International Olympic Committee
Heidi Klum
Nancy Lopez
John Madden
Joe Montana
Colin Montgomerie
Martina Navratilova
Greg Norman
Mark O'Meara
Arnold Palmer
Rugby World Cup
Serena Williams
Venus Williams
Tiger Woods
United States Golf Association

Selected Sports Academies

The David Leadbetter Golf Academy
IMG Hockey Academy
International Performance Institute
Nick Bollettieri Tennis Academy
The Soccer and Baseball Academies

Other Operations

IMG Golf Course Services (designs, manages, and markets golf courses worldwide)
Trans World International (sports television production)

COMPETITORS

Brillstein-Grey
Bull Run
Clear Channel Entertainment
CAA
Dentsu
Elite
the Firm
International Creative Management
Interpublic Group
Magnum Sports & Entertainment
TBA
United Talent
William Morris
WPP Group

HISTORICAL FINANCIALS

Company Type: Private

Income Statement FYE: December 31

	ESTIMATED REVENUE ($ mil.)	NET INCOME ($ mil.)	NET PROFIT MARGIN	EMPLOYEES
12/02	1,300	—	—	3,000
12/01	1,300	—	—	2,500
12/00	1,260	—	—	2,900
12/99	1,100	—	—	2,150
12/98	1,100	—	—	2,125
12/97	1,100	—	—	2,000
12/96	1,000	—	—	1,959
12/95	1,000	—	—	1,600
Annual Growth	3.8%	—	—	9.4%

Revenue History

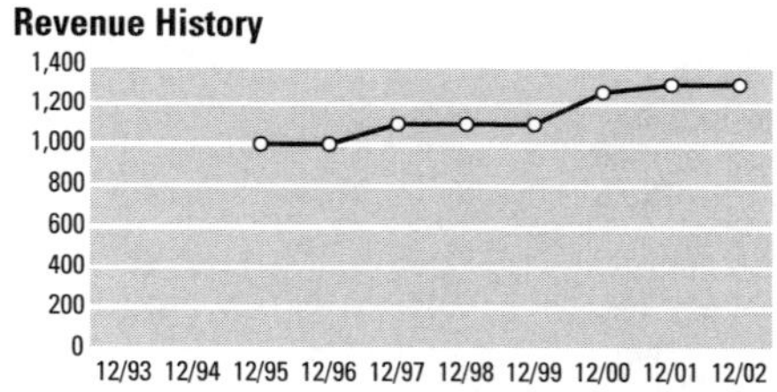

International Specialty Products Inc.

If you're washed, shaved, and groomed, then you've probably shared a chemical experience with the folks at International Specialty Products (ISP). The company makes about 300 types of specialty chemicals, which it breaks into three major market groupings: consumer, pharmaceutical and food and beverage, and performance and industrial. ISP also makes waterproofing agents, moisturizers, and preservatives for personal care products such as sunscreen and hair care products. Chairman and former corporate raider Samuel Heyman owns 100% of ISP now; after watching the company's stock dive in 2002, Heyman took the company private.

ISP makes pharmaceutical ingredients and chemicals used in toothpaste and denture adhesives. The company also makes butanediol (used in fibers and plastics) and mineral products (used in asphalt roofing shingles).

Suffering from stagnant sales, ISP has sold its filter products subsidiaries, and its pearlescent pigments business, and has shut down several plants (including two butanediol-manufacturing facilities) in an effort to cut costs and focus on core operations.

Heyman and ISP waged and lost, in July 2003, a proxy fight for control of Hercules, Inc., of which ISP owned 10%. ISP sold most of its shares in Hercules in September 2003.

EXECUTIVES

Chairman: Samuel J. Heyman, age 64
President, CEO, and Director: Sunil Kumar, age 53, $1,112,555 pay
EVP, Finance, Treasurer, and Director: Susan B. Yoss, age 44, $664,230 pay
EVP, General Counsel, Secretary, and Director: Richard A. Weinberg, age 43, $765,001 pay
SVP and CFO: Neal E. Murphy, age 46
SVP, Corporate Development and Strategy, and Director: Stephen R. Olsen, age 40, $317,360 pay
SVP and Commercial Director, Americas: Ron Brandt
SVP, Sales and Commercial Director, Europe, and Director: Roger J. Cope, age 58, $342,780 pay
SVP, Research and Development and Latin America: Lawrence Grenner, age 59, $302,125 pay
SVP, Sales, and General Manager, Asia: Warren Bishop
Global Marketing Director: Pierre Varin
SVP, Human Resources: Patricia Ippoliti
Auditors: KPMG LLP

LOCATIONS

HQ: 1361 Alps Rd., Wayne, NJ 07470
Phone: 973-628-4000 **Fax:** 973-628-4001
Web: www.ispcorp.com

International Specialty Products has operations in Asia, Canada, Europe, South America, and the US.

PRODUCTS/OPERATIONS

Selected Products

Fine chemicals
Food and beverage products
Industrial products
Minerals
Performance chemicals
Personal care products
  Hair care
  Skin care
Pharmaceuticals

COMPETITORS

3M
Albemarle
BASF AG
Bayer AG
Cambrex
Cognis
CPAC
Dow Chemical
DuPont Canada
Hercules
ICI
Lyondell Chemical
Noveon
Penford
Sigma-Aldrich
Stepan
Yule Catto

HISTORICAL FINANCIALS

Company Type: Private

Income Statement FYE: December 31

	REVENUE ($ mil.)	NET INCOME ($ mil.)	NET PROFIT MARGIN	EMPLOYEES
12/02	845	—	—	2,500
12/01	787	—	—	2,600
12/00	784	—	—	2,600
12/99	787	—	—	2,650
12/98	824	—	—	2,900
12/97	749	—	—	2,675
12/96	717	—	—	2,700
12/95	689	—	—	2,500
12/94	600	—	—	2,400
12/93	548	—	—	2,435
Annual Growth	4.9%	—	—	0.3%

Revenue History

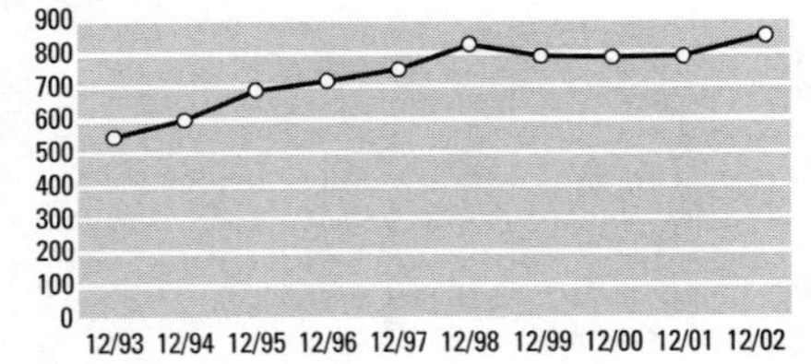

International Steel Group Inc.

The Darwinian concept of "survival of the fittest" has a steeling effect when it comes to International Steel Group. In March 2002, New York buyout firm W. L. Ross bought LTV's integrated steel operations for approximately $325 million in cash and debt to form International Steel Group (ISG). The company manufactures flat rolled steel through its plants located in Cleveland and East Chicago, Indiana, and a finishing plant in Illinois. ISG also runs a coke plant in Warren, Ohio. The company has purchased the steelmaking operations of Acme Metals for roughly $65 million. In 2003 ISG purchased the remaining steel assets of bankrupt Bethlehem Steel for about $1.5 billion.

With the purchase of Bethlehem Steel, ISG has become one of the largest steelmakers in the US, with shipments expected to be about 16 million tons per year.

EXECUTIVES

Chairman: Wilbur L. Ross Jr., age 65
President, CEO, and Director: Rodney B. Mott, age 51, $966,200 pay
COO: V. John Goodwin, age 59
CFO: Leonard M. Anthony, age 49
VP and Treasurer: Bruce Pole, age 48, $493,671 pay
VP Business Development: Gordon C. Spelich, age 45, $434,790 pay
VP External Affairs and Public Policy: Mitchell A. Hecht, age 43, $434,790 pay
John D. Lefler, age 57
VP Sales and Marketing: Jerome V. Nelson, age 42, $478,269 pay
Assistant VP and Corporate Manager, Human Resources: Karen A. Smith, age 49
Auditors: KPMG LLP

LOCATIONS

HQ: 3250 Interstate Dr., 2nd Fl., Richfield, OH 44286
Phone: 330-659-9100 **Fax:** 330-659-9135
Web: www.intlsteel.com

International Steel Group has 11 major manufacturing facilities in six states including integrated steelmakers in Cleveland; East Chicago, Indiana; Burns Harbor, Indiana; and Sparrows Point, Maryland.

PRODUCTS/OPERATIONS

Selected Products

Alloy plates
Carbon plates
Coated sheet
Cold-rolled sheets
Rail products
Semi-finished shapes
Tin mill products

COMPETITORS

AK Steel Holding Corporation
Arcelor
Corus Group
Dofasco
Ispat
Nippon Steel
Nucor
POSCO
Rouge Industries
Steel Dynamics
ThyssenKrupp
United States Steel
WCI Steel
Weirton Steel

HISTORICAL FINANCIALS

Company Type: Private

Income Statement FYE: December 31

	REVENUE ($ mil.)	NET INCOME ($ mil.)	NET PROFIT MARGIN	EMPLOYEES
12/02	933	70	7.5%	3,369

Interstate Battery System

Interstate Battery System of America offers a battery of batteries. The company can provide the electrical juice for everything from calculators and radios to automobiles and lawn equipment. Interstate Battery has distributors throughout the US, as well as in Canada, the Dominican Republic, Guam, and Puerto Rico. Consumers can purchase Interstate Battery's products at more than 200,000 retail locations, including a growing number of Interstate All Battery Centers. Interstate Battery also sponsors the Joe Gibbs Racing team on the NASCAR circuit. Chairman Norm Miller owns the company.

EXECUTIVES

Chairman: Norm Miller
President and CEO: Tommy Miller
EVP: Len Ruby
EVP: Carlos Sepulveda
VP and Controller: Lisa Huntsberry
VP, Advertising and Public Relations: Charles Suscavage
VP, Financial Services: Mike Hallick
VP, Human Resources and General Counsel: Walter Holmes
VP, Marketing, E-Commerce, and Retail Sales: Dennis Brown
Corporate Chaplain: Henry Rogers

LOCATIONS

HQ: Interstate Battery System of America, Inc.
12770 Merit Dr., Ste. 400, Dallas, TX 75251
Phone: 972-991-1444 **Fax:** 972-458-8288
Web: www.ibsa.com

Interstate Battery System of America has distributors in Canada, the Dominican Republic, Guam, Puerto Rico, and the US.

PRODUCTS/OPERATIONS

Selected Applications

Automotive/truck
Calculators
Camcorders
Cellular phones
Chargers
Commercial equipment
Computers/laptops
Cordless phones
Cordless tools
Flashlights
Household batteries
Lawn and garden
Marine/RV
Medical equipment
Motorcycles
Pagers
Photo batteries
Radio batteries
Sealed lead/SLA
Watches

COMPETITORS

Acme Electric
Active Power
C&D Technologies
Douglas Battery
Duracell
Eagle-Picher
East Penn
Energizer Holdings
Energy Conversion
EnerSys
Evercel
Exide
Furukawa Electric
General Cable
Imsa
Johnson Controls
Rayovac
Wilson Greatbatch

HISTORICAL FINANCIALS

Company Type: Private

Income Statement FYE: April 30

	REVENUE ($ mil.)	NET INCOME ($ mil.)	NET PROFIT MARGIN	EMPLOYEES
4/02	500	—	—	800
4/01	526	—	—	685
4/00	531	—	—	655
4/99	473	—	—	502
4/98	467	—	—	430
Annual Growth	1.7%	—	—	16.8%

Revenue History

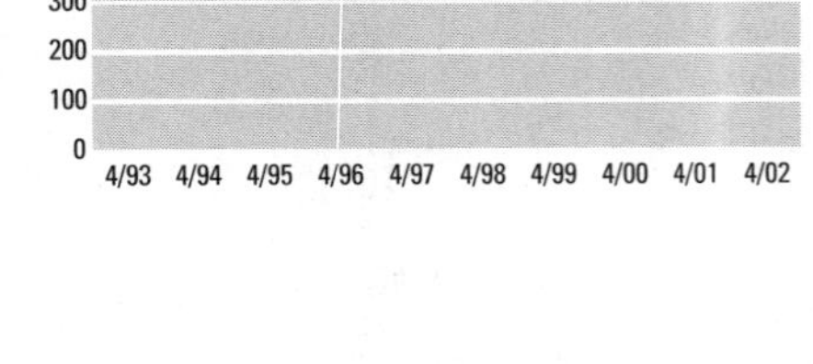

The Irvine Company Inc.

At The Irvine Company, everything is going according to plan. Master plan, that is. The company creates master-planned communities in well-heeled Orange County, of which the company owns some 50,000 acres (making it California's largest landowner). The company's land is called Irvine Ranch and includes the US's largest planned community, Irvine, with more than 150,000 residents; some 30,000 acres have been set aside for wildlife habitat and open spaces. Its core holdings are derived from the 120,000-acre Irvine Ranch, formed in the mid-1800s when James Irvine bought out the debts of Mexican land-grant holders. Chairman Donald Bren, one of America's wealthiest men, owns the company.

The Irvine Company's portfolio includes the Irvine Spectrum development, one of the nation's largest high-tech research and business centers, as well as two hotels, five marinas, and three golf courses.

The University of California, Irvine, is built on company-donated land.

The Irvine Company also owns Irvine Apartment Communities, a real estate investment trust (REIT) that owns some 75 apartment complexes in the Irvine Ranch area, as well as in San Diego, San Jose, and Los Angeles.

Chairman Donald Bren has continued the 35-year-old master plan created by the Irvine Foundation (the former parent of The Irvine Company), which calls for gradual development of rigorously planned communities. The plan — which has so far helped form the communities of Laguna Beach, Newport Beach, Orange, and Tustin, as well as centerpiece Irvine — has entered its final phase (set for completion around 2040), but the company faces increasing political opposition to its plans from area residents, who tend to become development-weary after they get their piece of the Irvine Ranch.

HISTORY

A wholesale merchant in San Francisco during the gold rush, James Irvine and two others assembled vast holdings in Southern California in the mid-1800s by buying out the debts of Mexican and Spanish land-grant holders. Irvine bought his partners' shares in 1876 and passed the ranch of 120,000 acres to his son, James II, upon his death in 1886. Eight years later James II incorporated the ranch as The Irvine Company and began turning it into an agribusiness empire, shifting from sheep ranching to cash crop farming.

James II owned the ranch and company until the 1930s, when the death of his son, James III, prompted him to transfer a controlling interest in the company to the not-for-profit Irvine Foundation. James III's wife, Athalie, and daughter, Joan, inherited 22% of Irvine.

In 1959 company president Myford Irvine, a grandson of James I and uncle to Joan, was found dead from two shotgun wounds. Officials ruled it a suicide, but others weren't so sure.

With Athalie and Joan's encouragement, the firm donated land in the early 1960s for the construction of the University of California, Irvine. The company would continue contributing to educational and philanthropic causes as well as donating property for green space to improve Orange County's suburban areas.

The 1960s also saw the Irvine Foundation forming its definitive master plan for pre-arranged communities and marked the company's entry into the real estate development sector. The plan was designed to anticipate and control growth, with provisions for green space and a mix of pricing levels.

Superrich firebrand Joan, who had long accused Irvine Foundation officers of serving their own interests at the expense of other stockholders, lobbied Congress in the late 1960s to change tax laws pertaining to the foundation. Along with a group of investors led by Donald Bren, Alfred Taubman, and Herbert Allen, Joan trumped a bid by Mobil Oil and in 1977 wrested control of the company from the foundation.

When California's real estate market went sour in 1983, Bren bought out his fellow shareholders, and increased his ownership stake from 34% to 95%. Joan returned to court to protest the price, gaining extra money when the court valued the land at $1.4 billion.

In 1993 Bren sought cash from his holdings by offering apartment developments as a real estate investment trust (REIT), Irvine Apartment Communities.

Orange County's record-setting bankruptcy in 1994 (the county lost $1.7 billion in risky investments) threatened the value of The Irvine Company's property portfolio, most of which is located in Orange County. Thanks in part to a frothy economy and settlements from brokerage firms, Orange County and The Irvine Company were spared another 1983-esque bust.

In 1996 Bren bought out the company's remaining stock. As part of its expansion into R&D, retail, and office properties in the Silicon Valley area, The Irvine Company opened an office in San Jose the next year, followed by its Eastgate Technology Park in San Diego in 1998. An industrywide slide in REIT stock prices prompted Bren to take Irvine Apartment Communities private in 1999.

The company continued to expand its retail and office holdings into the aughts — including the purchase of Century City's Fox Plaza. In 2002, the Irvine City Council approved The Irvine Company's plans to develop the last phase of the company's master plan (to be completed in 2040) — bringing over 12,000 homes, 730,000 sq. ft. of retail space, and 6.57 million sq. ft. of industrial space to the city's Northern Sphere area.

EXECUTIVES

Chairman: Donald L. Bren
Vice Chairman and COO: Michael D. McKee, age 57
Vice Chairman: Raymond L. Watson, age 76
Group SVP and CFO: Marc Ley, age 40
Group SVP, Environmental Affairs: Monica Florian
Group SVP, Entitlement and Public Affairs: Daniel Young
Group SVP, Corporate Communications: Larry Thomas
Group SVP, Urban Planning and Design: Robert N. Elliott
President, Investment Properties Group: Clarence W. Barker
President, Irvine Community Development: Joseph D. Davis
President, Apartment Communities, Investment Properties Group: Max L. Gardner, age 51
President, Office Properties, Investment Properties Group: William Halford
President, Resort Properties Group: L. K. Eric Prevette
VP, Commercial Land Sales, Investment Property Group: Larry Williams

LOCATIONS

HQ: 550 Newport Center Dr., Newport Beach, CA 92658
Phone: 949-720-2000 **Fax:** 949-720-2218
Web: www.irvinecompany.com

The Irvine Company owns and develops 54,000 acres of land in Orange County, California, including the City of Irvine and parts of Anaheim, Laguna Beach, Newport Beach, Orange, and Tustin. It also owns properties in Los Angeles, San Diego, and San Jose.

PRODUCTS/OPERATIONS

Selected Divisions

Investment Properties Group
Irvine Commercial Land Sales
Irvine Resort Properties (hotels, marinas, and golf courses)
Irvine Office Company (7 million sq. ft. of office space)
Irvine Retail Properties Company (6.3 million sq. ft. of shopping and retail space)
Irvine Apartment Communities
Irvine Community Development

COMPETITORS

Arden Realty
California Coastal Communities
C.J. Segerstrom & Sons
Corky McMillin
Intergroup
KB Home
Kilroy Realty
The Koll Company
Majestic Realty
MBK Real Estate
Mission West Properties
Newhall
Pan Pacific
Rancho Mission Viejo
Tejon Ranch

HISTORICAL FINANCIALS

Company Type: Private

Income Statement FYE: June 30

	REVENUE ($ mil.)	NET INCOME ($ mil.)	NET PROFIT MARGIN	EMPLOYEES
6/01	1,500	—	—	470
6/00	1,305	—	—	435
6/99	1,100	—	—	250
6/98	1,000	—	—	236
6/97	816	—	—	200
6/96	710	—	—	190
6/95	700	—	—	200
6/94	800	—	—	200
6/93	800	—	—	200
6/92	700	—	—	300
Annual Growth	8.8%	—	—	5.1%

Revenue History

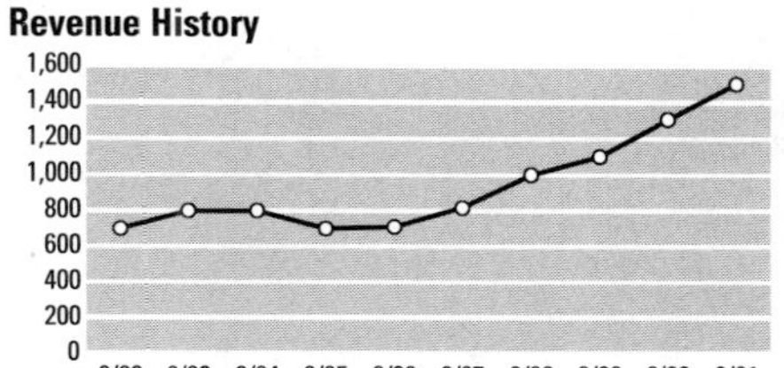

J. Crew Group, Inc.

The crews depicted in the flashy catalogs of the J. Crew Group are far from motley. Some 60% of J. Crew's sales come from classic-styled jeans, khakis, and other basic (but pricey) items sold to young professionals through its catalogs and Web site and in nearly 200 retail and factory outlets in the US. It also has about 70 outlets in Japan through a joint venture with ITOCHU. Asian contractors produce about 80% of the company's merchandise. Texas Pacific Group owns more than 60% of J. Crew; Emily Cinader Woods, daughter of founder Arthur Cinader, owns nearly 20%.

Almost two-thirds of J. Crew's sales come from retail and outlet; about 30% of sales are generated by the 32 catalog editions that reach more than 70 million people each year. Hemmed by the stagnant growth of its catalog operations, the New York City-based company has sold or closed two of its noncore catalog businesses, Popular Club Plan and Clifford & Wills, leaving it with only its namesake operations.

J. Crew has gone through some tough times since the Texas Pacific Group bought a majority stake in the family-run company in 1998. A plan to take the company public was shelved and the company has fallen farther behind rivals such as Abercrombie & Fitch and American Eagle Outfitters. In January 2003, heavy hitter Millard Drexler was brought in as chairman and CEO to try to turn the same successful trick that he did at his former company, The Gap.

EXECUTIVES

Chairman and CEO: Millard S. (Mickey) Drexler, age 58, $700,000 pay
President: Jeff Pfeifle, age 44, $760,000 pay
COO: Scott Gilbertson, age 34, $450,000 pay
EVP Human Resources: David F. Kozel, age 46
EVP Men's Business: Kathy Boyer, age 54
EVP Stores: Michael Dadario, age 44
SVP Manufacturing: Scott D. Hyatt, age 45, $354,000 pay
VP, Corporate Controller, and Interim CFO: Nicholas Lamberti, age 60
Auditors: KPMG LLP

LOCATIONS

HQ: 770 Broadway, New York, NY 10003
Phone: 212-209-2500 **Fax:** 212-209-2666
Web: www.jcrew.com

2002 Stores

	No.
California	23
New York	19
New Jersey	10
Pennsylvania	10
Illinois	9
Texas	9
Massachusetts	8
Florida	7
Michigan	7
Ohio	7
Virginia	7
Colorado	6
Connecticut	6
Georgia	6
Other states	60
Total	**194**

PRODUCTS/OPERATIONS

2003 Sales

	$ mil.	% of total
J. Crew Retail	408	53
J. Crew Direct	248	32
J. Crew Factory	76	10
Other	34	5
Total	**766**	**100**

COMPETITORS

Abercrombie & Fitch
American Eagle Outfitters
AnnTaylor
Benetton
Calvin Klein
Chadwick's of Boston
Coldwater Creek
Dillard's
Eddie Bauer
Federated
French Connection
Gap
Guess
Hartmarx
Intimate Brands
J. C. Penney
Lands' End
Lerner
Limited Brands
Liz Claiborne
L.L. Bean
Loehmann's
Marks & Spencer
May
Men's Wearhouse
Nautica Enterprises
Neiman Marcus
Nordstrom
Polo Ralph Lauren
Saks Inc.
Sears
Spiegel
Talbots
Target
Tommy Hilfiger

HISTORICAL FINANCIALS

Company Type: Private

Income Statement

FYE: Saturday nearest January 31

	REVENUE ($ mil.)	NET INCOME ($ mil.)	NET PROFIT MARGIN	EMPLOYEES
1/03	766	(41)	—	8,200
1/02	778	(11)	—	7,800
1/01	826	22	2.6%	7,600
1/00	717	(7)	—	8,400
1/99	824	(15)	—	8,900
1/98	834	(27)	—	6,200
1/97	809	13	1.5%	6,100
1/96	746	6	0.9%	5,600
1/95	738	15	2.0%	5,413
1/94	647	12	1.9%	4,479
Annual Growth	1.9%	—	—	7.0%

2003 Year-End Financials

Debt ratio: —
Return on equity: —
Cash ($ mil.): 19
Current ratio: 1.32
Long-term debt ($ mil.): 292

Net Income History

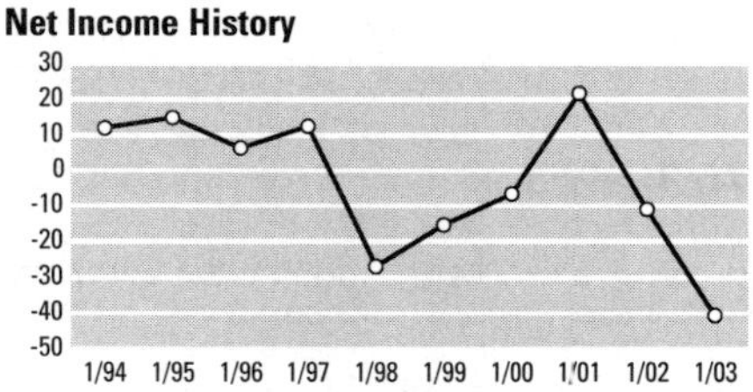

Jason Incorporated

Whether you're making the Sturgis run or just mowing your lawn, Jason Incorporated keeps your behind nice and comfy. The company's motor vehicle products segment has been the sole supplier of Harley-Davidson motorcycle seats for nearly 70 years, and it also makes seats for lawn care, construction, and agricultural equipment makers. The motor vehicle unit also makes fiber insulation for the automotive industry. The company's industrial products include power brushes, buffing wheels, and metal and wire components. Jason has been taken private by a management team headed by chairman Vincent Martin and CEO Mark Train (who together own about 40% of Jason).

Private equity firm Saw Mill Capital also has a stake in the company.

Co-founders Martin and Train concluded that high-tech stocks were drawing too much investor interest, and small cap manufacturing companies like Jason had little reason to remain public.

EXECUTIVES

Chairman: Vincent L. Martin, age 63
President and CEO: Mark Train
VP, Finance and Secretary: John Hengel
VP, Tax and Legal: Beth Klimczak
Controller: Scott Sannes

LOCATIONS

HQ: 411 E. Wisconsin Ave., Ste. 2120, Milwaukee, WI 53202
Phone: 414-277-9300 **Fax:** 414-277-9445
Web: www.jasoninc.com

Jason has operations in Brazil, Canada, China, Denmark, Germany, Mexico, Portugal, Romania, Sweden, Taiwan, the UK, and the US.

PRODUCTS/OPERATIONS

Selected Operations and Products

Industrial Products
JacksonLea (industrial buffing wheels and industrial buffing compound)
Jason Components Group (formed wire components, precision stamping)
Osborn International (industrial power brushes and maintenance brushes)

Motor Vehicle Products
Janesville Products (nonwoven fiber insulation for the automobile industry; moldable padding)
Milsco Manufacturing Co. (seating for motorcycles; agriculture, construction, and lawn/turf equipment)
Suroflex GmbH (acoustical insulation for the auto industry)

COMPETITORS

Carlisle Companies
Collins & Aikman
Foamex
Johnson Controls
Lear

HISTORICAL FINANCIALS

Company Type: Private

Income Statement FYE: Last Friday in December

	REVENUE ($ mil.)	NET INCOME ($ mil.)	NET PROFIT MARGIN	EMPLOYEES
12/02	450	—	—	3,000
12/01	450	—	—	3,000
12/00	450	—	—	3,400
12/99	424	—	—	3,600
12/98	391	—	—	3,250
12/97	481	—	—	3,111
12/96	443	—	—	3,099
12/95	407	—	—	2,790
12/94	357	—	—	2,953
12/93	235	—	—	2,140
Annual Growth	7.5%	—	—	3.8%

Revenue History

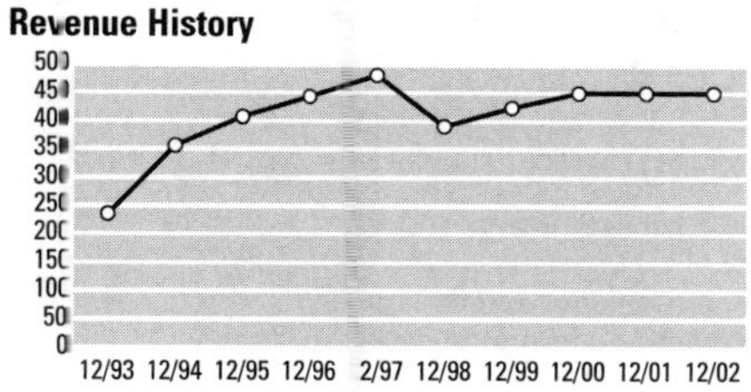

JELD-WEN, Inc.

JELD-WEN can improve your outlook — whether it's by providing new windows for your home, or by offering accommodations at a scenic resort. A leading maker of windows and doors, JELD-WEN owns more than 150 divisions in the Americas, Asia, and Europe. These divisions manufacture windows (Pozzi Wood Windows is part of JELD-WEN), interior and exterior doors, garage doors, door frames, moldings, and patio doors. JELD-WEN also sells time-shares at resorts such as Oregon's Eagle Crest and Running Y Ranch. Other interests include specialty wood products (including wood pellets used in fireplaces), real estate, marketing communications, and education. Chairman Richard Wendt and his siblings founded JELD-WEN in 1960.

JELD-WEN is bringing many of the products in its portfolio under the JELD-WEN brand. Products include wood, vinyl, and aluminum windows; wood and wood composite interior doors; and wood, steel, wood composite, and fiberglass exterior doors and entry systems.

EXECUTIVES

Chairman: Richard L. Wendt, age 72
Vice Chairman: Larry V. Wetter
President: Roderick C. (Rod) Wendt
CFO and Controller: Brent Cap
EVP: Robert Turner
SVP and Director: William Bernard Early
SVP: Douglas P. Kintzinger
VP Corporate Communications: Ted Abram
VP Marketing: Peter Dempsey
Treasurer: Karen Hoggarth
Director Human Resources: Eileen Harris

LOCATIONS

HQ: 401 Harbor Isles Blvd., Klamath Falls, OR 97601
Phone: 541-882-3451 **Fax:** 541-885-7454
Web: www.jeld-wen.com

JELD-WEN has divisions and companies in Argentina, Australia, Canada, Chile, France, Indonesia, Japan, Latvia, Lebanon, Malaysia, Morocco, Poland, Singapore, South Korea, Spain, Thailand, Turkey, the UK, and the US.

PRODUCTS/OPERATIONS

Selected Products

Doors
Exterior
Garage
Interior
Patio
Millwork
Columns
Posts
Spindles
Stair parts
Windows
Aluminum clad
Energy-efficient
Replacement
Wood

Resorts

Eagle Crest Resort (Oregon)
The Running Y Ranch Resort (Oregon)
Silver Mountain Ski Resort (Idaho)
Windmill Inns of America (Arizona, Oregon)

COMPETITORS

Andersen Corporation
Fairfield Resorts
Guardian Building Products
Lane Industries
Marshfield DoorSystems
Nortek
Owens Corning
Pella
Sierra Pacific Industries
Simonton Windows
Thermal Industries

HISTORICAL FINANCIALS

Company Type: Private

Income Statement FYE: December 31

	ESTIMATED REVENUE ($ mil.)	NET INCOME ($ mil.)	NET PROFIT MARGIN	EMPLOYEES
12/02	2,000	—	—	20,000
12/01	2,040	—	—	20,000
12/00	2,000	—	—	20,000
12/99	2,000	—	—	15,000
12/98	1,500	—	—	11,000
12/97	1,400	—	—	10,400
12/96	850	—	—	7,100
12/95	750	—	—	7,050
12/94	800	—	—	7,650
Annual Growth	12.1%	—	—	12.8%

Revenue History

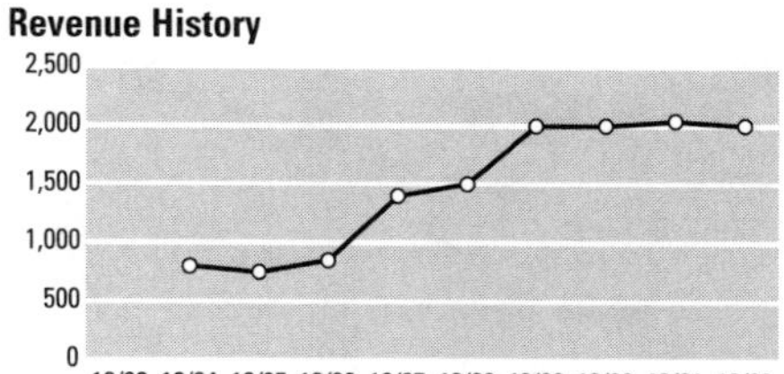

Jetro Cash & Carry Enterprises

Jetro Cash & Carry Enterprises serves up groceries, beverages, and tobacco products on the cheap to independent grocery stores and foodservice operators in California, Florida, Illinois, and the Northeast. The wholesaler operates 14 cash-and-carry warehouses stocking fresh meat, frozen foods, dry goods, and other items, many under the Red & White private label; it also provides support services. Jetro's Restaurant Depot unit (sort of a wholesale Home Depot for restaurateurs, caterers, and bar owners) sells groceries, cooking and serving equipment, and janitorial supplies online and from some 25 locations across the US. Jetro also has an export business serving the Caribbean. Founded in 1976, Jetro is owned by private investors.

EXECUTIVES

President and CEO: Stanley Fleishman
CFO: Bryan Emmert
Director of Human Resources: Stuart Kipilman

LOCATIONS

HQ: 15-24 132nd St., College Point, NY 11356
Phone: 718-762-8700 **Fax:** 718-661-9627
Web: www.jetro.com

2002 Jetro Stores

	No.
California	5
New York	4
Florida	1
Illinois	1
Maryland	1
New Jersey	1
Pennsylvania	1
Total	**14**

PRODUCTS/OPERATIONS

Selected Products

Automotive supplies
Baking ingredients
Beverages
Cleaning supplies
Condiments and dressings
Disposable products
Dry groceries
First-aid products
Food storage containers and wraps
Fresh meats
Frozen foods
Guest checks
Hardware
Health and beauty care products
Menu boards
Refrigerated foods
Restaurant supplies
School supplies
Seasonal products
Specialty foods
Tobacco products

COMPETITORS

Associated Wholesalers
C&S Wholesale
Cigarettes Cheaper
Costco Wholesale
Di Giorgio
Fleming Packaging
Gristede's Foods
Key Food
Krasdale Foods
Performance Food
SAM'S CLUB
Smart & Final
SUPERVALU
SYSCO
Wakefern Food

HISTORICAL FINANCIALS

Company Type: Private

Income Statement FYE: December 31

	ESTIMATED REVENUE ($ mil.)	NET INCOME ($ mil.)	NET PROFIT MARGIN	EMPLOYEES
12/01	430	—	—	1,000
12/00	420	—	—	1,000
12/99	415	—	—	1,000
12/98	420	—	—	1,000
12/97	420	—	—	1,000
12/96	360	—	—	1,000
Annual Growth	3.6%	—	—	0.0%

Revenue History

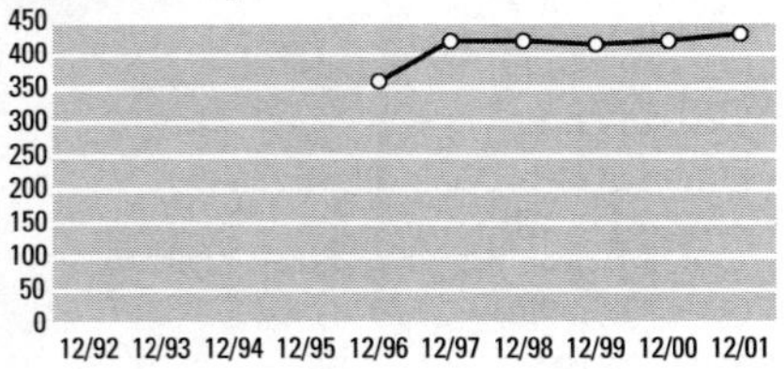

J.F. Shea Co., Inc.

J.F. Shea helped construct the Washington, DC, subway system, the Golden Gate Bridge, and the Hoover Dam, and now it wants to build your house. Its Shea Homes division builds single-family houses and planned communities. Flagship unit J.F. Shea Construction is involved in commercial and civil engineering projects and offers design/build services. The group's Heavy Civil Engineering division works on underground projects, including dams and tunnels, and its Redding division produces gravel, asphalt, and concrete products. Other interests include real estate property management, electrical contracting, and concrete guns and pumps. Founded as a plumbing company in 1876, J.F. Shea is still owned by the Shea family.

EXECUTIVES

President: John F. Shea
COO: Peter O. Shea Jr.
CFO and Secretary: James G. Shontere
VP; President, J.F. Shea Construction: Peter O. Shea
VP: Edmund H. Shea Jr.
VP Taxes: Ron Lakey
President, Shea Homes: Bert Selva

LOCATIONS

HQ: 655 Brea Canyon Rd., Walnut, CA 91789
Phone: 909-594-9500 **Fax:** 909-594-0935
Web: www.jfshea.com

PRODUCTS/OPERATIONS

Major Units

J.F. Shea Construction, Inc. (commercial buildings, subways, and civil engineering projects)
J.F. Shea Heavy Civil Engineering (bridges, tunnels, and transit systems)
Redding Construction (sand, gravel, asphalt, and concrete products; highway construction)
Reed Manufacturing (concrete guns and pumps and concrete-placing equipment)
Shasta Electric, Inc. (full-service electrical contractor for commercial and industrial projects)
Shea Homes (residential units, developed and master-planned communities)
Shea Mortgage (mortgage lender)
Shea Properties (apartment and industrial and commercial building management)
Venture Capital (investment firm)

COMPETITORS

Austin Industries
Bechtel
Black & Veatch
Centex
Del Webb
Dick Corporation
D.R. Horton
Granite Construction
Hyundai Engineering and Construction
Kajima Engineering and Construction
KB Home
Lennar
M.D.C. Holdings
Parsons
Peter Kiewit Sons'
Pulte Homes
Ryland
Shapell Industries
Standard Pacific
Tutor-Saliba
Washington Group

HISTORICAL FINANCIALS

Company Type: Private

Income Statement FYE: December 31

	REVENUE ($ mil.)	NET INCOME ($ mil.)	NET PROFIT MARGIN	EMPLOYEES
12/01	1,968	—	—	2,288
12/00	1,863	—	—	2,200
12/99	1,794	—	—	2,100
12/98	1,621	—	—	2,000
12/97	1,001	—	—	1,420
12/96	957	—	—	1,200
12/95	687	—	—	1,100
Annual Growth	19.2%	—	—	13.0%

Revenue History

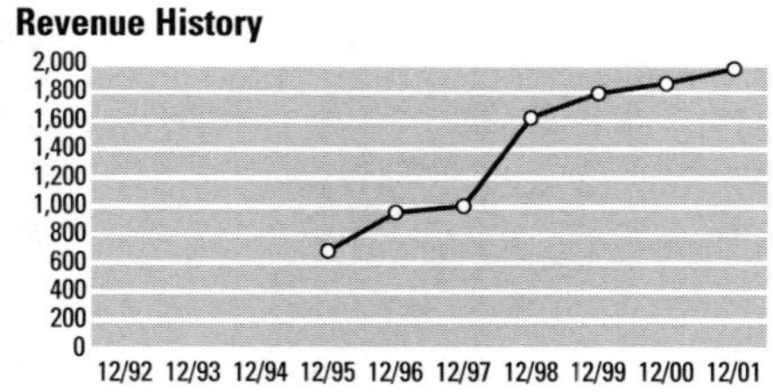

Jim Koons Automotive

Wheelin' and dealin' on the Web, Jim Koons Automotive Companies sells new and used cars the old-fashioned way and through the Internet. Its 18 locations in the Washington, DC, area (Virginia and Maryland) offer cars made by DaimlerChrysler, Ford, GM, Mazda, Toyota, and Volvo. Three locations specialize in used cars. Internet customers can obtain quotes, make appointments for parts and service, and access online coupons for oil changes and other services. CEO Jim Koons' father, John Koons Sr., the first auto dealer to enter the Automotive Hall of Fame, founded the company in 1964. The Koons family owns the company.

EXECUTIVES

CEO: James E. Koons
VP: Jim O'Connell
Corporate Controller: Ed Waugh
Systems Administrator: Robert Webb

LOCATIONS

HQ: Jim Koons Automotive Companies, Inc.
2000 Chain Bridge Rd., Vienna, VA 22182
Phone: 703-356-0400 **Fax:** 703-442-5765
Web: www.koons.com

COMPETITORS

Atlantic Automotive
Brown Automotive
Darcars
March/Hodge
Ourisman Automotive
Rosenthal Automotive

HISTORICAL FINANCIALS

Company Type: Private

Income Statement FYE: December 31

	ESTIMATED REVENUE ($ mil.)	NET INCOME ($ mil.)	NET PROFIT MARGIN	EMPLOYEES
12/01	993	—	—	1,400
12/00	941	—	—	1,400
12/99	800	—	—	1,300
12/98	650	—	—	1,200
12/97	550	—	—	1,200
12/96	550	—	—	1,200
12/95	565	—	—	1,200
12/94	560	—	—	1,100
12/93	500	—	—	1,300
Annual Growth	8.9%	—	—	0.9%

Revenue History

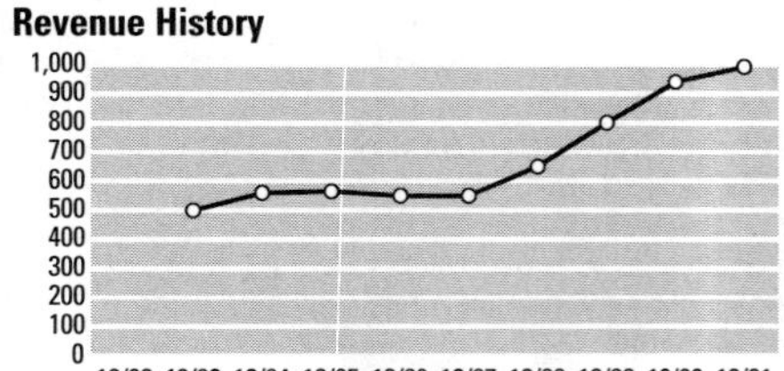

J. L. French Automotive Castings, Inc.

With a cast of customers like GM, Ford, Delphi, and Visteon, J. L. French Automotive Castings is sure to get rave reviews. The company provides automotive OEMs and Tier 1 suppliers with aluminum die cast engine and drivetrain components such as cam covers, oil pans, front engine covers, transmission cases, and timing chain covers. J. L. French supplies components for more than 20 Ford models (including top sellers like the F-Series pickup, Explorer, and Taurus), and also makes a number of parts for GM's Chevrolet S-10 trucks. Controlling shareholder Onex Corporation will continue to control J. L. French after its planned public offering.

EXECUTIVES

Chairman: Scott D. Rued, age 46
President, CEO, and Director: David S. Hoyte, age 55, $587,629 pay
EVP and CTO: Charles M. Waldon, age 53, $471,968 pay
Interim CFO and Director: Anthony Barone, age 53
General Manager, Ansola: Juan Manuel Orbea, age 50
Managing Director of Michigan Operations: Steven Moore
Managing Director of Wisconsin Operations: William J. Miller, $308,595 pay
Auditors: Deloitte & Touche

LOCATIONS

HQ: 4508 IDS Center, Minneapolis, MN 55402
Phone: 612-332-2335 **Fax:** 612-332-2012
Web: www.jlfrench.com

J.L. French Automotive Castings has production facilities in Kentucky, Michigan, and Wisconsin in the US, as well as in Mexico, Spain, and the UK.

2002 Sales by Origin

	$ mil.	% of total
US	443.3	81
UK	78.2	14
Spain	23.9	4
Mexico	5.0	1
Total	**550.4**	**100**

PRODUCTS/OPERATIONS

2002 Sales

	$ mil.	% of total
Medium to large aluminum castings		
Oil pans	174.7	32
Transmission cases	73.7	13
Engine front covers	54.3	10
Bedplates	48.0	9
Other medium to large castings	113.2	20
Small aluminum castings	81.3	15
Other products	5.2	1
Total	**550.4**	**100**

COMPETITORS

Atchison Casting
Citation
Grede Foundries
INTERMET

HISTORICAL FINANCIALS

Company Type: Private

Income Statement FYE: December 31

	REVENUE ($ mil.)	NET INCOME ($ mil.)	NET PROFIT MARGIN	EMPLOYEES
12/02	550	(272)	—	3,297
12/01	506	(7)	—	3,599
12/00	557	(10)	—	—
12/99	352	(14)	—	—
Annual Growth	16.1%	—	—	(8.4%)

2002 Year-End Financials

Debt ratio: —
Return on equity: —
Cash ($ mil.): 3
Current ratio: 1.02
Long-term debt ($ mil.): 398

Net Income History

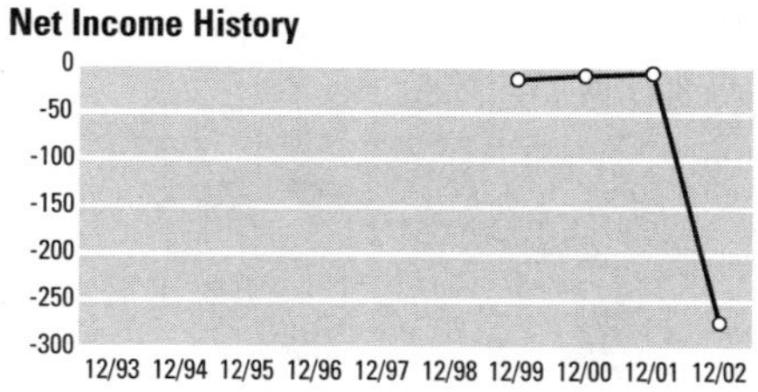

JM Family Enterprises, Inc.

Founder and honorary chairman Jim Moran and chairman Pat Moran (Jim's daughter) make JM Family Enterprises a family affair. JM, owned by the Moran family, is a holding company (Florida's second-largest private company, in fact, after Publix Super Markets) with about a dozen automotive-related businesses, including the nation's largest-volume Lexus retailer, JM Lexus, in Margate, Florida. JM's major subsidiary, Southeast Toyota Distributors, is the nation's largest Toyota distribution franchise, delivering Toyota cars, trucks, and SUVs to more than 160 dealers in Alabama, Florida, Georgia, and North and South Carolina.

Among JM Family's other subsidiaries, JM&A Group provides insurance and warranty services to retailers nationwide. World Omni Financial handles leasing, dealer financing, and other financial services for US auto dealers.

JM Family Enterprises is the largest woman-owned company in the US.

HISTORY

Jim Moran first became visible as "Jim Moran, the Courtesy Man" in Chicago TV advertisements in the 1950s. At that time he ran Courtesy Motors, where he was so successful as the world's #1 Ford dealer that *Time* magazine put his picture on its cover in 1961.

Moran had entered the auto sales business after fixing up and selling a car for more than three times the price he had paid for it. That profit was much better than what he made at the Sinclair gas station he had bought, so he opened a used-car lot. Later, he moved to new-car sales when he bought a Hudson franchise (Ford had rejected him).

Seeing the promise of TV advertising, in 1948 Moran pioneered the forum for Chicago car dealers, not only as an advertiser and program sponsor but also as host of a variety show and a country/western music barn dance. The increased visibility positioned Moran as Hudson's #1 dealer, but the sales tactics at Courtesy Motors earned an antitrust suit that was settled out of court.

In 1955 Moran started with Ford and, with his TV influence as host of *The Jim Moran Courtesy Hour,* he became the world's #1 Ford dealer in his first month.

He moved to Florida in 1966 after being diagnosed with cancer and given one year to live. Successfully fighting the disease, he bought a Pontiac franchise and later started Southeast Toyota Distributors. In 1969 he formed JM Family Enterprises.

Legal problems cropped up in 1973 when the IRS investigated a Nassau bank serving as a tax haven for wealthy Americans. Moran and three Toyota executives were linked to the bank, and in 1978 Moran was indicted for tax fraud. When an immunity deal fell through, Moran pleaded guilty to seven tax fraud charges in 1984 and was sentenced to two years (suspended), fined more than $12 million, and ordered to perform community service. Moran's legal problems threatened his association with Toyota and were blamed for causing his stroke in 1983.

JM's legal problems continued in the 1980s, partly because of the imposition of auto import restrictions. To get more cars to sell, some Southeast Toyota managers encouraged auto dealers to file false sales reports. Some North Carolina dealers resisted and one sued, settling out of court for $22 million. Other dealers alleged racketeering and fraud on the part of Southeast Toyota, and by the beginning of 1994, JM had paid more than $100 million in fines and settlements for cases stretching back to 1988. In spite of that, Toyota renewed its contract with the company in 1993, a year ahead of schedule.

Pat Moran succeeded her father as JM president in 1992. Between 1991 and 1994 three suits were filed against Jim and Southeast Toyota alleging racism against blacks in establishing Toyota dealerships. All three suits were settled.

Jim teamed with Wayne Huizenga in 1996 to launch a national chain of used-car megastores under the name AutoNation USA, which Jim expected would draw buyers to his own auto dealerships. (AutoNation USA's first store was built just two blocks from JM's Coconut Creek Lexus Dealership.) Jim's interest in AutoNation USA was converted into a small percentage (less than 5%) of Republic Industries stock after Huizenga merged AutoNation into waste hauler Republic Industries (now called AutoNation) in 1997.

In late 1998 JM embarked on a national strategy to expand its presence outside the Southeast, establishing an office in St. Louis that handles indirect consumer leasing.

In 2000 Jim became honorary chairman while Pat was given the chairman position and continued as CEO; COO Colin Brown was named president. Also that year the company was named the 51st Best Company to Work For in the United States by *Fortune* magazine. The company's rank in the Best Company to Work For list rose to 20th place in 2001.

In March 2003 Brown assumed the CEO title while Pat Moran continues as chairman.

EXECUTIVES

Honorary Chairman: James (Jim) M. Moran
Chairman: Patricia (Pat) Moran
President and CEO: Colin Brown, age 53
EVP: Louis Feagles
EVP and CFO: Corliss J. (Corky) Nelson
EVP and CIO: Scott Barrett
EVP, Human Resources: Gary L. Thomas
SVP: Jan Moran
Group VP, Corporate Communications: Tony Stromberg
VP: Larry McGinnes
VP, Community Relations: Rick Noland
VP, Corporate Communications: Lisa Kitei
VP, Government Relations: Kienan Moylan
VP, Human Resources: John Heins
VP, Human Resources Operations: Bruce Koeser
VP, Technology Delivery: Ken Yerves
VP, Sales and Strategic Alliances, JM&A Group: Mike Casey
Director, Corporate Safety: Claude Revels
Director, Corporate Security: Roger Robbins
Assistant VP and Chief Division Counsel: Caren Snead Williams

LOCATIONS

HQ: 100 Jim Moran Blvd., Deerfield Beach, FL 33442
Phone: 954-429-2000 **Fax:** 954-429-2300
Web: www.jmfamily.com

JM Family Enterprises operates auto retail, distribution, leasing, and financing businesses across the US, mainly in Alabama, Florida, Georgia, and North and South Carolina.

PRODUCTS/OPERATIONS

Selected Subsidiaries

Finance and Leasing
World Omni Financial Corp.
Centerone Financial Services

Insurance, Marketing, Consulting, and Related Companies
Fidelity Insurance Agency, Inc.
JM&A Group (auto service contracts, insurance)
Courtesy Administrative Services, Inc.
Courtesy Insurance Co.
Fidelity Insurance Agency, Inc.
Fidelity Warranty Services, Inc.
Jim Moran & Associates
J.M.I.C. Life Insurance Co.

Retail Car Sales
JM Lexus

Vehicle Processing and Distribution
SET Inland Processing
SET Parts Supply and Distribution
SET Port Processing
Southeast Toyota Distributors, LLC

COMPETITORS

CarMax
Gulf States Toyota
Hendrick Automotive
Holman Enterprises
Island Lincoln-Mercury
Morse Operations
United Auto Group

HISTORICAL FINANCIALS

Company Type: Private

Income Statement FYE: December 31

	REVENUE ($ mil.)	NET INCOME ($ mil.)	NET PROFIT MARGIN	EMPLOYEES
12/02	7,600	—	—	3,500
12/01	7,800	—	—	3,227
12/00	7,100	—	—	3,400
12/99	6,600	—	—	3,304
12/98	6,200	—	—	3,000
12/97	5,400	—	—	2,900
12/96	5,100	—	—	3,000
12/95	4,500	—	—	2,000
12/94	4,200	—	—	2,000
12/93	3,500	—	—	2,300
Annual Growth	9.0%	—	—	4.8%

Revenue History

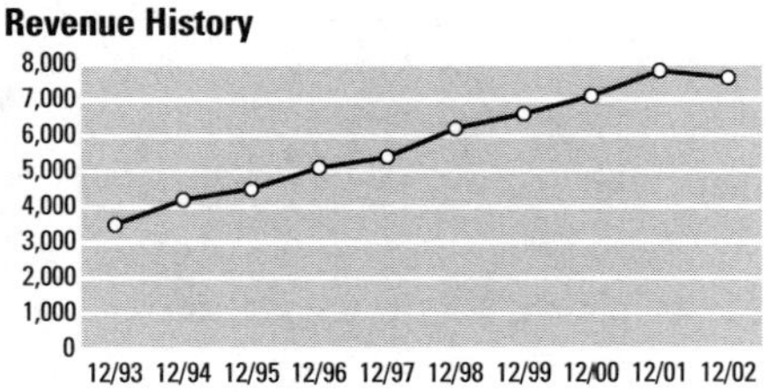

J. M. Huber Corporation

Toothpaste, paint, and tires — J. M. Huber claims to make them even better. Founded in 1883 by Joseph Maria Huber (and still owned by his heirs), the company makes specialty additives and minerals used to thicken and improve the cleaning properties of toothpaste, the brightness and gloss of paper, the strength and durability of rubber, and the flame retardant properties of wire and cable. The diverse company also makes oriented strand board (a plywood substitute). Huber manages a half-million acres of timberland in Maine and the southeastern US, and explores for and produces oil and gas in Texas, Colorado, Wyoming, and Utah.

EXECUTIVES

Chairman, President, and CEO: Peter T. Francis
Director, Corporate Communication: Robert Currie
Manager, Human Resources: Gary Crowell
Manager, Market Development, Sales and Product Management: Dianne Leipold

LOCATIONS

HQ: 333 Thornall St., Edison, NJ 08837
Phone: 732-549-8600 **Fax:** 732-549-2239
Web: www.huber.com

J. M. Huber Corporation has operations in Belgium, Canada, Denmark, Finland, France, India, Portugal, Sweden, and the US.

PRODUCTS/OPERATIONS

Selected Operations

Huber Energy (oil and gas acquisition, exploration, and production)
Huber Engineered Materials (engineered minerals and specialty chemicals)
Huber Engineered Woods (high-performance specialty woods, including oriented strand board)
Huber Timber (500,000 acres of timber)
JMH Financial Services (treasury services)
Noviant (carboxymethl cellulose)

COMPETITORS

Baker Hughes
Boise Cascade
Cabot
Georgia-Pacific Corporation
Marathon Oil
Minerals Technologies
Occidental Petroleum

HISTORICAL FINANCIALS

Company Type: Private

Income Statement FYE: December 31

	ESTIMATED REVENUE ($ mil.)	NET INCOME ($ mil.)	NET PROFIT MARGIN	EMPLOYEES
12/02	1,122	—	—	3,003
12/01	1,700	—	—	5,000
12/00	1,022	—	—	2,880
12/99	855	—	—	2,699
12/98	1,500	—	—	5,000
12/97	1,500	—	—	5,150
12/96	1,400	—	—	5,000
12/95	1,300	—	—	5,100
12/94	1,300	—	—	5,163
12/93	1,200	—	—	—
Annual Growth	(0.7%)	—	—	(6.5%)

Revenue History

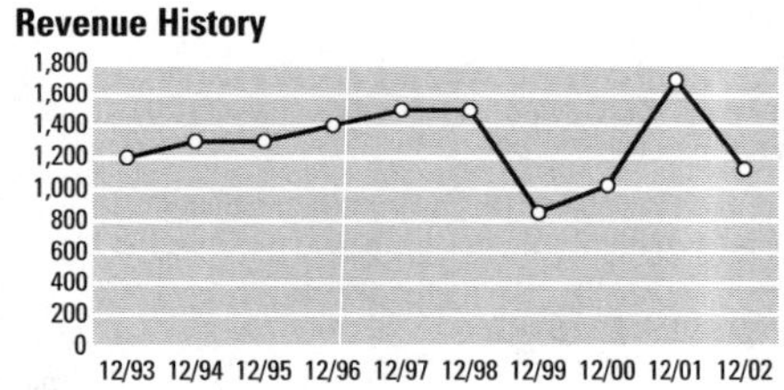

JMB Realty Corporation

JMB wants to make State Street a great street again and bring glitter back to the Steel City's Golden Triangle. A major US commercial real estate investment firm, JMB Realty owns, develops, and manages real estate projects throughout North America, including regional malls, hotels, planned communities, and office complexes. JMB is heavily involved in ambitious retail developments in Chicago's Loop and downtown Pittsburgh. JMB was founded in 1968 by Robert Judelson, Judd Malkin, and Neil Bluhm; Judelson (the "J" of JMB) is no longer involved with JMB, but Malkin remains as chairman and Bluhm is president.

EXECUTIVES

Chairman: Judd D. Malkin, age 64
President: Neil G. Bluhm
COO: Rigel Barber
CFO: Steve Lovelett
EVP Legal: Gary Nickele
VP Human Resources: Gail Silver
VP Marketing and Sales: Cindy Bodhe
Auditors: KPMG LLP

LOCATIONS

HQ: 900 N. Michigan Ave., Ste. 1100, Chicago, IL 60611
Phone: 312-440-4800 **Fax:** 312-915-2310

COMPETITORS

AXA Financial
DeBartolo
Helmsley
Inland Group
Lefrak Organization
Lincoln Property
Rouse
Tishman Realty
Trammell Crow

HISTORICAL FINANCIALS

Company Type: Private

Income Statement FYE: December 31

	ESTIMATED REVENUE ($ mil.)	NET INCOME ($ mil.)	NET PROFIT MARGIN	EMPLOYEES
12/01	1,000	—	—	—
12/00	1,000	—	—	—
12/99	1,000	—	—	—
12/98	1,000	—	—	—
12/97	1,000	—	—	—
12/96	1,000	—	—	—
12/95	1,000	—	—	—
12/94	1,100	—	—	—
12/93	975	—	—	—
Annual Growth	0.3%	—	—	—

Revenue History

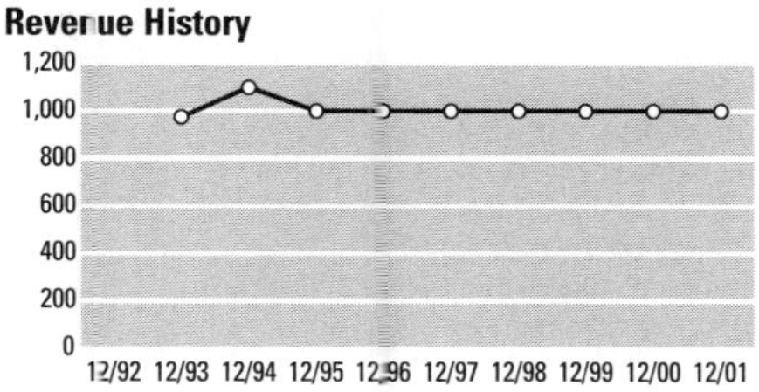

Jockey International

Jockey International has nothing to do with horses and everything to do with the classic men's brief (its invention). The firm makes men's, women's, and children's underwear and loungewear, sold through some 14,000 department and specialty stores. It licenses and distributes its products in more than 120 countries. Jockey International also holds licensing agreements. Chairman and CEO Debra Waller and her family own the company. Jockey International was founded in 1876 as a hosiery company intended to relieve lumberjacks of blisters and infections resulting from shoddy wool socks.

EXECUTIVES

Chairman and CEO: Debra Waller
President and COO: Edward C. (Ed) Emma
SVP, CFO, CIO: Frank Schneider
EVP, Jockey Brand Merchandising and Sales: John Brody
SVP, Customer Logistics: Edward (Ed) Gill
SVP, Jockey Brand Merchandising: Jim Noble
SVP, Manufacturing and Distribution: Brad Beal
VP, General Counsel, and Corporate Secretary: Mark Jaeger
VP, Human Resources: Michael (Mike) McDermott
VP, Marketing and Advertising: Jamie Lockard

LOCATIONS

HQ: Jockey International, Inc.
2300 60th St., Kenosha, WI 53141
Phone: 262-658-8111 **Fax:** 262-658-1812
Web: www.jockey.com

COMPETITORS

Calvin Klein
Danskin
Delta Galil Industries Ltd.
Fruit of the Loom
Maidenform
Sara Lee Branded
Victoria's Secret Stores
Warnaco Group

HISTORICAL FINANCIALS

Company Type: Private

Income Statement FYE: December 31

	ESTIMATED REVENUE ($ mil.)	NET INCOME ($ mil.)	NET PROFIT MARGIN	EMPLOYEES
12/01	550	—	—	5,000
12/00	600	—	—	5,000
12/99	600	—	—	5,400
12/98	545	—	—	5,400
12/97	525	—	—	5,400
12/96	500	—	—	5,200
12/95	450	—	—	4,500
12/94	425	—	—	5,000
12/93	450	—	—	—
Annual Growth	2.5%	—	—	0.0%

Revenue History

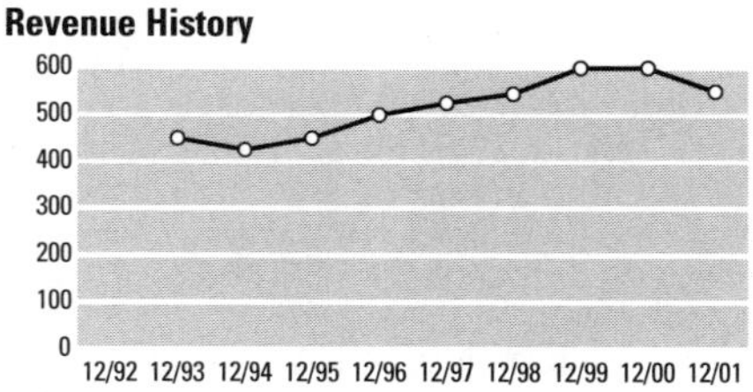

John Paul Mitchell Systems

From pomades to pompadours, John Paul Mitchell Systems does 'dos. The #1 privately owned hair care firm in the US makes more than 90 different hair care products that sell in about 100,000 hair salons worldwide. John Paul Mitchell was founded in Hawaii in 1980 by John Paul "J. P." DeJoria and the late Paul Mitchell. The company's signature white bottles with distinctive black lettering have attracted the attention of counterfeiters on more than one occasion. Chairman and CEO DeJoria, a former gang member who sports a black ponytail and beard (and is seen in company TV commercials), is a vocal supporter for consumer-product safety.

EXECUTIVES

Chairman and CEO: John Paul (J. P.) DeJoria
COO and Human Resources: Luke Jacobellis
VP Advertising and Public Relations: Nanette Bercu
VP Finance: Rick Battaglini

LOCATIONS

HQ: 9701 Wilshire Blvd., Ste. 1205,
Beverly Hills, CA 90212
Phone: 310-248-3888 **Fax:** 310-248-2780
Web: www.paulmitchell.com

COMPETITORS

Alberto-Culver
L'Oréal
Nexxus Products
SoftSheen/Carson
Stephan
Unilever
Wella

HISTORICAL FINANCIALS

Company Type: Private

Income Statement FYE: December 31

	ESTIMATED REVENUE ($ mil.)	NET INCOME ($ mil.)	NET PROFIT MARGIN	EMPLOYEES
12/01	600	—	—	100
12/00	600	—	—	100
12/99	600	—	—	97
12/98	200	—	—	110
12/97	185	—	—	100
12/96	165	—	—	89
Annual Growth	29.5%	—	—	2.4%

Revenue History

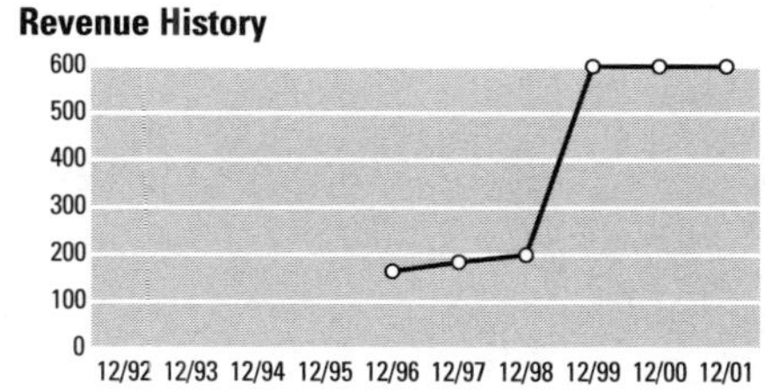

John Wieland Homes

John Wieland Homes & Neighborhoods (JW) develops land and builds cluster homes, townhomes, and more than 100 different types of upscale single-family homes in the Southeast US (in the metropolitan areas of Atlanta, Charleston, Charlotte, Raleigh, and Nashville). The company also provides remodeling and landscaping services. In cities where it builds, JW operates New Home Center design centers that provide interior and exterior design services. Wieland Financial Services offers mortgage lending to JW customers and others. CEO John Wieland owns the firm, which he founded in 1970.

EXECUTIVES

Chairman and CEO: John Wieland
President: Terry Russell
CFO: Doug Ray
EVP and General Counsel: Richard Bacon
SVP: John B. Gillespie
VP Construction: Dave Groff
VP Human Resources: John Wood
Secretary: Susan W. Wieland
Auditors: Birnbrey, Minsk & Minsk

LOCATIONS

HQ: John Wieland Homes & Neighborhoods, Inc.
1950 Sullivan Rd., Atlanta, GA 30337
Phone: 770-996-2400 **Fax:** 770-907-3481
Web: www.jwhomes.com

COMPETITORS

Beazer Homes
Centex
Del Webb
D.R. Horton
Engle Homes
M/I Schottenstein Homes
NVR
Oriole Homes
Pulte Homes

HISTORICAL FINANCIALS

Company Type: Private

Income Statement FYE: September 30

	ESTIMATED REVENUE ($ mil.)	NET INCOME ($ mil.)	NET PROFIT MARGIN	EMPLOYEES
9/02	500	—	—	900
9/01	502	—	—	900
Annual Growth	(0.4%)	—	—	0.0%

Revenue History

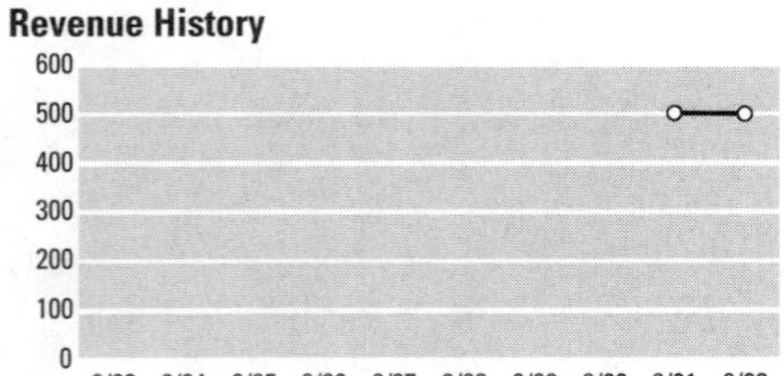

Johnson Publishing

Snubbed by advertisers when he founded his company 60 years ago, John Johnson has pushed his magazine company to the front of the pack. Led by its flagship publication, *Ebony,* family-owned Johnson Publishing Company is the largest black-owned publishing firm in the country. It also publishes *Jet* and operates a book division. In addition, Johnson Publishing produces a line of hair care products (Supreme Beauty) and cosmetics (Fashion Fair) marketed for African-American women, and each year it hosts the Ebony Fashion Fair, a traveling fashion show that raises money for scholarships and charities in cities across the US and Canada.

The company's book division features titles such as *The New Ebony Cookbook* and the more controversial *Forced Into Glory: Abraham Lincoln's White Dream.*

Johnson Publishing is owned and controlled by founder and chairman Johnson and his family. Johnson's daughter, Linda Johnson Rice, handles the day-to-day operations as president and CEO. His wife, Eunice, produces the Ebony Fashion Fair.

HISTORY

John H. Johnson launched his publishing business in 1942 while he was still in college in Chicago. The idea for a black-oriented magazine came to him while he was working part-time for Supreme Life Insurance Co. of America, where one of his jobs was to clip magazine and newspaper articles about the black community. Johnson used his mother's furniture as collateral to secure a $500 loan and then mailed $2 charter subscription offers to potential subscribers. He received 3,000 replies and used the $6,000 to print the first issue of *Negro Digest,* patterned after *Reader's Digest.* Circulation was 50,000 within a year.

Johnson started *Ebony* magazine in 1945 (which gained immediate popularity and is still the company's premier publication) and launched *Jet* in 1951, a pocket-sized publication containing news items and features. In the early days Johnson was unable to obtain advertising, so he formed his own Beauty Star mail-order business and advertised its products (dresses, wigs, hair care products, and vitamins) in his magazines. He won his first major account, Zenith Radio, in 1947; Johnson landed Chrysler in 1954, only after sending a salesman to Detroit every week for 10 years. For 20 years, *Ebony* and *Jet* were the only national publications targeting blacks in the US.

By the 1960s Johnson had become one of the most prominent black men in the US. He posed with John F. Kennedy in 1963 to publicize a special issue of *Ebony* celebrating the Emancipation Proclamation. US magazine publishers named him Publisher of the Year in 1972. Johnson launched *Ebony Jr!* (since discontinued) in 1973, a magazine designed to provide "positive black images" for black preteens. His first magazine, *Negro Digest* (renamed *Black World*), became known for its provocative articles, but its circulation dwindled from 100,000 to 15,000. Johnson retired the magazine in 1975.

Unable to find the proper makeup for his *Ebony* models, Johnson founded his own cosmetics business, Fashion Fair Cosmetics, that year, which carved out a niche beside Revlon (which introduced cosmetic lines for blacks) and another black cosmetics company, Johnson Products (unrelated) of Chicago. By 1982 Fashion Fair sales were more than $30 million.

The company got into broadcasting in 1972 when it bought Chicago radio station WGRT (renamed WJPC; that city's first black-owned station). It added WLOU (Louisville, Kentucky) in 1982 and WLNR (Lansing, Illinois; re-launched in 1991 as WJPC-FM) in 1985. By 1995, however, it had sold all of its stations.

Johnson and the company sold their controlling interest in the last minority-owned insurance company in Illinois (and Johnson's first employer), Supreme Life Insurance, to Unitrin (a Chicago-based life, health, and property insurer) in 1991. That year the company and catalog retailer Spiegel announced a joint venture to develop fashions for black women. The two companies launched a mail-order catalog called *E Style* in 1993 and an accompanying credit card the next year.

Johnson Publishing launched its South African edition of *Ebony* in 1995. Johnson was awarded the Presidential Medal of Freedom in 1996. The next year, however, circulation of *Ebony* fell 7% as mainstream magazines began covering black issues more thoroughly and a host of new titles appeared. In response, the company restructured its ventures and closed its *E Style* catalog. Johnson Publishing retired *Ebony Man* (launched in 1985) in 1998 and *Ebony South Africa* in 2000.

In 2002 John Johnson named his daughter Linda Johnson Rice as CEO of the company; Johnson remains as chairman and publisher.

EXECUTIVES

Chairman and Publisher: John H. Johnson, age 84
President and CEO: Linda Johnson Rice, age 45
Secretary and Treasurer; Producer and Director, EBONY Fashion Fair: Eunice W. Johnson
Executive Editor, EBONY Magazine: Lerone Bennett Jr.
SVP and General Counsel: June Acie Rhinehart
SVP Associate Publisher, Advertising: Jeff Burns Jr.
SVP, Fashion Fair Cosmetics: J. Lance Clark
VP and Associate Counsel: Christopher D. Benson
VP and Director of Promotions: Lydia J. Davis Eady
VP Finance: Treka Owens
Director of Circulation: Kenneth C. Brooks
Telecommunications Manager: Sheila Jenkins
Purchasing Manager: Ruth Wagner
Director Personnel: LaDoris Foster

LOCATIONS

HQ: Johnson Publishing Company, Inc.
820 S. Michigan Ave., Chicago, IL 60605
Phone: 312-322-9200 **Fax:** 312-322-0918
Web: www.ebony.com

PRODUCTS/OPERATIONS

Selected Operations

Fashion and Beauty Aids
Ebony Fashion Fair (traveling fashion show)
Fashion Fair Cosmetics (color cosmetics, fragrances, skincare)
Supreme Beauty Products (hair care)

Publishing
Books
Forced Into Glory: Abraham Lincoln's White Dream by Lerone Bennett Jr.
The New Ebony Cookbook by Charlotte Lyons
Magazines
Ebony
Jet

COMPETITORS

Advance Publications
Alberto-Culver
Avon
BET
Earl G. Graves
Essence Communications
Estée Lauder
Forbes
Hearst Magazines
LFP
L'Oréal
Mary Kay
Revlon
Time
Vanguarde Media

HISTORICAL FINANCIALS

Company Type: Private

Income Statement FYE: December 31

	REVENUE ($ mil.)	NET INCOME ($ mil.)	NET PROFIT MARGIN	EMPLOYEES
12/01	412	—	—	2,594
12/00	400	—	—	2,614
12/99	387	—	—	2,657
12/98	372	—	—	2,647
12/97	361	—	—	2,677
12/96	326	—	—	2,702
12/95	316	—	—	2,680
12/94	307	—	—	2,662
12/93	294	—	—	2,600
12/92	274	—	—	2,785
Annual Growth	4.6%	—	—	(0.8%)

Revenue History

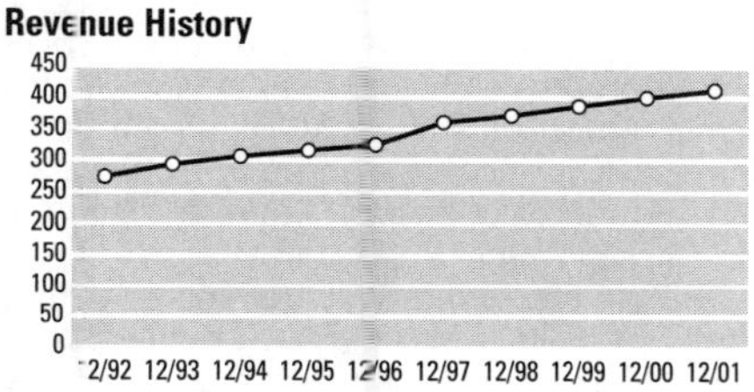

JohnsonDiversey

JohnsonDiversey is the industrial-strength version of S.C. Johnson & Son. Split off from the well-known private company in 1999, JohnsonDiversey consists of two units: Professional and Polymer. Professional provides commercial cleaning, hygiene, pest control, and food sanitation products to retailers, building service contractors, hospitality firms, and food service operators. Polymer produces acrylic resins used in printing, packaging, coatings, and adhesives. The Johnson family controls two-thirds of the company; Unilever controls the rest. The firm changed its name from S.C. Johnson Commercial Markets to JohnsonDiversey in 2002 after acquiring DiverseyLever, Unilever's industrial cleaning business.

The acquisition of DiverseyLever more than doubled the company's sales and made it the #2 industrial and institutional cleaning products firm, behind Ecolab, with a 13% market share. As part of the deal, the company took on considerable debt. JohnsonDiversey has an option to buy out Unilever's stake by 2007.

The company's cleaning products customers include ARAMARK, The Coca-Cola Company, McDonald's, and Wal-Mart; its polymer customers include ink makers Flint Ink and Sun Chemical.

JohnsonDiversey dates back to the 1930s, when S.C. Johnson became involved in commercial sales of cleaning products.

In April 2003 JohnsonDiversey created a SARS Control Center on its Web site in reaction to the worldwide spread of Severe Acute Respiratory Syndrome. The company uses the site to promote its own industrial sanitation products, especially its Virex and Forward lines of disinfectants, as potential weapons in the fight against SARS.

EXECUTIVES

Chairman: Samuel Curtis (Curt) Johnson III, age 47, $1,627,606 pay
President and CEO: Gregory E. Lawton, age 52, $2,380,274 pay
EVP and CFO: Michael J. (Mike) Bailey, age 49, $876,296 pay
EVP, Chief Administrative Officer, Secretary, and General Counsel: JoAnne Brandes, age 49, $888,016 pay
SVP and Group President: Mark Cross
SVP, Human Resources: Timothy Ransome, age 53
VP and CIO: Sue Leboza, age 48
VP and Treasurer: Francisco Sanchez
Auditors: Ernst & Young LLP

LOCATIONS

HQ: JohnsonDiversey, Inc.
8310 16th St., Sturtevant, WI 53177
Phone: 262-631-4001 **Fax:** 262-631-4282
Web: www.johnsondiversey.com

JohnsonDiversey has 51 manufacturing facilities in 29 countries.

2002 Sales

	$ mil.	% of total
North America	884	40
Europe	860	39
Japan	239	11
Asia/Pacific	128	6
The Americas	104	4
Adjustments	(19)	—
Total	**2,196**	**100**

PRODUCTS/OPERATIONS

2002 Sales

	$ mil.	% of total
Professional	1,951	88
Polymers	264	12
Adjustments	(19)	—
Total	**2,196**	**100**

Affiliated Businesses

Austo-C (manufactures commercial warewashing and laundry products)
The Butcher Company (manufactures and markets janitorial supplies)
US Chemical (manufactures labels for specialty cleaning products)
Whitmore Micro-Gen Research Laboratories (manufactures and supplies pesticides and related equipment)

COMPETITORS

Acuity Brands
Air Products
Arrow-Magnolia
Avecia
BASF AG
Clorox
Colgate-Palmolive
Dainippon Ink
Dow Chemical
Eastman Chemical
Ecolab
Kimberly-Clark
NCH
Procter & Gamble
Rohm and Haas
Surface Specialties

HISTORICAL FINANCIALS

Company Type: Private

Income Statement FYE: December 31

	REVENUE ($ mil.)	NET INCOME ($ mil.)	NET PROFIT MARGIN	EMPLOYEES
12/02	2,196	30	1.3%	13,530
12/01*	549	11	2.0%	14,500
6/01	1,133	33	2.9%	3,600
6/00	1,028	50	4.8%	3,500
6/99	980	15	1.5%	3,000
Annual Growth	22.4%	18.9%	—	45.7%

*Fiscal year change

2002 Year-End Financials

Debt ratio: 163.3%
Return on equity: 5.7%
Cash ($ mil.): 59
Current ratio: 1.19
Long-term debt ($ mil.): 1,360

Net Income History

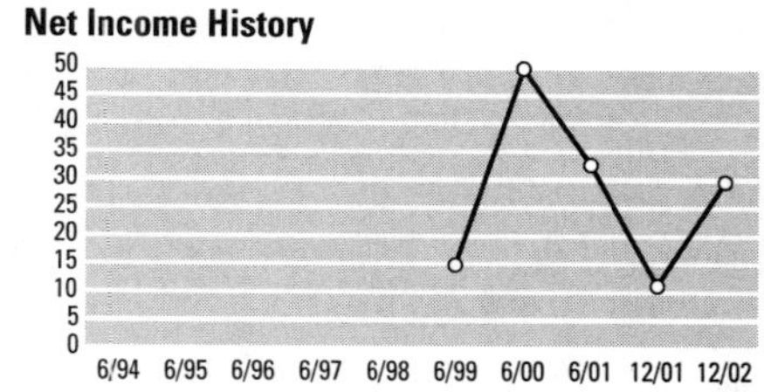

Jones Day

Legal leviathan Jones Day ranks as one of the world's largest law firms, providing counsel to about half of the *FORTUNE* 500 companies. It has more than 1,600 attorneys in some two dozen offices across the US, as well as in Asia and Europe. The firm's practice groups include litigation, tax, government regulation, and business. Jones Day has counted Bridgestone/Firestone, General Motors, IBM, RJR Nabisco, and Texas Instruments among its top clients. Other notable clients include America Online, Aventis, and BP Amoco. The firm traces its roots to the Cleveland law partnership founded by Edwin Blandin and William Rice in 1893.

EXECUTIVES

Managing Partner: Stephen J. Brogan
Administrative Partner: Mary Ellen Powers
CFO: Derald Hunt
Partner-in-Charge International Region: David F. Clossey
Partner-in-Charge, New York Office: Dennis W. LaBarre, age 60
Partner-in-Charge, Paris: Wesley R. Johnson Jr.
Chief Knowledge Officer: Terry L. Crum
Director of Administration: William Gaskill

LOCATIONS

HQ: Northpoint, 901 Lakeside Ave., Cleveland, OH 44114
Phone: 216-586-3939 **Fax:** 216-579-0212
Web: www.jonesday.com

Jones Day has US offices in Atlanta; Chicago; Cleveland; Columbus, Ohio; Dallas; Houston; Irvine, Los Angeles, and Menlo Park, California; New York City; Pittsburgh; and Washington, DC. The firm has international offices in Brussels; Frankfurt; Hong Kong; London; Madrid; Milan; Paris; Shanghai; Singapore; Sydney; Taipei, Taiwan; and Tokyo.

Jones Financial Companies

This is not your father's broker. Well, maybe it is. The Jones Financial Companies is the parent of Edward Jones (formerly called Edward D. Jones & Co.), an investment brokerage network catering to individual investors. Most of its clients are retired people and small-business owners in rural communities and suburbs. The "Wal-Mart of Wall Street" has thousands of satellite-linked offices in the US, Canada, and the UK. Brokers preach a conservative buy-and-hold approach, offering relatively low-risk investment vehicles such as government bonds, blue-chip stocks, and high-quality mutual funds.

Edward Jones' network of more than 8,800 offices — many of them with a single broker — makes it one of the largest brokerage networks in the world. The company also sells insurance and engages in investment banking for such clients as Wal-Mart and public agencies. The firm embraces technology, maintaining one of the industry's largest satellite networks (including a dish for each office).

Preferring to groom brokers internally, the firm accepts applicants with no previous experience, trains them extensively, and monitors investment patterns to prevent account churning and trading in risky low-cap stocks. Before they are given such luxuries as office space or assistants, new brokers must make 1,000 cold calls in their chosen community. Edward Jones' investment in training, backed by what's perceived to be old-school values and strong ethics, seems to be paying off: The firm has ranked on *Fortune* magazine's "100 Best Companies to Work For" for two consecutive years.

The Jones Companies is the only major financial services firm still organized as a partnership and managing partner John Bachmann has said it has no plans to go public. Meanwhile, it is plugging away at its goal to have at least 10,000 locations by 2004, an undertaking that has at least some brokers concerned about competition within the network and market saturation.

HISTORY

Jones Financial got its start in 1871 as bond house Whitaker & Co. In 1922 Edward D. Jones (no relation to the Edward D. Jones of Dow Jones fame) opened a brokerage in St. Louis. In 1943 the two firms merged.

Jones' son Edward "Ted" Jones Jr. joined the firm in 1948. Under Ted's leadership (and against his father's wishes), the company focused on rural customers, opening its first branch in the Missouri town of Mexico in 1955 and beginning its march across small-town America. Ted took over as managing partner in 1968, masterminding the company's small-town expansion. (The Wal-Mart comparison is apt; Ted Jones and Sam Walton were good friends.)

Almost from the start, the firm hammered home a conservative investment message focusing on blue-chip stocks and bonds. It expanded steadily throughout the years, adding offices with such addresses as Cedarburg, Wisconsin, and Paris, Illinois.

In the 1970s Edward D. Jones moved into underwriting with clients including Southern Co., Citicorp, and Humana. (It got burned in the mid-1980s on one such deal, when the SEC accused the company of fraud in a bond offering for life insurer D.H. Baldwin Co., which later filed for bankruptcy.)

The company's technological bent was spurred in 1978 after its Teletype network couldn't handle the demand generated by the firm's 220 offices. As a stopgap, the company nixed use of the Teletype for stock quotes, telling its brokers to call Merrill Lynch's toll-free number instead.

Managing partner John Bachmann took over from Ted Jones in 1980. (Bachmann started at the company as a janitor.) A follower of management guru Peter Drucker, Bachmann inculcated the company's brokers with Drucker's customer- and value-oriented principles.

Edward D. Jones began moving into the suburbs and into less-than-posh sections of big cities in the mid-1980s. In 1986 the company started a mortgage program, but the plan was never successful and was ended in 1988. The company weathered the 1987 stock market crash (many brokerages did not), albeit with thinner profit margins.

In 1990 Ted Jones died. The first half of the decade was a time of great expansion for the company as it doubled its number of offices. In 1993 the company opened an office in Canada.

In 1994 Jones Financial's acquisition of Columbia, Missouri-based thrift Boone National gave it the ability to offer trust and mortgage services to its clients, which helped sales as Jones started facing competition from Merrill Lynch in its small-town niche. The company's rapid expansion and relatively expensive infrastructure (all those one-person offices add up) began to eat at the bottom line, and in 1995 Bachmann stopped expansion so the firm could catch its breath.

In 1997 Edward Jones (which had unofficially dropped its middle "D" to boost name recognition) moved overseas, opening its first offices in the UK, a prime expansion target for the company. The next year the firm teamed up with Mercantile Bank to offer small-business loans. Jones resumed its expansionist push in 1999 and 2000, adding offices in all its markets, but continued to resist online trading.

EXECUTIVES

Managing Partner: John W. Bachmann, age 64, $211,870 pay
COO: Douglas E. (Doug) Hill, age 58, $186,870 pay
Chief Financial Officer: Steven Novik, age 53
General Partner, Human Resources: Michael R. Holmes, age 44
General Partner, Information Systems: Rich Malone, $169,370 pay
General Partner, Service Division: Darryl L. Pope, age 63
General Partner, Headquarters Administration: Robert (Bob) Virgil Jr., age 68
General Partner: James D. (Jim) Weddle, $169,370 pay
Principal, Canadian Operations: Gary D. Reamey, $144,370 pay
Principal, Product Review: William H. (Bill) Broderick III
Principal, Investment Banking: Daniel A. (Dan) Burkhardt
Principal, Fixed Income: Kevin N. Flatt
Principal, Equity Research: David G. Otto
Principal, Products and Services: Ray Robbins
Investment Representative, Member, Investment Policy Committee: Stephanie Simmons
Chief Market Strategist: Alan F. Skrainka
Head of Marketing: Dallas Kersey
Auditors: PricewaterhouseCoopers LLP

PRODUCTS/OPERATIONS

Selected Practice Areas

Antitrust
Bankruptcy
Environmental
Intellectual property
Labor
Real estate
Securities
Tax

Selected Clients

America Online
Aventis
BP Amoco
Bridgestone/Firestone
CBS
Citigroup
County of Los Angeles
Eastman Kodak
General Motors
Goldman Sachs
IBM
J. C. Penney
Johnson & Johnson
PepsiCo
Pfizer
Procter & Gamble
Texas Instruments
Tribune Company
The Washington Post Company

COMPETITORS

Akin, Gump
Baker & McKenzie
Cleary, Gottlieb
Clifford Chance
Holland & Knight
Latham & Watkins
Mayer, Brown, Rowe & Maw
Morgan, Lewis
Shearman & Sterling
Sidley Austin Brown & Wood
Skadden, Arps
White & Case

HISTORICAL FINANCIALS

Company Type: Partnership

Income Statement FYE: December 31

	REVENUE ($ mil.)	NET INCOME ($ mil.)	NET PROFIT MARGIN	EMPLOYEES
12/02	908	—	—	—
12/01	790	—	—	—
12/00	675	—	—	3,200
12/99	595	—	—	3,200
12/98	530	—	—	3,200
12/97	490	—	—	3,092
12/96	450	—	—	2,880
12/95	400	—	—	2,800
12/94	384	—	—	468
12/93	346	—	—	—
Annual Growth	11.3%	—	—	37.8%

Revenue History

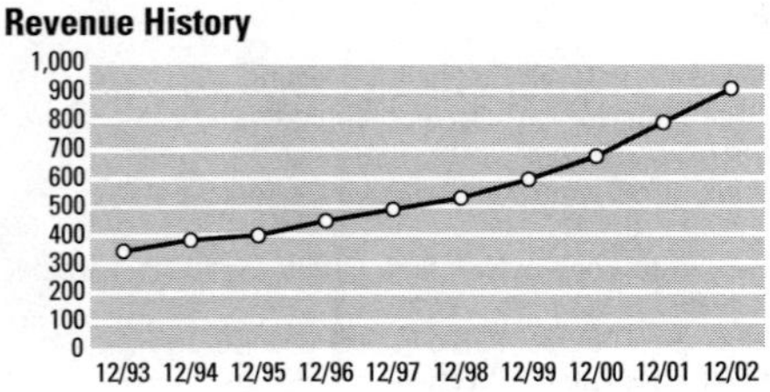

LOCATIONS

HQ: The Jones Financial Companies, L.L.L.P.
12555 Manchester Rd., Des Peres, MO 63131
Phone: 314-515-2000 **Fax:** 314-515-2622
Web: www.edwardjones.com

The Jones Financial Companies operates more than 8,800 offices in the US, Canada, and the UK.

PRODUCTS/OPERATIONS

Selected Subsidiaries

EDJ Holding Co., Inc.
EDJ Leasing Co., LP
Edward D. Jones & Co. Canada Holding Co., Inc.
Edward D. Jones & Co., LP (broker-dealer)
Edward D. Jones Ltd. (UK)
EJ Insurance Agency Holding LLC
EJ Mortgage LLC
Edward Jones Mortgage (50%)
LHC, Inc.
Unison Capital Corp., Inc.
Passport Research Ltd. (50%, money market mutual fund adviser)
Unison Investment Trust

COMPETITORS

A.G. Edwards
Charles Schwab
Citigroup
FleetBoston
Merrill Lynch
Morgan Stanley
National Financial Partners
Raymond James Financial
Baird
TD Waterhouse
UBS Financial Services
U. S. Bancorp Piper Jaffray
Wells Fargo

HISTORICAL FINANCIALS

Company Type: Partnership

Income Statement

FYE: December 31

	REVENUE ($ mil.)	NET INCOME ($ mil.)	NET PROFIT MARGIN	EMPLOYEES
12/02	2,270	143	6.6%	28,469
12/01	2,142	143	7.0%	26,460
12/00	2,212	230	10.4%	23,432
12/99	1,787	187	10.5%	20,541
12/98	1,450	193	13.7%	15,795
12/97	1,135	114	10.1%	13,691
12/96	952	93	9.8%	12,148
12/95	722	55	8.1%	11,717
12/94	661	54	8.2%	7,418
12/93	643	66	10.3%	8,330
Annual Growth	15.1%	9.4%	—	14.6%

Net Income History

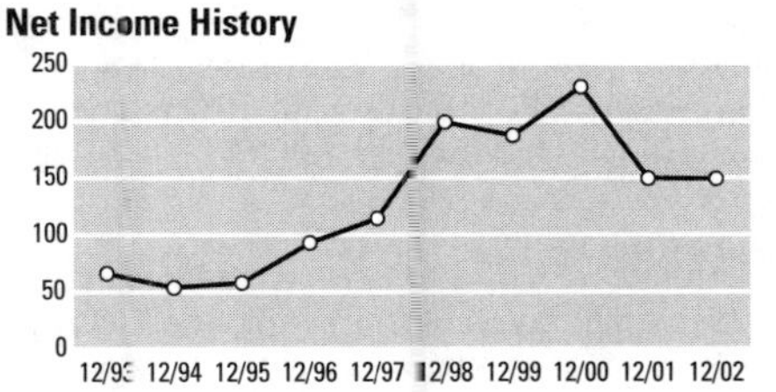

Jordan Industries, Inc.

It's not related to Michael, but with a name like Jordan Industries, it's no wonder this company does it all. Jordan is involved in markets as diverse as automotive products, bicycle reflector kits, software application development, electric motors, and specialty advertising products. It owns more than 20 companies, which are divided into five business units: Kinetek (electric motors and gears), Jordan Auto Aftermarket (torque converters), Jordan Specialty Plastics (plastic products), Specialty Printing and Labeling (promotional products), and Consumer and Industrial Products (orthopedic supports and gift items). Director David Zalaznick owns 20% of the company; chairman and CEO John W. Jordan II owns 18%.

EXECUTIVES

Chairman and CEO: John W. (Jay) Jordan II, age 55
President, COO, and Director: Thomas H. Quinn, age 55, $1,750,000 pay
SVP, Business Development: Joe Linnen
SVP, Finance and Accounting: Thomas C. Spielberger
SVP, International Business: Andrew W. Rice
VP, Assistant Secretary, and Director: Jonathan F. Boucher, age 46
General Counsel, Secretary, and Director: G. Robert Fisher, age 63
Auditors: Ernst & Young LLP

LOCATIONS

HQ: Arborlake Center, Ste. 550, 1751 Lake Cook Rd., Deerfield, IL 60015
Phone: 847-945-5591 **Fax:** 847-945-0198
Web: www.jordanindustries.com

Jordan Industries has facilities in Canada, France, Germany, Italy, Mexico, the UK, and the US.

2002 Sales

	$ mil.	% of total
US	638.7	89
Other countries	81.3	11
Total	**720.0**	**100**

PRODUCTS/OPERATIONS

Selected Products and Operations

Kinetek
Advanced D.C. Motors
Electrical Design & Control
FIR (electric motors)

Jordan Auto Aftermarket
Alma (remanufactured torque converters)
Atco (mobile air conditioning components)

Jordan Specialty Plastics
Beemak (point-of-purchase displays, brochure holders, sign holders)
Deflecto (injection-molded products)

Specialty Printing and Labeling
Seaboard (printed folding cartons and boxes, insert packaging, blister pack cards)
Valmark (graphic panel overlays, membrane switch control panels, adhesive-backed labels)

Consumer and Industrial Products
Cape Craftsmen (imports gifts, wooden furniture, framed art)
Cho-Pat (orthopedic sports medicine devices)

COMPETITORS

Aftermarket Technology
Baldor Electric
Bed Bath & Beyond
BorgWarner
HMI Industries
Multi-Color
Owosso
Red Man Pipe & Supply
Regal-Beloit
Seven Worldwide
Thomas Nelson
Twin Disc
Tyco International

HISTORICAL FINANCIALS

Company Type: Private

Income Statement

FYE: December 31

	REVENUE ($ mil.)	NET INCOME ($ mil.)	NET PROFIT MARGIN	EMPLOYEES
12/02	720	(64)	—	7,200
12/01	723	(58)	—	6,500
12/00	807	—	—	6,967
12/99	777	—	—	7,000
12/98	944	—	—	7,092
12/97	707	—	—	6,200
12/96	602	—	—	6,218
12/95	507	—	—	5,150
12/94	424	—	—	3,900
12/93	359	—	—	—
Annual Growth	8.1%	—	—	8.0%

2002 Year-End Financials

Debt ratio: —
Return on equity: —
Cash ($ mil.): 20
Current ratio: 1.67
Long-term debt ($ mil.): 716

Net Income History

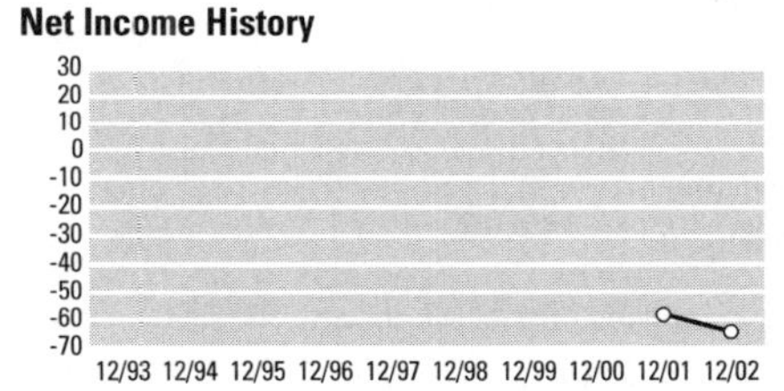

Jostens, Inc.

Are you *sure* you want to remember high school? Well, if you do, look to Jostens, the leading US producer of yearbooks and class rings. Class rings are sold on school campuses and through bookstores, retail jewelers, and the Internet, while Jostens' sports rings commemorate professional sports champions (it has made 24 of 36 Super Bowl rings). Jostens sells other graduation products including diplomas, announcements, caps, and gowns, and it takes and sells class and individual pictures for schools in the US and Canada. A private investment group led by Investcorp took Jostens private in May 2000. A CSFB fund plans to buy Jostens for nearly $500 million.

Printing and publishing account for more than 40% of Jostens' sales, mostly from yearbooks for all levels of schools from elementary through college. Representatives work closely with students and faculty advisors in all phases of yearbook creation — from planning, editing, and layout to production, printing, and distribution. The company also prints books, brochures, and promotional materials. Jostens exited the recognition business in 2001.

EXECUTIVES

Chairman and CEO: Robert C. Buhrmaster, age 55
Vice Chairman: Carl H. Blowers, age 62
President: Michael L. Bailey, age 46
VP, General Counsel, and Corporate Secretary: Paula R. Johnson, age 54
VP, Human Resources and Communications: Steven A. Tighe, age 50
CIO: Andrew W. Black, age 39
Treasurer: John L. (Jack) Larsen, age 44
Manager, Communications: Mark Cassutt
Auditors: PricewaterhouseCoopers LLP

LOCATIONS

HQ: 5501 Norman Center Dr., Minneapolis, MN 55437
Phone: 952-830-3300 **Fax:** 952-830-3293
Web: www.jostens.com

Jostens sells its products and services throughout North America through independent and employee sales representatives. It has manufacturing facilities in California, Illinois, Kansas, Massachusetts, Minnesota, New York, North and South Carolina, Pennsylvania, Tennessee, and Texas, as well in Canada.

2002 Sales

	$ mil.	% of total
US	716.1	95
Other countries	39.9	5
Total	**756.0**	**100**

PRODUCTS/OPERATIONS

Selected Products

Printing and publishing
Books
Commercial brochures
Promotional books and materials
Yearbooks (elementary, middle, and high schools; college)

Jewelry
Athletic rings
Class rings (high school and college)

Graduation products
Announcements
Caps and gowns
Diplomas

Photography
Class and individual school pictures
Prom and special events pictures
Senior portraits
Student ID cards

COMPETITORS

American Achievement
Lifetouch
Walsworth

HISTORICAL FINANCIALS

Company Type: Private

Income Statement FYE: Saturday nearest December 31

	REVENUE ($ mil.)	NET INCOME ($ mil.)	NET PROFIT MARGIN	EMPLOYEES
12/02	756	30	4.0%	6,700
12/01	737	4	0.6%	6,100
12/00	805	(19)	—	6,500
12/99	782	43	5.5%	6,700
12/98	771	42	5.4%	6,800
12/97	743	57	7.7%	6,500
12/96*	277	(1)	—	6,100
6/96	695	52	7.4%	5,600
6/95	665	50	7.6%	8,000
6/94	827	(16)	—	9,000
Annual Growth	(1.0%)	—	—	(3.2%)

*Fiscal year change

2002 Year-End Financials

Debt ratio: —
Return on equity: —
Cash ($ mil.): 11
Current ratio: 0.72
Long-term debt ($ mil.): 563

Net Income History

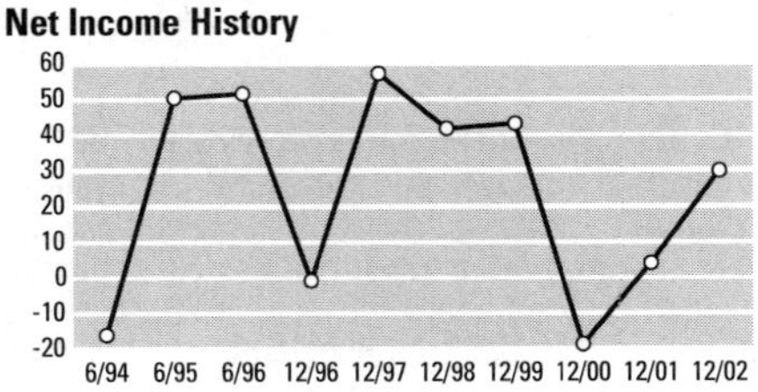

JPI

JPI can walk your dog or rent you a bike but what it does best is build and manage apartments. One of the largest luxury multifamily apartment developers in the US, JPI also manages more than 24,000 units in about a dozen states. The company typically buys underperforming properties in desirable areas and upgrades them with such features as parking garages, fitness centers, and 24-hour concierge services. JPI's student complexes include game rooms and fitness centers. Founded in 1976 as Jefferson Properties, Inc., JPI was a subsidiary of Southland Financial until the early 1990s when Hunt Realty invested in it.

EXECUTIVES

Chairman and CEO: J. Frank Miller III
President and COO: Robert D. Page
CFO: Frank B. Schubert
EVP, Senior Technology Services Partner: Tom Bumpass
SVP and Treasurer: Vanessa Hoffman
SVP, Accounting: Kirk Motsenbocker

LOCATIONS

HQ: 600 E. Las Colinas Blvd., Ste. 1800, Irving, TX 75039
Phone: 972-556-1700 **Fax:** 972-556-3889
Web: www.jpi.com

JPI has apartment or student housing properties in Arizona, California, Colorado, Florida, Georgia, Indiana, Kansas, Massachusetts, Michigan, Minnesota, Missouri, New Jersey, New York, North Carolina, Ohio, Oklahoma, Pennsylvania, Rhode Island, Tennessee, Texas, Virginia, Washington, Washington, D.C., and Ontario, Canada.

PRODUCTS/OPERATIONS

Services

Acquisitions
Construction
Development
Property management

COMPETITORS

AIMCO
Archstone-Smith Trust
Camden Property
Gables Residential Trust
Post Properties
Trammell Crow Residential

HISTORICAL FINANCIALS

Company Type: Private

Income Statement FYE: December 31

	REVENUE ($ mil.)	NET INCOME ($ mil.)	NET PROFIT MARGIN	EMPLOYEES
12/01	1,135	—	—	1,000
12/00	1,000	—	—	1,500
12/99	600	—	—	1,500
12/98	1,063	—	—	1,500
12/97	676	—	—	1,000
Annual Growth	13.8%	—	—	0.0%

Revenue History

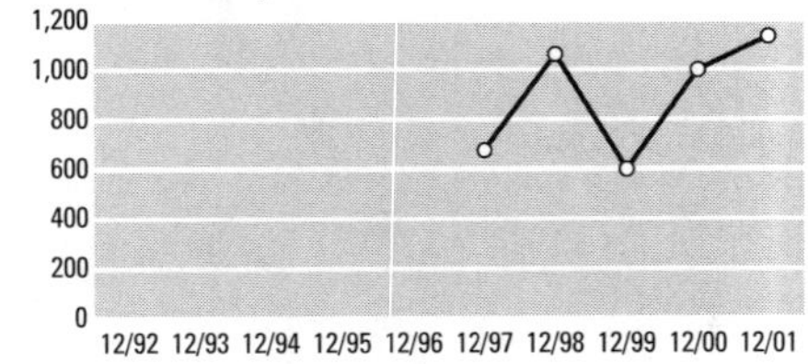

J.R. Simplot Company

J.R. Simplot hopes you'll have fries with that. Potato potentate J. R. "Jack" Simplot simply shook hands with McDonald's pioneer Ray Kroc in the mid-1960s, and his company's french fry sales have sizzled ever since. The company still remains the major french fry supplier for McDonald's and supplies Burger King and KFC as well. J.R. Simplot produces more than 2 billion pounds of french fries, hash browns, and nuggets annually, making it one of the world's largest processors of frozen potatoes. It offers its potato products mainly to food service and retail customers under its Simplot brand and private labels.

In addition to potatoes, J.R. Simplot also produces fruits and vegetables under the RoastWorks and Simplot Classic labels. The company's spuds sprouted other businesses as well, including cattle ranches and feedlots (which use feed made from potato peels). Its AgriBusiness Group mines phosphates (for fertilizer and feed) and silica. The company's Turf and Horticulture Group produces grass and turf seed and fertilizer.

Officially retired since 1994, J.R. Simplot remains one of the wealthiest Americans. After amassing a mountain of potato money, the spudillionaire moved on to semiconductors and invested heavily in Boise-based Micron Technology.

HISTORY

J.R. Simplot was born in Dubuque, Iowa, in 1909. His family moved to the frontier town of Declo, Idaho, about a year later. Frustrated with school and an overbearing father, Simplot dropped out at age 14 and moved to a local hotel, where he made money by paying cash for teachers' wage scrip, at 50 cents on the dollar. Simplot then got a bank loan using the scrip as collateral and moved into farming, first by raising hogs and then by growing potatoes. He met

Lindsay Maggart, a leading farmer in the area, who taught him the value of planting certified potato seed, rather than potatoes.

Simplot purchased an electric potato sorter in 1928 and eventually dominated the local market by sorting for neighboring farms. By 1940 his company, J.R. Simplot, operated 33 potato warehouses in Oregon and Idaho. The company moved into food processing in the 1940s, first by producing dried onions and other vegetables for Chicago-based Sokol & Co. and later by producing dehydrated potatoes. Between 1942 and 1945 J.R. Simplot produced more than 50 million pounds of dehydrated potatoes for the US military. During the war the company also expanded into fertilizer production, cattle feeding, and lumber. It moved to Boise, Idaho, in 1947.

In the 1950s J.R. Simplot researchers developed a method for freezing french fries. In the mid-1960s Simplot persuaded McDonald's founder, Ray Kroc, to go with his frozen fries, a handshake deal that practically guaranteed Simplot's success in the potato processing industry. By the end of the 1960s, Simplot was the largest landowner, cattleman, potato grower, and employer in the state of Idaho. He also had established fertilizer plants, mining operations, and other businesses in 36 states, as well as in Canada and a handful of other countries.

During the oil crisis of the 1970s, J.R. Simplot began producing ethanol from potatoes. However, Simplot's empire-building was not without its rough edges. In 1977 he pleaded no contest to federal charges that he failed to report his income, and the next year he was forced to settle charges that he manipulated Maine potato futures.

The company entered the frozen fruit and vegetable business in 1983. Other ventures included using wastewater from potato processing for irrigation and using cattle manure to fuel methane gas plants. Simplot set up a Chinese joint venture in the 1990s to provide processed potatoes to McDonald's and other customers in East Asia.

The company bought the giant ZX cattle ranch near Paisley, Oregon, in 1994. Simplot retired from the board of directors that year to become chairman emeritus; Stephen Beebe was named president and CEO. The 1995 acquisition of the food operations of Pacific Dunlop (now Ansell) led to the creation of Simplot Australia, one of the largest food processors in Australia. Its 1997 stock swap with I. & J. Foods Australia enlarged the subsidiary's frozen food menu.

In 1999 the company sold its Simplot Dairy Products cheese business to France's Besnier Group, and it teamed with Dutch potato processor Farm Frites to enter new markets. In 2000 it launched agricultural Web site planetAg, bought the turf grass seed assets of AgriBioTech, and added the US potato operations of food giant Nestlé to its pantry.

In 2001 the firm said it would build an $80 million potato-processing plant in Manitoba. Also that year the company said it would not increase the value of its contracts with growers struggling amid low prices in a glutted market.

In 2002 Simplot sold its Australian pudding maker Big Sister to the Fowlers Vacola Group and its Agrisource grain company to a private buyer. That same year Beebe retired and Lawrence Hlobik, president of the company's agribusiness unit, was named CEO.

The company closed its only meat-processing plant in September 2003.

EXECUTIVES

Chairman Emeritus: J. R. (Jack) Simplot
Chairman: Scott Simplot
CEO: Lawrence S. Hlobik
President and COO: Leigh Brinkerhoff
SVP Finance and CFO: Annette Elg
SVP Human Resources: Mike Vasilenko
SVP Sales & Marketing: Greg Ibsen
SVP and General Manager, Fertilizer Manufacturing and SVP and General Manager, Wholesale Marketing Group: Pat Avery
VP Public Relations: Fred Zerza
VP Special Projects: Rick Fisch
VP and General Manager, Turf and Horticulture Group: Joel Barker
VP and General Manager Grower Solutions Group: Dale Schmidt
President, Agribusiness Group: William J. Whitacre
Director, Energy: David Hawk
Manager, Transportation Services, Food Group: Paul Nagy

LOCATIONS

HQ: 1 Capital Center, 999 Main St., Ste. 1300, Boise, ID 83702
Phone: 208-336-2110 **Fax:** 208-389-7515
Web: www.simplot.com

PRODUCTS/OPERATIONS

Major Operating Groups

AgriBusiness Group
Nitrogen and phosphate fertilizers
Phosphate and silica ore mining

Corporate Group
Corporate Development Department
Corporate Information Systems
Simplot Aviation (in-company flight services)

Food Group (Simplot Foods)
Asparagus, avocadoes, broccoli, carrots, cauliflower, corn, peas, strawberries
Fresh potatoes (Blue Ribbon, Golden Classic)
Frozen fruits and vegetables
Frozen potato products (fries, nuggets, patties, sticks)
Roasted foods
Roasted vegetables and potatoes

Land and Livestock Group
Cattle feeding
Hay, corn, grain production for feedlots

COMPETITORS

Cargill	IMC Global
ConAgra	McCain Foods
ContiGroup	Michael Foods
Del Monte Foods	PCS
Golden State Foods	Pro-Fac
Heinz	Seneca Foods

HISTORICAL FINANCIALS

Company Type: Private

Income Statement FYE: August 31

	REVENUE ($ mil.)	NET INCOME ($ mil.)	NET PROFIT MARGIN	EMPLOYEES
8/02	3,000	—	—	13,000
8/01	3,000	—	—	13,000
8/00	2,700	—	—	12,000
8/99	2,730	—	—	12,000
8/98	2,800	—	—	12,000
8/97	2,800	—	—	12,000
8/96	2,700	—	—	13,000
8/95	2,200	—	—	10,000
8/94	2,100	—	—	10,000
8/93	1,700	—	—	9,000
Annual Growth	6.5%	—	—	4.2%

Revenue History

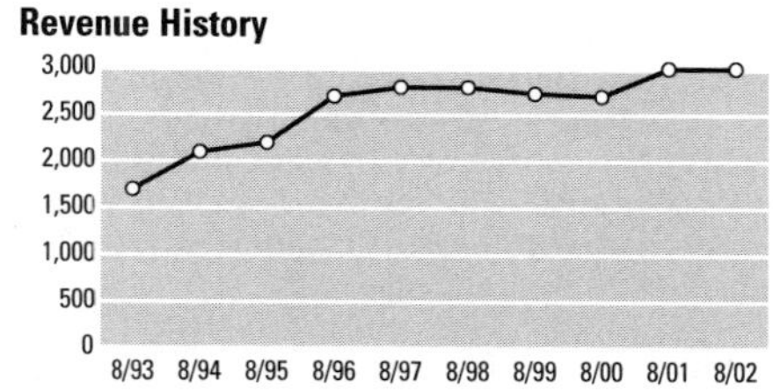

Kaiser Foundation Health Plan, Inc.

Kaiser Foundation Health Plan aims to be the emperor of the HMO universe. With more than 8 million members in nine states and the District of Columbia, it is one of the largest not-for-profit managed health care companies in the US. Kaiser has an integrated care model, offering both hospital and physician care through a network of hospitals and physician practices operating under the Kaiser Permanente name. Kaiser also sponsors the Permanente Medical Groups, associations consisting of about 12,000 doctors that provide medical care to Kaiser health plan subscribers. The company also runs a network of Kaiser Foundation hospitals.

California is the company's largest market, with about 75% of its members.

A string of losses due to skyrocketing costs and stiff competition from commercial providers of managed care have prompted Kaiser to raise rates and divest underperforming units. Kaiser sold its unprofitable operations in North Carolina (2000) and Kansas (2001).

Like many of its competitors, Kaiser faces the ever-rising costs of health care that threaten the gains it has made to get back in the black.

HISTORY

Henry Kaiser — shipbuilder, war profiteer, builder of the Hoover and Grand Coulee dams, and founder of Kaiser Aluminum — was a bootstrap capitalist who did well by doing good. A high school dropout from upstate New York, Kaiser moved to Spokane, Washington, in 1906 and went into road construction. During the Depression, he headed the consortium that built the great WPA dams.

It was in building the Grand Coulee Dam that, in 1938, Kaiser teamed with Dr. Sidney Garfield, who earlier had devised a prepayment health plan for workers on California public works projects. As Kaiser moved into steelmaking and shipbuilding during WWII (turning out some 1,400 bare-bones Liberty ships — one per day at peak production), Kaiser decided healthy workers produce more than sick ones, and he called on Garfield to set up on-site clinics funded by the US government as part of operating expenses. Garfield was released from military service by President Roosevelt for the purpose.

After the war, the clinics became war surplus. Kaiser and his wife bought them — at a 99% discount — through the new Kaiser Hospital Foundation. His vision was to provide the public with low-cost, prepaid medical care. He created the health plan — the self-supporting entity that would administer the system — and the group medical organization, Permanente (named after Kaiser's first cement plant site). He then endowed the health plan with $200,000. This health plan, the classic HMO model, was criticized by the medical establishment as socialized medicine performed by "employee" doctors.

But the plan flourished, becoming California's #1 medical system. In 1958 Kaiser retired to Hawaii and started his health plan there. But physician resistance limited national growth; HMOs were illegal in some states well into the 1970s.

As health care costs rose, Congress legalized HMOs in all states. Kaiser expanded in the 1980s; as it moved outside its traditional geographic areas, the company contracted for space in hospitals rather than build them. Growth slowed as competition increased.

Some health care costs in California fell in the early 1990s as more medical procedures were performed on an outpatient basis. Specialists flooded the state, and as price competition among doctors and hospitals heated up, many HMOs landed advantageous contracts. Kaiser, with its own highly paid doctors, was unable to realize the same savings and was no longer the best deal in town. Its membership stalled.

To boost membership and control expenses, Kaiser instituted a controversial program in 1996 in which nurses earned bonuses for cost-cutting. Critics said the program could lead to a decrease in care quality; Kaiser later became the focus of investigations into wrongful death suits linked to cost-cutting in California (where it has since beefed up staffing and programs) and Texas (where it has agreed to pay $1 million in fines).

In 1997 Kaiser and Washington-based Group Health Cooperative of Puget Sound formed Kaiser/Group Health to handle administrative services in the Northwest. Kaiser also tried to boost membership by lowering premiums, but the strategy proved *too* effective: Costs linked to an unwieldy 20% enrollment surge brought a loss in 1997 — Kaiser's first annual loss ever.

A second year in the red in 1998 prompted Kaiser to sell its Texas operations to Sierra Health Services. It also entered the Florida market via an alliance with Miami-based AvMed Health Plan. In 1999 Kaiser announced plans to sell its unprofitable North Carolina operations (it closed the deal the following year).

In 2000 Kaiser announced plans to charge premiums for its Medicare HMO, Medicare+Choice, to offset the shortfall in federal reimbursements. In 2001 the company's hospital division bought the technology and assets of defunct Internet grocer Webvan in an effort to increase its distribution activity. Also that year the son of a deceased anthrax victim sued a Kaiser facility for failing to recognize and treat his father's symptoms.

EXECUTIVES

Chairman, President, and CEO: George C. Halvorson
EVP, Health Plan Operations: Arthur M. Southam
SVP and CFO: Robert E. Briggs, age 55
SVP and CIO: Clifford Dodd
SVP, General Counsel, and Secretary: Kirk E. Miller
SVP and Chief Administration Officer: Robert M. Crane
SVP and Chief Compliance Officer: Dan Garcia
SVP, National Contracting Purchasing and Distribution: Joseph W. Hummel
SVP, Workforce Development: Leslie A. Margolin
SVP and Director for Care and Services Quality: Patricia B. Siegel
VP, National HIPAA Compliance and Kaiser Permanente Information Technology (KP-IT) Compliance: Mary Henderson
VP, Human Resources, Regions Outside California: Dresdene Flynn-White
President, Kaiser Permanente Northern California Region: Mary Ann Thode
President, Kaiser Permanente Southern California Region: Richard Cordova
Head of Annapolis Medical Center, Kaiser Permanente of the Mid-Atlantic States: Ruth A. Robinson
President, Mid-Atlantic Permanente Medical Group: Adrian E. Long
VP, Clinical Information System (CIS) Project: Bruce Turkstra
Executive Director, Columbia Gateway Medical Center, Kaiser Permanente of the Mid-Atlantic States: Susan Moriarty

LOCATIONS

HQ: 1 Kaiser Plaza, Oakland, CA 94612
Phone: 510-271-5800 **Fax:** 510-271-6493
Web: www.kaiserpermanente.org

Kaiser Foundation Health Plan operates in California, Colorado, Georgia, Hawaii, Maryland, Ohio, Oregon, Virginia, Washington, and the District of Columbia.

PRODUCTS/OPERATIONS

Selected Operations

Kaiser Foundation Health Plans (health coverage)
Kaiser Foundation Hospitals (community hospitals and outpatient facilities)
Permanente Medical Groups (physician organizations)

COMPETITORS

Aetna
Blue Cross
Catholic Health East
Catholic Health Initiatives
Catholic Healthcare Partners
Catholic Healthcare System
Catholic Healthcare West
CIGNA
HCA
Health Net
Humana
Oxford Health Plans
PacifiCare
Sierra Health
UnitedHealth Group
WellPoint Health Networks

HISTORICAL FINANCIALS

Company Type: Not-for-profit

Income Statement

FYE: December 31

	REVENUE ($ mil.)	NET INCOME ($ mil.)	NET PROFIT MARGIN	EMPLOYEES
12/02	22,500	70	0.3%	125,000
12/01	19,700	681	3.5%	111,000
12/00	17,700	590	3.3%	90,000
12/99	16,841	(6)	—	90,000
12/98	15,500	(288)	—	100,000
12/97	14,500	(270)	—	100,000
12/96	13,241	265	2.0%	90,000
12/95	12,290	550	4.5%	85,000
12/94	12,268	816	6.7%	84,845
12/93	11,930	848	7.1%	84,885
Annual Growth	7.3%	(24.2%)	—	4.4%

Net Income History

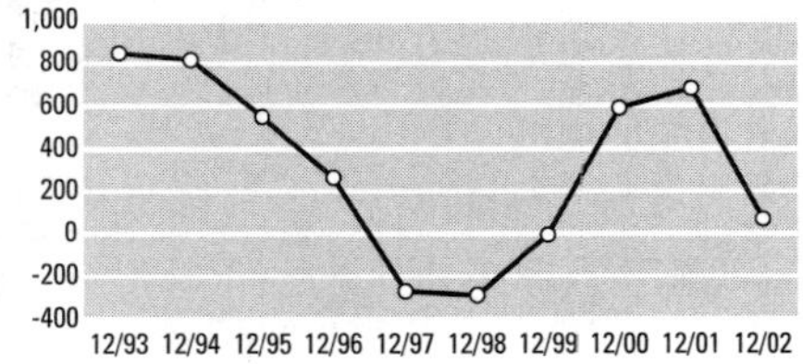

KB Toys

KB Toys hopes toy buyers will take their haul from the mall. One of the largest toy retailers in the US, KB Toys operates more than 1,300 stores under four main formats: KB Toys stores in malls, KB Toy Works neighborhood stores, KB Toy Outlets and KB Toy Liquidator in outlet malls, and KB Toy Express in malls selling close-out toys during the Christmas season. It has stores throughout the US and in Guam and Puerto Rico, and it sells toys online through KBtoys.com and eToys.com (KB Toys bought the inventory and rights to the defunct eToys business in 2001). It also offers a business-to-business gift program. The firm, founded as a wholesale candy company in 1922, is owned by private equity firm Bain Capital.

EXECUTIVES

President and CEO: Michael L. Glazer
EVP: Mark Scott
EVP and CFO: Robert J. Feldman
EVP, Strategic Business Development: Sal Vasta
SVP and COO, KBtoys.com: Michael J. Wagner
SVP, Stores: Stuart Lighton
VP and Controller: Joel Wiest
VP, General Counsel, and Secretary: Kenneth A. Grady
VP, Human Resources: Gerry Murray
VP, Marketing and Advertising: Bonnie Burton

LOCATIONS

HQ: 100 West St., Pittsfield, MA 01201
Phone: 413-496-3000 **Fax:** 413-496-3616
Web: www.kbtoys.com/kbhome.htm

KB Toys has distribution and fulfillment centers in Alabama, Arizona, Kentucky, Massachusetts, and New Jersey.

PRODUCTS/OPERATIONS

Store Formats

KB Toys Clearance Center (one store only, located in Wilmington, Delaware; more than 15,000 sq. ft., deeply discounted clearance and overstock toys, games, and collectibles)
KB Toys (more than 1,000 stores in malls; average size is 3,500 sq. ft.)
KB Toy Works (nearly 200 neighborhood stores; average size 7,500 sq. ft.)
KB Toy Outlet/Toy Liquidator (more than 100 stores in outlet malls)
KB Toy Express (temporary stores in malls operating from late October to late December)

COMPETITORS

Amazon.com
F.A.O.
FAO Schwarz
GameStop
Gymboree
Kmart
Sears
Target
Toys "R" Us
Wal-Mart
Zany Brainy

HISTORICAL FINANCIALS

Company Type: Private

Income Statement FYE: January 31

	REVENUE ($ mil.)	NET INCOME ($ mil.)	NET PROFIT MARGIN	EMPLOYEES
1/02	2,000	—	—	25,000
1/01	2,000	—	—	16,000
1/00	1,767	—	—	13,000
Annual Growth	6.4%	—	—	38.7%

Revenue History

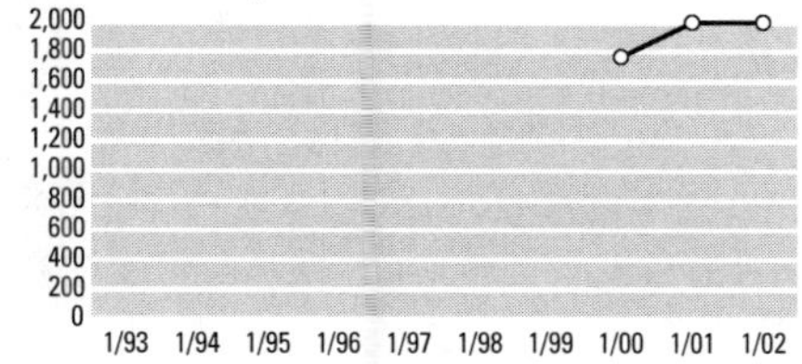

Kemper Insurance Companies

The Kemper Companies should be called The Scamper Companies since recent hard times have the company reeling. No longer writing new policies, the once-proud Kemper Insurance Companies has traditionally offered a wide array of personal, risk management, and commercial property & casualty products, mostly through its flagship Lumbermens brand. But the axe has come down on its service platform (sold to Platinum Equity), many of its mid-market lines such as worker's compensation and auto (sold to The St. Paul Companies), and much of its reinsurance arrangement with Berkshire Hathaway.

Over the past few years, Kemper had completed a realignment of its operations — selling its reinsurance operations and parts of its group captives business to The Hartford. However, losses from pre-1999 policies and investment difficulties during 2002 created a free-fall in income for 2002. (The company is one of the few troubled insurance outfits not to cite September 11 as even a partial explanation for its troubles.)

Opportunities to resurrect the company in any familiar form are evaporating, however. A deal to sell many remaining lines to Securitas Capital, Cypress Merchant Banking, and Gilbert Global Partners fell through in 2003.

HISTORY

James Kemper started Lumbermens Mutual in 1912 to provide workers compensation coverage to Illinois lumberyard owners. The 26-year-old insurance agent perceived a niche when yard owners complained that insurers were overcharging by lumping lumberyards in with the more dangerous logging business. The next year Kemper expanded into fire insurance for lumberyards by founding National Underwriters. Lumbermens began growing, adding offices in Philadelphia, Boston, and Syracuse, New York. By 1921 the company was based in Chicago.

Lumbermens was one of the first auto insurers in the US, and in 1926 it formed American Motorists Insurance Co. specifically for personal and commercial auto insurance. In the early 1930s the firm added boiler and machinery, surety bond, and inland marine coverage. After a receptionist began greeting callers with "Kemper Insurance," Lumbermens subsidiaries all began to be known as the "Kemper companies."

The Kemper family was active in philanthropy, founding a traffic safety institute at Northwestern University in the 1930s and endowing a scholarship fund.

In 1957 Lumbermens began offering marine coverage. The Kemper companies grew to include Federal Kemper Life Assurance in 1961 and American Protection Insurance the next year.

In 1967 Lumbermens, responding to concerns about how a mutual company could own so many subsidiaries, formed public holding company Kemperco (later Kemper Corp.) in which Lumbermens owned controlling interest. In 1981, at age 94, James Kemper died.

Like many other companies, Kemper Corp. set its sights in the 1980s on becoming a financial services powerhouse, buying three brokerages. As cyclic losses inherent in property/casualty insurance dragged down earnings growth, the company in 1989 began selling those operations back to Lumbermens for stock, decreasing Lumbermens' interest in Kemper Corp. (Property/casualty premiums had dropped from 60% of operating income in 1980 to 49% in 1981 and continued to fall until 1985.)

Additionally, reorganization gave separate management and boards of directors to Kemper Corp. and Kemper National Insurance Cos. (formed by Lumbermens Mutual Casualty Company, American Motorists Insurance Company, and American Manufacturers Mutual Insurance Company). In 1992 the companies' chairmanships were separated as well. Kemper Insurance (originally Kemper National) was formed just in time to be pummeled by the longest and costliest string of natural disasters in the 20th century.

Kemper Corp., meanwhile, became a financial services company with mutual fund offerings. In 1995 it sold its brokerage unit, and in 1996 it was bought by Insurance Partners and Zurich Insurance Group (now Zurich Financial).

Kemper Insurance, meanwhile, was devastated by the 1994 bond crash; earnings sank again in 1996 when the company bolstered environmental and asbestos reserves. Toward the end of the decade, the firm began realigning its insurance offerings, acquiring specialty coverage players (including Integrated DisAbility Management in 1997, Eagle Insurance in 1998, and Universal Bonding in 1999) and selling Kemper Reinsurance to GE Capital (1998). In 1999 Kemper took advantage of continuing deregulation when it announced plans to open LMC, a thrift serving Illinois. Kemper joined forces with Sumitomo Marine & Fire to sell discounted insurance products to Japanese corporations.

In 2000 Kemper bolstered its presence in the workers' compensation market when it acquired the policy renewal rights from the Superior National Insurance companies, which were under supervision by the California Insurance Department. The next year Kemper sold its Canadian subsidiary to UK-based Royal & Sun Alliance Insurance.

EXECUTIVES

Chairman and CEO: David B. Mathis, age 64
EVP, Capital Development: William A. Hickey
EVP, Client Services Group: Patricia A. Drago
SVP and CFO: Art Chandler
SVP and Chief Actuary: Frederick O. Kist
SVP, Corporate Planning and Administration: Mary Ann Eddy
SVP, Human Resources: Sue A. Coughlin
SVP and CFO, Lumbermens Mutual Casualty: Mural R. Josephson
VP, Marketing: Joel Borgardt
Treasurer: Michael A. Finelli Jr.
VP, Sales: Robert Gwinn
General Auditor: Kent L. Suarez
President and CEO, GreatLand Insurance Co.: W. (Mick) Taylor
President and CEO, Kemper Casualty Company; EVP, Lumbermens Mutual Casualty: Dennis P. Kane
President, Kemper Technology Services; SVP, Lumbermans Mutual Casualty Company: Jack E. Scott
Auditors: KPMG LLP

LOCATIONS

HQ: 1 Kemper Dr., Long Grove, IL 60049
Phone: 847-320-2000 **Fax:** 847-320-7992
Web: www.kemperinsurance.com

Kemper Insurance Companies has operations in Australia, Belgium, Canada, Germany, Japan, Singapore, and the US.

PRODUCTS/OPERATIONS

Subsidiaries and Affiliates

American Manufacturers Mutual Insurance Company
Eagle Insurance
Financial Insurance Solutions
GreatLand
Juris Prudent, Inc.
Kemper Alternative Risks
Kemper National Services, Inc.
Kemper Risk Management
Kemper Surety
KEMPES
Lumbermens Life Agency
NATLSCO

COMPETITORS

Acordia
Allstate
American Family Insurance
American Financial
AIG
American Safety Insurance
Chubb
CIGNA
CNA Financial
Liberty Mutual
Mutual of Omaha
New York Life
Prudential
Reliance Group
St. Paul Companies
Travelers

HISTORICAL FINANCIALS

Company Type: Mutual company

Income Statement FYE: December 31

	REVENUE ($ mil.)	NET INCOME ($ mil.)	NET PROFIT MARGIN	EMPLOYEES
12/02	1,000	(312)	—	5,000
12/01	2,848	121	4.3%	9,000
12/00	3,014	115	3.8%	8,500
12/99	2,913	168	5.8%	9,000
12/98	3,327	227	6.8%	9,000
12/97	3,380	222	6.6%	9,500
12/96	3,225	19	0.6%	10,068
12/95	3,283	169	5.1%	8,837
12/94	3,327	25	0.8%	8,295
12/93	—	119	—	9,000
Annual Growth	(13.9%)	—	—	(6.3%)

Net Income History

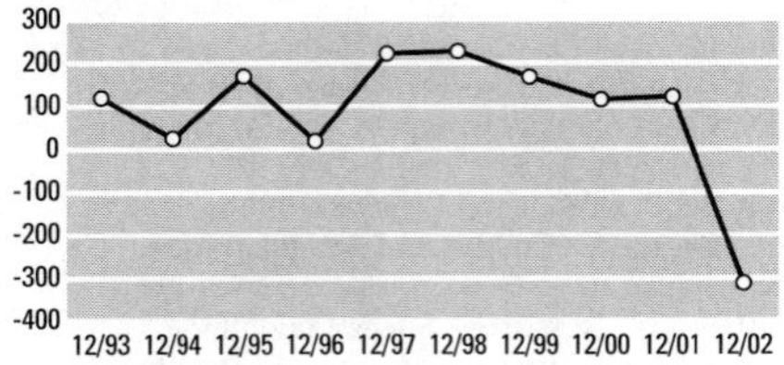

Kerr Drug, Inc.

Oh, you can buy knick-knacks and doo-dads at a Kerr Drug store, but the company that bills itself as "Carolina's Drugstore" puts its primary focus on pharmacy operations, which account for the majority of sales. Kerr Drug operates more than 130 stores in the Carolinas in several formats, ranging from upscale stores featuring cosmetologists, expanded gift sections, and even Starbucks coffee to the Smart Dollar Stores format offering more cleaning supplies, health and beauty aids, and soft goods. Founded by Banks Kerr in 1951, the chain was sold in 1995 to retailer J. C. Penney. A management group led by Kerr CEO Anthony Civello and CFO Richard Johnson took Kerr Drug private in 1996.

EXECUTIVES

Chairman, President and CEO: Anthony N. Civello
EVP and CFO: Richard D. Johnson
SVP, Merchandising and Marketing: William (Bill) Baxley
SVP, Operations: Buck Zawilla
SVP, Pharmacy and Logistics: Ralph Petri
VP and CIO: Joey Dorsett
VP, Human Resources: Briony Voorhees
Director of Customer Relations and Administration: Phyllis Patterson
Director of Facilities Planning: Jerry Root
Director of Marketing: Diane Eliezer
Director of Pharmacy: Mark Gregory

LOCATIONS

HQ: 2522 S. Tri-Center Blvd., Durham, NC 27713
Phone: 919-544-3896 **Fax:** 919-544-7138
Web: www.kerrdrug.com

Kerr Drug has more than 130 stores in North and South Carolina.

COMPETITORS

BJs Wholesale Club
CVS
Delhaize America
Eckerd
Kroger
Publix
Walgreen
Wal-Mart
Winn-Dixie

HISTORICAL FINANCIALS

Company Type: Private

Income Statement FYE: December 31

	ESTIMATED REVENUE ($ mil.)	NET INCOME ($ mil.)	NET PROFIT MARGIN	EMPLOYEES
12/01	750	—	—	3,500
12/00	650	—	—	3,500
Annual Growth	15.4%	—	—	0.0%

Revenue History

Key Food Stores

Key Food Stores Co-Operative unlocks buying power for independent New York grocers. Founded in 1937, the co-op helps about 115 independently owned food retailers in the New York City area compete with major supermarket chains by pooling buying power. Key Food's member-owners run stores mainly in Brooklyn and Queens, but also in the Bronx, Manhattan, and Staten Island and in Nassau County and Suffolk County. Among its members are Pick Quick Foods, Dan's Supreme Super Markets, Man-dell Food Stores, Gemstone Supermarkets, Queens Supermarkets, and Penguin Key Food Supermarkets. Distributor Grocery Haulers Inc. (GHI) bought the company's distribution business.

EXECUTIVES

CEO: Richard Pallitto
President: Lawrence Mandell
Treasurer: Sam Kristal
Controller: Ron Phillips

LOCATIONS

HQ: Key Food Stores Co-Operative, Inc.
1200 South Ave., Staten Island, NY 10314
Phone: 718-370-4200

COMPETITORS

Ahold USA
D'Agostino Supermarkets
Di Giorgio
General Trading
A&P
Gristede's Foods
King Kullen Grocery
Krasdale Foods
Pathmark

HISTORICAL FINANCIALS

Company Type: Cooperative

Income Statement FYE: April 30

	REVENUE ($ mil.)	NET INCOME ($ mil.)	NET PROFIT MARGIN	EMPLOYEES
4/02	445	—	—	400
4/01	433	—	—	400
4/00	487	—	—	425
4/99	500	—	—	425
4/98	550	—	—	425
4/97	550	—	—	425
4/96	515	—	—	480
4/95	541	—	—	500
4/94	600	—	—	500
4/93	600	—	—	—
Annual Growth	(3.3%)	—	—	(2.8%)

Revenue History

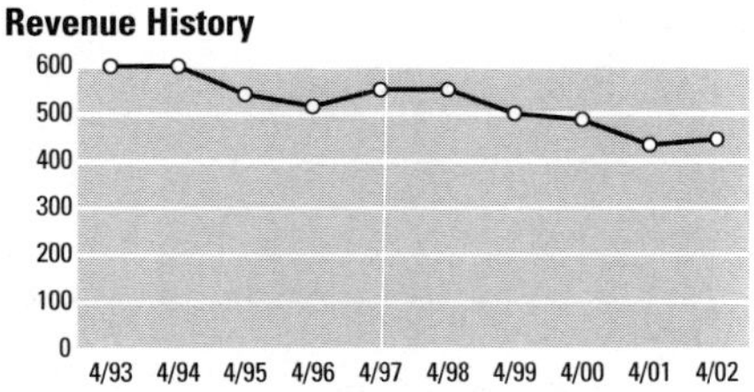

Key Plastics

If you unlock Key Plastics, you'll find a company that designs and makes plastic parts for cars and trucks around the world. Key Plastics' products include door handles, radio bezels, speaker grilles, air louvers, interior trim components, and pressurized bottles. The company's major customers are Ford, General Motors, and DaimlerChrysler. Other customers include suppliers to the carmakers. Key Plastics, which operates about 20 manufacturing facilities in Europe and North America, was acquired from bankruptcy protection in 2001 by Carlyle Management Group, a Dallas-based investment group (part of The Carlyle Group).

EXECUTIVES

Chairman and CEO: B. Edward Ewing
President: Daniel Ajamian
COO: David Benoit
SVP, Business Management: Doug Hollenshead
SVP, Human Resources and Legal Affairs: Rick Blough
VP, Business Management: Peter McElroy
VP, Finance: Skip Autry
President, Exterior Products Group: Tim Nelson
President, Underhood Products: Claire Walia

LOCATIONS

HQ: Key Plastics L.L.C.
21700 Haggerty Rd., Ste. 100 North,
Northville, MI 48167
Phone: 248-449-6100 **Fax:** 248-449-4105
Web: www.keyplastics.com

Key Plastics has manufacturing plants in Europe and North America. Its US plants are located in Indiana, Michigan, Ohio, and Pennsylvania.

PRODUCTS/OPERATIONS

Selected Products

Exterior/Underhood Products
Brake reservoirs
Degas bottles
Exterior and interior door handle assemblies
Exterior cladding and sail panels
Fuel door assemblies
Interior door handle assemblies
Mirror shells
Power steering bottles

Trim Products
Air bag covers
Air louvers
Flat appliqués
HVAC bezel assemblies
Ignition bobbins/spools
Ignition case assemblies
Instrument cluster assemblies
PRNDL bezels
Radio bezel assemblies
Seat trim
Speaker grilles

COMPETITORS

Donnelly
LDM Technologies
Lear
Siegel-Robert

HISTORICAL FINANCIALS

Company Type: Private

Income Statement FYE: December 31

	REVENUE ($ mil.)	NET INCOME ($ mil.)	NET PROFIT MARGIN	EMPLOYEES
12/02	525	—	—	6,600
12/01	502	—	—	6,500
12/00	376	—	—	6,413
12/99	537	—	—	6,726
12/98	372	—	—	5,000
12/97	306	—	—	3,730
12/96	217	—	—	2,780
12/95	179	—	—	1,600
12/94	194	—	—	1,960
12/93	150	—	—	1,580
Annual Growth	15.0%	—	—	17.2%

Revenue History

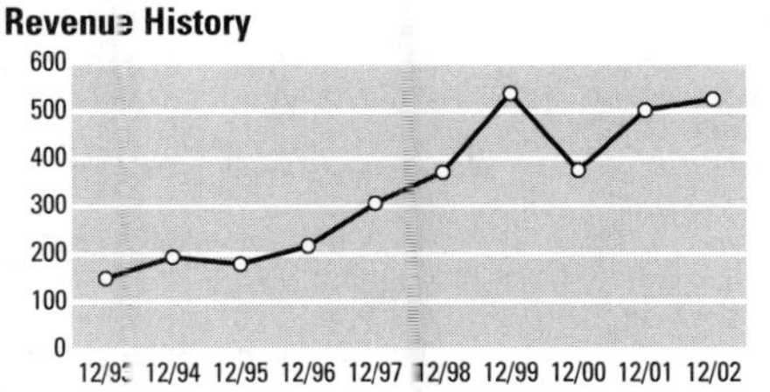

Keystone Foods LLC

Keystone Foods hopes you won't just have the salad. The company is one of the largest makers of hamburger patties and processed poultry. It's a major supplier to McDonald's restaurants; in the 1970s Keystone persuaded McDonald's to switch to frozen beef to reduce the health risks associated with fresh beef. Overseas, operations include McKey Food Services and MacFood Services (some are joint ventures). In addition to its worldwide meat processing plants, which produce millions of burgers daily, Keystone also operates M&M Restaurant Supply, and has begun to supply fresh beef to a US grocery retailer. Chairman and CEO Herbert Lotman owns the company, which began as a beef-boning business in the 1960s.

EXECUTIVES

Chairman and CEO: Herbert (Herb) Lotman, age 69
President and COO: Jerry Dean
VP, CFO: Paul McGarvie
VP, Human Resources: Jerry Gotro
VP, Sales: Jerry Wilson
Auditors: Ernst & Young LLP

LOCATIONS

HQ: 300 Barr Harbor Dr., Ste. 600,
West Conshohocken, PA 19428
Phone: 610-667-6700 **Fax:** 610-667-1460
Web: www.keystonefoods.com

Keystone Foods has operations in Asia, Australia, Europe, the Middle East, South America, and the US.

PRODUCTS/OPERATIONS

Selected Products

Beef
- Fajita strips
- Hamburger patties

Chicken
- Breaded patties
- Breast filets
- Diced
- Fajita strips
- Nuggets
- Wings

Fish
Pork

COMPETITORS

Anderson-DuBose
ConAgra
Gold Kist
Golden State Foods
Lopez Foods
Martin-Brower
McLane Foodservice
OSI
Perdue
Pilgrim's Pride
SYSCO
Tyson Foods
Tyson Fresh Meats
U.S. Foodservice

HISTORICAL FINANCIALS

Company Type: Private

Income Statement FYE: December 31

	ESTIMATED REVENUE ($ mil.)	NET INCOME ($ mil.)	NET PROFIT MARGIN	EMPLOYEES
12/01	2,700	—	—	6,700
12/00	2,650	—	—	6,700
12/99	2,594	—	—	6,700
12/98	2,342	—	—	4,300
12/97	2,184	—	—	4,300
12/96	1,900	—	—	4,000
12/95	1,700	—	—	2,000
12/94	1,600	—	—	—
12/93	1,500	—	—	—
Annual Growth	7.6%	—	—	22.3%

Revenue History

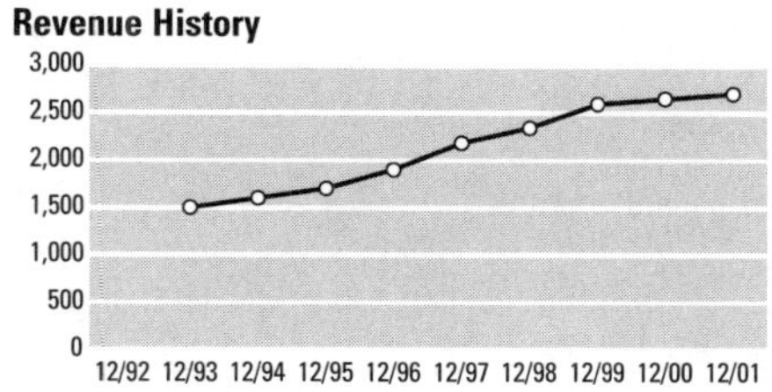

KI

KI can be found in cubicles, classrooms, cafeterias, and college dorms. Formerly known as Krueger International, KI makes ergonomic seating, cabinets, and other furniture used by businesses, health care organizations, schools, and government agencies. The company offers everything from desks to daybeds, not to mention tables, wall and storage systems, and even trash cans. KI operates manufacturing facilities in Canada, Italy, and the US, and markets its products through sales representatives, furniture dealers, architects, and interior designers. Founded in 1941, KI was bought in the 1980s by its managers, who later allowed their employees to buy company stock. The company is now 100% owned by employees.

EXECUTIVES

President and CEO: Richard J. Resch
CFO and Treasurer: Mark Olsen
VP Sales and Marketing: Mark Christopher
Director of Human Resources:
Kristine Hackbarth-Horn

LOCATIONS

HQ: 1330 Bellevue St., Green Bay, WI 54302
Phone: 920-468-8100 **Fax:** 920-468-0280
Web: www.ki.com

KI has manufacturing facilities in California, Kentucky, Mississippi, North Carolina, and Wisconsin, as well as in Canada and Italy.

PRODUCTS/OPERATIONS

Selected Products

Auditorium seating
Bookcases
Desks
File cabinets
Full-height movable walls
Lecterns
Modular furniture
Planters
Power and data connections
Receptacles
Residence hall furniture
Seating
Sleepers
Special events seating
Stools
Tables

Selected Operations

AGI (upscale upholstered wood-frame waiting room/lobby furniture)
Pallas Textiles (contract and residential textiles, wall coverings, panel fabrics)
Spacesaver (high-density mobile storage systems, steel shelving, and filing systems)

COMPETITORS

Falcon Products
Haworth
Herman Miller
HighPoint Furniture
HON INDUSTRIES
Kimball International
Knoll
La-Z-Boy
MITY
Shelby Williams
Steelcase
Virco Mfg.

HISTORICAL FINANCIALS

Company Type: Private

Income Statement FYE: December 31

	REVENUE ($ mil.)	NET INCOME ($ mil.)	NET PROFIT MARGIN	EMPLOYEES
12/02	600	—	—	3,500
12/01	625	—	—	3,500
12/00	631	—	—	4,517
12/99	606	—	—	4,500
12/98	550	—	—	4,265
12/97	450	—	—	2,800
12/96	420	—	—	—
Annual Growth	6.1%	—	—	4.6%

Revenue History

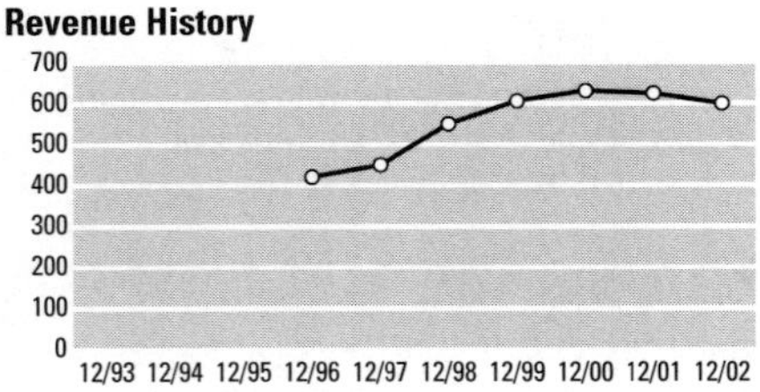

Kimball Hill Homes

Chicagoland's GI generation and their offspring, who have long thrived in the 'burbs, can thank lawyer-turned-builder D. Kimball Hill, a pioneer of the city's suburbs and founder of Kimball Hill Homes. The company builds single-family detached homes, townhomes, and condominiums in the Chicago area and in California, Florida, Nevada, Ohio, Oregon, Texas, Washington, and Wisconsin. Kimball Hill Homes mainly targets first-time and move-up buyers, but also builds homes up to 4,100 sq. ft. in size and $800,000 in price. Subsidiary KH Financial offers mortgage financing and refinancing of investment properties in five states. David Hill Jr., CEO and son of the founder, and other Hill family members own the company.

EXECUTIVES

Chairman and CEO: David K. Hill Jr.
President and COO: Isaac Heimbinder
CFO: Gene Rowehl
Director, Human Resources: Jo Ann Peterson
Director, Marketing: Brent Gustafson

LOCATIONS

HQ: 5999 New Wilke Rd., Ste. 504,
Rolling Meadows, IL 60008
Phone: 847-364-7300 **Fax:** 847-439-0875
Web: www.kimballhill.com

Kimball Hill Homes has principal operations in Austin, Dallas/Ft. Worth, and Houston, Texas; Chicago; Elk Grove, Sacramento, and Stockton, California; Bradenton, Naples, Sarasota, and Tampa, Florida; Las Vegas, Nevada; Cleveland, Ohio; Portland, Oregon; Vancouver, Washington; and Saint Francis (a Milwaukee suburb), Wisconsin.

COMPETITORS

Beazer Homes
Centex
David Weekley Homes
D.R. Horton
KB Home
Lennar
M.D.C. Holdings
Morrison Homes
Neumann Homes
Pulte Homes
Ryland
Schuler Homes
Town and Country Homes

HISTORICAL FINANCIALS

Company Type: Private

Income Statement FYE: September 30

	REVENUE ($ mil.)	NET INCOME ($ mil.)	NET PROFIT MARGIN	EMPLOYEES
9/03*	800	—	—	700
6/02	700	—	—	654
6/01	673	—	—	546
6/00	580	—	—	510
6/99	490	—	—	427
6/98	410	—	—	320
6/97	296	—	—	280
6/96	224	—	—	240
Annual Growth	19.9%	—	—	16.5%

*Fiscal year change

Revenue History

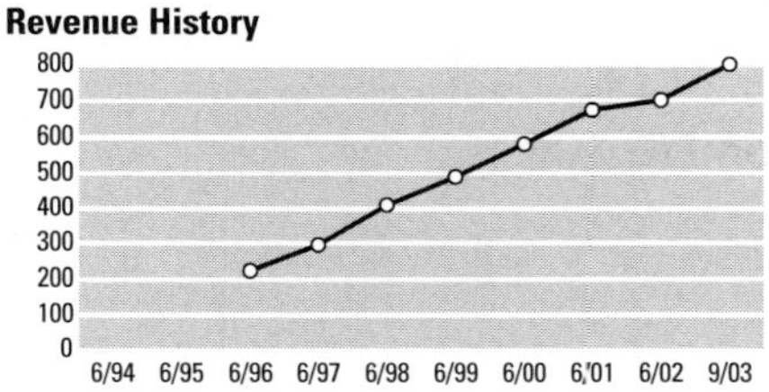

KinderCare Learning Centers, Inc.

KinderCare helps prepare the kids of today for the world of tomorrow. KinderCare Learning Centers, a leading US for-profit operator of preschool and child care facilities, provides child care and age-specific educational programs for kids from six weeks to 12 years old. Some 132,000 children are enrolled in about 1,270 centers in 39 states and two centers in the UK; the average weekly full-time tuition is around $145. Operations include KinderCare Learning Centers, KinderCare At Work, and Mulberry Child Care Centers. The company also runs high school distance learning programs. Affiliates of Kohlberg Kravis Roberts own a majority stake in KinderCare.

In addition to its programs for preschools and elementary-age children, KinderCare operates three programs for high school students through its KC Distance Learning subsidiary. These include Keystone National High School, the Learning and Evaluation Center (for make-up or extra-credit courses), and the Keystone eSchool (correspondence- and Internet-based courses).

KinderCare also has investments in Chancellor Beacon Academies, a charter school management company, and Voyager Expanded Learning, a developer of educational curricula.

EXECUTIVES

Chairman and CEO: David J. Johnson, age 56, $1,115,225 pay
SVP and Chief Development Officer: Bruce A. Walters, age 45, $320,157 pay
EVP and CFO: Dan R. Jackson, age 48, $321,092 pay
SVP, General Counsel and Secretary: Eva M. Kripalani, age 43, $305,558 pay
SVP, Human Resources: Edward L. Brewington, age 59
SVP, Operations: S. Wray Hutchinson, age 42
Auditors: Deloitte & Touche LLP

LOCATIONS

HQ: 650 NE Holladay, Ste. 1400, Portland, OR 97232
Phone: 503-872-1300 **Fax:** 503-872-1349
Web: www.kindercare.com

PRODUCTS/OPERATIONS

Selected Operations

KC Distance Learning
Keystone eSchool (online high school courses)
Keystone National High School (accredited correspondence-based high school)
Learning and Evaluation Center (high school subject extension, make-up, or extra credit classes)
KinderCare At Work (on-site or near-site corporate care centers for children six weeks to 12 years of age)
KinderCare Learning Centers (for children six weeks to 12 years of age)
Mulberry Child Care Centers (for children six weeks to 12 years of age)

Selected Educational Programs

Early Learning Curriculum (curriculum for children from 24 months to 26 months)
Hooked On Phonics (phonics-based reading and literacy program for children from three to five)
Journey to Discovery (kindergarten curriculum using materials from McGraw-Hill's DLM Early Childhood Program)
KC Imagination Highway (project-based curriculum for children from six to 12 years of age)
Kindergarten at KinderCare (private kindergarten)
Preschool at KinderCare (program for four-year-old children)
Preschool Readiness Curriculum (program for three-year-old children)
Summer Explorations (summer program for elementary school students)
Welcome to Learning (curriculum for children from six weeks to 24 months)

COMPETITORS

ARAMARK
Bright Horizons Family Solutions
Chancellor Beacon Academies
Child Development Schools
Childtime Learning Centers
Kaplan
Kiddie Academy International, Inc.
Knowledge Learning
La Petite Academy
Nobel Learning Communities
Security Capital
Sylvan Learning
YMCA

HISTORICAL FINANCIALS

Company Type: Private

Income Statement FYE: Friday closest to May 31

	REVENUE ($ mil.)	NET INCOME ($ mil.)	NET PROFIT MARGIN	EMPLOYEES
5/03	850	13	1.6%	25,000
5/02	829	17	2.0%	27,000
5/01	743	16	2.1%	28,000
5/00	697	20	2.9%	26,000
5/99	633	14	2.1%	25,400
5/98	597	3	0.6%	22,800
5/97	563	(13)	—	22,400
5/96	541	22	4.0%	23,000
5/95	507	22	4.4%	21,000
5/94	489	20	4.1%	21,500
Annual Growth	6.3%	(4.2%)	—	1.7%

2003 Year-End Financials

Debt ratio: 326.5%
Return on equity: 10.4%
Cash ($ mil.): 18
Current ratio: 0.52
Long-term debt ($ mil.): 441

Net Income History

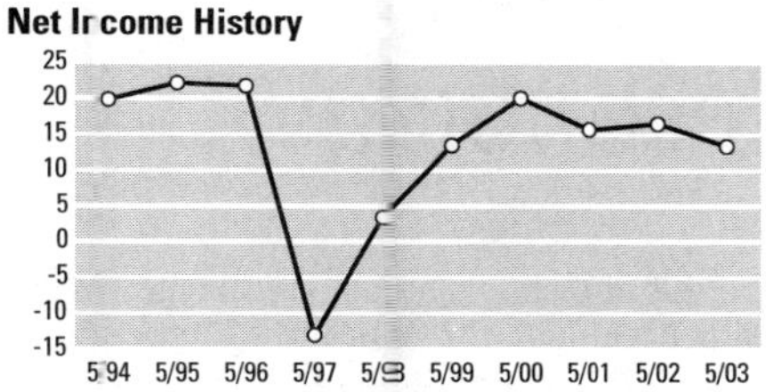

Kinetic Concepts, Inc.

Kinetic Concepts makes its bed and has no problems lying in it. The company makes beds for institutional and home use. Products include specialized mattresses and pressure relief and pulmonary care products to treat and prevent complications associated with patient immobility, such as pressure sores and the harmful buildup of fluid in the lungs. Kinetic Concepts also makes medical devices to help treat wounds and increase blood circulation, and has products that help caregivers move and treat obese patients. The company operates through more than 100 service facilities across the US and also markets its products in Australia, Canada, and Europe.

The company makes the BariKare line of specialized beds, the NuPulse system for treatment of diabetic-related wounds, and the PlexiPulse All In 1 pneumatic compression device.

The company's specialized medical beds, including the RotoRest Delta and the TriaDyne II, rotate on each side to prevent pressure sores from forming on bedridden patients.

EXECUTIVES

Chairman: Robert Jaunich II, age 63
President, CEO, and Director: Dennert O. (Denny) Ware, age 61, $809,991 pay
SVP, Secretary, and General Counsel: Dennis E. Noll, age 48, $556,916 pay
President, KCI USA: Christopher M. Fashek, age 53, $386,439 pay
President, KCI International: Jorg W. Menten, age 54
VP, Manufacturing: Michael J. Burke, age 55, $327,300 pay
VP, Human Resources: Rush E. Cone, age 52
VP, Finance, Acting CFO, and Corporate Controller: Martin J. Landon, age 43
VP, Corporate Development: G. Frederick Rush, age 53, $378,837 pay
Auditors: Ernst & Young LLP

LOCATIONS

HQ: 8023 Vantage Dr., San Antonio, TX 78230
Phone: 210-524-9000 **Fax:** 210-255-6998
Web: www.kci1.com

Kinetic Concepts, Inc., sells its products primarily in Australia, Canada, Europe, and the US.

COMPETITORS

Hillenbrand
Invacare
Medline Industries
Span-America Medical
Sunrise Medical

HISTORICAL FINANCIALS

Company Type: Private

Income Statement FYE: December 31

	REVENUE ($ mil.)	NET INCOME ($ mil.)	NET PROFIT MARGIN	EMPLOYEES
12/02	579	150	25.9%	3,400
12/01	456	24	5.2%	2,900
12/00	354	9	2.6%	2,400
12/99	321	(0)	—	2,100
12/98	331	12	3.6%	2,100
12/97	307	13	4.1%	2,100
12/96	270	39	14.4%	2,066
12/95	243	28	11.7%	2,016
12/94	270	64	23.6%	1,938
12/93	269	8	2.8%	2,460
Annual Growth	8.9%	39.5%	—	3.7%

2002 Year-End Financials

Debt ratio: —
Return on equity: —
Cash ($ mil.): 54
Current ratio: 2.31
Long-term debt ($ mil.): 491

Net Income History

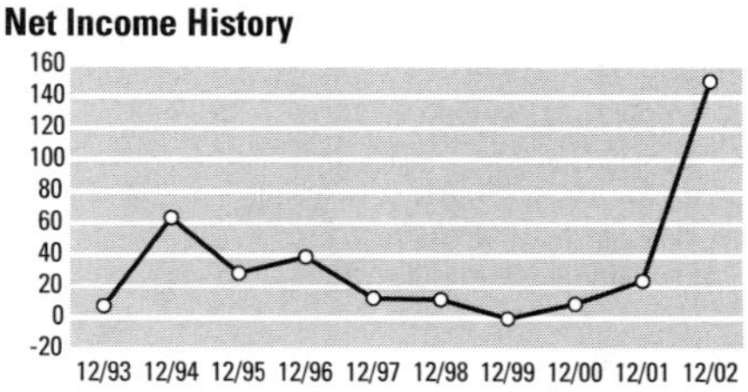

King Kullen Grocery

How's this for a crowning achievement? King Kullen Grocery Company claims to have been the originator of the supermarket format. Heralding itself as "America's first supermarket," the firm operates nearly 50 supermarkets, mainly on Long Island, New York. King Kullen also owns an 18,000-sq.-ft. Wild By Nature natural foods store (and plans to open more), and it offers a line of vitamins and supplements under the same name in some regular stores. Most stores average about 35,000 sq. ft., but it has a 62,000-sq.-ft. upscale market with features such as ethnic fare, catering, and a Wild By Nature section. Started in a Queens warehouse in 1930 by Michael Cullen, the firm is owned and operated by Cullen's relatives.

EXECUTIVES

Chairman and Co-CEO: Bernard D. Kennedy
Co-President and Co-COO: Brian C. Cullen
Co-President and Co-COO: J. D. Kennedy
VP, Government and Industrial Relations: Tom Cullen
Director of Human Resources: Thomas Nagle
Auditors: Grant Thornton LLP

LOCATIONS

HQ: King Kullen Grocery Company Inc.
185 Central Ave., Bethpage, NY 11714
Phone: 516-733-7100 **Fax:** 516-827-6325
Web: www.kingkullen.com

COMPETITORS

Ahold USA
C&S Wholesale
A&P
Gristede's Foods
IGA
Kmart
Man-dell Food Stores
Pathmark
Wakefern Food
Wal-Mart

HISTORICAL FINANCIALS

Company Type: Private

Income Statement FYE: September 30

	REVENUE ($ mil.)	NET INCOME ($ mil.)	NET PROFIT MARGIN	EMPLOYEES
9/02	790	—	—	4,800
9/01	782	—	—	4,579
9/00	720	—	—	4,400
9/99	714	—	—	4,100
9/98	725	—	—	4,500
9/97	750	—	—	4,400
9/96	724	—	—	4,500
9/95	706	—	—	4,500
9/94	718	—	—	4,500
9/93	720	—	—	4,500
Annual Growth	1.0%	—	—	0.7%

Revenue History

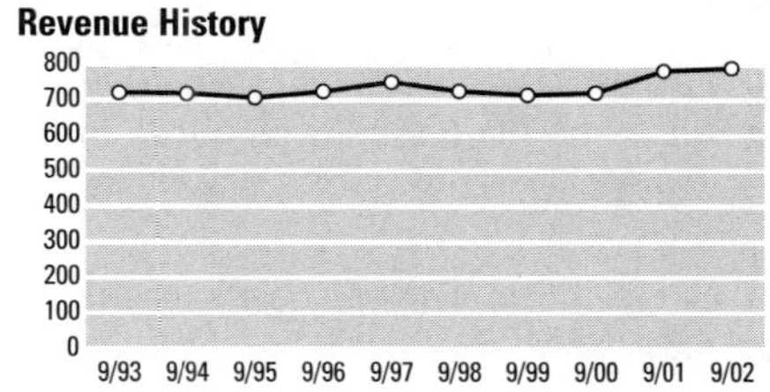

King Ranch, Inc.

Meanwhile, back at the ranch . . . the sprawling King Ranch, that is. King Ranch, founded in 1853, extends way beyond the original 825,000 acres that are still home to about 60,000 cattle and a wide variety of animal species. King Ranch oversees ranching and farming interests in Texas and Florida, but these days it also benefits from oil and gas royalties, farming (cotton, citrus, and sugar), and retail operations (designer saddles, leather goods). In addition, King Ranch also beefs up revenues with tourist dollars from birdwatchers, hunters, and sightseers who visit the Texas ranch. The descendants of founder Richard King own King Ranch.

Considered the birthplace of the American ranching industry, King Ranch has introduced the new highly fertile breed of beef cattle: the King Ranch Santa Cruz, which is one-fourth Gelbvieh, one-fourth Red Angus, and one-half Santa Gertrudis. Raising animals isn't the only thing King Ranch cottons to — this sprawl of four noncontiguous ranches is also one of the US's largest cotton producers.

Like a good western movie, some things ride into the sunset at King Ranch. The company sold its 670-acre Kentucky Thoroughbred breeding and racing farm, as well as most of its foreign ranches, and its primary oil and gas subsidiary.

The company's operations are managed from its Houston corporate headquarters.

HISTORY

King Ranch was founded in 1853 by former steamboat captain Richard King and his wife Henrietta, the daughter of a Brownsville, Texas, missionary. On the advice of his friend Robert E. Lee, King used his steamboating profits and occasional strong-arm tactics to buy land — miles of flat, brush-filled, coastal plain and desert south of Corpus Christi, Texas, valued at pennies an acre.

The next year King relocated the residents of an entire drought-ravaged village to the ranch and employed them as ranch hands, known ever after as *kineños* ("King's men"). The Kings built their homestead in 1858 at a site recommended by Lee.

King Ranch endured attacks from Union guerrillas during the Civil War and Mexican bandits after the war. Times were tough, but King was up to the challenge, always traveling armed and with outriders.

In 1867 the ranch used its famed Running W brand for the first time. After King's death in 1885, Robert Kleberg, who married King's daughter Alice, managed the 1.2 million-acre ranch for his mother-in-law. Henrietta died in 1925 and left three-fourths of the ranch to Alice. Before Robert's death in 1932, control of the ranch passed to sons Richard and Bob. In 1933 Bob negotiated an exclusive oil and gas lease with Houston-based Humble Oil, which later became part of Exxon.

While Richard served in Congress, Bob ran the ranch. He developed the Santa Gertrudis, the first breed of cattle ever created in the US, by crossing British shorthorn cattle with Indian Brahmas. The new breed was better suited to the hot, dry South Texas climate.

Bob made King Ranch a leading breeder of quarter horses, which worked cattle, and Thoroughbreds, which he raced. He bought Kentucky Derby winner Bold Venture in 1936 and a Kentucky breeding farm in 1946; that year a King Ranch horse, Assault, won racing's Triple Crown.

When Bob died in 1974, the family asked James Clement, husband of one of the founders' great-granddaughters, to become CEO and bypassed Robert Shelton, a King relative and orphan whom Bob had raised as his own son. Shelton severed ties with the ranch in 1977 over a lawsuit he filed against Exxon, and partially won, alleging underpayment of royalties.

Under Clement, King Ranch became a multinational corporation. In 1980 it formed King Ranch Oil and Gas (also called King Ranch Energy) to explore for and produce oil and gas in five states and the Gulf of Mexico. In 1988 Clement retired, and Kimberly-Clark executive Darwin Smith became the first CEO not related to the founders. Smith left after one year, and the reins passed to petroleum geologist Roger Jarvis and then to Jack Hunt in 1995.

With the help of scientists, in the early 1990s the company developed a leaner, more fertile breed of Santa Gertrudis called the Santa Cruz.

In 1998 Stephen "Tio" Kleberg, the only King descendant still actively working the ranch, was pushed from the saddle of daily operations to a seat on the board. King Ranch sold its Kentucky horse farm in 1998 and teamed up with Collier Enterprises that year to purchase citrus grower Turner Foods from utility holding company FPL Group. In 2000 King Ranch sold King Ranch Energy to St. Mary Land and Exploration Co. for $60 million.

EXECUTIVES

Chairman: James H. Clement
President and CEO: Jack Hunt
CFO: Bill Gardiner
VP Audit: Richard Nilles
VP Livestock: Paul Genho
Secretary and General Counsel: Frank Perrone
Director, Human Resources: Martha Breit
Director, Security and Wildlife: Butch Thompson

LOCATIONS

HQ: 3 River Way, Ste. 1600, Houston, TX 77056
Phone: 832-681-5700 **Fax:** 832-681-5759
Web: www.king-ranch.com

King Ranch operates ranching and farming interests in South Texas as well as in Florida.

Selected Agricultural Operations

Florida
- 3,100 acres (St. Augustine sod)
- 12,000 acres (sugar cane)
- 40,000 acres (orange and grapefruit groves)

Texas
- 60,000 acres (cotton and grain)

PRODUCTS/OPERATIONS

Selected Operations

King Ranch Museum
King Ranch Nature Tour Program
King Ranch Saddle Shop (leather products)
Consolidated Citrus Limited
Partnership (southern Florida citrus groves)

COMPETITORS

Alico
AzTx Cattle
Bartlett and Company
Cactus Feeders
Calcot
ContiGroup
Devon Energy
Friona Industries
Koch
Lykes Bros.
Southern States

HISTORICAL FINANCIALS

Company Type: Private

Income Statement FYE: December 31

	ESTIMATED REVENUE ($ mil.)	NET INCOME ($ mil.)	NET PROFIT MARGIN	EMPLOYEES
12/00	300	—	—	700
12/99	300	—	—	700
12/98	300	—	—	700
12/97	300	—	—	700
12/96	250	—	—	700
12/95	250	—	—	700
12/94	250	—	—	700
12/93	250	—	—	700
12/92	330	—	—	700
12/91	165	—	—	350
Annual Growth	6.9%	—	—	8.0%

Revenue History

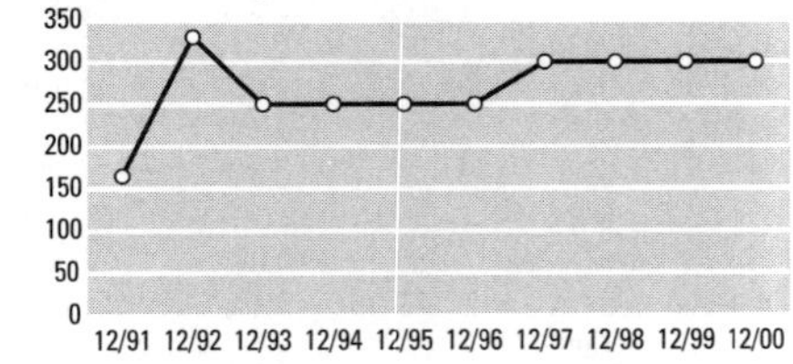

Kingston Technology

Kingston Technology cuts a regal figure in the realm of memory. The company is a top maker of memory modules — circuit boards loaded with DRAM (dynamic random-access memory) or other memory chips that increase the capacity and speed of printers and computers. Kingston also makes flash memory cards used in portable electronic devices such as digital cameras, wireless phones, and personal digital assistants. Kingston has taken on some manufacturing chores for its customers through its Payton Technology Project, a specialized factory that tests and packages memory chips before assembling them into customized memory modules. Founders John Tu (president and CEO) and David Sun (COO) own the company.

Tu and Sun promote a casual atmosphere and treat employees as members of an extended family. (Their work cubicles are identical to their employees'.) Since 1996 they have given over $100 million in bonuses to workers; in some cases the bonuses have amounted to three times the employees' annual salaries.

Kingston is also known for its friendliness to business partners. It is sometimes the first to receive scarce components during shortages, thanks to the good relations it enjoys with its suppliers. The company has inked a long-term deal with German chip heavyweight Infineon, under which Infineon is to supply much of Kingston's DRAM needs and Kingston is to provide Infineon with contract manufacturing and engineering services. Kingston has also made a $50 million investment in DRAM maker Elpida Memory.

EXECUTIVES

President and CEO: John Tu, age 61
COO: David Sun
CFO: Koichi Hosokawa
SVP, Sales and Marketing: Mike Sager
VP, Administration (HR): Daniel Hsu
VP, OEM Sales: Mark Pringle
Digital Storage Product Manager: Mike Kuppinger
Manager, Strategic Alliance Programs: Christina Patow
Memory Product Manager: Liesl Schwoebel

LOCATIONS

HQ: Kingston Technology Company, Inc.
17600 Newhope St., Fountain Valley, CA 92708
Phone: 714-435-2600 **Fax:** 714-435-2699
Web: www.kingston.com

Kingston Technology has operations in Australia, China, France, Germany, Ireland, Malaysia, Taiwan, the UK, and the US.

PRODUCTS/OPERATIONS

Selected Products

Flash memory cards (CompactFlash, DataFlash, MultiMediaCard, Solid State Floppy Disc Cards)
Memory modules and add-on boards
Standard memory modules (ValueRAM)

COMPETITORS

AMD
Amkor
ASE Test Limited
Centon
ChipPAC
Elpida
Hynix
Intel
Micron Technology
PNY Technologies
Samsung Electronics
SanDisk
Silicon Storage
SimpleTech
Unigen
Viking Components
Wintec

HISTORICAL FINANCIALS

Company Type: Private

Income Statement FYE: December 31

	REVENUE ($ mil.)	NET INCOME ($ mil.)	NET PROFIT MARGIN	EMPLOYEES
12/02	1,450	—	—	1,884
12/01	1,020	—	—	1,900
12/00	1,625	—	—	2,000
12/99	1,400	—	—	2,000
12/98	1,000	—	—	670
12/97	1,000	—	—	663
12/96	2,100	—	—	547
12/95	1,300	—	—	450
12/94	800	—	—	310
12/93	489	—	—	255
Annual Growth	12.8%	—	—	24.9%

Revenue History

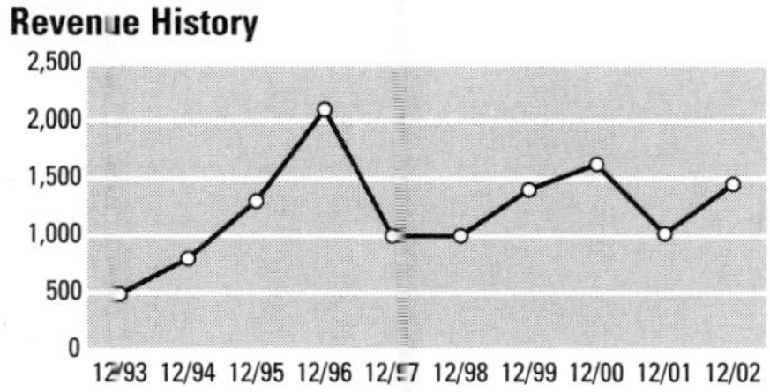

Kinko's, Inc.

Kinko's has come a long way since its founding as a college town copy shop. It operates more than 1,100 business service centers (open 24 hours a day) in Asia, Australia, Europe, and North America. Originally providing self-service copying, Kinko's now offers a full range of services, including binding and finishing services, color printing, document management, and Internet access. The company primarily serves small office/home office customers, but also provides digital document services to large companies. Kinko's allows customers to design products and place orders through its Kinkos.com Web site. Buyout firm Clayton, Dubilier & Rice owns about 73% of Kinko's.

Kinko's has continued to add services to its branch stores. The company added more than 200 sign and banner centers to stores in 2002. Kinko's also has formed strategic alliances with FedEx Corporation (in-store shipping for customers) and America Online (marketing and co-branding).

CEO Gary Kusin, a longtime Dallas businessman, relocated the company's headquarters to Dallas in early 2002. He cited the area's central location and low tax rate as reasons for uprooting the company. About 350 staffers lost jobs as a result of a restructuring of field support positions.

The company has purchased custom online printing firm, ImageX, for $16 million. J.P. Morgan Partners owns about 18% of Kinko's.

HISTORY

Kinko's is the creation of Paul Orfalea, who suffers from dyslexia and was inappropriately placed for six weeks in a school for the mentally retarded. The red-haired, Afro-sporting Orfalea (nicknamed Kinko) started selling pencils and spiral notebooks on the campus of UC Santa Barbara in 1970. When he saw a 10-cents-a-page photocopy machine in the library, he decided selling copies would be even better. The self-described hippie borrowed $5,000 that year and opened his first Kinko's shop in a former taco stand near the university. He sold school supplies and made copies on a wheeled copy machine that had to be moved outside because the shop was so small.

Orfalea opened a second California store in San Luis Obispo in 1972, and in the mid-1970s he started providing custom publishing materials for colleges. His innovative approach caught on, and by 1980 he had 80 stores in operation, mostly located near colleges.

In 1983 Kinko's opened its first store outside the US, in Canada, and in 1985 it opened its first 24-hour store, in Chicago. The company moved to Ventura, California, in 1988 and shifted its focus to the growing home office market in 1989 following the loss of a $1.9 million copyright-infringement suit for photocopying texts for professors. By 1990 Kinko's had 420 stores.

Kinko's began positioning itself as "Your Branch Office" in 1992. The next year it teamed up with telecommunications company Sprint and introduced videoconferencing services in 100 stores.

Kinko's opened an office in South Korea in 1995 and launched Kinkonet, its electronic communications network. The company teamed up with UUNET in 1996 to make Internet access available at its stores.

Until that year Orfalea was the sole owner of 110 stores and had partnership arrangements with more than 120 other entrepreneurs, a relationship that allowed Orfalea to control the company's rapidly growing network, while giving plenty of incentive for local expansion. This relaxed style of management also led to some unprofitable operations.

To remedy this, Kinko's went corporate in 1996, selling about 30% of the company to buyout firm Clayton, Dubilier & Rice for $219 million; the funds have been used for new technology and expansion. (The buyout firm later increased its stake to 42% and then again to 73%.) As part of the deal, Kinko's established a single, unified corporation, rolling into it all of the decentralized joint venture, corporate, and partnership companies operating under the Kinko's name.

In 1997 the company opened its first branch in China and made its first acquisition, document management company Electronic Demand Publishing, which became the core of Kinko's corporate document unit. In 1998 Kinko's opened its first stores in the UK (through a joint venture with the Virgin Group) and in the Middle East. The next year it began offering Internet-based custom printing services through an alliance with online print services firm iPrint.com.

In 2000 the company launched a new majority-owned Web firm, Kinkos.com, to offer Internet-based printing services. Orfalea resigned as chairman in 2000. In early 2001 Kinko's bought the rest of Kinkos.com (from Liveprint.com) and absorbed it into the company. Also that year Joseph Hardin Jr. (who had been CEO for more than three years) resigned from the company; Gary Kusin replaced him. The company relocated its headquarters to Dallas in 2002, a move that Orfalea criticized as unnecessary.

EXECUTIVES

Chairman: George Tamke Jr.
President, CEO, and Director: Gary M. Kusin, age 52
CFO: Mark A. Blinn
EVP and Chief Administration Officer: Daniel J. (Dan) Connors
EVP and Chief People Officer: Paul Rostron
EVP Operations: Mark Seals
SVP and General Manager, Western Region: Diana Ingram
SVP and President, Printing Division: James B. (Jim) McCurry, age 54
SVP, General Counsel, and Secretary: Frederic C. (Ric) Liskow
SVP Real Estate: Tom Carroll
SVP Sales: John McDonald
VP Finance and Controller: Curt McClellan
VP Global Sourcing: Steve Grupe
VP Leasing and Site Selection: Paul Myrick
VP Sales: Jennifer Goodwyn
Marketing Director: Heather Clark
Director of Environmental Affairs: Larry Rogero
Director of Public Relations: Maggie Thill
Corporate Communications: Chris Barnes

LOCATIONS

HQ: 13155 Noel Road, Ste. 1600, Dallas, TX 75240
Phone: 214-550-7000 **Fax:** 214-550-7001
Web: www.kinkos.com

Kinko's operates more than 1,100 stores in Australia, Canada, China, Japan, the Netherlands, South Korea, the UK, the United Arab Emirates, and the US.

PRODUCTS/OPERATIONS

Selected Products and Services

Binding and finishing services
Business and specialty papers
Computer rentals
Custom printing
Digital printing
E-mail
Fax services
FedEx services
Folding
Instant posters and banners
Internet access
Laminating
Laser printing
Office supplies
Overhead transparencies
Photocopying (black-and-white, color, full-service, self-service, oversize)
Pick up and delivery
Presentation materials
Scanning

COMPETITORS

Allegra
AlphaGraphics
Black Dot Group
Champion Industries
EagleDirect.com
Franchise Services
General Binding
IKON
Mail Boxes Etc.
Merrill
Office Depot
OfficeMax
On-Site Sourcing
Pitney Bowes
Staples
TRM
TVC Telecom
Xerox
Your Office USA

HISTORICAL FINANCIALS

Company Type: Private

Income Statement FYE: June 30

	ESTIMATED REVENUE ($ mil.)	NET INCOME ($ mil.)	NET PROFIT MARGIN	EMPLOYEES
6/02	2,100	—	—	20,000
6/01	2,200	—	—	25,000
6/00	2,000	—	—	26,000
6/99	1,800	—	—	25,000
6/98	1,600	—	—	24,000
6/97	1,500	—	—	24,000
6/96	1,350	—	—	23,000
6/95	1,100	—	—	19,000
Annual Growth	9.7%	—	—	0.7%

Revenue History

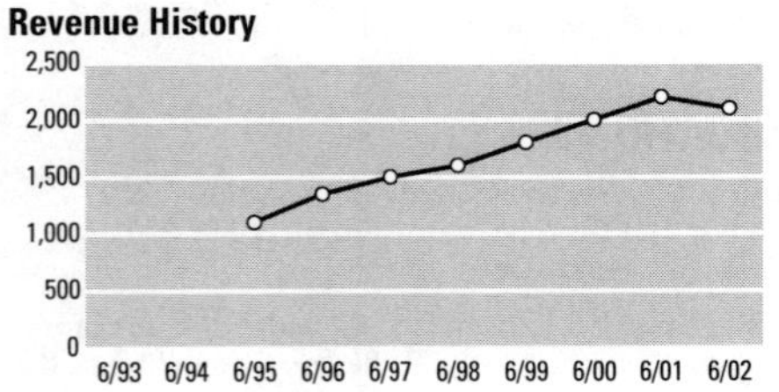

Kinray Inc.

Kinray, the US's largest privately held wholesale drug distributor, is nothing if not independent. It provides generic, branded, and repackaged drugs, health and beauty products, medical equipment, vitamins and herbals, and diabetes-care products; it also has a 600-item private-label program. The company serves nearly 2,000 pharmacies in seven northeastern US states. Kinray spearheaded the creation of the Wholesale Alliance Cooperative, a group of independent regional drug distributors that aims to help preserve the viability of independent pharmacies (who are customers to the wholesalers). The company was founded in 1944 by Joseph Rahr. His son, CEO and president Stewart Rahr, has owned the company since 1975.

EXECUTIVES

President and CEO: Stewart Rahr
General Manager: Bill Bodinger
Director Human Resources: Howard Hershberg

LOCATIONS

HQ: 152-35 10th Ave., Whitestone, NY 11357
Phone: 718-767-1234 **Fax:** 718-767-4388
Web: www.kinray.com

Kinray supplies pharmacies in Connecticut, Delaware, Massachusetts, New Jersey, New York, Pennsylvania, and Rhode Island.

COMPETITORS

Allou
AmerisourceBergen
Cardinal Distribution
The F. Dohmen Co.
McKesson
QK Healthcare

HISTORICAL FINANCIALS

Company Type: Private

Income Statement FYE: December 30

	REVENUE ($ mil.)	NET INCOME ($ mil.)	NET PROFIT MARGIN	EMPLOYEES
12/02	2,500	—	—	800
12/01	2,000	—	—	600
12/00	1,710	—	—	400
12/99	1,510	—	—	350
12/98	900	—	—	275
12/97	735	—	—	250
12/96	750	—	—	225
12/95	610	—	—	210
12/94	460	—	—	170
12/93	350	—	—	140
Annual Growth	24.4%	—	—	21.4%

Revenue History

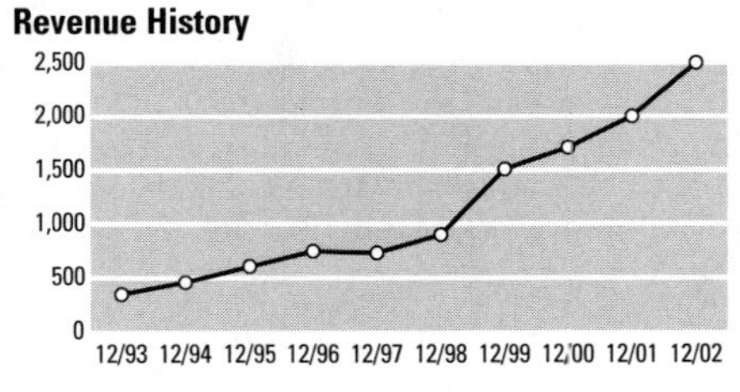

Kirkland & Ellis

Kirkland & Ellis is ready to go to court. The litigious law firm — home to former independent counsel Kenneth Starr — has been in the thick of several big courtroom battles, including defending Brown & Williamson Tobacco (it settled with the state of Minnesota for $6.5 billion in 1998). It serves other clients (General Motors, Dow Corning, Motorola) in areas such as intellectual property, antitrust, mergers and acquisitions, tort litigation, and employee benefits. Kirkland & Ellis has more than 900 lawyers in five US offices and one London office. Founded in 1908, the firm rose to prominence with the free speech and libel law strides made by firm namesakes Weymouth Kirkland and Howard Ellis.

EXECUTIVES

Firm Administrator: Douglas McLemore
CFO: Jay McAveeney
Director Media Relations: Joshua Peck
Manager Client Service: Maria Black
Human Resources: Wendy Cartland

LOCATIONS

HQ: Aon Center, 200 E. Randolph Dr., Chicago, IL 60601
Phone: 312-861-2000 **Fax:** 312-861-2200
Web: www.kirkland.com

Kirkland & Ellis has offices in Chicago, Los Angeles, New York City, San Francisco, and Washington, DC, as well as in London.

PRODUCTS/OPERATIONS

Selected Practice Areas

Antitrust
Employee benefits
Energy
Intellectual property
Litigation
Mergers and acquisitions
Real estate
Tax
Trusts and estates
Venture capital
White-collar crime

COMPETITORS

Baker & McKenzie
Cravath, Swaine
Jenner & Block
Jones Day
Mayer, Brown, Rowe & Maw
McDermott, Will
Sidley Austin Brown & Wood

HISTORICAL FINANCIALS

Company Type: Partnership

Income Statement FYE: January 31

	REVENUE ($ mil.)	NET INCOME ($ mil.)	NET PROFIT MARGIN	EMPLOYEES
1/03	611	—	—	—
1/02	530	—	—	—
1/01	470	—	—	—
1/00	410	—	—	700
1/99	310	—	—	600
1/98	255	—	—	552
1/97	229	—	—	504
1/96	220	—	—	—
1/95	215	—	—	—
1/94	180	—	—	—
Annual Growth	14.5%	—	—	11.6%

Revenue History

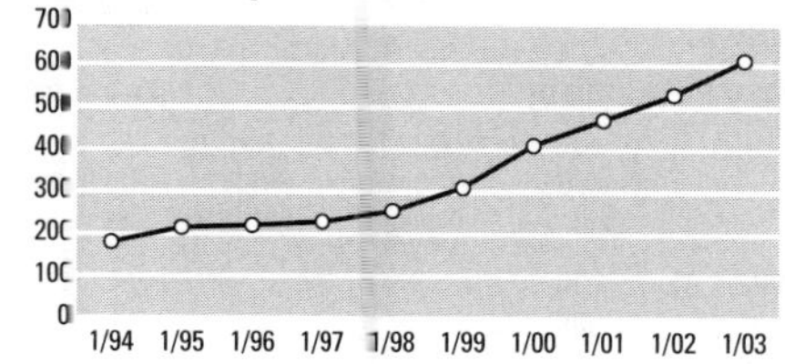

Kitchell Corporation

Not everything blooms in the Arizona desert, but Kitchell's building projects have. Operating primarily in the western US, Kitchell provides design, construction management, and real estate property development. It also builds custom luxury homes. It has worked on several North American projects (including casinos and business centers). Other commercial projects have included office parks, civic centers, malls, hospitals, and prisons. Kitchell also provides construction management for industrial facilities in Mexico and has created a transportation and logistics company to help its clients ship equipment to Mexico. German construction giant HOCHTIEF owns nearly 33% of Kitchell; the rest is held by employees.

EXECUTIVES

Chairman: Samuel F. Kitchell
President and CEO: William C. Schubert
Controller: William (Bill) Judge
EVP; President, Kitchell CEM: Gregory P. (Greg) Denk
President and COO, Kitchell Contractors: Mark Pendleton
President, Kitchell Custom Homes: Larry Butler
VP Marketing: Sandy Werthman
Director Communications: Barbara Bean
Director Human Resources: Kay Ellis
Auditors: Mayer Hoffman McCann P.C.

LOCATIONS

HQ: 1707 E. Highland Ave., Ste. 100, Phoenix, AZ 85016
Phone: 602-264-4411 **Fax:** 602-631-9112
Web: www.kitchell.com

Kitchell Corporation has offices in Arizona (Phoenix), California (Carlsbad, Sacramento, San Jose, and Visalia), Kansas (Kansas City), and Nevada (Las Vegas).

PRODUCTS/OPERATIONS

Selected Subsidiaries

American Refrigeration Supplies (formerly Arizona Refrigeration Supplies; wholesale refrigeration and air-conditioning)
Kitchell CEM (design and construction of public facilities)
Kitchell Contractors (general contracting and construction management)
NABERS Worldwide Logistics (logistics for industrial shipping to Mexico)
Kitchell Development Company (real estate development services)

COMPETITORS

Balfour Beatty
Gilbane
Jacobs Engineering
McCarthy Building
Perini
Sundt
Swinerton
Turner Corporation

HISTORICAL FINANCIALS

Company Type: Private

Income Statement FYE: December 31

	REVENUE ($ mil.)	NET INCOME ($ mil.)	NET PROFIT MARGIN	EMPLOYEES
12/02	463	—	—	850
12/01	475	—	—	900
12/00	500	—	—	1,000
Annual Growth	(3.8%)	—	—	(7.8%)

Revenue History

Klaussner Furniture Industries, Inc.

Klaussner Furniture Industries makes furniture for the couch potato in all of us. It is one of the US's largest makers of upholstered furniture. Klaussner sells fabric- and leather-upholstered sofas and recliners, chairs, ottomans, occasional tables, home entertainment, and dining furniture under the Distinctions, Realistic, Realistic Motion, Klaussner, and Klaussitalia brand names. It also offers sofas and chairs under the licensed Sealy name. Its 20 plants produce items exported to about 60 countries. Klaussner also owns about 20% of furniture retailer Jennifer Convertibles. Chairman Hans Klaussner has owned the company since 1979; it was founded in 1964 as Stuart Furniture Industries.

EXECUTIVES

Chairman: Hans Klaussner
President and CEO: J. B. Davis
CFO: Dave Bryant
VP Marketing: Jerry Bullins
VP Sales: Steve Brower
Information Systems Director: Bill Cook
Director Human Resources: Randy Timmerman

LOCATIONS

HQ: 405 Lewallen Rd., Asheboro, NC 27205
Phone: 336-625-6174 **Fax:** 336-625-8578
Web: www.klaussner.com

COMPETITORS

Ashley Furniture
Bassett Furniture
Berkline/BenchCraft
Chromcraft Revington
Ethan Allen
Flexsteel
Furniture Brands International
Haworth
Herman Miller
Hooker Furniture
La-Z-Boy
Natuzzi
Rowe Companies
Stanley Furniture
Steelcase
Badcock

HISTORICAL FINANCIALS

Company Type: Private

Income Statement FYE: December 31

	REVENUE ($ mil.)	NET INCOME ($ mil.)	NET PROFIT MARGIN	EMPLOYEES
12/01	955	—	—	6,900
12/00	1,057	—	—	7,000
12/99	815	—	—	6,800
12/98	750	—	—	6,600
12/97	738	—	—	6,570
12/96	716	—	—	6,900
12/95	717	—	—	6,950
12/94	658	—	—	6,955
Annual Growth	5.5%	—	—	(0.1%)

Revenue History

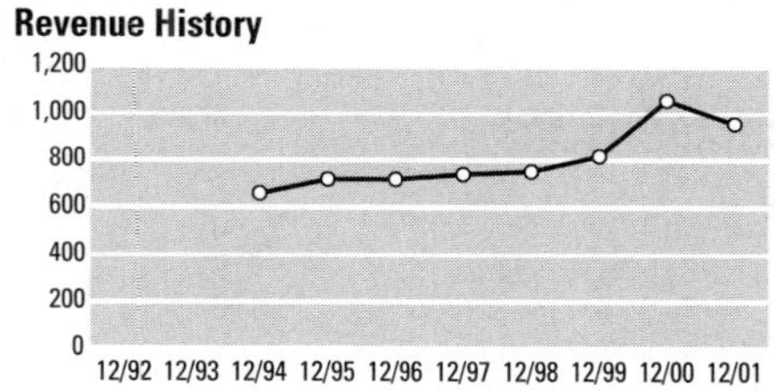

KMC Telecom Holdings, Inc.

KMC Telecom Holdings holds open the gate to a high-speed telecom pathway. The communications provider offers voice and broadband data services over fiber-optic networks in more than 35 Tier III markets (with populations between 100,000 and 750,000) in the southern, mid-Atlantic, and midwestern US. The company serves businesses, institutions, and telecom carriers seeking an alternative to the incumbent carrier. Its 3.6 million access and dedicated lines provide data services nationwide through agreements with other carriers. Among KMC Telecom's more than 15,300 customers are Texas A&M University, Wal-Mart, and Qwest. Chairman Harold Kamine, who founded KMC Telecom in 1995, owns about 70% of the company.

EXECUTIVES

Chairman and Founder: Harold (Hal) Kamine
Vice Chairman: Gary E. Lasher
Co-CEO and Director: William F. Lenahan
Co-CEO, COO, and Director: Roscoe C. Young II
EVP, CFO, and Director: William H. Stewart
EVP Network Operations: Larry Salter
SVP Human Resources: Charles Rosenblum
SVP National Markets: Kevin Bittner
SVP Private Network Group: Jamie Longino
SVP Staff Operations: Joe Ging
Auditors: Ernst & Young LLP

LOCATIONS

HQ: 1545 Route 206, Ste. 300, Bedminster, NJ 07921
Phone: 908-470-2100 **Fax:** 908-719-8775
Web: www.kmctelecom.com

KMC Telecom Holdings has operations in Alabama, Florida, Georgia, Indiana, Kansas, Louisiana, Maryland, Michigan, Minnesota, Mississippi, North Carolina, Ohio, South Carolina, Tennessee, Texas, Virginia, and Wisconsin.

PRODUCTS/OPERATIONS

Selected Services

Data
Frame relay and ATM (asynchronous transfer mode) transport
ISDN (Integrated Services Digital Network) connections
Network data switching

Voice
Centrex-type services
Local switched services
Long distance
Private lines and special access
Teleconferencing
Voicemail

COMPETITORS

AT&T
BellSouth
Covad Communications Group
Level 3 Communications
Qwest
SBC Communications
Sprint FON
Verio
Verizon
WorldCom

HISTORICAL FINANCIALS

Company Type: Private

Income Statement FYE: December 31

	REVENUE ($ mil.)	NET INCOME ($ mil.)	NET PROFIT MARGIN	EMPLOYEES
12/02	500	—	—	900
12/01	453	—	—	868
12/00	209	—	—	1,266
12/99	64	—	—	1,218
12/98	22	—	—	—
12/97	3	—	—	—
12/96	0	—	—	—
12/95	0	—	—	—
Annual Growth	—	—	—	(9.6%)

Revenue History

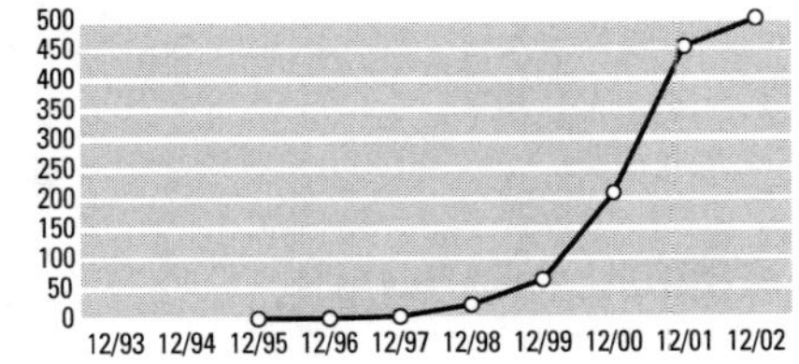

Knoll, Inc.

Designer cubicles make for happier workers, or so goes the gospel at Knoll. The company makes a variety of distinctively designed, curvilinear office furniture and related accessories, including office systems (a.k.a. cubicles) sold under such names as Equity, Dividends, and Currents. Other products include rolling chairs and other seating, tables, metal and wood desks, file cabinets, computer and desk accessories, textiles, and leather upholstery. Knoll management and investment firm Warburg Pincus own the company.

Some products are created by high-profile architects and designers such as Frank Gehry and Vietnam War Memorial architect Maya Lin.

Knoll markets its products through independent dealers in North and South America, Europe, and Asia. It has been increasing its sales force to grow its share of the middle to high-end office furniture market, with a focus on *FORTUNE* 500 companies.

EXECUTIVES

Chairman: Burton B. Staniar
CEO and Director: Andrew B. Cogan
President and CEO, Knoll North America, and Director: Kathleen G. Bradley
SVP, CFO, Treasurer, and Controller: Barry L. McCabe
SVP, Design: Carl G. Magnusson
SVP, General Counsel, and Secretary: Patrick A. Milberger
SVP, Operations: Stephen A. Grover
SVP, Sales and Distribution: Arthur C. Graves
VP, Human Resources: S. David Wolfe
Auditors: Ernst & Young LLP

LOCATIONS

HQ: 1235 Water St., East Greenville, PA 18041
Phone: 215-679-7991 **Fax:** 215-679-1755
Web: www.knoll.com

Knoll has three plants in Pennsylvania and Michigan in the US, two in Italy, and one in Canada.

COMPETITORS

Anderson Hickey
Bush Industries
Global Furniture
Haworth
Herman Miller
HighPoint Furniture
HON INDUSTRIES
Jami
KI
Kimball International
Natuzzi
Neutral Posture
Open Plan Systems
O'Sullivan Industries
Reconditioned Systems
Steelcase
Teknion
Virco Mfg.
Vitra

HISTORICAL FINANCIALS

Company Type: Private

Income Statement FYE: December 31

	REVENUE ($ mil.)	NET INCOME ($ mil.)	NET PROFIT MARGIN	EMPLOYEES
12/02	950	—	—	3,816
12/01	985	—	—	3,863
12/00	1,164	—	—	4,435
12/99	985	—	—	4,378
12/98	949	—	—	4,061
12/97	811	—	—	3,942
12/96	652	—	—	3,550
12/95	621	—	—	—
12/94	563	—	—	—
12/93	508	—	—	—
Annual Growth	7.2%	—	—	1.2%

2001 Year-End Financials

Debt ratio: —
Return on equity: —
Cash ($ mil.): 32
Current ratio: 1.02
Long-term debt ($ mil.): 485

Revenue History

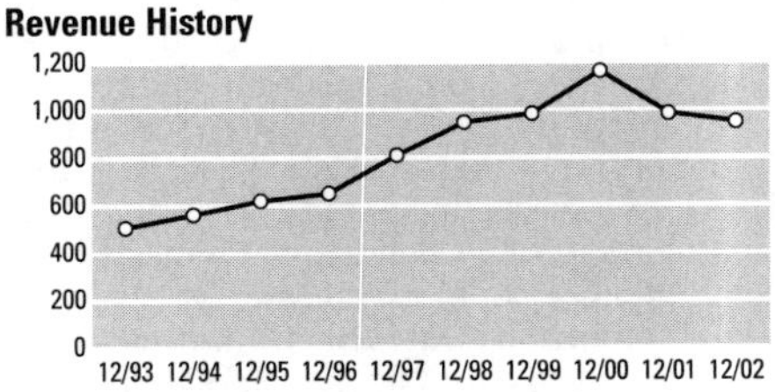

Koch Enterprises, Inc.

Koch gets straight A's. Koch Enterprises is a diversified company with interests including aluminum, automotive finishing systems, air-conditioning equipment, and adhesives. Subsidiaries include George Koch Sons (engineers, installs, and services a range of finishing systems for the automotive industry), Koch Air (distributes heating and air-conditioning equipment), Gibbs Die Casting (supplies automotive aluminum die-castings products), Brake Supply Company (repairs and replaces brakes and hydraulic systems for the automotive and mining industries), and Uniseal (makes adhesives and sealants for automobile manufacturers, as well as connectors for drain and waste pipes). The Koch family owns the company.

EXECUTIVES

President and CEO: Robert L. Koch II, age 64
CFO, Secretary, and Treasurer: Susan E. Parsons
EVP: James H. Muehlbauer, age 61

LOCATIONS

HQ: 14 S. 11th Ave., Evansville, IN 47744
Phone: 812-465-9800 **Fax:** 812-465-9613
Web: www.kochenterprises.com

Koch Enterprises operates facilities in Florida, Indiana, Kentucky, Michigan, Missouri, Nevada, Texas, Virginia, and Wyoming in the US, as well as in Brazil, Mexico, South Korea, and the UK.

PRODUCTS/OPERATIONS

Selected Subsidiaries

Audubon Metals (51%, aluminum alloy and automobile shredder residue processing)
Brake Supply Co. (brake and hydraulic system repair)
George Koch Sons, LLC (automotive finishing systems)
Gibbs Die Casting (parts manufacturing)
Koch Air LLC (distribution)
Uniseal, Inc. (parts manufacturing)

Selected Products and Services

Aluminum and magnesium die castings
Brake linings
Heating and air-conditioning equipment
Hydraulics
PIPECONX (pipe connectors)
Powder coating systems
Specialty sealants

COMPETITORS

Dana
Graco
Illinois Tool Works
Invensys
Kaiser Aluminum
Sun Hydraulics

HISTORICAL FINANCIALS

Company Type: Private

Income Statement FYE: December 31

	REVENUE ($ mil.)	NET INCOME ($ mil.)	NET PROFIT MARGIN	EMPLOYEES
12/02	550	—	—	3,050
12/01	540	—	—	3,400
12/00	617	—	—	3,400
12/99	561	—	—	3,500
12/98	520	—	—	2,800
Annual Growth	1.4%	—	—	2.2%

Revenue History

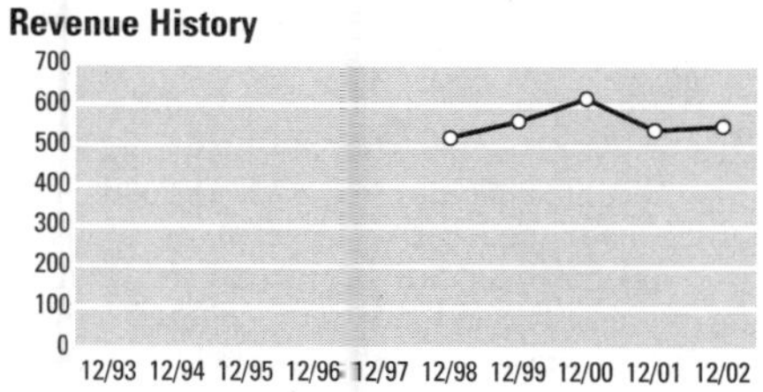

Koch Industries, Inc.

Koch Industries is the real thing when there's money to be made. Koch (pronounced "coke") is the second-largest private US company, after Cargill; it has extensive holdings in oil and gas, chemicals, minerals, ranching, and securities. Its two refineries process about 600,000 barrels of crude oil a day. Koch processes natural gas liquids, and operates gas gathering systems and a network of pipelines across North America. Its KoSa unit is a leading polyester producer. Other operations include commodity trading and transport, asphalt marketing, and the manufacture of chemical technology equipment for processing industries. Brothers Charles and David Koch control the company.

Koch's business activities focus on three core competencies: Trading (many Koch companies are well-established traders of a wide range of commodities); Operations (Koch companies strive to be industry leading, cost-efficient operators of their many plants and facilities); and Investments (Koch has equity investments in a variety of industries).

Koch combined its pipeline system and trading units with the power marketing businesses of electric utility Entergy in 2001 to form Entergy-Koch, a joint venture that ranks among the biggest energy commodity traders in the US.

In 2002 Koch acquired Valero Energy's 40% stake in a Mont Belvieu, Texas, natural gas liquids fractionator, boosting its ownership to 80%.

Ever alert for strategic acquisitions, Koch has named several top officers to a business development board to help identify growth opportunities.

HISTORY

Fred Koch grew up poor in Texas and worked his way through MIT. In 1928 Koch developed a process to refine more gasoline from crude oil, but when he tried to market his invention, the major oil companies sued him for patent infringement. Koch eventually won the lawsuits (after 15 years in court), but the controversy made it tough to attract many US customers. In 1929 Koch took his process to the Soviet Union, but he grew disenchanted with Stalinism and returned home to become a founding member of the anticommunist John Birch Society.

Koch launched Wood River Oil & Refining in Illinois (1940) and bought the Rock Island refinery in Oklahoma (1947). He folded the remaining purchasing and gathering network into Rock Island Oil & Refining (though later sold the refineries).

After Koch's death in 1967, his 32-year-old son Charles took the helm and renamed the company Koch Industries. He began a series of acquisitions, adding petrochemical and oil trading service operations.

During the 1980s Koch was thrust into various arenas, legal and political. Charles' brother David, also a Koch Industries executive, ran for US vice president on the Libertarian ticket in 1980. That year the other two Koch brothers, Frederick and William (David's fraternal twin), launched a takeover attempt, but Charles retained control, and William was fired from his job as VP.

The brothers traded lawsuits, and in a 1983 settlement Charles and David bought out the dissident family members for just over $1 billion. William and Frederick continued to challenge their brothers in court, claiming they had been shortchanged in the deal (the two estranged brothers eventually lost their case in 1998, and their appeals were rejected in 2000). In 1987 they even sued their mother over her distribution of trust fund money.

Despite this legal wrangling, Koch Industries continued to expand, purchasing a Corpus Christi, Texas, refinery in 1981. It expanded its pipeline system, buying Bigheart Pipe Line in Oklahoma (1986) and two systems from Santa Fe Southern Pacific (1988).

In 1991 Koch purchased the Corpus Christi marine terminal, pipelines, and gathering systems of Scurlock Permian (a unit of Ashland Oil). In 1992 the company bought United Gas Pipe Line (renamed Koch Gateway Pipeline) and its pipeline system extending from Texas to Florida.

To strengthen its engineering services presence worldwide, Koch acquired Glitsch International (a maker of separation equipment) from engineering giant Foster Wheeler in 1997. It also acquired USX-Delhi Group, a natural gas processor and transporter.

In 1998 Koch bought Purina Mills, the largest US producer of animal feed, and formed the KoSa joint venture with Mexico's Saba family to buy Hoechst's Trevira polyester unit. (Koch acquired the Saba family's stake in KoSa in 2001.) Lethargic energy and livestock prices in 1998 and 1999, however, led Koch to lay off several hundred employees, sell its feedlots, and divest portions of its natural gas gathering and pipeline systems. Purina Mills filed for bankruptcy protection in 1999 (later, it emerged from bankruptcy and held an IPO in 2000, and was acquired by #2 US dairy co-op Land O'Lakes in 2001).

William Koch sued Koch Industries in 1999, claiming the company had defrauded the US government and Native Americans in oil payments on Indian lands. A jury found for William, but he, Charles, and David agreed to settle the case in 2001 — and sat down to dinner together for the first time in 20 years.

In other legal matters, in 2000 Koch agreed to pay a $30 million civil fine and contribute $5 million toward environmental projects to settle complaints over oil spills from its pipelines in the 1990s. The company agreed to pay $20 million in 2001 to settle a separate environmental case concerning a Texas refinery.

EXECUTIVES

Chairman and CEO: Charles G. Koch, age 67
President, COO, and Director: Joseph W. (Joe) Moeller
EVP and Director: David H. Koch, age 63
EVP and Director: Richard H. Fink
EVP Operations and Director: Bill R. Caffey
SVP Joint Ventures: Cy S. Nobles
SVP Corporate Strategy: John C. Pittenger
CFO: Steve Feilmeier
VP Business Development: Ron Vaupel
VP, General Counsel, and Secretary: Paul Kaleta
Director of Corporate Compliance: Chris Wilkins
Director of Human Resources: Dale Gibbens
Controller: Kelly Bulloch
CIO: Randal Robison
Public Relations/Corporate Communications: Jay Rosser
President, Flint Hills Resources, LP: David L. Robertson
President, Koch Capital Markets: Sam Soliman
President and COO, Koch Chemical Technology Group, LLC: John M. Van Gelder
President, Koch Financial Corporation: Randall A. (Randy) Bushman
President, Koch Hydrocarbon, LP: Steve Tatum
President, Koch Materials Company: Rob Witte
President, Koch Mineral Services, LLC: Jeff Gentry
President, Koch Performance Roads, Inc.: Paul Wheeler
President, Koch Pipeline, LLC: Pat McCann
President, Koch Supply and Trading Company, LP: Steve Mawer
President, Koch Ventures Inc.: Ray Gary
Auditors: KPMG LLP

LOCATIONS

HQ: 4111 E. 37th St. N, Wichita, KS 67220
Phone: 316-828-5500 **Fax:** 316-828-5739
Web: www.kochind.com

Koch Industries has operations in Argentina, Australia, Belgium, Brazil, Canada, China, the Czech Republic, France, Germany, India, Italy, Japan, Luxembourg, the Netherlands, Poland, South Africa, Spain, Switzerland, the UK, the US, and Venezuela.

PRODUCTS/OPERATIONS

Selected Operations

Flint Hills Resources (formerly Koch Petroleum, crude oil and refined products)
- TrueNorth Energy LP (oil sands exploration and production)
- Koch Exploration Company, LLC

Koch Agriculture Group
- Matador Cattle Co.

Koch Chemicals Group
- Koch Chemicals (paraxylene)
  - KoSa (polyester)
- Koch Microelectronic Service Co. (semiconductor chemicals)
- Koch Specialty Chemicals (high-octane missile fuel)

Koch Chemical Technology Group (specialty equipment and services for refining and chemical industry)
- Brown Fintube Company
- Iris Power Engineering, Inc.
- The John Zink Company
- Koch-Glitsch, Inc.
- Koch Membrane Systems Inc.
- Koch Modular Process Systems, LLC
- Tru-Tec Services, Inc.

Koch Energy Group
- Entergy-Koch L.P. (50%)
  - Gulf South Pipeline Co. (50%)

Koch Financial Services, Inc.
- Koch Financial Corp.

Koch Gas Liquids Group
Koch Materials Co. (asphalt)
Koch Mineral Services (bulk ocean transportation and fuel supply)
- Koch Fertilizer Storage & Terminal Co.

Koch Pipeline Co. LP
Koch Supply & Trading, LLC
Koch Ventures LLC (investment in noncore businesses)

COMPETITORS

AEP
Aquila
ADM
Ashland
ATOFINA
Avista
BP
Cargill
CenterPoint Energy
ChevronTexaco
ConocoPhillips
ContiGroup
Duke Energy
Dynegy
Enron
EOTT
Exxon Mobil
Imperial Oil
Kerr-McGee
King Ranch
Lyondell Chemical
Marathon Oil
Motiva Enterprises
Occidental Petroleum
Peabody Energy
PEMEX
PG&E
Royal Dutch/Shell Group
Shell Oil Products
Southern Company
Sunoco
Tractebel
Williams Companies

HISTORICAL FINANCIALS

Company Type: Private

Income Statement FYE: December 31

	REVENUE ($ mil.)	NET INCOME ($ mil.)	NET PROFIT MARGIN	EMPLOYEES
12/02	40,000	—	—	11,000
12/01	40,000	—	—	11,000
12/00	40,000	—	—	11,500
12/99	33,050	—	—	12,500
12/98	35,000	—	—	16,000
12/97	36,200	—	—	15,600
12/96	30,000	—	—	13,000
12/95	25,200	—	—	12,500
12/94	23,725	—	—	12,000
12/93	20,000	—	—	12,000
Annual Growth	8.0%	—	—	(1.0%)

Revenue History

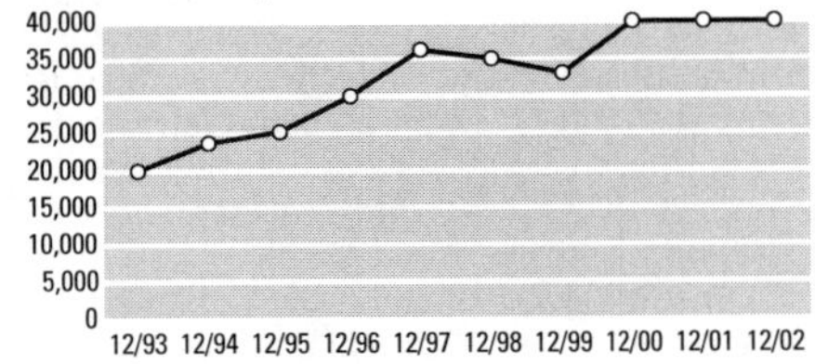

Kohlberg Kravis Roberts & Co.

The barbarians at the gate are now knocking politely. The master of the 1980s buyout universe, Kohlberg Kravis Roberts (popularly known as KKR) has shed its hostile takeover image for a kinder, gentler, buy-and-build strategy. KKR assembles funds from institutional and wealthy investors to buy low and sell high. An active investor, the firm supervises or installs new management and revamps strategy and corporate structure, selling underperforming units or adding new ones. KKR profits not only from its direct interest in these companies but also from fund and company management fees.

KKR's investments include stakes in publishing company PRIMEDIA (*Seventeen*, Channel One), diversified manufacturer Borden, and online mortgage lender Nexstar Financial. Kohlberg Kravis Roberts also has a joint venture with venture capital firm Accel to provide support for companies integrating online and brick-and-mortar businesses. Cousins Henry Kravis and George Roberts are the senior partners in KKR.

KKR is shopping in Europe, where bloated corporations are shedding noncore operations to streamline. Along with Wendel Investissement, KKR picked up French electrical product maker Legrand from Schneider Electric SA. Other European acquisitions include seven businesses spun off by German conglomerate Siemens. Some of the businesses are noncore operations such as Mannesmann Plastics Machinery and Demag Cranes & Components. KKR rolled up its acquisitions into a new company called Demag Holding upon completion of the transactions. The firm has also bought a 60% stake in the telephone directory subsidiaries of BCE in Canada.

Since 1976 KKR has invested $100 billion in more than 90 companies, with investors receiving returns of around 23%. As the economy cools, though, the firm is weathering its fair share of tumult. KKR is no longer the top fund raiser in the investment industry and has written off investments in such firms as Birch Telecom, which subsequently slid into bankruptcy.

HISTORY

In 1976 Jerome Kohlberg left investment bank Bear Stearns to form his own leveraged buyout firm; with him he brought protégé Henry Kravis and Kravis' cousin George Roberts. They formed Kohlberg Kravis Roberts & Co. (KKR).

Kohlberg believed LBOs, by giving management ownership stakes in their companies, would yield better results. KKR orchestrated friendly buyouts funded by investor groups and debt. The firm's first buyout was machine-toolmaker Houdaille Industries in 1979.

KKR lost money on its 1981 investment in the American Forest Products division of Bendix. But by 1984 the firm had raised its fourth fund and made its first $1 billion buyout: Wometco Enterprises.

The next year KKR turned mean with a hostile takeover of Beatrice. The deal depended on junk bond financing devised by Drexel Burnham Lambert's Michael Milken and on the sale of pieces of the company. KKR funded the buyouts of Safeway Stores and Owens-Illinois (1986), Jim Walter Homes (1987), and Stop & Shop (1988, sold in 1996).

Unhappy with the firm's hostile image, Kohlberg left in 1987 to form Kohlberg & Co. His suit against KKR over the alleged undervaluing of companies in relation to his departure settlement was resolved for an undisclosed amount.

The Beatrice LBO triggered a rash of similar transactions as the financial industry sought fat fees. The frenzy culminated in 1988 with the $31 billion RJR Nabisco buyout, which brought KKR $75 million in fees. As the US slid into recession in 1989, LBOs dwindled and KKR turned to managing its acquisitions.

The firm also did some bottom feeding. In 1991 KKR joined with what is now FleetBoston to buy Bank of New England. The next year it picked up 47% of what was then Advantica Restaurant Group (now just plain Denny's). It sold that holding in 1997.

KKR made its first international foray in 1993 with Russian truck maker Kamaz; it later stalled when Kamaz refused to pay management fees. The next year it freed itself from the RJR morass by swapping its investment in RJR for troubled food company Borden.

In the latter half of the decade, KKR reaped mixed results on its investments, including what is now Spalding Holdings (sporting goods and Evenflo baby products), supermarket chain Bruno's, and KinderCare Learning Centers. The $600 million KKR had sunk into magazine group K-III (now PRIMEDIA) between 1990 and 1994 didn't revive interest in the stock, and Bruno's filed for bankruptcy in 1998. Disgruntled investors complained about low returns, and in 1996 KKR booted activist megafund CalPERS from its investor ranks.

In 1998 KKR's niche buying continued when it joined with Hicks, Muse, Tate & Furst to buy Regal Cinemas, which it combined with Act III to form the biggest theater chain in the US. The chain's expansion left it on the brink of bankruptcy, and investor Philip Anschutz bought a chunk of its debt and possible control of the company in 2001.

The next year KKR departed from course and unveiled online mortgage lender Nexstar Financial, its first company built from the ground up.

Focused on Europe, in 2000 the firm claimed the telecommunications business of Robert Bosch (now Tenovis), UK private equity fund Wassall PLC, and Siemens' banking systems unit. The next year it bought the specialty chemicals and pigments operations of Laporte plc to create Rockwood Specialties.

Also in 2000, KKR joined with Internet VC firm Accel Partners to form Accel-KKR, Inc. to invest in companies that combine traditional business and Internet assets. It lost its place as the top fund-raiser to Thomas H. Lee, which closed a record-setting $6.[illegible] billion fund in early 2001. Kohlberg acquired major divisions from Laporte for about $1.175 billion in that same year.

EXECUTIVES

Founding Partner: Henry R. Kravis, age 59
Founding Partner, California: George R. Roberts, age 59
General Partner, London: Edward A. Gilhuly, age 43
General Partner: Perry Golkin, age 49
General Partner, California: James H. Greene (Jamie) Jr., age 52
General Partner, California: Robert I. MacDonnell, age 65
General Partner: Michael W. Michelson, age 52
General Partner: Paul E. Raether
General Partner: Scott M. Stuart, age 43
Managing Director, London: Johannes Huth
Chairman, Accel-KKR, Inc.: Paul M. Hazen, age 61
Office Manager: Sandy Cisneros
Auditors: Deloitte & Touche LLP

LOCATIONS

HQ: 9 W. 57th St., Ste. 4200, New York, NY 10019
Phone: 212-750-8300 **Fax:** 212-750-0003
Web: www.kkr.com

Kohlberg Kravis Roberts & Co. has offices in London; Menlo Park, California; and New York City.

PRODUCTS/OPERATIONS

Selected Investments

Accuride Corporation
Alea Group Holdings AG
Alliance Imaging, Inc.
Amphenol Corporation
Borden, Inc.
The Boyds Collection, Ltd.
Bristol West Insurance Group
Centric Software, Inc.
DPL Inc.
Evenflo Company, Inc.
FirstMark Communications Europe SA
IDEX Corporation
Intermedia Communications Inc.
KinderCare Learning Centers, Inc.
KKR.net AG
KSL Recreation Corporation
MedCath Incorporated
NewSouth Communications
Nexstar Financial Corporation
Owens-Illinois, Inc.
PRIMEDIA Inc.
Rockwood Specialties Inc
Shoppers Drug Mart Inc.
Spalding Holdings Corporation
Tenovis Holding GmbH
Walter Industries, Inc.
Willis Group Limited
Wincor Nixdorf Holding GmbH & Co.
WorldCrest Group
Zhone Technologies, Inc.
Zumtobel AG

COMPETITORS

AEA Investors
American Financial
Apollo Advisors
Bear Stearns
Berkshire Hathaway
Blackstone Group
Carlyle Group
Citigroup Global Markets
Clayton, Dubilier
CVC Capital Partners
Equity Group Investments
Forstmann Little
Goldman Sachs
Haas Wheat
Heico
Hicks, Muse
Interlaken Investment
Investcorp
Jordan Company
Lehman Brothers
Leonard Green
MacAndrews & Forbes
Merrill Lynch
Texas Pacific Group
Thomas Lee
Veronis Suhler Stevenson
Vestar Capital Partners
Wingate Partners

Kohler Co.

When plumbing powerhouse Kohler says profits are in the toilet, it's not complaining. Kohler makes bathroom products under the names Hytec, Kohler, and Sterling (plumbing products); Ann Sacks (ceramic tile, marble, stone products); and Kallista (bathroom fixtures). Brands in Europe include Jacob Delafon and Neomediam plumbing products and Sanijura bath cabinetry. Kohler also makes small engines, generators, electrical switchgear, and high-end furniture. Additionally, Kohler owns The American Club resort, golf courses, and other real estate; Kohler also breeds Morgan horses at Kohler Stables in Kentucky. Chairman Herbert Kohler Jr. and his sister Ruth Kohler, grandchildren of the founder, control the company.

Herbert has reorganized the company and has vowed it will never go public. The company is building a new manufacturing facility in Mexico and is expanding some of its US factories.

HISTORY

In 1873, 29-year-old Austrian immigrant John Kohler and partner Charles Silberzahn founded Kohler & Silberzahn in Sheboygan, Wisconsin. That year they purchased a small iron foundry that made agricultural products for $5,000 from Kohler's father-in-law. In 1880, two years after Silberzahn left the firm, its machine shop was destroyed by fire.

The company introduced enameled plumbing fixtures in the rebuilt factory in 1883. The design caught on, and the business sold thousands of sinks, kettles, pans, and bathtubs. By 1887, when Kohler was incorporated, enameled items accounted for 70% of sales. By 1900 the 250-person company received 98% of its sales from enameled iron products. That year, shortly after John Kohler began building new facilities near Sheboygan (which later became the company village of Kohler), he died at age 56. More trouble followed: Kohler's new plant burned down in 1901, and two of the founder's sons died — Carl at age 24 in 1904 and Robert at age 35 in 1905.

Eldest surviving son Walter built a boarding hotel to house workers and introduced other employee-benefit programs. He also set up company-paid workmen's compensation before the state made it law in 1917.

By the mid-1920s, when Kohler premiered colors in porcelain fixtures and added brass fittings and vitreous china toilets and washbasins to its line, it was the #3 plumbing-product company in the US. As a testament to the design quality of its products, Kohler items were displayed at the New York Museum of Modern Art in 1929. The company also began developing products that would grow in importance in later decades: electric generators and small gasoline engines. During the 1950s Kohler's engines virtually conquered Southeast Asia, where they were used to power boats, drive air compressors, and pump water for rice paddies in Vietnam and Thailand. While strikes against Kohler in 1897 and 1934 had been resolved quickly, a 1954 strike against the firm lasted six years. The strike gave Kohler the dubious honor of enduring the longest strike in US history.

Small-engine use grew in the US in the 1960s, and Kohler's motors were used in lawn mowers, construction equipment, and garden tractors. The founder's last surviving son, Herbert (a child from John Kohler's second marriage), died in 1968. Under the leadership of Herbert's son, Herbert Jr. (appointed chairman 1972), Kohler expanded its operations, buying Sterling Faucet (1984); Baker, Knapp & Tubbs (1986); and Jacob Delafon (1986). More recent acquisitions include Sanijura (bathroom furniture, France) in 1993; Osio (enamel baths, Italy) in 1994; Robern (mirrored cabinets) in 1995; Holdiam (baths, whirlpools, and sinks, France) in 1995; and Canac (cabinets, Canada) in 1996.

The company entered a growing plumbing market in China through four joint ventures formed in that country in 1996 and 1997. In 1998 several family and non-family shareholders claimed a reorganization plan unfairly forced them out and undervalued their stock. Legal battles over the stock's fair price continued in 1999, and a settlement was reached in 2000 that granted shareholders a fair price and Herbert and his sister Ruth gained firm control of the company. More legal battles continued in 2001 when the company sued Kohler International Ltd., a Canada-based company, for trademark infringement.

EXECUTIVES

Chairman and President: Herbert V. Kohler Jr., age 64
SVP Finance and CFO: Jeffery P. Cheney
SVP Human Resources: Laura Kohler
VP Marketing, Fixtures: Christopher Lohmann
Group President, Kitchen and Bath: David Kohler
Manager, Environmental Health and Safety Technology Resources: Paul Kubicek

LOCATIONS

HQ: 444 Highland Dr., Kohler, WI 53044
Phone: 920-457-4441 **Fax:** 920-457-1271
Web: kohlerco.com

Kohler Co. operates 44 manufacturing plants, 26 subsidiaries and affiliates, and sales offices worldwide.

PRODUCTS/OPERATIONS

Selected Operations

Engines
Commercial turf equipment engines
Consumer lawn and garden equipment engines
Industrial, construction, and commercial equipment engines
Recreational equipment engines

Furniture
Baker Furniture
McGuire Furniture Company
Milling Road Furniture

Generators
Kohler rental power
Marine generators
Mobile generators
On-site power systems
Automatic transfer switches
Switchgear
Residential generators
Small business generators

Kitchen and Bath Products
Canac (bathroom cabinetry)
Robern (lighting and mirrored bath cabinetry)
Sanijura (vanities and other bath furniture)

Plumbing products
Jacob Delafon (bathtubs, faucets, lavatories, and toilets)
Kohler (bath and shower faucets, baths, bidet faucets, bidets, body spa systems, glass showers and shower doors, kitchen and bathroom sinks and faucets, master baths, toilets, toilet seats, vanities, whirlpool baths)
Kallista (bathroom and kitchen sinks and faucets)
Sterling (bathing fixtures, faucets, sinks, tub/shower enclosures, vitreous china bath fixtures)

Tile and stone products
Ann Sacks (art tile, glazed tile, knobs and pulls, mosaics, terra cotta)

Real Estate
The American Club (resort hotel)
Blackwolf Run golf course
Inn on Woodlake
Kohler Stables
Whistling Straits golf course

COMPETITORS

American Standard
Armstrong Holdings
Armstrong World Industries
Bassett Furniture
Black & Decker
Briggs & Stratton
Carlson
Chicago Faucet
Cooper Industries
Crane
Dal-Tile
Dyson-Kissner-Moran
Elkay Manufacturing
Grohe
Geberit
Geberit Manufacturing
Gerber Plumbing Fixtures
Honda
Jacuzzi Brands
Klaussner Furniture
Leggett & Platt
Masco
Moen
Mueller Industries
Newell Rubbermaid
NIBCO
Samuel Heath
Starwood Hotels & Resorts
Tecumseh Products
TOTO
Villeroy & Boch
Waxman
Yamaha

HISTORICAL FINANCIALS

Company Type: Private

Income Statement FYE: December 31

	ESTIMATED REVENUE ($ mil.)	NET INCOME ($ mil.)	NET PROFIT MARGIN	EMPLOYEES
12/02	3,000	—	—	25,000
12/01	3,000	—	—	22,000
12/00	2,700	—	—	20,000
12/99	2,500	—	—	20,000
12/98	2,400	—	—	18,000
12/97	2,210	—	—	18,000
12/96	2,020	—	—	18,000
12/95	1,850	—	—	15,000
12/94	1,600	—	—	14,500
12/93	1,450	—	—	14,257
Annual Growth	8.4%	—	—	6.4%

Revenue History

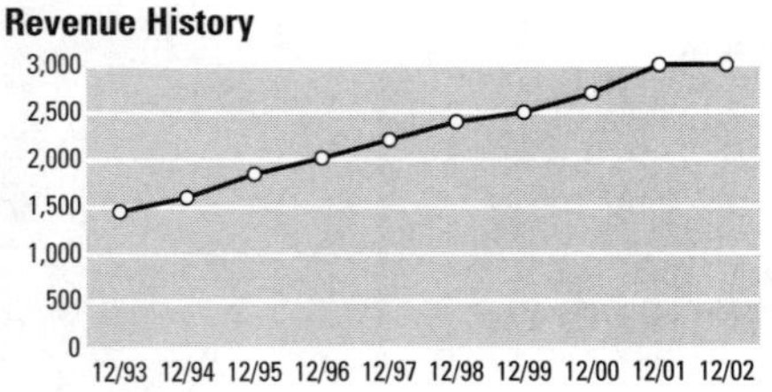

Koppers Industries, Inc.

Koppers treats wood right. Koppers Industries makes carbon compounds and treated-wood products for the chemical, railroad, aluminum, utility, construction, and steel industries around the world. Its carbon materials and chemicals unit makes materials for producing aluminum, polyester resins, plasticizers, and wood preservatives. The railroad and utility products unit supplies treated crossties and utility poles and treats wood for vineyard, construction, and other uses. Koppers indirectly owns 50% of KSA Limited Partnership, which produces about 140,000 concrete crossties annually. Koppers was formed in 1988. Private investment firm Saratoga Partners (New York) controls Koppers.

EXECUTIVES

Chairman: Robert Cizik, age 71
President, CEO, and Director: Walter W. Turner, age 56, $556,250 pay
VP and CFO: Donald E. Davis, age 46, $317,475 pay
VP, Australasian Operations: Ernest S. Byron, age 57
VP, European Operations, Kopper Europe: David Whittle, age 60, $355,770 pay
VP; General Manager, Carbon Materials and Chemicals: Kevin J. Fitzgerald, age 50, $176,400 pay
VP; General Manager, Global Marketing, Sales, and Development Group: Mark McCormack, age 43
VP; General Manager, Railroad Products and Services: Thomas D. Loadman, age 48, $268,949 pay
VP; General Manager, Utility and Construction Products: David T. Bryce
VP, Law and Human Resources; Corporate Secretary: Steven R. Lacy, age 47, $319,815 pay
VP, Safety, Health, and Environmental Affairs: Randall D. Collins, age 50
VP, Technology: Robert H. Wombles, age 51
Treasurer and Assistant Secretary: M. Claire Schaming, age 49
Auditors: Ernst & Young LLP

LOCATIONS

HQ: 436 7th Ave., Pittsburgh, PA 15219
Phone: 412-227-2001 **Fax:** 412-227-2333
Web: www.koppers.com

Koppers operates 39 facilities in Australia, Europe, Malaysia, New Zealand, South Africa, and the US.

2002 Sales

	$ mil.	% of total
US	511.4	70
Australia & Pacific Rim	118.9	16
Europe	100.0	14
Total	**730.3**	**100**

PRODUCTS/OPERATIONS

Selected Products

Carbon Materials and Chemicals
Carbon black
Carbon pitch
Coal tar distillates
Creosote
Furnace coke
Phthalic anhydride (PAA)
Refined tars
Roofing pitch

Railroad and Utility Products
Crossties (wood and concrete)
Pilings
Track and switch preassemblies
Utility poles

COMPETITORS

Cabot
Cytec
Kerr-McGee
KMG Chemicals
North American Technologies
RailWorks
Stepan

HISTORICAL FINANCIALS

Company Type: Private

Income Statement FYE: December 31

	REVENUE ($ mil.)	NET INCOME ($ mil.)	NET PROFIT MARGIN	EMPLOYEES
12/02	730	17	2.3%	2,057
12/01	708	13	1.9%	2,085
12/00	724	15	2.0%	2,155
12/99	664	24	3.6%	1,904
12/98	671	20	3.0%	1,927
12/97	593	(6)	—	1,990
12/96	589	14	2.4%	1,919
12/95	526	24	4.6%	2,104
12/94	476	11	2.3%	—
12/93	461	5	1.0%	—
Annual Growth	5.2%	15.0%	—	(0.3%)

2002 Year-End Financials

Debt ratio: —
Return on equity: —
Cash ($ mil.): 10
Current ratio: 1.41
Long-term debt ($ mil.): 209

Net Income History

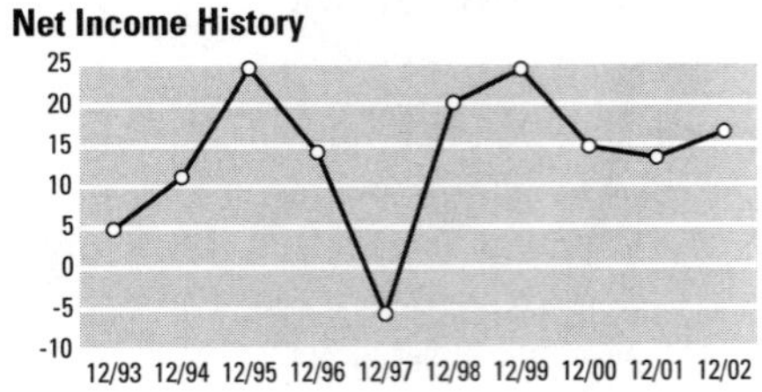

KPMG International

Businesses all over the world count on KPMG for accounting. The firm is the most geographically dispersed of accounting's Big Four, which also includes Deloitte Touche Tohmatsu, Ernst & Young, and PricewaterhouseCoopers. KPMG has reorganized its operations, transforming itself from a confederation of accounting firms into three more closely linked regional units: the Americas, Europe/Middle East/Africa, and Asia/Pacific. The firm's offerings include assurance, tax, and financial advisory services; its KLegal International network includes some 1,600 lawyers around the world.

After much regulatory pressure, KPMG separated its accounting and consulting operations; it sold a chunk of the consulting business to networking equipment maker Cisco Systems, then took it public and sold off its shares in 2002. The consulting unit, which in 2002 changed its name to BearingPoint, is buying KPMG's Austrian, German, and Swiss consulting businesses.

In 2003 the SEC charged the firm and four partners with fraud in relation to alleged profit inflation at former client Xerox in the late 1990s.

HISTORY

Peat Marwick was founded in 1911, when William Peat, a London accountant, met James Marwick during an Atlantic crossing. University of Glasgow alumni Marwick and Roger Mitchell had formed Marwick, Mitchell & Company in New York in 1897. Peat and Marwick agreed to ally their firms temporarily, and in 1925 they merged as Peat, Marwick, Mitchell, & Copartners.

In 1947 William Black became senior partner, a position he held until 1965. He guided the firm's 1950 merger with Barrow, Wade, Guthrie, one of the US's oldest firms, and built its consulting practice. Peat Marwick restructured its international practice as PMM&Co. (International) in 1972 (renamed Peat Marwick International in 1978).

The next year several European accounting firms led by Klynveld Kraayenhoff (the Netherlands) and Deutsche Treuhand (Germany) began forming an international accounting federation. Needing an American member, the European firms encouraged the merger of two American firms founded around the turn of the century, Main Lafrentz and Hurdman Cranstoun. Main Hurdman & Cranstoun joined the Europeans to form Klynveld Main Goerdeler (KMG), named after two of the member firms and the chairman of Deutsche Treuhand, Reinhard Goerdeler. Other members were C. Jespersen (Denmark), Thorne Riddel (Canada), Thomson McLintok (UK), and Fides Revision (Switzerland).

Peat Marwick merged with KMG in 1987 to form Klynveld Peat Marwick Goerdeler (KPMG). KPMG lost 10% of its business as competing client companies departed. Professional staff departures followed in 1990 when, as part of a consolidation, the firm trimmed its partnership rolls.

In the 1990s the then-Big Six accounting firms all faced lawsuits arising from an evolving standard holding auditors responsible for the substance, rather than merely the form, of clients' accounts. KPMG was hit by suits stemming from its audits of defunct S&Ls and litigation relating to the bankruptcy of Orange County, California (settled for $75 million in 1998). Nevertheless KPMG kept growing; it expanded its consulting division with the acquisition of banking consultancy Barefoot, Marrinan & Associates in 1996.

In 1997, after Price Waterhouse and Coopers & Lybrand announced their merger, KPMG and Ernst & Young announced one of their own. But they called it quits the next year, fearing that regulatory approval of the deal would be too onerous.

The creation of PricewaterhouseCoopers (PwC) and increasing competition in the consulting sides of all of the Big Five brought a realignment of loyalties in their national practices. KPMG Consulting's Belgian group moved to PwC and its French group to Computer Sciences Corporation. Andersen nearly wooed away KPMG's Canadian consulting group, but the plan was foiled by the ever-sullen Andersen Consulting group (now Accenture) and by KPMG's promises of more money. Against this background, KPMG sold 20% of its consulting operations to Cisco Systems for $1 billion. In addition to the cash infusion, the deal allowed KPMG to provide installation and system management to Cisco's customers.

Even while KPMG worked on the IPO of its consulting group (which took place in 2001), it continued to rail against the SEC as it called for relationships between consulting and auditing organizations to be severed. In 2002 KPMG sold its British and Dutch consultancy units to France's Atos Origin.

EXECUTIVES

Chairman, KPMG International and KPMG UK: Michael (Mike) Rake, age 55
CEO: Robert W. Alspaugh, age 56
COO: Colin Holland
CFO: Joseph E. Heintz
Chairman and CEO, KPMG LLP: Eugene D. O'Kelly, age 51
Chairman, Corporate Finance: David M. Beever, age 62
Chairman, Asian Anchor Practice: Marvin K.T. Cheung
Deputy Chairman, KPMG LLP: Jeffrey M. Stein, age 49
Vice Chairman, Assurance & Advisory Services, KPMG LLP: Timothy P. Flynn
Vice Chairman, Human Resources, KPMG LLP: Kathy H. Hannan
Vice Chairman, Marketing & Communications, KPMG LLP: Timothy R. Pearson
Vice Chairman, Tax Services, KPMG LLP: Richard Smith
CEO, KLegal International: Robert Glennie
National Partner in Charge, State and Local Tax Practice (SALT), KPMG LLP: Michael H. (Mike) Lippman
Partner in Charge, NY Financial Services, KPMG LLP: Robert F. Arning
Partner in Charge, Corporate Finance: Stephen Barrett
Managing Partner, Global Markets: Alistair Johnston
Managing Partner, Legal Services: Hartwich Lübmann
Managing Partner, Assurance: Rolf Nonnenmacher
General Counsel, KPMG LLP: Claudia L. Taft

LOCATIONS

HQ: 345 Park Ave., New York, NY 10154
Phone: 212-758-9700 **Fax:** 212-758-9819
Web: www.kpmg.com

KPMG International has offices in more than 150 countries.

2002 Sales

	$ mil.	% of total
Europe/Middle East/Africa	5,460	51
Americas	4,270	40
Asia/Pacific	990	9
Total	**10,720**	**100**

PRODUCTS/OPERATIONS

Selected Services

Assurance
- Financial statement audits
- Information risk management
- Management assurance services

Corporate Finance Advisory
- Insolvency services
- Investigations
- Restructuring and turnaround
- Forensic services
- Dispute resolution
- Intellectual property
- Litigation services
- Risk advisory

Tax and Legal
- Global transfer pricing services
- Indirect tax services
- International corporate tax services
- International executive services
- Mergers and acquisitions
- Trade and customs services

Transaction Services
- Stock exchange reporting
- Strategic and commercial intelligence
- Transaction evaluation
- Transaction structuring
- Vendor assistance

COMPETITORS

Aon
Bain & Company
Baker Tilly International
BDO International
Booz Allen
Deloitte Touche Tohmatsu
Ernst & Young
Grant Thornton International
H&R Block
Hewitt Associates
Marsh & McLennan
McKinsey & Company
PricewaterhouseCoopers
Towers Perrin
Watson Wyatt

HISTORICAL FINANCIALS

Company Type: Partnership

Income Statement

FYE: September 30

	REVENUE ($ mil.)	NET INCOME ($ mil.)	NET PROFIT MARGIN	EMPLOYEES
9/02	10,720	—	—	98,000
9/01	11,700	—	—	103,000
9/00	10,700	—	—	108,000
9/99	12,200	—	—	102,000
9/98	10,600	—	—	85,300
9/97	9,200	—	—	83,500
9/96	8,100	—	—	77,000
9/95	7,500	—	—	72,000
9/94	6,600	—	—	76,200
9/93	6,000	—	—	76,200
Annual Growth	6.7%	—	—	2.8%

Revenue History

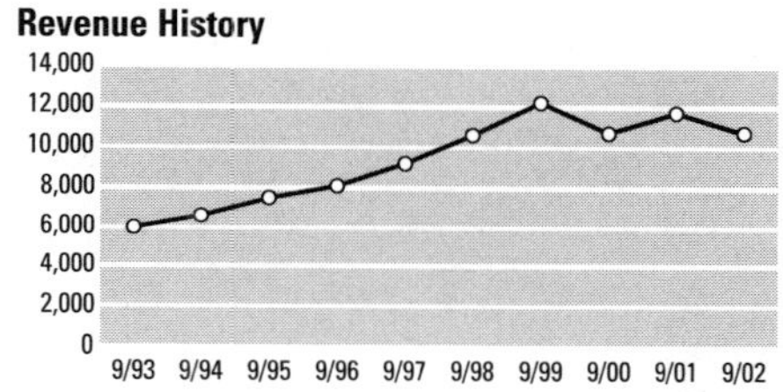

Krasdale Foods

Indirectly, Krasdale Foods has been supplying groceries to residents of the New York area for nearly 100 years. As a wholesale food distributor, the company serves about 3,900 independent clients, ranging from small corner stores to larger supermarkets. Customers include AIM, Bravo, C-Town (a former division of the company), Stop 1, and Shop Smart. Founded in 1908, the firm now distributes food to stores in Connecticut, Massachusetts, New Jersey, New York, and Pennsylvania under private and branded labels. The founding Krasne family, including CEO Charles Krasne (son of the company's founder), owns Krasdale Foods.

EXECUTIVES

President and CEO: Charles A. Krasne
EVP and COO: Robert Gewelb
CFO: Steve Silver
Director Human Resources: Ralph Zampini

LOCATIONS

HQ: Krasdale Foods, Inc.
65 W. Red Oak Ln., White Plains, NY 10604
Phone: 914-694-6400 **Fax:** 914-697-5225
Web: www.krasdalefoods.com

COMPETITORS

Associated Wholesalers
Bozzuto's
C&S Wholesale
Di Giorgio
Fleming Companies
Jetro Cash & Carry
Key Food
McLane
SUPERVALU
Wakefern Food

HISTORICAL FINANCIALS

Company Type: Private

Income Statement FYE: December 31

	REVENUE ($ mil.)	NET INCOME ($ mil.)	NET PROFIT MARGIN	EMPLOYEES
12/01	550	—	—	750
12/00	525	—	—	750
12/99	525	—	—	750
12/98	525	—	—	750
12/97	459	—	—	600
12/96	459	—	—	600
12/95	450	—	—	600
12/94	425	—	—	550
12/93	425	—	—	550
12/92	415	—	—	—
Annual Growth	3.2%	—	—	4.0%

Revenue History

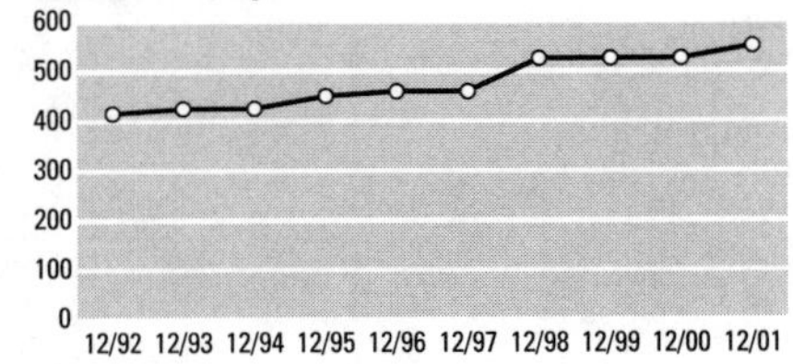

KRATON Polymers LLC

KRATON Polymers broke its bond with Royal Dutch/Shell Group but still has plenty of other bonds — both in the laboratory and with plastics makers. The company is the leading maker of styrenic block copolymers (SBCs), a family of polymers used in a variety of plastic, rubber, and chemical products, as well as for improving the stability of asphalt. More specifically, the KRATON family of polymers (D, G, FG, and IR) is used in adhesives, toys, and packaging, and to make shoe soles. The company has six manufacturing facilities in Asia, Europe, and North and South America. Private investment firm Ripplewood Holdings bought the company from Royal Dutch/Shell Group in 2001.

EXECUTIVES

CEO: Stephen M. Wood
VP, Americas and Director, KRATON G Polymers: Garret Davies
VP, Asia-Pacific: Issho Nakamura
VP, Europe, Africa, and Middle East and Director, KRATON D Polymers: Roger Morgan
VP, Finance and IT: Gary M. Spitz
VP, Operations: Rick Ott
VP, Technology: Bob Newman
General Legal Counsel: Joseph Waiter

LOCATIONS

HQ: 700 Milam St., North Tower, 13th Fl., Houston, TX 77002
Phone: 832-204-5400 **Fax:** 832-204-5460
Web: www.kraton.com

Manufacturing Facilities

Belpre, Ohio
Berre, France
Kashima, Japan
Paulinia, Brazil
Pernis, The Netherlands
Wesseling, Germany

COMPETITORS

BASF AG
Bayer AG
BP Chemicals
CPChem
Dow Chemical
DuPont
GE Plastics
ICI
NOVA Chemicals
Solvay

HISTORICAL FINANCIALS

Company Type: Private

Income Statement FYE: December 31

	ESTIMATED REVENUE ($ mil.)	NET INCOME ($ mil.)	NET PROFIT MARGIN	EMPLOYEES
12/02	600	—	—	1,000
12/01	600	—	—	1,000
Annual Growth	0.0%	—	—	0.0%

Revenue History

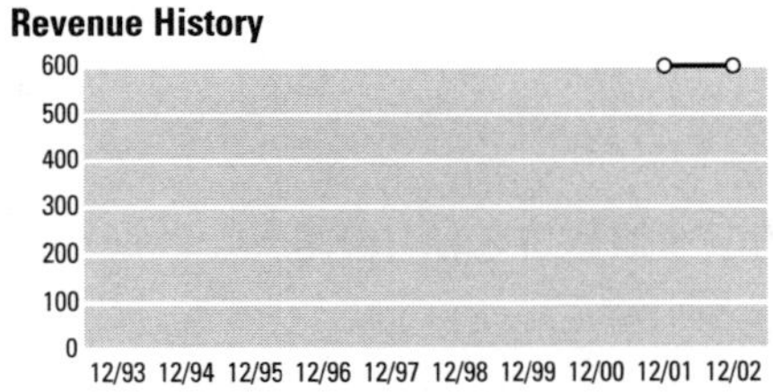

K-VA-T Food Stores, Inc.

What do you call a chain of supermarkets in Kentucky, Virginia, and Tennessee? How about K-VA-T Food Stores? K-VA-T is one of the largest grocery chains in the region, with about 85 supermarkets primarily under the Food City banner (and a handful of Super Dollar Supermarkets). Originally a Piggly Wiggly franchise with three stores, K-VA-T was founded in 1955. It has expanded by acquiring stores from other regional food retailers, opening new stores, and adding services such as more than 30 pharmacies, about 20 Gas'N Go gasoline outlets, and banking. Its Mid-Mountain Foods provides warehousing and distribution services. The founding Smith family owns a majority of K-VA-T; employees own the rest of the company.

EXECUTIVES

Chairman: Jack C. Smith
President and CEO: Steven C. Smith, age 45
EVP, Knoxville Division: Jody Helms
EVP, Tri-Cities Division: Johnny Cecil
SVP and COO: Jesse A. Lewis
SVP, Finance and Administration, CFO, Secretary, and Treasurer: Robert L. Neeley
SVP, Marketing: Tom Hembree
VP, Human Resources: Donnie Meadows

LOCATIONS

HQ: 201 Trigg St., Abingdon, VA 24210
Phone: 276-628-5503 **Fax:** 276-628-1592
Web: www.foodcity.com

PRODUCTS/OPERATIONS

Selected Departments

Bakery/Deli
Café
Dairy
Dry goods
Floral
Frozen foods
Gasoline
Meat
Pharmacy
Produce
Seafood
Video

COMPETITORS

Ahold USA
Albertson's
Alex Lee
AWG
Delhaize America
A&P
Houchens
Ingles Markets
Kmart
Kroger
Meijer
The Pantry
Ruddick
SUPERVALU
Ukrop's Super Markets
Wal-Mart
Winn-Dixie

HISTORICAL FINANCIALS

Company Type: Private

Income Statement FYE: December 31

	REVENUE ($ mil.)	NET INCOME ($ mil.)	NET PROFIT MARGIN	EMPLOYEES
12/02	1,063	—	—	9,300
12/01	1,000	—	—	8,700
12/00	963	—	—	8,690
12/99	880	—	—	7,100
12/98	760	—	—	6,500
12/97	712	—	—	6,300
12/96	691	—	—	6,000
12/95	634	—	—	4,000
12/94	592	—	—	3,752
12/93	562	—	—	3,673
Annual Growth	7.3%	—	—	10.9%

Revenue History

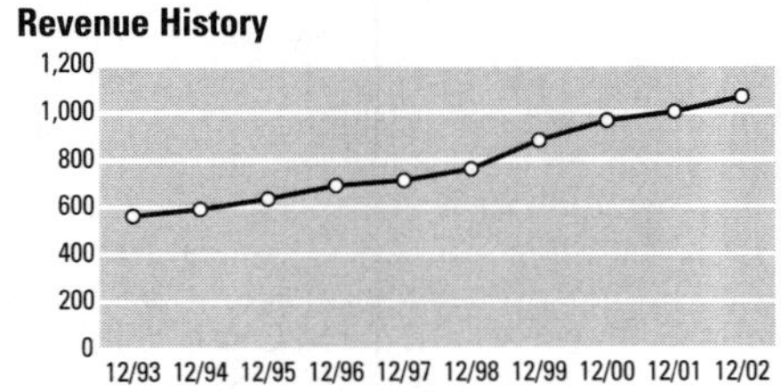

Land O'Lakes

Land O'Lakes butters up its customers, and goes to show you what life is like if everyone co-operates. Owned by and serving more than 7,000 dairy farmer members and 1,300 community co-operatives, Land O'Lakes is the #3 dairy co-op in the US (behind Dairy Farmers of America and California Dairies). It provides its members with wholesale fertilizer and crop protection products, seed, and animal feed. Its oldest product, LAND O' LAKES butter, is the #1 butter brand in the US. Land O'Lakes also produces packaged milk, margarine, sour cream, and cheese. The co-op's animal feed division is a leading animal and pet food maker.

In addition to its Land O'Lakes Farmland Feeds and Agriliance agronomy divisions, its Land O'Lakes swine division raises feeder pigs for members and sees the pigs to market. The co-op's subsidiary Land O'Lakes Finance provides financing services for beef, dairy, pork, and poultry producers.

In response to changes in the agriculture business and the rapidly consolidating dairy market, Land O'Lakes has positioned itself as a national player. Acquisitions and joint-ventures have helped it diversify beyond just butter and dairy commodities.

HISTORY

In the old days, grocers sold butter from communal tubs and it often went bad. Widespread distribution of dairy products had to await the invention of fast, reliable transportation. By 1921 the necessary transportation was available. That year about 320 dairy farmers in Minnesota formed the Minnesota Cooperative Creameries Association and launched a membership drive with $1,375, mostly borrowed from the US Farm Bureau.

The co-op arranged joint shipments for members; imposed strict hygiene and quality standards; and aggressively marketed its sweet cream butter nationwide, packaged for the first time in the familiar box of four quarter-pound sticks. A month after the co-op's New York sales office opened, it was ordering 80 shipments a week.

Minnesota Cooperative Creameries, as part of its promotional campaigns, ran a contest in 1924 to name that butter. Two contestants offered the winning name — Land O'Lakes. The distinctive Indian Maiden logo first appeared about the same time, and in 1926 the co-op changed its name to Land O'Lakes Creameries. By 1929, when it began supplying feed, its market share approached 50%.

During WWII civilian consumption dropped, but the co-op increased production of dried milk to provide food for soldiers and newly liberated concentration camp victims.

In the 1950s and 1960s, Land O'Lakes added ice cream and yogurt producers to its membership and fought margarine makers, yet butter's market share continued to melt. The co-op diversified in 1970 through acquisitions, adding feeds and agricultural chemicals. Two years later Land O'Lakes threw in the towel and came out with its own margarine. Despite the decreasing use of butter nationally, the co-op's market share grew.

Land O'Lakes formed a marketing joint venture, Cenex/Land O'Lakes Agronomy, with fellow co-op Cenex in 1987. As health consciousness bloomed in the 1980s, Land O'Lakes launched reduced-fat dairy products. It also purchased a California cheese plant, doubling its capacity. Land O'Lakes began ramping up its international projects at the same time: It built a feed mill in Taiwan, introduced feed products in Mexico, and established feed and cheese operations in Poland.

In 1997 the co-op bought low-fat cheese maker Alpine Lace Brands. Land O'Lakes took on the eastern US when it merged with the 3,600-member Atlantic Dairy Cooperative (1997), and it bulked up on the West Coast when California-based Dairyman's Cooperative Creamery Association joined its fold (1998).

During 2000 the co-op sold five plants to Dean Foods with an agreement to continue supplying the plants with raw milk. Also in 2000 Land O'Lakes combined its feed business with those of Farmland Industries to create Land O'Lakes Farmland Feed, LLC, with 69% ownership. That same year Cenex/Land O'Lakes Agronomy and Farmland Industries joined together their agronomy operations to create Agriliance LLC (now 50% owned).

In late 2001 the company spent $359 million to acquire Purina Mills (pet and livestock feeds). Purina Mills was folded into Land O'Lakes Farmland Feed and, as part of the purchase, Land O'Lakes increased its ownership of the feed business to 92%.

To take advantage of its nationally recognized brand, Land O'Lakes formed an alliance with Dean Foods in 2002 to develop and market value-added dairy products.

EXECUTIVES

Chairman: James D. (Jim) Fife
President and CEO: John E. (Jack) Gherty
EVP; COO Agricultural Services: Duane Halverson
EVP; COO Dairy Foods: Chris Policinski
SVP and CFO: Daniel E. Knutson, age 46
SVP Western Region, Dairy Foods Group: Jack Prince
VP, Foodservice Division: Kim Ewers
VP, General Counsel: John Rebane
VP, Human Resources: Karen Grabow
VP, Milk Supply Division: Gary A. Corbett, age 53
VP, Operations and Supply Chain, Dairy Foods: Fernando Palacios
VP, Planning and Business Development: Jim Wahrenbrock
VP, Public Affairs: Don Berg
VP, Research, Technology, and Engineering: David Hettinga
President, Land O'Lakes Farmland Feed: Robert D. (Bob) DeGregorio, age 46
Auditors: KPMG LLP

LOCATIONS

HQ: Land O' Lakes, Inc.
4001 Lexington Ave. North, Arden Hills, MN 55126
Phone: 651-481-2222 **Fax:** 651-481-2000
Web: www.landolakesinc.com

Land O'Lakes operates processing, manufacturing, warehousing, and distribution facilities across the US and internationally.

PRODUCTS/OPERATIONS

Selected Brands

Alpine Lace (low-fat cheese)
CROPLAN GENETICS (crop seed)
LAND O' LAKES (consumer dairy products)
Land O'Lakes (animal feed)
PMI Nutrition (animal feeds and pet foods)

Dairy Products

Butter
Cheese
Flavored butter
Light butter
Margarine
Milk
Sour cream

COMPETITORS

ADM
AMPI
California Dairies Inc.
Dairy Farmers of America
Dean Foods
Fonterra
Foremost Farms
Kraft Foods
National Dairy Holdings
Northwest Dairy
Parmalat
Pioneer Hi-Bred
Prairie Farms Dairy
Saputo
Schreiber Foods
Unilever
WestFarm Foods

HISTORICAL FINANCIALS

Company Type: Cooperative

Income Statement

FYE: December 31

	REVENUE ($ mil.)	NET INCOME ($ mil.)	NET PROFIT MARGIN	EMPLOYEES
12/02	5,847	99	1.7%	8,000
12/01	5,973	72	1.2%	8,600
12/00	5,756	103	1.8%	6,500
12/99	5,613	21	0.4%	6,500
12/98	5,174	69	1.3%	6,500
12/97	4,195	95	2.3%	5,500
12/96	3,486	119	3.4%	5,500
12/95	3,014	121	4.0%	5,500
12/94	2,859	75	2.6%	5,500
12/93	2,733	47	1.7%	5,700
Annual Growth	8.8%	8.6%	—	3.8%

2002 Year-End Financials

Debt ratio: 110.5%
Return on equity: 11.0%
Cash ($ mil.): 64
Current ratio: 1.18
Long-term debt ($ mil.): 1,007

Net Income History

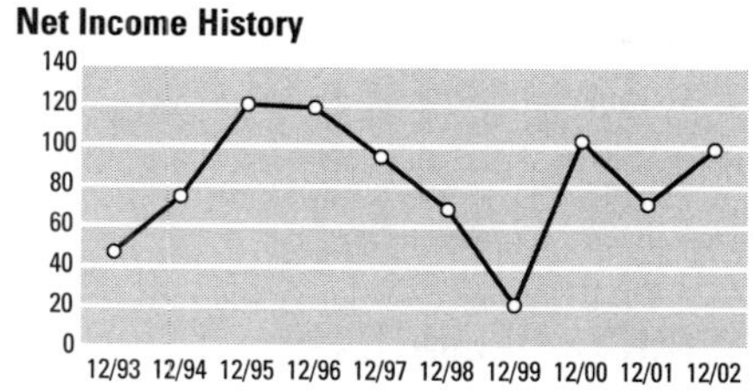

Landmark Communications

Landmark Communications' media properties are all over the map. Owner of cable station The Weather Channel, Landmark is also a leading community newspaper publisher. It publishes three metro newspapers (*The Virginian-Pilot, News & Record,* and *The Roanoke Times*) in North Carolina and Virginia and about 50 daily, semi-weekly, and weekly community papers in the East and Midwest. The company also publishes 70 free newspapers and special-interest publications, including some focusing on college sports. Chairman Frank Batten Jr. and his family own the company.

Landmark is 50% owner (with Cox Enterprises) of Trader Publishing, which prints classified advertising for motor vehicles, and owns about 50% of Capital-Gazette Communications, publisher of the *Washingtonian* magazine.

In addition to publishing, Landmark is big on the Internet. Its InfiNet unit (equally owned with partners Knight Ridder and Gannett) helps newspapers get online and operates Web sites for many of Landmark's properties. The company also owns CBS-affiliated TV stations in Las Vegas and Nashville, Tennessee. Its Landmark Education Services unit operates a handful of career schools.

EXECUTIVES

Chairman: Frank Batten Jr.
Chairman, Executive Committee: Frank Batten Sr.
Vice Chairman: Richard F. Barry III
President and COO: Decker Anstrom
EVP and CFO: Lemuel E. Lewis
EVP; President, Landmark Broadcasting: Donald H. Patterson Jr.
EVP, Secretary, and Corporate Counsel: Guy Friddell III, age 52
VP Human Resources: Charlie W. Hill

LOCATIONS

HQ: Landmark Communications, Inc.
150 W. Brambleton Ave., Norfolk, VA 23510
Phone: 757-446-2000 **Fax:** 757-446-2983
Web: www.landmarkcom.com

Landmark Communications has publications in Arkansas, Colorado, Florida, Illinois, Indiana, Iowa, Kentucky, Maryland, Mississippi, Nebraska, New Mexico, North Carolina, Ohio, Pennsylvania, South Carolina, Tennessee, West Virginia, and Virginia.

PRODUCTS/OPERATIONS

Broadcasting

KLAS-TV (Las Vegas)
Travel network (London)
The Weather Channel Networks
- Pelmorex, Inc. (50%, Canadian weather network)
- The Weather Channel
- weather.com

WTVF-TV (Nashville, TN)

Metro Newspapers

News & Record *(Greensboro, NC)*
The Roanoke Times *(VA)*
The Virginian-Pilot *(Norfolk, VA)*

COMPETITORS

Advance Publications
CNN
Community Newspaper Holdings
Cox Enterprises
Gannett
Hollinger International
Journal Communications
Knight-Ridder
Lamar Advertising
McClatchy Company
Media General
Meredith
New York Times
Stephens Media Group
Tribune
Washington Post

HISTORICAL FINANCIALS

Company Type: Private

Income Statement FYE: December 31

	ESTIMATED REVENUE ($ mil.)	NET INCOME ($ mil.)	NET PROFIT MARGIN	EMPLOYEES
12/01	732	—	—	5,000
12/00	805	—	—	5,000
12/99	730	—	—	5,000
12/98	650	—	—	4,500
12/97	573	—	—	4,500
12/96	550	—	—	4,500
12/95	501	—	—	4,500
12/94	467	—	—	4,500
12/93	437	—	—	—
12/92	407	—	—	—
Annual Growth	6.7%	—	—	1.5%

Revenue History

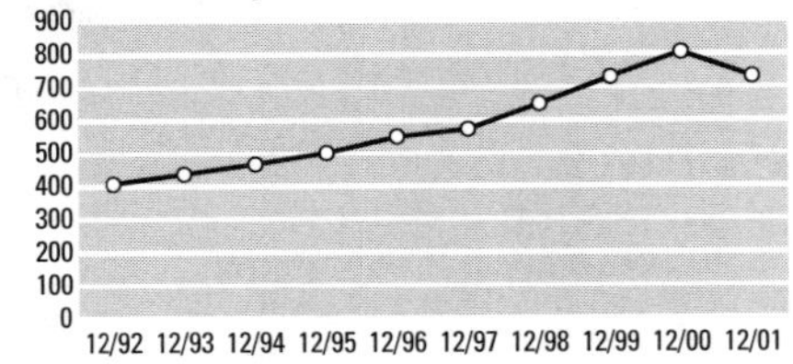

Lane Industries

From the seeds of a humble office machine and supplies manufacturer grew the mighty oak of Lane Industries. The diversified holding company's oldest investment is its nearly two-thirds stake in General Binding, a maker of binding and laminating equipment, marker boards, and paper shredders, founded by William Lane II in 1947. Lane Industries is also active in the lodging industry through Lane Hospitality, which owns or operates about 25 hotels, resorts, and time-share properties. Through Lane Security, the company owns Protection Service Industries, a security alarm firm in California, Arizona, and New Mexico. Lane Industries also has farming and ranching interests. The Lane family owns the company.

EXECUTIVES

President and CEO: Forrest M. Schneider, age 55
SVP: Richard R. Fabbrini
Chairman, President, and CEO, General Binding Corporation: Dennis J. Martin, age 52, $1,284,525 pay
President and CEO, Lane Hospitality: Bill DeForrest
Benefits Manager (HR): Linda Datz
MS Director, Lane Hospitality: Julio Castillo

LOCATIONS

HQ: Lane Industries, Inc.
1 Lane Center, 1200 Shermer Rd., Northbrook, IL 60062
Phone: 847-498-6789 **Fax:** 847-498-2104

COMPETITORS

Accor
ADT
Avery Dennison
Brink's
Fellowes
Fortune Brands
JELD-WEN
PolyVision
Protection One
Security Associates International
Standex
Starwood Hotels & Resorts
Tyco International

HISTORICAL FINANCIALS

Company Type: Private

Income Statement FYE: December 31

	REVENUE ($ mil.)	NET INCOME ($ mil.)	NET PROFIT MARGIN	EMPLOYEES
12/01	870	—	—	6,350
12/00	1,000	—	—	7,000
12/99	1,000	—	—	8,300
12/98	1,020	—	—	8,650
12/97	890	—	—	7,925
12/96	700	—	—	8,300
12/95	625	—	—	8,300
12/94	553	—	—	7,000
12/93	465	—	—	4,980
12/92	427	—	—	—
Annual Growth	8.2%	—	—	3.1%

Revenue History

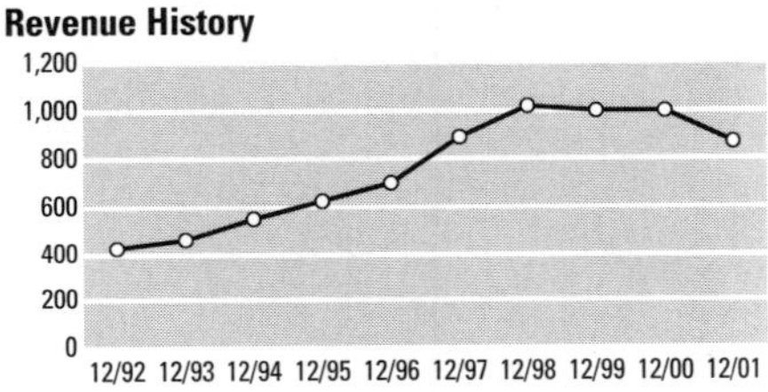

Lanoga Corporation

Lanoga is a lumbering giant. The company is one of the top US retailers of lumber and building materials, catering to professional contractors as well as consumers. Operating about 240 stores in 14 states, Lanoga has grown through dozens of small acquisitions. Its divisions include United Building Centers (Midwest and Rocky Mountain states), Lumbermens Building Centers (Northwest and Arizona), Spenard Builders Supply (Alaska), and the Home Lumber Company (Colorado). The firm bought 31 lumberyards and three manufacturing plants in Wisconsin and northern Michigan from Wickes. Lanoga was founded in the mid-1850s by the Laird and Norton families, who were cousins. Descendants of the company's founders own Lanoga.

EXECUTIVES

Chairman: Paul Brewer
President and CEO: Paul Hylbert
EVP, CFO, Secretary and Treasurer: William Brakken
EVP and COO: Mike Morehouse
VP, Market Development: George C. Finkenstaedt
President, Lumbermen's Building Centers: Dave Dittmer
President, Spenard Builders Supply: Ed Waite
President, United Building Centers: Dale Kukowski
IT Manager: Reba Mart

LOCATIONS

HQ: 17946 NE 65th St., Redmond, WA 98052
Phone: 425-883-4125 **Fax:** 425-882-2959
Web: www.lanogacorp.com

COMPETITORS

84 Lumber
Ace Hardware
Building Materials Holding
Home Depot
Lowe's
Menard
Stock Building Supply
TruServ
Wickes
Wolohan Lumber

HISTORICAL FINANCIALS

Company Type: Private

Income Statement FYE: December 31

	REVENUE ($ mil.)	NET INCOME ($ mil.)	NET PROFIT MARGIN	EMPLOYEES
12/02	1,450	—	—	7,000
12/01	1,400	—	—	5,500
12/00	1,300	—	—	5,360
12/99	1,251	—	—	5,125
12/98	1,030	—	—	4,085
12/97	990	—	—	4,147
12/96	842	—	—	3,730
12/95	760	—	—	3,600
12/94	746	—	—	3,400
12/93	657	—	—	2,975
Annual Growth	9.2%	—	—	10.0%

Revenue History

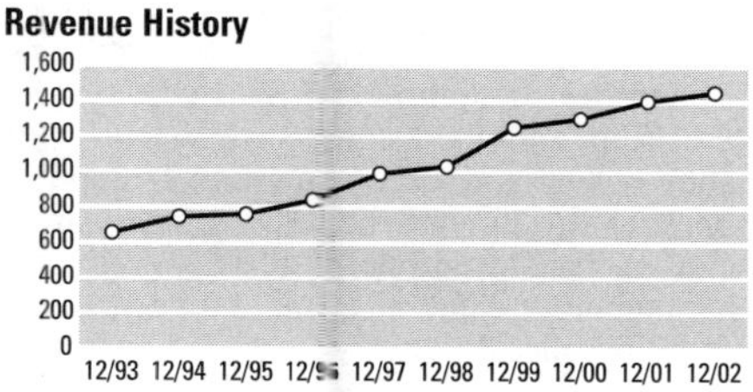

Larry H. Miller

You wouldn't hire the Larry H. Miller Group for your late night bebop, but the firm does know a little something about all that jazz. The company operates more than 35 auto dealerships in Arizona, Colorado, Idaho, New Mexico, Oregon, and Utah. Its dealerships sell Cadillac, Chevrolet, Honda, Lexus, Toyota, and other makes of cars. The company also owns the Utah Jazz, its home (the Delta Center arena), the WNBA's Utah Starzz, and Salt Lake City TV station KJZZ. In addition the Larry H. Miller Group operates two movie theaters with a total of about 30 screens in Salt Lake City and Sandy, Utah. Also in Sandy the company owns a 10-story office building. Owned by Larry H. Miller, the company was founded in 1979.

EXECUTIVES

CEO: Clark Whitworth
President: Karen G. Miller
SVP and Operations Manager: Bryant Henrie
Director of Human Resources: Linda Jeppesen

LOCATIONS

HQ: Larry H. Miller Group
9350 S. 150 East, Rte. 1000, Sandy, UT 84070
Phone: 801-563-4100 **Fax:** 801-563-4198
Web: www.lhm.com

Larry H. Miller Group owns and operates more than 35 automobile dealerships in Arizona, Colorado, Idaho, New Mexico, Oregon, and Utah.

COMPETITORS

AutoNation
Burt Automotive
DriveTime
Earnhardt's Auto Centers
Phil Long Dealerships
Ron Tonkin
United Auto Group
VT

HISTORICAL FINANCIALS

Company Type: Private

Income Statement FYE: December 31

	REVENUE ($ mil.)	NET INCOME ($ mil.)	NET PROFIT MARGIN	EMPLOYEES
12/01	1,550	—	—	—
12/00	1,367	—	—	—
12/99	1,361	—	—	—
12/98	1,200	—	—	—
12/97	1,019	—	—	—
12/96	842	—	—	—
12/95	926	—	—	—
12/94	700	—	—	—
12/93	688	—	—	—
12/92	500	—	—	—
Annual Growth	13.4%	—	—	—

Revenue History

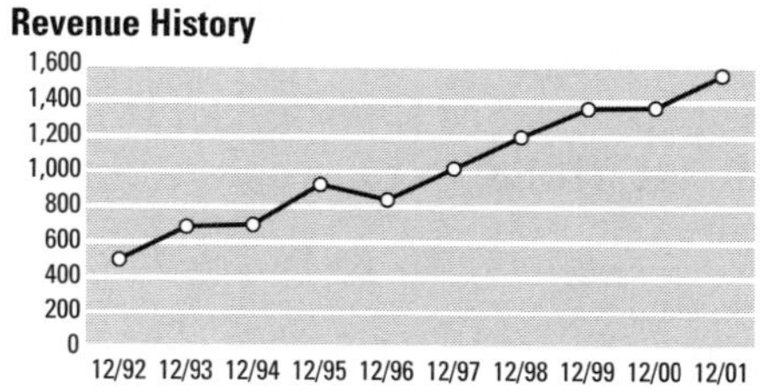

Las Vegas Sands

Rising from the ashes of the bulldozed Sands Hotel, the Venetian Casino Resort (owned and operated by Las Vegas Sands) brings a touch of Venice to the Las Vegas strip. Replete with gondoliers, the colonnades of Doge's Palace, and a replica of the Rialto Bridge, the Venetian offers a 116,000-sq.-ft. casino and a 3,000-room hotel (planned construction will add 1,000 hotel rooms). The facility also houses a shopping, dining, and entertainment complex. Las Vegas Sands operates the Venetian Congress Center conference facility that links the casino to the nearby Expo Center trade show and convention center (separately owned by an affiliate). Las Vegas Sands chairman and CEO Sheldon Adelson owns the company.

EXECUTIVES

Chairman and CEO: Sheldon G. Adelson, age 68
President and COO: William P. Weidner, age 56, $1,538,462 pay
EVP: Bradley H. Stone, age 47, $1,230,769 pay
SVP: Robert G. Goldstein, age 46, $1,153,846 pay
SVP Operations, The Venetian Resort: Paul Pusateri
VP Hotel Operations: Peter Walterspiel
Assistant to the Chairman and Secretary: David Friedman, age 45, $615,385 pay
VP Advertising: Scott Messinger
VP Casino Marketing: Howie Weiner
VP Finance: Harry D. Miltenberger, age 58
VP Human Resources, The Venetian Resort: David Newton
VP General Counsel, The Venetian Resort: Tom Smock
Auditors: PricewaterhouseCoopers LLP

LOCATIONS

HQ: Las Vegas Sands, Inc.
3355 S. Las Vegas Blvd., Las Vegas, NV 89109
Phone: 702-414-1000 **Fax:** 702-414-4884
Web: www.venetian.com

COMPETITORS

Boyd Gaming
Harrah's Entertainment
Mandalay Resort Group
MGM Mirage
Park Place Entertainment

HISTORICAL FINANCIALS

Company Type: Private

Income Statement FYE: December 31

	REVENUE ($ mil.)	NET INCOME ($ mil.)	NET PROFIT MARGIN	EMPLOYEES
12/02	572	(38)	—	4,000
12/01	524	(24)	—	4,000
12/00	590	16	2.7%	4,000
12/99	284	(66)	—	4,000
12/98	1	(30)	—	—
12/97	1	(1)	—	—
Annual Growth	263.6%	—	—	0.0%

2002 Year-End Financials

Debt ratio: —
Return on equity: —
Cash ($ mil.): 116
Current ratio: 1.31
Long-term debt ($ mil.): 1,216

Net Income History

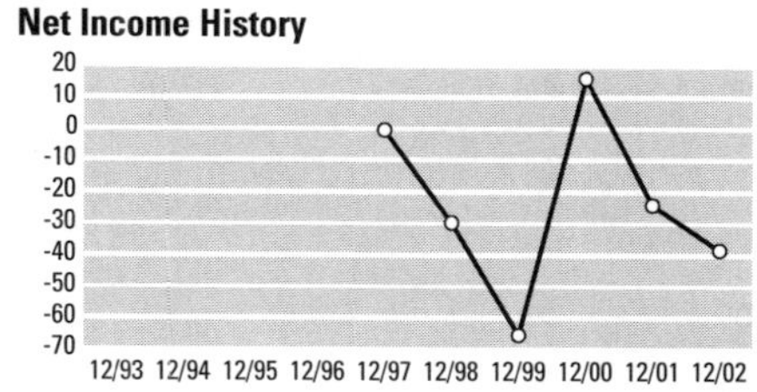

Latham & Watkins

Latham & Watkins' founders Dana Latham and Paul Watkins flipped a coin in 1934 to determine which of their names would go first on the company's shingle. From that coin toss, the law firm has grown into one of the largest in the US. With more than 1,500 lawyers, the firm ranks high in corporate finance, mergers and acquisitions, technology law, and litigation. Latham & Watkins was a key player in the financing for the Venetian Resort Hotel and Casino in Las Vegas and Gemstar's acquisition of TV Guide. Headquartered in Los Angeles, the firm has 21 locations worldwide. Latham & Watkins counts Amgen, Time Warner Inc., Lucent, and Morgan Stanley among its clients.

EXECUTIVES

Chairman and Managing Partner: Robert M. Dell
Financial Controller: Michael Eichenseer
Director Global Human Resources: Mimi Krumholz

LOCATIONS

HQ: 633 W. 5th St., Ste. 4000, Los Angeles, CA 90071
Phone: 213-485-1234 **Fax:** 213-891-8763
Web: www.lw.com

Latham & Watkins has offices in Boston; Chicago; Costa Mesa, Los Angeles, Menlo Park, San Diego, and San Francisco, California; Newark, New Jersey; New York City; Reston, Virginia; and Washington, DC; as well as in Brussels; Frankfurt and Hamburg, Germany; Hong Kong; London; Milan; Moscow; Paris; Singapore; and Tokyo.

PRODUCTS/OPERATIONS

Selected Practice Areas

Corporate
Environmental
Finance and real estate
International
Litigation
Tax

COMPETITORS

Baker & McKenzie
Davis Polk
Gibson, Dunn & Crutcher
O'Melveny & Myers
Paul, Hastings
Simpson Thacher
Skadden, Arps
Sullivan & Cromwell

HISTORICAL FINANCIALS

Company Type: Partnership

Income Statement FYE: December 31

	REVENUE ($ mil.)	NET INCOME ($ mil.)	NET PROFIT MARGIN	EMPLOYEES
12/02	906	—	—	—
12/01	770	—	—	—
12/00	643	—	—	2,647
12/99	582	—	—	2,297
12/98	502	—	—	2,287
12/97	421	—	—	—
12/96	363	—	—	—
12/95	300	—	—	—
12/94	263	—	—	—
12/93	234	—	—	—
Annual Growth	16.2%	—	—	7.6%

Revenue History

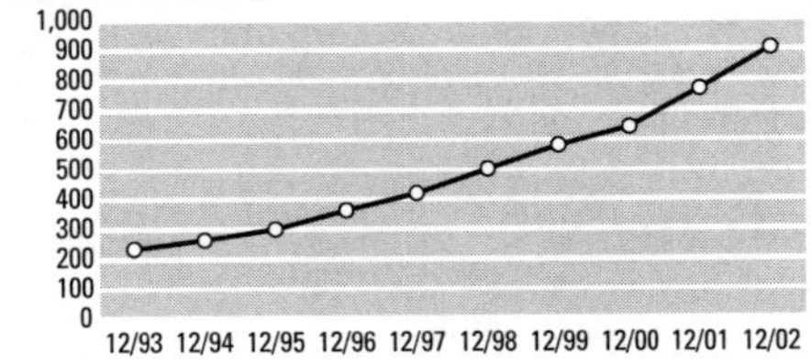

LDI, Ltd.

The "D" is definitely for "diversified" at LDI. The holding company, whose initials stand for Lacy Diversified Industries, deals in clothing, motorcycle parts, bicycle frames, and auto products. It owns Tucker Rocky Distributing, a distributor of apparel and aftermarket equipment for the watercraft, motorcycle, and snowmobile markets. LDI's Answer Products manufactures and distributes the Manitou brand of bicycle frames and suspension forks, as well as parts and apparel. LDI has a majority stake in FinishMaster, a leading auto paints and coating distributor in the US. LDI sold its Major Video Concepts video distribution business. Founded in 1912 as U.S. Corrugated-Fiber Box Co., LDI is owned by CEO Andre Lacy.

EXECUTIVES

Chairman and CEO: Andre B. Lacy, age 63
President and COO: David N. Shane
CFO: Michael P. Hutson
VP of Human Resources: Joyce Schooley
VP of Strategic Planning and Market Development: Paula Bachert

LOCATIONS

HQ: 54 Monument Circle, Ste. 800, Indianapolis, IN 46204
Phone: 317-237-5400 **Fax:** 317-237-2280
Web: www.ldiltd.com

COMPETITORS

BASF AG
Bell Industries
Cannondale
DuPont
Genuine Parts
Global Motorsport Group
RockShox
Trek

HISTORICAL FINANCIALS

Company Type: Private

Income Statement FYE: December 31

	REVENUE ($ mil.)	NET INCOME ($ mil.)	NET PROFIT MARGIN	EMPLOYEES
12/01	572	—	—	—
12/00	855	—	—	—
12/99	855	—	—	—
12/98	900	—	—	—
12/97	703	—	—	—
12/96	700	—	—	—
12/95	568	—	—	—
Annual Growth	0.1%	—	—	—

Revenue History

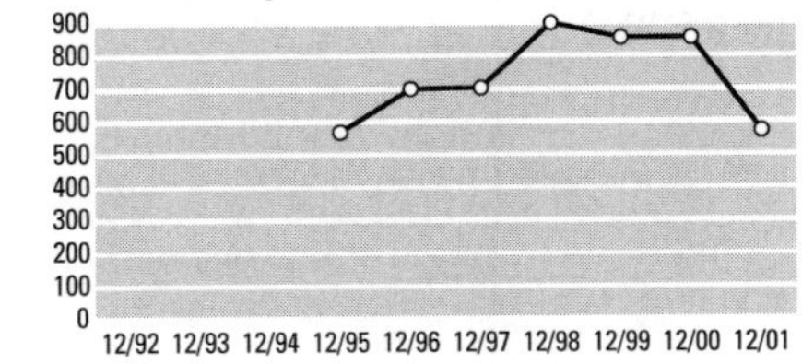

The Lefrak Organization

Horace Greeley said "Go west, young man!" and The Lefrak Organization listened — if you take the famous *New Yorker* comic strip's view that you're in the Midwest once you cross the Hudson. The Lefrak Organization is one of the US's largest private landlords, with more than 70,000 apartments in New York City and New Jersey, another 40,000 units under management, and millions of square feet of commercial space. Owned by the LeFrak family, the company also owns and manages a variety of commercial and retail properties throughout the New York City area, including flagship property 40 West 57th St.; tenants include Nautica, Bank of America, and Infinity Broadcasting.

Lefrak's flagship residential development, 5,000-unit Lefrak City in Queens, has been home to successive waves of ethnic groups seeking a better life.

The company is concentrating on its Newport development, a 400-acre community of apartments, office towers, and stores on the waterfront in Jersey City across the Hudson River from Manhattan. Lefrak has built half a dozen office towers (occupied by CIGNA, U.S. Trust, and UBS Financial Services, among others) on the site, and plans for further apartment developments and more office buildings are underway.

The company also has holdings in oil exploration (Lefrak Oil & Gas Organization, or LOGO) and entertainment (Lefrak Entertainment operates LMR, the record label that launched Barbra Streisand). It also owns stage and movie theaters and produces television programs, movies, and Broadway shows.

Chairman Samuel LeFrak, famed for his interpretation of the Golden Rule ("he who has the gold makes the rules"), passed away in April

2003. He was an active philanthropist, supporting the Guggenheim Museum and the American Museum of Natural History. He has also contributed to the oceanographic studies of the late sea explorer Jacques Cousteau.

HISTORY

Harry Lefrak and his father Aaron came to the US from Palestine (or France — there are many conflicting versions of the Lefrak family history — Aaron's father Maurice is said to have been a developer there in the 1840s) around 1900. They began building tenements in Brooklyn's Williamsburg neighborhood to house the flood of immigrants then pouring into New York City.

In 1901, Harry and Aaron started what is now known as The Lefrak Organization. It diversified into glass and for some time provided raw material for the workshops of Louis Comfort Tiffany. After WWI the glass factory was sold, and the company expanded into Brooklyn, where it developed housing and commercial space in Bedford-Stuyvesant, among other areas.

Samuel, Harry's son, began working in the business early, assisting tradesmen at building sites. He then attended the University of Maryland, and shunning a future career in dentistry (family lore claims his left-handedness would have required special tools), returned to the business. Samuel's first project was a 120-unit apartment building in Brooklyn's Midwood — it was 1938, and he was 20 years old and still a university student.

During WWII, the firm built camps and housing for the Army. After the war, business took off, as the company began building low-cost housing. Samuel took over the company in 1948. To keep costs down, Samuel bought clay and gypsum quarries, forests, and lumber mills and cement plants, eventually achieving 70% vertical integration of his operations. This included the creation of in-house architectural, engineering, and construction departments that handled all aspects of building the LeFrak empire's properties — from initial designs to general contracting — from the ground up.

The 1950s building boom was in part spurred by new laws in New York authorizing the issue of state bonds for financing low-interest construction loans, which Lefrak used to build more than 2,000 apartments in previously undeveloped coastal sections of Brooklyn. At its peak, Lefrak turned out an apartment every 16 minutes for rents as low as $21 per room.

In 1960 Lefrak broke ground for Lefrak City, a 5,000-apartment development built on 40 acres in Queens (after four years of negotiations with the trustees of the William Waldorf Astor estate over the sale price — $6 million), which featured air-conditioned units and rented for $40 per room.

The next decade brought a real estate slump that endangered the organization's next project, Battery Park. Lefrak issued public bonds to save it. Samuel also picked up a few more properties during this period, and he capitalized the "F" in his family name but not the company name. (He later said that he did this to distinguish himself from other Lefraks at his club who had been posted for nonpayment of dues, though a conflicting story states that his mother's French-born physician originally capitalized the "F" on Samuel's birth certificate.)

Samuel's son Richard became increasingly involved in the business in the 1980s as the organization began an even bigger project: the 600-acre Newport City development, begun in 1989 with plans for almost 10,000 apartments and retail and commercial space.

The company bought 200 oil fields in 1994 to build up its reserves of gas and home-heating oil.

Meanwhile, Lefrak City had "turned," as its original Jewish occupants sought greener fields. As occupancy dropped, the company relaxed its tenant screening, and the development deteriorated (it was subsequently tagged "Crack City"). In the 1990s, however, it began attracting a mix of African, Jewish, and Central Asian immigrants, whose tightly knit communities improved the development's safety and equilibrium.

Construction of the company's Newport project continued throughout the 1990s with construction of office buildings, apartments, and a hotel (completed in 2000) on the site. As a tight Manhattan office market drove up lease prices, Lefrak's new offices across the Hudson attracted companies in the finance and insurance sectors.

In 2001 the company's Gateway complex in Battery Park City was damaged in the World Trade Center terrorist attack. The tenants threatened a rent strike, prompting Lefrak to lower rents to compensate for the difficulties attributed to living near the site.

Samuel LeFrak passed away in April 2003 at the age of 85.

EXECUTIVES

President: Richard S. LeFrak, age 57
EVP and CFO: Richard N. Papert
EVP: Harrison LeFrak
EVP: James (Jamie) LeFrak
SVP Marketing and Public Relations: Edward Cortese
VP Commercial: Marsilia (Marcy) Boyle
VP Commercial: Irwin Granville
VP Construction and Engineering: Anthony Scavo
VP Finance and Administration and Treasurer: Mitchell Ingerman
General Counsel: Arnold S. Lehman
VP, Mid State Management: Charles Mehlman
Director, Human Resources: John Farrelly
Director, Residential Leasing: Tom Pichi
Auditors: Lewis Goldberg

LOCATIONS

HQ: 9777 Queens Blvd., Rego Park, NY 11374
Phone: 718-459-9021 **Fax:** 718-897-0688
Web: www.lefrak.com

The Lefrak Organization operates primarily in the New York metropolitan area.

Selected Properties

Commercial Space
Jersey City, New Jersey
Newport development
Manhattan
40 W. 57th St.
Gateway Plaza at Battery Park City
James Tower

Residential Apartments
Jersey City, New Jersey
Atlantic
East Hampton
James Monroe
Presidential Plaza
Riverside
Southampton
Towers of America
Manhattan
Gateway Plaza at Battery Park City
Queens
Lefrak City

Retail
Jersey City, New Jersey
Newport Centre Mall

PRODUCTS/OPERATIONS

Selected Operations

Energy
Lefrak Oil & Gas Organization

Entertainment
Lefrak Entertainment Co.

Real Estate
Commercial properties
Residential apartments
Residential co-op properties
Retail properties

COMPETITORS

Alexander's
Boston Properties
Equity Office Properties Trust
Hartz Mountain
Helmsley
Mack-Cali
Port Authority of NY & NJ
Reckson Associates Realty
SL Green Realty
Starrett Corporation
Tishman Realty
Trizec Properties
Trump
Vornado Realty Trust

HISTORICAL FINANCIALS

Company Type: Private

Income Statement

FYE: Last Sunday in November

	REVENUE ($ mil.)	NET INCOME ($ mil.)	NET PROFIT MARGIN	EMPLOYEES
11/00	3,800	—	—	16,200
11/99	3,200	—	—	16,110
11/98	2,750	—	—	16,000
11/97	3,400	—	—	18,000
11/96	3,500	—	—	17,500
11/95	3,300	—	—	17,400
11/94	3,100	—	—	17,500
11/93	3,200	—	—	18,000
11/92	3,200	—	—	18,000
11/91	3,100	—	—	18,000
Annual Growth	2.3%	—	—	(1.2%)

Revenue History

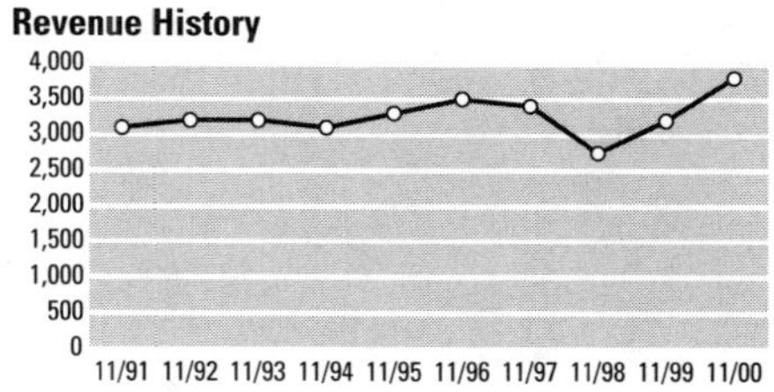

Leprino Foods

Don't try to butter up Leprino Foods — it's strictly into mozzarella, and finding things to do with all that leftover whey. The company is the world's largest maker of mozzarella cheese, which it sells to pizza chains (namely Pizza Hut) and food manufacturers. Leprino's other products include whey protein concentrate and lactose for use in animal feeds, baby formula, and baked goods. The firm gets its milk supply from the nation's large dairy co-ops. Leprino hopes to hitch its sales to the rising global popularity of pizza. It has acquired a stake in Glanbia — Europe's largest maker of pizza cheese. Italian immigrant Michael Leprino Sr. founded the company in 1950. It is still owned by the Leprino family.

EXECUTIVES

Chairman: James Leprino
President: Wesley J. Allen
SVP Administration: Ron Klump
SVP Business Development: Mike Reidy
VP Dairy Policy and Procurement: Sue Taylor
VP Personnel: Tom Deany
Controller: Paul Adams

LOCATIONS

HQ: Leprino Foods Company
1830 W. 38th Ave., Denver, CO 80211
Phone: 303-480-2600 **Fax:** 303-480-2605
Web: www.leprinofoods.com

Leprino Foods operates 11 plants in California, Colorado, Michigan, Nebraska, New Mexico, and New York.

COMPETITORS

Agri-Mark
Century Foods
Foremost Farms
Great Lakes Cheese
Kraft Foods
Saputo
Schreiber Foods

HISTORICAL FINANCIALS

Company Type: Private

Income Statement FYE: October 31

	ESTIMATED REVENUE ($ mil.)	NET INCOME ($ mil.)	NET PROFIT MARGIN	EMPLOYEES
10/03	1,900	—	—	3,350
10/02	1,750	—	—	3,000
10/01	1,700	—	—	2,500
10/00	1,650	—	—	2,800
10/99	1,550	—	—	2,800
10/98	1,250	—	—	2,300
10/97	1,000	—	—	2,300
10/96	1,200	—	—	2,200
10/95	1,100	—	—	2,200
Annual Growth	7.1%	—	—	5.4%

Revenue History

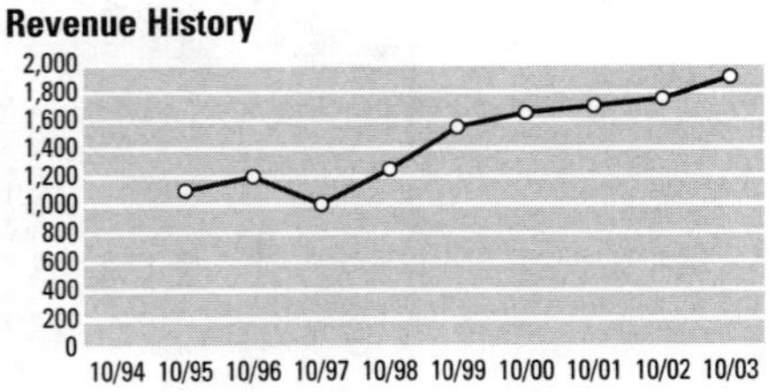

Lerner New York, Inc.

Lerner New York has taken a bite out of fashion's big apple. Lerner caters to women looking for city-style apparel (jeans, dresses, and coordinates) and accessories (sunglasses, costume jewelry, and hosiery) at moderate prices. The company sells name-brand and private-label fashions in about 520 mall-based Lerner New York and New York & Company stores in 43 states. Catalog retailer Brylane (like Lerner, a former subsidiary of Limited Brands) independently distributes Lerner catalogs, which offer different products than those found in Lerner's stores. Limited Brands acquired Lerner in 1985 and sold it in 2002 to an investor team led by Lerner's CEO, Richard Crystal, and including Bear Stearns Merchant Banking.

EXECUTIVES

President and CEO: Richard P. Crystal
EVP and National Sales Leader: Kevin Finnegan
EVP, Merchandising: Steven (Steve) Newman
EVP, Real Estate: John D. DeWolf III
Auditors: PricewaterhouseCoopers LLP

LOCATIONS

HQ: 450 W. 33rd St., 5th Fl., New York, NY 10001
Phone: 212-736-1222 **Fax:** 212-884-2396
Web: www.lernernewyork.com

COMPETITORS

AnnTaylor
bebe stores
Clothestime
Dillard's
Federated
Gap
J. Crew
J. C. Penney
Jones Apparel
Kohl's
Liz Claiborne
May
Spiegel
Target
TJX
Wet Seal

HISTORICAL FINANCIALS

Company Type: Private

Income Statement FYE: December 31

	REVENUE ($ mil.)	NET INCOME ($ mil.)	NET PROFIT MARGIN	EMPLOYEES
1/02	940	—	—	—
1/01	1,025	—	—	—
1/00	1,001	—	—	—
1/99	929	—	—	—
Annual Growth	0.4%	—	—	—

Revenue History

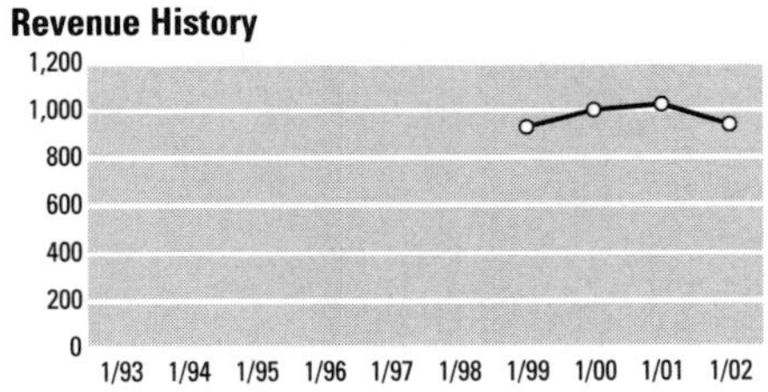

Les Schwab Tire Centers

If you need new tires after heeding Greeley's advice, go to Les Schwab Tire Centers. And it doesn't hurt that the owner wrote the bible of tire retailing: *Pride in Performance — Keep It Going.* Les Schwab Tire Centers prides itself on continued customer service; it sells tires and batteries and does alignment, brake, and shock work at some 365 stores in Alaska, California, Idaho, Montana, Nevada, Oregon, Utah, and Washington. With a story that rivals Moses', founder and chairman Les Schwab was reared in a logging camp and went to school in a converted boxcar. In 1952 he bought a tire shop that grew into Les Schwab Tire Centers. The firm, owned by Schwab and his family, plans to open about 20 new stores a year.

EXECUTIVES

Chairman: Les Schwab
President and CEO: Philip Wick
CFO: Tom Freedman
EVP: Dick Borgman
VP of Advertising and Marketing: Brian Capp
Director of Human Resources: Larry Smith

LOCATIONS

HQ: 646 NW Madras Hwy., Prineville, OR 97754
Phone: 541-447-4136 **Fax:** 541-416-5208
Web: www.lesschwab.com

COMPETITORS

Advance Auto Parts
AutoZone
Bridgestone
Commercial Tire
CSK Auto
Discount Tire
Goodyear
Pep Boys
Sears
Tire Centers
Wal-Mart

HISTORICAL FINANCIALS

Company Type: Private

Income Statement FYE: December 31

	ESTIMATED REVENUE ($ mil.)	NET INCOME ($ mil.)	NET PROFIT MARGIN	EMPLOYEES
12/01	1,000	—	—	6,000
12/00	800	—	—	6,000
12/99	800	—	—	5,500
12/98	750	—	—	5,300
12/97	850	—	—	5,300
12/96	700	—	—	4,800
12/95	525	—	—	4,225
12/94	500	—	—	4,000
12/93	450	—	—	3,500
Annual Growth	10.5%	—	—	7.0%

Revenue History

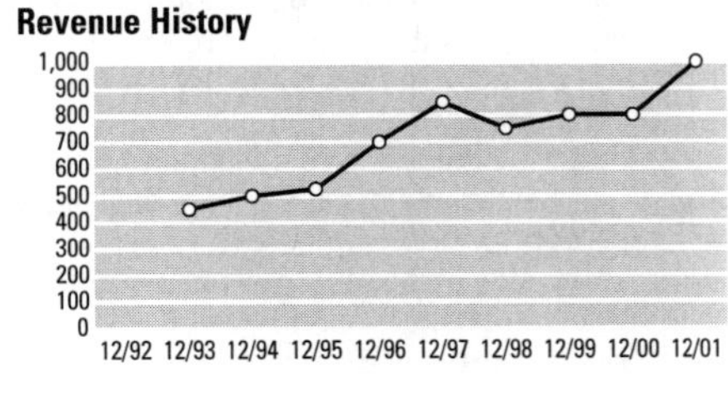

Levi Strauss

Levi Strauss & Co. (LS&CO.) is getting fancy with its pants while it tries to recapture the loyalty of America's tastemakers: teenagers. LS&CO., the world's #1 maker of brand-name clothing, sells jeans and sportswear under the Levi's, Dockers, and Slates names in more than 100 countries. Levi's jeans — department store staples — were once the uniform of American youth, but LS&CO. lost touch with the trends in recent years. To re-tap the youth market, LS&CO. is adding hip styles such as its unusually cut Engineered Jeans, the Superlow for women, and the Type 1 for the fashionista. The Haas family (relatives of founder Levi Strauss) owns LS&CO.

In late 2002, Levi Strauss overhauled its market strategy and, for the first time since the introduction of Dockers in 1986, rolled out a series of new brands. Varied and tiered in markets rather than relying on its basic one or two styles and brands, Levi's hopes they will help regain some of the market share lost to VF Corporation (makers of Lee and Wrangler) and others over the last decade.

Among a whole roster of new products, Levi's Superlow jeans and Levi Strauss Signature jeans were created for the mass market. Dockers Flat Front Mobile pants (with secret pockets for cell phones, PDAs, and other gadgets) and Dockers Go Khaki pants (with Stain Defender, a Teflon treatment preventing stains) target the 25 to 39 age group. Levi's Engineered Jeans were developed specifically for European and Asian markets and Levi's Vintage Clothing and Levi's Red were designated for the high-end market. Levi's Type 1, which made their debut at the 2003 Sundance Film Festival, were snatched up by Hollywood's most notable jeans-wearers.

Due to substantial drops in net sales over the last three years, the company has also taken measures to recoup some of its losses, including closing 37 of its factories worldwide and instead using independent contract manufacturers. The company is closing its remaining North American manufacturing facilities; its San Antonio operations will be closed by the end of 2003 and its three Canadian operations by March 2004. The closures will affect some 2,000 employees.

J.C. Penney Company represents 12% of overall sales.

HISTORY

Levi Strauss arrived in New York City from Bavaria in 1847. In 1853 he moved to San Francisco to sell dry goods to the gold rushers. Shortly after, a prospector told Strauss of miners' problems in finding sturdy pants. Strauss made a pair out of canvas for the prospector; word of the rugged pants spread quickly.

Strauss continued his dry-goods business in the 1860s. During this time he switched the pants' fabric to a durable French cloth called serge de Nimes, soon known as denim. He colored the fabric with indigo dye and adopted the idea from Nevada tailor Jacob Davis of reinforcing the pants with copper rivets. In 1873 Strauss and Davis produced their first pair of waist-high overalls (later known as jeans). The pants soon became *de rigueur* for lumberjacks, cowboys, railroad workers, oil drillers, and farmers.

Strauss continued to build his pants and wholesaling business until he died in 1902. Levi Strauss & Co. (LS&CO.) passed to four nephews who carried on their uncle's jeans business while maintaining the company's philanthropic reputation.

After WWII Walter Haas and Peter Haas (a fourth-generation Strauss family member) assumed leadership of LS&CO. In 1948 they ended the company's wholesaling business to concentrate on Levi's clothing. In the 1950s Levi's jeans ceased to be merely functional garments for workers: They became the uniform of American youth. In the 1960s LS&CO. added women's attire and expanded overseas.

The company went public in 1971. That year it added a women's career line and bought Koret sportswear (sold in 1984). By the mid-1980s profits declined. Peace Corps veteran-turned-McKinsey consultant Robert Haas (Walter's son) grabbed the reins of LS&CO. in 1984 and took the company private the next year. He also instilled a touchy-feely corporate culture often at odds with the bottom line.

In 1986 LS&CO. introduced Dockers casual pants. The company's sales began rising in 1991 as consumers forsook designer duds of the 1980s for more practical clothes. LS&CO. says seven out of every ten American men own a pair of Dockers. However, LS&CO. missed out on the birth of another trend: the split between the fashion sense of US adolescents and their Levi's-loving, baby boomer parents.

In 1996 the company introduced Slates dress slacks. That year LS&CO. bought back nearly one-third of its stock from family and employees for $4.3 billion. Grappling with slipping sales and debt from the buyout, in 1997 LS&CO. closed 11 of its 37 North American plants, laying off 6,400 workers and 1,000 salaried employees; it granted generous severance packages even to those earning minimum wage.

In 1998, citing improved labor conditions in China, LS&CO. announced it would step up its use of Chinese subcontractors. Further restructuring added a third of its European plants to the closures list that year. LS&CO.'s sales fell 13% in fiscal 1998. The next year LS&CO. closed 11 of 22 remaining North American plants. It also unleashed several new jeans brands that eschewed the company's one-style-fits-all approach of old.

In 1999 Haas handed his CEO title to Pepsi executive Philip Marineau.

In April 2002 LS&CO. announced it would close six of its last eight US plants and cut 20% of its worldwide staff (3,300 workers). In September 2003 it cut another 5% of its worldwide staff (650 workers). Also in September the company opened its first girls-only store located in Paris, France.

EXECUTIVES

Chairman: Robert D. (Bob) Haas, age 60, $1,148,077 pay
President and CEO: Philip A. Marineau, age 56, $1,450,000 pay
SVP and CFO: William B. Chiasson, age 50, $675,539 pay
SVP and CIO: David G. Bergen, age 47
SVP, General Counsel, and Assistant Secretary: Albert F. Moreno, age 58
SVP; President, Levi Strauss Asia Pacific: R. John Anderson, age 51, $546,413 pay
SVP; President, Levi Strauss Europe, Middle East, and Africa: Joseph (Joe) Middleton, age 46, $628,185 pay
SVP, US Customer Service: Scott LaPorta
SVP, Worldwide Human Resources: Fred Paulenich, age 38
SVP World Supply Chain: Paul Harrington
VP Merchandising, Development, and Marketing, Levi Strauss Signature: Mary Kwan, age 48
U.S. Brand President: Robert Hanson
Director of Internet Marketing: James (Jim) Stone
Director of Marketing (Canada): Julie Klee
Auditors: KPMG LLP

LOCATIONS

HQ: Levi Strauss & Co.
1155 Battery St., San Francisco, CA 94111
Phone: 415-501-6000 **Fax:** 415-501-7112
Web: www.levistrauss.com

Levi Strauss & Co. manufactures and sells its branded jeans, sportswear, and dress pants through retail locations and company-owned outlets in more than 100 countries.

2002 Sales

	$ mil.	% of total
Americas	2,692	65
Europe	1,093	26
Asia/Pacific	352	9
Total	**4,137**	**100**

PRODUCTS/OPERATIONS

Selected Brand Names

501
505
Dockers
Dockers K-1
Dockers Recode
Dockers Premium
Dress Mobile
Flat Front Mobile
Go Khaki
Levi's
Levi's Red
Levi's Engineered
Levi's Silvertab
Levi's Type 1
Pure Blue
Red Tab
Slates
Superlow

COMPETITORS

Abercrombie & Fitch
American Eagle Outfitters
Benetton
Calvin Klein
Diesel
Eddie Bauer
Fruit of the Loom
FUBU
Gap
Guess
Haggar
J. Crew
J. C. Penney
Jones Apparel
Limited Brands
Liz Claiborne
Nautica Enterprises
OshKosh B'Gosh
Oxford Industries
Polo Ralph Lauren
Tommy Hilfiger
Tropical Sportswear
VF
Warnaco Group

HISTORICAL FINANCIALS

Company Type: Private

Income Statement FYE: Last Sunday in November

	REVENUE ($ mil.)	NET INCOME ($ mil.)	NET PROFIT MARGIN	EMPLOYEES
11/02	4,137	25	0.6%	12,400
11/01	4,259	151	3.5%	16,700
11/00	4,645	223	4.8%	17,300
11/99	5,140	5	0.1%	30,000
11/98	5,959	103	1.7%	30,000
11/97	6,862	138	2.0%	37,000
11/96	7,136	465	6.5%	37,000
11/95	6,707	735	11.0%	37,700
11/94	6,074	558	9.2%	36,500
11/93	5,892	492	8.4%	36,400
Annual Growth	(3.9%)	(28.2%)	—	(11.3%)

2002 Year-End Financials

Debt ratio: —
Return on equity: —
Cash ($ mil.): 96
Current ratio: 1.53
Long-term debt ($ mil.): 1,752

Net Income History

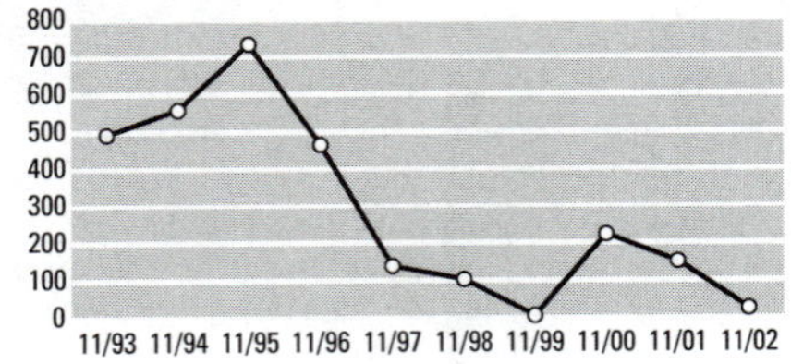

Levitz Home Furnishings, Inc.

The lamps stay lit at Levitz Home Furnishings, the holding company for Levitz Furniture Incorporated (LFI) and Seaman Furniture. LFI (parent company of the Levitz Furniture Corp. chain) has about 60 stores (half in California), while Seaman has more than 50 stores in the northeastern US. The creation of Levitz Home Furnishings in 2001 allowed LFI to emerge from Chapter 11 bankruptcy (originally filed in 1997), in part by distributing management of its 15 East Coast stores to Seaman. The alliance also combines the two companies' administration, advertising, distribution, merchandising, and warehousing efforts. Chairman James Rubin, also co-chairman of M.D. Sass Associates, controls Levitz Home Furnishings.

EXECUTIVES

Chairman: James B. Rubin
CEO: Alan Rosenberg
COO: Jay Carothers
CFO: Carl Landeck
VP, Advertising and Marketing: Esther Eaton
CTO: William (Bill) Kelly
Director of Human Resources: Michael (Mike) Rudman

LOCATIONS

HQ: 300 Crossways Park Dr., Woodbury, NY 11797
Phone: 516-496-9560 **Fax:** 631-927-1780
Web: www.levitz.com

COMPETITORS

Bombay Company
Cost Plus
Dillard's
Ethan Allen
Euromarket Designs
Federated
IKEA
J. C. Penney
Jennifer Convertibles
La-Z-Boy
Mattress Giant
May
Pier 1 Imports
Sleepy's
Williams-Sonoma

HISTORICAL FINANCIALS

Company Type: Private

Income Statement

FYE: April 30

	ESTIMATED REVENUE ($ mil.)	NET INCOME ($ mil.)	NET PROFIT MARGIN	EMPLOYEES
4/02	915	—	—	4,900
4/01	920	—	—	4,400
Annual Growth	(0.5%)	—	—	11.4%

Revenue History

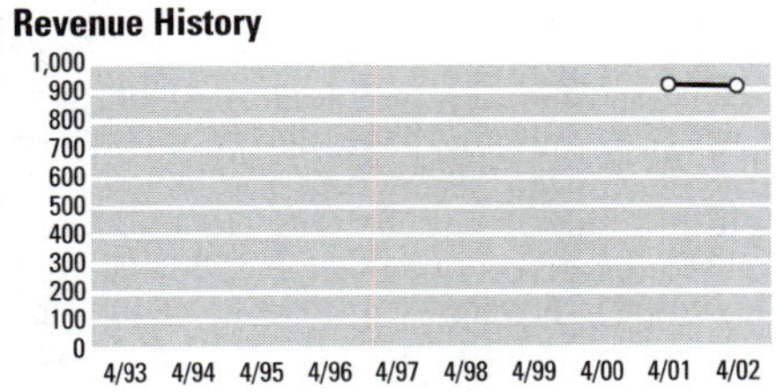

Liberty Mutual Insurance

Liberty Mutual wants more liberty. One of the largest workers' compensation insurers in the US, the firm gained more flexibility in dealing with rapidly changing markets by reorganizing as a mutual holding company. Liberty Mutual has alliances with health care providers to manage disability care and it also offers homeowners and auto insurance, retirement products, and group and individual life insurance. Other services include risk-prevention services (analyzing work sites and practices for safety), consulting, rehabilitation case management, and physical rehabilitation centers.

After failing to find a buyer, asset manager subsidiary Liberty Financial sold itself off little by little. Canadian insurer Sun Life acquired Keyport Life Insurance and mutual fund distributor Independent Financial Marketing Group. Liberty Financial's investment management segment (including subsidiaries Crabbe Huston, Stein Roe & Farnham, and Liberty Wanger Asset Management) was snapped up by FleetBoston. The company plans to spend the money it received from the sale of Liberty Financial on new acquisitions. Liberty Mutual has taken what is left of Liberty Financial private and merged it into one of its subsidiaries.

The company's diversification efforts include Liberty International, which provides insurance and occupational health and safety services in such countries as Canada, Japan, Mexico, Singapore, and the UK.

Liberty Mutual saw its results improve in 2002, thanks in part to rising insurance rates and the lack of natural disasters. The company also grew its international presence in areas such as South America and southern Europe. Strengthening its personal lines business, Liberty Mutual is buying Prudential's domestic property & casualty operations.

HISTORY

The need for financial aid to workers injured on the job was recognized in Europe in the late 19th century but did not make its way to the US until a workers' compensation law for federal employees was passed in 1908. Massachusetts was one of the first states to enact similar legislation. Liberty Mutual was founded in Boston in 1912 to fill this newly recognized niche.

Liberty Mutual followed the fire insurance practice of taking an active part in loss prevention. It evaluated clients' premises and procedures and recommended ways to prevent accidents. The company rejected the budding industry practice of limiting medical fees, instead studying the most effective ways to reduce the long-term cost of a claim by getting the injured party back to work.

In 1942 the company acquired the United Mutual Fire Insurance Company (founded 1908, renamed Liberty Mutual Fire Insurance Company in 1949). The next year it founded a rehabilitation center in Boston to treat injured workers and to test treatments.

In the 1960s and 1970s, Liberty Mutual expanded its line to include life insurance (1963), group pensions (1970), and IRAs (1975).

Seeking to increase its national presence, the company formed Liberty Northwest Insurance Corporation in 1983. It continued expanding its offerings, with new subsidiaries in commercial, personal, and excess lines and, in 1986, by moving into financial services by buying Stein Roe & Farnham (founded 1958).

The expansion/diversification strategy seemed to work. Earnings between 1984 and 1986 more than tripled. Then came the downturn: Recession was followed by a string of natural disasters, and Liberty Mutual's income fell sharply between 1986 and 1988. In 1992 and 1993 the firm lost suits to Coors and Outboard Marine for failing to back those companies in environmental litigation cases.

Liberty Mutual restructured in 1994, withdrawing from the group health business and reorganizing claims operations into two units: Personal Markets and Business Markets. The next year it gained a foothold in the UK when it received permission to invest in a Lloyd's of London syndicate management company.

The company expanded its financial services operations in 1995 and 1996, merging its Liberty Financial subsidiary with the already-public Colonial Group; it also acquired American Asset Management and Newport Pacific Management.

In a soft workers' compensation market, the company tried to build its position through key market acquisitions. In 1997 Liberty Mutual acquired bankrupt workers' comp provider Golden Eagle Insurance of California; the next year the firm bought Florida's Summit Holding Southeast. Mutual funds were also on the shopping list: Purchases included Société Générale's US mutual funds unit, led by international money dean Jean-Marie Eveillard. The firm also played suitor to high-performance trust fund SIFE; the $450 million proposal was rebuffed as ungenerous. In 1998 the company was slammed by increased claims — many related to a Condé Nast Building construction accident that shut down New York City's Times Square that summer. Liberty Mutual acquired erstwhile competitor Employers Insurance of Wausau that year.

In 1999 the company bought Guardian Royal Exchange's US operations. In a new international initiative that year, Liberty Mutual bought 70%

of Singapore-based insurer Citystate Holdings (to be renamed Liberty Citystate) as its foothold in Asia. The following year the company made plans to form a mutual holding company to raise funds for acquisitions.

Slumping property & casualty lines and the events of September 11 (the company paid out some $500 million in claims) hit Liberty Mutual in 2001.

EXECUTIVES

Chairman, President, and CEO: Edmund F. (Ted) Kelly, age 58
EVP, Auto, Home, and Life Markets: John B. Conners
EVP, Commercial Markets: Gary R. Gregg
EVP, Regional Agency Markets: Roger L. Jean
EVP, International Markets: Thomas C. Ramey, age 57
SVP and CFO: J. Paul Condrin III
SVP and CIO: Terry L. Conner
SVP and Chief Investment Officer: A. Alexander Fontanes
SVP and General Counsel: Christopher C. Mansfield
SVP, Human Resources and Administration: Helen E. R. Sayles
SVP, Communications: Stephen G. Sullivan
VP and Corporate Actuary: Robert T. Muleski
Auditors: Ernst & Young LLP

LOCATIONS

HQ: Liberty Mutual Insurance Company
175 Berkeley St., Boston, MA 02116
Phone: 617-357-9500 **Fax:** 617-350-7648
Web: www.libertymutual.com

Liberty Mutual Insurance has about 800 offices in the US, as well as in Argentina, Australia, Bermuda, Brazil, Canada, China, Colombia, Hong Kong, Ireland, Japan, Malaysia, Mexico, Portugal, Singapore, Spain, Thailand, the UK, and Venezuela.

PRODUCTS/OPERATIONS

Selected Product Lines

Annuities
Disability insurance
General liability
Individual and group auto and property insurance
Individual and group life
Investment advice and management
Mutual funds
Workers' compensation

Selected Operating Units

Liberty International
- Liberty ART SA (Argentina)
- Liberty Citystate (Singapore)
- Liberty International Canada
- Liberty International Underwriters
- Liberty Japan
- Liberty Mexico Seguros
- Liberty Mutual Insurance Company (Japan)
- Liberty Mutual Insurance Company (UK) Ltd.
- Liberty Paulista de Seguros (Brazil)
- Liberty Seguros SA (Colombia)
- Liberty Venezuela (merger between Seguros Panamerican and Seguros Caracas)

Liberty Mutual Group
- Colorado Casualty
- Golden Eagle Insurance Co.
- Indiana Insurance Company
- Liberty Northwest Insurance Corporation
- Merchants and Businessmen's Insurance Company
- Montgomery Mutual Insurance Company
- Peerless Insurance
- Summit Holding Southeast
- Wausau

COMPETITORS

21st Century
ACE Limited
AEGON USA
Allianz
Allstate
AIG
Charles Schwab
CIGNA
Citigroup
CNA Financial
Country Insurance and Financial Services
Fremont General
GenAmerica
The Hartford
ING
Lincoln National
MassMutual
MetLife
New York Life
Northwestern Mutual
Progressive Corporation
Prudential
SAFECO
St. Paul Companies
State Farm
T. Rowe Price
Travelers
USAA
Washington National Corporation

HISTORICAL FINANCIALS

Company Type: Mutual company

Income Statement

FYE: December 31

	ASSETS ($ mil.)	NET INCOME ($ mil.)	INCOME AS % OF ASSETS	EMPLOYEES
12/02	55,877	508	0.9%	35,000
12/01	29,375	(289)	—	35,000
12/00	30,264	403	1.3%	37,000
12/99	55,259	501	0.9%	37,440
12/98	26,254	245	0.9%	24,000
12/97	25,230	412	1.6%	23,000
12/96	22,690	474	2.1%	23,000
12/95	21,791	457	2.1%	23,000
12/94	20,644	451	2.2%	22,000
12/93	20,544	321	1.6%	22,000
Annual Growth	11.8%	5.2%	—	5.3%

2002 Year-End Financials

Equity as % of assets: 11.5%
Return on assets: 0.9%
Return on equity: 8.2%
Long-term debt ($ mil.): 1,250
Sales ($ mil.): 14,544

Net Income History

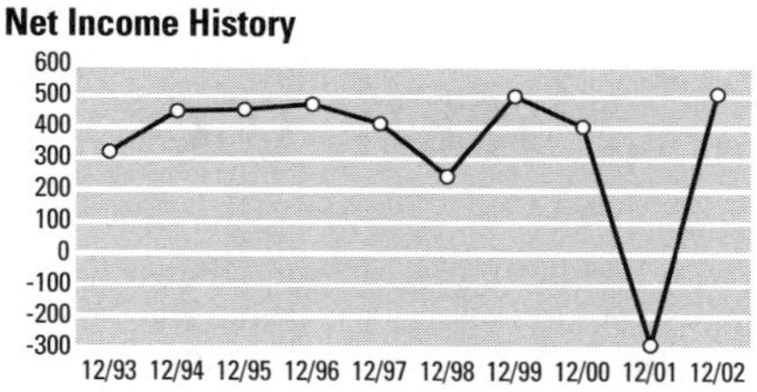

Lifetime Entertainment

Lifetime Entertainment Services hopes viewers make a long-term commitment to its television programs. The company operates three woman-oriented cable-TV networks (Lifetime, Lifetime Movie Network, Lifetime Real Women) offering original movies, talk shows, sports (including Women's National Basketball Association games), and syndicated shows. Its Lifetime channel reaches 85 million US households and is the highest-rated cable network in prime time. The Lifetime Online unit offers information and entertainment on the Web. The firm launched *Lifetime* magazine in 2003. Lifetime was formed by the merger of channels Daytime and Cable Health Network in 1984. It's jointly owned by Walt Disney (via ABC Cable) and Hearst.

EXECUTIVES

President and CEO: Carole Black
EVP and CFO: James Wesley
EVP and General Manager: Rick Haskins
EVP and General Manager, Lifetime Television Network: Lynn Picard
EVP Distribution and Business Development: Louise Henry Bryson
EVP Entertainment: Barbara Fisher
EVP Legal, Business Affairs, and Human Resources: Patricia Langer
EVP Public Affairs and Corporate Communications: Meredith Wagner

LOCATIONS

HQ: Lifetime Entertainment Services
309 W. 49th St., New York, NY 10019
Phone: 212-957-4610 **Fax:** 212-957-4449
Web: www.lifetimetv.com

PRODUCTS/OPERATIONS

Networks

Lifetime
Lifetime Movie Network
Lifetime Real Women

Selected Programming

Any Day Now
Caroline in the City
Designing Women
The Division
Golden Girls
Intimate Portrait
Lifetime Now
Strong Medicine

COMPETITORS

A&E Networks
CPB
Crown Media
Discovery Communications
Fox Entertainment
Harpo
iVillage
MSO
NBC
Oxygen Media
Paxson Communications
Rainbow Media
Viacom
Walt Disney

HISTORICAL FINANCIALS

Company Type: Joint venture

Income Statement

FYE: December 31

	REVENUE ($ mil.)	NET INCOME ($ mil.)	NET PROFIT MARGIN	EMPLOYEES
12/02	790	—	—	—
12/01	727	—	—	—
12/00	661	—	—	—
12/99	528	—	—	—
12/98	468	—	—	—
12/97	398	—	—	—
12/96	257	—	—	—
12/95	271	—	—	—
12/94	241	—	—	—
12/93	197	—	—	—
Annual Growth	16.7%	—	—	—

Revenue History

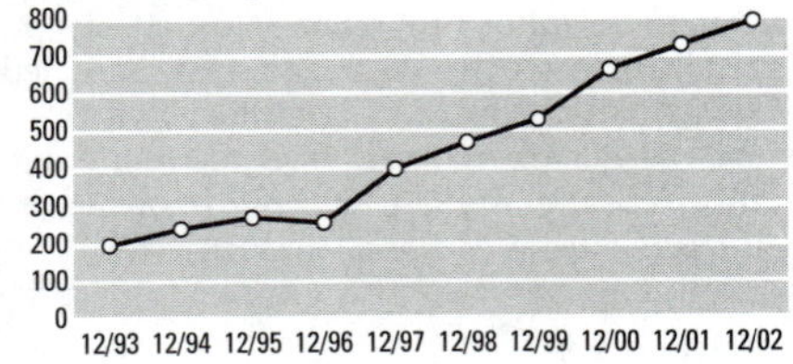

Lincoln Property

Lincoln Property is one of the US's largest diversified real estate companies — honest! Lincoln began by building apartments in the Dallas area, then expanded into commercial and retail projects. It now has residential properties comprising more than 140,000 units and has developed about 140 million sq. ft. of commercial properties nationwide (still managing 90 million). Lincoln has joint ventures with Lend Lease to develop commercial property and with Sam Zell's Equity Residential Properties to build apartments. Its joint venture with American International Group is active in Central Europe and Spain. CEO Mack Pogue cofounded Lincoln in 1965 with Trammell Crow, whose stake Pogue bought out in 1977.

EXECUTIVES

Chairman and CEO: A. Mack Pogue
VP, Secretary, and Treasurer: Nancy Davis
President and CEO, Commercial Division; Chairman, Lincoln Harris: William C. Duvall
President and CEO, Residential Division: J. Timothy Byrne
President, Lincoln Advisory Group: Gary Kobus
President, Lincoln Harris: John Harris
CFO, Residential Division: Dennis Streit
SVP and General Counsel, Residential Division: Dan M. Jacks
Human Resources Director: Luanne Hudson

LOCATIONS

HQ: Lincoln Property Company
3300 Lincoln Plaza, 500 N. Akard, Dallas, TX 75201
Phone: 214-740-3300 **Fax:** 214-740-3441
Web: www.lincolnproperty.com

Lincoln Property has US offices in Arizona, California, Colorado, Florida, Georgia, Illinois, Louisiana, Massachusetts, New Jersey, New York, North Carolina, Pennsylvania, Texas, Virginia, and Washington, DC. It has international offices in the Czech Republic, Germany, Hungary, Poland, and Spain.

PRODUCTS/OPERATIONS

Services

Corporate Property Services
Brokerage
Design and construction management
Facility management
Portfolio management

Investment Property Services
Accounting
Advisory
Design and construction management
Engineering
Financial
Leasing
Property management

COMPETITORS

AIMCO
Boston Properties
CB Richard Ellis
Cushman & Wakefield
Equity Residential
Grubb & Ellis
Inland Group
JMB Realty
Jones Lang LaSalle
Rouse
Simon Property Group
Tishman Realty
Trammell Crow Residential

HISTORICAL FINANCIALS

Company Type: Private

Income Statement FYE: June 30

	REVENUE ($ mil.)	NET INCOME ($ mil.)	NET PROFIT MARGIN	EMPLOYEES
6/02	1,766	—	—	5,000
6/01	1,352	—	—	4,900
6/00	1,251	—	—	4,900
6/99	1,462	—	—	4,900
6/98	1,399	—	—	4,529
6/97	1,165	—	—	4,054
6/96	1,115	—	—	4,025
6/95	1,100	—	—	4,191
6/94	1,000	—	—	4,200
Annual Growth	7.4%	—	—	2.2%

Revenue History

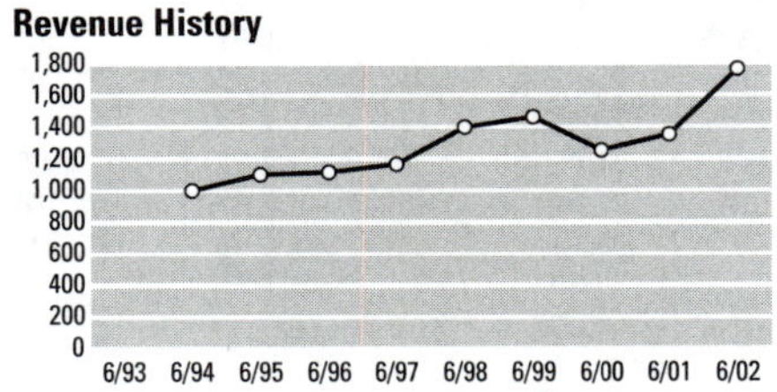

L.L. Bean, Inc.

With L.L. Bean, you can tame the great outdoors — or just look as if you could. The outdoor apparel and gear maker mails more than 200 million catalogs per year. Products include outerwear, sportswear, housewares, footwear, camping and hiking gear, fishing gear, and the Maine hunting shoe upon which the company was built. L.L. Bean also operates four retail and 15 factory outlets in the US, with nine additional stores in Japan. It also sells online through English- and Japanese-language Web sites. L.L. Bean was founded in 1912 by Leon Leonwood Bean and is controlled by his descendants.

From a pair of waterproof hunting boots in 1911, L.L. Bean's empire is based on catalogs mailed out under 95 different titles and advertising 16,000 products. Catalog sales account for 80% of L.L. Bean's revenue. L.L. Bean's flagship store in Freeport, Maine (known by locals as "the Bean") attracts 3 million visitors annually and is open 24 hours a day, 365 days a year. The company plans to open more retail outlets. Retail sales currently account for 20% of L.L. Bean's revenue; the company would like to see that number eventually rise to 50%. L.L. Bean also plans to scale back the number of catalog titles it offers.

L.L. Bean's famous customer service is exemplified by its liberal return policies and perpetual replacement of the rubber soles of its Maine Hunting Shoe. The company also offers seminars and events on such topics as fly fishing, sea kayaking, and outdoor photography.

In early 2003 L.L. Bean announced that it would cut about 500 jobs from its workforce and that its offer for early retirement had been accepted by an additional 200 employees. At around the same time, the company also began looking into the purchase of ailing Eddie Bauer, whose parent Spiegel filed for bankruptcy protection in early 2003. The buyout would expand Bean's retail stores business and strengthen overall sales.

HISTORY

Leon Leonwood Bean started out as a storekeeper in Freeport, Maine. Tired of wet, leaky boots, he experimented with various remedies and in 1911 came up with the Maine Hunting Shoe, a boot with rubber soles and feet and leather uppers. It became his most famous product.

From its outset in 1912, Bean's company was a mail-order house. The first batch of boots was a disaster: Almost all of them leaked. But Bean's willingness to correct his product's defects quickly, at his own expense, saved the company.

Maine's hunting licensing system, implemented in 1917, provided the company with a mailing list of affluent recreational hunters in the Northeast, and that year Bean opened a showroom to accommodate the customers stopping by his Freeport workshop.

Bean cultivated the image of the folksy Maine guide, offering durable, comfortable, weather-resistant clothes and reliable camping supplies. In 1920 Bean built a store on Main Street in Freeport. L.L. Bean continued to grow and add products, even during the Depression, and sales reached $1 million in 1937.

During WWII Bean helped design the boots used by the US military, and his company manufactured them, thus remaining afloat as the war years and rationing brought cutbacks in materials and outdoor activities. He began keeping the retail store open 24 hours a day in 1951, noting that he had "thrown away the keys." Bean added a women's department three years later.

Sales rose to $2 million in the early 1960s and were at $4.8 million when Bean died in 1967 at age 94. (He had resisted growing the business bigger, saying, "I'm eating three meals a day; I can't eat four.") The new president was Bean's grandson Leon Gorman, who had started with L.L. Bean in 1960. His early attempts at updating the mailing operations (mailing labels typed by hand and correspondence kept in cardboard boxes) had been vetoed by his grandfather. Gorman brought in new people and made improvements, including automating the mailing systems, improving the manufacturing systems, and targeting new, nonsporting markets (like women's casual clothes).

L.L. Bean continued its transition by targeting more of its classic customer profile — upper-middle-class college graduates — and sales grew about 20% annually for most of the 1980s. By 1989, however, sales had slowed and growth flattened as the national economy slumped and imitators carried away market share.

Unsolicited catalog orders had been coming in from Japan since the late 1980s, so in 1992 L.L. Bean began a joint venture with Seiyu and Matsushita Electric Industrial. Their first store opened that year (the company opened a catalog and service center in Japan in 1995). L.L. Kids began in 1993.

In 1996 the company began an online shopping service. Sparked by the success of its L.L. Kids division, which grew 300% in four years, the company opened a separate children's store in Freeport the next year. The company opened its second full-line store in 2000 near Washington, DC. L.L. Bean plans to continue opening retail stores in the eastern US.

L.L. Bean veteran Chris McCormick was named president and CEO in May 2001; Gorman remained chairman. McCormick is the first person outside of the Bean family to head the company.

In January 2002 L.L. Bean laid off 175 employees (about 4% of its workforce).

EXECUTIVES

Chairman: Leon A. Gorman, age 67
President and CEO: Chris McCormick, age 46
SVP and CFO: Mark Fasold
SVP and COO: Bob Peixotto
Senior Systems Analyst: Patrick Carroll
Director of Human Resources: Anne Sowles
Director of IT Operations: Stafford Soule
Senior Product Developer: Sandra Rossi
Advertising Manager: Denise Karkos

LOCATIONS

HQ: Casco Street, Freeport, ME 04033
Phone: 207-865-4761 **Fax:** 207-552-6821
Web: www.llbean.com

L.L. Bean sells through direct-mail catalogs and has retail stores and outlet stores in the US and Japan. It manufactures some of its merchandise in Maine.

PRODUCTS/OPERATIONS

Selected Catalogs

Corporate Sales (custom embroidered clothing and luggage)
Fly Fishing (equipment, outer wear, and accessories)
Home (linens, pillows, and decorating)
L.L. Bean
L.L. Bean Hunting
Outdoor Discovery Schools (classes and symposiums)
Outdoors (seasonal outdoor wear and accessories)
Traveler (clothing, luggage, and accessories)

Selected Products

Home and garden accessories
Men's, women's, and children's casual apparel
Outdoor classes
Outer wear
Shoes and boots
Sports gear and apparel
Travel apparel and luggage

COMPETITORS

Abercrombie & Fitch
American Eagle Outfitters
American Retail
Bass Pro Shops
Brylane
Cabela's
Coldwater Creek
Coleman
Columbia Sportswear
Dillard's
Eddie Bauer
Fast Retailing
Federated
Foot Locker
Gap
J. Crew
J. Jill Group
J. C. Penney
Johnson Outdoors
Lands' End
Levi Strauss
Limited Brands
Lost Arrow
May
Nautica Enterprises
Norm Thompson
North Face
Orvis Company
OshKosh B'Gosh
Polo Ralph Lauren
REI
Sears
Spiegel
Sports Authority
Sportsman's Guide
Talbots
Target
Timberland
Tommy Hilfiger

HISTORICAL FINANCIALS

Company Type: Private

Income Statement

FYE: February 28

	REVENUE ($ mil.)	NET INCOME ($ mil.)	NET PROFIT MARGIN	EMPLOYEES
2/02	1,140	—	—	4,500
2/01	1,100	—	—	4,700
2/00	1,100	—	—	4,000
2/99	1,070	—	—	4,000
2/98	1,068	—	—	3,600
2/97	1,040	—	—	3,500
2/96	1,078	—	—	3,800
2/95	976	—	—	3,800
2/94	867	—	—	3,500
2/93	743	—	—	3,500
Annual Growth	4.9%	—	—	2.8%

Revenue History

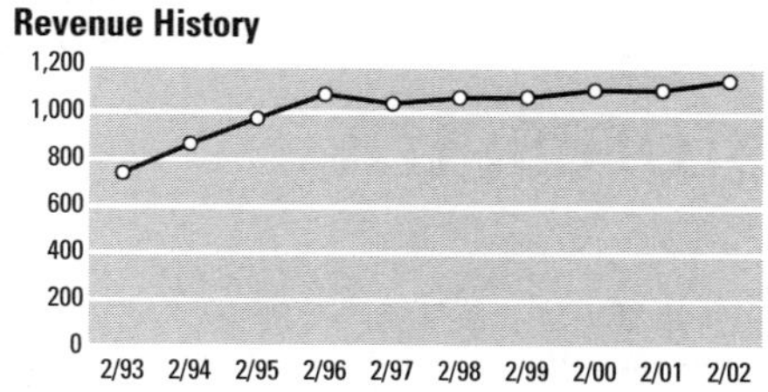

Loews Cineplex Entertainment

Running a theater chain has its highs and Loews. With more than 2,700 screens in some 280 theaters throughout the globe, Loews Cineplex Entertainment (the oldest theater circuit in North America) hopes to maintain the highs as one of the world's leading theater chains. The company operates under the Loews Theatres and Star Theatres names in 19 states, including major cities such as Boston, Chicago, New York, San Francisco, and Washington, DC. In addition, it owns and operates the Cineplex Odeon name in Canada and the Cinemex Theatres name in Mexico. Loews Cineplex also owns 50% stakes in theaters in Spain (Yelmo Cineplex) and South Korea (Megabox Cineplex).

Loews Cineplex was struggling in a US market overstuffed with theater seats and had operated under Chapter 11 bankruptcy protection in 2001. The company was not alone — many theater chains filed for bankruptcy protection that year in an industry-wide wave of red ink that was blamed on opening too many multiplex theaters while attendance dwindled at older locations. An investment group led by Onex Corporation acquired Loews Cineplex when it emerged from bankruptcy in 2002. Later that year the chain filed to go public. However, Loews has since postponed its IPO due to unsteady market conditions.

EXECUTIVES

President, CEO, and Director: Travis Reid, age 48, $518,559 pay
Chairman of Cineplex Odeon Canada: Allen Karp
President, US Division: Michael P. Norris, age 48
President of Cineplex Odeon Corporation, Canada: Sam DiMichele, age 48
SVP, CFO, and Treasurer: John J. Walker, age 49, $329,218 pay
SVP and Corporate Counsel: Michael Politi, age 35
SVP Marketing: John McCauley, age 37
VP Finance and Controller: Bryan Berndt, age 45
CEO, Grupo Cinemex: Miguel Angel Davila, age 36
Auditors: PricewaterhouseCoopers LLP

LOCATIONS

HQ: Loews Cineplex Entertainment Corporation
711 5th Ave., 11th Fl., New York, NY 10022
Phone: 212-833-6200 **Fax:** 212-833-6277
Web: www.loewscineplex.com

PRODUCTS/OPERATIONS

Selected Theater Brands

Cinemex (Mexico)
Cineplex Odeon (Canada)
Loews
Megabox Cineplex (50%, South Korea)
Star Theatres
Yelmo Cineplex (50%, Spain)

COMPETITORS

AMC Entertainment
Carmike Cinemas
CCG Holdings
Century Theatres
Cinemark
Famous Players
Hoyts Cinemas
National Amusements
Pacific Theatres
Regal Entertainment

HISTORICAL FINANCIALS

Company Type: Private

Income Statement

FYE: Last day in February

	REVENUE ($ mil.)	NET INCOME ($ mil.)	NET PROFIT MARGIN	EMPLOYEES
2/02	856	(188)	—	16,500
2/01	904	(436)	—	14,000
2/00	930	(51)	—	16,300
2/99	851	(6)	—	16,000
2/98	414	(0)	—	12,442
2/97	375	(0)	—	—
2/96	359	(3)	—	—
2/95	343	(5)	—	—
2/94	329	(4)	—	—
2/93	306	(1)	—	—
Annual Growth	12.1%	—	—	7.3%

2002 Year-End Financials

Debt ratio: —
Return on equity: —
Cash ($ mil.): 61
Current ratio: 0.09
Long-term debt ($ mil.): 32

Net Income History

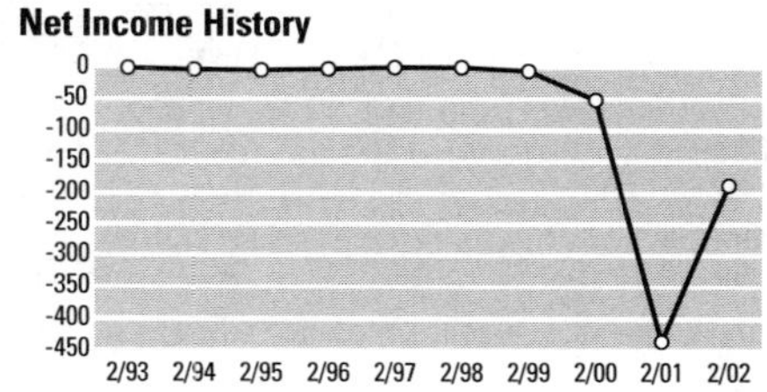

Longaberger Company

A tisket, a tasket, a Longaberger basket. The Longaberger Company is the #1 maker of handmade baskets in the US, selling nearly 10 million a year. The baskets are sold through in-home shows conducted by Longaberger's 71,000 independent sales associates. Baskets account for half of sales, but the company also sells fabrics, pottery, window treatments, and wrought-iron home accessories. Longaberger's home office is a seven-story rendition of a basket with two 75-ton handles on top. The company also owns a golf course, a hotel, and Longaberger Homestead (an events area with shops and restaurants). The family-owned firm is run by the daughters of the late Dave Longaberger, who founded the company in 1973.

EXECUTIVES

President and CEO: Tami Longaberger
CFO: Stephanie Imhoff
VP, Operations: Andy Neri
VP, Sales: Andrea Walters-Dowding
President, The Longaberger Foundation: Rachel Longaberger
CIO: Anne Dunlap
Director, Corporate Communications: Julie Moorehead
Public Relations: Jeanne M. Tiberio

LOCATIONS

HQ: The Longaberger Company
1500 E. Main St., Newark, OH 43055
Phone: 740-322-5000 **Fax:** 740-322-5240
Web: www.longaberger.com

The Longaberger Company has facilities in Dresden, Frazeyburg, Hartville, Newark, and Malta, Ohio.

COMPETITORS

Bed Bath & Beyond
Bombay Company
Cost Plus
Euromarket Designs
Garden Ridge
Hobby Lobby
Kirkland's
Linens 'n Things
Michaels Stores
Pier 1 Imports
Williams-Sonoma

HISTORICAL FINANCIALS

Company Type: Private

Income Statement FYE: December 31

	REVENUE ($ mil.)	NET INCOME ($ mil.)	NET PROFIT MARGIN	EMPLOYEES
12/02	906	—	—	7,300
12/01	970	—	—	7,000
12/00	1,000	—	—	8,000
12/99	819	—	—	7,500
12/98	700	—	—	7,000
12/97	611	—	—	5,800
12/96	520	—	—	5,100
12/95	410	—	—	5,026
12/94	340	—	—	4,500
Annual Growth	13.0%	—	—	6.2%

Revenue History

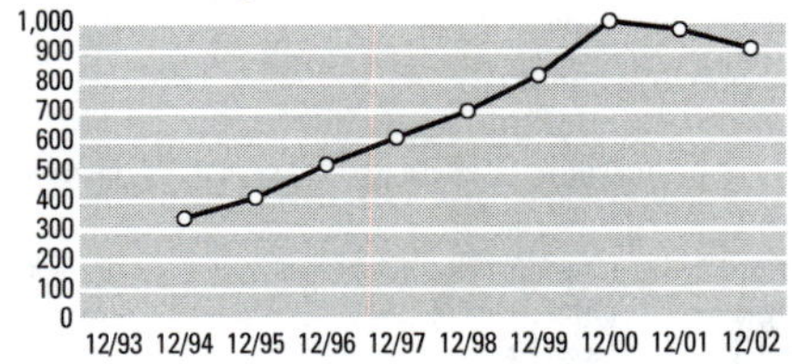

Love's Travel Stops & Country Stores, Inc.

If you're a trucker or RVer on the road, all you need is Love's. Love's Travel Stops & Country Stores operates more than 80 truck stops throughout a swath of about 23 states from California to Virginia, as well as around 70 convenience stores in Colorado, Kansas, New Mexico, Oklahoma, and Texas. Each travel stop includes a convenience store, a fast-food restaurant, (such as Taco Bell or Subway), and gas outlets for cars, trucks, and RVs. The travel stops also provide shower rooms, laundry facilities, game rooms, and mail drops. Love's Travel Stops & Country Stores is owned by the family of CEO Tom Love, who founded the company in 1964.

EXECUTIVES

Chairman and CEO: Tom Love
President and COO, Love's Development Companies: Greg Love
President, Love's Operating Companies: Frank Love
EVP and CFO: Doug Stussi
EVP, Store Operations: Tom Edwards
VP and CIO: Jim Xenos
VP, Construction: Terry Ross
Human Resources Director: Carl Martincich
Marketing Director: Mark Romig
Public Relations Director: Jenny Love Meyer

LOCATIONS

HQ: 10601 N. Pennsylvania, Oklahoma City, OK 73120
Phone: 405-751-9000 **Fax:** 405-749-9110
Web: www.loves.com

COMPETITORS

7-Eleven
Allsup's
ChevronTexaco
Exxon Mobil
E-Z Mart Stores
FFP Marketing
Flying J
Inland Resources
Marathon Oil
Petro Stopping Centers
Pilot
Racetrac Petroleum
Rip Griffin Truck Service Center
Royal Dutch/Shell Group
Stuckey's
TravelCenters of America
Valero Energy
Walgreen

HISTORICAL FINANCIALS

Company Type: Private

Income Statement FYE: December 31

	REVENUE ($ mil.)	NET INCOME ($ mil.)	NET PROFIT MARGIN	EMPLOYEES
12/02	1,300	—	—	3,800
12/01	1,086	—	—	3,200
12/00	894	—	—	3,150
12/99	614	—	—	2,500
Annual Growth	28.4%	—	—	15.0%

Revenue History

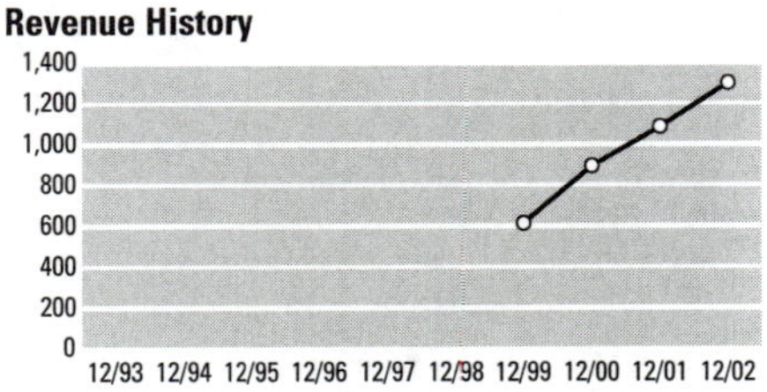

Lucasfilm Ltd.

The Force is definitely with Emperor George Lucas. With four of the 20 highest-grossing films of all time, Lucasfilm is one of the most successful independent production companies in the history of cinema. Owned by filmmaker George Lucas (the brains behind the *Star Wars* and *Indiana Jones* films), Lucasfilm's productions have won 17 Academy Awards. Its most recent movie is 2002's *Star Wars: Episode II — Attack of the Clones*; Lucasfilm's previous release, 1999's *Episode I — The Phantom Menace*, has grossed about $920 million worldwide and claims the #3 spot on the all-time list. Other subsidiaries in the Lucas empire are responsible for licensing, special effects, and software. Lucasfilm was created in 1971.

Lucasfilm consists of LucasArts (video games), Lucas Digital (special effects house Industrial Light + Magic and Skywalker Sound), and Lucas Licensing (consumer products). George Lucas also owns educational software firm Lucas Learning. In 2002 Lucas spun off digital sound systems firm THX as an independent company. In 2003 the company formed its Lucasfilm Animation unit to create digitally animated feature films. Lucasfilm is building a new headquarters and production center at the Presidio, a former Army base in San Francisco. A final sequel to the *Star Wars* series is slated for release in 2005.

HISTORY

After attending film school at the University of Southern California, George Lucas started his career as a documentary filmmaker, chronicling the production of Francis Ford Coppola's *Finian's Rainbow* in 1968. The two men became fast friends and founded American Zoetrope in 1969, which two years later released Lucas' feature film debut, the science-fiction film *THX 1138* (a full-length version of a student film he made at USC). The film flopped, and Coppola went into production on *The Godfather*. Lucas left American

Zoetrope and created his own company, Lucasfilm, in 1971.

Two years later Lucas released *American Graffiti* through Universal Pictures (with some financial help from Coppola). The film was a smash hit; it raked in $115 million in the US and made him a millionaire before the age of 30. It also gave him the clout to try and get his most ambitious project off the ground, a space opera called *Star Wars*. Universal, frustrated with cost overruns on *Graffiti*, wanted no part of Lucas' seemingly ridiculous idea, so he went to 20th Century Fox, which agreed to finance the $10 million film. Lucas gave up his directing fee for a percentage of the box-office take and all merchandising rights. He created Industrial Light + Magic (ILM) and Sprocket Systems (later Skywalker Sound) in 1975 to produce the visual and sound effects needed for the film.

Star Wars cost about $12 million, and almost everyone involved was sure it would bomb. Released in 1977, the movie shattered every box-office record, and the merchandising rights Lucas obtained made him a multimillionaire. With his take from *Star Wars,* Lucas was able to finance the film's sequel, *The Empire Strikes Back* (1980), out of his own pocket, meaning he would receive most of the profits (it grossed more than $220 million domestically). Lucasfilm's next production was *Raiders of the Lost Ark* (1981), directed by Lucas' friend Steven Spielberg. It went on to gross more than $380 million worldwide.

The next year Lucas began developing the THX sound system in preparation for the 1983 release of the third *Star Wars* film, *Return of the Jedi* (which hauled in more than $260 million domestically). He also founded LucasArts in 1982 to develop video games. Lucasfilm completed Skywalker Ranch (a facility housing many of its various companies in Marin County, California) in the mid-1980s and filled out the decade with two *Raiders* sequels — *Indiana Jones and the Temple of Doom* (1984, $333 million worldwide) and *Indiana Jones and the Last Crusade* (1989, $495 million worldwide).

Lucasfilm reorganized in 1993 by spinning off LucasArts into a separate company and regrouping ILM and Skywalker Sound into a new company called Lucas Digital. Lucasfilm won local government approval to build an $87 million film studio near Skywalker Ranch in 1996, and the following year it re-released the *Star Wars Trilogy* to theaters with new special effects in celebration of the 20th anniversary, adding another $250 million to its take. Anticipating the release of the first of three prequels to the *Star Wars Trilogy*, Lucasfilm started signing marketing agreements in 1998 (including deals with Hasbro and Pepsi) that resulted in advance licensing of nearly $3 billion.

Star Wars: Episode I — The Phantom Menace opened in May 1999 and has grossed about $920 million worldwide (it finished its initial run second only to *Titanic*). Later in 1999 Lucas announced plans to develop a $250 million digital arts center at the old Presidio army base in San Francisco to house ILM, LucasArts, Lucas Learning, Lucas Online, THX, and the George Lucas Educational Foundation.

The next film in the *Star Wars* series, *Episode II — Attack of the Clones,* opened in May 2002. In early 2003 the company reorganized, bringing in Lucas Digital, LucasArts Entertainment, and Lucas Licensing (which had been operating as independent companies) as subsidiaries under the Lucasfilm umbrella.

EXECUTIVES

Chairman and CEO: George W. Lucas Jr., age 58
COO: Micheline Chau, age 50
VP Marketing: Jim Ward
President, Lucas Digital: Jim Morris
President, LucasArts: Simon Jeffery
President, Lucas Licensing: Howard Rothman
SVP, Animation Development: Patty Blau
Director of Content Management Marketing: Steve Sansweet
Director of Special Programs: Kathleen Holliday

LOCATIONS

HQ: 3210 Kerner Blvd., San Rafael, CA 94912
Phone: 415-662-1800 **Fax:** 415-662-2437
Web: www.lucasfilm.com

PRODUCTS/OPERATIONS

Selected Productions

American Graffiti (1973)
Howard the Duck (1986)
Indiana Jones and the Last Crusade (1989)
Indiana Jones and the Temple of Doom (1984)
Labyrinth (1986)
More American Graffiti (1979)
Radioland Murders (1994)
Raiders of the Lost Ark (1981)
Star Wars: Episode I — The Phantom Menace (1999)
Star Wars: Episode II — Attack of the Clones (2002)
Star Wars: Episode III (2005)
Star Wars: Episode IV — A New Hope (1977)
Star Wars: Episode V — The Empire Strikes Back (1980)
Star Wars: Episode VI — Return of the Jedi (1983)
Tucker: The Man and His Dream (1988)
Willow (1988)
The Young Indiana Jones Chronicles (1992-96, TV movies)

COMPETITORS

Alliance Atlantis Communications
Artisan Entertainment
DreamWorks SKG
Fox Filmed Entertainment
Lions Gate Entertainment
MGM
New Line Cinema
Paramount Pictures
Pixar
Sony Pictures Entertainment
VUE
Disney Studios

HISTORICAL FINANCIALS

Company Type: Private

Income Statement FYE: March 31

	ESTIMATED REVENUE ($ mil.)	NET INCOME ($ mil.)	NET PROFIT MARGIN	EMPLOYEES
3/01	1,500	—	—	2,000
3/00	1,100	—	—	1,800
3/99	600	—	—	1,300
3/98	400	—	—	500
3/97	250	—	—	200
3/96	200	—	—	100
3/95	160	—	—	36
3/94	160	—	—	—
Annual Growth	37.7%	—	—	95.3%

Revenue History

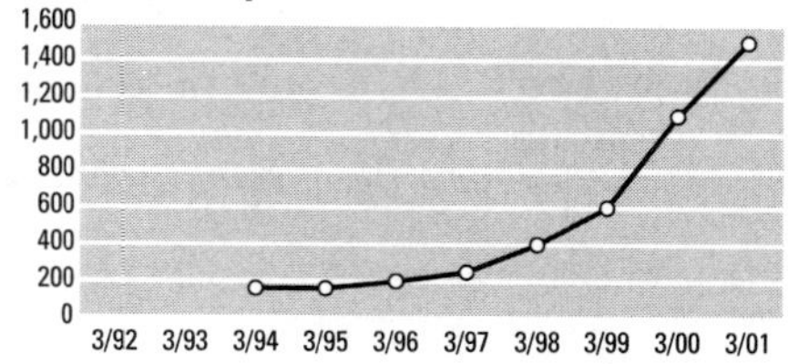

Lumbermens Merchandising

Membership has its privileges. Through Lumbermens Merchandising Corporation (LMC), lumber retailers in the eastern half of the US pool their buying resources to leverage volume discounts from vendors and increase their own efficiency. LMC's network of members includes more than 1,000 building material locations. The cooperative is the largest dealer-owned lumber building materials buying group in the US. It holds members to strict confidentiality, in part to safeguard vendor contracts. In addition to lumber and panel products, LMC also supplies its members with non-wood products, millwork, and hardware. LMC is planning to expand into the western portion of the US.

EXECUTIVES

CEO: Anthony J. DeCarlo
SVP Finance: David J. Gonze
SVP Purchasing: John Broomell
Auditors: Hege Kramer Connell Murphy & Goldkamp, P.C.

LOCATIONS

HQ: Lumbermens Merchandising Corporation
137 W. Wayne Ave., Wayne, PA 19087
Phone: 610-293-7000 **Fax:** 610-293-7098
Web: www.lmc.net

Lumbermens Merchandising Corporation services members in the eastern US.

PRODUCTS/OPERATIONS

Selected Members

Arch Creek Lumber
Kaufman Lumber
Masten Home Center
Peter Lumber
Short & Paulk Supply Co., Inc.

COMPETITORS

84 Lumber
Ace Hardware
Builder Marts
Do it Best
Guardian Building Products
Home Depot
Lowe's
TruServ

HISTORICAL FINANCIALS

Company Type: Cooperative

Income Statement FYE: September 30

	ESTIMATED REVENUE ($ mil.)	NET INCOME ($ mil.)	NET PROFIT MARGIN	EMPLOYEES
9/02	2,200	—	—	—
9/01	1,700	—	—	—
9/00	2,100	—	—	—
9/99	1,900	—	—	—
9/98	1,700	—	—	—
9/97	1,666	—	—	—
9/96	1,662	—	—	—
9/95	1,471	—	—	—
Annual Growth	5.9%	—	—	—

Revenue History

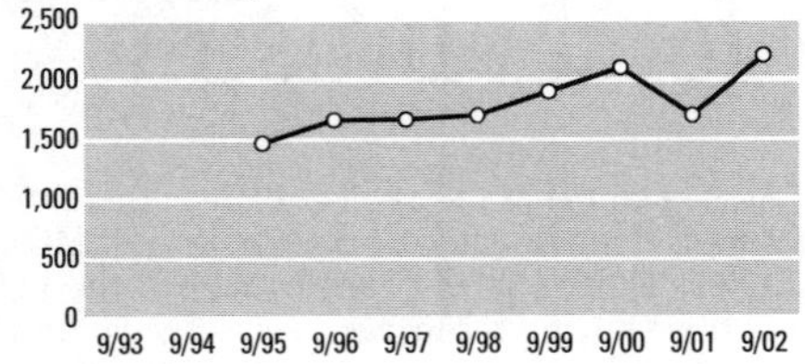

Lupient Automotive

Auto dealerships in Minnesota take a backseat to Lupient Automotive Group. The company, operating about 15 dealerships, is the largest auto dealer in the Land of 10,000 Lakes. Lupient Automotive sells a variety of models, including those made by General Motors, Kia, Nissan, Saturn, and Suzuki. The company is also one of the nation's leading dealerships in terms of fleet sales and offers title and license administration and nationwide delivery. Founded in 1968 by president and CEO James Lupient as an Oldsmobile dealership, Lupient Automotive also performs warranty, maintenance, and service work. The company boasts 50 ASE-trained technicians at Jim Lupient's Auto Mall in Golden Valley, Minnesota.

EXECUTIVES

Chairman: James W. (Jim) Lupient, age 68
CEO: Barbara Lupient
CFO: Keith Phillips

LOCATIONS

HQ: Lupient Automotive Group
750 Pennsylvania Ave., Golden Valley, MN 55426
Phone: 763-544-6666 **Fax:** 763-513-5517
Web: www.lupient.com

COMPETITORS

Jordan Automotive
PHH Arval
Russ Darrow

HISTORICAL FINANCIALS

Company Type: Private

Income Statement FYE: December 31

	REVENUE ($ mil.)	NET INCOME ($ mil.)	NET PROFIT MARGIN	EMPLOYEES
12/01	454	—	—	—
12/00	485	—	—	—
12/99	495	—	—	—
12/98	708	—	—	—
12/97	708	—	—	—
12/96	781	—	—	—
12/95	695	—	—	—
12/94	739	—	—	—
12/93	350	—	—	—
Annual Growth	3.3%	—	—	—

Revenue History

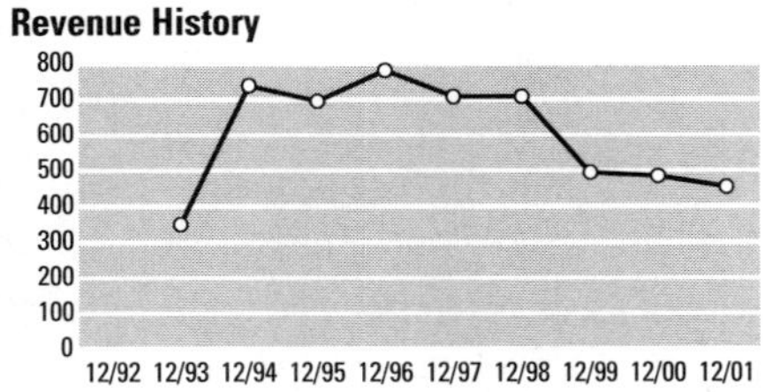

M. Fabrikant & Sons, Inc.

Diamonds have been around practically forever, and so has M. Fabrikant & Sons, a major US diamond wholesaler. Four generations of the Fabrikant and Fortgang families run the family-owned firm, which claims to be one of the oldest diamond and jewelry companies in the world (it was founded as a loose diamond wholesaler in New York City in 1895). Fabrikant purchases and sells loose and polished diamonds and other precious and semi-precious stones, plus diamond, gold, and silver jewelry. Customers include retailers such as Wal-Mart and major jewelry chains. Affiliates include Susan Fortgang's Royal Asscher Cut branded-diamond company, Japanese joint venture Leer Tokyo Pearl, and about 20% of jeweler Lazare Kaplan.

EXECUTIVES

Chairman: Charles Fortgang
President and CEO: Matthew Fabrikant Fortgang
COO: Michael Shaffet
CFO: Sheldon L. Ginsberg
VP Corporate Communications: Susan (Suzy) Boshwit
Human Resources: Susan Fortgang

LOCATIONS

HQ: 1 Rockefeller Plaza, 28th Fl., New York, NY 10020
Phone: 212-757-0790 **Fax:** 212-262-9757

PRODUCTS/OPERATIONS

Selected Stones

Diamonds
Emeralds
Opals
Pearls
Rubies
Sapphires

COMPETITORS

Atlas Pacific
Blue Nile
IWI Holding
Lazare Kaplan
LJ International
Michael Anthony Jewelers

HISTORICAL FINANCIALS

Company Type: Private

Income Statement FYE: July 31

	REVENUE ($ mil.)	NET INCOME ($ mil.)	NET PROFIT MARGIN	EMPLOYEES
7/02	900	—	—	800
7/01	930	—	—	800
7/00	1,000	—	—	800
7/99	820	—	—	800
7/98	780	—	—	800
7/97	745	—	—	825
7/96	751	—	—	875
7/95	650	—	—	850
7/94	600	—	—	750
7/93	560	—	—	700
Annual Growth	5.4%	—	—	1.5%

Revenue History

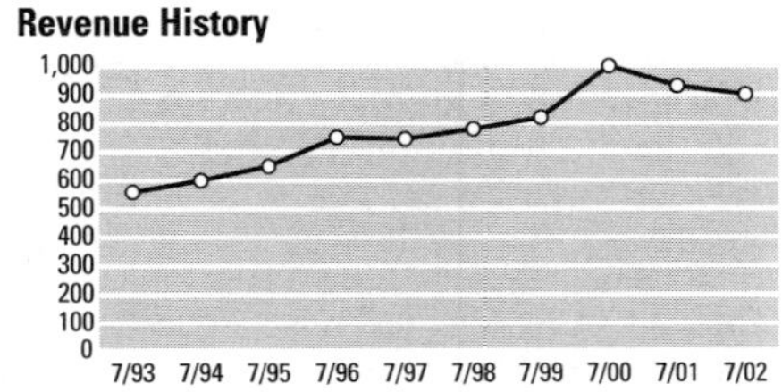

MA Laboratories

If you need a computer part, just ask your MA. Distributor MA Laboratories, one of the largest privately held companies in Silicon Valley, provides computer resellers and systems integrators with more than 3,000 high-tech gadgets and computer items. MA Labs specializes in memory modules but sells just about everything commonly found in or near a computer, including hard drives, motherboards, CD-ROMs, and video cards. Other products include monitors, software, fax modems, network cards, digital cameras, notebook computers, and accessories. Among MA's suppliers are 3Com, Advanced Micro Devices, Hewlett-Packard, IBM, Intel, Microsoft, Sony, and Toshiba. MA Labs was founded in 1983 by owner and CEO Abraham Ma.

EXECUTIVES

President and CEO: Abraham Ma
CFO: Ricky Chow
VP: Michael Ma
Director, Human Resources: Shareen Wu

LOCATIONS

HQ: MA Laboratories, Inc.
2075 N. Capitol Ave., San Jose, CA 95132
Phone: 408-941-0808 **Fax:** 408-941-0909
Web: www.malabs.com

PRODUCTS/OPERATIONS

Selected Products

CD and DVD drives
Computer components (keyboards, cooling fans, and other devices)
Data storage
Digital cameras
Hard drives
Input/output cards
Memory
Modems
Monitors
Motherboards
Multimedia (speakers, scanners, and other devices)
Networking
Notebook computers and accessories
Printers
Processors
Software
Video cards

COMPETITORS

Agilysys
Arrow Electronics
Avnet
Bell Microproducts
Ingram Micro
Kingston Technology
Merisel
N.F. Smith
Southland Micro
Supermicro Computer
Tech Data
Viking Components
Wintec

HISTORICAL FINANCIALS

Company Type: Private

Income Statement FYE: December 31

	REVENUE ($ mil.)	NET INCOME ($ mil.)	NET PROFIT MARGIN	EMPLOYEES
12/02	800	—	—	350
12/01	805	—	—	300
12/00	855	—	—	300
12/99	800	—	—	300
12/98	700	—	—	—
12/97	740	—	—	200
12/96	600	—	—	200
12/95	498	—	—	—
12/94	375	—	—	100
12/93	248	—	—	100
Annual Growth	13.9%	—	—	14.9%

Revenue History

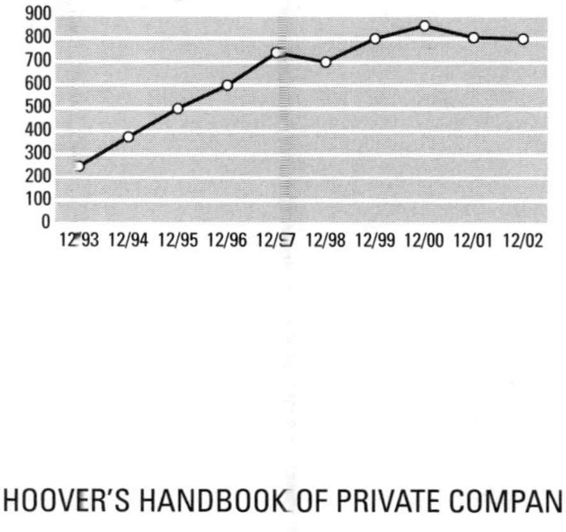

M. A. Mortenson

It's all bricks and mortar for M. A. Mortenson Company, one of the largest general contractors in the US. The company's services include planning, program and construction management, design/build delivery, and facility maintenance and operations. M. A. Mortenson builds aviation, education, health care, and sports facilities, as well as power plants and dams. It also builds and renovates military housing. Mortenson works primarily in the US, where its projects include a new arena for the NBA's Memphis Grizzlies and the Walt Disney Concert Hall, the new home for the Los Angeles Philharmonic Orchestra. The family-owned company was founded in 1954 by M. A. Mortenson Sr., whose son now serves as chairman and CEO.

EXECUTIVES

Chairman and CEO: M. A. Mortenson Jr.
President and COO: Thomas F. Gunkel
SVP and CFO: Peter A. Conzemius
SVP Operations: Bradley C. Funk
SVP: Paul V. Campbell
SVP: Paul I. Cossette
SVP: Daniel L. Johnson
SVP Business Development: Robert J. Nartonis
SVP: John V. Wood
VP: David Mortenson
Corporate Secretary: Mark A. Mortenson
Director Human Resources: Daniel R. Haag
Auditors: Deloitte & Touche LLP

LOCATIONS

HQ: M. A. Mortenson Company
700 Meadow Ln. North, Minneapolis, MN 55422
Phone: 763-522-2100 **Fax:** 763-520-3430
Web: www.mortenson.com

PRODUCTS/OPERATIONS

Selected Services

Construction management
Design/build delivery
Engineering, procurement, and construction (EPC)
General contracting
Maintenance and operations
Planning
Preconstruction services
Program management
Project development
Turnkey construction

COMPETITORS

AMEC
Barton Malow
Bovis Lend Lease
FaulknerUSA
Gilbane
Hensel Phelps Construction
Hoffman Corporation
Hunt Construction
McCarthy Building
Parsons
Perini
Skanska
Turner Corporation
Walbridge Aldinger
Walsh Group
Whiting-Turner
Zachry

HISTORICAL FINANCIALS

Company Type: Private

Income Statement FYE: December 31

	REVENUE ($ mil.)	NET INCOME ($ mil.)	NET PROFIT MARGIN	EMPLOYEES
12/02	1,455	—	—	1,800
12/01	1,128	—	—	1,800
12/00	1,080	—	—	2,153
12/99	968	—	—	1,920
12/98	904	—	—	1,873
12/97	803	—	—	1,700
12/96	786	—	—	1,500
12/95	781	—	—	1,650
12/94	775	—	—	1,600
12/93	798	—	—	1,700
Annual Growth	6.9%	—	—	0.6%

Revenue History

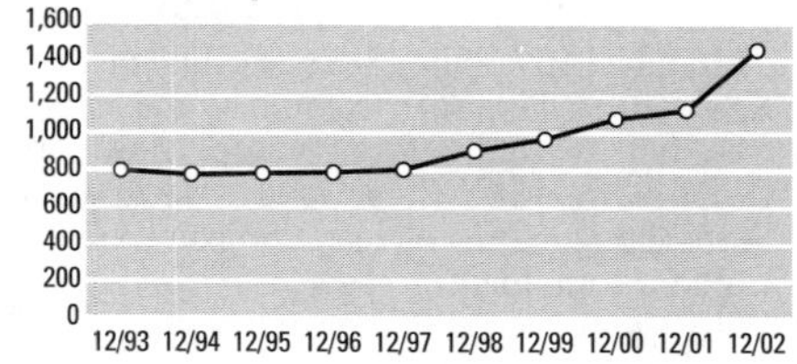

MacAndrews & Forbes Holdings

Through MacAndrews & Forbes Holdings, financier Ron Perelman is focused on makeup and money. The holding company has investments in an array of public and private companies, most notably 83%-owned Revlon (the #3 cosmetics company in the US), M&F Worldwide (licorice flavors), and WeddingChannel.com. Perelman is intent on reversing the fortunes of Revlon, which he has controlled since 1985. He did make a hefty profit when Consolidated Cigar Holdings (the #1 US cigar maker) was sold to French tobacco maker Seita in 1999.

MacAndrews & Forbes' other holdings include the drug development company TransTech Pharma (in which it is the largest shareholder); 83% of Panavision, the #1 provider of cameras for shooting movies and TV shows; and privately held Allied Security, one of the biggest providers of security guards and systems.

Perelman's holdings have dwindled in value since 1999. Most of the financier's business strategy involves improving his cash position and paying down debt — hence his IPO of Revlon (1996), the sale of The Coleman Company to American Household (formerly Sunbeam Corp., 1998), and the sale of two of Revlon's noncore units. Perelman has committed a $215 million debt-and-equity funding package to rescue Revlon, which is struggling with debt and dwindling market share.

Perelman is still a media curiosity, largely because of his very public courtship and wedding to wife #4, actress Ellen Barkin.

HISTORY

Ron Perelman grew up working in his father's Philadelphia-based conglomerate, Belmont Industries, but he left at the age of 35 to seek his fortune in New York. In 1978 he bought 40% of jewelry store operator Cohen-Hatfield Industries. The next year Cohen-Hatfield bought a minority stake in MacAndrews & Forbes (licorice flavoring). Cohen-Hatfield acquired MacAndrews & Forbes in 1980.

In 1984 Perelman reshuffled his assets to create MacAndrews & Forbes Holdings, which acquired control of Pantry Pride, a Florida-based supermarket chain, in 1985. Pantry Pride then bought Revlon for $1.8 billion with the help of convicted felon Michael Milken. After Perelman acquired Revlon, he added several other cosmetics vendors, including Max Factor and Yves Saint Laurent's fragrance and cosmetic lines.

In 1988 MacAndrews & Forbes agreed to invest $315 million in five failing Texas savings and loans (S&Ls), which Perelman combined and named First Gibraltar (sold to BankAmerica, now Bank of America, in 1993). The next year MacAndrews & Forbes bought The Coleman Company, a maker of outdoor equipment.

With a growing reputation for buying struggling companies, revamping them, and then selling them at a higher price, Perelman bought Marvel Entertainment Group (Marvel Comics) in 1989 and took it public in 1991. That year he sold Revlon's Max Factor and Betrix units to Procter & Gamble for over $1 billion.

MacAndrews & Forbes acquired 37.5% of TV infomercial producer Guthy-Renker and SCI Television's seven stations and merged them to create New World Television. That company was combined with TV syndicator Genesis Entertainment and TV production house New World Entertainment to create New World Communications Group, which Perelman took public in 1994. That year MacAndrews & Forbes and partner Gerald J. Ford bought Ford Motor's First Nationwide, the US's fifth-largest S&L at that time.

Subsidiaries Mafco Worldwide and Consolidated Cigar Holdings merged with Abex (aircraft parts) to create Mafco Consolidated Group in 1995. Following diminishing comic sales, Perelman placed Marvel in bankruptcy in 1996 and subsequently lost control of the company.

In 1997 First Nationwide bought California thrift Cal Fed Bancorp for $1.2 billion. In addition, Perelman sold New World to Rupert Murdoch's News Corp.

In 1998 Perelman orchestrated a $1.8 billion deal in which First Nationwide merged with Golden State Bancorp to form the US's third-largest thrift. Sunbeam Corp. (now American Household) bought Perelman's stake in Coleman that year, making Perelman a major American Household shareholder. Also in 1998 MacAndrews & Forbes bought a 72% stake in Panavision (movie camera maker, later increased to 91%), invested in WeddingChannel.com, and sold its 64% stake in Consolidated Cigar to French tobacco giant Seita (netting Perelman a smoking $350 million profit).

Still burdened by debt, Revlon sold its professional products business in 2000.

Perelman's stock in American Household was rendered worthless when the company initiated bankruptcy proceedings in February 2001. (It would emerge from bankruptcy, however, in December 2002.) He was also sued by angry shareholders after the board of M&F Worldwide, the licorice company he controls, bought Perelman's stock in Panavision at more than five times its market value. In order to settle the litigation surrounding the purchase, in 2002 M&F agreed to return Pereleman's 83% stake in Panavision to Mafco. Golden State Bancorp also left the MacAndrews fold in 2002 when it was acquired by Citigroup.

MacAndrews & Forbes Holdings acquired Allied Security, the largest independent provider of contract security services and products in the US, from Gryphon Investors in February 2003 for an undisclosed sum.

EXECUTIVES

Chairman and CEO: Ronald O. (Ron) Perelman, age 59
Co-Vice Chairman: Donald G. Drapkin, age 55
Co-Vice Chairman: Howard Gittis, age 68
SVP, Corporate Affairs: James T. Conroy
SVP, Human Resources: Herbert (Herb) Vallier
VP: Matthew Drapkin

LOCATIONS

HQ: MacAndrews & Forbes Holdings, Inc.
35 E. 62nd St., New York, NY 10021
Phone: 212-688-9000 **Fax:** 212-572-8400

MacAndrews & Forbes Holdings' consumer products operations are principally in the US.

PRODUCTS/OPERATIONS

Selected Holdings

Allied Security (leading provider of security guards and systems)
American Household (about 37%, small appliances and Coleman camping gear)
M&F Worldwide Corp. (32%, licorice extract)
Revlon Inc. (83%, cosmetics and personal care products)
TransTech Pharma (drug development company)
WeddingChannel.com

COMPETITORS

Alberto-Culver
Alticor
Avon
Body Shop
Brunswick
Chattem
Colgate-Palmolive
Dial
Estée Lauder
Guardsmark
Johnson & Johnson
Kellwood
L'Oréal USA
LVMH
Mary Kay
Procter & Gamble
Ulta
Unilever
Wackenhut

HISTORICAL FINANCIALS

Company Type: Private

Income Statement FYE: December 31

	REVENUE ($ mil.)	NET INCOME ($ mil.)	NET PROFIT MARGIN	EMPLOYEES
12/02	5,700	—	—	19,800
12/01	5,700	—	—	19,800
12/00	5,500	—	—	19,500
12/99	5,400	—	—	19,500
12/98	4,900	—	—	19,500
12/97	6,071	—	—	29,854
12/96	6,196	—	—	30,000
12/95	4,413	—	—	22,800
12/94	3,030	—	—	22,328
12/93	2,748	—	—	23,500
Annual Growth	8.4%	—	—	(1.9%)

Revenue History

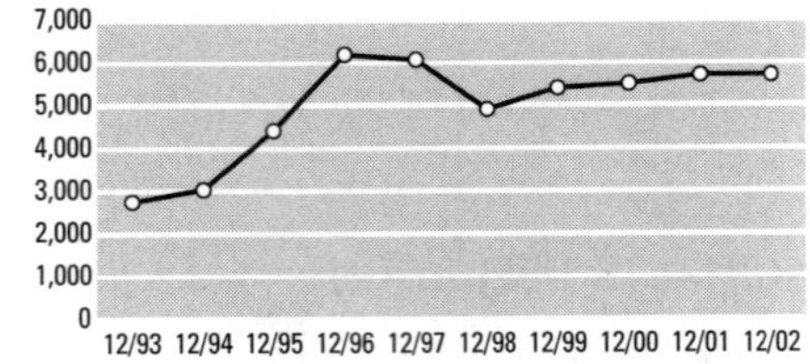

MACTEC, Inc.

This Big Mac is one of the largest engineering design companies in the US. MACTEC provides a full range of infrastructure and environmental engineering services to federal agencies, municipalities, and industrial customers, including construction management and facilities operation and management. A specialist in hazardous waste cleanups, the group provides decommissioning and demolition of nuclear facilities and remediation of brownfield sites. MACTEC, which has grown dramatically through acquisitions, doubled its size in 2002 by merging with environmental engineering firm Law Companies Group. Founded in 1975 as Management Analysis Company (MAC), MACTEC is majority-owned by private equity firm Nautic Partners.

EXECUTIVES

Chairman, President, and CEO: Bruce C. Coles
EVP and CFO: Robert B. Fooshee
SVP and CIO: Lawrence J. White
VP and Treasurer: Kendall H. Sherrill
VP and Director Human Resources: Jayne M. Dinan
VP: Reginald L. Sikes
General Counsel and Secretary: Keith C. Groen
Assistant Secretary: Bruce A. Duke
Marketing Manager: Janis Brown
Marketing Services Specialist: Vanessa Campbell

LOCATIONS

HQ: 1105 Sanctuary Pkwy., Ste. 300,
Alpharetta, GA 30004
Phone: 770-360-0600 **Fax:** 770-360-0580
Web: www.mactec.com

MACTEC has 126 offices throughout the US.

PRODUCTS/OPERATIONS

Selected Services

Air quality monitoring/engineering
Construction
Construction management
Emergency response/business resumption
Engineering design
Environmental assessments, management, and compliance
Facilities engineering and asset management
Geotechnical engineering and geoscience
Industrial hygiene and occupational health and safety
Natural and cultural resources
Nuclear decontamination, decommissioning, and demolition
Pollution prevention and control
Process safety and risk management
Radiological protection and engineering
Remedial construction
Turnkey telecom deployment
Value engineering and analysis
Water and wastewater treatment and design

COMPETITORS

AECOM
Bechtel
British Nuclear Fuels
CH2M HILL
Earth Tech
EG&G
ERM
MWH Global
Parsons
PSI
Shaw Group
Tetra Tech
USFilter
URS
Weston

HISTORICAL FINANCIALS

Company Type: Private

Income Statement FYE: December 31

	REVENUE ($ mil.)	NET INCOME ($ mil.)	NET PROFIT MARGIN	EMPLOYEES
12/02	486	—	—	4,000
12/01	500	—	—	4,000
12/00	325	—	—	2,400
Annual Growth	22.3%	—	—	29.1%

Revenue History

Madison Square Garden, L.P.

Like the city it calls home, Madison Square Garden is the entertainment company that never sleeps. The firm owns some of New York City's iconic institutions such as the NBA's New York Knicks, the NHL's New York Rangers, and their arena, Madison Square Garden, arguably the most famous sports venue in the world. Other holdings include regional sports networks Madison Square Garden Network and Fox Sports Net New York, and Radio City Music Hall, home of the leggy Rockettes. Madison Square Garden is owned by Regional Programming Partners, a joint venture between Cablevision's Rainbow Media (60%) and Fox Sports Networks (40%). The company also operates outside the Big Apple through Connecticut's Hartford Civic Center.

Madison Square Garden's revenues dropped about $34 million in 2001 for a variety of reasons. The 2001 terrorist attacks put a large dent in New York City's tourism dollars, which hurt the company's theater business. The Knicks early elimination from the NBA playoffs, as well as the Rangers' payment of expansion fees to the NHL, have also contributed to the decline. On the upside, Radio City Entertainment's touring Christmas show did well and Madison Square Garden's sports network affiliate fees increased.

EXECUTIVES

Chairman: James L. Dolan, age 47
Vice Chairman: Robert S. Lemle, age 50
President, Madison Square Garden and Radio City Entertainment: Seth Abraham
President, Sports Team Operations: Steve Mills
President, General Manager, and Head Coach, New York Rangers: Glen Sather, age 60
President and General Manager, New York Knicks: Scott Layden
SVP Communications: Barry Watkins
SVP Corporate Marketing: Betsy Bruce

LOCATIONS

HQ: 2 Pennsylvania Plaza, Ste. 14, New York, NY 10121
Phone: 212-465-6000 **Fax:** 212-465-6026
Web: www.thegarden.com

PRODUCTS/OPERATIONS

Selected Operations

Fox Sports Net New York (regional sports television network)
Hartford Civic Center (sports and entertainment venue)
Hartford Wolf Pack (minor league hockey team)
Madison Square Garden (sports and entertainment arena)
  Theater at Madison Square Garden (entertainment venue)
Madison Square Garden Network (regional sports television network)
New York Knicks (professional basketball team)
New York Liberty (professional women's basketball team)
New York Rangers (professional hockey team)
Radio City Entertainment
  Radio City Music Hall (entertainment venue)

COMPETITORS

Clear Channel Entertainment
ESPN
New Jersey Devils
New Jersey Nets
New York Giants
New York Islanders
New York Jets

HISTORICAL FINANCIALS

Company Type: Private

Income Statement FYE: December 31

	REVENUE ($ mil.)	NET INCOME ($ mil.)	NET PROFIT MARGIN	EMPLOYEES
12/02	790	—	—	—
12/01	842	—	—	—
12/00	876	—	—	—
Annual Growth	(5.1%)	—	—	—

Revenue History

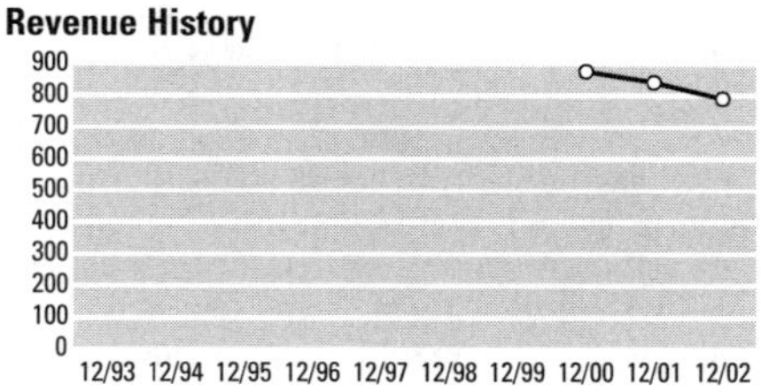

Main Street America Group

Who's your main insurance man? Main Street America Group provides a range of personal and commercial property & casualty products including coverage for small to midsized businesses and auto and homeowners insurance for individuals. The company does the majority of its business through its flagship subsidiary National Grange Mutual Insurance. Information Systems and Services Corporation offers third-party administration services such as broker management, policy processing, and underwriting services. Main Street America Group sells its products through independent agents.

EXECUTIVES

Chairman: Philip D. Koerner
President and CEO: Thomas M. Van Berkel
EVP Finance and Systems: Jeanne H. Eddy
VP and CIO: Joel Gelb
VP, Controller, and Treasurer: Edward J. Kuhl
VP and Secretary: William C. McKenna
VP Marketing: Kelly Stacy
Auditors: Ernst & Young LLP

LOCATIONS

HQ: 55 West St., Keene, NH 03431
Phone: 603-352-4000 **Fax:** 603-358-1173
Web: www.msagroup.com

Main Street America Group operates in Connecticut, Delaware, Florida, Georgia, Maine, Maryland, Massachusetts, New Hampshire, New York, North Carolina, Pennsylvania, Rhode Island, South Carolina, Tennessee, Vermont, and Virginia.

PRODUCTS/OPERATIONS

Selected Subsidiaries

Main Street America Assurance Company
Main Street America Financial Corporation
Main Street America Holdings, Inc.
MSA — Information Systems and Services Corporation
National Grange Mutual Insurance Company
Old Dominion Insurance Company

COMPETITORS

ACE Limited
Allstate
American Family Insurance
American Financial
AIG
Cincinnati Financial
Farmers Group
Fireman's Fund Insurance
GEICO
The Hartford
Liberty Mutual
Progressive Corporation
Prudential
Royal & SunAlliance USA
SAFECO
St. Paul Companies
State Farm
Travelers

HISTORICAL FINANCIALS

Company Type: Mutual company

Income Statement FYE: December 31

	REVENUE ($ mil.)	NET INCOME ($ mil.)	NET PROFIT MARGIN	EMPLOYEES
12/01	503	5	1.1%	—

Major League Baseball

It may be the national pastime, but Major League Baseball (MLB) is a big business whose troubled finances and disconnect with fans almost led it to yet another strike(out). MLB runs the game of professional baseball and oversees 30 franchises in 28 cities. Each team operates as a separate business but is regulated and governed by MLB. The league sets official rules, regulates team ownership, and collects licensing fees for merchandise. It also sells national broadcasting rights and distributes fees to the teams. (Regional broadcast rights are held by each franchise.) The MLB was formed when the rival National and American Leagues joined together in 1903.

MLB has enjoyed a resurgence in popularity, thanks in large part to Mark McGwire and Sammy Sosa's race to set a new home run record in 1998. Two years later the league tried to secure its financial future in 2000 when Fox Entertainment agreed to a six-year, $2.5 billion broadcasting contract. But the league and commissioner Bud Selig have made some tough decisions as financial disparity grows between small- and big-market teams.

The team owners and the league struggled throughout the 2002 season to negotiate a new labor agreement with players after the last contract, forged after a disastrous strike in 1994, expired at the end of the 2001 season. The cloud of the MLB's ninth work stoppage since 1972 hovered over the entire 2002 season, but another strike was narrowly avoided in late August at the 11th hour. The agreement forces the MLB to delay its plans to eliminate two teams until 2006 (the league had planned on contraction as early as 2003) and also places a luxury tax on teams with high payrolls. The money acquired from the tax will be distributed to smaller-market teams in an effort to allow those poorer clubs to compete with the high-priced talent of such teams as the New York Yankees.

Baseball fans became increasingly disgusted with both players and team owners as the threat of a strike loomed. But, now that a new labor agreement is in place, the MLB still has image problems that have to be addressed. Allegations that large amounts of players habitually abuse steroids is particularly troublesome, as was the disastrous 2002 All-Star game, which ended in embarrassment with Selig calling the tied contest in the 11th inning because both teams ran out of pitchers.

HISTORY

The first baseball team to field professional players was the Cincinnati Red Stockings in 1869. Teams in Boston, New York City, and Philadelphia followed suit. In 1876 eight professional teams formed the National League. Competing leagues sprang up and folded, but Ban Johnson's Western League (formed in 1892) seized on territory abandoned by the National League in 1900 and began luring National League players with higher salaries. Renamed the American League, it also began drawing away fans. The two leagues agreed to join forces in 1903 by having their champions meet in the World Series.

The sport flourished until the "Black Sox" scandal of 1919, in which eight Chicago White Sox players were accused of taking bribes to throw the World Series. The owners hired Judge Kenesaw Mountain Landis as baseball's first commissioner in 1921 to clean up the game's image. He served until his death in 1944. A joint committee of owners and players introduced more reforms in 1947, including a player pension fund.

The players formed the Major League Baseball Players' Association (MLBPA) in 1954 and signed the first collective-bargaining agreement with the owners in 1968. The players called their first strike in 1972, a 13-day walkout that won an improved pension plan. They won the right to free agency in 1976; another seven-week strike interrupted the 1981 season.

Salary increases slowed, and the free agent market dried up in the mid-1980s, prompting the MLBPA to sue the owners for collusion. The owners agreed to a settlement of $280 million in 1990. Baseball's eighth commissioner, Fay Vincent, resigned in 1992 after the owners effectively removed all power from the commissioner's office. An executive council of owners led by Milwaukee Brewers owner Bud Selig took control.

Prompted by the owners' decision to unilaterally restrict free agency and withdraw salary arbitration, the players started a 232-day strike in August 1994 that forced the cancellation of the World Series and stretched into the 1995 season. Revenue and income plummeted. Play resumed in 1995 when the owners and the MLBPA approved a new collective-bargaining agreement. Selig stepped down from the Brewers in 1998 to become the game's ninth commissioner.

Having alienated countless fans, baseball was resuscitated in 1998 by Mark McGwire and Sammy Sosa as they pursued Roger Maris' 37-year-old single-season home run record of 61. (McGwire's record of 70 only lasted until the 2001 season when the San Francisco Giants' outfielder Barry Bonds hit 72 homers.) The next year MLB umpires walked out for higher salaries, but the strategy backfired and 22 umpires lost their jobs. Later that year MLB signed a new six-year, $800 million TV contract with ESPN.

Sweeping changes took place in 2000 when owners, who had voted the previous year to eliminate the American and National league offices (centralizing power with the commissioner's office), also voted to restore the "best interests of baseball" powers to the commissioner, giving Selig full authority to redistribute wealth, block trades, and fine teams and players. The MLB also scored a financial home run when Fox Entertainment agreed to pay $2.5 billion for exclusive rights to televise all postseason contests through the 2006 season.

Due to the consistent financial disparity between large- and small-market teams, the league in 2001 voted to eliminate two teams before the start of the 2003 season. The next year Bob DuPuy was named president and COO of the league. (Former pres Paul Beeston resigned after talks over a new collective bargaining agreement stalled.) The following year another strike was avoided late in the season. The new labor agreement pushes back the league's contraction plans until 2006 and also places a luxury tax on teams with high payrolls, which is then distributed to small-market franchises.

EXECUTIVES

Commissioner: Allan H. (Bud) Selig, age 69
President and COO: Robert A. (Bob) DuPuy
EVP Administration: John McHale Jr.
EVP Baseball Operations: Sandy Alderson
EVP Business: Timothy J. Brosnan
EVP Labor and Human Resources: Rob Manfred
SVP and CFO: Jonathan D. Mariner, age 48
SVP Advertising and Marketing: Jaqueline Parkes
SVP Baseball Operations: Jimmie Lee Solomon
SVP International Business Operations: Paul Archey
SVP Licensing: Howard Smith
SVP Media Relations: Richard Levin
SVP Security and Facilities Management: Kevin M. Hallinan
VP Broadcasting: Bernadette McDonald
VP Community Affairs: Tom Brasuell
VP Corporate Sales and Marketing: Justin Johnson
VP Domestic Apparel Licensing, Headwear, and Sporting Goods: Steve Armus
VP Global Market Development: Jim Small
VP International Baseball Operations: Lou Melendez
VP Strategic Planning for Recruitment and Diversity: Wendy Lewis
President and CEO, MLB Advanced Media: Robert A. Bowman
Senior Manager of New Technology: Mike Napolitano
Director of Research: Dan Derian
Auditors: Deloitte & Touche LLP

LOCATIONS

HQ: 245 Park Ave., New York, NY 10167
Phone: 212-931-7800 **Fax:** 212-949-8636
Web: www.mlb.com

Major League Baseball has 30 franchises in 28 cities in the US and Canada.

PRODUCTS/OPERATIONS

Major League Franchises

American League
Anaheim Angels (1965, California)
  Los Angeles Angels (1961)
Baltimore Orioles (1952)
  St. Louis Browns (1902)
  Milwaukee Brewers (1901)
Boston Red Sox (1901)
Chicago White Sox (1901)
Cleveland Indians (1915)
  Cleveland Spiders (1889)
Detroit Tigers (1900)
Kansas City Royals (1969, Missouri)
Minnesota Twins (1961, Minneapolis)
  Washington Senators (1901; Washington, DC)
New York Yankees (1913, New York City)
  New York Highlanders (1903, New York City)
  Baltimore Orioles (1901)
Oakland Athletics (1968, California)
  Kansas City Athletics (1955, Missouri)
  Philadelphia Athletics (1901)
Seattle Mariners (1977)
Tampa Bay Devil Rays (1998)
Texas Rangers (1972, Arlington)
  Washington Senators (1961; Washington, DC)
Toronto Blue Jays (1977)

National League
Arizona Diamondbacks (Phoenix, 1998)
Atlanta Braves (1966)
  Milwaukee Braves (1953)
  Boston Braves (1912)
  Boston Beaneaters (1883)
  Boston Red Stockings (1871)
Chicago Cubs (1903)
  Chicago Orphans (1898)
  Chicago Colts (1884)
  Chicago White Stockings (1871)
Cincinnati Reds (1866)
Colorado Rockies (1993, Denver)
Florida Marlins (1993, Miami)
Houston Astros (1964)
  Houston Colt .45s (1962)
Los Angeles Dodgers (1958)
  Brooklyn Dodgers (1890, New York)
Milwaukee Brewers (1970; switched from American League, 1998)
  Seattle Pilots (1969)
Montreal Expos (1969)
New York Mets (1962, New York City)
Philadelphia Phillies (1883)
Pittsburgh Pirates (1887)
St. Louis Cardinals (1900)
  St. Louis Brown Stockings (1882)
San Diego Padres (1969)
San Francisco Giants (1958)
  New York Giants (1883, New York City)

COMPETITORS

AFL
FIFA
NASCAR
NBA
NFL
NHL
PGA
USSF
World Wrestling Entertainment

HISTORICAL FINANCIALS

Company Type: Association

Income Statement FYE: October 31

	REVENUE ($ mil.)	NET INCOME ($ mil.)	NET PROFIT MARGIN	EMPLOYEES
10/01	3,500	—	—	—
10/00	3,178	—	—	—
10/99	2,838	—	—	—
10/98	3,174	—	—	—
10/97	2,216	—	—	—
10/96	1,847	—	—	—
10/95	1,411	—	—	—
10/94	1,134	—	—	—
10/93	1,775	—	—	—
10/92	1,663	—	—	—
Annual Growth	8.6%	—	—	—

Revenue History

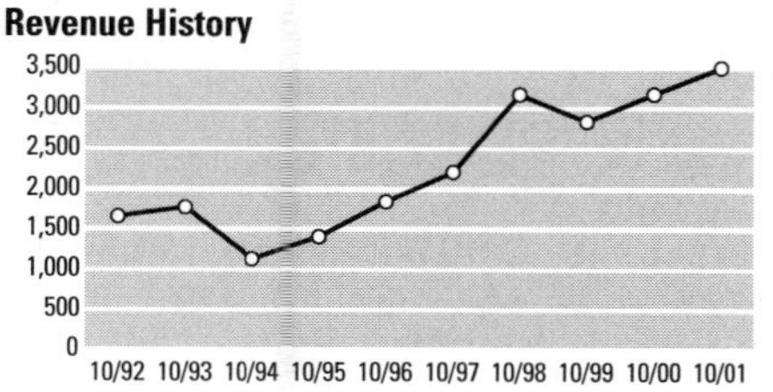

Marc Glassman

Marc Glassman wants to prove that low prices can lead to big things. The retailer operates about 55 drugstores, most of which are Marc's Discount Drug Stores in northeast Ohio, but also a handful of Xpect Discount Drugs in Connecticut. Marc Glassman's no-frills stores (sorry, credit cards not accepted) range in size from 18,000 sq. ft. to 48,000 sq. ft. Most have pharmacies and offer a constantly changing mix of closeout and excess merchandise in some 20 categories, including clothing, cosmetics, housewares, toys, and tools. The company specializes in seasonal products (Christmas, Halloween, lawn and garden). Owner and chairman Marc Glassman founded the company in Middleburg Heights, Ohio, in 1979.

EXECUTIVES

Chairman: Marc Glassman
CEO: Kevin Yaugher
CFO (HR): Beth Weiner

LOCATIONS

HQ: Marc Glassman, Inc.
5841 W. 130th St., Parma, OH 44130
Phone: 216-265-7700 **Fax:** 216-265-7737
Web: www.marcs.com

COMPETITORS

Ahold USA
Big Lots
CVS
Discount Drug
Dollar General
Dollar Tree
Family Dollar Stores
Giant Eagle
Kmart
Rite Aid
Target
Walgreen
Wal-Mart

HISTORICAL FINANCIALS

Company Type: Private

Income Statement FYE: December 31

	ESTIMATED REVENUE ($ mil.)	NET INCOME ($ mil.)	NET PROFIT MARGIN	EMPLOYEES
12/01	750	—	—	6,100
12/00	745	—	—	6,150
12/99	645	—	—	6,000
12/98	600	—	—	6,000
Annual Growth	7.7%	—	—	0.6%

Revenue History

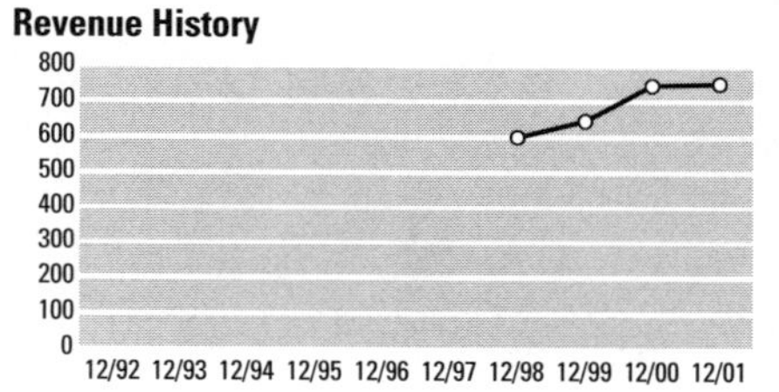

Maritz Inc.

Not only can Maritz send your employees on business trips, it can motivate them to go. With about 240 offices in more than 40 countries, Maritz offers travel, employee motivation, and marketing services. Its performance improvement and incentive programs help client companies improve workforce quality and customer satisfaction. The company is also one of the nation's largest custom market research companies. In addition, TQ3 Maritz Travel Solutions co-owns, with TUI AG, TQ3 Travel Solutions, Europe's top travel firm and a leading global agency with some 1,600 locations in more than 60 countries. The Maritz family owns the company.

The company's employee motivation and incentive programs help clients improve workforce quality and customer satisfaction. Its customers include a majority of the *Forbes* 500. Maritz is also one of the largest custom market research providers in the US, specializing in telecommunications and automotive research, and it provides syndicated buyer research services and conducts consumer surveys (Maritz Polls).

Facing heat from online incentive programs, Maritz launched its own online service, e-Maritz, in 2000. It also started Heybridge, an e-commerce subsidiary that helps small and midsized businesses sell over the Internet. In 2001 it purchased travel and incentive business McGettigan to add depth to its client offerings.

EXECUTIVES

Chairman and CEO: W. Stephen Maritz, age 44
SEVP and CFO: James W. Kienker, age 55
SVP Human Resources: Terry L. Goring
President, Maritz Travel Company: Jeffrey D. Reinberg
VP Community Affairs and Organizational Development: Tom Tener
CIO: Gil Hoffman
Business Development: Dennis Hummel
Marketing: Scott Bush

LOCATIONS

HQ: 1375 N. Highway Dr., Fenton, MO 63099
Phone: 636-827-4000 **Fax:** 636-827-3312
Web: www.maritz.com

Maritz operates 240 offices in Canada, France, Germany, Italy, Mexico, the Netherlands, South Africa, Spain, Turkey, the UK, and the US.

PRODUCTS/OPERATIONS

Services

Marketing Research
Custom marketing research
Customer satisfaction and customer value analysis
Data collection (focus groups, telephone interviews)
Maritz Polls and Maritz Research Reports
Syndicated buyer research
Telecommunications research

Performance Improvement
Communications
e-Learning
Fulfillment
Internet consulting
Loyalty marketing
Measurement and feedback
Rewards and recognition

Travel
Consulting services
Corporate travel management
Group travel services
Travel award programs

COMPETITORS

ACNielsen	J.D. Power
American Express	JTB
Carlson	Navigant International
Franklin Covey	NFO WorldGroup
Gallup	Opinion Research
Harris Interactive	Rosenbluth International
IMS Health	Thomas Cook AG
Information Resources	WorldTravel

HISTORICAL FINANCIALS

Company Type: Private

Income Statement FYE: March 31

	REVENUE ($ mil.)	NET INCOME ($ mil.)	NET PROFIT MARGIN	EMPLOYEES
3/02	1,500	—	—	6,000
3/01	1,318	—	—	6,200
3/00	1,325	—	—	6,500
3/99	2,200	—	—	6,500
3/98	2,170	—	—	6,500
3/97	2,010	—	—	7,500
3/96	1,795	—	—	7,000
3/95	1,078	—	—	6,410
3/94	1,442	—	—	6,080
3/93	1,260	—	—	6,000
Annual Growth	2.0%	—	—	0.0%

Revenue History

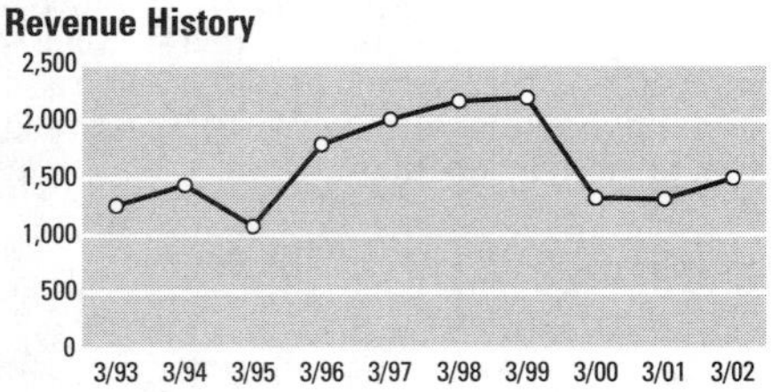

Mark IV Industries, Inc.

Mark IV Industries' engineered components and systems are on the mark when it comes to fluid-handling and power-steering uses. The company's automotive division manufactures idlers, pulleys, belts, power-steering and air-conditioning hoses, manifolds, and water pumps. Mark IV's powertrain division makes diesel and gasoline engines for automotive, industrial, agricultural, and marine uses. Other products include information display systems (for buses, aircraft, and railcars) and intelligent vehicle highway systems (traffic management and electronic toll products). European private equity firm BC Partners controls the company.

Since unloading its Purolator- and Facet-brand air- and fuel-filtration products, Mark IV has concentrated on divesting other product lines to further focus its product mix. The company has sold its Dayco Industrial Power Transmission (belts) unit to Carlisle Companies, and sold Dayco Industrial's fluid transfer and hydraulic hose unit to Parker Hannifin. The company's automotive division accounts for nearly 70% of sales.

EXECUTIVES

President: William P. Montague, age 56
SVP; President, Mark IV Automotive: Kurt J. Johansson
VP, Finance: Mark G. Barberio
VP; EVP, Mark IV Automotive: Giuliano Zucco
VP, Human Resources: Steve Kerns

LOCATIONS

HQ: 501 John James Audubon Pkwy.,
Amherst, NY 14226
Phone: 716-689-4972 **Fax:** 716-689-6098
Web: www.mark-iv.com

Mark IV Industries operates 37 manufacturing plants, 26 distribution and sales facilities, and nine technical centers in 16 countries.

2002 Sales

	% of total
North America	56
Europe, South America, & Asia	44
Total	**100**

PRODUCTS/OPERATIONS

Selected Automotive Products

Aftermarket products
Information display systems
Intelligent vehicle highway systems
OEM products
Powertrain products

COMPETITORS

BorgWarner
Dana
Delphi
Eaton
Gates Rubber
Goodyear
Tesma
Tomkins
Visteon

HISTORICAL FINANCIALS

Company Type: Private

Income Statement FYE: February 28

	REVENUE ($ mil.)	NET INCOME ($ mil.)	NET PROFIT MARGIN	EMPLOYEES
2/02	1,200	—	—	8,000
2/01	2,000	—	—	15,500
2/00	1,994	—	—	15,600
2/99	1,949	—	—	17,000
2/98	2,210	—	—	17,000
2/97	2,076	—	—	15,800
2/96	2,089	—	—	16,000
2/95	1,603	—	—	16,200
2/94	1,244	—	—	12,500
2/93	1,222	—	—	11,800
Annual Growth	(0.2%)	—	—	(4.2%)

Revenue History

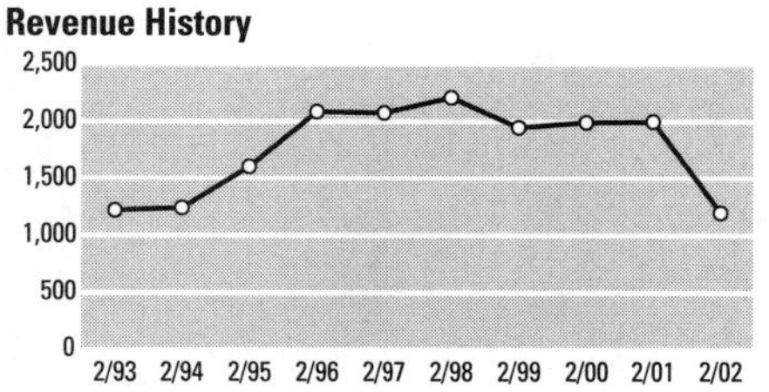

The Marmon Group, Inc.

With more monikers than most, The Marmon Group monitors a melange of more than 100 autonomous manufacturing and service companies. Marmon's manufacturing units make medical products, mining equipment, industrial materials and components, consumer products (including Wells Lamont gloves), transportation equipment, building products, and water-treatment products. Services include marketing and distribution and consumer credit information (Trans Union). Overall, Marmon companies operate 550 facilities in more than 40 countries. Chicago's Pritzker family (owners of the Hyatt hotel chain) owns The Marmon Group.

Each Marmon company works under its own management, and a small corporate office (fewer than 100 employees) oversees and pulls together the conglomerate, acting as combination CFO, tax lawyer, accountant, and broker to member companies.

Marmon continues to grow through acquisitions, largely to complement existing businesses in fields such as retail display equipment, fasteners and metal products, and consumer credit information.

HISTORY

Although the history of The Marmon Group officially begins in 1953, the company's roots are in the Chicago law firm Pritzker and Pritzker, started by Nicholas Pritzker in 1902. Through the firm the family made connections with First National Bank of Chicago, which A. N. Pritzker, Nicholas' son, used to get a line of credit to buy real estate. By 1940 the firm had stopped accepting outside clients to concentrate on the family's growing investment portfolio.

In 1953 A. N.'s son Jay used his father's connections to get a loan to buy Colson Company, a small, money-losing manufacturer of bicycles, hospital equipment, and other products. Jay's brother, Robert, a graduate of the Illinois Institute of Technology, took charge of Colson and turned it around. Soon Jay began acquiring more companies for his brother to manage.

In 1963 the brothers paid $2.7 million for about 45% of the Marmon-Herrington Company (whose predecessor, Marmon Motor Car, built the car that in 1911 won the first Indianapolis 500). The family now had a name for its industrial holdings — The Marmon Group.

It became a public company in 1966 when it merged with door- and spring-maker Fenestra. However, Jay began to take greater control of the group through a series of stock purchases, and by 1971 The Marmon Group was private once again.

A year earlier, in 1970, the group acquired a promising industrial pipe supplier, Keystone Tubular Service (which later became Marmon/Keystone). In 1973 Marmon began to acquire stock in Cerro Corp., which had operations in mining, manufacturing, trucking, and real estate; by 1976 the group had bought all of Cerro, thereby tripling its revenues. The brothers sold Cerro's trucking subsidiary, ICX, in 1977 and bought organ maker Hammond Corp., along with Wells Lamont, Hammond's glove-making subsidiary.

Marmon acquired conglomerate Trans Union in 1981. Trans Union brought many operations, including railcar and equipment leasing, credit information services, international trading, and water- and wastewater-treatment systems. Jay acquired Ticketmaster in 1982.

The Pritzkers made a foray into the airline business in 1984 by buying Braniff Airlines. After unsuccessfully bidding for Pan Am in 1987, they sold Braniff in 1988. Disappointments in other Pritzker businesses didn't slow Marmon, which added to its transportation equipment business in 1984 with Altamil, a maker of products for the trucking and aerospace industries.

To mark its 40th anniversary, the company sponsored a car, the Marmon Wasp II, at the 1993 Indianapolis 500. That year the Pritzkers sold 80% of Ticketmaster to Microsoft co-founder Paul Allen but retained a minority interest. Marmon sold Arzco Medical Systems in 1995 and Marmon/Keystone acquired Anbuma Group, a Belgian steel tubing distributor.

The Anbuma purchase and Marmon/Keystone's 1997 acquisition of UK tube distributor Wheeler Group exemplify Marmon's practice of building strength through acquisitions in its established markets. In 1998 Marmon purchased more than 30 companies and opened a business development office in Beijing.

Marmon splashed out more than $500 million in 1999 to make 35 acquisitions, including Kerite (power cables), OsteoMed (specialty medical devices), and Bridport (medical and aviation products). Jay died that year, and the company announced that his title of chairman will not be filled.

In 2000 Marmon spent another $500 million on more than 20 acquisitions, buying operations engaged in the production of retail display equipment, tank containers, and metal products, among others.

Former Illinois Tool Works chief John Nichols took over the Marmon CEO responsibilities from Robert Pritzker in 2001.

EXECUTIVES

President and CEO: John D. Nichols
EVP: Robert C. Gluth
SVP and CFO: Robert K. Lorch
SVP, Secretary, and General Counsel: Robert W. (Bob) Webb
SVP: Henry J. (Hank) West
VP Human Resources: Larry Rist
VP: Mike Hartley
Auditors: Ernst & Young LLP

LOCATIONS

HQ: 225 W. Washington St., Chicago, IL 60606
Phone: 312-372-9500 **Fax:** 312-845-5305
Web: www.marmon.com

PRODUCTS/OPERATIONS

Selected Member Companies

Automotive Equipment
Fontaine Modification Co.
Fontaine Trailer Co.
Marmon-Herrington Co.
Perfection HY-Test Co.

Building Products and Fasteners
Anderson Copper and Brass Co.
Atlas Bolt & Screw Company
Shepherd Caster Corporation
Shepherd Products Inc.

Consumer Products, Marketing, and Financial Services
Beijing Huilian Food Co., Ltd.
Getz Bros. & Co., Inc.
Great Lakes Consulting Group, Inc.
MarCap Corp.
Wells Lamont Corporation

Credit Data and Information Management
Trans Union LLC

Industrial Products
Amarillo Gear Co.
Bridport Aviation

Medical Products
American Medical Instruments, Inc.
B.G. Sulzle, Inc.
Medical Device Technologies, Inc. (MD Tech)
Pearsalls Limited
Surgical Specialties Corporation

Metal Products and Materials
Cerro Copper Products Co.
Cerro Metal Products Co.
Penn Aluminum International, Inc.

Pipe and Tube Distribution
Marmon/Keystone Corporation
Future Metals, Inc.
M/K Huron Steel

Railway and Transportation Services
Exsif Worldwide, Inc.
Penn Machine Co.
Railserve, Inc.
Trackmobile, Inc.
Union Tank Car Co.

Retail and Food Service Equipment
L.A. Darling Co.
Store Opening Solutions, Inc.
Thorco Industries, Inc.

Seat Belts and Cargo Restraints
Am-Safe Inc.
Bridport Aviation

Water Treatment Systems
Ecodyne Limited
EcoWater Systems, Inc.
Spectrum Labs, Inc.

Wire and Cable Products
Cable USA, Inc.
Comtran Corporation
Hendrix Wire & Cable, Inc.
The Kerite Co.
Owl Wire and Cable, Inc.
Rockbestos-Surprenant Cable Corp.

COMPETITORS

Alcatel
Balfour Beatty
Cable Design Technologies
Eaton
Equifax
GE
Illinois Tool Works
Ingersoll-Rand
ITT Industries
LEONI
Masco
Nexans
Pirelli & C.
Superior TeleCom
Terex
USG
Wolverine Tube

HISTORICAL FINA[illegible]

Company Type: Private

Income Statement

	REVENUE ($ mil.)	[illegible]	[illegible]	[illegible]
12/02	5,756	[illegible]	[illegible]	[illegible]
12/01	6,414	—	—	[illegible]
12/00	6,786	—	—	40,000
12/99	6,530	—	—	40,000
12/98	6,032	—	—	35,000
12/97	6,003	—	—	33,000
12/96	5,776	—	—	35,000
12/95	6,083	—	—	30,000
12/94	5,302	—	—	28,000
12/93	4,319	—	—	27,700
Annual Growth	3.2%	—	—	0.9%

Revenue History

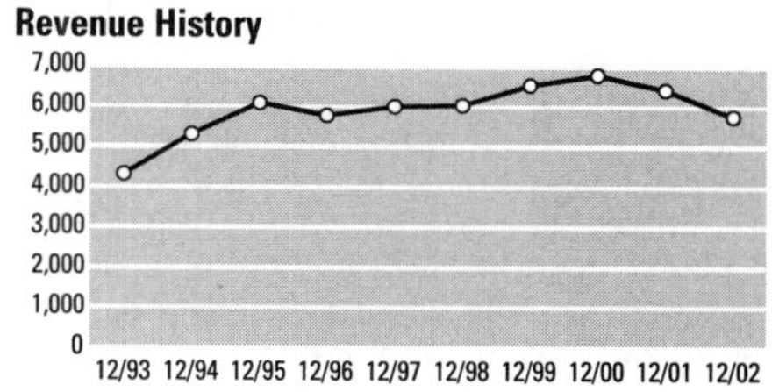

Mars

Mars knows chocolate sales are nothing to snicker at. The #2 US candy maker (behind Hershey) makes such worldwide favorites as M&M's, Snickers, and the Mars bar. Its other products include 3 Musketeers, Dove, Milky Way, Skittles, Twix, and Starburst sweets; Combos and Kudos snacks; Uncle Ben's rice; and pet food under the names Pedigree, Sheba, and Whiskas. Mars also makes drink vending equipment and electronic automated payment systems. The Mars family (including siblings Forrest Mars Jr., president and CEO John Mars, and VP Jacqueline Badger Mars) owns the highly secretive firm — making the Mars family one of the richest in the country.

Mars also offers ice-cream versions of several of its candy bars. Its automated payment systems include electronic coin changers and bill acceptors. In 2003 the company made an all-share offer for Japanese vending machine parts manufacturer Nippon Conlux. The offer was Mar's first takeover venture in Japan.

The company, surpassed in candymaking in the US by Hershey, is ahead of its rival internationally. Mars stays virtually debt free and uses its profits for international expansion. It now sells its products in more than 100 countries on five continents.

Mars agreed to buy French pet food company Royal Canin in July 2001. In summer 2002 the two companies agreed to sell five pet food brands in order to gain regulatory approval. Upon the EU's approval of the sale, Mars will acquire a 10% stake in Royal Canin; it hopes to acquire full control of the company sometime in 2003.

Also in 2003 Mars announced that it will make an energy bar to be called Snickers Marathon that tastes like its Snickers candy bar.

k Mars invented the Milky Way candy bar 923 after his previous three efforts at the ndy business left him bankrupt. After his es-ranged son, Forrest, graduated from Yale, Mars hired him to work at his candy operation. When Forrest demanded one-third control of the company and Frank refused, Forrest moved to England with the foreign rights to Milky Way and started his own company (Food Manufacturers) in the 1930s. He made a sweeter version of Milky Way for the UK, calling it a Mars bar. Forrest also ventured into pet food with the 1934 purchase of Chappel Brothers (renamed Pedigree). At one point he controlled 55% of the British pet food market.

During WWII Forrest returned to the US and introduced Uncle Ben's rice (the world's first brand-name raw commodity) and M&M's (a joint venture between Forrest and Bruce Murrie, son of the then-Hershey president). The idea for M&M's was borrowed from British Smarties, for which Forrest obtained rights (from Rowntree Mackintosh) by relinquishing similar rights to the Snickers bar in some foreign markets. The ad slogan "Melts in your mouth, not in your hand" (and the candy's success in non-air-conditioned stores and war zones) made the company an industry leader. Mars introduced M&M's Peanut in 1954. It was one of the first candy companies to sponsor a television show — *Howdy Doody* in the 1950s.

Forrest merged his firm with his deceased father's company in 1964, after buying his dying half sister's controlling interest. (He renamed the business Mars at her request.) The merger was the end of an alliance with Hershey, who had supplied Frank with chocolate since his Milky Way inception.

In 1968 Mars bought Kal Kan. (The division now oversees all pet food operations.) In 1973 Forrest, then 69 years old, delegated his company responsibility to sons Forrest Jr. and John. Five years later the brothers, looking for snacks to offset dwindling candy sales from a more diet-conscious America, bought the Twix chocolate-covered cookie brand. During the late 1980s they bought ice-cream bar maker Dove Bar International and Ethel M Chocolates, producer of liqueur-flavored chocolates, a business their father had begun in his retirement.

Hershey passed Mars as the US's largest candy maker in 1988 when it acquired Cadbury Schweppes' US division (Mounds and Almond Joy). In response to the success of Hershey's Symphony Bar, Mars introduced its dark-chocolate Dove bar in 1991.

While Hershey chose to stick close to home, Mars ventured abroad. The company entered the huge confectionery market of India in 1989 by building a $10 million factory there. In 1996 the company opened a confectionery processing plant in Brazil. Back home, the company expanded its Starburst candy line in 1996 and in 1997 launched new ad campaigns, including M&M's spots featuring a trio of animated M&M candies. Mars introduced Uncle Ben's Rice Bowl frozen meals in the late 1990s.

Forrest Sr. died in 1999, spurring rumors that Mars would go public or be sold. Instead, the company dismantled most of its sales force, opting to use less costly food brokers. Also in 1999 Forrest Jr. retired, leaving brother John as president and CEO. Still far behind its rival, Mars received a modest boost in US market share when Hershey experienced computer troubles.

In 2000 the company established a subsidiary, Effem India, to market Mars' products in India. In 2003 Mars acquired French pet food producer Royal Canin. That same year its Mexican subsidiary, Effem Mexico SA de CV, merged with Mexican confectioner, Grupo Matre, to form a partnership to produce candy for Hispanic markets.

EXECUTIVES

Chairman, President, and CEO: John Franklyn Mars, age 71
VP: Jacqueline Badger Mars, age 63
VP and Secretary: D. M. Newby
VP and Treasurer: R. E. Barnes
President, Americas: Paul S. Michaels
President, Masterfoods South America: Eduardo Senf
President, Masterfoods USA: Bob Gamgort
VP, Licensing Masterfoods USA: Michele Brown
VP, Marketing Masterfoods USA: Mark Mattia
VP, Marketing Services Masterfoods USA: Peter Littlewood
Director, In-Store Solutions Masterfoods USA: Dena R. Clem
Director, Licensing Masterfoods USA: Lynn Scott
Director, Marketing Masterfoods Pet Food: Chris Jones
Director, Media Masterfoods: Barbara King
Director, Marketing Masterfoods USA: Brain Zeug
Director, National Sales Masterfoods USA: Larry Lupo

LOCATIONS

HQ: Mars, Incorporated
6885 Elm St., McLean, VA 22101
Phone: 703-821-4900 **Fax:** 703-448-9678
Web: www.mars.com

PRODUCTS/OPERATIONS

Selected Products

Candy
3 Musketeers
Bounty
Dove
Ethel M Chocolates
Maltesers
M&M's
Mars
Milky Way
Opal Fruit
Revels
Skittles
Snickers
Starburst
Twix

Ice-Cream Bars
3 Musketeers
DoveBars
M&M Cookie Ice Cream Sandwiches
Milky Way
Snickers
Starburst Ice Bars

Pet Food
Bounce
Brekkies
Cesar
Chappie
Dine
Frolic
KiteKat
Loyal
My Dog
Pedigree
Sheba
Trill
Waltham
Whiskas

Snacks
Combos
Kudos

Rice and Other Food and Drinks
Dolmio sauces
Flavia drinks
Masterfoods condiments and sauces
Suzi Wan Chinese food
Uncle Ben's Rice

Other Products
Coin changers
Flavia office beverage systems
Klix beverage vending equipment
Smart card payment systems

COMPETITORS

Archibald Candy
Barry Callebaut
Barry Callebaut USA
Brach's
Cadbury Schweppes
Campbell Soup
Lindt & Sprüngli
Colgate-Palmolive
ConAgra
Grupo Corvi
CSM
Doane Pet Care Company
Ezaki Glico
Ferrara Pan Candy
Ferrero
General Mills
Guittard
Hershey
Heinz
Kraft Foods
Meiji Seika
Nestlé
Riviana Foods
Rocky Mountain Chocolate
Russell Stover
See's Candies
Thorntons
Tootsie Roll
Unilever
Wrigley
World's Finest Chocolate

HISTORICAL FINANCIALS

Company Type: Private

Income Statement FYE: December 31

	ESTIMATED REVENUE ($ mil.)	NET INCOME ($ mil.)	NET PROFIT MARGIN	EMPLOYEES
12/02	15,000	—	—	30,000
12/01	15,500	—	—	30,000
12/00	15,400	—	—	30,000
12/99	15,200	—	—	28,500
12/98	15,500	—	—	30,000
12/97	14,400	—	—	28,500
12/96	14,000	—	—	28,000
12/95	13,000	—	—	28,000
12/94	12,500	—	—	28,000
12/93	13,000	—	—	27,000
Annual Growth	1.6%	—	—	1.2%

Revenue History

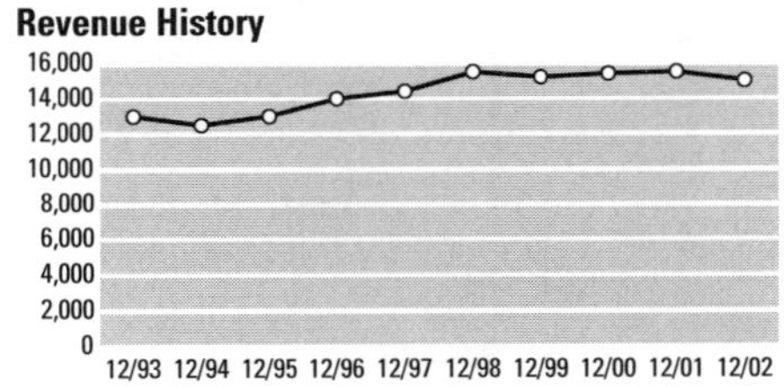

Martin-Brower

McDonald's is worth its weight in gold(en arches) to The Martin-Brower Company. Martin-Brower is the largest supplier of distribution services to the McDonald's restaurant chain. The company is the exclusive distributor to about 44% of the McDonald's restaurants in the US and all of its outlets in Brazil, Canada, and Central America, supplying such items as crew hats, first-aid kits, lightbulbs, and trash bags. The company operates about 30 distribution centers in seven countries. Martin-Brower changed hands in 1998 when privately owned food and beverage distributor Reyes Holdings purchased the company from UK-based Sygen International (previously PIC International).

EXECUTIVES

Co-Chairman: J. Christopher (Chris) Reyes
Co-Chairman and CEO: M. Jude Reyes, age 48
CFO: John Roussel
VP, Human Resources: Phil Menzel

LOCATIONS

HQ: The Martin-Brower Company, L.L.C.
9500 West Bryn Mawr Ave., Ste. 700,
Rosemont, IL 60018
Phone: 847-227-6500 **Fax:** 847-227-6550

COMPETITORS

Anderson-DuBose
Golden State Foods
Keystone Foods
SYSCO
U.S. Foodservice

HISTORICAL FINANCIALS

Company Type: Private

Income Statement FYE: December 31

	REVENUE ($ mil.)	NET INCOME ($ mil.)	NET PROFIT MARGIN	EMPLOYEES
12/02	3,000	—	—	2,900
12/01	2,800	—	—	2,900
12/00	2,500	—	—	2,200
12/99*	2,400	—	—	2,200
6/98	2,305	—	—	2,200
6/97	2,709	—	—	—
6/96	2,603	—	—	—
Annual Growth	2.4%	—	—	7.2%

*Fiscal year change

Revenue History

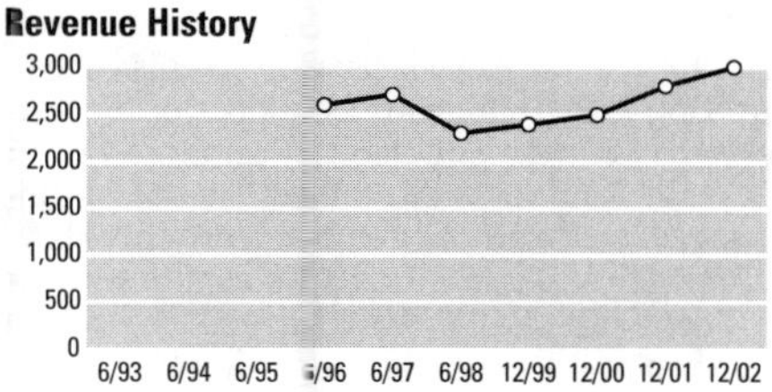

Marty Franich Auto Center

Fleet customers can sail on into Marty Franich Auto Center dealerships. Founded in 1948, the company consists of two full-service dealerships in Watsonville, California, that sell Chrysler, Dodge, Ford, Jeep, Lincoln, and Mercury vehicles. The dealer also sells used vehicles, and it operates parts and service departments. The company specializes in sales to fleet buyers and sells to rental outfits nationwide, including Hertz and Avis Group. President and CEO Steven Franich is the son of founder Martin (Marty) Franich, whose family owns the company.

EXECUTIVES

President and CEO: Steven (Rocky) Franich, age 56
Customer Relations Director: Abbie Romandia
Finance Manager: Tim Liebel
General Manager: Doug Inman
General Sales Manager: Leyton Felix
Used Car Manager: Steve Phillips
Internet Sales Manager, Marty Franich Chrysler Dodge Jeep: Jonathan Barr

LOCATIONS

HQ: 550 Auto Center Dr., Watsonville, CA 95076
Phone: 831-722-4181 **Fax:** 831-724-1853
Web: www.franichford.com

COMPETITORS

AutoNation
Kuni Automotive
Prospect Motors
Sonic Automotive
Tasha Inc.
United Auto Group

HISTORICAL FINANCIALS

Company Type: Private

Income Statement FYE: December 31

	REVENUE ($ mil.)	NET INCOME ($ mil.)	NET PROFIT MARGIN	EMPLOYEES
12/02	800	—	—	108
12/01	815	—	—	100
12/00	925	—	—	100
12/99	859	—	—	100
12/98	946	—	—	104
Annual Growth	(4.1%)	—	—	0.9%

Revenue History

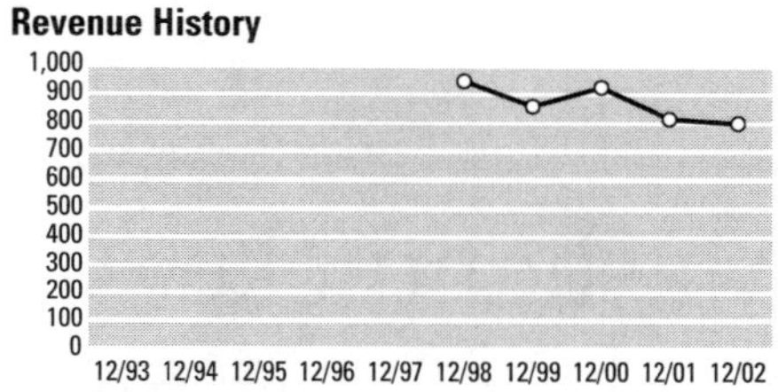

Mary Kay Inc.

Celebrating its 40th anniversary in 2003, Mary Kay is in the pink (and in Avon's shadow) as the US's #2 direct seller of beauty products. It sells more than 200 products in eight product categories: body care, cosmetics, facial skin care, fragrances, men's skin care, nail care, nutritional supplements, and sun protection. More than 1 million independent sales consultants demonstrate Mary Kay products in the US and some 34 other countries. Consultants vie for awards each year, ranging from jewelry to the company's trademark pink Cadillacs (first awarded in 1969). The family of founder Mary Kay Ash owns most of the company.

Founded by a woman for women, Mary Kay has an overwhelmingly female independent sales force. Although the company stands by Mary Kay's original goal of providing financial and career opportunities for women, much of the company's executive population is male. Ash's son Richard Rogers (chairman and CEO) runs the company.

Mary Kay works hard to retain the feel of a small company, despite its more than 1-million-strong independent sales force and the firm's growing international reach. As part of this initiative, each beauty consultant receives the option to buy her own Web site to use for selling to clients.

During her lifetime, Mary Kay Ash was known for her religious nature as well as her generosity. She founded the Mary Kay Ash Charitable Foundation in 1996. She suffered a debilitating stroke later that year and died on Thanksgiving Day 2001.

HISTORY

Before founding her own company in 1963, Mary Kay Ash worked as a Stanley Home Products sales representative. Impressed with the alligator handbag awarded to the top saleswoman at a Stanley convention, Ash was determined to win the next year's prize — and she did. Despite that accomplishment and having worked at Stanley for 11 years, a male assistant she had trained was made her boss after less than a year on the job. Tired of not receiving recognition, Ash and her second husband used their life savings ($5,000) to go into business for themselves. Although her husband died of a heart attack shortly before the business opened, Ash forged ahead with the help of her two grown sons.

She bought a cosmetics formula invented years earlier by a hide tanner. (The mixture was originally used to soften leather, but the tanner noticed how the formula made his hands look younger, and he began applying the mixture to his face, with great results.) Ash kept her first line simple — 10 products — and packaged her wares in pink to compliment the typically white bathrooms of the day. Ash also enlisted consultants, who held "beauty shows" with five or six women in attendance. Mary Kay grossed $198,000 in its first year.

The company introduced men's skin care products in 1965. Ash bought a pink Cadillac the following year and began awarding the cars as prizes three years later. (By 1981 orders were so large — almost 500 — that GM dubbed the color "Mary Kay Pink.")

Ash became a millionaire when her firm went public in 1968. Mary Kay grew steadily through the 1970s. Foreign operations began in 1971 in Australia, and over the next 25 years the company entered 24 more countries, including nations in Asia, Europe, Central and South America, and the Pacific Rim.

Sales plunged in the early 1980s, along with the company's stock prices (from $40 to $9 between 1983 and 1985). Ash and her family reacquired Mary Kay in 1985 through a $375 million LBO. Burdened with debt, the firm lost money in the late 1980s. Mary Kay took a number of steps to boost sales and income, doing a makeover on the cosmetics line and advertising in women's magazines again (after a five-year hiatus) to counter its old-fashioned image. The company also introduced recyclable packaging and lipstick in a tube (replacing brush-on palettes). In 1989 Avon rebuffed a buyout offer by Mary Kay, and both companies halted animal testing.

In 1993 Mary Kay opened a subsidiary in Russia, which later became the company's fourth-largest international market (behind Mexico, China, and Canada). Ash suffered a debilitating stroke in 1996.

In 1998 Mary Kay began selling through retail boutiques in China because of a government ban on direct selling. Changing with the times, Mary Kay added a white sport utility vehicle and new shades of pink to its fleet of 10,000 GM cars that year.

Chairman John Rochon was named CEO in 1999. Also in 1999 Mary Kay launched *Women & Success* (a magazine for consultants) and Atlas (its electronic ordering system).

In June 2001 Richard Rogers, the company

chairman and son of Ash, replaced Rochon as CEO. A month later Mary Kay introduced the Velocity Products line, targeting girls ages 14 to 24. Ash died on Thanksgiving Day 2001.

Mary Kay Poland, headquartered in Warsaw, became the company's 34th international market in mid-2003.

EXECUTIVES

Chairman and CEO: Richard R. Rogers, age 59
President and COO: David Holl
President, Global Sales and Marketing: Tom Whatley
EVP and CIO: Kregg Jodie
EVP, Global Manufacturing: Dennis Greaney
EVP, Global Marketing/R&D: Myra O. Barker
EVP, Global Human Resources and Operations: Darrell Overcash
SVP, Finance: Terry Smith
VP, Global Corporate Communications: Randall Oxford
President, Mary Kay Europe: Tara Eustance
General Counsel: Brad Glendening
General Manager, Mary Kay Poland: Ewa Kudlinska-Pyrz
Project Manager, Information Services Technology: Lou Silvey
Corporate Communications: Diana Gold
Corporate Communications: Shannon Summers

LOCATIONS

HQ: 16251 Dallas Pkwy., Addison, TX 75001
Phone: 972-687-6300 **Fax:** 972-687-1609
Web: www.marykay.com

Mary Kay's independent sales force of more than 1 million sells the company's products in more than 33 markets in Asia, Australia, Europe, North America, and South America.

PRODUCTS/OPERATIONS

Selected Product Lines

Body care
Cosmetics
Facial skin care
Fragrances
Men's skin care
Nail care
Nutritional supplements for men
Nutritional supplements for women
Sun protection

COMPETITORS

Alberto-Culver
Allou
Alticor
Avon
Bath & Body Works
BeautiControl Cosmetics
Body Shop
Clarins
Colgate-Palmolive
Coty
Del Labs
Dial
Estée Lauder
Helen of Troy
Herbalife
Intimate Brands
John Paul Mitchell
Johnson & Johnson
L'Oréal
L'Oréal USA
Merle Norman
New Dana Perfumes
Nu Skin
Perrigo
Procter & Gamble
Reliv'
Revlon
Schwarzkopf & DEP
Scott's Liquid Gold
Shaklee
Shiseido
Sunrider
Unilever
Wella

HISTORICAL FINANCIALS

Company Type: Private

Income Statement FYE: December 31

	REVENUE ($ mil.)	NET INCOME ($ mil.)	NET PROFIT MARGIN	EMPLOYEES
12/02	1,560	—	—	3,600
12/01	1,300	—	—	3,600
12/00	1,200	—	—	3,600
12/99	1,000	—	—	3,250
12/98	1,000	—	—	3,500
12/97	1,050	—	—	3,500
12/96	1,000	—	—	3,000
12/95	950	—	—	2,800
12/94	850	—	—	2,400
12/93	737	—	—	2,400
Annual Growth	8.7%	—	—	4.6%

Revenue History

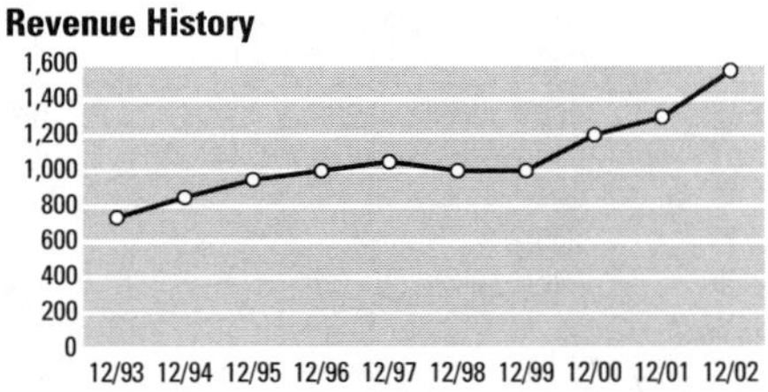

Mashantucket Pequot Gaming Enterprise Inc.

Mashantucket Pequot Gaming Enterprise has propelled the Mashantucket Pequot Tribal Nation (with roughly 600 members) from the depths of intense poverty to its lofty position as the wealthiest Native American tribe in the US. It owns and operates Foxwoods Resort Casino, one of the largest casinos in the world and, many believe, the most profitable. The complex offers more than 6,400 slot machines and 350 gaming tables in six casinos, three hotels (Grand Pequot Tower, Great Cedar Hotel, Two Trees Inn), 24 restaurants, live entertainment, and a string of retail shops.

The Mashantucket Pequot reservation is a sovereign nation, and the Pequot tribe is not obligated to pay local property or business taxes, or reveal all of its finances. However, estimates of Foxwoods' annual revenues exceed $1 billion. The state of Connecticut receives 25% of the casino's slot machine revenues.

In addition to its gaming operations, the Mashantucket Pequot Tribal Nation owns Fox Navigation (high-speed ferry service) and the Pequot Pharmaceutical Network (mail-order and discount pharmaceuticals). It also owns three Connecticut hotels (Hilton Mystic, Norwich Inn & Spa, Randall's Ordinary Inn) and two golf courses (Foxwoods Golf & Country Club at Boulder Hills and Pequot Golf Club). The Mashantucket Pequot Tribal Nation has even established the Mashantucket Pequot Museum and Research Center dedicated to the tribe's life and history.

Two books released in 2000 and 2001, which questioned the authenticity of the Mashantucket Pequot tribe and claimed that the government was duped into giving them more land for their reservation than they were entitled to, sparked a series of lawsuits from neighboring communities. In early 2002 the Mashantucket Pequot tribe announced it had withdrawn its application to annex 165 acres of land close to its Foxwood Resort Casino, ending nearly 10 years of legal battles.

HISTORY

Once a powerful tribe, the Pequots were virtually wiped out in the 17th century by disease and attacks from colonists. More than 350 years later, Richard "Skip" Hayward, a pipefitter making $15,000 a year, led the fight for federal recognition of his nearly extinct Mashantucket Pequot tribe. He was elected tribal chairman in 1975, and the US government officially recognized the tribe in 1983.

The Indian Gaming Regulatory Act of 1988 opened the door for legal gambling on reservations, but tribes still had to negotiate with state governments for authorization. Hayward hired G. Michael "Mickey" Brown as a consultant and lawyer. Brown took the tribe's legal battle to the US Supreme Court, which eventually ruled that the Pequots could build a casino. When some 30 banks turned down the Pequots for a construction loan, Brown introduced Hayward and his tribe to Lim Goh Tong, billionaire developer of the successful Gentings Highlands Casino resort in Malaysia. Tong invested approximately $60 million, and the Foxwoods casino opened in 1992.

Brown brought in Alfred J. Luciani to serve as president and CEO of Foxwoods. Luciani stayed less than a year, however, resigning because of what he called philosophical differences with tribe leadership. Brown took over as CEO in 1993. Although Foxwoods grew rapidly, Brown often wrestled with members of the tribal council over how the business should be run. The next year Brown rehired Luciani to oversee the development of the Grand Pequot Tower hotel.

Brown resigned and Luciani was fired in 1997 after it was revealed that Brown had not fully disclosed his ties with Lim Goh Tong and that, in 1992, Luciani had accepted a $377,000 loan from Gamma International, a vendor that provided keno services to Foxwoods. The Pequots considered these actions to be conflicts of interest. A new management team was brought in, and Floyd "Bud" Celey, a veteran of Hilton Hotels, was appointed CEO.

The Pequots opened the Mashantucket Pequot Museum and Research Center in 1998. When tribal elections were held later that year, Kenneth Reels was elected chairman of the Pequot's tribal governing body, ousting Hayward from the position he had held for more than 20 years. Hayward was elected vice chairman. Mashantucket Pequot Gaming Enterprise concentrated on improving financial accountability in 1999, and the tribe began cutting costs by shuttering unprofitable holdings, including Pequot River Shipworks, its shipbuilding business.

Former COO William Sherlock replaced Celey as CEO in 2000. That year the first of two books (the second was published in 2001), which questioned the tribe's legitimacy, created some controversy for the group. A federal audit in 2000 revealed that the tribe's pharmaceutical firm was giving discount drugs intended for Native Americans to its non-Native American employees. In 2002 the tribe withdrew its application to annex 165 acres of land close to its Foxwood Resort Casino after nearly 10 years of legal battles.

EXECUTIVES

Chairman, Tribal Council: Kenneth Reels
Vice Chairman, Tribal Council: Richard A. (Skip) Hayward
President and CEO: William Sherlock
COO: Robert Sheldon
EVP Marketing: Robert De Salvio
SVP Administration: Bryce Kirchner
SVP Finance: John O'Brien
SVP Human Resources: Joanne Franks
Director, Public Relations: Arthur Henick
Director, Public Relations: Toni Parker-Johnson
Media Relations Manager: Bryce MacDonald

LOCATIONS

HQ: Rte. 2, Mashantucket, CT 06339
Phone: 860-312-3000 **Fax:** 860-312-1599
Web: www.foxwoods.com

The Mashantucket Pequot Gaming Enterprise has holdings in Connecticut and Rhode Island.

PRODUCTS/OPERATIONS

Selected Operations

Foxwoods Resort Casino
Foxwoods Golf & Country Club at Boulder Hills (Richmond, RI)
Grand Pequot Tower
Great Cedar Hotel
Two Trees Inn

Selected Mashantucket Pequot Tribal Nation Holdings

Fox Navigation (ferry service)
Hilton Mystic (Mystic, CT)
Mashantucket Pequot Gaming Enterprise (Foxwoods Resort Casino; Ledyard, CT)
Mashantucket Pequot Museum and Research Center (Mashantucket, CT
Norwich Inn & Spa (Norwich, CT)
Pequot Golf Club (Stonington, CT)
Pequot Pharmaceutical Network (mail-order and discount pharmaceuticals)
Randall's Ordinary Inn (North Stonington, CT)

COMPETITORS

Aztar
Connecticut Lottery
Harrah's Entertainment
Kerzner International
Mohegan Tribal Gaming
New York State Lottery
Park Place Entertainment
Trump Hotels & Casinos

HISTORICAL FINANCIALS

Company Type: Private

Income Statement FYE: September 30

	ESTIMATED REVENUE ($ mil.)	NET INCOME ($ mil.)	NET PROFIT MARGIN	EMPLOYEES
9/02	1,000	—	—	11,500
9/01	1,500	—	—	11,500
9/00	1,300	—	—	11,500
9/99	1,200	—	—	11,500
9/98	1,000	—	—	11,500
9/97	1,000	—	—	11,180
9/96	1,100	—	—	12,000
9/95	1,030	—	—	11,000
9/94	1,000	—	—	10,000
9/93	1,000	—	—	9,100
Annual Growth	5.2%	—	—	4.8%

Revenue History

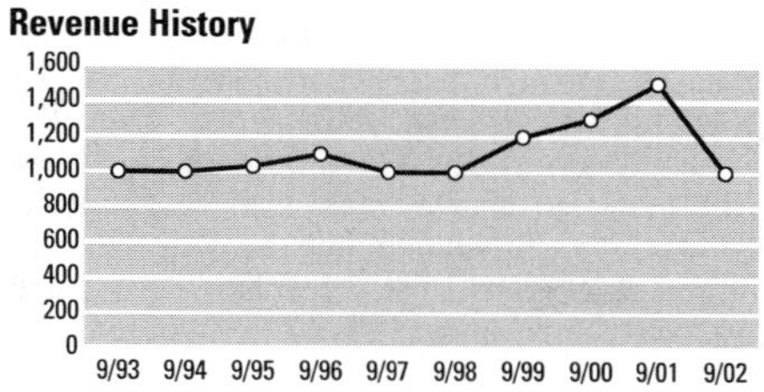

Massachusetts Institute of Technology

The Massachusetts Institute of Technology (MIT) really takes the prize. A leading research institution, the school is granted more patents annually than any other university and 55 people associated with MIT are Nobel Prize recipients. Blending that science and engineering acumen with a top business program, MIT graduates have started more than 4,000 companies — Campbell Soup, Hewlett-Packard, and Intel to name just a few. Tuition for MIT's more than 10,000 students runs about $28,000 a year. The faculty of the 27 academic departments includes over 960 professors. Founded in 1865, MIT is privately endowed.

EXECUTIVES

President: Charles M. Vest, age 62
Chancellor: Phillip Clay
Provost: Robert A. Brown
EVP: John R. Curry
VP for Research and Associate Provost: Alice Gast
VP Information Systems and Professor of Electrical Engineering: James D. Bruce
Director Corporate Relations: Karl F. Koster
VP Human Resources: Laura Avakian, age 57
Auditors: PricewaterhouseCoopers LLP

LOCATIONS

HQ: 77 Massachusetts Ave., Cambridge, MA 02139
Phone: 617-253-1000 **Fax:** 617-253-8000
Web: www.mit.edu

PRODUCTS/OPERATIONS

Schools and Selected Areas of Study

School of Architecture and Planning
Architecture
Urban studies and planning

School of Engineering
Aeronautics and astronautics
Civil and environmental engineering
Materials science
Nuclear engineering
Ocean engineering

School of Humanities, Arts and Social Science
Economics
Foreign languages and literatures
History
Literature
Music and theater arts
Political science

School of Science
Biology
Chemistry
Mathematics
Physics

Sloan School of Management
Whitaker College of Health Sciences and Technology

HISTORICAL FINANCIALS

Company Type: School

Income Statement FYE: June 30

	REVENUE ($ mil.)	NET INCOME ($ mil.)	NET PROFIT MARGIN	EMPLOYEES
6/02	1,665	—	—	9,400
6/01	1,465	—	—	8,700
6/00	2,191	—	—	8,400
6/99	1,549	—	—	6,985
6/98	1,480	—	—	8,500
6/97	1,447	—	—	8,000
6/96	1,360	—	—	8,100
6/95	1,231	—	—	10,000
6/94	1,186	—	—	10,826
6/93	1,251	—	—	—
Annual Growth	3.2%	—	—	(1.8%)

Revenue History

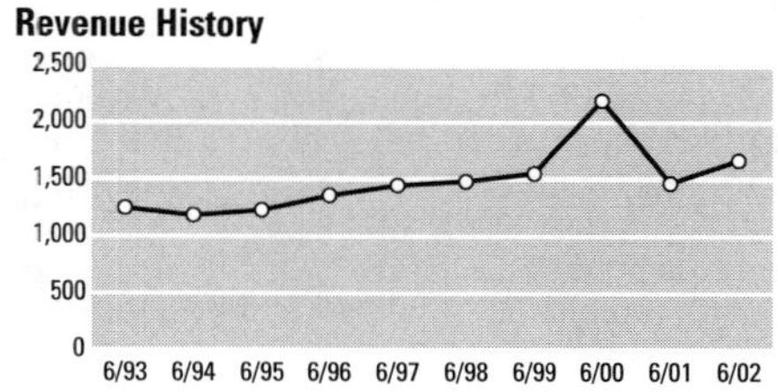

Massachusetts Mutual Life

After flirting with the possibility of demutualizing, Massachusetts Mutual Life Insurance (MassMutual) has decided to stay the course. Founded in 1851, MassMutual sells individuals and small businesses a variety of life insurance and pension products through more than 1,300 offices in the US. Its Financial Services Group offers retirement plans for individuals and businesses, annuities, and trust services (through The MassMutual Trust Company). Other subsidiaries include OppenheimerFunds (mutual funds), David L. Babson & Co. (investor services), and Cornerstone Real Estate (real estate equities).

Like so many other insurance firms, MassMutual is determined to transform into a financial services firm. However, you won't catch the firm issuing stock to get the job done; the management of MassMutual has decided to keep things collective despite pressure from some policyholders.

MassMutual International is exporting the company's operations worldwide, having established subsidiaries in Argentina, Bermuda, Chile, Hong Kong, Japan, Luxembourg, and Taiwan. It focuses on new product development (the majority of sales come from products or channels developed within the last couple of years) and broadened distribution.

MassMutual posted a $1.4 billion net profit in 2002, spearheaded by its worldwide insurance sales, which grew more than 30% compared to 2001.

HISTORY

Insurance agent George Rice formed Massachusetts Mutual in 1851 as a stock company based in Springfield. The firm converted to a mutual in 1867. For its first 50 years MassMutual sold only individual life insurance, but after 1900 it branched out, offering first annuities (1917) and then disability coverage (1918).

The early 20th century was rough on MassMutual, which was forced to raise premiums on new policies during WWI, then faced the high costs of the 1918 flu epidemic. The firm endured the Great Depression despite policy terminations, expanding its product line to include income insurance. In 1946 MassMutual wrote its first group policy, for Jack Daniel's maker Brown-Forman Distillers. By 1950 the company had diversified into medical insurance.

MassMutual began investing in stocks in the 1950s, switching from fixed-return bonds and mortgages for higher returns. It also decentralized and in 1961 began automating operations. By 1970 the firm had installed a computer network linking it to its independent agents. During this period, whole life insurance remained the core product.

With interest rates increasing during the late 1970s, many insurers diversified by offering high-yield products like guaranteed investment contracts funded by high-risk investments. MassMutual resisted as long as it could, but as interest rates soared to 20%, the company experienced a rash of policy loans, which led to a cash crunch. In 1981, with its policy growth rate trailing the industry norm, MassMutual developed new products, including UPDATE, which offered higher dividends in return for adjustable interest on policy loans.

In the 1980s MassMutual reduced its stock investment (to about 5% of total investments by 1987), allowing it to emerge virtually unscathed from the 1987 stock market crash.

The firm changed course in 1990 and entered financial services. It bought a controlling interest in mutual fund manager Oppenheimer Management. MassMutual announced in 1993 that, with legislation limiting rates, it would stop writing new individual and small-group policies in New York.

The next year the company targeted the neglected family-owned business niche; in 1995 it sponsored the American Alliance of Family-Owned Businesses and rolled out new whole life products aimed at this segment. That year it bought David L. Babson & Company, a Massachusetts-based investment management firm, and opened life insurance companies in Chile and Argentina.

In 1996 MassMutual merged with Connecticut Mutual. It also acquired Antares Leveraged Capital Corp. (commercial finance) and Charter Oak Capital Management (investment advisory services). The next year MassMutual sold its Life & Health Benefits Management subsidiary.

Still in the mood to merge, the company entered discussions with Northwestern Mutual in 1998, but culture clashes terminated the talks. Also that year the company helped push through legislation that would allow insurers to issue stock through mutual holding companies, a move which MassMutual itself contemplated in 1999.

MassMutual expanded outside the US at the turn of the century. In 1999 it issued securities in Europe, opened offices in such locales as Bermuda and Luxembourg, and bought the Argentina operations of Jefferson-Pilot. A year later it expanded into Asia when it bought Hong Kong-based CRC Protective Life Insurance (now MassMutual Asia). In 2001 the company entered the Taiwanese market, buying a stake in Mercuries Life Insurance (now MassMutual Mercuries Life Insurance) and acquired Japanese insurer Aetna Heiwa Life (a subsidiary of US health insurer Aetna).

EXECUTIVES

Chairman, President, and CEO: Robert J. O'Connell
EVP and CFO: Howard E. Gunton
EVP and CIO: Christine M. Modie
EVP and Chief Investment Officer; Chairman and CEO, David L. Babson & Company: Stuart H. Reese
EVP and General Counsel: Lawrence V. Burkett Jr.
EVP, Human Resources, Services, Communications, and State Government Relations: Susan A. Alfano
EVP, Individual Insurance Group, Product, Sales, and Marketing: Matthew E. Winter
EVP, Individual Insurance Group, Shared Services and Large Corporate Markets: James E. Miller
EVP, Retirement Services: Frederick C. Castellani
EVP; Chairman, President, and CEO, OppenheimerFunds: John V. Murphy
SVP, Corporate Communications: Frances B. Emerson
SVP, Corporate Financial: Michael T. Rollings
SVP, Corporate Human Resources: Nancy M. Roberts
SVP, Corporate Services: Colin C. Collins
SVP, Corporate Tax: Richard D. Bourgeois
Auditors: PricewaterhouseCoopers LLP

LOCATIONS

HQ: Massachusetts Mutual Life Insurance Company
1295 State St., Springfield, MA 01111
Phone: 413-788-8411 **Fax:** 413-744-6005
Web: www.massmutual.com

Massachusetts Mutual Life Insurance operates in Argentina, Bermuda, Chile, Hong Kong, Japan, Luxembourg, Taiwan, and the US.

PRODUCTS/OPERATIONS

Major Subsidiaries

Antares Capital Corporation (commercial finance)
C.M. Life Insurance Company
Cornerstone Real Estate Advisers, Inc. (real estate equities)
David L. Babson and Company, Inc. (institutional investment services)
MassMutual International, Inc.
MassMutual Trust Company, F.S.B.
MML Bay State Life Insurance Company
MML Investors Services, Inc.
OppenheimerFunds, Inc. (mutual funds)

COMPETITORS

AIG American General
Allianz
Allstate
American Financial
AIG
AXA Financial
Charles Schwab
CIGNA
Citigroup
CNA Financial
Conseco
FMR
Guardian Life
The Hartford
Jefferson-Pilot
John Hancock Financial Services
Liberty Mutual
Mellon Financial
Merrill Lynch
MetLife
Nationwide
New York Life
Northwestern Mutual
Principal Financial
Prudential
Retirement System Group
St. Paul Companies
State Farm
TIAA-CREF
Torchmark
UBS Financial Services

HISTORICAL FINANCIALS

Company Type: Mutual company

Income Statement FYE: December 31

	ASSETS ($ mil.)	NET INCOME ($ mil.)	INCOME AS % OF ASSETS	EMPLOYEES
12/02	84,102	1,408	1.7%	9,000
12/01	78,934	791	1.0%	9,000
12/00	73,739	740	1.0%	8,000
12/99	70,586	441	0.6%	7,900
12/98	66,979	359	0.5%	7,885
12/97	61,069	262	0.4%	—
12/96	55,752	239	0.4%	—
12/95	38,632	159	0.4%	—
12/94	35,720	93	0.3%	—
12/93	34,699	139	0.4%	—
Annual Growth	10.3%	29.3%	—	3.4%

2002 Year-End Financials

Equity as % of assets: 7.3%
Return on assets: 1.7%
Return on equity: 25.0%
Long-term debt ($ mil.): —
Sales ($ mil.): 16,253

Net Income History

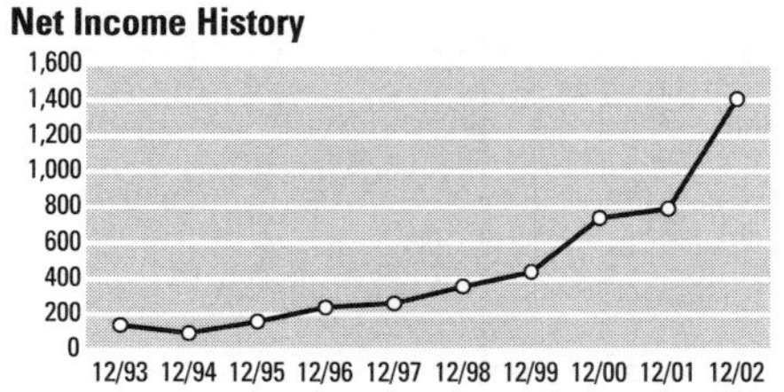

MasterCard Incorporated

Surpassing Visa in market share — *that* would be priceless. MasterCard is the US's #2 payment system and is owned by its 25,000 financial institution members worldwide. It markets the MasterCard (credit and debit cards) and Maestro (debit cards) brands, provides the transaction authorization network, and collects fees from members. Its cards are accepted at more than 30 million global locations. MasterCard also operates the Cirrus ATM network and Mondex International, a chip-based smart card subsidiary. In 2002 MasterCard acquired Europay International and renamed it MasterCard Europe, a wholly owned subsidiary through which most of its European business is now conducted.

Citigroup, J.P. Morgan Chase, and BANK ONE each own about 7% of MasterCard.

Long considered more downmarket than Visa, MasterCard is working to add affluent users (the World MasterCard offers 24-hour concierge services).

The company is working amid growing competition to make its electronic smart card (single-use or refillable chip-based cards used as cash) the industry standard through Mondex. Smart cards are common in Europe, but have met consumer resistance in the US. MasterCard is launching smart card initiatives in Asia and moving into wireless e-commerce; it is teaming up with Oberthur Card Systems to develop secure methods to make purchases over wireless devices. And in December 2002 the company initiated a market test of MasterCard PayPass, a new "contactless" radio frequency chip solution enabling users to tap or wave their payment card over a terminal.

MasterCard's quest for market share led to its merger with Europay, the firm's European counterpart, in mid-2002. European members now own about a third of the newly created holding company, MasterCard Inc. While consolidating Maestro's ownership (Europay and MasterCard had owned it 50-50) has given MasterCard control of the world's largest debit card network, it continues to trail Visa in credit cards.

The company hopes to continue growing by increasing the number of places MasterCard is accepted, focusing specifically on mobile and electronic commerce, fast-food restaurants, and public sector payments such as taxes, fines, and tolls.

HISTORY

A group of bankers formed The Interbank Card Association (ICA) in 1966 to establish authorization, clearing, and settlement procedures for bank credit card transactions. This was particularly important to banks left out of the rapidly growing BankAmericard (later Visa) network sponsored by Bank of America.

By 1969, ICA was issuing the Master Charge card throughout the US and had formed alliances in Europe and Japan. In the mid-1970s ICA modernized its system, replacing telephone transaction authorization with a computerized magnetic strip system. ICA had members in Africa, Australia, and Europe by 1979. That year the organization changed its name (and the card's) to MasterCard.

In 1980 Russell Hogg became president when John Reynolds resigned after disagreeing with the board over company performance and direction. Hogg made major organizational changes and consolidated data processing in St. Louis. MasterCard began offering debit cards in 1980 and traveler's checks in 1981.

MasterCard issued the first credit cards in China in 1987. The next year it bought Cirrus, then the world's largest ATM network. It also secured Eurocard (now Europay) to supervise MasterCard's European operations and help build the brand.

Hogg resigned in 1988 after disagreements with the board, and was succeeded by Alex Hart. In 1991 the Maestro debit card was unveiled.

The 1990s were marked by trouble in Europe: The Europay pact hadn't resulted in the boom MasterCard had hoped for, customer service was below par, and competition was keen. Alex Hart retired in 1994 and was succeeded by Eugene Lockhart, who tackled the European woes. Lockhart considered ending the relationship but eventually worked things out with Europay. By the end of the decade, Europay was locked in a vicious battle to undercut Visa's market share through lower fees.

MasterCard in 1995 invested in UK-based Mondex International, maker of electronic, set-value, refillable smart cards. But US consumer resistance to cash cards and competition in the more advanced European market delayed growth in this area.

In October 1996 a group of merchants, including Wal-Mart and Sears, filed class-action lawsuits against both MasterCard and Visa, challenging the "honor all cards" rule. Because usage fees are higher, merchants don't want to accept consumers' MasterCard- or Visa-branded off-line, or signature-based debit cards, and claim the card issuers are violating antitrust laws by tying acceptance of debit to that of credit. (In a dramatic twist, minutes before the trial was set to begin in 2003, MasterCard announced an undisclosed settlement.)

Lockhart resigned in 1997 and was succeeded by former head of overseas operations Robert Selander. The next year the Justice Department sued MasterCard and Visa for prohibiting member banks from issuing competing credit cards, such as American Express' Optima. That year MasterCard and Visa came under scrutiny for attempting to create a debit card monopoly.

Yet another management upheaval began in 1999 as the company moved to streamline its organizational structure and shift away from geographical divisions. It also said member banks could boost visibility by putting their logos on card fronts and moving MasterCard's logo to the back.

In 2000 the Justice Department charged MasterCard and Visa with antitrust practices stemming from the companies' cross-ownership structure and an alleged noncompetitive alliance between them. The next year a federal judge ordered the two companies to allow their member banks to issue rival credit cards, but the order has been stayed pending appeal.

In 2002 MasterCard merged with Europay, the Belgium-based card company with which it already had close ties. As part of the transaction, holding company MasterCard Inc. was formed; MasterCard International became its main subsidiary and Europay became its Europe Region.

EXECUTIVES

Chairman Emeritus: Donald L. Boudreau, age 62
Chairman: Lance L. Weaver, age 48
President and CEO: Robert W. Selander, age 52, $3,283,000 pay
President, Asia/Pacific Region: André Sekulic
President, Europe Region: Peter Hoch
President, Latin America/Caribbean Region: Jean F. Rozwadowski
President, MasterCard Canada: Walter M. Macnee
President, North American Region: Ruth Ann Marshall
President, South Asia/Middle East/Africa Region: Sonny Sannon
SEVP, Customer Group: Alan J. Heuer, $1,475,000 pay
SEVP, Global Development: Christopher D. Thom, $1,200,000 pay
SEVP, Global Technology and Operations: Jerry McElhatton, $1,400,000 pay
EVP, CFO, and Treasurer: Denise K. Fletcher, age 54, $825,000 pay
EVP and Chief e-Business Officer, Global Development: Arthur D. Kranzley
EVP and Chief Marketing Officer: Lawrence (Larry) Flanagan
EVP, Central Resources: Michael W. Michl
EVP, Global Account Management: Gary Flood
EVP, MasterCard Advisors: G. Henry Mundt III
SVP and Business Finance Officer, Global Development: Spencer Schwarz
SVP and Controller: Chris A. McWilton
SVP, General Counsel, and Secretary: Noah J. Hanft
SVP and Assistant General Counsel: Joshua L. Peirez
VP, Global Communications: Sharon Gamsin
Auditors: PricewaterhouseCoopers LLP

LOCATIONS

HQ: 2000 Purchase St., Purchase, NY 10577
Phone: 914-249-2000 **Fax:** 914-249-4206
Web: www.mastercardintl.com

MasterCard has US offices in California, Delaware, Florida, Georgia, Illinois, Missouri, New York, and Washington, DC. It has international offices in Argentina, Australia, Belgium, Brazil, Canada, Chile, China, Colombia, Hong Kong, India, Indonesia, Japan, Malaysia, Mexico, the Philippines, Singapore, South Africa, South Korea, Taiwan, Thailand, the United Arab Emirates, the UK, and Venezuela. It provides services in more than 210 countries.

PRODUCTS/OPERATIONS

Products

Cirrus Card
Corporate Fleet MasterCard Card
Corporate MasterCard Card
Gold MasterCard Card
Maestro Card
MasterCard BusinessCard Card
MasterCard Corporate Executive Card
MasterCard Corporate Multi Card
MasterCard Corporate Purchasing Card
MasterCard Executive BusinessCard Card
MasterCard mc2
MasterCard travelers cheques
Mondex Card
Platinum MasterCard Card
Prepaid programs
Standard MasterCard Card
World MasterCard Card

COMPETITORS

American Express
Morgan Stanley
Visa

HISTORICAL FINANCIALS

Company Type: Holding company

Income Statement FYE: December 31

	ASSETS ($ mil.)	NET INCOME ($ mil.)	INCOME AS % OF ASSETS	EMPLOYEES
12/02	2,261	116	5.1%	4,000
12/01	1,486	142	9.6%	3,300
12/00	1,182	118	10.0%	3,100
12/99	973	86	8.9%	2,700
12/98	841	57	6.8%	2,400
12/97	651	40	6.1%	2,357
12/96	—	72	—	2,025
12/95	—	22	—	2,000
12/94	—	12	—	1,975
12/93	—	—	—	1,300
Annual Growth	28.3%	33.1%	—	13.3%

2002 Year-End Financials

Equity as % of assets: 45.3%
Return on assets: 6.2%
Return on equity: 14.3%
Long-term debt ($ mil.): 80
Sales ($ mil.): 1,892

Net Income History

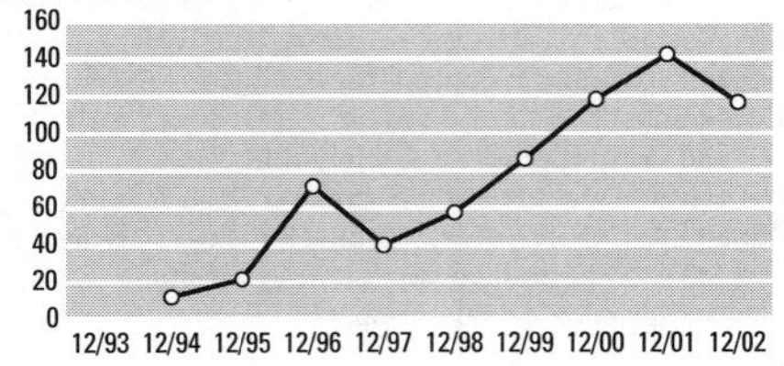

Mayer, Brown, Rowe & Maw

Practicing law is a supreme calling for many attorneys at Mayer, Brown, Rowe & Maw (formerly Mayer, Brown & Platt). One of the largest law firms in the US, Mayer, Brown was one of the first to specialize in arguing cases before the Supreme Court. The firm has over 1,300 lawyers at its 13 offices in the US and Europe, offering their expertise in corporate and securities law and litigation, global trade, and real estate. Founded in 1881 in Chicago, the firm has represented clients such as Dow Chemical, America Online (now Time Warner Inc.), and BMW.

Mayer, Brown is also noted for being one of the first of the top 20 law firms to elect a woman as managing partner (1991) and for having a large percentage of female lawyers.

EXECUTIVES

Chairman: Tyrone C. Fahner
Executive Director: Steven R. Wells
CFO: Alan S. Cohen
Director Human Resources: Coleen Callahan

LOCATIONS

HQ: 190 S. LaSalle St., Chicago, IL 60603
Phone: 312-782-0600 **Fax:** 312-701-7711
Web: www.mayerbrownrowe.com

The firm has US offices in Charlotte, North Carolina; Chicago; Houston; Los Angeles; New York City; Palo Alto, California; and Washington, DC. International offices include Brussels; Cologne and Frankfurt, Germany; London and Manchester, UK; and Paris.

PRODUCTS/OPERATIONS

Selected Practice Areas

Bankruptcy
Corporate and securities
Environmental
Government relations
International trade
Labor
Litigation
Real estate
Taxation
Venture capital

COMPETITORS

Baker & McKenzie
Jenner & Block
Jones Day
Katten Muchin
Kirkland & Ellis
Latham & Watkins
McDermott, Will
Sidley Austin Brown & Wood
Skadden, Arps
White & Case
Winston & Strawn

HISTORICAL FINANCIALS

Company Type: Partnership

Income Statement FYE: December 31

	REVENUE ($ mil.)	NET INCOME ($ mil.)	NET PROFIT MARGIN	EMPLOYEES
12/02	705	—	—	—
12/01	573	—	—	—
12/00	534	—	—	1,000
12/99	464	—	—	820
12/98	400	—	—	816
12/97	340	—	—	695
12/96	325	—	—	643
12/95	274	—	—	550
12/94	263	—	—	550
12/93	253	—	—	533
Annual Growth	12.1%	—	—	9.4%

Revenue History

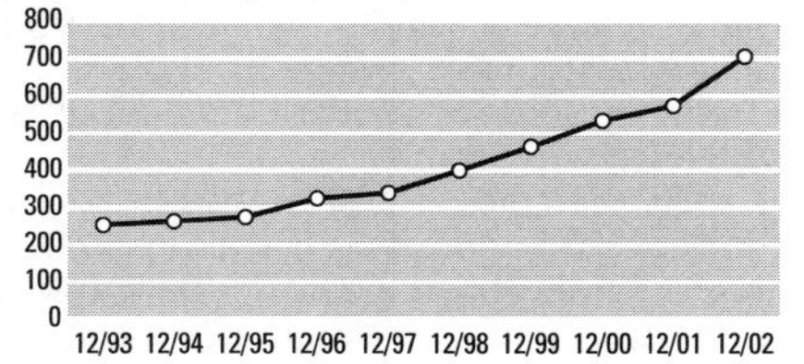

Mayo Foundation

Mayo can whip up a medical miracle. The not-for-profit Mayo Foundation provides health care, most notably for difficult medical conditions, through its renowned Mayo Clinic in Rochester, Minnesota. Its multidisciplinary approach to care attracts some 500,000 patients a year, including such notables as Ronald and Nancy Reagan and the late King Hussein of Jordan. The Mayo Health System is a network of 13 affiliated community hospitals and clinics in several select states. The Mayo Foundation also conducts research and trains physicians, nurses, and other health professionals. The Mayo Foundation dates back to a frontier practice launched by William Mayo in 1863.

In addition to the Mayo Clinic, the foundation operates two other Rochester hospitals — Saint Mary's and Rochester Methodist. It has clinics in Arizona and Florida and operates 13 hospitals in Iowa, Minnesota, and Wisconsin. At the University of Minnesota, the foundation's education programs include the Mayo Graduate School of Medicine and the Mayo School of Health-Related Sciences.

With managed care limiting patients' ability to use its facilities, Mayo forms referral alliances with hospital groups, HMOs, and other groups. Its charter prevents it from raising prices to compensate for rising health care costs, so the foundation commercializes medical technology, publishes medical literature, and invests in other medical startups to increase income. Also, affluent patients who can pay — well — for treatment (and who may contribute to the endowment) help subsidize care for those who can't pay.

HISTORY

In 1845 William Mayo came to the US from England. He was a doctor, veterinarian, river boatman, surveyor, and newspaper editor before settling in Rochester, Minnesota, in 1863.

When a tornado struck Rochester in 1883, Mayo took charge of a makeshift hospital. The Sisters of St. Francis offered to replace the hospital that was lost in the disaster if Mayo would head the staff. He agreed reluctantly. Not only were hospitals then associated with the poor and insane, but his affiliation with the sisters raised eyebrows among Protestants and Catholics.

Saint Marys Hospital opened in 1889. Mayo's sons William and Charles, who were starting their medical careers, helped him. After the elder Mayo retired, the sons ran the hospital. Although the brothers accepted all medical cases, they made the hospital self-sufficient, attracting paying patients by pioneering in specialization at a time when physicians were jacks-of-all-medical-trades.

This specialization attracted other physicians, and by 1907 the practice was known as "the Mayo's clinic." The brothers, in association with the University of Minnesota, established the Mayo Foundation for Medical Research (now the Mayo Graduate School of Medicine), the world's first program to train medical specialists, in 1915.

In 1919 the brothers transferred the clinic properties and miscellaneous financial assets, primarily from patient care profits, into the Mayo Properties Association (renamed the Mayo Foundation in 1964). Under the terms of the endowment, all Mayo Clinic medical staff members became salaried employees. In 1933 the clinic established one of the first blood banks in the US. Both brothers died in 1939.

Part of the association's mission was to fund research. In 1950 two Mayo researchers won a Nobel Prize for developing cortisone to treat rheumatoid arthritis. The foundation opened its second medical school, the Mayo Medical School, in 1972.

As insurers in the 1980s pressured to cut hospital admissions and stays, the foundation diversified with for-profit ventures. In 1983 Mayo began publishing the *Mayo Clinic Health Letter*, its first subscription publication for a general audience, and the *Mayo Clinic Family Health Book*. It also began providing specialized lab services to other doctors and hospitals. The addition of Rochester Methodist Hospital (creating the largest not-for-profit medical group in the country) was also a response to financial pressures. Following the money south as affluent folks retired, the foundation opened clinics in Jacksonville (1986); Scottsdale, Arizona (1987); and in nearby Phoenix (1998).

Seeking to expand in its home market, Mayo in 1992 formed the Mayo Health System, a regional network of health care facilities and medical practices. In 1996 former patient Barbara Woodward Lips left $127.9 million to the foundation, the largest bequest in its history.

In the late 1990s the foundation increasingly looked to corporate partnerships to help defray costs and to expand research activities. In 1998 and 1999 Mayo boosted its presence overseas with nonmedical regional offices. Mayo scientists in 2000 announced they had regrown or repaired nerve coverings in mice; this type of damage in humans (caused by such conditions as multiple sclerosis) had been considered irreparable. The Mayo Foundation continues to push for breakthroughs in medical science.

EXECUTIVES

Chairman: Bert A. Getz, age 64
President and CEO: Michael B. Wood
CFO and Treasurer, Mayo Foundation; Chair Department of Finance: David R. Ebel
VP and Director for Education: Thomas Berquist
VP, Chief Administrative Officer, and Secretary: Robert K. Smoldt
VP: Denis A. Cortese
Chair, Human Resources: Marita Heller
General Counsel: Jonathan Oviatt
Chief Development Officer: James Schroeder
Director for Development: E. Rolland Dickson
Administrator, Mayo Clinic Scottsdale: James G. Anderson
Chair, Board of Governors, Mayo Clinic Jacksonville: George B. Bartley
Chair, Department of Radiation Oncology, Mayo Clinic Scottsdale: Michele Y. Halyard
Chair, Board of Governors, Mayo Clinic Rochester: Hugh C. Smith
Chair, Department of Surgery, Mayo Clinic Scottsdale: Victor F. Trastek
Vice Chair, Board of Governors, Mayo Clinic Rochester: Sylvester Sterioff
Director, Mayo Clinic Cancer Center: Franklyn G. Prendergast, age 57

LOCATIONS

HQ: 200 1st St. SW, Rochester, MN 55905
Phone: 507-284-2511 **Fax:** 507-284-0161
Web: www.mayo.edu

The Mayo Foundation operates facilities in Rochester, Minnesota; Jacksonville; and Phoenix and Scottsdale, Arizona, it also has a network of community health care providers in Iowa, Minnesota, and Wisconsin.

PRODUCTS/OPERATIONS

Principal Divisions

Charter House, Rochester (retirement community)
Mayo Clinic Hospital, Phoenix
Mayo Clinic Jacksonville
Mayo Clinic Rochester
Mayo Clinic Scottsdale
Mayo Health System (network of clinics and hospitals in Iowa, Minnesota, and Wisconsin)
Rochester Methodist Hospital
Saint Marys Hospital, Rochester
St. Luke's Hospital, Jacksonville

Selected Mayo Publications:

Publications for Patients
Inside Mayo Clinic *(Rochester)*
The Mayo Checkup *(Jacksonville)*
Mayo Clinic Complete Book of Pregnancy & Baby's First Year
Mayo Clinic Family Health Book
Mayo Clinic Guide to Self-Care
Mayo Clinic Health Letter
Mayo Clinic Heart Book
Mayo Clinic on Arthritis
Mayo Clinic on High Blood Pressure
The Mayo Clinic Williams-Sonoma Cookbook
Mayo Clinic Women's HealthSource
Perspectives on Mayo
Update *(Scottsdale)*

Publications for Physicians
Clinical Update
Dialogue
Mayo Clinic Cardiology Review
Mayo Clinic Proceedings
Mayo Medical Laboratories Communique
Mayo Medical Laboratories Interpretive Handbook
Medical Update *(Jacksonville)*

COMPETITORS

Allina Hospitals
Ascension
Catholic Health Initiatives
Catholic Healthcare Partners
Detroit Medical Center
HCA
Health Management Associates
HEALTHSOUTH
Henry Ford Health System
Johns Hopkins Medicine
Memorial Sloan-Kettering
Methodist Health Care
New York City Health and Hospitals
Rush System for Health
Scripps
SSM Health Care
Tenet Healthcare
Trinity Health
Universal Health Services

HISTORICAL FINANCIALS

Company Type: Not-for-profit

Income Statement FYE: December 31

	REVENUE ($ mil.)	NET INCOME ($ mil.)	NET PROFIT MARGIN	EMPLOYEES
12/02	4,425	—	—	41,527
12/01	4,135	—	—	45,536
12/00	3,710	—	—	44,000
12/99	2,750	—	—	41,265
12/98	2,370	—	—	32,531
12/97	2,566	—	—	30,497
12/96	2,348	—	—	28,671
12/95	2,189	—	—	25,433
12/94	1,873	—	—	21,856
12/93	1,579	—	—	21,770
Annual Growth	12.1%	—	—	7.4%

Revenue History

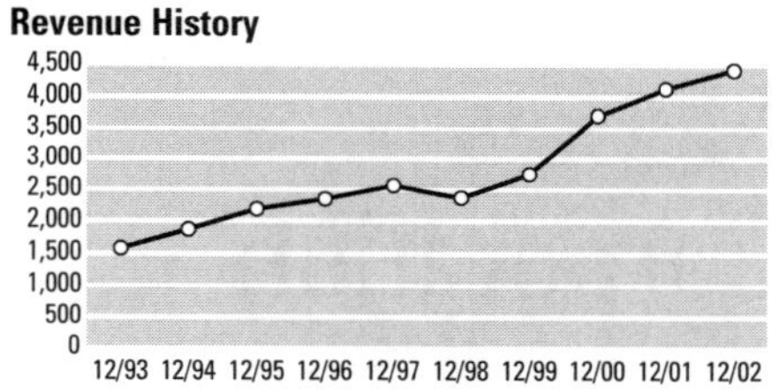

MBM Corporation

What's on the menu at your favorite restaurant? Just ask MBM Corporation, one of the leading privately owned custom food service distributors in the US. The company specializes in providing food to national restaurant chains such as Arby's, Burger King, Chick-fil-A, and Darden Restaurants (Red Lobster, Olive Garden, Bahama Breeze). MBM fills its customers' orders through its network of about 30 distribution centers across the US. J. R. Wordsworth founded the company about 50 years ago as a retail food distributor. MBM made the transition to its present role in restaurant food distribution after Wordsworth's children bought the business in the 1970s.

EXECUTIVES

Chairman and President: Jerry L. Wordsworth
CFO: Jeff Kowalk
Director of Human Resources: Tim Ozment

LOCATIONS

HQ: 2641 Meadowbrook Rd., Rocky Mount, NC 27802
Phone: 252-985-7200 **Fax:** 252-985-7241

COMPETITORS

Ben E. Keith
Clark Products
Golden State Foods
Gordon Food Service
Martin-Brower
McLane
McLane Foodservice
Performance Food
Reyes Holdings
Sodexho
SYSCO
U.S. Foodservice

HISTORICAL FINANCIALS

Company Type: Private

Income Statement FYE: December 31

	REVENUE ($ mil.)	NET INCOME ($ mil.)	NET PROFIT MARGIN	EMPLOYEES
12/02	4,236	—	—	3,500
12/01	4,236	—	—	3,500
12/00	3,823	—	—	2,500
12/99	2,700	—	—	2,364
12/98	2,500	—	—	1,600
12/97	2,000	—	—	1,500
12/96	1,800	—	—	—
Annual Growth	15.3%	—	—	18.5%

Revenue History

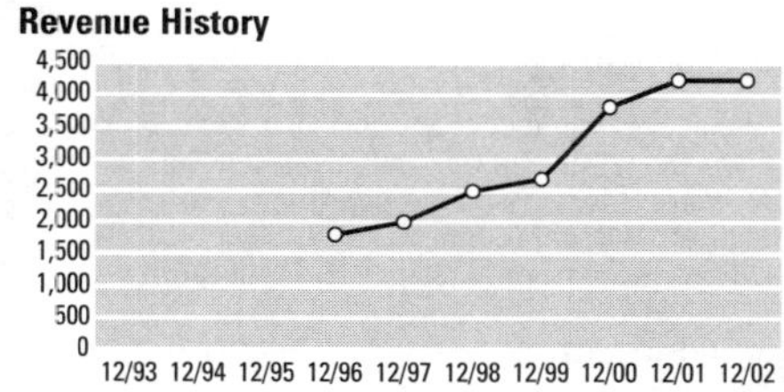

McCarthy Building

A company that was in construction before Reconstruction, McCarthy Building Companies is one of the oldest privately held builders in the US. The general contractor and construction manager has projects worldwide and ranks among the top builders of health care facilities in the US.

Contracts include heavy construction projects (bridges and water and waste-treatment plants), industrial projects (biopharmaceutical, food processing, and microelectronics facilities), commercial projects (retail and office buildings), and institutional projects (airports, prisons, and schools).

Timothy McCarthy founded the firm in 1864. His great-grandson, chairman emeritus Michael McCarthy, sold the firm to its employees in 2002.

EXECUTIVES

Chairman Emeritus: Michael M. McCarthy, age 65
Chairman and CEO: Michael D. Bolen, age 54
President, COO and Director: Michael D. Hurst, age 51
EVP, CFO, Treasurer and Director: George F. Scherer, age 58
SVP, General Counsel, Secretary and Director: James A. Staskiel, age 47
VP Human Resources: Jan Kraemer
Director Corporate Communications: Michael (Mike) Lenzen
Auditors: Ernst & Young LLP

LOCATIONS

HQ: McCarthy Building Companies, Inc.
1341 N. Rock Hill Rd., St. Louis, MO 63124
Phone: 314-968-3300 **Fax:** 314-968-3037
Web: www.mccarthy.com

McCarthy Building Companies has offices in Dallas; Newport Beach, Sacramento, and San Francisco, California; Las Vegas; Phoenix; and St. Louis. It also has operations in Canada, Egypt, Japan, Malaysia, Mexico, Panama, Saudi Arabia, and the US Virgin Islands.

PRODUCTS/OPERATIONS

2003 Sales

	% of total
Commercial	31
Health care	20
Science & technology	14
Education	9
Institutional	9
Heavy/civil	7
Parking	6
Industrial	4
Total	**100**

Selected Projects

Anaheim Entertainment Parking Structure (California)
Arizona Department of Corrections (Perryville)
Blue Water Bridge (Port Huron, MI)
Bridgeport Hospital (Connecticut)
Children's Hospital of Wisconsin (Milwaukee)
Grand Glaize Waste Treatment (Valley Park, MO)
Hewlett Packard Fast Fab Facility (Corvallis, OR)
Hilton Hotel & Vertical Expansion (Bridgeport, CT)
Hollywood & Highland Academy Awards Theatre (Los Angeles)
Houston Intercontinental Airport
King County Regional Justice Center (Kent, WA)
Lambert-St. Louis International Airport — East Parking
Port of Houston's Port Terminal Railroad Lead Track (Deer Park, TX)
Sky Harbor International Airport — Rental Car Garage (Phoenix)
Space Needle Renovations (Seattle)
St. Joseph's Hospital (Marshfield, WI)
St. Louis City Justice Center
St. Louis Public Schools
United Parcel Service (Redmond, WA)
University Hospital (Denver)

COMPETITORS

Barton Malow
Bechtel
Bovis Lend Lease
Centex
DPR Construction
Gilbane
Hensel Phelps Construction
Peter Kiewit Sons'
Skanska
Swinerton
Turner Corporation

HISTORICAL FINANCIALS

Company Type: Private

Income Statement FYE: March 31

	REVENUE ($ mil.)	NET INCOME ($ mil.)	NET PROFIT MARGIN	EMPLOYEES
3/03	1,024	—	—	2,000
3/02	1,050	—	—	2,500
3/01	1,205	—	—	2,500
3/00	940	—	—	2,500
3/99	1,200	—	—	2,000
3/98	1,134	—	—	2,000
3/97	1,059	—	—	1,300
3/96	795	—	—	1,000
3/95	950	—	—	525
3/94	705	—	—	450
Annual Growth	4.2%	—	—	18.0%

Revenue History

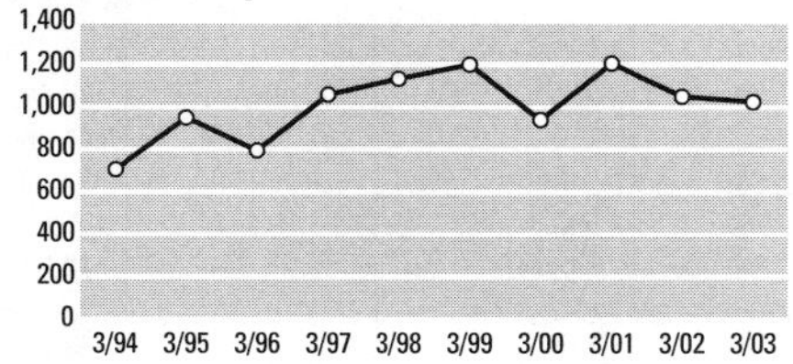

McCoy Corporation

Even though it's battling building supply retail leaders The Home Depot and Lowe's, McCoy still has time for a day off. The company owns and operates about 90 McCoy's Building Supply Centers located primarily in Texas, but also in Arkansas, Louisiana, Mississippi, New Mexico, and Oklahoma. McCoy's locations adhere to the retailer's steadfast tradition of keeping stores closed on Sundays. In addition, McCoy is an affiliate of the TruServ hardware cooperative. In 2001 Mike McCoy and his sister Brenda sold their interest in the business to their brother Brian. Their grandfather, Frank, founded a roofing company in 1923, which their father, Emmett, combined with McCoy Supply to form the current company.

EXECUTIVES

President, CEO, and Director: Brian F. McCoy
EVP, CFO, and Director: C.R. Churchwell III
VP and Controller: Rick Neal
VP of Business Development: John Meeks
VP of Human Resources: Kent Williams
VP of Information Technology: Dennis Strong
VP of Marketing: Dan Stauffer
VP of Operations: James Lewallen
VP of Purchasing: Greg Pannell
VP of Store Development: Art Johnson
Secretary: Nancy Rodriguez
Auditors: Lolley & Fontenot, P.C.

LOCATIONS

HQ: 1200 IH-35 North, San Marcos, TX 78666
Phone: 512-353-5400 **Fax:** 512-395-6608
Web: www.mccoys.com

COMPETITORS

84 Lumber
Ace Hardware
Building Materials Holding
Foxworth-Galbraith Lumber
Home Depot
Lowe's
Stock Building Supply
Sutherland Lumber
TruServ

HISTORICAL FINANCIALS

Company Type: Private

Income Statement FYE: December 31

	REVENUE ($ mil.)	NET INCOME ($ mil.)	NET PROFIT MARGIN	EMPLOYEES
12/02	452	—	—	2,200
12/01	450	—	—	2,200
12/00	467	—	—	2,500
12/99	504	—	—	2,500
12/98	454	—	—	1,816
12/97	420	—	—	1,700
12/96	432	—	—	1,700
12/95	441	—	—	1,700
12/94	400	—	—	1,600
12/93	370	—	—	1,300
Annual Growth	2.2%	—	—	6.0%

Revenue History

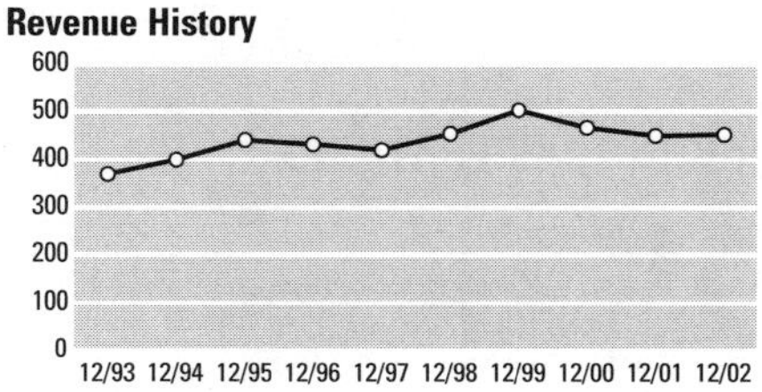

McDavid Auto Group

McDavid Auto Group has plenty of horsepower for the Lone Star State. The company, a part of Asbury Automotive Group, is one of the largest vehicle vendors in Texas, with about a dozen dealerships in Austin, Houston, and Dallas. McDavid Auto Group sells new cars made by Acura, Ford, General Motors, Honda, Kia, Nissan, and Suzuki. It also sells used cars and provides parts and service. The company was originally named for its founder and former CEO, David McDavid, who started his first car dealership in 1962 at age 19; he is a former minority owner of the Dallas Mavericks basketball team. McDavid sold 70% of the company to Asbury in 1998.

EXECUTIVES

President and CEO: Michael Kane
CFO: Jay Torda
VP, Operations: David McDavid Jr.
VP, Operations: Jimmy McDavid
Payroll and Human Resources Director: Kristy Pyatt

LOCATIONS

HQ: 3700 W. Airport Fwy., Irving, TX 75062
Phone: 972-790-6100 **Fax:** 972-986-5689
Web: www.mcdavid.com

COMPETITORS

Allen Samuels Enterprises
Ancira
AutoNation
CarMax
CarsDirect.com
Don Davis Auto Group
Gillman
Group 1 Automotive
Gulf States Toyota
Gunn Automotive
Huffines Automotive
McCombs Automotive
McCombs Enterprises
Sonic Automotive
VT

HISTORICAL FINANCIALS

Company Type: Private

Income Statement FYE: December 31

	REVENUE ($ mil.)	NET INCOME ($ mil.)	NET PROFIT MARGIN	EMPLOYEES
12/02	600	—	—	1,100
12/01	700	—	—	1,200
12/00	596	—	—	1,100
12/99	575	—	—	1,050
12/98	550	—	—	1,000
12/97	542	—	—	1,000
12/96	512	—	—	930
12/95	500	—	—	928
12/94	420	—	—	870
Annual Growth	4.6%	—	—	3.0%

Revenue History

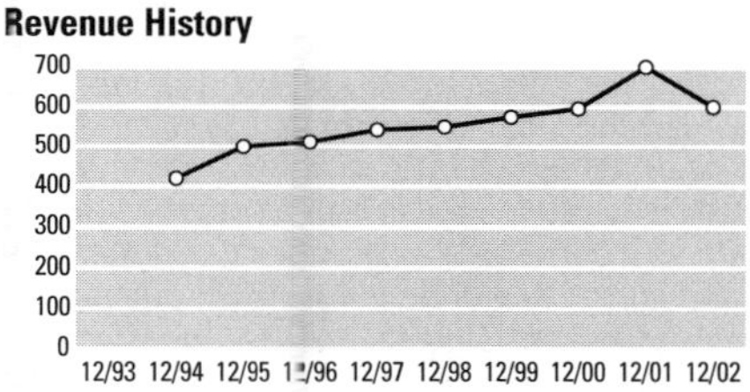

McDermott, Will & Emery

Not only is McDermott, Will & Emery one of the largest law firms in the US, it was also one of the first law firms to admit a female to its partnership ranks. The firm has more than 900 attorneys in eight US offices and international offices in London and Düsseldorf and Munich, Germany. McDermott, Will & Emery's multiple practice areas include antitrust, corporate, employee benefits, estate planning, health law, intellectual property, international, regulation and government affairs, tax, and trial law. The firm has represented clients such as the City of Anaheim, California (in a case related to Orange County's bankruptcy); Ford; and Chiquita Brands International. E. H. McDermott founded the firm in 1934.

EXECUTIVES

Chairman: Lawrence (Larry) Gerber
Vice Chairman: Alan J. Olson
Executive Director of Administration: Louis Covotsos
Executive Director of Operations: Lewis Liszt
Director of Finance: David Alexander
Director of Human Resources: Donna Daly
Director of Practice Development: Amy Nigrelli
Director of Professional Development: Sharon Abrahams
Information Technology Partner: Jeffrey C. Schwarz

LOCATIONS

HQ: 227 W. Monroe St., Chicago, IL 60606
Phone: 312-372-2000 **Fax:** 312-984-7700
Web: www.mwe.com

McDermott, Will & Emery has US offices in Boston; Chicago; Irvine, Los Angeles, and Palo Alto, California; Miami; New York City; and Washington, DC. The firm has international offices in London; and Düsseldorf and Munich, Germany.

COMPETITORS

Baker & McKenzie
Hogan & Hartson
Jenner & Block
Jones Day
Katten Muchin
Kirkland & Ellis
Lord, Bissell
Mayer, Brown, Rowe & Maw
Sidley Austin Brown & Wood
Skadden, Arps
Sonnenschein Nath
Winston & Strawn

HISTORICAL FINANCIALS

Company Type: Partnership

Income Statement FYE: December 31

	REVENUE ($ mil.)	NET INCOME ($ mil.)	NET PROFIT MARGIN	EMPLOYEES
12/02	628	—	—	2,000
12/01	563	—	—	1,970
12/00	503	—	—	2,004
12/99	445	—	—	1,900
12/98	390	—	—	1,831
12/97	334	—	—	2,032
12/96	281	—	—	—
12/95	237	—	—	—
12/94	207	—	—	—
12/93	180	—	—	—
Annual Growth	14.9%	—	—	(0.3%)

Revenue History

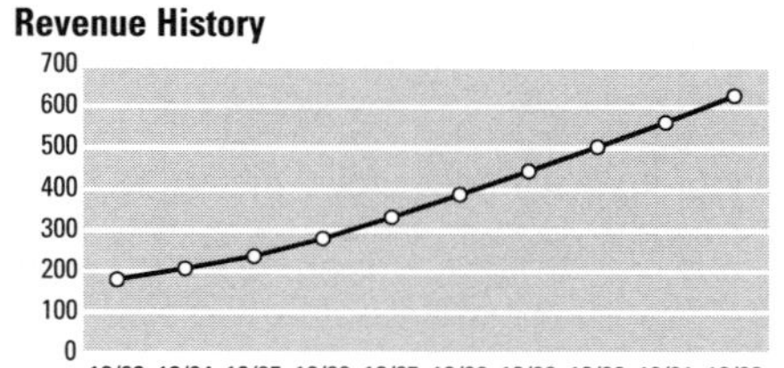

McJunkin Corporation

It's fitting that McJunkin is a pipeline for many gas and oil companies. The company is a nationwide distributor of steel, pipe, valves and fittings, and drilling, electrical, and mining supplies. Its McJunkin Appalachian unit distributes gas and oil products throughout the Appalachian basin. In addition to providing technical support, McA Target Oil Tools distributes and sells drilling tools. McJunkin Controls provides valve cleaning and rebuilding services. The company operates in Mexico and Latin America through its Trottner-McJunkin joint venture. Clients include power, pulp and paper, mining, and automotive companies. Founded in 1921, the firm is still owned by descendants of the McJunkin family.

The company will continue to look for acquisitions that complement its core activities. McJunkin has signed a letter of intent to acquire Indiana-based CIGMA, a joint venture of Vectren Utility Services, and Citizens By-Products, which acts as an integrated supplier and distributor for the utility, pipeline construction, and related industries. The acquisition will give McJunkin a larger gas and oil product presence in its Midwest region. The company will also look to expand its Nigeria and Venezuela operations.

EXECUTIVES

Chairman and CFO: Michael H. Wehrle, age 47
President and CEO: H. Barnard (Bernie) Wehrle III
SVP, National Accounts: Rory Isaac
SVP, Sales: Stephen D. Wehrle
VP, Communications: Lynne Zande
VP, Marketing: Scott Vuchetich
CTO: Jim Underhill
Manager, Human Resources: Pam Young

LOCATIONS

HQ: 835 Hillcrest Dr., Charleston, WV 25311
Phone: 304-348-5211 **Fax:** 304-348-4922
Web: www.mcjunkin.com

McJunkin Corporation operates through more than 125 locations in Mexico, Nigeria, the US, and Venezuela.

PRODUCTS/OPERATIONS

Selected Products

Carbon steel pipe
Carbon steel and corrosion resistant fittings and flanges
Electrical products
Engineered products
Gas distribution and transmission products
Stainless steel and corrosion resistant tubular products
Valves

COMPETITORS

Amcast Industrial
American Cast Iron pipe
CIRCOR International
Cooper Cameron
McWane
National-Oilwell
Shaw Group
Swagelok
Tyco International
USFilter
Wilson Industries

HISTORICAL FINANCIALS

Company Type: Private

Income Statement FYE: December 31

	REVENUE ($ mil.)	NET INCOME ($ mil.)	NET PROFIT MARGIN	EMPLOYEES
12/02	830	—	—	1,600
12/01	830	—	—	1,600
12/00	741	—	—	1,399
12/99	655	—	—	1,245
12/98	731	—	—	1,600
12/97	700	—	—	1,300
12/96	682	—	—	1,300
12/95	667	—	—	1,300
12/94	627	—	—	1,306
12/93	550	—	—	1,372
Annual Growth	4.7%	—	—	1.7%

Revenue History

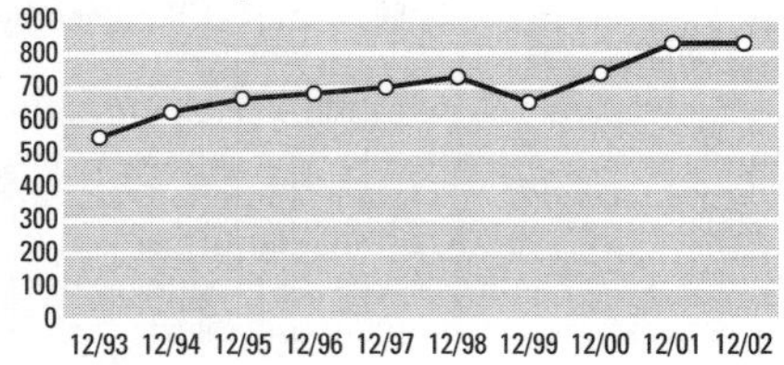

McKee Foods Corporation

When Little Debbie smiles up out of your lunch bag, you know you are loved. McKee Foods' Little Debbie is the US's leading brand of snack cake, named for and featuring the smiling face of the company's founders' granddaughter. The company makes snack cakes, creme-filled cookies, crackers, and candy. McKee Foods also sells granola bars, fruit snacks, and cereals under its Sunbelt brand. Low prices and family packs of individually wrapped treats have driven sales. McKee Foods is the largest independent bakery in the US. The company started in 1934 with founder O. D. McKee and his wife, Ruth, selling nickel cakes from the back seat of their car. The company is still owned and operated by the McKee family.

The company has a fleet of trucks and brings home extra money through "backhauling" for other customers after delivering Little Debbie products. Employees who have worked for more than two years are eligible for profit-sharing bonuses. New product development is key in the highly competitive snack market, and McKee Foods steadily puts out variations such as its Cosmic Crispy bars with chocolate chips.

Ellsworth and Jack McKee, sons of the founders, are chairman and CEO, respectively. And, while Debbie herself doesn't hold an executive position with the company, third-generation Mike McKee is president.

EXECUTIVES

Chairman: Ellsworth D. McKee
CEO: Jack C. McKee
President: Mike McKee
CFO: Barry Patterson
VP, Human Resources: Eva L. Disbro
Manager, Corporate Communications and Public Relations: Ruth Garren

LOCATIONS

HQ: 10260 McKee Rd., Collegedale, TN 37315
Phone: 423-238-7111 **Fax:** 423-238-7101
Web: www.mckeefoods.com

McKee Foods has baking facilities in Arkansas, Tennessee, and Virginia.

PRODUCTS/OPERATIONS

Selected Products

Little Debbie Brand
Breakfast pastries (coffee cakes, honey buns, muffin loaves)
Candy (Peanut Cluster, Star Crunch)
Cookies and pies (Marshmallow Supremes, Nutty Bars, Oatmeal Creme Pies)
Crackers (Toasty Crackers with Peanut Butter)
Seasonal snacks (holiday-themed cakes and cookies)
Snack cakes (Devil Squares, Swiss Cake Rolls)

Sunbelt Brand
Cereal bars (with fruit filling)
Cereals (granola, low-fat, fruit & nut)
Fruit snacks
Granola bars (chewy, fudge-dipped)

COMPETITORS

Chattanooga Bakery
FlowersFoods
General Mills
Grist Mill Company
Interstate Bakeries
Kellogg
Kellogg Snacks
Lance
Otis Spunkmeyer
Saputo
Tasty Baking
Weston Foods

HISTORICAL FINANCIALS

Company Type: Private

Income Statement FYE: Friday nearest June 30

	REVENUE ($ mil.)	NET INCOME ($ mil.)	NET PROFIT MARGIN	EMPLOYEES
6/03	978	—	—	6,500
6/02	970	—	—	6,500
6/01	900	—	—	6,000
6/00	865	—	—	5,450
6/99	855	—	—	5,393
6/98	831	—	—	5,350
6/97	825	—	—	5,346
6/96	735	—	—	5,000
6/95	680	—	—	4,550
6/94	640	—	—	4,400
Annual Growth	4.8%	—	—	4.4%

Revenue History

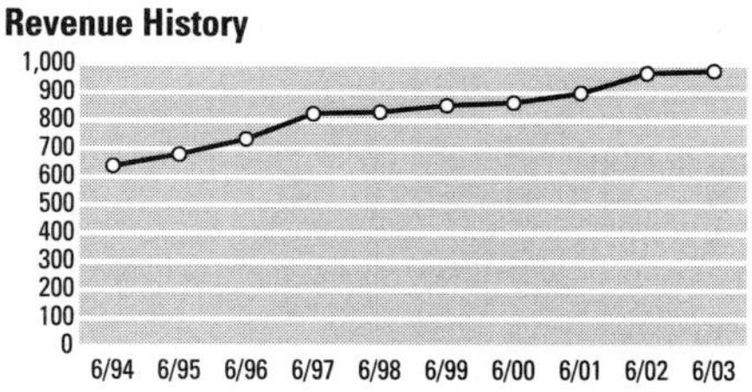

McKinsey & Company

Focusing on the big picture has made McKinsey & Company a big success. It is one of the world's top management consulting firms with some 82 offices in 44 countries. The company provides a full spectrum of consulting services (finance, technology management, strategy) primarily to private companies. Recruiting the top graduates from business schools, it uses Darwinian "move up or get out" policies to weed out all but the best and still build a large network of former employees. McKinsey's reputation comes from a few basic ideals: The client's interests come first; be discreet; be honest; don't overextend yourself. Alumni include former American Express chairman Harvey Golub and former CBS chief Michael Jordan.

The Firm (as it is known to insiders) provides services in strategy, organization, corporate finance, marketing, and is beefing up its capabilities in information technology, an area on which the consulting industry is increasingly focused. Although its customers are mostly private companies, McKinsey also serves government organizations, foundations, and associations. Additionally, the company runs the McKinsey Global Institute, an independent group that generates original research on economic, social, and geopolitical issues.

McKinsey's cachet comes from its devotion to the bottom line, meticulous data-gathering, discretion, and a carefully cultivated mystique. Its partners must survive a rigorous up-or-out weeding process in which failure to advance to higher levels means dismissal. The economic downturn has taken its toll on the consulting industry, and McKinsey has found itself competing fiercely with other firms for fewer clients and having more consultants on its hands (employees are staying put instead of leaving for Internet startups and venture capital firms).

The company has also faced scrutiny for its ties to and consulting done for such troubled companies as Enron, Global Crossing, and Kmart.

McKinsey is owned by its partners and led by its managing director.

HISTORY

McKinsey & Company was founded in Chicago in 1926 by University of Chicago accounting professor James McKinsey. The company evolved from an auditing practice of McKinsey and his partners, Marvin Bower and A. T. Kearney, who began analyzing business and industry and offering advice. McKinsey died in 1937; two years later, Bower, who headed the New York office, and Kearney, in Chicago, split the firm. Kearney renamed the Chicago office A. T. Kearney & Co., and Bower kept the McKinsey name and built up a practice structured like a law firm.

Bower focused on the big picture instead of on specific operating problems, helping boost billings to $2 million by 1950. He hired staff straight out of prestigious business schools, reinforcing the firm's theoretical bent. Bower implemented a competitive up-or-out policy requiring employees who are not continually promoted to leave the firm. Only 20% of associates become partners.

Before becoming president in 1953, Dwight

Eisenhower asked McKinsey to find out exactly what the government did.

By 1959 Bower had opened an office in London, followed by others in Amsterdam; Dusseldorf, Germany; Melbourne; Paris; and Zurich. In 1964 the company founded management journal *The McKinsey Quarterly*. When Bower retired in 1967, sales were $20 million, and McKinsey was the #1 management consulting firm. During the 1970s it faced competition from firms with newer approaches and lost market share. In response, then-managing director Ronald Daniel started specialty practices and expanded foreign operations.

The consulting boom of the 1980s was spurred by mergers and buyouts. By 1988 the firm had 1,800 consultants, sales were $620 million, and 50% of billings came from overseas.

The recession of the early 1990s hit white-collar workers, including consultants. McKinsey, scrambling to upgrade its technical side, bought Information Consulting Group (ICG), its first acquisition. But the corporate cultures did not meld, and most ICG people left by 1993.

In 1994 the company elected its first managing director of non-European descent, Indian-born Rajat Gupta. Two years later the traditionally hush-hush firm found itself at the center of that most public 1990s arena, the sexual discrimination lawsuit. A female ex-consultant in Texas sued, claiming McKinsey had sabotaged her career (the case was dismissed).

In 1998 McKinsey partnered with Northwestern University and the University of Pennsylvania to establish a world-class business school in India. The following year graduating seniors surveyed in Europe, the UK, and the US named the company as their ideal employer.

Also in 1999 the company created McKinsey to help "accelerate" Internet startups. The next year it increased salaries and offered incentives to better compete with Internet firms for employees. In 2001 the company expanded its branding business with the acquisition of Envision, a Chicago-based brand consultant.

In 2003 Ian Davis was elected as managing director of the firm, succeeding Rajat Gupta who served as managing director for 9 years (the firm imposes a term limit on the position). Davis had previously served as the head of the firm's UK office.

EXECUTIVES

Managing Director: Ian Davis, age 52
Director of External Relations, North and South America: Michael Stewart
Director of Finance: Jack Murrin
Director of Personnel: Jerome Vascellaro
President, McKinsey New York: Michael Patsalos-Fox
Managing Partner, Amsterdam: Robert Reibestein
Managing Partner, Dusseldorf: Jurgen Kluge
Managing Partner, Seoul: Dominic Barton, age 41

LOCATIONS

HQ: 55 E. 52nd St., New York, NY 10022
Phone: 212-446-7000 **Fax:** 212-446-8575
Web: www.mckinsey.com

PRODUCTS/OPERATIONS

Selected Areas of Practice

Automotive
Banking and securities
Chemicals
Consumer industries and packaged goods
Corporate finance
Corporate strategy
High tech
Insurance
Marketing
Operational effectiveness
Payors and providers
Pharmaceuticals and medical products
Pulp and paper
Retail
Telecommunications
Travel and logistics

COMPETITORS

Accenture
A.T. Kearney
Bain & Company
BearingPoint
Booz Allen
Boston Consulting
Computer Sciences
Deloitte Consulting
IBM
Mercer
PA Consulting
Perot Systems

HISTORICAL FINANCIALS

Company Type: Private

Income Statement FYE: December 31

	REVENUE ($ mil.)	NET INCOME ($ mil.)	NET PROFIT MARGIN	EMPLOYEES
12/02	3,300	—	—	12,000
12/01	3,400	—	—	13,000
12/00	3,400	—	—	13,000
12/99	2,900	—	—	10,500
12/98	2,500	—	—	10,000
12/97	2,200	—	—	8,500
12/96	2,100	—	—	7,100
12/95	1,800	—	—	6,050
12/94	1,500	—	—	6,000
12/93	1,300	—	—	5,560
Annual Growth	10.9%	—	—	8.9%

Revenue History

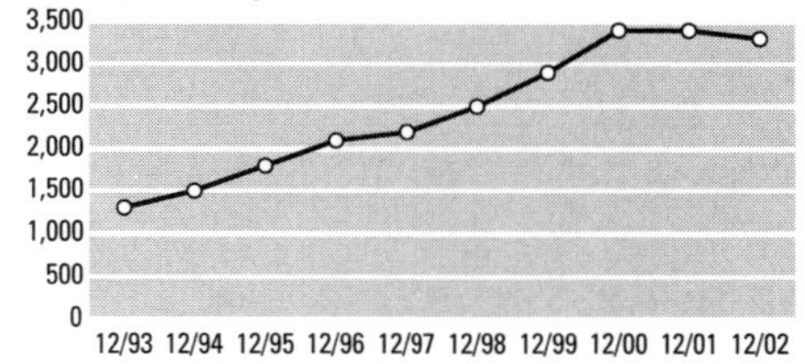

McWane Corp.

As a leading manufacturer of fire hydrants, McWane may just be a dog's best friend. Through its many divisions, McWane makes a variety of fluid control devices that include fire hydrants, industrial valves, pipes, and flanges. With the acquisition of Amerex in Trussville, Alabama, McWane has become one of the world's leading makers of fire extinguishers and fire suppression systems. Through its Manchester Tank division, the company also produces gas grills as well as propane tanks for recreational vehicles. Its M&H Valve Company, which makes industrial valves with waste-water applications and fire hydrants, has been in operation since 1854. McWane was founded in 1921 and continues to be family-owned.

EXECUTIVES

Chairman: C. Phillip McWane, age 45
President: Ruffner Page
CFO: Charles (Charley) Nowlin

LOCATIONS

HQ: 2900 Hwy. 280, Ste. 300, Birmingham, AL 35223
Phone: 205-414-3100 **Fax:** 205-414-3180
Web: www.mh-valve.com

McWane has operations in Alabama, Iowa, New Jersey, New York, Ohio, Texas, and Utah.

PRODUCTS/OPERATIONS

Selected Operations

Amerex Corporation (industrial and commercial fire extinguishers)
Clow Valve Company (fire hydrants and valves)
Clow Water Systems Company (ductile iron pipe and fittings)
Kennedy Valve (fire hydrants and valves)
M&H Valve Company (fire hydrants, gears and casings, stem guides, valves)
McWane Cast Iron Pipe Company
Pacific States Cast Iron Pipe Company (ductile iron pipe)
Tyler Pipe Company (cleanouts, drains, fittings, valves)

COMPETITORS

American Cast Iron pipe
Atchison Casting
Citation
Henry Technologies
Indeck
INTERMET
Kidde
Margate Industries
McJunkin
Metallurg
Northwest Pipe
Walter Industries

HISTORICAL FINANCIALS

Company Type: Private

Income Statement FYE: December 31

	ESTIMATED REVENUE ($ mil.)	NET INCOME ($ mil.)	NET PROFIT MARGIN	EMPLOYEES
12/02	750	—	—	5,200
12/01	750	—	—	5,200
12/00	630	—	—	5,170
12/99	625	—	—	4,400
12/98	585	—	—	4,350
12/97	575	—	—	5,700
12/96	525	—	—	5,650
12/95	500	—	—	5,500
12/94	475	—	—	5,400
Annual Growth	5.9%	—	—	(0.5%)

Revenue History

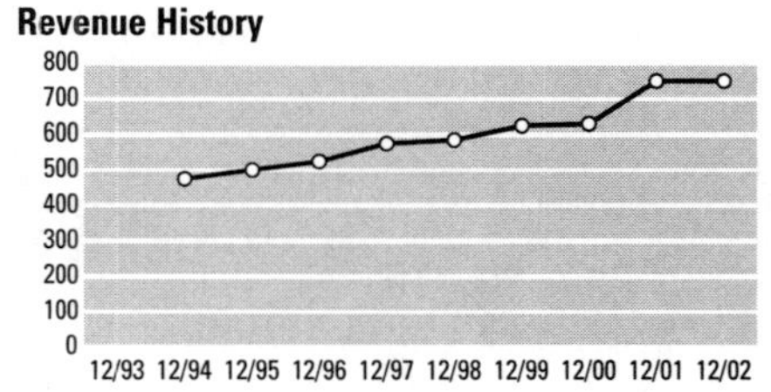

MediaNews Group, Inc.

Paper cuts can really hurt, especially when they're made by newspaper predator MediaNews Group. Known for ruthlessly cutting staff at unprofitable newspapers, the company publishes 50 dailies (including *The Denver Post* and *The Salt Lake Tribune*) and about 120 non-dailies in a dozen states. It also operates Web sites for most of its daily papers and operates a small number of radio and television stations. The company is a joint venture of vice chairman and CEO Dean Singleton and chairman Richard Scudder, who began buying newspapers together in 1983.

Considered one of the nation's top 10 newspaper firms, MediaNews owns newspapers with a combined daily circulation of more than 4 million. *The Denver Post* is part of the Denver Newspaper Agency, a joint operating agreement (JOA) with E. W. Scripps (owner of the *Rocky Mountain News*) that combines the business operations of both papers. The company's other media holdings include radio stations in Texas and Alaska and a TV station in Anchorage, Alaska (KTVA).

MediaNews focuses on building newspaper clusters in specific geographic regions. Following its strategy, the company added to its Northern California cluster with its 2002 purchase of *The Reporter* newspaper in Vacaville, California. The company struck a deal with Gannett in 2003 to form the Texas-New Mexico Newspaper Partnership, comprising six daily and about a dozen non-daily papers.

The Salt Lake Tribune is also run under a similar joint operating agreement with The Deseret News Publishing Company (owner of the *Deseret News*). A legal dispute with the previous owners of The Salt Lake Tribune has resulted in a court order forcing the company to offer the Utah newspaper back to the McCarthey family.

MediaNews is owned by the families of Singleton and Scudder.

EXECUTIVES

Chairman: Richard B. Scudder, age 88
Vice Chairman and CEO: William D. (Dean) Singleton, age 50, $990,500 pay
President: Joseph J. (Jody) Lodovic IV, age 40, $719,300 pay
EVP and COO: Gerald E. (Jerry) Grilly, age 54, $1,102,187 pay
SVP Operations: Anthony F. Tierno, age 56, $475,000 pay
VP and CFO: Ronald A. (Ron) Mayo, age 39, $223,100 pay
VP Human Resources: Charles M. Kamen
Secretary: Patricia Robinson
Treasurer: James L. McDougald, age 47
Auditors: Ernst & Young LLP

LOCATIONS

HQ: 1560 Broadway, Ste. 2100, Denver, CO 80202
Phone: 303-563-6360 **Fax:** 303-894-9327
Web: www.medianewsgroup.com

MediaNews Group publishes newspapers in Alaska, California, Colorado, Connecticut, Massachusetts, New Mexico, Pennsylvania, Texas, Utah, Vermont, and West Virginia. It also owns a radio station and television station in Alaska and radio stations in Texas.

PRODUCTS/OPERATIONS

Operating Divisions

Alaska Broadcasting Group
ANG Newspapers (54%, part of the California Newspapers Partnership)
Charleston Newspapers
Connecticut Newspapers Group
Denver Newspapers
Graham Newspapers
Los Angeles Newspaper Group
New England Newspapers Group
Texas-New Mexico Newspaper Partnership
North Central California Newspaper Group
Northern California Newspapers Group
South Eastern Pennsylvania Newspapers Group
Utah Newspaper

COMPETITORS

Copley Press
Eagle-Tribune Publishing
E. W. Scripps
Freedom Communications
Gannett
Hearst
Hearst Newspapers
Journal Register
Knight-Ridder
Lee Enterprises
Liberty Group Publishing
New Times
New York Times
Pulitzer
Tribune
Village Voice Media

HISTORICAL FINANCIALS

Company Type: Private

Income Statement

FYE: June 30

	REVENUE ($ mil.)	NET INCOME ($ mil.)	NET PROFIT MARGIN	EMPLOYEES
6/02	712	12	1.7%	11,200
6/01	853	25	3.0%	11,200
6/00	947	130	13.8%	8,939
6/99	1,010	—	—	8,997
6/98	850	—	—	8,800
6/97	620	—	—	8,000
6/96	545	—	—	7,000
6/95	375	—	—	4,500
6/94	495	—	—	4,300
6/93	575	—	—	7,950
Annual Growth	2.4%	(69.2%)	—	3.9%

2002 Year-End Financials

Debt ratio: 15.7%
Return on equity: 28.6%
Cash ($ mil.): 2
Current ratio: 0.99
Long-term debt ($ mil.): 942

Net Income History

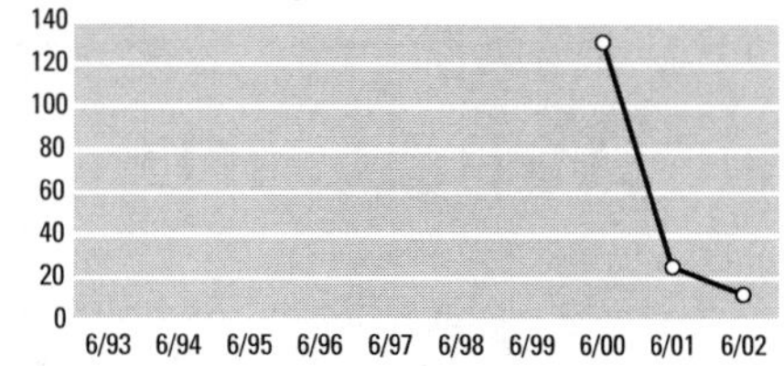

Medline Industries, Inc.

Medline Industries, a private medical equipment distributor and manufacturer, goes toe-to-toe with the bigger guns, selling more than 100,000 products, such as furnishings for hospital rooms, exam equipment, housekeeping supplies, and surgical gloves and garments. The company manufactures about 70% of its products and then distributes them to such customers as hospitals, extended care facilities, and home health care providers. Marketing efforts are handled by Medline's some 650 sales representatives and roughly 25 distribution centers. The company is owned by the Mills family, which founded Medline in 1910 as a manufacturer of nurses' gowns.

EXECUTIVES

CEO: Charles S. (Charlie) Mills
President: Andy Mills
COO: Jim Abrams
CFO: Bill Abington
VP, Human Resources: Joseph Becker
VP, National Accounts: Steve Heintze
President, Sales: Ray Swaback
President, Operating Room Division: James Spann

LOCATIONS

HQ: 1 Medline Place, Mundelein, IL 60060
Phone: 847-949-5500 **Fax:** 800-351-1512
Web: www.medline.com

Medline Industries sells its products in more than 20 countries.

PRODUCTS/OPERATIONS

Selected Product Categories

Bed and bath products
Central supply
Enteral products
Equipment and furnishings
Exam and diagnostics
Gloves
Housekeeping
Incontinence products
Nursing
Rehabilitation
Respiratory
Skin care
Surgery and O.B.
Urology
Wound care

COMPETITORS

Allegiance
Hillenbrand
Kimberly-Clark
Maxxim Medical
McKesson
Owens & Minor
Sunrise Medical
Tyco Healthcare

HISTORICAL FINANCIALS

Company Type: Private

Income Statement FYE: December 31

	REVENUE ($ mil.)	NET INCOME ($ mil.)	NET PROFIT MARGIN	EMPLOYEES
12/02	1,450	—	—	3,800
12/01	1,231	—	—	3,500
12/00	1,016	—	—	3,277
12/99	905	—	—	2,600
12/98	756	—	—	2,300
12/97	655	—	—	2,700
12/96	600	—	—	2,383
12/95	560	—	—	2,200
12/94	476	—	—	2,000
12/93	413	—	—	—
Annual Growth	15.0%	—	—	8.4%

Revenue History

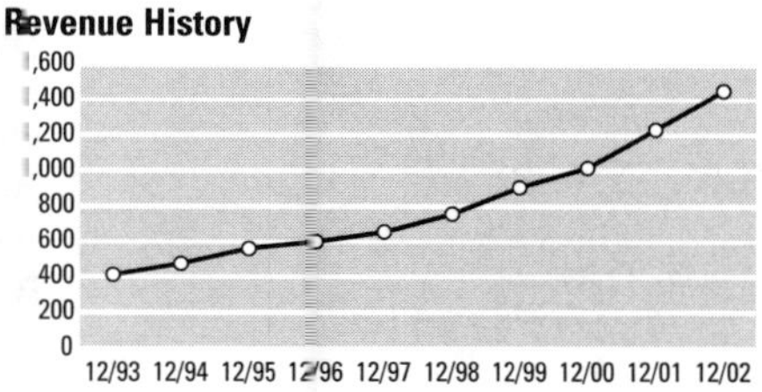

MedStar Health

Whether you've been knocked out and are seeing stars or you're just plain sickly, MedStar Health can cater to you. The not-for-profit organization runs seven hospitals in Baltimore and Washington, DC. With more than 4,000 affiliated physicians, MedStar offers such services as acute care, rehabilitation, assisted living, hospice, long-term care, and emergency services. Its MedStar Physician Partners contracts with private physicians in the Baltimore/Washington, DC area. MedStar also manages an independent practice association, which includes both primary and specialty care physicians. The company also conducts medical research through its MedStar Research Institute.

EXECUTIVES

Chairman: James R. Hyde
Vice Chairman: Robert Gladstone
CEO and Director: John P. McDaniel, age 60
President and COO: Kenneth A. Samet
EVP and CFO: Michael A. Curran
EVP, Corporate Services: Michael C. Rogers
EVP, Medical Affairs: William L. Thomas
SVP and CIO: B. Alton Brantley
SVP and General Counsel: Robert J. Ryan
Corporate Director, Communications and Public Affairs: John A. Marzano
Director of Human Resources: David Noe
Auditors: PricewaterhouseCoopers LLP

LOCATIONS

HQ: 5565 Sterrett Place, 5th Fl., Columbia, MD 21044
Phone: 410-772-6500 **Fax:** 410-715-3905
Web: www.medstarhealth.org

Baltimore Hospitals
Franklin Square Hospital
Good Samaritan Hospital
Harbor Hospital Center
Union Memorial Hospital

Washington, DC, Hospitals
Georgetown University Hospital
National Rehabilitation Center
Washington Hospital Center

COMPETITORS

Ascension
Bon Secours Health
Christiana Care
Inova
Johns Hopkins Medicine
Trinity Health

HISTORICAL FINANCIALS

Company Type: Not-for-profit

Income Statement FYE: June 30

	REVENUE ($ mil.)	NET INCOME ($ mil.)	NET PROFIT MARGIN	EMPLOYEES
6/02	2,110	—	—	22,000
6/01	1,990	—	—	21,700
6/00	1,800	—	—	21,466
6/99	1,600	—	—	21,233
6/98	1,400	—	—	21,000
6/97	643	—	—	7,000
6/96	600	—	—	6,000
6/95	571	—	—	6,500
6/94	522	—	—	—
6/93	521	—	—	—
Annual Growth	16.8%	—	—	19.0%

Revenue History

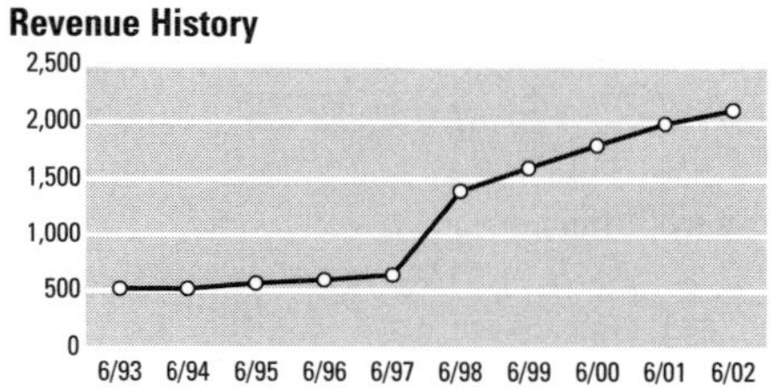

Meijer, Inc.

Meijer (pronounced "Meyer") is the green giant of retailing in the Midwest. The company operates nearly 160 combination grocery and general merchandise stores; about half are in Michigan, while the rest are in Illinois, Indiana, Kentucky, and Ohio. Its huge stores (which average 200,000 to 250,000 sq. ft. each, or about the size of four regular grocery stores) stock about 120,000 items, including Meijer private-label products. Customers can choose from about 40 departments, including hardware, apparel, toys, and electronics. Most stores also sell gasoline, offer banking services, and have multiple in-store restaurants. Founder Hendrik Meijer opened his first store in 1934; the company is still family-owned.

Although the discount superstore format is most often referred to in conjunction with its rival Wal-Mart, Meijer is its pioneer. But that hasn't stopped the world's #1 retailer from muscling in on Meijer's markets. Wal-Mart has 14 supercenters in Michigan; eight in communities that also have a Meijer store. Meijer is responding by cutting prices, putting some expansion plans on hold, and renovating some older stores. It is also cutting jobs — some 350 positions were eliminated in September 2003 — to become more efficient.

On the other hand, Kmart's woes are giving Meijer a boost. With 35 of Kmart's recent store closings within 10 miles of a Meijer store, the company has begun filling prescriptions for former Kmart customers.

HISTORY

Dutch immigrant and barber Hendrik Meijer owned a vacant space next to his barbershop in Greenville, Michigan. Because of the Depression, he couldn't rent it out. So in 1934 he bought $338.76 in merchandise on credit and started his own grocery store, Thrift Market, with the help of his wife, Gezina; son, Fred; and daughter, Johanna; he made $7 the first day. Meijer had 22 competitors in Greenville alone, but his dedication to low prices (he and Fred often traveled long distances to find bargains) attracted customers. In 1935, to encourage self-service, Meijer placed 12 wicker baskets at the front of the store and posted signs that read, "Take a basket. Help yourself."

A second store was opened in 1942. The company added four more in the 1950s. In 1962 Meijer — then with 14 stores — opened the first one-stop shopping Meijer Thrifty Acres store, similar to a hypermarket another operator had opened in Belgium a year earlier. By 1964, the year that Hendrik died and Fred took over, three of these general merchandise stores were operating. The company entered Ohio in the late 1960s.

In the early 1980s Meijer bought 14 Twin Fair stores in Ohio, 10 in Cincinnati. It sold the stores by 1987, however, after disappointing results. Meijer had greater success in Columbus, Ohio, where it opened one store that year and immediately captured 20% of the market. In 1988 the company began keeping most stores open 24 hours a day.

Meijer annihilated competitors in Dayton, Ohio, in 1991, when it opened four stores that year. The company entered the Toledo market in 1993 with four stores; after one year it had taken 11.5% of the market. A foray into the membership warehouse market was abandoned in 1993, just a few months after they had opened, when Meijer said it would close all seven SourceClubs in Michigan and Ohio.

The company entered Indiana in 1994, opening 16 stores in less than two years; it also reached an agreement with McDonald's to open restaurants in several stores. The first labor strike in Meijer's history hit four stores in Toledo that year, leading to pickets at 14 others. Union officials accused the company of using intimidation tactics by its hiring of large, uniformed men in flak jackets and combat boots as security guards. After nine weeks Meijer agreed to recognize the workers' newly attained union affiliation.

In 1995 the company opened 13 stores, including its first in Illinois. It reentered the Cincinnati market in 1996, announcing the opening of two new stores there by mailing 80,000 videos to residents. By the end of the year, Meijer had a total of five stores in Cincinnati and had entered Kentucky.

Meijer opened a central kitchen in Indiana to prepare deli salads and some vegetables and process orange juice for its stores in 1997. It opened its first two stores in Louisville, Kentucky, the following year. Meijer broke into the tough Chicago-area market with its first store in 1999.

The next year Meijer opened several "village-style" stores — scaled-down versions (about 155,000 sq. ft.) of its larger stores. Later in 2000 Meijer unveiled what it claims is the largest superstore in North America. The 255,000-sq.-ft. behemoth (compared to a Wal-Mart Supercenter, which averages about 183,106 sq. ft.) features a gourmet coffee shop, a card shop, a bank open seven days a week, and restaurants serving pizza and sushi.

In February 2002 co-chairman Hank Meijer was named CEO, succeeding Jim McClean, who had run the company since 1999. The retailer launched a "reinvented superstore format" at six Dayton, Ohio-area stores in late 2002. The makeover emphasizes discount fashion (featuring brands such as Levi's, Dockers, and Gotcha) in a department store atmosphere.

EXECUTIVES

Chairman Emeritus: Fred Meijer, age 82
Co-Chairman: Doug Meijer, age 48
Co-Chairman and CEO: Hendrik G. (Hank) Meijer, age 50
President and COO: Paul Boyer, age 56
SVP, Finance and Administration, and CFO: Jim Walsh
SVP, Human Resources: Wendell (Windy) Ray
SVP, Merchandising: Larry Zigerelli
SVP, Public and Consumer Affairs: Brian Breslin
Division VP, Foods Merchandising: Dave Perron
Division VP, Hardlines: Terry Griffith
Group VP, Fashion Merchandising: Jo Ann Ogee
Group VP, Grocery Merchandising: Ralph Fischer
Group VP, Perishables Merchandising: Dave Prostko
VP, Pharmacy: Mike Major
VP, Real Estate: Mike Kinstle
VP, Service Operations: Carole Morgan
Regional VP: Scott Seling
Regional VP: Ken Wright
Director, Community and Customer Relations: John Zimmerman
Director, Marketing/E-Commerce Group: Michael Ross
Director, Promotions and Partnerships: Cathy Cooper
Market Director: Frank Curnutte
Regional Market Director: Jackie Martini
Community Relations Manager: Steve VanWagoner
Manager, Marketing and Promotions: Brian Hauenstein
Project Manager, Healthy Living: Nicola MacGuire

LOCATIONS

HQ: 2929 Walker Ave. NW, Grand Rapids, MI 49544
Phone: 616-453-6711 **Fax:** 616-791-2572
Web: www.meijer.com

2003 Stores

	No.
Michigan	78
Ohio	36
Indiana	25
Illinois	9
Kentucky	8
Total	**156**

PRODUCTS/OPERATIONS

Selected Meijer Store Departments

Apparel
Auto supplies
Bakery
Banking
Books
Bulk foods
Coffee shop
Computer software
Dairy
Delicatessen
Electronics
Floral
Food court
Gas station
Hardware
Health and beauty products
Home fashions
Jewelry
Lawn and garden
Music
Nutrition products
Paint
Pets and pet supplies
Pharmacy
Photo lab
Portrait studio
Produce
Service meat and seafood
Small appliances
Soup and salad bar
Sporting goods
Tobacco
Toys
Wall coverings
Wine

COMPETITORS

Albertson's
ALDI
CVS
D&W Food Centers
Dollar General
Dominick's
Eagle Food
Family Dollar Stores
Fleming Companies
Giant Eagle
A&P
Home Depot
IGA
Kmart
Kroger
Marsh Supermarkets
Penn Traffic
Retail Ventures
Roundy's
Schnuck Markets
Schottenstein Stores
Spartan Stores
SUPERVALU
Target
Walgreen
Wal-Mart
Winn-Dixie

HISTORICAL FINANCIALS

Company Type: Private

Income Statement

FYE: January 31

	ESTIMATED REVENUE ($ mil.)	NET INCOME ($ mil.)	NET PROFIT MARGIN	EMPLOYEES
1/03	10,900	—	—	83,402
1/02	10,600	—	—	83,402
1/01	10,000	—	—	80,000
1/00	9,500	—	—	80,000
1/99	8,300	—	—	80,000
1/98	6,900	—	—	77,000
1/97	6,000	—	—	73,000
1/96	5,640	—	—	65,000
1/95	5,160	—	—	70,000
1/94	4,250	—	—	65,000
Annual Growth	11.0%	—	—	2.8%

Revenue History

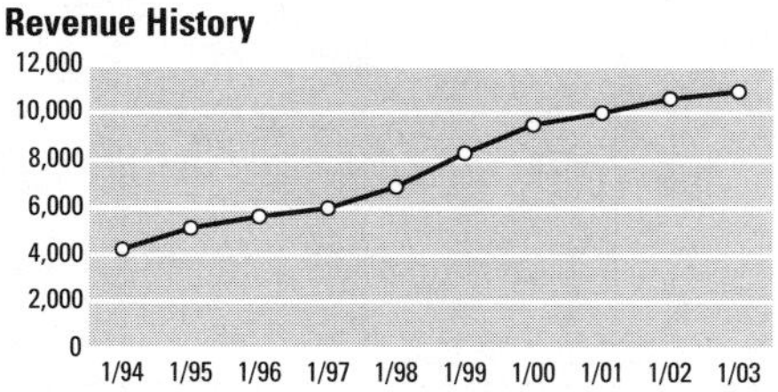

Memorial Sloan-Kettering Cancer Center

Ranked as one of the nation's top cancer centers, Memorial Sloan-Kettering Cancer Center includes Memorial Hospital for pediatric and adult cancer care and the Sloan-Kettering Institute for cancer research activities. The cancer center specializes in bone-marrow transplants and chemotherapy and offers programs in cancer prevention, treatment, research, and education. Memorial Sloan-Kettering offers inpatient and outpatient services to more than 10,000 patients every year. Other services include pain management, rehabilitation, and psychological programs.

EXECUTIVES

Co-Chairman: Douglas A. (Sandy) Warner III, age 56
Honorary Co-Chairman: Laurance S. Rockefeller
Co-Chairman: James D. Robinson III, age 67
Vice Chairman; Chairman, Sloan-Kettering Institute: Louis V. Gerstner Jr., age 61
Vice Chairman; Chairman, Board of Managers, Memorial Hospital: Richard I. (Dick) Beattie, age 64
President, CEO, and Director: Harold Varmus
President Emeritus and Director: Paul A. Marks
Physician-in-Chief, Memorial Hospital: Robert E. Wittes, age 58
SVP and Hospital Administrator: Kathryn Martin
SVP Finance and Assistant Treasurer: Michael P. Gutnick
VP Human Resources: Michael Browne
VP Marketing: Ellen Miller Sonet

LOCATIONS

HQ: 1275 York Ave., New York, NY 10021
Phone: 212-639-2000 **Fax:** 212-639-3576
Web: www.mskcc.org

COMPETITORS

Carilion Health System
Columbia University
Detroit Medical Center
Johns Hopkins Medicine
Mayo Foundation
New York City Health and Hospitals
Partners HealthCare
Rush System for Health
University of Texas

HISTORICAL FINANCIALS

Company Type: Not-for-profit

Income Statement

FYE: December 31

	REVENUE ($ mil.)	NET INCOME ($ mil.)	NET PROFIT MARGIN	EMPLOYEES
12/02	1,088	(81)	—	7,953
12/01	959	(120)	—	7,609
12/00	876	64	7.3%	7,296
12/99	790	222	28.1%	7,133
12/98	747	204	27.3%	6,618
12/97	694	207	29.8%	6,142
12/96	648	178	27.5%	5,799
12/95	650	191	29.4%	6,050
12/94	637	21	3.4%	6,034
12/93	607	39	6.4%	6,203
Annual Growth	6.7%	—	—	2.8%

Net Income History

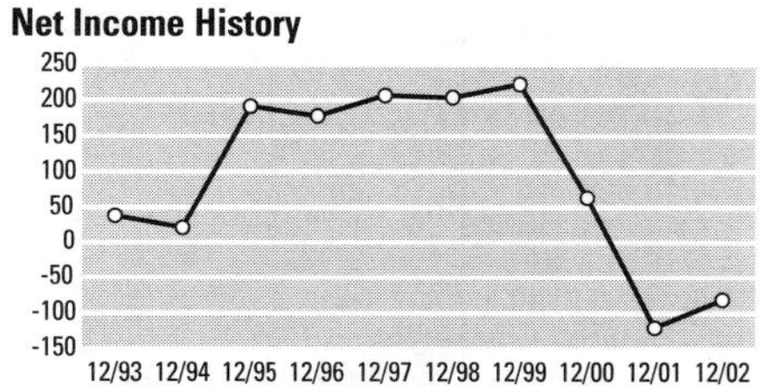

Menard, Inc.

If sticks and stones break bones, what can two-by-fours and 2-in. nails do? That is what Menard is wondering now that its biggest rivals (#1 home improvement giant The Home Depot and #2 Lowe's) are hammering away at its home turf. The third-largest home improvement chain in the US, Menard has more than 170 stores in Illinois, Indiana, Iowa, Michigan, Minnesota, Nebraska, North and South Dakota, and Wisconsin. The stores sell home improvement products, such as floor coverings, hardware, millwork, paint, and tools. Unlike competitors, all the company's stores have full-service lumberyards. Menard is owned by president and CEO John Menard Jr., who founded the company in 1972.

Although Menard outlets are typically smaller than those of Home Depot, they offer a similar selection of products by building large warehouses adjacent to stores and then quickly restocking merchandise when it's sold. The company is increasing its average store size to 225,000 sq. ft.

The company's products are laid out on easy-to-reach, supermarket-styled shelves. To help keep expenses low and prices cheap, Menard makes some of its merchandise, including doors and trusses.

Besides billionaire founder and owner John Menard running the chain, other family members are engaged in its everyday operations. John Menard also owns Team Menard, an Indy car-racing team.

HISTORY

John Menard was the oldest of eight children on a Wisconsin dairy farm. To pay for attending the University of Wisconsin at Eau Claire, he and some fellow college students built pole barns in the late 1950s. Learning that other builders had trouble finding lumber outlets open on the weekends, Menard began buying wood in bulk and selling it to them. He added other supplies in 1960 and sold his construction business in 1970 as building supply revenues became his chief source of income.

He founded Menard in 1972 as the do-it-yourself craze was beginning, but he wanted an operation run more like mass merchandiser Target, with easy-to-reach shelves, wide aisles, and tile floors rather than the cold, cumbersome layout used by lumberyards. To realize that concept, Menard built warehouses and stockrooms behind the stores so he could restock merchandise quickly.

Menard's vision worked, and he began building his midwestern empire, often acquiring abandoned retail sites that were inexpensive and in good locations. By 1986 Menard was in Iowa, Minnesota, North and South Dakota, and Wisconsin, and by 1990 it had 46 stores. In the early 1990s Menard began enlarging its operations to serve the ever-growing number of stores, opening a huge warehouse and distribution center and a manufacturing facility that made doors, Formica countertops, and other products. Menard entered Nebraska in 1990 and opened its first store in Chicago the next year. By 1992 there were more than 60 stores.

That year Menard made the National Enquirer with a story about the firing of a store manager who had built a wheelchair-accessible home for his 11-year-old daughter with spina bifida, violating a company theft-prevention policy forbidding store managers to build their own homes. The company insisted that the man was fired in part because of poor work performance.

Menard continued to expand to new areas, operating stores in Indiana and Michigan by 1992. As it continued expanding in the Chicago area, it offered varying store formats, ranging from a full line of building materials to smaller Menards Hardware Plus stores. By 1994 Menard had 85 stores, many bigger than 100,000 sq. ft.

In 1995 and 1996 the company was plagued with lawsuits filed by customers charging false arrest and imprisonment for shoplifting. An on-duty police officer apprehending a shoplifting suspect at a store was even stopped and searched.

Competition also heated up during that time. The Home Depot's push into the Midwest — including opening several stores directly across the street from Menard — spurred Menard to fight back by lowering prices and opening nearly 40 stores. The fight forced smaller chains like Handy Andy out of business.

In 1997 Menard and his company were fined $1.7 million after dumping bags of toxic ash from its manufacturing facility at residential trash pick-up sites rather than at properly regulated outlets (it had been fined for similar violations in 1989 and 1994). In response to a price war initiated by Home Depot, in 1998 Menard dropped sales prices by 10%.

In 1999 competitor Lowe's began moving into Menard's biggest market, Chicago. Menard began opening larger stores in 2000 (about 162,000 sq. ft., or some 74,000 sq. ft. bigger than the older stores). In 2001 it began beefing up its lines of home appliances, adding more washers, dryers, dishwashers, refrigerators, and ranges.

Menard opened a 225,000 sq. ft. store — the company's new prototype, larger by 50 sq. ft. than the original — in Bloomington, Indiana, in April 2003.

EXECUTIVES

President and CEO: John R. Menard Jr., age 62
CFO and Treasurer: Earl R. Rasmussen
VP of Merchandising: Ed Archibald
VP of Operations: Larry Menard
CTO: Dave Wagner
Payroll Manager: Terri Jain
General Counsel: Dawn M. Sands

LOCATIONS

HQ: 4777 Menard Dr., Eau Claire, WI 54703
Phone: 715-876-5911 **Fax:** 715-876-2868
Web: www.menards.com/nindex.html

Menard owns home improvement stores in Illinois, Indiana, Iowa, Michigan, Minnesota, Nebraska, North Dakota, South Dakota, and Wisconsin.

PRODUCTS/OPERATIONS

Stores

Menards (home improvement stores)
Midwest Manufacturing (product manufacturing)

Selected Departments

Appliances
Building materials
Electrical (wiring, lighting)
Floor coverings
Hardware
Lumberyard
Millwork (doors, cabinetry, molding)
Plumbing
Seasonal (Christmas, lawn and garden)
Tools
Wall coverings (wallpaper, paint)

COMPETITORS

84 Lumber
Ace Hardware
Carter Lumber
Do it Best
Fastenal
Home Depot
Lanoga
Lowe's
Primus
Sears
Seigle's
Sherwin-Williams
Stock Building Supply
Sutherland Lumber
TruServ
Wal-Mart
Wickes
Wolohan Lumber

HISTORICAL FINANCIALS

Company Type: Private

Income Statement FYE: January 31

	ESTIMATED REVENUE ($ mil.)	NET INCOME ($ mil.)	NET PROFIT MARGIN	EMPLOYEES
1/02	5,300	—	—	9,200
1/01	5,000	—	—	7,600
1/00	4,500	—	—	7,000
1/99	4,000	—	—	7,000
1/98	3,700	—	—	7,000
1/97	3,200	—	—	7,000
1/96	2,700	—	—	6,534
1/95	2,300	—	—	5,800
1/94	1,750	—	—	5,000
1/93	1,400	—	—	—
Annual Growth	15.9%	—	—	7.9%

Revenue History

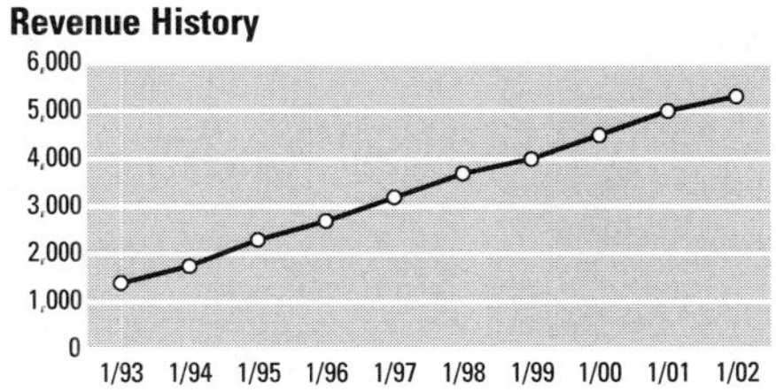

Menasha Corporation

Menasha has the whole package. Founded in 1849 as a woodenware business, the holding company now owns businesses that make packaging and paperboard, returnable material handling systems, product labels, and promotional materials. Each company is independently operated. The company's main subsidiaries are Menasha Packaging Company (corrugated packaging), ORBIS Corporation (returnable materials handling products), Poly Hi Solidur (polymers), and Promo Edge Company (printing). It also has investments in other manufacturing companies. Menasha operates nearly 70 facilities across the US and in seven other countries. Descendants of founder Elisha Smith own a majority of Menasha.

EXECUTIVES

Chairman: Thomas J. Prosser, age 66
President, CEO, and Director; CEO, Promo Edge: Harold R. Smethills Jr.
VP, CFO, and Treasurer: Arthur Huge
VP and CIO: Ed Wojciechowski
VP and General Counsel: James Sarosiek
Director, Corporate Development and Strategic Planning: Lindsay A. Gardner
Human Resources: Cindy Heindel

LOCATIONS

HQ: 1645 Bergstrom Rd., Neenah, WI 54956
Phone: 920-751-1000 **Fax:** 920-751-1825
Web: www.menasha.com

Menasha and its subsidiaries have operations in Australia, Brazil, Canada, France, Germany, India, Japan, Mexico, the Netherlands, Singapore, South Africa, Switzerland, the UK, and the US.

PRODUCTS/OPERATIONS

Selected Operations

Menasha Material Handling Corporation
Menasha Packaging Company
Poly Hi Solidur Group
Polymer Technologies Group
Promotional and Informational Graphics Group

COMPETITORS

Boise Cascade
Longview Fibre
Shorewood Packaging
Smurfit-Stone Container
Sonoco Products
Unisource
Valspar

HISTORICAL FINANCIALS

Company Type: Private

Income Statement FYE: December 31

	REVENUE ($ mil.)	NET INCOME ($ mil.)	NET PROFIT MARGIN	EMPLOYEES
12/02	1,100	—	—	5,500
12/01	1,100	—	—	5,400
12/00	1,121	—	—	6,046
12/99	991	—	—	5,759
12/98	952	—	—	6,000
12/97	933	—	—	5,759
12/96	915	—	—	5,584
12/95	916	—	—	5,100
12/94	779	—	—	4,900
12/93	674	—	—	4,600
Annual Growth	5.6%	—	—	2.0%

Revenue History

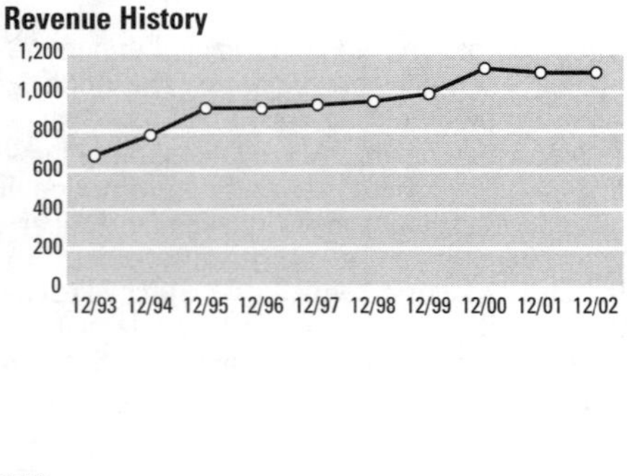

Meridian Automotive

From bumper to bumper, Meridian Automotive Systems has the line on what it takes to keep a vehicle together. The auto parts company operates three business segments: Exterior Composites (body panels, fenders, tailgates); Interiors and Exterior Lighting (floor consoles, fog lamps, instrument panels, signal lamps); and Front and Rear End Modules (bumpers, energy absorbing foam, plastic fascias). Meridian's major customers include Ford, General Motors, and DaimlerChysler. The company operates 20 primary manufacturing plants in North and South America. Meridian is owned by Windward Capital Partners, Capital d'Amerique CDPQ Inc., Credit Suisse First Boston, and Northwestern Mutual Life Insurance.

EXECUTIVES

Chairman: Robert H. Barton III, age 69
President, CEO, and Director: H. H. (Buddy) Wacaser, age 53
EVP and CFO: Richard Newsted, age 45
EVP, Engineering and Product Development: Jon Baker, age 58
SVP, Secretary, and General Counsel: Dean Vanek, age 44
VP, Human Resources: Thomas C. (Tom) Eggebeen, age 51
VP, Sales: David White, age 52
Auditors: PricewaterhouseCoopers LLP

LOCATIONS

HQ: Meridian Automotive Systems, Inc.
550 Town Center Dr., Ste. 475, Dearborn, MI 48126
Phone: 313-336-4182 **Fax:** 313-253-4026
Web: www.meridianautosystems.com

Meridian Automotive Systems has 20 principal manufacturing facilities in Brazil, Canada, Mexico, and the US.

PRODUCTS/OPERATIONS

Selected Products

Exterior Composites
Body panels
Fenders
Hood assemblies
Pickup truck boxes
Tailgates

Interiors and Exterior Lighting
Cupholders
Decorative trim panels
Door panels
Floor consoles
Fog lamps
Glove boxes
Instrument panels
Signal lamps
Tail lamps

Front and Rear End Modules
Chrome-plated and painted stamped steel bumpers
Energy absorbing foam
Plastic fascias
Steel rollform beams

COMPETITORS

A.G. Simpson
Delphi
Dura Automotive
Faurecia
Tower Automotive

HISTORICAL FINANCIALS

Company Type: Private

Income Statement FYE: December 31

	REVENUE ($ mil.)	NET INCOME ($ mil.)	NET PROFIT MARGIN	EMPLOYEES
12/02	1,100	—	—	5,500
12/01	977	—	—	5,900
12/00	803	—	—	—
12/99	468	—	—	—
Annual Growth	32.9%	—	—	(6.8%)

2001 Year-End Financials

Debt ratio: —
Return on equity: —
Cash ($ mil.): 1
Current ratio: 1.50
Long-term debt ($ mil.): 524

Revenue History

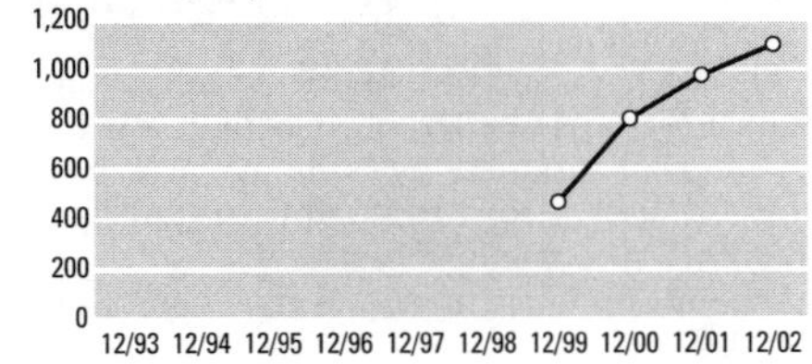

Meritage, Inc.

Meritage was founded in 1999, but it has a long heritage. The company was formed by combining three long-established North American factory automation and machine tool sales, engineering, and service companies — Hartwig, Ellison Machinery, and Robert E. Morris Company. Meritage distributes and services factory automation equipment such as machine tools, robotics products, and metrology equipment. Meritage, which is run by a six-member executive committee that includes the heads of the three founding companies, operates through 35 service and distribution locations in the US.

EXECUTIVES

CEO: Jim Ellison
Member of Executive Committee: Gary Hartwig
Member of Executive Committee: Lee Morris
CFO: Charles A. Cusumano
CIO: Craig Allen
EVP: David Goodfellow
Human Resources: Faye Lao

LOCATIONS

HQ: 9880 S. Pioneer Blvd., Santa Fe Springs, CA 90670
Phone: 562-949-8311 **Fax:** 562-949-1600
Web: www.meritageinc.com

Meritage has 35 distribution and service locations in the US.

COMPETITORS

Cameron & Barkley
DXP Enterprises
JLK Direct Distribution
MSC Industrial Direct
Production Tool Supply
Reynolds Machine & Tool
WESCO International
W.W. Grainger

HISTORICAL FINANCIALS

Company Type: Private

Income Statement FYE: December 31

	ESTIMATED REVENUE ($ mil.)	NET INCOME ($ mil.)	NET PROFIT MARGIN	EMPLOYEES
12/02	460	—	—	600
12/01	460	—	—	600
Annual Growth	0.0%	—	—	0.0%

Revenue History

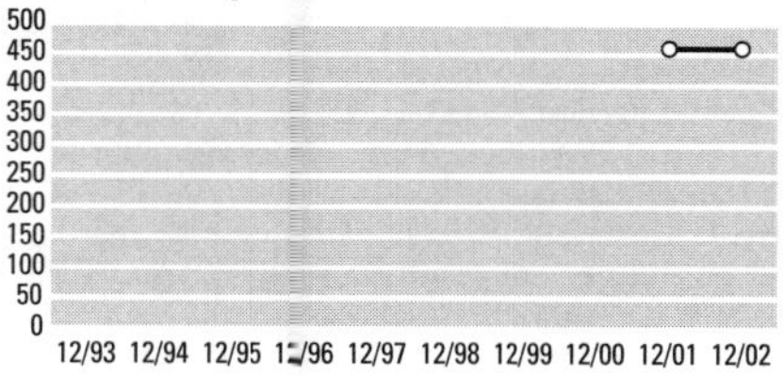

Merrill Corporation

This company merrily manages documents and provides data and printing services. Merrill Corporation is among the largest document management firms in the US and a leading provider of financial document services, such as preparing and delivering electronic filings to the SEC, producing annual reports, and creating other time-sensitive documents. It also provides software and services to help its clients manage electronic documents and maintains data centers at a number of client sites. In addition, Merrill provides corporate communication materials and traditional printing services. The company, controlled by Credit Suisse First Boston, has nearly 50 offices worldwide.

With its stock price flagging, the company in 1999 agreed to a buyout by affiliates of Donaldson, Lufkin & Jenrette (later acquired by Credit Suisse First Boston). However, a weak market for financial document services seriously impinged the company's ability to pay down its growing debt load in 2000 and Merrill's lenders declared the company in default the next year. A recapitalization plan completed in 2002 helped the company to get back on track.

EXECUTIVES

CEO: John W. Castro, age 54
President and COO: Rick R. Atterbury
EVP and CFO: Robert H. Nazarian
VP and Controller: Dean A. Niehus
VP DataSite Services: Paul Hartzell
President, Document Management Services: Allen J. (Al) McNee
President, Financial Document Services: Mike James
Senior Account Manager: Kenneth J. Green
Sales, Financial Document Services Division: Tom Chorske

LOCATIONS

HQ: 1 Merrill Circle, St. Paul, MN 55108
Phone: 651-646-4501 **Fax:** 651-646-5332
Web: www.merrillcorp.com

Merrill has offices in Australia, Canada, France, Germany, the UK, and the US. It has affiliate offices in Africa, Asia, Australia, Europe, Latin America, and the Middle East.

PRODUCTS/OPERATIONS

Selected Products and Services

Document management services
- Copying
- Desktop publishing
- Fax management

Financial document services
Merrill Print Group
- Commercial printing
- Creative design services
- Digital prepress services
- Printing

Strategic communication services
- Brochures
- Business cards
- Letterhead
- Newsletters
- Point-of-purchase materials
- Print delivery systems
- Retail forms

COMPETITORS

ADP
Banta
Bowne
Cadmus Communications
Consolidated Graphics
Kinko's
Mail-Well
Moore Corporation
Premier Print Holdings
Quad/Graphics
R. R. Donnelley
St. Ives
Service Point
Standard Register
Workflow Management

HISTORICAL FINANCIALS

Company Type: Private

Income Statement FYE: January 31

	REVENUE ($ mil.)	NET INCOME ($ mil.)	NET PROFIT MARGIN	EMPLOYEES
1/02*	603	—	—	4,086
1/00	588	—	—	4,157
1/99	510	—	—	3,933
1/98	460	—	—	3,838
1/97	354	—	—	2,804
1/96	245	—	—	2,253
1/95	237	—	—	1,739
1/94	182	—	—	1,601
1/93	148	—	—	1,041
1/92	125	—	—	831
Annual Growth	19.1%	—	—	19.4%

*Irregular reporting interval

Revenue History

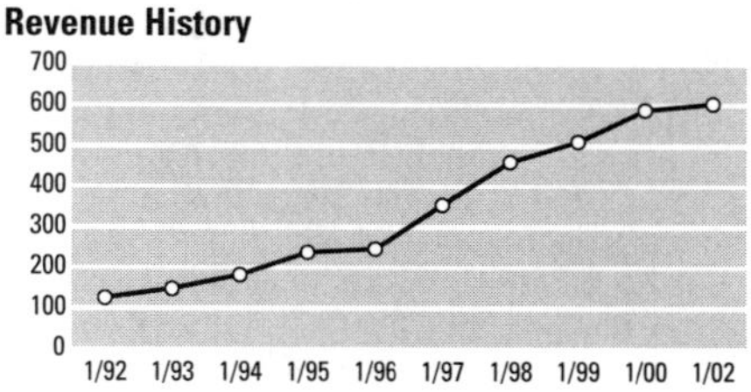

Metaldyne Corporation

Whether you're cruising down the highway or being towed, Metaldyne products may be involved. The metal-forming and -machining company's Chassis Group, Engine Group, and Driveline Group make automotive components for passenger cars and commercial vehicles. Products include components and assemblies for engines, noise and vibration control, transmissions, wheels, suspensions, axles, and drivelines. Metaldyne, now part of Heartland Industrial Partners, was formed through the consolidation of MascoTech, Simpson Industries, and Global Metal Technologies.

EXECUTIVES

Chairman, President and CEO: Timothy D. Leuliette, age 53, $2,650,000 pay
EVP and CFO: William M. (Bill) Lowe Jr., age 49, $577,112 pay
Group President, Chassis Group: Joseph Nowak, age 52
Group President, Driveline and Transmission Group: Bruce Swift
Group President, Engine Group: George Thanopoulos, age 39, $537,381 pay
VP, Human Resources: Jim Strahley
VP, Sales and Marketing: Chuck Pestow
Director of Corporate Communications: Kurt Ruecke
Corporate Legal Counsel: Jeff Pollock
Auditors: PricewaterhouseCoopers LLP

LOCATIONS

HQ: 47659 Halyard Dr., Plymouth, MI 48170
Phone: 734-207-6200 **Fax:** 734-207-6500
Web: www.metaldyne.com

Metaldyne operates more than 50 manufacturing and technology centers in 11 countries.

2002 Sales

	$ mil.	% of total
North America		
US	1,473	82
Other countries	62	4
Europe	247	14
Australia	11	—
Total	**1,793**	**100**

PRODUCTS/OPERATIONS

Selected Products

Axles and drivelines
Engine parts
Noise, vibration, and harshness products
Transmission and transfer case products
Wheel-end and suspension products

COMPETITORS

American Axle & Manufacturing
ArvinMeritor, Inc.
Dana
Delco Remy
Delphi
Eaton
GKN
NGK INSULATORS
Raytech
Robert Bosch
SPS Technologies
Sypris Solutions
Visteon

HISTORICAL FINANCIALS

Company Type: Private

Income Statement FYE: December 31

	REVENUE ($ mil.)	NET INCOME ($ mil.)	NET PROFIT MARGIN	EMPLOYEES
12/02	1,793	(62)	—	7,100
12/01	2,128	(43)	—	12,500
12/00	1,650	56	3.4%	11,600
12/99	1,680	92	5.5%	9,500
12/98	1,636	98	6.0%	9,200
12/97	922	115	12.5%	9,000
12/96	1,281	52	4.0%	5,100
12/95	1,678	59	3.5%	10,800
12/94	1,702	(220)	—	12,700
12/93	1,583	48	3.0%	12,200
Annual Growth	1.4%	—	—	(5.8%)

2002 Year-End Financials

Debt ratio: 111.3%
Return on equity: —
Cash ($ mil.): 19
Current ratio: 0.85
Long-term debt ($ mil.): 669

Net Income History

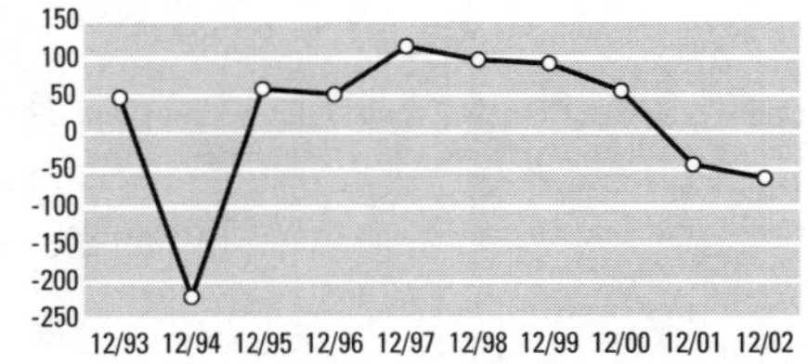

Metromedia Company

Metromedia Company has a lot of irons in a lot of fires. The global media and communications giant is one of the US's largest private companies. Through Metromedia International Group it has interests in telecommunications ventures in Eastern Europe and the former Soviet Union. These include cable TV, wireless and land-based phone systems, radio stations, and toll-calling services. Metromedia also controls Metromedia Fiber Network, which operates fiber-optic networks in urban areas. Its Metromedia Energy is an energy broker and provider of long-distance telephone services. Metromedia Restaurant Group owns or franchises some 1,000 Ponderosa, Bennigan's, Bonanza, and Steak and Ale restaurants worldwide.

In 2002 Metromedia Fiber Network filed for Chapter 11 bankruptcy, citing a lower than expected demand for broadband connections in large cities. John Kluge resigned from the Metromedia Fiber Network board late that year.

Billionaire investors John Kluge (chairman of Metromedia Company) and Stuart Subotnick (EVP) run the company through a partnership.

HISTORY

German immigrant John Kluge, born in 1914, came to Detroit at age eight with his mother and stepfather. He later worked at the Ford assembly line. At Columbia University he studied economics and (to the chagrin of college administrators) poker, building a tidy sum with his winnings by graduation. Kluge worked in Army intelligence during WWII. After the war he bought WGAY radio in Silver Spring, Maryland, and went on to buy and sell other small radio stations.

Kluge began to diversify, entering the wholesale food business in the mid-1950s. In 1959 he purchased control of Metropolitan Broadcasting, including TV stations in New York and Washington, DC, and took it public. He renamed the company Metromedia in 1960.

Metromedia added independent stations — to the then-legal limit of seven — in other major markets, paying relatively little compared to network affiliate prices. The stations struggled through years of infomercials but thrived in the late 1970s and early 1980s. Metromedia's stock price rose from $4.50 in 1974 to more than $500 in 1983. The company also acquired radio stations, the Harlem Globetrotters, and the Ice Capades.

In 1983 Kluge bought paging and cellular telephone licenses across the US. He later acquired long-distance carriers in Texas and Florida. In 1984 Metromedia went private in a $1.6 billion buyout and began to sell off its assets in 1985. It sold its Boston TV station to Hearst and its six other TV stations to Rupert Murdoch for a total of $2 billion. In 1986 it sold its outdoor advertising firm, nine of its 11 radio stations, and the Globetrotters and Ice Capades. Kluge then sold most of the company's cellular properties to SBC Communications. In 1990 it sold its New York cellular operations to LIN Broadcasting and its Philadelphia cellular operations to Comcast.

Building what Kluge envisioned as his steak house empire, the firm bought the Ponderosa steak house chain (founded in the late 1960s) in 1988 from Asher Edelman and later added Dallas-based USA Cafes (Bonanza steak houses, founded 1964) and S&A Restaurant Corp. (Steak and Ale, founded 1966; Bennigan's, founded 1976). Also in 1988 Kluge rescued friend Arthur Krim, whose Orion Pictures was threatened by Viacom, by buying control of the filmmaker.

Kluge's grand steak house vision did not come to fruition. Increased competition squeezed profits at Ponderosa and Bonanza. The restaurant group also was plagued by management shake-ups, aging facilities, food-quality issues, and even bad press. (Bennigan's was ranked the worst casual dining chain in the US in a 1992 Consumer Reports poll.)

In 1989 Kluge merged Metromedia Long Distance with the long-distance operations of ITT. Renamed Metromedia Communications in 1991, the company merged with other long-distance providers to become MCI WorldCom. (Kluge sold his 16% of MCI WorldCom to the public in 1995.)

Kluge created Metromedia International Group in 1995 by merging Orion Pictures, Metromedia International Telecommunications, MCEG Sterling (film and television production), and Actava Group (maker of Snapper lawn mowers and sporting goods — sold 2002). Metromedia Restaurant Group announced a $190 million refinancing agreement for S&A Restaurant Corp. in 1998 to expand and refurbish its restaurants; it closed 28 unprofitable restaurants that year and launched a franchise program to grow its Bennigan's and Steak and Ale chains.

Metromedia expanded its Bennigan's units in South Korea in 1999 and the next year announced it would build 65 new restaurants in the US and expand to more than 200 units internationally. In 2001 Verizon Communications invested nearly $2 billion in Metromedia Fiber Network, but the latter company was forced to declare Chapter 11 bankruptcy the following year. It blamed lower than expected demand for its metropolitan Internet services due to stiff competition, which drove down prices.

EXECUTIVES

Chairman and President: John W. Kluge, age 87
EVP; President and CEO, Metromedia International Group: Stuart Subotnick, age 61
SVP Finance and Treasurer: Robert A. Maresca
SVP, Secretary, and General Counsel: David A. Persing
SVP: Silvia Kessel
VP and Controller: David Gassler
VP Financial Reporting: Vincent D. Sasso Jr., age 42
VP: Mario P. Catuogno
Manager Human Resources: Jamie Smith-Wagner
Manager Pension and Profit Sharing: Patti Ann Kletz
Auditors: KPMG LLP

LOCATIONS

HQ: 1 Meadowlands Plaza, East Rutherford, NJ 07073
Phone: 201-531-8000 **Fax:** 201-531-2804

PRODUCTS/OPERATIONS

Selected Subsidiaries and Affiliates

Metromedia Energy (energy and long-distance telephone service)
Metromedia Fiber Network, Inc. (competitive local-exchange carrier)
Metromedia International Group, Inc. (telecommunications)
Metromedia Restaurant Group (Bennigan's, Bonanza, Ponderosa, Steak and Ale)

COMPETITORS

Applebee's
AT&T
Brinker
BT
Buffets
Carlson Restaurants
Darden
Deutsche Telekom
Hellenic Telecommunications
Level 3 Communications
Lone Star Steakhouse
O'Charley's
Outback Steakhouse
Perkins
Rostelecom
Ryan's
Sprint FON
Verizon
WorldCom
Worldwide Restaurant Concepts

HISTORICAL FINANCIALS

Company Type: Private

Income Statement FYE: December 31

	ESTIMATED REVENUE ($ mil.)	NET INCOME ($ mil.)	NET PROFIT MARGIN	EMPLOYEES
12/02	1,450	—	—	29,500
12/01	1,400	—	—	28,500
12/00	1,500	—	—	29,500
12/99	1,610	—	—	32,000
12/98	1,500	—	—	62,700
12/97	1,950	—	—	63,000
12/96	1,900	—	—	—
12/95	1,900	—	—	—
12/94	2,000	—	—	—
12/93	1,900	—	—	—
Annual Growth	(3.0%)	—	—	(14.1%)

Revenue History

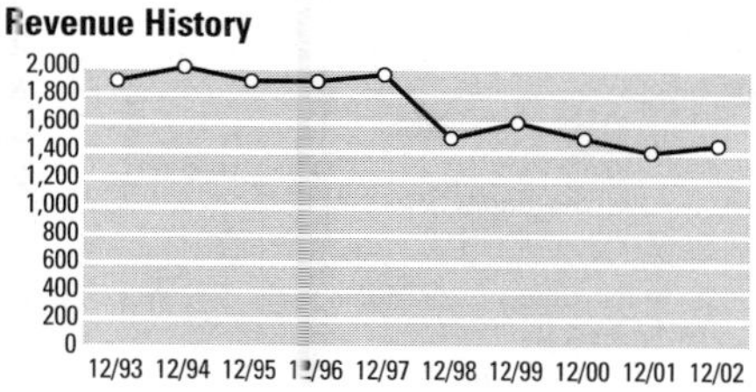

Metropolitan Transportation Authority

No Sigma Chi or Chi Omega chapter has anything on New York City's Metropolitan Transportation Authority (MTA) — it rushes millions of people on an average day. The largest public transportation system in the US, the government-owned MTA moves more than 2.3 billion passengers a year. The MTA's New York City Transit Authority runs a fleet of about 5,100 buses in New York City's five boroughs, provides subway service to all but Staten Island, and operates the Staten Island Railway. Other MTA units offer bus and rail service to Connecticut and Long Island and maintains the Triborough system of toll bridges and tunnels.

The MTA, a public-benefit corporation chartered by the New York Legislature, is working to become more self-sufficient. It has cut expenses through more efficient administration and maintenance. The agency also has introduced electronic fare collection (MetroCard) and toll collection (E-Z Pass), and the once-ubiquitous subway token has been phased out. But operating deficits have persisted, and the MTA has increased fares and taken advantage of low interest rates to restructure its debt.

In addition, the MTA has announced plans to restructure its bus operations by combining the bus units of three of its operating entities: the New York City Transit Authority, the Metropolitan Suburban Bus Authority, and the Manhattan and Bronx Surface Transit Operating Authority.

HISTORY

Mass transit began in New York City in the 1820s with the introduction of horse-drawn stagecoaches run by small private firms. By 1832 a horse-drawn railcar operating on Fourth Avenue offered a smoother and faster ride than its street-bound rivals.

By 1864 residents were complaining that horsecars and buses were overcrowded and that drivers were rude. (Horsecars were transporting 45 million passengers annually.) In 1870 a short subway under Broadway was opened, but it remained a mere amusement. Elevated steam railways were built, but people avoided them because of the smoke, noise and danger from explosions. Cable cars arrived in the 1880s, and by the 1890s electric streetcars became important.

Construction of the first commercial subway line was completed in 1904. The line was operated by Interborough Rapid Transit (IRT), which leased the primary elevated rail line in 1903 and had effective control of rail transit in Manhattan and the Bronx. In 1905 IRT merged with the Metropolitan Street Railway, which ran most of the surface railways in Manhattan, giving the firm almost complete control of the city's rapid transit. Public protests led the city to grant licenses to Brooklyn Rapid Transit (later BMT), creating the Dual System. The two rail firms covered most of the city.

By the 1920s the transit system was again in crisis, largely because the two lines were not allowed to raise their five-cent fares. With the IRT and BMT in receivership in 1932, the city decided to own and operate part of the rail system and organized the Independent (IND) rail line. Pressure for public ownership and operation of the transit system resulted in the city's purchase of all of IRT's and BMT's assets in 1940 for $326 million.

In 1953 the legislature created the New York City Transit Authority, the first unified system. In 1968, two years after striking transit workers left the city in a virtual gridlock, the Metropolitan Transit Authority began to coordinate the city's transit activities with other commuter services.

The 1970s and 1980s saw the city's transit infrastructure and service deteriorate as crime, accidents, and fares rose. But by the early 1990s a modernization program had begun to make improvements: Subway stations were repaired, graffiti was removed from trains, and service was extended. By 1994 the agency said subway crime was down 50% from 1990, and ridership had increased.

The MTA set up a five-year plan in 1995 to cut expenses by $3 billion. Only 18 months later and already two-thirds of the way to reaching the goal, the authority said it would cut another $230 million and return the savings to customers as fare discounts. The agency agreed in 1996 to sell Long Island Rail Road's freight operations. The next year it began selling its one-fare/free-transfer MetroCard Gold.

In 1998 the MTA capital program completed the $200 million restoration of the Grand Central Terminal. The next year the MTA ordered 500 new clean-fuel buses. But the agency suffered a setback when New York State's $3.8 billion Transportation Infrastructure Bond Act, which included $1.6 billion for MTA improvements, was rejected by voters in 2000.

MTA subway lines in lower Manhattan suffered extensive damage from the September 11, 2001, terrorist attacks that destroyed the World Trade Center's twin towers. The attacks left the MTA (which was already seeking billions of dollars for improvements) faced with $530 million worth of damage.

Facing a budget gap for the 2003 fiscal year, the MTA authorized the sale of nearly $2.9 billion worth of transportation bonds, the largest bond issue in the agency's history. The MTA had hoped the eventual proceeds from the bonds would help stave off a fare increase, but in 2003 the agency raised subway and bus fares from $1.50 to $2, among other fare and toll increases.

EXECUTIVES

Chairman: Peter S. Kalikow
Vice Chairman: Edward B. (Ted) Dunn
Vice Chairman: David S. Mack
Executive Director and COO: Katherine N. Lapp
Deputy Executive Director, Administration: Linda Kleinbaum
Deputy Executive Director, Corporate Affairs and Communications: Christopher P. Boylan
Deputy Executive Director, General Counsel, and Secretary: Catherine A. Rinaldi
President, MTA Bridges and Tunnels: Michael C. Ascher
President, MTA Long Island Bus: Neil S. Yellin
Acting President, MTA Long Island Railroad: James J. (Jim) Dermody
President, MTA Metro-North Railroad: Peter A. Cannito
President, MTA New York City Transit: Lawrence G. Reuter
Director Budgets and Financial Management: Gary G. Caplan
Auditor General: Paul Spinelli
Chief of Staff: Maureen E. Boll
Director of Security: William A. Morange
Auditors: Deloitte & Touche LLP

LOCATIONS

HQ: 347 Madison Ave., New York, NY 10017
Phone: 212-878-7000 **Fax:** 212-878-0186
Web: www.mta.nyc.ny.us

MTA New York City Transit operates buses in all five New York City boroughs and provides subway service to all but Staten Island. It also maintains seven bridges and two tunnels in New York City. The MTA Staten Island Railway extends from the Staten Island Ferry landing 14 miles south to Tottenville. MTA Metro-North Railroad has rail lines to outlying counties in New York and Connecticut. MTA Long Island Bus operates buses in Nassau, Queens, and Suffolk counties. MTA Long Island Rail Road has rail lines to Nassau and Suffolk counties.

PRODUCTS/OPERATIONS

2002 Sales

	% of total
Passengers	74
Tolls	23
Other	3
Total	**100**

Selected Operating Units

The Long Island Rail Road Company (MTA Long Island Rail Road)
Metro-North Commuter Railroad Company (MTA Metro-North Railroad)
Metropolitan Suburban Bus Authority (MTA Long Island Bus)
New York City Transit Authority (MTA New York City Transit)
Staten Island Rapid Transit Operating Authority (MTA Staten Island Railway)
Triborough Bridge and Tunnel Authority (MTA Bridges and Tunnels)

COMPETITORS

BostonCoach
Coach USA
Laidlaw International
Amtrak
Port Authority of NY & NJ
SuperShuttle International

HISTORICAL FINANCIALS

Company Type: Government-owned

Income Statement

FYE: December 31

	REVENUE ($ mil.)	NET INCOME ($ mil.)	NET PROFIT MARGIN	EMPLOYEES
12/02	4,053	360	8.9%	64,138
12/01	4,052	390	9.6%	64,169
12/00	4,033	(386)	—	62,800
12/99	5,590	(489)	—	58,000
12/98	5,707	(7)	—	57,551
12/97	5,511	(93)	—	57,563
12/96	5,381	440	8.2%	56,551
12/95	5,005	(154)	—	58,201
12/94	5,189	(156)	—	65,465
12/93	5,036	(136)	—	64,838
Annual Growth	(2.4%)	—	—	(0.1%)

Net Income History

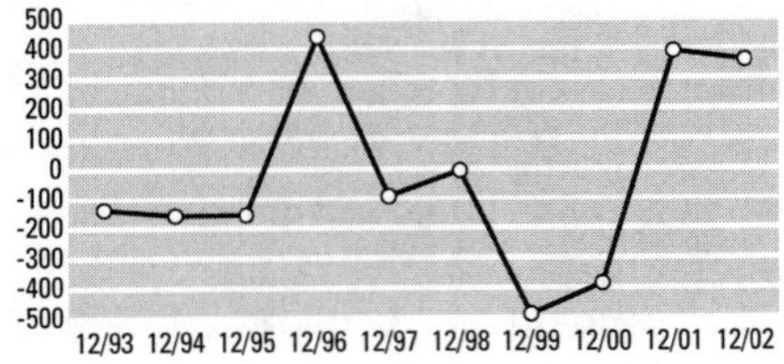

MFA Incorporated

Begun in 1914 when seven Missouri farmers got together to buy 1,150 pounds of binder twine, agricultural cooperative MFA today ties together 45,000 farmers in Missouri and adjacent states.

MFA, the US's oldest regional co-op, supplies its member-owners with manufacturing, distribution, and purchasing services. It runs retail service centers and works with independent dealers. MFA produces and markets beef, dairy, horse, and swine feeds, as well as soybean, corn, wheat, grass, grain, and alfalfa seeds.

The co-op also provides crop-protection services, animal-health products, and farm supplies.

EXECUTIVES

President: Don Copenhaver
SVP Corporate Operations: David Jobe
SVP Corporate and Member Services (HR): Janice Schuerman
SVP Agri Services Division: Bill Streeter
VP, CFO, and Treasurer: Allen Floyd
VP, Corporate Secretary, and General Counsel: J. Brian Griffith
VP Crop Protection, Farm Supply, and Seed Marketing: Ron Utterback
VP Distribution: Bruce Hanson
VP Feed Manufacturing and Marketing: Joe Powell
VP Livestock Operations: Kent Haden
VP Plant Foods Marketing: Charles Cott

LOCATIONS

HQ: 201 Ray Young Dr., Columbia, MO 65201
Phone: 573-874-5111 **Fax:** 573-876-5430
Web: www.mfaincorporated.com

COMPETITORS

Ag Processing
Ag Services
Alabama Farmers Cooperatives
Andersons
ADM
Cargill
CHS
ConAgra
Farmland Industries
Gold Kist
GROWMARK
Southern States
Tennessee Farmers
Wilbur-Ellis

HISTORICAL FINANCIALS

Company Type: Cooperative

Income Statement FYE: August 31

	REVENUE ($ mil.)	NET INCOME ($ mil.)	NET PROFIT MARGIN	EMPLOYEES
8/02	692	3	0.4%	1,400
8/01	621	7	1.2%	1,350
8/00	561	8	1.5%	1,300
8/99	563	—	—	1,300
8/98	644	—	—	1,400
8/97	706	—	—	1,800
8/96	667	—	—	1,200
8/95	593	—	—	—
Annual Growth	2.2%	(19.7%)	—	2.7%

2002 Year-End Financials

Debt ratio: 67.5%
Return on equity: 2.8%
Cash ($ mil.): 4
Current ratio: 1.48
Long-term debt ($ mil.): 74

Net Income History

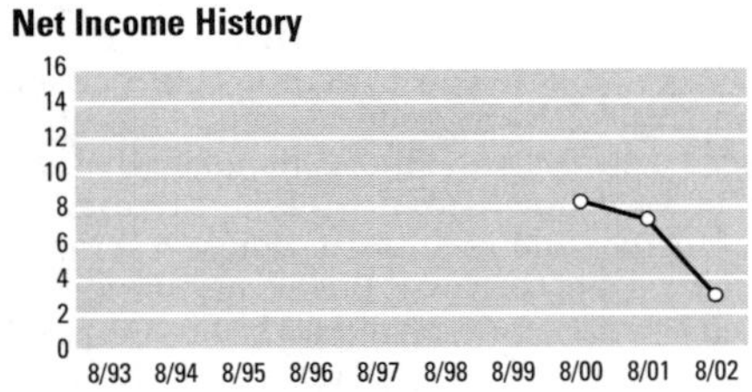

Michael Foods

With the help of 13 million hens, Michael Foods is the leading US producer of egg products (frozen, pre-cooked, dried). The food processor and distributor has several divisions, but eggs account for over half of its sales. Its Northern Star division pre-shreds and mashes potatoes. The company also packages cheese and distributes refrigerated foods. Customers include food processors, food service distributors, and grocery stores. The company is selling its dairy products division (ice cream mixes, coffee creamers) to dairy giant Dean Foods. It is also considering selling its egg products division. Thomas H. Lee has agreed to buy the company from the Michael family and investors for $1.05 billion.

EXECUTIVES

Chairman, President, and CEO: Gregg A. Ostrander, age 50, $1,170,000 pay
EVP, CFO, and Treasurer: John D. Reedy, age 57, $513,300 pay
Assistant Treasurer and Secretary: Mark D. Witmer, age 45
President, Potato Products, Dairy Products, and Refrigerated Distribution Divisions: James D. Clarkson, age 50, $513,300 pay
President, Egg Products: Bill L. Goucher, age 56, $513,300 pay
EVP of Corporate Development, Egg Products Division: Bradley L. Cook, age 47, $322,396 pay
Auditors: PricewaterhouseCoopers LLP

LOCATIONS

HQ: Michael Foods, Inc.
401 Carlson Pkwy., Ste. 300, Minnetonka, MN 55305
Phone: 952-258-4000 **Fax:** 952-258-4911
Web: www.michaelfoods.com

Michael Foods has production facilities in Canada and the US; it distributes its products in the US, with some sales in Europe, the Far East, and South America.

PRODUCTS/OPERATIONS

Selected Products

Dairy Products
Coffee creamer
Ice cream mix
Ultra-pasteurized dairy products

Egg Products
Dried eggs
Egg substitutes (Better 'n Eggs, All Whites)
Extended shelf-life liquid eggs (Easy Eggs, Table Ready)
Fresh eggs
Frozen eggs
Precooked eggs (hard boiled, patties, omelets)

Refrigerated Potato Products
Hash browns
Mashed potatoes
Specialty potato products

COMPETITORS

Cal-Maine Foods
Cargill
ConAgra
Dean Foods
Heinz
JR Simplot
Kraft Foods
Land O'Lakes
McCain Foods
Primera Foods
Rose Acre Farms
Sargento

HISTORICAL FINANCIALS

Company Type: Private

Income Statement FYE: Saturday nearest to December 31

	REVENUE ($ mil.)	NET INCOME ($ mil.)	NET PROFIT MARGIN	EMPLOYEES
12/02	1,168	30	2.5%	4,371
12/01	1,161	4	0.4%	4,050
12/00	1,081	45	4.1%	4,100
12/99	1,053	44	4.2%	4,530
12/98	1,021	40	3.9%	4,160
12/97	956	32	3.4%	3,870
12/96	616	(3)	—	2,700
12/95	537	18	3.3%	2,600
12/94	506	15	3.0%	2,700
12/93	475	(16)	—	2,550
Annual Growth	10.5%	—	—	6.2%

2002 Year-End Financials

Debt ratio: 275.3%
Return on equity: 17.9%
Cash ($ mil.): 21
Current ratio: 1.34
Long-term debt ($ mil.): 494

Net Income History

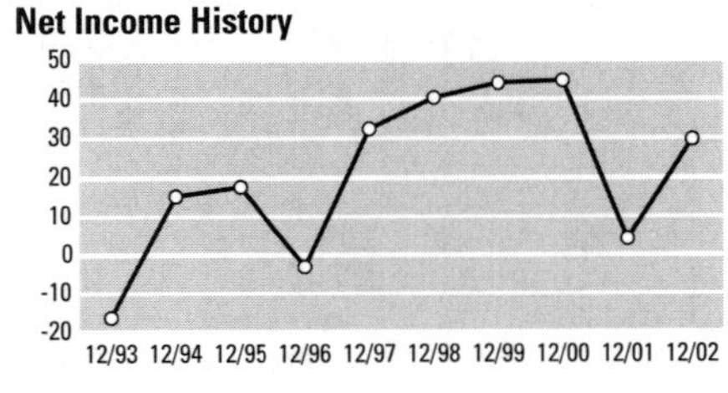

Micro Warehouse, Inc.

Micro Warehouse has undergone a not-so-micro sale. A direct-to-consumer computer products seller, the company markets its products through catalogs, the Internet, and telemarketers. Serving individual, corporate, education, and government customers, Micro Warehouse offers more than 30,000 items, including computers, hardware, software, peripherals, and networking equipment. The company was bought by an investor group (including CEO Jerome York) in 2000. Hit hard by competition and heavy debt, in September 2003 Micro Warehouse sold its North American operations to computer retailer CDW Corporation and filed for Chapter 11 bankruptcy protection.

Increased competition from manufacturers (such as Compaq, Dell, and Gateway) that market their products directly forced Micro Warehouse to restructure across the board. It streamlined business, dumping unprofitable operations (including its European headquarters and North American operations) and trimming its workforce. The company retains a distribution center in the US and operations in Europe. The company's European operations are up for sale.

EXECUTIVES

Chairman, President, and CEO: Jerome B. (Jerry) York, age 64
EVP Corporate Affairs and General Counsel: Larry Midler
EVP E-Commerce and CIO: Nihad Hafiz
EVP Finance and CFO: Lori Schmalkuche
EVP Marketing: Brian Burch
SVP Human Resources and Learning & Development: Laurie Kalman
VP Commercial Sales: Sean McGilloway
VP Marketing: Omer Artun
VP Sales Operations: Hilary Hirche

LOCATIONS

HQ: 535 Connecticut Ave., Norwalk, CT 06854
Phone: 203-899-4000 **Fax:** 203-899-4203
Web: www.warehouse.com

Micro Warehouse has operations in France, Germany, the Netherlands, the UK, and the US (distribution center only).

COMPETITORS

Apple Computer
ASI Corp.
Best Buy
Beyond
Black Box
BUY.COM
CDW
Comark
CompuCom
CompUSA
Computacenter
Cyberian Outpost
Dell
Fry's Electronics
GameStop
Gateway
GTSI
Insight Enterprises
MCSi
Micro Electronics
Office Depot
OfficeMax
PC Connection
PC Mall
PC Warehouse
Provell
SARCOM
Software Spectrum
Systemax
Tech Data
Zones

HISTORICAL FINANCIALS

Company Type: Private

Income Statement FYE: December 31

	REVENUE ($ mil.)	NET INCOME ($ mil.)	NET PROFIT MARGIN	EMPLOYEES
12/02	2,000	—	—	1,700
12/01	2,200	—	—	2,700
12/00	2,600	—	—	3,000
12/99	2,400	—	—	3,200
12/98	2,220	—	—	3,595
12/97	2,126	—	—	4,133
12/96	1,916	—	—	3,481
12/95	1,308	—	—	3,100
12/94	776	—	—	2,300
12/93	450	—	—	1,496
Annual Growth	18.0%	—	—	1.4%

Revenue History

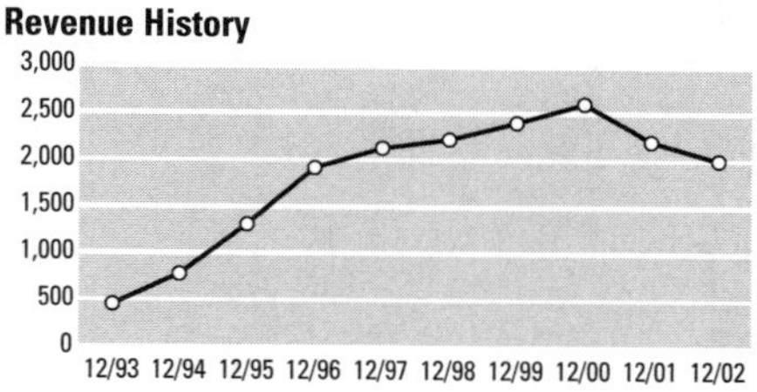

MidAmerican Energy Holdings

There's a new kind of twister tearin' up Tornado Alley. MidAmerican Energy Holdings generates, transmits, and distributes electricity to more than 680,000 customers and distributes natural gas to 660,000 customers in four Midwest states through subsidiary MidAmerican Energy Company. Its UK regional distribution subsidiaries, Northern Electric and Yorkshire Electricity, serve about 3.6 million electricity customers. MidAmerican Energy Holdings also has independent power production, real estate, and gas exploration, production, and pipeline operations. Warren Buffett's Berkshire Hathaway and other investors own the company.

MidAmerican Energy Company distributes electricity in Iowa, South Dakota, and Illinois, and it distributes natural gas in those three states plus Nebraska. It also generates 4,600 MW of electricity (primarily from coal-fired plants) and sells wholesale energy to other utilities and marketers. MidAmerican Energy Holdings' residential real estate brokerage, HomeServices of America (formerly HomeServices.Com), operates in 15 states in the US. Subsidiary CalEnergy has nearly 1,600 MW of capacity from independent power projects in the US and the Philippines.

MidAmerican Energy Holdings, which once focused on building and operating geothermal, hydroelectric, and natural gas power plants worldwide, now gets most of its revenues from its energy distribution operations. While deregulation led many regulated utilities into the independent power production business, MidAmerican Energy Holdings diversified by purchasing regulated utilities in the US and abroad. The company has also expanded its gas transportation operations through acquisitions; it operates nearly 18,000 miles of pipeline.

MidAmerican Energy Holdings was purchased by Warren Buffett's Berkshire Hathaway and other investors in 2000. Because of regulatory restrictions on utility ownership, Berkshire owns the majority of MidAmerican Energy Holdings' stock but has less than 10% of its voting control. Buffett business partner and Berkshire director Walter Scott controls a majority of MidAmerican Energy Holdings' voting rights.

HISTORY

Amid oil shortages, polluted air, and concerns about the safety of nuclear power plants, Charles Condy formed California Energy in 1971 to sell oil and gas partnerships and to consult on the development of geothermal power plants.

In 1978 Congress passed the Public Utility Regulatory Policies Act (PURPA) to wean the US from foreign oil by encouraging efficient use of fossil fuels and development of renewable and alternative energy sources. Grasping the potential of the changing energy environment, CalEnergy signed a 30-year deal with the US government in 1979 to develop the geothermal Coso Project, northeast of Los Angeles. In the 1980s CalEnergy focused entirely on geothermal development and started producing power at the Coso Project in 1987, the year the company went public.

Omaha, Nebraska-based construction firm Peter Kiewit Sons' injected some much-needed capital when it began buying a stake in the company in 1990. CalEnergy restructured in 1991, moving its headquarters from San Francisco to Omaha. It also acquired Desert Peak and Roosevelt Hot Springs geothermal areas in the US and made plans to enter markets in Asia. In 1993 the Philippine government contracted CalEnergy to develop geothermal projects. CalEnergy also obtained the rights to exploit geothermal fields in Indonesia. In 1994 the company opened a geothermal plant in Yuma, Arizona.

In 1996 CalEnergy doubled its size by acquiring rival Magma Power, and it began geothermal projects in the Salton Sea and the Imperial Valley in California. It also took advantage of the growing deregulation trend in the UK by acquiring a controlling stake in Northern Electric, a major British regional electricity company with about 1.5 million customers in northeast England and Wales.

Completing its transformation into a global power player, CalEnergy acquired gas plants in Poland and Australia in 1997. It also attracted 300,000 new gas customers in the UK. The company bought back Kiewit's stake that year. In 1998 CalEnergy subsidiary CalEnergy International Ltd. was part of a consortium (the PowerBridge Group) that won a contract to develop, synchronize, and transmit up to 1,000 MW of electricity from Lithuania to Poland, at an estimated cost of $400 million.

The next year CalEnergy bought MidAmerican Energy Holdings, an electric utility, for about $2.4 billion. CalEnergy then took the MidAmerican name and moved its headquarters to Des Moines, Iowa. Subsidiary MidAmerican Realty Services went public as HomeServices.Com; MidAmerican Energy Holdings retained a majority stake. In 2000 Warren Buffett's Berkshire Hathaway led an investor group, which included MidAmerican Energy Holdings CEO David Sokol, in purchasing MidAmerican Energy Holdings for about $2 billion and $7 billion in assumed debt.

In 2001 MidAmerican Energy Holdings bought out minority shareholders in HomeServices.Com, making it a wholly owned subsidiary. It also traded Northern Electric's electricity and gas retail supply operations for Innogy's Yorkshire Electricity distribution business in 2001.

The following year the company purchased The Williams Companies' Kern River Gas Transmission subsidiary, which operates a 926-mile interstate pipeline in the western US, in a $960 million deal. Also in 2002 MidAmerican Energy Holdings purchased the Northern Natural Gas pipeline from Dynegy for $928 million plus $950 million in assumed debt.

EXECUTIVES

Chairman and CEO: David L. Sokol, age 46
President, COO, and Director: Gregory E. Abel, age 40
SVP and CFO: Patrick J. Goodman, age 36
SVP and Chief Administrative Officer: Keith D. Hartje, age 53
SVP and General Counsel: Douglas L. Anderson, age 45
President and CEO, HomeServices of America: Ronald J. Peltier
President and COO, Northern Electric: P. Eric Connor, age 52
President, CalEnergy Generation: Edward J. Heinrich
President, CalEnergy Generation Philippines: David A. Baldwin
President, Kern River Gas: Robert L. Sluder
President, Northern Natural Gas: Mark Hewett
Auditors: Deloitte & Touche LLP

LOCATIONS

HQ: MidAmerican Energy Holdings Company
666 Grand Ave., Des Moines, IA 50309
Phone: 515-242-4300 **Fax:** 515-281-2389
Web: www.midamerican.com

MidAmerican Energy Holdings has energy operations in Illinois, Iowa, Nebraska, and South Dakota, and in Australia, the Philippines, Poland, and the UK.

PRODUCTS/OPERATIONS

2002 Sales

	$ mil.	% of total
MidAmerican Energy Co.	2,241	45
HomeServices	1,138	23
CE Electric UK	795	16
CalEnergy Generation	365	7
Northern Natural Gas	177	4
Kern River	127	3
Corporate & other	125	2
Total	**4,968**	**100**

Selected Subsidiaries

CalEnergy Generation (independent power production, Philippines and US)
CalEnergy Gas (Holdings) Limited (exploration and production, Australia, Poland, and UK)
CE Electric UK Funding
  Northern Electric plc
    Northern Electric Distribution Ltd (electricity distribution, UK)
  Yorkshire Power Group Ltd.
    Yorkshire Electricity Distribution plc (electricity distribution, UK)
HomeServices of America, Inc. (formerly HomeServices.Com, real estate brokerage)
Kern River Gas Transmission Company (natural gas pipeline)
MidAmerican Energy Company (electricity and natural gas distribution)
Northern Natural Gas Company (natural gas pipeline)

COMPETITORS

AES
Alliant Energy
Ameren
Aquila
Calpine
Dynegy
Edison International
El Paso
Entergy
International Power
Mirant
National Power
Nebraska Public Power
Nicor
Peoples Energy
Scottish and Southern Energy
Scottish Power
TXU Europe

HISTORICAL FINANCIALS

Company Type: Private

Income Statement FYE: December 31

	REVENUE ($ mil.)	NET INCOME ($ mil.)	NET PROFIT MARGIN	EMPLOYEES
12/02	4,968	380	7.6%	10,985
12/01	5,337	143	2.7%	9,780
12/00	5,103	133	2.6%	9,550
12/99	4,399	167	3.8%	9,700
12/98	2,555	127	5.0%	3,703
12/97	2,166	(84)	—	4,300
12/96	519	93	17.8%	4,400
12/95	355	63	17.9%	593
12/94	155	37	23.8%	278
12/93	132	47	35.7%	249
Annual Growth	49.6%	26.1%	—	52.3%

2002 Year-End Financials

Debt ratio: 308.5%
Return on equity: 19.0%
Cash ($ mil.): 895
Current ratio: 1.12
Long-term debt ($ mil.): 7,077

Net Income History

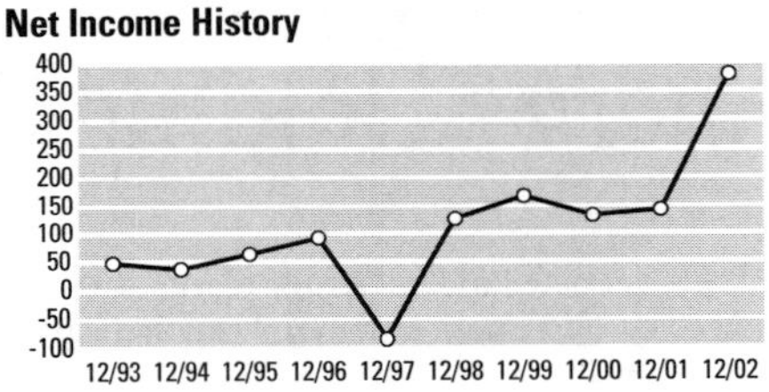

Milliken & Company Inc.

Milliken & Company makes textiles and chemicals used in products ranging from art supplies to space suits. One of the world's largest textile companies, Milliken produces finished fabrics for rugs and carpets, as well as other synthetic fabrics used in such goods as apparel, automobiles, tennis balls, and specialty textiles. It also makes chemicals and petroleum products. Milliken's colorants infuse products such as Crayola markers, its clarifying agents make plastics clear, and its various other chemical products are used in the automotive, consumer products, and turf markets. Milliken operates about 65 manufacturing operations worldwide. The Milliken family controls the company.

Roger, a billionaire who is actively campaigning against the US trade policy, has led Milliken since 1947.

HISTORY

Seth Milliken and William Deering formed a company in 1865 to become selling agents for textile mills in New England and the southern US. Deering left the partnership, and in 1869 he founded Deering Harvester (now Navistar).

Milliken set up operations in New York before the turn of the century, began buying the accounts receivable of cash-short textile mill operators, and invested in some of the companies.

In his position as agent and financier, Milliken was able to spot failing mills. He bought out the distressed owners at a discount and soon became a major mill owner himself. In 1905 Milliken and his allies waged a bitter proxy fight and court case to win control of two mills, earning Milliken a fearsome reputation.

H. B. Claflin, a New York dry-goods wholesaler that also operated department stores, owed money to Milliken. When Claflin went bankrupt in 1914, Milliken got some of the stores, which became Mercantile Stores. The Milliken family retained about 40% of the chain (sold to Dillard's in 1998).

Roger Milliken, grandson of the founder, became the president of the company in 1947 and has ruled with a firm hand. He fired brother-in-law W. B. Dixon Stroud in 1955, and none of Roger's children, nephews, or nieces has ever been allowed to work for the company. The workers at Milliken's Darlington, South Carolina, mill voted to unionize in 1956. The next day Milliken closed the plant, beginning 24 years of litigation that ended at the US Supreme Court. Milliken settled with its workers for $5 million.

In the 1960s the company introduced Visa, a finish for easy-care fabrics. Milliken launched its Pursuit of Excellence program in 1981; the program stressed self-managed teams of employees and eliminated 700 management positions. Tom Peters dedicated his 1987 bestseller, *Thriving on Chaos,* to Roger.

Away from that limelight, Milliken is (and has always been) a secretive, closely held business. In 1989 that secrecy and family control were threatened when members of the Stroud branch of the family sued the company in the Delaware courts and then sold a small number of shares to Erwin Maddrey and Bettis Rainsford, executives of Milliken competitor Delta Woodside. The courts ruled in favor of Milliken in 1992; Maddrey and Rainsford were required to sign confidentiality agreements before receiving Milliken information. Roger financially backed opponents of NAFTA in 1993.

Milliken is known by competitors for its unofficial motto: "Steal ideas shamelessly." Woven-filament maker NRB sued Milliken in 1997 for corporate spying and the following year industrial textile maker Johnston Industries filed a similar lawsuit. Milliken settled both cases out of court.

In 1999 Milliken began using its Millitron dye technology to produce residential carpets and rugs. It also introduced new brands of patterned rugs (including Royal Dynasty, Prestige, American Heritage). In 2000 the company built a manufacturing facility in South Carolina to expand its production of Millard-brand clarifying agents. Milliken announced that it would close its Union and Saluda plants by the first half of 2004.

EXECUTIVES

Chairman and CEO: Roger Milliken, age 87
Vice Chairman: Thomas J. (Tom) Malone
President and COO: Ashley Allen
CFO: Jerry Pribanic
VP, Human Resources: Curtis Pressley
President, Milliken Chemical: John Rekers
Director, Public Affairs: Richard Dillard

LOCATIONS

HQ: 920 Milliken Rd., Spartanburg, SC 29304
Phone: 864-503-2020 **Fax:** 864-503-2100
Web: www.milliken.com

Milliken & Company has about 65 manufacturing facilities worldwide, including operations in Australia, Belgium, Brazil, Denmark, France, Germany, Japan, Spain, the UK, and the US.

PRODUCTS/OPERATIONS

Selected Products

Chemicals
Carpet cleaner (Capture)
Clarifying agents for plastics (Millard)
Colorants and tints (ClearTint, Liquitint, Palmer, Reactint)
Electroconductive powders (Zelec)
Resin intermediates
Specialty chemicals
Textile chemicals (Lubestat, SynFac, SynStat, Versatint)
Turf maintenance chemicals

Fabrics, Carpet, and Rugs
Area rugs
Automotive fabrics
Carpet and carpet tiles
Drapery fabrics
Knit and woven apparel fabrics
Mats (Milliken KEX)
Mops (Milliken KEX)
Pool table cloth
Table linen fabrics
Tennis ball felt
Towels
Upholstery fabric

COMPETITORS

Asahi Kasei
Avondale Incorporated
Beaulieu of America
Burlington Industries
Collins & Aikman
Crompton
Dixie Group
Dow Chemical
DuPont
Galey & Lord
Guilford Mills
Interface
Johnston Industries
Mohawk Industries
Reliance Industries
Shaw Industries
Springs Industries
WL Gore

HISTORICAL FINANCIALS

Company Type: Private

Income Statement

FYE: November 30

	ESTIMATED REVENUE ($ mil.)	NET INCOME ($ mil.)	NET PROFIT MARGIN	EMPLOYEES
11/02	3,600	—	—	14,000
11/01	3,900	—	—	20,000
11/00	4,000	—	—	21,000
11/99	3,500	—	—	18,000
11/98	3,100	—	—	16,000
11/97	3,200	—	—	16,000
11/96	3,000	—	—	15,000
11/95	2,800	—	—	13,500
11/94	2,706	—	—	13,500
11/93	2,707	—	—	14,000
Annual Growth	3.2%	—	—	0.0%

Revenue History

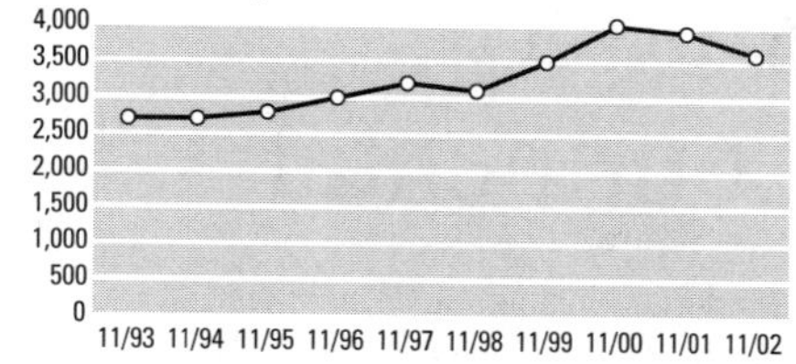

Minnesota Mutual

With 10,000 lakes in their state, Minnesotans have learned to be careful. Minnesota Mutual's flagship Minnesota Life Insurance Company helps them take care, with individual and group life and disability insurance and annuities. Other business units include Advantus Capital Management, which provides asset management. Two other subsidiaries, Securian Holding and Securian Financial (offering advisory programs, mutual funds, and annuities), were created by the conversion of Minnesota Mutual Life into the mutual holding company Minnesota Mutual Companies.

EXECUTIVES

Chairman, President, and CEO: Robert L. Senkler
EVP and Director: Robert E. Hunstad
EVP, Secretary, and General Counsel: Dennis E. Prohofsky
EVP, Individual and Retirement Services: Randy F. Wallake
SVP and CFO: Gregory S. Strong
SVP, Human Resources and Corporate Services: Keith M. Campbell
SVP, Group Insurance: James E. Johnson
SVP, Individual Insurance: Terrence M. Sullivan
SVP, Asset Management, Treasurer, and Director: William N. Westhoff
Auditors: KPMG LLP

LOCATIONS

HQ: Minnesota Mutual Companies, Inc.
400 Robert St. North, St. Paul, MN 55101
Phone: 651-665-3500 **Fax:** 651-665-4488
Web: www.minnesotamutual.com

Minnesota Mutual Companies operates nationwide.

COMPETITORS

American United
Conseco
Guardian Life
MetLife
MONY
National Western
New York Life
Northwestern Mutual
Pacific Mutual
Prudential

HISTORICAL FINANCIALS

Company Type: Private

Income Statement

FYE: December 31

	ASSETS ($ mil.)	NET INCOME ($ mil.)	INCOME AS % OF ASSETS	EMPLOYEES
12/02	17,695	4	0.0%	4,400
12/01	17,711	70	0.4%	4,400
12/00	17,900	—	—	4,400
12/99	18,354	—	—	4,400
12/98	16,434	—	—	4,400
12/97	14,402	—	—	2,187
12/96	12,443	—	—	1,950
12/95	—	—	—	1,792
12/94	—	—	—	1,716
Annual Growth	6.0%	(39.6%)	—	12.5%

2002 Year-End Financials

Equity as % of assets: 10.5%
Return on assets: 0.0%
Return on equity: 0.2%
Long-term debt ($ mil.): 137
Sales ($ mil.): 1,696

Net Income History

MMI Products

MMI Products wants to fence you in. MMI operates in two segments: fencing products and concrete construction products. The company's Merchants Metals fencing products include residential and commercial chain-link security fencing, aluminum and die-cast galvanized steel fencing fittings, and ornamental iron fence products. MMI sells its fencing products primarily to fence wholesalers and residential and commercial contractors. The company's concrete construction products include wire mesh and other products used to install reinforcing bars and grids. These products have applications in the construction of concrete pipe, bridges, and roads. Citicorp Venture Capital controls about 50% of MMI.

EXECUTIVES

Chairman: Julius S. Burns, age 70, $393,134 pay
President, CEO, and Director: John M. Piecuch, age 54, $561,070 pay
VP, CFO, and Secretary: Robert N. Tenczar, age 53, $208,922 pay
VP; President, Ivy Steel and Wire Division: James M. McCall, age 60, $245,650 pay
VP; President, Meadow Burke Products Division: Davy J. Wilkes, age 65, $252,050 pay
VP, Merchants Metals: Mike Fink
VP Sales, Merchants Metals: Dan Tinker
Director, Human Resources: Gary Hoffpauir
National Sales Manager, Merchants Metals: Matt R. McMurrough
Sales Manager, Wood and PVC Products, Merchants Metals: Steve Colley
Auditors: Ernst & Young LLP

LOCATIONS

HQ: MMI Products, Inc.
515 W. Greens Rd., Ste. 710, Houston, TX 77067
Phone: 281-876-0080 **Fax:** 281-876-1648
Web: www.merchantsmetals.com

MMI Products has 75 manufacturing and distribution centers throughout the US.

PRODUCTS/OPERATIONS

Selected Products

Aluminum die-cast fittings
Commodity building mesh
Galvanized chain-link fence fabric
Galvanized pressed-steel fittings
Ornamental iron fence products
Pipe mesh
Structural mesh
Vinyl-coated chain-link fence fabric
Vinyl-coated colored pipe
Vinyl fencing

COMPETITORS

Associated Materials
CertainTeed
Dayton Superior
Insteel
Keystone Consolidated
Oklahoma Steel and Wire
Universal Forest Products

HISTORICAL FINANCIALS

Company Type: Private

Income Statement

FYE: Saturday closest to December 31

	REVENUE ($ mil.)	NET INCOME ($ mil.)	NET PROFIT MARGIN	EMPLOYEES
12/02	505	(2)	—	2,400
12/01	502	10	2.0%	2,500
12/00	530	19	3.6%	2,590
12/99	481	19	3.9%	2,700
12/98	418	11	2.6%	2,200
12/97	347	8	2.2%	1,800
12/96	283	6	2.2%	1,400
12/95	201	—	—	1,282
12/94	150	—	—	1,000
12/93	150	—	—	1,000
Annual Growth	14.4%	—	—	10.2%

2002 Year-End Financials

Debt ratio: —
Return on equity: —
Cash ($ mil.): 3
Current ratio: 2.48
Long-term debt ($ mil.): 225

Net Income History

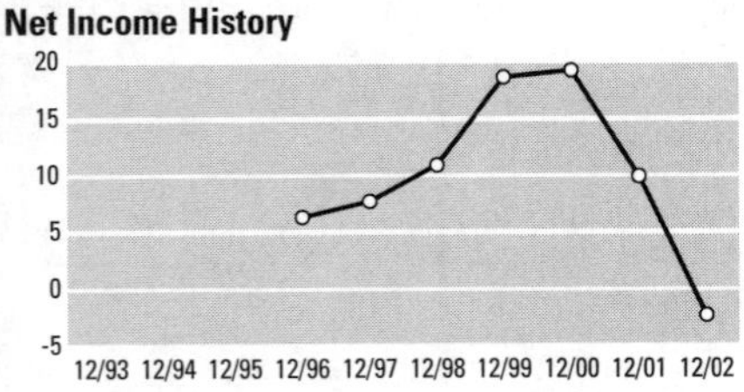

Modern Continental

Modern Continental Companies is a modern concern with Old World values. Italian immigrant Lelio (Les) Marino founded the company in 1967 after he and co-worker Kenneth Anderson left a Boston construction firm. A heavy construction leader in New England, Modern Continental Companies focuses on highways, mass transit systems, and other infrastucture projects. Its most notable current job is on Boston's Central Artery Tunnel, "The Big Dig," The company also develops residential, commercial, and marina projects; Marino's personal interests have led the company to dabble in health care, restaurant operation, organic farming, and tourism. Marino owns 75% of the company; Anderson, 25%.

EXECUTIVES

CEO: Lelio (Les) Marino
CFO: Peter Grela
EVP: Charles F. (Charlie) Madden
Director Human Resources: Edward Burns
Director Marketing: Lorraine Marino
President, Modern Continental Construction: John Pastore
Auditors: Darmody, Merlino & Co.

LOCATIONS

HQ: Modern Continental Companies, Inc.
600 Memorial Dr., Cambridge, MA 02139
Phone: 617-864-6300 **Fax:** 617-864-8766
Web: www.moderncontinental.com

Modern Continental Companies has offices in California, Georgia, Massachusetts, New York, New Jersey, North Carolina, South Carolina, and Utah in the US and abroad in Brazil and the West Indies.

PRODUCTS/OPERATIONS

Selected Construction Activities

Airports
Buildings and foundations
Design/build
Heavy civil
Highways and bridges
Mass transit and rail
Treatment facilities and utilities
Tunneling and microtunneling

Selected Subsidiaries and Affiliates

Boston Harbor Cruises (sightseeing and commuter)
Boston Yacht Haven (marina complex)
Marino Center for Progressive Health (nonprofit medical clinic)
The Marina at James Landing (marina)
Marino Lookout Farm (tourist attraction)
Modern Health Store (vitamins and health products)
Paul Revere Transportation (commuter and luxury buses)
Ristorante Marino (Italian Restaurant)

COMPETITORS

Alberici
Bechtel
Bovis Lend Lease
Centex
Clark Enterprises
Fluor
Granite Construction
HBG
Kraus-Anderson
M. A. Mortenson
McCarthy Building
PCL
Perini
Peter Kiewit Sons'
Skanska
Suffolk Construction
Swinerton
TIC Holdings
Turner Corporation
Tutor-Saliba
Walsh Group
Whiting-Turner

HISTORICAL FINANCIALS

Company Type: Private

Income Statement

FYE: June 30

	REVENUE ($ mil.)	NET INCOME ($ mil.)	NET PROFIT MARGIN	EMPLOYEES
6/02	1,117	—	—	4,823
6/01	1,118	—	—	5,700
6/00	792	—	—	5,200
6/99	665	—	—	4,750
Annual Growth	18.9%	—	—	0.5%

Revenue History

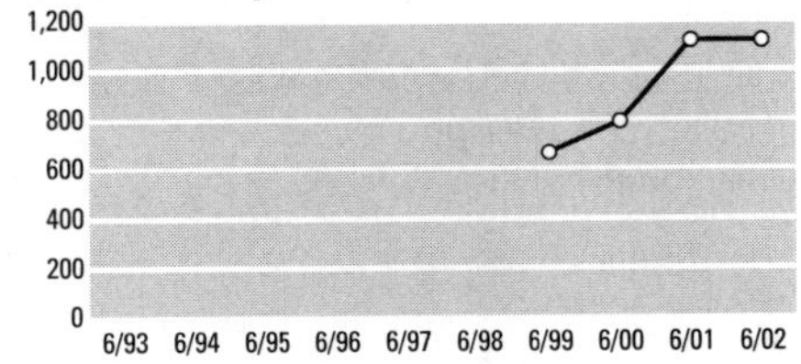

Modus Media International

The meaning of life is mysterious, so Modus Media keeps its customers fulfilled in another sense. The company provides outsourced manufacturing, fulfillment, and distribution services for such hardware and software firms as Sun Microsystems, Dell, Sony, and Microsoft. Modus Media has more than 20 globally linked supply centers in a dozen countries. In addition, it offers online transaction services such as e-commerce Web site design, payment processing, and fulfillment. Modus Media also provides customer relations services. The company was spun off from Stream International in 1998.

EXECUTIVES

Chairman: Terence M. (Terry) Leahy
CEO: R. Scott Murray
SVP and CFO: Timothy M. Adams
SVP and CIO: Jerry Kelly
SVP and General Counsel: Sheila M. Flaherty
SVP Client Services: Kate Morgans
SVP Human Resources: William H. (Bill) Shupert III
President, Americas: Dan Beck
President, Asia: Ken Southerland
President, Europe: David Tanner
Director Corporate Communications: Donna Tolley

LOCATIONS

HQ: Modus Media International, Inc.
690 Canton St., Westwood, MA 02090
Phone: 781-407-2000 **Fax:** 781-407-3800
Web: www.modusmedia.com

PRODUCTS/OPERATIONS

Selected Services

Content Manufacturing
Fulfillment and distribution
Inventory management
Procurement
Production and assembly

e-Fulfillment
Customer response centers
Return, refund, and rebate processing
Transaction processing
Web site development

COMPETITORS

Banta
Bertelsmann
Cinram
Convergys
Printech
Quebecor
Rainmaker Systems
StarTek
Sykes Enterprises
Zomax

HISTORICAL FINANCIALS

Company Type: Private

Income Statement FYE: December 31

	REVENUE ($ mil.)	NET INCOME ($ mil.)	NET PROFIT MARGIN	EMPLOYEES
12/01	606	—	—	3,860
12/00	682	—	—	4,800
12/99	698	—	—	4,500
12/98	630	—	—	4,550
12/97	685	—	—	—
12/96	812	—	—	—
12/95	912	—	—	—
Annual Growth	(6.6%)	—	—	(5.3%)

Revenue History

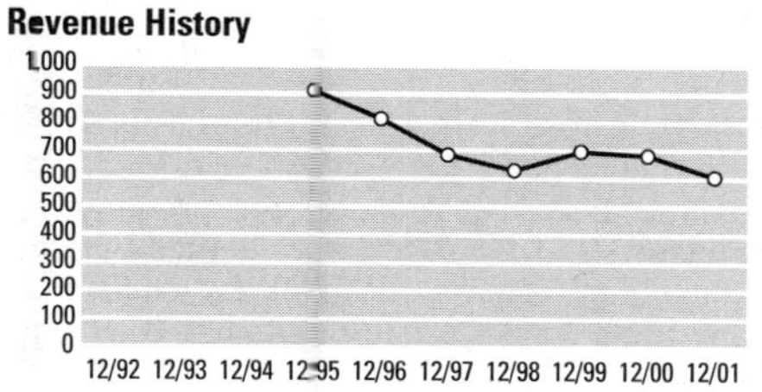

Mohegan Tribal Gaming Authority

The sun also rises at Mohegan Sun Casino, a complex run by the Mohegan Tribal Gaming Authority for the Mohegan Tribe of Indians of Connecticut. The Native American-themed facility's 315,000 sq. ft. of gaming space in the Casino of the Earth and Casino of the Sky enclose more than 6,100 slot machines, 240 gaming and 42 poker tables, and simulcast horse race wagering. The facility also includes a 1,200-room luxury hotel, a 10,000-seat arena, a 300-seat cabaret, and dozens of stores and restaurants. Gambling revenues go to after-school and cultural programs for the tribe, financial assistance to other tribes, and college education for tribal members; a quarter of the slots revenue goes to the state.

EXECUTIVES

Chairman: Mark F. Brown
President and General Manager: William J. Velardo, $1,053,000 pay
Vice Chairman: Peter Schultz
EVP Finance and CFO: Jeffrey E. Hartmann, $559,000 pay
EVP Marketing: Mitchell G. Etess, $627,000 pay
SVP Hotel Sales and Marketing: Jon Arnesen
VP Human Resources: Kevin Bogel
VP Sports and Entertainment: Paul Munick
Auditors: PricewaterhouseCoopers LLP

LOCATIONS

HQ: 1 Mohegan Sun Blvd., Uncasville, CT 06382
Phone: 860-862-8000 **Fax:** 860-862-7167
Web: www.mohegansun.com

The Mohegan Tribal Gaming Authority operates the Mohegan Sun Casino in southeastern Connecticut.

PRODUCTS/OPERATIONS

Table Games

Baccarat
Blackjack
Caribbean stud poker
Craps
Pai Gow poker
Roulette

COMPETITORS

Aztar
Harrah's Entertainment
Mashantucket Pequot Gaming
Park Place Entertainment
Trump Hotels & Casinos

HISTORICAL FINANCIALS

Company Type: Private

Income Statement FYE: September 30

	REVENUE ($ mil.)	NET INCOME ($ mil.)	NET PROFIT MARGIN	EMPLOYEES
9/02	1,042	100	9.6%	10,203
9/01	787	205	26.0%	7,583
9/00	740	146	19.7%	6,202
9/99	682	(39)	—	5,703
9/98	575	(332)	—	5,065
9/97	466	37	7.9%	4,500
Annual Growth	17.5%	22.2%	—	17.8%

2002 Year-End Financials

Debt ratio: —
Return on equity: —
Cash ($ mil.): 85
Current ratio: 0.38
Long-term debt ($ mil.): 1,052

Net Income History

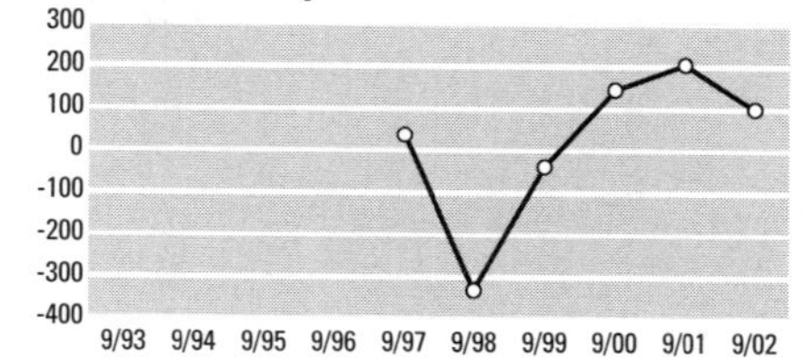

Morris Communications

What we have here is *not* a failure to communicate. Morris Communications' small-market media empire — which stretches from coast to coast — includes some 55 daily, non-daily, and free community newspapers; nearly 30 radio stations; two radio networks; 20 magazines and specialty publications; 27 tourist publications; and two book publishers; as well as online services, outdoor advertising, and printing and marketing operations. Morris has grown through acquisitions, although the company has been selling some newspapers as it consolidates operations. The firm began in 1945 when William Morris Jr. bought *The Augusta Chronicle,* a newspaper founded in 1785. The Morris family owns the company.

EXECUTIVES

Chairman and CEO: William S. Morris III, age 68
President: William S. Morris IV
VP, CFO, Secretary, and Treasurer: Craig S. Mitchell, age 44
VP, Controller, and Secretary: Darrel K. Fry
President, Fairway Outdoor Advertising: Mark E. Moyer
Marketing Director: A. Mark Smith
Director Human Resources: Martha Jean McHaney
Director of Market Research and Direct Marketing: James E. Smith
Corporate Communications: Jo Ann S. Hoffman

LOCATIONS

HQ: Morris Communications Corporation
725 Broad St., Augusta, GA 30901
Phone: 706-724-0851 **Fax:** 706-722-7125
Web: www.morriscomm.com

Morris Communications has publishing and broadcasting operations in the US and Europe.

PRODUCTS/OPERATIONS

Business Units

Book Publishing and Distribution
Broadcasting
Commercial Printing
Direct and Events Marketing
Magazines and Specialty Publications
Newspaper Publishing
Online & Computer Services
Outdoor Advertising
Radio Networks
Tourist Publications

COMPETITORS

Advance Publications
Clear Channel
Community Newspaper Holdings
Cox Enterprises
Dow Jones
Emmis Communications
Gannett
Hollinger International
Knight-Ridder
Media General
New York Times
Stephens Media Group
Tribune

HISTORICAL FINANCIALS

Company Type: Private

Income Statement FYE: December 31

	REVENUE ($ mil.)	NET INCOME ($ mil.)	NET PROFIT MARGIN	EMPLOYEES
12/01	570	—	—	6,000
12/00	601	—	—	6,000
12/99	579	—	—	5,800
12/98	539	—	—	5,600
12/97	481	—	—	5,400
12/96	439	—	—	5,400
12/95	425	—	—	5,400
12/94	416	—	—	5,140
12/93	399	—	—	—
Annual Growth	4.6%	—	—	2.2%

Revenue History

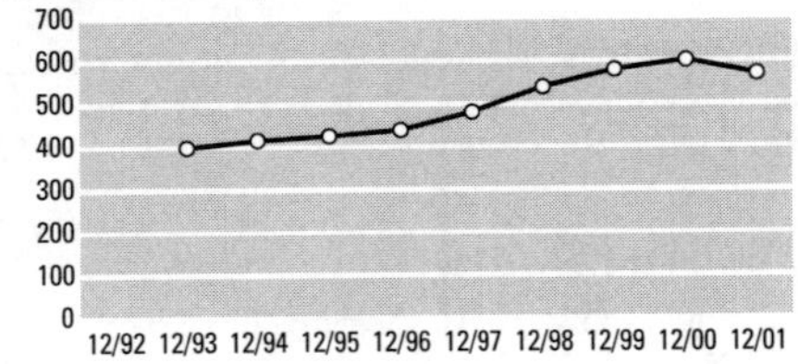

Morrison & Foerster LLP

The City by the Bay is home to some pretty steep hills, but San Francisco law firm Morrison & Foerster knows the legal lay of the land. Morrison & Foerster is known for its intellectual property and corporate finance expertise, having lent a hand in some of the most splashy Internet IPOs (EarthWeb, Netscape, uBid). Its nearly 1,000 attorneys also practice in areas such as litigation, labor and employment, and taxation. Morrison & Foerster has 12 US offices, and six offices in Europe and Asia. The firm traces its roots to a San Francisco law firm founded by Alexander Morrison and Thomas O'Brien in 1883.

EXECUTIVES

Chair: Keith Wetmore
Managing Partner for Operations: Pamela Reed
Managing Partner for Operations: Frederick Lodge
Managing Partner for Operations: Laurie Hane
CFO: William Twomey
CTO: Jo Haraf
Senior Manager of Human Resources: Kathleen Dykstra
Communications Manager: Kerry Efigenio
Communications Manager, Asia: Grace Hung
Communications Manager, Europe: Rosemary Hall
Communications Manager, New York: Casey Lawlor

LOCATIONS

HQ: 425 Market St., San Francisco, CA 94105
Phone: 415-268-7000 **Fax:** 415-268-7522
Web: www.mofo.com

Morrison & Foerster has US offices in Denver; Irvine, Los Angeles, Palo Alto, Sacramento, San Diego, San Francisco, and Walnut Creek, California; McLean, Virginia; New York City; and Washington, DC. The firm has international offices in Beijing, Brussels, Hong Kong, London, Singapore, and Tokyo.

PRODUCTS/OPERATIONS

Selected Practice Areas

Communications and mass media
Finance
Financial services
Intellectual property
International
Investment management
Labor and employment
Land use, environmental, and energy
Litigation and dispute resolution
Mergers and acquisitions
Real estate
Tax

COMPETITORS

Baker & McKenzie
Cooley Godward
Fenwick & West
Gray Cary
Heller, Ehrman
Littler Mendelson
Orrick, Herrington
Pillsbury Winthrop
Skadden, Arps
Wilson Sonsini

HISTORICAL FINANCIALS

Company Type: Partnership

Income Statement FYE: December 31

	REVENUE ($ mil.)	NET INCOME ($ mil.)	NET PROFIT MARGIN	EMPLOYEES
12/02	505	—	—	—
12/01	490	—	—	—
12/00	437	—	—	—
12/99	322	—	—	1,800
12/98	274	—	—	1,664
12/97	242	—	—	1,404
12/96	220	—	—	1,397
12/95	203	—	—	1,358
12/94	200	—	—	1,400
12/93	202	—	—	—
Annual Growth	10.7%	—	—	5.2%

Revenue History

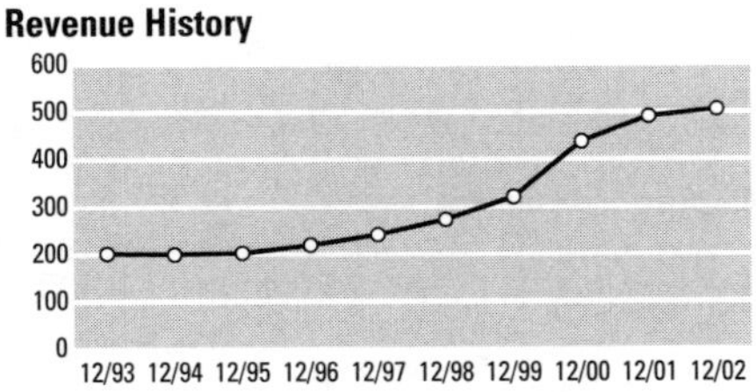

Motiva Enterprises LLC

Making money is a major motive behind Motiva Enterprises, which operates the eastern and southeastern US refining and marketing businesses of Royal Dutch/Shell's Shell Oil unit and Saudi Aramco. The company operates four refineries with a total capacity of 860,000 barrels a day, and it sells fuel at 13,000 Shell and Texaco branded gas stations. Motiva and sister company Shell Oil Products US (formerly Equilon), which operates in the West and Midwest, together make up the #1 US gasoline retailer. Motiva is a 50-50 joint venture of Shell and Saudi Aramco.

Via a long-term agreement with Saudi Aramco for crude oil supply, Motiva has holdings in almost 50 product terminals and operates three refineries on the Gulf Coast and one in Delaware.

Motiva was formed in 1998 to combine the eastern and southeastern US refining and marketing businesses of Texaco, Shell Oil, and Saudi Aramco. Texaco and Saudi Aramco each owned 35% of Motiva, and Shell owned 30%. In 2001 Texaco agreed to sell its stakes in Motiva (to Shell and Saudi Aramco) and Equilon (to Shell) to gain regulatory clearance to be acquired by Chevron. The deals were completed in 2002. Shell took full ownership of Equilon, which was renamed Shell Oil Products US.

HISTORY

Although Motiva was not created until 1998, two of its key players, Texaco and Saudi Aramco, had been doing business together in various ventures since 1936. But they had never tried anything on the scale of the Star Enterprise joint venture approved by Texaco CEO James Kinnear and Saudi Oil Minister Hisham Nazer in late 1988. The deal, valued at nearly $2 billion, was the largest joint venture of its kind in the US.

The agreement to create Star Enterprise sprang, in part, from Texaco's tumultuous ride following its purchase of Getty Oil in 1983. Texaco was sued by Pennzoil for pre-empting Pennzoil's bid for Getty, and Pennzoil won a $10.5 billion judgment in 1985. Texaco filed for bankruptcy in 1987 and eventually settled with Pennzoil for $3 billion.

In 1988 Texaco emerged from bankruptcy after announcing a deal with Saudi Aramco at a stockholder meeting. Texaco got a much-needed injection of cash, and Saudi Aramco gained a steady US outlet for its supply of crude. The Saudis had been at odds with their OPEC partners for several years, and in late 1985 then-Saudi Oil Minister Sheikh Yamani and Saudi Aramco began increasing production, leading to an oil price crash in 1986. Nazer replaced Yamani and changed Saudi Aramco's strategy. To secure market share, the Saudis started signing long-term supply contracts.

The deal with Texaco gave Saudi Aramco a 50% interest in Texaco's refining and marketing operations in the East and on the Gulf Coast — about two-thirds of Texaco's US downstream operations — including three refineries and its Texaco-brand stations. In return, the Saudis paid $812 million cash and provided three-fourths of Star's initial inventory, about 30 million barrels of oil. They also agreed to a 20-year, 600,000-barrel-a-day commitment of crude. Each company named three representatives to Star's management.

The new company soon initiated a modernization and expansion program: It acquired 65 stations, built 30 new outlets, and remodeled another 172 during 1989. In 1994 it began franchising its Texaco-brand Star Mart convenience stores. By mid-1995 it had sold 30 franchises.

Facing a more competitive oil marketing environment in the US, Shell Oil approached Texaco in 1996 with the possibility of merging some of their operations. In 1998 Shell and Texaco formed Equilon Enterprises, a joint venture that combined their western and midwestern refining and marketing activities.

Later that year Shell and Texaco/Saudi Aramco (Star Enterprises) formed Motiva to merge the companies' refining and marketing businesses on the East Coast and Gulf Coast. Shell and Texaco also formed two more Houston companies as satellite firms for Motiva and Equilon: Equiva Trading Company, a general partnership that provides supplies and trading services, and Equiva Services, which provides support services. L. Wilson Berry, the former president of Texaco Refining and Marketing, took over as CEO of Motiva.

In 1999 Motiva and Equilon together bought 15 product terminals from Premcor. To boost profits, the Motiva board appointed Texaco downstream veteran Roger Ebert as its new CEO in 2000, replacing Berry, who announced his resignation after a Motiva board meeting.

US government regulators in 2001 required that Texaco sell its Motiva and Equilon stakes in order to be acquired by Chevron. That year Texaco veteran John Boles replaced Ebert (who retired) as CEO. Shell and Saudi Aramco agreed to buy Texaco's stake in Motiva, and Shell agreed to buy Texaco's stake in Equilon. The deals were completed in 2002.

EXECUTIVES

President and CEO: John Boles
CFO: William M. Kaparich
VP Commercial Marketing and Distribution: Ralph Grimmer
VP Human Resources and Corporate Services: Bruce Culpepper
VP Refining: Carmine Falcone
General Manager Wholesale: Hugh Cooley
Chief Diversity Officer: John Jefferson
General Counsel: Rick Frazier

LOCATIONS

HQ: 1100 Louisiana St., Houston, TX 77002
Phone: 713-277-8000 **Fax:** 713-277-9099
Web: www.motivaenterprises.com

Motiva operates gas stations in the northeastern and southeastern US. It has refineries in Convent and Norco, Louisiana; Delaware City, Delaware; and Port Arthur, Texas.

Major Operations

Alabama
Arkansas
Connecticut
Delaware
Florida
Georgia
Louisiana
Maryland
Massachusetts
Mississippi
New Hampshire
New Jersey
New York
North Carolina
Pennsylvania
Rhode Island
Tennessee
Texas
Vermont
Virginia

COMPETITORS

7-Eleven
BP
CITGO
Cumberland Farms
Exxon Mobil
Gulf Oil
Marathon Ashland Petroleum
Racetrac Petroleum
Sunoco
Valero Energy
Wawa

HISTORICAL FINANCIALS

Company Type: Joint venture

Income Statement

FYE: December 31

	REVENUE ($ mil.)	NET INCOME ($ mil.)	NET PROFIT MARGIN	EMPLOYEES
12/02	16,700	—	—	3,800
12/01	18,000	—	—	5,000
12/00	19,446	—	—	8,000
12/99	12,196	—	—	6,000
12/98	5,371	—	—	3,750
Annual Growth	32.8%	—	—	0.3%

Revenue History

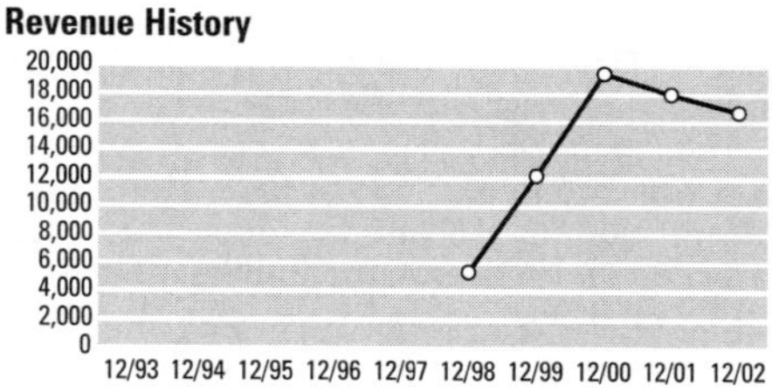

Motor Coach Industries

Do you know what NFL analyst John Madden and inmates of the Los Angeles County jail have in common? Both of them take a bus — a bus made by Motor Coach Industries International (MCII). The company builds luxury buses under the MCII and Dina brands. MCII's buses are up to 45 feet long and, if you buy one like Madden's, offer such creature comforts as full kitchens and marble bathtubs (inmates enjoy fewer amenities). The company's commuter coaches feature vacuum flush toilets and six-monitor video systems. MCII also makes ISTV prison buses and offers motor coach service, financing, and refurbishing. Investment firm Joseph Littlejohn & Levy owns more than 60% of MCII; Mexico's Gómez-Flores family owns the rest.

EXECUTIVES

CEO: Stephen K. Clough
President and COO: Tom Sorrells III
CFO: Allan Swanson
VP and General Manager, Financial Services: Michael Denny
VP, Corporate Marketing: Patricia Ziska
VP, General Counsel and Secretary: Timothy J. Nalepka
VP, Human Resources: Pete Tully
VP, Sales and Marketing: Gregory Berg

LOCATIONS

HQ: Motor Coach Industries International, Inc.
1700 E. Golf Rd., Schaumburg, IL 60173
Phone: 847-285-2000 **Fax:** 847-285-2079
Web: www.mcicoach.com

Motor Coach Industries International's three manufacturing plants are in North Dakota, Canada, and Mexico. It operates service centers in California, Illinois, New Jersey, and Texas in the US, and in Quebec, Canada.

PRODUCTS/OPERATIONS

Selected Products

Charter and tour coaches
Commuter and transit coaches
Conversion shells
Inmate Security Transportation Vehicles (ISTVs, prison buses)

COMPETITORS

Coachmen
Fleetwood Enterprises
Freightliner
Mayflower
Monaco Coach
Rexhall
Supreme Industries
Thor Industries
Winnebago

HISTORICAL FINANCIALS

Company Type: Private

Income Statement

FYE: December 31

	REVENUE ($ mil.)	NET INCOME ($ mil.)	NET PROFIT MARGIN	EMPLOYEES
12/01	700	—	—	4,200
12/00	692	—	—	4,200
12/99	911	—	—	4,600
12/98	932	—	—	4,500
Annual Growth	(9.1%)	—	—	(2.3%)

Revenue History

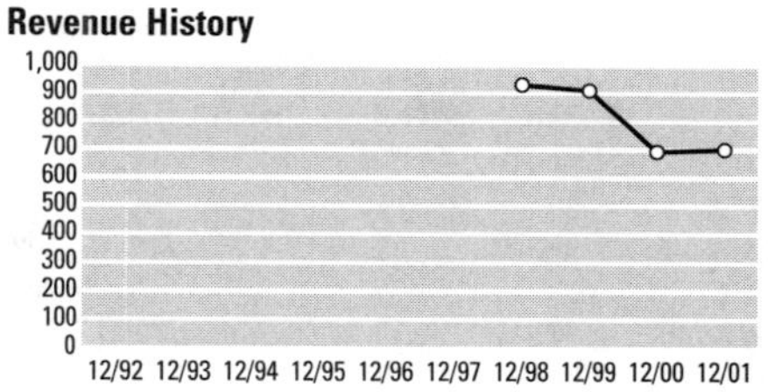

MSX International

MSX International (MSXI) never tires of steering its clients into the driver's seat. The company provides staffing, engineering, and other business services to clients primarily from the auto industry. MSXI generates the majority of its sales by providing services to automotive companies, including DaimlerChrysler, Ford, and GM. Among its offerings are temporary and permanent staffing, executive search, training, product engineering, program management, supply chain management, and custom communications. Citigroup owns about 75% of the company.

Although MSXI has concentrated heavily on the auto industry, the company wants to expand its presence in such industries as health care, consumer products, and financial services.

EXECUTIVES

Chairman: Erwin H. (Bill) Billig, age 76
Vice Chairman and CEO: Thomas T. (Tom) Stallkamp, age 56
EVP and CFO: Frederick K. (Fred) Minturn, age 45
SVP Sales and Account Management: Lorne Hamilton
SVP Supply Chain Management: H. James (Jim) Carleton
VP Human Resources and Intellectual Capital Services: Paul J. Wagner
VP Marketing and Corporate Communications: Bruce Wagner
Auditors: PricewaterhouseCoopers LLP

LOCATIONS

HQ: MSX International, Inc.
22355 W. Eleven Mile Rd., Southfield, MI 48034
Phone: 248-299-1000 **Fax:** 248-829-6250
Web: www.msxi.com

MSX International has 117 locations in 26 countries.

COMPETITORS

Adecco
ADP
Bowne
CDI
EDS
IBM
ICG Commerce
Keane
Kelly Services
Kforce
Lason
Manpower
Monster
Pininfarina
Randstad
Volt Information
Xerox

HISTORICAL FINANCIALS

Company Type: Private

Income Statement FYE: Sunday nearest December 31

	REVENUE ($ mil.)	NET INCOME ($ mil.)	NET PROFIT MARGIN	EMPLOYEES
12/02	807	(63)	—	7,923
12/01	929	1	0.1%	10,142
12/00	1,035	15	1.4%	14,000
12/99	760	10	1.3%	9,594
12/98	1,081	3	0.3%	7,899
12/97	565	(3)	—	—
12/96	228	4	1.7%	—
12/95	216	6	3.0%	—
12/94	185	5	2.9%	—
Annual Growth	20.3%	—	—	0.1%

2002 Year-End Financials

Debt ratio: —
Return on equity: —
Cash ($ mil.): 11
Current ratio: 1.02
Long-term debt ($ mil.): 231

Net Income History

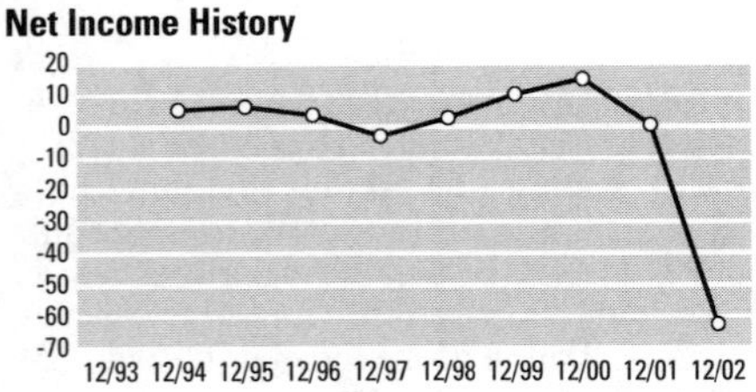

MTS

Whether pop music rocks your world or Broadway tunes set your feet a-tappin', MTS offers a tower of choices. MTS — owner of Tower Records — is one of the largest specialty retailers of music in the US with nearly 120 company-owned music, book, and video stores in five countries; its franchise agreements encompass nine additional countries. MTS also runs WOW! stores (a joint venture with electronics retailer The Good Guys) and publishes several free music magazines. International operations account for more than 40% of sales (expected to drop dramatically following the 2002 sale of its Japanese operations). Founder and chairman Russell Solomon and his son and CEO Michael, own 99% of MTS.

Russell Solomon has described himself as an "aging hippie" who scorns corporate stuffiness and is known for confiscating neckties from visiting executives and displaying them outside his office. MTS was named for his son, Michael T. Solomon.

Though it helped pioneer specialty retailing's superstore concept, MTS has fewer stores than other major music chains; it is known for broad selection and high volume. Unlike other specialty retailers, managers at each store are granted discretion in maintaining the level and mix of their inventories.

The chain has faced increasing competition from discounters such as Wal-Mart, from industry consolidation, and from online retailers. Big losses prompted the company to adopt a restructuring plan, and it has indefinitely postponed the idea of going public. MTS announced in May 2003 that it is looking to sell the Tower Records chain.

HISTORY

Russell Solomon began selling used jukebox records in 1941 in his father's Tower Cut Rate Drug Store at age 16. He joined the Army after dropping out of high school and went back to work in his father's store after his 1946 discharge. In 1952 he took over the record inventory from his father's store and began wholesaling, setting up record departments in drugstores and department stores.

Solomon's record wholesaling business went broke and creditors forced him to liquidate in 1960. Days later, with $5,000 from his father, Solomon incorporated MTS (named after his son Michael T.) and soon opened the first Tower Records in Sacramento, California. A month later a second Sacramento store was born. The first Tower Books opened in 1963, adjacent to one of the record stores.

By the 1967 "Summer of Love," Solomon was noticing the diverse musical tastes of the flower children who hung out in his stores. With the music business exploding, he figured serving the market would require stocking stores with a huge selection. In 1968 the first store outside Sacramento was opened, Tower Records' landmark Columbus Street store in San Francisco. At the time it was the largest record store in the US.

In 1970 Tower Records opened in Los Angeles on the Sunset Strip. The company started expanding outside California in 1976 (mainly in the West) and overseas in 1979 (Japan). The first Tower Video opened in Sacramento in 1981; three more opened the next year. The East Coast got its first Tower Records in 1983 (New York City); at the time the 35,000-sq.-ft. store was the world's largest. That year the company debuted *Pulse!* magazine, an in-store freebie with record reviews and artist interviews. The company's real expansion began in 1989; by 1994 Tower Records, with 127 outlets, had more than doubled its stores. That year it opened its first multimedia store, offering books, videos, records, and CD-ROMs under one roof.

MTS opened the largest record shop in the world (an eight-floor megastore in Tokyo) and the first WOW! store (a joint venture with electronics retailer The Good Guys) in Las Vegas in 1995. That year it started selling CDs on the Internet via America Online; it added its own online store in 1996. In 1998 MTS sold $110 million in bonds to raise money for expansion. Also in 1998 president and CEO Russell Solomon passed his Tower-guarding duties and his titles to son Michael.

To counteract growing losses, MTS began several experiments in 2000, including digital-downloading kiosks that allow customers to download songs and burn their own CDs. A similar project allows customers to pay for music from Tower's Web site and then immediately download it.

In 2001 MTS adopted a restructuring plan that included closing and liquidating most standalone and combination bookstores and selling the company's operations in Argentina, Hong Kong, Taiwan, and Singapore and converting them to franchises. It also decided to shut down its operations in Canada. The company's large losses in fiscal 2001 were attributed mostly to the restructuring and the closure of some of its international operations.

As part of the September 2002 settlement of a CD price-fixing case, MTS is one of three music retailers and five recording companies that agreed to pay more than $67 million to compensate consumers. The companies will also distribute more than $75 million worth of CDs to US public entities and nonprofits. In October 2002 MTS sold off the entirety of its Japanese operations.

As a way of addressing the growing digital music distribution market, MTS helped found Echo, a joint venture started in January 2003 by Best Buy, Trans World Entertainment, Virgin Entertainment (a part of Virgin Group), and Wherehouse Music. The consortium's goal is to devise a technology and licensing platform for the delivery of digital music to its retail members.

EXECUTIVES

Chairman: Russell M. Solomon, age 77, $932,780 pay
President, CEO, and Director: Michael T. Solomon, age 54, $460,400 pay
EVP, CFO, Secretary, Treasurer, and Director: DeVaughn D. Searson, age 58, $328,106 pay
SVP, European Operations: Andy D. Lown, age 37
SVP, Far East Operations: Keith Cahoon, age 46, $199,917 pay
SVP, Online Operations: Kevin Ertell
SVP, Technology and Supply Chain and CIO: William (Bill) Baumann, age 40
VP, Marketing: Russell (Russ) Eisenman
Director of Human Resources: Shauna Pompei
Auditors: PricewaterhouseCoopers LLP

LOCATIONS

HQ: MTS, Incorporated
2500 Del Monte St., West Sacramento, CA 95691
Phone: 916-373-2500 **Fax:** 916-373-2535
Web: www.towerrecords.com

US Locations

Arizona	Massachusetts
California	Nevada
Colorado	New Jersey
Connecticut	New York
District of Columbia	Oregon
Georgia	Pennsylvania
Hawaii	Tennessee
Illinois	Texas
Louisiana	Virginia
Maryland	Washington

PRODUCTS/OPERATIONS

Selected Operations

Internet
TowerRecords.com

Music magazines
Bounce (Japan)
Pass (Taiwan)
Pulse! (US)
Pulse Latino (Latin America)
Top (UK)

Stores
Tower
WOW! (jointly operated with The Good Guys)

COMPETITORS

Amazon.com	Hollywood Entertainment
Barnes & Noble	Kmart
Bertelsmann	Movie Gallery
Best Buy	MP3.com
Blockbuster	Musicland
BMG Entertainment	Target
Books-A-Million	Trans World Entertainment
Borders	Virgin Group
CDnow	Wal-Mart
Columbia House	WHSmith
Costco Wholesale	Wherehouse Entertainment
EMI Group	
Hastings Entertainment	
HMV	

HISTORICAL FINANCIALS

Company Type: Private

Income Statement

FYE: July 31

	REVENUE ($ mil.)	NET INCOME ($ mil.)	NET PROFIT MARGIN	EMPLOYEES
7/02	983	(57)	—	4,828
7/01	1,080	(90)	—	6,795
7/00	1,100	(10)	—	7,158
7/99	1,026	(8)	—	7,500
7/98	1,008	10	1.0%	7,200
7/97	992	4	0.4%	6,800
7/96	1,001	10	1.0%	—
7/95	951	15	1.6%	—
7/94	809	17	2.1%	—
7/93	699	15	2.1%	—
Annual Growth	3.9%	—	—	(6.6%)

2002 Year-End Financials

Debt ratio: —
Return on equity: —
Cash ($ mil.): 37
Current ratio: 0.77
Long-term debt ($ mil.): 116

Net Income History

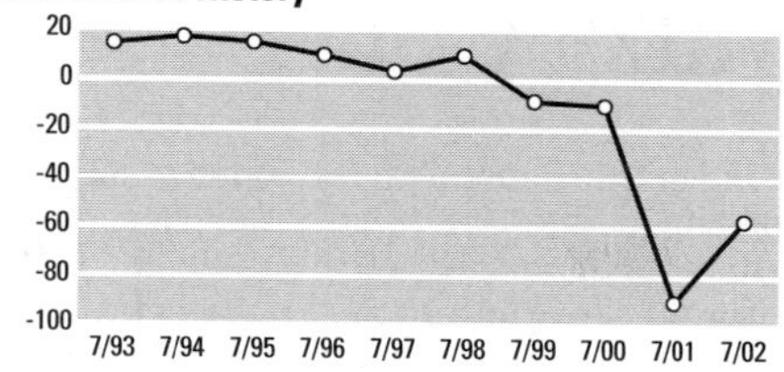

Mutual of Omaha

In the wild kingdom that is today's insurance industry, The Mutual of Omaha Companies wants to distinguish itself from the pack. The company provides individual health and accident coverage (via subsidiary Mutual of Omaha Insurance); its United of Omaha unit offers life insurance and annuities. The firm also offers personal property/casualty lines (homeowners, boat, auto, and flood coverage), disability coverage, brokerage services, pension plans, and mutual funds. Mutual of Omaha, which is owned by its policyholders, offers its products mainly through agent networks.

Increased cost-mindedness among clout-wielding managed care organizations has put traditional indemnity insurers — which have less power to bargain for lower-cost services — at a disadvantage, as have state laws mandating coverage for persons regardless of underwriting policy. Mutual of Omaha is exiting the health business in some areas and is adding managed care services. The company is focused on growing its health care networks internally, rather than by acquisition, to ensure its standards are met. These networks are largely in underserved rural areas, where the firm has kept a strong presence. The insurer is also working to increase sales of its life insurance and annuities products.

Mutual of Omaha is involved in wildlife conservation and protection. Starting with sponsorship of the long-running *Mutual of Omaha's Wild Kingdom,* this interest has evolved into a grant and scholarship program run by the company's Wildlife Heritage Center. Focusing on its core individual and employer-based lines, the company is selling its property & casualty and flood insurance operations to Fidelity National Financial.

HISTORY

Charter Mutual Benefit Health & Accident Association got its start in Omaha, Nebraska, in 1909. A year later, half of its founders quit, leaving a group headed by pharmaceuticals businessman H. S. Weller in charge. He tapped C. C. Criss as principal operating officer, general manager, and treasurer. Criss brought in his wife, Mabel, and brother Neil to help run the business.

Formed to offer accident and disability protection at a time when there were many fraudulent benefit societies, Charter Mutual Benefit Health faced consumer resistance that slowed growth in its first 10 years. By 1920 it was licensed in only nine states. Experience helped it refine its products and improve its policies' comprehensibility. By 1924 the firm had more than doubled its penetration, gaining licensing in 24 states.

The US was nearing the depths of the Depression when Weller died in 1932. Criss succeeded him as president. The stock crash had brought a steep decline in the value of the firm's asset base, and premium income dropped (accompanied by an increase in claims). Even so, Mutual Benefit Health expanded its agency force, the scope of its benefits, and its operations. It went into Canada in 1935 and began a campaign to obtain licensing throughout the US.

By 1939 the company was licensed in all 48 states. During WWII it wrote coverage for civilians killed or injured in acts of war in the US (including Hawaii) and Canada. With paranoia running high and consumer goods in short supply, the insurance industry boomed during the war (and payouts on stateside act-of-war claims were low to nonexistent). Criss retired in 1949.

Gearing up its post-war sales efforts, in 1950 the company changed its name to Mutual of Omaha and adopted its distinctive chieftain logo. During the 1950s it added specialty accident and group medical coverage. In 1963 it made an advertising coup when it launched *Mutual of Omaha's Wild Kingdom.* Hosted by zoo director Marlin Perkins and, later, naturalist sidekick Jim Fowler, the show was one of the most popular nature programs of all time. Later that decade the company added investment management to its services.

Changes in the health care industry during the 1990s led Mutual of Omaha to de-emphasize its traditional indemnity products in favor of building managed care alternatives. In 1993 it joined with Alegent Health System to form managed care company Preferred HealthAlliance. Mutual of Omaha also stopped writing new major medical coverage in such states as California, Florida, New Jersey, and New York, where state laws made providing health care onerous. This led the company to cut its workforce by about 10% in 1996.

In 1999 it bought out Alegent's interest in their joint venture and entered the credit card business (offering First USA Visa cards). The firm also lifted its $25,000 limit for coverage of AIDS-related illnesses (its standard limit is $1 million); the company had been sued over the policy.

EXECUTIVES

Chairman and CEO: John W. (Jack) Weekly, age 72
President and Director: Daniel P. Neary
EVP and Chief Investment Officer; President, Mutual of Omaha Investor Services: Richard A. (Rick) Witt
EVP, Treasurer, and Comptroller: Tommie D. Thompson
EVP and Chief Actuary: Cecil D. Bykerk
EVP and Executive Counsel: Lawrence F. Harr
EVP and General Counsel: Thomas J. McCusker
EVP, Corporate Services and Corporate Secretary: M. Jane Huerter
EVP, Government Affairs: William C. Mattox
EVP, Individual Financial Services; President, Companion Life Insurance: Randall C. Horn
EVP, Information Services: James L. Hanson
SVP, Human Resources: John Brown
President and CEO, Innowave: Thomas P. Weekly
President and CEO, Kirkpatrick, Pettis, Smith, Polian: L.C. (Jack) Petersen
President and CEO, Omaha Property and Casualty Insurance: Martin W. Dourney
Auditors: Deloitte & Touche LLP

LOCATIONS

HQ: The Mutual of Omaha Companies
Mutual of Omaha Plaza, Omaha, NE 68175
Phone: 402-342-7600 **Fax:** 402-351-2775
Web: www.mutualofomaha.com

The Mutual of Omaha Companies operate throughout the US.

PRODUCTS/OPERATIONS

Selected Services and Products

Annuities
Dental insurance
Disability insurance
Individual life and health insurance
Long-term-care insurance
Major medical
Mutual funds
Property/casualty coverage

Selected Subsidiaries and Affiliates

Companion Life Insurance Company
innowave Incorporated (water purification products)
Kirkpatrick, Pettis, Smith, Polian Inc. (brokerage)
Mutual of Omaha Insurance Company
Mutual of Omaha Investor Services (mutual funds)
Omaha Property and Casualty Insurance Company
United of Omaha Life Insurance Company
United World Life Insurance Company

COMPETITORS

Aetna
Allstate
American National Insurance
Assurant Group
AXA Financial
Blue Cross
CIGNA
CNA Financial
Guardian Life
John Hancock Financial Services
Liberty Mutual
MassMutual
MetLife
MONY
Morgan Stanley
New York Life
Northwestern Mutual
Prudential
State Farm
USAA

HISTORICAL FINANCIALS

Company Type: Mutual company

Income Statement FYE: December 31

	ASSETS ($ mil.)	NET INCOME ($ mil.)	INCOME AS % OF ASSETS	EMPLOYEES
12/02	15,203	(14)	—	6,600
12/01	11,533	31	0.4%	6,600
12/00	14,465	156	1.1%	7,000
12/99	13,959	90	0.6%	7,000
12/98	13,231	117	0.9%	7,111
12/97	12,639	181	1.4%	7,309
12/96	11,726	105	0.9%	7,047
12/95	10,659	122	1.1%	8,163
12/94	9,551	82	0.9%	8,330
12/93	8,600	94	1.1%	7,665
Annual Growth	6.5%	—	—	(1.6%)

2002 Year-End Financials

Equity as % of assets: 10.5%
Return on assets: —
Return on equity: —
Long-term debt ($ mil.): —
Sales ($ mil.): 4,353

Net Income History

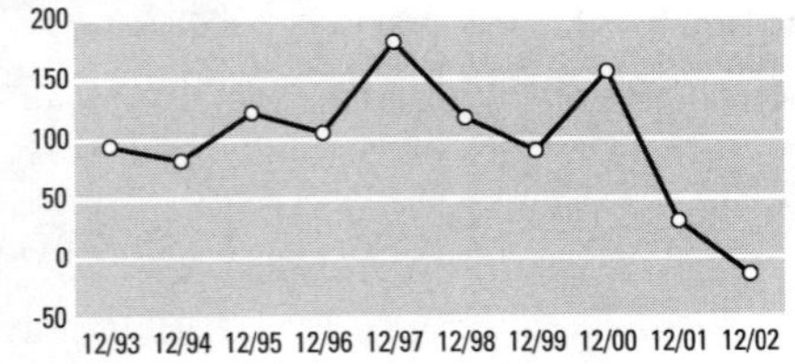

Muzak LLC

The hills are alive with the sound of Muzak. The king of canned music, Muzak offers more than 60 programs delivered via satellite, local broadcast transmission, tapes, and CDs. The company counts retailers, grocery stores, hotels, office buildings, and factories among its 350,000 customers, and an estimated 100 million people hear Muzak tunes each day. In addition to providing music from genres such as classical, country, Latin, oldies, and contemporary, the company also sells, installs, and maintains sound systems, intercoms, telephone messaging systems, closed circuit television, and other communications systems. Investment firm ABRY Partners owns about 64% of the company.

Music delivered via satellite accounts for 75% of Muzak's business. The company made numerous acquisitions in the late 1990s and hopes to restore profitability by renewing its focus on its core services. Radio station giant Clear Channel owns about 21% of Muzak.

HISTORY

George Squier patented a system for transmitting phonograph music over electrical lines in 1922. He sold the rights to utility North American Company, and together they formed a subsidiary to begin testing the system in Cleveland. In 1934 Squier coined the term Muzak ("muz" from music and "ak" from Kodak, his favorite company) before he died that year. The company moved to New York in 1936.

During the 1930s Muzak was used in then-newfangled elevators to calm riders (hence the term "elevator music"). In 1938 Warner Bros. bought the company but sold it the next year to US Senator William Benton. Experiments showed that music could increase productivity, and during WWII Muzak systems were installed in factories.

After the war the company continued to work on Stimulus Progression — the idea of regulating worker productivity through music. In 1972 Teleprompter bought the company and began distributing its music via satellite. Westinghouse bought Teleprompter in 1981 and sold it to Marshall Field V in 1986. Field bought Seattle-based Yesco, a producer of "foreground" music for retailers, and merged the two the next year. Led by Yesco's management, Muzak began updating its sound to appeal to baby boomers. Field sold Muzak to its management and New York investment firm Centre Capital in 1992.

In 1996 the company called off plans to go public. Saddled with debt from the buyout and mounting losses, it ousted CEO John Jester in 1997 and replaced him with William Boyd, who refocused the company on its core music business. During 1998 the company began buying competitors and its own independent affiliates. In 1999 Muzak merged with Audio Communications Network, a Muzak franchiser owned by media investment firm ABRY Partners, and the Muzak affiliates owned by Capstar (Capstar later became part of AMFM, which was subsequently acquired by radio station owner Clear Channel). Later that year Muzak made a string of acquisitions, including Data Broadcasting's (now Interactive Data Corporation) InStore Satellite Network, a music and ad business.

In 2000 Muzak moved its headquarters to Fort Mill, South Carolina. Extending its acquisitive streak, the company acquired Telephone Audio Productions (audio marketing and messaging) and Muzak franchisee Vortex Sound Communications.

EXECUTIVES

Chairman and CEO: William A. (Bill) Boyd, age 61, $300,023 pay
President: Lon Otremba
COO, CFO, and Treasurer: Stephen P. Villa, age 39, $212,117 pay
SVP Brand: Alvin Collis
SVP Owned Operations: Michael K. (Mike) Hoeltke, age 40, $351,705 pay
SVP Owned Operations and Marketing: Kenneth F. (Kenny) Kahn, age 40, $159,923 pay
SVP Technical Operations: David M. Moore, age 39, $119,995 pay
VP: Royce G. Yudkoff, age 46
VP, General Counsel, and Assistant Secretary: Michael F. Zendan II, age 39, $125,000 pay
VP and Secretary: Peni Garber, age 40
VP Administration: Page Walker
VP Marketing: Kimberly Wolff
VP Operations: Paul Ziegler
VP Team Member Services (HR): Frank Messana
Controller: Mark Williams
Financial Reporting Manager: Catherine Walsh
Auditors: PricewaterhouseCoopers LLP

LOCATIONS

HQ: 3318 Lakemont Blvd., Fort Mill, SC 29708
Phone: 803-396-3000 **Fax:** 803-396-3357
Web: www.muzak.com

Muzak offers its services in 15 countries.

PRODUCTS/OPERATIONS

Selected Products

Audio Architecture (music programming)
Voice (music and messages for phone systems)

Selected Music Genres

Classical
Country
Jazz
Latin
Mature adult
Oldies
Popular contemporary
Popular contemporary instrumentals
Specialty
Urban

COMPETITORS

DMX MUSIC
PlayNetwork
Sirius Satellite Radio
TM Century

HISTORICAL FINANCIALS

Company Type: Private

Income Statement FYE: December 31

	REVENUE ($ mil.)	NET INCOME ($ mil.)	NET PROFIT MARGIN	EMPLOYEES
12/02	218	(30)	—	1,491
12/01	203	(44)	—	1,347
12/00	192	(44)	—	1,395
12/99	130	(22)	—	1,324
12/98	100	(12)	—	1,041
12/97	91	(13)	—	667
12/96	87	(11)	—	751
12/95	87	(6)	—	715
12/94	83	(7)	—	—
12/93	59	(4)	—	—
Annual Growth	15.7%	—	—	11.1%

2002 Year-End Financials

Debt ratio: 249.6%
Return on equity: —
Cash ($ mil.): 2
Current ratio: 1.03
Long-term debt ($ mil.): 295

Net Income History

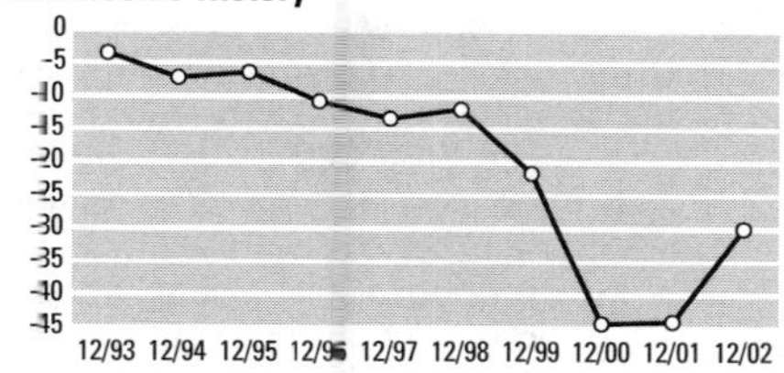

MWH Global

MWH Global's initials tell the story of this energy and environmental engineering, construction, and water resource management firm formed by the 2001 merger of Montgomery Watson and HARZA Engineering. Montgomery Watson has brought water, wastewater, and environmental specialties to the table, while HARZA has added its expertise in power plant design to the mix. MWH Global offers design, construction, finance, operation, and maintenance services for infrastructure projects in more than 30 countries in the Americas, Europe, the Middle East, and the Asia/Pacific Rim. The new company has deep roots: Montgomery Watson was founded in 1945, and HARZA was founded in 1920. MWH Global employees own the company.

EXECUTIVES

Chairman: Murli Tolaney
Vice Chairman: Refaat A. Abdel-Malek
President and CEO: Robert B. (Bob) Uhler
CFO: David J. D. Harper
EVP; President, MW Enterprises: Don Evenson
President, MWH Americas: Don Smith
President, MWH Asia: Michael Oswell
President, MWH Constructors: Mark Swatek
President, MWH Europe, Middle East, Africa and India: Richard N. (Rich) Walkmuller
Corporate Counsel: David A. Taggert
Director Human Resources: Gary R. Melillo
Auditors: PricewaterhouseCoopers LLP

LOCATIONS

HQ: MWH Global, Inc.
380 Interlocken Crescent, Ste. 200,
Broomfield, CO 80021
Phone: 303-533-1900 **Fax:** 303-533-1901
Web: www.mw.com

PRODUCTS/OPERATIONS

Selected Services

Construction
Energy plant design
Facilities development
Government relations
Water and environment services

COMPETITORS

AECOM
Bechtel
Black & Veatch
Bouygues
CET Environmental
CH2M HILL
Dick Corporation
EA Engineering
Earth Tech
Fluor
Foster Wheeler
Halliburton
Jacobs Engineering
Peter Kiewit Sons'
Severn Trent
Suez
Tetra Tech
USFilter
WS Atkins
Zachry

HISTORICAL FINANCIALS

Company Type: Private

Income Statement FYE: September 30

	REVENUE ($ mil.)	NET INCOME ($ mil.)	NET PROFIT MARGIN	EMPLOYEES
12/02*	856	—	—	6,000
9/01	722	—	—	5,500
9/00	550	—	—	3,500
9/99	510	—	—	3,600
9/98	482	—	—	3,500
9/97	442	—	—	3,200
9/96	433	—	—	3,500
9/95	405	—	—	3,300
9/94	336	—	—	3,100
9/93	261	—	—	—
Annual Growth	14.1%	—	—	8.6%

*Fiscal year change (since changed back to September)

Revenue History

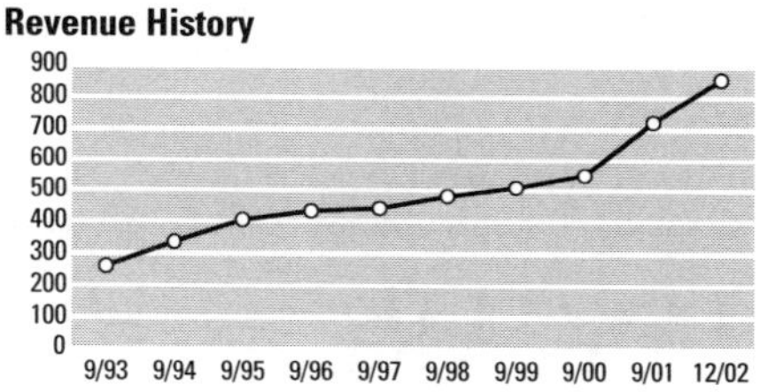

NASD

Bull market or bear, NASD will be there. NASD (formerly The National Association of Securities Dealers) is parent of the #3 US stock market, the American Stock Exchange (AMEX), and former parent of the #2 market, Nasdaq. (The Nasdaq Stock Market was spun off through a series of private sales and now trades OTC; NASD still holds 55% of its stock.) Since Nasdaq's spinoff was completed in 2002, NASD has coped with its emptier nest by concentrating on its regulatory functions. Per SEC orders, NASD Regulation oversees over-the-counter securities trading and disciplines traders; virtually all US securities dealers are members. NASD has agreed to sell AMEX to GTCR Golder Rauner.

Even without stock market subsidiaries, NASD has plenty to keep it busy. More than 5,000 brokerages and some 650,000 registered securities representatives are under its jurisdiction. NASD writes rules, conducts investigations, and disciplines firms or individuals that don't comply. NASD also operates arbitration and mediation programs and offers educational services to industry professionals and to investors.

HISTORY

NASD was founded in 1939 as a self-regulating entity for over-the-counter (OTC) securities traders who traded directly with companies or with market makers authorized to trade their stock. Traders shopped by phone to get the best price from the market makers, and up-to-date OTC quotes were unobtainable. NASD set trading qualifications, administered licensing tests, set standards for underwriting compensation, and disciplined wayward traders.

In 1963 the SEC asked the NASD to develop an automated OTC quotations system. Work began in 1968 on facilities in Trumbull, Connecticut, and Rockville, Maryland. The system went online in 1971 and soon turned into an electronic trading medium because it made dealer quotes more competitive and instantly visible. By 1972 volume exceeded 2 billion shares, and two years later the Nasdaq claimed a share volume nearly one-third of the New York Stock Exchange's. By 1980 it reported having almost 60% of the NYSE's volume, although Nasdaq counted both sides of many trades.

In 1975 Congress gave NASD responsibility for regulating the municipal securities market and asked the SEC to develop a national market system for share trading. The SEC handed the task to NASD. The market started trading in 1982 with 40 stocks, establishing a two-tier system: one for the crème de la crème, such as MCI (now WorldCom) and Microsoft, and one for smaller or newer issues. The system is continually updated; new technology made it a model for other markets.

To improve responsiveness to small investors, NASD instituted the SOES (small order entry system) after the 1987 stock crash, when many traders bailed themselves out before executing customer sell orders. So-called SOES bandits (dealers who used the system to make frequent small trades) increased the market's volatility and made Nasdaq vulnerable to NYSE's contention that auction exchanges were fairer to investors. An SEC investigation resulted in a requirement that dealers execute small customer orders along with their own and at the best prices. In 1997 the new rules were phased in and spreads dropped by an average of 35% without affecting volume.

But NASD teetered between appeasing the public and looking out for its own. A 1997 proposal to cap investor arbitration awards at $750,000, regardless of actual damages, met with criticism, since arbitration had been instituted in 1987 because the parties could receive remedies comparable to those available in court.

Reform-minded Wall Streeter Frank Zarb took over in 1997. Nasdaq and the American Stock Exchange (AMEX) merged the next year. NASD reluctantly complied when the SEC asked it to join the NYSE in real-time trade price reporting.

With for-profit, around-the-clock competitors like The Island ECN and Archipelago in mind, NASD prepared in 1999 to spin off Nasdaq as a for-profit market (overwhelmingly approved in 2000). Nasdaq also extended official pricing to 6:30 p.m. (Eastern time) and agreed to share listings with the Hong Kong Stock Exchange.

In 2000 Nasdaq converted stock prices from fractions to decimals, mandated by regulators. That year it joined with SOFTBANK to build Nasdaq Japan, an Internet-based market of primarily Japanese tech companies. In 2001 the flaccid economy led Nasdaq to trim about 10% of its staff — its first job cuts since just after the 1987 crash. Zarb also retired that year.

In the wake of the terrorism attacks that shook Wall Street and the nation in 2001, Nasdaq and the NYSE began discussing a disaster plan under which the two would cooperate should a future incident cripple either market. It also continued to refine its focus toward regulation, with plans to dispose of AMEX, and a series of private stock sales that would ultimately separate Nasdaq from NASD in 2002.

EXECUTIVES

Chairman and CEO: Robert R. Glauber, age 64, $2,100,000 pay
Vice Chairman and President, NASD Regulatory Policy and Oversight: Mary L. Schapiro, age 47
President, Regulatory Services & Operations: Douglas H. Shulman
SEVP and Chief Administrative Officer: Michael D. Jones
President, Dispute Resolution, EVP, and Chief Hearing Officer: Linda D. Fienberg
EVP and General Counsel: T. Grant Callery
EVP and CTO: Martin P. Colburn
EVP and CFO: Todd T. DiGanci
EVP, Member Regulation: Robert C. Errico
EVP and Director of Dispute Resolution: George H. Friedman
EVP, Enforcement: Barry R. Goldsmith
EVP, Disclosure Policy and Review, Regulatory Policy and Oversight: R. Clark Hooper
EVP, Registration & Disclosure: Derek W. Linden
EVP, Market Regulation and US Exchange Solutions: Stephen I. Luparello
EVP, Member Services: M. Ann Short
EVP, Regulatory Policy & Programs: Elisse Barbara Walter
SVP, Human Resources: Andrew C. Goresh
Auditors: Ernst & Young LLP

LOCATIONS

HQ: 1735 K St. NW, Washington, DC 20006
Phone: 202-728-8000 **Fax:** 202-293-6260
Web: www.nasd.com

NASD has regulation and dispute resolution offices throughout the US.

PRODUCTS/OPERATIONS

2002 Sales

	% of total
Nasdaq	53
NASD	30
Amex	17
Total	**100**

Selected Subsidiaries & Affiliates

The American Stock Exchange, LLC
NASD Dispute Resolution, Inc.
NASD Regulation, Inc.

COMPETITORS

Bloomberg
CBOT
E*TRADE Financial
Goldman Sachs
Instinet
Investment Technology
Knight Trading
LaBranche & Co
NYSE

HISTORICAL FINANCIALS

Company Type: Not-for-profit

Income Statement FYE: December 31

	REVENUE ($ mil.)	NET INCOME ($ mil.)	NET PROFIT MARGIN	EMPLOYEES
12/02	1,238	(4)	—	2,087
12/01	1,539	112	7.3%	3,200
12/00	1,555	114	7.3%	3,200
12/99	1,177	154	13.1%	3,000
12/98	740	47	6.4%	2,900
12/97	634	36	5.7%	2,200
12/96	556	55	9.9%	2,218
12/95	438	17	3.9%	2,000
12/94	372	21	5.6%	2,328
12/93	332	39	11.7%	2,145
Annual Growth	15.7%	—	—	(0.3%)

2002 Year-End Financials

Debt ratio: 36.6%
Return on equity: —
Cash ($ mil.): 474
Current ratio: 2.57
Long-term debt ($ mil.): 430

Net Income History

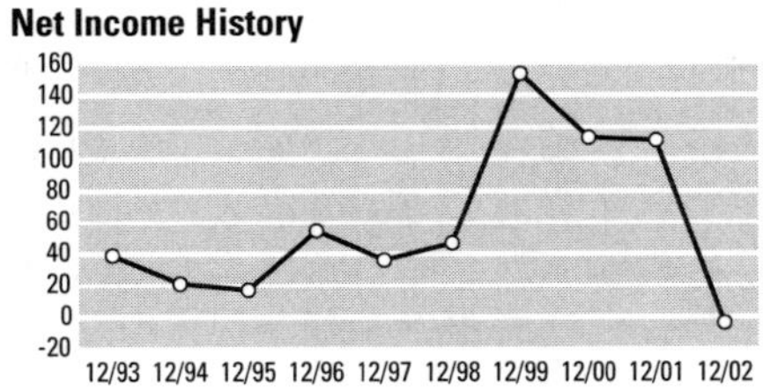

NASCAR

In the race for respectability in the sports world, NASCAR is on the right track. The National Association for Stock Car Auto Racing is one of the fastest-growing spectator sports in the US, appealing to all demographics. NASCAR runs about 90 races each year in 25 states through three racing circuits: the Busch, Craftsman Truck, and its signature Winston Cup Series. The Winston Cup, featuring popular drivers like Jeff Gordon and Dale Jarrett, alone draws more than 6 million race fans each year. NBC, FOX, and Turner Broadcasting have taken note, paying $2.4 billion a year for broadcast rights (until 2008). NASCAR was founded in 1948 by Bill France Sr. and is still owned by the France family.

Even though the networks have lost money on the first two years of the NASCAR contract, they still have plenty of reason to be optimistic about the future of the partnership. NASCAR ratings for NBC are up about 72% after two years, and Turner and TNT have acquired 40 new sponsors for the Winston Cup series. In addition, as a younger generation of drivers begin to pull in new viewers, the company's popularity has begun making inroads into parts of the country beyond its traditional fan base of the southern US.

NASCAR does have its share of headaches, though. The company is moving races out of some of the smaller markets starting with the 2004 season, which has drawn loud protests from racetrack owner and rival Speedway Motorsports. The France family also controls publicly traded International Speedway Corporation, the largest racetrack owner in the US. The reschedulings benefit International Speedway tracks, and a Speedway Motorsports shareholder has filed a lawsuit against NASCAR on antitrust grounds.

And in a surprise move, R.J. Reynolds dropped out as the sponsor for the title Wiston Cup series. The tobacco company's wallet has seen better days thanks to tobacco lawsuits and restricted advertising. Reynolds had been the sponsor of the title race since 1971. Cell phone company Nextel signed a massive 10-year, $750 million deal with NASCAR to become the new title sponsor for the race, starting in 2004. The agreement should silence any critics of the racing circuit's longevity, as the Nextel deal is the biggest sports sponsorship deal in history.

HISTORY

Bill France Sr. founded the National Championship Stock Car Circuit (NCSCC) in 1947 as a place for ex-Prohibition-era moonshine runners to show off their driving skills. France, the son of a Washington, DC, banker, was a skilled mechanic and racecar builder. In 1934 he moved his family to Daytona Beach, Florida, which was nirvana for racecar drivers who used the hard beach as a speedway.

The City of Daytona Beach in 1938 approached France, who by then owned a successful gas station and mechanic shop frequented by racers, and asked him to organize a race. France rounded up drivers and solicited local businesses to donate prizes such as beer and cigars. The event drew 4,500 fans. He organized another race the following year and turned a profit of a few thousand dollars.

WWII interfered with France's racing career when he was drafted and sent to work in a shipyard. Upon his return, lacking the money to put another race together in Florida, he sponsored a national championship race for stock cars (cars with standard auto bodies not specially designed for racing) in North Carolina. Since there was no national body governing the races and setting rules, France's championship idea drew little enthusiasm. So, in 1947 he formed the NCSCC and set up a point system for drivers and a fund for prize money. Seeking to expand NCSCC's powers, France in 1948 gathered 35 prominent racing figures from all over the US and they organized to form the National Association for Stock Car Auto Racing (NASCAR), of which France was elected president.

France tirelessly promoted the sport with the help of racetrack owners wanting NASCAR to make their races official, and as a result the sport grew rapidly in the 1950s and 1960s. Racetrack owners began upgrading their facilities or building new ones with paved tracks to replace the older dirt tracks. France in 1957 convinced Daytona Beach to allow him to replace the city's original beach track with a 2.5-mile paved raceway. It opened two years later to a crowd of 42,000.

In 1972, as France got more involved in operating specific tracks and having less time to focus on NASCAR, he passed the business on to his son, Bill France Jr. Bill Jr. signed R.J. Reynolds as a major sponsor in 1971, and NASCAR held the Winston 500 (the first incarnation of today's Winston Cup series) in Talladega, Alabama.

The company's first televised race, the Daytona 500, aired on the CBS Television Network in 1979 and drew about 16 million viewers. Cable sports network ESPN also began airing races in 1981. The inherent danger of stock car racing began to hit home with the racing related deaths of popular drivers such Adam Petty in 2000 and

Dale Earnhardt in 2001.

In 2003 Bill France Jr. handed reins of the company to son Brian France by promoting him to chairman and CEO. Bill Jr. remains vice chairman.

EXECUTIVES

Chairman and CEO: Brian Z. France, age 41
Vice Chairman: William C. (Bill) France Jr., age 70
Vice Chairman, EVP, and Secretary: Jim France
President: Mike Helton
SVP and COO: George Pyne
VP Broadcasting: Paul Brooks
VP Corporate Administration: Ed Bennett
VP Corporate Communications: Jim Hunter
VP Corporate Marketing: Brett Yormark
VP Finance: Doris Rumery
VP Licensing and Consumer Products: Mark Dyer
President and CEO, NASCAR Images: Jay Abraham
Corporate Counsel: Gary Crotty
Treasurer: Tom Bledsoe
Assistant Secretary: Betty Jane France
Managing Director of Brand and Consumer Marketing: Roger VanDerSnick
Managing Director of Broadcasting and New Media: Jeffrey N. Pollack
Managing Director of Licensing: Blake Davidson
Director of Human Resources: Starr George
Director of Multimedia Marketing: Dan Lynch
Director of New Business and Industry Relations: Andrew Feit

LOCATIONS

HQ: National Association for Stock Car Auto Racing
1801 W. International Speedway Blvd.,
Daytona Beach, FL 32115
Phone: 386-253-0611 **Fax:** 386-681-4041
Web: www.nascar.com

PRODUCTS/OPERATIONS

Selected Races

Busch Series
Food City 250
Ford 300
Hardee's 250
Pepsi 300
Tropicana Twister 300

Craftsman Truck Series
Chevy Silverado 150
Craftsman 200
Florida Dodge Dealers 250
NASCAR Craftsman Truck Series 250

Winston Cup Series
Coca-Cola 600
Daytona 500
Gatorade 125s
Pontiac Excitement 400
Subway 400

COMPETITORS

AFL
CART
Indy Racing League
Major League Baseball
NBA
NFL
NHL
World Wrestling Entertainment

HISTORICAL FINANCIALS

Company Type: Private

Income Statement

FYE: December 31

	ESTIMATED REVENUE ($ mil.)	NET INCOME ($ mil.)	NET PROFIT MARGIN	EMPLOYEES
12/02	3,000	—	—	450
12/01	2,500	—	—	400
12/00	2,000	—	—	350
12/99	1,500	—	—	300
12/98	2,000	—	—	—
Annual Growth	10.7%	—	—	14.5%

Revenue History

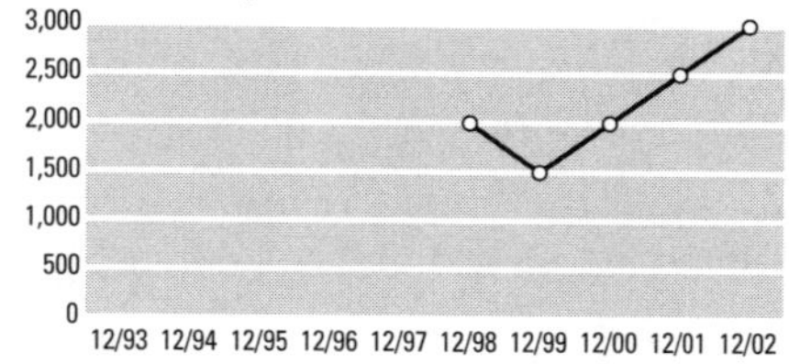

National Basketball Association

The National Basketball Association has shot a lot fewer airballs lately. The NBA is shaking off its fiscal and image problems with a little magic from Michael Jordan, who came out of retirement and played two seasons with the Washington Wizards. The prospect of seeing Jordan play again boosted fan interest as well as attendance throughout the league. (Jordan retired for the third, and likely final, time in 2003.) The 29-team NBA is divided into Eastern and Western Conferences and includes one Canadian team. The league also operates the WNBA (women's basketball), which features 13 teams. In 2003 it launched NBA TV, a cable channel devoted to all things basketball.

After a less than stellar 1998-99 season that saw a contentious lockout and the second retirement of Jordan, the NBA had seen its attendance figures and TV ratings decline dramatically. Add to that a host of on- and off-court image problems (such as boring play and a laundry list of player scandals), and 19-year commissioner David Stern has his work cut out for him to return the league to its glory days of the 1980s.

Despite the attendance and ratings declines, the league still manages to bring in the dough through lucrative merchandising deals and TV contracts. In 2002 the NBA cut a new six-year TV contract with Walt Disney's ABC and ESPN, and Time Warner's Turner Sports worth a reported $4.6 billion. Some fans are unhappy with the new TV contract as it puts a majority of the league's games almost exclusively on cable. The NBA further milked the new TV contract by expanding the first round of the playoffs from a best-of-five to a best-of-seven format. But the league's ratings for the 2003 NBA Finals were the worst in the history of the championship series due largely to the fact that the teams, the San Antonio Spurs and New Jersey Nets, don't have much of a national following.

Expansion is also still very much alive for the NBA. After the Charlotte Hornets moved to New Orleans for the 2002-03 season, the league voted to give the city another franchise that will begin play in 2004-05. Robert Johnson, founder of BET, is the majority owner of the new Charlotte Bobcats. He is the first black owner of a major league sports team.

The NBA has also decided to rethink its strategy regarding the WNBA. The league has restructured the previous ownership rules for a WNBA franchise that dictated only the current owners of NBA clubs could own a sister team. The move allows the league to expand into cities where there isn't already an NBA franchise.

HISTORY

Dr. James Naismith, a physical education teacher at the International YMCA Training School in Springfield, Massachusetts, invented basketball in 1891. Naismith nailed peach baskets at both ends of the school's gym, gave his students a soccer ball, and one of the world's most popular sports was born.

In the beginning many YMCAs deemed the game too rough and banned it, so basketball was limited to armories, gymnasiums, barns, and dance halls. To pay the rent for the use of the hall, teams began charging spectators fees for admission, and leftover cash was divided among the players. The first pro basketball game was played in 1896 in Trenton, New Jersey.

A group of arena owners looking to fill their halls when their hockey teams were on the road formed the Basketball Association of America in 1946. It merged with the midwestern National Basketball League in 1949 to form the 17-team National Basketball Association (NBA).

Six teams dropped out in 1950. The league got an unexpected boost the next year when a point-shaving scandal rocked college basketball. The bad publicity for the college game made the pros look relatively clean, and it helped attract more fans. Another boost came through innovation when the league introduced the 24-second shot clock in 1954, which sped up the game and increased scoring.

Basketball came into its own in the late 1950s and 1960s, thanks to the popularity of such stars as Wilt Chamberlain, Bill Russell, and Bob Cousy. A rival league, the American Basketball Association (ABA), appeared on the scene in 1967 with its red, white, and blue basketball. Salaries escalated as the two leagues competed for players. The leagues merged in 1976.

By the early 1980s the NBA was suffering major image problems (drugs, fighting, racial issues) and began to wane in popularity. The league was resuscitated by exciting new players such as Magic Johnson, Larry Bird, and Michael Jordan, and, in 1984, a new commissioner, David Stern. Although increased commercialism drove some purists crazy, big-name players and big-time rivalries helped sell the NBA's most important commodity — sport as entertainment.

Stern went to work cleaning up the league's image and financial problems, pushing through a strict anti-drug policy and a salary cap (the first such cap in major US sports). He also signed big marketing deals with such sponsors as Coca-Cola and McDonald's. The NBA added its first two non-US teams in 1995, the Toronto Raptors and the

Vancouver Grizzlies. (The Grizzlies moved to Memphis in 2001.) The league also created the Women's NBA (WNBA) in 1996.

On July 1, 1998, the NBA owners voted to lock out players, leading to the first work stoppage in the NBA's 52-year history. The dispute lasted six months, and the NBA's 1998-99 season was pared down to 50 games from the standard 82.

Concerned with the rash of players either leaving college early or skipping it entirely for the NBA, the league announced the formation of a developmental league (akin to baseball's minor leagues) in 2000, which started play in 2001. Also in 2001 the NBA got a much-needed shot in the arm when Michael Jordan came out of retirement for a second time to play for the Washington Wizards.

The following year the league signed a new TV contract. Former owner NBC decided not to pursue the league after its $1.3 billion bid failed to measure up to a six-year, $4.6 billion deal offered by Walt Disney's ABC and ESPN, and Time Warner's Turner Sports.

EXECUTIVES

Commissioner: David J. Stern, age 61
Deputy Commissioner and COO: Russell T. Granik
EVP Global Media Properties and Marketing Partnerships: Heidi Ueberroth
SVP Basketball Operations: Stu Jackson
SVP Business Affairs: Harvey E. Benjamin
SVP Communications: Timothy P. Andree
SVP Event and Attractions Group, NBA Entertainment: Ski Austin
SVP Finance: Robert Criqui
SVP Global Merchandising: Sal LaRocca
SVP International: Andrew Messick
SVP Marketing and Team Business Operations: Bernie Mullin
SVP New League Development: Rob Levine
SVP Operations and Technology: Steve Hellmuth
VP Interactive Marketing: Brenda Spoonemore
VP International Basketball Operations: Kim Bohuny
VP Marketing and Media: Ron Erskine
VP Marketing Partnerships: Jonathan Press
VP Team Marketing Services: Bill Sutton
Human Resources: Patrica E. Swedin
President, National Basketball Development League: Phillip Evans
President and COO, NBA Entertainment: Adam Silver
President, NBA Television and New Media Ventures: Ed Desser
President, Women's National Basketball Association: Valerie B. Ackerman
EVP Programming and Executive Producer, NBA Entertainment: Gregg Winik
SVP and COO, WNBA: Paula Hanson

LOCATIONS

HQ: Olympic Tower, 645 5th Ave., New York, NY 10022
Phone: 212-407-8000 **Fax:** 212-754-6414
Web: www.nba.com

PRODUCTS/OPERATIONS

Eastern Conference

Atlantic Division
Boston Celtics
Miami Heat
New Jersey Nets
New York Knicks
Orlando Magic
Philadelphia 76ers
Washington Wizards

Central Division
Atlanta Hawks
Chicago Bulls
Cleveland Cavaliers
Detroit Pistons
Indiana Pacers
Milwaukee Bucks
New Orleans Hornets
Toronto Raptors

Western Conference

Midwest Division
Dallas Mavericks
Denver Nuggets
Houston Rockets
Memphis Grizzlies
Minnesota Timberwolves
San Antonio Spurs
Utah Jazz

Pacific Division
Golden State Warriors
Los Angeles Clippers
Los Angeles Lakers
Phoenix Suns
Portland Trail Blazers
Sacramento Kings
Seattle SuperSonics

COMPETITORS

AFL
CART
Major League Baseball
Major League Soccer
NASCAR
NFL
NHL
PGA
World Wrestling Entertainment

HISTORICAL FINANCIALS

Company Type: Association

Income Statement FYE: August 31

	REVENUE ($ mil.)	NET INCOME ($ mil.)	NET PROFIT MARGIN	EMPLOYEES
8/00	2,164	—	—	—
8/99	956	—	—	800
8/98	1,874	—	—	1,000
8/97	1,664	—	—	850
8/96	1,403	—	—	650
8/95	1,259	—	—	550
8/94	1,030	—	—	450
8/93	999	—	—	—
8/92	843	—	—	—
8/91	606	—	—	—
Annual Growth	15.2%	—	—	12.2%

Revenue History

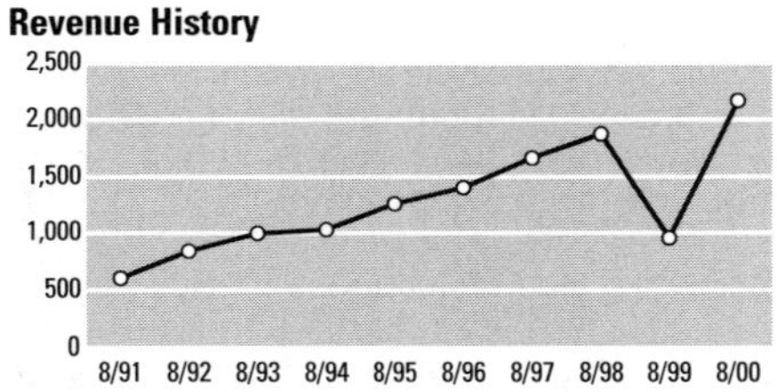

National Cooperative Refinery

Cooperation is a refined art and refining a cooperative art for the National Cooperative Refinery Association (NCRA), which provides three farm supply cooperatives (Cenex Harvest States, GROWMARK, and MFA Oil) with fuel through its oil refinery in Kansas. In 1943, five regional farm supply cooperatives, tired of wartime fuel shortages, created the NCRA to buy the Globe oil refinery in McPherson, Kansas. The refinery's production capacity ia about 75,000 barrels per day. Fuel from the refinery is allocated to member-owners on the basis of ownership percentages. In addition to the refinery, NCRA owns Jayhawk Pipeline, minority interests in two other pipeline companies, and an underground oil storage facility.

EXECUTIVES

President: James Loving
VP Finance: John Buehrle
VP Supply and Trading: Galen Menard
Auditors: PricewaterhouseCoopers LLP

LOCATIONS

HQ: National Cooperative Refinery Association
1391 Iron Horse Rd., McPherson, KS 67460
Phone: 620-241-2340 **Fax:** 620-241-5531
Web: www.ncrarefinery.com

COMPETITORS

ChevronTexaco
Premcor
Valero Energy

HISTORICAL FINANCIALS

Company Type: Cooperative

Income Statement FYE: August 31

	ESTIMATED REVENUE ($ mil.)	NET INCOME ($ mil.)	NET PROFIT MARGIN	EMPLOYEES
8/02	962	—	—	534
8/01	800	—	—	560
8/00	700	—	—	600
8/99	700	—	—	600
8/98	700	—	—	560
8/97	773	—	—	540
8/96	760	—	—	560
8/95	596	—	—	—
Annual Growth	7.1%	—	—	(0.8%)

Revenue History

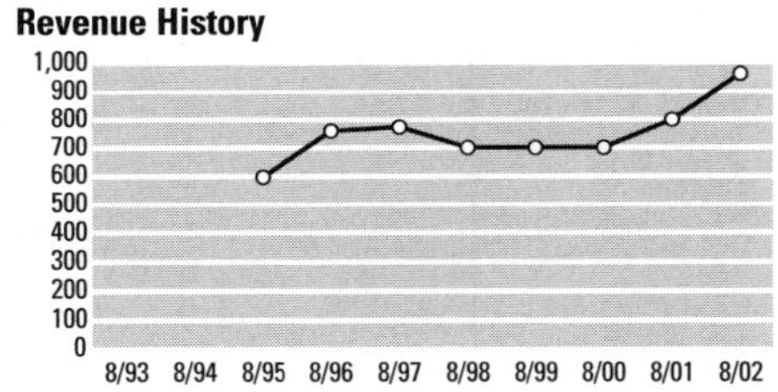

National Distributing

National Distributing Company strives to live up to its name, distributing beverages in Washington, DC and nine US states. With operations primarily on the east coast, but also in Colorado, New Mexico, and Ohio, NDC is the fourth largest wholesale wine, and spirits vendor in the US. A private firm founded in the 1900s by Chris Carlos (joined by Alfred Davis in 1942), NDC distributes brands such as Bacardi rum, Jack Daniels whiskey, Jose Cuervo tequila, Korbel wine, and Finlandia vodka. The Carlos and Davis families own and operate National Distributing.

EXECUTIVES

Chairman and CEO: Jay M. Davis
Vice Chairman and Secretary: Jerry Rosenberg
Vice Chairman and Treasurer: John A. Carlos
President and COO: Charles Andrews
EVP: Chris Carlos
SVP and Director of Operations: Steve Feldman
President and Regional Director, Florida: Jim Smith
President and Regional Director, Georgia: Fred Bleiberg
VP, Human Resources: Bruce E. Carter
Chief Administrative Officer: Greg Johnson

LOCATIONS

HQ: National Distributing Company, Inc.
1 National Dr. SW, Atlanta, GA 30336
Phone: 404-696-9440 **Fax:** 404-505-1013
Web: www.ndcweb.com/home

National Distributing Company operates in Colorado, Florida, Georgia, Maryland, New Mexico, Ohio, South Carolina, Virginia, and Washington, DC.

COMPETITORS

Bacardi USA
Charmer Industries
Constellation Brands
Gambrinus
Geerlings & Wade
Georgia Crown Distributing
Glazer's Wholesale Drug
Johnson Brothers
Molson
Southern Wine & Spirits
Sunbelt Beverage
Wirtz
Young's Market

HISTORICAL FINANCIALS

Company Type: Private

Income Statement FYE: December 31

	ESTIMATED REVENUE ($ mil.)	NET INCOME ($ mil.)	NET PROFIT MARGIN	EMPLOYEES
12/01	1,700	—	—	2,500
12/00	1,600	—	—	2,500
12/99	1,500	—	—	2,000
12/98	1,300	—	—	2,000
12/97	1,025	—	—	1,700
12/96	995	—	—	1,700
12/95	875	—	—	1,500
12/94	855	—	—	1,500
12/93	830	—	—	2,300
12/92	805	—	—	2,300
Annual Growth	8.7%	—	—	0.9%

Revenue History

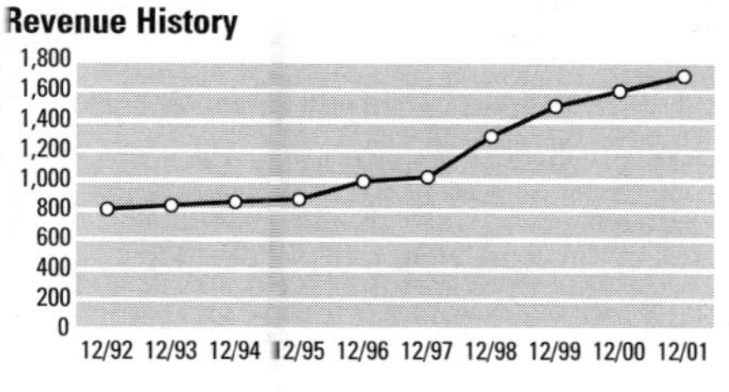

National Envelope

Pushing the envelope is this company's business. National Envelope makes some 160 million envelopes each day, ranging from regular office envelopes to customized envelopes for direct-mail use. Products under its Printmaster brand include envelopes with windows, translucent envelopes, booklet-style envelopes, envelopes with clasps, and presentation portfolios. National Envelope serves paper distributors and wholesalers throughout Canada and the US. The company's divisions include New York Envelope, Williamhouse, and Old Colony Envelope, a supplier of fine paper products. William Ungar owns National Envelope, which he founded in 1952.

EXECUTIVES

Chairman and CFO: Nathan F. Moser
CEO and COO: Leslie F. (Les) Stern
EVP and Director of Marketing: Bernard W. Mathiew
VP Information Technology: Mark Mogul
Director of Human Resources: Karen Schreck

LOCATIONS

HQ: National Envelope Corporation
29-10 Hunters Point Ave.,
Long Island City, NY 11101
Phone: 718-784-0505 **Fax:** 718-706-7663
Web: www.nationalenvelope.com

National Envelope Corporation has more than 20 manufacturing and distribution facilities throughout California, Colorado, Georgia, Illinois, Kansas, Massachusetts, Missouri, New Jersey, New York, Pennsylvania, Texas, Washington, and Wisconsin, as well as Ontario, Canada.

PRODUCTS/OPERATIONS

Selected Products

Durable mailers
Envelopes (traditional, translucent, commercial, window, booklet, clasp, jumbo-sized)
Fine papers
Open end and open side envelopes
Presentation portfolios
Printed papers (announcements, invitations, awards, certificates, reports)

COMPETITORS

Avery Dennison
Gould Paper
Mail-Well
Moore Corporation
National Service Industries
Newark
Polyair Inter Pack
Reynolds Food Packaging
Stora Enso Oyj
Unisource
UPM-Kymmene
Wausau-Mosinee Paper
Workflow Management

HISTORICAL FINANCIALS

Company Type: Private

Income Statement FYE: December 31

	ESTIMATED REVENUE ($ mil.)	NET INCOME ($ mil.)	NET PROFIT MARGIN	EMPLOYEES
12/02	640	—	—	5,000
12/01	625	—	—	5,000
12/00	450	—	—	4,000
12/99	400	—	—	3,500
12/98	350	—	—	2,800
12/97	300	—	—	2,800
12/96	330	—	—	—
12/95	300	—	—	—
12/94	300	—	—	2,800
12/93	250	—	—	—
Annual Growth	11.0%	—	—	7.5%

Revenue History

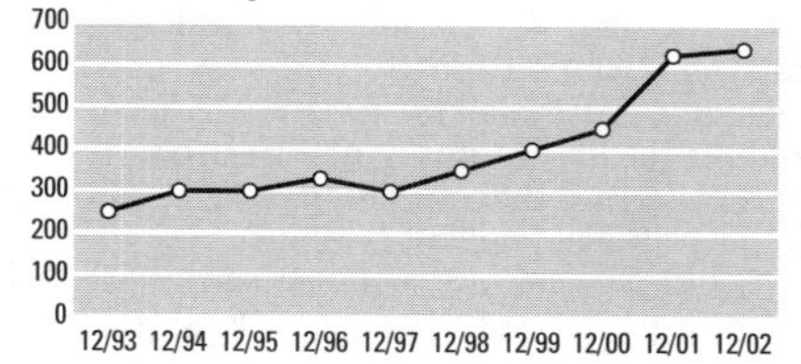

National Football League

In the world of professional sports, the National Football League (NFL) is blitzing the competition. The organization oversees America's most popular spectator sport, acting as a trade association for 32 franchise owners. The teams operate as separate businesses but share much of the revenue generated through broadcasting and merchandising. The NFL was founded as the American Professional Football Association in 1920. The league reorganized its two conferences, the AFC and NFC, for the 2002-03 season when the Houston Texans joined the league as the latest, and probably last, expansion team. Fans initially protested the realignment, but quieted once it was clear the reorganization made more geographic sense.

The NFL's primary operations consist of subsidiaries NFL Properties, which generates billions through merchandising and licensing, and NFL Enterprises, the entity that negotiates national broadcasting rights for the teams. The league's current eight-year, $17.6 billion TV contract with FOX, CBS, ESPN, and ABC was struck in 1998. In 2002 the NFL also extended for another five years its exclusive deal with DIRECTV to broadcast NFL Sunday Ticket. The package allows DIRECTV subscribers to view any of the 14 Sunday telecasts, regardless of their local market. The announcement of the $2 billion deal is bad news for some cable channels, which were hoping to gain rights to certain NFL games for national distribution. The NFL is also launching the NFL Channel, a 24-hour football network in late 2004. So far, only DIRECTV has agreed to carry the channel, and the league hopes to have agreements with cable carriers before the launch.

Other subsidiaries include NFL Charities and NFL Films. The league is also capitalizing on the Internet as a revenue source, signing a four-year $300 million deal with SportsLine.com, AOL, and CBS in 2001 to promote and maintain the league's NLF.com site.

HISTORY

Descended from the English game of rugby, American football was developed in the late 1800s by Walter Camp, a player from Yale University who is generally credited with introducing new rules for downs and scoring. Professional teams sprang up in the 1890s, but football remained relatively unorganized until 1920, when George Halas and college star Jim Thorpe helped organize the American Professional Football Association. The new league featured 14 teams from the Midwest and East, including Halas' Staleys (now the Chicago Bears) and the Racine Cardinals (now the Arizona Cardinals). In 1922 the association changed its name to the National Football League.

The new league suffered many growing pains over the next decade, but by the 1930s the NFL had settled on 10 teams including the Green Bay Packers (joined in 1921), the New York Giants (1925), and the Philadelphia Eagles (1933). Interest in the game remained somewhat regional, however, until the late 1940s and 1950s. In 1946 the Cleveland Rams moved to Los Angeles, and in 1950 the NFL expanded with three teams joining from the defunct All-American Football Conference. Television showed its potential in 1958 when that year's championship game, the first to be televised nationally, kept audiences riveted with an overtime victory by the Baltimore Colts over the Giants. In 1962 the NFL signed its first league-wide television contract with CBS for $4.65 million.

The 1960s brought a new challenge in the form of the upstart American Football League (AFL). Concerned that the AFL would steal players with higher salaries and draw away fans, NFL commissioner Pete Rozelle negotiated a deal in 1966 to combine the leagues. That season concluded with the first AFL-NFL World Championship Game, which was renamed the Super Bowl in 1969. When the merger was completed in 1970, the new NFL sported 26 teams.

Football's popularity exploded during the 1970s, helped by the rise of franchise dynasties such as the Pittsburgh Steelers (four Super Bowl wins) and the Dallas Cowboys (five NFC titles). In 1982 the Oakland Raiders moved to Los Angeles after a jury ruled against the NFL's attempts to keep the team in Oakland. The decision prompted other teams to relocate in search of better facilities and more revenue. (The Raiders returned to Oakland in 1995.) Rozelle stepped down in 1989 and was replaced by Paul Tagliabue.

During the 1990s the league expanded to 30 teams, adding the Carolina Panthers and Jacksonville Jaguars in 1995. The next year Art Modell moved his Cleveland Browns franchise to Baltimore to become the Ravens (the city of Cleveland held onto the rights to the Browns name and history and the franchise was revived in 1999), and in 1997 the Houston Oilers defected to Tennessee and were renamed the Titans. The next year brought new television deals worth $17.6 billion over eight years.

The NFL made plans for new expansion in 1999, awarding a franchise to Robert McNair of Houston, who paid a record $700 million franchise fee and $310 million for a new stadium. Named the Houston Texans, the team began play in 2002. (The NFL realigned the NFC and AFC in 2002, shifting to eight divisions with four teams each.)

EXECUTIVES

Commissioner: Paul J. Tagliabue, age 62
EVP and COO: Roger Goodell
EVP and General Counsel: Jeff Pash
EVP Communications and Government Affairs: Joe Browne
EVP Labor Relations; Chairman, NFL Management Council: Harold R. Henderson
EVP New Media and Enterprises: Thomas E. Spock
SVP Broadcast Planning: Dennis Lewin
SVP Business Affairs: Frank Hawkins
SVP Consumer Products: Mark Holtzman
SVP Events: Jim Steeg
SVP Marketing and Sales: John Collins
SVP New Media: Christopher J. Russo
SVP and Managing Director, NFL International: Douglas Quinn
VP Communications: Greg Aiello
VP Consumer Products: Gene Goldberg
VP Corporate Sponsorship: Steve Phelps
VP Football Development and Operations: John Beake
VP Human Resources and Administration: Nancy Gill
VP Media Sales: Chris Fuller
VP NFL International: Gordon Smeaton
VP Player and Employee Development: Mike Haynes
VP Security: Milt Ahlerich
VP and Head of Marketing: Shawn Dennis
Controller: Joe Siclare
President, NFL Films: Steve Sabol
Executive Director, NFL Player's Association; Chairman, PLAYERS INC: Gene Upshaw, age 58
Managing Director, NFL Europe: Jim Connelly
Auditors: Deloitte & Touche LLP

LOCATIONS

HQ: National Football League, Inc.
280 Park Ave., New York, NY 10017
Phone: 212-450-2000 **Fax:** 212-681-7599
Web: www.nfl.com

The National Football League oversees 32 franchises in 31 cities. It also has six franchises in Europe.

PRODUCTS/OPERATIONS

National Football League Franchises

American Football Conference
Baltimore Ravens (1996)
Cleveland Browns (1944, joined the NFL from the AAFC in 1950)
Buffalo Bills (1959, joined the NFL from the AFL in 1970, New York)
Cleveland Browns (1999)
Cincinnati Bengals (1968, joined the NFL from the AFL in 1970)
Denver Broncos (1959, joined the NFL from the AFL in 1970)
Houston Texans (2002)
Indianapolis Colts (1984)
Baltimore Colts (1953)
Jacksonville Jaguars (1995, Florida)
Kansas City Chiefs (1963, joined the NFL from the AFL in 1970, Missouri)
Dallas Texans (1959)
Miami Dolphins (1966, joined the NFL from the AFL in 1970)
New England Patriots (1971; Foxboro, MA)
Boston Patriots (1959, joined the NFL from the AFL in 1970)
New York Jets (1959, joined the NFL from the AFL in 1970)
Oakland Raiders (1995, California)
Los Angeles Raiders (1982)
Oakland Raiders (1959, joined the NFL from the AFL in 1970)
Pittsburgh Steelers (1940)
Pittsburgh Pirates (1933)
San Diego Chargers (1961, joined the NFL from the AFL in 1970)
Los Angeles Chargers (1959)
Tennessee Titans (1998, Nashville)
Tennessee Oilers (1997, Memphis)
Houston Oilers (1959, joined the NFL from the AFL in 1970)

National Football Conference
Arizona Cardinals (1994, Phoenix)
Phoenix Cardinals (1988)
St. Louis Cardinals (1960)
Chicago Cardinals (1922)
Racine Cardinals (1901, Chicago)
Morgan Athletic Club (1898, Chicago)
Atlanta Falcons (1966)
Carolina Panthers (1995; Charlotte, NC)
Chicago Bears (1922)
Chicago Staleys (1921)
Decatur Staleys (1920, Illinois)
Dallas Cowboys (1960)
Detroit Lions (1934)
Portsmouth Spartans (1930, Ohio)
Green Bay Packers (1919, Wisconsin)
Minnesota Vikings (1961, Minneapolis)
New Orleans Saints (1967)
New York Giants (1925)
Philadelphia Eagles (1933)
St. Louis Rams (1995)
Los Angeles Rams (1946)
Cleveland Rams (1937)
San Francisco 49ers (1946, joined the NFL from the AAFC in 1950)
Seattle Seahawks (1976)
Tampa Bay Buccaneers (1976)
Washington Redskins (1937; Washington, DC)
Boston Redskins (1933)
Boston Braves (1932)

Selected Business Units

NFL Charities
NFL Enterprises (media development)
NFL Films (highlight packages)
NFL Properties (licensing, marketing, promotions, and publishing)

COMPETITORS

CART
FIFA
Major League Baseball
NASCAR
NBA
NHL
PGA
World Wrestling Entertainment

HISTORICAL FINANCIALS

Company Type: Association

Income Statement FYE: March 31

	REVENUE ($ mil.)	NET INCOME ($ mil.)	NET PROFIT MARGIN	EMPLOYEES
3/01	4,200	—	—	450
3/00	3,602	—	—	450
3/99	3,271	—	—	400
3/98	2,448	—	—	400
3/97	2,331	—	—	—
3/96	2,059	—	—	—
3/95	1,730	—	—	—
3/94	1,753	—	—	—
Annual Growth	13.3%	—	—	4.0%

Revenue History

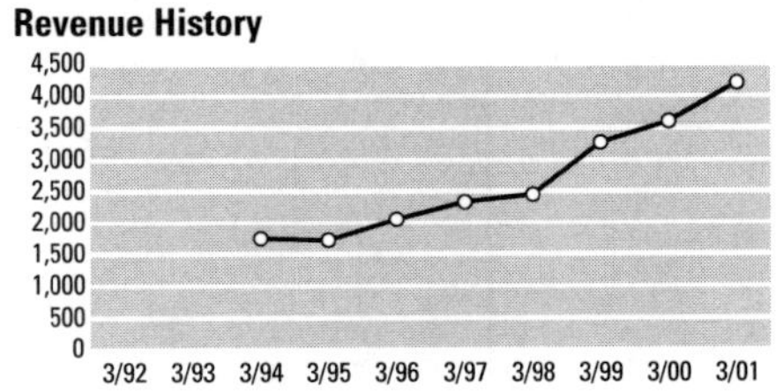

National Geographic Society

It's not your father's National Geographic Society anymore. Still publishing its flagship *National Geographic* magazine, the not-for-profit organization with some 10 million members has expanded into an array of venues to enhance our knowledge of the big blue marble. For-profit subsidiary National Geographic Ventures is fortifying the organization's presence on television and the Web and in map-making and retail. The organization owns part of the National Geographic Channel, a cable channel it operates jointly with NBC and FOX. The National Geographic Society also supports geographic expeditions (it has funded more than 7 000 scientific research projects) and sponsors exhibits, lectures, and education programs.

As competition from relative newcomers such as Discovery Communications intensifies, the commercialization of the National Geographic Society has been accelerating.

HISTORY

In 1888 a group of scientists and explorers gathered in Washington, DC, to form the National Geographic Society. Gardiner Hubbard was its first president. The organization mailed the first edition of its magazine, dated October 1888, to 165 members. The magazine was clothed in a brown cover and contained a few esoteric articles, such as "The Classification of Geographic Forms by Genesis." The organization's tradition of funding expeditions began in 1890 when it sent geologist Israel Russell to explore Alaska. It began issuing regular monthly editions of *National Geographic* in 1896.

Following Hubbard's death in 1897, his son-in-law, inventor Alexander Graham Bell, became president. Aiming to boost the magazine's popularity, he hired Gilbert Grosvenor (who later married Bell's daughter) as editor. Grosvenor turned the magazine from a dry, technical publication to one of more general interest.

Under Grosvenor the magazine pioneered the use of photography, including rare photographs of remote Tibet (1904), the first hand-tinted colored photos (1910), the first underwater color photos (1920s), and the first color aerial photographs (1930).

The organization sponsored Robert Peary's trek to the North Pole in 1909 and Hiram Bingham's 1912 exploration of Machu Picchu in Peru. National Geographic expanded into cartography with the creation of a maps division in 1915. Grosvenor became president in 1920.

By 1930 circulation was 1.2 million (up from 2,200 in 1900). Grosvenor's policy of printing only "what is of a kindly nature . . . about any country or people" resulted in two articles that were criticized for their kindly portrayal of prewar Nazi Germany (however, National Geographic maps and photographs were used by the US government for WWII intelligence). That policy eased over the years, and in 1961 a *National Geographic* article described the growing US involvement in Vietnam.

Grosvenor retired in 1954. His son Melville Bell Grosvenor, who became president and editor in 1957, accelerated book publishing and created a film unit that aired its first TV documentary in 1965. Melville retired in 1967.

Melville's son Gilbert Melville Grosvenor took over as president in 1970. The organization debuted its *National Geographic Explorer* television series in 1985. National Geographic branched into commercial ventures in 1995 when it created for-profit subsidiary National Geographic Ventures to expand its presence on television, the Internet, maps, and retail.

Grosvenor became chairman in 1996, and Reg Murphy took over as president. Murphy shook up the organization by laying off nearly a quarter of its staff and stepping up its profit-making activities. National Geographic branched into cable television in 1996 when it partnered with NBC to launch a documentary channel (FOX bought into the partnership three years later).

John Fahey replaced Murphy as president in 1998. The following year National Geographic unveiled its *Adventure* magazine. To fight a circulation decline, the organization began offering *National Geographic* on newsstands for the first time in 1999. In 2000 National Geographic Ventures acquired recreational topographic map company Wildflower Productions. As part of an agreement to buy 30% of travel portal iExplore, National Geographic also agreed to license the use of its name for the first time in the organization's history. In 2002 National Geographic began using IBM software and hardware to digitize thousands of its culture and nature images to sell online.

EXECUTIVES

Chairman, Board of Trustees: Gilbert M. Grosvenor, age 71
Vice Chairman, Board of Trustees: Reg Murphy
President and CEO: John M. Fahey Jr., age 50
EVP and CFO: Christopher A. Liedel
EVP: Terrence B. Adamson
EVP: Terry D. Garcia
EVP; President, Books and School Publishing Group: Nina D. Hoffman
EVP; President, Magazine Publishing Group: John Q. Griffin
SVP Communications: Betty Hudson
SVP Human Resources: Thomas Sablo
SVP International: Robert W. Hernandez
SVP School Publishing: Ericka Markman
VP: Bernard B. Callahan
VP: Kitty Carroll Colbert
VP and Controller: Michael J. Cole
VP and Publisher, *National Geographic*: Steve Giannetti
VP and Treasurer: H. Gregory Platts
Chairman, Committee for Research and Exploration: Peter Raven
President, National Geographic Channel, International: David Haslingden
President, National Geographic Enterprises: Linda Berkeley
President, National Geographic Maps: William L. Stoehr
President, National Geographic Television: Timothy T. Kelly
President, National Geographic Ventures: Dennis Patrick
President, NationalGeographic.com: Mitchell Praver
Executive Director, Education Foundation: Lanny M. Proffer
Editor in Chief, *National Geographic*: William L. (Bill) Allen

LOCATIONS

HQ: 1145 17th St. NW, Washington, DC 20036
Phone: 202-857-7000 **Fax:** 202-775-6141
Web: www.nationalgeographic.com

PRODUCTS/OPERATIONS

Selected Operations

Books
- *Cuba*
- *Eyewitness to the 20th Century*
- *Last Climb: The Legendary Everest Expeditions of George Mallory*
- *Return to Midway*
- *The World of Islam*

Education products
Magazines
- *Adventure*
- *National Geographic*
- *Traveler*
- *World*

Maps and atlases
Sponsorship of expeditions, lectures, and education programs
Television
- National Geographic Channel (25%, cable channel)
- *National Geographic Explorer*
- PBS specials
  - *Really Wild Animals*
  - *Tales from the Wild*

COMPETITORS

DeLorme
Discovery Communications
Educational Insights
Encyclopaedia Britannica
ESRI
Lonely Planet
MapQuest.com
Rand McNally
Time
Time Warner

HISTORICAL FINANCIALS

Company Type: Not-for-profit

Income Statement

FYE: December 31

	REVENUE ($ mil.)	NET INCOME ($ mil.)	NET PROFIT MARGIN	EMPLOYEES
12/01	476	—	—	1,500
12/00	500	—	—	1,500
12/99	600	—	—	1,450
12/98	537	—	—	1,410
12/97	489	—	—	1,214
12/96	401	—	—	1,300
12/95	423	—	—	1,551
12/94	419	—	—	1,493
12/93	423	—	—	1,700
12/92	453	—	—	2,005
Annual Growth	0.6%	—	—	(3.2%)

Revenue History

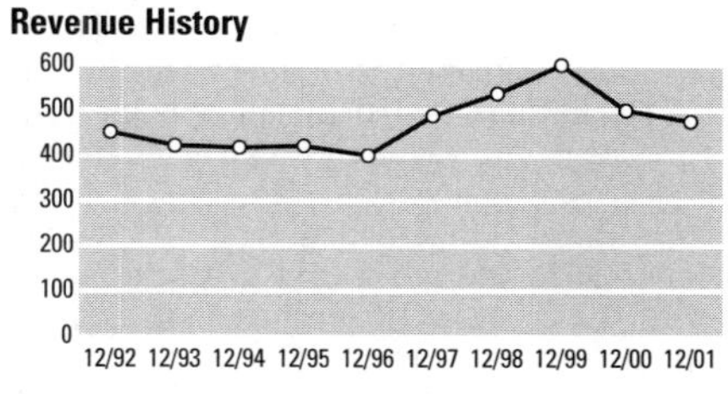

National Hockey League

Contrary to popular humor, you don't have to go to a fight to see a hockey match break out in the National Hockey League. Nevertheless, for the NHL's 30 US and Canadian teams, there's plenty of opportunity for fisticuffs in each game. The clubs are organized into two conferences with three divisions each. Seven minor and semi-pro hockey leagues also fly under the NHL banner. Two expansion teams started play in the 2000-01 season (Columbus Blue Jackets, Minnesota Wild), which was also the first year of the league's current $600 million five-year TV deal with ABC and ESPN, secured by commissioner Gary Bettman.

Despite the increase in league revenue over the past few seasons, the NHL still has a long way to go to catch up to the other professional sports leagues in popularity. Bettman's top priorities have included implementing rule changes that sped up the pace of the game. He has also had to help two teams, the Ottawa Senators and the Buffalo Sabres, maneuver their way out of bankruptcy proceedings, something that is still pretty rare among professional sports franchises.

Free agency has also drastically changed the game in the past few seasons, and has helped teams like the Mighty Ducks of Anaheim, which made it to the Stanley Cup Finals in 2003. And while there is no salary cap yet in hockey, the players' current collective bargaining agreement expires right in time for the start of the 2003-04 season. League owners are expected to push hard for a cap, which might lead to another players' strike. The NHL will also likely have to endure tough negotiations for a new television broadcasting agreement when renewal talks kick in about mid-2003. Ratings have been down on both ESPN and ABC, which might force the league to seek out different partners or reduce their price.

HISTORY

The National Hockey League traces its heritage to 1893, when the Stanley Cup (donated by Lord Stanley, Governor General of Canada) was first awarded to the Montreal Amateur Athletic Association hockey club of the Amateur Hockey Association of Canada. The National Hockey Association (NHA) was the first professional league to award the Cup (a large silver chalice with a new layer added each year, passed to the winning team and engraved with the names of that team's players) in 1910. The NHA folded in 1917 when feuding brought the need for a new image. That year Frank Calder, a British scholar and former sports journalist who came to Canada to be a soccer player, decided to keep the NHA's teams intact, rename the organization the National Hockey League (NHL), and appoint himself president. The league consisted of four teams that played a 22-game schedule.

The original Ottawa Senators (the team went under in 1934 and reemerged as an expansion team in 1992) were the league's first dynasty, winning four Cups from 1920-27. The NHL added its first US team in 1925 when the Boston Bruins joined the league. The 1920s saw continued expansion, but the NHL remained amorphous as many teams joined up and dropped out during the decade. Hordes of players went to WWII, forcing the NHL to field teams whose players were too young, too old, or barely able to skate. The league almost shut down, but the Canadian government encouraged play to continue, claiming it boosted national morale.

The Montreal Canadiens (winners of 24 Stanley Cups, more than any other franchise by far) dominated the NHL for most of the next three decades. The NHL, after representing a small number of teams for many years, launched its largest expansion in league history in 1967 when six US-based franchises joined up. The league expanded to 21 teams in 1979 by absorbing its rival professional league, the World Hockey Association. US interest in the sport stagnated for many years, however, as it was largely considered a Canadian sport, and its reputation for brutal violence turned off many fans. The NHL tried to put an end to its slugfest image by implementing new rules in 1992, reducing violent play and emphasizing a quicker game based on skill and style.

Several expansion teams (Anaheim, Florida, Tampa Bay, Ottawa, San Jose) were added to the NHL throughout the 1990s, a decade marred by the only major labor dispute in the league's history. Team owners instituted a player lockout in 1994 and delayed the season but ultimately failed in their goal of implementing a salary cap (the current contract between the players' union and owners runs through 2004). In 1997 the NHL added four new expansion teams (Atlanta; Columbus, Ohio; Minnesota; and Nashville), introducing them over a four-year period.

The league's plan to boost popularity by using pro players in the 1998 Winter Olympics games in Nagano, Japan, was thwarted by limited, late-night coverage. Later that year NHL team owners agreed to a $600 million, five-year television contract with Walt Disney's ABC and ESPN starting with the 2000-01 season. That season also marked further expansion as the Minnesota Wild and the Columbus Blue Jackets took to the ice. The league got a shot in the arm from the 2002 Winter Olympics in Salt Lake City which featured many NHL players in a hotly contested US vs. Canada final. The Canadians took the gold medal with a 5-2 victory.

EXECUTIVES

Commissioner: Gary B. Bettman, age 51
EVP and COO: Jon Litner
EVP and CFO: Craig Harnett
EVP and Chief Legal Officer: William Daly
EVP and Director of Hockey Operations: Colin Campbell
EVP Legal and Business Affairs and General Counsel, NHL Enterprises: Richard Zahnd
SVP Finance: Joseph DeSousa
SVP Hockey Operations: James Gregory
SVP New Business Development and President, NHL Interactive CyberEnterprises: Keith Ritter
SVP Security: Dennis Cunningham
SVP Television and Media Ventures: Doug Perlman
SVP and General Counsel: David Zimmerman
VP Broadcasting and Programming: Adam Acone
VP Club Marketing: Scott Carmichael
VP Communications: Bernadette Mansur
VP Consumer Products Marketing: Jim Haskins
VP Strategic Development: Susan Cohig
Group VP Consumer Products Marketing: Brian Jennings
Group VP Corporate Marketing: Andrew Judelson
Group VP Events and Entertainment: Frank Supovitz
Group VP Information Technology: Peter DelGiacco
Group VP and Managing Director, NHL International: Ken Yaffe
President, NHL Enterprises: Ed Horne
Director of Human Resources: Janet A. Meyers
Director of Officiating: Andy van Hellemond
Auditors: PricewaterhouseCoopers LLP

LOCATIONS

HQ: 1251 Avenue of the Americas, 47th Fl., New York, NY 10020
Phone: 212-789-2000 **Fax:** 212-789-2020
Web: www.nhl.com

The National Hockey League has 24 teams in the US and six in Canada.

PRODUCTS/OPERATIONS

Eastern Conference

Atlantic Division
New Jersey Devils
New York Islanders
New York Rangers
Philadelphia Flyers
Pittsburgh Penguins

Northeast Division
Boston Bruins
Buffalo Sabres
Montreal Canadiens
Ottawa Senators
Toronto Maple Leafs

Southeast Division
Atlanta Thrashers
Carolina Hurricanes
Florida Panthers
Tampa Bay Lightning
Washington Capitals

Western Conference

Central Division
Chicago Blackhawks
Columbus Blue Jackets
Detroit Red Wings
Nashville Predators
St. Louis Blues

Northwest Division
Calgary Flames
Colorado Avalanche
Edmonton Oilers
Minnesota Wild
Vancouver Canucks

Pacific Division
Mighty Ducks of Anaheim
Dallas Stars
Los Angeles Kings
Phoenix Coyotes
San Jose Sharks

Minor and Semi-Pro Leagues

American Hockey League
Central Hockey League
East Coast Hockey League
International Hockey League
United Hockey League
West Coast Hockey League
Western Professional Hockey League

COMPETITORS

AFL
CART
Indy Racing League
Major League Baseball
Major League Soccer
NASCAR
NBA
NFL
PGA

HISTORICAL FINANCIALS

Company Type: Association

Income Statement

FYE: June 30

	REVENUE ($ mil.)	NET INCOME ($ mil.)	NET PROFIT MARGIN	EMPLOYEES
6/03	1,927	—	—	—
6/02	1,875	—	—	—
6/01	1,769	—	—	—
6/00	1,566	—	—	—
6/99	1,285	—	—	—
6/98	1,141	—	—	289
6/97	1,105	—	—	257
6/96	936	—	—	200
6/95	568	—	—	150
6/94	732	—	—	110
Annual Growth	11.3%	—	—	27.3%

Revenue History

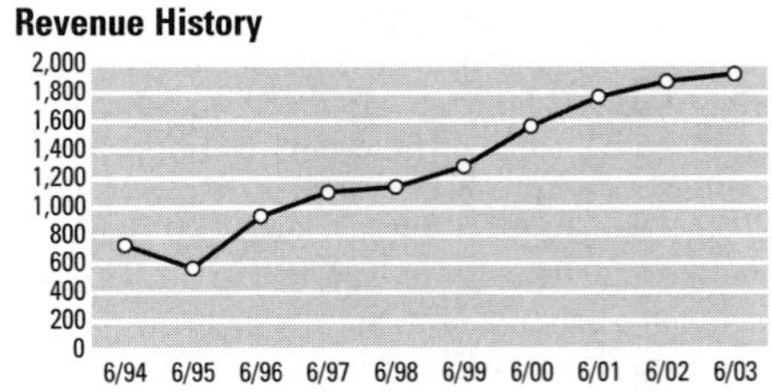

National Life Insurance

Founded in 1848, National Life Insurance Company is one of the oldest life insurance firms in the US. Through its subsidiaries, the company offers a full range of individual life insurance and annuity products and has shifted its status from that of an insurance outfit to that of a financial services company by increasing its investment services segment. Affiliates include Life Insurance Company of the Southwest (annuities) and the Sentinel Companies (investment products and services). National Life is a mutual company owned by its policyholders.

EXECUTIVES

Chairman and CEO: Thomas H. MacLeay, age 53
President, COO, and Director: James A. Mallon
VP, Human Resources: Jane Bowman
Chief Investment Officer: Rodney A. Buck
Auditors: PricewaterhouseCoopers LLP

LOCATIONS

HQ: National Life Insurance Company
1 National Life Dr., Montpelier, VT 05604
Phone: 802-229-3333 **Fax:** 802-229-9281
Web: www.natlifeinsco.com

PRODUCTS/OPERATIONS

Selected Subsidiaries

American Guaranty & Trust
Equity Services, Inc.
Life Insurance Company of the Southwest
National Life Insurance Company
National Retirement Plan Advisors Inc.
NL Capital Management, Inc.
The Sentinel Companies

COMPETITORS

AIG American General
AXA Financial
CIGNA
Citigroup
CNA Financial
FMR
John Hancock Financial Services
MassMutual
MetLife
New York Life
Ohio National Financial Services
Principal Financial
Prudential

HISTORICAL FINANCIALS

Company Type: Mutual company

Income Statement FYE: December 31

	ASSETS ($ mil.)	NET INCOME ($ mil.)	INCOME AS % OF ASSETS	EMPLOYEES
12/02	10,739	26	0.2%	1,000
12/01	10,161	48	0.5%	1,000
12/00	9,618	61	0.6%	950
12/99	9,356	57	0.6%	900
12/98	9,206	20	0.2%	750
12/97	8,814	36	0.4%	750
12/96	8,304	17	0.2%	960
12/95	—	—	—	1,000
12/94	—	—	—	1,016
12/93	—	—	—	944
Annual Growth	4.4%	7.2%	—	0.6%

2002 Year-End Financials

Equity as % of assets: 9.4%
Return on assets: 0.2%
Return on equity: —
Long-term debt ($ mil.): 70
Sales ($ mil.): 1,079

Net Income History

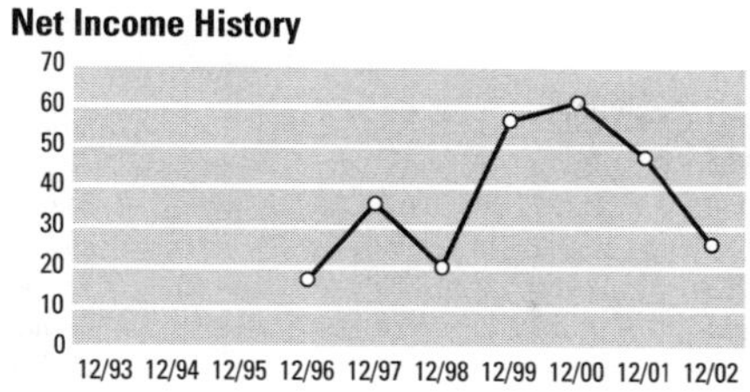

National Railroad Passenger Corporation

Fueled by government dollars, Amtrak keeps on chugging, hoping to operate under its own steam. The National Railroad Passenger Corporation, better known as Amtrak, carries more than 23 million passengers a year in 46 states. A for-profit company that has never been profitable, Amtrak is almost wholly owned by the US Department of Transportation and receives large subsidies from the federal government, which wants Amtrak to be self-sufficient. But Amtrak may not have the chance to do so — the Amtrak Reform Council has proposed to Congress that the company be broken up and that competition be allowed on some passenger routes.

Under new CEO David Gunn, Amtrak has moved to cut costs by reducing its workforce. Nevertheless, the railroad needs subsidies to maintain its operations. For fiscal 2003, Amtrak asked for $1.2 billion from the federal government — more than twice what the Bush administration proposed — and received $1.05 billion, after extensive negotiations in Congress. Amtrak officials, who had said long-distance routes would be shut down if the company didn't receive the requested $1.2 billion, said the grant approved by lawmakers would allow service to be maintained through September, the end of the federal fiscal year.

Still pending in Washington is a recommendation from the Amtrak Reform Council, which was established under 1997 legislation that set a December 2002 deadline for the carrier to be financially self-sufficient. The council has proposed to Congress that Amtrak be divided into three parts: a federal agency to oversee national rail programs, a company to manage tracks, and another company to manage rail service. It also calls for Amtrak's monopoly on rail passenger service to end, allowing competition within two to three years on certain routes.

HISTORY

US passenger train travel peaked in 1929, with 20,000 trains in operation. But the spread of automobiles, bus service, and air travel cut into business, and by the late 1960s only about 500 passenger trains remained running in the US. In 1970 the combined losses of all private train operations exceeded $1.8 billion in today's dollars. That year Congress passed the Rail Passenger Service Act, which created Amtrak to preserve America's passenger rail system. Although railroads were offered stock in the corporation for their passenger equipment, most just wrote off the loss.

Amtrak began operating in 1971 with 1,200 cars, most built in the 1950s. Although the company lost money from the outset ($153 million in 1972), it continued to be bankrolled by Uncle Sam, despite much criticism. Amtrak ordered its first new equipment in 1973, the year it also began taking over stations, yards, and service staff. The company didn't own any track until 1976, when it purchased hundreds of miles of right-of-way track from Boston to Washington, DC.

After a 1979 study showed Amtrak passengers to be by far the most heavily subsidized travelers in the US, Congress ordered the company to better utilize its resources. The 1980s saw Amtrak leasing its rights-of-way along its tracks in the Northeast corridor to telecommunications companies, which installed fiber-optic cables, and beginning mail and freight services for extra revenue.

In the early 1990s Amtrak faced a number of challenges: Midwest flooding, falling airfares, and safety concerns over a number of rail accidents, particularly the 1993 wreck of the Sunset Limited near Mobile, Alabama, in which 47 people were killed (the worst accident in Amtrak's history). In 1994 Amtrak's board of directors (at Congress' behest) adopted a plan to be free of federal support by 2002. In 1995 the company began planning high-speed trains for its heavily traveled East Coast routes.

In 1997 Amtrak finalized agreements to buy the high-speed cars and locomotives central to its self-sufficiency plan. It also began increasing its freight hauling and had its first profitable product line: the Metroliner route between New York and Washington, DC.

Amtrak's board of directors was replaced by Congress in 1997 with a seven-member Reform Board appointed by President Clinton. Chairman and president Thomas Downs resigned that year, and Tommy Thompson, then governor of Wisconsin, took over as chairman. Former Massachusetts governor Michael Dukakis was named vice chairman, and George Warrington stepped in as Amtrak's president and CEO.

Technical problems in 1999 delayed Amtrak's introduction of the Acela high-speed train in the Northeast until late 2000, when service began in the Boston-Washington, DC, corridor. In 2001 Amtrak pitched a 20-year plan, involving an annual outlay of $1.5 billion in federal funds, for expanding and modernizing its passenger service to help alleviate highway and airport congestion nationwide.

Thompson left the Amtrak board in 2001 after he was named US secretary of health and human services.

Realizing Amtrak would not meet its December 2002 deadline to be self-sufficient, in 2002 the Amtrak Reform Council sent a proposal to Congress that Amtrak be divided into three groups: one to oversee operations and funding, a second to maintain certain Amtrak-owned tracks and properties, and a third to operate trains. It also called for competition to be allowed on some passenger routes within two to three years.

Also in 2002 Warrington resigned and was replaced by David Gunn, who formerly headed the metropolitan transit systems in New York and Toronto. Gunn began moving to cut costs, and he worked to secure new federal money to avert a threatened shutdown of rail service in July 2002.

EXECUTIVES

Chairman: John Robert Smith
Vice Chairman: Michael S. Dukakis
President and CEO: David L. Gunn
CFO: Deno Bokas
EVP Marketing and Sales: Barbara J. Richardson
SVP Operations: William L. (Bill) Crosbie
VP Government Affairs: Joe McHugh
VP Human Resources: Lorraine A. Green
VP Labor Relations: Joseph M. Bress
VP Operations: Edward V. Walker
VP Planning and Business Development: Gilbert O. (Gil) Mallery
VP Procurement: Michael Rienzi
VP and Counsel, Business Diversity and Strategic Initiatives: Gerri Mason Hall
President, Amtrak Mail & Express: Lee H. Sargrad
General Manager, Eastern Business Group: Bill Lerch
Chief Engineer: David Hughes
Chief Operations Planning Officer: John Tucker
Chief of Sales, Distribution, and Customer Service: Matt Hardison
Corporate Secretary: Alicia Serfaty
Auditors: KPMG LLP

LOCATIONS

HQ: 60 Massachusetts Ave. NE, Washington, DC 20002
Phone: 202-906-3000 **Fax:** 202-906-3306
Web: www.amtrak.com

PRODUCTS/OPERATIONS

2002 Sales

	$ mil.	% of total
Passenger-related	1,468.2	66
Commuter	295.2	13
Mail & express	124.7	6
Other	340.1	15
Total	**2,228.2**	**100**

COMPETITORS

America West
AMR
Burlington Northern Santa Fe
Continental Airlines
CSX
Delta
Greyhound
Norfolk Southern
Northwest Airlines
Southwest Airlines
UAL
Union Pacific
US Airways

HISTORICAL FINANCIALS

Company Type: Government-owned

Income Statement FYE: September 30

	REVENUE ($ mil.)	NET INCOME ($ mil.)	NET PROFIT MARGIN	EMPLOYEES
9/02	2,228	(1,132)	—	22,000
9/01	2,109	(1,248)	—	24,600
9/00	2,111	(768)	—	25,000
9/99	2,042	(702)	—	25,000
9/98	2,285	(353)	—	24,000
9/97	1,674	(762)	—	23,000
9/96	1,555	(764)	—	23,000
9/95	1,497	(808)	—	24,100
9/94	1,413	(986)	—	24,000
9/93	1,403	(731)	—	24,000
Annual Growth	5.3%	—	—	(1.0%)

Net Income History

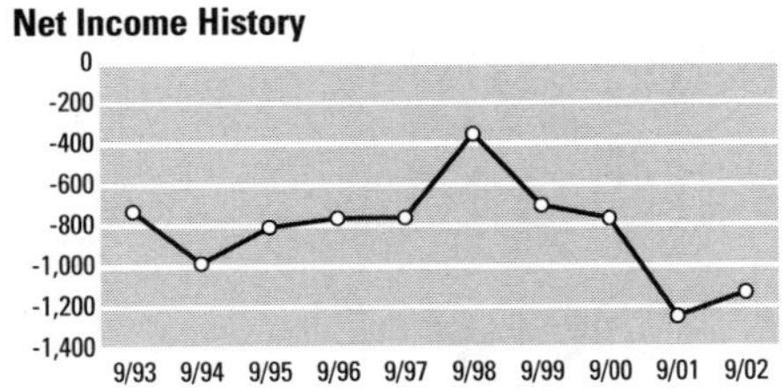

National Rural Utilities Cooperative

Cooperation may work wonders on Sesame Street, but in the real world it takes money to pay the power bill. The National Rural Utilities Cooperative Finance Corporation, or CFC, provides financing for electrical and telephone projects throughout the US. Owned by its more than 1,000 members, most of which are electrical co-operatives, the CFC supplements the government loans that traditionally fueled rural electric utilities by selling commercial paper, medium-term notes, and collateral trust bonds for its loans. The CFC was formed in 1969 by the National Rural Electric Cooperative Association, a lobby representing the nation's electric co-ops.

EXECUTIVES

President and Director: Stephen R. Louder, age 51
VP and Director: Robert A. Caudle, age 58
Secretary-Treasurer and Director: James P. Duncan, age 56
Governor and CEO: Sheldon C. Petersen, age 50, $582,970 pay
SVP, Member Services and General Counsel: John J. List, age 56, $314,844 pay
SVP and CFO: Steven L. Lilly, age 53, $363,282 pay
SVP, Operations: John T. Evans, age 53, $314,844 pay
SVP, Corporate Relations: Richard E. Larochelle, age 50
SVP, Rural Telephone Finance Cooperative: Lawrence Zawalick, age 45, $262,774 pay
SVP, Credit Risk Management: John M. Borak, age 59
VP and Controller: Steven L. Slepian
Auditors: Ernst & Young LLP

LOCATIONS

HQ: National Rural Utilities Cooperative Finance Corporation
2201 Cooperative Way, Herndon, VA 20171
Phone: 703-709-6700 **Fax:** 703-709-6778
Web: www.nrucfc.org

National Rural Utilities Cooperative Finance Corporation provides financing throughout the US and its territories.

PRODUCTS/OPERATIONS

Selected Subsidiaries and Affiliates

National Cooperative Services Corporation (debt refinancing and lending to electric co-ops)
Rural Telephone Finance Cooperative (rural telecommunications lending)

COMPETITORS

AgAmerica
AgFirst
GE

HISTORICAL FINANCIALS

Company Type: Cooperative

Income Statement FYE: May 31

	ASSETS ($ mil.)	NET INCOME ($ mil.)	INCOME AS % OF ASSETS	EMPLOYEES
5/03	20,974	652	3.1%	222
5/02	20,343	107	0.5%	215
5/01	19,999	133	0.7%	200
5/00	17,083	115	0.7%	186
5/99	13,925	76	0.5%	182
5/98	10,683	62	0.6%	164
5/97	9,058	55	0.6%	200
5/96	8,054	49	0.6%	—
5/95	7,081	45	0.6%	—
5/94	6,224	33	0.5%	—
Annual Growth	14.5%	39.2%	—	1.8%

2003 Year-End Financials

Equity as % of assets: 4.4%
Return on assets: 3.2%
Return on equity: 103.5%
Long-term debt ($ mil.): 16,001
Sales ($ mil.): 1,071

Net Income History

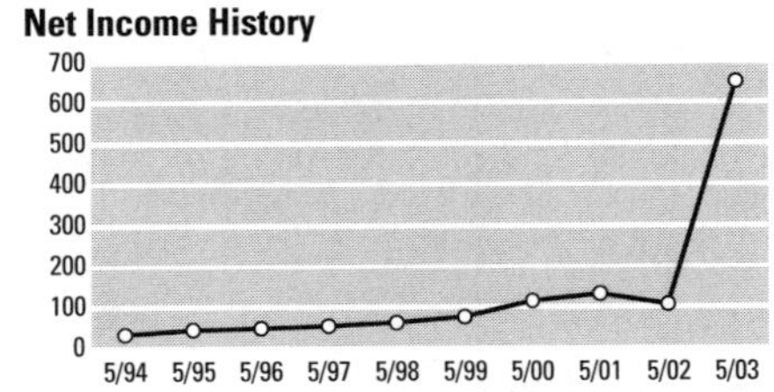

National Service Industries, Inc.

National Service Industries (NSI) won't throw in the towel when it comes to pushing the envelope. The company operates two segments, linen rental and envelope manufacturing. Its National Linen Service unit rents linens and related products to the restaurant, lodging, and health care industries, primarily in the southeastern US. Its other subsidiary, Atlantic Envelope, makes custom envelopes and other office products. In late 2001 NSI spun off Lithonia Lighting Group (residential, commercial, industrial, and institutional lighting fixtures) and NSI Chemicals Group into a new company named Acuity Brands. The company merged with NS Acquisition Corp. in 2003 and went private.

Prior to the spin-off, NSI's National Linen Service and Atlantic Envelope units accounted for only about 20% of the company's sales. The much smaller NSI is adjusting to its smaller stature by reducing the size of its board, selling its old corporate headquarters building, and flattening its hierarchy.

EXECUTIVES

Chairman, President, and CEO: Brock A. Hattox, age 54, $600,000 pay
EVP; President, National Linen Service: Richard LeBer, age 44, $387,500 pay
EVP; President, Atlantic Envelope Company: J. Randolph (Randy) Cook, age 57, $406,588 pay
CFO, SVP, and Treasurer: Chester J. (Chet) Popkowski, age 51, $261,000 pay
SVP, General Counsel, and Secretary: Carol Ellis Morgan, age 48, $261,252 pay
Auditors: PricewaterhouseCoopers LLP

LOCATIONS

HQ: 1420 Peachtree St., NE, Atlanta, GA 30309
Phone: 404-853-1000 **Fax:** 404-853-1015
Web: www.nationalservice.com

PRODUCTS/OPERATIONS

Selected Operations

Textile Rental (National Linen Service)
Bar towels
Bath towels
Blankets
Mats
Mops
Napkins
Restroom supplies
Scrubs and surgical drapery
Table and bed linens

Envelopes
Courier envelopes
Custom business envelopes
Specialty filing products

COMPETITORS

ARAMARK
Cintas
G&K Services
Georgia-Pacific Corporation
Hotelworks.com
Mail-Well
Murray Envelope
National Envelope
Reynolds Food Packaging
Steiner
UPM-Kymmene

HISTORICAL FINANCIALS

Company Type: Private

Income Statement FYE: August 31

	REVENUE ($ mil.)	NET INCOME ($ mil.)	NET PROFIT MARGIN	EMPLOYEES
8/02	532	(32)	—	7,100
8/01	563	27	4.8%	7,700
8/00	2,566	100	3.9%	20,000
8/99	2,219	124	5.6%	19,700
8/98	2,031	109	5.4%	16,700
8/97	2,036	107	5.3%	16,100
8/96	2,014	101	5.0%	20,600
8/95	1,971	94	4.8%	21,100
8/94	1,882	83	4.4%	22,000
8/93	1,805	75	4.2%	22,200
Annual Growth	(12.7%)	—	—	(11.9%)

2002 Year-End Financials

Debt ratio: 0.5%
Return on equity: —
Cash ($ mil.): 21
Current ratio: 1.78
Long-term debt ($ mil.): 1

Net Income History

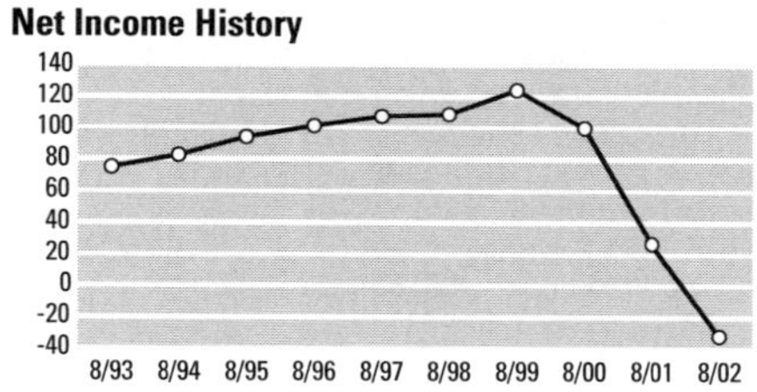

National Textiles, L.L.C.

Have you heard the one about National Textiles? Boy, has this company got a yarn to spin. National Textiles makes open-end and ring-spun cotton, cotton-polyester blend yarns, knit fabrics, finished tubular fabrics, and cut parts. Sara Lee (maker of Hanes) is the company's primary customer for use in brands such as Just My Size, Hanes Beefy-Ts, Hanes Her Way, and Champion. It has about 10 production facilities, acquired from Sara Lee, and a cotton distribution center in the southern US; its Georgia location is among the world's largest spinning plants and its Tennessee location is a leading US ring-spun facility. Chairman Marty Granoff and his son, Michael, own most of the company.

EXECUTIVES

Chairman: Martin J. (Marty) Granoff
President and CEO: Jerry D. Rowland
CFO: Keith G. Huskins
VP, Human Resources: David V. Shirlen
CIO: Barry Markus

LOCATIONS

HQ: 480 Hanes Mill Rd., Winston-Salem, NC 27105
Phone: 336-714-8400 **Fax:** 336-714-8786
Web: www.nationaltextiles.com

National Textiles has plants in Georgia, North Carolina, South Carolina, Tennessee, and Virginia.

Selected Plant Locations

Advance, North Carolina (cotton and yarn warehouse)
China Grove, North Carolina (ring spun)
Eden, North Carolina (knitting)
Forest City, North Carolina (knitting)
Galax, Virginia (finishing and cutting)
Gastonia, North Carolina (ring spun)
Greenwood, South Carolina (fleece and jersey fabrics)
Mountain City, Tennessee (ring spun)
Rabun Gap, Georgia (spinning mill)
Sanford, North Carolina (spun yarn)

COMPETITORS

Avondale Incorporated
Galey & Lord
Mount Vernon Mills
Nisshinbo
Parkdale Mills
Toyobo

HISTORICAL FINANCIALS

Company Type: Private

Income Statement FYE: June 30

	REVENUE ($ mil.)	NET INCOME ($ mil.)	NET PROFIT MARGIN	EMPLOYEES
6/02	700	—	—	4,325
6/01	800	—	—	5,038
6/00	728	—	—	5,157
6/99	727	—	—	4,217
Annual Growth	(1.3%)	—	—	0.8%

Revenue History

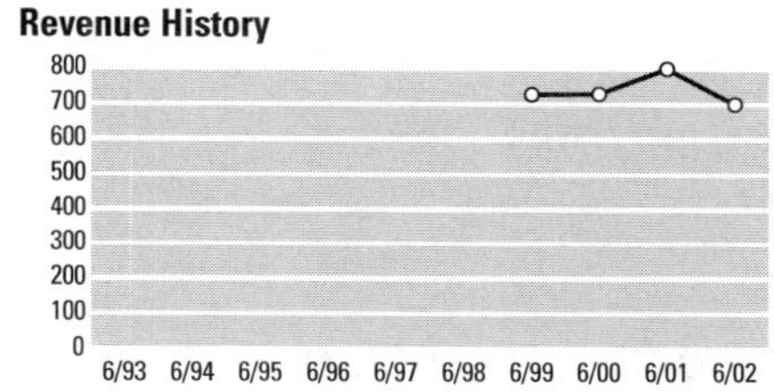

National Wine & Spirits, Inc.

Bartender to the nation's breadbasket, National Wine & Spirits is one of the Midwest's largest wine and liquor distributors. Serving 36,000 locations, the company distributes to restaurants, liquor stores, and retailers in Illinois, Indiana, and Michigan and owns an interest in a Kentucky distributor. The company's suppliers include Fortune Brands (Jim Beam), Diageo (Bailey's), and Beringer Blass Wine Estates. The company operates through several wholly owned subsidiaries. CEO James LaCrosse and director Norma Johnston own National Wine & Spirits, which was founded in 1934.

Major changes among suppliers of distilled spirits have National Wine & Spirits and other alcohol distributors across the country reevaluating how they do business.

For example, Diageo is conducting a state-by-state review to determine the companies that have exclusive rights to distribute its products. In Illinois, it has not granted such rights to National Wine & Spirits; two other suppliers, Future Brands and Canandaigua Wine Company, also have ended the company's Illinois distribution rights. As a result, National Wine & Spirits is scaling back operations and about 300 jobs in that state and forming a strategic alliance with Glazer's Wholesale Drug Company.

However, in Michigan and Indiana, National Wine & Spirits does have exclusive rights to distribute Diageo products, which is likely to boost business in those areas.

To broaden its offerings, the company also sells imported and specialty beers through a subsidiary and in some markets sells cigars.

EXECUTIVES

Chairman, President, CEO, and CFO: James E. LaCrosse, age 70, $407,000 pay
COO and Secretary: John J. Baker, age 33
EVP, Sales and Marketing: Gregory J. Mauloff, age 51, $309,615 pay
EVP and Director: J. Smoke Wallin, age 36, $297,231 pay
VP and General Manager, NWS-Indiana: Patrick J. Hurrle, age 53, $319,550 pay
President, US Beverage: Joseph J. Fisch, age 54, $392,500 pay
Treasurer and Corporate Controller: Patrick A. Trefun, age 43
Auditors: Deloitte & Touche LLP

LOCATIONS

HQ: 700 W. Morris St., Indianapolis, IN 46206
Phone: 317-636-6092 **Fax:** 317-685-8810
Web: www.nwscorp.com

COMPETITORS

Glazer's Wholesale Drug
Johnson Brothers
Southern Wine & Spirits

HISTORICAL FINANCIALS

Company Type: Private

Income Statement FYE: March 31

	REVENUE ($ mil.)	NET INCOME ($ mil.)	NET PROFIT MARGIN	EMPLOYEES
3/02	682	8	1.1%	1,618
3/01	661	15	2.3%	1,521
3/00	626	6	0.9%	1,550
3/99	553	—	—	1,550
3/98	521	—	—	1,517
3/97	491	—	—	—
3/96	443	—	—	—
3/95	427	—	—	—
3/94	396	—	—	—
Annual Growth	7.0%	15.5%	—	1.6%

2002 Year-End Financials

Debt ratio: 475.4%
Return on equity: 30.7%
Cash ($ mil.): 12
Current ratio: 2.08
Long-term debt ($ mil.): 110

Net Income History

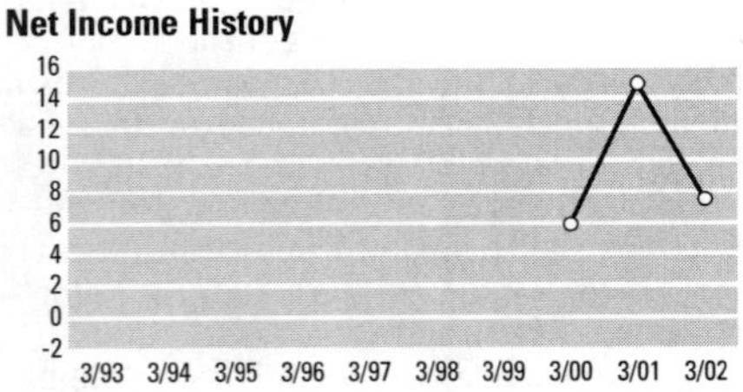

NationsRent

NationsRent has found a new lease on life since reorganizing its operations to lift itself out of bankruptcy. The equipment rental company, which emerged from Chapter 11 protection in 2003, serves construction and industrial customers and supplies nearly everything from garden tools to backhoes and bulldozers. It also sells new and used equipment and parts and offers repair services. The company, which has expanded rapidly through acquisitions, has more than 250 locations in 26 states in the US. NationsRent is controlled by The Baupost Group and Phoenix Rental Partners.

EXECUTIVES

Co-Chairman: Bryan T. Rich
Co-Chairman: Douglas M. Suliman
CEO and Director: Thomas J. (Jeff) Putman, age 52
CFO: Thomas J. Hoyer
VP Information Services: James J. Domanski
Regional VP, Central/West Region: Francis X. Hassis
Regional VP, Midwest/Northeast Region: Timothy C. (Tim) Stommel
Regional VP: Ron Halchishak
Regional VP: John Jackson
Regional VP: Fernando Pinera
Regional VP: William (Bill) Stewart
Auditors: Ernst & Young LLP

LOCATIONS

HQ: NationsRent, Inc.
450 E. Las Olas Blvd., Ste. 1400,
Fort Lauderdale, FL 33301
Phone: 954-760-6550 **Fax:** 954-760-6565
Web: www.nationsrent.com

NationsRent has more than 245 locations in Alabama, Arizona, California, Colorado, Connecticut, Florida, Georgia, Indiana, Kentucky, Louisiana, Maine, Massachusetts, Michigan, Nevada, New Hampshire, New Jersey, New York, North Carolina, Ohio, Pennsylvania, Rhode Island, South Carolina, Tennessee, Texas, Utah, and West Virginia.

PRODUCTS/OPERATIONS

Selected Equipment Rented and Sold

Air tools and accessories
Compaction equipment
Concrete equipment
Crane trucks
Demolition equipment
Dozers
Drilling equipment
Excavator trucks
Floor care equipment
Forklifts
Graders
Hoists and jacks
Lasers and measuring equipment
Light towers
Loaders and backhoes
Paving equipment
Plumbing equipment
Sandblasting equipment
Scrapers
Skidsteer loaders and attachments
Sweepers, brooms, and scrubbers
Truck loaders
Trenchers
Turf equipment
Welders
Wheel loaders

COMPETITORS

Aggreko
Atlas Lift Truck Rentals
Hertz
National Equipment Services
Neff
RDO Equipment
Rental Service
United Rentals
Western Power

HISTORICAL FINANCIALS

Company Type: Private

Income Statement FYE: December 31

	REVENUE ($ mil.)	NET INCOME ($ mil.)	NET PROFIT MARGIN	EMPLOYEES
12/02	462	(161)	—	3,191
12/01	595	(942)	—	3,146
12/00	669	(74)	—	3,000
12/99	558	32	5.7%	3,430
12/98	236	13	5.4%	2,300
12/97	9	1	10.8%	1,000
Annual Growth	118.4%	—	—	26.1%

2002 Year-End Financials

Debt ratio: —
Return on equity: —
Cash ($ mil.): 7
Current ratio: 1.53
Long-term debt ($ mil.): 1,147

Net Income History

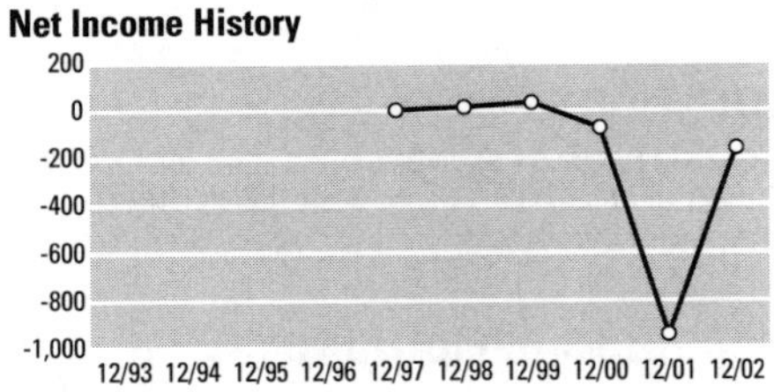

Nationwide

Call it truth in advertising — Nationwide has offices throughout the US. The company is a leading US property & casualty insurer that, though still a mutual firm, operates in part through publicly held insurance subsidiary Nationwide Financial. In addition to personal and commercial property & casualty coverage, life insurance, and financial services, Nationwide offers surplus lines, professional liability, workers' compensation, managed health care, and other coverage. The company sells its products through such affiliates as Farmland Insurance, GatesMcDonald, Scottsdale Insurance, and asset manager Gartmore.

Focusing on personal and small business lines in the US, Nationwide is buying specialty auto insurer THI from Prudential. Nationwide Financial also bought Provident Mutual Life Insurance (now Nationwide Provident); the acquisition made the company the fourth-largest US provider of variable life insurance.

Although Nationwide Financial and its Strategic Investments segment underperformed in 2002, the company swung to a net profit, helped in part by improved underwriting results by its insurance subsidiaries.

HISTORY

In 1919 members of the Ohio Farm Bureau Federation, a farmers' consumer group, established their own automobile insurance company. (As rural drivers, they didn't want to pay city rates.) To get a license from the state, the company, called Farm Bureau Mutual, needed 100 policyholders. It gathered more than 1,000. Founder Murray Lincoln headed the company until 1964.

The insurer expanded into Delaware, Maryland, North Carolina, and Vermont in 1928, and in 1931 it began selling auto insurance to city folks. It expanded into fire insurance in 1934 and life insurance the next year.

During WWII growth slowed, although the company had operations in 12 states and Washington, DC, by 1943. It diversified in 1946 when it bought a Columbus, Ohio, radio station. By 1952 the firm had resumed expansion and changed its name to Nationwide.

The company was one of the first auto insurance companies to use its agents to sell other financial products, adding life insurance and mutual funds in the mid-1950s. Nationwide General, the country's first merit-rated auto insurance firm, was formed in 1956.

Nationwide established Neckura in Germany in 1965 to sell auto and fire insurance. Four years later the company bought GatesMcDonald, a provider of risk, tax, benefit, and health care management services. It organized its property/casualty operations into Nationwide Property & Casualty in 1979.

The company experienced solid growth throughout the 1980s by establishing or purchasing insurance firms, among them Colonial Insurance of California (1980), Financial Horizons Life (1981), Scottsdale (1982), and, the largest, Employers Insurance of Wausau (1985). Wausau wrote the country's first workers' compensation policy in 1911.

Earnings were up and down in the 1990s as the company invested in Wausau and in consolidating office operations. Nationwide set up an ethics office in 1995, a time of increased scrutiny of insurance industry sales practices, and made an effort to hire more women as agents. In 1996 the Florida Insurance Commission claimed the company discriminated against customers on the basis of age, gender, health, income, marital status, and location. Nationwide countered that the allegations originated from displeased agents.

In 1997 the company settled a lawsuit by agreeing to stop its redlining practices (it avoided selling homeowners' insurance to urban customers with homes valued at less than $50,000 or more than 30 years old, which allegedly discriminated against minorities). It also dropped a year-old sales quota system that was under investigation.

As the century came to a close, Nationwide began to narrow its focus on its core businesses. It spun off Nationwide Financial Services so the unit could have better access to capital, and it expanded both at home and abroad through such purchases as ALLIED Group (multiline insurance), CalFarm (agricultural insurance in California), and AXA subsidiary PanEuroLife (asset management in Europe). It jettisoned such operations as West Coast Life Insurance, its Wausau subsidiary, and its ALLIED Life operations. The company's discrimination woes came back to haunt it in 1999, and it created a $750,000 fund to help residents of poor Cincinnati neighborhoods buy homes.

At the end of 2000 Nationwide Health Plans asked regulators for permission to exit the profit-poor HMO business. The division plans to maintain its more popular PPO operations. The next year Nationwide's expansion in Europe continued with the purchase of UK fund manager Gartmore Investment Management.

EXECUTIVES

Chairman and CEO: William G. (Jerry) Jurgensen, age 51
EVP, CFO, and Chief Investment Officer: Robert A. Rosholt, age 52
EVP, General Counsel, and Secretary: Patricia R. (Pat) Hatler, age 48
EVP and Chief Administrative Officer: Donna A. James, age 45
EVP and CIO: Michael C. Keller, age 43
EVP and Chief Strategic Officer; President, Nationwide Strategic Investments: Douglas C. Robinette, age 48
President and Managing Director, Nationwide Global Holdings: Richard D. Headley, age 54
President and CEO, Gartmore Group: Paul J. Hondros
President and COO, Nationwide Insurance: Galen R. Barnes, age 55
President and COO, Nationwide Financial, Nationwide Life Insurance, and Nationwide Life & Annuity Insurance: Joseph J. Gasper, age 59
President and COO, Allied Insurance: Steve S. Rasmussen
President and COO, Scottsdale Insurance Companies: R. Max Williamson
Auditors: KPMG LLP

LOCATIONS

HQ: One Nationwide Plaza, Columbus, OH 43215
Phone: 614-249-7111 **Fax:** 614-249-7705
Web: www.nationwide.com

Nationwide operates in more than 35 countries around the world.

PRODUCTS/OPERATIONS

Selected Subsidiaries and Affiliates

Gartmore Group (UK)
GatesMcDonald
Nationwide Agribusiness
  Farmland Insurance
Nationwide Federal Credit Union
Nationwide Financial
  401k Company
  National Deferred Compensation
  Nationwide Advisory Services
  Nationwide Home Mortgage Company
  Nationwide Retirement Plan Services, Inc.
  Nationwide Retirement Solutions
  PEBSCO Nationwide Retirement Solutions
  Pension Associates, Inc.
  Villanova
Nationwide Global
  PanEuroLife
Nationwide Insurance
  Allied Insurance
  CalFarm Insurance
  Nationwide Health Plans
Nationwide Realty Investors
Scottsdale Insurance

COMPETITORS

ACE Limited
AIG
Allstate
American Financial
AXA
AXA Financial
Blue Cross
CIGNA
Citigroup
CNA Financial
Guardian Life
The Hartford
John Hancock Financial Services
Liberty Mutual
MassMutual
MetLife
New York Life
Northwestern Mutual
Pacific Mutual
Principal Financial
Prudential
St. Paul Companies
State Farm
Travelers
UnitedHealth Group
USAA

HISTORICAL FINANCIALS

Company Type: Mutual company

Income Statement

FYE: December 31

	ASSETS ($ mil.)	NET INCOME ($ mil.)	INCOME AS % OF ASSETS	EMPLOYEES
12/02	117,930	252	0.2%	30,000
12/01	113,463	(295)	—	35,000
12/00	117,040	331	0.3%	35,000
12/99	115,760	526	0.5%	35,000
12/98	98,280	963	1.0%	32,815
12/97	83,214	1,031	1.2%	29,051
12/96	67,624	250	0.4%	33,184
12/95	57,420	183	0.3%	32,949
12/94	47,696	445	0.9%	32,600
12/93	42,213	501	1.2%	32,583
Annual Growth	12.1%	(7.3%)	—	(0.9%)

2002 Year-End Financials

Equity as % of assets: 6.6%
Return on assets: 0.2%
Return on equity: 3.2%
Long-term debt ($ mil.): 1,439
Sales ($ mil.): 29,421

Net Income History

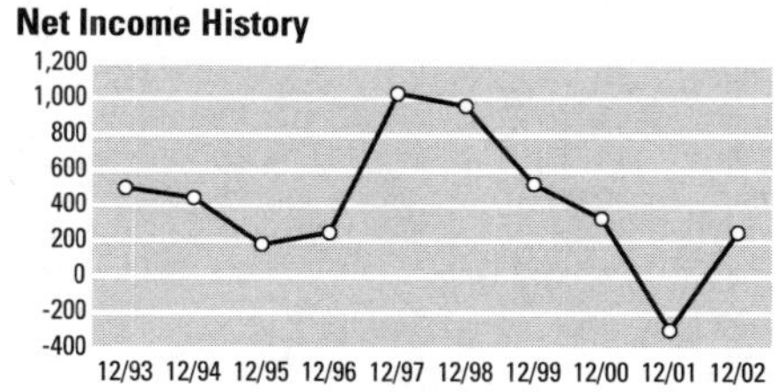

Navy Federal Credit Union

"Once a member, always a member," promises Navy Federal Credit Union (NFCU). This policy undoubtedly helped NFCU become one of the nation's largest credit unions, claiming more than 2 million members. Formed in 1933, NFCU provides US Navy and Marine Corps personnel and their families with checking and savings accounts, mortgages, IRAs, and a variety of loans (including auto and student loans). Members (who can retain their credit union privileges even after discharge from the armed services) get access to ATMs in Visa's PLUS Network and the Armed Forces Financial Network. NFCU has some 90 locations in the US and about 25 more overseas.

EXECUTIVES

Chairman: John A. Lockard
President and CEO: Brian L. McDonnell
Auditors: PricewaterhouseCoopers LLP

LOCATIONS

HQ: 820 Follin Ln., Vienna, VA 22180
Phone: 703-255-8000 **Fax:** 703-255-8741
Web: www.navyfcu.org

Selected US Service Center Locations

California
Florida
Georgia
Illinois
Louisiana
Maryland
Mississippi
New Jersey
New York
North Carolina
Ohio
Pennsylvania
South Carolina
Tennessee
Texas
Virginia
Washington, D.C.

COMPETITORS

Bank of America
BANK ONE
Citibank
FleetBoston
U.S. Central Credit Union
USAA
Wachovia
Wells Fargo

HISTORICAL FINANCIALS

Company Type: Not-for-profit

Income Statement FYE: December 31

	ASSETS ($ mil.)	NET INCOME ($ mil.)	INCOME AS % OF ASSETS	EMPLOYEES
12/02	17,585	181	1.0%	4,000
12/01	15,107	157	1.0%	4,000
12/00	12,413	185	1.5%	3,500
12/99	11,188	128	1.1%	3,100
12/98	10,793	113	1.0%	3,100
12/97	9,709	95	1.0%	3,597
12/96	8,922	—	—	3,423
12/95	8,723	—	—	3,304
12/94	—	—	—	3,185
12/93	—	—	—	3,102
Annual Growth	10.5%	13.8%	—	2.9%

2002 Year-End Financials

Equity as % of assets: 90.9%
Return on assets: 1.1%
Return on equity: 1.2%
Long-term debt ($ mil.): 184
Sales ($ mil.): 1,201

Net Income History

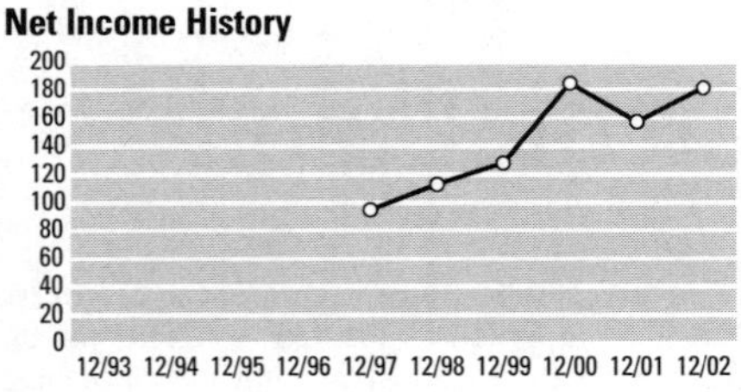

NCH Corporation

NCH Corporation has been cleaning up for years. The company makes and sells about 450 chemical, maintenance, repair, and supply products for customers in more than 60 countries. NCH markets its products — including many types of cleaners — through a direct sales force to the agricultural, home-improvement, industrial, recreational, and utility industries. Specialty chemical products, including cleaning and water treatment chemicals, deodorizers, lubricants, paints and paint strippers, patching compounds, and flooring and carpet treatments, account for the majority of sales. Other products include fasteners, welding supplies, and plumbing parts. Descendants of founder Milton Levy own the company.

EXECUTIVES

Chairman and President: Irvin L. Levy
EVP: John I. Levy
EVP: Lester A. Levy Jr.
EVP: Robert M. Levy
EVP: Walter M. Levy
SVP, CFO, and Controller: Tom F. Hetzer, age 64
SVP: Earl Nicholson
VP and Treasurer: Glen Scivally
VP and Secretary: Joe Cleveland
VP, Human Resources: Neil Thomas
Director, Marketing: Mike Benton
Auditors: Grant Thornton LLP

LOCATIONS

HQ: 2727 Chemsearch Blvd., Irving, TX 75062
Phone: 972-438-0226 **Fax:** 972-438-0186
Web: www.nch.com

NCH Corporation has roughly 20 manufacturing facilities in Asia, the Americas, and Europe, and office and warehouse facilities in Europe and the Americas.

PRODUCTS/OPERATIONS

Selected Operations and Products

Chemical Specialties
Cleaning chemicals
Deodorizers
Floor and carpet care products
HVAC products
Lubricants
Oil production facility chemicals
Paint
Paint removers
Water-treatment chemicals

Plumbing Products Group
Plumbing products for new construction
Plumbing repair and replacement parts

Partsmaster Group
Cutting tools
Electrical products
Fasteners
Welding alloys

Landmark Direct
First-aid supplies
Workplace signage and productivity products

COMPETITORS

Cintas
Danaher
Detrex
Ecolab
H.B. Fuller
Hercules
Hughes Supply
Illinois Tool Works
JohnsonDiversey
Lawson Products
Pioneer
Quaker Chemical
Safety-Kleen
Smart & Final
Snap-on
SYSCO
Vallen
WD-40

HISTORICAL FINANCIALS

Company Type: Private

Income Statement FYE: April 30

	REVENUE ($ mil.)	NET INCOME ($ mil.)	NET PROFIT MARGIN	EMPLOYEES
4/02	650	—	—	8,000
4/01	680	—	—	8,404
4/00	728	—	—	9,330
4/99	787	—	—	10,093
4/98	784	—	—	10,373
4/97	767	—	—	10,458
4/96	773	—	—	10,543
4/95	735	—	—	10,569
4/94	680	—	—	10,378
4/93	680	—	—	10,089
Annual Growth	(0.5%)	—	—	(2.5%)

Revenue History

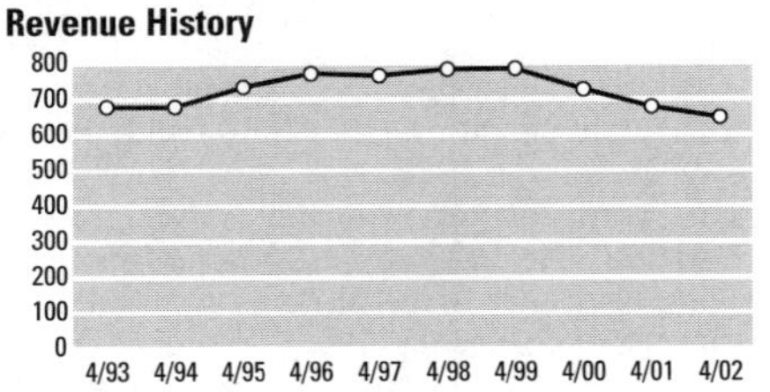

Nelnet, Inc.

Got Ivy League tastes on a community college budget? Nelnet may be able to help. The company, more formally known as National Education Loan Network, serves students, universities, and lenders in all aspects of the student loan process. It originates loans for itself and its partners, 99% of which are originated under the Federal Family Education Loan Program (FFELP). It also manages a nearly $10 billion student loan portfolio (making it one of the nation's leaders in total student loan assets managed), and services or provides servicing software for some $36 billion in student loans.

EXECUTIVES

Chairman and Co-CEO: Michael S. Dunlap, age 39, $1,125,198 pay
Vice Chairman and Co-CEO: Stephen F. Butterfield, age 51, $1,125,198 pay
President and Director: Don R. Bouc, age 56, $700,000 pay
CFO and Executive Director: Terry J. Heimes, age 39, $329,167 pay
Executive Director and CIO: Raymond J. Ciarvella, age 46, $750,000 pay
Executive Director and Chief Marketing Officer: David A. Bottegal, age 46, $329,167 pay

Executive Director, Investor Relations: Cheryl Watson, age 42
Executive Director, Legal, Policy Support, Facilities, and Purchasing; and Secretary: Edward P. Martinez, age 49
Executive Director, Portfolio Management: Richard H. Pierce, age 60, $1,080,000 pay
Auditors: KPMG LLP

LOCATIONS

HQ: 121 S. 13th St., Ste. 201, Lincoln, NE 68508
Phone: 402-458-2370 **Fax:** 402-458-2399
Web: www.nelnet.net

Nelnet is headquartered in Lincoln, Nebraska, and has offices in Albany, New York; Boise, Idaho; Denver, Colorado; Indianapolis, Indiana; Jacksonville, Florida; Phoenix, Arizona; Portland, Maine; St. Paul, Minnesota; Tulsa, Oklahoma; and Washington, DC.

PRODUCTS/OPERATIONS

2002 Sales

	$ mil.	% of total
Interest income		
Loan interest	405.1	74
Investment interest	20.8	3
Noninterest income		
Loan servicing & other fee income	103.9	19
Software services & other income	21.9	4
Total	**551.7**	**100**

COMPETITORS

Bank of America
BANK ONE
Citigroup
education lending group
J.P. Morgan Chase
KeyCorp
Nellie Mae
PHEAA
Sallie Mae
Student Loan
Wells Fargo

HISTORICAL FINANCIALS

Company Type: Private

Income Statement FYE: December 31

	ASSETS ($ mil.)	NET INCOME ($ mil.)	INCOME AS % OF ASSETS	EMPLOYEES
12/02	9,767	49	0.5%	1,890
12/01	8,135	7	0.1%	—
12/00	—	5	—	—
Annual Growth	20.1%	228.3%	—	—

2002 Year-End Financials

Equity as % of assets: 1.1%
Return on assets: 0.5%
Return on equity: 56.3%
Long-term debt ($ mil.): 9,448
Sales ($ mil.): 552

Net Income History

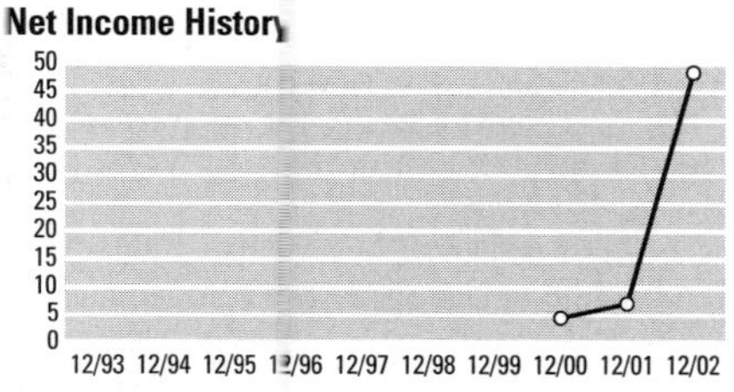

NESCO, Inc.

NESCO doesn't take diversification lightly. The holding company's operations include industrial equipment manufacturing, real estate investment, and staffing services. NESCO's industrial group includes material handlers Continental Conveyor (conveyor systems for the mining industry) and Goodman Conveyor (bulk conveyor equipment). Other industrial group companies include ACC Automation, which makes dip molding equipment for manufacturing everything from rubber gloves to condoms, Penn Union (copper and aluminum electrical connectors), NESCO Service Co. (staffing), and Rogers Company (trade show exhibits). Founder and president Robert Tomsich owns the company, which is not related to Oklahoma-based NESCO, a specialty contractor.

EXECUTIVES

Chairman and President: Robert J. Tomsich
VP, Finance: Frank Rzicznek
President and CEO, Continental Conveyor and Equipment Company: C. E. Bryant Jr.
President, Goodman Conveyor Company: Doug Markham
EVP, Continental Conveyor and Equipment Company: James L. (Jim) Smothers

LOCATIONS

HQ: 6140 Parkland Blvd., Mayfield Heights, OH 44124
Phone: 440-461-6000 **Fax:** 440-449-3111
Web: www.nescoinc.com

PRODUCTS/OPERATIONS

Selected Subsidiaries

ACC Automation (custom machinery and engineering systems)
Continental Conveyor & Equipment Co. (conveyor equipment and systems)
Goodman Conveyor Co. (conveyor equipment and systems)
NESCO Service Co. (clerical, industrial, and technical staffing)
Penn Union (electrical connectors)
Rogers Co. (marketing exhibits)

COMPETITORS

Babcock International
Briggs & Stratton
FKI
Heidelberg
Ingersoll-Rand
Jervis B. Webb
Kelly Services
MAN
Manpower
Molex
RWE
Thomas & Betts

HISTORICAL FINANCIALS

Company Type: Private

Income Statement FYE: December 31

	REVENUE ($ mil.)	NET INCOME ($ mil.)	NET PROFIT MARGIN	EMPLOYEES
12/02	1,050	—	—	9,500
12/01	1,065	—	—	9,500
12/00	1,200	—	—	10,250
12/99	1,100	—	—	10,250
12/98	1,065	—	—	700
12/97	1,000	—	—	10,000
12/96	1,000	—	—	6,000
12/95	420	—	—	3,400
12/94	320	—	—	—
Annual Growth	16.0%	—	—	15.8%

Revenue History

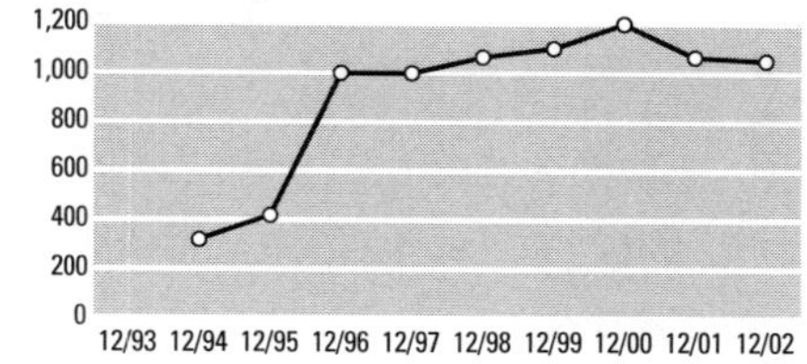

New Balance Athletic Shoe

New Balance Athletic Shoe's everyman appeal is what gives it a boost. Unlike rivals NIKE and adidas-Salomon, the company shuns celebrity endorsers; its lesser-known athletes show its emphasis on substance versus style. The approach attracts a clientele of aging boomer jocks who are less fickle than the teens chased by other shoe firms. New Balance is known for its wide selection of shoe widths. Besides men's and women's shoes for running, cross-training, basketball, tennis, hiking, and golf, the company offers fitness apparel and kids' shoes and owns leather boot maker Dunham. Founded in 1906 to make arch supports, owner, chairman, and CEO Jim Davis bought New Balance on the day of the 1972 Boston Marathon.

EXECUTIVES

Chairman and CEO: James S. (Jim) Davis, age 59
President and COO: Jim Tompkins
President Emeritus: John E. Larson
CFO and EVP: John Gardner
EVP Administration: Anne Davis
EVP Manufacturing and Procurement: Herb Spivak
VP and Corporate Controller: John Withee
VP Corporate Human Resources: Carol O'Donnell
VP Global Marketing: Paul Heffernan
VP International: Edward (Ed) Haddad

LOCATIONS

HQ: New Balance Athletic Shoe, Inc.
Brighton Landing, 20 Guest St., Boston, MA 02135
Phone: 617-783-4000 **Fax:** 617-787-9355
Web: www.newbalance.com

COMPETITORS

Adidas-Salomon
Brooks Sports
Converse
Fila USA
K-Swiss
Mizuno
NIKE
PUMA
Reebok
Roots
Saucony

HISTORICAL FINANCIALS

Company Type: Private

Income Statement FYE: December 31

	REVENUE ($ mil.)	NET INCOME ($ mil.)	NET PROFIT MARGIN	EMPLOYEES
12/02	1,200	—	—	2,400
12/01	1,160	—	—	2,400
12/00	1,100	—	—	2,400
12/99	890	—	—	2,000
12/98	630	—	—	1,600
12/97	560	—	—	1,500
12/96	483	—	—	1,300
12/95	380	—	—	1,200
Annual Growth	17.9%	—	—	10.4%

Revenue History

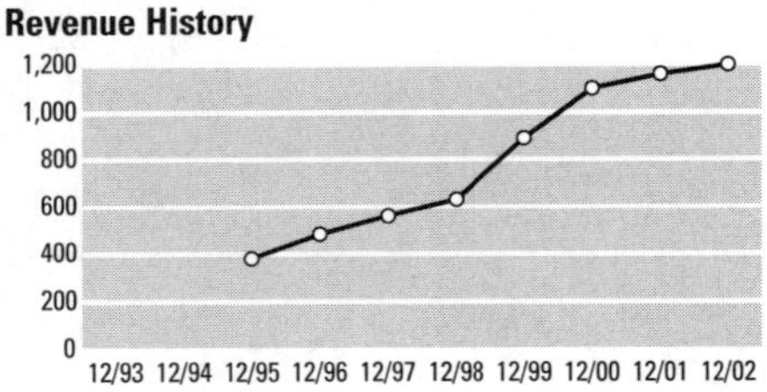

New NGC, Inc.

New NGC, Inc., doing business as National Gypsum Company, produces an array of wall supplies and is the second-largest gypsum wallboard manufacturer in the US, behind USG Corporation. The company sells wallboard under the Gold Bond and Durabase brand names. It also produces joint treatment compounds (ProForm), cement board (PermaBase), plaster, and framing systems and tests acoustical, fire, and structural properties of building materials. National Gypsum sells its products worldwide to the construction industry. Delcor Inc., a subsidiary of Golden Eagle Industries, owns the company.

Although National Gypsum never manufactured products that contained asbestos, the company has negotiated an agreement that will, upon federal approval, protect New NGC from any future asbestos liability claims related to its 1993 purchase of assets of Asbestos Claims Management Corporation (ACMC). (ACMC filed for Chapter 11 bankruptcy protection in 2002.)

New NGC will pay $347 million to the NGC Bodily Injury Trust for protection against all asbestos claims related to National Gypsum.

In 2003 president and CEO Thomas Nelson was named vice chairman of the policy advisory board for Harvard University's Joint Center for Housing Studies. Also that year, *Occupational Hazards* magazine named National Gypsum as one of "America's Safest Companies."

EXECUTIVES

Chairman: C. D. (Dick) Spangler Jr.
President and CEO: Thomas C. Nelson
SVP, Business Development and Technology: Page Odom
SVP, Operations: Gerard (Jerry) Carroll
SVP, Sales and Marketing: Craig Weisbruch
VP and CFO: William D. (Bill) Parmelee
VP and General Counsel: Sam Schiffman
VP, Human Resources: Nick Rodono
Director, Communications: Nancy H. Spurlock
Director, Marketing: David Drummond
Auditors: PricewaterhouseCoopers LLP

LOCATIONS

HQ: 2001 Rexford Rd., Charlotte, NC 28211
Phone: 704-365-7300 **Fax:** 704-365-7579
Web: www.national-gypsum.com

New NGC operates 31 plants, eight mines and quarries, four paper mills, and two research facilities in Canada and the US.

PRODUCTS/OPERATIONS

Selected Products and Brands

Ceiling systems (Gridstone, Seaspray, and High Strength)
Cement board (PermaBase)
Gypsum wallboard (Gold Bond and Durabase)
Joint compounds, spray textures, and tape
Manufactured housing products (wallboard, ceiling board, spray texture, and construction guides)
Plaster, plaster base, and finishes
Prefinished gypsum wallboard and panels (Durasan)
Shaftwall and area separation wall (H-stud and I-stud systems)
Wallboard and plaster base (Hi-Abuse and Hi-Impact)

COMPETITORS

Centex Construction Products
Johns Manville
Lafarge North America
Temple-Inland
USG

HISTORICAL FINANCIALS

Company Type: Private

Income Statement FYE: December 31

	ESTIMATED REVENUE ($ mil.)	NET INCOME ($ mil.)	NET PROFIT MARGIN	EMPLOYEES
12/02	1,300	—	—	2,600
12/01	1,300	—	—	2,600
12/00	1,510	—	—	2,650
12/99	1,410	—	—	2,600
Annual Growth	(2.7%)	—	—	0.0%

Revenue History

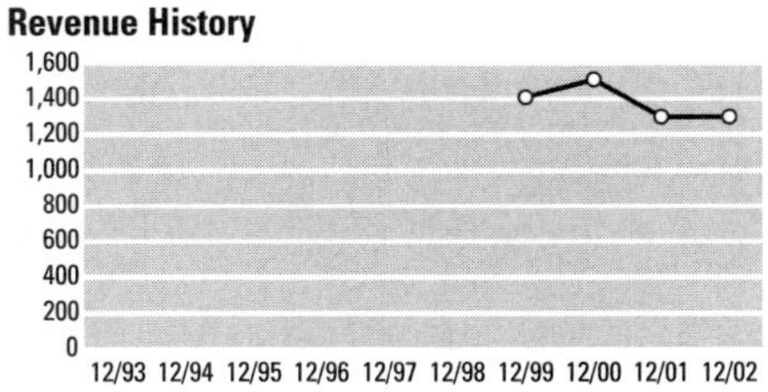

New United Motor Manufacturing

What do you get when a Japanese production process meets a California lifestyle? New United Motor Manufacturing, Inc. (NUMMI), a 50-50 joint venture between General Motors (GM) and Toyota. NUMMI makes Tacoma pickup trucks and Corolla sedans for Toyota. The Tacoma pickup is made only at the NUMMI plant in Fremont, California. The company also makes GM's Pontiac division's Vibe sport wagon. NUMMI can produce 220,000 cars and 150,000 pickups a year. Together GM and Toyota are researching alternative-fuel vehicles to meet strict emissions requirements.

In addition to the Vibe, NUMMI has also debuted the Voltz — a right-hand-drive car that is exported to Japan for Toyota. NUMMI began as an experiment to see if Japanese management techniques emphasizing team decision-making would work in the US. The experiment has been a success story. Toyota's strategy to build more vehicles in the markets it serves (rather than transport them) helps the company reduce costs. NUMMI's production methods are considered to be among the world's most efficient.

HISTORY

Rivals General Motors (GM) and Toyota applied the old adage, "If you can't beat 'em, join 'em," in forming their 50-50 joint venture New United Motor Manufacturing, Inc. (NUMMI). During the early 1980s, GM was sagging in the small-car market, and Japan's Toyota wanted to build cars in the US to ease trade tension. GM head Roger Smith and Toyota chairman Eiji Toyoda met in 1982 to discuss ways to achieve their goals.

After a year of negotiations, the two companies announced their partnership at GM's plant (which GM had closed in 1982) in Fremont, California. Toyota put up $100 million, and GM provided the plant (valued at $89 million) and $11 million cash. The companies also raised $350 million to build a stamping plant.

To gain FTC approval, the companies agreed to limit the venture to 12 years (extended later), make no more than 250,000 cars a year for GM, and refrain from sharing strategic information. In 1984 the FTC approved the deal and NUMMI was born.

The Fremont plant had a reputation for poor labor relations, and Toyota originally refused to rehire any of the workers from the plant; after prolonged negotiations with the United Auto Workers (UAW), it agreed to hire 50% plus one of the former workers. From the outset NUMMI was different, with fewer management layers and a blurred distinction between blue- and white-collar workers.

NUMMI's first car, a Chevy Nova, rolled off the assembly line in late 1984. The company began producing the Corolla FX, a two-door version of the four-door Nova, in 1986. NUMMI earned kudos for high worker morale and productivity and was selected that year as a case study on positive labor-management relations for the International Labor Organization Conference.

Despite its success on some fronts, NUMMI's sales slid during the late 1980s. It had earned a reputation for high-quality cars, but it struggled with high overhead and weak Nova sales. In 1988 NUMMI halted Nova and Corolla FX production to build Geo Prizm and Corolla sedans.

By late 1989 NUMMI's production numbers had begun to rebound. In 1990 NUMMI began a major expansion as it geared up to build Toyota's half-ton pickup. Its first Toyota 4X2 pickup (the Toyota Hi-Lux) rolled off the assembly line in 1991, followed by the Toyota 4X4 pickup the next year.

In 1993 the FTC approved an indefinite extension of the original 12-year GM-Toyota agreement. Also that year NUMMI began building the Toyota Xtracab (an extended version of Toyota's pickup), and it began constructing a plastics plant to build bumper coverings for Prizms and Corollas. It also expanded the paint, body welding, and assembly plant facilities.

Although Toyota had produced half of its North America-bound pickups in Japan and half in the US for years, it shifted all compact truck production to the NUMMI plant with the 1995 launch of the Tacoma. NUMMI built its 3 millionth vehicle in 1997 and marked the event by donating three vehicles to charitable agencies in the Fremont area.

In 1998 Toyota introduced an updated Tacoma compact pickup, and GM changed the name of the Geo Prizm to the Chevrolet Prizm. The companies agreed in 1999 to a five-year partnership to develop and possibly produce alternative-fuel vehicles. GM alluded to the possible discontinued production of the Prizm in 2000; it could be replaced by a next-generation model.

EXECUTIVES

Chairman, President, CEO, and CFO: Yuki Azuma
VP Finance and Purchasing and Treasurer: Toshiki Amano
VP, Human Resources and Legal, and Corporate Secretary: Patricia Salas Pineda, age 50
VP, Manufacturing Operations: Ernesto Gonzalez-Beltram
General Manager Purchasing: Linda McClogan

LOCATIONS

HQ: New United Motor Manufacturing, Inc.
45500 Fremont Blvd., Fremont, CA 94538
Phone: 510-498-5500 **Fax:** 510-770-4116
Web: www.nummi.com

PRODUCTS/OPERATIONS

Selected Models

Pontiac Vibe (sport wagon)
Toyota Corolla (sedan)
Toyota Tacoma (pickup)
Voltz (right-hand drive sport wagon)

COMPETITORS

DaimlerChrysler
Fiat
Ford
Fuji Heavy Industries
Honda
Isuzu
Kia Motors
Mack Trucks
Mazda
Nissan
Peugeot Motors of America, Inc.
Saab Automobile
Suzuki Motor
Volkswagen

HISTORICAL FINANCIALS

Company Type: Joint venture

Income Statement FYE: December 31

	ESTIMATED REVENUE ($ mil.)	NET INCOME ($ mil.)	NET PROFIT MARGIN	EMPLOYEES
12/02	—	—	—	5,500
12/01	—	—	—	5,000
12/00	—	—	—	4,600
12/99	—	—	—	4,700
12/98	4,699	—	—	4,800
12/97	4,600	—	—	4,800
12/96	4,700	—	—	4,700
12/95	4,500	—	—	4,800
12/94	3,700	—	—	4,500
12/93	2,700	—	—	4,300
Annual Growth	11.7%	—	—	2.8%

Revenue History

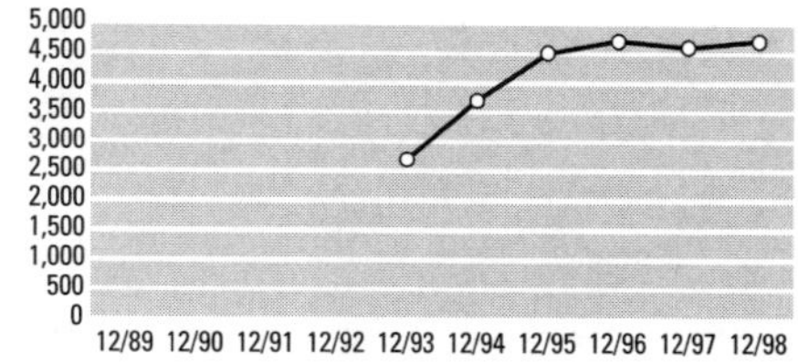

New York City Health and Hospitals

New York City Health and Hospitals Corporation (HHC) takes care of the Big Apple. HHC has facilities in all five boroughs of New York City. As one of the largest municipal health service systems in the United States, HHC operates a healthcare network consisting of 11 acute care hospitals (including Bellevue, the nation's oldest public hospital), community clinics, diagnostic and treatment centers, long-term care facilities, and a home health care agency. HHC also provides medical services to New York City's correctional facilities, and operates MetroPlus, a health maintenance organization.

In recent years HHC has lost paying patients to newer, better-equipped facilities, and is left caring for a deluge of medically indigent and Medicaid patients, who tend to be sicker than the general population since they wait longer to seek care.

To streamline, HHC has slashed jobs, worked to reduce the average length of stay of patients, and cut back on unnecessary facilities.

HISTORY

The City of New York in 1929 created a department to manage its hospitals for the poor. During the Depression, more than half of the city's residents were eligible for subsidized care, and its public hospitals operated at full capacity.

Four new hospitals opened in the 1950s, but the city was already having trouble maintaining existing facilities and attracting staff (young doctors preferred private, insurance-supported hospitals catering to the middle class). Meanwhile, technological advances and increased demand for skilled nurses made hospitals more expensive to operate. The advent of Medicaid in 1965 was a boon for the system because it brought in federal money.

In 1969 the city created the New York City Health and Hospitals Corporation (HHC) to manage its public health care system — and, it was hoped, to distance it from the political arena. But HHC was still dependent on the city for funds, arousing criticism from those who had hoped for more autonomy. A 1973 state report claimed "the people of New York City are not materially better served by the Health and Hospitals Corporation than by its predecessor agencies."

City budget shortfalls in the mid-1970s led to cutbacks at HHC, including nearly 20% of staff. Later in the decade, several hospitals closed and some services were discontinued. Ed Koch became mayor in 1978 and gained more control over HHC's operations. Struggles between his administration and the system led three HHC presidents to resign by 1981. That year Koch crony Stanley Brezenoff assumed the post and helped transform HHC into a city pseudo-department.

The early 1980s brought greater prosperity to the system. Reimbursement rates and collections procedures improved, allowing HHC to upgrade its record-keeping and its ambulatory and psychiatric care programs. In the late '80s, sharp increases in AIDS and crack addiction cases strained the system, and a sluggish economy decreased city funding. Criticism mounted in the early 1990s, with allegations of wrongful deaths, dangerous facilities, and lack of Medicaid payment controls. HHC lost patients to managed care providers, and revenues plummeted. In 1995 a city panel recommended radically revamping the system.

Faced with declining revenues and criticism from Mayor Rudolph Giuliani that HHC was "a jobs program," the company began cutting jobs and consolidating facilities in 1996. Under Giuliani's direction, HHC made plans to sell its Coney Island, Elmhurst, and Queens hospital centers. In 1997 the New York State Supreme Court struck down Giuliani's privatization efforts, saying the city council had a right to review and approve each sale. In 1998 Giuliani continued to seek to restructure HHC, and the agency itself contended it was making progress toward its restructuring goals, which were aimed at giving HHC more autonomy as well as more fiscal responsibility. In anticipation of a budget shortfall that year, the system laid off some 900 support staff employees. In 1999 the state court of appeals ruled HHC could not legally lease or sell its hospitals.

In 2000 HHC launched its effort to improve its physical infrastructure, by beginning the rebuilding and renovation of facilities in Brooklyn, Manhattan, and Queens. The organization also began converting to an electronic (and thus more efficient) clinical information system. In 2001 HHC forged ahead with further restructuring initiatives. It introduced the Open Access plan, a cost-cutting measure designed to expedite the processes involved in outpatient visits.

EXECUTIVES

President, CEO, and Director: Benjamin K. Chu
Vice Chairman: Edward J. Rappa
SVP, Finance: Marlene Zurack
SVP Corporate Planning, Community Health, and Intergovernmental Relations: LaRay Brown
SVP Operations: Frank J. Cirillo

SVP, North Brooklyn Health Network; Executive Director, Woodhull Medical and Mental Health Center: Lynda D. Curtis
SVP Medical and Professional Affairs: Van Dunn
SVP, Central Brooklyn Family Health Network; Executive Director, Kings County Hospital Center: Jean Leon
SVP, North Bronx HealthCare Network; Executive Director, Jacobi Medical Center and North Central Bronx Hospital: Joseph S. Orlando
SVP, South Manhattan Healthcare Network; Executive Director, Bellevue Hospital Center: Carlos Perez
SVP, Generations Plus Northern Manhattan Health Network; Executive Director, Lincoln Medical and Mental Health Center, and Metropolitan Hospital Center: Jose R. Sanchez
SVP, Queens Health Network; Executive Director, Elmhurst Hospital Center: Pete Velez
SVP, South Brooklyn/Staten Island Health Network; Executive Director, Coney Island Hospital: William P. Walsh
SVP and General Counsel: Alan D. Aviles
Auditors: KPMG LLP

LOCATIONS

HQ: New York City Health and Hospitals Corporation
125 Worth St., Ste. 514, New York, NY 10013
Phone: 212-788-3321 **Fax:** 212-788-0040
Web: www.ci.nyc.ny.us/html/hhc

HHC Networks

Brooklyn Staten Island Family Health Network
- Coney Island Hospital
- Dr. Susan Smith McKinney Nursing and Rehabilitation Center
- East New York Diagnostic & Treatment Center
- Kings County Hospital Center
- Sea View Hospital Rehabilitation Center and Home

Generations Plus Northern Manhattan Health Network
- Harlem Hospital Center
- Lincoln Medical and Mental Health Center
- Metropolitan Hospital Center
- Morrisania Diagnostic & Treatment Center
- Renaissance Diagnostic & Treatment Center
- Segundo Ruiz Belvis Diagnostic & Treatment Center

North Bronx Network
- Jacobi Medical Center
- North Central Bronx Hospital

North Brooklyn Health Network
- Cumberland Diagnostic & Treatment Center
- Woodhull Medical and Mental Health Center

Queens Health Network
- Elmhurst Hospital Center
- Queens Hospital Center

South Manhattan Healthcare Network
- Bellevue Hospital Center
- Coler/Goldwater Memorial Hospital
- Gouverneur Nursing Facility and Diagnostic & Treatment Center

COMPETITORS

Catholic Healthcare System
Columbia University
Cornell University
Memorial Sloan-Kettering
Montefiore Medical
Mount Sinai NYU Health
NYU
North Shore-Long Island Jewish Health System
Saint Vincent Catholic Medical Centers

HISTORICAL FINANCIALS

Company Type: Government-owned

Income Statement FYE: June 30

	REVENUE ($ mil.)	NET INCOME ($ mil.)	NET PROFIT MARGIN	EMPLOYEES
6/02	4,300	—	—	31,544
6/01	4,300	—	—	32,385
6/00	4,100	—	—	33,500
6/99	4,131	—	—	33,403
6/98	3,835	—	—	31,600
6/97	4,069	—	—	33,000
6/96	4,461	—	—	35,000
6/95	4,134	—	—	41,711
6/94	3,949	—	—	45,000
6/93	3,468	—	—	—
Annual Growth	2.4%	—	—	(4.3%)

Revenue History

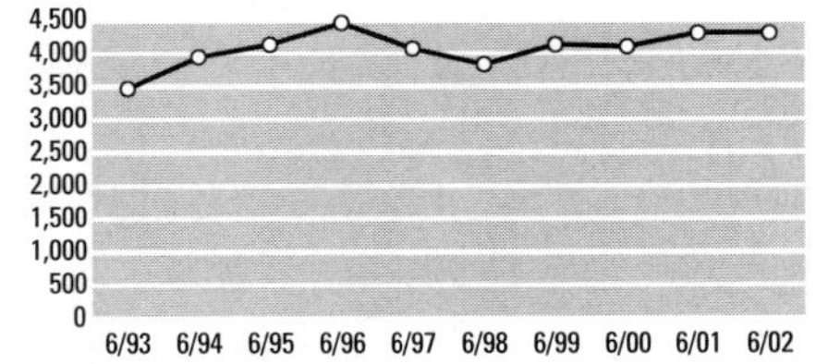

New York Life Insurance

New York Life Insurance has been in the Big Apple since it was just a tiny seed. The company (the top mutual life insurer in the US) is adding products but retaining its core business: life insurance and annuities. Its New York Life International is reaching out geographically, where the life insurance market is not yet mature. New York Life has added such products and services as mutual funds and securities brokerage for individuals. It also offers its asset management services to institutional investors. Other lines of business include special group policies sold through AARP and to federal government contractors.

After state legislators failed to approve a mutual holding company structure, New York Life announced it would not follow its rivals in demutualizing for fear of being gobbled up in a merger. The insurer will instead use its considerable war chest to further build international (the company is expanding into Asia) and asset management operations.

Streamlining operations, New York Life has put all of its asset management operations under one umbrella (New York Life Asset Management).

The company had a strong year in 2002 for its core life insurance operations; domestic sales grew by more than 40%.

HISTORY

In 1841 actuary Pliny Freeman and 56 New York businessmen founded Nautilus Insurance Co., the third US policyholder-owned company. It began operating in 1845 and became New York Life in 1849.

By 1846 the company had the first life insurance agent west of the Mississippi River. Although the Civil War disrupted southern business, New York Life honored all its obligations and renewed lapsed policies when the war ended. By 1887 the company had developed its branch office system.

By the turn of the century, the company had established an agent compensation plan that featured a lifetime income after 20 years of service (discontinued in 1991). New York Life moved into Europe in the late 1800s but withdrew after WWI.

In the early 1950s the company simplified insurance forms, slashed premiums, and updated mortality tables from the 1860s. In 1956 it became the first life insurer to use data-processing equipment on a large scale.

In the 1960s New York Life helped develop variable life insurance, which featured variable benefits and level premiums; it added variable annuities in 1968. Steady growth continued into the late 1970s, when high interest rates led to heavy policyholder borrowing. The outflow of money convinced New York Life to make its products more competitive as investments.

The company formed New York Life and Health Insurance Co. in 1982. It acquired MacKay-Shields Financial, which oversees its MainStay mutual funds, in 1984. The company's first pure investment product, a real estate limited partnership, debuted that year. When limited partnerships proved riskier than most insurance customers bargained for, investors sued New York Life; in 1996 the company negotiated a plan to liquidate the partnerships and reimburse investors.

Expansion continued in 1987 when it bought a controlling interest in a third-party insurance plan administrator and group insurance programs. The company also acquired Sanus Corp. Health Systems.

New York Life formed an insurance joint venture in Indonesia in 1992 and entered South Korea and Taiwan. The next year it bought Aetna UK's life insurance operations.

In 1994 New York Life grew its health care holdings, adding utilization review and physician practice management units. Allegations of churning (agents inducing customers to buy more expensive policies), led New York Life to overhaul its sales practices in 1994; it settled the resulting lawsuit for $300 million in 1995. Soon came claims that agents hadn't properly informed customers that some policies were vulnerable to interest-rate changes and that customers might be entitled to share in the settlement. Some agents lashed out, saying New York Life fired them so it wouldn't have to pay them retirement benefits.

As health care margins decreased and the insurance industry consolidated, New York Life in 1998 sold its health insurance operations and said it would demutualize — a plan ultimately foiled by the state legislature.

In 2000 the company bought two Mexican insurance firms, including the nation's #2 life insurer, Seguros Monterrey. It received Office of Thrift Supervision permission to open a bank, New York Life Trust Company. Also that year, the company created a subsidiary to house its asset management businesses and entered the Indian market through its joint venture with Max India. In 2002 New York Life entered into a joint life insurance venture with China's Haier Group.

EXECUTIVES

Chairman and CEO: Seymour (Sy) Sternberg, age 59
Vice Chairman; Chairman and CEO, New York Life International: Gary G. Benanav, age 57
President and Director: Frederick J. Sievert
EVP and CFO: Michael E. Sproule
EVP and Secretary: George J. Trapp
EVP and Chief Distribution Officer: Phillip J. Hildebrand
EVP; Chairman and CEO, New York Life Investment Management LLC: Gary E. Wendlandt
SVP and CIO: Judith E. Campbell
SVP and Chief Actuary: Joel M. Steinberg
SVP and Chief Investment Officer: Anne F. Pollack
SVP, General Auditor, and Chief Privacy Officer: Thomas J. Warga
SVP and General Counsel: Shelia K. Davidson
SVP and Treasurer: Jay S. Calhoun
SVP and Chief of Staff: Sandra J. Kristoff
SVP, Corporate Governance, Assistant Secretary, and Deputy General Counsel: David A.K. Harland
SVP, Human Resources: Leonard J. Elmer
SVP, Agency Department; President and CEO, NYLEX Benefits: Albert J. (Bud) Schiff
Chairman and CEO, MacKay Shields; Vice Chairman, New York Life Investment Management: Ravi Akhoury
Chairman, McMorgan & Company: Terry O'Toole
CEO, McMorgan & Company: Robert R. Barron
President and COO, New York Life Investment Management: Stephen C. Roussin
EVP and COO, New York Life International: Cynthia Y. Valko
Auditors: PricewaterhouseCoopers LLP

LOCATIONS

HQ: New York Life Insurance Company
51 Madison Ave., New York, NY 10010
Phone: 212-576-7000 **Fax:** 212-576-8145
Web: www.newyorklife.com

New York Life Insurance Company operates in Argentina, China, Hong Kong, India, Indonesia, Mexico, the Philippines, South Korea, Taiwan, Thailand, the US, and Vietnam.

PRODUCTS/OPERATIONS

2002 Assets

	$ mil.	% of total
Cash & equivalents	6,650	5
Bonds	78,311	61
Stocks	2,789	2
Mortgage loans	10,068	8
Policy loans	6,267	5
Assets in separate account	12,915	10
Other assets	12,340	9
Total	**129,340**	**100**

Individual Operations
New York Life Insurance and Annuity Corporation (individual life insurance and annuities)

International Operations
New York Life International, Inc.

Special Markets
NYLIFE Administration Corp. (long-term care and other specialty programs)
New York Life Benefit Services, Inc. (retirement benefits administration)

Asset Management
New York Life Asset Management LLC
MacKay Shields LLC
Madison Square Advisors LLC
MainStay Management LLC,
Monitor Capital Advisors LLC
New York Life Benefit Services LLC

COMPETITORS

AEGON
AIG American General
Allianz
Allstate
AIG
American National Insurance
AXA
AXA Financial
Charles Schwab
CIGNA
Citigroup
CNA Financial
Fortis
Guardian Life
The Hartford
Jefferson-Pilot
John Hancock Financial Services
Kemper Insurance
MassMutual
Merrill Lynch
MetLife
MONY
Morgan Stanley
Mutual of Omaha
Northwestern Mutual
Principal Financial
Prudential
State Farm
T. Rowe Price
TIAA-CREF
UBS Financial Services

HISTORICAL FINANCIALS

Company Type: Mutual company

Income Statement FYE: December 31

	ASSETS ($ mil.)	NET INCOME ($ mil.)	INCOME AS % OF ASSETS	EMPLOYEES
12/02	129,340	1,016	0.8%	12,000
12/01	109,961	1,086	1.0%	11,800
12/00	97,101	1,205	1.2%	11,800
12/99	94,979	555	0.6%	7,349
12/98	90,367	753	0.8%	13,000
12/97	84,067	650	0.8%	12,570
12/96	78,809	579	0.7%	12,190
12/95	74,281	625	0.8%	8,442
12/94	68,926	404	0.6%	8,130
12/93	66,791	368	0.6%	—
Annual Growth	7.6%	11.9%	—	5.0%

2002 Year-End Financials

Equity as % of assets: 11.5%
Return on assets: 0.8%
Return on equity: 8.6%
Long-term debt ($ mil.): 2,602
Sales ($ mil.): 24,721

Net Income History

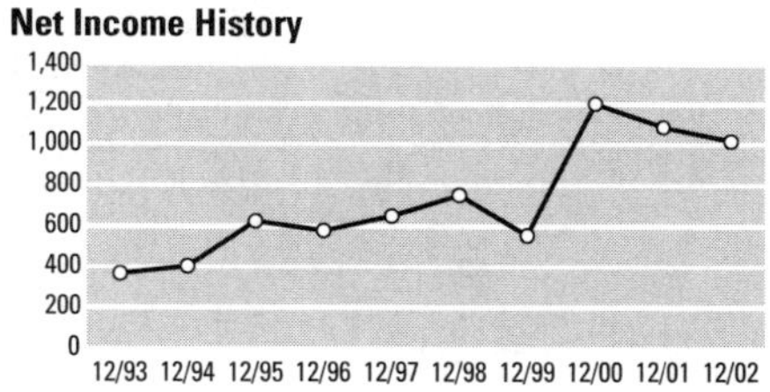

New York State Lottery

Winning the New York State Lottery could make you king of the hill, top of the heap. The New York State Lottery is one of the largest and oldest state lotteries in the US (only New Hampshire's lottery is older). It offers players both instant-win games, as well as the multimillion-dollar jackpots of its lotto games. In addition, the New York lottery operates Quick Draw, a Keno-style game in which numbers are picked every five minutes. The lottery sells tickets through more than 15,000 retailers and some 14,000 online terminals (maintained by GTECH Holdings).

The New York State Lottery has raised more than $20 billion for state educational programs (which get 33% of sales) since its inception. In addition to education, proceeds from the lottery have helped pay for the construction of New York City Hall, as well as bridges and roads for the state. The lottery returns more than half the money it takes in as prizes; 2% of sales are used to cover administrative costs, while retailers get 6%.

New York's legislature had resisted approving a multistate game, but finally caved late in 2001 and authorized a bill allowing New Yorkers to buy Powerball tickets. The New York State Lottery joined up with the nine-state Big Game Group in 2002 to launch the Mega Millions game.

HISTORY

In the mid-1960s the New York state legislature succeeded in sending a lottery amendment to voters, and 60% of New Yorkers voted in favor of the amendment in 1966. Lottery sales began in 1967 with a raffle-style drawing game. In its first year of operation, the lottery contributed more than $26 million to the state's education fund.

New York introduced its first instant game in 1976, with sales topping $18 million the first week. The state debuted its six-of-six lotto game two years later. Sales were slow until 1981, when Louie "the Light Bulb" Eisenberg — the state's first lottery celebrity — won $5 million, the largest single-winner prize at that time.

GTECH Holdings won the contract to operate New York's lottery terminal sales in 1987. The Quick Pick option — through which a terminal chooses a player's numbers — was introduced in 1989, as was a new lotto game and the state's first online computer terminal game. Autoworker Antonio Bueti set a record for the largest individual prize, winning $35 million in 1990. A jackpot of $90 million was split among nine players in 1991.

Through the mid-1990s, however, lackluster lottery sales were blamed on the Persian Gulf War, the recession, and poor publicity. During 1993 and 1994, lottery management revamped the state's lottery infrastructure and redesigned some games. The investment paid off in October 1994 when lotto fever pushed a jackpot to $72.5 million. During the height of the frenzy, sales reached $46,000 a minute.

Quick Draw, which lets players choose numbers every five minutes, was added in 1995. Sales of the game topped $1 million on the second day and soon it was grossing nearly $12 million a week. Real estate mogul Donald Trump unsuccessfully sued to stop Quick Draw, claiming that it was more addictive than (his) casinos and would encourage organized crime. That year the New York State Lottery became the first to reach $3 billion in sales in a single year.

In 1996 the state pulled its Quick Draw advertising after critics complained it encouraged compulsive gambling. Lottery officials replaced enticing ads with advertising stressing the lottery's benefits to state education. The lottery was the subject of a sting operation that year led by Governor George Pataki to crack down on lottery vendors selling tickets to minors. In 1997 the lottery spawned its own game show with the debut of *NY Wired,* a half-hour weekly program pitting vendor representatives against each other for cash prizes given to audience members and schools.

With sales slipping, the state left longtime ad partner DDB Needham Worldwide (now DDB Worldwide) in 1998 and signed a $28 million contract with Grey Advertising. Lottery director Jeff Perlee resigned the next year. He was replaced by Margaret DeFrancisco, who helped drum up sales with Millennium Millions, which paid out a record $100 million prize to Johnnie Ely, a cook from the South Bronx, on the eve of 2000. Two players shared a record $130 million jackpot later in the year.

After holding out for years, the New York legislature in late 2001 authorized a bill that would allow state residents to participate in the multistate Powerball lottery. In 2002 the New York Lottery joined with the nine-state Big Game Group to launch the Mega Millions game, which replaced the Big Game established in 1996.

EXECUTIVES

Director: Margaret R. DeFrancisco
Director of Financial Administration: Gerald (Jerry) Woitkoski
Director Marketing and Sales: Connie H. Laverty
Director of Operations: Daniel J. Codden
Director Human Resources: Charles Titus
Auditors: KPMG LLP

LOCATIONS

HQ: 1 Broadway Center, Schenectady, NY 12301
Phone: 518-388-3300 **Fax:** 518-388-3368
Web: www.nylottery.org

PRODUCTS/OPERATIONS

Selected Games

Numbers games
New York Lotto
Numbers
Pick 10
Quick Draw
Take Five
Win 4

Instant-win games
Blackjack
Cash Flurries
Fortune Cookie
Go for the Green
Ho Ho Doubler
Hot Shots
Loose Change
Lucky 7s
Pot o' Gold
Red Hot Hearts
Take 5
Top 10
Win 4

COMPETITORS

Connecticut Lottery
Massachusetts State Lottery
Multi-State Lottery
New Hampshire Lottery
New Jersey Lottery
Pennsylvania Lottery
Vermont Lottery

HISTORICAL FINANCIALS

Company Type: Government-owned

Income Statement FYE: March 31

	REVENUE ($ mil.)	NET INCOME ($ mil.)	NET PROFIT MARGIN	EMPLOYEES
3/01	4,185	1,447	34.6%	350
3/00	3,674	1,365	37.2%	350
3/99	3,831	1,413	36.9%	345
3/98	4,185	1,529	36.5%	350
3/97	4,136	1,543	37.3%	340
3/96	3,752	1,400	37.3%	310
3/95	3,028	1,244	41.1%	239
3/94	2,369	1,011	42.7%	241
3/93	2,360	1,001	42.4%	233
3/92	2,063	867	42.0%	231
Annual Growth	8.2%	5.9%	—	4.7%

Net Income History

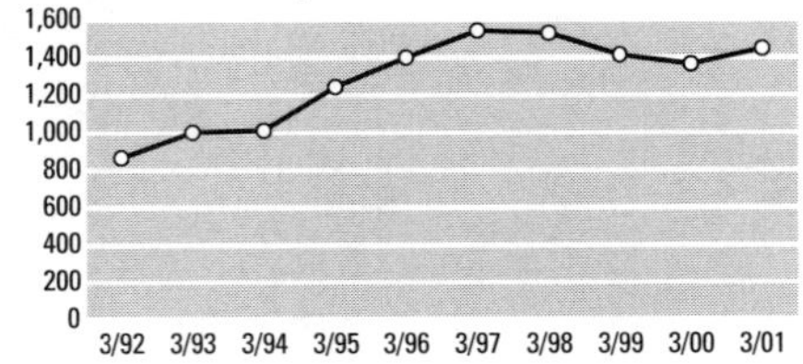

New York Stock Exchange, Inc.

It's not called the Big Board for nothing: The New York Stock Exchange (NYSE) is one of the US's oldest and the world's largest stock market. The member-owned, not-for-profit group lists nearly 2,800 companies, including most of the largest US corporations; it also recruits foreign companies seeking the liquidity available only in US markets. The NYSE is an auction exchange, meaning that stock prices are set largely by a throng of traders in an area the size of a football field, where the opening and closing of the day's action is punctuated by the NYSE's famous bell.

NYSE touts its people-driven exchange against the electronic market run by archrival Nasdaq. The Big Board also faces competition from foreign exchanges and such electronic communications networks (ECNs) as The Island (now owned by Instinet). Even though the NYSE argues that ECN trades hamper investors' ability to see the big picture, the exchange accommodates brokers making large-block trades off the floor.

To better compete, the NYSE has boosted technology spending to improve execution times and has begun offering more and more new products, including ETFs (exchange-traded funds), such as the Qs. It also launched Open Book, a product that offers traders real-time access to specialist firms' buy and sell order information.

The company owns two-thirds of Securities Industry Automation Corporation (SIAC), which provides communications, data processing, and clearing services primarily to the NYSE and to the American Stock Exchange, which owns the remainder of SIAC.

The exchange had also bandied about plans to go public as a for-profit company, but has shelved the idea.

NYSE Chairman Richard Grasso, who earned a reputation as something of a hero in the months following the 2001 terrorist attacks on New York City, resigned under fire two years later when his $140 million pay package was revealed. During the furor over Grasso's pay, the SEC launched an investigation, and many officials — including the heads of top pension funds — called for his resignation. Grasso had worked his way up through the exchange's ranks, starting as a clerk in the late 1960s.

Former Citigroup Chairman John Reed was named interim chairman and CEO following Grasso's departure.

HISTORY

To prevent a monopoly on stock sales by securities auctioneers, 24 New York stockbrokers and businessmen agreed in 1792 to avoid "public auctions," to charge a commission on sales of stock, and to "give preference to each other" in their transactions. The Buttonwood Agreement, named after a tree on Wall Street under which they met, established the first organized stock market in New York. The Bank of New York was the first corporate stock traded under the Buttonwood tree.

Excluded traders continued dealing on the streets of New York until 1921 and later formed the American Stock Exchange.

In 1817 the brokers created the New York Stock & Exchange Board, a stock market with set meeting times. The NYS&EB began to require companies to qualify for trading (listing) by furnishing financial statements in 1853. Ten years later the board became the New York Stock Exchange.

Stock tickers began recording trades in 1867, and two years later the NYSE consolidated with competitors the Open Board of Brokers and the Government Bond Department. Despite repeated panics and recessions in the late 1800s, the stock market remained unregulated until well into the 20th century.

In the 1920s the NYSE installed a centralized stock quote service. Post-war euphoria brought a stock mania that fizzled in the crash of October 1929. The subsequent Depression brought investigation and federal regulation to the securities industry.

The NYSE registered as an exchange in 1934. In 1938 it reorganized, with a board of directors representing member firms, nonmember brokers, and the public; it also hired its first full-time president, member William McChesney Martin. As a self-regulating body, the NYSE policed the activities of its members.

The NYSE began electronic trading in the 1960s; in 1968 it broke 1929's one-day record for trading volume (16 million shares). It became a not-for-profit corporation in 1971.

Despite upgrades, technology was at least partly to blame for the crash of 1987: A cascade of large sales triggered by computer programs fueled the market's fall. NYSE's income suffered, leading to a $3 million loss in 1990.

In 1995 Richard Grasso became the first NYSE staff employee named chairman. The NYSE followed the other US stock markets in 1997 by switching trade increments from one-eighth point to one-sixteenth point (known as a "teenie" by arbitrageurs). New circuit-breaker rules halted trading on October 27 when the Dow Jones Industrial Average dropped 550 points in a day (the NYSE increased the trigger to 1,050 points in 1999).

The NYSE used a veiled threat to move to New Jersey to win itself the promise of some growing space. In 1999 the exchange named Karen Nelson Hackett as its first woman governor.

The Big Board in 2000 announced plans to go public, but the move stalled, then died altogether. It also extended its official pricing until 6:30 p.m. (Eastern). In the wake of the terrorism attacks that shook Wall Street and the nation, the NYSE and Nasdaq in 2001 began discussing a disaster plan that would see the two cooperating should a future incident cripple either market. Also that year, the NYSE moved entirely to decimal pricing, in accordance with SEC mandates.

EXECUTIVES

Interim Chairman and CEO: John S. Reed, age 64
Executive Vice Chairman, President and Co-COO: Robert G. (Bob) Britz, age 52
Executive Vice Chairman, President and Co-COO: Catherine R. Kinney, age 51
Vice Chairman: David F. Komansky, age 63
Senior Advisor to the Chairman: William R. Johnston
Group EVP, Regulation: Edward A. Kwalwasser, age 62
Group EVP, International: Bryant W. Seaman III, age 50
EVP and General Counsel: Richard P. (Rich) Bernard, age 51
EVP, Corporate Listings & Compliance: Noreen M. Culhane, age 51
EVP, Enforcement: David P. Doherty, age 62
EVP: Richard A. Edgar, age 56
EVP, Communications: Robert T. Zito, age 49
Senior Managing Director, International: Georges Ugeux, age 56
SVP, Floor Operations: Anne E. Allen
SVP and Chief Economist: Paul B. Bennett, age 51
SVP and CTO: Roger Burkhardt, age 41
SVP, International Corporate: Dorothy A. Carey
SVP, Strategy & Planning: James L. Cochrane, age 59
SVP and Associate General Counsel: James F. Duffy, age 53
SVP and CFO: Keith R. Helsby, age 59
SVP, Market Structure and New Market Initiatives: Robert J. McSweeney, age 50
SVP, International Relations: Alain Y. Morvan, age 64
SVP, Market Surveillance: Regina C. Mysliwiec
SVP, Government Relations: Richard L. Ribbentrop, age 56
VP, Communications: Richard C. Adamonis, age 48
VP, Human Resources: Dale B. Bernstein, age 48
VP, Marketing Communications: Michael H. Cohen, age 40
Auditors: PricewaterhouseCoopers LLP

LOCATIONS

HQ: 11 Wall St., New York, NY 10005
Phone: 212-656-3000 **Fax:** 212-656-2126
Web: www.nyse.com

PRODUCTS/OPERATIONS

2002 Sales

	$ mil.	% of total
Listing fees	286.1	27
Data processing	224.6	21
Market data fees	168.8	16
Trading fees	152.8	14
Regulatory fees	120.8	11
Facility & equipment fees	52.6	5
Membership fees	12.8	1
Other	47.4	5
Total	**1,065.9**	**100**

COMPETITORS

AMEX
Archipelago
CBOE
Chicago Mercantile Exchange
Deutsche Börse
E*TRADE Financial
Instinet
Investment Technology
Island ECN
Knight Trading
London Stock Exchange
Nasdaq Stock Market
NYFIX
TRADEBOOK

HISTORICAL FINANCIALS

Company Type: Not-for-profit

Income Statement FYE: December 31

	REVENUE ($ mil.)	NET INCOME ($ mil.)	NET PROFIT MARGIN	EMPLOYEES
12/02	1,066	28	2.6%	1,500
12/01	884	32	3.6%	1,500
12/00	815	73	8.9%	1,500
12/99	736	75	10.2%	1,500
12/98	729	101	13.9%	1,500
12/97	639	86	13.5%	1,475
12/96	562	74	13.3%	1,475
12/95	501	57	11.3%	1,450
12/94	452	44	9.7%	1,450
12/93	445	54	12.1%	1,500
Annual Growth	10.2%	(7.0%)	—	0.0%

Net Income History

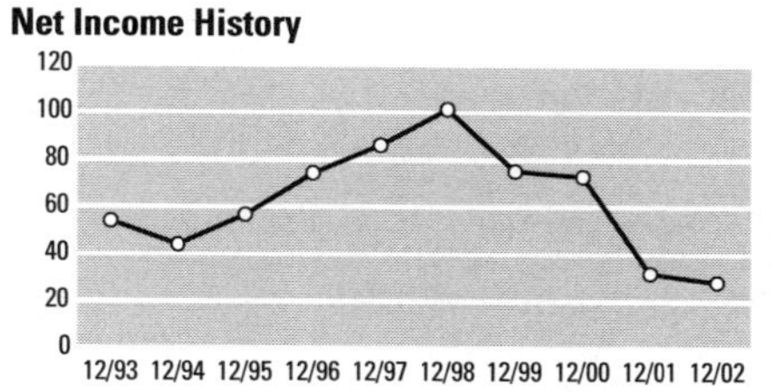

The Newark Group, Inc.

The Newark Group is proof that one man's trash is another man's treasure. The company, founded in 1912, is a major producer of paper products from recycled materials. Its recycled fibers division operates paper mills across the US and converts the 2.5 million tons of wastepaper it collects annually into several grades of paper and fiber products, including envelopes, corrugated cardboard, and newspaper. The paperboard division produces 1.3 million tons of paperboard per year from its 15 US mill sites. Recycled paperboard ends up in such products as books, puzzles, gameboards, and packaging.

The company's brands include BreezeBoard (100% recycled paperboard), NewKote (boxboard), and Stress Relief (separator stock).

EXECUTIVES

Chairman and CEO: Fred G. von Zuben
Vice Chairman: Edward K. Mullen
President and COO: Robert H. Mullen
VP, Finance: Joseph Byrne
VP, Human Resources: Carl R. Crook
VP and Controller: Lynn M. Herro
VP, General Counsel: David Ascher

LOCATIONS

HQ: 20 Jackson Dr., Cranford, NJ 07016
Phone: 908-276-4000 **Fax:** 908-276-2888
Web: www.newarkgroup.com

The Newark Group operates plants in Canada, France, Spain, and the US. The group sells its products in these countries as well as the Pacific Rim region.

PRODUCTS/OPERATIONS

Selected Products

Recycled Fibers
Corrugated products
Envelopes
Newspapers
Printing grades
Roll stock

Recycled Paperboard
Boxboard
Clay-coated folding board
Separator stock
Tube and core grades

COMPETITORS

Caraustar
Field Container
Georgia-Pacific Corporation
Green Bay Packaging
International Paper
Oji Paper
Parsons & Whittemore
Rock-Tenn
Smurfit-Stone Container
Sonoco Products
Southern Container
Stora Enso North America
Weyerhaeuser

HISTORICAL FINANCIALS

Company Type: Private

Income Statement FYE: April 30

	REVENUE ($ mil.)	NET INCOME ($ mil.)	NET PROFIT MARGIN	EMPLOYEES
4/02	800	—	—	4,200
4/01	883	—	—	4,150
4/00	864	—	—	4,500
4/99	800	—	—	3,900
4/98	715	—	—	3,200
4/97	690	—	—	3,000
4/96	700	—	—	3,000
4/95	700	—	—	2,700
4/94	490	—	—	2,900
4/93	480	—	—	2,700
Annual Growth	5.8%	—	—	5.0%

Revenue History

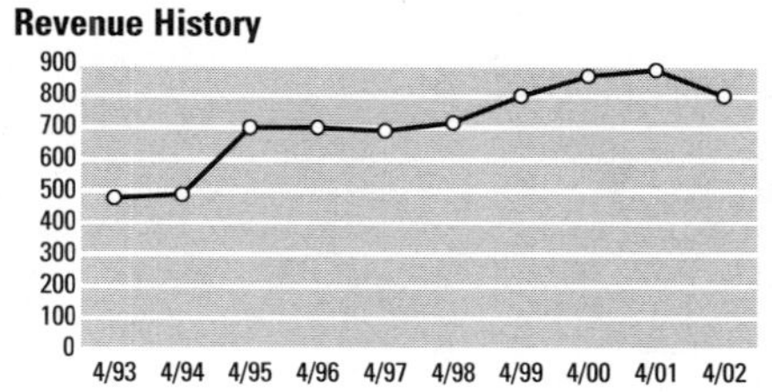

NextiraOne, LLC

A next step toward convergence, NextiraOne specializes in voice and data systems integration, network infrastructure assessment and outsourcing, and call center applications. The company also offers specialized consulting services focusing on strategic technology, business protection, and education advisory services. NextiraOne operates a global network and teams up with such technology partners as Nortel Networks, Cisco Systems, and Alcatel to serve its more than 400,000 clients. The company is owned by Platinum Equity Holdings, which formed NextiraOne in 2001 by combining a group of companies that included the network services unit of Williams Communications Group (now WilTel) and assets from Alcatel.

EXECUTIVES

President and CEO: Michael S. (Mike) Ruley, age 43
EVP and CFO: Robert (Bob) Buhay
EVP, Business and Process Improvement: Stephanie Barter
EVP, Human Resources and General Counsel: Ted O'Neal
SVP, Business Development and Strategy: Michael Mecham
SVP, Sales: Robert Vrij
SVP, Service Operations: Charles Copeland Jr.
VP and CIO: Loren Tobey
Chief Marketing Officer: Todd W. Brinegar
Manager, Corporate Communications: Kathy Bradley

LOCATIONS

HQ: 2800 Post Oak Blvd., Ste 200, Houston, TX 77056
Phone: 713-307-4000 **Fax:** 713-307-4914
Web: www.nextiraone.com

NextiraOne has headquarter operations in Houston and Paris.

PRODUCTS/OPERATIONS

Selected Services

Alarm monitoring and notification
Configuration management
Convergence readiness assessment
Data installation
Data network design
LifeCycle services (planning, design, implementation, management, and support)
Network discovery and documentation
Network performance baseline
PBX traffic and security assessment and analysis
Staging and configuration
Strategic consulting
Systems integration
Voice network design

COMPETITORS

Accenture
AT&T
Avaya
CIBER
Computer Sciences
Convergys
Deloitte Consulting
Deutsche Telekom
DiData
EDS
Greenwich Technology
HP Services
IBM
Keane
Perot Systems
SBC Communications
Sprint
Verizon

HISTORICAL FINANCIALS

Company Type: Private

Income Statement

FYE: December 31

	REVENUE ($ mil.)	NET INCOME ($ mil.)	NET PROFIT MARGIN	EMPLOYEES
12/02	2,500	—	—	13,000
12/01	1,000	—	—	6,500
Annual Growth	150.0%	—	—	100.0%

Revenue History

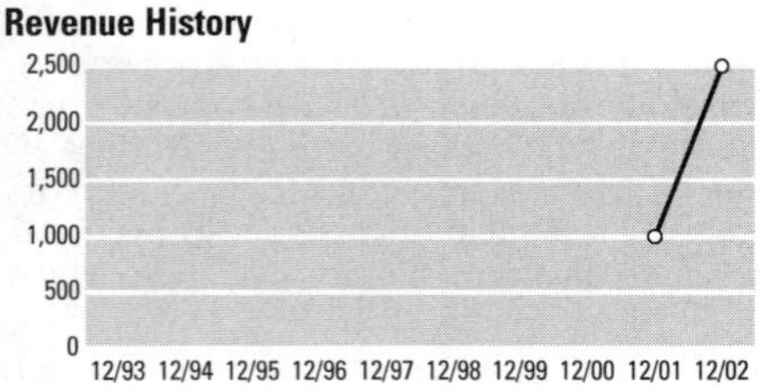

Nikken Global

Nikken Global wants to attract you — and your friends and relatives — to buy and sell magnetic therapeutic devices through its global distribution network (think Amway). The company has pulled in independent distributors to sell its magnetic "wellness" products, such as pillows, sleep masks, support wraps, shoe inserts, jewelry, and blankets. Nikken tugs at Fido and Fluffy, too, offering pet products such as blankets and vitamins. It also provides human nutritional supplements and skin care products. The company does business in more than 20 countries in the Asia/Pacific region, Europe, and North America. Nikken is owned by Isamu Masuda, who founded the company in Japan in 1975.

EXECUTIVES

Chairman and CEO: Toshizo (Tom) Watanabe
President and COO: Kendall Cho
VP Sales, Nikken North America: Eric Marchant
World Ambassador: Larry Proffit
Human Resources Manager: Rick Knudson

LOCATIONS

HQ: Nikken Global, Inc.
52 Discovery Rd., Irvine, CA 92618
Phone: 949-789-2000 **Fax:** 800-669-8856
Web: www.nikken.com

PRODUCTS/OPERATIONS

Selected Products

Magnetic
Elastomag Headband
Elastomag Shoulder Wrap
Intelli-Rest Pillow
Jewelry
Kenko Dream Deluxe Mattress
Kenko Pet Pad
Kenko Sleep Mask
KenkoPillow
Kenkoseat Plus (seat pad)
Magsteps (insoles)
PiMag Water System
Solitens (TENS - Transcutaneous Electrode Nerve Stimulator)
ThermoWear Clothing

Skin Care
Bio-Directed CM Complex Skin Cream
Swiss Soflöwer Skin Care products
ThalassoKea Skin Therapy

COMPETITORS

Amway
Biomagnetics
Magnetherapy
The Nautilus Group
Shaklee

HISTORICAL FINANCIALS

Company Type: Private

Income Statement

FYE: December 31

	ESTIMATED REVENUE ($ mil.)	NET INCOME ($ mil.)	NET PROFIT MARGIN	EMPLOYEES
12/02	1,500	—	—	—
12/01	1,500	—	—	—
12/00	1,500	—	—	—
12/99	1,500	—	—	—
12/98	1,500	—	—	250
12/97	1,500	—	—	171
Annual Growth	0.0%	—	—	46.2%

Revenue History

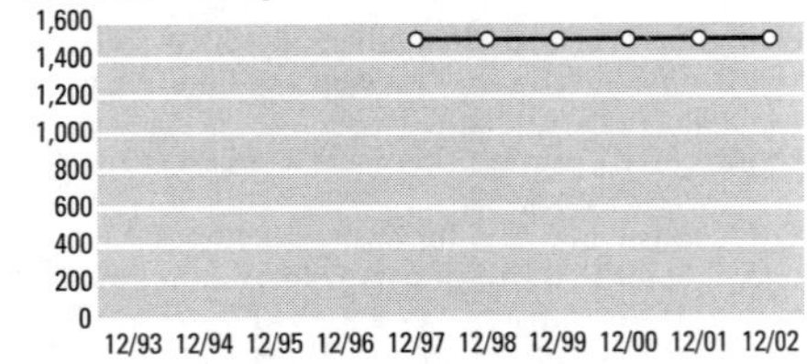

Nortek Holdings, Inc.

Nortek Holdings (formerly Nortek, Inc.), through its subsidiaries, makes and distributes building products for the residential and commercial construction, do-it-yourself, remodeling, and renovation markets. Products include kitchen-range hoods, bath cabinets, windows, and doors. The company also makes HVAC systems for commercial and residential use, including the manufactured-housing market. It sells residential HVAC products under such brands as Frigidaire and Tappan. Nortek sold some of its door and window businesses, as well as its Hoover Treated Wood Products subsidiary. Affiliates of private equity firm Kelso & Company (New York) and Nortek management investors have taken the company private.

Nortek, Inc. was reorganized as holding company Nortek Holdings in 2002 in order for it to be acquired. Kelso & Company and certain members of Nortek Holdings' management, including chairman and CEO Richard Bready, completed the acquisition in January 2003. Richard Bready's equity interest in the company was reduced from about 35% to 16%.

EXECUTIVES

Chairman, President, and CEO: Richard L. Bready, age 58
EVP and COO: Robert Ractliffe
VP, Controller, and CFO: Almon C. Hall III
VP, General Counsel, and Secretary: Kevin W. Donnelly
VP and Treasurer: Edward J. Cooney
Director, Human Resources: Jane White
President and CEO, Nordyne: David LaGrand
President and CEO, Ply Gem Industries: Lee D. Meyer
President, Variform: John Wayne
Auditors: Ernst & Young LLP

LOCATIONS

HQ: 50 Kennedy Plaza, Providence, RI 02903
Phone: 401-751-1600 **Fax:** 401-751-4610
Web: www.nortek-inc.com

Nortek has manufacturing operations in Canada, China, France, Italy, and the US.

PRODUCTS/OPERATIONS

Selected Products

Air-Conditioning and Heating
Air conditioners
Furnaces
Heat pumps

Windows, Doors, and Siding
Aluminum trim coil
Skylights
Steel and fiberglass entry doors
Sunrooms
Vinyl decking
Vinyl fencing
Vinyl patio doors
Vinyl siding
Vinyl windows
Wood windows

COMPETITORS

AAON
American Standard
Andersen Corporation
Associated Materials
Black & Decker
Bocenor
Carrier
GE Interlogix
Goodman Manufacturing
JELD-WEN
Lapeyre
Lennox
Masco
Masonite International
MasterBrand Cabinets
Mohawk Industries
NCI Building Systems
Novar
Owens Corning
Pella
Royal Group Technologies
Simpson Manufacturing
Stanley Works
ThermoView Industries
York International

HISTORICAL FINANCIALS

Company Type: Private

Income Statement

FYE: December 31

	REVENUE ($ mil.)	NET INCOME ($ mil.)	NET PROFIT MARGIN	EMPLOYEES
12/02	1,888	63	3.3%	9,750
12/01	1,856	8	0.4%	9,900
12/00	2,195	42	1.9%	12,200
12/99	1,993	49	2.5%	12,100
12/98	1,738	35	2.0%	9,640
12/97	1,134	21	1.9%	9,262
12/96	970	22	2.3%	6,497
12/95	776	15	1.9%	6,423
12/94	737	18	2.4%	5,317
12/93	744	(21)	—	5,640
Annual Growth	10.9%	—	—	6.3%

2002 Year-End Financials

Debt ratio: 309.8%
Return on equity: 21.2%
Cash ($ mil.): 295
Current ratio: 2.49
Long-term debt ($ mil.): 984

Net Income History

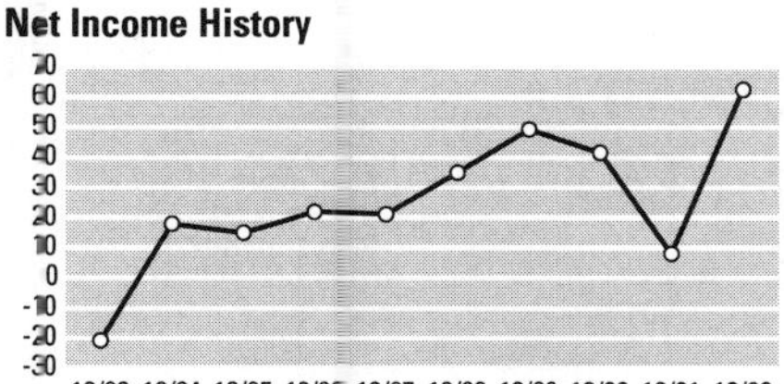

North Carolina Electric

It's a cooperative effort: North Carolina Electric Membership (NCEMC) generates and transmits electricity to 26 of 27 of the state's electric cooperatives. The co-op owns two peaking generators (30 MW of capacity) and a 28% stake (640 MW) in the Catawba Nuclear Station in South Carolina. It also buys power from Progress Energy, American Electric Power, and other for-profit utilities. NCEMC's member cooperatives serve more than 800,000 businesses and homes (or about 2.4 million people) in North Carolina. The wholesale co-op also operates an energy operations center and offers training programs, engineering and construction management, and power supply planning to all 27 cooperatives.

EXECUTIVES

President; President and CEO, Piedmont EMC: R. G. (Randy) Brecheisen
EVP and CEO: Charles W. (Chuck) Terrill
COO: Richard K. Thomas
VP Finance: Lark S. James
SVP Competitive Strategies: Carolyn Watts
VP; EVP and CEO, Roanoke Electric Cooperative: Curtis Wynn
Secretary and Treasurer; CEO, Jones-Onslow EMC: J. Ronald McElheney
Director Corporate Communications: Jane Pritchard
Auditors: Grant Thornton LLP

LOCATIONS

HQ: North Carolina Electric Membership Corporation
3400 Sumner Blvd., Raleigh, NC 27616
Phone: 919-872-0800 **Fax:** 919-878-3970
Web: www.ncemcs.com

PRODUCTS/OPERATIONS

Subsidiaries

North Carolina Association of Electric Cooperatives (NCAEC, training programs)
The Tarheel Electric Membership Association, Inc. (TEMA, purchasing and materials supply)

COMPETITORS

AEP
Dominion Resources
Duke Energy
MEAG Power
Progress Energy
SCANA
Santee Cooper
TVA

HISTORICAL FINANCIALS

Company Type: Cooperative

Income Statement

FYE: December 31

	REVENUE ($ mil.)	NET INCOME ($ mil.)	NET PROFIT MARGIN	EMPLOYEES
12/02	750	—	—	148
12/01	660	—	—	146
12/00	665	—	—	151
12/99	636	—	—	150
12/98	645	—	—	149
12/97	630	—	—	150
12/96	650	—	—	150
12/95	711	—	—	150
Annual Growth	0.8%	—	—	(0.2%)

Revenue History

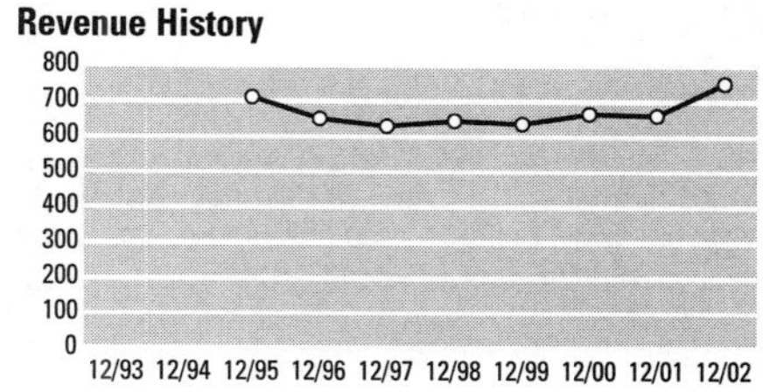

North Pacific Group, Inc.

Paneling, poles, pilings, pipes and all, North Pacific Group (NOR PAC) is building on the construction industry. The company is one of North America's largest wholesale distributors of building materials. Employee-owned since the 1986 retirement of its founder, Doug David, NOR PAC distributes wood, steel, agricultural, and food products. Wood products, which make up the majority of its business, include lumber, millwork, poles, and logs. NOR PAC sells its products to furniture makers, retailers, and metal fabricators. Its more than 30 subsidiaries and divisions include Saxonville USA, Landmark Building Products, and Cascade Imperial Mills. David founded NOR PAC in 1948.

EXECUTIVES

Chairman and CEO: Thomas J. Tomjack
COO: David Hughes
President, Schultz, Snyder & Steele: Tom LeVere
President, Southern Business Unit: Frank Johnston
EVP, Burns Lumber: John Stembridge
EVP, Hardwood Business Unit: Jack Clark
EVP, Specialty Products Business Unit: Phil Myers
Corporate Secretary: Tacy Lind
CFO and Treasurer: Christopher D. Cassard
Director, Marketing: Monique Bauer
VP, Human Resources: Karen Austin
Auditors: KPMG LLP

LOCATIONS

HQ: 815 NE Davis St., Portland, OR 97232
Phone: 503-231-1166 **Fax:** 503-238-2641
Web: www.north-pacific.com

PRODUCTS/OPERATIONS

Selected Subsidiaries

Allen Timber (wholesales softwoods and hardwoods)
Burns Lumber Company (wholesales forest products)
Cascade Imperial Mills (wholesales Canadian wood products)
Castle Pacific (wholesales hardwood lumber and plywood)
Century Flooring (sales of solid oak flooring)
Delta Forest Products (wholesales engineered wood products)
Landmark Building Products (sales of forest products and building materials)
North Pacific Composites (sales of fiberglass poles)
Pacific Vermillion (joint-venture engaged in sales of dimension hardwood products and hardwood flooring in the US and Europe)
Saxonville USA (general partnership that distributes panel products in the northeast US)
Schultz, Snyder & Steele Lumber Company (distributes building materials in Michigan, Ohio, and Indiana)

COMPETITORS

ABC Supply
Boise Cascade
Bradco Supply
Georgia-Pacific Corporation
Guardian Building Products
Huttig Building Products
Louisiana-Pacific
MAXXAM
PrimeSource Building
Sierra Pacific Industries
Simpson Investment
Temple-Inland
Weyerhaeuser

HISTORICAL FINANCIALS

Company Type: Private

Income Statement FYE: December 31

	REVENUE ($ mil.)	NET INCOME ($ mil.)	NET PROFIT MARGIN	EMPLOYEES
12/02	1,140	—	—	850
12/01	1,100	—	—	850
12/00	1,200	—	—	840
12/99	1,128	—	—	746
12/98	970	—	—	850
12/97	1,126	—	—	860
12/96	1,027	—	—	840
12/95	1,012	—	—	600
12/94	948	—	—	560
12/93	840	—	—	465
Annual Growth	3.5%	—	—	6.9%

Revenue History

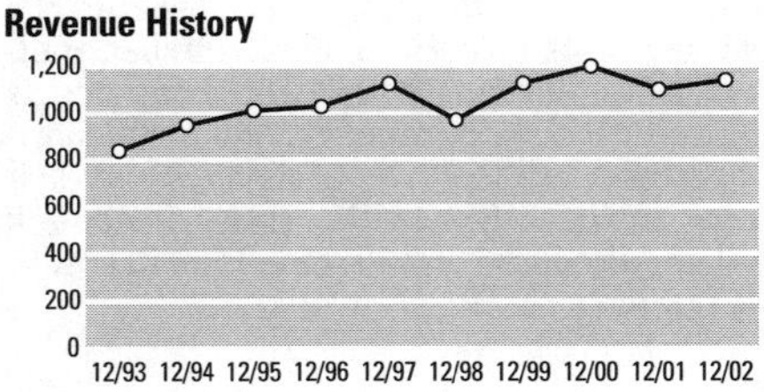

North Shore-Long Island Jewish Health System

This hospital system has a scope that stretches long beyond Long Island. The product of a merger between the North Shore Health System and Long Island Jewish Medical Center, North Shore-Long Island Jewish Health System (NS-LIJ) runs 18 hospitals in Long Island and New York's outer boroughs; several of these are affiliated with regional medical schools (including New York University and the Albert Einstein College of Medicine).

The system has a mental health facility, long-term care facilities, trauma centers, rehabilitation, and outpatient surgery centers, and also offers home care and hospice services.

NS-LIJ is also part of the Biomedical Research Alliance of New York, which conducts biomolecular and gene therapy research and conducts clinical cancer trials.

EXECUTIVES

Chairman; Co-Chairman, North Shore LIJ Health System Foundation: Roy J. Zukerberg
Co-Chairman: John S. T. Gallagher, age 71
President, CEO, and Director: Michael J. Dowling
COO: Michael D. Israel
SVP and CFO: Bob Shapiro
SVP and General Counsel: Keith Tompson
SVP and Chief Administrative Officer: Charles M. Trunz III
VP Human Resources: Ronald Stone
Chief of Staff: Mark J. Solazzo
Chief Medical Officer: Jon R. Cohen

LOCATIONS

HQ: 145 Community Dr., Great Neck, NY 11021
Phone: 516-465-8100 **Fax:** 516-465-8396
Web: www.nslij.com

PRODUCTS/OPERATIONS

Hospitals

Central Suffolk Hospital (Riverhead, NY)
Eastern Long Island Hospital (Greenport, NY)
Franklin Hospital Medical Center (Valley Stream, NY)
Huntington Hospital (acute care, sports medicine; New York)
Long Island Jewish (LIJ) Medical Center (New Hyde Park, NY)
North Shore University Hospital (Forest Hills, NY)
NSUH at Glen Cove (community hospital; New York)
NSUH at Manhasset (New York)
NSUH at Plainview (acute-care community hospital, New York)
NSUH at Syosset (specialty facility, amubulatory surgery, pain management, multiple sclerosis; New York)
Peninsula Hospital Center (teaching hospital, acute care; Far Rockaway, NY)
Schneider Children's Hospital (teaching hospital, pediatrics; New Hyde Park, NY)
Southampton Hospital (New York)
Southside Hospital (community hospital; Bay Shore, NY)
Staten Island University Hospitals (two facilities, associated with State University of New York; Brooklyn and Staten Island, NY)
Zucker Hillside Hospital (psychiatric hospital; Glen Oaks, NY)

COMPETITORS

Catholic Healthcare System
New York City Health and Hospitals
New York Health Care
Saint Vincent Catholic Medical Centers

HISTORICAL FINANCIALS

Company Type: Not-for-profit

Income Statement FYE: December 31

	REVENUE ($ mil.)	NET INCOME ($ mil.)	NET PROFIT MARGIN	EMPLOYEES
12/01	3,200	—	—	30,000
12/00	2,310	—	—	35,000
12/99	2,331	—	—	28,400
12/98	2,165	—	—	27,000
12/97	2,124	—	—	27,000
12/96	1,976	—	—	—
12/95	—	—	—	—
Annual Growth	10.1%	(4.0%)	—	2.7%

Revenue History

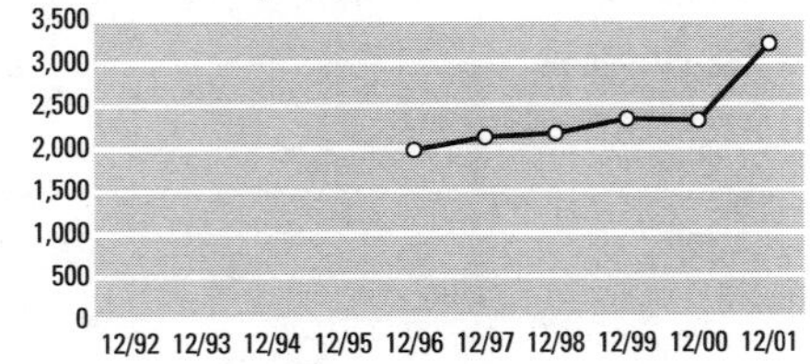

Northern Tool & Equipment

Serious do-it-yourselfers put their kids to sleep with bedtime stories from the catalogs of Northern Tool & Equipment. The company sells snowblowers, log splitters, pressure washers, power generators, and other heavy-duty tools and equipment, primarily to construction contractors, landscape crews, auto shops, and the do-it-yourself crowd. Most of the company's sales are through its catalogs, but it also sells through its Web site and in more than 45 retail stores in 10 states. Northern Tool & Equipment makes about 10% of the products it sells. CEO Donald Kotula and his family own the company. Kotula started the business in 1981 as a mail-order shop out of his garage.

EXECUTIVES

Chairman and CEO: Donald L. Kotula, age 54
President: Chuck Albrecht
CFO: John Manning
VP of Human Resources: Jean Erath
VP of Information Systems: Todd Wermerson
VP of Retail Operations: Roger Bunn
VP of Sales and Marketing: Terry Knoploh

LOCATIONS

HQ: Northern Tool & Equipment Company
2800 Southcross Dr. West, Burnsville, MN 55306
Phone: 952-894-9510 **Fax:** 952-882-6927
Web: www.northerntool.com

Northern Tool & Equipment Company has stores in Florida, Georgia, Iowa, Minnesota, North Carolina, South Carolina, Tennessee, Texas, Virginia, and Wisconsin.

PRODUCTS/OPERATIONS

Selected Products

Air compressors
Augers
Hoists
Lawn mowers
Log splitters
Power generators
Pressure washers
Sandblasters
Sanders
Small engines
Snowblowers
Spray guns
Tractors
Winches

COMPETITORS

Ace Hardware
Builder Marts
Do it Best
Home Depot
Lowe's
McCoy
Tractor Supply
TruServ

HISTORICAL FINANCIALS

Company Type: Private

Income Statement FYE: December 31

	ESTIMATED REVENUE ($ mil.)	NET INCOME ($ mil.)	NET PROFIT MARGIN	EMPLOYEES
12/01	750	—	—	2,400
12/00	650	—	—	2,375
Annual Growth	15.4%	—	—	1.1%

Revenue History

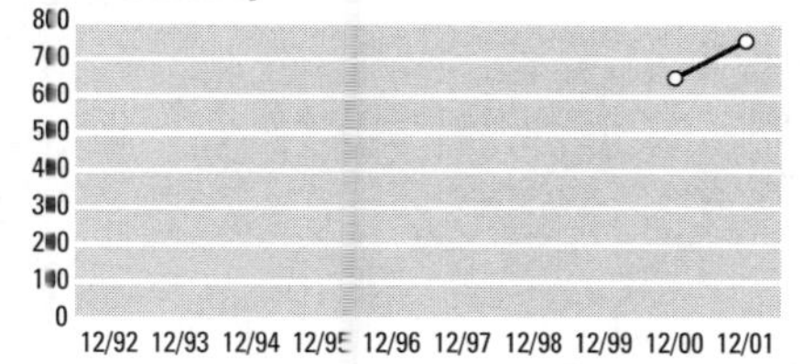

Northwestern Mutual

Making sure it's not all quiet on the Northwestern front, Northwestern Mutual's 7,800 agents (meticulously recruited and trained) sell a lineup of life and health insurance and retirement products, including fixed and variable annuities and mutual funds to a clientele of small businesses and prosperous individuals. Other lines of business include midwestern investment bank Robert W. Baird & Co. and pension manager Frank Russell Company (known for the Russell 2000 stock index). The company also operates its own trust services subsidiary, Northwestern Mutual Trust.

Northwestern Mutual would "enter the 21st century as we left the 19th," according to its former chairman and CEO, John Ericson (who retired in mid-2001).

Well, not exactly. Although the company has resisted the industry trend of demutualizing and remains committed to ownership by its about 3 million policyholders, The Quiet Company has begun blowing its own horn — in a diffident, upper Midwest way. Reorganized to highlight its wealth management products, life insurance still accounts for the majority of the company's revenue. The company targets wealthy individuals over 55.

Northwestern Mutual managed to grow premium volume in 2002 but heavy investment losses dragged its net results down.

HISTORY

In 1854, at age 72, John Johnston, a successful New York insurance agent, moved to Wisconsin to become a farmer. Three years later Johnston returned to the insurance business when he and 36 others formed Mutual Life Insurance (changed to Northwestern Mutual Life Insurance in 1865). From the beginning the company's goal was to be better, not just bigger.

The company continued to offer level-premium life insurance in the 1920s, while competitors offered new types of products. This failure to rise to new demands brought a decline in market share that lasted into the 1940s.

Northwestern automated in the late 1950s. In 1962 it introduced the Insurance Service Account, whereby all policies owned by a family or business could be consolidated into one monthly premium and paid with pre-authorized checks. In 1968 Northwestern inaugurated Extra Ordinary Life (EOL), which combined whole and term life insurance, using dividends to convert term to paid-up whole life each year. EOL soon became the company's most popular product.

Suffering from a low profile, in 1972 the insurer kicked off its "The Quiet Company" ad campaign during the summer Olympics. Public awareness of Northwestern jumped. But even in advertising, the company was staid; a revamped Quiet Company campaign made a return Olympic appearance 24 years later in another effort to raise the public's consciousness.

During the 1980s Northwestern began financing leveraged buyouts, gaining direct ownership of companies. Investments included two-thirds of flooring maker Congoleum (with other investors); it also bought majority interests in Milwaukee securities firm Robert W. Baird (1982; now 64%) and mortgage guarantee insurer MGIC Investment (1985; now 11%).

The firm stayed out of the 1980s mania for fast money and high-risk diversification. Instead, it devoted itself almost religiously to its core business, despite indications that it was a shrinking market.

In the early 1990s new life policy purchases slowed and the agency force declined — ominous signs, since insurers make their premium income on retained policies, and continued sales are crucial to growth. Northwestern reversed the trend, adding administrative support for its agents, using database marketing to target new customers, and increasing the cross-selling of products among existing customers. The result was a record-setting 1996.

With the financial services industry consolidating, Northwestern in 1997 moved into the mutual fund business by setting up its nine Mason Street Funds.

In the 1990s many large mutuals sought to demutualize, and in 1998 Northwestern, politically influential in Wisconsin, successfully lobbied for legislation to permit demutualization, citing the need to be able to move quickly in shifting markets.

The next year the company acquired Frank Russell Co., a pension management firm. The acquisition gave Northwestern a foothold in global investment management and analytical services (the Russell 2000 index).

The company followed up with an all-out reorganization, separating the office of president from the duties of chairman and CEO, and naming, for the first time, an EVP of marketing. In 2001 the firm opened Northwestern Mutual Trust, a wholly owned personal trust services subsidiary.

EXECUTIVES

President and CEO: Edward J. Zore, age 57
COO and Chief Compliance Officer: John M. Bremer
Chief Insurance Officer: Peter W. Bruce
EVP, Agencies: William H. Beckley
EVP, Planning and Technology: Deborah A. Beck, age 55
EVP, Marketing: Bruce L. Miller
SVP and CFO: Gary A. Poliner
SVP and CIO: Barbara F. Piehler
SVP and Chief Investment Officer: Mason G. Ross
SVP and Chief Actuary: William C. Koenig
SVP, Annuity and Accumulation Products: Leonard F. Stecklein
SVP, Corporate and Government Relations: Frederic H. Sweet
SVP, Investment Products and Services: Charles D. Robinson
SVP, Life Insurance: Richard L. Hall
SVP, Public Markets: Mark G. Doll
SVP, Securities and Real Estate: John E. Schlifske, age 43
VP, Human Resources: Susan A. Lueger
Auditors: PricewaterhouseCoopers LLP

LOCATIONS

HQ: 720 E. Wisconsin Ave., Milwaukee, WI 53202
Phone: 414-271-1444 **Fax:** 414-299-7022
Web: www.northwesternmutual.com

PRODUCTS/OPERATIONS

Selected Subsidiaries

Frank Russell Company (investment management and securities brokerage)
Mason Street Funds (mutual funds)
Robert W. Baird & Co. Incorporated (asset management)

COMPETITORS

AIG American General
Alliance Capital
AIG
AXA Financial
CIGNA
Citigroup
CNA Financial
Conseco
FMR
Fortis
GenAmerica
Guardian Life
The Hartford
John Hancock Financial Services
Liberty Mutual
MassMutual
Merrill Lynch
MetLife
MONY
Morgan Stanley
Mutual of Omaha
Nationwide
New York Life
Pacific Mutual
Principal Financial
Prudential
T. Rowe Price
TIAA-CREF

HISTORICAL FINANCIALS

Company Type: Mutual company

Income Statement FYE: December 31

	ASSETS ($ mil.)	NET INCOME ($ mil.)	INCOME AS % OF ASSETS	EMPLOYEES
12/02	102,935	158	0.2%	4,200
12/01	98,392	650	0.7%	4,100
12/00	92,125	1,829	2.0%	3,900
12/99	85,985	1,337	1.6%	3,700
12/98	77,995	809	1.0%	4,117
12/97	71,081	689	1.0%	3,818
12/96	62,680	620	1.0%	3,513
12/95	54,876	459	0.8%	3,344
12/94	48,112	279	0.6%	3,300
12/93	44,061	330	0.7%	3,500
Annual Growth	9.9%	(7.9%)	—	2.0%

2002 Year-End Financials

Equity as % of assets: 7.0%
Return on assets: 0.2%
Return on equity: 2.2%
Long-term debt ($ mil.): 5,559
Sales ($ mil.): 16,024

Net Income History

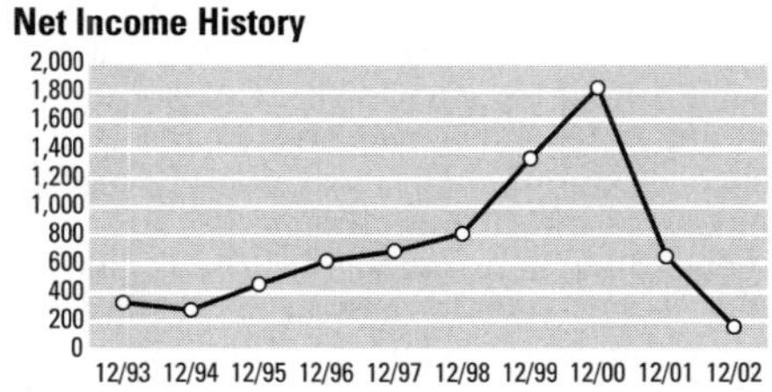

Northwestern University

Near the City of Big Shoulders is a place that shapes broad minds. With its main campus in the Chicago suburb of Evanston, Northwestern University serves its 17,000 students through 11 schools and colleges such as the McCormick School of Engineering and Applied Sciences and the Medill School of Journalism. Its Chicago campus houses the schools of law and medicine, as well as several hospitals of the McGaw Medical Center. Northwestern is home to several research centers, continuing education services, and community outreach programs. The university also supports 19 intercollegiate athletic programs. Founded in 1851, Northwestern is the only private institution in the Big 10 conference.

With tuition and fees running more than $27,200 a year, about 60% of undergraduates receive some form of financial aid from the school.

Among Northwestern's top-ranked programs are its law school, medical school, and its engineering program. Its J. L. Kellogg Graduate School of Management is ranked first in the nation by *Business Week.* Its journalism and drama programs produced such alumni as Charlton Heston, Gary Marshall, and Julia Louis-Dreyfus. Current US Supreme Court Justice John Paul Stevens is also a former Wildcat.

The school's endowment has swelled to about $3.5 billion, and it has exceeded its original Campaign Northwestern fund-raising goal of $1 billion by more than $15 million. The money will be used to increase endowment for student scholarships and fellowships, to help repair and build facilities, and fund more faculty positions.

HISTORY

Northwestern University's Methodist founders met in 1850 to create an institution of higher learning serving the original Northwest Territory. The university was chartered in 1851, and two years later it acquired 379 acres of property north of Chicago on Lake Michigan. The town of Evanston was later named after John Evans, one of the school's founders.

Classes began in the fall of 1855 with two professors and 10 students. By 1869 Northwestern had more than 100 students and began to admit women. In 1870 Northwestern signed an affiliation agreement with the Chicago Medical College (founded 1859), and three years later it joined with the original University of Chicago (no relation to the current institution) to create the Union College of Law. When the University of Chicago closed in 1886 due to financial difficulties, Northwestern took control of the law school. The university reorganized in 1891, consolidating its affiliated professional schools (dentistry, law, medicine, and pharmacy) into the university.

By 1900 Northwestern had become the third-largest university in the US (after Harvard and Michigan), with an enrollment of 2,700. During the 1920s the university created the Medill School of Journalism, named for Joseph Medill, founder of the *Chicago Tribune.* In 1924 the school's athletic teams adopted the nickname Wildcats, and two years later the university completed the primary buildings that form its Chicago campus. Northwestern suffered a drop in enrollment during the Depression, but after WWII it saw student numbers swell as veterans took advantage of the GI Bill. Expansion continued throughout the 1960s and 1970s.

In 1985 the school and the City of Evanston began developing a research center to attract more high-tech industries to the area. The university's graduate school of business achieved national prominence in 1988 after it was ranked #1 in the US by *Business Week.* In 1995 Henry Bienen, a dean at Princeton, became the school's 15th president. That year Northwestern's football team, forever the doormat of the Big 10, achieved national fame when it won the conference championship.

In 1998 faculty member Professor John Pople won the Nobel Prize in Chemistry, the first Nobel Prize awarded to a faculty member while teaching at the university. To help pay for needed expansion, Bienen launched Campaign Northwestern that year with the goal of raising $1 billion. Northwestern won a significant legal battle in 1998 when a judge ruled that the university was not obligated to pay a faculty member simply because he had been granted tenure. Encouraged by its successful efforts, the college in 2000 raised its fund-raising goal to $1.4 billion from $1 billion.

The university's dental school closed its doors the following year, citing the difficulties posed for private schools in providing a competitive dental education.

EXECUTIVES

President: Henry S. Bienen
Provost: Lawrence B. Dumas
SVP Business and Finance: Eugene S. Sunshine
VP and General Counsel: Thomas G. Cline
VP Administration and Planning: Marilyn McCoy
VP Information Technology: Morteza A. Rahimi
VP Research: Lydia Villa-Komaroff
VP Student Affairs: William J. Banis
VP University Relations: Alan K. Cubbage
Interim VP University Development: Jonathan R. Heintzelman
Associate VP Human Resources: Guy E. Miller
Director Media Relations: Charles R. Loebbaka
Investor Relations: Clarke L. Caywood

LOCATIONS

HQ: 633 Clark St., Evanston, IL 60208
Phone: 847-491-3741 **Fax:** 847-491-8406
Web: www.nwu.edu

Northwestern University has one campus in Chicago and one in Evanston, Illinois.

PRODUCTS/OPERATIONS

Selected Undergraduate Colleges and Schools

Medill School of Journalism
Robert McCormick School of Engineering and Applied Sciences
School of Education and Social Policy
School of Music
School of Speech
Weinberg College of Arts and Sciences

Selected Graduate Schools

The Graduate School
J. L. Kellogg Graduate School of Management
Medical School
Medill School of Journalism
Robert McCormick School of Engineering and Applied Sciences
School of Education and Social Policy
School of Law
School of Music
School of Speech

Selected Research Centers and Institutes

Banking Research Center
Center for Biotechnology
Center for Catalysis and Surface Science
Center for Mathematical Studies in Economics and Management Science
Center for Quality Engineering and Failure Prevention
Center for Quantum Devices
Center for Reproductive Science
Center for Sleep and Circadian Biology
Center for the Study of Ethical Issues in Business
Heizer Center for Entrepreneurial Studies
Institute for Environmental Catalysis
Institute for Health Services Research and Policy Studies
Institute for Neuroscience
Institute for Policy Research
Kellogg Environmental Research Center
Materials Research Center
Program of African Studies
Traffic Institute
Transportation Center

HISTORICAL FINANCIALS

Company Type: School

Income Statement FYE: August 31

	REVENUE ($ mil.)	NET INCOME ($ mil.)	NET PROFIT MARGIN	EMPLOYEES
8/02	989	—	—	6,800
8/01	959	—	—	5,700
8/00	875	—	—	5,700
8/99	782	—	—	5,700
8/98	816	—	—	5,985
8/97	721	—	—	5,978
8/96	779	—	—	5,800
8/95	708	—	—	5,800
8/94	676	—	—	5,650
8/93	628	—	—	5,650
Annual Growth	5.2%	—	—	2.1%

Revenue History

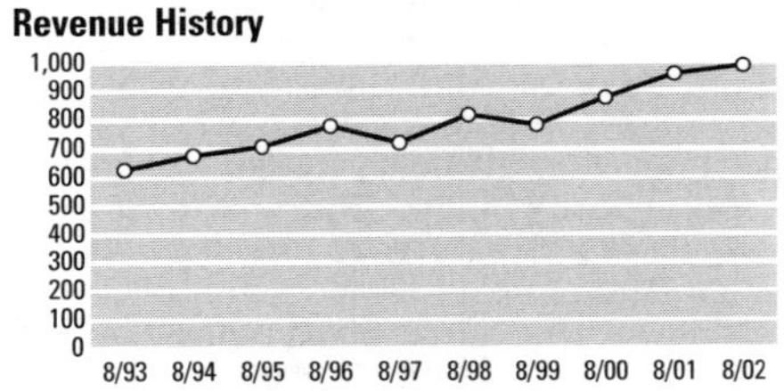

Noveon, Inc.

Polymers and additives add up to big business for Noveon. The specialty chemical maker, formerly the Performance Materials segment of what is now Goodrich Corporation, was spun off as PMD Group in early 2001 and renamed Noveon that May. Products include performance polymers and additives (colorants, fragrance enhancers) used in food and beverages, personal and home care products, and pharmaceuticals. Noveon's additives also are found in paints, coatings, water treatments, lubricants, and rubber. In addition, the company makes post-chlorinated polyvinyl chloride (CPVC) resins and compounds, and thermoplastic polyurethanes (TPUs). Noveon is owned by AEA Investors, DLJ Merchant Banking, and DB Capital Partners.

EXECUTIVES

Chairman: H. William Lichtenberger, age 67
President, CEO, and Director:
Steven J. (Steve) Demetriou, age 44, $1,200,000 pay
EVP and CFO: Michael D. Friday, age 51, $516,328 pay
SVP and General Manager, Personal Care and Pharmaceuticals Global Business Unit:
William B. Sedlacek, age 48, $408,964 pay
SVP, Corporate and Business Development:
Kumar Shah, age 54, $280,000 pay
SVP, General Counsel, and Secretary:
Christopher R. Clegg, age 45, $412,484 pay
SVP, Human Resources, Strategic Sourcing, and Information Technology: Sarah R. Coffin, age 50, $509,093 pay
Auditors: Ernst & Young LLP

LOCATIONS

HQ: 9911 Brecksville Rd., Cleveland, OH 44141
Phone: 216-447-5000 **Fax:** 216-447-5669
Web: www.noveoninc.com

Noveon has 27 manufacturing facilities, most of which are in the US, but also in Belgium, China, France, Germany, India, Malaysia, the Netherlands, South Korea, Spain, and the UK.

2002 Sales

	% of total
US	63
Europe	18
Other regions	19
Total	**100**

PRODUCTS/OPERATIONS

Selected Products

Consumer Specialties
Performance Coatings
Specialty Materials (Polymers)

COMPETITORS

ATOFINA
BASF AG
Bayer
Caffaro
Celanese
Ciba Specialty Chemicals
Clariant International
Cognis
CP Kelco ApS
Croda
Crompton
Degussa
Dow Chemical
DSM
DuPont
FMC
Georgia Gulf
Great Lakes Chemical
Hercules
Hoffmann-La Roche
Huntsman International
ISP
Nippon Carbide Industries
OMNOVA Solutions
Reichhold
Repsol YPF
Rhodia
Rohm and Haas
Royal Dutch/Shell Group
Sekisui Chemical
Sensient
Sumitomo Chemical
Surface Specialties
Tessenderlo Chemie
Velsicol Chemical

HISTORICAL FINANCIALS

Company Type: Private

Income Statement FYE: December 31

	REVENUE ($ mil.)	NET INCOME ($ mil.)	NET PROFIT MARGIN	EMPLOYEES
12/02	1,069	35	3.2%	2,800
12/01	1,063	(34)	—	2,790
Annual Growth	0.6%	—	—	0.4%

2002 Year-End Financials

Debt ratio: 169.5%
Return on equity: 8.7%
Cash ($ mil.): 80
Current ratio: 1.95
Long-term debt ($ mil.): 847

Net Income History

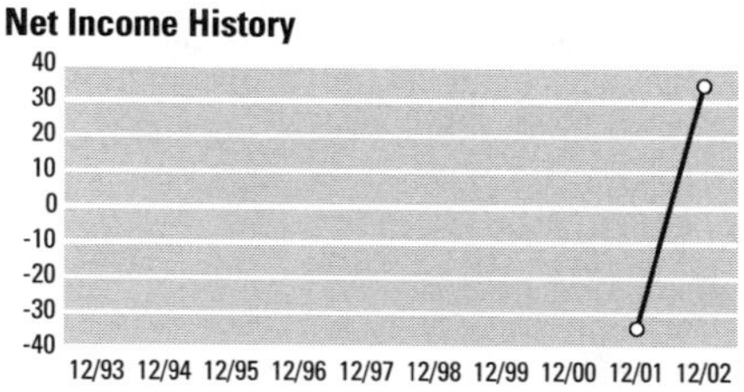

NPC International

In Pizza Hut's deep-dish empire, NPC International is the prince of pepperoni. NPC is the world's largest franchisee of Pizza Hut restaurants, with more than 800 of the red-roofed restaurants and delivery kitchens in 27 states. Its slice of the pizza-peddling pie accounts for a significant chunk of the Pizza Hut franchises and of the entire Pizza Hut system (which is owned by fast-food giant YUM! Brands). Most of NPC's units are located in the South. The company also owns a 20% stake in Romacorp, which operates the Tony Roma's casual dining chain. CEO Gene Bicknell was one of the original Pizza Hut franchisees, opening his first pizza restaurant in 1962. He led an investors group that took NPC private in 2001.

EXECUTIVES

Chairman and CEO: O. Gene Bicknell, age 70
President and COO: James K. Schwartz, age 41
SVP, CFO, Treasurer, and Secretary: Troy D. Cook, age 40
VP Pizza Hut Operations, Eastern Division:
Robert R. Greene, age 43
VP Pizza Hut Operations, Southern Division:
L. Bruce Sharp, age 45
VP Pizza Hut Operations, Western Division:
D. Blayne Vaughn, age 46
VP and Director of Human Resources:
LaVonne K. Walbert, age 39
VP Marketing: Linda K. Lierz, age 34
Auditors: KPMG LLP

LOCATIONS

HQ: NPC International, Inc.
720 W. 20th St., Pittsburg, KS 66762
Phone: 913-327-5555 **Fax:** 913-327-5850
Web: www.npcinternational.com

NPC International operates more than 800 Pizza Hut restaurants in Alabama, Arizona, Arkansas, Colorado, Delaware, Florida, Georgia, Illinois, Indiana, Iowa, Kansas, Kentucky, Louisiana, Minnesota, Mississippi, Missouri, Nevada, North Carolina, North Dakota, Oklahoma, Oregon, South Carolina, South Dakota, Tennessee, Texas, Utah, and Washington.

COMPETITORS

AmeriKing
Burger King
Chick-fil-A
CKE Restaurants
Subway
Domino's
Little Caesar's
McDonald's
Noble Roman's
Papa John's
Pizza Inn
PJ United
Round Table Pizza
RPM Pizza
RTM Restaurant Group
Sbarro
Sydran Services
Triarc
United States Beef
Wendy's

HISTORICAL FINANCIALS

Company Type: Private

Income Statement FYE: December 31

	REVENUE ($ mil.)	NET INCOME ($ mil.)	NET PROFIT MARGIN	EMPLOYEES
12/02*	425	—	—	17,000
3/02	536	—	—	18,700
3/01	505	—	—	16,800
3/00	456	—	—	15,200
3/99	401	—	—	15,000
3/98	455	—	—	13,400
3/97	295	—	—	9,300
3/96	323	—	—	11,500
3/95	316	—	—	10,300
3/94	337	—	—	8,400
Annual Growth	2.6%	—	—	8.1%

*Fiscal year change

Revenue History

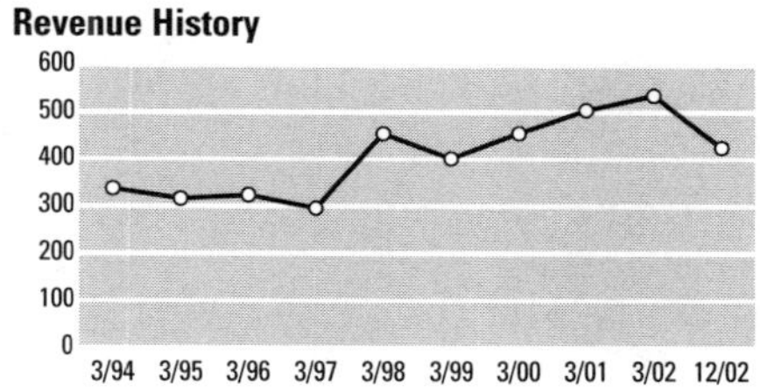

NRT Incorporated

NRT is Not a Realty Trust anymore. The #1 residential real estate company in the US began life in 1996 as National Realty Trust, established by real estate franchisor HFS (now Cendant) to own the nearly 400 real estate offices that came with the purchase of Coldwell Banker. Cendant and a subsidiary of Apollo Advisors restructured the trust in order to snap up successful independent realtors in hot metropolitan markets and rebrand them under Cendant's franchise names (Coldwell Banker and ERA). The realtor has more than 850 offices in about 25 markets. Subsidiary Coldwell Banker Commercial NRT lists commercial and investment properties. NRT has purchased New England brokerage firm The DeWolfe Companies.

EXECUTIVES

President and CEO: Robert M. (Bob) Becker
EVP and General Sales Manager: Michael R. Good
SVP and CFO: Kevin Greene
SVP and CEO, Coldwell Banker Residential Real Estate, Florida: Judith Green
SVP and Chief Administrative Officer: Ross D. Anthony
SVP and General Counsel: Ken Hoffert
SVP Human Resources: Matt Henson
SVP Marketing: Kristine Miklusek Santucci

LOCATIONS

HQ: 339 Jefferson Rd., Parsippany, NJ 07054
Phone: 973-240-5000 **Fax:** 973-240-5241
Web: www.nrtinc.com

NRT's corporate offices are in Parsippany, NJ, and Mission Viejo, CA. It owns residential and commercial real estate brokerages in about 25 metropolitan areas in the US.

Selected Locations

Atlanta
Baltimore
Boston
Chicago
Cincinnati
Columbus, Ohio
Dallas
Denver
Harrisburg, Pennsylvania
Los Angeles
Miami
Minneapolis
Milwaukee
New York
Orlando
Pittsburgh
Sacramento
Salt Lake City
San Diego
San Francisco
St. Louis
Stamford, Connecticut
Tampa
Washington D.C.

COMPETITORS

Baird & Warner
CB Richard Ellis
Colliers International
Cushman & Wakefield
HomeServices
Marcus & Millichap
Prudential
RE/MAX

HISTORICAL FINANCIALS

Company Type: Private

Income Statement

FYE: December 31

	ESTIMATED REVENUE ($ mil.)	NET INCOME ($ mil.)	NET PROFIT MARGIN	EMPLOYEES
12/02	4,039	—	—	52,801
12/01	3,159	—	—	51,000
12/00	2,800	—	—	37,000
12/99	2,600	—	—	32,000
Annual Growth	15.8%	—	—	18.2%

Revenue History

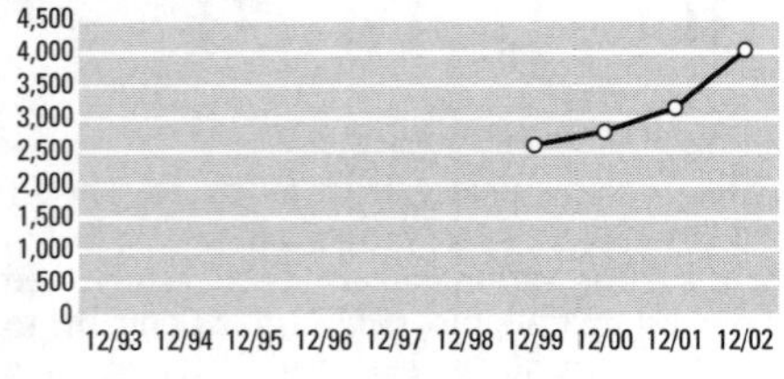

Nypro Inc.

Nypro is a real pro when it comes to injection molding. The company makes plastic parts used in devices that range from cell phones, electric razors, and seat belts to inkjet printer cartridges and personal computers. Customers in the electronics and telecommunications industries together account for nearly half of sales. Although custom-precision plastic-injection molding is Nypro's core business, the company also offers assembly services to other manufacturers. Nypro's products can be found around the world; however, North America accounts for more than half of its sales. Co-chairman Gordon Lankton sold Nypro to employees in 1999 through an employee stock ownership plan.

EXECUTIVES

Chairman: Gordon B. Lankton
Co-Chairman: Nicholas D. (Nick) Aznoian
President and Director: Brian S. Jones
VP, Information Technology, Chief Supply Chain Officer, and Director: Michael C. MacKenty
VP, Marketing and Business Development and Director: Randall S. (Randy) Barko
VP and General Manager, East Region: Gregory G. Adams
VP, China and India: James R. Buonomo
VP, Contract Manufacturing: Louis Gaviglia
VP, Engineering: Richard J. Hoeske
President, Nypro Latin America: Samuel Landol
VP, Treasurer, CFO, and Director: Theodore E. Lapres III
Auditors: PricewaterhouseCoopers

LOCATIONS

HQ: 101 Union St., Clinton, MA 01510
Phone: 978-365-9721 **Fax:** 978-368-0236
Web: www.nypro.com

Nypro has operations in 27 plants in Asia, Europe, and North and South America.

2002 Sales

	% of total
North America	54
China & India	21
Latin America	13
Europe	8
Southeast Asia	4
Total	**100**

PRODUCTS/OPERATIONS

2002 Sales by Industry

	% of total
Electronics & telecommunications	48
Health care	26
Consumer industrial	11
Automation, robotics & tooling	8
Automotive	7
Total	**100**

COMPETITORS

Atlantis Plastics
Berry Plastics
Carlisle Engineered Products
Deswell Industries
Hoffer Plastics
Omni Industries
Tuthill

HISTORICAL FINANCIALS

Company Type: Private

Income Statement

FYE: June 30

	REVENUE ($ mil.)	NET INCOME ($ mil.)	NET PROFIT MARGIN	EMPLOYEES
6/02	590	30	5.1%	9,000
6/01	495	32	6.4%	8,000
6/00	591	25	4.3%	7,000
Annual Growth	(0.1%)	8.7%	—	13.4%

2002 Year-End Financials

Debt ratio: 79.0%
Return on equity: 19.0%
Cash ($ mil.): 128
Current ratio: 2.05
Long-term debt ($ mil.): 138

Net Income History

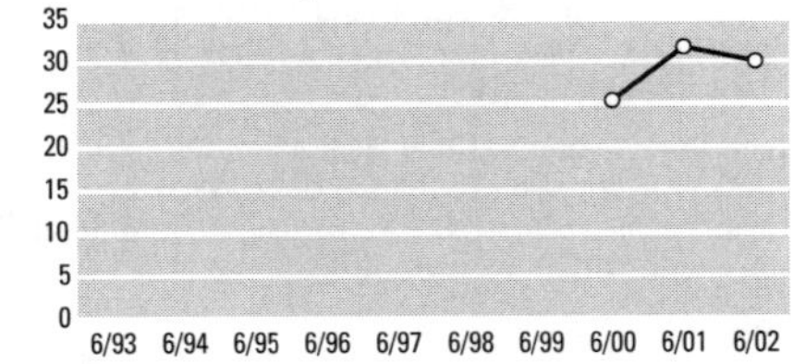

Ocean Spray Cranberries, Inc.

Ocean Spray Cranberries has transformed cranberries from turkey sidekick to the stuff of everyday beverages, cereal, and mixed drinks. Known for its blue-and-white wave logo, the company controls more than half of the US cranberry drink market. A marketing cooperative owned by more than 900 cranberry and citrus growers in the US and Canada, Ocean Spray produces its line of juices by blending the cranberry with fruits ranging from apples to tangerines. It also makes other cranberry products (sauce, snacks), grapefruit juice, and Ocean Spray Premium 100% juice drinks.

In recent years, surplus harvests of cranberries, competition from store brands, and drought in some areas have cut into its market share and forced layoffs. Competition from industry giants such as Coca-Cola and Pepsi, both of which are trying to increase market share in the non-carbonated drinks sector, also have hurt the company.

To expand beyond the berry's traditional role, Ocean Spray has turned the fruit into a chewy snack (Craisins), and cranberries now show up in cobranded cookies and cereal. It has also introduced a "white juice" made from preripened cranberries that have a less tart taste. Promotion efforts have been aided by research showing that cranberry juice can reduce urinary tract infections.

Ocean Spray's Ingredient Technology Group processes fruit into juice ingredients.

In February 2003 rival Northland Cranberries made a cash and stock bid to take over the juice business of Ocean Spray. The company rejected the offer that same month. Upset by their lack of input in the decision, cranberry growers voted in March to revamp the Ocean Spray board, reducing its size from 15 to 12 members and keeping just three of the board's previous members. Soon after, Ocean Spray laid off about 60 people, including several executives. The cooperative has hired Morgan Stanley to review strategic options for the company, including a possible sale of the business.

HISTORY

Ocean Spray Cranberries traces its roots to Marcus Urann, president of the Cape Cod Cranberry Company. In 1912 Urann, who became known as the "Cranberry King," began marketing a cranberry sauce that was packaged in tins and could be served year-round. Inspired by the sea spray that drifted off the Atlantic and over his cranberry bogs, Urann dubbed his concoction Ocean Spray Cape Cod Cranberry Sauce.

It didn't take long for other cranberry growers to make their own sauces, and rather than compete, the Cranberry King consolidated. In 1930 Urann merged his company with A.D. Makepeace Company and with Cranberry Products, forming a national cooperative called Cranberry Canners. During the 1940s it added growers in Wisconsin, Oregon, and Washington and, to reflect its new scope, changed its name to National Cranberry Association.

Canadian growers were added to the fold in 1950. Urann retired in 1955, and two years later the co-op introduced its first frozen products. To take advantage of the popular Ocean Spray brand name, in 1959 the company changed its name to Ocean Spray Cranberries.

Two weeks before Thanksgiving that year, the US Department of Health mistakenly announced that aminotriazole, a herbicide used by some cranberry growers, was linked to cancer in laboratory rats. Sales of what consumers called "cancer berries" plummeted, and Ocean Spray nearly folded. However, the US government came to the rescue with subsidies in 1960, and the company stayed afloat.

The scare convinced Ocean Spray it needed to cut its dependence on seasonal demand, and it began to diversify more aggressively into the juice business, introducing a heavily promoted new line of juices blending cranberries with apples, grapes, and other fruits.

Ocean Spray allowed Florida's Indian River Ruby Red grapefruit growers to join the co-op in 1976. The company acquired Milne Food Products, a manufacturer of fruit concentrates and purees, in 1985, and three years later it signed a Japanese distribution deal.

To maintain its edge in a growing but increasingly competitive market, Ocean Spray automated plants and allied with food giants to create cranberry-flavored treats such as cookies (Nabisco, 1993) and cereal (Kraft Foods, 1996). In 1998 it unsuccessfully sued to block PepsiCo's purchase of juice maker Tropicana on grounds that it would interfere with PepsiCo's distribution of Ocean Spray's drinks. Ocean Spray also introduced a line of 100% juice blends to compete with rivals such as former co-op member Northland Cranberries.

Bumper harvests from 1997 through 1999 led to lower cranberry prices. As a result, in 1999 the company announced its third round of layoffs since 1997 (bringing the total to 500, or nearly one-fifth of its workforce). It also suspended its practice of buying back the stock of its growers, who must buy shares to join the co-op.

Amid criticism that it has been unable to compete effectively with for-profit rivals, Ocean Spray hired former Pillsbury executive Robert Hawthorne as CEO in 2000. Grower-owners voted not to explore a sale of the company at its 2001 annual meeting, a vote of confidence for the new management. The company supported a 32% crop reduction to help eliminate the crop surpluses that cause depressed prices. Ocean Spray also sold its interest in Nantucket Allserve (Nantucket Nectars) to Cadbury Schweppes, which folded Nantucket's brands into its Snapple unit.

In 2002 Hawthorne resigned. Barbara S. Thomas, a board member and former president of Warner Lambert's consumer health care division, was named interim CEO.

In February 2003 Northland Cranberries made a bid to take over the juice business of Ocean Spray: The bid was quickly rejected. President and COO Randy Papadellis was named CEO in June.

EXECUTIVES

CEO: Randy Papadellis
CFO and SVP: Tim C. Chan
VP, Human Resources: Katie Morey
Chief Marketing Officer: Stewart Gallagher
Senior Manager, Corporate Communications and Public Affairs: Chris Phillips
Auditors: Deloitte & Touche

LOCATIONS

HQ: 1 Ocean Spray Dr., Lakeville-Middleboro, MA 02349
Phone: 508-946-1000 **Fax:** 508-946-7704
Web: www.oceanspray.com

Ocean Spray Cranberries has seven receiving stations and eight processing and bottling plants in Florida, Massachusetts, Nevada, New Jersey, Oregon, Texas, Washington, Wisconsin, and British Columbia, Canada.

PRODUCTS/OPERATIONS

Selected Products

Cranberry Juice Cocktails
Cranberry Juice Cocktail
Cranberry Juice Cocktail with Calcium

Cranberry Juice Drinks
Cran Apple
Cran Cherry
Cran Grape
Cran Mango
Cran Raspberry
Cran Strawberry
Cran Tangerine

Craisins Sweetened Dried Cranberries
Cherry Flavor Sweetened Dried Cranberries
Orange Flavor Sweetened Dried Cranberries
Original Sweetened Dried Cranberries

Fresh Fruits and Sauces
Citrus
Cranberries
Grapefruit
Jellied Cranberry Sauce
Whole Berry Cranberry Sauce

Light Cranberry Juice Drinks
Light Cranberry Juice Cocktail
Light Cran Grape
Light Cran Raspberry
Light White Cranberry

Premium 100% Cranberry Juices
Cranberry Blend
Cranberry and Concord Grape
Cranberry and Georgia Peach
Cranberry and Mixed Berry
Cranberry and Pacific Raspberry
Cranberry and Red Delicious Apple
White Cranberry Blend

Premium 100% Grapefruit Juices
Pink Grapefruit
Ruby Red Grapefruit
White Grapefruit

Ruby Grapefruit Juice Drinks
Ruby Lemonade Grapefruit Juice Drink
Ruby Mango Grapefruit Juice Drink
Ruby Red Grapefruit Juice Drink
Ruby Strawberry Grapefruit Juice Drink
Ruby Tangerine Grapefruit Juice Drink

White Cranberry Juice Drinks
White Cranberry
White Cranberry and Apple
White Cranberry and Peach
White Cranberry and Strawberry

COMPETITORS

Altria
Cadbury Schweppes
Campbell Soup
Chiquita Brands
Clement Pappas & Co.
Cliffstar
Coca-Cola
Dole
Florida's Natural
Gatorade/Tropicana
Hansen Natural
Smucker
National Grape Cooperative
Northland Cranberries
Odwalla
Pepsi-Cola North America
Sunkist

HISTORICAL FINANCIALS

Company Type: Cooperative

Income Statement FYE: August 31

	REVENUE ($ mil.)	NET INCOME ($ mil.)	NET PROFIT MARGIN	EMPLOYEES
8/02	1,068	115	10.8%	2,000
8/01	1,104	143	13.0%	2,200
8/00	1,400	—	—	2,000
8/99	1,360	—	—	2,000
8/98	1,480	—	—	2,350
8/97	1,438	—	—	2,300
8/96	1,433	—	—	2,300
8/95	1,361	—	—	2,300
8/94	1,221	—	—	2,300
8/93	1,168	—	—	2,300
Annual Growth	(1.0%)	(8.9%)	—	(1.5%)

2002 Year-End Financials

Debt ratio: 119.9%
Return on equity: 86.3%
Cash ($ mil.): 54
Current ratio: 2.21
Long-term debt ($ mil.): 202

Net Income History

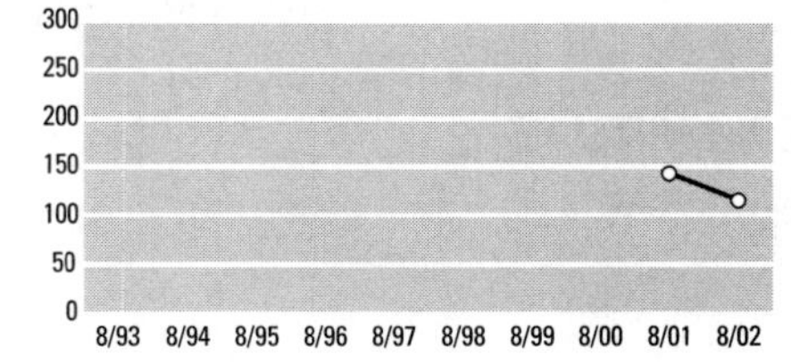

Oglethorpe Power

Not-for-profit Oglethorpe Power Corporation is one of the largest electricity cooperatives in the US, with contracts to supply wholesale power to 39 member/owners (making up most of Georgia's electric distribution cooperatives) until 2025. Oglethorpe's member/owners, which also operate as not-for-profits, serve about 1.5 million residential, commercial, and industrial customers, and the co-op; Oglethorpe trades power on the wholesale market. The company, which was formed in 1974, has a generating capacity of nearly 3,700 MW (primarily from coal-fired and nuclear power plants). In addition, Oglethorpe also has power contracts with other suppliers that account for nearly 20% of its energy supply.

EXECUTIVES

Chairman: Benny W. Denham, age 72
Vice Chairman: J. Sam L. Rabun, age 71
President and CEO: Thomas A. (Tom) Smith, age 48, $435,349 pay
COO: Michael W. (Mike) Price, age 42, $266,797 pay
SVP and Group Executive, Administration and Risk Management: W. Clayton (Clay) Robbins, age 56, $231,551 pay
SVP, Operations: Clarence D. Mitchell
VP and Group Executive, Planning, Rates, and Analysis: Elizabeth Bush (Betsy) Higgins, age 34, $194,815 pay
VP, Finance and Treasurer: Anne F. Appleby
Director, Public Relations: Greg Jones
Auditors: PricewaterhouseCoopers LLP

LOCATIONS

HQ: Oglethorpe Power Corporation
2100 E. Exchange Place, Tucker, GA 30085
Phone: 770-270-7600 **Fax:** 770-270-7325
Web: www.opc.com

PRODUCTS/OPERATIONS

2002 Sales

	$ mil.	% of total
Members	1,127	97
Non-members	36	3
Total	**1,163**	**100**

2002 Energy Mix

	% of total
Coal	35
Nuclear	27
Purchased	15
Hydro	15
Gas & oil	8
Total	**100**

COMPETITORS

AGL Resources
FPL Group
MEAG Power
Progress Energy
PS Energy
Southern Company
TVA

HISTORICAL FINANCIALS

Company Type: Cooperative

Income Statement FYE: December 31

	REVENUE ($ mil.)	NET INCOME ($ mil.)	NET PROFIT MARGIN	EMPLOYEES
12/02	1,163	18	1.5%	173
12/01	1,139	18	1.6%	175
12/00	1,199	20	1.7%	160
12/99	1,176	20	1.7%	144
12/98	1,144	21	1.8%	125
12/97	1,048	22	2.1%	170
12/96	1,101	22	2.0%	—
12/95	1,150	22	1.9%	—
12/94	1,056	23	2.2%	—
12/93	1,101	12	1.1%	—
Annual Growth	0.6%	3.9%	—	0.4%

2002 Year-End Financials

Debt ratio: 878.8%
Return on equity: —
Cash ($ mil.): 151
Current ratio: 1.44
Long-term debt ($ mil.): 3,267

Net Income History

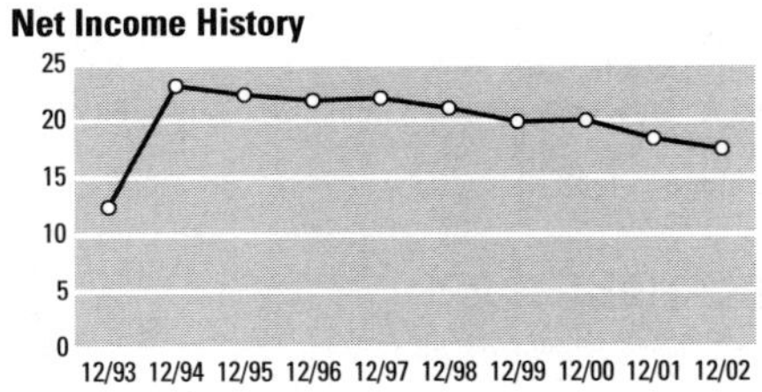

Ohio National Financial Services

Ohio National Financial Services subsidiary Ohio National Life Insurance sells individual and group life insurance, disability insurance, pension plans, and annuities.

Other company subsidiaries include Ohio National Equities and O.N. Equity Sales, which offer wholesale and retail brokerage services, and Ohio National Investments, an investment adviser to the ONE Fund series mutual fund.

The firm's products are sold in 47 states, the District of Columbia, and Puerto Rico. The company expanded into New York with the acquisitions of asset manager Suffolk Capital Management and First ING Life Insurance Company of New York (renamed National Security Life and Annuity).

EXECUTIVES

Chairman, President, and CEO: David B. O'Maley, age 56
Vice Chairman: John J. Palmer
EVP, CFO, and Director: Ronald J. Dolan
EVP Agency and Group Distribution and Director: D. Gates Smith
SVP and General Counsel: Michael F. Haverkamp
SVP and Actuary: David W. Cook
SVP Administration: Howard C. Becker
SVP Corporate Relations and Communications: Diane S. Hagenbuch
President and COO, ONECO: Barbara A. Turner
VP and Counsel: William C. Price
VP Human Resources and Corporate Services: Anthony G. Esposito
Auditors: KPMG LLP

LOCATIONS

HQ: 1 Financial Way, Cincinnati, OH 45242
Phone: 513-794-6100 **Fax:** 513-794-4504
Web: www.ohionatl.com

PRODUCTS/OPERATIONS

Selected Subsidiaries

National Security Life and Annuity
Ohio National Equities, Inc. (wholesale brokerage)
Ohio National Investments, Inc. (investment adviser)
Ohio National Life Assurance Corporation (ONLAC)
The Ohio National Life Insurance Company (ONLIC)
Ohio National Seguros de Vida, S.A. (Chile)
Suffolk Capital Management (asset management)

COMPETITORS

American Family Insurance
AIG
American United
AXA Financial
Great American Financial Resources
Guardian Life
The Hartford
John Hancock Financial Services
Lincoln National
MassMutual
MetLife
Minnesota Mutual
National Life Insurance
Nationwide
New York Life
Northwestern Mutual
Principal Financial
Prudential
StanCorp Financial Group

HISTORICAL FINANCIALS

Company Type: Mutual company

Income Statement FYE: December 31

	ASSETS ($ mil.)	NET INCOME ($ mil.)	INCOME AS % OF ASSETS	EMPLOYEES
12/02	11,620	51	0.4%	700
12/01	9,924	76	0.8%	700
12/00	8,092	79	1.0%	700
12/99	7,573	89	1.2%	650
12/98	6,862	68	1.0%	600
12/97	6,331	67	1.1%	575
12/96	5,782	60	1.0%	—
Annual Growth	12.3%	(2.7%)	—	4.0%

2002 Year-End Financials

Equity as % of assets: 8.1%
Return on assets: 0.5%
Return on equity: 5.5%
Long-term debt ($ mil.): 281
Sales ($ mil.): 761

Net Income History

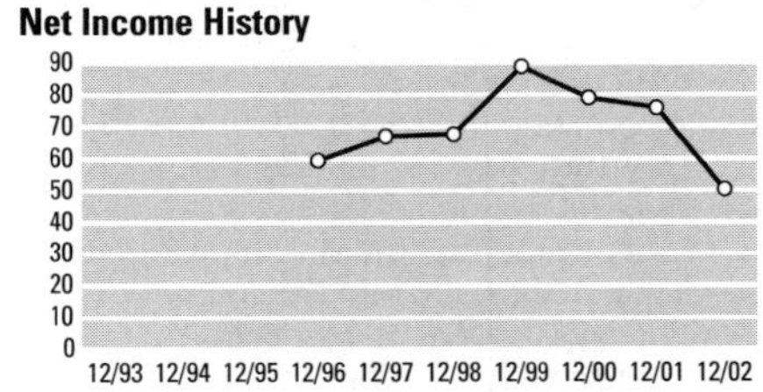

The Ohio State University

The first student body of Ohio State University (OSU) had 24 students. Today the university is Ohio's largest institution of higher learning and has the nation's second-largest single-campus enrollment (about 48,000 students at its Columbus campus), behind The University of Texas at Austin. It also has four regional campuses and two agricultural institutes. OSU's approximately 3,000 faculty members offer instruction in more than 170 undergraduate and 200 graduate programs. Its colleges and schools range from the Austin E. Knowlton School of Architecture to the College of Medicine and Public Health to the Fisher College of Business. The school was established in 1870 as Ohio Agricultural and Mechanical College.

Noteworthy university alumni include astronaut Nancy Sherlock Currie, golfer Jack Nicklaus, author John Jakes, and Olympian Jesse Owens.

Near the close of 2000, OSU unveiled a five-year academic plan under which the university will spend $750 million to advance its national academic standing.

HISTORY

In 1870 the Ohio legislature, prompted by Governor Rutherford B. Hayes, agreed to establish the Ohio Agricultural and Mechanical College in Columbus on property provided by the Morrill Act of 1862 (the land-grant institution act, which gave land to states and territories for the establishment of colleges).

After a heated battle over whether the college should teach only agricultural and mechanical arts or foster a broad-based liberal arts curriculum, the college opened in 1873 offering agriculture, ancient languages, chemistry, geology, mathematics, modern languages, and physics courses. Two years later the school appointed its first female faculty member. The Ohio State University became the school's name in 1878; that year it graduated its first class. OSU graduated its first female student the next year.

OSU grew dramatically, adding schools of veterinary medicine (1885), pharmacy (1885), law (1891), and dairy sciences (1895). It awarded its first Masters of Arts degree in 1886.

The university continued to expand in the early 20th century, with enrollment surpassing 3,000 in 1908; by 1923 it had reached 10,000. New schools were added in education (1907), medicine and dentistry (1913), and commerce and journalism (1923). During WWI Ohio State designated part of its campus as training grounds and established the only college schools in the nation for airplane and balloon squadrons. Ohio Stadium was dedicated in 1922.

During the Great Depression Ohio State cut back salaries and course offerings. In the 1940s the school geared for war once again by establishing radiation and war research labs, as well as programs and services for students who were drafted. OSU captured its first national football championship in 1942.

The 1950s ushered in the era of legendary OSU football coach Woody Hayes. Hayes led his beloved Buckeyes to three national championships and nine Rose Bowl appearances before he was discharged for striking a Clemson player in 1978. The 1950s also saw the addition of four regional campuses at Lima, Mansfield, Marion, and Newark.

In the early 1960s the university was engaged in internal free-speech battles. By the end of that decade, enrollment had surpassed 50,000. OSU opened its School of Social Work in 1976.

In 1986 OSU and rival Michigan shared the Big 10 football conference title. Enrollment at OSU topped 54,000 in 1990 but then began declining. In response, the university tried to cut costs and beef up revenues. One way was through alliances: In 1992 it teamed with research group Battelle to develop a testing system for new drugs for the Food and Drug Administration. But when more savings were needed in 1995 and 1996, the university began streamlining operations, merging journalism and communications, and consolidating several veterinary departments. However, it also approved the creation of a new school of public health to provide education in environmental health, epidemiology, and health care management and financing.

But sports were not forgotten, and in 1996 OSU broke ground on the $84 million Schottenstein Center, a multipurpose facility for the university's basketball and ice hockey teams. In 1997 president Gordon Gee announced that he was leaving OSU for Brown University. The next year William Kirwan from the University of Maryland came on board as president.

In 2000 the university's "Affirm Thy Friendship" contribution campaign came to a close. The campaign increased OSU's endowment from $493 million in 1993 to $1.3 billion in 2000. Ohio State won the national football championship in early 2003.

EXECUTIVES

President: Karen A. Holbrook
EVP and Provost (Interim): Barbara Snyder
SVP Business & Finance and CFO: William Shkurti
VP Agricultural Administration and University Outreach: Bobby D. Moser
VP Research: C. Bradley Moore
VP Student Affairs: William H. Hall
VP University Relations: Lee Tashjian
VP Research (Interim): Thomas J. (Tom) Rosol
Vice Provost Minority Affairs: Mac A. Stewart
CIO: Ilee Rhimes
Secretary of the Board of Trustees, Special Assistant to the President for Government Relations: William Napier
Controller: Greta J. Russell
Executive Assistant to the President and General Counsel: Virginia M. (Ginny) Trethewey
Associate VP Human Resources: Larry M. Lewellen
Auditors: Deloitte & Touche LLP

LOCATIONS

HQ: 1800 Cannon Dr., Columbus, OH 43210
Phone: 614-292-3980 **Fax:** 614-292-4818
Web: www.osu.edu

The Ohio State University has campuses in Columbus, Lima, Mansfield, Marion, and Newark. It has two agricultural centers in Wooster, Ohio.

PRODUCTS/OPERATIONS

Selected Colleges and Schools

Austin E. Knowlton School of Architecture
College of Biological Sciences
College of Dentistry
College of Education
College of Engineering
College of Food, Agricultural, and Environmental Sciences
College of Human Ecology
College of Humanities
College of Law
College of Mathematical and Physical Sciences
College of Medicine and Public Health
College of Nursing
College of Optometry
College of Social and Behavioral Sciences
College of Social Work
College of the Arts
College of Veterinary Medicine
Graduate School
Max M. Fisher College of Business
School of Natural Resources
University College

HISTORICAL FINANCIALS

Company Type: School

Income Statement FYE: June 30

	REVENUE ($ mil.)	NET INCOME ($ mil.)	NET PROFIT MARGIN	EMPLOYEES
6/01	1,661	—	—	32,000
6/00	1,554	—	—	31,302
6/99	1,923	—	—	29,502
6/98	1,749	—	—	31,268
6/97	1,630	—	—	29,000
6/96	1,531	—	—	29,266
6/95	1,575	—	—	29,500
6/94	1,506	—	—	29,658
6/93	1,409	—	—	29,576
6/92	1,656	—	—	29,565
Annual Growth	0.0%	—	—	0.9%

Revenue History

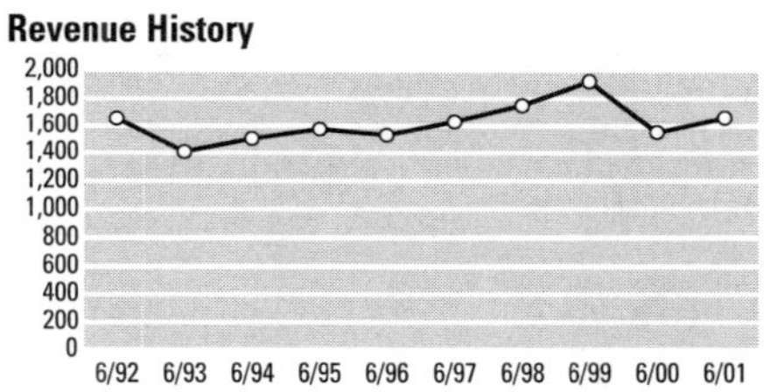

The Okonite Company

Thomas Edison had a bright idea, but it was The Okonite Company that prevented it from being too shocking. Okonite, founded in 1878, was one of the first US makers of insulated electrical wire and cable. Early customers included not only Edison but also telegraphy pioneer Samuel Morse. Still a leader in the wire and cable industry, Okonite specializes in control, distribution, instrumentation, power, signal, communication transmission, and special purpose wire and cable products. The company has plants across the US and equips chemical plants, electric utilities, paper mills, railroads, and refineries. Okonite has been employee-owned since 1976.

EXECUTIVES

Chairman and CEO: Victor Viggiano
President and COO: Alfred Coppola
CFO and Treasurer: David Sokira
VP, Human Resources: Thomas (Tom) Scanlon
Director, Management Information Systems: William Blowers
Manager of Personnel: Paulette Vita
Benefits Administrator: Kathy Cuomo

LOCATIONS

HQ: 102 Hilltop Rd., Ramsey, NJ 07446
Phone: 201-825-0300 **Fax:** 201-825-3524
Web: www.okonite.com

The Okonite Company operates manufacturing facilities in California, Kentucky, New Jersey, Rhode Island, and South Carolina.

PRODUCTS/OPERATIONS

Selected Products

Control cables
High-voltage cables
Low-voltage cables
Special-purpose products
Cable guides
Cable-slitting saws
Channel-lock pliers
Hacksaw blades
Tubing cutters

COMPETITORS

Anixter International
Cable Design Technologies
CommScope
General Cable
Graybar Electric
International Wire
Pirelli & C.
Sumitomo Electric
Superior TeleCom
Volex

HISTORICAL FINANCIALS

Company Type: Private

Income Statement FYE: December 31

	ESTIMATED REVENUE ($ mil.)	NET INCOME ($ mil.)	NET PROFIT MARGIN	EMPLOYEES
12/01	500	—	—	1,400
12/00	500	—	—	1,400
12/99	500	—	—	1,400
12/98	300	—	—	1,400
12/97	300	—	—	1,000
12/96	250	—	—	1,400
12/95	260	—	—	1,400
12/94	200	—	—	1,000
12/93	150	—	—	1,000
12/92	190	—	—	1,000
Annual Growth	11.4%	—	—	3.8%

Revenue History

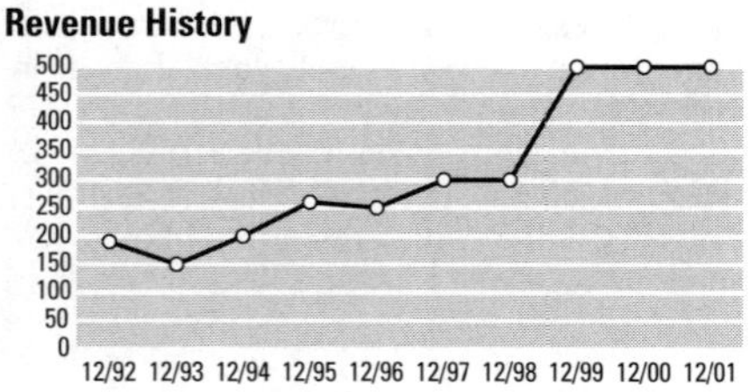

Olan Mills, Inc.

The picture is changing for Olan Mills, the world's leading producer of family portraits. The company operates through two divisions: Church Directories (its top revenue generator) and Studio Portraits (about 550 studios in Kmart stores, 125 free-standing studios in the US and Puerto Rico, and some 100 stores in the UK). Olan Mills once had over 1,000 studios but closed many locations to focus on its Kmart operations. The company later lost more studios when the beleaguered Kmart began closing stores. Olan Mills hopes to open new locations in surviving Kmart locations, as well as in other retail stores. Olan and Mary Mills founded the company in 1932; their son, Olan Mills II, owns the company.

EXECUTIVES

Chairman: Olan Mills II
President and CEO: Robert L. (Bob) McDowell
CFO: Laura Carden
VP Human Resources: A. V. (Terry) Blunt

LOCATIONS

HQ: 4325 Amnicola Hwy., Chattanooga, TN 37422
Phone: 423-622-5141 **Fax:** 423-629-8128
Web: www.olanmills.com

COMPETITORS

CPI Corp.
Hallmark
Lifetouch
PCA International

HISTORICAL FINANCIALS

Company Type: Private

Income Statement FYE: December 31

	ESTIMATED REVENUE ($ mil.)	NET INCOME ($ mil.)	NET PROFIT MARGIN	EMPLOYEES
12/01	450	—	—	5,500
12/00	400	—	—	5,000
12/99	400	—	—	5,000
12/98	500	—	—	6,000
12/97	600	—	—	12,000
12/96	625	—	—	14,000
12/95	600	—	—	15,000
12/94	550	—	—	15,000
12/93	475	—	—	13,300
Annual Growth	(0.7%)	—	—	(10.5%)

Revenue History

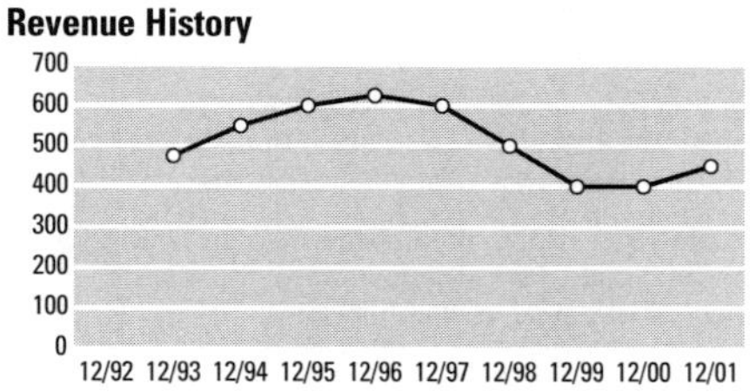

Old World Industries, Inc.

Old World Industries is taking a progressive lead in the production of chemicals. The company is the #2 US antifreeze maker (after Honeywell, maker of Prestone) and the only vertically integrated antifreeze producer. Old World's antifreezes include Peak and Sierra (the latter is marketed to parents and pet owners as a safer alternative antifreeze), as well as private labels. Old World also makes deicers, pickup bed liners (Herculiner), windshield wiper blades (SmartBlade), and spark plugs (SplitFire). The company's chemicals unit is a leading maker of ethylene glycol (used in antifreeze), ethylene oxide, and liquid caustic soda. Chairman and CEO Tom Hurvis and Riaz Waraich own Old World.

EXECUTIVES

Chairman and CEO: J. Thomas Hurvis
President: James (Jim) Bryan
CFO: Brian Schweigel
VP, Marketing: Jeff Stauffer
VP, Retail: Jerry Riccioni
President, Auto Division: Richard Jago
Manager, Human Resources: Dori Cullotta

LOCATIONS

HQ: 4065 Commercial Ave., Northbrook, IL 60062
Phone: 847-559-2000 **Fax:** 847-559-2266
Web: oldworld.quietgiant.com

Old World Industries has operations in Pasadena, Texas, and offices in Northbrook, Illinois.

PRODUCTS/OPERATIONS

Selected Products

Antifreeze (Peak, Fleet, Sierra, private-label)
Chemicals (diethylene glycol, ethylene glycol, ethylene oxide, methanol, polyethylene glycol, triethylene glycol, and liquid caustic soda)
Deicer and ice remover (for windshields, streets, sidewalks, and runways)
Pickup bed liner (Herculiner)
Spark plugs and wire sets (SplitFire)
Windshield wiper blades (SmartBlade)

COMPETITORS

Ashland
BASF AG
Dow Chemical
Durakon
Equistar Chemicals
Formosa Plastics USA
Honeywell International
Huntsman International
Lancaster Colony
Robert Bosch
Shell Chemicals
Ziebart

HISTORICAL FINANCIALS

Company Type: Private

Income Statement FYE: December 31

	ESTIMATED REVENUE ($ mil.)	NET INCOME ($ mil.)	NET PROFIT MARGIN	EMPLOYEES
12/02	500	—	—	150
12/01	500	—	—	150
12/00	500	—	—	147
12/99	325	—	—	200
12/98	300	—	—	150
12/97	300	—	—	152
12/96	280	—	—	150
12/95	275	—	—	135
Annual Growth	8.9%	—	—	1.5%

Revenue History

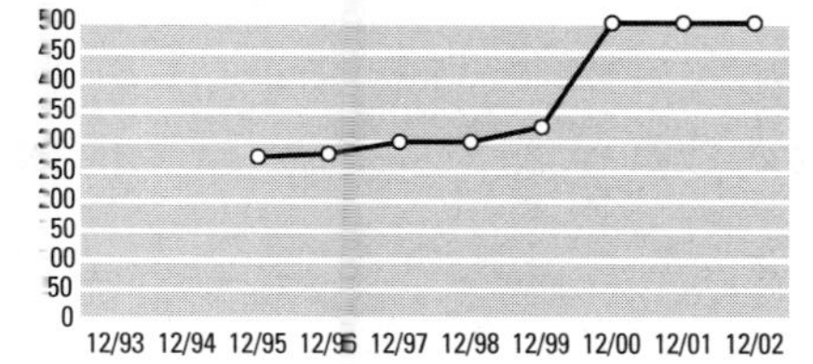

Omega World Travel

Omega is the last word in travel. Omega World Travel is one of the largest travel agencies in the US, with more thatn 200 locations in 30-plus states and the District of Columbia, as well as in Japan and the UK. The company specializes in corporate travel arrangements (more than half of its business) but also handles government contracts, group travel, and plain old vacationers. It also serves clients though an online travel site. Most of Omega's sales come from airline reservations. In addition, the company offers discounts on all major cruise lines at its CRUISE.COM Web site and provides travel agent training through its Omega Travel School. President Gloria Bohan founded the company in 1972.

EXECUTIVES

President: Gloria Bohan
COO: Daniel (Dan) Bohan
CFO: Michael Peranio
EVP Sales and Client Service: Goran Gligorovic
VP Corporate Operations: Diane Bozicevich
VP Field Sales: Stan Brown
VP Government Operations: Patt Hall
VP Regional Sales: Peter Buckingham
VP Vendor Relations: Rick Singer
Managing Director, UK Operations: Ranka Daniels
Director Human Resources: Betsy Amos

LOCATIONS

HQ: 3102 Omega Office Park, Fairfax, VA 22031
Phone: 703-359-0200 **Fax:** 703-359-8880
Web: www.owt.net

COMPETITORS

American Express
Carlson Wagonlit
Maritz
Navigant International
Rosenbluth International
Sabre
Thomas Cook AG
Travel and Transport
WorldTravel

HISTORICAL FINANCIALS

Company Type: Private

Income Statement FYE: December 31

	REVENUE ($ mil.)	NET INCOME ($ mil.)	NET PROFIT MARGIN	EMPLOYEES
12/01	750	—	—	1,000
12/00	710	—	—	1,000
12/99	612	—	—	1,000
12/98	556	—	—	1,000
12/97	620	—	—	700
Annual Growth	4.9%	—	—	9.3%

Revenue History

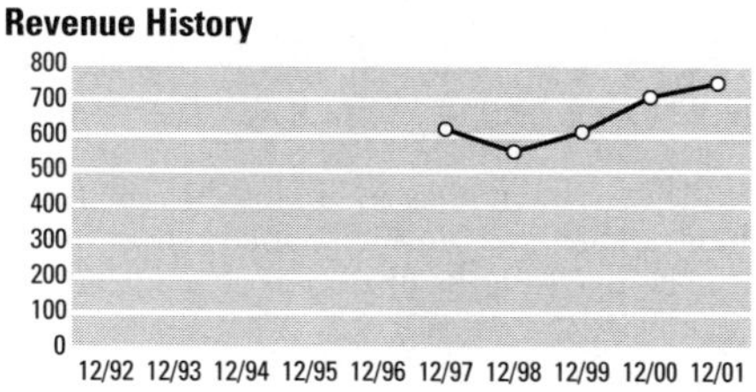

O'Melveny & Myers LLP

O'Melveny & Myers is more than happy to play the role of legal guardian angel. Founded in 1885, O'Melveny & Myers is one of the oldest law firms in Los Angeles, and it has developed strong ties to the media and entertainment industry. Sony Pictures Entertainment, Walt Disney, and Time Warner Inc. are among the firm's clients. It also is known for political clout: Former US Secretary of State Warren Christopher is a senior partner. O'Melveny & Myers' practice areas include communications, entertainment and media, and real estate. The firm is expanding its services for high-tech companies, which include legal advice related to software licensing, intellectual property, and venture capital investments.

EXECUTIVES

Chairman and CEO: Arthur B. Culvahouse Jr.
CFO: James De Guelle
COO: Bruce Boulware
Director Human Resources: Beth Naples

LOCATIONS

HQ: 400 S. Hope St., Ste. 1500, Los Angeles, CA 90071
Phone: 213-430-6000 **Fax:** 213-430-6407
Web: www.omm.com

PRODUCTS/OPERATIONS

Selected Practice Areas

Asia Practice
Banking and financial institutions
Bankruptcy
Communications
Employee benefits
Entertainment and media
Environmental
Health care
Internet law
Labor and employment
Litigation
Real estate
White-collar crime

COMPETITORS

Akin, Gump
Baker & McKenzie
Davis Polk
Gibson, Dunn & Crutcher
Latham & Watkins
Paul, Hastings
Skadden, Arps
Sullivan & Cromwell

HISTORICAL FINANCIALS

Company Type: Partnership

Income Statement FYE: January 31

	REVENUE ($ mil.)	NET INCOME ($ mil.)	NET PROFIT MARGIN	EMPLOYEES
1/03	563	—	—	2,200
1/02	490	—	—	1,900
1/01	401	—	—	1,500
1/00	373	—	—	1,500
1/99	328	—	—	1,450
1/98	284	—	—	1,400
1/97	260	—	—	1,350
1/96	253	—	—	1,314
1/95	257	—	—	1,334
1/94	232	—	—	1,130
Annual Growth	10.4%	—	—	7.7%

Revenue History

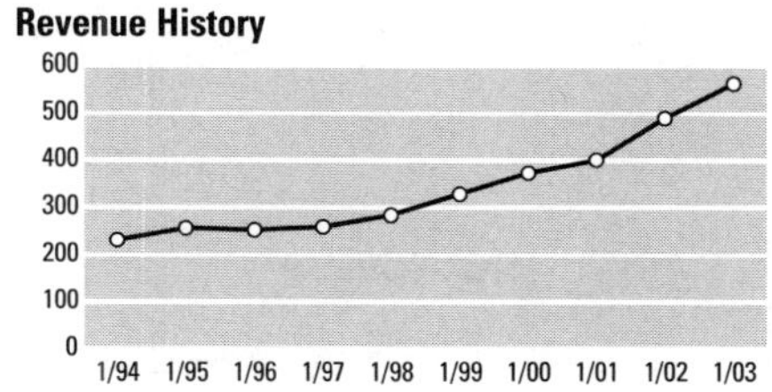

OmniSource Corporation

OmniSource lives on scraps. Irving Rifkin founded the private, family-owned scrap-metal processor and trader in 1943 to supply scrap for WWII. OmniSource was a pioneer in adopting formal quality-control programs and in turning scrap into briquettes for foundry and steel-mill furnace use. Today the company rates as one of the largest scrap recycling firms in North America. Through a network of six brokerage offices, it tracks national and international scrap prices and activities. OmniSource operates 32 processing facilities, a secondary aluminum smelting plant, and a heavy-media separation facility. The founder's son, Leonard Rifkin, is chairman and CEO.

EXECUTIVES

Chairman and CEO: Leonard I. Rifkin, age 48
President and COO: Daniel Rifkin
EVP and CFO: Gary Rohrs
EVP, Administration: Ben Eisbart
EVP, Ferrous Group: John Marynowski
EVP, Non-Ferrous: Martin Rifkin
EVP, Non-Ferrous: Richard Rifkin
SVP, Ferrous Sales: Donald Jarrell Sr.
SVP, Industrial Sourcing: Thomas Tuschman
VP, Ohio Ferrous Group: Joel Beren
CIO: Dave Parlette
Manager, Atlanta Office: Howard Smith

LOCATIONS

HQ: 1610 N. Calhoun St., Fort Wayne, IN 46808
Phone: 260-422-5541 **Fax:** 260-423-8500
Web: www.omnisource.com

OmniSource operates numerous sites in the eastern US and Ontario, Canada.

PRODUCTS/OPERATIONS

Selected Products

Aluminum
Ferrous and nonferrous scrap
Steel briquettes

Selected Service

Metal brokerage

COMPETITORS

Cargill Steel
Commercial Metals
David J. Joseph
International Briquettes
Keywell
Metal Management
Roanoke Electric Steel
Stelco
Tang Industries

HISTORICAL FINANCIALS

Company Type: Private

Income Statement FYE: September 30

	ESTIMATED REVENUE ($ mil.)	NET INCOME ($ mil.)	NET PROFIT MARGIN	EMPLOYEES
9/02	840	—	—	1,350
9/01	820	—	—	1,400
9/00	835	—	—	1,350
9/99	825	—	—	1,500
9/98	680	—	—	1,150
9/97	600	—	—	960
9/96	550	—	—	800
9/95	500	—	—	800
9/94	430	—	—	700
Annual Growth	8.7%	—	—	8.6%

Revenue History

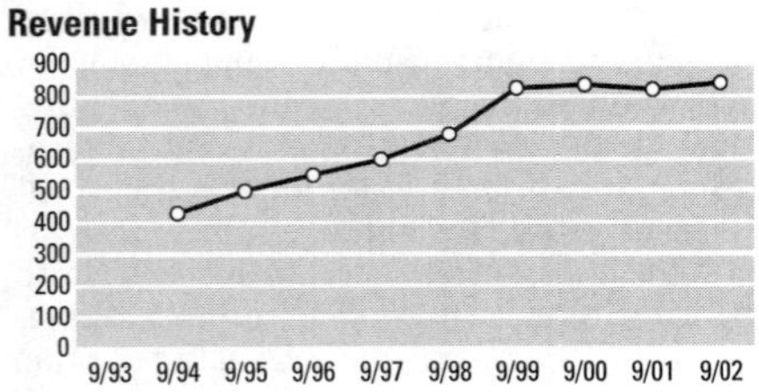

O'Neal Steel, Inc.

O'Neal Steel has an angle on the steel industry. One of the US's leading private metals service companies, O'Neal sells a full range of metal products — including angles, bars, beams, coil, pipe, plate, and sheet — made from steel, aluminum, brass, and bronze. Its Weldment Fabrication Division makes subassemblies, bracket weldments, and precision parts for the mining and the mobile crane industries. Founded by Kirkman O'Neal in 1922 in Alabama, the company has expanded largely through mergers and acquisitions. It is still owned and run by the O'Neal family.

The company operates around 40 plants in southeastern, midwestern, southwestern, and mountain states, from which it offers such metal-processing services as forming, laser cutting, machining, oxy-fuel and plasma burning, shearing, tube bending, and sawing.

O'Neal's Masonry Arts division was involved in rebuilding the Pentagon after it was destroyed on September 11, 2001, by hijackers. The company provided such supplies as angles, beams, flats, tubing, and aluminum and stainless sheet to assist in completing the project as scheduled.

EXECUTIVES

Chairman: Emmet O'Neal
President and CEO: Bill Jones
COO: Terry Taft
VP and CFO: Mary Valenta
VP, Human Resources: Shawn Smith
Controller/Comptroller: Gayle Morgan
Director Marketing: Henley Smith
Director Purchasing: Holman Head
IS/IT: Michael Gooldrup
Inside Sales Representative: Tom Mayo
Outside Sales Representative: Tommy Harris

LOCATIONS

HQ: 744 41st St. North, Birmingham, AL 35222
Phone: 205-599-8000 **Fax:** 205-599-8037
Web: www.onealsteel.com

O'Neal Steel operates metal processing facilities in about 40 locations in the midwest, southeast, southwest, and mountain area.

PRODUCTS/OPERATIONS

Selected Products

Alloy bars
Coil
Cold finished bars
Grating
Hot rolled bars
Pipe
Structural shapes
Tubing

Selected Processing Services

Coil processing
Cutting
Forming
Machining
Notching
Punching and drilling
Rolling
Sawing
Shearing
Tube bending
Welding

COMPETITORS

Canam Manac
Cargill Steel
Earle M. Jorgensen
IPSCO
Metalcraft
Metals USA
Quanex
Reliance Steel
Russel Metals
Ryerson Tull
Worthington Industries

HISTORICAL FINANCIALS

Company Type: Private

Income Statement FYE: December 31

	REVENUE ($ mil.)	NET INCOME ($ mil.)	NET PROFIT MARGIN	EMPLOYEES
12/02	750	—	—	2,500
12/01	742	—	—	2,500
12/00	941	—	—	2,950
12/99	941	—	—	2,900
12/98	930	—	—	2,675
12/97	755	—	—	2,200
12/96	651	—	—	2,000
12/95	687	—	—	—
12/94	581	—	—	—
Annual Growth	3.2%	—	—	3.8%

Revenue History

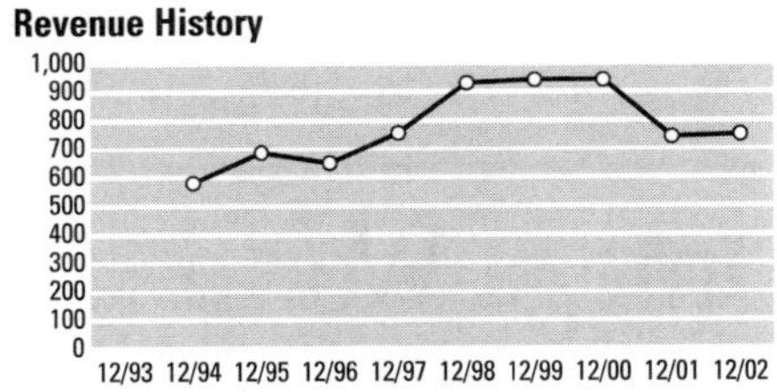

Opus Corporation

This Opus can be heard from coast to coast. Founded in 1953 as Rauenhorst Construction Company, the commercial real estate development and management firm builds custom facilities (office buildings, warehouses, and malls) for purchase or lease and develops business parks. The company also offers architecture, engineering, construction, property management, and financing and leasing. Opus operates through five independent operating companies and has several subsidiaries that provide support functions. The company has nearly 30 offices across the US. The Gerald Rauenhorst family owns the company.

EXECUTIVES

Founding Chairman: Gerald Rauenhorst
Chairman: Keith Bednarowski
President and CEO: Mark H. Rauenhorst, age 50
SVP and CFO: Ronald W. Schiferl
SVP and Chief Investment Officer: Andrew C. (Andy) Deckas
SVP, Secretary, and General Counsel: Dan F. Nicol
SVP Tax: Luz Campa
VP, Human Resources: Janet A. Maistrovich

LOCATIONS

HQ: 10350 Bren Rd. W, Minnetonka, MN 55343
Phone: 952-656-4444 **Fax:** 952-656-4529
Web: www.opuscorp.com

Opus has offices in Allentown, Pennsylvania; Atlanta; Austin, Texas; Chicago; Columbus, Ohio; Dallas; Denver; Detroit; Fort Lauderdale, Florida; Houston; Indianapolis; Kansas City, Kansas; Los Angeles; Milwaukee; Minneapolis; Orange County, California; Orlando, Florida; Pensacola, Florida; Philadelphia; Phoenix; Portland, Oregon; Sacramento, California; San Francisco; San Jose, California; Seattle; St. Louis; and Tampa, Florida.

PRODUCTS/OPERATIONS

Subsidiaries

Opus Architects & Engineers, Inc.
Opus East, L.L.C.
Opus National, L.L.C.
Opus North Corporation
Opus North Management Corporation
Opus Northwest Management, L.L.C.
Opus Northwest, L.L.C.
Opus Properties, L.L.C.
Opus South Corporation
Opus South Management Corporation
Opus West Corporation
Opus West Management, L.L.C.

COMPETITORS

Alter Group
Brookfield Properties
Castle & Cooke
Forest City Enterprises
Hines Interests
Irvine Company
Lincoln Property
Structure Tone
Trizec Properties

HISTORICAL FINANCIALS

Company Type: Private

Income Statement FYE: December 31

	ESTIMATED REVENUE ($ mil.)	NET INCOME ($ mil.)	NET PROFIT MARGIN	EMPLOYEES
12/02	967	—	—	1,275
12/01	1,200	—	—	1,400
12/00	1,400	—	—	1,250
12/99	1,100	—	—	1,250
12/98	900	—	—	1,250
12/97	575	—	—	1,200
12/96	450	—	—	600
Annual Growth	13.6%	—	—	13.4%

Revenue History

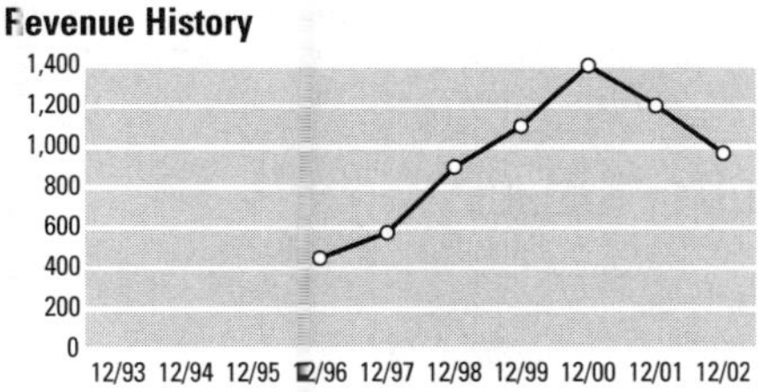

Ormet Corporation

Ormet's canny business skills have made it one of the US's leading producers of aluminum. Through its Ormet Primary Aluminum subsidiary, the company smelts aluminum ore (bauxite) and manufactures aluminum ingot, billet (pressed bars), sheet, foil, and other products for the fabrication, extrusion, and conversion markets. The company's Ormet Aluminum Mill Products subsidiary further processes the aluminum into auto trim, cans, gift wrap, packaging, and other products. Ormet operates nine plants (including alumina plants, rolling mills, recycling facilities, and marine terminals), primarily in the midwestern US. CEO Emmett Boyle owns the company, which was founded in Hannibal, Ohio, in 1954.

EXECUTIVES

Chairman and CEO: R. Emmett Boyle
President and COO: Michael S. Williams
VP, Finance and CFO: Rich Caruso
VP Ormet Aluminum Mill Products Operations: Ned Damron
VP Primary Operations and Cast Products: Zeno DeMori
Director, Corporate Communications: Laurie Leonard
Director, Personnel: Lisa Riedle
Hannibal Rolling Mill Division Manager: Steve Jorris

LOCATIONS

HQ: 1233 Main St., Ste. 4000, Wheeling, WV 26003
Phone: 304-234-3900 **Fax:** 304-234-3929
Web: www.ormet.com

Ormet operates in the US from nine facilities in seven states, including sites along the Mississippi and Ohio Rivers.

PRODUCTS/OPERATIONS

Selected Products

Alumina
Aluminum foil
Aluminum sheet
Primary aluminum

COMPETITORS

Alcan
Alcoa
Corus Group
SEPI
Hydro Aluminium
Kaiser Aluminum
MAXXAM
Mitsubishi Chemical
Nippon Light Metal
Norsk Hydro
Pechiney
Rio Tinto

HISTORICAL FINANCIALS

Company Type: Private

Income Statement FYE: December 31

	REVENUE ($ mil.)	NET INCOME ($ mil.)	NET PROFIT MARGIN	EMPLOYEES
12/02	650	—	—	2,750
12/01	700	—	—	3,000
12/00	700	—	—	3,000
12/99	690	—	—	3,300
12/98	780	—	—	3,300
12/97	910	—	—	3,300
12/96	830	—	—	3,300
12/95	960	—	—	3,300
12/94	880	—	—	3,300
12/93	819	—	—	2,500
Annual Growth	(2.5%)	—	—	1.1%

Revenue History

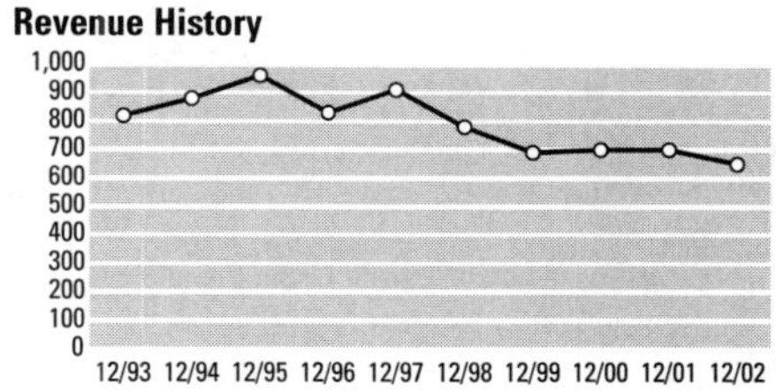

Ourisman Automotive

Whether your preference is for American or foreign, Ford or Chevy, Ourisman Automotive Enterprises can satisfy your vehicular proclivity. Serving the Washington, DC, area, Ourisman Automotive operates 14 dealerships throughout Maryland and Virginia. The company's Chevrolet, Chrysler, Dodge, Ford, Honda, Mitsubishi, Plymouth, Suzuki, and Toyota dealerships sell both new and used vehicles. Ourisman Automotive also sells parts and offers service and financing. The Ourisman family, which owns the company, founded Ourisman Automotive Enterprises in 1921.

EXECUTIVES

Chairman: Mandell J. Ourisman, age 76
President: John Ourisman
CFO: Mohamed Reshed
General Manager: Abbas Khademi

LOCATIONS

HQ: Ourisman Automotive Enterprises
4400 Branch Ave., Marlow Heights, MD 20748
Phone: 301-423-4028 **Fax:** 301-423-5725
Web: www.ourisman.com

COMPETITORS

Atlantic Automotive
Brown Automotive
Hall Auto World
Jim Koons Automotive
March/Hodge
Pohanka Automotive
Rosenthal Automotive
Sheehy Auto

HISTORICAL FINANCIALS

Company Type: Private

Income Statement FYE: December 31

	REVENUE ($ mil.)	NET INCOME ($ mil.)	NET PROFIT MARGIN	EMPLOYEES
12/01	656	—	—	1,000
12/00	622	—	—	1,000
12/99	549	—	—	950
12/98	535	—	—	973
12/97	520	—	—	1,025
12/96	518	—	—	1,001
12/95	520	—	—	949
12/94	491	—	—	949
12/93	396	—	—	916
Annual Growth	6.5%	—	—	1.1%

Revenue History

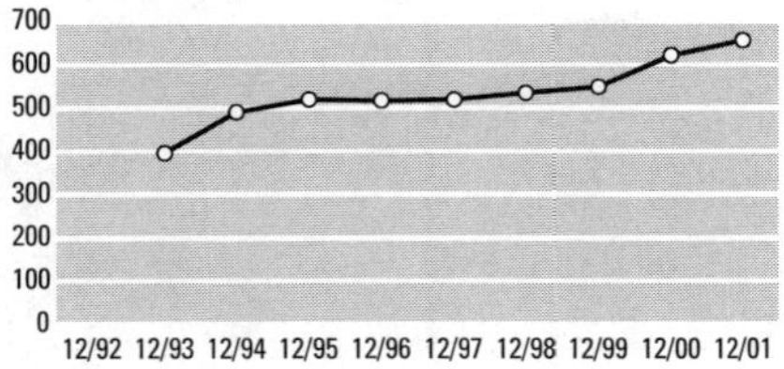

Outsourcing Solutions Inc.

Pay now or deal with Outsourcing Solutions (OSI) later. The accounts-receivable management firm provides a variety of collection, portfolio purchasing, and outsourcing services to its customers, which include credit card, financial, utility, and health care companies, as well as education, government, and retail clients. The acquisitive company operates some 65 offices in about 25 states; it also offers its services in Canada, Mexico, and Puerto Rico. Services include providing call centers for credit authorization and customer service. OSI also purchases new and delinquent accounts from creditors. OSI, which is majority owned by Madison Dearborn Partners, has filed for Chapter 11 reorganization protection.

EXECUTIVES

Chairman: Paul R. Wood, age 49
President and CEO: Kevin T. Keleghan, age 44
EVP and President, TSI Business Services Group: Michael A. DiMarco, age 45, $342,915 pay
EVP and President, Financial Services Business Group: Bryan K. Faliero, age 37, $269,304 pay
EVP and President, Telecom/Utilities Business Services Group: Michael B. Staed, age 56, $265,818 pay
EVP, Sales: Michael G. Meyer
EVP and CFO: Gary L. Weller, age 42, $292,508 pay
SVP, General Counsel, and Secretary: Eric R. Fencl
SVP, Human Resources: C. Bradford McLeod
Corporate Communications Manager: Aimee Muldrow

LOCATIONS

HQ: 390 S. Woods Mill Rd., Ste. 350, Chesterfield, MO 63017
Phone: 314-576-0022 **Fax:** 314-576-1867
Web: www.osi.to

PRODUCTS/OPERATIONS

Selected Subsidiaries and Affiliates

Coast-to-Coast Consulting, LLC
Greystone Business Group, LLC
Jennifer Loomis & Associates, Inc.
Medical Accounting Service
North Shore Agency, Inc.
OSI Collection Services, Inc.
OSI Education Services, Inc.
OSI Outsourcing Services, Inc.
OSI Portfolio Services, Inc.
Qualink, Inc.
RWC Consulting Group, LLC
Transworld Systems Inc.
University Accounting Services, LLC

COMPETITORS

Asta Funding
Deluxe
Encore Capital Group, Inc.
Equifax
GC Services
IntelliRisk Management
National Processing
NCO Group
Portfolio Recovery Associates
Rampart Capital

HISTORICAL FINANCIALS

Company Type: Private

Income Statement FYE: December 31

	REVENUE ($ mil.)	NET INCOME ($ mil.)	NET PROFIT MARGIN	EMPLOYEES
12/02	592	—	—	7,200
12/01	612	—	—	9,000
12/00	543	—	—	7,600
12/99	504	—	—	7,000
12/98	479	—	—	7,000
12/97	272	—	—	5,000
12/96	106	—	—	—
12/95	30	—	—	—
12/94	39	—	—	—
12/93	24	—	—	—
Annual Growth	43.0%	—	—	7.6%

Revenue History

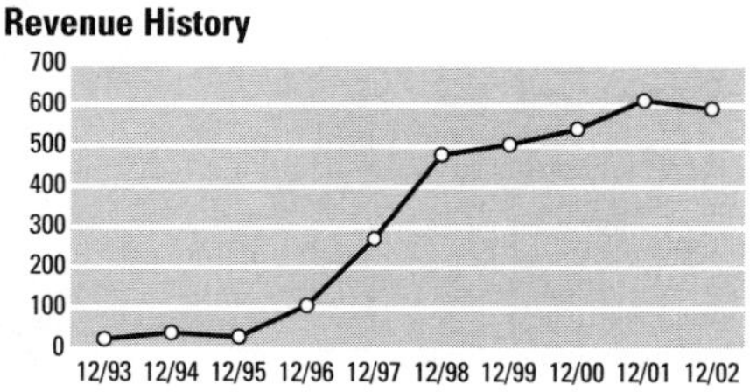

Oxbow Corporation

Oxbow is bullish on energy and mining. The diversified firm's Oxbow Carbon & Minerals unit produces and markets coke, coal, petroleum, and carbon products. Other company operations include Oxbow Power, which builds and operates power plants (it currently has two plants in Costa Rica); Oxbow Energy, which is developing a natural gas site in Colorado; and Oxbow Realty Services, which develops and manages commercial and residential real estate projects. Oxbow is controlled by William Koch, an America's Cup winner who founded Oxbow in 1983 after being ousted from the family business (Koch Industries) by brothers Charles and David. A series of lawsuits between Oxbow and Koch Industries has been settled.

EXECUTIVES

President: William I. Koch
VP, General Counsel, and Director: Richard P. Callahan
VP, Finance: Zachary Shipley
President and COO, Oxbow Carbon & Minerals: Brian Acton
President, Gunnison Energy Corporation; President, Oxbow Power Corporation: Vince Zodiaco
President, Oxbow Realty Services: Kenneth A. Swanson
EVP, Oxbow Carbon and Minerals: Lawrence H. Black
EVP, Oxbow Realty Services: Russell J. Burke
Director of Corporate Communications: Brad Goldstein
Director of Human Resources: Kathy Flaherty
Auditors: PricewaterhouseCoopers LLP

LOCATIONS

HQ: 1601 Forum Place, Ste. 1400, West Palm Beach, FL 33402
Phone: 561-697-4300 **Fax:** 561-640-8747
Web: www.oxbow.com

Oxbow has offices in Brazil, Canada, China, Costa Rica, Mexico, the UK, and the US.

PRODUCTS/OPERATIONS

Selected Operations

Gunnison Energy (development of natural gas resources at North Fork Valley, Colorado)
Oxbow Carbon & Minerals (mining and marketing of coal, petroleum coke, metallurgical coke, steel, gypsum, industrial minerals, and combustion ash)
Oxbow Power (development and operation of geothermal and hydroelectric utilities in Costa Rica)
Oxbow Realty Services (commercial and residential real estate development and management, primarily in New England)

COMPETITORS

Alliance Resource Partners
Black Hills
Drummond
Duke Energy
Dynegy
Enron
Horizon Natural Resources
Kinder Morgan Energy Partners
Koch
MidAmerican Energy
ONEOK
Sunoco
Westmoreland Coal

HISTORICAL FINANCIALS

Company Type: Private

Income Statement FYE: December 31

	ESTIMATED REVENUE ($ mil.)	NET INCOME ($ mil.)	NET PROFIT MARGIN	EMPLOYEES
12/02	450	—	—	500
12/01	450	—	—	500
12/00	450	—	—	500
12/99	440	—	—	500
12/98	475	—	—	800
12/97	500	—	—	700
12/96	450	—	—	900
12/95	425	—	—	900
12/94	720	—	—	1,600
12/93	1,100	—	—	1,600
Annual Growth	(9.5%)	—	—	(12.1%)

Revenue History

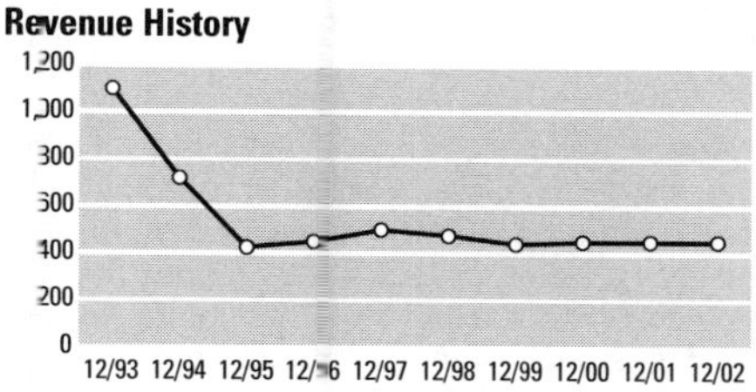

Oxford Automotive, Inc.

Oxford Automotive, a supplier of metal car and truck components, is riding the sport utility vehicle (SUV) boom all the way to the bank. The company manufactures suspension and structural systems, leaf springs, and other components for the automotive manufacturing industry. A majority of those components roll out on SUVs, minivans, and light trucks made by such companies as GM, Ford, Renault, Peugeot, and DaimlerChrysler. The company's products can be found on Ford's F-Series pickups and on DaimlerChrysler's Ram pickups. Chairman Selwyn Isakow controls the company.

EXECUTIVES

Chairman: Selwyn Isakow, age 51
Vice Chairman: Rex E. Schlaybaugh Jr.
President and CEO: John W. Potter
EVP and CFO: Martin E. Welch III
SVP, Human Resources: Dennis Bemis
President, North American Division: Jeffrey W. Wilson
Director, Corporate Communications: Liz Pinto
Auditors: PricewaterhouseCoopers LLP

LOCATIONS

HQ: 850 Stephenson Hwy., Troy, MI 48083
Phone: 248-577-4900 **Fax:** 248-577-4998
Web: www.oxauto.com

Oxford Automotive has operations in Argentina, Canada, France, Germany, Italy, Mexico, Turkey, the US, and Venezuela.

PRODUCTS/OPERATIONS

Selected Products

Mechanisms
Handbrakes
Hood and trunk
Jacks
Seat latches
Sliding door mechanisms

Structures
Body side assemblies
Cargo doors
Door assemblies
Floor plan assemblies
Front engine compartment
Rail assemblies (front and rear)
Rear compartment
Tailgate assemblies

Suspension
Coil springs
Control arm subassemblies
Multi-leaf conventional springs
Rear suspension modules
Spring mounting hangers and shackles

COMPETITORS

Active Tool & Manufacturing
A.G. Simpson
American Axle & Manufacturing
ArvinMeritor, Inc.
Dana
Lear
Magna International
Mayflower
Midway Products Group
SANLUIS
Shiloh Industries
ThyssenKrupp Budd
Tower Automotive
Trianon Industries
Wagon plc

HISTORICAL FINANCIALS

Company Type: Private

Income Statement FYE: March 31

	REVENUE ($ mil.)	NET INCOME ($ mil.)	NET PROFIT MARGIN	EMPLOYEES
3/02	800	—	—	7,000
3/01	824	—	—	7,400
3/00	809	—	—	5,500
3/99	592	—	—	5,100
3/98	410	—	—	3,800
3/97	137	—	—	—
3/96	85	—	—	—
3/95	75	—	—	—
3/94	65	—	—	—
Annual Growth	36.8%	—	—	16.5%

Revenue History

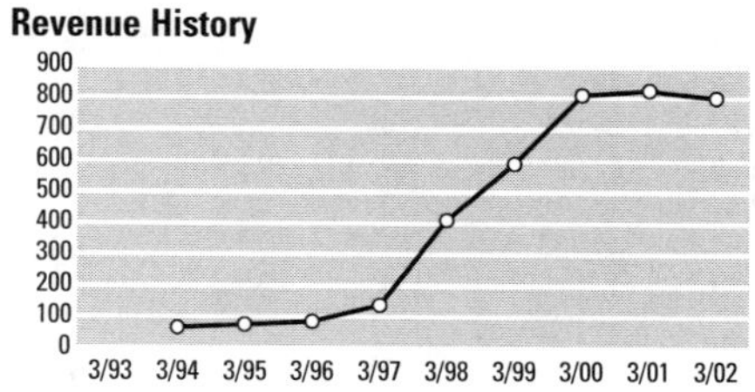

Pacific Mutual

Life insurance is Pacific Mutual Holding's stock-in-trade. Pacific Mutual owns stock company Pacific LifeCorp, which, through its primary subsidiary Pacific Life Insurance, is the largest California-based life insurance outfit. Pacific Life offers fixed and variable life insurance policies, annuities, and pension plans; other subsidiaries manage health plans and provide real estate advice. Through Pacific Select Distributors, the company markets such investment products as annuities, mutual funds, and index funds. Pacific Mutual also owns almost a third of Allianz Dresdner Asset Management of America (formerly PIMCO Advisors), a major investment management firm majority-owned by insurer Allianz.

Pacific Mutual's conversion from a pure mutual to a mutual holding company gives it more flexibility and the option of an IPO; meanwhile, policyholders retain ownership of the company, but hold no stock.

Targeting individuals and small businesses, the company has opted out of the reinsurance business. It sold UK-based World-Wide Reassurance to Scottish Annuity & Life in exchange for a nearly 25% stake in the annuity reinsurer. Rate hikes in the insurance industry and a strong year for its mutual funds and annuities segment helped the company's results in 2002. Like many of its rivals, Pacific Mutual was adversely affected by the slumping markets.

HISTORY

Pacific Mutual began business in 1868 in Sacramento, California, as a stock company. Its board was dominated by California business and political leaders, including three of the "Big Four" who created the Central Pacific Railroad (Charles Crocker, Mark Hopkins, and Leland Stanford) and three former governors (Stanford, Newton Booth, and Henry Huntley Haight). Stanford (founder of Stanford University) was the company's first president and policyholder.

By 1870 Pacific Mutual was selling life insurance throughout most of the western US. Expansion continued in the early 1870s into Colorado, Kentucky, Nebraska, New York, Ohio, and Texas. The company ventured into Mexico in 1873 but sold few policies. It had more luck in China, accepting its first risk there in 1875, and in Hawaii, where it started business in 1877. In 1881 Pacific Mutual moved to San Francisco.

Leland Stanford died in 1893. His widow and eponymous university, though rich in assets, found themselves struggling through a US economic depression. The benefit from Stanford's policy kept the university open until the estate was settled.

In 1905 Conservative Life bought the firm. The Pacific Mutual name survived the acquisition just as its records survived the fire that ravaged San Francisco after the 1906 earthquake. Pacific Mutual then relocated to Los Angeles.

The company squeaked through the Depression after a flood of claims on its noncancellable disability income policies forced Pacific Mutual into a reorganization plan initiated by the California insurance commissioner (1936). After WWII, Pacific Mutual entered the group insurance and pension markets.

After 83 years as a stock company and an eight-year stock purchasing program, Pacific Mutual became a true mutual in 1959.

Pacific Mutual relocated to Newport Beach in 1972. During the 1980s it built up its financial services operations, including its Pacific Investment Management Co. (PIMCO, founded 1971). The company was in trouble even before the stock crash of 1987 because of health care costs and over-investment in real estate. That year it brought in CEO Thomas Sutton, who sold off real estate and emphasized HMOs and fee-based financial services.

In the 1990s the firm cut costs and increased its fee income. PIMCO Advisors, L.P. was formed in 1994 when PIMCO merged with Thomson Advisory Group. The merger gave Pacific Mutual a retail market for its fixed-income products, a stake in the resulting public company, and sales that offset interest rate variations and changes in the health care system.

The company assumed failed Confederation Life Insurance Co.'s corporate-owned life insurance business and merged insolvent First Capital Life into Pacific Life as Pacific Corinthian Life in 1997. That year Pacific Mutual became the first top-10 US mutual to convert to a mutual holding company, thus allowing it the option of issuing stock to fund acquisitions. Because the firm remained partially mutual, however, policyholders retained ownership but got no shares of Pacific LifeCorp, its new stock company.

To compete with one-stop financial service behemoths such as Citigroup, Pacific Mutual began selling annuities through a Compass Bank subsidiary in 1998. The next year it bought controlling interests in broker-dealer M.L. Stern and investment adviser Tower Asset Management. In 2000 the world's #2 insurer, Allianz, bought all of PIMCO Advisors other than the interest retained by Pacific Mutual when it spun off the investment manager.

EXECUTIVES

Chairman and CEO, Pacific Mutual Holding, Pacific LifeCorp, and Pacific Life: Thomas C. Sutton, age 61
President, Pacific Life: Glenn S. Schafer, age 54
EVP and CFO, Pacific Life: Khanh T. Tran, age 46
EVP, Pacific Life: Lynn C. Miller
EVP, Pacific Life, Annuities and Mutual Funds Division; Chairman and CEO, Pacific Select Distributors: Gerald W. (Bill) Robinson
EVP, Pacific Life, Group Insurance Division: David W. Gartley
EVP, Pacific Life, Institutional Products Division; EVP and Chief Credit Officer, Pacific Financial Products: Mark W. Holmlund
EVP, Pacific Life, Real Estate Division: Michael S. Robb
EVP, Pacific Life, Securities Division; EVP and Chief Credit Officer, Pacific Financial Products: Larry J. Card
SVP and General Counsel, Pacific Life: David R. Carmichael
SVP, Administration, Pacific Life, Annuities and Mutual Funds Division: Robert C. Hsu
SVP, Finance and Administration, Pacific Life, Life Insurance Division: S. Gene Schofield
SVP, Guaranteed Products, Pacific Life, Institutional Products Division: John E. Milberg
SVP, Human Resources, Pacific Life: Anthony J. Bonno
SVP, Public Affairs, Pacific Life: Robert G. Haskell
SVP, Risk and Financial Management, Pacific Life, Institutional Products Division: Henry M. McMillan
SVP, Marketing Operations, Pacific Life, Life Insurance Division: Michael A. Bell
SVP, Sales, Pacific Life, Annuities and Mutual Funds Division: Dewey P. Bushaw
SVP, Strategic Planning and Development, Pacific Life: Marc S. Franklin
SVP, Pacific Select Distributors: Peter S. Deering
SVP, Finance, Pacific Life, Group Insurance Division: W. Douglas Lehman
Auditors: Deloitte & Touche LLP

LOCATIONS

HQ: Pacific Mutual Holding Company
700 Newport Center Dr., Newport Beach, CA 92660
Phone: 949-219-3011 **Fax:** 949-219-7614
Web: www.pacificlife.com

Pacific Mutual Holding has insurance operations throughout the US (except in New York).

PRODUCTS/OPERATIONS

2002 Assets

	$ mil.	% of total
Cash & equivalents	619	1
Bonds	20,986	37
Stocks	762	1
Mortgage loans	3,123	5
Policy loans	5,115	9
Other investments	3,335	6
Assets in separate account	19,241	34
Other assets	4,124	7
Total	**57,305**	**100**

Selected Subsidiaries and Affiliates
Allianz Dresdner Asset Management of America L.P. (31%)
Associated Securities Corp.
Aviation Capital Group
M.L. Stern & Co., LLC
Mutual Service Corporation
Pacific Financial Products, Inc.
Pacific Life & Annuity Company
Pacific LifeCorp.
Pacific Life Insurance Company
Pacific Select Distributors, Inc.
PMRealty Advisors, Inc.

COMPETITORS

Acordia
Aetna
AXA Financial
Blue Cross
Charles Schwab
CIGNA
Citigroup
GenAmerica
Guardian Life
Hartford Life
Health Net
John Hancock Financial Services
Liberty Mutual
Lincoln National
MassMutual
MetLife
MONY
Nationwide
Nationwide Provident
New York Life
Northwestern Mutual
PacifiCare
Principal Financial
Prudential
St. Paul Companies
StanCorp Financial Group
State Farm
USAA
WellPoint Health Networks

HISTORICAL FINANCIALS

Company Type: Mutual company

Income Statement FYE: December 31

	ASSETS ($ mil.)	NET INCOME ($ mil.)	INCOME AS % OF ASSETS	EMPLOYEES
12/02	57,305	50	0.1%	3,700
12/01	56,055	247	0.4%	3,600
12/00	54,784	995	1.8%	3,600
12/99	50,123	371	0.7%	3,799
12/98	39,884	242	0.6%	2,700
12/97	34,009	176	0.5%	3,422
12/96	27,065	167	0.6%	2,750
12/95	17,589	85	0.5%	2,700
12/94	14,728	81	0.5%	2,400
12/93	13,346	119	0.9%	2,400
Annual Growth	17.6%	(9.2%)	—	4.9%

2002 Year-End Financials

Equity as % of assets: 7.5%
Return on assets: 0.1%
Return on equity: 1.2%
Long-term debt ($ mil.): 1,080
Sales ($ mil.): 3,816

Net Income History

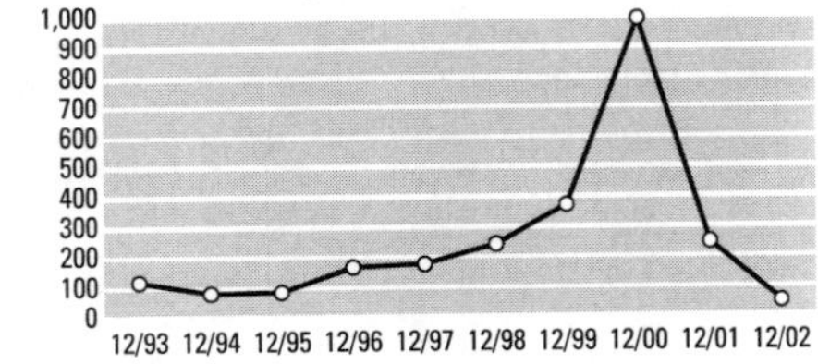

Pameco Corporation

Pameco's business blows hot and cold. The company distributes heating, ventilation, and air-conditioning (HVAC) systems and equipment and refrigeration products throughout the US. Pameco serves mainly small to medium-sized independent contractors through its network of about 300 branches throughout the US and Guam. Pameco distributes central air conditioners, heat pumps, and furnaces, as well as walk-in coolers and ice machines. The company also serves the repair and replacement market. Pameco closed about 50 branches in 2000 in its efforts to restructure. Pameco is owned by Littlejohn & Co. and Quilvest American Equity, which bought the company in 2001.

EXECUTIVES

President and CEO: Dixon R. Walker
SVP and CFO: Steve Lister
SVP Branch Operations: Pete Koury
SVP Sales and Marketing: Steve Wing
SVP Supply Chain: Kevin Nohelty
VP and CIO: Thomas E. Cook
VP Human Resources: John Monarck
Corporate Counsel: Joe Ellsworth
Auditors: Ernst & Young LLP

LOCATIONS

HQ: 651 Corporate Circle, Ste. 200, Golden, CO 80401
Phone: 303-568-1200 **Fax:** 303-568-1232
Web: www.pameco.com

COMPETITORS

Ferguson Enterprises
Gensco-Albina
Hughes Supply
Ingersoll-Rand Climate Control
Johnstone Supply
Lennox
Noland
Watsco

HISTORICAL FINANCIALS

Company Type: Private

Income Statement FYE: Last day in February

	REVENUE ($ mil.)	NET INCOME ($ mil.)	NET PROFIT MARGIN	EMPLOYEES
2/02	500	—	—	1,600
2/01	400	—	—	1,600
2/00	604	—	—	1,493
2/99	625	—	—	1,691
2/98	484	—	—	1,587
2/97	379	—	—	1,300
2/96	335	—	—	—
2/95	323	—	—	—
2/94	338	—	—	—
2/93	300	—	—	—
Annual Growth	5.8%	—	—	4.2%

Revenue History

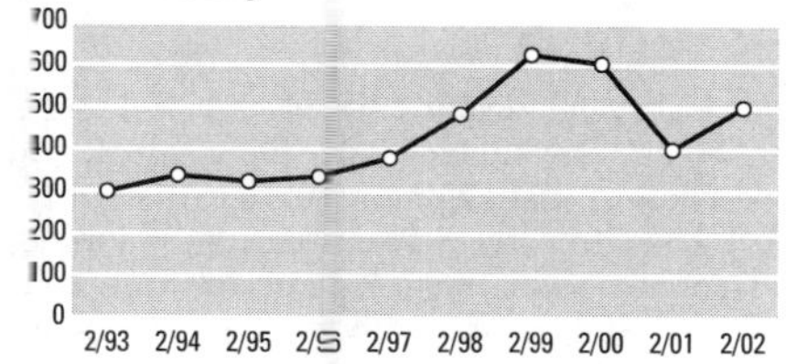

The Pampered Chef, Ltd.

Got a hankerin' for crinkle-cut watermelons, perfectly wedged apples, or artfully zested lemons? Then call The Pampered Chef, a direct seller of about 150 gourmet kitchen gadgets, cookware, cookbooks, and foodstuffs. The company has more than 71,000 independent sales reps who hock their wares at in-home kitchen parties (à la Tupperware) throughout the US, the UK, Germany, and Canada. The reps demonstrate product use and care and share recipes. As incentive (à la Mary Kay), reps can ultimately "earn" jewelry, as well as trips. Founded in 1980 by home economist and educator Doris Christopher, The Pampered Chef was sold to Berkshire Hathaway, the conglomerate controlled by billionaire Warren Buffett, in 2002.

EXECUTIVES

Chairman and Founder: Doris K. Christopher, age 57
President and COO: Marla Gottschalk, age 43
EVP and Chief Administrative Officer: Rick Geu
SVP Corporate Communications: Jane Edwards
SVP International: Rick Voke
SVP Legal and Global Human Resources: Catherine Landman
SVP Marketing: Susan Gustasson
SVP Operations: Rick McCall
SVP Sales: Jean Jonas
Public Relations Manager: Carol Marino

LOCATIONS

HQ: 1 Pampered Chef Ln., Addison, IL 60101
Phone: 630-261-8900 **Fax:** 630-261-8622
Web: www.pamperedchef.com

PRODUCTS/OPERATIONS

Selected Product Lines

Baking Basics (pizza rollers)
Cook's Library (original recipes)
Cutting Edge (knives, graters, blades)
Family Heritage Stoneware (baking stoneware, pans, bowls)
Generation II (cookware)
Kitchen Companions (cooking tools)
The Pampered Chef Pantry (specialty foods)

COMPETITORS

Amazon.com
Bed Bath & Beyond
Euromarket Designs
Kmart
Lifetime Hoan
Linens 'n Things
MSO
Sears
Target
Tastefully Simple
Tupperware
Wal-Mart
Williams-Sonoma
Wilton Industries
WKI Holding

HISTORICAL FINANCIALS

Company Type: Private

Income Statement FYE: December 31

	REVENUE ($ mil.)	NET INCOME ($ mil.)	NET PROFIT MARGIN	EMPLOYEES
12/02	730	—	—	1,000
12/01	740	—	—	1,110
12/00	709	—	—	1,125
12/99	590	—	—	970
12/98	500	—	—	800
12/97	420	—	—	630
12/96	328	—	—	500
12/95	225	—	—	400
Annual Growth	18.3%	—	—	14.0%

Revenue History

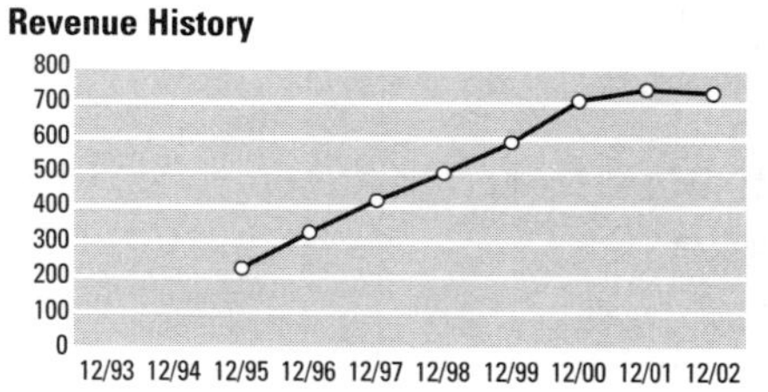

Parkdale Mills

Like that nice, soft-spun cotton in your undies? Thank Parkdale Mills. Parkdale, founded in 1916, is the largest independent yarn spinner in the US. The company manufactures cotton and cotton-polyester blend yarns and specializes in spun yarn that winds up in consumer goods such as sheets, towels, underwear, and hosiery. Parkdale has customers worldwide, including Jockey International, Lands' End, Fieldcrest Cannon, L.L. Bean, and Springmaid. The company operates and owns 66% of Parkdale America, a joint venture with polyester and nylon yarn maker Unifi. It also operates mills in Mexico through a joint venture with Burlington Industries. Chairman Duke Kimbrell owns about half of Parkdale.

EXECUTIVES

Chairman: W. Duke Kimbrell, age 78
President and CEO: Anderson D. Warlick, age 46
CFO: Dan Wilson
VP, Marketing: Charles F. (Charlie) Dickinson
VP, Sales: John Smeak
Director of Human Resources: Reid Baker

LOCATIONS

HQ: Parkdale Mills, Inc.
P.O. Box 1787, Gastonia, NC 28053
Phone: 704-874-5000 **Fax:** 704-874-5176
Web: www.parkdalemills.com

The company has manufacturing facilities in North Carolina and Virginia. Its fiber distribution facilities are located in North Carolina.

COMPETITORS

Avondale Incorporated
Burke Mills
Fuji Spinning
Guilford Mills
National Textiles
Nisshinbo

HISTORICAL FINANCIALS

Company Type: Private

Income Statement FYE: September 30

	ESTIMATED REVENUE ($ mil.)	NET INCOME ($ mil.)	NET PROFIT MARGIN	EMPLOYEES
9/02	900	—	—	3,500
9/01	1,001	—	—	3,650
9/00	1,000	—	—	3,600
9/99	934	—	—	3,600
9/98	850	—	—	3,200
9/97	960	—	—	3,000
9/96	550	—	—	2,600
Annual Growth	8.6%	—	—	5.1%

Revenue History

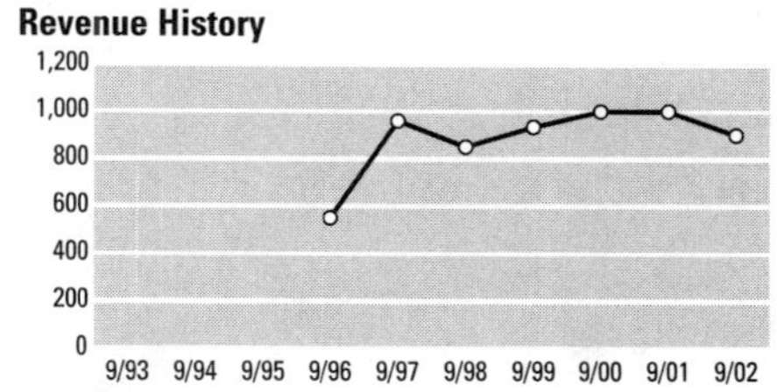

Parsons & Whittemore

Parsons & Whittemore is one of the world's largest producers of market pulp, the raw material used in papermaking. It is also a supplier of bleached kraft pulp, which is used to make paper bags, butcher wrap, newsprint, strong bond and ledger paper, and tissue. Parsons & Whittemore has pulp mills in Alabama and in Canada. It also produces newsprint through its Alabama River Newsprint joint venture with Canada's Abitibi-Consolidated, the world's largest newsprint maker. Chairman George Landegger and his family own the company. Landegger's father, Karl, came to the US from Austria in 1938 and bought Parsons & Whittemore, then a small pulp-trading firm founded in 1909.

EXECUTIVES

Chairman, President, and CEO: George Landegger
CFO: Steven Sweeney
Director, Human Resources: Suzanne Henry

LOCATIONS

HQ: Parsons & Whittemore, Incorporated
4 International Dr., Rye Brook, NY 10573
Phone: 914-937-9009 **Fax:** 914-937-2259

Parsons & Whittemore operates pulp mills in Alabama and Canada.

COMPETITORS

Boise Cascade
International Paper
Louisiana-Pacific
Pope & Talbot
Potlatch
Smurfit-Stone Container
Tembec
Weyerhaeuser

HISTORICAL FINANCIALS

Company Type: Private

Income Statement FYE: March 31

	ESTIMATED REVENUE ($ mil.)	NET INCOME ($ mil.)	NET PROFIT MARGIN	EMPLOYEES
3/02	1,100	—	—	2,500
3/01	1,100	—	—	2,500
3/00	1,045	—	—	2,500
3/99	790	—	—	2,500
3/98	825	—	—	2,500
3/97	780	—	—	2,500
3/96	800	—	—	2,000
3/95	1,600	—	—	2,000
3/94	1,181	—	—	1,800
3/93	870	—	—	1,500
Annual Growth	2.6%	—	—	5.8%

Revenue History

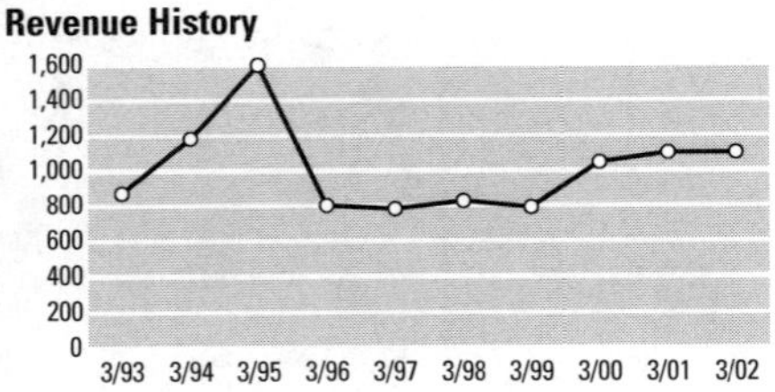

Parsons Brinckerhoff

After converting the US, Parsons Brinckerhoff is spreading its word around the globe. A leading US transportation engineering firm, the company provides planning, design, construction and program management, and consulting services for construction projects worldwide. It specializes in transit systems, tunnels, bridges, highways, and airports but also works on telecommunications, energy, and environmental projects. Founded in 1885 by William Barclay Parsons, the firm designed New York City's first subway. Recent projects range from designing Kentucky's William H. Natcher Bridge to recycling stockpiled munitions for the U.S. Army. Employee-owned Parsons Brinckerhoff operates about 200 offices worldwide.

EXECUTIVES

Chairman: Morris Levy
President and CEO: Thomas J. (Tom) O'Neill
EVP and CFO: Richard A. Schrader
EVP and Director Corporate Development: Michael I. Schneider
CIO: William G. Reddan
Director Human Resources: John J. Ryan
Director Public Relations: Thomas W. (Tom) Malcolm
Auditors: Ernst & Young

LOCATIONS

HQ: Parsons Brinckerhoff, Inc.
1 Penn Plaza, New York, NY 10119
Phone: 212-465-5000 **Fax:** 212-465-5096
Web: www.pbworld.com

PRODUCTS/OPERATIONS

Selected Subsidiaries

Company 39 (visual communications and information technology)
Parsons Brinckerhoff Australia Pty Limited (formerly PPK Environment & Infrastructure Pty Ltd; transport and environmental services in Asia and Australia)
Parsons Brinckerhoff Limited (engineering services for infrastructure projects)
Parsons Brinckerhoff Quade & Douglas, Inc.
PB Aviation, Inc.
PB Buildings, Inc.
PB Constructors Inc.
PB Farradyne Inc. (transportation systems design)
PB Telecommunications, Inc.
PBConsult Inc. (management consulting services)

COMPETITORS

AECOM
BE&K
Black & Veatch
CH2M HILL
Granite Construction
HNTB
Jacobs Engineering
Louis Berger
Parsons
Skidmore Owings
STS Consultants
STV
Tutor-Saliba
URS
Washington Group

HISTORICAL FINANCIALS

Company Type: Private

Income Statement FYE: October 31

	REVENUE ($ mil.)	NET INCOME ($ mil.)	NET PROFIT MARGIN	EMPLOYEES
10/02	1,350	—	—	9,294
10/01	1,193	—	—	9,289
10/00	1,083	—	—	8,588
10/99	945	—	—	7,700
10/98	760	—	—	7,000
10/97	613	—	—	5,320
10/96	541	—	—	5,024
10/95	493	—	—	4,834
10/94	470	—	—	4,800
10/93	393	—	—	3,700
Annual Growth	14.7%	—	—	10.8%

Revenue History

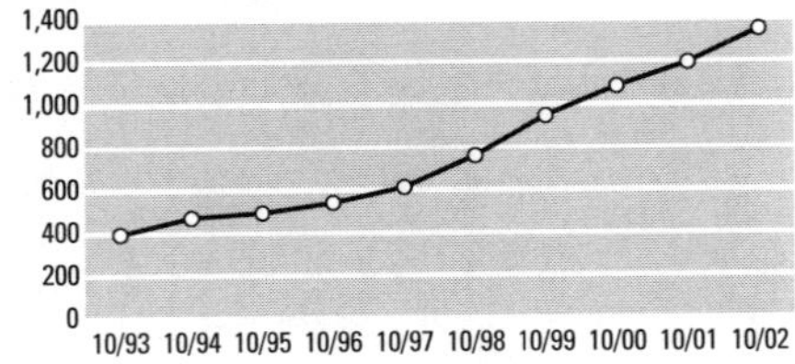

Parsons Corporation

Almost evangelically, Parsons carries its message — and its engineering, procurement, and construction management services — worldwide. The company provides design, planning, and construction management through four main operating groups: advanced technologies, commercial technology, infrastructure and technology, and transportation. Among its many projects, Parsons has designed power plants; built dams, resorts, and shopping centers; and provided environmental services such as the cleanup of hazardous nuclear wastes. Parsons has also added improvements to airports and rail systems, bridges, and highways. Customers of the employee-owned company include government agencies and private industries.

The company, which is owned by its employees, has diversified in order to compete in every major region of the world. It has even provided vehicle emissions and inspections as part of its advanced technologies offerings. Through its commercial technology group it provides services to a broad range of communications, industrial, and technology customers, such as telecom carriers, equipment manufacturers, state and federal government agencies, pharmaceutical firms, defense contractors, and transportation agencies.

Among Parsons' projects has been its participation since 1998 in the US Army's programs for alternative technologies for chemical weapons disposal. The company established the Parsons Fabrication Facility in Pasco, Washington, to test process systems for chemical weapon and bulk agent disposal. The events of September 11, 2001, prompted the US Army to accelerate the destruction of its chemical weapons, and Parsons' Newport, Indiana, chemical agent disposal facility has been developing a plan for speedy neutralization of the weapons. Parsons has also provided engineering management support for the construction of the Russian Chemical Weapons Destruction Complex.

Parsons has been developing its security services and has been selected to a team of companies that will be providing homeland security services at the Ports of New Jersey and New York to track containers.

Another project is the first major suspension bridge to be built in the US in more than 35 years. Parsons, which has been involved in the design and construction of more than 20 recent suspension bridges, is providing final design and engineering support during construction for the Carquinez Bridge near San Francisco.

HISTORY

Ralph Parsons, the son of a Long Island fisherman, was born in 1896. At age 13 he started his first business venture, a garage and machine shop, which he operated with his brother. After a stint in the US Navy, Parsons joined Bechtel as an aeronautical engineer. The company changed its name to Bechtel-McCone-Parsons Corporation in 1938. However, Parsons later sold his shares in that company and left in 1944 to start his own design and engineering firm, the Ralph M. Parsons Co., after splitting with partner John McCone (who later headed the CIA).

Parsons Co. expanded into the chemical and petroleum industries in the early 1950s. During that decade it oversaw the building of several natural gas and petroleum refineries overseas, including the world's largest, in Lacq, France.

In the early 1960s the company began working in Kuwait, which later proved to be one of its biggest markets. By 1969 Parsons had built oil refineries for all of the major oil companies, designed launch sites for US missiles, and constructed some of the largest mines in the world. In 1969 the company went public. With annual sales of about $300 million, it ranked second only to Bechtel in the design and engineering field. Ralph Parsons died in 1974.

The company built oil and gas treatment and production plants in Alaska in the 1970s and reorganized itself into The Parsons Corporation and RMP International in 1978. It went private in 1984 as The Parsons Corporation, taking advantage of a new tax law that favored corporations with employee stock ownership plans (ESOPs). Not all employees were happy, though. Several groups sued, maintaining that the plan disproportionately benefited executives, and that the buyout left the ESOP with all of the debt but no decision-making power. A Labor Department investigation later exonerated Parsons executives.

Parsons had just finished work on a power plant in Kuwait when Iraq invaded in 1990. Several employees were detained by the Iraqis but were released shortly before the Persian Gulf War. Two years later the company returned to Kuwait to rebuild some of the country's demolished infrastructure.

James McNulty, who had led the company's infrastructure and technology group, replaced Leonard Pieroni as CEO in 1996 after Pieroni died in the Bosnia plane crash that also claimed the life of US Secretary of Commerce Ronald Brown. Later that year a Parsons-led consortium won a $164.5 million contract for infrastructure projects in Bosnia.

Parsons restructured in 1997 to focus on energy, transportation, and infrastructure projects. The next year Parsons was chosen to manage construction of a $5 billion refinery in Bahrain, a $1.4 billion gas plant in Saudi Arabia, and a $1 billion polyethylene project in Abu Dhabi.

Parsons partnered with TRW in 2000 to create TRW Parsons Management & Operations to bid on the DOE's Yucca Mountain site in Nevada, a potential repository for the US's high-level radioactive waste and spent nuclear fuel. It also was awarded a three-year contract to help rebuild the war-torn Serbian province of Kosovo and the next year was awarded a similar contract for Bosnia-Herzegovina.

In 2001 the company won a US Federal Aviation Agency contract to upgrade air traffic control towers and other equipment and systems. That year the company's joint venture with construction giant Fluor was awarded a contract to design and engineering work for the first offshore oil field in Kazakhstan.

The next year Parsons won a contract from Dallas Area Rapid Transit (DART) to provide systems engineering and construction management services for the second phase of the buildout for the light-rail system, the largest expansion of its kind in North America. In 2003 it also won a contract for final design and construction management of the first light-rail system in Charlotte, North Carolina.

EXECUTIVES

Chairman and CEO: James F. (Jim) McNulty
President and COO: Frank A. DeMartino
EVP and CFO: Curtis A. Bower
SVP and General Counsel: Gary L. Stone
SVP, Government Relations: James E. Thrash
VP, Human Resources: David R. Goodrich
VP and General Manager, Asset Management: Ronald L. (Ron) Freeland
President, Parsons Advanced Technologies: Clifford E. Eby
President, Parson Commercial Technology: Charles L. (Chuck) Harrington
President, Parsons Energy and Chemicals Group: William E. Hall
President, Parsons Infrastructure and Technology Group: John A. (Jack) Scott
President, Parsons Transportation: James R. (Jim) Shappell
President, Parsons Water and Infrastructure Inc. (PWI): David L. Backus
SVP, Parsons Infrastructure and Technology Group: Milton Hunter
SVP and Manager, Bridge and Tunnel Division: Craig Finley Jr.
SVP and Manager, Rail/Transit Division: James Rollings
VP, Parsons Infrastructure & Technology Group, Energy Sector, SDS Division: Willie Clark
VP, Parsons Transportation: Nicholas C. LaRocco Jr.
Manager, Project Development Division (Transportation Markets): Brigid Hynes-Cherin
VP Corporate Relations: Erin Kuhlman
Director Business Development, Bridge & Tunnel Division: T. A. (TAG) Goodwin
Director Business Development, Energy Sector, Systems, Defense, and Security Division: Karen L. Kimball

LOCATIONS

HQ: 100 W. Walnut St., Pasadena, CA 91124
Phone: 626-440-2000 **Fax:** 626-440-2630
Web: www.parsons.com

Parsons Corporation provides heavy construction services in all states in the US and 80 other countries in Africa, Europe, Latin America, the Middle East, and Southeast Asia.

PRODUCTS/OPERATIONS

Selected Markets and Services

Parsons Advanced Technologies Group
Call centers
Criminal justice
Energy market data
Environmental data management
Revenue collection and management systems
Transportation data management
Vehicle inspection and compliance

Parsons Commercial Technology Group
Cable and component assembly
Equipment testing and system commissioning
Network planning and installation
Physical plants
Procurement, planning, and logistics
Project management
Remediation
Wireless and wireline network management systems

Parsons Infrastructure and Technology Group
Commercial and institutional facilities
Entertainment
Infrastructure
Mobile source air quality
Water resources

Parsons Transportation Group
Aviation
Bridges
Highways
Railroads
Systems Engineering
Tunneling
Urban transport

COMPETITORS

ABB
AECOM
BE&K
Bechtel
Black & Veatch
Bouygues
Day & Zimmermann
Fluor
Foster Wheeler
Gilbane
Granite Construction
Halliburton
Hyundai Engineering and Construction
Jacobs Engineering
Lend Lease
Louis Berger
M. A. Mortenson
Michael Baker
Peter Kiewit Sons'
Stone & Webster
TIC Holdings
Turner Corporation
Tutor-Saliba
URS
Washington Group

HISTORICAL FINANCIALS

Company Type: Private

Income Statement FYE: December 31

	REVENUE ($ mil.)	NET INCOME ($ mil.)	NET PROFIT MARGIN	EMPLOYEES
12/02	2,400	—	—	9,100
12/01	1,500	—	—	9,500
12/00	2,400	—	—	13,500
12/99	1,800	—	—	11,000
12/98	1,600	—	—	11,000
12/97	1,263	—	—	10,400
12/96	1,600	—	—	10,000
12/95	1,467	—	—	10,600
12/94	1,597	—	—	9,500
12/93	1,547	—	—	10,000
Annual Growth	5.0%	—	—	(1.0%)

Revenue History

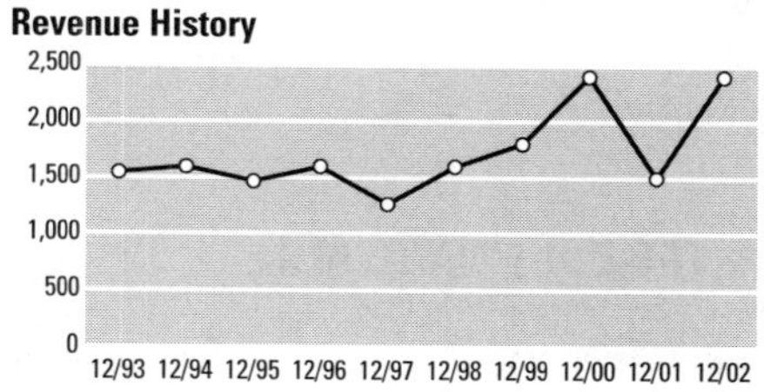

Partners HealthCare

Partners HealthCare System runs Massachusetts' biggest hospital group. Formed in 1994 by Brigham and Women's Hospital and Massachusetts General Hospital, the not-for-profit organization offers primary and specialist care, acute-care hospitals, and other services. Affiliated institutions include the Harvard Medical

School, Dana-Farber/Partners CancerCare (a collaboration between the Dana-Farber Cancer Institute and Partners hospitals), and Partners Community HealthCare (a physician network encompassing more than 1,000 practitioners). The organization also sponsors research programs and community health outreach programs.

EXECUTIVES

Chairman: John M. Connors
President and CEO: Samuel O. Thier, age 65
CFO: Peter Markel
VP Human Resources: Dennis Colling
Secretary and General Counsel: Ernest M. Haddad

LOCATIONS

HQ: Partners HealthCare System, Inc.
800 Boylston St., Ste. 1150, Boston, MA 02199
Phone: 617-278-1000 **Fax:** 617-278-1049
Web: www.partners.org

PRODUCTS/OPERATIONS

Selected Member Institutions

Brigham and Women's Hospital
Brigham and Women's/Faulkner Hospital
Dana-Farber/Partners CancerCare
Massachusetts General Hospital
McLean Hospital
MGH Institute of Health Professions (graduate school)
Newton-Wellesley Hospital
North Shore Medical Center
Charter Professional Services
North Shore Children's Hospital
Salem Hospital
Shaughnessy-Kaplan Rehabilitation Hospital
Union Hospital
Visiting Nurse Association of Greater Salem
Partners Community HealthCare, Inc.
Cambridge Hospital
Emerson Hospital
Lawrence Memorial Hospital
Melrose-Wakefield Hospital
Spaulding Rehabilitation Hospital

COMPETITORS

Baystate Health Systems
CareGroup
HCA
Tenet Healthcare

HISTORICAL FINANCIALS

Company Type: Not-for-profit

Income Statement FYE: September 30

	REVENUE ($ mil.)	NET INCOME ($ mil.)	NET PROFIT MARGIN	EMPLOYEES
9/02	4,218	56	1.3%	30,000
9/01	3,773	32	0.8%	30,000
9/00	3,317	123	3.7%	30,000
9/99	2,873	28	1.0%	20,000
9/98	2,434	54	2.2%	19,407
9/97	2,209	90	4.1%	19,132
9/96	2,107	—	—	24,900
9/95	1,773	—	—	24,878
9/94	1,664	—	—	—
Annual Growth	12.3%	(9.2%)	—	2.7%

2002 Year-End Financials

Debt ratio: 38.9%
Return on equity: 2.0%
Cash ($ mil.): 198
Current ratio: 2.56
Long-term debt ($ mil.): 1,075

Net Income History

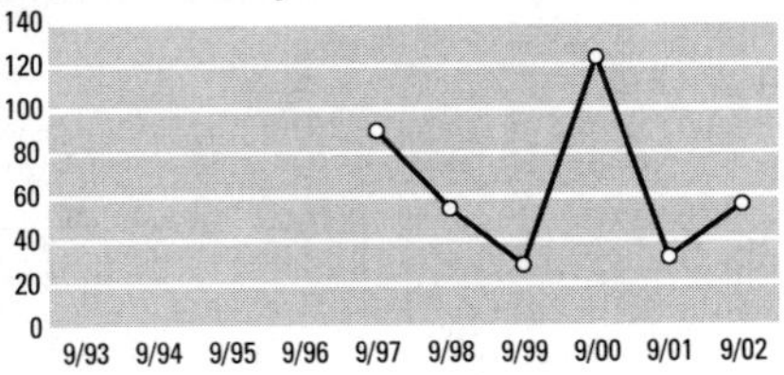

Paul, Hastings, Janofsky & Walker LLP

Got a discrimination problem? Paul, Hastings, Janofsky & Walker may suit your needs. The law firm has built a solid reputation in employment law. Paul Grossman, a partner specializing in employment law, co-authored *Employment Discrimination Law* (the official treatise of the American Bar Association). Clients such as UPS and Hughes Aircraft have turned to Paul, Hasting for their expertise in the field. Real estate also is an area of strength for the firm. Other practice areas include business law, litigation, and tax. Founded in 1951, Paul, Hastings has seven offices in the US and four in Europe and Asia.

EXECUTIVES

Chairman: Seth Zachary
Managing Partner: Greg M. Nitzkowski
CFO: Timothy (Tim) Wright
CIO: Mary Odson
Human Resources Officer: Jeanne Gervin

LOCATIONS

HQ: 515 S. Flower St., 25th Fl., Los Angeles, CA 90071
Phone: 213-683-6000 **Fax:** 213-627-0705
Web: www.paulhastings.com

Paul, Hastings, Janofsky & Walker has offices in Atlanta; Costa Mesa, Los Angeles, and San Francisco, California; Stamford, Connecticut; and Washington, DC. It also has offices in Beijing, Hong Kong, London, and Tokyo.

PRODUCTS/OPERATIONS

Selected Practice Areas

Business law
Employment law
Litigation
Real Estate
Tax

COMPETITORS

Gibson, Dunn & Crutcher
Latham & Watkins
Littler Mendelson
O'Melveny & Myers
Orrick, Herrington

HISTORICAL FINANCIALS

Company Type: Partnership

Income Statement FYE: January 31

	REVENUE ($ mil.)	NET INCOME ($ mil.)	NET PROFIT MARGIN	EMPLOYEES
1/03	488	—	—	—
1/02	456	—	—	—
1/01	389	—	—	—
1/00	286	—	—	1,500
1/99	267	—	—	1,500
1/98	219	—	—	1,260
1/97	179	—	—	1,055
1/96	164	—	—	1,100
1/95	157	—	—	1,100
1/94	145	—	—	1,000
Annual Growth	14.5%	—	—	7.0%

Revenue History

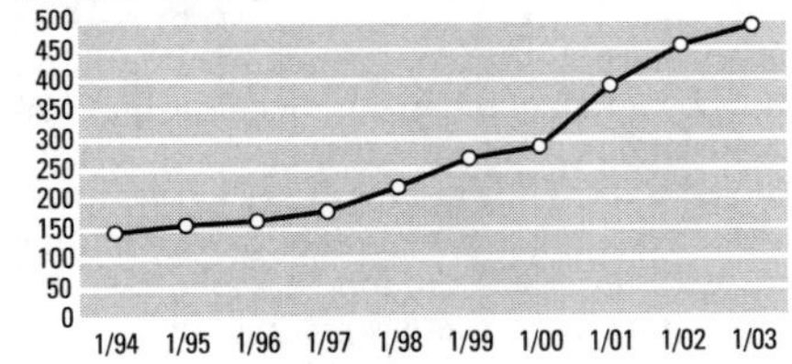

P.C. Richard & Son

P.C. Richard & Son aims to short out Circuit City. Founded in 1909 by Dutch immigrant milkman and jack-of-all-trades Peter Christiään Richard, the family-owned company has more than 40 stores in the New York City metropolitan area. Once a hardware store, P.C. Richard now gets about half of its sales from appliances (microwaves, vacuum cleaners), and it also sells home electronics (DVD players, TVs) and computers. The firm is operated by fourth-generation Richard family members. P.C. Richard attempted to go public in 1993 but withdrew its offering after a tepid response. In 2003 the company acquired the name, trademark, and customer lists of bankrupt electronics chain Nobody Beats The Wiz.

EXECUTIVES

Chairman: Alfred J. Richard
President and CEO: Gary Richard
EVP: Peter Richard Sr.
VP and CFO: Tom Pohmer
VP, Merchandising and Operations: Gregg Richard
CTO: Chuck Fichtner
Director, Advertising: Alan Meschkow
Director, Human Resources: Bonni Rondinello

LOCATIONS

HQ: 150 Price Pkwy., Farmingdale, NY 11735
Phone: 631-843-4300 **Fax:** 631-843-4309
Web: www.pcrichard.com

COMPETITORS

Best Buy
Circuit City Stores
Harvey Electronics
Home Depot
J & R Electronics
Lowe's
REX Stores
Sears
Wal-Mart

HISTORICAL FINANCIALS

Company Type: Private

Income Statement FYE: January 31

	ESTIMATED REVENUE ($ mil.)	NET INCOME ($ mil.)	NET PROFIT MARGIN	EMPLOYEES
1/03	993	—	—	2,200
1/02	925	—	—	2,134
1/01	880	—	—	2,173
1/00	740	—	—	2,073
1/99	625	—	—	2,000
1/98	520	—	—	1,700
1/97	515	—	—	1,500
1/96	425	—	—	1,500
1/95	400	—	—	1,500
1/94	400	—	—	1,500
Annual Growth	10.6%	—	—	4.3%

Revenue History

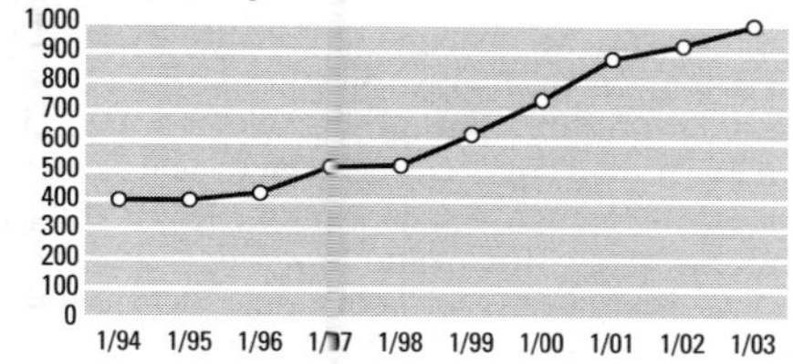

PeaceHealth

PeaceHealth serves residents in Alaska, Washington, and northern Oregon. The health system includes six acute care hospitals with a total of some 900 beds, as well as physician practices, community health clinics, chemical dependency rehabilitation clinics, and other outpatient care facilities and services.

EXECUTIVES

President and CEO: John Hayward
SVP of Organizational Development and COO: Judy Hodgson
SVP of Healthcare Improvement and CIO: John Haughom
SVP of Healthcare Improvement and CIO: Jim Scott
SVP of Business Development and CFO: H.W. (Skip) Kriz
SVP, Legal Services: Stuart Hennessey

LOCATIONS

HQ: 15325 SE 30th Pl., Ste. 300, Bellevue, WA 98007
Phone: 425-747-1711 **Fax:** 425-649-3825
Web: www.peacehealth.org

HISTORICAL FINANCIALS

Company Type: Not-for-profit

Income Statement FYE: June 30

	REVENUE ($ mil.)	NET INCOME ($ mil.)	NET PROFIT MARGIN	EMPLOYEES
6/02	769	—	—	6,230

Peerless Importers, Inc.

Peerless Importers has some of the most beloved liquid assets around. The company, founded in 1943, distributes wine and spirits in New York and Connecticut. Its spirits catalog includes blends, brandy and cognac, cordials and liqueurs (including Baileys Irish Cream), gin, rum, scotch (including J&B), and vodka. Wines are imported from Australia, Chile, and Western Europe. Unfortunately, Peerless Importers does have peers and has, in the past, lost business from liquor giants Diageo and Bacardi Limited to New York rivals like Charmer Industries. The Magliocco family (through its Quaker Equities holding company) owns and operates Peerless Importers and its Johnny Barton subsidiary.

EXECUTIVES

Chairman: John T. Magliocco
President and CEO: Nino Magliocco
VP: Joseph Magliocco
Controller: Mario Gottesmann
Manager, Human Resources: Debbie Andruk

LOCATIONS

HQ: 16 Bridgewater St., Brooklyn, NY 11222
Phone: 718-383-5500 **Fax:** 718-389-5708
Web: www.peerimp.com

COMPETITORS

Allied Domecq
Bacardi
Brown-Forman
Charmer Industries
Constellation Brands
Diageo
Gallo
Johnson Brothers
LVMH

HISTORICAL FINANCIALS

Company Type: Private

Income Statement FYE: December 31

	REVENUE ($ mil.)	NET INCOME ($ mil.)	NET PROFIT MARGIN	EMPLOYEES
12/01	710	—	—	1,200
12/00	690	—	—	1,200
12/99	660	—	—	1,200
12/98	620	—	—	1,200
12/97	605	—	—	1,200
12/96	590	—	—	1,200
12/95	635	—	—	1,400
12/94	585	—	—	1,200
12/93	535	—	—	1,200
Annual Growth	3.6%	—	—	0.0%

Revenue History

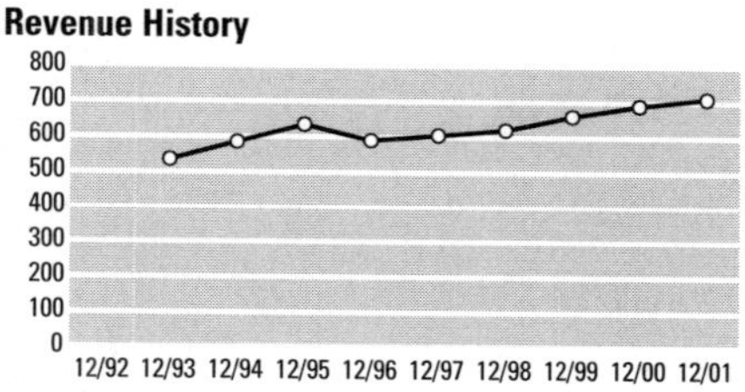

Pella Corporation

Window and door maker Pella got out of a jamb by offering its products through retailers. Originally Pella focused on upscale homeowners, builders, and designers, marketing its products through a network of distribution centers and high-end Pella Window Stores retail outlets. The company has expanded its market, allowing do-it-yourselfers to buy its ProLine windows and doors through building supply stores. Pella's products include sliding French and contemporary doors and awning, clad casement, and bay windows. Pella was founded in 1925 as Rolscreen Company (after its first product, a roll-up window screen). The descendants of founder Pete Kuyper own the company.

Pella's plan for growth includes expanding its storm door, entry systems, and window product offerings. The company unveiled its Impervia window and door product line, manufactured from its exclusive Duracast five-layer fiberglass composite material, at the International Builders' Show in January 2003. The material is stated to be nine times stronger than vinyl and twice as strong as aluminum in tensile strength tests. The product line includes single-hung, sliding, and fixed window units and is expected to be available in certain southern and western markets in the US in 2003, expanding into other regions later the next year.

In 2003 Pella was distinguished by *FORTUNE* magazine as one of the "100 Best Companies to Work For."

EXECUTIVES

President and CEO: Mel Haught
SVP, CFO, and Secretary: A. Jacqueline (Jackie) Dout, age 48
SVP Finance: Herbert Liennenbrugger
SVP Sales and Marketing: Chris Simpson
VP Human Resources: Karin Peterson
Corporate Public Relations: Kathy Krafka Harkema
Director of Sales and Marketing, Advanced Materials Division: Duane Putz

LOCATIONS

HQ: 102 Main St., Pella, IA 50219
Phone: 641-628-1000 **Fax:** 641-628-6070
Web: www.pella.com

Pella has manufacturing plants in Carroll, Pella, Shenandoah, Sioux City, and Story City, Iowa, and in Gettysburg, Pennsylvania.

PRODUCTS/OPERATIONS

Selected Products

Doors
In-swing French
Out-swing French
Sliding contemporary
Sliding French

Windows
Awning
Bow/bay
Casement
Circlehead
Clad frame
Cornerview
Double-hung
Replacement
Single-hung

COMPETITORS

Andersen Corporation
Atrium
Bocenor
International Aluminum
JELD-WEN
Marshfield DoorSystems
Nortek
Pacesetter
Sierra Pacific Industries
Simonton Windows
Thermal Industries
Therma-Tru
ThermoView Industries
Tomkins

HISTORICAL FINANCIALS

Company Type: Private

Income Statement FYE: November 30

	ESTIMATED REVENUE ($ mil.)	NET INCOME ($ mil.)	NET PROFIT MARGIN	EMPLOYEES
11/02	900	—	—	6,945
11/01	900	—	—	6,800
11/00	910	—	—	6,300
11/99	900	—	—	6,755
11/98	600	—	—	6,000
11/97	600	—	—	4,500
11/96	475	—	—	3,500
11/95	450	—	—	3,500
11/94	425	—	—	3,126
11/93	400	—	—	—
Annual Growth	9.4%	—	—	10.5%

Revenue History

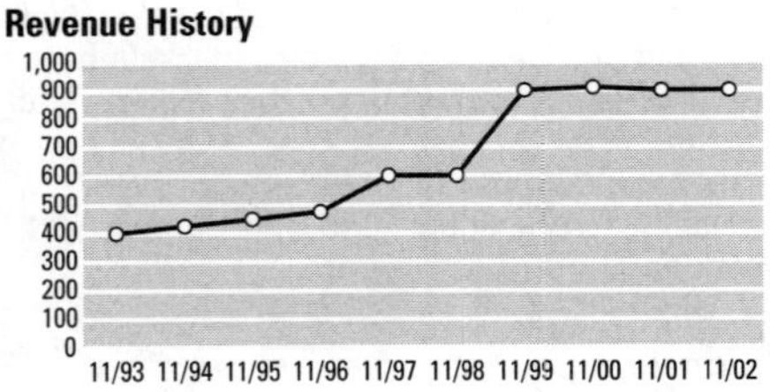

Penn Mutual Life Insurance

Founded in 1847, Penn Mutual Life Insurance offers life insurance, annuities, and investment products. The company has five main subsidiaries, including Penn Insurance and Annuity and brokerages Janney Montgomery Scott and Hornor, Townsend & Kent. Penn sells its products to high-net-worth individuals, professionals, and small businesses. Products include term, whole life, universal life, variable universal life, and disability income insurance policies, as well as a full range of deferred and immediate annuity products. The company also provides trust services and asset management to individuals and institutions.

EXECUTIVES

Chairman and CEO: Robert E. Chappell Jr., age 65
President, COO, and Director: Daniel J. Toran
EVP and CFO: Nancy S. Brodie
EVP and Chief Marketing Officer: Larry L. Mast
EVP and Chief Investment Officer: Peter M. Sherman
SVP, Systems and Service: John M. Albanese
SVP, Human Resources: Michael A. Biondolillo
SVP, Market Conduct and General Auditor: Nina M. Mulrooney
SVP, Independence Financial Network: Bill D. Fife
VP, Marketing Communications: Patricia Beauchamp

LOCATIONS

HQ: Penn Mutual Life Insurance Co.
600 Dresher Rd., Horsham, PA 19044
Phone: 215-956-8000 **Fax:** 215-956-8347
Web: www.pennmutual.com

Penn Mutual Life Insurance operates throughout the US.

PRODUCTS/OPERATIONS

Subsidiaries
Hornor, Townsend & Kent, Inc. (NASD broker/dealer)
Independence Capital Management, Inc. (asset management)
Janney Montgomery Scott LLC (stock brokerage)
The Penn Insurance and Annuity Company (life insurance)
The Pennsylvania Trust Company (trusts and estates)

COMPETITORS

Aetna
American National Insurance
AXA Financial
CIGNA
The Hartford
John Hancock Financial Services
MassMutual
MetLife
MONY
Nationwide Provident
New York Life
Pacific Mutual
Prudential
Union Central

HISTORICAL FINANCIALS

Company Type: Mutual company

Income Statement FYE: December 31

	ASSETS ($ mil.)	NET INCOME ($ mil.)	INCOME AS % OF ASSETS	EMPLOYEES
12/02	11,335	73	0.6%	1,100
12/01	10,833	97	0.9%	1,100
12/00	10,708	139	1.3%	950
12/99	10,583	80	0.8%	850
12/98	10,086	58	0.6%	850
12/97	9,367	73	0.8%	848
12/96	8,757	49	0.6%	800
Annual Growth	4.4%	7.0%	—	5.5%

2002 Year-End Financials

Equity as % of assets: 13.6%
Return on assets: 0.7%
Return on equity: 5.1%
Long-term debt ($ mil.): 5,190
Sales ($ mil.): 1,026

Net Income History

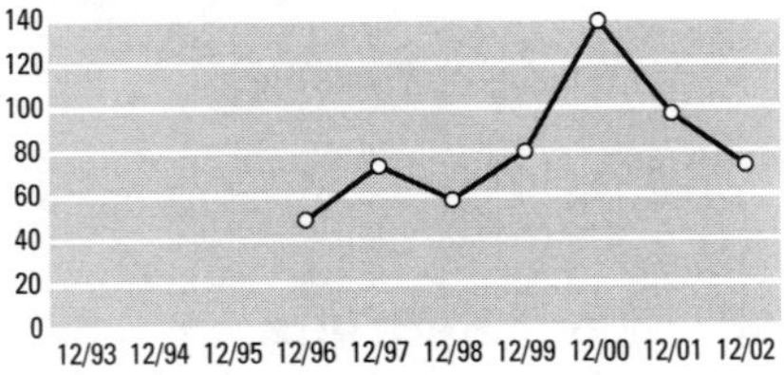

Penske Corporation

Penske, headed by race-car legend Roger Penske, seems to be on the right track as a diversified transportation firm. Closely held Penske has a 21% stake in Penske Truck Leasing Company, the US's #2 commercial truck rental operation, after Ryder, with more than 700 locations. GE Equipment Management owns the other 79%. Penske Automotive operates six car dealerships in California and owns 40% of publicly traded United Auto Group (UAG), which runs about 190 franchised dealerships in 19 states, Brazil, Puerto Rico, and the UK. Truck-Lite makes safety lights for boats, buses, cars, commercial trucks, construction equipment, and recreational vehicles. Roger Penske is the majority owner of the company.

The company's relationship with Kmart became strained after the retailer filed Chapter 11 early in 2002. Penske eventually responded by closing its 560-plus Penske Auto Centers at Kmart locations nationwide.

Penske just can't seem to resist that new car smell. The company has sold its racetrack interests and upped its stake in the struggling UAG. Roger Penske personally visited most of UAG's dealerships to help return the chain to profitablity. He now heads UAG. Penske has sold its 49% stake in heavy-duty truck engine maker Detroit Diesel to DaimlerChrysler. However, Penske plans to take joint control with DaimlerChrysler of a Detroit Diesel unit in Italy, VM Motori. Penske souped-up its Penske Truck Leasing unit with the purchase of Rollins Truck Leasing, which was the US's third-largest truck rental and leasing player.

HISTORY

As a teen Roger Penske earned money by repairing and reselling cars. At age 21 Penske entered his first auto race; he was running second when his car overheated. His winning ways, however, were soon apparent, and in 1961 *Sports Illustrated* named him race car driver of the year.

Nonetheless, in 1965 Penske went looking for a day job. With a $150,000 loan from his father, he bought a Chevrolet dealership in Philadelphia and retired from racing to avoid loading his balance sheet with steep life-insurance premiums for the CEO. Penske teamed with driver Mark Donohue in 1966 to form the Penske Racing Team. Donohue died in a crash in 1975, but team Penske continued.

In 1969 Penske started a regional truck-leasing business, incorporated under the name

Penske. The company established auto dealerships in Pennsylvania and Ohio in the early 1970s. In 1975 the company bought the Michigan International Speedway. Penske and fellow racing team owner Pat Patrick started the race-sponsoring organization Championship Auto Racing Teams (CART) in 1978.

In 1982 Penske's truck-leasing business formed a joint venture with rental company Hertz to form Hertz Penske Truck Leasing. Penske expanded its auto dealerships in the 1980s by acquiring dealerships in California, including Longo Toyota in 1985.

Racing legend Al Unser Sr. surprised Indy 500 watchers in 1987 by driving a car borrowed from an exhibition in a hotel lobby to a first-place finish for the Penske Racing Team.

In 1988 Penske bought 80% of GM's Detroit Diesel engine-making unit, which had a market share of only 3% and had lost some $600 million over the previous five years. Penske trimmed $70 million from the unit's budget by firing 440 salaried employees, streamlining manufacturing processes, and cutting administration expenses. Detroit Diesel's market share doubled in its first two years as a Penske unit. Also in 1988 Penske purchased Hertz's stake in Hertz Penske Truck Leasing, which it later combined with the truck-rental division of appliance maker General Electric to create Penske Truck Leasing.

By 1993 Detroit Diesel's market share had grown to more than 25%. That year the engine maker went public. Penske bought 860 Kmart auto centers for $112 million in 1995. The company's racing business, Penske Motorsports, went public in 1996, but Penske retained a 55% stake in the company. Also that year Penske bought Truck-Lite, Quaker State's automotive lighting unit.

Penske Truck Leasing formed Penske Logistics Europe in 1997 to offer information systems and other integrated logistics services on that continent. The next year it formed a logistics joint venture with Brazil-based Cotia Trading to serve US-based clients in the South American market, and Penske Logistics Europe opened a pan-European transport routing center in the Netherlands.

Penske sold its Penske Motorsports operations, which included racetracks in California, Michigan, North Carolina, and Pennsylvania, to International Speedway in 1999. The same year Penske invested about $83 million for a 38% stake in car retailer United Auto Group and Roger Penske became CEO of Penske. In 2000 the company sold its 48.6% stake in Detroit Diesel to DaimlerChrysler.

The following year Penske Corp. added three additional dealerships. Later in 2001 Penske Truck Leasing acquired Rollins Truck Leasing (then the US's third-largest player behind Ryder and Penske) for $754 million.

After Kmart filed Chapter 11 early in 2002, Penske expressed a "wait and see" strategy about the fate of its Penske Auto Centers business. Later that year Penske's Truck-Lite Industries bought Federal-Mogul's lighting business for $23 million.

Early in April 2002 Penske had waited long enough, and didn't like what it saw. It closed its 560-plus Penske Auto Centers at Kmart locations nationwide.

EXECUTIVES

Chairman and CEO: Roger S. Penske, age 67
President and Director: Robert H. Kurnick Jr., age 41
EVP, Administration: Paul F. Walters
EVP and CFO: J. Patrick Conroy
Director; Chairman, Truck-Lite, Inc.; Managing Partner, Birmingham Capital Partners: Richard J. Peters, age 55
VP, Human Resources: Randall W. Johnson

LOCATIONS

HQ: 3270 W. Big Beaver, Ste. 130, Detroit, MI 48084
Phone: 248-648-2000 **Fax:** 248-614-1127
Web: www.penske.com

Penske operations include Penske Automotive, with six dealerships in southern California; Penske Truck Leasing, with more than 700 rental locations in the US and Canada; and United Auto Group, with about 190 franchise dealerships in 19 states, Brazil, Puerto Rico, and the UK.

PRODUCTS/OPERATIONS

Selected Subsidiaries and Affiliates

Davco Technology (fuel filters and engine accessories)
Penske Automotive (retail auto sales)
Penske Truck Leasing Co. LP (21%, truck rental and leasing)
Truck-Lite (automotive lighting)
United Auto Group (40%, retail auto sales)

COMPETITORS

AMERCO
Asbury Automotive
AutoNation
DaimlerChrysler
Fiat
General Motors
Group 1 Automotive
Isuzu
Mack Trucks
Navistar
PACCAR
Prospect Motors
Ryder
Sonic Automotive
Tasha Inc.
Volvo

HISTORICAL FINANCIALS

Company Type: Private

Income Statement FYE: December 31

	REVENUE ($ mil.)	NET INCOME ($ mil.)	NET PROFIT MARGIN	EMPLOYEES
12/02	12,000	—	—	36,000
12/01	11,000	—	—	36,000
12/00	10,000	—	—	34,000
12/99	6,400	—	—	34,000
12/98	6,000	—	—	28,000
12/97	5,800	—	—	28,000
12/96	5,200	—	—	25,000
12/95	3,900	—	—	16,700
12/94	3,287	—	—	16,000
12/93	3,250	—	—	11,500
Annual Growth	15.6%	—	—	13.5%

Revenue History

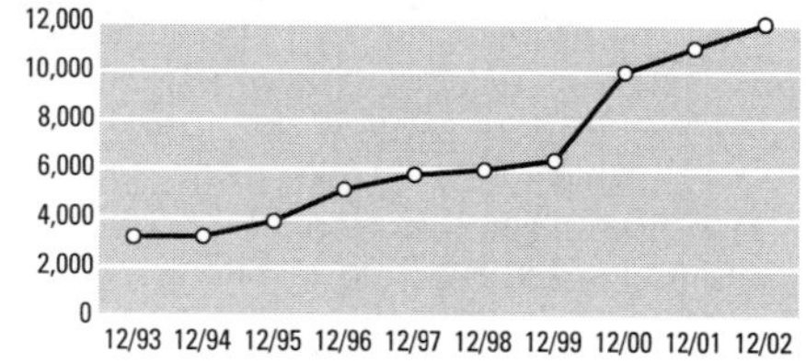

Pepper Construction

Although Pepper Construction Group sprinkles buildings across the US, it mainly spices up the construction landscape in the US Midwest. A top general contractor and construction manager in the region, Pepper constructs commercial buildings, hospitals, hotels, malls, and schools. Commercial, health care, and retail markets account for most of its sales. The firm outsources design and engineering tasks but can perform concrete, drywall, masonry, and millwork jobs; it offers hazardous waste services through Pepper Environmental Technologies. Recent projects include headquarters for Tellabs and Chicago Tribune Interactive. Founded by Stanley F. Pepper in Chicago in 1927, the company is owned and run by his family.

EXECUTIVES

Chairman: Richard S. Pepper
President and CEO: J. David Pepper
CFO: Joel D. Thomason
VP IT: Howie Piersma
EVP and General Counsel: Thomas M. O'Leary
SVP and Secretary; President, Pepper Environmental Technologies, Inc.: Richard H. Tilghman
SVP Human Resources: John Beasley
VP and Treasurer: Gordon B. Marshall
Director of Communications: Shannon Blagg

LOCATIONS

HQ: Pepper Construction Group, LLC
643 N. Orleans St., Chicago, IL 60610
Phone: 312-266-4700 **Fax:** 312-266-2792
Web: www.pepperconstruction.com

Pepper Construction Group has offices in Barrington, Chicago, and Tinley Park, Illinois; Austin and Houston, Texas; Indianapolis; and Irvine, California.

PRODUCTS/OPERATIONS

Selected Subsidiaries

Pepper Construction Company
Pepper Construction Company of Indiana, LLC
Pepper Construction Co. Pacific
Pepper-Lawson Construction, LP
Pepper Environmental Technologies, Inc.

COMPETITORS

AMEC Construction Management
Barton Malow
Bovis Lend Lease
Centex
Charles Pankow Builders
Clark Enterprises
Gilbane
Graycor
M. A. Mortenson
Power Construction
Turner Corporation
Walbridge Aldinger
Walsh Group

HISTORICAL FINANCIALS

Company Type: Private

Income Statement FYE: September 30

	REVENUE ($ mil.)	NET INCOME ($ mil.)	NET PROFIT MARGIN	EMPLOYEES
9/02	816	—	—	1,250
9/01	834	—	—	1,250
9/00	723	—	—	1,250
9/99	690	—	—	1,257
9/98	623	—	—	1,335
9/97	494	—	—	1,200
9/96	426	—	—	833
9/95	460	—	—	908
9/94	485	—	—	921
9/93	405	—	—	800
Annual Growth	8.1%	—	—	5.1%

Revenue History

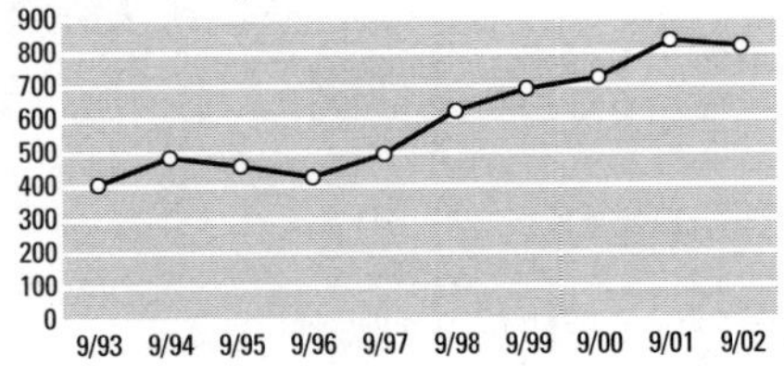

Perdue Farms Incorporated

James Perdue makes Big Bird nervous. His family's company is one of the largest in the US poultry market, selling 48 million pounds of distinctly yellow chicken products and nearly 4 million pounds of turkey products each week. Vertically integrated, Perdue Farms sees its birds from the egg to the supermarket meat case. Perdue is expanding its value-added chicken parts and food service products and has established a plant in China through a joint venture. It also processes grain and makes vegetable oils and pet food ingredients. Founded by Arthur Perdue (James' grandfather) in 1920, the company sells its products in the East, Midwest, and South, and it exports to more than 50 countries.

While the company breeds and hatches the eggs, it ships the chicks off to supervised contract growers, who then send back fully grown birds. The company processes grain to make its own feeds and vegetable oils, and turns poultry by-products into pet food ingredients. In addition, in a joint venture with AgriRecycle, it makes fertilizer from used chicken litter.

James Perdue, who — like his famous father, Frank, had before him — appears in its advertisements. Perdue produces its own breed of chicken, the skin of which is a distinct yellow color, resulting from a diet that includes marigold petals.

HISTORY

If asked which came first, the chickens or the eggs, the Perdue family will tell you the eggs did. Arthur Perdue, a railroad express worker, bought 23 layer hens in 1920 and started supplying the New York City market with eggs from a henhouse in his family's backyard in Salisbury, Maryland. His son Frank joined the business in 1939.

The Perdues sold broiling chickens to major processors, such as Swift and Armour, in the 1940s and pioneered chicken crossbreeding to develop new breeds. The family started contracting with farmers in the Salisbury area in 1950 to grow broilers for them. Frank became president of the company in 1952. The next year it began mixing its own feed.

Frank persuaded his father to borrow money to build a soybean mill in 1961. (Arthur had not willingly gone into debt in his previous 40-plus years in the poultry industry.) The soybean mill was part of Frank's plan to vertically integrate the company — with grain storage facilities, feed milling operations, soybean processing plants, mulch plants, hatcheries, and 600 contract chicken farmers — to counter the threat of processors buying chickens directly from farmers rather than through middlemen like the Perdues. To differentiate their products, the Perdue name was applied to packages on retail meat counters in 1968.

Two years later the company began a breeding and genetic research program. During the following years Frank transformed himself from country chicken salesman to media poultry pitchman when the company decided to use him as spokesperson in its print, radio, and TV ads. Catchy slogans ("It takes a tough man to make a tender chicken") combined with Frank's whiny voice and sincere face helped sales. As Perdue Farms expanded geographically into new eastern markets such as Philadelphia, Boston, and Baltimore, it acquired the broiler facilities of other processors.

In 1983 James Perdue, Frank's only son, joined the company as a management trainee. In 1984 Perdue added processors in Virginia and Indiana and introduced turkey products. Two years later it acquired Intertrade, a feed broker, and FoodCraft, a food equipment maker. However, after enjoying a rising demand for poultry by a health-conscious society in the 1970s and early 1980s, the company found its sales leveling off in the late 1980s. When North Carolina fined Perdue for unsafe working conditions in 1989, the company increased its emphasis on safety.

James, who had become chairman of the board in 1991, replaced his folksy father in 1994 as the company's spokesman in TV ads. In the early 1990s Perdue's management determined future sales growth lay in food service and international sales; therefore, the poultry company quietly began laying the groundwork to support these new markets.

Perdue launched its Cafe Perdue entrée meal kits in 1997. The following year it purchased food service poultry processor Gol-Pak and, through a joint venture, opened a poultry processing plant in Shanghai, China.

Settlements to chicken catchers and line workers in 2001 and 2002 cost the company over $12 million in back wages. Also in 2002 Perdue announced it would be shuttering a deboning plant purchased only three years earlier, and put its money-losing Italian entrée De Luca business (purchased in 1998) up for sale.

EXECUTIVES

Chairman, CEO, and CFO: James A. Perdue
President and COO: Robert (Bob) Turley
SVP of Retail, Sales, and Marketing: Steve Evans
SVP of Supply Chain Management: Larry Winslow
VP of Human Resources: Rob Heflin
President and General Manager, Specialty Foods: Randy Day
President and General Manager, Grain and Oilseed Division: Dick Willey
Director of Public Relations: Tita Cherrier
Director of Environmental Service: John Chlada

LOCATIONS

HQ: 31149 Old Ocean City Rd., Salisbury, MD 21804
Phone: 410-543-3000 **Fax:** 410-543-3292
Web: www.perdue.com

Perdue Farms has operations in Alabama, Connecticut, Delaware, Florida, Indiana, Kentucky, Maryland, New Jersey, North Carolina, Pennsylvania, South Carolina, Tennessee, Virginia, and West Virginia.

PRODUCTS/OPERATIONS

Selected Poultry Products and Brands

Fresh Poultry
Chicken parts (Prime Parts)
Cornish hens
Ground chicken
Roasters and turkeys (Oven Stuffer)
Seasoned chicken
Skinless, boneless poultry cuts (Fit 'N Easy)
Turkey burgers
Turkey sausage

Fully Cooked Poultry
Cutlets
Nuggets (Fun Shapes)
Rotisserie-style chicken (Tender Ready)
Tenders

Other Products
Pet food ingredients
Vegetable oils

Other Brands

Chef's Choice
Cookin' Good
Gol-pak
Shenandoah
Short Cuts

COMPETITORS

AJC International
Allen Family Foods
Cagle's
Cargill
ConAgra
Cooper Farms
Gold Kist
Hormel
Keystone Foods
Murphy-Brown
Pilgrim's Pride
Sanderson Farms
Townsends
Tyson Foods

HISTORICAL FINANCIALS

Company Type: Private

Income Statement FYE: March 31

	REVENUE ($ mil.)	NET INCOME ($ mil.)	NET PROFIT MARGIN	EMPLOYEES
3/02	2,700	—	—	20,000
3/01	2,700	—	—	19,500
3/00	2,501	—	—	19,500
3/99	2,515	—	—	20,500
3/98	2,200	—	—	18,000
3/97	2,200	—	—	18,000
3/96	2,100	—	—	19,000
3/95	1,700	—	—	18,600
3/94	1,600	—	—	18,600
3/93	1,300	—	—	13,300
Annual Growth	8.5%	—	—	4.6%

Revenue History

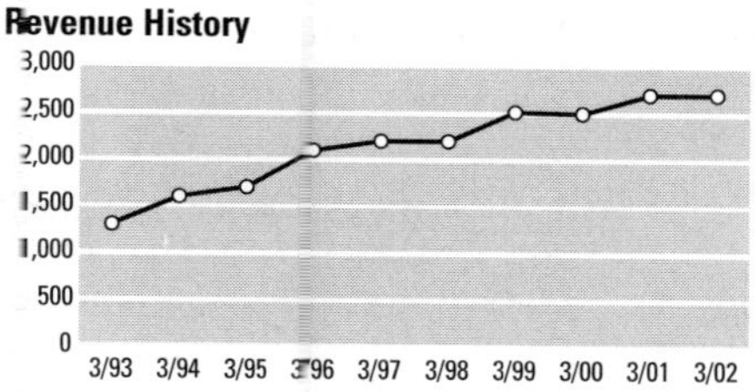

Peter Kiewit Sons', Inc.

By building everything from tunnels to high-rises, Peter Kiewit Sons' has become a heavyweight in the heavy construction industry. The employee-owned firm is one of the largest general contractors in the US, having projects in nearly 40 states, as well as in Canada and Puerto Rico. A transportation specialist, Kiewit builds bridges, highways, railroads, airports, and mass transit systems. Transportation contracts account for half of Kiewit's sales. It also works on projects such as commercial buildings, mining infrastructure, waste-disposal systems, and telecommunications infrastructure. The company is owned by current and former employees and Kiewit family members.

With most of its contracts dedicated to large-scale transportation projects, the company leads the US in highway construction projects, which have included work for the Winter Olympics in Salt Lake City and for Denver's interstate highway system. It ranks first in dollar volume for federal highway contracts.

The group also ranks highly in the hydropower, water supply, sanitary and storm sewer, and transmission line and cable construction markets. Kiewit specializes in design/build projects and often works through joint ventures. Public contracts account for nearly 65% of total revenues.

The construction business has the undivided attention of Kiewit these days. It has spun off its asphalt and ready-mix concrete business as Kiewit Materials and has created a unit to focus on construction for the offshore drilling industry. The company also continues to provide construction for telephone and data network operator Level 3 Communications, although it divested the telecom business in 1998.

HISTORY

Born to Dutch immigrants, Peter Kiewit and brother Andrew founded Kiewit Brothers, a brickyard, in 1884 in Omaha, Nebraska. By 1912 two of his sons worked at the yard, which was named Peter Kiewit & Sons. When Peter Kiewit died in 1914, his son Ralph took over, and the firm took the name Peter Kiewit Sons'. Another son, Peter, joined Ralph at the helm in 1924 after dropping out of Dartmouth and later took over.

During the Depression, Kiewit managed huge federal public works projects, and in the 1940s it focused on war-related emergency construction projects.

One of the firm's most difficult projects was top-secret Thule Air Force Base in Greenland, above the Arctic Circle. For more than two years 5,000 men worked around the clock, beginning in 1951; the site was in development for 15 years. In 1952 the company won a contract to build a $1.2 billion gas diffusion plant in Portsmouth, Ohio. It also became a contractor for the US interstate highway system (begun in 1956).

Peter Kiewit died in 1979, after stipulating that the largely employee-owned company should remain under employee control and that no one employee could own more than 10%. His 40% stake, when returned to the company, transformed many employees into millionaires. Walter Scott Jr., whose father had been the first graduate engineer to work for Kiewit, took charge. Scott made his mark by parlaying money from construction into successful investments.

When the construction industry slumped, Kiewit began looking for other investment opportunities, and in 1984 it acquired packaging company Continental Can Co. (selling off noncore insurance, energy, and timber assets). Continental was saddled with a 1983 class action lawsuit alleging that it had plotted to close plants and lay off workers before they were qualified for pensions. In 1991 Kiewit agreed to pay $415 million to settle the lawsuit. In the face of a consolidating packaging industry, the company sold Continental in the early 1990s.

In 1986 Kiewit loaned money to a business group to build a fiber-optic loop in Chicago; by 1987 it had launched MFS Communications to build local fiber loops in downtown districts. In 1992 Kiewit split its business into two pieces: the construction group, which was strictly employee-owned; and a diversified group, to which it added a controlling stake in phone and cable TV company C-TEC in 1993. That year Kiewit took MFS public; by 1995 it had sold all its shares, and the next year MFS was bought by telecom giant WorldCom.

In 1996 Kiewit assisted CalEnergy (now MidAmerican Energy) in a hostile $1.3 billion takeover of the UK's Northern Electric. Kiewit got stock in CalEnergy and a 30% stake in the UK electric company, all of which it sold to CalEnergy in 1998.

That year Kiewit spun off its telecom and computer services holdings into Level 3 Communications. Scott, who had been hospitalized the year before for a blood clot in his lung, stepped down as CEO, and Ken Stinson, CEO of Kiewit Construction Group, took over Peter Kiewit Sons'.

In 1999 Kiewit acquired a majority interest in Pacific Rock Products, a construction materials firm in Canada. Kiewit spun off its asphalt, concrete, and aggregates operations in 2000 as Kiewit Materials. Also that year the company created Kiewit Offshore Services to focus on construction for the offshore drilling industry. In 2001 the company acquired marine construction firm General Construction Company (GCC). The next year it expanded its offshore business further by buying a Canadian subsidiary from oil and gas equipment services company Friede Goldman Halter, which was trying to emerge from bankruptcy.

Kiewit made history in 2002 for the fastest completion of a project of its type when it completed the rebuilding of Webbers Falls I-40 Bridge in Oklahoma at the end of July. The bridge collapsed in May after being hit by a pair of barges, resulting in 14 fatalities.

EXECUTIVES

Chairman Emeritus: Walter Scott Jr., age 72
Chairman and CEO, Peter Kiewit Sons' and Kiewit Construction: Kenneth E. Stinson, age 60, $4,768,274 pay
President, COO, and Director: Bruce E. Grewcock, age 49, $1,015,000 pay
EVP and Director; EVP, Kiewit Pacific: Richard W. Colf, age 59, $1,215,000 pay
EVP and Director; EVP, Kiewit Pacific: Allan K. Kirkwood, age 59, $1,215,000 pay
EVP and Director: Douglas E. Patterson, age 52, $542,400 pay
VP, CFO, and Treasurer: Michael J. Piechoski, age 49
SVP, General Counsel, and Secretary: Tobin A. Schropp, age 40
VP, Human Resources and Administration: John B. Chapman, age 57
VP: Ben E. Muraskin, age 39
VP: Gerald S. Pfeffer, age 57
VP: Jerry C. Porter, age 59
VP: James E. Rowings, age 50
VP; Area Manager, Kiewit Pacific: Lawrence J. Cochran, age 47
Controller: Gregory D. Brokke, age 40
Auditors: KPMG LLP

LOCATIONS

HQ: Kiewit Plaza, Omaha, NE 68131
Phone: 402-342-2052 **Fax:** 402-271-2939
Web: www.kiewit.com

Peter Kiewit Sons' has 21 principal operating offices in North America.

PRODUCTS/OPERATIONS

Selected Subsidiaries

Ben Holt Company
Bentson Contracting Company
Bibb and Associates, Inc.
Bighorn Walnut, LLC
CMF Leasing Co.
GSC Contracting, Inc.
General Construction Company
Gilbert/CBE Indonesia L.L.C.
Gilbert Central Corp.
Gilbert Frontier, Inc.
Gilbert/Healy, L.P.
Gilbert Industrial Corporation
Gilbert Marine L.L.C.
Gilbert Network Services, L.P.
Gilbert Southern Corp.
Gilbert Texas Corp.
Gilbert Western Corp.
Global Surety & Insurance Co.
Guernsey Construction Company
Gulf Marine Fabricators, Inc.
K-G Leasing Company
K-G-W Leasing Company
KP Leasing Company
KT Mining, LP
KiEnergy, Inc.
Kiewit Alabama Mining Company
Kiewit Construction Company
Kiewit Construction Group Inc.
Kiewit Constructors Inc.
Kiewit Engineering Co.
Kiewit Engineering Canada Ltd.
Kiewit Financial Services B.V.
Kiewit/Holt Indonesia L.L.C.
Kiewit/Holt-Philippines, L.P.
Kiewit Industrial Co.
Kiewit Industrial Canada Ltd.
Kiewit International Inc.
Kiewit International Services Inc.
Kiewit International Services Ltd.
Kiewit Management Limited
Kiewit Mining Services Inc.
Kiewit Network Services Co.
Kiewit Offshore Services, Ltd.
Kiewit Pacific Co.
Kiewit Pipelines Ltd.
Kiewit Venezuela Inc.

Kiewit Western Co.
ME Holding Inc.
Mass. Electric Securities Corp., Inc.
Midwest Agencies, Inc.
Newsham Hybrids (USA), Inc.
PT Kiewit International
Peter Kiewit Sons Co. Ltd.
Seaworks, Inc.
Twin Mountain Construction Company
Twin Mountain Construction II Company
V.K. Mason Construction Ltd.
Walnut Creek Mining Company

COMPETITORS

ABB
Balfour Beatty Construction Inc.
Bechtel
Black & Veatch
Bovis Lend Lease
Fluor
Foster Wheeler
Granite Construction
Halliburton
ITOCHU
Jacobs Engineering
Parsons
Perini
Raytheon
Skanska USA Civil
Turner Corporation
Tutor-Saliba
Washington Group
Whiting-Turner
Williams Companies

HISTORICAL FINANCIALS

Company Type: Private

Income Statement FYE: Last Saturday in December

	REVENUE ($ mil.)	NET INCOME ($ mil.)	NET PROFIT MARGIN	EMPLOYEES
12/02	3,699	193	5.2%	15,000
12/01	3,871	175	4.5%	16,000
12/00	4,463	179	4.0%	11,146
12/99	4,013	165	4.1%	20,300
12/98	3,403	288	8.5%	16,200
12/97	2,764	155	5.6%	16,200
12/96	2,904	221	7.6%	14,000
12/95	2,902	244	8.4%	14,300
12/94	2,991	110	3.7%	14,000
12/93	2,179	261	12.0%	10,620
Annual Growth	6.1%	(3.3%)	—	3.9%

2002 Year-End Financials

Debt ratio: 2.4%
Return on equity: 21.1%
Cash ($ mil.): 275
Current ratio: 1.79
Long-term debt ($ mil.): 24

Net Income History

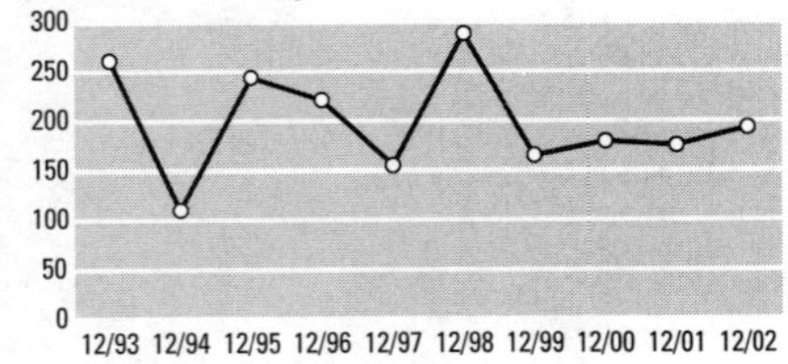

Petro Stopping Centers, L.P.

Petro Stopping Centers is the center of attention for truckers who need a petro stop. The firm operates some 60 truck stops (about a third of them franchised) in 31 states. Its truck stops sell Mobil-brand diesel fuel, gas, and travel merchandise such as food, toiletries, truck accessories, and electronics. (Fuel accounts for almost 75% of sales.) The centers also provide Petro:Lube facilities (preventive maintenance services), showers, laundry services, game rooms, and Iron Skillet restaurants (home-style cooking). The company is run by chairman and CEO Jack Cardwell, who founded it in 1975, and his son, COO Jim Cardwell. Volvo Petrol Holdings owns more than 50% of Petro Stopping Centers.

EXECUTIVES

Chairman and CEO: James A. (Jack) Cardwell Sr., age 70, $420,000 pay
COO and Director: James A. (Jim) Cardwell Jr., age 42, $247,115 pay
CFO, Treasurer, and Assistant Secretary: Edward Escudero, age 32
CIO: Richard Tisdale
VP, General Counsel, and Secretary: Nancy C. Santana, age 46, $218,845 pay
VP, Fuel Islands: Keith Kirkpatrick
VP, Iron Skillet: Bill Webbon
VP, Petro:Lube: David Latimer, age 44, $148,048 pay
Director of Human Resources: Walter Kalinowski
Auditors: KPMG LLP

LOCATIONS

HQ: 6080 Surety Dr., El Paso, TX 79905
Phone: 915-779-4711 **Fax:** 915-774-7382
Web: www.petrotruckstops.com

PRODUCTS/OPERATIONS

2002 Sales

	$ mil.	% of total
Fuel	684.9	74
Non-fuel	172.9	19
Restaurant	65.1	7
Total	**922.9**	**100**

COMPETITORS

Bowlin Travel Centers
ChevronTexaco
Exxon Mobil
FFP Marketing
Flying J
Love's Country Stores
Pilot
Rip Griffin Truck Service Center
TravelCenters of America
Valero Energy

HISTORICAL FINANCIALS

Company Type: Private

Income Statement FYE: December 31

	REVENUE ($ mil.)	NET INCOME ($ mil.)	NET PROFIT MARGIN	EMPLOYEES
12/02	923	7	0.8%	4,202
12/01	914	(14)	—	4,108
12/00	981	(5)	—	4,186
12/99	720	2	0.3%	4,208
12/98	637	(9)	—	3,902
12/97	686	(13)	—	3,691
12/96	637	(9)	—	3,529
12/95	533	4	0.7%	—
Annual Growth	8.2%	9.1%	—	3.0%

2002 Year-End Financials

Debt ratio: 655.1%
Return on equity: —
Cash ($ mil.): 8
Current ratio: 0.59
Long-term debt ($ mil.): 175

Net Income History

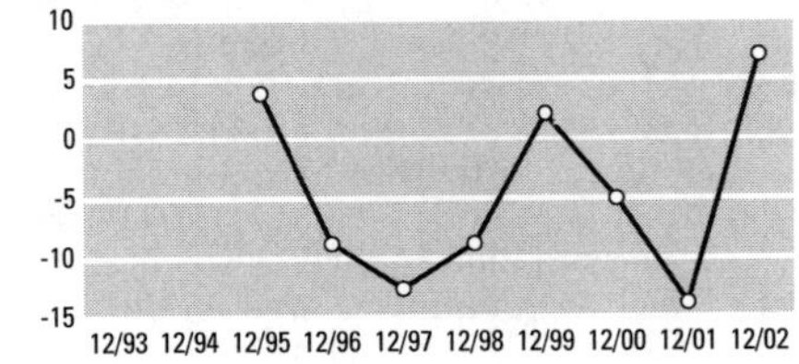

Pilot Corporation

Pilot offers a salve to those suffering from white-line fever. Catering to truckers and travelers alike, Pilot operates about 300 travel centers in 37 states (through a joint venture with Marathon Ashland Petroleum); each features one or more national food chains, such as Subway, Dairy Queen, Wendy's, and Taco Bell. Pilot features fuel islands large enough to service several 18-wheelers at a time and private showers for its customers. Pilot also operates about 70 convenience stores in Tennessee and Virginia. James Haslam II got Pilot off the ground in 1958 as a gas station that sold cigarettes and soft drinks; now his son, CEO James Haslam III, pilots the firm. The Haslam family owns the company.

In February 2003 Pilot Travel Centers LLC — a joint venture of Pilot Corporation and Marathon Ashland Petroleum — acquired 60 Williams TravelCenters in 15 states, primarily in the Midwest, Southeast, and Southwest. Pilot is rebranding the locations as Pilot Travel Centers, which will raise the store count to 295 locations in 37 states.

EXECUTIVES

Chairman: James A. Haslam II
CEO: James A. Haslam III, age 49
President: William E. Haslam, age 44
EVP Direct Sales and Development: Mark A. Hazelwood
VP Finance, CFO, and CIO: Jeffrey L. (Jeff) Cornish, age 51
VP Operations: Mark A. Rowan
Manager, Pilot University: Jaymi Damron

LOCATIONS

HQ: 5508 Lonas Rd., Knoxville, TN 37909
Phone: 865-588-7487 **Fax:** 865-450-2800
Web: www.pilotcorp.com

Pilot operates about 300 travel centers in 37 states through a joint venture with Marathon Ashland and about 70 convenience stores in Tennessee and Virginia.

PRODUCTS/OPERATIONS

Operations

Convenience stores (groceries, gas and diesel, and assorted merchandise)
Travel centers (groceries, showers, gas and diesel, restaurants, and assorted merchandise)

COMPETITORS

7-Eleven
ChevronTexaco
Exxon Mobil
FFP Marketing
Flying J
Love's Country Stores
Motiva Enterprises
Petro Stopping Centers
Rip Griffin Truck Service Center
Royal Dutch/Shell Group
Stuckey's
TravelCenters of America

HISTORICAL FINANCIALS

Company Type: Private

Income Statement FYE: December 31

	REVENUE ($ mil.)	NET INCOME ($ mil.)	NET PROFIT MARGIN	EMPLOYEES
12/01	1,700	—	—	7,200
12/00	1,768	—	—	7,209
12/99	1,312	—	—	7,800
12/98	2,000	—	—	7,000
12/97	1,388	—	—	5,724
12/96	1,265	—	—	5,363
12/95	1,257	—	—	3,854
12/94	1,010	—	—	3,803
12/93	599	—	—	2,664
Annual Growth	13.9%	—	—	13.2%

Revenue History

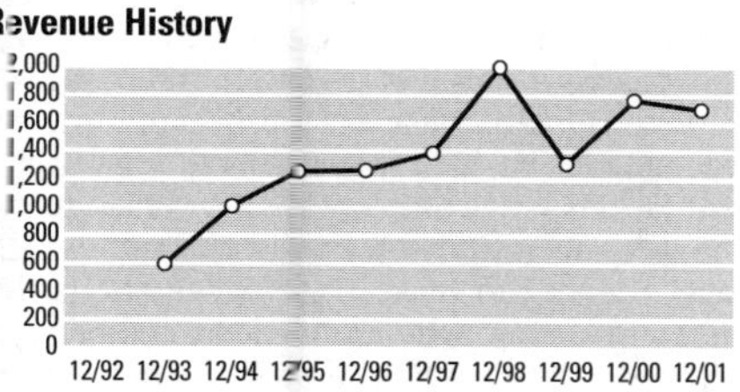

Plains Cotton Cooperative

Plainly speaking, the Plains Cotton Cooperative Association (PCCA) is one of the nation's largest cotton handlers. The farmer-owned marketing cooperative has about 26,000 members in Oklahoma, Kansas, and Texas. PCCA markets about 3 million bales of cotton each year through TELCOT, its computerized trading system that continually updates cotton prices, buyer data, and other information. The co-op has cotton warehouses in Texas and Oklahoma and denim mills in Texas (Levi Strauss is a major customer). The co-op was formed in 1953 to enable cotton farmers to obtain the most competitive price for their cotton.

EXECUTIVES

Chairman: Jackie Mull
President and CEO: Van May
VP of Administration and Human Resources: Jim Taylor
VP of Finance: Sam Hill
VP of Information Systems: Joe Tubb
VP, Marketing: David Stanford
VP, Marketing Fabric Sales: Jack Mathews
VP, Operations: Darryl Lindsey
Director of Communications: John Johnson
Personnel Manager: Lee Phenix
Auditors: Robinson Burdette Martin & Cowan, L.L.P.

LOCATIONS

HQ: Plains Cotton Cooperative Association
3301 E. 50th St., Lubbock, TX 79408
Phone: 806-763-8011 **Fax:** 806-762-7333
Web: www.pcca.com

COMPETITORS

Alabama Farmers Cooperatives
Avondale Incorporated
Burlington Industries
Calcot
Cargill
Cone Mills
Dan River
Dunavant Enterprises
Greenwood Mills
Parkdale Mills
Southwestern Irrigated Cotton
Staplcotn

HISTORICAL FINANCIALS

Company Type: Cooperative

Income Statement FYE: June 30

	REVENUE ($ mil.)	NET INCOME ($ mil.)	NET PROFIT MARGIN	EMPLOYEES
6/02	800	—	—	1,000
6/01	620	—	—	1,000
6/00	774	—	—	—
6/99	633	—	—	—
6/98	925	—	—	1,350
6/97	836	—	—	800
6/96	785	—	—	800
6/95	1,014	—	—	800
6/94	798	—	—	800
Annual Growth	0.0%	—	—	2.8%

Revenue History

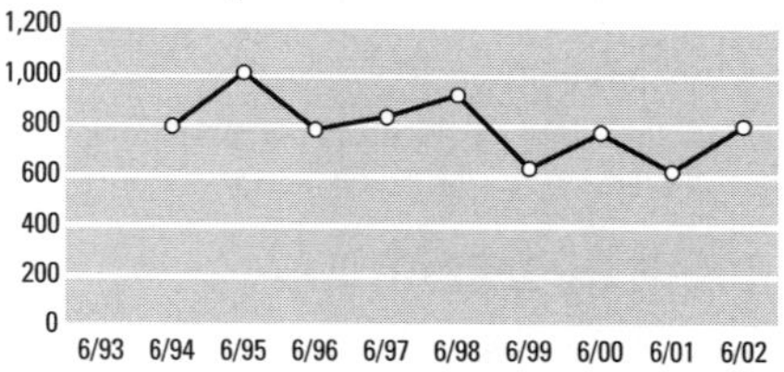

Planet Automotive

Expect a lot of iron, glass, and rubber on the surface of Planet Automotive Group. Formerly Potamkin Manhattan, the company coalesced from a network of auto dealerships owned by the Potamkin family. The company's 40-plus dealerships operate primarily in Florida, but also in California, Illinois, Iowa, Massachusetts, New York, Pennsylvania, and Texas. It has grown through acquisitions of new- and used-car dealerships. The company's dealerships also offer parts and service departments. The late Victor Potamkin opened his first dealership in 1946, and his two sons, Robert and Alan, now run the company.

EXECUTIVES

Co-Chairman and Co-CEO: Alan Potamkin
Co-Chairman and Co-CEO: Robert Potamkin
President and COO: Joe Herman
CFO: David Yusko
EVP, Mergers and Acquisitions: George McCabe
SVP, Field Operations: John Hawkins
SVP, Financial Operations: Joe Suitt
SVP, Staff Operations: Andy Pfeifer

LOCATIONS

HQ: Planet Automotive Group, Inc.
2333 Ponce De Leon Blvd., Ste. 600,
Coral Gables, FL 33134
Phone: 305-774-7690 **Fax:** 305-774-7697
Web: www.planetautomotive.com

COMPETITORS

AutoNation
Hendrick Automotive
Holman Enterprises
JM Family Enterprises
March/Hodge
Morse Operations
Pacifico
United Auto Group

HISTORICAL FINANCIALS

Company Type: Private

Income Statement FYE: December 31

	REVENUE ($ mil.)	NET INCOME ($ mil.)	NET PROFIT MARGIN	EMPLOYEES
12/01	1,411	—	—	1,600
12/00	1,350	—	—	1,600
12/99	1,306	—	—	1,600
12/98	1,300	—	—	1,800
12/97	1,200	—	—	2,000
12/96	1,218	—	—	2,360
12/95	1,290	—	—	2,500
12/94	1,400	—	—	—
12/93	1,185	—	—	—
12/92	850	—	—	—
Annual Growth	5.8%	—	—	(7.2%)

Revenue History

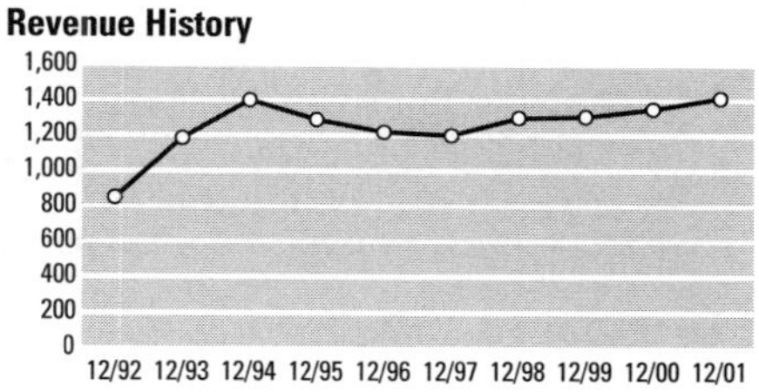

Plastech Engineered Products

Plastech Engineered Products is helping automakers mold the future. The company is a maker of blow-molded and injection-molded plastic products, primarily for the automotive industry. Products include automotive interior trim, wiring harnesses, and cockpit modules. Plastech also engages in component painting and metal stamping. The company has added a facility in Louisville, Kentucky, to make interior trim for Ford Motor's Ford Explorer and Mercury Mountaineer SUVs. Plastech also is 51% owner of Automotive Modular Concepts, a wiring harness joint venture with Delphi Corporation. Former Ford Motor product engineer Julie Brown founded the company in 1988 and is its owner and CEO.

EXECUTIVES

Chairperson and CEO: Julie Nguyen Brown
VP, Engineering: Darwin Baker
VP, Operations: Don Coates
General Manager: Jeff Hemer
Manager, Human Resources: Danita Reece

LOCATIONS

HQ: 835 Mason St., Dearborn, MI 48124
Phone: 313-791-3001 **Fax:** 313-792-2729
Web: www.plastecheng.com

Plastech Engineered Products has facilities in Kentucky, Indiana, and Michigan.

COMPETITORS

Clarion Technologies
Dura Automotive
Siegel-Robert
Venture Industries

HISTORICAL FINANCIALS

Company Type: Private

Income Statement FYE: December 31

	ESTIMATED REVENUE ($ mil.)	NET INCOME ($ mil.)	NET PROFIT MARGIN	EMPLOYEES
12/01	560	—	—	2,562
12/00	550	—	—	2,562
Annual Growth	1.8%	—	—	0.0%

Revenue History

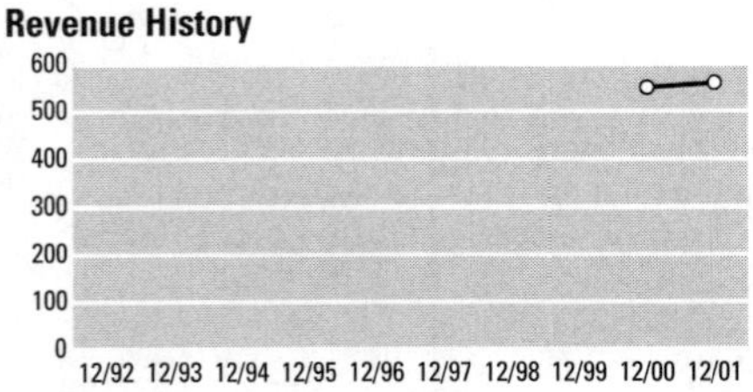

Plastipak Holdings, Inc.

Plastipak Packaging likes to keep things bottled up. The company supplies plastic containers for products such as carbonated and noncarbonated beverages, food, cleaning products, distilled spirits, and processed juices. It makes high-density polyethylene (HDPE) resins and polyethylene terephthalate (PET) at its plants in the US and South America. In conjunction with Canada-based Husky Injection Molding Systems, Plastipak has pioneered a molding process, EXI-PAK, that allows products that were once confined to glass or metal containers to be packaged in plastic. It also licenses its technologies to manufacturers, including customers in Brazil, Germany, and New Zealand. The Young family owns and runs Plastipak.

The company's two largest business segments, which make containers for carbonated and noncarbonated beverages and the consumer cleaning industries, bring in about 85% of its revenue.

Procter & Gamble is the company's largest customer, accounting for 25% of its sales. Plastipak is the exclusive supplier of plastic containers for Procter & Gamble's liquid laundry detergents (Tide, Cheer, Era, and Gain) and other products like Bounce and Febreze; it is also the largest supplier of plastic containers for Kraft Foods salad dressing, barbecue sauces, and grated cheeses.

The company's Whiteline subsidiary serves 70% of Plastipak's transportation needs with a fleet of 275 tractors and 900 trailers. Its Clean Tech subsidiary, a plastics recycling firm, provides much of the company's raw material needs.

EXECUTIVES

Chairman, President, and CEO: William C. Young, age 62, $812,145 pay
VP, Finance; CFO, Treasurer, and Assistant Secretary: Michael J. Plotzke, age 45, $395,915 pay
VP, International Sales and Marketing: Frank Pollock
VP, Operations and Manufacturing: William Slat, age 55, $383,005 pay
VP, Sales and Marketing: Gene W. Mueller, age 45, $336,660 pay
President, Clean Tech: Thomas Busard, age 51, $11,333,962 pay
CIO: David Daugherty
Corporate Legal Counsel and Secretary: Leeann M. Underhill, age 57
Auditors: Grant Thornton LLP

LOCATIONS

HQ: 9135 General Court, Plymouth, MI 48170
Phone: 734-455-3600 **Fax:** 734-354-7391
Web: www.plastipak.com

Plastipak Packaging has manufacturing facilities in Brazil and the US.

PRODUCTS/OPERATIONS

Selected Operations

Package development services
Plastic container manufacturing
High-density polyethylene (HDPE) resins
Polyethylene terephthalate (PET)
Technology licensing and equipment
EXI-PAK preform over-molding process technology (employs multi-layer, barrier, and post-consumer plastic technologies in PET bottles)
G.E.M. PAK container molding system

COMPETITORS

Ball Corporation
CPChem
Constar International
Crown
Graham Packaging
Husky Injection Molding Systems
PolyOne
PVC Container
Sidel
Silgan

HISTORICAL FINANCIALS

Company Type: Private

Income Statement FYE: Saturday closest to October 31

	REVENUE ($ mil.)	NET INCOME ($ mil.)	NET PROFIT MARGIN	EMPLOYEES
10/02	812	9	1.1%	3,700
10/01	810	—	—	3,300
10/00	566	—	—	3,000
Annual Growth	19.8%	—	—	11.1%

Revenue History

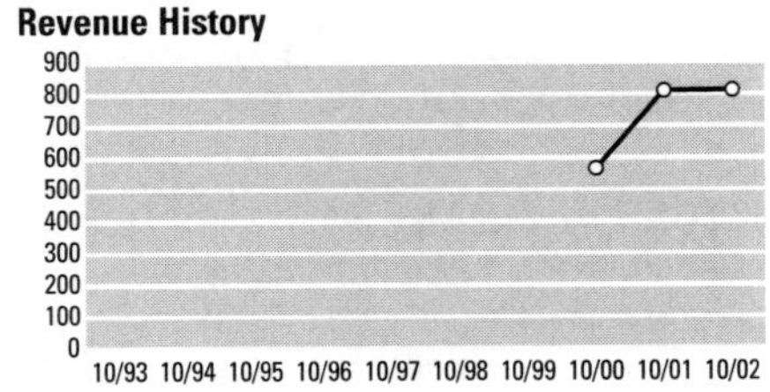

Pleasant Holidays, LLC

What's more pleasant than a holiday? Pleasant Holidays has traditionally specialized in offering wholesale tour packages to Hawaii, and has added excursions to Australia, the Caribbean, Fiji, New Zealand, Mexico, Tahiti, and several other exotic destinations. The company has also taken to cyberspace, operating a Web site through which travel agents can make travel reservations. Ed and Lynn Hogan, who founded the company in 1959, own Pleasant Holidays. The couple began to sell vacations to the island state shortly after Hawaii became part of the US. The company also owns four Hawaiian hotels — Kahana Beach Resort, Royal Lahaina Resort, Royal Kona Resort, and Kauai Coconut Beach Resort.

EXECUTIVES

Founder and Chairman: Edward J. (Ed) Hogan, age 74
President and CEO: Tim Irwin
EVP, COO, and CFO: Ron Krueger
VP E-Commerce: Todd Castor
VP Human Resources: Christine Bogdan
VP Information Systems: Delmar Steurmer
VP Marketing: Michael Gardiner
VP Operations: Jim Barsch
VP Product Development: Bob Froio
VP Sales: Jerry Healy
Manager Group Sales: JoAnne Bryan

LOCATIONS

HQ: 2404 Townsgate Rd., Westlake Village, CA 91361
Phone: 818-991-3390 **Fax:** 805-495-4972
Web: www.pleasantholidays.com

COMPETITORS

American Express
Carlson Wagonlit
Liberty Travel
Maritz
priceline.com
Rosenbluth International
WorldTravel

HISTORICAL FINANCIALS

Company Type: Private

Income Statement FYE: December 31

	REVENUE ($ mil.)	NET INCOME ($ mil.)	NET PROFIT MARGIN	EMPLOYEES
12/02*	487	—	—	710
12/00	450	—	—	1,000
12/99	400	—	—	1,700
12/98	350	—	—	1,700
12/97	320	—	—	1,700
12/96	320	—	—	1,600
12/95	320	—	—	1,700
12/94	300	—	—	1,793
12/93	320	—	—	1,700
Annual Growth	5.4%	—	—	(10.3%)

*Irregular reporting interval

Revenue History

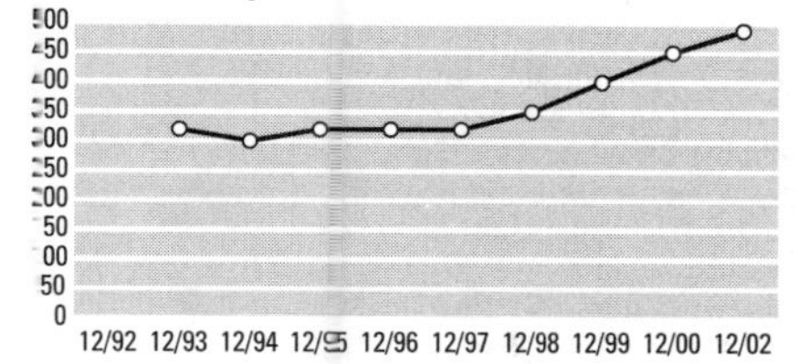

Pliant Corporation

Pliant is flexible when it comes to packaging. The company makes flexible packaging products and value-added films for a variety of uses. In the US Pliant produces specialty films used to make diapers, incontinence products, and sterile packaging. It also produces industrial films such as stretch films (used to bundle palletized loads during shipping), PVC films (used to wrap food products), medical films, and converter films. Pliant's International unit sells films in Asia, Canada, Europe, and Mexico. Its Pliant Solutions unit includes the decorative and surface coverings business acquired from Decora Industries. The Durham family and J.P. Morgan Partners own about 28% and 61% of the company, respectively.

EXECUTIVES

Chairman: Edward A. Lapekas, age 60
President, CEO, and Director: Harold C. Bevis
EVP and CFO: Brian E. Johnson, age 47, $307,128 pay
EVP and President, Flexible Packaging: Len Azzaro, age 53
EVP and President, Pliant International: Elise H. Scroggs, age 41, $238,389 pay
EVP and President, Pliant USA (Pliant Films): Stanley B. Bikulege, age 39, $294,176 pay
EVP, Procurement and Strategic Sourcing: Douglas W. Bengtson, age 55, $257,647 pay
SVP and President, Pliant Solutions: Ronald A. (Ron) Artzer, age 59, $263,062 pay
VP, Human Resources: Larry Shepler
Director of Corporate Communications: John McCurdy
Auditors: Ernst & Young LLP

LOCATIONS

HQ: 1515 Woodfield Rd., Ste. 600, Schaumburg, IL 60173
Phone: 847-969-3300 **Fax:** 847-969-3338
Web: www.pliantcorp.com

Pliant Corporation has manufacturing facilities in Australia, Canada, Germany, Mexico, Singapore, and the US.

PRODUCTS/OPERATIONS

2002 Sales

	$ mil.	% of total
Pliant US		
Converter films	221	25
Printed & barrier films	207	24
Industrial films	159	18
Specialty films	156	18
Pliant International	108	12
Pliant Solutions	28	3
Total	**879**	**100**

COMPETITORS

AEP Industries
Griffon
Pactiv
Polymer Group
Reynolds Food Packaging
Sealed Air
Spartech

HISTORICAL FINANCIALS

Company Type: Private

Income Statement FYE: December 31

	REVENUE ($ mil.)	NET INCOME ($ mil.)	NET PROFIT MARGIN	EMPLOYEES
12/02	879	(43)	—	3,250
12/01	840	(2)	—	3,500
12/00	844	(51)	—	3,150
12/99	814	18	2.2%	3,800
12/98	681	8	1.2%	3,000
Annual Growth	6.6%	—	—	2.0%

Net Income History

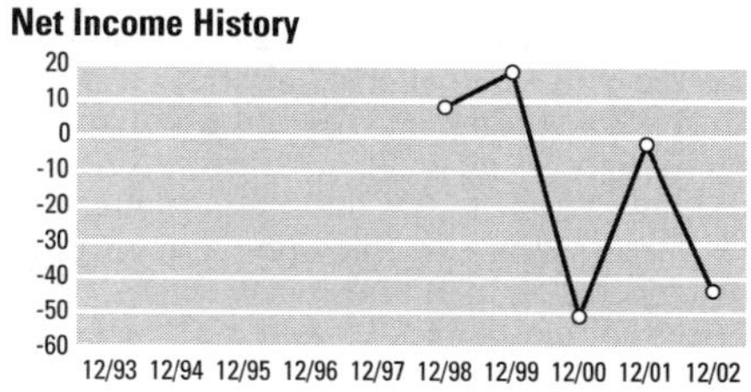

PMC Global, Inc.

PMC Global makes Teletubbies brand kiddie soap *and* the pipe that drains the suds away. The diversified international company produces memory chips, connectors, film, packaging, plastics, plastic-molding equipment, and specialty chemicals, among other things. It operates through more than a dozen specialized divisions such as ASC Group (electronics), Cosrich (children's bath, cosmetics, and toiletry products, including Disney brands), PMC Specialties Group (specialty chemicals), and VCF Films (PVC and acrylic films). CEO Philip Kamins (who owns the company) founded PMC (Plastic Management Corporation) in 1971 as an outgrowth of a small plastics scrap yard he founded in 1964.

EXECUTIVES

President and CEO: Philip E. Kamins
CFO: Thian C. Cheong
EVP and Treasurer: Lori Johnson
President, Austin Semiconductor: Ken Buckley
President, Continental Connector: Michael Sexton
President, Futura Coatings: Charles Zajaczkowski
President, General Plastics Corporation: Robert Scher
President, Komo: Tom Azzarelli
VP, Operations, Austin Semiconductor: Chris Imhof
VP, Sales and Marketing, Austin Semiconductor: Bob Heppel
VP and General Manager, Komo: Michael Verdon
VP, Sales and Marketing, Komo: Jeff Erickson
Controller: Brad Barton
Director, Human Resources: Karen Ferguson

LOCATIONS

HQ: 12243 Branford St., Sun Valley, CA 91352
Phone: 818-896-1101 **Fax:** 818-897-0180
Web: www.pmcglobalinc.com

PMC Global comprises subsidiaries with operations throughout the US and in Belgium, Canada, France, Germany, Italy, Japan, Luxembourg, the Netherlands, Singapore, Spain, and the UK.

PRODUCTS/OPERATIONS

Selected Operations

ASC Group, Inc. (electronic components)
- Austin Semiconductor (memory chips)
- Continental Connector (electrical connectors)
- Gentape (electrical connectors)
- North Penn Technology (memory packages)
- Secure Communication Systems (ruggedized computers)

Cosrich Group, Inc. (children's bath products and play cosmetics)
Futura Coatings, Inc. (reaction spray elastomers)
General Plastics Group, Inc. (high-performance coatings)
Gusmer Machinery Group, Inc. (equipment for foams, high-performance coatings and elastomers, composites, and fiberglass)
Komo Machine, Inc. (computer numerically controlled routers)
Plastics Color Corporation (color and additive concentrates used in plastics)
Plastic Services & Products, Inc. (polyurethane drainage pipe)
PMC Specialties Group, Inc. (chemical intermediates and specialty products)
PSC Industries, Inc. (design and fabrication of non-metallic materials)
VCF Specialty Films, Inc (pvc and acrylic films)
Winkler Forming, Inc. (PET products)

COMPETITORS

BASF AG
Bayer AG
BP
Carpenter
Cohesant Technologies
Colgate-Palmolive
Crompton
Dow Chemical
DuPont
E.ON
Huntsman International
Inteplast
Johnson & Johnson
Pactiv
Sealed Air
Teknor Apex
TT electronics
Unilever

HISTORICAL FINANCIALS

Company Type: Private

Income Statement FYE: December 31

	REVENUE ($ mil.)	NET INCOME ($ mil.)	NET PROFIT MARGIN	EMPLOYEES
12/02	800	—	—	4,300
12/01	800	—	—	4,300
12/00	784	—	—	4,300
12/99	877	—	—	5,130
12/98	859	—	—	5,100
12/97	828	—	—	5,125
12/96	876	—	—	4,299
12/95	780	—	—	5,130
12/94	709	—	—	4,100
12/93	715	—	—	3,756
Annual Growth	1.3%	—	—	1.5%

Revenue History

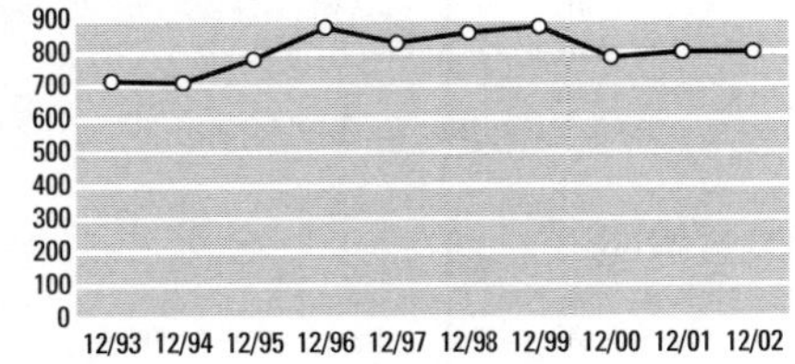

The Port Authority of New York and New Jersey

The Port Authority of New York and New Jersey bridges the often-troubled waters between the two states — and helps with many of the region's other transportation needs. The bi-state agency operates and maintains airports, tunnels, bridges, a commuter rail system, shipping terminals, and other facilities within the Port District, an area surrounding the Statue of Liberty. A self-supporting public agency, the Port Authority receives no state or local tax money but relies on tolls, fees, and rents. The governors of the two states each appoint six of the 12 members of the agency's board and review the board's decisions.

The Port Authority's facilities include such international symbols of transportation and commerce as the George Washington Bridge, the Holland and Lincoln tunnels, and LaGuardia and John F. Kennedy airports. The Port Authority Trans-Hudson (PATH) rapid-transit system provides commuter rail service between New York and New Jersey.

The World Trade Center was among the agency's most visible assets before its twin towers and much of the rest of the complex were destroyed in terrorist attacks on September 11, 2001. The Port Authority is working with other agencies, government officials, and real estate interests on the rebuilding of the 16-acre site in Lower Manhattan.

HISTORY

New York and New Jersey spent much of their early history fighting over their common waterways. In 1921 a treaty creating a single, bistate agency, the Port of New York Authority, was ratified by the New York and New Jersey state legislatures.

The agency struggled at first, although its early projects, such as the Goethals Bridge (1928, linking Staten Island to New Jersey), were far from timid. It merged with the Holland Tunnel Commission in 1930, which brought a steady source of revenue. In 1931 the George Washington Bridge (spanning the Hudson River from Manhattan to New Jersey) was completed. The Lincoln Tunnel (also linking Manhattan to New Jersey) opened in 1937.

After WWII the Port Authority broadened its focus to include commercial aviation. In 1947 the agency took over LaGuardia Airport, and the next year it dedicated the New York International Airport (renamed John F. Kennedy International Airport in 1963).

As trucking supplanted railroads in the late 1950s, The Port Authority experimented with more efficient ways of transferring cargo. In 1962 it built the first containerport in the world. That year the agency acquired a commuter rail line connecting Newark to Manhattan, which became the Port Authority Trans-Hudson (PATH).

In the early 1970s the Port Authority completed the World Trade Center. The agency changed its name to The Port Authority of New York and New Jersey in 1972 to reflect its role in mass transit between the two states. Critics, however, frequently assailed the agency for inefficiency and pork-barrel politics. In 1993 terrorists detonated a truck bomb in one of the World Trade Center towers, but within a year the building had largely recovered.

George Marlin became executive director in 1995. He cut operating expenses for the first time since 1943 and through budget cuts and layoffs, saved $100 million in 1996 and avoided hikes in tolls and fares. A privatization proponent, Marlin sold the World Trade Center's Vista Hotel to Host Marriott and arranged for the sale of other nontransportation businesses. He stepped down in 1997, and Robert Boyle took the post. That year the agency broke ground on the $1.2 billion Terminal 4 at JFK International Airport.

In 1998 the Port Authority authorized a $930 million design and construction contract for a light-rail line to JFK International Airport. New York City mayor Rudolph Giuliani proposed legislation in 1999 to place the Port Authority's LaGuardia and JFK airports under City Hall jurisdiction.

An 18-month standoff between the governors of New York and New Jersey regarding disputes over leases and agency spending was settled in 2000, which allowed the Port Authority to move forward with projects that had been blocked. Also in 2000 Boyle announced plans to resign. Neil Levin, New York's state insurance superintendent and a former Goldman Sachs vice president, replaced him the next year.

After the Port Authority and Vornado Realty Trust in 2001 failed to finalize an agreement for Vornado to lease the World Trade Center, the Port Authority that year signed a 99-year, $3.2 billion deal to lease portions of the World Trade Center's office space to a group led by Silverstein Properties while leasing the retail space to Westfield America.

Less than two months later, the World Trade Center's twin towers were destroyed when terrorists hijacked passenger jets and flew them into the buildings. Levin was killed, and 83 other Port Authority employees were listed as dead or missing.

The cleanup of the World Trade Center site, known as "Ground Zero," was completed in 2002, eight months after the attacks.

EXECUTIVES

Chairman, The Port Authority of New York and New Jersey, Port Authority Trans-Hudson, Newark Legal and Communications Center Urban Renewal, and New York and New Jersey Railroad: Anthony R. Coscia, age 43

Vice Chairman, The Port Authority of New York and New Jersey, Port Authority Trans-Hudson, Newark Legal and Communications Center Urban Renewal, and New York & New Jersey Railroad: Charles A. Gargano

Executive Director, The Port Authority of New York and New Jersey, Port Authority Trans-Hudson, Newark Legal and Communications Center Urban Renewal, and New York & New Jersey Railroad: Joseph J. Seymour

Deputy Executive Director: Michael R. DeCotiis

COO: Ernesto L. Butcher

CFO: Charles F. McClafferty

Chief Administrative Officer: Louis J. LaCapra

Chief Engineer: Frank Lombardi, age 54

Treasurer: Bruce F. Bohlen

Comptroller: Margaret R. Zoch

Special Advisor to Executive Director and Secretary: Karen E. Eastman

Director, Audit: John D. Brill

Director, HR: Michael Massiah

Director, Public Affairs: Kayla Bergeron

General Counsel; VP and Secretary, New York & New Jersey Railroad: Jeffrey S. Green

Auditors: Deloitte & Touche LLP

LOCATIONS

HQ: 225 Park Ave. South, 15th Fl., New York, NY 10003

Phone: 212-435-7000 **Fax:** 212-435-6670

Web: www.panynj.gov

The Port Authority of New York and New Jersey operates primarily in the five boroughs of New York City, four suburban New York counties, and eight counties in northern New Jersey.

PRODUCTS/OPERATIONS

Selected Operations

Air Terminals

Downtown Manhattan Heliport (New York)
John F. Kennedy International Airport (New York)
LaGuardia Airport (New York)
Newark Liberty International Airport (New Jersey)
Teterboro Airport (New Jersey)

Interstate Transportation

Bayonne Bridge (Staten Island to Bayonne, New Jersey)
George Washington Bridge (Manhattan to Ft. Lee, New Jersey)
George Washington Bridge Bus Terminal
Goethals Bridge (Staten Island to Elizabeth, New Jersey)
Holland Tunnel (Manhattan to Jersey City, New Jersey)
Lincoln Tunnel (Manhattan to Union City, New Jersey)
Outerbridge Crossing (Staten Island to Perth Amboy, New Jersey)
Port Authority Bus Terminal (Manhattan)
The Port Authority Trans-Hudson System (PATH, rail transportation between New York and New Jersey)

Port Commerce
Auto Marine Terminal (Bayonne, New Jersey)
Brooklyn-Port Authority Marine Terminal (New York)
Elizabeth Marine Terminal (New Jersey)
Howland Hook Marine Terminal (New York)
Port Newark (New Jersey)
Red Hook Container Terminal (New York)

Economic and Waterfront Development
Bathgate Industrial Park (Bronx, New York)
Essex County Resource Recovery Center (municipal waste-to-energy electric generation plant; Newark, New York)
Industrial Park at Elizabeth (Elizabeth, New Jersey)
Newark Legal & Communications Center (office development; Newark, New Jersey)
Queens West (mixed-use waterfront development; Queens, New York)
Hoboken South (mixed-use waterfront development; Hoboken, New Jersey)
The Teleport (communications center; Staten Island, New York)

COMPETITORS

Coach USA
Covanta
Helmsley
Lefrak Organization
MTA
Amtrak
Reckson Associates Realty
Tishman Realty
Trump

HISTORICAL FINANCIALS

Company Type: Government agency

Income Statement FYE: December 31

	REVENUE ($ mil.)	NET INCOME ($ mil.)	NET PROFIT MARGIN	EMPLOYEES
12/02	2,671	740	27.7%	7,000
12/01	2,715	216	7.9%	7,000
12/00	2,648	372	14.1%	7,000
12/99	2,548	314	12.3%	7,200
12/98	2,361	299	12.7%	7,200
12/97	2,206	282	12.8%	7,500
12/96	2,154	199	9.2%	8,100
12/95	2,083	177	8.5%	9,250
12/94	1,980	153	7.7%	9,200
12/93	1,921	108	5.6%	9,350
Annual Growth	3.7%	23.8%	—	(3.2%)

2002 Year-End Financials

Debt ratio: 123.2%
Return on equity: 13.3%
Cash ($ mil.): 41
Current ratio: 1.18
Long-term debt ($ mil.): 7,294

Net Income History

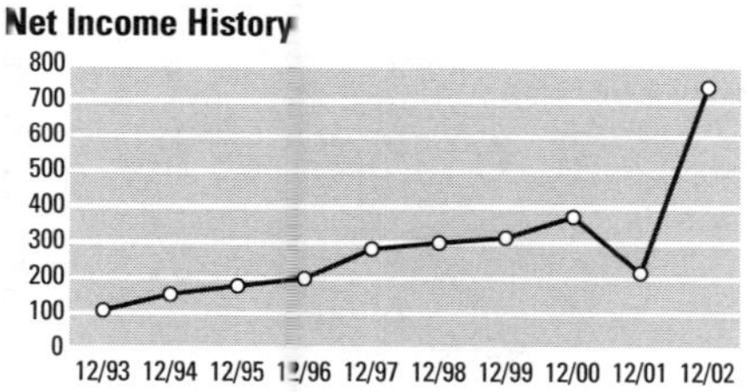

Power Authority of the State of New York

Question authority? Well, without question, authority for power lies in the Power Authority of the State of New York (commonly referred to as the New York Power Authority, or NYPA). The company generates and transmits more than 20% of New York's electricity, making it the largest state-owned public power provider in the US. It is also New York's only statewide electricity supplier. NYPA owns hydroelectric and fossil-fueled generating facilities that produce about 5,700 MW of electricity, and it operates more than 1,400 circuit-miles of transmission lines.

The authority sells power to government agencies, municipal systems, rural cooperatives, private companies, private utilities (for resale), and neighboring states. Its clients include some of the largest electricity users in the US, including the New York City government and the Metropolitan Transportation Authority. NYPA receives no state funds or tax credits. Instead, it finances new projects through bond sales.

Following its shift from a regulated monopoly to a competitor in an open power market, NYPA is aiming to grow by reducing the cost of the energy it provides and by developing electric transportation (such as electric cars) and other energy-efficiency projects, such as installing emergency power generators in metropolitan buildings. It is also working to improve the state's transmission grid and increase its generating capacity.

HISTORY

The Power Authority of the State of New York (aka New York Power Authority, or NYPA) was established in 1931 by Gov. Franklin Roosevelt to gain public control of New York's hydropower resources. The utility's major power plants came on line with the opening of the St. Lawrence-Franklin D. Roosevelt Power Project (1958) and the Niagara Power Project (1961). The Blenheim-Gilboa Pumped Storage Power Project opened in 1973.

In the mid-1970s NYPA shifted to nuclear power when it opened the James A. FitzPatrick Nuclear Power Plant (1975) and the Indian Point 3 Nuclear Power Plant (1976). The company then opened gas- and oil-powered plants: the Charles Poletti Power Project (1977) and the Richard M. Flynn Power Plant (1994).

In 1998 the authority allocated low-cost electricity to five companies that planned to invest $104 million in business expansions in western New York. The company suffered a loss in 1999 in part from reduced hydro generation and a drop in investment earnings. In 2000 NYPA sold its two nuclear plants (1,800 MW of capacity) to utility holding company Entergy for $967 million.

The company completed the installation of 11 gas-powered turbines at various locations in New York City and on Long Island in 2001; the program was initiated to prevent against expected energy shortages that summer, but it also helped maintain power in areas of the city during the September 11 terrorist attack.

EXECUTIVES

Chairman: Louis P. Ciminelli
Vice Chairman: Frank S. McCullough Jr.
President and CEO: Eugene W. Zeltmann
EVP, Secretary, and General Counsel: David E. Blabey
EVP Business Services and Administration: Vincent C. Vesce
EVP Power Generation and Project Operations: Robert A. Hiney
SVP and CFO: Michael H. Urbach
SVP Energy Services and Technology: Robert L. Tscherne
SVP Marketing, Economic Development, and Supply Planning: Louise M. Morman
SVP Public and Governmental Affairs: Peter A. Barden
SVP Transmission: H. Kenneth Haase
VP Energy Risk Assessment and Control and Chief Risk Officer: Thomas H. Warmath
VP and Controller: Arnold M. Bellis
CIO: Dennis Eccleston
Acting Treasurer: Michael Brady
Auditors: PricewaterhouseCoopers LLP

LOCATIONS

HQ: 123 Main St., White Plains, NY 10601
Phone: 914-681-6200 **Fax:** 212-468-6360
Web: www.nypa.gov

Selected Operations

Transmission Control Facility
Frederick R. Clark Energy Center (Oneida County)

Fossil-Fueled Plants
Charles Poletti Power Project (New York City)
Richard M. Flynn Power Plant (Suffolk County)
PowerNow! Turbines (11 units in New York City and Long Island)

Hydropower Plants
Blenheim-Gilboa Pumped Storage Power Project (Schoharie County)
Niagara Power Project (Niagara County)
St. Lawrence-Franklin D. Roosevelt Power Project (St. Lawrence County)

Small Hydropower Plants
Ashokan Project (Ulster County)
Crescent Plant (Albany and Saratoga Counties)
Gregory B. Jarvis Plant (Oneida County)
Kensico Project (Westchester County)
Vischer Ferry Plant (Saratoga and Schenectady counties)

PRODUCTS/OPERATIONS

2002 Sales

	$ mil.	% of total
Power sales	1,643	80
Wheeling charges	274	13
Transmission charges	143	7
Total	**2,060**	**100**

COMPETITORS

CH Energy
Con Edison
Dynegy
Enbridge
Energy East
Entergy
KeySpan Energy
Rochester Gas and Electric
TransCanada

HISTORICAL FINANCIALS

Company Type: Government-owned

Income Statement FYE: December 31

	REVENUE ($ mil.)	NET INCOME ($ mil.)	NET PROFIT MARGIN	EMPLOYEES
12/02	2,060	84	4.1%	1,600
12/01	2,016	18	0.9%	1,600
12/00	2,034	170	8.3%	1,531
12/99	1,458	(233)	—	—
12/98	1,484	63	4.2%	—
12/97	1,481	106	7.1%	3,259
12/96	1,430	69	4.8%	3,200
12/95	1,413	—	—	3,300
12/94	1,460	—	—	3,500
12/93	1,430	—	—	3,500
Annual Growth	4.1%	3.3%	—	(8.3%)

2002 Year-End Financials

Debt ratio: 138.2%
Return on equity: 5.1%
Cash ($ mil.): 0
Current ratio: 1.29
Long-term debt ($ mil.): 2,326

Net Income History

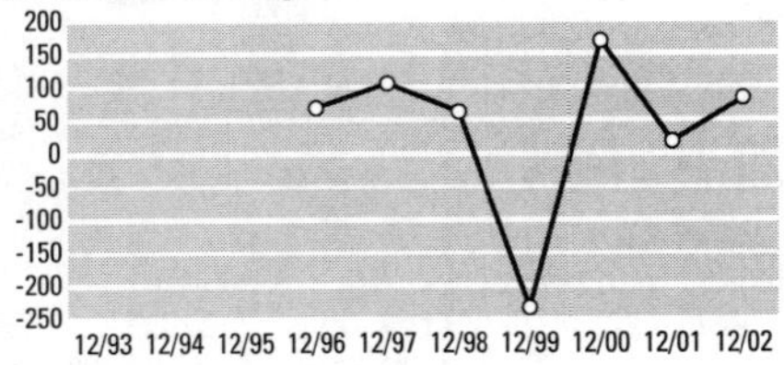

PQ Corporation

PQ Corporation minds its Ps and Qs when producing inorganic industrial chemicals. The company is one of the world's largest producers of sodium silicates (a glass product made from sand), marketing more than 40 silica-based products. Glass-bead products made by subsidiary Potters Industries are used in highway striping to reflect headlights. PQ's glass beads also are used to grind and process pigments for paints, coatings, inks, and cosmetics. Its potassium silicates are used in welding rods, soaps, and detergents. PQ's magnesium sulfate (Epsom salt crystals) is used in animal feed, packaging products, and pharmaceuticals. PQ is owned by descendants of the founding Elkinton family, management, and retirees.

EXECUTIVES

President and CEO: Stanley W. Silverman
CFO: William Levy
EVP; President and CEO, Potters Industry, Inc.: Jerry Sheridan
EVP: Michael Imbriani
CIO and Director, Information Technology: R. W. Fabrizio
Manager, Human Resources and Organizational Development: W. F. Rathberger III
Treasurer: Amy E. Ard
Group Manager, Magnesium Sulphate: Dan Dougherty
Group Manager, Industrial Chemicals: Mark Vincent

LOCATIONS

HQ: 1200 W. Swedesford Rd., Berwyn, PA 19312
Phone: 610-651-4200 **Fax:** 610-651-4435
Web: www.pqcorp.com

PQ Corporation operates roughly 65 chemical and glass-bead plants in about 20 countries throughout Asia, Australia, Europe, and North and South America.

PRODUCTS/OPERATIONS

Selected Subsidiaries and Affiliates

Akzo-PQ Silica (joint venture)
Ashai-PQ Silica Co., Ltd. (Japan) (joint venture)
National Silicates, Ltd. (Canada)
Potters Industries, Inc.
Productos Quimicos Panamericanos, S.A. (Columbia) (joint venture)
Vitro-PQ Quimica, S.A. de C.V. (Mexico) (joint venture)
Zeolyst International (joint venture with Royal Dutch Shell Group)

COMPETITORS

Brenntag
Electroglas
ExxonMobil Chemical
Ferro
IMC Global
Jilin Chemical
Millennium Chemicals
Nippon Chemical Industrial
Nippon Denko
OxyChem
Univar USA

HISTORICAL FINANCIALS

Company Type: Private

Income Statement FYE: December 31

	ESTIMATED REVENUE ($ mil.)	NET INCOME ($ mil.)	NET PROFIT MARGIN	EMPLOYEES
12/02	500	—	—	1,600
12/01	500	—	—	1,600
12/00	500	—	—	—
12/99	500	—	—	1,600
Annual Growth	0.0%	—	—	0.0%

Revenue History

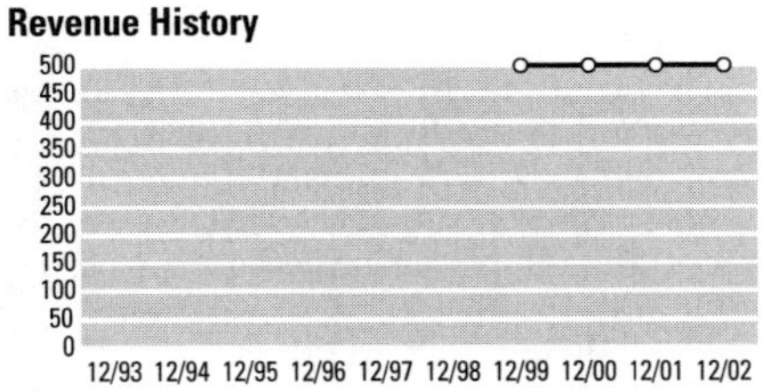

Presbyterian Healthcare

Established in the early 1900s as a sanatorium for tuberculosis patients, not-for-profit Presbyterian Healthcare Services (PHS) now cares for more than 400,000 New Mexicans. PHS's Presbyterian Health Plan serves individuals, spouses, and dependents, covering everything from preventive to emergency care. PHS hospitals offer small group plans for companies with less than 50 employees and group health plans with HMO and point-of-service options. Enrollees include the State of New Mexico, University of New Mexico, and Intel. The PHS network of eight hospitals and about 15 community health centers and clinics stretches from Cimarron to Ruidoso.

EXECUTIVES

President and CEO; Chairman, Presbyterian Health Plan: James H. Hinton
SVP and COO: Mark Reifsteck
SVP and CFO: Liz Alhand
SVP Legal Services: Diane Fisher
SVP Strategic Planning: Peter Snow
VP Human Resources: Renee Reimer
VP Information Services: Bob Skinner
VP Marketing and Communications: Michelle Campbell
President, Presbyterian Health Plan: David R. Scrase
CFO, Presbyterian Health Plan: Dale Maxwell

LOCATIONS

HQ: Presbyterian Healthcare Services
2501 Buena Vista SE, Albuquerque, NM 87106
Phone: 505-841-1234 **Fax:** 505-923-6141
Web: www.phs.org

Hospital, Clinic, and Community Health Care Center Locations

Albuquerque
Angel Fire
Belen
Carrizozo
Cimarron
Clovis
Espanola
Portales
Rio Rancho
Ruidoso
Socorro
Springer
Tucumcari

COMPETITORS

Banner Health
Catholic Health Initiatives
CIGNA
Triad Hospitals

HISTORICAL FINANCIALS

Company Type: Not-for-profit

Income Statement FYE: December 31

	REVENUE ($ mil.)	NET INCOME ($ mil.)	NET PROFIT MARGIN	EMPLOYEES
12/01	1,007	52	5.2%	7,253
12/00	1,000	—	—	7,500
12/99	444	—	—	7,500
12/98	348	—	—	7,500
12/97	402	—	—	7,400
12/96	405	—	—	—
12/95	314	—	—	—
12/94	304	—	—	—
12/93	281	—	—	—
Annual Growth	17.3%	—	—	(0.5%)

Revenue History

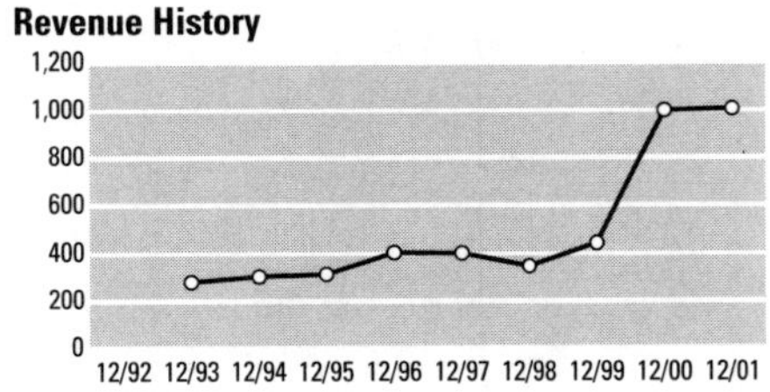

PricewaterhouseCoopers

Not merely the firm with the longest one-word name, PricewaterhouseCoopers (PwC) is also the world's largest accountancy, formed when Price Waterhouse merged with Coopers & Lybrand in 1998, passing then-leader Andersen. The firm has offices around the world, providing clients with services in three lines of business: Assurance and Business Advisory Services (including financial and regulatory reporting), Tax and Legal Services, and Corporate Finance and Recovery. The company serves some of the world's largest businesses, as well as smaller firms.

PwC puts its heft to good use: Global clients make up about 40% of the firm's sales. Its bottom line, though, changed significantly in 2002, when PwC sold its consulting arm to IBM. A separation had been under consideration for years in light of SEC concerns about conflicts of interest when firms perform auditing and consulting for the same clients. The collapse of Enron and concomitant downfall of Enron's auditor and PwC's erstwhile peer Andersen undoubtedly hastened plans to spin off PwC's consultancy via an IPO, which was scrapped in favor of the IBM deal.

Like the other members of the (now) Big Four, PwC picked up business and talent as scandal-felled Andersen was winding down its operations in 2002. The former Andersen organization in China and Hong Kong joined PwC, accounting for about 70% of the approximately 3,500 Andersen alumni that came aboard.

In 2003 former client AMERCO (parent of U-Haul) sued PwC for $2.5 billion, claiming negligence and fraud in relation to a series of events that led to AMERCO restating its results.

HISTORY

In 1850 Samuel Price founded an accounting firm in London and in 1865 took on partner Edwin Waterhouse. The firm and the industry grew rapidly, thanks to the growth of stock exchanges that required uniform financial statements from listees. By the late 1800s Price Waterhouse (PW) had become the world's best-known accounting firm.

US offices were opened in the 1890s, and in 1902 United States Steel chose the firm as its auditor. PW benefited from tough audit requirements instituted after the 1929 stock market crash. In 1935 the firm was given the prestigious job of handling Academy Awards balloting. It started a management consulting service in 1946. But PW's dominance slipped in the 1960s, as it gained a reputation as the most traditional and formal of the major firms.

Coopers & Lybrand, the product of a 1957 transatlantic merger, wrote the book on auditing. Lybrand, Ross Bros. & Montgomery was formed in 1898 by William Lybrand, Edward Ross, Adam Ross, and Robert Montgomery. In 1912 Montgomery wrote *Montgomery's Auditing,* which became the bible of accounting.

Cooper Brothers was founded in 1854 in London by William Cooper, eldest son of a Quaker banker. In 1957 Lybrand joined up to form Coopers & Lybrand. During the 1960s the firm expanded into employee benefits and internal control consulting, building its technology capabilities in the 1970s as it studied ways to automate the audit process.

Coopers & Lybrand lost market share as mergers reduced the Big Eight accounting firms to the Big Six. After the savings and loan debacle of the 1980s, investors and the government wanted accounting firms held liable not only for the form of audited financial statements but for their veracity. In 1992 the firm paid $95 million to settle claims of defrauded investors in MiniScribe, a failed disk-drive maker. Other hefty payments followed, including a $108 million settlement relating to the late Robert Maxwell's defunct media empire.

In 1998 Price Waterhouse and Coopers & Lybrand combined PW's strength in the media, entertainment, and utility industries, and Coopers & Lybrand's focus on telecommunications and mining. But the merger brought some expensive legal baggage involving Coopers & Lybrand's performance of audits related to a bid-rigging scheme involving former Arizona governor Fife Symington.

Further growth plans fell through in 1999 when merger talks between PwC and Grant Thornton International failed. The year 2000 began on a sour note: An SEC conflict-of-interest probe turned up more than 8,000 alleged violations, most involving PwC partners owning stock in their firm's audit clients.

As the SEC grew ever more shrill in its denunciation of the potential conflicts of interest arising from auditing companies that the firm hoped to recruit or retain as consulting clients, PwC saw the writing on the wall and in 2000 began making plans to split the two operations. As part of this move, the company downsized and reorganized many of its operations.

The following year PwC paid $55 million to shareholders of MicroStrategy Inc., who charged that the auditing firm defrauded them by approving the client firm's inflated earnings and revenues figures.

EXECUTIVES

Global Chairman: Andrew Ratcliffe
Global CEO and Global Board Member: Samuel A. DiPiazza
Global CFO: Geoffrey E. Johnson
Global Board Member, France: Pierre B. Anglade
Global Board Member, Netherlands: Paul R. Baart
Global Board Member, South Africa: Colin Beggs
Global Board Member, Australia: Paul V. Brasher
Global Board Member, US: Jay D. Brodish
Global Board Member, Brazil: Raimundo L.M. Christians
Global Board Member, Switzerland: Edgar Fluri
Global Board Member, UK: Alec N. Jones
Global Board Member, Germany: Jan Konerding
Global Board Member, US: Keith D. Levingston
Global Board Member, US: Dennis J. Lubozynski
Global Board Member, US: Donald A. McGovern
Global Board Member, Canada: Israel H. Mida
Global Board Member, Japan: Dean A. Yoost
Managing Partner, Global Markets: Willem L.J. Bröcker
Managing Partner, Global Operations: Amyas C.E. Morse, age 53
Global General Counsel; Acting US General Counsel: Lawrence Keeshan
Global Human Capital Leader: Amy DiGeso, age 49
Global Industries, Markets and Strategic Planning Leader: Rocco J. Maggiotto
Global Human Resources Solutions Leader: John Kaplan
Human Resources, Learning, and Education Leader (US): Bob Daugherty
Marketing Leader (US): Dean Kern

LOCATIONS

HQ: 1301 Avenue of the Americas, New York, NY 10019
Phone: 646-471-4000 **Fax:** 646-394-1301
Web: www.pwcglobal.com

PricewaterhouseCoopers has offices in about 150 countries.

2002 Sales

	% of total
Europe, Middle East & Africa	45
North America	38
Asia/Pacific	13
South & Central America	4
Total	**100**

PRODUCTS/OPERATIONS

Selected Services

Audit, Assurance, and Business Advisory Services
Accounting and regulatory advice
Attest and related services
Audit
Corporate training
Performance measurement and corporate reporting
Public services audit and advisory
Specialized services for growing and middle market companies

Global Risk Management Solutions
Audit and compliance services
Behavioral transformation (services related to human resources)
Operational advisory
Risk and value management
Security and technology services
Sustainability services

Financial Advisory (called Corporate Finance & Recovery outside the US)
Business recovery services
Corporate finance
Dispute analysis and investigations (forensics)
Specialized services relating to infrastructure, government, and utilities
Valuation and strategy

Global Tax Services
Customs and duties
E-business services
Finance and treasure
Global VAT solutions
Global visa solutions
International assignment solutions
Mergers and acquisitions
Personal financial services
Tax compliance and outsourcing
Transfer pricing

Selected Industry Specializations

Consumer and Industrial Products and Services
Automotive
Energy and utilities
Industrial products
Pharmaceuticals
Retail and consumer
Services (including public sector)

Financial Services
Banking and capital markets
Insurance
Investment management
Real estate

Technology InfoComm and Entertainment
Entertainment and media
Information and communications
Technology

COMPETITORS

Bain & Company
BDO International
Booz Allen
Boston Consulting
Deloitte Touche Tohmatsu
Ernst & Young
H&R Block
Hewitt Associates
KPMG
Marsh & McLennan
McKinsey & Company
Towers Perrin
Watson Wyatt

HISTORICAL FINANCIALS

Company Type: Partnership

Income Statement FYE: June 30

	REVENUE ($ mil.)	NET INCOME ($ mil.)	NET PROFIT MARGIN	EMPLOYEES
6/02	13,800	—	—	124,563
6/01	24,000	—	—	160,000
6/00	21,500	—	—	150,000
6/99	15,300	—	—	155,000
6/98	15,000	—	—	140,000
6/97	5,630	—	—	60,000
6/96	5,020	—	—	56,000
6/95	4,460	—	—	53,000
6/94	3,980	—	—	50,122
6/93	3,890	—	—	48,781
Annual Growth	15.1%	—	—	11.0%

Revenue History

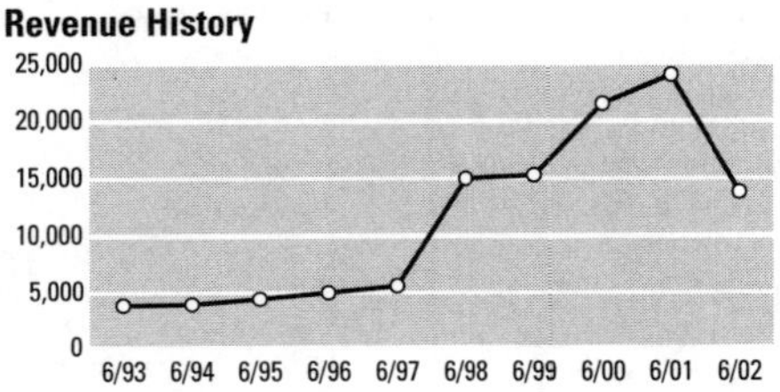

Primus, Inc.

You Win some, you Win some more. So it goes for Primus, which has invested in some 425 small to medium wholesale distributors in about 40 states that sell plumbing, heating, air-conditioning, electrical, and other supplies to contractors and other professional customers. The companies are easily recognizable by their Win-prefixed names, such as Columbia Winnelson (plumbing products), Salt Lake Windustrial (pipes and valves), and Dayton Winfastener (specialty fasteners). Primus supports these companies, through units Dapsco and Distro, with bulk purchasing, warehousing, accounting, and data processing. Primus is owned by heirs of the investors who founded Primus in 1956.

EXECUTIVES

President: Richard W. Schwartz
CIO/CTO: Jeffrey Dana
Treasurer/Comptroller: Jack W. Johnston
Director, Corporate Communications and Secretary: Bruce Anderson
Director, Finance: Ward Allen
Director, Human Resources: Thomas Snow

LOCATIONS

HQ: 3110 Kettering Blvd., Dayton, OH 45439
Phone: 937-294-6878 **Fax:** 937-293-9591
Web: www.winholesale.com

PRODUCTS/OPERATIONS

Selected Businesses

Winair (heating, ventilation, air conditioning, and refrigeration)
Winfastener (specialty fasteners)
Winholesale (piping, commercial valves, and fittings)
Winlectric (electrical supplies and products)
Winpump (pumps and accessories)
Wintronic (electronic parts and equipment)
Winwater Works (waterworks and utility supplies)

COMPETITORS

Fastenal
Ferguson Enterprises
Gensco-Albina
Groeniger & Company
Hajoca Corporation
Home Depot
Hughes Supply
Johnstone Supply
Lowe's
MSC Industrial Direct
Noland
W.W. Grainger

HISTORICAL FINANCIALS

Company Type: Private

Income Statement FYE: January 31

	REVENUE ($ mil.)	NET INCOME ($ mil.)	NET PROFIT MARGIN	EMPLOYEES
1/02	1,001	—	—	3,195
1/01	1,040	—	—	3,093
1/00	931	—	—	3,037
1/99	780	—	—	2,175
Annual Growth	8.7%	—	—	13.7%

Revenue History

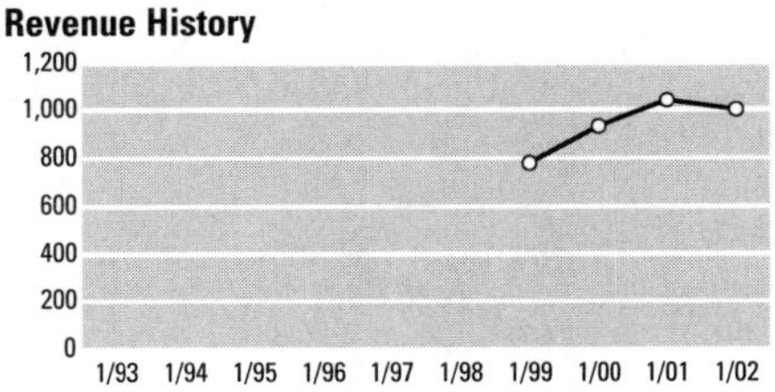

Princeton University

Princeton rules the Ivy League. The highly selective university accepts about 11% of those who apply. Founded in 1746, Princeton is one of the US's richest universities, with an endowment of more than $8 billion (behind Harvard, Yale, and Texas). It offers degrees in 35 departments. Princeton's more than 6,300 students pay a tuition of more than $27,000 a year; 50% receive some financial aid. Nobel prize winners associated with Princeton include Woodrow Wilson (who was Princeton's president before becoming US president), writer Toni Morrison, and physicist Richard Feynman. The university also is loosely affiliated with the Institute for Advanced Study where Albert Einstein once taught.

EXECUTIVES

President: Shirley M. Tilghman
Provost: Amy Gutmann
SVP Administration: Charles F. Kalmbach Jr.
VP Campus Life: Janet Smith Dickerson
VP Facilities: Kathleen Mulligan
VP Information Technology and CIO: Betty Leydon
VP Public Affairs: Robert K. Durkee
VP and Secretary: Thomas H. Wright Jr.
VP Development: Brian J. McDonald
CFO and Treasurer: Christopher McCrudden
General Counsel: Peter G. McDonough
Auditors: Deloitte & Touche LLP

LOCATIONS

HQ: 1 Nassau Hall, Princeton, NJ 08544
Phone: 609-258-3000 **Fax:** 609-258-1294
Web: www.princeton.edu

PRODUCTS/OPERATIONS

2002 Sales

	$ mil.	% of total
Government grants & contracts	178.2	21
Tuition & fees	168.4	20
Private gifts, grants & contracts	70.7	9
Other	417.9	50
Adjustment	(85.1)	
Total	**750.1**	**100**

HISTORICAL FINANCIALS

Company Type: School

Income Statement FYE: June 30

	REVENUE ($ mil.)	NET INCOME ($ mil.)	NET PROFIT MARGIN	EMPLOYEES
6/02	750	—	—	12,238
6/01	639	—	—	11,754
6/00	594	—	—	14,965
6/99	544	—	—	11,169
6/98	519	—	—	11,124
6/97	986	—	—	—
6/96	1,113	—	—	—
6/95	866	—	—	—
6/94	690	—	—	—
6/93	541	—	—	—
Annual Growth	3.7%	—	—	2.4%

Revenue History

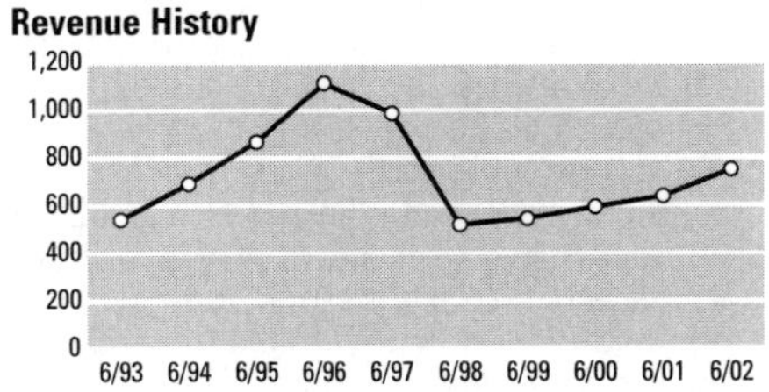

Printpack, Inc.

Printpack wraps its flexible packaging around salty snacks, confections, baked goods, cookies, crackers, and cereal, as well as tissues and paper towels. The company's packaging includes plastic film, aluminum foil, metallized films and paper with specialized coatings, and cast and blown monolayer and co-extruded films. Customers include Frito-Lay, Georgia Pacific, General Mills, and Quaker Oats. Printpack manufactures packaging materials at about 20 plants in the US, Mexico, and the UK. The founding Love family owns and manages the company, which was founded in 1956.

EXECUTIVES

Chairman: Gay M. Love, age 72
President, CEO, and Director: Dennis M. Love, age 47, $802,674 pay
VP, Finance and Administration: R. Michael Hembree, age 52, $299,706 pay
VP, Human Resources: Nicklas D. Stucky, age 55, $250,633 pay
VP, Engineering: August Franchini Jr., age 58
VP, General Manager, and Director: James E. Love III, age 44, $426,774 pay
VP and General Manager: Michael A. Fisher, age 54
VP and General Manager: James J. Greco, age 57, $443,275 pay
VP and General Manager: William E. Lewis, age 57
VP and General Manager: John N. Stigler, age 53
Auditors: PricewaterhouseCoopers LLP

LOCATIONS

HQ: 4335 Wendell Dr., Atlanta, GA 30336
Phone: 404-691-5830 **Fax:** 404-699-7122
Web: www.printpack.com

Printpack operates 20 manufacturing plants in the US, Mexico, and the UK.

PRODUCTS/OPERATIONS

Selected Customers

Frito-Lay
General Mills
Georgia Pacific
Hershey
Keebler
Kellogg
Mars
Nabisco
Nestle
Quaker Oats

COMPETITORS

AEP Industries
Alcoa
Bemis
Madeco
Pechiney
Pliant
PMC Global
Reynolds Food Packaging
Sealed Air

HISTORICAL FINANCIALS

Company Type: Private

Income Statement FYE: Saturday nearest June 30

	REVENUE ($ mil.)	NET INCOME ($ mil.)	NET PROFIT MARGIN	EMPLOYEES
6/02	1,100	—	—	4,300
6/01	1,027	—	—	3,800
6/00	907	—	—	3,800
6/99	846	—	—	3,600
6/98	832	—	—	3,500
6/97	782	—	—	3,500
6/96	443	—	—	2,330
6/95	455	—	—	2,663
6/94	407	—	—	3,000
6/93	378	—	—	—
Annual Growth	12.6%	—	—	4.6%

Revenue History

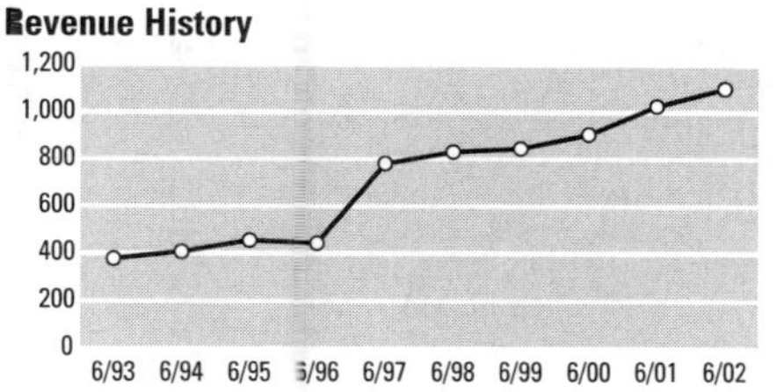

Providence Health System

Sisterhood is powerful in health care. The order of the Sisters of Providence runs not-for-profit Providence Health System in the Pacific Northwest (with outposts in Alaska and California). The system operates more than 20 acute care hospitals, as well as long-term care and assisted-living facilities and primary care centers. In addition the company offers health plans, low-income housing, and home health, hospice, and various community outreach services. The Sisters were founded in 1843 in Montreal; their work in the US began in 1856, when five members of the order established a mission in what was then Washington Territory.

EXECUTIVES

Chairman: Kay Stepp
President and CEO: Henry G. (Hank) Walker, age 55
COO: John F. Koster
CFO: Michael Butler
VP, General Counsel, and Secretary: Jeffrey W. Rogers
VP, Human Resources: Sue Byington
VP, Planning and Policy Development: Claudia Haglund
Treasurer: Lynn Chappell
System Director, Public Relations: Cheryl Sjoblom
System Director, Providence International Missions Program: Mark Koenig

LOCATIONS

HQ: 506 2nd Ave., Ste. 1200, Seattle, WA 98104
Phone: 206-464-3355 **Fax:** 206-464-3038
Web: www.providence.org

Providence Health System operates in Alaska, California, Oregon, and Washington.

Selected Facilities

Alaska
Providence Alaska Medical Center (Anchorage)
Providence Horizon House (assisted living, Anchorage)
Providence Kodiak Island Medical Center (Kodiak Island)
Providence Seward Medical Center (Seward)

California
Little Company of Mary Hospital (Torrance)
Providence Holy Cross Medical Center (Mission Hills)
Providence St. Joseph Medical Center (Burbank)
San Pedro Peninsula Hospital (San Pedro)

Oregon
Providence Hood River Memorial Hospital (Hood River)
Providence Medford Medical Center (Medford)
Providence Milwaukie Hospital (Milwaukie)
Providence Newburg Hospital (Newburg)
Providence Portland Medical Center (Portland)
Providence St. Vincent Medical Center (Portland)
Providence Seaside Hospital (Seaside)

Washington
Providence Centralia Hospital (Centralia)
Providence St. Peter Hospital (Olympia)
Providence Everett Medical Center (Everett)
Providence Toppenish Hospital (Teppensih)
Providence Yakima Medical Center (Yakima)

COMPETITORS

Adventist Health
Catholic Healthcare West
HCA
Legacy Health System
Los Angeles County Health Department
Memorial Health Services
PacifiCare
Sisters of Charity of Leavenworth
Sutter Health
Tenet Healthcare
Triad Hospitals
UniHealth

HISTORICAL FINANCIALS

Company Type: Not-for-profit

Income Statement FYE: December 31

	REVENUE ($ mil.)	NET INCOME ($ mil.)	NET PROFIT MARGIN	EMPLOYEES
12/02	3,529	58	1.6%	33,920
12/01	3,274	95	2.9%	32,929
12/00	3,229	162	5.0%	32,238
12/99	3,000	—	—	27,000
12/98	2,709	—	—	23,000
12/97	2,346	—	—	21,800
12/96	2,137	—	—	20,368
12/95	1,579	—	—	17,956
12/94	1,503	—	—	17,362
Annual Growth	11.3%	(4.2%)	—	8.7%

Net Income History

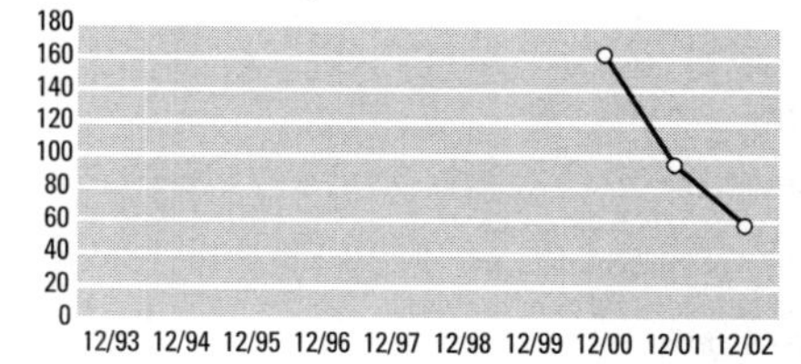

Public Broadcasting Service

More than just a showcase for a certain purple Teletubby, Public Broadcasting Service (PBS) serves up educational content to public TV stations across the country. A private, non-profit organization owned and operated by about 350 US public TV stations, PBS provides TV programming and related services such as distribution, fundraising support, and technology development. Programs include *NOVA*, *This Old House*, and *Masterpiece Theater*. Revenues come from underwriting, membership dues, federal funding (including grants from the not-for-profit Corporation for Public Broadcasting), royalties, license fees, and product sales. The organization was founded in 1969 to provide cultural and educational programming.

In early 2003 the station group laid off 14 staff members due to lower-than-expected subscriber revenue and corporate underwriting. Subsequently, PBS's board of directors voted to accept 30-second ad spots from corporate sponsors.

EXECUTIVES

President and CEO: Patricia (Pat) Mitchell, age 60, $393,125 pay
EVP and COO: W. Wayne Godwin
EVP PBS Business and Development: Judy L. Harris
SVP and Co-Chief Program Executive: John F. Wilson
SVP and Co-Chief Program Executive: Jacoba (Coby) Atlas
SVP and General Counsel: Katherine Lauderdale
SVP Brand Management, Promotion, and Media Relations: Lesli Rotenberg

SVP Business Affairs: James F. Guerra
SVP Development and Corporate Relations: Robert Altman
SVP Technology and Operations: Edward P. Caleca
Director, Corporate Communications and Speechwriter: Patricia Murphy
Auditors: PricewaterhouseCoopers LLP

LOCATIONS

HQ: 1320 Braddock Place, Alexandria, VA 22314
Phone: 703-739-5000 **Fax:** —
Web: www.pbs.org

PRODUCTS/OPERATIONS

Selected Programming

Antiques Roadshow
Austin City Limits
Barney
Frontier House
Frontline
Great Performances
In The Mix
Juila Child: Lessons with Master Chefs
Lawrence Welk Show
Live from Lincoln Center
Masterpiece Theater
McLaughlin Group
Mister Rogers' Neighborhood
Mystery!
Nature
The NewsHour with Jim Lehrer
The New Yankee Workshop
NOVA
Now with Bill Moyers
P.O.V.
Sesame Street
Teletubbies
This Old House
Victory Garden
Washington Week
ZOOM

COMPETITORS

A&E Networks
BBC
Discovery Communications
NBC
National Geographic
Universal Television

HISTORICAL FINANCIALS

Company Type: Not-for-profit

Income Statement

FYE: June 30

	REVENUE ($ mil.)	NET INCOME ($ mil.)	NET PROFIT MARGIN	EMPLOYEES
6/02	534	—	—	500
6/01	542	—	—	—
Annual Growth	(1.4%)	—	—	—

Revenue History

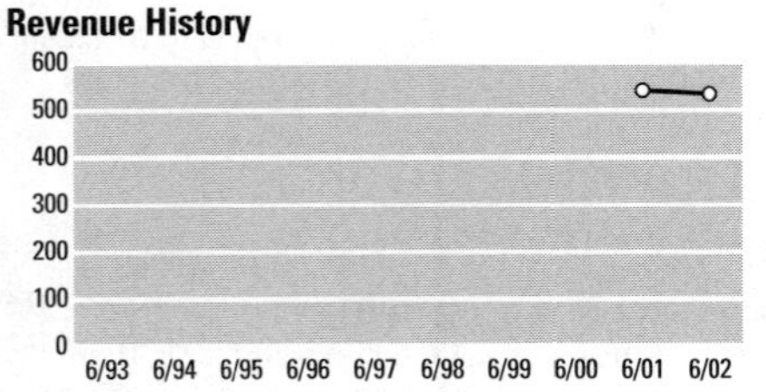

Publix Super Markets, Inc.

Shoppers at Publix shouldn't have to worry about being checked out — although with its share of gender and race discrimination lawsuits, they might wonder. Publix Super Markets is the #1 privately owned supermarket chain in the US. Most of its 740-plus stores are in Florida, but it also operates in Alabama, Georgia, South Carolina, and Tennessee. Publix makes some of its own deli, bakery, and dairy goods, and many stores offer flowers, housewares, and pharmacies. Founder George Jenkins began offering stock to Publix employees in 1930. Employees own about 27% of Publix, which is still run by the Jenkins family.

By emphasizing service and a family-friendly image rather than price, Publix has grown faster and been more profitable than Winn-Dixie Stores and other rivals. While winning Florida's shoppers, Publix has lost a few legal battles brought by its employees. It has settled three suits (over gender and race discrimination) but currently is embroiled in another suit alleging it discriminated against Hispanics. Despite the lawsuits, Publix was named to *FORTUNE* magazine's "Most Admired Companies" list.

Publix is moving into the convenience store/gas station business with its "Pix" convenience stores. It has two stores in Polk County, Florida, and is opening two more in Deltona and Kissimmee. Publix opens about 30 new supermarkets each year. About 75% of the the company's stores are in Florida.

HISTORY

George Jenkins, age 22, resigned as manager of the Piggly Wiggly grocery in Winter Haven, Florida, in 1930. With money he had saved to buy a car, he opened his own grocery store, Publix, next door to his old employer. The small store (named after a chain of movie theaters) prospered despite the Depression, and in 1935 Jenkins opened another Publix in the same town.

Five years later, after the supermarket format had become popular, Jenkins closed his two smaller locations and opened a new, more modern Publix Market. With pastel colors and electric-eye doors, it was also the first US store to feature air conditioning.

Publix Super Markets bought the All-American chain of Lakeland, Florida (19 stores), in 1944 and moved its corporate headquarters to that city. The company began offering S&H Green Stamps in 1953, and in 1956 it replaced its original supermarket with a mall featuring an enlarged Publix and a Green Stamp redemption center. Publix expanded into South Florida in the late 1950s and began selling stock to employees.

As Florida's population grew, Publix continued to expand, opening its 100th store in 1964. Publix was the first grocery chain in the state to use bar-code scanners — all its stores had the technology by 1981. The company beat Florida banks in providing ATMs and during the 1980s opened debit card stations.

Publix continued to grow in the 1980s, safe from takeover attempts because of its employee ownership. In 1988 the company installed the first automated checkout systems in South Florida, giving patrons an always-open checkout lane.

Publix stopped offering Green Stamps in 1989, and most of the $19 million decrease in the chain's advertising expenditures was attributed to the end of the 36-year promotion. That year, after almost six decades, "Mr. George" — as founder Jenkins was known — stepped down as chairman in favor of his son Howard. (George died in 1996.)

In 1991 Publix opened its first store outside Florida, in Georgia, as part of its plan to become a major player in the Southeast. Publix entered South Carolina in 1993 with one supermarket; it also tripled its presence in Georgia to 15 stores.

The United Food and Commercial Workers Union began a campaign in 1994 against alleged gender and racial discrimination in Publix's hiring, promotion, and compensation policies.

Publix opened its first store in Alabama in 1996. That year a federal judge allowed about 150,000 women to join a class-action suit filed in 1995 by 12 women who had sued Publix charging that the company consistently channeled female employees into low-paying jobs with little chance for good promotions. The case, said to be the biggest sex discrimination lawsuit ever, was set to go to trial, but in 1997 the company paid $82.5 million to settle and another $3.5 million to settle a complaint of discrimination against black applicants and employees.

Publix promised to change its promotion policies, but two more lawsuits alleging discrimination against women and blacks were filed in 1997 and 1998. The suit filed on behalf of the women was denied class-action status in 2000. Later that year the company settled the racial discrimination lawsuit for $10.5 million. Howard Jenkins stepped down as CEO in mid-2001; his cousin Charlie Jenkins took the helm.

In mid-2002 Publix made an equity investment in Florida-based Crispers, a chain of 13 quick-serve restaurants targeting health-conscious diners. Also that year, Publix entered the Nashville, Tennessee, market with the purchase of seven Albertson's supermarkets, a convenience store, and a fuel center.

In mid-2003 Publix pulled the plug on its online store PublixDirect, which offered delivery service in parts of Florida, citing disappointing sales.

EXECUTIVES

Chairman: Howard M. Jenkins, age 50
Vice Chairman: Hoyt R. (Barney) Barnett, age 59, $324,600 pay
CEO and Director: Charles H. (Charlie) Jenkins Jr., age 59, $466,093 pay
President and Director: W. Edwin (Ed) Crenshaw, age 52, $401,088 pay
CFO and Treasurer: David P. Phillips, age 43, $263,743 pay
SVP and CIO: Daniel M. Risener, age 62, $269,160 pay
SVP and Director: Tina P. Johnson, age 43
SVP, Supply Chain: James J. (Jim) Lobinsky, age 63
SVP: Thomas M. O'Connor, age 55
VP, Atlanta Division: Robert H. Moore, age 60
VP and Assistant Secretary: Linda Kane, age 37
VP and Controller: G. Gino DiGrazia, age 40
VP and Controller: Sandra J. (Sandy) Woods
VP, Distribution: Richard J. Schuler, age 47
VP, Facilities: David S. Duncan, age 49
VP, Human Resources and Compliance: James H. Rhodes II, age 58
VP, Human Resources and Employment Law: Joseph W. Carvin, age 51
VP, Internal Audit: Linda S. Hall, age 43
VP, Jacksonville Division: Todd Jones
VP, Lakeland Division: Thomas M. McLaughlin, age 52
VP, Manufacturing: R. Scott Charlton, age 44
VP, Marketing: Mark R. Irby, age 47
VP, Operations, Miami Division: William V. (Bill) Fauerbach, age 56

VP, Product Business Development, Fresh Product: David E. Bridges, age 53
VP, Product Business Development, Grocery/Non-Foods: David E. Bornmann, age 45
VP, Public Affairs: M. Clayton Hollis Jr., age 46
VP, Real Estate: John R. Frazier, age 53
VP, Retail Business Development: Dale S. Myers, age 50
VP, Risk Management: Edward T. Shivers, age 63
General Counsel and Secretary: John A. Attaway Jr., age 44
Auditors: KPMG LLP

LOCATIONS

HQ: 3300 Airport Rd., Lakeland, FL 33811
Phone: 863-688-1188 **Fax:** 863-284-5532
Web: www.publix.com

Publix Super Markets operates about 740 grocery stores in Alabama, Florida, Georgia, South Carolina, and Tennessee. The company also has three dairy processing plants (Deerfield Beach and Lakeland, Florida, and Lawrenceville, Georgia) and a deli plant and a bakery in Lakeland. Publix operates eight distribution centers in Florida (Boynton Beach, Deerfield Beach, Jacksonville, Lakeland, Miami, Orlando, and Sarasota) and Georgia (Lawrenceville).

2002 Stores

	No.
Florida	565
Georgia	137
South Carolina	28
Alabama	7
Tennessee	4
Total	**741**

PRODUCTS/OPERATIONS

Selected Supermarket Departments

Bakery
Banking
Dairy
Deli
Ethnic foods
Floral
Groceries
Health and beauty care
Housewares
Meat
Pharmacy
Photo processing
Produce
Seafood

Foods Processed

Baked goods
Dairy products
Deli items

COMPETITORS

Albertson's
ALDI
BI-LO
Bruno's Supermarkets
Costco Wholesale
CVS
Delhaize America
Fleming Companies
IGA
Ingles Markets
Kerr Drug
Kmart
Kroger
Nash Finch
The Pantry
Rite Aid
Royal Ahold
Ruddick
Sedano's
Smart & Final
Walgreen
Wal-Mart
Whole Foods
Winn-Dixie

HISTORICAL FINANCIALS

Company Type: Private

Income Statement

FYE: Last Saturday in December

	REVENUE ($ mil.)	NET INCOME ($ mil.)	NET PROFIT MARGIN	EMPLOYEES
12/02	16,027	632	3.9%	123,000
12/01	15,370	530	3.5%	126,000
12/00	14,724	530	3.6%	126,000
12/99	13,069	462	3.5%	120,000
12/98	12,067	378	3.1%	117,000
12/97	11,224	355	3.2%	111,000
12/96	10,431	265	2.5%	103,000
12/95	9,393	242	2.6%	95,000
12/94	8,665	239	2.8%	90,000
12/93	7,473	184	2.5%	82,000
Annual Growth	8.8%	14.7%	—	4.6%

2002 Year-End Financials

Debt ratio: 0.0%
Return on equity: 21.9%
Cash ($ mil.): 214
Current ratio: 1.07
Long-term debt ($ mil.): 0

Net Income History

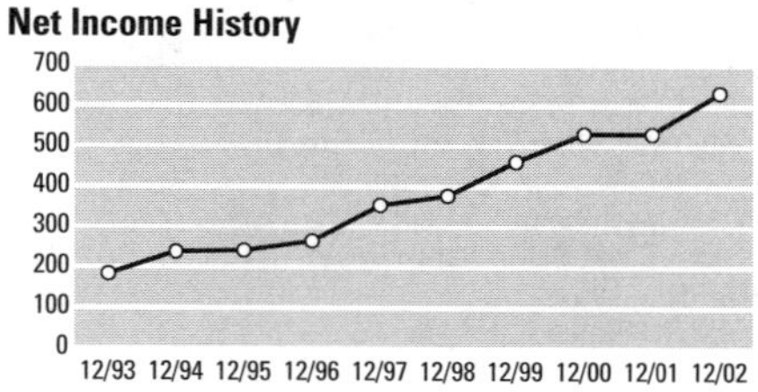

Purdue Pharma

Purdue Pharma makes drugs, not boilers. The company, (formerly Purdue Frederick), known for OTC medicines like Betadine (an antiseptic) and Senokot (a laxative), concentrates its research and development on pain management and cancer. Prescription drugs include pain relievers MS Contin and OxyContin. It is also developing cardiac and respiratory therapies, as well as inhaled drug delivery systems. The firm markets products from other manufacturers in addition to its own products. Purdue Pharma also sponsors the pain control organization Partners Against Pain. Founded in 1892, the firm is part of a network of affiliates with operations in Asia, North and South America, and Europe.

EXECUTIVES

Chairman and Co-CEO: Mortimer D. Sackler
Co-CEO: Raymond R. Sackler
President: Richard S. Sackler
EVP and COO: Michael Friedman
EVP and CFO: Edward B. Mahony
EVP and General Counsel: Howard R. Udell
EVP and International General Counsel: Stuart Baker
EVP, Manufacturing: Edward Albright
EVP, Worldwide Research and Development: Paul D. Goldenheim
VP, Human Resources: David Long
VP, Sales and Marketing: James Lang
Executive Director, Public Affairs: Robin Hogen

LOCATIONS

HQ: Purdue Pharma L.P.
201 Tresser Blvd., Stamford, CT 06901
Phone: 203-588-8000 **Fax:** 203-588-8850
Web: www.purduepharma.com

Purdue Pharma operates facilities in Stamford, Connecticut; Cranbury and Totowa, New Jersey; Ardsley, New York; Wilson, North Carolina; and Coventry, Rhode Island.

PRODUCTS/OPERATIONS

Selected Alliances

3M Drug Delivery Systems
Abbott Laboratories
Celltech Group plc
Corixa Corporation
Genzyme Molecular Oncology

COMPETITORS

Abbott GmbH
Aventis
Bayer AG
Bristol-Myers Squibb
Elan Corporation
Endo Pharmaceuticals
Johnson & Johnson
Merck
Novartis
Pfizer

HISTORICAL FINANCIALS

Company Type: Private

Income Statement

FYE: December 31

	REVENUE ($ mil.)	NET INCOME ($ mil.)	NET PROFIT MARGIN	EMPLOYEES
12/01	1,500	—	—	3,000
12/00	1,200	—	—	3,000
12/99	812	—	—	—
12/98	603	—	—	—
Annual Growth	35.5%	—	—	0.0%

Revenue History

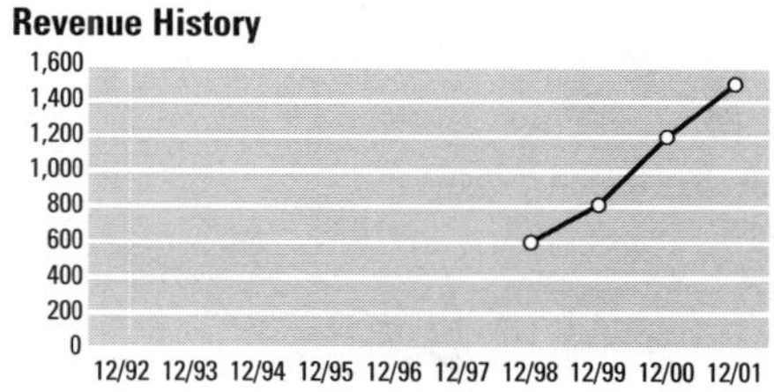

Purity Wholesale Grocers, Inc.

Untainted by grocery retailing, Purity Wholesale Grocers (PWG) sticks to getting the goods to grocers. The company takes advantage of the discounts granted to large wholesalers and retailers (and of the promotional pricing offered in certain regions) by purchasing items and selling them to retailers not privy to those discounts. PWG moves groceries, health and beauty care items, pharmaceutical products, dairy foods, and dry goods to US grocery chains, drugstores, and convenience stores. PWG's marketing network is made up of about a dozen independently operated food distributors, marketers, and transportation firms in the US and Puerto Rico. The company is owned by Jeff Levitetz, who founded PWG in 1982.

EXECUTIVES

Chairman: Jeff Levitetz
President and CEO: Salvatore Ricciardi
CFO: Alan Rutner
SVP, Operations: John Tarr
Controller: Tom Jankus
Director of Human Resources: Karen McGrath

LOCATIONS

HQ: 5400 Broken Sound Blvd. NW, Ste. 100, Boca Raton, FL 33487
Phone: 561-994-9360 **Fax:** 561-241-4628
Web: www.pwg-inc.com

COMPETITORS

Dot Foods
Eby-Brown
Fleming Companies
Nash Finch
Spartan Stores
SUPERVALU
SYSCO

HISTORICAL FINANCIALS

Company Type: Private

Income Statement FYE: June 30

	REVENUE ($ mil.)	NET INCOME ($ mil.)	NET PROFIT MARGIN	EMPLOYEES
6/02	1,600	—	—	490
6/01	1,450	—	—	440
6/00	1,300	—	—	650
6/99	1,500	—	—	650
6/98	1,200	—	—	600
6/97	1,000	—	—	400
6/96	700	—	—	300
6/95	650	—	—	275
Annual Growth	13.7%	—	—	8.6%

Revenue History

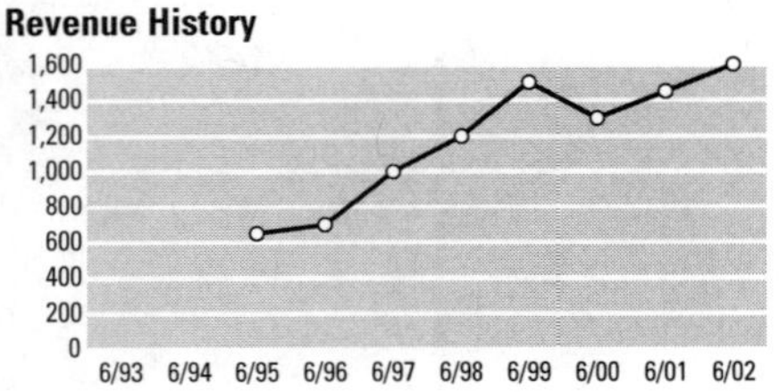

Quad/Graphics

Your mailbox may be filled with Quad/Graphics' handiwork. One of the largest privately held printers in the US, the company prints catalogs, magazines, books, direct mail, and other items. It offers a full range of services, including design, photography, desktop production, printing, binding, wrapping, and (through subsidiary Parcel/Direct) distribution and transportation. At its printing facilities — five of which are in Wisconsin — the company prints catalogs for Bloomingdale's and Victoria's Secret, among others, as well as periodicals such as *People, Newsweek, National Geographic,* and *Sports Illustrated.* Company employees and relatives of the founding Quadracci family own Quad/Graphics.

Quad is one of the most employee- and community-oriented companies in the industry. The firm has been recognized for its fun work atmosphere, and it provides on-site day care centers, health clubs, and medical clinics. In addition, it sponsors sports leagues (softball, bowling), awards college scholarships to employees' children, and provides interest-free auto loans. Quad/Graphic's Windhover Fund manages the philanthropic distribution of 5% of the company's pretax profit for social, cultural, and educational projects.

Founder and company president Harry Quadracci died at age 66 in 2002 in an accidental drowning. His brother, Tom, who has served as a board member and EVP, was appointed president of the company.

EXECUTIVES

President and CEO: Thomas A. Quadracci
VP Finance and CFO: John C. Fowler
VP and Controller: Linda Larson
VP Customer Service: Ron Nash
VP East Coast Sales: Bob Wachtendonk
VP Midwest Sales: Timothy Ohnmacht
VP Print Sales: Joel Quadracci
VP Transportation: Bill Deja
VP West Coast Sales: Renee Lekan
CIO: Steve Jaeger
Public Relations: Claire Ho

LOCATIONS

HQ: Quad/Graphics, Inc.
W224 N3322 Duplainville Rd., Pewaukee, WI 53072
Phone: 414-566-6000 **Fax:** 414-566-4668
Web: www.qg.com

Quad/Graphics has production plants in Georgia, New York, West Virginia, and Wisconsin. It also operates joint ventures in Argentina, Brazil, and Poland.

PRODUCTS/OPERATIONS

Selected Services

Binding and finishing
Color correction
Design
Desktop production
Direct mailing
Imaging and photography
Ink jetting
Integrated circulation
Mailing and distribution
Mailing list management
Parcel fulfillment
Printing
Scanning

COMPETITORS

Anderson Lithograph
Applied Graphics
Arandell
Banta
Berlin Industries
Black Dot Group
Champion Industries
Consolidated Graphics
Dai Nippon Printing
Merrill
Quebecor World
Queens Group, Inc.
R. R. Donnelley
Taylor Corporation
Toppan Printing
Vertis

HISTORICAL FINANCIALS

Company Type: Private

Income Statement FYE: December 31

	REVENUE ($ mil.)	NET INCOME ($ mil.)	NET PROFIT MARGIN	EMPLOYEES
12/02	1,800	—	—	11,000
12/01	1,700	—	—	10,500
12/00	1,800	—	—	14,000
12/99	1,500	—	—	13,000
12/98	1,400	—	—	11,000
12/97	1,200	—	—	11,000
12/96	1,042	—	—	9,500
12/95	1,002	—	—	8,444
12/94	801	—	—	7,500
12/93	703	—	—	6,800
Annual Growth	11.0%	—	—	5.5%

Revenue History

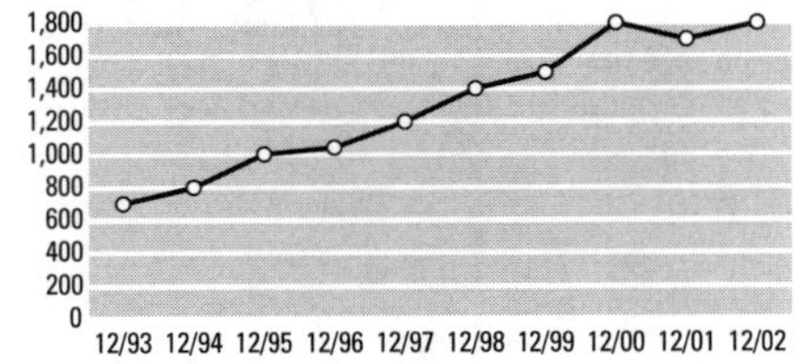

Quality Distribution

As far as bulk carriers go, Quality Distribution is the bulkiest: It's the largest tank truck operator in North America. Its main subsidiary, Quality Carriers, transports bulk chemical products in the US and Canada. Other operating units include TransPlastics and Levy Transport. Overall, the company's fleet consists of about 3,100 tractors and 7,700 trailers. Clients have included Procter & Gamble, PPG Industries, Dow Chemical, and DuPont. Quality Distribution also provides dry bulk hauling, transloading, tank cleaning, intermodal transport, and logistics services. A unit of Leon Black's Apollo Advisors owns 86% of the company, which was founded in 1965.

EXECUTIVES

Chairman, President, and CEO:
Thomas L. (Tom) Finkbiner, age 50
EVP Affiliate Relations: Michael A. Grimm, age 56
EVP and General Manager: Virgil T. (Bo) Leslie, age 48
SVP Corporate: Dennis R. (Denny) Copeland
SVP Finance and CFO: Samuel (Sam) Hensley, age 42
SVP Performance Planning: Keith J. Margelowsky
VP Internal Audit: Lorrel Margelowsky, age 48
VP Management Information Systems:
Siamak Azmoudeh
VP Marketing: Bob Kelly
SVP Operations, Quality Carriers: Randy Sheeler
Manager, Corporate Administration: Diane Helland

LOCATIONS

HQ: Quality Distribution Inc.
3802 Corporex Park Dr., Tampa, FL 33619
Phone: 813-630-5826 **Fax:** 813-630-1537
Web: www.qualitydistribution.com

COMPETITORS

Burlington Northern Santa Fe
Chemical Logistics Corporation
Groendyke Transport
J. B. Hunt
Landstar System
Manfredi Motor Transit
Schneider National
Stolt-Nielsen
Superior Carriers
Trimac
Union Pacific

HISTORICAL FINANCIALS

Company Type: Private

Income Statement FYE: December 31

	REVENUE ($ mil.)	NET INCOME ($ mil.)	NET PROFIT MARGIN	EMPLOYEES
12/02	517	(45)	—	4,431
12/01	511	(13)	—	—
12/00	557	(42)	—	—
Annual Growth	(3.7%)	—	—	—

2002 Year-End Financials

Debt ratio: —
Return on equity: —
Cash ($ mil.): 1
Current ratio: 1.27
Long-term debt ($ mil.): 394

Net Income History

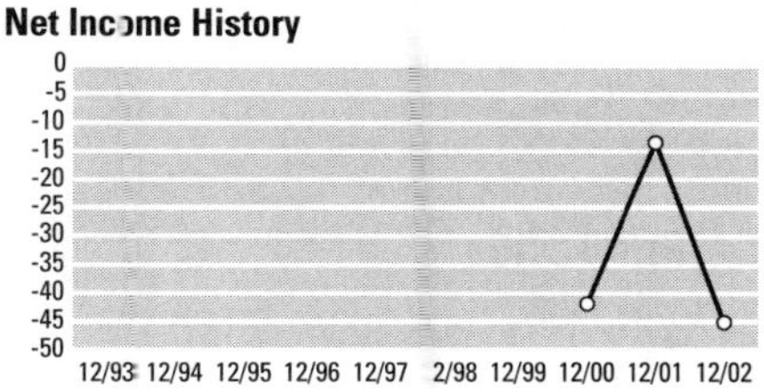

Quality King Distributors Inc.

Quality King Distributors rules a gargantuan gray market empire. It buys US name-brand products that have been exported to overseas markets, re-imports them, then sells them below suggested retail prices. The practice, deeply disliked by US manufacturers, but has been ruled legal by the Supreme Court. Quality King distributes groceries and hair, health, and beauty care products to pharmacy and grocery chains, grocery distributors, and wholesale clubs throughout the US. Bernard Nussdorf and his wife Ruth founded Quality King in 1960 in Queens, New York. The Nussdorf family still owns the company, which has transferred its pharmaceutical distribution business to affiliate QK Healthcare prior to spinning it off.

EXECUTIVES

Chairman: Glenn Nussdorf
CFO: Dennis Barkey
VP, Human Resources: Jane Midgal
VP, Data Processing: Marc Garrett

LOCATIONS

HQ: 2060 9th Ave., Ronkonkoma, NY 11779
Phone: 631-737-5555 **Fax:** 631-439-2388
Web: www.qkd.com

The company has warehouse facilities in Ronkonkoma, New York.

COMPETITORS

Allou
AmerisourceBergen
Cardinal Health
C.D. Smith Healthcare Inc
D & K Healthcare Resources
Henry Schein
Kinray
McKesson

HISTORICAL FINANCIALS

Company Type: Private

Income Statement FYE: October 31

	REVENUE ($ mil.)	NET INCOME ($ mil.)	NET PROFIT MARGIN	EMPLOYEES
10/02	2,450	—	—	1,400
10/01	2,400	—	—	1,300
10/00	2,050	—	—	1,200
10/99	1,800	—	—	1,000
10/98	1,400	—	—	1,000
10/97	1,200	—	—	1,000
10/96	950	—	—	900
10/95	880	—	—	700
10/94	850	—	—	660
10/93	860	—	—	650
Annual Growth	12.3%	—	—	8.9%

Revenue History

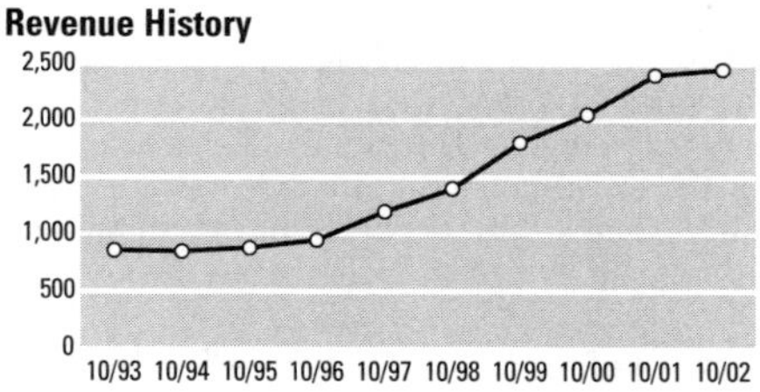

Quexco Incorporated

Quexco gets the lead out and puts it back in. A leading secondary lead producer, this private holding company recycles scrapped lead acid batteries into refined lead and lead products. Quexco's RSR Corporation subsidiary is one of the largest lead smelters in the US, with operations in California, Indiana, New York, and Texas. Quexco also owns Eco-Bat Technologies plc, a UK-based battery recycler with operations in Europe and South Africa. The company's RSR Technologies subsidiary (formerly its R&D unit) offers technology and product development services to the metals industry. Chairman and CEO Howard Meyers, who also heads Bayou Steel Corporation, controls Quexco.

EXECUTIVES

Chairman, President, and CEO: Howard M. Meyers, age 60

LOCATIONS

HQ: 2777 N. Stemmons Fwy., Dallas, TX 75207
Phone: 214-688-4000 **Fax:** 214-630-5864

Quexco has operations in the US, Europe, and South Africa.

PRODUCTS/OPERATIONS

Selected Operations

Eco-Bat Technologies plc (battery recycling, UK)
  STMC Holdings
RSR Corporation
  Bestolife Corporation (pipe thread compounds and lubricants for the oil exploration industry)
  Quemetco Metals Limited (electro-winning anodes for the copper industry)
  Revere Smelting & Refining (lead recycling)
RSR Technologies Inc. (recycling industry R&D services)
West Morris Properties, Inc.

COMPETITORS

Exide
Noranda
Renco

HISTORICAL FINANCIALS

Company Type: Private

Income Statement FYE: December 31

	ESTIMATED REVENUE ($ mil.)	NET INCOME ($ mil.)	NET PROFIT MARGIN	EMPLOYEES
12/02	2,000	—	—	7,000
12/01	2,000	—	—	7,000
Annual Growth	0.0%	—	—	0.0%

Revenue History

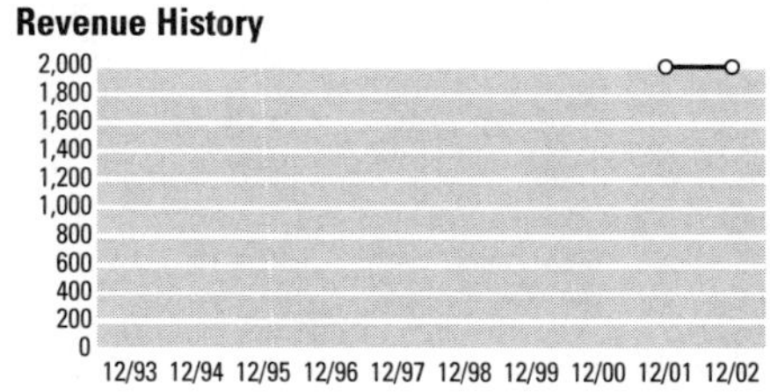

QuikTrip Corporation

QuikTrip provides a quick fix for people on the go. QuikTrip (QT) owns and operates some 400 gasoline and convenience stores primarily in the Midwest. QT stores, which average 4,500 to 5,000 sq. ft., feature the company's own brand of gas, as well as brand-name beverages, candy, and tobacco, and QT's own Quik 'n Tasty and HOTZI lines of sandwiches. QuikTrip travel centers offer CAT scales, food, fuel, showers, and other services for truckers. The company's FleetMaster program offers commercial trucking companies detailed reports showing drivers' product purchases, amounts spent, and odometer readings. QuikTrip was co-founded in 1958 by chairman Chester Cadieux and partners. His son Chet runs the company.

EXECUTIVES

Chairman: Chester Cadieux
President, and CEO: Chester (Chet) Cadieux Jr.
SVP, Finance: Terry Carter
Director, Human Resources: Kim Owen
Manager, Public and Government Affairs: Mike Thornbrugh

LOCATIONS

HQ: 4705 S. 129th East Ave., Tulsa, OK 74134
Phone: 918-615-7700 **Fax:** —
Web: www.quiktrip.com

QuikTrip owns stores in Arizona, Georgia, Illinois, Iowa, Kansas, Missouri, Nebraska, Oklahoma, and Texas.

COMPETITORS

7-Eleven
Casey's General Stores
ChevronTexaco
CITGO
Exxon Mobil
E-Z Mart Stores
Hale-Halsell
Krause Gentle
Motiva Enterprises
Racetrac Petroleum

HISTORICAL FINANCIALS

Company Type: Private

Income Statement FYE: April 30

	REVENUE ($ mil.)	NET INCOME ($ mil.)	NET PROFIT MARGIN	EMPLOYEES
4/02	3,050	—	—	6,575
4/01	2,929	—	—	6,045
4/00	2,347	—	—	5,248
4/99	1,804	—	—	4,796
4/98	1,830	—	—	4,635
4/97	1,730	—	—	4,400
4/96	1,423	—	—	4,075
4/95	1,195	—	—	2,501
4/94	985	—	—	2,200
4/93	827	—	—	2,500
Annual Growth	15.6%	—	—	11.3%

Revenue History

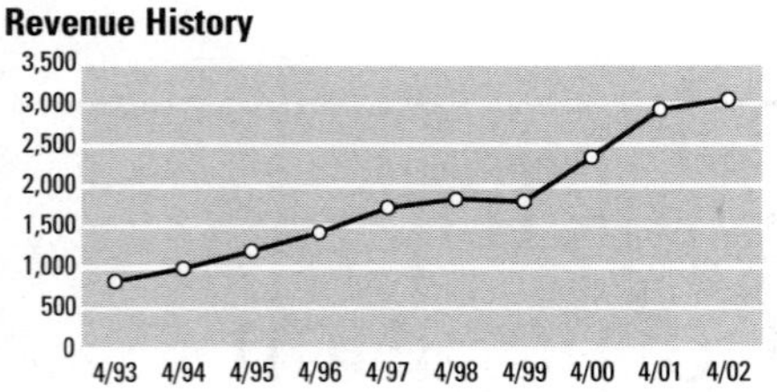

Quintiles Transnational

Quintiles Transnational has plenty to CRO about. One of the world's top contract research organizations (CROs), it provides services to help drug and medical device companies develop and sell their products. The firm's Product Development Services unit offers preclinical research and conducts clinical trials. The CRO's Commercialization unit offers regulatory consulting, as well as sales and marketing consulting, hiring, and training to get a product to buyers. Quintiles' PharmaBio Development unit teams with emerging health care firms to get new products approved and on the market by exchanging its R&D services for royalties. A group led by chairman Dennis Gillings took the firm private in September 2003.

The CRO's Verispan joint venture with McKesson provides health care information products. Verispan, formed in 2002, brought McKesson's Kelly/Waldron unit together with Quintiles-owned Scott-Levin, a preeminent pharmaceutical industry market research company, and SMG Marketing Group. By bringing these marketing services firms under one umbrella, Quintiles can stay involved in a product's life span longer.

Quintiles, which operates in almost 50 countries, has suffered the double-whammy of pharmaceutical industry consolidation, which has trimmed its client list, and industry cost-cutting efforts. More drugmakers are bringing R&D work in-house to keep down expenses; the firm's top client, Aventis, accounts for only 11% of sales.

Its PharmaBio Development and Verispan operations are among the company's attempts to continue to grow, even though they're in the risky business of pinning their hopes on drugs that may not make it onto the market. For instance, PharmaBio inked a deal with Eli Lilly to help market the as-yet-unapproved antidepressant Cymbalta, which it thinks could bring in a significant portion of the company's future revenues.

Quintiles ended its nearly 10-year stint as a public company in hopes that once it casts off the burden of meeting and beating Wall Street expectations, the CRO will have the freedom to grow its business as it chooses. The move brings founder Gillings back into the driver's seat; riding shotgun is financial backer BANK ONE's One Equity Partners. The returning CEO envisions Quintiles as an investor in the products it helps develop. However, the company loaded up on debt as part of its leap from NASDAQ.

EXECUTIVES

Chairman and CEO: Dennis B. Gillings, age 58, $680,067 pay
EVP and CFO: James L. Bierman, age 50, $431,706 pay
EVP, General Counsel, Secretary, and Head of Global Human Resources: John J. Russell Jr., age 56, $307,944 pay
SVP, Strategic Planning and Investor Relations: Greg Connors
SVP, Global Business Development: Tracy K. Tsuetaki, age 41
VP, Medical and Scientific Services: David Frakes
VP, Corporate Communications: Pat Grebe
Auditors: PricewaterhouseCoopers LLP

LOCATIONS

HQ: Quintiles Transnational Corp.
4709 Creekstone Dr., Ste. 200, Durham, NC 27703
Phone: 919-998-2000 **Fax:** 919-998-2094
Web: www.quintiles.com

Quintiles Transnational operates in 48 countries worldwide.

2002 Sales

	$ mil.	% of total
The Americas:		
US	695	35
Other countries	43	2
Europe & Africa:		
UK	344	17
Other countries	317	16
Asia/Pacific	193	10
Reimbursed service costs	400	20
Total	**1,992**	**100**

PRODUCTS/OPERATIONS

Selected Subsidiaries

Action International Marketing Services Limited (UK)
Benefit Holding, Inc.
Clin Data International (PTY) Limited (South Africa)
G.D.R.U. Limited (UK)
Innovex, L.P.
Laboratorie Novex Pharma Sarl (France)
The Lewin Group, Inc.
Medical Informatics KK (Japan)
Minerva Ireland Limited
PharmaBio Development, Inc.
Quintiles (Israel) Ltd.
Quintiles Hong Kong Limited
Source Informatics European Finance, Inc.
Spectral Laboratories Limited (India)
Transforce, S.A. de C.V. (Mexico)
Verispan, L.L.C.

COMPETITORS

Battelle Memorial
Covance
Healthworld Communications
IMS Health
Kendle
Life Sciences Research
NDCHealth
Nelson Communications
PAREXEL
Pharmaceutical Product Development

HISTORICAL FINANCIALS

Company Type: Private

Income Statement FYE: December 31

	REVENUE ($ mil.)	NET INCOME ($ mil.)	NET PROFIT MARGIN	EMPLOYEES
12/02	1,992	127	6.4%	15,548
12/01	1,620	(34)	—	17,224
12/00	1,660	419	25.2%	18,219
12/99	1,607	109	6.8%	20,453
12/98	1,188	84	7.0%	15,520
12/97	815	55	6.8%	10,900
12/96	538	4	0.8%	7,375
12/95	156	11	7.2%	2,000
12/94	90	7	7.4%	1,200
12/93	62	4	6.2%	900
Annual Growth	47.1%	47.7%	—	37.2%

2002 Year-End Financials

Debt ratio: 1.2%
Return on equity: 8.3%
Cash ($ mil.): 644
Current ratio: 2.09
Long-term debt ($ mil.): 19

Net Income History

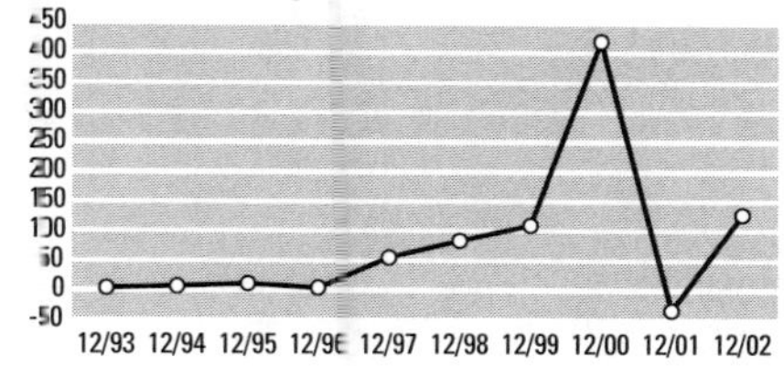

R.A.B. Holdings

R.A.B. Holdings holds the reins on two fast-growing grocery segments: kosher foods and health foods. It owns one of the top US kosher food makers, The B. Manischewitz Company, which makes matzos and other foods. It also operates Millbrook Distribution Services, which distributes specialty and natural foods, health and beauty care products, and general merchandise items to retailers in 42 states. R.A.B. has increased sales of its products by offering items such as rice pilafs and soup mixes to attract health-conscious non-Jewish consumers. The company also offers merchandising services to its retailers through Millbrook Retail Solutions. Founder, chairman, president, and CEO Richard Bernstein owns 40% of R.A.B.

EXECUTIVES

Chairman, President, and CEO: Richard A. Bernstein, age 57
Vice Chairman: Lewis J. Korman, age 58
EVP, CFO, Treasurer, and Director: Steven M. Grossman, age 42, $295,750 pay
EVP; President and CEO, Millbrook Distribution, and Director: Robert A. Sigel, age 49, $475,000 pay
SVP, Legal Affairs; Secretary; and Director: James A. Cohen, age 57, $234,000 pay
SVP: Ira A. Gomberg, age 59
President and CEO, The B. Manischewitz Company; and Director: Bruce W. Glickstein, age 57, $250,844 pay
EVP, Marketing, Millbrook Distribution Services: William Paul
SVP, Human Resources, Millbrook Distribution Services: Pete Schmidt
Auditors: Deloitte & Touche LLP

LOCATIONS

HQ: R.A.B. Holdings, Inc.
444 Madison Ave., New York, NY 10022
Phone: 212-688-4500 **Fax:** 212-888-5025
Web: www.millbrookds.com

PRODUCTS/OPERATIONS

2003 Sales

	$ mil.	% of total
Millbrook	459.5	90
Manischewitz	62.1	10
	(13.5)	—
Total	**508.1**	**100**

Selected Products and Brands

Distribution
Ethnic and specialty foods (Manischewitz, Horowitz Margareten, Goodman's, Gold Boat, Season, Guiltless Gourmet)
General merchandise items
Health and beauty care items
Natural foods

Kosher Foods
Cake mixes
Cookies
Crackers
Gefilte fish
Matzos
Noodles
Soups

COMPETITORS

AWG
Distribution Plus
Fleming Companies
Frito-Lay
Haddon House
Hain Celestial
Nash Finch
SUPERVALU
Tree of Life
United Natural
Wessanen

HISTORICAL FINANCIALS

Company Type: Private

Income Statement FYE: March 31

	REVENUE ($ mil.)	NET INCOME ($ mil.)	NET PROFIT MARGIN	EMPLOYEES
3/03	508	(33)	—	1,520
3/02	596	(7)	—	1,770
3/01	652	(5)	—	2,340
3/00	581	11	1.9%	2,660
3/99	511	(7)	—	2,120
3/98	470	1	0.3%	2,330
Annual Growth	1.6%	—	—	(8.2%)

2003 Year-End Financials

Debt ratio: —
Return on equity: —
Cash ($ mil.): 6
Current ratio: 1.81
Long-term debt ($ mil.): 165

Net Income History

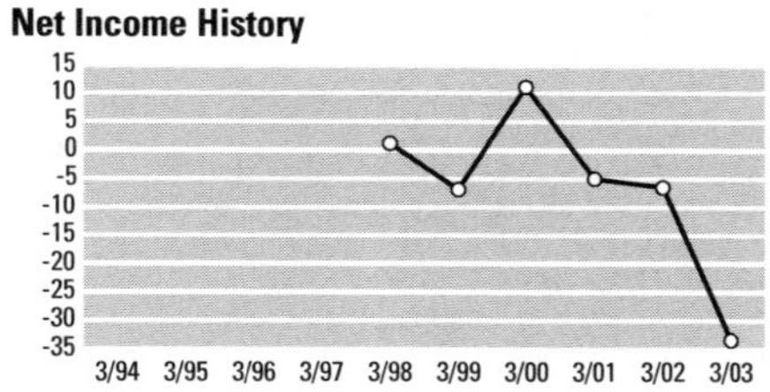

RaceTrac Petroleum, Inc.

RaceTrac Petroleum hopes it is a popular pit stop for gasoline and snacks in the Southeast. The company operates about 500 company-owned and franchised gas stations and convenience stores in Alabama, Arkansas, Florida, Georgia, Kentucky, Louisiana, Mississippi, North Carolina, South Carolina, Tennessee, Texas, and Virginia under the RaceTrac and Raceway names. Carl Bolch founded RaceTrac in Missouri in 1934. His son, chairman and CEO Carl Bolch Jr., moved the company into high-volume gas stations with long, self-service islands that can serve many vehicles at once. RaceTrac's convenience stores also sell fresh deli food, rent videos, and offer some fast-food fare. The Bolch family owns the company.

EXECUTIVES

Chairman and CEO: Carl E. Bolch Jr.
President: Max Lenker
CFO: Robert J. Dumbacher
SVP, Operations: Ben Tison
VP, Human Resources: Allison Moran

LOCATIONS

HQ: 300 Technology Ct., Smyrna, GA 30082
Phone: 770-431-7600 **Fax:** 770-431-7612
Web: www.racetrac.com

COMPETITORS

7-Eleven
ChevronTexaco
Cumberland Farms
Exxon Mobil
E-Z Mart Stores
Gate Petroleum
Motiva Enterprises
The Pantry
Pilot
QuikTrip

HISTORICAL FINANCIALS

Company Type: Private

Income Statement FYE: December 31

	REVENUE ($ mil.)	NET INCOME ($ mil.)	NET PROFIT MARGIN	EMPLOYEES
12/02	3,000	—	—	3,820
12/01	2,942	—	—	3,850
12/00	2,811	—	—	4,932
12/99	1,846	—	—	3,700
12/98	1,500	—	—	3,800
12/97	1,005	—	—	3,612
12/96	1,340	—	—	3,000
12/95	1,056	—	—	2,700
12/94	909	—	—	2,300
12/93	795	—	—	2,100
Annual Growth	15.9%	—	—	6.9%

Revenue History

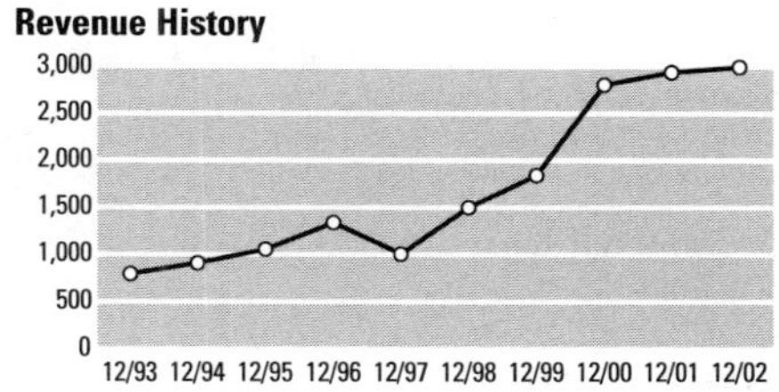

RailWorks Corporation

RailWorks tries to stay on track by providing rail system services and products across the US and Canada. RailWorks companies build, repair, maintain, and operate tracks; install communications and signaling systems; and oversee rail electrification. Customers include short-line railroads, transit authorities and commuter railroads, municipalities, and manufacturing and power plants. Nonrail services include electrical contracting and providing bridge and highway support structures. RailWorks had been streamlining operations before filing for bankruptcy in 2001. The group emerged from bankruptcy in 2002 as a private company whose primary owners include two private investment groups and RailWorks employees.

EXECUTIVES

Chairman: Albert W. (Ab) Rees
CEO: Jim Kimsey
VP and CFO: Kenneth J. (Ken) Bauer
President, RailWorks Transit, Inc; EVP, L.K. Comstock & Co.: Ben D'Alessandro
President, Track Products and Services: William R. (Bill) Donley
President, Transit Systems: C. William (Bill) Moore
VP and General Counsel: Michael (Mike) Rivera
Corporate and Marketing Communications: Kathy Simpson
Auditors: PricewaterhouseCoopers LLP

LOCATIONS

HQ: 1 N. Lexington Ave., White Plains, NY 10601
Phone: 914-323-3051 **Fax:** 410-580-6099
Web: www.railworks.com

RailWorks operates from more than 30 offices in the US and Canada.

PRODUCTS/OPERATIONS

Selected Subsidiaries

Breaking Technology & Equipment, Inc.
CPI Concrete Products, Inc.
Dura-Wood LLC
Hovey Industries, Ltd.
HSQ Technology
L.K. Comstock & Company, Inc.
M-Track Enterprises, Inc.
Midwest Construction Services, Inc.
National Rail Contractors, Inc.
Neosho Central America, Inc.
Pacific Northern Rail Contractors, Inc.
PNR Leasing, Ltd.
RailWorks Canada, Inc.
RailWorks Track Services, Inc.
RailWorks Transit, Inc.
RailWorks Wood Products, Inc.
RWKS Construction, Inc.
U.S. Railway Supply, Inc.
Wood Waste Energy, Inc.

COMPETITORS

ALSTOM
AMSTED
L. B. Foster
Meridian Rail
MYR Group
Parsons
Washington Group

HISTORICAL FINANCIALS

Company Type: Private

Income Statement FYE: December 31

	REVENUE ($ mil.)	NET INCOME ($ mil.)	NET PROFIT MARGIN	EMPLOYEES
12/01	617	—	—	3,850
12/00	614	—	—	3,320
12/99	468	—	—	2,500
12/98	213	—	—	2,000
12/97	253	—	—	1,748
Annual Growth	24.9%	—	—	21.8%

Net Income History

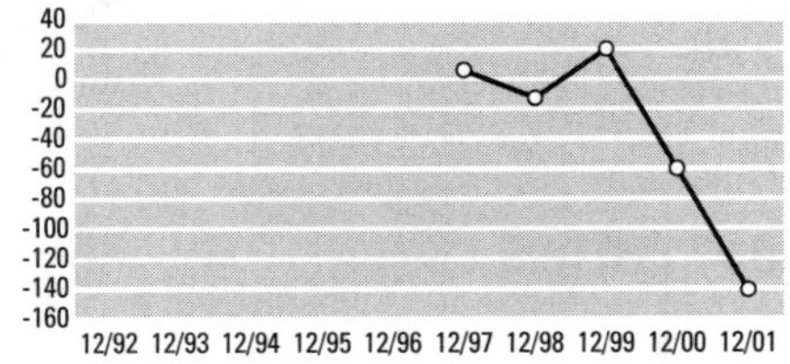

Raley's Inc.

Raley's has to stock plenty of fresh fruit and great wines — it sells to the people that produce them. The company operates about 135 supermarkets and larger-sized superstores, mostly in Northern California, but also in Nevada and New Mexico. In addition to its flagship Raley's Superstores, the company operates Bel Air Markets, Nob Hill Foods (an upscale Bay Area chain), and a discount warehouse chain, Food Source. Raley's stores typically offer groceries, natural foods, liquor, and pharmacies. Readers of *Consumer Reports* named Raley's the #1 supermarket chain in the US in 2000. Founded during the Depression by Tom Raley, the company is owned by Tom's daughter Joyce Raley Teel and is run by the family.

EXECUTIVES

Co-Chairman: James E. Teel
Co-Chairman: Joyce Raley Teel, age 72
President: William J. Coyne
COO: David W. (Dave) D'Arezzo, age 44
EVP and CFO: William Anderson
SVP, Human Resources: Jeffrey D. Szczesny
SVP, Sales and Marketing: Dennis Ferguson
VP, Superstores: Rick Kaiser
CIO: Eric F. G. Wilson
Director, General Merchandise Sales and Merchandising: John Raley
General Counsel: Jennifer Crabb
Corporate Communications Specialist: Nicole Townsend

LOCATIONS

HQ: 500 W. Capitol Ave., West Sacramento, CA 95605
Phone: 916-373-3333 **Fax:** 916-371-1323
Web: www.raleys.com

2003 Stores

	No.
California	113
Nevada	12
New Mexico	9
Total	**134**

PRODUCTS/OPERATIONS

2003 Stores

	No.
Raley's Superstores	83
Nob Hill Foods	26
Bel Air Markets	18
Food Source	7
Total	**134**

COMPETITORS

Albertson's
Costco Wholesale
Food 4 Less
Kroger
Longs Drug
Ralphs
Safeway
Save Mart
Trader Joe's Co
Wal-Mart
Whole Foods
Wild Oats Markets
WinCo Foods

HISTORICAL FINANCIALS

Company Type: Private

Income Statement FYE: June 30

	REVENUE ($ mil.)	NET INCOME ($ mil.)	NET PROFIT MARGIN	EMPLOYEES
6/02	3,200	—	—	17,000
6/01	3,000	—	—	17,000
6/00	2,849	—	—	16,800
6/99	3,000	—	—	15,000
6/98	2,193	—	—	15,000
6/97	1,957	—	—	12,900
6/96	1,912	—	—	11,000
6/95	1,810	—	—	7,500
6/94	1,800	—	—	7,150
6/93	1,850	—	—	—
Annual Growth	6.3%	—	—	11.4%

Revenue History

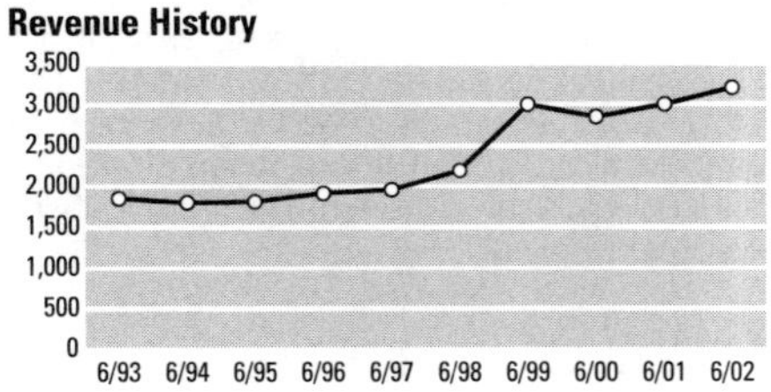

Rand McNally & Company

Rand McNally lets you know where you stand. The largest commercial mapmaker in the world, the company is famous for its flagship Rand McNally Road Atlas —the best-selling product in the history of mapmaking. In addition, the company produces travel-related software (TripMaker, StreetFinder) and educational products for classrooms (globes, atlases). Rand McNally also operates a Web site and makes mileage and routing software for the transportation industry. Founded in 1856, Rand McNally was owned by the McNally family until AEA Investors bought a controlling interest in 1997.

The company makes maps for the Canadian market through its Rand McNally Canada unit. It sells its products online and through some 50,000 retail outlets across the US, including 25 Rand McNally stores.

Although it created a Web site in 1996, the company didn't really begin focusing on the Internet until 1999, years later than online rivals such as MapQuest.com. In 2000 Rand McNally relaunched its Web site in hopes of catching up with its online competitors.

In early 2003 Rand McNally filed for Chapter

11 bankruptcy protection. The company exited bankruptcy within two months, with buyout firm Leonard Green & Partners as its new majority owner with a 50% stake.

HISTORY

Rand McNally was founded by William Rand and Andrew McNally in 1856. In 1864 the pair bought the job-printing department of the *Chicago Tribune,* and they expanded into the printing of railroad tickets and schedules. They published their first book, a Chicago business directory, in 1870.

In 1872 the company printed its first map for the *Railway Guide.* Rand McNally later expanded into publishing paperback novels (popular among train travelers), and by 1891 annual sales topped $1 million.

During the 1890s McNally bought Rand's share of the business, and the company branched into printing school textbooks. Rand McNally's first photo auto guide was issued in 1907, and the company introduced its first complete US road atlas in 1924.

When Hitler invaded Poland in 1939, Rand McNally's New York stock of European maps sold out in one day. WWII necessitated the revision of a number of maps — a challenge that the company continued to face throughout the 20th century.

Although the company had abandoned adult fiction and nonfiction in 1914, it reentered the field in 1948 when a company official persuaded explorer Thor Heyerdahl to write a book for the company about his adventures. First published in 1950, Heyerdahl's *Kon-Tiki* sold more than a million copies in its first six years.

Rand McNally produced its first four-color road atlas in 1960, and during the 1970s it began publishing travel guides for Mobil Oil. The next decade the company published several new road atlases to fill the void created when gas stations discontinued their practice of giving away free road maps. Rand McNally sold its textbook publishing business to Houghton Mifflin in 1980, and five years later it began computerizing its cartography operation.

In 1993 the company acquired Allmaps Canada Limited (now Rand McNally Canada). It introduced *TripMaker,* a CD-ROM vacation-planning program, the next year. Also in 1994 Rand McNally won a contract to create maps for a *Reader's Digest* atlas. The company debuted its StreetFinder street-level software in 1995 and created its Cartographic and Information Services division in 1996. It also established a Web site that year.

The next year, as part of a plan to focus on mapmaking and providing geographic information, Rand McNally sold a number of its subsidiaries (Book Services Group, DocuSystems Group). AEA Investors bought a controlling interest in the company later in 1997, bringing an end to more than 140 years of McNally family control (though it did retain a minority stake). While Rand McNally was still profitable, the sale to AEA underscored the challenges facing the company: Growth in earnings had slowed, and technological changes (Internet maps and software) had altered the mapmaking industry.

Rand McNally expanded in 1999 with acquisitions of mapmakers Thomas Bros. Maps and King of the Road Map Service. Later that year Henry Feinberg resigned as chairman and CEO. Richard Davis was appointed CEO, and John Macomber became chairman.

In 2000 the company relaunched its Web site with additional trip planning capabilities. Also that year it became the primary North American distributor of *National Geographic* maps and COO Norman Wells replaced Davis as CEO.

In 2001 Michael Hehir was named CEO, Wells replaced Macomber as chairman, and Macomber remained as a director on the board.

EXECUTIVES

Chairman: Norman E. Wells
President, CEO, and Director: Michael Hehir
EVP Operations: Kevin Harold
SVP and CFO: Norman Smagley, age 42
SVP and Chief Administrative Officer: Dean Haskell
SVP and CTO: Ken Levin
SVP Business Development: Jim Welch
SVP Consumer Travel: Victoria (Vicki) Donnowitz
SVP Geographic Information Services: Joel Minster
SVP Supply Chain Management: Tom Anderson
VP Business Operation: Alan Yefsky
VP Sales and Distribution: Dennis FitzPatrick
Director, Educational Publishing: Pat Riley
Director, Retail Stores and Internet: David Rickabaugh
General Manager, Transportation Data Management: Bob Simmons
Group Controller: David Jones
Editorial Director: Laurie Borman
Director of Marketing: Amy Krouse
Corporate Communications and Media Relations: Jennifer Chrzastek
Media Relations: Christina Goodwin

LOCATIONS

HQ: 8255 N. Central Park Ave., Skokie, IL 60076
Phone: 847-329-8100 **Fax:** 847-329-6361
Web: www.randmcnally.com

Rand McNally operates in the US and Canada. It has retail stores in California, Florida, Illinois, Massachusetts, Michigan, Minnesota, Missouri, New Jersey, New York, Pennsylvania, Texas, Virginia, and Washington, DC.

PRODUCTS/OPERATIONS

Selected Print Products

Business Travelers' Briefcase Atlas
Motor Carriers' Road Atlas
Rand McNally Pocket City Atlas
Rand McNally Road Atlas
The Thomas Guides

Selected Sales Channels

Rand McNally (retail stores)
randmcnally.com (e-commerce)

Selected Software

New Millennium World Atlas Deluxe Edition
Rand McNally StreetFinder Deluxe
Rand McNally TripMaker Deluxe

COMPETITORS

AAA
Analytical Surveys
DeLorme
ESRI
Expedia
Globe Pequot
Lonely Planet
MapInfo
MapQuest.com
Michelin
National Geographic
Piersen Graphics
R. L. Polk
TravRoute

HISTORICAL FINANCIALS

Company Type: Private

Income Statement FYE: December 31

	REVENUE ($ mil.)	NET INCOME ($ mil.)	NET PROFIT MARGIN	EMPLOYEES
12/01	200	—	—	1,000
12/00	200	—	—	1,000
12/99	179	—	—	920
12/98	175	—	—	1,000
12/97	175	—	—	1,000
12/96	163	—	—	1,000
12/95	469	—	—	4,650
12/94	438	—	—	4,200
12/93	395	—	—	4,000
12/92	342	—	—	4,000
Annual Growth	(5.8%)	—	—	(14.3%)

Revenue History

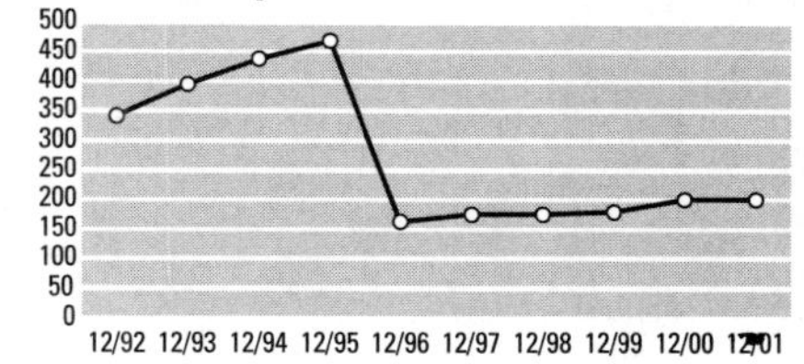

R. B. Pamplin

Founded by a man of the cloth, R. B. Pamplin casts a wide net. The family-owned conglomerate, started in 1957 by minister and company CEO Robert Pamplin Jr. (Robert Sr. is chairman), has operations ranging from entertainment to retail stores to manufacturing interests (asphalt, concrete, and textiles). The company's Mount Vernon Mills is one of the largest denim producers in the US. Pamplin's entertainment concerns include radio broadcasting, newspapers, and record labels in the northwestern US. The company's other units are as diverse as retail stores offering Christian products to Columbia Empire Farms, which grows berries and grapes used in preserves and wine, then sold through its Your NorthWest stores.

EXECUTIVES

Chairman: Robert Pamplin Sr.
President and CEO: Robert Boisseau (Bob) Pamplin Jr.
President and COO, Mount Vernon Mills: Roger W. Chastain

LOCATIONS

HQ: R. B. Pamplin Corp.
805 SW Broadway, Ste. 2400, Portland, OR 97205
Phone: 503-248-1133 **Fax:** 503-248-1175
Web: www.pamplin.org

COMPETITORS

Avondale Incorporated
Burlington Industries
CEMEX
Cone Mills
Gannett
Greenwood Mills
Holcim
Plains Cotton
Salem Communications
Springs Industries
U.S. Concrete
WestPoint Stevens

HISTORICAL FINANCIALS

Company Type: Private

Income Statement FYE: Saturday closest to Dec. 31

	REVENUE ($ mil.)	NET INCOME ($ mil.)	NET PROFIT MARGIN	EMPLOYEES
12/02	800	—	—	8,500
12/01	800	—	—	8,500
12/00*	890	—	—	7,584
5/99	844	—	—	7,500
5/98	843	—	—	7,000
5/97	802	—	—	6,500
5/96	800	—	—	6,500
5/95	835	—	—	6,250
5/94	695	—	—	5,728
5/93	675	—	—	—
Annual Growth	1.9%	—	—	5.1%

*Fiscal year change

Revenue History

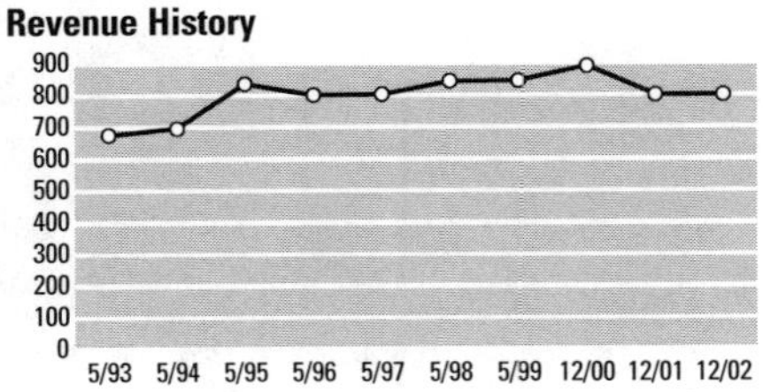

RDO Equipment

RDO Equipment herds Deere in a big way. RDO distributes, sells, rents, services, and finances equipment and new and used trucks to agricultural, construction, manufacturing, transportation, and warehousing industry customers. The company operates about 45 retail stores in nine states, almost 40 of which are Deere stores, making RDO one of the largest Deere dealership networks in North America. New Deere products generate 45% of sales. RDO also sells heavy-duty trucks through Volvo and Mack truck centers. RDO sold its 80%-owned RDO Rental Co. to United Rentals. Chairman Ronald Offutt founded the company in 1968, took it public in 1997, and returned it to private ownership, which he controls, in 2003.

EXECUTIVES

Chairman, President, CEO, and Director: Ronald D. Offutt, age 60
COO and Director: Christi J. Offutt, age 33
CFO: Steven B. Dewald, age 42
EVP, Project/Process Management: Kenneth J. (Skip) Horner Jr.
SVP, Special Projects: Larry E. Scott
Director, Information Systems: Dave Green
Chief People Officer: Jeff Antonelli
Secretary and Director: Allan F. Knoll, age 59
Auditors: PricewaterhouseCoopers LLP

LOCATIONS

HQ: RDO Equipment Co.
2829 S. University Dr., Fargo, ND 58103
Phone: 701-297-4288 **Fax:** 701-271-6328
Web: www.rdoequipment.com

RDO Equipment has about 45 dealerships in Arizona, California, Minnesota, Montana, Nebraska, North Dakota, South Dakota, Texas, and Washington.

PRODUCTS/OPERATIONS

2003 Sales

	% of total
New equipment & truck sales	51
Used equipment & truck sales	20
Product support (parts & service)	29
Total	**100**

COMPETITORS

AGCO
Caterpillar
CLARK Material
CNH Global
Crown Equipment
DaimlerChrysler
Financial Federal
Ford
Ingersoll-Rand
JCB
Kobe Steel
Komatsu
Navistar
Nissan
PACCAR
Ritchie Bros. Auctioneers
Toyota

HISTORICAL FINANCIALS

Company Type: Private

Income Statement FYE: January 31

	REVENUE ($ mil.)	NET INCOME ($ mil.)	NET PROFIT MARGIN	EMPLOYEES
1/03	535	3	0.6%	1,182
1/02	550	(2)	—	1,325
1/01	680	(19)	—	1,429
1/00	689	7	0.9%	1,602
1/99	579	2	0.3%	1,554
1/98	429	13	3.1%	1,214
1/97	302	11	3.7%	800
1/96	224	5	2.1%	663
1/95	184	10	5.3%	—
1/94	144	6	4.0%	—
Annual Growth	15.7%	(7.1%)	—	8.6%

2003 Year-End Financials

Debt ratio: 5.7%
Return on equity: 3.4%
Cash ($ mil.): 2
Current ratio: 1.41
Long-term debt ($ mil.): 5

Net Income History

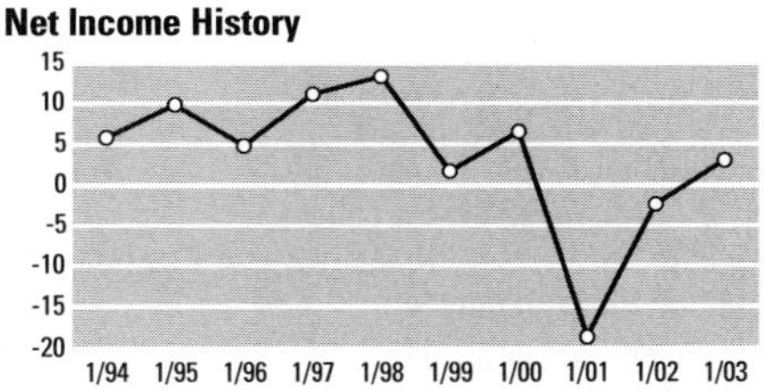

Recreational Equipment, Inc.

Outdoor gear and clothing from Recreational Equipment, Inc. (REI) outfits everyone from mountain climbers to mall walkers. The company is one of the nation's largest consumer co-operatives, with about 2 million member-owners. Through about 60 outlets in 24 states, REI sells high-end gear, clothing, and footwear (including private-label goods) for adventurous outdoor activities such as climbing, kayaking, and skiing, as well as for hiking, bicycling, and camping. The company also repairs gear, and it sells merchandise online and through occasional catalogs.

REI's community and environmental involvement includes youth program support, community service, and designating a portion of its operating budget to environmental restoration projects. The company operates an adventure travel service, REI Adventures, and through its partnership with US Bank (a subsidiary of U.S. Bancorp) offers members the REI Visa card.

REI stores feature product demonstrations, educational seminars, and gift registries. The company's MSR (Mountain Safety Research) subsidiary makes mountaineering equipment, outdoor clothing, and camping products. Customers can become co-op members by paying a one-time fee; its privileges include getting about 10% of their annual purchases refunded in the form of patronage dividends.

EXECUTIVES

Chairman: Tom Harville
Vice Chairman: Frances M. (Fran) Conley, age 60
President and CEO: Dennis Madsen
EVP and COO: Sally Jewell
SVP, CFO, and Corporate Treasurer: Brad Johnson
SVP, Merchandising: Matt Hyde
VP, Finance, Acting SVP, Marketing: Atsuko Tamura
VP, General Counsel, and Corporate Secretary: Pam Myers
VP, Human Resources: Glen Simmons
VP, Retail: Brian Unmacht
Director, Public Affairs: Michael Collins

LOCATIONS

HQ: 6750 S. 228th St., Kent, WA 98032
Phone: 253-395-3780 **Fax:** 253-395-4352
Web: www.rei.com

PRODUCTS/OPERATIONS

Selected Products and Services

Bicycles and accessories
Books and maps
Camping gear
Canoes, kayaks, and related gear
Climbing gear
Clothing (children's, men's, and women's)
Fitness gear
Footwear
Gift registry
Racks (bike, boat, and ski mounts)
REI photo service (with PhotoWorks)
REI repair service
Sleeping bags
Snow sports gear
Tents
Travel accessories

COMPETITORS

Academy
Bass Pro Shops
Big 5
Cabela's
Coleman
Dick's Sporting Goods
Eastern Mountain Sports
Galyans Trading
G.I. Joe's
Hibbett Sporting Goods
Johnson Outdoors
Lands' End
L.L. Bean
Lost Arrow
North Face
Spiegel
Sport Chalet
Sports Authority
Sportsman's Guide

HISTORICAL FINANCIALS

Company Type: Cooperative

Income Statement FYE: December 31

	REVENUE ($ mil.)	NET INCOME ($ mil.)	NET PROFIT MARGIN	EMPLOYEES
12/01	740	8	1.0%	6,000
12/00	698	(11)	—	7,000
12/99	621	10	1.7%	6,000
12/98	587	14	2.4%	6,000
12/97	536	15	2.8%	5,100
12/96	484	16	3.2%	4,800
12/95	448	13	2.8%	—
12/94	432	14	3.2%	—
Annual Growth	8.0%	(5.3%)	—	4.6%

2001 Year-End Financials

Debt ratio: 58.2%
Return on equity: 3.9%
Cash ($ mil.): 126
Current ratio: 1.42
Long-term debt ($ mil.): 117

Net Income History

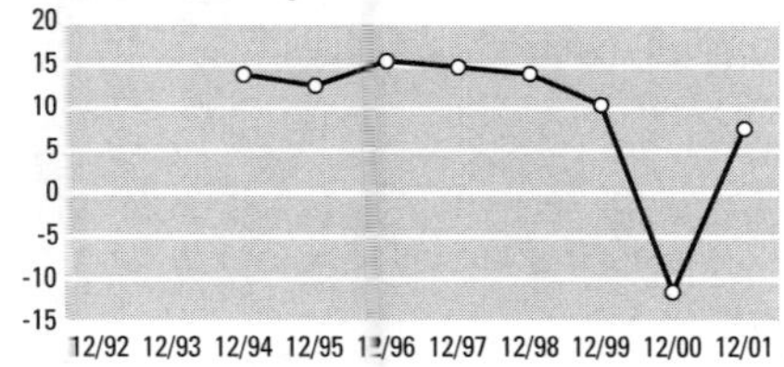

Red Apple Group, Inc.

Red Apple Group sells apples (and more) in the Big Apple. Subsidiary United Refining, which processes 72,000 barrels of oil a day, distributes fuel to its 400 KwikFill/Red Apple gas stations/convenience stores in New York, Pennsylvania, and Ohio. Red Apple controls Gristede's Foods, a leading New York City supermarket chain. It also has real estate, aircraft leasing, and newspaper operations. CEO John Catsimatidis owns the Red Apple Group, which lost out to Russian oil giant LUKOIL in a bid to acquire East Coast gasoline retailer Getty Petroleum Marketing. Red Apple owns and operates regional gas retailer Country Fair (68 gas stations).

EXECUTIVES

Chairman, President, and CEO, Red Apple Group and Gristede's Foods; Chairman and CEO, United Refining Company: John A. Catsimatidis, age 54
CFO, Gristede's Foods: Gary Pokrassa, age 55
EVP, Finance and Administration, Secretary, and Director, Gristede's Foods: Kishore Lall, age 55

LOCATIONS

HQ: 823 11th Ave., New York, NY 10019
Phone: 212-956-5803 **Fax:** 212-247-4509
Web: www.jacny.com

The Red Apple Group operates gasoline stations in New York, Ohio, and Pennsylvania. It owns commercial property in Florida, New Jersey, New York, and the Virgin Islands. The company also operates supermarkets in the New York City area.

COMPETITORS

7-Eleven
Ahold USA
Amerada Hess
D'Agostino Supermarkets
Getty Petroleum Marketing
A&P
King Kullen Grocery
Man-dell Food Stores
Motiva Enterprises
Pathmark
Premcor
Sunoco
TOTAL
Wakefern Food

HISTORICAL FINANCIALS

Company Type: Private

Income Statement FYE: February 28

	ESTIMATED REVENUE ($ mil.)	NET INCOME ($ mil.)	NET PROFIT MARGIN	EMPLOYEES
2/03	2,100	—	—	7,500
2/02	2,000	—	—	7,000
2/01	1,100	—	—	3,117
2/00	1,000	—	—	3,082
2/99	820	—	—	3,200
2/98	850	—	—	2,700
2/97	2,200	—	—	4,200
2/96	2,150	—	—	4,300
2/95	2,250	—	—	2,425
2/94	2,500	—	—	2,425
Annual Growth	(1.9%)	—	—	13.4%

Revenue History

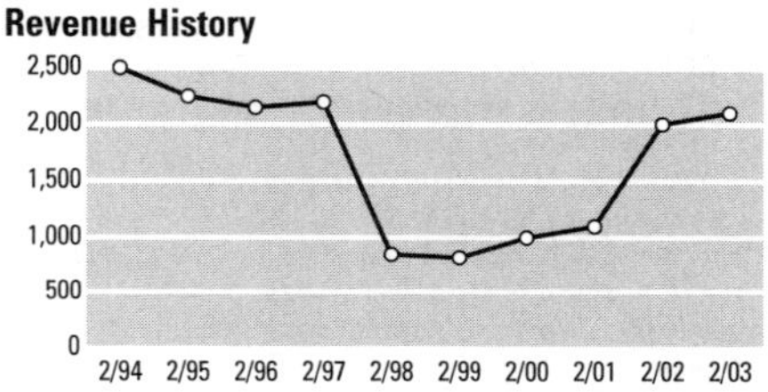

Red Chamber Group

The Red Chamber Group does more than dream about fish. The fourth-largest seafood supplier in North America (after ConAgra, Star-Kist, and Marine Harvest), Red Chamber Group imports and exports all manner of seafood — from shrimp to fish to lobster — around the world. It also operates aqua farms. Red Chamber Group serves as an umbrella for a number of companies on both coasts, including Red Chamber Co. (which started as a small family-owned restaurant in Los Angeles), Aqua Star, Neptune Foods, Mid-Pacific Seafoods, OFI Markesa International, and Tampa Bay Fisheries. The Kou family owns and operates Red Chamber.

EXECUTIVES

Chairperson and CEO: Shan Chun Kou
President and Director: Shu Chin Kou
COO and Director: Ming Bin Kou
SVP: Tony Neves
EVP and CFO: Ming Shin Kou
President, OFI Markesa International: Brent Church
President, Neptune Foods: Howard Choi

LOCATIONS

HQ: 1912 E. Vernon Ave., Vernon, CA 90058
Phone: 323-234-9000 **Fax:** 323-231-8888
Web: www.redchamber.com

PRODUCTS/OPERATIONS

Selected Operations

Aqua Star
Blue Pataya Foods
Kitchens Seafood
Mid-Pacific Seafoods
Neptune Foods
OFI Markesa International
Tampa Bay Fisheries

COMPETITORS

Dulcich
Kyokuyo
Maruha
Nichiro
Nippon Suisan Kaisha
Star-Kist
Trident Seafoods

HISTORICAL FINANCIALS

Company Type: Private

Income Statement FYE: December 31

	REVENUE ($ mil.)	NET INCOME ($ mil.)	NET PROFIT MARGIN	EMPLOYEES
12/02	680	—	—	—
12/01	680	—	—	—
12/00	665	—	—	—
Annual Growth	1.1%	—	—	—

Revenue History

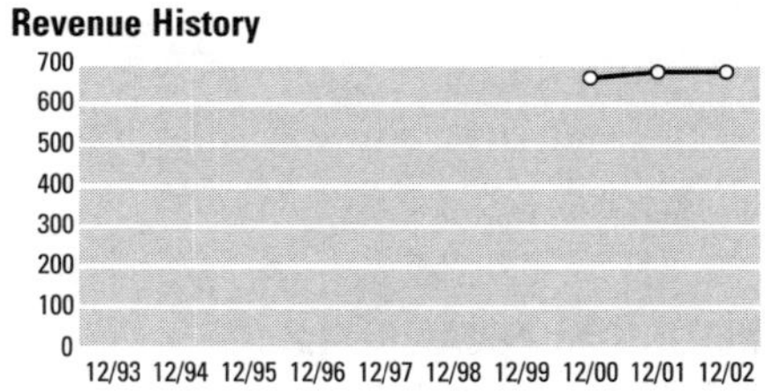

Renco Group

Renco Group is a holding company for a diverse bunch of businesses. Its AM General subsidiary makes the HUMVEE, an extra-wide all-terrain vehicle used by the military, and the HUMMER, the HUMVEE's civilian counterpart. Renco Steel and WCI Steel manufacture, fabricate, and distribute steel. Renco was established in 1980 and is owned by industrialist Ira Rennert, a former business consultant whose Long Island, New York, home is double the size of the White House and is said to include 29 bedrooms, 42 bathrooms, a 100-car garage, and an English pub.

Other Renco Group companies include Doe Run, the world's #2 lead smelter; coal miner Rencoal; and Consolidated Sewing Machine, which makes industrial sewing machines.

EXECUTIVES

Chairman, President, and CEO: Ira Leon Rennert, age 68
EVP and COO: Patrick G. Tatom, age 52
EVP: Marvin Koenig
VP Finance; VP Finance and CFO, Renco Steel: Roger L. Fay, age 57
VP Commercial: David A. Howard, age 43
Vice Chairman, President, and CEO, Doe Run: Jeffrey L. Zelms, age 57
President and CEO, WCI Steel: Ed Caine
VP Finance and CFO, Renco Steel: John P. Jacunski, age 37
Secretary and General Counsel: Justin W. D'Atri

LOCATIONS

HQ: Renco Group, Inc.
30 Rockefeller Plaza, New York, NY 10112
Phone: 212-541-6000 **Fax:** 212-541-6197

PRODUCTS/OPERATIONS

Selected Subsidiaries

AM General (manufactures the High Mobility Multipurpose Wheeled Vehicle known as the HUMVEE and the HUMMER, and diesel engines)
Consolidated Sewing Machine Corp. (manufactures industrial sewing machines, specialty machines, cutting machines, and motors)
Doe Run Company (lead smelter)
Renco Steel Holdings, Inc. (steel producer)
Rencoal, Inc. (coal miner)
WCI Steel, Inc. (steel producer)

COMPETITORS

AK Steel Holding Corporation
ASARCO
Nippon Steel
Nucor
Oshkosh Truck
Peugeot
RSR
Singer
United States Steel

HISTORICAL FINANCIALS

Company Type: Private

Income Statement FYE: October 31

	REVENUE ($ mil.)	NET INCOME ($ mil.)	NET PROFIT MARGIN	EMPLOYEES
10/02	2,175	—	—	13,500
10/01	2,150	—	—	14,000
10/00	2,500	—	—	15,000
10/99	2,500	—	—	15,000
10/98	2,550	—	—	11,000
10/97	2,520	—	—	10,500
10/96	1,800	—	—	7,150
10/95	1,650	—	—	6,995
10/94	1,650	—	—	7,000
10/93	1,500	—	—	6,000
Annual Growth	4.2%	—	—	9.4%

Revenue History

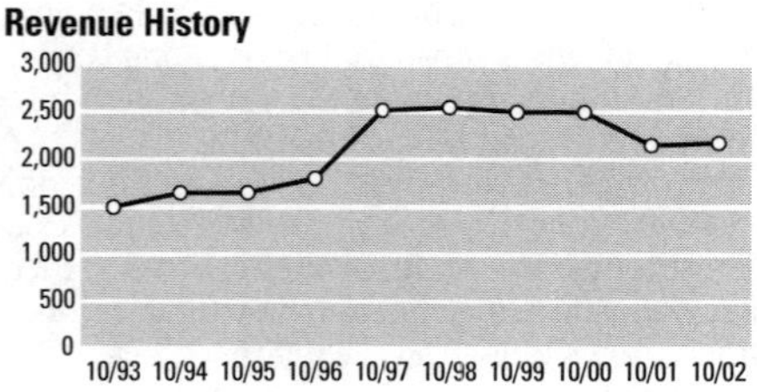

Republic Engineered Products LLC

Republic Engineered Products (formerly Republic Technologies International) has set the bar higher after once being under Chapter 11 bankruptcy protection. The company is one of the largest producers of special bar quality (SBQ) used to make automobiles, heavy equipment, and similar products. Customers — including DaimlerChrysler, Ford, GM, and their suppliers — turn the company's steel into components such as bearings, crankshafts, and spark plug shells. Through Blue Bar Holdings, private investment firms KPS Special Situations Fund L.P. (New York) and Hunt Investment Group L.P. (Dallas) own the company.

EXECUTIVES

Chairman and Managing Director: Michael G. Psaros, age 35
President, CEO, and Director: Joseph F. Lapinsky, age 53, $631,250 pay
CFO, VP Finance, and Controller: Joseph A. Kaczka, age 55, $180,000 pay
EVP, Technology and Quality Assurance: John G. Asimou, age 57, $236,250 pay
VP and General Manager, Lorain (Ohio) Operations: James T. Kuntz, age 64, $180,000 pay
VP, Hot Roll Bar Operations: Noel J. Huettich, age 57, $213,370 pay
VP, Human Resources: John Willoughby, age 55
VP, Marketing: James T. Thielens Jr., age 44
VP, Sales: Charles T. Cochran, age 48
Auditors: Deloitte & Touche LLP

LOCATIONS

HQ: 3770 Embassy Pkwy., Akron, OH 44333
Phone: 330-670-3000 **Fax:** 330-670-7031
Web: www.republicengineered.com

Republic Engineered Products operates facilities in Indiana, Ohio, and New York.

PRODUCTS/OPERATIONS

Selected Products

Hot-rolled engineered bar
Merchant-quality bar
Reinforcing bar

COMPETITORS

AK Steel Holding Corporation
Arcelor
Chaparral Steel
Corus Group
Gerdau AmeriSteel
Macsteel Service Centers USA
Niagara Corporation
North Star Steel
Nucor
Quanex
Rouge Industries
Timken
United States Steel

HISTORICAL FINANCIALS

Company Type: Private

Income Statement FYE: December 31

	REVENUE ($ mil.)	NET INCOME ($ mil.)	NET PROFIT MARGIN	EMPLOYEES
12/02	912	(81)	—	2,494
12/01	994	(183)	—	2,500
12/00	1,265	(287)	—	3,889
12/99	1,033	(328)	—	5,019
12/98	473	(114)	—	—
12/97	243	(45)	—	—
Annual Growth	30.3%	—	—	(20.8%)

2002 Year-End Financials

Debt ratio: 256.5%
Return on equity: —
Cash ($ mil.): 2
Current ratio: 0.75
Long-term debt ($ mil.): 80

Net Income History

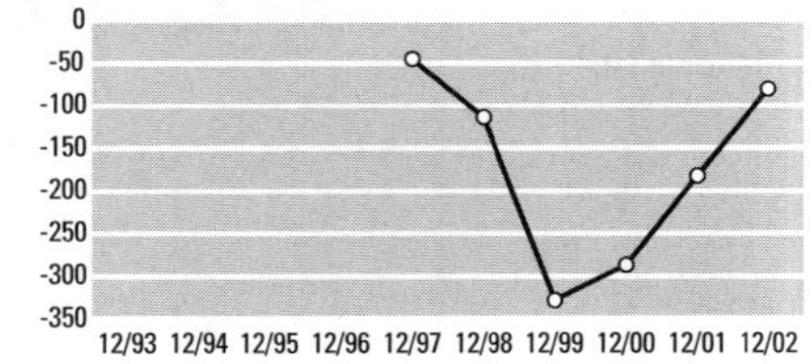

Resolution Performance Products LLC

The name Resolution Performance Products (RPP) is beginning to resin-ate throughout the chemical industry. Once the Resins and Versatics business of Shell Chemicals, the unit was sold to private investment firm Apollo Management in 2000 and renamed. RPP is the world's leading maker of epoxy resins, which are used in coatings, adhesives, and printed circuit boards because of their insulating and adhesive properties. While RPP gets two-thirds of its sales from epoxy resins, it also produces versatic acids — used in pharmaceuticals, personal care products, and coatings — and bisphenol-A, a chemical intermediate used in making epoxy resins. Apollo Management owns about 90% of the company; Shell Oil owns nearly 8%.

EXECUTIVES

Chairman and CEO: Marvin O. Schlanger, age 54
President and COO: Jeffrey M. Nodland, age 47
EVP, CFO, and Secretary: J. Travis Spoede, age 51
VP and CIO: Hanna M. Lukosavich, age 46
VP and General Counsel: Mark S. Antonvich, age 42
VP: James H. Melloan Jr., age 59
VP, Global Business Development and Asia Pacific: Dany Subrata, age 39
VP, Global Sales: Wouter W. Jongepier, age 40
VP, Human Resources: Dennis F. White, age 51
Treasurer: Thomas P. Bausch, age 55
Auditors: PricewaterhouseCoopers LLP

LOCATIONS

HQ: 1600 Smith St., Ste. 2400, Houston, TX 77002
Phone: 832-366-2300 **Fax:** 832-366-2584
Web: www.resins.com

Manufacturing Facilities

Argo, IL
Barbastro, Spain
Deer Park, TX
Lakeland, FL
Moerdijk, the Netherlands
Norco, LA
Pernis, the Netherlands
Stanlow, UK
Wesseling, Germany
Yokkaichi City, Japan

PRODUCTS/OPERATIONS

Selected Products

Basic versatic acids
Bisphenol-A (BPA)
Cardura
Epichlorohydrin (ECH)
Epoxy resins
VeoVa

COMPETITORS

Asahi Denka Kogyo
Ashland Specialty Chemical
Dainippon Ink
Dow Chemical
ExxonMobil Chemical
Mitsubishi Chemical
Mitsui Chemicals
Nan Ya Plastics
Nippon Kayaku
Sunoco Chemicals

HISTORICAL FINANCIALS

Company Type: Private

Income Statement

FYE: December 31

	REVENUE ($ mil.)	NET INCOME ($ mil.)	NET PROFIT MARGIN	EMPLOYEES
12/02	740	(7)	—	994
12/01	863	15	1.7%	940
Annual Growth	(14.3%)	—	—	5.7%

2002 Year-End Financials

Debt ratio: —
Return on equity: —
Cash ($ mil.): 4
Current ratio: 1.54
Long-term debt ($ mil.): 565

Net Income History

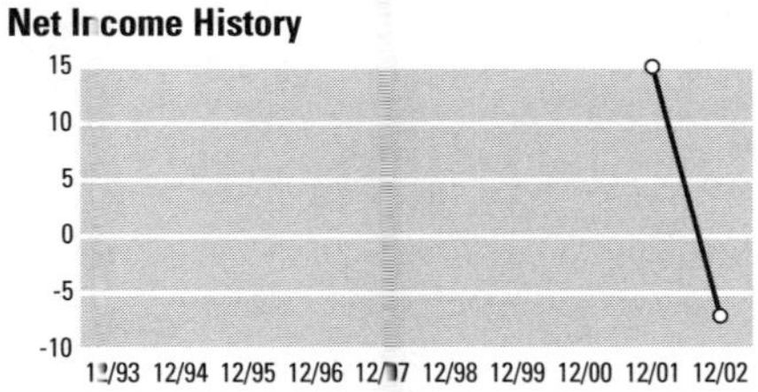

Retail Brand Alliance, Inc.

Given a food court and some kiosks, Retail Brand Alliance could open its own shopping mall. The holding company operates more than 1,000 mostly mall-based women's apparel shops in about 45 states under the Casual Corner, August Max, and Petite Sophisticate banners. The company also owns 160-store chain Brooks Brothers (men's and women's clothing) which is returning to its classic roots and expanding internationally. Carolee Designs (jewelry and accessories) and Adrienne Vittadini, a womenswear designer, are also in the company's portfolio. President and CEO Claudio Del Vecchio owns Retail Brand Alliance, which he acquired from his father's company, Luxottica Group (operator of LensCrafters and Sunglass Hut).

EXECUTIVES

President and CEO: Claudio Del Vecchio, age 44
COO: Mark Shulman
CFO: Brian K. Baumann
SVP; President and CEO, Carolee Designs: Carolee Friedlander
Chief Store Operations Officer: Kathy Self
VP Human Resources: Susan Eyvazzadeh
Chief Merchandising Officer: Eraldo Poletto
VP of Management Information System: Stefano Gaggion

LOCATIONS

HQ: 100 Phoenix Ave., Enfield, CT 06082
Phone: 860-741-0771 **Fax:** 860-745-9714

PRODUCTS/OPERATIONS

Selected Stores

Adrienne Vittadini
August Max
Brooks Brothers
Casual Corner
Carolee Designs
Petite Sophisticate

COMPETITORS

AnnTaylor
Dillard's
Federated
Gap
J. C. Penney
Limited Brands
LVMH
May
Men's Wearhouse
Pinault-Printemps-Redoute
Richemont
Saks Inc.
Talbots

HISTORICAL FINANCIALS

Company Type: Private

Income Statement

FYE: July 31

	REVENUE ($ mil.)	NET INCOME ($ mil.)	NET PROFIT MARGIN	EMPLOYEES
7/02	1,500	—	—	10,036
7/01	900	—	—	10,000
Annual Growth	66.7%	—	—	0.4%

Revenue History

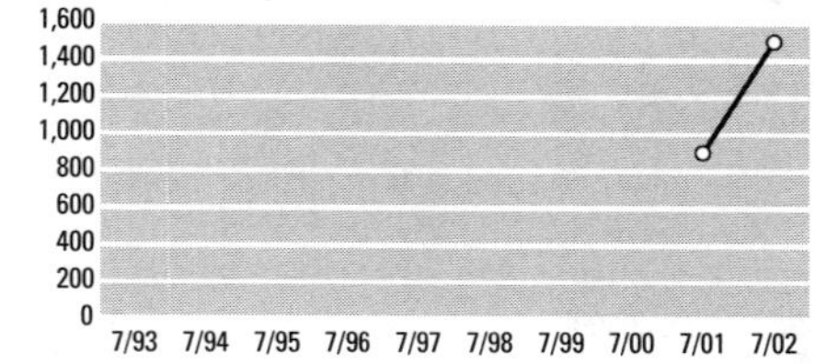

Reyes Holdings

Closely held Reyes Holdings has a kingly grasp over two things that are often held closely together — food and beer. Through its subsidiary companies Reyes Holdings distributes products throughout North, Central, and South America. One of these, The Martin-Brower Company, supplies McDonald's restaurants in the US and Canada, as well as serving Brazil, Central America, and Puerto Rico. Reyes Holdings also counts Premium Distributors of Virginia, Chicago Beverage Systems, and California's Harbor Distributing among the wholesalers it owns. The company operates more than 35 distribution centers in the US and six other countries. Chairman Chris Reyes, vice chairman Jude Reyes, and VP David Reyes own the company.

EXECUTIVES

Chairman: J. Christopher (Chris) Reyes, age 49
Vice Chairman: M. Jude Reyes, age 48
EVP, Business Development: Dean H. Janke, age 48
SVP and CFO: Daniel P. (Dan) Doheny, age 41
SVP, Human Resources: Phil Menzel
SVP, IT: Joe Crenshaw
SVP, Operations: Ray Guerin
VP: David K. Reyes, age 47

LOCATIONS

HQ: Reyes Holdings LLC
9500 West Bryn Mawr Ave., Ste. 700,
Rosemont, IL 60018
Phone: 847-227-6500 **Fax:** 847-227-6550

PRODUCTS/OPERATIONS

Selected Wholesalers

Chicago Beverage Systems
Harbor Distributing
The Martin-Brower Company
Premium Distributors of Virginia

COMPETITORS

Alex Lee
Anderson-DuBose
Ben E. Keith
Clark Products
Golden State Foods
Gordon Food Service
Keystone Foods
MBM
McLane Foodservice
Performance Food Services Group
SYSCO
U.S. Foodservice

HISTORICAL FINANCIALS

Company Type: Private

Income Statement FYE: December 31

	REVENUE ($ mil.)	NET INCOME ($ mil.)	NET PROFIT MARGIN	EMPLOYEES
12/02	4,180	—	—	3,994
12/01*	3,900	—	—	3,877
9/00	3,500	—	—	4,200
9/99	2,375	—	—	—
Annual Growth	20.7%	—	—	(2.5%)

*Fiscal year change

Revenue History

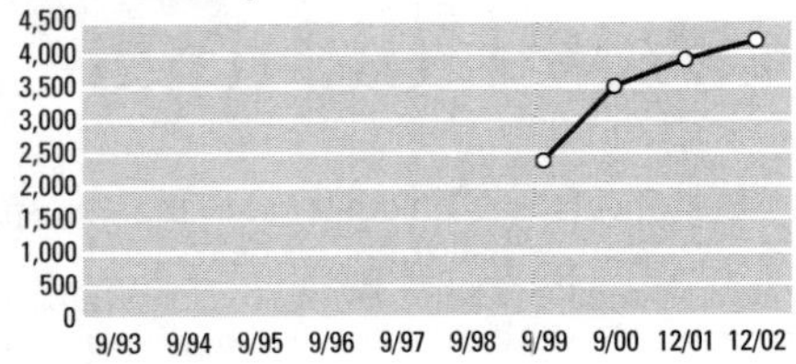

Ricart Automotive Inc.

If you can't find a car that's fast enough at Ricart Automotive, you might ask the staff if they know of any good planes for sale. Ricart Automotive serves the Columbus, Ohio, area with four dealerships, including the 66-acre Ricart Mega Mall, that offer new and used vehicles, vans, and RVs. Ricart sells Ford and DaimlerChrysler cars, as well as a boatload of Asian imports — about 16,000 cars annually. The company offers service, parts, and financing. Other Ricart business ventures are Ricart Aviation, which buys and sells reconditioned airplanes, and Ricart Mortgage. Brothers and co-CEOs Fred Ricart and Rhett Ricart took over for their father, Paul, who opened a small Ford lot in 1953.

EXECUTIVES

Co-CEO: Paul F. (Fred) Ricart Jr.
Co-CEO: Rhett C. Ricart
COO: Greg Dryden
CFO: Chris Pustelak
Director of Human Resources: Terry DeRammelaere

LOCATIONS

HQ: 4255 S. Hamilton Rd., Groveport, OH 43125
Phone: 614-836-6265 **Fax:** 614-836-6563
Web: www.ricart.com

PRODUCTS/OPERATIONS

Selected makes

Chrysler
Ford
Hyundai
Isuzu
Jeep
Kia
Lincoln
Mazda
Mercury
Mitsubishi
Nissan

COMPETITORS

AutoNation
General RV Center
March/Hodge
Sonic Automotive
Spitzer
United Auto Group

HISTORICAL FINANCIALS

Company Type: Private

Income Statement FYE: December 31

	REVENUE ($ mil.)	NET INCOME ($ mil.)	NET PROFIT MARGIN	EMPLOYEES
12/02	400	—	—	1,000
12/01	426	—	—	1,030
12/00	441	—	—	1,000
12/99	492	—	—	1,000
12/98	507	—	—	1,000
12/97	503	—	—	889
12/96	573	—	—	968
12/95	582	—	—	1,100
12/94	500	—	—	500
Annual Growth	(2.8%)	—	—	9.1%

Revenue History

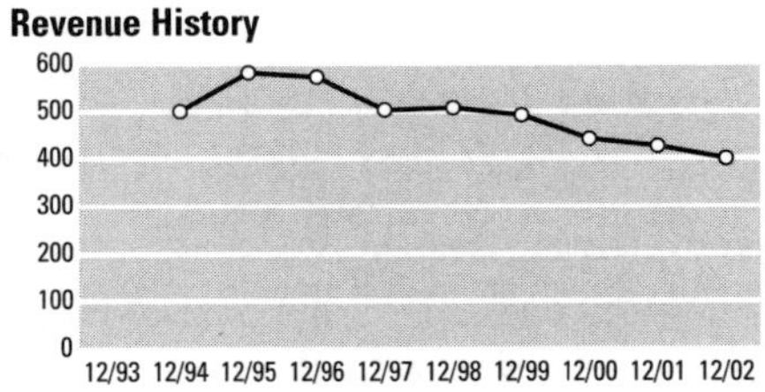

Rich Products Corporation

Starting in 1945 with "the miracle cream from the soya bean," Rich Products has grown from a niche maker of soy-based whipped toppings and frozen desserts to a major US frozen foods manufacturer. Since the 1960s the company has developed new products, such as Coffee Rich (non-dairy coffee creamer), and expanded through acquisitions to include frozen bakery and pizza doughs and ingredients for the food service and in-store bakery markets, plus SeaPak (seafood) and Byron's (barbecue). Rich Products markets some 2,300 products in about 80 countries. The company, owned and operated by the founding Rich family, also owns the Wichita Wranglers and Buffalo Bisons minor league baseball teams.

In a move to grow its dessert offerings, Rich acquired Mother's Kitchen (gourmet cakes and cheesecakes) in 2003. Continuing to add to these offerings, that year Rich also acquired Morningstar Foods' brand frozen whipped topping and creamer lines from Dean Foods.

EXECUTIVES

Chairman: Robert E. Rich Sr.
President: Robert E. Rich Jr., age 61
COO: William G. Gisel Jr.
CFO: Charles R. Trego
EVP, Sales: Kevin Malchoff
SVP, Human Resources: Brian Townson
SVP, Legal and Communication: Maureen O. Hurley
President, Food Service: Dennis Janesz
Secretary: David E. Rich

LOCATIONS

HQ: 1150 Niagara St., Buffalo, NY 14213
Phone: 716-878-8000 **Fax:** 716-878-8765
Web: www.richs.com

PRODUCTS/OPERATIONS

Selected Products

Bagels
Barbecue
Brownies
Cakes
Cheesecakes
Donuts
Dough
Bread
Cookie
Dry mixes
Eclairs and puffs
Fillings
Icings
Muffins
Pies
Pizza
Pretzels
Pudding
Sweet rolls
Topping

COMPETITORS

Aurora Foods
ConAgra
Dawn Food Products
FlowersFoods
International Multifoods
Kraft Foods
Nestlé
Schwan's
Unilever

HISTORICAL FINANCIALS

Company Type: Private

Income Statement FYE: December 31

	REVENUE ($ mil.)	NET INCOME ($ mil.)	NET PROFIT MARGIN	EMPLOYEES
12/01	1,702	—	—	6,500
12/00	1,620	—	—	7,000
12/99	1,515	—	—	6,500
12/98	1,400	—	—	6,000
12/97	1,300	—	—	6,000
12/96	1,200	—	—	6,000
12/95	1,100	—	—	6,500
12/94	1,000	—	—	7,000
12/93	990	—	—	7,000
12/92	940	—	—	—
Annual Growth	6.8%	—	—	(0.9%)

Revenue History

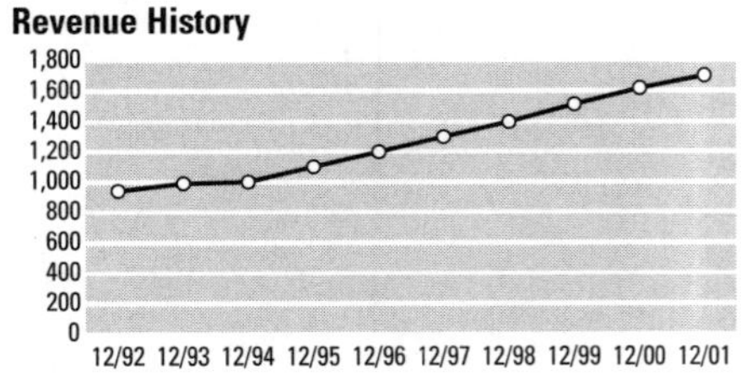

Ritz Camera Centers, Inc.

Ritz Camera Centers began as a one-man portrait studio and developed into the largest photographic chain in the US. More than 1,300 stores nationwide offer one-hour photofinishing, cameras, film, and related photographic and optical products and services. Stores operate under the Ritz, Camera Shop, Kits, Inkley's, and Wolf names; the company also sells online. Subsidiary Boater's World Marine Centers has more than 100 stores nationwide that offer gear and clothing for fishing and boating. CEO David Ritz owns Ritz Camera, which was founded in 1918. His cousin, Chuck Wolf, owned Wolf Camera (#2 photo chain in the US), which Ritz Camera bought in 2001. Still focused on growth, Ritz bought Camera World in 2002.

EXECUTIVES

Chairman, President; and CEO; Chairman, Ritz Interactive: David M. Ritz
Vice Chairman: Charles R. (Chuck) Wolf
CFO: Jay Sloan
President and CEO, Ritz Interactive: Fred H. Lerner
Director of Human Resources: Alan MacDonald
Public Relations Manager: Brooke Ritz

LOCATIONS

HQ: 6711 Ritz Way, Beltsville, MD 20705
Phone: 301-419-0000 **Fax:** 301-419-2995
Web: www.ritzcamera.com

Ritz Camera Centers operates more than 1,350 stores throughout the US. The company also operates more than 100 Boater's World Marine Centers in more than 25 states.

PRODUCTS/OPERATIONS

Selected Merchandise and Services

Boater's World Marine Centers
Apparel
Electronics
Fishing
Watersports

Ritz Camera Centers
Albums and frames
Binoculars
Camera attachments
Cameras
Cellular phones
Darkroom equipment and supplies
Digital imaging accessories
Digital imaging services
Film and processing
Lenses
One-hour photofinishing
Personalized photo products
Printers and scanners
Projectors and accessories
Studio lighting and accessories
Telescopes

COMPETITORS

Best Buy
Circuit City Stores
Costco Wholesale
CVS
Eckerd
MarineMax
MOTO Franchise
PhotoWorks
Travis Boats & Motors
Walgreen
Wal-Mart
West Marine

HISTORICAL FINANCIALS

Company Type: Private

Income Statement FYE: December 31

	ESTIMATED REVENUE ($ mil.)	NET INCOME ($ mil.)	NET PROFIT MARGIN	EMPLOYEES
12/01	1,350	—	—	12,000
12/00	800	—	—	7,000
12/99	800	—	—	7,000
12/98	650	—	—	6,500
12/97	625	—	—	7,000
Annual Growth	21.2%	—	—	14.4%

Revenue History

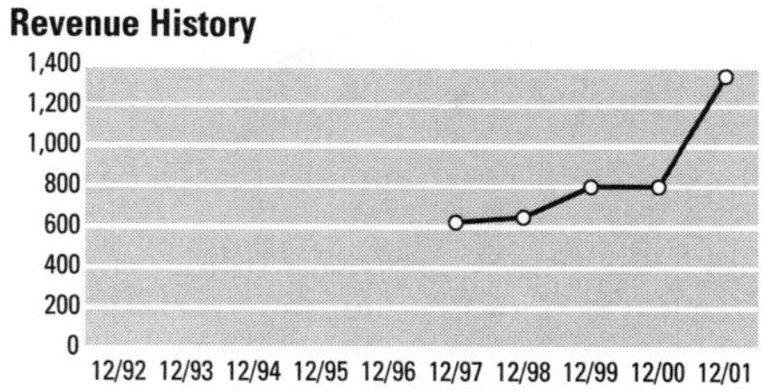

The Robert Wood Johnson Foundation

The Robert Wood Johnson Foundation uses its wealth to improve your health. The foundation is the nation's largest charitable organization devoted exclusively to health care issues. In 2001 it donated about $561 million to about 1,140 grant and contract recipients working in three primary areas: access to health care, substance abuse, and chronic care. The Johnson Foundation supports such programs and initiatives as training, policy analysis, public education, and the gathering of health statistics. The foundation has an endowment with more than $9 billion in assets.

In 2001 the foundation announced it would add a fourth major initiative to its funding goals, community health issues. Jumpstarting its new initiative, the Johnson Foundation made its largest grant to date that year, a $100 million donation to faith-based volunteer group Faith in Action. The foundation's namesake, Robert Wood Johnson, endowed the organization with stock in his family's business, health care products company Johnson & Johnson.

EXECUTIVES

Chairman: Robert E. Campbell, age 69
President and CEO: Risa J. Lavizzo-Mourey, age 48
Senior Financial Officer: Rona Smyth Henry
EVP: Lewis G. Sandy
SVP and Director, Health Group: J. Micheal McGinnis
VP, General Counsel, and Secretary: J. Warren Wood III
VP and Treasurer: Peter Goodwin
VP, Communications: David J. Morse
CIO: Brian S. O'Neill
Controller: G. Russell Henshaw Jr.
Director, Human Resources: David L. Waldman
Auditors: PricewaterhouseCoopers LLP

LOCATIONS

HQ: Rte. 1 and College Rd. East, Princeton, NJ 08543
Phone: 888-631-9989 **Fax:** 609-627-6422
Web: www.rwjf.org

2002 Grants

	% of total
Middle Atlantic	28
South Atlantic	26
Pacific	13
Northeast central	12
New England	11
Other areas	10
Total	**100**

PRODUCTS/OPERATIONS

2002 Grants

	% of total
General health care	24
Substance abuse	23
Chronic health care	20
Community health	18
Other philanthropic programs	15
Total	**100**

Health Care Group
Coverage
Clinical care management
End of life
Priority populations
Supportive services

Health Group
Alcohol and illegal drugs
Community health
Health and behavior
Population health science and policy
Tobacco

Other programs
Children's health issues
Health care professionals and career development
Training and education

HISTORICAL FINANCIALS

Company Type: Foundation

Income Statement FYE: December 31

	REVENUE ($ mil.)	NET INCOME ($ mil.)	NET PROFIT MARGIN	EMPLOYEES
12/02	428	—	—	150
12/01	468	—	—	150
12/00	930	—	—	150
12/99	647	—	—	150
12/98	616	—	—	150
12/97	528	—	—	145
12/96	430	—	—	135
12/95	421	—	—	—
Annual Growth	0.2%	—	—	1.8%

Revenue History

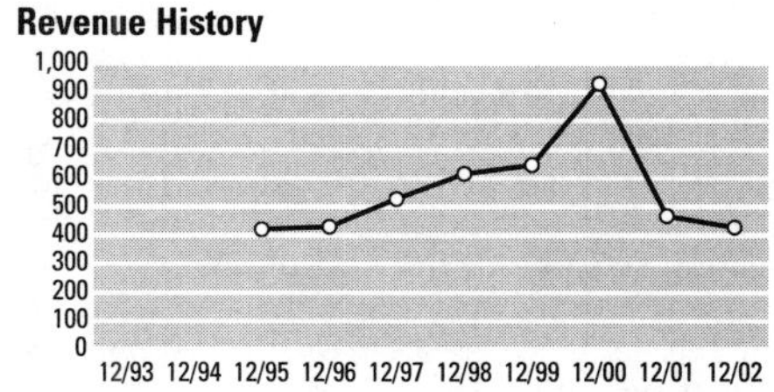

The Rockefeller Foundation

The Rockefeller Foundation is one of the nation's oldest private charitable organizations. It supports grants, fellowships, and conferences for programs that try to identify and alleviate need and suffering around the world. These programs (or themes) include initiatives to foster fair implementation of health care, job opportunities for America's urban poor, creative expression through the humanities and arts, and agricultural policies that ensure food distribution to people in developing countries. The foundation's cross theme of global inclusion binds its programs to a global focus, ensuring that globalization gets doled out democratically and helps populations typically alienated from the global economy.

President Gordon Conway has introduced the reorganization focusing on the role of globalization in aiding the poor. The foundation's former divisions — such as Agricultural Sciences, Equal Opportunity, and Health Sciences — now come under the themes of Food Security, Working Communities, and Health Equity. Its non-New York City offices (Bangkok; Mexico City; Nairobi, Kenya; Harare, Zimbabwe; and San Francisco) are taking on increasing responsibility in carrying out the group's global mission. The foundation maintains no ties to the Rockefeller family or its other philanthropies. An independent board of trustees sets program guidelines and approves all expenditures.

HISTORY

Oil baron John D. Rockefeller, one of America's most criticized capitalists, was also one of its pioneer philanthropists. Before founding The Rockefeller Foundation in 1913, he funded the creation of The University of Chicago (with $36 million over a 25-year period) and formed organizations for medical research (1901), the education of southern African-Americans (1903), and hookworm eradication in the southern US.

Rockefeller turned the control of the foundation over to his son John D. Rockefeller Jr. in 1916. The younger Rockefeller separated the foundation from the family's interests and established an independent board. (The board later rejected a proposal from John Sr. to replace school textbooks that he claimed promoted Bolshevism.)

In the mid-1920s the foundation started conducting basic medical research. In 1928 it absorbed several other Rockefeller philanthropies, adding programs in the natural and social sciences and the arts and humanities. During the 1930s the foundation developed the first effective yellow fever vaccine (1935), continued its worldwide battles against disease, and supported pioneering research in the field of biology. Other grants supported the performing arts in the US and social science research. During WWII it supplied major funding for nuclear science research tools (spectroscopy, X-ray diffraction).

After the war, with an increasing number of large public ventures modeled after the foundation (e.g., the UN's World Health Organization) taking over its traditional physical and natural sciences territory, the organization dissolved its famed biology division in 1951. The following year emphasis swung to agricultural studies under chairman John D. Rockefeller III. The organization took wheat seeds developed at its Mexican food project to Colombia (1950), Chile (1955), and India (1956); a rice institute in the Philippines followed (1960). The Green Revolution sprouted 12 more developing-world institutes.

In the 1960s the foundation began dispatching experts to African and Latin American universities in an effort to raise the level of training at those institutions. The long bear market of the 1970s caused the foundation's assets to drop to a low of $732 million (1977).

In 1990 the organization established the Energy Foundation, a joint effort with the MacArthur Foundation and the Pew Charitable Trusts, to explore alternate energy sources.

In the mid-1990s the Republican-led Congress launched three probes into the foundation and several other not-for-profits over allegations of political activities that could jeopardize their tax status.

In 1998 Gordon Conway, a British agricultural ecologist, became the foundation's 12th (and first foreign) president. He implemented a retooling of the organization's programs in 1999. He also led an effective campaign against bioengineering giant Monsanto's (now part of Pfizer) plan to market "sterile seeds" that do not regenerate. In 2000 James Orr III, a Rockefeller board member and CEO of Boston's United Asset Management Corporation, succeeded Alice Ilchman as chairman of the board of trustees. In 2001 the foundation pledged $5 million for disaster relief efforts in New York City following the September 11 terrorist attacks. The Rockefeller Foundation launched a multi-year initiative to promote fair intellectual property policies to the poor in 2002.

EXECUTIVES

Chairman: James F. Orr III
President: Gordon R. Conway
EVP for Strategy: Lincoln C. Chen
VP, Administration and Communication: Denise Gray-Felder
VP: Robert W. Herdt
VP and Acting Director, Working Communities: Julia I. Lopez
Associate VP: Joyce L. Moock
Corporate Secretary: Lynda Mullen
Treasurer and Chief Investment Officer: Donna J. Dean
CTO: Fernando Mola-Davis
Comptroller: Charles J. Lang
Director, Health Equity: Timothy Evans
Director, Human Resources: Robert Giacometti
Director, Creativity and Culture: Raymond Paredes
Director, Global Inclusion: Robert Bach
Associate Director, Population, The Cairo Agenda: George Brown
Manager, Office Services: Cora L. Springer
Manager, Fellowships and Special Projects: Joseph R. Bookmyer
Auditors: Ernst & Young LLP

LOCATIONS

HQ: 420 Fifth Ave., New York, NY 10018
Phone: 212-869-8500 **Fax:** 212-764-3468
Web: www.rockfound.org

The Rockefeller Foundation has field offices in Kenya, Mexico, Thailand, Zimbabwe, and the US, and maintains the Bellagio Study and Conference Center in northern Italy.

PRODUCTS/OPERATIONS

Themes

Creativity & Culture (Renews and preserves the cultural heritage of people excluded from the globalizing economy; promotes public exchanges of ideas;
supports diversity and creativity in humanities and arts.)
Food Security (Generates agricultural institutions, policies, and innovations to help rural poor in developing countries.)
Global Inclusion (Seeks to ensure that globalization processes are carried out fairly and democratically, benefiting those most in need.)
Health Equity (Seeks to improve the implementation of health care in developing countries.)
Working Communities (Seeks to increase employment, improve schools, and encourage democratic participation in poor urban neighborhoods in the US.)

HISTORICAL FINANCIALS

Company Type: Foundation

Income Statement FYE: December 31

	REVENUE ($ mil.)	NET INCOME ($ mil.)	NET PROFIT MARGIN	EMPLOYEES
12/01	104	—	—	250
12/00	127	—	—	230
12/99	680	—	—	220
12/98	388	—	—	150
12/97	510	—	—	149
12/96	413	—	—	152
12/95	319	—	—	130
12/94	21	—	—	137
12/93	208	—	—	147
12/92	198	—	—	142
Annual Growth	(6.9%)	—	—	6.5%

Revenue History

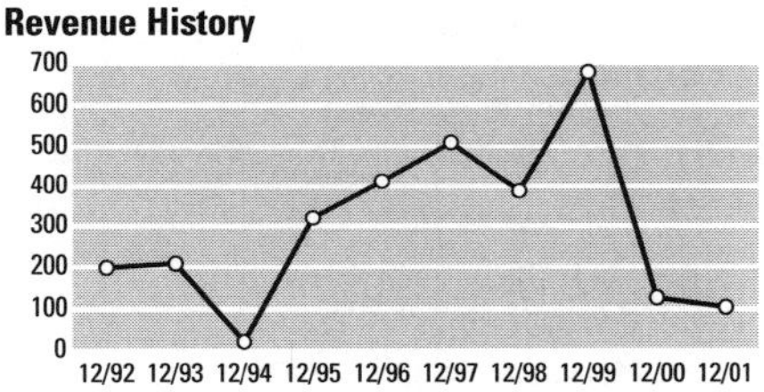

Rockwood Specialties Inc.

The more Rockwood Specialties adds, the more it makes. The company gets most of its sales from producing additives, including pigments, wood preservation chemicals, smectite-based chemicals, and additives for water. In addition to additives, Rockwood Specialties has two other divisions: electronics (specialty chemicals for semiconductors and printed circuit boards) and compounds (AlphaGary and Gomet), which prepare plastics for a variety of uses. A leader or #2 in many of its niches, the firm is Europe's largest silicon wafer recycler. The company was created in 2000 when Kohlberg Kravis Roberts & Co. bought several divisions from Laporte.

EXECUTIVES

Chairman and CEO: Seifi Ghasemi
VP and CFO: Robert J. Zatta
VP, Law and Administration: Thomas J. Riordan
CIO: Mark J. Yankowskas
Treasurer: Scott G. Smith
President, Cyantek: Gary Grossklaus
President, Exsil: Roy Cutler
President, Rockwood Electronic Materials, Electrochemicals: Moeries Elias
Auditors: Deloitte & Touche LLP

LOCATIONS

HQ: 100 Overlook Center, Princeton, NJ 08540
Phone: 609-514-0300 **Fax:** 609-514-8720
Web: www.rockwoodspecialties.com

Rockwood Specialties operates about a dozen units in all, with operations in North America, Asia, and Europe.

PRODUCTS/OPERATIONS

Selected Operations and Products

Advantis Technologies (pool, spa, and water surface chemicals)
AlphaGary Corp. (compounding of plastics)
American Silicon Products (wafer reclaim)
Chemical Specialties Inc. (CSI, wood preservation chemicals)
Compugraphics (photomasks)
Cyantek (specialty chemicals for semiconductors)
Electrochemicals (chemicals for printed circuit boards)
Exsil, Inc. (silicon test wafers)
Garnet (compounding and molding of plastics)
Mineral Research and Development (MRD)
Rockwood Additives, Ltd. (smectite-based additives)
Rockwood Electronic Materials (ultra-pure chemicals and wafer reclaim)
Rockwood Pigments (iron oxide pigments)
Southern Clay Products (smectite-based additives)
Southern Color Company (pigments for the construction industry)

COMPETITORS

DuPont Photomasks
Ferro
Kingboard
LNP
OM Group
Ondeo Nalco
Photronics
PolyOne
Rohm and Haas
Trio-Tech

HISTORICAL FINANCIALS

Company Type: Private

Income Statement FYE: December 31

	ESTIMATED REVENUE ($ mil.)	NET INCOME ($ mil.)	NET PROFIT MARGIN	EMPLOYEES
12/02	760	—	—	2,500
12/01	800	—	—	2,700
Annual Growth	(5.0%)	—	—	(7.4%)

Revenue History

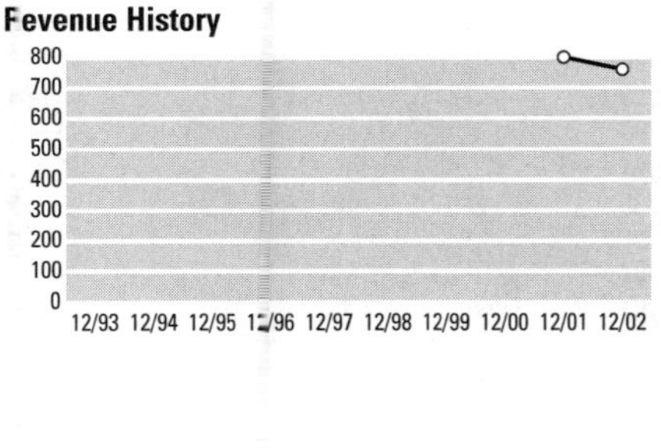

Roll International

Churning out collectible family heirlooms (or flea market fodder) is the primary business of Stewart and Lynda Resnick's Roll International. The centerpiece of their empire is The Franklin Mint, the world's largest collectibles company, with operations in 15 countries. The Franklin Mint sells goods by mail order, through its Web site, and in about 50 company-owned and independent retail stores. It also operates The Franklin Mint Museum, which has displayed such authentic items as a Jacqueline Kennedy Onassis necklace and a Princess Diana gown. Other Roll operations include Paramount Farms (pistachios and almonds), Paramount Citrus (citrus products), and Teleflora (floral delivery service).

The Franklin Mint (no connection to the US Mint) develops about 1,200 products each year and has sold everything from *Gone With the Wind* figurines and *Star Trek* chess sets to limited-edition Monopoly games and even the Elvis Presley commemorative .45 automatic. The Franklin Mint produces many of its wares under licensing agreements with the likes of the Vatican, The Coca-Cola Company, and Harley-Davidson, among others.

EXECUTIVES

Co-Chairman, President, and CEO; President, Paramount Farms: Stewart A. Resnick, age 66
Co-Chairman: Lynda R. Resnick
CFO: Robert A. Kors
VP and General Counsel: Jean Cooper
VP Finance and Accounting: Peter R. Gurney
President and CEO, Teleflora: Gregg Coccari

LOCATIONS

HQ: Roll International Corporation
11444 W. Olympic Blvd., 10th Fl.,
Los Angeles, CA 90064
Phone: 310-966-5700 **Fax:** 310-914-4747

PRODUCTS/OPERATIONS

Selected Product Categories

Clocks
Collectible knives and weapons
Collector eggs
Die-cast vehicle scale models
Games
Jewelry
Plates
Pocket watches
Porcelain and pewter sculptures
Porcelain and vinyl dolls
Tankards

Selected Franklin Mint Licenses

The Coca-Cola Company
Graceland
Harley-Davidson
House of Fabergé
Mercedes-Benz
Metro-Goldwyn-Mayer
National Football League
Oleg Cassini
Paramount
Rolls-Royce
The Vatican

COMPETITORS

1-800-FLOWERS.COM
Action Performance
AgraQuest
Blue Diamond Growers
Boyds Collection
Brown-Forman
Calcot
Department 56
Dow AgroSciences LLC
Enesco Group
FTD
Hallmark
John Sanfilippo & Son
King Ranch
Maisto
Marian
MSO
ML Macadamia Orchards
RC2
Security Capital
Sun Growers
Village Farms
Zindart

HISTORICAL FINANCIALS

Company Type: Private

Income Statement FYE: December 31

	ESTIMATED REVENUE ($ mil.)	NET INCOME ($ mil.)	NET PROFIT MARGIN	EMPLOYEES
12/01	800	—	—	5,100
12/00	825	—	—	5,100
12/99	700	—	—	5,000
12/98	725	—	—	7,500
12/97	1,511	—	—	7,500
12/96	1,280	—	—	7,500
12/95	1,360	—	—	7,700
12/94	1,300	—	—	7,500
12/93	1,180	—	—	7,500
12/92	960	—	—	7,500
Annual Growth	(2.0%)	—	—	(4.2%)

Revenue History

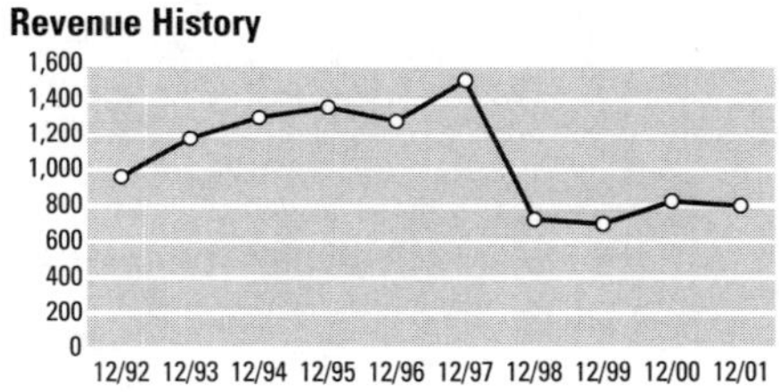

Rooms To Go

Need that sofa, recliner, table, and lamp in a hurry? Rooms To Go — with about 90 stores in Florida, Georgia, North Carolina, South Carolina, Tennessee, and Texas — has transformed itself into the top-selling furniture retailer in the US. The company markets its limited selection of furniture to brand-conscious, time-pressed customers. It packages low- to moderately priced furniture and accessories and offers discounts for those willing to buy a roomful. Rooms To Go also operates a Rooms to Go Kids chain with nearly 20 stores in the Southeast, Texas, and Puerto Rico. President and owner Jeffrey Seaman and his father, Morty, founded the firm in 1990 after selling Seaman Furniture Company.

EXECUTIVES

President and CEO: Jeffrey Seaman
COO: Steve Buckley
CFO: Lou Stein
VP Advertising: Richard Scobey
IT Director: Russ Rossen
Director Human Resources: Linda Garcia

LOCATIONS

HQ: Rooms To Go, Inc.
11540 Hwy. 92 East, Seffner, FL 33584
Phone: 813-623-5400 **Fax:** 813-620-1717
Web: www.roomstogo.com

COMPETITORS

Bassett Furniture	J. C. Penney
Bombay Company	La-Z-Boy
Ethan Allen	Pier 1 Imports
Furniture.com	Rowe Companies
Havertys	Sears
IKEA	

HISTORICAL FINANCIALS

Company Type: Private

Income Statement FYE: December 31

	REVENUE ($ mil.)	NET INCOME ($ mil.)	NET PROFIT MARGIN	EMPLOYEES
12/01	1,260	—	—	5,500
12/00	1,040	—	—	4,834
12/99	860	—	—	4,000
12/98	720	—	—	3,500
12/97	600	—	—	3,314
12/96	450	—	—	—
Annual Growth	22.9%	—	—	13.5%

Revenue History

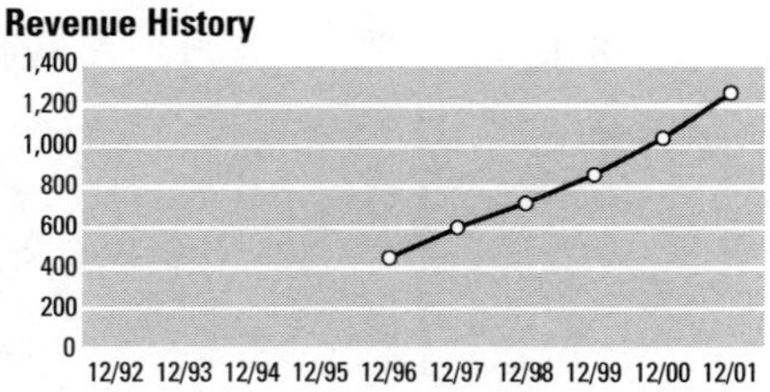

Rooney Brothers

Film star Mickey isn't the only Rooney to have landed big contracts. Rooney Brothers, through its Manhattan Construction unit, builds hospitals, government buildings (George Bush Presidential Library in Texas), offices, highways, and sports arenas (Reliant Stadium in Houston). It offers construction management, general contracting, and design/build services to its clients, located mainly in the southwestern and mid-Atlantic states. Rooney Brothers also makes construction materials, operates building supply stores, and manufactures electronics. Family-owned Rooney Brothers was organized in 1984 to acquire Manhattan Construction, which was founded by patriarch L. H. Rooney in 1896.

EXECUTIVES

Chairman: L. Francis Rooney III, age 49
President and COO, Manhattan Construction: Timothy P. (Tim) Rooney
SVP Construction, Manhattan Construction: Curtis Ferguson
SVP and CFO, Manhattan Construction: Kevin P. Moore
VP Marketing: Jessica Klassen
President, Dallas Division, Manhattan Construction: John W. Dixon
Secretary and Treasurer: Jim Lawson
Human Resources, Manhattan Construction: Jackie Proffitt
President, Rooney Insurance Agency: Jim Geisinger
Auditors: Ernst & Young LLP

LOCATIONS

HQ: Rooney Brothers Company
5601 S. 122nd East Ave., Tulsa, OK 74146
Phone: 918-583-6900 **Fax:** 918-592-4334
Web: www.rooneybrothers.com

Rooney Brothers' Manhattan Construction unit has offices in Dallas and Houston; Fairfax, Virginia; Oklahoma City and Tulsa, Oklahoma; and Mexico City.

PRODUCTS/OPERATIONS

Selected Construction Areas

Airport and aviation
Corporate and commercial
Corrections
Entertainment
Government
Health care
Hospitality and leisure
Institutional and academic
Special projects
Sports and entertainment

Selected Operations

Hope Lumber & Supply Company
Manhattan Construction Company
Manhattan Environmental
M.J. Lee Construction
Moore's Lumber
OAI Electronics

COMPETITORS

Austin Industries	Home Depot
Barton Malow	Jacobs Engineering
Bechtel	Lowe's
Beck Group	M. A. Mortenson
Fluor	Siemens
Foster Wheeler	Turner Corporation
Hensel Phelps Construction	Washington Group

HISTORICAL FINANCIALS

Company Type: Private

Income Statement FYE: September 30

	REVENUE ($ mil.)	NET INCOME ($ mil.)	NET PROFIT MARGIN	EMPLOYEES
9/02	1,201	—	—	2,500
9/01	1,053	—	—	2,400
9/00	1,002	—	—	2,400
9/99	925	—	—	2,400
9/98	769	—	—	2,000
9/97	611	—	—	1,800
9/96	500	—	—	1,800
9/95	230	—	—	750
9/94	214	—	—	—
Annual Growth	24.1%	—	—	18.8%

Revenue History

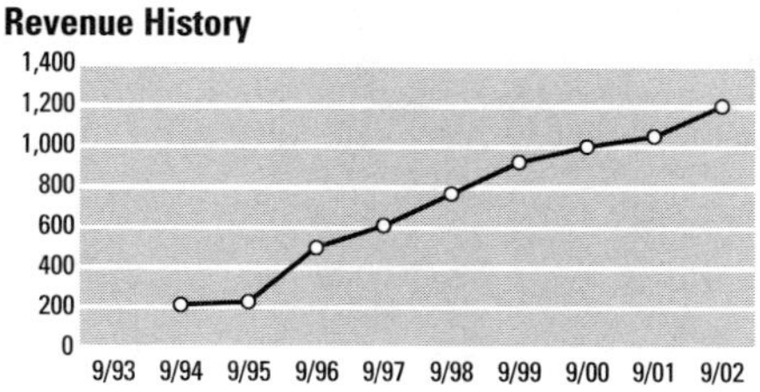

Roseburg Forest Products Co.

With roots in a Depression-era sawmill, Roseburg Forest Products has branched out with a comprehensive line of wood products. The company produces specialty panels (melamine, particleboard, and vinyl laminates), and plywood products such as concrete forming panel and siding. Its standard lumber offerings include pine, Douglas fir, and Hemlock products. Roseburg manages nearly 800,000 acres of land in northern California and southern Oregon. The company is owned by the heirs of philanthropist Kenneth Ford, who established the Ford Family Foundation.

EXECUTIVES

Chairman, President, and CEO: Allyn Ford
CFO: Ron Burgess
VP Human Resources: Hank Snow

LOCATIONS

HQ: Old Hwy. 99 South, Roseburg, OR 97470
Phone: 541-679-3311 **Fax:** 541-679-9543
Web: www.rfpco.com

Roseburg Forest Products has operations and timberlands in California and Oregon.

PRODUCTS/OPERATIONS

Selected Products

Plywood Products
Concrete forming
Hardwood plywood
Industrial grades
Sanded fir plywood
Sheathing
Siding
Underlayment

Specialty Panels
Foil overlays
Melamine
Particleboard
Prefinished
Shelving
Vinyl laminates

Lumber
Douglas fir
Hemlock/white fir
Pine
Premier stud

COMPETITORS

Columbia Forest Products	MAXXAM
Georgia-Pacific Corporation	Potlatch
Hampton Affiliates	Sierra Pacific Industries
Louisiana-Pacific	Simpson Investment
	Weyerhaeuser

HISTORICAL FINANCIALS

Company Type: Private

Income Statement FYE: December 31

	ESTIMATED REVENUE ($ mil.)	NET INCOME ($ mil.)	NET PROFIT MARGIN	EMPLOYEES
12/02	750	—	—	3,600
12/01	750	—	—	3,600
12/00	730	—	—	3,600
12/99	850	—	—	4,000
12/98	850	—	—	4,000
12/97	775	—	—	3,950
12/96	850	—	—	3,050
12/95	750	—	—	3,300
12/94	620	—	—	3,500
12/93	600	—	—	3,400
Annual Growth	2.5%	—	—	0.6%

Revenue History

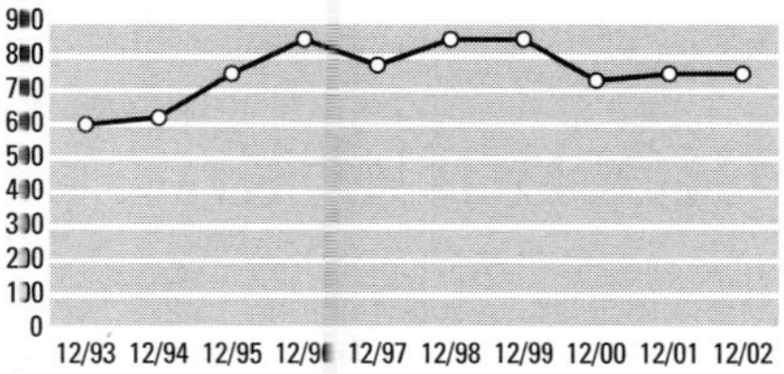

Rosenbluth International

In the mood for a trip? Rosenbluth International will help you unravel the travel scene. A leading travel management company, Rosenbluth emphasizes services for corporate clients (ChevronTexaco, J.P. Morgan Chase, NIKE). With locations in more than 50 countries worldwide, the company is known for staying abreast of evolving travel technology and offers its services with the aid of travel systems such as its Discount Analysis Containing Optimal Decision Algorithms (DACODA, maximizes savings on airlines tickets). Founded in 1892 by Marcus Rosenbluth, the company still is owned and operated by his family, including his great-grandson, chairman and CEO Hal Rosenbluth.

In addition to providing traditional travel services (airline, hotel and car rental reservations), Rosebluth has branched into virtual travel management, offering its clients services such as Web conferencing.

Rosenbluth International makes billions by keeping its customers second. The company, whose corporate philosophy was revealed in chairman and CEO Hal Rosenbluth's 1992 book *The Customer Comes Second* (after employees), is a leader in travel management services. The company's mascot is a salmon, because of its ability to successfully swim upstream against the tide.

In 2003, American Express signed an agreement to acquire Rosenbluth International.

HISTORY

In 1892 Marcus Rosenbluth began selling immigration packages from his storefront shop to neighbors in Philadelphia's Brewerytown. After collecting $50 in various currencies, he would arrange passage for an immigrant family's European relative to Ellis Island, often greeting the American-to-be personally and helping complete forms in the new language.

Rosenbluth's travel company rode out the ups and downs of two world wars and the emerging commercial airline industry. By the time Rosenbluth's great-grandson Hal Rosenbluth came aboard in 1974, the mostly consumer leisure travel agency was making more than $20 million a year. In the year of airline deregulation (1978), a lightbulb went on as Hal Rosenbluth observed reservation agents working on the company's corporate accounts. He soon demoted himself from vice president to reservations agent and began steering the company toward corporate accounts.

Before deregulation, airlines focused on service; fares were regulated by law and rarely changed. Businesses were interested mostly in who could deliver their tickets the fastest. With deregulation, fares changed with dizzying frequency. Yield management replaced service. Travelers needed help sorting through the confusion, and Rosenbluth saw the opportunity to meet their needs.

In the early 1980s accounts with Bethlehem Steel and DuPont helped Rosenbluth gain a national presence. A less than ecstatic reception in Atlanta in 1985 motivated the company to upgrade its high-tech pricing and reservations system and lure corporate accounts with promises of savings and good service. Hal Rosenbluth became CEO in 1987, and the next year Rosenbluth sought to grow overseas by forming Rosenbluth International Alliance (RIA), a network of independent business travel agencies.

Hal Rosenbluth's book, *The Customer Comes Second,* was published in 1992. Rosenbluth abandoned RIA in 1993 (buying some of the businesses and setting up new ones) when it found it could not control the quality of service it offered to multinationals. Crunched by low air fares, the company began reorganizing operations in 1994 by breaking up the company into 100-plus branches serving specific clients and regions. It also laid off about 10% of its workforce.

In 1997 the company geared itself for global growth by forming a strategic alliance with The SABRE Group to integrate SABRE's technology into its travel reservations systems. One year later Rosenbluth bought Swedish travel firm Business Express.

Rosenbluth acquired travel services firm Aquarius Travel in 1999. Later that year the company expanded into Web-based travel services when it bought a majority of Internet travel services company biztravel.com. In 2000 Rosenbluth unveiled Rosenbluth Everywhere, a custom online and wireless travel service. The company also expanded into non-travel call center services and made headlines when biztravel.com offered travelers refunds for flights that arrived late (biztravel.com folded the next year in the wake of the September 11th terrorist attacks).

The company continued to seek out partnerships in 2001, adding large Chinese travel agency China Comfort to its list of business affiliates. In 2002 Rosenbluth landed another major corporate client, US publisher McGraw-Hill.

EXECUTIVES

Chairman and CEO: Hal F. Rosenbluth, age 51
President and COO: Alex Wasilov
CFO: Thomas Sukay
SVP Marketing: Michael Boult
SVP North America: Ron DiLeo
SVP Upstream: Jerry Johnson
VP and Corporate Controller: Jeff Petrick
VP and General Counsel: Thomas Knoblauch
VP Business Development, Upstream: Joe Terrion
VP Marketing and Business Development North America: Gordon Locke
VP Human Resources Development: Cecily Carel
VP Central US: Yma Sherry
VP Western US: R. Timothy (Tim) Small
CIO: John Dabek
Director Corporate Development: Mara Pagotto
Director Sales, Western Europe: Ton Maanicus
Director Supplier Relations, Western Europe: Richard Lovelock
Director Western European Operations: Nanette Tobin
Regional Director, UK: Steven Busby

LOCATIONS

HQ: 2401 Walnut St., Philadelphia, PA 19103
Phone: 215-977-4000 **Fax:** 215-977-4028
Web: www.rosenbluth.com

PRODUCTS/OPERATIONS

Selected Products and Services

Rosenbluth (business travel management system)
Custom-Res (global reservation system)
Discount Analysis Containing Optimal Decision Algorithms (DACODA, system for maximizing savings on airline tickets)
E-Ticket Tracking Solution (electronic ticket tracking system)
Global Distribution Network (electronic reservation system)
Res-Monitor® (low-fare search system)
Rosenbluth's Electronic Messaging Services (e-mail-based travel management system)
Travelution (discount airline tickets Web site)

COMPETITORS

American Express
Carlson Wagonlit
Expedia
JTB
Kuoni Travel
Maritz
MyTravel
Pleasant Holidays
priceline.com
Travelocity
TUI
WorldTravel

HISTORICAL FINANCIALS

Company Type: Private

Income Statement FYE: December 31

	REVENUE ($ mil.)	NET INCOME ($ mil.)	NET PROFIT MARGIN	EMPLOYEES
12/01	6,000	—	—	5,200
12/00	5,500	—	—	5,500
12/99	4,500	—	—	4,500
12/98	3,500	—	—	4,500
12/97	4,000	—	—	4,500
12/96	3,500	—	—	4,500
12/95	3,200	—	—	—
Annual Growth	11.0%	—	—	2.9%

Revenue History

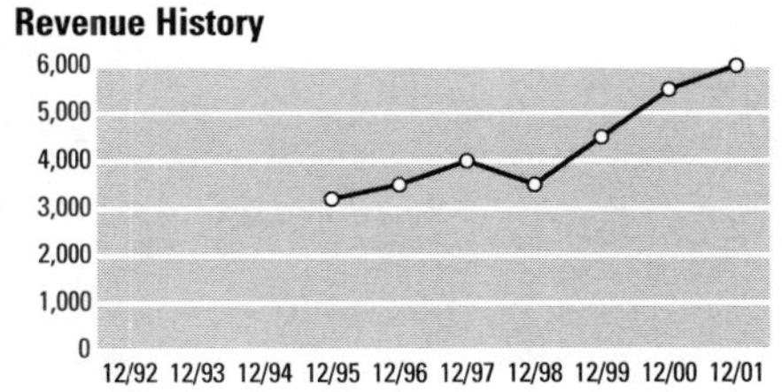

Rosen's Diversified, Inc.

Rosen's Diversified has the goods to make the grass greener for the cows it slaughters. The agricultural holding company has interests including Rosen's Incorporated which distributes agricultural chemicals, including fertilizers, for farms in the upper Midwest. Its beef-slaughtering operations consist of four meatpacking plants with the capacity to slaughter about 4,000 head of cattle a day. Rosen's Diversified processes meat for restaurants, government customers, and food manufacturers in the US. The company was founded in 1946 by brothers Elmer and Ludwig Rosen. CEO Thomas Rosen (the son of Elmer) and other family members share ownership of Rosen's Diversified.

EXECUTIVES

CEO: Thomas J. Rosen, age 55
CFO: Rob Hovde
General Counsel, Director of Human Resources: Dominick Driano
President, Rosen's Incorporated: Ivan R. Wells

LOCATIONS

HQ: 1120 Lake Ave., Fairmont, MN 56031
Phone: 507-238-4201 **Fax:** 507-238-9966
Web: www.rosens.com

COMPETITORS

American Foods
Cargill
Farmland Industries
Smithfield Foods
Swift
Tyson Foods

HISTORICAL FINANCIALS

Company Type: Private

Income Statement FYE: September 30

	ESTIMATED REVENUE ($ mil.)	NET INCOME ($ mil.)	NET PROFIT MARGIN	EMPLOYEES
9/02	950	—	—	2,000
9/01	800	—	—	2,000
9/00	700	—	—	1,800
9/99	620	—	—	1,500
9/98	560	—	—	1,200
9/97	550	—	—	1,200
9/96	500	—	—	900
9/95	500	—	—	900
Annual Growth	9.6%	—	—	12.1%

Revenue History

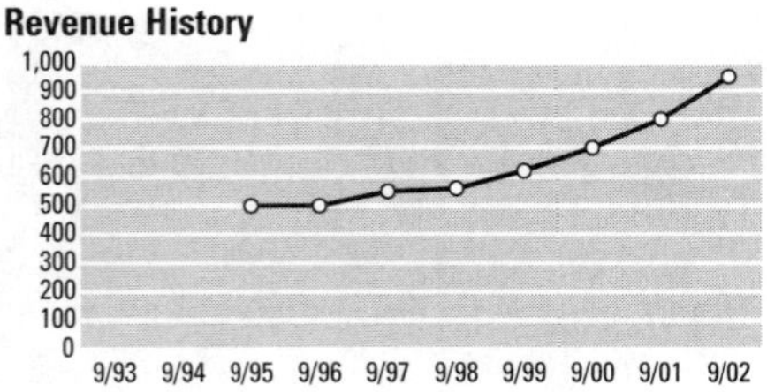

Rosenthal Automotive

A dealer of wheels in a city of wheeler-dealers, Rosenthal Automotive operates about 15 auto dealerships in the Washington, DC, area. Rosenthal's dealerships sell more than 22,000 new cars a year, including Acuras, Chevrolets, Hondas, Jaguars, Mazdas, Nissans, Toyotas, Volkswagens, and Volvos. The company also sells used cars and has wholesale and fleet operations. Chairman and owner Robert Rosenthal founded Rosenthal Automotive in 1954 when he opened his first Chevrolet dealership in Arlington, Virginia. In 1997 Rosenthal joined other dealers in the Washington, DC, area to form Capital Automotive REIT, the first automotive-only real estate investment trust in the US.

Robert Rosenthal owns more than 11% of Capital Automotive REIT.

EXECUTIVES

Chairman: Robert M. Rosenthal, age 75
COO: Don Bavely
CFO: Michael Baron
Director of Human Resources: Jeraldine Mendez

LOCATIONS

HQ: Rosenthal Automotive Organization
1100 S. Glebe Rd., Arlington, VA 22204
Phone: 703-553-4300 **Fax:** 703-553-8435

COMPETITORS

Atlantic Automotive
AutoNation
Brown Automotive
CarMax
Darcars
Jim Koons Automotive
March/Hodge
Ourisman Automotive
Sheehy Auto

HISTORICAL FINANCIALS

Company Type: Private

Income Statement FYE: December 31

	REVENUE ($ mil.)	NET INCOME ($ mil.)	NET PROFIT MARGIN	EMPLOYEES
12/02	900	—	—	1,500
12/01	862	—	—	1,500
12/00	825	—	—	1,625
12/99	791	—	—	1,600
12/98	823	—	—	1,600
12/97	786	—	—	1,500
12/96	846	—	—	1,600
12/95	846	—	—	1,600
12/94	785	—	—	1,500
12/93	643	—	—	1,400
Annual Growth	3.8%	—	—	0.8%

Revenue History

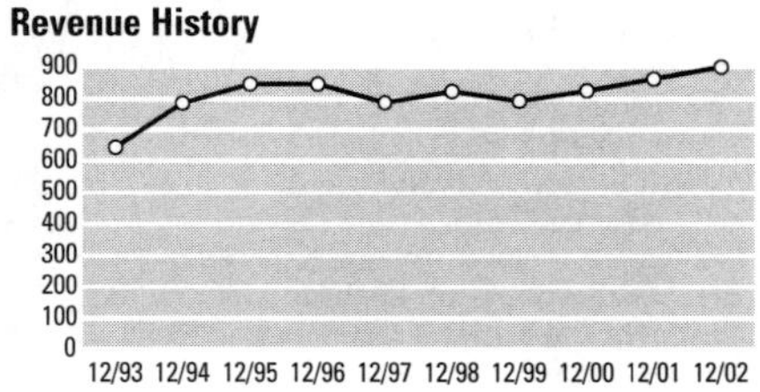

Rotary International

The rotary phone may be gone, but Rotary International is still going strong. The service organization addresses issues such as AIDS, hunger, and illiteracy, and includes about 30,000 clubs in more than 160 countries with a membership of nearly 1.2 million (predominantly men, although women are its fastest-growing segment). Its not-for-profit Rotary Foundation invests in international education and humanitarian programs (funds are raised through voluntary contributions). Rotary International also sponsors Interact clubs for secondary school students, as well as a network of more than 6,900 Rotaract clubs for members ages 18-30. It is governed by a 19-member board and maintains offices globally.

Membership in Rotary clubs is by invitation only. Each club strives to include representatives from major businesses, professions, and institutions in its community. The organization's name arose from the early practice of rotating meetings among members' offices. Originally all male, women were first admitted into the organization in 1989.

HISTORY

On February 23, 1905, lawyer Paul Harris met with three friends in an office in Chicago's Unity Building. Inspired by the fellowship and tolerance of his boyhood home in Wallingford, Vermont, Harris proposed organizing a men's club to meet periodically for the purpose of camaraderie and making business contacts. The new endeavor was organized as the Rotary Club of Chicago and had 30 members by the end of the year.

As additional clubs followed, the organization assumed its role as a civic and service organization (the installation of public comfort stations in Chicago's City Hall was one of its first projects). At the first convention of the National Association of Rotary Clubs in 1910, Harris was elected president. International clubs soon followed, and by 1921 there were Rotary clubs on each continent.

In 1932, while struggling to revive a company with financial difficulties, Rotarian Herbert Taylor devised a statement of business ethics that later became the Rotarian mantra. Taylor's "4-Way Test" consisted of the following questions: "Is it the truth? Is it fair to all concerned? Will it build goodwill and better friendships? Will it be beneficial to all concerned?"

During WWI Rotary clubs promoted war relief and peace fund efforts. Following WWII the clubs assisted in efforts to aid refugees and prisoners of war. The extent of Rotarian involvement in international issues became clear when 49 members assisted in drafting the United Nations Charter in 1945.

The first significant contributions to The Rotary Foundation followed Harris' death in 1947. These funds formed the bedrock for the foundation's programs, and in 1965 the foundation created its Matching Grants and Group Study Exchange programs. Rotary International also welcomed younger members in the 1960s by creating its Interact and Rotaract clubs in 1962 and 1968, respectively.

The largest meeting of Rotarians occurred in

1978 when almost 40,000 members attended the organization's Tokyo convention. But controversy was fast approaching the male-only organization. In 1978 a California Rotary club defied the male-only requirement and admitted two women. Claiming that the club had violated the organization's constitution, Rotary International revoked the club's charter. A lengthy court battle ensued, and a series of appeals landed the issue on the docket of the US Supreme Court. In 1987 the court ruled that the all-male requirement was discriminatory. Two years later Rotary International officially did away with its all-male status.

In the 1990s membership in Rotary clubs grew, but at a slower pace than in the organization's past. Mary Wolfenberger was appointed the organization's first female CFO in 1993 (resigned 1997). In 1998 Rotary International joined with the United Nations to launch a series of humanitarian service projects in developing areas. In 1999 the organization spearheaded events to help flood victims in North Carolina and refugees in the Balkans. In 2000 the group created a program specializing in peace and conflict resolution. Rotary International established its first Internet-based Rotary club in early 2002. Also that year the group founded the Rotary Centers for International Studies which selects 70 scholars a year to study in master's-level programs in peace studies.

EXECUTIVES

Chairman of the Rotary Foundation: Gen W. Kinross
President: Jonathan Majiyagbe
President-elect: Glenn E. Estess
VP: Frank C. Collins
Treasurer: Gennaro M. Cardinale
General Secretary: Edwin H. Futa
Controller: Mark A. Vieth
Director Human Resources: Carolyn Engblom
Communications Services General Manager: Kathy Kessenich
Membership Services General Manager: Theresa Nissen
Rotary Foundation General Manager: Duane Sterling
Corporate Services Manager: Andrew McDonald
Public Relations Manager: Susan Ross

LOCATIONS

HQ: 1 Rotary Center, 1560 Sherman Ave., Evanston, IL 60201
Phone: 847-866-3000 **Fax:** 847-328-8281
Web: www.rotary.org

Rotary International has clubs in more than 160 countries.

PRODUCTS/OPERATIONS

Selected Issues Addressed

AIDS
Concern for the aging
Drug-abuse prevention
Environment
Hunger
Literacy
Polio
Service to women
Urban violence prevention
Youth

Selected Programs

Educational programs
Ambassadorial Scholarships
Grants for University Teachers
Group Study Exchange (GSE)
Rotary World Peace Scholarships
Humanitarian grants
Discovery Grants
Grants for Rotary Volunteers
Matching Grants
New Opportunities Grants
Peace Program Grants
PolioPlus Program
Polio Eradication Advocacy
Polio Eradication Private Sector Campaign
PolioPlus Partners

HISTORICAL FINANCIALS

Company Type: Not-for-profit

Income Statement FYE: June 30

	REVENUE ($ mil.)	NET INCOME ($ mil.)	NET PROFIT MARGIN	EMPLOYEES
6/02	56	(6)	—	500
6/01	62	—	—	500
6/00	61	—	—	450
6/99	61	—	—	450
6/98	73	—	—	400
6/97	72	—	—	400
6/96	62	—	—	400
6/95	60	—	—	350
6/94	59	—	—	450
6/93	52	—	—	617
Annual Growth	0.8%	—	—	(2.3%)

Revenue History

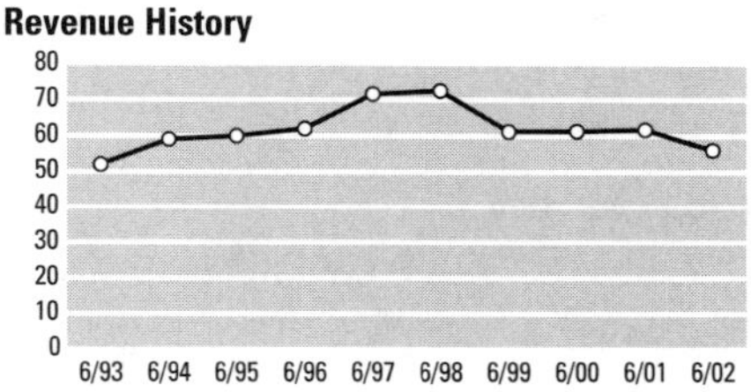

Roundy's, Inc.

Roundy's rounds up name-brand and private-label goods and distributes them to warehouse and grocery stores throughout the Midwest. The company also owns 64 retail stores — 56 in Wisconsin and eight elsewhere in the Midwest. Roundy's also services nearly 800 independent and licensee stores. Roundy's offers its members and customer stores support services, including accounting and inventory control, advertising, and store financing. Roundy's is a leading Wisconsin food retailer, with supermarket chains operating under the Pick 'n Save and Copps Food Centers banners. Roundy's was founded in 1872. Private investment firm Willis Stein & Partners bought Roundy's in 2002.

Forty-five percent of Roundy's sales come from its distribution business to independent grocery stores across 14 states. To boost its sales and profits, Roundy's has been acquiring independent stores, most recently seven Pick 'n Save supermarkets in Wisconsin from Prescott's Supermarkets.

In 2003 the company agreed to acquire seven Kohl's grocery stores from The Great Atlantic & Pacific Tea Company. The stores, located in Madison, Wisconsin, will operate under the Copps banner. It also agreed to purchase 40 Minneapolis-St. Paul-located Rainbow Foods stores from Fleming.

HISTORY

Migration from the eastern US and overseas was boosting Milwaukee's ranks when William Smith, Judson Roundy, and Sidney Hauxhurst formed grocery wholesaler Smith, Roundy & Co. in 1872. Smith left the firm in 1878 for his first of two terms as Wisconsin's governor, and William Peckham joined the enterprise, which was then renamed Roundy, Peckham & Co. Two years later Charles Dexter joined the company, by then operating in five midwestern states and running a manufacturing business.

The wholesaler became Roundy, Peckham & Dexter Co. in 1902, following the death of Hauxhurst (Roundy died in 1907). The company introduced its first private-label product — salt — in 1922. In 1929 Dexter (then 84) came up with a plan to publicize the Roundy's name by handing out cookbooks that called for the company's goods.

Roy Johnson, who joined the company in 1912, was named president near the end of the Depression. In the 1940s the wholesaler acquired smaller companies in the region. The company became Roundy's in 1952 when Roundy, Peckham & Dexter was bought by a group comprising hundreds of Wisconsin grocery retailers. Johnson remained head of the new company until his death in 1962. James Aldrich led the company for the next 11 years.

In 1970 Roundy's started Insurance Planners, which offered insurance to retailers. Vincent Little became president of the company in 1973. Two years later Roundy's began a real estate subsidiary (Ronco Realty) and opened its first Pick 'n Save Warehouse Foods store.

The company expanded in the mid-1980s through the purchase of distributors. But expansion hurt profits, and dividends were suspended in 1984 and 1985. In the late 1980s several Pick 'n Save stores opened throughout Wisconsin and other midwestern states. Owners grew suspicious of Little's accounting practices and the special treatment given a Roundy's-owned store run by his son, and in 1986 they forced him out of his president and CEO positions. John Dickson replaced him.

By 1994 Pick 'n Save had vastly upgraded its image — one store sold $1,000 cognac and featured an $18,000 cappuccino machine. However, sales dropped off for the third straight year. COO Gerald Lestina was named CEO in 1995, replacing Dickson, who continued as chairman. Dickson died later that year.

Roundy's did not pay its members a dividend in 1995 as it made an effort to offset losses in Michigan and Ohio. To ease those losses, in 1997 the company closed 12 poorly performing stores in those states. A year later a fire destroyed its Evansville, Indiana, warehouse; the company rebuilt the facility in 1999. Also in 1999 Roundy's purchased three supermarkets in Indiana from Kroger and The John C. Groub Company.

The Mega Marts and Ultra Mart chains, which together operate 24 Pick 'n Save stores, primarily in Wisconsin, were acquired by Roundy's in 2000. In 2001 Roundy's launched an online grocery shopping service, called Pick 'n Save Online Shopping, in two test stores in Wisconsin (the plan was eventurally scuttled). Also in 2001 the company purchased its competitor, The Copps Corporation, acquiring 21 stores in north and central Wisconsin and a wholesale business that distributes to retailers in Wisconsin and northern Michigan.

Chicago-based Willis Stein & Partners bought Roundy's in June 2002. In October Roundy's completed the acquisition of four Gold's Pick 'n Save stores in northeastern Milwaukee for $26 million. It also acquired three Rainbow stores from Fleming in December of that year.

EXECUTIVES

Chairman, President, and CEO: Robert A. Mariano, age 52
EVP and CFO: Darren W. Karst, age 43
Group VP, Human Resources: Colleen J. Stenholt, age 52
Group VP, Marketing: Andrew A. Abraham, age 39
Group VP, Supply Chain: Donald S. Rosanova, age 53
Group VP, Wholesale Development & Real Estate: Michael J. Schmitt, age 54, $275,250 pay
VP, Advertising: Londell J. Behm, age 51
VP, Loss Prevention & Security: Michael J. Santimauro, age 56
VP, Management Information Systems: Larry C. Goddard, age 48
VP, Retail Operations and Customer Satisfaction: Gary L. Fryda, age 50, $332,500 pay
VP, Secretary, and Treasurer: Edward G. Kitz, age 49
VP and Controller: Randy T. Benz, age 41
Director of Natural and Organic Foods: Robert E. Carlson
Media Contact: Lynn Guyer
Auditors: Ernst & Young

LOCATIONS

HQ: 23000 Roundy Dr., Pewaukee, WI 53072
Phone: 262-953-7999 **Fax:** 262-953-7989
Web: www.roundys.com

Roundy's distributes its goods from eight wholesale distribution centers in four Midwestern states to about 800 licensee and independent retail operations in the Midwest.

PRODUCTS/OPERATIONS

Selected Private and Controlled Labels

Buyers' Choice
IGA
Old Time
Roundy's Quality
Shurfine

Product Lines

Bakery goods
Dairy products
Dry groceries
Fresh produce
Frozen foods
General merchandise
Meats

Selected Services

Centralized bakery purchasing
Business development
Financing
Group advertising
Insurance
Inventory control
Market analysis
Merchandising
Ordering assistance
Point-of-sale support
Pricing services
Purchasing reports
Retail accounting
Retail training

COMPETITORS

Albertson's
ALDI
AWG
Central Grocers Cooperative
Certified Grocers Midwest
Costco Wholesale
Dominick's
Eagle Food
Fleming Companies
A&P
GSC Enterprises
Hy-Vee
IGA
Kroger
McLane
Meijer
Nash Finch
S. Abraham & Sons
Spartan Stores
SUPERVALU
Topco Associates
Wal-Mart

HISTORICAL FINANCIALS

Company Type: Private

Income Statement

FYE: Saturday nearest December 31

	REVENUE ($ mil.)	NET INCOME ($ mil.)	NET PROFIT MARGIN	EMPLOYEES
12/02	3,638	31	0.9%	13,151
12/01	3,450	26	0.7%	13,451
12/00	2,984	21	0.7%	9,071
12/99	2,717	18	0.6%	5,617
12/98	2,579	12	0.5%	5,193
12/97	2,611	11	0.4%	5,071
12/96	2,579	10	0.4%	5,481
12/95	2,488	9	0.4%	4,839
12/94	2,462	7	0.3%	4,775
12/93	2,480	8	0.3%	4,884
Annual Growth	4.3%	16.4%	—	11.6%

2002 Year-End Financials

Debt ratio: 167.1%
Return on equity: 12.4%
Cash ($ mil.): 140
Current ratio: 1.24
Long-term debt ($ mil.): 560

Net Income History

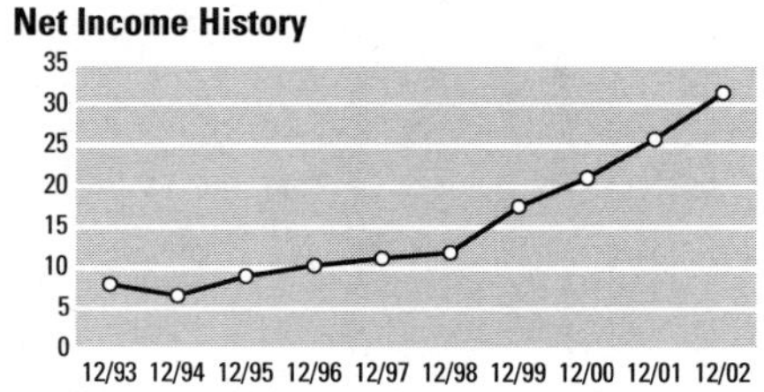

Royster-Clark

Royster-Clark has been spreading it on thick for more than 125 years. The company makes fertilizer and crop-protection products. It processes seed for leading seed companies and sells seed under its own label. Operations include granulation, blending, and seed-processing plants, 400 retail farm supply centers, and a network of distribution terminals and warehouses. The company offers such agronomic services as custom blending and spreading and soil sampling. Chairman and CEO Francis Jenkins owns 38% of the company. Investment firm 399 Venture Partners (a Citigroup affiliate) owns 32%.

Royster-Clark operates in the eastern, southern, and midwestern US.

Another major investor is CTT Partners, which has about a 6% stake.

EXECUTIVES

Chairman and CEO: Francis P. Jenkins Jr., age 60, $699,990 pay
President and COO: G. Kenneth Moshenek, age 51, $424,981 pay
CFO: Paul M. Murphy, age 58, $200,577 pay
Senior Managing Director, International: Max Baer, age 70
Managing Director, Human Resources: Kenneth W. (Ken) Carter, age 57
Managing Director and Controller: Joel F. Dunbar, age 54
Auditors: KPMG LLP

LOCATIONS

HQ: Royster-Clark, Inc.
1251 Avenue of the Americas, Ste. 900, New York, NY 10020
Phone: 212-332-2965 **Fax:** 212-332-2999
Web: www.roysterclark.com

Royster-Clark operates primarily in the eastern, southeastern, and midwestern US. The company has production facilities in Alabama, Florida, Georgia, Illinois, North Carolina, Ohio, South Carolina, Tennessee, Virginia, and Wisconsin.

PRODUCTS/OPERATIONS

Selected Products

Crop Nutrients
Bagged and bulk dry fertilizers
Custom-blended fertilizers
Fertilizer materials
Granulated fertilizers
Lime and landplaster
Liquid fertilizers
Specialty fertilizers

Crop Protection
Fungicides
Herbicides
Insecticides

Seeds
Soybean
Wheat

COMPETITORS

Agrium
Cargill
CHS
ConAgra
Dow Chemical
DuPont
Farmland Industries
FMC
IMC Global
Monsanto
Southern States
Terra Industries
Terra Nitrogen
Tractor Supply
Wilbur-Ellis

HISTORICAL FINANCIALS

Company Type: Private

Income Statement

FYE: December 31

	REVENUE ($ mil.)	NET INCOME ($ mil.)	NET PROFIT MARGIN	EMPLOYEES
12/02	898	(5)	—	3,130
12/01	954	(9)	—	3,130
12/00	913	(5)	—	3,130
12/99	715	7	0.9%	—
Annual Growth	7.9%	—	—	0.0%

2002 Year-End Financials

Debt ratio: 450.1%
Return on equity: —
Cash ($ mil.): 1
Current ratio: 2.11
Long-term debt ($ mil.): 343

Net Income History

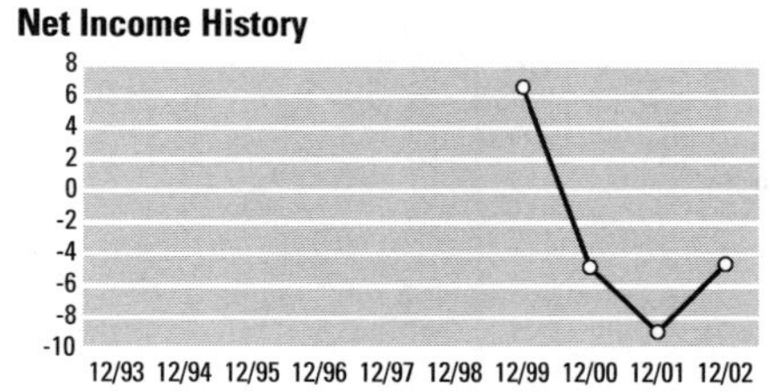

RTM Restaurant Group

RTM is motivated by roast beef. RTM Restaurant Group is the largest franchise group in the US operating and franchising more than 1,000 restaurants in 22 states. The company is the nation's largest operator of Arby's restaurants, with more than 780 units franchised from Triarc. The quick service restaurants are known for their roast beef sandwiches and other burger alternatives. In addition, the company has a stake in Winners International, the franchisor of Mrs. Winner's Chicken & Biscuits. RTM was founded in 1973 by CEO Russ Umphenour. He retains majority ownership in the company.

To focus on its Arby's operations, the company sold its stake in Lee's Famous Recipe Chicken in 2003. Jeff Miller, formerly an executive with DenAmerica (later Phoenix Restaurant Group) and a veteran KFC franchisee, bought the chain of 150 quick-service restaurants.

Umphenour worked his way to the top of the food chain after starting out at a Michigan Arby's in 1967. He started RTM (which stands for Results Thought Motivation) with 11 Arby's restaurants in Georgia and Alabama. The company's holdings expanded to 100 locations by 1980, and in 1997 RTM acquired more than 350 Arby's units from Triarc. It acquired its stake in Mrs. Winners in 1989.

EXECUTIVES

Chairman: Dennis Cooper
CEO: Russell V. Umphenour Jr.
President: Tom Garrett
SVP Finance and CFO: Doug Benham
SVP and Secretary: Russ Welch
SVP and CIO: Patti Reilly
SVP Corporate Communications and Public Relations: John Gray
SVP Human Resources and General Counsel: Sharron Barton
SVP Marketing: Debbie Pike
SVP Operations: Ray Biondi

LOCATIONS

HQ: 5995 Barfield Rd., Atlanta, GA 30328
Phone: 404-256-4900 **Fax:** 404-256-7277
Web: www.rtmrestaurantgroup.com

COMPETITORS

AFC Enterprises
AmeriKing
Blimpie
Burger King
Chick-fil-A
CKE Restaurants
Subway
Dairy Queen
Jack in the Box
McDonald's
NPC International
Quizno's
Schlotzsky's
Sonic
Wendy's
YUM!

HISTORICAL FINANCIALS

Company Type: Private

Income Statement FYE: May 31

	REVENUE ($ mil.)	NET INCOME ($ mil.)	NET PROFIT MARGIN	EMPLOYEES
5/03	751	—	—	25,000
5/02	735	—	—	25,000
5/01	675	—	—	25,000
5/00	605	—	—	25,000
5/99	685	—	—	23,000
5/98	647	—	—	23,000
5/97	405	—	—	20,000
Annual Growth	10.8%	—	—	3.8%

Revenue History

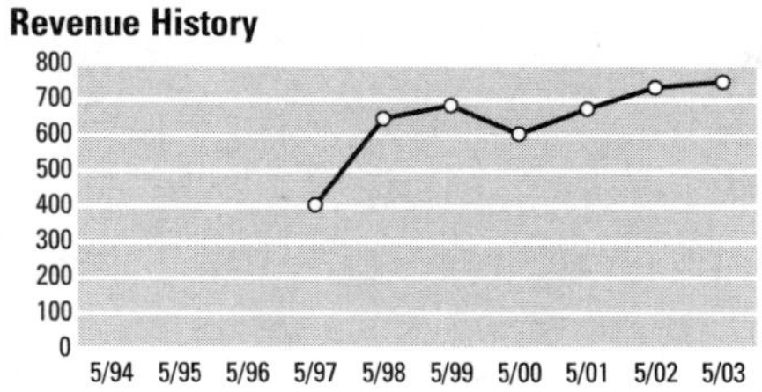

Rudolph and Sletten, Inc.

Rudolph and Sletten builds on shaky ground in California, but the force is with it. The firm built Lucasfilm's Skywalker Ranch production facility and is a leading player in the Silicon Valley, where it raised corporate campuses for Apple Computer, Microsoft, and Sun Microsystems, among others. Acting as on-site general contractor or construction manager, the company specializes in projects for the health care, high-tech research and manufacturing, biotechnology, and entertainment industries; it also takes on such unique projects as the Monterey Bay Aquarium. Onslow "Rudy" Rudolph, father of president and CEO Allen Ruldoph, founded the company in 1960 and was joined by former chairman Kenneth Sletten in 1962.

EXECUTIVES

President and CEO: Allen A. Rudolph
Chief Administrative Officer: Karen M. Rudolph
EVP and COO: Dennis R. Giles
EVP and Chief of Estimating/Preconstruction: Gary L. Walz
CFO: James F. (Jim) Evans
VP and General Counsel: Paul A. Aherne
Director Human Resources: Barbara Duncan
Business Development, Marketing, and Sales Executive: Dianna Wright
Auditors: KPMG LLP

LOCATIONS

HQ: 989 E. Hillsdale Blvd., Ste. 100, Foster City, CA 94404
Phone: 650-572-1919 **Fax:** 650-577-1558
Web: www.rsconstruction.com

Rudolph and Sletten has offices in Foster City, Irvine, Sacramento, and San Diego, California.

PRODUCTS/OPERATIONS

Selected Customers

3Com
Amgen
Apple Computer
Bayer Corporation
Genentech
Microsoft
Monterey Bay Aquarium
Shaklee Corporation
Stanford University
Sun Microsystems

Major Markets

Biotechnology
Corporate campuses
Entertainment
Health care
High-tech
Pharmaceutical

COMPETITORS

Beck Group
Devcon Construction
DPR Construction
Hathaway Dinwiddie Construction
Hensel Phelps Construction
Hoffman Corporation
Kitchell Corporation
S. J. Amoroso Construction
Swinerton
Turner Corporation
Webcor Builders
Whiting-Turner

HISTORICAL FINANCIALS

Company Type: Private

Income Statement FYE: June 30

	REVENUE ($ mil.)	NET INCOME ($ mil.)	NET PROFIT MARGIN	EMPLOYEES
6/02	1,002	—	—	800
6/01	852	—	—	1,200
6/00	675	—	—	1,200
6/99	565	—	—	1,000
6/98	600	—	—	900
6/97	500	—	—	767
6/96	453	—	—	815
6/95	350	—	—	641
6/94	276	—	—	570
6/93	300	—	—	500
Annual Growth	14.3%	—	—	5.4%

Revenue History

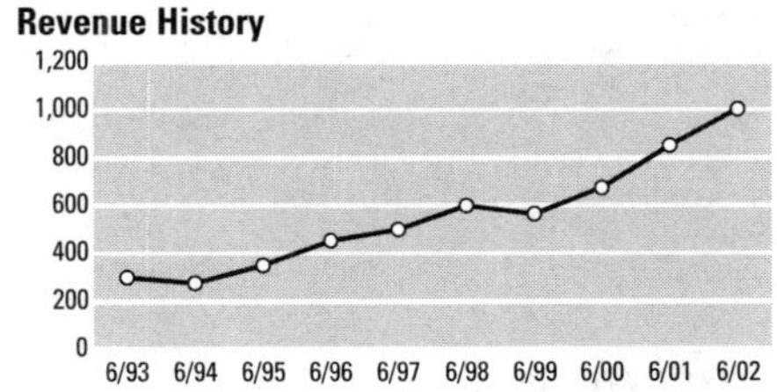

Russell Stover Candies Inc.

For Russell Stover Candies, life *is* a box of chocolates. The largest US maker of boxed chocolates is protecting its sweet position. Faced with growing competition as Hershey and Mars invade the boxed-chocolate arena, it has countered with a chocolate bar by packaging its version of that popular campfire treat — the s'more (graham cracker, marshmallow, chocolate). It also sells bagged candy, but boxed treats — especially Whitman's Sampler and Pangburn's Millionaires — are its main business. For diabetics and others the company offers sugar-free candy, including a sugarless version of Millionaires. The company is owned by the founding Ward family and led by co-presidents and brothers Tom and Scott Ward.

Russell Stover is hoping to attract younger customers through the use of licensed characters (Elvis, Looney Tunes, Peanuts) in conjunction with its chocolate products. It also produces individually wrapped candy-bar aisle treats. Its Whitman's affiliate makes the famous Whitman's Sampler.

Russell Stover's candies are sold by supermarkets, card and gift shops, drugstores, mass merchandisers (it has more than 40,000 wholesale customers), and more than 50 Russell Stover Candies retail stores throughout all 50 states, as well as in Canada and Puerto Rico.

EXECUTIVES

Co-President and COO: Thomas S. Ward
Co-President: Scott H. Ward, age 46
CFO and Chief Administrative Officer: Dick Masinton
SVP, Information Systems: David Copas
VP Human Resources: Robinn S. Weber
VP Logistical Operations and Product Scheduling: Robert G. Maack
VP Marketing: John O'Hara
VP Sales: Mark Frame

LOCATIONS

HQ: 4900 Oak St., Kansas City, MO 64112
Phone: 816-842-9240 **Fax:** 816-561-4350
Web: www.russellstover.com

Russell Stover Candies has factories in Colorado, Kansas (2), Tennessee, and Texas.

PRODUCTS/OPERATIONS

Selected Products

Almond Delights
Assorted Chocolates
Caramels
Cherry Cordials
Chocolate Covered Nuts
French Chocolate Mints
Fruit Flavored Jellies
Lemon Squares
Millionaires (regular and sugar free)
Miniature Chocolates
Mint Patties
Orange Patties
PB & Grape Jelly Cup
Pecan Delights
Sugar Free Milk Chocolate
Toffee
Traditional S'mores Candy Bar
Truffles

COMPETITORS

Archibald Candy
Barry Callebaut
Brach's
Cadbury Schweppes
Campbell Soup
Chase General
Lindt & Sprüngli
DFG Confectionery
Ferrero
Hershey
Jelly Belly Candy
Just Born
Mars
Nestlé
Rocky Mountain Chocolate
See's Candies
Sherwood Brands
Tootsie Roll
World's Finest Chocolate

HISTORICAL FINANCIALS

Company Type: Private

Income Statement FYE: February 28

	ESTIMATED REVENUE ($ mil.)	NET INCOME ($ mil.)	NET PROFIT MARGIN	EMPLOYEES
2/02	471	—	—	6,000
2/01	600	—	—	5,200
2/00	620	—	—	6,200
2/99	500	—	—	6,300
2/98	510	—	—	6,000
2/97	442	—	—	5,900
Annual Growth	1.3%	—	—	0.3%

Revenue History

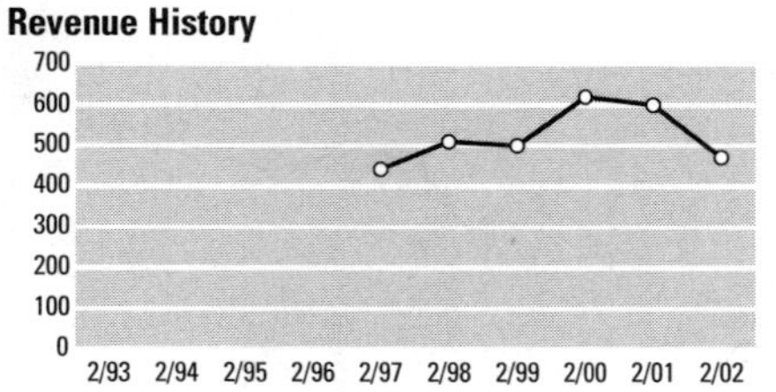

S. Abraham & Sons, Inc.

Impudence won't get you anywhere in the grocery business, but SAS might. Regional wholesale food distributor S. Abraham & Sons (SAS) serves convenience stores and small grocers in seven midwestern states. The company distributes name-brand groceries, health and beauty aids, snacks, store supplies, and tobacco. SAS offers private-label products such as Smart Choice health and beauty aids and Red & White groceries; its fast-food programs include Beantown (coffee), Salubre (pizza), and Subsations (sandwiches). SAS also provides services such as category management (shelf management). Founded in 1927 by Sleyman Abraham, SAS is family-owned and operated.

EXECUTIVES

President and CEO: Alan Abraham
SEVP: Jerry Abraham
VP Distribution: Larry Derdaele
VP Human Resources: Keith Anderson
VP Information Technology: Will Tesch
VP Loss Prevention and Safety: Clarence Petzold
VP Marketing: W. James Anderson
VP Sales: Barry Latham
VP and Controller: James Leonard
VP and General Manager — Heartland: Bill Burgess

LOCATIONS

HQ: 4001 Three Mile Rd., Grand Rapids, MI 49501
Phone: 616-453-6358 **Fax:** 616-453-9346
Web: www.sasinc.com

S. Abraham & Sons has distribution centers in Grand Rapids, Michigan; Louisville, Kentucky; and Milwaukee, Wisconsin.

COMPETITORS

AWG
Certified Grocers Midwest
Clark Products
Eby-Brown
Fleming Companies
H.T. Hackney
McLane
Nash Finch
Roundy's
Shurfine International
Spartan Stores
SUPERVALU

HISTORICAL FINANCIALS

Company Type: Private

Income Statement FYE: December 31

	REVENUE ($ mil.)	NET INCOME ($ mil.)	NET PROFIT MARGIN	EMPLOYEES
12/01	850	—	—	1,000
12/00	776	—	—	991
12/99	750	—	—	1,205
12/98	693	—	—	1,100
Annual Growth	7.0%	—	—	(3.1%)

Revenue History

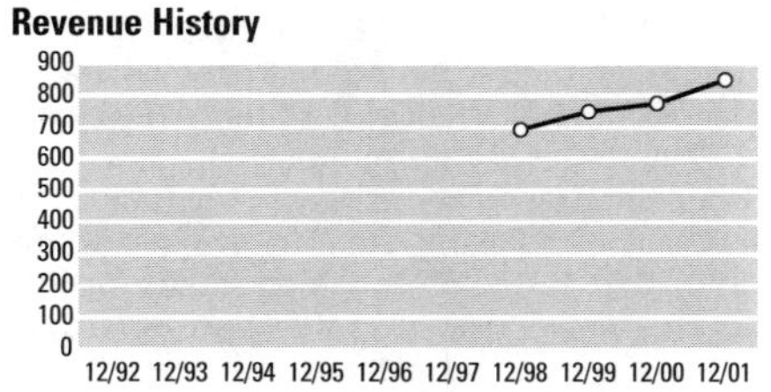

Safelite Group

Safelite Group has the answer to what blew into your windshield. The company, the US's largest auto glass retailer, serves more than 2 million customers each year through Safelite AutoGlass, Jiffy Lube, and Pep Boys service centers. It makes its own windshields at a factory in Kansas and another in North Carolina. Safelite also operates two national call centers for auto glass service scheduling and claims processing. Heavy debt led Safelite to file for Chapter 11 bankruptcy in 2000; later that year it emerged from bankruptcy and restructured. Founded in 1947, Safelite merged with rival Vistar in 1997. Safelite is 90%-owned by a 35-bank syndicate.

EXECUTIVES

Chairman and CEO: John F. Barlow
EVP and COO: Dan Wilson
EVP and CFO: Douglas A. (Doug) Herron
SVP, Manufacturing, Distribution, and Purchasing: Douglas A. Maehl
SVP, Marketing, Strategic Planning, and Human Resources: Elizabeth A. Wolszon
SVP, National Sales: Thomas M. (Tom) Feeney
VP, Finance: Poe A. Timmons
CIO/CTO: Tim Plazk
VP, Marketing, Safelite Glass: Denise Klapper
Auditors: Deloitte & Touche LLP

LOCATIONS

HQ: Safelite Group, Inc.
2400 Farmers Dr., 5th Fl., Columbus, OH 43216
Phone: 614-210-9000 **Fax:** 614-210-9451
Web: www.safelite.com

PRODUCTS/OPERATIONS

Subsidiaries

Safelite Fulfillment, Inc. (retail and wholesale auto glass)
Safelite Glass Corp. (windshield manufacturing)
Safelite Solutions LLC (claims management outsourcing)

COMPETITORS

Apogee Enterprises
Asahi Glass
Donnelly
Guardian Industries
Pilkington
PPG
Vitro America, Inc.

HISTORICAL FINANCIALS

Company Type: Private

Income Statement FYE: Saturday nearest March 31

	REVENUE ($ mil.)	NET INCOME ($ mil.)	NET PROFIT MARGIN	EMPLOYEES
3/02	634	33	5.2%	6,000
3/01	725	—	—	6,300
3/00	859	—	—	6,100
3/99	877	—	—	6,300
3/98	214	—	—	6,800
3/97	483	—	—	6,500
3/96	438	—	—	—
3/95	372	—	—	—
3/94	357	—	—	—
3/93	328	—	—	—
Annual Growth	7.6%	—	—	(1.6%)

Revenue History

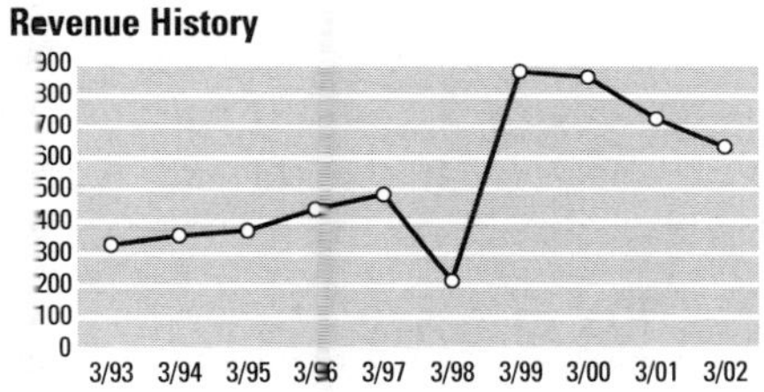

Salvation Army

The largest civil army in the land, the Salvation Army is about 2 million strong. Its programs assist alcoholics, drug addicts, the homeless, the handicapped, the elderly, prison inmates, people in crisis, and the unemployed through a range of services. These include day-care centers, programs for people with disabilities, substance abuse programs, and educational facilities for at-risk students. It also provides disaster relief in the US and abroad. The Salvation Army USA is a national unit of the Salvation Army, an international body based in London, which oversees Army activities in more than 100 countries.

The name Salvation Army may only ring a bell with you around Christmas, but Salvation Army USA is always working. Active as a church and a charity, the organization serves nearly 37 million people a year. It also provides disaster relief in the US and abroad. The Salvation Army usually tops the list of US not-for-profits in terms of donations received: In 2001 contributions reached about $555 million.

Along with promoting charity, the Salvation Army seeks to save souls. As an evangelical church, it preaches the message of salvation through Jesus Christ. Before joining the organization and becoming a soldier (a lay member), one must sign an agreement known as the "Articles of War," a commitment to the avoidance of gambling, debt, and profanity and to abstention from alcohol, tobacco, and other recreational drugs. The US organization includes some 450,000 soldiers, more than 1 million volunteers, and nearly 5,400 officers, who are also ordained ministers.

Officers are expected to wear their uniforms at all times and to work full-time for the Salvation Army. They receive no salary; instead, they are provided with room and board and given a limited stipend.

The Salvation Army USA is only one of scores of national Salvation Army organizations around the world, which report to the group's global leader, General John Larsson, at its international headquarters in the UK.

HISTORY

William Booth (1829-1912) started preaching the gospel as a Wesleyan Methodist in the UK, but the church expelled him because he insisted on preaching outside and to everyone, including the poor. In 1865 he moved to the slums of London's East End and attracted large crowds with his volatile sermons. Opposition to his message of universal salvation for drunks, thieves, prostitutes, and gamblers often caused riots. In fact, the first women in the organization wore bonnets designed with a dual purpose in mind — warmth and protection from flying objects.

At a meeting in 1878, a sign was used referring to the "Salvation Army." Booth adopted the reference as both the name and the style of his organization. Members became soldiers, evangelists were officers, and Booth was referred to as "General." Prayers became knee drills, and contributions were called cartridges.

The Salvation Army marched across the Atlantic to the US in 1880, led by seven women and one man. Women have always played an active role in the Salvation Army, both as officers and soldiers. Booth's wife, Catherine Mumford, was a leading suffragette, and Booth advocated equal rights for women.

In 1891 a crab pot was placed on a San Francisco street to collect donations, with a sign reading "Keep the Pot Boiling." The idea led to the Salvation Army's annual Christmas kettle program.

During WWI the organization became famous for the doughnuts that it served the doughboys fighting on the front lines. After some internal dissension, the Salvation Army took its only public political stance in 1928 with the endorsement of Herbert Hoover for his support of Prohibition during his presidential campaign. The charity opened its first home for alcoholics in 1939, in Detroit.

After WWII the Salvation Army began using such radio and TV programs as *Heartbeat Theater* and *Army of Stars* to spread its message.

Over the years the Salvation Army has provided assistance to victims of hurricanes, floods, and earthquakes. Volunteers rendered almost 70,000 service hours in the aftermath of the Oklahoma City bombing in 1995, counseling more than 1,600 victims and family members, helping with funeral arrangements, and providing food, clothing, and travel assistance. Indicative of the organization's readiness and extensive reach, its volunteers were helping victims in Guam within minutes of the 1997 Korean Air plane crash. The Salvation Army was quickly on the scene after a Jonesboro, Arkansas, shooting incident in 1998 when four students and one teacher were killed by fellow students. Late that year the organization received the largest donation in its history — $80 million from Joan Kroc, wife of McDonald's co-founder Ray Kroc.

In 2000 General Paul Rader retired, and with incoming General John Gowans the organization initiated its first reform in more than 100 years by allowing officers to marry outside the ranks. Following the September 11 attacks in 2001, the Salvation Army provided assistance to rescue workers and families affected by the tragedy through its Disaster Relief Fund.

EXECUTIVES

Chairman National Advisory Board: Edsel Ford
General (International Director): John Larsson
Commissioner (National Commander): Todd Bassett
Lieutenant Colonel (National Treasurer and Secretary Business Administration): Don McDougald
Colonel (National Chief Secretary): Thomas C. Lewis
Colonel (National Secretary for Personnel): Myrtle V. Ryder
Commissioner (Eastern Territory): Lawrence Moretz
Commissioner (Southern Territory): Philip Needham
Commissioner (Central Territory): Kenneth Baillie
Commissioner (Western Territory): Linda Bond
Commissioner (National President Women's Organizations): Carol Bassett
Auditors: PricewaterhouseCoopers LLP

LOCATIONS

HQ: The Salvation Army National Corporation
615 Slaters Ln., Alexandria, VA 22313
Phone: 703-684-5500 **Fax:** 703-684-3478
Web: www.salvationarmyusa.org

Salvation Army USA operates service centers, local churches, and social service programs and facilities throughout the US and provides disaster relief worldwide.

PRODUCTS/OPERATIONS

Selected Services

Alcohol and drug treatment centers
Clinics and hospitals
Convalescent homes
Counseling
Crisis counseling
Food distribution centers
Handicapped housing
Homeless shelters
Institutes for the blind
Leprosy clinics
Military canteens and hostels
Nurseries and day care centers
Occupational centers
Prison ministry
Probation housing
Refugee centers
Science and trade schools
Student housing
Welfare aid

HISTORICAL FINANCIALS

Company Type: Not-for-profit

Income Statement FYE: September 30

	REVENUE ($ mil.)	NET INCOME ($ mil.)	NET PROFIT MARGIN	EMPLOYEES
9/02	2,497	—	—	40,000
9/01	2,313	—	—	45,000
9/00	1,803	—	—	45,096
9/99	1,707	—	—	43,318
9/98	2,078	—	—	39,883
9/97	2,525	—	—	40,770
9/96	2,070	—	—	44,626
9/95	1,421	—	—	38,999
9/94	1,355	—	—	39,591
9/93	1,398	—	—	—
Annual Growth	6.7%	—	—	0.1%

Revenue History

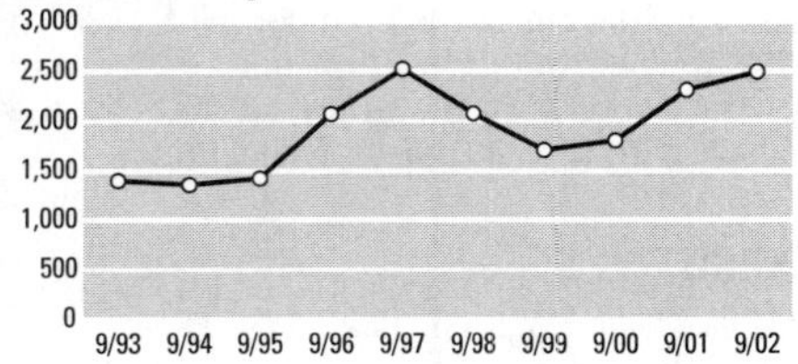

Sam Swope Auto Group, LLC

Sam Swope Auto Group would like to park its cars in front of every Kentucky home. The company owns about 20 automobile dealerships in Kentucky. (Most dealerships are at one location in Louisville.) In 1952 founder and chairman Sam Swope parlayed his love of cars into his first dealership, which sold Plymouth and Dodge cars, in Elizabethtown, Kentucky. Swope dealerships sell General Motors cars, including Buicks, Cadillacs, GMC trucks, Pontiacs, and Saturns. Other company dealerships sell BMW, Honda, Infiniti, Lexus, Mitsubishi, and Toyota models. The company also sells used cars. Sam Swope Auto Group, owned by the Swope family, offers parts and service departments, as well as a body repair center.

EXECUTIVES

Chairman: Samuel G. Swope, age 76
President: Richard (Dick) Swope
EVP and CFO: Michael Sanderson
VP, Marketing and Promotions: Patricia (Patti) Swope
Systems Administrator: Charlie Booher
CRM and Systems Manager: Andy Stottmann
Human Resources Assistant: Michelle Frank

LOCATIONS

HQ: I-64 & S. Hurstbourne Pkwy., Louisville, KY 40299
Phone: 502-499-5000 **Fax:** 502-499-5009
Web: www.swope.com

PRODUCTS/OPERATIONS

Selected Makes

BMW
Buick
Cadillac
GMC
Honda
Infiniti
Lexus
Mitsubishi
Pontiac
Saturn
Toyota
Volvo

COMPETITORS

AutoNation
Jeff Wyler Automotive
Sonic Automotive
United Auto Group

HISTORICAL FINANCIALS

Company Type: Private

Income Statement FYE: December 31

	REVENUE ($ mil.)	NET INCOME ($ mil.)	NET PROFIT MARGIN	EMPLOYEES
12/02	470	—	—	—
12/01	476	—	—	—
12/00	445	—	—	—
12/99	375	—	—	—
12/98	300	—	—	—
12/97	405	—	—	1,087
12/96	466	—	—	—
Annual Growth	0.1%	—	—	—

Revenue History

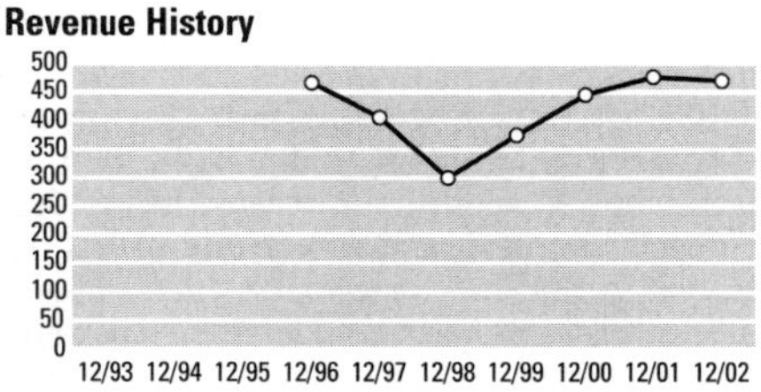

Sammons Enterprises, Inc.

Sammons Enterprises summons its revenues from several sources. The diversified holding company's interests include insurance (Midland National Life Insurance and North American Company for Life and Health Insurance) and water bottling (Mountain Valley Spring). Sammons Enterprises also owns The Grove Park Inn Resort in Asheville, North Carolina. The company has sold industrial equipment distribution unit Briggs-Weaver in order to focus on its core niche businesses. The late Charles Sammons, an orphan who became a billionaire philanthropist, founded the company in 1962. His estate still owns the company, and his widow, Elaine Sammons, serves as chairman.

EXECUTIVES

Chairman: Elaine Sammons
President and CEO: Robert W. Korba
SVP Finance and Treasurer: Joseph A. Ethridge
SVP, Secretary, and General Counsel: John Washburn
VP Organization Development: Bob Kendall
VP Real Estate: Bill Daves
Controller: Laura Gullo
Director, Benefit Plans: Carol Cochran

LOCATIONS

HQ: 5949 Sherry Ln., Ste. 1900, Dallas, TX 75225
Phone: 214-210-5000 **Fax:** 214-210-5099
Web: www.sammonsenterprises.com

Sammons Enterprises has operations all across the US.

COMPETITORS

CIGNA
MetLife
Nestlé
New York Life
Principal Financial
Prudential
Suntory
Vermont Pure

HISTORICAL FINANCIALS

Company Type: Private

Income Statement FYE: December 31

	REVENUE ($ mil.)	NET INCOME ($ mil.)	NET PROFIT MARGIN	EMPLOYEES
12/02	1,950	—	—	3,200
12/01	1,510	—	—	3,000
12/00	1,934	—	—	3,000
12/99	2,000	—	—	2,300
12/98	1,725	—	—	3,250
12/97	1,580	—	—	2,300
12/96	1,600	—	—	2,300
12/95	1,300	—	—	3,300
12/94	1,300	—	—	1,640
12/93	1,308	—	—	4,000
Annual Growth	4.5%	—	—	(2.4%)

Revenue History

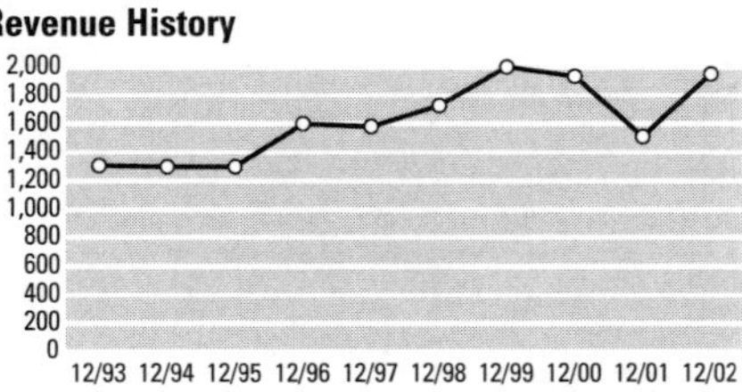

SARCOM, Inc.

Despite the military-sounding name, SARCOM isn't a military contractor. The company sells, installs, and maintains computers for large corporations. SARCOM, which has branches in a dozen states mostly located across mid-America, offers asset management, product procurement, consulting, integration, and help desk support, among its services. The company has a corporate training unit called The Abreon Group (formerly SARCOM Enterprise Education). SARCOM works with such vendors as Computer Associates, McAfee, Palm, and Sony. The company was founded in 1983.

SARCOM is short for Sara and Randy's computers. The company was funded as a computer store by its namesake and former CEO Randy Wilcox, who incorporated his wife's name in the company moniker. SARCOM changed CEOs in 2002, bringing in former WorldCom exec Jeff Sturgeon. The company also completed a $102 million debt-for-equity swap in 2002, led by BNP Paribas and company shareholders.

EXECUTIVES

Chairman, SARCOM Holdings: Chuck Sweet
Chairman: Randy Wilcox
CEO: Jeff Sturgeon
SVP, Services: John Strauss
VP, Finance and Secretary: Kevin Iler
VP, Operations: Elli Workum
VP, Sales: Joe Chick
Director, Information Services: Dan Schneider
Human Resources: Stephanie Murray

LOCATIONS

HQ: 8337 Green Meadows Dr. North,
Lewis Center, OH 43035
Phone: 614-854-1300 **Fax:** 614-854-1555
Web: www.sarcom.com

SARCOM has offices in California, Florida, Idaho, Indiana, Kentucky, Maryland, Michigan, Ohio, Oregon, Pennsylvania, Tennessee, and Texas.

PRODUCTS/OPERATIONS

Services

Asset management
Consulting
Electronic commerce purchasing (SARCOMDirect)
Handheld device support
Help desk support
Installation
Integration
Maintenance
Product procurement and planning
Software licensing
Technology selection

COMPETITORS

Accenture
AlphaNet Solutions
Avnet
Comark
CompuCom
EDS
En Pointe
Hartford Computer
Ingram Micro
Manchester Technologies
Merisel
Micro Warehouse
Pacific Magtron
PC Warehouse
Pomeroy IT
Softmart

HISTORICAL FINANCIALS

Company Type: Private

Income Statement FYE: December 31

	REVENUE ($ mil.)	NET INCOME ($ mil.)	NET PROFIT MARGIN	EMPLOYEES
12/02	447	—	—	1,500
12/01	485	—	—	1,600
12/00	700	—	—	1,700
12/99	700	—	—	2,300
12/98	688	—	—	2,300
12/97	400	—	—	1,400
12/96	230	—	—	800
12/95	200	—	—	710
12/94	100	—	—	550
Annual Growth	20.6%	—	—	13.4%

Revenue History

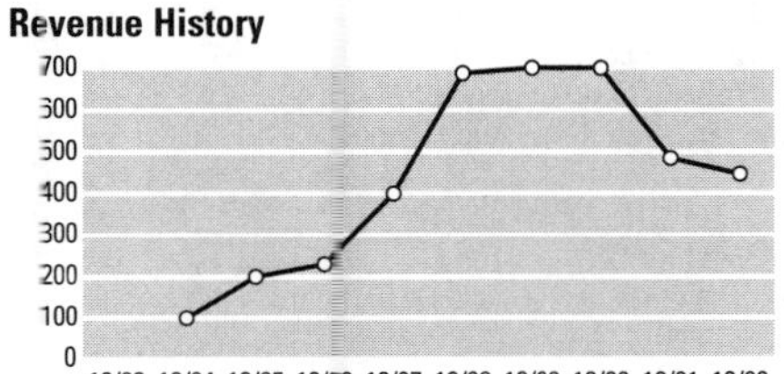

Sargento Foods

Sargento Foods doesn't milk the cows or stir the curds, but it does shred, package, and market mozzarella, cheddar, and other cheeses made to its own specifications and those of retail customers. By turning cheese into value-added products such as recipe-ready shredded cheese blends and sliced cheeses for sandwiches, Sargento has been successful in the shadow of cheese giant Kraft Foods. Its food service product line includes appetizers, cheese ingredients, and sauces. It also sells high-end specialty cheeses via catalog and the Internet. Historically innovative (it was the first to package shredded cheese), Sargento was founded in 1953 and is owned and operated by the Gentine family.

EXECUTIVES

Chairman and CEO: Louis P. Gentine
SVP Finance: George Hoff
EVP: Mark Rhyan
Executive Director of Human Resources: Karri Neils
President, Consumer Products Division:
Robert Clouston
President, Food Ingredients Division:
Michael (Mike) Gordy
President, Food Service Division:
Lawrence J. (Larry) Gentine
VP, Food Service Sales & Marketing: Sam Colson
VP, Corporate & Marketing Communications:
Barbara Gannon

LOCATIONS

HQ: Sargento Foods, Inc.
1 Persnickety Place, Plymouth, WI 53073
Phone: 920-893-8484 **Fax:** 920-893-8399
Web: www.sargentocheese.com

Sargento Foods has four facilities in Wisconsin.

COMPETITORS

ConAgra
Kraft Foods
Land O'Lakes
Lucille Farms
Marathon Cheese
Saputo
Schreiber Foods

HISTORICAL FINANCIALS

Company Type: Private

Income Statement FYE: Saturday nearest June 30

	REVENUE ($ mil.)	NET INCOME ($ mil.)	NET PROFIT MARGIN	EMPLOYEES
6/03	534	—	—	1,300
6/02	550	—	—	1,300
6/01	484	—	—	1,100
6/00	400	—	—	1,000
6/99	335	—	—	1,000
6/98	330	—	—	1,000
Annual Growth	10.1%	—	—	5.4%

Revenue History

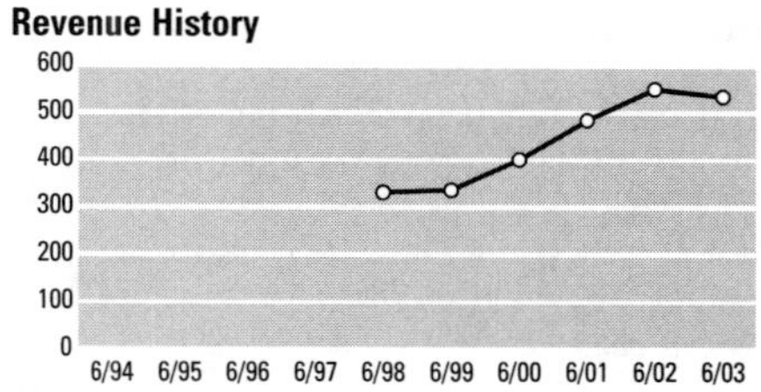

SAS Institute

Don't talk back to this company about business intelligence. SAS (pronounced "sass"), the world's largest privately held software company, leads the market in data warehousing and data mining software used to gather, manage, and analyze enormous amounts of corporate information. Clients such as Maytag, Air France, and the US Department of Defense use its software to find patterns in customer data, manage resources, and target new business. Founded in 1976, SAS also offers industry-specific integrated software and support packages. Chairman, president, and CEO James Goodnight owns about two-thirds of the company; co-founder and EVP John Sall owns the remainder.

The company continues to grow both its revenue (the company has reported some 26 consecutive years of increased sales numbers) and its product offerings. SAS introduced a variety of financial management software packages reflecting the trend, and need, for companies to maintain accurate financial records. The acquisition of ABC Technologies and event-triggering and behavioral tracking technology from Verbind, as well as the formation of the SAS Performance Management Division in 2002 support the company's goal to lead the growth of the performance management market. SAS is also looking to marketing analysis software for future growth. The company created its Marketing & Customer Analytics business unit to develop marketing-analysis software, in addition to its existing SAS Marketing Automation program. Along with its new products, SAS continues to expand its existing business intelligence offerings.

Known for its tight-knit community, SAS offers its employees perks including two on-site child-care centers, atrium-like cafeterias, a gym, a swimming pool, walking trails, a health care center, and free M&Ms in every break room.

EXECUTIVES

Chairman, President, and CEO:
James H. (Jim) Goodnight
EVP and Chief Administrative Officer:
W. Greyson Quarles Jr.
EVP: John Sall
SVP and CTO: Keith V. Collins
SVP and Chief Marketing Officer: Jim Davis
VP, General Counsel, and Secretary: John Boswell
VP, Financial Services Practice: Mark Moorman
President, SAS Canada: Carl Farrell
President, SAS International: Art Cooke

LOCATIONS

HQ: SAS Institute, Inc.
100 SAS Campus Dr., Cary, NC 27513
Phone: 919-677-8000 **Fax:** 919-677-4444
Web: www.sas.com

SAS Institute has nearly 140 offices worldwide and customers in approximately 120 countries.

2002 Customers

	% of total
Business	71
Education	18
Government	11
Total	**100**

PRODUCTS/OPERATIONS

Selected Software

Customer relationship management
Data analysis
Data mining
Data warehousing
E-commerce
Enterprise performance management
Experimental design
Financial management
Human resources management
Information technology systems management
Patent discovery and analysis
Portfolio analysis
Project planning and management
Risk management
Statistical analysis
Supply chain analysis
Web traffic analysis

COMPETITORS

Accrue Software
Ascential Software
Brio Software
Business Objects
Cognos
Computer Associates
Crystal Decisions
E.piphany
Hummingbird
Hyperion
Information Builders
Insightful
IBM
Microsoft
MicroStrategy
Oracle
SPSS
Sybase
Teradata

HISTORICAL FINANCIALS

Company Type: Private

Income Statement FYE: December 31

	REVENUE ($ mil.)	NET INCOME ($ mil.)	NET PROFIT MARGIN	EMPLOYEES
12/02	1,180	—	—	9,023
12/01	1,130	—	—	8,636
12/00	1,120	—	—	8,500
12/99	1,020	—	—	6,400
12/98	871	—	—	5,400
12/97	750	—	—	5,108
12/96	653	—	—	4,500
12/95	562	—	—	4,138
12/94	482	—	—	3,260
12/93	420	—	—	2,897
Annual Growth	12.2%	—	—	13.5%

Revenue History

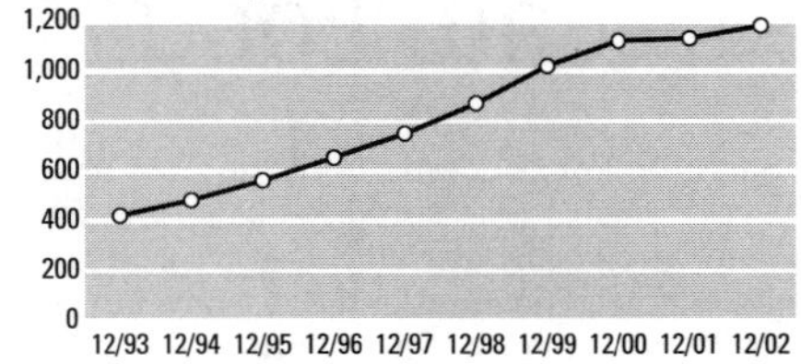

Sauder Woodworking

Sauder Woodworking takes the fear out of furniture and makes furniture for the God-fearing. The firm is the #1 US maker of ready-to-assemble (RTA) furniture (ahead of Bush Industries and O'Sullivan Industries) and, through Sauder Manufacturing, is also a top maker of church furniture and institutional seating. RTA products include computer workstations, desks, entertainment centers, and wardrobes. Subsidiary Archbold Container makes corrugated packaging and displays. Sauder's products are sold through retailers in more than 70 countries. In 2001 Sauder acquired Progressive Furniture, which makes fully assembled furniture. The company was founded in 1934 by Erie Sauder and is still family owned and operated.

EXECUTIVES

Chairman: Maynard Sauder
President and CEO: Kevin Sauder
EVP, Finance and CFO: Arnold Moshier
EVP, Marketing and Sales: John Yoder
EVP, Operations: Garrett Tinsman
VP, Administration: Elvin O. (Ed) Yoder
VP, Human Resources: Steve Webster
VP, Merchandising: Susan Dountas
VP, Sales: Brent Gingerich

LOCATIONS

HQ: Sauder Woodworking Co.
502 Middle St., Archbold, OH 43502
Phone: 419-446-2711 **Fax:** 419-446-3692
Web: www.sauder.com

PRODUCTS/OPERATIONS

Selected Products

Bedroom furniture
Entertainment furniture
Kitchen/utility furniture
Office/computer furniture
Shelving/storage

COMPETITORS

Bassett Furniture
Bush Industries
Chromcraft Revington
DMI Furniture
Dorel Industries
Furniture Brands International
Haworth
Herman Miller
HON INDUSTRIES
IKEA
Jami
O'Sullivan Industries
Stanley Furniture
Steelcase

HISTORICAL FINANCIALS

Company Type: Private

Income Statement FYE: December 31

	REVENUE ($ mil.)	NET INCOME ($ mil.)	NET PROFIT MARGIN	EMPLOYEES
12/02	700	—	—	3,500
12/01	700	—	—	3,500
12/00	700	—	—	3,950
12/99	565	—	—	3,900
12/98	545	—	—	3,200
12/97	500	—	—	3,300
12/96	500	—	—	3,200
12/95	467	—	—	3,200
12/94	445	—	—	3,200
Annual Growth	5.8%	—	—	1.1%

Revenue History

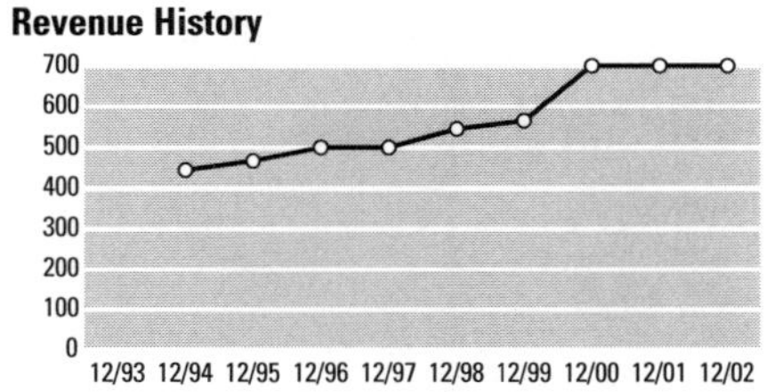

Save Mart Supermarkets

Save Mart Supermarkets is one of the big wheels in the California grocery business. A sponsor of the NASCAR Dodge/Save Mart 350, the company has about 100 grocery stores in Northern and Central California. Its supermarkets and warehouse stores operate under the S-Mart, Save Mart Foods, and Food Maxx banners. The chain has been trying out different formats, including an upscale prototype with its own coffeehouse and expanded offerings of ethnic and organic foods and its popular private-label salad mix line, Fresh Favorites. Save Mart also owns distributor SMART Refrigerated Transport. CEO Robert Piccinini owns most of Save Mart, which was founded in 1952 by his father, Mike Piccinini, and uncle, Nick Tocco.

EXECUTIVES

Chairman and CEO: Robert M. (Bob) Piccinini, age 61
President and COO: Bob Spengler
VP, CFO and CIO: Ron Riesenbeck
VP, Human Resources and Law: Mike Silveira
VP, Real Estate: Jim Watt
VP, Operations: Art Patch
Controller: Steve Ackerman
Director, Marketing: Sally Sanborn

LOCATIONS

HQ: 1800 Standiford Ave., Modesto, CA 95350
Phone: 209-577-1600 **Fax:** 209-577-3857

PRODUCTS/OPERATIONS

2002 Stores

	No.
Conventional supermarkets	20
Superstores	62
Warehouse stores	14
Total	**96**

COMPETITORS

Albertson's
Costco Wholesale
Kroger
Longs Drug
Raley's
Ralphs
Rite Aid
Safeway
Smart & Final
Trader Joe's Co
Vons
Wal-Mart

HISTORICAL FINANCIALS

Company Type: Private

Income Statement FYE: March 31

	REVENUE ($ mil.)	NET INCOME ($ mil.)	NET PROFIT MARGIN	EMPLOYEES
3/02	1,600	—	—	7,300
3/01	1,524	—	—	7,200
3/00	1,468	—	—	7,000
3/99	1,452	—	—	7,200
3/98	1,300	—	—	7,003
3/97	1,200	—	—	6,400
3/96	1,135	—	—	5,864
3/95	1,130	—	—	6,062
3/94	1,130	—	—	6,265
3/93	1,100	—	—	7,000
Annual Growth	4.3%	—	—	0.5%

Revenue History

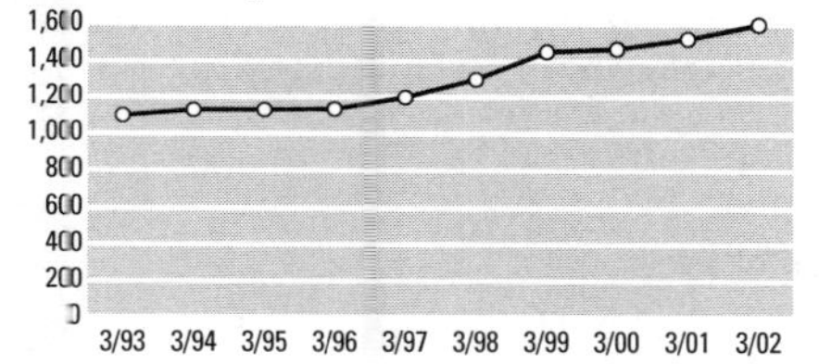

S.C. Johnson & Son, Inc.

S.C. Johnson & Son helped consumers move from the flyswatter to the spray can. The company is one of the world's largest makers of consumer chemical products. These include Drano-brand drain cleaner, Glade air freshener, Johnson floor wax, OFF! insect repellent, Pledge furniture polish, Raid insecticide, Shout stain remover, Windex window cleaner, and Ziploc plastic bags. The founder's great-grandson and one of the richest men in the US, chairman emeritus Samuel Johnson, and his immediate family own about 60% of S.C. Johnson; descendants of the founder's daughter own about 40%.

Many of S.C. Johnson's products have been and remain top sellers in their market categories. The company has operations in nearly 70 countries and its products are available in more than 100.

In 2003, *Working Mother* magazine recognized S.C. Johnson as one of the 100 best companies for working mothers.

The company's commercial products division (Johnson Wax Professional and Johnson Polymer) has been spun off as a private company owned by the Johnson family. The company has also sold most of its personal care line.

HISTORY

Samuel C. Johnson, a carpenter whose customers were as interested in his floor wax as in his parquet floors, founded S.C. Johnson in Racine, Wisconsin, in 1886. Forsaking carpentry, Johnson began to manufacture floor care products. The company, named S.C. Johnson & Son in 1906, began establishing subsidiaries worldwide in 1914. By the time Johnson's son and successor, Herbert Johnson, died in 1928, annual sales were $5 million. Herbert Jr. and his sister, Henrietta Lewis, received 60% and 40% of the firm, respectively. The original section of S.C. Johnson's headquarters, designed by Frank Lloyd Wright and called "the greatest piece of 20th-century architecture" in the US, was finished in 1939.

In 1954, with $45 million in annual sales, Herbert Jr.'s son Samuel Curtis Johnson joined the company as new products director. Two years later it introduced Raid, the first water-based insecticide, and soon thereafter, OFF! insect repellent. Each became a market leader. The company unsuccessfully attempted to diversify into paint, chemicals, and lawn care during the 1950s and 1960s. The home care products segment prospered, however, with the introduction of Pledge aerosol furniture polish and Glade aerosol air freshener.

After Herbert Jr. suffered a stroke in 1965, Samuel became president. In 1975 the firm banned the use of the chlorofluorocarbons (CFCs) in its products, three years before the US government banned CFCs. Samuel started a recreational products division that was bought by the Johnson family in 1986. That company went public in 1987 as Johnson Worldwide Associates, with the family retaining control.

The company launched Edge shaving gel and Agree hair products in the 1970s but had few products as successful in the 1980s. It moved into real estate with Johnson Wax Development (JWD) in the 1970s, but sold JWD's assets in the late 1980s.

S. Curtis Johnson, Samuel's son, joined the company in 1983. In 1986 S.C. Johnson bought Bugs Burger Bug Killers, moving into commercial pest control; in 1990 it entered into an agreement with Mycogen to develop biological pesticides for household use.

In 1993 it bought Drackett, bringing Drano and Windex to its product roster along with increased competition from heavyweights such as Procter & Gamble and Clorox. That year S.C. Johnson sold the Agree and Halsa lines to DEP. In 1996 it launched a line of water-soluble pouches for cleaning products that allow work to be done without touching hazardous chemicals. President William Perez became CEO the next year.

S.C. Johnson bought Dow Chemical's DowBrands unit, maker of bathroom cleaner (Dow), plastic bags (Ziploc), and plastic wrap (Saran Wrap), for $1.2 billion in 1998. It then sold off other Dow brands (cleaners Spray 'N Wash, Glass Plus, Yes, and Vivid) to the UK's Reckitt & Colman to settle antitrust issues.

A year later S.C. Johnson sold its skin care line, including Aveeno, to health care products maker Johnson & Johnson, and spun off its commercial products unit as a private firm owned by the Johnson family. Boosting its home cleaning line, in 1999 it introduced two new products: AllerCare (for dust mite control) and Pledge Grab-It (electrostatically charged cleaning sheets).

In 2000 S.C. Johnson pulled its AllerCare carpet powder and allergen spray from store shelves after some consumers had negative reactions to the fragrance additive in the products. That year H. Fisk Johnson succeeded his father (who became chairman emeritus) as chairman.

In 2001 the company was fined $950,000 for selling banned Raid Max Roach Bait traps in New York after agreeing to pull them from store shelves. Also that year S.C. Johnson's Japanese subsidiary agreed to buy that country's leading drain cleaner brand, Pipe Unish, from Unicharm. In October 2002 the company acquired the household insecticides unit of German drug giant Bayer AG for $734 million.

EXECUTIVES

Chairman Emeritus: Samuel C. Johnson, age 75
Chairman: H. Fisk Johnson, age 44
President, CEO, and Director: William D. (Bill) Perez, age 55
President, North America: David L. May
President, Europe, Africa, and Near East: Steven P. Stanbrook, age 45
EVP, Americas: Pedro Cieza
SVP, General Counsel and Secretary: David Hecker
SVP, Worldwide Corporate Affairs: Jane M. Hutterly
SVP, Worldwide Human Resources: Gayle P. Kosterman
SVP, Worldwide Manufacturing and Procurement: Nico J. Meiland
SVP, Worldwide Research, Development & Engineering: Darcy D. Massey
SVP and CFO: W. Lee McCollum, age 53
VP, Air Care Business and Canadian Operations: Gregory J. Barron
VP, Corporate Tax Counsel: Robert S. Randleman
VP, Enterprise Resource Planning: David C. Henry
VP, Finance – North America: Mark H. Eckhardt
VP, Finance and Information Systems – EurAFNE: Francis Foin
VP, Home Cleaning Business: John Rote
VP, Human Resources, Asia/Pacific: Wesley A. Coleman, age 53
VP, Insect Control and Shave Business: William C. Thompson
VP, Marketing Services – Worldwide: Ralph D. Perry
VP, North American Sales: Darwin Lewis
VP, Research, Development and Engineering – Global Air Care: Richard S. Hutchings
VP and Area Director – Asia: Frank F. Guerra
VP, Human Resources Asia/Pacific: Jeffrey M. Waller
VP and CIO: Daniel E. Horton
VP and Corporate Treasurer: William H. Van Lopik
VP and Group Managing Director – Europe: Filippo Meroni

LOCATIONS

HQ: 1525 Howe St., Racine, WI 53403
Phone: 262-260-2000 **Fax:** 262-260-6004
Web: www.scjohnson.com

S.C. Johnson & Son has operations in nearly 70 countries worldwide.

PRODUCTS/OPERATIONS

Selected Products and Brands

Air Care
Air freshener (Glade, Glade Duet)
Pillow and mattress covers (AllerCare)

Home Cleaning
Bathroom/drain (Drano, Scrubbing Bubbles, Vanish, Dow)
Cleaners (Fantastik, Windex, Windex Multi-Surface Cleaner with Vinegar)
Floor care (Pledge, Pledge Grab-It, Johnson)
Furniture care (Pledge, Pledge Wipes, Pledge Grab-it Dry Dusting Mitts)
Laundry/carpet care (Shout)

Home Storage
Plastic bags (Ziploc)
Plastic wrap (Handi-Wrap, Saran Wrap)

Insect Control
Insecticides (Raid, Raid Max)
Repellents (Deep Woods OFF!, OFF!, OFF! Mosquito Lamp, OFF! Skintastic)

COMPETITORS

3M
Alticor
Blyth
Church & Dwight
Clorox
Colgate-Palmolive
Dial
DuPont
Gillette
Henkel
IWP International
Procter & Gamble
Reckitt Benckiser
Shaklee
Unilever
United Industries
Yankee Candle

HISTORICAL FINANCIALS

Company Type: Private

Income Statement FYE: Friday nearest June 30

	ESTIMATED REVENUE ($ mil.)	NET INCOME ($ mil.)	NET PROFIT MARGIN	EMPLOYEES
6/02	5,000	—	—	9,500
6/01	4,500	—	—	9,500
6/00	4,200	—	—	9,500
6/99	4,200	—	—	9,500
6/98	5,000	—	—	13,200
6/97	4,300	—	—	12,500
6/96	4,000	—	—	12,100
6/95	4,000	—	—	13,400
6/94	3,800	—	—	13,100
6/93	3,550	—	—	13,100
Annual Growth	3.9%	—	—	(3.5%)

Revenue History

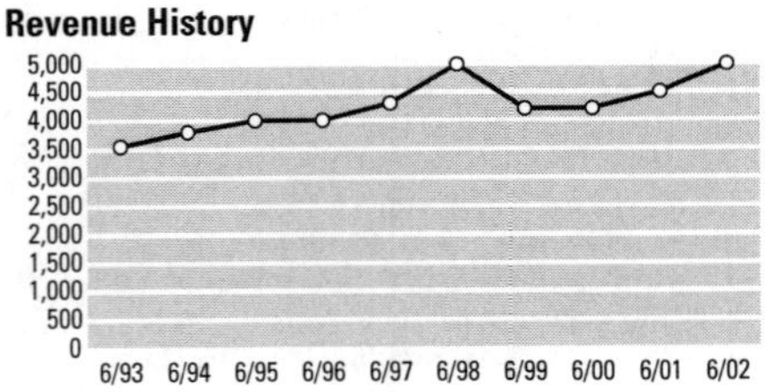

Schenectady International

Schenectady International came to life by bringing good varnishes to life for General Electric. Founded by Howard Wright in 1906, the company was established to develop insulating varnishes for GE's early electrical devices. Today Schenectady International still makes chemical coatings for insulating copper and aluminum magnet wire, as well as friction material resins for use in making brake linings and clutch facings. The company's other products include chemicals used in the production of semiconductors, imaging products, rubber compounds, agrochemicals, dyes, fuel additives, and flavoring agents. Descendants of Wright still own the company.

EXECUTIVES

Chairman and CEO: Wallace A. Graham
President and COO: Robert Carr
SVP, Financial and CFO: John C. Obst
VP, Electrical Coatings Division: Gregg W. Brown
VP, Sales and Marketing, Chemical Division: Charles H. Griswold
Corporate Controller: David M. Bartkoski
Director, Business Planning: Howard Picard
Director, Human Resources: J. Richard Wyles
Manager, Corporate Communications: Kimberly A. Perone
Auditors: KPMG LLP

LOCATIONS

HQ: Schenectady International, Inc.
2750 Balltown Rd., Schenectady, NY 12304
Phone: 518-347-4200 **Fax:** 518-346-3111
Web: www.siigroup.com

Schenectady International has 25 plants in Australia, Brazil, Canada, China, France, Germany, India, Japan, Korea, Mexico, South Africa, Switzerland, the UK, and the US.

PRODUCTS/OPERATIONS

Selected Products
Alkylcresols and xylenols
Antioxidants
Bectron coatings for electronics
Coating and adhesive resins
Di- and tri-alkylphenols
Electronic chemicals
Friction materials
Imaging products
Mono-alkylphenols
Pyridines
Rubber compound resins

COMPETITORS

BASF AG
Clariant International
Dow Chemical
Eastman Resins
DuPont
Ferro
Mitsui Chemicals
PolyOne
Spraylat
Texas Petrochemicals

HISTORICAL FINANCIALS

Company Type: Private

Income Statement FYE: December 31

	ESTIMATED REVENUE ($ mil.)	NET INCOME ($ mil.)	NET PROFIT MARGIN	EMPLOYEES
12/01	600	—	—	2,500
12/00	650	—	—	2,800
Annual Growth	(7.7%)	—	—	(10.7%)

Revenue History

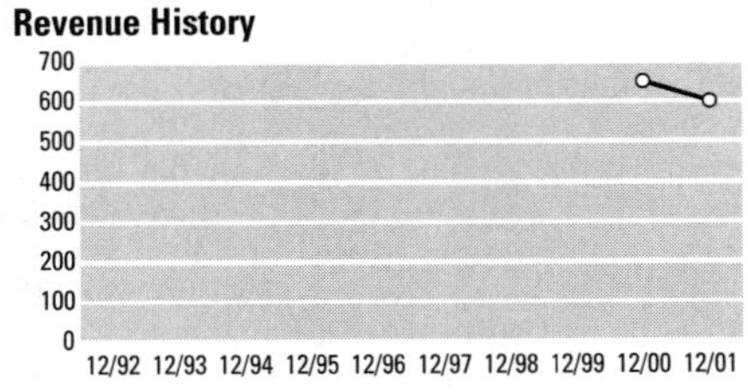

Schneider National, Inc.

If you think that's the Great Pumpkin behind you, look again. With its signature bright-orange fleet of 14,000 trucks and more than 40,000 trailers, Schneider National is one of the top truckload carriers in the US. The company's Schneider National Carriers unit provides truckload service throughout North America, including one-way van, expedited, dedicated, and intermodal offerings, as well as truck brokerage. Schneider Bulk Carriers transports liquid chemicals, and Schneider Specialized Carriers concentrates on the industrial glass industry. The company's Schneider Finance unit sells and leases commercial truck equipment. Schneider Logistics offers supply chain management services.

Not content to rely on its truckload business, Schneider National is expanding its intermodal offerings — freight transportation by a combination of road and rail — through a partnership with Burlington Northern Santa Fe. The company hopes to include other railroads in its intermodal business.

Schneider National is known for being an early adopter of new transportation technology — it was one of the first carriers to link all its trucks by two-way satellite. More recently, the company has invested in an in-cab e-mail system to help drivers stay in touch with their families. Schneider National plans to install global positioning units in its trailers in order to keep closer track of shipments.

Chairman and former CEO Don Schneider, son of the company's founder, is among its shareholders. He doesn't disclose how much of the company he owns.

HISTORY

A. J. "Al" Schneider bought a truck in 1935 with money earned from selling the family car. He drove the truck for three years, got another, and then leased them both to another firm. Becoming general manager of Bins Transfer & Storage in 1938, Schneider bought the company that year and changed the name to Schneider Transport & Storage. In 1944 Schneider stopped storing household goods and continued as an intrastate carrier in Wisconsin through the 1950s, transporting food and household goods. The Interstate Commerce Commission granted its first interstate license to Schneider in 1958.

Al's son Donald joined the company as general manager in 1961, and in 1962 the company dropped "Storage" from its name to become Schneider Transport. The 1960s also saw the first of many acquisitions. Donald became CEO in 1973, overseeing more acquisitions and the creation of Schneider National as a holding company for the organization. Donald also saw to the installation of computerized control systems, the first of many technical innovations Schneider would use in its trucks.

With the Motor Carrier Act's passage in 1980, restrictions eased and interstate shipping opened up. Schneider (and its competitors) saw the sky as the limit and founded Schneider Communications, a long-distance provider, in 1982. Eager to escape the Teamsters' thrall but choosing not to go head-to-head with the powerful union, Schneider formed Schneider National Carriers as a nonunion company out of three 1985 acquisitions, which signed on new recruits, while Schneider Transport remained unionized. Schneider focused on guaranteeing on-time delivery in the deregulated market: In 1988 Schneider became the first trucking company to install a satellite-tracking system in its trucks, setting the industry standard.

Schneider further expanded its services in the 1990s, starting with Schneider Specialized Services for carrying difficult items. It moved into Canada and Mexico in 1991. By 1993 some two-thirds of *FORTUNE* 500 companies used Schneider, and the company formed Schneider Logistics to help companies streamline their shipping operations. It sold Schneider Communications to Frontier Communications in 1995. The company moved into Europe in 1997.

It continued buying other US trucking firms, including Landstar Poole and Builder's Transport (both in 1998), mainly to acquire their drivers for its expanding fleet. In 1999 Schneider acquired the glass-transportation business of A. J. Metler & Rigging.

In 2000 Schneider acquired the freight payment services of Tranzact Systems and further boosted its e-commerce offerings through alliances with ContractorHub.com and Paperloop.com. The company also made plans to spin off Schneider Logistics and sell part of it to the public, but unfavorable market conditions put the IPO on hold. Schneider added expedited services to its portfolio in 2001 to provide time-definite delivery in Canada, Mexico, and the US.

Christopher Lofgren's promotion to president and CEO in 2002 made him the first person outside the founding family to lead Schneider National.

EXECUTIVES

Chairman: Donald J. (Don) Schneider, age 67
President and CEO: Christopher B. (Chris) Lofgren
CFO: Thomas A. (Tom) Gannon
VP Capacity Development and Safety: Don Osterberg
VP Corporate Marketing: Thomas (Tom) Nightingale
VP Human Resources: Tim Fliss
VP Technology Services: Paul Mueller
President, Financial Services: Richard Palmieri
President, Schneider Logistics: Thomas I. (Tom) Escott
President, Transportation Services: Scott Arves
VP and General Manager, Schneider Brokerage: Mark Rourke
VP, Schneider Logistics Payment Services: Philip Morse
VP Sales, Transportation Services: Mark DePrey
Area VP of Sales, Transportation Services: Greg Sanders
Regional VP of Sales: Mark Aurig
Regional VP of Sales: Mark Coleman
Regional VP of Sales: Chris Knauss
CIO: Steve Matheys
VP Sales, Mexico: Will Chang
Product Development Director, Mexico: Rafael Moreno
General Manager, Schneider National Bulk Carriers: Jim Van Hefty
Director, Business Development, Schneider Logistics: Todd Callahan
Director, Business Development, Schneider Logistics: Michael Detampel
Regional Account Manager: Damon Detry, age 34
Regional Account Manager: Efrain Cantu Delgado

LOCATIONS

HQ: 3101 S. Packerland Dr., Green Bay, WI 54306
Phone: 920-592-2000 **Fax:** 920-592-3063
Web: www.schneider.com

Major North American Operating Centers

Akron, Ohio
Charlotte, North Carolina
Chicago
Dallas
Des Moines, Iowa
Detroit
Evergreen, Alabama
Green Bay, Wisconsin
Harrisburg, Pennsylvania
Houston
Indianapolis
Los Angeles
Memphis
St. Louis
Toronto

PRODUCTS/OPERATIONS

Selected Operating Units

Schneider Finance (commercial financing and leasing services)
Schneider Logistics, Inc. (supply chain management services)
Schneider National Bulk Carriers (liquid chemical transport services)
Schneider National Carriers (full-truckload service, including intermodal, brokerage, expedited services, dedicated transport, and one-way van transport)
Schneider Specialized Carriers (open equipment transportation, specializing in industrial glass transport)

COMPETITORS

Burlington Northern Santa Fe
Cannon Express
Celadon
C.H. Robinson Worldwide
CSX
J. B. Hunt
Landstar System
Norfolk Southern
Roadway
Ryder
Swift Transportation
Union Pacific
Werner Enterprises

HISTORICAL FINANCIALS

Company Type: Private

Income Statement FYE: December 31

	REVENUE ($ mil.)	NET INCOME ($ mil.)	NET PROFIT MARGIN	EMPLOYEES
12/02	2,627	—	—	20,756
12/01	2,388	—	—	19,349
12/00	3,089	—	—	18,775
12/99	3,000	—	—	19,000
12/98	2,711	—	—	17,000
12/97	2,510	—	—	16,500
12/96	2,156	—	—	17,550
12/95	1,700	—	—	15,500
12/94	1,325	—	—	15,300
12/93	1,175	—	—	13,950
Annual Growth	9.4%	—	—	4.5%

Revenue History

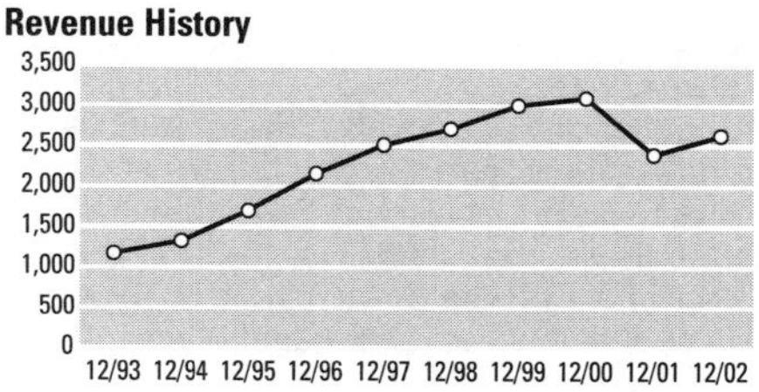

Schnuck Markets, Inc.

If you'll meet me in St. Louis, then chances are there'll be a Schnuck Market in sight. The region's largest food chain, Schnuck Markets operates about 100 stores, mostly in the St. Louis area, but also in other parts of Missouri and in Illinois, Indiana, Mississippi, Tennessee, and Wisconsin. All stores offer a full line of groceries, and most have pharmacies, video rental outlets, in-store banking, and florist shops. Although most stores operate under the Schnuck banner, the company also runs several Logli supermarkets and a Sentry Drug in Illinois. The company acquired 12 Seessel's stores in Memphis from Albertson's in 2002. Founded in 1939, the company is owned by the Schnuck family.

EXECUTIVES

Chairman and CEO: Craig D. Schnuck, age 54
President and COO: Scott C. Schnuck
CFO: Todd R. Schnuck
SVP, Logistics, Manufacturing and Information Technology: Bob Drury
SVP, Marketing and Merchandising: Randy Wedel
SVP, Store Operations: Bill Bredenkoetter
VP, Human Resources: William (Bill) Jones
Secretary and General Counsel: Mary Moorkamp, age 40
Director, Communication: Lori Willis

LOCATIONS

HQ: 11420 Lackland Rd., St. Louis, MO 63146
Phone: 314-994-9900 **Fax:** 314-994-4465
Web: www.schnucks.com

2002 Stores

	No.
Missouri	74
Illinois	21
Tennessee	12
Wisconsin	6
Indiana	4
Total	**117**

COMPETITORS

7-Eleven
AWG
CVS
Dierbergs Markets
Dominick's
Eagle Food
Hy-Vee
Kmart
Kroger
Meijer
SUPERVALU
Walgreen
Wal-Mart

HISTORICAL FINANCIALS

Company Type: Private

Income Statement FYE: October 31

	ESTIMATED REVENUE ($ mil.)	NET INCOME ($ mil.)	NET PROFIT MARGIN	EMPLOYEES
10/02	2,107	—	—	18,000
10/01	2,000	—	—	16,000
10/00	2,100	—	—	17,000
10/99	2,010	—	—	16,000
10/98	1,800	—	—	16,000
10/97	1,800	—	—	16,000
10/96	1,700	—	—	16,000
10/95	1,600	—	—	15,500
10/94	1,200	—	—	12,000
10/93	1,225	—	—	7,958
Annual Growth	6.2%	—	—	9.5%

Revenue History

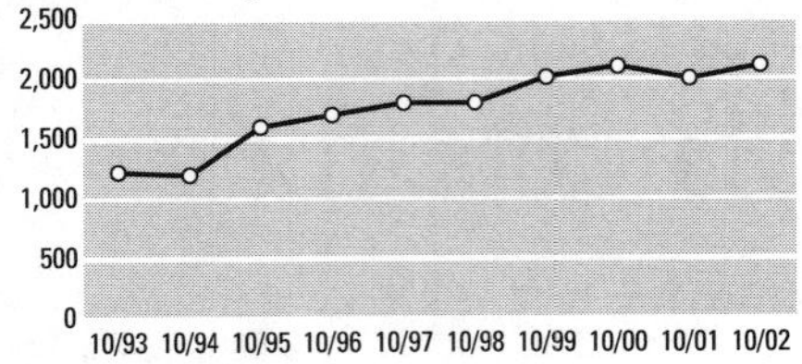

Schreiber Foods

If you order cheese on that burger, you might well get a taste of Schreiber Foods. The cheese processor is a major supplier of the cheese used on hamburgers by US fast-food restaurants. Schreiber primarily produces private-label processed and natural cheese to retailers, food service distributors, and food manufacturers. Its few brands include American Heritage, Cache Valley, Cooper, and Clearfield. Subsidiary Green Bay Machinery makes cheese-slicing and -wrapping equipment. The company sold off its frozen food plant, and has bought up smaller cheese operations to expand it geographic reach. Founded in 1945, Schreiber opted in 1999 to transfer its ownership into an employee stock ownership plan.

EXECUTIVES

Chairman: Jack Meng
President and CEO: Larry P. Ferguson
CFO: Brian Liddy
SVP, Human Resources: Jeff Ottum
SVP, Information Services: Frederick Parker
VP, Industrial & Regulatory Affairs: Deborah Van Dyk
President, Raskas Foods: Heschel Raskas

LOCATIONS

HQ: Schreiber Foods, Inc.
425 Pine St., Green Bay, WI 54301
Phone: 920-437-7601 **Fax:** 920-437-1617
Web: www.sficorp.com

Schreiber Foods has production facilities in Arizona, Georgia, Missouri, Pennsylvania, Texas, Utah, and Wisconsin, as well as in Germany, Brazil, and Mexico. It sells cheese in more than 45 countries.

PRODUCTS/OPERATIONS

Brands

American Heritage
Cache Valley
Clearfield
Cooper
Raskas
Schreiber

COMPETITORS

AMPI
Bongrain
Dairy Farmers of America
Foremost Farms
Fromageries Bel
Great Lakes Cheese
Kraft Foods
Land O'Lakes
Leprino Foods
Lucille Farms
Saputo
Sargento
WestFarm Foods

HISTORICAL FINANCIALS

Company Type: Private

Income Statement FYE: September 30

	ESTIMATED REVENUE ($ mil.)	NET INCOME ($ mil.)	NET PROFIT MARGIN	EMPLOYEES
9/02	1,450	—	—	4,400
9/01	1,350	—	—	3,100
9/00	1,300	—	—	3,000
9/99	1,160	—	—	2,600
9/98	1,100	—	—	2,600
9/97	1,400	—	—	2,600
9/96	1,375	—	—	2,300
9/95	1,320	—	—	2,400
9/94	1,300	—	—	2,400
9/93	1,250	—	—	2,800
Annual Growth	1.7%	—	—	5.2%

Revenue History

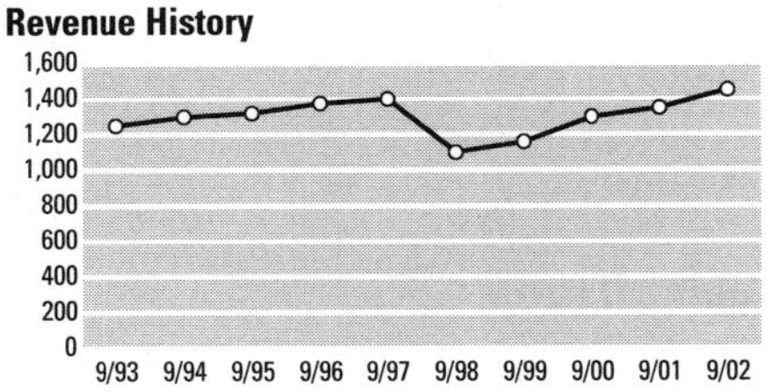

The Schwan Food Company

Frozen pizza is the flashy part of The Schwan Food Company (formerly Schwan's Sales Enterprises). With pizza brands such as Tony's, Red Baron, and Freschetta, the company is the #2 frozen-pizza maker in the US, behind Kraft Foods. Schwan is also a top supplier to the institutional frozen-pizza market and has operations in Europe. But pizza isn't the only slice in the company's revenue — its core business is a fleet of home-delivery trucks. Schwan delivers casseroles, ice cream, and frozen foods to homes in the continental US. The family of late founder Marvin Schwan owns the company.

With its unintentionally retro-hip freezer delivery trucks, The Schwan Food Company is definitely cool. The company maintains a home-delivery system that brings more than 300 frozen food products directly to customers in 48 mainland states. Orders can include bagels or pancakes, and Schwan's ice cream has a devoted following.

The company's frozen pizza has almost 30% of the US market share (Kraft has almost 40%). Schwan's pizza is aboard Air Force One. In addition to its US pizza market, Schwan sells Freschetta and Chicago Town pizzas in Western Europe and supplies schools and other institutional cafeterias with frozen pizza and sandwiches. Another Schwan unit produces food manufacturing equipment and systems to convert vehicles to using liquid propane.

In conjunction with its Red Baron pizza brand, Schwan owns and operates the #1 civilian airshow act in the world, featuring the Red Baron Stearman Squadron, a formation aerobatics team that performs using vintage Stearman bi-planes.

The Schwan family is notoriously secretive (Marvin Schwan himself gave no interviews after 1982).

HISTORY

Paul Schwan bought out his partner in their dairy in 1948 and began manufacturing ice cream using his own recipes. His son, Marvin Schwan, made deliveries for the dairy for a few years. After attending a two-year college, Marvin came back in 1950 to work at the dairy full-time. Two years later he began using his delivery experience to take advantage of the increase in homes with freezers. He bought an old truck for $100 and began a rural route selling ice cream to farmers. He quickly developed a loyal customer base and expanded to two routes the following year.

In the 1960s the company diversified with two acquisitions: a prepared sandwich company and a condensed fruit juice company. A new holding company, Schwan's Sales Enterprises, was established in 1964. Schwan's began delivering pizza the next year. Paul died in 1969.

Deciding that frozen pizza was not a fad, Marvin bought Kansas-based Tony's Pizza in 1970 and quickly rose to the top of the new industry. In the late 1970s Schwan's entered the commercial leasing business, and it later added more leasing companies under the Lyon Financial Services umbrella (sold 2000).

The company entered the institutional-pizza market in the mid-1980s and bought out competitors Sabatasso Foods and Better Baked Pizza. Schools liked Schwan's use of their government surplus cheese to make pizzas, which the company then sold to the schools at a discount.

In 1992 the company bought two Minnesota-based food companies: Panzerotti, a stuffed pastry business, and Monthly Market, a specialty retailer that sells groceries to fund-raising groups. It also began selling its pizzas in the UK. The next year Schwan's bought Chicago Brothers Frozen Pizza, a San Diego-based company specializing in deep-dish pizza.

Marvin died of a heart attack in 1993 at age 64, with his worth estimated at more than $1 billion. The previous year he had willed two-thirds of the company's stock to a charitable Lutheran trust, which was to be bought out by Schwan's after his death. In 1994 his brother, Alfred, and Marvin's friend Lawrence Burgdorf made arrangements to have the company repurchase the foundation's shares for a total of $1.8 billion. But Marvin's four children filed a lawsuit in 1995 against their uncle and Burgdorf over the action. They claimed the men did not have the financial health of the company at heart and were divided in their loyalty. The children, on the other hand, were called money-hungry and callous to their father's last wishes. (The case was settled in 1997, but no information was released.)

In 1994 more than 200,000 people in 28 states contracted salmonella food poisoning after eating *E. coli*-tainted Schwan's ice cream. The company's insurance company eventually paid out nearly $1 million to about 6,000 affected customers in exchange for their signing releases promising they would not sue Schwan's.

Lenny Pippin became the company's fourth CEO in 1999, replacing Alfred, who stayed on as chairman. Schwan's exited the Canadian market at the end of 1999 due to perennial losses. In 2000 Schwan's introduced irradiated frozen ground-beef patties, struck an agreement with another company to electronically pasteurize some of its products, and sold the assets and trademarks of its Chicago Brothers food operations.

In mid-2001 Schwan's expanded its offerings by acquiring frozen-dessert maker Edwards Fine Foods from private equity firm Ripplewood Holdings. In early 2002 the company sold off its Orion Food Systems fast-food subsidiary to Kohlberg Investors. That year Schwan joined the food industry trend toward handheld convenience foods by introducing a microwaveable, single-serve pizza slice designed to be eaten on the go.

The company began a reorganization of its business units and changed its name from Schwan's Sales Enterprises to The Schwan Food Company in early 2003.

In April 2003 Schwan acquired the frozen-dessert business of Mrs. Smith's Bakeries from Flowers Foods for $240 million in cash. Flowers retained the frozen bread and roll dough segment of Mrs. Smith. The pies, cakes, cobblers, and pie crusts fits in well with Schwan's other products.

EXECUTIVES

Chairman: Alfred Schwan
President and CEO: M. Lenny Pippin
EVP, Finance and CFO: Tracy Burr
EVP and Chief Marketing Officer: Michael Ziebell
EVP, Technology: Doug Olsem
SVP and General Manager, Food Service: Greg Flack
VP, Administration and General Counsel: Dave Paskach
VP, Human Resources: Sue Beary
VP, Public Relations: Howard Miller
VP and CFO of Operations: Harry Leonardi
President, Schwan's University: Arnie Strebe
President and COO, Food Service: Larry A. Oberkfell, age 48
President and COO, Global Consumer Brands: John Beadle
Director, Corporate Communications: John Nabholz
Director, Customer Marketing Consumer Brands, North America: Mark Rehborg
Director, Internet and Advanced Technology Marketing: Glenn Bader
Director, Marketing Consumer Brands North America: Darci Eckermann
Director, Retail Marketing Edward's Baking: Connie Day
Brand Manager, Freschetta: Tom Bierbaum
Brand Manager, Tony's: Laura Daley
Associate Brand Manager, Red Baron Pizza: Amy Ruegg
Senior Technologist, Product Development: David Rettey

LOCATIONS

HQ: 115 W. College Dr., Marshall, MN 56258
Phone: 507-532-3274 **Fax:** 507-537-8226
Web: www.schwans.com

The Schwan Food Company has manufacturing facilities in the US and in Europe; its products are sold in the 48 contiguous states and Western Europe.

PRODUCTS/OPERATIONS

Selected Consumer Brands

Chicago Town (frozen pizza, UK)
Edward's Fine Foods (desserts)
Freschetta
Larry's (frozen potato side dishes)
Pagoda Café (frozen Oriental foods)
Red Baron
Tony's

COMPETITORS

Aurora Foods
Ben & Jerry's
Blue Bell
Celentano Brothers
Colorado Prime
ConAgra
Domino's
Dreyer's
Kraft Foods
Kraft Foods North America
Little Caesar's
Luigino's
Nation Pizza Products
Nestlé
Omaha Steaks
Papa John's
SYSCO
YUM!

HISTORICAL FINANCIALS

Company Type: Private

Income Statement FYE: December 31

	ESTIMATED REVENUE ($ mil.)	NET INCOME ($ mil.)	NET PROFIT MARGIN	EMPLOYEES
12/02	3,500	—	—	24,000
12/01	3,000	—	—	22,000
12/00	3,100	—	—	6,000
12/99	3,350	—	—	6,000
12/98	2,875	—	—	6,000
12/97	2,900	—	—	6,000
12/96	2,500	—	—	6,000
12/95	2,350	—	—	6,000
12/94	2,200	—	—	6,000
12/93	2,100	—	—	6,000
Annual Growth	5.8%	—	—	16.7%

Revenue History

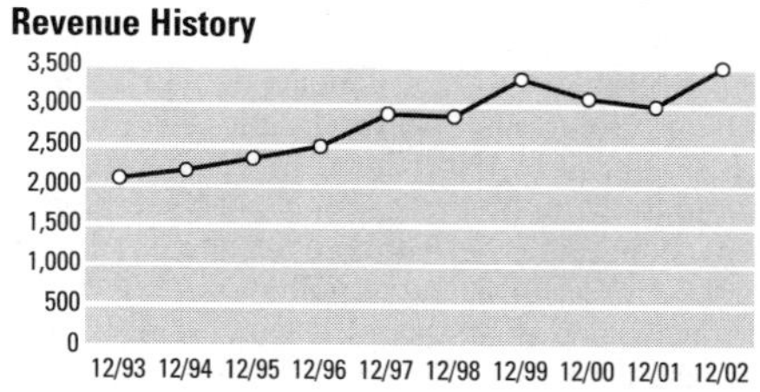

Schwarz Paper Co.

Schwarz is always up for a promotion. Founded in 1907, the printing, packaging, paper, and distribution company makes a wide array of products, including bags, boxes, and other packaging materials used by retailers (such as The Gap and McDonald's) for promotional purposes. The commercial packaging group provides inventory management and distribution of corrugated packaging, tapes, strapping, tubes, cushioning, and cleaning supplies. The printing division prints tray liners and placemats, for example, for customers including restaurants and airlines. Chairman and CEO Andrew McKenna owns the company.

EXECUTIVES

Chairman and CEO: Andrew J. McKenna Sr., age 73
President and COO: Andrew J. (Andy) McKenna Jr., age 46
CFO: Warren Kelleher
VP, Human Resources: Susan H. Bondy
Technology: Thomas J. Lammers
Treasurer: Susan L. Donatello
Operations: Keith R. Hutchison
Sales Manager: Courtney D. Wright

LOCATIONS

HQ: 8338 Austin Ave., Morton Grove, IL 60053
Phone: 847-966-2550 **Fax:** 847-966-1271
Web: www.schwarz.com

Schwarz's operations include facilities throughout the US and in the UK.

PRODUCTS/OPERATIONS

Selected Operations

Commercial Packaging Group (sourcing, inventory management, and distribution of packaging products)
Printing Division (printer and converter of specialty tray liners, placemats, and specialty bags)
Retail Services (packaging materials and supplies for retail chains)

COMPETITORS

Badger Paper Mills
Boise Cascade
Chesapeake Corporation
Field Container
Inland Paperboard
Insignia Systems
MOD-PAC
Rock-Tenn
Shorewood Packaging
Simon Worldwide
Smurfit-Stone Container
Stora Enso North America

HISTORICAL FINANCIALS

Company Type: Private

Income Statement FYE: September 30

	REVENUE ($ mil.)	NET INCOME ($ mil.)	NET PROFIT MARGIN	EMPLOYEES
9/02	450	—	—	350
9/01	454	—	—	850
9/00	435	—	—	820
9/99	363	—	—	765
9/98	322	—	—	715
9/97	302	—	—	650
9/96	271	—	—	610
9/95	240	—	—	565
9/94	209	—	—	520
9/93	176	—	—	—
Annual Growth	11.0%	—	—	(4.8%)

Revenue History

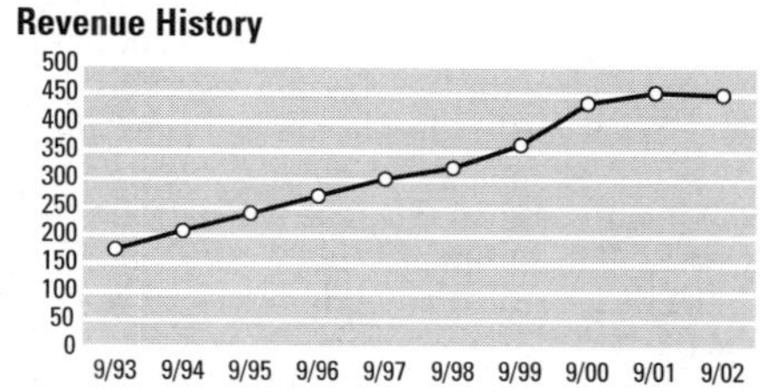

Science Applications International

It definitely pays to have a rich Big Brother, or an Uncle Sam with deep pockets. Science Applications International Corporation (SAIC) is a leading provider of systems integration, engineering, and R&D services to the US government, which accounted for more than 90% of revenues in fiscal year 2003. SAIC also provides professional services to the commercial sector, including consulting, software implementation, and network engineering. Its Telcordia Technologies subsidiary (formerly the research arm of the Baby Bells) supplies a variety of software and services to the telecommunications sector. SAIC is the nation's largest employee-owned research and engineering company.

Following the terrorist attacks of September 11, 2001, the company has seen increased demand for homeland security-related projects, prompting it to install an emergency telecommunications system in New York, develop a training program for US sky marshals, and build a communications network for the US Central Command. SAIC also has its hands in undersea data collection and space systems engineering.

Together with Boeing, SAIC has inked various multi-million dollar deals with the US Army. Together, those companies are developing practices for the $14.9 billion Future Combat Systems (FCS) program that will reshape the US Army operations.

In April of 2003 SAIC acquired the rights to various threat-analysis Information Sharing and Analysis Centers (ISACs) from Predictive Systems. The ISACs were created in 1997 to encourage private companies to share information about threats and warnings as a way to reduce their vulnerability to terrorist attacks.

Also in the beginning of 2003 SAIC engaged in talks to sell its 60% interest in Venezuelan joint venture Informática, Negocios y Tecnologa, S.A., (INTESA) to partner Petróleos de Venezuela, S.A. (PDVSA). The political climate in that country put a temporary damper in the negotiations.

The company also inked a $48 million contract to provide engineering services to NASA's Orbital Space Plane (OSP) project. The project is developing strategies to safely transport the International Space Station crew to and from orbit. SAIC will provide NASA with technical services in the areas of vehicle engineering, crew survival and escape, and systems engineering.

Founder, chairman, and CEO Robert Beyster — who has guided the company to record revenues for each of the last 32 years — asserts that employee ownership has been key to the company's success, and has shown little interest (or need) in pursuing an IPO. The company last received $200,000 from private investors in 1970. But the omnipresent and self-described workaholic Beyster retired as CEO in November 2003. Former General Dynamics VP Kenneth Dahlberg stepped in as his replacement; Beyster will remain as chairman until 2004.

HISTORY

Physicist Robert Beyster, who worked at Los Alamos National Laboratory in the 1950s, was hired by General Atomic in 1957 to establish and manage its traveling wave linear accelerator. When the company was sold to Gulf Oil in 1968, research priorities changed and Beyster left. He founded Science Applications Inc. (SAI) the following year and built his business from consulting contracts with Los Alamos and Brookhaven National Laboratories.

During the first year Beyster instituted an employee ownership plan that rewarded workers that brought onboard new business with stock in SAI. Beyster's idea was to share the success of SAI and to raise capital.

In 1970 the company established an office in Washington, DC, to court government contracts. Despite a recession, SAI continued to grow during the 1970s, and by 1979 sales topped $100 million. The following year SAI restructured, becoming a subsidiary of Science Applications International Corporation (SAIC), a new holding company.

During the 1980s defense buildup, an emphasis on high-tech weaponry and SAIC's high-level Pentagon connections (directors have included former defense secretaries William Perry and Melvin Laird and former CIA director John Deutch) brought in contracts for submarine warfare systems and technical development for the Strategic Defense Initiative ("Star Wars").

As defense spending slowed with the end of the Cold War, SAIC began casting a wider net. By 1991 computer systems integration and consulting accounted for 25% of sales, which surpassed the $1 billion mark.

SAIC made several purchases during the mid-1990s, including transportation communications firm Syntonic, Internet domain name registrar Network Solutions, Inc. (NSI), and government think tank Aerospace Corp. In 1997 SAIC acquired Bellcore (the research lab of the regional Bells, now Telcordia Technologies), and reduced its stake in NSI through a public offering. SAIC formed several alliances in 1998, including a joint venture with Rolls-Royce to service the aerospace, energy, and defense industries.

The next year SAIC expanded its information technology (IT) expertise with the acquisition of Boeing's Information Services unit. It also acquired the call center software operations of Elite Information Group. SAIC in 2000 realized a significant gain on its $5 million purchase of NSI when e-commerce software maker VeriSign bought the minority-owned (23%) subsidiary for $17 billion.

In 2001 SAIC signed a variety of large contracts, including an outsourcing agreement with BP to manage that company's North American application and hosting services, as well as a $3 billion deal to provide support (in conjunction with Bechtel Group) for the US Department of Energy's civilian radioactive waste management program.

EXECUTIVES

Chairman: J. Robert Beyster, age 78, $1,988,898 pay
CEO: Kenneth C. Dahlberg, age 58
EVP: D. H. Foley, age 58
EVP: Steve D. Rockwood, age 59
EVP: William A. Roper Jr., age 57
EVP; Executive Chairman, ANXeBusiness: John E. Glancy, age 56
EVP and CFO: Thomas E. Darcy, age 53, $925,015 pay
EVP and Operations Manager, Washington, DC: Robert A. Rosenberg, age 68
EVP and Secretary: J. Dennis Heipt, age 60, $1,010,014 pay
EVP: Randy I. Walker, age 38
EVP Commercial Outsourcing: Art L. Slotkin, age 56
EVP Federal Business: Duane P. Andrews, age 58, $1,067,322 pay
EVP Strategic Initiatives: Joseph P. (Joe) Walkush, age 50
EVP Systems Integration: John H. Warner Jr., age 62, $878,359 pay
EVP Telecommunications Sector: Neil E. Cox, age 53
SVP and Controller: Peter N. Pavlics, age 42
SVP and General Counsel: D. E. Scott, age 46
SVP and Manager, Applied Software Systems Engineering Technology Group: Beverly J. Kitaoka
SVP and Manager, Global Telecommunications Group: Robert K. (Bob) Young
SVP and Manager, Information Technologies Integration Group: Bryan Bebb
SVP and Manager, Information Technology Services Group: Gerry Anderson
SVP and Manager, Integrated Network Engineering and Operations Group: Peter Dube
SVP and Manager, Space, Earth and Atmospheric Sciences Group: Neil Hutchinson
SVP and Program Manager, Safety, Reliability, and Quality Assurance: Frank L. Culbertson Jr.
SVP Human Resources: Bernard Theull
Director of Community Relations: Gerald E. Connolly
Auditors: Deloitte & Touche LLP

LOCATIONS

HQ: Science Applications International Corporation
10260 Campus Point Dr., San Diego, CA 92121
Phone: 858-826-6000 **Fax:** 858-826-6800
Web: www.saic.com

Science Applications International has offices in more than 150 cities worldwide.

PRODUCTS/OPERATIONS

Selected Practice Areas

Biomedical research
Criminal justice
Customer relationship management
Data mining and warehousing
Distributed enterprise management
E-business systems
Energy
Environmental consulting
Financial services
Imagery
Information security
Information technology
Knowledge management
Maritime systems
National security
Outsourcing
Software development
Space systems
Supply chain management
Systems integration and program management
Telecommunications
Training programs
Transportation
Wireless communications

Selected Products

Aviation vehicles
Computer hardware
Inspection technology
Safety and security systems
Simulators
Software
Transportation systems

Selected Technologies

Abacus (aerial imagery analysis)
AgentMiner (data mining and information collection)
OMEGA (weather prediction)
Quava (software development)

COMPETITORS

Accenture
AMS
Anteon
Battelle Memorial
CACI International
Cap Gemini
Computer Sciences
EDS
General Dynamics
Hewlett-Packard
Hughes Electronics
IBM
ITT Industries
Keane
Lockheed Martin
ManTech
MITRE
Northrop Grumman
Perot Systems
Titan
Unisys
Veridian

HISTORICAL FINANCIALS

Company Type: Private

Income Statement FYE: January 31

	REVENUE ($ mil.)	NET INCOME ($ mil.)	NET PROFIT MARGIN	EMPLOYEES
1/03	5,903	246	4.2%	38,700
1/02	6,095	19	0.3%	40,400
1/01	5,896	2,059	34.9%	41,500
1/00	5,530	620	11.2%	39,078
1/99	4,740	151	3.2%	35,200
1/98	3,089	85	2.7%	30,300
1/97	2,402	64	2.7%	22,600
1/96	2,156	57	2.7%	21,100
1/95	1,922	49	2.6%	20,500
1/94	1,671	42	2.5%	17,800
Annual Growth	15.1%	21.9%	—	9.0%

2003 Year-End Financials

Debt ratio: 44.7%
Return on equity: 10.9%
Cash ($ mil.): 2,197
Current ratio: 2.26
Long-term debt ($ mil.): 897

Net Income History

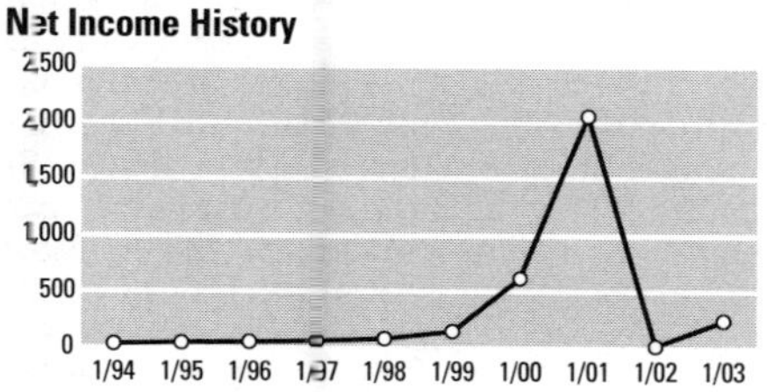

The Scoular Company

The people who grow the wheat aren't usually the ones who grind it. The Scoular Company handles the process that goes on between the two groups. The company is best known for grain marketing, trading more than 400 million bushels of grain and more than 1 million tons of grain byproducts (used for animal feed) annually throughout North America. Other divisions offer fishmeal products for animal and aquaculture feeds, ingredients for food manufacturing, truck freight brokering, and livestock marketing. Founded in 1892 to run grain elevators, employee-owned Scoular operates elevators in Colorado, Nebraska, and South Dakota.

EXECUTIVES

Chairman: Marshall E. Faith
CEO: Randal L. Linville
CFO: Roger L. Barber
SVP, Administration, Development, and Finance: John M. Heck
SVP, Corporate Development and Shareholder Relations: David M. Faith
SVP, Secretary and General Counsel: Joan C. Maclin
Director, Human Resources: Yvonne Lutz

LOCATIONS

HQ: 2027 Dodge St., Omaha, NE 68102
Phone: 402-342-3500 **Fax:** 402-342-5568
Web: www.scoular.com

Scoular has facilities in 16 US states, as well as in Canada and Mexico.

PRODUCTS/OPERATIONS

Selected Operations

Commodity Marketing Division (grain by-product and feed ingredient trading)
Country Elevator Division (grain elevators)
Grain Marketing Divisions (grain trading)
Industrial Food Ingredients (food ingredients)
International Proteins Corporation (fishmeal for feed)
TSC Container Freight (truck freight logistics)

COMPETITORS

Ag Processing
Agway
ADM
Bartlett and Company
Bunge Limited
Cargill
CHS
ConAgra
DeBruce Grain
Farmland Industries
GROWMARK
Southern States

HISTORICAL FINANCIALS

Company Type: Private

Income Statement FYE: May 31

	REVENUE ($ mil.)	NET INCOME ($ mil.)	NET PROFIT MARGIN	EMPLOYEES
5/03	1,900	—	—	330
5/02	2,100	—	—	330
5/01	2,098	—	—	400
5/00	2,015	—	—	379
5/99	1,729	—	—	400
5/98	1,606	—	—	267
5/97	1,900	—	—	278
5/96	1,955	—	—	285
5/95	1,130	—	—	225
5/94	1,121	—	—	250
Annual Growth	6.0%	—	—	3.1%

Revenue History

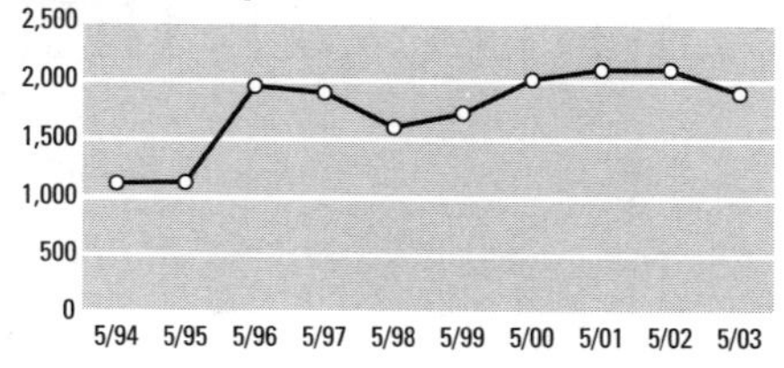

Sealy Corporation

Sealy is a slumbering giant. The company, North America's #1 maker of bedding products, manufactures mattresses and box springs and sells them in more than 7,000 stores. Its brands include Sealy, Barrett, and Stearns & Foster. Sealy's customers include sleep shops, furniture and department stores, warehouse clubs, and mass merchandisers, as well as the hospitality industry. Sealy also licenses its name to makers of other bedding products (pads, pillows) and home furnishings (sofas, futons). The company runs about 30 factories in Argentina, Brazil, Canada, France, Italy, Mexico, Puerto Rico, and the US. Boston-based investment firm Bain Capital, along with company management, owns Sealy.

While the majority of Sealy's sales come from the US, the firm also has licensees and sales operations worldwide. Sealy is making acquisitions and building plants to expand its business in the Latin American region.

EXECUTIVES

Chairman: Ronald L. (Ron) Jones, age 60, $678,462 pay
President and CEO: David J. (Dave) McIlquham, age 48, $636,552 pay
Corporate VP and CFO: James B. (Jim) Hirshorn, age 36
Corporate VP, General Counsel, and Secretary: Kenneth L. Walker, age 54
Corporate VP Human Resources: Jeffrey C. Claypool, age 55, $310,001 pay
Corporate VP Marketing: Mark Hobson, age 43
Corporate VP Sales: Al Boulden, age 56
President, International Bedding Group: Lawrence J. Rogers, age 54, $371,565 pay
Auditors: PricewaterhouseCoopers LLP

LOCATIONS

HQ: Sealy Drive, 1 Office Pkwy., Trinity, NC 27370
Phone: 336-861-3500 **Fax:** 336-861-3501
Web: www.sealy.com

Sealy has about 30 manufacturing facilities in Argentina, Brazil, Canada, France, Italy, Mexico, Puerto Rico, and 17 US states. It has licensees in Australia, the Bahamas, the Dominican Republic, Israel, Jamaica, Japan, New Zealand, Saudi Arabia, South Africa, Thailand, and the UK.

PRODUCTS/OPERATIONS

Selected Brand Names

Bassett
Bed Time
Carrington-Chase
Meyer
Sealy
Sealy Back Saver
Sealy Correct Comfort
Sealy Kids
Sealy Posture Premier
Sealy Posturematic
Sealy Posturepedic
Stearns & Foster

COMPETITORS

Mattress Giant
Premier Bedding Group
Select Comfort
Serta
Simmons
Spring Air
TWI Holdings
Badcock

HISTORICAL FINANCIALS

Company Type: Private

Income Statement FYE: Sunday nearest November 30

	REVENUE ($ mil.)	NET INCOME ($ mil.)	NET PROFIT MARGIN	EMPLOYEES
11/02	1,189	17	1.4%	6,480
11/01	1,197	(21)	—	6,410
11/00	1,102	30	2.7%	6,077
11/99	986	16	1.6%	5,460
11/98	891	(34)	—	5,193
11/97	805	7	0.9%	5,456
11/96	698	(1)	—	4,875
11/95	654	20	3.0%	4,520
11/94	698	29	4.2%	4,345
11/93	683	26	3.8%	4,844
Annual Growth	6.4%	(4.6%)	—	3.3%

2002 Year-End Financials

Debt ratio: —
Return on equity: —
Cash ($ mil.): 27
Current ratio: 1.29
Long-term debt ($ mil.): 720

Net Income History

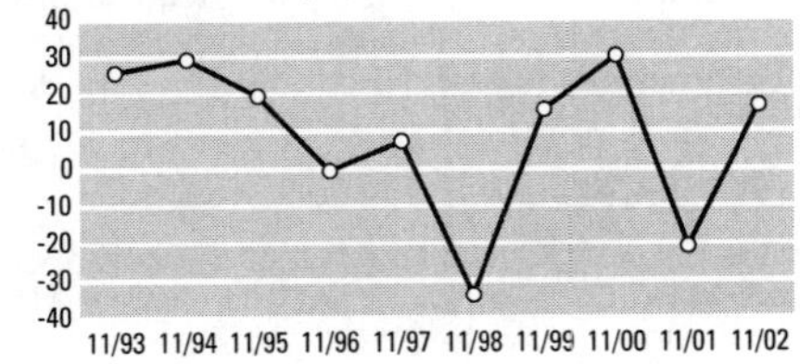

Security Benefit Group

Security Benefit Group of Companies is the largest life insurer in the Jayhawk State. The group operates through Security Benefit Life Insurance Company, which offers variable life insurance, annuities, mutual funds, and asset management services through about 16,500 sales representatives. Security Benefit is highlighting its asset management skills by opening several new funds. After more than 100 years as a mutual company, the company made plans to convert to stock ownership but never followed through on those plans. Security Benefit's roots go back to the Knights and Ladies of Security, a benefit society begun in 1892 in Topeka, Kansas.

EXECUTIVES

Chairman: Howard R. Fricke, age 67
President and CEO: Kris Robbins
SVP, CFO, and Treasurer: Donald Schepker
SVP and CIO: David Keith
SVP and Chief Marketing Officer: Kal Bakk
SVP, Customer Management: Venette K. Davis
SVP, Human Resources: Craig Anderson
VP, Marketing and Communications: Jennifer Purvis
Auditors: Ernst & Young LLP

LOCATIONS

HQ: Security Benefit Group of Companies
1 Security Benefit Place, Topeka, KS 66636
Phone: 785-438-3000 **Fax:** 785-438-5177
Web: www.securitybenefit.com

PRODUCTS/OPERATIONS

Selected Subsidiaries

Security Benefit Life Insurance Company
Security Distributors, Inc.
Security Management Company, LLC

COMPETITORS

Aetna
American United
Americo
CIGNA
CNA Financial
FMR
John Hancock Financial Services
Kansas City Life
Mutual of Omaha
Principal Financial
Prudential
Thrivent Financial
UnitedHealth Group

HISTORICAL FINANCIALS

Company Type: Private

Income Statement FYE: December 31

	ASSETS ($ mil.)	NET INCOME ($ mil.)	INCOME AS % OF ASSETS	EMPLOYEES
12/02	7,325	6	0.1%	700
12/01	7,463	31	0.4%	600
12/00	7,872	70	0.9%	—
12/99	8,310	69	0.8%	—
12/98	7,429	58	0.8%	—
12/97	6,403	52	0.8%	—
12/96	5,748	44	0.8%	—
12/95	4,914	37	0.8%	—
12/94	4,202	34	0.8%	—
12/93	3,883	33	0.8%	—
Annual Growth	7.3%	(17.6%)	—	16.7%

2002 Year-End Financials

Equity as % of assets: 6.1%
Return on assets: 0.1%
Return on equity: 1.3%
Long-term debt ($ mil.): —
Sales ($ mil.): 2,067

Net Income History

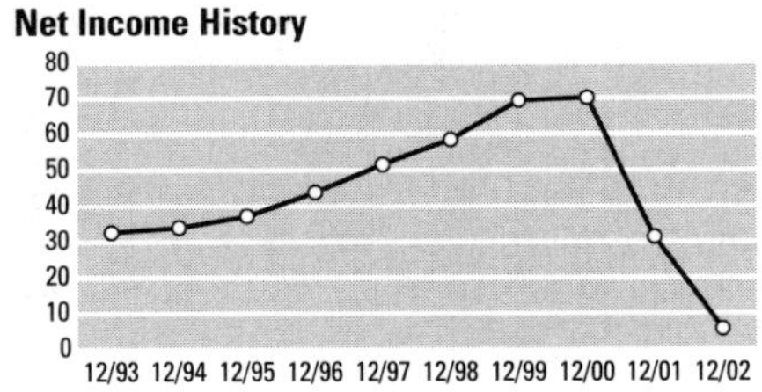

SEMATECH, Inc.

SEMATECH (from "semiconductor manufacturing technology") is more than semantics. The not-for-profit research consortium, which does business as International SEMATECH, pursues advances in design, lithography, interconnect, and other facets of chip manufacturing. It also provides custom wafer processing and publishes technical reports for its members. The group is funded by member dues; employees from its members' companies — Agere, Advanced Micro Devices, Hewlett-Packard, IBM, Infineon, Intel, Motorola, Philips, Taiwan Semiconductor, and Texas Instruments — carry out research at its Texas site.

International SEMATECH is credited with updating the equipment used in American factories and helping US chip makers recover their global dominance.

The consortium has lost some of its original US members in recent years — in part because of the US chip industry's return to dominance, in part because of its inclusion of non-US firms — but continues to tackle difficult technological issues related to the shrinking size of chips and use of new materials. The organization has more recently lost two foreign members — Hynix and STMicroelectronics — both citing budgetary reasons.

Amid a harsh downturn in the semiconductor industry and an increasingly difficult funding environment, International SEMATECH is teaming up with other international research organizations, including Selete, its Japanese counterpart. The consortium also announced plans to lay off about 60 employees — a tenth of its workforce — in response to smaller budgets and in the face of a sharp downturn across the semiconductor industry. However the company has also announced plans to establish another research campus in Albany, New York — dubbed International SEMATECH North — with funding from New York State and IBM.

HISTORY

In 1986 Japan surpassed the US to become the leading maker of semiconductors. The Semiconductor Industry Association (SIA), a US chip industry trade group, formed SEMATECH in 1987 with the help of five years' worth of funding from the US Defense Department's Defense Advanced Research Projects Agency, along with another $100 million per year from 14 member companies. Intel co-founder (and chip industry legend) Robert Noyce became the consortium's first CEO.

Former Xerox research executive Bill Spencer became CEO of SEMATECH after Noyce's death in 1990. Despite its technological advances, critics complained that the organization primarily benefited its largest members. In the early 1990s Micron Technology and LSI Logic (its smallest members) and Harris Corp. dropped out.

SEMATECH's government funding was extended (although at a lower level) in 1992. When the US regained its world chip manufacturing title that year, many credited SEMATECH for the turnaround.

In 1994 SEMATECH began phasing out federal backing. Citing the main challenge to US chip makers as technology limits rather than foreign competition, the organization in 1996 invited European and Asian manufacturers to join an initiative to convert semiconductor wafers from eight to 12 inches (300mm). When government funding came to an end in 1996, SEMATECH formed an international branch and increased its dues to cover lost funding.

In 1997 Mark Melliar-Smith was named CEO. (Spencer remained chairman until 2000, when O. B. Bilous succeeded him.) In 1998 five companies from Asia and Europe formed the new International SEMATECH. That year National Semiconductor left SEMATECH, citing financial difficulties.

In 1999 Motorola, concerned about the organization's international push, gave the required two years notice that it would withdraw. Compaq

— which had become a member when it acquired Digital Equipment (but not that company's chip operations) in 1997 — also made plans to leave.

By 2000 SEMATECH and International SEMATECH became a single entity (and began using International SEMATECH as its trade name). That year SEMATECH accelerated its international involvement through pacts with Selete, the organization's Japanese counterpart, and Belgium research agency IMEC.

In 2001 Bob Helms, a Texas Instruments engineer and Stanford University emeritus professor, succeeded Melliar-Smith as the consortium's president and CEO. In 2003 Helms stepped down as president and CEO and was replaced by IBM veteran Michael Polcari.

EXECUTIVES

Chairman: O. B. Bilous
President and CEO: Michael R. Polcari
VP and COO, Advanced Technology: Betsy Weitzman
VP and COO, Manufacturing Operations and Technology: John Schmitz
Chief Administrative Officer: David Saathoff
Director, Interconnect: Navjot Chhabra
Co-Director, Lithography: Giang Dao
Co-Director, Lithography: Anthony (Tony) Yen
Associate Director, Interconnect: Ken Monnig
Program Manager, Extreme Ultraviolet Lithography: Kevin Kemp
Program Manager, Mask Strategy: Kurt R. Kimmel
Manager, Productivity Analysis: Tim Stanley
Manager, Wafer Services Group: Brent Ames
Technical Account Representative, Wafer Services Group: Yvette Jorgenser
Technical Account Representative, Wafer Services Group: Vangie Lopez
Technical Account Representative, Wafer Services Group: Lesli Roush
Technical Account Representative, Wafer Services Group: Reuben Santana
Wafer Services Process Engineering, Wafer Services Group: Rich Berger
Development Contracts: Debora Kalens
Volunteer Activities/Donations: Christi Cochren
Media Relations Contact: Dan McGowan
Auditors: PricewaterhouseCoopers LLP

LOCATIONS

HQ: 2706 Montopolis Dr., Austin, TX 78741
Phone: 512-356-3500 **Fax:** 512-356-3086
Web: www.sematech.org

SEMATECH includes members from Germany, the Netherlands, Taiwan, and the US.

PRODUCTS/OPERATIONS

Research and Development Programs

Advanced technical development facilities and facilities design
Front-end processes
Interconnect
Lithography
Manufacturing methods and productivity

SEMATECH Members

Advanced Micro Devices
Agere
Hewlett-Packard
IBM
Infineon
Intel
Motorola
Philips
Taiwan Semiconductor Manufacturing Corp.
Texas Instruments

COMPETITORS

Intel
IBM
MIT
Research Triangle Institute
SAIC
Southwest Research Institute
SRI International
University of California

Seminis, Inc.

Seminis doesn't put up with any bad seeds. Seminis is the world's largest developer, grower, and marketer of fruit and vegetable seeds. Some of its seeds are genetically engineered to be disease and insect resistant; some are plain old hybrids. The company sells seeds under primary brands Asgrow, Bruinsma, Genecorp, Petoseed, and Royal Sluis. Its customers include grower, dealers, distributors, and wholesales in countries worldwide. Formed in 1994, Seminis has grown by acquiring other seed companies. Formerly a subsidiary of publicly traded Savia, Seminis (which was also publicly but separately traded) went private in 2003.

The company holds the world's largest germ plasm bank (which stores genetic information on seeds). Its research in genetic engineering has drawn negative attention from Greenpeace and eco-terrorists in the US.

Seminis produces about 4,000 varieties of fruit and vegetable seeds, which it sells in more than 150 countries. Asia is its fastest-growing sales region.

EXECUTIVES

Chairman, CEO, President, and COO: Alfonso Romo Garza, age 52, $800,233 pay
SEVP, Worldwide Commercial: Bruno Ferrari, age 41
SVP, Asia: Oscar Javier Velasco, age 48
SVP, Research and Development: Charles Edward Green, age 59
VP, Human Resources and Information Technology: Mateo Mazal
VP, Worldwide Corporate Comptroller: Gaspar Alvarez Martinez, age 47, $228,057 pay
Secretary: Jorge Barrera Guiterrez, age 64
Manager, Corporate Communications: Gary Koppenjan
Auditors: PricewaterhouseCoopers LLP

LOCATIONS

HQ: 2700 Camino del Sol, Oxnard, CA 93030
Phone: 805-485-7317 **Fax:** 805-918-2545
Web: www.seminis.com

Seminis sells seeds in more than 150 countries. It has 49 research and development operations in 17 countries and production facilities in more than 25.

PRODUCTS/OPERATIONS

Full-line Brands

Asgrow (beans, broccoli, carrots, tomatoes, melons, onions, peas, cucumbers, squash, and sweet peppers)
Petoseed (broccoli, cucumbers, tomatoes, hot peppers, lettuce, melons, tomatoes, squash, and sweet peppers)
Royal Sluis (beans, cabbage, lettuce, radishes, and spinach)

Selected Regional and Specialty Brands

Bruinsma (vegetables, Europe)
California (fruits and vegetables, Middle East)
Choong Ang (fruits and vegetables, South Korea)
Horticeres (vegetables, Brazil)
Hungnong (vegetables, South Korea)

COMPETITORS

Cargill
Delta and Pine Land
Dow Chemical
DuPont
Exelixis Plant Sciences
Limagrain Holdings
Pioneer Hi-Bred
Sakata Seed Corporation
Syngenta

HISTORICAL FINANCIALS

Company Type: Private

Income Statement

FYE: September 30

	REVENUE ($ mil.)	NET INCOME ($ mil.)	NET PROFIT MARGIN	EMPLOYEES
9/02	453	16	3.6%	2,702
9/01	450	(135)	—	2,993
9/00	474	(81)	—	3,800
9/99	531	(4)	—	3,900
9/98	428	7	1.6%	3,000
9/97	380	62	16.4%	—
9/96	381	(50)	—	—
Annual Growth	2.9%	—	—	(2.6%)

2002 Year-End Financials

Debt ratio: 67.6%
Return on equity: 4.9%
Cash ($ mil.): 37
Current ratio: 2.42
Long-term debt ($ mil.): 228

Net Income History

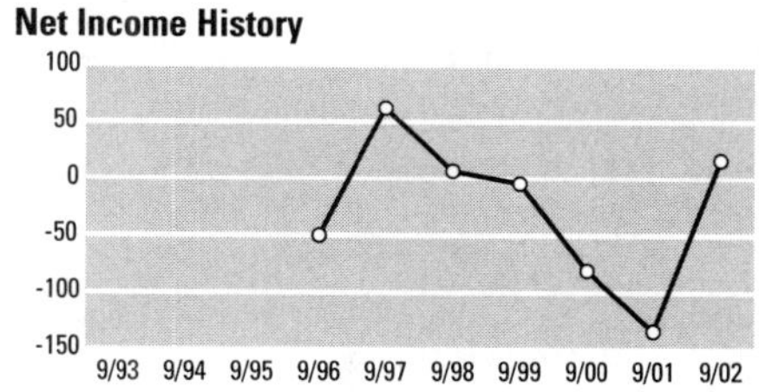

Seminole Electric Cooperative, Inc.

This Seminole is not only a native Floridian, but it has also provided electricity in the state since 1948. Seminole Electric Cooperative (SECI) generates and transmits electricity for 10 member distribution cooperatives that serve about 750,000 residential and business customers in 45 Florida counties. SECI has more than 1,800 MW of primarily coal-fired generating capacity. The cooperative also buys electricity from other utilities and independent power producers, and it owns 400 miles of transmission lines. SECI was formed to aggregate the power demands of its members and is governed by a board of trustees representing the 10 member utilities.

EXECUTIVES

President, Board of Trustees: Wilson G. Sheppard
VP, Board of Trustees: John W. Drake
EVP and General Manager: Richard J. Midulla
VP, Financial Services and Assistant Treasurer: John W. Geeraerts
VP, Energy Delivery: Floyd J. Welborn
VP, Energy Production: James R. Duren
VP, Strategic Services and Assistant Secretary: Timothy S. Woodbury
Director, Operations: Steve Wallace
Secretary and Treasurer: William T. Mulcay Jr.
Auditors: PricewaterhouseCoopers LLP

LOCATIONS

HQ: 16313 N. Dale Mabry Hwy., Tampa, FL 33618
Phone: 813-963-0994 **Fax:** 813-264-7906
Web: www.seminole-electric.com

PRODUCTS/OPERATIONS

Members

Central Florida Electric Cooperative
Clay Electric Cooperative
Glades Electric Cooperative
Lee County Electric Cooperative
Peace River Electric Cooperative
Sumter Electric Cooperative
Suwannee Valley Electric Cooperative
Talquin Electric Cooperative
Tri-County Electric Cooperative
Withlacoochee River Electric Cooperative

COMPETITORS

Duke Energy
Florida Public Utilities
FPL Group
JEA
Progress Energy
Southern Company
TECO Energy

HISTORICAL FINANCIALS

Company Type: Cooperative

Income Statement FYE: December 31

	REVENUE ($ mil.)	NET INCOME ($ mil.)	NET PROFIT MARGIN	EMPLOYEES
12/02	714	2	0.3%	468
12/01	669	2	0.4%	455
12/00	583	—	—	438
Annual Growth	10.7%	(4.2%)	—	3.4%

2002 Year-End Financials

Debt ratio: 964.7%
Return on equity: 3.1%
Cash ($ mil.): 24
Current ratio: 1.59
Long-term debt ($ mil.): 756

Net Income History

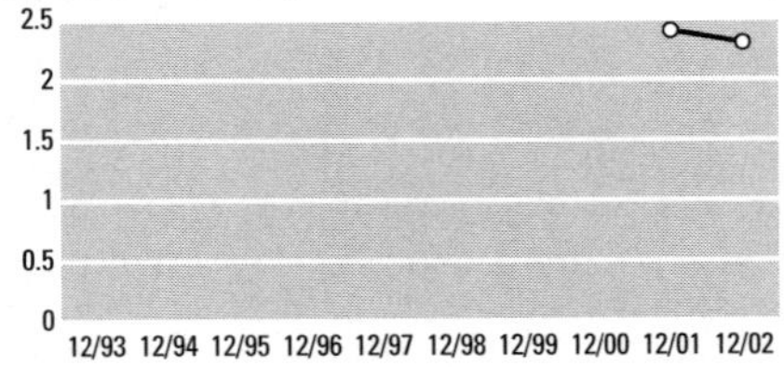

Sentara Healthcare

Health care's a beach for Sentara Healthcare. The not-for-profit organization provides medical services for about 2 million residents of southeastern Virginia and northeastern North Carolina. The system includes six hospitals, nine assisted-living centers, more than 30 primary care offices, an integrated outpatient health care campus, and several fitness centers. Sentara's Optima Health Plan provides HMO coverage to more than 250,000 members. The organization also provides home health services, ground and air medical transport, community health education programs, and mobile diagnostic vans.

EXECUTIVES

CEO: David L. Bernd
President: Howard P. Kern
CFO: Rob Broerman
Corporate VP and Chief Medical Officer: Rod Hochman
VP, Information Technology and CIO: Bertram S. Reese
VP, Human Resources: Michael Taylor

LOCATIONS

HQ: 6015 Poplar Hall Dr., Norfolk, VA 23502
Phone: 757-455-7000 **Fax:** 757-455-7964
Web: www.sentara.com

Sentara operates in northeastern North Carolina and southeastern Virgina.

Hospitals

Sentara Bayside Hospital (Virginia Beach, VA)
Sentara CarePlex Hospital (Hampton, VA)
Sentara Leigh Hospital (Norfolk, VA)
Sentara Norfolk General Hospital (Norfolk, VA)
Sentara Virginia Beach General Hospital (Virginia Beach, VA)
Sentara Williamsburg Community Hospital (Williamsburg, VA)

PRODUCTS/OPERATIONS

Facilities

Assisted-living centers
Fitness centers
Hospitals
Nursing centers
Outpatient campus
Primary care practices

COMPETITORS

Bon Secours Health
Carilion Health System
Mid Atlantic Medical
Novant Health
Wake Forest University Baptist Medical Center

HISTORICAL FINANCIALS

Company Type: Not-for-profit

Income Statement FYE: April 30

	REVENUE ($ mil.)	NET INCOME ($ mil.)	NET PROFIT MARGIN	EMPLOYEES
4/03	1,530	—	—	15,200
4/02	1,600	—	—	15,200
Annual Growth	(4.4%)	—	—	0.0%

Revenue History

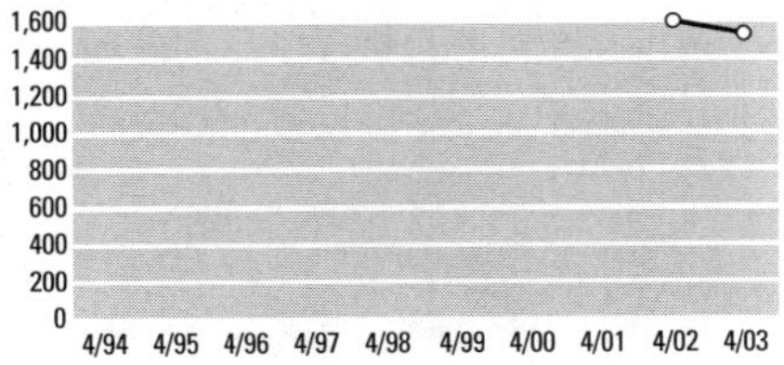

Sentry Insurance

Vigilant for its policyholders, Sentry Insurance (of the famous Minuteman statue logo) offers a variety of insurance coverage, including life, group health, auto, and property/casualty insurance. The mutual company (owned by its policyholders) offers coverage through several subsidiaries. Sentry also provides specialized insurance to small and large businesses, including manufacturers and retailers. The company's Sentry Equity Services offers mutual fund services through its Sentry Fund. Sentry was founded in 1904 to provide insurance to members of the Wisconsin Retail Hardware Association.

EXECUTIVES

Chairman, President, and CEO: Dale R. Schuh
VP and COO: Jim Clawson
VP, Secretary, and General Counsel: William M. O'Reilly
VP, Finance: William J. Lohr
VP, Human Resources: Greg Mox
VP, Investments: Jim Weishan
Senior Director and Controller: Carol Sanders
Auditors: PricewaterhouseCoopers

LOCATIONS

HQ: Sentry Insurance, a Mutual Company
1800 North Point Dr., Stevens Point, WI 54481
Phone: 715-346-6000 **Fax:** 715-346-7516
Web: www.sentry.com

Sentry Insurance has offices throughout the US.

PRODUCTS/OPERATIONS

Selected Subsidiaries
Dairyland County Mutual of Texas
Dairyland Insurance Company
Middlesex Insurance Company
Parker Services, L.L.C.
Patriot General Insurance Company
Sentry Casualty Company
Sentry Equity Services Inc.
Sentry Life Insurance Company
Sentry Life Insurance Company of New York
Sentry Select Insurance Company

COMPETITORS

Allstate
AIG
CIGNA
CNA Financial
Cobalt
MetLife
Nationwide
New York Life
Prudential
Reliance Group
State Farm

HISTORICAL FINANCIALS

Company Type: Mutual company

Income Statement FYE: December 31

	ASSETS ($ mil.)	NET INCOME ($ mil.)	INCOME AS % OF ASSETS	EMPLOYEES
12/02	6,945	46	0.7%	4,400
12/01	6,587	80	1.2%	4,300
12/00	6,499	217	3.3%	4,200
12/99	6,409	107	1.7%	4,200
12/98	—	134	—	4,000
12/97	5,648	147	2.6%	4,479
12/96	5,363	115	2.1%	4,750
12/95	5,162	188	3.6%	3,909
12/94	4,852	—	—	4,041
12/93	4,670	—	—	4,500
Annual Growth	4.5%	(18.1%)	—	(0.2%)

2002 Year-End Financials

Equity as % of assets: 28.3%
Return on assets: 0.7%
Return on equity: 2.4%
Long-term debt ($ mil.): 1,886
Sales ($ mil.): 1,898

Net Income History

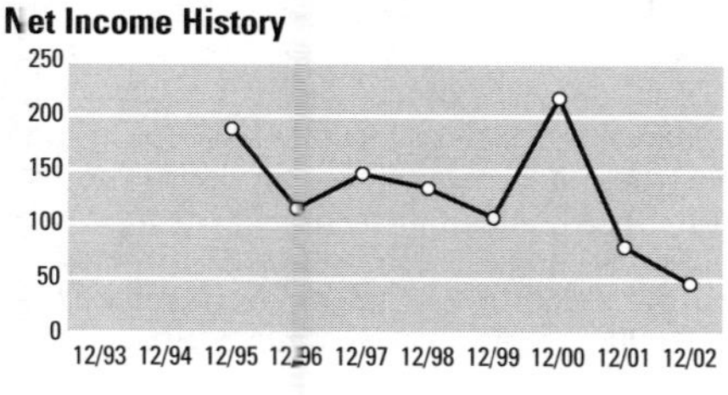

Serta, Inc.

Serta, the #2 mattress manufacturer in the world (behind Sealy), hopes to keep the competition awake at night. It is the nation's #1 mattress supplier to hotels and motels; its Perfect Sleeper mattress line, which it has been selling since the 1930s, is the best-selling premium mattress in the US. Serta's top-of-the-line mattress collection is sold under the Perfect Night name. Founded in 1931 by 13 mattress makers who licensed the Serta name, the company is now owned by eight independent licensees; each licensee has separate marketing, manufacturing, and sales operations. The group has 27 factories in the US, four in Canada, and another 27 throughout Asia, Europe, the Middle East, and South America.

EXECUTIVES

Chairman, President, and CEO: Edward F. (Ed) Lilly
Group VP and Managing Director, International Division: Al Klancnik
VP and Controller: Kevin Bayer
VP, Advertising and Chief Brand Officer: Susan Ebaugh
VP, Information Systems: Mark VanDenburgh
VP, Manufacturing Services: Bob Sabalaskey
VP, Marketing: Bob Malin
VP, Sales: Jeff Van Tuyle
VP and Brand Manager, Masterpiece: Chad Megard

LOCATIONS

HQ: 325 Spring Lake Dr., Itasca, IL 60143
Phone: 630-285-9350 **Fax:** 630-285-9330
Web: www.serta.com

COMPETITORS

The Nautilus Group
Premier Bedding Group
Sealy
Select Comfort
Simmons
Spring Air
TWI Holdings

HISTORICAL FINANCIALS

Company Type: Private

Income Statement FYE: December 31

	REVENUE ($ mil.)	NET INCOME ($ mil.)	NET PROFIT MARGIN	EMPLOYEES
12/01	870	—	—	4,800
12/00	858	—	—	4,800
12/99	834	—	—	4,800
12/98	764	—	—	4,800
12/97	670	—	—	4,000
12/96	578	—	—	4,000
12/95	552	—	—	2,500
12/94	470	—	—	2,000
12/93	380	—	—	—
Annual Growth	10.9%	—	—	13.3%

Revenue History

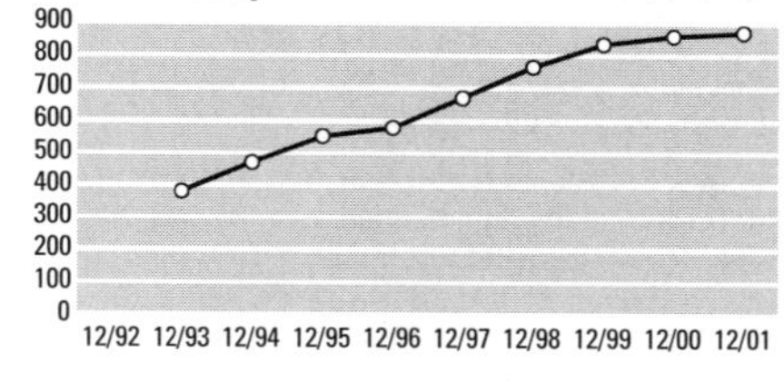

Services Group of America

Though it bears a rather vague company name, Services Group of America's operations are pretty specific. Its subsidiary, Food Services of America, is a food service distributor, supplying hospitals, restaurants, and schools in 15 western and midwestern states. Its McCabe's Quality Foods business supplies fast-food and casual-dining chain restaurants in the western US. Services Group's other operations include fresh fruit and vegetable marketing, commercial real estate development and management, and natural Black Angus beef production and marketing. The company, formed in 1985, has agreed to buy the West Coast food-distribution operations of Marriott International, which will be absorbed by McCabe's.

EXECUTIVES

Chairman and CEO: Thomas J. Stewart
CFO: Peter Smith
VP, Corporate Communications: Gary L. Odegard
Director, Human Resources: Lanett Draper

LOCATIONS

HQ: 4025 Delridge Way SW, Ste. 500, Seattle, WA 98106
Phone: 206-933-5225 **Fax:** 206-933-5247
Web: www.fsafood.com

Services Group of America has operations in Anchorage, Alaska; Billings, Montana; Fargo and Minot, North Dakota; Fresno, California; Everett, Kent, Seattle, and Spokane, Washington; Boise, Idaho; Omaha, Nebraska; and Portland, Oregon.

COMPETITORS

Gordon Food Service
McLane Foodservice
Performance Food
Reyes Holdings
Smart & Final
SYSCO
U.S. Foodservice

HISTORICAL FINANCIALS

Company Type: Private

Income Statement FYE: January 31

	ESTIMATED REVENUE ($ mil.)	NET INCOME ($ mil.)	NET PROFIT MARGIN	EMPLOYEES
1/02	1,650	—	—	3,300
1/01	1,480	—	—	3,300
1/00	1,202	—	—	2,900
1/99	1,400	—	—	2,500
1/98	1,350	—	—	2,300
1/97	1,350	—	—	2,500
1/96	1,200	—	—	2,500
1/95	1,030	—	—	2,500
1/94	950	—	—	2,500
1/93	1,275	—	—	3,000
Annual Growth	2.9%	—	—	1.1%

Revenue History

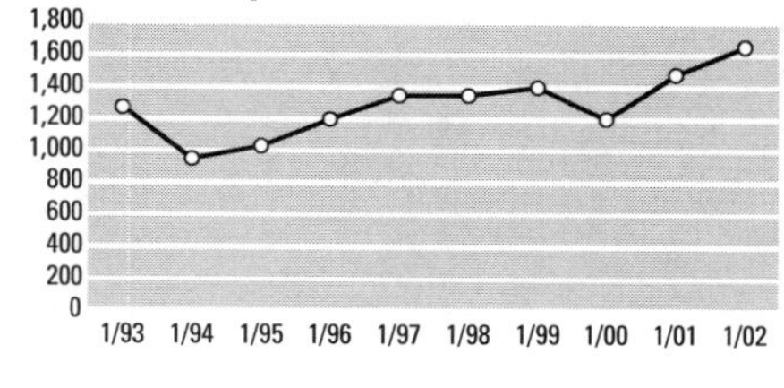

The SF Holdings Group, Inc.

The words "Can I get that to go?" are like money in the bank for the SF Holdings Group. Through subsidiaries the company produces disposable paper and plastic cups, plates, cutlery, and food packaging sold under brand names such as Centerpiece, Hoffmaster, Lily, Preference, and Sweetheart. Its Sweetheart Cup subsidiary accounts for almost 75% of sales and primarily sells its wares to institutional food service customers such as restaurant chains, schools, theaters, and airlines. The Fonda Group, another subsidiary, also sells to institutional food service customers and to consumer markets, as well as through supermarkets and warehouse clubs. Chairman and CEO Dennis Mehiel owns about 72% of SF Holdings.

EXECUTIVES

Chairman and CEO, Sweetheart Holdings, Sweetheart Cup, CEG Group, and Fonda: Dennis Mehiel, age 60, $892,212 pay
Vice Chairman, SVP, and Director; EVP Sweetheart Holdings, Sweetheart Cup; EVP, Fonda: Thomas Uleau, age 58, $523,366 pay
SVP, CFO, and Treasurer: Hans H. Heinsen, age 49, $351,848 pay
Secretary and General Counsel: Harvey L. Friedman, age 59, $402,850 pay
SVP; President of Sweetheart Holdings and Sweetheart Cup: Michael Hastings, $298,846 pay
SVP; President and COO, Fonda: Robert Korzenski, age 47, $384,543 pay
VP, Human Resources, Sweetheart Holdings and Sweetheart Cup: Jeffery Seidman, age 46
Auditors: Deloitte & Touche LLP

LOCATIONS

HQ: 373 Park Ave. South, New York, NY 10016
Phone: 212-779-7448 **Fax:** 212-779-9562

The SF Holdings Group has manufacturing and warehousing facilities in Canada, Mexico, and the US.

PRODUCTS/OPERATIONS

Selected Products

Consumer Products
Foam, paper, and plastic bowls, cups, and plates
Plastic cutlery and straws

Food Service Products
Foam dinnerware and lids
Paper and plastic cold cups and lids
Paper and plastic containers and lids
Paper containers and lids
Paper hot cups and lids
Plastic cutlery, stirrers, straws, and toothpicks

COMPETITORS

Amscan
Dart Container
Huhtamäki
Pactiv
Silgan
Solo Cup

HISTORICAL FINANCIALS

Company Type: Private

Income Statement FYE: Last Sunday in September

	REVENUE ($ mil.)	NET INCOME ($ mil.)	NET PROFIT MARGIN	EMPLOYEES
9/02	1,277	—	—	6,370
9/01	1,317	—	—	8,234
9/00	1,277	—	—	8,200
9/99	1,200	—	—	8,050
9/98	844	—	—	6,700
9/97	886	—	—	6,700
9/96	960	—	—	7,500
9/95	987	—	—	8,600
9/94	899	—	—	8,600
9/93	830	—	—	8,500
Annual Growth	4.9%	—	—	(3.2%)

Revenue History

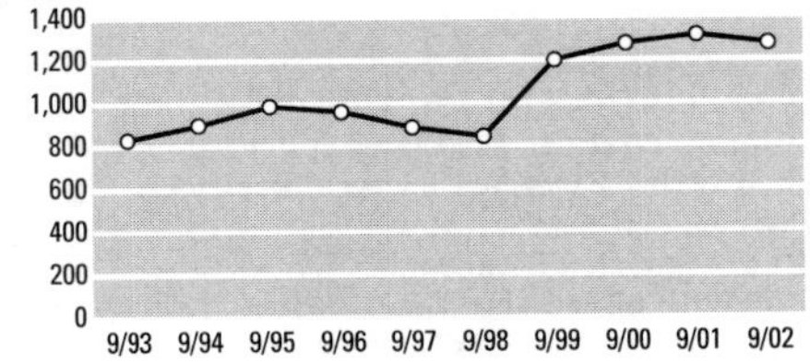

Shamrock Foods Company

Milk does a business good too. Thanks to that udder delight, Shamrock Foods has fortified itself from a mom-and-pop dairy into the fourth-largest independent food service distributor in the US serving supermarkets, convenience stores, restaurants, and institutional clients in 10 states in the West and Southwest, including Southern California, Colorado, and Texas. The company's Shamrock Farms division processes dairy products, including milk, cottage cheese, and sour cream. Production of the company's ice cream is outsourced. Its products are sold under the Shamrock Farms and Sunland brands, as well as under private labels. Started in 1922, Shamrock Foods is owned and run by the founding McClelland family.

EXECUTIVES

Chairman & CEO: Norman McClelland
President and COO: Kent McClelland
SVP and CFO: F. Phillips Giltner III, age 78
VP, Human Resources: Robert (Bob) Beake
Secretary and Treasurer: Frances McClelland

LOCATIONS

HQ: 2540 N. 29th Ave., Phoenix, AZ 85009
Phone: 602-233-6401 **Fax:** 602-233-2791
Web: www.shamrockfoods.com

Shamrock Foods does business in 10 states: Arizona, California, Colorado, Kansas, Nebraska, Nevada, New Mexico, Texas, Utah, and Wyoming.

PRODUCTS/OPERATIONS

Selected Products

Beverages
Canned goods
Dairy products
Fresh produce
Fresh and frozen meat
Fresh and frozen poultry
Fresh and frozen seafood
Sanitation products
Tabletop and equipment

COMPETITORS

Berkeley Farms
California Dairies Inc.
Dairy Farmers of America
Dean Foods
Land O'Lakes
McLane Foodservice
SYSCO
U.S. Foodservice

HISTORICAL FINANCIALS

Company Type: Private

Income Statement FYE: September 30

	REVENUE ($ mil.)	NET INCOME ($ mil.)	NET PROFIT MARGIN	EMPLOYEES
9/02	1,093	—	—	2,143
9/01	1,100	—	—	2,196
9/00	1,177	—	—	2,426
9/99	1,081	—	—	2,337
9/98	995	—	—	2,284
9/97	892	—	—	2,168
9/96	818	—	—	2,064
9/95	703	—	—	1,783
9/94	609	—	—	1,500
9/93	550	—	—	1,200
Annual Growth	7.9%	—	—	6.7%

Revenue History

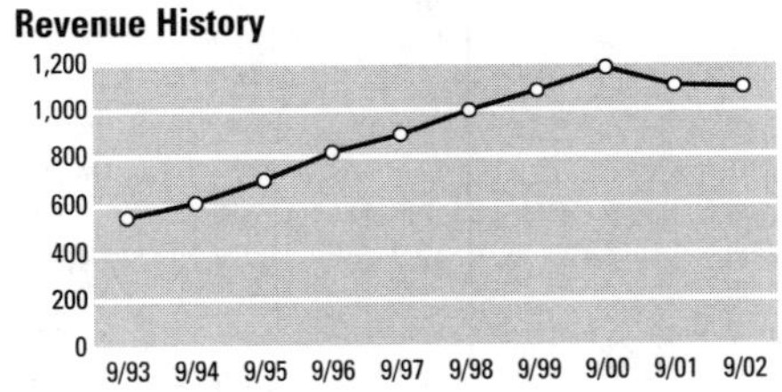

Shapell Industries, Inc.

Shapell Industries shapes its business around constructing homes for Californians. The real estate development firm builds luxury townhouses and single-family homes in Northern and Southern California that range in price from $400,000 to more than $1 million. Shapell also provides home financing and interior design services for its customers and develops shopping centers and offices near its home communities. The company, which began as S&S Construction Company in 1955, has built more than 60,000 homes since it was founded by Nathan Shapell, his brother David, and brother-in-law Max Webb. A Holocaust survivor, Nathan Shapell constructed homes in Germany for displaced Jews after WWII before he moved to the US.

EXECUTIVES

Chairman and CEO: Nathan Shapell
CFO: Margaret Leong
CTO: Bill Bailey
Human Resources Director: Eileen Ho
Auditors: PricewaterhouseCoopers LLP

LOCATIONS

HQ: 8383 Wilshire Blvd., Ste. 700,
Beverly Hills, CA 90211
Phone: 323-655-7330 **Fax:** 323-651-4349
Web: www.shapellnc.com

Shapell Industries has housing communities in Castro Valley, Danville, Gilroy, the San Francisco Bay Area, San Jose, and San Roman in Northern California and in Laguna Niguel, Porter Ranch, Thousand Oaks, and Yorba Linda in Southern California.

PRODUCTS/OPERATIONS

Selected Divisions and Subsidiaries

S&S Construction Co.
Westminster Mortgage Company

COMPETITORS

Barratt Developments
Capital Pacific
Centex
D.R. Horton
J.F. Shea
KB Home
Lennar
Pulte Homes
Ryland
Standard Pacific
Toll Brothers
William Lyon Homes

HISTORICAL FINANCIALS

Company Type: Private

Income Statement FYE: December 31

	ESTIMATED REVENUE ($ mil.)	NET INCOME ($ mil.)	NET PROFIT MARGIN	EMPLOYEES
12/02	500	—	—	400
12/01	500	—	—	400
12/00	600	—	—	400
12/99	575	—	—	400
12/98	554	—	—	400
12/97	529	—	—	400
12/96	475	—	—	300
12/95	425	—	—	300
12/94	390	—	—	300
Annual Growth	3.2%	—	—	3.7%

Revenue History

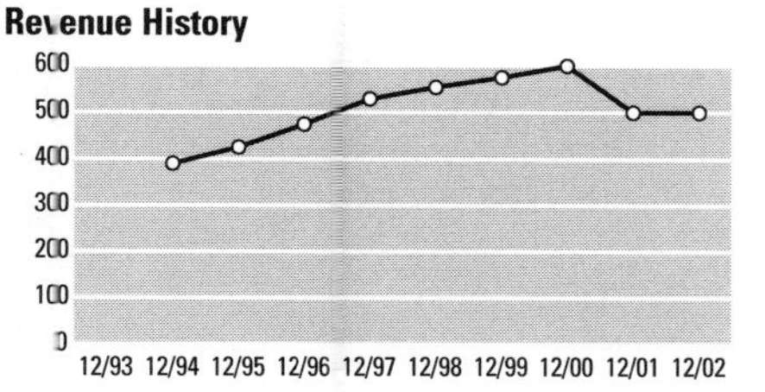

Shearman & Sterling

Law firm Shearman & Sterling has secured its place in history. Founded in 1873, the firm helped railroad baron Jay Gould fight for control of US railroads, aided in brokering a deal to free hostages in Iran, and represented women suing the Citadel military academy for admission. Today Shearman & Sterling has more than 1,000 lawyers in 18 domestic and international offices. Its practice areas include antitrust, bankruptcy, capital markets, intellectual property, litigation, mergers and acquisitions, project development and finance, and tax. Shearman & Sterling clients have included Viacom, Citigroup, and France Telecom.

EXECUTIVES

Senior Partner: David Heleniak
Managing Partner: Robert C. Treuhold
Executive Director, New York: Kimberly Gardner
Director Finance, New York: Kenneth W. Johnsen
Director Global Human Resources: Kathleen Weslock
Director Administrative Human Resources: Barbara Gannet
Director Professional Development: Halle Schargel
Media and Communications Manager: Dara McQuillan

LOCATIONS

HQ: 599 Lexington Ave., New York, NY 10022
Phone: 212-848-4000 **Fax:** 212-848-7179
Web: www.shearman.com

Shearman & Sterling has offices in Menlo Park and San Francisco, California; New York City; and Washington, DC; as well as Abu Dhabi, UAE; Beijing; Brussels; Düsseldorf, Frankfurt, Mannheim, and Munich, Germany; Hong Kong; London; Paris; Rome; Singapore; Tokyo; and Toronto.

PRODUCTS/OPERATIONS

Selected Practice Areas

Antitrust
Bank finance
Executive compensation and benefits
Global capital markets
Intellectual property
International trade
Litigation and dispute resolution
Mergers and acquisitions
Project development and finance
Restructuring and bankruptcy
Tax

COMPETITORS

Cleary, Gottlieb
Clifford Chance
Cravath, Swaine
Davis Polk
Debevoise & Plimpton
Jones Day
Kelley Drye
Milbank, Tweed
Proskauer Rose
Simpson Thacher
Skadden, Arps
Sullivan & Cromwell
Wachtell, Lipton

HISTORICAL FINANCIALS

Company Type: Partnership

Income Statement FYE: December 31

	REVENUE ($ mil.)	NET INCOME ($ mil.)	NET PROFIT MARGIN	EMPLOYEES
12/02	700	—	—	—
12/01	620	—	—	—
12/00	590	—	—	—
12/99	491	—	—	1,900
12/98	426	—	—	1,800
12/97	356	—	—	1,760
12/96	324	—	—	—
12/95	284	—	—	—
12/94	268	—	—	—
12/93	256	—	—	—
Annual Growth	11.8%	—	—	3.9%

Revenue History

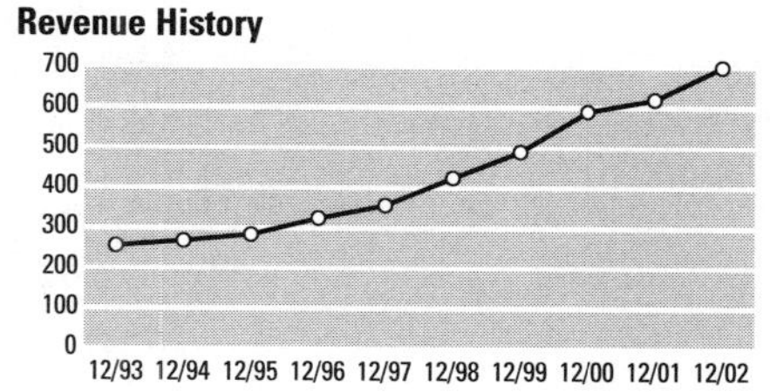

Sheehy Auto Stores

Don't blame Sheehy Auto Stores (formerly VinCo Management) for heavy traffic on the beltway around the nation's capital. Sheehy just sells cars; *people* drive. Sheehy Auto Stores operates 17 Sheehy auto franchises in the Washington, DC, area: seven in Maryland and nine in Virginia. The company's dealerships sell new Chevrolet, Dodge, Ford, Honda, Isuzu, Kia, Mitsubishi, and Nissan vehicles. All Sheehy dealerships sell used cars and offer financing, leasing, and service. Customers can order parts and make service appointments online through the company's Web site. President Vince Sheehy owns the company.

EXECUTIVES

President: Vincent A. (Vince) Sheehy, age 44
CFO: Michael Larkin
Operations Manager: Neil Desmond
Marketing Manager: Kevin Scrimgeour
Director of Training Center: Dane Basl

LOCATIONS

HQ: 12450 Fair Lakes Circle, Ste. 380, Fairfax, VA 22033
Phone: 703-802-3480 **Fax:** 703-802-3481
Web: www.sheehy.com

COMPETITORS

Atlantic Automotive
Brown Automotive
Hall Auto World
Jim Koons Automotive
March/Hodge
Ourisman Automotive
pohanka automotive
Rosenthal Automotive

HISTORICAL FINANCIALS

Company Type: Private

Income Statement FYE: December 31

	REVENUE ($ mil.)	NET INCOME ($ mil.)	NET PROFIT MARGIN	EMPLOYEES
12/01	600	—	—	—
12/00	500	—	—	—
12/99	368	—	—	—
12/98	292	—	—	—
12/97	343	—	—	—
12/96	323	—	—	—
Annual Growth	13.2%	—	—	—

Revenue History

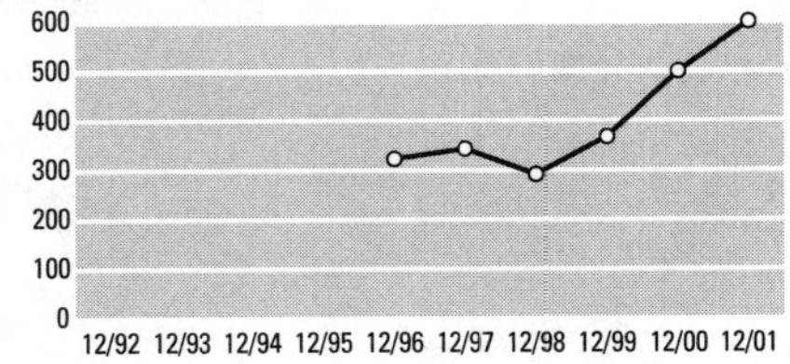

Sheetz, Inc.

You might say Sheetz is to the convenience store business what Wal-Mart is to discount shopping. Noted for being exceptionally large (stores average 4,200 sq. ft., nearly twice the size of the average 7-Eleven, but new stores are planned to be 4,700 sq. ft.), Sheetz stores sell groceries, fountain drinks, baked goods, and made-to-order sandwiches and salads, as well as discount gas and cigarettes. The company operates about 280 combination convenience stores and gas stations, mostly in small and midsized towns in Pennsylvania, but also in towns throughout Maryland, Ohio, Virginia, and West Virginia. Founded in 1952 by Bob Sheetz, the company is owned and run by the Sheetz family.

EXECUTIVES

Chairman: Stephen G. Sheetz, age 55
President and CEO: Stanton R. Sheetz, age 47
EVP Marketing: Louie Sheetz
EVP Operations: Dan McMahon
VP Finance: Joseph S. Sheetz
VP and General Counsel: Mike Cortez
VP Human Resources: Phil Freeman
VP Marketing: Bill Reilly
VP Petroleum Supply: Mike Lorenz
VP Real Estate: Joseph M. Sheetz

LOCATIONS

HQ: 5700 6th Ave., Altoona, PA 16602
Phone: 814-946-3611 **Fax:** 814-946-4375
Web: www.sheetz.com

PRODUCTS/OPERATIONS

Selected Products

Dot'z Bakery items
MTO (Made to Order) sandwiches
Nachos
Salads
Schmuffin breakfast sandwiches

COMPETITORS

7-Eleven
BP
Convenience USA
Cumberland Farms
Exxon Mobil
Giant Eagle
Kroger
Motiva Enterprises
Sunoco
Uni-Marts
Wawa

HISTORICAL FINANCIALS

Company Type: Private

Income Statement FYE: September 30

	REVENUE ($ mil.)	NET INCOME ($ mil.)	NET PROFIT MARGIN	EMPLOYEES
9/02	1,920	—	—	8,500
9/01	1,900	—	—	7,500
9/00	1,620	—	—	7,000
9/99	1,161	—	—	6,200
9/98	952	—	—	4,950
9/97	877	—	—	5,500
9/96	756	—	—	4,900
9/95	750	—	—	4,525
9/94	689	—	—	4,100
9/93	577	—	—	3,600
Annual Growth	14.3%	—	—	10.0%

Revenue History

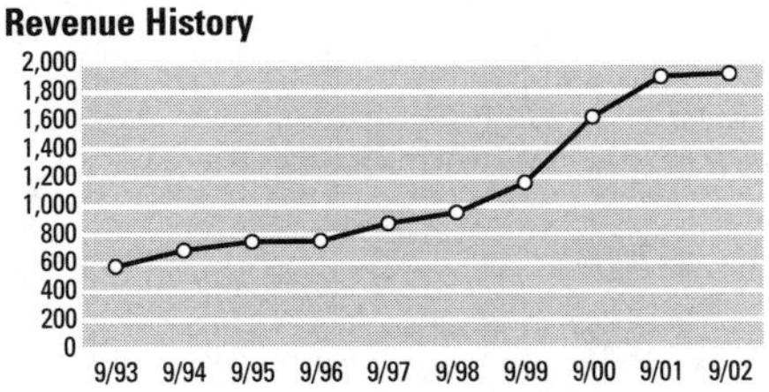

Sherwood Food Distributors

They don't slaughter the cows or grind the sausage, but Sherwood Food Distributors (SFD) will deliver the meat. The company is one of the largest wholesale distributors of meat and poultry in the US. SFD ships over 12 million pounds of meat from packers such as Cargill, Hormel, and Perdue Farms, and delivers it to grocery retailers, food manufacturers, and food service distributors in the Midwest and eastern US. The company operates distribution centers in Detroit, Cleveland, and Cincinnati. SFD was formed in 1987 by the merger of the food distribution operations of Orleans International and Regal Packaging, each of which owns half of the company.

EXECUTIVES

Managing Partner: Earl Ishbia
Managing Partner: J. Lawrence (Larry) Tushman
CFO: Lon Makanoff
Operations Director: Phil Walega
Human Resource Manager: Carole Stearn

LOCATIONS

HQ: 18615 Sherwood St., Detroit, MI 48234
Phone: 313-366-3100 **Fax:** 313-366-8825
Web: www.sherwoodfoods.com

COMPETITORS

Colorado Boxed Beef
Empire Beef
Gordon Food Service
Stock Yards Packing
Wolverine Packing

HISTORICAL FINANCIALS

Company Type: Private

Income Statement FYE: October 31

	REVENUE ($ mil.)	NET INCOME ($ mil.)	NET PROFIT MARGIN	EMPLOYEES
10/02	762	—	—	700
10/01	830	—	—	700
10/00	750	—	—	500
10/99	725	—	—	500
10/98	750	—	—	500
10/97	750	—	—	500
10/96	750	—	—	500
10/95	645	—	—	500
10/94	499	—	—	480
10/93	453	—	—	254
Annual Growth	6.0%	—	—	11.9%

Revenue History

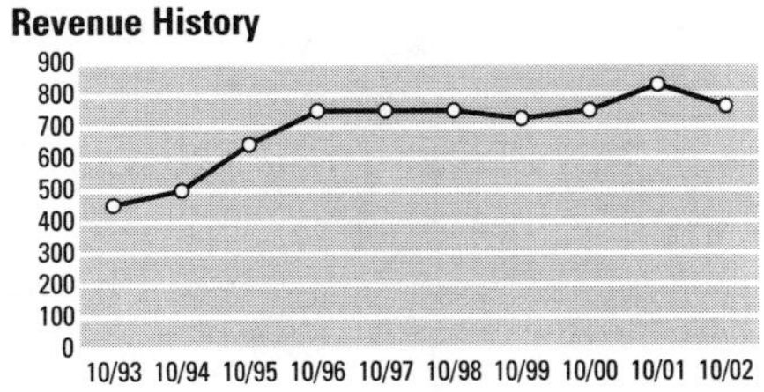

Shorenstein Company LLC

Shorenstein helps businesses shore up in new places. The company is one of the US's largest and oldest privately owned real estate firms, owning interests in or managing some 20 million sq. ft. of office space. It is also one of the largest office landlords in San Francisco, where about 7 million sq. ft. of its properties are located. Shorenstein invests in large, high-quality office buildings that it operates and manages itself; a subsidiary manages office properties for institutional investors. The firm also offers a line of closed-end funds that invest in office properties. Founded by Walter Shorenstein after WWII, the company is now owned by his son, chairman and CEO Douglas Shorenstein.

EXECUTIVES

Chairman Emeritus and Founder: Walter H. Shorenstein
Chairman and CEO: Douglas W. Shorenstein
President: Glenn A. Shannon
Managing Director and CFO: Richard A. Chicotel
SEVP: Stanley L. Berger
EVP and Senior Investment Manager: Thomas W. Hart
EVP and Director, Finance and Accounting: Debra H. Paul
Public Relations: Sarah Keaton
Auditors: Deloitte & Touche LLP

LOCATIONS

HQ: Bank of America Center, 555 California St., 49th Fl., San Francisco, CA 94104
Phone: 415-772-7000 **Fax:** 415-398-6682
Web: www.shorenstein.com

Shorenstein manages or owns properties in Charlotte, North Carolina; Chicago; Kansas City, Missouri; New Orleans; New York; Oakland, California; Philadelphia; Phoenix; Sacramento, California; San Francisco; Somers, New York; and Waltham, Massachusetts.

COMPETITORS

Alexandria Real Estate Equities
AmeriVest
Bedford Property
Boston Properties
CarrAmerica
Equity Office Properties Trust
London Merchant
Mission West Properties
Silverstein Properties
SL Green Realty
Witkoff Group

HISTORICAL FINANCIALS

Company Type: Private

Income Statement FYE: December 31

	ESTIMATED REVENUE ($ mil.)	NET INCOME ($ mil.)	NET PROFIT MARGIN	EMPLOYEES
12/01	750	—	—	550
12/00	750	—	—	550
12/99	750	—	—	620
12/98	750	—	—	620
12/97	750	—	—	620
12/96	600	—	—	700
12/95	545	—	—	700
12/94	550	—	—	650
Annual Growth	4.5%	—	—	(2.4%)

Revenue History

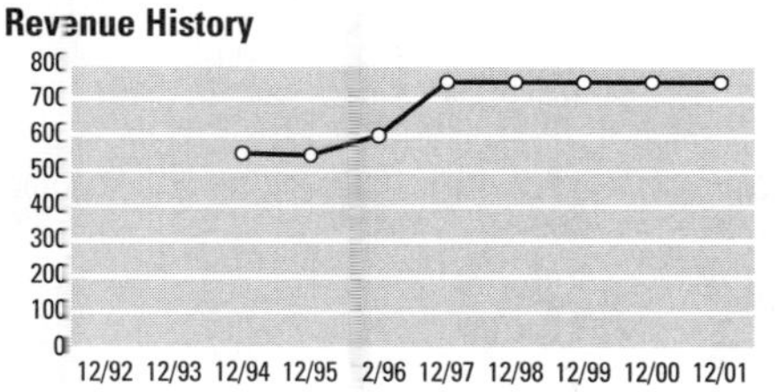

Sidley Austin Brown & Wood

Sidley Austin Brown & Wood aims to be a one-stop shop for corporate clients needing legal help. The law firm was created in 2001 by the merger of Chicago-based Sidley & Austin (founded by Norman Williams and John Thompson in 1866) and Wall Street-based Brown & Wood (established in 1914 in New York City). The firm employs more than 1,500 attorneys around the world, including Chicago and five other US cities. The firm's practices include financial transactions, antitrust, bankruptcy, intellectual propety and taxes. Clients have included AT&T and Citigroup.

The World Trade Center office was destroyed by terrorist attacks in 2001; new space was leased.

EXECUTIVES

Chairman Executive Committee: Thomas A. Cole
Chairman Management Committee: Charles W. Douglas
Vice Chairman Management Committee: Thomas R. Smith Jr., age 65
Executive Director: Timothy Bergen
CIO: Nancy Karen
Chief Marketing Officer, Chicago: Nancy Villano
Chief Marketing Officer, New York: Jan Zagorin
Director Human Resources, Firmwide: Michael Prapuolenis
Controller: Christian Cooley

LOCATIONS

HQ: Sidley Austin Brown & Wood LLP
Bank One Plaza, 10 S. Dearborn St.,
Chicago, IL 60603
Phone: 312-853-7000 **Fax:** 312-853-7036
Web: www.sidley.com

Sidley & Austin has US offices in Chicago, Dallas, Los Angeles, New York City, San Francisco, and Washington, DC. It has international offices in Beijing, Geneva, Hong Kong, London, Shanghai, Singapore, and Tokyo.

PRODUCTS/OPERATIONS

Selected Practice Areas

Antitrust and trade regulation
Banking and finance
Corporate
Cyberlaw
Employee benefits
Entertainment finance
Environmental
Intellectual property
Litigation
Real estate
Securities
Tax
Telecommunications

COMPETITORS

Baker & McKenzie
Jenner & Block
Jones Day
Katten Muchin
Kirkland & Ellis
Latham & Watkins
Mayer, Brown, Rowe & Maw
McDermott, Will
Morgan, Lewis
Skadden, Arps
White & Case
Winston & Strawn

HISTORICAL FINANCIALS

Company Type: Partnership

Income Statement FYE: December 31

	REVENUE ($ mil.)	NET INCOME ($ mil.)	NET PROFIT MARGIN	EMPLOYEES
12/02	831	—	—	2,913
12/01	715	—	—	3,000
12/00	670	—	—	3,000
12/99	446	—	—	2,000
12/98	421	—	—	2,000
12/97	360	—	—	1,952
12/96	303	—	—	1,848
12/95	277	—	—	1,623
12/94	255	—	—	1,606
12/93	252	—	—	1,613
Annual Growth	14.2%	—	—	6.8%

Revenue History

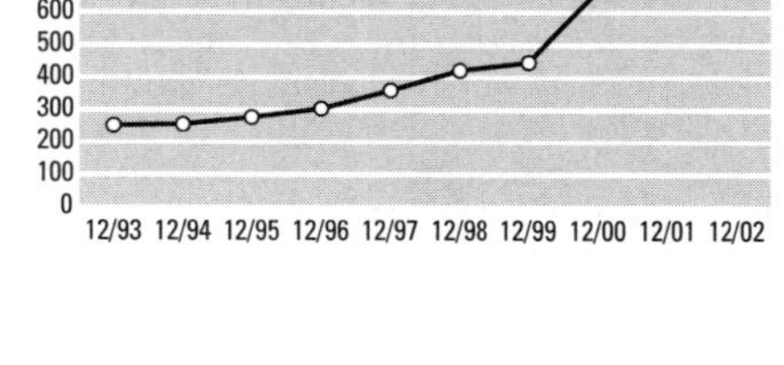

Siegel-Robert

Siegel-Robert is molding the future of plastic automotive components. The company is a leading maker of injection-molded plastic products for the automotive industry, as well as a diversified range of other manufacturers. The automotive division makes such items as door handles, emblems, radiator grilles, interior trim components, and side moldings. The company's diversified products division makes items such as texturized computer housings, light housings, and decorative faucet assemblies. Siegel-Roberts also offers chrome plating, painting, and assembly services for the products it makes.

EXECUTIVES

President and CEO: David A. Adams
VP and Treasurer: Robert Bowron
Director, Recruiting: Tom Barry

LOCATIONS

HQ: Siegel-Robert, Inc.
12837 Flushing Meadows Dr., St. Louis, MO 63131
Phone: 314-965-2444 **Fax:** 314-544-8472
Web: www.srob.com

Siegel-Robert operates eight manufacturing facilities in Arakansas, Georgia, Kentucky, Missouri, and Tennessee, and maintains sales offices in Mexico, and the UK.

PRODUCTS/OPERATIONS

Selected Products

Automotive Components
Body side moldings
Door handles
Consoles and seat trim
Emblems
Exterior mirrors
Headlamp housings
Instrument panels
Interior trim components
Knobs, levers, and buttons
Modular front end assemblies
Nameplates
Radiator grilles
Side moldings
Tail lamp housings
Wheelcovers

Diversified Products
Computer housings
Electrical cable assemblies
Decorative faucet assemblies
Decorative nameplates
Painted furniture fixtures
Plumbing fixtures
Shower spray head assemblies

COMPETITORS

A. Schulman
Balda
Collins & Aikman
Donnelly
Dura Automotive
Gentex
JPE
Key Plastics
Lacks Enterprises
McKechnie
Nippon Light Metal
Plastic Omnium
Summa Industries
Venture Industries

HISTORICAL FINANCIALS

Company Type: Private

Income Statement FYE: December 31

	REVENUE ($ mil.)	NET INCOME ($ mil.)	NET PROFIT MARGIN	EMPLOYEES
12/02	550	—	—	4,500
12/01	540	—	—	4,500
12/00	500	—	—	4,000
12/99	500	—	—	3,500
12/98	485	—	—	3,100
Annual Growth	3.2%	—	—	9.8%

Revenue History

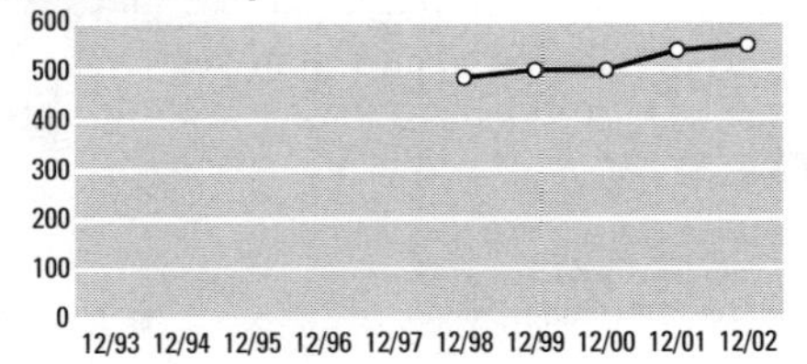

Sierra Pacific Industries

Sierra Pacific Industries (SPI) isn't your run-of-the-mill company. One of the largest US landowners, it manufactures millwork products and lumber in Northern California. Subsidiary Sierra Pacific Windows makes aluminum clad and wood patio doors and specialty windows. It also owns 1.5 million acres of California timberlands. SPI's cogeneration plants recycle wood waste into electricity that is used to power its plants; excess electricity is sold to local utilities and energy service providers. SPI traces its roots to a company started in the late 1920s by R. H. "Curly" Emmerson, father of CEO Red Emmerson. The third generation of the Emmerson family owns and operates Sierra Pacific.

Protests in the 1980s against logging on public land prompted the company to begin buying its own forested areas, a practice the company continues. However, SPI has announced plans to sell 30,000 to 50,000 acres of forestland to the US Forest Service for preservation. The company is also embarking on a new operation — property development. SPI has determined that some of its acquired land tracts are better suited for residential or commercial development than for growing trees.

EXECUTIVES

President: A. A. (Red) Emmerson
VP, Financial: Mark Emmerson
VP, Sales and Marketing: George Emmerson
President, Sierra Pacific Foundation: Carolyn Emmerson Dietz
Data Processing Manager: Steve Gaston
Director, Human Resources: Ed Bond

LOCATIONS

HQ: 19794 Riverside Ave., Anderson, CA 96007
Phone: 530-378-8000 **Fax:** 530-378-8109
Web: www.spi-ind.com

PRODUCTS/OPERATIONS

Selected Products

Aluminum-clad windows and doors
Cedar fencing
Chips for pulp mills
Decorative bark
Dimension lumber
Douglas Fir timbers
Millwork
Poles
Shavings for particleboard
Wood windows and doors

COMPETITORS

Atrium
Georgia-Pacific Corporation
International Paper
Louisiana-Pacific
Marshfield DoorSystems
MAXXAM
North Pacific Group
Simpson Investment
Weyerhaeuser

HISTORICAL FINANCIALS

Company Type: Private

Income Statement FYE: December 31

	ESTIMATED REVENUE ($ mil.)	NET INCOME ($ mil.)	NET PROFIT MARGIN	EMPLOYEES
12/02	1,300	—	—	3,900
12/01	1,315	—	—	3,700
12/00	1,500	—	—	3,600
12/99	1,450	—	—	3,600
12/98	1,100	—	—	3,000
12/97	1,000	—	—	3,200
12/96	1,000	—	—	3,200
12/95	950	—	—	3,100
12/94	770	—	—	3,000
12/93	733	—	—	2,800
Annual Growth	6.6%	—	—	3.8%

Revenue History

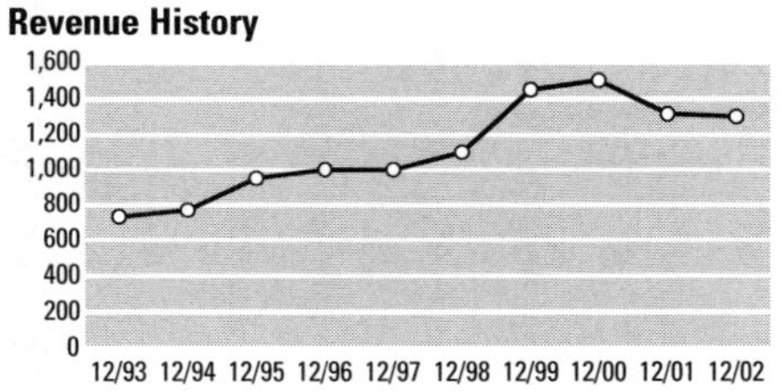

Sigma Plastics Group

The plastic sheeting and film business is not Greek to Sigma Plastics. Having grown through acquisitions, the company (one of the largest of its kind in North America) produces plastic film and sheet for industrial, institutional, and government markets. Sigma's Zeta Consumer Products subsidiary filed for bankruptcy and was then sold, marking the end of Sigma's foray into the housewares business. The company manufactures its diverse range of plastic products on 700 extrusion lines at its plants in 23 North American locations. Chairman and CEO Alfred Teo owns Sigma.

EXECUTIVES

Chairman and CEO, Sigma Plastics, Zeta Consumer Products, and Bio Starr; Chairman and Co-CEO, Aargus; Chairman, FlexSol Holding: Alfred S. Teo, age 57
President and COO, Sigma Stretch Film: Robert Nocek
CEO, FlexSol Holding: Brian Stevenson
CFO, Zeta Consumer Products Corp.: John Reier
Director, Human Resources: Debra Barbour

LOCATIONS

HQ: Page & Schuyler Ave., Bldg. #8, Lyndhurst, NJ 07071
Phone: 201-933-6000 **Fax:** 201-933-6429

Sigma has 23 manufacturing facilities throughout North America.

COMPETITORS

Bemis
DuPont
Huntsman International
Inteplast
Pactiv
Raven Industries
Sealed Air
Sonoco Products
Spartech
Tyco International

HISTORICAL FINANCIALS

Company Type: Private

Income Statement FYE: October 31

	REVENUE ($ mil.)	NET INCOME ($ mil.)	NET PROFIT MARGIN	EMPLOYEES
10/02	750	—	—	3,100
10/01	765	—	—	3,100
10/00	720	—	—	2,400
10/99	720	—	—	2,400
10/98	765	—	—	3,000
10/97	485	—	—	2,500
10/96	400	—	—	2,150
10/95	325	—	—	1,800
10/94	265	—	—	1,200
10/93	112	—	—	—
Annual Growth	23.5%	—	—	12.6%

Revenue History

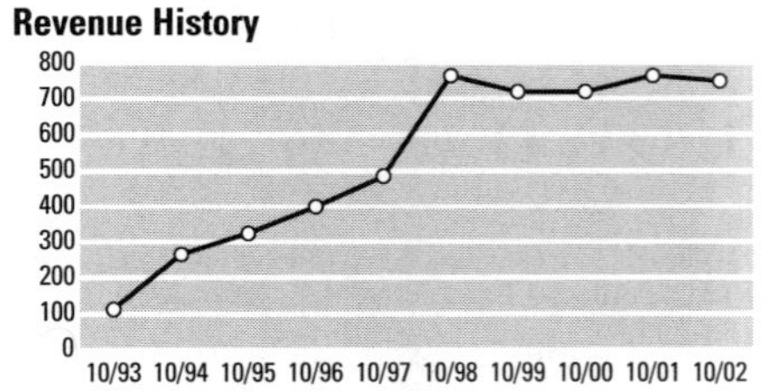

Silver Line Building Products

At Silver Line Building Products, when employees look out the window, it's not daydreaming — it's their job! Silver Line is one of the largest manufacturers of vinyl windows in the US. The company targets the new-construction and replacement markets with a range of designs, from double-hung and picture windows to custom-made octagonal and quarter-round window styles. It also makes sliding-glass patio doors. Customers include building-supply stores such as The Home Depot, specialty window dealers, and lumberyards. Silver Line offers its American Craftsman line through Home Depot, its largest customer. The company was founded in 1947 by Arthur Silverman; today it is run by his son, Kenneth Silverman.

EXECUTIVES

President and CEO: Kenneth Silverman
CFO: Kathleen Bloch
VP Administration: Mark Steinbauer
Director, Human Resources: Robert Perez

LOCATIONS

HQ: Silver Line Building Products Corporation
1 Silverline Dr., North Brunswick, NJ 08902
Phone: 732-435-1000 **Fax:** 732-418-0190
Web: www.silverlinewindow.com

Silver Line Building Products operates manufacturing facilities in Georgia, Illinois, New Jersey, and Texas.

PRODUCTS/OPERATIONS

Selected Products

Awning windows
Basement hopper windows
Bay and bow windows
Casement windows
Double-hung windows
Garden windows
Picture windows
Single-hung windows
Sliding glass doors
Sliding windows

COMPETITORS

Andersen Corporation
Associated Materials
Atrium
Butler Manufacturing
JELD-WEN
Nortek
Owens Corning
Pella
Sierra Pacific Industries
Thermal Industries
Therma-Tru

HISTORICAL FINANCIALS

Company Type: Private

Income Statement FYE: December 31

	ESTIMATED REVENUE ($ mil.)	NET INCOME ($ mil.)	NET PROFIT MARGIN	EMPLOYEES
12/02	500	—	—	6,000
12/01	500	—	—	4,600
Annual Growth	0.0%	—	—	30.4%

Revenue History

Simmons Company

Simmons sleeps tight as the #3 US mattress maker, behind Sealy and Serta. The firm makes and distributes mattresses and accessories under the BackCare, Beautyrest, Deep Sleep, DreamScapes, Olympic Queen, and Simmons labels. It licenses its trademarks for retail stores and to makers of beds and sleeping aids. Simmons sells through nearly 8,000 furniture outlets, department stores, and specialty shops. Simmons also owns nearly 70 retail World of Sleep and Mattress Gallery outlets in the US. Directors Peter Lamm, Richard Dresdale, and Mark Genender, through investment firm Fenway Partners, own about 85% of Simmons; Simmons' employees and Investcorp own the rest. Zalmon Simmons founded the firm in 1871.

EXECUTIVES

Chairman and CEO: Charles R. Eitel, age 53, $1,141,122 pay
President and Director: Robert W. (Bob) Hellyer, age 43, $569,915 pay
EVP and COO: Mark A. Parrish, age 37, $474,929 pay
EVP, CFO, Assistant Treasurer, Assistant Secretary, and Director: William S. Creekmuir, age 47, $549,758 pay
EVP Human Resources and Assistant Secretary: Rhonda Rousch, age 48, $273,761 pay
SVP, General Counsel, and Secretary: Kristen K. McGuffey, age 37
SVP Marketing: Donald J. Hofmann, age 50
SVP Sales: Kevin Damewood, age 46
Auditors: PricewaterhouseCoopers LLP

LOCATIONS

HQ: One Concourse Pkwy., Ste. 800, Atlanta, GA 30328
Phone: 770-512-7700 **Fax:** 770-392-2560
Web: www.simmons.com

PRODUCTS/OPERATIONS

Selected Brands

BackCare
Beautyrest
DeepSleep
DreamScapes
Olympic Queen
Simmons

COMPETITORS

DUX
The Nautilus Group
Premier Bedding Group
Sealy
Select Comfort
Serta
Spring Air
TWI Holdings

HISTORICAL FINANCIALS

Company Type: Private

Income Statement FYE: Last Saturday in December

	REVENUE ($ mil.)	NET INCOME ($ mil.)	NET PROFIT MARGIN	EMPLOYEES
12/02	670	24	3.6%	2,900
12/01	680	(1)	—	2,800
12/00	727	(11)	—	3,300
12/99	620	(9)	—	2,700
12/98	601	—	—	2,800
12/97	550	—	—	2,800
12/96	530	—	—	2,700
12/95	490	—	—	2,600
Annual Growth	4.6%	—	—	1.6%

2002 Year-End Financials

Debt ratio: —
Return on equity: —
Cash ($ mil.): 6
Current ratio: 1.33
Long-term debt ($ mil.): 242

Net Income History

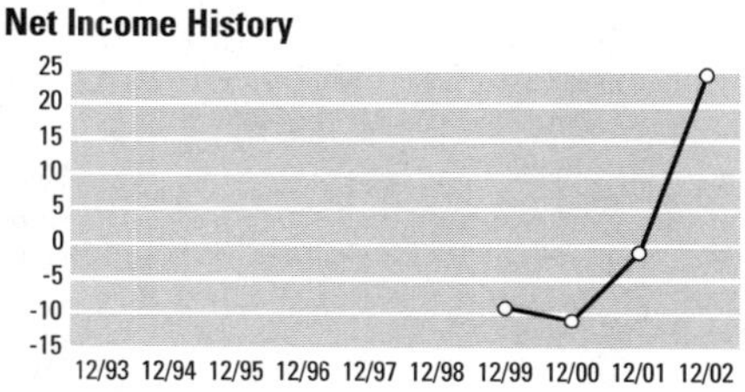

Simpson Investment Company

Simpson Investment Company is one of the oldest privately owned forest products companies in the northwestern US. The holding company makes paper and lumber products through its subsidiaries, Simpson Timber and Simpson Paper. Simpson Timber owns timberlands and operates converting facilities in California, Oregon, and Washington, where it produces dimension lumber and plywood; its Simpson Door Company makes stile and rail wood-panel doors. Simpson Paper, through subsidiary Simpson Tacoma Kraft, makes bleached and unbleached kraft pulp and linerboard used in packaging (boxes and grocery bags). Simpson Paper also recycles cardboard into paper. The Simpson family has controlled the firm since its founding in 1890.

EXECUTIVES

Chairman and CEO: Colin Moseley
CFO: Allan F. Trinkwald
Human Resources Manager: Linda Cronin

LOCATIONS

HQ: 1301 Fifth Ave., Ste. 2800, Seattle, WA 98101
Phone: 206-224-5000 **Fax:** 206-224-5060
Web: www.simpson.com

Simpson Investment Company has operations in the US in California, Oregon, and Washington.

PRODUCTS/OPERATIONS

Selected Products

Doors
Kraft papers
Lumber (Douglas fir, hemlock, and coastal redwood)
Plywood
Recycled cardboard
Wood chip and sawdust products (used to make fuel, landscaping products, and paper)

COMPETITORS

Boise Cascade
Georgia-Pacific Corporation
International Paper
Louisiana-Pacific
North Pacific Group
Rayonier
Roseburg Forest Products
West Fraser Timber
Weyerhaeuser

HISTORICAL FINANCIALS

Company Type: Private

Income Statement

FYE: December 31

	ESTIMATED REVENUE ($ mil.)	NET INCOME ($ mil.)	NET PROFIT MARGIN	EMPLOYEES
12/02	800	—	—	4,300
12/01	800	—	—	4,300
12/00	785	—	—	4,300
12/99	1,400	—	—	4,300
12/98	1,500	—	—	4,500
12/97	1,400	—	—	4,200
12/96	1,500	—	—	4,500
12/95	1,700	—	—	6,600
12/94	2,000	—	—	8,000
12/93	1,100	—	—	7,600
Annual Growth	(3.5%)	—	—	(6.1%)

Revenue History

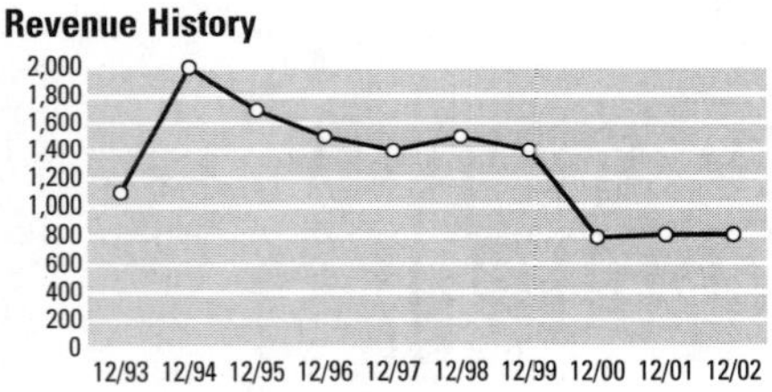

Simpson Thacher & Bartlett

When the urge to merge strikes corporate America, Simpson Thacher & Bartlett is ready to serve. It is one of the largest law firms in New York and a leader in assisting clients in mergers and acquisitions; the firm has had a hand in the Exxon-Mobil merger and America Online's acquisition of Time Warner. Other practice areas include capital markets, government investigations, intellectual property, labor, real estate, and tax. Simpson Thacher, which was founded in 1884, has offices in New York City and Los Angeles and Palo Alto, California, as well as Hong Kong, London, Singapore, and Tokyo.

EXECUTIVES

Chairman of the Executive Committee: Richard I. (Dick) Beattie, age 64
Director of Finance: Christopher Conroy
Director of Legal Employment: Dee Pifer
Business Development: Susan Bussy

LOCATIONS

HQ: 425 Lexington Ave., New York, NY 10017
Phone: 212-455-2000 **Fax:** 212-455-2502
Web: www.simpsonthacher.com

PRODUCTS/OPERATIONS

Selected Practice Areas

Antitrust
Capital markets and securities
Credit and banking
Exempt organizations
Government investigations and business crimes
Intellectual property
Labor and employment
Litigation
Mergers and acquisitions
Personal planning
Real estate
Tax

COMPETITORS

Cahill Gordon
Cleary, Gottlieb
Cravath, Swaine
Davis Polk
Debevoise & Plimpton
Proskauer Rose
Shearman & Sterling
Skadden, Arps
Sullivan & Cromwell
Wachtell, Lipton
Weil, Gotshal

HISTORICAL FINANCIALS

Company Type: Partnership

Income Statement

FYE: December 31

	REVENUE ($ mil.)	NET INCOME ($ mil.)	NET PROFIT MARGIN	EMPLOYEES
12/02	544	—	—	—
12/01	516	—	—	—
12/00	500	—	—	—
12/99	434	—	—	1,500
12/98	386	—	—	1,400
12/97	315	—	—	1,300
12/96	280	—	—	—
12/95	254	—	—	—
12/94	216	—	—	—
12/93	209	—	—	—
Annual Growth	11.2%	—	—	7.4%

Revenue History

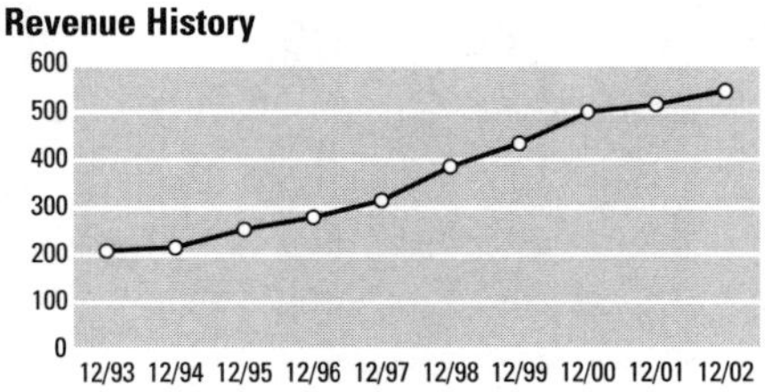

Sinclair Oil Corporation

Way out west, where fossils are found, brontosaur signs litter the ground. They belong to Sinclair Oil's more than 2,600 service stations and convenience stores in 22 western and midwestern US states. The company also operates three oil refineries, two pipelines (one jointly owned with ConocoPhillips), exploration operations, and a trucking fleet, all in the western US. It owns the Grand America Hotel, the Little America hotel chain, and two ski resorts (Sun Valley in Idaho and Snowbasin in Utah). Snowbasin was a venue of the 2002 Winter Olympics. The man behind all of this is Earl Holding, whose storied company, founded in 1916 by Harry Sinclair, was a central figure in the infamous Teapot Dome scandal.

EXECUTIVES

President and CEO: R. Earl Holding, age 76
VP Finance and Treasurer: Charles Barlow
VP Human Resources: Lowell Hardy
VP: Clint Ensign
General Manager Retail: Larry Rogers
Auditors: PricewaterhouseCoopers LLP

LOCATIONS

HQ: 550 E. South Temple, Salt Lake City, UT 84102
Phone: 801-524-2700 **Fax:** 801-524-2848
Web: www.sinclairoil.com

Sinclair Oil's operations include marketing offices in Colorado, Kansas, Minnesota, Missouri, and Texas; refineries in Oklahoma and Wyoming; trucking terminals in Colorado, Idaho, Iowa, Kansas, Missouri, Nebraska, Oklahoma, and Wyoming; and Little America hotels and resorts in Arizona, California, Idaho, Utah, and Wyoming.

PRODUCTS/OPERATIONS

Selected Operations

Oil and Gas
- Marketing
- Pipelines
- Product Terminals
- Refineries
- Trucking

Little America Hotels & Resorts

COMPETITORS

BP
Cendant
ConocoPhillips
Exxon Mobil
Giant Industries
Hilton
Marriott International
Royal Dutch/Shell Group
Vail Resorts
Valero Energy
Winter Sports

HISTORICAL FINANCIALS

Company Type: Private

Income Statement FYE: December 31

	ESTIMATED REVENUE ($ mil.)	NET INCOME ($ mil.)	NET PROFIT MARGIN	EMPLOYEES
12/01	2,300	—	—	6,900
12/00	1,900	—	—	6,500
12/99	1,200	—	—	5,600
12/98	1,300	—	—	5,600
12/97	1,700	—	—	5,600
12/96	1,400	—	—	5,600
12/95	1,225	—	—	—
12/94	1,050	—	—	—
12/93	1,385	—	—	—
12/92	1,385	—	—	—
Annual Growth	5.8%	—	—	4.3%

Revenue History

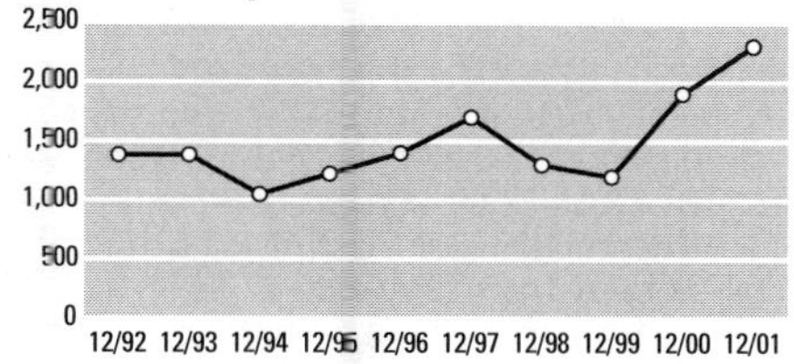

SIRVA, Inc.

Whether you're moving across the street, across town, or across the ocean, SIRVA will get your belongings where they need to be. One of the largest moving and relocation services companies in the world, SIRVA operates in more than 40 countries in Asia, Australia, Europe, and North America. Among its brands are SIRVA Relocation, Allied Van Lines, Global Van Lines, North American Van Lines, Pickfords, Allied Pickfords, Maison Huet, and Scanvan. Relocation services can include records management and home sale, purchase, and mortgage services, in addition to moving. Other SIRVA operations include logistics and insurance. Funds managed by investment firm Clayton, Dubilier & Rice own 81% of SIRVA.

EXECUTIVES

Chairman: James W. (Jim) Rogers, age 52
President, CEO, and Director: Brian P. Kelley, $444,822 pay
SVP and CFO: Joan E. Ryan, age 47
SVP and CIO: Ann M. Harten, age 41
SVP, General Counsel, and Secretary: Ralph A. Ford, age 56, $351,101 pay
SVP Human Resources: Todd W. Schorr, age 46
SVP Sales and Marketing: Tim Callahan
President, Moving Services: Michael P. Fergus, age 51, $446,232 pay
President , Network Services: Lawrence A. Writt, age 46, $373,539 pay
President, U.S. Moving and Specialized Transportation: John M. Dupuy, age 47 $348,133 pay
Auditors: PricewaterhouseCoopers LLP

LOCATIONS

HQ: 700 Oakmont Ln., Westmont, IL 60559
Phone: 630-570-3000 **Fax:** 630-570-3606
Web: www.sirva.com

PRODUCTS/OPERATIONS

2002 Sales

	$ mil.	% of total
Relocation		
North America	1,544.4	71
Europe & Asia/Pacific	408.0	18
Network Services	125.0	6
Transportation	108.2	5
Total	**2,185.6**	**100**

Selected Operating Companies

Allied International (moving services)
Allied Special Products (logistics)
Allied Van Lines (moving services)
Global Van Lines (moving services)
Maison Huet (moving services, France)
midiData (logistics, Germany)
National Association of Independent Truckers (insurance)
northAmerican Logistics
North American Van Lines (moving services)
Pickfords (moving services, UK)
Scanvan (moving services, Scandinavia)
SIRVA Logistics
SIRVA Relocation
TransGuard (insurance)

COMPETITORS

AMERCO
Atlas World Group
Bekins
Cendant
Graebel
Mayflower
Penske Truck Leasing
Prudential
Royal & Sun Alliance Insurance
UniGroup

HISTORICAL FINANCIALS

Company Type: Private

Income Statement FYE: December 31

	REVENUE ($ mil.)	NET INCOME ($ mil.)	NET PROFIT MARGIN	EMPLOYEES
12/02	2,186	21	1.0%	7,500
12/01	2,249	(17)	—	7,795
12/00	2,379	(22)	—	7,000
Annual Growth	(4.1%)	—	—	3.5%

2002 Year-End Financials

Debt ratio: 470.3%
Return on equity: 23.4%
Cash ($ mil.): 45
Current ratio: 0.98
Long-term debt ($ mil.): 572

Net Income History

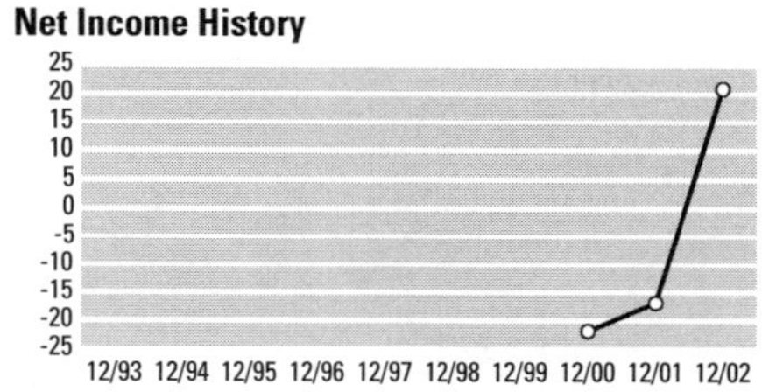

Skadden, Arps, Slate, Meagher & Flom LLP

Have you heard about the law firm that sued the business information publisher for a profile that opened with a wickedly clever lawyer joke? Neither have we, and we would like to keep it that way. Skadden, Arps, Slate, Meagher & Flom, the largest US law firm and one of the largest in the world, employs about 1,800 attorneys in 22 offices around the world. Founded in 1948, the firm offers counsel for corporate dealings, litigation, and international concerns. Skadden, Arps, Slate, Meagher & Flom has first-rate bankruptcy, litigation, and securities practices.

Widely known for its mergers and acquisitions (M&A) practice, Skadden, Arps is a giant in the field; between 1990 and 1999, the firm handled more than 1,000 deals. For example, the firm represented Germany's Mannesmann in the largest merger in history when it was acquired by Vodafone Group for about $180 billion.

HISTORY

Marshall Skadden, Leslie Arps, and John Slate hung out their shingle in New York City on April Fool's Day, 1948. Skadden and Arps came from a Wall Street law firm, and Slate had been counsel to Pan American World Airways. Without the reputation and connections of the established New York law firms, the firm found work one case at a time from referrals, handling mainly commercial, corporate, and litigations work. Marshall Skadden died in 1958.

Denied the luxury of steady clients, the firm was forced to be innovative and, at times, unorthodox. Joe Flom, who had joined as the firm's first associate, specialized in corporate law and proxy fights. During the 1960s, when tender offers and hostile takeovers increased, many of the more venerable firms referred clients engaged in the undignified corporate raids to Flom to preserve their gentlemanly reputations. With "white shoe" lawyers on Wall Street hesitant to tread into the uncivilized region of corporate takeovers, Skadden, Arps went for it, and the firm virtually pioneered the business of mergers and acquisitions (M&A) under Flom.

When Congress passed the Williams Act in 1968, which "legitimized" tender offers by providing regulation, other law firms started to get in on the act. Skadden, Arps was way ahead of the game, however, and as corporations and lawyers realized that aggressive legal tactics helped win corporate takeover battles, it also became apparent that Joe Flom was the expert. As takeover fights became more frequent in the early 1970s, the firm earned more than just respect. Earnings came not just from some of the highest hourly rates in the industry, but from hefty retainers (now a common practice at many firms) on the theory that association with Flom would scare raiders off. The only other name that could strike such fear in people's hearts was Marty Lipton of rival takeover specialists Wachtell, Lipton, Rosen & Katz. From the late 1970s through the 1980s, Skadden, Arps was involved in almost every important M&A case in the US.

The firm used its success in mergers and acquisitions to build its practice in other areas. In the early 1980s it branched into bankruptcy, product liability, and real estate law. By then it had opened offices in Boston; Chicago; Los Angeles; Washington, DC; and Wilmington, Delaware. Les Arps died in 1987.

With the boom in mergers and acquisitions activity and bankruptcies in the late 1980s, the firm grew to almost 2,000 lawyers by 1989. Then came the recession, and M&A work virtually dried up. Skadden, Arps responded by shedding more than 500 lawyers between 1989 and 1990. It also scrambled to diversify and expand internationally. As takeover activity rebounded in the mid-1990s, the diversification strategy actually began to work against Skadden, Arps because profits didn't skyrocket like those of M&A specialist firms.

The firm opened an office in Singapore in 1995 to coordinate its Asian business, signaling that city's growing importance as a financial center. Two years later two-thirds of the firm's Beijing team defected to a rival firm. Headquarters shrugged it off and flew in replacements. Skadden, Arps won one of its highest profile cases in 1998 when the sexual harassment suit brought against President Clinton by Paula Jones was thrown out.

With its M&A practice in full swing again, Skadden, Arps was involved in 70 announced M&A deals in 1999, including the $75 billion merger of oil companies Exxon and Mobil. It also became the first US law firm to reach $1 billion in revenue in 2000. (It passed the $1 billion mark again in 2001.) The company announced an alliance with Italian law firm Studio Chiomenti in mid-2001. The firm took part in three of the top ten M&A deals of 2002.

EXECUTIVES

Executive Partner: Robert C. Sheehan
Finance Director: Carol Sawdye
Director, Associate Development: Jodie R. Garfinkel
Director, Human Resources: Laurel Henschel
Director, Legal Hiring: Carol Lee H. Sprague
Director, Marketing & Communications: Sally Feldman
Director, Technology: Harris Z. Tilevitz
Senior Partner: Joseph H. Flom
Senior Partner, Corporate Practice: Roger S. Aaron
Senior Partner Litigation: William P. Frank
Managing Partner, Boston: Louis A. Goodman
Managing Partner, Chicago: Wayne W. Whalen
Managing Partner, Houston: Lyndon C. Taylor
Managing Partner, Los Angeles: Rand S. April
Managing Partner, New York: Irene A. Sullivan
Managing Partner, Palo Alto: Kenton J. King
Managing Partner, Reston: Ronald Barusch
Managing Partner, Washington: Michael P. Rogan
Managing Partner, Wilmington: Steven J. Rothschild
Managing Partner, Asian Practice: Phyllis G. Korff
Managing Partner, European Practice: Bruce M. Buck

LOCATIONS

HQ: 4 Times Square, New York, NY 10036
Phone: 212-735-3000 **Fax:** 212-735-2000
Web: www.skadden.com

US Offices

Boston
Chicago
Houston
Los Angeles
New York City
Newark, NJ
Palo Alto, CA
San Francisco
Washington, DC
Wilmington, DE

International Offices

Beijing
Brussels
Frankfurt
Hong Kong
London
Moscow
Paris
Singapore
Sydney
Tokyo
Toronto
Vienna

PRODUCTS/OPERATIONS

Selected Practice Areas

Antitrust
Banking and institutional investing
Corporate finance
Government affairs
Health care
Insurance
Intellectual property
International trade
Internet and e-commerce
Labor and employment law
Litigation
Mass torts and insurance litigation
Mergers and acquisitions
Real estate
Tax
Trusts and estates
White-collar crime

COMPETITORS

Baker & McKenzie
Cleary, Gottlieb
Clifford Chance
Cravath, Swaine
Davis Polk
Debevoise & Plimpton
Jones Day
Latham & Watkins
Mayer, Brown, Rowe & Maw
Paul, Weiss, Rifkind
Shearman & Sterling
Sidley Austin Brown & Wood
Simpson Thacher
Sullivan & Cromwell
Wachtell, Lipton
Weil, Gotshal
White & Case

HISTORICAL FINANCIALS

Company Type: Partnership

Income Statement

FYE: December 31

	REVENUE ($ mil.)	NET INCOME ($ mil.)	NET PROFIT MARGIN	EMPLOYEES
12/02	1,310	—	—	4,500
12/01	1,225	—	—	4,350
12/00	1,154	—	—	4,235
12/99	1,025	—	—	3,600
12/98	890	—	—	3,200
12/97	826	—	—	3,000
12/96	710	—	—	3,150
12/95	635	—	—	3,000
12/94	582	—	—	3,100
12/93	478	—	—	3,200
Annual Growth	11.9%	—	—	3.9%

Revenue History

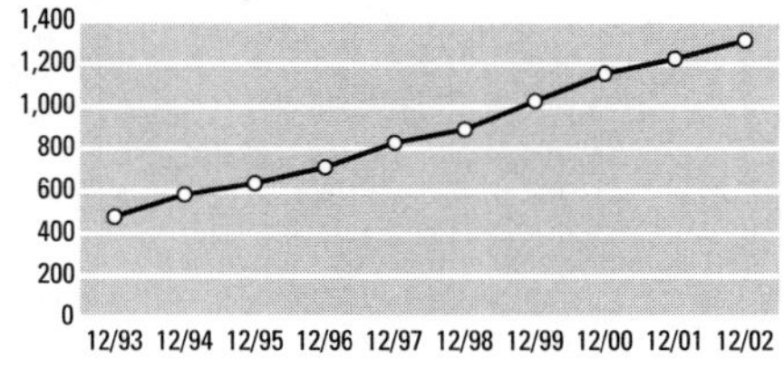

Smead Manufacturing Company

Smead Manufacturing wants to keep its customers organized. Accordingly, it makes a variety of paper-related and software products to organize and manage offices. Smead's first product, a bandless, expandable file, is still among the more than 5,000 items it makes for retail sale in office supply stores nationwide (including Office Depot and OfficeMax). Smead products range from hanging folders, labels, and binder covers to the more advanced Smeadlink software package, which manages hard copy and computerized documents. Products are sold worldwide. CEO Sharon Hoffman Avent owns Smead, which was founded in 1906 by her grandfather Charles Smead; her mother, Ebba Hoffman, ran the company for more than 40 years.

The company has acquired subsidiaries of The Lindegaard Group, a Norwegian maker of filing and organization products, desk accessories, and stationery products. The subsidiaries, which will help Smead expand into Eastern Europe, are in Denmark, Estonia, Finland, France, Norway, Sweden, and the UK.

EXECUTIVES

President and CEO: Sharon L. Hoffman Avent
SVP Sales and Marketing: David Fasbender
VP Finance and CFO: Dale Olson
VP Human Resources: Dean Schwanke
VP Information Services: Joseph Vossen
VP Marketing: Albert Arends
VP Operations: Walter (Wally) Glashan
VP Sales: Thomas Sullivan
President and Managing Director, Smead Europe: Simon Feenstra
Manager Marketing and Communications: Michael Buckley

LOCATIONS

HQ: 600 Smead Blvd., Hastings, MN 55033
Phone: 651-437-4111 **Fax:** 651-437-9134
Web: www.smead.com

Smead Manufacturing sells its products in more than 50 countries around the world. It has production and distribution facilities in California, Georgia, Minnesota, Ohio, South Carolina, Texas, Utah, and Wisconsin, and it has three manufacturing plants and eight sales offices in Europe.

PRODUCTS/OPERATIONS

Selected Products

Accessories (desktop, filing)
Binders and report covers
Color-coded folders and X-ray jackets
Custom-made products
End tab products
Expanding pockets
Hanging products
Poly products
Self-adhesive labels
Shelving
Top tab products

COMPETITORS

American Tissue
Avery Dennison
Cardinal Brands
Esselte
Fellowes
Fortune Brands
TAB Products

HISTORICAL FINANCIALS

Company Type: Private

Income Statement FYE: April 30

	REVENUE ($ mil.)	NET INCOME ($ mil.)	NET PROFIT MARGIN	EMPLOYEES
4/02	497	—	—	2,800
4/01	488	—	—	3,200
4/00	450	—	—	3,200
4/99	433	—	—	2,900
4/98	315	—	—	2,500
4/97	310	—	—	2,300
Annual Growth	9.9%	—	—	4.0%

Revenue History

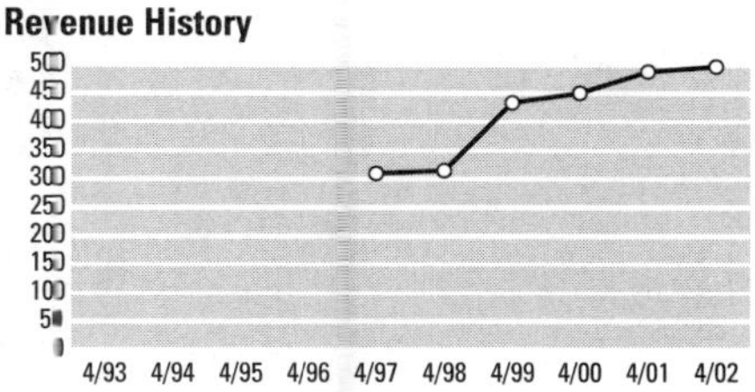

Smithsonian Institution

The Smithsonian Institution wears many hats, from the one worn by Harrison Ford in the Indiana Jones Trilogy to the one worn by Abraham Lincoln the night he was assassinated. The world's largest museum, the Smithsonian houses more than 140 million pieces in 16 museums and galleries. More than 35 million people every year come view its exhibits on art, music, TV and film, science, history, and other subjects. Admission to its museums, most of which are located on the National Mall in Washington, DC (two are in New York City), is usually free. The Smithsonian also operates the National Zoo and a handful of research facilities. The Smithsonian receives 57% of its operating revenue from the federal government.

The Smithsonian's exhibits display items such as the Declaration of Independence, the ruby slippers worn by Judy Garland in *The Wizard of Oz*, and the Wright Brothers' first airplane. A board of regents that includes Vice President Richard Cheney, Chief Justice William Rehnquist, six members of Congress, and nine private citizens leads the institution.

HISTORY

English chemist James Smithson wrote a proviso to his will in 1826 that would lead to the creation of the Smithsonian Institution. When he died in 1829, he left his estate to his nephew, Henry James Hungerford, with the stipulation that if Hungerford died without heirs, the estate would go to the US to create "an Establishment for the increase and diffusion of knowledge among men." Hungerford died in 1835 without any heirs, and the US government inherited more than $500,000 in gold.

Congress squandered the money after it was received in 1838, but perhaps feeling pangs of guilt, covered the loss. The Smithsonian was finally created in 1846, and Princeton physicist Joseph Henry was named as its first secretary. That year it established the Museum of Natural History, the Museum of History and Technology, and the National Gallery of Art. The Smithsonian's National Museum was developed around the collection of the US Patent Office in 1858. The Smithsonian continued to expand, adding the National Zoological Park in 1889 and the Smithsonian Astrophysical Observatory in 1890.

The Freer Gallery, a gift of industrialist Charles Freer, opened in 1923. The National Gallery was renamed the National Collection of Fine Arts in 1937, and a new National Gallery, created with Andrew Mellon's gift of his art collection and a building, opened in 1941. The Air and Space Museum was established in 1946.

More museums were added in the 1960s, including the National Portrait Gallery in 1962 and the Anacostia Museum (exhibits and materials on African-American history) in 1967. The Kennedy Center for the Performing Arts was opened in 1971. The Collection of Fine Arts was renamed the National Museum of American Art and the Museum of History and Technology was renamed the National Museum of American History in 1980.

The Smithsonian placed its first-ever contribution boxes in four of its museums in 1993. A planned exhibit featuring the Enola Gay — the plane that dropped the atomic bomb on Hiroshima — created a firestorm in 1994 with critics charging that the exhibit downplayed Japanese aggression and US casualties in WWII. The original exhibit was canceled in 1995, the director of the Air and Space Museum resigned, and a scaled-down version of the exhibit premiered.

Large contributions from private donors continued in the 1990s; the Mashantucket Pequot tribe gave $10 million from its casino operations in 1994 for a planned American Indian museum and prolific electronics inventor Jerome Lemelson donated $10.4 million in 1995. The museum celebrated its sesquicentennial in 1996 amid news that $500 million in repairs were needed over the next 10 years.

California real estate developer Kenneth Behring gave the largest cash donation ever to the museum in 1997 — $20 million for the National Museum of Natural History. Short of funds, the Smithsonian had to cut back on its 150th anniversary traveling exhibit that year. The Smithsonian announced a $26 million renovation for the National Museum of Natural History in 1998. Two years later Kenneth Behring quadrupled his record breaking 1997 donation of $20 million by giving $80 million to the National Museum of American History. Catherine Reynolds withdrew most of her $38 million gift in 2002 after the Smithsonian Institution refused to implement her ideas for an exhibit at the National Museum of American History.

EXECUTIVES

Secretary: Lawrence M. Small, age 61
CFO: Alice Maroni
Undersecretary, American Museums and National Programs: Sheila Burke
CEO, Smithsonian Business Ventures: Gary Beer
Director, International Art Museums Division: Thomas W. Lentz, age 48
Director, Government Relations: Nell Payne
Director, Human Resources: Carolyn E. Jones
Director, National Programs: Herma Hightower, age 58
Director, Communications: David J. Umansky
Director, Policy and Analysis: Carole Neeves
Director, American Art Museum: Elizabeth Broun
Director, National Air and Space Museum: John Dailey
Director, National Portrait Gallery: Marc Pachter
Director, National Zoological Park: Lucy H. Spelman, age 37
Director, Hirshhorn Museum: Ned Rifkin
Director, Planning, Management, and Budget: Bruce Dauer
General Counsel: John E. Huerta, age 57
Director National Museum of American History: Brent D. Glass

LOCATIONS

HQ: 1000 Jefferson Dr. SW, Washington, DC 20560
Phone: 202-357-2700 **Fax:** 202-786-2377
Web: www.smithsonian.org

The Smithsonian Institution has museums and galleries located in New York City and Washington, DC; its research centers are located in the US and Panama.

PRODUCTS/OPERATIONS

Museums and Research Centers

Anacostia Museum and Center for African American History & Culture
Archives of American Art
Arthur M. Sackler Gallery
Arts and Industries Building
Center for Folklife Programs and Cultural Heritage
Conservation and Research Center
Cooper-Hewitt, National Design Museum (New York City)
Freer Gallery of Art
Hirshhorn Museum and Sculpture Garden
National Air and Space Museum
National Museum of African Art
National Museum of American History
National Museum of Natural History
National Museum of the American Indian (New York City)
National Portrait Gallery
National Postal Museum
National Zoological Park
Smithsonian American Art Museum
Renwick Gallery
Smithsonian Astrophysical Observatory
Smithsonian Center for Latino Initiatives
Smithsonian Center for Materials Research and Education
Smithsonian Environmental Research Center
Smithsonian Institution Building (The Castle)
Smithsonian Marine Station at Fort Pierce
Smithsonian Tropical Research Institute

HISTORICAL FINANCIALS

Company Type: Not-for-profit

Income Statement FYE: September 30

	REVENUE ($ mil.)	NET INCOME ($ mil.)	NET PROFIT MARGIN	EMPLOYEES
9/02	691	—	—	—
9/01	665	—	—	—
9/00	604	—	—	6,500
9/99	563	—	—	6,400
9/98	775	—	—	—
9/97	729	—	—	6,469
9/96	703	—	—	6,487
9/95	750	—	—	6,600
9/94	605	—	—	6,671
9/93	730	—	—	6,800
Annual Growth	(0.6%)	—	—	(0.6%)

Revenue History

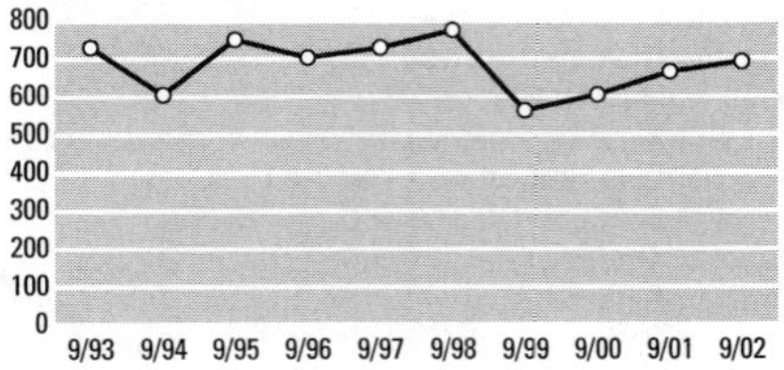

Soave Enterprises

Soave Enterprises is suave enough to manage multiple lines of business. The company provides capital to small businesses. Its diverse interests are divided into four groups: Industrial (including demolition and waste collection services), Metals Recycling (metals shredding and recycling), Real Estate (including residential, industrial, and recreational projects in six states), and Diversified (ranging from auto dealerships to beer distribution, hydroponic tomato gardening, ground transportation around Detroit Metro Airport, and insurance sales). The bulk of Soave's operations are in Michigan. President and CEO Anthony Soave, who founded the company in 1961, owns Soave Enterprises.

EXECUTIVES

President and CEO: Anthony L. Soave
EVP: Yale Levin
EVP: Peter C. Saputo
VP and CFO: Michael L. Piesko
VP: Kathleen B. McCann
Director, Human Resources: Marcia Moss

LOCATIONS

HQ: Soave Enterprises L.L.C.
3400 E. Lafayette St., Detroit, MI 48207
Phone: 313-567-7000 **Fax:** 313-567-0966
Web: www.soaveenterprises.com

Soave Enterprises operates primarily in Michigan, but the company also has businesses in Florida, Kansas, Illinois, Missouri, Ohio, Tennessee, Virginia, and Ontario, Canada.

PRODUCTS/OPERATIONS

Selected Operations

Industrial
City Concrete and Asphalt Crushing, LLC (portable concrete crushing services)
Inland Waters Pollution Control, Inc. (hazardous and non-hazardous waste collection and transportation)
M & M Contracting, L.L.C. (demolition services)
Power Vac Services, Inc. (waste hauling)

Materials Recycling
Autoshred of Michigan, Inc. (scrap steel shredder)
Far Western Trucking Company, Ltd. (raw materials transport, Canada)
SLC Recycling Industries, Inc. (nonferrous metals recycler)
Zalev Bros. Co. (scrap steel recycler)

Real Estate
Bay Dunes (golf course, Florida)
Brambleton (residential community, Virginia)
Cocahatchee (resort community, Florida)
The Dunes (condominium community, Florida)
The Regatta (residential resort community, Florida)
Trident Properties, Inc. (real estate developer with projects in Florida, Illinois, Michigan, and Virginia)

Other
Checker Cab Company (Detroit cab company)
Chicago Beer Distributing Co. (Anheuser-Busch distributor, Illinois)
City Aviation Services, Inc. (aircraft rental company)
Commuter Express (service ground transportation company near Detroit Metro Airport)
Great Northern Hydroponics (greenhouse tomato farm)
Heritage Motors (automobile dealership)
Independence Honda, Inc. (automobile dealership)
Independence Lincoln-Mercury, Inc. (automobile dealership)
Lakeshore Agency, Inc. (insurance agency)

COMPETITORS

Chaparral Steel
Continental Motors
David J. Joseph
KB Home
Lennar
Nucor
Republic Services
Russ Darrow
Ryerson Tull
Ryland
Schnitzer Steel
Steel Technologies
Tang Industries
Tube City
VT
Waste Management

HISTORICAL FINANCIALS

Company Type: Private

Income Statement FYE: December 31

	REVENUE ($ mil.)	NET INCOME ($ mil.)	NET PROFIT MARGIN	EMPLOYEES
12/01	900	—	—	2,000
12/00	878	—	—	1,835
12/99	807	—	—	2,100
12/98	625	—	—	1,400
12/97	533	—	—	1,000
Annual Growth	14.0%	—	—	18.9%

Revenue History

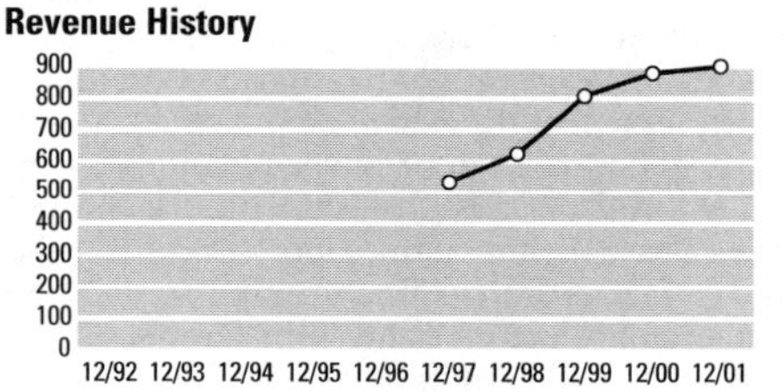

Software House International

Software House International (SHI) wants to put software in houses across the globe. The company distributes more than 100,000 hardware and software products from suppliers such as Adobe, Corel, Microsoft, and IBM. SHI also offers professional services such as systems integration and application development through its Software House Enterprise Solutions division. The company counts Agilent, AT&T, Boeing, and Hewlett-Packard among its clients. Founded in 1982, SHI has grown from a company with less than $1 million in annual revenue in 1989, when entrepreneur Thai Lee assumed ownership, to a company with more than $1 billion in annual revenues.

EXECUTIVES

Chairman and Co-CEO: Leo Koguan, age 48
President and Co-CEO: Thai Lee, age 45
CFO: Paul Ng
Human Resources: Anthony Salina

LOCATIONS

HQ: Software House International, Inc.
2 Riverview Dr., Somerset, NJ 08873
Phone: 732-764-8888 **Fax:** 732-764-8889
Web: www.shi.com

Software House International has offices in Canada, France, Hong Kong, the UK, and the US.

PRODUCTS/OPERATIONS

Selected Products

Cameras
Copiers
Fax machines
Hubs
Modems
Motherboards
Notebooks
PCs
Power supplies and surge protection equipment
Printers
Processors
Scanners
Servers
Software
Storage products
Switchers and routers

Selected Services

Application development
Asset management
Contract staffing
Desktop installation
E-commerce
Network consulting
Security management
Systems integration
Technical support

COMPETITORS

Arrow Electronics
ASI Corp.
Avnet
Bell Microproducts
CDW
Comark
CompuCom
GE Access
Ingram Micro
ICG
Merisel
Micro Warehouse
Pacific Magtron
SARCOM
Softmart
Supercom
Tech Data

HISTORICAL FINANCIALS

Company Type: Private

Income Statement FYE: December 31

	REVENUE ($ mil.)	NET INCOME ($ mil.)	NET PROFIT MARGIN	EMPLOYEES
12/02	1,797	—	—	900
12/01	1,730	—	—	1,000
12/00	1,390	—	—	1,000
12/99	909	—	—	1,000
Annual Growth	25.5%	—	—	(3.5%)

Revenue History

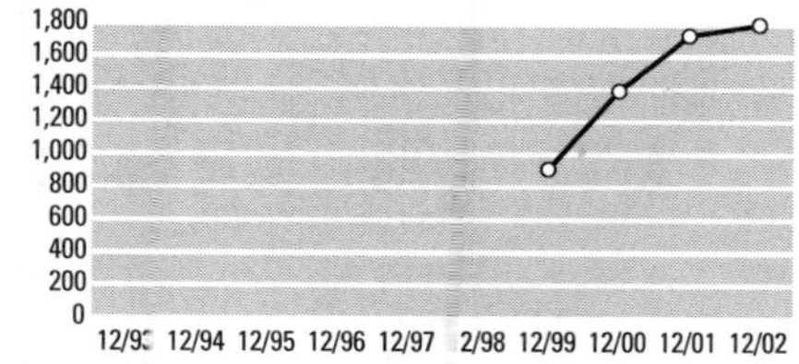

Solo Cup

Solo Cup's goodies are best enjoyed in the company of others. A leader in the disposable product market, the company makes cups, plates, bowls, storage containers, cutlery, and drinking straws. In addition to mass-market retailers Solo Cup's items are sold to end users, including restaurants, schools, hospitals, and coffee shops. The company has 14 manufacturing facilities and about a dozen warehouses. The firm's plastic, paper, and foam goods are sold, soiled, and thrown out around the world. Leo J. Hulseman founded the Paper Container Manufacturing Company in 1936; it became Solo Cup in 1946, named for the cone-shaped paper cup that made it famous. His descendants own and operate the company.

EXECUTIVES

CEO: Robert L. Hulseman
COO and CFO: Ronald L. Whaley
VP, Human Resources: Kathleen Wolf

LOCATIONS

HQ: Solo Cup Company
1700 Old Deerfield Rd., Highland Park, IL 60035
Phone: 847-831-4800 **Fax:** 847-831-5849
Web: www.solocup.com

Solo Cup sells its products in 50 countries around the world. It has distributors in Africa, Asia, the Caribbean, Europe, Latin America, the Middle East, the South Pacific, and the US.

PRODUCTS/OPERATIONS

Selected Products and Brands

Consumer Products Division
Cozy Cups
Party Line (plastic plates, bowls, cups)
SignatureColors (plastic plates, bowls, cups)
Solo Bathroom Cups
Solo Kitchen Cups
Storables (disposable storage containers)
Ultra Clear (clear and colored plastic cups)

Food Service Products Division
Cutlery
Dispensers
Foam containers
Paper plates, bowls, cups
Plastic plates, bowls, cups, lids, deli and food containers
Straws

COMPETITORS

American Greetings
Amscan
Berry Plastics
Dart Container
EarthShell
Huhtamäki
Pactiv
Rexam
Reynolds Food Packaging
SF Holdings

HISTORICAL FINANCIALS

Company Type: Private

Income Statement FYE: December 31

	ESTIMATED REVENUE ($ mil.)	NET INCOME ($ mil.)	NET PROFIT MARGIN	EMPLOYEES
12/01	900	—	—	4,700
12/00	833	—	—	4,700
Annual Growth	8.0%	—	—	0.0%

Revenue History

Southern States Cooperative

Founded in 1923 to provide affordable, high-quality seed to Virginia farmers, Southern States Cooperative serves about 321,000 members, mainly in midwestern and southern states. The co-op offers its farmer-owners feed and fertilizer manufacturing, seed processing, grain marketing, and petroleum and propane services, as well as wholesale farm supplies. Its Southern States and GardenSouth stores sell farm supplies, garden products, and fuel through about 740 outlets. Other services include GrowMaster Crop Services, sales financing, and an aquaculture program. Southern States Cooperative merged with Michigan Livestock Exchange in 1998 and purchased Agway Inc.'s consumer wholesale dealer business.

EXECUTIVES

Chairman: John Henry Smith, age 51
President and CEO: Thomas Scribner
EVP, Business Development: Joseph Koch
EVP and CFO: Leslie Newton
SVP, General Counsel, and Secretary:
N. Hopper Ancarrow Jr., age 56, $166,897 pay
VP and COO: Wesley Wright
VP and CIO: Karen Lankford
VP, Finance: Lee Whitney
VP, Human Resources: Jerry Walker
VP, Marketing and Independent Markets:
Steve Patterson
Director, Corporate Communications, Member Relations, and Public Affairs: Jim Erickson
Auditors: PricewaterhouseCoopers LLP

LOCATIONS

HQ: Southern States Cooperative, Incorporated
6606 W. Broad St., Richmond, VA 23230
Phone: 804-281-1000 **Fax:** 804-281-1413
Web: www.southernstates-coop.com

Southern States Cooperative has operations in Alabama, Arkansas, Delaware, Florida, Georgia, Indiana, Kentucky, Louisiana, Maryland, Michigan, Mississippi, North Carolina, Ohio, Pennsylvania, South Carolina, Texas, Virginia, and West Virginia.

COMPETITORS

Ag Processing
Ag Services
Agway
Andersons
ADM
CHS
ConAgra
Farmland Industries
GROWMARK
Scoular
Tractor Supply

HISTORICAL FINANCIALS

Company Type: Cooperative

Income Statement FYE: June 30

	REVENUE ($ mil.)	NET INCOME ($ mil.)	NET PROFIT MARGIN	EMPLOYEES
6/02	1,463	(68)	—	5,000
6/01	1,739	(15)	—	5,700
6/00	1,547	5	0.3%	5,425
6/99	1,366	(2)	—	6,000
6/98	1,120	11	1.0%	3,800
6/97	1,216	28	2.3%	3,800
6/96	1,123	28	2.5%	3,800
6/95	1,014	18	1.8%	3,800
6/94	950	7	0.8%	3,539
6/93	937	—	—	—
Annual Growth	5.1%	—	—	4.4%

2002 Year-End Financials

Debt ratio: 209.3%
Return on equity: —
Cash ($ mil.): 12
Current ratio: 1.84
Long-term debt ($ mil.): 267

Net Income History

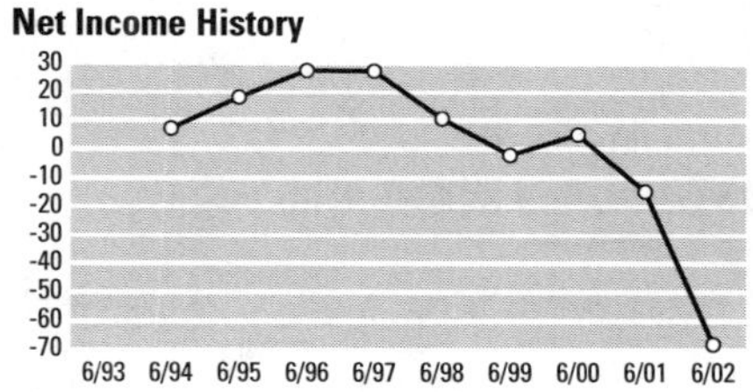

Southern Wine & Spirits

Fueled by alcohol and nicotine, Southern Wine & Spirits of America delivers market dominance. The firm is the #1 US distributor of wine and spirits, serving eleven states. In addition to importing and distributing wine and spirits, it distributes imported brews, such as Grolsch and Steinlager; cigars, such as Don Diego and Montecristo; and nonalcoholic beverages, including Clamato and Rose's Lime Juice. The company also owns large stakes in both Pacific Wine & Spirits (part of Terlato Wine Group) and Romano Bros.

Beverage, the largest spirits wholesaler in Illinois; it is also entering new markets elsewhere. Chairman and CEO Harvey Chaplin and his secretive family own more than 50% of the company.

EXECUTIVES

Chairman and CEO: Harvey Chaplin
President and COO: Wayne Chaplin
SVP, President of Wine Division: Melvin (Mel) Dick
First VP and Treasurer: Steven Becker
National Director of Human Resources: Mark Krauss
Director of Human Resources, Miami: Manny Chacon

LOCATIONS

HQ: Southern Wine & Spirits of America, Inc.
1600 NW 163rd St., Miami, FL 33169
Phone: 305-625-4171 **Fax:** 305-625-4720
Web: www.southernwineandspirits.com

Southern Wine & Spirits of America distributes products from 15 warehouses in Arizona, California, Colorado, Florida, Hawaii, Illinois, Kentucky, Nevada, New Mexico, Pennsylvania, and South Carolina. The company has exclusive rights to distribute Allied Domecq brands in California and Hawaii.

PRODUCTS/OPERATIONS

Selected Products

Beer
Cigars
Nonalcoholic beverages and mixes
Spirits
Wines

COMPETITORS

Altadis
Bacardi
Banfi Vintners
Ben E. Keith
Sunbelt Beverage
Constellation Brands
Geerlings & Wade
Georgia Crown Distributing
Glazer's Wholesale Drug
Johnson Brothers
National Distributing
National Wine & Spirits
Peerless Importers
Rémy Cointreau
Synergy Brands
Topa Equities
UST
Wirtz
Young's Market

HISTORICAL FINANCIALS

Company Type: Private

Income Statement

FYE: December 31

	REVENUE ($ mil.)	NET INCOME ($ mil.)	NET PROFIT MARGIN	EMPLOYEES
12/02	4,400	—	—	7,100
12/01	3,750	—	—	5,680
12/00	3,500	—	—	5,600
12/99	3,100	—	—	5,400
12/98	2,600	—	—	4,500
12/97	2,450	—	—	4,500
12/96	2,200	—	—	4,000
12/95	2,125	—	—	4,000
12/94	1,985	—	—	3,925
12/93	1,620	—	—	3,675
Annual Growth	11.7%	—	—	7.6%

Revenue History

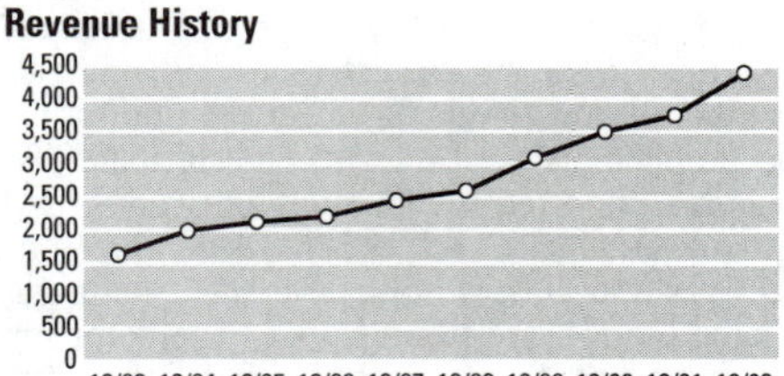

Southwire Company

Southwire hopes everyone's cable-ready. One of the world's largest cable and wire manufacturers, Southwire makes building wire and cable, utility cable products, industrial power cable, telecommunications cable, copper and aluminum rods, and cord products. The company also provides engineering and machining and fabrication services. Its Forte Power Systems subsidiary provides turnkey services for high-voltage systems using extruded-dielectric cable. Founded in 1950 by Roy Richards Sr. (the chairman's father), Southwire is owned by the Richards family.

Southwire will continue to build on its core operations, as evidenced by its purchase of General Cable Corporation's building wire assets, which made Southwire one of North America's largest producers of building wire. The company is also expanding its base of operations in Asia, such as the copper rod system deal with China's Jiangxi Copper Products Company that includes a furnace system complete with a loader, melter, holder and launder system, casting machine, and automatic metal pouring system.

EXECUTIVES

Chairman: Roy Richards Jr.
President and CEO: Stuart Thorn
VP, Finance: J. Guyton Cochran Jr.
VP, ITS: Lee Hunter
VP, Human Resources: Mike Wiggins
VP, Legal: Stanley Tate
VP, Operations: Jeff Herrin
VP, Sales and Marketing, Energy Division: Steve McClendon
Manager, Communications: Gary Leftwich

LOCATIONS

HQ: One Southwire Dr., Carrollton, GA 30119
Phone: 770-832-4242 **Fax:** 770-832-4929
Web: www.southwire.com

Southwire operates manufacturing plants in the US and sales offices in Hong Kong, Mexico City, and Paris.

PRODUCTS/OPERATIONS

Selected Products

Aluminum rod
Building wire
Communication cable
Copper rod
Electrical wire and cable
High voltage cable
Magnet wire
Specialty wire
Transit cable
Wire-making machinery

COMPETITORS

AFC Cable
Alcan
Alcatel
Alpine Group
Anixter International
Balfour Beatty
Belden
Bridon
Cable Design Technologies
Capro
Carlisle Companies
Encore Wire
General Cable
International Wire
Nexans
Phelps Dodge
Pirelli & C.
Showa Electric Wire & Cable
Sumitomo Electric
Superior TeleCom
Volex

HISTORICAL FINANCIALS

Company Type: Private

Income Statement

FYE: December 31

	ESTIMATED REVENUE ($ mil.)	NET INCOME ($ mil.)	NET PROFIT MARGIN	EMPLOYEES
12/02	1,700	—	—	3,400
12/01	1,500	—	—	3,300
12/00	1,500	—	—	3,000
12/99	1,300	—	—	4,000
12/98	1,400	—	—	4,500
12/97	1,700	—	—	4,900
12/96	1,700	—	—	5,000
12/95	1,900	—	—	5,200
12/94	1,600	—	—	5,000
12/93	1,300	—	—	5,000
Annual Growth	3.0%	—	—	(4.2%)

Revenue History

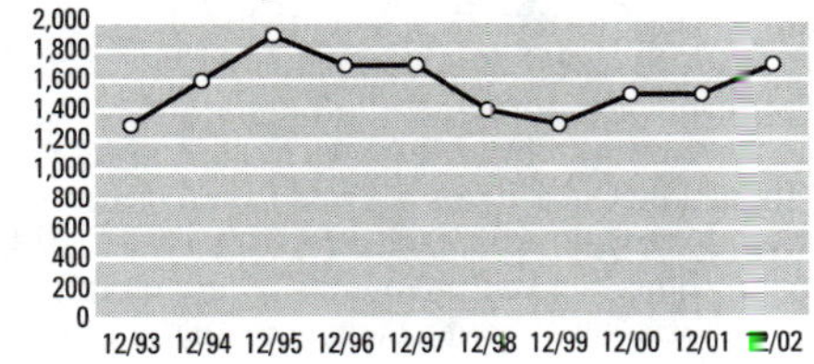

Spring Air Company

Spring Air is calling you to bed. The mattress company offers the Back Supporter, Four Seasons, and Comfort Caress Collection lines featuring amenities such as asthma and allergy sensitive fabrics and silk and wool blend mattresses to control body temperature. Selling products worldwide through furniture retailers, department stores, and bedding stores, Spring Air is the #4 US mattress manufacturer (behind Sealy, Serta, and Simmons). Spokespersons for Spring Air include game show hostess Vanna White and a live Kodiak bear which tests mattresses. Spring Air was founded in 1926 by mattress innovator Francis Karr, who introduced an offset-coil that adjusts to sleepers' weight. Spring Air Partners owns the company.

EXECUTIVES

Chairman: Eric Spitzer
President and CEO: James (Jim) Nation
CFO: Vince Zupkus
EVP Sales and Marketing: Randy Lobeig
EVP: Cleve Murphy
SVP Manufacturing: Steve Bryant
VP Sales: Ron Hayes

LOCATIONS

HQ: 2980 River Rd., Des Plaines, IL 60018
Phone: 847-439-4399 **Fax:** 847-439-4322
Web: www.springair.com

Spring Air Company manufactures its products in Argentina, Australia, Canada, Ireland, Mexico, the Middle East, the UK, and the US.

COMPETITORS

DUX
Premier Bedding Group
Sealy
Select Comfort
Serta
Simmons
TWI Holdings

HISTORICAL FINANCIALS

Company Type: Private

Income Statement FYE: December 31

	REVENUE ($ mil.)	NET INCOME ($ mil.)	NET PROFIT MARGIN	EMPLOYEES
12/01	475	—	—	1,600
12/00	420	—	—	1,600
12/99	414	—	—	1,600
12/98	386	—	—	2,000
12/97	381	—	—	1,400
12/96	375	—	—	1,315
12/95	366	—	—	1,500
12/94	330	—	—	1,500
12/93	275	—	—	—
Annual Growth	7.1%	—	—	0.9%

Revenue History

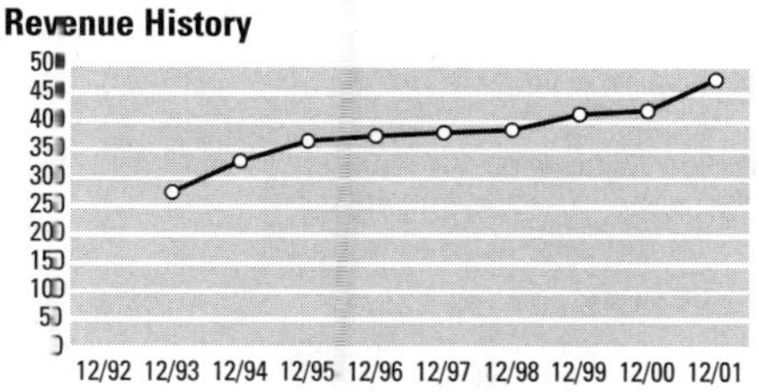

Springs Industries, Inc.

Springs Industries wants to cozy up in your bedroom. The company makes bath rugs, bedspreads, pillows, sheets, shower curtains, and towels under the Springmaid and Wamsutta brands. Springs also makes baby bedding, fabrics, hardware, infant apparel, and window blinds (Bali, Graber brands). The firm makes private-label items for Wal-Mart and Target, and licensed brands such as Harry Potter and NASCAR. Springs sells through catalogs, department stores, and mass retailers. The Close family, descendants of co-founder Leroy Springs, owns about 55% of Springs. Heartland Industrial Partners, with which the Close family took the firm private, owns the remaining 45%.

Wal-Mart represents about 25% of Springs' sales. The company also sells through about 60 of its own outlet stores. Historically an apparel textile maker, Springs has spent the last decade refocusing on home fashions through sales and acquisitions. In 2003 Springs acquired Charles D. Owen Manufacturing, the company's blanket supplier.

HISTORY

Springs Industries began in 1887 as Fort Mill Manufacturing Co., a cotton miller organized by Samuel Elliott White and a group of investors, including Leroy Springs, White's future son-in-law. Springs later founded his own cotton mill, Lancaster Cotton Mills, in 1895 and gained control of Fort Mill Manufacturing in 1914, three years after White died.

Leroy's only son, Elliott Springs, became president in 1931 when his father died. Left with massive debt and six aging cotton mills, Elliott rejuvenated the company by modernizing mill equipment and consolidating the plants into the Springs Cotton Mills (1933). During WWII the company's seven mills made fabric for military use.

In 1945 Springs started the Springmaid line of bedding and fabrics. Elliott's satiric, risqué, but effective ads (beginning in 1948) helped the company become a leading producer of sheets.

Elliott died in 1959 and his son-in-law, William Close, became president. With profits sharply declining, the company went public as Springs Mills in 1966.

The first non-family member to be president, Peter Scotese from Federated Department Stores, was hired in 1969. The next year Springs began working with designer Bill Blass. It diversified into synthetic fabrics in 1971 by buying a minority interest in a Japanese textile plant producing Ultrasuede for apparel and cars.

Springs acquired Graber Industries (window-decorating products) in 1979 and three years later changed its name to Springs Industries. In 1985 it acquired M. Lowenstein, which made Wamsutta home furnishings; the deal also gave it Clark-Schwebel Fiber Glass (industrial fabrics). Springs added Carey-McFall (Bali blinds) in 1989.

Declining economic conditions throughout the textile industry in the late 1980s and early 1990s forced Springs to close plants and trim its weakened finished-fabrics segment (the downsizing continued into 1993). A $70 million charge in 1990 led to a $7 million loss, its first in 25 years as a public company.

Historically a maker of apparel fabrics, Springs had grown vulnerable to imports and launched a long-term plan to focus on home furnishings through sales and acquisitions. In 1991 the company set up a bath group with the purchase of C. S. Brooks. Springs became a leading seller of home textiles in Canada the next year by buying the marketing and sales units of C. S. Brooks Canada and Springmaid distributor Griffiths-Kerr. A hostile takeover bid for rival Fieldcrest Cannon was rebuffed in 1993.

Expanding in 1995, Springs acquired Dundee Mills (baby and health care products, towels), Dawson Home Fashions (bath accessories, shower curtains), and Nanik Window Coverings (blinds, shutters). In 1996 the company sold its Clark-Schwebel subsidiary and the following year purchased half of American Fiber Industries (pillows, mattress pads, comforters).

Crandall Close Bowles became the eighth president of Springs in 1997. The next year she took over the chairman and CEO posts from Walter Elisha.

To further focus on its home furnishings business, in 1998 the company sold its UltraSuede business (but kept its UltraLeather business) and its industrial products division. In 1999 Springs finally exited the apparel fabrics business when it sold its Springfield division to a management group, then it purchased Regal Rugs (bath and accent rugs) and the remaining 50% of American Fiber Industries.

In April 2001 the Close family agreed to partner with private equity firm Heartland Industrial Partners to take Springs private. In September the deal was completed, increasing the family's stake to 55%, with Heartland owning the remaining 45%.

In March 2002 Springs acquired the rug division of Beaulieu Group, followed in April by its purchase of the sourced quilt division of Ultima Enterprises. In June Springs completed another acquisition, taking control of Burlington Industries' window treatments and bedding consumer products businesses.

In May 2003 Springs completed its acquisition of Charles D. Owen Manufacturing, one of the last remaining blanket makers in the US.

EXECUTIVES

Chairman and CEO: Crandall Close Bowles, age 53, $637,504 pay
EVP and CFO: Kenneth E. Kutcher
EVP and CIO: Ray E. Greer
EVP, Operations: Dean Riggs
EVP; President, Sales and Marketing Group: Thomas P. (Tom) O'Connor, age 54, $396,672 pay
SVP and Chief Purchasing Officer: John R. Cowart
SVP and President, National Sales: Rick Canter
SVP, General Counsel, and Secretary: C. Powers Dorsett
SVP, Global Sourcing and International Marketing: Charles M. Metzler
SVP, Human Resources: Gracie P. Coleman
VP and Treasurer: Samuel J. Ilardo
VP, Corporate Communications and Public Affairs: Ted Matthews
VP, Creative Development: Nancy W. Webster
President, Basic Bedding Division: Randy Spence
Director of Juvenile Sales: Thomas McCaffrey
Business Manager, Freestanding Windows: Gary Kitchens
Auditors: Deloitte & Touche LLP

LOCATIONS

HQ: 205 N. White St., Fort Mill, SC 29715
Phone: 803-547-1500 **Fax:** 803-547-1636
Web: www.springs.com

Springs Industries operates about 40 manufacturing plants in 12 U.S. states, Canada, and Mexico.

PRODUCTS/OPERATIONS

Selected Brand Names

Home Furnishings
Daisy Kingdom
Dundee
Performance
Regal
Springmaid
Texmade (in Canada)
Wabasso (in Canada)
Wamsutta

Window Furnishings and Related Hardware
Bali
CrystalPleat
FashionPleat
Graber
Maestro
Nanik

COMPETITORS

Avondale Incorporated
Burlington Industries
Carter's
Coats
Croscill
Crown Crafts
Dan River
Galey & Lord
Gerber Childrenswear
Guilford Mills
Hollander Home Fashions
Hunter Douglas
Milliken
Mohawk Industries
National Textiles
Newell Rubbermaid
Pillowtex
R. B. Pamplin
WestPoint Stevens

HISTORICAL FINANCIALS

Company Type: Private

Income Statement FYE: Saturday nearest December 31

	REVENUE ($ mil.)	NET INCOME ($ mil.)	NET PROFIT MARGIN	EMPLOYEES
12/02	2,100	—	—	17,000
12/01	1,800	—	—	17,000
12/00	2,275	—	—	18,200
12/99	2,220	—	—	18,500
12/98	2,181	—	—	17,500
12/97	2,226	—	—	19,500
12/96	2,243	—	—	20,700
12/95	2,233	—	—	23,700
12/94	2,069	—	—	20,500
12/93	2,023	—	—	20,300
Annual Growth	0.4%	—	—	(2.0%)

Revenue History

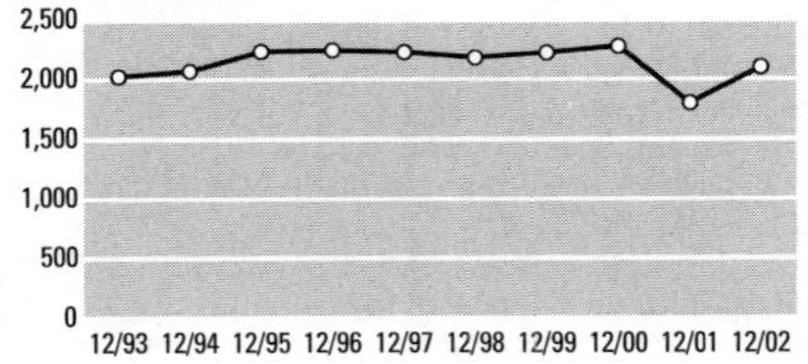

SRI International

Business Week magazine has called SRI International "Silicon Valley's soul." The not-for-profit think tank ponders advances in biotechnology, chemicals and energy, computer science, electronics, and public policy — and ways to commercialize those advances. SRI focuses on technology research and development, business strategies, and issues analysis. It has more than 800 patents and patent applications in such areas as information sciences, software development, communications, robotics, and pharmaceuticals. Among SRI's clients are Visa, Samsung, NASA, and the US Department of Defense. Originally founded in 1946 as Stanford Research Institute, SRI became fully independent of Stanford University in 1970.

The organization has conceived such innovations as the computer mouse, magnetic encoding for checks, the videodisc, and high-definition television, not to mention some of the foundations of personal computing, the Internet, and stealth technology. Its 1,400 scientists, researchers, policy experts, and support staff work at research centers worldwide.

SRI has two for-profit subsidiaries: Sarnoff (formerly a unit of General Electric) specializes in creating and commercializing electronic, biomedical, and information technologies, and SRI Consulting focuses on such issues as organizational management, marketing technologies, and the commercialization of processes. SRI and Sarnoff have together spun off more than 20 companies (*Business Week* has also called SRI "Spin-Off City").

HISTORY

In the 1920s Stanford University professor Robert Swain envisioned a research center devoted to chemistry, physics, and biology. Swain received support from university president Ray Lyman and alumnus Herbert Hoover, but the Great Depression and WWII postponed the venture. Finally, in 1946, the Stanford Research Institute was formed in conjunction with the university. That year the David Sarnoff Research Center invented the color TV tube under the wing of RCA Laboratories.

During Stanford Research's early years, it worked on such projects as logistics for Disneyland, magnetic ink for character recognition, and strategies for combating air pollution. The think tank was the focus of student protests in the 1960s because of its defense work. In 1969 Stanford Research Institute was one of four nodes on the first computer network, the ARPANET. It became fully independent in 1970 as SRI International.

During the 1960s and 70s, SRI won large contracts from the US Department of Defense for research in such areas as radar, speech recognition, and noise cancellation technologies. It got a tremendous boost in 1987 when longtime client General Electric gave SRI the Sarnoff Research Center (as a tax write-off) plus $250 million in business, along with $65.2 million in cash.

In 1993 SRI founded Pangene to commercialize gene cloning and analysis technology. The next year it founded GeneTrace to develop genetics-related products for biomedical research and Nuance Communications to commercialize speech recognition products. Intuitive Surgical, which develops minimally invasive surgical technologies, was formed in 1995.

SRI developed two key components for use in an improved mail sorting program, which the US Postal Service announced in 1997 it would use to save millions in processing costs. The David Sarnoff Research Center changed its name to Sarnoff Corporation that year. SRI joined Motorola in 1997 to make semiconductors for digital TVs.

In 1998 SRI and the National Science Foundation teamed to develop innovative science and math teaching programs. The following year SRI began working with network equipment leader Cisco Systems and the US Army to develop a voice and multimedia communications system for the military. In 2001 SRI partnered with SPEEDCOM Wireless to co-develop wireless technology.

EXECUTIVES

Chairman: Samuel H. Armacost, age 64
President and CEO: Curtis R. Carlson
SVP and CFO: Thomas J. Furst
VP, Biopharmaceutical Division: Glenn Rice
VP, Engineering and Systems Division: John W. Prausa
VP, Information and Computing Sciences: William Mark
Acting VP, Information, Telecommunications, and Automation Division and Director, Advanced Automation Technology Center: Prasanna Mulgaonkar
VP, Intellectual Property and Strategic Planning: Steven Weiner
VP, Global Business Development: Leonard Polizzotto
VP, Legal and Business Affairs and General Counsel: Richard Abramson
VP, Corporate Business Development in Biotechnology: Michael Tracy
VP, Physical Sciences: Lawrence H. Dubois
VP, Policy Division: Dennis Beatrice
VP, Ventures and Strategic Business Development: Norman Winarsky
President and CEO, SRI Holdings: Alan Herzig, age 68
Senior Director, Corporate and Marketing Communications: Alice R. Resnick
Senior Director, Human Resources: Jean E. (Jeanie) Tooker
Senior Director, Vaccine and Biotherapeutics Development: Rae Lyn Burke

LOCATIONS

HQ: 333 Ravenswood Ave., Menlo Park, CA 94025
Phone: 650-859-2000 **Fax:** 650-326-5512
Web: www.sri.com

SRI International has offices in Denmark, Japan, and South Korea, and throughout the US.

PRODUCTS/OPERATIONS

Business Areas

Automation and Robotics
Automotive and Commercial Equipment Technologies
Biopharmaceutical Development
Chemistry, Materials, and Applied Physics
Communications Technologies
Defense and Intelligence
Information Science and Software Development (human-computer interaction)
Medical Devices
Pharmaceutical Discovery
Policy (analysis of social, technological, and economic changes)
Product Engineering
Sensors and Measurement Systems
Systems and Services

Subsidiaries

Sarnoff Corporation (commercialization of innovative electronics, biomedical, and information technologies)
SRI Consulting (management consulting)

Selected SRI Spinoffs

AlterEgo Networks (wireless networking device services)
AtomicTangerine (information security consulting)
Intuitive Surgical, Inc. (technologies and techniques for minimally invasive surgery)
Nuance Communications, Inc. (speech recognition technology)
Pangene Corp. (genetic engineering technology)

Selected Sarnoff Spinoffs

Delsys Pharmaceutical Corp. (drug manufacturing and delivery technologies)
DIVA Systems Corporation (interactive video-on-demand services)
Orchid BioSciences, Inc. (gene analysis products and services)
Pyramid Vision Technologies (real-time video image systems)
Sarcon Microsystems, Inc. (infrared and chemical sensing technologies used in laboratory analysis, industrial monitoring, and commercial security applications)
Sarif (polysilicon active-matrix liquid crystal light valves for projection displays and head-mounted systems)
Secure Products (anticounterfeiting and anti-diversion systems)
Songbird Hearing, Inc. (development of a disposable hearing aid)

COMPETITORS

Aerospace Corporation
Andersen
Battelle Memorial
Bayer
Booz Allen
CACI International
Charles Stark Draper Laboratory
DaVinci Institute
Educational Testing Service
DuPont
Kendle
LECG
MIT
McKinsey & Company
Mission Research
MITRE
PAREXEL
Quintiles Transnational
RAND
Research Triangle Institute
SAIC
Southwest Research Institute
Teknowledge
University of California
Wellcome Trust
Westat

HISTORICAL FINANCIALS

Company Type: Not-for-profit

Income Statement FYE: December 31

	REVENUE ($ mil.)	NET INCOME ($ mil.)	NET PROFIT MARGIN	EMPLOYEES
12/02	199	—	—	1,400
12/01	180	—	—	1,400
12/00	164	—	—	1,400
12/99	160	—	—	1,400
12/98	174	—	—	1,500
12/97	363	—	—	2,783
12/96	326	—	—	2,700
12/95	320	—	—	1,900
12/94	312	—	—	1,973
12/93	312	—	—	2,170
Annual Growth	(4.9%)	—	—	(4.8%)

Revenue History

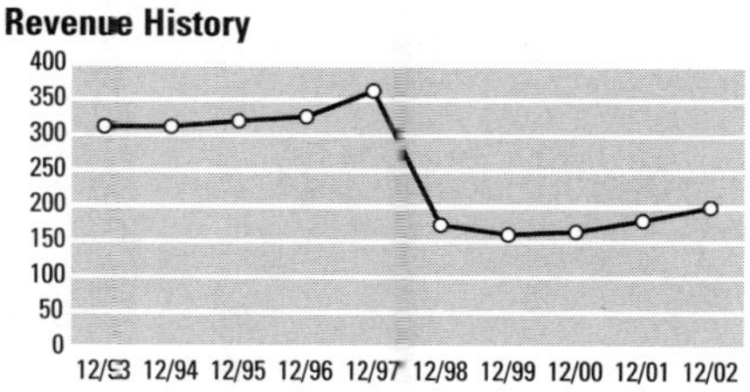

SSM Health Care System Inc.

The health care mission of SSM Health Care System began with five nuns who fled religious persecution in Germany in 1872 only to arrive in St. Louis in the midst of a smallpox epidemic. They formed their first hospital there in 1877 and later became pioneers in bringing health care to the rural frontier, founding the Oklahoma Territory's first hospital in 1898. Today the not-for-profit, sponsored by the Franciscan Sisters of Mary, owns and operates some 20 acute care hospitals with more than 5,000 licensed beds. The company also operates nursing homes and rehabilitation clinics, and offers home health and hospice care. SSM's facilities are located in Illinois, Missouri, Oklahoma, and Wisconsin.

EXECUTIVES

President and CEO: Sister Mary J. Ryan
EVP and COO: William C. Schoenhard
SVP Human Resources: Steven M. Barney
SVP Stewardship: Rev. Dennis A. Brodeur
SVP Strategic Development and Acting CFO: William P. Thompson
VP, Employee Benefits: Susan E. Goldberg
President and CIO, SSM Information Center: Thomas K. Langston
Senior System Executive: Sister Mary E. Sloan

LOCATIONS

HQ: 477 N. Lindbergh Blvd., St. Louis, MO 63141
Phone: 314-994-7800 **Fax:** 314-994-7900
Web: www.ssmhc.com

Selected Facilities

Illinois
Good Samaritan Regional Health Center (Mt. Vernon)
St. Francis Hospital & Health Center (Blue Island)
St. Mary's Hospital (Centralia)

Missouri
Pike County Memorial Hospital (Louisiana)
St. Francis Hospital & Health Services (Maryville)
St. Mary's Health Center (Jefferson City)
SSM Cardinal Glennon Children's Hospital (St. Louis)
SSM DePaul Health Center (Bridgeton)
SSM St. Joseph Health Center (St. Charles)
SSM St. Joseph Hospital of Kirkwood
SSM St. Joseph Hospital West (Lake St. Louis)
SSM St. Mary's Health Center (St. Louis)
Villa Marie Skilled Nursing Facility (Jefferson City)

Oklahoma
Bone & Joint Hospital (Oklahoma City)
St. Anthony Hospital (Oklahoma City)

Wisconsin
St. Clare Hospital and Health Services (Baraboo)
St. Clare Meadows Care Center (Baraboo)
St. Mary's Care Center (Madison)
St. Mary's Hospital Medical Center (Madison)

COMPETITORS

Advocate Health Care
Allina Hospitals
BJC HealthCare
Greenville Hospital System
HCA
Mayo Foundation
Rush System for Health
Sisters of Mercy
Tenet Healthcare

HISTORICAL FINANCIALS

Company Type: Not-for-profit

Income Statement FYE: December 31

	REVENUE ($ mil.)	NET INCOME ($ mil.)	NET PROFIT MARGIN	EMPLOYEES
12/01	1,705	47	2.8%	22,000
12/00	1,459	—	—	20,500
12/99	1,321	—	—	20,500
12/98	1,285	—	—	20,500
12/97	1,285	—	—	19,439
12/96	2,070	—	—	19,200
12/95	1,856	—	—	19,000
12/94	1,001	—	—	17,000
12/93	1,000	—	—	16,051
12/92	859	—	—	—
Annual Growth	7.9%	—	—	4.0%

Revenue History

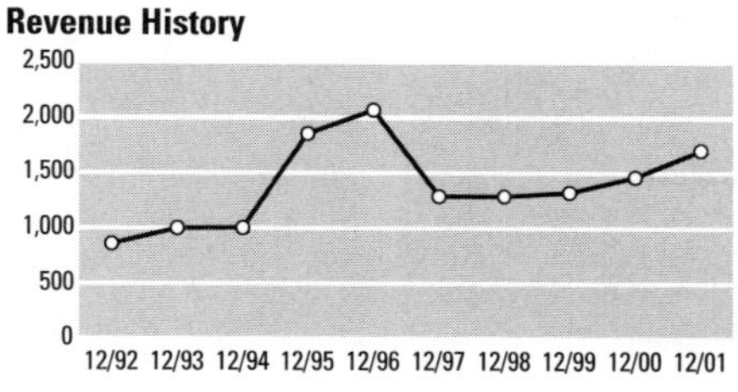

St. Joseph Health System

St. Joseph Health System (SJHS) operates 15 not-for-profit hospitals, three home health centers, clinics, hospices, and many other health care delivery organizations. Founded in 1920 as a ministry of The Sisters of St. Joseph of Orange, SJHS has facilities in California, eastern New Mexico, and West Texas.

EXECUTIVES

Chairman: Sister Katherine (Kit) Gray
President and CEO: Richard J. Statuto
SVP and COO: Jeff Flocken
SVP and CFO: Joseph Randolph
SVP and CIO: Ben Williams

LOCATIONS

HQ: 500 S. Main St., Ste. 1000, Orange, CA 92868
Phone: 714-347-7500 **Fax:** 714-347-7540
Web: www.stjhs.org

COMPETITORS

Catholic Health Initiatives
Catholic Healthcare West
HCA
Sutter Health
Tenet Healthcare

HISTORICAL FINANCIALS

Company Type: Not-for-profit

Income Statement FYE: June 30

	REVENUE ($ mil.)	NET INCOME ($ mil.)	NET PROFIT MARGIN	EMPLOYEES
6/02	2,514	31	1.2%	18,930
6/01	2,378	30	1.3%	18,000
Annual Growth	5.7%	2.3%	—	5.2%

Net Income History

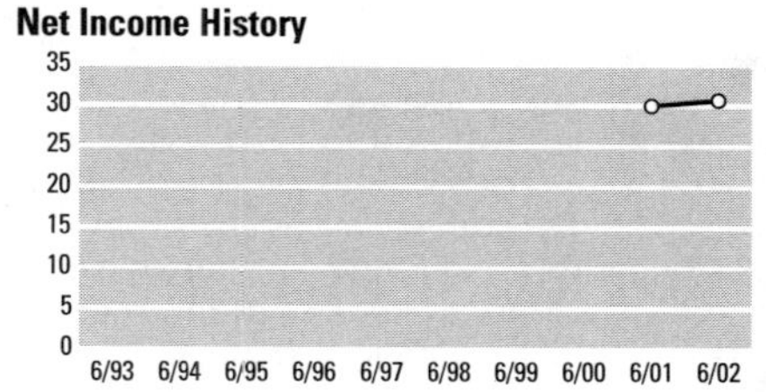

Stanford University

Prospectors panning for gold in higher education can strike it rich at Stanford University. The school is one of the premier educational institutions in the US, boasting respected programs in business, engineering, law, and medicine, among others. Its campus is home to more than 14,000 students as well as 1,700 faculty members. A private institution, Stanford supports its activities through an $8 billion endowment, one of the largest in the US. The university was founded in 1885 by Leland Stanford Sr. and his wife, Jane, in memory of their son, Leland Jr.

Stanford is also widely recognized as one of the top US research universities and sports a host of laboratories and research centers, including the Stanford Institute for Economic Policy Research and the Stanford Linear Accelerator Center. Its faculty members include 17 Nobel Prize winners and 21 National Medal of Science winners.

In 2000 the school welcomed its 10th president, former provost John Hennessy, who launched a campaign to raise $1 billion, the largest drive ever undertaken by a university. It quickly reached half that goal thanks to donations from such alumni as Jerry Yang (cofounder of Yahoo!), Charles Schwab, and Texas billionaire Robert Bass. However, its alumni ranks lost a prominent member in 2001 when William Hewlett (of Hewlett-Packard) died.

HISTORY

In 1885 Leland Stanford Sr. and his wife, Jane, established Leland Stanford Junior University in memory of their son Leland Jr., who had died of typhoid at age 15. Stanford made his fortune selling provisions to California gold miners and as a major investor in the Central Pacific Railroad, one of the two companies that built the first transcontinental railway. It was Stanford who connected the tracks laid eastward by Central Pacific and westward by Union Pacific with a gold railway spike in 1869. He also served as California's governor and as a US senator.

The Stanfords donated more than 8,000 acres of land from their own estate to establish an unconventional university, one that was coeducational and nondenominational with a focus on preparing students for a profession. Stanford opened its doors in 1891 to a freshman class of 559 students. It awarded its first degrees four years later, and among the graduates was future US president Herbert Hoover.

Leland Stanford Sr. died in 1893, and in 1903 Jane Stanford turned the university over to the board of trustees. After weathering significant damage in the 1906 Great San Francisco Earthquake, the university established a law school in 1908 and its medical school five years later.

During WWI the university mobilized half of its students into the Students' Army Training Corps. The School of Education was established in 1917, followed by the School of Engineering and Graduate School of Business eight years later. In 1933 a rule limiting the number of women admitted to Stanford was abolished.

Wallace Sterling, who became president of the university after WWII, initiated the transformation of Stanford into a world-class institution with a reputation for teaching and research. Under Sterling the university initiated development on the Stanford Research Park.

In 1958 Stanford opened its first overseas campus (near Stuttgart, Germany), and the Stanford Medical Center was completed the following year. The university created a computer science department in 1965 and two years later opened the Stanford Linear Accelerator Center dedicated to physics research.

Donald Kennedy became president in 1980. The next year students voted to abandon the university's official mascot, the "Indians," in response to concerns raised by Native American students. The nickname "Cardinal" was adopted in its place. The term refers to the school's color, cardinal red.

Also during Kennedy's tenure, it was revealed that Stanford had overcharged the Office of Naval Research for indirect costs associated with research. The scandal led to Kennedy's resignation in 1992, and in 1994 the Office of Naval Research and the university settled a related lawsuit for $1.2 million and a stipulation that Stanford had not committed any wrongdoing. Gerhard Casper succeeded Kennedy as president.

In 1997 Stanford and the University of California at San Francisco combined their teaching hospitals in a public/private merger. Two years later after the controversial experiment had harmed both hospitals' financial picture, the merger was terminated, and the two hospitals agreed to go their separate ways.

In 1999 Casper announced his intention to resign as president. The school tapped provost John Hennessy as his replacement. Soon after his appointment in 2000, Hennessey launched a campaign to raise $1 billion. Former Stanford professor and Netscape co-founder Jim Clark donated $150 million (the largest single donation since its founding grant) later that year to support Stanford's biomedical engineering and sciences program. The school also launched a new company, SKOLAR, which developed an online search engine for the medical industry.

EXECUTIVES

President: John L. Hennessy, age 50
Provost: John W. Etchemendy
VP Public Affairs: Gordon Earle
VP Development: John B. Ford
VP Business Affairs and CFO: Randall (Randy) Livingston
President Stanford Alumni Association: Howard Wolf
VP and General Counsel: Deborah Zumwalt
Associate VP and Director University Communications: Alan Acosta
Executive Director Human Resources: John Cammidge
Executive Director Information Technology Systems and Services: Christopher Handley

LOCATIONS

HQ: 857 Serra St., Stanford, CA 94305
Phone: 650-723-2300 **Fax:** 650-725-0247
Web: www.stanford.edu

PRODUCTS/OPERATIONS

Selected Schools

Undergraduate
School of Earth Sciences
School of Engineering
School of Humanities and Sciences

Graduate
School of Business
School of Earth Sciences
School of Engineering
School of Education
School of Humanities and Sciences
School of Law
School of Medicine

Selected Interdisciplinary Research Centers

Center for Computer Research in Music and Acoustics
Center for Integrated Facility Engineering
Center for Integrated Systems
Stanford Integrated Manufacturing Association

Selected Laboratories, Centers, and Institutes

Center for Research on Information Storage Materials
Center for the Study of Language and Information
Edward L. Ginzton Laboratory
Institute for International Studies
Institute for Research on Women and Gender
Stanford Center for Buddhist Studies
Stanford Humanities Center
Stanford Institute for Economic Policy Research
W.W. Hansen Experimental Physics Laboratory

Selected Medical Research Facilities

Center for Biomedical Ethics
Center for Research in Disease Prevention
Human Genome Center
Richard M. Lucas Center for Magnetic Resonance Spectroscopy & Imaging
Sleep Disorders Center

Other Selected Research Facilities

Hoover Institution on War, Revolution and Peace
Hopkins Marine Station
Martin Luther King, Jr. Papers Project
Stanford Linear Accelerator Center

HISTORICAL FINANCIALS

Company Type: School

Income Statement FYE: August 31

	REVENUE ($ mil.)	NET INCOME ($ mil.)	NET PROFIT MARGIN	EMPLOYEES
8/01	2,940	—	—	—
8/00	1,957	—	—	—
8/99	1,749	—	—	—
8/98	1,558	—	—	—
8/97	1,474	—	—	—
8/96	1,416	—	—	—
Annual Growth	15.7%	—	—	—

Revenue History

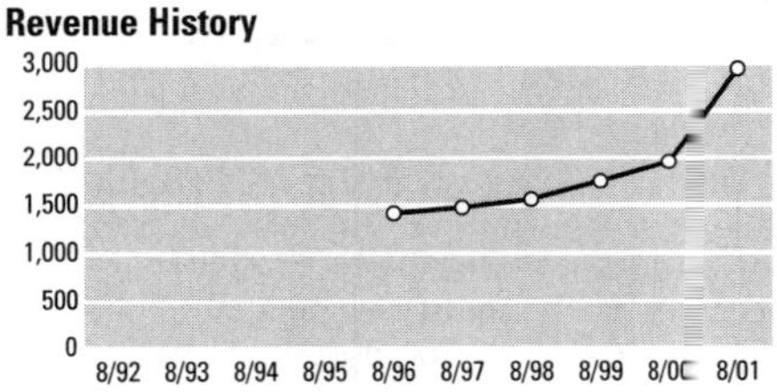

Staple Cotton Cooperative

Wear underwear? Chances are Staplcotn had a hand in it. Staple Cotton Cooperative Association, best known for its Staplcotn cotton marketing arm, serves more than 12,000 member-owners in 41 states. Founded in 1921 by Mississippi cotton producer Oscar Bledsoe and 10 Delta growers, it sells about 3 million bales of cotton annually. Most of the yield is sold to the US textile industry to make men's knit underwear, T-shirts, sheets, towels, and denim. Customers include Fruit of the Loom and Levi Strauss & Co. The co-op's Stapl-discount subsidiary offers low-interest loans for equipment, buildings, and land. Staplcotn is represented worldwide by Amcot, which also represents three other US cotton co-ops.

EXECUTIVES

Chairman; Chairman, Stapldiscount:
William A. Percy II, age 63
President and CEO; President & CEO, Stapldiscount:
Woods E. Eastland, age 58
VP and Treasurer; VP and Treasurer, Stapldiscount:
Mack L. Alford
VP Human Resources and Secretary; VP Human Resources & Secretary, Stapldiscount:
Eugene A. (Gene) Stansel Jr.
VP Marketing: Meredith B. Allen
VP, Sales Operations: David Camp
General Counsel; General Counsel, Stapldiscount:
Kenneth E. Downs

LOCATIONS

HQ: Staple Cotton Cooperative Association
214 W. Market St., Greenwood, MS 38930
Phone: 662-453-6231 **Fax:** 662-453-6274
Web: www.staplcotn.com

COMPETITORS

Agway
Alabama Farmers Cooperatives
Calcot
Cargill
Dunavant Enterprises
Plains Cotton
Southern States
Tennessee Farmers

HISTORICAL FINANCIALS

Company Type: Cooperative

Income Statement FYE: August 31

	REVENUE ($ mil.)	NET INCOME ($ mil.)	NET PROFIT MARGIN	EMPLOYEES
8/02	1,220	—	—	248
8/01	1,050	—	—	230
8/00	1,041	—	—	230
8/99	850	—	—	200
8/98	705	—	—	197
8/97	657	—	—	156
8/96	640	—	—	—
8/95	664	—	—	—
8/94	520	—	—	—
8/93	520	—	—	—
Annual Growth	9.9%	—	—	9.7%

Revenue History

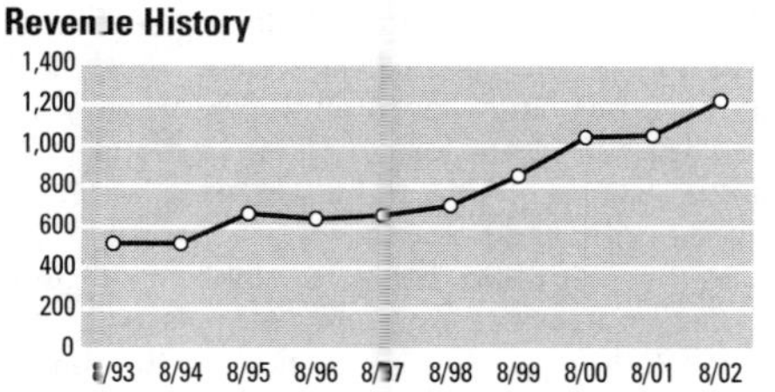

Starrett Corporation

From King Kong to the Queen of Mean, the stories of Starrett's buildings are interwoven into New York's history. Founded in 1922, the company provides a variety of real estate development and construction management services, primarily in the New York City area. Affiliate and former subsidiary HRH Construction generally serves as construction project manager for Starrett; among its notable Manhattan projects is the Empire State Building, which was subleased by Leona Helmsley from Donald Trump. Starrett also manages residential properties through subsidiary Grenadier Realty. New York-based Blackacre Capital Management owns a majority stake in Starrett.

EXECUTIVES

Chairman: Gregory Cuneo, age 43
President and CEO: Robert J. Birnbach
CFO: Frank Jones
SVP, General Counsel, and Secretary: Stephen Salup
SVP: Felice Michetti

LOCATIONS

HQ: 2 Park Ave., New York, NY 10016
Phone: 212-616-3100 **Fax:** 212-616-3200
Web: www.starrettcorp.com

COMPETITORS

CB Richard Ellis
Cushman & Wakefield
Dyson-Kissner-Moran
Forest City Enterprises
Gilbane
Grubb & Ellis
Lefrak Organization
Louis Dreyfus
Mack-Cali
Perini
Reckson Associates Realty
Simon Property Group
Structure Tone
Tishman Realty
Trump

HISTORICAL FINANCIALS

Company Type: Private

Income Statement FYE: December 31

	REVENUE ($ mil.)	NET INCOME ($ mil.)	NET PROFIT MARGIN	EMPLOYEES
12/01	500	—	—	600
12/00	515	—	—	570
12/99	515	—	—	—
12/98	350	—	—	—
12/97	250	—	—	—
12/96	167	—	—	—
12/95	138	—	—	1,486
12/94	141	—	—	1,100
12/93	122	—	—	1,100
12/92	112	—	—	1,435
Annual Growth	18.1%	—	—	(9.2%)

Revenue History

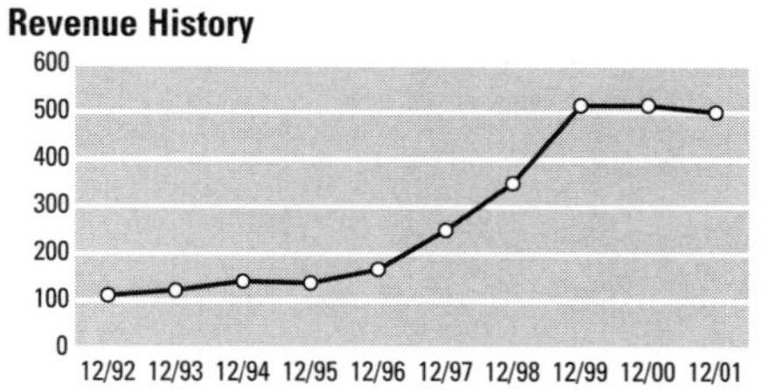

State Farm Insurance

Like an enormous corporation, State Farm is everywhere. One of the US's largest personal lines property & casualty companies, State Farm Insurance Companies provides auto insurance, as well as homeowners, nonmedical health, and life insurance through some 16,000 agents. Competition has increased with the fall of barriers between the banking, securities, and insurance industries. State Farm's not-so-secret weapon is a federal savings bank charter (State Farm Financial Services) that offers deposit accounts, CDs, mortgages, and auto and home equity loans by phone and on the Internet.

The company is expanding its financial services, but insurance is still its main source of income. State Farm insures about 20% of the automobiles on US roads; auto insurance accounts for almost 70% of the company's property & casualty premiums.

Taking advantage of the currently lucrative insurance climate, State Farm has formed Bermuda-based reinsurer Da Vinci Re together with RenaissanceRe. The company stopped writing new homeowners policies in some 15 states in an effort to improve profitability.

Although total revenue increased in 2002, State Farm experienced underwriting losses in its health, homeowners, and property & casualty segments. Slumping equity markets also brought the company's net results down.

Since its founding, the group's companies have been run by only two families, the Mecherles (1922-54) and the Rusts (1954-present).

HISTORY

Retired farmer George Mecherle formed State Farm Mutual Automobile Insurance in Bloomington, Illinois, in 1922. State Farm served only members of farm bureaus and farm mutual insurance companies, charging a one-time membership fee and a premium to protect an automobile against loss or damage.

Unlike most competitors, State Farm offered six-month premium payments. The insurer billed and collected renewal premiums from its home office, relieving the agent of the task. In addition, State Farm determined auto rates by a simple seven-class system, while competitors varied rates for each model.

State Farm in 1926 started City and Village Mutual Automobile Insurance to insure nonfarmers' autos; it became part of the company in 1927. Between 1927 and 1931 it introduced borrowed-car protection, wind coverage, and insurance for vehicles used to transport schoolchildren.

State Farm expanded to California in 1928 and formed State Farm Life Insurance the next year. In 1935 it established State Farm Fire Insurance. George Mecherle became chairman in 1937, and his son Ramond became president. In 1939 George challenged agents to write "A Million or More (auto policies) by '44." State Farm saw a 110% increase in policies.

During the 1940s State Farm focused on urban areas after most of the farm bureaus formed their own insurance companies. In the late 1940s and 1950s, it moved to a full-time agency force.

Homeowners coverage was added to the insurer's offerings under the leadership of Adlai Rust, who led State Farm from 1954 until 1958, when Edward Rust took over. He died in 1985 and his son, Edward Jr., currently holds the top spot.

Between 1974 and 1987 the insurer was hit by several gender-discrimination suits (a 1992 settlement awarded $157 million to 814 women). State Farm has since tried to hire more women and minorities.

In the early 1990s serial disasters, including Hurricane Andrew and the Los Angeles riots, proved costly. The 1994 Northridge earthquake alone generated more than $2.5 billion in claims and contributed to a 72% decline in earnings.

State Farm — the top US home insurer since the mid-1960s — canceled 62,500 residential policies in South Florida in 1996 to cut potential hurricane loss an estimated 11%. In response, Florida's insurance regulators rescinded a previously approved rate hike. That year the company agreed to open more urban neighborhood offices to settle a discrimination suit brought by the Department of Housing and Urban Development, which accused State Farm of discriminating against potential customers in minority-populated areas.

Legal trouble continued. In 1997 State Farm settled with a California couple who alleged the company forged policyholders' signatures on forms declining coverage and concealed evidence to avoid paying earthquake damage claims. That year a policyholder sued to keep State Farm from "wasting company assets" on President Clinton's legal defense against Paula Jones' sexual harassment charges (Clinton held a State Farm personal liability policy).

Relations with its sales force already rocky, State Farm in 1998 proposed to reduce up-front commissions and cut base pay in favor of incentives for customer retention and cross-selling. Reduced auto premiums and increased catastrophe claims from across the US eroded State Farm's bottom line that year. A federal thrift charter obtained in 1998 let the company launch banking operations the next year.

State Farm is appealing a 1999 Illinois state court judgment that it pay $1.2 billion to policyholders for using aftermarket parts in auto repairs. In 2000 the company was hit with a class-action lawsuit about its denial of personal-injury claims; previous suits had been individual cases.

In 2002, State Farm Indemnity withdrew from the New Jersey auto insurance market.

EXECUTIVES

Chairman and CEO: Edward B. (Ed) Rust Jr., age 52
Vice Chairman, President, and COO: Vincent J. Trosino, age 62
SEVP, Chief Administrative Officer, and Director: James E. Rutrough
SEVP, Chief Agency and Marketing Officer, and Director: Charles R. Wright
EVP and General Counsel: Kim M. Brunner
EVP, Financial Services: Jack W. North
EVP: Brian V. Boyden
EVP: John P. Coffey
EVP: Barbara Cowden
EVP: William K. King
SVP, CFO, and Treasurer: Michael L. Tipsord
SVP, Investments: Paul N. Eckley
SVP, Investments: Kurt G. Moser
VP, Corporate Secretary, and Counsel: Laura P. Sullivan
VP, Human Resources: Arlene Hogan
President and CEO, State Farm Federal Savings Bank: Stanley R. Ommen
SVP and Chief Administrative Officer, Life Company Affiliates: Susan D. Waring
Systems VP: Richard Shellito
Auditors: PricewaterhouseCoopers LLP

LOCATIONS

HQ: State Farm Insurance Companies
1 State Farm Plaza, Bloomington, IL 61710
Phone: 309-766-2311 **Fax:** 309-766-3621
Web: www.statefarm.com

State Farm Insurance Companies has operations in Canada and throughout the US.

PRODUCTS/OPERATIONS

Group Companies

State Farm County Mutual Insurance Company of Texas (high-risk auto insurance)
State Farm Federal Savings Bank
State Farm Fire and Casualty Company (homeowners, boat owners, and commercial insurance)
State Farm Florida Insurance Company (homeowners and renters insurance)
State Farm General Insurance Company (property insurance)
State Farm Indemnity Company (auto insurance in New Jersey)
State Farm Life Insurance Company
State Farm Mutual Automobile Insurance Company (auto and health insurance)

COMPETITORS

ACE Limited
Allstate
American Family Insurance
AIG
Berkshire Hathaway
Chubb
CNA Financial
Country Insurance and Financial Services
GEICO
The Hartford
Liberty Mutual
MetLife
Nationwide
Progressive Corporation
Prudential
SAFECO
Travelers
USAA
Zurich Financial Services

HISTORICAL FINANCIALS

Company Type: Mutual company

Income Statement FYE: December 31

	ASSETS ($ mil.)	NET INCOME ($ mil.)	INCOME AS % OF ASSETS	EMPLOYEES
12/02	113,043	(2,800)	—	79,400
12/01	117,162	(5,000)	—	79,400
12/00	119,602	408	0.3%	79,300
12/99	80,114	1,033	1.3%	79,300
12/98	88,366	996	1.1%	76,257
12/97	82,296	3,581	4.4%	—
Annual Growth	6.6%	—	—	1.0%

2002 Year-End Financials

Equity as % of assets: —
Return on assets: —
Return on equity: —
Long-term debt ($ mil.): —
Sales ($ mil.): 49,700

Net Income History

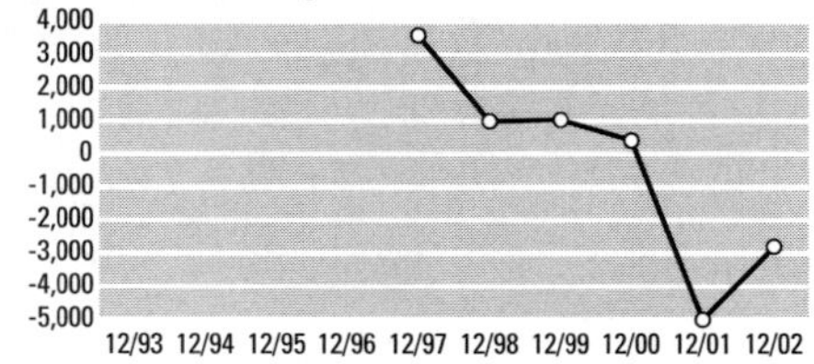

State University of New York

SUNY days are ahead for many New Yorkers seeking higher education. With nearly 390,000 students, the State University of New York (SUNY) is running neck-and-neck with California State University for the title of largest university system in the US. The school maintains 64 campuses around New York State, including 13 university colleges and four university centers, 30 community colleges, five technical colleges, and three health centers. Its institutions offer some 5,100 programs of study, including accounting, journalism, bioengineering, and computer science. The university system hands out some 70,000 diplomas each year, including nearly 9,000 post-graduate degrees.

Most students are residents of New York State (about a third of all New York State high school graduates enroll at SUNY institutions) and pay about $3,400 a year in tuition. SUNY is also top-notch in research, boasting more than $700 million in federal, state, and local grants and contracts. Its laboratories have helped pioneer magnetic resonance imaging, implantable heart pacemakers, and supermarket bar code scanners.

Chancellor Robert King is challenging SUNY administrators and the state to increase levels of funding to help keep the university competitive against other top-flight institutions. New York Governor George Pataki has pledged a $2 billion multi-year construction program for SUNY's facilities.

HISTORY

The State University of New York was organized in 1948, but it traces its roots back to several institutions founded in the 19th century. In 1844 the New York state legislature authorized the creation of the Albany Normal School, which was charged with educating the state's secondary school teachers. Two years later, the University of Buffalo was chartered to provide academic, theological, legal, and medical studies. More normal schools later were founded between 1861 and 1889 in Brockport, Buffalo, Cortland, Fredonia, Geneseo, New Paltz, Oneonta, Oswego, Plattsburgh, and Potsdam.

In the early 1900s the state established several agricultural colleges, including schools in Canton (1907), Alfred (1908), Morrisville (1910), Farmingdale (1912), and Cobleskill (1916). New York also set up several schools as units of Cornell University, including colleges of veterinary medicine (1894), agriculture (1909), home economics (1925), and industrial and labor relations (1945).

After WWII, veterans began to fill US colleges and universities, taking advantage of the GI Bill to secure a college education. The legislature set up SUNY in 1948 to consolidate 29 institutions under a single board of trustees charged with meeting the growing demand. The board coordinated the state colleges into a single body and established four-year liberal arts colleges, professional and graduate schools, and research centers. During the 1950s and 1960s, new campuses were created at Binghamton, Stony Brook, Old Westbury, Purchase, and Utica/Rome, and enrollment began to take off, jumping from 30,000 in 1955 to 63,000 in 1959.

By the early 1970s SUNY had more than

320,000 students at 72 institutions. But budget constraints later that decade led to higher tuition, reduced enrollment goals, and employment cutbacks. In 1975 eight New York City community colleges were transferred to City University. SUNY's enrollment began growing again during the 1980s, reaching more than 400,000 by 1990. Early in the decade, the institution began implementing SUNY 2000, a plan that called for increasing access to education and diversifying undergraduate studies. Following his election in 1994, Governor George Pataki proposed more than $550 million in cuts to the SUNY system.

In 1997 John Ryan replaced Thomas Bartlett as chancellor. The following year SUNY became the exclusive sponsor of The College Channel, a guide to colleges and college life aimed at high school juniors and seniors and broadcast by PRIMEDIA's Channel One. In 1999 the governor's budget director, Robert King, was named chancellor to replace the retiring Bartlett. In 2000 SUNY faced rising budget shortfalls at its teaching hospitals, in part because money was being siphoned off to other areas. That year King announced a set of initiatives to raise an additional $1.5 billion in federal research grants and $1 billion in private donations over five years.

In 2001 the university announced its intention to keep tuition at $3,400 a year for the seventh year in a row.

EXECUTIVES

Chancellor: Robert L. King
Provost and Vice Chancellor Academic Affairs: Peter D. Salins
Vice Chancellor and COO: Richard P. Miller Jr.
Vice Chancellor and CFO: David Richter
Vice Chancellor Community Colleges: Robert T. Brown
Vice Chancellor Business and Industry Relations: R. Wayne Diesel
Vice Chancellor Legal Affairs and University Counsel: D. Andrew Edwards Jr.
Vice Chancellor and Secretary; President, Research Foundation of the State University of New York: John J. O'Connor
University Controller: Patrick J. Wiater
University Auditor: C. Kevin O'Donoghue
Assistant Vice Chancellor for Employee Relations: Joyce Villa
Director of Employee Relations: Raymond (Ray) Haines
Associate Director of Employee Relations: Pam Williams
Auditors: KPMG LLP

LOCATIONS

HQ: State University Plaza, Albany, NY 12246
Phone: 518-443-5500 **Fax:** 518-443-5387
Web: www.suny.edu

PRODUCTS/OPERATIONS

Selected Institutions

Colleges of Technology
Alfred
Canton
Cobleskill
Delhi
Morrisville
University Colleges of Technology

Health Science Centers
Brooklyn
Syracuse

Statutory Colleges
College of Agriculture and Life Sciences at Cornell University
College of Ceramics at Alfred University
College of Human Ecology at Cornell University
College of Veterinary Medicine at Cornell University
School of Industrial and Labor Relations at Cornell University

University Centers
Albany
Binghamton
Buffalo
Stony Brook

University Colleges
Brockport
Buffalo State
Cortland
Empire State
Fredonia
Geneseo
New Paltz
Old Westbury
Oneonta
Oswego
Plattsburgh
Potsdam
Purchase

HISTORICAL FINANCIALS

Company Type: School

Income Statement

FYE: June 30

	REVENUE ($ mil.)	NET INCOME ($ mil.)	NET PROFIT MARGIN	EMPLOYEES
6/02	3,476	—	—	—
6/01	5,211	—	—	—
6/00	5,076	—	—	—
6/99	4,629	—	—	65,000
6/98	4,564	—	—	65,000
6/97	4,244	—	—	56,135
6/96	4,136	—	—	55,000
6/95	4,167	—	—	52,000
6/94	4,018	—	—	48,194
6/93	3,692	—	—	47,574
Annual Growth	(0.7%)	—	—	5.3%

Revenue History

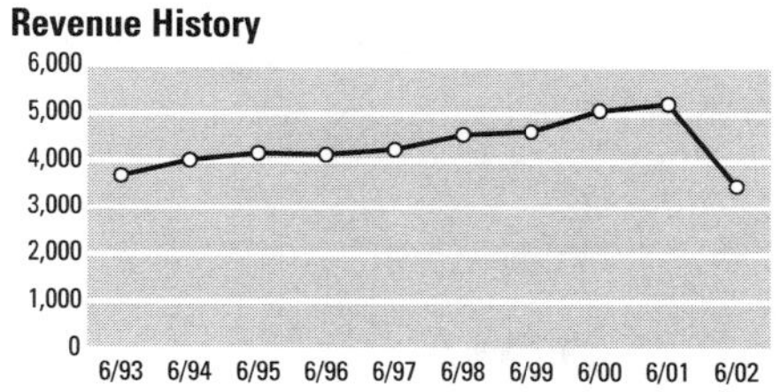

Stater Bros. Holdings Inc.

Stater Bros. Markets has no shortage of major league rivals, operating in the same Southern California markets as Ralphs, Albertson's, and Safeway-owned Vons. Stater Bros. Holdings has about 155 Stater Bros. Markets, mostly in Riverside and San Bernardino counties. It also has stores in Kern, Los Angeles, Orange, and San Diego counties. In 1999 the company converted about 45 outlets it bought from Albertson's to the Stater Bros. Market name. It also has a 50% stake in milk and juice processor Santee Dairies. Stater Bros. is owned by La Cadena Investments, a general partnership consisting of Stater Bros. CEO Jack Brown and other company executives.

Competition from the grocery giants, and the purchase of the stores from Albertson's, has put a strain on the company's profits. To distinguish itself from rivals, the chain refuses to offer promotional games and frequent shopper cards, boasting everyday low prices instead. Kroger owns the other 50% of Santee Dairies; Santee serves Stater Bros. Markets and Ralph's, as well as independent grocers.

Stater Bros. Holdings is the largest privately held supermarket chain in Southern California. The company plans to open one to five new stores per year.

HISTORY

In 1936, at age 23, Cleo Stater and his twin brother, Leo, mortgaged a Chevrolet to make a down payment on a modest grocery store where Cleo had been working for five years in their hometown of Yucaipa, California. Later that year the brothers bought their second grocery in the nearby community of Redlands. Their younger brother, Lavoy, soon joined them to help build the company. In 1938 the brothers opened the first Stater Bros. market in Colton; by 1939 they had a chain of four stores.

The small, family-owned grocery chain continued to grow. In 1948 Stater Bros. opened its first supermarket (which was several times larger than its other stores and had its own parking lot) in Riverside. By 1950 the company had 12 stores.

Stater Bros. consolidated its offices and warehouse in Colton in the early 1960s and continued its expansion into nearby communities. By 1964 it operated 27 supermarkets in 18 cities in Los Angeles, Orange, Riverside, and San Bernardino counties. In 1968 the brothers sold the company's 35 stores to Long Beach, California-based petroleum services provider Petrolane for $33 million. Lavoy succeeded Cleo as president.

As a division of Petrolane, Stater Bros. kept growing. In the 1970s the company introduced a new store design that expanded sales area but required less land and a smaller building. The number of stores more than doubled (to over 80) between 1968 and 1979, when Lavoy retired.

Ron Burkle, VP of Administration for Petrolane, and his father, Joe, president of Stater Bros., attempted to buy the chain for $100 million in 1981. Infuriated by the low bid, Petrolane fired Ron and demoted his father, who left that year. Jack Brown was named president in his place. Petrolane sold the chain in 1983 to La Cadena Investments, a private company that included Brown and other top Stater Bros. executives.

Leo died in 1985. That year the company went public to reduce debt from the 1983 LBO and to provide funds for an extensive expansion plan. It also incorporated as Stater Bros. Inc. In 1986 a proxy fight for control of the company erupted between Brown's La Cadena group and chairman Bernard Garrett, who owned about 41% of Stater Bros. Brown had been suspended as president and CEO (Joe Burkle returned in his place), but Los-Angeles based investment firm Craig Corp. bought Garrett's stake and Brown returned; he was later elected chairman. That year Stater Bros. also became a co-owner in Santee Dairies with Hughes Markets (now part of Kroger).

The next year Craig and Stater Bros. executives took the grocery chain private again. Burkle bought a 9% stake in Craig in 1989 through Yucaipa Capital Partners. Also in 1987 Craig reduced its stake in Stater Bros., transferring some stock to La Cadena. Stater Bros. Holdings was created as a parent company for the grocery chain.

Stater Bros. expressed an interest in buying rival Alpha Beta stores when they were put up for sale, but Yucaipa Companies bought them in 1991. Craig considered selling its stake in Stater Bros. in 1992; it finally sold its half of the company to La Cadena in 1996.

In 1999 Stater Bros. acquired 33 Albertson's

and 10 Lucky stores, as well as one store site. (The FTC required Albertson's to sell the stores in order to acquire American Stores, Lucky's parent.) The acquisition and the early retirement of debt resulted in its 1999 losses. In September 2001 company co-founder Cleo Stater died.

In early 2002 the company announced a partnership with Krispy Kreme Doughnuts to offer the treats at selected Stater Bros. supermarkets.

EXECUTIVES

Chairman, President and CEO: Jack H. Brown, age 63, $1,188,000 pay
Vice Chairman: Thomas W. Field Jr., age 68
EVP and COO: Donald I. (Don) Baker, age 61, $473,000 pay
SVP and CFO: Phillip J. Smith, age 55, $202,000 pay
SVP, Retail Operations: Edward A. Stater, age 51, $182,000 pay
Group SVP Administration: A. Gayle Paden, age 65, $338,000 pay
Group SVP of Marketing: Dennis L. McIntyre, age 42, $192,000 pay
Group SVP of Retail Operations: James W. (Jim) Lee, age 51
VP, Construction and Maintenance: Scott Limbacher
VP, Corporate Affairs: Susan Atkinson
VP, Human Resources: Kathy Finazzo
Secretary and Director: Bruce D. Varner, age 66
Property Development Manager: Mike McCasland
Auditors: Ernst & Young LLP

LOCATIONS

HQ: 21700 Barton Rd., Colton, CA 92324
Phone: 909-783-5000 **Fax:** 909-783-3930
Web: www.staterbros.com

Stater Bros. Holdings operates one distribution center and about 155 supermarkets in Southern California.

2002 Stores

	No.
San Bernardino County	47
Riverside County	40
Orange County	30
Los Angeles County	27
Northern San Diego County	10
Kern County	2
Total	**156**

PRODUCTS/OPERATIONS

Selected Departments and Products

Bakery
Dairy products
Delicatessen
Fresh produce
Frozen foods
General merchandise
Health & beauty aids
Liquor
Meats
Seafood

COMPETITORS

Albertson's
Arden Group
Costco Wholesale
Longs Drug
Ralphs
Smart & Final
Trader Joe's Co
Vons
Walgreen
Wal-Mart
Whole Foods

HISTORICAL FINANCIALS

Company Type: Private

Income Statement

FYE: Last Sunday in September

	REVENUE ($ mil.)	NET INCOME ($ mil.)	NET PROFIT MARGIN	EMPLOYEES
9/02	2,666	12	0.4%	13,400
9/01	2,574	8	0.3%	12,600
9/00	2,418	(6)	—	12,100
9/99	1,830	(9)	—	12,700
9/98	1,726	3	0.1%	8,700
9/97	1,718	14	0.8%	8,900
9/96	1,705	16	0.9%	8,900
9/95	1,580	7	0.4%	9,800
9/94	1,540	9	0.6%	10,000
9/93	1,526	6	0.4%	9,800
Annual Growth	6.4%	8.4%	—	3.5%

2002 Year-End Financials

Debt ratio: —
Return on equity: —
Cash ($ mil.): 81
Current ratio: 1.64
Long-term debt ($ mil.): 470

Net Income History

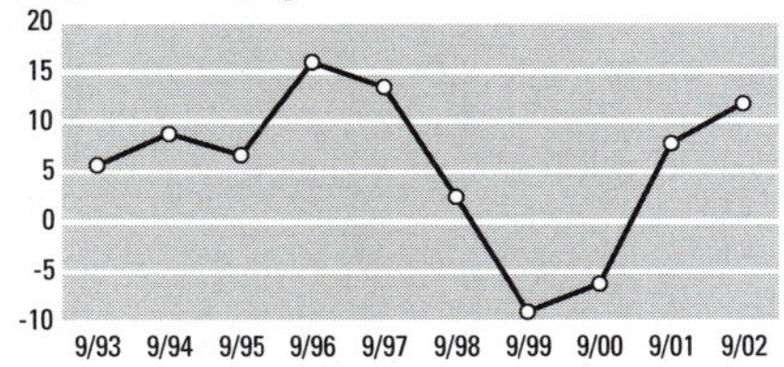

Sterling Chemicals, Inc.

Having emerged from bankruptcy in 2002, Sterling Chemicals (formerly Sterling Chemicals Holdings) has plotted a new course for fiscal solvency. Sterling is focusing on its core petrochemical business, which includes the production of styrene, used to make Styrofoam, and acetic acid. As part of its bankruptcy reorganization plan, Sterling sold its wood pulp chemicals business (sodium chlorate/chlorite) to pay off debt; it also transferred its acrylic fibers business to local management for a nominal fee. Sterling and its US subsidiaries filed for bankruptcy in 2001; its foreign operations were not included in the filing.

An industrywide price drop and the economic slowdown have contributed to Sterling's struggles. To recoup, the company focused on strategic alliances and long-term supply arrangements with major customers (it supplies chemicals to BP Chemicals, which accounts for about 10% of sales, and BASF Corporation). Sterling also decided to withdraw from its money-losing commodity textile business. The changes, however, couldn't thwart the bankruptcy filing. Sterling sold its pulp chemicals operations to Canada-based Superior Propane Inc. for about $375 million; the sale included five plants in Canada and one in Georgia.

Before filing for bankruptcy, former directors Rolf Towe and Frank Hevrdejs owned 16% and 7% of Sterling, respectively. Koch Industries owned 9%. Sterling now is owned by Resurgence Asset Management, L.L.C. and its creditors.

Upon emerging from bankruptcy, the company reduced its debt load from roughly $1 billion to about $20 million.

EXECUTIVES

Chairman: Robert W. Roten, age 68
CEO; President; EVP, Operations; and Director: Richard K. Crump, age 56, $535,990 pay (prior to title change)
VP, Finance and CFO: Paul G. Vanderhoven, age 49, $331,867 pay
VP, Human Resources and Administration: Wayne R. Parker
VP and General Counsel: Kenneth M. Hale, age 40
Auditors: Deloitte & Touche LLP

LOCATIONS

HQ: 1200 Smith St., Ste. 1900, Houston, TX 77002
Phone: 713-650-3700 **Fax:** 713-654-9551
Web: www.sterlingchemicals.com

Sterling Chemicals has plants in Texas.

2002 Sales

	% of total
US	66
Other	34
Total	**100**

PRODUCTS/OPERATIONS

Selected Products

Petrochemicals and Fibers
Acetic acid (sold exclusively to BP Chemicals)
Acrylonitrile (used in making acrylic fibers)
DSIDA (herbicide)
Methanol
Plasticizers (sold exclusively to BASF Corporation)
Sodium cyanide
Styrene
TBA (used in pesticides, solvents, and synthetic rubber)

COMPETITORS

ATOFINA
BASF AG
BP
Celanese
CPChem
Degussa
Dow Chemical
Eastman Chemical
DuPont
Formosa Plastics USA
Lyondell Chemical
Methanex
Millennium Chemicals
NOVA Chemicals
Shell Chemicals
Solutia
Sunoco Chemicals

HISTORICAL FINANCIALS

Company Type: Private

Income Statement

FYE: September 30

	REVENUE ($ mil.)	NET INCOME ($ mil.)	NET PROFIT MARGIN	EMPLOYEES
9/02	629	(36)	—	871
9/01	744	(221)	—	923
9/00	1,078	(87)	—	1,180
9/99	721	(110)	—	1,180
9/98	823	(49)	—	1,500
9/97	909	(28)	—	1,700
9/96	791	32	4.0%	1,200
9/95	1,030	150	14.6%	1,200
9/94	701	—	—	—
9/93	519	—	—	—
Annual Growth	2.2%	—	—	(4.5%)

2002 Year-End Financials

Debt ratio: —
Return on equity: —
Cash ($ mil.): 23
Current ratio: 1.22
Long-term debt ($ mil.): 15

Net Income History

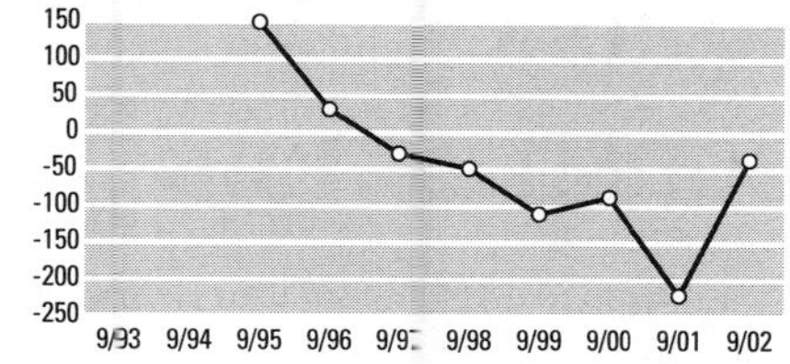

Stevedoring Services of America

On a ship, "port" means left, "starboard" means right, and "stevedoring" means heavy lifting, which is what Stevedoring Services of America (SSA) does. The largest marine terminal operator in the US, SSA loads and unloads ships at ports from Seattle to New Zealand. The company handles a variety of cargo, including steel, coal, and cars. It also provides rail terminal services, warehousing, and shipment tracking. SSA's Tideworks Technology division offers administrative and operational software and technology services for terminal operators. Founded in the 1880s, SSA has been owned by the Smith and Hemingway families since 1949; president Jon Hemingway is the third generation of his family to head the company.

EXECUTIVES

President: Jon Hemingway
SVP: Dan Flynn
SVP: Claude Stritmatter
SVP; COO, SSA Terminals: Ed DeNike
SVP, Finance: Charles Sadowski
SVP, Information Technology: Mike Schwank

LOCATIONS

HQ: 1131 SW Klickitat Way, Seattle, WA 98134
Phone: 206-623-0304 **Fax:** 206-623-0179
Web: www.ssofa.com

Stevedoring Services of America has operations in Africa, the Asia/Pacific region, North America, and South America.

COMPETITORS

Alexander & Baldwin
Associated British Ports
Evergreen Marine
Hutchison Whampoa
Mitsubishi Logistics
P&O
TMM

HISTORICAL FINANCIALS

Company Type: Private

Income Statement FYE: January 31

	ESTIMATED REVENUE ($ mil.)	NET INCOME ($ mil.)	NET PROFIT MARGIN	EMPLOYEES
1/02	1,046	—	—	10,000
1/01	1,000	—	—	6,000
1/00	950	—	—	6,000
1/99	850	—	—	6,000
1/98	850	—	—	7,500
1/97	800	—	—	6,000
1/96	700	—	—	5,000
1/95	500	—	—	4,200
1/94	500	—	—	4,200
Annual Growth	9.7%	—	—	11.5%

Revenue History

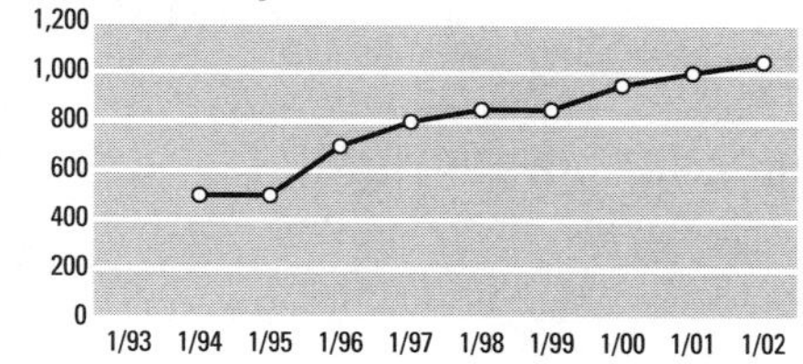

Stewart's Shops

I scream, you scream, we all scream for Stewart's ice cream, especially if we live in upstate New York or Vermont, home to more than 300 Stewart's Shops. Stewart's Shops (formerly known as Stewart's Ice Cream Company) runs a chain of convenience stores selling some 3,000 different products, including dairy items, groceries, food to go (chili and soup), beer, gasoline, and, of course, ice cream. Stewart's makes its own ice cream — more than 50 flavors both hand-dipped and packaged — and dairy products, and it has several private-label products. It also sells national brands. The founding Dake family owns about two-thirds of the company; employee compensation plans own the rest of Stewart's Shops.

EXECUTIVES

President and CEO: William (Bill) Dake
SVP: Nancy Trimbur
VP, Manufacturing: Gary C. Dake
Treasurer: David A. Farr
Director, HR: Jim Botch
Director, Marketing and Public Relations: Susan Dake

LOCATIONS

HQ: Stewart's Shops Corp.
2907 Route 9, Balston Spa, NY 12020
Phone: 518-581-1200 **Fax:** 518-581-1209
Web: www.stewartsicecream.com

PRODUCTS/OPERATIONS

Selected Products and Services

Banking terminals
Beer
Dairy products
Food to go
Gasoline
Groceries
Hand-dipped ice cream
Lottery sales
Packaged ice cream
Soda

COMPETITORS

7-Eleven
Allied Domecq
Ben & Jerry's
Brigham's
Cumberland Farms
Exxon Mobil
Golub
Kroger
Pathmark
Penn Traffic
Royal Ahold
Sunoco
TravelCenters of America

HISTORICAL FINANCIALS

Company Type: Private

Income Statement FYE: Last Sunday in December

	REVENUE ($ mil.)	NET INCOME ($ mil.)	NET PROFIT MARGIN	EMPLOYEES
12/02	730	—	—	3,200
12/01	700	—	—	3,000
12/00	648	—	—	2,990
Annual Growth	6.1%	—	—	3.5%

Revenue History

Strategic Hotel Capital LLC

Strategic Hotel Capital (SHC) strategically invests capital in hotels. The private investment group owns more than 30 hotel properties, which operate on a "fee for service" basis, in the US, Europe, and Mexico. Its affiliated brands include Four Seasons, Hilton, Marriott, and Ritz-Carlton, as well as trophy properties such as Manhattan's Marriott East Side and Essex House Westin and San Diego's Hyatt Regency. In early 2002 SHC began considering an IPO but plans seemed to fizzle as the economy headed south that summer. The company receives funding from Goldman Sachs and Prudential; CEO Laurence Geller also owns a stake in the company.

EXECUTIVES

Chairman and CEO: Laurence S. Geller, age 55
EVP and COO: Laurence B. Lacaff
EVP Corporate Strategy: Vernis D. Deming
SVP Development: Steven Kisielica
SVP Finance: Jayson C. Cyr
SVP and General Counsel: Patricia A. Needham
VP Acquisitions — Europe: Tanya Geller
Human Resources: Jan Peterson

LOCATIONS

HQ: 77 W. Wacker Dr., Ste. 4600, Chicago, IL 60601
Phone: 312-658-5000 **Fax:** 312-658-5799
Web: www.shci.com

PRODUCTS/OPERATIONS

Selected Hotel Brands

Embassy Suites
Four Seasons
Hilton
Hilton International
Hotel Inter-Continental
Hyatt
Loews
Marriott
Renaissance
Ritz-Carlton
Sheraton
Westin

COMPETITORS

Accor
Fairmont Hotels
Four Seasons Hotels
Helmsley
Hilton
Hyatt
Marriott International
Starwood Hotels & Resorts
Wyndham

HISTORICAL FINANCIALS

Company Type: Private

Income Statement FYE: December 31

	REVENUE ($ mil.)	NET INCOME ($ mil.)	NET PROFIT MARGIN	EMPLOYEES
12/01	1,000	—	—	50
12/00	1,000	—	—	47
12/99	860	—	—	—
Annual Growth	7.8%	—	—	6.4%

Revenue History

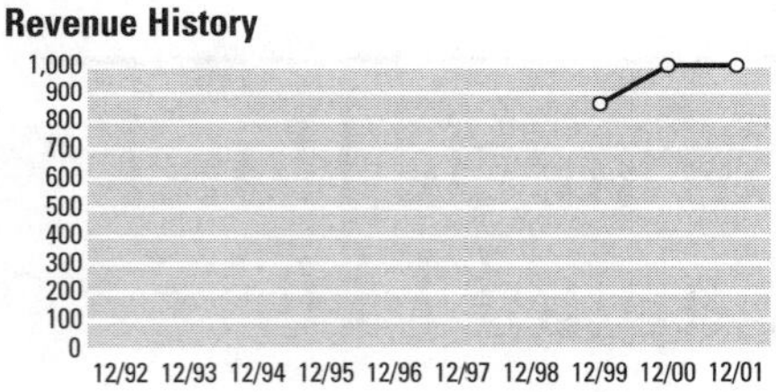

Structure Tone

Structured to set the right tone for its clients, The Structure Tone Organization develops corporate and commercial properties for major clients down the block and around the world. Through four main companies, the group provides general contracting, construction management, and project management services for building construction, interior fit-outs and renovations, and infrastructure upgrades. A top builder in the New York City area (it is a leader in telecommunications projects there as well), the company also works in Asia, Europe, and South America. Structure Tone was founded to focus on building interiors in 1971 by Lou Marino and Patrick Donaghy, whose family now owns the company.

EXECUTIVES

Chairman: James Donaghy
Vice Chairman: Brian Donaghy
President and COO: Anthony Carvette
CFO: Ray Froimowitz
SVP Human Resources: Robert Yardis
VP Marketing: Kevin Jackson
Director of Management Information Systems: Steven Barber
Director Human Resources: Tony Tursy

LOCATIONS

HQ: The Structure Tone Organization
770 Broadway, 9th Fl., New York, NY 10003
Phone: 212-481-6100 **Fax:** 212-685-9267
Web: www.structuretone.com

The Structure Tone Organization has offices in Colorado, Connecticut, Florida, Massachusetts, New Jersey, New York, Puerto Rico, Texas, and Virginia in the US. It also has locations in France, Germany, Hong Kong, Ireland, Italy, Spain, and the UK.

PRODUCTS/OPERATIONS

Companies

Constructors & Associates, Inc.
Pavarini Construction
ST TECH Services, Inc.
Structure Tone International
Structure Tone Inc.

Sectors

Commercial
Convention centers
Correctional facilities
Cultural centers
Educational
Entertainment
Health care
Hospitality
Interiors
Residential
Retail
Sports

COMPETITORS

AMEC Construction Management
Bovis Lend Lease
Clark Enterprises
Devcon Construction
DPR Construction
Foster Wheeler
Gilbane
Hunt Construction
Kajima Engineering and Construction
Opus
PCL
Perini
Peter Kiewit Sons'
Skanska USA Building
Tishman Realty
Turner Corporation
Walsh Group
Washington Group
WorkPlaceUSA

HISTORICAL FINANCIALS

Company Type: Private

Income Statement FYE: October 31

	ESTIMATED REVENUE ($ mil.)	NET INCOME ($ mil.)	NET PROFIT MARGIN	EMPLOYEES
10/02	2,100	—	—	1,600
10/01	2,100	—	—	1,600
10/00	2,000	—	—	1,300
10/99	1,600	—	—	1,000
Annual Growth	9.5%	—	—	17.0%

Revenue History

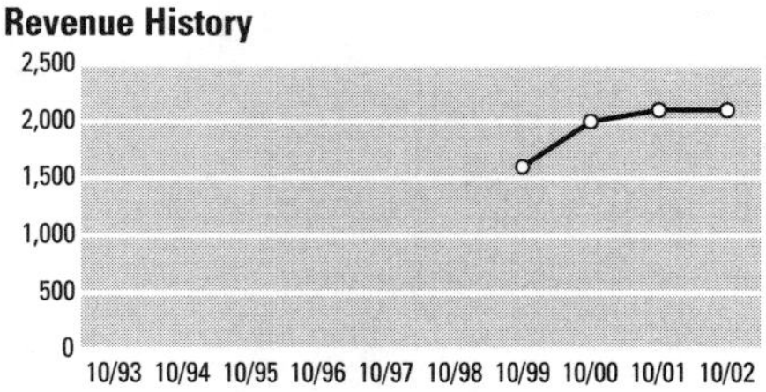

Suffolk Construction

The bricks fly at Suffolk Construction. The company provides general contracting, construction management, preconstruction, and design/build services to clients in the public and private sectors across the US. Commercial and residential projects include university halls, senior housing, hotels (Marriott, Hilton), corporate offices, and retail facilities.

A top Boston contractor, Suffolk Construction is owned by president John Fish and his father Edward, who created Suffolk Construction in 1982. It also operates in Florida and California.

The Fish family has been in the construction business for four generations (since the 1890s). Another construction company is owned by John's brother Ted Fish.

EXECUTIVES

Chairman: Edward A. Fish
President and Treasurer: John F. Fish
CFO: Mike Azarela
SVP, California Division: Michael Archibald
SVP, Florida Operations: Rex Kirby
Director Business Development, Florida: Steve Gelb
Director Operations, Special Projects Division: Mark DiNapoli
Human Resources: Jodi Grant
Auditors: Ziner, Kennedy, & Lehan LLP

LOCATIONS

HQ: Suffolk Construction Company, Inc.
65 Allerton St., Boston, MA 02119
Phone: 617-445-3500 **Fax:** 617-445-2343
Web: www.suffolk-construction.com

Suffolk Construction has offices in Boston; Irvine, California; and West Palm Beach, Florida. It has projects throughout the US.

PRODUCTS/OPERATIONS

Selected Services

Construction Management
Permit processing assistance
Physical construction supervision
Project schedule preparation and maintenance
Requisition processing and submission
Systems operation training

Design/Build Process
Project team direction
Architect hire

General Contracting
Hard bids
Project schedules
Project specific safety plans
Staging and sequencing plans

Preconstruction
Design and permitting assistance
Preconstruction and construction schedule development
Recommendation of long lead item purchases

COMPETITORS

Bovis Lend Lease
Centex
Clark Enterprises
Kraus-Anderson
McCarthy Building
Modern Continental Companies
Pepper Construction
Perini
Swinerton
Turner Corporation
Walsh Group
Whiting-Turner

HISTORICAL FINANCIALS

Company Type: Private

Income Statement FYE: August 31

	REVENUE ($ mil.)	NET INCOME ($ mil.)	NET PROFIT MARGIN	EMPLOYEES
8/02	702	—	—	487
8/01	663	—	—	460
8/00	574	—	—	425
8/99	556	—	—	401
Annual Growth	8.1%	—	—	6.7%

Revenue History

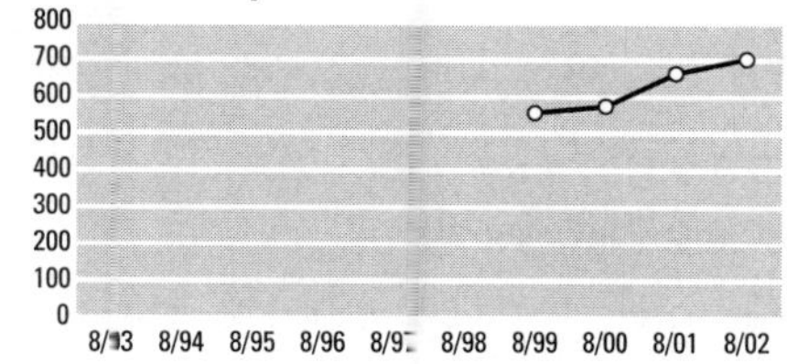

Sullivan & Cromwell LLP

Sullivan & Cromwell has a long and storied history. Founded in 1879 by Algernon Sullivan and William Cromwell, the firm was on hand for the foundation of both General Electric in 1882 and United States Steel in 1901. Today, Sullivan & Cromwell has about 700 lawyers in four US and eight international offices. It focuses on corporate law for industrial, commercial, and financial clients, more than half of which are located abroad. Sullivan & Cromwell's major clients include investment and banking giant Goldman Sachs and Microsoft (which the firm has represented in its antitrust battle with the US Justice Department).

EXECUTIVES

Chairman: H. Rodgin Cohen
Executive Director: Arthur Gurwitz
Director Finance: Larry Tsaousis
Director Legal Personnel: Andrea Locklear

LOCATIONS

HQ: 125 Broad St., New York, NY 10004
Phone: 212-558-4000 **Fax:** 212-558-3588
Web: www.sullcrom.com

Sullivan & Cromwell has offices in Beijing; Frankfurt; Hong Kong; London; Los Angeles and Palo Alto, California; Melbourne; New York City; Paris; Sydney; Tokyo; and Washington, DC.

PRODUCTS/OPERATIONS

Selected Practice Areas

Banking
Commercial real estate
Corporate and financial
Estates and personal
Litigation
Mergers and acquisitions
Project finance
Tax

COMPETITORS

Baker & McKenzie
Clifford Chance
Cravath, Swaine
Davis Polk
Jones Day
Latham & Watkins
Skadden, Arps
Wachtell, Lipton
Williams & Connolly

HISTORICAL FINANCIALS

Company Type: Partnership

Income Statement FYE: December 31

	REVENUE ($ mil.)	NET INCOME ($ mil.)	NET PROFIT MARGIN	EMPLOYEES
12/02	624	—	—	—
12/01	568	—	—	—
12/00	517	—	—	—
12/99	474	—	—	2,000
12/98	427	—	—	2,000
12/97	395	—	—	2,000
12/96	346	—	—	—
12/95	318	—	—	—
12/94	298	—	—	—
12/93	299	—	—	—
Annual Growth	8.5%	—	—	0.0%

Revenue History

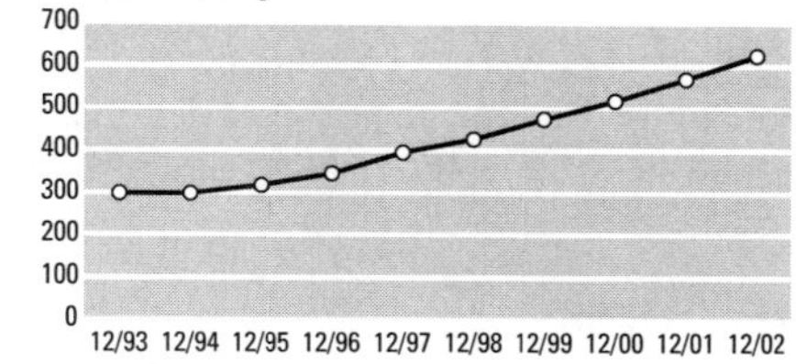

The Sundt Companies, Inc.

Arizona is the land of sun and the home of Sundt. Through Sundt Construction and other subsidiaries, The Sundt Companies offers construction management, general contracting, and design/build services for its commercial, governmental, and industrial clients. It also can finance, own, and lease projects back to the customer. Sundt's projects include commercial buildings, highways, flood control, pipelines, senior housing, and fiber-optic cable installation. A builder of military housing, in 1943 the company developed the top-secret town of Los Alamos, New Mexico, where the first atomic bomb was built. Founded in 1890 by Norwegian immigrant carpenter Mauritz Sundt, the company is now employee-owned.

EXECUTIVES

Chairman and CEO, The Sundt Companies and Sundt Construction: J. Doug Pruitt
EVP and CFO: Raymond C. Bargull
SVP Human Resources: Richard Condit
SVP and General Counsel: Peter Johnson
President, C.R. Fedrick: Dee Fedrick
President and COO, Sundt Construction Northern California: Robert Earl
President, Heavy Construction Division, Sundt Construction: John Cluff
President and COO, Southern California, Sundt Construction: Thomas R. (Tom) Remensperger
President, Texas Division, Sundt Construction: Brice Hill

LOCATIONS

HQ: 4101 E. Irvington Rd., Tucson, AZ 85714
Phone: 520-748-7555 **Fax:** 520-750-6295
Web: www.sundt.com

The Sundt Companies and its subsidiaries have offices in Dallas; Novato, Sacramento, and San Diego, California; and Tempe and Tucson, Arizona.

PRODUCTS/OPERATIONS

Selected Services

Competitive bid
Construction management
Design/assist
Develop/leaseback
General contracting
Project management
Tenant improve/renovation
Turnkey

COMPETITORS

Austin Industries
Centex
Charles Pankow Builders
D. L. Withers
DPR Construction
Granite Construction
Hunt Building
Hunt Construction
Kitchell Corporation
McCarthy Building
Meadow Valley
O'Neil Industries
Perini
Peter Kiewit Sons'
Swinerton
Target General
Weitz

HISTORICAL FINANCIALS

Company Type: Private

Income Statement FYE: September 30

	REVENUE ($ mil.)	NET INCOME ($ mil.)	NET PROFIT MARGIN	EMPLOYEES
9/02	464	—	—	4,360
9/01	500	—	—	1,929
9/00	550	—	—	1,300
9/99	525	—	—	1,300
9/98	450	—	—	1,400
9/97	436	—	—	1,375
9/96	417	—	—	—
Annual Growth	1.8%	—	—	26.0%

Revenue History

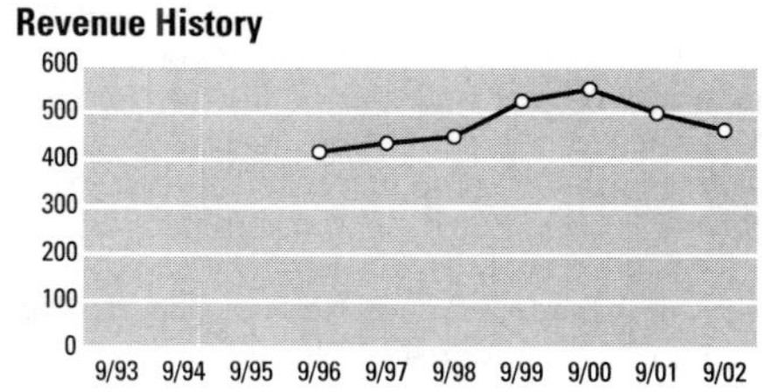

Sunkist Growers

Perhaps the US enterprise least susceptible to an outbreak of scurvy, Sunkist Growers is a cooperative owned by 6,000 citrus farmers in California and Arizona. Sunkist markets fresh oranges, lemons, grapefruit, and tangerines in the US and overseas. Fruit that doesn't meet fresh market standards is turned into juices, oils, and peels for use in food products. The Sunkist brand is one of the most recognized names in the US; through licensing agreements the name also appears worldwide on dozens of beverages and other products, from vitamins to fruit rolls.

Sunkist is one of the 10 largest marketing cooperatives in America and the largest cooperative in the world's fruit and vegetable industry. More than 20% of Sunkist's sales volume is exported; Sunkist's biggest export customers are Canada, Hong Kong, Japan, and South Korea. Sunkist has licensing agreements with companies in more than 55 countries.

In order to keep up with a changing market and consumer demand, in 2003 Sunkist announced that it would begin offering precut bagged fruit to consumers and restaurants.

HISTORY

Sunkist Growers was founded in the early 1890s as the Pachappa Orange Growers, a group of California citrus farmers determined to control the sale of their fruit. Success attracted new members, and in 1893 the Southern California Fruit Exchange was born. The name "Sunkissed" was coined by an ad copywriter in 1908, and it was soon reworked into "Sunkist" and registered as a trademark, becoming the first brand name for a fresh produce item. Eventually the co-op renamed itself after its popular brand: It became Sunkist Growers in 1952. Sunkist began licensing its trademark to other companies in the early 1950s.

As early as 1916, efforts to increase citrus consumption included designing and marketing glass citrus juicers and encouraging homemakers to "Drink an Orange." The co-op also promoted the practice of putting lemon slices in tea or water and funded early research on the health benefits of vitamins (vitamin C in particular). In 1925 tissue wrappers gave way to stamping the Sunkist name directly on each piece of fruit.

Although Sunkist pioneered bottled orange juice in 1933, its juice marketing efforts were never as successful as those of its Florida competitors. Florida oranges are drippy and dowdy and thus better suited for juicing. Capitalizing on this aspect, Florida growers dominated the market for fresh and frozen juice.

In 1937 Congress created a system of citrus shipment quotas and limits (known as "marketing orders") that ultimately proved most beneficial to large citrus cooperatives. By the early 1990s the marketing order system was under political attack, and in 1992 the Justice Department filed civil prosecution against Sunkist, alleging that the co-op had reaped unfair extra profits by surpassing its lemon shipment limits. In 1994, after much legal wrangling, the quotas were abolished and the Justice Department dropped its case against Sunkist.

Inconveniently warm weather and increasing competition from imported citrus marked the harvests of 1996. That year the co-op had trouble maintaining discipline among its members; some undercut Sunkist price levels, while others flooded the market to sell their fruit at the higher early market prices, creating a supply surplus. Also that year the co-op relinquished the marketing of all Sunkist juices in North America to Florida-based Lykes Bros. in a licensing agreement.

The co-op agreed in 1998 to distribute grapefruit from Florida's Tuxedo Fruit, providing Sunkist with winter grapefruit supply and increasing its year-round consumer a-peel. Also in 1998 Russell Hanlin, Sunkist president and CEO since 1978, was succeeded by Vince Lupinacci. Lupinacci, who had held positions with Pepsi and Six Flags, became the first person from outside the citrus business to hold Sunkist's top post.

In 1998 the company sold 90 million cartons of fresh citrus — the greatest volume in its history — despite increased competition from imported Latin American, South African, and Spanish crops, a damaging California freeze, and the ill effects of El Nino. The next year production was almost halved because of adverse weather.

Lupinacci resigned in 2000, citing personal and family reasons. Chairman Emeritus James Mast then took the helm as acting president. Although the company grew its market through exports to China in 2000, its profits were squeezed that year by increasing foreign competition, a citrus glut, and lessened demand. In mid-2001 Jeff Gargiulo replaced Mast as Sunkist's president and CEO.

EXECUTIVES

Chairman: Al Williams
President Emeritus: Russell L. Hanlin
President and CEO: Jeffrey D. (Jeff) Gargiulo
VP and COO: James A. (Jim) Padden
VP, Corporate Relations: Michael J. Wootton
VP, Finance and Treasurer: Richard G. French
VP, Domestic Sales: John B. McGuigan
VP, International Sales and Sales Operations: Russell L. Hanlin II
VP, Law and General Counsel: Thomas M. Moore
VP, Licensing/International Business Development: Ashok D. Patel
VP, Marketing and Sales Promotion: Robert J. Verloop
VP, Processed Products, Research/Technical Services: Owen W. Belletto
Corporate Secretary: Linda D. Shepler
Director, Human Resources: John R. McGovern
Auditors: KPMG LLP

LOCATIONS

HQ: Sunkist Growers, Inc.
14130 Riverside Dr., Sherman Oaks, CA 91423
Phone: 818-986-4800 **Fax:** 818-379-7405
Web: www.sunkist.com

2002 Sales

	$ mil.	% of total
Domestic Sales	585	61
Export Sales	215	22
Other	164	17
Total	**964**	**100**

COMPETITORS

Alico
Chiquita Brands
Coca-Cola North America
Dole
Florida's Natural
Fresh Del Monte Produce
Gatorade/Tropicana
Louis Dreyfus Citrus
UniMark Group
Vitality Beverages

HISTORICAL FINANCIALS

Company Type: Cooperative

Income Statement FYE: October 31

	REVENUE ($ mil.)	NET INCOME ($ mil.)	NET PROFIT MARGIN	EMPLOYEES
10/02	964	(2)	—	—
10/01	993	4	0.4%	—
10/00	847	(4)	—	—
10/99	862	6	0.7%	—
10/98	1,069	6	0.6%	875
10/97	1,075	—	—	813
10/96	1,025	—	—	878
10/95	1,096	—	—	1,150
10/94	1,005	—	—	1,138
10/93	1,093	—	—	1,200
Annual Growth	(1.4%)	—	—	(6.1%)

2002 Year-End Financials

Debt ratio: 97.4%
Return on equity: —
Cash ($ mil.): 13
Current ratio: 1.32
Long-term debt ($ mil.): 48

Net Income History

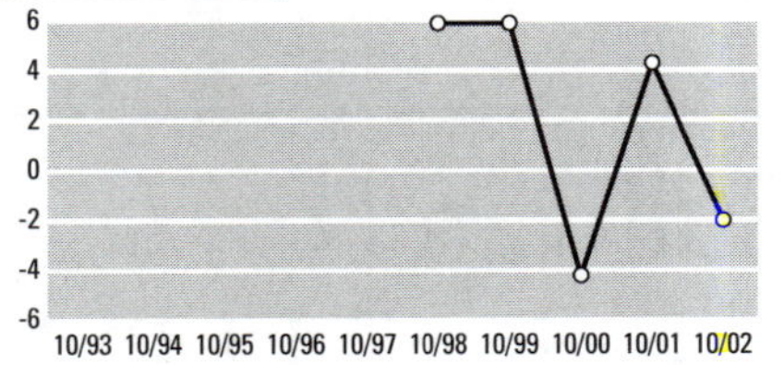

Superior Group

Metal-centric holding company Superior Group makes and sells tubing through subsidiaries Fine Tubes (precision tubing), Superior Tube (small metal tubing), Swepco Tube (corrosion-resistant tubing and pipe), and Western Pneumatic Tube (thin-walled tubing). Its TW Metals subsidiary is a metals distributor and processor for such customers as Air France, FedEx, and United Airlines. Superior's Drever Group designs and sells industrial furnaces to steel mills and metal manufactures, while Sharp Corp. makes consumer-friendly packaging for pharmaceuticals such as carded blister packaging and child-resistant bottles. SGI Capital is Superior's investment arm. Superior is owned by the Warden family, heirs of its founder.

EXECUTIVES

CEO: William G. Warden IV
President: Peter G. Gould
Director Employee Relations: Tom Pezick
President, SGI Capital: Tom Balderston
President and CEO, Sharp: George K. Burke Jr.
President, Swepco Tube: Kenneth J. Schultz Jr.
President and CEO, TW Metals: Dennis M. Oates
President and CEO, Western Pneumatic Tube: R. Dirk Fanning

LOCATIONS

HQ: Superior Group, Inc.
3 Radnor Corporate Center, Ste. 400,
Radnor, PA 19087
Phone: 610-964-2000 **Fax:** 610-964-2001
Web: www.superior-group.com

Through its subsidiaries, Superior Group operates through more than 40 facilities in Europe and the US.

PRODUCTS/OPERATIONS

Selected Products

Metal Distribution Market
Fittings
Pipe
Tubing

Specialty Market
Anneal furnaces
Bright annealing furnaces
Continuing annealing furnaces
Pickle furnaces
Sintering furnaces
Strip packaging
Tube annealing furnaces

Tube Manufacturing Market
Coil tube
Light wall welded tubing
Nickel-based alloys
Precision tubing
Small diameter metal tubing
Straight length tube
Stainless steels
Structural shapes
Titanium alloys
Tubing
Welded pipe

COMPETITORS

American Cast Iron pipe
Connell Limited Partnership
Earle M. Jorgensen
Field Container
Inductotherm
Lone Star Technologies
Maverick Tube
Novamerican Steel
RPC Group
Special Metals
Wolverine Tube

HISTORICAL FINANCIALS

Company Type: Private

Income Statement

FYE: December 31

	ESTIMATED REVENUE ($ mil.)	NET INCOME ($ mil.)	NET PROFIT MARGIN	EMPLOYEES
12/02	750	—	—	3,400
12/01	800	—	—	3,400
12/00	750	—	—	3,400
Annual Growth	0.0%	—	—	0.0%

Revenue History

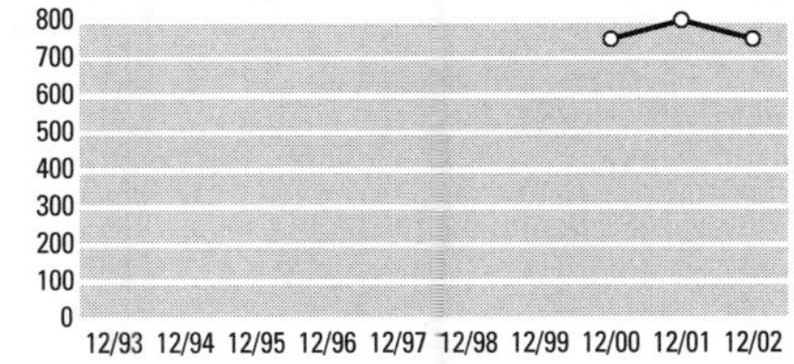

Sutherland Lumber

The West is best for Sutherland Lumber. The company operates some 60 lumber and home-improvement stores in 15 western and midwestern states. Sutherland's stores range in size from 50,000 to 190,000 sq. ft. They sell lumber, paints, tools, and building packages for houses, sheds, garages, and farm buildings. In addition the stores sell lawn and garden equipment, plumbing supplies, and materials for hobbies and crafts. The company, which is owned and operated by the Sutherland family, was founded in 1917 as an oilfield supplier. The family also has holdings in ranching, farmland, timber, and manufacturing.

EXECUTIVES

CEO and CFO: Steve Scott
President and CEO, Housemart.com: Chris Sutherland Jr.
President, Sutherland Lumber and Home Center: Chris Sutherland
Human Resources Director: Shanna Wilson
Data Processing Manager: Bill Bryan
Marketing Manager: Tina Keller

LOCATIONS

HQ: Sutherland Lumber Company, L.P.
4000 Main St., Kansas City, MO 64111
Phone: 816-756-3000 **Fax:** 816-756-3594
Web: www.sutherlands.com

Sutherland Lumber has stores in Arizona, Arkansas, Colorado, Iowa, Kansas, Louisiana, Mississippi, Missouri, Nebraska, New Mexico, Ohio, Oklahoma, Texas, Utah, and Wyoming.

COMPETITORS

84 Lumber
Ace Hardware
Amazon.com
Do it Best
Foxworth-Galbraith Lumber
Home Depot
Hope Lumber & Supply
Lowe's
McCoy
Menard
TruServ
Wickes

HISTORICAL FINANCIALS

Company Type: Private

Income Statement

FYE: December 31

	ESTIMATED REVENUE ($ mil.)	NET INCOME ($ mil.)	NET PROFIT MARGIN	EMPLOYEES
12/01	850	—	—	2,300
12/00	825	—	—	2,300
12/99	800	—	—	2,300
12/98	780	—	—	3,000
12/97	740	—	—	3,000
12/96	910	—	—	3,000
12/95	925	—	—	3,000
12/94	900	—	—	3,000
12/93	850	—	—	3,000
Annual Growth	0.0%	—	—	(3.3%)

Revenue History

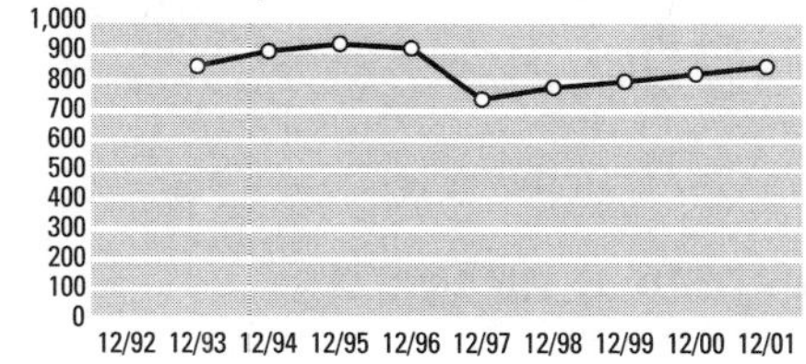

Sutter Health

Sutter Health is one of the nation's largest not-for-profit health care systems. It was organized in 1996 through the merger of Sutter Health and California Healthcare System. Today the company caters to residents in more than 100 northern California communities. Its services are provided through the firm's approximately 3,600 affiliated doctors, from facilities of various types, including acute care hospitals, home health/hospice networks, medical groups, occupational health services centers, and skilled nursing facilities. Sutter Health's network also boasts several research institutes.

EXECUTIVES

Chairman: Ralph E. Andersen
President, CEO, and Director: Van R. Johnson
EVP and COO: Patrick E. Fry
SVP and CFO: Robert D. Reed
SVP, Chief Medical Officer, and Clinical Integration Officer: Gordon C. Hunt Jr.
SVP and General Counsel: Gary Loveridge
SVP, Administrative Services: Joel Grey
SVP, Public Affairs: Cyndi Kettmann
VP, Human Resources: Ken Buback
Auditors: Ernst & Young LLP

LOCATIONS

HQ: 2200 River Plaza Dr., Sacramento, CA 95833
Phone: 916-733-8800 **Fax:** 916-286-6841
Web: www.sutterhealth.org

PRODUCTS/OPERATIONS

Hospitals

Alta Bates Medical Centers (Berkeley, CA)
California Pacific Medical Centers (San Francisco)
Eden Medical Center (Castro Valley, CA)
Kahi Mohala, A Behavioral Healthcare System (Ewa Beach, HI)
Marin General Hospital (San Rafael, CA)
Memorial Hospital Los Banos (CA)
Memorial Medical Center (Modesto, CA)
Novato Community Hospital (CA)
Peninsula Medical Center (Burlingame, CA)
Summit Medical Center (Oakland, CA)
Sutter Amador Hospital (Jackson, CA)
Sutter Auburn Faith Hospital (CA)
Sutter Center for Psychiatry (Sacramento, CA)
Sutter Coast Hospital (Crescent City, CA)
Sutter Davis Hospital (CA)
Sutter Delta Medical Center (Antioch, CA)
Sutter Lakeside Hospital (Lakeport, CA)
Sutter Maternity & Surgery Center of Santa Cruz (CA)
Sutter Medical Center of Santa Rosa (CA)
Sutter Medical Center, Sacramento (CA)
Sutter Roseville Medical Center (CA)
Sutter Solano Medical Center (Vallejo, CA)
Sutter Tracy Community Hospital (CA)

COMPETITORS

Adventist Health	Providence Health
Catholic Healthcare West	Stanford University Medical
HCA	Tenet Healthcare
Memorial Health Services	

HISTORICAL FINANCIALS

Company Type: Not-for-profit

Income Statement FYE: December 31

	REVENUE ($ mil.)	NET INCOME ($ mil.)	NET PROFIT MARGIN	EMPLOYEES
12/01	4,216	101	2.4%	36,000
12/00	3,500	111	3.2%	35,000
12/99	2,919	51	1.7%	35,000
12/98	2,881	39	1.3%	35,000
12/97	2,663	60	2.3%	35,000
12/96	2,453	24	1.0%	35,000
12/95	2,226	—	—	—
12/94	1,940	—	—	—
12/93	958	—	—	—
Annual Growth	20.3%	33.3%	—	0.6%

Net Income History

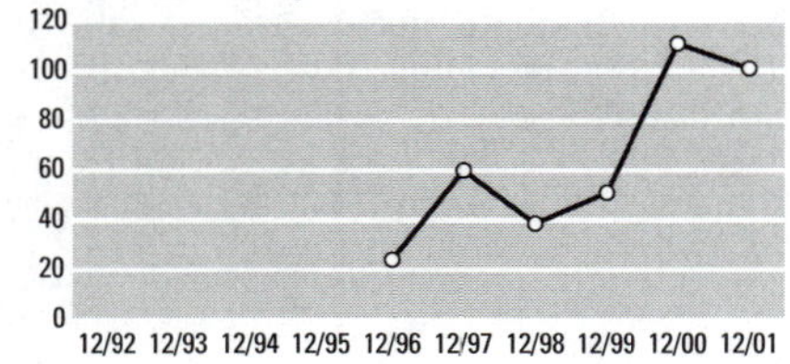

Swagelok Company

With sales partners worldwide, Swagelok Company has to speak many languages, *fluidly*. The company makes fluid system components, which include plug, pinch, and radial diaphragm valves, sanitary fittings, and welding systems. Its products are used by bioprocessing and pharmaceuticals research companies and in the oil and gas, power, and semiconductor industries. Swagelok has more than 200 manufacturing, research, sales, and distribution facilities worldwide. Founded in 1947 by Fred Lennon in his kitchen, the company requires all prospective sales people and their families to tour company facilities for two months before coming on board. The Lennon family still controls the company.

Swagelok is expanding the product base in its biopharmaceutical line of valves and related supplies through the introduction of new equipment and acquisitions. The company has also expanded its line of pressure gauges.

EXECUTIVES

Chairman and CEO: William R. Cosgrove
President and COO: Arthur F. (Art) Anton
CFO: Frank J. Roddy
VP, Corporate Communications: Franziska H. Dacek
VP, Engineering: Carl E. Meece
VP, Human Resources: James L. Francis
VP, Information Systems: David E. O'Connor
VP, Marketing: Michael R. Butkovic
VP, Operations: Kennan J. Malec
VP, Planning and Development: Michael L. MacKay
Corporate Communications: Dennis Grantham

LOCATIONS

HQ: 29500 Solon Rd., Solon, OH 44139
Phone: 440-248-4600 **Fax:** 440-349-5970
Web: www.swagelok.com

PRODUCTS/OPERATIONS

Selected Products

Filters	Quick connects
Fittings	Regulators
Gauges	Sample cylinders
Hoses	Tube benders and cutters
Leak detectors	Valves
Lubricants and sealants	Weld systems
Manifolds	

COMPETITORS

Amcast Industrial	ITT Industries
CIRCOR International	Shaw Group
Consolidated Stainless	T3
Crane	Tyco International
Hughes Supply	Walter Industries

HISTORICAL FINANCIALS

Company Type: Private

Income Statement FYE: December 31

	ESTIMATED REVENUE ($ mil.)	NET INCOME ($ mil.)	NET PROFIT MARGIN	EMPLOYEES
12/02	1,000	—	—	3,000
12/01	1,000	—	—	3,000
12/00	1,200	—	—	3,300
12/99	1,050	—	—	2,000
12/98	1,030	—	—	5,000
12/97	1,200	—	—	2,500
12/96	1,100	—	—	2,500
12/95	1,000	—	—	2,500
12/94	1,000	—	—	2,500
12/93	600	—	—	1,900
Annual Growth	5.8%	—	—	5.2%

Revenue History

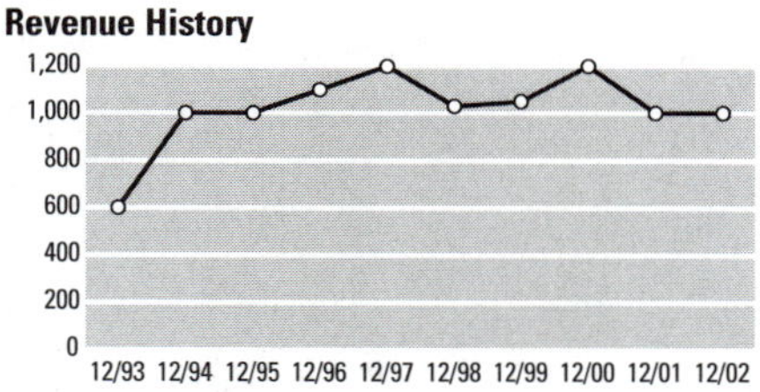

Swift & Company

Swift & Company has a hoof up on other newcomers to the meat industry. Once the meat processing business of ConAgra, the company was spun off and is now 54% owned by an investment group led by Hicks, Muse, Tate & Furst and Booth Creek Management. ConAgra has kept 46% of Swift and still obtains fresh beef, pork, and lamb from its former subsidiary, but only accounts for 9% of its sales. With operations in Australia as well as the US, the company is the #3 US beef processor — behind Tyson's IBP Fresh Meats and Cargill's Excel unit. Swift & Company is focused on fresh, branded, and value-added meats.

In 2003 Swift partnered with Specialty Foods Group to produce deli meats (dry sausages, smoked and cooked meats, and deli sticks and loaves) under the Swift Premium name.

EXECUTIVES

Chairman: George N. Gillett Jr., age 64
President, CEO, and Director: John N. Simons Jr., age 42, $600,000 pay
President, North American Red Meats: Dennis Henley, age 57, $400,000 pay
VP, CFO: Danny Herron, age 48, $300,000 pay
VP, Beef Operations: Marshall Ernst, age 51, $375,000 pay
VP, General Counsel: Donald F. Wiseman, age 57, $275,000 pay
VP, Communications: Jim Herlihy
VP, Human Resources: Jack Shandley
Auditors: PWC

LOCATIONS

HQ: 1770 Promontory Circle, Greeley, CO 80634
Phone: 970-506-8000 **Fax:** 970-506-8307
Web: www.swiftbrands.com

Swift & Company has operations in the US and Australia.

PRODUCTS/OPERATIONS

2003 Sales

	% of total
Swift Beef	67
Swift Pork	19
Swift Australia	14
Swift Lamb	—
Total	**100**

COMPETITORS

Cargill
ContiGroup
Greater Omaha Packing
Hormel
Smithfield Foods
Tyson Foods
Tyson Fresh Meats
U.S. Premium Beef
Wolverine Packing

HISTORICAL FINANCIALS

Company Type: Private

Income Statement FYE: Last Sunday in May

	REVENUE ($ mil.)	NET INCOME ($ mil.)	NET PROFIT MARGIN	EMPLOYEES
5/03	8,432	58	0.7%	21,300
5/02	8,476	76	0.9%	21,400
5/01	9,060	66	0.7%	—
5/00	8,963	36	0.4%	—
5/99	8,040	10	0.1%	—
5/98	7,997	(61)	—	—
Annual Growth	1.1%	—	—	(0.5%)

2003 Year-End Financials

Debt ratio: 131.7%	Current ratio: 1.98
Return on equity: 6.7%	Long-term debt ($ mil.): 620
Cash ($ mil.): 65	

Net Income History

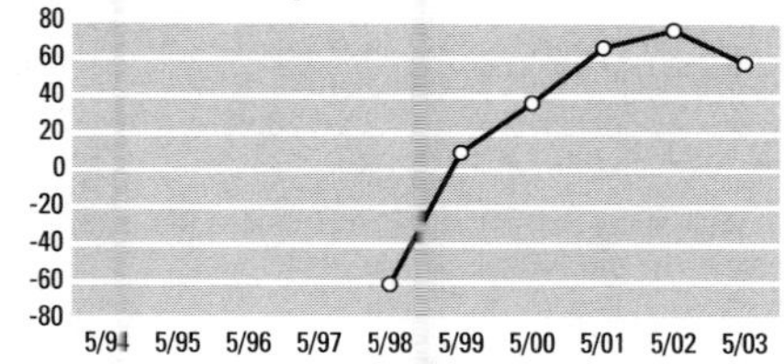

Swinerton Incorporated

Swinerton is building up the West just as it helped rebuild San Francisco after the 1906 earthquake. The construction group, formerly Swinerton & Walberg, builds commercial, industrial, and government facilities, including resorts, subsidized housing, public schools, Hollywood soundstages, hospitals, and airport terminals. Through subsidiaries Swinerton offers general contracting, construction and program management, and design/build services. It also provides property management for conventional, subsidized, and assisted living residences. The employee-owned company, which has been expanding in the past decade in the Northwest and Southwest, traces its family tree to 1888.

EXECUTIVES

Chairman and CEO: David H. (Dave) Grubb Sr.
President: James R. (Jim) Gillette
EVP and CFO: Michael Re
EVP Business Development: Jeffrey C. Hoopes
VP Business Development: Lee Ploszaj
VP (San Diego): Christopher Day
VP Human Resources: Paul Smolinski
Communications Coordinator: Sara Hall
Auditors: PricewaterhouseCoopers

LOCATIONS

HQ: 260 Townsend St., San Francisco, CA 94107
Phone: 415-421-2980 **Fax:** 415-984-1204
Web: www.swinerton.com

Swinerton's group of companies has offices in seven western states in the US: Arizona, California, Colorado, Oregon, Texas, Utah, and Washington.

PRODUCTS/OPERATIONS

Selected Services

Construction Services
Construction management
Design/build
General contracting
Specialty construction

Consultant Services
Loan administration
Surety services

Property Services
Construction and renovation management
Owner representation and consulting
Property assessment
Property management

Selected Markets

Education and research
Entertainment
Health care
Hotels
Office buildings
Public facilities
Recreational facilities
Renovation and restoration
Retail
Technology
Tenant improvement
Transportation

COMPETITORS

Bechtel
Beck Group
Bovis Lend Lease
Charles Pankow Builders
Devcon Construction
DPR Construction
Gilbane
Hathaway Dinwiddie Construction
Hensel Phelps Construction
J.F. Shea
Kitchell Corporation
Rudolph & Sletten
S. J. Amoroso Construction
Skanska USA Building
Sundt
Turner Corporation
Tutor-Saliba
Webcor Builders
Whiting-Turner

HISTORICAL FINANCIALS

Company Type: Private

Income Statement FYE: December 31

	REVENUE ($ mil.)	NET INCOME ($ mil.)	NET PROFIT MARGIN	EMPLOYEES
12/01	1,549	—	—	1,200
12/00	1,550	—	—	1,450
12/99	1,150	—	—	1,400
12/98	902	—	—	1,500
12/97	792	—	—	1,400
12/96	501	—	—	1,300
12/95	412	—	—	1,000
12/94	389	—	—	1,200
12/93	290	—	—	1,100
12/92	250	—	—	—
Annual Growth	22.5%	—	—	1.1%

Revenue History

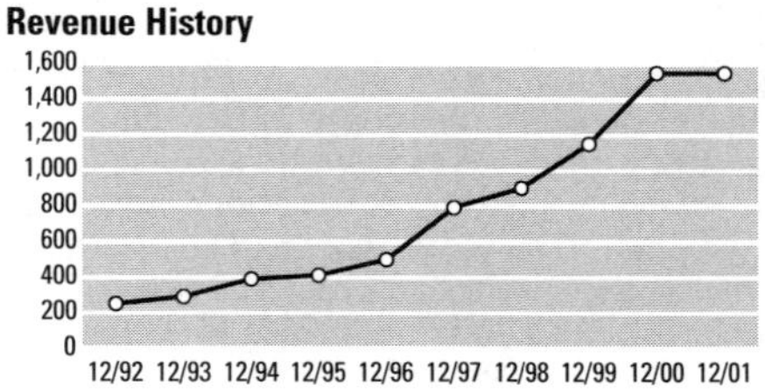

TAC Worldwide Companies

TAC Worldwide wants to be a permanent fixture in the temporary staffing business. The company offers contract and temporary staffing services through 150 offices in all 50 states and in 22 countries throughout Europe, North America, and Southeast Asia. TAC offers staffing in fields such as information technology, engineering, office support, and entertainment. Each year it places 50,000 contract and temporary employees with more than 6,500 companies. Chairman Salvatore Balsamo, who controls TAC Worldwide, founded the company as Technical Aid Corporation in 1969.

EXECUTIVES

Chairman: Salvatore A. (Sal) Balsamo
President and CEO: Gary T. DiCamillo, age 52
EVP: Jim Fabiano
CIO: Steve Morin
Director Human Resources: Bob Moritz

LOCATIONS

HQ: 888 Washington St., Dedham, MA 02026
Phone: 781-251-8000 **Fax:** 781-251-8064
Web: www.1tac.com

PRODUCTS/OPERATIONS

Selected Operations

EDP Contract Services (IT staffing)
TAC Automotive Group (automotive staffing)
TAC Engineering Resources (computer-related engineering staffing)
TAC Entertainment Staffing (entertainment staffing)
TAC Nationwide Staffing (technical and engineering staffing)
TAC Staffing Services (clerical, accounting, and customer services staffing)
TECH/AID (technical staffing)
Technical Aid Europe (engineering and IT staffing in Europe)

COMPETITORS

Adecco
Bartech
CDI
Kelly Services
Manpower
MPS
MSX International
Randstad
Robert Half
Spherion
Trans Global Services
Vedior
Volt Information

HISTORICAL FINANCIALS

Company Type: Private

Income Statement FYE: December 31

	REVENUE ($ mil.)	NET INCOME ($ mil.)	NET PROFIT MARGIN	EMPLOYEES
12/01	850	—	—	1,150
12/00	1,100	—	—	1,298
12/99	1,000	—	—	1,150
12/98	737	—	—	1,075
12/97	648	—	—	1,075
12/96	566	—	—	1,060
12/95	390	—	—	1,090
Annual Growth	13.9%	—	—	0.9%

Revenue History

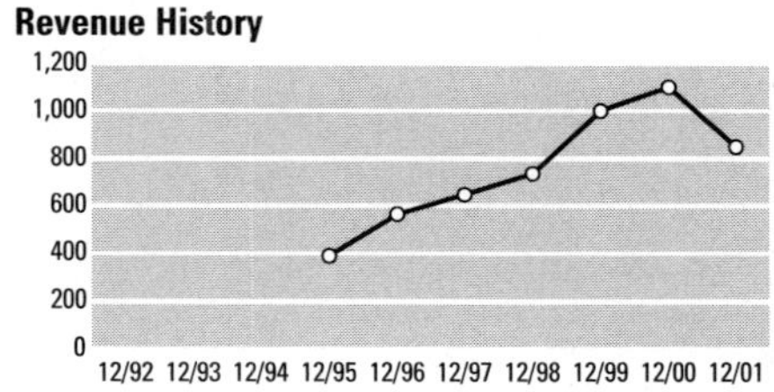

Tang Industries

Although it's not a good source of Vitamin C, Tang Industries *is* a diversified holding company. Its largest subsidiary, National Material, is a metal-fabricating and -distributing company that engages in steel stamping and recycles and trades aluminum and scrap metal. Another subsidiary, SKD Automotive Group, supplies tooling operations aimed at the automobile industry. Tang Industries also has steel operations in China. The company's holdings include real estate, manufacturer GF Office Furniture, and Curatek Pharmaceuticals, which specializes in niche markets overlooked by large drugmakers. The company was founded in 1964 by Chinese immigrant Cyrus Tang after he bought a small metal-stamping shop in Illinois.

EXECUTIVES

Chairman, President, and CEO: Cyrus Tang
Treasurer and Secretary: John Chen
VP, Legal and Administration and General Counsel, National Material LP: Vytas Ambutas
Asst. Treasurer: Kurt R. Swanson

LOCATIONS

HQ: Tang Industries, Inc.
3773 Howard Hughes Pkwy., Ste. 350N,
Las Vegas, NV 89109
Phone: 702-734-3700 **Fax:** 702-734-6766
Web: www.tangindustries.com

Tang Industries has more than 50 facilities in Canada, Mexico, and the US.

PRODUCTS/OPERATIONS

Selected Operations

Curatek Pharmaceuticals
GF Office Furniture, Ltd. (steel and wooden office furniture)
  Office Suites, Inc. (wooden office furniture)
National Material, LP (industrial manufacturing)
  Cox Metal Processing Co.
  Interstate Steel Co.
  National Coating Technology
  National Lamination Co.
Taber Extrusions
  SKD Industries (stamped and welded automotive components)

COMPETITORS

Abbott Labs
Alcoa
Bristol-Myers Squibb
Commercial Metals
Haworth
Herman Miller
Metalcraft
OmniSource
Ryerson Tull
Steelcase

HISTORICAL FINANCIALS

Company Type: Private

Income Statement FYE: December 31

	ESTIMATED REVENUE ($ mil.)	NET INCOME ($ mil.)	NET PROFIT MARGIN	EMPLOYEES
12/02	1,270	—	—	3,750
12/01	1,250	—	—	3,700
12/00	1,250	—	—	3,700
12/99	1,230	—	—	3,600
12/98	1,200	—	—	3,500
12/97	975	—	—	3,770
12/96	1,100	—	—	4,000
12/95	1,300	—	—	3,800
12/94	1,100	—	—	3,700
12/93	878	—	—	3,500
Annual Growth	4.2%	—	—	0.8%

Revenue History

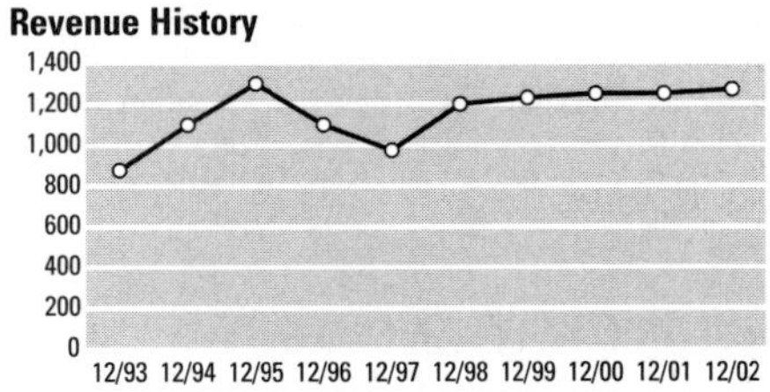

TAP Pharmaceutical

TAP Pharmaceutical Products taps into hot drug industry trends. The joint venture between Abbott Laboratories and Takeda Chemical Industries develops and sells drugs in the US and Canada. The company's products target cancer, gastroenterology, gynecology, and urology. TAP's Lupron Depot was developed to treat advanced prostate cancer, but can also treat endometriosis in women and central precocious puberty in children. The company also markets Prevacid, which is used to treat acid reflux disease and ulcers, with Abbott and has gained FDA approval for antibiotic Spectracef.

The company's pipeline includes drugs for hormone replacement therapy, obesity, and gout. Although erectile dysfunction treatment Uprima won European approval, TAP withdrew it from FDA consideration after questions arose over its efficacy and safety. It is continuing to improve the drug for resubmission.

TAP agreed to pay a record-setting $875 million to settle criminal and civil charges over its pricing and marketing of Lupron; a few executives and former executives have been indicted on allegations of criminal conspiracy.

EXECUTIVES

President: H. Thomas Watkins
EVP: Shinji Honda
VP, Human Resources: Denise Kitchen
VP, Research and Development: Xavier Frapaise
Ethics and Compliance Officer: L. Stephan Vincze
Controller: Kevin Dolan
Public Relations: Kim Modory

LOCATIONS

HQ: TAP Pharmaceutical Products Inc.
675 North Field Dr., Lake Forest, IL 60045
Phone: 847-582-2000 **Fax:** 800-830-6936
Web: www.tap.com

TAP Pharmaceutical Products has facilities in California, Georgia, Illinois, New Jersey, and Texas.

PRODUCTS/OPERATIONS

Products

Lupron/Lupron Depot (endometriosis, prostate cancer)
Prevacid (gastric acid inhibitor)
Prevpac (Prevacid plus antibiotics)
Spectracef (antibiotic)
Uprima (erectile dysfunction treatment)

COMPETITORS

AstraZeneca
Bone Care International
GlaxoSmithKline
Hawker Resources
ICOS
Pfizer
PRAECIS PHARMACEUTICALS
Zonagen

HISTORICAL FINANCIALS

Company Type: Joint venture

Income Statement FYE: December 31

	REVENUE ($ mil.)	NET INCOME ($ mil.)	NET PROFIT MARGIN	EMPLOYEES
12/02	4,037	—	—	3,000
12/01	3,787	—	—	3,000
12/00	3,539	—	—	2,500
12/99	2,928	—	—	2,300
12/98	2,063	—	—	2,000
12/97	1,566	—	—	1,500
12/96	1,129	—	—	1,250
12/95	750	—	—	1,000
Annual Growth	27.2%	—	—	17.0%

Revenue History

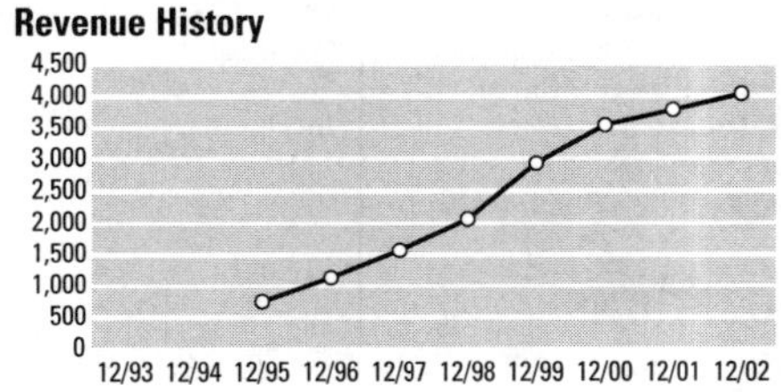

Taylor Corporation

Taylor Corporation is wedded to invitations. One of the largest specialty printers in the US, Taylor was founded in 1951 as wedding invitation printer Carlson Craft. Taylor operates through some 80 firms in Australia, Europe, and North America. Its subsidiaries print wedding invitations, Post-it Notes, and graduation announcements, among other items.

The company also owns greeting card company Current and offers direct marketing, office supplies, and online sales of printed products.

Chairman Glen Taylor — who bought the company in 1975 — has relinquished his CEO title to spend more time on philanthropy, agribusiness, and basketball (Taylor is majority owner of the Minnesota Timberwolves).

Current is one the largest direct marketers of paper products, gifts, and home decorating items in the US. Current's products include address labels, greeting cards, note cards, gift wrap, and personalized items such as stamps and stickers. Current laid off more than 10% of its workforce in 2002, blaming a downturn in the economy.

Its Carlson Craft unit is the nation's top maker of personalized wedding invitations. In addition, it personalizes birth announcements, holiday cards, party invitations, business stationery, and other items.

EXECUTIVES

Chairman: Glen A. Taylor, age 61
CEO: Bradley Schreier
Director of Human Resources: Jenny Miller

LOCATIONS

HQ: 1725 Roe Crest Dr., North Mankato, MN 56003
Phone: 507-625-2828 **Fax:** 507-625-2988

PRODUCTS/OPERATIONS

Selected Subsidiaries

Apex Business Systems
Carlson Craft Commercial
Current
Direct Marketing Resources
James Tower
Labelworks
Marketing General
Original Smith Printing
Promo Direct
Regency Thermographers
Royal Imprints
Stationery House
Thayer Publishing
Travel Tags
Web Graphics

COMPETITORS

American Achievement
American Greetings
Arandell
BCT International
Black Dot Group
Champion Industries
CSS Industries
Hallmark
Quad/Graphics
Quebecor World
R. R. Donnelley

HISTORICAL FINANCIALS

Company Type: Private

Income Statement FYE: December 31

	ESTIMATED REVENUE ($ mil.)	NET INCOME ($ mil.)	NET PROFIT MARGIN	EMPLOYEES
12/01	1,300	—	—	14,000
12/00	1,310	—	—	14,000
12/99	1,300	—	—	11,000
12/98	1,000	—	—	11,000
12/97	900	—	—	12,000
12/96	750	—	—	10,000
12/95	650	—	—	8,000
12/94	600	—	—	6,500
12/93	460	—	—	—
12/92	460	—	—	—
Annual Growth	12.2%	—	—	11.6%

Revenue History

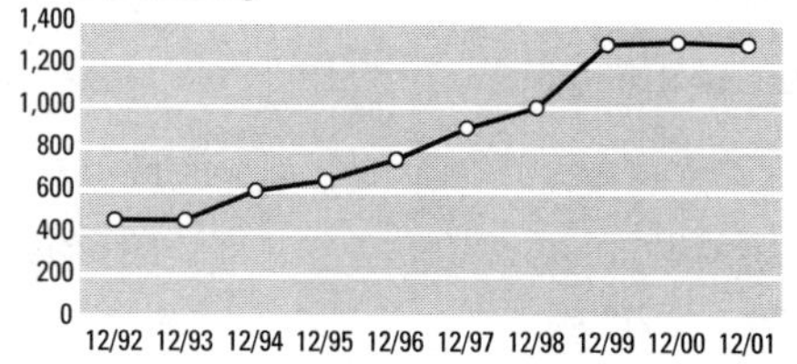

TIAA-CREF

It's punishment enough to write the name *once* on a blackboard. Teachers Insurance and Annuity Association — College Retirement Equities Fund (TIAA-CREF) is one of the US's largest, if not longest-named, private pension systems, providing for some 2.5 million members of the academic community and for investors outside academia's ivied confines. It also serves some 15,000 institutional investors. TIAA-CREF's core offerings include financial advice, investment information, retirement accounts, pensions, annuities, individual life and disability insurance, tuition financing, and trust services (through savings bank TIAA-CREF Trust). The system also manages its own line of mutual funds.

TIAA-CREF — one of the nation's heftiest institutional investors, with more than $260 billion in assets under management — has not been afraid to throw its weight around corporate boardrooms. The organization is known for active and choosy investing, and is a vocal critic of extravagant executive compensation packages. With an increasing share of its investment assets overseas, TIAA-CREF is also leading the crusade for global corporate governance standards.

TIAA-CREF exited the group life and disability business, selling its operations to StanCorp Financial Group.

HISTORY

With $15 million, the Carnegie Foundation for the Advancement of Teaching in 1905 founded the Teachers Insurance and Annuity Association (TIAA) in New York City to provide retirement benefits and other forms of financial security to educators. When Carnegie's original endowment was found to be insufficient, another $1 million reorganized the fund into a defined-contribution plan in 1918. TIAA was the first portable pension plan, letting participants change employers without losing benefits and offering a fixed annuity. The fund required infusions of Carnegie cash until 1947.

In 1952 TIAA CEO William Greenough pioneered the variable annuity, based on common stock investments, and created the College Retirement Equities Fund (CREF) to offer it. Designed to supplement TIAA's fixed annuity, CREF invested participants' premiums in stocks. CREF and TIAA were subject to New York insurance (but not SEC) regulation.

During the 1950s, TIAA led the fight for Social Security benefits for university employees and began offering group total disability coverage (1957) and group life insurance (1958).

In 1971 TIAA-CREF began helping colleges boost investment returns from endowments, then moved into endowment management. It helped found a research center to provide objective investment information in 1972.

For 70 years retirement was the only way members could exit TIAA-CREF. Their only investment choices were stocks through CREF or a one-way transfer into TIAA's annuity accounts based on long-term bond, real estate, and mortgage investments. In the 1980s CREF indexed its funds to the S&P average.

By 1987's stock crash, TIAA-CREF had a million members, many of whom wanted more protection from stock market fluctuations. After the crash, Clifton Wharton (the first African-American to head a major US financial organization) became CEO; the next year CREF added a money market fund, for which the SEC required complete transferability, even outside TIAA-CREF. Now open to competition, TIAA-CREF became more flexible, adding investment options and long-term-care plans.

John Biggs became CEO in 1993. After the 1994 bond crash, TIAA-CREF began educating members on the ABCs of retirement investing, hoping to persuade them not to switch to flashy short-term investments and not to panic during such cyclical events as the crash.

In 1996 it went international, buying interests in UK commercial and mixed-use property. TIAA-CREF filed for SEC approval of more mutual funds in 1997. Although Federal tax legislation took away TIAA-CREF's tax-exempt status in 1997, the change was made without decreasing annuity incomes for the year.

The status change let TIAA-CREF offer no-load mutual funds to the public in 1998. A trust company and financial planning services were added; all new products were sold at cost, with TIAA-CREF waiving fees. TIAA-CREF in 1998 became the first pension fund to force out an entire board of directors (that of sputtering cafeteria firm Furr's/Bishop's). Also that year TIAA-CREF's crusade to curb "dead hand" poison pills (an antitakeover defense measure) found favor with the shareholders of Bergen Brunswig (now AmerisourceBergen), Lubrizol, and Mylan Laboratories. Late in 1999, the organization sold half of its stake in the Mall of America to Simon Property Group, keeping 27%. The next year it made a grab for more market share when it launched five new mutual funds.

Biggs retired in 2002, and was succeeded by Herbert Allison.

EXECUTIVES

Chairman, President, and CEO: Herbert M. Allison, age 60
Vice Chairman and Chief Investment Officer: Martin L. Leibowitz
EVP and CFO: Elizabeth A. (Betsy) Monrad
EVP and CTO: Susan Kozik
EVP, Information Technology: C. Victoria Apter
EVP, CREF Investments: Scott C. Evans
EVP; President, TIAA-CREF Investment Products: Martin E. Galt III
EVP, Finance and Planning: Richard L. Gibbs
EVP, Public Affairs: Steven Goldstein
EVP, External Affairs: Don Harrell
EVP, Financial Operations and Facilities: Ira J. Hoch
EVP, Human Resources: Matina S. Horner, age 63
EVP and Chief Actuary: Harry I. Klaristenfeld
EVP and General Counsel: George W. Madison, age 49
EVP, Retirement Services Administration: Frances Nolan
EVP; President, TIAA-CREF Life Insurance Company: Bertram L. Scott, age 51
EVP, Marketing: Deanne J. Shallcross
EVP, Consulting Services: David A. Shunk
EVP, TIAA Investments: John A. Somers

EVP; President, Shared Services: Mary Ann Werner
EVP; President, Retirement Services: James A. Wolf
SVP and Chief Counsel for Corporate Governance: Peter C. Clapman
VP; President, TIAA-CREF Trust Company: Joseph J. Gazzoli
VP and Corporate Secretary: E. Laverne Jones
Auditors: Deloitte & Touche LLP

LOCATIONS

HQ: 730 3rd Ave., New York, NY 10017
Phone: 212-490-9000 **Fax:** 212-916-4840
Web: www.tiaa-cref.com

Offices

Atlanta
Bloomington, MN (Minneapolis-St. Paul)
Boston
Chicago
Denver
Dublin, OH (Columbus)
Indianapolis
Kirkland, WA (Seattle)
Las Colinas, TX (Dallas)
Morrisville, NC (Raleigh-Durham)
New York
Newport Beach, CA (Los Angeles)
Philadelphia
Phoenix
Pittsburgh
Rochester, NY
San Francisco
Southfield, MI (Detroit)
Tampa
Washington, DC

PRODUCTS/OPERATIONS

Selected Subsidiaries and Units

Teachers Personal Investors Services, Inc. (mutual fund management)
TIAA-CREF Individual & Institutional Services, Inc. (broker-dealer)
TIAA-CREF Institute (think tank)
TIAA-CREF Institutional Mutual Funds (investment company)
TIAA-CREF Life Insurance Company (insurance and annuities)
TIAA-CREF Mutual Funds (investment company)
TIAA-CREF Trust Company, FSB (trust services)
TIAA-CREF Tuition Financing, Inc. (state tuition savings program management)

COMPETITORS

Aetna
AIG American General
AIG
AXA Financial
Bank of New York
Berkshire Hathaway
CalPERS
Charles Schwab
CIGNA
Citigroup
FMR
John Hancock Financial Services
J.P. Morgan Chase
MassMutual
Merrill Lynch
MetLife
New York Life
Northwestern Mutual
Principal Financial
Prudential
T. Rowe Price
U.S. Global Investors
USAA
Vanguard Group

HISTORICAL FINANCIALS

Company Type: Not-for-profit

Income Statement FYE: December 31

	ASSETS ($ mil.)	NET INCOME ($ mil.)	INCOME AS % OF ASSETS	EMPLOYEES
12/02	261,252	—	—	6,500
12/01	274,390	—	—	6,700
12/00	281,383	—	—	5,000
12/99	289,248	—	—	5,000
12/98	249,715	—	—	5,000
12/97	214,296	—	—	4,920
12/96	182,612	—	—	4,490
Annual Growth	6.2%	—	—	6.4%

Asset History

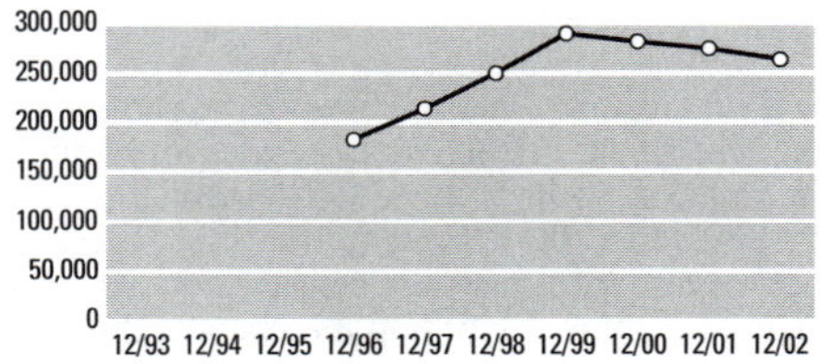

Team Health

Team Health hopes to score some points with its outsourced physician services. It has contracts with nearly 400 hospitals in about 40 states to provide medical staffing, management, administrative, and other support services. With some 2,200 physicians in its network, the firm specializes in emergency medicine, radiology, pediatrics, anesthesia, and hospitalists (hospital physicians who coordinate care during patients' stays with their primary physicians and other medical professionals). It operates through physician-managed regional affiliates. A group of emergency physicians founded Team Health in 1979. Cornerstone Equity Investors and Madison Dearborn Capital Partners each own nearly 40% of the company.

Team Health plans to grow by increasing its presence in the market for staffing military hospitals, and by obtaining business with hospitals which currently do not outsource their hospital staffing functions.

EXECUTIVES

President and CEO: Lynn Massingale, age 50, $624,835 pay
COO: Michael L. Hatcher, age 52, $377,161 pay
CFO: David Jones, age 35
EVP and General Counsel: Robert Joyner, age 55, $288,129 pay
EVP, Finance and Administration: Robert Abramowski, age 52, $383,922 pay
EVP, Radiology: Abraham (Jay) Bronner
EVP, Billing and Reimbursement: Stephen Sherlin, age 57, $328,203 pay
Corporate VP, Human Resources: Lisa Courtney
Chief Medical Officer: Gar LaSalle
Auditors: Ernst & Young LLP

LOCATIONS

HQ: Team Health, Inc.
1900 Winston Rd., Knoxville, TN 37919
Phone: 865-693-1000 **Fax:** 865-539-8003
Web: www.teamhealth.com

PRODUCTS/OPERATIONS

2002 Sales

	$ mil.	% of total
Fee-for-service	908	74
Contracts	293	24
Other	30	2
Total	**1,231**	**100**

COMPETITORS

Aveta Health
EmCare
Per-Se Technologies
PhyAmerica
RehabCare
Sheridan Healthcare

HISTORICAL FINANCIALS

Company Type: Private

Income Statement FYE: December 31

	REVENUE ($ mil.)	NET INCOME ($ mil.)	NET PROFIT MARGIN	EMPLOYEES
12/02	1,231	16	1.3%	6,800
12/01	965	—	—	3,500
12/00	919	—	—	1,804
12/99	852	—	—	1,500
12/98	548	—	—	1,388
Annual Growth	22.4%	—	—	48.8%

Revenue History

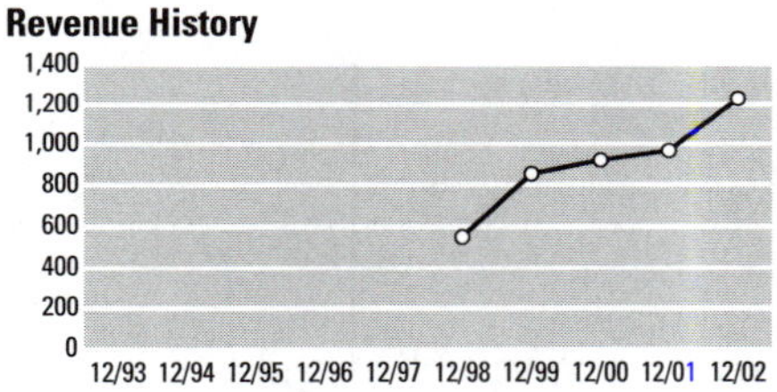

Tekni-Plex, Inc.

Tekni-Plex's hoses aren't for hosers. The company's consumer packaging segment makes irrigation hoses, garden hoses, gaskets, and precision tubing. Tekni-Plex's healthcare segment makes blister packages, cap liners, medical tubing, and vinyl compounds for pharmaceuticals and medical devices. The company's food segment produces egg cartons and processor trays for the poultry and meat industries. Tekni-Plex also makes vinyl resins used in a variety of industrial products. Over 90% of the company's sales are in the US; Wal-Mart stores account for 10% of sales. Dr. F. Patrick Smith (chairman and CEO), Kenneth Baker (president), and Arthur Witt (director) control the company through Tekni-Plex Partners.

EXECUTIVES

Chairman and CEO: F. Patrick Smith
President, COO, and Principal Accounting and Financial Officer: Kenneth W.R. Baker
VP, International: Michael Franklin
Director, Human Resources: Joe Bruno
Auditors: BDO Seidman, LLP

LOCATIONS

HQ: 201 Industrial Pkwy., Somerville, NJ 08876
Phone: 908-722-4800 **Fax:** 908-722-4967
Web: www.tekni-plex.com

Tekni-Plex has manufacturing facilities in the US and abroad in Argentina, Belgium, and Singapore.

PRODUCTS/OPERATIONS

Selected Products

Consumer Packaging and Products
Garden hose
Irrigation hose
Precision tubing and gaskets

Healthcare
Blister packaging
Cap liners and seals
Coated film
Co-extrusions
Flexible film
Laminations
Medical tubing
Rigid packaging film
Semi-rigid film
Vinyl compounds

Food Packaging
Egg cartons
Processor trays

Specialty Resins and Compounds
Vinyl resins

COMPETITORS

BASF Corporation
CCL Plastic Packaging
Crown
Huntsman International
RPC Group
Sealed Air
Shorewood Packaging
Smurfit-Stone Container
Sonoco Products
Teknor Apex

HISTORICAL FINANCIALS

Company Type: Private

Income Statement

FYE: Friday nearest June 30

	REVENUE ($ mil.)	NET INCOME ($ mil.)	NET PROFIT MARGIN	EMPLOYEES
6/03	611	3	0.6%	3,300
6/02	578	(7)	—	3,090
6/01	526	(19)	—	3,000
6/00	507	(21)	—	2,900
6/99	489	15	3.1%	2,950
6/98	310	9	2.8%	2,800
6/97	145	(12)	—	—
6/96	81	1	1.2%	—
6/95	45	0	0.4%	—
Annual Growth	38.7%	42.5%	—	3.3%

2003 Year-End Financials

Debt ratio: —
Return on equity: —
Cash ($ mil.) 48
Current ratio: 3.27
Long-term debt ($ mil.): 713

Net Income History

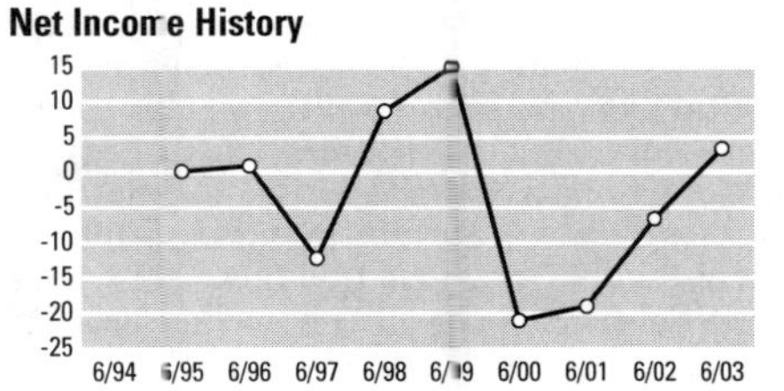

telcobuy.com

telcobuy.com helps the phone company make a connection. The company operates an online business-to-business marketplace for the telecommunications industry. Its site includes more than 500,000 telecommunications infrastructure products and services representing some 3,000 suppliers. telcobuy also provides electronic procurement, technical consulting, and contract manufacturing, among other services. Its major clients include SBC Communications and Verizon. Founders David Steward (chairman) and James Kavanaugh (CEO) control telcobuy through an entity called World Wide Technology.

EXECUTIVES

Chairman: David L. Steward
CEO: James P. Kavanaugh
President and COO: Mark J. Catalano
CFO: Thomas W. Strunk
VP Business Operations: Julene J. Tojo
VP Business Systems Services: Chris Scaglione
VP E-Business: Alan T. Hirabayashi
VP Human Resources: Ann W. Marr
CTO: Robert M. Olwig
Auditors: KPMG LLP

LOCATIONS

HQ: telcobuy.com LLC
60 Weldon Pkwy., St. Louis, MO 63043
Phone: 314-569-7000 **Fax:** 314-569-8310
Web: www.telcobuy.com

telcobuy.com has facilities in California, Maryland, Missouri, and Texas.

COMPETITORS

Anixter International
Graybar Electric
Verticalnet
WESCO International

HISTORICAL FINANCIALS

Company Type: Private

Income Statement

FYE: December 31

	REVENUE ($ mil.)	NET INCOME ($ mil.)	NET PROFIT MARGIN	EMPLOYEES
12/02	750	—	—	400
12/01	604	—	—	400
12/00	610	—	—	400
12/99	246	—	—	97
12/98	53	—	—	—
12/97	19	—	—	—
12/96	4	—	—	—
12/95	3	—	—	—
Annual Growth	122.3%	—	—	60.4%

Revenue History

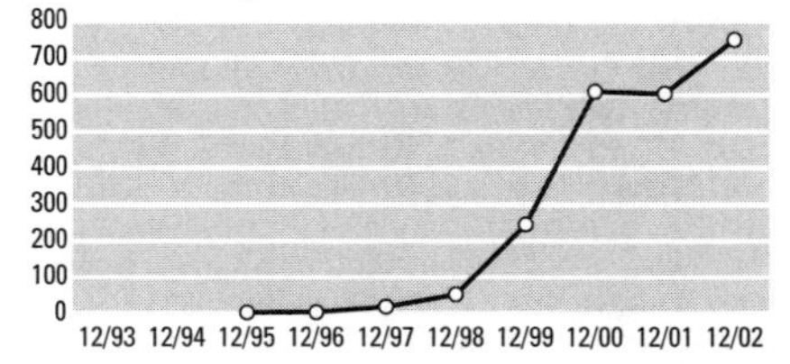

Tenaska, Inc.

Tenaska is tenacious when it comes to generating electricity. The employee-owned company develops, owns, operates, and maintains power plants in North America and Latin America. It has interests in generation facilities (primarily hydroelectric and fossil-fueled) that generate 7,700 MW of capacity. Tenaska also develops plants for third parties, providing engineering and construction, site development, financing, and management services. Other operations include electricity and natural gas marketing and trading, and fuel supply and transportation contracting. Tenaska was founded in 1987 by CEO Howard Hawks and VP Thomas Hendricks.

EXECUTIVES

Chairman and CEO: Howard L. Hawks
VP, CFO, and Secretary: Ronald N. Quinn
VP and Controller: Jerry Crouse
VP Acquisitions: Marc L. Peterson
VP Business Development: Thomas E. Hendricks
VP Business Development: Darrell W. Bevelhymer
VP Corporate Development; CEO, Tenaska International: Paul G. Smith
VP Engineering, Construction, and Operations: Mike Lebens
VP Finance and Treasurer: Mike Lawler

LOCATIONS

HQ: 1044 N. 115th St., Ste. 400, Omaha, NE 68154
Phone: 402-691-9500 **Fax:** 402-691-9575
Web: www.tenaska.com

Tenaska owns operating power projects in Alabama, Georgia, Texas, and Washington in the US, as well as in Bolivia. It also has plants under construction in Alabama, Oklahoma, and Virginia.

COMPETITORS

AES
Calpine
Covanta
Edison Mission Energy
International Power
Mirant
National Energy & Gas Transmission
NRG Energy
Reliant Resources
Sithe Energies
Texas Genco

HISTORICAL FINANCIALS

Company Type: Private

Income Statement

FYE: December 31

	REVENUE ($ mil.)	NET INCOME ($ mil.)	NET PROFIT MARGIN	EMPLOYEES
12/02	2,231	—	—	460
12/01	2,665	—	—	450
Annual Growth	(16.3%)	—	—	2.2%

Revenue History

Tennessee Valley Authority

Although the Tennessee Valley Authority (TVA) may not be an expert on Tennessee attractions like Dollywood and the Grand Ole Opry, it is an authority on power generation. TVA is the largest government-owned power producer in the US, with more than 31,500 MW of generating capacity. The federal corporation transmits electricity to 158 local distribution utilities, which in turn serve 8.3 million consumers. It also provides power for industrial facilities and government agencies, and it manages the Tennessee River system for power production and flood control.

TVA is the sole power wholesaler, by law, in an 80,000-sq.-mi. territory that includes most of Tennessee and portions of six neighboring states (Alabama, Georgia, Kentucky, Mississippi, North Carolina, and Virginia). Generating and transmitting power to local distribution utilities accounts for 86% of TVA's sales.

Most of TVA's power comes from traditional generation sources, but the company is also exploring alternative energy technologies: It is offering green choice options through its distribution affiliates, and it is developing a fuel cell facility in Mississippi.

TVA has also agreed to produce tritium, a radioactive gas that boosts the power of nuclear weapons, for the US Department of Energy (a first for a civilian nuclear power generator). The company is making modifications at its Watts Bar and Savannah River plants to produce and extract the gas; it plans to begin producing tritium by 2007.

TVA's rates are among the nation's lowest, which would-be competitors attribute to its exemption from federal and state income and property taxes. To prepare for deregulation, the authority is trying to reduce its $25 billion debt.

HISTORY

In 1924 the Army Corps of Engineers finished building the Wilson Dam on the Tennessee River in Alabama to provide power for two WWI-era nitrate plants. With the war over, the question of what to do with the plants became a political football.

An act of Congress created the Tennessee Valley Authority (TVA) in 1933 to manage the plants and Tennessee Valley waterways. New Dealers saw TVA as a way to revitalize the local economy through improved navigation and power generation. Power companies claimed the agency was unconstitutional, but by 1939, when a federal court ruled against them, TVA had five operating hydroelectric plants and five under construction.

During the 1940s TVA supplied power for the war effort, including the Manhattan Project in Tennessee. During the postwar boom between 1945 and 1950, power usage in the Tennessee Valley nearly doubled. Despite adding dams, TVA couldn't keep up with demand, so in 1949 it began building a coal-fired unit. Because coal-fired plants weren't part of TVA's original mission, in 1955 a Congressional panel recommended the authority be dissolved.

Though TVA survived, its funding was cut. In 1959 it was allowed to sell bonds, but it no longer received direct government appropriations for power operations. In addition, it had to pay back the government for past appropriations.

TVA began to build the first unit of an ambitious 17-plant nuclear power program in Alabama in 1967. However, skyrocketing costs forced it to raise rates and cut maintenance on its coal-fired plants, which led to breakdowns. In 1985 five reactors had to be shut down because of safety concerns.

In 1988 former auto industry executive Marvin Runyon was appointed chairman of the agency. "Carvin' Marvin" cut management, sold three airplanes, and got rid of peripheral businesses, saving $400 million a year. In 1992 Runyon left to go to the postal service and was replaced by Craven Crowell, who began preparing TVA for competition in the retail power market.

TVA ended its nuclear construction program in 1996 after bringing two nuclear units on line within three months, a first for a US utility. The next year it raised rates for the first time in 10 years, planning to reduce its debt. In response to a lawsuit filed by neighboring utilities, it agreed to stop "laundering" power by using third parties to sell outside the agency's legally authorized area.

In 1999 the authority finished installing almost $2 billion in scrubbers and other equipment at its coal-fired plants so that it could buy Kentucky coal along with cleaner Wyoming coal. That year, however, the EPA charged TVA with violating the Clean Air Act by making major overhauls on some of its older coal-fired plants without getting permits or installing updated pollution-control equipment. It ordered TVA to bring most of its coal-fired plants into compliance with more current pollution standards. The next year TVA contested the order in court, stating compliance would jack up electricity rates.

TVA was fined by the US Nuclear Regulatory Commission in 2000 for laying off a nuclear plant whistleblower. Crowell resigned in 2001, and Glenn McCullough Jr. was named chairman.

EXECUTIVES

Chairman: Glenn L. McCullough Jr.
President and COO: Oswald J. (Ike) Zeringue
EVP Financial Services and CFO: David N. Smith
EVP and General Counsel: Maureen Dunn
EVP Administration: D. LeAnne Stribley
EVP Communications and Government Relations: Ellen Robinson
EVP Customer Service and Marketing: Mark O. Medford
EVP Fossil Power Group: Joseph R. Bynum
EVP Human Resources: John E. Long Jr.
EVP River System Operations and Environment: Kathryn J. Jackson
EVP Transmission and Power Supply: Terry Boston
EVP TVA Nuclear and Chief Nuclear Officer: John A. Scalice
SVP Economic Development: John J. Bradley
SVP Information Services: Diane Bunch
SVP Performance Initiatives: Ronald A. Loving
SVP Power Resources and Operations Planning: Jack A. Bailey
SVP Strategic Planning and Analysis: Theresa A. Flaim, age 52
VP Bulk Power Trading: Amy T. Bums
VP External Communications: Tracy Williams
VP Investor Relations: Sylvia H. (Sissy) Caldwell
Acting VP, Performance Initiatives: Anda A. Ray
Senior Manager Industrial Development: Charles E. Shoopman Jr.
Senior Manager Industrial Recruitment: David Hooks
Senior Manager Minority and Small Business Development: Ella Rogers
Senior Manager Technical Services: James E. Allen
Manager Community Development: Phil Scharre
Freedom of Information Act Officer: Denise Smith
Privacy Act Officer: Wilma H. McCauley
Auditors: PricewaterhouseCoopers LLP

LOCATIONS

HQ: 400 W. Summit Hill Dr., Knoxville, TN 37902
Phone: 865-632-2101 **Fax:** 865-632-2270
Web: www.tva.gov

The Tennessee Valley Authority's service area covers most of Tennessee and parts of Alabama, Georgia, Kentucky, Mississippi, North Carolina, and Virginia.

PRODUCTS/OPERATIONS

2002 Sales

	$ mil.	% of total
Electricity		
Municipalities & cooperatives	5,856	86
Industries	732	11
Federal agencies & other	159	2
Other	88	1
Total	**6,835**	**100**

HISTORICAL FINANCIALS

Company Type: Government-owned

Income Statement

FYE: September 30

	REVENUE ($ mil.)	NET INCOME ($ mil.)	NET PROFIT MARGIN	EMPLOYEES
9/02	6,835	73	1.1%	13,000
9/01	6,999	(3,311)	—	13,000
9/00	6,762	24	0.4%	13,400
9/99	6,595	119	1.8%	13,322
9/98	6,729	233	3.5%	13,818
9/97	5,552	8	0.1%	14,500
9/96	5,693	61	1.1%	16,021
9/95	5,375	10	0.2%	16,559
9/94	5,401	151	2.8%	19,027
9/93	5,276	311	5.9%	18,974
Annual Growth	2.9%	(14.9%)	—	(4.1%)

2002 Year-End Financials

Debt ratio: 3,108.9%
Return on equity: 10.5%
Cash ($ mil.): 397
Current ratio: 0.32
Long-term debt ($ mil.): 21,358

Net Income History

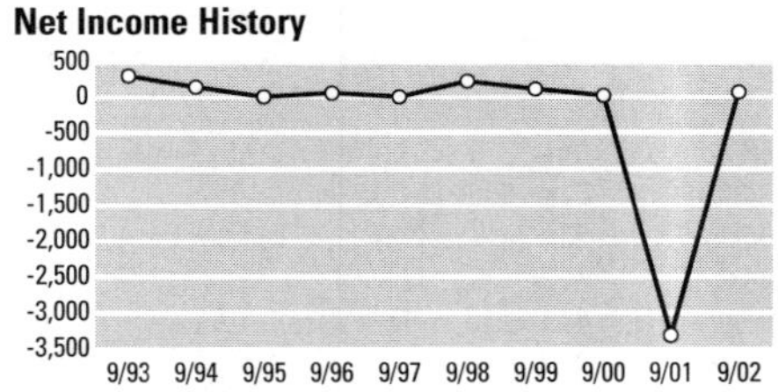

Texas A&M

Everything is bigger in Texas, even its universities. With more than 97,000 students at nine institutions, The Texas A&M University System ranks among the largest in the US. Its flagship school at College Station is well-known not only for its programs in engineering and agriculture, but also for its long-held traditions and school spirit. Other system institutions include Tarleton State University and Prairie View A&M. The system also runs eight state extension agencies and a health sciences center. Texas A&M was founded in 1876 as the Agricultural and Mechanical College of Texas. The A&M system was formed in 1948. It is funded in part by a $7.7 billion state endowment (shared with the University of Texas).

Texas A&M in College Station is the largest campus in the system, with an enrollment exceeding 44,000.

In the wake of a bonfire collapse which took the lives of 12 students in 1999, A&M has been charged by outsiders with trying to conceal the university's involvement in the accident. Still others have called on A&M to loosen some of its traditions. However, the school, students, and alumni have all stood fast against the tide. A&M has also embarked on a mission to renovate its facilities, announcing a $2 billion capital spending campaign.

HISTORY

The Texas Constitution of 1876 created an agricultural and mechanical college and stated that "separate schools shall be provided for the white and colored children, and impartial provisions shall be made for both." The white school, the Agricultural and Mechanical College of Texas (later Texas A&M), began instruction that year. Texas A&M was a men's school at first, and membership in its Corps of Cadets was mandatory. The Agricultural and Mechanical College of Texas for Colored Youth (later Prairie View A&M) opened in 1878.

To help fund the agricultural colleges and The University of Texas, the Legislature established the Permanent University Fund in 1876 to hold more than one million acres of land in West Texas as an endowment. An additional one million acres was added in 1883. The Santa Rita well on the university land struck oil in 1923 and money flowed into the Permanent University Fund's coffers. Under the provisions of the constitution, The University of Texas got two-thirds of the income, and A&M got the rest.

In 1948 The Texas A&M College System was established to oversee Texas A&M, Prairie View A&M, Tarleton State, and Arlington State (which left the system in 1965 and is now The University of Texas at Arlington). By 1963 enrollment system-wide had reached 8,000. That year the system changed its name to The Texas A&M University System, the same year that Texas A&M went co-ed.

By the mid-1980s enrollment had surpassed 35,000 students. The system grew quickly in 1989 when it added Texas A&I University (now Texas A&M University-Kingsville), Corpus Christi State (now Texas A&M University-Corpus Christi), and Laredo State University (now Texas A&M International). West Texas State College in Canyon joined the system in 1990 and became West Texas A&M University in 1993.

The 91-year-old Baylor College of Dentistry (in Dallas) and East Texas State University, well-known for training future teachers, joined the A&M system in 1996 (East Texas State was divided into Texas A&M University-Commerce and Texas A&M-Texarkana). In 1997 the system opened the first portion of the $82 million George Bush Presidential Library and Museum.

In early 1998 the system signed an alliance with the private South Texas College of Law in Houston, which was opposed by the Texas Higher Education Coordinating Board. (In 1999 a judge ruled that the two schools had to discontinue their affiliation.) That year Texas Instruments donated $5.1 million to the system (one of the largest donations in the institution's history) for the creation of an analog technology program. Chancellor Barry Thompson announced he would retire in 1999. The system appointed former Army general Howard Graves as the new chancellor (he passed away in September 2003).

Tragedy struck the College Station campus in 1999 when logs being stacked for the annual bonfire celebrating The University of Texas/Texas A&M football game collapsed and killed 12 people. Clinging to the 90-year tradition, many Aggies past and present insisted the bonfire go on in future years. In 2000 Graves announced a $2 billion, five-year capital improvement plan. In 2002 Robert Gates, former interim dean of Texas A&M University's George Bush School of Government and Public Service, was named president of the university system.

EXECUTIVES

Chairman, Board of Regents: Erle Nye, age 66
Vice Chairman: Dionel E. Avilés
President: Robert M. Gates, age 60
Deputy Chancellor: Jerry Gatson
Vice Chancellor of Academic and Student Affairs: Leo Sayavedra
Vice Chancellor of Agriculture and Life Sciences: Edward A. Hiler
Vice Chancellor of Business Services (CFO): Tom D. Kale
Vice Chancellor of Governmental Affairs: Stanton C. Calvert
Vice Chancellor of Health Affairs; President, The Texas A&M University System Health Science Center: Nancy W. Dickey
Associate Vice Chancellor of Human Resources: Patti Couger
Associate Vice Chancellor of Budgets and Accounting: B. J. Crain
Associate Vice Chancellor and Treasurer: Greg Anderson
Associate Vice Chancellor of Planning and Institutional Research: Glenn Dowling
Associate Vice Chancellor of Distance Learning and Information Technology: LeAnn McKinzie
President, Tarleton State University: Dennis P. McCabe
President, Texas A&M International University: Ray Keck III
President, Texas A&M University-Commerce: Keith McFarland
President, Texas A&M University-Corpus Christi: Robert R. Furgason, age 67
President, Texas A&M University-Kingsville: Rumaldo Juarez
President, Texas A&M University-Texarkana: Stephen R. Hensley
President, West Texas A&M University: Russell Long
General Counsel: Delmar Cain
Director Communications: Bob Wright
Auditors: Texas State Auditor

LOCATIONS

HQ: The Texas A&M University System
John B. Connally Bldg., 301 Tarrow, 3rd Fl., College Station, TX 77840
Phone: 979-458-6000 **Fax:** 979-845-2490
Web: tamusystem.tamu.edu

PRODUCTS/OPERATIONS

Selected Texas A&M University System Components

Health Science Center
Baylor College of Dentistry
College of Medicine
Graduate School of Biomedical Sciences
Institute of Biosciences and Technology
School of Rural Public Health

State Agencies
Texas Agricultural Experiment Station
Texas Agricultural Extension Service
Texas Engineering Experiment Station
Texas Engineering Extension Service
Texas Forest Service
Texas Transportation Institute
Texas Veterinary Medical Diagnostic Laboratory
Texas Wildlife Damage Management Service

Universities
Prairie View A&M University
Tarleton State University
Texas A&M International University
Texas A&M University
Texas A&M University-Commerce
Texas A&M University-Corpus Christi
Texas A&M University-Kingsville
Texas A&M University-Texarkana
West Texas A&M University

HISTORICAL FINANCIALS

Company Type: School

Income Statement FYE: August 31

	REVENUE ($ mil.)	NET INCOME ($ mil.)	NET PROFIT MARGIN	EMPLOYEES
8/02	2,254	—	—	25,000
8/01	1,928	—	—	24,000
8/00	2,620	—	—	23,000
8/99	1,792	—	—	23,000
8/98	1,695	—	—	23,300
8/97	1,550	—	—	22,800
8/96	1,425	—	—	22,600
8/95	1,299	—	—	20,000
8/94	1,287	—	—	16,367
8/93	1,212	—	—	15,966
Annual Growth	7.1%	—	—	5.1%

Revenue History

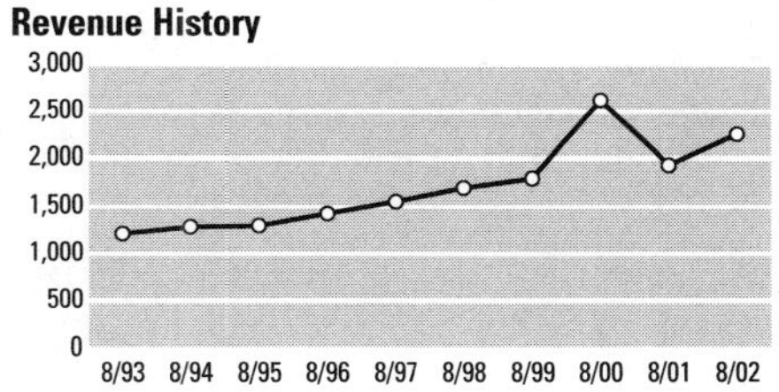

Texas Lottery Commission

The eyes of Texas are watching the lotto jackpot. The Texas Lottery Commission oversees one of the country's largest state lotteries, which has pumped more than $10 billion into state coffers since it was created in 1991. About 57% of lottery sales are paid out in prize money, while more than 30% goes to the state's Foundation School Fund; the remainder covers administration costs and commissions to retailers. The lottery offers four numbers games (Lotto Texas, Pick 3, Cash 5, and Texas Two Step) and several instant-win games sold through retailers around the state. Retailers such as grocery stores, gas stations, and liquor and convenience stores make a small commission on tickets they sell.

The Lone Star lottery seems to be rebounding, with rising sales after two years of losses. The company discontinued its slumping Texas Million lottery game in 2001. It also changed its Texas Lotto game so that customers must match six numbers out of 54 numbers instead of 50. The extra four numbers changed the odds of winning from about one in 16 million to one in 26 million.

HISTORY

A state lottery had been an issue in Texas for years before it was discussed in earnest in the mid-1980s. Falling oil and gas revenue had plunged the state into a recession, raising the specter of tax increases. In 1985 the state budget had a shortfall of $1 billion; that figure tripled by 1987. Adding fuel to the fire, the Texas Supreme Court ruled in 1989 that Texas had to change the way it funded public schools to avoid penalizing poor school districts. The ruling forced the state to seek new sources of revenue. In 1991 Governor Ann Richards called a special session of the legislature to deal with the fiscal crisis, and House Bill 54 was passed, creating the state lottery. The measure was approved by 64% of voters.

In May 1992 Richards bought the symbolic first ticket at an Austin feed store (it was not a winner). Fourteen hours later Texans had spent nearly $23 million on tickets — breaking the California Lottery's first-day sales record — and had won $10 million in prizes. More than 102 million tickets were sold the first week. GTECH Holdings was awarded a five-year contract that year for lotto operations. Lotto Texas started in November with a winner taking nearly $22 million. By the end of the year, lotto sales in Texas had topped $1 billion. In its first 15 months, it contributed $812 million to the state's coffers.

In March 1994 five winners split a record $77 million jackpot. By that autumn sales from the lottery's beginning had surpassed $5 billion. In November a Mansfield, Texas, gas station owner picked up the largest single-winner jackpot, $54 million. By the end of 1994, Texas had the largest state lottery in the US. Cumulative sales topped $8 billion in mid-1995. In its first 37 months of operation, the Texas Lottery contributed $2.5 billion to the state's general fund. Cash 5 debuted that year, and instant ticket vending machines were installed at some sites.

In 1996 lottery director Nora Linares was dismissed following allegations that one of her friends received $30,000 from GTECH as a "hunting consultant." When a GTECH official was convicted in New Jersey of taking kickbacks from a lobbyist, questions were raised concerning payments to GTECH's Texas lobbyist, former Texas Lieutenant Governor Ben Barnes. In 1997 Texas canceled its contract with GTECH to operate the lottery through 2002 and reopened bidding; GTECH filed suit to enforce the contract. Executive director Lawrence Littwin later was dismissed by the commission. Littwin sued GTECH, claiming the company had gotten him fired (the case was settled in 1999). Linda Cloud, his replacement, reinstated GTECH's contract. That year the Texas legislature voted to increase the amount going to the state and to reduce prize payouts.

Lottery sales fell sharply in 1998, due in part to the reduced prize money. To combat suffering sales, the legislature reversed itself the next year and restored the level of prize payouts. The commission proposed lengthening the odds of winning to create larger jackpots, but public outcry scuttled the plan. In 2000 the commission agreed to change the wording on its scratch tickets after a San Antonio College professor and his students argued that breaking even is not winning. The following year it introduced its first new lottery game in about three years, Texas Two Step, and discontinued Texas Million following slumping sales. The commission changed its Lotto Texas game in 2003, lengthening the odds to about one in 48 million.

EXECUTIVES

Chairman: C. Thomas Clowe
Acting Executive Director: Gary Grief
Director Communications: Keith Elkins
Director Financial Administration: Bart Sanchez
Director Human Resources: Jim Richardson
Director Marketing: Toni Smith
Director Security: Mike Pitcock
General Counsel: Kimberly Kiplin

LOCATIONS

HQ: 611 E. Sixth St., Austin, TX 78701
Phone: 512-344-5000 **Fax:** 512-344-5080
Web: www.txlottery.org

PRODUCTS/OPERATIONS

Selected Games

Lottery Games
Cash 5
Lotto Texas
Pick 3
Texas Two Step

Scratch-off Games
$25,000 Hearts
$50,000 Fortune
Big Bonus Bucks
Cattle Drive Cash Round Up
Cold Hard Cash
Deal Me In
Deluxe 7-11-21
Double Lucky Number
Prairie Dog Dollars
Ride to Riches
Star of Texas
Texas Trails
Treasure Hunt
Wild Cash
Wizard of Odds

COMPETITORS

Georgia Lottery
Multi-State Lottery
New Mexico Lottery
 Authority

HISTORICAL FINANCIALS

Company Type: Government-owned

Income Statement FYE: August 31

	REVENUE ($ mil.)	NET INCOME ($ mil.)	NET PROFIT MARGIN	EMPLOYEES
8/02	2,966	64	2.2%	—
8/01	2,826	87	3.1%	—
8/00	2,658	(116)	—	335
8/99	3,156	(118)	—	300
8/98	3,106	1,213	39.0%	335
8/97	3,761	1,421	37.8%	304
8/96	3,449	1,101	31.9%	325
8/95	3,052	1,014	33.2%	325
8/94	2,772	932	33.6%	325
8/93	1,863	660	35.4%	325
Annual Growth	5.3%	(22.8%)	—	0.4%

Net Income History

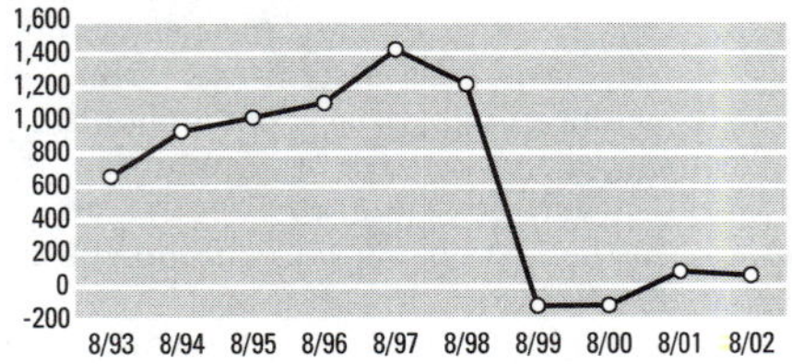

Texas Pacific Group

Yee-hah! Let's round us up some LBOs. Investment firm Texas Pacific Group (TPG) has staked its claim on the buyout frontier with a reputation for roping in companies other firms wouldn't touch with a ten-foot pole. TPG is an active investor, often taking control of the firms in which it invests. It profits not only from the rise in value of its holdings, but also from fund management. Like investor Warren Buffett, TPG invests in brands, buying and resuscitating consumer and *luxe* labels, as well as less-recognizable technology and telecommunications companies.

TPG goes where other firms fear to tread, targeting perennial losers that offer the potential for big payoffs such as US Airways, of which it planned to buy almost 40% as a part of that airline's Chapter 11 reorganization. TPG was upstaged, however, when The Retirement Systems of Alabama stepped in and offered the airline a better deal. With buying opportunities drying up in the US, the firm is looking for bargain prices on European firms. In the volatile Latin American market, however, TPG is curbing the size and pace of its investments.

TPG's holdings include Oxford Health Plans, Magellan Health Services, Ducati Motor, J. Crew, Del Monte, Motorola, and ON Semiconductor. Its venture capital affiliate TPG Ventures invests in telecommunications and technology companies. TPG is leading a group of investors, including Bain Capital, in buying US-based Burger King from British firm Diageo. Co-founder and partner David "Bondo" Bonderman is known for turning around Continental Airlines. TPG usually holds onto a company for at least five years, although consistent moneymakers are likely to be kept indefinitely.

Affiliated funds include the Newbridge partnerships (overseas investments) and Colony Capital (real estate). Newbridge, which is also owned by Blum Capital Partners, is poised to take a share of China-based Shenzhen Development Bank in a landmark foreign investment in mainland China.

HISTORY

The story of Texas Pacific Group is largely the story of David "Bondo" Bonderman. The magna cum laude Harvard law grad — an ardent Democrat and former law professor — built a reputation as an adviser who helped Texas billionaire Robert Bass rack up triple-digit returns.

After a decade with Bass, Bonderman struck

out on his own in 1992. James Coulter, recruited to the Bass organization out of Stanford University's business school, went with him. William Price, a former Bain & Company consultant who advised Bonderman on some of his Bass deals, joined them, as did Richard Schifter (airlines background) and David Stanton (technology expertise).

Bonderman raised eyebrows in 1993 when TPG affiliate Air Partners recapitalized Continental Airlines, then in its second bankruptcy. At the time the airline industry was losing billions, and Bonderman was a little-known quantity. After an extensive restructuring and management shakeup, Bonderman turned Continental into the US's #5 airline, logging record profits for four consecutive quarters.

This type of deal would become Bonderman's modus operandi: jumping into troubled waters shunned by others, turning the company around then (often) selling his interest for a profit. Of the head-rolling that frequently occurs after buyouts, Bonderman once said, "Generally speaking, you like to dance with the girl that brung you, and if you can't, sometimes you have to shoot her." In 1994 Bonderman worked his magic with America West Airlines. As with Continental, TPG sold shares in a second offering that made millions.

While the health care industry was debating reform in 1994, Bonderman seized the opportunity to buy a majority share in managed care company PPOM (sold 1997). In 1995 affiliated fund Colony Capital teamed up with Virgin Group to buy 116 MGM Cinemas and bring the multiplex boom to the UK.

Taking a cue from Robert Mondavi, TPG in 1996 bought Nestlé's debt-ridden Wine World Estates (with help from investment group Silverado Partners), renamed it Beringer Wine Estates Holdings, and took it public in 1997 in an IPO twice as big as Mondavi's.

In 1997 TPG bought clothier J. Crew Group. In an era of falling petroleum prices, the firm gambled on Appalachian energy company Belden & Blake and teamed with Genesis Health Ventures and Cypress Group to buy a stake in ailing elder care operator Multicare. It also bought Del Monte Foods, the world's #1 maker of canned fruits and vegetables (taking it public in 1999).

Bonderman and Air Partners in 1998 sold their interest in Continental to Northwest Airlines. Following its strategy of buying turnarounds, TPG threw lifelines to HMO Oxford Health Plans (1998) and Magellan Health Services (1999). It also built its technology holdings, investing in integrated circuits maker ZiLOG (1998) and leading a management buyout of a Motorola unit that is now ON Semiconductor.

The group jumped into a European investment hotbed, taking a majority stake in Punch Taverns Group, which bought 3,600 pubs from Allied Domecq. In 1999 TPG bought the Bally fashion house and a stake in Italian scooter maker Piaggio. It failed, however, to turn around Favorite Brands, selling the marshmallow and candy maker to Nabisco. In 2000 TPG said it would buy a stake in French smart-card maker Gemplus and would sell more than 4 million of its 23 million shares of GlobeSpan Virata at about $100 per share. (TPG's original investment was about $850,000.)

In 2002 TPG took off and picked up Gate Gourmet, an airline catering company, from the bankrupt Switzerland-based Swissair Group. It also exited its participation in ZiLOG upon completion of that company's reorganization. TPG dropped its 51% holding of Denbury Resources down to 38% for about $7 million. It also sold about 33% of its stake in motorcycle company Ducati, but it smelled a good deal and bought Burger King Corporation.

TPG is prepared for flight again in 2003 with US Airways by investing $200 million in the new equity of the airline once out of chapter 11. The airline believes TPG's investment will be added to $1 billion collateralized loan supported by the federal guarantee, which has been approved with conditions by the Air Transportation Stabilization Board (ATSB).

EXECUTIVES

Managing Partner: David Bonderman, age 60
CFO: Jim O'Brien
VP: John Viola
Treasurer: Michelle Reese
General Partner, TPG Ventures for European Investment: Badri Nathan
Human Resources Manager: Jennifer Dixon

LOCATIONS

HQ: 301 Commerce St., Ste. 3300,
Fort Worth, TX 76102
Phone: 817-871-4000 **Fax:** 817-871-4001

Texas Pacific Group has offices in Fort Worth, Texas; San Francisco; Washington, DC; and London.

PRODUCTS/OPERATIONS

Selected Holdings

America West Airlines
Bally Management (shoes and accessories)
Belden & Blake Corp. (oil and gas)
Burger King Corporation (restaurant)
Del Monte Foods Company
Denbury Resources Inc. (oil and gas)
Ducati Motor SpA
Gate Gourmet (airline catering)
Genesis Health Ventures Inc.
GlobeSpan (semiconductors)
J. Crew Group Inc.
Magellan Health Services Inc.
MEMC Electronic Materials (silicon wafers for semiconductors)
ON Semiconductor
Oxford Health Plans, Inc.
Paradyne Networks, Inc. (broadband accessory devices)
Piaggio
Punch Taverns Ltd.
Ryanair Holdings (airlines)
Zhone Technologies (data networking equipment)

COMPETITORS

AEA Investors
Apollo Advisors
Berkshire Hathaway
Blackstone Group
Carlyle Group
Clayton, Dubilier
Goldman Sachs
Haas Wheat
Heico
Hicks, Muse
Jordan Company
Keystone
KKR
Oaktree Capital
Sevin Rosen
Thomas Lee
Wingate Partners

Texas Petrochemicals

The road does get bumpy, doesn't it? Texas Petrochemicals (TPC) had been motoring along thanks to the US Clean Air Act of 1990, which requires an oxygenate be added to gasoline in heavily populated areas. The company had been getting about half its sales from the production of MTBE, the predominate oxygenate used in the US; however, it is reducing its dependence on MTBE following several contamination incidents. (MTBE is on its way to being banned by many states.) The company's reliance on MTBE coupled with a national movement away from use of the additive forced Texas Petrochemicals to file for Chapter 11 bankruptcy protection in July 2003. Several investment firms and officers own the company.

Live by the environmental sword and you might die by it as well, it seems. The Clean Air Act generated a lot of business for Texas Petrochemicals. But concern for the environment has caused a severe reduction in MTBE demand, and many states are in the process of banning the gasoline additive. TPC filed for Chapter 11 in July 2003 because it would not be able to meet the interest payments on its bonds. The company will restructure, following which it will phase out MTBE production and focus on its core specialty chemicals businesses.

TPC's product line now focuses on C4 hydrocarbons, including butadiene (for synthetic rubber), butene-1 (used in the production of ethylene), high-purity isobutylene (an intermediate for lube oils and specialty resins), and di-isobutylene (a raw ingredient for surfactants). Texas Petrochemicals operates its own cogeneration power plant and sells the excess capacity.

EXECUTIVES

Chairman: Arthur W. Peabody Jr.
President and CEO: Carl S. Stutts, age 55, $317,398 pay (prior to promotion)
SVP, Finance and CFO: E. Joseph Grady
SVP, Operations: John P. Yoars, age 59, $222,770 pay
SVP, Secretary, and General Counsel: Stephen R. Wright, age 54, $267,286 pay
VP, C4 Olefins: Jerry Law
VP, Finance: Brian Bourque
Director, Human Resources: Jimmy Rhodes
Auditors: Deloitte & Touche LLP

LOCATIONS

HQ: Texas Petrochemicals LP
3 Riverway, Ste. 1500, Houston, TX 77056
Phone: 713-627-7474 **Fax:** 713-626-3650
Web: www.txpetrochem.com

Texas Petrochemicals' main manufacturing facilty is located in Houston, Texas. It also owns storage facilities in Louisiana and Texas.

PRODUCTS/OPERATIONS

Selected Products

C4 olefins
Butadiene

Specialty chemicals
Butene-1
Isobutylene

Fuel products
Alkylate (gasoline blend component)
Butylene (ingredient in making alkylate)
Methyl tertiary butyl ether (MTBE)
Polyisobutylene

COMPETITORS

Braskem
Dow Chemical
Enterprise Products
Equistar Chemicals
Huntsman International
JLM Industries
Lyondell Chemical
Methanex
Millennium Chemicals
Octel
Tauber Oil
Valero Energy

HISTORICAL FINANCIALS

Company Type: Private

Income Statement FYE: June 30

	REVENUE ($ mil.)	NET INCOME ($ mil.)	NET PROFIT MARGIN	EMPLOYEES
6/02	600	0	0.1%	323
6/01	859	6	0.7%	316
6/00	745	17	2.2%	294
6/99	448	1	0.3%	308
6/98	515	(1)	—	328
6/97	490	(13)	—	319
6/96	497	18	3.6%	—
6/95	475	33	6.8%	—
6/94	352	34	9.6%	—
6/93	411	28	6.8%	—
Annual Growth	4.3%	(39.6%)	—	0.2%

2002 Year-End Financials

Debt ratio: 331.0%
Return on equity: 0.4%
Cash ($ mil.): 12
Current ratio: 1.05
Long-term debt ($ mil.): 248

Net Income History

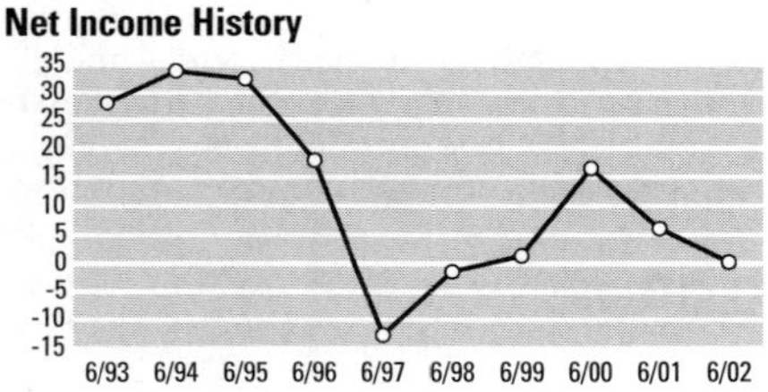

Thrivent Financial for Lutherans

The Spirit has moved Aid Association for Lutherans (AAL) to merge with Lutheran Brotherhood. The resulting entity was christened Thrivent Financial for Lutherans, now a 3 million member-strong fraternal organization. The merger brings under one steepled roof some $55 billion in assets under management in mutual funds, bank and trust services (AAL Bank and Trust and LB Community Bank & Trust merged into Thrivent Financial Bank), and other financial services. Thrivent Financial, which operates all over the US, also has about $150 billion in life insurance in force.

EXECUTIVES

Chairman: John O. Gilbert
President, CEO, and Director: Bruce J. Nicholson, age 57
EVP and CFO: Laurence W. (Larry) Stranghoener, age 48
EVP, Financial Services Operations: Jon M. Stellmacher
EVP, Integration: Walter S. Rugland
SVP and General Counsel: Woodrow E. Eno
SVP, Marketing: Pamela J. (Pam) Moret
CIO: Larry Robbins
Auditors: Ernst & Young LLP

LOCATIONS

HQ: 625 4th Ave. South, Minneapolis, MN 55415
Phone: 612-340-7000 **Fax:** 612-340-4070
Web: www.thrivent.com

PRODUCTS/OPERATIONS

2002 Sales

	$ mil.	% of total
Investment income	2,180	52
Premiums	1,311	31
Contract charges	529	13
Mutual fund & other	175	4
Realized investment losses	(324)	—
Total	**3,871**	**100**

COMPETITORS

American Express
Citigroup
FMR
MetLife
New York Life
State Farm
TIAA-CREF

HISTORICAL FINANCIALS

Company Type: Not-for-profit

Income Statement FYE: December 31

	ASSETS ($ mil.)	NET INCOME ($ mil.)	INCOME AS % OF ASSETS	EMPLOYEES
12/02	47,892	(292)	—	3,420
12/01	23,478	139	0.6%	3,733
12/00	22,112	228	1.0%	2,086
12/99	21,158	226	1.1%	3,914
12/98	19,418	134	0.7%	1,751
12/97	17,975	210	1.2%	1,596
12/96	16,671	130	0.8%	1,559
12/95	—	—	—	—
12/94	—	—	—	—
12/93	—	—	—	—
Annual Growth	19.2%	—	—	14.0%

2002 Year-End Financials

Equity as % of assets: 11.8%
Return on assets: —
Return on equity: —
Long-term debt ($ mil.): 10,836
Sales ($ mil.): 3,871

Net Income History

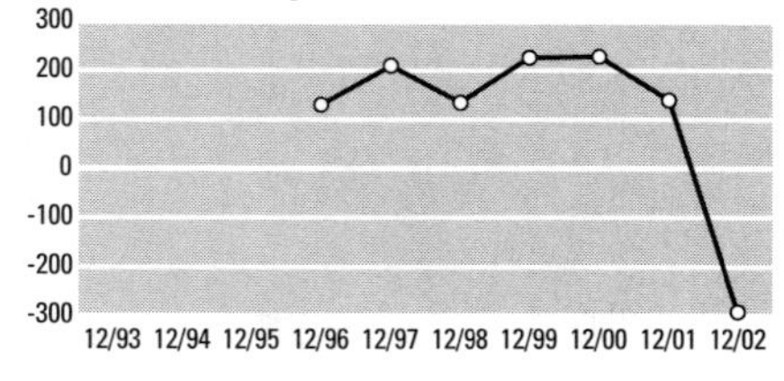

TIC Holdings

TIC Holdings doesn't flinch when it comes to constructing heavy industrial projects. Founded in 1974, the holding company offers services including civil engineering, heavy equipment erection, pipeline construction, and electrical installation. Main subsidiary TIC — The Industrial Company provides industrial construction services in the US through several regional units. Subsidiary Western Summit Constructors focuses on water and wastewater projects. TIC also has an international unit. The management-owned firm ranks among leading contractors in the wastewater, petrochemical, power, refining, mining, and industrial process markets, as well as in the electrical and instrumentation and pulp and paper sectors.

EXECUTIVES

CEO: Ronald W. (Ron) McKenzie
CFO: Jim Kissane
CEO, TIC: Gary McKenzie
SVP Business Development, TIC: Al Knapp
VP Business Development, TIC: Brad Lawson
VP Business Development, TIC: Thomas G. (Tom) Stapleton
Human Resources: Barbara Judd
Public Relations: Gary Bennett

LOCATIONS

HQ: TIC Holdings, Inc.
2211 Elk River Rd., Steamboat Springs, CO 80487
Phone: 970-879-2561 **Fax:** 970-879-6078
Web: www.tic-inc.com

TIC Holdings has offices in California, Colorado, Connecticut, Georgia, Kansas, Michigan, Minnesota, Oregon, Texas, and Wyoming. It also has an international location in Mexico City and in Edmonton, Canada.

PRODUCTS/OPERATIONS

Selected Subsidiaries

TIC — The Industrial Company
TIC — International, Inc.
TIC — Wyoming, Inc.
Western Summit Constructors, Inc.

COMPETITORS

ABB Lummus Global
aker Kvaerner
Bechtel
Black & Veatch
Chicago Bridge and Iron
Day & Zimmermann
Dick Corporation
Earth Tech
Fluor
Foster Wheeler
Gilbane
M. A. Mortenson
McDermott
Parsons
Peter Kiewit Sons'
Philipp Holzmann
Shaw Group
Skanska
Turner Corporation
Washington Group
Whiting-Turner
Zachry

HISTORICAL FINANCIALS

Company Type: Private

Income Statement FYE: December 31

	REVENUE ($ mil.)	NET INCOME ($ mil.)	NET PROFIT MARGIN	EMPLOYEES
12/02	1,221	—	—	7,000
12/01	1,123	—	—	5,000
12/00	998	—	—	6,000
12/99	745	—	—	5,000
12/98	500	—	—	5,000
12/97	516	—	—	5,000
12/96	462	—	—	5,000
12/95	456	—	—	5,000
Annual Growth	15.1%	—	—	4.9%

Revenue History

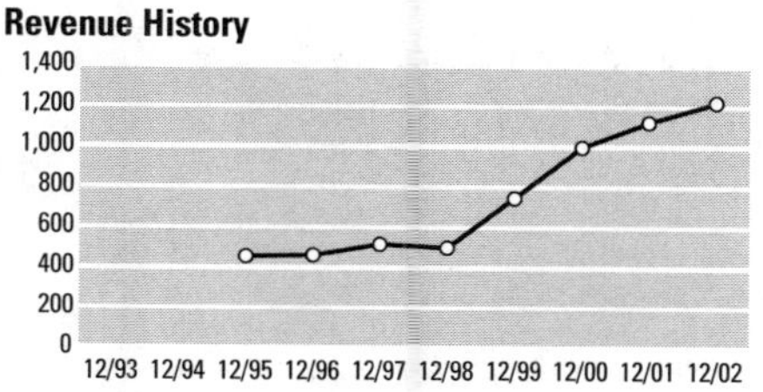

TNP Enterprises

The sleepy little utility from the Southwest has made a big splash in its industry. TNP Enterprises' regulated utility unit, Texas-New Mexico Power (TNMP), transmits and distributes electricity to nearly 250,000 customers in Texas and New Mexico. Nonregulated subsidiary First Choice Power competes in the Texas retail electric supply market, which was deregulated in 2002. The company has sold its 300-MW power plant. TNP Enterprises was acquired in 2000 by a private investor group in the first LBO of a US electric utility. Industry veteran William Catacosinos of Laurel Hill Capital Partners led the buyout and became TNP's CEO. Other investors include CIBC World Markets.

EXECUTIVES

Chairman, President, and CEO: William J. Catacosinos, age 72, $1,905,869 pay
CFO: Theodore A. (Ted) Babcock, age 48, $301,799 pay
Secretary: Kathleen A. Marion, age 48, $131,217 pay
Treasurer; President, First Choice Power: Manjit S. Cheema, age 48, $571,167 pay
Chairman, President, and CEO, TNMP: Jack V. Chambers Jr., age 53, $751,831 pay
SVP and COO, TNMP: W. Douglas Hobbs, age 59, $359,431 pay
VP and Treasurer, TNMP: Patrick L. Bridges, age 44, $330,000 pay
VP and General Counsel, TNMP: Michael D. Blanchard, age 52, $330,000 pay
VP Human Resources, TNMP: Melissa D. Davis, age 45, $330,000 pay
VP Power Resources, TNMP: Larry W. Dillon, age 48, $330,001 pay
Auditors: Deloitte & Touche LLP

LOCATIONS

HQ: TNP Enterprises, Inc.,
4100 International Plaza, Tower II,
Fort Worth, TX 76109
Phone: 817-731-0099 **Fax:** 817-737-1343
Web: www.tnpe.com

TNP Enterprises provides electric service to customers along the Gulf Coast of Texas, north-central and West Texas, and south-central and southwestern New Mexico.

PRODUCTS/OPERATIONS

2002 Sales

	$ mil.	% of total
FirstChoice	505.3	64
TNMP		
Residential	102.5	13
Commercial	94.0	12
Industrial	42.1	5
Other TNMP	11.5	1
Other	39.7	5
Adjustments	(107.7)	—
Total	**687.4**	**100**

COMPETITORS

AEP
Brazos Electric Power
Cap Rock Energy
CenterPoint Energy
Centrica
El Paso Electric
LCRA
Pedernales Electric
PNM Resources
Reliant Resources
Southern Union
TXU

HISTORICAL FINANCIALS

Company Type: Private

Income Statement FYE: December 31

	REVENUE ($ mil.)	NET INCOME ($ mil.)	NET PROFIT MARGIN	EMPLOYEES
12/02	687	32	4.7%	742
12/01	659	9	1.4%	786
12/00	644	1	0.2%	836
12/99	576	30	5.2%	823
12/98	587	19	3.3%	885
12/97	585	30	5.1%	1,305
12/96	503	23	4.6%	935
12/95	486	42	8.5%	894
12/94	478	(17)	—	1,051
12/93	474	12	2.4%	1,086
Annual Growth	4.2%	12.0%	—	(4.1%)

2002 Year-End Financials

Debt ratio: 576.4%
Return on equity: 38.1%
Cash ($ mil.): 17
Current ratio: 0.44
Long-term debt ($ mil.): 519

Net Income History

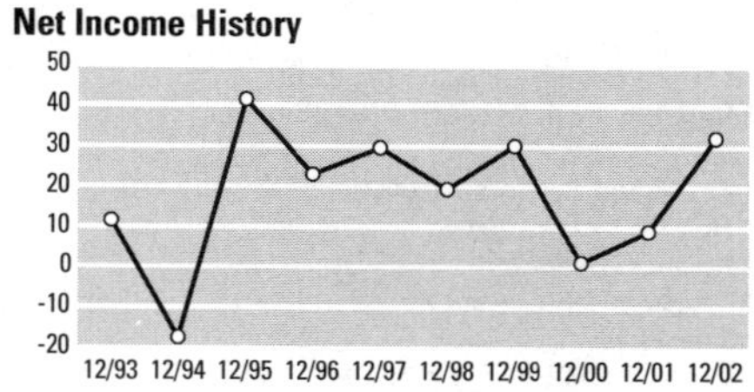

Topa Equities

Holding company Topa Equities casts a wide net. Owned by John Anderson, Topa has about 40 businesses involved in automobile dealerships (Silver Star Automotive), beer distribution, insurance, real estate, and more. Topa's beverage operations include Ace Beverage, Mission Beverages, and Paradise Beverages; the firm dominates the Hawaiian and Caribbean beer markets and serves California. Brands sold include all major US brews and leading US imports Guinness, Heineken, and Labatt, among others. Anderson started in 1956 as a distributor of Hamm's beer. UCLA's Anderson School of Business, to which Anderson donated $15 million, is named for him.

EXECUTIVES

Chairman, President and CEO: John E. Anderson, age 86
CFO: Brenda Seuthe
VP, Office and Retail Leasing: Darren Bell
Director Human Resources: Virginia Flores
IT: Roland Garcia
President and CEO, Topa Insurance Co.: Noshirwan Marfatia
VP, CFO, and Treasurer, Topa Insurance Co.: Daniel Sherrin
VP, Personal Lines, Topa Insurance Co.: H. Edward Good
VP, Claims, Topa Insurance Co.: James Kalupa

LOCATIONS

HQ: Topa Equities, Ltd.
1800 Avenue of the Stars, Ste. 1400,
Los Angeles, CA 90067
Phone: 310-203-9199 **Fax:** 310-557-1837

COMPETITORS

AutoNation
Beauchamp Distributing
CarrAmerica
CB Richard Ellis
Citigroup
Galpin Motors
Nationwide
Penske Automotive
Prospect Motors
Southern Wine & Spirits
State Farm
Tuttle-Click
Young's Market

HISTORICAL FINANCIALS

Company Type: Private

Income Statement FYE: December 31

	REVENUE ($ mil.)	NET INCOME ($ mil.)	NET PROFIT MARGIN	EMPLOYEES
12/02	986	—	—	2,025
12/01	946	—	—	1,949
12/00	865	—	—	1,600
12/99	776	—	—	1,400
12/98	754	—	—	1,300
12/97	752	—	—	1,310
12/96	675	—	—	1,300
12/95	656	—	—	1,100
12/94	607	—	—	1,141
12/93	559	—	—	1,179
Annual Growth	6.5%	—	—	6.2%

Revenue History

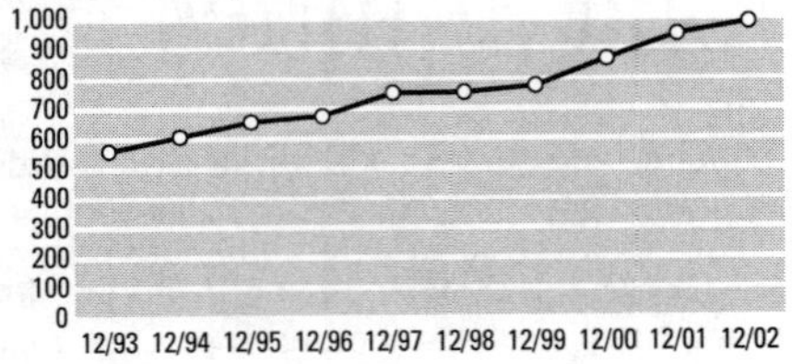

Topco Associates

Topco Associates is principally into private-label procurement. Topco uses the combined purchasing clout of more than 50 member companies (mostly supermarket operators) to wring discounts from suppliers. Serving grocery wholesalers, retailers, and food service firms, Topco markets more than 5,000 private-label items, including fresh meat, dairy and bakery goods, and health and beauty aids. Its brands include Food Club, Shurfine, and a line of "Top" labels such as Top Crest. In 2001 Topco Associates, Inc. merged operations with Shurfine International to form Topco Associates LLC. The new entity is 86%-owned by Topco Holdings, Inc. (formerly Topco Associates).

Holding company Shurfine International owns 14% of the merged entity, which also has members in Israel and Japan. But most of Topco's member companies are in the consolidating US market, where many stores have been bought by giant chains.

Topco's cost-saving scheme goes beyond product offerings; its buying power cuts costs for its members' stores. Its warehouse equipment purchase and a financial services program also create savings for members.

In addition to the Shurfine, Food Club, and Top Crest brands, Topco distributes Ultimate Choice and Shurfresh products. Topco also helps members market their own brands.

HISTORY

Food Cooperatives was founded in Wisconsin in 1944 to procure dairy bags and paper products during wartime shortages. A few years later it merged with Top Frost Foods, with which it had some common members. In 1948 the name Topco Associates was adopted (created by combining the word "Top" from Top Frost with the "Co" in Cooperatives). The member companies involved in the merger included Alpha Beta, Big Bear Stores, Brockton Public Market, Fred Meyer, Furr's, Hinky Dinky, Penn Fruit Company, and Star Markets.

Topco initially sold basic commodities to private-label retailers, but then it added fresh produce in 1958. It expanded its product line further in 1960, moving into general merchandise, health and beauty care items, and store equipment. In 1961, when the company moved its headquarters to Skokie, Illinois, revenues topped the $100 million mark. In the 1960s other leading supermarkets, including Giant Eagle, King Soopers, McCarty-Holman, and Tom Thumb, joined Topco.

Also that decade it came under attack from the Justice Department when it was accused of antitrust activity in granting its members exclusive distribution rights for Topco-branded products. In 1972 the Supreme Court ruled against Topco. It then agreed to sell products under the private labels of its members.

In the late 1970s the company introduced Valu Time, the first nationally marketed line of branded generic products. This concept was then adopted by many US supermarkets. By 1979 Topco surpassed $1 billion in annual revenues.

By the end of the 1980s, Topco's membership had expanded to include Randall's, Riser Foods, Pueblo International, Schnuck Markets, and Smith's Food & Drug Centers. In 1988 it introduced World Classics, a premium line of high-volume, high-margin products promoted as national brands.

During the early 1990s Topco ran through a number of CEOs. In 1990 Robert Seelert replaced 10-year CEO Marcel Lussier. In 1992 John Beggs took over, and the next year Steven Rubow was handed the reins.

The early 1990s also saw rapid growth, with 20 new members bringing the company's total to 46 by 1995 (its membership later declined in number through acquisition and consolidation). Topco also expanded internationally, with the membership of Oshawa Group in Canada and the associate membership of SEIYU in Japan in 1995. Also that year the company lured upscale Kings Super Markets away from distributor White Rose.

Topco began offering members utility accounting and natural gas services through Illinova Energy Partners in 1998. The company expanded its Top Care line of personal care products in 1999, using a variety of packaging designed to resemble several name brands within a single category. CEO Rubow retired late that year and was replaced by Steve Lauer. Topco took aim at consumers who prefer natural foods in 2000, launching the Full Circle line of organically grown items.

In November 2001 Topco combined operations with co-op operator Shurfine International and re-formed as a limited liability company. Topco Associates, Inc. and Shurfine International became holding companies with stakes in Topco Associates LLC. Lauer, the CEO of Topco Associates, Inc., was named president and CEO of the new company.

EXECUTIVES

Chairman: Joseph V. Fisher
Vice Chairman: Steven C. Smith, age 45
President, CEO, and Director: Steven K. (Steve) Lauer
SVP and Chief Procurement Officer: Jeffrey Posner
SVP and President, Wholesale Channel: John Stanhaus
SVP Center Store: Daniel F. Mazur
SVP Cost Containment Programs/Support Services: Ian Grossman
SVP Member Development: Kenneth H. Guy
SVP Perishables: Russel Wolfe
SVP World Brands: Michael Ricciardi
VP Best Practices and Cost Containment: David McMurray
VP Brand and Product Innovation: Maryruth Wilson
VP Dairy: Laird Snelgrove
VP Finance: Deborah (Debbie) Byers
VP Grocery: Dennis Dangerfield
VP Non-Foods: Curt Maki
VP Produce and Floral Operations: Bert Boyd
VP Sales and Marketing, Wholesale Channel: Mike Nugent
Director Creative Services: Karen Vorwald
Manager Human Resources: Dennis Pieper
Auditors: KPMG LLP

LOCATIONS

HQ: Topco Associates LLC
7711 Gross Point Rd., Skokie, IL 60077
Phone: 847-676-3030 **Fax:** 847-676-4949
Web: www.topco.com

Topco Associates purchases products on behalf of its members in the US, Israel, Japan, and Puerto Rico.

PRODUCTS/OPERATIONS

Selected Private-Label Brands

Food Club
Full Circle
Pet Club
Price Saver
Savers Choice
Shurfine
Shurfresh
Shurtech
Top Care
Top Crest
Ultimate Choice

Selected Member Companies

Ace Hardware
Acme
Ahold USA
Alex Lee
Associated Grocers, Inc.
Big Y Foods
Blue Square-Israel
Eagle Food Centers
F.A.B. Inc.
Food City
Fred W. Albrecht Grocery Co.
Fresh Brands (Piggly Wiggly)
Furr's Supermarkets
Giant Eagle
Haggen
Harris Teeter
Hy-Vee
Kings Super Markets
K-VA-T Food Stores
Meijer
Penn Traffic Company
Piggly Wiggly Carolina
Pueblo International
Raley's Supermarkets
Schnuck Markets
THE SEIYU
Ukrop's Super Markets
Unipro Food Service
Wegmans
Weis Markets

COMPETITORS

Ahold USA
C&S Wholesale
Kroger
SUPERVALU
SYSCO
Wakefern Food
Wal-Mart

HISTORICAL FINANCIALS

Company Type: Cooperative

Income Statement FYE: December 31

	REVENUE ($ mil.)	NET INCOME ($ mil.)	NET PROFIT MARGIN	EMPLOYEES
12/02	4,000	—	—	300
12/01*	3,300	—	—	300
3/00	3,400	—	—	275
3/99	4,000	—	—	359
3/98	3,900	—	—	365
3/97	3,700	—	—	400
3/96	3,900	—	—	390
3/95	3,700	—	—	375
3/94	3,500	—	—	400
3/93	3,000	—	—	375
Annual Growth	3.2%	—	—	(2.4%)

*Fiscal year change

Revenue History

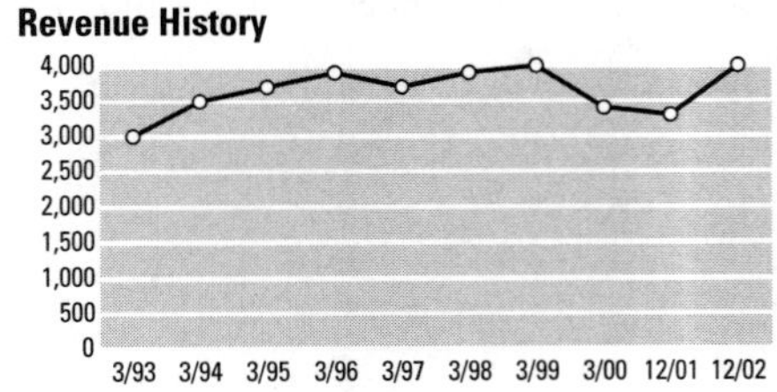

Toresco Enterprises, Inc.

Auto malls — what a concept! Donald Toresco, owner of Toresco Enterprises, helped pioneer the idea. The company's largest unit, Autoland of New Jersey, sells Chrysler, Dodge, Ford, Jeep, and Toyota. Five other locations, also in New Jersey, sell Chevrolet, Kia, Lexus, Lincoln-Mercury, and Mazda models in addition to those listed above. In all, the six locations sell more than 14,000 new cars annually. The dealerships also sell used cars and offer service, financing, and fleet sales. Chairman Toresco founded his company in 1965 as a used-car dealership; he also has interests in the real estate and insurance industries.

EXECUTIVES

Chairman: Donald Toresco
EVP: Andrea Karsian
Director of Human Resources, Autoland: Lisa Cesaro

LOCATIONS

HQ: 170 Route 22 East, Springfield, NJ 07081
Phone: 973-467-2900 **Fax:** 973-467-1824
Web: www.1800autoland.com

COMPETITORS

AutoNation
Holman Enterprises
Hometown Auto
Planet Automotive Group
Sansone Auto Network

HISTORICAL FINANCIALS

Company Type: Private

Income Statement FYE: December 31

	REVENUE ($ mil.)	NET INCOME ($ mil.)	NET PROFIT MARGIN	EMPLOYEES
12/02	498	—	—	692
12/01	530	—	—	682
12/00	550	—	—	682
12/99	495	—	—	700
12/98	500	—	—	750
12/97	463	—	—	598
12/96	437	—	—	650
12/95	430	—	—	782
12/94	412	—	—	585
12/93	400	—	—	—
Annual Growth	2.5%	—	—	2.1%

Revenue History

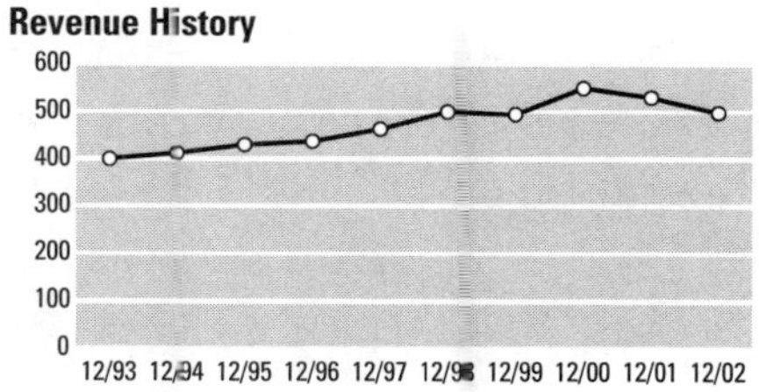

Towers Perrin

Refusing to live in an ivory tower, this company aims to offer practical advice. One of the leading management consulting firms in the world, Towers Perrin serves an extensive list of corporate clients, including more than 700 of the *FORTUNE* 1000 companies. The firm's core focus is on human resources consulting. Its Tillinghast-Towers Perrin unit focuses on risk management and actuarial services to financial companies, and its Towers Perrin Reinsurance serves clients primarily as a reinsurance intermediary. In addition to consulting, the company produces several publications and surveys investigating business trends and challenges.

After guiding its clients through the downsizing and consolidating 1990s, Towers Perrin has been working to streamline its own operations. The company has pared down its client roster, keeping mainly its biggest customers. At the same time it has been creating new business by expanding into new practice areas, such as public relations and corporate communications.

Towers Perrin was founded by four partners in 1934. It now has more than 630 partners.

EXECUTIVES

Chairman and CEO: Mark Mactas
CFO: Mark L. Wilson
Managing Director and Chief Administration Officer: Garrett L. Dietz
Managing Director Executive Compensation and People Advisory Services: Donald L. (Don) Lowman
Managing Director Global Marketing: Sharon Clark
Managing Director Global Markets: Michael (Mike) Ponicall
Managing Director Human Resources: Anne Donovan Bodnar
Director Sales, Strategy, and Operations: Christopher Michalak
General Counsel and Secretary: Kevin Young

LOCATIONS

HQ: One Stamford Plaza, 263 Tresser Blvd., Ste. 700, Stamford, CT 06901
Phone: 203-326-5400 **Fax:** 203-326-5499
Web: www.towers.com

Towers Perrin has 78 offices in 23 countries worldwide.

PRODUCTS/OPERATIONS

Selected Operations

Tillinghast-Towers Perrin
Financial Reporting
Mergers, Acquisitions, and Restructuring
Products, Markets, and Distribution
Risk Management
Value-Based Management

Towers Perrin
Administration Solutions
Change Management
Communication
Executive Compensation
Global Databases and Surveys
Health and Welfare
HR Delivery Solutions
Mergers, Acquisitions, and Restructuring
Retirement Services
Rewards and Performance Management
Sales Compensation
Superannuation in Australia

COMPETITORS

Accenture
Aon
A.T. Kearney
Bain & Company
Booz Allen
Boston Consulting
Deloitte Touche Tohmatsu
Drake Beam Morin
Ernst & Young
Gallup
Hewitt Associates
KPMG
Marsh & McLennan
Marsh
McKinsey & Company
PricewaterhouseCoopers
Right Management
Watson Wyatt

HISTORICAL FINANCIALS

Company Type: Private

Income Statement FYE: December 31

	REVENUE ($ mil.)	NET INCOME ($ mil.)	NET PROFIT MARGIN	EMPLOYEES
12/02	1,400	—	—	8,000
12/01	1,469	—	—	9,009
12/00	1,448	—	—	8,919
12/99	1,338	—	—	8,600
12/98	1,125	—	—	6,314
12/97	1,000	—	—	6,350
12/96	855	—	—	6,361
12/95	822	—	—	5,050
12/94	767	—	—	5,000
12/93	709	—	—	5,000
Annual Growth	7.9%	—	—	5.4%

Revenue History

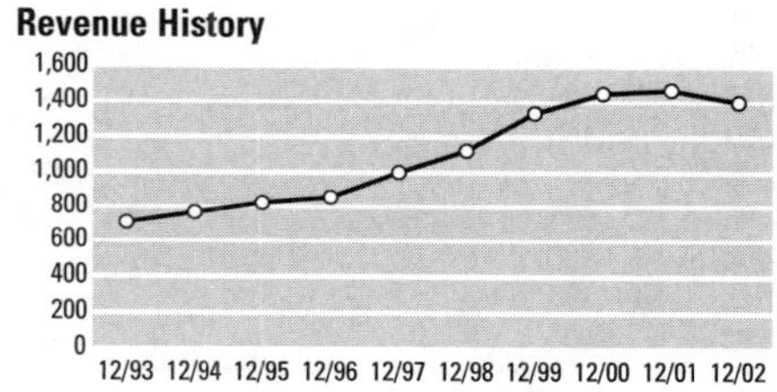

Transammonia

Fertilizer, liquefied petroleum gas (LPG), and petrochemicals form the lifeblood of international trader Transammonia. The company trades, distributes, and transports these commodities around the world. Transammonia's fertilizer business includes ammonia, phosphates, and urea. Transammonia's Sea-3 subsidiary imports and distributes propane to residential, commercial, and industrial customers in the northeastern US and in Florida. The company's Trammochem unit trades in petrochemicals, specializing in aromatics, methanol, methyltertiary butyl ether (MTBE), and olefins. Trammo Petroleum trades oil products including gasoline, heating oil, jet fuel, and naphtha from its office in Houston.

EXECUTIVES

Chairman and CEO: Ronald P. Stanton
VP and CFO: Edward G. Weiner
CIO: Benjamin Tan
Director Human Resources: Marguerite Harrington

LOCATIONS

HQ: Transammonia, Inc.
350 Park Ave., Ste. 400, New York, NY 10022
Phone: 212-223-3200 **Fax:** 212-759-1410
Web: www.transammonia.com

Transammonia operates offices in 18 countries, with major trading centers in Darien, Connecticut; Tampa; and Houston in the US and in Amman, Jordan; Beijing; Switzerland; Hong Kong; Lachen; London; and Paris.

COMPETITORS

Cargill
CF Industries
ConAgra
Dynegy
EOTT
Farmland Industries
HELM
Magellan Midstream
Norsk Hydro
Terra Industries

HISTORICAL FINANCIALS

Company Type: Private

Income Statement FYE: December 31

	REVENUE ($ mil.)	NET INCOME ($ mil.)	NET PROFIT MARGIN	EMPLOYEES
12/01	2,434	—	—	237
12/00	2,447	—	—	218
12/99	1,480	—	—	205
12/98	1,380	—	—	249
12/97	2,100	—	—	262
12/96	2,480	—	—	235
12/95	2,469	—	—	200
12/94	1,330	—	—	207
12/93	1,350	—	—	190
12/92	1,400	—	—	—
Annual Growth	6.3%	—	—	2.8%

Revenue History

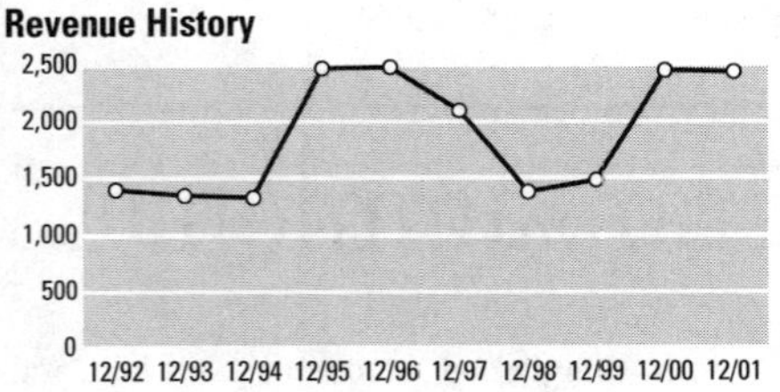

Trans-Resources

Better gardening through chemicals. Trans-Resources, Inc. (TRI) makes specialty plant nutrients as well as industrial and organic chemicals for businesses worldwide. Through Haifa Chemicals, TRI is the world's largest producer of agricultural-grade potassium nitrate, a specialized growth nutrient for produce and tobacco, and propanil, a rice herbicide. (Haifa Chemicals has about two-thirds of the world market for potassium nitrate.) Other TRI subsidiaries make fertilizers and herbicides. TRI defaulted on some high-yield bonds in 2001. Two of its subsidiaries, Cedar Chemical and Vicksburg Chemical, have filed for chapter 11 bankruptcy protection. Chairman Arie Genger and family own the company.

EXECUTIVES

Chairman and CEO: Arie Genger, age 57
President and COO: William Dowd
CFO: John M. Jureller
VP and Controller: Ray Keller
VP, Human Resources: Thomas Murphy
Chairman, Haifa Chemicals: Avi D. Pelossof
Managing Director, Haifa Chemicals: Gabi Politzer
Managing Director, TRI Chemicals: Gyorgy Pinter

LOCATIONS

HQ: Trans-Resources, Inc.
375 Park Ave., 11th Fl., New York, NY 10152
Phone: 212-515-4100 **Fax:** 212-515-4111
Web: www.trans-resources.com

Trans-Resources has operations in Argentina, Belgium, Brazil, Canada, China, France, Greece, Hungary, India, Israel, Italy, Japan, Luxembourg, Mexico, the Netherlands, South Africa, Spain, Thailand, the UK, and the US.

PRODUCTS/OPERATIONS

Selected Subsidiaries

Elgo (Israel, irrigation equipment)
Haifa Chemicals Limited (Israel, specialty fertilizers)
NA-CHURS/ALPINE Solutions (liquid starter fertilizers)
North Hungarian Chemical Works Ltd. (Hungary, herbicides)
Plant Products Co. Ltd. (Canada, soluble fertilizers)

COMPETITORS

Dow AgroSciences LLC
IMC Global
Mississippi Chemical
Monsanto
Phibro Animal Health
SQM

HISTORICAL FINANCIALS

Company Type: Private

Income Statement FYE: December 31

	REVENUE ($ mil.)	NET INCOME ($ mil.)	NET PROFIT MARGIN	EMPLOYEES
12/02	497	—	—	1,700
12/01	500	—	—	1,700
12/00	500	—	—	1,700
12/99	497	—	—	1,700
12/98	424	—	—	1,500
12/97	377	—	—	840
12/96	412	—	—	1,000
12/95	386	—	—	1,500
12/94	334	—	—	1,400
12/93	326	—	—	1,500
Annual Growth	4.8%	—	—	1.4%

Revenue History

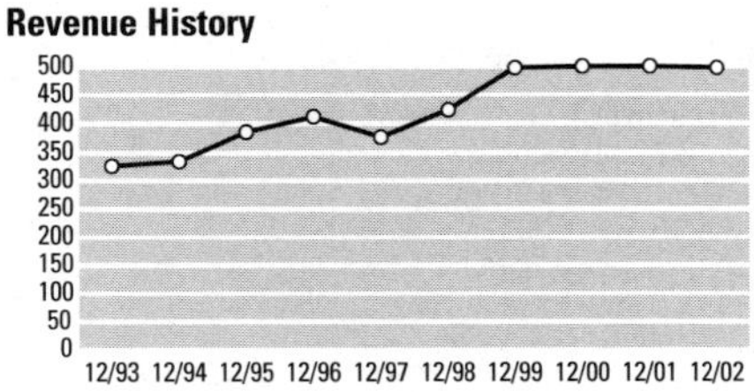

TravelCenters of America, Inc.

TravelCenters of America is in the food, fuel, and relaxation business for the long haul. The company's network of about 150 interstate highway travel centers in 40 states is the nation's largest. Company-owned and franchised truck stops provide fuel, fast-food and sit-down restaurants (Country Pride, Buckhorn Family), convenience stores, and lodging. With professional truck drivers accounting for most of the customers, some outlets also offer "trucker-only" services such as laundry and shower facilities, telephone and TV rooms, and truck repair services. The company is owned by a group of investors led by Oak Hill Capital Partners, Freightliner, and company officers.

EXECUTIVES

Chairman, President, and CEO: Edwin P. Kuhn, age 59, $861,000 pay
SVP, CFO, and Secretary: James W. (Jim) George, age 51, $516,250 pay
SVP, Marketing: Timothy L. Doane, age 45, $516,250 pay
SVP, Sales: Michael H. Hinderliter, age 53, $516,250 pay
VP and General Counsel: Steven C. Lee, age 39, $262,625 pay
VP, Human Resources: Bruce Sebera
Director, Public Relations and Advertising: Michael O'Connor
Auditors: PricewaterhouseCoopers LLP

LOCATIONS

HQ: 24601 Center Ridge Rd., Ste. 200,
Westlake, OH 44145
Phone: 440-808-9100 **Fax:** 440-808-3306
Web: www.tatravelcenters.com

PRODUCTS/OPERATIONS

2002 Sales

	% of total
Fuel	66
Non-fuel	33
Other	1
Total	**100**

COMPETITORS

Bowlin Travel Centers
ChevronTexaco
Exxon Mobil
Flying J
Love's Country Stores
Marathon Ashland Petroleum
Petro Stopping Centers
Pilot
Rip Griffin Truck Service Center
Royal Dutch/Shell Group
Stuckey's

HISTORICAL FINANCIALS

Company Type: Private

Income Statement FYE: December 31

	REVENUE ($ mil.)	NET INCOME ($ mil.)	NET PROFIT MARGIN	EMPLOYEES
12/02	1,870	1	0.1%	10,000
12/01	1,935	(10)	—	10,255
12/00	2,060	(38)	—	10,635
12/99	1,455	(25)	—	11,000
12/98	924	(15)	—	9,800
12/97	1,039	(6)	—	8,000
12/96	696	5	0.8%	—
12/95	456	10	2.2%	—
12/94	467	10	2.1%	—
12/93	349	8	2.2%	—
Annual Growth	20.5%	(20.1%)	—	4.6%

2002 Year-End Financials

Debt ratio: 3,440.1%
Return on equity: 7.1%
Cash ($ mil.): 14
Current ratio: 1.17
Long-term debt ($ mil.): 525

Net Income History

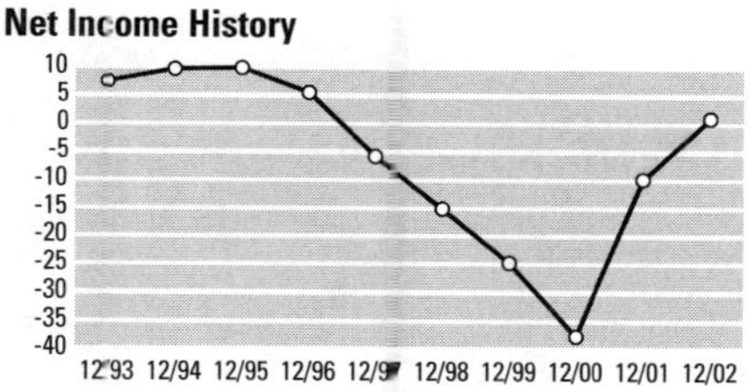

Trinity Health

Trinity Health is really more of a duo than a trio; the not-for-profit company is the result of a coupling between Mercy Health Services and Holy Cross Health System. Trinity Health runs nearly 50 hospitals and more than 360 outpatient facilities, as well as long-term care facilities, home health agencies, and hospice programs, in seven states. Its subsidiary, Trinity Health Plans, operates the Care Choices HMO in some 10 Michigan counties. Trinity Health sold its majority stake in GNA, formerly its rehabilitation therapy subsidiary. Catholic Health Ministries sponsors the organization.

EXECUTIVES

Chairman: James Hendricks
President and CEO: Judith C. Pelham, age 57
COO: Edgar T. Carlson
CFO: James H. Combes
EVP, Legal: Daniel Hale
EVP, Eastern Division: Michael A. Slubowski
EVP, Western Division: Marsha Casey
SVP, Human Resources: William (Bill) Anderson
SVP, Mission Integration: Sister M. Gretchen Elliot
SVP, Strategic Planning and Support: Bruce Goldstrom
VP, Corporate Communications and Public Relations: Steve Shivinsky

LOCATIONS

HQ: 27870 Cabot Dr., Novi, MI 48377
Phone: 248-489-5004 **Fax:** 248-489-6039
Web: www.trinity-health.org

Selected Facilities

California
Saint Agnes Medical Center (Fresno)

Idaho
Saint Alphonsus Regional Medical Center (Boise)

Indiana
Saint Joseph's Regional Medical Center (South Bend)

Iowa
Mercy Medical Centers (Clinton, Des Moines, Dubuque, Mason City, New Hampton, Sioux City)

Maryland
Holy Cross Health (Silver Spring)

Michigan
Mercy Hospital (Cadillac)
Saint Joseph Mercy Health System (Ann Arbor)
Saint Mary's Mercy Medical Center (Grand Rapids)
St. Joseph Mercy — Oakland (Pontiac)

Ohio
Ambulatory Management Services (Westerville)
Mount Carmel Health System (Columbus)

COMPETITORS

Ascension
Beverly Enterprises
Blue Cross (MI)
Detroit Medical Center
HCA
Henry Ford Health System
Mayo Foundation
Triad Hospitals
William Beaumont Hospital

HISTORICAL FINANCIALS

Company Type: Not-for-profit

Income Statement FYE: June 30

	REVENUE ($ mil.)	NET INCOME ($ mil.)	NET PROFIT MARGIN	EMPLOYEES
6/02	4,800	—	—	44,500
6/01	4,500	—	—	45,700
6/00	4,100	—	—	45,700
6/99	3,300	—	—	36,000
6/98	2,534	—	—	26,436
6/97	2,399	—	—	27,510
6/96	2,303	—	—	30,000
6/95	2,201	—	—	26,584
6/94	1,704	—	—	24,362
6/93	1,576	—	—	—
Annual Growth	13.2%	—	—	7.8%

Revenue History

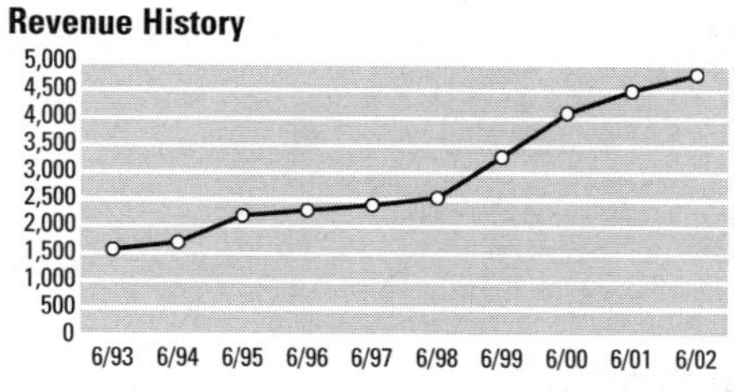

Tri-State Generation and Transmission

Tri-State Generation and Transmission Association supplies wholesale electricity to 44 rural distribution utilities that serve about 500,000 customers in Colorado, Nebraska, New Mexico, and Wyoming. The member-owned cooperative has a generating capacity of more than 1,800 MW, primarily from interests in fossil-fueled power plants, and it owns or operates 5,300 miles of transmission lines. Tri-State also purchases power and sells its excess supply to other utilities. Formed in 1952, Tri-State entered New Mexico through its 2000 acquisition of Plains Electric Generation and Transmission Cooperative.

EXECUTIVES

Chairman: Harold (Hub) Thompson
Vice Chairman: Rick Gordon
EVP and General Manager: Frank R. Knutson
EVP and General Manager: J. M. Shafer
SVP, Power Management and Generation: Charles Crane
VP and CFO: Charles L. (Chuck) Yetzbacher
VP, Administration and Human Resources: Sara Rivenburgh
Auditors: Ernst & Young LLP

LOCATIONS

HQ: Tri-State Generation and Transmission Association, Inc.
1100 W. 116th Ave., Westminster, CO 80234
Phone: 303-452-6111 **Fax:** 303-254-6007
Web: www.tristategt.org

COMPETITORS

Aquila
Basin Electric Power
El Paso Electric
Nebraska Public Power
Omaha Public Power
PNM Resources
Xcel Energy

HISTORICAL FINANCIALS

Company Type: Cooperative

Income Statement FYE: December 31

	REVENUE ($ mil.)	NET INCOME ($ mil.)	NET PROFIT MARGIN	EMPLOYEES
12/02	617	33	5.3%	855
12/01	633	17	2.7%	985
12/00	563	—	—	942
Annual Growth	4.7%	90.1%	—	(4.7%)

2002 Year-End Financials

Debt ratio: 622.3%
Return on equity: 15.7
Cash ($ mil.): 105
Current ratio: 1.05
Long-term debt ($ mil.): 1,392

Net Income History

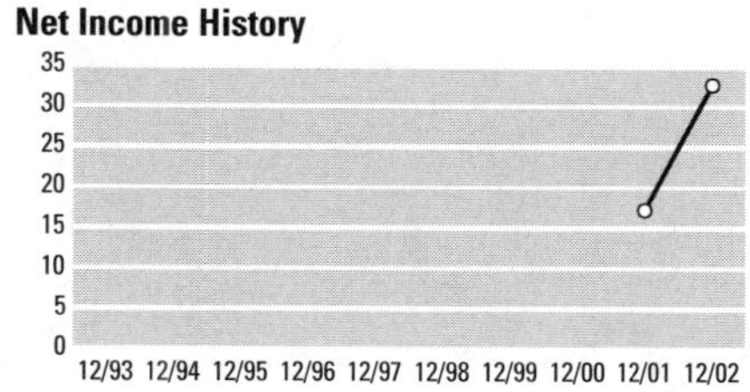

The Trump Organization

When it comes to betting on big business, The Donald always pulls out a Trump card. Through The Trump Organization, Donald Trump can claim several pieces of prime real estate in the Big Apple, including Trump International Hotel and Tower, Trump Tower (26 floors of it, anyway), and 40 Wall Street. Trump also owns 47% of publicly traded Trump Hotels & Casino Resorts and is operator of three Atlantic City casinos (Trump Taj Mahal, Trump Plaza, and Trump Marina), a tribal casino in California, and a riverboat casino in Indiana. Other holdings include a Florida resort and 50% of the Miss USA, Miss Teen USA, and Miss Universe beauty pageants (CBS owns the rest).

The Donald continues to excel on the strength of his deal-making prowess; the flamboyant tycoon is renowned for setting up real estate partnerships in which other firms put up most of the cash while he retains most of the control. In the Trump World Tower, for example, he invested $6.5 million, while Korean firm Daewoo pumped in more than $58 million.

Trump also has profited from his famous moniker — which he has trademarked — and his public image: Developers now can pay to co-brand their properties using the Trump name, as long as they meet Trump's super-luxury standard.

Trump dumped his stake in the now-tallest building in New York City. His interest in the Empire State Building leasehold brought in only a paltry $2 million per year. He's also been ordered by the courts — after a lengthy legal battle — to sell his 50% stake in the General Motors Building to co-owner Conseco; the two parties have agreed to sell the building.

Trump is currently renovating New York City's landmark Delmonico Hotel into luxury condos that will be rechristened Trump Park Avenue and is planning on providing Canada with its tallest building — Toronto's Trump International Hotel & Tower.

HISTORY

The third of four children, Donald Trump was the son of a successful builder in Queens and Brooklyn. After graduating from the Wharton School of Finance in 1968, his first job was to turn around a 1,200-unit foreclosed apartment complex in Cincinnati that his father had bought for $6 million with no money down. Managing the Cincinnati job gave Trump a distaste for the nonaffluent; he wanted to get to Manhattan to meet all the right people.

Operating as The Trump Organization, he took options on two Hudson River sites in 1975 for no money down and began lobbying the city to finance his construction of a convention center. The center was built, but not by Trump, who nevertheless got about $800,000 and priceless publicity. He and hotelier Jay Pritzker turned the Commodore Hotel near Grand Central Station into the Grand Hyatt Hotel in 1975. Trump married fashion model Ivana Zelnicek two years later.

In 1981 he built the posh Trump Tower on Fifth Avenue and proceeded to wheel and deal himself into '80s folklore. In 1983 he joined with Holiday Inn to build the Trump Casino Hotel (now Trump Plaza) in Atlantic City using public-issue bonds (he bought out Holiday Inn's interest in 1986), and he bought the Trump Castle from Hilton in 1985. In 1987 he ended up with the unfinished Taj Mahal in Atlantic City, then the world's largest casino, after a battle with Merv Griffin for Resorts International (Griffin won). He bought the Plaza Hotel in Manhattan in 1988, and the Eastern air shuttle (renamed the Trump Shuttle) the next year.

As the 1990s dawned, though, Trump's balance sheet was loaded with about $3 billion in debt. At the same time, his marriage to Ivana broke up in a splash of publicity. Trump's 70 creditor banks consolidated and restructured his debt in 1990. He married Marla Maples in 1993. (They divorced in 1998.)

In 1995 Trump formed Trump Hotels & Casino Resorts and took it public. He also paid a token $10 for 40 Wall St. (now home to American Express). The next year he sold his half-interest in the Grand Hyatt Hotel to the Pritzker family and unloaded more than $1.1 billion in debt by selling the Taj Mahal and Trump's Castle to Trump Hotels. That year Trump bought the Miss Universe, Miss USA, and Miss Teen USA beauty pageants.

In 1997 he published *The Art of the Comeback*, a follow-up to *The Art of the Deal* (1987), and started work on Trump Place, a residential development on New York's Upper West Side. He teamed with Conseco in 1998 to buy the famed General Motors Building for $800 million. In 1999 he began building the Trump World Tower — a 90-story residential building near the United Nations complex. Residents of nearby high rises brought lawsuits in 2000, claiming that the new building would block their view and lower their property value. The court sided with Trump.

The following year Trump and publisher Hollinger International announced plans to transform the former riverfront headquarters of the *Chicago Sun-Times* into a residential and commercial development. Originally planned to be the world's tallest skyscraper, the development would have returned to Chicago the lofty title it lost to the Petronas Towers (Kuala Lumpur, Malaysia). Trump decided to scale back the project in the wake of terrorist attacks on the World Trade Center.

EXECUTIVES

Chairman, President, and CEO: Donald J. Trump, age 56
CFO: Allen Weisselberg
EVP Acquisitions and Finance: Abraham Wallach
EVP: George Ross
VP Finance: John P. Burke, age 53
VP Public Relations and Human Resources: Norma Foerderer
VP Purchasing: Harry Geruldsen
Corporate Secretary: Rhona Graff-Riccio
General Counsel: Bernard Diamond

LOCATIONS

HQ: 725 Fifth Ave., New York, NY 10022
Phone: 212-832-2000 **Fax:** 212-935-0141
Web: www.trumponline.com

PRODUCTS/OPERATIONS

Trump Hotels & Casino Resorts, Inc.

Trump 29 Casino (tribal casino; Twentynine Palms Reservation, CA)
Trump Indiana (mooring for a 37,000-sq.-ft. yacht casino; Buffington Harbor, IN)
Trump Marina (casino resort; Atlantic City, NJ)
Trump Plaza (hotel/casino; Atlantic City, NJ)
Trump Taj Mahal (hotel/casino; Atlantic City, NJ)

Other Holdings

40 Wall Street
Briar Hall Country Club (Westchester County, NY)
General Motors Building at Trump International Plaza
Mar-A-Lago (private club; Palm Beach, FL)
Miss Teen USA pageant
Miss Universe pageant
Miss USA pageant
Ocean Trails Golf Course (private club; Ranchos Palos Verdes, CA)
Trump International Golf Club (West Palm Beach, FL)
Trump International Hotel and Tower
Trump Palace
Trump Parc
Trump Place
Trump Tower
Trump World Tower

COMPETITORS

Alexander's
American Real Estate Partners
Aztar
Boston Properties
Harrah's Entertainment
Helmsley
Hyatt
Lefrak Organization
Marriott International
Mashantucket Pequot Gaming
MGM Mirage
Park Place Entertainment
Port Authority of NY & NJ
Ritz-Carlton
Rouse
Tishman Realty
Vornado Realty Trust

HISTORICAL FINANCIALS

Company Type: Private

Income Statement FYE: December 31

	ESTIMATED REVENUE ($ mil.)	NET INCOME ($ mil.)	NET PROFIT MARGIN	EMPLOYEES
12/02	8,500	—	—	22,000
12/01	8,500	—	—	22,000
12/00	8,000	—	—	22,000
12/99	7,000	—	—	22,000
12/98	6,800	—	—	22,000
12/97	6,500	—	—	22,000
12/96	6,000	—	—	19,000
12/95	4,000	—	—	19,000
12/94	2,750	—	—	15,000
12/93	2,000	—	—	15,000
Annual Growth	17.4%	—	—	4.3%

Revenue History

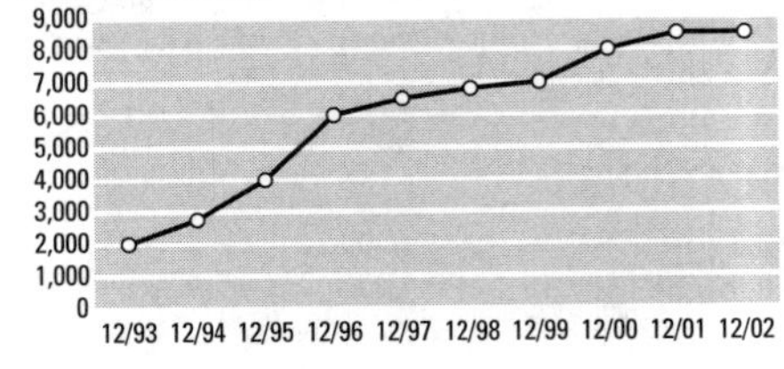

TruServ Corporation

To survive against home improvement giants such as The Home Depot and Lowe's, TruServ is relying on pure service. Formed by the merger of Cotter & Company (which was the supplier to the True Value chain) and ServiStar Coast to Coast, the cooperative serves some 6,800 retail outlets, including its flagship True Value hardware stores. The company, which is the third-largest hardware cooperative in the US behind Do It Best and Ace Hardware, sells building, home improvement, and garden supplies, as well as appliances, housewares, sporting goods, and toys. TruServ also manufactures its own brand of paints and the necessary applicators.

Additionally, the firm operates the Taylor Rental and Grand Rental Station chains and serves the Home & Garden Showplace chain.

The merger of Cotter & Company and ServiStar Coast to Coast (operator of Coast to Coast and ServiStar hardware stores, most of which converted to the True Value banner) gave members — many of them mom-and-pop outlets — more buying clout to compete against the do-it-yourself mega-retailers, plus retail advice and advertising support. TruServ has been growing its business in the rental and maintenance, repair, and operation (MRO) arenas. At the store level, TruServ is developing "lite" or smaller versions of its signature programs, such as Platinum Paint Shop, for the co-op's stores (more than half) that are less than 6,000 sq. ft.

Already serving about 150 international members in more than 50 countries, TruServ is also expanding its opportunities abroad.

HISTORY

Noting that hardware retailers had begun to form wholesale cooperatives to lower costs, John Cotter, a traveling hardware salesman, and associate Ed Lanctot started pitching the wholesale co-op idea in 1947 to small-town and suburban hardware retailers, and by early 1948 they had enrolled 25 merchants for $1,500 each. Cotter became chairman of the new firm, Cotter & Company.

The co-op created the Value & Service (V&S) store trademark in 1951 to emphasize the advantages of an independent hardware store. Acquisitions included the 1963 purchase of Chicago-based wholesaler Hibbard, Spencer, Bartlett, giving Cotter 400 new members and the well-known True Value trademark, which soon replaced V&S signs. Four years later Cotter broadened its focus by buying the General Paint & Chemical Company (Tru-Test paint). The V&S name was revived in 1972 for a five-and-dime store co-op, V&S Variety Stores.

Cotter died in 1989. By that time there were almost 7,000 True Value Stores. Cotter moved into Canada in 1992 by acquiring hardware distributor and store operator Macleod-Stedman (275 outlets).

Juggling variety-store and hardware merchandise and delivering very small amounts of merchandise to a lukewarm co-op membership did not allow for economies of scale, so in 1995 the company quit its manufacturing operations and its US variety stores (though it still serves variety stores in Canada, operating as C&S Choices), tightened membership requirements, and introduced new services.

Two years later Cotter formed TruServ by merging with hardware wholesaler Servistar Coast to Coast. ServiStar had its origins in the nation's first hardware co-op, American Hardware Supply, which was founded in Pittsburgh in 1910 by M. R. Porter, John Howe, and E. S. Corlett. By 1988, the year it changed its name to ServiStar, the co-op topped $1 billion in sales.

ServiStar expanded in the upper Midwest and on the West Coast in 1990 when it acquired the assets of the Coast to Coast chain (founded in 1928 as a franchise hardware store in Minneapolis); ServiStar brought Coast to Coast out of bankruptcy two years later, making it a co-op. Merging its 1992 acquisition of Taylor Rental Center with its Grand Rental Station stores in 1993 made ServiStar the #1 general rental chain. In 1996 it consolidated Coast to Coast's operations into its own and changed its name to ServiStar Coast to Coast.

President Don Hoye became CEO of the company in 1999. That year TruServ slashed 1,000 jobs and declared it would convert all its hardware store chains to the True Value banner. But TruServ lost $131 million in 1999 over bookkeeping gaffs, and co-op members received no dividends. Of 2,800 ServiStar dealers, only 1,900 raised the True Value flag. Others either declined to switch or were never offered the change because other True Value stores already shared their market area. In addition, stores began deserting the co-op because of inventory and other problems. In late 2000 the company sold its lumber and building materials business.

As competition continued to increase in 2001, the company was facing falling sales, lawsuits from shareholders, and accusations by retailers of unfair practices intended to pressure them into adopting the cooperative's flagship True Value banner. TruServ also had to confront a $200 million loan default. It made cuts in its corporate staff and divested its Canadian interests. In July 2001 Hoye resigned. The company's CFO and COO, Pamela Forbes Lieberman, was named the new CEO that November.

In April 2002 the company reported a net loss of $50.7 million during 2001, which it attributed to restructuring charges, inventory write-downs, and finance fees. Also that month the company announced that it had received $200 million in long-term financing. TruServ, under SEC investigation for alleged inventory, accounting, and other internal-control problems, was one of several companies that failed in August 2002 to meet a government requirement to swear by their past financial results.

In January 2003 TruServ received about $125 million in financing from investment firm W. P. Carey & Co. in a sale-leaseback deal on seven of TruServ's distribution centers. In March 2003 TruServ settled the SEC's allegations, without admitting or denying them, and agreed to follow measures intended to ensure compliance with securities laws.

EXECUTIVES

Chairman: Bryan R. Ableidinger, age 54
Vice Chairman: Peter G. Kelly, age 59
President, CEO, and Director:
Pamela Forbes Lieberman, age 48, $1,174,750 pay
SVP and CFO: David A. Shadduck, age 42, $472,235 pay
SVP, General Counsel, and Secretary: Cathy Anderson, age 53
SVP, Merchandise Supply Chain: William F. Godwin, age 48, $443,916 pay
SVP, Sales and Manufacturing: Michael D. Rosen
VP and Corporate Treasurer: Barbara L. Wagner
VP, Human Resources: Amy Mysel, age 50
VP, Maintenance, Repair, and Operations: Fred Kirst
VP, Marketing and Advertising: Carol Wentworth, age 45
VP, Retail Development: Brian Kiernan
VP, Retail Finance: Jon Johnson
Chief Administrative Officer, General Counsel, and Secretary: Robert Ostrov, $439,756 pay
CIO: Leslie Weber
Director, Commodities: Debbie Randall
Director, International: Mimi Apelqvist
Director, Member Relations: Dave Feuerhelm
Sales Director, Specialty Businesses: Michelle Finnigan
General Manager, Rental: Dick Detmer
Auditors: PricewaterhouseCoopers LLP

LOCATIONS

HQ: 8600 W. Bryn Mawr Ave., Chicago, IL 60631
Phone: 773-695-5000 **Fax:** 773-695-6516
Web: www.truserv.com

PRODUCTS/OPERATIONS

Selected Operations

Grand Rental Station
Grill Zone
Home & Garden Showplace
Induserve Supply
Party Central
Taylor Rental

COMPETITORS

84 Lumber
Ace Hardware
Akzo Nobel
Benjamin Moore
Do it Best
Fastenal
Hertz
Home Depot
Kmart
Lanoga
Lowe's
McCoy
Menard
Northern Tool
Réno-Dépôt
Sears
Sherwin-Williams
Stock Building Supply
Sutherland Lumber
United Rentals
Valspar
Wal-Mart
Wickes
Wolohan Lumber

HISTORICAL FINANCIALS

Company Type: Cooperative

Income Statement

FYE: December 31

	REVENUE ($ mil.)	NET INCOME ($ mil.)	NET PROFIT MARGIN	EMPLOYEES
12/02	2,176	21	1.0%	3,200
12/01	2,619	(51)	—	4,000
12/00	3,994	34	0.9%	4,300
12/99	4,502	(131)	—	5,500
12/98	4,328	21	0.5%	6,500
12/97	3,332	43	1.3%	5,800
12/96	2,442	52	2.1%	3,825
12/95	2,437	59	2.4%	4,186
12/94	2,574	60	2.3%	4,200
12/93	2,421	57	2.4%	4,400
Annual Growth	(1.2%)	(10.4%)	—	(3.5%)

2002 Year-End Financials

Debt ratio: 126.3%
Return on equity: 23.4%
Cash ($ mil.): 9
Current ratio: 1.21
Long-term debt ($ mil.): 125

Net Income History

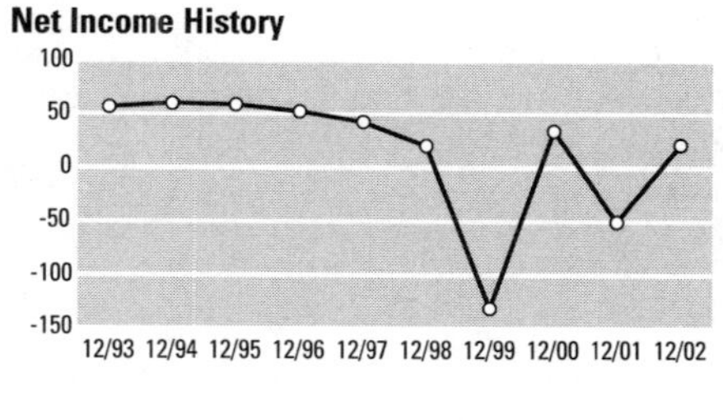

Trustmark Insurance

Trustmark Insurance was established in 1913 as the Brotherhood of All Railway Employees to provide disability coverage to railroad workers. Trustmark is licensed in all 50 states and covers more than 2.5 million people from all walks of life. Operations include group and individual health coverage (medical, dental, disability, and life insurance) and voluntary insurance products (specialty products through voluntary payroll deductions). Subsidiary Starmark markets health plans to small businesses. Other subsidiaries combat health-care fraud and offer third-party administration and cost management of health care plans. A mutual company, Trustmark is owned by its policyholders.

EXECUTIVES

Chairman and CEO, Trustmark Insurance and Trustmark Mutual Holding: J. Grover Thomas Jr.
President, Trustmark Insurance and Trustmark Mutual Holding: David M. McDonough
CFO: Brink Marcuccili
SVP, General Counsel, and Secretary: Frank G. Gramm
SVP Investments: Jerry Hitpas
SVP and Chief Marketing Officer, Trustmark Mutual Holding: James K. Derleth
VP Human Resources: Robert R. Worobow

LOCATIONS

HQ: Trustmark Insurance Company
400 Field Dr., Lake Forest, IL 60045
Phone: 847-615-1500 **Fax:** 847-615-3910
Web: www.trustmarkinsurance.com

PRODUCTS/OPERATIONS

Selected Subsidiaries

CoreSource
MultiBenefit Services
The Sentinel Group
Star Marketing and Administration, Inc. (Starmark)
Trustmark Health Resources

COMPETITORS

Aetna
AXA Financial
Blue Cross
CIGNA
Citigroup
CNA Financial
MetLife
Prudential

Company Type: Mutual company

Income Statement

FYE: December 31

	REVENUE ($ mil.)	NET INCOME ($ mil.)	NET PROFIT MARGIN	EMPLOYEES
12/02	1,100	—	—	3,500
12/01	1,393	—	—	3,400
12/00	1,322	—	—	3,500
12/99	1,167	—	—	3,500
12/98	1,058	—	—	3,300
12/97	972	—	—	2,600
12/96	890	—	—	1,575
12/95	765	—	—	1,555
12/94	711	—	—	1,419
12/93	662	—	—	—
Annual Growth	5.8%	—	—	11.9%

Revenue History

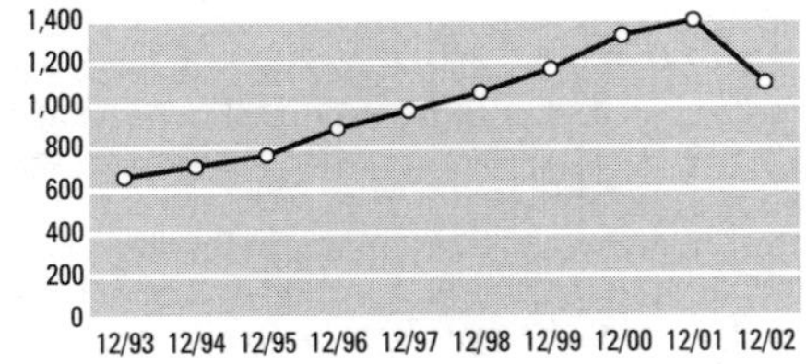

TTI, Inc.

TTI is passionate about passives. Each year the company distributes more than 1.7 million electronic components, including passive components such as resistors and capacitors, and interconnects such as cables, sockets, and filter connectors. Suppliers of its 160,000 line items include 3M, Amphenol, Philips, and Vishay Intertechnology. TTI also offers services such as component packaging and supply chain management. TTI, which owner and CEO Paul Andrews founded in 1971 as a supplier to the military, serves manufacturers of aerospace and defense systems, computers, telecom equipment, medical devices, and industrial products.

EXECUTIVES

Chairman and CEO: Paul E. Andrews Jr.
SVP, Asia: John Davidson
SVP, Finance: Nick M. Kypreos
SVP, Global Product Marketing: Mike Morton
SVP, Global Sales and Marketing: Craig Conrad
SVP, Information Services: David Minter
SVP, Operations: J. D. Beasley
Director, Human Resources: Myran Dill
Corporate Communications Coordinator: Cathy Walensky

LOCATIONS

HQ: 2441 Northeast Pkwy., Fort Worth, TX 76106
Phone: 817-740-9000 **Fax:** 817-740-9898
Web: www.ttiinc.com

TTI has offices in Canada, China, Denmark, France, Germany, Hong Kong, Italy, Mexico, Singapore, Spain, Sweden, Switzerland, Taiwan, the UK, and the US.

PRODUCTS/OPERATIONS

Selected Products

Capacitors
Circuit protectors
Connectors
EMI filters
Frequency controllers
Magnetic/inductors
Passive integrators
Relays
Resistors
Switches
Transformers

Selected Suppliers

3M
Amphenol
Cornell Dubilier
Glenair
KEMET
KOA
Littelfuse
Molex
Philips
Pulse Engineering
Raychem
Spectrum Control
Tyco Electronics
Vishay Intertechnology

COMPETITORS

All American Semiconductor
Arrow Electronics
Avnet
Electrocomponents
Future Electronics
Jaco Electronics
N.F. Smith
Nu Horizons Electronics
Premier Farnell
ROHM
Sager Electrical

HISTORICAL FINANCIALS

Company Type: Private

Income Statement

FYE: December 31

	REVENUE ($ mil.)	NET INCOME ($ mil.)	NET PROFIT MARGIN	EMPLOYEES
12/02	630	—	—	1,100
12/01	750	—	—	1,550
12/00	955	—	—	1,050
12/99	555	—	—	1,055
12/98	461	—	—	985
12/97	450	—	—	933
12/96	411	—	—	819
Annual Growth	7.4%	—	—	5.0%

Revenue History

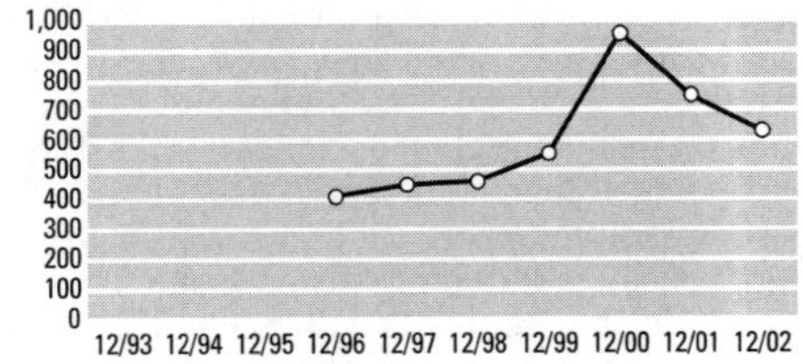

TTX Company

TTX Company keeps the railroad industry chugging by leasing railcars to railroad companies in the US and Canada. Rail companies generally prefer to rent railcars as needed rather than buy them because the cars are often switched and traded along the tracks. With 127,000 railcars, TTX's fleet includes three types of railcars (intermodal, autorack, and general use) designed to carry containers, autos, farm and construction equipment, and lumber and steel products. It has distribution centers in Illinois and Washington and maintains its fleet through three repair centers (in California, Florida, and South Carolina) and 31 inspection centers in the US. TTX is owned by the largest railroads in the US and Canada.

EXECUTIVES

President and CEO: Andrew F. Reardon
SVP Equipment: Robert S. Hulick
SVP Fleet Management: Thomas F. Wells
VP Business and Market Planning: Harold J. Cerveny
VP Finance and Treasurer: Thomas D. (Tom) Marion
VP Information Technology: John M. Braly
Assistant VP and Director Human Resources: Michelle Pomeroy
Controller: Frank J. Previti
General Counsel and Corporate Secretary: Patrick Loftus
Auditors: KPMG LLP

LOCATIONS

HQ: 101 N. Wacker Dr., Chicago, IL 60606
Phone: 312-853-3223 **Fax:** 312-984-3790
Web: www.ttx.com

TTX Company has distribution centers in Illinois and Washington; division repair facilities in California, Florida, and South Carolina; intermodal terminal repair sites in Alabama, Arkansas, California, Colorado, Florida, Illinois, Maryland, Minnesota Missouri, New Jersey, Oregon, Tennessee, Texas, Virginia, and Washington; and repair tracks in California, Illinois, Kansas, and Texas.

PRODUCTS/OPERATIONS

Selected Equipment Types

Bi-level auto rack car
Bulkhead flat car
Chain tie-down car
Double-stack container car
General service flat car
Gondola
Plain box car
Tri-level auto rack car

COMPETITORS

Andersons
Capital Finance
GATX
Genesee & Wyoming
Greenbrier
Joseph Transportation
Pacer International
Pioneer Railcorp
XTRA

HISTORICAL FINANCIALS

Company Type: Private

Income Statement FYE: December 31

	REVENUE ($ mil.)	NET INCOME ($ mil.)	NET PROFIT MARGIN	EMPLOYEES
12/02	918	—	—	1,285
12/01	983	—	—	1,400
12/00	1,020	—	—	1,614
12/99	985	—	—	1,975
12/98	937	—	—	2,000
12/97	880	—	—	2,000
12/96	859	—	—	1,965
12/95	864	—	—	1,985
12/94	810	—	—	2,000
12/93	730	—	—	—
Annual Growth	2.6%	—	—	(5.4%)

Revenue History

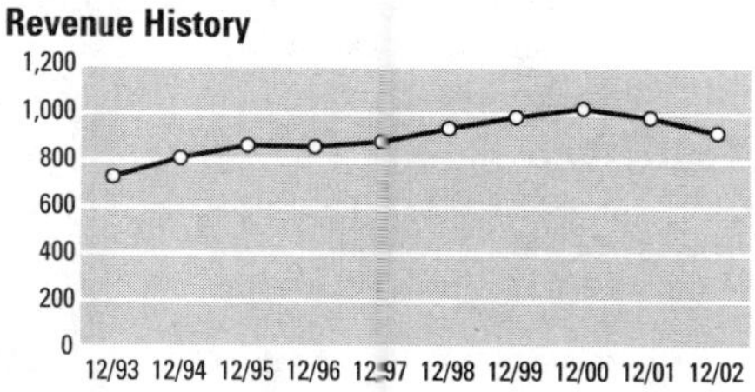

Tube City, Inc.

Tube City can do just about anything with industrial leftovers. A steel-mill service company, Tube City provides raw materials and services that help mills and foundries profit from their scrap. The company, which has operations in 16 states in the US, primarily processes and brokers steel scrap. Its processing services include burning, breaking, shearing, shredding, and bailing. As a major regional scrap metal broker, Tube City brokers and processes more than 6 million tons of scrap annually. It also provides transportation (trucking and rail), equipment leasing, and maintenance and machine shop services. David Coslov founded the family-owned company in 1926.

EXECUTIVES

Chairman and CEO: Michael Coslov
President and COO: Joseph Curtin
EVP Finance and Administration and General Counsel: Tom Lippard
SVP Finance: Daniel Rosati
Human Resources Manager: Jeannie DeCarlo
Marketing Manager: Gary Henkel

LOCATIONS

HQ: 12 Monongahela Ave., Glassport, PA 15045
Phone: 412-678-6141 **Fax:** 412-678-2210
Web: www.tubecity.com

Tube City has operations in Alabama, Arkansas, California, Georgia, Illinois, Indiana, Michigan, Nebraska, New Jersey, Ohio, Oklahoma, Pennsylvania, South Carolina, Tennessee, Texas, and Virginia.

COMPETITORS

Commercial Metals
David J. Joseph
Keywell
Metal Management
OmniSource

HISTORICAL FINANCIALS

Company Type: Private

Income Statement FYE: December 31

	REVENUE ($ mil.)	NET INCOME ($ mil.)	NET PROFIT MARGIN	EMPLOYEES
12/02	600	—	—	500
12/01	550	—	—	500
12/00	600	—	—	500
12/99	580	—	—	500
12/98	550	—	—	500
12/97	520	—	—	492
12/96	524	—	—	475
12/95	466	—	—	375
12/94	403	—	—	221
Annual Growth	5.1%	—	—	10.7%

Revenue History

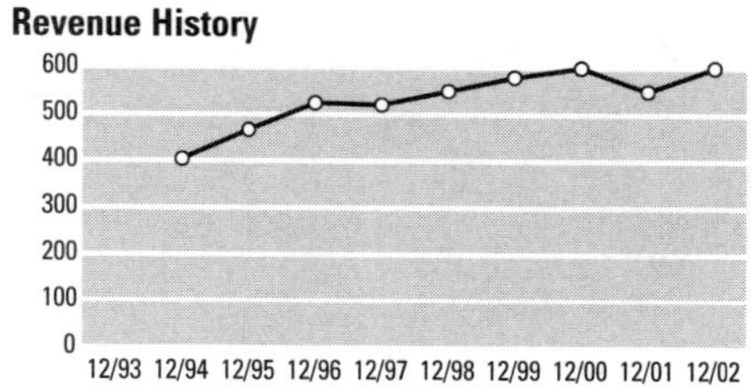

Tufts Associated Health Plans

Managed health care headaches in the New England states have made times tough for Tufts Associated Health Plans. The not-for-profit company provides management, administrative, and marketing services for its affiliates and subsidiaries, including Tufts Associated Health Maintenance Organization (TAHMO), Total Health Plan, and Tufts Benefit Administrators. Its provider network serves more than 900,000 members. Tufts Associated Health Plans offers HMO, health maintenance organization, PPO, point-of-service, and other health care plans to its customers.

EXECUTIVES

President and CEO: Nancy L. Leaming
CFO: Andy Hilbert
SVP and Chief Medical Officer: Philip R. Boulter
SVP and CIO: Tricia Trebino
SVP and Corporate General Counsel: James Roosevelt Jr.
SVP, Planning and Development: Jon M. Kingsdale
SVP, Sales, Marketing, and Member Services: Kevin J. Counihan
Manager, Human Resources: Sally Morrissey
Auditors: Ernst & Young LLP

LOCATIONS

HQ: Tufts Associated Health Plans, Inc.
333 Wyman St., Waltham, MA 02454
Phone: 781-466-9400 **Fax:** 781-466-8583
Web: www.tufts-healthplan.com

PRODUCTS/OPERATIONS

Health Plans

HMO
POS (point-of-service)
EPO (exclusive provider option)
PPO (preferred provider organization)
Secure Horizons Tufts Health Plan for Seniors (Medicare)

COMPETITORS

Aetna
Blue Cross (MA)
CIGNA
ConnectiCare
Harvard Pilgrim
Prudential
UnitedHealth Group

HISTORICAL FINANCIALS

Company Type: Not-for-profit

Income Statement FYE: December 31

	REVENUE ($ mil.)	NET INCOME ($ mil.)	NET PROFIT MARGIN	EMPLOYEES
12/02	2,000	—	—	2,500
12/01	2,000	—	—	2,500
12/00	2,000	—	—	3,000
12/99	2,000	—	—	3,000
12/98	1,600	—	—	2,500
12/97	1,210	—	—	2,341
12/96	865	—	—	1,200
12/95	670	—	—	1,128
12/94	542	—	—	—
12/93	456	—	—	—
Annual Growth	17.9%	—	—	12.0%

Revenue History

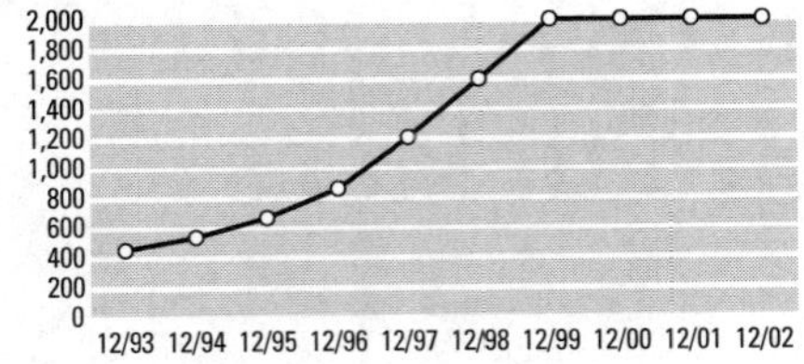

Tulane University

Tulane University may be in the Big Easy, but its classes are anything but. The school is a private, research-based institution with 11 schools and colleges. Its almost 12,400 students are enrolled in either graduate or undergraduate programs including law, medicine, architecture, engineering, and liberal arts and sciences, among others. Tulane's New Orleans campus houses most of its facilities, but the school also has satellite campuses in two other Louisiana towns, as well as one Mississippi location. Founded in 1834, the schools original name was the Medical College of Louisiana. It took on the Tulane moniker in 1884.

EXECUTIVES

Chairman: John E. Koerner III, age 60
President: Scott S. Cowen, age 56
SVP Academic Affairs and Provost: Lester A. Lefton
SVP External Affairs: Yvette Jones
SVP Health Sciences: Paul K. Whelton
SVP Operations and CFO: Anthony P. Lorino
VP and Chief of Staff: Anne Baños
VP Human Resources: Andrew Heck
VP University Communications: Deborah L. Grant
General Counsel: Victoria Johnson
Auditors: Deloitte & Touche LLP

LOCATIONS

HQ: 6823 St. Charles Ave., New Orleans, LA 70118
Phone: 504-865-5000 **Fax:** 504-862-8713
Web: www2.tulane.edu

HISTORICAL FINANCIALS

Company Type: School

Income Statement FYE: June 30*

	REVENUE ($ mil.)	NET INCOME ($ mil.)	NET PROFIT MARGIN	EMPLOYEES
12/02	563	—	—	—
12/01	546	—	—	—
Annual Growth	3.2%	—	—	—

*Fiscal year change

Revenue History

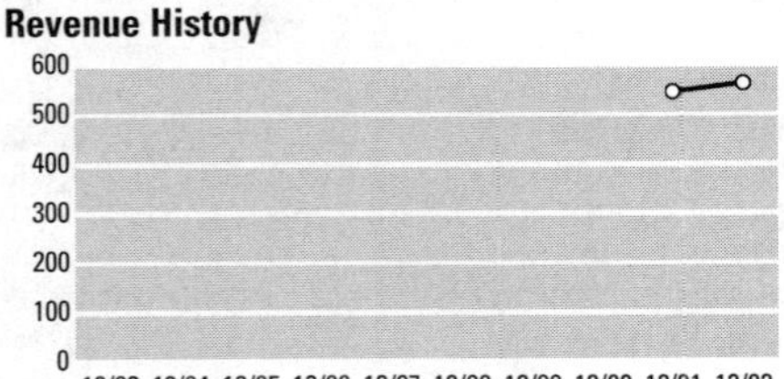

Turner Industries, Ltd.

Turner Industries turns out industrial services. Founded in 1961, the company is a top US player in industrial construction, contract maintenance, and outsourcing. Its customers include oil refiners, petrochemical companies, power generators, and pulp and paper mills. Through 16 subsidiaries, Turner Industries provides such services as equipment rental, environmental remediation, heavy hauling and rigging, pipe fabrication, and tank cleaning. Turner Industries also provides maintenance and materials management and training workshops and staffing services. Founder and chairman emeritus Bert Turner is principal shareholder of the company.

EXECUTIVES

Chairman Emeritus: Bert S. Turner
Chairman and CEO: Roland Toups
President: Thomas H. Turner
VP Finance, CFO, Secretary, and Treasurer: Lester J. (Les) Griffin Jr.
VP and CIO: Lowell K. Vice
Director Human Resources: Russell Gauthreaux

LOCATIONS

HQ: 8687 United Plaza Blvd., Ste. 500, Baton Rouge, LA 70809
Phone: 225-922-5050 **Fax:** 225-922-5055
Web: www.turner-industries.com

Turner Industries operates from more than 30 offices in Alabama, Louisiana, and Texas.

PRODUCTS/OPERATIONS

Selected Services

Bundle extraction
Construction
Contract maintenance
Environmental remediation
Equipment rental
Heavy hauling
Hydroblasting
Painting
Pipe fabrication
Preventive maintenance
Procurement
Rigging
Scaffolding
System integration
Tank cleaning

COMPETITORS

ABB
aker Kvaerner
APi Group
Austin Industries
Bechtel
Black & Veatch
Centerline Piping
CH2M HILL
Chicago Bridge and Iron
Fluor
Foster Wheeler
Halliburton
Jacobs Engineering
McDermott
Parsons
Peter Kiewit Sons'
Philip Services
Shaw Group
TIC Holdings
Zachry

HISTORICAL FINANCIALS

Company Type: Private

Income Statement FYE: October 31

	ESTIMATED REVENUE ($ mil.)	NET INCOME ($ mil.)	NET PROFIT MARGIN	EMPLOYEES
10/02	800	—	—	12,000
10/01	790	—	—	11,000
10/00	741	—	—	12,000
10/99	673	—	—	10,000
10/98	600	—	—	9,800
10/97	553	—	—	10,500
10/96	500	—	—	10,000
10/95	486	—	—	8,100
10/94	400	—	—	600
10/93	400	—	—	—
Annual Growth	8.0%	—	—	45.4%

Revenue History

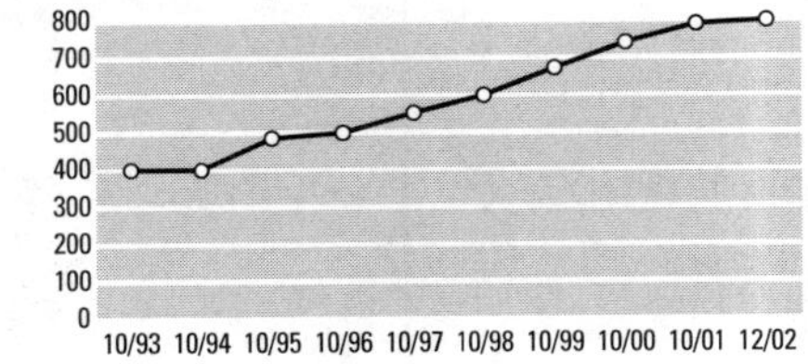

Tutor-Saliba Corporation

Beneath California's glamour, Tutor-Saliba is making tracks. A key player in US transportation construction, it was the lead builder of Los Angeles' new subway system and San Francisco's BART extension to the airport. The construction and engineering company, which offers construction management and design/build services, is known for its California public works projects, including work on the Los Angeles Central Library and the San Francisco Main Post Office. The company's owner, president and CEO Ronald Tutor, is also chairman of Perini, a joint venture partner of Tutor-Saliba. Ronald Tutor and Naseeb Saliba founded the firm.

EXECUTIVES

Chairman, President, and CEO: Ronald N. Tutor, age 63
SVP and CFO: William (Bill) Sparks
SVP Operations: Pat Henderson
VP Asian Operations: Tom Anderson
Payroll Supervisor: Charen Smith
Director Human Resources: Sylvia Aguilar
Auditors: PricewaterhouseCoopers

LOCATIONS

HQ: 15901 Olden St., Sylmar, CA 91342
Phone: 818-362-8391 **Fax:** 818-367-5379
Web: www.tutorsaliba.com

PRODUCTS/OPERATIONS

Selected Projects

Alameda Corridor, Los Angeles
Bank One Ballpark, Phoenix
BART Line Trackway, San Francisco International Airport
Emergency Command Control Communications System Centers, Los Angeles
Federal Office Building, Los Angeles
Folsom Prison
International Terminal, San Francisco International Airport
Moscone Convention Center, San Francisco
San Diego Convention Center
San Francisco Main Post Office
Tom Bradley International Terminal, Los Angeles International Airport

COMPETITORS

Bechtel
Clark Enterprises
Dick Corporation
Granite Construction
Hensel Phelps Construction
J.F. Shea
Kajima Engineering and Construction
M. A. Mortenson
Modern Continental Companies
Parsons Brinckerhoff
Parsons
Peter Kiewit Sons'
Walsh Group
Washington Group

HISTORICAL FINANCIALS

Company Type: Private

Income Statement FYE: December 31

	REVENUE ($ mil.)	NET INCOME ($ mil.)	NET PROFIT MARGIN	EMPLOYEES
12/01	457	—	—	2,400
12/00	642	—	—	2,400
12/99	728	—	—	2,400
12/98	673	—	—	2,490
12/97	619	—	—	2,400
12/96	515	—	—	2,200
12/95	346	—	—	1,500
12/94	316	—	—	985
12/93	257	—	—	—
Annual Growth	7.5%	—	—	13.6%

Revenue History

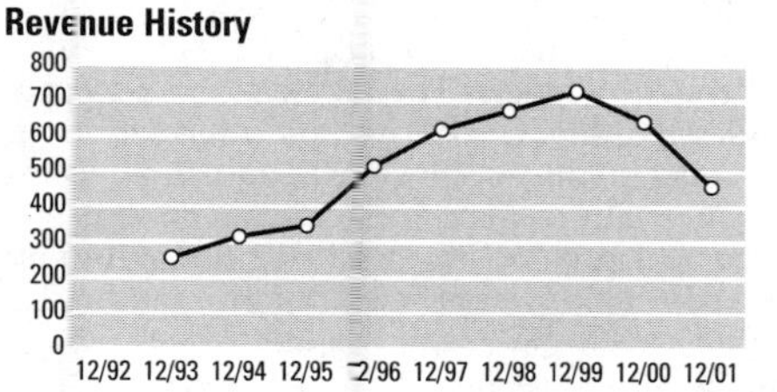

Tuttle-Click Automotive

Despite its connections to the Republican Party, Tuttle-Click Automotive Group does sell cars to Democrats. The firm operates about 10 new- and used-car dealerships throughout Orange County, California, and in Tucson, Arizona. The firm's dealerships sell Ford, DaimlerChrysler, Mitsubishi, and Hyundai cars and trucks. It also operates Ford and Chrysler auto service centers. The company was founded by Holmes Tuttle, who sold Ronald Reagan a car in 1946 and ended up a prominent GOP fundraiser; he even persuaded Reagan to run for governor of California in 1966. Tuttle's son, co-CEO Robert Tuttle (a White House aide under Reagan), and Arizona-based co-CEO James Click own the company.

EXECUTIVES

Co-CEO: James H. Click
Co-CEO: Robert H. (Bob) Tuttle, age 59
CFO: Chris Cotter
Director of Personnel: Angie Mejia

LOCATIONS

HQ: Tuttle-Click Automotive Group
14 Auto Center Dr., Irvine, CA 92618
Phone: 949-598-4800 **Fax:** 949-830-0980
Web: www.tuttleclick.com

PRODUCTS/OPERATIONS

Selected Automobile Brands

Chrysler
Dodge
Eagle
Ford
Hyundai
Jeep
Mitsubishi
Plymouth

COMPETITORS

AutoNation
David Wilson's
Earnhardt's Auto Centers
Ford of Santa Monica
Larry H. Miller Group
Lithia Motors
Marty Franich
Prospect Motors
Sonic Automotive
Southern California Auto Group
Vista

HISTORICAL FINANCIALS

Company Type: Private

Income Statement FYE: December 31

	REVENUE ($ mil.)	NET INCOME ($ mil.)	NET PROFIT MARGIN	EMPLOYEES
12/02	669	—	—	1,350
12/01	687	—	—	1,400
12/00	718	—	—	1,400
12/99	700	—	—	1,380
12/98	665	—	—	1,310
12/97	585	—	—	1,400
12/96	608	—	—	1,400
12/95	582	—	—	1,284
12/94	561	—	—	1,400
Annual Growth	2.2%	—	—	(0.5%)

Revenue History

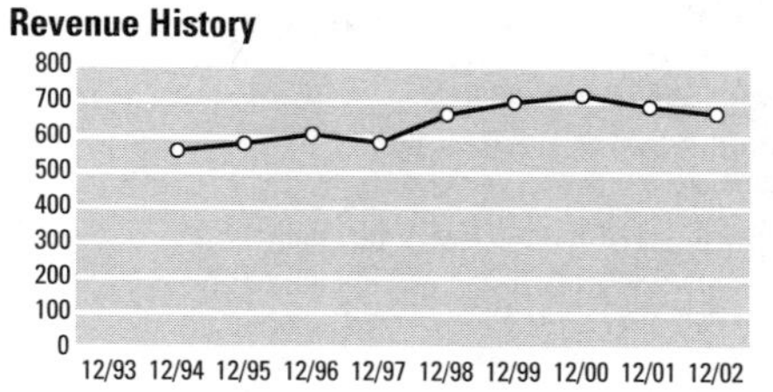

Ty Inc.

Take some fabric, shape it like an animal, fill it with plastic pellets, and you, too, could own luxury hotels. That's the lesson taught by Ty Warner, sole owner of Ty Inc., the firm behind Beanie Babies and their worldwide cult following — popular with kids and adults alike. Since 1993 Ty has produced more than 365 different Beanie Babies with colorful names such as Punxsutawney Phil (current) and Cheeks the baboon (retired). Other products include Beanie Buddies (bigger versions of traditional Beanies), Ty Classics (stuffed animals), Beanie Boppers (preteen dolls), and Punkies (squeezable beanbag pals). Beanie bucks enabled Warner to buy three luxury hotels (in New York and California) in recent years.

Ty's marketing smarts have kept Beanies popular for years rather than for a single holiday season, à la Furby or Tickle Me Elmo. The company limits production so that supply never outstrips demand, keeping only 40 or 50 Beanie Babies in circulation at any one time. Ty's "retirement" of a Beanie can cause its price among collectors to skyrocket from its $5-$7 retail debut to hundreds or even thousands of dollars.

Rather than flood the market with Beanies through the likes of Toys "R" Us and Wal-Mart, Ty sells them only through specialty toy and gift retailers.

In addition, the firm doesn't advertise, relying instead on the word of mouth that is rampant in Beanie culture. Books, magazines, newsletters, and Web sites stoke collectors' enthusiasm. This collectors' market — which Ty frowns upon (officially, anyway) — shows signs of fading, however.

HISTORY

Ty Warner, the son of a plush-toy salesman, started his toy career selling stuffed animals to specialty shops for stuffed-bear manufacturer Dakin. Warner left Dakin in 1980, moved to Europe for a few years, and in the mid-1980s returned to the US and founded Ty Inc. The company first designed a line of $20, understuffed Himalayan cats.

Beanie Babies first debuted at a 1993 trade show. In January 1994 the first nine Beanies went on sale — at prices low enough for kids to afford — in Chicago specialty stores. As Warner had learned at Dakin, selling stuffed animals through specialty retailers rather than through mass merchandisers meant bigger profits for suppliers and longer-term popularity.

By 1995 there were about 30 different Beanies, and Ty's estimated sales were $25 million. The popularity of Beanies exploded in 1996, first in the Midwest, then along the East Coast, and then across the US. By midyear, Beanies — along with the public's mania for getting them before they sold out — were receiving widespread media coverage. Ty heightened the frenzy among collectors when it started announcing Beanie retirements on its Web site in 1997.

McDonald's got on the bandwagon in 1997: The fast-food giant issued some 100 million "teenie" Beanie Babies in a Happy Meal promotion. McDonald's ran out of the toys and had to end the promotion early, causing a public relations mess. McDonald's doubled its toy order in 1998 and teamed up with Ty again in 1999 and 2000.

In 1998 Warner paid $10 million for a 7% stake in marketing company Cyrk. In return,

Cyrk developed the Beanie Babies Official Club, which turned stores that sell Beanies into "official headquarters" offering club membership kits. Ty introduced its Attic Treasures and Beanie Buddies lines that year.

By spring 1998 Beanies had become a customs issue at the Canadian border, where Ty's limit of one imported Beanie per person into the US resulted in tears and fisticuffs. (The company later raised the personal limit to 30.) That summer the crowds at Major League Baseball games featuring Beanie giveaways were 26% bigger than average.

Warner bought the Four Seasons hotel in New York City in 1999. He also provided auditing documents and correspondence to *The New York Post* indicating that Ty had 1998 profits of more than $700 million — more than Hasbro and Mattel combined.

After an August 1999 announcement that it would retire the Beanies at the end of the year, the company held a New Year's vote to determine their fate. In the most shocking outcome since *Rocky IV,* the public voted overwhelmingly in favor of continuing the Beanies. Ty introduced its humanoid Beanie Kids line in early 2000. Later that year Warner bought the Four Seasons Biltmore Hotel and the San Ysidro Ranch — the hostelry where JFK and Jackie honeymooned; both are near Santa Barbara, California.

In 2001 Ty debuted its pre-teen Beanie Boppers (boy and girl dolls designed for kids from 8 to 12 years of age). In an effort to round out his Four Seasons Biltmore Hotel and Coral Casino properties in California, Warner, in late 2002, began plans to purchase nearby Sandpiper Golf Course.

EXECUTIVES

President and CEO: H. Ty Warner
EVP and CFO: Michael W. Kanzler
VP: Tania Lundeen
Director, Human Resources: Nancy Pena

LOCATIONS

HQ: 280 Chestnut Ave., Westmont, IL 60559
Phone: 630-920-1515 **Fax:** 630-920-1980
Web: www.ty.com

PRODUCTS/OPERATIONS

Selected Products

Attic Treasures
Baby Ty
Beanie Babies
Beanie Boppers
Beanie Buddies
Beanie Kids
Pluffies
Punkies
Teenie Beanie Boppers
Ty Classics

COMPETITORS

Applause
Boyds Collection
Build-A-Bear
Enesco Group
Hasbro
Imperial Toy
Mattel
North American Bear
Pleasant
Russ Berrie
Vermont Teddy Bear

HISTORICAL FINANCIALS

Company Type: Private

Income Statement FYE: December 31

	ESTIMATED REVENUE ($ mil.)	NET INCOME ($ mil.)	NET PROFIT MARGIN	EMPLOYEES
12/02	750	—	—	600
12/01	750	—	—	650
12/00	850	—	—	1,000
12/99	1,250	—	—	1,000
12/98	1,000	—	—	1,000
12/97	400	—	—	500
12/96	250	—	—	200
12/95	25	—	—	50
Annual Growth	62.6%	—	—	42.6%

Revenue History

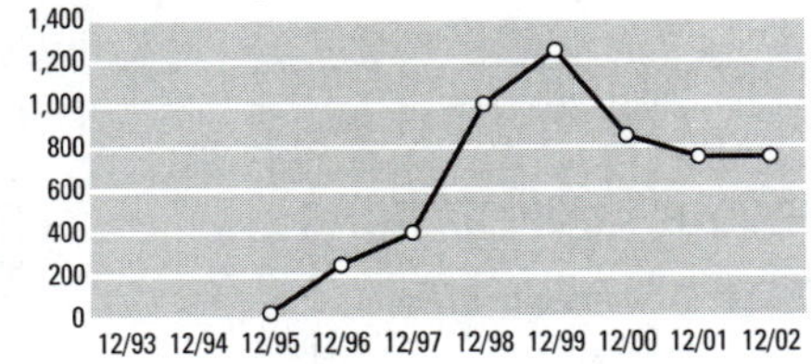

UIS, Inc.

Once the maker of candy bars and parts for cars, UIS has abandoned auto parts in favor of candy hearts. UIS's automotive subsidiaries included Champion Laboratories (oil filters), Neapco (transmission parts), Wells Manufacturing (ignition and electrical components), and Pioneer (auto specialty supplier) and were sold to The Carlyle Group for $800 million. UIS's remaining operations include New England Confectionery Company (Sweethearts, NECCO wafers, Clark Bar) and Hurd Millwork (window and patio doors). Founder Harry Lebensfeld started the company in 1945 with the purchase of an Indiana desk maker. UIS is owned by a trust for Lebensfeld's only child (who is married to EVP Richard Pasculano) and her children.

EXECUTIVES

Chairman, President, and CEO: Andrew E. Pietrini
EVP and Treasurer: Joseph F. Arrigo
EVP: Richard Pasculano

LOCATIONS

HQ: 15 Exchange Place, Ste. 1120, Jersey City, NJ 07302
Phone: 201-946-2600 **Fax:** 201-946-9325

PRODUCTS/OPERATIONS

Selected Operations

Hurd Millwork Company, Inc.
Window and patio door systems

New England Confectionery Company
Confectionery products including Sweethearts, NECCO wafers, and Clark Bars

COMPETITORS

Andersen
Hershey
Mars

HISTORICAL FINANCIALS

Company Type: Private

Income Statement FYE: December 31

	REVENUE ($ mil.)	NET INCOME ($ mil.)	NET PROFIT MARGIN	EMPLOYEES
12/02	1,000	—	—	8,800
12/01	1,056	—	—	8,820
12/00	1,087	—	—	8,910
12/99	1,081	—	—	8,800
12/98	1,020	—	—	8,614
12/97	986	—	—	8,600
12/96	928	—	—	8,300
12/95	871	—	—	8,255
12/94	830	—	—	8,100
12/93	745	—	—	7,258
Annual Growth	3.3%	—	—	2.2%

Revenue History

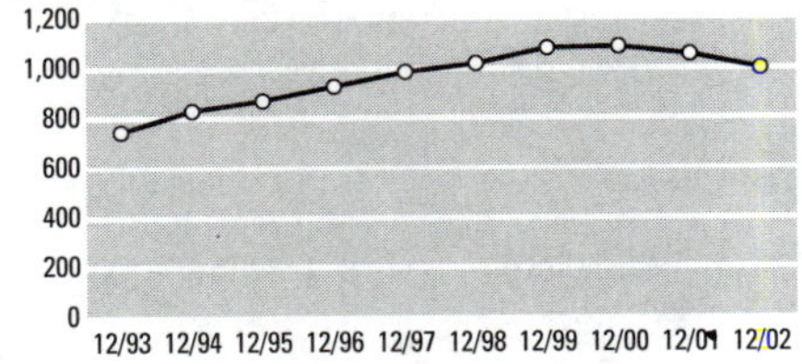

Underwriters Laboratories

Billions of products proudly wear the mark of Underwriters Laboratories (UL). More than 65,000 manufacturers — including makers of toys, industrial controls, and telephone equipment — pay to have their products tested by the not-for-profit laboratory. Products with the ubiquitous UL mark typically sell better than untested products. The organization also provides seasonal safety tips and information on product recalls to consumers and audits compliance with product certification requirements. Founded in 1894, UL expanded worldwide by first partnering with other certification organizations and then (beginning in the mid-1990s) by acquiring facilities outside the US.

Alliances with other standards-and-testing organizations allow UL to help US and foreign manufacturers take their products to other markets. The organization has laboratory, testing, and certification facilities in more than 70 countries and serves customers in nearly 90 countries.

UL's corporate members (not manufacturers of products subject to UL coverage) elect trustees, who approve capital projects and corporate acquisitions.

EXECUTIVES

Chairman: Fred R. Marcon
President, CEO, and Director: Loring W. Knoblauch
EVP; COO, International: Joe Bhatia
EVP; COO, North America: Don Mader
SVP and CFO: Michael Saltzman
SVP and Chief Administrative Officer: Ken Melnick
SVP and CIO: Mark Sklenar
SVP, Global Human Resources: Jim Austgen

SVP, Global Marketing and Sales: Stuart Paul
VP and CTO: Ted V. Hall
VP and General Counsel: John Verscaj

LOCATIONS

HQ: Underwriter Laboratories, Inc.
333 Pfingsten Rd., Northbrook, IL 60062
Phone: 847-272-8800 **Fax:** 847-272-8129
Web: www.ul.com

Underwriters Laboratories has offices in Argentina, Brazil, Canada, China, Denmark, France, Germany, Hong Kong, India, Italy, Japan, Malaysia, Mexico, the Netherlands, Singapore, South Korea, Spain, Sweden, Taiwan, the UK, and the US.

PRODUCTS/OPERATIONS

Selected Product Areas

Alarm systems
Audio/video products
Distributed generation equipment
Electrical control equipment
Electric vehicle components
Fire equipment
Food service equipment
Industrial control equipment
Information technology equipment
Lasers
Local-area network (LAN) cable
Marine products
Medical devices
Programmable electronics/software
Refrigerants/HVAC
Telecommunications equipment
Water system components

Service Areas

Drinking water compliance testing
Electromagnetic compatibility (EMC)
Energy verification
Environmental and public health
Field evaluations
Flammability training
Food safety
International compliance
Large-scale fire testing
Machinery assessment
Management system registration
NEBS testing
Source verification and inspection

COMPETITORS

Bureau Veritas
Canadian Standards Association
Consumers Union
Exponent
Intertek
J.D. Power
Methode Electronics
National Technical Systems
SGS

Revenue History

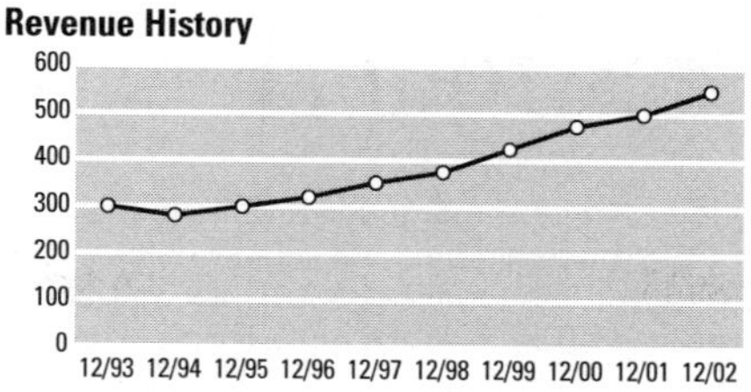

Unified Western Grocers, Inc.

Unified Western Grocers guarantees that food and general merchandise reach about 3,700 mostly independent grocery stores in nine western states and several countries in the South Pacific. The food wholesaler and cooperative supplies a full line of groceries, as well as its own bakery and dairy goods. In addition to name-brand items, its offerings include private labels Better Buy, Cottage Hearth, and Western Family. The co-op also provides member support services such as store remodeling, financing, and insurance. Unified serves about 670 patrons, many of whom own shares in the company. It was formed in 1999 when Certified Grocers of California merged with United Grocers of Oregon.

Consolidation and the trend toward self-distribution among food retailers has hurt wholesale grocery distributors. The two co-ops merged to match the buying power afforded to large supermarket chains and wholesalers.

Unified is helping independent grocers capture an increasing share of the Hispanic market in places like Los Angeles by supplying ethnic foods and targeted marketing campaigns to its member stores.

The co-op is selling or closing all 12 of its company-owned SavMax Foods stores as part of its plan to exit its unprofitable retail business and focus on its wholesale division (95% of total sales).

HISTORY

Certified Grocers of California evolved from a group of 15 independent Southern California grocers that formed a purchasing cooperative in 1922 to compete against large grocery chains. Certified Grocers of California incorporated in 1925 and issued stock to 50 members.

The co-op merged with a small retailer-owned wholesale company called Co-operative Grocers in 1928. It acquired Walker Brothers Grocery in 1929 and nearly tripled the previous year's sales. By 1938 the co-op had grown to 310 members and 380 stores, and sales passed $10 million.

Certified launched a line of private-label products under the Springfield name in 1947. In the early 1950s it added nonfood items and began processing its own private-label coffee and bean products. The co-op added delicatessen items in 1956. During the 1960s and 1970s, Certified added a meat center, a frozen food and deli warehouse, a produce distribution center, a creamery, a central bakery, and a specialty foods warehouse.

In 1989 the co-op opened several membership warehouse stores called Convenience Clubs. The Save Mart and Boys Markets chains left the fold in 1991. The co-op lost about 30% of its business during the next two years, including the Bel Air and Williams Bros. chains. After disappointing returns, in 1992 Certified sold its warehouse stores, cut staff, and consolidated warehouses.

CFO (and former Atlantic Richfield executive) Al Plamann was appointed CEO in 1994, succeeding Everett Dingwell. In 1996 the co-op began to convert its customers' older retail stores to Apple Markets in Southern California. Revenues began to dip in 1997 as the result of reduced purchases from some supermarkets and the sale the previous year of one of its subsidiaries, Hawaiian Grocery Stores.

Member chain Stumps converted to the Apple Markets banner in 1998. Faced with a declining customer base, in 1999 Certified merged with United Grocers of Oregon to form Unified Western Grocers.

Dr. R. Norton, F. L. Freeburg, and A. C. Brinckerhoff founded United Grocers of Oregon in 1915 as a way for grocers in Portland to cooperate in purchasing merchandise. By the next year the co-op had 35 members. In the 1950s United formed a trucking department and established a general merchandise division. It also grew rapidly in the 1950s through acquisitions, buying Northwest Grocery Company and the Fridegar Grocery Company. In 1963 United formed its frozen food department when it purchased Raven Creamery.

By 1975 the company's Northwest Grocery Company subsidiary had 14 Cash and Carry warehouses that sold goods to small grocers and restaurants. In 1995 United bought California food distributor Market Wholesale. Three years later the company sold its Cash and Carry warehouse-style stores to Smart & Final.

Upon completion of the merger in 1999, Certified's president and CEO, Plamann, was named to head the new organization. Soon after, Unified consolidated warehouse operations, eliminated duplicate personnel, and combined its private labels. Also in 1999 the company acquired California-based Gourmet Specialties.

The next year it bought the specialty foods business of J. Sosnick and Son, another California company, and Central Sales of Washington State. The company attributed net losses during 2001 to delays in moving the source for northern California specialty merchandise from southern to northern California and to the costs of entering the Washington marketplace, among other factors.

In 2002 Unified closed seven retail stores in Northern California and Oregon (under the Apple Markets and SavMax Foods banners) that accounted for sales of about $140 million as part of its plan to reduce debt and focus on wholesaling.

HISTORICAL FINANCIALS

Company Type: Not-for-profit

Income Statement FYE: December 31

	REVENUE ($ mil.)	NET INCOME ($ mil.)	NET PROFIT MARGIN	EMPLOYEES
12/02	550	—	—	5,900
12/01	500	—	—	6,000
12/00	475	—	—	5,938
12/99	425	—	—	5,500
12/98	375	—	—	5,258
12/97	352	—	—	4,200
12/96	320	—	—	4,000
12/95	300	—	—	3,900
12/94	281	—	—	3,900
12/93	300	—	—	4,100
Annual Growth	7.0%	—	—	4.1%

EXECUTIVES

President and CEO: Alfred A. (Al) Plamann, age 60, $500,000 pay
EVP, Finance and Administration and CFO: Richard J. Martin, age 57, $277,019 pay
EVP, General Counsel, and Secretary: Robert M. Ling Jr., age 45, $271,422 pay
SVP Distribution: Rodney L. VanBebber, age 47
SVP Procurement: Philip S. Smith, age 52, $201,058 pay
SVP Retail Support Services, Perishables, and Retailer Services; President, SavMax Foods: Daniel J. Murphy, age 56, $208,269 pay
VP and CIO: Gary S. Herman
VP and Controller: William O. Cotè, age 45
VP and Treasurer: David A. Woodward, age 59
VP, Human Resources: Don Gilpin

VP, Insurance: Joseph A. Ney, age 54
President, Southern California: Luis de la Mata
Auditors: Deloitte & Touche LLP

LOCATIONS

HQ: 5200 Sheila St., Commerce, CA 90040
Phone: 323-264-5200 **Fax:** 323-265-4006
Web: www.uwgrocers.com

Unified Western Grocers distributes to about 3,700 member stores in Arizona, California, Colorado, Hawaii, western Idaho, Nevada, Oregon, Utah, Washington, and several countries in the South Pacific and elsewhere.

PRODUCTS/OPERATIONS

Selected Co-op Members

Alamo Market
Andronico's Markets
Bales For Food
Berberian Enterprises, Inc.
Bristol Farms Markets, Inc.
Estacada Foods, Inc.
Evergreen Markets, Inc.
Gelson's Markets
Goodwin & Sons, Inc.
Howard's On Scholls
Joe Notrica, Inc.
K. V. Mart Co.
Mar-Val Food Stores, Inc.
Mollie Stone's Markets
Pioneer Super Save, Inc.
Pokerville Select Market
Pro & Son's, Inc.
Sentry Market
Stump's Market, Inc.
Super A Foods, Inc.
Super Center Concepts, Inc.
Sweet Home Thriftway
Tresierras Bros. Corp.
Wright's Foodliner

Selected Support Services

Financing
Information technology
Insurance
Private labels
Real estate development
Store design
Transportation

COMPETITORS

Associated Food
Associated Grocers
Fleming Companies
Nash Finch
Shurfine International
SUPERVALU
Topco Associates
Wal-Mart
WinCo Foods

HISTORICAL FINANCIALS

Company Type: Cooperative

Income Statement FYE: Saturday nearest September 30

	REVENUE ($ mil.)	NET INCOME ($ mil.)	NET PROFIT MARGIN	EMPLOYEES
9/02	2,793	(39)	—	3,600
9/01	2,930	(13)	—	4,200
9/00	3,067	(11)	—	4,000
9/99	1,894	3	0.1%	3,945
9/98	1,832	3	0.2%	2,200
9/97	1,927	2	0.1%	2,400
9/96	1,949	2	0.1%	2,400
9/95	1,823	1	0.0%	2,470
9/94	1,874	(2)	—	2,600
9/93	2,007	0	—	2,500
Annual Growth	3.7%	—	—	4.1%

2002 Year-End Financials

Debt ratio: 330.7%
Return on equity: —
Cash ($ mil.): 10
Current ratio: 1.52
Long-term debt ($ mil.): 288

Net Income History

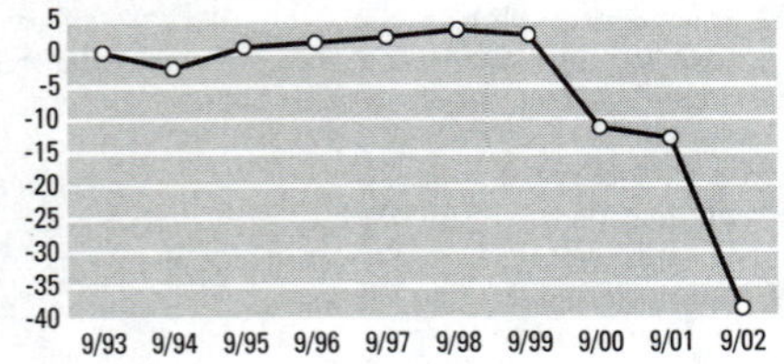

UniGroup, Inc.

Moving household goods has made many of UniGroup's companies household names. The moving service company transports household goods and other items in more than 100 countries through subsidiaries United Van Lines and Mayflower Transit. Its Total Transportation Services unit sells and leases trucks and trailers and provides moving supplies, and its Vanliner Group offers insurance to movers. Subsidiary UniGroup Worldwide offers relocation management and assistance, and Insite Logistics provides third-party logistics services. Founded in 1987, UniGroup is owned by a 250-person group that includes agents of United Van Lines and Mayflower Transit and company managers.

EXECUTIVES

Chairman: Gerry Stadler
President and COO: Richard P. (Rich) McClure
CFO: James G. (Jim) Powers
SVP and CIO: Randall C. Poppell
President Transportation Services Group: Patrick Larch
President UniGroup Worldwide: Michael Kranisky
President Vanliner Group: John Temporiti
Director Human Resources: Sherry Fagin

LOCATIONS

HQ: 1 Premier Dr., Fenton, MO 63026
Phone: 636-326-3100 **Fax:** 636-326-1106
Web: www.unigroupinc.com

COMPETITORS

AMERCO
Atlas World Group
Bekins
Budget
Graebel
Nelson Westerberg
SIRVA

HISTORICAL FINANCIALS

Company Type: Private

Income Statement FYE: December 31

	REVENUE ($ mil.)	NET INCOME ($ mil.)	NET PROFIT MARGIN	EMPLOYEES
12/02	1,708	—	—	1,335
12/01	1,896	—	—	1,400
12/00	2,009	—	—	1,871
12/99	1,878	—	—	1,800
12/98	1,800	—	—	1,600
12/97	1,749	—	—	1,650
12/96	1,626	—	—	1,600
12/95	1,406	—	—	1,000
12/94	995	—	—	950
12/93	912	—	—	950
Annual Growth	7.2%	—	—	3.9%

Revenue History

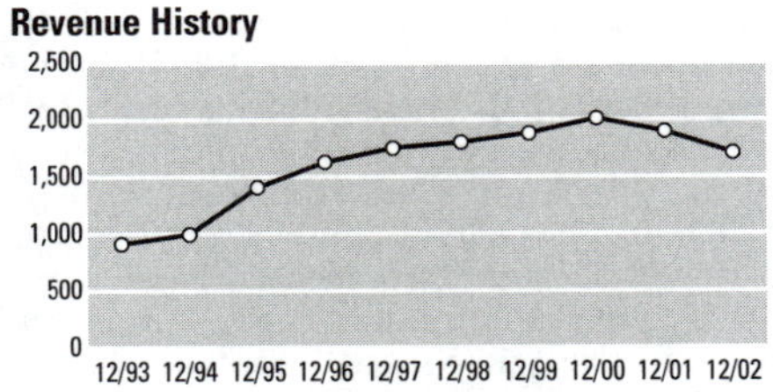

Unimin Corporation

Mining company Unimin Corporation produces industrial minerals and provides global transportation services. Unimin supplies mineral products to a broad range of industries, which include the glass, fiberglass, ceramic, semiconductor, quartz lighting, paint and coatings, fiberoptics, foundry, and oil and gas industries. Other industries served include the construction, paper and paperboard, plastics, rubber, refractory, and metallurgical industries. Unimin has operations in the Americas, Scandinavia, and Australia. The company was founded in 1970.

EXECUTIVES

President: Kevin F. Crawford
EVP: Thomas M. Kilroy Jr.
SVP: Joseph C. Shapiro
VP: H. Frederick Barnard III
VP: Dick Benck
VP: Andrew Bradley
VP: Thomas Hiscox
VP: Craig Johnson
VP: Andrew Kachele

LOCATIONS

HQ: 258 Elm St., New Canaan, CT 06840
Phone: 203-966-8880 **Fax:** 203-966-3453
Web: www.unimin.com

PRODUCTS/OPERATIONS

Selected Products

Ball clay
Barium sulfate
Bentonite clay
Calcium carbonate
Dolomite
Feldspar
High-purity quartz
Kaolin
Magnetite
Microcrystalline silica
Nepheline syenite
Olivine
Silica sand
Talc

HISTORICAL FINANCIALS

Company Type: Private

Income Statement FYE: December 31

	ESTIMATED REVENUE ($ mil.)	NET INCOME ($ mil.)	NET PROFIT MARGIN	EMPLOYEES
12/02	550	—	—	4,000

Union Central Life Insurance

Next stop for insurance, Union Central. Union Central Life Insurance Company is a mutual life insurance company that operates in all 50 states and the District of Columbia. The company offers a range of individual life and disability insurance, investment products, annuities, group retirement plans, and group insurance. Union Central also offers employee and executive benefit planning, estate planning, and retirement planning. Union Central's investments are mainly in bonds and collateralized mortgage obligations, of which mortgage investments accounted for about 20%. Union Central was founded in 1867.

EXECUTIVES

Chairman, President, and CEO: John H. Jacobs
EVP, CFO, and Corporate Actuary: James L. Livingston Jr.
EVP, General Counsel, and Secretary: David F. Westerbeck
EVP, Individual Insurance and Annuities: Gary T. Huffman
SVP, Employee Benefits: Dale D. Johnson
SVP, Information Systems and Human Services: Mark Quinlan
Auditors: Ernst & Young LLP

LOCATIONS

HQ: The Union Central Life Insurance Company
1876 Waycross Rd., Cincinnati, OH 45240
Phone: 513-595-2200 **Fax:** 513-595-5418
Web: www.unioncentral.com

Union Central Life Insurance operates throughout the US.

PRODUCTS/OPERATIONS

Selected Subsidiaries

Carillon Investments, Inc.
Payday of America
PRB Administrators, Inc.
Summit Investment Partners

COMPETITORS

AIG American General
Allstate
American National Insurance
Citigroup
John Hancock Financial Services
MassMutual
MetLife
New York Life
Northwestern Mutual
Penn Mutual Life
Principal Financial
Protective Life
Prudential

HISTORICAL FINANCIALS

Company Type: Mutual company

Income Statement FYE: December 31

	ASSETS ($ mil.)	NET INCOME ($ mil.)	INCOME AS % OF ASSETS	EMPLOYEES
12/02	6,411	(26)	—	900
12/01	6,119	0	0.0%	900
12/00	5,507	35	0.6%	800
12/99	5,604	19	0.3%	800
12/98	5,088	31	0.6%	800
12/97	4,784	51	1.1%	755
12/96	4,430	39	0.9%	743
12/95	4,091	24	0.6%	750
12/94	3,780	21	0.5%	870
12/93	3,534	20	0.6%	994
Annual Growth	6.8%	—	—	(1.1%)

2002 Year-End Financials

Equity as % of assets: 9.1%
Return on assets: —
Return on equity: —
Long-term debt ($ mil.): 4,060
Sales ($ mil.): 487

Net Income History

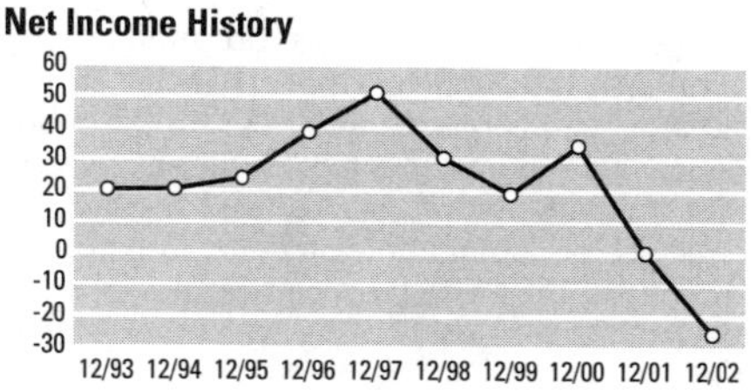

United Industries

Many a bug has bitten the dust due to United Industries. Its Spectrum Brands unit makes insecticides, insect repellents, lawn and garden pesticides, herbicides, and fertilizers. Its brands include Hot Shot, Real-Kill, Spectracide, and Cutter. The Home Depot, Lowe's, and Kmart account for about 74% of sales. United Industries' products are sold in the US, Canada, and the Caribbean. Founded in 1969 as a bolt maker, United moved into insect control via acquisitions, including Unilever's Chesebrough-Ponds in 1988. In 2002 United Industries bought the Schultz Company, a lawn and garden company, and WPC Brands, an outdoor health and safety company. The Thomas H. Lee Equity Fund IV owns about 84% of United.

EXECUTIVES

Chairman, President, and CEO: Robert (Bob) Caulk, age 51, $820,000 pay
EVP, CFO, and Director: Daniel J. Johnston, age 44, $510,205 pay
SVP, Business Development: Steven D. Schultz, age 55
SVP, Marketing: Kent J. Davies, age 39, $311,495 pay
SVP, Operations: John F. Timony, age 53, $346,172 pay
VP, Corporate Development: Robert S. Rubin, age 36, $306,383 pay
VP, Secretary, and General Counsel: Louis N. Laderman, age 51
VP, Human Resources: Rick K. Spurlock
Auditors: PricewaterhouseCoopers LLP

LOCATIONS

HQ: United Industries Corporation
2150 Schuetz Rd., St. Louis, MO 63146
Phone: 314-427-0780 **Fax:** 314-253-5978
Web: www.spectrumbrands.com

United Industries has manufacturing plants in Jackson, Wyoming; Orrville, Ohio; Sylacauga, Alabama; and Vinita Park, Missouri. It has distribution centers in Allentown, Pennsylvania; Bridgeton, Missouri; Earth City, Missouri; Gainesville, Georgia; Ontario, California; Orrville, Ohio; and Sylacauga, Alabama. It has a warehouse in Vinita Park. It has a storage facility in Homesville, Ohio, and a temporary-storage facility in Bridgeton.

PRODUCTS/OPERATIONS

Selected Brands

Atwater Carey (first aid kits)
Cutter (insect repellant)
Expert Gardener (fertilizers and controls)
Garden Safe (natural plant care products)
Hot Shot (household insect control)
Multi Cote (plant foods)
No-Pest (household insect control)
Peters (lawn and garden fertilizers)
Potable Aqua (water purification tablets)
Real-Kill (household insect control)
Repel (insect repellant)
Schultz (plant foods and potting soils)
Spectracide (outdoor insecticides and herbicides)
Spectracide Terminate (termite control)
Sting-Eze (insect bite relief sticks)
Vigoro (lawn and garden fertilizers)

COMPETITORS

Bayer AG
Central Garden & Pet
Clorox
S.C. Johnson
Scotts
U.S. Home & Garden

HISTORICAL FINANCIALS

Company Type: Private

Income Statement FYE: December 31

	REVENUE ($ mil.)	NET INCOME ($ mil.)	NET PROFIT MARGIN	EMPLOYEES
12/02	480	25	5.3%	725
12/01	273	7	2.5%	800
12/00	266	1	0.5%	800
12/99	285	(12)	—	800
12/98	283	47	16.5%	800
Annual Growth	14.2%	(14.2%)	—	(2.4%)

2002 Year-End Financials

Debt ratio: —
Return on equity: —
Cash ($ mil.): 10
Current ratio: 1.62
Long-term debt ($ mil.): 395

Net Income History

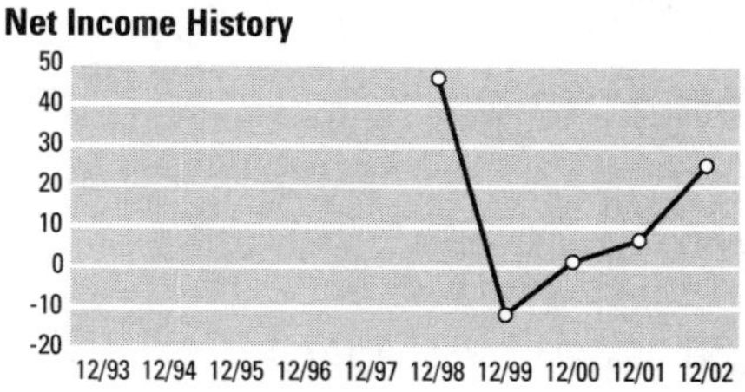

United Space Alliance

USA! United Space Alliance (USA) is a space-race heavyweight (each of the Space Shuttles — Discovery, Atlantis, and Endeavour — weighs 173,000 pounds). A joint venture between Lockheed Martin and Boeing, USA was established in 1996 to consolidate NASA's various Space Shuttle contracts under a single entity. As prime contractor, the company is involved in astronaut and flight controller training, flight software development, Shuttle payload integration, and vehicle processing, launch, and recovery operations. USA also provides training and operations planning for the International Space Station. Its main operations are at the Johnson Space Center (Texas) and Kennedy Space Center (Florida).

As goes the Shuttle program, so goes United Space Alliance. In light of the Columbia disaster of 2003, Shuttle launches will be curtailed for the foreseeable future; at worst, the second disaster in 113 launches (a 1.8% failure rate) could lead to the end of the program as many wonder if it's too costly — in both human and financial terms — to continue. If the current Shuttle program ends, its work will likely be taken up by unmanned rockets, which cost a tiny fraction of a Shuttle launch and risk no lives, and by a next-generation reusable shuttle, which would take advantage of more advanced materials and technologies than do the Shuttles, which were designed in the 1970s. Nevertheless, President Bush's 2004 budget — written before the Columbia disaster — earmarks $3.9 billion for the Space Shuttle program, a 22% increase from the 2003 budget.

EXECUTIVES

CEO: Michael J. (Mike) McCulley
CFO: Bill Caple
CIO: Kathy Tamer
VP and Program Manager, Space Flight Operations: Howard DeCastro
Space Station Program Manager: James F. Buchli
Director of Security: Ed Wilson

LOCATIONS

HQ: 600 Gemini St., Houston, TX 77058
Phone: 281-212-6000 **Fax:** 281-212-6177
Web: www.unitedspacealliance.com

United Space Alliance has operations in Alabama, California, Florida (Kennedy Space Center), Texas (Johnson Space Center), and Washington, DC.

COMPETITORS

Arianespace
BAE SYSTEMS
EADS
Honeywell Aerospace
Northrop Grumman
Raytheon

HISTORICAL FINANCIALS

Company Type: Joint venture

Income Statement FYE: December 31

	ESTIMATED REVENUE ($ mil.)	NET INCOME ($ mil.)	NET PROFIT MARGIN	EMPLOYEES
12/02	1,400	—	—	10,000
12/01	1,200	—	—	10,000
Annual Growth	16.7%	—	—	0.0%

Revenue History

United States Postal Service

Through snow, rain, heat, and gloom of night, the United States Postal Service (USPS) handles more than 40% of the world's cards and letters. Overall, the USPS delivers more than 200 billion pieces of mail a year to about 138 million addresses. The independent government agency relies on postage and fees to fund operations. Though it has a monopoly on delivering nonurgent letters, the USPS faces competition for services such as package delivery. The US president appoints nine of the 11 members of the board that oversees the USPS. The presidential appointees select the postmaster general, who, along with the deputy postmaster general, is a board member.

A challenge for the agency is the growing use of the Internet, which the USPS expects will cause the volume of "snail mail" to decline. To keep pace, the USPS is launching e-commerce initiatives such as computerized postage. The agency has also tapped into online shopping with its priority mail, merchandise return, and delivery confirmation services. It has formed limited alliances with express delivery companies, including a deal in which FedEx provides air transportation for express mail, priority, and first-class mail shipments (but doesn't deliver the mail).

With an eye on its bottom line, the USPS has scaled down its construction program and accelerated the pace of its rate increases, although officials hope to delay the next increase until 2006. In addition, the agency is reducing its workforce through attrition and cutting hours of operation at some post offices.

A commission appointed by President Bush has recommended that the USPS adopt some private-sector management practices in order to ensure the agency's long-term financial health and to preserve universal mail service. The Bush administration expects the commission's recommendations to lead to the most significant revamp of postal operations since the early 1970s.

HISTORY

The second-oldest agency of the US government (after Indian Affairs), the Post Office was created by the Continental Congress in 1775 with Benjamin Franklin as postmaster general. The postal system came to play a vital role in the development of transportation in the US.

At that time, postal workers were riders on muddy paths delivering letters without stamps or envelopes. Letters were delivered only between post offices. Congress approved the first official postal policy in 1792: Rates ranged from six cents for less than 30 miles to 25 cents for more than 450. Letter carriers began delivering mail in cities in 1794.

First based in Philadelphia, in 1800 the Post Office moved to Washington, DC. In 1829 Andrew Jackson elevated the position of postmaster general to cabinet rank — it became a means of rewarding political cronies. Mail contracts subsidized the early development of US railroads. The first adhesive postage stamp appeared in the US in 1847.

Uniform postal rates (not varying with distance) were instituted in 1863, the year free city delivery began. The start of free rural delivery in 1896 spurred road construction in isolated US areas. Parcel post was launched in 1913, and new mail-order houses such as Montgomery Ward and Sears, Roebuck flourished.

The famous pledge beginning "Neither snow nor rain . . . " — not an official motto — was first inscribed at the main New York City post office in 1914. Scheduled airmail service between Washington, DC, and New York City began in 1918, stimulating the development of commercial air service. The ZIP code was introduced in 1963.

As mail volume grew, postal workers became increasingly militant under work stress. (Franklin's pigeonhole sorting method had barely changed.) A work stoppage in the New York City post office in 1970 spread within nine days to 670 post offices, and the US Army was deployed to handle the mail. Later that year the Postal Reorganization Act was passed. The new law established a board of governors to handle postal affairs and choose the postmaster general, who became CEO of an independent agency, the United States Postal Service (USPS). The next year USPS negotiated the first US government collective-bargaining labor contract. Express mail service began in 1977, and USPS stepped up automation efforts.

In 1995 USPS launched Global Package Link, a program to expedite major customers' shipments to Canada, Japan, and the UK. The next year it overhauled rates, cutting prices for larger mailers who prepared their mail for automation and raising prices for small mailers who didn't.

Postmaster General Marvin Runyon — whose six-year tenure took the agency from the red into the black — retired in 1998 and was succeeded by USPS veteran William Henderson. The next year a one-cent hike in the price of first-class postage took effect. (Another one-cent increase took effect in 2001, and the rate rose once again the following year.) In a nod to the Internet, USPS in 1999 contracted with outside vendors to enable customers to buy and print stamps online.

In 2001 USPS formed a strategic alliance with rival FedEx through which FedEx agreed to provide air transportation for USPS mail, in return for the placement of FedEx drop boxes in post offices.

Henderson stepped down at the end of May 2001, and EVP Jack Potter was named to replace him. That year several postal workers in a Washington, DC, branch office were exposed to anthrax-tainted letters.

EXECUTIVES

Chairman: S. David Fineman
Vice Chairman: John F. Walsh
Postmaster General and CEO: John E. (Jack) Potter
Deputy Postmaster General: John Nolan
EVP and COO: Patrick R. Donahoe
EVP and CFO: Richard J. Strasser Jr.
SVP and Chief Marketing Officer: Anita J. Bizzotto
SVP Government Relations: Ralph Moden
SVP Human Resources: Suzanne Medvidovich
SVP Intelligent Mail and Address Quality: Charles E. (Charlie) Bravo
SVP Operations: John A. Rapp
VP and CTO: Robert L. (Bob) Otto
VP and Consumer Advocate: Francia G. Smith
VP Delivery and Retail: Henry A. Pankey
VP Diversity Development: Murray Weatherall
VP Employee Resource Management: Dewitt Harris
VP Engineering: Thomas G. Day
VP Facilities: Rudolph K. Umscheid
VP Finance and Controller: Donna M. Peak
VP and General Counsel: Mary Gibbons
VP International Business: James P. Wade
VP Labor Relations: Anthony Vegliante
VP Network Operations Management: Paul Vogel
VP Pricing and Classification: Stephen M. Kearney
VP Product Development: Nicholas F. (Nick) Barranca
VP Public Affairs and Communications: Azeezaly S. Jaffer
Acting VP Sales: Steven Hernandez
VP Service and Market Development: John R. Wargo
Acting VP Strategic Planning: Julie Moore
VP Supply Management: A. Keith Strange
VP and Treasurer: Robert J. Pedersen
Chief Postal Inspector: Lee Heath
Auditors: Ernst & Young LLP

LOCATIONS

HQ: 475 L'Enfant Plaza SW, Washington, DC 20260
Phone: 202-268-2500 **Fax:** 202-268-4860
Web: www.usps.com

PRODUCTS/OPERATIONS

Selected Services

Certified mail
Collection-on-delivery (COD)
Delivery confirmation (via Web)
Digital Certificate (proof of identification for electronic transactions)
Express mail
First-class mail
Free mail for the blind and handicapped
International mail
Mail forwarding
Merchandise return (downloadable return-mail labels)
Money orders
Passport applications
PC Postage
Periodicals
Post office boxes
Postage meters
Priority mail
Registered mail
Return receipt
Special delivery
Standard mail

COMPETITORS

BAX Global
DHL
FedEx
Mail Boxes Etc.
Roadway
UPS

HISTORICAL FINANCIALS

Company Type: Government-owned

Income Statement FYE: September 30

	REVENUE ($ mil.)	NET INCOME ($ mil.)	NET PROFIT MARGIN	EMPLOYEES
9/02	66,463	(676)	—	854,376
9/01	65,834	(1,680)	—	797,795
9/00	64,540	(199)	—	787,538
9/99	62,726	363	0.6%	800,000
9/98	60,072	550	0.9%	792,041
9/97	58,216	1,264	2.2%	765,174
9/96	56,402	1,567	2.8%	760,966
9/95	54,294	1,770	3.3%	753,384
9/94	49,252	(914)	—	728,944
9/93	47,418	(1,765)	—	691,723
Annual Growth	3.8%	—	—	2.4%

2002 Year-End Financials

Debt ratio: —
Return on equity: —
Cash ($ mil.): 1,156
Current ratio: 0.15
Long-term debt ($ mil.): 7,300

Net Income History

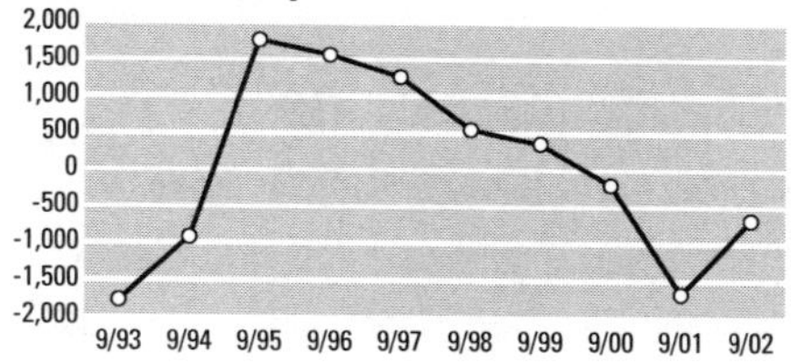

United Supermarkets

From Muleshoe up to Dalhart and on over to Pampa, United Supermarkets keeps the Texas Panhandle well fed. The grocer has more than 40 supermarkets, mostly in rural towns. Its stores feature deli, floral, and bakery shops, as well as groceries, pharmacies, and gas at some locales. The company's larger format, Market Street, stocks more specialty foods. United Supermarkets runs its own distribution facility. H. D. Snell founded the firm in Sayre, Oklahoma, in 1916 as United Cash Store. He bucked the norms of the day — when grocers sold on credit — by selling for cash at lower prices. United Supermarkets is owned and run by the Snell family. (President Gantt Bumstead is the great-great-grandson of the founder.)

EXECUTIVES

President: Gantt Bumstead
SVP and CEO: Kent Moore
VP and COO: Bert Short
VP and CFO: Keith Mann
VP and CIO: Scott Gilmour
VP, Customer and Community Service: Matt Bumstead
VP, Human Resources: Phil Pirkle
Chief Marketing Officer: Dan Sanders
Controller: SuzAnn Kirby

LOCATIONS

HQ: United Supermarkets, Ltd.
7830 Orlando Ave., Lubbock, TX 79423
Phone: 806-791-0220 **Fax:** 806-791-7491
Web: www.unitedtexas.com/myunited

COMPETITORS

Albertson's
H-E-B
Homeland Stores
IGA
Kroger
Minyard Food Stores
Randall's
Wal-Mart

HISTORICAL FINANCIALS

Company Type: Private

Income Statement FYE: January 31

	ESTIMATED REVENUE ($ mil.)	NET INCOME ($ mil.)	NET PROFIT MARGIN	EMPLOYEES
1/03	700	—	—	7,000
1/02	600	—	—	5,000
1/01	575	—	—	5,000
1/00	570	—	—	4,500
1/99	560	—	—	4,000
1/98	520	—	—	4,000
1/97	450	—	—	4,000
1/96	400	—	—	3,300
1/95	350	—	—	3,000
1/94	330	—	—	2,600
Annual Growth	8.7%	—	—	11.6%

Revenue History

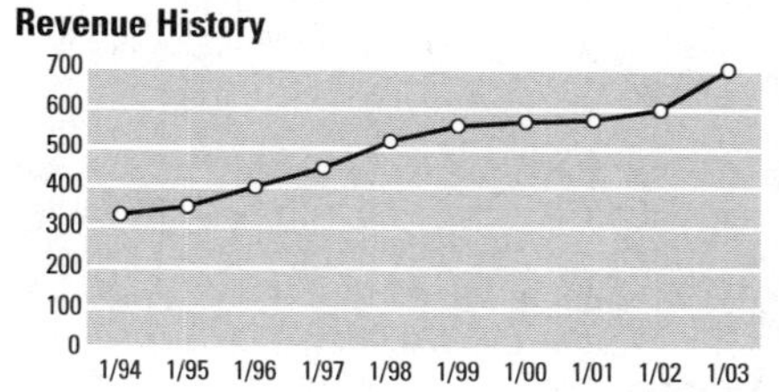

United Way of America

United Way of America (UWA) has been described as a mutual fund for charitable causes, and with thousands of agencies receiving financial support from UWA's 1,400 local organizations, the epithet seems fitting. The not-for-profit organization focuses on health and human services causes. Its local organizations help to fund a multitude of endeavors, including the American Cancer Society, Big Brothers/Big Sisters, Catholic Charities, Girl Scouts and Boy Scouts, and The Salvation Army. During a fund-raising campaign that began in 2000, UWA raised about $3.9 billion (some 50% from employee contributions and about 23% from corporations). Its administrative expenses average 13% of funds raised.

Each of the local organizations is an independent entity governed by local volunteers, and UWA acts as a national services and training center, supporting the local organizations with services such as national advertising and research. To advance the understanding of its role, UWA has launched an initiative to raise awareness of how it serves local communities.

HISTORY

The first modern Community Chest was created in 1913, laying the foundation for the practice of allocating funds among multiple causes. Five years later, representatives from 12 fund-raising organizations met in Chicago and established the American Association for Community Organizations, the predecessor of the present-day United Way. By 1929 more than 350 Community Chests had been established.

Payroll deductions for charitable contributions debuted in 1943. In 1946 the United Way's predecessor organization initiated a cooperative relationship with the American Federation of Labor and the Congress of Industrial Organizations (which merged to become the AFL-CIO in 1955); the two groups agreed to provide services to members of organized labor. (The relationship continues today, with the organizations collaborating on projects such as recruiting members of organized labor to lead health and human services organizations.)

The Uniform Federal Fund-Raising Program was created by order of President Dwight Eisenhower in 1957, enabling federal employees to contribute to charities of their choice. (The program later evolved into the Combined Federal Campaign.) Six years later Los Angeles became the first city to adopt the United Way name when more than 30 local Community Chests and United Fund organizations merged. The national organization, which had been operating under the United Community Funds and Councils (UCFCA) name, adopted the United Way of America (UWA) name in 1970. It established its headquarters in Alexandria, Virginia, the next year.

Congress made its first grant for emergency food and shelter to the private sector in 1983, and UWA was selected as its fiscal agent. UWA created its Emergency Food and Shelter National Board Program the same year. In 1984 UWA created the Alexis de Tocqueville Society to solicit larger donations from individuals (it attracted such members as Bill Gates and Walter Annenberg).

In 1992 William Aramony, UWA's president for more than two decades, resigned after coming under fire for his lavish expenditures. Former Peace Corps head Elaine Chao was tapped to replace him, and in 1995 Aramony was sentenced to seven years in prison for defrauding the organization of about $600,000. Former UWA CFO Thomas Merlo and Stephen Paulachak (former president of a UWA spinoff) were convicted on related charges. After four years spent burnishing UWA's tarnished image, Chao resigned in 1996 and was succeeded the next year by Betty Beene, who had headed UWA operations in Houston and New York City's Tri-State area.

In an effort to stress the manner in which its local organizations benefit their communities, UWA launched a brand-initiative campaign in 1998. The following year UWA's local organization in Santa Clara, California, found itself in serious financial straits when donations began slipping despite its location in the wealthy Silicon Valley. Infoseek (now Walt Disney Internet Group's GO.com) founder Steve Kirsch and Microsoft founder Gates chipped in $1 million and $5 million, respectively, to help keep the organization afloat.

Beene, who drew the ire of some chapters for suggesting a national pledge-processing center and national standards, stepped down in January 2001. That same year UWA began funneling more funds into smaller community projects instead of national charities. In 2002 Brian Gallagher took over as president and CEO.

EXECUTIVES

Chairman: Len Roberts
President and CEO: Brian A. Gallagher
CFO: Edward J. Christie Jr.
VP External Communications: Ann Andrews
CIO: Michael Schreiber
Controller: W. Vernon McHargue Jr.
Director Public Relations: Philip Jones
Legal Counsel: Patti Turner
Human Resources: Evelyn Amador

LOCATIONS

HQ: 701 N. Fairfax St., Alexandria, VA 22314
Phone: 703-836-7112 **Fax:** 703-683-7840
Web: national.unitedway.org

United Way of America has 1,400 local organizations across the US.

PRODUCTS/OPERATIONS

Selected Recipients of United Way Funds

American Cancer Society
American Red Cross
Big Brothers/Big Sisters of America
Boy Scouts of America
Catholic Charities USA
Girl Scouts of the United States of America
The Salvation Army
The Urban League

HISTORICAL FINANCIALS

Company Type: Not-for-profit

Income Statement FYE: December 31

	REVENUE ($ mil.)	NET INCOME ($ mil.)	NET PROFIT MARGIN	EMPLOYEES
12/02	5,000	—	—	15,166
12/01	4,000	—	—	8,500
12/00	3,910	—	—	—
12/99	3,770	—	—	—
12/98	3,580	—	—	—
12/97	3,400	—	—	—
12/96	3,250	—	—	—
12/95	3,148	—	—	—
12/94	3,078	—	—	—
12/93	3,050	—	—	—
Annual Growth	5.6%	—	—	78.4%

Revenue History

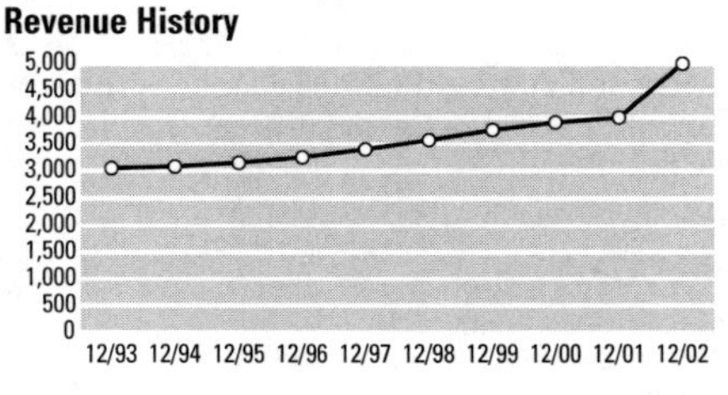

University of California

The University of California (UC) system has nearly 200,000 students at its nine campuses (which include three law schools and five medical schools) located in Berkeley, Davis, Irvine, Los Angeles (UCLA), Riverside, San Diego, San Francisco, Santa Barbara, and Santa Cruz. The schools offer areas of study in more than 150 disciplines ranging from the arts to bioengineering. The university's 10th campus, UC Merced, is scheduled to open in 2004. UC also operates three US Department of Energy research labs in California and New Mexico.

In wake of the 1996 approval of California's Proposition 209, which eliminated state affirmative-action programs, enrollment of minorities and the hiring of female faculty both dropped in the UC system. To help restore minority admissions to pre-Prop 209 levels, UC guarantees admission to the top 4% of students at each California high school and operates outreach programs aimed at low-income students. Beginning in 2004, high school students falling between the top 4% and 12.5% will be eligible for admission to UC after completing a transfer program at a California community college. State budget cuts proposed in 2003 could sharply decrease the amount of money spent on minority outreach.

HISTORY

The founders of California's government provided for a state university via a clause in the state's constitution in 1849. The origins of the College of California, opened in Oakland in 1869, date back to the Contra Costa Academy, a small school established by Yale alumnus Henry Durant in 1853. Durant ran Contra Costa, and then the college, until 1872. Women were allowed to enter the school in 1870. The college moved to Berkeley and graduated its first class (12 men) in 1873.

As California's economy and population grew, so did its university system. Renamed University of California (UC) in 1879, it had 1,000 students by 1895. Agriculture, mining, geology, and engineering were among its first fields. A second campus was established at Davis in 1905, followed by campuses in San Diego (1912) and Los Angeles (1919).

The Depression brought cutbacks in funding for UC, but the system rebounded in the 1940s. It opened its fifth campus (Santa Barbara) in 1944, and during WWII it also began gaining recognition for research. Between 1945 and 1965 enrollment quadrupled, spurred by GI Bill-sponsored veterans and a population shift to the West. The state legislature formulated the Master Plan for Higher Education in 1960, which reorganized university administration and established admission requirements. Campuses were established at Irvine and Santa Cruz in 1965.

The first of several important demonstrations in the 1960s at UC Berkeley came in 1964 over the university's attempts to ban political activity on a strip of UC-owned land. The People's Park riot of 1969, touched off when UC tried to close a parcel of land in Berkeley that students had turned into a kind of playground for the counterculture, left one dead and more than 50 wounded.

Aware of the changing demographics of its student body, especially its growing Asian enrollment (28% in 1990), UC Berkeley gave the chancellor's job to Chang-Lin Tien in 1990 — the first person of Asian descent to hold that position at a major US university (Tien served as chancellor until 1997). A California recession in the early 1990s resulted in budget cuts for UC. Strapped for cash, the university launched a for-profit entity in 1992 to tap its extensive library of patents.

UC San Diego chancellor Richard Atkinson succeeded Jack Peltason as UC president in 1995, the same year the UC Board of Regents approved a new campus — the university's 10th — in the San Joaquin Valley. That year it voted to phase out race- and sex-based affirmative action. The board, in an effort to be competitive with other top universities in recruiting faculty, voted to offer health benefits to the partners of gay employees in 1997. Also that year UC created the California Digital Library and began putting its library collection online.

Entrepreneur Alfred Mann donated $100 million to UCLA in 1998 for biomedical research. Also that year admissions of non-Asian-American minorities to the fall freshman classes of UCLA and UC Berkeley fell sharply. The following year the UC system began guaranteeing admission to the top 4% of students in each of the state's high schools. UC took some heat in 1999 and 2000 for two separate instances of security breaches at the Los Alamos National Laboratory.

Robert Dynes, previously chancellor of UC San Diego, became president of the UC system in October 2003.

EXECUTIVES

Chairman: John J. Moores
President: Robert C. Dynes
Provost and SVP, Academic Affairs: C. Judson King, age 69
SVP, Business and Finance: Joseph P. Mullinix
SVP, University Affairs: Bruce B. Darling
Treasurer and VP, Investments: David H. Russ
VP, Financial Management: Anne C. Broome
VP, Educational Outreach: Winston C. Doby
VP, Health Affairs: Michael V. Drake
VP, Agriculture and Natural Resources: W. R. (Reg) Gomes
VP, Clinical Services Development: William H. Gurtner
VP, Budget: Lawrence C. (Larry) Hershman
VP, Laboratory Management: John P. McTague
Secretary: Patricia L. Trivette
General Counsel and VP, Legal Affairs: James E. Holst
Associate VP, Human Resources & Benefits: Judith Boyette
Auditors: PricewaterhouseCoopers LLP

LOCATIONS

HQ: 1111 Franklin St., Oakland, CA 94607
Phone: 510-987-0700 **Fax:** 510-987-0894
Web: www.universityofcalifornia.edu

Campuses

UC Berkeley
UC Davis
UC Irvine
UC Los Angeles (UCLA)
UC Riverside
UC San Diego
UC San Francisco
UC Santa Barbara
UC Santa Cruz

PRODUCTS/OPERATIONS

Department of Energy Laboratories

Ernest Orlando Lawrence Berkeley National Laboratory (Berkeley, CA)
Lawrence Livermore National Laboratory (Livermore, CA)
Los Alamos National Laboratory (New Mexico)

HISTORICAL FINANCIALS

Company Type: School

Income Statement FYE: June 30

	REVENUE ($ mil.)	NET INCOME ($ mil.)	NET PROFIT MARGIN	EMPLOYEES
6/02	15,980	—	—	114,282
6/01	15,887	—	—	108,827
6/00	14,048	—	—	103,767
6/99	13,074	—	—	99,890
6/98	9,375	—	—	130,000
6/97	9,022	—	—	130,000
6/96	8,363	—	—	137,874
6/95	7,958	—	—	131,660
6/94	7,895	—	—	132,964
6/93	7,548	—	—	131,661
Annual Growth	8.7%	—	—	(1.6%)

Revenue History

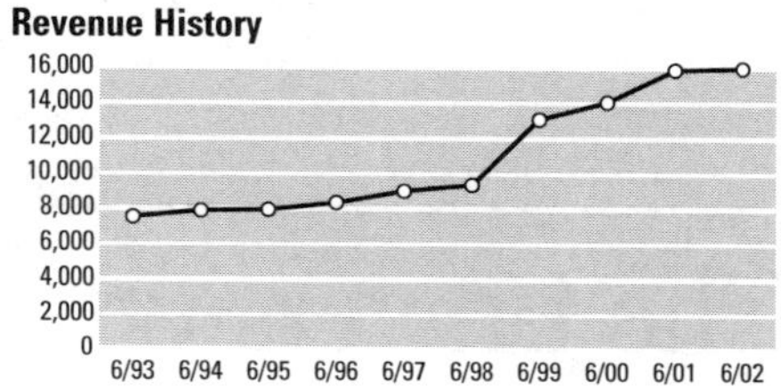

The University of Chicago

The University of Chicago ranks as one of the world's youngest and most-esteemed major universities. Its undergraduate branch, The College, offers a core curriculum based on the "Great Books." The school is associated with more than 70 Nobel Prize recipients, including Enrico Fermi, Milton Friedman, and Saul Bellow. Undergraduates can major in more than 50 areas. Among the U of C's graduate programs are the University of Chicago Law School and Graduate School of Business, both of which are ranked in the top 10 by *U.S. News & World Report.* Founded in 1890 by John D. Rockefeller, the university has an endowment of about $3.5 billion. The U of C has 13,000 students and more than 2,100 faculty.

The University of Chicago has steadfastly stood its ground against trendiness in education curricula. All students take courses that expose them to the social, biological, and physical sciences, as well as humanities, mathematics, and language. Rare is the student who is not versed in Thucydides. While the university's list of those who graduated is impressive, the list of those who did not is equally prominent, including Oracle's Larry Ellison and author Kurt Vonnegut.

Students attending the U of C study primarily at its 200-acre main campus on the South Side of Chicago, but the university's Graduate School of Business also maintains campuses in downtown Chicago; Barcelona, Spain; and Singapore. Among the many institutions affiliated with the U of C are the University of Chicago Medical Center, the Enrico Fermi Institute, the Argonne National Laboratory, and the Yerkes Observatory. The University of Chicago Press publishes 250-300 new titles each year, as well as more than 50 journals, and is the largest university press in the US.

HISTORY

The University of Chicago took its name from the first U of C, a small Baptist school that operated from 1858-1886. The school, incorporated in 1890, was born when William Rainey Harper, the man who was to become the University's first president, convinced Standard Oil's John D. Rockefeller to provide a founding gift of $600,000. Members of the American Baptist Education Society chipped in another $400,000, and department store owner Marshall Field donated the land for the campus.

The university opened in 1892 with a faculty of 103 and 594 students. As it grew, the university took over property that had been used in the Columbian Exposition of 1892-93, eventually surrounding the fair's former midway. (The school's football team later earned the nickname "Monsters of the Midway" while being coached by the legendary Amos Alonzo Stagg; this was before withdrawing from intercollegiate play in 1939.) Legend has it that the university retains the right to rejoin the Big Ten.

Only four years after its founding, the university's enrollment of 1,815 exceeded Harvard's. By 1907, 43% of its 5,000 students were women. Robert Maynard Hutchins, president from 1929 to 1951, revolutionized the university and American higher education by insisting on the study of original sources (the Great Books) and competency testing through comprehensive exams. He organized the college and graduate divisions into their present structure, reaffirming the role of the university as a place for intellectual exploration rather than vocational training. In 1942 the U of C ushered in the nuclear age when Enrico Fermi created the first controlled nuclear chain reaction in the school's abandoned football stadium.

From the 1950s through the 1970s, the university purchased and restored Frank Lloyd Wright's famed Robie House and built the Joseph Regenstein Library (1970). In 1978 Hanna Holborn Gray became the first woman to be named president of a major university. Gray abolished the decade-old Lascivious Costume Ball, a major social event (some would say the only social event) at the university. Hugo Sonnenschein succeeded Gray in 1993. The beginning of his tenure coincided with a period of financial difficulty for the school as increases in costs outpaced revenue growth. In 1996 Sonnenschein announced plans to boost enrollment by as much as 30% in order to invigorate the school's finances.

U of C graduate and former professor Myron Scholes shared the Nobel Prize in economics in 1997. The next year the school announced plans for a $35 million athletics center to be named after Gerald Ratner, a former student who donated $15 million toward construction of the facility. The university later signed an agreement to supply content to Internet distance-learning startup UNext.com, founded by trustee Andrew Rosenfield. (This agreement was controversial within the university community.) Cardean University, UNext.com's online university, began operating in 2000.

Sonnenschein resigned in 2000 and was replaced by Don Randel, former provost of Cornell University. That year the University of Chicago Graduate School of Business opened a campus in Singapore, and U of C economist James Heckman was awarded the Nobel Prize for his work in microeconomics.

EXECUTIVES

President: Don Michael Randel, age 63
Provost: Richard P. Saller
VP Administration and CFO: Donald J. Reaves, age 55
VP Community and Government Affairs: Henry S. Webber
VP Development and Alumni Relations: Randy L. Holgate
VP and CIO: Gregory A. Jackson
VP and Chief Investment Officer: Philip Halpern
VP and Dean College Enrollment: Michael C. Behnke
VP and Dean of Students in the University: Stephen P. Klass
VP and General Counsel: Beth A. Harris
Associate VP Human Resources Management: G. Chris Keeley
Comptroller: William J. Hogan Jr.
Auditors: KPMG LLP

LOCATIONS

HQ: 5801 S. Ellis Ave., Chicago, IL 60637
Phone: 773-702-1234 **Fax:** 773-702-4155
Web: www.uchicago.edu

The University of Chicago has campuses in the Hyde Park area of Chicago; downtown Chicago; Barcelona, Spain; and Singapore.

PRODUCTS/OPERATIONS

The College (Undergraduate)

Biological Sciences Collegiate Division
Humanities Collegiate Division
New Collegiate Division
Physical Sciences Collegiate Division
Social Sciences Collegiate Division

Selected Affiliated Institutions

Argonne National Laboratory
Center for Gender Studies
Center for Middle Eastern Studies
Chapin Hall Center for Children and the Laboratory Schools
Enrico Fermi Institute
James Franck Institute
The MacLean Center for Clinical Medical Ethics
Oriental Institute

Selected Graduate Schools and Programs

Divinity School
Graduate School of Business
Graham School of General Studies
Harris Graduate School of Public Policy Studies
Law School
Pritzker School of Medicine
School of Social Service Administration

Selected Libraries

D'Angelo Law Library
Eckhart Library (mathematics, mathematical statistics, and computer science)
Harper Memorial Library for the College
John Crerar Library (natural sciences, medicine, and technology)
Joseph Regenstein Library (humanities and social sciences)
School of Social Service Administration Library
Yerkes Observatory Library (astronomy and astrophysics)

HISTORICAL FINANCIALS

Company Type: School

Income Statement FYE: June 30

	REVENUE ($ mil.)	NET INCOME ($ mil.)	NET PROFIT MARGIN	EMPLOYEES
6/01	1,617	—	—	12,000
6/00	1,639	—	—	11,900
6/99	848	—	—	11,900
6/98	892	—	—	12,869
6/97	1,377	—	—	12,000
6/96	1,395	—	—	12,000
6/95	1,313	—	—	10,954
6/94	1,217	—	—	11,400
6/93	1,150	—	—	11,800
6/92	1,113	—	—	—
Annual Growth	4.2%	—	—	0.2%

Revenue History

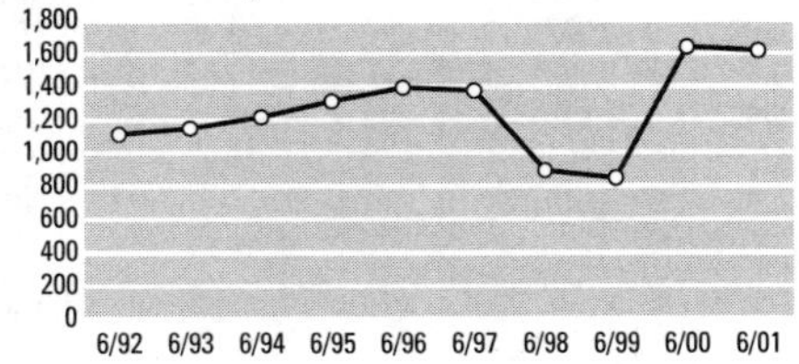

The University of Iowa

The University of Iowa Hawkeyes see clearly from their perch as Iowa's largest university. Founded in 1847, the university has nearly 30,000 students (about two-thirds of which are undergraduates) on its Iowa City campus. The university is home to 11 colleges spanning a variety of majors and disciplines, including distinguished programs in audiology, print making, creative writing, speech pathology, and nursing. Among the University of Iowa's distinguished alumni are Al Jarreau, John Irving, Flannery O'Connor, Gene Wilder, and Tennessee Williams.

EXECUTIVES

President: David J. Skorton, $281,875 pay
Provost: Jon Whitmore
VP Student Services and Dean of Students: Phillip E. Jones
VP Finance and University Services and Treasurer: Douglas K. True
CIO: David Dobbins
General Counsel: Mark E. Schantz
Associate VP and Director Human Resources: Susan (Sue) Buckley

LOCATIONS

HQ: 249 IMU, Iowa City, IA 52242
Phone: 319-335-3500 **Fax:** 319-335-0860
Web: www.uiowa.edu

PRODUCTS/OPERATIONS

Selected Colleges and Programs

College of Business
College of Dentistry
College of Education
College of Engineering
College of Law
College of Liberal Arts
College of Medicine
College of Nursing
College of Pharmacy
College of Public Health
Division of Continuing Education
Graduate College
Interdisciplinary Programs
International Programs

HISTORICAL FINANCIALS

Company Type: School

Income Statement FYE: June 30

	REVENUE ($ mil.)	NET INCOME ($ mil.)	NET PROFIT MARGIN	EMPLOYEES
6/02	1,721	—	—	12,000
6/01	1,611	—	—	11,813
6/00	1,531	—	—	16,006
6/99	1,531	—	—	16,576
6/98	1,241	—	—	17,129
6/97	1,344	—	—	28,161
6/96	1,200	—	—	20,000
6/95	1,144	—	—	23,000
6/94	1,119	—	—	22,410
6/93	984	—	—	—
Annual Growth	6.4%	—	—	(7.5%)

Revenue History

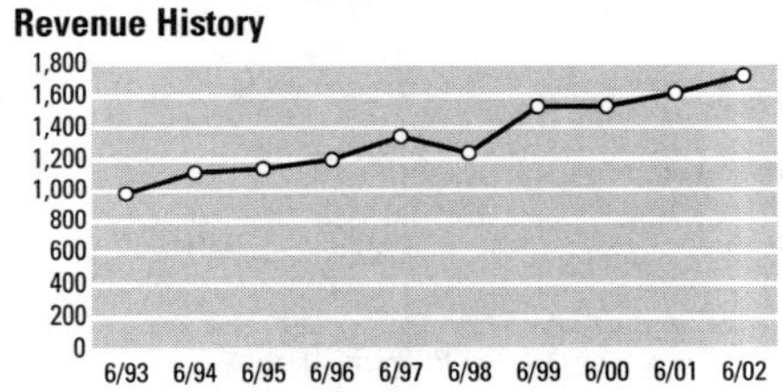

The University of Michigan

Michigan — it's shaped like a mitten, and higher education fits the state like a glove. The University of Michigan has been a leader in the state's education effort since its founding in 1817. With about 53,000 students and more than 5,000 faculty members scattered across three campuses (Ann Arbor, with about 38,000 students; Dearborn; and Flint), the university's diverse academic units span such areas of study as architecture, dentistry, education, law, medicine, music, and social work. Notable alumni include Gerald Ford (the university is home to the Gerald R. Ford Library and the Ford School of Public Policy) and playwright Arthur Miller.

EXECUTIVES

President: Mary Sue Coleman
Interim Provost and EVP Academic Affairs: Paul N. Courant
EVP and CFO: Robert A. Kasdin
VP Development: Susan K. Feagin
VP and General Counsel: Marvin Krislov
VP Research: Fawwaz T. Ulaby
VP and Secretary: Lisa A. Tedesco
Associate VP Human Resources and Affirmative Action and Chief Human Resource Officer: Barbara S. Butterfield
Auditors: Ernst & Young LLP

LOCATIONS

HQ: 3074 Fleming Administration Bldg., Ann Arbor, MI 48109
Phone: 734-764-1817 **Fax:** 734-764-4546
Web: www.umich.edu

PRODUCTS/OPERATIONS

Selected Academic Units

Architecture and urban planning
Art and design
Business administration
Dentistry
Education
Engineering
Kinesiology
Law
Literature, science, and the arts
Medicine
Music
Natural resources and environment
Nursing
Pharmacy
Public health
Public policy
Social work

HISTORICAL FINANCIALS

Company Type: School

Income Statement FYE: June 30

	REVENUE ($ mil.)	NET INCOME ($ mil.)	NET PROFIT MARGIN	EMPLOYEES
6/02	2,944	—	—	—
6/01	2,696	—	—	—
6/00	4,609	—	—	—
6/99	3,334	—	—	—
6/98	2,881	—	—	23,000
6/97	2,630	—	—	23,000
6/96	2,444	—	—	22,596
6/95	2,348	—	—	—
6/94	2,252	—	—	—
6/93	2,162	—	—	—
Annual Growth	3.5%	—	—	0.9%

Revenue History

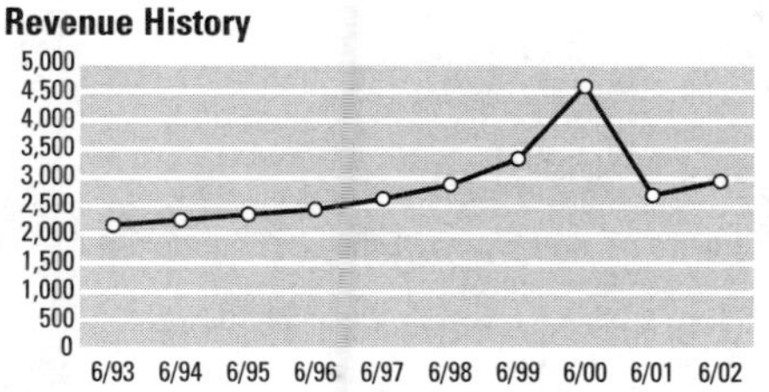

University of Missouri System

"Show-Me" the education! The University of Missouri, founded in 1839 (it was the first publicly supported institution of higher education created in the Louisiana Territory), educates more than 56,500 students at four campuses and through a statewide extension program; some 24% of the students are in graduate or professional programs. Nicknamed "Mizzou," the university's cadre of campuses includes flagship UM-Columbia (home to some 23,700 students, 20 schools and colleges, and the University of Missouri Health Sciences Center), UM-Kansas City, UM-Rolla, and UM-St. Louis. Offering fields of study ranging from journalism to law to fine arts, the university has a nearly 9,800-member faculty and research staff.

EXECUTIVES

President, Board of Curators: Paul W. Steele
VP, Board of Curators: John A. Mathes
President: Manuel T. Pacheco, age 61
EVP and Director Cooperative Extension: Ronald J. Turner
VP Information Systems: Ralph J. Caruso Jr.
VP Human Resource Services: R. Kenneth Hutchinson
VP Academic Affairs: Stephen W. Lehmkuhle
VP Finance and Administration: Natalie R. Krawitz
Treasurer: Shirley S. DeJarnette
General Counsel: Marvin E. (Bunky) Wright
Auditors: Deloitte & Touche LLP

LOCATIONS

HQ: 321 University Hall, Columbia, MO 65211
Phone: 573-882-2121 **Fax:** 573-882-2721
Web: www.system.missouri.edu

The University of Missouri has campuses in Columbia, Kansas City, Rolla, and St. Louis.

PRODUCTS/OPERATIONS

Selected Colleges and Schools

Accountancy
Agriculture
Arts and Science
Business
Education
Engineering
Fine Arts
Food and Natural Resources
Graduate School
Health Related Professions
Honors College
Human Environmental Sciences
Information Science and Learning Technology
Journalism
Law
Medicine
Natural Resources
Nursing
Social Work
Veterinary Medicine

Campuses

University of Missouri-Columbia (about 23,700 students)
University of Missouri-Kansas City (about 13,000 students)
University of Missouri-Rolla (about 4,900 students)
University of Missouri-St. Louis (about 15,000 students)

HISTORICAL FINANCIALS

Company Type: School

Income Statement FYE: June 30

	REVENUE ($ mil.)	NET INCOME ($ mil.)	NET PROFIT MARGIN	EMPLOYEES
6/02	1,253	—	—	26,316
6/01	1,446	—	—	27,914
6/00	1,356	—	—	32,870
6/99	1,487	—	—	20,000
6/98	1,396	—	—	15,818
6/97	1,336	—	—	15,283
6/96	1,226	—	—	17,400
6/95	1,164	—	—	18,997
6/94	1,060	—	—	20,958
6/93	990	—	—	17,060
Annual Growth	2.7%	—	—	4.9%

Revenue History

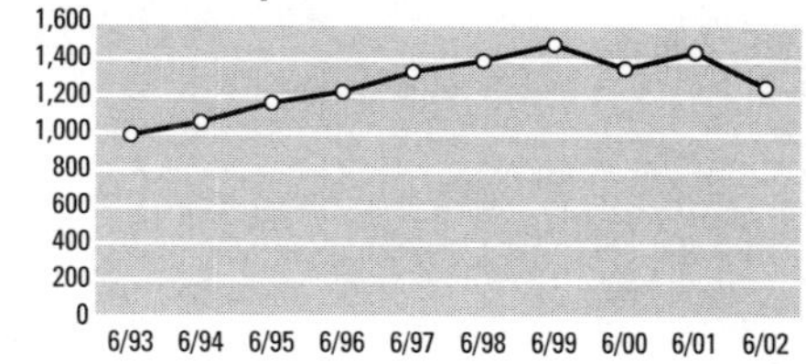

The University of Nebraska

The University of Nebraska has sprouted four campuses out in the fields of the Cornhusker State. Founded in 1869, the state university system offers bachelor's, master's, and doctoral degrees in such programs as agriculture, business, education, and engineering at its campuses in Kearney, Lincoln, and Omaha. The university's Medical Center in Omaha trains doctors, performs research, and is affiliated with a 700-bed teaching hospital. The University of Nebraska also operates research and extension services across the state. Nearly 47,000 students attend classes in the university system, which is recovering from a severe 1997 enrollment drop caused by tighter admissions standards.

EXECUTIVES

President: L. Dennis Smith
EVP and Provost: Jay Noren
VP External Affairs and Corporation Secretary: Kim M. Robak, age 47
VP Business and Finance: David E. Lechner
VP and General Counsel: Richard Wood
CIO: Walter Weir
Assistant VP and Director Communications: Joe Rowson
Assistant VP and Director Finance: Michael Justus
Assistant VP and Director Human Resources: Ed Wimes
Auditors: Deloitte & Touche

LOCATIONS

HQ: 3835 Holdrege St., Lincoln, NE 68583
Phone: 402-472-2111 **Fax:** 402-472-1237
Web: www.uneb.edu

PRODUCTS/OPERATIONS

University Campuses

The University of Nebraska at Kearney (6,400 students)
The University of Nebraska-Lincoln (23,000 students)
The University of Nebraska Medical Center (Omaha, 2,800 students)
The University of Nebraska at Omaha (14,500 students)

Selected Colleges and Programs

Agricultural Science and Natural Resources
Architecture
Arts and Sciences
Business Administration
Dentistry (University of Nebraska Medical Center)
Engineering and Technology
Fine and Performing Arts
Graduate Studies
Human Resources and Family Science
Law
Medicine (University of Nebraska Medical Center)
Nursing (University of Nebraska Medical Center)
Pharmacy (University of Nebraska Medical Center)
Teachers College

HISTORICAL FINANCIALS

Company Type: School

Income Statement FYE: June 30

	REVENUE ($ mil.)	NET INCOME ($ mil.)	NET PROFIT MARGIN	EMPLOYEES
6/02	1,133	—	—	11,530
6/01	1,157	—	—	—
6/00	1,071	—	—	—
6/99	1,016	—	—	—
6/98	1,249	—	—	—
6/97	1,270	—	—	16,000
6/96	1,100	—	—	15,000
6/95	1,081	—	—	15,000
6/94	1,145	—	—	—
6/93	839	—	—	—
Annual Growth	3.4%	(28.0%)	—	(3.7%)

Revenue History

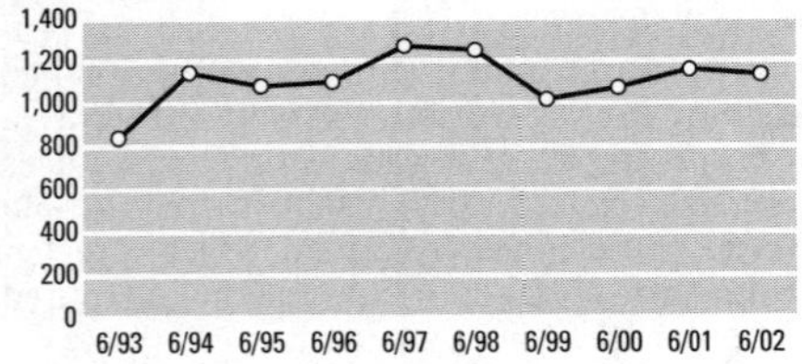

University of Pittsburgh

Now this is a school that really needs a nickname. The University of Pittsburgh of the Commonwealth System of Higher Education (whew! — Pitt for short) has some 32,000 students spread across its five campuses. Its flagship Pittsburgh campus has more than 23,000 students. The Pitt Panthers pursue their studies in 18 schools and colleges, including arts and sciences, engineering, and business. Pitt also is affiliated with the UPMC Health System, which operates a network of hospitals and an insurance company, manages physicians' offices, and offers long-term care and in-home services. The university was founded in 1787 and has an endowment exceeding $1 billion.

EXECUTIVES

Chairperson: William S. Dietrich II, age 65
Chancellor and CEO: Mark A. Nordenberg, age 54
Executive Vice Chancellor: Jerome Cochran
Senior Vice Chancellor and Provost: James V. Maher
Senior Vice Chancellor Health Sciences: Arthur Levine
Vice Chancellor Budget and Controller: Arthur Ramicone
Vice Provost Graduate Studies: Elizabeth U. Baranger
Vice Provost Research: George E. Klinzing
Associate Vice Chancellor Human Resources: Ronald W. (Ron) Frisch
Auditors: Deloitte & Touche LLP

LOCATIONS

HQ: University of Pittsburgh of the Commonwealth System of Higher Education
4200 5th Ave., Pittsburgh, PA 15260
Phone: 412-624-4141 **Fax:** 412-624-7282
Web: www.pitt.edu

The University of Pittsburgh of the Commonwealth System of Higher Education has campuses in Bradford, Greensburg, Johnstown, Pittsburgh, and Titusville, Pennsylvania.

PRODUCTS/OPERATIONS

Selected Schools and Colleges

Arts and Sciences
Business
Dental Medicine
Education
Engineering
General Studies
Health and Rehabilitation Sciences
Honors College
Information Sciences
Law
Medicine
Nursing
Pharmacy
Public and International Affairs
Public Health
Social Work

HISTORICAL FINANCIALS

Company Type: School

Income Statement FYE: June 30

	REVENUE ($ mil.)	NET INCOME ($ mil.)	NET PROFIT MARGIN	EMPLOYEES
6/02	1,146	—	—	10,000
6/01	1,097	—	—	10,000
6/00	1,033	—	—	10,000
6/99	984	—	—	10,000
6/98	888	—	—	9,600
6/97	820	—	—	9,453
6/96	872	—	—	9,621
6/95	844	—	—	9,671
6/94	817	—	—	9,299
6/93	801	—	—	—
Annual Growth	4.1%	—	—	0.9%

Revenue History

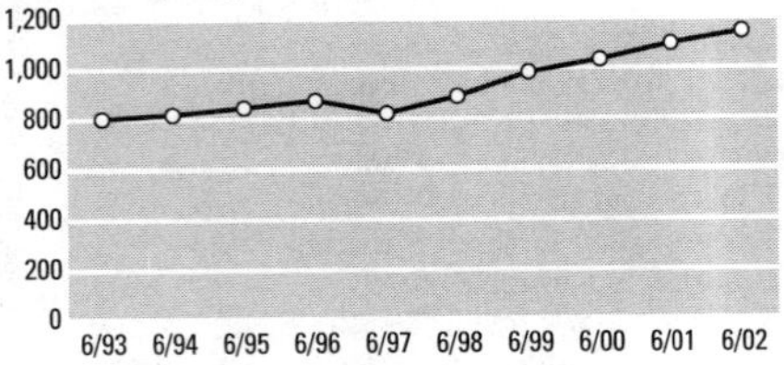

University of Rochester

The buzz about the University of Rochester is music to some ears. The private, upstate New York institution is nationally recognized for its programs in medicine, engineering, and business, and its Eastman School of Music (founded by Eastman Kodak creator George Eastman) is one of the top music schools in the US. The university, which has an endowment of more than $1.1 billion, offers about 175 bachelor's, master's, and doctoral degrees to its more than 8,200 full- and part-time students. Undergraduate tuition runs more than $25,000. Founded as a Baptist-sponsored institution in 1850, the university is nonsectarian today.

EXECUTIVES

President: Thomas H. Jackson
Provost: Charles E. Phelps
SVP Administration and Finance, CFO, and Treasurer: Ronald J. Paprocki
SVP Institutional Resources: Douglas W. Phillips
SVP and Vice Provost for Health Affairs: Jay H. Stein
VP and General Secretary: Paul J. Burgett
Vice Provost and CIO: Amelia Tynan
Auditors: KPMG LLP

LOCATIONS

HQ: Administration Bldg., Rochester, NY 14627
Phone: 585-275-2121 **Fax:** 585-275-0359
Web: www.rochester.edu

PRODUCTS/OPERATIONS

Selected Schools

Eastman School Campus
Eastman School of Music
Medical Center
Eastman Dental Center
School of Medicine and Dentistry
School of Nursing
Strong Memorial Hospital
River Campus
Margaret Warner Graduate School of Education and Human Development
William E. Simon Graduate School of Business Administration

Other Operations

C. E. K. Mees Observatory (Bristol Hills, NY)
Center for Optoelectronics and Imaging
Laboratory for Laser Energetics
Memorial Art Gallery
Mt. Hope Campus

HISTORICAL FINANCIALS

Company Type: School

Income Statement FYE: June 30

	REVENUE ($ mil.)	NET INCOME ($ mil.)	NET PROFIT MARGIN	EMPLOYEES
6/02	1,427	—	—	11,200
6/01	1,419	—	—	12,242
6/00	1,340	—	—	13,656
6/99	1,160	—	—	12,968
6/98	1,061	—	—	12,568
6/97	865	—	—	11,859
6/96	822	—	—	11,801
6/95	846	—	—	11,956
6/94	804	—	—	11,653
6/93	764	—	—	11,249
Annual Growth	7.2%	—	—	(0.0%)

Revenue History

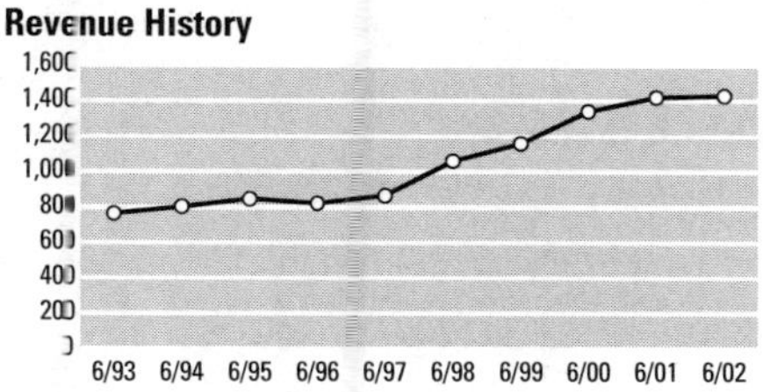

The University of Southern California

This Trojan horse, filled with more than 28,000 students, is more than welcome at the University of Southern California (USC). Founded in 1880, the private university (home of the Trojans) grew up with the city of Los Angeles. It offers 77 undergraduate majors and 139 postgraduate degrees. Recognized for distinguished programs in business, engineering, film, law, medicine, public administration, and science, USC boasts two Los Angeles campuses and a string of research centers and health care facilities. The university also supports medical staffs at five Los Angeles hospitals. USC is the largest private employer in Los Angeles.

The university's focus on fund raising under current president Steven Sample has resulted in four individual donations of $100 million or more for his efforts to improve USC's undergraduate programs and medical school, as well as to attract top-flight teachers.

EXECUTIVES

President: Steven B. Sample, age 61
SVP Academic Affairs and Provost: Lloyd Armstrong Jr.
SVP Administration: Dennis F. Dougherty
SVP University Advancement: Alan Kreditor
SVP Medical Care: Stephen J. Ryan, age 62
SVP University Relations: Martha Harris
VP, General Counsel, and Secretary: Todd R. Dickey
CIO: Jerry D. Campbell
Auditors: PricewaterhouseCoopers LLP

LOCATIONS

HQ: University Park, Los Angeles, CA 90089
Phone: 213-740-2311 **Fax:** 213-740-5229
Web: www.usc.edu

PRODUCTS/OPERATIONS

Schools and Programs

Annenberg School for Communication
College of Letters, Arts and Sciences
Graduate School
Independent Health Professions
Keck School of Medicine
The Law School
Leonard Davis School of Gerontology
Marshall School of Business
Rossier School of Education
School of Architecture
School of Cinema-Television
School of Dentistry
School of Engineering
School of Fine Arts
School of Pharmacy
School of Policy, Planning, and Development
School of Social Work
School of Theatre
Thornton School of Music

Campuses

Health Sciences Campus
University Park Campus

Health Facilities

Childrens Hospital Los Angeles
Doheny Eye Institute
Los Angeles County+USC Medical Center
USC University Hospital
USC/Norris Comprehensive Cancer Center

HISTORICAL FINANCIALS

Company Type: School

Income Statement FYE: June 30

	REVENUE ($ mil.)	NET INCOME ($ mil.)	NET PROFIT MARGIN	EMPLOYEES
6/02	1,480	—	—	17,000
6/01	1,399	—	—	17,000
6/00	1,186	—	—	17,000
6/99	1,142	—	—	17,000
6/98	1,307	—	—	17,000
6/97	1,239	—	—	17,000
6/96	1,233	—	—	17,100
6/95	1,152	—	—	17,000
6/94	971	—	—	17,000
6/93	932	—	—	17,000
Annual Growth	5.3%	—	—	0.0%

Revenue History

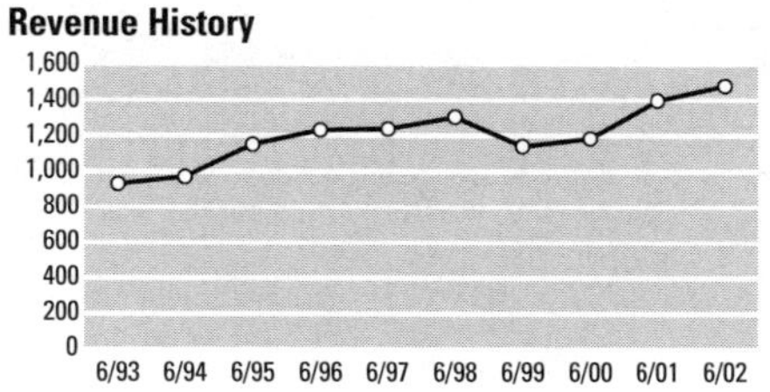

The University of Texas System

These students are hooked on higher education. The University of Texas System runs nine universities throughout the Lone Star State with a total enrollment of nearly 170,000 students, making it one of the largest university systems in the US. (Its flagship school in Austin, with some 50,000 students, ranks as the largest campus population in the nation.) UT also runs six health centers and four medical schools and receives more than $1 billion a year for research. Its $10 billion endowment fund (managed by the University of Texas Investment Management Co.) is the third largest in the country (after Harvard and Yale). Established in 1876, UT Austin opened in 1883. The UT System was formally organized in 1950.

With the bulging ranks of Generation Y looming on the horizon, the UT System expects its enrollment to swell to 250,000 by the end of the decade. To accommodate the increase, the system has laid out plans for nearly $3 billion in capital spending for new and improved facilities. It also hopes the improvements will put it on par with research institutions such as California State.

HISTORY

The Texas Declaration of Independence (1836) admonished Mexico for having failed to establish a public education system in the territory, but attempts to start a state-sponsored university were stymied until after Texas achieved US statehood and fought in the Civil War. A new constitution in 1876 provided for the establishment of "a university of the first class," and in 1883 The University of Texas (UT) opened in Austin. Eight professors taught 218 students in two curricula: academics and law.

The school's first building opened in 1884, and in 1891 the university's medical school opened in Galveston. By 1894 UT-Austin had 534 students and a football team. UT opened a Graduate School in 1910 and various other colleges over the years. The university added its first academic branch campus when the Texas State School of Mines and Metallurgy (opened in 1914 in El Paso) became part of the system in 1919.

UT's financial future was secured in 1923 when oil was found on West Texas land that had been set aside by the legislature as an education endowment. The income from oil production, as well as the proceeds of surface-use leases, became the Permanent University Fund (PUF), from which only interest and earnings on the revenues can be used: two-thirds by UT and one-third by Texas A&M University. UT continued to grow, thanks to the PUF, which topped $100 million by 1940.

UT sported the black eye of racial prejudice (as did many other institutions at the time) when it refused to admit Heman Sweatt, a black student, to its law school in 1946. The Supreme Court ordered UT to admit him in 1950, the same year the UT System was officially organized. Sixteen years later, in one of the nation's most highly publicized crimes, Charles Whitman killed 14 people and wounded 31 others with a high-powered rifle fired from atop the UT-Austin administration tower. The observation deck wasn't closed until

1975, however, after a series of suicides. (It was later reopened in 1999.)

In the meantime, UT added a medical center in Dallas and several graduate schools in Austin. The 1960s through the 1980s were a time of geographic expansion for the system as it absorbed other institutions, started several new campuses, and expanded its network of medical centers. In 1996 the UT System became the first public university to establish a private investment management company (University of Texas Investment Management Co.) to invest PUF money (by that time over $9 billion) and other funds.

The race issue reared its head again in 1996 when a Federal court ruled in the Hopwood decision (named for the plaintiff) that the UT System could no longer use race to determine scholarships and admissions. Minority enrollments declined the following year, prompting the Texas Legislature to enact a law granting admission to the top 10% of graduates from any Texas high school to the state university of their choice. Chancellor William Cunningham announced plans in 2000 to expand the UT System by 100,000 students over the decade. After he resigned that year, R. D. Burck took over as his successor. In 2001 UT received a $50 million donation, the largest gift in its history, from Texas businessman and Minnesota Vikings owner Red McCombs. The following year Burck stepped down and was replaced by Mark Yudof, former president of the University of Minnesota.

EXECUTIVES

Chairman, Board of Regents: Charles Miller
Vice Chairman, Board of Regents: Rita C. Clements
Vice Chairman, Board of Regents: Woody L. Hunt
Vice Chairman, Board of Regents: A. W. (Dub) Riter Jr.
Counsel and Executive Secretary, Board of Regents: Francie A. Frederick
Chancellor: Mark G. Yudof
Executive Vice Chancellor Academic Affairs: Teresa Sullivan
Executive Vice Chancellor Business Affairs: Kerry L. Kennedy
Acting Executive Vice Chancellor Health Affairs: James C. Guckian
Vice Chancellor and General Counsel: Cullen M. Godfrey
Vice Chancellor Administration: Tonya Brown
Vice Chancellor Development and External Relations: Shirley B. Perry
Vice Chancellor Educational System Alignment: Edwin R. Sharpe Jr.
Vice Chancellor Federal Relations: William H. Shute
Vice Chancellor Governmental Relations: Tom A. Scott
Vice Chancellor Special Engineering Programs: Charles Sorber
President, University of Texas at Arlington: Robert E. Witt
President, University of Texas at Austin: Larry R. Faulkner
President, University of Texas at Brownsville: Juliet V. García
President, University of Texas at Dallas: Franklyn G. Jenifer, age 64
President, University of Texas at El Paso: Diana S. Natalicio, age 63
President, University of Texas Pan American: Miguel A. Nevárez
President, University of Texas of the Permian Basin: W. David Watts
President, University of Texas at San Antonio: Ricardo Romo
President, University of Texas at Tyler: Rodney H. Mabry
Executive Director Public Affairs: Michael L. Warden
Director Human Resources: John Poole
Auditors: Texas State Auditor

LOCATIONS

HQ: 601 Colorado St., Austin, TX 78701
Phone: 512-499-4200 **Fax:** 512-499-4218
Web: www.utsystem.edu

PRODUCTS/OPERATIONS

University of Texas System Component Institutions

Academic Institutions
The University of Texas at Arlington (established 1895; 19,148 students)
The University of Texas at Austin (1883; 50,010)
The University of Texas at Brownsville (1991; 9,094)
The University of Texas at Dallas (1961; 10,137)
The University of Texas at El Paso (1914; 14,695)
The University of Texas-Pan American (Edinburg; 1927; 12,520)
The University of Texas of the Permian Basin (Odessa; 1969; 2,222)
The University of Texas at San Antonio (1969; 18,607)
The University of Texas at Tyler (1971; 3,392)

Health Institutions
The University of Texas Health Science Center at Houston (established 1972; 3,170 students)
The University of Texas Health Science Center at San Antonio (1959; 2,557)
The University of Texas Health Center at Tyler (1947)
The University of Texas M.D. Anderson Cancer Center (Houston, 1941)
The University of Texas Medical Branch at Galveston (1891; 1,952)
The University of Texas Southwestern Medical Center at Dallas (1943; 1,554)

HISTORICAL FINANCIALS

Company Type: School

Income Statement FYE: August 31

	REVENUE ($ mil.)	NET INCOME ($ mil.)	NET PROFIT MARGIN	EMPLOYEES
8/02	4,806	—	—	65,689
8/01	6,461	—	—	63,054
8/00	5,943	—	—	79,430
8/99	4,131	—	—	78,000
8/98	5,244	—	—	77,112
8/97	4,803	—	—	75,517
8/96	4,624	—	—	74,364
8/95	4,300	—	—	72,395
8/94	4,030	—	—	70,000
8/93	3,744	—	—	67,985
Annual Growth	2.8%	—	—	(0.4%)

Revenue History

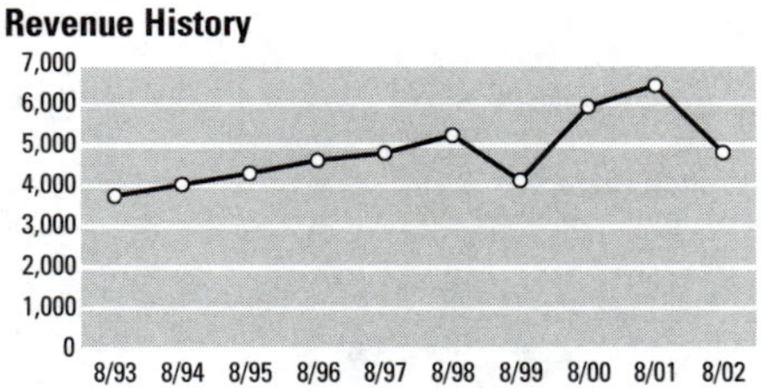

University of Washington

The University of Washington (UW) is Husky indeed, with more than 37,400 students enrolled at its main Seattle campus. Founded in 1861 as the Territorial University of Washington, UW (pronounced "U-dub" by those on campus) also has smaller branches in Tacoma and Bothell. The university maintains 17 schools and colleges for both undergraduate and graduate students (more than 70% of students on the main campus are undergrads). It also operates a health sciences center and an academic medical center, which includes the University of Washington Medical Center and Harborview Medical Center.

EXECUTIVES

President: Richard L. McCormick, age 53
EVP: Weldon E. Ihrig
Provost and VP Academic Affairs: Lee L. Huntsman
VP Student Affairs: Ernest R. Morris
VP Medical Affairs and Dean School of Medicine: Paul G. Ramsey
VP University Relations: Jack H. Faris
Treasurer of the Board of Regents: V'Ella Warren
Director Human Resources: Elizabeth Coveney
Auditors: KPMG LLP

LOCATIONS

HQ: 301 Gerberding Hall, Ste. 400, Seattle, WA 98195
Phone: 206-543-2560 **Fax:** 206-543-5651
Web: www.washington.edu

The University of Washington has campuses in Bothell, Seattle, and Tacoma, Washington.

PRODUCTS/OPERATIONS

Schools and Colleges

The College of Architecture and Urban Planning
The College of Arts and Sciences
The College of Education
The College of Engineering
The College of Forest Resources
The College of Ocean and Fishery Sciences
The Graduate School
The Graduate School of Public Affairs
Information School
The School of Business Administration
The School of Dentistry
The School of Law
The School of Medicine
The School of Nursing
The School of Pharmacy
The School of Public Health and Community Medicine
The School of Social Work

Health and Medical Centers

Academic Medical Center
Alcohol and Drug Abuse Institute
Center on Human Development and Disability
Harborview Medical Center
Institute on Aging
Regional Primate Research Center
Research Center in Oral Biology
University of Washington Medical Center

Warren G. Magnuson Health Sciences Center
Department of Environmental Health and Safety
Hall Health Primary Care Center

HISTORICAL FINANCIALS

Company Type: School

Income Statement FYE: June 30

	REVENUE ($ mil.)	NET INCOME ($ mil.)	NET PROFIT MARGIN	EMPLOYEES
6/02	1,814	—	—	23,680
6/01	2,647	—	—	23,462
6/00	2,696	—	—	25,917
6/99	2,456	—	—	25,281
6/98	1,748	—	—	34,757
6/97	1,615	—	—	32,080
6/96	1,990	—	—	30,000
6/95	1,785	—	—	22,655
6/94	1,783	—	—	21,536
6/93	1,260	—	—	—
Annual Growth	4.1%	—	—	1.2%

Revenue History

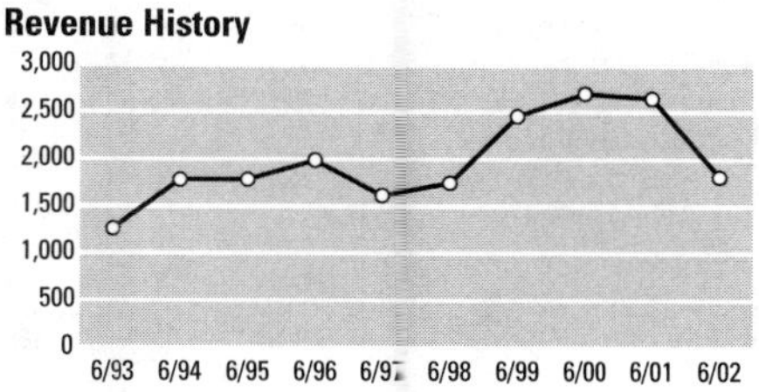

The University of Wisconsin System

There is no School of Cheese in the University of Wisconsin System, but there are 13 four-year universities, 13 two-year campuses, and a statewide extension program. The University of Wisconsin System is one of the largest public university systems in the US, with some 157,000 students. Its top school is the University of Wisconsin at Madison, which offers undergraduate, graduate, and doctoral degrees and regularly ranks as one of the top public schools in the US. It has some 40,900 students and a nationally recognized graduate program in sociology. The system's other major campus is the University of Wisconsin at Milwaukee, with more than 23,800 students.

The University of Wisconsin System is ranked in the top 10 of US public schools by *U.S. News & World Report*. One-third of the UW System's annual budget comes from state funds. Student fees, federal grants, fund raising, and other sources account for the remainder.

HISTORY

When Wisconsin became a state in 1848, its constitution called for the establishment of a state university. A board of regents was named, and it first established a preparatory school because regents felt Wisconsin's secondary schools were not advanced enough to prepare students for university studies. The school began classes in 1849 with 20 students in the Madison Female Academy Building. The University of Wisconsin's first official freshman class began studies in the fall of 1850. A campus was established a mile west of the state capitol in Madison. By 1854, when it held its first commencement (with two graduates), the school had 41 students.

Enrollment dipped during the Civil War (all but one of the school's senior class joined the army) but soon rebounded, and by 1870 the university had almost 500 students. Meanwhile, it established a school of agriculture (1866) and a school of law (1868). The state established normal schools (teachers colleges) in Platteville (1866), Whitewater (1868), Oshkosh (1871), and River Falls (1874).

There was also a teachers' course for women at the university in Madison. However, when John Bascom became president in 1874, he transformed the university into a truly coeducational institution, putting women "in all respects on precisely the same footing" with the men.

While the university at Madison remained Wisconsin's primary seat of learning, the state continued to establish normal schools. It opened institutions in Milwaukee (1885), Superior (1893), Stevens Point (1894), La Crosse (1909), and Eau Claire (1916). The nine normal schools eventually became a system of state colleges called Wisconsin State Universities.

The university at Madison also continued to grow, and by the late 1920s it had almost 9,000 students. WWII brought a drop in enrollment, but afterward it took off, jumping from about 7,000 in 1945 to over 22,000 by the late 1950s. The University of Wisconsin-Milwaukee branch was founded in 1956. Other branch campuses were established in Green Bay (1965) and Kenosha (1968).

The Madison campus became a focal point for student protests during the Vietnam War. Events came to a head in 1970 when President Fred Harrington resigned during a four-day standoff between students and the National Guard. War protesters also placed a bomb outside Sterling Hall, which housed the Army Math Research Center; the explosion killed one student and injured three others.

The state legislature merged the University of Wisconsin and the Wisconsin State Universities in 1971 to create The University of Wisconsin System. By the early 1980s it had an enrollment of nearly 160,000. Later that decade, however, it tightened admission standards, and enrollment began to fall.

A property-tax reform bill passed by the legislature in 1994 cut into The University of Wisconsin System's funding the next year. The system announced it would cut 500 jobs in 1997, use more part-time instructors, and increase class sizes to deal with the $43 million it lost in the budget cuts.

UW-Madison broke ground on the $22 million Fluno Center for Executive Education in 1998, a 100-room dorm, classroom building, and dining hall rolled into one. The next year enrollment at The University of Wisconsin System's two-year colleges broke 10,000 for the first time in five years. The licensing of technologies invented at the UW-Madison campus was expanded to include all four-year universities in the UW System in 2000. The System's mandatory student-fee policy was ruled unconstitutional later that year.

EXECUTIVES

President: Katharine C. Lyall, age 62
SVP Academic Affairs: Cora B. Marrett
SVP Administration: David W. Olien
VP Finance: Deborah A. Durcan
VP University Relations: Linda Weimer
Assistant VP Administrative Services: Ellen James
Assistant VP Academic Affairs, Senior Advisor of President, Multicultural Affairs: Andrea-Teresa (Tess) Arenas
Assistant VP Capital Planning and Budget: Nancy J. Ives
Associate VP Academic Affairs: Ron Singer
Associate VP Budget and Planning: Freda Harris
Associate VP Human Resources: George H. Brooks
Associate VP Learning and Information Technology: Edward Meachen
Associate VP Policy Analysis and Research: Frank Goldberg
Director Budget Planning: Melissa Kepner
Director Information Services: Nancy Crabb
Director Internal Audit: Ronald L. Yates
General Counsel: Patricia Brady
Auditors: State of Wisconsin Legislative Audit Bureau

LOCATIONS

HQ: Van Hise Hall, 1220 Linden Dr., Madison, WI 53706
Phone: 608-262-2321 **Fax:** 608-262-3985
Web: www.uwsa.edu

University Campuses

UW-Baraboo/Sauk County (two-year college, 653 students)
UW-Barron County (two-year college, 570)
UW-Eau Claire (four-year university; 10,643)
UW-Fond Du Lac (two-year college, 684)
UW-Fox Valley (two-year college; 1,776)
UW-Green Bay (four-year university; 5,558)
UW-La Crosse (four-year university; 9,092)
UW-Madison (four-year university; 40,877)
UW-Manitowoc (two-year college, 647)
UW-Marathon County (two-year college; 1,292)
UW-Marinette (two-year college, 535)
UW-Marshfield/Wood County (two-year college, 643)
UW-Milwaukee (four-year university; 23,835)
UW-Oshkosh (four-year university; 10,929)
UW-Parkside (four-year university; 5,016)
UW-Platteville (four-year university; 5,511)
UW-Richland (two-year college, 496)
UW-River Falls (four-year university; 5,822)
UW-Rock County (two-year college, 981)
UW-Sheboygan (two-year college, 768)
UW-Stevens Point (four-year university; 8,735)
UW-Stout (four-year university; 7,780)
UW-Superior (four-year university; 2,787)
UW-Washington County (two-year college, 939)
UW-Waukesha (two-year college; 2,245)
UW-Whitewater (four-year university; 10,471)

HISTORICAL FINANCIALS

Company Type: School

Income Statement FYE: June 30

	REVENUE ($ mil.)	NET INCOME ($ mil.)	NET PROFIT MARGIN	EMPLOYEES
6/02	3,059	—	—	25,000
6/01	3,160	—	—	24,000
6/00	2,922	—	—	23,981
6/99	2,558	—	—	25,889
6/98	2,543	—	—	25,500
6/97	2,399	—	—	25,399
6/96	2,612	—	—	28,626
6/95	2,556	—	—	30,410
6/94	2,442	—	—	30,341
6/93	2,309	—	—	30,269
Annual Growth	3.2%	—	—	(2.1%)

Revenue History

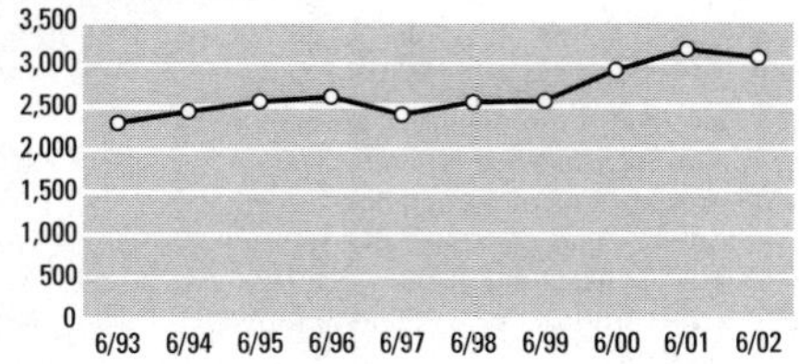

U.S. Can

U.S. Can doesn't want to stop the flow of new products into the marketplace — it only hopes to contain them. The company makes steel and plastic nonbeverage containers in the US and Europe that hold everything from food to paint. Its aerosol containers, which account for the largest portion of sales, are used to package household, automotive, paint, hygiene, and industrial products. Besides standard containers the company offers custom and specialty products such as decorative tins, stampings, and collectible items like metal signs, as well as containers used to store chemicals. Private investment firm Berkshire Partners owns 77% of U.S. Can.

U.S. Can's approximately 5,000 customers include Gillette and Sherwin-Williams.

The company is the leading seller of aerosol cans in the US and holds the #2 position in Europe. The company expanded into South America when it bought about 37% of Argentina's Fornametal SA, an aerosol can plant.

EXECUTIVES

Chairman: Carl Ferenbach, age 60
CEO and Director: John L. Workman, age 51, $469,723 pay
SVP and CFO: Sandra K. Vollman, age 45
SVP, Aerosol, Paint, and General Line: Thomas A. Scrimo, age 54, $287,677 pay
SVP, General Counsel, and Secretary: Larry S. Morrison
SVP, Human Resources: Roger B. Farley, age 59, $274,069 pay
SVP, International and President, European Operations: Francois Vissers, age 42, $302,157 pay
SVP, North American Sales and Channel Development: James J. Poehling, age 55, $322,292 pay
VP, Group Marketing and CIO: Sheleen Quish, age 54
Auditors: Deloitte & Touche LLP

LOCATIONS

HQ: U.S. Can Corporation
700 E. Butterfield Rd., Ste. 250, Lombard, IL 60148
Phone: 630-678-8000 **Fax:** 630-678-8131
Web: www.uscanco.com

U.S. Can has plants in Argentina, Denmark, France, Germany, Italy, Spain, UK, and the US.

2002 Sales

	$ mil.	% of total
US	555.3	70
Europe	241.2	30
Total	**796.5**	**100**

PRODUCTS/OPERATIONS

Selected Products

Aerosol containers
Custom and specialty containers
Paint, plastic, and general line cans

COMPETITORS

Ball Corporation
BWAY
CCL Industries
Crown
Owens-Illinois
Silgan
Sonoco Products

HISTORICAL FINANCIALS

Company Type: Private

Income Statement FYE: December 31

	REVENUE ($ mil.)	NET INCOME ($ mil.)	NET PROFIT MARGIN	EMPLOYEES
12/02	797	(72)	—	2,400
12/01	772	(40)	—	2,600
12/00	810	(12)	—	2,700
12/99	714	21	3.0%	3,000
12/98	710	(16)	—	3,195
12/97	739	(32)	—	4,478
12/96	761	12	1.5%	4,065
12/95	627	4	0.6%	3,678
12/94	563	19	3.3%	3,500
12/93	455	8	1.6%	2,745
Annual Growth	6.4%	—	—	(1.5%)

2002 Year-End Financials

Debt ratio: —
Return on equity: —
Cash ($ mil.): 12
Current ratio: 1.24
Long-term debt ($ mil.): 524

Net Income History

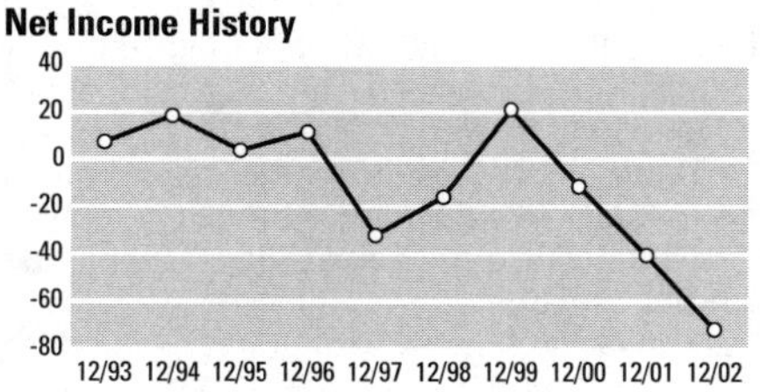

U.S. Central Credit Union

United credit unions stand in U.S. Central Credit Union, a cooperative "central bank" for a network of about 30 corporate (or regional) credit unions. These, in turn, represent more than 10,000 consumer credit unions nationwide. The cooperative performs a variety of liquidity and cash management functions, such as funds transfer, settlement services, risk management, and custody services. Subsidiary CU Investment Solutions provides investment advisory services to the corporate credit unions, while majority-owned Corporate Network eCom offers bill payment and technology services to the network and its members.

Another subsidiary, Network Liquidity Acceptance Company, works as a liquidity facility by purchasing loans originated by the credit union community.

EXECUTIVES

Chairman: Edward J. Fox
Vice Chairman: David A. (Dave) Preter
President and CEO: Dan Kampen
Secretary and Director: Robert W. (Bob) Thurman
Treasurer and Director: Tom Kuehl
SVP and CFO: Kathryn (Kathy) Brick
SVP and General Counsel: François G. Henriquez II
Director, Sales: Nicole Hinken
Director, Human Resources: Linda Pfingsten
Auditors: Deloitte & Touche LLP

LOCATIONS

HQ: 9701 Renner Blvd., Ste. 100, Lenexa, KS 66219
Phone: 913-227-6000 **Fax:** 913-438-1564
Web: www.uscentral.org

PRODUCTS/OPERATIONS

2002 Sales

	$ mil.	% of total
Interest		
Investment securities	581.3	75
Securities purchased under agreements to resell	64.1	8
Federal funds sold	37.8	5
Loans	30.9	4
Time deposits & other short-term investments	28.6	3
Stock of the Central Liquidity Facility	20.6	3
Fee income	15.6	2
Total	**778.9**	**100**

COMPETITORS

A.G. Edwards
Bear Stearns
BISYS
Charles Schwab
CheckFree
Concord EFS
DST
EDS
First Data
Fiserv
Fiserv Securities
Jack Henry
Merrill Lynch
NOVA
Online Resources
PrimeVest
Private Business
SEI

HISTORICAL FINANCIALS

Company Type: Cooperative

Income Statement FYE: December 31

	ASSETS ($ mil.)	NET INCOME ($ mil.)	INCOME AS % OF ASSETS	EMPLOYEES
12/02	31,808	59	0.2%	230
12/01	32,221	48	0.1%	200
12/00	22,759	45	0.2%	186
12/99	26,218	43	0.2%	219
12/98	25,709	38	0.1%	190
12/97	18,087	30	0.2%	179
12/96	17,925	29	0.2%	149
12/95	19,305	28	0.1%	151
12/94	18,681	—	—	164
Annual Growth	6.9%	11.3%	—	4.3%

2002 Year-End Financials

Equity as % of assets: 90.7%
Return on assets: 0.2%
Return on equity: 0.2%
Long-term debt ($ mil.): 356
Sales ($ mil.): 779

Net Income History

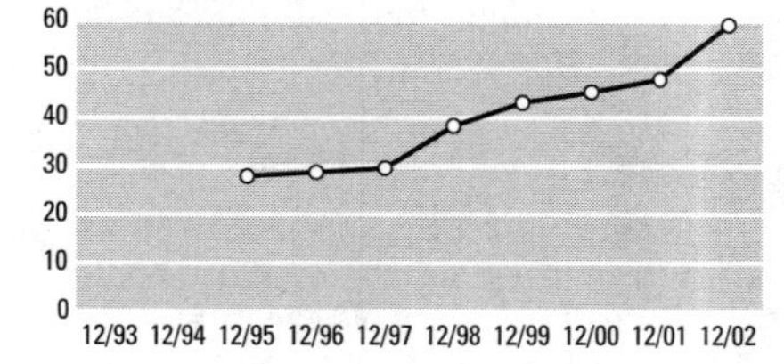

U.S. Oil Co., Inc.

U.S. Oil Co. supplies refined oil products to US residents in the Midwest, and does a lot more. In addition to the wholesale distribution of oil products (its largest revenue generator), the company operates gas stations, and installs gas pumps, tanks, and other petroleum-related equipment. It also provides plumbing and heating services, operates a laboratory for environmental analysis, and collects used waste oil to be processed into burner fuel. Founded in the 1950s as Schmidt Oil by the sons of local fuel distributor Albert Schmidt, U.S. Oil Co. is still controlled by the Schmidt family.

EXECUTIVES

President and CEO: Thomas A. Schmidt
CFO and Treasurer: Paul Bachman
Director Human Resources: Gretchen Leverson
Director Information Systems: Fred Pennings
Corporate Secretary: Joe Kaufman
General Counsel: Marjorie Young

LOCATIONS

HQ: 425 S. Washington St., Combined Locks, WI 54113
Phone: 920-739-6101 **Fax:** 920-788-0531
Web: www.usoil.com

U.S. Oil has operations in Illinois, Michigan, Minnesota, Missouri, and Wisconsin.

PRODUCTS/OPERATIONS

Major Operations

Design Air (heating and air conditioning equipment)
Express Convenience Centers (gas stations and car washes)
NEW Energy, LLC, U.S. Oil (fuel oil and gasoline)
U.S. Lubricants (motor oil and related products)
U.S. Petroleum Equipment (petroleum-related equipment installation)
U.S. Petroleum Laboratory (environmental and used oil testing and analysis)
U.S. Petroleum Operations (gasoline, fuel oil, and natural gas)
U.S. Plumbing & Heating (commercial and residential plumbing and heating services)
U.S. Tire & Exhaust (exhaust pipe manufacturing and autoparts distribution)

COMPETITORS

Apex Oil
Motiva Enterprises
Premcor
Sunoco

HISTORICAL FINANCIALS

Company Type: Private

Income Statement FYE: July 31

	REVENUE ($ mil.)	NET INCOME ($ mil.)	NET PROFIT MARGIN	EMPLOYEES
7/03	1,166	—	—	670
7/02*	753	—	—	730
12/00	765	—	—	850
Annual Growth	23.5%	—	—	(11.2%)

*Fiscal year change

Revenue History

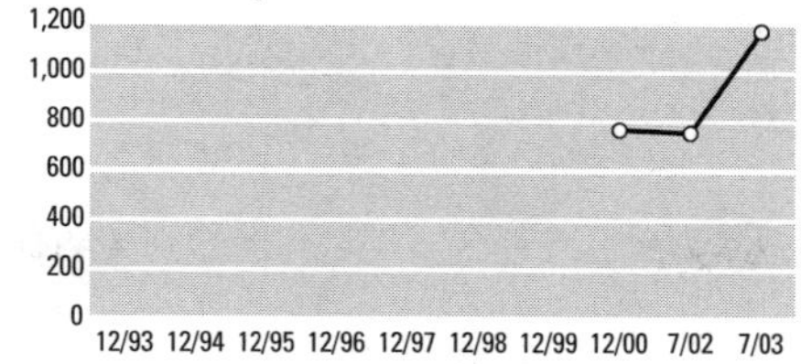

USAA

USAA has a decidedly military bearing. The mutual insurance company serves some 5 million customers, primarily military personnel and their families. Its products and services include property & casualty (sold only to military personnel) and life insurance, banking, discount brokerage, and investment management. USAA relies largely on technology and direct marketing to sell its products, reaching clients via the telephone and Internet. The company also has a large mail-order catalog business (computers, furniture, jewelry, and home and auto safety items), and it offers long-distance telephone service, travel services, and Internet access to its members.

The company is expecting its membership to continue growing, projecting it to nearly double by 2010. In an attempt to increase revenue, the company has entered new markets by making efforts to target people less affluent than military officers.

Facing rising claims and a decline in value of its investments, USAA has streamlined operations by reducing staff and closing down divisions (including mailing, printing, and information technology offices).

In 2002, USAA's decreased investment income was offset by higher insurance rates, improved credit card sales, and increased loan volumes.

HISTORY

In 1922 a group of 26 US Army officers gathered in a San Antonio hotel and formed their own automobile insurance association. The reason? As military officers who often moved, they had a hard time getting insurance because they were considered transient. So the officers decided to insure each other. Led by Major William Garrison, who became the company's first president, they formed the United States Army Automobile Insurance Association.

In 1924, when US Navy and Marine Corps officers were allowed to join, the company changed its name to United Services Automobile Association. By the mid-1950s the company had some 200,000 members. During the 1960s the company formed USAA Life Insurance Company (1963) and USAA Casualty Insurance Company (1968).

Robert McDermott, a retired US Air Force brigadier general, became president in 1969. He cut employment through attrition, established education and training seminars for employees, and invested in computers and telecommunications (drastically cutting claims-processing time). McDermott added new products and services, such as mutual funds, real estate investments, and banking. Under McDermott, USAA's membership grew from 653,000 in 1969 to more than 3 million in 1993.

During the 1970s, in an effort to go paperless, USAA became one of the insurance industry's first companies to switch from mail to toll-free (800) numbers. In the early 1980s the company introduced its discount purchasing program, USAA Buying Services. In 1985 it opened the USAA Federal Savings Bank. USAA began installing an optical storage system in the late 1980s to automate some customer service operations.

McDermott retired in 1993 and was succeeded by Robert Herres. The following year USAA Federal Savings Bank began developing a home banking system, offering members information and services over advanced screen telephones provided by IBM.

In the early 1990s USAA's real estate activities increased dramatically. In 1995 USAA restructured its interest in the Fiesta Texas theme park in San Antonio in order to focus on previously developed properties in geographically diverse areas. That year Six Flags Theme Parks (now Six Flags, Inc.) assumed operation and management of Fiesta Texas (which purchased it from USAA in 1998).

In 1997 USAA began including enlisted military personnel as members. It also started to experiment with a "plain English" mutual fund prospectus. In 1998 USAA also began offering Choice Ride in Orlando, Florida. For about $1,100 per quarter and a promise not to drive except in emergencies, the pilot program provided 36 round trips and a 90% discount on car insurance, in hopes of keeping older drivers from unnecessarily getting behind the wheel.

Also in 1998, as part of its new Financial Planning Network, USAA began offering retirement and estate planning assistance aimed at 25- to 55-year-olds for a yearly $250 fee. In 1999 claims doubled largely due to the impact of Hurricane Floyd and spring hail storms hitting military communities in North Carolina and Virginia.

USAA also moved in 1999 to consolidate its customers' separate accounts (such as mutual fund holdings, stocks and bonds, and life insurance products) into one main account to strengthen customer relationships and reduce operational costs. The next year, after completing a number of technology projects, it laid off workers for the first time in its history.

In 2002, Robert Herres resigned as chairman and was succeeded by CEO Robert Davis.

EXECUTIVES

Chairman, President, and CEO: Robert G. (Bob) Davis
EVP, CFO, and Corporate Treasurer: Josue (Joe) Robles Jr.
EVP, Corporate Secretary, and General Counsel: Bradford W. Rich
EVP, Corporate Communications: Wendi E. Strong
EVP, Corporate Services: David H. Garrison
SVP, Enterprise Business Operations: Robert T. Handren
EVP, Financial Planning Services: Dawn M. Johnson
EVP, Human Resources: Elizabeth D. Conklyn
EVP, Marketing: Karen B. Presley
President and CEO, USAA Alliance Services: Donna M. Bhatia
President and CEO, USAA Federal Savings Bank: Mark H. Wright

President and CEO, USAA Investment Management: Christopher W. Claus
President and CEO, USAA Life Insurance: James M. Middleton
President and CEO, USAA Real Estate and La Cantera Development: Edward B. Kelley
President, USAA Information Technology: Stephen E. Yates, age 55
President, USAA Property and Casualty Insurance: Henry Viccellio Jr.
Auditors: KPMG LLP

LOCATIONS

HQ: 9800 Fredericksburg Rd., San Antonio, TX 78288
Phone: 210-498-2211 **Fax:** 210-498-9940
Web: www.usaa.com

USAA has major regional offices in Arizona, California, Colorado, Florida, Texas, and Virginia. It maintains international offices in London and Frankfurt, Germany.

PRODUCTS/OPERATIONS

Selected Operations

USAA Alliance Services Company (merchandising & member services)
USAA Federal Savings Bank
USAA Investment Management Company (mutual funds, investment and brokerage services)
USAA Property & Casualty (including automobile, home, boat, and flood insurance)
USAA Real Estate Company

COMPETITORS

21st Century
AIG American General
Allstate
American Express
American Financial
AIG
AXA Financial
Berkshire Hathaway
Charles Schwab
Chubb
CIGNA
Citigroup
CNA Financial
FMR
Guardian Life
The Hartford
John Hancock Financial Services
Kemper Insurance
Liberty Mutual
MassMutual
MetLife
Morgan Stanley
Mutual of Omaha
Nationwide
New York Life
Northwestern Mutual
Pacific Mutual
Prudential
St. Paul Companies
State Farm
T. Rowe Price
UBS Financial Services

HISTORICAL FINANCIALS

Company Type: Mutual company

Income Statement

FYE: December 31

	ASSETS ($ mil.)	NET INCOME ($ mil.)	INCOME AS % OF ASSETS	EMPLOYEES
12/02	38,203	500	1.3%	22,000
12/01	33,829	604	1.8%	22,000
12/00	32,794	669	2.0%	22,000
12/99	30,323	765	2.5%	21,795
12/98	28,831	980	3.4%	20,120
12/97	25,007	1,189	4.8%	17,967
12/96	23,622	855	3.6%	16,571
12/95	22,244	730	3.3%	15,677
12/94	19,548	564	2.9%	15,233
12/93	18,494	676	3.7%	15,905
Annual Growth	8.4%	(3.3%)	—	3.7%

2002 Year-End Financials

Equity as % of assets: 20.8%
Return on assets: 1.4%
Return on equity: —
Long-term debt ($ mil.): 4,491
Sales ($ mil.): 9,222

Net Income History

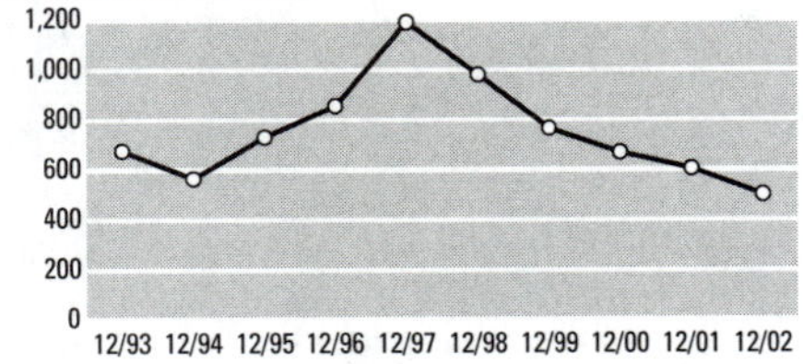

Utica Mutual Insurance

One of the 25 largest mutual insurance groups in the US, Utica Mutual Insurance has been providing commercial and personal property & casualty and life insurance coverage since 1914. The company (also known as Utica National) operates through a host of subsidiaries including Graphic Arts Mutual Insurance, Republic-Franklin Insurance, Utica National Life, and Utica National Insurance Company of Texas. Commercial products include specialty coverage for auto shops, financial institutions, physicians, and retail stores; Utica Mutual also offers personal home business, computer, life, and auto coverage. Selling its products nationwide, the company is represented by some 1,200 independent agents.

EXECUTIVES

Chairman: W. Craig Heston
President and CEO: J. Douglas Robinson
EVP: Brian P. Lytwynec
SVP and CFO: Anthony C. Paolozzi
SVP, Marketing and Sales; President and COO, UticaLIFE: David C. Cunningham
SVP and Director of Human Resources: Clarke Peterson
VP and General Counsel: Thomas P. Bonaros
Auditors: PricewaterhouseCoopers LLP

LOCATIONS

HQ: Utica Mutual Insurance Company
180 Genesee St., New Hartford, NY 13413
Phone: 315-734-2000 **Fax:** 315-734-2680
Web: www.uticanational.com

PRODUCTS/OPERATIONS

Selected Subsidiaries

Graphic Arts Mutual Insurance Company
Republic-Franklin Insurance Company
Utica Lloyd's of Texas
Utica National Assurance Company
Utica National Insurance Company of Texas
Utica National Life Insurance Company
Utica Specialty Risk Insurance Company

COMPETITORS

ACE Limited
Allstate
American Financial
AIG
AXA Corporate Solutions Insurance Company
Farmers Group
The Hartford
Kemper Insurance
Liberty Mutual
PMA Capital
Prudential
SAFECO
St. Paul Companies
State Farm
Travelers
USAA
White Mountains Insurance Group

HISTORICAL FINANCIALS

Company Type: Mutual company

Income Statement

FYE: December 31

	ASSETS ($ mil.)	NET INCOME ($ mil.)	INCOME AS % OF ASSETS	EMPLOYEES
12/02	2,035	15	0.8%	1,500
12/01	1,972	(103)	—	1,500
Annual Growth	3.2%	—	—	0.0%

2002 Year-End Financials

Equity as % of assets: —
Return on assets: 0.8%
Return on equity: —
Long-term debt ($ mil.): —
Sales ($ mil.): 643

Net Income History

Utility Trailer Manufacturing

Utility Trailer Manufacturing is spreading reefer madness. Utility Trailer is one of the US's largest manufacturers of refrigerated trailers, or reefers, as they are known in the business. The company also produces dry freight trailers, flatbeds, and curtain-sided trailers at five plants in the US. Its refrigerated trucks include special designs for the whole food distribution and fast-food markets, such as a truck with separate chambers for frozen and dry goods. The company's trailers are distributed throughout Canada, Mexico, the US, and to a lesser extent in Argentina. Two brothers, H.C. and E.W. Bennett, founded the company in 1914 and their descendants still own it.

EXECUTIVES

CEO: Paul Bennett
CFO: Arthur Goolsbee
SVP, Marketing and Sales: Craig Bennett
Director, Data Processing: Richard Vaughn
Director, Human Resources: John Stanton

LOCATIONS

HQ: Utility Trailer Manufacturing Co.
17295 E. Railroad St., City of Industry, CA 91748
Phone: 626-965-1541 **Fax:** 626-965-2790
Web: www.utilitytrailer.com

Utility Trailer Manufacturing operates seven manufacturing facilities throughout the US.

PRODUCTS/OPERATIONS

Selected Products

Dry freight trailers
Flatbeds
Refrigerated trailers (reefers)
Curtain-sided trailers
Used trailers

COMPETITORS

Great Dane
Lufkin Industries
RailAmerica
Wabash National

HISTORICAL FINANCIALS

Company Type: Private

Income Statement FYE: December 31

	REVENUE ($ mil.)	NET INCOME ($ mil.)	NET PROFIT MARGIN	EMPLOYEES
12/02	600	—	—	3,200
12/01	650	—	—	3,400
12/00	680	—	—	3,400
12/99	650	—	—	2,900
12/98	584	—	—	2,600
12/97	483	—	—	2,550
12/96	429	—	—	2,500
12/95	515	—	—	—
12/94	400	—	—	—
12/93	300	—	—	—
Annual Growth	8.0%	—	—	4.2%

Revenue History

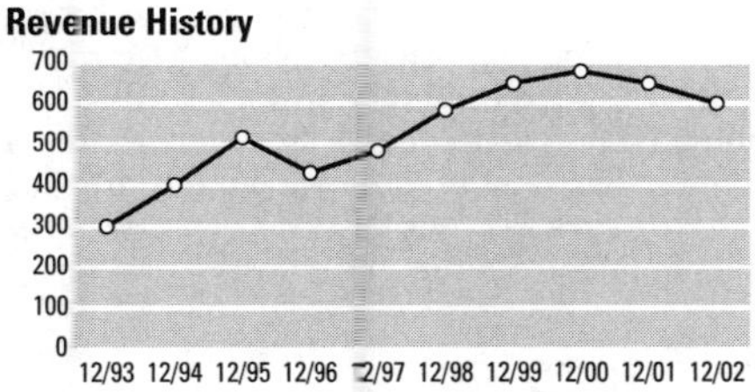

Vanderbilt University

The house that Cornelius built, private Vanderbilt University was founded in 1873 with a $1 million grant from industrialist Cornelius Vanderbilt. The university's endowment has grown to about $2 billion, and the campus today is a haven for nearly 10,500 students and 1,900 full-time faculty. Vanderbilt has 10 schools and colleges; its Owen Graduate School of Management and its medical school rank near the top of national surveys. A major research university, Vanderbilt receives millions a year in sponsored awards to fund its facilities. Vanderbilt offers graduate and professional degrees, as well as undergraduate programs in areas such as education and human development, engineering, and the arts and sciences.

EXECUTIVES

Chairman: Martha R. Ingram, age 67
Vice Chairman: Rebecca W. Wilson
Vice Chairman: Dennis C. Bottorff
Chancellor: E. Gordon Gee, age 59
Provost and Vice Chancellor Academic Affairs: Nicholas S. Zeppos
Vice Chancellor Administration and CFO: Lauren J. Brisky
Vice Chancellor Investments and Treasurer: William T. Spitz
Vice Chancellor Public Affairs: Michael J. Schoenfeld
Vice Chancellor Student Life and University Affairs, General Counsel, and Secretary: David Williams II
Interim Associate Vice Chancellor Human Resources: Jerry Fife
Auditors: KPMG LLP

LOCATIONS

HQ: 2201 West End Ave., Nashville, TN 37235
Phone: 615-322-7311
Web: www.vanderbilt.edu

PRODUCTS/OPERATIONS

Selected Schools and Colleges

Blair School of Music
College of Arts and Science
Divinity School
Graduate School
Law School
Owen Graduate School of Management
Peabody College
School of Engineering
School of Medicine
School of Nursing

HISTORICAL FINANCIALS

Company Type: School

Income Statement FYE: June 30

	REVENUE ($ mil.)	NET INCOME ($ mil.)	NET PROFIT MARGIN	EMPLOYEES
6/02	1,590	—	—	16,679
6/01	1,419	—	—	15,427
6/00	1,280	—	—	16,532
6/99	1,181	—	—	16,161
6/98	1,246	—	—	13,993
6/97	1,125	—	—	13,739
6/96	1,121	—	—	12,937
6/95	1,021	—	—	12,040
6/94	993	—	—	11,781
6/93	907	—	—	—
Annual Growth	6.4%	—	—	4.4%

Revenue History

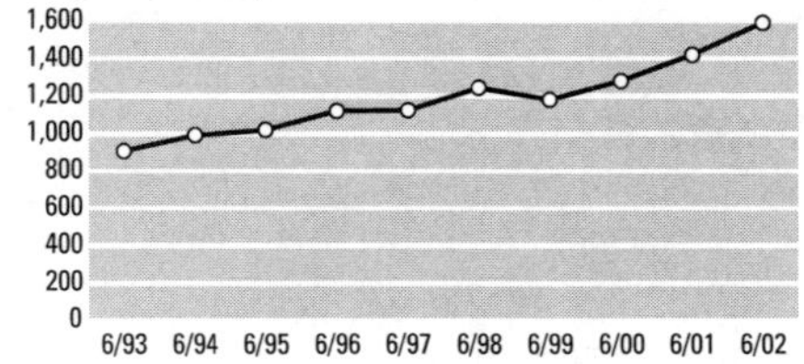

Vanguard Group

If you buy low and sell high, invest for the long term, don't panic, and generally disapprove of those whippersnappers at Fidelity, then you may end up in the Vanguard of the financial market. The Vanguard Group offers individual and institutional investors a line of highly sought-after mutual funds and brokerage services; it is the #2 fund manager after FMR (aka Fidelity), but is closing the gap, claiming more than $590 billion of assets under management. Vanguard's fund options include more than 100 stock, bond, mixed, and international offerings, as well as variable annuity portfolios; its Vanguard 500 Index Fund is one of the largest in the US.

The company is known as much for its puritanical thriftiness and conservative investing (it actively discourages short-term investing with redemption fees, defining "short-term" as three years) as for its line of index funds, which track the performance of such groups of stock as the S&P 500.

Unlike other funds, Vanguard is set up like a mutual insurance company. The funds (and by extension, their approximately 17 million investors) own the company, so fees are low to nonexistent; funds are operated on a tight budget so as not to eat into results. The company spends next to nothing on advertising, relying instead on strong returns and word-of-mouth.

And despite its no-broker, no-load background, Vanguard has developed cheap ways to dole out advice, especially through the use of toll-free numbers and the Internet and by quietly touting its online brokerage service.

HISTORY

A distant cousin of Daniel Boone, Walter Morgan knew a few things about pioneering. He was the first to offer a fund with a balance of stocks and bonds, serendipitously introduced early in 1929, months before the stock market collapsed. Morgan's balanced Wellington fund (named after Napoleon's vanquisher) emerged effectively unscathed.

John Bogle's senior thesis on mutual funds impressed fellow Princeton alum Morgan, who hired Bogle in 1951. Morgan retired in 1967 and picked Bogle to replace him. That year Bogle engineered a merger with old-school investment firm Thorndike, Doran, Paine and Lewis. After culture clashes and four years of shrinking assets, the Thorndike-dominated board fired Bogle, who appealed to the mutual funds and their separate board of directors. The fund directors decided to split up the funds and the advisory business.

Bogle named the fund company The Vanguard Group, after the flagship of Lord Nelson, another Napoleon foe. Vanguard worked like a cooperative; mutual fund shareholders owned the company, so all services were provided at cost. The Wellington Management Company remained Vanguard's distributor until 1977, when Bogle convinced Vanguard's board to drop the affiliation. Without Wellington as the intermediary, Vanguard sold its funds directly to consumers as no-load funds (without service charges). In 1976 the company launched the Vanguard Index 500, the first index fund. These measures attracted new investors in droves.

Vanguard rode the 1980s boom. Its Windsor fund grew so large the company closed it, launching Windsor II in 1985. Vanguard weathered the 1987 crash and began the 1990s as the US's #4 mutual fund company. The actively managed funds of FMR (better known as Fidelity), most notably its Magellan fund, led the market then. The retirement of legendary Magellan manager Peter Lynch and the fund's consequential underperformance spurred a rush to index funds. Vanguard moved up to #2.

Vanguard played against type in 1995 when it introduced the Vanguard Horizon Capital Growth stock fund, an aggressively managed fund designed to vie directly with Fidelity's funds.

In 1997 Vanguard added brokerage services and began selling its own and other companies' funds on the Internet to allow clients to consolidate their financial activities. In 1998 Bogle passed the chairmanship to CEO John Brennan, a soft-spoken technology wonk. Walter Morgan died that year at age 100.

Investors were ruffled when 70-year-old Bogle announced that corporate age limits would force him to leave the board of directors at the end of 1999. (Bogle retains an office at Vanguard headquarters, and remains popular on the speaker circuit.)

Despite Vanguard's stated commitment to the little guy, by late 2002 the company was forced to mitigate realities of the economy and started courting investors with bigger bankrolls; it also raised fees for some customers with smaller accounts.

EXECUTIVES

Chairman and CEO: John J. Brennan
Chief Investment Officer: George U. (Gus) Sauter
Managing Director, Legal Department, and General Counsel; Secretary, Vanguard Fiduciary Trust Company: R. Gregory Barton
Managing Director, Direct Investor Services: James H. Gately
Managing Director, Human Resources: Kathleen C. Gubanich
Managing Director, Institutional Investor Group: F. William McNabb III
Managing Director, Planning and Development Group: Michael S. Miller
Managing Director, Finance Group: Ralph K. Packard
Managing Director, IT: Mortimer J. Buckley

LOCATIONS

HQ: The Vanguard Group
100 Vanguard Blvd., Malvern, PA 19355
Phone: 610-648-6000 **Fax:** 610-669-6605
Web: www.vanguard.com

The Vanguard Group has offices in Malvern, Pennsylvania; Charlotte, North Carolina; and Scottsdale, Arizona; as well as in Brussels, London, Melbourne, and Tokyo.

COMPETITORS

Alliance Capital Management
American Century
AIG
AMVESCAP
Charles Schwab
FMR
Franklin Resources
Janus Capital
Legg Mason
MFS
Merrill Lynch
Putnam
T. Rowe Price
USAA

HISTORICAL FINANCIALS

Company Type: Private

Income Statement FYE: December 31

	ASSETS ($ mil.)	NET INCOME ($ mil.)	INCOME AS % OF ASSETS	EMPLOYEES
12/02	560,000	—	—	10,000
12/01	590,000	—	—	11,000
12/00	—	—	—	11,000
12/99	—	—	—	11,000
12/98	—	—	—	10,000
12/97	—	—	—	5,000
Annual Growth	(5.1%)	—	—	14.9%

Asset History

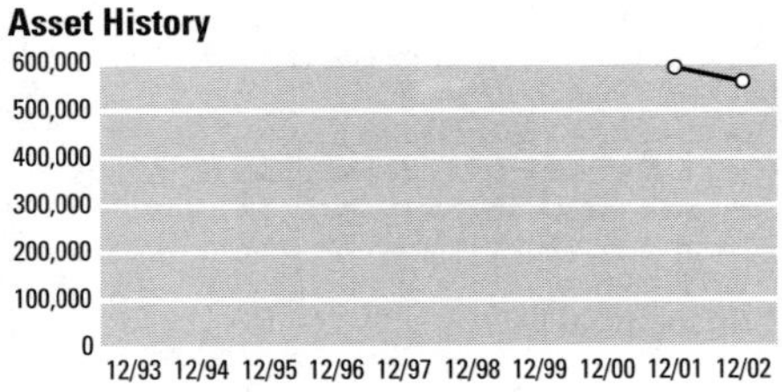

Variety Wholesalers

Variety is not only the spice of life — it's also a major purveyor of discount retail goods. With about 500 stores in 14 states from Louisiana to Delaware, Variety Wholesalers has survived even Wal-Mart's march through rural America. The company, which has aggressively bought other chains while closing poorly performing stores, tends to set up shop in small towns where the retail giants fear to tread. The company's retail outlets include Bargain Town, Maxway, Rose's, Super 10 (which prices all items at or below $10), Super Dollar, Super Saver, and Value-Mart. Variety Wholesalers was founded in 1932 by James Pope; the Pope family, including chairman and CEO John Pope, owns and leads the company.

EXECUTIVES

Chairman, President, and CEO: John W. Pope Sr.
Vice Chairman, SEVP, and CFO: Art Pope
EVP, Stores and Merchandising: Wilson Sawyer
Human Resources Manager: Frances Burger

LOCATIONS

HQ: Variety Wholesalers, Inc.
3401 Gresham Lake Rd., Raleigh, NC 27615
Phone: 919-876-6000 **Fax:** 919-790-9526

COMPETITORS

Big Lots
Bill's Dollar Stores
Dollar General
Dollar Tree
Family Dollar Stores
Fred's
Kmart
Target
Wal-Mart

HISTORICAL FINANCIALS

Company Type: Private

Income Statement FYE: December 31

	ESTIMATED REVENUE ($ mil.)	NET INCOME ($ mil.)	NET PROFIT MARGIN	EMPLOYEES
12/01	800	—	—	8,300
12/00	691	—	—	8,300
12/99	782	—	—	10,100
12/98	820	—	—	10,500
12/97	1,000	—	—	12,000
Annual Growth	(5.4%)	—	—	(8.8%)

Revenue History

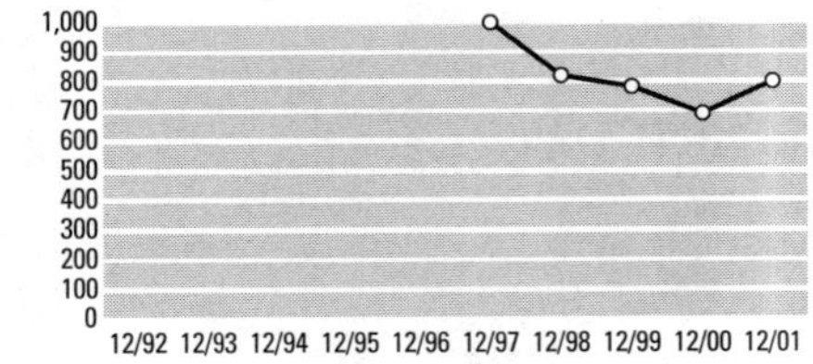

VarTec Telecom

Actors and comedians employed promoting 10-10 calling plans can thank VarTec Telecom, a pioneering provider of "dial-around" long-distance service. VarTec provides residential and business calling plans, as well as Internet access and 800-number service. The company was founded in 1989 by president Joe Mitchell and his wife, chief administrative officer Connie Mitchell, along with Ray Atkinson, president of international operations. Holding company Telephone Electronics Corp. owns a majority stake in VarTec, which acquired Dallas-based long-distance retailer Excel Communications in 2002. VarTec has dropped plans to merge with business telecom services reseller Lightyear Communications.

EXECUTIVES

Chairman and CEO: A. Joe Mitchell Jr.
COO; President, Consumer Markets: Ron Hughes
EVP and CFO: Kevin W. McAleer
EVP Legal and Regulatory Affairs and Chief Legal Officer: Michael Hoffman
Chief Administrative Officer; President, VarTec Properties: Connie Mitchell
President, International Operations Division: Ray Atkinson

LOCATIONS

HQ: VarTec Telecom, Inc.
1600 Viceroy Dr., Dallas, TX 75235
Phone: 214-424-1000 **Fax:** 214-424-1555
Web: www.vartec.com

VarTec Telecom has switching facilities in Atlanta; Chicago; Colorado Springs, Colorado; Dallas; Frankfurt; London; Los Angeles; New York; Orlando, Florida; Pittsburgh; and Seattle.

PRODUCTS/OPERATIONS

Selected Subsidiaries

eMeritus Communications, Inc. (integrated telecommunications services)
EurExce (integrated telecommunications, UK)
Excel Telecommunications (long-distance reseller)
VarTec Telecom Europe, Ltd. (telecommunications customer services, UK)

COMPETITORS

9278 Communications
AT&T
DigiTEC 2000
Matrix Telecom
McLeodUSA
Qwest
Sprint FON
Talk America
WorldCom

HISTORICAL FINANCIALS

Company Type: Private

Income Statement FYE: December 31

	REVENUE ($ mil.)	NET INCOME ($ mil.)	NET PROFIT MARGIN	EMPLOYEES
12/02	1,400	—	—	2,700
12/01	1,040	—	—	1,793
12/00	995	—	—	1,276
12/99	960	—	—	2,238
12/98	913	—	—	1,460
12/97	850	—	—	1,200
12/96	470	—	—	—
12/95	125	—	—	—
Annual Growth	41.2%	—	—	17.6%

Revenue History

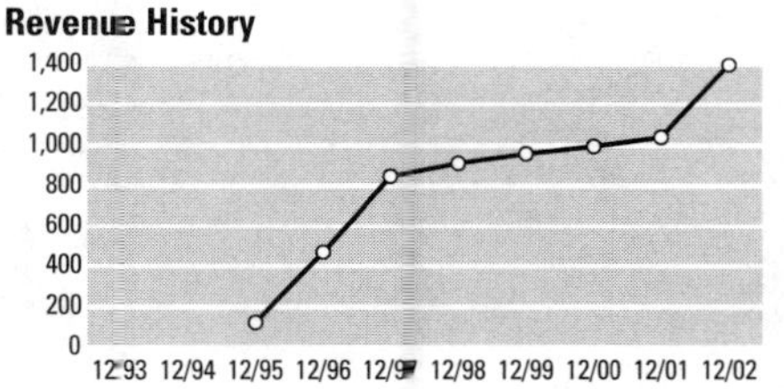

Vertis Inc.

Although it has changed its name, Vertis still hopes its advertising business will blossom. The company (formerly Big Flower Holdings) provides integrated marketing and advertising services to more than 3,000 clients. In 2002 the company unified its three operating units under the Vertis name. The company's services include advertising production, direct marketing, digital production, and media planning. Vertis operates the largest digital photography network dedicated to the ad industry and produces newspaper inserts such as color comics, TV magazines, and supplements. An investor group led by Thomas H. Lee Company and Evercore Partners owns Vertis.

In addition to its advertising services Vertis also provides digital services, online marketing, and strategic consulting, as well as direct mailing, response management, Internet integration, and database management.

Vertis has undergone significant restructuring in recent years. It began relying less and less on its traditional commercial printing business in the late 1990s as it expanded into areas of marketing and advertising. Later it consolidated its three primary divisions (all the better to create cross-selling opportunities), took itself private, moved its headquarters from New York City to Baltimore (headquarters of its TC Advertising division), and changed its name from Big Flower Holdings to Vertis. In 2002 the company consolidated all its operations (LTC Group, TC Advertising, and Webcraft) under the Vertis name.

EXECUTIVES

Chairman and CEO: Donald E. Roland, age 60, $966,325 pay
COO, Vertis North America: Herbert W. Moloney III, age 52, $710,661 pay
CFO: Dean D. Durbin, age 50, $592,576 pay
SVP and General Counsel: John V. Howard Jr., age 40, $408,513 pay
SVP Human Resources: Catherine S. Leggett, age 52, $408,513 pay
SVP Vertis Advertising Production Services: Tom Conti
Auditors: Deloitte & Touche LLP

LOCATIONS

HQ: 250 W. Pratt St., 18th Fl., Baltimore, MD 21201
Phone: 410-528-9800 **Fax:** 410-528-9287
Web: www.vertisinc.com

Vertis operates through more than 120 locations in the US and Europe.

PRODUCTS/OPERATIONS

Divisions

Retail and Newspaper Services
Direct Marketing Services
Ad Technology Services
Vertis Europe

COMPETITORS

ACG Holdings
Acxiom
ADVO
Applied Graphics
Experian
Harte-Hanks
Moore Corporation
Quebecor World
R. R. Donnelley
Schawk
Seven Worldwide
Valassis

HISTORICAL FINANCIALS

Company Type: Private

Income Statement FYE: December 31

	REVENUE ($ mil.)	NET INCOME ($ mil.)	NET PROFIT MARGIN	EMPLOYEES
12/02	1,675	(120)	—	8,700
12/01	1,851	(55)	—	9,000
12/00	1,986	(25)	—	10,000
12/99	1,800	—	—	10,000
12/98	1,740	—	—	10,000
12/97	1,377	—	—	8,500
12/96	1,202	—	—	6,410
12/95	532	—	—	4,000
12/94	565	—	—	3,200
12/93	555	—	—	—
Annual Growth	13.1%	—	—	13.3%

2002 Year-End Financials

Debt ratio: —
Return on equity: —
Cash ($ mil.): 6
Current ratio: 0.92
Long-term debt ($ mil.): 1,096

Net Income History

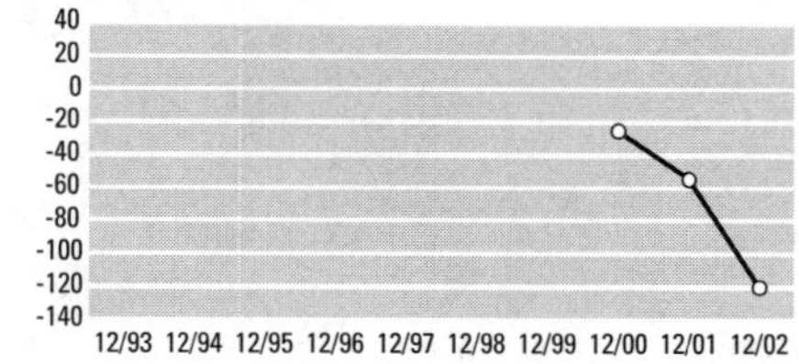

Viasystems Group, Inc.

Viasystems counts on electronics makers' desire to build their systems via contract manufacturing. The company is a contract manufacturer of printed circuit boards (PCBs), backpanel assemblies used to connect PCBs, wire harnesses, custom enclosures, and cable assemblies. While most sales are to telecom and networking customers, Viasystems also serves automotive, computer, and industrial manufacturers. Telecom equipment giant Lucent is a top customer. Chairman Thomas Hicks and his investment firm Hicks, Muse, Tate & Furst own 57% of the company, which has emerged from Chapter 11 bankruptcy a leaner organization.

Viasystems has used acquisitions — including units from Lucent and Marconi — to expand its international operations. The company has also sold businesses in order to streamline operations.

EXECUTIVES

CEO: David M. Sindelar, age 45
President and COO: Timothy L. (Tim) Conlon, age 51
President, Asia/Pacific: Steven S. L. Tang, age 47
SVP and CFO: Joseph S. Catanzaro, age 50
SVP, Sales and Marketing: John McAlister
SVP, Supply Chain Management: Jerry Sax
VP and CIO: David Egbert
VP, Human Resources: Bailey Hurley
Auditors: PricewaterhouseCoopers LLP

LOCATIONS

HQ: 101 S. Hanley Rd., Ste. 400, St. Louis, MO 63105
Phone: 314-727-2087 **Fax:** 314-746-2233
Web: www.viasystems.com

Viasystems Group has facilities in Canada, China, Hong Kong, Mexico, the Netherlands, the UK, and the US.

PRODUCTS/OPERATIONS

Services

After-sales support (including repair and upgrades)
Design and prototyping
Full system assembly
Packaging and distribution
Supply chain management
Systems assembly and test

Products

Backpanel assemblies
Cable assemblies
Custom enclosures
Multilayer printed circuit boards
Single-layer printed circuit boards
Wire harnesses

COMPETITORS

Benchmark Electronics	Photocircuits
Celestica	Plexus
DDi Corp.	Sanmina-SCI
Flextronics	SMTC
Manufacturers' Services	Solectron
Merix	SYNNEX

HISTORICAL FINANCIALS

Company Type: Private

Income Statement FYE: December 31

	REVENUE ($ mil.)	NET INCOME ($ mil.)	NET PROFIT MARGIN	EMPLOYEES
12/02	900	—	—	18,000
12/01	1,207	—	—	18,800
12/00	1,605	—	—	24,700
12/99	1,102	—	—	18,500
12/98	1,032	—	—	19,350
12/97	900	—	—	7,200
12/96	872	—	—	7,100
12/95	728	—	—	—
12/94	565	—	—	—
Annual Growth	6.0%	—	—	16.8%

Revenue History

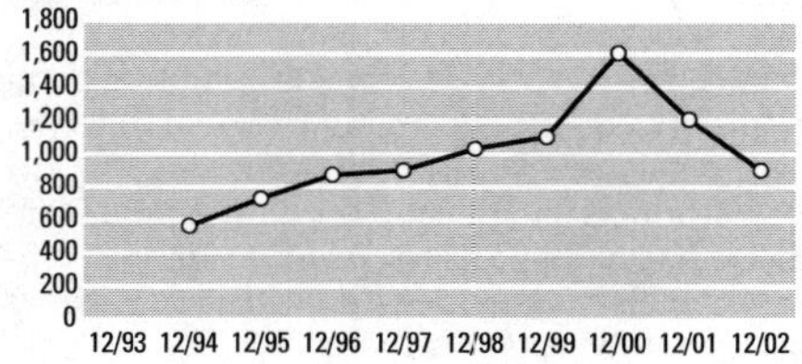

ViewSonic Corporation

ViewSonic has a display for every occasion. The company makes CRT and LCD computer displays, including the Professional Series for high-end computer-aided design, desktop publishing, and graphic design; the Graphics and E2 lines for homes and small offices; and the A Series for replacing monitors included in bundled systems. ViewSonic also offers plasma TVs, high-definition televisions (HDTV), LCD projectors, handheld computers, and tablet PCs. CEO James Chu, who founded ViewSonic in 1987, is the company's majority owner. ViewSonic has also received financing from the venture capital arm of chip giant Intel, which has partnered with the company to develop inexpensive chipsets for high-definition TV.

EXECUTIVES

Chairman and CEO: James Chu
CFO: James Morlan
SVP; Managing Director, ViewSonic Europe: Christopher Franey
SVP, Advanced Technology Group: Marc McConnaughey
VP and General Counsel: Robert Ranucci
VP, Information Services: Robert Lee Moon
VP, Marketing: Tony Dowzall
VP, US Sales: Brian Igoe

LOCATIONS

HQ: 381 Brea Canyon Rd., Walnut, CA 91789
Phone: 909-444-8888 **Fax:** 909-468-1202
Web: www.viewsonic.com

ViewSonic has offices in Australia, Canada, China, Denmark, Finland, France, Germany, Italy, Japan, the Netherlands, Norway, Russia, Singapore, Spain, Sweden, Taiwan, the UK, and the US.

PRODUCTS/OPERATIONS

Selected Products

LCD projectors
Monitors (CRT, LCD)
Personal digital assistants
Tablet PCs
Televisions (high-definition, plasma)

COMPETITORS

Acer	Mitsubishi Corporation
ADI Systems	NEC
Apple Computer	Palm
Dell	Princeton Graphic Systems
Fujitsu	Samsung Electronics
Gateway	Sharp
Handspring	Sony
Hewlett-Packard	
InFocus	

HISTORICAL FINANCIALS

Company Type: Private

Income Statement FYE: December 31

	REVENUE ($ mil.)	NET INCOME ($ mil.)	NET PROFIT MARGIN	EMPLOYEES
12/02	1,000	—	—	600
12/01	1,000	—	—	600
12/00	1,371	—	—	800
12/99	1,040	—	—	700
12/98	941	—	—	700
12/97	826	—	—	675
12/96	510	—	—	600
12/95	350	—	—	550
12/94	200	—	—	120
12/93	100	—	—	80
Annual Growth	29.2%	—	—	25.1%

Revenue History

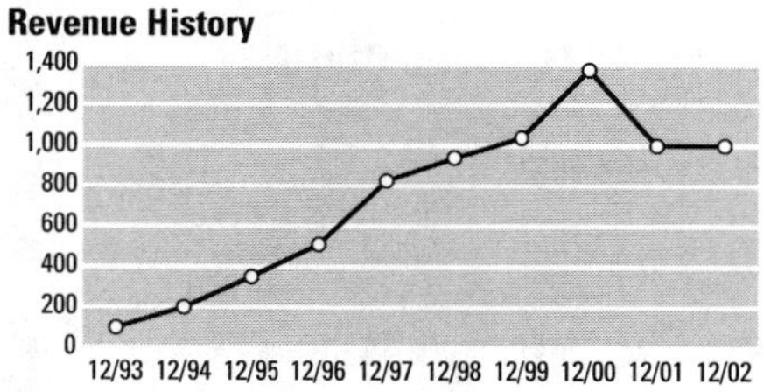

Vinson & Elkins

Even the law firms are big in Texas. Vinson & Elkins has more than 860 attorneys in five US offices (three in Texas) and four international offices. The firm is a specialist in international energy law and litigation. It has one of the largest health care practices in the US as well. In addition, Vinson & Elkins operates in almost all areas of civil law, including antitrust, intellectual property, international, and securities law. It serves a broad range of government, corporate, and individual clients. Vinson & Elkins, which James Elkins and William Vinson founded in Houston in 1917, has garnered some unwanted attention as outside law firm for another Houston institution — Enron.

EXECUTIVES

Managing Partner: Joseph C. (Joe) Dilg
CFO: John Spire
Director Attorney Employment: Patty Calabrese
Legal Media Strategist: Mark Curriden
Media Relations Specialist: Melissa Carroll

LOCATIONS

HQ: Vinson & Elkins L.L.P.
2300 1st City Tower, 1001 Fannin,
Houston, TX 77002
Phone: 713-758-2222 **Fax:** 713-758-2346
Web: www.velaw.com

Vinson & Elkins has US offices in Austin, Dallas, and Houston, Texas; New York City; and Washington, DC. The firm also has offices in Beijing, London, Moscow, and Singapore.

PRODUCTS/OPERATIONS

Selected Practice Areas

Antitrust litigation and counseling
Business and finance
Corporate securities
Energy
Government and international procurement
Health industry practice and experience
Insurance litigation
Intellectual property and technical litigation
International trade
Internet/e-commerce
Labor and employment law
Litigation
Public finance
Real estate
Securities and shareholders litigation
Tax
Telecommunications
White-collar criminal defense

COMPETITORS

Akin, Gump	Fulbright & Jaworski
Andrews & Kurth	Jenkens & Gilchrist
Baker Botts	Skadden, Arps
Bracewell & Patterson	

HISTORICAL FINANCIALS

Company Type: Partnership

Income Statement FYE: December 31

	REVENUE ($ mil.)	NET INCOME ($ mil.)	NET PROFIT MARGIN	EMPLOYEES
12/02	457	—	—	—
12/01	455	—	—	—
12/00	387	—	—	2,000
12/99	328	—	—	2,000
12/98	282	—	—	1,900
12/97	255	—	—	1,800
12/96	232	—	—	—
12/95	217	—	—	—
12/94	211	—	—	—
12/93	203	—	—	—
Annual Growth	9.5%	—	—	3.6%

Revenue History

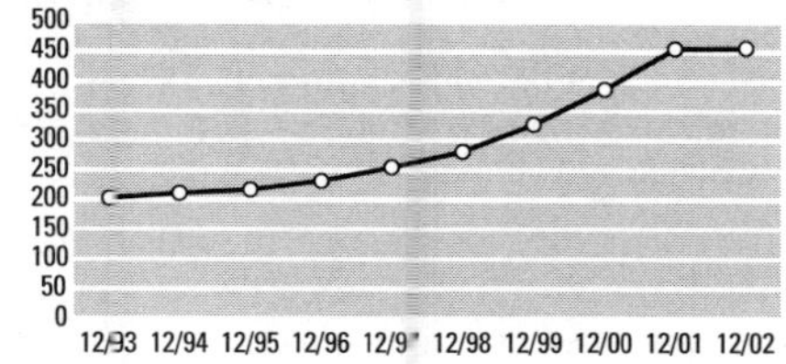

Visa International

Paper or plastic? Visa International hopes you choose the latter. Visa operates the world's largest consumer payment system (ahead of MasterCard and American Express) with more than 1 billion credit and other payment cards in circulation. The company is owned by 21,000 financial institutions, each of which issues and markets its own Visa products. They all participate in the VisaNet payment system, which provides authorization, transaction processing, and settlement services for purchases from 24 million merchants worldwide. In addition to credit cards, Visa also provides its customers with debit cards, Internet payment systems, value-storing smart cards, and traveler's checks.

Visa International operates through six autonomous regional organizations: Asia/Pacific; Canada; Central & Eastern Europe, Middle East & Africa (CEMEA); European Union (EU); Latin America & Caribbean; and the US. It also owns Inovant, an information technology and processing subsidiary.

Visa is accelerating its push to introduce chip cards over magnetic stripe technology, and it is maneuvering its Open Platform technology into position against the MasterCard-supported Mondex platform and Microsoft's Smart Card for Windows. Winner takes all in this contest, with losers having to adapt to new systems or face a shrinking market share.

Both Visa U.S.A. and MasterCard International were recently in some 4 million retailers' sights. Led by retail giant Wal-Mart, the merchants claimed Visa and MasterCard violated antitrust laws and attempted to monopolize a legally defined market for debit cards. The plaintiffs sought up to $200 billion in damages in their class-action suit. Just as the 1996 lawsuit was to go to trial in early 2003, Visa settled, agreeing to pay $2 billion (twice that of co-defendant MasterCard) over the next decade. Both agreed to pay $25 million immediately, as well as reduce the fee merchants pay for signature-based debit cards. At the time of settlement, some 129 million consumers carried the Visa debit card.

HISTORY

Although the first charge card was issued by Western Union in 1914, it wasn't until 1958 that Bank of America (BofA) issued its BankAmericard, which combined the convenience of a charge account with credit privileges. When BofA extended its customer base outside California, the interchange system controlling payments began to falter because of design problems and fraud.

In 1968 Dee Hock, manager of the BankAmericard operations of the National Bank of Commerce in Seattle, convinced member banks that a more reliable system was needed. Two years later National BankAmericard Inc. (NBI) was created as an independent corporation (owned by 243 banks) to buy the BankAmericard system from BofA.

With its initial ad slogan, "Think of it as Money," the Hock-led NBI developed BankAmericard into a widely used form of payment in the US. A multinational corporation, IBANCO, was formed in 1974 to carry the operations into other countries. People outside the US resisted BankAmericard's nominal association with BofA, and in 1977 Hock changed the card's name to Visa. NBI became Visa USA, and IBANCO became Visa International.

By 1980 Visa had debuted debit cards, begun issuing traveler's checks, and created an electromagnetic point-of-sale authorization system. Visa developed a global network of ATMs in 1983; it was expanded in 1987 by the purchase of a 33% stake in the Plus System of ATMs, then the US's second-largest system. Hock retired in 1984 with the company well on its way to realizing his vision of a universal payment system.

The company built the Visa brand image with aggressive advertising, such as sponsorship of the 1988 and 1992 Olympics, and by co-branding (issuing cards through other organizations with strong brand names, such as Blockbuster and Ford).

In 1994 Visa teamed up with Microsoft and others to develop home banking services and software. Visa Cash was introduced during the 1996 Olympics. Visa pushed its debit cards in 1996 and 1997 with humorous ads featuring presidential also-ran Bob Dole and showbiz success story Daffy Duck.

Visa expanded its smart card infrastructure in 1997. It published, with MasterCard, encryption and security software for online transactions. The gloves came off the next year as the companies vied to convince the world to rally around their respective e-purse technology standards.

During the 1990s, Visa fought American Express' attempts to introduce a bank credit card of its own by forbidding Visa members in the US from issuing the product; the Justice Department responded with an antitrust suit against Visa and MasterCard. The case went to trial in 2000 with the government claiming that Visa and MasterCard stifle competition and enjoy an exclusive cross-ownership structure.

Also that year, the company made a deal with Gemplus, the French smart card company, to enable payments over wireless networks; Visa also inked a billing deal with wireless technology company Aether Systems, as well as e-commerce agreements with telecommunications companies Nokia and Ericsson.

The company continued its technology push in 2000 with a deal with Financial Services Technology Consortium to test biometrics — the use of fingerprints, irises, and voice recognition to identify cardholders. The company also launched a pre-paid card, Visa Buxx, targeted at teenagers.

That year the European Union launched an investigation into the firm's transaction fees, alleging that the fees could restrict competition. The following year Visa International agreed to drop its fee to 0.7% of the transaction value over five years.

In 2001 a federal judge ordered Visa and MasterCard to allow member banks to issue rival credit cards, but the card firms are appealing.

EXECUTIVES

President and CEO: Malcolm Williamson, age 63
CFO: Ken Sommer
EVP, Human Resources: Elizabeth Rounds
EVP and General Counsel: Guy Rounsaville
EVP, Global Marketing Partnerships and Sponsorships: Tom Shepard
SVP, Public Policy: Mark MacCarthy
President, Inovant: John Partridge
President and CEO, Visa Asia/Pacific: Rupert G. Keeley
President, Visa Canada: Derek A. Fry
President, Visa Central and Eastern Europe, Middle East, and Africa Region: Anne L. Cobb
President, Visa European Union (EU): Johannes I. (Hans) van der Velde
President, Visa Latin America and Caribbean: Eduardo Eraña
President and CEO, Visa U.S.A.: Carl F. Pascarella, age 58
EVP and COO, Visa U.S.A.: William H. (Bill) Ott Jr.
EVP and CFO, Visa U.S.A.: Victor W. Dahir
EVP, Brand Marketing, Visa U.S.A.: Rebecca Saeger, age 47
EVP, Corporate Relations, VISA U.S.A.: Douglas (Doug) Michelman
EVP, General Counsel, and Secretary, Visa U.S.A.: Paul A. Allen
EVP, Human Resources, Visa U.S.A.: Jan van der Voort
EVP, Operations and Risk Management, Visa U.S.A.: Steve Ruwe
EVP, Product Management, Visa U.S.A.: Anthony N. (Tony) McEwen
EVP, Sales and Integrated Solutions, Visa U.S.A.: John T. Gardner Jr.
EVP, Systems Group and CTO, Visa U.S.A.: Scott Thompson
VP, Public Affairs, Visa U.S.A.: Kelly Presta

LOCATIONS

HQ: 900 Metro Center Blvd., Foster City, CA 94404
Phone: 650-432-3200 **Fax:** 650-432-7436
Web: www.visa.com

Visa cards are accepted at 24 million locations in more than 130 countries.

PRODUCTS/OPERATIONS

Products and Services

ATMs (almost 650,000 locations)
Electron (debit card outside of US)
Interlink (debit card)
smartVisa card (computer-chip-embedded card that is accepted worldwide)
Visa Business card (for small businesses and professionals)
Visa Cash (smart cards)
Visa Classic card (credit/debit card issued by Visa's 21,000 member banks)
Visa Corporate card (for travel and entertainment expenses)
Visa Debit card (accesses bank account for immediate settlement of payments)
Visa Gold card (higher spending limits)
VisaNet (electronic transaction processing network)
Visa Purchasing card (for corporate purchases)
Visa Travelers Cheques
Visa TravelMoney (prepaid card in any currency)

COMPETITORS

American Express
Citigroup
MasterCard
Morgan Stanley

HISTORICAL FINANCIALS

Company Type: Private

Income Statement FYE: September 30

	ESTIMATED REVENUE ($ mil.)	NET INCOME ($ mil.)	NET PROFIT MARGIN	EMPLOYEES
9/02	4,800	—	—	6,000
9/01	3,600	—	—	6,000
9/00	3,000	—	—	5,000
9/99	2,800	—	—	5,000
9/98	2,550	—	—	5,000
9/97	2,050	—	—	5,000
9/96	1,650	—	—	4,800
9/95	1,330	—	—	4,000
9/94	1,260	—	—	3,500
9/93	1,040	—	—	3,000
Annual Growth	18.5%	—	—	8.0%

Revenue History

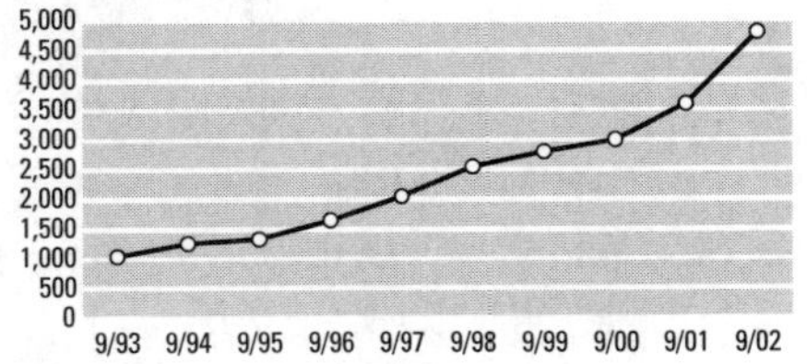

Vought Aircraft Industries, Inc.

The skies are fraught with Vought; Vought Aircraft Industries is one of the world's largest aerostructures subcontractors. Products include fuselage subassemblies (doors and fuselage panels), nacelles, thrust reversers, empennage structures, wings, and other components for military and commercial aircraft. The company's primary customers include Boeing, Gulfstream Aerospace, Lockheed Martin, and Northrop Grumman. Vought also does subcontract work for military cargo planes (C-17), bombers (B-2), and fighters (F-14 and F/A-18). The Carlyle Group owns about 90% of Vought, which also provides spare parts, maintenance, repair, and overhaul services.

EXECUTIVES

President and CEO: Tom Risley
EVP and CFO: William J. (Bill) McMillan
VP and General Counsel: W. Bruce White Jr.
VP, Boeing Commercial Programs: Stephen A. (Steve) Davis
VP, Business Management: Randy Smith
VP, Controller, and Treasurer: Cletus C. Glasener Jr.
VP, Human Resources, Administration, and Information Services: Judith W. (Judy) Northup

LOCATIONS

HQ: 9314 W. Jefferson Blvd., Dallas, TX 75211
Phone: 972-946-2011 **Fax:** 972-946-3465
Web: www.voughtaircraft.com

Vought Aircraft Industries has facilities in Hawthorne, California; Stuart, Florida; Milledgeville, Georgia; and Dallas.

PRODUCTS/OPERATIONS

Selected Products

Doors
Empennage and flight control surfaces
Fuselage panels
Nacelles
Wings

Selected Commercial Programs

Boeing 737
Boeing 747
Boeing 757
Boeing 767
Boeing 777
Gulfstream IV
Gulfstream V
Hawker 800

Selected Military and NASA Programs

B-2
C-17 Globemaster III
E-2C Hawkeye
E-8C/JSTARS
EA-6B Prowler
F-14 Tomcat/Super Tomcat
F/A-18E/F Super Hornet
Global Hawk
P-3C Orion
S-3A/B Viking
T-38 Talon
V-22 Osprey

COMPETITORS

CPI Aerostructures
Goodrich
LMI Aerospace
NORDAM
TransTechnology

HISTORICAL FINANCIALS

Company Type: Private

Income Statement FYE: December 31

	REVENUE ($ mil.)	NET INCOME ($ mil.)	NET PROFIT MARGIN	EMPLOYEES
12/02	1,200	—	—	5,245
12/01	1,400	—	—	5,000
12/00	1,000	—	—	5,000
Annual Growth	9.5%	—	—	2.4%

Revenue History

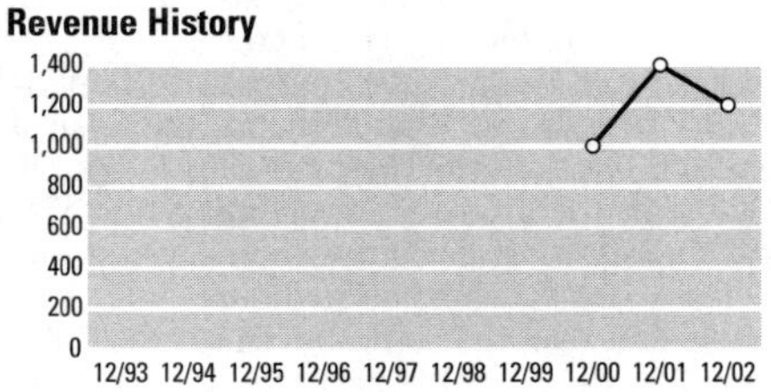

VT Inc.

VT is in pursuit of the pole-position as one of the top three US car dealers. The company operates more than 30 dealerships in some 10 states, primarily Texas and Missouri; it sells more than 120,000 new cars per year. It offers nearly 20 brands of new and used cars (and RVs) made by General Motors, Ford, Honda, Isuzu, and Nissan, among others. VT also engages in fleet sales and receives a significant portion of its revenue from back-shop operations such as parts and service and body shop sales. Founder and co-CEO Cecil Van Tuyl began his automotive empire in 1955. He owns the company with son and co-CEO Larry Van Tuyl.

EXECUTIVES

President and Co-CEO: Cecil Van Tuyl
Co-CEO: Larry Van Tuyl
VP Personnel: John A. Morford
Secretary and Treasurer: Robert J. Holcomb

LOCATIONS

HQ: 8500 Shawnee Mission Pkwy., Ste. 200, Shawnee Mission, KS 66202
Phone: 913-895-0200 **Fax:** 913-789-1039
Web: www.vanenterprises.com

VT has dealerships in Arizona, Florida, Illinois, Indiana, Kansas, Missouri, Nebraska, New Mexico, and Texas.

COMPETITORS

Asbury Automotive
AutoNation
CarMax
Hendrick Automotive
Jordan Automotive
United Auto Group

HISTORICAL FINANCIALS

Company Type: Private

Income Statement FYE: December 31

	REVENUE ($ mil.)	NET INCOME ($ mil.)	NET PROFIT MARGIN	EMPLOYEES
12/01	5,299	—	—	7,000
12/00	4,300	—	—	6,000
12/99	3,600	—	—	5,805
12/98	2,587	—	—	5,000
12/97	2,423	—	—	5,000
12/96	2,075	—	—	4,300
12/95	1,755	—	—	3,950
12/94	1,681	—	—	3,874
12/93	1,356	—	—	3,682
12/92	1,088	—	—	2,500
Annual Growth	19.2%	—	—	12.1%

Revenue History

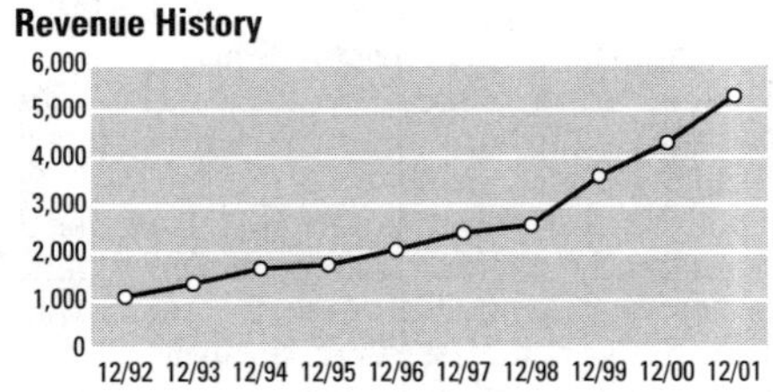

Vulcan Inc.

Even with all his Vulcan logic, could Spock invest like *this?* Brainy billionaire Paul Allen organizes his business and charitable ventures under Vulcan (formerly Vulcan Northwest). Vulcan includes Allen's slim stake in the industry-defining juggernaut Microsoft, as well as holdings in dozens of companies providing computer, technology, multimedia, and communications products and services. Vulcan holds stakes in some six charitable organizations. Allen also owns professional sports teams like the

NBA's Portland Trail Blazers and the NFL's Seattle Seahawks.

Vulcan's charities support the arts, medical research, land conservation, and other causes. Allen, who co-founded Microsoft with Bill Gates, promotes a "wired world" vision, in which everyone is united through interconnecting communications, entertainment, and information systems. His Vulcan Ventures finds investment opportunities. CEO Jody Patton, Allen's sister, oversees both his business and charitable ventures. He has also paid for a sponsorship of the OneWorld Challenge yachting team that will compete in the famous America's Cup race in 2003.

Many of Allen's investments in the "wired world" took a beating with the stock market downturn. He even saw his own personal wealth take a dip, but that hasn't stopped him from looking for ways to wring goodness out of technological advances. Among his latest projects is the Final Encyclopedia. Straight out of a sci-fi novel, the project is looking to put together the ultimate reference source in a form accessible to everyone.

HISTORY

Paul Allen and Bill Gates first worked together on computer projects as schoolmates in Seattle. They developed a program to determine traffic patterns and launched Traf-O-Data, an operation that failed because the state provided the information for free. When Allen saw an article on the MITS Altair 8800 minicomputer in 1975, the two realized it needed a simplified programming language to make it useful. They offered MITS a modified version of BASIC they had written for Traf-O-Data. The company set them up in an office in Albuquerque, New Mexico. They then began their biggest collaboration of all: Microsoft. While Gates concentrated on business, Allen focused on technical issues.

They moved to Bellevue, a Seattle suburb, in 1979. The next year IBM asked them to create a programming language for a PC project. Allen bought Q-DOS (quick and dirty operating system) from Seattle Computer; the pair tweaked it and renamed it MS-DOS. Allen and Gates made a key decision to structure their contract with IBM to allow clones. They also helped design many aspects of the original IBM PC.

Allen developed Hodgkin's disease in 1982. Facing his own mortality, he ended his daily involvement in Microsoft (keeping a chunk of the company and a board seat) and began to play more (traveling and playing the electric guitar). With his cancer in remission in 1985, Allen founded multimedia software company Asymetrix. The next year he set up Vulcan to hold his diversified interests and Vulcan Ventures. He also began helping startups, indulging his interests (buying the NBA's Portland Trail Blazers in 1988 and donating some $60 million to build a museum honoring his musical idol, Jimi Hendrix, and other Pacific Northwest artists). He has also funded Seattle-area civic improvements.

In 1990 Allen hired William Savoy to help organize his finances; Savoy later became president of Vulcan Ventures. Seeing a need for more R&D in the US, Allen in 1992 started Interval Research. He also invested in America Online (sold 1994). In 1993 Allen bought 80% of Ticketmaster (sold 1997), and in 1995 he invested in DreamWorks SKG, the multimedia company of Steven Spielberg, Jeffrey Katzenberg, and David Geffen.

Allen made a rare buy outside the entertainment and high-tech worlds through a 1996 investment in power turbine maker Capstone Turbine. To prevent the Seattle Seahawks from moving to California, Allen bought the team in 1997 and made plans for a new stadium. He consolidated his management operations under Vulcan and dissolved Paul Allen Group (founded 1994), keeping Vulcan Ventures.

Allen moved into cable in 1998 and 1999; his Charter Communications eventually became the #4 US cable firm. In 1999 several Allen investments (Charter Communications, Vulcan Ventures, RCN, High Speed Access, and Go2Net) joined to form wired-world venture Broadband Partners.

In 2000 it was nearly impossible to ignore Allen's influence on Seattle as several major projects took shape or were completed, including the new Seahawks' arena, the rock 'n' roll museum, and the renovation of a 90-year-old train station as part of a complex that will include Vulcan's new headquarters. That year he provided a $100 million infusion to struggling Oxygen Media. In 2001 Vulcan Ventures bought sports games Web site operator Small World Media to boost its sports holdings.

Vulcan is invested in RCN, a provider of high-speed internet services, which sold Non-Strategic New Jersey Cable Systems in 2003. Vulcan also has a stake in Drugstore.com, which partnered with AC Lens (contact lenses), FTD, 1-800-Wheelchair.com and Comexia (a global delivery company) to increase business worldwide.

EXECUTIVES

Chairman: Paul G. Allen, age 50
CEO: Jody Patton
CFO: Joseph Franzi
President, Vulcan; President, Vulcan Ventures: William D. Savoy, age 38
VP and General Counsel: Richard Leigh
VP Art, Design, and Construction: John H. Thomas
VP Corporate Communications: Steven C. Crosby
VP, Corporate Leadership: Denise Wolf
VP Finance: Buster Brown
VP Information Management Services: Chris Purcell
VP Investment Management: Nathan Troutman
VP Media Development: Richard E. Hutton
VP Real Estate: Ada M. Healey

LOCATIONS

HQ: 505 5th Ave. South, Ste. 900, Seattle, WA 98104
Phone: 206-342-2000 **Fax:** 206-342-3000
Web: www.vulcan.com

PRODUCTS/OPERATIONS

Selected Holdings

800.com (online consumer electronics retailer)
Alventive (Internet application services)
Charter Communications (cable-TV system)
Click2learn, Inc. (multimedia development software)
Colorado Microdisplay (display technologies)
Command Audio (audio-on-demand service)
CyberSource (ecommerce transaction services)
Dick's Clothing & Sporting Goods (online retailer)
Digeo Broadband Inc. (broadband services)
DreamWorks SKG (entertainment company)
Drugstore.com (online retailer)
e-steel (Internet marketplace)
eStyle, Inc. (online retailer)
Fantasma Networks, Inc. (wireless services)
HealthAnswers, Inc. (health care communications)
High Speed Access Corp. (digital-subscriber-line provider)
IFILM (film industry online content provider)
imandi.com (online marketplace)
Instantiations, Inc. (Java-based software developer)
iVAST (broadband content provider)
Kestrel Solutions (optical fiber networking)
Metricom, Inc. (wireless data-transmission products)
Microsoft Corporation
myplay, inc. (digital music services)
NETSchools Corp. (educational technology equipment and services)
Oxygen Media (Internet and television content provider)
Paraform Inc. (3D computer graphics provider)
Portland Trail Blazers (professional basketball team)
RCN Corporation (broadband fiber-optic networks)
Replay TV, Inc. (television programming technology provider)
Sandbox.com (online sports and entertainment content provider)
ScienceMedia (science and health online products)
Seattle Seahawks (professional football team)
Sharewave Inc. (digital wireless technology)
Small World (online fantasy sports)
The Sporting News (print and online sports magazine)
Stamps.com (online postage retailer)
Telescan, Inc. (online investor information)
TiVo (television programming technology provider)
Transmeta (microprocessors)
Triscend Corporation (configurable system-on-chip devices)
USA Networks (broadcasting and other media, retail, and Internet services)
Versata, Inc. (business software)
Vulcan Ventures, Inc. (investments)
Wavtrace (wireless technology)

COMPETITORS

Accel Partners
Austin Ventures
Benchmark Capital
Boston Ventures
Draper Fisher Jurvetson
Flatiron Partners
Harris & Harris
Hummer Winblad
Institutional Venture Partners
Kleiner Perkins
Matrix Partners
Mayfield Fund
Menlo Ventures
Microsoft
SOFTBANK
Sutter Hill
Trinity Ventures
US Venture Partners
Venrock Associates
Veronis Suhler Stevenson

The Wackenhut Corporation

Wackenhut battles the perils of modern life by providing a variety of security services. The company's offerings include armed guards, background investigations, consulting, and security for airports, nuclear power plants, and US embassies. Wackenhut's security services include armed guards, security consulting and program development, background investigations, fire and rescue services, and specialized security for airports, nuclear power plants, and US embassies. The company is a subisidiary of Group 4 Falck, the world's #2 security company (after Securitas).

Wackenhut was acquired by Denmark's Group 4 Falck in 2002. In the deal, Group 4 Falck also gained control of Wackenut's 57% stake in Wackenhut Corrections (now named The GEO Group). However, in 2003 WCC bought back the shares that Group 4 Falck gained control over, severing its ties to both the Wackenhut and Group 4 Falck families.

Through its Wackenhut Services subsidiary, the company provides security services to the US government. Excluding its government service operations, the company has reorganized its US operations into three divisions: commercial, nuclear, and consulting and investigation.

EXECUTIVES

CEO: Gary A. Sanders, age 50
CEO, Wackenhut Services: James L. (Jim) Long, age 54
President, Consulting and Investigations Division: William T. Hill, age 63
President, Nuclear Division: Richard A. (Rich) Michau, age 52
SVP, Commerical Division: Drew Levine, age 41
CIO: Brian McCabe
Auditors: KPMG C. Jespersen; PricewaterhouseCoopers

LOCATIONS

HQ: 4200 Wackenhut Dr., Palm Beach Gardens, FL 33140
Phone: 561-622-5656 **Fax:** 561-627-2041
Web: www.wackenhut.com

PRODUCTS/OPERATIONS

Selected Subsidiaries

American Guard and Alert, Inc.
Wackenhut Airline Services, Inc.
Wackenhut Educational Services, Inc.
Wackenhut Resources, Inc. (Oasis)
Wackenhut Services, Incorporated

COMPETITORS

Command Security
Guardsmark
Securicor
Securitas

HISTORICAL FINANCIALS

Company Type: Private

Income Statement FYE: Sunday nearest December 31

	REVENUE ($ mil.)	NET INCOME ($ mil.)	NET PROFIT MARGIN	EMPLOYEES
12/02	—	—	—	40,000
12/01	2,809	—	—	57,000
12/00	2,505	—	—	65,000
12/99	2,152	—	—	76,000
12/98	1,755	—	—	70,000
12/97	1,127	—	—	56,000
12/96	906	—	—	51,000
12/95	797	—	—	39,000
12/94	748	—	—	37,000
12/93	664	—	—	33,000
Annual Growth	19.8%	—	—	2.2%

Revenue History

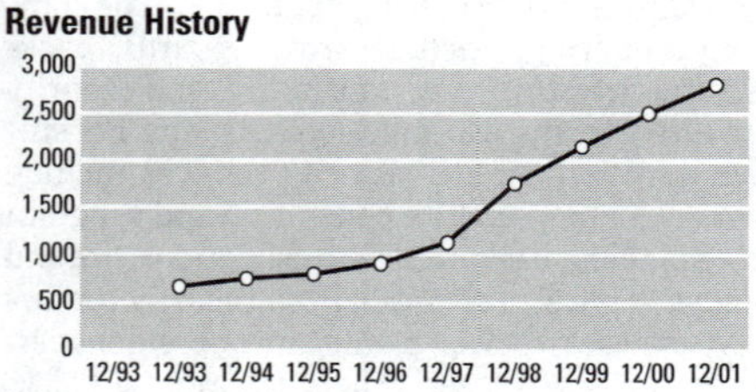

Wakefern Food Corporation

Started by seven men who each invested $1,000, Wakefern Food has grown into the largest retailer-owned supermarket cooperative in the US. The co-op is owned by 38 independent grocers who operate about 190 ShopRite supermarkets in Connecticut, Delaware, New Jersey (where it is a leading chain), New York, and Pennsylvania. More than half of ShopRite stores offer pharmacies. In addition to name-brand and private-label products (ShopRite, Chef's Express, Reddington Farms), Wakefern supports its members with advertising, merchandising, insurance, and other services. Wakefern's ShopRite Supermarkets subsidiary acquired the assets of Florida-based Big V Supermarkets, which filed for bankruptcy in 2000.

Wakefern Food is remodeling, upgrading technology, and expanding product selection at the newly acquired Big V stores.

The company provides members and other customers with more than 20,000 name-brand items, including groceries, dairy and meat products, produce, frozen foods, and general merchandise. It also sells more than 3,000 items under the ShopRite label.

All members are given one vote in the co-op, regardless of size.

HISTORY

Wakefern Food was founded in 1946 by seven New York- and New Jersey-based grocers: Louis Weiss, Sam and Al Aidekman, Abe Kesselman, Dave Fern, Sam Garb, and Albert Goldberg (the company's name is made up of the letters of the first five of those founders). Like many cooperatives, the association sought to lower costs by increasing its buying power as a group.

They each put in $1,000 and began operating a 5,000-sq.-ft. warehouse, often putting in double time to keep both their stores and the warehouse running. The shopkeepers' collective buying power proved valuable, enabling the grocers to stock many items at the same prices as their larger competitors.

In 1951 Wakefern members began pooling their resources to buy advertising space. A common store name — ShopRite — was chosen, and each week co-op members met to decide which items would be sale priced. Within a year, membership had grown to over 50. Expansion became a priority, and in the mid-1950s co-op members united in small groups to take over failed supermarkets. One such group, called the Supermarkets Operating Co. (SOC), was formed in 1956. Within 10 years it had acquired a number of failed stores, remodeled them, and given them the ShopRite name.

During the late 1950s sales at ShopRite stores slumped after Wakefern decided to buck the supermarket trend of offering trading stamps (which could then be exchanged for gifts), figuring that offering the stamps would ultimately lead to higher food prices. The move initially drove away customers, but Wakefern cut grocery prices across the board and sales returned. The company also embraced another supermarket trend: stocking stores with nonfood items.

The co-op was severely shaken in 1966 when SOC merged with General Supermarkets, a similar small group within Wakefern, becoming Supermarkets General Corp. (SGC). SGC was a powerful entity, with 71 supermarkets, 10 drugstores, six gas stations, a wholesale bakery, and a discount department store. Many Wakefern members opposed the merger and attempted to block the action with a court order. By 1968 SGC had beefed up its operations to include department store chains as well as its grocery stores. In a move that threatened to break Wakefern, SGC broke away from the co-op, and its stores were renamed Pathmark.

Wakefern not only weathered the storm, it grew under the direction of chairman and CEO Thomas Infusino, elected shortly after the split. The co-op focused on asserting its position as a seller of low-priced products. Wakefern developed private-label brands, including the ShopRite brand. In the 1980s members began operating larger stores and adding more nonfood items to the ShopRite product mix. With its number of superstores on the rise and facing increased competition from club stores in 1992, Wakefern opened a centralized, nonfood distribution center in New Jersey.

In 1995, 30-year Wakefern veteran Dean Janeway was elected president of the co-op. The company debuted its ShopRite MasterCard, co-branded with New Jersey's Valley National Bank, in 1996. The following year the co-op purchased two of its customers' stores in Pennsylvania, then threatened to close them when contract talks with the local union deteriorated. In 1998 Wakefern settled the dispute, then sold the stores.

The company partnered with Internet bidding site priceline.com in 1999, offering customers an opportunity to bid on groceries and then pick them up at ShopRite stores. Big V, Wakefern's biggest customer, filed for Chapter 11 bankruptcy protection in 2000 and said it was ending its distribution agreement with the co-op. In July 2002, however, Wakefern's ShopRite Supermarkets subsidiary acquired all of Big V's assets for approximately $185 million in cash and assumed liabilities.

EXECUTIVES

Chairman and CEO: Thomas (Tom) Infusino
President and COO: Dean Janeway
CFO: Ken Jasinkiewicz
EVP, Marketing: Joseph Sheridan
SVP, Administrative Support: Natan Tabak
VP Corporate and Consumer Affairs: Mary Ellen Gowin
VP Human Resources: Ernie Bell
President and COO ShopRite Supermarkets: Kevin Mannix
Director, Advertising: Karen McAuvic

LOCATIONS

HQ: 600 York St., Elizabeth, NJ 07207
Phone: 908-527-3300 **Fax:** 908-527-3397
Web: www.shoprite.com

Wakefern Food's 38 members operate nearly 200 ShopRite supermarkets in Connecticut, Delaware, New Jersey, New York, and Pennsylvania.

PRODUCTS/OPERATIONS

Major Members

Foodarama Supermarkets
Inserra Supermarkets
Village Super Market

Selected Private Labels

Black Bear (deli items)
Chef's Express
Reddington Farms (poultry)
ShopRite

COMPETITORS

C&S Wholesale
Di Giorgio
Fleming Companies
A&P
IGA
King Kullen Grocery
Kings Super Markets
Krasdale Foods
Pathmark
Royal Ahold
Shurfine International
Stop & Shop
SUPERVALU
Wal-Mart

HISTORICAL FINANCIALS

Company Type: Cooperative

Income Statement FYE: September 30

	REVENUE ($ mil.)	NET INCOME ($ mil.)	NET PROFIT MARGIN	EMPLOYEES
9/02	6,200	—	—	50,000
9/01	5,900	—	—	—
9/00	5,800	—	—	—
9/99	5,500	—	—	—
9/98	5,000	—	—	—
9/97	4,613	—	—	—
9/96	4,304	—	—	—
9/95	3,700	—	—	—
9/94	3,740	—	—	—
Annual Growth	6.5%	—	—	—

Revenue History

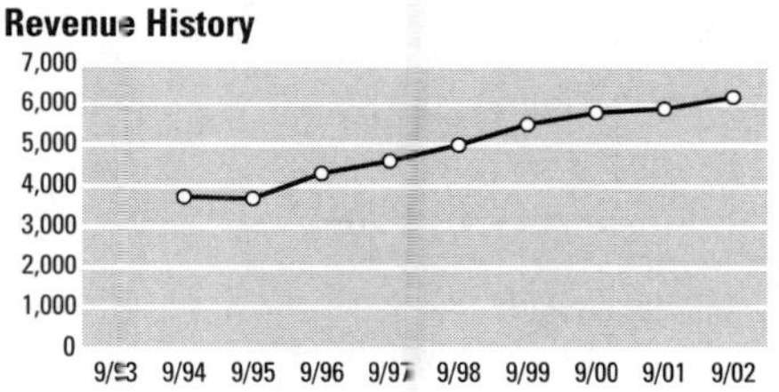

Walbridge Aldinger

The Motor City has been home to Motown Records, Madonna, and . . . Walbridge Aldinger? Walbridge Aldinger, a top 50 US contractor, provides design, engineering, construction management, and plant operation and maintenance. Much of its business is tied to Michigan's automotive industry, but the company serves several markets through three groups: commercial, industrial, and heavy civil special projects. Units include rigging and equipment installer Belding Walbridge, automotive construction joint ventures DEVCON Industrial Group and Walbridge Tilbury, and building installation services firm Walbridge Specialty Services. In 1975 the father of CEO John Rakolta bought Walbridge Aldinger, which was founded in 1916.

EXECUTIVES

Chairman and CEO: John Rakolta Jr.
Vice Chairman: Ronald L. (Ron) Hausmann
President and COO: Richard J. (Rick) Haller
EVP: Michael R. (Mike) Haller
SVP Business Development: Dave Hanson
VP and CFO: Vince DeAngelis
VP Human Resources: Terry Merritt
Auditors: Doeren & Mayhew

LOCATIONS

HQ: Walbridge Aldinger Company
613 Abbott St., Detroit, MI 48226
Phone: 313-963-8000 **Fax:** 313-963-8150
Web: www.walbridge.com

Walbridge Aldinger operates from offices in Chicago, Detroit, and Tampa in the US. It also has offices in Canada (London and Windsor), Mexico (Mexico City), and the UK (Birmingham).

PRODUCTS/OPERATIONS

Selected Services

Construction management
Consulting
Design/build delivery
General contracting
Ironworker and boilermaker services
Facility management
Machinery and equipment moving and installation
Millwright and machinist services
Program management
Transportation, heavy haul, logistical, and forwarding services

COMPETITORS

Alberici
Barton Malow
Bechtel
Clark Enterprises
EllisDon Construction
Fluor
Foster Wheeler
Halliburton
Hensel Phelps Construction
Jacobs Engineering
M. A. Mortenson
Parsons
Pepper Construction
Peter Kiewit Sons'
Skanska USA Building
Turner Corporation
Washington Group
Whiting-Turner

HISTORICAL FINANCIALS

Company Type: Private

Income Statement FYE: December 31

	REVENUE ($ mil.)	NET INCOME ($ mil.)	NET PROFIT MARGIN	EMPLOYEES
12/02	925	—	—	1,500
12/01	810	—	—	1,300
12/00	750	—	—	1,000
12/99	775	—	—	700
12/98	675	—	—	643
12/97	630	—	—	600
12/96	675	—	—	500
12/95	660	—	—	500
12/94	503	—	—	500
12/93	405	—	—	612
Annual Growth	9.6%	—	—	10.5%

Revenue History

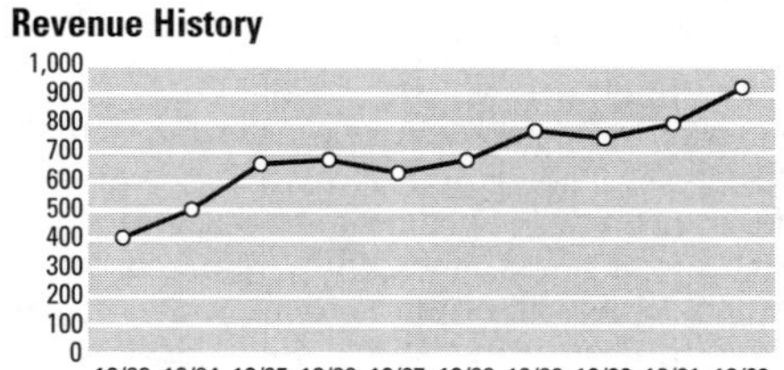

The Walsh Group

The Walsh Group erects walls, halls, malls, and more. Walsh provides design/build and construction services for industrial, public, and commercial projects throughout the US. Its projects range from prisons to skyscrapers to shopping malls. The group consists of Walsh Construction of Chicago and Archer Western Contractors of Fort Lauderdale, Florida. Operating from 13 regional offices, Walsh provides complete project management services, from planning and demolition to general contracting and finance. It is a major player in bridge and highway construction and also renovates and restores buildings and provides interior construction and design services. The Walsh family still owns the firm, founded in 1898.

EXECUTIVES

Chairman; CEO, Walsh Construction: Matthew M. Walsh
President: Daniel J. Walsh
CFO, Secretary, and Treasurer: Larry J. Kibbon
VP Business Development: Patrick M. Donley
Executive Secretary: Marilyn Honkisz
Human Resources Manager: Rhonda Hardwick
Auditors: Wolf & Company, P.C.

LOCATIONS

HQ: 929 W. Adams St., Chicago, IL 60607
Phone: 312-563-5400 **Fax:** 312-563-5466
Web: www.walshgroup.com

The Walsh Group's Archer Western Contractors has offices in Atlanta; Arlington, Texas; Englewood, Colorado; Jacksonville, Florida; Phoenix; San Diego; and Virginia Beach, Virginia. Its Walsh Construction Company has offices in Boston; Chicago; Detroit; LaPorte, Indiana; Pittsburgh; and Pleasanton, California.

PRODUCTS/OPERATIONS

Projects

Apartment complexes
Correctional facilities
Data centers
Education facilities
Health-care facilities
Highways and bridges
Hotels
Industrial parks
Interiors
Laboratories
Parking garages
Renovations
Retail centers
Senior housing
Skyscrapers
Treatment plants

COMPETITORS

Balfour Beatty Construction Inc.
Barton Malow
Bechtel
Bovis Lend Lease
Dunn Industries
Fluor
Granite Construction
Hunt Construction
Jacobs Engineering
M. A. Mortenson
McCarthy Building
Pepper Construction
Peter Kiewit Sons'
Skanska
TIC Holdings
Turner Corporation

HISTORICAL FINANCIALS

Company Type: Private

Income Statement FYE: December 31

	REVENUE ($ mil.)	NET INCOME ($ mil.)	NET PROFIT MARGIN	EMPLOYEES
12/01	1,450	—	—	3,000
12/00	1,304	—	—	2,600
12/99	1,080	—	—	1,000
12/98	1,170	—	—	3,500
12/97	992	—	—	2,000
12/96	740	—	—	1,500
12/95	604	—	—	1,000
12/94	450	—	—	4,000
12/93	345	—	—	—
Annual Growth	19.7%	—	—	(4.0%)

Revenue History

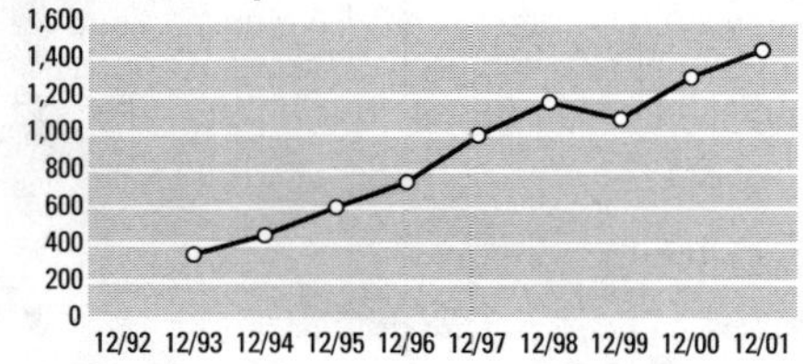

Warren Equities

Warren Equities fills car tanks and stomachs in the US Northeast. The holding company sells fuel and groceries from over 400 service stations and convenience stores from Maine to Virginia operating under the Xtra Mart brand. Warren's distribution companies supply those stores, as well as independent outlets, with gasoline, grocery, and tobacco products. Other Warren companies trade and store petroleum, provide environmental testing services, and make promotional signs and clothing. Chairman and owner Warren Alpert founded the company in 1950 after Standard Oil awarded him a distributorship. His foundation gives annual grants to medical researchers; he has donated more than $20 million to Harvard Medical School.

EXECUTIVES

Chairman: Warren Alpert, age 82
Vice Chairman: Edward M. Cosgrove
President and CEO: Herbert Kaplan
CFO and Treasurer: John Dziedzic
EVP: Francis K. La Forge
Controller and Assistant Treasurer: Richard J. Sawicki
Director Human Resources: Thomas Palumbo
Auditors: KPMG LLP

LOCATIONS

HQ: Warren Equities, Inc.
27 Warren Way, Providence, RI 02905
Phone: 401-781-9900 **Fax:** 401-461-7160
Web: www.warreneq.com

Warren Equities operates in Connecticut, Maine, Maryland, Massachusetts, New Hampshire, New York, Pennsylvania, Rhode Island, and Virginia.

PRODUCTS/OPERATIONS

Subsidiaries

Auburn Merchandise Distributors, Inc. (wholesale marketing)
Convenient Graphics (promotional products)
Drake Petroleum Company, Inc. (wholesale gasoline)
Kenyon Oil Company, Inc. (retail gasoline and convenience stores)
MidValley Oil Company (retail gasoline and convenience stores)
Warex Terminals Corporation (wholesale marketing)
Xcel Environmental, Inc. (environmental services)

COMPETITORS

7-Eleven
BP
Casey's General Stores
Crown Central Petroleum
Cumberland Farms
Getty Petroleum Marketing
Global Companies
Motiva Enterprises
Sunoco
SUPERVALU
Wawa

HISTORICAL FINANCIALS

Company Type: Private

Income Statement FYE: May 31

	REVENUE ($ mil.)	NET INCOME ($ mil.)	NET PROFIT MARGIN	EMPLOYEES
5/02	1,000	—	—	2,200
5/01	984	—	—	2,200
5/00	797	—	—	2,100
5/99	587	—	—	2,100
5/98	620	—	—	2,100
5/97	700	—	—	2,300
5/96	900	—	—	2,100
5/95	786	—	—	1,600
5/94	701	—	—	1,600
5/93	650	—	—	1,560
Annual Growth	4.9%	—	—	3.9%

Revenue History

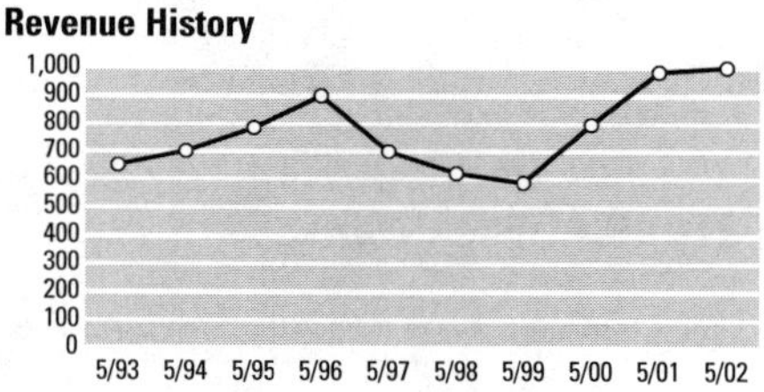

Washington University in St. Louis

Washington University in St. Louis is the gateway to higher education for more than 12,000 students. Founded in 1853, the private university is renowned for its academic programs in business, law, medical research, occupational therapy, physical therapy, and social work. Students can also explore fields of study such as architecture, art, and engineering. Faculty members include a US poet laureate, a Nobel prize winner, and five recipients of the National Medal of Science. A leader in research, the university receives substantial research funding from the National Science Foundation and the National Institutes of Health.

EXECUTIVES

Chancellor: Mark S. Wrighton, age 53
Executive Vice Chancellor and Dean, Arts and Sciences: Edward S. Macias
Executive Vice Chancellor Medical Affairs and Dean, Medical School: William A. Peck, age 69
Executive Vice Chancellor: Richard A. Roloff
Vice Chancellor for Finance and CFO: Barbara Feiner
Executive Vice Chancellor and General Counsel: Michael R. Cannon
Vice Chancellor Public Affairs: M. Fredric Volkmann
Auditors: PricewaterhouseCoopers LLP

LOCATIONS

HQ: 1 Brookings Dr., St. Louis, MO 63130
Phone: 314-935-5000 **Fax:** 314-935-7088
Web: www.wustl.edu

PRODUCTS/OPERATIONS

Selected Schools and Colleges

College of Arts and Sciences
George Warren Brown School of Social Work
Graduate School of Arts and Sciences
John M. Olin School of Business
School of Architecture
School of Art
School of Engineering and Applied Science
School of Law
School of Medicine
University College

HISTORICAL FINANCIALS

Company Type: School

Income Statement FYE: June 30

	REVENUE ($ mil.)	NET INCOME ($ mil.)	NET PROFIT MARGIN	EMPLOYEES
6/02	1,342	—	—	8,000
6/01	1,278	—	—	8,000
6/00	1,024	—	—	7,963
6/99	1,053	—	—	8,000
6/98	942	—	—	8,017
6/97	935	—	—	7,735
6/96	918	—	—	7,400
6/95	887	—	—	7,100
6/94	1,180	—	—	7,054
6/93	1,046	—	—	7,162
Annual Growth	2.8%	—	—	1.2%

Revenue History

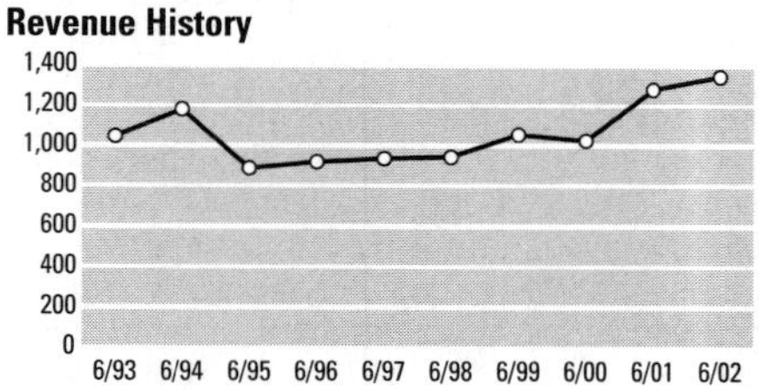

Wawa, Inc.

It's not baby talk — when folks say they need to go to the Wawa, they need groceries. Wawa runs more than 540 Wawa Food Markets in Delaware, Maryland, New Jersey, Pennsylvania, and Virginia. Wawa stores are noted for their coffee and their salad and deli offerings, including hoagie sandwiches; about 100 stores sell gas. Unlike many convenience store chains, Wawa has its own dairy, supplying Wawa stores and about 1,000 hospitals, schools, and other institutions. The company opened its first store in 1964, but its roots go back to an iron foundry begun in 1803 by the Wood family; food operations began in 1902 when George Wood started a dairy in Wawa, Pennsylvania. The Wood family owns 52% of the company.

EXECUTIVES

President and CEO: Richard D. Wood Jr.
EVP: Howard B. Stoeckel
EVP, Finance and Administration: There du Pont
SVP Law: Vincent P. Anderson
SVP Operations: Harry McHugh
VP Human Resources: Karen Casale
CIO: Neil McCarthy
Manager Public Relations: Lori Bruce

LOCATIONS

HQ: 260 W. Baltimore Pike, Wawa, PA 19063
Phone: 610-358-8000 **Fax:** 610-358-8878
Web: www.wawa.com

PRODUCTS/OPERATIONS

Selected Products and Private-Label Brands

Bakery (Wawa)
Cold beverages (Wawa)
Coffee (Freshly Brewed Coffee)
Hoagies (Built-to-Order, Shorti)
Hot breakfast sandwiches (Sizzli)
Ready-to-eat foods (Wawa Express)
Wawa Dairy Division
- 100% orange juice (All Florida)
- Butter
- Eggs
- Fruit juices and drinks
- Margarine
- Milk (including lactose-free, chocolate, and strawberry)
- Spring water (Deer Park)
- Tea
- Yogurt (Dannon)

COMPETITORS

7-Eleven
Albertson's
Amerada Hess
ChevronTexaco
Cumberland Farms
Subway
Exxon Mobil
Foodarama Supermarkets
Genuardi's Family Markets
Getty Realty
A&P
Kroger
Motiva Enterprises
Rutter's Dairy
Sheetz
Uni-Marts
Village Super Market
Warren Equities
Wegmans

HISTORICAL FINANCIALS

Company Type: Private

Income Statement FYE: December 31

	REVENUE ($ mil.)	NET INCOME ($ mil.)	NET PROFIT MARGIN	EMPLOYEES
12/01	2,010	—	—	13,000
12/00	1,500	—	—	13,000
12/99	1,398	—	—	12,000
12/98	1,000	—	—	12,000
12/97	1,010	—	—	12,500
12/96	959	—	—	12,000
12/95	901	—	—	10,000
12/94	838	—	—	—
12/93	786	—	—	—
12/92	715	—	—	—
Annual Growth	12.2%	—	—	4.5%

Revenue History

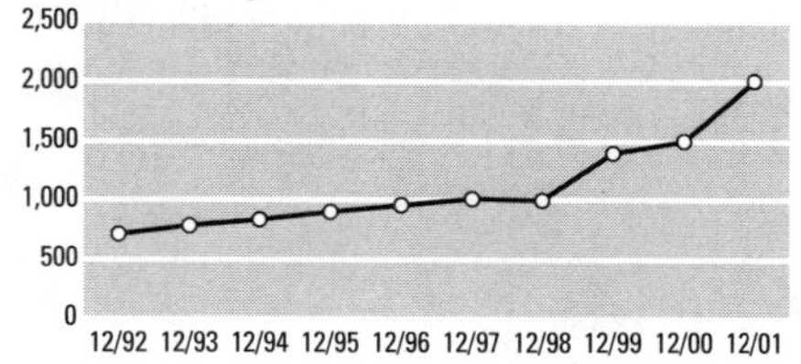

WB Television

Ah, The WB Television Network — broadcasting's fount of teen angst. With Generation Y-oriented hits like *Gilmore Girls* and *Charmed,* the upstart network that took to the airwaves in 1995 has developed a reputation for luring the younger demographic. (The network took a hit in the ratings following the defection of popular *Buffy the Vampire Slayer* to rival UPN. Buffy is no longer on the air.) The WB Network broadcasts prime-time programming six nights a week. Under the guise of Kids' WB!, the network also provides weekday morning, afternoon, and Saturday morning children's programming, including the popular *Pokémon* series. Time Warner owns 66% of The WB, Tribune Company owns 22%, and WB executives own 11%.

EXECUTIVES

Co-Chairman and Co-CEO: Jamie Kellner, age 57
Co-Chairman: Garth Ancier
Co-CEO: Jordan Levin
President and COO: Jed Petrick
EVP, Finance and Operations: Mitch Nedick
EVP, Current Programming and Primetime Scheduling: John Litvack
EVP General Counsel: John Maatta
EVP Marketing: Suzanne Kolb
EVP Media Sales: Bill Morningstar
EVP Network Communications: Brad Turell

LOCATIONS

HQ: The WB Television Network
4000 Warner Blvd., Bldg. 34R, Burbank, CA 91522
Phone: 818-977-5000 **Fax:** 818-977-6771
Web: www.thewb.com

PRODUCTS/OPERATIONS

Selected Programs

7th Heaven
Angel
Charmed
Everwood
Gilmore Girls
Grounded for Life
The Jamie Kennedy Experiment
Reba
Smallville

COMPETITORS

ABC
CBS
FOX Broadcasting
MBC
NBC
UPN

HISTORICAL FINANCIALS

Company Type: Joint venture

Income Statement FYE: December 31

	REVENUE ($ mil.)	NET INCOME ($ mil.)	NET PROFIT MARGIN	EMPLOYEES
12/02	589	—	—	400
12/01	450	—	—	340
12/00	453	—	—	—
12/99	384	—	—	—
12/98	260	—	—	—
12/97	136	—	—	—
12/96	87	—	—	—
Annual Growth	37.5%	—	—	17.6%

Revenue History

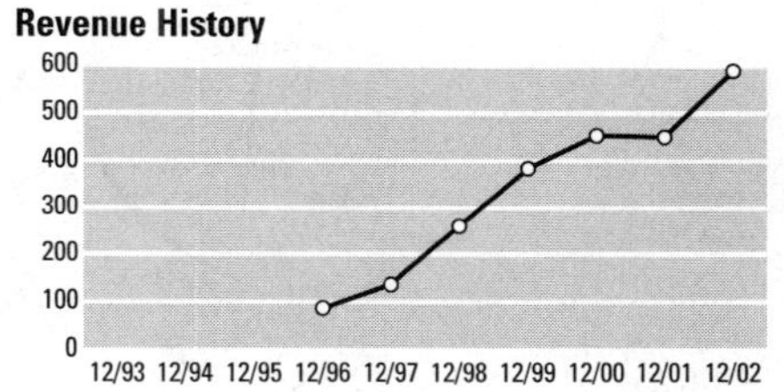

Webcor Builders, Inc.

The core of Webcor Builders is commercial building in Silicon Valley and Northern California. The company constructs mid- and high-rise office buildings, residential and medical facilities, hotels, and parking structures. Known for its focus on high-tech projects, the builder has worked on headquarters for Oracle and Adobe Systems and a headquarters compound for Lucas Digital's Industrial Light + Magic and LucasArts Entertainment. The company also provides interior construction and renovation services, seismic upgrades, concrete construction, and telecommunications networking and technology consulting. The surviving entity of a 1994 merger with A.J. Ball Construction, Wecor is owned by president Andrew Ball.

EXECUTIVES

Chairman: David R. Boyd
President and CEO: Andrew J. (Andy) Ball
EVP: Richard Lamb
SVP Concrete: Rosser Edwards Jr.
SVP Estimating: Chet Brians
SVP Interiors: Bill Kalff
SVP Business Development: Glenn Gabel
VP Finance: Dave Fisher
Director Administration and Human Resources: Kaela Hanrahan
Director Marketing: Kerry Boyd
Auditors: S.J. Gallina LLP

LOCATIONS

HQ: 951 Mariners Island Blvd., 7th Fl., San Mateo, CA 94404
Phone: 650-349-2727 **Fax:** 650-524-7399
Web: www.webcor.com

Webcor Builders has offices in Hayward, Los Angeles, San Francisco, and San Mateo, California.

PRODUCTS/OPERATIONS

Selected Subsidiaries

Webcor Concrete
Webcor Interior Construction Group (ICG)
Webcor Technologies

COMPETITORS

Beck Group
Charles Pankow Builders
Clark Enterprises
DPR Construction
Hathaway Dinwiddie Construction
Hensel Phelps Construction
S. J. Amoroso Construction
Skanska USA Building
Turner Corporation
Washington Group
Whiting-Turner

HISTORICAL FINANCIALS

Company Type: Private

Income Statement FYE: December 31

	REVENUE ($ mil.)	NET INCOME ($ mil.)	NET PROFIT MARGIN	EMPLOYEES
12/02	1,340	—	—	800
12/01	1,155	—	—	800
12/00	760	—	—	840
12/99	636	—	—	400
12/98	541	—	—	377
12/97	526	—	—	337
12/96	411	—	—	203
12/95	83	—	—	250
12/94	69	—	—	255
12/93	46	—	—	270
Annual Growth	45.5%	—	—	12.8%

Revenue History

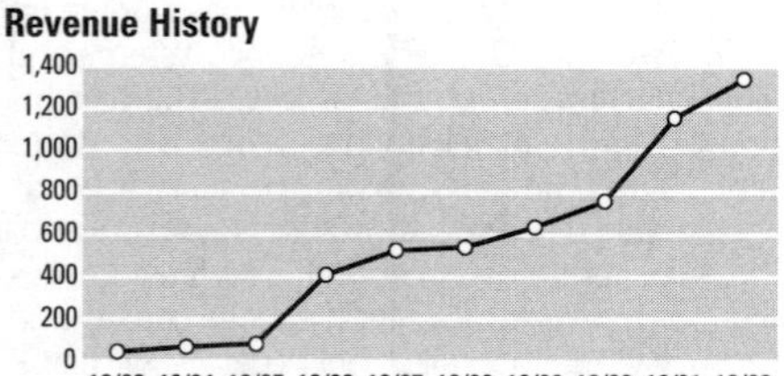

Wegmans Food Markets, Inc.

One name strikes fear in the hearts of supermarket owners in New York, Pennsylvania, and New Jersey: Wegmans Food Markets. The supermarket chain owns more than 60 stores, but they are hardly typical. Much larger than most supermarkets (up to 120,000 sq. ft.), they offer specialty shops such as huge in-store cafes, cheese shops with some 400 different varieties, and French-style pastry shops with exotic desserts. The company is known for its gourmet cooking classes and an extensive employee-training program.Wegmans also runs about 15 Chase-Pitkin Home & Garden home-improvement stores. Founded in 1916, the company is still owned by the family of founder John Wegman. His nephew, Robert Wegman, is CEO.

Wegmans plans to open its first store in Virginia in February 2004.

EXECUTIVES

Chairman and CEO: Robert B. Wegman
President: Daniel R. (Danny) Wegman
EVP, Operations: Jack DePeters
SVP and CFO: Jim Leo
SVP, Consumer Affairs: Mary Ellen Burris
SVP, Distribution: Mike Bargmann
SVP, Information Technology: Don Reeve
VP, Marketing: Colleen Wegman
Director, B2B: Marianne Timmons
Director, Human Resources: Gerald Pierce

LOCATIONS

HQ: 1500 Brooks Ave., Rochester, NY 14624
Phone: 585-328-2550 **Fax:** 585-464-4664
Web: www.wegmans.com

PRODUCTS/OPERATIONS

Selected Products and Services

Bulk foods
Coffee/cappuccino bar
Cooking classes
Dry cleaning
Gift and fruit baskets
Kosher deli
Market café
Nature's Marketplace (organic health and food items)
Organic produce
Pharmacy
Photo processing and photo enlarging
Sushi bar
UPS parcel service

COMPETITORS

Ahold USA
Albertson's
Foodarama Supermarkets
Foodtown
Giant Eagle
Golub
A&P
Home Depot
IGA
Kmart
Penn Traffic
Safeway
SUPERVALU
Wal-Mart
Wawa

HISTORICAL FINANCIALS

Company Type: Private

Income Statement FYE: December 31

	ESTIMATED REVENUE ($ mil.)	NET INCOME ($ mil.)	NET PROFIT MARGIN	EMPLOYEES
12/02	3,000	—	—	30,000
12/01	2,920	—	—	29,072
12/00	2,800	—	—	29,826
12/99	2,670	—	—	28,766
12/98	2,450	—	—	25,000
12/97	2,340	—	—	25,000
12/96	2,250	—	—	25,000
12/95	2,130	—	—	—
12/94	2,000	—	—	—
12/93	1,813	—	—	—
Annual Growth	5.8%	—	—	3.1%

Revenue History

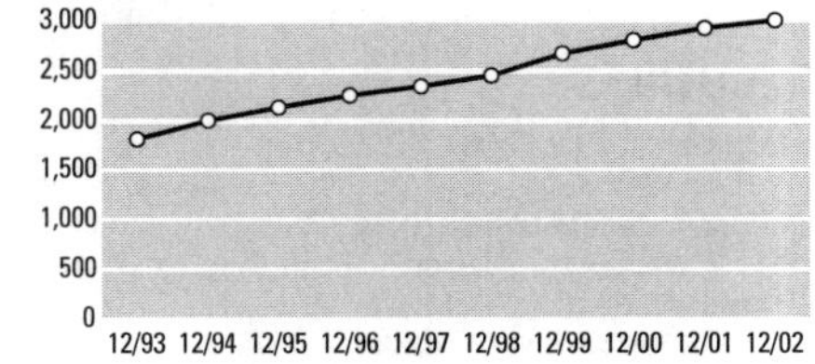

Weil, Gotshal & Manges LLP

The seeds of Weil, Gotshal & Manges (WGM) may have been planted in New York City, but its branches have grown globally. Founded in 1931, the law firm has 15 offices worldwide. WGM strives to integrate the expertise of its more than 1,000 lawyers across all practice areas for the benefit of clients such as General Electric, Hicks, Muse, Tate & Furst, and CBS. Its office in Washington, DC, for example, lends legislative support and its Silicon Valley office offers technology know-how. WGM is well-known for its business finance and restructuring practice; other practice areas include energy, real estate, tax law, and trusts and estates.

EXECUTIVES

Chairman and Executive Partner: Stephen J. Dannhauser
Executive Director: John W. Neary
CFO: Norman W. LaCroix
CIO: Jim McGinnis
Chief Marketing Officer: Katherine D'Urso
Associate Executive Director: Rob Singer
Associate Relations Director: Brad Scott
Auxiliary Legal Services Director: Kevin Curtin
Human Resources Director: Pat Bowers

LOCATIONS

HQ: 767 5th Ave., New York, NY 10153
Phone: 212-310-8000 **Fax:** 212-310-8007
Web: www.weil.com

Weil, Gotshal & Manges has U.S. offices in Boston; Dallas; Houston; Menlo Park, California; Miami; New York City; and Washington, DC. It has international offices in Brussels; Budapest, Hungary; Frankfurt; London; Paris; Prague, Czech Republic; Singapore; and Warsaw, Poland.

PRODUCTS/OPERATIONS

Selected Practice Areas

Business finance and restructuring
Corporate
Energy
Litigation
Real estate
Securities
Tax
Technology
Trade practices and regulatory law
Trusts and estates

COMPETITORS

Cleary, Gottlieb
Clifford Chance
Cravath, Swaine
Paul, Weiss, Rifkind
Proskauer Rose
Shearman & Sterling
Sidley Austin Brown & Wood
Simpson Thacher
Skadden, Arps
Sullivan & Cromwell
Wachtell, Lipton
White & Case

HISTORICAL FINANCIALS

Company Type: Partnership

Income Statement FYE: December 31

	REVENUE ($ mil.)	NET INCOME ($ mil.)	NET PROFIT MARGIN	EMPLOYEES
12/02	688	—	—	—
12/01	581	—	—	—
12/00	506	—	—	—
12/99	440	—	—	1,800
12/98	400	—	—	1,700
12/97	354	—	—	1,600
12/96	322	—	—	—
12/95	306	—	—	—
12/94	311	—	—	—
12/93	315	—	—	—
Annual Growth	9.1%	—	—	6.1%

Revenue History

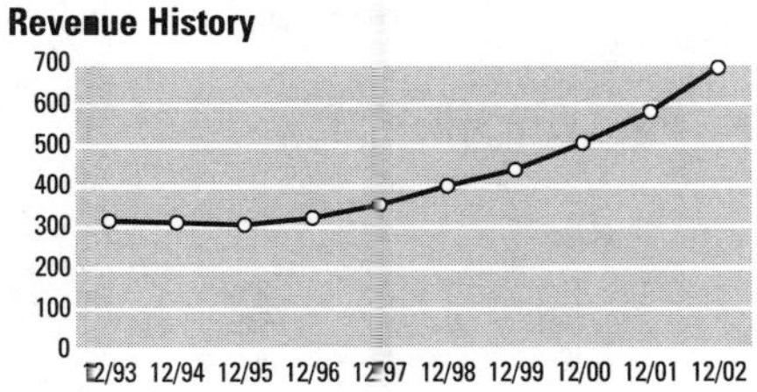

The Weitz Group, LLC

It took wits for The Weitz Group to become a top US general building contractor. Founded in 1855 by carpenter Charles H. Weitz, the company was run by the Weitz family for four generations before becoming employee-owned. It provides general contracting, construction management, and design/build services, constructing everything from office buildings, industrial plants, senior communities, and schools to hotels, golf courses, supermarkets, and malls. Weitz entered the homebuilding market with its 2001 purchase of Colorado-based Norris Associates, which constructs multimillion-dollar homes in well-heeled resort areas. Weitz builds supermarkets and warehouse/distribution centers through its Hy-Vee Weitz unit.

EXECUTIVES

Chairman, President, and CEO: Glenn H. De Stigter
COO: James (Jim) Simmons
CFO: Craig Damos
CIO: Mark Federle
VP Human Resources: Kris Jensen
SVP, Colorado Division: Gary D. Meggison, age 45
SVP, National Division: Fran Snook
General Counsel and Secretary: David Strutt
Auditors: KPMG Peat Marwick

LOCATIONS

HQ: Capital Square, 400 Locust St., Ste. 300, Des Moines, IA 50309
Phone: 515-698-4260 **Fax:** 515-698-4299
Web: www.weitz.com

The Weitz Group has offices in Arizona, Colorado, Florida, Iowa, Kansas, and Nebraska.

PRODUCTS/OPERATIONS

Selected Clients & Projects

Arizona Biltmore Hotel
The Breakers Hotel
Iowa State University
Rosenblatt Stadium
The Nicklaus Golf Club at LionsGate
The Principal Financial Group
Twentieth Century Fox

COMPETITORS

Barton Malow
Bovis Lend Lease
Brasfield & Gorrie
Centex
Charles Pankow Builders
Choate Construction
Clark Enterprises
David Weekley Homes
Dunn Industries
Gilbane
Graycor
H.J. Russell
Hunt Construction
Peter Kiewit Sons'
Skanska
Structure Tone
Sundt
Turner Corporation
Walsh Group
Webcor Builders
Whiting-Turner

HISTORICAL FINANCIALS

Company Type: Private

Income Statement FYE: December 31

	REVENUE ($ mil.)	NET INCOME ($ mil.)	NET PROFIT MARGIN	EMPLOYEES
12/01	810	—	—	1,104
12/00	650	—	—	1,322
12/99	657	—	—	1,104
12/98	577	—	—	909
Annual Growth	12.0%	—	—	6.7%

Revenue History

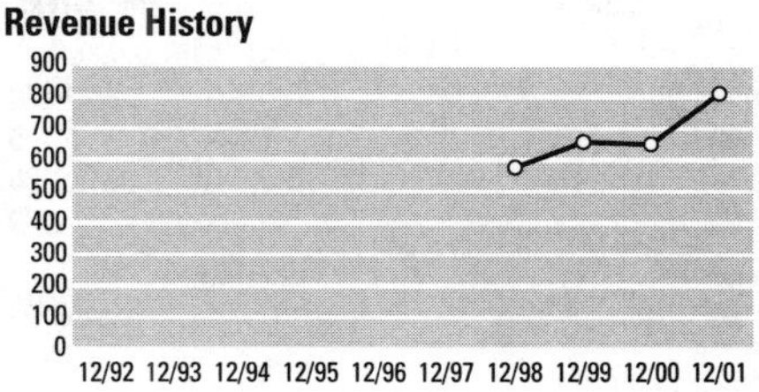

Wells' Dairy, Inc.

From the five-quart tub of Cherry Nut ice cream to red, white, and blue Bomb Pops, Wells' Dairy spans the frozen treat spectrum. Best known for its Blue Bunny brand of ice cream and frozen novelties, Well's Dairy sells its products in convenience stores, restaurants, supermarkets, schools, and vending machines. Its Contract Manufacturing Division produces fluid, cultured, and frozen dairy products for third parties. Founded as a small town dairy in 1913 by the late Fred H. Wells, the company grew through acquisitions to become a strong regional ice cream player with a presence in markets across the US and 20 countries. It is still owned and managed by the Wells family.

EXECUTIVES

CEO: Gary M. Wells
President: Dan Wells
COO: Doug Wells
CFO: Larry Heemstra
EVP: Mike Wells
VP, Human Resources: Mac Rothenbuhler
VP, Information Services: Kim Norby
VP, Marketing: Jim Reynolds
Director of Public Relations: Dave Smetter

LOCATIONS

HQ: 1 Blue Bunny Dr., Le Mars, IA 51031
Phone: 712-546-4000 **Fax:** 712-546-1782
Web: www.wellsdairy.com

Wells' Dairy has production facilities in Iowa, Nebraska, and Utah and additional facilities in Arizona, Kansas, and Texas.

PRODUCTS/OPERATIONS

Selected Products

Cottage cheese
Fresh yogurt
Frozen yogurt
Ice cream
Ice cream novelties
Juice
Milk
Sherbet
Snack dip
Sour cream

COMPETITORS

Allied Domecq QSR
Blue Bell
Dairy Farmers of America
Dean Foods
Dreyer's
Marigold foods
Nestlé
Quality Chekd
Schwan's
Unilever
YoCream

HISTORICAL FINANCIALS

Company Type: Private

Income Statement FYE: December 31

	REVENUE ($ mil.)	NET INCOME ($ mil.)	NET PROFIT MARGIN	EMPLOYEES
12/01	650	—	—	2,450
12/00	580	—	—	2,400
12/99	600	—	—	2,200
12/98	525	—	—	2,200
Annual Growth	7.4%	—	—	3.7%

Revenue History

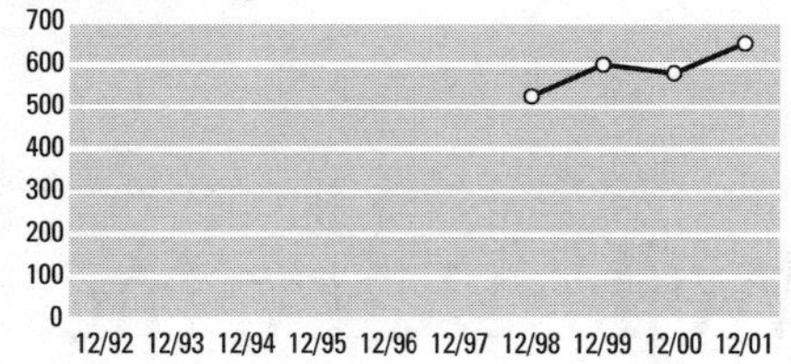

Werner Co.

If a man's reach exceeds his grasp, perhaps he should buy a Werner — the company claims to be the world's #1 producer of ladders. For the do-it-yourselfer, Werner makes extension, step, attic, and platform ladders made of wood, fiberglass, or aluminum; professional products include work platforms and stages, planks, and ladder jacks. The remainder comes from Werner's extruded products division, which makes aluminum products such as pneumatic cylinders, bracket systems, shelving, and components for material handling machinery. Investcorp controls Werner (through Werner Holding Co., Inc.), but the former has been looking to sell the . . . ladder.

Ladders and related products account for about 85% of sales.

EXECUTIVES

Chairman: Donald M. Werner, age 69
Vice Chairman: Michael E. Werner, age 43
President, CEO, and Director: Dennis G. Heiner, age 59, $1,258,265 pay
SVP, Operations: Peter R. O'Coin, age 55, $448,320 pay
SVP, Sales: Edward W. Gericke, age 45
VP, CFO, and Treasurer: Larry V. Friend, age 56, $407,307 pay
VP, Secretary, and General Counsel: Eric J. Werner, age 40, $392,385 pay
Human Resources Manager: John Guyton
Auditors: PricewaterhouseCoopers LLP

LOCATIONS

HQ: 93 Werner Rd., Greenville, PA 16125
Phone: 724-588-8600 **Fax:** 724-588-0315
Web: www.wernerco.com

Werner Co. has manufacturing locations in Alabama, California, Illinois, Kentucky, and Pennsylvania.

PRODUCTS/OPERATIONS

2002 Sales

	$ mil.	% of total
Climbing products	444.3	85
Extruded products	76.1	15
Total	**520.4**	**100**

COMPETITORS

Aarque
Columbus McKinnon
Danaher
JLG Industries
Nippon Light Metal
Terex

HISTORICAL FINANCIALS

Company Type: Private

Income Statement FYE: December 31

	REVENUE ($ mil.)	NET INCOME ($ mil.)	NET PROFIT MARGIN	EMPLOYEES
12/02	520	27	5.3%	2,800
12/01	536	16	2.9%	3,000
12/00	545	12	2.3%	3,100
12/99	485	11	2.3%	3,400
12/98	436	0	0.0%	—
12/97	416	(91)	—	—
12/96	367	19	5.3%	—
12/95	329	6	1.9%	—
12/94	329	11	3.4%	—
12/93	278	5	1.7%	—
Annual Growth	7.2%	21.9%	—	(6.3%)

2002 Year-End Financials

Debt ratio: —
Return on equity: —
Cash ($ mil.): 43
Current ratio: 1.97
Long-term debt ($ mil.): 234

Net Income History

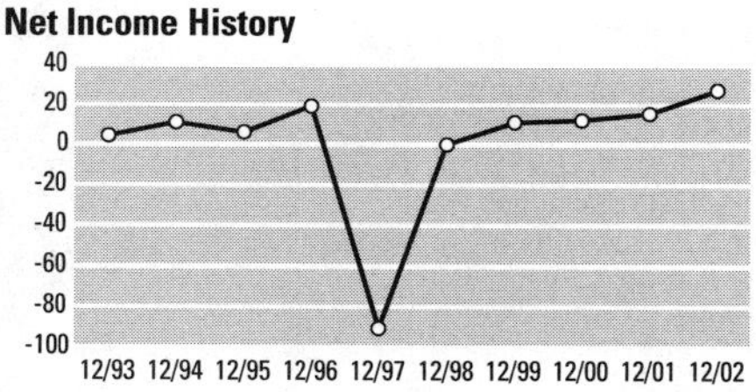

Westcon Group

Westcon Group is no con — it's pro-global. The company's three divisions, Comstor, Westcon, and Voda One, resell networking equipment made by Cisco Systems (about 55% of sales), Avaya, Nortel Networks, and other top manufacturers. Networking servers, switches, and routers; network security systems; and virtual private network systems top Westcon's product list. The company also provides a variety of support services, including training, network design, logistical support, and others. Chairman Thomas Dolan and EVP Philip Raffiani founded Westcon in 1985. South Africa-based networking company Datatec Ltd. owns 90% of the company, which has acquired Dutch networking products distributor Landis Group.

EXECUTIVES

Chairman: Thomas (Tom) Dolan
President and CEO: Alan Marc Smith
EVP and General Manager: Philip Raffiani, $408,334 pay
VP, Finance and CFO: John P. O'Malley III
VP, Marketing and Investor Relations: Jenny Pappas
Director of Business Solutions: Duncan Craven
Corporate Counsel: Jeanne Horan
Human Resources: David Deluke
Auditors: Deloitte & Touche

LOCATIONS

HQ: Westcon Group, Inc.
520 White Plains Rd., Ste. 100,
Tarrytown, NY 10591
Phone: 914-829-7000 **Fax:** 914-829-7137
Web: www.westcongroup.com

Westcon Group has operations in Australia, Austria, Belgium, Brazil, Canada, Denmark, Germany, Ireland, the Netherlands, Norway, Singapore, Spain, Sweden, the UK, and the US.

2002 Sales

	% of total
North America	64
Europe	29
Other regions	7
Total	**100**

PRODUCTS/OPERATIONS

Selected Products

Data caching servers
Integrated communication systems
Internet servers
Network security systems
Network switches and routers
Videoconferencing systems
Virtual private network systems
Wireless network access systems

Selected Services

Inventory management
Logistics
Network design and consulting
Support
Technical services
Training

COMPETITORS

Avaya
CDW
Cisco Systems
Comark
CompuCom
En Pointe
Ingram Micro
Nortel Networks
Pomeroy IT
Resilien
ScanSource
Tech Data

HISTORICAL FINANCIALS

Company Type: Private

Income Statement FYE: February 28

	REVENUE ($ mil.)	NET INCOME ($ mil.)	NET PROFIT MARGIN	EMPLOYEES
2/03	1,627	—	—	1,400
2/02	1,670	—	—	1,300
2/01	1,939	—	—	1,059
2/00*	1,168	—	—	1,057
3/99	587	—	—	—
3/98	334	—	—	—
Annual Growth	37.2%	—	—	9.8%

*Fiscal year change

Revenue History

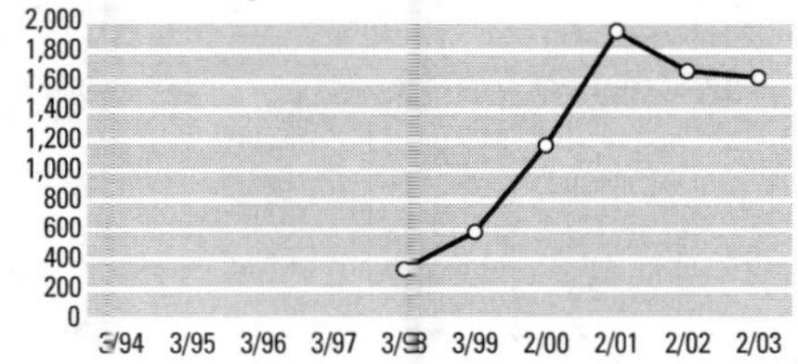

Western Family Foods, Inc.

From mayo to mops, Western Family Foods supplies private-label products to more than 3,500 independent grocery retailers in 23 mostly western states. It also sells in Asia, Russia, and Latin America. Its main brands are Western Family and Shurfine (no relation to competitor Shurfine International). Western Family coordinates with manufacturers and wholesalers to produce more than 6,000 products. The company helps retailers develop private labels, and it is part of a consortium that buys general merchandise and sells it to independent retailers. Wholesalers Affiliated Foods, Associated Food Stores, Associated Grocers, Olean Wholesale, Unified Western Grocers, and URM Stores own Western Family, founded in 1934.

EXECUTIVES

President and CEO: Ronald S. King
CFO: Russ Jones
SVP, Procurement: Robert Cutler
SVP Sales and Marketing: David (Dave) Hayden
VP, Data Processing: Gregg Florence
VP, International: Charlie Rotta
VP, Quality Assurance: Roy Besand
Manager Human Resources: Michelle Baker

LOCATIONS

HQ: 6700 SW Sandburg St., Tigard, OR 97223
Phone: 503-639-6300 **Fax:** 503-684-3469
Web: www.westernfamily.com

Western Family Foods serves customers in 23 states, and it exports products to Chile, China, Fiji, Guam, Hong Kong, Indonesia, Japan, Malaysia, Mexico, Micronesia, Panama, the Philippines, Russia, Singapore, South Korea, Taiwan, Thailand, and Vietnam.

PRODUCTS/OPERATIONS

Selected Private Labels

Better Buy
Market Choice
Shur Saving
Shurfine
Western Family

COMPETITORS

Fleming Companies
Nash Finch
SUPERVALU
Topco Associates

HISTORICAL FINANCIALS

Company Type: Private

Income Statement FYE: April 30

	ESTIMATED REVENUE ($ mil.)	NET INCOME ($ mil.)	NET PROFIT MARGIN	EMPLOYEES
4/02	560	—	—	75
4/01	500	—	—	74
4/00	500	—	—	74
4/99	500	—	—	74
4/98	500	—	—	70
Annual Growth	2.9%	—	—	1.7%

Revenue History

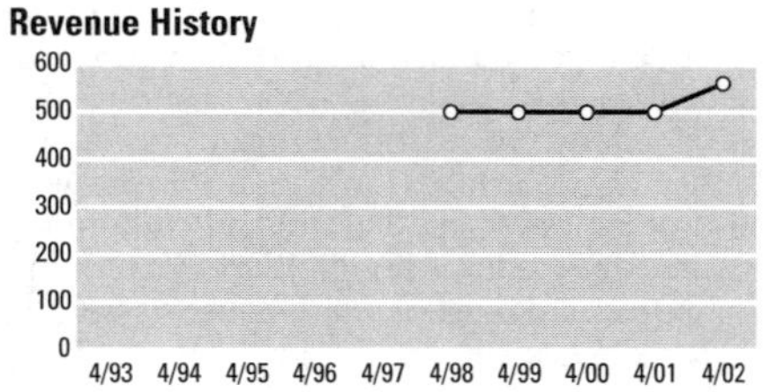

Westfield Group

Westfield Group (formerly Ohio Farmers Insurance) has plowed beyond the crop and cattle biz. Through its affiliates, including First Patriot Insurance, Old Guard Insurance, Westfield Insurance, and Westfield National, the company offers such standard personal lines as auto and homeowners insurance; its niche products include fidelity and surety bonds and specialty coverage for farmers, auto repair shops, and religious organizations. The insurer has opened Westfield Bank, offering personal and business banking services through a referral program involving independent insurance agents in northeastern Ohio.

EXECUTIVES

Chairman: Cary Blair
CEO: Robert J. Joyce
CFO and Treasurer: Robert Krisowaty
President, Westfield Bank: Jon Park
Corporate Counsel and Secretary: Brooks Rorapaugh
Controller: Bambi Beshire
Chief Human Resources Officer: Debra Cummings
Senior Executive, Marketing: Kent Daugherty

LOCATIONS

HQ: 1 Park Circle, Westfield Center, OH 44251
Phone: 330-887-0101 **Fax:** 330-887-0840
Web: www.westfield-cos.com

Ohio Farmers Insurance operates in about 20 states nationwide.

PRODUCTS/OPERATIONS

Selected Affiliates

American Select Insurance Company
First Delaware Insurance Company
First Patriot Insurance Company
Ohio Farmers Insurance Company
Old Guard Insurance Company
Westfield Insurance Company
Westfield National Insurance Company

COMPETITORS

Allstate
AIG
CNA Financial
The Hartford
MetLife
Nationwide
New York Life
Prudential
State Farm
Travelers

HISTORICAL FINANCIALS

Company Type: Private

Income Statement FYE: December 31

	REVENUE ($ mil.)	NET INCOME ($ mil.)	NET PROFIT MARGIN	EMPLOYEES
12/02	1,200	—	—	2,000
12/01	745	—	—	2,000
12/00	800	—	—	2,000
12/99	840	—	—	2,000
12/98	854	—	—	2,037
12/97	900	—	—	2,300
12/96	892	—	—	2,290
12/95	856	—	—	2,200
12/94	724	—	—	2,092
12/93	638	—	—	1,840
Annual Growth	7.3%	—	—	0.9%

Revenue History

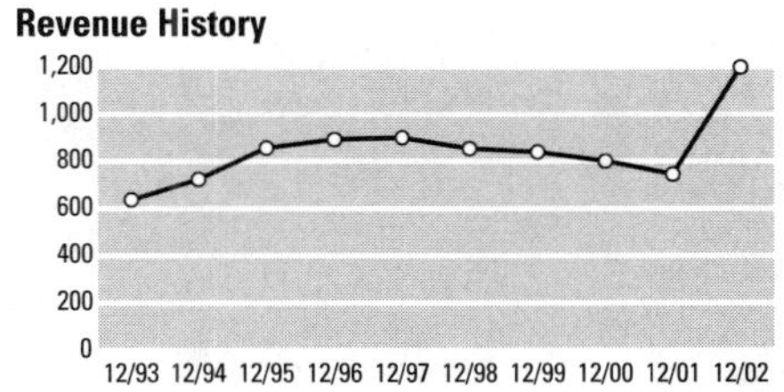

Whataburger

When you see that familiar orange and white roof, you know you're in for a Whataburger. With more than 580 owned and franchised outlets, the company operates a popular fast-food chain in Texas, Oklahoma, and a half dozen other southern states. Whataburger restaurants are typically open 24 hours a day and serve burgers and fries along with breakfast items (taquitos, pancakes), fajitas, chicken, and salads. About 230 of the company's restaurants are franchised. Loyal Whataburger fans can don the company's line of apparel sporting the chain's logo. The late Harmon Dobson founded Whataburger in Corpus Christi, Texas, in 1950. His family (including Dobson's son, chairman and CEO Thomas Dobson) owns the company.

Despite the fact that Whataburger has a much smaller presence than its national competitors, the chain is nevertheless a powerful player in its native Texas because of the intense loyalty of its customers.

The company is expanding primarily though new franchising agreements.

EXECUTIVES

Chair Emeritus: Grace Dobson
Chairman and CEO: Thomas E. (Tom) Dobson
President and COO: Timothy P. (Tim) Taft
EVP and CFO: John M. McLellan
SVP Operations: Robert R. Moore
Chief Accounting Officer: Wendy A. Beck
Group Director of Human Resources: Sandee Pritchard
Group Director of Marketing: Rodney J. Martin
Auditors: KPMG LLP

LOCATIONS

HQ: Whataburger, Inc.
1 Whataburger Way, Corpus Christi, TX 78411
Phone: 361-878-0650 **Fax:** 361-878-0473
Web: www.whataburger.com

Whataburger has more than 580 fast-food restaurants in Alabama, Arizona, Florida, Louisiana, New Mexico, Oklahoma, and Texas, and a small number in Mexico.

COMPETITORS

AFC Enterprises
Burger King
Checkers Drive-In
Chick-fil-A
CKE Restaurants
Deli Management
Subway
Dairy Queen
Jack in the Box
Krystal
McDonald's
Quizno's
Schlotzsky's
Sonic
Taco Bueno
Taco Cabana
Triarc
Braum's
Wendy's
YUM!

HISTORICAL FINANCIALS

Company Type: Private

Income Statement FYE: September 30

	REVENUE ($ mil.)	NET INCOME ($ mil.)	NET PROFIT MARGIN	EMPLOYEES
9/03	460	—	—	12,000
9/02	448	—	—	11,000
9/01	395	—	—	9,500
9/00	352	—	—	8,800
9/99	309	—	—	8,400
9/98	291	—	—	8,800
9/97	265	—	—	8,000
9/96	248	—	—	7,500
9/95	240	—	—	7,200
9/94	250	—	—	7,500
Annual Growth	7.0%	—	—	5.4%

Revenue History

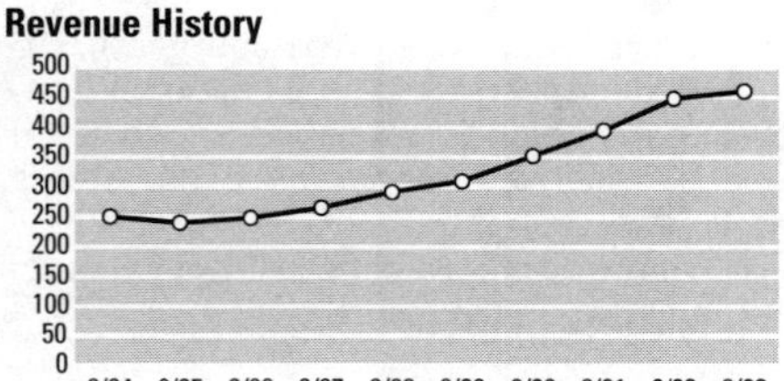

Wherehouse Entertainment

Wherehouse Entertainment wants to be where it's at for music and video lovers. The company operates about 150 stores mostly under the Wherehouse Music, Tu Musica, and XChange names. The stores sell music, videocassettes, DVDs, video games, and accessories. Many of its stores also rent videos and games and buy and sell used CDs. Wherehouse became one of the largest US music retailers after its 1998 purchase of Blockbuster Music from Viacom; however, declining sales have led the company to file for Chapter 11 bankruptcy protection (for the second time in less than 10 years) and close more than half of its stores. Trans World Entertainment purchased most of Wherehouse's assets in October 2003.

EXECUTIVES

Chairman, President and CEO: Jerry M. Comstock Jr., age 49
Interim CFO, Chief Administrative Officer: Mark A. Velarde, age 46, $274,862 pay
EVP and General Merchandise Manager: Lewis S. Garrett, age 52
SVP, Store Operations: Barbara C. Brown, age 50, $177,556 pay
VP, Treasurer, General Counsel and Assistant Secretary: Charles M. Fuertsch
VP and Controller: Mehdi Mahdavi, $166,616 pay
VP, Human Resources: Toni Caputo
Auditors: Deloitte & Touche LLP

LOCATIONS

HQ: Wherehouse Entertainment, Inc.
19701 Hamilton Ave., Torrance, CA 90502
Phone: 310-965-8300 **Fax:** 310-538-8798
Web: www.wherehousemusic.com

PRODUCTS/OPERATIONS

Selected Store Names

GameSpace
Odyssey
Tu Musica
Wherehouse
Wherehouse Entertainment
Wherehouse Music
Wherehouse Outlet
Xchange

COMPETITORS

Best Buy
Blockbuster
Borders
CD Warehouse
CDnow
Circuit City Stores
DVD.com
Hastings Entertainment
Hollywood Entertainment
Kmart
MTS
Target
Trans World Entertainment
Wal-Mart

HISTORICAL FINANCIALS

Company Type: Private

Income Statement FYE: January 31

	REVENUE ($ mil.)	NET INCOME ($ mil.)	NET PROFIT MARGIN	EMPLOYEES
1/02	604	(54)	—	5,260
1/01	706	(22)	—	6,330
1/00	766	(1)	—	6,721
1/99	497	7	1.4%	8,038
1/98	327	8	2.4%	3,625
1/97	366	(30)	—	5,450
1/96	433	(44)	—	7,100
1/95	500	(162)	—	2,700
1/94	472	(42)	—	2,700
1/93	449	(6)	—	6,600
Annual Growth	3.4%	—	—	(2.5%)

2002 Year-End Financials

Debt ratio: 86.2%
Return on equity: —
Cash ($ mil.): 2
Current ratio: 0.96
Long-term debt ($ mil.): 22

Net Income History

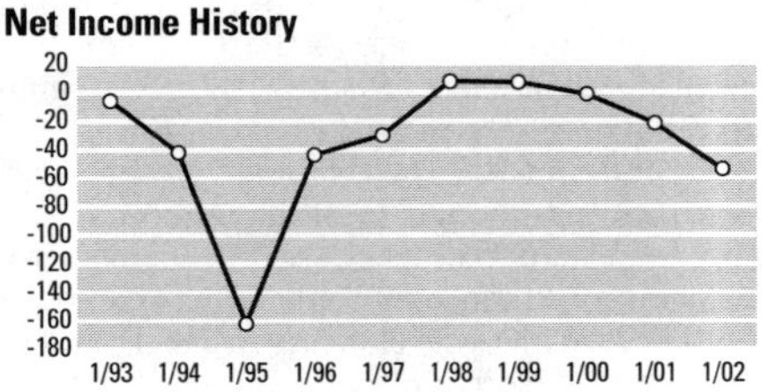

White & Case

What do you call a law firm with some 1,500 lawyers? Well, the safe answer would be White & Case. One of the world's largest law firms, White & Case has buoyed its global reputation by establishing 35 international offices in locations such as Bangkok; Budapest, Hungary; Istanbul, Turkey; London; Paris; Riyadh, Saudi Arabia; and Warsaw, Poland (the firm also maintains six US offices, including its New York City headquarters). Among White & Case's practice areas are bankruptcy, corporate, intellectual property, litigation, project finance, and tax. The firm's client list has included Deutsche Bank and Royal Ahold. White & Case was founded in 1901.

EXECUTIVES

Managing Partner: Duane D. Wall
Administrative Partner: David N. Koschik
CFO: James Lotchford
Chief Knowledge Officer: Eugene Stein
Chief Marketing Officer: Liz Pava
Senior Manager, Media Relations and External Communications: Roger J. Cohen
Director Human Resources: Jill Connors

LOCATIONS

HQ: White & Case LLP
1155 Avenue of the Americas, New York, NY 10036
Phone: 212-819-8200 **Fax:** 212-354-8113
Web: www.whitecase.com

White & Case has 41 offices in Africa, the Americas, Asia, Europe, and the Middle East.

PRODUCTS/OPERATIONS

Selected Practice Areas

Antitrust
Arbitration and alternative dispute resolution
Bankruptcy and reorganization
Corporate
Employee benefits
Insurance
Intellectual property
Litigation
Mergers and acquisitions
Project finance
Public finance
Tax
Telecommunications

COMPETITORS

Akin, Gump
Baker & McKenzie
Clifford Chance
Holland & Knight
Jones Day
Latham & Watkins
Mayer, Brown, Rowe & Maw
Morgan, Lewis
Sidley Austin Brown & Wood
Skadden, Arps
Weil, Gotshal

HISTORICAL FINANCIALS

Company Type: Partnership

Income Statement FYE: December 31

	REVENUE ($ mil.)	NET INCOME ($ mil.)	NET PROFIT MARGIN	EMPLOYEES
12/01	603	—	—	—
12/00	491	—	—	—
12/99	405	—	—	—
12/98	352	—	—	—
12/97	318	—	—	—
12/96	282	—	—	—
12/95	247	—	—	—
12/94	233	—	—	—
12/93	210	—	—	—
12/92	197	—	—	—
Annual Growth	13.3%	—	—	—

Revenue History

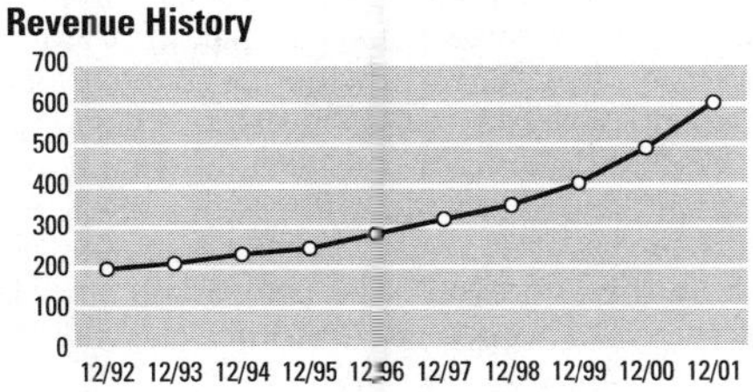

White Castle System, Inc.

The treasure room of this fast food fortress contains Slyders. White Castle System owns and operates about 380 hamburger joints known for their little square burgers called Slyders. The burgers are steamed over a bed of onions rather than grilled and served on a steamed bun with a single slice of pickle. Patrons typically consume a sack of Slyders at a time. White Castle restaurants can be found in about a dozen states, primarily in the Midwest. The company also sells frozen Slyders through supermarket chains. The first fast food chain in the US, White Castle was founded by Walter Anderson and real estate broker E. W. "Billy" Ingram in 1921. The Ingram family continues to control the company.

Little has changed at White Castle over the years, from its Slyders to its castle-shaped buildings. That has helped the chain establish strong loyalty among both customers and employees. However, its reluctance to franchise and lack of television advertising has allowed the venerable chain to fall far behind fast food giants such as McDonald's and Burger King. The chain does sell branded items (caps, mugs, and shirts) to keep its loyal fans happy and engaged.

In addition to its hamburger business, White Castle System owns PSB Company, a subsidiary that makes metal products and equipment, including fixtures and cooking tools needed at the restaurants. PSB also makes lawn spreaders under the PrizeLAWN brand.

EXECUTIVES

Chairman, President, and CEO: Edgar W. (Bill) Ingram III, age 52
VP, CFO, and Treasurer: William A. Blake
VP, General Counsel, and Secretary: G. Roger Post
VP Marketing and Site Development: Kim Kelly-Bartley
Senior Director of Training and Human Resources: John Kelly
Director of Marketing: Jamie Richardson
Assistant Secretary and Corporate Counsel: Nicholas W. Zuk
Human Resources: Heather Ward

LOCATIONS

HQ: 555 W. Goodale St., Columbus, OH 43215
Phone: 614-228-5781 **Fax:** 614-464-0596
Web: www.whitecastle.com

White Castle Systems operates about 380 fast food restaurants in Illinois, Indiana, Kentucky, Michigan, Minnesota, Missouri, New Jersey, New York, Ohio, Tennessee, and Wisconsin.

COMPETITORS

AFC Enterprises
Back Yard Burgers
Blimpie
Burger King
Checkers Drive-In
Chick-fil-A
CKE Restaurants
Culver's
Subway
Dairy Queen
Jack in the Box
Krystal
McDonald's
Quizno's
Sonic
Steak n Shake
Triarc
Wendy's
YUM!

HISTORICAL FINANCIALS

Company Type: Private

Income Statement FYE: December 31

	REVENUE ($ mil.)	NET INCOME ($ mil.)	NET PROFIT MARGIN	EMPLOYEES
12/02	490	—	—	12,900
12/01	472	—	—	12,500
12/00	473	—	—	12,100
12/99	439	—	—	12,100
12/98	418	—	—	11,300
12/97	384	—	—	11,000
12/96	360	—	—	—
12/95	350	—	—	—
12/94	325	—	—	—
Annual Growth	5.3%	—	—	3.2%

Revenue History

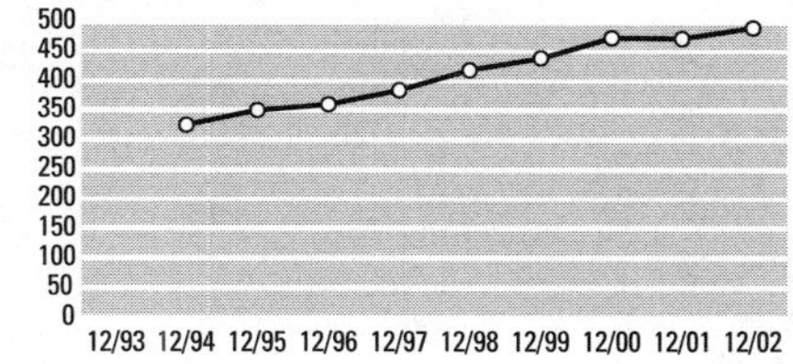

Whiting-Turner Contracting

Whiting-Turner Contracting is a big fish in an ocean of builders. The employee-owned firm provides construction management, general contracting, and design/build services, primarily for large commercial, institutional, and infrastructure projects in the US. It subcontracts about 85% of its volume, but its in-house activities include mechanical and electrical work, concrete forming, and foundation services. A key player in retail construction, the company also undertakes such diverse projects as biotech clean rooms, schools, stadiums, and corporate headquarters for clients like AT&T, General Motors, and the US Army. G. W. C. Whiting and LeBaron Turner founded the company in 1909 to build sewer lines.

EXECUTIVES

President and CEO: Willard Hackerman
EVP Finance and CFO: Charles Irish
SVP (Baltimore): Gino Gemignani
SVP (Irvine): Len Cannatelli
SVP (New Haven, CT): Daniel (Dan) Bauer
SVP (Washington, DC): Richard Vogel
VP Marketing: David Boucher
Director Human Resources: Edward Spaulding
Auditors: PricewaterhouseCoopers LLP

LOCATIONS

HQ: The Whiting-Turner Contracting Company
300 E. Joppa Rd., Baltimore, MD 21286
Phone: 410-821-1100 **Fax:** 410-337-5770
Web: www.whiting-turner.com

The Whiting-Turner Contracting Company has offices in Allentown, Pennsylvania; Atlanta; Baltimore; Boston; Chantilly, Virginia; Charlotte, North Carolina; Cleveland; Dallas; Fort Lauderdale, Florida; Irvine, California; Las Vegas; New Haven, Connecticut; Newark, Delaware; Orlando, Florida; Richmond, Virginia; San Francisco; Somerset, New Jersey; Tampa, Florida; and Washington, DC.

PRODUCTS/OPERATIONS

Selected Services

Bid packaging
Budgeting
Constructibility reviews
Estimating
Mechanical and electrical assistance
Planning and scheduling
Procurement
Project control
Purchasing
Siting
Value analysis
Value engineering

Selected Markets

Biotechnology and pharmaceutical
Clean room and high-technology
Education
Entertainment
Health care and senior living
Industrial and manufacturing
Lodging and hospitality
Mission critical facilities
Offices
Parking
Retail
Sports
Transportation
Utility
Warehouse and distribution

COMPETITORS

Barton Malow
Bechtel
Bovis Lend Lease
Choate Construction
Clark Enterprises
DPR Construction
Dunn Industries
Fisher Development
Fluor
Gilbane
Hensel Phelps Construction
Hoffman Corporation
Kitchell Corporation
McCarthy Building
Perini
Peter Kiewit Sons'
Skanska
Suffolk Construction
Swinerton
Turner Corporation
Weitz

HISTORICAL FINANCIALS

Company Type: Private

Income Statement FYE: December 31

	ESTIMATED REVENUE ($ mil.)	NET INCOME ($ mil.)	NET PROFIT MARGIN	EMPLOYEES
12/01	2,400	—	—	2,100
12/00	1,646	—	—	2,000
12/99	1,418	—	—	2,000
12/98	1,260	—	—	1,800
12/97	1,050	—	—	1,500
12/96	800	—	—	1,000
12/95	700	—	—	800
12/94	600	—	—	800
12/93	600	—	—	800
12/92	500	—	—	900
Annual Growth	19.0%	—	—	9.9%

Revenue History

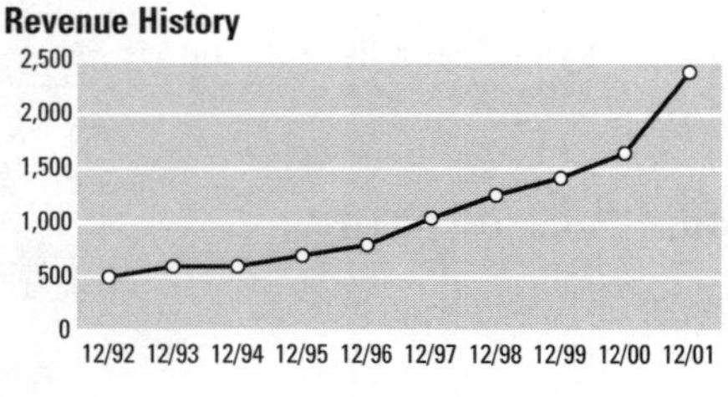

Wilbur-Ellis Company

Helpful hint: Don't stand downwind of the Wilbur-Ellis Company. A distributor for major chemical companies, Wilbur-Ellis sells animal feed, fertilizer, insecticides, seed, and machinery through outlets in North America. Subsidiary Connell Brothers exports and distributes chemicals and feed throughout the Pacific Rim. Additionally, Wilbur-Ellis provides consulting, pesticide spraying, and other agriculture-related services. It also owns Knox McDaniels, a supplier of vitamin and mineral premix products in the western US. Brayton Wilbur Sr. and Floyd Ellis founded the company in 1921 as a fish-oil supplier; it is still owned by the Wilbur family.

EXECUTIVES

Chairman: Brayton Wilbur Jr.
Vice Chairman: Carter P. Thacher
President and CEO: Herbert B. Tully
EVP, Agribusiness: Daniel R. Vradenburg
VP, Connell Division: Theodore Eliot
VP, Feed Division: Ron Salter
VP, Treasurer, and CFO: Jim Crawford
Legal Counsel: Robert Schmalz
Manager, Human Resources: Anne Cleary

LOCATIONS

HQ: 345 California St., 27th Fl., San Francisco, CA 94104
Phone: 415-772-4000 **Fax:** 415-772-4005
Web: www.wilbur-ellis.com

PRODUCTS/OPERATIONS

Selected Products

Agricultural chemicals
Animal feed
Fertilizer
Fungicide
Herbicide
Insecticides
Machinery
Seed protectants
Sprayers

Selected Services

Crop consulting
Fertilizer application
Pesticide application
Product development

COMPETITORS

Agrium
Agway
ADM
Cargill
CF Industries
CHS
ConAgra
Farmland Industries
GROWMARK
JR Simplot
Terra Industries

HISTORICAL FINANCIALS

Company Type: Private

Income Statement FYE: December 31

	ESTIMATED REVENUE ($ mil.)	NET INCOME ($ mil.)	NET PROFIT MARGIN	EMPLOYEES
12/02	1,200	—	—	2,500
12/01	1,185	—	—	2,500
12/00	1,131	—	—	2,000
12/99	1,300	—	—	2,500
12/98	1,100	—	—	2,500
12/97	1,200	—	—	2,100
12/96	900	—	—	1,900
12/95	870	—	—	1,800
12/94	918	—	—	1,800
12/93	900	—	—	1,800
Annual Growth	3.2%	—	—	3.7%

Revenue History

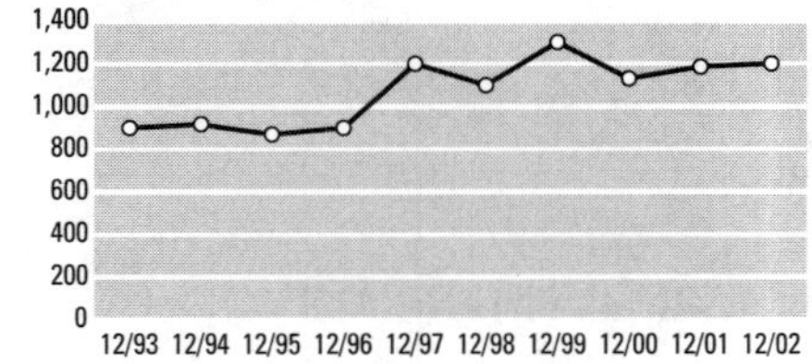

William Blair & Company, L.L.C.

William Blair & Company looks to the past when forging ahead. Driven by both tradition and progress, the private investment banking firm provides financing and brokerage services worldwide to corporate, institutional, and private investors. Its offerings include portfolio management, sales and trading, investment banking services, mutual funds, and venture capital financing. Its research department publishes reports on more than 250 companies. Founded during the Depression, the company financed the growth of many Chicago businesses. William Blair & Company is employee-owned.

EXECUTIVES

Chairman: Edgar D. (Ned) Jannotta
Vice Chairman and CEO: E. David (Dave) Coolidge III
President and COO: John R. Ettelson
CFO: Timothy L. (Tim) Burke
General Counsel: Arthur J. Simon
Chief Human Resources Officer: Kenneth Moss
Media Relations: Tony Zimmer
Auditors: Ernst & Young LLP

LOCATIONS

HQ: 222 W. Adams St., Chicago, IL 60606
Phone: 312-236-1600 **Fax:** 312-368-9418
Web: www.williamblair.com

The company has operations in Chicago; Hartford, Connecticut; London; San Francisco; Tokyo; Vaduz, Liechtenstein; and Zurich.

COMPETITORS

Banc of America Securities
Friedman, Billings, Ramsey Group
Keefe, Bruyette & Woods
KeyCorp
Baird
Roth Capital Partners
U. S. Bancorp Piper Jaffray

HISTORICAL FINANCIALS

Company Type: Private

Income Statement FYE: December 31

	REVENUE ($ mil.)	NET INCOME ($ mil.)	NET PROFIT MARGIN	EMPLOYEES
12/01	460	—	—	900
12/00	355	—	—	949
12/99	340	—	—	844
12/98	275	—	—	759
12/97	270	—	—	697
12/96	250	—	—	635
12/95	200	—	—	595
12/94	150	—	—	555
12/93	150	—	—	—
Annual Growth	15.0%	—	—	7.2%

Revenue History

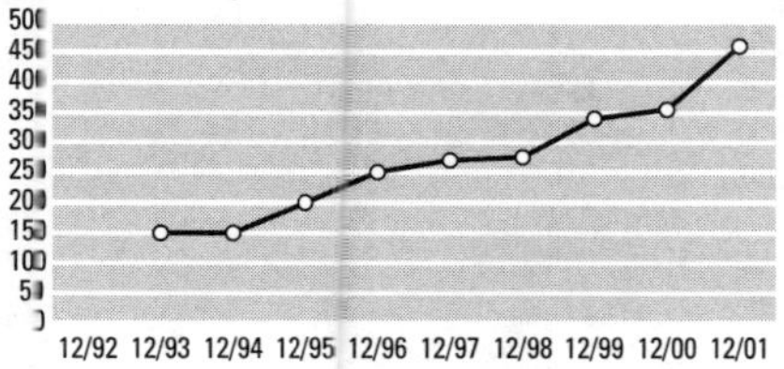

Williamson-Dickie Manufacturing

Appreciated by the working class and the sophomore class alike, Williamson-Dickie Manufacturing makes Dickies-brand khaki pants, bib overalls, jeans, and women's and children's apparel. It also produces Workrite safety uniforms. Founded in 1922, the company makes work clothes that were originally tailored with the blue-collar set in mind; in recent years the Dickies look has also fallen into favor with fashionable teens. Williamson-Dickie's work clothes portfolio includes Dickies T-shirts, which are made extra long to prevent the display of "plumber's crack" by squatting workmen. Dickies products are sold worldwide through retailers and directly to businesses. The founding Williamson family owns the company.

EXECUTIVES

Chairman, President, and CEO: Philip C. Williamson, age 39
Vice Chairman: Gail Williamson-Rawl
COO and CFO: Britt Ingebritson
VP Human Resources: Marett Cobb
VP Marketing: Jon Ragsdale

LOCATIONS

HQ: Williamson-Dickie Manufacturing Company
509 W. Vickery Blvd., Fort Worth, TX 76104
Phone: 800-336-7201 **Fax:** 817-877-5027
Web: www.dickies.com

PRODUCTS/OPERATIONS

Selected Licensed Products

Backpacks
Belts
Boots, shoes
Gloves
Hats, caps
Medical uniforms
Socks
Sunglasses
Wallets
Watches

COMPETITORS

Carhartt
Fruit of the Loom
FUBU
Levi Strauss
Mossimo
OshKosh B'Gosh
Phat
Tommy Hilfiger
VF

HISTORICAL FINANCIALS

Company Type: Private

Income Statement FYE: December 31

	REVENUE ($ mil.)	NET INCOME ($ mil.)	NET PROFIT MARGIN	EMPLOYEES
12/01	845	—	—	6,300
12/00	820	—	—	6,300
12/99	780	—	—	5,600
12/98	690	—	—	6,000
12/97	633	—	—	5,450
12/96	550	—	—	6,200
12/95	485	—	—	5,446
12/94	450	—	—	6,000
12/93	400	—	—	6,000
12/92	300	—	—	—
Annual Growth	12.2%	—	—	0.6%

Revenue History

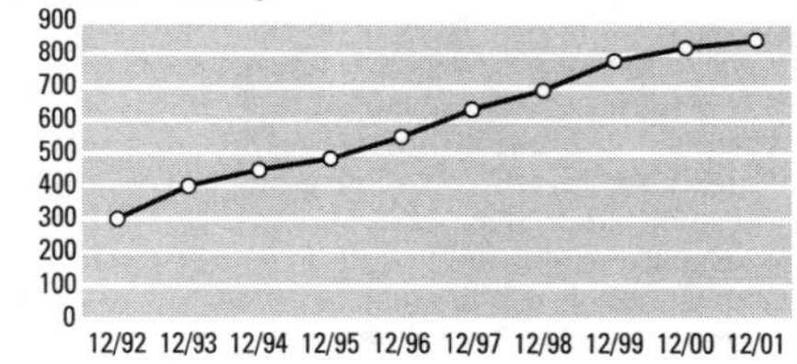

WinCo Foods

WinCo Foods isn't just big on self-service — it's giant. Inside the immense stores (average size is 85,000 sq. ft.) of this mostly employee-owned supermarket chain, customers shop for food in bulk and bag their own groceries. The company's 40-plus stores also feature pizza shops, bakeries, health and beauty products, and organic foods. WinCo Foods, formerly known as Waremart Foods, was renamed as a shortened version of "winning company." The name is also an acronym for its states of operation, which include Washington, Idaho, Nevada, California, and Oregon. Founded in 1968, WinCo Foods formerly operated stores under the Cub Foods and Waremart names. Employees own more than 80% of the company.

EXECUTIVES

Chairman and CEO: William D. (Bill) Long
President and COO, Director: Scott Preece
CFO and Secretary, Director: Gary R. Piva
VP, Advertising: Sharon Kadell
VP, Engineering: Dick VanderLinden
VP, Information Technology: Glen Reynolds
VP, Labor & Human Resources: Roger Cochell
VP, Marketing & Promotions: Dave Strausborger
VP Public and Legal Affairs: Michael Read

LOCATIONS

HQ: WinCo Foods, Inc.
650 N. Armstrong Place, Boise, ID 83704
Phone: 208-377-0110 **Fax:** 208-377-0474
Web: www.wincofoods.com

2003 Stores

	No.
Oregon	16
California	9
Idaho	8
Washington	6
Nevada	2
Total	**41**

PRODUCTS/OPERATIONS

Selected Store Departments

Bakery
Bulk foods (more than 500 items)
Delicatessen
Fresh meat
Health and beauty aids
Organic products
Pizza shop
Produce
Seafood

COMPETITORS

Albertson's
Associated Food
AWG
Costco Wholesale
Fred Meyer Stores
Haggen
Raley's
Safeway
Stater Bros.
Unified Western Grocers
Wal-Mart

HISTORICAL FINANCIALS

Company Type: Private

Income Statement FYE: March 31

	REVENUE ($ mil.)	NET INCOME ($ mil.)	NET PROFIT MARGIN	EMPLOYEES
3/02	1,540	—	—	6,500
3/01	1,300	—	—	5,300
3/00	1,160	—	—	5,000
3/99	940	—	—	4,900
Annual Growth	17.9%	—	—	9.9%

Revenue History

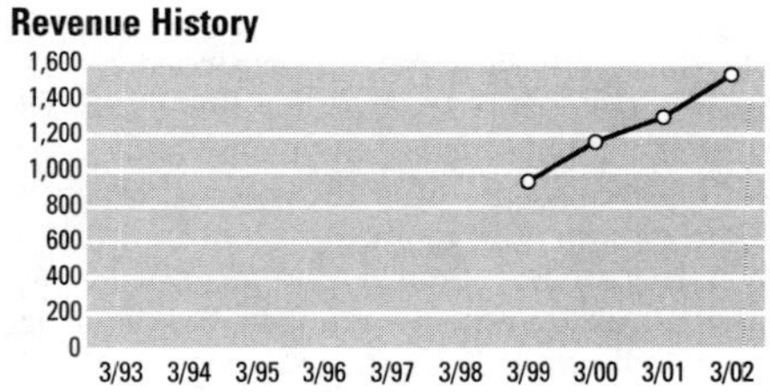

W.K. Kellogg Foundation

Charitable grants from W.K. Kellogg Foundation are gr-r-reat! Founded in 1930 by cereal industry pioneer Will Keith Kellogg, the foundation provides about $220 million in grants each year to programs focused on youth and education, as well as health issues. It also funds many rural development and agricultural projects and works to foster greater volunteerism. Most of its grants go to initiatives in the US, though it also makes grants throughout Latin America and Africa. The foundation's work is funded primarily from its nearly $6 billion trust.

W.K. Kellogg Foundation is guided by its founder's desire "to help people help themselves" and prefers funding programs that offer long-term solutions rather than quick handouts. In 1934 Kellogg donated $66 million in stock to the foundation, which now ranks as one of the largest charitable organizations in the world.

W.K. Kellogg Foundation, which owns nearly a third of the Kellogg Company, is governed by an independent board of trustees.

HISTORY

Born in 1860, Will Keith Kellogg's early jobs included those of stock boy and traveling broom salesman. He also worked as a clerk (and, later, bookkeeper and manager) at the Battle Creek Sanitarium, a renowned homeopathic hospital where his older brother, John Harvey Kellogg, was physician-in-chief. The brothers' experiments to improve vegetarian diets led to a happy accident in 1894 that resulted in the first wheat flakes. In 1906 W.K. Kellogg started the Battle Creek Toasted Corn Flake Company. Through marketing genius and innovative products, Kellogg's company became a leader in the industry.

A philanthropist by inclination, Kellogg established the Fellowship Corporation in 1925 to build an agricultural school and a bird sanctuary, as well as to set up an experimental farm and a reforestation project. He also gave $3 million to hometown causes, such as the Ann J. Kellogg School for disabled children, and for the construction of an auditorium, a junior high school, and a youth recreation center.

After attending a White House Conference on Child Health and Protection, Kellogg established the W.K. Kellogg Child Welfare Foundation in 1930. A few months later he broadened the focus of the charter and renamed the institution the W.K. Kellogg Foundation. That year the foundation began its landmark Michigan Community Health Project (MCHP), which opened public health departments in counties once thought too small and poor to sustain them. In 1934 Kellogg placed more than $66 million in Kellogg Company stock and other investments in a trust to fund his foundation.

During WWII the foundation expanded its programming to Latin America, funding advanced schooling for dentists, physicians, and other health professionals. After the war, it broadened its programming to include agriculture to help war-torn Europe. It funded projects in Germany, Iceland, Ireland, Norway, and the UK. Following Kellogg's death in 1951, the organization began providing support for graduate programs in health and hospital administration, as well as for rural leadership and community colleges.

During the 1970s the foundation lent its support to the growing volunteerism movement and to aiding the disadvantaged, with a special emphasis on programs for minorities. A review of operations in the late 1970s led the Kellogg Foundation to reassert its emphasis on health, education, agriculture, and leadership. The foundation also expanded its programs to southern Africa.

In 1986 The Kellogg Foundation began funding the Rural America Initiative — a series of 28 projects meant to develop leadership, train local government officials, and revitalize rural areas. William Richardson became president and CEO of the foundation in 1995, leaving his post as president of The Johns Hopkins University. Also during the 1990s, the foundation supported the Community-Based Public Health Initiative, which assisted universities in educating public health professionals by presenting community-based approaches to students and faculty.

In 1998 the organization announced a five-year, $55 million plan to bring health care to the nation's poor and homeless. Also that year it gave Portland State University a $600,000 grant to develop its Institute for Nonprofit Management. In 1999 the Kellogg Foundation started its first geographically based program, pledging $15 million in grants for development of Mississippi River Delta communities in Arkansas, Louisiana, and Mississippi. In 2001 the foundation pledged an additional $20 million to support economic growth in the region through the Emerging Markets Partnership. In 2002 the Kellogg Foundation awarded about $2 million in grants to SPARK (Supporting Partnerships to Assure Ready Kids) to help prepare low-income children for starting school. The organization funded a national campaign to improve men's health in 2003.

EXECUTIVES

President and CEO: William C. Richardson, age 62
SVP and Corporate Secretary: Gregory A. Lyman
SVP Programs: Anne C. Petersen
VP and Chief Investment Officer: Paul J. Lawler
VP Finance and Treasurer: La June Montgomery-Tally
VP Programs: Richard M. Foster
VP Programs: Marguerite M. Johnson
VP Programs: Robert F. (Bob) Long
VP Programs: Gail D. McClure
Director Human Resources: Norm Howard
Director Marketing and Communications: Karen E. Lake
Director Technology: Tim Dechant
Controller: Gloria Dickerson
Senior Counsel and Assistant Corporate Secretary: Mary C. Cotter
Auditors: PricewaterhouseCoopers LLP

LOCATIONS

HQ: 1 Michigan Ave. East, Battle Creek, MI 49017
Phone: 269-968-1611 **Fax:** 269-968-0413
Web: www.wkkf.org

2002 Grants

	$ mil.	% of total
US	184.6	83
Africa	16.0	7
Latin America & the Caribbean	22.5	10
Total	**223.1**	**100**

PRODUCTS/OPERATIONS

2002 Grants

	$ mil.	% of total
Youth & education	39.7	19
Health	36.0	16
Food systems & rural development	30.9	14
Latin America & the Caribbean	22.5	10
Program activities	22.4	10
Special opportunities	20.3	9
Philanthropy & Volunteerism	16.6	7
Africa	16.0	7
Recurring grants	7.6	3
Greater Battle Creek	7.4	3
Cross program initiative	3.7	2
Total	**223.1**	**100**

HISTORICAL FINANCIALS

Company Type: Foundation

Income Statement FYE: August 31

	REVENUE ($ mil.)	NET INCOME ($ mil.)	NET PROFIT MARGIN	EMPLOYEES
8/02	250	—	—	200
8/01	223	—	—	209
8/00	277	—	—	250
8/99	327	—	—	290
8/98	330	—	—	286
8/97	374	—	—	280
8/96	298	—	—	276
8/95	271	—	—	264
8/94	235	—	—	—
8/93	256	—	—	—
Annual Growth	(0.2%)	—	—	(3.9%)

Revenue History

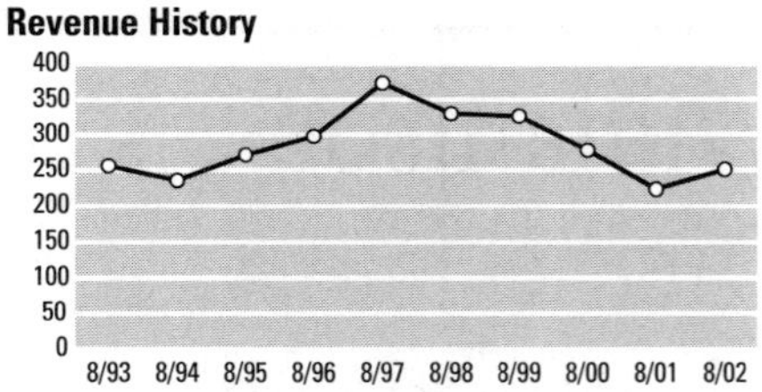

WKI Holding Company, Inc.

WKI Holding has cooked up a kitchen kingpin. The holding company's World Kitchen subsidiary (formerly Corning Consumer Products) makes some of the most popular kitchenware and tableware in the US. Its brands include Corelle, CorningWare, Pyrex, Revere, and Visions. The company doubled its size with its 1999 purchases of houseware firms EKCO Group (Farberware, Baker's Secret) and General Housewares (Chicago Cutlery, OXO); it adopted the WKI Holding name in 2000. Buyout firm Kohlberg Kravis Roberts bought most of the company in 1998 from optical fiber and high-performance glass maker Corning. WKI Holding filed for Chapter 11 bankruptcy protection in 2002; the firm emerged from Chapter 11 in February 2003.

EXECUTIVES

Chairman: John L. Mariotti, age 61
President and CEO: James A. (Jim) Sharman, age 42, $248,910 pay
SVP and CFO: Joseph W. McGarr, age 50, $300,205 pay
SVP, Human Resources: Joseph Galligher
VP and CIO: John Conklin
VP, Secretary, and General Counsel: Raymond J. Kulla, age 55, $235,000 pay
President, OXO International: Alexander (Alex) Lee, age 41, $346,500 pay
Director, Corporate Communications: David Lanzillo
Auditors: Deloitte & Touche LLP

LOCATIONS

HQ: 11911 Freedom Dr., Ste. 600, Reston, VA 20190
Phone: 703-456-4700 **Fax:** 607-377-3411
Web: www.worldkitchen.com

WKI Holding has factories and distribution facilities in Asia, Australia, and North and South America.

PRODUCTS/OPERATIONS

Selected Brands

Bakeware
Baker's Secret
CorningWare
Cuisinart
EKCO
Farberware
Pyrex

Cutlery
Chicago Cutlery
Regent Sheffield
Revere

Dinnerware
Corelle

Kitchen and Household Tools
EKCO
OXO

Precision Cutting Tools
Olfa

Rangetop Cookware
EKCO
Magnalite
Revere Ware

COMPETITORS

ARC International
Gibson Overseas
Lifetime Hoan
Newell Rubbermaid
Oneida
Pampered Chef
SEB
Tupperware
Wilton Industries

HISTORICAL FINANCIALS

Company Type: Private

Income Statement FYE: December 31

	REVENUE ($ mil.)	NET INCOME ($ mil.)	NET PROFIT MARGIN	EMPLOYEES
12/01	746	(133)	—	4,200
12/00	828	(150)	—	5,200
12/99	618	(35)	—	5,250
12/98	533	(36)	—	3,200
12/97	573	14	2.4%	—
12/96	632	3	0.5%	—
Annual Growth	3.4%	—	—	9.5%

2001 Year-End Financials

Debt ratio: —
Return on equity: —
Cash ($ mil.): 67
Current ratio: 0.34
Long-term debt ($ mil.): 9

Net Income History

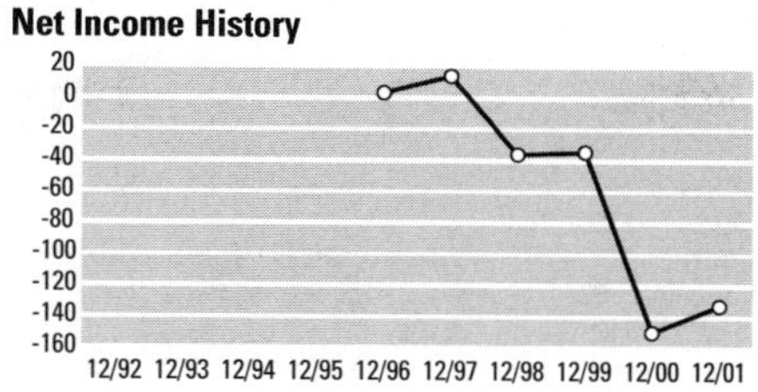

W. L. Gore & Associates, Inc.

W. L. Gore & Associates would like your clothing to take a deep breath. The company makes a variety of fluoropolymer products; best known is its breathable, waterproof, and windproof GORE-TEX fabric. Product uses range from clothing and shoes to guitar strings, dental floss, space suits, and sutures. In addition to its apparel (popular among hikers and hunters), W. L. Gore makes insulated wire and cables, filtration products, and sealants. Fabrics are offered under such brands as AIRVANTAGE, DRYLOFT, and WINDSTOPPER. The Gore family owns about 75% of the company; Gore associates own the rest.

W. L. Gore is known for its unusual style of management — the lattice system. There is no fixed authority, as the company has "sponsors," not bosses, and all employees are considered associates. Company goals and tasks are determined by consensus.

EXECUTIVES

Chairman: Robert W. Gore
President and CEO: Charles E. Carroll
Associate CIO: Justin Kershaw
Director, Human Resources: Sally Gore

LOCATIONS

HQ: 555 Papermill Rd., Newark, DE 19711
Phone: 302-738-4880 **Fax:** 302-738-7710
Web: www.gore.com

W. L. Gore & Associates operates manufacturing facilities in China, Germany, Japan, Scotland, and the US, with sales and customer service offices in those countries as well as in Argentina, Australia, Austria, Brazil, Finland, France, Greece, Hong Kong, India, Italy, Korea, Malaysia, the Netherlands, New Zealand, Poland, Russia, Singapore, Spain, Sweden, and Taiwan.

PRODUCTS/OPERATIONS

Divisions

Consumer Products
Electronics
Fabrics
Medical and Health Care
Membrane Filtration and Separations
Sealants and Fibers Technologies

COMPETITORS

Belden
Burlington Industries
CardioTech
Donaldson
Kellwood
Malden Mills
Milliken
Superior TeleCom
Thoratec Corp
Timberland

HISTORICAL FINANCIALS

Company Type: Private

Income Statement FYE: March 31

	REVENUE ($ mil.)	NET INCOME ($ mil.)	NET PROFIT MARGIN	EMPLOYEES
3/03	1,200	—	—	6,000
3/02	1,230	—	—	6,000
3/01	1,400	—	—	6,600
3/00	1,350	—	—	5,888
3/99	1,280	—	—	7,000
3/98	1,150	—	—	6,600
3/97	1,064	—	—	6,100
3/96	958	—	—	5,860
3/95	825	—	—	5,700
3/94	804	—	—	5,170
Annual Growth	4.6%	—	—	1.7%

Revenue History

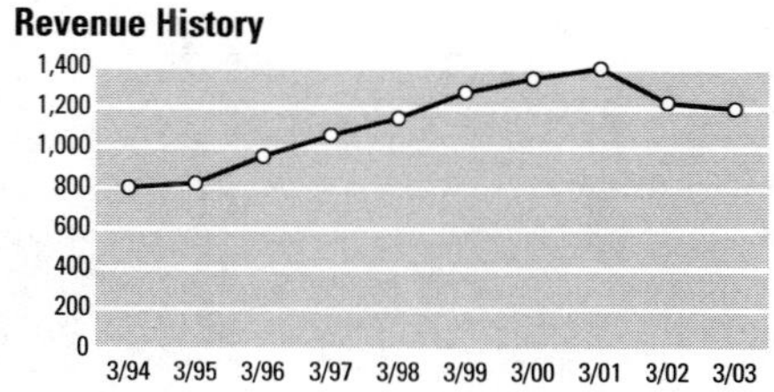

WL Homes LLC

WL Homes, doing business as John Laing Homes, is one of the largest homebuilders in Southern California. John Laing Homes builds homes and communities for first-time to luxury homebuyers. It operates divisions in California and Colorado. The company offers financing through JLH Mortgage. WL Homes was created from the 1998 merger of John Laing Homes (UK) and Watt Homes in the US. In 2001 John Laing Homes (UK) sold more than half of its stake in the company (retaining 22%) to an investor group led by chairman Ray Watt and CEO Larry Webb. WL Homes ranked 28th among the top 400 homebuilders in *Professional Builder* magazine's 2002 list.

EXECUTIVES

Chairman: Ray Watt
CEO: H. Lawrence (Larry) Webb
CFO: Wayne J. Stelmar
EVP Sales and Marketing: William B. (Bill) Probert
VP People: Beverly Newton
VP Sales and Marketing: Marianne Browne
Treasurer: Shahram Gheysari

LOCATIONS

HQ: 895 Dove St., Ste. 200, Newport Beach, CA 92660
Phone: 949-265-2400 **Fax:** 949-265-2500
Web: www.johnlainghomes.com

WL Homes operates divisions in California (Inland Empire, Los Angeles/Ventura; South Coast, Orange County/San Diego; Laing Luxury, Southern California; and Sacramento) and in Colorado Springs and Denver, Colorado.

COMPETITORS

Brookfield Homes
Centex
D.R. Horton
Hovnanian Enterprises
Lennar
NVR
Pulte Homes
Ryland
Toll Brothers

HISTORICAL FINANCIALS

Company Type: Private

Income Statement FYE: December 31

	REVENUE ($ mil.)	NET INCOME ($ mil.)	NET PROFIT MARGIN	EMPLOYEES
12/02	701	—	—	—
12/01	600	—	—	—
12/00	603	—	—	—
Annual Growth	7.8%	—	—	—

Revenue History

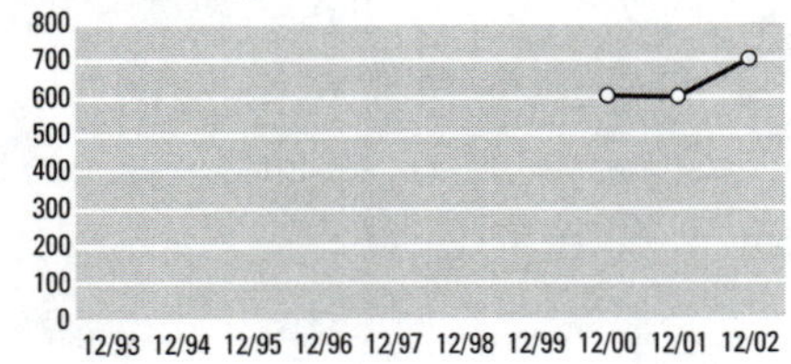

Wolverine Packing

If Mary lost her little lamb anywhere near Detroit, it probably ended up at Wolverine Packing. The wholesale meat packer and distributor is one of the largest lamb processors in the US. The company slaughters, processes, trims, and packs veal and lamb and sells frozen beef, pork, and poultry to retailers and the food service industry. Wolverine Packing also produces Halal meats (in accordance with Muslim dietary laws) and portion control and patty products, and markets its veal as Bonnie Maid Premium Veal. The company was founded in 1937 and has operations in Detroit's historic Eastern Market district. The founding Bonahoom family owns and operates Wolverine Packing.

EXECUTIVES

President & CEO: Alfred J. (Jim) Bonahoom
Marketing: Alfred J. (Jay) Bonahoom Jr.
CFO: Brian Bartes
VP and Treasurer: Roger Bonahoom
Director of Human Resources: Denise Goodrich

LOCATIONS

HQ: Wolverine Packing Company
2535 Rivard St., Detroit, MI 48207
Phone: 313-259-7500 **Fax:** 313-568-1909
Web: www.wolverinepacking.com

COMPETITORS

Cattleman's
Colorado Boxed Beef
Empire Beef
Sherwood Food
Showcase Foods
Stock Yards Packing
Swift
Tyson Fresh Meats
U.S. Foodservice

HISTORICAL FINANCIALS

Company Type: Private

Income Statement FYE: December 31

	REVENUE ($ mil.)	NET INCOME ($ mil.)	NET PROFIT MARGIN	EMPLOYEES
12/01	574	—	—	250
12/00	610	—	—	250
12/99	560	—	—	175
12/98	370	—	—	150
12/97	300	—	—	—
Annual Growth	17.6%	—	—	18.6%

Revenue History

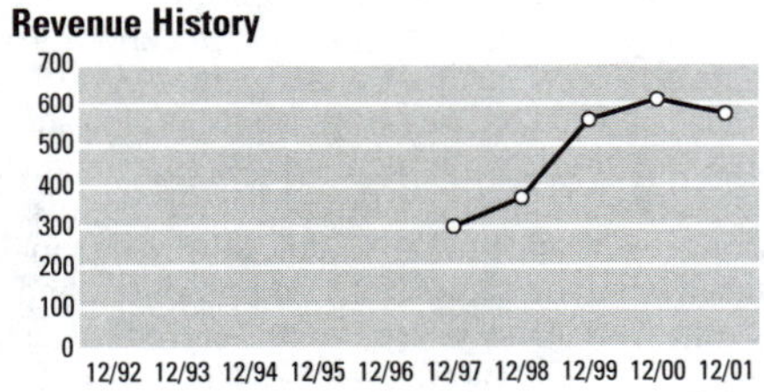

WorkPlaceUSA

Striving to be the "Wal-Mart of real estate," WorkPlaceUSA offers end-to-end services for commercial real estate projects. Founded in 1989 by CEO and owner John Amend as The Amend Group, the company has evolved from a tenant brokerage firm into a one-stop shop for real estate, design, construction, and technology consulting services. The group offers services such as architecture and engineering, general contracting, construction and project management, interior design, real estate finance information systems, and tenant brokerage. WorkPlaceUSA's engineering group designs mechanical, electrical, plumbing, and fire protection systems for corporate office and technical infrastructure real estate projects.

EXECUTIVES

Chairman, President, and CEO: John T. Amend, age 52
Vice Chairman: Teresa Amend, age 50
CFO: David Amend
SVP Project Management: Don Altwein
SVP Project Management: Rick Montgomery
SVP Project WorkPlaceUSA: Edward (Ed) Ulbricht
SVP Tenant Brokerage: Jay Ballou
SVP and CTO: David Gordon
VP Sales and Marketing: Jennifer Hatton

LOCATIONS

HQ: Workplace USA, Inc.
8150 N. Central Expwy., Ste. 1100, Dallas, TX 75206
Phone: 214-696-6900 **Fax:** 214-696-0037
Web: www.workplaceusa.com

WorkPlaceUSA offers services to corporations across the US.

COMPETITORS

Beck Group
CB Richard Ellis
Centex
Cushman & Wakefield
Hensel Phelps Construction
HOK
Integrated Electrical Services
Kennedy-Wilson
Gensler
Trammell Crow
Turner Corporation

HISTORICAL FINANCIALS

Company Type: Private

Income Statement FYE: December 31

	ESTIMATED REVENUE ($ mil.)	NET INCOME ($ mil.)	NET PROFIT MARGIN	EMPLOYEES
12/01	640	—	—	120

WorldTravel BTI

Instead of phoning home, E.T. could have called WorldTravel BTI. WorldTravel has grown from a small travel agency to #3 in the US (behind American Express and Carlson Wagonlit). Clients include many large US corporations such as PepsiCo, Deloitte Touche, and De Beers. WorldTravel has over 1,600 ticketing locations and more than 50 affiliates across the US; through Business Travel International (BTI) it offers another 3,000 locations in more than 80 countries. Its WorldTravelNet offers personalized travel information and services, including real-time flight status, hotel rates, weather, and maps. Chairman John Fentener van Vlissingen owns a majority stake in the company through BCD Holdings.

EXECUTIVES

Chairman: John A. Fentener van Vlissingen
CEO: Michael A. (Mike) Buckman, age 53
President: Danny Hood
COO: John Snyder
CFO: Thomas (Tom) Barham
EVP: Dee Runyon
VP Human Resources: Nancy Pavey
VP Information Technology/Network Services: Brian Slynn
Director Communications and Media Relations: Amy Berk

LOCATIONS

HQ: 1055 Lenox Park Blvd., Ste. 420, Atlanta, GA 30319
Phone: 404-841-6600 **Fax:** 404-814-2983
Web: www.worldtravel.com

PRODUCTS/OPERATIONS

Selected Services

Air Program Manager
BTI Global Hotel Programme
Corporate Fulfillment
Corporate Hotel Program
Leisure Travel
Web-based and Desktop Reporting
WorldTravel BTI Concierges
WorldTravelNet

COMPETITORS

American Express
Carlson Wagonlit
JTB
Kuoni Travel
Maritz
Rosenbluth International
World Travel Specialists

HISTORICAL FINANCIALS

Company Type: Private

Income Statement FYE: December 31

	ESTIMATED REVENUE ($ mil.)	NET INCOME ($ mil.)	NET PROFIT MARGIN	EMPLOYEES
12/01	3,800	—	—	5,175
12/00	3,800	—	—	5,800
12/99	3,500	—	—	5,000
12/98	3,300	—	—	5,000
12/97	3,000	—	—	5,000
12/96	2,500	—	—	3,000
Annual Growth	8.7%	—	—	11.5%

Revenue History

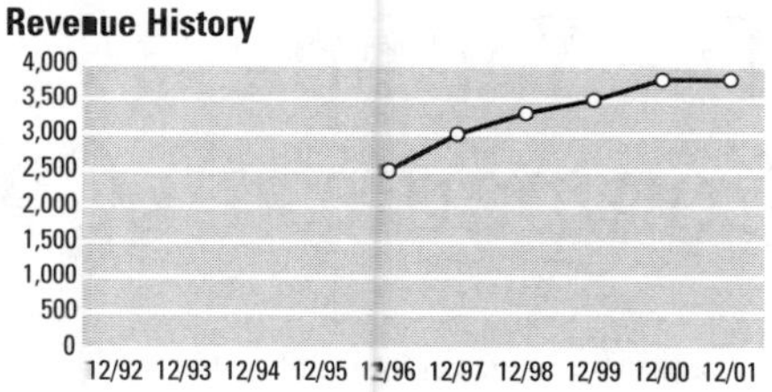

Yale University

What do President George W. Bush, writer William F. Buckley Jr., and actress Meryl Streep have in common? They are all Yalies. Yale University is one of the nation's most prestigious private liberal arts institutions, as well as one of its oldest (founded in 1701). Its $10.4 billion endowment ranks second only to Harvard's in the US. Yale comprises an undergraduate college, a graduate school, and 10 professional schools. Programs of study include architecture, law, medicine, and drama. Its 12 residential colleges (a system borrowed from Oxford) serve as dormitory, dining hall, and social center. The school has more than 11,100 students and some 3,000 faculty members.

EXECUTIVES

President: Richard C. Levin
Provost: Alison F. Richard
VP and Secretary: Linda Koch Lorimer, age 51
VP and General Counsel: Dorothy K. Robinson
VP Development: Charles J. Pagnam
VP Finance and Administration: Robert L. Culver
VP New Haven and State Affairs: Bruce D. Alexander
Director of Placement and Staff Relations: Katherine F. (Kitty) Matzkin
Director of the Yale University Investments Office: Alan S. Forman
Auditors: PricewaterhouseCoopers LLP

LOCATIONS

HQ: 246 Church St., New Haven, CT 06520
Phone: 203-432-2331 **Fax:** 203-432-2334
Web: www.yale.edu

PRODUCTS/OPERATIONS

Colleges and Schools

Graduate School of Arts and Sciences
School of Architecture
School of Art
School of Divinity
School of Drama
School of Forestry & Environmental Studies
School of Law
School of Management
School of Medicine
School of Music
School of Nursing
Yale College (undergraduate studies)

HISTORICAL FINANCIALS

Company Type: School

Income Statement FYE: June 30

	REVENUE ($ mil.)	NET INCOME ($ mil.)	NET PROFIT MARGIN	EMPLOYEES
6/02	1,467	—	—	7,577
6/01	1,353	—	—	7,398
6/00	1,264	—	—	10,800
6/99	1,150	—	—	10,318
6/98	1,083	—	—	9,685
6/97	992	—	—	10,000
6/96	931	—	—	9,200
6/95	948	—	—	10,000
6/94	902	—	—	9,600
6/93	852	—	—	8,500
Annual Growth	6.2%	—	—	(1.3%)

Revenue History

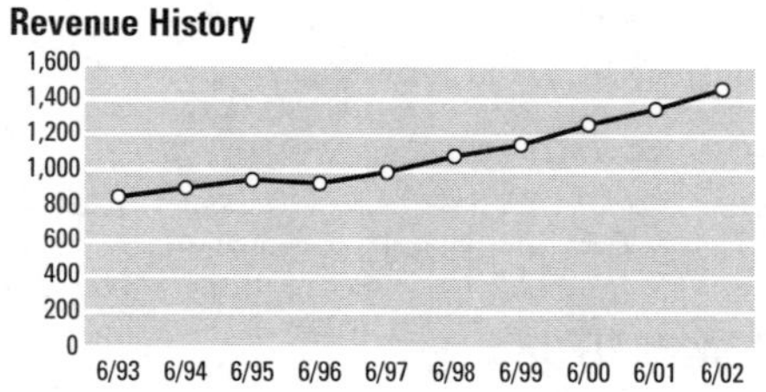

The Yates Companies

The Yates Companies is the extended family of W.G. Yates & Sons Construction Company. The commercial and heavy construction builder has been cashing in on casino projects and has won federal contracts for military facilities. Other family members are Mississippi-based JESCO and Tennessee-based Blaine Construction. The group, which operates mostly in the Southeast and along the East Coast, provides a broad range of construction-related services, including engineering, electrical and mechanical construction, millwrighting, and steel fabrication. The company is owned by the Yates family, including president and CEO Bill Yates, who co-founded it in 1964 with his father, the late William Gully Yates.

EXECUTIVES

Chairman, President, and CEO: William G. (Bill) Yates Jr.
CFO and Treasurer: Marvin B. Blanks III
EVP, Gulf Coast Division, W.G. Yates & Sons: William G. Yates III
General Counsel: Kenny Bush
President, JESCO: Jerry Stubblefield
President, Blaine Construction: Dorman Blaine
Director of Business Development and Marketing Manager: Jody Tidwell

LOCATIONS

HQ: The Yates Companies, Inc.
1 Gully Ave., Philadelphia, MS 39350
Phone: 601-656-5411 **Fax:** 601-656-8958
Web: www.wgyates.com

W.G. Yates & Sons Construction Company has offices in Alabama, Florida, Mississippi, and Tennessee.

PRODUCTS/OPERATIONS

Selected Services

Casino construction
Construction management
Design/build
Engineering
Forest products
General construction
Heavy commercial construction
Marine construction
Renovation
Retail construction
Utility construction

COMPETITORS

Brasfield & Gorrie
Choate Construction
Clark Enterprises
Dunn Industries
Fluor
Hunt Construction
Jacobs Engineering
Perini
Turner Corporation
Whiting-Turner

HISTORICAL FINANCIALS

Company Type: Private

Income Statement FYE: December 31

	ESTIMATED REVENUE ($ mil.)	NET INCOME ($ mil.)	NET PROFIT MARGIN	EMPLOYEES
12/02	1,023	—	—	3,000
12/01	750	—	—	3,000
12/00	740	—	—	3,000
12/99	700	—	—	3,000
Annual Growth	13.5%	—	—	0.0%

Revenue History

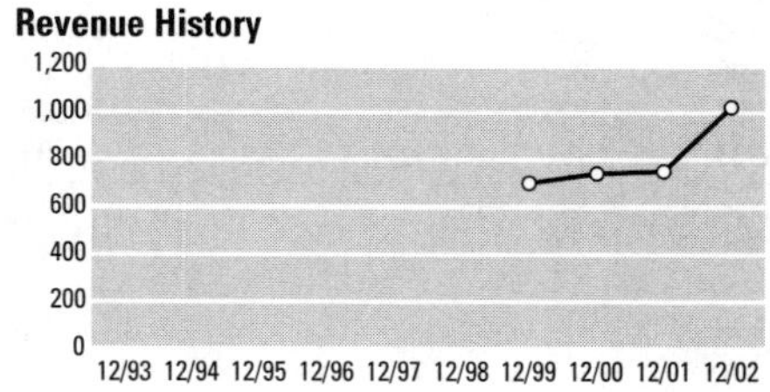

YMCA

If the Village People can be believed, it's fun to stay at the YMCA. One of the nation's largest not-for-profit community service organizations, YMCA of the USA assists the more than 2,400 individual YMCAs across the country and represents them on both national and international levels. YMCAs serve some 18 million people across the US. One of the largest child-care providers in the US, YMCAs also offer programs in areas such as aquatics, arts and humanities, health and fitness, and teen leadership. The first YMCA in the US was established in 1851 as an outgrowth of the YMCA movement launched by George Williams in the UK in 1844.

EXECUTIVES

Chairman: Tom Beerntsen
Vice Chairman: David Epperson
National Executive Director: Kenneth L. Gladish
CFO: Kate Spencer
CIO: Jeff Bundy
General Counsel: Jan Koran
Director Human Resources: Sharon Rakowski
Director International Group: Jerry Prado Shaw
Chief Marketing Officer: JoAnna Taylor

LOCATIONS

HQ: YMCA of the USA
101 N. Wacker Dr., Chicago, IL 60606
Phone: 312-977-0031 **Fax:** 312-977-9063
Web: www.ymca.net

PRODUCTS/OPERATIONS

Selected YMCA Programs

Aquatics
Arts and humanities
Camping
Child-care
Community development
Family
Health and fitness
International
Older adults
SCUBA
Sports
Teen leadership

HISTORICAL FINANCIALS

Company Type: Not-for-profit

Income Statement FYE: December 31

	REVENUE ($ mil.)	NET INCOME ($ mil.)	NET PROFIT MARGIN	EMPLOYEES
12/01	4,000	—	—	25,000
12/00	3,907	—	—	25,000
12/99	3,500	—	—	20,240
12/98	3,137	—	—	30,000
12/97	2,719	—	—	27,000
12/96	2,332	—	—	23,500
12/95	2,070	—	—	20,000
12/94	1,935	—	—	20,000
12/93	1,762	—	—	10,299
Annual Growth	10.8%	—	—	11.7%

Revenue History

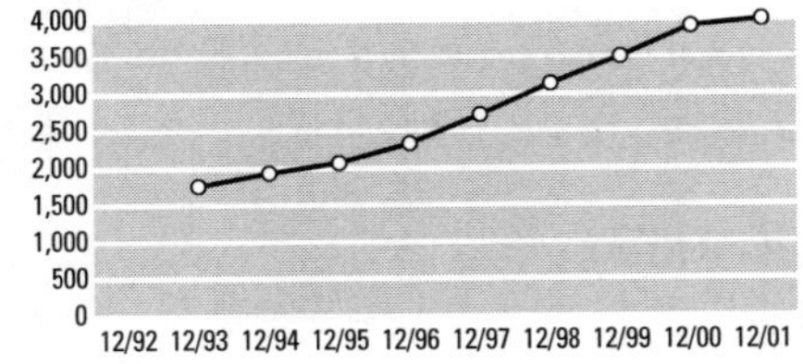

Young's Market Company, LLC

Although no longer young, Young's Market Company is in high spirits. Young's Market is one of the largest distributors of beer, wine, and distilled spirits in the US. The company is a major supplier along the Pacific coast. It also operates in Hawaii through its Better Brands subsidiary. Young's Market distributes products for Bacardi, Brown-Forman, and other distillers and winemakers. It distributes all Chalone Wine Group wines in California. John Young founded the company in 1888, which at one time included grocery retailing and specialty food distribution. The Underwood family, relatives of the Young's, bought Young's Market in 1990.

EXECUTIVES

Chairman and CEO: Vernon O. Underwood Jr.
EVP and Assistant to the President: Paul Vert
SVP and CFO: Dennis J. Hamann
VP, Corporate MIS: Steven G. Schaad
VP, Human Resources: Naomi Buenaslor
Corporate Secretary: Janet Underwood Smith

LOCATIONS

HQ: 2164 N. Batavia St., Orange, CA 92865
Phone: 714-283-4933 **Fax:** 714-283-6175
Web: www.youngsmkt.com

Young's Market Company primarily distributes to Alaska, California, Hawaii, Oregon, and Washington.

COMPETITORS

Beauchamp Distributing
Glazer's Wholesale Drug
National Distributing
National Wine & Spirits
Southern Wine & Spirits
Topa Equities
WinterBrook Beverage

HISTORICAL FINANCIALS

Company Type: Private

Income Statement FYE: February 28

	REVENUE ($ mil.)	NET INCOME ($ mil.)	NET PROFIT MARGIN	EMPLOYEES
2/02	1,490	—	—	1,700
2/01	1,300	—	—	1,700
2/00	1,100	—	—	1,700
2/99	1,090	—	—	1,600
2/98	1,000	—	—	1,500
2/97	960	—	—	1,400
2/96	1,000	—	—	1,600
2/95	910	—	—	1,650
2/94	900	—	—	1,600
2/93	910	—	—	1,500
Annual Growth	5.6%	—	—	1.4%

Revenue History

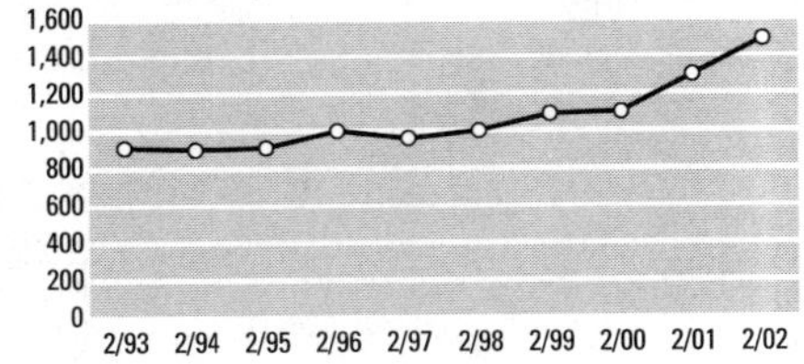

The Yucaipa Companies LLC

Yucaipa has a hungry eye for picking out ripe bargains in different industries, but made its name with grocery stores. The investment company forged its reputation as the ultimate grocery shopper, executing a series of grocery chain mergers and acquisitions that put the company on the supermarket map. The Yucaipa Companies owns Jurgensen's, Falley's, and Alpha Beta, among other chains. The company's chairman, billionaire Ron Burkle, is a prominent Democratic activist and fundraiser; former president Bill Clinton and the Rev. Jesse Jackson serve on the company's board.

Yucaipa maintains a 70% stake in Golden State Foods, one of McDonald's largest suppliers; 9% of Fleming, a major food distributor; and 2% of Kroger. It maintains a link to the food industry through a minority stake in Simon Worldwide (formerly Cyrk), a promotional marketing company whose largest customer is McDonald's. Yucaipa's portfolio also includes Alliance Entertainment (a distributor of music, videos, and games) and a 6% interest in Kmart Corporation.

Some of its investments have run into bumps in the road: Kmart filed for bankruptcy in 2002, and Simon faced numerous lawsuits stemming from a scandal after an employee allegedly rigged its client McDonald's Monopoly games and stole the cash.

Yucaipa is teaming up with California Public Employees' Retirement System (CalPERS) to form Yucaipa American Funds, which will seek to raise funds from union pensions and invest in labor-friendly businesses.

HISTORY

Ronald Burkle launched his career in the grocery industry as a box boy at his dad's Stater Bros. grocery store. By age 28 Burkle had moved up to SVP of administration, but he was fired after botching a buyout of the company in 1981.

Burkle and former Stater Bros. colleagues Mark Resnik and Douglas McKenzie founded Yucaipa (named after Burkle's hometown of Yucaipa, California) in 1986 when they bought Los Angeles gourmet-grocery chain Jurgensen's. The next year Yucaipa bought Kansas-based Falley's, which had 20 Food 4 Less stores in California.

In 1989 Yucaipa merged with Breco Holding, operator of 70 grocery stores, and bought Northern California's Bell Markets. It acquired ABC Markets in Southern California in 1990. The next year the company bought the 142-store chain Alpha Beta. Thirty-six Yucaipa stores were damaged in the 1992 Los Angeles riots, but Yucaipa rebuilt, working with unions to keep workers employed until the stores were operational.

The company acquired the 28-store Smitty's Super Valu chain (now Fred Meyer Marketplace) in 1994. The following year Yucaipa bought the 70-year-old family-owned chain Dominick's Finer Foods. Later in 1995 Yucaipa's Food 4 Less chain merged with Los Angeles competitor Ralphs Grocery (founded in 1873 by George Ralphs), making Yucaipa #1 in Southern California.

Yucaipa sold Smitty's to Utah-based Smith's in 1996, acquiring a minority stake in Smith's (Burkle became Smith's CEO). Dominick's went public in 1996, and Yucaipa retained a minority stake. The next year Fred Meyer bought Smith's for $1.9 billion. Burkle became the acquired company's chairman, and Yucaipa gained a 9% interest in Fred Meyer.

In 1998 Fred Meyer bought Ralphs and 155-store Quality Food Centers (QFC). Yucaipa and Wetterau Associates, a management firm, bought Golden State Foods, giving Yucaipa a 70% stake in the McDonald's food supplier. Yucaipa sold Dominick's to Safeway.

After Kroger bought Fred Meyer in 1999, Yucaipa turned away from the consolidating grocery industry and moved into cyberspace. That year Burkle and former Walt Disney president Michael Ovitz launched CheckOut Entertainment Network, which operated CheckOut.com, an entertainment Web site at which Web surfers could buy books, music, and videogames. Yucaipa hired Richard Wolpert, former president of Disney Online, to oversee its Internet and technology activities.

Yucaipa added to its portfolio in 1999 by taking stakes in GameSpy (online games), Talk City (later LiveWorld, online chat service), OneNetNow (online communities), ClubMom (Web site for mothers), and Cyrk (now Simon Worldwide, promotional marketing). Yucaipa also bought music, video, and games distributor Alliance Entertainment. The company also holds a minority stake in Simon Worldwide.

Music and video retailer Wherehouse Entertainment became a 50%-owner of CheckOut.com after it merged its online retailing operations with CheckOut.com in 1999. (As the Internet economy faltered, Yucaipa sold CheckOut.com in 2001.)

In 2000 the company digressed from its focus on the Web to invest in Kole Imports, an importer of merchandise sold in discount stores.

EXECUTIVES

Managing Partner: Ronald W. (Ron) Burkle, age 50
CFO: Steve Mortensen
Senior Advisor: William J. Clinton, age 57
Partner: Carlton J. Jenkins, age 47
Partner: Erika Paulson, age 27
Partner: Ed Renwick
Partner: Scott Stedman
Partner: Nick Tasooji
Partner: Ira Tochner
Chief Administration Officer and Human Resources Director: Bill Bailey
Legal: Robert P. Bermingham
Public Relations/ Corporate Communications: Ari Swiller
Investor Relations and Business Development: Adrienne Gaines

LOCATIONS

HQ: 9130 W. Sunset Blvd., Los Angeles, CA 90069
Phone: 310-789-7200 **Fax:** 310-228-2873

PRODUCTS/OPERATIONS

Selected Investments

Alliance Entertainment (music, videos, and game distribution)
Fleming Companies (9%, wholesale food distributor)
Golden State Foods (70%, McDonald's supplier)
Kmart Corporation (6%, discount retailer)
Kole Imports (minority stake, discount merchandise importer)
The Kroger Co. (2%, grocery stores)
Simon Worldwide (20%, promotional marketing)

COMPETITORS

Bain Capital
Berkshire Hathaway
Blackstone Group
Carlyle Group
Hicks, Muse
KKR
Leonard Green
Texas Pacific Group
Thomas Lee

Zachry Construction

H. B. Zachry began building roads and bridges in 1924, and now his son and grandsons are running the show. Zachry Construction builds and maintains power and chemical plants, steel and paper mills, refineries, roadways, dams, airfields, and pipelines. Operating mostly in Texas and the southeastern US, Zachry has built facilities for companies such as Alcoa, BP Chemicals, DuPont, and Samsung. It also works internationally and reconstructed the US Embassy in Moscow. In addition, Zachry owns interests in ranches and in oil exploration, cement, hospitality, and realty companies, as well as a stake in the San Antonio Spurs basketball team. The Zachry family owns the firm.

EXECUTIVES

Chairman and CEO: Henry Bartell Zachry Jr.
President: John B. Zachry
SVP and Controller: Joe J. Lozano
SVP Corporate Business Development: Keith D. Manning
SVP Power: Robert Kalt
SVP: Ken Oleson
VP, General Counsel, and Secretary: Murray Johnston
VP Employee Relations: Steve Hoech
VP Community Relations: Cathy Obriotti Green
Auditors: Ernst & Young

LOCATIONS

HQ: Zachry Construction Corporation
527 Logwood, San Antonio, TX 78221
Phone: 210-475-8000 **Fax:** 210-475-8060
Web: www.zachry.com

COMPETITORS

aker Kvaerner
Alberici
Austin Industries
Barton Malow
Bechtel
Black & Veatch
Dick Corporation
Fluor
Foster Wheeler
Gilbane
Granite Construction
Halliburton
Hensel Phelps Construction
Hoffman Corporation
Holloman
Krupp Polysius
M. A. Mortenson
McCarthy Building
MWH Global
Parsons
Peter Kiewit Sons'
Sumitomo Mitsui Construction
TIC Holdings
Turner Industries
Washington Group

HISTORICAL FINANCIALS

Company Type: Private

Income Statement FYE: December 31

	REVENUE ($ mil.)	NET INCOME ($ mil.)	NET PROFIT MARGIN	EMPLOYEES
12/01	1,940	—	—	14,000
12/00	1,400	—	—	14,000
12/99	1,195	—	—	11,000
12/98	670	—	—	7,500
12/97	660	—	—	7,500
12/96	775	—	—	7,625
12/95	780	—	—	10,100
12/94	750	—	—	10,000
12/93	792	—	—	8,000
12/92	769	—	—	—
Annual Growth	10.8%	—	—	7.2%

Revenue History

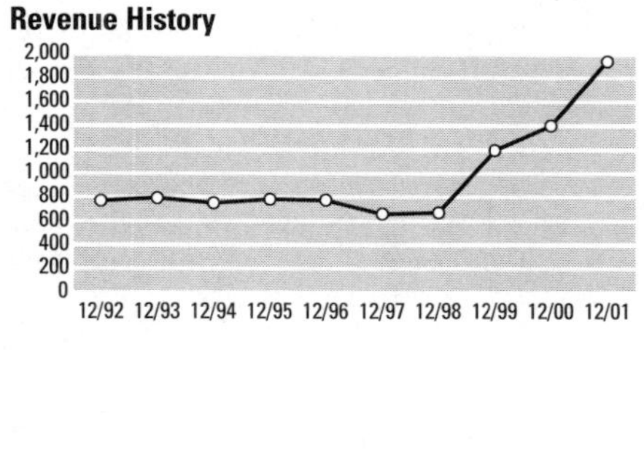

Hoover's Handbook of

Private Companies

The Indexes

Index by Industry

INDUSTRY CATEGORIES

AEROSPACE & DEFENSE

AGRICULTURE

AUTOMOTIVE & TRANSPORT

BANKING

BEVERAGES

BUSINESS SERVICES

TRANSPORTATION SERVICES

Index by Headquarters

NORTH CAROLINA

NORTH DAKOTA

OHIO

OKLAHOMA

OREGON

PENNSYLVANIA

Index of Executives

B

C

D

E

G

H

I

J

L

M

N

O

P

Q

R

S

T

U

V

W

X

Y

Z